INDONESIA
HANDBOOK

4TH EDITION

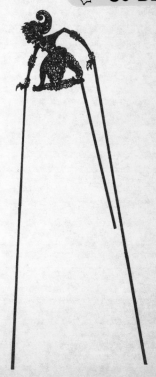

INDONESIA HANDBOOK

4TH EDITION

BILL DALTON

moon PUBLICATIONS

INDONESIA HANDBOOK

Published by
Moon Publications
722 Wall Street
Chico, California 95928, USA
tel. (916) 345-5473/5413

Printed by
Colorcraft Ltd., Hong Kong

© Copyright Bill Dalton **1988**

Please send all comments,
corrections, additions,
amendments and critiques to:

**BILL DALTON
MOON PUBLICATIONS
722 Wall Street
Chico, CA 95928, USA**

PRINTING HISTORY
1st Edition 1977
2nd Edition 1980
3rd Edition 1985
4th Edition 1988

Library of Congress Cataloging in Publication Data

Dalton, Bill.
  Indonesia Handbook / Bill Dalton —4th ed.
    p.   cm.
  Bibliography: p.
  Includes index.
  ISBN 0-918373-12-3 : $17.95
  1. Indonesia — Description and travel — 1981 — Guide-books.
I. Title.
DS614.D34 1988   88-21613
915.98'0438 — dc19   CIP

To my daughters
Sri and Ari

ACKNOWLEDGEMENTS

Countless people have contributed their skills and insights into this 4th edition of *Indonesia Handbook* over the past 7 years. For all their support and their encouragement, I give immeasurable thanks. My gratitude goes first to my editors Deke Castleman, Mark Morris, and Asha Johnson who labored long and hard through dozens of drafts to help make this the best guide to Indonesia yet published. Sincere thanks also goes to Dave Hurst, our art director, who worked so doggedly in re-designing the cover art and typography for not only my guide but our whole line of guides. To Collin Ross, Todd Clark, Rachel Photenhauer, Peggy Ponton, all of whom gave a helping hand in the pasteup—good work! Thanks also to Andrea Greenbaum and Christa Jorgensen who completed so many niggling yet necessary tasks. Louise Foote, Moon's cartographer, deserves high praise for creating fine maps out of barely decipherable field sketches, with assistence from Alex Foote, Diana Lasich, and Anita Neef. I am also grateful to Asha Johnson, our typesetter-cum-editor, for her perseverence in turning out reams of typeset galleys, literally hundreds of corrections and corrections of corrections! My thanks also goes to our sales manager, Donna Galassi, who is largely responsible for getting our guides better known among booksellers and travelers, and for turning our sales department into one of the best in the business. I am grateful to Virginia Michaels, our publicity manager, for her promotional efforts in launching *Indonesia Handbook*. Effusive thanks also to artists Gordy Ohliger, Diana Lasich, and Louise Foote for their line and tonal drawings. And bravo to Rick Johnson, our shipping and fulfillment manager, who gets the books out the door!

This guide would not have the depth nor the ring of personal experience it does without the hundreds of readers who have sent in information over the years. I'm also indebted to the scores of tourist office officials who helped me with literature, transportation, tips, advice. The following is only a partial list of all those who have made contributions: Robert Kennington, Andy Johnson, Ido Damsura, Rob Cornelisse, J.D. McEwan, Syafruddin Bustami, Michael Wollman, Eddie Schindler, Hunt Kooiker, Pat Jevne, Kare Smith, Piet Veel, Harry Pariser, Stephanie Wheeler, Wim Wolters, Graham Simmons, Chaidir Zitom, Peter White, Pyers Croft, Wayne Pease, Bill Weir, Carl Parkes, Steve McGuiness, Joseph S. Brown, Rob Wallace, Helmy Ali, Bob Thomson, Yanricoh, Benno Grzimek, Richard Lewell, Duana Ogle, Lamon Rutten, Dr. Krommenhoek, Mykl Meagher, Ray Steen, Bob Nilsen, Harvey Arden, Made Wijaya, A. Pasaribu, H. Amir Husin, Harry Soeharman, Laura L. Babcock, Rusniah Marjuni, Siti Baizura Hussein, G. Braman, D. Yost, Christian Kallen, Tilly Soukotta, George M. Kdise, Wiwiek P. Yusuf, Buddy Datunsolang, J.C. Parera, H. Usman, A.J. Lake, Ros Bulo, Kaye and John Dickson, Edy Batubara, Oka Kartini, Suteja Neka, Somadi, S.N. Adnyana, Chamdi, Wiyoso, Boedisanyoto, B. Mariso, Ira Bashkow, Laura Tjokrodipo, Handoyo, Maumun Rustina, Soerjanto, S. Heryanadi, Gilah Hirsch, David Lebrun, Hasanuddin, David Mussry, Maman Alibasya Pane, Steven Solter, Sutedjo Hardjo Prawiro, Zulkifli, Donna Mackiewicz, plus scores of others who didn't want their names to appear in this book.

PHOTO AND ILLUSTRATION CREDITS

front cover: Rich MacDonald. **illustrations:** Bill Dalton—page 561; Louise Foote—page 620; David Hurst—pages 117, 817; Diana Lasich-Harper—pages 254, 279, 295, 305, 315, 318, 320, 332, 370, 494, 628, 649, 683, 686, 778, 898, 971; William Marschall—page 897; Jean Moreno—pages 209, 377, 739; Gordon Ohliger—pages 100, 119, 127, 145, 147, 177, 383, 586, 691, 704, 723 (left), 752, 586, 951, 954; **black and white photos:** Air New Zealand, photo by Walter Imber—page 819; Field Museum of Natural History—page 959; Royal Tropical Institute, Amsterdam—pages 570, 614, 333, 363, 395, 408, 463, 735, 742, 804 (left), 965, 998; Bill Weir—pages 827, 841, 845, 858

CONTENTS

SUMATRA . . . 471

NUSATENGGARA . . . 647

KALIMANTAN . . . 735

LIST OF MAPS

INDONESIAN GEOGRAPHIC ABBREVIATIONS
USED IN TEXT AND ON MAPS

D. — *Danau* (lake)
G. — *Gunung* (mountain)
Jl. — *Jalan* (street)
Kb. — *Kebun* (garden, plantation, estate)
Kec. — *Kecamatan* (district)
Kep. — *Kepulauan* (archipelago, islands)
L. — *Laut* (sea)

Ma. — *Muara* (mouth of river, delta)
P. — *Pulau* (island)
Sel. — *Selat* (strait)
S. — *Sungai* (river)
Tel. — *Teluk* (bay)
Tg. — *Tanjung* (cape, point)

TEXT ABBREVIATIONS

a/c — air-conditioned
C — Centigrade
C. — Century
d — double occupancy
E — east
L — left
N — north

OW — one way
Peng. — *penginapan* (hotel)
pp — per person
R — right
RM — *Rumah Makan* (restaurant)

RR — railroad
RS — *Rumah Sakit* (hospital)
RT — roundtrip
S — south
s — single occupancy
t — triple occupancy
W — west

PREFACE

NIMBIN
—17th to 28th of April, 1973

Since 1973, Moon Publications of Chico, California, has specialized in guidebooks for independent, adventurous travelers. How the company has grown, from its beginnings on a windy hilltop in southeastern Australia to the permanent niche it occupies in the travel book market today, is an adventure in itself. After traveling around the world for 7 years to over 70 countries, I entered Australia from Indonesia in 1973 with $20 in my pocket. I got a job as a gardener in the Cairns public works department and moved into the Cairns Youth Hostel. One evening at the hostel I was typing out some travel notes for some Germans when a crusty old New Zealand journalist peered over my shoulder, "You should publish that information, not just give it away!" he advised. It was just the spark I needed.

Rumors had been circulating around the country for weeks about an arts festival in a small town called Nimbin in the hills of New South Wales. Communes, hippies, and travelers were converging on the site from all over Australia. Taking the old Kiwi's suggestion to heart, I mimeographed 800 copies of 6 typewritten pages and crude maps, titled it "A Traveler's Notes: Indonesia," stuffed them into my rucksack, and hitched a ride south in a car that had NIMBIN OR BUST spelled out in dust on its rear window. Driving deep into the countryside, we at last arrived at Nimbin. A fountain of red paint spurted above a storefront, psychedelic motifs ran from building to building all along the main street, and outlandishly dressed people emerged barefoot from all manner of wheeled contraptions. As I surveyed the scene, I realized that I had happened upon an Australian Woodstock, a landmark event of the 1970s, a brilliant once-in-a-lifetime experience.

Nimbin was perched on top of a small hill. Below was a broad valley cut in two by a winding river. Scattered across the valley floor were hundreds of teepees, tents, multicolored domes, makeshift plastic shelters, vans, and RVs, all under tall bushy eucalyptus trees. I was invited to stay in a huge communal plastic orange igloo with a gang of bikers. Late into the first night, chillums sparked in the darkness as a New Zealand organist pierced the night air with Christian rock music. The next morning I woke to the sound of flutes and chanting Hare Krishnas. Peeking out of the igloo, a heavy mist encircled the trees and drifted over a sea of bodies crashed everywhere on the damp grass. Smoke puffed above a small aborigine tribe from cen-

tral Australia camped on a nearby hill where they performed dances and told stories. The aborigines considered Nimbin a holy place inhabited by departed spirits and refused to pay the entrance fee to land they felt had been stolen from them.

That day hundreds of celebrants—each one a character—arrived. Fred Robinson, an amazing white-haired 83-year-old Moses figure from Perth, gave talks on the Grand Order of the Universe, flying saucers, and Right Diet in order to save the world by 1978—which promised to be a very heavy year. In a nearby field, peddling furiously, a man attempted to get an absurd spiral-shaped flying machine off the ground. As the crowds swelled, a mushroom-eating greeter called out "Hello Bruce!" to everyone. Webster, a sexual activist, revolutionary, and spiritualist, enthused on his soapbox in his faultless British accent: "What we need is not a new Christ but a new Robin Hood! Not pie in the sky! Pie now!" A bedraggled band of crazy long-haired flautists and bongo drummers from Melbourne, who called themselves "The White Company," poured out of a long white bus. All shared food and whatever else they had; at the communal privies, guys and girls—complete strangers—shared the toilets and took showers together. Everyone was repeating "It's working, it's working!" Nimbin was to become a metaphor for a whole generation of Australians.

The whole hilltop was swarming with people and humming with activity. Rock concerts, be-ins, peak experiences, spontaneous dances swirled around us. Shops sold oatmeal cookies and stir-fry vegies on paper plates (the locals called wholewheat flour "hippie flour" and brown rice "hippie rice.") At the Learning Exchange were workshops on silversmithing, Transcendental Meditation, instrument- and batik-making, mime by the White Company, and others such as "Sex—The Virile Sport." A massage tent had opened up, and in the afternoon at the Butter Factory vehement diatribes were underway on racism, Gay and Feminist Liberation, radical sociology, and anti-psychiatry. At the Nimbin Pub, packed with freaks and farmers from 10 a.m. to 10 p.m., the till was white hot. And the din! A few doors down, a poetry group was reading Yevtushenko by candlelight in the middle of the street. Dollar Brand, an African pianist, was playing a wild improvisation in Nimbin Hall, taking the audience to a crescendo then into the nadirs. In the Central Cafe, the New Zealand jug band Blertha sent a hundred people rockin' with their shivering electric guitars. It was a scene of mind-boggling freshness and innocence.

Each morning for a week, as groups gathered in the small town park for breakfast, I set up my stack of booklets and put up my sign: GYPSY GUIDE—50 CENTS on the sidewalk. Word spread far and fast, as if a famous author were autographing his bestseller! A few travelers looked at the cover and reached immediately for coins. Some read the whole booklet and bought; some read it and didn't. Some told me I should charge a dollar, some tried to bargain me down to a quarter, and some said it was an outright ripoff. Questions came thick and fast: Are there trains on Java? Can you change Australian money in Indonesia? Do the police hassle female travelers? Isn't it spoiled by now? A few old Asia hands put me through an hour's grilling before they'd put their hands in their pockets. I told everyone it was the freshest information around about Indonesia and that it made excellent reading to boot. Someone wanted the address of Moon Publications—I answered, "Nimbin!" Another guy scanned it and exclaimed, "I have a photographic memory, thanks a lot." Yet another complimented, "Well penned, mate!" One girl told me about an underground press in Sydney, Tomato Press, on Glebe Point Road. "If you make a little staple-bound book out of this, then the bookstores will take it," she advised. (I immediately made note of that! Bless her, wherever she is!) Old friends and I were reunited: Leslie from Goa (now with a new baby girl), Allen from an opium den in Penang, Luis from a brothel in Bangkok. By the sixth day I had sold 400 copies and started to show a profit. Amazing! And it kept on selling. It occurred to me that I had stumbled upon something.

By the 10th day, the media got hold of the event and turned it into a real circus. Straight tourists walked down the main street warily like they were in a lion park. Keeping their kids close to their sides, they stood agape at the goings-on, laughing nervously. Plainclothesmen drove the dirt roads and notices circulated with their license plate numbers. Cameramen worked the throngs. An official-looking man asked me "Where's the main attraction?" Later that morning, news spread of an orgiastic be-in on the soccerfield. It started as a snake-like procession winding in and out of all the tents—a freak parade with everyone singing and playing musical toys. In the center the crowd danced and gyrated, a naked free-spirited frenzy, while a shaggy bare-ass photographer with an oversized 16mm movie camera recorded the climax for posterity. In that Australian Summer of Love of 1973, this was the Flower Children's penultimate moment.

The next day the tents in the valley started to thin. Ride notices appeared on the bulletin board of the Info Office and hitchhikers were strung out along the road out of town with city signs on top of backpacks, heading for Lismore and points south. On the last night, a night of the full moon, a farewell bonfire was lit on top of a nearby mountain. The next morning, with an horrendous hangover and a pocket full of Australian dollars, I met a gregarious English-Australian who was headed for Sydney on a 350 Suzuki. "Got room for me?" "How big's your pack?" Showed him with my hands. "Yeah, think so." "Far out!" Within a week I had a bed in the offices of Tomato Press, right over the clanking press downstairs, and was completing a new edition of "A Traveler's Notes," now a 16-page stapled booklet. Over the coming months, I tramped the streets of Sydney, Melbourne, and Adelaide selling the latest edition at flea markets and sidewalk fairs, on university campuses, on King's Cross, to bookstores, to anyone I met. I used it instead of money. The 2,000-copy printrun sold out in 2 months. People began to seek me out to give me additional travel information on Indonesia, which I dutifully wrote down. My knowledge and my notes grew. Soon I had enough to publish a 32-page booklet, which kept on selling. *Indonesia Handbook,* the mammoth grandchild of those seminal information sheets sold on a sidewalk in Nimbin, has gone on to sell over 250,000 copies. What began as scribbled notes in a travel journal 15 years ago grew into a publishing organization with 23 titles (so far!) and distribution in over 30 countries.

Bill Dalton (left), flogging "A Traveler's Notes: Indonesia" at Nimbin, NSW, in April 1973

IS THIS BOOK OUT OF DATE?

Although we have done everything in our power to make the information in *Indonesia Handbook* as accurate as possible, the task is sometimes too much for us. You can help us out. If some prices have gone up, if some services have been discontinued or are unacceptable for some reason, if certain suggestions are misleading, or if you have shortcuts, warnings, transportation tips, new museums and sights, bureaucratic hassles, arts and crafts buys, new cultural performances, money-saving tips and strategies, write us so we can let other readers know. If you get off the beaten track and come across a special place or have some favorite restaurants and hotels we don't mention, we'd be grateful to hear about them. Women travelers sometimes run into situations which warrant special attention, so if you let us know about them, we'll pass the information on. We also value highly letters from resident expatriates, hikers, and outdoor enthusiasts. Letters from Indonesians themselves, with their impressions of *Indonesia Handbook,* are particularly welcome.

Although we try to make our maps as accurate as possible, we would appreciate readers pointing out any omissions or inaccuracies. If you can improve a map, add a map of your own, or have high-quality artwork that you'd like to see in the next edition, send it too. When writing or drawing, always try to be as specific and accurate as possible. Notes written on the spot are always more concise than those put down on paper later. Write comments into the margins of your copy of *Indonesia Handbook* as you go along, then send us a summary when you get home. Or we'd be happy to replace your marked-up correction copy with a fresh copy.

This guide is updated at every reprint and completely revised every 2 years, so your contributions will eventually be shared with thousands of others traveling in Indonesia. This guide is a sounding board and a clearinghouse for travelers, so please help us to keep in the avant garde of adventurous, independent travel by writing to us. Address your letters to:

Bill Dalton
c/o Moon Publications
722 Wall Street
Chico CA 95928 USA

NOTE TO PHOTOGRAPHERS

Amateur and professional photographers are invited to submit photos for consideration of publication in the next edition of *Indonesia Handbook*. Good photos from our readers always get preference over stock photos from agencies. Please send only good-quality duplicate color slides or black-and-white prints (color prints are of little use). The scenes depicted in all photos must be specifically identified if they are to be useable. Photographers will be acknowledged in the photo credits and receive a free copy of the edition in which their photo first appears. By submitting photos, it's understood that the photographer is thereby granting Moon Publications the non-exclusive right to publish the photo(s) under the above terms. The publisher is not responsible and cannot, in most cases, undertake to return this material.

FREE MOON BOOK FOR CONTRIBUTORS

For those who send us substantial information, we will send a free copy of the next edition of *Indonesia Handbook* or any other Moon Publications guide you wish. We reserve the right, however, to determine what is "substantial." Thank you for your help.

INTRODUCTION

A country of incredible and diverse beauty, Indonesia stretches across one-seventh of the globe between Malaysia and Australia. This sprawling island chain encompasses mind-stupefying extremes: 5,000-meter-high snowcapped mountains of Irian Jaya, sweltering lowland swamps of eastern Sumatra, open eucalyptus savannahs of Timor, lush rainforests of W. Java, with lava-spewing volcanos the whole length. After exisiting as a Dutch colony for over 300 years, Indonesia fought for and won its independence in 1949. The archipelago, astride both the Indian and Pacific oceans, has been the seedbed of unique Asian and Australasian tropical marine, animal, and plant forms. The most complex single nation on Earth, each of Indonesia's 6,000-plus inhabited islands has customs, native dress, architecture, dialects, ethnology, and geography all its own. Its wayang puppets, unearthly gamelan music, exquisite textiles, matchless and varied cuisines, hundreds of tribes, ancient ruins and historical sites, wildlife and nature reserves and friendly people make Indonesia one of Asia's last travel discoveries.

THE PHYSICAL SETTING

The outer limits of this 6,400-km stretch of islands (*"Dari Sabang ke Merauke"* or "From Sabang to Merauke") are as far as California is from Bermuda or as far as Perth, Australia, is from Wellington, New Zealand. Indonesia has a total area of 5 million sq km (about 1 million sq km more than the total land area of the U.S.), of which more than 2 million sq km are land. Its sea area is 3 times larger than its land area, and Indonesians are one of the few peoples in the world who include water within the boundaries of their territory, calling their country *Tanah Air Kita,* which means literally "Our Land and Water" (or "Our Native Land"). Of the 10 largest islands in the world, Indonesia claims the better part of 3 (New Guinea, Borneo, and Sumatra); in addition there are about 30 small archipelagos, each containing literally thousands of islands. Of the 13,677 islands that make up its territory, some 6,000 are named and only 992 are permanently settled.

Volcanos
Most Indonesians live and die within sight of a volcano. This archipelago sprawls through a part of the western Pacific known as The Ring of Fire. Registering up to 3 earthquakes per day, this region is home to over 400 volcanos, 70-80 of which are still active. The islands are the site of the earth's 2 greatest volcanic cataclysms in history (Krakatoa and Tambora); each year there's an average of 10 major eruptions. All this volcanic activity not only destroys, but also brings gigantic benefit by aiding growth and life. The ancient Hindu monuments constructed for over

750 years on Java were mostly built from cooled lava rock, ideal for carving. The whitish ash produced by an eruption, rich in chemicals, reaches a wide area of surrounding land. Rivers carry ash even farther by way of irrigation canals to the crops. Thus Indonesia has some of the most fertile land on the planet. In places it's said you can shove a stick in the ground and it'll sprout leaves. A serious pursuit not to be missed in Indonesia is volcano climbing—Keli Mutu, Rinjani, Agung, Bromo, Merapi, Papandayan, Sibayak—each offering hauntingly desolate landscapes, cold invigorating hikes, and often a hot or cold springs bath after. Numerous remote and wildly pristine high mountain lakes were made by volcanic cataclysms eons ago.

Climate
Indonesia straddles the equator and the days are all the same length. This country has a typical equatorial climate with only 2 seasons: wet and hot. The hot season is slightly hotter and not quite so wet as the wet season, while the wet season is slightly wetter and not quite so hot as the hot season. The wet season lasts from about Nov. to Mar. or Apr., and the hot season May-October. Sometimes it rains so hard it's like falling into a swimming pool; with a roar the skies upend, spilling a solid wall of water on the earth below, flattening plants and flowers to the soaked earth. Locales E of Solo (C. Java) have sharply defined dry seasons, the duration increasing the closer the area is to Australia. In the far southeastern islands such as Timor and Roti, the dry season can last up to

7 months. Sumatra and Kalimantan, lying closer to the equator and farther from Australia, have *no* dry seasons. But don't put off your trip just because it's the wet season. When it rains the dust on the roads is kept down, flowers are bursting, it's fresher and cooler, and everywhere it's green like bright wet paint. If you're caught out in the rain, just cut down a banana leaf to make an ideal umbrella, or in Irian Jaya, use grass. In many places good umbrellas (Rp2000) are made from bamboo coated with wax paper and pig fat; slips easily into the top of a pack.

In Indonesia it's always hot, but due to mountain breezes and altitude, there's roughly one degree of cooling for every 90 m in elevation. Humidity is always high. Asians have a different appreciation of climate than people in the West. The mere hint of a breeze is always the signal for Indonesians to tighten scarves, close up windows, and turn up collars, lest *masuk angin,* i.e. one is "entered by the wind" (catches cold or flu). On the other hand, warmth is associated with "hard work, pain, terror, bad," while in the West we think "pleasant, cozy, secure, healthy." Most Indonesians socialize and promenade in the cool of the evening.

AGRICULTURE

Indonesia is an agricultural nation. Four out of five Indonesians work the soil. The *desa* is the entire productive community of a small village. In the Western sense, the *desa* is an authoritarian, undemocratic system. It can be likened to a sort of oriental kibbutz. Wooden or bamboo houses are loosely scattered around vegetable plots and fruit trees—papaya, mango, guava, coconut, *kapok* and various palms—with narrow pathways winding in every direction. Sometimes there are also a commmunity meeting place, barns and fishponds. The *desa* is often surrounded by dry or wet ricefields, hedges, bamboo groves, with forests beyond. People work hard all day, then return home to pray, sing, dance, smoke *kretek,* gossip, watch *wayang* or TV, sleep, then rise at 0400 to labor again in the fields. Controlling every activity in the *desa* is a council of elected villagers. The headman is called the *kepala desa.* An ancient cooperative system *(gotong royong),* in which everyone lends a hand, manages parceling out land, community seed beds, growing crops, and the irrigation and storage of rice. There are mainly 2 systems of cultivation used in Indonesia, *ladang* and *sawah.*

Ladang

Ladang means shifting or swidden cultivation, a method of agriculture characterized by prodigious human labor using uncomplicated, pre-industrial implements. It's estimated that as much as ½ of all Indonesians still work *ladang.* This method of farming was practiced in Europe during the Middle Ages when Europe was underpopulated, its inhabitants, dressed in animal skins, beating back the forests. The practice of *ladang* can be very complex—a stable, well-balanced system in which man and his environment co-exist in harmony. Basically, it's an imitation of nature itself. Unirrigated, arable land is prepared by slashing and burning jungle, clearing it, then planting and harvesting a wide variety of quick-growing, predominantly food crops. Cultivators plant in rows, working usually uphill over fallen trees and rough ground. The men poke holes with sharpened sticks, the women follow behind dropping in unhusked rice seeds, a few per hole. After some days green shoots appear from 99% percent of the holes. *Ladang* is usually practiced on the nonvolcanic, less fertile soil of the outer islands, and the soil soon becomes exhausted. The plot is then abandoned. At least l0 years is needed for the jungle to overgrow the cultivated plot and replenish the soil. The *ladang* farmer is then able to return and cultivates the plot for another 2 years, repeating the cycle. If the cycle is shortened and the forest doesn't take root again, tenacious *alang-alang* grass takes hold and depletes the soil of all nourishment, rendering it useless for *any* kind of farming.

The *ladang* system requires roughly 10 times the area needed for wet-rice growing because large tracts of land are held by relatively small numbers of farmers. In most parts of the world, this shifting-farming means moving villages and a nomadic existence, but in Indonesia most *ladang* farmers live in permanent villages. *Ladang* usually fosters clans or genealogical communities as are found on Flores, Sulawesi, and Timor. Because of the pressure of population and the introduction of improved agricultural methods, this dry-fields cultivation is giving way all over Indonesia to the more intensive wet-rice cultivation, called *sawah.*

Sawah

This type of wet-rice cultivation is a spectacular form of agriculture which often looks like a soft green stairway climbing into the sky. Although it can be utilized up to l600 m above sea level, *sawah* is commonly found in the monsoon areas of the low-lying plains—the water supply being more plentiful and more regular. Because such complicated irrigation systems have always needed a despot to manage them efficiently, *sawah* cultivation has given rise in Indonesia's history to strong territorial agrarian communities supporting an aristocratic hierarchy headed by kingships who based their rule on divine right. Technically very intricate and delicate to manage, this system of complex waterworks is more economical than *ladang* in terms of rice output per acre, able to support some of the highest rural population densities in the world. Nowhere has *sawah* been better perfected than on Java and Bali, because nowhere is there so little land available to accommodate the high birthrate. Two or three ricecrops a year may sometimes be planted, and *sawah* has the capacity to produce undiminished yields year after year.

Water is of supreme importance in *sawah* growing: it decomposes and aerates the soil, checks weed growth, and generally works like an aquarium. During the wet season, *sawah* is planted with rice, and during the dry the same fields are often planted with corn and cassava. Backbreaking planting, weeding, plowing, and harvesting are all done by hand, elbow and knee deep in mud, with iron and wood tools. Plows to turn the soil are worked by *kerbau* (water buffalos) except on smaller fields close to the edges of the terraces. By using a hoe, the farmer can in effect transfer the food the buffalo would eat directly to himself. In the southeastern islands, the water buffalo is driven over the fields, turning them to a slushy mire; in effect, the animal acts as the plow itself.

Many animist rites practiced today persist from the old time when people were bound by strong religious ties to their communal land. When rice is planted on Java or Bali, a small plaited figure of a fertility goddess is placed under an umbrella and incense is burned in her honor so that there will be good crops the following season. This rice goddess, *Dewi Sri,* is believed to literally dwell in the rice stalks. At harvest time the stalks must be cut in a certain way so as not to offend her. Wood-mounted, razor-like handblades *(ani ani)* are used by women who deftly conceal them in their palms so the goddess won't see them. Only 3-4 stalks at a time are cut so the rice soul will not be frightened. This method is also useful in reaping the largest percentage of yield while leaving the greatest amount of harvested crop on the field to refertilize it. Though it's grueling work, rice harvesting is a happy time.

FAUNA AND FLORA

Animal Life
There are 40 different species of mammals scattered throughout the archipelago and 150 state-supervised game parks and nature reserves. Also, if you can handle the *karma,* many hunting areas. Among its mammals are great apes such as the orangutan with its blazing orange shaggy coat, deep-black wild cattle, 35-cm-high miniature deer, clouded leopards, mountain goats *(serow),* wild wart hogs, the sun bear with a large white circle on its chest, long-snouted tapirs which gallop like stallions, tossing their heads and whinnying. The fauna of Irian Jaya (western New Guinea) resembles that of Australia: vividly colored birds of paradise, spiny anteaters, mouse-like flying possums, bandicoots. Reptiles include giant monitor lizards, the reticulated python (world's longest snake, up to 9 m long), deep croaking geckos.

Bird species number in the thousands: peacocks, pheasants, partridges, turkey-sized pigeons, jungle fowl which incubate their eggs in volcanic steam, black ibis flying in V-formations, and the hornbill of the Kalimantan jungle which sounds like a puffing locomotive when it flies. Insect forms number in the hundreds of thousands: fabulously colored butterflies, aquatic cockroaches, praying mantises like bright green banana leaves beetles in the shape of violins, submarine-diving grasshoppers, the world's most extraordinary moth, the Atlas, whose wing span measures 25 cm across, spiders which catch and devour small birds in giant webs. In Indonesia's seas are found the world's most expensive shell (The Glory of the Seas), crabs *(birgus)* which can clip down coconuts and open them on the ground, freshwater dolphins, and fish that climb mango trees looking for insects!

Plantlife
Due to its extreme geographic fragmentation, Indonesia is richer in plant species than either the American or African tropics. Its total number of flowering plant species number more than 35,000. To cite only a sample of Indonesia's floral wealth, there are 250 species of bamboo, 150 species of palm, and in the more fertile areas flowers are rampant—hibiscus, jasmine, allamanda, frangipani, bougainvillea, lotus lilies ½ m wide. Java alone has 5,000 plant species, and there are twice as many species of plants on Borneo as in all of Africa. The tall, hardwood rainforest trees of Irian Jaya rival the giant sequoias of California; banyan trees planted outside the royal cities of C. Java are connected with authority and are populated by hordes of spirits; the Corpse Plant of Sumatra smells like putrefying animal flesh; the largest bloom in the world, the *rafflesia* (1m wide), inhabits Sumatra; the luxurious vegetation of Borneo hosts the seductive colors of orchids, which glow in the perpetual twilight of the jungle. Because of the unbelievable humidity, strong sunlight, and fecund volcanic soil, when you build a fence in Indonesia 6 months later it is not a fence. It is a living wall of vegetation!

Nature Reserves
The most expedient and best way to view Indonesia's wild plant and animal life is to visit one of its 150 state-run reserves. To gain entry to these reserves, you must have permission in advance from Dinas Perlindungan dan Pengawetan Alam (the Forest Authority, or PPA for short) which has offices in Bogor (Jl. Juanda), W. Java, and in all the major towns throughout Indonesia. The authorities are loosening up, and increasingly you are even able to obtain the permits in the reserve itself. One outstanding reserve is the Ujung Kulon nature park in far western Java where you can see wild oxen, tigers, leopards, gibbons, and possibly even one of the last 1,000 remaining Javan rhinoceros. The largest of Indonesia's reserves is the

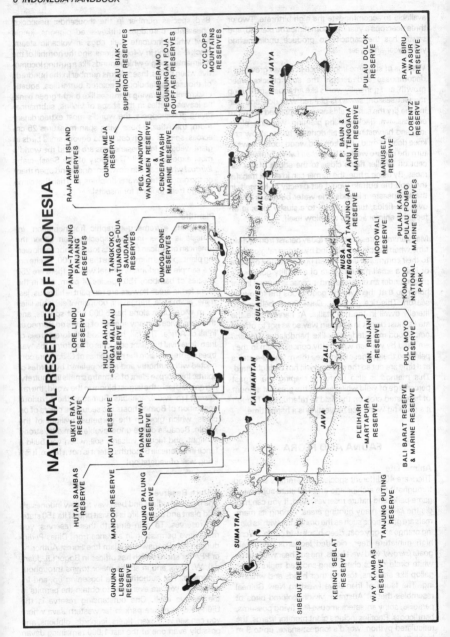

NATIONAL RESERVES OF INDONESIA

CYCLOPS MOUNTAINS RESERVES

IRIAN JAYA

PULAU DOLOK RESERVE

RAWA BIRU –WASUR RESERVE

MEMBERAMO PEGUNUNGAN FOJA ROUFFAER RESERVES

PULAU BIAK– SUPERIORI RESERVES

GUNUNG MEJA RESERVE

PEG. WANDIWOI/ WANDAMEN RESERVE & CENDERAWASIH MARINE RESERVE

P. BAUN & ARU TENGGARA MARINE RESERVE

LORENTZ RESERVE

MANUSELA RESERVE

MALUKU

RAJA AMPAT ISLAND RESERVES

PANUA–TANJUNG PANJANG RESERVES

TANGKOKO –BATUANGAS–DUA SAUDARA RESERVES

DUMOGA BONE RESERVES

PULAU KASA –PULAU POMBO MARINE RESERVES

TANJUNG API RESERVE

MOROWALI RESERVE

SULAWESI

NUSA TENGGARA

KOMODO NATIONAL PARK

LORE LINDU RESERVE

HULU–BAHAU –SUNGAI MALINAU RESERVE

GN. RINJANI RESERVE

BALI

PULO MOYO RESERVE

BUKIT RAYA RESERVE

KUTAI RESERVE

PADANG LUWAI RESERVE

KALIMANTAN

JAVA

PLEIHARI MARTAPURA RESERVE

BALI BARAT RESERVE & MARINE RESERVE

HUTAN SAMBAS RESERVE

MANDOR RESERVE

GUNUNG PALUNG RESERVE

TANJUNG PUTING RESERVE

SUMATRA

GUNUNG LEUSER RESERVE

KERINCI SEBLAT RESERVE

WAY KAMBAS RESERVE

SIBERUT RESERVES

mighty Leuser Nature Reserve of N. Sumatra, which still has extensive tracts of land classified as "unexplored." The largest lizard in the world, the Komodo Dragon *(Varanus Komodoensis)* lives in sanctuaries on Komodo and adjacent islands in the Flores Sea E of Bali between Flores and Sumbawa.

In addition to these wildlife parks are also many bird sanctuaries. Chief among them are the small coastal islets of Dua, Rambut, and Bokor, all within easy reach of Jakarta. Second best to seeing these reserves and sanctuaries is to visit one of the country's zoos, the best of which are found in Jakarta, Yogya, Bandung, and Surabaya on Java. If paleozoology is your interest, in the Sangiran area around Solo (C. Java), ancient fossils of rhinoceros and elephant are found in great abundance. It was along C. Java's Solo River where skeletal remains of the erect ape man, *pithecanthropus erectus,* were found in the 19th C., a discovery which rewrote Darwin's theory of evolution.

HISTORY

When you read Indonesian history, you read world history. This country is a subtle blending of every culture that ever invaded it—Chinese, Indian, Melanesian, Portuguese, Polynesian, Arabian, English, Dutch, and American. Indonesia's history is a story of wave after wave of migrations of peoples who either absorbed earlier arrivals, killed them off, or pushed them into less favorable regions such as deep forests, high mountains, or remote islands (where many tribes are found to this day). This ongoing and unending process explains Indonesia's astounding ethnic diversity.

Prehistory

Java was one of the earliest places in the world where man lived. In I891 the fossil skull of an ape man was discovered at Trinil in C. Java. This erect near-man lived at a time when Europe was under ice, most of Indonesia was a part of Asia, and the Sunda Shelf was above water. He walked to Java, which was then a high mountainous island covered in wild jungle. This species of very early man ranged from Africa all the way N to the glacial border of Europe and E to China some 500,000 years ago at the very beginning of the Pleistocene Period. Charcoal and charred bones indicate he used fire and made crude flint heads. This *Homo erectus* was not an ancestor of present-day Indonesians but a race all its own that has vanished; either he couldn't adapt or was wiped out by more advanced incoming species. Excavations at Sangiran (N of Solo, C. Java) uncovered an even more primitive type than *Homo erectus.* In 1931, at Ngandong (near Trinil), 11 skullcaps were found; more advanced than *Homo erectus,* these were the so-called Solo Man. All 11 skullcaps had been deliberately cracked open at their bases: Solo Man was probably a brain-eating cannibal. Found with him was an astonishingly rich fossil bed of 23,000 mammalian bones, mostly of extinct oxen, elephants, and hippos. Also uncovered were scrapers, borers, choppers, and stone balls used in slings.

Negritos, a pygmy people who began to radiate through the islands some 30,000 years ago, were the first known human migrants into Indonesia. No one knows from where they came. There are still genetic traces of these short, woolly haired, round-headed people in the jungles of E. Sumatra, the uplands of the Lesser Sundas (Nusatenggara), and in the remote highlands of Irian Jaya (western New Guinea). More advanced than the Negritos were the 2 human skulls found at Wajak along the Brantas River in E. Java. The first true ancestor of present-day Indonesians, the Wajak Man was the earliest known *Homo sapiens* found on Java; he lived about 10,000-12,000 years ago. Wajak Man, who replaced the Negritos, might have been an Australoid type.

The Ancient Peoples

Ancestors of the present-day Malay peoples of Indonesia had been living in what is now Kampuchea and Vietnam and were pushed toward Indonesia by population pressure from the north. Anthropologists say they came in 2 great waves, spreading through Sumatra, Borneo, Celebes, and Java. First came the so-called proto-Malayans (caucasoid Malays), possessing a neolithic-level culture. They are represented today by the Batak of Sumatra, the Toraja of Sulawesi, and the Dayak of interior Borneo. Next the deutero-Malays (more of a mongoloid type) arrived. These were carriers of a more developed Bronze Age civilization from Indochina. The deutero-Malays are represented in all the ports and coasts of the Greater Sunda Islands of Sumatra and Java. Both waves originate from the same stock of people, but the proto-Malays were thought to be a culturally retarded stock who fled Indochina before they learned civilization. Today, generally speaking, the proto-Malays occupy the agricultural interiors while the deutero-Malays settled the coastal regions. These 2 types in turn greatly mixed with the earlier Australoid immigrants.

Even before Christ was born, Indonesian life was already well established. Bronze and iron have been in use in some parts of these islands since at least 2500 B.C.; neolithic peoples made huge bronze drums and chopping hoes. They knew how to grow rice, use bamboo pipes for irrigation and buffalos for drawing plows. There were matriarchal societies and

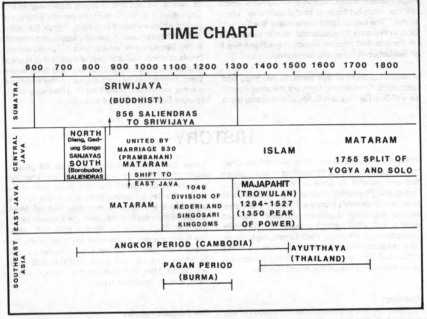

TIME CHART

	600 700 800 900 1000 1100 1200 1300 1400 1500 1600 1700 1800
SUMATRA	**SRIWIJAYA** **(BUDDHIST)** **856 SALIENDRAS TO SRIWIJAYA**
CENTRAL JAVA	**NORTH** Dieng, Gedung Songo **SANJAYAS** **SOUTH** (Borobudor) **SALIENDRAS** / **UNITED BY MARRIAGE 830 (PRAMBANAN) MATARAM** SHIFT TO / **ISLAM** / **MATARAM** **1755 SPLIT OF YOGYA AND SOLO**
EAST JAVA	**MATARAM** EAST JAVA **1049 DIVISION OF KEDERI AND SINGOSARI KINGDOMS** / **MAJAPAHIT (TROWULAN) 1294-1527 (1350 PEAK OF POWER)**
SOUTHEAST ASIA	**ANGKOR PERIOD (CAMBODIA)** **AYUTTHAYA (THAILAND)** **PAGAN PERIOD (BURMA)**

organized villages under *adat* law. These ancient Indonesians could navigate by the stars as far as India, they had animist beliefs and worshipped ancestors, there was puppetry, music, coil pottery, cloth, fighting arts. They absorbed war fleets, political systems, and religions.

THE HINDU/BUDDHIST PERIOD

Indian chroniclers wrote of Java as early as 600 B.C., and the ancient Hindu epic, the *Ramayana*, also gives mention of Indonesia. By the 2nd century A.D. Indian traders had arrived in S. Celebes, Sumatra, and Java. By this time the stage was set for Hinduism. Bronze Age Indonesians had many culturally similar traits that could make the Indian culture easier to absorb; they could assimilate Indian civilization and religion without feeling hopelessly backwards. At the time of its colonializing efforts, India, considered the pinnacle of civilization, was at the apex of its cultural vigor. The local rulers of Indonesian feudal states most likely invited high-caste and learned Brahmans to migrate and work as a literate bureaucracy. Indian influences touched only the ruling classes; there was no significant impact on the rural people, who have always leaned more toward animism. By the 4th C., Indonesians were using the S. Indian Pallava script to carve Mahayana Buddhist inscriptions.

Sanskrit loan words found in the Indonesian language today indicate the specific contributions Indians made during their period of influence in the archipelago, which lasted 1400 years (200 to 1600 A.D.): healing practices, astronomy, navigation techniques, the potter's wheel, horses and elephants, textile dyeing, plank boats and wheeled carts, figure sculpture and decorative arts, written literature, monumental architecture, spices for cooking (tumeric and cardamom). Many legal practices were also carried to Indonesia, as well as numerous titles relating to social rank and regal pomp. The Indians spread the use of wet-rice cultivation, which the Tamils themselves had mastered by 450 B.C. Sanskrit words such as *angsa* (duck) and *gembala* (shepherd) show that they introduced techniques of animal husbandry. Glass was also brought by the Indians: *kaca*, or mirror, is a Sanskrit word.

But their most far-reaching and significant exports were metaphysics, philosophy, and the Hindu concept of a divine ruler with unchecked powers. The Indians practiced a more integrated religious system than Indonesians at the time, a heirarchy of Gods with specific roles to play. By the 5th C., Brahmanist cults worshipping Shiva had sprung up on Java and temples were built to confirm the authority of Hindu religious beliefs. By the 9th C., syncretism appeared on Java, a belief system which regarded both Shiva and Buddha as incarnations of the same being. In the 10th C. students were sent to the great Buddhist University of Nalanda in NE India, and Indonesians even went as far as Tibet for learning and philosophy. The Sriwijaya Hindu Kingdom rose in southern Sumatra during the 12th and 13th centuries and exercised a wide sphere of influence over all of SE Asia. On Java, early Hindu states rose and fell—Pajajaran, Saliendra, Kediri, Singosari. Most of them, although very rich and powerful, were mainly coastal empires.

Advent Of Buddhism

Indian missionaries took Buddhism to Indonesia at a time when it was declining in India itself. Indonesians were ready to go beyond the confines of their indigenous religions. Though adherents of Hinduism and Buddhism were hard and fast enemies in India, in most instances in Indonesia followers of these 2 religions lived side-by-side in peace, blending with and borrowing from one another. On the fertile ground of SE Asia, Mahayana Buddhism evolved into a new kind of polytheism. Sumatra remained primarily Buddhist, but Hinduism eventually took over on Java. Extant races of Buddhist temples are found in the Padanglawas complex in S. Tapanuli, S. Sumatra, in Buddhist *candi* scattered throughout Java (Mendut, Pawon, Sari, Jago), culminating in the largest Buddhist monument in the world, the imposing Borobudur stupa of C. Java built in the 9th century by Buddhist Saliendras.

The Majapahit

The Indonesian-Indian era reached its apogee in the 14th C. Javanese Majapahit Empire, the Golden Age of Indonesian history. Though it thrived for barely 100 years (1292-1398), Majapahit was Indonesia's greatest state because it aimed at Indonesian unification and an Indonesian identity. Gaja Mada, the famous prime minister of this E. Javanese empire, worked so hard in his life to unite all the islands that it took 4 officials to do his job when he died. During this last mighty Java-Hindu kingdom, Indonesian sculpture and architecture suddenly veered away from Indian prototypes and a revitalized native folk art emerged. When Islamic traders arrived in the 15th and 16th centuries, they found all the great islands of Indonesia to be a complex of well-established Indianized kingdoms.

Even though Indian cultural traditions had ostensibly disappeared from the island of Java by the 16th C. (as a result of Islamization), much is still visible from Buddhist-Hindu times. The *kraton* courts of Solo and Yogya are today hardcore enclaves of Java-Hindu culture. The religion and culture of Bali, the *gamelan* orchestra, and the 5-note scale were also inherited from India. *Bopati* was the term used by the old Hindu aristocracy for a governor of a province, and the Indonesian *bupati* holds this power to this day. Many motifs and styles of the previous Hindu-Javanese culture permeate Indonesian art: all over Java you can see gates leading to the mosques and cemeteries of

the Islamic high saints constructed in Hindu-style. Indian epic poems have been adapted into living Indonesian theater and Indian mythic heros dominate the plots. Place names of Indian derivation are found all over Indonesia. Indian scripts persisted until Indonesian was latinized in the 20th C., and Sanskrit words still abound in many Indonesian regional languages. Indonesia's present state motto is a Sanskrit phrase. And even the national emblem of Indonesia, the largest and most populated Muslim state in the world, is the mythical bird Garuda—the mount of the Hindu God Vishnu!

ISLAM

Arabs started arriving in Indonesia as far back as the 4th century A.D., even before the birth of Mohammed (about 571 A.D.), to take part in the trade between the great civilizations of the Mediterranean, India, SE Asia, and China. In the 14th C. the Mohammedans consolidated their hold on Gujerat in India and began to expand their trade considerably in Indonesia. This was the beginning of the Islamic period in the archipelago. Islam caught on in far northern Sumatra first, then spread to Java. The capture of Melaka by the Portuguese in 1511 scattered Muslim merchants all over insular SE Asia, taking their faith with them and spreading Islam even farther afield. Islam first took hold most solidly in those areas of Indonesia which had been least affected by the Hindu civilizations of the past: the north-central Java coast, Banten in W. Java, and the Aceh and Minangkabau regions of N. and W. Sumatra. The Hindu princes of Java were probably first converted to Islam by a desire for trade, wealth, and power. Principalities on the N. Java coast employed skillful Arab harbormasters to run shipping warehouses for them.

The *raja* would be converted first, then the people would take up the faith of their ruler en masse. The converted rulers adjusted to indigenous pre-literary sentiments by permitting sultans to be worshipped as saints after death. Pre-Islamic signal towers became Muslim minarets and the native Indonesian meeting hall was transformed into a mosque. Rulers placed their royal *gamelan* in the mosques and people came to listen, then stayed to be converted to the new religion. Demak was the first important Javanese city to turn Muslim (in 1477), followed by Cirebon (in 1480). In 1487, a coalition of Muslim princes attacked what was left of the Hindu Majapahit Empire. By the end of the 15th C. there were 20 Muslim kingdoms over the entire archipelago and Islam was here to stay.

The Lure Of Islam

Indonesia is one of the few countries where Islam didn't supplant the existing religion purely by military conquest. Its appeal was first and foremost psychological. Radically egalitarian and possessing a scientific spirit, when Islam first arrived in these islands it was a forceful revolutionary concept that freed the common man from his Hindu feudal bondage. Until Islam arrived, he lived in a land where the king was an absolute monarch who could take away his land and even his wife at whim. Islam, on the other hand, taught that all men in Allah's eyes are made of the same clay, that no man shall be set apart as superior. There were no mysterious sacraments or initiation rites, nor was there a priest class. With its direct and personal relationship between man and God, Islam possessed great simplicity. *Everyone* could talk to Allah. Though Mohammed was His only Prophet, each follower was an equal of Mohammed. Islam is ideally suited to an island nation; it is a trader's religion which stresses the virtues of prosperity and hard work. It allows for high individual initiative and freedom of movement in order to take advantage of trade opportunities everywhere. The religion is tied to no locality and God can be worshipped anywhere, even on the deck of a ship. It was (and is) an easy religion to join. All that was needed was a simple declaration of faith, the *syahadat*: "There is no God but Allah and Mohammed is His only Prophet." It compelled a man to bathe and to keep clean, encouraged him to travel out to see the world (to Mecca), and, in short, exerted a democratizing, modernizing, civilizing influence over the peoples of the archipelago. Islam also had a great political attraction. It was first adopted by coastal princes as a counter to the threat of Portuguese and Dutch Christianity, as a rallying point of identity. Islam really caught on in the early 16th C. as a force against Portuguese colonial domination, then 100 years later as a force against the Dutch, always spreading just ahead of the foreign overlords.

Islam And The Arts

During the process of Islamicization in the 15th and 16th centuries, the arts were deeply affected. The Indian period is known for its emphasis on the performing arts, but during the Islamic period the emphasis shifted more to the written arts. Arabic literary styles (and many themes) provided models upon which a local literature could be based. Stimulated by the sultans of the new central and north coast Javanese Islamic states, the textile-decorating arts and armoury flourished, as well as some high-quality decoration in plaster, stone and brick (at Sendangduwar, near Bojonegoro; at Mantingan, near Jepara). *Wayang* and *gamelan* went through their most refined development during the fully Islamic 18th century. Because Islam prohibited the worship of idols (most of the seated Buddha heads at Borobudur were knocked off by Muslim vandals) and portraits of human beings, early Islamic art was made to be stiff and formal. Only trees and flowers could be represented, never living creatures. This prohibition has been the main source of uniqueness and intrigue in Indonesian art forms, and even on today's *batik* you often see the wings of birds and the antlers of deer, but not the outlines of the animals themselves. On the debit side, because of the puritanism of Islam, Indonesia has a short tradition in anatomical painting and the public still finds nude drawing and painting offensive.

THE PORTUGUESE PERIOD

The Portuguese were the first bearers of European civilization to Indonesia. Carrying their God with them to be embraced by the heathens, these vigorous and bold southern Europeans arrived in Indonesia a full 100 years before the Dutch. The Portuguese period lasted only about 150 years, from about 1512. Portuguese was the *lingua franca* of the archipelago in the 16th C. and initially even Dutch merchants had to learn the language in order to trade. Portuguese involvement was largely commercial and did not involve territorial expansion; they set up fortified outposts in sheltered harbors of islands to guard their trade routes and to offer respite and repair facilities for their fleets. Keeping the upper hand by virtue of their superior striking power, weaponry, and navigation techniques, the Portuguese were at first simply pirates who acquired tribute and booty, exploiting whatever commodities they came upon: slaves, gold, textiles, spices, ivory. The Portuguese period was of small significance economically and had little effect on the great intra-Asian trade route that stretched like a giant artery from Arabia to Nagasaki. In 1570, they murdered the sultan of Ternate in the hopes that they would gain more favors with his successor. The inhabitants revolted and threw them off the island, the beginning of Portuguese decline in Indonesia. The sun set permanently on Portuguese possessions in the area when Portugal decolonized East Timor in 1974. Indonesian troops invaded, occupied, and subjugated that last anachronistic stronghold of Portuguese culture in December 1975.

What did the Portuguese leave behind? For their small numbers and brevity of their tenure, the Portuguese had a deep impact. Much musical influence is evident: *kroncong* music, named after the sound of a guitar strumming, is still a popular folk entertainment in Jakarta. The Indonesian language is sprinkled with hundreds of other Portuguese loan words; *mentega* (butter), *pesta* (festival), *garpu* (fork), *sepatu* (shoe), *gereja* (church), *meja* (table); as well as many geographic locations (Flores, Roti, Pombo, etc.). Tobacco was first brought from the New World by these medieval adventurers in the 16th century. Portuguese shipbuilding techniques and designs are still adhered to in Sulawesi and in many shipyards of Nusatenggara. Old Portuguese helmets and spears

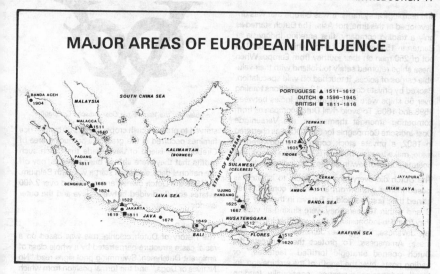

MAJOR AREAS OF EUROPEAN INFLUENCE

PORTUGUESE ▲ 1511–1612
DUTCH ● 1596–1945
BRITISH ■ 1811–1816

BANDA ACEH 1904
MALAYSIA
SOUTH CHINA SEA
MALACCA 1511 1640
SUMATRA
PADANG 1811
KALIMANTAN (BORNEO)
TERNATE 1512 1605 TIDORE
STRAIT OF MAKASSAR
SULAWESI (CELEBES)
CERAM
AMBON 1511
JAYAPURA
IRIAN JAYA
BENGKULU 1685 1824
UJUNG PANDANG
BANDA SEA
JAVA SEA
1522
JAKARTA 1619 1811
1625 1667
1678 JAVA 1849
NUSATENGGARA 1512
ARAFURA SEA
BALI
FLORES 1512 1620

are kept as family heirlooms by descendants. Large numbers of Florinese and Amboinese have Portuguese blood. Scores of 16th and 17th C. Portuguese forts are scattered around Maluku and other eastern islands.

THE ENGLISH PERIOD

In the early part of the 17th C. the English were direct rivals to the Dutch in the exploitation of the East Indies. The 2 great maritime powers even kept outposts alongside each other in Banten, Makassar, Jakarta, and on Ambon. Although treaties made in Europe dictated that cooperation between the 2 chartered companies were to be peacefully regulated, in the actual theater of conflict they were far from amicable partners. The underlying rivalry and enmity erupted at last on the island of Ambon in 1623 when all the personnel of the English factory were tortured and executed. This "Ambon Massacre" was heatedly blown up by the diplomatic circles of the time and vivid woodcut illustrations were printed in the popular press which enraged the English public.

Almost 200 years later during the Napoleonic Wars, Java was occupied (1811-1816) by English Expeditionary Forces and the sultan's *kraton* in Yogya (C. Java) was stormed and subdued. The young and energetic Lord Raffles, founder of Singapore, was then appointed governor. He immersed himself enthusiastically in the history, culture and customs of Indonesia, uncovering the famous Borobudur temple and even meticulously recording the cannibalistic

habits of the Batak of northern Sumatra. But because England wanted to prepare Holland against attack by France and Prussia, most of the Indies were again handed over to the Dutch in 1816. Raffles tried to perpetuate British interests in the islands (principally in Bengkulu, SW Sumatra), but eventually the English abandoned Indonesia altogether and by 1824 had shifted their focus of power to Singapore. The English made another brief and ignominious appearance on Java in 1945 to accept the official Japanese surrender of the islands and to keep order, but within several months they were accused (accurately) by the Indonesians and the world of being pawns of the Dutch and had embarrassingly extricated themselves from their awkward role by 1946.

It is a fiction of English historical scholarship that during the English period many significant, long-lasting economic, land, and humanitarian reforms were introduced. The English presence lives on today in hundreds of words of English derivation found in *Bahasa Indonesia: stop* (stop), *bis* (bus), *mobil* (car), *universitas* (university), *pena* (pen); and in the name of Yogya's main street, Malioboro, a corruption of Marlborough, a victorious English general in the Napoleonic Wars.

THE DUTCH PERIOD

By the time European traders reached the East Indies in the late 16th C., it had government, cities, monumental temples, irrigation systems, handicrafts, orchestras, shipping, art, literature, cannon-fire, harems, and astrological systems. It was Europe that was undeveloped at this time, not Asia. The Dutch started as only a trading company, first entering Indonesia at Banten in 1596 with just 4 ships which had lost 145 out of 250 men on their journey from Europe. When these ships returned safely to Holland with their valuable cargos of spices, it touched off wild speculation. Backed by private companies, 12 expeditions totaling over 65 ships were sent to the East Indies between 1598 and 1605. To avoid rival Dutch companies from competing amongst themselves, the Vereenigde Oost-Indische Compagnie (or the VOC) was chartered in 1602, a private stock company empowered to trade, make treaties, build forts, maintain troops, and operate courts of law in all the East Indies lands.

The Dutch did everything they could to isolate this closed insular world from all outside contact. They gained their first foothold in Batavia in the early 17th C. and within 10 years they were sinking all vessels they found in Indonesian waters, whether Indian, Malay, Javanese, Portuguese, Japanese, Chinese, Siamese, Ammanese. To protect their interests the Dutch opened strategic fortified "factories," or trading posts, over the length of the archipelago. Internal Indonesian dynasties, continually feuding amongst themselves, were easy prey for such a strong external force, and by the mid-17th C. the Dutch found themselves the new masters of huge amounts of unintended and unexpected territory. When sultans asked for Dutch arms and assistance to help put down a rival sultan or usurper, the Dutch would always assist—gaining more land in the bargain. Using a combination of arms, treaties, treachery, and puppets, they became increasingly more involved in the internal affairs of Indonesian states.

Dutch Hegemony

Not content with mere trading as middlemen and carriers, the Dutch began to seek control of the very sources of production. New crop plants were introduced and a plantation agriculture was established and expanded. During their efforts to develop a coffee crop in W. Java in 1723, the Dutch appointed supervisors to organize production, the beginning of a Dutch administrative system in Indonesia. With the bankruptcy of the VOC in 1799 because of corruption and mismanagement, it was gradually replaced by institutionalized imperialism in the form of a huge bureaucracy of colonial civil servants. The commercial enterprise had become a colonial empire. An infamous forced cultivation system, the Culture System, was instituted by the Dutch in 1830, and soon not only coffee, but also sugar, indigo, pepper, tea and cotton were raised to supply the demand in Europe. During this period virtually all of Java was turned into a vast state-owned labor camp run somewhat like the 17th C. slave plantations of southeastern United States. Javanese farmers were even

emblem for the Vereenigde Oost-Indische Compagnie

starved to produce cash crops: in 1849-50 serious rice famines occurred in the great rice-producing area of Cirebon. The island of Java made the Dutch such profits that they were able to build railways, pay off the national debt, and even start a war with Belgium. By 1938 the Dutch owned and controlled over 2,400 estates equally divided between Java and the outer islands.

Colonial Rule

The history of Dutch colonial rule was based on a racial caste structure perpetrated by a whole class of emigrant Dutchmen. Swimming pool signs read "No Natives or Dogs," and the formal position from which to address a Dutch master was from the floor. The Dutch regarded Indonesians as "half-devil, half-child"; they carried their White Man's Burden with pride. In exchange for the natives' work and for the wealth of their land, the Dutch would bestow upon the Indonesians all the benefits of white civilization: their education, technology, social order, arts, even let the Indonesians love their God. Less aloof than the French or British, the Dutch ruled their 68 million subjects (in 1940) rigidly and efficiently, paying the peasants meager wages, and doing little to educate the people. Under Dutch rule no higher education was available until the 1920s when 3 colleges were finally established. By 1940, about 90% of the people were illiterate, only 2 million children were in schools in a country of 68 million, and only 630 Indonesians had graduated from high school. The Dutch, running their immense island empire with just 30,000 government officials, lived in big, stolid, 1-story houses and plantation homes maintained by numerous servants. They washed down huge lunches with vast quantities of beer and gin, wore native costume around the house, and freely intermarried with the natives. The Netherlanders could point to Indonesians with pride as a happy people weaned from savagery, reared to a prosperous independence by a system so well-understood by the Dutch—a paternal despotism.

The hangover of the Dutch 300-year presence is still with the people to this day. This is especially evident on Java which was colonized for the longest period. Tourists are still greeted with *Belanda! Belanda!*, a Portuguese word which originally meant "Hollander," but now has come to mean any white person. And boys still call male travelers by the honorific *Om,* which is Dutch for "uncle." The imperiousness of Dutch administration began to soften in the early 20th C. with the implementation of their humanitarian-inspired Ethical Policy which showed more of a desire to begin a true partnership with the Indonesian people. But the colonialists never really considered handing these regions over to the indigenous peoples. As a governor-general of the Netherlands Indies solemnly pronounced in the 1930s: "We Dutch have been here for 300 years, and we shall remain here for another 300!"

NATIONALISM

Intellectuals and aristocrats were the earliest nationalists; the peasants have always accepted authority in Indonesian history, no matter whose. Diponegoro, the eldest son of a Javanese sultan, was the country's first nationalist leader. In 1825, after the Dutch had built a road across his estate and committed various other abuses, he embarked on a holy war against them. The man was a masterful guerrilla tactician, and both sides waged a costly war of attrition and scorched-earth policy in which 15,000 Dutchmen and 250,000 Indonesians died, mostly from diseases. At one point during this war the Dutch even considered pulling out of Java. Diponegoro fought for 5 years until he was treacherously lured into negotiations and arrested. His face is now on coins and street signs, and an Army Division is even named after him. Certainly he became one of the nationalists' most important symbols. But it was the daughter of a nobleman, Raden Kartini, who first expressed publicly, at the beginning of this century, the right of Indonesians to have the same access to knowledge and Western ideas as Europeans had. Although filled with self-pity at being a pampered princess, her *Letters* (first published in 1911) written to a literate Dutch couple were sensitive, visionary, and full of fire. They caused people in both Europe and Asia to wake up to the new spirit that was in the air. Kartini, also celebrated as Indonesia's first woman's emancipationist, died in childbirth at age 24. Her memory and ideals are kept alive each 21 April when parades, programs, and social activities are held in her honor all over Indonesia.

Early 20th C. Nationalism

Indonesians knew that something was in the wind for Asia when little Japan defeated the colossus Russia in 1905. Indonesia didn't pass completely into Dutch hands until 1911, and as soon as the Dutch got it all together, they started to lose it. In the mistaken belief that to-know-us-is-to-love-us, selected Indonesians from high-bred families were sent to Holland for higher education. Many of these same Western-educated Indonesians later became fiery nationalists: by

providing education for Indonesians, the Dutch had made themselves redundant. By the time WW I came along, a number of nationalist organizations had sprung up suddenly and almost simultaneously, revealing the extreme dissatisfaction and impatience the Javanese masses had for the colonial regime. The Javanese were secretly waiting for a *Ratu Adil,* a Righteous Prince who would free them from their oppressors.

Budi Utomo (High Endeavor), formed in 1908, was a society whose members came largely from the Western-educated Javanese elite. A religious organization called Muhammadiyah followed in 1912, an attempt to blend Western technology and culture with Islamic thought. But these were intellectuals' societies and had little to do with the ordinary man. An organization of middle-class traders started the Sarekat Islam (Muslim Society) on a nation-wide basis in 1912. Originally intended to help Indonesian *batik* and textile businessmen meet growing Chinese competition, Sarekat Islam grew at a spectacular rate into the first mass political organization in Indonesia; by 1917 it had 800,000 members. Momentum was building.

The PNI (Indonesian National Party) was started in 1926, an ex-engineer named Sukarno as its chairman. With his oratorical power and dominating, charismatic style, Sukarno soon emerged as Indonesia's most forceful political personality. PNI wanted complete independence for the Indonesian people, a government elected by them and responsible to them. It advocated achieving this right through Gandhi-style non-cooperation. But with the world depression of 1929, the Dutch were in no mood to bargain. They were determined to make up for all their losses by increasing the exploitation of Indonesia's natural resources. A police state, enforced by a ruthlessly efficient secret police, was imposed throughout the islands. Increasingly repressive measures against nationalist leaders were becoming effective as men like Sukarno, Hatta, and Sjahrir were rounded up, exiled, released, then rearrested. The Dutch broke up political parties and waived petitions. Anti-Dutch feelings grew. In 1940, after the Germans invaded the low countries, the capitulation of Holland had a shocking, sobering effect on the Dutch community in Indonesia. To the Indonesians the Dutch suddenly didn't seem so powerful anymore. But instead of beginning to improve relations with Indonesians to present a united front against a possible Japanese invasion, the Dutch continued to be resolutely repressive.

Invasion Of The Indies

With the crippling of the U.S. Pacific Fleet at Pearl Harbor, the subsequent conquest of the Philippines and the capture of Singapore, the Japanese had brought the war right to the doorstep of the Dutch East Indies. And the loss of the British destroyers — the *Prince of Wales* and *Repulse* — left the Netherlands East Indies wide open for attack. The whole of the Indies suddenly became militarized. In January 1942 Japanese landed troops on Celebes and Borneo. In Batavia, the Bank of Java—largest and most powerful bank in SE Asia—moved the contents of its vaults on to the cruiser *Sumatra* which sailed for the Dutch West Indies. By February of that year, starting with a parachute assault on Palembang, the Japanese launched a full-scale invasion of Sumatra. The crucial battle for Java was joined on 27 Feb. when a small force of 14 Allied ships went out to meet a superior Japanese invasion fleet in the Sunda Strait and were blown out of the ocean. On 1 March 1942, Japanese forces landed in Batavia practically without a fight. The last transmission from the Indies was a commercial radio broadcast from Java: "We are closing down now," the voice quavered. "Goodbye 'til better times. Long Live the Queen!" By mid-March the Japanese had overrun Java and the Dutch Commander-in-Chief surrendered. Overnight Dutch power and prestige plummeted in the eyes of Indonesians.

The Japanese Occupation

The Indonesians were at first gratified that their Asian brothers had freed them by overthrowing the Dutch. The Japanese immediately backed the nationalists and orthodox Muslims, the 2 groups most opposed to Dutch rule. The new masters even spoke reassuringly of one day granting Indonesia its own independence. But the Japanese soon showed themselves to be even more ruthless, fascist, and cruel than the Dutch had ever been. Without even being at war with Japan, Indonesia suffered terribly at the hands of the conquerors. They were an occupying military power; workers were made to bow to Japanese soldiers and forced to wear identification tags. To work in the jungles of Burma and Malaysia as slave laborers, the invaders conscripted 270,000 young men, of which only 70,000 returned. The Japanese also routinely rounded up Indonesian women to serve as prostitutes in their army camp brothels; 10,000 children were produced in liasons between Japanese soldiers and white Dutch women. Indonesia was included in the "Greater Southeast Asia Co-Prosperity Sphere," which in reality meant it was to be exploited of every possible resource. The islands were plundered of all raw materials: oil, rubber, rice, and other products, and their cities were stripped clean of gold, jewels, as well as tons of wrought-iron fences and ornament, shipped to Japan and smelted down to make pig iron for the war machine.

During their occupation, the Japanese also encouraged Indonesian nationalism and allowed political boards to form, but only with the intention of using these for their own war aims. Sukarno, who was retained by the Japanese to help them govern, cleverly used every opportunity to educate the masses, inculcating in them a nationalist consciousness and fervor. At first it was forbidden to speak in public any other language but Japanese and Indonesians were forced

A stamp issued in 1944 during the Japanese occupation of Indonesia (1942-45), stating "Sacrifice for the Great Struggle." An extra 10 sen was added to the price of the stamp as a contribution to the war fund of the Japanese Imperial Forces to pay for warplanes.

to learn it. But when the Japanese realized how difficult this was to implement, they began to promote *Bahasa Indonesia*, which was eventually used to spread their propaganda out to the smallest villages. The language grew to become a gigantic symbol, disseminated on an ever wider basis, further unifying the islands. The Japanese also created an armed homeguard, later to become the core of a revolutionary militia which would fight the Dutch upon their return. As the war progressed and the Japanese began losing the battles, more and more power passed into the hands of Indonesians.

The British Role

Eleven days after Hiroshima, on 17 Aug. 1945, Sukarno and Hatta declared independence in Jakarta and the Republic of Indonesia was born. Many Indonesians believed that the bomb was heaven-sent as it caused Japan's sudden surrender and prevented so much suffering in Indonesia. The war ended and fearing the return of the Dutch, the Indonesians desperately tried to secure as many Japanese weapons as they could, and even engaged in small-scale battles against the Japanese. Meanwhile, remnants of a shattered Dutch colonial army, weakened by the war, tried to regain a foothold on their precious islands; many Indonesians feared that armed Dutch troops would infiltrate back into Indonesia under the British flag. The British, who first arrived in Jakarta as early as 29 Sept. 1945, were charged with the thankless task of disarming Japanese troops, shipping them back to Japan, and maintaining order. Duped into fighting for the Dutch, they got more than they bargained for in bloody running street battles with Indonesian fighters, culminating in the furious month-long Battle of Surabaya. Convinced that the republic was supported wholeheartedly by the Indonesian masses, the British informed the Republican government that they were responsible for law and order inland. This constituted de facto recognition of the new Indonesian government by the British.

The Revolution

The Dutch were back and they intended to start up just where they had left off. But they were mistaken; it was not going to be business as usual. Once the Japanese army left their posts, bands of politically aligned young people (laskar) sprang up. The total strength of these irregular armed troops surpassed many times the strength of the official Republican army. During the internal revolution against the Dutch (1945-1949), communications were non-existent and the provinces were on their own, administratively and militarily. Internationally, in the early years of the struggle, the Indonesians were almost alone in their fight against the Dutch. It was the independent Asian states, the Soviet Union, Poland, and the Arab states who gave the new republic their support, not the U.S. and other Western powers who always tried to put forth compromises and watered-down solutions. United Nations resolutions were ignored, that world body's role a fiasco.

In January 1946, Sukarno considered Jakarta too vulnerable and moved the Republic's capital to Yogya where he could depend more upon Yogya's powerful sultan for support. In April of that year negotiations began between the Dutch and the Indonesians to decide the question of independence. The Dutch only used the resulting pacts and treaties to buy time, consolidate their positions, and try to gain international support. Dutch troops embarked on "pacification" exercises, attacking many key cities on Java and Sumatra in July 1947 and butchering hundreds. In 1948 an ultra-conservative government was voted into power in Holland which felt that even a so-called "free Indonesia" should be linked as closely as possible to the Netherlands—an irreconcilable position to the Republicans. In late 1948 the Dutch considered further negotiations with the Republic futile. In December, Yogya was bombed and strafed, then occupied by Dutch shock paratroopers. Sukarno and most of the members of the revolutionary cabinet were taken into "protective" custody, but 3 divisions

of the Republican army evaporated into the countryside to avoid a head-on clash.

In spite of Dutch military successes in the cities, the countryside was controlled by Republicans. Endless guerrilla attacks were launched against the Dutch. Soon, outraged world opinion rallied behind the new Republic and the UN applied real pressure. It was also realized that the amount the Dutch were spending to regain the islands and crush the patriots was embarrassingly close to the sum which the U.S. had given Holland in war reconstruction aid under the Marshall Plan. The U.S. Congress decided such backing was against their principles, withdrawing its support. Indonesian Republicans controlled the highways, the food supply, the villages; what they could not control, they burned or blew up. Merdeka! (Freedom!) was on everybody's lips. Finally, on the eve of a new decade, a high drama was played out all over Indonesia when the Dutch red, white, and blue flag was hauled down and the red and white flag of Indonesia was raised in its place. The Dutch transferred sovereignty to a free Indonesia on 27 Dec. 1949. Today, all over Indonesia, military museums commemorate with photos, dioramas, weaponry, documents and uniforms the struggle against the Dutch.

POST INDEPENDENCE

On 16 Dec. 1949, the House and the Senate unanimously elected Sukarno as President of the new Federal State of Indonesia, and on 17 Dec. Sukarno was solemnly sworn in. Indonesia was quickly recognized by most of the important states of the world and the UN admitted it as its 60th member. After all the suffering, sacrifice, and fighting, it was now time to build up the nation again. "It was not enough to have won the war," Hatta had said. "Now we must take care not to lose the peace." It would not be easy: when the Dutch were at last ousted in 1949, the Indonesians had nothing—no teachers, no higher-level civil service class, no national income. The mills and factories were closed or destroyed. There was serious fighting against secessionists, communists, and religious fanatics. As a constitutional democracy in the early 1950s, politicians who put the good of their party over the good of the country scrambled after power. The new Republic turned over cabinets every 6 months, and there was chaotic bickering and dissension among the military, religious, left-wing and conservative factions in the embryonic government. In 1955, there were 169 political parties fighting for only 257 seats!

To stop the chaos, Sukarno declared in 1956 his policy of "Guided Democracy" and the creation of a National Council made up of members he would handpick himself. Sukarno stated that the age-old In-

President Sukarno triumphantly announcing Indonesia's UN membership in 1950. A hero's burial was awarded this ex-engineer, double Gemini, lecherous leader of Indonesia from 1949 to 1965. When he was a young political activist on Java the Dutch called him "The Fighting Cock." Sukarno was a mad jumble of contradictions—prophetic powers, immense charm and learning, with a dangerous totalitarian leaning. Appointing himself a crusader against the economic and political might of the post-industrial Western nations, he initiated aggressive territorial expanionist policies against Malaysia in his Konfrontasi campaign of 1962-65. Known affectionately as Bung Karno, he had spellbinding oratorial powers, championing the cause of the ordinary man. Yet he was a preposterous hypocrite who owned 19 motorcars, kept scores of mistresses, and used to hover in his helicopter over streams where naked women bathed. It was Sukarno who inspired most of Jakarta's super-kitsch monumental architecture. The man was adulated as a god, a reincarnation of Vishnu, the ancient Hindu god. Starting shortly after the 1965 coup, in which he was implicated, the army began to systematically dismantle Sukarno's power up until his death in 1970. On the night Sukarno died, Indonesians say you could see his face in the moon and that there were electrical storms for 3 days.

donesian tradition of *gotong royong* (decision through consensus) would be best suited for Indonesia as a way of hastening the cumbersome decision-making process. Political parties and legislative bodies were abolished. The Outer Islands continued to prove unruly, claiming rightfully that the central government was neglecting them, and that Jakarta was becoming too lenient toward the communists. In Feb. 1958, W. Sumatra and N. Celebes revolted against the Jakartan centralist government, demanding more outer-island Muslim-oriented autonomy. By calling themselves anti-communists they received aid, equipment, and arms from the United States. A full-scale, though lackadaisical, civil war was under way and 70 army battalions had to be mobilized to suppress the insurgents. Sukarno landed troops on the eastern coast of Sumatra and by 17 April 1958 central government troops took Padang, W. Sumatra. On 5 May Bukittinggi fell. The Irian Jaya question was brought to a head in 1961 when the Indonesian president ordered amphibian landings and paratroop drops into this Dutch-controlled territory of West New Guinea. These forays stirred the UN to action; the Netherlands turned that territory over to Indonesian administration in 1962.

"Pariah Among Nations"

By the late 1950s, Sukarno was augmenting more and more power, press censorship was introduced, politicians and intellectuals were jailed. During the early 1960s, Sukarno's government left the UN and grew violently anti-Western and militant. In order to prevent Sabah and Sarawak, the British-controlled sections of North Borneo, from joining the proposed Malaysian federation, Sukarno initiated an aggressive *konfrontasi* military campaign. Raiders were sent to attack the Malaysian peninsula and skirmishes broke out in northern Borneo between Indonesians, British, and Australian troops. Sukarno aligned himself with Communist China, parroting their official anti-imperialist line, even cutting ties with the UN.

For 20 years this visionary and mesmerizing leader had welded the islands together by adroitly playing off powerful groups against one another, his government a hectic marriage of widely disparate political ideologies. When he told his people that Marxism, nationalism, and Islam were all reconciled in one political philosophy, "Sukarnoism," they embraced it. Sukarno had squandered billions on colossal stadiums, conference halls, and Soviet-style statuary. The inflation rate was running at 650% per year; mammoth foreign debts had accumulated; opposed factions of the military, communists, Muslims, and other groups were grappling for control of the government. The political polarization between Army generals on the one side and the Indonesian Communist Party (PKI) on the other was nearing the breaking point.

The 1965 "Coup"

What happened before dawn on 1 Oct. 1965 and all the events that followed have come under increasing scrutiny over the last 20 years. The official Suharto-regime version and Western conventional scholarship would have the world believe that the PKI attempted a coup early that morning. Accumulating evidence, however, points to the possibility that it was Suharto, other Indonesian army leaders, and the CIA that actually engineered the coup. On the night of 30 Sept.

1965, 6 top generals and their aides were abducted and brutally murdered. What followed was one of the most massive retaliatory bloodbaths in modern world history. An unknown general named Suharto, with alleged secret U.S. backing, mobilized the army strategic reserve (KOSTRAD) against "the communist conspirators." The Indonesian army had never forgiven the communists for an attempted coup in 1948. While the armed forces stood aside, fanatical Muslim youth groups burned the PKI headquarters in Jakarta to the ground. Over the following months all of Java ran amuck, resulting finally in the organized mass political murdering of as many as half a million people who were shot, knifed, strangled, and hacked to death, while tens of thousands of others were imprisoned without trial. The Communist Party was obliterated. The army assumed leadership of the country, eventually developing a system of authoritarian domination and repression without precedent in Indonesia, a system which only now shows signs of slackening.

After the coup, a complete ideological and economic reversal took place, which continues to this day. In 1966 Indonesia's militant *konfrontasi* campaign with Malaysia was called off and a neutralist foreign policy was adopted. The Indonesian congress announced plans to rejoin the UN. Although his implication in the plot was never made clear, Sukarno's power was systematically undermined by the new regime until his death in June 1970. Pragmatic, shrewd, reliable Suharto is today Indonesia's head of state, a man born of humble parents in 1921 in a village near Yogya (C. Java). A family man with 6 children, Suharto is a mild-mannered speaker and keeps a low profile, a style which stands out in stark contrast to his flamboyant and magnetic predecessor. For more about the myth of the communist coup, read *Indonesia: Law, Propaganda and Terror* (Zed Press, UK) by Julie Southwood and Patrick Flanagan, and *The Indonesian Tragedy* (Graham Brash Pty. Ltd. Singapore) by Brian May.

GOVERNMENT

Indonesia is easily the most broken-up country in the world, and its sheer expanse and diversity alone make it awesomely difficult to govern. There have been revolts in one part of the archipelago or the other for the past 25 years (presently in W. Kalimantan, E. Timor, and Irian Jaya). The approximately 60,000 political prisoners also point out how below the surface and deep this country's social disunity and differences are. On the state crest are the old Sanskrit words *Bhinneka Tunggal Ika,* "We are many but we are one." This line is played hard by the country's leaders who try to bring unity to the country and spread a national consciousness by invoking nationalistic ceremonies, by claiming a mystical, divine mandate to rule, and through their national fitness program, *senam pagi* (morning exercise), practiced every morning in even the most remote hill villages. The Indonesian language is another great unifying force. And there is definitely a shared feeling of being an Indonesian, a pride in things characteristically Indonesian (Sukarno called it *Indonesianasii),* and in their vast and beautiful native land.

To bring all the diverse people of this sprawling island nation together within the political and geographic entity called "Indonesia" is still and will always be the greatest single problem facing its leaders. Along with such typical fundamental problems of a Third World developing nation as overpopulation, unemployment, corruption, dependence on world markets for key export commodities, lack of an industrial base and technical expertise, and a history of runaway inflation, the widely dispersed group of 13,000 islands has an uneven population and an unequal distribution of natural wealth. This fragmented archipelago is also

very exposed militarily—no navy or air force to speak of, and an army of only 350,000. In addition, it is a massive job trying to usher a basically feudal society into the 20th C. overnight, a job which requires constant vigilance and indoctrination. The gigantic conservatism, the low-key Indonesian temperament, the resignation of the masses—and the help of the army—keep the government in power. Resignation is in fact the Indonesians' greatest asset, giving the people the patience to take such a succession of demogogic, inept, and unjust rulers. But when one understands Indonesian attitudes toward authority, whether the Indonesian government is an authoritarian one or not isn't seen as particularly important. Indonesians instead look at whether their government satisfies them or not—food in their bellies, a roof over their heads, and cloth to cover them. They look at its substance rather than its form.

SYSTEM OF GOVERNMENT

Indonesia is now a military oligarchy run by President Suharto, but through history Indonesia has tried them all, practically every political persuasion—absolute kingship, extreme cultural conservatism, outlandish noisy political radicalism, noble revolution, Stalinist mass political butchering, parliamentary democracy, civil war, total anarchy, a hero against international aggression, and now generals with modern weaponry. You can't talk about any of Indonesia's beliefs, practices, ideals or institutions as being modern or old-fashioned because at the same time Indonesia is a very progressive and a very backward state—believ-

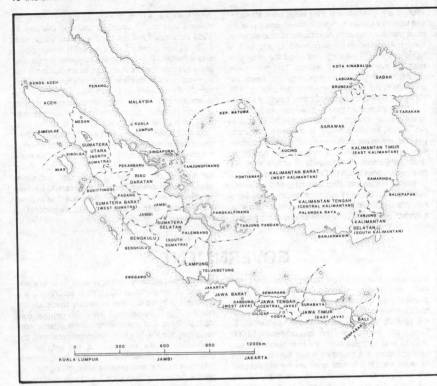

ing in myths, false messiahs, Marxist prophecy, solid traditional customs, archaic magic, chilling rationality, ultra-futuristic technology.

Pancasila

In modern times, the concept of *Pancasila* (Five Principles) has become the basis of civilized rule. The government urges all Indonesians to accept this state ideology as their fundamental philosophy, crucial to national unity. Displayed on practically every government building, the 5 *sila,* or principles, are: 1) Belief in One Supreme God; 2) a Just and Civilized Humanity; 3) Nationalism, the Unity of Indonesia; 4) Democracy, guided by the wisdom of unanimity arising from discussion *(musjawarah)* and mutual assistance *(gotong royong)*; 5) Social Justice, the equality of political rights and the rights of citizenship, as well as social and cultural equality. Since 1985, all social and political organizations have been required to adopt the *Pancasila* principles as their basic platform. Rather than hard and fast guidelines, each regime tends to interpret these 5 concepts in a way that will further its political goals. The present regime, for example, is

utilizing the Five Principles to override the legal system and impose harsh restrictions on political and religious dissent.

The State Organs

According to the text of the country's constitution, supposedly still in effect, the nation has the form of a republic with sovereignty residing in the people. The functions of the government include executive, legislative, and judicial. There is no specific separation of powers, no system of checks and balances in government. The constitution provides for a strong presidency. The highest governmental executive, the president serves a term of 5 years, and apparently may be re-elected indefinitely. In March 1988, President Suharto was re-elected to serve yet another 5 years. The cabinet, appointed by the president, with a current membership of 22, is responsible only to the president.

The president himself is directly responsible only to the MPR (Majellis Permusyawaratan Rakyat), the People's Consultative Assembly. This assembly has 980

INDONESIA'S 27 PROVINCES

members consisting of farmers, workers, students, businesspersons, clergy, the intelligentsia, armed forces, and other special interest groups, a heterogeneous body meant to represent a cross-section of society. Although empowered by the constitution with the highest authority of the state, in reality the assembly is your classic rubber-stamp parliament which meets rarely and does not decide on important issues. The president has the right to appoint members of the MPR, the very body that elects him—at least 60% of its members work for the government party and nearly 200 are either admirals, generals, or air marshalls. It's more or less a perpetuation of the colonial political structure. According to the original 1945 Constitution, elections for the MPR are to take place every 5 years when it goes into a sort of queen bee-like paroxysm of activity for 2 weeks, masquerading as a decision-making body. The last was held in 1987.

The 460-member Dewan Perwakilan Rakyat (DPR), or the House of Representatives, is the legislative branch of the state, sitting at least once a year. Although every statute should require the approval of the DPR, it is equally as impotent as the MPR. Finally, in the judiciary branch of government, the Supreme Court cannot impeach nor can it rule on the constitutionality of legislation or decrees. Administratively, Indonesia is divided into 27 provinces, each headed by a governor nominated by a provincial legislature and appointed by the central government. Akin to the U.S. states and state capitals, each province has its own capital. The provinces are further divided into regencies, subdistricts, and municipalities.

Political Parties

There are only 3 political parties of any strength in Indonesia: the government's Golkar party, the Muslim's Unite: Development Party (PPP), and the Sukarnoist/Christian Indonesian Democratic Party (PDI). The government political machine, Golkar, is all-powerful. It is a body formed to represent the armed forces, the bureaucracy, farmers, women's organizations, students, and many other "functional groups" (or Golongan Karya). Except during elections, only Golkar

1987 GENERAL ELECTIONS

General elections function essentially as pro-forma exercises to give the current regime the appearance of legitimacy within Indonesia as well as in the international community. The electoral mechanism, which functions better and more efficiently with each new election, is less an election than a "training exercise" in democracy (the president's own words). And there are definite signs that Indonesian voters are evolving into a more politically mature electorate. Even though 50,000 or more participated in frenetic party rallies in the big cities, the 3-week campaign of 1987 which led up to elections went relatively smoothly, without major rioting or bloodshed (60 had died in election-related deaths in 1982). The flags of each party — yellow for Golkar, red for PDI, and green for PPP — fluttered from crowded trucks as wild campaigners on motorcycles sped by flashing the party sign: 3 fingers for Golkar, 2 for PDI, and 1 for PPP. Everyone knew who was going to win, so the opposing parties were tolerated. At political rallies and on TV, candidates from the other parties were not allowed to criticize the president or his policies (and were pulled from the podium if they did). They also had to refrain from addressing religious, ethnic, regional, or international matters. In this election the PPP was barred from using its traditional symbol, the *Kaaba*, the building in Mecca containing the sacred black stone and regarded as the House of God.

The enthusiasm with which the opposing parties were received caught the government unawares, signaling a desire in large segments of the population for change. Even the ghost of Sukarno still haunts the Indonesian political landscape; the small Indonesian Democratic Party (PDI) exploited Sukarno's charismatic image to the maximum in the '87 elections, with surprising effect. The PDI is a shaky ragbag of Christian and nationalist parties with Sukarno's old Indonesian Nationalist Party as standard bearer. The dead dictator still holds a spell over the youth of Indonesia; thousands in Sukarno T-shirts paraded at PDI rallies in an explosion of *pemuda* (youth) power. Largest minority political party in Indonesia, the Muslim-backed United Development Party (PPP) campaigned aggressively, but was no match for Golkar. The government party was 50 times better financed than its rivals and had the use of nationwide government broadcast networks, taking over 70% of the vote. As for the outlawed PKI (Partai Komunis Indonesia), once the largest communist party outside Russia, government authorities concede in private that there is no evidence of a resurgence. Just to make sure, though, before each election it executes a few sad old communists whom they incarcerated 20 years ago to show the people that they had better vote for Golkar or the commie bugaboos might get in again.

can organize down to the village level, so if you don't vote for Golkar you don't get the new village school or ag co-op. Golkar even installs the candidates for the other 2 major parties (in 1987 picking a particularly unpopular one for the PPP). Regardless of the views of the majority of voters, in every election since the early 1970s the army has mounted an extensive campaign to guarantee that Golkar wins all levels of central and provincial legislatures. Golkar has a virtual monopoly on the political loyalty of all senior ministers, as well as Indonesia's vast civil service of 2 million. Since they are on the government payroll, and since Golkar membership is often necessary to win licenses, contracts, and promotions, civil servants owe the ruling party their unequivocal support. With brazen, uncanny precision, Golkar usually predicts that it will win so and so many votes in an upcoming election. Their prediction for April 1987 was spot on. Golkar won over 70% of the vote, while PDI surprised itself by achieving nearly 11%, and the PPP around 27%.

ADMINISTRATION— LOCAL AND FEDERAL

Gotong Royong

Gotong royong means the joint responsibility and mutual cooperation of the whole community to each of its members, all of whom work together to achieve a common end. Having its origins in much earlier times, this is an all-important principle in Indonesian life. Indonesia is made up of tens of thousands of villages and the tradition of *gotong royong* is the real grass-roots basis of political rule. Whenever fire, flood, earthquake, volcanic eruption strike, when pipelines carrying water break down or a new dam needs building or an old dam needs repairing, *gotong royong* goes immediately into effect. Men usually work with their own tools and without pay. Sometimes neighboring villagers are expected to help. If a village follows this communal organization, no household will be without land to work, employment to subsist, and food to eat. Anyone in trouble will receive help.

The system revolves around thousands of village headmen (*lurah* or *kepala desa*) throughout the land, who coordinate *gotong royong* programs and carry out government policies. These *lurah* rule by assigning friends and assistants to tasks, a sort of administration by relationships; loyalties to family, village, and friends are more important than self-advancement. The government greatly stresses this sort of "village socialism" because it makes their job so much easier, enabling the country to almost run itself. The government, for example, can't afford the enormous expense of building roads across this vast archipelago. So when roads have to be constructed in an area the government goes out to the villages and explains the advantages of having roads and asks if the locals want to do it themselves. In this way, with the villagers supplying the labor and the government the equipment and materials, thousands of kilometers of roads have been built all over Indonesia.

Musjawarah And *Mufakat*

The native political process is built on ancient customs of Javanese origin. *Musjawarah* (deliberation) and *musfakat* (agreement) are methods of resolving political, policy, and personal differences by prolonged discussion ending in unanimous decision. These methods are used both in the highest legislative body of the state (the MPR) and at the humblest village meetings. The village council of elders is the foundation on which the Indonesian version of democracy is based. Indonesia is not heir to the democratic tradition and Indonesians don't believe in and even scorn Western-style democracy where the majority of 50-plus-one or more gets their way—a virtual dictatorship of the majority. They believe that this system isn't fair to the remaining 49 or less percent of the voters. The will of the minority is just as important as that of the majority (or at least it should be), so the council just talks itself out until all parties come to an accord, too exhausted or too hoarse to discuss the issue any further. It is each person's responsibility to state his feelings, taking part in all negotiations. This technique goes very slowly, but all points of view are eventually brought together in one compromise agreement. The ideal is not always followed: even though the MPR is supposed to uphold the traditions of *musjawarah,* with all its decisions and decrees taken unanimously, in practice it tends to follow the chief executive's direction without hesitation.

The Bureaucracy

You'll find ample opportunity to observe at close quarters Indonesia's ponderous, octopus-like bureaucracy. In the out areas, you will often have to seek out information or aid from the local *camat,* or apply for a *surat jalan* from the office of the *bupati* (mayor) office. Petty officials proliferate: Indonesia is a land of a million little dictators who hold people's lives in their hands. In the higher levels, many officials, like the brilliant German-educated minister for state research and technology, Jusuf Habibie, and the dynamic minister for tourism, Joop Ave, are invaluable assets to their country. The bureaucracy is a privileged class; positions in local government carry prestige, job security, and steady pay, and openings are hotly sought after. Local authorities in Indonesia's 3,500 subdistricts and 62,900 villages function as extensions of the central government, attempting to impose Jakarta's tight political and administrative grip on local affairs. But in spite of its hierarchal appearance, the real glue which holds the whole structure of this nation's bureaucracy together is the phenomenon of *bapakism,* a father figure, the *bapak,* supervising a circle of loyal followers in a given bureaucratic office.

The Indonesians came to independence in 1949 without any experience with or concept of an indigenous and traditional structure of national power. Over the 3 centuries of their occupation, the Dutch had given Indonesians virtually no skills in administration and government service above junior levels. Indonesian officials were always allowed to decide the more inconsequential departmental matters, but for the weightier decisions in affairs of high finance and politics the Dutch decided for them. Over a period of 300 years there evolved a tradition of invariably allowing the more important decisions to always go to the top and to settle only minor problems lower down the hierarchy, a time-honored tradition which has resulted in the extreme paternalism and painfully slow decision-making process in the Indonesian bureaucracy today. The penchant for uniforms also seems to have been inherited from the Dutch because everyone has one—harbormasters, agricultural students, parking lot attendants, etc.

THE ARMED FORCES

Indonesia's armed forces, the most powerful institutionalized base of support for the country's leadership, is under the direct control of the Javanese President (Suharto) and the Ministry of Defense. As is the case in many developing countries, Indonesia is a warrior's society. Dads love to dress their little sons up in generals' uniforms adorned with medals and braids, and half the streets are named after soldiers or revolutionary heros. As was learned when the army soundly defeated the Dutch, national defense had to be built on the deterrent of a strong army that would never surrender even if it meant continuous territorial guerrilla warefare. But over the last decade the military has been streamlining its ranks, as U.S. arms merchants supply it with state-of-the-art military toys such as Harpoon and Rapier missles, A-4 Skyhawk, F-5 Tiger jets, and even the advanced F-16s. Although their soldiery often display a banana-republic appearance and lack of professionalism, the military appears to be this nation's only credible political power at present, the power structure's best source of educated and disciplined manpower. The service provides the country with its president, half of its ambassadors, two-thirds of its regional governors, half its ministers. The army calls itself the "New Order" and it isn't likely that it will soon loosen its heavy-handed grip on the reins of state.

The Army's Role

The army's continuing power and prestige in national and political affairs is a legacy of its role in the early days of the republic when it fought against the Dutch. Since the army won independence and also saved the country from both the 1948 and 1965 communist uprisings, it looks upon itself as having a sacred right and duty to monitor and safeguard that independence. Everywhere you turn in nearly every village of Indonesia you find the inevitable memorial to the brave martyrs of the revolution, as if the government never wants the people to forget to whom they owe their gratitude for freeing them. One wonders how all these dead heroes would view the present corrupt and self-seeking military regime which perceives it their god-given right to rule over Indonesia's civilian population.

The Dutch occupation of West Irian, as well as the retaliatory takeover in 1957 of Dutch businesses and property, served to greatly expand the army's role in the economy. These seizures left army officers managing plantations, mines, factories, import companies, all of which supplemented the meager funding available to the army through conventional channels. Today the Javanese "financial generals" of Indonesia own corporations, monopolies, shipping lines, hotels, mines, plantations, oil wells. These old army cronies of Suharto's hold key military slots for terms much longer than what is written into law. A number of them have even been commissioned purely for their connections with Chinese businessmen. You could say it is the "Indonesian situation," but the military is doing little to privatize its numerous holdings. See the "Economy" section.

The Army Bureaucracy
The army also considers itself a socio-political force which stabilizes the state and defines its objectives. The army sees this role enshrined in the concept of dwi-fungsi, or dual function, which calls for an army level of command corresponding to each function of the civil government from the province right down to the village. Since the majority of local officials at all levels are in some way attached to the military, dwi-fungsi ensures that the army permeates civilian life through a network of military watchdogs running parallel to the whole civilian bureaucracy, prodding their civilian counterpart when necessary. All 12 territorial military commands in the Outer Islands are under the jurisdiction of Java-based officers. But as anyone knows, politics is much too serious a business to leave up to mere generals. The army is only a microcosm of Indonesia and it's just as regionalist and corrupt as Indonesia's civil service and the business sector. Everywhere in Indonesia you see army officers in their Mercedes or shiny jeeps cruising past the burdened, impoverished peasants: aristocrats with a new face. Every facility the army owns or occupies is surrounded by barbed wire, giving Indonesia the appearance of a country that is occupied by its own government.

At its best, the army is the people's friend. At its worst, it's a terrorizing and intimidating secret police. Between 1982 and 1985, death-squad operations were launched against gangs of criminals in Java and Sumatra. Slugs recovered from the bullet-riddled bodies showed that the weapons used were the same as army and police handguns. Up to 4000 clandestine executions were reported, most believed to be free of political motivation, and the crime rate plunged dramatically. Indonesian newspapers referred to the incidences as "mysterious killings" until the government ordered the strictly controlled press to stop reporting such cases in 1985.

How The Army Rules
Students have frequently demonstrated over corruption, unequal income distribution, unemployment, and rising prices. Riots could also be staged by a powerful general to discredit his rival. The army has a long history of organizing or manipulating street mobs of civilians or student demonstrators to get its way. This is how it usually works. When the opposition wants something they "plan" a demonstration. The whole affair is planned down to which town, village, and city is to take part, who is to be paid off, who is to get it and who is not, what is to be burned and what is not. The idea perhaps would be to have a 5-day riot. Then a group of generals might have to back down because they would realize that they cannot contain the rebellion once it starts. This explains why the government, the army, cannot allow students any more than limited freedom, because it would all just get out of hand. And this is why the army comes down so hard on the students. Army clashes with students usually result in a few deaths, mass arrests, and the harsh repression of all student political activity, as well as the muzzling of newspapers which tactlessly report the "incidents." In 1986, retired general Hartono Dharsono was sentenced to 10 years in prison for questioning the official account given in 1984 of the alleged Muslim extremist riots in Jakarta's port of Tanjung Priok. As a traveler you'll notice definite fascist tendencies such as the requirement that you register with the neighborhood police or the R.T. (Rukun Tetangga) within 24 hours if you stay as a guest of an Indonesian family. Reason? To avoid suspicion (and a Rp50,000 fine). The government is paranoid of subversives and you could be one. During the 1987 elections, foreigners residing in Indonesia were were not allowed to travel or to gather in groups of over 8 without permission.

CENSORSHIP, PROPAGANDA, AND CIVIL LIBERTY

Social, political, and cultural censorship is almost taken for granted in Indonesia. Censorship takes many forms. If you go to a movie and wonder why the main character suddenly vanishes, that's the long finger of the government. The hero was too anti-social, amoral, or the film too sexually explicit. Films of primitive, traditional Indonesian peoples such as the

Asmat of Irian Jaya are not allowed to be shown in Indonesia even though the films are sympathetic and sensitive. The authorities believe that they show Indonesia to Indonesians in a bad light. Also, the government makes sure that the masses don't hear the "wrong" information about radical theocratic societies such as Iran's, news of which might trigger a chain reaction that could jeopardize the privileges of its ruling class. In fact, the only reliable way to know what's really going on in Indonesia is to read what they say *isn't* going on. If an official is quoted in the paper as denying something, read it with extra suspicion and caution. After the Finance Minister, for example, has just signed a big export deal and is quoted in giant headlines in the papers as saying "WE WILL NOT SELL OUR COUNTRY!"—that means he just did. And right up until the time of the last big devaluation in Sept. 1986, there were bold headlines: WE WILL NEVER DEVALUE! This was an attempt by the government-controlled press to head off money speculation. Get your facts from denials, and always read carefully between the lines. It is the Javanese way to maintain a calm appearance, to continue smiling while withdrawing so that the issue may be taken up more peaceably later.

In the West, freedom of the press is a universal right. But in Indonesia, due to the variety of its cultures and the stage of its economic development, freedom of the press is regarded as less important than stability and harmony among the people. Indonesian domestic newpapers routinely stretch or omit the truth, or outright lie. In Oct. 1987, *Sinar Harapan,* a leading Jakarta daily, was shut down for leaking a proposed economic program, and in June 1987 *Prioritas* was silenced for committing some other editorial indiscretion. Pages critical of Indonesia are often blacked out of such imported weeklies as *Far Eastern Economic Review, Time* and *Newsweek.* Still, offending articles in the print media can be found and photocopies made everywhere easily and cheaply. Since it's virtually impossible for the authorities to prevent the circulation of banned material, one wonders why the censors even bother. The VCR recorder is another engine of social change. The VCR is, in effect, a printing press, able to grind out copy after copy of banned tapes which can easily be smuggled across borders. Porno movies are sometimes shown on the night buses of Sumatra and sizzling Hong Kong films are the rage of the Chinese community. Foreign reporters are tossed out if they are too candid in their reporting. In mid-1986 a whole planeload of Australian tourists was barred from entry because of scathing editorial in the *Sydney Morning Herald* that compared President Suharto with Marcos and accused Suharto, his family, and business associates of "waxing fat on government capital, credit, and concessions, and accumulating $2-3 billion." This front-page article caused the most serious crisis in Australian-Indonesian relations since the 1960s.

Liberties

Indonesia's military bureaucratic state can best be described as an open patriarchal dictatorship. Don't think that to live in Indonesia, Big Brother is always watching. And Indonesia's government and religious system are not unremittingly oppressive, requiring the loss of many personal freedoms. The Javanese come from a softer civilization than North Korea's or Saudi Arabia's. There is authoritarianism, but not mind control. A citizen—or a visitor—is actually quite inept if he can't arrange to pay or otherwise get his own way in the system. The rule of formal, court-upheld law doesn't exist here, since it would be unenforcible if it did. Customary *(adat)* law, which covers even criminal and civil cases, is the most powerful social force of all. Legal rules are made up day by day according to each situation. Police in Indonesia don't even know how to process an arrest or how to properly report a crime. Not only that, but in many cases you have to pay *the police* if you get robbed. To report a robbery in Jakarta you usually have to pay a fee and you can only go on Mon. and Wed. mornings between 1000 and 1200!

So, what does a "lawless" Indonesia mean? Well, has anything really unpleasant happened to you in Indonesia? Got in a fight lately? Ever been sued or arrested? It's rare that a person ever gets arrested, that a situation gets so out of hand that it's taken to that extreme. Because the *adat* affords so much latitude and reinterpretation, the extent of personal liberty in practice is actually astonishingly high. Government controls which are actually felt by the people are extremely limited compared to places like the U.S. or Germany where the power and tax systems of the government touch every individual every day. Regulations can be stretched much more in Indonesia than they can in the West and problems can almost always be worked out before they come to a confrontation. If you rock the boat they come up and say, "Please don't rock the boat." And if you rock the boat again, they say, "Really, we'd rather you didn't rock the boat." And if you do it again they say, "Look, what do you *want?*" And if you go on, then they'll finally have to put you in jail. The golden rule: just don't talk politics to the wrong people, dress properly, and above all respect the *adat.*

JAKARTAN CENTRALISM

The government is centered on the centrally located, middle-sized island of Java, and it is also intensely Java-centered. Indonesia's is not a truly representative government; the Javanese are in effect the new colonialists of the archipelago. An elite of perhaps 2,000 men manipulate Indonesian politics. With only a dozen or so exceptions, they all speak English, drive new Japanese cars, live in Jakarta, and are Javanese. There has always been tension and conflict between the seafaring, mercantile Muslim states of Indonesia's Outer Islands and the bureaucratic, powerful, Hindu-ized forces of Java. Many of the Outer Islands have come to resent Java's heavy-handed overlordship of all the islands of Indonesia. Colonialism, whether by white Dutch Europeans or brown Javanese Asians, is equally unacceptable to Indonesia's Outer Island peoples, most of whom would prefer a looser federa-tion to ensure a more just distribution of the national wealth and power. Civil servants must wait for their promotions—or demotions—from Jakarta. Gover-nors can be summarily dismissed by the Javanese without even consulting the regional legislature (DPRD), even though they had been elected by that body. The Javanese hold an overwhelming represen-tation among senior officers in the national armed forces, over 80 percent! Not a single Outer Island ter-ritorial command is held by a native son, whereas the commands of West, Central, and East Java are all held by native sons.

The Threat Of Separatism

The threat of separatism always looms large in this scattered island nation. Java's 90 million people couldn't possibly survive on their own and if any of the resource-rich Outer Islands gets uppity, Java sends bombers into the sky and assault troops ashore to quell at once any secessionist uprisings. There were serious revolts in 1959 in Sumatra and N. Celebes because Java took too much of the revenues those regions were earning for its own enrichment and improvement. It's now a deliberate government (Javanese) policy to constantly rotate all governors, provincial chiefs of police, as well as heads of military districts throughout Indonesia. This is aimed at pre-venting too much power from becoming consoli-dated in one man ("Bapakism") and to check the pos-sibility of any further costly challenges to the central Javanese government as occurred in 1959. The army maintains this same method of constantly changing command posts of its field officers in order to keep too much provincial army power from becoming concen-trated in popular army commanders. Suharto has also made sure that the commander of KOSTRAD (the Ar-my Strategic Reserve), the rank from which he was catapulted to power during the 1965 "coup," con-stantly changes hands.

In spite of all these measures, violent opposition to the Suharto government has nevertheless taken place in ongoing separatist insurgencies in the remote prov-inces of Irian Jaya and E. Timor. Indonesia took over Irian Jaya from the Dutch in 1962 after a brief military campaign, a land grab which resulted in a spectacular 25% territorial gain for Indonesia. As a result of native Papuan grievances against oppressive Indonesian rule, forced acquisition of land, and the central gov-ernment's transmigration policy, a guerrilla force was

guerillas of the OPM resistance movement in Irian Jaya

formed in Irian Jaya called the OPM (Organisasi Papua Merdeka). Following the withdrawal of Por-tugal from E. Timor in 1975, the Indonesian govern-ment bloodily intervened to prevent Fretilin, the in-dependence movement there, from taking control. Both the U.S. and Australia, which gave their tacit ap-proval to the invasion, shared Indonesia's fear that Fretilin would make the territory a second Cuba. In July 1976 Indonesia annexed E. Timor as the 27th province of Indonesia. News of fighting in these ter-ritories is seldom made public as the national press is tightly censored by the Javanese centralists. First-hand sources, however, have reported that fighting has died down and that the guerrillas are no real threat to the occupying power.

INTERNATIONAL POLITICS

Indonesia founded the nonaligned movement at the historic Asia-Africa conference in Bandung in 1955, and Indonesia's foreign minister recently announced that his country will assume the 101-member non-aligned movement's chair after Zimbabwe's term ends in 1988. During the pre-1965 Sukarno years, In-donesia developed close ties with China and the Soviet Union and was openly aggressive against what Sukarno called the Old Established Forces (the West) and even initiated foreign military adventures against Irian Jaya and Malaysia. Although Indonesia is today officially nonaligned, since Suharto stepped into power the government has aligned itself much closer to the West. This growing dependence has also resulted in a new foreign policy. Indonesia suspended its relations with China after accusing Peking of engineering an abortive communist coup in Indonesia in 1965. Almost simultaneously, diplomatic relations with Malaysia, which had been thrown into chaos by Sukarno's *konfrontasi* campaign, were reestablished. Since Suharto's takeover in 1967, Indonesia has been the recipient of a massive range of diplomatic, economic, ideological, and military support from the U.S., totaling about $300 million a year. American arms pouring into Indonesia—about $40 million yearly—go to preserve a liaison with the military through Suharto's regime. It is important to note that the biggest Indonesian embassy in the world is in Washington D.C., and the biggest American embassy in the world is in Jakarta. Japan provides the world's largest share of Indonesia's foreign development capital, and lesser but still substantial sums come from W. Germany, the Netherlands, France, and Australia.

But more than humanitarian interest has motivated the West's investment and interest in the region. Indonesia sits on the largest and richest oil reserves in SE Asia, is an influential member of OPEC, and its vast island network controls the Straits of Malacca and other passages the Soviet Navy must use to get from its Pacific bases into the Indian Ocean and the shipping lanes of the Persian Gulf. Although no country in their right mind would ever launch a land invasion of this scattered archipelago, with thousands of islands offering sanctuary for guerrilla resistance, the West *does* want this tremendously important strategic gateway firmly in its camp, or at least not under Moscow's thumb. Maintaining Indonesia's strength as the largest country in SE Asia, and perhaps the only one with the potential of becoming a major world power, is of prime importance to the stability of the entire region. Indonesia is currently a member of the Association of South East Asian Nations (ASEAN), and Jakarta hosted a meeting of ASEAN in Oct. 1986.

Although Indonesia's policies fit in nicely with U.S. policy toward SE Asia, Indonesia espouses Asian neutralism and all the aid money given by the West does not guarantee Indonesian support in the international arena. Even though the government is anti-communist, its backing for the U.S.-supported effort by ASEAN to get Vietnam's occupation forces out of Cambodia has been lukewarm. The Indonesian Foreign Minister has said that it is only a question of time before his country normalizes relations with China, and progress was begun in 1985 with a visit to Jakarta of China's foreign minister. But contemporary public sentiment has shown that Indonesians consider China, a nation the U.S. has befriended, a greater threat to peace in Asia than Russia. And, even though

the U.S. would like to keep the 13,700-island archipelago under its influence, the USSR has begun to make overtures to improve relations. Soviet leader Gorbachev described Indonesia in 1985 as "one of the world's great nations," and has openly declared his country's willingness to expand economic and cultural ties.

THE NEW ORDER

The soft-spoken Suharto rose to power in 1965-66 because he controlled a key position in the Indonesian army during a crisis. Over the past 20 years the army has played the central role in the nation's development, and has given Suharto his all-pervasive base of power. During this period, Suharto has been consummate in handling internal army politics and in clever political maneuverings, accumulating and reinforcing his power by gathering around him powerful people. Not only the armed forces, but also the civilian bureaucracy and the technocrats, foreign investors and creditors, ethnic Chinese businessmen, Muslim landowners, and educated Christians are all solidly behind him. Purges during 1965-68 wiped out most of his left-leaning opponents and all remaining Sukarno supporters in the military. With the government assiduously monitoring dissent, and the PKI banned more than 20 years ago, "communist" purges even continued into late 1985 when an old communist leader was executed and several oil companies were ordered to dismiss more than 1,500 employees said to have been associated with the PKI.

Despite the apparent drift toward a more dictatorial and obscurantist system, Suharto generally receives high marks for guiding the country through the turbulence of the 1960s, and for the aggressive political, economic, and social reforms of the 1970s. Officially called the "Father of Development"—the contemporary equivalent of a Javanese king—Suharto is credited with establishing the mainstays of the Indonesian economy: the massive export of oil and natural gas. "The government has laid the foundations," the president has said of his achievements. "Future generations need only continue." The increase in the power of the state under Suharto has also made the political and economic climate more stable and the rule of law firmer. For those who lived through the turbulent Sukarno years, this is no insignificant gain. But it comes with a price.

Opposition
With the untold wealth and influence he has gained over the past 20 years working hand in hand with foreign multi-national corporations, Suharto has gradually neutralized all potential opposition with either money, positions, or promotions. But since the

early 1980s, opposition to President Suharto's New Order government has been increasing. Many prominent national figures have openly voiced criticism and opponents guilty of ideological crimes are jailed. The harsh prison terms handed down serve as a warning to all who dissent. Rising unemployment, student unrest, the politically frustrated masses, and the widening inequality between the urban and rural sectors all add to the tensions. These tensions led to violence during the parliamentary election campaign in May 1982, when opponents of the government attempted to disrupt what they believed were rigged polls in which outcomes were meaningless. Troops fired on rioters and were ordered to "shoot on the spot" anyone who attempted to disturb the polling. In Benteng Square rioters hurled rocks and burned automobiles. There were tanks and soldiers in full battle fatigues on the streets, and the toll was 60 dead, 1,334 injured. Admiral Sudomo, national security head, told a group of ASEAN journalists on the eve of the elections, "We will shoot very cautiously, for this is a democracy." In 1984 there were more riots, bombings, and show trials were staged in 1986. All through the first half of 1986, student demonstrations protesting incompetent rectors and tuition fees exploded all over Indonesia. But Suharto remains firmly in control through it all. He was re-elected unopposed for his fifth 5-year term in March 1988. But the opposition does not go away.

The Islamic Bloc

Indonesia is the largest Muslim nation in the world, and the Islamic movement poses the greatest potential threat to the present regime. While the 350,000-member armed forces have become the ultimate power factor in Indonesia under Suharto, the Muslims have faded to an even more inferior position than during Sukarno's period of "Guided Democracy." In 1972, Suharto forced the 4 Muslim parties to merge into one Development Union Party (PPP). The PPP has been forced to pledge allegiance to the principles of Pancasila, which in effect has turned the Pancasila state ideology into an alternative state religion. Over the past several years, Islamic fundamentalists, accused of goading the masses to anti-government acts, have been given prison terms of up to 3 years. In Sept. 1984 there were bloody Muslim riots at Jakarta's port when troops clashed with extremists, leaving hundreds dead. Muslim radicalism has started to send down deep roots here, and many fear that the political environment, modernization, the influx of Western culture, combined with economic injustices and rampant corruption at the highest levels of government, may push even more alienated youths increasingly in that direction. Many young people see Islam—the professed religion of 90% of the population—as their best prospect for a voice in the future, the closest thing to a formal and potentially mass-based political opposition. Although a Muslim himself, Suharto has lately favored Christian officers in vital commands as they help keep the powerful fundamentalist Muslim factions in check. Christians are a minority and it would be impossible for them to overthrow him and become President.

Suharto, now a jowly 66 years old and getting soft around the middle, is no longer the trim, tough-minded military chief who led a guerrilla band in the war against the Dutch. Re-elected unopposed for a 5th term in March 1988, Suharto will remain president—health permitting—into at least the early 1990s. Who will succeed him? Whoever fills the position of vice-president is seen as the President's political heir. Key figures for the vice-presidency are the state secretary and Golkar chair Sudharmono and the head of the armed forces Benny Moerdani. But with the unpredictability and intrigue of Indonesia's political scene, with ministers falling in and out of favor with the first family, no one is placing bets. But the question of leadership of this sprawling SE Asian nation—the 5th most populous in the world—is indeed a matter of frightening moment.

THE ECONOMY

Before WW II, Indonesia exported substantial percentages of the world's rubber, tin, petroleum, pepper, cloves, nutmeg, quinine, coffee, tea, palm oil, and copra. But by 1965, 15 years after independence, President Sukarno's disastrous economic policies had left the Indonesian economy in chaos with a foreign debt of $1630 million. The population was among the poorest in the world (the average annual per capita income dropped from US$73 in 1960 to US$65 in 1963). Since Suharto ousted Sukarno from power in 1966, there is no doubt that the new government has pushed the nation upward after its near economic collapse. Following the crisis of the '60s, Suharto's New Order changed a badly managed economy to a liberal market economy backed by foreign investment and state planning. Within 3 years of Sukarno's overthrow, a complete turnabout of economic policy was accomplished. The new regime first managed to get the nation's debt, which had soared to $2.4 billion, under control. By balancing the budget and controlling the money supply, Suharto was able to bring down inflation from 639% in 1966 to under 15% in 1969 (now hovering around 10%). Resources were redirected from wasteful prestige projects to producing food and clothing, and to the building of roads and harbors. Through a fortuitous combination of good management and good luck, the economy was put on track again and Suharto's tough rule has brought years of stability, so crucial to economic development. Suharto has recently confidently slashed development spending to defray the oil crises which hammered the economy in 1985/86, and at the ASEAN meeting hosted by Jakarta in Oct. 1986, President Aquino of the Philippines even discussed with Suharto the economic strengthening of ASEAN into a European-style common market.

The Berkeley Mafia

The new administration wholeheartedly adopted Western development concepts and strategies largely through the efforts of an economic clique trained at the University of California that became known as "the Berkeley Mafia." These powerful technocrats encouraged foreign investment with major incentives such as tax exemptions and assurances of free profit. With billions of dollars in Western aid and food imports pouring into the country, they made Indonesia a model of a successful developing nation. And even after the oil-price collapse in 1986 brought about a drastic reduction in petroleum revenues, accompanied by a price slump of 34% in tin, rubber, and other commodities, the technocrats came to the rescue again, saving Indonesia's economy from the fate that befell Mexico, Venezuela, and Nigeria. The economy is doing so well that international lending agencies like the World Bank agreed in June 1987 to loan Indonesia yet another $3.2 billion. The 1987 budget was US$13.9 billion, 6.4% larger than the previous year's budget.

Evidence is everywhere of Indonesia's new-found wealth. You see antennae breaking the skylines in every Indonesian city now, health-care centers have been set up all over the archipelago, farmers are subsidized with lime and fertilizers, poor students are sent to the university. Another sign is the dynamic growth of domestic tourism: groups of young people can be seen all over rural Java, packs on their backs, hiking to nature reserves and resorts, sleek a/c sightseeing buses speed down highways, and long lines of cars return from a weekend of recreation. There are snarling traffic jams on the outskirts of all the big cities, new roads, highways, and bridges have multiplied, and the volume of transport vehicles and the amount of consumer goods available have increased 3-fold in the past 10 years. A cigarette seller on the streets of Jakarta can make Rp6000 a day, and even a *becak* driver can now afford small portions of meat and egg with his bowl of rice.

Obstacles To Development

But signs of social and economic woes surface everywhere beyond the high-rise glitter of Jakarta, the capital. Indonesia is still one of the poorest countries of SE Asia, and with the 1986/87 drop in oil prices is suffering its worst economic crises in its 42-year history. The main problems of this overpopulated, impoverished agricultural nation are that too many of its people are concentrated in only certain fertile areas, and that its wealth is distributed too unevenly. Gov-

ernment graft on epic scales compounds the waste of resources; the 1986-87 budget was the first in 17 years that cut government spending. In 1987, its foreign debt was US$42.6 billion with debt service consuming 11% of the country's GDP. According to the World Bank, Indonesia has an estimated per capita income of only US$520. On teeming Java, the anchor-island of this archipelagic nation, 40% of the populace lives in "absolute poverty," even by Third World standards, and Indonesia ranks in the bottom 20% of the world's 160 nations. Life expectancy in 1985 was 56 years (up from 47 in 1980). Between 1980 and 1985, infant mortality dropped from 107 for every thousand births to 80.

The gap between rich and poor is growing; the vast wealth created by oil and other resources over the past decade has gone to a privileged elite. The strong link between political and economic power and the existence of a huge corrupt bureaucracy make equitable economic development nearly impossible. Government and foreign-financed development programs are plagued by the bungling incompetence of government managers. Tensions between the military-backed government of President Suharto and unemployed, rebellious young people are growing, breeding fears that the young may turn increasingly to Muslim radicalism. The government has even taken the drastic step of banning TV advertising primarily aimed at the urban affluent in the (probably correct) belief that it only raises expectations, creates envy and social unrest. Relentless population pressures mount regardless of efforts at birth control. Nationwide, more than 35% of the work force is unemployed or stuck in low-paying, poverty-sharing jobs. About 2.8 million Indonesians join the labor force each year (400,000 young men in Jakarta alone). Estimates are that Indonesia's population, 5th largest in the world, could double in 35 years, which would create catastrophic social turmoil.

FOREIGN MONEY

Indonesia views itself as a pretty girl who is well-endowed, with a lot of dirty rich old men lurking about. On the face of it, the potential for foreign investment in Indonesia seems enormous: vast stores of raw materials, especially oil (the world's 12th largest producer); a strategic location straddling vital waterways between the Pacific and Indian oceans; a labor pool of 168 million people; and 20 years of relative political and social stability. Since 1967, Indonesia has been able to acquire billions in aid from 12 nations acting together as the Inter-Governmental Group on Indonesia (IGGI), the so-called donor countries—Japan, U.S., Australia, Canada, Belgium, France, Germany, Italy, Holland, New Zealand, Switzerland, and the UK. However, starting in 1985 when world oil prices dropped from $25 a barrel to less than

$10 Indonesia's foreign earnings have been deeply gouged. In Sept. 1986, the government was forced to devalue the Indonesian *rupiah* 31%, a direct result of the oil-price collapse and reduced government receipts from that critical export commodity. Harried by exhorbitant transportation and utilities costs, high interest rates, red tape, and wide-scale government graft, scores of foreign investors abandoned Indonesia. The level of total foreign investment plummeted from US$2.8 billion in 1983 to US$1.1 billion in 1984 to just over US$800 million in 1986. In response to this catastrophic flight of capital, the country faces the most painful austerity measures in more than a decade, the government slashing its development budget in 1986 by US$3 billion. To regain lost ground, the government in May 1986 unveiled a new economic reform policy which offers perks for new investors, opening up 297 sectors from which they were previously banned.

Foreign Aid

International financial institutions have also contributed substantial development sums over the 20 years since Suharto came to power. Since 1966, the U.S. alone has provided nearly $3 billion in direct aid to Indonesia, mostly in the form of loans, and at least as much again in funds that have been channeled by way of the World Bank and other organizations. The catch is that the U.S. and Indonesia's other principal-aid donor countries dictate which financial controls are to be instituted and for how long, while Indonesia's aid indebtedness grows ever higher. The hard fact is that foreign aid is only a vehicle for creating a favorable infrastructural framework needed to effectively exploit manufacturing, forestry, and mining products—commodities which are vital to the industrialized U.S., Western Europe, and Japan. Some aid projects, such as the government's *transmigrasi* schemes, have drawn international rebuke. In this controversial program, 698,200 families were moved between 1950 to 1986, many to areas where rainforests and wildlife had been cleared, only to leave the soil too poor to support agriculture. The project is now being scaled down enormously by the loss of oil revenues and the government's inability to pay its share of the costs.

INDUSTRY

Though in large part an agricultural country, Indonesia has made significant progress in recent years in developing a modern infrastructure and an industrial base related in large measure to its abundant natural resources. Industry in Indonesia employs only about 7% of the people, and includes oil refineries; fertilizer, cement, steel, liquified natural gas (LNG)

plants; mineral, timber and wood-processing projects. Light manufacturing, concentrated overwhelmingly on Java, focuses on tires, furniture, shoes, textiles, electronics, drugs, cigarettes. Automobile assembly plants make European, Japanese, and Australian models, and Indonesia has even has gotten into the high-tech aerospace industry—a state-owned company (IPTN) in Bandung (W. Java) manufactures a 35-seat passenger aircraft and helicoptors. As a rule, though, the Indonesian economy relies much too heavily on oil, timber, rubber, and other highly localized industrialization programs. Foreign exchange is generated through the sale of raw natural resources extracted mostly by Japanese and American multinational corporations. Periodic 5-year plans (Bappenas) have attempted to diversify the economy, stressing the traditional agricultural sector and the more labor-intensive industries.

Opposition demands are increasing to privatize most of the 215 giant state monopolies that control such crucial commodities as oil, cloves, and palm oil, as well as hotels, banking, travel agencies, and numerous other industries that compete with the private sector. More than 50% of Indonesia's annual corporate tax revenues are derived from these over-bureaucratized state-run concerns that have been criticized for being mismanaged and run with too high overheads, and for consistently turning in inadequate profits. Such lumbering giants as the state oil monopoly, and the national railways and airlines, will not be affected.

Oil And LNG

Although agriculture dominates domestic activity, the driving force behind the Indonesia economy over the past 10 years has always been petroleum, which until 1985 accounted for over two-thirds of the country's gross export earnings and about 60% of total budget revenues. When oil prices quadrupled during 1973-74, Indonesia's export earnings doubled. This period of abundance was soon eclipsed by the global recession as well as the political scandal and near bankruptcy in 1976 of Pertamina, the state-owned oil and gas company. A crony of the president, General Ibnu Sutowo had expanded Pertamina's activities into steel, petrochemicals, real estate, telecommunications, shipping and air transport. But when Pertamina failed to meet a payment on a short-term debt in March 1975, an investigating team found that the oil company had amassed debts of US$10.5 billion!

More than 90% of Indonesian crude oil production comes from fields worked by American oil companies. Indonesia currently produces around 1.2 million barrels per day (a quota set by OPEC). However, because of the dramatic drop in oil revenues since 1986, Indonesia is now experiencing the most serious economic downturn of the past 20

FUELS, METALS AND MINERALS OF INDONESIA

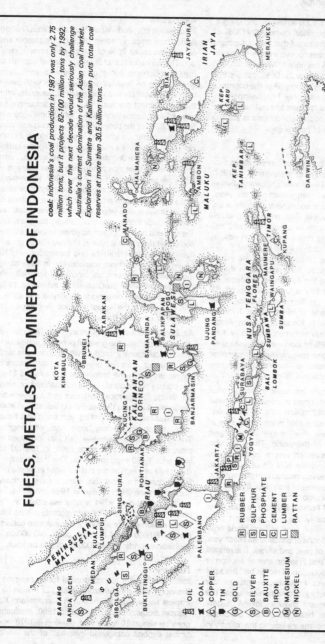

coal: Indonesia's coal production in 1987 was only 2.75 million tons, but it projects 82-100 million tons by 1992, which over the next decade would seriously challenge Australia's current domination of the Asian coal market. Exploration in Sumatra and Kalimantan puts total coal reserves at more than 30.5 billion tons.

oil: The price for Indonesia's benchmark Minas crude was US$17.56 per barrel for the first 6 months of 1988. Indonesia, which has faithfully fulfilled the production quota assigned to it at the Vienna OPEC meeting in May of 1988, has suggested sanctions against OPEC members who have violated their production quotas. "Otherwise what's the use of having an organization," says Indonesia's Mining and Energy Minister Ginandjar.

illegal goldmining: Illegal goldmining began to grow in 1983 and 1984 after the rupiah devaluation, when the public saw gold as "better to save than money. "The government's main targets for stopping illegal miners are N. Sulawesi, all provinces of Kalimantan (50,000 in C. Kalimantan alone), Jambi, and Bengkulu. If illegal miners did not cease their activities by 1 July 1988, they were arrested. Local residents who pan gold traditionally are not considered illegal miners.

OIL
COAL
COPPER
TIN
GOLD
SILVER
BAUXITE
IRON
MAGNESIUM
NICKEL

R RUBBER
S SULPHUR
P PHOSPHATE
C CEMENT
L LUMBER
  RATTAN

years. Since the government is so heavily and dangerously dependent on this critical commodity (70% of its gross receipts), it's estimated that Indonesia loses US$350 million in revenues for every dollar the barrel of oil falls. By April 1988 the price of Minas crude was about $14 per barrel, far below the OPEC cartel's $18 a barrel benchmark. But with only 34 of the country's 60 oil basins explored and only 14 developed, Indonesia's recoverable oil reserves will last her well into the 21st century. In addition, Indonesia is still the world's largest exporter of natural gas.

Heavy Metals

Non-petroleum mineral production has increased substantially since the change in government in 1967. Although the legends of Indonesia's huge and diverse mineral riches have been exaggerated over the years, the nation does possess major mineral deposits of tin, copper, bauxite, and nickel. Coal production, which has shown a big drop from its pre-war level of 2 million tons, is undergoing major revitalization now in the country's principal coal- mining region of S. Sumatra. Latest estimates of coal reserves are put at 15,000 million metric tons. Indonesia lies in the tin belt of the world, being the 4th largest producer. Its measured tin reserves in the Lingga Group off SE Sumatra are around 1 million tons. Bauxite, from which aluminum is made, is mined (about 1 million tons yearly) entirely on P. Bintan in Riau by Alcoa; another major reserve has been confirmed in W. Kalimantan. At present, 90% of Indonesia's bauxite is exported to Japan. A joint-venture aluminum smelter was completed at the massive Asahan industrial complex in N. Sumatra in the mid-'80s.

But the most spectacular increases in heavy metal have been in nickel and copper production. Indonesia has reserves of over 40 million tons of nickel ore, enough to last 47 years. Nickel is mined by Inco at Soroako in C. Sulawesi, also the site of the largest nickel smelting plant in the world. There are also significant nickel reserves on several island groups between Halmahera and the NW tip of Irian Jaya. Copper is almost exclusively produced in the high and rugged Ertsberg Mountains of Irian Jaya by Freeport Copper Co., the first corportation to take advantage of the generous 1967 Foreign Investment Law. This mine represents probably the world's largest base metal reserve (33.5 million tons of high-grade ore), producing over 56,000 tons of concentrates each year (plus small quantities of gold and silver). The refined ore's value is so high that Freeport earned enough in the first 2 years of production to regain half the total financing of the project. Presently, because of low 1986/87 market prices, high production costs, and the generally poor investment climate, dozens of new mining projects have been postponed or closed down, and mining concerns are leaving the country in droves.

Agriculture

Indonesia is still predominantly an agricultural nation. Agriculture employs about 60% of the people and contributes about 25% of the gross domestic product. The agricultural sector enjoys the full support of President Suharto, son of a rice farmer from C. Java, who is seen on television talking more with *petani* than with assembly-line workers or bureaucrats. With the oil boom of the early '70s, the Indonesians increased their agricultural output, which now accounts for over 80% of the country's non-oil export earnings. Indonesia is the world's 2nd largest producer of rubber (¼ of the world's market), the 4th biggest coffee producer, and the 3rd largest producer of rice. Farmers increased their rice production by an average of 6.6% per year between 1977 and 1987. Indonesia is the world's 5th largest cacao producer. Indonesia also ranks 5th in soybean production, having doubled its output in the past 5 years. Other significant cash exports include copra, palm oil, sugar, bananas, tea. These gains have not been achieved without skirting ecological disaster because of the overuse of government-subsidized fertilizers and pesticides—Rp365 billion and Rp42 billion, respectively, in 1986 alone. Indonesian plantations are renowned for their mismanagement; their productivity is estimated to be 40% below that of neighboring Malaysia's. In spite of this, Indonesia is the largest producer (and largest importer!) of cloves in the world.

Although Indonesia has twice as many fishermen as Japan and perhaps the greatest potential fish stock of any tropical country, productivity is about one-tenth that of Japan. Salt fish provides the main source of animal protein in the Indonesian diet (around 11 kg per person per annum). Large mechanized commercial fleets, for the most part joint-ventures with the Japanese, dominate the sea-fishing industry; in some cases this has caused conflict with traditional fishermen who angrily destroy boats, nets, and engines. The total catch of saltwater fish has increased by more than 5% per year since 1968; in 1981/82 the yield was 1,490 thousand tons. The inland catch is about half as much as the total brought in by sea fishing. Indonesia's new 200-nautical-mile exclusive economic zone (EEZ) ratified in 1983 should lead to tighter control over what is now essentially an "archipelagic state" set in its own gigantic private lake. Half a million people all over Indonesia also cultivate fish in 180,000 ha of brackish ponds, 40,000 ha of freshwater ponds, and 80,000 ha of rice paddies.

Forestry

Indonesia has the largest tropical forest reserves in the world after the Amazon, about 122 million ha in tropical hardwoods (55 million in Sumatra and Kalimantan alone). Between 1970 and 1980, production grew by almost 10% per year, peaking in 1978 when timber exports comprised over half of the world's

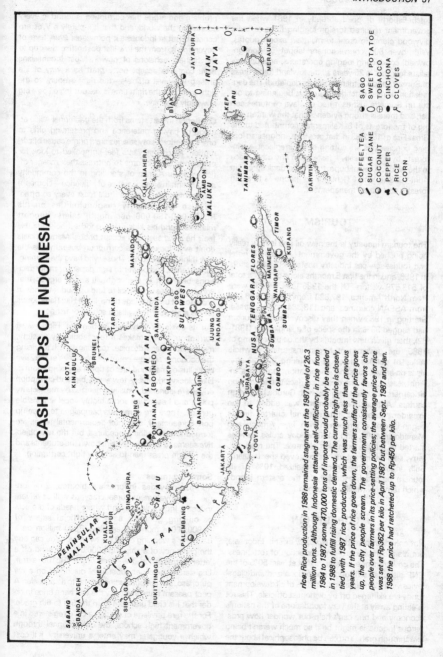

CASH CROPS OF INDONESIA

SAGO
SWEET POTATOE
TOBACCO
CINCHONA
CLOVES

COFFEE, TEA
SUGAR CANE
COCONUT
PEPPER
RICE
CORN

rice: Rice production in 1988 remained stagnant at the 1987 level of 26.3 million tons. Although Indonesia attained self-sufficiency in rice from 1984 to 1987, some 470,000 tons of imports would probably be needed in 1988 to fulfill rising domestic demand. The current high price is closely tied with 1987 rice production, which was much less than previous years. If the price of rice goes down, the farmers suffer; if the price goes up, the city people scream. The government consistently favors city people over farmers in its price-setting policies; the average price for rice was set at Rp362 per kilo in April 1987 but between Sept. 1987 and Jan. 1988 the price had ratcheted up to Rp450 per kilo.

total. Exports dropped abruptly in 1981 when the government required foreign logging firms to build plywood plants in order to maintain export quotas. With over 500 concessioners (about 60 foreign-owned) conducting logging operations, environmentalists fear that in 20 years all the lowland forest areas of Sumatra and Kalimantan will be depleted. The degradation of river catchment areas is beginning to occur on Sumatra just as it had on Java centuries earlier, and there is strong evidence that the wanton raping of the forests of E. Kalimantan contributed to the Great Fire of 1982-83 in that province. Indonesian logging concessions are cutting down irreplacable rainforests by 1% annually — faster than any other place in the world. A ray of hope: the World Bank agreed in April 1988 to lend $31 million to Indonesia to aid in forestry and estate management.

TOURISM

The tourism industry is the new oil and is now really being pushed by the government. A dynamic hotel and tourist-services industry hosted 693,447 visitors in 1986, and in the first 6 months alone of 1987 a total of 513,579 visitors. Of the 1986 total, 56,231 were from North America, 197,828 from Europe, 166,020 from ASEAN countries, and 113,384 from Australia. Starting in 1983 when they discovered that tourism had sagged 33% in the space of a single year (1981-82), then given new impetus by the oil-price slump of 1986, the government began instituting a whole series of policies aimed at bolstering the industry: visas-on-arrival, clearing immigration formalities inflight, easier customs clearance, facilities for foreign air carriers, and joint services with Garuda by foreign carriers. A tourism department was added to the President's cabinet, international charter flights began landing at airports in Irian Jaya, Ambon, and Manado in 1984, and $100-per-day cruise services started to tap the upmarket clientele. The road, rail, ferry, ship infrastructure has improved spectacularly. Still, Indonesia hasn't even realized 10% of its tourism potential, especially in the eastern islands which remain virtually untouched.

CORRUPTION

Not only does corruption *(korupsi)* exist in Indonesia, but it's a complex art — the perfection of rottenness. The government even admits that at least 50% of the GNP disappears through institutionalized and illegal levies, and it's estimated that 30% of all development funds are skimmed off by dishonest officials. This rot is eating away at the very foundations of the nation's economy and one can't help but wonder how prosperous Indonesia might be if so much weren't being lost through graft. You can be philosophical about the

problem and argue that corruption is found in every country in the world, and that it's purely a Western concept. But in Indonesia it permeates every level of government, from the lowliest post office clerk up to the highest echelons of power. Most Indonesians have come to accept petty graft as a way of life among low-level officials — the right amount to the right person at the right time is like putting oil on a big unwieldly machine.

Corruption in part stems from the traditional Asian attitude of paying deference and presenting gifts to one's superiors. Low salaries are a prime cause of corruption, as civil servants feel compelled to look for other sources of income to buttress their meager official wages. A man of standing in the community must maintain an appearance of affluence — clothes, a car, comfortable home, a ritual feast every so often. He also has weighty responsibilities on his Rp120,000-180,000 per month salary: support relatives, send his kids off to good schools, etc. He feels he *must* seek and accept bribes. Many officials don't even look at it as corruption but rather as the way things *ought* to be. Those who have the learning, competence, and power to sign papers or make decisions believe it is their right. It's also argued that *korupsi* enables an official to find off-budget funds in order to get useful things done, like a Hari Raya bonus for his staff or a new village school or fishpond.

But its costs far outweigh its benefits. Higher-level corruption, which makes a few fabulously wealthy, most Indonesians despise, realizing that it's ruining the economy and the country's morale. Yet they live in disillusionment and fear of doing anything about it. Like clockwork, every few years big anti-corruption drives are launched, usually organized by the security police and headed by some highly vocal and visible general. There are numerous campaigns to clean up port bureaucracy, and inter-departmental teams are formed to streamline procedures, but the real objective seems to be more to calm down the students and the foreign press than to actually fight corruption.

Some Examples

Korupsi pervades Indonesia's bloated, 2-million-member government bureaucracy, as well as private industry. Indonesia is a land where heads of projects or oil-king generals earn an official salary of Rp900,000 a month, then blow Rp30 million on a daughter's wedding or on a new Volvo. You can buy the captaincy of a ship (Rp1,000,000), or send off a letter extra-fast at the post office (Rp100 extra). Legislators, who get substantial discounts on a car purchase, sell the purchasing permit to a car dealer. A poor peasant must even pay the teacher a bribe in order that his child graduate from the 5th to 6th grade. For the rare privilege of getting a child registered in a government high school, the only channel through which a youngster may enter a university, it'll cost

Rp200,000 in Surabaya, Rp150,000 in C. Java, and as high as Rp500,000 (Rp1,000,000 if you're Chinese) in Jakarta. If a family has put together its last *rupiah* to educate a son for a career, he can't get work at the end of his schooling unless he has a paid "sponsor" in the government. You meet countless young men who've studied everything from aircraft engineering to clerical procedures who are at home doing nothing; they don't yet have "sponsors." Also, few can get a job in the city without "papers" from police and other powers that be, stating that the person concerned is not a radical or communist in sympathies. Each "paper" costs about Rp50,000.

Even the judicial system is not immune to graft. Indonesians say that the best way to tip the scales of justice is to first tip the judge who is trying your case, whether it be for a traffic ticket or murder. In fact, people don't even *use* the legal system unless they have the money. Bribes of US$100,000 are not uncommon in important cases, and during preliminary negotiations the verdict may go first one way and then the other as rival bids are put in. The tax department is another notorious hotbed of corruption. If a firm seeks approval to carry forward a US$1 million loss as an offset against future profits, a 10% personal payment to the right tax official will expedite the necessary approval. Customs officials in particular feel payoffs are their due, often in the form of confiscated shipments. The president in 1985 commissioned a Swiss accounting firm to assess custom duties, a move which cut import and export costs by an estimated 20%. In the state banks, as well as public and private local banks, corruption is rife.

Big-league business corruption involves the acquisition and assignment of major industrial contracts; the finance minister himself is rumored to receive a 1% cut of *all* business transactions in Indonesia. For any capital project, whether financed by private funds or foreign aid, 10-15% of the investment routinely goes to bribes and kickbacks for officials whose signatures are required to advance the paperwork another step up the ladder. Many big projects get stalled while companies or aid organizations find ways to justify the huge overruns without revealing that they had been caused by bribes. Companies make sizable contributions to charitable organizations and it is not just a coincidence that a certain high official's wife heads the charity. Sums involved can be astonishing. When a $12,000-a-year official of the state-run oil monopoly died, he had $80 million in the bank!

The Chinese Connection

The paths of corruption always lead inexorably to the top and all campaigns against corruption always have their upper limits where investigators may go no higher. Any informed person in the street can quote off-hand at least a half-dozen proven examples where members of Suharto's family have used their well-placed connections with "Pak Harto" to gain favors and positions in industries spanning the whole spectrum of the Indonesian economy. Using Chinese middlemen who handle most of the money, the president's 3 sons — Sigit, Bambang, Hutomo — have been awarded virtual monopolies in key industries such as insurance, steel, plastics, telecommunications. Mr. Liem Sioe Liong, the richest man in Indonesia, has used his close ties with the president to receive a monopoly on the multi-million dollar clove-import business. Mr. Liem's group is also the biggest shareholder in Indonesia's largest privately owned bank. In another celebrated incident, the government in 1985 bought US$350 million worth of shares in Indocement, a failing concern owned by Liem and now the main producer of cement in Indonesia.

THE PEOPLE

There has been such an influx of peoples into Indonesia from China, Arabia, Polynesia, SE Asia, Indochina, and later from Portugal and Holland, that you can't say that Indonesia has produced one people. The country is in fact an ethnological goldmine, the variety of its human geography (336 ethnic groups) without parallel on Earth. Welded together by a unifying *lingua franca* and intermarrying freely, Indonesia has all the Asian cultures, races, and religions; they worship Allah, Buddha, Shiva, and the Christian God — and in some places an amalgam of all four. Shades of skin vary from yellow to coal black. Indonesians strive to discover how all these differences can unite all Indonesians in beautiful harmony. The motto clasped in the talons of Garuda, the menacing eagle that is the state crest, is *Bhinneka Tunggal Ika* ("Unity in Diversity").

Being a collection of local archipelagic nations, many Indonesians identify themselves in local terms: *Orang Toraja, Orang Sawu, Orang Mentawai*, etc. This sense of local identity for one's tribe has fostered an attitude of tolerance toward other cultures summed up in the Indonesian expression *"Lain Desa, lain adat"* or "Other villages, other customs." And get along they must, as there are regional differences (between the devout matrilineal Minangkabau and the syncretic hierarchal Javanese); class conflicts (animist villager and orthodox Muslim landlord); racial minorities (Chinese, Eurasians, Indians, Negritos); religious minorities (Christians, Buddhists, Hindus); and local minorities (Kupang Buginese, Surabaya Madurese, Jakartan Ambonese). If Indonesia didn't already exist, no way in hell would anyone ever invent it.

DEMOGRAPHIC MAP OF INDONESIA

In 1930, this island country had only 7 cities with more than 100,000 people, 6 of them on Java. By 1961, it possessed 21 — 11 on Java, 6 on Sumatra, and 2 on Borneo and Sulawesi. Containing already some of the most densely inhabited areas on Earth, Indonesia's population is expected virtually to double — to 250 million — by the year 2000. It has the worst possible combination: one of the highest growth rates, a high population density, and a very large population base. A vigorous government birth control program is hardly slowing the rate.

INHABITANTS PER SQ. KM.

- UNDER 10
- 11-19
- 20-39
- 40-79
- 80-119
- 300-599
- 600-799
- 8000 (JAKARTA RAYA)

0   500 km

Population

Indonesia has the 5th largest population in the world — about 173 million — which equals the combined population of all other SE Asian countries. Better health care, falling infant mortality (80 per thousand births in 1985) and longer life expectancy (averaging 56 years in 1985) are keeping more people alive. The population of Java, about the size of New York state, has quadrupled this century to 91 million, well over a third of the population of the U.S. The population of Jakarta, a city of traffic-choked streets and stinking canals, has now swollen to 8 million. In Banjaran (W. Java) is the largest condom factory in SE Asia, producing 130 million condoms a year, yet birth control efforts have not been able to stem the country's 2.1% annual population growth.

The country's controversial *transmigrasi* policy has also failed to reduce Indonesia's overcrowded urban populations, the totals estimated to increase from today's 35 million to 130 million by 2025. The idea of this scheme, started in 1969, is to move people from the overcrowded islands of Java (1,500 people per sq km) to sparsley populated islands like Sumatra (182 per sq km), Kalimantan (38 per sq km) and Irian Jaya (8.5 per sq km) where there is more space for them to farm or to work in small industries. More than 3.5

million people have been relocated, but critics have charged that the scheme amounts to cultural genocide — the biggest colonization program in history that has led to disastrous ecological deterioration. From the Indonesian point of view — since they are all one nation — transmigration is integration, not colonization. The locals often don't mind transmigrants because they bring with them money and skills to develop the land, creating employment opportunities and clients for regional businesses into the bargain. From 1980 to 1985, the program created more than 500,000 jobs and new *transmigrasi* settlements produced a respectable 5% of Indonesia's rice.

The Indonesian Family

Ever since nomadic Malay hunter-gatherers settled and started cultivating rice in the fertile ashes of burned forests and on the slopes of volcanos some 4,500 years ago, rice has been at the very center of Indonesian culture. Grown virtually everywhere in the country, the structure and pressure of this intensive cultivation has given rise to very close-knit families all over Indonesia, especially on the island which supports the bulk of the population — the rural villages of Java. The heart and soul of Indonesia is the village. Eighty percent of the people live in 60,000 agricultural communities throughout the archipelago. Village life has changed only superficially over the past thousands of years. The village council of elders is the foundation on which the Indonesian version of democracy is based and village and family loyalties come before all others. City dwellers, only 20% of the total population, are the exception. Even Jakarta, the capital of Indonesia with a population of 8 million, has all the habits and manners of a village—or actually, of thousands of villages.

The extended family is a sophisticated structure which makes alliances and friendships, keeps people happy, and offers a superbly supportive environment for children, elders, etc. A family could include grandparents, grandchildren, father's relatives, mother's relatives, nieces, nephews, cousins, all living under the same roof. The nation as a whole is looked upon as a family: the president, *bupati*, and schoolmasters are often referred to as *Bapak* or *Pak* (father) by the public. A school mistress or *warung* proprietor is addressed as *ibu* (mother) by children, and don't be surprised when an Indonesian friend seems to refer to scores of his peers as "brothers." Most Indonesians have never slept in a room where they couldn't hear someone else's breathing.

Cultural Differences

Many of Indonesia's ethnic pockets have remained isolated because of the archipelago's size, jungles, swamps, highlands, complex customs. You can find ways of life which are 5,000 years apart—a journey through time. Cross-sections of the people live in the Neolithic, Bronze, Middle, and Nuclear ages. Some Indonesians wear rings and rats' ribs in their noses, others read the *Asian Wall Street Journal* and break dance. If they have mingled at all, it's taken place near the sea. Many of the mountain tribes have never recovered from past invasions or migrations when they were scattered into the hills by conquerors who took over the richer valleys and coasts. The Kubu and Mamak tribes of Sumatra, the Punan of Kalimantan, and the Alfuro of Maluku are all descendants of the so-called Veddoids from Central Asia who drifted into the archipelago between 7000 and 8000 B.C. They are still considered uncivilized by the present coastal inhabitants of these areas. A theme in much Indonesian folklore and *wayang* is the constant struggle between dark-complexioned highlanders and lowlanders, or between the noble princes and the "black giants" (the aboriginals of the jungles and mountains). Indonesians can be quite color conscious and many are outright segregationists. Village women and their little girls smear white powder on their faces to "beautify," and Indonesian women take all possible precautions against exposing their skin to the sun to prevent a fieldworker's complexion. It's thought that the darker the skin, the more primitive the person, and the lower his or her class. People from Biak look down upon the Papuans from the mainland, urban Timorese regard the mountain people as inferior, and Jakartans hold themselves above the farmers of the countryside.

Adat

Meaning customary law, this is the word Indonesians utter when you ask them a question about a custom which they practice but don't know why or how it began. They just say, "It is *adat*." The closest thing to *adat* we have in the West is Common Law. Although it might not be obvious to the casual observer, this unwritten, unspoken traditional village law covers the actions and behavior of each inhabitant in every village and city *kampung* in Indonesia. Evolving from a distant time when villages were largely self-governing, its dictates and taboos decide what foods are eaten and when, ceremonies and duties to the ill or dead, ownership of land and irrigation systems, architecture of family houses and granaries, criminal and civil cases such as theft and rights of inheritance, relations between older and younger brothers and sisters, the order in which daughters will marry, whom they will marry, how they will marry, how guests are to be treated—everything, the total way of life. Being a self-contained law-of-the-village, *adat* is especially forcible in times of economic or political instability. *Adat* helps to ensure peace and tolerance between all the various religious communities because they all have *adat* in common. *Adat* even serves as a sort of social welfare organization for new migrants to the city.

Adat is rooted in religion, yet it is not a religion. Indonesians say, "Religion comes in from the sea, but customs come down from the mountains." The incoming Islamic religion was in many instances radically modified to fit in with local *adat* law. Rules and behavior from imported religions have also become a part of *adat*. Some say that *adat* is a stranglehold on the people because it encourages superstition instead of reasoning, and that there is no progress because all actions are based on precedents. The product of centuries of habit, most of the more elaborate and cultic *adat* have been forgotten and those left now cover mostly the basic necessities and social functions of life. The original meaning of many acts and gestures may be lost, yet are rigorously performed without question. Change from within Indonesian society is very slow.

THE CHINESE

Indonesia's most important ethnic minority and largest alien group. Although they comprise only about 2% (5 million) of Indonesia's total population, the Chinese control about 75% of the country's private domestic capital. They succeed in all fields: as professionals, bankers, tour guides, traders, shopkeepers, plantation overseers, machine shop workers,

ETHNIC MAP OF INDONESIA

MALAYS

1 ACEHNESE
4 MINANGKABAU
6 EAST SUMATRAN
6a SOUTH SUMATRAN
7 SUDANESE
8 JAVANESE
9 MADURESE
10 BANJARS
13 } MAKASSARESE
   { BUGIS

PROTO-MALAYS

2 GAYOS and ALAS
3 BATAK
11 DAYAK
14 TORAJAN

INDO-AUSTRONESIANS

5 KUBU
12 PUNAN

PAPUANS

15 ARFAK
16 MARIND-ANIM

MIXED RACES

17 MOUNTAIN PAPUAN

TRACES OF PAPUAN BLOOD

MIXED PAPUAN-MALAY

Indonesia contains at least 17 major entho-linguistic groups (each with a million or more members), plus around 200 smaller groups. Coexisting within this island nation's boundaries are Neolithic tribes, sophisticated urban dwellers, isolated hunter-gatherers, skilled Arab mariners, rustic slash-and-burn mountaineers, Chinese merchants. "Like the harmonious beauty of a multi-colored rainbow," President Suharto himself has rhapsodized. Scholars have attributed Indonesia's astounding range of racial types to a series of racial migrations made by dozens of groups arriving from the Asian mainland over several millenia.

mechanics. Though contacts had been recorded between China and W. Java as early as the 5th C., overseas Chinese were first brought in by the Dutch during early colonial times to work as coolies. They eventually worked their way into the bureaucratic and merchant classes, becoming tax collectors, moneylenders, and entrepreneurs. Although forbidden to own land, they still enjoyed many more privileges in the Dutch multi-caste society than Indonesians enjoyed. In the 20th C., nationalist fighters remember with bitterness the indifference or opposition with which most Chinese viewed the revolutionary struggle. This very class of native Indonesians today form the civil bureaucracy and officer corp in the army. The Chinese are also resented for their alien religion, wealth, and business skills, in spite of the fact that wealthy Chinese businessmen *(cukong)* work closely with high-placed Indonesians—even up to the president himself—advising and financing them, and giving them a cut of the profits. Even though Indonesia broke diplomatic ties with Communist China in 1967, the Chinese are naively suspected of being ultimately loyal to Peking, not Jakarta.

The Jews Of SE Asia

Because Indonesians resent and envy the Chinese, they have been traditionally ostracized from the mainstream of Indonesian society. Periodic purges—economic, social, violent—are perpetrated against them. In an uprising in Jakarta in 1740, thousands of Chinese were slaughtered, and after the 1965 coup as many as 200,000 lost their lives. If your father is Chinese, you are Chinese until you die; Indonesia and Korea are the only countries in Asia that base nationality entirely on paternal lineage. The government prevents Chinese from settling in rural areas in large numbers, and Chinese are not allowed to run their own schools, publish their own newspapers, or form political parties. Chinese characters have been erased, by government decree, from all of Indonesia's Chinatowns and even blacked out of photographs in magazines. Chinese-language foreign publications are banned. The authorities have even outlawed their physical fitness exercise, *tai chi,* which employs a few Mandarin words and some soothing Chinese music. Chinese may not keep dual citizenship and must take on Indonesian surnames *(taiji).* Often they choose high-class *priyayi* names which enrages the Javanese even more!

The *Peranakan*

Meaning "Children of the Indies," these Chinese-Indonesians have lived in Indonesia for generations and have become thoroughly Indonesianized. *Peranakan* have intermarried with Indonesians and are completely illiterate in Chinese languages. This group has evolved its own customs, *adat,* dialect and cuisine *(Nonya* cooking). *Peranakan*-Chinese have lost more of their Chinese-ness than have most of the world's 30 million or so overseas Chinese; they are looser, funkier, less inhibited and reserved than Singaporean or Taiwanese Chinese, for example. *Totok,* on the other hand, are Indonesia's more Chinese-oriented Chinese, concentrated in business districts like Jakarta Kota in typical shophouse dwellings as are found in SE China.

LANGUAGE

Such is the diversity of tongues in Indonesia (250 speech forms, each with its own regional dialects) that often the inhabitants of the same island don't speak the same native language. On the tiny island of Alor alone there are over 70 different dialects, and on Sulawesi 62 languages have been identified. Fortunately, one language, *Bahasa Indonesia,* is taught in all schools from the elementary grades. Indonesian is by no means the native language in all parts of the archipelago. Though it's almost universally known as a second language, *Bahasa Indonesia* is the only cultural element that unifies the entire population. First used mainly as a political tool in 1927 with the cry "One Nation, One Country, One Language!", it's the only language used in broadcasting, in official and popular publications, advertisements, and on traffic signs. All the films shown in Indonesia are required by law to be dubbed in standardized, modern Indonesian. Most of the country's regional languages change forms and endings to show deference to the one addressed, but *Bahasa Indonesia* does not. Thus, Indonesian has been one of the main forces behind the democratization of all the different classes and races of Indonesia.

Indonesian, or a dialect of it, is the native language in the following areas: throughout Sumatra (especially the E coast); the coasts of Borneo; Manado and environs; in scattered locales around the Lesser Sunda Islands and Maluku; and in large urban centers such as Jakarta and Semarang. Indonesian has a tremendous amount of dialectical variation and each ethnic group speaks its own accented form: the Javanese speak it very slowly and monotonously, the Sundanese speak it in a sing-song manner, while the Irianese use an archaic form taught only by missionaries. But all dialects are intelligible. On Java, many people over 40 speak Dutch, but not many are Dutch-speaking on the Outer Islands except for Ambon and N. Sulawesi.

HISTORY

Bahasa Indonesia started as a trader's language for use throughout the archipelago, a prototype of the old *Melayu* (Malay) language which you can still hear spoken in its almost pure form in the small Riau and Lingga archipelagos off the east-central coasts of Sumatra. Sumatra's 12th C. Sriwijaya Empire spread the language far and wide through its early influence in the region. Then came the enemy languages: over the past millenium, the Indonesian language has been infused with literally thousands of "foreign" words: not only Polynesian but also Tagalog, Visayan, and Ilocano from the Philippines, and later Portuguese, Dutch, Spanish, English, and French. The earliest Malay dictionary and phrasebook was published in Europe in 1603 by Frederick de Houtman who had been present during the first European contact with Indonesians off the coast of Banten in 1596. The Dutch, during their 300-year occupation of the archipelago, did not wish the Indonesians to speak Dutch so they used Malay from the start as the native language of government.

In the early part of the 20th C., Indonesian nationalists quickly realized the need for a national language when they found themselves addressing their revolutionary meetings in Dutch! In 1928, *Bahasa Indonesia* was adopted as the future national language at the Second Indonesian Youth Congress. Also during the 1920s a new literature came into existence with native poets such as Yamin, Effendi, and Pane writing traditional sonnets but using Indonesian. When the Japanese army occupied Indonesia from 1942-45, the invaders found it impossible to substitute their own language. For this and purely political reasons—in order to disseminate their propanganda throughout the islands—they encouraged the use of Indonesian, a language that most Indonesians could speak or at least understand. When the war ended, the Proclamation of Independence was written and broadcast to the world in Indonesian. When Indonesia achieved nation-status in the 1950s, a modern version of the language was quickly developed and expanded to apply to all the higher requirements of a fully modernizing, developing country—technical, scientific, abstract, literary—as well as serving the needs of administration, law, scholarship, and commerce.

Modern Indonesian

In its history Indonesian has devoured thousands of words from Indonesia's local languages, as well as from Arabic, Chinese, Dutch, Portuguese, Sanskrit, Tamil, French, English and American. Many words of Western origin which have found their way into *Bahasa Indonesia* have obvious roots. Whether you realize it or not, you're already familiar with a good number of Indonesian words, among which are *hotel, doktor, polisi, cigaret, musik, paspor, revolusi, subversif* and *lego jangkar* (drop anchor). The process of coining new words gains currency in the colloquial language among intellectuals first, many of the newly adopted words being terms used in the field of some advanced technology, politics, sports, economics, or military science. Sanskrit-derived words such as *kapas* (cotton) still have wide use in the archipelago, and Chinese forms are also readily recognizable. Portuguese loan words include *nyonya (senhora)* and *garpu* (from the Portuguese word for fork, *garfo*). Words which are Arabic in origin include the days of the week such as *Jumat* (Friday), *Sabtu* (Saturday); also *jaman* (from the Arabic *zaman,* for period) and *ijin* (*izin,* or permit.)

At least 7000 Dutch words are found in Indonesian: *meubel* (from the Dutch word for furniture, *meublen),* *universitas,* (from the Dutch for university, *universiteit)* and *mobil,* (from the Dutch, *automobiel).* *Kecamatan* (district) and *kabupaten* (regency) are words left from the system by which the Japanese divided administrative areas during their occupation in the 1940s. Javanese and Sundanese, spoken by over 90 million people, have also had a significant impact on the development of the *lingua franca* of Indonesia. An exceedingly onomatopoetic language, *layang-layang* means kite, and *cemplung* means to drop into the water, derived from the sound cars make when heaved into canals by students in Jakartan riots. It is a poetic language—*matahari* means sun or literally the "eye of the day." And it's picturesque—*bunga uang* means bank interest (from *bunga* or flower and *uang* or money). Other words you may have run across include *Tuan* (master), *amok* (blind terror), *sarong* (Malay skirt), and *topi* (hat), as well as the familiar *bambu* (bamboo).

LEARNING

If you're traveling in a foreign land it's impossible to understand the culture unless you have some knowledge of the language. Language teaches culture, not the other way around. Learning the language is also the miracle drug to help minimize culture shock. Using a phrasebook is OK, so long as you realize that you're not really using the language, but merely holding up verbal signs: WHERE IS THE TOILET? God forbid that you get back something not in the phrasebook. If you can make the phrasebook work, fine; but an interchange of ideas is difficult. The most important sentence in phrasebook-speak is "I don't speak the language." *Then* you can ask your question. If you don't get the idea across that you're a nonspeaker of the language, the respondent is likely to produce an outpouring of verbiage impossible to comprehend. But what if you *really* want to learn the language? To have even a basic operational skill will take 6 months of intensive work. Here're some pointers:

1) First learn the numbers and the time and calendar systems, the mastering of which will spare you much frustration and money.

2) For anyone serious about picking up some *Pasar Melayu* ("market talk"), it's best to commence traveling in Sumatra where Indonesian is spoken with flawless pronunciation as the native language, and probably worst to start in E. Java where after several months you may be speaking better Indonesian than many natives (try asking a Surabayan *becak* driver the root of the verb *bertemakan).*

3) Avoid Indonesians who try to speak to you in English; they're your most formidable obstacle to learning their language. The only way to learn another language is to never speak your own. If you live with a non-English-speaking family, you'll be semi-fluent in a month. You have to learn it—to *survive!*

4) Concentrate at first on just listening and speaking. It takes only a few weeks to learn the sound system properly, then you're on your own. You must hear Indonesian spoken and speak it every chance you get. Immerse yourself in it. Listen and constantly repeat words and phrases, impressing them on your memory. Take the word *menandatangani,* a bit of a stumbler, meaning "to sign something." Have Indonesians teach you how to pronounce it. The more times you use it, the quicker you'll learn to pronounce it correctly, and the quicker it will become a part of your vocabulary. Only after you've learned the pronunciation should you take on the written language. If you learned the language initially from books at the high school or college level, you were not taught the language, you were taught *about* the language.

5) Don't worry about making grammatical errors or common mistakes; this self-consciousness is a tremendous block to learning. You *have* to make mistakes to learn. Children are quite willing to be wrong and that's why they're able to learn a foreign language so quickly. They don't care if it comes out grammatically correct. "Perfect" Indonesian is also of little concern to Indonesians, who will always give you the benefit of the doubt. And you still get points for trying!

6) Although at first you may not have a substantial vocabulary, try to use what words you *do* know skillfully. You'll be flabbergasted what you can say with a vocabulary of only 500 or so words. You can get along for weeks with just *makan, tidur, mandi, terlambat, sebentar lagi, sekarang, belum, sudah* ("eat, sleep, wash, too late, in a little while, now, already, not yet"). Infinite combinations of sentences! In one month of diligent work you'll be speaking the "market talk" or *Pasar Melayu* — all that you'll need for bargaining, getting around, and relating to people.

7) After awhile you reach a certain point where you're actually understanding. The plateau to strive for is being able to ask questions in Indonesian, and quickly integrate the answers. The most important phrases toward this end are "What is this called in Indonesian?" *(Apa namanya ini di Bahasa Indonesia?)* and "How do you say this in Indonesian?" *(Bagaimana anda menyebutnya?)*

8) *Warung,* bus stops, markets, kiosks, offices are the best classrooms in the land. While waiting for a friend, bus, train, for a *wayang* or movie to begin, or for some bureaucratic hassle, head toward any *warung* or group of bystanders and start up a conversation. Educated Indonesians in any gathering will make themselves known, and they delight in teaching you. They are very patient, repeating and writing words out, teaching you idioms, and breaking sentences down for you. Indonesians are also very encouraging, crying *"Wah, pintar sekali!"* ("Wow, very smart!") the moment you utter just a few intelligible words. These daily, regular Indonesian lessons with the people are easily the equal of any $1200 Berlitz Total Immersion Course. And one good way to capitalize on the Indonesians who constantly approach you is to just make up your mind to learn 5 new words from every new Indonesian you meet.

9) If you move around and stay with the people, all you really need is a good dictionary. Never go anywhere without it and never stop asking questions. Listen to the radio. Translate songs, labels, posters, signs, banners, newspapers, tickets, handouts. Ask, ask, ask questions.

10) If you're learning a regional Indonesian language, use *Bahasa Indonesia* as your learning medium. Always ask for the Indonesian word for the *Bahasa Daerah* (local language) word.

Indonesian Language Tapes

Language/30 Indonesian is an excellent introductory, self-taught language tape program which will put you in tune with the language after about 6 hours of listening. Based on the US Army speed-up language learning method, this concise course stresses only conversationally useful words and phrases. You get 2 cassettes (about 1½ hours) of guided greetings, introductions, requests and general conversation at hotels, restaurants, places of business and entertainment. Using only natives speaking flawless Indonesian, all conversations are spoken in both Indonesian and English. To order, write Educational Services Corp., 1725 K Street, NW #408, Washington D.C. 20006, tel. (202) 298-8424.

Beginning Indonesian Through Self-Instruction is an extensive 58-tape set of 60- and 90-minute study tapes. This expensive, extensive language course focuses on drill with tapes accompanied by a text (US$40) which serves as backup to supplement the oral training. This text and tapes are now the standard works for Indonesian language teaching in the English-speaking world. To order, call Tape Sales, DMLL Language Laboratory, 009 Morrill Hall, Cornell University, Ithaca NY 14853 (tel. 607-255-7394). In Europe, Linguaphone Institute Ltd., Beaver Lane, Hammersmith, London, W69AR, sells a home-study *Bahasa Indonesia* language tape course.

Books

Find a dictionary that suits you. Bilingual dictionaries in English, German, French, Dutch, and Japanese can be bought in Indonesia's large cities. Dictionaries may be bought cheaper in Indonesia than in the West, but the editorial standard and the binding are not very good. Far and away the best dictionary for the truly serious Indonesianist (although it's a bit heavy to lug around), is the brilliantly-compiled, 449-page *An Indonesian-English Dictionary* (US$39.50), by John M. Echols and Hassan Shadily, 2nd Ed., 1963. The companion volume is the 660-page *An English-Indonesian Dictionary* (US$34.50), Echols and Shadily, 1975. Both are available from the Publications Office, SE Asia Program, 120 Uris Hall, Ithaca, NY 14853, tel. (607) 255-8038.

The Echols & Shadily Indonesian-English lexicon still contains the old spelling and it's doubtful now if the new edition will ever come out because Echols died in 1982. However, a new 388-page dictionary: *Contemporary Indonesian-English Dictionary* (US$17.95), by A. Ed. Schmidgall-Tellings and Alan M. Stevens (1981) is an "update" on Echols' 1963 classic and contains only material not given in it. It isn't meant to be used as an independent comprehensive dictionary, but it's up-to-date and very good as Indonesian dictionaries go. Order it from the Ohio University Press, Scott Quadrangle, Athens, OH 45701, tel. (614) 594-5505/594-5852. The only pocket-size dictionary available in North America is *Van Goor's Concise Indonesian Dictionary, English-Indonesian* and *Indonesian-English*, by A.L.N. Kramer, Sr. (US$8.95), by far the most portable for the hardcore traveler and student of Indonesian culture. This hardcover dictionary measures only 12 x 15 cm so you can easily carry it in your shoulder bag. It's all you really need. Order it from Charles E. Tuttle Co., Box 410, Rutland, VT 05701-05701-0410, tel (802) 773-8930. If you're staying for a month or less, the best phrasebook available is *Say it in Indonesian*, ($3.50). Order it from Dover Publications, 31 E. Second St., Mineola, NY 11501, tel. (516) 294-7000. A slightly less expensive alternative is *Indonesia Phrasebook* (US$2.95) sold by Lonely Planet Publications, 112 Linden St., Oakland,

CA 94607, tel. (415) 893-8555. If you memorize this little booklet, it'll be quite adequate for a short 30-day-or-less stay.

Other Language Aids

Use your dictionary in combination with a good deal of conversation practice, a good oral-method book, and a good grammar study book. Australian high school texts are very often top-notch. *Teach Yourself Indonesian* by J.B. Kwee ($6.95), available from Fodor's Travel Publications, 201 E. 50th St., New York, NY 10022 tel. (212) 872-8254, contains carefully-graded lessons which take the reader through pronunciation and word order, parts of speech and grammar. A cheap, fairly competent study book which can be bought in bookshops in the big cities of Indonesia is A.M. Almatsier's *How To Master the Indonesian Language*, Penerbit Djambatan, 1978. Children's Indonesian language readers, available in bookshops all over Indonesia, are well suited for foreigners because they are scaled down from the 8th or 9th grades to the first grade level. The language used is idiomatic and has everyday applications; these readers also contain much information about Indonesia's culture and history. The lower the number (1B opposed to 3A), the simpler the text. Some you can almost read by following the pictures. They usually cost only Rp500 to Rp1000.

BODY LANGUAGE

Such aggressive gestures and postures as crossing your arms over your chest or standing with your hands on your hips while talking, in particular with older people, are regarded as insulting; this is the traditional posture of defiance and anger in *wayang* theater. Anger is not usually shown openly. Loud voices are particularly offensive and the more important and vehement the subject under discussion, the quieter an Indonesian voice is likely to become. The feet are considered the lowliest part of the body and, especially on Java, it's a serious offense to sit with the soles of your feet pointing at people (such as propping them up on a table). It's also impolite to use your toes for pointing as when indicating something displayed on the ground in the *pasar*. Also, to beckon anybody with the crooked index finger is rude. If you need to call to someone (e.g. a passing *becak* driver), extend your right hand and make a motion using the cupped fingers turned downward. Neither should you point with your forefinger, but use instead your right thumb for pointing. Since Asians consider the left hand unclean, never use it to touch someone or to give and receive things. If you should use your left hand, say *maaf* ("excuse me"). When giving or receiving something from someone older or in a high office, extend your right arm (but not too far), bring your left arm across the front of your body, then touch your fingers to your right elbow. When passing in front of an elder or high-born person or person of equal rank whom you don't know, bend your body slightly, particularly if that person is sitting. Avoid blowing your nose into a handkerchief (especially loudly). Make a point of asking a guest to eat or drink when food is served since he will wait until you verbally offer it by saying *silahkan* ("please"). Conversely, it's polite to wait until you are given permission before you eat or drink.

RELIGION

All the great religions have come to these islands over the centuries and Indonesians have absorbed each one. In some cases they have made these incoming religions even more complex, in other instances modified them so drastically as to make them almost unrecognizable. Religion holds a gigantic importance in Indonesian life. Religious Affairs comes under the Department of Religion, headed by a cabinet minister who works with the assistance of officials answerable to each of the recognized religious communities: Islam, Christianity, Hinduism, and Buddhism. National law requires that religion be an academic subject in all schools from the elementary through the first 2 years of university. Each religious community develops its own curriculum for use in the schools, and each student must study and pass an examination on the religion of his family. Your religious faith is also required to provide you with an identification card. Of the world's 900 million Muslims, Indonesia has the largest concentration — the professed religion of at least 90% of the population. However, there are meaningful differences in the degree of orthodoxy practiced by Indonesia's Islamic groups. Take for example the chasm between the staunchly Islamic Acehnese of N. Sumatra or the Sundanese of W. Java, and the much more lax Sasaks of Lombok. Or consider the typically orthodox Malays of E. Sumatra and coastal Kalimantan, and the Central Javanese whose Islam has been considerably influenced by Hindu-Java mysticism.

Minority Religions

Despite Protestant and Catholic missionary proselytizing for centuries, there are only 12.5 million Christians in various pockets throughout Indonesia, about 7% of the population. Although the Dutch colonials favored the Christians above Islamic Indonesians, openly supporting Protestant and Catholic churches and schools, during the revolution Christian guerrilla bands distinguished themselves fighting the Dutch,

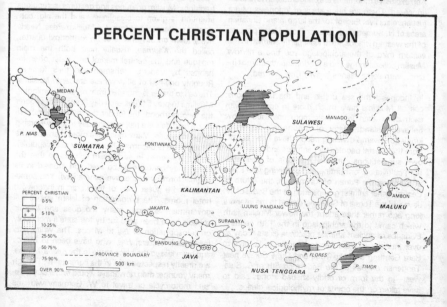

PERCENT CHRISTIAN POPULATION

PERCENT CHRISTIAN
- 0-5%
- 5-10%
- 10-25%
- 25-50%
- 50-75%
- 75-90%
- OVER 90%

- - - - PROVINCE BOUNDARY

0   500 km

MEDAN
P. NIAS
SUMATRA
PONTIANAK
KALIMANTAN
SULAWESI
MANADO
JAKARTA
UJUNG PANDANG
SURABAYA
BANDUNG
JAVA
AMBON
MALUKU
P. FLORES
NUSA TENGGARA
P. TIMOR

earning the respect of their Muslim counterparts. In 1976, there were an estimated 2.7 million Roman Catholics in Indonesia; in Flores, which has had strong Portuguese influences, the *majority* are Catholic. In Minahasa, N. Sulawesi, 90% are Christian; in both Ambon, S. Maluku, and the Mentawai Islands off the W. coast of Sumatra, 50%. The Chinese of Indonesia are either Christian, Taoist, Confucianist, or Buddhist. Most Indonesian Buddhists live on Java, made up of the Chinese, Tenggerese (SE of Surabaya), and various Buddhist sects in Solo, Cirebon, and Yogya. The Badui of W. Java are Buddhists in some of their beliefs, and other scattered Buddhist elements are found throughout Java. Bahais and Jehovah's Witnesses are not allowed to organize. The 3 million people of Bali are Hindu, or to be more precise, Bali-Hindu.

Animism

Animism, the belief that every object has a hidden power, influences everything Indonesians do and think, no matter what their professed religion. All over Indonesia people are strongly influenced by the spirits of ancestors, rice, trees, rocks, rivers, mists, the sun, rain, and other natural phenomena. These animists believe that the entire universe is mysteriously present in every place and at every instant. Mountains, the source of fertilizing water and soil, are the border between the human world and the world of the dead. And explosive mountains are dangerous, always to be appeased. There are huge areas of Indonesia where just animists live. Except for the large inland Christian areas of N. Sumatra, the interior Proto-Malay peoples of the western islands are at least partly animist. In the eastern third of the archipelago you find a narrow Muslim coastal fringe and a predominantly animist interior, with some islands heavily Christianized.

In Indonesia the sea unites and the land divides; coastal Muslims have much more in common with each other than with their more animistic fellow believers inland. Many of Indonesia's highland, jungle, or swamp-dwelling people have been cut off from the coastal peoples for centuries and retain their own superstitions, singular methods of slash-and-burn cultivation, or hunting and gathering (the Kubu of Sumatra, the Punan of Kalimantan, the Alfuro of Ceram). Other animist groups such as the Badui of W. Java and the Toraja of Sulawesi retired to the interiors long ago rather than adopt the newer Muslim faith which came to the archipelago in the 13th century. Evidence of ancient animist practices exists today all over Indonesia—from Kereta Kencana in E. Java to Batu Gantung on Lake Toba and Outje Seraya near Tengenan on Bali to the Bada megalith of C. Sulawesi—in the form of oddly shaped stones said to have taken on the spirits of mythological dieties.

ISLAM IN INDONESIA

Arrival

Islam reached Indonesia more than 600 years after its birth in the Middle East. It was first carried into the region by peaceful Gujerati merchants from India, not by fanatical Arabs. Islam, in fact, had mellowed out considerably by the time it reached Indonesia, dipping into Persian and Indian philosophies along the way. It arrived a much less austere form than was found in the Middle East—a more personal, mystical, salvation-conscious sect from Persia (present-day Iran) called Sufism, which practiced a more emotional approach to God. Not until 1869, with the opening of the Suez Canal, did orthodox Islam finally enter Indonesia. More Indonesians could then visit Mecca, bringing back the Arabic way of life, and setting up theological seminaries (*pesantren*) upon their return from the *haj*. At first, spreading Islam was toughgoing because Java-Hinduism was so firmly entrenched. The areas in Indonesia today which practice the most orthodox forms of Islam—Ternate in Maluku, the N. coast of Java, Banten in W. Java, Aceh Province on the N tip of Sumatra, and the Minangkabau region of the W. Sumatra—are still located far from the regions where the ancient Hindu-Javanese civilizations were most developed.

Today, all aspects of Indonesian life reflect Muslim traditions: Muslim greetings and gestures, scrupulous attention is given to cleanliness, and the pig, considered unclean, is not found in Muslim areas. Nearly every town on Java has a *santri* (orthodox) quarter, called the *Kauman*, usually near both the main mosque and the central market and most often inhabited by traders, craftsmen and their families. Roughly one-half of all Javanese are *santri* Muslims. The call to prayer is sounded from minarets reminding Muslims to pray 5 times each day (it seems the poorer the neighborhood, the louder the loudspeakers). Friday, a holy day, is a half working day to allow worship in the mosques. Many men have more than one wife (though this is becoming increasingly unacceptable). Arabic is learned in all Muslim schools so that the *Koran* may continue to be read and studied in its original form by successive generations. You sometimes find a guest copy of the *Koran* in Indonesian hotel rooms. The propagation of Islam enjoys full government support: many mosques and Islamic schools have been paid for by the state's monopoly on transportation of *haj* to Mecca. The white *peci* (headgear) wearers, *Haji*, who have been to Mecca and have kissed the black stone in the *Kaaba* 7 times, are greatly respected men in the community. Though many younger men nowadays would rather buy a Suzuki motorcycle or travel to W. Germany with the

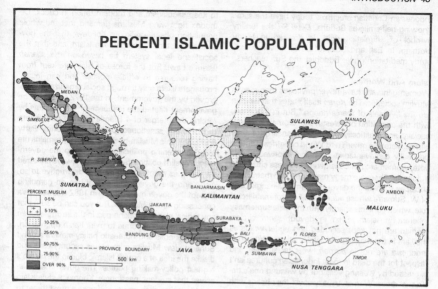

PERCENT ISLAMIC POPULATION

PERCENT MUSLIM
- 0-5%
- +/+ 5-10%
- 10-25%
- 25-50%
- 50-75%
- 75-90%
- OVER 90%

— — — PROVINCE BOUNDARY

0   500 km

MEDAN, P. SIMEULUE, P. SIBERUT, SUMATRA, JAKARTA, BANDUNG, SURABAYA, BALI, JAVA, BANJARMASIN, KALIMANTAN, P. FLORES, P. SUMBAWA, NUSA TENGGARA, SULAWESI, MANADO, AMBON, MALUKU, TIMOR

money, others diligently save for this pilgrimage. About 76,000 Indonesians perform the *Haj* each year (432 died in 1981 — from heat exposure).

Orthodoxy Vs. Secularism

There has always been conflict in Indonesia over those who want to see the country turned into a more fundamentalist Islamic state and those who want to promote modern life. Two of the most serious armed rebellions since Indonesia gained independence have been incited by Muslims, and on several occasions Islamic extremists were nearly successful in attempts to assassinate former President Sukarno. In Suharto's Indonesia of today, the Islamic movement poses the greatest potential threat to the regime. Since the rise of Khomeini in Iran in 1979, there's been a renewed interest in Islam in Indonesia. Fiery Moslem literature is circulated and, increasingly, normally apathetic young Muslims are turning to religion as a form of protest. As in other Muslim countries, fundamentalism has an appeal for young middle-class Indonesians disillusioned with the corrupt, materialistic, Westernized ways of their parents. Also joining the groundswell are members of the *asli* Muslim merchant bourgeoisie whose economic power has declined because of the type of capitalism that has been imposed on Indonesia by its secular government. The recent economic recession due to sharply declining oil prices has also contributed greatly to the revival of Islam.

Every year or so, like clockwork, the disillusionment erupts in violence. In March 1981, hijackers took over an Indonesian domestic aircraft and flew it to Bangkok. After Indonesian commandos stormed the plane, freeing 40 hostages, the government claimed that the hijack was the work of an extremist group known as *Islamic Jihad*. In Sept. of 1984 troops clashed with Muslim rioters in Jakarta's port of Tanjung Priok, killing hundreds, and later that year there was a rash of bombings aimed at wealthy Chinese businessmen affiliated with Suharto. Between Jan. and Apr. 1985, the courts convicted 37 Muslims on various charges, from incitement of the Sept. 1984 riots to civil crimes. Most were fined but some were jailed up to 3 years.

Islam/Buddhism/Hinduism

Java was a Hindu-Buddhist island for well over 1,000 years, and there are traces left everywhere of Indian Buddhism and Shivaism. The Indonesian word for prayer, *sembahyang*, comes from the Buddhist *sembah* which describes the hands pressed together with the fingers extended, touching the chest, lips or forehead. *Puasa*, the Indonesian word for the Muslim fast, is actually a Sanskrit word still used in India. Even though E. Java is overwhelmingly Muslim, you see at every turn the split-temple gateway *(candi bentar)* which is patterned after ancient Hindu structures. Although Hindu-Buddhist syncretism reached its zenith during the 15th C. Majapahit Empire, the faces on

Indonesian Christian crucifixes today have the same knowing half-smile as Buddha. *Dewi Sri*, the fertility symbol of animistic origin, is dressed in Hindu clothing. In Bali and Solo (C. Java), travelers may study meditation under Buddhist and Sufi teachers.

Islam And Women

Women generally have fewer privileges than men in Muslim societies. The *Koran* itself states that women are the "vessels of men's honor." But in Indonesia, with the exception of Palestinians, women are more socially and politically advanced than any of their Islamic sisters in other Third World countries. Though politically disadvantaged by being deprived of the vote, women are not considered 2nd-class citizens in Indonesia. There are many matrilineal and matriarchal societies such as the devoutly Islamic Minangkabaus of W. Sumatra whose *adat* laws allow for matriarchal rule, which conflicts sharply with the male supremacy inherent in Islam. Even in devout *santri* circles, women are not kept secluded and under wraps as they are in the majority of Islamic nations. Women in Indonesia are not in *purdah* (wear facial veils), and respect for the dead in most Indonesian cultures isn't expressed by wearing veils but by wearing one's traditional dress. Women usually cover their heads with a scarf which is often colorful and worn with a low-cut blouse and skin-tight *sarung*, to bring out the best in a woman's figure.

Except in houses of worship, women in Indonesia are not segregated, and sometimes special mosques are built for women. Indonesian women are set against their men taking on more than one wife. When a woman is kept as a second wife, she is often divorced from her husband but still maintained until all the formalities are carried out, or until she can gain financial independence. Army personnel in Indonesia are rigorously discouraged from taking a second wife, which doesn't look good on their record and promotions suddenly become hard to acquire. The wife even initiates divorce proceedings in Indonesia, a heresy in every other Islamic country. This agreement between spouses is part of the marriage contract. Women are active in business and government, and have sat on the Indonesian Supreme Court. One of the most dynamic Muslim women's movements in the world is the Aisjijah of Muhammadijah. Among Indonesia's most significant holidays is Kartini Day honoring Mother Kartini, a Javanese princess whose writings initiated an early 20th C. movement to modernize the status and image of Indonesian women.

Islam In Indonesian Politics

Even though the carefully worded first *sila* in the Five Principles *(pancasila)* gives Christians, Buddhists, and Hindus equal status with the Muslim majority, divorcing Islam from politics simply isn't possible in Indonesia. After all, this is the largest Muslim country in the world. Islam is viewed by the faithful as a means to keep secularism and modernization in check. Orthodox right-wing Muslims demand that the whole population observe religious holidays, that the government protect and encourage Islam, and that the social and legal system be based on the *shariah* (Islamic Law). But the forces of Islam are kept from having recourse to official politics and can legally propagate Islam only through social organizations approved by the government. In the 1972 elections, the government diluted the influence of the Muslims by forcing the merger of 4 Islamic political parties into the officially sanctioned Development Unity Party (PPP). Still, this Muslim-backed PPP party remains the most threatening political opposition to the government. Muslim political factions have always criticized gambling as mentally and morally destructive to society, and the government's total ban on gambling (except the government lottery) in 1982 was seen as a concession to the Muslims. But you can be sure that any radical elements taking part in the struggle for an Islamic state will continue to meet harsh oppression. Senior generals and domestic policy-makers around Suharto view Muslim militants as security risks and dislike the idea of a potent Islamic bloc in the nation's highest policy-making bodies. The government perceives that strident, passionate, Khomeini-style Islam would weaken their power and pose a great threat to the nation's development, political stability, and unity.

Indonesian-style Islam

Unlike Iran, where fundamentalist Shiite Muslims predominate, most of Indonesia's Muslims follow the more moderate Sunni branch. Yet in each region of this country, Islam is practiced with a peculiar twist of its own. Dogma has never had as much importance to Indonesians as the ritual and social aspects of religion. Today, numerous communities conform more to pre-Islamic animist and Hindu-Buddhist ways of life than they do to the formal precepts of the *Koran*. Even in a strongly Islamicized city such as Palembang, S. Sumatra, you see sizzling posters advertising softcore (though heavily edited) Italian porno movies. Though the official state religion is Islam, many Christians sit on the cabinet and hold high army commands, while the Christian holy day, Sunday, is the official government holiday. Many Indonesian mosques lack minarets and instead have onion-shaped cupolas. Few Indonesians actually understand Arabic. Only portions of the Javanese Islamic population strictly perform all the precepts of Islam—5 prayers a day, almsgiving, fasting, pilgrimages, etc.

Islam And Mysticism

Indonesians are preoccupied with mystical and devotional matters, their spiritualism eclipsing the basic rationalism of Islam. Indonesia is a country where even its president believes in a Javanese brand of mysticism and omens. Because the Indonesian masses are so spiritually vulnerable, subversive groups have often masked themselves behind religious sects to foment rebellions or gain political influence. Surantika Samin (1859-1914) was a Javanese mystical leader in the Blora region who rejected all forms of external authority; in 1914, the Dutch government, fearing a revolt, exiled Samin to Palembang where he died. The Kutil Movement of 1945 was a social revolution attributed to a semi-religious guru figure, and in the extraordinary Sawito Kartowibowo affair of Oct. 1976 a Javanese mystic succeeded in securing the signatures of such prominent figures as Dr. Hatta, the co-signer of the Proclamation of Independence, in order to give authority to his cause. Even high Javanese public officials (including Suharto) still seek *wahyu* (divine revelation and guidance from above) through meditation and seclusion. His regime shaken during 20 years at the top by such omens as earthquakes, plots against the government, and continuing student unrest, Suharto won re-election in 1988 in an attempt to restore *kerukunan,* a sense of harmony to his heavenly mandate to rule.

Mysticism is alive and well in E. and C. Java, where the Sultan of Yogya is still looked upon as a god and where there's a brisk market in newly published or reprinted old editions of Javanese esoteric wisdom and other mystico-religious books. Ritual meals (*sela-*

matan) are attended by neighbors and friends to appease the spirits during important transitional events.

Army generals helicopter into the camps of mystics in E. Java (Blitar) for spiritual consultations. Witch doctors *(dukun)* exorcize evil spirits from granaries, temples, cars, hotels, swimming pools. Thieves use black magic to rob houses. There are devils and satans, ghosts which steal children *(wewe),* and lure young men *(puntianak).* There are daylight spirits *(banaspati),* angels of God, and even one angel who went astray, *Idyadril.* In isolated Kalimantan, as in 5th C. Europe, wraiths of smoke are taken for ghosts and among some Islamic groups of Sumatra mysticism is connected with trance dances. On Ambon, white-magic priests *(mawang)* work harmoniously alongside the Christian or Muslim religious leaders of a village. The staunchly Islamic Makassarese of S. Sulawesi worship ancient pieces of regalia such as large stones, flags, swords, umbrellas, and plows, presenting regular offerings of food and betelnut, and on important occasions animals are even sacrificed to them. Catholics of Yogya use *gamelan* music to celebrate mass, and some Christians of Kalimantan pay homage to God by spitting, and the Christians of Torajaland (Sulawesi) sacrifice bulls to the memory of a dead *raja.* It's far easier to learn when religions began in Indonesia than it is to know when they ended.

ARTS AND CRAFTS

With its giddy variety of insular environments, Indonesia is unique as a place where so many beautiful traditional crafts have been made for thousands of years. Superb craftsmanship and the longest traditions are best seen in the simplest crafts: the palm weaving of Bali, the flutemaking of the Torajans, the basketry of the Rotinese, the lizard motifs on Batak magic wands and houses, and infinite other examples of traditional domestic and cultic art. Indonesian arts and crafts lend themselves especially to attractive decorative items and furnishings for contemporary Western homes. *Batik,* king of Indonesian art forms, can be fashioned into upholstery, and the superb *ikat* textiles of the archipelago can make unique wall hangings. Shopping in Indonesia is a real hit-or-miss treasure hunt; you must doggedly search every corner of a shop to find what you are looking for. Indonesians have different tastes, so look for that item which strikes your fancy. Many villages or city *kampung* specialize in their own crafts. If you want to know what crafts an area or city specializes in, just ask the locals what gifts they take to out-of-town relatives when they visit. This way, you find out what is cheap, unique, or rare about that place. If the plastic arts interest you, always head for ASRI (School of Fine

Arts), art centers in the larger cities where painting, drawing, graphics, sculpture, and the decorative arts are taught. For shipping crafts home, see the "Communications" chapter.

Ancient Art
Because of the tropical climate, stone temples and megaliths are the only remnants of their ancient art—the art of rajas, priests, sultans, and aristocrats. The art of the common people—everyday objects in cloth, papyrus, palm leaf, and wood—have long since disintegrated. But the motifs and symbols survive as nothing is destroyed and everything is preserved in Indonesia. Designs and techniques of prehistoric painters and sculptors are still widely used in textiles, metal *objets d'art,* and woodcarvings on houses and *prahu.* Fish with human faces which were carved on Prambanan stone reliefs a millenium ago can be seen today in S. Balinese paintings. Primitive art, such as that practiced by the Asmat and Tanimbar islanders, uses models and themes found in ancester worship. Today you can purchase replicas of small *terra cotta* figurines at Trowulan (near Mojokerto, E. Java) and heavy stonecarved images of ancient Hindu gods at Batubulan (S. Bali) and on the road out to Borobudur.

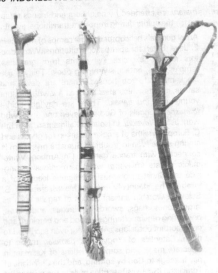

mandau: *A traditional Dayak weapon made of bronze or steel—a combination of axe, sword, and machete—which possessed a powerful spirit. Exquisite handles, sheaths, and hilts were made of ivory, ebony, or staghorn and decorated with very detailed carvings of crocodiles, lizards, deer, turtles, fish, toads, and frogs, and sometimes human heads with oiled and well-combed tufts of hair on the ends. One side of the mandau is 7 mm thick to give it weight, while it's curved razor-sharp edge is ideal for beheading. Head-taking was looked upon as a sacrifice to supernatural deities and spirits as well as an initiation rite into manhood.*

Buying And Trading

Crafts in shops are acquired either by middlemen who travel to crafts areas or from people in need of money who approach the shop with family heirlooms. You will often find shops selling similar goods located in a particular neighborhood or all in a row on a certain street or stretch of road. Locations of shops may be scattered and inconvenient, and hours of operation uncertain. Because of the helter-skelter location of shops and markets, and Indonesia's wide cultural and geographic diversity, it's best to narrow your focus to a particular craft or artform, then design your itinerary. For example, if primitive art interests you, get a Garuda "Domestic Discounted Fare" (see "Internal Transport") and fly to Medan, Lake Toba, Rantepao, southern Maluku, and Irian Jaya. If it's *batik* you want, plan a route through Java that takes in the *batik* centers of Jakarta, Cirebon, Yogya, Solo, and Pekalongan. Or you can simply wander around Indonesia sampling all its different crafts. But be forewarned that if you stick to the Lake Toba-Yogya-Bali tourist rut, you will be exposed to crafts which use the same themes and techniques *ad nauseum*.

The best buys are usually in the town or island where a particular craft is produced because there's a much wider selection and the artisans are often more agreeable to bargaining than city shopkeepers who pay higher overheads. This is not always the case, however, because even in remote areas you are regarded as a rich foreigner and peer pressure from other villagers could escalate prices. So consider how much your trip to these out areas will cost because in the end you could actually save money by just making your purchases in reputable shops in the large cities of Medan, Jakarta, and Denpasar, even if prices are expensive. On the other hand, Torajan crafts from Sulawesi and Batak crafts from Sumatra are not widely available in Jakarta and Bali, so you should take advantage of the availability of regional crafts while you're in a given area.

When shopping for crafts, prices fluctuate from shop to shop, from stall to stall, and from hour to hour, depending upon the cash flow of the seller and your bargaining skills. Be ready for some irrational merchants who don't understand Western supply-and-demand pricing logic; the exceptions are Chinese, Minangkabau, and Batak vendors who are willing to strike bargains to realize incremental profits. For buying anything from coconuts to stone carvings at village and souvenir markets, the morning price is often the lowest of the day because the sellers believe that if they make a sale right off, then the day will go well for them. If you let third parties take you into a shop, a commission will very often be tacked onto the price you pay, and they sometimes make a nuisance of themselves demanding their cut. Shops working on a low overhead don't want anything to do with them.

Bring Western clothes specially for trading. T-shirts, especially ones with cartoons or messages or emblems on them, you can sell or swap quite easily. Parisian T-shirts go over the best for trading. Also Western jewelry and flashy but inexpensive wristwatches are well received. Your safari-style jean jacket could fetch as much as Rp14,000 in Indonesia, either in cash or in trading value, but jean trousers don't have such a high barter value any longer because everyone's got them.

Tailors And Seamstresses

You can buy ready-made clothes but they tend to fade, wrinkle maddeningly, and finally fall apart because of the cheap material. Colors also tend to be very loud, and successful patterns are overproduced with the same designs over and over. Large and extra-large sizes are in chronic short supply. It's better to have a tailor or seamstress sew your clothes. Take just several changes of clothes because eventually you'll replace all your clothing with really cheap and lovely Indonesian-style garments which you can design yourself. Tailoring costs only Rp3000 for a dress, Rp2000 for a skirt, and Rp2000 for a shirt. Like the Thais, Indonesians are very skilled at copying from an already sewn piece or from a photo in a fashion magazine. Take a shirt, skirt or pair of trousers which fits you very well from which the tailor will make a paper pattern. Be sure to explain *everything* (their tastes are different from ours), specifying even the buttons to be used, the pant length, and all modifications. Names and addresses of competent local tailors and seamstresses can always be had from fabric shops and tourists offices. One of the few natural, traditional, inexpensive cotton fabrics left on Java is *lurik*, available in meter lengths from Pasar Klewar in Solo (C. Java) or Toko Terang Bulan, Jl. Taman Siswa 55, Yogya. Also coming on the scene are *jumputan*, the tie-dye fabrics of Java, and Balinese *endek*, an alternative fabric to age-old *batik*.

TEXTILES

The scattered isles of Indonesia offer probably the world's greatest collection of traditional textiles. Incorporating unique patterns, designs, and colors, you'll find everything from the primitive barkcloths of C. Sulawesi and Irian Jaya, sophisticated weft and warp *ikat* designs using natural dyes of the Lesser Sundas, color-rich *lurik* of C. Java, and dazzling *songket* textiles of Sumatra. At one time over much of Indonesia, textiles had a religious significance. Sundanese women of W. Java weren't allowed to marry until they had woven a *samping*, and Pekalongan women of the N coast used to spend half the night meditating and burning incense before starting work on a *batik*. Organic dyes were sometimes ritually made from the blood of human sacrifices. Even today *sarung* are often wrapped around the bride and bridegroom to symbolize unity, spread over a seriously ill person to increase his power of resistance, and the dead are honored by being covered with precious textiles. For most visitors, these labor-intensive textiles are brought to best advantage as wall hangings and upholstery coverings rather than as material for clothes.

Batik

Indonesian artists love animal motifs: buffalos, elephants, crocodiles, snakes, lizards, as well as dragons, lion birds, and other mythological creatures. You can see these motifs vividly represented in In-

batik tulis: *Hand-drawn batik in which hot wax is poured into a small copper crucible called a canting (pictured above). With 1, 2, or 3 spouts of varying thicknesses, the canting is used like a pencil to apply a wax pattern upon a fabric. In this wax-resist method, all parts of the cloth not covered in wax take up the dye. Although several "wax-writings" inscribed with a canting date back to the 16th C., batik did not reach its zenith until high-quality white cotton was first introduced from European factories. The technique achieved its highest level in Central and E. Java during the early 20th C. with the making of batik of unbelievable detail and quality. Today, in the kraton courts of Java (Cirebon, Solo, Yogya), see priceless old batik on soft worn silk behind glass cases.*

an example of a batik *motif derived from creeping plants, in this case the trumpet-shaped chili pepper* (lombok)

donesia's most renowned textile craft, *batik*. These beautiful hand-done works of art on cloth are made by using a "wax-resist" method whereby wax is applied to the cloth in order to resist the dye. The wax can be applied by hand *(tulis)*, or with a metal stamp *(cap)*. In *batik tulis*, hot wax is poured into a small, 12-mm-wide copper crucible called a *canting*. With 1, 2 or even 3 spouts of varying thicknesses, a *canting* is used like a pencil to apply a wax pattern upon a fabric; all parts of the cloth not covered in wax take up the dye. On *batik tulis* work the colors on both sides of the cloth are equally vibrant because the wax is applied to both sides, whereas in *cap batik* the inside colors are duller because the wax has been applied to one side only.

The quality of the cloth used is always an important determinant of the price. Although several "wax-writings" inscribed with a *canting* date back to the 16th C., *batik* did not reach its zenith until high-quality white cotton was first introduced from European factories beginning in the late 19th and early 20th centuries. During this period, *batik* of unbelievable detail and quality was produced in a number of private workshops of C. Java. Today the main *batik*-producing centers are still found in the cities of Cirebon, Yogya, Solo, and Pekalongan on Java, although *batik* is also produced as far N as Jambi (S. Sumatra) and as far E as Madura (E. Java). A fine art form, *batik* painting, has also been developed in the last decade. In this wax-resist technique, the wax is applied by using either the traditional *canting* or a brush (as in oil painting). To view a large selection of *batik* paintings, visit ASRI (Academy of Fine Arts) on Jl. Gampingan, as well as the many galleries around the *kraton* of Yogya.

Weaving

First brought from India, weaving retains heavy Hindu influences. In these islands, fabrics aren't only woven in 2 directions but sometimes in 3 and 4, and some fabrics *(songket)* are even interwoven with gold thread. Each completed, handloomed fabric represents a colossal amount of human labor and now most of these tribal, agricultural crafts only survive in the more remote parts of the archipelago (the interiors of the islands of Nusatenggara, Kalimantan, Sulawesi) where imported printed cloth isn't so readily available. There are many regional and island differences: the ancient applique technique of the Dayak, the magnificent "Ships of the Dead" textiles of the Krui country of S. Sumatra, brilliant flaming *ikat* cloths of the Bali Aga villages of E. Bali, the pure silk *sarung* of Samarinda (E. Kalimantan) that can last 20 years.

Information

To really grasp the range and understand the workmanship and techniques behind Indonesian woven cloths and *batik*, a visit to Jakarta's Textile Museum on Jl. Satsuit Tubun (near Tanah Abang Bus Station) is mandatory. Besides its fabulous textile collection, the museum displays looms and *batik*-making tools and also has a library. In the *kraton* courts of Solo and Yogya (C. Java) you may see priceless old *batik* on soft worn silk behind glass cases. For more antique textiles, visit the shop of Caecil Papadiminitriou, Jl. Pasuruan 3, Jakarta Pusat (tel. 377953), near the antique stalls on Jl. Surabaya. Also refer to the booklist in the backmatter for some excellent books on Indonesian textiles. In Yogya, where there are over 900 *batik* factories, you can study *batik*-making in workshops under Javanese masters. For more about *batik*, see Java's "Intro."

ANTIQUES

The markets and shops of Indonesia are a hidden mine for antique hunters. There are marvelous ice-shaving machines, Ming China, old VOC coins, bottles and ink-wells, embroideries, 300-year-old trading beads, as well as antique brass lamps, Delftware, pewterware, canopied beds, old chests, enameled bedpans, and a wealth of other period artifacts left over from the Dutch years. The best antique flea markets are on Java, in particular Solo and on the N coast (Jakarta, Cirebon, Semarang, Surabaya). Most antique shops are cluttered and disorganized so you really have to dig around. Learn as much as you can beforehand so you can discern the gems from the junk. Visit museums, take tours, and be sure to attend cultural lectures sponsored by Jakarta's Ganesha Society, a very culturally active organization run by the American Women's Association; their events are usually publicized well in advance in the special-interest sections of the local press. Jakarta's City Museum and National Museum offer excellent examples of the various antiques and regional styles found in Indonesia. The most famous row of antique shops in Indonesia is along Jakarta's Jl. Surabaya, dominated for the most part by shrewd Minang merchants.

Some warnings. Beware of sellers-on-foot of old coins. Back in the 1970s, you could buy old VOC coins for as little as Rp100, then sell them for 100 marks apiece back in Germany, paying for your trip to Indonesia. Not anymore. The price asked for these coins nowadays is usually just too low (Rp30,000 for a silver 12½ guilder piece) for them to be real. The vendor's story usually is that he or she is in desperate need of money. Although these fakes are extremely convincing, don't fall for it! Also be wary of paying antique prices for textiles which vendors claim are "very old" (anywhere from 2 weeks to 150 years!). Best to stick to reputable established sellers who know a great deal about textiles.

wayang: *A Javanese word meaning literally "shadow" or "ghost." Indonesians believe that drama is the shadow of life and that man is a mere puppet of God. Wayang is the main vehicle of drama in Indonesia, using live people or puppets to enact stories from the lives of Javanese ancestors or from the Hindu epics. This art is at least 1,000 years old and on Java you may see figures on 13th C. bas-reliefs similar to those used in wayang today. Some wayang forms have completely died out. These are only a few of the more than 200 diverse characters: gods, nobles, cruel kings and princes, demons, giants, vile monsters, beautiful princesses, wise men, servants, lovable clowns and fools. The almond-eyed, slant-nosed, chalky-faced ones are the heros and the pop-eyed, bulbous-nosed ones are the villains. All characters win approval no matter what their personality or appearances. Everyone watches and enjoys wayang, from becak drivers to cabinet ministers. It's a mixture of mysticism, slapstick, comedy, morality play, social commentary, and magical myth-making—all in one. Audiences sit up all night watching live plays in immense bamboo theaters, following every word with laughter or boos, tense silence, or crying. Wayang is also used to effect social change; clowns, for example, ad lib about family planning. Movies, TV, and rock groups only provide more themes.*

CARVING

Indonesia's hundreds of ethnic groups produce some of the world's most sought-after and exciting primitive art. You can find almost any form of woodcarving: *si gale gale,* life-sized wooden puppets which the Bataks of N. Sumatra jerk to life when a child dies; eerie 2-m-high ancestor figures of the Leti Islands in Maluku; menacing demons, *naga,* and human-like fish of the Javanese; handsomely grained ebony animal figures of Bali; posts, house gables, and window shutters of the Sumbanese and Alorese; frightening masks, war shields, and spears of the Irianese. Decorated with beads and feathers, Dayak shields and baby carriers make superb wall pieces in Western homes. Jepara, on the N coast of C. Java, is famous for its ornately carved furniture and panels. Mas is the woodcarving center of Bali.

Basically, Indonesian carving falls into 2 categories: the ancient Dongson style which dates from 350 B.C. and derives from Indochina, and the "high" Hinduized style of the Balinese and Javanese *kraton.* On Java and Bali, the original Dongson culture gave way to the more sophisticated import of ideas from India. Dongson-influenced art forms are found more in the Outer Islands while Hinduized art forms are found on Java and Bali where dragons and other Hindu mythological creatures are popular on gong stands, prows of boats, beams of houses, and temples. The wood available to both styles is mostly teak, ironwood, and young ebony. Many traditional handicrafts would have disappeared long ago if it weren't for tradition-loving tourists. And tourism is also why they've become so expensive. A good Balinese carved statue now costs up to US$250.

Other Carving Media

The detail on other popular carving media—buffalo horn, bone, ivory or hornbill beak—can be so extreme you need a magnifying glass to see the work. For the best and cheapest carved tortoise shell and seashells, go to Ambon and Ternate in Maluku. For stonework, using smooth lava rock, go to Yogya (C. Java) and Batubulan (S. Bali). Leatherwork is done mainly on a crude grade of buff-colored buffalo hide. On Jl. Malioboro in Yogya, the capital of leather carving in Indonesia, sidewalk vendors sell luggage, briefcases, lampshades, pendants, belts, purses, sandals. Examine these articles carefully as the workmanship is generally shoddy, the leather is odoriferous, and the styles old-fashioned. Another major leather carving center, particularly for footwear, is Bandung, W. Java. The best-known carvings in hide, usually goatskin, are gilded shadow puppets used in the *wayang kulit* of C. and E. Java. These *wayang,* which represent different characters in the Hindu *Ramayana* epic, make excellent decorative wall pieces. So strongly stylized that they look barely human, the eyes, nose, and mouth are carved out last "to break open" the puppet, i.e. to give it life.

METALWORK

Metalworking in bronze, brass, and tin still thrives in

rumah gadang: *The "big house" of the Minangkabau people of W. Sumatra has inspired a national architectural style exemplified in the graceful buildings of the ITB campus of Bandung, W. Java. Resting on 20-30 wooden pillars, traditional roofs are made of thick layers of black palm-tree fibers (ijuk). The structure is able to accommodate a number of families. Each daughter is entitled to a room where she'll receive her husband when she marries; extra extensions ("horns") are built onto the high roofs for each son-in-law the mother or grandmother acquires. In front are richly decorated rice sheds (lumbung) identical to the big house but on a smaller scale. The more rice sheds, the wealthier the family. The Minangkabau expression derived from their house-building, "It doesn't crack in the heat or rot in the rain," is used to express durability, tenacity, integrity.*

areas where Hindu influence was once strongest: the prosperous seaports of Java, Bali, S. Sulawesi, coastal Borneo, and W. Sumatra. The most spectacular examples of ancient Dongson influence are the magnificent bronze kettle drums *(moko)* of the Pantar and Alor islands of eastern Nusatenggara. Artistic tinwork, decorated with delicate scroll lines, is produced from tin extracted from the islands of Bangka and Billiton (off the SE coast of Sumatra). Probably the most popular metal artifact for visitors is the legendary *kris,* the ornamental dagger worn by Javanese and Balinese to ceremonies. The sacred blade can be straight or curved, and the hilts and scabbards beautifully decorated. Old bejeweled specimens can cost well over US$1000, though souvenir varieties with wooden handles can be found for less than US$10. Indonesian artists also excel in precious-metal crafts such as silversmithing, and setting semiprecious stones such as quartz, agate, pearls, purple amethyst, moonstone, onyx, jasper, and carnelian in silver and gold. The indigenous black opal is of particular interest to international rock hounds. Stones are seldom polished so as to preserve their natural look and sometimes even nut casings or shiny green beetle wings are set in gold—for the beauty of it, not for the "value." Precious metals are often mixed with other metals to obtain different nuances of color (and to save money). In Aceh Province, far northern Sumatra, acid is used to discolor and embellish ornamental gold.

Jewelry

Banjarmasin in S. Kalimantan is a major domestic center for rings set with stones as well as for Dayak polished stone beads. In the shops of Kuta Beach on Bali contemporary jewelry is displayed, and in the high-class hotels of Jakarta visit the Spiro family chain of shops, each run by a different member of the family—Joyce Spiro in the Sari Pacific, J. Spiro in the Hilton, Linda Spiro in the Borobudur Intercontinental. While in Jakarta, visit the workshop of P.D. Pelangi Indonesian Opal & Jewelry Center, Jl. Gatot Subroto (tel. 583051/587981). Silver, contrary to popular belief, is quite cheap, especially the way they cut it in Indonesia. No matter what the silversmiths of Bali, Yogya, and Bukittinggi try to tell you about all the excruciating handtooled work it took to make a particular piece, don't pay more than Rp4500 for a ring, small brooch or pendant. Silver centers: Ujung Pandang (S. Sulawesi), Kota Gadang (N. Sumatra), Kota Gede (C. Java, near Yogya), Culuk and Mas (S. Bali).

MISCELLANEOUS

A large and unique variety of toys, knives, hats, mats, and other traditional crafts is available in Indonesia's markets. Also be on the lookout for musical instruments—gongs made in Bogor and Solo, Batak string instruments, Asmat drums, Torajan flutes, Sundanese *angklung*, Javanese xylophonic *gamelan* instruments, the singing tops and bird whistles of Bali. Stuffed animals are sold in the Penanjung Game Park (Pangandaran) in W. Java, mounted butterflies at the Bogor Botanic Gardens (60 km S of Jakarta) and at Bantimurung (S. Sulawesi), and the island of Japen off the northern coast of Irian Jaya is the center for illegal bird-of-paradise skins. Bird markets are found in all the large cities of Java. Gili Air and Gili Trawangan off the NW coast of Lombok offer perhaps the archipelago's best shell collecting. For wild and hybridized orchids and shells, a visit to Clara Bundt's Orchid Garden & Shell Collection (Jl. Mochtar Lufti 15, Ujung Pandang) is a must, as are the natural history collections in both the National Museum of Jakarta and the Zoological Museum of Bogor.

Plaiting

Indonesia's oldest craft. Woven containers are still made where tin and plastics haven't yet penetrated. Bamboo, rattan, sisal, *nipah*, or *lontar* palm are ingeniously utilized all over Indonesia, probably most creatively by the Sundanese of W. Java, Dayak of Kalimantan, and the Balinese. Many consider the palm-leaf offerings set outside the houses and temples of Bali greater works of art than the island's copycat world-famous paintings and carvings. Bamboo tubes are used to store tobacco or as life-preservers, to make arrows, quivers, jars, bridges, knife sheaths, fishing rods, betelnut boxes, walking canes, flutes, animal cages. Split bamboo is made into nets, hats, wickerwork, mats, umbrella frames. Since "modern" tools such as iron hatchets, axes, machetes, small planes and knives are needed to gather bamboo and to work it, the plaiting crafts are best developed among the more advanced cultures of western Indonesia and least developed among the more inaccessible, archaic tribes of eastern Indonesia.

Ceramics

Since plentiful bamboo is so easily crafted into vessels, ceramic firing techniques have never developed into advanced crafts in these islands. Glazed ceramics are crafted in Kasongan village near Yogya, Plered in W. Java, the Ceramics Research Center of Bandung (W. Java); Pejaten (near Tabanan) and Batu Jimbar (Sanur) on Bali; Banyumolok and Kediri in W. Lombok (large vases and water pots). Indonesia was once a big center for Chinese pottery and you can find well-preserved pieces in the far reaches of the archipelago: dug out of old Chinese graves on Sumba, in the Dayak longhouses of Borneo, in the dusty souvenir shops of Ambon. As well as the finer courtware, you will also find "Kitchen Ming," so named because it was utilized for everyday use by the Chinese 300-400 years ago. The farther away from the tourist centers, the cheaper. Giant Tang vases cost Rp500,000 in Ambon, and whole sets of Kitchen Ming perhaps as little as Rp250,000 in Samarinda. Transport this venerable and expensive china *on your lap* on the plane home.

Paintings

Not until the late 19th C. did an Indonesian painter, the Javanese Raden Saleh (1814-1880), attain fame in the European art world. Devoted mainly to landscape painting, most of the Indonesian art of this period merely imitated Western styles and was devoid of originality in concept or design. Just before WW II, such art associations as Pelukis Rakyat and Seniman Indonesian Muda sprang up, which developed a genuine Indonesian expression through the adoption of Western techniques. Affandi, one of the leaders of that early effort, maintains a studio today near the Ambarrukmo Palace Hotel in Yogya. Other famous Indonesian artists, who create oil and *batik* paintings, prints, and posters, have galleries in Yogya, Jakarta, and Bali. In Yogya, visit ASRI, Jl. Gampingan; in Jakarta, the best are the Harris Art Gallery, (Jl. Cipete 41) and Oet's Gallery (Jl. Palatehan 133), both in Kebayoran Baru. The Ubud area is the painting hub of Bali; visit the Neka Museum in Campuan and the Agung Rai Gallery in Peliatan. For a history of Balinese painting, see Bali's "Introduction."

EVENTS

Ninety percent of Indonesians are nominal Muslims, so Islamic religious holidays dominate the festival calendar. Because of the heat, Indonesians celebrate most of their holidays early in the morning or late at night. To find out about events, first get the *Indonesia Calendar of Events*, covering festivals, holidays, and events throughout the archipelago for the current year. Pick this booklet up at Garuda offices in any of Indonesia's large cities, or at Indonesian embassies or Garuda offices overseas. Also, as soon as you arrive in an area, head for the tourist office and inquire about any festivals taking place. Some regional tourist offices might also hand out a list of annual local events, but oftentimes the personnel at these offices won't even think to tell you that an event is going on in a nearby village or even in the same city.

A good Javanese calendar has most of the important observations shown on it. Since their calendar is based on the lunar year (354 days), their festivals move backwards through the solar months, the dates varying from one year to the next by approximately 11 days. The Balinese calendar is based on yet a different system. Being Hindu, Bali has festivals all its own. And this goes for nearly every major ethnic group of Indonesia—each holds its own celebrations, ceremonies and commemorative occasions. On Good Friday, Portuguese descendants on Flores carry a statue of the Virgin Mary in a barefoot procession while wearing grass pompoms, black costumes, and triangular-shaped caps—a tropical slant on this Roman event. The mountain-dwelling Tenggerese of E. Java throw live bulls and chickens into a molten crater once a year to placate the gods in the famous Kasada Festival. And on remote Sumba Island, mock battles and jousting matches are held each April, harkening back to an era of internecine warfare.

Religious holidays could cause some inconvenience to travelers. For example, during the holy month of *Ramadan,* which is practiced with varying intensity throughout the islands, usually the only places to eat in orthodox Islamic areas are dark secretive *warung,* hidden away in back alleys. Traveling the week before other big holidays, such as *Leberan,* can be exhausting on Java: about 90 million Javanese cross the island to visit their families during this time! Certainly you won't feel lonely. Reservations for trains or buses should be made at least a week before, and it can be nearly impossible to find an empty seat on an intraisland flight or ship. Some of the more important, Java-oriented holidays are:

Ramadan (Or Puasa)

A month-long fast in the 9th month of the Javanese calendar. It's preceded on Java by *Padusan,* a cleansing ceremony to prepare the spirit for the coming fast. Islamic fasting is less drastic than the Hindu custom of total abstinence from all food and drink, Gandhistyle. Muslims are more into a moon cycle. The whole family rises at 0300 or 0400, gorges themselves, then eats nothing during the daylight hours. Many visit family graves and royal cemeteries (Kota Gede and Imogiri in C. Java) where they recite prayers, strew flowers and holy water, burn incense. Special prayers are said at mosques and at home. Brand new velvet *peci* are sold everywhere on the street. The fasting month ends when you can properly sight the crescent of the new moon with the naked eye.

Lebaran

Also called *Hari Raya* (or in Arabic, *Idul Fitri).* The first day of the 10th month of the Arabic calendar, this marks the end of the Muslim fast, an outburst of celebrations climaxing a month of pent-up tension and austerity. After tom-toms and firecrackers all night long, the festivities usually begin at 0700 when everyone turns out for an open-air service in the village *alun-alun.* Mass prayers are held the first morning, followed by 2 days of continuous feasting and public holidays. Women dress in white, like nuns. A householder buys new clothing for his children and servants, verses are sung from the holy *Koran,* and sometimes there are religious processions. This is a joyous time for mutual forgiveness when pardon is asked for all wrongs of the past year. *Leberan* is like Christmas, Valentine's Day, and the New Year's resolutions all rolled into one! With everyone dressed in their finery, Muslim Indonesians all day long visit and revisit neighbors and relatives, bringing gifts of specially prepared food, the best the family can afford. At each house a cup of tea is served with helping after helping of sweet doughy cake and bright cookies until you burst. *Lebaran* continues until all the visits to relatives are ended. A large extended family could celebrate *Lebaran* for as long as a week.

Other Religious Holidays

Al'qur'an is a sacrificial ceremony which corresponds to the Arabian event. In Yogya, it's called *Garebeg Besar. Al'qur'an* is celebrated on a lesser scale in Solo, Jakarta, Cirebon, and Demak (centering around Demak's ancient mosque) on Java. In Medan, N. Sumatra, the Sultan of Deli takes part in ceremonies at a traditional Malay court. *Idul Adha* is the Muslim day of sacrifice held on the 10th day of the llth month of the Arabic calendar when devotees visit the mosque. Those who are able attend special ceremonies in

pencak silat: *This fighting skill can also be a beautiful art form. Found all over Indonesia, the word silat has more to do with the physical culture side of it while pencak is more the art side. The martial art has a number of origins: in it, Nepalese music, Hindu and Arabian weapons, and Siamese costumes are all utilized. Priests, who studied the actions and skills of animals to learn how to defend themselves, invented the combative techniques. Though derived from Sumatra, this fighting style reached its technical zenith on Java, where today you find the majority of the many styles. By the 14th C., pencak silat had become a highly polished, very technical, and deadly art practiced only by the Majapahit sultans and their court officials. Commoners were forbidden from learning its tactics. Today, the styles are used as a basis for self-defense by the Indonesian army. One characteristic of the many forms is the ability to go from a standing position to a sitting posture, then springing up to tear, grab, and rip like a wild monkey. Another characteristic is its natural easy-flowing circular graceful movement, with or without weapons. Sometimes trances are used during training. Hypnosis can be employed against an enemy, i.e., at close quarters taking the knife out of an enemy's hand as he blinks. Many practitioners are deft puppeteers, exercising their fingers to improve their fighting skills. The enemy is seldom despised, but "loved," even in combat.*

Mecca. **Maulid Nabi Mohammed** is the birthday of Mohammed held on the 12th day of the new year on the Arabic calendar. Also called *Hari Natal.* **Mi'raj Nabi Mohammed** celebrates the Ascension of The Prophet Mohammed.

Proklamasi Kemerdekaan

Independence Day. A public holiday which marks the anniversary of Indonesian independence from Holland, declared in 1945 and won in 1949. On 17 August each year, celebrations take place all over Indonesia. This is the biggest Indonesian national holiday, celebrated differently on each island. In Aceh (N. Sumatra), there are Arab ceremonies; in Wamena (Irian Jaya), Papuan tribal dancing and athletic events; in Manado (N. Sulawesi), parade floats applaud the growth of industry; in Tenggarong (E. Kalimantan), Dayak blowpipe competitions. Wherever the venue, there are dances, public entertainment, speeches, parades, and performances. The tradition is for kids and youth organizations to take part in the festivities with parades and marches, and for the older generation to look on. Go out to the *kampung* where village sports and games take place. Many of the resort towns and hill stations are crowded with domestic tourists at this time.

Bersih Desa

Takes place at the time of the rice harvest. Houses and gardens are cleaned, fences whitewashed, village roads and paths repaired. Once enacted to remove evil spirits from the village, *Bersih Desa* has lost most of its ritualistic significance. In some Indonesian societies, it expresses gratitude to such fertility figures as *Dewi Sri*, the rice goddess.

Kartini Day

Raden Kartini (1879-1903) was Indonesia's first women's emancipationist, whose memory is celebrated on 21 April. Her collection of published "Letters," written to close Dutch friends at the turn of the century, are now a modern classic. In them she poured out her feelings about the restrictions imposed on her by the feudal Javanese *adat* system.

The daughter of the Regent of Jepara, she had a formal Dutch high school education and was offered a Dutch scholarship, but instead of continuing her education, she was given in marriage. Kartini died in childbirth at age 24. There are parades, lectures, programs, and social activities attended by women, schoolgirls, university teachers, female workers, members of women's organizations, all wearing their gorgeous regional dress. Like Mother's Day, mothers aren't allowed to work; kids and fathers do the cooking, washing, housecleaning, etc. Many busloads of pilgrims pay their respects at the grave of Kartini near Rembang (C. Java).

Christmas
This national public holiday, held 25 December, is enthusiastically celebrated among the Minahasans of N. Sulawesi, the Batak of N. Sumatra, the Catholics of Flores, and among other Christian pockets throughout Indonesia.

ACCOMMODATIONS

If you're paying more than US$5 per day for a room, you're being culturally deprived of first-hand experience with the Indonesian people, the *rakyat*, the masses. You can live in neo-colonialist splendor relatively cheaply in Indonesia, but the more money you're spending the more distance is created, and the less of an Indonesian experience your visit will be. Instead of insulating yourself in large and glitzy international-class hotels, stay in native-style accommodations like *losmen, penginapan, wisma* or Chinese hotels which are friendly, crowded, and noisy as zoos. Even in these low-priced hotels, there's sometimes a row of more expensive rooms with a/c, balconies, and showers. In the accommodations sections of this guide, the low-cost, native places are always given first, working up in price to luxury-class accommodations.

Cities differ greatly in the availability of low-cost accommodations; Yogya has a multitude of *losmen* while Surabaya has few. Choose your *losmen* carefully because how good a time you have in a place frequently depends on the friendliness and location of the *losmen* or hotel you stayed in. Don't get stuck in an airless, mosquito-filled room, kept awake all night by traffic. Other travelers are the greatest source of the best places to stay, or ask at bus or train stations immediately upon arrival for cheap places to stay. *Becak* and taxi drivers often know these places, too. In the smaller villages ask the *hansip* (district civilian militia) about homes that put up travelers. The same person who tells you that a hotel or *losmen* in this book no longer exists will also be able to tell you where another good one is. In many cases, the names of Indonesian hotels indicate the origins or passions of their proprietors, as in "Losmen Banda" or "Hotel Anggrek." The nationality of the people who stay in Indonesia's accommodations depends on the season; if it's Dec., it's the Australians, if it's April, it's the Dutch, if it's July or Aug., it's the French and Belgians.

Indonesian-style Accommodations
Be prepared. Many low-priced accommodations are located near mosques so strains of the Muslim call to prayer over blaring loudspeakers are an automatic alarm which wakes you up at the crack of dawn. If the *losmen* has electricity there will probably be more noise since radios and TVs are often played at full volume, blasting through paper-thin walls. Increasingly, the proprietor and his family will spend evenings sitting like zombies in the other room mesmerized by the color TV. Roosters, babies crying, children playing, and loud music all begin promptly at 0600, so if you've got a full day ahead of you make sure you turn in early. Indonesian hotels are usually very conscientious about waking you up early to catch a train, bus, or plane.

Indonesians are ardent, life-long energy conservationists. Many inexpensive *penginapan* and *losmen* turn off the electricity during the daylight hours and turn it on again only when it's really needed at around 1700 or 1800 till 2300 or 2400. This means that often the electricity is out in the mornings so anything that requires sight—like packing—you should do the night before. You might also want to substitute a 100-watt bulb for the 25-watt, as lighting is so terribly dim. Kerosene lamps are more attuned to the slow-paced tropical setting in places like Bali and also extend your night's sleep. If there are prostitutes in residence it will probably prove noisier at night and you have to keep a closer watch on your gear. It's also common in cheap *losmen* for the boys who work there, and even the manager himself, to have hidden, long-established peepholes so that couples and single women can be spied upon.

Most of the typical low-cost Indonesian-style places have short beds (max. 1.8 m or 6 feet) and low doorways, both painfully undersized for larger-framed Westerners. The more expensive hotels and *wisma* are well screened, but few cheap hotels provide mosquito nets so bring your own or use mosquito coils. Mattresses, often without a top sheet, may be so thin that you have to pile one on top of the other to get a good night's rest. Indonesian-style cheaper accommodations ordinarily offer only a cold-water outside toilet with no toilet seat. To relieve yourself, put your feet in footrests and squat down over a hole in the cement, then flush with water from a plastic scoop. Sewerage systems don't always work well and waves of stench could pass through the coziest of places. Many *losmen*, homestays, and *penginapan* offer laundry service with a price list posted. It's OK to leave your room service tray out in the hallway once you're finished.

Some *losmen* owners seem not to be keen on accommodating white travelers. Sometimes they say they are full when there are obviously plenty of rooms unoccupied. The reason is that they often balk at the required police paperwork or perhaps the police try to hit them up for *uang rokok* ("cigarette money") which could reduce the profit on a Rp2500 single room to practically nothing. If you go directly to the police and ask them to help you find accommodations, they will take you right back to the reluctant *losmen* and you're in!

Holding Down Costs

Most of the following remarks apply only to economy-class, native-style accommodations. Room tariffs throughout the islands can vary considerably; the same class of accommodations in remote places like Ambon can be 4 times more expensive than Bali. What it costs depends on which island or city you go to. If you follow the well-worn travelers' trail through Sumatra, Java, and Bali (or vice versa), Indonesia could be one of the cheapest places in all of SE Asia. Because of the competition between *losmen* and the high concentration of tourists, Bali has by far the best accommodations anywhere in Indonesia for the money — even as low as Rp1000 per night. In the past few years prices have really gone up in the outlying islands; for an economy room the average is now Rp4000-8000. On Java, a Rp3500 hotel room in a small town will be much more of a bargain than a Rp3500 hotel room in a bigger city like Bandung or Jakarta. If the town is small enough, the very best joint in town will cost only Rp6000-8000. Mountain resort accommodations are expensive but the farther down the slopes of the mountain the accommodations are located, the cheaper they tend to be. It makes quite a difference in expenses if 2 people travel together and split the cost of a room. A double room could cost Rp3500 while a single may cost Rp3000! In many hotels you pay a flat rate for the room no matter how many people occupy it. Parents with 2 kids make the perfect traveling team: all 4 fit in a room, at a restaurant table, or into a taxi. Usually the medium-priced rooms in a hotel, *wisma*, or *pasanggrahan* are better value than the lowest or highest priced rooms.

Each class of rooms, and even *individual* rooms, are priced according to its particular asset or drawback. Some rooms are definitely better than others, so check several before deciding, as Indonesians' criteria are different from ours. You'll often find that Indonesians attach importance and value in amenities that you don't find necessary or even comfortable. For example, a large, dark, dingy room could cost thousands of *rupiah* more than a small, cramped, clean room. Or a foam mattress might be more expensive than a *kapok* mattress, even though *kapok* is cooler than foam. Or they feel fluorescent lighting is more desirable — and expensive — than single bulb lighting. Or because the room has a balcony which faces the (noisy) street, it should cost more. A price is also attached to each "extra": a fan is invariably Rp1000-1500 or more extra, a/c is Rp5000 extra, or a private *kamar mandi* up to Rp5000 extra.

Indonesians will always show you the most expensive rooms first, but you'll be surprised how a cheaper class of rooms somehow materializes once you begin to show a lack of interest in the rooms shown or the prices quoted. You can bargain with hotels, especially if they have a lot of empty rooms or if it's the slow season. To get a better price for a room and make it easier for the proprietor to save face, ask "Do you give a student discount or do you have a student's room?" Everyone knows that students don't have a lot of money. During holiday seasons such as *Hari Raya*, which lasts for 7 days, all prices go up and accommodations throughout Indonesia fill to capacity. Also, over Christmas in the hill stations outside the big cities of Java, room prices can quadruple.

At airport taxi desks, clerks always try to push upscale hotels (in the Rp25,000 range) or any hotel they get a commission from. Touts in Jakarta and other city airports like Kupang and Pontianak approach you showing color brochures and offering "special package rates" for hotels. These are sometimes good deals, sometimes bad. Sometimes the special-rate rooms are all filled up when you finally arrive at the hotel. But what's good about these offers are the free rides into the city, whether you take them up on their offer or not.

Room Taxes

It's important to remember that a 10% government *and* a 10% service tax might sometimes mysteriously be added onto your bill. Again, this extra cost is often hidden and the customer is not aware of it until the bill is handed to him! Make sure that there are not 2 *dafter tarip* (hotel tariff card), one showing taxes and the other not. Read all the small print. These extra charges should always be prominently posted and if they're not, you shouldn't have to pay. It doesn't hurt each time to ask first off if they exist. Taxes are usually in effect only in the higher-priced hotels.

Baggage Storage

If you're only going to be in town for an afternoon while waiting for your bus, train, or *bemo* to leave, try to work a deal with a *losmen* or *penginapan* proprietor to take a room on an hourly basis. Then you can rest up in peace and quiet, read, arrange your things, get washed up, and pay only three-quarters or one-third of the rate. Indonesians are hospitable and they could be amenable to this type of short-term arrangement. Alternatively, you can also leave your pack at the bus station office *(terminal bis)*, tourist office *(Kantor Pariwisata)*, mayor's office *(Kantor Bupati)*, or in the home of the village chief *(Rumah Kepala Desa* or *Rumah Kepala Kampung)*, depending upon which is the friendliest or most convenient. It is very common for *losmen* frequented by travelers to offer to store your gear while you're traveling around in exchange for staying with them again upon your return.

Mandi

Losmen, penginapan and *pasanggrahan* all over the archipelago ordinarily do not possess running water, and even *wisma*-class accommodations may not have a *mandi* with piped-in water. The verb *mandi* means to bathe or wash; the noun means the place where you bathe or wash. A *mandi* could be a bamboo-partitioned enclosure along the riverbanks of Sumatra or Halmahera; ornate, tiled washrooms with jacuzzis in high-priced hotels; open-air, shoulder-high cement bathing enclosure in a Balinese courtyard. Usually it is a special room, either inside the accommodations or built outside, equipped with a large water tank complete with frogs, fish, and moist lichen-covered walls. Bobbing in the middle of the water is a plastic or metal scoop with which you throw water over yourself, elephant-fashion. Do not climb in the tank and bathe, which fouls it. Instead, soap yourself down and rinse yourself off while standing on the *mandi* floor. The water is warm to cool and you will welcome its refreshing tingle after spending a day in the humid tropical sun. In mountain resorts or those *losmen* or *penginapan mandi* fed by underground wells, the water could be icy cold. In these cases, wait until the hottest part of the day to bathe. All over this volcanic region there are also hotsprings *(air panas)* where you're welcome to bathe, often with local Indonesians. Western-style toilets, bathtubs and showers are generally found only in the homes of rich, Westernized Indonesians, or in expensive, international-style hotels.

WC

Pronounced "WEE-CEE." This abbreviation stands for "water closet," the basic European designation for toilet. Other Indonesian phrases for toilets are either *kamar mandi,* or *kamar kecil* ("little room"). Sometimes the WC is located in the *mandi* room itself, but more often it's a separate, darkened enclosure. If you just need to urinate, it is quite socially acceptable to use the floor of the *mandi;* just rinse the floor down afterwards. An Indonesian WC consists of 2 footpads and a drainage hole made of molded cement. One squats on the pads and afterwards cleans by splashing water from a nearby can. Fill the can

either from the *mandi* water, faucet, or river. Slowly, this Asian-style WC is giving way in the more expensive hotels to Western-style sit-down toilets, especially in highly touristed places like Bali. Which is a shame because there is not a more comfortable, orthopedically sound, and physiologically natural position in which to relieve yourself than squatting on your haunches. Also, using water instead of paper is a more hygienic method of cleaning yourself than toilet paper. In fact, not only is toilet paper expensive and hard to find, but squat toilets are not designed to flush paper products. Westerners, who are reluctant to do as the Romans, often clog up *losmen* WCs with their copious use of toilet paper.

TYPES OF ACCOMMODATIONS

Places to sleep are limited only by your imagination. For example, if you're really stuck in a remote area it's often possible to sleep on a *warung* bench without charge if you eat at these. Also, you most probably would be able to stay on the floor of the local school or church *(gareja kristen)*. Church keepers, after obtaining permission from the *pendata,* are usually most helpful.

Staying With People

In Indonesia, someone is always inviting you home to meet their family. Muslims take care of strangers; it's part of the Islamic tradition of hospitality. Even if your *enemy* comes to your front door, you must shelter, feed, and succor him. Indonesians themselves when they travel always stay with relatives. If you stay with a family in a *kampung*, it's polite to drop in on the *kepala kampung* or the *kepala desa* (headman) to introduce yourself and register (sometimes pay a charge of Rp100-200). His house is usually the largest one in the village, with a big verandah for holding meetings. Often, as a foreign visitor, you're obliged to stay with the *kepala desa* and not in a lesser-ranking household. If the village is very small and you have no other place to stay, the *kepala* will fix you up for free or for a nominal charge (maybe Rp2000). In someone's home, don't expect a room to yourself; you'll most likely get just a bed (no privacy) plus several meals per day. It's a nice gesture to bring notebook paper, pens and pencils, coins or stamps from your country for the children, and cigarettes, soap or perfume for the adults. Make it known that these gifts are not compensation but meant as a kindness. Travelers coming after you will benefit from your thoughtfulness.

Homestays

The phenomenon of "homestays," or staying in licensed private homes in tourist villages, is found mainly on Bali but is also popping up in resorts like Pangandaran (W. Java) and Gili Trawangan (NW Lombok). Often named after the family who offers the accommodation (e.g. "Homestay Wijaya"), they share many of the characteristics of *losmen* and *penginapan* except that they are more homey and familiar; you mix more with the family and meals are more apt to be shared with them.

The Police

If places are too expensive or if there are none, go to the police and ask for their help in finding a place to stay. Some hotels might refuse to put you up even though they have vacant rooms because there are too many police forms to fill out and too many hassles and even suspicions if they do; or perhaps they must pay the police too much of a cut for putting up tourists. In these cases, since they're causing all the inconvenience, go to the police and request accommodations. If you throw yourself on their doorstep like this they will usually be extremely obliging. In exchange for entertainment, English-speaking practice, and endless examination of your passport, sleep for free on their floor, in a cell, or pitch your tent in the station's backyard.

Camping

You can legally and safely camp at police stations (with permission), in reserves (such as P. Pombo, Maluku), and high on the slopes or in the craters of volcanos (such as G. Rinjani, Lombok). There are a few bonafide campgrounds (such as Tawangmangu, E. Java), and if you're hard up you may crash on village *balai* platforms or in fields at the side of the road (but because of wild animals, never in Sumatra). If you're driving your own car, it's also possible to camp in the isolated agricultural estates of Java if you ask permission of the *kepala perkebunan* (plantation manager). When available, facilities for visitors in reserves or game parks are often quite basic. Bring food with you, something to sleep in or on, and some kind of shelter from the rain. In some areas it may be necessary to pack in water. Take along a small, portable, one-burner kerosene stove; kerosene is available in even the smallest villages. Cheap, strong, locally made plastic serves well as a ground cover or as a shelter when tied onto a pole framework.

Don't underestimate either the terrain or the temperature, especially if visiting mountain reserves. Trails where they exist are seldom marked. Don't expect to explore reserves by car; on foot or by boat is more common. Sometimes horses are available. Good shoes or boots, cold weather clothing, compass, maps, and a guide may be essential. You may camp in designated areas, but at some (such as the Arai Canyon in E. Sumatra) you may not. At other reserves (Pangandaran in SW Java) there are cheap *losmen* in the immediate vicinity. Permits are necessary to visit some reserves, obtainable either from Direktorat Perlindugan dan Pengawetan Alam (PPA), Jl. Juanda, 9, Bogor, W. Java, or at the forestry dept. offices in the nearest large town.

Penginapan

A lodging house with very basic facilities—table, chair, bed, thin walls, and a single low-powered light bulb hanging from a cord. Even more basic than a *losmen*, but often even cheaper. See them all over Indonesia down little back lanes, sometimes with just a sign PENG-X, with the owner's name. Like country roadhouses, *penginapan* are found in hill stations, coastal towns, and deep in the interiors of Indonesia's islands. The differences between *penginapan* and *losmen* are becoming blurred; they are essentially just different names for the same class of accommodation.

Losmen

A cheaply run hotel but still quite livable. Often concentrated around train, *bemo*, and bus stations. Bathrooms are usually shared. You can be woken up as early as 0530 by water poured down your *mandi* chute, honking geese, roosters crowing, *bemo* sputtering outside your window, babies crying, or kids going off to school. Room service depends on the particular *losmen* or on the *ibu* (your hostess, meaning "mother"). Here's where you find the most interesting people—itinerant merchants, students, *pegawi*, other budget travelers. *Losmen* prices differ from Sumatra right on through to Irian Jaya (the most expensive); they run anywhere from Rp1500-10,000. On Bali, staying at a *losmen* means living with a family. In Jakarta and other places on Java, a *losmen* could mean a brothel and they are considered somewhat degrading. You'll seldom find *losmen* in the hill stations of Java where more expensive *wisma* and guesthouses are more common.

Wisma

A *wisma* is an Indonesian lodge or small guesthouse, with pretensions of grandeur in the high-sounding name. Usually it's one story, efficiently run, privately or family owned. The *wisma*-class hotels are actually some of the best accommodations for the money in Indonesia. Running usually about Rp4500-12,000, they are comfortable, homey, and the service is first-class. *Wisma* often have flush toilets, and a simple breakfast is frequently included in the price of a room. The name *wisma* is also used for ordinary buildings or office blocks. Falling in this same category are *pondok* (private lodges) and tourist guesthouses like the remarkable and high-standard row of 20 guesthouses on Jl. Prawirotaman in Yogya (C. Java).

Pastoran

The Catholic priest's residence. In Outer Island cities like Tual in the Kais and Dobo in the Arus, stay as a guest in the local *pastoran* for only Rp2000 per day including meals. Though the food isn't the greatest, it's still a tremendous deal because you sit down with the brothers in the evenings and listen to the day's stories. These men are extremely well informed about the area and you learn a great deal.

Hotels

Hotel associations, with government backing, are really cracking down on the heretofore loose use of the term, and now won't let anyone call themselves a "hotel" without meeting certain standards. Whenever the front desk clerk starts speaking English to you, you're probably in a hotel. All over Indonesia, aging Dutch colonial-era and Sukarno-era hotels are slowly but surely giving way to a whole set of newer and slicker hotels. The grand old spacious hotels still retain their distinct charm and glamour, but they are slowly turning musty, dank, foul-smelling and run-down with age. Though many refused to face reality and lower their rates, with the rise of the new generation of hotels the older ones have gone out of business or been forced down in price. The traveler can sometimes find real bargain accommodations in these bygone relics—Rp3500-6500 for gigantic rooms with anteroom, dressing room, verandah (but atrocious plumbing!). Realizing the tourist's love of colonial nostalgia, a modern annex with a/c rooms and full facilities at exorbitant rates is often found behind or in front of the original hotel, which is being completely remodeled.

Youth Hostels

There are only 3 legitimate youth hostels in Indonesia: Wisma Taruna in Denpasar (Jl. Gedung 17), Wisma Delima in Jakarta (Jl. Jaksa 5), and Kopo International Youth Hostel in the Puncak (Jl. Raya 502, 70 km from Jakarta). With the exception of Kopo, they are small, plain, more regimented but in the same price range as *losmen* or *penginapan*. Modern showcase youth hostels *(Graha Wisata Remaja)* at Ancol and Taman Mini Indonesia in Jakarta function essentially as student or youth-group dormitories and are booked months in advance by Javanese students.

Asrama

Student dormitory or 2-or-more-to-a-room accommodation. You might find spare beds for hire in an *asram*, particularly during school holidays. Or stay there free as a guest of a student. *Asrama* can also mean a detention center; the jail for visa overextensions and dope peddlers on Bali is called Asrama Tahanan Imigrasi.

Pasanggrahan

Also known as *rumah-rumah kehutanan.* These are government forestry huts or lodges in parks, nature or wildlife reserves, their functions nearly interchangeable. They operate mostly in the Outer Islands of Maluku, Sulawesi, Kalimantan, Sumatra, though they are also found on overcrowded Java. Travelers may stay in them if they are not occupied by government people. *Pasanggrahan* are usually quite cheap, sometimes even free. There could be several of them in one locale, so by asking just for a *rumah-rumah kehutanan* you may be directed to a different one than the one you're looking for. *Pasanggrahan* could also mean a commercial lodging house, frequently in more out-of-the-way places.

International-class Hotels

About 30 of these American-style hotels are already operating, divided among the country's big cities and provincial capitals (even in such remote places as Balikpapan in E. Kalimantan where the Hotel Benakutai charges US$92 single!). Most feature all the mod cons including a/c, coffee shops, continental and Japanese restaurants, swimming pools. Jakartan hotels like the new Aryaduta Hyatt and the Jakarta Hilton even have international direct dialing, jacuzzis, fitness rooms, and running tracks! Bali has the nation's swankiest international-class hotels, located mostly within the Sanur-Nusa Dua-Kuta Beach tourist triangle. A Club Med has even opened up in Nusa Dua. For a listing of these 3-, 4-, and 5-star deluxe hotels, their rates, addresses and facilities, refer to the "Pacific Hotel Directory" in *Pacific Travel News,* published each June and December. Contact either the Directorate General of Tourism (Jl. Kramat Raya 81, Jakarta) or any of the Indonesian tourist offices in the countries listed in the "Information" chapter. Alternatives to the international-style hotels are the small business hotels that have sprung up all over Indonesia in the wake of the country's new-found prosperity. In these hotels—the Sultan instead of the fancy Eka Doray in Banda Aceh, the Marco Polo instead of the plush Mandarin in Jakarta—are often much better value than the big hotels and you get more local flavor.

While exploring the Asmat area of the SW coast of Irian Jaya, you may be invited to stay overnight in an Asmat dwelling (left). The semi-nomadic Asmat live in an extensive river country of low, muddy land covered in eternally green forests. Since stone is at a premium in their region, knives and daggers are made from cassowary leg bones and spears and arrows are fashioned from bamboo and wood—Mesolithic Age practices. The Asmat carve large squatting ancestor figures with upward-bent arms and other 3-dimensional woodcarvings. The Asmat are still greatly feared because of their headhunting, cannibalism, and unending tribal warfare in former times.

FOOD

Indonesia has one of the world's great cuisines, a cuisine which has not yet been given the recognition it deserves. Its influences originate from all corners of the globe. Located at the crossroads of the ancient world, astride the great trade routes between the Middle East and Asia, wave after wave of traders, adventurers, pirates, and immigrants have, since the Middle Ages, been drawn by the riches of the Spice Islands. Thus, nature and history have conspired to give Indonesia a cuisine as varied and highly seasoned as its thousands of islands and its hundreds of ethnic groups. From India came curries, cucumber, eggplant, Indian mustard, cowpeas. Incoming Chinese brought the *wok* and stir-frying, Chinese mustard, and such vegetables as brassica and Chinese cabbage. From Arabia have come typical Middle-Eastern gastronomic techniques and ingredients such as kebab and flavorful goat stews. Peanuts, avocado, pineapple, guava, papaya, tomato, squash, pumpkin, cacao, and soybeans have all been introduced by Europeans. During their occupation of Indonesia in WW II, the Japanese showed the Javanese how to stock flooded fields with fish and introduced improved methods of planting rice. To this day, each culinary art of foreign origin is distinguishable in Indonesian cooking, yet each is blended creatively with the islands' own cooking secrets. **note:** Refer to the glossary in the backmatter for the restaurant and market food vocabulary.

Fasting Month

This is not the time of year to enjoy the best cooking in Indonesia's many Islamic areas. Usually the only places to eat during *bulan puasa* or *Ramadan* (fasting month) are dark, hidden, secretive back-alley *warung*. During this time, you're forced to eat in more expensive Chinese restaurants. The great majority of Indonesia's Chinese aren't Islamic and it's business as usual. You're also restricted in the variety of the meals available. If you can't get a meal, eat fruit or fried tofu or chew a trail mix of dried fruit and peanuts during the day to keep your strength up. The month-long fast lasts all day until 1700 or 1800 when a bell rings or a siren screams to signal the end of the daily fast. The date of the fasting month changes each year according to the Islamic calendar.

INGREDIENTS

Nasi

The basic diet on most of the islands is rice, lots of it, supplemented with vegetables, a bit of fish, often fried, and once in a while, savory meat and eggs. Any-

thing with the word *nasi* in front of it means that it's prepared or served with rice. All traditional Indonesian food is designed to complement or be complemented by rice, a plentiful crop grown on the country's terraced paddyfields. For Indonesians, the whiter the rice, and the more it's been culled and slipped, the tastier it is (although all the nutrients have been taken out). Because rice production gets most of the attention by focusing work, irrigation channels, and fertilizers to produce several crops a year, it's taking up more and more land previously used for other, generally higher protein-staples such as groundnuts, soybeans, sweet potatoes and maize. As a result, the average rural diet has actually worsened.

an Indonesian kitchen

Soybeans

The soybean is known as the yellow vegetable cow of Indonesia. Because of this wonderful bean, the country folk often eat a lot more nutritiously than the rich who gorge themselves and their children on such status foods as meat, bread, beer, soda and chocolate, and other high-carbohydrate luxuries. Rural people, on the other hand, eat such hearty soybean-based organic foods as *tahu* (soybean cake), *tempe* (fermented soybeans), or coconut candy and cane syrup—all poor man's food—and much more healthy. *Tempe* is found in the greatest abundance and variety on Java, each small cake wrapped in shiny pieces of banana leaf.

Other Ingredients

Abundant vegetation and few edible animals in the tropics have led its inhabitants to adopt a semi-vegetarian diet. Many temperate-zone vegetables were derived from Europe (even cauliflower!). Other main sources of protein in rural Indonesia are fish, poultry, and eggs. Beef products are consumed mostly by urbanites, and almost all the really high-grade meat is imported. Rural consumption of beef is kept in check by the need to maintain buffaloes as draught animals and cows as milk producers. Pork is produced and consumed by the Hindu Balinese, the mainly urban Chinese, and the non-Malay population. Goats, bred all over Muslim Indonesia, are the Muslim Staff of Life. Due to its high protein value, *tempe* is considered the meat of the poor.

Leaves of bamboo, mangos, papayas, cassava, and beans are also used in cooking. Coconut, coconut milk, chilies, ginger, and peanuts are used more in Indonesian cooking than in other Asian cuisines. Coconut is used in nearly every shape and form but mostly to add richness to curries and sauces. Indonesians can do wonders with freshly grated coconut which is first kneaded and sieved, then blended with water. As it cooks, the coconut milk thickens and with the addition of flour or corn starch it becomes a sauce. Peanut sauces made with chilies and unsweetened coconut cream top the delicacies most enjoyed by Westerners. In the tropics it's better to stick to a light diet of rice and fish, which gives you all the protein you need. Lighten up on meat, you don't need all that fat and protein overload. The idea of fat is to keep you warm and you're trying to do the opposite here, to refrigerate yourself from the inside.

Spices

Indonesia taught the world the use of exotic spices and herbs. Indonesian cuisine is known for its deliberate combination of contrasting flavors and textures: spicy, sour, sweet, and other flavor-assertive spices. The carefully orchestrated contrasts and counterpoints will catch your taste buds by surprise. The most ramshackle *warung* can bring forth an array of exquisite foods with flavors, textures, aromas that you never dreamed existed. There are tingling ginger sautees, rich and creamy peanut sauces, spice-laden chili *sambal* toppings that will fire the palate. Turmeric, a yellow root of the ginger family that resembles a small carrot, is often used in Indonesian recipes. Indonesians can develop unending original gastronomic themes using lemon-grass and laos, cardamon and chilies, tamarind and turmeric, plus many other seasonings that *must* be experienced on your trip through these islands. All find their way into delightfully and sometimes scorchingly hot dishes. Surprisingly, one seldom comes across the spices — nutmeg, pepper, mace, and cloves — that gave the "Spice Islands" their name and spurred Columbus to accidentally discover America. In general, Indonesian cooking spices are used less than in the curries of India, yet more than in Chinese food. Some areas of Indonesia lack spices altogether in their cooking, such as in many locales of Kalimantan or southern Maluku where the food tends to be bland and unappetizing. To these areas of Indonesia, bring dehydrated food, spices, hot sauce, salt.

Hot Spices

Chilies and hot soybean sauce *(kecap)* are widely popular. When in doubt as to whether the dish is spicy hot or not, ask *Pedas atau tidak?* ("Hot or not?"). There are many kinds of hot chili sauces *(sambal)* and spiced chili pastes; the ones from Padang, W. Sumatra, are some of the hottest in the world. Almost every dish has its own kind of *sambal,* and each Indonesian family makes its own a little differently, and the Chinese make theirs differently still. But don't get the idea that all Indonesian food is hot. Many, many dishes are quite mild and palatable to the Westerner. Compare the subtle and refined cuisine of the Javanese with the unfussy and straightforward cooking of the Minangkabau. Central Java's food is sweet and spicy, while E. Java's is more salty and hot. Sumatran food is very spicy hot. If the dish is too hot, just squeeze a little lemon with some salt over the dish to make it less so. *Kretek* cigarettes also help cool down your throat after a chili burning.

Fish And Seafood

Indonesia, comprised mostly of ocean, offers a staggering amount of fresh seafood: tuna, shrimp, lobster, crab, anchovies, carp, prawns, sea slugs. Prepared most competently by the Bugis and Makassarese of S. Sulawesi, try exotic fish and shellfish dishes which you probably can't often afford in your own country. Fish and shellfish dinners in Indonesia's homey restaurants and roadside *warung* cost about half the Singapore price and about one-tenth the United States or European price (average Rp2500-4500). The Irianese serve some of the best baked fish *(ikan bakar)* in Indonesia. The country's rice farmers raise a supplementary fish crop by letting fish loose to spawn in flooded ricefields; dinner is caught by opening up a sluice gate or scooping up fish in a net. *Belut* (eel) are also caught at night in the ricefields; buy a good-sized bunch of this crisp delicacy wrapped in newspaper for only dimes. Some freshwater fish such as the buttery *belanak* (gray mullet) are bred in compounds; take the bones out, mix with coconut milk and spices, then wrap it into its skin and bake. Sea slugs are another delicacy, a textural experience. Cook them with chicken or some other kind of meat, and the slugs take on the flavor of meat. Since sea slugs are the magic mushrooms of the ocean — you'll have that night the most extraordinary hallucinogenic dreams!

MENUS

National Dishes

The following dishes are found all over Indonesia. Curries and noodle dishes, found at roadside stalls for Rp750-1250, are among the most popular everyday foods — each with an Indonesian touch. Other national dishes include smooth and steamy leaf-wrapped *hors d'oeuvres,* soft and crunchy fried rice dishes (nasi goreng). Mie goreng (fried noodles) means noodles fried in coconut oil with eggs, meat, tomato, cucumber, and shrimp paste, spices and chilies added. Both nasi goreng and mie goreng are common breakfast dishes in Indonesia. If istimewa ("special") is written after either dish, it means it comes with egg on top. Sate are marinated strips of chicken, beef, mutton, or pork impaled on veins of coconut palm and grilled over charcoal and then dipped into a spicy peanut sauce.

Another widespread nourishing dish is the Chinese cap cai, a kind of Indonesian meat and vegetable chop suey. Soto means that thick santen (coconut cream) is added to a soup; this is also a breakfast dish. Sop is more similar to a meat and vegetable stew; it means only that water is added. A frequently encountered Indonesian dish left over from Dutch times and found mostly in hotel restaurants is the rijstaffel ("rice table"), a sort of Indonesian smorgasbord. In colonial days, a ceremonial rijstaffel could embrace as many as 350 courses. Today, 5 to 10 courses is more the norm! The total meal offers a variety of tastes, some sweet, others spicy, all to be eaten with steaming hot rice and condiments. Today you can experience a basic rijstaffel in less elaborate form in nasi padang restaurants (see below).

Regional Foods

Each region of Indonesia has its own characteristic specialties rarely, if ever, found in other parts of Indonesia. In addition, there are tribal foods from isolated groups and ceremonial foods which are cooked only on festive occasions. The aboriginal Punan of S. Kalimantan eat roast lizard, while a single python can feed a whole village of inland Irianese. The Minangkabau of N. Sumatra serve nasi kunyit and singgang ayam only at weddings or memorial celebrations. Though rice is the staple for most Indonesians, rice is replaced by maize and the root of the cassava plant in the eastern island groups, and sago in Maluku and New Guinea. Cassava, which looks like a shriveled turnip, has a ridiculously low protein count (1% as compared to 10% in rice); it's a starchy, unappetizing, fibrous mass which millions of Indonesians subsist on. Westerners know it only in its refined form as tapioca. Sago is sometimes served in unusual ways such as Ambon's glue-like papeta. Santri (orthodox) Indonesians abhor pork but love lamb. You never see pork in Muslim areas, but the meat is a favorite of the Chinese and the Hindus of Bali. Pigs run all over Bali, but are absent on Java.

Always sample the home cooking in each area. In some regions such as Minahasa, mice and dog are considered savory delicacies. Tritis, a specialty of the Karo of N. Sumatra is partially digested grass taken from a cow's stomach. The Torajans of C. and S. Sulawesi cook meat or fish in buffalo or pig's blood inside bamboo sections. The Sundanese of W. Java

specialize in cooking goldfish, while the specialty of the Madurese (off E. Java) is a tantalizing thick soup called soto madura. The Balinese cook ducks and pigs to perfection, and are very fond of sweet and/or sticky foods made of rice (lontog and ketan). Dishes like kalderado and bolu made by the Florinese find their counterparts in small markets throughout Portugal on the other side of the world. Gado-gado, which refuses to flourish outside of Jakarta, is a healthy Javanese vegetable salad combining potatoes and other vegetables, a rich peanut sauce, and a prawn-and-rice cracker called krupuk. Peanut butter-loving Americans are particularly fond of gado-gado because it's served with a good quantity of peanut sauce on top.

Ordering Food

The traditional way to eat is with the fingers of the right hand touching the food; fingers taste better than metal. Always eat with the right hand; the left hand is used in the toilet. (At one time the right hand was cut off thieves, thereby preventing them from ever eating in public again.) In the country, warung meals are often served cold on a banana leaf, which tastes better than plastic or glass. If you want a dish served (temperature) hot, say Yang masih panas. The appearance of the dish is also important. If it doesn't look good, Indonesians won't eat it. Great care is taken at markets to make the food attractive to catch the shopper's eye: flowers are sprinkled over fruit, dishes are brightly garnished, and green leaves are spread under vegetables.

In restaurants, write down your order on the slip of paper provided. So that there be no misunderstanding, write down the price of the dish too. Learn the ingredients that go into the various dishes before you try ordering in a restaurant. For example, soto babat telor is a soup prepared with the intestines of a cow. Quite good if you like this sort of thing, but if you don't, understanding the words soto (soup) and telor (egg) is obviously not enough. And whenever you order any meat dish, specify whether you want the flesh (daging) of the chicken or cow, or the innards (isi perut or babat) of the animal. Never assume anything because Indonesians will continually serve you the gizzards, liver, brain, or kidneys unless you tell them otherwise—in their own language. Imported foods are expensive. Save money by following the eating and drinking habits of the area through which you're traveling; eat krupuk and rice instead of bread and potatoes, replace whiskey with brem (mild rice wine).

VENDORS

Indonesia's streets are filled with beverage vendors pushing carts full of poisonous-looking concoctions and walking restaurants dangling from pikulan. The sate man comes with his whole kitchen on his shoul-

tukang sate

ders. Listen for the sound of his feet rhythmically hitting the mud. He squats in the gutter and fans the embers of his charcoal brazier until it glows red hot, then turns out sizzling skewered beef, pork, chicken, turtle meat or mutton with different sauces, the culinary style varying from place to place. If you take up residence in Indonesia, ask around for the different vendors who service the homes in your neighborhood. They cut pork Western-style and could even have mild-cured hams. They will also deliver chickens, streaky bacon, crab, frog legs, and who knows what else.

Krupuk

The Indonesian pretzel, a big, crispy, oversized cracker made from fish flakes, crab claws, shrimp paste, or fruit mixed with rice, dough, or *sago* flour. After being dried to look like thin, hard, colored plastic, when fried in oil the *krupuk* unfolds and blossoms. Served cold, it's very tangy. To keep the crackers fresh, the barefoot *krupuk* man carries on a bamboo pole 2 huge insulated containers which look like big milk cans. Since bread is seldom eaten, being too expensive and not to their taste, Indonesians use *krupuk* for bread. Some people like to dip *krupuk* into their tea as Westerners do cookies into milk. *Krupuk*

are also used as scoops for curry or *gado-gado,* just as Westerners use potato chips with dips. When hungry, grab some delicious *krupuk:* it'll tide you over until you can get a proper meal. As a snack, it's very nutritious, the reason why so many malnourished Indonesians are able to function at all.

Warung

When you get hungry, just follow your nose toward the day and night markets *(pasar malam)* on the perimeters of bus, minibus, and train stations, where you'll discover a collection of smokey ramshackle *warung.* Indonesian food is delicious at all levels, and by far the best food for the money is served in these makeshift foodstalls—the poor-man's restaurant— glowing with hissing gas lamps with plastic canopies, hardwood benches or stools, and sometimes $30,000 BMWs parked out front. Hundreds line the streets, markets, and town squares of Indonesia's cities, towns, and villages, especially at night. They also serve the Businessman's Lunch of Indonesia and do a very brisk business at noontime. *Warung* offer pure Indonesian cuisine and usually specialize in *soto, sate, nasi goreng, mie goreng, lontong,* or *cap cai,* which you eat with a cheap aluminum spoon and much banter from your fellow diners. Also available are such snacks as *krupuk* (fish or shrimp chips), *pisang goreng* (fried bananas), fried *tempe,* etc.

If you're sitting in one *warung,* it doesn't mean that you can't order from other ones nearby; choose one with the friendliest atmosphere, then walk around to the various neighboring *warung* and order different food items: 10 sticks of *sate* from one tent, a *sop sayur* from another, a *gado-gado* from a third, all the while pointing back toward your table. Even if you don't speak *Bahasa Indonesia,* it's possible to simply point to anything that looks good. After eating and before paying your bill, ask how much and make sure that it's figured correctly. If you eat US$3 worth of this roadside food you're making an absolute glutton of yourself. *Warung* that serve only coffee *(kopi)* and biscuits *(kue)* are exclusively for menfolk who sit around, gossip, read the daily newspaper or listen to the transistor radio. They often stop here when returning home and exchange news. Thus, *warung* are an important source of information, and they make excellent language labs for learning Indonesian. These coffee shops also sell domestic supplies such as kerosene, lamps, batteries, needles, buttons, medicine, dried fish, and salt. At night it could be the only well-lit place in the whole village.

Restaurants

Be wary when handed a menu written in English, which is a menu meant for tourists. These tourist restaurants are typified by Western cassette music, menus in English featuring Western-style dishes, uninspired food, bright neon lights, overpricing. Most tone down the spicy hotness and eliminate many of the "funny-tasting" spices in order to make the food more palatable for travelers who go there to listen to the great tapes. Restaurants or *warung* catering exclusively to tourists are not always bad value. Take, for example, the amazing fish dinner for under US$1 you get at Bus Sis in Yogya and the authentic Indonesian dishes served at Made's Warung on Kuta Beach (Bali). You can usually project the prices in a restaurant by the price of their *nasi goreng;* if that dish is overpriced, other dishes will probably be too. Too many Western-style restaurants charge up to Rp2000 for a *mie goreng* or *nasi goreng* without *udang, telor, daging*—just fried white rice with microscopic bits of vegetables in it. Restaurants also shouldn't be charging for hot tea *(tea pahit),* Rp100 for hot scented water! For generally more authentic food stick to the streets, and eat in *warung* or *rumah makan. Rumah makan* just means "eating place" and it could be good. As anywhere, the number of people who patronize the restaurant is a signal of its quality.

Chinese Restaurants

Generally, if prices aren't given on the menu, it's a Chinese restaurant. Most major towns and cities have Chinese restaurants (often called *restoran)* which are generally more expensive than Indonesian-style eating places but offer more variety and culinary sophistication. A typical Chinese-style restaurant now charges about Rp6000-7000 pp minimum for a large meal, including beer, and as high as Rp10,000 if in a large city. Bear in mind that if you ask for a *mie goreng* in a Chinese restaurant, although it could be superior to that found in a *warung* or in a *rumah makan,* it's not authentic Indonesian cooking. If you feel that Indonesian or Islamic food lacks vegetables, head for a Chinese restaurant which usually serves an abundance of fresh vegetables with their dishes as standard fare. The Chinese eat meat but they are a little fussy, taking only small, gourmet-cooked portions. It's best to visit Chinese restaurants in a group so that a wide variety of tasty dishes can be sampled. During the fasting month, Chinese *restoran* are the only ones open during the daytime.

Nasi Padang

The Minangkabaus from W. Sumatra turn out some of the best cooks in Indonesia, and it is in one of their *nasi padang* restaurants where you'll experience the most bonafide, tastiest—and spiciest—Indonesian cooking. A *rumah makan Padang* is sure to be found amongst the many restaurants on the main street of any town or village in Indonesia, no matter what the size. If you're in a hurry, Padang restaurants offer the quickest service of any eatery. Although they are on the whole the best in Indonesia, Padang restaurants are also some of the most expensive. A cup of *kopi susu* may cost you up to Rp800, meals could easily run Rp5000-6000 pp in a city, perhaps Rp3000 in a country town. Once seated, waiters bring for refreshment a cold napkin, a free glass of hot tea, a lit candle to keep flies away, and a glass of hot water holding and semi-sterilizing your eating utensils. No menu is needed. All you have to do to initiate an overwhelming cascade of food is utter just one word: *nasi,* while pointing to the window filled with great basins of spicy hot food. Waiters will then glide forward with up to 10 small dishes balanced precariously up and down each arm, setting them all straightaway before you. You pay only for those dishes you eat, so get the prices straight for *each* dish before diving in, otherwise the bill could be a shocker. The sauce from each is free so if you find a restaurant that gives plenty of rice, eat only a couple of the dishes and use the sauce from the rest, as Indonesians do. Afterwards, you'll be given a fingerbowl and a hot napkin to clean yourself.

The vegetable dishes are always the cheapest. Meat dishes can really run up the tab as they may cost up to Rp1250 per portion. Stick with the ol' standbys—fried fish *(ikan goreng),* the curries, fresh vegetables *(sayur),* or branch out to something more exotic such as spiced prawns or steamed sweet potato leaves. These W. Sumatrans are especially fond of curries of which there are about 10 variations, plus eggs with chilies, and a great number of *kambing* (goat), *ayam* (chicken) or *lembu* (beef) dishes. There could be 2 or 3 kinds of eggs (duck eggs, hen eggs, dove eggs), 3 kinds of fish; chicken fried, boiled and roasted; bowls of liver, brains, hearts, kidneys, tripe, plus all sorts of vegetables like cabbage, beans, carrots. *Rendang,* a wonderfully flavored meat and sauce dish, is prepared not only with beef but also with chicken, heart, or liver. Rice is either on the house or you are charged a nominal price (all you can eat for Rp500). *Nasi padang* restaurants don't usually carry bread but often have fluffy, crispy *krupuk.*

Nasi Campur

Cover your table with dishes if you're in a group but if you're alone just ask for *nasi campur*—a mini version served on one plate of *nasi padang* cuisine—which is often cheaper than asking for all the *a la carte* dishes to be set before you. A *nasi campur* is a filling plate of steamed rice with either fish, beef, chicken, or mutton, plus a mixture of eggs and/or vegetables, roasted peanuts and shredded coconut heaped on top. A thick sauce covers it all. A good *nasi campur* at Rp850-1500 (depending upon what you have on top of your rice) is the best-value eating in Indonesia. Get your best *nasi campur* before the lunch crowd starts coming in at around 1100, when there's the widest selection from which to choose.

FRUITS

Discovering the new tastes of the local fruits, delicately crisp and bursting with juices, is one of the delights of traveling in Indonesia. Many of this country's fruits are found nowhere else on Earth. A serving of fruit is the customary dessert for most Indonesians; fruit vendors and stands are found at almost every step along the busy streets of Indonesia's towns and villages. The local markets offer an even greater variety. Stands selling fruits and/or juice stay open long after most other *warung* close down, so you can find fruit to snack on until late at night. All fresh fruit and vegetables should be washed and peeled before eating. There are pineapples *(nanas),* pomelo *(citrus decumana,* the best from Cirebon, W. Java), mangos, melons, guavas. Pineapple is refreshing and rich in vitamin C; helps digestion too. The citrus *(jeruk)* family is also well represented on the islands: tangerines, really cheap oranges, grapefruits, lemons, limes. Sweet *jeruk* run about Rp1500 per kg. There are also *salak, rambutan,* lychees, jackfruit *(nangka),* breadfruit *(campedak),* and papaya. The delicious mango tastes different on every island, and the varieties here are distinct from the rest of SE Asia. The unripe mango may be substituted for apples in pies, the ripe fruit for peaches. Some of these exotic tropical fruits are available canned in oriental food stores and Chinatowns in the United States, Australia, and Europe. Fresh lychees, guavas, and starfruit can sometimes be found in such stores seasonally. But the most spectacular fruits cannot be found anywhere except in Indonesia.

Endemic Fruits
Try these splendid delicacies as you may never get another chance. The mangosteen *(manggis)* is hailed by some as the most perfect of fruits. Its outside is round and purple, its inside is like an orange, but creamy, cool, and melts on the tongue. The mangosteen was enjoyed and lauded by Queen Victoria. The smelly, infamous *durian* (family *Sterculiuceae),* spiked like a gladiator's weapon, tastes simultaneously like onions and caramel fluff. It is a fruit much enjoyed by those who are not put off by its evil aroma. Believed to be an aphrodisiac an old Malay expression goes, "When the *durians* are down, the *sarungs* are up." The fruit is named for its prickles or *duri.* Durian on Java cost as much as Rp1500 for select large ones, but it's often difficult to find a good one (sellers seem almost eager to sell you rotten ones!).

The lychee-like *rambutan* has a prickly rind of a pale rose color. Within, the *rambutan* holds a dark green transparent jelly, somewhat like a grape in taste, but far more keenly luscious. Don't be alarmed by the *rambutan's* hairy exterior; this is an easy fruit to love. Gently squeeze open the fruit and enjoy the sweet, translucent flesh inside. *Salak* is commonly called the snake-fruit because of the remarkable pattern of its skin; carefully peel and enjoy. It's similar in taste to an apple, but not quite.... The amazing array continues: the tiny, delicious *blimbing* is another favorite; *gambu* (Rp1000 for 10) is a cousin of the *blimbing* and equally as delectable. The bell-shaped *jambu air* fruit *(genus Eugenia),* though tasteless, is an effective thirst-quencher. The *sawo* is shaped like a potato but tastes like a ripe, honey-flavored peach or pear. The unbelievably juicy *Zirzak* (or *sirzak;* means "sour sack" in Dutch) is unforgettable. Then there are sweet, gooey, sumptuous fruits such as the *langsat* and the *marquisa.* When you bite into the jelly-like *tuih* fruit, it tastes like sweet, fine coconut milk.

The Banana Family
The pride of place among all Indonesian fruits must go to the cheap and ubiquitous banana *(pisang).* Indonesia has 42 varieties in all shapes, flavors, textures, sizes, from the tiny finger-like *pisang tuju* to the prized ½-m-long *pisang raja* ("King Banana") for frying which grows upwards instead of down. Some bananas are big and fat and red-skinned; others have edible skins; then there are seedless ones and ones with big black seeds; wild species; and some varieties that are only edible when cooked. One of the sweetest varieties is the small "golden banana" *(pisang mas),* with its thin skin and incomparable taste; its leaves are used to wrap rice. *Pisang susu* ("milk banana") is not too sweet, just the right size, and one of the nicest tasting. Bananas are also used frequently to season meats and stews, and plantains are sometimes cut into very small cubes to resemble *nasi goreng* and prepared in the same way as fried rice. Bananas seldom cost more than Rp100 apiece.

DRINKS AND DESSERTS

Thirsty foreigners are provided, in most cases, with boiled water from their *losmen* and thus don't have to be paranoid about drinking unclean water. If traveling in the Outer Islands, or even onboard a ship, give the *losmen* or the ship's galley a pot on your arrival. They will fill it with boiling water to cool overnight so it can be put into your water bottles. About the only drink that Indonesians themselves take with meals is a variety of warm or cold China tea, excellent without milk or sugar (for unsweetened tea, say *teh pahit).* In a *restoran* or *rumah makan,* you shouldn't be charged for *teh pahit.* Plain iced tea *(teh es)* should cost only Rp100 or so. Tea helps stimulate the appetite and digestion and will keep you awake after a heavy lunch. Powerful coffee, a crop originally introduced by the Dutch in 1699, is grown widely on Java, Bali, and Sumatra. The best is cultivated S of Semarang, C. Java. Indonesian *kopi* is sometimes laced with chicory or chocolate. Served pitch-black, sweet, thick, and rich, with grounds still floating on top, in most places it costs only Rp500-600 for a tall glass.

Since there are so many mineral and vitamin-rich natural fruit drinks here, both hot and cold, many derived from fruits found nowhere else in the world, it's insane to drink Fanta or Coca Cola. Instead, quench your thirst at ice juice stands *(warung es jus)* or at carts selling liquid tubs of poisonous hue bobbing with ice which line Indonesia's streets. These sometimes contain delicious, though overly sweetened, natural drinks like citrus juices *(air jeruk)*, *es zirzak*, or the incredible avocado drink blend, *es pokat*. *Bajigur* is a drink made of coconut milk thickened with rice and sweetened with palm sugar. *Es soda gembira* is like an American ice cream soda without the ice cream.

Because fresh milk is often considered unsafe to drink, Indonesians use powdered whole milk. Sterilized milk (Ultramilk), as well as canned evaporated milk, are also available and safe to drink, although more expensive. (It shouldn't be difficult to find a wet nurse for your baby; Indonesians believe it's spiritual and magical that a part of themselves forever becomes a part of your child.) Or drink coconuts as a form of sterile milk, and to help rehydrate yourself. Coconuts contain adequate potassium and are a great source of glucose. *Kopyor* is a lighter coconut than the *kelapa muda*, and its subtle, velvety flavor is much in demand. You can tell a *kopyor* coconut by shaking it to feel if it's gone a little "bad." The man who can culture *kopyor* coconuts is a rich man indeed, since the phenomenon can't occur other than naturally. Out of 100 coconut trees perhaps only 2 will be *kopyor* coconuts.

Alcoholic Drinks

Is it just a happy coincidence that Dutch beer goes so well with Indonesian food? Heineken of Holland taught Indonesians how to brew Indonesia's ubiquitous Bintang lager beer (0.6 liter bottles), the best accompaniment to Indonesia's hot, spicy food. Guiness Stout has started to make inroads all over Indonesia, and Irish whiskey is served in the bars of Kuta and Denpasar. For native brews, mildly alcoholic *tuak* (palm wine), brewed a month before it's drunk, gives you a mellow slow-motion high. *Brem* is rice wine made from glutinous rice and coconut milk. Old *brem* (more than 3 days old) is sour and has more alcoholic content; new *brem* (under 3 days old) has a sweet taste and lower alcoholic content. Either type of *brem* costs Rp1200-2000 per bottle. *Badek* is another fermented liquor obtained from rice, and the tipple *arak* is an insidiously potent rice-spirit distilled by the Chinese.

Desserts

Bananas steamed, deep-fried, or boiled cost about Rp100 each, and are found everywhere. Many desserts are derived from rice. *Ketan* is rice pudding cooked in coconut milk and sugar syrup. Indonesians love their sweetmeats and you'll see them everywhere: lentil pastes, coconut cakes, gaily colored rice pastries, crunchy peanut cookies, sticky banana cakes, mung-bean soups, and other bizarre munchies. *Lontong*, used in *gado-gado*, is rice cooked in banana leaves and tastes somewhat like cold Cream of Wheat. *Bubur santen* is rice porridge cooked in palm sugar and coconut milk. After cooking rice, what sticks to the bottom of the pot turns brown, crunchy, and sticky. This rice is as much coveted by the children of an Indonesian family as cake icing is in an American family or pigskin rinds are in a Danish family. Ice cream comes in all the usual flavors plus *durian*, coconut cream, and lychee fruit flavors; sweet corn kernel ice cream is another Indonesian treat. Often bakeries specialize in their own homemade ice cream, or you can stick with (safer) locally manufactured brands such as Peters and Diamond. The latest rage in Indonesia is deep-fried ice cream, imported from Adelaide, which remains frozen on the inside because of a special kind of flour.

Indonesians love sweets and you're in a constant battle against sugar intake as everywhere you go coffee and tea are served in glasses already ⅓ filled with sugar and sweet condensed milk. *Warung* offer a great variety of sweets and snacks kept in big glass jars; help yourself and let the owner know afterwards how many you ate of each item (prices are standard, usually Rp125-250 per). *Es campur* is the Indonesian equivalent of the banana split and this is why many travelers become real aficionados of this dessert. *Es campur* are made differently all over Indonesia but a typical one consists of sweetened water, milk, syrup, gelatin, cubes of sweet bread, *tape* (cassava root dessert, or tapioca), and other nameless coagulated brightly colored pulpy substances; they run anywhere from Rp500-900. There are also many special holiday desserts. During *Hari Raya*, pastries and a cornucopia of cookies are served. On Asjura, a Muslim holiday on the 10th day of the first month in the Islamic calendar, a rice porridge *(bubur asjura)* with peanuts, eggs, and sweet beans is prepared.

MONEY

The Indonesian monetary unit is called the *rupiah*, issued in notes of Rp100, Rp500, Rp1000, Rp5000, Rp10,000, and in coins of Rp5, Rp10, Rp25, Rp50 and Rp100—all of different sizes. Study Indonesian currency and coins until you're familiar with all the denominations. You'll seldom use the Rp5 and Rp10 coins; just keep them as souvenirs. Bills are all the same size but different colors. Be very careful with the old Rp10,000 notes which still circulate; they are maddeningly similar to Rp5000 notes. If you don't recognize the difference, this is a real quick way to lose 3½ bucks. They've got a new Rp10,000 note now that's cobalt, so no problem. When changing large amounts, banks usually give you Rp10,000 notes which could make it difficult to get your wallet or moneybelt shut! But changing even a Rp10,000 bill in the outlying provinces of Indonesia could prove troublesome. If heading for the outliers, the best is just to accept Rp1000 and Rp5000 notes. Technically, visitors are not allowed to take in or take out more than Rp50,000. When leaving the country, your *rupiah* may be exchanged for foreign currencies, so be sure to always keep your exchange receipts.

APPROXIMATE CURRENCY EQUIVALENTS

Currency	Country	Indonesian Equivalent
US$1	USA	Rp1635
A$1	Australia	Rp1165
UK1	United Kingdom	Rp2626
NZ$1	New Zealand	Rp975
S$1	Singapore	Rp784
Mal$1	Malaysia	Rp649
HK$1	Hong Kong	Rp213
Fr1	Switzerland	Rp1025
Kr1	Sweden	Rp180
Fr1	France	Rp262
NF1	Netherlands	Rp774
DM1	W. Germany	Rp873
C$1	Canada	Rp1250
100Y	Japan	Rp1091

Attitudes

To swagger with your money in Indonesia is against your interests—you'll just be asking to be taken advantage of. To the man in the street a dollar's worth of *rupiah* has the same emotional impact as $10 has to us; US$2,000 is enough to keep a rural Indonesian family of 4 for a year. In Indonesia a price is put on everything "extra"—a better seat on the bus, for extra sugar or ice in your drink, to urinate at the market, for the use of a fan, for each and every application form at a government office (Rp100-200 apiece), and even a fee (Rp20) just to pick up letters at a *post restante*—everything. On holidays in Indonesia the prices are double or triple what they usually are. In the mountain resort of Bandungan (C. Java), a room that normally goes for Rp8000 fetches Rp20,000 at Christmas-time. On Bali in the evenings minibus and *bemo* prices go up by Rp25-50 ("evening service")! The marketing concept of the "giant economy size" is absent in Indonesia. The smallest size here is nearly always the best value. Three *martabak* at Rp350 each are twice as much food as one of the Rp800 sizes; same thing goes for laundry soap or *ikat* blankets. Neither do Indonesian retailers value the "return customer" idea; they want your money now, up front, not sometime in the future.

EXPENSES

Don't ask how much Indonesian currency is worth in "real money"; it's just as real as American or Australian currency. Don't make the mistake of always translating Indonesian prices into U.S. or European currency—think in *rupiah*. It doesn't cost "just" 50 American cents, it costs 700 damn *rupiah!* How much money you spend per day depends upon your tastes, the level of comfort you demand, where you want to go and how you get there. If you're on the move, buying tickets on buses, taxis, and trains, count on living for about US$8-12 a day. In places like Jakarta, Irian Jaya, and Maluku, where prices for transport, accommodations, and food are much higher, expect more like US$12-18 per day. If you're staying put, much less. There are tens of thousands of villages where you can live for US$3 per day or less—if you do it like the villagers. Mountain tourist resorts and big cities are the most expensive. There's also a significant price difference between Jakarta and the other cities of Indonesia. It takes you Rp15,000 to get 15 km into the city by taxi from Jakarta's Soekarno-Hatta Airport, whereas in Surabaya the same trip costs only Rp400 in a *bemo*.

Due to the intense competition, the cheapest places are right along the traveler's trail—Bali, Yogya, Lake Toba, etc. But don't think that because it's so cheap in the tourist ghettoes, you won't get extravagant; you may spend *more*. Instead of buying just one of an item, you buy three. Don't pay an entrance or parking fee without getting an official receipt (unless only a "donation" is requested, then Rp100-200 is acceptable). If you can spare it, give something; in many cases the attendants make their living from tourists. Often "guards" *(penjaga* or *juru kunci)* try to make you pay a fee to enter a parking lot, historical site, temple, or museum; plus Rp100-250 extra for your camera. If you can't afford it, put the camera in a bag, go around the side, and get in free. There will also be beggars outside and inside holy places *(tempat kramet)* because it's believed that people have a bigger heart when they visit a holy place.

Tipping

A few annoying Western customs have caught on. Never tip on the Outer Islands or on Bali. Don't contribute to this cancer! Expect to tip for individual service only in the big hotels. Airport porters and bellhops in Jakarta generally expect a tip of Rp500-1000, except at Denpasar's or Ujung Pandang's airport where Rp2000 is more in order! Hire-car drivers *(sopir)* may be tipped Rp1000-2000—but only if they've earned it. Taxi drivers are never tipped, although in Jakarta they could be pushy about tips. As in Europe, high-priced hotels usually add a 10% service charge, plus 11% government tax. Leading restaurants also may add a service charge, and additional tipping may be expected.

Bribes

You can pay your way out of almost anything in Indonesia: for forgetting a cholera shot at Bali airport, Rp5000; for a dope bust on Java, Rp500,000; for killing a man in Medan, Rp1,000,000, and so forth (prices subject to inflation). Perhaps as much as 30% of the salaries of civil servants come from bribes, the majority by businesses trying to start up. You know when it's coming: "The official is out right now...", or " The matter must be referred to another department...", or "No more forms." A good technique is to put a Rp10,000 (or whatever you think is called for) note inside your passport when you hand it over to an official. If he's offended, just explain that's where you usually keep your money. If your eyes meet and he takes it, it worked. It is unlikely that travelers will ever need to resort to bribery, but often you may not even know if you've just paid a bribe because it is often masked behind some official fee or charge. With the launching of the anti-graft campaign Opstib ("Operation Order") in 1988, the Indonesians seem determined to curb lower-level corruption. They might even make it this time, but it will take time.

EXCHANGE

Banks

U.S. dollars, known and accepted all over Indonesia since WW II, are still the most useful foreign currency to carry while traveling in Indonesia. U.S. currency has the most fixed rate of exchange because the *rupiah* is based on it. Though the dollar could have a more favorable exchange rate than other currencies, it's possible to cash other well-known currencies as Australian dollars, Deutschmarks, Netherlands florin, French and Swiss francs. Canadian dollars are a bit more difficult. To find the rough U.S. dollar equivalent of a large amount of *rupiah*, merely divide by 15,000 and you come out roughly with the amount of money in increments of US$10. For example, if a plane ticket costs Rp37,000, this means it's roughly $25 (15,000 into Rp37,000). Cash can be exchanged for your traveler's cheques at branches of the Bank Expor Impor Indonesia, Bank Negara Indonesia, and Bank Rakyat Indonesia, all of which have branches virtually the length and breadth of the country. Bank hours are generally Mon. to Fri. 0800-1200, Sat. 0800-1100, but get there early to avoid lines. You'll need your passport for each exchange transaction. Gold is freely and legally traded in Indonesia and there are a good number of gold shops in every good-sized Indonesian city.

Moneychangers

Moneychangers (and banks) charge a set fee for their services, so each time you change money, it costs you. The minimum you should exchange on a routine basis should be the most you can afford to lose. Banks seldom post rates of exchange, though official moneychangers often do. Moneychangers, found anywhere tourists congregate, are often open much later than banks. Their rates vary from good to bad, yet could offer a much more favorable exchange than banks. Rates fluctuate daily. You'll be able to find a plethora of moneychangers on the main roads of Kuta and Sanur on Bali; you'll also find that their rates are very similar to Denpasar's banks but their service is much quicker. Also, check with the moneychangers in Penang (Malaysia), and in Singapore's Change Alley, Raffles Place, and Battery Road before you go to Indonesia; they could give an excellent *rupiah* rate for Australian or United States cash (up to Rp1600 per U.S. dollar).

Changing Money

Bear in mind that the exchange rates for the various currencies are different all over Indonesia. For example, the exchange rate for the German mark is 10% better in Jakarta than in Sumatra. In Jakarta, the U.S. dollar is worth around Rp1500, in Bukittinggi Rp1320,

The most widely used "people's money" is the Rp100 bill. The image is that of the revolutionary war hero, General Sudirman (1912-50), was a gifted military tactician. Suffering from tuberculosis, he was carried on a stretcher from battle to battle, dying soon after the transfer of sovereignty by Holland to Indonesia. The Rp1000 note is the most useful. The image is that of Prince Diponegoro (1787-1855). Declaring a holy war against the Dutch in 1825, Diponegoro carried out a relentless guerrilla war which dragged on for 5 years and cost the Dutch 15,000 men.

in Prapat Rp1400. Medan is said to offer better rates than anywhere else, for whatever reason. Not only are there regional differences, but the rates for foreign currencies depend on the bank and even on *the branch* of the bank. Rates sometimes vary so much from one bank to the next that the right choice could save 2-4 percent. Bank Bumi Daya consistently gives good rates all over Java. Bank Negara Indonesia seems at least as good as the competition, though for larger amounts it's still worth shopping around if you've got more time than money. In order to encourage tourism, the best rates in Indonesia are usually found in the tourist towns. In the far reaches of Indonesia the exchange rates could be downright criminal, or there could be no banks at all. Go to such outlying areas, where they might not have ever heard of a Swiss franc, with plentiful Indonesian cash in small denominations. Avoid, if you can, exchanging money at airports, train stations, and leading hotels. Wherever it's most convenient to change money, it's also the most costly. If you arrive in Indonesia at an airport where the rates too high, exchange only US$20 or so, enough to get you a hotel room and a meal that night. If you exchange money at your hotel desk, you get at least 5% below the rate offered by the state banks.

CASH, TCs, AND CCs

Cash

It's foolish to travel to Indonesia carrying only cash since there's no black market. For safety, it's better to bring a widely accepted brand of traveler's cheques such as American Express. No one seems really interested in foreign cash anyway, certainly not at anything better than bank rates for traveler's cheques. But always carry some US$5s, US$10s and US$20s in case you need quick money if banks are closed. And if you're going to outlying areas of Indonesia,

carry proportionally more U.S. cash because at times it's very inconvenient to locate banks, if there are any. Indonesian banks, even on Bali, absolutely refuse to touch foreign banknotes which are dirty, soiled, or physically damaged (listen to the Ugly Australian complain in Denpasar about getting stuck with the $20 note because of the torn corner!). In the Outer Islands paper currency tends to stay in circulation longer, so Indonesian banknotes start to take on the appearance of filthy scraps of torn cloth. This worn money will not be accepted, so you shouldn't allow it to be passed on to you. Also, don't carry coins across a border (such as from Irian Jaya into PNG), since most banks won't exchange them. Either use them up, convert them to paper bills, or give them away to kids. But if you intend to return to the country, some loose change will come in handy.

Traveler's Cheques

American Express, First National City Bank, Barclays, and Thomas Cook's traveler's cheques are accepted all over Indonesia. Amex checks are the best of all; they are the fastest to give a refund. All these companies have branches in Jakarta or Singapore in case you lose your checks. Some of Australia's savings banks and other lesser-known banks without agents in Asia will let you starve before they replace your lost TCs. The major Indonesian banks such as Bank Bumi Daya, Bank Expor Impor, Bank Rakyat Indonesia, and Bank Negara Indonesia all take most Aussie and the better-known TCs. It usually takes only about 20 min. to cash your TCs at a bank. If you come across a bank that won't accept your brand of TCs, it might help to ask for the person in charge or the bank manager. Major hotels and some shops will also take TCs (at lousy rates). If you're having trouble trying to cash TCs in a small business, volunteer to go to the bank with someone and cash your check. There are even cases (Ternate?) where the only banks you come across will just accept certain brands of TCs, such as only Amex.

And it's unbelievable that you can still have trouble changing English pound TCs in Indonesia, even in a city the size of Malang (E. Java). Here, they can't or won't change them and will tell you to go up to Surabaya.

Credit Cards

Indonesia is very much a cash-oriented society. Plastic credit cards can be utilized in Indonesia but only in the big cities such as Jakarta, Surabaya, Palembang, Medan, Aceh—and then limitedly. Take a list of your credit card numbers and phone numbers to call so you can cancel the cards if you lose them; leave a duplicate list with a friend back home. When charging, be sure to verify the total amount charged, sign the charge slip, and retain the customer copy (charge slips could be altered and used to defraud by adding an extra zero). Don't discard the slips until the charges have been filed and paid. Ask hotels, restaurants, and shops to convert the total amounts into dollars and cents, then write the amount on the charge slip. This way, in spite of currency fluctuations, you'll know exactly what is owed your credit card company. Your passport number and your credit card are needed for all transactions.

Acceptance of the American Express card is becoming more and more widespread and using it is a wonderful way to husband your valuable TCs and cash. Personal checks are usually useless, with one exception. It's easy as pie to cash your personal check for any amount up to US$1000 upon presentation of your American Express card at the main American Express office in Jakarta (Arthaloka Bldg., Jl. Jen. Sudirman, Mon.-Fri. 0815-1400, Sat. 0815-1100, tel. 587-401). This way, you don't have to take that much cash with you on the first leg of your journey through Nusatenggara or Sumatra, then halfway through your trip in Jakarta you can replenish your cash supply. Don't count on using your Amex or other credit cards anywhere but in the swankiest hotels, international airlines offices, and big city restaurants. Some travel agencies will also accept them, which is convenient because you can pay for a car rental or a tour through them. Different branches of the same store will have different policies; for example, Sarinah's 5th floor won't accept Amex but its 1st floor will!

Wire Transfers

Also called remittance orders. Take enough money with you in the first place ($2000 for 2-5 months of budget travel should be sufficient) so you won't have to go through the hassle of having money wired, which costs up to US$15 for the service. Travelers who've been caught short have found that it may take several weeks to get money remitted by wire from Australia, North America, or Europe. Then there's the horror story of the Indonesian bank that kept the money wired to them for a month and invested it! If you're really stuck, a telex is a much faster way to transfer money than ordinary telegrams or money-grams. Before you go, get your bank's telex number. A slower way is to wire home and ask for an international money order. You'd think that your own country's consulate or embassy would help you out in emergencies, but they usually care more about promoting commerce than they do about helping individual travelers. If you're repatriated by your embassy, you'll probably have to repay the money lent you before you're allowed to travel abroad again.

BARGAINING

Bargaining is the process by which you come to an agreement on a price with the seller before you make a purchase or receive a service. Try to get the lowest price the seller will accept. The more Indonesians overcharge, the less interaction there is, the less respect there is, and the more impoverished the communication becomes. So always bargain hard for everything everywhere, including medicine in drugstores, hospitalization, immigration fees, entrance charges to museums or temple sites, no matter what type of establishment it is, even "fixed-price" shops. Buying and bargaining in Indonesia can be good-humored or it can be infuriating, a game won by technique and strategy, not by anger or threats. The price is always made in consideration of the merchant's need on that day, his assessment of the potential buyer, how much he or she likes you, plus the sporting spirit of the exchange. Bargaining isn't a one-way process at all—Indonesians enjoy it. It's a pleasurable way Indonesians have to relate with you. It should be leisurely and friendly.

Some Techniques

Bargaining is an invaluable skill developed through getting burned many times. Indonesians don't really cheat, you just have to listen real hard. In the hopes that you'll be over-generous, when you ask Indonesians "How much?", they are very fond of replying, "It's up to you." Find out the price of the item first; don't ever assume a price or take a (perhaps biased) bystander's word for it. Before you go out shopping, ask your hotel proprietor, houseboy, driver, or someone else who is uninvolved with the shop, what the *correct* price is. Indonesians themselves are always swapping price information as a way of keeping their costs down. Don't stop and buy at the very first stall, vendor, or shop you come across; compare prices first, learn about the quality and the differences. Do all your heavy crafts-buying your last week in Indonesia when you are the most knowledgable. For luxury items like carvings, jewelry, paintings, start out with ¼ the price they ask, then inch up; for services like *becak* and laundry, start out with ½ the price they ask; for essentials like canned groceries, soap, room rental, even restaurant meals, start off at ¾ the price they ask—roughly. Remain flexible.

Avoid asking the seller the price; he will start out too high. The bargainer should initiate with a reasonable price so the whole exchange gets off to a realistic start. When they smile, it means they know you know its value. Cut their first offer and then go up begrudgingly in small increments; fight for every decimal. When they frown, the bargaining is reaching its conclusion. When you offer the highest price you're willing to pay, don't budge. As a last resort, try "The Walk Away," as feigned disinterest will make for many a good deal. Your position is strongest when you appear not to care. This is almost always necessary with *becak* drivers, but *before* climbing in. Just smile, shrug your shoulders, and walk slowly away with cocked ears. Often the driver or seller will call you back, agreeing to your last bid. Another hint is not to hover around or fondle the item you really want; never give a clue of your *true* interest. If you show any enthusiasm for it, they will not budge in price. Instead, include the item with other articles you want, as if it's a second thought. Or throw it in at the last minute before clinching your negotiations: "Oh, how much for this too?"

Another trick is to bid for goods early in the day just as the vendor/store/stall opens for business. A seller believes that making a sale right off will give him or her good luck for the rest of the day, so they're willing to take a lower price just to get the day off to a good start. There is even a verb *(penglaris)* which means "selling the first article cheap early in the morning in order to stimulate further sales." Thus the expression, "morning price." If you have an Indonesian friend buy your tickets for boats, flights, buses, vehicle charters, as well as fruits, food, etc., they can get better prices than you and you won't need to bargain. Expat residents always send their houseboys and cooks to the markets to do the food shopping. Also try asking for the *harga belajar* (student's price) or asking "Could I have the Rp1000 size (or portion)?" and they'll often come up with a cheaper "size," and it saves face. There is much more incentive for the budget traveler to learn the language than for the more affluent traveler. The traveler realizes that he can save lots of money and make friends easier if he knows how to bargain in Indonesian. If you speak Indonesian, natives assume you already know the prices and usually won't charge you as much or will give in to your price more quickly.

Bargaining Etiquette

It's bad manners to continue to bargain after a deal has been struck, a service has been rendered, or an item has been bought. Bargaining is most critical in markets, with anyone who quotes you a ridiculous price, when taking *becak* and Sumatran buses, and with beach or street vendors of tourist items that the natives themselves seldom buy. It's really challenging to try to get the same price as the neighborhood locals. There is a second (higher) price for out-of-town Indonesians, and still a third and higher price for Chinese, *orang besar* ("big man"), Indonesians from other islands, and foreigners like you. The foreign tourist, thought to be the most ignorant and richest of all, gets overcharged constantly. You pay according to your station in life. If you say you're poor, they laugh. (If you're so poor, how come you're here?) Always try to be a bit more patient than the seller. If you stand around and watch locals buy something and pay, go up and pay the same.

Admittedly, being overcharged gets very tiresome after awhile. Though it's only a matter of pennies, the practice manages to annoy every Westerner eventually, as a matter of principle. But sometimes you just can't cut the price down too much. Stubborn and aggressive, some travelers just won't pay that extra Rp200. Here they've traveled halfway around the world to become livid over a lousy 15 cents. The Indonesian won't make a million; he's got to feed a family of six. If you think it's going to cause an argument, just give that little bit extra. The vendor may not be overcharging you and it's just not worth the ill will. In certain places you can reduce the price, but Indonesians work very hard and must maintain a profit margin. There's a vast difference between the opportunistic tourist-oriented stores, markets, and street sellers, and those businesses that offer goods and services mostly to Indonesians. Also, you tend not to get overcharged as much in the country as in the cities.

Fixed Price

Fixed prices *(harga pasti)* are a growing trend now in tourist shops. The posting of a *HARGA PASTI* sign is supposed to prevent you from bargaining, but it shouldn't. Particularly if you buy more than one item you should qualify for a "bulk-purchase discount" of at least a portion of the price off each item. On a large bulk purchase or multiple luxury purchase, many thousands of *rupiah* should be taken off the retail total. Bargaining can be a prolonged exchange lasting days and even weeks. Often if you wait the seller out, you'll get a substantial discount. Get to know the seller and his family, go back again and again, have tea, and keep it friendly. He or she might be in a better mood or need the money more in a few days or weeks. Sometimes the price is actually unbargainable with no discounts or reductions. This is most often the case in high-priced hotels and restaurants, department stores, and tourist shops; they know they'll get it. A general rule: if you see a price posted or attached to an item, it's a fixed-price shop. But if they say it's *harga pasti* and nothing is posted, there's room for haggling.

Bring digital watches, dainty Western jewelry, flashy shirts, and other trendy Western clothes for trading, making it possible to strike up some good deals for artwork, fabrics, jewelry, etc. Even wool is coveted, such as wool baby caps. T-shirts with slogans, Western logos, mottos, or scenes on them are good trading value. Bring fantastic, phantasmagoric, psychedelic, or SciFi posters—young Indonesians love them. (Also refer to the "Trading" section under "Crafts" for more swappable items to take.)

VISAS

For many nationalities, tourist visas are no longer required to enter Indonesia. Tourists and those attending conventions receive a "tourist pass" or "entry stamp" upon arrival that allows them to stay up to 2 months anywhere in Indonesia (except E. Timor). This policy, instituted in 1983, was aimed at bolstering the country's sagging tourism industry (a drop of more than 33% in number of visitors from 1981 to 1982). As long as they make their exit and entry through certain air and seaports, nationals of the following 26 countries do not need a visa beforehand:

Australia	Malaysia
Austria	Netherlands
Belgium	New Zealand
Canada	Norway
Denmark	Philippines
Finland	Singapore
France	South Korea
Great Britain	Spain
Greece	Sweden
Iceland	Switzerland
Italy	Thailand
Japan	USA
Luxemburg	West Germany

Visitors from other countries can obtain a tourist visa from any Indonesian Embassy or consulate; 2 photos are required and a small fee is charged. All visitors must possess a passport valid for at least 6 months after arriving in Indonesia. A tourist must also have an onward ticket by plane or boat out of Indonesia, or a letter from an air carrier, shipping or cruise company, or travel agency confirming the purchase of those tickets. The 2-month tourist pass cannot be extended. If you want to stay longer your only option is to leave the cheapest way possible, then re-enter for another 2 months. To fulfill the onward-journey requirement, or to leave the country cheaply and return, the shortest, cheapest exit/re-entry points are: Medan, N. Sumatra, to Penang, Malaysia (by air or sea); from Jakarta, W. Java, to Singapore (by air or sea); from Pontianak, W. Kalimantan, to Kucing, E. Malaysia (by air); from Tarakan, E. Kalimantan, to Tawau, E. Malaysia (by air or speedboat). See also "Re-entry" below.

Restrictions

If you have an entry pass in Indonesia, it's impossible to change the status of your visa unless you do it outside of Indonesia. Apply for other types of visas months (years?) in advance in your country of origin. Citizens of Israel, Portugal, and S. Africa may not enter Indonesia on their passports. Immigration officials also reserve the right to deny entry to any visitor who, in their opinion, is not properly dressed or groomed, lacks the proper funds, or (in their words) "may endanger the country's security, peace, and stability or the public health and morals." For these unfortunate undesirables, a transit visa is issued at the airport upon their arrival which allows them to hang out at the airport until the departure of the aircraft they arrived on or the first available flight to their desired destination.

KINDS OF VISAS

Kinds Of Visas

Ordinary tourists entering through designated sea and airports do not need visas, but if you enter via other points or have a reason to stay in Indonesia longer than 2 months there are several other stay permits available. A business visa, for example, can be obtained on application; extensions are at the discretion of the immigration authorities in Indonesia's 27 provincial capitals. In all these *kantor imigrasi* offices of Indonesia, the prices for visas are becoming standardized, varying only slightly. A fixed price list is usually posted on the walls so you know exactly what you should pay. Probably the best place to get visas approved is right in the heart of the beast: Jakarta. To accommodate all the extra stamps required for special visas, when you apply for your passport try to get additional pages put in at no extra charge. In the U.S., ask for a "businessman's passport." Extra pages will save you time-consuming trips to officious U.S. consulates overseas when you run out of blank pages in your passport.

If you stay over 3 months in Indonesia on *any* visa, you must "register as an alien," pay Rp1500 (plus Rp400 for 2 forms) and be fingerprinted. After residing in Indonesia 6 months, any foreign resident (both adults and children) wishing to leave the country must now obtain an exit permit and pay a "foreign fiscal tax" of Rp150,000. This tax constitutes an advance payment of one's income tax. Only the diplomatic corps, members of international organizations, airline personnel, and government-sponsored people are exempt.

KINDS OF VISAS

Visitor's Visa

Unfortunately, this type of visa isn't given out as much as it used to be—only in special cases. You must have either a legitimate reason to travel (relatives in Indonesia? study a martial art? academic research?), or be involved in an accredited study program. You must apply in advance in your country of origin for this type of visa. A special application form must be filled out and you must show a letter of invitation from an influential sponsor or guarantor in Indonesia (a government official, high-ranking military officer, respected *non-Chinese* business-owner, for example). And it's not always certain you'll get it. Even requests for special consideration from your embassy with stamps and state seals and everything might not cut it. Return or onward tickets (airline/ship) are still requested by Indonesian *imigrasi* officials upon arrival. Visitor's Visas are normally given for a 4- or 5-week initial stay but they can be extended up to 5 times for one or more month's duration each time, for a total of 6 months.

Extensions are granted at the sole discretion of *Kantor Imigrasi* personnel. To apply, you'll need your sponsor's extension request letter, sponsor's ID card copy, and the application for visa extension. Then keep your fingers crossed that it will all work! You also need a good measure of serenity—even a saint would lose patience with the *imigrasi* people. Typical is when they ask you to wait a few minutes to see an official. An hour later, you're told that the man will be in his meeting until 1400 (the time the office closes). Then comes the oft' heard "come back tomorrow." Finally, it turns out you never had to see that official in the first place. Apply early because it might take as little as 2 days or as much as 3 weeks to get an extension, and you might have to go back 4 or more times. *Imigrasi* likes you to bring an Indonesian friend because they *hate* to speak English. It gets more difficult for stays beyond 3 months, and small offices (like Padang) refuse to handle it. You may need to be fingerprinted and fill out additional forms. Also, your sponsor may have to write new letters.

When you have used up your 6 months limit, the words "FINAL EXTENSION" are stamped in your passport. It's generally easier for Europeans to get Visitor's Visa extensions than it is for N. Americans or Australians. Australians are processed with the most prejudice because they make it difficult for Indonesians to enter Australia and remain there for any length of time. It's a way of hitting back at Australia's lingering White Australia Policy. Dutch travelers are given a lot of slack because of nostalgic historical/cultural ties between the 2 countries. Indonesians seem to go out of their way to show the Dutch that they hold no grudge. Dutch travelers even have a better chance if the *imigrasi* officer speaks their language (sometimes the case!). In order to study their religious discipline, spiritual organizations like Sumarah in Solo, C. Java, have been known to make it easier for travelers to get Visitor's Visa extensions.

Business Visa

A Business Visa, available at Indonesian Consulates, allows a stay of up to 30 days and can be extended to 3 months. It's for single entry and costs US$4.80. Submit forms in duplicate with 2 photos, plus a letter in duplicate from a business firm or employer stating the purpose of your visit and giving financial guarantees. Under certain circumstances, this type of visa might be easier to obtain than a Visitor's Visa. A business manager or firm owner must vouch for the fact that you are carrying out some service for him in Indonesia. Some foreigners, in order to export handicrafts and textiles, start up a company with an Indonesian, then "the company" sponsors them. Still, whether you get one or not depends on the *imigrasi* department. For a businessman who intends to remain in Indonesia less than 6 weeks, it makes more sense just to enter with a tourist pass. If you're a writer, journalist, or photographer, don't say so.

PORTS OF ENTRY AND DEPARTURE

Only the following are officially designated as ports of entry and departure:

Medan, N. Sumatra: Polonia Airport; Belawan seaport
Pekanbaru, E. Sumatra: Simpang Tiga Airport
Riau, E. Sumatra: Batubesar Airport or Batu Ampon seaport on P. Batam (S of Singapore)
Jakarta: Cengkareng Airport; Tanjung Priok seaport
Surabaya: Tanjung Perak seaport
Bali: Ngurah Rai Airport; Benoa seaport; Padangbai seaport (E. Bali)
Timor, E. Nusatenggara: Eltari Airport, Kupang
W. Kalimantan: Pontianak Airport

Sulawesi: Sam Ratulangi Airport, Manado; Bitung seaport, E. of Manado. An interesting connection to here is Garuda's Guam-Manado flight.
Maluku: Pattimura Airport, Ambon; Ambon Harbor
Irian Jaya: Frans Kaisiepo Airport, Biak. Travelers arriving from the USA may get off here and begin their visit to Indonesia by touring the eastern islands first.

Bear in mind that if you enter Indonesia at any point not listed above, such as Jayapura (Irian Jaya) or Tg. Pinang (Riau), you're required to have a proper visa and will receive only 28 days upon arrival. If you enter Indonesia overland from PNG or North Borneo (E. Malaysia), or take a boat from the southern Philippines to E. Kalimantan, you are entering Indonesia illegally. If you're caught, Indonesian immigration officials may put you in jail or right back on the plane.

ENTRY POINTS OF INDONESIA

However, their policies about entering Indonesia from neighboring countries seem to be constantly changing, subject to aimless bureaucratic caprice. Sometimes you get the impression that regulations are trumped up right on the spot when they tell you that clearances/permits are required to enter points in E. and W. Kalimantan, Maluku, Irian Jaya, Aceh, and Riau. For example, practically every Indonesian embassy and consulate in the world insists that you need a permit from Jakarta to travel in the interior of Irian Jaya. This is a persistent myth. In Jayapura's police station permits *(surat jalan)* for the interior are issued routinely while you wait (more time if you don't have 4 passport photos). On the other hand, East Timor, which was occupied by the Indonesians in 1975, is definitely off-limits and you may not even visit West Timor's most easterly district bordering E. Timor without a *surat jalan* (which are never issued).

OVERSTAYING AND RETURNS

Sometimes, if you show *kantor imigrasi* your ticket, you can get an extension over your 60-day maximum stay in order to meet a ship or plane. They routinely grant a 3-day overstay, particularly if you're leaving by ship. For an overstay longer than 3 days, the only legitimate excuse is that you've lost your passport or are in the hospital or can bring a note from a doctor or hospital verifying a medical problem. Or you might find that when leaving the country after having overstayed 2 or even 3 days, they'll just let it go without re-

quiring you to go to an *imigrasi* office. If your flight is booked up to 2 weeks after your last day, you also should be able to get an extension from an *imigrasi* officer for the waiting time. It will probably require a letter from your travel agency explaining the situation. Some desperate individuals even "lose" their passport, claim it's been stolen, or take a swim in the sea with their passport. The bureaucratic paperwork resulting in a lost passport could prolong their stays in Indonesia by weeks.

Re-entry

If you use up your 2-month maximum stay but want to spend more time in Indonesia, one answer is to leave the country, return, and get a new tourist pass stamp in your passport. Most people in this situation spend US$160 on a RT ticket from Jakarta to Singapore, spend a few days in Singapore shopping, then fly right back to Jakarta. Cheaper is to leave Indonesia at certain points as close as possible to neighboring countries from where you can re-enter. Some obvious exit points are not that reliable. For example, be forewarned that Indonesian authorities may not allow you to exit Jayapura (capital of Irian Jaya) for Wewak, PNG (the eastern half of the island of New Guinea). The following are the most convenient, least expensive routes out:

1) by air from Medan, N. Sumatra, to Penang, northern peninsular Malaysia
2) by air from Pekanbaru (E. Sumatra) to Melaka (Malaysia), then by taxi to Kuala Lumpur

SELECTED INDONESIAN EMBASSIES AND CONSULAR OFFICES ABROAD

Australia
Indonesian Embassy
8 Darwin Ave.
Yarralumla
Canberra ACT 2600
tel. 72 3222

Indonesian Consulate
22 Coronation Drive, Stuart Park
Darwin N.T. 5790
tel. 819352

Indonesian Consulate
52 Aloert Road, 3rd Floor
South Melbourne
Victoria 3205
tel. (031) 6907811

Indonesian Consulate
133 St. George's Terrace
Perth WA 6000, tel. 219821

Indonesian Consulate
Piccadilly Court, 3rd Floor
222 Pitt Street, Sydney
tel. 264 2976/2195/2323

Canada
Indonesian Embassy
287 Maclaren Street
Ottawa, Ontario K2P OL9
tel. (613) 236 7403/7404

Indonesian Consulate
425 University Ave., 9th Floor
Toronto, Ontario M56 156
tel. (416) 5916461/2

Indonesian Consulate
526 Granville
Vancouver B.C. V6C IV5
tel. 682 8855/58

Great Britain & Ireland
Indonesian Embassy
38 Grosvenor Square
London WIX 9 AAD
tel. 01 499 7661

Hong Kong
Indonesian Consulate
127-129 Leighton Road
6-8 Koswick Street
Causeway Bay
tel. HK (5) 7904421/8

Italy
Indonesian Embassy
53 Via Campania, Rome
tel. 475 9251

Japan
Indonesian Embassy
2-9 Higashi Gotanda, 5 Chome
Shinagawa-ku, Tokyo
tel. 441 4201/9

Malaysia
Indonesian Embassy
Jl. Tun Razak 233
Kuala Lumpur
tel. 421011/411141/421228

Indonesian Consulate
Coastal Road, Karamunsing
Kota Kinabalu, Sabah
E. Malaysia
tel. 64100/54245/55110/54459/
53571

Indonesian Consulate
Jl. Burmah 467, Penang
tel. 25162/25163/25164/25168

New Zealand
Indonesian Embassy
70 Glen Road
Kelburn, Wellington
tel. 758695

Netherlands
Indonesian Embassy
8 Tobias Asserlaan
2517 KC's Graven Hage
tel. 070 469796

Papua New Guinea
Indonesian Embassy
Sir John Guisa Drive
Sel 410, Lot 182, Waigoni
tel. 253116/18 253544

Philippines
Indonesian Embassy
Salcedo Street
Lagaspi Village 185/187
tel. 85 50 61/68

Singapore
Indonesian Embassy
7 Chatsworth Road
Singapore 1024
tel. 7377422

Sweden
Indonesian Embassy
47/V Strandvagen 11456
Stockholm, tel. 635470/4

United States of America
Indonesian Embassy
2020 Massachusetts Ave.
Washington D.C. 20036
tel. (202) 293 1745

Indonesian Consulate
233 North Michigan Ave.,
Ste. 1422
Chicago IL 60601
tel. (312) 9380101

Indonesian Consulate
1990 Post Oak Blvd., Ste. 1900
Houston TX 77056
tel. (713) 626 3291

Indonesian Consulate
Pri Tower
Honolulu HI 96842
tel. 524 4300

Indonesian Consulate
3457 Wilshire Blvd.
Los Angeles CA 90010
tel. (213) 383 5126

Indonesian Consulate
5 E. 68th Street
New York NY 10021
tel. (212) 879 0600

Indonesian Consulate
351 California Street, Ste. 700
San Francisco CA 94104
tel. (415) 474 9571

West Germany
Indonesian Embassy
Bernkasteler Strasse 2
5300 Bonn 2
tel. 0228 310091

3) by river ferry from Pekanbaru (E. Sumatra) via Tg. Pinang to Singapore

4) by air or ship from Jakarta (W. Java) to Singapore

5) by air from Pontianak (W. Kalimantan) to Kucing (Sarawak, E. Malaysia)

6) by air from Tarakan (E. Kalimantan) to Tawau (Sabah, E. Malaysia), or by boat from Nunukan (E. Kalimantan, N of Tarakan) to Tawau. The boat connection is sometimes on, sometimes off

7) by air from Kupang (Timor, E. Nusatenggara) to Darwin (Northern Territory, Australia)

SUGGESTED ITINERARIES

To get the most out of a long-term visit to Indonesia, to see as many high-quality places as possible over a 4-month (one re-entry) period, many travelers take one of the following overland-and-sea routes. Both are less expensive alternatives and save the hassle of flying back and forth between Indonesia and any of its neighboring countries more than once.

Sumatra-Java-Bali

First fly or take a boat from Penang, peninsular Malaysia, to Medan, N. Sumatra. Northern Sumatra is the most scenic and one of the richest parts of the island from a cultural/tourist's point of view. Spend an adequate 6-7 weeks in the wilds of Aceh province, on beautiful Lake Toba, and in and around Bukittinggi. When you're ready to leave, go out through Pekanbaru where you can get a river boat for only Rp7500 to P. Batam or Tg. Pinang, insular Riau. Then from either of these ports off the E coast of Sumatra it costs about Rp7000 and takes 3-4 hours aboard a motor launch to Singapore. Spend a few days there, relax, clean up any health problems, pick up your mail, go shopping, then return to Tg. Pinang and continue down to Jakarta by ship or plane. Spend another 2 months on colorful Java and Bali. This way you don't backtrack but keep on a southerly course, losing none of your momentum and getting to see the whole western part of the archipelago. It costs about the same as if you'd taken the Rp16,000 Padang-Jakarta boat or the punishing overland trip through the southern portion of Sumatra, which isn't the most attractive part of the island anyway. Boats leave every day from Pekanbaru to P. Batam or Tg. Pinang, from where it's easy to find a launch to Singapore.

Outer Island Route

First leave Bali for Surabaya, then make your way for 2 months by boat or plane through Sulawesi and Kalimantan, exiting Indonesia at Tarakan (E. Kalimantan) for Tawau (E. Malaysia). Spend some time going across E. Malaysia (northern Borneo), then come down on the regular Merpati flight from Kucing to Pontianak in W. Kalimantan (getting a new Indonesian tourist pass in your passport). Experience W. Kalimantan, then from Pontianak board the Bouraq

flight to Singapore or take a ship from Pontianak to Tg. Pinang in insular Riau, E. Sumatra. Next, board one of the launches to Singapore, come back and get a new stamp on P. Batam where you can board an ocean-going *kapal* to Pekanbaru, E. Sumatra. From Pekanbaru take a bus up to Bukittinggi, Lake Toba, finally exiting at the top of the island through Medan to Penang. Variations can be worked on this theme. For instance: Darwin-Kupang-Nusatenggara-Bali-Java-P. Batam-Singapore-P. Batam (with new entry stamp)-Pekanbaru-Bukittinggi-Lake Toba-Medan-Penang.

Easterly Route

If you intend to enter Indonesia from PNG (Wewak to Jayapura), Indonesian officials may not give you a tourist pass stamp when you arrive in Jayapura, so you'll need a Indonesian visa from the Indonesian Embassy in Port Moresby, PNG (Sir John Guisa Drive, tel. 253116). Get the very latest news about restrictions from travelers you meet along the way. Travelers taking the Garuda's direct Los Angeles-Jakarta flight from the U.S. W coast get off at Biak (northern Irian Jaya), then work their way W through the eastern islands to Bali, Java, and Sumatra—the "back-door" approach.

SELECTED DIPLOMATIC OFFICES IN JAKARTA

If you have trouble in Indonesia, it might be worthwhile to visit your embassy or consulate. Some countries which trade heavily with Indonesia have not only embassies but also several consulates scattered through the islands. Besides its embassy in Jakarta, the U.S. has 3 full-sized consular offices in Medan, Surabaya, and Bali. On Bali the office consists of just one woman at Sanur; motorcycle accidents and lost passports provide most of her work. A full listing can be obtained from any of the Indonesian Government Tourist Offices in all the main provincial capitals of Indonesia. The following is a partial list:

Australia Embassy of Australia
Jl. Thamrin 15 tel. 323109

Canada Embassy of Canada
Wisma Metropolitan I, 5th Floor Jl. Jen. Sudirman, Kav. 29 tel. 510709/514022

Denmark Royal Danish Embassy
Jl. Abdul Musi 34 tel. 346615

West Germany
Jl. Thamrin 1 tel. 323908/324292/324357

Great Britain Her Britannic Majesty's Embassy
Jl. Thamrin 75 tel. 330904

Japan Embassy of Japan
Jl. Thamrin 24 tel. 324308/324948/325396

Malaysia Embassy of Malaysia
Jl. Imam Bonjol 17 tel. 332170/336438/332864

Indonesia's
coat of arms

Pancasila: The "Five Principles" put forth by the state as a foundation of political and social rule, comparable to the U.S.'s Bill of Rights and England's Magna Carta. They are: 1) Belief in one of the four great universal religions. The mass support of this principle made the killing of a million "atheist" communists in 1965 much easier. Symbol: star. 2) Nationalism. Symbol: the head of a wild buffalo. 3) Indonesian democracy. Distinct from Western-based democracy. Takes place on the village level to promote mutual help, discussion, agreement. Symbol: banyan tree. 4) Humanitarianism. Indonesia takes its place among the family of nations. Symbol: chain, the unbroken unity of mankind. 5) Social Justice. A just and prosperous society that will give adequate supplies of food, clothing, and shelter for all. Symbol: sprays of rice and cotton.

Pancasila is a synthesis of all the main intellectual movements of the modern world, another expression of the famous blending of philosophic and religious ideologies which have been operating in Indonesia for thousands of years. Intended to promote the unity of the Indonesian people, different political groups have always interpreted the Five Principles to serve their own purposes.

Netherlands Embassy of the Kingdom of Netherlands
Jl. Rasun Said, Kav. S-3, 12950 tel. 511515

New Zealand New Zealand Embassy
Jl. Diponegoro 41 tel. 330552/330620/330680

Singapore Embassy of the Republic of Singapore
Jl. Proklamasi 23 tel. 348761/347783

Sweden Embassy of the Kingdom of Sweden
Jl. Taman Cut Mutiah 12 tel. 333061

United States of America Embassy of the USA
Jl. Merdeka Selatan 5 tel. 360360

CUSTOMS REGULATIONS

Indonesian Customs
Mellow. Customs procedures have become even more relaxed with the installation of green and red routes at international airports. Tourists with nothing to declare use the green route with no baggage inspection. Duty-free items that may be imported are: 200 cigarettes or 50 cigars and 2 pounds of tobacco; cameras (no limit) and reasonable amounts of film; 2 liters of liquor; a reasonable amount of perfume for personal use. All weapons and ammunition, anything that can be considered pornographic (such as a copy of *Playboy*), narcotics, as well as video cameras, TV sets, radio/cassette recorders and books with Chinese characters in them are forbidden entry into Indonesia (though Customs officials are very relaxed about enforcement). Technically, used radios, typewriters, and record players should be listed on your passport, and must be taken out upon departure, but officials hardly ever notice. Technically, books and printed matter using Indonesian languages are prohibited (or must be cleared by the Minister of Culture first). If you need medication, get a letter from your doctor. Importing animals is not recommended. Because there is no rabies in Indonesia, the import of dogs and cats is strictly controlled. Owners must prove that pets were inoculated against rabies at most 6 months before arrival, and a good health certificate is required from a veterinarian in your country of origin.

U.S. Customs
Because of the illegal drug trade from Asia, U.S. officials in West Coast ports keep a watchful eye out. Los Angeles International Airport is slow, but Hawaii is perhaps the slowest port of entry. Most flights from Indonesia make Honolulu or Los Angeles their main ports of entry to the U.S., so booking a flight to avoid Honolulu is your only salvation. Returning from Indonesia, business travelers report fewer hassles than tourists. If you state that you were traveling on business, U.S. Customs will usually ask about your trip, have a look at your ticket, and request a business card, so have one handy. As a returning U.S. resident, you may bring $400 worth (fair retail value) of duty-free articles acquired in Indonesia. If shipped, the goods should be accompanied by a commerical invoice. Bona fide, unsolicited gifts are allowed to enter duty free by mail if their fair retail value does not exceed $25 and the recipient does not receive more than $25 worth of gifts on the same day. Serious shoppers of antiquities, Chinese porcelains, coins, and ethnographic artifacts should consult export regulations prior to purchase.

Australian Customs

Batik tulis and hand-embroidered designs on natural cloth (like cotton) are duty free; they come under "handicrafts" at the Australian customs gate. Have the seller verify on the receipt that the goods were hand-drawn. For plain white cotton and for handwritten designs on synthetics (dacron, nylon, orlon, etc.), you pay duty. The highest tax is paid on satin and velvet. You can often get around paying your home-country duty when importing Indonesian goods by sending them airmail or seamail in one-kg packages. Be aware when buying crafts in Irian Jaya or in the eastern islands of Indonesia that feathers, bows and arrows, mud (as on masks), untreated cowhide (lampshades of Yogya), or anything with shells embedded in it, won't be let into Australia (Australia doesn't have hoof and mouth disease yet).

INFORMATION

Travel Information

The really valuable and up-to-date travel information you'll get from other travelers along the way—cheapest and friendliest *losmen,* where to eat and drink (in detail), best beaches, most beautiful walks, where to meet other travelers, the most unusual things to do. The many Indonesians you inevitably meet can tell you of any *wayang,* dance, or folk dramas happening, where to get crafts, medicine, etc. This book will fill in the rest. Thirteen thousand islands should keep you busy for awhile.

Tourist Offices

Tourist offices go by the designation *BAPPARDA, DIPARDA, KANWIL DEPPARPOSTEL,* or you can simply ask for the *kantor pariwisata* (tourist office). In large provincial capitals, these offices are usually found in or near the governor's office *(Kantor Gubernor* or *Gubernoran).* In the smaller cities, the *kantor pariwisata* is very often situated in the best hotel or the biggest travel agency in town (like NITOUR) or, if not, they would definitely know where it is. Many are located out of town because of the cheap rents. In small towns, the Department of Education and Culture (Kantor Pendidikan dan Kebudayaan) is the next best place to go for tourist information.

The usefulness of tourist offices is very uneven throughout the country—it's all a matter of meeting the right person with a happy combination of enthusiasm, experience, contacts, and knowledge. Tourist offices in big tourist centers like Jakarta, Yogya, Solo, and Bali are the most efficient, providing outstanding information and brochures. Though they are supposed to dispense free information and advice, many may not always be that helpful. Woefully underfunded, the staff could be uninformed, not conversant in English, their files neglected, or they could be either out of brochures and maps or have only one left, an "office copy" (which you can ask to borrow to make a quick photocopy). Literature, most of which is sent to overseas embassies from Jakarta, is often rationed and not on display. Publications go out of print quickly and are seldom reprinted, so always get into the habit of asking if anything is available and snap it up. Some of these regional offices publish excellent booklets and pamphlets like the *East Java Visitors Guide Book* issued by the East Java Government Dept. of Tourism; the *Bali Tourist Guide* (free from hotels) the *Bali Path Finder* (Rp1000) issued by the Ubud Tourist Office (C. Bali). If available, get ahold of the pamphlet called *Calendar of Events* which lists all the major religious holidays and annual cultural events, as well as the *Tourist Map of Indonesia.*

One of the best information centers in the world on things Indonesian is the Directorate General of Tourism, Jl. Kramat Raya 81 (PO Box 409), Jakarta, see page 201. The DGT publishes brochures, books, maps covering all 27 provinces. Also well-informed and fluent in English are the people at the Visitor Information Center, Jakarta Theatre Building, Jl. Thamrin 9 (opp. Sarinah Dept. Store), with a wide selection of publications and maps. Here is where you get ahold of really useful copies of *Jakarta Bus Routes and Train Services* and *Jakarta General Information.* For a selected list of Indonesian embassies and consulates overseas, see the "Visa" chapter in the introduction. Many have a tourist promotion office attached, as well as a Garuda office.

Other Sources

If the tourist office fails to provide you with complete info, you might do better to go to the local Garuda, Merpati, or Bouraq airlines offices which, although not strictly in the tourist information business, may employ personnel who are more knowledgeable than those in official government tourist offices. Personnel in travel agencies also could be extremely helpful; many have photo albums of destination areas and conduct private tours on the side. Ask. For inquiries of a historical or cultural nature, the offices of the PDK (Office of Education and Culture), found in even the smallest towns, might have informed and dedicated people who can tell you the exact locations of old ruins, and may even have maps and literature (in Indonesian) on old sites and artforms. The American Women's Association (AWA), Agape House, Jl. Wijaya 11/72, Kebayoran, Jakarta, is very active in welcoming newcomers. The AWA sponsors events

PROVINCIAL GOVERNMENT TOURIST OFFICES

SUMATRA

Aceh: Jl. Sultan Alaidin Mahmudsyah no. 2,
   tel. 22146/22221, Banda Aceh
North Sumatra: Jl. Durian,
   tel. 26793/26785, Medan
West Sumatra: Jl. Veteran no. 93,
   tel. 21819/27874/23176, Padang
Riau: Jl. Cut Nyak Dien,
   tel. 23740/23188, Pekanbaru
Jambi: Jl. Telanaipura,
   tel. 27003/23190, Jambi
Bengkulu: Jl. Basuki Rakhmat 2,
   tel. 31789/31798, Bengkulu
South Sumatra: Jl. Kapten A. Rivai,
   tel. 20434/21657, Palembang
Lampung: Jl. Cut Mutia,
   tel. 41491, Teluk Betung

JAVA

Jakarta: Jl. M.H. Thamrin 81,
   tel. 344117/332641, Jakarta
West Java: Jl. Soekarno-Hatta 198,
   tel. 411285/421988, Bandung
Yogyakarta: Jl. K.H. Ahmad Dahlan 4,
   tel. 3022, Yogya
Central Java: Jl. Pemuda 136,
   tel. 26001, Semarang

East Java: Jl. Jawa 2-4,
   tel. 44209, Surabaya

OTHER PROVINCES

Bali: Jl. Melati 23,
   tel. 8365/2811, Denpasar
W. Kalimantan: Jl. Sutan Sahrir 5,
   tel. 2771/2960, Pontianak
C. Kalimantan: Jl. Brigjen. Katamso,
   tel. 21178/21227, Palangkaraya
S. Kalimantan: Jl. Basuki Rakhmat,
   tel. 2053, Banjarbaru
E. Kalimantan: Jl. Jen. A. Yani,
   tel. 21073, Samarinda
C. Sulawesi: Jl. R.A. Kartini,
   tel. 21121/21221, Palu
N. Sulawesi: Jl. Sam Ratulangi 9,
   tel. 52923/3052, Manado
S.E. Sulawesi: Jl. Imam Bonjol 78, Kendari
W. Nusatenggara: Jl. Udayana 14,
   tel. 22525, Mataram
E. Nusatenggara: Jl. Palapa 18,
   tel. 21294, Kupang
Maluku: Jl. Dr. Latumetten,
   tel. 2331, Ambon
Irian Jaya: Jl. Sumatra, Blok IV,
   tel. 41138/22138, Jayapura

and provides a wealth of information about living in Indonesia including an excellent handbook called *Introducing Indonesia*.

LIBRARIES AND ARCHIVES

To broaden your knowledge of Indonesia and better prepare yourself before arriving, reading is the answer. The more knowledge you bring of Indonesia to Indonesia, the more knowledge you'll take away with you. The world nexus for cultural, historical and ethnographic research on Indonesia shifted during the 1960s from Holland to Australia, then in recent years to the USA. Now the world's largest bibliographic and archival collections of Indonesiana are in the USA, a country which has more than 100 performing *gamelan* orchestras as well as 25 clubs devoted solely to various forms of *pencak silat*. Holland, however, is still the repository of almost all the prewar printed literature and of the majority of the official archives of the Dutch East Indies colonial government. The Australian National University of Canberra

still puts out a monthly acquisitions list of all publications relating to Indonesia; they are sent material by a full-time agent who travels around Indonesia and does nothing but acquire books, pamphlets, and periodicals.

Special Collections

The Mitchell Library in Sydney (Australia) has one of the world's largest collections of books on Indonesia (and Australasia). But the Wason Collection of the Olin Library (Room 107) on the campus of Cornell University in Ithaca, New York State, is the finest and largest library of Indonesiana in the world. Obtain a pass first from the front desk and descend into the subterranean stacks consisting of 8 long, ceiling-high shelves of books in Indonesian, English, French, and Dutch about Indonesia, plus several long aisles of large format books. Cornell University also sponsors the Modern Indonesian Project which publishes semiyearly journals (such as *Indonesia*), studies, bibliographies, and dictionaries. The Koninklijk Institut Voor de Tropen (Royal Tropical Institute), 63 Mauritskade, 1092 AD Amsterdam, has very fine and large collections of books and old photos on Indonesia. Once called the Colonial Institute, generations of Indonesian scholars who spent their whole lives in the Indies used to work here although now most of the old professors have died. The Royal Tropical Institute is now in the hands of a younger, more politicized staff who are preoccupied with world hunger agrinomics and birth control in Africa and South America. Another huge, famous Indonesiana collection is housed at the University of Leiden in Holland (Witte Singel, Leiden) in the Koninklijk Instituut voor Taal-, Land- en Volkenkunde (KITLV—a truly magnificent pre-war collection of books and periodicals on Indonesia.

PRINT MEDIA

Newspapers And Magazines

English-language dailies published in Jakarta include *The Indonesian Times* (morning), Jl. Pejambon 7 (tel. 348170), and *The Indonesian Observer* (afternoon), Jl. A.M. Sangaji 11 (tel. 344642), as well as the *Jakarta Post*. The English-language *Surabaya Post* is published in Surabaya, E. Java, while the *Bali Post* is published in Denpasar, Bali. These newspapers, each costing around Rp300, have limited world coverage and both accept classified ads. Besides a number of powerful Indonesian state newspapers, virtual house magazines of Indonesia's ruling class, local newsstands also sell overseas editions of the *Asian Wall Street Journal, London Times, Bangkok Post,* and the *International Herald Tribune* (which costs Rp2500!), *Straits Times* and *The Australian.* Reading Indonesian newspapers is one good method of improving your Indonesian; the Catholic newspaper *Kompas* and the Jakarta daily *Sinar Harapan* are both recommended. *Indonesia Magazine* (Jl. Diponegoro 59, Jakarta) contains English-language articles of interest to travelers. *Runo Magazine,* Jl. Pulo Raya III/13, Jakarta Pusat, is a sort of Indonesian-language *National Geographic. Time* and *Newsweek* magazines are also readily available, though sections critical of the government are sometimes heavily censored with big blotches of black ink.

Specialty Publications

Antara Kita is a small booklet issued 3 times a year containing notes and progress reports on the latest research taking place in Indonesia by scholars from around the world—academics helping academics. The periodical also publishes very useful bibliographies, essays, and notices of cultural and social events happening in the community of Indonesianists. For a subscription (US$3 students, US$4.50 individuals, US$6 institutions), write to Joel Kuipera, Editor, Dept. of Sociology and Anthropology, Seton Hall University, South Orange, NJ

07079, USA, tel. (201) 761-9170. The weekly magazine *Asiaweek* is an excellent source of the latest news highlights from Indonesia, with an emphasis on the economy. For a subscription (US$90 for 50 weeks), write to: Asiaweek Ltd., 7th Fl., Toppan Bldg., 22 Westlands Rd., Quarry Bay, Hong Kong.

Inside Indonesia is a hard-hitting newsletter published in Australia which contains privileged insights into Indonesian politics, new technologies, lifestyles, culture, and the business community. For a subscription, write to Box 190, Northcote, Victoria 3070, Australia. *Indonesia Reports* is a current news digest compiled by leading journalists, business executives, government officials, and Indonesia specialists in universities and colleges worldwide—probably the most exhaustive summary of the Indonesian press available. For a subscription to this and other reports, issued each month, write Indonesia Publications, North College Park Station, Box 895, College Park, MD 20740, tel. (301) 474-0712.

Specialty Publishers

The most active publisher of both reprints and new titles on Indonesia is Oxford University Press (Walton St., Oxford OX2 6DP, London, England, or 16-00 Pollitt Drive, Fair Lawn NJ 07410 USA). Oxford carries at least 20 titles on Indonesia in their famous and exciting "Oxford in Asia" series. Topics range from a discussion of the *prahu* to nostalgic rambles of 19th C. adventurers, from social customs and history to the natural wonders of Asia. Selected for the quality of the writing, the individual books in the series are also fine specimens of contemporary bookmaking and design. Of a more scholarly persuasion are the historical papers and publications of the Cornell Modern Indonesia Project (102 West Avenue, Ithaca NY 14850); anyone interested in Indonesian military politics should read their *Suharto And His Generals* by David Jenkins. Ask for a complete list of publications. Another reputable university press dealing with Asian subjects is the University of Hawaii Press (2840 Kolowalu St., Honolulu HI 96822).

E. J. Brill (Postbus 9000, 2300 PA Leiden, tel. (071) 312624, Holland) publishes a large stock of Dutch-, English-, German-, and French-language reprints of old out-of-print classics on Indonesia like F.M. Schnitger's *Lost Kingdoms of Sumatra* (originally published in 1939) and A. Hoogerwerf's *Udjung Kulon: The Land of the Last Javan Rhinoceros* (1970). Ask for their "South and East Asia" catalog. Brill has an office in the USA (W.S. Heinman Inc., 1780 Broadway, Ste. 1004, New York NY 10019, tel. 212-757-7628) but they don't always stock some of the more esoteric titles carried in their general catalog. AMS Press, Inc. (56 East 13th St., New York NY 10003) publishes a fascinating selection of reprints of such arcane classics as Claire Holt's *Dance Quest in*

Celebes and *The Community of Erai (Wetar)*. Ask for their "SE Asia" mail order catalog. In Singapore, *The Indonesian Tragedy* and a reprint of Wallace's *The Malay Archipelago* are available from Graham Brash (Pte) Ltd. (36-C Prinsep St., Singapore 0718) who specializes in the Malay region.

Bookstores

Jakarta and other major cities are the best places to buy foreign publications of all kinds at any number of good bookstores. Prices for imported books, paperbacks, and magazines are high and selections are limited. Books published in Indonesia are cheaper in Jakarta than at tourist sites such as Borobudur or Denpasar. Bring half a dozen good paperbacks (which can always be easily traded for other travelers' books later), plus your basic reference/travel books. In Jakarta, try the following outlets: Gunung Agung, Jl. Kwitang 6 (the largest bookshop in Indonesia), has a wide selection of paperbacks in English and books, guides, and maps about Indonesia. Also check out the Gramedia bookshops at Jl. Melawai IV/13, Blok M, and Jl. Gajah Mada 109; the bookshop at Sarinah Dept. Store, and the usually excellent selections at such hotel bookshops and newstands as the Hotel Indonesia newsstand. An assortment of foreign newspapers and magazines is sold on the newsstand at Hero Supermarket in Barito Plaza (Kebayoran Baru) and at Toko Wiratafami on the 2nd Floor of Ratu Plaza (Senayan). In Medan (N. Sumatra), try Toko Buku Pustaka Mimbar. There are a number of bookshops in Kuta (Kuta Beach Road and Jl. Legian), Legian, and Sanur on Bali where you can find ample reading material. On the road in Asia you'll always meet people who will have books to trade. Save some of your very best paperbacks for trading; don't let go of the gems for an inferior book. For a selected list of books and magazine articles covering every aspect of Indonesian life, refer to the "Booklist" in the backmatter. For books on learning *Bahasa Indonesia,* refer to the "Language" chapter of the introduction.

In Singapore, Select Books Pte. Ltd., 19 Tanglin Road 03-15, Tanglin Shopping Centre, 3rd Floor, Singapore 1024, tel. 732 1515, has the largest collection of books on SE Asia currently in print in the world. For out of print books on Indonesia, head for Antiques of the Orient downstairs in the same building. Address: 02-40 Tanglin Shopping Center, Singapore 1024, tel. 734 9351. The huge Toppan Bookstore in the Orchard Plaza Shopping Centre on Orchard Road and MPH Bookstore (71-77 Stanford Road) both have very respectable Indonesiana collections as well. The big Singaporean chain bookstores tend to have a wider selection of books on Indonesian history, culture, politics, anthropology, language study, travel than many bookshops in Indonesia itself. In Holland, Ge Nabrink & Son Booksellers, Korte Korsjespoortsteeg

8, 1012 TC Amsterdam (only a 5 min. walk from central train station), tel. 020-223058, specializes in Indonesiana. About 85% of their publications are in Dutch, the rest in English, German, and French. First send for catalog, place your order, then they will send a pro forma invoice. Ge Nabrink charges high prices (US$150 for a rare book is not unusual). For bargains, check out Amsterdam's flea markets and other antiquarian bookshops.

Lending Libraries In Indonesia

For English-language books, try the British Consul, Jl. Jen. Sudirman 56, and the gigantic Indonesian/American Cultural Center, Jl. Pramuka Kav. 30, Jakarta Timur, and the American Woman's Club, Jl. Pakubuwono VI/20c, Kebayoran Baru, which all operate lending libraries. The Dutch Cultural Center Erasmus Huis, Jl. Menteng Raya 25 (tel. 772325), has a library of over 10,000 volumes, mostly in Dutch. (This library contains the most information about Indonesia of all the other cultural centers of Jakarta.) Goethe Institute, Jl. Mataram Raya 23, Jakarta Timor, has a 7,500-volume library (mostly German). Centre Cultural Francais, Jl. Salemba Raya 25, has a 5,000-volume library plus films and slides. The Australian Cultural Centre, Citibank Bldg. on Jl. Thamrin, has an English-language collection of 6,000 books and 250 periodicals. The Japan Cultural Centre, Jl. Cemara 1, also offers a library open to the public. All the above cultural centers require a reasonable membership fee, and their libraries are only a part of the many services and activities they offer.

Major Libraries In Indonesia

These include the Arsip National Republik Indonesia, Ampera Raya, Cilandak III, Jakarta Selatan, W. Java, tel. 781851; Library of Hasanuddin University, Perpustakaan Pusat, Universitas Hasanuddin, Kampus Beraya, Ujung Pandang, S. Sulawesi, tel. 3029; Perpustakaan Jujasan Hatta (Hatta Foundation Library), Malioboro 85, Yogya, C. Java; Perpustakaan Negara (State Library), Malioboro, Yogya, C. Java; Perpustakaan Pusat Institut Teknologi Bandung (Central Library of Bandung Institute), Jl. Ganesya I0, Bandung, W. Java, tel. 83814; Perpustakaan Museum Nasional (Library of the National Museum), Merdeka Barat 12, Jakarta, W. Java, tel. 360551. These are only the very largest collections. There are dozens of other university, government, religious, corporate/business, public and special libraries throughout Indonesia. Inquire at each provincial tourist office.

ARCHIVES AND OTHER RESOURCES

Film

Check your nearest major library for films and videos on Indonesia. See the movies *The Year of Living*

Dangerously and *Max Havalaar,* the first Australian and the second Dutch, both before and after you visit Indonesia. Anthropological film archives may have copies of Margaret Mead's *Island of Bali;* the strong, primitive feeling of this 1930s' film no longer exists on Bali. *Pray For Death* and *Arctic Heat* are other film classics possibly available through your library. *The Sky Above and the Mud Below* is a splendid documentary made by a Dutch-French expedition, the first to cross what was then the Netherlands New Guinea, walking from the Arafura Sea to the N coast. An exciting whitewater river video is Sobek Adventure's *River of the Red Ape,* the first descent of Sumatra's Alas River through the world's largest orangutan rainforest. Indonesia fever swept America in mid-1988 with the broadcasting on public television of Lorne and Lawrence Blair's brilliant 4-part "Ring of Fire" series which recorded an adventurous 12-year exploration of the Indonesian archipelago. Now available in video. For more films, the Harvard Institute for International Development (1737 Cambridge St., Cambridge MA 02138, tel. 617-495-3482) has published *Film on Indonesia: The State of the Art,* a listing of all known documentary films on Indonesia (except Irian Jaya), with a short resume for each. A catalog of films on Indonesia has been compiled by Toby Volkman; send US$5 (which includes shipping) to the Council of Southeast Asian Studies, Yale Univerity, 85 Trumbull St., 13A Yale Station, New Haven, CT 06520.

Culture

The Menara Hotel in Ubud, S. Bali, is the headquarters of the one-room Mudraswara Foundation, which features a collection of books on the Balinese arts, some for loaning. They charge a small fee to join, or you can read on the premises. Theo & Arjan Productions is a multi-media company specializing in SE Asia with an accent on Indonesia. They make socialcultural documentaries for radio and television, audiovisuals, write articles, and put on photo exhibits and lectures. Connected with them is Trans Asian Press, a group of free lance photographers with a combined photo archive of over 250,000 slides and photographs (many on Indonesia) as well as music recordings (ask about their delightful "Bali: Eternal Circle 1" tape). A more modest slide and tape library on Indonesia can be found at the Third World Teaching Resource Center, University of California, Santa Cruz, CA 95060, tel. (408) 429-2119. TWTRC has a collection of more than 1,000 individual slides on Indonesia, 50 cassette tapes of Indonesian music and language, and 6 slide shows with scripts and tapes. Contact the director, Sjamsir Sjarif. For commercial use, the Koninklijk Instituut Voor de Tropen, Mauritskade 63, 1092 AD Amsterdam, Netherlands, tel. 020 924949, has a gigantic collection of slides and photos (especially strong on prewar material). In the Photography Department of the Field Museum of Natural History (Roosevelt Road at Lake Shore Drive, Chicago, IL 60605) the emphasis is on b/w prewar photos of the Dutch East Indies.

The Lincoln Center for the Performing Arts in New York has a very fine collection of books, manuscripts, and artifacts on Asian dance—the only multi-media dance archive on Asian dance in the world. There are some 3,418 books and periodicals on Asian dance, over 5,000 photographs and slides, 125 volumes of manuscripts, and over 400 hours of film and videotapes. Of these, there are more than 800 films and videotapes of Indonesian dancers, audio recordings of Javanese and Balinese dance masters, photos, and other documents provided by the Claire Holt Collection on Indonesian dance.

MAPS

The best folded maps of Indonesia available are the APA Roadmaps: *Bali* (scale 1:180,000), *Sumatra* (1:1,500,000), *Java and West Nusatenggara* (1:1,500,000), *Kalimantan* (1:1,500,000), etc. Costing US$6.95 each, these beautiful maps feature vivid 8-color printing, topographic features in realistic relief, and major city plans in close-up margin inserts. Another high-quality folded map is *Hildebrand's Travel Map of Western Indonesia,* which covers Sumatra at 1:3,570,000, Java at 1:1,887,000, and Sulawesi at 1:3,226,000. At US$5.95, this up-to-date map clearly presents the country's topography, roads, towns and cities. The Bartholomew World Travel Map series puts out *Asia, South-East,* an attractively colored contour map of SE Asia (area: Hong Kong to Java and from Burma to New Guinea) at a scale of 1:5,800,000 (US$6.95).

Domestic Sources

Indonesian tourist offices and travel agencies dispense country-wide, regional, and local maps of Indonesia, but don't rely on their accuracy or up-to-dateness. *Indonesia Tourist Map* is a high-quality 2-color map given out free by the Directorate General of Tourism and distributed all over Indonesia and in tourist promotion offices abroad. Regional tourist offices also give away town plans of the main cities of Sumatra, Java, and Bali. Many of the hotels, airlines offices, travel agencies, police stations, tourist and *camat* offices of Indonesia display wall maps, probably the best area maps available. Be careful of some maps you buy in Indonesia itself. For example, PT Starnico's (Jl. Cempeka Baru 1A, Jakarta Pusat, tel. 411829) big wall maps of Kalimantan, Maluku, and Irian Jaya (at Rp5000 apiece) are a joke. If you try to use them, you become convinced that they determine village locations by throwing darts at the map; Starnico's maps of Sumatra and Java are better. PT Pembina (Jl. Pajaitan 45, Jakarta, tel. 813886) also publishes a series of regional maps of Sumatra, Java, Bali, and the Outer Islands, complete with distance charts. Both the Starnico and Pembina series may be bought at big bookstores, or directly from the publishers.

The Directorat Topografi Angkatan Darat in Jakarta has more up-to-date and comprehensive maps, but they probably won't sell them to tourists as topo maps are classified in most of SE Asia. Any you see will be stamped *Terhard* (Restricted), with a long warning from the Indonesian army stating that users "should not let the maps fall into unauthorized hands." You may have better luck at Seksi Publikasi (Publications Section), open 0800-1200), Geological Survey of Indonesia, Geological Museum, Jl. Diponegoro 57, Bandung (W. Java), which has on file the 1962 series (1:50,000) of full-color U.S. Army Mapping Service (AMS) maps as well as geologic maps.

Overseas Sources
The most extensive stocks of maps for sale in Australia are at: Angus and Robertsons, 107 Elizabeth St., Melbourne; Sydney's Angus and Robertsons on Pitt St.; Dymock's on George St., Sydney; as well as the Rex Map Centre in Sydney (412 Pacific Highway, Artaron, NSW). Topografische Dienst, Westvest 9, Delft, Netherlands, has more maps of Indonesia than even the University of Leyden. Very helpful proprietor. This is *the* address to write to if you want a copy of a map on, say, Wetar Island or the Talaud Archipelago. Most of his maps are old, but up-to-date maps on Indonesia's outlying islands are nearly impossible to find. Keep in mind that, despite the passing of years, maps based on topographic survey work by the Dutch are still very informative. Roads on the maps may no longer be roads on the ground, but you nearly always find something there. Most old Dutch maps are usually available as dyeline (diazo) copies only.

TPC maps
Probably the best available maps you can buy are the USAF Tactical Pilotage Charts (TPC) at 1:1/2 m. These cost only about US$5 each and are available from Distribution Center CH4, National Ocean Survey, Riverdale MD 20737; Air Touring Shop, Elstrea Aerodrome, Hertfordshire UK; and the Rex Map Centre, 412 Pacific Highway, Artaron, NSW, Australia. TPC maps are good on coastlines and rivers, but urban areas are very out of date. They can be obtained in Indonesia or Malaysia too, but difficult to find in Singapore.

U.S. Army Maps
Good topographic maps of all the main Indonesian islands can also be purchased from the U.S. Army Topographic Command, Washington D.C. The trouble is that these maps are made strictly from aerial and satellite photos with very little local input so that fairly important towns may be shown as little villages and little villages as larger towns—also, roads are not current. These maps can be found in any good map room of any sizable library, so just blow them up or copy them on a photocopier.

Nautical Maps
Ask in libraries for Operational Navigational Charts (or ONC charts), scale 1:1,000,000. James Cook University of North Queensland (Townsville) publishes *Indonesian Ports: An Atlas-Gazetteer* by Gale Dixon (Monograph '6, 1982), which identifies a larger number of Indonesian ports than has previously been available from a single source, including some no more than a copra shed on a river and ports where the maximum depth of water alongside is less than a meter.

U.S.
The Abbott collection at the National Museum of Natural History building, Smithsonian Institution, Washington D.C. has a huge collection of 6,000 well-documented Indonesian artifacts. Abbott built and outfitted a schooner in Singapore in 1899 and began a 10-year entirely self-financed labor of love, sailing through the Dutch East Indies collecting birds, mammals, reptiles, fish, mollusks, crustaceans, insects. Unfortunately, the collection is difficult to use because in many cases the labels and documentation have become separated from the artifacts. To view the collection, make inquiries to Collections Manager, Processing Lab, Dept. of Anthropology, NHB Stop 112, Smithsonian Institution, Washington D.C. 20560, tel. (203) 357-2681 at least 2 weeks in advance. For those interested in the textile arts, the Textile Museum, 2320 S Street, NW, Washington D.C. 20008, possesses 10,000 textiles as well as 1,000 rugs, with a good representation of Indonesian textiles. The museum also houses a shop with an extensive collection of textile and carpet-related publications, gift items, plus a library of 7,000 books and periodicals. Call (202) 667-0441 for hours.

Museums In Indonesia
In all there are 28 museums in Indonesia. The best are: the National Museum, Jl. Medeka Barat 12, Jakarta (ceramics, ethnography, prehistory, archaeology, anthropology); the Jakarta City Museum (or Jakarta Museum), in the Kota section of the city (history of the city of Jakarta, especially strong on colonial history); Museum Radya Pustaka, Kraton, Solo, C. Java (decorative arts, royal heirlooms); Bali Museum, Paputan Square, Denpasar, Bali (archaeology, local arts, crafts and folkarts, masks, theatrical arts); Museum Puri Lukisan, Ubud, Bali (collection of modern Balinese paintings and some sculpture); Gedung Pengabidian on the campus of Cendrawasih University, Abepura (6 km from Jayapura), Irian Jaya (sculpture, pottery, garments, spears, masks, and other anthropological artifacts, and a 45,000-volume library).

Atlases
In Washington D.C., the Library of Congress Geography and Map Division has cataloged over 48,000

atlases, the largest such collection in the world. The official pre-war atlas of all the tropical Netherlands territories (Atlas van tropisch Nederland, Batavia, or Topographical Survey of the Netherlands Indies) was printed in 1938. Many of its social, economic, and political assertions have long been outdated. Yet, for Outer Island Indonesia, it's still one of the few complete sources. This atlas, as well as a few quadrangle topo maps, can be found in both the Sydney and Melbourne university libraries. Another useful sourcebook is the 975-page *Gazeteer of Place Names of Indonesia and Portuguese Timor* (1978), published by the U.S. Army Topographic Command, Washington D.C. Updated every 10 years, this unbelievably detailed tome gives the exact coordinates and the old and new spellings of tens of thousands of place names throughout Indonesia. The *Gazeteer* is cross-referenced and also contains 32 maps of 1:1 million scale and 1:250,000 (needed for Java and Bali because of all the cultural detail). Write them for a publication list, prices, and shipping details.

MUSEUMS

A great number of museums in Indonesia and abroad with sizable collections of Indonesiana show life as it was before modern machinery, cars, and tourists arrived to undermine the old-world traditions of these islands. These "colonial museums" house collections of arts, crafts, traditional technology, theatrical props, and archaeological artifacts from a bygone world.

Holland

The Royal Tropical Institute (Koninklijk Instituut Voor de Tropen) occupies a large old building at 63 Mauritskade in Amsterdam 1092, Holland, tel. 020 924949. This institute specializes in the tropical areas of the world, and is involved in present-day economic development programs in Indonesia. On display is an impressive Indonesian collection of artifacts including a huge number of old *batik*, a Javanese country house, Hindu Javanese antiquities, puppetry, 3-D slides, as well as a big library. Though not open to the general public (they don't have the display space), the Natural History Museum in Leiden has an impressive collection of archipelic lifeforms. It's primarily a reference collection, a taxonomical assemblage of stuffed specimens (the *Pithecanthropus erectus* skull that Duboise found is here). Much scientific work is being

carried out, and you can come in contact with congenial and informative ex-colonists who still have all the old colonial attitudes—a dying breed. For anthropologists, there is also the Volkerenkunde Museum in Leiden; the Indonesian and Irian Jaya collections are particularly good. Again, there's only a portion exhibited but if you have a good enough reason you could see the collection. Work your way in. The famous Museum voor Land-en Volkenkunde in Rotterdam displays a Cirebon *batik* acquired in 1860—one of the oldest *batik* specimens in existence.

West Germany

Indonesian collections are found in the Rautenstrauch-Joest Museum (Museum Fur Volkerkunde) of Cologne, Ubierring 45, 5000 Koln, tel. 0221/3111065-66 (Asmat, Batak, and Dayak carvings, art from the Bandas and Tanimbars); Museum Fur Volkerkunde, Schaumainkai 29, 6000 Frankfurt 70, tel. 0611/2125391; Hamburgisches Museum Fur Volkerkunde, Rothenbaumchaussee 64, 2000 Hamburg 13, tel. 040/44195505; Volkerkundemuseum Der Von Portheimstiftung, Hauptstr. 235, 6900 Heidelberg, tel. 06221/817828; Obergunzburg (Bayern) Heimatmuseum, Marktplatz 1, 8953 Obergunzburg, tel. 08372/1311; Deutsches Ledermuseum Mit Deutschem Schuhmuseum, Frankfurterstr. 86, 6050 Offenbach, tel. 0611/813021; Linden-Museum Stuttgart, Hegelplatz 1, 7000 Stuttgart 1, tel. 0711/2050, 3230; and Volkerkundliches Museum, Steinstr. 19, 3430 Witzenhausen, tel. 05542/3203 (emphasis on New Guinea).

Poland

Since 1973 Poland's capital city, Warsaw, has had a thriving center for the study of SE Asian artifacts. Now located at 24 Solec St., 00-403 Warsaw, tel. 29 67 24, it's called the Asia and Pacific Museum. The accent is on Indonesia since the initial contribution for the institute was a donation of 3,046 objects made by Andrzej Wawrzyniak, a specialist on Indonesia, who remains the museum's director. The collection now numbers 9,000 pieces, comprised mostly of ancient sculptures, Balinese temple paintings, weapons, ritual masks, puppets, textiles, musical instruments, contemporary paintings. Also has an 8,000 volume library and microfilm archive.

BEFORE DEPARTURE: WHAT TO TAKE

Papers

You'll need a passport to cross borders, exchange currency, cash traveler's cheques, pick up mail at *poste restante* (General Delivery) or at American Express, sign in at a hotel, and whenever the police or immigration officials ask to see it. If entering Indonesia through an unofficial gateway (see "Visas"), you'll need an Indonesian visa from an Indonesian consulate or embassy in your home country or a neighboring country before flying into Indonesia. Write down your passport number, traveler's cheque numbers, vital contact addresses, and any other pertinent information. Make two copies. One copy you should carry with your luggage, leave the other with a friend or family back home, contactable via phone call or cable. Register all valuables such as cameras and tape recorders in your passport. If these items are insured before you leave your home country and they are registered in your passport, that is valid proof if the items are stolen. It would also be wise to jot down in a little notebook the plane ticket numbers, place and date of issue, and how tickets were paid for (credit card number, cash, personal check); this information is invaluable if the ticket is lost or stolen, and could save you enormous hassles. It's also advisable to travel with a copy of your birth certificate in case you lose your passport or for repatriation purposes.

If you wear glasses or contacts, or take medication on a regular basis, make sure you carry a copy of the prescription in case you lose any of these items. Have your doctor make out prescriptions using scientific names that are internationally understood. Unless you are entering Indonesia from an infected area, you won't be asked for your International World Health Certificate. Take 6 or so passport photos with you, then have 30-40 more printed from the negative in Singapore, Penang, Hong Kong, or Indonesia where prints are cheaper than in the West. Passport photos are crucial when filling out forms, applying for a *surat jalan,* or to give out as gifts—you'll use up dozens on a trip through Asia.

The International Student Identification Card (ISIC) could be useful for getting discounts of up to 25% on rail and flight tickets, as well as entrance fees to museums. To apply, write (including date of birth, citizenship, and name of school or university where you are a full-time student) to: CIEE Student Travel, 205 East 42nd St., New York NY 10017, tel. (212) 661-1414. Counterfeit ones on Bali sell for US$6, plus US$3 for each yearly stamp; cards are also for sale for 300 baht at the Atlanta Hotel and the Malaysia Hotel in Bangkok (be very careful not to accept poor forgeries). Obtain an International Driver's Permit with

motorcycle endorsement (Aus$15 or US$20) if you want to rent a motorcycle on Bali or in Sulawesi (a license on Bali costs US$30!). Don't leave home without a small, light, thin address book to fill with the names of new friends and to refer to when you write home. Indonesia only has 3 official youth hostels (one each in Jakarta, Denpasar, and the Puncak Pass), so you really don't need a Youth Hostel Card here. Just pay the few dollars extra.

Packing

Pack light. A week before, gather up everything you're thinking of taking, put it all in your pack and go for a long walk. How will it feel maneuvering that much weight through jostling, crowded Indonesian rail and bus stations under a humid 95-degree F (36-degree C) tropical sun? Be sure to fill your pack only one-half or two-thirds full because you'll find yourself gradually replacing all your drab Western clothes with colorful Indonesian garments. To keep your pack from throwing you off balance, make sure it has a hip belt. Several packs on the market feature hideaway harness systems which would make you "invisible" crossing borders, so you don't have to be concerned about the stigma of "hippie!" Choose a sturdy, well-designed pack with heavy-duty zippers, non-corrosive Fastex and Dacron thread, which carries an original owner lifetime warrantee against defects in materials and workmanship. Always put an identifying badge or mark on your pack; this will prevent someone from picking it up and will also keep you from picking up someone else's. Bring as well a light tent and a portable one burner kerosene stove (kerosene is available everywhere) if you'll be camping in Indonesia's numerous camping areas *(tempat kemahan)* and national reserves. Instead of sleeping on grimy mats and mattresses, run a seam down a washable cotton double bedsheet to make a light sleeping bag (Indonesia is too hot for your standard sleeping bag).

CLOTHING

Choose patterned or dark-colored fabrics that won't show wear or soil as quickly. In a tropical climate, cotton clothes are the most comfortable to wear (nylon doesn't breathe in the heat). But since 100% cotton needs ironing, bring along a few changes of half-cotton, half-synthetic, wrinkle-free garments for visits to bureaucratic offices. Indonesia is too hot for Western-style sportcoats, so either buy a light *batik* sportcoat or just an attractive *batik* long-sleeved shirt for formal occasions—quite acceptable and very fashionable. Denim is also generally too hot for Indonesia and takes too long to dry when it gets wet; perhaps bring one pair for high-altitude trekking or cycling, or bring along a pair of much less suffocating corduroys or light summer trousers. Take along a warm light sweater or cardigan for the higher altitudes such as Kintamani (C. Bali), Bandungan (C. Java), and the Baliem Valley (Irian Jaya). The temperature drops about 3 degrees F for every 325 m higher in altitude, and heavy cloud cover in mountain climes can bring on even a sharper fall in temperature (see "Climate" for info on Indonesia's seasons). Take a water-resistant jacket which packs light and, worn over sweaters, keeps you warm as it will help hold in your body heat. Long-sleeved shirts can be worn on cool evenings and as protection against sunburn or insects, with the sleeves rolled up when it gets hot. The wearing of shorts by men is generally considered inappropriate for anything except the roughest manual work, long-distance cycling, or for going to and from the bathroom or beach. Recommended also is a cloth or khaki fisherman-style hat, deep enough to stay on your head in heavy winds, with a brim to protect you from rain or the ferocity of the sun. Spray it with water repellent. It may be frumpy looking, but it will do the job. A helmet is very wise equipment for motorcyclists; get one with a bubble to protect your face from rain, sleet, insects. Before you go, ask your local clothes shops if they'd like you to send back beautiful *batik* or material (tacking on your commission, of course).

Women's Dress

Take only clothes which are lightweight, easily rinsed, brushed, and renovated. Women should take long-sleeved blouses and longish skirts. Skimpy clothing, backless dresses, shorts, and even slacks can be offensive in this Muslim country, particularly if worn in mosques, temples, churches, in the classroom, or on formal occasions. Your bikini will not be thought offensive provided it is worn only at the swimming pool or on Kuta or Sanur Beach (Bali). Experienced female travelers replace nightgowns with T-shirts, and bathing suits can double for underwear if they're easy to wash, quick-drying, light, and comfortable. Also substitute a bikini top for a bra if possible. Fifteen minutes in the sun is all it takes to dry out a suit after swimming or washing. Take one wrinkle-proof dress which is easy to wash and dress up or down. Dresses of double-knit cotton T-shirt material are excellent. Clothes shops of Medan, Toba, Jakarta, Yogya, Solo, Denpasar, and especially Kuta Beach (Bali) have a wide selection of economically priced dresses, shawls, kimonos, jackets, skirts, blouses, pants, *sarung*, shirts (you name it). Closely scrutinize the quality of the sewing. The American Women's Association publication *Introducing Indonesia* lists for 20 pages the names and addresses of stores and shops where men's, women's, and children's wear can be

bought. Consider packing a light shawl if most of your tops are shoulderless. Scarves are stylish, lightweight, compact, and versatile and can be used as belts, shawls, sashes for temples; scarves replace jewelry, transforming one outfit into many. Don't take many dresses as its better to complete your travel wardrobe on arrival. To avoid poorly sewn, ready-made clothes, you should employ one of Indonesia's tens of thousands of seamstresses to sew a dress (Rp3000), shirt (Rp2000), skirt (Rp2000). A *batik* shop can recommend a dressmaker. All you need to do is give them one of your best-fitting garments from which they will make a paper pattern; they are also skilled at sewing a garment from a photograph.

The National Dress

Provided you buy the right *batik* colors and wear the garments properly on the right occasions, the Javanese will take it as a compliment if you wear Indonesian traditional dress. Get expert local advice before sallying forth in your *sarung, peci, kain* and *kebaya* (see glossary). The *sarung* is a simple oblong (2½ m x 1½ m) of *batik* waxed cloth, often cotton, or *ikat* cloth wrapped around the waist and falling in a single fold in front. Dyed in rich and delicate designs of brilliant colors, the *sarung* is sometimes held in place by a tight sash *(selempang)*. On the slim and graceful bodies of the Javanese, the *sarung* is respectable and pretty, but when worn on some of the robust figures of Westerners it looks ludicrous. The *sarung* has a multitude of uses: as a sunshade, baby carrier, sheet at night when it's cool, or to cover a filthy bed. A towel is bulky to carry, so learn to substitute an absorbent cotton *sarung* and go out and air dry in the sun.

A *kain* is a length of cloth measuring approx. 2 X 1 m, made of cambric-based *batik* or *lurik* (a Javanese cotton weaving) and worn as a wrap-around, ankle-length skirt. This cloth could be interwoven with silk or metallic threads on Bali, or heavy silk interwoven with gold metallic thread on Sumatra. The *kebaya* is a long-sleeved blouse worn over the *kain* or skirt-wrapping, and it comes in various lengths ranging from mid-hip to the knees. The short *kebaya* can be made from flowered or plain cotton, silk, brocade, lame, synthetic fabrics, lace, *lurik* and white organdy trimmed with cutwork embroidery or lace. The longer version is most attractive in lace, flowered voile, or embroidered nylon. To complete this woman's costume, a long stole *(selendang)* is draped over one shoulder. Evening shoes and light, matched jewelry provide the accessories. You'll even find thousands of professional *kretek* cigarette-rollers wearing this formal dress in the sweatshop factories of C. Java!

Laundry

Could be really expensive; you either have to find an *ibu* (literally "mother," but figuratively any older woman) who does washing, or take laundry to Chi-

MISCELLANEOUS CHECKLIST

- sunscreen cream or lotion
- hidden moneybelt or mobile office
- light sleeping bag (or run a seam down a washable cotton double bed sheet)
- cheap butane lighter and candle (in case of power outages)
- good English/Indonesian, Indonesian/English dictionary
- bicycle-locking chain and padlock, especially if you bring your own bike or know you'll rent one there
- roll of black electrician's tape to cover up peepholes in walls of cheap hotels
- flashlight or penlight to keep you from falling in open ditches or into one of Indonesia's notorious drain holes in the cities, a good way to chip a tooth or bruise a shinbone
- leave jewelry at home; while in Indonesia take advantage of Balinese, Yogyanese, or Minangkabau jewelry
- tampax or tampons; available only in large population centers like Medan, Palembang, Jakarta, Yogya, Surabaya, Denpasar
- Alarm wrist watch or clock to wake you up for early buses or trains (although many Indonesian accommodations do provide reliable wake-up service)
- razor with stainless steel blades
- an efficient, hand-held fan
- rolling papers (difficult to find in Indonesia)
- medicine and/or first aid kit. Also water purification tablets or kit, and prescription glasses (take one spare set)
- tin foil to reflect oil lamps, candles, and other weak lighting
- goggles or diving mask for underwater sports, bicycle, and motorcycle rentals (bad pollution in some places)
- mosquito net with plenty of loops. If desired, pack dome-shaped tent posts for your mosquito net when there are no nails on walls to hang it on
- umbrella that folds down or buy a pigfat-coated Chinese one there
- sewing kit (needles, thread, spare buttons)
- toiletries: your portable washroom can be either assembled before departure or after arrival as many brand-name toiletries are available in Indonesia. Nail file could be useful. To save space, use hand soap for your hair instead of shampoo
- food bag: can opener, Swiss Army knife (with bottle opener, can opener, corkscrew, scissors, tweezers), fork, spoon, metal camp cup and plate, immersion heater
- bags: a fishnet bag or large open bag can double as a knapsack for 3-day excursions, or to carry souvenirs, sun oil, towels, and other easily replaced items. Plastic bottles contain liquids. Plastic bags hold food, carry soiled or damp clothes, protect clothes from rain while backpacking
- earplugs: If you're senstive to noise, these are useful on planes and in noisy hotels; get the easy-to-mold variety
- compass: an important travel asset, particularly if the area you're traveling in (Irian Jaya?) has few signs
- light canteen to fill with potable water
- small notebooks and ballpoint pens; pencils as gifts for kids
- temple scarf to wear when entering Balinese temples. Rent them at temple gates (Rp200) or buy one (Rp800)
- 20-30 b/w passport photos of yourself to give away as gifts and for necessary applications, registrations, permissions, etc.

nese laundries which will charge Rp400-2000 (depending on the article) per piece *and* take 2-3 days. It's twice as cheap in the West using a laundromat (there are no laundromats in Indonesia). Your hotel will almost always offer a laundry service; guests may also wash their clothes in the sinks or in the *mandi* in *losmen* or *penginapan* courtyards. Buy laundry soap, Rp400 per packet. An inexpensive, light nylon clothesline or length of rope, plus a few clothes pegs to hang clothes up with, are smart items to take to Indonesia.

Footwear
Bring one pair of shoes, one pair of rubber sandals, and one pair of sneakers. Don't leave home, however, with brand new footwear; they should already be broken in and comfortable. A good pair of sneakers or Reeboks can add hours of sightseeing or hiking to

your day, especially in the cities where you might be doing a fair amount of walking on hard pavement. Change the laces on your shoes or boots before going to Indonesia so you don't have to take a spare set along. If you intend to buy footwear there, be aware that European-sized ready-made footwear (and clothing) is not easy to find in Indonesia. The international chain, Bata, sells inexpensive shoes in leather, canvas, or plastic, but a U.S. 9 is the largest size they make. Bata has many outlets (open 0900-2000) in the main cities of Java.

Gifts
Colorful foreign stamps are the lightest, least expensive, most appreciated, simplest gifts to carry. Kids always ask for coins. Bring pens and notebooks (school children often have to pay for their own school supplies). Teenagers love bizarre mottoed

T-shirts. Lighters, tiny camper's can openers, gift catalogs (like Sears), and packaged flower seeds from home all make great gifts for a foreign host. Color photographs of yourself, your family and especially your children are always in high demand. Postcards of your country or your business card are also valuable for trading and as "gifts." Big fluffy heavy-duty cotton towels, and wool garments, are loved by Indonesians.

GETTING TO INDONESIA

The prices and air routes into Indonesia change constantly. As soon as the "Official Airlines Guide" is published each month, it's already out of date. Check the latest and cheapest means of getting to Indonesia in the Sunday travel section of a major metropolitan newspaper near you. IATA (International Air Traffic Association) is a cartel of air carriers which artificially fixes high fares for all participating carriers so you pay the same inflated amount no matter which airline you use. Avoid paying full IATA fares by not patronizing the actual airlines offices which must charge full IATA fares. Instead, buy your tickets from consolidators. These discount agencies, some even IATA members, often sell "gray-market" tickets much cheaper than the airlines, sometimes at rates not allowed to be advertised. For example, the Singapore-Jakarta flight usually costs S$270 RT, but sometimes you can get in on the Singapore-Jakarta UTA or KLM flight at a much lower RT price in Singapore or Penang. Also, officially, the London-Jakarta fare is UK350 OW but it's possible to buy a non-IATA ticket to England in Jakarta for as low as UK250. Also consider buying a OW ticket from Europe or the U.S. direct to Bangkok, Singapore, or Hong Kong, points from where it's inexpensive to fly onward to Indonesia.

To obtain an Indonesian entry stamp you are required to have a ticket not only into but also out of Indonesia. This rule, which the Indonesian authorities are very sticky about, causes inconvenience for people who want to leave Indonesia by boat from Medan to Penang or from Nunukan to Tawau (N. Borneo), but there's really no way to get around it.

Gateways
You can fly into Indonesia from all over the world. The 3 main international gateways by air are Jakarta, the national capital; Denpasar, Bali's capital; and Medan, N. Sumatra. Even though the island of Bali is overwhelmingly Indonesia's most popular tourist destination, for years the national flag-carrier of Indonesia (Garuda) held a virtual monopoly on all international flights into Bali, and no cut-rate chartered aircraft were allowed into Indonesia. But thanks to new management, the skies over Indonesia are becoming increasingly open. Several carriers have contracted joint services with Garuda to Bali's Ngurah Rai Airport near Denpasar: Singapore Airlines from Singapore, Cathay Pacific from Hong Kong, Malaysian Airline System from Kuala Lumpur, and China Airlines from Taipei—all offering at least twice-weekly services.

As Manila is for the Philippines and Tokyo is for Japan, by far the largest number of flights arrive in Jakarta's international Cengkareng Airport, 20 km W of Jakarta. From Jakarta make your way to Bali and beyond by sea, land, or air. Only Papua New Guinea and E. Malaysia share borders with Indonesia. You'll need a visa to enter Indonesia from PNG but no visa is required to enter West Kalimantan (bordering E. Malaysia); refer to the Irian Jaya and Kalimantan sections to find out how. Unbelievably, except on expensive cruise ships or by private yacht, it's really difficult to reach this island nation by water. There are only 2 regular entry points by ship. Ferries depart Penang (Malaysia) for Medan (N. Sumatra) and a daily ferry connects Singapore with P. Batam in the Riau Archipelago from where you can board another ferry to Pekanbaru, E. Sumatra. Oceanliners and cruise ships of the Holland American Lines, Garuda's Spice Island Cruises, and Lindblad Travel call at remote Indonesian ports at luxury prices. These upmarket tour companies offer fly/cruise arrangements whereby you're flown to Bali or Medan, then meet up with your cruise vessel from there.

Hitch A Yacht
Every year about 300 yachts sail from the U.S. West Coast to Tahiti and beyond. Most sail around the Pacific for a year or so, while a small percentage continue around the world. It pays to pick out the hard-core yachties from the maze of others in the yacht clubs of Sydney and Los Angeles. Yachts are almost invariably crewed by men or couples and are perpetually short of crew for the longer passages. You'll cook, help with the lines at the docks, take turns as lookout. Expect to share food and lodging costs (about $50 per week); the yacht owner handles all harbor dues, oil, propane, etc. When approaching the skipper, assure him that you don't get seasick, that you have the money to pay your share, *and* are able to put up the cost of an emergency flight home. At the end ask for a letter of recommendation which will help you get on with the next skipper. From Panama to Tahiti, check at the clubs on both sides of the canal in Jan., Feb., or March for rides to the Galapagos, the Marquesas, Tuamotus, and Tahiti. From Tahiti in

June, July, or Aug., it's possible to hitch rides to Indonesia, New Zealand, and Australia via Tonga or Fiji. Yachts also leave for Indonesia from such Asian ports as Phuket (Thailand), Penang, Hong Kong, Singapore, and even Papua New Guinea. From Australia, if you're persistent, it's also possible to catch rides to Bali on yachts heading to South Africa (via Mauritius) or Sri Lanka (via Singapore). Try the Sydney Yacht Club in May, or Cairns and Darwin in June, July, or August. Each Aug. a yacht race takes place from Darwin to Ambon, Central Maluku.

Circle-Pacific Fares
Using a combination of airlines out of the U.S. — Air New Zealand, Qantas, MAS, Singapore Airlines — travelers can spend up to a year circling the Pacific and SE Asia. A typical itinerary may include 7 or even 8 stopovers: Los Angeles, Honolulu, Papeete, Cook Islands, Fiji, New Zealand, Australia, Indonesia (Jakarta or Denpasar), Singapore, Hong Kong, Australia, Japan. Additional stopovers cost US$100-200 extra. Some require that you use all your tickets within 12 months, others give only 6 months. If you go to your travel agent, a low-season ticket could cost over $2000. So be sure to have your travel agent do business through an Orient consolidator. Or if you call the consolidator directly you could get it down to US$1400 (Overseas Tours, 1-800-323-8777) or even US$1200 (OC Tours, 1-800-632-4739). A down payment of US$200-500 is due within 10 days of placing your reservation, the balance within 30-45 days of departure. Three percent extra is charged if you use your credit card.

Round-The-World Tickets
Indonesia may be included as a stopover on many RTW tickets. The numerous possible variations in RTW itineraries depend on which of the 3 basic ticketing alternatives the traveler selects. The best and most expensive is the full-fare, full-service ticket — you can go where you like on almost any airline. If you wish to visit a few areas only, you can give up some flexibility and save substantially by buying one of the RTW packages offered by individual airlines or specific groups of airlines. It's cheaper still to string together several discount tickets, acquired in such bargain centers as London, Bangkok, and Hong Kong. There is considerable variation in price (from U.S. US$1500-2500, from Australia around A$2800, from London around UK1000); length of validity (80-365 days); and number of stopovers permitted (3 to open). If your RTW ticket does not offer a stop in Indonesia, try to get as close as possible (Singapore or Bangkok), then just jog down to the archipelago. Airlines to try for RTWs: Qantas, Singapore Airlines, Northwest Orient/Garuda.

FROM MALAYSIA AND EAST MALAYSIA

From Penang
Malaysia is a good place to buy cheap air tickets. Popular with travelers is the low-priced hop from Penang across the Melaka Strait to Medan, N. Sumatra. From the Prangin Road Bus Station in Penang, take a bus every hour (0700 to 1000, M$1.20) out to Penang's airport (allow 1 hour). The MAS flight leaves Penang's airport at 1030 daily and takes just 20 min. to Medan (M$105 OW, M$150 RT). A regular ferry sails from Penang at 1830 on Mon. and Wed., arriving in Medan's port of Belawan at 0800. Buy tickets at Penang's Tourist Association Office on Jl. Syed Barakhbah, at Sanren Delta Marine on Jl. Leboh Ferquhar (tel. 379325), or at any number of travel agencies and hotels along Chulia Street. Tickets cost M$55 2nd Class, M$65 1st Class (berths in 4-person staterooms).

At Langli Tours & Travel, 340 Chulia St., a Singapore-Jakarta-Sydney-Singapore ticket costs M$1650 RT. French Airlines (UTA) tickets are available from King's Travel Service, Chulia St.: Singapore-Jakarta-Noumea-Sydney, back to Noumea, then to Auckland-Noumea-Papeete-Los Angeles. On the open market this ticket is worth about US$925 (S$1850), but you can buy it in Malaysia (Penang) for around US$700; check out MSL Travel, Hotel Ming Court, H1, 202 Macalister Rd., tel. 24748/9. In Kuala Lumpur, try MSL Travel, South East Asia Hotel, 69 Jl. Haji Hussein, tel. 2989722. An occasional hydrofoil leaves Kelang (Kuala Lumpur's port) for Medan. Sometimes boats carrying charcoal (and passengers) depart Melaka (Malaysia) to Dumai (E. Sumatra) for M$30, taking 1 day; from Dumai travel by road to Pekanbaru, E. Sumatra. Garuda offers a flight Singapore-Jakarta-Yogya-Denpasar-Sydney for US$396; buy this ticket at Jay's Travel Agency near the Malaysia Hotel, Bangkok.

From E. Malaysia
Because of the activity of alleged communist insurgents, it's illegal to enter the Indonesian territory of Kalimantan from Sabah or Sarawak by Landrover, jeep, *longbot*, or overland walking. But flying is OK. One oft-used approach is from Kucing (Sarawak) to W. Kalimantan Province. First hop a Straits Steamship Co. ship or fly MAS (M$170) from Singapore to Kucing, then from Kucing grab the Merpati flight down to Pontianak for Rp97,700. From Pontianak, it is possible but very arduous and expensive to do a trans-Borneo trek up the Kapuas River into E. Kalimantan Province (see "W. Kalimantan" section). There's also an irregular flight between (E. Kalimantan Province) from Tawau, Sabah (E. Malaysia) and

Tarakan (E. Kalimantan) with Bali Air for around M$100 (4 times weekly). It's sometimes full or cancelled, so allow a few extra days before your visa expires. You need an Indonesian visa beforehand because Tarakan is an unofficial entry point into Indonesia.

FROM SINGAPORE

By Air

The most popular and convenient departure point from which to reach Jakarta is Singapore. Remember that 30-day excursion fares are usually much cheaper than regular fares. The cramped office of Airmaster Travel Center, Room 1, 36-B, Prinsep Street (tel. 3383942/3376838/3386383/3389752), Singapore 0718, sells a 30-day S$260 excursion fare Singapore-Jakarta-Denpasar for US$270 RT. Other Airmaster Singapore-Jakarta RT fares: S$240 with KLM (1 month), S$255 with UTA (1 year), S$340 with Thai (1 year), S$310 with Garuda (1 month), and S$470 with Garuda (1 year). A Singapore-Jakarta-Denpasar ticket with Airmaster costs S$375 OW with Garuda; a Singapore-Denpasar ticket with a stopover in Yogya sells for S$550 OW (1 month) or S$750 OW (1 year). From Singapore to Medan, S$230 OW or S$330 RT. From Singapore to Pekanbaru, S$172 RT. Check around for even cheaper fares. Many travel agencies are advertised in the *Straits Times,* though the very cheapest deals are passed from traveler to traveler.

Airline offices: Cathay Pacific, Ocean Bldg., Collyer Quay, tel. 91 1811); Garuda, 101 Thomson Rd., Goldhill Square (tel. 250 5888); KLM, Mandarin Hotel, 333 Orchard Rd., tel. 737 7211; MAS, Singapore Shopping Centre, Clemenceau Ave., tel. 336 6777; Qantas, Mandarin Hotel, 333 Orchard Rd., tel. 737 3744; Singapore International Airlines, 77 Robinson Rd., tel. 223 8888; UTA, Ming Court Hotel, Tanglin Rd., tel. 737 7166.

Consider flying all the way from Singapore to Sydney (Australia) for around S$1000 OW, S$1850 RT; Singapore-Darwin, S$880 OW; Singapore-Yogya-Perth, Rp650 OW (or Rp1500 RT). For an extra S$125 or so, a stopover in Bali may be written into any of these tickets. Also check out the latest price of the popular UTA Singapore-Jakarta-Sydney-Noumea-Auckland-Papeete-Los Angeles ticket for around S$1750, valid for 1 year. Student discount tickets (ID card needed) are available from Singapore to Jakarta for around S$275-300 RT or S$200 OW; from Singapore to Denpasar, with a stopover in Yogya, runs about S$600 RT. Check with Student Travel Australia (STA), 12 Mezzanine Fl., Ming Court Hotel, corner of Tanglin and Orchard roads, tel. 734 5681. Garuda (Goldhill Square, Thomson Rd., tel. 2502888/ 2505666) also serves Pontianak from Singapore. MAS has nonstop daily flights from Singapore to

Kucing departing 0935 and 1745 (arriving 1945). From Kucing, Merpati flights leave every Fri. at 1115, arriving at 1210 in Pontianak. Singapore Airlines (SIA) and Garuda both offer daily flights to Medan, leaving in the morning. The SIA flight departs at 0845, the Garuda at 1140. The fares are the same, around S$230 OW, S$330 RT.

By Sea

Take note that Singapore is an hour ahead of Indonesian time. Travelers are able to reach the Riau Archipelago, 3-4 hours S of Singapore, on their own by taking a ferry from Singapore to the port of Sekupang on P. Batam. The launch for Tg. Pinang leaves from Finger Pier, Prince Edward Road (Singapore) at 0815, 1015, 1215, 1415, 1615, and costs S$20. From Singapore to Tg. Pinang direct is S$65, though it's cheaper in the other direction (Rp33,000). A cheaper way to get to Tg. Pinang, and better if you want to see more, is to take a bus from Sekupang to Nagoya (Rp500) on P. Batam, then a taxi from Nagoya to Kabil (Rp8000, or cheaper if you share a taxi). From Kabil, boats leave about every 20 min. all day long to Tg. Uban on P. Bintan (Rp2000). From Tg. Uban take a bus to Tg. Pinang (Rp1850). From Tg. Pinang's dock, boats sail up the Siak River 36 hours to Pekanbaru, E. Sumatra, for Rp12,500 Deck Class, Rp17,000 for cabin including food (rice and fish). Take care of your belongings; many thieves. This journey has been highly praised by readers for its scenery and adventure—a unique and increasingly popular way to enter Sumatra. From Pekanbaru, numerous buses leave for Bukittinggi and points north. To Pekanbaru there are 3 Garuda flights weekly for around S$300.

FROM SINGAPORE TO EAST MALAYSIA

By Air

From Tawau (Sabah, E. Malaysia), the traveler can reach E. Kalimantan by sea or air, and from Kucing (Sarawak) he can reach Pontianak (W. Kalimantan) only by air (Rp97,700). There's no direct flight to Tawau from Singapore; you have to fly to E. Malaysia's Kota Kinabalu first. Flights from Singapore to Kota Kinabalu cost S$375 OW, S$610 RT. Or Singapore-Kucing is S$185 OW, S$285 RT; then from Kucing to Tawau it's a total of S$265 OW. Yet from Singapore to Tawau via Kota Kinabalu it costs S$355, and Tawau via Kucing is S$345. Bouraq (Bali Air) flies from Tawah to Tarakan (E. Kalimantan) for M$100. Take note that flights to E. Malaysia are usually S$20-40 cheaper out of Johore Bahru, a city just across the narrow strait separating Singapore from the Malay peninsula. Also ask about MAS advance purchase fares and their night flights; MAS even provides free transport from their downtown Singapore office to the Johore Bahru airport.

By Sea

Interisland ships are on the way out, so grab your chance. Mansfield Travel in the Ocean Building (tel. 732 0088) on Collyer Quay (Singapore) arranges passages to E. Malaysia. Singapore Straits Steamship Co. sails from Singapore to Tawau OW for S$400; only 1st class available. Four meals a day, takes 5 days, 10 days RT, 12 passengers only, sharing a cabin for 3. It's wise to book 1-2 weeks before embarkation. The ship to Brunei costs S$400, 1st class only. These boats don't depart at specific times; call SSSC and they'll tell you when the next one is sailing. It's also possible to get a SSSC ship from Singapore 1-2 times weekly to Sabah. Ships carrying passengers aren't always available to Kucing, though they could call at Kucing on the way.

FROM AUSTRALIA AND PNG

Both Qantas and Garuda offer frequent services to Bali from Australia's main cities of Sydney, Melbourne, Darwin, Perth, and Port Hedland (W. Australia). Only Garuda offers the Darwin and Port Hedland service, while both Garuda and Qantas operate all the other services. But even Economy Class tickets are expensive, currently A$989 from Sydney to Jakarta, A$910 from Sydney to Denpasar (Bali), and A$810 from Perth to Darwin. Merpati flights depart Darwin (Northern Territory) for Denpasar (W. Timor) each Thurs. and Sat. at 0930. For A$175 OW (2 hours to Kupang), this ticket allows 7 stops: Darwin-Kupang-Maumere-Ruteng-Labuhanbajo-Bima-Ampenan-Denpasar. Or you can fly direct from Darwin to Kupang for only A$125 (A$175 RT) and begin island-hopping W through the eastern islands.

STA (Student Travel Australia) offices in Australia: 55A O'Connell St., North Adelaide, tel. (08) 267-1304, Adelaide; Shop 2, Societe Generale House, 40 Creek Street, tel. (07) 221-9629, Brisbane; Concessions Bldg., ANU, tel. (062) 47-0800, Canberra; 220 Faraday St., Carlton, tel. (03) 347-6911, Melbourne; 424 Hay St., Subiaco, tel. (09) 382-3977, Perth; 1A Lee St., Railway Square, tel. (02) 212-1255, Sydney; 100 Stanley St., tel. (077) 727-382, Townsville.

APEX Fares

The best deals are the advance purchase excursion fares. These must be reserved and paid for at least 3 weeks before departure, with substantial penalty if you cancel. Always buy these tickets in the off-season (Feb.-Nov.) when rates are lower. For example, from Sydney to Bali in the high season (Dec.-Jan.) is only A$500, just A$400 in the low season. From Perth to Bali in the high season is A$295 but only A$255 in the low season. Also check out the 7-28 day excursion fares to Bali (A$656 to A$820) offered by many travel/tour agencies. Garuda sells a RT ticket from Darwin to Denpasar for A$320. Natrabu, in the Smith Street Mall under the Victoria Pub, is the travel agent in Darwin representing Garuda. This agent is particularly informative about Nusatenggara.

From Perth

Fly from this Western Australian city to Jakarta for A$350 (peak), A$278 (low), and even cheaper if you bought an advance purchase ticket. Other sample fares: Jakarta, A$345 OW (peak), A$282 OW (low); Jakarta A$525 RT (peak), A$425 RT (low). Seven to 28-day excursion fares to Bali, A$420-578. Flights (DC10s) between Perth-Denpasar-Jakarta leave twice weekly. Cathay Pacific charges A$308 from Perth to Jakarta; a morning flight, only 4 hours, good meal, free grog. If you have an International Student ID card, check out Student Travel Australia (STA) flights from Perth to Jakarta. There are also STA charter flights to Kuala Lumpur (with connecting flights to Indonesia) and to Denpasar. For cruises to Indonesia out of Freemantle, Western Australia, see "Group Tours" section below.

From Darwin

Another way to get to Indonesia is to hitch to Darwin via Townsville, or take a train from Sydney or Melbourne with student discount (50% off) to Alice Springs, then hitch to Darwin in 1-2 days. (If you intend to fly from Darwin to Indonesia during the Australian university vacation Dec.-Jan., you better book 1-2 months ahead.) From Darwin, Merpati flies to Kupang (W. Timor) for A$125 OW or A$175 RT. A visa is no longer required to enter Timor; you get a 2-month entry stamp at the airport upon arrival. The flight leaves each Sat. morning at 0900 and takes just 2 hours; from Kupang flights leave for Darwin at 1430 on Fridays. Alternatively, the flight from Darwin to Denpasar (Bali) is a preposterous A$375 OW. This twice-weekly flight can be slightly cheaper than flights out of Australia's E. coast cities but unless you have extraordinary luck hitching and snag a ride straight through to Darwin, you must consider how much you'll spend on food and accommodations getting to Darwin. It's even more dismal a prospect during the wet season. From Darwin there are sometimes cattle boats for US$150-300 OW, or private yachts a bit cheaper that shuttle irregularly between Darwin and the Indonesian islands, but you can't count on them. A good place to stay in Darwin is the Darwin Rest House, 11 Houston St., tel. 811-638.

From PNG

Land or sea approaches from PNG to Irian Jaya are illegal. For K143, Air Niugini flies weekly across the international border (via Vanimo) from Wewak (northern PNG) to Jayapura, the provincial capital of Irian Jaya (W. New Guinea). Departure tax is K10. Before arriving, get an Indonesian visa at the Indonesian Embassy in Port Moresby (Sir John Guisa Drive, Sel 410, Lot 182, Waigoni, tel. 253-116/18-253544) because Jayapura is not an official entry point into Indonesia. Even with a visa, you may be limited to the number of days you may stay or you may be only given a transit visa and not allowed to leave Jayapura. It all depends how relations between Indonesia and PNG are at the time of travel.

Group Tours

One of the cheapest ways to get to Indonesia from Australia is to join a group tour, which can cost even less than APEX fares. Even though you pay for places and services sight unseen, the prices are unbeatable: Sydney to Bali, A$655 (peak), A$510 (low); Sydney to Jakarta, A$785 (peak), A$635 (low); Perth to Bali, A$410 (peak), A$320 (low); Perth to Jakarta, A$470 (peak), A$389 (low). Prices on these packaged tours include hotel vouchers which you exchange for accommodations in Indonesia; other vouchers you can use in restaurants or even to rent bicycles or motorcycles. Many travelers just take advantage of the cheap airfares and end up not using the vouchers which can only be used for standard accommodations sometimes out-of-the-way and/or have expensive food. Look for the best deals in the travel sections of Australia's big city newspapers where ticket agencies advertise "Cheap Tours to Indonesia." If you've got the money, investigate soft-class cruises from Australia. The spectacular and expensive Lindblad cruise from New Zealand sails up through Australia's Great Barrier Reef and through the beautiful islands of eastern Indonesia to Bali.

FROM OTHER POINTS IN ASIA

The easiest is to take the flight from Manila to Kota Kinabalu for US$250 (Royal Brunei Airlines). There's much discussion of flights operating between Mindanao to Tarakan or Sabah, but none are operating yet. Merpati operates a very irregular charter from Manila to Bali "X" number of times a month. Check with YSTAPHIL, 4227, Tomas Claudio St. (beside Excelsior Hotel, Roxas Blvd.), tel. 832-0680, Philippines. A number of travel agents in Bangkok offer cheap tickets which are usually paid for in Penang, issued in Kuala Lumpur, and collected in Bangkok! Always fetch your ticket from the same office on the same day or at the same time you pay for it. Fares and departure dates fluctuate, and getting a straight answer to a seemingly simple question is like trying to bite the wind. Near the Malaysia Hotel in Bangkok are about 5 travel agencies which sell cheap tickets; some also sell fake student ID cards for US$6. Walk between them and compare prices. One with a questionable reputation is J's Travel Agency; several other agencies are located along Sukhumvit Road. Also try

Onward Travel, Khao San Rd., and K Travel has a good reputation among travelers. S.T.A. in Viengtai Hotel is expensive but honest: sample price Bangkok-Bali-Jakarta-Singapore-Bangkok for US$420. It does pay to shop around and there are discounts for off-season and student flights, as well as package deals offering no-frills indirect flights to your destination.

From Japan And Korea

Tokyo is a better place to buy air tickets than is generally realized. In addition to the local market, there's a large population of *gaijin*, most of whom are required by Japanese immigration to periodically leave the country and re-enter rather than extend their visas in Tokyo. This requirement has created a ready market for cheap excursion fares, and you see many discount travel agencies advertised in the *Japan Times* and *Tokyo Journal*. Tokyo is a very big place, so it's best to phone around and compare prices. The following agencies are worth checking into: STA, Sandem Bldg., 5th Floor, Room 5A 5-5, 3 Chome Koji-Machi Chiyoda-Ku, Tokyo, tel. 221 1043; A.B.C. Air Bank Co., tel. 233-1177; Asahi International Travel, tel. 584-5732; E.H.L., tel. 351-2131; M.I.C., tel. 370-6577; N.L.C., tel. 988-7801. The only non-stop flight from Tokyo to Bali (Denpasar) is offered by Garuda on their DC10 wide-body jets. Discount fares are not available from South Korea; travelers usually fly out of Tokyo. The travel agent in the USO Club outside the gates of the Yongsan U.S. Army Garrison is worth trying (104, Kalwol-dong, Yongsan-gu, Seoul, tel. 792 3063/792 3028). He sells mostly RT tickets to Asian destinations for GIs and their dependents.

From Taiwan

Taipei-Manila costs as little as US$135 OW. For discount travel agencies, see the notice board at the Taipei Hostel which is near the Lai Lai Sheraton Hotel (from the main entrance, go R, first L, first R, and the hostel is on the 6th floor of the last building on the L-hand side of the street).

From Hong Kong

Hong Kong is just as cheap as Bangkok and Penang for air tickets in SE Asia with direct flights to Jakarta (and connections to Bali) for as little as HK$2400, and to Denpasar for HK$2800. Return flights are even better bargains. Many discount travel agencies advertise in the English-language morning newspapers such as the *Hong Kong Standard,* the *South China Morning Post,* as well as the monthly magazine *Business Traveler* (available at newstands or at 200 Lockhart Rd., 13th floor). A little shopping around should prove worthwhile, but the following agencies are consistently good: Student Travel Bureau (HKSTB), Star House, 10th Floor, Room 1020, Tsimshatsui, Kowloon, tel. 3-7213269; STB, 30 Queen's Rd., Central

Hong Kong, tel. 5-8107272; and Traveller's Hostel, Chungking Mansions, 16th Floor, Nathan Rd., Tsimshatsui, Kowloon. HK$120 airport tax in Hong Kong.

From Sri Lanka

Air Lanka has added Colombo-Jakarta service with departures from Colombo on Mon., Thurs., and Sat., returning on Tues., Thurs., and Saturday. All flights stop over in Singapore. Discount fares are also available. Try Walkers Tours Ltd., 130 Glennie St., tel. 21101; Ceylon Luxury Tours, 13/1 Lloyds Bldg., Sir Baron Jayatilaka Mawatha, Colombo, tel. 240060.

FROM THE U.S. AND CANADA

American-based airlines serving Indonesia include Hong Kong Airlines, Garuda Indonesia, Japan Airlines, China Air, Lufthansa, KLM, Qantas, Pan Am, Sabena, and TWA. Most airlines have toll-free numbers which can be called at no cost from any part of the United States. An hour or so spent calling around to these free numbers will provide the most up-to-date info on current airfares, timetables, connections, etc. Toll-free numbers are often busy during business hours so it's easier to try in the evening. Call the toll-free information number (tel. 1-800-555-1212) 24 hours a day, 7 days a week, to find out the numbers of the airlines you're interested in. If you work through a travel agent, always have him contact an Orient consolidator for the very best fares. High season is June-Sept., and December.

Garuda Indonesia

Since 1986, the national carrier of Indonesia has operated twice-weekly direct flights between Los Angeles and Bali, departing both Los Angeles and Denpasar on Fri. and Sunday and on the way refueling in Honolulu and Biak, a small island off the northern coast of Irian Jaya. The DC10, often only ⅓ full, takes off at 1000 and flies first to Hawaii (6 hours), then to Biak, then 4 more hours to Bali. You then change to another plane for the final leg to Jakarta. Total time in the air: 23 hours. Good liquor and food, table linen, enthusiastic crew. The fare from L.A. to Jakarta is about US$1000 RT (or just to Biak, US$800 RT), with no discounted tickets. Just buy the cheaper ticket to Biak, the easternmost gateway to Indonesia, then start island hopping through Maluku, Sulawesi, and Kalimantan—the backdoor approach to Indonesia. This is an excellent way to enter Indonesia from W. Coast U.S. because you enter the best part of Indonesia—the Outer Islands. Alternatively, Garuda's flight from Honolulu to Bali stops over at Biak (9 hours from Honolulu), then it's another 3½ hours to Bali.

Garuda has North American offices at: 3457 Wilshire Blvd., Los Angeles, CA 90010 (for reservations and info call (800) 332-2223 inside California or (800) 826-2829 outside California); 360 Post St. Ste. 804, San Francisco, CA 94108, tel. (415) 788-2626; 51 E. 42nd St., Ste. 616, New York, NY 10017 (for reservations call (800) 248-2829 outside New York or (212) 370-0707 inside eastern region); 1040 W. Georgia St., Vancouver B.C., Canada V6E 4H1, tel. (604) 681-3699; 1600 Kapiolani Blvd., Ste. 632, Honolulu HI 96814, tel. (808) 947-9500. It's worth checking into a number of "Orient Tour" packages, for 5, 10, 15-plus days, also offered by Garuda. Their price depends largely upon which hotel you stay in. Their upmarket Nusa Dua package costs around US$1200 RT, while the package with accommodations at Alit's Beach Bungalows (Kuta) costs US$1100 RT. Ask about the special Garuda student rate (US$800 or so).

West Coast Flights

The travel sections of the Los Angeles Times and the San Francisco Chronicle-Examiner are full of ads for cheap trans-Pacific flights. Be sure to investigate the APEX RT fares; stopovers usually aren't permitted. Los Angeles-Washington-London-Jakarta-Honolulu-Los Angeles for US$675 OW or US$1436 RT. Korean Airlines (1-800-421 8200) is usually extremely reasonable; you can fly from Los Angeles to Hong Kong (US$900 RT Sun.-Thurs., or US$600 OW if purchased 21 days before departure). From Hong Kong, take Garuda to Denpasar (coach, $989 OW; 1st Class, $1,579 OW). Singapore Airlines (1-800-742 3333) has a flight direct from San Francisco to Singapore for US$600 (or US$1000 RT), 7-day advance purchase, no minimum stay, stop for free in Honolulu but any other stop is $50. They feed you steak, lobster, lamb dinners, salmon croquettes, free champagne, beer, cognac—the works! Book 21 days in advance. Any travel agency in the U.S. will sell you this ticket, but during June, July, and Aug. it goes up to US$650 OW, US$1100 RT. Once in Singapore, Jakarta is only US$150 away by plane. A cheap way to get to Bangkok is on Philippines Airline's (1-800-435 9725) 21-day ticket from the West Coast for US$659 OW, stopover in Manila for only US$50. Their low-season fare is US$559 OW. If you get a ticket just to Jakarta, you can exit through northern Sumatra, travel up to Bangkok, and then back to the States with Korean Airlines (US$425) which stops in Hong Kong, Taiwan, Korea, Hawaii, Los Angeles, and San Francisco.

From The East Coast

Other possible routings start from New York. KLM (1-800-556 7777) flies to Jakarta (via Amsterdam), then take Garuda to Denpasar (OW coach fare is $1,234; 1st class is $2,059 OW). From Tokyo to Denpasar, Garuda (1-800-332 2223) charges $1,021 OW for coach fare; $1,752 OW for 1st Class. Scan the New York Times for cut-rate airfares to SE Asia, then get down to Indonesia by yourself. And don't forget the good ol' Icelandic Airways (1-800-223 5500) connection from New York across the Atlantic (US$159 to Luxembourg), then from Europe fly to Asia with one of the cut-rate European charters (see "From London").

Cheap Travel Agencies In The U.S.

For easy mail-order ticketing, **OC Tours**, 110 E. 25th Ave., San Mateo, CA 94403 (call toll free 1-800-632-4739 in California, or 1-800-222-5292 outside CA) offers Garuda tickets for US$485 OW (US$869 RT) to Jakarta as well as to other Asian cities. **Overseas Tours**, 475 El Camino Real, Ste. 206, Millbrae, CA 94030 (tel. 1-800-323-8777 in CA, or 1-800-222-5292 outside California) claims they can match any advertised ticket price to the Orient. In the spring of 1988 they were selling a Los Angeles-Hondolu-Sydney-Denpasar-Singapore-Hong Kong-Tokyo-Los Angeles for only $1399 with 2 "free" stopovers in Auckland, Fiji, or the Cook Islands. Overseas represents 20 scheduled airlines, 300 tours, and 500 hotels in Asia. **Community Travel Service**, 5237 College Ave., Oakland, CA 94618, tel. (415) 653-0990, also has great prices to Asia; for example, they sell a RT ticket for $952 to Jakarta with stops in Tokyo both ways on Japan Airlines. **OE Tours**, 275 Post St., 4th Fl., San Francisco, CA 94108, boasts low airfares to Asia: Hong Kong for US$418 OW, $736 RT; Bangkok, $562 OW or $744 RT.

Council Travel Services, 2511 Channing Way, Berkeley, CA, tel. (415) 848-8604, is another well-known discounter. **Student Travel Network** is a budget ticket agency with offices at 166 Geary St. Ste. 702, San Francisco, CA 94108, tel. (415) 391-8407; tel. (213) 670-9698; 2500 Wilshire Blvd., Ste. 507, Los Angeles CA 90057, tel. (213) 380-2184; 7204 Melrose Ave., West Hollywood, (213) 934-8722; 920 Westwood Blvd., Los Angeles CA 90024, tel. (213) 824-1574; 17 East 45th St., New York, NY, tel. (212) 986-9470. **Pan Express Travel** (209 Post St., Ste. 921, San Francisco, CA 94108, tel. (415) 989-8282) sells a US$475 OW (US$830 RT) ticket San Francisco-Honolulu-Biak-Denpasar-Yogya-Jakarta. Then all you have to do is buy a MAS Airlines ticket from Medan to Penang (US$96) to fulfill the onward ticket requirement (or get a refund in Jakarta).

Vayatour USA Inc.

This 21-year-old Indonesian-based tour company and ticket agent has overseas offices in Singapore, Amsterdam, Hong Kong, Tokyo, Canada, and the U.S. (6420 Wilshire Blvd. Ste. 420, Los Angeles, CA 90048, tel. 213-655-3851). Outside California, call 1-800-992-8291. Among their many tours, Vayatours offers a 7-day "Bali-Flores Overland Tour" (US$820), a 4-day "Krakatau Adventure" tour (US$460), a 9-day "Exotic Java Bali Tour" (US$479). Prices do not include airfares. They can also design any adventure or special-interest tour to fit your group's needs. With

offices or associates on every major island in Indonesia, the traveler can confidently make travel arrangements anywhere in the archipelago.

From Canada

Canada is not a particularly good place to buy air tickets, but with persistence some good bargains can be found. In Vancouver try to find a Filipino, Chinese, or some other "ethnic" travel agency, then telephone OC Tours (above) to compare prices. Look up **Travel Cuts**, the Canadian student travel bureau, 187 College St., Toronto, Ontario M5T 1P7, tel. (416) 979-2406. They sell a ticket for US$850 OW (C$1340 RT) to Jakarta; Travel Cuts has offices in Vancouver (1516 Duranleau St., 604-687-6033), Halifax, Montreal, Ottawa, Winnipeg, Calgary, Edmonton, etc. (see Yellow Pages). They sell consistently inexpensive fares. Still, it may be cheaper to fly to SE Asia from a nearby city in the U.S., though naturally the expense of obtaining information and the ease and expense of getting to the U.S. airport from Canada must be taken into consideration.

FROM LONDON

London is famous for its low air fares to the Orient—the best place in Europe to buy air tickets. This is because of the many discount ticket outlets called "bucket shops." Each shop may or may not have their own advance purchase requirements and cancellation penalties, and cheaper tickets may not be available at peak periods when airlines can fill their planes at higher prices. When buying a ticket through a "bucket shop," don't pay more than a deposit before receiving the ticket, since these agencies have a high rate of closure. Garuda Indonesia, notorious for their monopolistic practices and high prices, even takes part in the slashed airfares business in London. An appealing option is to fly London-Hong Kong for which fares are cut-throat, then—after a trip into China perhaps—buy a RT Hong Kong-Jakarta. On your return fly on to anywhere from Hong Kong.

Sample Airfares

Fares from London to Jakarta run about UK275 OW or UK475 RT. Compare prices on Aeroflot, Pakistan, and Air Lanka airlines to Asia. (Garuda now operates flights from Bangkok to Jakarta and from Colombo, Sri Lanka, to Jakarta.) There are also various low-cost London-Australia and London-New Zealand flights available for about UK500-800 RT, with very inexpensive stopovers in either Singapore or Bali. Start inquiries at London's Garuda office (35 Duke St., London W1M 5DF, tel. 4863011), but inquiries only—Garuda must charge full fares. The fewer the stopovers, the cheaper the ticket. Round-the-World tickets are also available out of London for as cheap as

UK1105-1500. Reliable travel agencies for cut-rate tickets: Trailfinders Travel Centre, 46 Earls Court Rd., London W8 6EJ; Student Travel Australia, 74 Old Brompton Rd., South Kensington SW7 (tel. 01-581 1022) or at 117 Euston Rd, London NW1. Also try Far East Travel Centre, 32 Shaftsbury Ave., London W1, and ISTS Student Flights, Earls Court Underground Station, London SW5.

Useful Publications
The weekly *Time Out* (available at London newsstands or from Tower House, Southampton St., London WC2E 7HD) contains ads for many bargain airfares and bucket shops. The publications *Trailfinder, The News and Travel Magazine* and the excellent monthly magazine *Business Traveller* (available from newsstands or direct from 60/61 Fleet St., London EC4Y 1LA) may also prove useful. Current issues of the above publications are often found lying around hotel lobbies. In W. Berlin, all the cheapest flights are advertized in the fortnightly entertainment magazine *Zitty*.

FROM OTHER POINTS IN EUROPE

You may still save money buying your ticket in London rather than on the continent, especially if you hitchhike to London. It's just a question of the length of your trip, convenience, and your exact itinerary. But Indonesia has become quite a popular destination for Europeans, so it won't be that difficult to find low discount fares in Brussels, Amsterdam, Paris, Zurich, Frankfurt, Basel, Vienna, and Rome either. Fares are so cheap now that even retired people are making the 16-hour flight direct from Europe to Bali (with stopovers perhaps in Medan and Jakarta). In Brussels, check the Yellow Pages for the addresses of the Nouvelles and Wirtz agencies. Belgium's Sabena flies Brussels-Manila. Antwerp is another bargain center for low airfares; try Wats, de Keyserlei 44, Antwerp, Belgium. Also plenty of cheap flights leaving Athens, Greece.

West Germany
There's a big market for cheap airfares to Asia in Germany—almost every other traveler you meet in Indonesia is a German! Recommended are the following travel agencies and ticket offices: Alternativ Tours, Wilmersdorfer Str. 94, tel. 030-8812080/89, Berlin (the cheapest); Aquator, Hohenzollernstr. 93, tel. 089/2711350, Munich; Travel Overland, Barerstrasse 73, tel. 089/2716447, Munich; Asien-Reisen, Europapal 20, tel. 0711/7156091, Stuttgart; Asien-Reisen, Haselnubweg 37, tel. 0221/796037, Koln. Also check out RDS offices: RDS, Rentzelstr. 16, tel. 442363, Hamburg; RDS, Asternstr. 34, tel. 702454, Hannover; and RDS, Hindenburgplatz 64, tel. 832098,

Munster. Student travel offices: SSTS/ONTEJ, Kaiserstrasse 13, D-600 Frankfurt/Main, tel. (069) 281915; ARTU, Hardenbergstrasse 9, Berlin 12, tel. (030) 310771. Approx. sample RT fares from Frankfurt: Jakarta, DM1900; Denpasar, DM2000; Bangkok, DM1500; Singapore, DM1700. Interflug, the East German carrier, has cheap (DM825 OW) flights to Beijing, China, and Singapore (DM725), booked by any travel agent in West Germany too. No airport tax from East Berlin—the originating point of both flights—but DM5 transit visa must be purchased at the border. These flights depart Schonefeld Airport outside East Berlin. Direct bus every 30 min. from main West Berlin bus station to Schonefeld is DM7 OW. Interflug is much better than the Soviet Union's Aeroflot.

Austria
All the Okista offices have reliably cheap airfares: Okista, Turkenstr. 4, tel. 3475260, Vienna; Okista, Brandhofgasse 16, tel. 32482, Graz; Okista, Josef-Hirn Str. 7, tel. 28997, Innsbruck; Okista, Neuer Platz 2, tel. 56400, Klagenfurt; Okista, Pfarrplatz 8, tel. 275893, Linz; Okista, Hildmannplatz 1a, tel. 46769, Salzburg.

Switzerland
Get ahold of a recent issue of the best Swiss travelers magazine, *Globetrotter-Magazin,* Postfach, tel. 01-211 20 23/24, 8023 Zurich, which lists loads of cheap airlines (and good booklists). Ticket agencies offering budget fares to Asia are: Stohl Travel, tel. 022 316560, Geneva; SOF Travel, tel. 01 301 3333, Zurich; Globetrotter, Rennweg 35, tel. 01-2117780, Zurich; Globetrotter, Munzgraben 4, tel. 031-211121, Bern; Globetrotter, Freie Str. 47, tel. 061-257766, Basel. The SSR offices are also outlets for cheap Indonesia-bound tickets: SSR, Theaterstr. 10, tel. 228868, Basel; SSR, Hallerstr. 4, tel. 240312, Bern; SSR, Goldgasse 12, tel. 224665, Chur; SSR, 8 Rue de la Barre, tel. 203975, tel. 203975, Lausanne; SSR, 3 Rue Vignier, tel. 299733, Genf; SSR, Leonhardstr. 10, tel. (01) 242 3000, Zurich.

From Amsterdam
Fly from Amsterdam to Singapore at very reasonable prices; could be even cheaper than flying from Sydney to Singapore! Cheapest flight from Holland to Indonesia could be with Czechoslovakian Airlines: Amsterdam-Prague-Obidabi-Bombay-Singapore-Jakarta; takes 20 hours. KLM and Garuda now have a weekly B747 joint service between Amsterdam and Bali or Jakarta for around US$800. Much cheaper is NBBS, Dam 17; and Malibu Travel, Damrak 30, 1012 LJ Amsterdam, tel. 020-234912. Malibu offers the cheapest flights for adults; NBBS would be cheaper for holders of student ISIC card. Sample Malibu fares (US$1 = 1.85 Dutch guilders) in Dutch guilders: Jakar-

ta, 1740 eastbound, 2095 westbound; 2415 eastbound, 2415 westbound with UTA Airlines; 2575 eastbound via Micronesia; 3250 eastbound, 3250 westbound via Easter Island. Malibu tickets are non-refundable, non-reroutable, and non-transferable. You don't have the freedom to travel from any European city, only from Amsterdam. Smaller than Malibu and more likely to give personalized service is Amber Reiseburo, Da Costastraat 77, 1053 ZG, Amsterdam, tel. 851155. Another discount agent is Eureka, Rokin 10, 1012 KR Amsterdam, tel. 020-256597, selling a RT ticket to Jakarta for 1660 guilders, RT to Bali for 1990 guilders. This company is in the same office as Budget Bus, which sells the cheapest bus fares to all over Europe. An excellent Outer Island tour specialist is Wereld Orientalie Reizen, Dr. Letteplein 1, 3731 JR De Bilt, Holland.

From Italy And France

Nouvelles Frontieres of Italy and France offers the cheapest airfares from France and Italy to the Far East; their Rome-Jakarta ticket costs only LIT950,000 RT (US$1 = LIT1,400). Offices: NF, Via lo del Divino Amore, 18, tel. (06) 6785841/2/3/4/5, Rome; NF, Via Vincenzo Stefano Breda, tel. (049) 25033-22544, Padua; NF, c/o Ciocco Travels, Via Cavour, 166, tel. (055) 579294, Florence. Also check out CTS, Via Genova 16, tel. (06) 479931 and ESTC, Largo Brancaccio 55, tel. (06) 7316161. In France, NF offices are at 37 Rue Violet 75015, tel (00331) 5786540, Paris; and at 24 Av. G. Clemenceau 06000, tel (003393) 2503322544, Nice. Voyages et Decouvertes, 21 Rue Cambon, 75001, Paris (tel. 42961680) is another agency selling discounted tickets.

CRUISES

The trouble with cruises is that passengers are only able to stop for 3-4 hours at some ports (such as Nias).

But the luxury and service is undeniable. In addition to around-the-world cruises that may call at a single Indonesian port, at least 4 cruise lines will sail the Java Sea in 1988 and 1989. Royal Cruise Line's *Golden Odyssey* departs Bangkok for Semarang, Yogya, and Bali on its way to Hong Kong. Pearl Cruises' *Bangkok, Bali & Beyond* itinerary visits Jakarta, Semarang (for a trip to Borobudur), and Bali. Royal Viking's Jewels of the Orient cruise aboard the *Royal Viking Star* departs Singapore and Bangkok for Bali, and their *Sea Goddess I* also calls on several Indonesian ports (departs Freemantle, Australia). Inquire at your travel agency for departure times and prices.

Adventure Cruises

Those cruisers who prefer a more localized experience may be interested in the *Island Explorer* operated by Spice Island Cruises and marketed in the U.S. by Salen Lindblad. In spring 1972, the *Island Explorer* made her first visit to the eastern archipelago, visiting islands whose last contact with Westerners was before WW II and in some cases never before in living memory. Today the tradition is carried on by the *Island Explorer*. Built to yacht specifications, the ship on its 14-day cruise carries 36 passengers and 20 crew and visits such out-of-the-way destinations as Flores, Komodo, Ambon, Nias, and other islands E of Bali and W of Irian Jaya (US$4260). Facilities on board include satellite telephones, hobie cats, windsurfers, a glass-bottom boat, water skis, and a complete scuba-diving facility. Spice Island Cruises has also announced its newest seagoing venture, a 22-passenger high-performance dive ship. For cabin costs and complete details on their winter and summer voyages, contact Salen Lindblad Cruising Inc., 133 E. 55th St., New York, NY 10022, tel. 1-800-223-5688.

INTERNAL TRANSPORT

Nothing is easy in Indonesia, especially traveling. There are 2 ways to travel here: the tourist way and the native way. Monied tourists, or those with limited time, hire cars and minibuses, use taxis and planes, and join package tour groups; these modes of transport are all covered below. But for speed, mobility, economy, and firsthand contact with the people, the native way can't be beat. The choice of native transport available, particularly on Java, will amaze you. The most common means of local transport is the bicycle. Crowded inter-island mass transit systems are not yet adequate to meet all of the needs of the people, but Indonesians make do and, given enough time, everyone gets where they're going. By

Western standards, public transport in the big cities—ranging from hire cars to man-driven tricycles—is also overburdened and inadequate. Besides taxis, which are the most convenient and the most expensive, there are *bemo, helicak, bajaj, becak,* and other contraptions used for short distances. Often, the only way to travel between the majority of Indonesia's thousands of Outer Islands is by air or sea.

The obstacles against smooth, leisurely travel are formidable. Road conditions are often deplorable, seas are rough, flights frequently delayed or cancelled, and schedules change constantly. Difficult as it is to travel in Indonesia, if you're stuck there's always a way out. Simplify and travel light. You don't really need a sleeping bag because rooms are so cheap. Minimize clothing—when your shirt gets dirty, wash it. (The Indonesian fiery sun will dry a light cotton shirt in 7 minutes flat!) Get down to one piece of luggage and a shoulder bag if you can. Not only does little luggage cut down chances of loss and theft, but it changes your whole philosophy of travel. When you arrive in a town it relieves you of having to set up a base right away. You're light on your feet, better able to walk around and sightsee. And, if you don't like the place, just blow through. Flag a vehicle down, ask people the way, or start walking or hitching—your luck will change.

Best Time To Travel

The most important thing to understand about travel in Indonesia is the concept of *jam karet,* or "rubber time." Like the Mexican philosophy of *manana,* times of departures are stretched or contracted depending on the whim of the driver, pilot, or captain and how full or empty the passenger seating is. So don't be in a hurry. No one else is! As far as comfort is concerned, the best time of day to travel is from 0600 to about noon, or else after the sun goes down. Because Indonesia's climate is tropical, people travel here all seasons of the year. But the least desirable time to travel is at the end of the rainy season in Jan. and Feb. when roads, bridges, railroad tracks, and airfields could be washed out, or closed indefinitely. If traveling to a difficult-to-reach village in the Outer Islands, just wait for market day (once or twice a week) when it's easier to get out and back.

Avoid traveling during religious holidays such as Idul Fitri (the end of the Islamic fasting month), when millions of Indonesians hit the road to visit relatives. You must compete with them for transport and tourist facilities and prices skyrocket. On Friday, the Muslim holy day, many offices are closed and transportation almost stops at 1100 or so when Muslims can go to pray at the *mesjid.* If it's a holiday such as *Hari Raya,* or a particularly busy tourist season such as Aug. on Bali, or something or other is going on that prevents you from getting a seat on a long-distance night bus or train, just take local transportation instead—*oplet, bemo,* minibus, short-run trains—in 40- to 50-km segments. For example, if you can't get a seat but really want to leave Denpasar for Surabaya, just get on a local colt for Gilimanuk, cross the strait, then flag down a ride on a *bemo* or colt from Ketapang on the other side to Situbondo, Besuki, Probolinggo, and on to Surabaya. You'll get there paying just about the same amount as you would if you were to take a night bus, though it will take you longer.

Travel Info

Tourists who don't speak *Bahasa Indonesia* well will have difficulty communicating with drivers/operators, but what a wonderful incentive to learn! Refer to the appendix for phrases in *Bahasa Indonesia* which will help you get around. Tourist offices in the cities dispense info, brochures, and maps, and may also be useful for booking hotels, arranging tours, transport and boat charter, train tickets, etc. They are plugged into many of the local travel service vendors and many actually function as mini-travel agencies. Also, don't hesitate to avail yourself of the army or the police when trying to find places to stay, eat, vehicles to charter, or if you need help in any way. Usually, they are extremely friendly and helpful.

Asking Directions

When you reach a town and want to find the bus, *oplet,* or minibus station in order to continue on to your destination, just ask *Dimana stasiun...?* with the name of your destination put after. When asking directions, if people give the answer or say yes too quickly it probably means "maybe" or else "I don't know." It's sometimes difficult to get the right information from Indonesians because of their infuriating habit of only wanting to tell you what they think you want to hear, whether they have the information or not. (Indonesian domestic tourists, as well as foreign visitors, meet with this same problem.) Often the integrity of the relationship is more important than the objectivity, so if you're lied to it probably means that Indonesians just want to please you. Minimize this by asking very specific questions. If you're driving your own car, be prepared to lean out of your window and ask *Dimana Sukamade?* (Where is Sukamade?). No doubt you will get the traditional reply, *"Terus"* (straight on) regardless. Or *Terus, kiri* or *Terus, kanan* (right, left) which will cover all options. (How silly we travelers are, needing such precise directions!) Interpret rather *the way* they say it to determine what they really mean.

Another tip: never ask a leading question such as, "This is the right way, isn't it?" but instead, *"Which* is the right way?" Ask at least 3 people, then take a mean average. If it's an obscure place, keep asking as you go along and eventually you'll get there. Try to single out the man or woman with a khaki, light gray, or deep blue safari uniform. This is a *pegawai,* one of the nation's 2 million plus civil servants. They are often better educated and more articulate at giving directions. Indonesians also tend to give distances less than they really are; if it's 500 m, they say 100, if it's 7 km, they say 2 km. Names are shortened frequently: Cibadak becomes "Badak," Sukabumi becomes "Bumi," Cilegon becomes "Egon"—all cried out to solicit passengers as the *bemo* speeds down the road or through the market. Indonesians could also use an altogether different name than the official public name, such as "Badung" for Denpasar. Another aspect of finding your way that's confusing is the several different names given to a single street. Indonesia has many heros to commemorate so there might be 4 or 5 different names covering a single street's entire length. As for maps, don't rely on them—even those published by the government! Although judging from a map it might appear that Indonesia has a superb road system, in truth many of the roads haven't existed since Dutch times or else are *planned* for the future. If you trust a map completely, you could get stuck walking 2 days through a mosquito-infested, rain-drenched jungle.

Transport Costs

A rough guide would be about Rp30 per km—a bit less than this in Java's mainstream bus system, a bit more on Sumatra's public buses, and up to 2 or even 3 times as much for end-of-the-line minibus or *bemo* segments way, way up into the mountains. You eventually develop a sense of what's the correct price to pay, a feeling that a Rp1000 *becak* ride offer is really worth only Rp500. Some Indonesians take advantage of your ignorance by overcharging, so you must constantly exercise your bargaining powers—part of understanding Indonesia. Catch them at it, then have a laugh together over it. It's all in your attitude. When riding in any private native-style transportation, one way of learning the correct charge is to first ask the passengers the usual, standard fare *(harga biasa)*. Settle on the price *before* you get in the vehicle (do this without exception) and, if necessary, bargain each and every time. Often, when you're traveling with a large backpack on a *bemo* or small bus, you're asked to pay another adult fare as your pack takes up another place and they lose out on the fare. You are expected to understand this. Often there's a day price and a night price (sometimes double the day price). On big national or religious holidays such as *Hari Raya*, transport companies always try to raise the price of each seat. Don't get out of the *bemo, becak,* or cab without receiving your correct change first.

Ticket Touts/Guides

Though some are downright unsavory types, you don't necessarily have to be paranoid about the touts hanging around the bus stations and the harbors of Indonesia who want to help you. They claim to have special connections with the ship's captain, stationmaster, harbormaster, or whoever. Actually, this may be the case and these touts could save you a lot of trouble and money if you learn how to work with them and tell the good ones from the bad ones. Be open. They could help you get a ticket when all other channels are closed. Their "fee," tacked on to the base price—if not ridiculously high—might be worth it. The same thing goes for self-appointed multilingual guides who attach themselves onto you at airports, in the cities or in villages at the base of volcanos. These contacts could lead to exciting experiences. Local guides are a part of the regional color and the personality of a new place. Their rates can be quite reasonable, around US$3, $5, or at most $10 per day. Some of these freelance guides check out flight manifests at airports to see who's flying in, or hang around tourist information offices or traveler's hotels in order to meet customers. They seem to have friends everywhere; they may work for a tour company on the side. Guides often don't have telephones (too expensive) and can only be contacted through their friends working in a tourist agency, tourist office, or hotel. Specialized, "official" guides are also available to do tours of museums, temples, mosques, palaces, tea plantations, etc.

Paperwork/Permits

While traveling within Indonesia, always carry your passport; police will often ask for it. International student ID cards can be used for discounts on ferries or trains; get them cheap in Bangkok. An International Driver's License is available from your local motorist's association; when hiring a bicycle it can be used as a substitute when asked to deposit your passport. Permits are necessary to visit many reserves and national parks in Indonesia such as Bukit Lawang, N. Sumatra, the Baluran Game Park of E. Java, and Komodo Island, Nusatenggara. Costing around Rp1500, these permits are usually available from a Directorate of Nature Conservation (PPA) officer in the park itself, or in a PPA office in the town nearest the reserve. Or you could even apply at an Indonesian consulate before leaving for Indonesia. A *surat jalan* is a letter which the traveler is required to carry in order to present on demand to army, police, immigration or custom officials while traveling in the Outer Islands. Obtainable only from local/regional police stations, this advance permission is often necessary to help with connecting transportation. *Surat jalan* are by no means required in most parts of Indonesia but only in really outlying or restricted areas such as the OFM trouble spots of Irian Jaya and in far western West Timor. Consult individual travel chapters as to current requirements; it is highly unlikely your travel agent will be able to advise you.

Hitchhiking

There are not that many privately owned vehicles in Indonesia. Hitching is slow but enjoyable on Java, N. Sumatra, and S. Sulawesi. Hitching is easiest of all on Bali. Meet the people. Practice your Indonesian. Engineers, the military, merchandisers, truckies, foreign aid workers, tourists will pick you up in jeeps, trucks, cars, Landrovers, motorcycles, bicycles. *Ojek* is a bicycle (motorized or not) used as a *becak* by taking a passenger on the back seat. There's even a story of an oil company helicopter landing by a highway in S. Sumatra to pick up a hitchhiker. On Bali you're at least not bothered by the crowds of people which tend to congregate around you on Java and Sumatra—one reader counted 130 standing around him at a road junction in Sulawesi. Be prepared: hitching could be as bad or as good as you've encountered anywhere.

MOTORCYCLES

A fast and inexpensive way of getting around, and often the only way to negotiate dirt roads in the rainy season. Indonesians call a motorcycle simply *honda*, as in *naik honda* ("by honda" or "by motorcycle"). A bike is super-convenient to use; on Bali, for example, you can travel N all the way to Singaraja via Mengwi in just 1 day on a motorcycle. Ride one with great caution as serious motorcycle accidents on Indonesia's often congested, madcap roads are all too common. Indonesia is not the place to learn to ride a motorcycle. Chickens, dogs, and children dart out unexpectedly into the road, there are giant potholes, big trucks lumber down the road straddling both lanes, and cars travel at night without using their headlights. Bring warm clothes because in the highlands the temperature drops considerably. An International Driver's License (endorsed for motorcycles) is usually required before you can rent one. Even then, you still need to get a special local license on Bali. Here you're fingerprinted, photographed, and given a written and driving test, costing in all over US$30! International Driving Permits are available at automobile clubs such as your local AAA office (take 2 photos); valid for one year.

Traveling With A Motorcycle

For long term, the best is to buy one of the local Hondas for Rp300,000-500,000, then resell it later for maybe half what you paid for it. If you travel intraisland with your own bike, make sure it's a lightweight machine because you might have to load and unload it frequently. Freighting costs aren't that high. For example, it'll cost you around Rp125,000 to transport your motorcycle by ship from Surabaya all the way to Timor, or about US$350 from Jakarta to Australia. Petrol is cheap at Rp600 per liter. You need a *carnet*, which is a deposit you leave with your automotive association at home to ensure that you don't sell the bike in Indonesia. The adventurous motorcyclist could start out from Singapore by ship, first carrying his bike through the customs building in Singapore harbor. Shippers could charge you US$15-25 each time for handling (lifting and lowering) because there are no cranes. While traveling through the islands by ship, always get a customs clearance for the bike the day before and get a pass from the harbormaster *(syahbandar)* to enter the harbor, then just show up with your ticket. When arriving at dockside, to avoid getting bogged down by hours of paperwork at customs, try driving off the ship and right through the gate saying hello to everyone without stopping. You might make it!

Rentals

Motorcycles may be rented in Yogya, Kuta Beach, and Denpasar for Rp5000-8000 per day, or cheaper by the week. Most are 90-125cc, and you don't really need anything heavier or more powerful. The longer the rental period the lower the rate, and the newer and more powerful the higher the rate (trail bikes are the most expensive). Most are rented out by private parties, usually young men trying to make the bike pay for itself. Some places don't have motorcycle rentals, even though they're on the tourist trail. On Bali it's a big business; a *losmen* saves up all its money so it can buy a motorbike to rent out. Check not only *losmen* but restaurants, travel agents, and clothing shops with signs out front stating MOTORCYCLE FOR HIRE. On Bali approach the groups of young men you see lounging around their bikes on street corners. Check the battery, oil, brakes, cables, clutch, *et al* carefully before you agree to a rental fee. You should take at least a crude knowledge of motorcycle mechanics to Indonesia if you plan to rent a bike there, and also bring some simple tools—a screwdriver, wrench, and pliers. For example, one scenario is to be in a thunderstorm on the unlit road from Parangtritis back to Yogya when your headlight bulb burns out, and you can't find anyone who owns a screwdriver.

Honda Sikap

Another method of motorcycle transport is called *ojek* or *honda sikap* ("holding tight" in Javanese) in which you pay a driver for the privilege of riding on the back of his motorcycle to your destination. This type of travel is offered by the locals out to the Belahan Temple group in E. Java, from Lemahabang to Bandungan in C. Java, in the Tanjung Isui area of E. Kalimantan, and in many other Outer Island locales. If you're really stuck, try asking for the *honda sikap* arrangement anywhere, or try hitching motorcycles at the side of the road. Bicycle riders can be approached for *ojek* rides too. When riding double on a bicycle, females are expected to sit side-saddle while holding onto the pack rack—a real trick! You have to make a running leap and settle into position while the bike is in motion. The *ojek* driver, for both motorcycles and bicycles, is called *pengojek*.

BICYCLE RIDING IN INDONESIA

Besides walking, the cheapest form of transport possible. Bicycles here serve as packmule, jalopy for dating, family car, vendor's shop, and what kids use until they can afford a motorcycle. For the traveler, few other modes of transport offer such versatility. A bicycle can be ridden, carried by almost every other form of transport from outrigger canoes to jets, and can even be lifted on one's shoulders across streams or over lava-strewn volcanos. Cycling offers virtually

Family Outing *by Otto Djaja, 1956*

no transport costs, complete freedom from schedules, and next to walking unsurpassed closeness to nature. From a bicycle you can hear the birds singing, see clouds float over volcanic peaks, cruise by vignettes of village life, hear little tykes shout "I love you," find a Balinese temple festival or suddenly come upon a Javanese Whip Dance—really *experience* Indonesia.

Road Conditions

Bicycling on Java and Bali is probably more rewarding than in Western countries but it is also more demanding. Because they are Indonesia's most densely populated and developed islands, these islands also have Indonesia's best road systems—good quality roads reaching to every corner of each island. All but the most minor roads are sealed. By contrast, long stretches of roads in the Outer Islands of Nusatenggara, Sulawesi, and Sumatra can be unpaved, potholed, and washed away. Where roads are nonexistent, ride in motorcycle ruts or along footpaths. Because of their scale and topo features, the Apa/Nelles Verlag maps are the best ones to use. Since it could be dangerous to ride a bicycle on the more heavily trafficked roads, most main roads on Java have cycle paths. Where there are no tracks, motorists seem to be more aware of cyclists than in the West (in Indonesia, cyclists are the majority and motorists are the minority!). You must get used to judging the different speeds of traveling vehicles on these roads, adjusting to oxcarts, *becak*, motorcycles, buses, and cars (in order of speed). Perhaps the greatest danger is erratic cycling by the locals and *becak* drivers. Keep to the smaller roads wherever possible. The signposting is fairly good.

At first it seems there are *no* traffic rules except for the one that says "Yield to those who are bigger and faster than you." But after awhile you learn that the rules are just different. In doing a right hand turn, for example, you turn onto the R hand side of the road first, then cycle *against* the traffic until there's a gap in the traffic before crossing over to your side of the road (see diagram). If you want to go straight ahead at intersections, put your hand straight out in front of you while keeping eye contact with the oncoming drivers. At really busy intersections, you should dismount and walk your bike across. Cyclists who won't get off the road for anybody should not ride in Asia. Be prepared to pull off the road if large vehicles are coming straight at you or from behind. The physical shock of riding long distances over the washboard roads of Indonesia's Outer Islands or back areas can be a huge strain. If you're not a physical fitness freak and if you grow tired of the torment of the highway, load your bicycle on top of a bus or minibus for the long hauls to the main centers of interest so you don't arrive too hot and exhausted to enjoy cycling around the local attractions once there.

Equipment And Repair

If you're an ardent cyclist, you should consider taking your own bike. For long-distance touring, it's all important to buy a thoroughly robust machine. The Dawes Super Galaxy (US$700), with its wide wheels and indestructible frame, would be ideal. Airlines are surprisingly lenient about accepting one as luggage, often free (as on Qantas), but check first. For air travelers, the easiest is to have a bike that disassembles and can be carried in a bag. The bicycle should have low gears and be 100% reliable. Avoid bikes with skinny 1" and 1-1/8" tires; 1 ¼" or 1-3/8" are stronger and more shock-absorbing. Make sure all parts conform to accepted international specifications to make finding replacement threads, wheels, spokes, and gears easier. Bring the best quality, strongest back panniers because they will take a lot of punishment. If you're renting a local bike, a carrier rack *(bagase)* over the rear fender is quite adequate for carrying your shoulder bag or knapsack, fastened with a couple of elastic "spider" shock cords with hooks.

Tires and tubes are available in the urban centers in all the usual sizes, though other high-tech 10-speed parts and tools might prove difficult to obtain. If you take your own machine, bring a small, comprehensive tool kit containing any special tools (including a spoke key and block-and-chain rivet removers). A critical accessory is a horn or very loud bell. Indonesian pumps are too clumsy to carry around, so bring your own or have flats repaired there. Since bikes are used so much in everyday life by the Indonesians themselves, even the smallest villages have bike shops or someone whose specialty it is to fix bikes. Called a *tukang sepeda* (bicycle repairer), he sets up shop usually in the corner of the street. His labor charges are low, mending your puncture while you wait for only Rp200 or so, using only rubber from old inner tubes, a pot of glue, and a hammer with which to bang on the patch.

Traveling By Bike

Buy the highest-quality equipment before you set out as Indonesian manufactured goods are shoddy and don't last. Don't carry a lot of gear because you may want to park and explore an area by foot. In this case, you must either find someone like a headman or *warung* owner to safeguard your gear or carry it all with you. Take along a T-shirt and a nicer shirt for temple festivals. Bring zinc oxide or a sunhat for protection against hours of riding under the ferocious tropical sun. A good helmet, with its abundant padding and insulation, would be even better. A rear-view mirror, reflectors, and a dynamo light give added protection. In remote regions, carry a sharp stick to be used against vicious dogs. Many local bikes are equipped with a claw-like key lock which locks around the wheel and guards against petty theft, but a heavy-duty hacksaw-proof steel cable lock *(kunci)* offers much more security. At most public places—post offices, markets, schools, big stores—leave your bike at the *titipan sepeda* (bicycle parking area) where the attendant who guards the bikes gives you a ticket which corresponds to a stub on your bike. Some *titipan sepeda* are provided as a service for students or customers, but at others you have to pay Rp50-100. Camping gear is not needed as the distances are not great between towns on Java and Bali and the *losmen* and *penginapan* are so inexpensive. Bring your bike inside your room, or ask the proprietor where the safest place is. If no accommodations are available when night falls, police stations or churches are usually hospitable. There are, however, some nice places to camp in seashore, mountain, or remote areas, so essential items include: a lightweight tent; sleeping bag, pad, and ground sheet; a light and efficient Optimus petrol stove; a plastic survival bag for storing luggage at night; plastic water bottles; compass; altimeter; Swiss Army knife; flashlight; medical kit; small presents like balloons and postcards of home, etc.

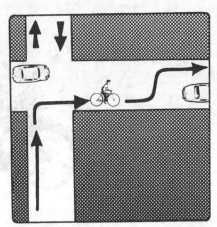

It seems at first there are no traffic rules in Indonesia, but after a while you learn that the rules are just different. When executing a R-hand turn, for example, turn onto the R-hand side of the road first, then cycle against traffic before crossing over.

Bicycle Check

Volcanos offer unbelievably steep climbs and dizzying descents. Never go into the mountains without good brakes. Both front and rear brakes must be able to stop your bike alone in case one of the brakes fails while going downhill. Brake shoes *(karet rem)*, which cost only Rp500 a pair, should be symmetrically positioned and show plenty of rubber. The best test is whether or not each brake pair can stop your bike and hold it while you push forward with all your might. Before renting or buying a bike, turn it upside down and spin the wheels to see if the rims have any deep rust spots which could cause the wheel to buckle under stress. Observe the wheel as it passes by the brake shoe; if it wobbles more than 6 mm, you might get shimmying. Also, examine carefully for loose or broken spokes.

Don't rent or buy pushbikes with bald or soft tires *(ban)*; the shop will promptly pump them up for you but so will you every day after that. A bell *(bel)* and light *(lampu)* are both essential. Spin the wheel with the generator *(dinamo)* engaged to make sure that the light works. A back reflector *(stopan)* is another important safety feature. If your bicycle seat *(sadal sepon)* is uncomfortable, so will you be during your whole tour. Buy a new soft, padded seat (Rp5000-7000) or at least a tie-on foam seat cover (Rp2000). These can be bought at any good bike shop. Adjust the seat so you can straighten your legs and touch the lower pedal with your heel. If you're really tall, you may have to outfit your bike with an extra-long seat tube *(pepa sadal panjang)*. Lightly oil all moving parts before setting out each day, and check that all nuts and bearings are tight (seat, brake linkage cables, brake rims, etc.).

Renting Vs. Buying Bicycles

For long-distance touring, your bike must be in top mechanical condition. Most Indonesian machines will definitely not win you a place in the Tour de France. At the places in Indonesia where it's most pleasant to ride a bicycle (Yogya and Solo in C. Java, Kuta and Legian in S. Bali), they are plentiful and cheap to rent. In other places such as Telukdalam on Nias, Parangtritis in W. Java, Bukittinggi in W. Sumatra, it takes some looking to find bikes to rent, and more looking to find one that works! Rental choices run from one-speed clunkers with terrible seats to one-speed clunkers with terrible seats, no reflectors, bell, lights, or brakes. Most are sturdy black-painted machines which resemble 2-wheeled tanks.

An alternative to renting would be to buy a used bicycle. Toko Sepeda (bike shops) in the cities sell cheap 10-speed Taiwanese models, a few Japanese mountain bikes, and kids BMX bikes. If you're going to be in the area for a month or more, try to work out a "special arrangement" with the bike shop whereby you buy a good used bike for around Rp60,000-80,000 and undertake to repair and upgrade it if the shop guarantees to buy it back when you leave for 20-25% less than what you initially paid. This, in the long run, results in a very low daily rental cost. For straight rentals, count on a normal rate of Rp1000-1500 per day or Rp5000-6000 per week. Another approach: instead of agreeing to pay the full amount in cash, bargain to improve the bike and deduct the cost from the rental cost.

INTER- AND INTRA-CITY TRANSPORT

Most of the following native transport systems make regular stops at terminals, street corners, or intersections, but they also frequently pick up passengers anywhere they find them. Occasionally, they also make detours to let you off where you want to go. If the driver tries to renegotiate the fare halfway to your destination, ask to be let out and insist upon paying the fare only up to that point. Faced with the reality of losing the whole fare, the driver will go back to his original price.

Helicak

A cheaper alternative to taxis, these are motorized 3-wheeled vehicles consisting of a tinted plastic bubble-cabin mounted on a motorcycle, sheltered from the sun or rain. A *helicak* can fit 2 passengers who sit in the bubble in front of the driver. Quite common in Jakarta, they cost Rp500-1000 for short distances.

Bajaj

Making inroads into the traditional pedicab *(becak)* market in many cities is the *bajaj*, a 2-seat, 3-wheeled vehicle that could be described as the motorized version of the *becak*. *Bajaj* transport can be hired in almost all the big towns. It's a bit comfier and moves a lot faster than the *becak*, though they often have engine trouble (repaired in about 10 seconds).

Bemo

Short for *becak motor*. There are 3 ways you can die in a *bemo*: a head-on collision, suffocation, or fright. Bigger than a *bajaj*, this is an open-backed pickup truck. Made in several sizes, it is outfitted with 2 rows of low, wooden passenger benches down the sides. Built more for Asians than for larger Western frames, the smaller, 3-wheeled ones (which look like a cross between a pickup truck and a golf cart) usually pack 6-8 passengers, while the large, 4-wheeled ones can carry 12-16 people. Both are usually overcrowded; the driver will not leave until he's convinced that nobody else can be stuffed in, with everyone shoulder to shoulder (particularly on busy market days). You will also intimately learn the driver's music preference as he will play his favorite tapes at full volume for hours on end. Though they have irregular schedules, *bemo* operate on fixed routes like buses, but they can also be hired for short or long-distance trips (see "Private Vehicles"). Since they're always stopping for and dropping off passengers, they will stop anywhere you want them to. Hail them over as they run along all the main routes of a city or on main highways between towns. Prices vary from region to region, but are usually higher on less frequented routes. Count on about Rp75 per km with a minimum of Rp100; Rp200-300 for a 1- to 3-km ride is the usual charge. *Bemo* often go up at least Rp50-100 in price at night, especially in popular tourist areas. Determine the correct fare before climbing in (good-natured bickering might be necessary); also ask the driver, his assistant, or passengers for confirmation to make sure you — or they — know where you're going. In over-touristed areas such as Bali, *bemo* drivers and their assistants can be really *kasar* as they get all the business they can handle. The old-style *bemo* is gradually giving way all over Indonesia to Japanese-made minibuses.

Oplet

Small motorized vehicles (bigger than *bemo*), seating for 6-10 passengers, costing Rp150-300, depending on the distance. *Oplet* generally operate on specific routes, and also in between cities and nearby towns. Flag them down at any point along the road. In Sumatra, an *oplet* is a multi-colored Chevrolet bus or minibus, reminiscent of the Filipino *jeepney*, while on Java it's a canopied pickup truck with seats. In bigger cities such as Jakarta, *oplet* are being slowly replaced with *Microlet*, light blue vehicles that have the same fares and run on the same routes. Anytime a *bemo* or an *oplet* stops and a cabin passenger's seat becomes vacant, you have a perfect right to occupy it (this front window seat is the best for photography). Anyone else getting in (up to 3 people) should allow you to continue to sit at the window seat. Drivers often put you up front out of deference (you get a lot of mileage out of your white skin in Asia) or to show you off. If you're carrying a lot of luggage you're often charged an extra fare. See "Private Vehicles" about hiring *oplet* for group touring or day-tripping.

Minibuses

Also called colts (pronounced KOLL). Assembled in Mitsubishi's Surabaya plant and from there spewed out all over Indonesia, minibuses have 11 seats holding up to 20 people with the conductor hanging out the side almost as a permanent fixture. The name colt also applies to *all* minibuses, not just Mitsubishi colts. These small vans travel all the middle-distance runs on most of the major and secondary roads throughout the archipelago, shuttling passengers back and forth between neighboring cities such as Kuta-Singaraja, Yogya-Solo, Malang-Surabaya, Ujung Padang-Pare Pare, Ambon-Passo, Biak-Bosnik, Jayapura-Abepura. Operating the shorter, highly trafficked routes more frequently than the big public buses do, minibuses are in fact replacing buses on many transport routes. Private minibuses are more expensive than buses because they're not controlled by the government as buses are, so they can almost charge anything—as long as it's competitive. Though they cost up to Rp400-1000 more than buses, minibuses are considerably faster (also more likely to crash) and are a lot more convenient and comfortable, especially if you can reserve your own seat. For reserved seat passengers, the driver will often take you right to your doorstep or at least near your destination; this is well worth the extra money that would otherwise be spent hassling for a *becak* or *bemo*. Also, because minibuses carry fewer passengers, they fill up faster and depart more often than do the larger buses. Fares are not really fixed but may vary Rp50-100 from the usual, depending upon the hour of day, weather conditions, and number of passengers. It's best to ask the officials at bus and minibus stations what the correct fare is. Before taking off, your minibus driver might circle around the town or city for 20 min. soliciting passengers to fill all remaining seats and only depart once they're full. Midway through your minibus journey you might be asked to board another minibus that will take you the rest of the way. Minibuses can also be chartered for your personal use at rates oftentimes cheaper than taxis.

Horse-drawn Carts

Though slow, horse-drawn carts and carriages are a delightful little adventure. And you can brag about the experience to your grandchildren! They come in a variety of shapes and styles, each a pleasant mode of travel in many towns and villages. These horse carriages stand in rows near train stations, around the grassy *alun alun*, or on the edge of town waiting for their fares. The 2-wheeled kind (one horse) are called *dokar* or *sado*, and they can carry up to 4 people. You have to balance yourself and your gear so the total weight won't strain the horse. When darkness falls, the drivers light the wicks on polished oil lamps on the coach. *Dokar* are very much part of the scene in and around such regional centers as Bandung, Bogor, and Yogya, but you'll be hard-pressed to find one in or around Jakarta. If you travel farther E to Yogya, Solo, Malang, Surabaya, the carriages are larger with 4 wheels, drawn by 2 horses, and able to accommodate up to 8 people. These are called *andong* or *bendi*. In Kuta Beach, *dokar* run down to Legian, catering to yuppie tourists at inflated fares. On Lombok, they're called *cidomo*. Fares are set by bargaining, the average Rp600-1400. Some owners of horse-drawn vehicles operate on a fixed-fee basis, particularly when they offer local sightseeing trips. But if you want to hire one for specific journeys that involve going out of town, then it's always better to agree on the fare first.

BECAK

All over Indonesia you find the pedal-powered *becak* (trishaw) which looks like a big painted rocking chair on wheels. A *becak* (nearest pronunciation is BEH-jack) is best described as a manpowered tricycle-taxi, an enjoyable form of transport for 2 ordinary-sized people. Quite often a *becak* is the most convenient and readily available form of transport to get you and your rucksack from the bus or train station to your hotel or *losmen* in a new town. Passengers sit side by side in front of the driver *(tukang becak)*, a canvas or cloth canopy giving some measure of protection from the sun, exhaust fumes, and dust. When it rains, the protection is augmented by a large flap of transparent plastic. Truly one of the great experiences of Asia is to ride in a *becak*. At the flick of the wrist you can signal a turn to the L or right. In the evenings glide under starlight, trees, street lamps with just the sound of 3 rubber tires rolling on the pavement. If you're traveling beside a lake or low canal it feels like you're skimming along the surface of the water in a boat. No other form of conveyance combines all the viewing advantages of walking-pace travel with the comforts of a city taxi. In the gaudily painted *becak*, you'll drink in more sights, become more immersed in the local atmosphere, even carry on conversations with passersby as you roll along. A *becak* driver can take you to places completely inaccessible to cars and taxis.

Few work harder for their bowl of rice than the *becak* driver. Though he speaks rudimentary English at best, you won't find a better guide than your *tukang becak;* he knows where to change money, where the best craft shops, entertainment districts, and the cheapest hotels are. He will walk you up hills, pushing you from behind. You may expect this, it's normal, but if the hill is too steep, get out and walk to give the guy a break. His thighs are enormous, his shirt is wet with sweat, his lifespan averages 40 years, most dying of an overworked, enlarged heart. Not many men make it their first choice. The number of *becak* is a barometer of a city's poverty and unemployment level. Look at the scarcity of *becak* on Bali where so many tourists (and money) are concentrated. But on an island as densely populated as Java, any kind of gainful occupation is better than none. Yet *your* driver is one of the lucky ones in that you've given him a (probably) overcharged fare. For 10 minutes' labor he can sit down and eat a full-course meal. Many also earn commissions for leading tourists into crafts shops. In Yogya (C. Java), when *becak* drivers offer to take you around to *batik* factories for 2 hours for only Rp200-300, they are after sales commissions.

Fares

Becak are usually leased by the drivers. Since up to ⅓ of the fare goes to the *becak* owner, *becak* are often more expensive than *bemo.* Costing Rp300-600 for a 1- to 5-km ride, *becak* are considered by Indonesians slightly extravagant. They are most often used on nights out, by the Chinese, by children going to school (up to 6 at a time!), by people on their way back from the market when they have a heavy burden. It costs Rp400 by *becak* from the Blitar (E. Java) bus station to a hotel, whereas the same Rp400 gets you by bus all the way to Tulungagung, 33 km down the road! If you want to walk instead of taking a *becak,* you can save yourself the price of a meal. So use *becak* prudently. There are no fixed fares; they vary according to the distance, how hungry the driver is for a fare, his ulterior motives, and on your bargaining skills. Find out the approximate fare to a place from a shopkeeper, hotel proprietor, or bystander. Also be aware that the fare is 20-30% more for 2 people. Fares could also be higher at night or when it's raining. Don't have a *becak* driver wait, he'll charge you extra for his time. There's no shortage of *becak,* so let him go, just get another when you're ready to leave. If you have many errands or stops to make, *becak* can be hired at about Rp600-1000 per hour (expect the lower end in impoverished areas such as E. Java and the higher end in cities such as Jakarta). An advantage of hiring a *becak* by the hour is that you can stop anytime you want, observe, talk to people, ask questions, shop at markets, take photographs.

If you can take the *becak* driver out of earshot of his cronies, he'll be more likely to agree to a *harga biasa* (normal fare). Don't try to bargain with "tourist" *becak* at bus stations and outside of popular tourist and travelers hotels and sites. Just walk a block away in any direction and look for another one (it really helps to know Indonesian). Try to choose an older *becak* driver over a younger one; they know better the true value of money, are not as savvy, and can be bargained with more easily. The younger, more ambitious drivers want up to Rp1500-2000 an hour. The "walk-away" technique works really well with *becak* drivers. There are always 10 or more drivers to step into his place if he doesn't accept your offer. Haggle for a moment, it's part of the game. Never give anything to your *becak* driver that will lead him to expect more, or else there will be a big argument over money. Since generosity is so often confused with abundance, it may cause problems if you give cigarettes, drinks, or whatever away. **Note:** Though pedicabs are easy to find in most towns and cities, they are usually restricted to operating only on the peripheries of Indonesia's really big cities. Those areas in which pedicabs are prohibited are called Daerah Bebas Becak or DBB (pronounced DE-BE-BE).

Paying

Never pay till the end. Get change before the ride because drivers very often won't give you, or genuinely don't have, the exact change. If you tell him you have to go looking for change, suddenly he remembers he has some. Never hand a driver a large bill (over Rp1000), believing that he will fetch you the correct change; always assume he'll run off with the money. If you don't have it, go and get the money changed yourself at the nearest vendor, restaurant, or from someone in the street. Let him do the waiting, not you. It may take 5 minutes or so to get your change but at least you won't be taken. Have him put the correct change into your hand first, then pay him. If he raises a stink about the amount he receives, it's hardly worth an altercation. Just hand him that little extra money (what, 20 cents?!). If you agreed to the fare before you climbed in and afterwards he wants more, ask him if he'd like to go to the police with you. That usually ends it. When hiring a *becak* driver (or a porter), a good rule of thumb to use when determining what to pay is to first make inquiries as to the normal full-day's wage for a day laborer (Rp2000-3000 per day in Indonesia), then pay no more than twice that.

TAXIS

Taxis—licensed and metered, as we know them in the West—are available only in Jakarta. In the rest of Indonesia private cars are customarily used as taxis, for which you pay an agreed-upon or fixed amount. You can usually find taxis on certain streets in inner areas of the city, or outside the larger hotels. Or you can call the nearest taxi company. With the notable exception of Jakarta, highly trafficked profitable routes, such as between airports and major cities, are seldom serviced by buses or other modes of transport. In these cases, taxis are the only game in town. To save in taxi costs from airports into cities (sometimes as far as 25 km!), befriend someone on the plane or wait at the taxi desk for someone to share the costs with. It is also frequently possible just to walk 1 or 2 kilometers outside the airport gate to a main highway and flag down a *bemo* or minibus into town. When heading from cities out to the airport, always hire local transport vehicles such as *bemo, kijang, bajai* or minibuses which charter at much cheaper rates than taxis. When arriving in large Indonesian cities (for example, Semarang, Yogya, Solo, or Medan), hire a taxi at designated desks in the airport terminal. In Jakarta, go outside and climb into one of the taxis which constantly pass in front of the terminal (Rp15,000 into the city). Bear in mind that taxi (and *bajai*) drivers speak little English and often know only the names of major streets.

Fares

Though taxis are a near-at-hand mode of transport and very convenient, they are expensive if you travel alone. If you have friends to share the fare with, taxis could be better value than even public transport. Licensed taxis equipped with a meter usually charge Rp500 for the first km plus Rp150 for each additional km. Taxis may also be chartered at about Rp4500-5000 per hour, or by the day or week. For longer distances, shared taxis are a comfortable, streamlined way to travel. Get a group of up to 5 people together and call 2 days in advance. Shared taxi companies operate between Jakarta and Bandung, Cirebon, Tasikmalaya and Semarang, or between Solo, Semarang and Yogya. Shared taxi companies also operate in Medan (N. Sumatra) and Padang (W. Sumatra).

PRIVATE VEHICLES

Privately Owned Hire Cars

Private, unlicensed "taxis" found in many provincial towns are for the most part older vehicles. Their rate is approximately Rp3500-5000 per hour, depending on how well you can bargain, how badly they need the fare, the type or newness of the car, length of hire, and distance. In many cases, a friendly bout of haggling can quickly produce very acceptable results. Two hours is usually the minimum period. Cars which have been in junkyards for 20 years in America are still alive and well here. These privately owned vehicles, crammed full of people, animals, and goods, shuttle back and forth over short distances. Even in the outskirts of Jakarta, 1950's Austins and Chevrolets are still used for city-fringe transportation needs. These

old cars, with heavy-gauge steel bodies, seem to run forever. Indonesians are ingenious at fashioning spare parts or rendering outlandish repairs to keep their cars running almost indefinitely. In some cases they actually tool parts like carburetors themselves or substitute Japanese spare parts. In the cities, the cars used tend to be newer-generation Japanese compacts. The number of cars has increased, but still only 20% of the people own a car.

Bemo Hire

A handy means of sightseeing for a small (4-5) group of people. It's frequently easier and cheaper to hire an *oplet, bemo,* minibus, or private car in each place you visit than to go to the trouble and expense of dealing with a taxi or an official car rental agency. There's hardly a road in Indonesia which is not traveled regularly by *oplet* or *bemo;* some roads are so deplorable you wouldn't touch them with a car! If you hire a *bemo,* they not only cost less than a rented Landrover, jeep, or car but in most instances the owner pays for the gas. And you don't have to pay for the driver's food and accommodation either, since you can quickly find a new *bemo* to hire by the day in each new town you visit. To hire a *bemo* for a whole day (0800-1700), count on between Rp20,000-25,000 (including driver). If chartering by the hour (Rp3000-5000), make it clear that each quarter of an hour beyond the estimated number of hours will be charged at ¼ of the hourly rate because they often expect you to "round it off." Write down the starting time on a piece of paper and put it up on the dashboard. Don't let the driver and helper jam 16 of their friends in once you start your charter. Bear in mind that smaller *bemo* hire out for less than larger *bemo,* and that *bajai* are the cheapest of all (perhaps Rp3000 per hour).

If you want to travel from point A to B, hiring a *bemo* could work out cheaper or equal to the cost of doing the same run in sections. For example, if 5 of you wanted to go from Yogya to Borobudur you would first have to take a bus to Muntilan (Rp700 pp), then a public *bemo* from Muntilan to the temple for another Rp400 pp. The total of Rp5500 your group would spend is perhaps more than it would've cost to hire a *bemo* direct from Yogya to Borobudur. To determine how much a charter is worth, estimate how much the vehicle would earn if it were transporting passengers during the same time period you want to charter it for. In other words, you have to compensate for its "down time," plus a little bit extra.

Car Rentals

There are numerous car rental agencies, including Avis (Jl. Diponegoro 25, tel. 341964/349206, Jakarta). Daily rates are around US$70 per day; lowest self-drive rate is US$77 (for a Ford Laser). National Car Rental (Kartika Plaza Hotel, Jl. Thamrin 10, tel.

332006/322849, Jakarta) offers cheaper rates. It's also possible to rent by the hour. Avis in Jakarta and Bali offer chauffeur-driven cars starting at US$10 per hour for a 4-seat Toyota. There's usually no tax, gasoline is included, and you must be at least 25 years old (19 for National). An International Driver's License is usually not necessary; any valid license is sufficient.

Nitour (Jl. Majapahit 2, tel. 340955, Jakarta 10160) and Pacto Ltd. (Jl. Surabaya 8, tel. 347457, Jakarta 10320), Indonesian-based companies found in all the bigger towns, are trustworthy car rental agencies. In Bali, hotels and travel agencies arrange car rentals. If you go through an agency and hire a Landrover, get the long-chassis model with the wide wheel base as passengers are really jounced around on rough roads in the model with the short wheel base.

Sopir

Unlike many other Asian countries such as India, Pakistan, or even Thailand, Westerners in Indonesia often drive themselves. However, when hiring cars most newcomers to Indonesia think it wise to use a chauffeur or driver *(sopir)* because they don't know the language and are not used to the country's crowded and hazardous road conditions (left-hand drive, for example). Remember that the streets in most Indonesian cities, and also the main roads between cities, are very busy from dawn to dusk, especially on Java. If you are not happy in a sea of thick, fast-moving traffic—everything from buzzing mopeds, trucks, and buses to plodding oxcarts, *becak*, and pedestrians—it's best to leave your first car trip in the hands of a capable local driver. Oftentimes, you don't have a choice in the matter, as private vehicles are usually not rented without an accompanying driver. An Indonesian driver can probably get you to your destination hours faster (and safer) than if you drove, including time for a picnic along the way. And if there's an accident, your driver will be responsible, not you. If you hit a pedestrian, invariably the attitude of the villagers will be hostile, the motorist *ipso facto* guilty.

This probably won't happen, but a *sopir* often is used less to explain things to you than to explain you to the people! A driver-guide frees you from always explaining that you're not an invader; he helps Indonesians get over the surprise. *Sopir* also clean and maintain the car. Though drivers are not that expensive, a rented car could still be more expensive than a taxi. Expect a lot of parking and entrance fees if you hire a car; the driver could be in collusion with parking lot attendants or the keeper of the gate and you could be charged numerous unnecessary and inflated fees. Where do you find a good driver? Your hotel proprietor or the local tourist office can probably recommend one.

MOTORING IN INDONESIA

Drive Your Own Car

A personal car for sightseeing, shopping, and trips to the mountains or seashore adds a great deal of convenience and independence. Until very recently the Indonesian government restricted the import of privately owned vehicles to diplomatic passport holders. But now you can bring your own car into Indonesia, as long as you take it out again when the visit is over. Importing a car for personal use is tax-free and, provided international documents are produced (obtainable in the visitor's home country), the procedures are simple. For people bringing in their own vehicle, the following documents are required: an International Certificate of Insurance; motor vehicle registration book or ownership (called *Buku Pemilik Kendaraan Bermotor)*, obtainable from the police; and a *Carnet de Passage*, which is a letter of guarantee that the motor vehicle will be exported after completion of visit or proof that an onward passage has been booked for the motor vehicle.

Alternatively, you can buy a car while there. Be forewarned, however, that cars are very expensive by U.S. standards. Road taxes, depending on the car size, can run from US$500 to $900 per year. Insurance is a necessity; companies, all with offices in Jakarta, include: PT Asuransi Bintat (specializes in car insurance); Union Insurance Society of Canton, Ltd. (a UK company offering all types of insurance); the American Insurance Company (under U.S. management, offering comprehensive coverage worldwide); and American International Underwriters Ltd. (also provides comprehensive coverage). Insurance rates run from US$500-$800 per year. An International License is obtained in your country upon presentation of a valid license. On Bali, you must get a local license and take a road test. The drawback to driving your own car is that you might not truly experience Indonesia, only drive through it. Only when and if you step from the metal box will you taste Indonesia firsthand. So just use a car to get places—then start walking or biking.

Tips

Roads and bridges are being improved and new roads and superhighways built at a frenetic pace in Indonesia. Depending on the season and local road conditions, it's possible to drive from Jakarta to the eastern tip of Java (over 1,200 km) in 2 or 3 days. On the archipelago's smaller outer islands few roads are asphalted, and road conditions are utterly unpredictable. One year a road is excellent and well paved, the next it's no more than a bumpy river bed. On Sumatra and Sulawesi, roads are frequently washed out or wiped out by landslides; while traffic piles up to either side of the huge hole in the road, everyone waits for someone to come along who wants to get across worse than they do. Agricultural estate roads are rarely asphalted but they usually have a good all-weather gravel surface. On jungle roads, the rain can be so dense it clatters on your hood like nails and steams up the interior until you run with sweat. Because of heat, dust, and traffic fumes, most people prefer their cars air-conditioned. On long journeys, take iced drinks or water and snack foods that don't require refrigeration. When traveling by car, remember that maps can be misleading as to the size, importance, and conditions of roads. Much signposting is left over from Dutch times. Should you follow the wrong road to an unexpected or unfamiliar destination, seek assistance from the local government office. The *kepala kampung* (village headman), *bupati* (district head), or *lurah* (area head) can help you find the right road or accommodations for the night. If you're stopped by a cop, talk to him a few minutes to make sure he's serious. If he is, nip it in the bud and pay him Rp10,000 right away. Don't hand over your license and registration or it'll cost you Rp60,000-70,000 in legal costs to get them back.

Called benzine or *premium* in Indonesia, gas costs around Rp600 per liter. Only the state-owned Pertamina Company may sell gasoline. Both high-and lower-octane gasolines are sold (standard U.S. 6-cylinder or low compression 8-cylinder cars operate adequately on it). If you're renting a car or *oplet* with a driver, be sure that it's understood which party is to pay for the gas. It's not necessary to carry extra gasoline while motoring in Java, but since stations are often few and far between, fill your tank when you see one. Car repair (labor costs only) averages Rp4000 per hour.

BUS TRAVEL

Buses are cheaper and slower—but with assigned seating slightly less crowded—than a *bemo* or minibus. There's generally more elbow room (except on the legendary Sumatran buses) than a minibus offers. On a bus you're also high above the road so you can take in more of the countryside. Seats in the front of the bus, particularly just behind the driver, tend to be somewhat bigger and more comfortable than rear seats. Pick buses that seat 4 across (pay Rp500 extra) which are more comfortable than 5-across buses. The most comfortable seats on the whole bus, as far as riding out the bumps go, are in the middle *(di tengah)*, but not over the wheel. Children sit wherever there is a small space, which might be beside the already-flattened traveler. Depending on the weather, you might want to sit by the open door for free air conditioning. Local public buses are frequent and very useful for the short sightseeing jaunts. Daytime travel on buses on congested roads is slow and exhausting; they go much faster in the cool of the night. On long-distance buses you take about an hour to cover 40 km; use this formula to calculate roughly the length of time it takes to get somewhere. Some itineraries are more picturesque to travel by bus than by train, such as from Karangpanjang to Lubuklinggau, S. Sumatra. There are other segments where it's more expedient to take a bus because fleets of them leave constantly: for example, from Jakarta to Bogor or from Denpasar to Surabaya. On many routes (such as ¾ of Sumatra), there are no rail connections; you have no choice but to take buses. There is a widespread bus system on Java, yet buses still aren't as cheap as 3rd Class rail, and for the longer distances on Java it's generally more relaxing to take trains.

Local Buses

Local buses offer slow but frequent service between, and can even be used for exploring around, most small towns and cities. Destinations are posted above the front windshield. At big city bus stations there will usually be a row of buses with their engines running, ready to pull out. If the first bus is full, just climb on the one behind which will be ready to leave within minutes. Once these local buses are on the road, however, anywhere you're standing when the bus comes by, *that's* the bus stop. Often there's standing room only. Be extra careful with your money and valuables—lots of pickpockets.

Bis Kota

These inexpensive intra-city buses are available only in such major cities as Jakarta, Bandung, Yogya, Semarang, and Surabaya, with fares of Rp100-200 no matter your destination in town. *Bis kota*, which only stop at designated bus stops, tend to be very crowded, noisy, hot, and uncomfortable. City bus route maps are not available except in Jakarta, so go up to the guys in the white shirts and ask directions. In some cities, like Jakarta, *bis kota* stop only at designated bus stops. In other cities, like Yogya, just flag them down at the side of the street.

Bis Malam

Longer distances between major cities are often connected by *bis malam* (night buses). These specialized nonstop buses usually leave in the late afternoon or early evening and arrive the next morning or afternoon, with a limited number of stops (about once every 3 hours) for light meals. The Indonesian equivalent of U.S.'s Greyhound and Australia's Pioneer bus systems, *bis malam* are safer, cooler, faster, and more expensive than regular day buses. The journey from Jakarta to Bali, for example, takes 3 days, with transfers at Semarang and Surabaya. There is even a *bis malam* service across the whole of western Indonesia, from Denpasar (Bali) all the way to Aceh on the northern tip of Sumatra (though you have to change buses 4 or 5 times). Ask around amongst other travelers and *losmen* proprietors as to which bus companies are currently the best; they could also advise you where to book seats. Some of the longer routes are serviced by Mercedes deluxe a/c buses (these tend to be smaller than European Mercedes, though they hold just as many passengers). Some bus companies keep brand-new Mercedes buses out in front of their offices to lure you in, then when you show up for your 30-hour journey, it's in an old crate crammed full of as many people as is humanly possible.

Except in big cities like Jakarta where all passengers alight at the Pulo Gadung Bus Station, the new generation of *bis malam* with airline seats, onboard toilets, and full a/c will even drop you off wherever you wish once you arrive at your destination. A *nasi padang* meal, snack, and drinks are sometimes included in the price of a ticket. Your money and valuables should be kept in your shoulder or handbag which you should lean against or sleep on while traveling. If your rucksack is put on the roof, personally see that it's properly tied down (some travelers even habitually padlock and chain it to the roof rack!). No standing passengers are usually allowed, so get your ticket the morning of the day you want to depart (tickets are often sold out by 1300). Even better, buy your ticket the day before departure so you can be assured of getting a hand-picked seat which will accommodate your long legs. If you roll into a town or city during the day and buy your tickets in advance, you may store your things safely in a *bis malam* company office or even a local bus station office while you wander around until departure time.

Fares

Buses are the cheapest way to get around within Indonesia. You can figure out what the fare should be if you know the distance: by government regulation, bus companies in Indonesia can't charge more than Rp15 per km for good roads, Rp17 per km for bad roads. Bear in mind that in Kalimantan, Irian Jaya, and Sulawesi, fares run a little higher. Fares for short distances (especially on Java and Bali) are extraordinarily cheap. Few local 20-km-plus rides ever cost more than one U.S. dollar and it's unbelievably exhausting to do more than Rp10,000 worth of bus travel in one day. With minibuses you can often haggle about the price, but on the big express buses there's usually a standard fare which is fixed and unarguably cheap. Fares are almost always posted on the ticket window *(loket)* in the bus station. Children ages 4-11 are usually charged ½ the adult ticket; under 4, free. Excess baggage is often charged at least ¼ of adult fare. You hear of some travelers succeeding in getting a student's discount; it might be worth a try.

TRAIN TRAVEL

Sadly, Indonesia's unique state railway system (PJKA) has been neglected, while stinking, noisy *bemo, oplet,* and minibuses continue to proliferate. Indonesian railways date back to the late 19th C; at one time, the Java State Railway held a world record for the longest nonstop narrow guage running between Batavia and Surabaya. In those days all trains ceased running at dusk because of "hazards of the jungle." During the Japanese occupation, most of the country's motive power and rolling stock was removed to Manchuria. There are now 7,891 km of track, all on Java, Madura, and Sumatra. Java's rail system, the most extensive in Indonesia, runs the whole length of the island, connecting the E coast with the ferry for Bali and the W coast with the ferry to Sumatra. In Sumatra, trains connect the port of Telukbetung with Palembang and Lubuklinggau in the S, while other tracks connect Padang (W. Sumatra) with inland Lake Singkarak and the port of Belawan to Medan in the north.

A decade ago Java was still the equivalent of a wildlife sanctuary for rare engines, with over 700 active steam locomotives made up of no less than 69 classes. No steam engines were ever built on Java, and those that are now retired are all of unique design from European manufacturers. As of spring 1987, all of the huge, black, lumbering, coal-burning locomotives have been phased out of passenger operation. A few of the country's steam locomotives — museum pieces in the West — can still be seen hauling freight and sugar in E. Java and two are left in Medan. Now India and China are more relevant destinations for rail enthusiasts. Occasionally you can see locos puffing out of the railyards in Madiun (E. Java); these yards should be visited sooner rather than later. Behemoths such as Mallets or Hartmanns, their smokestacks belching steam and soot, can also be seen hauling rolling stock up severe gradients in the vicinity of Bandung at Cibatu. Another big draw for rail buffs is the open-air museum at Ambarawa in C. Java (S of Semarang) where 22 steam locomotives (B2220, C2821, C2407, C2728, C1801, etc.) have been let out to pasture. Charter groups can enjoy the thrill of a steam-hauled ride aboard a vintage Swiss-built cogwheel tank loco from Ambarawa to Bedono through scenic hilly terrain; book through the PJKA office, Jl. Thamrin 3, Semarang. In 1988, aficionados may join one of 5 groups expected to take part in a 14-day rail tour. The program starts in Jakarta and goes all the way by train to Bandung, Yogya, Surabaya, and Banyuwangi; the highlight of the W. Suma-

double mallet gathering steam, Madiun's railyard, E. Java

tra segment is the spectacular 5-hour trip on a cog railway between Padang and Batu Tebal (Lake Singkarak). For more information, contact Pacto Ltd., Jl. Surabaya 8, Jakarta 10320, tel. 347457/347433/347426/347919.

Advantages

For the longer distances, trains are slower though less tiring and more comfortable than buses, minibuses or *bemo*. Trains are also cheaper, provide refreshments, and offer color and scenery without the numbing discomfort and moments of utter terror which typify a long-distance bus or minibus ride. On trains you're sitting in relative comfort, there's fresh air coming in, you can get up and stretch your legs, vendors walk up and down the aisles selling refreshments, you can read your newspaper or book, and it's easy to strike up conversations with other passengers. Another big advantage to train travel is the convenience of journeying from city center to city center with no transfer fares to pay, no weather delays or road obstacles. On Java you can travel from Jakarta to Surabaya by fast, diesel-fueled a/c express trains day or night; the *Bima* passes through Yogya and Solo, while the *Mutiara* takes the northern route through Semarang. The *Parahyangan* offers 4 services daily between Jakarta and Bandung, taking only 4 hours. The bigger cities such as Surabaya and Jakarta have several different stations serving W-, S-, and E-bound trains. Your hotel clerk or the tourist office can advise you as to which city station is for you and the easiest way to get to it.

Practicalities

Regular day trains make more stops than night trains, have no a/c, but offer an ever-changing view of rural Java for a cheaper rate. However, many travelers opt for cooler nighttime travel, particularly on the long and medium-distance hauls. Most trains in Indonesia don't run to their timetables, and schedules change frequently. Arriving later than expected can be a nuisance, and many trains arrive 1-2 hours early as well. For example, try getting into Lubuklinggau (Sumatra) at 0300 instead of at the promised 0600. In these instances, just stay at the station, find the buffet, drink coffee and eat bananas until dawn. It's wise to take your own food and water since the food on trains and/or train platforms is often bland, expensive, and made without much care. Have a couple of *nasi campur* (Rp1000-1500) made up for you at a good private *warung* prior to boarding; they keep the night. Fruit, snacks, and drinks may be purchased from vendors. For meeting people, the dining car is the best place to hang out.

Fares

Fares are not posted in most train stations but schedules often are. Student discounts are given at the ticket window *(loket)* and differ as much as 10-25%; they usually only apply to the cheaper economy 3rd Class day trains. Trains have different prices at different times of day. Fares vary from train to train too, as well as by class. There are many different types of trains. Some are decrepit, slow, noisy, with hard seats; others are sleek, fast, comfortable, and expensive. An economy-class seat on the a/c *Bima II* from Jakarta to Surabaya costs Rp19,700, while a 3rd Class seat on the *GBM Selatan* for the same run costs only Rp6800. Special night express trains, such as the *Mutiara Utara*, and day express trains such as the *Ekspres Siang*, connect Bandung and Surabaya via Yogya. The *Bima* and the *Mutiara Utara* of Java are the luxury trains, linking Jakarta and Surabaya; the *Bima* is the only one which has sleepers. The *GBM Cepat* ("Fast") and *Senja* trains are lumbering and crowded. It's best to travel in the more expensive but infinitely superior trains (even 3rd

Class is OK). For anyone used to train fares in many other parts of the world — Europe, for example — the cost of rail travel in Indonesia is astonishingly cheap. Where else, except for India, can you travel in comfort at express speeds for 3 hours for a fare of around US$1.00? Try it, between Jakarta and Bandung, on the fast *Parahyangan* trains (5 departures daily). Fares range from only US$12-25 for the journey all the way from Jakarta-Yogya-Semarang, depending on the class of travel and category of train. **Note:** If your ticket costs Rp200-400 more than the fare you see listed, a "station fee" *(bea stasiun)* has been added; the amount of the fee depends on the ticket price.

Reservations/Buying Tickets

Obtaining a train ticket can be an infuriating experience in Indonesia. As trains are heavily booked, it's often difficult to obtain tickets at the last minute. Double-check schedules. If you board a train without a reserved seat, you'll end up standing and swaying the whole way. Seat reservations at some stations and for some trains are available only one day in advance; in other cities tickets can be bought 3 days before departure; in yet other cities, only 1 hour before departure! In Jakarta, tickets can be bought only on the day of departure so rise early, get in line, and expect to wait for as long as 2-3 hours. Observe Weber's Rule: the longer you stand in line, the more likely it is the wrong line. Also tickets could be sold out before you reach the agent. If this happens, it sometimes helps to make a direct appeal at the Kantor Kepala Stasiun (Stationmaster's Office) where they possibly could conjure up an extra ticket or 2 for *pegawi* and frustrated Westerners (at Jakarta's Gambir Station, there's even a special window serving foreigners). A roundtrip by train cannot be booked; return reservations must be made at the point of departure. To save the hassle of getting to a station and waiting in line, reservations may be made 1-3 days in advance through a travel agency for a small charge.

BY AIR

For internal destinations, surface transportation is much cheaper and in some cases more easily available than flights. However, you'll find that often the only alternative to a lengthy land or sea passage — particularly in the Outer Islands — is to take scheduled flights (such as between Bali-Lombok; Gorontalo-Palu, C. Sulawesi; Palembang-Bengkulu; Ambon-Banda; Padang-Jakarta). This means that, given the limited 2 months you have in Indonesia, if you want to see the Outer Islands beyond Java, Sumatra, and Bali, flying is almost unavoidable. Flying in Indonesia is a breeze; the skies are empty (and safer) and the weather usually clear. There are 45 private or semi-

private airlines, some foreign-controlled, and some involved primarily with mineral development, flying a zany collection of aircraft. State-run Garuda Indonesia is the largest Indonesian airline, and offers both domestic and international services. Other airlines, offering mainly domestic flights, include Merpati (owned by Garuda), Mandala, Bouraq, Sempati, Pelita, and Seulawah, all of whose services average 15-25% cheaper than Garuda. These alternative airlines concentrate in the low-traffic, outer fringe areas of the archipelago on sectors not covered by Garuda. Most big towns in Indonesia are connected to Jakarta by air.

Costs/Practicalities

There could be quite a difference in the fares offered by different airlines between the same 2 points. Check Mandala and Bouraq airlines; they may well be cheaper. Also, if you've decided where you'll be flying to in Indonesia, tickets may be cheaper to buy in Australia, Japan, or Bangkok before you go. For example, it's possible to make bookings in Australia for Garuda flights within Indonesia. Always compare your home-country prices against the *rupiah* prices. Most airlines only give student discounts to Indonesian students, and then only with special letters from school registrars, *plus* much stuffing about. ASEAN students, and on occasion Western students, might get a 25-30% reduction in airfares upon presentation of their student ID if they talk hard and long enough. A charter aircraft costs US$300-800 per hour, depending on the type of aircraft.

At the main airline offices or tourist information centers in Indonesia's big cities, get ahold of the various airline timetables *(tarip penumpang)* which give routes, fares, flight frequencies, and addresses of all the provincial offices of each airline. Always confirm flight availability and book a seat at the local airline office in your city of departure. This is especially important in the eastern islands where flights are less frequent and seats tend to fill up quickly. Merpati is less adept than Garuda when it comes to confirming tickets; expect your name not to appear on the passenger list. When ordering or confirming airline tickets through hotels or travel agencies, for their legwork they could charge Rp2000-2500 extra per ticket. Airport tax ranges from Rp1000 to Rp2000 for internal flights, and Rp6000 for external flights. Baggage allowances are from 10 kg (on smaller planes such as the 16-passenger Fokker Friendship) up to 20 kg (normal allowance); excess baggage charge is about Rp1500 per kg (if they even bother to charge you). If you are carrying a lot of gear, you have to grit your teeth and pay for it. Avoid paying too much by maxing out your carry-on allowance. If you know you're returning to the same airport, most have luggage storage facilities (Rp500-1000 per day).

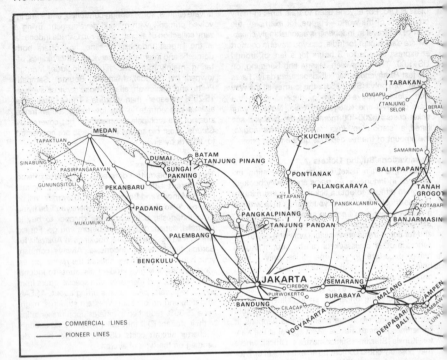

COMMERCIAL LINES
PIONEER LINES

Try to get a seat in front of the wings so you can enjoy some of Indonesia's spectacular volcanic and marine scenery during your flight. The pilots and other crew members on Indonesian aircraft can be incredibly accommodating and hospitable. For example, if you're a pilot you could get invited into the open cockpit, and there are stories of Indonesian pilots swooping low over volcanos at the special request of the passengers. But be loose. Your flight to Ujung Pandang or Medan is very likely to be late *after* you've arrived at the airport the required 2 hours early. And perhaps the plane won't take off at all. Or you could be asked to move to the front of the plane for some inexplicable, slightly foreboding, reason. Garuda is the exception. Of the 33 flights I took with Garuda over a 60-day period in 1987, only 1 flight was postponed, a dozen flights were delayed 10-15 minutes, and only 2-3 flights were over an hour late.

Arriving/Airport Transport
A good number of Indonesia's provincial airfields—particularly in the eastern islands—are served only by Skyvans and consist of just a grassy strip. Goats and cows must be chased off before planes can land, and the "terminal" might consist of a thatch hut with a single wooden table. In the Outer Islands airstrips are often far from town but you can usually hitch a ride in with the crew, the airlines may provide transport, or you can walk out to the nearest road and hail a passing *bemo*, minibus, or motorcycle. In the larger cities taxis into town are often available through the taxi desk in the terminal. The fares are always fixed. In places like Ambon, Torajaland, and Jayapura, astronomical fares (Rp15,000!) are demanded for relatively short distances. If it's a private taxi, wait until most of the other passengers have left, then he may come down in price. Or just walk several kilometers out to the main highway and hitch or take a *bis kota*. Frequently you can get a free ride in from the airport by choosing a hotel which will pay your taxi fare if you stay there. Look for signs on the wall or for men holding up placards. Places to stay are also suggested by the airport tourist or taxi booths, with free rides into town often thrown in.

Merpati
Means "pigeon." Merpati is the second national carrier and flies turboprop aircraft to about 110 destinations within Indonesia as well as some border-crossing flights to Australia and Eastern Malaysia.

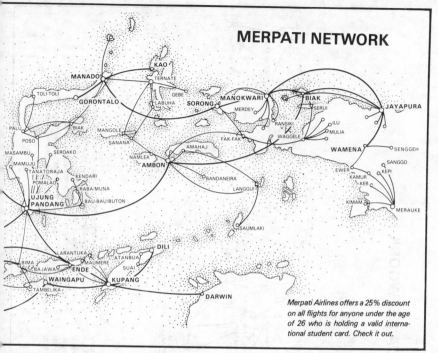

MERPATI NETWORK

Merpati Airlines offers a 25% discount on all flights for anyone under the age of 26 who is holding a valid international student card. Check it out.

Owned by Garuda, the understanding is that Merpati service remote destinations and not compete for customers with Garuda on the higher-profit, heavily trafficked routes. Providing an air bridge for the people of remote areas to district centers and provincial capitals, Merpati flies to virtually all parts of the country. It is particularly active in eastern Indonesia (like from Ambon to Langgur in the Kais, Rp84,600) and to really isolated corners of the archipelago such as the Baliem Valley (Irian Jaya), Palu (C. Sulawesi), and Longbawan (E. Kalimantan). In Western New Guinea alone, Merpati serves 40 airstrips. Merpati operates a laughable variety of outlandish aircraft including Vanguards, 707s, Viscounts, Skyvans, Twin Otters. Getting your money out of Merpati if a flight is canceled is like getting water out of a rock. They are also notorious for making it difficult to replace lost tickets. Head office: Jl. Angkasa 2, Jakarta; tel. 413608/417404.

Garuda Indonesia

The flag carrier of Indonesia, 40-year-old Garuda is the largest of all the Indonesian airlines, flying long-distance international routes to major Asian, European, and Australian cities, as well as a wide-ranging domestic network of 35 destinations. Whereas most other domestic airlines use only propeller-driven planes, Garuda uses modern jet-powered DC-9s, DC-10s, 747s, A300 Airbuses, and F-28 jets. Named after Vishnu's legendary mount in the Hindu *Ramayana* epic, Garuda is more efficient and more modernly equipped than other Indonesian airlines. Their planes are usually half full and you can grab any seat you want. Curiously, the lack of competition has not meant poor service; subsidized and well-funded by the government, Garuda's staff is courteous, its pilots professional, its aircraft well-maintained, and its ticketing and seat reservations service fully computerized. They are also about 15-20% more expensive. Unlike other Indonesian airlines, Garuda offers direct flights from Jakarta to destinations of commercial or tourist importance in the archipelago; it also offers shuttle flights to Surabaya and Semarang several times daily. Garuda's international service (28 cities in 5 continents) is even higher grade because they have to compete with other crack international airlines (their international flights are dearer than most). Garuda has also expanded its operations to include "exotic holidays for independent travelers," i.e. tours of Jakarta, Bandung, Yogya, Solo, Surabaya, Bali, Lake Toba, as well as "golfing holidays" and "nature

GARUDA NETWOORK

airlines, history: The Dutch parent company, KLM, established the KNILM to provide air links for mail and the military in the Dutch East Indies in 1928. The first service began between Batavia and Semarang and Batavia and Bandung with a Fokker F-VII (a single-engine, 8-seat monoplane). KNILM also operated the first regional air network in South and SE Asia with the initiation of services from Batavia to Singapore and Medan in 1931.

While the Indonesians were struggling for their independence from 1945 to 1949, several Indonesian air force officers established Indonesian Airways in Rangoon, Burma, on 28 Jan. 1949 — the first airline representing the newly formed Republic. This airline was dissolved in 1950 and the government established Garuda. From its formation in 1949 until 1962, Garuda was the only carrier serving Indonesian domestic markets.

packages.'' Bookings may be made through any Garuda sales office.

In Indonesia, Garuda's head office is at Jl. Ir. H. Juanda 15, Jakarta; tel. 370709. They also have offices in 34 other Indonesian cities, from Merauke (Irian Jaya) to Banda Aceh (N. Sumatra). International offices are located in **Australia:** 144 North Terrace, tel. 217 3333, Adelaide; Corner Todd and Person Sts., tel. 50 5211/50 5236, Alice Springs; Corner Adelaide and Greek Sts., tel. 33 2011/31 0311, Brisbane; Alinga St., Civic Centre, tel. 48 8433/46 021, Canberra; 16 Benner St., tel. 816422/811103, Darwin; 45 Bourke St., tel. 654 2522, Melbourne; AMP Bldg., 140 St. George St., tel. 481 0963/322 4000, Perth; 4 Bligh St., Capel Court, Bligh House, tel. 323 6044, Sydney; in **North America** 360 East Randolf, Ste. 2704, Chicago; Indonesian Consulate General Bldg., 3457 Wilshire Blvd., tel. 387 3323/387 0651, Los Angeles; 51 East 42nd St., Ste. 413-415, tel. 370 0707/826 2829, New York; KLM, 327 Bay St., tel. 366 9041, Toronto; in **Europe:** Singel 540, tel. 272 626, Amsterdam; Poststrasse 2-4, tel. 2380688, Frankfurt; Bureau de Swissair, Voyages Aeriens, Gare de Cornavin, tel. 982121, Geneva; Hermanstrasse 40, tel. 327450/59, Hamburg; 35 Duke Street, tel. 4863011/9353780, London W1M 5DF; 17 Ave. Hoche, 3rd Fl., tel. 45624545, Paris; Via Berberini 103, tel. 4755813/15, Rome; Kungsgaten 35, tel. 218811/218830, Stockholm.

Domestic Discounted Fares

It was a great blow to travelers and tourists when Garuda terminated its "Visit Indonesia Airpass" program in October of 1988. Garuda still offers a discount program which you should take advantage of if you'll be doing a lot of flying around Indonesia. It's more complicated than the VIAP, so have a qualified travel agent help you figure out your most cost-effective itinerary.

1) A 50% discount to domestic sector fares is applied for passengers from Europe, Australia, USA, Hong Kong or Japan to points in Sulawesi, Maluku, and Irian Jaya.

2) A 25% discount to domestic sector fares is applied for passengers originating from points in Europe, Australia, USA, Hong Kong, and Japan to other islands in Indonesia (Java, Bali, Sumatra, Timor, Lombok, Kalimantan).

3) A 25% discount to domestic sector fares is applied for passengers originating from points other than Europe, Australia, USA, Hong Kong, and Japan to Sulawesi, Maluku, and Irian Jaya.

4) A 25% discount on domestic sector fares is applied for passengers originating from points other than Europe, Australia, USA, Hong Kong, and Japan to other islands (Java, Bali, Sumatra, Timor, Lombok, and Kalimantan).

5) A 50% discount on domestic sector fares is applied for passengers originating from Singapore and Malaysia for the sectors Medan to Banda Aceh and from Medan to Padang.

Bouraq Airlines

A private company offering mostly domestic air services linking Jakarta and other points on Java; Denpasar, Maumere, Kupang, and Waingapu in Nusatenggara; many points in Kalimantan (their specialty); between Tawau (Sabah, E. Malaysia) and Tarakan (E. Kalimantan); Manado, Gorontalo, Palu, and Ujung Pandang on Sulawesi; and to and from Ternate in N. Maluku. Bouraq has 29 offices in Indonesia (head office: Jl. Angkasa 1-3, Jakarta; tel. (021) 629 5150/659 5179/659 5194). Bali Air is a subsidiary of Bouraq and is used for charter flights only.

Others

Sempati (Jl. Merdeka Timur 7, tel. 348760/367743, Jakarta) is a passenger and cargo service airline operating between Jakarta and Japan, Malaysia, Philippines, and Singapore; they have one Boeing 707, 3 Fokker F-27s; also Trislanders, Islanders, and Cessnas. Mandala (Jl. Veteran I/34, tel. 368107, Jakarta) operates 4-engine prop planes in the far reaches of Sumatra, Kalimantan, Sulawesi, and Irian Jaya, with connecting flights to Java. Many companies, such as Seulawah (Jl. Patrice Lumumba 18BD, tel. 354207, Jakarta) are involved in mining in Indonesia and operate their own planes internally. Also check out Pelita Air Service, Jl. Abdul Muis 52, tel. 275908. These private companies can fly where official domestic airlines do not, and sometimes have to renew their permits to fly *every week*. On the Outer Islands you could be lucky and get a free ride with a lone charter, but you should expect to pay. In Sumatra, Irian Jaya, and Kalimantan, you may have to use the sometimes more expensive missionary or oil company aircraft. Missionary aircraft are the only means by which to penetrate deep into the interior of E. Kalimantan.

BY SEA

Sea transportation—in one form or the other—is available to and from all the inhabited islands of Indonesia. Since inter-island passage on large seagoing ships *(kapal laut)* is still seriously deficient for an archipelic nation of this size (there are only 8 ocean ports with a loading capacity of 40,000 metric tons per day), one must often use smaller boats and *prahu* which can sail virtually anywhere, even up to 900 km inland from the mouths of rivers (as in Kalimantan). The most reliable oceangoing shipping company is stateowned Pelni, which has 6 new German ships sailing from one end of the archipelago to the other (Banda

Aceh to Sorong) on fixed schedules. Pelni ships are fast, modernly equipped, and designed to carry 1,000-1,500 passengers in a/c in 4 classes. Other shipping lines like Samudra and Trikora Lloyd also have vessels working the archipelago, but are principally cargo carriers. Check with a *syahbandar* (harbor-master) in the thousands of ports of Indonesia about the coming and going of boats and their prices. Or ask around the harbor first to find a ship sailing where you want to head, then go to the shipping company office. This is when knowing Indonesian really pays off.

Indonesia's small wooden sailboats or outriggers *(prahu)*, large sailing boats such as the Makassarese and Bugis schooners *(kapal layar)*, and small, motorized coasters *(kapal motor)* are sometimes the only reasonable means to get to really hard-to-reach places. Frozen as they are in a 19th C. time warp, it's an unforgettable experience riding on Indonesian vessels. A passage on a ship is also an ideal language-learning opportunity as other passengers frequently don't speak European languages. Unless you're planning a time-consuming, adventurous trip and have at least a month left on your visa, taking passage on a *kapal layar* (sailing vessel) is not usually recommended. These native cargo-carrying craft usually have limited room, the passengers just a pleasant after-thought. Kalimantan has its own genera of river boats: canopied boats with outboard motors *(klotok)*, small and narrow rowboats *(sampan)*, motorboats *(spetbot)*, bulky river ferries, and fast riverboats with bench seats, often with several outboard motors *(longbot)*. There are even outboard motor-powered outrigger canoes which skim across the from E. Kalimantan to Sawah, E. Malaysia, and from W. Lombok's port of Bangsal to offshore islands.

Yachts

For private yachts, try the port of Benoa on Bali in Aug., Sept., or Oct.; you could possibly hitch a ride to the Outer Islands, Singapore, Australia, or even Sri Lanka, Capetown, Brazil, or the W. Indies. It is rare to find yachties who simply cruise the Indonesian islands; most sailors you meet are circumnavigators who want to clear the area as fast as possible because of government red tape and the threat of piracy. Most are on their way from Australia to the Indian Ocean and on to the Red Sea or the Cape of Good Hope. If arriving in Indonesia by sea, government regulations require that all yacht crew members and ships' passengers have valid passports, visas, and inoculations (health certificates).

Costs

You can't buy Pelni tickets through travel agencies, only direct through a Pelni office in each of Indonesia's most important 32 ports. Pelni's child fares are normally half the adult fares. Food is includ-

ed in the price. If you cancel your Pelni ticket, you lose 25% *plus* the runaround. Be ready for illogical pricing structures and irregularities, i.e. different prices charged for the same boat on the same route. Don't ask why the price from Bitung (N. Sulawesi) to Ternate (N. Maluku) is different from the price for Ternate to Bitung, or why the Jayapura-Ambon fare is the same as the Sorong-Ambon fare. Don't fall for an agent's pitch for *asuransi;* by the time you collect this insurance you'll be too old to enjoy it. Usually there are no student discounts on vessels, but always try (especially in Nusatenggara and Sulawesi). As soon as you get onboard the larger ships, one of the ship's hands will ask you if you want to rent out his cabin. Expect to pay around Rp15,000-20,000 (women have been known to get them for free). The cabin is usually reasonably clean, the portholes let in fresh air, you have some privacy, you don't have to watch your gear all the time, and you get to use the shower or toilet when you want.

On the smaller *kapal motor,* such as from Padang (W. Sumatra) to Nias, there might be just 2 classes. First Class means you're under a canopy on the upper deck, while Deck Class means you're on the uncovered lower deck scorched by the sun. On the smaller boats, try going directly to the captain himself and paying him your fare; it's often more expensive to deal with a shipping office. If you go through a ticket agent it could work out 10-15% more, but could save you a lot of running around. Just have the ticket seller itemize for you each "extra" charge on your ticket, or you may end up paying for his lunch. It might be difficult to buy your ticket from an office or even an agent, so always be prepared to buy it second-hand from sharks who add at least Rp1000-2000 onto the original fare.

Pelni

Pelni (Pelayaran Nasional Indonesia) is the national shipping company with over 70 ships connecting all the country's major and provincial harbors. Pelni gets to just about everywhere at 2-3 week intervals. Get ahold of their latest schedule (head office: Jl. Angkasa 18, tel. 416262/417136/417137/417319, Jakarta). Some ships of the Pelni fleet should have been torpedoed years ago—the dirtiest, stinkingest rust-buckets ever to sail the 7 seas. Fortunately, these blemishes on the good name of Pelni are being retired one by one and replaced by showpiece ships, all based in Jakarta. Indonesians are extremely proud of Pelni's new German-built fleet of 6 ships like the KM *Kerinci* which sails from Sibolga (N. Sumatra) to Java, avoiding the long, tortuous bus ride through S. Sumatra. Fares on all of these ships are standardized and very reasonable; in 4th Class you sleep in an 8-berth cabin with your own locker; in 3rd Class, there are 6 beds; in 2nd Class, 4 beds, and 1st Class, 2 beds. First

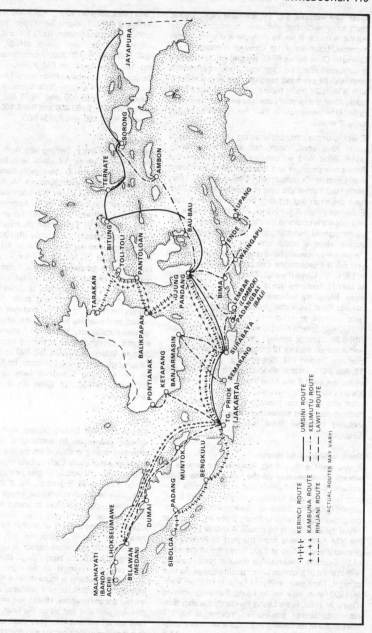

PELNI NETWORK

-·|-·|-· KERINCI ROUTE
++++ KAMBUNA ROUTE
-·-·-·- RINJANI ROUTE
— — — UMSINI ROUTE
-·—·—· KELIMUTU ROUTE
········· LAWIT ROUTE

(ACTUAL ROUTES MAY VARY)

Class fare includes a/c, TV, day and night videos, bathrooms with hot showers, comfortable beds, palatable meals. If you're a couple and want to stay together, book either 1st Class or Economy Class. Economy Class bunks 50-60 people; you're assigned a numbered space on long, low, wooden platforms, each with its overhead baggage rack. Arrive at dockside at least 3-4 hours before sailing to secure a good bunk. Always take your valuables with you during fire drills. One drawback is that the roundtrip usually takes 2 weeks.

Check with the other big shipping companies which could have small, clean, fast ships with friendly crews, good food, yet cheaper fares than Pelni. Use Pelni's fare structure as a reference when bargaining with captains. Or consult with a travel agency. There are at least 9 other shipping companies of note which have ships running regularly between Sumatra-Java, E. Sumatra-Riau (Tg. Pinang), Maluku-Irian Jaya, up and down the coasts of Kalimantan, Sulawesi, as well as throughout Nusatenggara. Perintis Lines, for instance, charges about one half Pelni's fares (but Perentis ships usually have only 2 small lifeboats, and you risk the catastrophe that befell the *Tampomas II* in 1981). Sriwijaya Raya (Jl. Tiang Bendera 52, Jakarta Barat) offers intra-island cargo and passenger services. Samudera Indonesia (Jl. Kali Besar Barat 43, Jakarta Kota) is another private company to investigate, as well as Trikora Lloyd (Jl. Malaka 1, Box 1076/DAK, Jakarta Kota). Jakarta Lloyd (Jl. Haji Agus Salim 28, Jakarta) services the U.S., Europe, Japan, and Australia with its 12 cargo vessels. Ocean Transport and Trading Ltd. (Speed Bldg., Jl. Gajah Mada 18, Box 3421, Jakarta) also has regular worldwide services. But even if you have the captain's permission, it's very difficult to leave the country by ship as you must also clear your passage with immigration, the harbormaster, and sometimes naval authorities. This includes container ships leaving Tg. Pinang for Singapore.

Sample Ships And Routes

If you want a truly long, leisurely sea voyage (2 weeks), book passage on the KM *Kambuna* which embarks Belawan (Medan's port, N. Sumatra) for Tanjung Priok (Jakarta), Surabaya, Ujung Pandang, Balikpapan, Bitung (N. Sulawesi), Balikpapan, Ujung Pandang, Surabaya, Tanjung Priok, Belawan. Inquire at any of the above ports for details. A shorter voyage on the KM *Kerinci* sails from the port of Padang (W. Sumatra) every Mon. at 2200 down the whole coast of W. Sumatra, volcano after volcano, finally passing within sight of Krakatoa which could be spewing lava at night. The *Kerinci* arrives in Tanjung Priok on Tues. at 1600, then sails on to Ujung Pandang, arriving Thurs. at 1300. From Ujung Pandang, the ship then returns to Jakarta, arriving Sat. morning at 1000. It then embarks for Padang at 2100 the same day, arriving on Mon. at 0600. Approximate Economy and 1st

Class fares: Jakarta-Padang, Rp22,500 and Rp50,740 (3 days, 2 nights); Jakarta-Balikpapan, Rp41,700 and Rp95,200; Jakarta-Sorong, Rp72,600 and Rp173,200; Jakarta-Bau Bau (an island off SE Sulawesi), Rp42,500 and Rp100,200. Approximate Economy and 1st Class fares on KM *Kelimutu* (Semarang-Banjarmasin-Surabaya-Padangpai-Lembar-Ujung Pandang-Bima-Waingapu-Ende-Kupang): Semarang-Banjarmasin, Rp25,000 and Rp51,400; Semarang-Ujung Pandang, Rp53,400 and Rp94,400; Semarang-Kupang, Rp81,400 and Rp134,900.

Ferries

Regular ferries link P. Sabang with Aceh in far northern Sumatra, Merak (W. Java) with Bakauheni (S. Sumatra); Surabaya (E. Java) with Kamal (Madura); Ketapang (E. Java) with Gilimanuk (W. Bali); Padangbai (SE Bali) with Lembar (W. Lombok), Sumbawa and Flores (stopping off at P. Komodo en route), Sorong to Jeffman (Irian Jaya), up and down the Kapuas River in W. Kalimantan, plus many more. One of the most remote is the daily (Rp1000 OW) ferry from Langgur on Kai Kecil to Elat on Kai Besar in the Kai Islands of SE Maluku. All ferries run either a number of times daily or several times weekly, are reasonably priced, and take motorcycles, bicycles, and vehicles. Their frequency obviates the need for spending time in connecting ports. On the main islands the ferries for channel and river crossings are owned by the railway system; this is why connections between railheads, rivers, and channels are so smooth. Crossings take anywhere from 40 min. (E. Java to Bali) to 4-5 hours (SE Bali to W Lombok). Fares range from Rp450 Economy, Rp7000 1st Class on the Ketapang Gilimanuk ferry up to Rp3200 Economy, Rp4550 1st Class on the Padangbai-Lembar ferry.

Prahu

Known for their beauty, speed, and strength, Indonesia possesses an astounding variety of indigenous sailing craft known by the generic term *prahu* (or *kapal layar*). Each cultural region handcrafts its own design: the *pinisi* (Bugis), *janggolan* (Madura), *lambo* (Bali), *nade* (Sumatra), etc. If the world's oil wells were to dry up tommorow, goods and people in Indonesia would continue to move from place to place just as they always have. See a number of superb specimens lying at anchor in Sundakelapa (near Pasar Ikan) in Jakarta, the port of Kalimas in Surabaya, and at Paotare harbor in Ujung Pandang. Getting on one of the bigger Bugis-style cargo boats as a paying passenger to the Outer Islands from Surabaya or Jakarta is more difficult than imagined. Indeed, it is somewhat of a privilege, as passengers are but encumberances. Unless you show up with all your luggage and just sit on the boat, a lot of times they sail off without you. They make enough money as it is shipping their cargos and don't really need the

Bugis **pinisi:** Since the 1500s, the Bugis were feared pirates who attacked ships and sold slaves as far as Melaka; the English word "boogeyman" is derived from "Bugis." Using their sleek pinisi, they collected trepang on the coast of northern Australia as early as the 1800s and over the centuries have set up trading colonies in every Indonesian port. The Bugis pinisi is the most versatile and the largest of Indonesia's traditional sailing craft (ranging from 120 to 200 tons). They make up one of the world's major surviving sailing fleets. A copy of the Western schooner of the mid-19th C., the pinisi is immediately recognized by its tall ketch rig of 7 sails (including 2 topsails to catch the slightest breeze), 3 jibs, and fixed gaffs. The hearth consists of a 1-by 2-m box filled with mud which is moved about the deck (the crew subsists mainly on rice), water is stored in jerry cans, and the toilet overhangs the stern. Without benefit of mechanical wharf aids, pinisi dock in the most crowded corners of the harbor; coolies unload cargo holds by trudging along narrow, bouncing gangplanks under crushing loads of barbed wire, bags of cement, cans of kerosene, lumber, kapok mattresses, furniture, motorbikes, sacks of rice and salt, coils of lantana vine, for wages of Rp2000 per day. Possibly catch a ride on a pinisi lying at anchor at Sundakelapa (Jakarta), Paotare (Ujung Pandang), and Ujung (Surabaya).

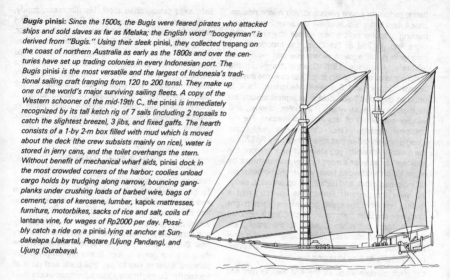

piddly Rp15,000 or Rp20,000 taking you from Surabaya to Ujung Pandang or wherever. Besides, you might prove more trouble than you're worth. These huge motorless boats, which look like fat, round-bilged sailing hippopotami with enormous and unwieldy lateen sails, are sometimes stuck on a windless sea for a week. There could be a tremendous storm with lightning everywhere, big waves and driving rain—you could get sick or washed overboard. It's much easier to get on the big sailing boats on the Outer Islands to *other* Outer Islands (from Flores to Sumbawa, for example), where the captain depends more on passenger fares. If you have the ability to endure cramped, rolling conditions for 3 or more days, do try to get on one just for the sheer medieval thrill of it. You'll play bottlecap checkers or Indonesian dominoes with the crew, catch up on your letter-writing, learn the Bugis alphabet or how to cook curried fish and rice. Under a full moon you can sometimes see dolphins riding the bow wave above a luminous night sea. A little grass and a bottle of Chinese wine are enough to guide you in the night like the north star.

Boat Hire

To visit such remote places as the Krakatoa Volcano, the bird islands off W. Java, the pearl-diving islands of the Arus, or the resort islands of Makassar Bay, it's necessary to hire a boat from a fisherman or charter agency. Though you can rent just about anything that floats in Indonesia, suitable boats would include open-decked trawlers or rugged, well-equipped *kapal*

motor with a skilled captain and crew. A hotel or tourist office can often suggest, if not arrange, a reputable captain and a reliable boat; if a high-standing *pegawi* accompanies you, it can also help your bargaining position. Or have a *kepala desa* recommend a certain boat and its captain. If you don't have a referral, shop around for the best boat at the cheapest price. Make it clear exactly what you're paying for: does the price include gas and return trip? Food? Cover everything so there won't be any misunderstandings. Rent it for the trip rather than by the hour or within a set period of time as the engine could die and the boat drift overnight, or lose a rudder—both of which would render the promise unfulfilled. Be sure to bring some plastic along to cover your gear in case it rains; also take along plenty of food, water, or bottled drinks. To hire a boat to take you out to sea to take pictures of *prahu* under full sail, fix the price beforehand (but not by the hour). You'll also need permission from the harbormaster as every Indonesian port is considered a naval installation and thus a restricted area.

Sea Travel

You definitely must be flexible with your schedule if traveling by sea; in other words, don't have one. Indonesians call it *jam karet* (rubber time). Sometimes you wait 30 hours on deck for your *kapal motor* to even leave the port. And if it's the Indonesian school holidays (2nd or 3rd week of June) or a religious holiday, you have no hope in hell of finding a place on a large intra-island ship. Most smaller boats don't carry flares, radios, or spare parts and you might ride anchor 4 days in the middle of the Makassar Strait with a missing propeller before help comes. If you pay a bit more and go 2nd or 1st Class, the Indonesian archipelago is still a place where you can experience leisurely, luxurious 19th C.-style travel in the staterooms of oceangoing ships just as in the days of Joseph Conrad and Somerset Maugham. As it is often so crowded belowdecks, foreigners usually exile themselves aloft where it's cooler, cleaner, and windier and bereft of rats and cockroaches. For the cheapest passage—Deck Class *(kelas dek)*—take along a woven rattan mat *(tikar,* costs only Rp1200 in the *pasar),* with which you stake out your territory; the *tikar* serves as your carpet by day and mattress by night. Or on a crowded boat, you might be better off taking a hammock and hanging it up on deck, swaying with the current. Sometimes you can rent a folding bed from the crew, or crew members might even rent out their own cabin. Deck Class is not only the cheapest but often superior to the small, hot, sometimes windowless cabins. Except for the new Pelni ships, even 1st- and 2nd-Class cabins can often be too stuffy to stay in during the day.

On such modern ships as the KM *Kerinci* and KM *Kambuna,* which call at the main ports of Java, Sulawesi, Sumatra, and Kalimantan, 1st and 2nd Class cabins have a/c, hot and cold water, TV and videos each night, and 4 respectably prepared meals per day. Economy Class has replaced Deck Class; instead of a deck you get long platforms divided into numbered 2-m-wide sleeping spaces with luggage racks. But these fine ships are exceptions. On other shipping lines if traveling Deck Class during the wet season you can get drenched, so a small tent is great to have. The toilets may reek of ammonia—like squatting above an open vial of tear gas—until later in the voyage they begin to mellow out with quite a different odor. Don't plan on washing as the *mandi* may consist of one leaky pipe. To save money on hotels, ask the captain if you may sleep onboard while the ship is in harbor. On many of the bigger ships, go onboard early or the night before to get a good place and keep from sleeping amongst masses of people; also, much of the available space could be taken up by merchandise. As a Westerner, you may be able to use the officers' toilet and shower.

Food
On non-Pelni ships, unless you fancy chunky white rice and fishheads, or rice and an egg twice a day, bring your own food. On Pelni's KM *Kambuna* and KM *Kerinci* you get rice, fish or meat, vegetables, and a hard-boiled egg, served on a cardboard tray. Some smaller boats serve fresh-caught fish, but many give you salted dehydrated fish which smells like wet dog fur. For sustenance and diversity through the voyage, bring fresh fruits and vegetables, canned cheese and

fish, *sago* cakes, dried toast, biscuits, nuts, candy, coffee, tea, sweetener or honey. There's always hot water. Cork up a couple of bottles of drinking water. Bring your own tin cup, plate, and eating utensils, as these are usually in short supply. On bigger ships sometimes you can slip the 2nd-Class kitchen or the officer's mess some money or a shirt and they'll deliver meals to you even if you're traveling Deck Class. Sample the first couple of meals to see if they're really that superior to Deck Class vittles instead of paying a lump price for meals for the whole voyage.

PACKAGE TOURS

Foreign Tour Companies
To get to hard-to-reach places such as Ujong Kulon and Komodo within the time at your disposal, some find it necessary to sign on with a tour. And when you're paying top dollar for the tour, and the promotional material promises it, you should expect the very best. But be cautious. Many tour companies advertise the stars but don't deliver. Some are simply pinchpennies. (Best is just to use this book and do it all yourself!) You might see a tour advertised out of New York City or Sydney, for example, "A Borneo Jungle Safari." You might even have a real good group of people and have a great time, but these tours starting from the U.S., Australia, or Europe could cost up to US$1800 for the airfare alone plus another $3,200 for the ground arrangements. At this level of touring you have a perfect right to expect the absolute tops in hotels when in the big cities. But when you arrive in Jakarta, you could get shunted into the tatty old Hotel Indonesia instead of the much newer Mandarin, or not get to stay at the Ambarrukmo in Yogya, and in Surabaya not at the Majapahit but be billeted at a seedy resort hotel up in Tretes. In other cases you may have to rely totally on the offices of a completely disastrous Western tour leader, a freeloader who may not even feel at home in a 1st Class hotel. There is usually an Indonesian ground operator involved; the big rich Western company hires a local agency to lay it all on, they mark it up plenty, send along a tour leader to act as guide, and all the work is done by the local crew, who usually turn out to be wonderful. But it could be ripoff.

A trustworthy tour operator in the U.S.? Award-winning Vayatours Inc. has just opened their first sales office in North America at 6420 Wilshire Blvd., Ste. 420, Los Angeles CA 90048, tel. (213) 655-3851. Universal Travel, 8888 Clairemont Mesa Blvd., Ste. A, San Diego CA 92123, tel. (619) 569-5060 (or out-of-state 1-800-272-7888), puts on an exclusive 17-day tour of Bali, Lombok, and Yogya for US$1,695. You can also sign up for package tours in Singapore; try German Asian Travels (Pte) Ltd., 9 Battery Road 14-03

Propelled by engines, wind, muscle, or the current, on Kaliman-tan are found dozens of different vessels, the local names chang-ing from river to river. The longbot (sometimes called ketinting), pictured above, is a specialized craft which lies so flat and shallow in the water that underwater obstacles are easily avoid-ed. If you run into rapids, the boat has to be pulled along the banks by ropes tied to trees. In E. Kalimantan, river taxis travel regularly up the Mahakam River as far as Long Bagun, but from there to authentic Dayak villages farther upriver you'll have to hire a longbot. It costs, for example, Rp350,000 to hire one from Long Bagun to Long Tuyuk. Although permits have not been re-quired when traveling upriver since 1986, some police will still stop you. It's still a good idea to report at each local police station.

Straits Trading Building, tel. 533-5466. The agent for Pacto Ltd., a reputable company offering unusual tours to all over Indonesia, is represented in the U.S. by Sobek Expeditions Inc., Angels Camp, CA 95222, tel. (209) 736-4524. Contact the Indonesian embassy or consulate in your country (see "Visa" section) for additional tour companies specializing in Indonesia.

Adventure/Special Interest Tours

Indonesian companies are really starting to get into the adventure/special-interest travel market. The following are some major inbound operators whose services and reliability are top-notch. Pacto Ltd. (Jl. Surabaya 8, tel. 347457/347433, Jakarta 10320, with branches all over Indonesia), in partnership with the famous California-based Sobek Expeditions Inc., of-fers rafting trips on the remote Alas River of northern Sumatra. Operating out of Medan, tours begin in May and run for 6 days (about US$420) or 4 days (about US$330). Sobek Expeditions Inc. (Angels Camp, CA 95222, tel. 209-736-4524) conducts a 3-week foray for a limit of 12 people into the highlands of West New Guinea. Land cost from Jayapura is US$3500; cost in-cluding airfares from Los Angeles is US$4400. PT Tomaco (Jakarta Theatre Bldg., Jl. Thamrin 9, tel. 320087/332907/347453) does 5-day adventure tours on E. Kalimantan's Mahakam River for US$450-500 pp, depending upon the number of people in your group. Tomaco has a branch office in Hotel Benakutai, Jl. P. Antasari, Balikpapan, E. Kalimantan, tel. 21747/22747).

Agaphos (Jl. Gajah Mada 16, tel. 351333/359659, Jakarta 10130) gives tours to C. and S. Sulawesi, Kalimantan, Irian Jaya, as well as diving trips to Maluku. Melati Djuwantara (Jl. Wahid Hasyim 76, tel. 332729/326039/330531, Jakarta 10340) specializes in tours to Kalimantan, Irian Jaya, and Maluku. Raptim Indonesia, Jl. Cut Mutiah 8, tel. tel. 337704/335585,

Jakarta 10350) specializes in Irian Jaya. Tambora Pariwisata Indah, Jl. Sultan Hasanuddin 70, tel. 774657/773543, Jakarta 12160, offers tours to Irian Jaya, Maluku, C. Sulawesi, and Kalimantan. Satriavi (Jl. Prapatan 32, tel. 353543/355438, Jakarta 10410) does a botanical tour taking in the Bogor Gardens, the tea plantations and factory of Gunung Mas in Cisarua (W. Java). Scores of other companies do volcano climbing tours, historical tours, diving tours, cultural tours. The Surabaya-based PT Wisata Bahari Indah (Jl. Tanjung Priok 6, tel. 031-29133/293313) charters specially outfitted traditional *pinisi* sailing vessels for a 16-day cruise to Bali and Lombok (US$500) or a 35-day itinerary with ports of call including Komodo, Flores, Tanimbar, and Ambon (US$1200). Each of In-donesia's regional tourist offices (see "Information") can help in selecting the right tour company for you.

Local Tours

Mainstream tour agencies like Natrabu or Jaya Tours tend to be more standardized and predictable, so don't miss the opportunity to take some weird, off-beat local tour. You'll bump into a self-proclaimed guide at your hotel or at the local tourist office who could take you out to his village to see a circumcision ceremony or wedding or ramfight. PT Sumber Budi of Ambon offers an incredible lobster-catching tour on the neighboring island of Saparua, or you can go jungle-tripping with Uncle Didi in the vicinity of Bukit-tinggi (N. Sumatra). A local *losmen* owner in Lovina Beach (N. Bali) can take you on a snorkeling outing, and at The Westerners in Solo (C. Java) you could meet Abdul who takes tourists on a fantastic bicycle tour. You'll have the time of your life! Official local cultural tours, like the 2-hour free guided tour of Jakarta's National Museum (each Mon. and Wed. at 0930) and of Jakarta's mammoth Istiqlal Mosque for only Rp1000, are also very good value.

CONDUCT

If you fly into Jakarta from Los Angeles, Munich, or Perth, and have never been to Indonesia before, you might go into immediate shock. It might be dark, you can't see where you are, it's crowded, noisy and unbelievably humid, and you might suspect that everyone is out for your money or is going to rob you. Not trusting the buses, you take a Bluebird taxi from the Soekarno/Hatta International Airport 20 km into Jakarta, costing 15 bucks. You may be the only foreign guest in the hotel, with nothing softening the shock of being in a completely foreign place—like Mexico was ten years ago! The family will be watching TV, everyone looking like zombies. In the middle of the night the Muslim loudspeakers start blaring. You feel totally alien (with a touch of excitement). It is time to start adjusting and adapting.

Traveling In Indonesia

Try to suspend judgment instead of getting mad. You can't get mad at 173 million people. To lessen the initial impact, spend a little bit extra in the beginning and stay in a comfortable hotel. Once you start meeting other Western travelers, you become part of the traveling community, and you won't feel so alone. It also helps to go to Indonesia the first time with a set purpose. Go there to learn something like dance, jewelry-making, painting, *batik, gamelan,* or to study classical Hindu monuments or to climb volcanos. You've got to use imagination, energy, daring, and style to avoid following the well-worn paths of other travelers. And you've got to stay a week in a *kampung* before you can get the faintest glimpse of what it's like to be an Indonesian. Only by opening yourself up to help and advice from Indonesians can you start to understand them. But don't remake your whole personality and temperament for them. If you're really the outrageous and flamboyant type, observe their most important social etiquette but then go ahead and show them who *you* are. These cultures aren't as fragile and delicate as many tourists make them out to be; there's at least 8 civilizations buried under their soil. They will love you for providing them with your own brand of street theater. Besides, there are plenty of *kasar* people around, great characters and not really frowned upon. These types usually qualify for the gesture of the forefinger held vertically in front of the nose and between the eyes which means that the character is mad, stupid, or "does not speak his brain." Most Indonesians leave outrageous behavior to the village idiot, the traveling gypsy theater, *becak* drivers, and those inscrutable Westerners!

Always being scrutinized, in Indonesia you have to learn to live with the idea of being a freak. Be prepared for treatment we would consider rude in the West; if your hat flies off or you stumble, people will probably laugh. If a Western male travels with an Indonesian girl through Indonesia, expect a lot of hassles. She has to report to the police in most towns and many hotel owners won't allow you to sleep together in the same room. It opposes Islamic law and makes his hotel look like a brothel. Normally, if a couple is unmarried there is no problem sleeping together in the same room, so long as they're both from the West. If you're traveling with a child in Indonesia, especially a fair-complexioned male child, the problem is not finding a free babysitter for the day. The problem is getting your child *back* from the babysitter. Don't bring any sentimental attachments toward animals with you. This is Asia. Indonesian children jump up and down with glee while dogs die horribly from rifle shot or drowning.

Indonesian Attitudes

Tourists must first get it out of their heads that the man in front of them is "only an Indonesian" and stop thinking that "he's so small and I'm so big." Most Indonesians have split personalities, split between Western logic and Eastern feeling. The Hindus taught them how to escape, the Muslims taught them how to accept, and the Dutch taught them how to fight. Indonesians usually hide such negative feelings as jealousy, envy, or anger. If a Westerner quarrels with an Indonesian, he is assertive, confronts the Indonesian, deals with the situation honestly and openly, and expresses his anger directly (but not violently). But the angrier the Westerner becomes, the quieter and softer the Indonesian will become. The Indonesian has been trained to cope with stressful interpersonal situations entirely differently. He will be nonassertive and continue to smile, he will maintain a calm appearance and withdraw from the quarrel. He will choose probably to deal with the issue later through a third person. When Indonesians avoid your gaze it doesn't necessarily mean that they are afraid of you. Under most circumstances, eye contact is avoided as such contact, particularly if it's prolonged, may be interpreted as a challenge, and may anger the other person. A subordinate always refrains from direct eye contact with a superior.

When under intolerable stress, the normal Indonesian reaction is to retreat deeply into himself so that he seems no longer to inhabit his body, he cuts himself off from the outside world and its unbearable pressure. On Bali after a fatal automobile accident, groups of Balinese can be seen sleeping at the accident site. When pushed beyond this temporary catatonic state, an Indonesian may "run amok" (blind anger), an extreme cultural reaction to intolerable stress. Indonesians rarely show anger but when they do, they run amok and go stick a knife in someone. Indonesians believe that Westerners get angry so quickly because they eat too much meat, take themselves too seriously, and don't know how to laugh at themselves.

Stereotypes

According to the Australian stereotype, Indonesians are a friendly, sweet, charming, delightful people who are polite (often too polite), but unfuriatingly inefficient, slow-moving, and unreliable. Indonesians on the other hand see the average Australian as rich, loud, *kasar,* ill-mannered, pushy, selfish, immoral. Stereotypical traits such as these are reinforced again and again whenever Australians and Indonesians meet. Bear in mind, however, that there are important differences between Indonesian subcultures, just as there are between Australian subcultures. It can even be argued that the differences between a Javanese and an upriver Dayak are in many ways greater than the difference between Dayaks and Australians. Here are the most important differences:

Australia
1. Much importance placed on privacy and respect for an individual's space. Strong personal friendship bonds are formed, but social obligations are not as strongly felt. Individuals stick with their own ethnic groups or people of the same skin color.

2. More importance is placed on the individual than on the group. Each person is responsible for his or her's own actions and initiative.

3. Much emphasis is placed on efficiency and completing tasks with the minimum of waste.

4. Very direct and open manner. Such *kasar* values as bluntness, arrogance, suspicion, and denigration of refinement and education enshrined in the ocker image of Australian manhood stands diametrically opposed to the *alus* values embodied in the general Indonesian culture.

Indonesia
1. Much emphasis placed on mutual togetherness, and on physical and emotional closeness to others of the same sex.

2. Greater importance is placed on the group than on the individual. It is the individual's duty to obey the will of the group and the group leader.

3. Much emphasis placed on maintaining a lifestyle that is smooth, graceful and refined.

4. An overriding concern for correct form and politeness.

Individual Vs. The Group

There's no place in this society for the individual like there is in the West. Indonesians seek the security and support of others, and individuals aren't admired and are even laughed at. The ideal is that each individual feels at one with a group, his self-identity deriving from his group identity. Indonesians think that the man or woman who stands alone is unnatural and a little absurd. If you say you're over 20 years old and don't have any children, Indonesians pity you. In fact, to answer with an outright "No!" is too blunt; say instead *belum* (not yet). Loyalties to family, village and friends are much more important than self-advancement. Indonesians are accustomed to sharing their beds with other family members and they may feel lonely and frightened when sleeping alone. A family member who brings disgrace to the family, even through no fault of her own (e.g. rape) will be cast out in order to maintain the dignity of the family.

Time

Many Indonesians place little importance on time. One of the most valuable gifts you can be given here as a Westerner is a new way to structure your time. You learn not only that time is not money, but that life is better than money. Slow-moving *wayang* shows, circumcision feasts, *gamelan* music, a happy *selamatan,* and lovely *batik* give more pleasure than getting rich (and ulcers) in the heart-attack machine. In Indonesia, you discover how to wait and be patient, how to observe and know. You start to realize what it's like to be an Asian.

Sex And Intimacy

Westerners tend to show their feelings and affections—as between a boyfriend and girlfriend or husband and wife—very demonstratively. There is more body contact in Western societies. But Indonesians of the opposite sex are not openly affectionate with each other. Though in Western societies it's considered homosexual behavior, Indonesian males and females frequently touch, link arms, or hold hands with their peers. The whole nation seems to be involved in a conspiracy of intimacy. This is quite unaffected and casual, considered a mark of friendship and sociability, not sex. The rule in Australia is for men not to touch other men in public (except to shake hands), while the rule in Indonesia is *do* touch other men in public. This is why Indonesians sometimes perceive Australian men as unfriendly when they don't allow themselves to be touched, while Australians perceive Indonesian men as effeminate when they do allow themselves to be touched! But this touching never occurs between people of the opposite sex, especially lovers, and to do so would bring shame to those involved. Thus, Westerners should never kiss in public. Not even relatives. Indonesian exchange students in Australia are shocked when Australian female student friends kiss them in public each time they see them. Also, don't do extreme dances in Indonesia. The modern Indonesian youth who has received Western education has no objection but the older generation considers modern dancing in which couples touch each other blatant and vulgar sexuality.

Prolonged eye contact between young unmarried people of the opposite sex is avoided as it may be interpreted as a sexual invitation and as such is disapproved. Single traveling women are much more likely to get raped in the U.S. or Australia than in Indonesia, but you can expect men and boys to touch you indecently. (Unsavory types tend to hang around train and bus stations, movie theatres, and ferry docks.) If this happens just spit out at him, *Kau babil* ("You pig!"), which will get his and the crowd's attention, the aim being to humiliate him in public so he doesn't do it again.

Hygiene
Westerners often take a shower once daily; Indonesians bathe at least twice daily (early in the morning and after school or work). In Indonesia, don't jump into the bath water; it's for throwing over you. The bathroom floor gets very wet, and that's OK. Many Indonesians are surprised when they see Westerners always trying to keep their bathroom floors dry. If you have to defecate in the open, do it in running water. If males need to urinate in populated places, just squat down in a ditch with knees spread to give you cover. About 1000 million people in 3rd World countries piss in this manner onto the earth. In Indonesia, people don't blow their nose in front of others, but sniffing is OK. Westerners clean the house once or twice a week; Indonesians clean the house every day. Indonesians usually wash their clothes every day and thus do not bring many clothes with them when they travel. Many Australian students are smokers—both male and female. In Indonesia, smoking cigarettes is common for male students but uncommon for female students.

Dealing With The Bureaucrats
Rule-breaking tourists make it hard for those who follow, so you should be law-abiding. However, don't always assume you need to ask permission or get clearance to do something or go somewhere. The more questions you ask, the more questions will be asked of you. Just go ahead and do it. Since government offices are so busy, you have to be aggressive and not let anyone cut in front of you. Once you reach the official, open with a friendly exchange, then bring up business, "Oh, by the way..." When confronting the Immigration Department, be *extra* respectful. "And what do *you* recommend in this matter?" Play the game. If you're trying to get some paperwork through immigration, or get something cleared through customs, be courteous but volunteer as little information as possible. Use the telephone whenever you can; it's cheaper than waiting months for a letter to arrive. Frequently an important letter can get stuck on someone's desk and never move, and a telephone call can get the ball rolling again. Never get angry, despite long and frustrating waits. In places unaccustomed to tourists (such as parts of Sulawesi, Kalimantan, and Nusatenggara), the police can be almost harassing at times. As well as wanting to know who you are and what you're doing all alone in their territory, they will quickly let you know that they run the place, then grab the chance to show off their English, especially if there are other functionaries around who have no command of *Bahasa Inggeris.* If you get into any hassles with annoyingly officious cops, customs, or *imigrasi* officials, just act stupid, meek, friendly, and innocent. In most cases, they just want you to acknowledge the fact that they are real and have power over you. Bypass petty officials if you can and go right to the top; often these higher-placed men are more intelligent, reasonable, and understanding.

Religion
Respect their religions. Religion plays a central role in the lives of Indonesians. Indonesians aren't offended easily, but they have opinions. Don't tell everybody you're an atheist; people will react with confusion, disbelief, even scorn, thinking you're a godless communist. For them, it would be like discovering that a person could be alive without a heartbeat. Ninety percent of Indonesians are Muslims. While the Islamic holy book, the *Koran,* is being read, don't drink or smoke; never put a book or anything else on it. Remove your shoes when you enter a mosque. Some Muslims must not touch dogs; others must not touch wet dogs. An Indonesian might bathe a much-loved dog every day while wearing gloves. Friends and neighbors will not enter an Indonesian's house if a dog also lives in the house, considering the place unclean. Fear of ghosts and spirits is very real for some Indonesians, especially people from country areas, and some wear charms on their bodies to ward off evil spirits.

Chinese temples are used for religious worship and ceremonies by those practicing Confucianism, Taoism, and Buddhism, and should be given the same respect as mosques. Scarves should be worn around the waist when entering Balinese temples. Don't pat a child on the head, especially if he's Buddhist. In fact, never touch anybody's head. Most Indonesians see the head as the seat of the soul and therefore sacred.

Dress And Grooming
You'll be the object of constant scrutiny. Indonesians are very conservative, so be neat, clean, and fairly careful about what you wear. Wearing shorts, singlets, braless jerseys, strapless tops, and thongs in the main streets of even the smallest village could be insulting, something only the lower-class people, such as fieldworkers and *becak* drivers, do. A *sarong* tied above the breasts is only acceptable on the way to bathe. Long hair is no problem because many Indo-

nesian freedom fighters vowed not to cut their hair until they had won independence from the Dutch (the struggle went on for 5 years!). If you wear a beard you'll be known as *Bapak Jenggot*, "Father Beard." Indonesians want to know how you keep from getting food caught in it, mothers will tell their children you'll eat them up, and others will think you're angry all the time, like a *raksasa*. Whether you wear a beard or not, children—and older people too—will often be afraid of you, though they'll try not to show it. Children only see white men when they punch, shoot and kill in the movies; this is why many start crying and running the moment they see you.

Interactions

Don't get too annoyed about constantly being asked where you're going. Think up some zany answers, or use the standard ones, like exactly where you *are* going, if you know, or just *jalan jalan* which means roughly "out walking" and covers everything from just wandering to heading for the toilet. Or try the Malay response, *Saya makan angin*, "I'm eating the wind." One of the most important phrases you can learn, it also helps to get rid of those *becak* drivers who won't leave you alone.

This custom of questioning is carried on from the time when you called out who you were and where you were going as you walked through a strange village, to assure people everything was all right, and maybe you could carry a message for them on the way. If people join you on the path or road, make conversation; they're (usually) not latching onto you forever. Youngsters still call Western tourists by the Indonesian word for Dutchman *(Belanda)*. So when you hear *Belanda!* behind you, turn around and come back with *Bukan Belanda! Saya orang Selandia Baru!* (I'm not Dutch! I'm a New Zealander!) or some such reply. The fixed look of suspicion turns into surprise or a smile at being spoken to in roughly recognizable Indonesian, and news of who you are seems to travel on far ahead of you. Try not to spoil the children. If small children offer their services as guides, you can give "payment" in various ways other than handing out money or candy (rots their teeth). Give instead a look through your binoculars, some pencils, or a small notebook. If an adult Indonesian does a favor, he could ask for some *uang rokok* (literally, "cigarette money," or pocket change).

Hassles

Don't freak out if a pickpocket probes your jeans or shoulder bag for money, just take the strange fingers out, point at him and announce to everyone, *Pencopet!* (Pickpocket!). In the countryside, a crowd sometimes wrestles a thief to the ground and holds him until a policeman hauls him away in handcuffs! On occasion in S. Sumatra, Flores, or Sulawesi, you could get taunted by young boys who just want to see how you'll react. It's absolutely essential not to get angry—this is what most delights them. One method is to ask bystanders where one of the boys' father is, then go to him and complain of his son's disrespectful behavior. With all the neighbors looking on, the father must uphold his honor in the *kampung*, and the boy will be taken care of, perhaps right there before your very eyes. In some outlying towns of Indonesia—such as Lahat, S. Sumatra or Gorontalo, N. Sulawesi—you could get into a situation where a jeering crowd starts following you around, teasing, taunting and verbally abusing you. In these cases, try to find a public official *(pegawai)* or policeman with whom you can establish a respectful rapport. Or enter a really outlying, untouristed area only with an authority figure to set the tone for encounters with rude individuals. Often you have surprise on your side and you're gone before a crowd can even gather.

With the disarming smile of a little girl, many Indonesians are skilled at coaxing you into doing things that you don't really want to do. If you don't want to do what someone asks you to do, just say simply, *Bukan adat kami*, "It's not our custom." Inhabiting over 6,000 islands and surrounded by hundreds of dissimilar ethnic groups, Indonesians understand well that different people practice different customs. In tourist locales like Bali, Lake Toba, and Yogya, street sellers can be unbelievably pushy and will stick to you like glue. Always be polite at first, expressing your disinterest. But if they persist and follow you and aggressively hound you, make a stand, turn around and face them, stating firmly and unequivocally that you don't want it. Keep repeating this in Indonesian and in English, while looking them straight in the eye, until they back off. Usually this works quite well, but if it doesn't say vehemently *Silahkan pergi!* (Please go!). Another technique found to be effective for use with a nagging crafts vendor is to just make him an offer that is so ridiculously low that he gives you up for a lost cause (but be careful, he could accept it!). Also be wary of predatory touts who offer to show you around different arts and crafts shops, expecting a commission from the owners. The ultimate hassle in Indonesia is getting busted for selling dope, an offense which Indonesians take very seriously. In 1986 an Australian horse trainer was sentenced to life imprisonment by an Indonesian court after being convicted of possessing 26 pounds of marijuana. Right now there are Westerners in jail for possession in Takingon (Aceh) and Denpasar (Bali).

Staying With People

Conversations on buses, trains, and boats often lead to great places to stay. You may never have to stay in a hotel if you're friendly, humble, and patient with yourself and others. But staying with a family means absolutely no privacy, sometimes even sharing a bed.

This could get old fast since you're always in the spotlight. As a visitor you must take on many unwilling roles, acting somebody you're not. All friends and relatives will come to see you, and anyone in the *kampung* who speaks English will come around to practice. You'll be invited to do things with the family so that they can parade you around the village or city street, showing you off to everyone. On occasion you're only used as a vehicle to boost someone's standing amongst his peers or to somehow increase that person's status in the community. When you go off for the day, bring back an *oleh-oleh*, a small edible gift for those you're staying with.

Conversation

Indonesians will always ask you if you like Indonesia, if you would come back. They are very proud of their country. Education seems to be taking hold and a sense of national identity has been created. *Do* talk politics (except with the army and police). Who else is going to tell them? But remember that a high value is placed on deferential or submissive behavior in Indonesia. It is the duty of the individual to obey the communal law and to defer to established group elders, those in whom the group authority is invested. The West's idea of democracy would never work in this country, composed as it is of so many divisive forces, so don't try to foist Jeffersonian democratic principles on them. People like to talk politics in private, but *only* in private. More polite conversation will be initiated by the usual exchange of greetings, then the inevitable, "What country are you from?" Children will always yell "HELLO M-R-R-R-R!!" and "HELLO MI-S-S-S-S!" and other calls from the lexicon of tourist greetings, and you could simply answer *Pergi ke mana?* (Where are you going?) or *Dimana jalan kaki?* (Where is the footpath?). Watching wide-eyed as you walk by, they will think that the foreigner can greet, so perhaps he can also understand. Learn the traditional greetings in the local languages of each region you visit. In the West when members of the same family in the same house greet each other with "Hi," "Hello," or "How are you?" Indonesians feel it is very formal. People in the same house in Indonesia instead launch straightaway into conversation, e.g. when you come home from school your mother asks "Are you tired?"

Table Manners

An Indonesian always offers to share the meal he is eating when a visitor arrives at his house, office, or park bench. If you are invited to eat or drink, watch your Indonesian host; a guest may not start if not invited to do so by the host with *Silakan* (Please begin), sometimes 20 min. later! Never eat with the left hand—it's used with water instead of toilet paper.

Take a small helping the first time around because your host will be offended if you don't eat a second helping. It's polite to keep pace with your host. (And if you empty your plate, it means you want more.) Don't ask for salt, pepper, soy sauce, or *sambal*. This is an insult, implying that the cook did not know which spices to add to the dish. Many Indonesians don't use a knife or fork at home but instead are accustomed to using a spoon and fork, chopsticks, or their fingers. Westerners go out for dinner at least once a week, but Indonesian families eat out only on festive occasions such as birthdays. Be careful not to offend your Indonesian friends, 90% of whom are Muslims, who are forbidden to eat pork. In their company never ask for or offer dishes prepared with pork or lard. Indonesians are also unaccustomed to eating uncooked food such as salads, cold meats, and dairy products, and sometimes Western food can even upset their stomachs. In Indonesia, fruit is always served with a knife and a plate. In Australia, it delights Indonesians to take big bites out of apples in public (they never get to do this at home), but eating just sandwiches for lunch makes them hungry (it's seldom enough). Westerners rarely eat the insides of cattle or sheep (for pets only), but in Indonesia every part of an animal is eaten except its eyes. Many traditional families in Indonesia do not talk during meals; conversation starts only after the meal. Cover your mouth with your hands when picking your teeth; only animals should show their fangs.

Visiting

It is an Indonesian tradition to make unannounced visits early in the evening. The best time to visit Indonesians in their homes is betwen 1600 and 1800 after work, food, and siesta, and in Islamic areas, before the evening prayers. Visitors are never turned away. If you are kept waiting for your host to appear, it's a compliment: he's changing into nice clothes to receive you. Conversely, he'd be offended if you visited him only in a *sarung* or a T-shirt. It's polite to introduce yourself when meeting strangers without waiting for someone else to do the introductions. *Do* shake hands when greeting people; both men and women will offer their hands. Respect is shown by bowing from the waist when passing in front of people, especially older people. Share your cigarettes around and if you've been into town bring back some biscuits for the kids (if you have the money). Travelers should also be prepared to forego an occasional night's sleep. Make of the night, the day. Many forms of entertainment, prayers, and religious festivals run all night long. In some places people stay up the whole night of the full moon simply for the coolness and the magic of it. There's plenty of magic left in Indonesia.

THEFT

Budget travelers are more vulnerable to theft than the more affluent tourists who take planes, taxis, and rented cars from place to place. There are thieves the width and breadth of Indonesia—snatch thieves, pickpockets, cat burglars, con artists, and on Sumatran buses travelers have even been drugged in order to make them easier to rob. Since they have to carry all their money and valuables on or about their persons, travelers are prime targets, a natural for thieves to single out. Suspicion and wariness which demand constant effort are not very agreeable states of mind, but they do prevent thefts, which would be even more unpleasant. Reports of theft can be exaggerated. Paranoia breeds paranoia. However, take all imaginable precautions because practically anything you have, they want. Wet wash is stolen from the line, and shower shoes from in front of your door. Indonesians borrow things—surfboards, sunglasses, rings, guitars, books, and "forget to return them" (pinjam lagi, trus hilang). The Indonesians you are forced to move among traveling on the cheap frequently confuse generosity with abundance, taking advantage of your good nature and your desire to be friendly. Indonesians themselves are seldom stolen from. At night they accord their motorcycles the ultimate honor: they put them in bedrooms. Travelers also rip off other travelers, so exercise just as much caution around Westerners, especially in dormitory-style accommodations such as are found in Jakarta and Surabaya.

Don't Leave Home Without Them

The best preventative of all is to travel through these islands without jewelry, watch, or camera. The less you travel with, the less there is to be stolen. Also the less resentment is aroused; see what happens to your bargaining position if you flash money or showy jewelry around. Never carry a lot of cash, only US$50 or so at a time, enough to see you through the week. Whether it's English pounds, U.S. or Australian dollars, keep all your money in small denominations or traveler's cheques. TCs are cashable at banks, shops, and in restaurants at night in Bali, Yogya, Surabaya, or Jakarta. Even if you have to go to the bank twice a week to cash TCs, it's better than losing all your money (although some would argue the point).

Festivals And Stealing

All over Indonesia theft increases dramatically as holiday seasons approach. Indonesians themselves take extraordinary precautions to prevent theft of their homes during these times. The stealing gets so bad that for several weeks prior to the 30-day-long Muslim fast Ramadan the Javanese customarily turn their houses into fortresses. This is because poorer Indonesians are trying to get ahold of money and goods before the fast begins when they must forgo all. Indonesians are also under great pressure to buy gifts for their friends and relatives at the end of the fast (Hari Raya), a cash outlay as financially devastating as our Christmas. Java is the most notorious during this time, but there's also a big increase in stealing prior to some of the more important festivals on Bali.

DISCOURAGING THEFT

All the following precautions should quickly become second nature to you. Almost all hotel rooms have doors with locks. Use them. Even better is to take your own lock and key along to prevent "inside" jobs perpetrated by hotel boys or maids. If a door doesn't close tightly or if the lock seems flimsy, jam a chair underneath the door handle at night to make it difficult to open. If you have the slightest doubts about your hotel security, it's best to stay in a more expensive hotel. Never take a room without strong bars on the windows. If you do, either take all your valuables with you when you go out, or ask if you can store them in the proprietor's quarters. Or spend that Rp2000-3000 extra for a safer hotel with bars on the windows, a penjaga (guard), the manager always around, and a good high stone wall with barbed wire or broken glass on top. The general public must be prevented from entering the compound area; this is essential. Your room window shouldn't face an alley or a side street but face toward the interior of the hotel. Beware of leaving bags on floors which can be hooked with a line or pole and pulled to the window.

If you're staying with Indonesians, as much as you'd like to trust them, the word that a Westerner (connotes "rich") is in town spreads instantly throughout the whole kampung. Quick and quiet, thieves will enter your room through the window while you sleep and steal the camera from the hook above your head or the backpack from underneath your very bed. Don't set anything valuable near an open window or on a curbside table while dining al fresco. When you're sailing onboard a Pelni ship, be sure to take all your valuables with you when there's a lifeboat drill. When trains stop at stations, never leave anything valuable unattended on the seats or on the table while the window is open. Don't leave valuables in a vehicle; to show that you haven't, leave the glove compartment open. Also take care with anyone coming up to you dressed a little too slickly and talking English a little too glibly; he could be a con-artist. Muggings are practically unheard of except in the wrong part of Jakarta and Surabaya at the wrong times of day. If you go into a red-light district, go sober; most muggings occur when you're drunk. Carry the minimum amount of cash you'll need for the night in your shoe. Finally, if you're going hiking, you can always leave any belongings or gear with the local cops in exchange for a ½-hour passport inspection and/or English conversation practice.

PICKPOCKETS

If your mind is not on your money, you'll be vulnerable to pickpockets. Like a mosquito, you don't know you've been bit until after the itching starts. Heed signs AWAS COPET (Beware of Pickpockets). There's even a school for pickpockets in Cirebon, W. Java. Graduates of this school are said to be able to remove your wallet from your back pocket while you're sitting down or extract money deep inside front trouser pockets. Be wary of minor accidents— being shoved or bumped, or having your foot stepped on. When big interisland ships dock, avoid passenger crushes. If you're being pushed around in a crowd, drop your arms and turn to face the person bumping you. A pickpocket will usually turn his head and move away smartly. Don't be taken in by commotions or distractions of any kind. Whenever a fight breaks out, leave as quickly and unobtrusively as possible.

One big advantage of traveling with somebody else is that you are less likely to get ripped off; you can keep an eye on each other and on each other's gear. On Bali, sit in the "traveler's seat" in the back of bemo with your R or L side next to the cab, rendering your pockets and bags more difficult to get into. Keep your pack against the bemo cab with your eye on it, pockets facing the wall. Be extra wary of the bemo of Bali; travelers get ripped off by young pickpockets dressed as schoolkids who work in groups: 1 or 2 divert you while another steals. On the buses of Jakarta, a gang of young hooligans may surround you and pick your pocket while you're standing. Though you may even realize what is happening, there's little you can do about it, squashed as you are. The other passengers, with Jakarta's heavy gangsterism, will probably be too scared to help.

Wallets, Purses, Shoulder Bags, Rucksacks

If you're traveling on the cheap in Indonesia, the whole concept of the wallet in the hip pocket must be discarded. Pickpockets have wallets and purses in shoulderbags clocked—they know exactly how to get at them. Never put purses in coat pockets, in shopping bags, or on counters. The only safe way for a woman to carry her purse is to hug it tightly against her side away from the street, protected by her arm. The less you open your bag in public, the better.

Avoid zipper-type shoulder bags because you don't always close the zipper all the way, leaving room enough for a hand to reach inside. Instead use a latch or snap which fastens the bag, or use a bag with a very small opening which you have to pry apart yourself in order to get into it. In Yogya (C. Java), thieves specialize in slitting open moneybelts, clothes, and packs with razors. Don't put valuables in a camera case; thieves have caught onto this practice. Try not to carry cameras hanging around your neck; thieves will be tempted to pull them off. Be wary of approaching motorbikes; purses and bags could be snatched from your shoulder by rear-riders on cycles as you walk along (this is a Surabaya specialty). To avoid these motorcycle snatch thieves, don't walk in the street; if you do, walk with your bag held tightly under the shoulder nearest the sidewalk. Leave your address book, traveler's cheque serial numbers, passport number, photographs, heavy money, air tickets, and other hard-to-replace papers in the bowels of your rucksack, to be taken out in the privacy of your own room only as you need them. Your rucksack offers the most security because it either remains in your room or it's riding on your back, making it difficult for a thief to get deep inside it without being discovered. Keep only those possessions you can do without in side pockets or on the top layer of rucksacks or packs.

Lost Air Tickets/Passports

It's a good idea to write down your ticket number, flight number, issuing agent, date of issue, and method of payment. Having all this information at the ready will make your ticket easier to refund in case of loss. You still have to pay a non-refundable $10 or more fee to the airline to replace your lost or stolen ticket. Since the airline wants to be sure tickets haven't been used, tickets can only be refunded at least 4 months after their expiration date. Try not to put your passport and money in the same place; if stolen, you've lost everything at once. Report passport loss immediately to the nearest police station and ask for a letter of reported theft/loss. Without this letter, required negotiations with *imigrasi* can be

difficult. New passports or letters of travel can be obtained through consulates and embassies. Your embassy or consulate most likely can be found in Jakarta (unless you come from Botswana), but many of Indonesia's major trading partners also maintain embassies or consulates in Surabaya (E. Java), Bali, and Medan (N. Sumatra).

Reporting To Police

If your goods are ever stolen, try and put word out on the street (verbally or with posters) that you will pay a reward to get your gear back. It can either be helpful or futile to go to the police. In some instances, using them can end up costing you *more*. Before an investigation the police may ask to talk about it over dinner, which *you* pay for. Other accounts tell of travelers appealing to the police upon theft of a cassette recorder; when the police recover it by sheer accident they ask for the traveler to donate Rp5000 "for finding it." On the other hand, a policeman can end up being your only friend in case of a psychologically devastating loss of a moneybelt. He might console you, feed you, then start up a collection to get you back safely to "your friends." This happened to me once in Padangpai (E. Bali) after my moneybelt got stolen aboard the ferry from Lombok.

Money Belts

Designed to go *under* your clothes, moneybelts are recommended for Indonesia, and particularly if you're going beyond (Burma? India?). Keep your TCs, passport and other documents in plastic so they don't become soiled with sweat, thus unreadable and troublesome to use. Make canvas money pouches slit-proof with steel-lined backing or leather reinforcement. If you hang a compact pouch on a leather strap around the neck, that dangles under your shirt just above your waist, be aware it can be yanked off in crowds. Better is a tight moneybelt fastened around your waist under your clothing and next to your skin. Highly durable, water-repellent, cotton-blend, field-tested moneybelts, with heavy-duty zippers, are available for only $8.95 plus $1.25 shipping directly from Moon Publications, 722 Wall St., Chico, CA 95927, U.S.A., tel. (916) 345-5473.

COMMUNICATIONS

POWER AND MEDIA

Electricity

In the past, current has been 110V, 50 cycles AC, but most areas are now changing over to 220-240 volts 50 cycles AC. Some houses may even have both 110 and 220. Power is fairly reliable, but "brown-outs" are not uncommon. If you're renting a home it's wise to get one with its own start-up generator; in the cities you already have to put thousands of dollars down and pay up to 2 years in advance rent for a house with all the Western conveniences, so a few thousand extra shouldn't hurt. Electricity in the *kampung* and even in some larger towns can be minimal — you'll get used to solitary dim bulbs (which you can replace with higher-wattage bulbs) and oil lamps. Street lighting is also haphazard. Since the sidewalks and streets of Indonesia are full of pitfalls and debris, always carry a flashlight.

Always check to make sure which current is installed before plugging in expensive electrical appliances. If you're planning to rent a house and live in Indonesia for awhile, it's best to buy appliances when you get there. All 110V, 50-cycle appliances will operate on a transformer but will run slower and less efficiently. Transformers are readily available and are reasonably priced, as are 220V appliances. Bottled gas *(elpigi)* is used here and most choose to use gas stoves (without an electric starting device which leaves you stoveless during power outages) and gas clothes dryers. Repair shops are located all over; most better appliance establishments will give a guaranteed repair, if you don't mind bringing it back several times.

Television

Television, video tapes, and the movies are starting to make Indonesians as self-conscious as Westerners. There's even video sets on the buses! Televisi Republik Indonesia (TVRI) is a government-operated nationwide TV network. Jakarta TVRI, connected via domestic satellite and microwave, covers most of Indonesia. Television, broadcast some 6 hours a day, is expanding rapidly in Indonesia, with many outlying cities constructing their own local broadcast facilities. The medium is a tool of the state and programming consists of pro-government Indonesian-language local and national news, educational and religious programs, sports and special events, Indonesian music and dramas, nationalistic documentaries and reports, and about 1½ hours of English-language car-

toons and old syndicated American re-runs, usually played late at night.

American TV sets aren't compatible with Indonesian signals. American black-and-white sets can easily be converted locally, but for color it's best to buy a set locally or rent one. Many long-term U.S. expats bring their sets for use with video cassettes and games. Local TV sets are OK quality but more expensive than sets in most other countries and are used for viewing Indonesian TVRI and PAL-system video cassettes. Rental rates are quite expensive, averaging Rp45,000 per month. Don't bring stereo equipment from the U.S. because it must be adjusted and is difficult to have it re-adjusted back to the American speed. Just buy your stereo there and sell it when you leave.

Radio

Radio Republik Indonesia (RRI) has 45 stations which comprise the national system. Radio is still important and keeps most of the population informed and entertained. RRI broadcasts news and commentary in English about an hour a day (early morning and evening). In addition, many private radio stations broadcast RRI news and Indonesian and Western music on AM and FM. Short wave reception includes English-language programs such as BBC, Voice of America, and American Top Forties.

POSTAL SERVICES

Sending Letters

Indonesia has a fairly efficient postal service *once* your missive is mailed, but it can be maddening *getting* it mailed! In the post office, go to the window having a scale first because your letter has to be weighed and given a stamp value. Then take it to another window for stamps. Go up to the clump of people and push your letter as far as possible through the barred window to gain the attention of the postal clerk. Then try to squeeze your money into some gap between all the other hands. These are acceptable manners at Indonesian post offices. After getting your stamps, take them over to the glue stands and reglue them because the glue used on Indonesian stamps is too weak. Rates within the country: under 1000 grams, Rp385; 1000-3000 grams, Rp750; 3000-5000 grams, Rp1000; 5000-10,000 grams, Rp1500.

Not all of Indonesia's postal branches offer complete postal services; some do not, for example, accept parcels. Post offices in the big cities and tourist centers are fast and efficient, using the latest digital scales. Stamps can also be purchased at shops selling postcards, and most of the larger hotels sell stamps and collect letters for mailing which saves you time standing in line at crowded post offices. If possible, watch the stamps being cancelled or else they could get stolen. For philatelists, commemorative stamps and First Day Covers are available at Jakarta's main post office on Jl. Pos Utara.

Registration

Register anything of value. The charge for registering your letter *(surat tercatat)* is about equal to the charge of postage, but the chances are improved—though not guaranteed—that your letter will reach its destination. Letters bound for overseas or domestic delivery may be registered at any post office branch. A signed form should be returned to the sender indicating that the letter was received by the addressee.

First Class

There are 2 forms of express service available for domestic mail: blue envelopes marked *Kilat* and stickers ensure Air Mail Service, while yellow envelopes marked *Kilat Khusus* are the equivalent of Air Mail Special Delivery. These envelopes, as well as aerograms, are available at all post offices. Express service costs an extra Rp65, usually saves at least 1-2 days, and it's a service you should always use. "Kilat" letters, like ordinary letters, may be put into a mailbox along the street.

Overseas

Always use the express service *(Kilat)* for international mail which gets letters over to the Americas, Europe, or Australia in 5-7 days. Airmail costs for postcards are Rp600 to the U.S., Rp400 to Europe, and Rp300 to Australia. A normal letter costs Rp1550 to the U.S. Handy and fast aerograms cost Rp750. Use a strong envelope (bring with you to Indonesia) to make sure your exposed film or letter arrives safely.

Incoming Mail

Most travelers use *poste restante* service in either Jakarta or on Bali. Have your mail sent to either one of Jakarta's 2 main post offices: Central Post Office *(Kantor Pos Pusat)*, Jl. Pos Utara, open Mon.-Sat. 0800-1600, and in Kebayoran at Jl. Kapt. Tendean 43, open Mon.-Thurs. 0800-1600, Fri. 0800-1100, and Sat. 0800-1230. Bali's main post office is inconveniently located in the new administrative district of Denpasar, or you can have your mail sent to any of the branch offices in Kuta, Ubud, or Singaraja. Since letters are frequently missorted (such as under "P" when they should be under "B"), all mail should be addressed to you with your last name in caps and underlined, using only your first and middle initials. You also might be able to locate a missorted letter under your first name. Your name should go first, then Kantor Pos, the town name, the island name, then Republik Indonesia. A small fee of Rp50 is charged to pick up a letter at any *post restante*.

Sending goods out of Indonesia is getting safer, but receiving goods is still risky. Stories are rife, such as the priest who was sent cassette music. When he opened his parcel he found that all the tapes had been substituted with cheap Indonesian tapes, plus a few items were stolen. Or copies of *National Geographic* that arrive dogeared a month late. Approximately half the things mailed to you in Indonesia get ripped off, especially medicine, books, and magazines. If magazines are sent, make sure they're mailed in a plain cover or envelope, then they might get through (copies of *Life* sold at Medan Airport have had their covers torn off, which once had sombody's name on them).

PAKET POS (PACKET POST)

Mailing packages from Singapore by seamail is just about the same price as from Indonesia, and reports have it that mailing from Singapore isn't any safer (though it is definitely cheaper). Only the larger Indonesian post offices offer parcel service; they often have a special room around the side of the building or a completely separate building *(Paket Pos)* that processes parcels for surface post. Overseas-bound packages may be posted, insured, and registered *(tercatat)*. At the post office the parcel will be opened for customs inspection, so don't bother sealing it up. Sample seamail rates from Indonesia to: U.S., up to 1 kg, Rp7250; over 1 kg but less than 3 kg, Rp12,350; over 3 kg but less than 5 kg, Rp17,550; over 5 kg but less than 10 kg, Rp28,900. To Europe: up to 1 kg, Rp8000; over 1 kg but less than 3 kg, Rp10,250; over 3 kg but less than 5 kg, Rp13,050; over 5 kg but less than 10 kg, Rp17,750.

When sending packages, always max out your parcel to 10 kg because you're paying for the 5-kg to 10-kg rate anyway. Likewise, on the 3- to 5-kg rate, max out to 5 kg. Put your name and address on a slip of paper inside the package as well as outside, in case of damage. Provincial post offices may not have the proper custom forms, or they may be out of stamps—be prepared for this. Bring spare carbon paper because you'll be required to fill out copies of forms; often the post office runs out of carbon. International seamail can take up to 6 months, but it usually takes 2-3 months. And if you have a lot to send back this is one way to go instead of going through an even more expensive shipping company.

Wrapping And Packaging

Shops will usually wrap your purchases in a flimsy layer of newspaper, binding the whole in plastic twine with a convenient carrying handle, an arrangement

continued on p. 130

PHOTO TIPS

With its lush landscapes, colorful markets, architectural and historical sites, and above all its friendly people, Indonesia is an endlessly photogenic country with thousands of subjects popping up constantly on every island. But in order to enhance the photographic experience and ensure the quality of your shots, some advance preparation is necessary. First of all, pack light. If you're struggling with 2 bags full of still-camera photographic equipment, all you'll be doing is worrying about your gear (and you *should* worry). Two SLR camera bodies (in case one should fail), plus about 3 lenses, are the maximum you should carry. Be sure that both bodies are in good working order and that the meters have fresh batteries. In case your camera breaks down, the standard of repair services in Indonesia is extremely uneven. You could get charged Rp25,000 for a lightmeter adjustment only to discover that your meter is as faulty as it was before you took it in. With the new generation of 35mm, fully automatic, auto-focusing subcompacts on the market, travelers in droves are now starting to leave home their clunkier, heavier, changeable-lens 35mm SLRs. Ricoh's remarkable, full-featured TF-500 is an example.

Equipment

The range of subjects and lighting conditions in Indonesia requires good equipment. Considering the sharp light and shadow contrasts of the tropics, a camera with through-the-lens metering is essential. Beginners should start with an inexpensive model made by one of the major manufacturers, then later when you're ready to advance to a more sophisticated model you can still use your old lenses. Wealthier travelers also take an instant Polaroid camera to the country's outlying areas, which causes great delight with the local populace. As an emergency camera, some travelers carry a high-quality underwater camera such as the Nikonos. Designed with the typical Nikon durability for underwater photography, the camera's shutter and film carrier mechanisms are housed in an inner body sealed by gaskets. These gaskets keep out not only the sea but also protect the camera's working parts from such traveler's hazards as frost, sand, tropical humidity, and dust for that climb through Bromo's sandsea or for that wet ride up an upper tributary of the Mahakam River in E. Kalimantan. And at the end of each day of heavy traveling, just stick it under a faucet and rinse it off.

Accessories

Take fresh batteries (for both camera and flash) and try to keep it down to 2 lenses. A 24-mm wide angle and a 80-200 zoom will probably handle about 80% of the situations you'll face (as well as lighten your load). Zoom lenses aren't very fast so you should also take along a basic 50-55mm lens for available-light photography using fast film. Take the smallest camera bag that will hold your gear. Use a Skylight filter (1A or 1B) to reduce the bluish haze of scenes in color, and a yellow, orange, or red filter to add tone and contrast to b & w photography. Filters also protect your expensive lenses. A lens hood is also highly recommended in the tropics to keep direct sun off the lens.

Camera And Film Care

The heat and humidity of Indonesia's climate can easily ruin your film and camera. Heat gives color film a greenish-yellow tone which is impossible to eradicate in normal processing. Silica gel packets, stored and carried with your equipment, should help significantly in keeping moisture at a minimum (dry tea leaves are also effective). Never leave your camera and film in the sun or in any hot place for any length of time. When you take your camera suddenly out of an a/c environment and enter the heated air outside it will sweat, so allow a few minutes for natural defogging of external and internal lens surfaces. Condensation on the inside of the camera should be allowed to evaporate by its own accord instead of wiping and smearing it. Also, don't allow film to sit in your camera for more than a week as the emulsion will stick and sweat, resulting in wavy lines in your pictures. Keep taking pictures steadily to prevent this from happening. Tropical mildew growth can also be a problem for cameras and slides. Storage in cool locations (like inside of rucksacks) will cut down on this; check periodically for mildew buildup and use silica gel. Also, insist on hand inspection of your carry-on camera bag and film at domestic airport security checkpoints.

Film

One of the finest films in the world for tropical photography is Kodachrome 64, but you should also take along faster 200 ASA film and even some 400 (or higher) ASA film for use in poor light situations. (Recommended: 70% of your film should be Kodachrome 64, 20% ASA 200, 10% ASA 400 or above.) To bring out the colors, get in the habit of punching up your ASA rating (which are all overated by the manufacturers on the film carton anyway); this will also eliminate the need, in some cases, to use your flash. Take more film than you think you'll need. Film in Indonesia is expensive and, with the suffocatingly humid climate, you never know how it has been cared for and stored. Shops, particularly in the Outer Islands, may not have or may be out of the film you want in the size you want. Just decide in advance on what film you think you'll need and carry enough with you. Keep spare film rolls in a lead-coated or plastic film bag in your backpack.

Hong Kong, Bangkok, Singapore, or the mail-order photo supply outfits in New York are all good places to stock up on inexpensive film. If you do run out of film, color film is widely available throughout Indonesia. The most popular 35mm brand is Fuji, available everywhere in a full range of ASA/DIN ratings and selling at about the same price as overseas. Although Kodachrome slide film is for sale in Jakarta and Bali at a cost of around Rp18,000 for film and processing, the processing is unreliable. By contrast, a 36-exposure roll of Fujicolor print film costs around Rp5000. Always check the expiry date on the film box, especially if you come across the film in Indonesia's outer areas. Film is sold at shops and hotels in towns and cities, with the best selections in Jakarta and Bali. Larger stores in major cities also stock other leading world brands such as Agfa, Polaroid, and b & w films, as well as film in larger formats (9mm), Super 8 movie film, and video tapes, but prices tend to be higher than back home. The Bali Foto Center on Kuta Beach carries more than 50 film brands, kept in a special a/c showcase.

When To Shoot

Light diffusion on the equator is different from the temperate zones so beware of the intense sunlight and haze that occurs from 1000 to 1500 which causes color film to flatten and wash out. Sometimes you can increase the vibrancy of your daytime pictures by deliberately underexposing by at least a ½ f-stop. Polarizing filters also help a great deal in reducing the haze. The *very* best light for rich, warm color photos under the tropical sun is usually between 0700 and 1000 a.m. The sun is straight overhead by around 1100 which usually causes a bluish cast. Try to rise with the Indonesians at the early hours for cleaner air and crisper light and colors. Purposeful but careful underexposure by 1 f-stop or so will help put wispy clouds back in the sky. Remember also that lush tropical green of *sawah* or jungle usually photographs better if backlit by the sun. Shadows are harsh and strong in the tropics, especially at midday, causing high contrasts. Find those films which show more shadow detail or take careful light readings from the shadows if such detail is desired (highlighted areas will be slightly overexposed but acceptable). Or use a flash to fill in the shadows; if you don't have a flash, you need *at least* ASA 200 film for Borobudur. Sidelighting also helps to achieve greater depth to most subjects. Tropical sunsets will have the most exotic colors if the exposure reading is taken of the sky without the bright sun, then shoot straight into the sunset. A powerful flash is often the only means by which to capture the night-time dances of Bali or the beautiful Ramayana Dance Ballet at Prambanan (although the use of flash is terribly distracting to the audience). Always be mindful of scale; when you shoot a picture of an immense volcanic crater, without a tree or human figure it will look like a scale model made of sand and mud!

Shooting People

Indonesians are polite and congenial and usually willing to have you record them and their ceremonies on film. In fact, one big problem is keeping bystanders and city crazies *out* of the composition if you are trying to shoot just one subject. The Baliem Valley of Irian Jaya and possibly Torajaland of S. Sulawesi will probably be the only places where you'll be asked for money. Among traditional peoples it's common for them to believe that you will capture their souls if you photograph them. The Sakai of the Dumai area of S. Sumatra are downright hostile or terrified if you try to take their picture, Toba Batak women are sometimes too shy, and in some orthodox Islamic areas such as Aceh there are religious prohibitions against taking photos of people in prayer. It's also impolite to photograph people bathing in streams or rivers. As a courtesy, first ask for permission with the word *permisi*, or expressive hand gestures making your intention clear. Please respect refusals. The discreet use of a telephoto lens obviates having to ask permission. In street photography, one technique is to hire a *becak* for use as a blind in order to shoot families out walking, sellers and vendors, etc. Be aware of the sacredness of many of the ceremonies you may witness; act accordingly when using flash or maneuvering for shots. Disrespect for monuments and being pushy will make it not only unpleasant for you but also for photographers who follow.

Shooting Objects

Unless there happens to be a particular festival or service taking place inside and outside, always ask first before photographing the interiors of mosques, churches, or temples. It's highly unlikely that permission will be refused. If you wish to take photos of government buildings, museums, monuments, etc., a modest fee is often charged for a camera and a higher one for a movie or video camera. This fee may apply to the exterior, interior, and even surrounding grounds. In some exhibits or museums (such as the Textile Museum and National Museum of Jakarta), the use of flash fades the priceless exhibits and is prohibited. All over Indonesia it's forbidden to take pictures of airports, military barracks, bridges, RR stations, harbors, and port or military installations without the necessary papers (the asking for which may arouse suspicion!). If you're in doubt, ask officials or guards, or your film might be confiscated.

Processing

Color print film is developed and printed locally in just 1 hour (if busy), only 30 min. (if not). Slide film takes around 2-3 days, and video film in 7 days. At only around Rp200 per print, color print costs are considerably lower than in most Western countries. Instamatic film runs about Rp600 to develop plus Rp150 per print. Developing b & w film in the outliers of Indonesia could be a real problem, with the film having to be sent to Jakarta in some cases (a 10-day wait). The quality is generally good at the better shops and photo studios, but on the whole it varies widely, even for b & w film processing. And no processing facilities for Agfa exist in Indonesia. An alternative is to just store your exposed film, which can keep up to 2 months before processing, or send your exposed film via airmail to processing centers back home. Mail-order processing is convenient, low-priced, and guarantees quality processing. One of the risks, though, is loss or damage in the mail. To reduce this risk, put your name and address right on the film cartridge with transparent tape. You can use one of the high-volume processors advertised in such U.S. magazines as *Popular Photography*.

For more reliable processing, use Kodak mailers, small yellow envelopes selling for around US$8-10 (for both film and mailer) over the counter in many drugstores and camera shops, or for only US$7-8 using mail order houses in New York (get toll-free numbers in photo magazines). Using mailers is especially recommended if you work with Kodachrome. Since the mailers are prepaid, just write the address of a certified Kodak processing facility on the front of the envelope and airmail your exposed slide film back from anywhere in Indonesia. Then all your processed slide film will be waiting back home when you arrive, and the processing 95% of the time is quite good. If you pre-address your mailers before your trip, arrange them in numerical order. Just insert your first roll of exposed film in the lowest number, then they will all be in chronological order when you get back. Keep the detachable serialized tag on the envelope as a record of each dispatch.

that would never withstand the rigors of travel. To protect your wares for overseas shipping, the best padding in Indonesia is foam carpet backing available from carpet stores. For sending goods seamail, buy very sturdy bamboo or rattan baskets which cost only Rp1000 or so for a large one. Found in dozens of shapes and sizes, these baskets have lids, can hold up to 10 kg (the limit for overseas parcels) tightly packed, and their interlocking construction can withstand almost any kind of punishment (except crushing, and penetration by sharp objects). Again, cheap colorful Chinese *tali*, plastic twine, is used to bind them.

The contents of parcels must be inspected at the post office before mailing, so don't wrap your package until it's inspected. In big city post offices often there are men who will wrap your package in a nylon jacket for a fee of Rp900-1200 per package. Chances are that after you buy the paper and string and get together everything you need, you will have spent that amount yourself (plus lots of running around). Using this service also tends to move it along faster through the system. These men are available only in the main cities where the volume makes it worth their while.

Parcels By Bus

To transport goods from one part of Indonesia to another, overland bus companies offer quite cheap freight-only charges. These services are used by many firms and individuals. All have offices in Jakarta and throughout Indonesia. Elteha is located on Jl. Tanah Abang Timur 16 A, Jakarta, or right behind the Denpasar Post Office on Bali, with branches in all main towns. Also on Bali, Balimas, Jl. Hasanudin 27, Denpasar, charges about Rp10,000 to transport 200 kg from Denpasar to Jakarta. Also check out Usaha Express and Titipan Kilat.

Shipping Arts And Crafts

There are specialized air express companies on Bali, so if you're buying crafts in the Outer Islands wait until you get to Bali to airfreight them. Airfreight companies based on Bali are expensive, charging about US$8-10 per kg (min. 5 kg) total cost, and taking 7-10 days. Try PT Golden Bali Express, JL. Kartini 52, Denpasar, one of the most competent of the air express companies operating on the island. If you pack it yourself you might get the price down. Also, check on the "unaccompanied baggage" rates on your flight home. At about US$3.50 per kg, these rates may be much cheaper than airfreight. Seamail (surface post), on the other hand, is the cheapest way of all to send your goods home (see above). It will cost you a trip to the Kantor Paket Pos (usually near the GPO) of a large city, take 1-2 hours of your time, and average out to about US$1-1.50 per kilo. Usually there's a weight limit of 10 kg. You'll need to fill out forms CP2 (5 copies) and C2/CP3, then pack and seal the parcel in front of post clerks to ensure that you're not sending any antiquities home. Surface post to N. America or to Europe often takes 3 months.

TELEPHONES, TELEGRAMS, CABLES, AND TELEX

Local Calls

Jakarta has largely shed its reputation for having one of the most agonizingly frustrating phone systems in all of Asia. Overloading of the telephone system used to be so severe that it was almost *impossible* to place a call during normal business hours. Now you can routinely place both domestic and international calls. Public pay phones (Rp50 per local call) are found here and there, but are frequently out of order. Local calls (Rp100 per call) are easier to place in hotel lobby pay phones in the large cities.

Intercity Calls

Dial long-distance within Indonesia by first dialing the city code number (Malang 0341, Banda Aceh 0851, etc.), then the local number. The archipelago is divided up into 5 zones and calls are priced according to zone. The rate from Jakarta ranges from Rp300-500 per minute for Zone V calls (Java, Sumatra, Sulawesi, Nusatenggara, and Kalimantan), to Rp1000 per minute for Zone I calls (Biak, Nabire, and Manokwari). Fees are computed also according to the speed you want your call put through: *biasa* (ordinary), or *segara* (express).

International Telecommunications

International calls are handled by Indosat, a state-owned enterprise that uses the International Satellite system. For International Direct Dialing, go to the Kantor Telepon & Telegrap in Indonesia's bigger cities and dial the country code (U.S. 001, Australia 006143, etc.), then the local number. Now there are 20 cities—such as Jakarta, Bogor, Bandung, Medan, Surabaya, Denpasar, Semarang, the Torajan area, and even remote Nabire, Irian Jaya—which offer International Direct Dialing. Completely computerized, the system has links with 127 countries. Where direct-dialing overseas connections is not available, operator assistance can be accessed by dialing 101 throughout Indonesia or 104 in Jakarta. The reception is usually quite good.

Telephone credit-card calls are honored, but collect calls are only accepted now between Indonesia and Europe, America, and Australia. Sample (station-to-station) rates from Jakarta to: U.S., Rp13,650 for 3 min, Rp4550 for each additional min.; Europe, Rp18,540 for 3 min., Rp6180 for each additional min.; Asian countries, Rp10,400 for 3 min., Rp5200 for each additional min.; Caribbean, South Asia, Rp13,650 for 3 min., Rp4550 for each additional minute. Person-to-person calls are about twice the rate of station-to-station calls (reduced rates on Sundays). A 25% discount is given on calls made between 2100 and 0600 to ASEAN countries, Hong Kong, Taiwan, Japan, Australia, New Zealand, India, and the Middle East.

Although it's a wonderful feeling dialing direct in minutes to a friend in New York from your a/c hotel room overlooking the Surabaya skyline, hotels levy a preposterously high surcharge for calls made by guests. Instead, just take a *becak* down to the city telephone office. In Jakarta and other larger cities, it's open 24 hours a day, 7 days a week. For overseas cables, allow 36 hours. A 15-word full-rate cable to the U.S. runs Rp8050, telex about Rp10,000. Cables sent to points within Indonesia are much cheaper.

Photocopying/High Tech

Shops offering cheap photocopies are found in every urban center. Copyright laws are totally ignored so that you are able to have a whole book copied, bound in hard cover in the color paper of your choice, in only 1 hour. Even government documents marked CONFIDENTIAL will be copied without hesitation. It's virtually impossible for the Indonesian authorities to prevent the circulation of banned material, and censored articles from contraband copies of the *Far Eastern Economic Review* and *Newsweek* are not that difficult to come by. Prices for photocopies vary: in Yogya, Rp15 per copy; in Bali, Rp20; and in the "Executive Center" in Jakarta's Borobudur Hotel, Rp200 (no wonder foreign businessmen find Indonesia so expensive!).

In a reverse of Third World exploitation, Indonesians are into computer piracy in a big way. Software is outrageously cheap. Hundreds of programs—DBase III, Pagemaker, Multiplan, Flight Simulator, Visicalc—can be bought for about Rp8000 per disc, which includes the pirated manual. If you plan to bring into Indonesia any computers and other high-tech equipment, you must declare it and deposit the purchase price at Indonesian customs. Customs may or may not return your deposit and may even hold your equipment for several months! The solution here is to buy your video equipment, hardware, or whatever, in Jakarta.

TIME

There are 3 time zones in Indonesia. West Indonesia Standard Time (Java, Bali) is Greenwich Mean Time plus 7 hours; Central Indonesia Standard Time (Lombok, Nusatenggara) is GMT plus 8 hours; East Indonesia Standard Time (Maluku, Irian Jaya) is GMT plus 9 hours. What this means is (daylight savings time excluded), at midnight in London, it's 0700 in Jakarta and Denpasar, 0800 in Lombok and 0900 in Ambon. (It's also 1000 in Sydney, 1600 in Los Angeles, and 1900 in New York.) In Jakarta, for the correct time, dial 103. Most of Indonesia is on or so close to the equator that the days and nights are about the same length. On Bali, about midpoint in the archipelago, the sun rises at 0500 and sets at 1700.

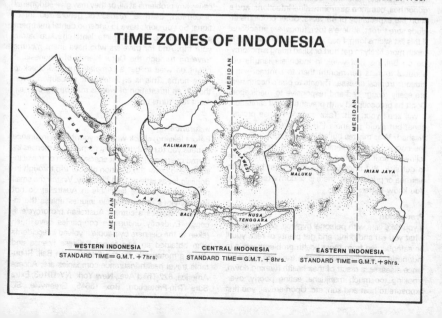

TIME ZONES OF INDONESIA

WESTERN INDONESIA	CENTRAL INDONESIA	EASTERN INDONESIA
STANDARD TIME= G.M.T. +7hrs.	STANDARD TIME= G.M.T. +8hrs.	STANDARD TIME= G.M.T. +9hrs.

Business Hours

Very flexible, depending on numerous variables. The work week in Indonesia is convoluted because of mixing the 2 religious schemes. The Islamic calendar is used simultaneously with the Gregorian calendar. Banks, offices, and schools close early on Friday because it's the Sabbath, but in order to fit in with the world at large, Sunday is also observed as a day of rest. Saturday, meanwhile, is a partial work day, so their work week consists of 4 full days and 2 partial days (they get the worst of both worlds). During major religious holidays such as the month-long Muslim fast (puasa), restaurants in Islamic areas are most likely closed during the daylight hours.

Generally speaking, government offices open at 0800 Mon.-Sat., closing at 1500 or 1600 Mon.-Thurs., 1130 on Fri., and 1400 on Saturday. Always get an early start for government offices, before the lines get long and the day grows hot. Banks are open 0800-1200 Mon.-Fri., and 0800-1100 on Sat.; bank branches in hotels, however, often remain open into the afternoon, and moneychangers in the tourist centers stay open at night. Shops operate from 0900 to 1800 or later, 6 days a week. Shopping centers, department stores, and supermarkets in the big cities frequently remain open until 2100. Expect business to take midday lunch breaks of an hour or more during which time no one answers the phone, even in Jakarta.

HEALTH

Traveling in Indonesia can be medically safe, if you get the appropriate immunizations, and take precautionary steps regarding food, drink, and cleanliness. In fact, if you work it right, you could return in better health than before you left! The West poses at least as many dangers to one's health as Indonesia, but in the West illnesses are more insidious and long-term, arising from tensions, unrestrained self-indulgence, environmental pollution, chemical additives in food, and so on. There's no Indonesian national disease, but the most common ailments are dysentery, hepatitis, hookworm, tapeworm, roundworm, amoebas, enteric parasites, cholera, trachoma, tuberculosis, gonorrhea, common gastrointestinal infections, and a short life expectancy of 49 years. Other problems include sore throat, athlete's foot, fungal ear infections. If this list seems long, keep in mind that the traveler is much more likely to get hurt or killed riding a motorcycle on Bali his first week in Indonesia (snuffs out about 3 tourists per month) than to contract some hideous tropical disease. Threats to one's health here are easily recognized and responsive to medication. Don't be preoccupied with prevention and sanitation; it will spoil your visit. Take common-sense precautions, but avoid paranoia ("How were these dishes washed? Was this tea boiled long enough?"). Even in the swank hotels hygienic techniques aren't always followed, so if it's your turn to get sick, you're gonna get sick. But once you have your first bout with diarrhea or prickly heat, there is seldom a reccurence. You know better.

Prevention

If you take care with personal hygiene, use caution in what you eat and drink, and get plenty of rest, you'll be safeguarded from most health problems while in Indonesia. Most illnesses among travelers are resistance diseases, a result of their health running down, smoking too much marijuana, eating poorly, overexposure to heat and sun, etc. Upon arrival, you first owe it to yourself to become acclimated to the tropical environment: maintain adequate fluid and salt intakes, avoid fatigue, dress light. Jet lag may change your sleeping patterns and eating habits, so at first plan extra rest. Being informed about what and where the risks are and how to avoid them is your very best protection. If you hear there's a cholera epidemic in Cirebon, stay away. What's wrong with walking barefoot in the tropics? Several different types of infections, such as tetanus and Cutaneous Larra Mirgnas, which can enter the body through the skin, thrive in the tropics. They don't need a cut as a doorway, but can burrow in through the skin itself. These may not cause any problems at all, or they may give abdominal discomfort, diarrhea, rashes, or generalized infections. So you don't have to undergo dental treatment in Indonesia, go for a complete dental checkup before your trip. And for travelers who have spent months traveling through the Outer Islands of Indonesia, it might be wise to get a complete medical checkup once home. This is an intelligent precaution, even though an infestation of worms may be the only ailment that turns up.

Insurance

Before leaving, check whether your health insurance entitles you to reimbursement of medical expenses incurred overseas. If not, get special health or travel insurance to cover the duration of your trip through Indonesia for as little as US$3 per day. Watch the small print—some policies (available in Australia) do not pay damages on motorcycle injuries unless the insured possesses a current Australian motorcycle license. Evidently, insurance companies have been taken to the cleaners by people involved in accidents who obtained an easy-to-get Balinese license and drove a motorcycle for the first time on Bali. Reputable travel health insurance companies are: Access America, 622 Third Ave., New York, NY 10163; Extra Sure Trip-Protection, Box 16645, Greenville, SC

29606, tel. (808) 242-4154; Health Care Abroad, 923 Investment Bldg., 1511 K St. NW, Washington, D.C. 20009, tel. (202) 393-5500; and Traveller's Medical Service, Golden Square, Petworth, West Sussex GU28 OAP, tel. (0798) 43383.

IMMUNIZATIONS

Pre-travel immunizations give partial protection. Tetanus, polio, and yellow-fever vaccines are very effective, but others, such as cholera, are not. First have a look at the latest World Immunization Chart of IAMAT (International Assoc. for Medical Assistance to Travelers), 350 Fifth Ave., Suite 5620, New York, NY 10001, or find out from an official vaccine center which immunizations are currently required for travel to Indonesia (double-check with the Indonesian Embassy). Another good place to check in the U.S. is the Center for Disease Control in Atlanta, tel. (404) 639-3311. To keep your arms from falling off, get your immunizations over a couple of months rather than having every one of them done in a rush shortly before you leave. The whole series never has to be repeated but you should receive boosters for any immunization for which the effective period has elapsed. Most Westerners have had polio immunizations as children, and therefore need only a booster. You should be protected against tetanus, which is more prevalent in the tropics. A yellow-fever vaccination is only required for those arriving within 6 days after leaving or transiting a yellow fever locale. It's a good idea to be minimally vaccinated against cholera. Typhoid and paratyphoid vaccinations are optional but advisable; it's better to be over-protected, as a serious illness can spoil your trip. Tuberculosis is common in Indonesia, and many countries advise getting the BCG skin test before your trip to establish that you have a negative reaction, then get retested about 2 months after you return home. Consult your doctor concerning immunizations for children which may include triple antigen (DPT), polio, measles, rubella (German measles), and mumps. You should get immunized against measles if you've never had one, or were vaccinated against it before 1969. A gamma-globulin injection will give you about 6 months protection against hepatitis; this shot, however, only gives protection against infectious hepatitis and not serum hepatitis, which is caught from injections using unclean hypodermic needles. Rabies vaccinations are unnecessary unless you are likely to be playing with bats, working as a zookeeper at a wild rodent park, or as a temple guard on Bali.

Vaccination Centers
Since no vaccinations or inoculations are at present required except for visitors arriving from infected areas, you won't even be asked for your *Buku Kuning* ("yellow booklet"). This is the International Certificate

of Vaccination, required by law for international travel, which records all immunizations and vaccinations. The booklet is available from designated vaccination centers around the world or direct from your doctor. In the U.S., many local public-health departments give shots for free, charging only a small fee for the stamp in your vaccination certificate. In Australia, contact the Commonwealth Office Health Centers. In Indonesia itself, cholera and yellow-fever vaccinations are dispensed at Jakarta's Soekarno/Hatta Airport in Cengkareng, though the cheapest place to get immunizations in Jakarta is Dinas Kesehatan, Jl. Kesehatan 10.

FOOD AND DRINK

Food and water-borne infections are one of the greatest threats to the traveler in the tropics. Bacterial infections (typhoid, paratyphoid, cholera, salmonella, shigella), infectious hepatitis, and such lovely parasitic infections as guineaworm, bilharzia, bacillary dysentery, amoebic dysentery, worms, and giardiasis can all be transmitted by contaminated food, water, and ice cubes. As dairy products are often made with untreated water and unpasteurized milk, they are outstanding media for the breeding of many pathogenic bacteria. So it's advisable not to drink local fresh milk or eat ice cream sold by street vendors. Stick to dairy products labeled as pasteurized. Diamond, Peters, and Campina are quality brand-name ice cream products sold locally. Also, hotel ice creams are usually safe. All milk should be boiled before it's drunk to cut down drastically on your chances of catching dysentery, typhoid, brucellosis, or even polio. Also, drink your milk right after you boil it as germs will immediately start breeding again. Yogurt, being relatively more acidic, is considered safer, and in fact is a remedy for upset stomach.

All vegetables and fruit eaten raw should be thoroughly washed, rinsed, and peeled before eating. Vegetables used in raw salads may have been fertilized with "night soil" (human excrement) and the contaminating organisms may remain on the vegetable surface. Lettuce and cabbage are particularly difficult to clean. Salad dressings (such as mayonnaise) may be a potential source of bacterial infection, especially if it's been sitting out. All meat and fish should be very well cooked or you stand the chance of being infested by worms. Seafood should be eaten while fresh and shellfish should always be thoroughly cooked. Cold meats provide an excellent media for the multiplication of bacteria, particularly in the heat and humidity of the tropics. Stick to well-cooked meals served hot; don't eat rare meats, and avoid cold buffets.

Contaminated Water
One of the biggest culprits in transmitting disease.

Diseases which may be transmitted by water include cholera, typhoid fever, bacillary dysentery, giardiasis. The water (well water, tap water, and water used for making ice) in most tropical countries must be considered unsafe to drink because of poor sewage disposal and improperly treated water supplies. Bottled water from a reputable firm or water you have treated yourself (see below) should be the only water considered safe to drink. Avoid ice cubes, unless they have been made from boiled water. Hot beverages carry fewer disease-causing organisms than cold beverages. Non-carbonated bottled drinks may or may not be safe to drink, but use carbonated, bottled, or boiled water instead of tap water for brushing your teeth. In restaurants unboiled water is often used for washing dishes and cooking certain foods. The freezing of water does not kill the organisms, nor does the alcohol in a drink! There are several practical methods to make water safe to drink. If you boil it briskly for 10 min., all the major disease organisms will be killed. But don't transfer it to a container which hasn't been sterilized by rinsing with boiled water. Chemical sterilization, such as water purification tablets like Halazone, is popular, but watch for side effects. Another chlorine-based method is to add sufficient laundry bleach so that a slight chlorine odor is detectable in the water after mixing thoroughly in a clean container. Let stand for 30 min. before drinking. Adding 5-10 drops of tincture of iodine per liter also works well; let stand for 20 minutes.

Salt

When your body sweats under the tropical sun you lose salt, so more should be added to your diet. Initial jet lag and fatigue might simply be caused by salt deprivation. Loss of body fluids as a result of diarrhea or dysentery also calls for an increased consumption of salt. Salt tablets are not really necessary, but after heavy physical exercise you might add a little extra salt to your food. If trekking into remote areas of Indonesia, take along ordinary salt. A mixture of salt and water also serves as a mild antiseptic. If you have a sore throat gargle with this solution.

EXHAUSTION AND HEAT EXPOSURE

Travelers need to adjust to a climate that is extreme by Western standards, possibly producing fatigue and loss of appetite for the new arrival. Acclimating to the enervating heat and humidity could take weeks. First, slow down the pace. Don't overdo activity and get overtired. No one else does. Get plenty of sleep. Persuade yourself to follow the Indonesian custom of *tidur siang* (napping) sometime between 1200 and 1600, the hottest part of the day, or at least lie low during this time when only mad dogs and Dutchmen are out. Drink increased amounts of water with fresh lemon and lime juice, and make sure there's salt in your diet. Restrict alcohol and smoking. Avoid rich, fatty foods. Don't eat too much fruit as this can cause stomachaches and diarrhea. Adapt yourself to exposure to the sun gradually; you'll be able to stay out in it more and more. Use suntan creams or zinc oxide. Small children should be especially careful. Wear loose cotton clothing, light in color and weight. Wear a floppy hat and walk in the shade. Or carry an umbrella as Indonesians do and you'll walk in the shade all the time. Indonesian women put rice powder on their faces to protect their skins from the sun and to keep their complexions from turning dark. Travel in really hot areas only at dawn or dusk, and prevent travel exhaustion by breaking up marathon trips with stopovers. Some Indonesians will take a *mandi* up to 3 times a day to stay cool by keeping the surface temperature of their bodies low.

Heatstroke Prevention

Heatstroke is caused by the breakdown of the body's sweating mechanism. Symptoms are a marked increase in body temperature to over 40 degrees C (105 degrees F) accompanied by reduction in perspiration, and sometimes nausea or vomiting. Avoid heatstroke by drinking adequate fluids, taking in enough salt, wearing sensible and naturally made clothing, and moderating your intake of alcohol. Though rare, heatstroke is an emergency. The victim should be taken to a cool room, doused with cold water, his body fanned and sponged until his temperature drops to at least 39 degrees C (102 degrees F), at which point the sponging should stop. Keep patient at rest.

DIARRHEA

Travelers' diarrhea constitutes 90% of travel health problems, affecting about half of the 5 million visitors to the tropics each year. Diarrhea often begins within a few days of arrival in a tropical climate. Many stomach troubles are a result of sudden changes of climate, food, and water, rather than poor hygiene during food preparation. Travelers are exposed to organisms they're not used to. This is equally true for travelers from the tropics who are visiting the West. Emotional upsets or the stress of travel may also play a role in causing simple diarrhea. It generally is a self-limiting disease lasting only 1-3 days. If it persists for more than 5 days, see a doctor. People frequently refer to acute diarrhea as dysentery but this is a misnomer. Dysentery is a serious disease characterized by blood mucus and/or pus in the stool. So if you have severe diarrhea which lasts more than 2-3 days, accompanied by fever, black-colored stools or painful stomach cramps, you may have amoebic or bacillary dysentery. Seek medical attention as this disease can cause severe damage to the intestines and to general health. Diarrhea is much more common than dysentery. If you're eliminating more than a liter an hour, be sure to drink that much water because it could be cholera; you might need intravenous feeding.

SUGGESTED MEDICAL TREATMENTS

MINOR TREATMENTS

Cuts

Since bacteria breed so quickly in this climate, the tiniest cut or sore could soon become a festering ugly tropical ulcer which necessitates prolonged antibiotic treatment. Most tropical ulcers and sores are due to mosquito bites. The most painful and difficult bites to heal are on the feet and ankles. Rub your feet and ankles with good repellent or wear woolen socks and long jeans. To protect against insects, use mosquito netting. The cheaper hotels don't usually provide mosquito netting, but mosquito coils work quite effectively. Wear long sleeves and long trousers at sundown, apply insect repellent after dark, cover legs and wear protective foot gear when walking through tall grass. If you're breaking in a new pair of sandals, protect your skin against abrasions by wearing bandaids.

Whenever the skin is broken, it requires much more attention than in colder climates. First, clean the opening with soap and water, apply some antiseptic cream, and cover it well with a bandaid. Re-clean the cut and change the bandaid every day, more often if it gets damp or wet. If it's a large cut or wound, use a non-stick sterile gauze dressing after cleansing the wound carefully with soap and water. If you can't have it sutured, at least try to join the skin's edges. If the wound is bleeding badly, apply direct pressure and dressings, or a clean handkerchief or T-shirt until the bleeding stops. As long as you have open wounds, avoid the beach. Swimming in the sea is also best avoided. If you can't resist the beautiful beaches, immediately after leaving the ocean wash the wound and apply a new dressing. If an infection sets in (inflammation and pain after 2 days), soak the wound in hot water for at least 15 min., cover with a sterile dressing, then take an antibiotic pill once every 6 hours on an empty stomach.

Food Poisoning

Food poisoning lasts about 3 days and little can be done for this awful illness. Avoid foods not adequately refrigerated, including shellfish, salads, mayonnaise, and custard-filled pastries served under unsanitary conditions.

Fungal Infections

These include athlete's foot and ringworm. Avoid them by using only your own towel, wearing flip-flops to bathe, using open sandals, and not wearing nylon or other synthetic garments. Ringworm is not really a worm but a fungal infection which produces a red-ringed patch, usually on the trunk of the body, accompanied by itching, pain, and scaling. When it's cured it just leaves a small red spot; within a year new skin appears. Dab on a Chinese medicine called 3-Leg-Brand Ringworm Cure. One application is enough. Go into a Chinese apothecary and point at the fungus; they'll know

what you need. Or use a benzoic acid compound. Tinaderm, available in the UK, is a cream applied at night. In the U.S., try Micatin, a broad spectrum anti-fungal; Selsun dandruff shampoo can also be used in the treatment of fungal infections. First wet the area, rub shampoo on like soap, leave for 5-10 min., then rinse off with water. Treat this way 2-3 times. In Indonesia, buy the wide-spectrum anti-fungus Mycolog. You need the cream or lotion, and powder in case infected areas get soaked with sweat. In the case of vaginal infections, fungus is caused by a bacterial imbalance. Yogurt is a bacterial culture, so yogurt on a tampon neutralizes the fungus and soothes the itch.

Infections And Skin Ailments

In a tropical climate, you need to be more careful about personal hygiene. Bacteria thrive in hot humid areas, causing an increase in a variety of infections. Bacteria can enter the body through wounds or insect bites, especially those which have been scratched. Extra care should be taken in drying yourself, particularly around the ears, after bathing or swimming, so rashes won't develop. Phisohex is effective for cleaning rashes and sores. Corn starch, baby powder, or arrowroot powder help keep the skin dry, preventing rashes which tend to develop if you're always splashing your anus with water from Indonesian toilets. Cutaneous larva migrans is a skin infection caused most frequently by the larval form of dog and cat hookworms and is picked up by direct skin contact with contaminated soil. These larvae penetrate the skin; they don't grow to maturity but travel a tortuous path just under the skin, leaving a tiny trail behind them, progressing about 2-5 cm a day. The presence of the larvae often produces severe itching at the site; secondary infection, introduced by scratching, may be a problem. Always wear enclosed shoes or flippers covering the whole foot when entering water; never walk in bare feet on coral. Avoid *all* contact with cone shells in reefs and shallow waters, as these inject a dangerous venom. Handle only with forceps. Don't put live cone shells in your pocket.

Leeches

Usually a problem only above 1,200 m altitude, leeches wait insidiously at the sides of trails, cling to trees, or hang from leaves overhead along dense jungle tracks used by deer and wild pigs. They smell human perspiration, then wait to fall onto your hair, beard (they love moist darkness) or neck, push their suckers through boot eyelets, get under your belt and into the groin area, and even penetrate the anus. They also attack at night while you're sleeping. Clothes only offer a catchhold for leeches; you might try walking barefoot and half naked like the Dayaks of Kalimantan who cover their bodies with mud while hiking. Also effective is to apply a mixture of tobacco juice and water on your skin and let it dry. If you're naked you can flick them off as you see them. They usually can't be felt until they drop off saturated with blood, or you feel a trickle of blood or a warm sticky spot under your clothes or inside your boot. If they've attached themselves, either hold a lighted match or cigarette to them or apply salt or iodine to make them fall off, then stick on a cigarette paper to help stop the flow of blood as they inject an anti-coagulant. Don't tear them off as the head remains embedded and bites could become inflamed.

Aches

Indonesians think it ludicrous that Westerners take aspirin for a headache when the only sensible thing to do is to get a massage. The Danis of Irian Jaya tie smoked charmed grasses around the neck, and some Indonesians wear little white tapes containing an anesthetic on their temples. There's also a green paste to smear on the forehead to cure headaches. The *krok*-treatment consists of rubbing I Ching coins on the muscles in combination with eucalyptus oil to produce a friction rash so the pores open to let out the pain and heat (and evil). *Kayumanis* is a stick which is chewed for throat ailments; it tastes sweet but is expensive at Rp4000 a bundle.

Plants

Don't be too quick to blame insects when you return from a hike with your hand or leg swollen or tingling with a rash. A great variety of plants harbor toxic chemicals in their leaves, or sprout nasty nettles. Merely brushing against them results in nagging skin irritations. Some people are more sensitive than others. Exercise caution with garden and house plants, particularly when children are around; some are poisonous if eaten. Carry an antihistamine cream to soothe severe skin irritations.

Prickly Heat

An intensely irritating skin rash quite frequently encountered in the tropics, usually soon after arrival. Red pimples or blisters break out on areas of the body that are always moist from sweating—under a tight-fitting belt, in the armpits or crotch area, and behind the knees. Your chances of getting it can be lessened by wearing loose-fitting cotton clothing and by avoiding nylon and synthetic materials that don't "breathe." To treat it, splash cold water on the rash to cool it, dab it dry, then apply a dusting powder. Calamine lotion can also be used to soothe the skin. In severe cases, when the rash keeps you awake at night, use an antiseptic powder and even an antihistamine. To keep it from acting up, cut down on your use of soap.

Snakebite

Of Indonesia's 450 species of snakes, only 5 are considered dangerously poisonous. Cobras need to be treated with great caution, since they are venomous (pythons are not), and can even be found in cities. Other common poisonous snakes are the *krait,* easily recognized by alternate black-and-white bands, and a small gray snake with an attractive pink head. Snakebite treatment consists of having the victim lie down at complete rest. Immobilize the limb and apply firm pressure over bitten area with a roller bandage. If bitten on the foot or ankle, bind one leg to the other for sup-

port; if bitten on the hand or wrist, use an improvised splint. If victim becomes unconscious, turn him on to the side and keep airway clear. Alert the nearest hospital immediately, while keeping the victim as calm and as immobile as possible. Don't wash, cut, or suck the bite site. Do *not* apply a tourniquet.

Venereal Disease

Two cases of AIDS were reported in 1986. Both Dutch tourists, one succumbed to the disease in the General Hospital in Denpasar on Bali. His companion, who tested positive, left the country together with the remains of his friend. Being a seafaring nation, gonorrhea has spread to most ports of the archipelago. Syphillis is much less common. In the cities, the higher-paid hotel call girls are less likely to be infected. Silir, outside of Solo (C. Java), and Perloah outside of Brastagi (N. Sumatra), are compounds established to keep better control over prostitution; in these and other "special" villages, the prostitutes are regularly examined by doctors and given antibiotic shots once weekly. Using a condom will give you the best available protection. You should also urinate after intercourse and wash your genitals with soap and water. You see innumerable carts selling all manner of pills, ointments, and antibiotics on the streets of such brothel districts as Bungunrecho in Surabaya, but these might only relieve the symptoms and usually will not wipe out the infection. You may have unhappily acquired more than one kind of VD and if you treat just one, it might mask the effects of another. Frequenters of brothels swear by Bactarim (Roche, Switzerland) as a preventative (20 tablets for Rp2200). If you *do* get gonorrhea, it's only serious if ignored or not recognized. It's somewhat like getting a runny nose, except a lot easier to clear up. Don't try treating it yourself; you should have a full lab test in a *rumah sakit* (public hospital). The treatment given in an outpatient clinic is often much cheaper than that given in a private doctor's office. A public hospital usually charges you around Rp5000 for an injection of penicillin or tetracycline. You need 2 injections plus a course of ampicillin. A private hospital or one run by a church group could charge you up to Rp25,000 for this very routine and simple treatment.

Worms

Worm *(caci)* infestations are common in warm countries like Indonesia where rainfall is plentiful. Hookworm eggs are passed into the soil in human or animal feces. Eggs hatch in the soil and the larval form enters the bloodstream when the skin comes in contact with this contaminated soil. Severe itching and burning may occur at the site where the parasite enters the body (often the area between the toes). Once inside, the larvae travels via the circulatory system, through the lungs, eventually arriving at the intestines where it attaches itself to the wall of the bowel. Feeding on minute amounts of blood from its human host, the hookworm develops into an adult, shaped like a tiny hook. It may cause no symptoms at all, or in heavy infections may produce anemia, especially in children. A roundworm infection may occur when you eat vegetables that have been fertilized with human feces. The eggs hatch in the stomach, from where the larvae enter the blood and may migrate to affect other organs of the body. No symptoms may be evident, or the worms may cause abdominal discomfort, diarrhea, and sometimes a generalized rash. Pinworm infestations are also common. Their eggs are often swallowed, then hatch in the stomach from where they enter the intestines and ultimately the anus where they lay their sticky white eggs. Pinworms (also called threadworms), about .5 cm long, are easy to detect in the area around the anus. Roundworms, hookworms, and pinworms are common infections which are easily spread, so all members of a traveling group should simultaneously take worm medicine. To prevent worms, wear footwear. In Indonesia, one extremely effective non-prescription anti-worm medicine is Combantrin (Rp3000 for 10 tablets). To find out if you have worms, stool lab exams are widely available, even in remote Rantepao, S. Sulawesi.

SERIOUS DISEASES

Hepatitis
One must exercise all the same precautions against this water-borne disease as one does in preventing dysentery and diarrhea. Unsanitary eating utensils and unwashed salads and fruits are prime suspects. Hepatitis is a debilitating liver disease which turns the skin and the whites of the eyes yellow, the feces whitish, and the urine deep orange or brown. These symptoms—as well as sleepiness, nausea, depression, dramatically diminished appetite—appear around 3 weeks after infection. *See a doctor*. To cure it, take liver-fortifying pills, eat nutritious foods, relax in the shade of a hill climate. Never drink alcohol, use tobacco, or take antibiotics while under treatment. Though it doesn't prevent the disease, a gammaglobulin shot beforehand ameliorates the symptoms if you *do* get hepatitis.

Cholera
Amongst travelers who stay in tourist accommodations along the most popular itineraries and who avoid potentially contaminated food and water, the risk of cholera is very small. Sometimes you hear stories of whole Javanese villages being wiped out in a cholera epidemic but in the Indonesian press you would read of "only 10 deaths—an isolated incident." In the summer of 1983 there was a big cholera epidemic in Banda Aceh; 500 people were hospitalized and 30 people died. It's around, but it would be really bad luck if a traveler contracted it (there have been only 9 confirmed cases among all U.S. travelers in the last 17 years). The ultimate preventative is to eat only cooked foods which are still hot, and drink only carbonated bottled soft drinks or beer, and boiled or safely treated water. Cholera vaccine is only about 40% effective and should not be relied upon; most countries don't require the vaccination now anyway.

Malaria
This disease strikes more than 150 million people in the world each year with more than a million deaths. In 1987, two Australians died of malaria while traveling in Indonesia.

Malaria is an acute and sometimes chronic infectious disease caused by protozoan parasites within red blood cells, resulting in various derangements of the digestive and nervous systems. The parasite is transmitted to humans by the bite of the female anopheles mosquito. Symptoms include high fever, headaches and body aches, sweating and shivering, with progressive anemia and splenic enlargement. Falciparum, cerebral malaria, is a vicious form which attacks the brain, a killer strain which is unfortunately found in Indonesia. Being bad for business, the Indonesian government doesn't want to scare off tourists by emphasizing the risks, even though the traveler could easily protect himself if he were given the proper info. Check with the Center for Infectious Diseases, Parasitic Diseases Division, Atlanta GA 30333, tel. (404) 639-3311 before leaving. The malarial season in Indonesia lasts all year and the whole country is affected below 1,200 m altitude (though Jakarta and Surabaya and their surroundings are without risk). Malaria has greatly decreased on Java but it is still found on the Outer Islands such as Nias, Flores, Kai, etc.

For the average tourist entering a malarial zone, the mainstay of protection is chloroquine phosphate (brand names: Avoclor, Reochin, and Aralen). It's essential to take your malarial-suppressant 2 weeks before arrival *and* for 4 weeks after leaving. If you take your medicine faithfully, you most likely won't be stricken. But remember no anti-malarial is 100% effective. In areas of Indonesia where malaria and other insect-borne diseases are endemic, sleep in a room with screened windows, keep well-covered after dusk, use insect repellents (surprisingly difficult to find in Indonesia), mosquito nets, and coils which don't kill mosquitos but drug them. Snake-shaped mosquito coils are jade-green in color, the heads of the 2 coils interlocked in the center. In the best tradition of Chinese puzzles, it's maddeningly difficult to divide the 2 coils without breaking them. If you're living in Indonesia, mosquitos must be deprived of their breeding areas. Do away with clogged drains, standing water, water in dishes under flower pots. **Note:** In some areas of Indonesia, such as E. Kalimantan and Irian Jaya, some malarial strains have developed immunity to chloroquine. Consult your physician to make sure your malaria-suppressant is effective against all strains of malaria. One option is to supplement a weekly dose of 300 mg chloroquine with 100 mg of proguanil taken daily, or take proguanil instead of chloroquine. Pregnant women should seek advice before taking any malaria prophylactic.

Bilharzia (Schistosomiasis)
Although you can catch bilharzia by drinking infected water, you're more likely to be infected swimming in still or slow-moving freshwater in areas where the disease is known to exist. Tiny snails breed in the water and serve as hosts to parasitic worms or "flukes" which penetrate the skin. If in doubt, rub off the water with a towel right after bathing because evidence indicates that the worms burrow into the skin only after the infected water has evaporated. Symptoms: blood in urine, diarrhea, blood and mucus in the stools, general feeling of ill health.

Prevention

Don't overconsume fruits, especially during Dec. and Jan.; even the Balinese get the infamous "Bali Belly" during this epidemic season. Avoid all obvious sources of contaminated food and drink. Before you consider eating in a *warung* or restaurant, look closely at the faces and hands of the cooks and people who will be serving you. They also eat the food they sell. If their faces reflect ill-health, their fingernails are dirty, and their establishment is generally unkempt and unsanitary, walk on by. Eat hot chili peppers with your meals—tourists get the shits so often because they don't eat the hot spicy food which kills most of the bacteria. If you're unused to highly seasoned meals, break yourself in to it gradually. Also follow the advice in the "Food and Drink" section of this chapter.

Diet

If diarrhea strikes, you lose a considerable amount of fluid and salt. These *must* be replenished by immediately drinking lots of fluids (but not alcohol or strong coffee) to avoid dehydration. Take in clear fluids such as water, weak tea with sugar, juice, clear soup or broth (no milk) or soda that has stood awhile so the carbonation is gone. The very best liquid is an oral rehydration solution, available in pharmacies everywhere, which contains the necessary salts. Experienced travelers who go into remote areas often carry their own special preparation: combine a teaspoon salt, ½ teaspoon baking soda, 4 teaspoons cream of tartar, and 6 teaspoons sugar. Add this to a liter of water. You can prepare the dry mixture ahead of time and pack it along in case you need it. Gradually add such plain foods as biscuits, boiled rice, bread, boiled eggs, adding other solid foods until you recover. Indonesians, if they eat at all, drink *jamu* and eat the young *jambu* fruit and plain rice. Bananas are good because they're bland and contain the binding agent pectin. Pawpaw is also useful, and since the fruit is an enzyme, it's easily digested. Avoid fatty, spicy foods and stick to bland foods while under treatment. Add milk products last. Often, after a serious diarrhea attack, your body is dehydrated and there could be painful muscular contractions in the stomach; fruit juice or cola with a teaspoon of salt dissolved in it will counteract this.

Medicine

Against mild dysentery or fever, 10 drops of tincture of opium in a small amount of water, up to 5 times daily, works marvelously. Or 10 papaya or pumpkin seeds a day should also do it. Another native cure is to eat the skin of the papaya or small brown pills made from papaya skin by the Balinese (this cure has no constipation afterwards). Isogel is a natural vegetable material which soothes and regulates the stomach. It comes in large packets which you can, with any liquid, decant into smaller plastic bottles. If you believe in white man's medicine, and if your immune system can handle it, a well-tried and effective remedy is

codeine-phosphate, available only by prescription. An over-the-counter drug sold in Indonesia which clears up diarrhea is Diatabs. One ounce of Pepto Bismol liquid taken every 30 min. provides symptomatic relief for most people with diarrhea. Enterovioform and Mexaform are dangerous (cause eye and nerve damage) and should be avoided. Lomotil, minuscule white tablets, works outstandingly well, but should not be used for more than a day or 2 since it has the potential of locking in the infection. Another surefire remedy is to take one 250 mg tetracycline capsule at the first signs of diarrhea; symptoms should disappear in a matter of hours. More difficult cases may require 4 capsules a day for 1-2 days. Remember that many of the remedies for the shits (Lomotil, Imodium, Kaolin, Diocalm, Isogel, tetracycline, or paregoric) should be used sparingly as they only relieve the symptoms and do not actually cure the disease. Diarrhea could be the symptom of a wide variety of diseases. Don't use these medicines if you have high fever or chills, or with persistent or bloody diarrhea.

MEDICAL TREATMENT IN INDONESIA

Jamu

The great Dutch botanist Rumphius (1628-1702) was one of the first to recognize the curative powers of *jamu* in his remarkable work *The Ambonese Herbal* (1741). These over-the-counter herbal medicines are derived from the forests of Indonesia—hidden pharmacies of potent medicines in the form of plants, grasses, minerals, fungi, roots, barks, parts of mammals, birds, reptiles. They come in pills, capsules, powders, beans, peas, flat seeds, or can look like tea leaves. Today you see tri-colored *jamu* stalls in the markets, painted up like barber poles with row upon row of small packages, little jars and bottles lining the shelves. You need no doctor's prescription. Explain your problem to the vendor and he'll know what you'll need. Follow the dosage directions on the packet or bottle. *Jamu* is cheap (about Rp300-500 per packet); the "super" is served with an egg, 2 sorts of wine, a cup of sweet tea and a piece of candy afterwards, all for Rp1500-2000. Most *jamu* brands have real bizarre names like Rooster *(Cap Jago)* or the Fountain of Youth *(Air Mancur)*.

There are hundreds of different *jamu*, one for seemingly every conceivable malady. Javanese women look astonishingly well preserved after having 6 kids because new mothers take up to 10 *jamu* internally and externally over a period of 40 days after delivery to remove any excess blood from the body, to contract uterine muscles, for slimming, to restore vigor, and to reinforce sex appeal. *Patmosari*, or *Jamu Galian Singset*, makes women between 20 and 50 younger looking, tightens the vagina, revitalizes and slims. Women over 40 drink a special *jamu* to keep themselves from getting too thin. *Jelok Temu* is given to 1-year-old babies for strength. *Jantung* fortifies the heart. *Lular* paste, made from rice mixed with pulverized bark and flowers, slows the wrinkling and aging process. *Mangir* is a yellow powder put on the skin to make it clear, fragrant, refined. *Ginjal* is for inflamed appendix, making an operation unnecessary. *Kumis Kucing* (cat whiskers) is for urinary tract infections. *Beras Kencur* peps you up all day. If you're tired, feeling really depressed, take a 40-day course of the antidepressant *Colasan,* which really blasts you right out of whatever is hanging you up.

Other *jamu* treat colds, tightness or dizziness in the head, runny nose, sore throat, bronchitis, flu, "starry eyes"; there are anti-cough herbs, and others for sore bones, backaches, and listlessness. There are men's tonics to increase strength. If rubbed on at night, all feelings of tiredness and stiffness are gone by morning. They've even got a special *jamu* for *becak* drivers and for other laborers who do extreme physical labor, as well as herbs that strengthen and increase the health of hard-working women. *Jamu* can quickly smooth out wrinkled skin, cure bloodshot eyes and hangovers, intestinal tapeworms, stomach sickness, indigestion and overeating, pimples, skin diseases and rashes. Young girls take *Kokok* after menstruation, which cleanses the blood, beautifies, makes the eyes and face bright again. Specific *jamu* are for late menstruation or taken before to ensure that the cycle comes on time (but may cause abortions if 1-2 months pregnant). Special aphrodisiac *jamu* are available to increase fertility. If women, especially mothers with many children, take "Magic Formula No. 125," they will find that their husbands will become more considerate.

Pharmacies

You can buy most medicines in the pharmacies *(apotik)* of Indonesia without a prescription; in smaller pharmacies feel free to bargain. Most international-standard hotels have pharmacies. American drug companies have manufacturing subsidiaries in Indonesia, particularly in Jakarta, so many U.S. medications are available and are just as expensive as they are in the West. Because brand names might be different, it helps to know the medicine's generic name. If you can't read Indonesian, be sure to have the pharmacist explain the proper dosage, which might be different than what you're accustomed to. Get ahold of the pharmaceutical directory *Iso Indonesia* (Rp7000), which gives an explanation of what each drug is and what it's used for (also available in English). If you require a particular medicine over a long period of time, you better bring your own supply. This includes birth control pills, vitamins, blood pressure medication, and thyroid or estrogen hormones. Keep all medicines out of reach of Indonesians; pills are like candy to them.

Doctors

Although doctors in Indonesia charge only Rp5000-10,000 per visit, they can make some big mistakes. They often pretend they know everything but they do not. To make up for their dearth of diagnostic skill, they tend to prescribe a standard recipe of antibiotics, antihistamines, tranquilizers, and vitamins for 3 days. They figure this recipe covers about anything that could go wrong with you. And whatever it is, the Indonesian doctor is going to stick you with a needle. If you're ill, insist on a blood test because they seldom order one. Better than taking pills and needles is to choose a natural treatment of *jamu* (the finest herbalists are in Solo, C. Java). As a general rule, if you have to go to a doctor at all, go to a Chinese doctor in the cities. The proprietor of any hotel or *losmen* can come up with the name of a reliable and reasonably priced *dokter* or two. If you feel that language will be a problem, get the names of English, German, or French-speaking doctors from your respective embassy or consulate. Or call representatives of a shipping company or airline from your home country; they can often suggest names of good doctors. Although there are English-speaking doctors, there are no foreign doctors with private practices in Indonesia. The government no longer issues work permits to foreign physicians.

Specialists

Routine dental care such as cleaning and fillings can be performed in all the main cities. Locate a good *dokter gigi* (dentist) through your embassy or consulate, but complicated root canal therapy, surgery, or bridge contruction and repair is often referred to specialists in Singapore. No certified orthodontists work in Jakarta. Dental floss is hard to find in Indonesia, so bring an ample supply. It's wise to attend to all your dental needs before arriving in Indonesia. Jakarta optometrists do satisfactory lenswork, but take an extra pair of glasses and lens prescription, contact lens cleaning and storage fluids.

Hospitals

If you're seriously ill, go to Jakarta, Semarang, Bandung, Surabaya, Medan, or Singapore—major cities which have the best-equipped hospitals, many with 24-hour emergency service. All reports indicate that Bali has really substandard medical services (not one X-ray machine on the whole island) and that malpractice is widespread. Jakarta has Indonesia's best medical services, although adequate medical coverage is also offered in other cities on Java—Bethesda Hospital, Yogya, C. Java, tel. 22812; RS Baptist, Jl. Mauni Kediri, E. Java, tel. 809 (run by Americans, English-speaking staff), and the Catholic Hospital St. Vicentius a Laulo, Surabaya, E. Java (tel. 7562). Hospitals are reluctant to bill; it's either cash on the line or at least part payment in advance. Equipment is generally pretty rustic. Their fees usually include meals, but the Indonesian custom is for families to supplement these. Many Indonesian hospitals have no buzzer system which summons a nurse, so relatives must sleep beside the bed to give attention. In many of the Outer Islands and remote areas of Indonesia, the only treatment available is at small, foreign-supported missionary clinics or crowded, poorly staffed and outfitted government health centers *(puskesma)*. If you've been struck by a *bemo*, a clinic won't take you; only a *rumah sakit* (hospital) can accept emergency cases. In some areas, you are hours away from medical treatment: on Samosir Island in the middle of Lake Toba (N. Sumatra), the only contact to the mainland—and the nearest hospital—is by radio. Major medical clinics in Jakarta include:

The Medical Scheme, Setiabudi Building, Jl. H. Rasuna Said Kuningan, tel. 513 367. Their staff speaks either English or Dutch. Consulting hours Mon.-Fri. 0830-1530; 24-hour emergency service.

The Metropolitan Clinic, Wisata Office Tower, 2nd Floor, Hotel Wisata (behind Hotel Indonesia), Jl. Thamrin, tel. 320 408. This large private clinic has 16 departments including lab, X-ray, physical therapy. Over 65 physicians and dentists in group practice. Consulting hours vary so call for an appointment. Info pamphlet available.

S.O.S. Medika, tel. 733 014. Offers both daily clinic services and 24-hour home visit service. Their house call service includes doctor, other necessary staff, plus special emergency medical equipment. Their 24-hour ambulance service charges around Rp45,000 per hour. S.O.S. Medika also arranges medical evacuations from Indonesia to Singapore or elsewhere. All 30 doctors speak English; some also speak Dutch, French, German.

St. Carolus Hospital, Jl. Salemba Raya 41, tel. 883 091. A private hospital with an excellent reputation. Accepts emergencies on a space available basis (ask for extension 264).

DUKUN

The Indonesian folk doctor. Long-established opponents of Western medicine, these barefoot doctors have used locally made remedies and treatments for thousands of years. Though most of the *dukun's* medicines have never been laboratory tested, many have a sound scientific basis in modern medicine *(dukun* were the first to use quinine to cure malaria). Whenever one of these old men die, it's like a library has burned down, knowledge never to be recovered. Great numbers of Indonesia's 173 million (mostly rural) people put their faith in the *dukun*. For the villager he's cheap and on the spot; they will go to him before a hospital or clinic. In the cities often you see *dukun* standing or squatting in parks or on street corners in the middle of circles 5 people deep, shouting out the wondrous properties of medicines spread out on blankets before them. The *dukun* often receives no consultation fee but gets his income from the sale of his herbs and potions only.

It's believed that some *dukun* are men of supernatural powers who contain souls of dead people who talk through them, speaking in tongues or in Old Javanese. Among them are witch doctors who can exorcize evil spirits from houses and heal illnesses by faith. They claim to be able to cure people who have been secretly poisoned or purge them of spells cast on them by less powerful *dukun*. These native medicos believe that mind rules over matter; for psychosomatic sicknesses they dispense psychosomatic cures. Secret Islamic sayings and prayers are written on pieces of paper, then dunked in a glass of water. When drunk, the patient is cured of his ailment. *Dukun* can also improve a client's sex appeal. A "diamond blown onto the lips" by a *dukun* will give his customer an irresistible smile and fascination for the opposite sex. A great many *dukun* are also quacks.

COMFORT

Do what Indonesians do to maintain comfort. Notice while relaxing they wear cool *sarung* and *kain*, ideal for this climate. Besides its most common use as a colorful wrap-around skirt, a *sarung* is also an all-purpose garment used to carry fruit, babies, or to cover yourself while bathing. It also serves as a nightgown or bedcover, umbrella, baby hammock, comfortable informal wear tied over the breasts, etc. Man-made chemical fabrics (nylon, rayon, etc.) are too hot and sticky in this climate, so just wear drip-dry, loose-fitting, light-colored cotton clothes. If caught in a passing torrential downpour, there's no need to change clothes. The heat from the sun and from your body will dry out your clothing quickly. If your room is damp, clammy and dark, air out all your bedding on a line in the sterilizing sun as a regular habit before going off; Indonesians do. Also, you can get another day out of a sweaty shirt or blouse simply by hanging it out all day in the scorching Indonesian sun, making it fragrant and wearable again. If you lay your mattress out in strong sunlight, bedbugs will vacate it. Take a *mandi* as frequently as you need to stay cool. Use a dipper to throw cold water over your red-hot skin (though if it's too hot, a shockingly cold *mandi* might give you a headache).

When you're too hot, bring your inner body temperature up to the outside temperature by drinking water or hot tea; ice-cold cokes just make you thirstier. It's healthy to be out in the sun's torrid heat for a while during the day; it has a purifying, acclimatizing effect. At night Indonesians of all ages love to cuddle a long, skinny, sausage-shaped pillow, the *bantul guling* (nicknamed the "Dutch Wife"), which looks like a long, soft, punching bag. This pillow absorbs the sweat so that you can sleep sounder, and it delightfully fits the contours of arms and legs. If a "Dutch Wife" isn't available, use any other piece of cloth such as a *sarung* for absorbing sweat from delicate areas. In cheap hotels keep mosquitos off by moving your bed under a fan or by using mosquito coils *(obat nyamuk)*, which are quite effective, slightly nauseating, slightly dangerous (you hear of mattresses burning), and can be bought anywhere for Rp400-500. Very few travelers use a mosquito net for sleeping, yet you can buy them in single or family-size for a song. They only weigh 100-200 grams; if you buy one with the strings long enough, you can put it up practically anywhere. Makes sleeping in the tropics great!

Mandi And Toilets

Most bathrooms are Indonesian-style with tiled floors and a tub in one corner filled with cool water. You bathe by standing beside the tub and pouring water over yourself with a dipper *(gajung)*. These "splash baths" can be a little chilly in the mornings but they are very refreshing when you get used to it. There are 2 types of toilets, the raised sit-down Western one, and the floor-level squat-down one. Finding Western-style toilets is often difficult; try flash restaurants and hotels, fancy shops, pharmacies. Indonesian-style toilets are found in bus and train stations, people's homes, and native-style accommodations like *losmen* and *penginapan*. Indonesians don't normally use toilet paper (many consider it unhygienic), and the plumbing isn't designed to cope with large amounts of it. Covered buckets are sometimes provided in tourist areas for the disposal of toilet paper and tampons. It's a good idea to adopt the Indonesian custom of splashing yourself with a dipper after using the toilet. The tub dipper and toilet dipper should be kept separate, but often are not; a small cement trough is found next to the squat-down toilet to provide water for the toilet dipper. When you take a crap in one of these toilets, throw in at least 3 full dippers of water to wash it down. Unless you have water boiled for you, hot water is never available in the lower-priced accommodations. A haircut will cost you in most places on Java Rp500 and maybe you can get a shave for an extra Rp300. Or just wear a beard instead of shaving.

MEDICAL KIT

A medicine kit takes on extra importance if you're planning some rugged trips to remote areas such as Kalimantan and Irian Jaya. The contents of the kit listed below will prepare you for almost any problem. Tablets are always more convenient than liquids when traveling; keep your medicines in small hard-to-break plastic bottles. Label each thoroughly with a full description of its purpose and dosage. If you suffer from any medical problem (allergies, reactions to medications, etc.), take a letter from your doctor and a written medical history to assure proper treatment in an emergency. Many of the following supplies can be bought in Jakarta after your arrival—if you want to go through the trouble and sometimes the extra expense. Generic names are used whenever possible.

Pepto Bismol
In case of stomach trouble, use Pepto Bismol or antacids. In emergencies, sodium bicarbonate will also neutralize acidity.

Tinactin Or Micatin
Available in the U.S. without a prescription (Desenex also works well), used to treat prickly heat, jock itch, athlete's foot, ringworm. Native herbal skin treatments include *bajamaduri* (spiny spinach) for treating burns, and Cap Pagoda Cream for tropical ulcers.

Analgesics
Aspirin (at least 5 grain, 325 mg) to relieve minor pain, for lowering the temperature, and for symptomatic relief of colds and respiratory infections, especially if you're going to the Outer Islands. Alka-Seltzer (merely buffered, fizzy aspirin) is another common painkiller. Codeine is a more powerful drug used for the relief of pain and cough.

Antihistamine Tablets
Eases and soothes the debilitating symptoms of allergies, hay fever, colds, vomiting, irritating skin conditions, insect bites, rashes. The cream is also effective for jellyfish stings. For motion sickness and nausea, 1-2 antihistamine tablets such as meclizine (Antivert) can help prevent and relieve the discomfort or non-prescription Dramamine (could cause drowsiness 3-4 hours later). If you don't have a prefered brand, try chlorpheniramine maleate tablets. In Canada, try Gravol; in UK, try Sea-Legs. It also helps motion sickness to chew glucose-based tablets (also effective if you need energy).

Clove Oil
For toothaches. Cotton wool soaked in *arak* serves almost as well in relieving tooth and gum pain.

Anti-Diarrhetics
Highly concentrated tincture of opium or less-concentrated camphorated tincture of opium are superb remedies against diarrhea; paregoric or charcoal tablets are also effective. Brand-name drugs include Stop Trot (add one packet to a glass of water) in the UK, Kaopectate in the U.S. More powerful medications such as Lomotil or Imodium (Streptotriad in UK) should be used sparingly. Lomotil, a prescription drug, also helps to ease abdominal cramps, nausea, chills, and low-grade fever that are frequently by-products of diarrhea. Any anti-diarrhea drug is contraindicated if the diarrhea is persistent, associated with high fever, blood in

stools, jaundice, or drowsiness. Beware: Enterovioform, sold over the counter virtually everywhere in Indonesia (including remote *warung* on top of volcanos), has been found to cause neurological damage.

Antibiotics

If in remote areas carry antibiotics (penicillin or tetracycline) for emergencies (skin or urinary tract infections), but bear in mind that they could cause some complex side effects. Since antibiotics break down your resistance, use only after you've exhausted every other means of treatment. Don't take more than one antibiotic at a time, and don't stop the full course of treatment just because the symptoms have gone away (the usual course is at least 7 days). Many different varieties (from cheapest to most expensive): tetracycline, penicillin G tablets, penicillin V tablets, ampicillin or amoxicillin capsules, and broad-spectrum cephalexin capsules. If you're allergic to penicillin, don't take amoxicillin or ampicillin.

Topical Eye Antibiotics

Very useful for treatment of eye irritations and conjunctivitis. Avoid penicillin products as you are more likely to become allergic to them if they are used on the skin. Good antibiotic eye creams include those that contain bacitracin, neomycin, or polymixin.

Antiseptics

Handy for minor cuts and scrapes (Indonesian mercurochrome doesn't even sting!). Savlon is a great antiseptic cream available in the UK (Cetavlon in the rest of the world). Outstanding ointments to use against tropical ulcers are F.G. Ointment (Meiji) and Neosporin or Polysporin ointments. Antibiotic Cicatran Cream or Betadine are good for cuts and mosquito bites gone septic. Sepsotupf from Germany heals small cuts by morning. Bacitracin is a very good bacterial ointment available in Indonesia.

Anti-Insect

Take some preventatives against insects; roll-ons or sprays are not readily available. Take a can of OFF to mosquito areas, such as on river trips in S. Sumatra and Kalimantan, and backpacking trips to remote or inaccessible areas. Works for 4 hours. These are usually only necessary for campers, trekkers, and hardcore bathers, otherwise go into any *apotik* and get *Minyak Sereh* mosquito repellent (contains citronella). Comes in thick, small glass bottles (Rp500) and really works (but doesn't last as long as OFF). Cutter's is another reliable repellent. Use Kwell (not available in Indonesia) or Pyrinate shampoo to combat head lice and scabies.

Leech Repellent

Dibutyl Phthalate, if applied to the skin, is effective for 4 hours. If sprayed on your clothes, it's effective for up to 2 weeks. Skin coated in a mixture of tobacco juice and water repels leeches. Clothes soaked in a concentrated salt solution also ward off leeches. Many insect repellents are also effective.

Sunscreens

Expensive in Indonesia, so bring your own. Paba or zinc oxide, an opaque ointment, is widely available. Reapply after heavy sweating. Hat and sunglasses are critical items to carry in the tropics. Use a lip salve like Chapstick (comfrey cream also works well) to replace loss of essential lip oils which can be surprisingly painful.

Tiger Balm

Relieves itching from insect bites, soothes headaches and muscle pains if massaged vigorously into the skin. The red variety is the strongest.

Laxative

Metamucil, a mild, bulk-producing laxative with natural dietary fiber, aids digestion and combats constipation, but is bulky to carry.

Vitamins

Vitamin tablets are fiendishly expensive and of dubious pedigree when found in Indonesia. The country's fruits and vegetables should instead provide all the vitamins you need. Because of the lack of dairy products, however, take iron and calcium. An iron supplement is important for women. If you feel rundown or have trouble with menstruation, take 1 ferrous sulfate tablet (200 mg) per day or eat liver in *nasi padang* restaurants until you feel better. If you eat too much rice, you'll lack Vitamin B; take Bitamin B12 and B6 because they work as catalysts for each other. Beriberi is a severe thiamine (B1) deficiency that often appears in the tropics among people who subsist for the most part on polished white rice.

First-Aid

Assorted bandaids are light, take up little room, and make fantastic gifts out in the villages. More practical, however, are the ectoplast strips which can be cut to any variety of sizes and shapes. Bring 1 roll of sterile cotton gauze and a roll of adhesive surgical tape. Elastic bandage for strains and sprains, and moleskin felt padding with adhesive backing for prevention of blisters (adhesive tape can be used as substitute). Also bring disinfectant, soap, cotton swabs, thermometer in hard case, tweezers, scissors, safety pins, needles, a sterile razor blade, plastic dropper bottles for your tincture of opium. For rinsing out cuts or tooth and gum infections, use sodium bicarbonate, which is like a toothpaste, soap, and deodorant all in one tube. Rinsing with hydrogen peroxide 3 times a day is equally effective.

Others

An anti-fungal powder; calamine lotion to soothe itching; eyedrops for infections (choloromycetin available in N. America, Albucid in the UK—both in liquid or ointment). Nose spray (phenylephrine HCL, ½ %) or nasal decongestant for sinuses and stuffed noses. Water purification tablets such as tetraglycine hydroperiodide, halogen, iodine in various forms, or Potable-Aqua. Chlorine compounds such as Halazone are ineffective against amoebas. Chloroquine or chloroquine-substitute to prevent malaria attacks.

JAVA

When fossil remains of the erect ape Pithecanthropus erectus were found on Java in 1891, scientists surmised that Java was the original location of the Garden of Eden. The most famed of all of Indonesia's islands, Java is still one of the richest, lushest, most densely populated on Earth, and ranks among the loveliest regions anywhere. Deep purple, fiery volcanos tower majestically over a land of intense green plains, twisting mountain passes, cool hillside resorts, remote crater lakes, extraordinary Hindu temples, wild game parks, botanical gardens, serene beaches, dense rainforests, savannah, thick bamboo groves, stands of teak, and squalling, teeming cities. It is Indonesia's easiest island to get around; along with Bali's, its inhabitants are most likely to understand English. Java is both young and old. It was the genesis of Indonesia's powerful maritime and agricultural kingdoms, and contains the best-preserved and highest number of monuments, many completed centuries before Columbus discovered America.

INTRODUCTION

Though Java is the smallest (129,625 sq km) of the Greater Sunda Islands, it is inhabited by the bulk of Indonesia's population (65%, or 110 million). Yet the island comprises only 7% of the country's land area. Here live most of the country's urban population, as well as the majority of its poorest peasantry. Many areas of Java resemble India because of the congestion, the rice paddies, the explosive colors: "I see India everywhere, but I do not recognize it," said the great Bengali poet Tagore when he visited Java in 1927.

The Dutch concentration of all their resources on Java for several hundred years greatly increased the differences between it and Indonesia's other islands, which the Javanese still consider "Outer Islands." Educationally, it's the most advanced. Java's universities and technological institutions form the backbone of Indonesia's tertiary education. Java is topheavy with industry, processing, and modern transport and telecommunication facilities, the island of opportunity where young men flock from the Outer Islands to find jobs. Java also processes raw materials from Indonesia's productive horticultural regions: tobacco, foods, beverages, rubber, timber, textiles, machinery. Yet, because of its giant population, Java could never survive if it were left to its own resources; it would be like a head without a body.

THE LAND

Java's total land area is 129,625 sq km. The island is 1,000 km long and its width varies between 60 and 200 km. A chain of volcanic mountains extends the whole length of the island; 15 volcanos are above 3,000 m high (where it drops to freezing at night) and 44 are between 2,000 and 3,000 m. With an average population density of 800 people per sq km, and hosting 8 of Indonesia's deadliest volcanos, Java is the archipelago's most overcrowded danger zone. There's a vast contrast between the sluggish, muddy, isle-enclosed Java Sea of the N coast, and the wild deserted southern shoreline which borders the Indian Ocean. Here, the continental shelf drops off sharply and tremendous waves crash against steep, dangerous beaches.

Though the island's original lowland and coastal vegetation have virtually disappeared after hundreds of years of intensive land use, there are still areas of mangroves on the coasts, rainforests in the W, monsoon forests in the E, some *casuarina* woodlands and savannah lowlands, as well as pristine montane forest on the slopes of some of its volcanos (especially in the east). All these various ecosystems, in spite of intense population pressure, are generally well represented in the island's 84 conservation areas (the most outstanding is the Ujung Kulon Reserve of far western Java).

Agriculture

Java's level of fertility and agricultural productivity is without parallel in any other equatorial land, and most of its people make their living by farming. Because of Java's miraculously rich volcanic soil—with loam so dark it looks like melted chocolate—farmers often harvest 2 or even 3 rice crops a year; maize matures in

7 weeks, and a banana tree in 10. Shifting cultivation is almost unknown, while wet-rice cultivation *(sawah)* is extensive, irrigated by water systems over 2,000 years old. Terraces, often only one m wide, are etched in steep hillsides with wooden handtools. Everything that grows on Java has its use; nothing is thrown away unless it's made into compost or used to feed chickens or goats. From planting time to harvest, the rice crop is watched with the same love and concern as one would the life of a child. Rocks and stones are removed by hand and stray soil on the roadside is swept up with brooms and returned to the paddy. What we in the West call "perishables" are recycled on Java almost endlessly.

Who Owns The Land?

In principle, land is village-owned, and established villagers have a right to work land which was cultivated by their ancestors. However, there just isn't enough land to go around. Since large families are common, land is split up many times among sons. With each generation, the size of family farms—already small—grows ever smaller as the land is divided down among the male heirs. Because Java's population density is among the highest in the world, the island's landholdings are among the smallest. Javanese farmers must make a living for their families of 5-6 children from the same area that an average Australian farm family uses to park its cars and tractors. Javanese work an average farm of less than 0.6 ha (about 2 acres) and a farmer with 2 ha is considered a big landowner. Of this 0.6 ha, half is set aside for rice; the rest the family uses for fruit and vegetable gardens, house, and stables. Plots too small to farm are sold (often to the rich), and more and more families become landless. Present surveys show that about 50% of Java's population are landless, another 25% nearly so—tragic figures for a predominantly rural farming society.

The Green Revolution

In some areas, export crops are even given emphasis over food crops; in E. Java the government uses as much as 30% of the land for sugarcane cultivation, a lopsided practice carried over from the Dutch colonial period. Traditional village welfare and harvesting institutions once ensured that the poor would have at least a necessary minimum to eat, but population pressure, modernization, and socio-economic inequalities are rapidly rendering these important and time-honored institutions ineffective.

The much-heralded Green Revolution, with its new strains of rice so responsive to high-tech fertilizers and irrigation systems, was supposed to be the answer to feeding the exploding population. Between 1968 and 1978 rice production jumped 50% and yields are still 36% higher than the average of all other rice producers in SE Asia. And in spite of population growth, average per capita rice consumption has increased by 25% from 90 to 113 kg a year. Yet these figures are misleading because the per capita food consumption *among the poor* has steadily diminished, and the chasm between the rich and poor continues to widen. The truth is that the modern agricultural technologies benefit primarily that small group of landed gentry with the money or credit to afford them and the skills to use them, and the accompanying mechanization has left large numbers of poor farmers without work.

The Future

Many prominent Indonesian and Western observers fear that Java is careening inexorably toward an ecological disaster that will undercut food production before its theoretical agronomic goal can be reached. Under the enormous pressure of population expansion, deforestation is progressing at a frightening pace with thousands of stands of trees cut down each year. East Java alone is consuming 14 million cubic meters of firewood per annum, equal to ⅔ the peak lumber export of both Sumatra and Kalimantan. No more forests can be cleared for farming or firewood without further silting up the island's reservoir and irrigation systems, some of the most extensive, intricate, and delicate in the world—the lifeline of the country's rice cultivation. The cycle of floods and droughts also has taken its toll on lowland ricefields, causing serious food shortages.

Indonesia is already involved in a race against time. The funds earmarked for reforestation and extensive terracing get siphoned off as they travel down the long, corrupt pipeline of bureaucracy. The Javanese farmer can't begin terracing a whole hillside for Rp50,000! Meanwhile, the topsoil of Java is sliding into the sea. The whole island might be a desert by the year 2050.

Climate

It's a myth of temperate peoples that the tropics have perpetual blue skies. Since this island is so mountainous (121 volcanos), it makes for a variety of climates, and it's often cloudy. Though the sun doesn't stay hidden for long, bright clear days are rare. From Dec. to March it's rainy, especially in western Java, which has one of the highest levels of precipitation in the country. It rains heaviest in Feb., and there is a distinct dry season at the far eastern end of Java. Although violent thunderstorms occur, there are no true hurricanes. Java's "winter" is June, July, and Aug., one of the most pleasant times to visit.

FAUNA AND FLORA

Fauna

Though Java's fauna are of the Indo-Malay type, sig-

MAJOR RESERVES OF JAVA

1. Pulau Dua P. Rambut bird sanctuaries
2. Ranca Danau Reserve
3. Ujung Kulon Reserve
4. Gungung Halimun Reserve
5. Gunung Gede Pangrango National Park
6. Pananjung Pangandaran Reserve
7. Dieng Plateau Lake Reserves
8. Arjuno-Lalijiwo Reserve
9. Gunung Semeru Reserve
10. Yang Plateau Reserve
11. Baluran National Park
12. Ijen-Merapi Reserves
13. Nusa Barung Reserve
14. Meru Betiri Reserve
15. Banyuwangi Selatan Reserve

nificant differences occur between the fauna of Sumatra and Java. Even though the strait between the 2 islands is only 15 km wide, no clouded leopards, *siamang*, orangutans, sun bears, tapirs, or elephants are found on Java, and no *banteng*, leopards, or *rusa* are native to Sumatra. For millions of years Java was covered with rich tropical jungle and mountains, an animal zoo in which *Homo sapiens* was the prey. Since man and beast shared the island for eons, it is little wonder that Javanese myths and legends are filled with animals and animal-like creatures, whose common enemy was the threat of volcanic eruptions. But as man multiplied and cut down the jungle slopes, the animals started losing out.

Even as late as 1940 tigers still lived on the outskirts of Bandung, but today perhaps 6 Javan tigers survive in the small Meru Betiri Reserve (Sukamade), SW of Banyuwangi in E. Java, a number which the World Wildlife Fund doubts is a viable breeding population. The Javan one-horned rhinoceros virtually died out in the early part of this century, though a few still live in the forests of Ujung Kulon in the western tip of Java. The number of place names with *Badak* (rhinoceros) suggests they were once widespread; the mammoth tracks ancient rhinoceroses made can still be seen near the craters of some volcanos (for example, on the top of G. Ciremai in W. Java). *Banteng* (wild oxen) have been reduced to a few herds in the reserves of Ujung Kulon, Pangandaran, and Baluran. The black panther, being nocturnal and fairly adaptable, may be more common than is generally thought, but as soon as one is found it is shot, and the future for this

magnificent beast looks bleak. Wild boar and deer are restricted to the reserves. Other creatures—anteaters, deer, monkeys, and birds—do not require such extensive habitats, and have retreated into what jungle remains.

Forty species of birds live on Java. Since Indonesians are avid hunters (deduced by the number of guns you see on a Sunday), many of the smaller species of birds and pigeons have been killed off. In coastal areas dwell swifts whose nests go to make that prized delicacy, bird's-nest soup. Larger birds such as eagles, hawks, several species of jungle fowl, and green peacocks have retreated into the mountains. There are still 100 varieties of snakes, but crocodiles no longer exist anywhere on Java. Java's frogs sound like birds, and giant iguana, up to 2 m long with thick bodies and eerie humanoid hands, are still found near Bandung on the Citarum River. Colonies of lizards can be observed on some of the islands of Kep. Seribu; they also live on P. Krakatau and P. Sangiang off W. Java, and in the caves of Pelabuhan Ratu. Another animal which invades *kampung* after chickens is a kind of civet cat called a *musang* (or *careuh*), a delightful cross between a raccoon and a badger, about 2 times larger than a cat. One does not have to sit for long in the rainforest to see thousands of insects—species you never dreamed existed.

Flora

The native vegetation forms a dense tropical forest in western Java, with a few stands left of timber trees including teaks, gigantic fig trees, various palms, and bamboos. But over vast areas below an altitude of 2,000 m, all primary forests have been destroyed to clear land for agricultural purposes. At least 5,000 plant species grow on Java, including 35 species of fruit, 20 of them found nowhere else. There are giant strawberries, turpentine mangos, scarlet hibiscus *(Kembang sepatu),* moonlight orchids, water lilies, frangipani, and the lotus *(padmasna)* flower. Gossamer beards hang down from *kapok* trees, showers of brilliant flowers sit atop *cassieas* and trees-of-fire. In high forest regions grow tree ferns, azaleas, wild rhododendrons, yew trees, heather, lily-of-the-valley, myrtle, honeysuckle, even edelweiss. The island's extensive plantations grow coffee, tea, cacao, sugar, tobacco, indigo, tapioca, cinchona (quinine), *kapok,* cloves, and rubber for export.

HISTORY

Java is the physical center of all the islands, and has always been the trading focus and the metropolitan island of the archipelago. It is the golden mean in both size and location, long the most favored of all the archipelic islands for human habitation and thus the most politically powerful. Java's history is long. Compared to the poor archaeological record on the Outer Islands, the island has a fantastic wealth of documents and monuments. On all the major Indonesian islands but Java, the main centers of population and power have always been located in coastal areas. But because of the wealth generated by huge surpluses obtained from wet-rice cultivation throughout its history, great pre-colonial inland empires have come to power on this island: Majapahit, Singosari, Kediri, and Mataram. Ancient Java was a land of peasants and princes, with the peasants producing and laboring for the palace cities and temples, providing the massive agricultural wealth to fuel the empire's maritime trade.

Written history began in Indonesia with the coming of Hinduism. For centuries Hindu culture overwhelmed Java, and is still very much in evidence today—mystic vocabularies, trains (the *Bima),* even noodles are named after the heroes of the Indian epics. Buddhist and Hindu religious symbols remain everywhere you turn. Starting in the 14th C., another import from India (Gujerat) made its appearance: Islam. The new religion first entrenched itself in Demak and Gresik on Java's N coast. These first strongholds eventually grew into a series of powerful commercial Islamic city-states. But with the arrival of Europeans in the 16th and 17th centuries, the days of these kingdoms were numbered.

Colonialization

While Shakespeare was still alive, the Dutch took possession of the island. For a period of 200 years, beginning in about 1723, Java became the key island in the Dutch East Indies empire, paying its shareholders in Europe an average dividend of 18% per annum. Under Dutch rule Java became known as the finest garden of the tropics, one of the best-governed tropical islands in the world. It was a wonder of colonial management, a land of railroads, schools, swank resorts, vast well-run estates. You could telephone any point on the island from your hotel, and travel on some of the best-paved roads in the Orient. Batavia (present-day Jakarta)—with steep white-walled mansions lining canals, overhanging roofs of red tiles, signs all in Dutch—could easily be mistaken for a street in Rotterdam or The Hague. For 40 years during the 19th C., while the peasants starved, all of Java was turned into a huge work farm, run by a system of enormously profitable forced deliveries of cash crops. The Javanese have said that the Dutch had good heads but cold hearts, and claim that they lost all their lands because it was exactly the reverse with them.

ARCHAEOLOGY

Irrigation farming long ago created an intensely cooperative society in which villages were grouped together under strong district rulers who were needed to control the flow of water. The ability to support such luxurious pastimes as immortalizing oneself or one's god by erecting impressive stone monuments, requiring decades to build with massive human toil and suffering, indicates a gigantic agricultural wealth. For more than 750 years (A.D. 732 to about 1405), starting with the advent of Indian culture, temples were built all the way from the Dieng Plateau in C. Java to Candi Kedaton, near Bondowoso, in E. Java. Ruins are *still* being unearthed. The highest concentration and the best-preserved Hindu-Buddhist temples have been uncovered in C. and E. Java, a region comparable to ancient Egypt's "Realm of the Dead." Most of the art of the early Hindu period has perished and relatively little is known of its development until the 8th C., the beginning of the Hindu-Indonesian period. Because of the tropical climate, only the work of the stone sculptors and the megalith builders has survived, leaving remains of temples not only on Java but all over Sumatra, on Sulawesi, and even as far as Borneo. **Note:** When searching for ancient ruins on Java, a sign on the roadway almost always points the way to the monument.

Candi

This word is derived from the Sanskrit *Chandgrika* (House of the Goddess of Death) or *Candika,* another name for Durga (Goddess of Death). Regardless of the temple's purpose or its symbolic religious source, the present-day meaning of *candi* is roughly "temple." Outwardly, *candi* do not differ from temples serving for regular worship of Hindu deities, but many Javanese *candi* were dedicated to the cult of the dead or linked to the idea of an afterlife. Evident on supposedly "Hindu" temples on Java is a combination of Hindu symbols and deities, plus a monument to a god-king, ancient nobleman, ancestor sire or teacher whose ashes were buried underneath or in a niche of the *candi*. In some temples (such as Mendut) the dead king is actually depicted as a Hindu god, his spirit presiding in a statue of a god which can be contacted ritually. Thus, *candi* were magic centers radiating power.

The *candi* you see today were once surrounded by flowering trees, high walls, and tall gates opening on inner courtyards. All around these sumptuous temple complexes were shady lanes, ricefields, and the bamboo homes of the people stretching to the horizon. The long-lasting stone *candi* were rich Brahmans' structures; the temples of the people were built of wood and bamboo and never survived. Seldom do you see any of Java's ruined classical temples venerated in the present day. Indeed, compared to the temples of India, which are crowded and throb with life, Java's temples are archaeological specimens only maintained in order to promote tourism. (Exceptions are ancient classical bathing places sometimes still used by the locals to wash themselves and their clothes.)

But the temple builders created the seeds of their own destruction. Working the peasants too hard may have been the reason that the population shifted from E. Java in the 10th C. and did not return until the 16th century. Temple construction had all but stopped by the end of the 15th C., with the Mt. Lawu Group being one of the last remnants in stone of the Java-Hindu period.

Candi Construction

It is believed that plans of most temple construction in Indonesia originated in India, though this has never been proven: no monuments in India are quite like the *candi* of Java. Indonesian artisans and sculptors struck out on their own, coming up with a new way of building, sometimes even surpassing the artistry of the motherland. Hindu-Java religion, cosmology, monotheism, and aboriginal cult worship have all come together in these monuments. The ground plan of many complexes reproduces the human body lying face down on the earth—the foot, body, and head. This is related to the parallelism between the microcosm and macrocosm—in the very small is found the very large.

Many *candi* were built in the shape of the Buddhist sacred mountain, Meru. In their simplest form, these sepulchral monuments consist of 3 parts: base, temple, and temple roof, forming a cube-like terraced pyramid usually with a platform for walking around to view the carved pictures. A stairway often leads up to the terrace. In the more elaborate *candi* are more platforms, niches, porches, and bases. Hindu-Javanese temples were frequently enlarged long after they were first built, their foundations replaced or annexes added. This happened so often that it makes for much confusion among scholars.

One striking characteristic of classical Hindu-Javanese stone architecture is that the amount of hewn stone required for walling in space is often very large. Often the enormous masses of stone making up the straight-walled temple body contain just one small inner chamber *(cella)* in which is placed the cult image of the god or ancestor in whose memory the whole structure was erected (these images are almost always missing). At the entrance of the *cella* space was provided for only a single priest to pray. Javanese techniques of construction make little use of pillars or true arches. Mass is always given more emphasis than space, the structure often piled high with heavy, overlapping layers of big stone blocks. Borobudur is a stunning example of this, a huge ponderous heap of stone covering the top of a hill, with only a small room in its central *dagob* (the highest pinnacle) where the holy relics were kept.

Reliefs

The characters and themes from Indian epic poems on temple bas-reliefs in Java are very common because in the 12th C. a courtly *kakawin* poem was written (inspired by the Indian version) which became immensely popular, greatly stimulating the plastic arts of Java. These Indonesian versions of the great narrative Hindu poems carved in relief aren't nearly as sexually explicit as in India, but the everyday life of ancient tropical Java is clearly depicted with pots, pans, ropes, small lizards, birds robbing grain bins, fruit markets, parading priests. Archaeologists can derive the date of a monument by "reading" certain animals somewhere on the structure, such as 3 frogs, 2 crabs, 3 iguanas, and an eel, which somehow add up to A.D. 1455! Highly durable "diamond plaster" enabled carvers to add extreme detail, helped to preserve the carvings, and provided a base on which to paint colors.

Equatorial wind and rain have worn smooth the now exposed carvings and ornamentation to such an extent that many reliefs have lost much of their vividness and definition even in the mere 40-odd years since they were first photographed in the '20s and '30s. The most superb example of Hindu-Java art, Borobudur, has been eaten by lichen, cracked by seeping water, all its classical carvings becoming more and more illegible. The finest bas-reliefs and sculpture of the C. Javanese period today make up part of the royal collections in Bangkok, presented by the Dutch colonial government to the visiting king of Thailand in 1896. Other outstanding collections are found in Leiden and Amsterdam.

The *Kraton*

When the temple-city concept arrived from India, the *kraton* developed as the Indonesian counterpart. These walled fortified palaces of Javanese rulers became the centers of political power and culture. Containing several thousand people, each of these self-contained regent mini-cities was tied to a dynasty, and each new dynasty founded a new *kraton*. The most famous *kraton* of Java are in Yogya and Solo, C. Java. The farther away from the *kraton*, the more indigenous customs and animism held sway among the rural population.

As in India, these fortresses incorporated all that the surrounding region would need in the way of commerce, art, religion. They contained banks, baths, shops, temples, massage and meditation chambers, schools, workshops, scribes, concubine quarters—everything, for both body and soul, that the royalty had a use for. Only the *kraton* was open to all the new values and attractions which the imported Indian civilization had to offer. The *kraton* adopted and then modified first the caste system of Hinduism, then the philosophical structure of Islam. Being the home of the leisured aristocracy, only these courts possessed enough wealth for the arts and crafts to flourish. Handcrafted objects were made as ornaments and utensils for the king and members of the court. Though the *kraton* was their origin, crafts eventually spread beyond their walls and into the villages and the countryside.

Dance also found a home in the *kraton.* Each of the princely courts of Solo and Yogya created their dance dramas, and their dance styles all evolved differently. During the colonial period, for the most part a time of peace on Java, when money wasn't going to war, artistic expression flowered even more intensively. The princes, though politically powerless, were still extremely wealthy and indulged in all the more pompous, grandiose ceremonial occasions. The finest *wayang* puppets, masks, and dance costumes in Indonesia were (and are) produced in and for the *kraton*.

During the years of the Forced Cultivation Period (approx. 1830-69), the twin *kraton* regents of Java were partners with the Dutch in the ruthless exploitation of their own people. Yet the *kraton* have always been regarded as the center of the world for the masses, the reservoirs of spiritual power. They were even built in such a way as to represent a microcosm of the universe. The titles of the hereditary rulers who live in them today testify to their supernatural cosmic function: the Susuhunan of Solo is called Paku Buwana ("Axis of the World"); and the Sultan of Yogya is called Hamengko buwana ("He who cradles the World in His Lap"). The cities of Solo and Yogya have even grown up around these cities within a city.

Chinese Temples

Called *klinteng* or *klenteng* in Indonesian, the largest, best preserved, and best known are located on the N coast of Java, and date from as early as the 16th century. Chinese temples are not high, but are like the Chinese themselves "down to earth," always larger in the horizontal plane than in the vertical. The large and often beautiful curved roof, sitting on short columns or pillars, is their main feature. As far as possible the whole complex is laid out symmetrically. Chinese temples in Indonesia were often founded by grounded Chinese sea captains or rich merchants who had successfully established themselves on Java, took Javanese wifes, and eventually dedicated a temple to a deity to whom they attributed their good fortune. Stone tablets in niches inside often record the founders' names and the year the temple was established. Outstanding *klinteng* are found in Jakarta, Cirebon, and Semarang.

THE PEOPLE

With their light brown skin, straight black hair, high cheekbones, small and slender builds, the Javanese originally belonged to the Oceanic branch of the Mongoloid race. But the Javanese "race" is actually a blending of every race that ever established itself on the island. Java's more than 110 million people belong to primarily 4 major cultural-lingual ethnic groups: the Sundanese of W. Java (about 30 million), the Javanese of C. and E. Java (about 80 million), the Tenggerese from the area in E. Java around G. Bromo (300,000), and the Madurese inhabiting the long island of Madura NE of Surabaya in E. Java. Of these, the Javanese are numerically the largest group and, in terms of cultural and political influence, the most important.

Population

Population is a Javanese (and to a lesser extent, Balinese) problem. Thus, it's an Indonesian problem. Sixty-five percent of Indonesia's total population is concentrated on this 1,000-km-long, grossly overpopulated island, its land area amounting to only 7% of the total land surface of Indonesia. Java's population leaps ahead of measures to limit it and is fast approaching the danger point. The absence of a welfare system or of any social security program in Indonesia almost necessitates having children (especially sons) who will care for you when you grow old.

With the island's population growing by over 2 million per year, Java is a precise working model of the Malthusian Theory in which death operates to keep the total population within the means of subsistence. In 1805, Java's population was only 5 million. While Asia as a whole doubled its population between 1800 and 1950, Java's increased 7 times.

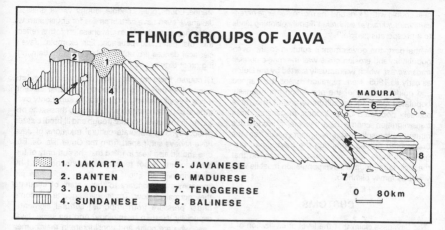

ETHNIC GROUPS OF JAVA

MADURA

1. JAKARTA
2. BANTEN
3. BADUI
4. SUNDANESE
5. JAVANESE
6. MADURESE
7. TENGGERESE
8. BALINESE

0   80km

Now Java has 110 million people in an area about the size of the state of New York. Or to put it another way, Australia is 60 times larger than Java but has one-sixth the population.

Java is one vast village. Though the island has Indonesia's biggest and most crowded cities, 85% of it is rural. With over 800 people per sq km, this is the densest agricultural population in the world. Because the countryside is so economically depressed, the Javanese surge into the cities. But even the countryside is now feeling the population pressure, and the incredible absorption capacity of the Javanese village is finally starting to break down.

If population growth and urban immigration levels continue at the current rate, Java will most likely double its present population in 30 years, becoming a virtual island city. Jakarta's population alone is expected to grow to more than 21 million by the end of this century. Even if the birth rate drops to 1% growth annually, by the year 2000 Java's population will have increased to around 150 million and Indonesia's total population will have increased to 250 million. This would give Java an average density of almost 1,100 per sq km, a figure greater than the present density of the most urbanized centers of Western Europe. With 60% of Java's land already cultivated and with the burgeoning population overflowing onto what is now farmland, what will all these extra people eat? Gigantic problems with education and natural resources in the years to come will result.

Poverty-sharing

Because of Java's unbelievable population density, a phenomenon known as "shared poverty" is often seen. It means that for what jobs do exist, far too many people are there to fill them. This results in

many people undertaking a job that takes few. Half a dozen people may work on a car, 3 men milk a goat, bales of tobacco are shared by buyers as a way of spreading risks if the tobacco isn't sold quickly, *becak* drivers share territories, and stall owners haggle and peddle intensively, or else trade goods constantly to keep business and money circulating at all times. Everybody survives just below or just above the poverty line by dividing, for example, the per-hectare gains when there's a declining ratio of rice-growing land per family as population increases. In Solo, C. Java, many university teachers are allowed to teach only 4 hours each per week, or full-time only 8 hours per week. Top professors are so scarce that they are flown around the Outer Island universities for lectures. This unique system is able to absorb most everyone in need of work, providing all with at least some kind of work to earn their daily bread. Instead of some being really poor, everybody is just a little poor.

The Future

The Suharto government, realizing that a runaway population could undo even its most far-reaching development efforts, began family planning programs soon after it took power. The program's success can be attributed in large part to the thousands of village-level family planning associations throughout Java. Folk traditions are also used to limit family size, with all the village *ibu* meeting once monthly to coordinate efforts. In some Javanese villages elections for the "King of the Condom" and "Queen of the IUD" are even held. Signs are attached to the fronts of houses proclaiming that the occupant is enrolled in the program, stating the type of contraceptive used, and the proud results achieved! The Rp5 coin, the lowest monetary unit circulated widely among the rural masses, has on the reverse side a neat couple with 2 kids and the motto *Keluarga berencana menuju rakyat sejahtera* ("Family planning leads to a prosperous people").

In the past, the government's solution to the overpopulation and erosion crisis was the magic cure-all *transmigrasi*, which was actually started by the Dutch as early as 1905. Transmigration means the planned and guided shifting of the population from densely populated Java to agricultural areas of the more sparsely populated Outer Islands. In general, these transmigration schemes have never really worked. It's rather like transplanting a malignant cancer from the breast onto the leg. Although the *transmigrasi* program continues, it is now generally recognized that the main cure for Java's overpopulation must lie with vigorous family planning.

CUSTOMS

The Javanese claim that the level of civilization of a people can be measured by the refinement of its system of etiquette. So strongly do they feel this, that the Javanese commonly refer to etiquette as the *busananing bangsaa*, "the garments of a nation." And by this measurement, the Javanese pride themselves on being one of the most refined, polite, and cultivated peoples on Earth. This cultivation has stemmed from the *priyayi* tradition. *Priyayi* is the gentry class of Java, the old Hindu-Javanese aristocracy who guard and hold such values and ethics as extreme politeness, deference to the aged, soft-spokenness, proper conduct, sophistication, social arts and graces, and artistic skills (dance, drama, music, and verbal eloquence). This official class eventually became the civil servant class under the Dutch, and today they are white-collar workers, businessmen, the newly educated, the civil administrators. As a class they consider manual labor undignified—if you can read and write, then you must "have clean hands."

Priyayi Etiquette

On this overpopulated island everyone would be at each other's throats if people were too intimate, too loud, too vulgar, or too blunt. It's a virtue not to say what you really mean, i.e., "to talk Javanese." The granny won't ask outright for her cup of tea if someone has forgotten it, but will only say "It's awfully hot and dusty, isn't it?" Even *priyayi* children are awesomely well behaved. Mastery of formal etiquette is given so much emphasis that a child who has not yet learned the subtleties of etiquette is often said to be *durung Jawa*, or "not yet Javanese."

Priyayi values still have a strong hold on people of all ages on Java and you often see written on·signs or hear people say, "People must have etiquette-feeling." Complicated Javanese etiquette dictates eye direction, position of hands, and the way one sits, stands, points, greets people, laughs, walks, dresses. Javanese even have certain smiles for anger, sorrow, suffering, and grief. Most Javanese art forms reflect this discipline and patience. For example, Java's classical dances are unbelievably intricate, demanding great dignity and perfect self-control.

Of course, there are other ways of viewing *priyayi* etiquette. Like the English Oxford or "educated" accent, it is a way of wielding an oppressive superiority over others, of denying status and power to those who originate in the lower or *kasar* (rough and ill-bred) classes of society. The elaborate cultural traditions of Java have always set it apart from the Outer Islands. But one should also bear in mind that the authority of formal etiquette is not recognized everywhere and by every individual. Even scrupulously polite people sometimes act contrary to the system of etiquette they normally follow. Traditional etiquette has come under pressure from imported cultural elements, especially Western technology. And the same Javanese who are polite and considerate in their homes are among the world's most rude and inconsiderate drivers, or are grossly *kasar* to a Western woman at a bus station.

Rules Of Etiquette

Four principal elements make up *priyayi* etiquette: **1)** The ability to recognize and honor age and rank. In a word, you may not differ with your elders. **2)** The ability to avoid shocking and offending others. This skill is manifested most superbly in the Javanese art of conversation, characterized by its indirectness and mildness. The cultivated man or woman always tries to put others at ease and ensure no unexpected shock or offense to a listener. Since open dislike or disagreement would give rise to a strained or uneasy atmosphere, which the true *priyayi* would prefer to avoid by any means at his disposal, it's very common for Javanese to express agreement with something they do not agree with. Thus, when a Javanese says "yes," interpret *the way* he says it to determine what he really means. **3)** The ability to conceal one's real feelings. The Javanese approach possibly delicate subjects in a roundabout fashion and rarely speak bluntly or frankly. No one looks for disturbance; everyone seeks peace. **4)** The ability to exercise an almost catatonic self-control, to not only avoid startling others but also because jerkiness, irregularity, and unpredictability are signs of a lack of inner refinement. The less refined a person is seen to be, the more he falls in the eyes of his peers. Loud voices, flamboyant behavior, bragging, roars of laughter, wails of sorrow are all considered ill-mannered. Passion or anger is expected only of children, wild animals, peasants, the retarded, and foreigners. The Javanese keep it all inside; you only see the placid exterior and the seemingly calm smile.

Language
The Javanese language is far more complicated than the other languages of the archipelago. As a direct result of the strong influence of the Indian caste system on Javanese life, the Javanese language is the most intricate device ever created to show social rank. Many Javanese in fact prefer to speak *Bahasa Indonesia* because then they won't have to speak up or down to people. Because of its dense population, people are organized into a tight hierarchy on Java. When Javanese first meet, a sort of extended introduction takes place in which classification of an individual according to his ethnic group, rank, and place in society is a ritual which must be performed before social interaction may begin. Thus the Javanese spend an inordinate amount of time classifying each other and some conversations never get beyond this.

It's impossible to speak Javanese without expressing the speaker's view of his social status as it relates to the listener. The Javanese lexicon contains a great number of honorific speech forms which, if used correctly, demand an extreme awareness of the proper respect due to age and rank. There are high, middle, and low levels of speaking to your inferior, to your equal, and to your superior. Separate languages include one for the gods and ritual feasts, an ancient poetic language, a classical Old Javanese *(Kawi)* which is a sort of Latin of the Javanese language, and even special formal vocabularies for the royal court. A sultan always uses the low language and servants the high language when talking to each other. Village schoolteachers address pupils in low *nongko* while pupils answer back in high *nongko*. Another level of *nongko* is only used when you're angry.

Their language also shows the Javanese obsession with politeness. Politeness is an instrument for making others as well as yourself feel peaceful within. Thus, you never ask a tailor outright "How much?" but instead "What will it be in exchange for the thread?" For your wife you say "friend in the back of the house." In addition, several different speech tones, *alus* (polite) and *kasar* (crude) are used. One is soft, slow, tender; the other loud, rough, rapid.

RELIGION

Once again, out of sheer numbers, the religion of Java is beyond doubt the most potent political and social force in Indonesia. *Agama Jawa* (The Religion of Java) has evolved into an incredible blending of doctrines and practices: in the Javanese story of creation, all the world's major religions have been taken into account. An estimated 148 religious sects exist on Java, mainly in E. and C. Java.

For centuries Javanese feudalism was the true religion, not the law of the *Koran*. From its early years, Javanese Islam has been a merger of Sufism (Islamic mysticism), Hinduism, and native superstition. Only in the 19th and 20th C. did Islam penetrate rural Java so deeply as to upset the traditional patterns of authority. Today Islam is the professed religion of 90% of its inhabitants. But the Javanese differ widely in the intensity of their beliefs. Only 5-10% adhere to a relatively purist form of Islam *(santri),* some 30% to a syncretic and Javanized version of Islam, while most of the remaining consider themselves only nominal Muslims. The latter group is known as *abangan,* professed adherents of Islam, but whose practices and thinking are closest to the old Javanese mysticism, animism, and Indo-Javanese traditions. There are vast parts of Java, especially C. Java, that are still Hindu-Buddhist.

Mysticism
The recent widespread *abangan* cultural awakening was brought about in part because of the aggressiveness of organized politicized Islam on Java, in which orthodox Islamic views and ways of life were pushed upon the majority of the population. The unorthodox *abangan* groundswell is not only popular among the poor and powerless, but also among the powerful. Although calling themselves Muslim, the Javanese ruling class is preoccupied with mystical religious views and metaphysical philosophy. Traditionally, many of Java's kings became hermits when they grew old, and today a strong *abangan* undercurrent runs through the military leadership of Indonesia, including the president himself (born in a poor Javanese village, the son of a *petani*). Numerous peasant revolts under charismatic mystic leaders have occurred such as Diponegoro in the 1830s, the Kutil Movement of 1945, and the extraordinary Sawito Kartowibowo Affair of 1976.

The Javanese today practice their own form of Islam, permeated with animistic rites and superstitions. The *wayang* theater is almost completely non-Islamic, its roots reaching deep into myths and sagas of ancient Javanese heroes. Javanese *pamong* (tutors), black magicians, mystic teachers, and *dukun* (healers), famous for their oracular powers, have often influenced powerful politicians. Incense is burned before beautiful works of art such as a *topeng* mask, a *kris,* a gong, or a famous bronze *gamelan.* Worshipped by individual families or by whole villages, these *pusaka* (talismanic heirlooms) often form legends around themselves. *Pusaka* are said to be able to charm people, ward off sickness and evil, make the rains come on time.

BATIK

Java produces the world's finest *batik.* A traditional method of decorating cloth, *batik* is an art of great antiquity. The word is derived from a Javanese word meaning "fine point," though in everyday usage it means "wax printing" or "wax-resist painting." *Batik* is traditionally used for clothing; even on formal occasions one may wear open-necked *batik* shirts, blouses *(kebaya),* skirts *(saura),* or dresses. Formerly, *batik* fabrics were used mainly to make *sarung,* women's skirts, scarves, and men's headgear; cloth even had a strong cultic function. Nowadays *batik* is used in housecoats, long dresses, blouses, ties, belts, slippers, hats, umbrellas, sportjackets, as well as in interior decorating and fashion: wall and carpet designs, lampshades, tablecloths, napkins, bedspreads, shopping bags, briefcases, fans. Even school uniforms in Indonesia have subdued *batik* patterns in them.

Most Javanese women cannot afford to wear traditional dress every day (also not appropriate to wear while bicycling) but don instead cheaper Western clothes. During national holidays you see all the women and girls wearing the traditional *sarung-kebaya* outfit, the national dress of Indonesia. A great domestic demand for *batik* always has existed on Java, so it isn't just because of the tourists that *batik-*making has survived and prospered. But the tourists have undoubtedly accounted for an increase in the making of *alus,* or high-quality, hand-done *(batik tulis)* pieces.

Several stock sizes of *batik* are available. *Kain panjang* is 2½ times its width. A *dodot* is used for high court ceremonies; its length is 4 times its width. The *sarung* is 2 times its width, sewn into a cylindrical shape and worn as a skirt. The *slendang* is a breast and shoulder cloth worn by women. The *kain kepala* is a head cloth worn by men.

History

Indonesia has been trading in *batik* since the days of the Arab and Indian merchant fleets of the early 16th century. The craft was probably introduced into Indonesia during the 12th C., though no one knows exactly from where. Possibly it originated in Turkey or Egypt. Most "modern" (after 1840) *batik* can be traced back to Javanese influence and some believe that it evolved on Java and Madura out of an ancient way of textile painting. Statues covered with typical *batik* motifs have been found in Javanese temples dating back 1,200 years. The earliest evidence of *batik-*making dates back to the courts of C. Java. *Batik* centers later developed on the N coast, and then spread to other parts of Java. Each area produced a distinctive design and color.

At one time, only persons of royal rank were allowed to wear some patterns; *batik* kerchiefs *(kain kepala)* are still draped over the tombs of Javanese royalty and Islamic saints. The art was considered a spiritual discipline and the making of *batik* was once strictly the pursuit of ladies of the nobility. *Batik* as a folk art was nearly destroyed by the import of Japanese cotton prints in the 1930s and '40s. Today's principal *batik* centers of Java are Yogya, Solo, Pekalongan, Cirebon, Tasikmalaya, Indramayu, Garut, and Lasem.

Batik Tulis

The most prized and expensive *batik,* designs of *batik tulis* are usually drawn on fine cotton, linen, or (for those who can afford it) silk. Finely detailed designs are sometimes drawn first free-hand with a pencil on the textile, then hot liquid wax, impervious to dye, is applied with a pen-like instrument called a *canting,* with one, 2, or 3 spouts and a small bowl on top which is dipped into the hot wax. The areas *not* to be colored are filled in with wax. The cloth is then passed through a vat of the desired colored dye, such as blue. The wax is then removed from the parts of the dried material that are still to be dyed in the next step by soaking the cloth in hot water and scraping the wax off. Next, the areas to be kept blue are waxed over. This process is repeated during each phase of the coloring up to 4 or more times until the overall pattern and effect are created.

Batik *is a striking patterned cloth made by a wax and dye technique. Indonesia—and particularly Java—produces the highest quality in the world. For 700 years this art was practiced solely by women of royal families. Since it took many arduous months to produce a single fabric, batik-making was once considered a spiritual discipline and a form of meditation. To design and dye a piece took great inward concentration: one would "draw the batik* design on the heart." *Copper stamps* (cap), *devised in 1840, are much in use today and cap-printed* batik *is much less expensive and painstaking than the older hand-done method. Yogya and Solo (C. Java) are still the twin capitals of both kinds of batik. The designs pictured above are a few of many thousands of different designs and color variations. To see the process of batik-making, visit the Batik and Handicraft Research Center, Jl. Kusumanegara 2, Yogya.*

Women generally do the designing and waxing, which require great care and skill. Men normally do the dyeing itself. A *batik tulis* could take up to 40 days to complete. Really high-grade pieces can take as long as 6 months, especially if deep-toned vegetable dyes are used (rarely now), which take time for the colors to come out. Until recently there's been a tendency away from the time-consuming, painstaking *batik tulis* work towards the quicker but usually inferior stamped-process *(batik cap)* which can be produced on a larger commercial scale. But as the knowledge and sensitivity of tourists towards Indonesian art forms increases, the demand for expensive, hand-drawn *batik* grows steadily along with it.

If you want older, used *batik sarung*, vendors can be found in the markets of such C. Javanese towns as Yogya and Solo. However, it would be more effective to place yourself in a village and put the word out that you want to buy. Then sit back and see what turns up (as low as Rp3000 a piece). Otherwise, the old, really well-done pieces can be quite difficult to find.

Cap

Pronounced "chop." This is a faster and cheaper method of *batiking*, which uses the same traditional patterns. Copper stamps *(cap)* are used to impress wax patterns onto the fabric. *Cap* are made from strips of metal and wire meticulously soldered together, and are themselves collectors' items and art objects. In use since 1840, this process is making *batik* more and more a craft practiced by young men. Though generally resulting in a lessening of fine detail, some *cap batik* can be far superior to *batik tulis* work using simple and imitative designs.

Designs

Batik designs are as infinite and variegated as Indonesian society itself. You find crazy quilt patterns, circles, ovals, rosette shapes, stars, flowering tendrils, checkered and round patterns, rhombuses, wavy lines, S-like flourishes, swastikas, and bird tails. Even partly completed *batik*, such as a cream or white background with some unfinished patterns, is very striking. Sometimes the waxed cloth is even crackled by hand to create a shattered effect. Indigenous designs abound, such as the *sawat* pattern which forms the wings and tail of Garuda or the Siliwangi tiger. Some designs are non-symmetrical, others are more rigid, while the free-form variety is endless. Most artisans copy from patterns but the more talented designers can draw intricate floral, geometric, and wildlife patterns from memory—flowing designs filled with stunning colors.

In traditional *batik*, 3 basic types of designs are used: horizontal (called "soft rain"), vertical, and diagonal. Diagonal motifs are considered less harsh than either vertical or horizontal. The designs for the courts of Yogya and Solo were basically indigenous, although some influence from India is seen on the higher-quality cloth. In these C. Javanese sultanates certain patterns symbolize the position of the wearer. Court officials, bridal couples, and public figures wear a special *sarung (dodot)* which is much larger than that worn by commoners.

Batik designs offer a fascinating window onto the history and mythology of Indonesia. The introduction in Java of Islam, which forbade depicting lifelike figures, led to stylized patterns without direct representation of human or animal forms. Chinese and European influences are evident in the design and color combinations of Pekalongan and Cirebon *batik*, where bright colors, and filigree-like birds, flowers, trees, all form part of the pattern. The motifs of C. Java vary greatly from those on the N coast. Other regions and cities prefer Western motifs, and still others have ancient stylized motifs which are very simple yet so mysterious.

Colors

Historically, natural organic dyes were used, though today their use is disappearing. Indigo, made from the plant, is the oldest dye, and human blood was once a prized natural dye. Europeans in the 19th C. introduced synthetic dyes which are now widely used. If chemical dyes are used (usually really bright colors), *batik* lasts 25-30 years; organic dyed cloths, which fade into a rich deep color, last 45-50 years. In those places (such as Nusatenggara) where natural dyes are still in use, the fabric must be dipped into the dye up to 25 times.

Colors still very much differentiate certain regions: turkey red in Sumatra, blue-black from Indramayu. The C. Javanese *kraton* courts of Yogya and Solo (the main centers for *batik*) hold to the "official" court colors: indigo, dark browns, deep blues, and maroon *(soga)*—colors of dignity. Mauve is suitable only for young unmarried girls. West Javanese *batik* is punctuated by golden yellows and light browns with rich, dark, blackish-blue backgrounds. In the Northern coastal districts and on Madura, bright reds, yellows, glowing russets, and greens are dominant. Modern *batik* makes use of multicolored combinations: crimson, yellow and green mixed with blue, yellow, and black are the main colors used. *Batik* looks brilliant in summer sunshine. Darker colors look stunning next to dark complexions or deeply tanned skin.

The *Indische*

The word *Indische*, which has no English equivalent, was used to describe a remarkable class of people of European or Eurasian descent who had lived for generations in the old Dutch East Indies before Indonesians gained their independence in 1949. The *Indische* were usually half-Dutch and half-Javanese, though they could also be part French, Arabian, Chi-

a Javanese Kris

The kris, Indonesia's traditional dagger is an organic part of this culture and unique to Indonesia There are 40 different types. It's used as a weapon, an ornament, a cult object, or it could be a family's coat of arms, an enshrined heirloom, or stand proxy for a bridegroom marrying a girl of lower caste. It's wavy, snake-like blade makes it easier to bypass bones and ribs (like a saw) and because of the shape of the puncture the wound doesn't close. Its presence brings luck, relieves the pain of women in labor; it rattles in its sheath when danger is near, averts fire and flood. A prince's kris can affect the destiny of a whole nation. At one time a kris was something every adult Javanese male had to possess, and different handles stood for different classes of people. You still see this dagger as part of the uniform in the C. Javanese kraton, but now the rarest and most beautiful specimens are in museums or in the possession of old priyayi families. Masterfully made kris blades inlaid with gold and meteorite metal cost around 3 million in antique shops. Rare and prized noblemen's kris handles, sculpted of gold and set with rubies, diamonds, and sapphires, could cost 10 million rupiah. Souvenir models start at about Rp5000. The pande-caste (kris-makers) are now mostly panel-beaters in automotive garages.

nese, or even pure European—anyone who had lived long enough in the Indies to wholeheartedly adapt to native ways.

Among this enterprising and multilingual people were a small group of *batikers* who established a half-dozen or so commercial *batik* factories. Most of these compounds were founded over a period of 70 years (approximately 1870-1940) in the N-central Javanese town of Pekalongan. These workshops, which turned out only hand-drawn *(tulis)* work using natural dyes, produced *batik* pieces of such extraordinary quality that they have never been equaled. When you find pieces today, they are seldom for sale. For the most part the *batik* was produced for wealthy colonials, or for their own group on occasions of weddings and circumcision ceremonies. Newlyweds would receive 6, 12, even 24 pieces of matching *batik:* the richer the gift-giver, the more pieces and the higher their quality.

Outstanding among the *Indische* was Eliza van Zuylen (1863-1947) who established a *batik kampung* in the 1800s in Pekalongan. Her pieces were exorbitant even then, costing the equivalent of US\$500. Van Zuylen's specialty was flower arrangements and bouquets with soft pastel-colored edges against solid backgrounds; butterflies or birds often flitted around the flowers. No one has ever duplicated the precision and fineness of her work.

Memorable *Indische* flower and geometric motifs were often inspired or drawn from Dutch botany texts or tourist postcards. None of the designs originated on Java and are no longer used today: a whole group of children playing, 2 magnificent swans floating on the water with huge lilies in the background, a whole *sarung* of flapping, fighting cocks. One technique used was to remove the wax from the cloth by boiling

after each dyeing, which created knife-sharp, cleanly delineated edges. Another was to boil off the wax but leave a one-mm-thick coat, then pound the piece with huge wooden mallets to beat the wax in. Ground betelnuts were sometimes added to the dyes to soften the colors.

Though *Indische* reputations were based on their use of soft natural colors such as peach, pink, light blue, and mauve, which simply could not be imitated, by the early 1900s Chinese *batik* factories using synthetic dyes were starting to seriously compete with the *Indische batikers.* With the invasion of the Japanese in 1942, this influential and unusual era in the history of *batik* came to an end.

KRIS

A magical, wavy-bladed dagger. At one time all Javanese men, from the age of 3, were required to wear a *kris.* Indonesians in Java, Sumatra, and other islands still have a fondness for wearing these ceremonial daggers, and the *kris* is often worn formally by the groom at weddings and by a young man to his circumcision ceremony. Rank is denoted by the method of wearing the *kris,* and it must be worn according to set rules: on Java, for example, it must be stuck in the belt in back so that the end of the sheath points to the L and the hilt points to the right.

On the best *kris,* hilts often have exquisite carving in ivory or metalwork, decorated with *raksasa* figures (demonic images that drive off evil spirits), little gnome-like men, snakes, or monkeys. The grips of noblemen's *kris* were often sculpted of gold and set with rubies, diamonds, and sapphires. The Majapahit Kris, dating from the Majapahit Period (A.D.

1293-1478), of which you see only facsimilies nowadays, has both the blade and hilt forged out of a single piece of metal. The ornaments on the blade also provide protection: delicate leaves, *garuda*, or *kala*-figures and very frequently a *naga* (serpent). *Kris* blades sometimes have up to 31 (though usually just 7 or 9) *lok* (undulations) and over 30 motifs. These waves are designed to "saw" flesh for a deeper, ripping stab, and also make the wound difficult to close and thus to heal. An odd number of *lok* assures good luck.

Mystical Qualities

A high mystic value is given to this instrument of death. Traditionally, old *kris pusaka* are part of the family's heirlooms kept in the back of the house and stored in silk with other objects of the cult of ancestors. In an elaborate rite still practiced in C. Java, once a year the *kris* is taken out and cleaned, a sacrifice is shown to it, and incense is burned, prayers are offered, and the blade is rubbed with ointments. Carved out of gold and silver and studded with precious gems, a *kris* was at one time the exclusive possession of the noble class. A *kris* had to suit the wearer's disposition and character exactly — the ideal alter-ego. The number of times it had drawn blood added to its power. Before a battle or assassination, the lethal poison *warangan* (arsenic) was applied to the blade to assure a fatal wound. The owner would even bake the blade in the entrails and brains of snakes and scorpions to increase its power. A *kris* has a spirit and is capable of sorcery: it can talk, fly, swim, turn into a snake, even father human children. Designs on the blade were intended to ward off demons and render the wearer invulnerable. If pointed at someone or if stabbed into the shadow or footprint of an intended victim, the invisible venom of the *kris* could kill a man. When danger is near, *kris* have been known to rattle in their sheaths.

Kris-making

The *kris* is a work of great craftsmanship. This unique weapon was made by the *empu* or *pande* (smiths and armorers) who exercised a secret and holy craft. Though he usually came from a poor and humble family, the *pande* was addressed as an honored lord. The smithy was a hallowed place and the *empu* never failed to carry out a very detailed ritual before work was begun on each *kris*.

These deadly weapons were forged by beating and folding alternate layers of meteorite iron and nickel *(pamor)*. The blade was polished and treated for weeks with lemon juice, coconut water, and arsenic. Then a cryptic formula would blacken the iron and whiten the nickel to create a strange pattern of rivulets. The art of cutting and folding these contrasting metals is now lost; the best nickelous iron from several meteorites embedded on Java was ex-

hausted 100 years ago. The metals later used were of inferior quality. Gradually over the 19th C., the superior arms of the Dutch made the *kris* obsolete in battle. Sacred blades are seldom created now; the unwritten skills have been lost. Nowadays, the *kris* serves only to complete ceremonial dress, is kept as a family heirloom, or is treasured by collectors.

Bronze Work

Blacksmiths have always been highly revered members of the Javanese community. According to Javanese mythology, a blacksmith named Panji is the primal ancestor of the Javanese people. The Javanese were renowned for their skills in metalworking during their Bronze Age (2500-1000 B.C.). These skills included the making of large bronze kettledrums which were probably used for the mystical purpose of rainmaking. Some of these instruments have been unearthed in recent times, for example near Semarang (C. Java), and on the island of Alor megalithic bronze kettledrums *(moko)* have been used until quite recently as ceremonial and dowry objects. But by far the crowning achievement of Javanese bronze work is the great bronze *gamelan* orchestras of C. Java, made up of 70-80 instruments.

FOLK THEATER

Drama

Each locality of Java boasts its own exciting folk drama. The best place to see this popular theater is in small villages where the admission is low and relaxed performances are spiced with lots of humor. In the cities people have been conditioned by modern films and fast-paced life and want their entertainment *hebat* (violent, sensational). For villagers who can't read and don't own a TV, these dramatizations of folk tales, proverbs, and poems give them new ways of thinking and behaving. Also used as a political vehicle, almost all troupes nowadays are financed by pro-Suharto regime army officers.

When an entertainment troupe arrives in a small village, it's a big night. Actors and actresses barely make a living from their profession, traveling like gypsies with their pots, pans, bedding, and children in tow. Most come from poor families, have had little education, and work at unskilled jobs when not touring. As they seldom have time to rehearse, these actors have become professional improvisors. The director distributes the roles and gives a brief sketch of the story about an hour before the performance. The gradual but steady appearance of communal TV sets in even the remotest villages is slowly eroding the popular demand for these traveling theater troupes. Folk drama does survive, however, in People's Amusement Parks (THRs) in all of the biggest cities of Java, where the following forms are regularly staged.

Ludruk

A modern-day, mostly E. Javanese, transvestite musical theater form. Plays aren't based solely on Javanese mythology and history but are taken as well from everyday life, with many satirical allusions to contemporary events. There's no definite repertoire. All roles are improvised by male actors renowned for their flawless ability in imitating women. In the countryside, *ludruk* performances cost as little as Rp250 to enter. Get backstage if you can, where you can see the performers apply their makeup, don their costumes, and put on their falsies.

Ketoprak

A folk melodrama originating in Yogya. A more traditional theater form than *ludruk*, *ketoprak* is more movie-like and more costly to stage, often utilizing technical devices. *Ketoprak* is most often performed in the Javanese language accompanied by *gamelan*. Dancing and singing are used in the beginning and at the end, but not in the middle. A show usually starts at 2100 and ends at 0100. Serials are frequently divided into 7 installments, lasting throughout the week. This genre takes its stories mostly from E. Javanese folklore and history, as well as from Chinese and Arab sources. Traditional moral lessons with contemporary social commentary are woven into the plot; *ketoprak* informs, instructs, and entertains at the same time, passing on new trends and ideas in subtle ways.

This performed literature tells much about current Javanese society. Past, present, and future are all incorporated into the story line—kings, court scenes, enchanted rings, magic incantations, village doctors, political elections, bandits, dwarves, battle scenes on man-powered horses—you could see *anything!* Even the Christmas story or *Hamlet* may be enacted, with traditional Javanese dress and mannerisms, and all kinds of local elements mixed in to "Javanize" it so it will be a box office success. Clowns perform hilarious mimicry of the courtly *Serimpi* dancers, including all the simpering expressions, as audiences roar with laughter at this slapstick comedy. *Ketoprak* is sometimes so popular that local authorities must close the shows down because villagers are spending too much money, neglecting family responsibilities and local taxes. It's truly a theater of the people.

GAMELAN

Gamelan is the broad name for many varieties of xylophonic orchestras with bronze, wooden, or bamboo keys on wooden or bamboo bases or resting on tubular resonators, balanced on pegs or suspended. This type of percussion ensemble is found in other forms in Thailand, the Philippines, Madagascar, Kampuchea. *Gamelan* orchestras are the most widespread type of orchestra in the archipelago, especially on

Java and Bali. The most sophisticated of these orchestras is the native Javanese *gamelan,* usually composed of about a dozen musicians and used as accompaniment in *wayang* and dance performances. But in its complete modern form, a *gamelan* orchestra could comprise 70-80 instruments. With it as well are solo vocalists *(pasinden)* and up to 15 choir *(gerongan)* members. Native *gamelan* seldom play outside Indonesia because of the transportation expenses.

The ethereal sound of the *gamelan* is created when rows of small bronze kettle-shaped discs of varying sizes, with raised nipples, are hit with cudgel-like sticks. These bronze instruments give the *gamelan* its highly distinctive musical range, from thin tinkles to deep booming reverberations. *Gamelan* music can't be compared with the compositions of the West's great polyphonic composers such as Bach, whose music is so mathematically laid down. *Gamelan* is much looser, freer, more flighty and unpredictable. Some feel *gamelan* music is curiously melancholy, even disturbing.

Aficionados of this art should subscribe to *Balungan* ($8 for 3 issues per year), a publication dedicated to *gamelan* in all its forms. Write to: *Balungan,* Mills College Station, Oakland CA 94613 USA.

History

The bronze kettledrum originated from the Dongson culture of N. Vietnam, then spread to China in the middle of the 1st millenium B.C., reaching the archipelago around the 3rd century B.C. String instruments were probably influenced by a similar contact with people from ancient India and the Middle East. Gongs were certainly imported into Java and the rest of the major islands during the Sriwijaya Dynasty, whose empire dominated SE Asia in the 9th century. In that period *gamelan,* together with drums and blown conch shells, were used for ceremonial occasions. You can even find these predecessors of the *gamelan* on 10th C. Borobudur bas-reliefs. *Gamelan* as we know it today attained the pinnacle of its refinement in the C. Javanese *kraton* of the 18th and 19th centuries. Although strange to the European ear, the inimitable quality of *gamelan* has attracted Western composers ever since Claude Debussy first "discovered" it at the end of the 19th century.

Tonal Scales

The Javanese *gamelan* owes its origin to the influx of peoples from SE Asia who brought with them the *pelog* scale. A complete *gamelan* consists of 2 almost identical-looking sets of instruments, with some gongs and drums common to both sets. One set is tuned to the 5-tone *slendro* scale and one to the 7-toned *pelog* scale. No 2 orchestras are tuned exactly alike.

Each tone system has a different feeling. Generally, the *slendro* is more festive and cheerful while the *pelog* is more solemn and sad. Scales are divided into unfamiliar intervals and scales can be constructed to fit any kind of performance. Modulations aren't found, melodies aren't based on a fixed key note, and the tonal material is very flexible. Though *gamelan* is more rigidly structured, as in jazz there's no written score. Neither is there as much solo playing as in Western bands, but more of an integration of sounds. The playing technique is handed down through suc-

cessive generations, and *gamelan* orchestras hundreds of years old often carry such proper names as "Venerable Dark Cloud," "Flowering Success," and "Drifting in Smiles."

Instruments

The main theme is carried by the *saron,* a set of convex metallic resonating keys which are beaten with small mallets. These are the most striking instruments; *saron* look like a number of round, bell-shaped pudding dishes with covers. This sound is given more

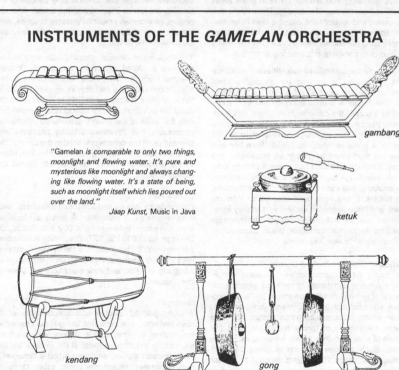

INSTRUMENTS OF THE *GAMELAN* ORCHESTRA

gambang

"Gamelan *is comparable to only two things, moonlight and flowing water. It's pure and mysterious like moonlight and always changing like flowing water. It's a state of being, such as moonlight itself which lies poured out over the land."*

Jaap Kunst, Music in Java

ketuk

kendang

gong

Gamelan, *the native orchestra of Indonesia, has a 1,500-year history. The names of the instruments suggest the sounds and rhythms of this remarkable music-making group. Certain instruments have the role of carrying the main theme, others play counter melodies and keep the tempo, while gongs do the musical paraphrasing. The leaders are the drummers, the most skilled musicians of the group. The beat of the* kendang *drum usually follows the movement of the dancers or puppets, serving in the role of conductor in Western orchestras. The* demung *has rows of small bronze slabs, while the* gambang *has blocks of resonant wood*

which are beaten with sticks to make a snapping, cracking sound. The kenong is like an overturned brass bowl with a raised nipple, set in a red, blue, or gold frame and beaten with small mallets to produce a sharp metallic ring. The total sound of the gamelan is like the beating of insect wings or the sound of a river trickling over rocks at night. It is said to stimulate the growth of flowers. Keep your eye out for KOKAR, music academies where you can study gamelan and other regional instruments as well as watch dance rehearsals.

depth and is paraphrased by the xylophone-like *gender,* a row of resonant tubes. The *ketuk* has short, flat, dull accents, while the *kenong* has deep resounding notes. The various gong tones and subtle beats are difficult to distinguish at first. The gongs reverberate with shimmering, echoing notes. The *kendang* provides the beat for the melody, accelerating or lowering the tempo as the composition requires. The beat of the *keprak* (wood block) provides the rhythm for the dancers. The sorrowful violin-like 2-stringed *rebab,* similar to a Persian viol, accompanies the chorus who sing in unison or recite in nasal tones speeches from the plot of a *wayang.* There might also be a zither, and several light, magical reed flutes *(suling),* the only wind instruments in the *gamelan,* paraphrasing the nuclear theme in a higher key. Half a dozen drums complete this amazing ensemble.

There are numerous regional specialties and modifications. East Java is famous for its high-pitched *gamelan* in which plucked zithers play a prominent role. The *kecapi* is a unique Sundanese instrument used as a part of the *gamelan* in W. Java. This boat-shaped plucked zither often has a *suling* or vocal accompaniment. The *angklung,* very popular in W. Java, is a portable instrument made from bamboo tubes cut to different lengths freely suspended in a frame. Although restricted to 4 notes, a strange xylophonic sound is produced when the frame is shaken. The *angklung* was used in ancient times for marching into battles. It has now been adapted to Western scales and large *angklung* orchestras can play European as well as Indonesian songs. The *gamelan angklung* orchestra combines these bamboo instruments with gongs and drums.

Gamelan With Dance And Drama

The music which accompanies a *wayang* performance remains constantly in harmony with the sequence of events unfolding on stage. There is appropriate music for each of the different main characters, music which accompanies battle scenes and love scenes, melancholy or tender music played at the demise of a hero, spiritual music, heroic music, dance music. Such a close relationship exists between *gamelan* and dance that when a dance is broadcast on the radio, listeners are able to follow and visualize perfectly the movements of the dancers.

DANCE

Since the split of the Mataram Kingdom into the vassal states of Yogya and Solo in 1775, the art of court dancing has evolved differently in each of these C. Javanese *kraton.* These cultural capitals have always been artistic rivals: Solo considers Yogyanese dancers too stiff and Yogya thinks Solonese dancers are too slack and casual. The differences today in the 2 schools are still recognizable, though unimportant.

In court dancing, the emphasis is on angular graceful poses and smooth subtle gestures. This type of dancing is far removed from Western theories of art and reflects the ultra-refinement of Javanese courts. Having evolved at a time of warring states, classical dancing is executed with all the deliberation of a slow march and the precision of a drill maneuver. Sometimes years of arduous muscular training is required to execute certain gestures such as arching the hand until the fingers touch the forearm (to imitate the opening of flower petals). Dancers are incredibly detached, yet their inaction and long periods of immobility are just as important as the action. All these pauses, silences, and motions arrested in space, with lowered eyes and meditative poses, make Javanese dance hypnotic to watch.

The tradition of classical dancing was once looked upon as a sacred legacy by the courts. Dancers selected from the lower-class families of the *kraton* population could take part only in supporting roles in the royal plays. It wasn't until 1918 in Yogya when the Krida Beksa Wirama Dance School was founded outside the walls of the *kraton,* established in order to perpetuate the Javanese arts by teaching *any* talented pupil the dances practiced in the courts. The royal monopoly on dancing was at last broken. Many village groups have since imitated and diluted the courtly style.

Dance Hire

Private dance groups perform for anniversaries, wedding receptions, or *selematan.* A group can be hired from anywhere between Rp50,000 and Rp600,000 (average Rp60,000-150,000.) If you hire a troupe to perform, you'll thus repay the family you're staying with for their kindness, their prestige in the village or *kampung* will rise, and their neighbors will share in the pleasure.

Serimpi

A slow, graceful, disciplined classical dance of C. Java perfected over centuries, using super-controlled movements of arms, hands, fingers, and head. Its sources are the same as those of the *Bedaya,* the old *Amir Hamzah* stories, depicting a battle between 2 rival princesses. Impersonal poise, subtle restraint, and an intense inward meditation are maintained throughout, with the face tilting downward, staring fixedly at the floor. The dancers carry out such unrealistic movements as a fish flowing through the water, or dancers tiptoeing over the floor and gliding (called "flying"), with a dagger in one hand and a fluttering scarf in the other—a sort of stylized combat. Dancers' heads move slowly from side to side in a regal manner while executing "bird movements" or "make-up miming," the hips arching back slightly, the torso leaning forward. Hands usually stay at hip level, elbows slightly bent. *Serimpi* ends in a sitting position with a Hindu blessing.

Bedaya

Many different versions. One of the oldest and most sacred forms is *Bedaya ketawang,* performed on the second day of the month *Ruwah* on the Javanese calendar—the anniversary of the Susuhunan of Solo's ascension to the throne. Originating over 400 years ago, this dance is dedicated to the dreaded South Sea Goddess Nyai Loro Kidul, who was said to have appeared to the first ruler of the dynasty, Sultan Agung (1613-45), expressing her love for him by dancing and singing before him. The 9 dancers, also called *Bedaya,* are traditionally selected from families related to the sultan. They belong to the innermost ceremonial circle of the *kraton,* where this dance form has reached its highest development. Performances are kept secret, and no photographs are taken so as not to anger the South Sea Goddess who is invisible but present; if the dance displeases her, it's feared she might carry one of the dancers off to the bottom of the sea. You might get in on one of the rehearsals, which last a week.

The dancers' period of training is long and they must also sing. The dancers (girls aged 15-16 years) are dressed like brides with their hair piled up in a bun, wearing beautiful intricate haircoils of gold, precious stones, and jasmine buds. They must fast before the dance to purify mind and body, and none may be in her menses. The dance lasts 90 minutes. First, offerings to the gods *(sajen)* are made. While a female choir sings a litany, dancers move languidly, their movements punctuated by chanting hypnotic bell-like sounds, flicks of long sashes, gentle kicks beneath long swirling trains, while incense permeates the air. Dancers are like priestesses in their detachment and solemnity, their gowns undulating like sea waves. Showers of petals are thrown over the audience.

Reyog

A *wayang topeng* masked dance in which a great leering tiger's head or a monster's headmask with peacock feathers on top is worn(see a specimen in Surabaya's tourist office on Jl. Pemuda). Sometimes weighing 50 kg and up to 50 cm tall, the mask rests on the nape of the neck and is held in place by the teeth. Though they have small builds, *reyog* dancers have incredibly strong neck muscles due to dancing many hours wearing this heavily decorated headpiece. It's said to be impossible to strangle these dancers by hand.

The *reyog* story is about a local king desiring the daughter of a neighboring king. In an effort to discourage the unwanted suitor, the princess assigns her prospective husband an impossible task: to dig a tunnel from his palace to her father's palace. The Balinese *Barong* dance might have been derived from the *reyog.* You may be bored by the story of the success of good over evil, but the average villager sits enthralled and wide-eyed for up to 12 straight hours. This trance dance originated in Ponorogo, E. Java, and occasionally *reyog* dances are held in Ponorogo's Kantor Kabupaten on Jl. Kabupaten, N of the *alun-alun.* You can hire a whole performance for Rp150,000-250,000. To attract tourists, *reyog ponorogo* is also sponsored by the East Java Tourist Development Board, headquartered in Surabaya.

Kuda Kepong (Kuda Lopeng)

East Java's famous horse-trance dance in which one, 4, 6, or 8 performers ride black cut-out bamboo-weave hobbyhorses to the rhythm of drums, gongs, and flutes, while a man beats a steel pipe with a hammer. Many variations of *Kuda Kepong* are found in different parts of Java in which more masked players, monsters, and mysterious rites are involved. (In a Chinese-influenced version, there's even a role for a dragon.) No stage or enclosure is needed for this dance. It can be dangerous and requires the presence and aid of a *dukun* (medicine man or mystic teacher) who uses mantras to control the dancers. Drugs, hypnosis, or alcohol are never used. Sometimes there's a sham battle, then suddenly one of the dancers becomes *jadi* (possessed), believing he's a horse. This state is usually induced by the pain caused by cracking each other with whips, sometimes drawing blood. The entranced dancer gallops, canters, rears, and prances like a circus pony. There's a bundle of hay in a corner which the "horse" chews. A dancer often loses control while behaving like a horse—shrieking, twitching, slurping water from a pail, running wild and whinnying, rolling in the grass, charging with stiff body and voided expression. The *dukun* finally calms the performer and brings him out of the trance with incense and incantations.

WAYANG

A Javanese word meaning literally "shadow" or "ghost," *wayang* is a theatrical performance of living actors, 3-dimensional puppets, or shadow images held before a screen lit from behind. The word can also refer to the puppets themselves. In most forms, the dialogue is in Javanese or Sundanese; sometimes the Indonesian language is used. Most often the chants are in *Kawi* (Old Javanese), as archaic a language today as Shakespearean English.

Wayang drama forms reflect all aspects of Javanese culture. Characters are judged not by their actions but by their devotion to what is appropriate to their castes, and by their predetermined roles in the drama. Gestures are appreciated more than common sense, style more than content. Courage, loyalty, and refinement always win out in the end, and fate is accepted without question. The *wayang* plays do not just show the direct victory of good over evil, but also weakness as well as greatness in all its characters and, by implication, in society as a whole.

Wayang performances are staged when some transitional event occurs in a person's life: birthdays, weddings, important religious occasions, or as ritual entertainment during family feasts or *selamatan*. Coming of age (puberty), a circumcision, promotions in rank, even the building of a new swimming pool—all could be excuses for a show. While providing entertainment, the *wayang* media also teach the meaning and purpose as well as the contradictions and anomalies of modern life. The policies of the military government are even explained in terms of *wayang* theater, not only by the puppet-masters, but also in newspaper editorials and even in government statements.

History

These art forms date from before the 9th century. *Wayang* came before Indian influence, the present-day heroes having evolved from ancestral spirits. In ancient pre-Hindu times, *wayang* puppets were perhaps portraits of deceased ancestors who came down to earth to visit and communicate with their descendants during the performance. *Wayang's* function was to placate and please the gods so as to increase fertility or to exorcise or propitiate various ghosts and evil spirits. Since the moving, flickering silhouettes were considered the very souls of the dead, the puppeteer *(dalang)* was probably first a shamanistic priest, a medium between the dead and the living.

With the arrival of Hinduism from India sometime after the 1st century A.D., the exciting and dramatic Hindu epic stories of the *Ramayana* and *Mahabharata* were incorporated into existing Indonesian ritual stories. During the time of intense Hindu influence (8th-15th C.), Hindu teachers used *wayang* as a vehicle to propagandize and popularize their religion. Indian epic heroes, gods, demons, and giants eventually began to supplant all the ancestor figures (except the clowns), and Indonesian backgrounds were given to the Indian epics. Records tell of a remote King Airlangga enjoying puppet performances at his court in Java in the 11th century.

These shows also had a strong influence on Java-Hindu sculpture. On 13th C. bas-reliefs you can see figures similar to *wayang* puppets of the time, portraying all the same characters and events as *wayang* does today. When Hinduism started to give way to Islam in the 13th C., Indonesian Muslims simply made heroes of the Islamic literary figures and turned them into puppet characters. Shadow plays were used by sultans to flatter themselves and their courts, to glorify and perpetuate the feudalistic court ritual of the Javanese royalty. *Wayang*, by reinforcing the class system, has always kept everyone in his place. Because Muslims banned the reproduction of the human form, both good and evil puppets were made ugly and grotesque so that they wouldn't resemble living beings, and the puppets' faces, coloring, hairdos, clothes, and jewelry are still so strongly stylized that they are more symbols than actual human figures. *Wayang* puppets are the only figural representations left over from the graphic arts of the early Islamic period.

The Audience

As a foreigner you won't be able to follow all the stories, but you can't help but be infected by the atmosphere. The audience is the best show of all. Twenty to a thousand Javanese sit up all night long in a theater reeking of clove cigarette smoke and packed to overflowing. Babies fall asleep on mothers' laps, people tip off chairs in hysterical laughter, kids alternately sleep and come awake and giggle in front of or behind the screen until dawn. The audience already knows all the stories and roles backwards and forwards and though they are constantly moving around eating, sleeping, and talking, they never lose the thread. This 3,000-year-old mythology still applies today; it's living and dynamic—much more of an elective and kinetic exchange than the movies could ever be. A show is like eavesdropping on neighbors, or more accurately, on friends and relatives. The audience loses all sense of time as the gods themselves—not their shadows—are actually on the screen.

Wayang Characters As Role Models

The *wayang* repertoire also serves as a character chart by which to judge people. Javanese sometimes use proper names from the Indian epic poems to refer to people they meet. "He's a Suyudana," the ambitious and deceitful leader of the 99 Korawa brothers; or "He's just like Gatutkaca" (brave). The shape of a person's face and body can also typecast him: "He walks like a Raksasa!" (threatening and lumbering). Arjuna typifies tenacity and dedication to duty; Yudistira is pure, righteous, and compassionate; Krishna exemplifies clairvoyance and magic powers, and so on. *Wayang* characters also provide types to be emulated, giving the young a clear audio-visual message as to which qualities and virtues to strive for and which to avoid. The heroes and villains of these stories are well known to the public not only through all forms of *wayang* theater, but also through millions of comic books. Children grow up surrounded by the physical, psychological, and ethical traits of the *wayang* characters.

Forms Of *Wayang*

With the exception of the Sunda region of W. Java, today there are more than 10,000 individual performers of the *wayang kulit* shadow play on Java and Bali. (The Sundanese of W. Java prefer *wayang golek*, carved wooden puppets, to the intricately

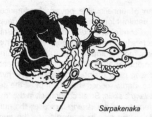
Sarpakenaka

carved flat leather figures of the *wayang kulit.)* In addition to these well-known forms of *wayang,* there are a few rare, vestigial forms such as *wayang beber,* a narrated presentation in which drawings are unrolled, and new forms like Jakarta's *wayang karya* which features a large puppet stage. In Pamekasan on the island of Madura off E. Java, one troupe of *Wayang Orang Madura* wears masks which cover only the top part of their faces so that the players' mouths are exposed to speak freely. The Chinese of Java have their own form of *wayang golek,* which is performed only in a temple. It is believed that *wayang golek* is the last development of all the native *wayang* forms.

Wayang Emigrates

Javanese colonialists have gradually transmitted *wayang* and its ethical system all over the archipelago. *Wayang* has even made its way overseas, carried by Javanese and Sundanese who have emigrated to all parts of the world. In Malaysia, Javanese laborers were recruited by the English to construct roads in the 19th C., and during WW II Javanese slave laborers *(romusha)* were indentured by the Japanese to serve the empire, taking their culture with them. *Wayang* is even found in New Caledonia and in all the former Dutch territories of the world, such as Surinam in S. America where 40,000 ethnic Javanese settled at the beginning of this century. These emigrants from Java were not trained artists and *dalang,* but farmers. But on Java they grew up with the *wayang* forms, so they fashioned puppets and put on their own frontier versions of the *Mahabharata* and *Ramayana* epics, which naturally became modified over the years under the influence of the adopted country. Thus the overseas *wayang* forms are unique, using puppets which are crudely carved, performed to homemade and unorthodox *gamelan.*

Museums

The Wayang Museum in Jakarta (Jl. Pintu Besar Utara 27) may not be the largest *wayang* collection in the world but it is certainly one of the most comprehensive. Exhibited are specimens of *wayang* forms from not only numerous provinces of Indonesia, including the Outer Islands, but also puppetry from all over the world. Outstanding collections of different kinds of *wayang* are also found in Amsterdam, Rotterdam, Leiden, and The Hague in the Netherlands, but mainly those museums concentrate on the Sundanese, Javanese, and Balinese forms only. Several *wayang* collections are also in the Musee Guimnet and the Musee L'Homme, Paris; in the Dallem Museum of W. Berlin; and in the museums of Hamburg, Offenbach, and Munich in W. Germany.

Lakon

The plot of a *wayang* performance. The *lakon* is usually divided into 3 principal, escalating phases, each with many scenes. Lasting from 4 to 10 hours, *wayang* plays are more exciting and spectacular than tragic or funny. Everything is illusion, symbolism, dream, fairytale, and mysticism. The true origins of the plots are almost untraceable after having been put into the Indonesian cultural blender. Stories are a combination of old sacred myths, the adventures of noblemen, various historical plays, ancient Javanese folk poetry, and the newer Indian epic tales of gods and princesses. Or the theme could be extremely contemporary with liberated women, problems of marriage, social issues, etc. acted out. Despite the differences, all themes emphasize absolute good against absolute evil. Western and Chinese cinema have had a strong influence on all forms of *wayang* theater (kung-fu fighting in the battle scenes). And in spite of the inroads TV has made in the villages, *wayang's* popularity remains strong.

Some plots *(Wayang Menak)* are drawn from an old Arab story, the *Menak* cycle, but have been completely Javanized and "improved" upon; even old Javanese folk tales such as the *Panji* cycle have been worked over extensively and presented in *Wayang Gedog.* There are *wayang* plays about the shrewd, brave little mouse-deer *(wayang kancil),* who outwits the stronger animals of the jungle. Mystics use *wayang* to propagate their cult; *Wayang Madya* plays are based on the 19th C. epic poetry of Ranggawarsita, who recorded the reign of an E. Javanese prophet-king, Jayabaya (this form has now been confined to the Solo court and is rarely performed). *Wayang Josuf* is about Joseph of the Bible, and his brothers. Plots became more politicized after WW II during the independence struggle when the need arose to politically indoctrinate the masses *(Wayang Suluh).* *Wayang* was then used to applaud heroism in guerilla warfare, and the communists even had Arjuna use the hammer and sickle as a weapon. In *Wayang Panca Sila,* the history of the republic is glorified: the 5 Pandava brothers from the *Mahabharata* symbolize the 5 *Panca Sila* principles of government. *Wayang* plays have also been utilized to explain the meaning of 5-year economic plans to the people.

Epic Indian Poems

By far the most popular form of *wayang* is that based

Dasarata

on the Indian classical poems, the *Ramayana* and the *Mahabharata*. The original epics were brought from India and translated over 1,000 years ago. They were only adapted for Javanese theater in the 19th century. For many Indonesians these classic stories are the holy books, not the *Koran*. In fact, the *wayang* mythology has been called "the Bible of Java" because they allude to a time when the gods were still on Earth, a time when they established the great rules and traditions of life.

Themes are usually variations of the struggles between the gods and demons with men choosing sides *(Bhrata-yuddha)*. Man either shares the glory with the gods or is destroyed, or helps the gods ward off demons' attacks *(Arjuna Wiwaha)*. The plot gives guidance for the development of one's life from the inconclusive struggles of youth (the swaying back and forth in the first act of the play), through the struggle to understand oneself and conquer one's own passions (the conquering of the demons and giants in the wilderness, which usually takes place in the second act), to the mature ability to control oneself and solve one's own and the community's problems (the final resolution of the plot in the third act).

The Dalang

The *wayang* puppeteer. The *dalang* is the playwright, producer, principal narrator, conductor, and director of this shadow world. He's an expert in languages and highly skilled in the techniques of ventriloquism. Some *dalang* (or their wives) even carve their own puppets, maintaining a cast of up to 200 which are kept in a big wooden box *(katok)*. He must be familiar with all levels of speech according to the *dramatis personae*, modulating his voice and employing up to 9 tonal and pitch variations to suit each of the puppets' temperaments. The *dalang* has a highly developed dramatic sense and if he has a good voice, his chants are beautiful and captivating to hear. He must also be intimately versed in history, including complex royal genealogies; music (melodies, modes, phrases, songs); recitation (both *gamelan* and spoken); eloquence (an extempore poet creating a warm or terrifying atmosphere); possess a familiarity with metaphysics, spiritual knowledge, and perfection of soul. Traveling from village to village and city to city, he has as many fans as a film star.

A man of unbelievable physical endurance (some chew betelnut for strength) and amazing detachment and self-control, he must be able to work his many characters for 9 hours or longer, keeping as many as 6 puppets moving and talking at the same time. With movements of arms, hands, fingers, feet, and voice, the *dalang* must maintain different body rhythms all at once. Battle scenes show best of all the degree of the *dalang's* skills. Small children sit in the front rows and sometimes the *dalang* increases the number of battles in the plot in proportion to the number of children in the audience. In ancient times he was nothing less than a priest officiating at a religious ritual. On Java the *dalang* retains to this day vestiges of his role as a priest, particularly in the *Ruwatan* performance (a ritual warding off of evil from a vulnerable child). On Hindu Bali the *dalang* is still seen as a sacred storyteller and is called *pamangku-dalang* (priest-storyteller).

Once passed down from father to son, the puppeteer's art is now taught only in special schools in C. Java. The working *dalang's* fees depend on his reputation and popularity. It is common for *dalang* of the first rank, such as Nartosado of Yogya (Solo-style), Amamsoroto, Durmoko, and Supraman of Solo, to demand 2 million *rupiah* (US$2000) for one night's work. And a special appearance can incur additional costs because of all the *extra* expenses. When a first-class *dalang* performs, only the very best orchestra can be hired. If the *gamelan* is second or third rate it will not do the *dalang* justice.

Characters

The easiest way to pick out the speaker is to watch the puppets' or actors' arms. If they stretch out, they are speaking; if they hang down, they are silent. Javanese can tell the good and evil characters as easily as an American can discern the bad guys in any cowboy film. They look for such things as the placement and shape of eyes, nose, mouth, the absence or presence of body hair or chin whiskers, the pose of the head, the coiffure, the headgear, clothing, jewelry—all or each of these immediately identify the character. Soft or raging voices also assist in picking out specific character-types. The most easily recognizable *wayang* are those of the Hindu epics: Brahma and Vishnu (the gods who create and sustain life), Shiva (the Great Teacher), Durga (consort to Shiva), and Ganesha (the elephant-headed son of Shiva). Each of these heroes has his own melody played for him at his appearance.

Six facial and body colors also indicate individual character, temperament, and mood. Vishnu's face is black, Shiva's face is gold, and Krishna's enemy brother Baladewa has a red face. White depicts noble descent, youth, beauty; a blue or green face means cowardice. Black stands for inner maturity, adulthood, virtue, calmness; gold indicates beauty or royal-

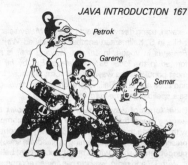

ty or glory. A black face with gold body indicates a refined warrior in a state of determination. Red shows uncontrolled passions and desires. A dozen shapes of mouths express emotion, and about 25 varieties of stylized coiffures and headgear denote priests, princes, warriors, queens, deities, high kings, or gods. At least 3 types of hair bun delineate different characters. Arjuna and his twin brothers Makula and Sadewa wear their hair in an upward curl like a scorpion's tail or a lobster's claw, indicative of their royalty. Gods wear a long cloak, shawl, and footwear; kings wear a pleated *kain.* Warriors often wear a belt for their *kris.* Priests and high nobility have eyes almost closed.

The size of each puppet depends on whether they be demons, giants, gods, or just ordinary people. Puppets representing the highest deities are smaller than those of the noble heroes, who in turn are smaller than their opponents. The bulky demons are the largest puppets of all. (This same proportion is followed in the classical relief sculpture on ancient Javanese temples.) Large sizes like Bima and Kumbakarna are an indication of physical power but not necessarily of greatness, passion, or violence. Generally, the large villain figures belong to the negative "left" side of the screen or stage, while the smaller good guys belong to the positive "right" side, though exceptions abound.

The posture with the legs held wide apart is found in warriors and rough characters, while females are shown with legs close together. Different shapes of eyes and noses denote nobility, patience, crudeness, steadfastness, power, loyalty, clownishness, wisdom. Basically, almond eyes and pointed noses mean benevolent puppets, while bulging round eyes and bulbous noses identify crude ones with their pompous display of ornamentation and the cocky angle of their heads, typified by characters like Burisrawa. Arjuna epitomizes aristocracy and refinement with his almond-shaped eyes, finely turned long-pointed nose in a straight line from the tip to forehead, slightly bowed head showing humility, no moustache, and absolutely no jewelry or finery. Finally, witches, animals, and demons — exempt from the ceremonial behavior of noble humans — have license to adopt hilarious styles of their own, and often provide an element of raucous comedy.

Panakawan

The deformed *panakawan* (clowns) Semar, Gareng, and Petruk are the trusted and loving servants of the heroes. But they are much more. With their short legs, ugly shapes, fat stomachs, sagging breasts, jutting jaws, whether limping or trickstering or fighting, they are *wayang's* most laughable and lovable characters. Genealogically speaking, Semar is the father of all the clowns. Many in the audience look upon him as a deity, the chief of all the gods, and actually worship him as such. When he meets with the gods they always use honorific language when addressing him; he in turn speaks *down* to them. Every once in a while Semar loses his temper, goes up to the heavens and starts knocking heads about. He has even gotten away with throwing the great god Brahma down a well. The gods apologize and defer to him, because Semar is there to lead as well as to serve. This is the crux in understanding the Javanese view of what god really is. God should be the strongest force there is, yet he is available — like a servant — to anyone who needs him. Semar represents the common people — the source of his awesome power — the *real* voice of god.

Semar is as well a comic, a symbol of wisdom and humor, and he invokes laughter. He is a figure of great and abiding mystery. When he comes on stage, the chorus sings a song of praise, "Who is Semar? *What* is Semar? He has the genitals of a man, yet the dress of a woman. He is a midget, and yet he is very big. He is very old, yet he wears his hair like a child...." Because of his spectacular magic tricks, Semar gets terrific audiences. This clown even goes around as a sort of spy, eavesdropping and looking for information. He could be in disguise, for example, as a sleight-of-hand magician — but he uses *real* magic. In many of the stories the princes try to prevent him from having his way, but if the tide goes against him he merely changes into another one of his infinite godlike aspects, such as that of a bold young knight. Even though his role, appearance, and voice change, the audience knows very well that it is still Semar. He can do no wrong in their eyes!

WAYANG KULIT

A "shadow play" using 2-dimensional puppets chiseled by hand out of buffalo or goat parchment, with the appearance of paper dolls but with arms that swivel. This shadow play can be likened in the English audiences' mind to a combination "Punch and Judy Show" and "Shadow Graph." Since a *wayang kulit* puppet is a stylized exaggeration of a human shape, it's really a shadow of a shadow. Many different styles of *wayang kulit* exist. Palembang performs its own version, using its own dialect (a sort of Melayu slang), while in S. Kalimantan another style called *Wayang Banjar* is in vogue. In Jakarta, *wayang kulit* is performed in the local *Batawi* dialects. But by far the most popular is the *wayang kulit* form practiced in C. and E. Java and on Bali, where it has been developed as a spellbinding medium for storytelling.

Other forms of *wayang*, such as *wayang golek* and *wayang orang*, find *wayang kulit* difficult to compete with. For one thing, it's the cheapest *wayang* form to present, requiring no costuming or elaborate sets, just puppets and a sheet with a bright electric light behind it. With TV and radio, *wayang* has spread economically to a much wider audience. These media are not killing *wayang kulit* as many people maintain. If anything, the mass media are increasing *wayang kulit's* exposure to the people. Although some *dalang* may lose work because of the widespread sale and use of cassettes, there are also some positive effects: students may learn the *dalang's* art through the cassettes, and *dalang* and musicians practice with cassettes. Cassettes are everywhere, in all the villages, and they're definitely cheaper. One night's performance using cassettes runs about Rp20,000, whereas Rp100,000 is the lowest a village can pay for a live performance. Moreover, a performance put on by a well-known *dalang* costs as much as 2-3 million *rupiah*.

Wayang Broadcasts

In all of Java's major cities you can easily tune in on *wayang kulit* performances on the national radio network (RRI). These performances, with just the voice of the *dalang* and the *gamelan* music, usually air from 2100-0500. On the first Sat. night of each month a performance is broadcast from Semarang's radio station, the second Sat. from Yogya's, the third from Solo's, the fourth from Jakarta. On those months with 5 Saturdays, a performance also originates from Surabaya or Madiun. In Bandung, not only a *wayang kulit* but a *wayang golek* troupe performs on the RRI; from Cirebon, *Wayang Golek Cirebon* is put on the air. Amateur troupes in Jakarta and in other cities of Java broadcast *wayang kulit* programs for the sole purpose of recording cassettes (8 or 9 for a single performance) at about Rp20,000 per set.

History

The Javanese have been cultivating the shadow play for more than 2,000 years. This sophisticated theater is one of the strongest cultural traits to have survived throughout Indonesia's recorded history. Originally, it was connected with ancestor worship and from its very beginnings has had religious significance. South India was probably the original source of Indonesian *wayang kulit*. Recorded in *Pali* canons, it existed there as far back as the first century. Forms related to *wayang kulit* are found today from the *Nang* plays of

Thailand all the way to Turkey. In Indonesia, *wayang kulit* was established by migrating Hindus who adapted the native shadow play to their own stories of adventure and war, the *Ramayana* and *Mahabharata*. The earliest written record in Indonesia of a shadow play is found on a stone inscription in C. Java dated A.D. 907, a performance of dance, music, buffoonery, and song dedicated to Bima. The present plays, the product of a long evolution, are based on the Indian epics, native Javanese legends, and stories adopted from Arabic tales.

Wayang-making

A complete set of *wayang kulit,* including duplications of a single character to show different ages and moods, could number 350-400 puppets, the smallest only 23 cm high and the tallest over one meter. The *Penatah,* the *wayang*-making artist, first cuts out contours from buffalo leather or, in the last decade, goatskin. All the cutting and coloring is executed with the help of a special pattern book using 12 different motifs which help make the figures more recognizable. Before painting, the hide is rubbed smooth, then given a plain white background. Next, gold or yellow paint is applied to give puppets the effect of gilding. Of delicate and grotesque design, stiffened with glue and colored with bright acrylics, the best seem worked in delicate lace filigree.

During a performance, each leather figure is held by a flexible rod of split buffalo horn which has been cut, heated, and stretched along the torso of each puppet. The sharp bottom end of the rod, when not in use, is stuck into a banana trunk. Stick-like horn rods are also attached to the puppets' elbows and shoulder joints so that the arms may be manipulated. Faces of the puppets are always in profile, the body turned to the front and both feet turned in the same direction as the facial profile. Performances are uncannily realistic with the characters jabbing each other in the chests and waving their arms about to punctuate the action or to fit the type of character who's speaking or acting. The puppets can tilt, advance, retreat, fall, pivot, dance, fight, rise, hover, come down from the sky, fly up like a bird. For an otherwordly effect the puppets are moved toward or away from the screen, the shadows themselves becoming sharp black outlines or blurry grays, always fading and wavering. Small boys love to sit in back on the *dalang's* side of the screen to watch his deft hands and to better appreciate the designs and colors of the puppets.

Lakon

Predominantly 2 types of repertoires. *Wayang Gedok* features heroes who date from the late Java-Hindu era and stories that revolve around the E. Javanese legends of Prince Panji. This form is most popular in E. Java, rarely seen in C. Java. *Wayang Purwa* draws its themes from episodes and heroes of Indonesia's prehistory and the Hindu *Mahabharata* and *Ramayana* epic poems. These mythological tales are the most frequently seen and best known shadow plays. All the themes share the same plots and the same typology of heroes runs through them all. The setting is always Java. The traditional 10-hour performance is divided into 3 principal parts. In each of these periods a different *gamelan* musical pitch heightens the mood. The leading character seldom appears before midnight, usually a little after. Only then can the audience be sure which story is being staged.

The first time period, from about 0800-1200, is said to stand for the youthful period of human life, from infancy to adolescence. The *dalang* takes this opportunity to instruct on refinement of manners and give ethical advice. At midnight there's always a great climax *(gara-gara)*, a clash between good and evil forces. After this, the second period opens and lasts until around 0300. In this period the clowns play a large part, giving relief as the heavy plot unfolds. This phase symbolizes the young adult's struggle in society. Finally, the *gamelan* switches the mood (third phase) to a lighter-pitched music as the hero slays his enemies, good triumphs over evil, and peace is regained. There's a joyous victory dance *(tajungan)* by Bima or his father Blaju (God of the Wind). Then the sun comes up both on and off stage, in *both* worlds. This last period represents the wisdom and maturity of old age.

WAYANG GOLEK

Puppets-in-the-round. Since *wayang golek* is the imitation by human actors of the movements of the shadow puppets, the 3-dimensional *wayang golek* puppets imitate human beings imitating the shadow puppets. These puppets are much more like our Western ones except that rods are used to manipulate them, not strings. No shadow or screen is used. The audience faces the *dalang* and watches realistic people in miniature. Different *gamelan* musical pitches set the mood. This *wayang* form is most often performed in the daytime. Traditional *wayang golek* has a less ceremonial, less magical, more worldly atmosphere than the shadow puppets.

To see one of the top new *dalang* in action, with incredible use of characterization and ventriloquism, attend a show at Lingkung Seni Wayang Golek in the village of Giri Harja III, Asep Sunandar Sunarya, Keluarga Jelekong, Ciparay, Bandung District. Here, the *dalang* is really jazzed, keeping his audience in a constant uproar. Pyrotechnic techniques are even used to compete with the movies: heads pop up from bodies, real blood spills, characters smoke cigarettes, and there's real smoke and fire! Modern, highly topical themes and social issues are played out, with actual exchanges taking place between the *golek* puppets and the audience. By contrast, tourist performances of *wayang golek* in Yogya tend to be dispirited, poorly produced, the puppets almost paralytic.

History

The existence in Indonesia of a set of 13th C. Chinese doll puppets suggests that the original source of *wayang golek* was China over 2,000 years ago. The idea for this most recent form of *wayang* might have been borrowed from the round puppets of the Chinese communities on Java's northern coastal ports where, in the 15th C., mention is first made of wooden doll puppets. It's known that in the great mercantile centers on the N coast of Java such as Banten, Cirebon, Demak, and Gresik (near modern Surabaya) lived a mixed population of Arab and Chinese traders as well as urbanized Javanese. In these areas, *wayang golek* first took hold among the common people, gradually evolving a wide repertoire of plays to suit the varied cultural and ethnic tastes of its audience. Later, *wayang golek* was used extensively by Moslem propagandists who subtly modified the Hindu elements to reflect the encroaching Islamic faith. The origin of the modern form dates from the 16th C., invented by an important historical figure, Sunan Kalidjaga. This brigand-turned-Moslem-saint used the puppet play to make converts and was rewarded by becoming himself one of the *wayang golek* characters!

Puppet-making

No room for innovation exists in the sculpting of a modern *golek* puppet; the artisans are strict copyists. Puppets consist of a trunk and head plus arms that rotate at the shoulder and elbow joints, moved from beneath by means of thin rods attached to the palms. Puppets are batiked, enameled, and bejeweled and have surprisingly human features. Since a *dalang* must stand for so long with his arms upraised, the puppet is carved from strong but light *arbasia*-wood. The neck is elongated and the head swivels on a central bamboo pole hidden under the flowing *kain* or *sarung*, the real clothing of the figure. Puppets are dressed by the local seamstress, often the wife of the carver. Costumes include court dress of a European lord of the 18th C., or perhaps a dashing Arabian knight.

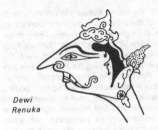

Dewi
Renuka

The shape and color of the head, face, and headdress follow the same conventions as the leather puppets, though *golek* are less stylized and more individualistic. *Golek* faces are like masks, meticulously painted, showing the full range of expressions: smiles, hideous mean-tempered scowls, foolish dumb stares, and haughty composures. See the puppets pant and shake with fright, their heads turning in all directions and their arms going a mile a minute. Prices for souvenir models vary enormously, depending on the quality. A 18-cm-high (7-inches) miniature might cost Rp6500-8500; one 45 cm tall (1 ½ feet), Rp8500-12,000. Solo's Pasar Triwindu on Jl. Diponegoro is a good place to shop for *golek* puppets.

Lakon
Wayang golek is something of a morality play, a social commentary, and magical myth-making—all in one. Stories have not always appeared in the polite guise of the mannered Indian epics; this *wayang* form's origins were proletarian rather than aristocratic. *Wayang golek* plays are tied in closely with the history of the penetration of Islam into Indonesia and were used in propaganda campaigns introducing the new religion. In C. Java, this form is based also on the adventures of Mohammed's uncle, the Arabian prince Amir Hamzah. Stories could also be about the chivalrous Prince Menak who prepares the world for Mohammed. All these Arabian folk tales were brought by the Moslem settlers, with plots and characters similar to those of Aladdin, Sinbad, and Harona-El-Rashid of *A Thousand and One Nights*. The *Panji* stories, which tell of the life of the mythical Prince Panji and other legendary Javanese kings, could also be portrayed in *wayang golek*. In W. Java the stories derive more from the *Mahabharata* and *Ramayana* legends (*purwa* repertory), and the *wayang golek* performed in this region is meant more as entertainment.

WAYANG TOPENG

Masked theater which mimes the stories of the *wayang golek*, employing dancing by men acting like puppets. Dance masks are an important part of the Indonesian culture, known all over Java and Bali. Sometimes the dancers themselves speak their roles, other times the *dalang* speaks for them with the actors just marching on and off stage. Although classical Javanese language (*Kawi*) is most often used, it's spoken in a less stylized form than in *wayang orang*. Troupes on Java consist of male dancers; female roles are taken by boys from ages 8-14, before their voices change.

Masks are often similar to the heads of *golek* puppets. Older masks from both Java and Bali had pronounced sculptural qualities; the actor did not speak since masks were held in position by the actor biting a leather strap or wooden prong. Carved out of light wood, today the masks are flatter, features tend to be painted rather than carved, and a strap around the head is used, freeing the mouth for speech. The eyes are mere slits which require the dancer to throw back his head in order to see—giving his movements a birdlike quality. On stage the shiny beautiful masks with big mysterious eyes seem suspended in the air. An entire *wayang topeng* troupe consists of perhaps 20-25 people, and a set of *topeng* contains traditionally 40-80 pieces. Some masks are rare and prized, guarded as *pusaka*, and found only in collections of princes and in museums. The acclaimed *Reni* masks on display at the Sonobudoyo Museum in Yogya attain this classic standard.

Each region of Java features a different style of *topeng* masks, costuming, and dancing. The most active *topeng* centers are in E. Java and on Bali. The Cirebon-style dance masks are more reserved. Javanese masks have tapered faces, sharp noses, and small mouths, while Balinese masks have full oval faces, broad noses, and heavy lips. The Javanese have a few standard comic masks, whereas Balinese comic masks are limited only by the carver's imagination. Many of the Balinese masks are elaborately decorated, with real hair or hair-like fibers, bright colors, bulging eyes, and hinged jaws. In all *topeng* forms, face, hair, and headdresses are painted in a color appropriate to the character. Faces are generally round, the shape and size and shape of the nose depending upon the stature of the personage. White masks are usually reserved for the king and his queen, features calm and elongated, with half-open lips showing the front teeth. A red *topeng* often depicts a powerful rival, with a fuller face and larger features.

History
This theater form probably stems from the ancient Javanese practice of masked dancers performing at primitive death rites. The *wayang kulit* repertoire naturally influenced *wayang topeng*. When Islam finally became entrenched on Java in the 16th C., masked dances were banned from ritual life but persisted in folk plays put on by wandering masked players in the villages. For 3 centuries *wayang golek* flourished in the towns of northern Java; it was Islamic and popular, a robust parody of the formal

splendor of the *wayang kulit* as performed in the inland *kraton*. Even today, *wayang topeng* persists more as a popular theater form than as a court tradition.

Lakon

Though stylistically influenced by Hinduism, the plays depict the intrigues of the royal courts of Java and Bali. The plots are derived mainly from the *Panji* cycle, centering on the legendary prince of Jenggala. Try to see the *Topeng Tua*, which portrays the wistful, meditative movements and attitudes of an old man usually involving 3-4 actors and up to 40 fascinating masks.

WAYANG ORANG

Called *wayang wong* in Javanese, these are abstract, symbolic dance plays, with or without masks, employing actor-dancers who dress up like *golek* puppets. Masks are usually only worn by actors playing animals: monkeys, birds, or monster roles (for example, the King of Demons in the *Ramayana*). A *dalang* may recite and chant, but the dialogue is most often spoken by live actors and actresses wearing shiny costumes of gold and black, and rich deep-colored *batik* silks. Because of its hilarious antics, *wayang orang* is more intelligible and more of a spectacle to Westerners than other *wayang* forms. But *wayang orang* is also by far the most expensive to stage. A boxful of leather or wooden puppets is much cheaper to maintain than a whole troupe of live actors who have to be fed, clothed, transported, and paid. Consequently, *wayang orang* is also the rarest—a real treat to see if you ever get the chance.

History

Wayang orang has an ancient pre-Islamic source as perhaps a cremation celebration, male initiation rite, war dance, or chant recital, with the *dalang* acting as a kind of priest. The modern form first flowered in the 18th and 19th centuries, and was put on solely for the aristocracy. The form reached its peak in the years 1900-1940 when huge performances were presented in the royal courts of C. Java. Presided over by the sultan, Javanese and Dutch dignitaries and splendidly dressed court ladies and gentlemen would sit in long rows attending an opulent feast and glittering dance drama lasting up to 3 days. Now only the 4-day dance festivals at Prambanan in C. Java and at Pandaan in E. Java each year from June to Oct. can compare with those magnificent bygone extravaganzas.

Dancers

Wayang orang's highly controlled and stylized dance style so closely imitates the gestures and movements of the leather cut-out marionettes that the dancer, especially the male, seems to move on a 2-dimensional plane; feet, knees, and thighs are separated at extreme angles so that his body appears flat. Thus the term *wayang orang*, or "human puppets." Many other parallels exist between *wayang orang* and *wayang kulit*. The actors' waiting room is called a *kotak*, the same as the chest in which the *dalang* of *wayang kulit* keeps his puppets. The shape of the stage is similarly long and narrow. The dancers usually show only their profiles to the audience, just as the *wayang kulit* puppets do. The postures, costumes, and make-up of the actors are also very similar. *Wayang orang* actors are so exquisitely and elaborately costumed and made up that their faces look as if they have a coat of enamel over them. Dressing for the *Tari Gatutkaca*, a dance portraying manhood, can take as long as 2 hours. Observe the lavish jewelry and tall headdresses, the same shapes as those worn by the *wayang kulit* shadow puppets.

During the performance, almost complete impassivity of facial expression is required. Limited strictly to 3 levels, each level expresses different states of the soul. Likewise, strong emotion and moods are expressed within a particular mode of dance; you don't see inner conflicts. Dancers have to learn a painstakingly meticulous iconography. Each mode of dancing is adjusted to the physique of an individual dancer and characters can be picked out by just the way they walk. A small man will play the part of a smooth, flowing, slow-moving, and soft-speaking dancer, the *alus* style, whereas a big, round-faced man is chosen for a hostile, crude, and booming-voiced part, the brusque *kasar* style. In the battles, all combatants fight in strictly their own styles. An actor always remains "in character," with even the movements of monsters strictly choreographed.

The crux of the male style is the snappiness and angularity in which all movements are carried out, the hands forming the Hindu *mudras*. Female dancers play subtle, graceful parts, always dancing with legs held close together, the steps small and tight-fitting, with knees slightly bent. Fingers are at times extended by fingernails to accentuate their dramatic impact. Arms and shoulders are covered with a fine yellow powder. Dance scarves *(sampur)* are used to express sadness or to symbolically topple an enemy. Love scenes are enacted powerfully without players even touching each other; all the tension and passion is put across sheerly through stances and eye contact.

The Javanese *wayang orang* comic servants *(panakawan)*—Semar, Petruk, Gareng, and Bagong—are not found in the more faithful and sedate Indian original of the *Mahabharata* by Valmiki; they are a pure Javanese animist creation. The Hindu god Shiva is often played by a woman, diligently taught from age five. Taunted by bearded devils and other demonic creatures, she glides, dances, fights, makes speeches, cries, sings—and always wins in the end.

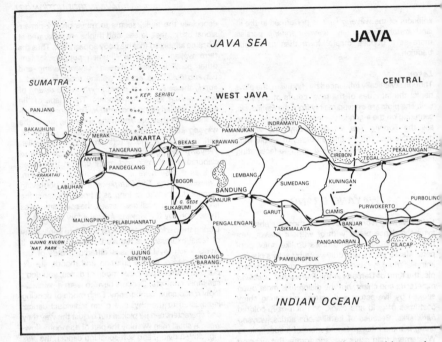

JAVA

JAVA SEA

SUMATRA

CENTRAL

KEP. SERIBU

WEST JAVA

PANJANG

BAKAUHUNI

PAMANUKAN

INDRAMAYU

MERAK

JAKARTA

BEKASI

KRAWANG

CIREBON

TEGAL

PEKALONGAN

TANGERANG

ANYER

PANDEGLANG

BOGOR

LEMBANG

SUMEDANG

KUNINGAN

PURBOLINO

KRAKATAU

LABUHAN

G. GEDE

SUKABUMI

CIANJUR

BANDUNG

PURWOKERTO

MALINGPING

PELABUHANRATU

GARUT

CIAMIS

BANJAR

PENGALENGAN

TASIKMALAYA

PANGANDARAN

CILACAP

UJUNG KULON
NAT. PARK

UJUNG
GENTING

SINDANG
BARANG

PAMEUNGPEUK

INDIAN OCEAN

Lakon

Plots are taken mostly from the same sources as in *wayang kulit. Wayang orang* combines the glamorous mythology of the Hindu epics with classical Javanese dance, both interwoven with many tribal myths. As in a good Shakespearean play there's a little something for everyone—clowns, demons, magic, juggling, tricks, bawdy jokes—a mixture of circus vaudeville and the grace of ballet. The dialogues are spoken in High Javanese, intoned with melodic, almost ecclesiastical monotony except for the extremely stylized high-pitched cackle of mockery or a sudden roar of anger. Fifty different scenes are sometimes played out and *wayang orang* can last from 6 hours to 3 days. Nowadays you could see a girl putting on makeup, a boy flying a kite, a woman weaving, a couple arguing, an infatuated hero falling into a state of hallucination—anything could happen in *wayang orang!*

TRANSPORT

No problem getting around. Java's conveyances are often packed to overflowing, but the traveler can choose from a wide variety. Since people live everywhere on the island, there's transportation to everywhere—you move along on one contraption after another through the day and night. There are city buses, local buses, night (express) buses, plus minibuses, *oplet, bemo,* trains, taxis, and rental cars. Each district has its own type of cart, wagon, gig, carriage, bus, *oplet,* and pedicab, with distinctive harnesses, markings, colors. Bicycles are for rent in Yogya and Solo for around Rp1000 per day, horses can be hired in many of the hill stations for Rp2000-3000 per hour, and horsedrawn carts such as *dokar, andong* and *delman* can be hired in the rural towns. Hitchhiking is fair to good on Java, though some vehicles (including motorcycles and private cars) will stop, thinking you're flagging them down as a paying passenger. Another confusing aspect of travel on Java is place name duplication: there are several towns by the name "Karanganyar" and "Kadupandak," and innumerable "Cipanas."

Java has ¾ of all the tarred roads in Indonesia, even roads which climb up to the craters of volcanos (Bromo and Tangkuban Prahu). Most are ludicrously inadequate, overloaded, and congested. An asphalted 2-lane (4 lanes around the big cities) highway extends for over 1,534 km between Jakarta and Denpasar, Bali, and a super-highway runs between Jakarta and Bogor and Jakarta and Merak in W. Java. Ring roads girdle the giant port of Surabaya, E. Java. New toll roads *(jalan tol)* are being built all the time, usually linking a large city (like Surabaya and Semarang) with its airport.

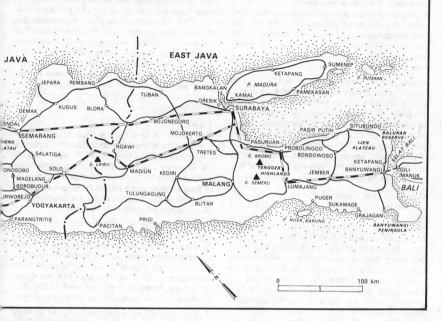

JAVA　　　　　　　　EAST JAVA

Local Buses

Bus and taxi stations are often referred to by their old Dutch name: *stanplatz*. Between cities, buses are generally faster and more punctual than trains, and for out-of-the-way places local buses are more convenient as they reach places trains don't. Most of the time you can just stand to the side of the road and flag a bus down heading in your direction (except in the big cities). Sitting on narrow wooden seats built for Asian physiques, daytime travel on these big lumbering local buses is slow and hot, but cheap. Buses are also slightly safer than taking minibuses.

Ask the attendants at the bus station's information office about which buses go where and when—they are most helpful and they will even store your gear. If you don't have a ticket and want to be assured a seat (necessary if you're over 5½ feet tall), always board your bus at the station. If the bus to your destination is leaving just as you arrive at the station and it's too full for your liking, take the one behind loading up—it's half-full but will probably depart within 15 minutes.

On some bus journeys (unless it's a long-distance *ekspres* bus), one sometimes has to change buses. This happens when there aren't enough passengers to pay for the gas and oil, let alone the salaries for the driver and attendants. Often the driver or ticket-seller won't tell you (because they often don't know themselves) that 2 hours down the road you'll be put on a different bus (sometimes 20 years older).

In Java's main cities city buses *(bis kota)* run extensively, stopping only at designated bus stops and charging a flat rate of only Rp100-200 to all corners of the city, but *bis kota* are very crowded and their routes are confusing for the first-time visitor. In Jakarta, gangs of youths work the city buses pickpocketing and robbing tourists, so it's recommended that you use more expensive private bus companies (Patas buses), taxis or *bajai* (motorized 3-wheelers for 2 people).

Long-distance Buses

Ekspres or *bis malam* (night bus) travel non-stop on all the major roads linking all the big cities and towns of Java. It costs only Rp15,000 to traverse the entire 1,000-km-long island by bus (allow at least 3 days) More expensive than local buses, you get a reserved seat and meals; snacks and drinks are often included in the fare. *Bis malam* usually depart in the late afternoon or early evening, traveling faster, cooler, and more comfortably on less congested roads, but you sacrifice sightseeing for speed. As drivers drive like madmen, long-distance bus travel can be nerve wracking and exhausting. While waiting for your bus to depart, often you may leave your gear safely at the bus terminal office.

Minibuses, *Helicak, Bemo, Oplet*

Minibuses travel the short distances between cities, towns, and villages at frequent intervals; they are more comfortable and expensive than local buses. Just like a private taxi, they often drop you off right at your door. Minibuses travel Java's mountainous areas where the big buses can't.

Rugged *bemo* (a canopied pickup truck with bench seats down each side) and *oplet* (small truck or bus) also travel Java's country backroads at very reasonable fares; these roads represent the most extensive transport network on the island. They seldom depart before they have a full complement of paying passengers, so you often get a free ride all over town for 20 min. looking for passengers. Local transport vehicles such as these usually stop running in the early evening, so plan for this.

Helicak and *bajai* are motorbikes with enclosed cars to the side or behind. These are the cheapest and quickest transport around Java's cities—as little as Rp300-500 per km. Hundreds of bicycle rickshaws *(becak)* are found in all fair-sized to large towns on the island. *Becak* cost around Rp400 per km, but in the rural towns they are even cheaper. During the day, *becak* are frequently banned from the downtown areas of Java's big cities. On all vehicles like the above, which you hire on a one-time basis, always always agree on the fare to a specific destination before climbing in.

Taxis/Rental Cars

Metered taxis are available only in Jakarta. Taxi stands are usually found in some downtown locations, around hotels and markets, at the airport, and around train and bus terminals. Except for Jakarta, which has a superb luxury bus service from the new Sukarno/Hatta Airport to points downtown (for only Rp2000!), usually a fixed fare is in force, varying from as low as Rp3500 in Solo up to Rp9000 in Surabaya. Taxis may be rented for around Rp4500 per hour (count on Rp1000 more per hour if a/c), always with a minimum of 2 hours; in Jakarta, Blue Bird is the best taxi company. Share-taxis or intercity taxi companies such as Media, Parahiyangan, and "4848," offer services between all large cities such as Jakarta and Bandung; you meet at their office and they'll drop you off right at your destination. See "Jakarta" for addresses.

Rental car companies such as Avis, Hertz, and National are based in all the main cities (addresses under city coverages), but cost US$70-90 per day. Cheaper than rental cars are minibuses and *bemo* which run around Rp25,000-30,000 per day to "charter." Unlike Bali, it's customary on Java for a driver to be included in the cost of the rented vehicle, and you are expected to pay for the driver's food and lodging en route (perhaps Rp8000-10,000 daily), plus a full tank of gas so that he can return to his point of origin. Private cars

rent for around Rp25,000 per day (with driver), the price depending upon the year, make, size, and condition of the car; whether it has a/c or not; and upon the linguistic abilities of the driver. The local tourist office can always make arrangements, or perhaps your hotel proprietor can help you find a good deal. Gasoline here is Rp350 per liter at Pertamina gas stations *(pompa benzin),* found at intervals on highways all over Java. Gas dispensed from roadside drums is more expensive (perhaps Rp450-500) and probably watered down to boot.

Trains

Two parallel rail lines run the whole length of Java: one along the N coast, the other through the island's center via Bogor and Yogya. In the W, the line ends at Merak where you catch the ferry across the Selat Sunda to Sumatra, and in the E it ends at Ketapang (N of Banyuwangi), where you catch the ferry across the Bali Strait to Bali. No point on the island is more than 80 km from a RR station.

While bus stations are often located 2-6 km out of town, train stations *(stasiun kereta api)* are often right downtown. Reasonable accommodations, and good transport connections, are frequently found near the station. In really large cities like Jakarta, which has 5 train stations, some stations are more convenient than others. Always try to find out which station you'll be departing from and which one you'll be arriving at.

Trains, especially for the longer hauls, can be more comfortable than tiresome and hot day buses. Every class of train is represented. Java's luxury-class a/c trains, such as the *Bima* and the *Mutiara Utara,* have sleepers and dining cars, and are reasonably fast, while the cheaper trains are slow and crowded, with wooden seats and holes-in-the-floor for toilets. The inexpensive *Senya* (dusk) trains lumber out of Surabaya and Jakarta around 1800 and reach the middle of Java (Yogya) the next day around 0800 or 1000; they then leave at dusk for Jakarta and Surabaya. The *Senya Utama* express between Jakarta and Yogya-Solo in C. Java offers reclining seats in non a/c but fan-cooled coaches. Another useful express service is the *Parahyangan,* which links Jakarta and Bandung and vice versa in just 3 hours. Some lines, such as the one from Yogya-Bandung and Bandung-Jakarta, are incredibly beautiful. Others, such as the electric-line from Jakarta to Bogor, is crammed with commuters during the early morning and late afternoon peak hours. For all the main train routes through Java, refer to the transport sections of Jakarta and Surabaya.

Fares for the exact same journey, on the same class, might differ widely from train to train; fares (and schedules) are posted in most stations. To get a good seat and avoid waiting in line, buy your ticket early on the day of departure. Except for the deluxe *Bima* or *Mutiara* trains, you're usually not allowed to buy your ticket the day or night before. For these 3rd Class

SAMPLE TRANSPORT FARES ON JAVA

(US$ = Rp1635)

BY TRAIN

From	To	Train	Depart	Arrive	Class
Jakarta	Bandung	Parahyangan II	0515/Kota	0830	Rp4500 2nd
Jakarta	Cirebon	GBM Utaru II	1730/Senen	2126	Rp3400 3rd
Jakarta	Merak	Cepat	1630/Kota	1425	Rp1100 3rd
Jakarta	Yogya	Bima II	1600/Kota	1130	Rp18,700 2nd
Jakarta	Surabaya	Mutiara Utara	1630/Kota	0650	Rp22,000 1st
Bandung	Jakarta	Parahyangan III	0610	0935	Rp4500 2nd
Bandung	Surabaya	Express Siang	0510	2205	Rp5400 3rd
Semarang	Jakarta	Seja Semarang	2000	0445	Rp5000 3rd
Surabaya	Banyuwangi	Mutiara Timur	1000	1730	Rp2400 3rd
Surabaya	Malang	Cepat	1700	1955	Rp1100 3rd

BY BUS

From	To	Distance (km)	Standard	A/c and reclining seats
Jakarta	Bandung	187	Rp2000	Rp3000
Jakarta	Cirebon	259	Rp2250	Rp3200
Jakarta	Pangandaran	427	Rp3700	Rp5200
Jakarta	Solo	602	Rp5200	Rp7400
Jakarta	Surabaya	878	Rp7550	Rp10,800
Bandung	Bogor	157	Rp1350	Rp1500
Yogya	Cilicap	210	Rp1800	Rp2600
Yogya	Banyuwangi	631	Rp5450	Rp7750
Surabaya	Semarang	379	Rp3250	Rp4650
Surabaya	Kudus	364	Rp3150	Rp4500

BY AIR

From	To	Airline	Flights per week	Fare
Jakarta	Cilicap	Merpati	daily (1000)	Rp46,100
Jakarta	Cirebon	Merpati	twice daily	Rp28,800
Jakarta	Semarang	Merpati	daily (1530)	Rp39,600
Yogya	Surabaya	Merpati	daily (0700)	Rp25,500
Bandung	Yogya	Merpati	3 times weekly	Rp40,000
Cilicap	Jakarta	Merpati	twice daily	Rp28,800
Malang	Jakarta	Merpati	daily (1500)	Rp65,000
Semarang	Bandung	Merpati	daily (1315)	Rp41,400
Surabaya	Jakarta	Merpati	daily (1430)	Rp63,500
Surabaya	Bandung	Bouraq	daily (1300)	Rp58,700
Yogya	Bandung	Bouraq	daily (1420)	Rp43,400
Jakarta	Surabaya	Bouraq	daily (1500)	Rp73,000

trains, just show up an hour before departure and try to grab the best seat possible. On the deluxe trains, certain travel agencies (such as Carnation Tours & Travel, Jl. Menteng Raya 24, tel. 344027 in Jakarta) specialize in booking train tickets up to 3 days before departure, but charge Rp1000 or so for the service. Incidentally, student discounts of 10 to 25% are easy to get but tend to be granted only on the cheap trains.

Train schedules are unreliable and change frequently. For *all* classes of trains, expect both arrivals and departures to be late. Timetables are helpful in planning your journey; ask for the free pamphlet *Jadwal Perjalanan* at the tourist offices or stationmaster's office at the train station. It lists major and local train service all over Java, as well as connecting ferries to Bali and Sumatra. If you can't read the timetable or if you're having any trouble making yourself understood, the *kepala stasiun* (stationmaster) can usually help.

Fly

To save time, you might decide to fly the island's air network at prices as much as 10 times more than the bus. Jakarta, Yogya, Semarang, and Surabaya have many scheduled daily flights, plus small aircraft and helicoptors fly to Pelabuhan Ratu (S coast of W. Java) and to Pulau Seribu N of Jakarta. Shuttle services, linking the big cities, depart up to 12 times daily; no advance booking and tickets must be bought with cash at the window. Some segments might be heavily booked, so always try to reserve your seat in advance at the airline office, or with a travel agent who usually charges a Rp1000-1500 fee. Sample (Garuda) fares: Jakarta-Surabaya, Rp86,000; Jakarta-Yogya, Rp65,000 (30 min.); Surabaya-Solo, Rp35,000;

Surabaya-Semarang, Rp40,000. Merpati and Bouraq fares are about 10% cheaper. Be prepared to pass over some lofty volcanos.

Boats And Ships

On Java you can't get more than 160 km from the sea. Catch seagoing motorized craft *(kapal motor)* and ships *(kapal laut)* to the Outer Islands from dozens of N coast ports. The national inter-island shipping company, Pelni, has modern passenger ships leaving Jakarta and Surabaya for all the Outer Islands at the phenomenal cost of only Rp28,000 per day 1st Class. The MV *Rinjani,* for example, leaves Jakarta's port of Tanjung Priok on Wed. at 0800 and arrives in Ambon (Maluku) on Sun. at 1300. Most northern ports also have sailing vessels *(prahu layar),* which you may board after striking a deal with the captain and obtaining permission from the harbormaster *(syahbandar).* To enter the harbor area, first ask the chief of the harbor police who will just wave you through the gate or issue you a temporary permit. Photography is forbidden because all of Indonesia's harbors are naval security areas.

Regular interisland ferries leave from: Merak, W. Java, to Bakauhuni, S. Sumatra; Ketapang, E. Java, to Gilimanuk, W. Bali; Surabaya, E. Java, to Kamal, Madura; Panarukan, E. Java, to Kalianget, Madura. There is also an excellent and exciting short ferry service on the S coast from Cilicap, C. Java, to Kalipucang, W. Java. If traveling between Yogya and the seaside resort of Pangandaran in W. Java, this segment is far superior to the bus. Daily shuttles also depart from Jakarta to the resort island of P. Bidadari in Pulau Seribu in the Bay of Jakarta.

Chicken Market Bridge

JAKARTA

INTRODUCTION

Also known as the *Ibu Kota,* the "Mother City," this teeming metropolis of 8 million is Indonesia's capital, the brain and nerve center of the country. The world's ideas, technology, and fashions first touch Indonesia here. It's the literary center and headquarters for the mass media; all of Indonesia's newspapers are printed here. The city has a film industry, modern theater academy, prestigious university, and the oldest medical school and the oldest clubhouse in SE Asia. Jakarta is where all the big contracts are signed, the strings pulled, the rake-offs happen. Eighty percent of all foreign investments come through here, and most of the money stays here. The chief drama of this city is its contrasts, a fascinating collision of East and West where air-conditioned diesels hurtle by the peddler and sleek office towers throw shadows across cardboard hovels. It has Indonesia's most expensive buildings and its murkiest slums—great rivers of steel, glass, and granite winding through endless expanses of one-story *kampung.* Here live the most and least educated people of Indonesia. Jakarta is Indonesia's most dynamic, problem-ridden city.

Attractions

Since its founding in 1619, Jakarta has had a reputation for being run-down and hectic, a city of stinking canals, shantytowns, blaring horns, traffic-tangled, grimy streets—Asia's most overcrowded, underplanned and least-visited capital. However, the Indonesianist cannot afford to bypass this giant nerve center, especially those with an interest in culture and history. Jakarta's National Museum has one of the finest collections of Orientalia in the world, and virtually *all* government departments have their head offices here. Travelers' expenses will be 2 to 3 times more here than anywhere else in Indonesia. A thin slice of pineapple could put you back Rp200, a second-rate Western movie Rp2500, while cheap hotel rooms are in the Rp6000-10,000 range. Another hard reality are the audacious pickpockets on Jakarta's bus routes, with regularly occurring tales of gangs of 5 or 6 youths relieving travelers of all their possessions at knifepoint (to avoid this, take only taxis or the streamlined Patas buses). Serious street crime has been cut drastically by vigilante groups who, starting in 1985, have executed criminals with the tacit sanction of the authorities. Political violence (even during the 1987 general elections) is almost non-existent.

Climate

Hot. This flat coast of Java can be suffocatingly humid (as high as 95%!) with few breezes. The temperature drops dramatically within 20 min. on the drive from Jakarta to Bogor and into the hills toward Bandung. Everyone tries to escape to these climes on the weekends and traffic could be backed up 2 hours. Nov. to May can be drenching wet. Because of the city's outdated sewer and drainage system, two-thirds of Jakarta is flooded then. All government offices close down, traffic snarls, vehicles stall, gas is scarce, and thousands of people are in need of shelter.

HISTORY

Jakarta has the longest continuous history of any modern Indonesian city (Hindu inscriptions dating from A.D. 5 have been found near Tanjung Priok). For centuries merchants met near the mouth of the Ciliwung River (now the Kali Besar area), a site destined to be conquered later by empire-mad Dutch, opportunistic English, and Japanese expansionists. When the Portuguese made the first European contact with a Javanese kingdom in 1522, Jakarta was called Sundakelapa. The Hindu raja's control of Sundakelapa was broken by Islamic troops on 22 June 1527, a date still celebrated as the city's birthday. The conquering Muslim prince, Fatahillah, then renamed this small Javanese settlement Jayakarta—"City of Victory."

The Dutch Era

In the early 1600s, Dutch traders established a fortified trading post in Jayakarta. In 1619, they overcame the Bantenese rulers and burned the village to the ground. The Dutch then built a small garrison which withstood 2 assaults (1628 and 1629) by a mighty army of 80,000. Repelling subsequent attacks, the Dutch became more and more entrenched. Renaming the site Batavia for a medieval Germanic tribe that once occupied the lowlands of Holland and Belgium, they built a completely new city of intersecting canals, small houses with tiny windows and red-tiled roofs—a Little Holland in the tropics. Batavia (pop. 32,000 in 1619) soon became the trade center for the Dutch East India Co., from where Dutch governors sent voyagers out to open new trading routes. Batavia became known as the "Pearl of the Orient," with massive agricultural wealth flowing through its port, which Captain Cook called "the best marine yard in the world." These same European ships also carried malaria to the once healthy seaport, turning it into one of the worst pestholes of the world. Known for 100 years as "the Graveyard of Dutchmen," its silted-up canals became ideal breeding grounds for diseases. (From 1735-1780, more Europeans died in Jakarta than lived there as permanent residents.) By the mid-18th C., many families had moved to the new suburb of Weltevreden (meaning "Well-contented") in the healthier southern reaches of the city. Batavia's outskirts were dotted with spacious country estates occupied by the Dutch elite. From 1811-1816 Jakarta was the base for Sir Stamford Raffles, Java's English administrator when the British occupied the Indies during the Napoleonic Wars. Many of Jakarta's modern (post-1700s) relics and architecture have survived. Thus in Jakarta, more than anywhere else in Indonesia, you can see and feel the effect of the Dutch, Portuguese, and English presence.

The Twentieth Century

With the proclamation of Indonesian independence in 1945, the name Jakarta—an abbreviation of its native name Jayakarta—was readopted. Most historical buildings remained standing at the end of WW II, though many had been looted by the Japanese military. During the Sukarno era, Jakarta was a collection of villages barely held together by the slogans of bombastic nationalism, but in the subsequent Suharto years the main avenues were widened and buildings shot up in all directions. Still not a particularly pretty city, it's improving. The better-known sections of Jakarta are relatively new. Menteng is largely the product of the early 20th century; Kebayoran Baru was laid out by the Dutch after WW II. In 1966, Jakarta was officially named the "Special Capital District." Over the last 15 years, the government has begun to revitalize Jakarta's rich collection of historical attractions: colonial fortifications, country estates, graveyards, mosques, and Chinese temples. The old Dutch section of Kota has undergone restoration along with a number of Jakarta's classical architecture and monuments, reopened as museums and memorial halls. In addition, the establishment of greenbelts, parks, offshore resorts, and an ultra-modern international airport has begun to draw tourist revenue away from more popular Asian destinations such as Bangkok and Hong Kong. For a more thorough discussion of Jakarta's historical remains, read *Historical Sites of Jakarta* by A. Heuken (Yayasan Cipta Loka Caraka, 1982).

THE PEOPLE

From the beginning, the Dutch were highly suspicious of the local people. These new rulers carefully limited the number of Sundanese and Javanese permitted to live in their city. For labor they imported many slaves, chiefly from their Burmese possession (then called Arakan); later they brought in thousands of Balinese, mostly female slaves. To serve as a merchant class, a great many Chinese were also imported. Frequently mistreated and forced to live outside the city walls, the Chinese nevertheless were important to the Dutch and to the development and prosperity of the local economy because of their skills as middlemen, craftsmen, and cultivators. All immigrants as well as natives were set apart by ethnic groupings into *kampung*, an arrangement still very much in evidence. Jakarta is to this day a city of a thousand villages, each with its own shops, schools, police, and customs. The city epitomizes the Indonesian national motto, "Unity in Diversity"; it has been a melting pot for Javanese, Chinese, Balinese, Batak, Minangkabaus, Maluku Islanders, Europeans. The population is so mixed that it comprises a separate race of people (the Dutch called them "Batavians"). Jakartans even speak their own vivid dialect, Jakartanese. Despite a 1971 edict declaring Jakarta a "closed city," over 200,000 migrants enter Jakarta each year from Java's economically depressed countryside and Indonesia's outlying islands.

Four-fifths of these newcomers make their living as laborers, *becak* drivers, one-man manufacturers, hawkers, servants, *warung* cooks, etc.—all contributing to the substratum world of its bazaar economy. One-fourth of Jakarta's people are squatters, sticking close to shopping centers for income or close to the rivers and ditches for washing. Thousands who sleep in the streets are known as *orang gelandangan*, "people on the move." Beware of *Buaya Kemayoran* ("Kemayoran Crocodiles"), the riffraff operating in the Kemayoran district.

SIGHTS

Jakarta's Neighborhoods

Jakarta lies on a N-S axis. The ubiquitous Indonesian army occupies all the prime real estate—veritable palaces! Fronting the city's main drag, Jl. Thamrin, are many of its largest office buildings, major hotels, theaters, banks, etc. At Jl. Thamrin's southern end is the new suburb of Kebayoran Baru; at the northern end is Lapangan Merdeka (Freedom Square) with the towering National Monument. To the N are Kota and Sundakelapa, sites of the city's Dutch beginnings and oldest remains. Posh Menteng, Gondangdia, and Cikini (where the diplomats now live) were the most exclusive Dutch residential areas; you still see villas with white stucco walls, tiled roofs and floors, and shaded porches. See also the millionaires' row of Kemang, and along Jl. Iman Bonjol and Jl. Diponegoro. Tanjung Priok, Jakarta's port, is constantly being modernized; it handles 70% of Indonesia's imports and a high percentage of exports. Tour the city on Sundays, when Jakarta's streets have 30-40% less traffic.

KOTA (OLD BATAVIA)

With its Old World atmosphere, this is the oldest part of the city. Originally, this relatively small northern area was the waterfront swamp where the Dutch first settled—and remained for 330 years! Surrounded by a moat and thick wall, Old Batavia stretched from Pasar Ikan S to Jl. Jembatan Batu/Jl. Asmeka. In this neighborhood the Dutch stored their spices in warehouses along the harbor, and from majestic buildings surrounding a cobblestone-paved square they administered a vast mercantile empire. Old Batavia's heart was where the Jakarta City Museum is today. From Jl. Thamrin, take bus no. 70 (Rp200) or PATAS bus 16 (Rp350) to Terminal Bis Kota, also called Stanplatz.

Sightseeing

Most of the sights of Kota are within walking distance from Stanplatz. Easily visit all the museums (Museum Wayang, Museum Bahari, Jakarta City Museum, and Balai Seni Rupa) in one morning. Near Stanplatz on Jl. Nelayan Barat see the one remaining 17th C. drawbridge, which marked the SW corner of the old Dutch fort. From Museum Wayang on Jl. Pintu Besar cross the drawbridge over the Kali Besar to see the only 17th C. building left, the shop owned by P.T. Satya Niaga. Through the 18th C., ships could sail under the drawbridge, and continue up the Ciliwung River.

Glodok

Go wandering (in the daytime) around Glodok, the immediate area around Jl. Pintu Besar, Jakarta's Chinatown. The Dutch architecture in the nearby neighborhoods contrasts strikingly with the Chinese buildings. Glodok is now a banking, trade, and entertainment center. Hunt for temples along the narrow back streets, lined with Chinese food vendors and shops. Near the new 2-story shopping center only a few old Chinese houses remain; most were demolished to fill in mosquito-infested canals and to acquire building blocks for the "new town" farther south. Beside Museum Bahari are *bajai* which will take you back to Terminal Bis Kota for Rp300; get back into the city from here for another Rp100.

Gedung Syahbandar

Near Museum Bahari is a tower-like building which overlooks Pasar Ikan, a good point to begin your tour. Early in the 17th C., the Javanese erected a military post on this spot to control the mouth of the Ciliwung River and keep an eye on the Dutch who, in 1610, had been given permission to build some houses and a *go-down* (warehouse). Within months of signing the contract, the unruly Dutch violated it by changing the building material to stone. By 1618, through a series of similarly deceitful moves, the Dutch were firmly entrenched in Jayakarta, their cannons trained on their host's *kraton*. This watchtower, built in 1839 by the VOC, who by then were in nearly complete control of Java, is one of the few remains of Kastel Batavia, completed in 1652. Gedung Syahbandar or Menara Syahbandar (Harbormaster's Building) was once a light-

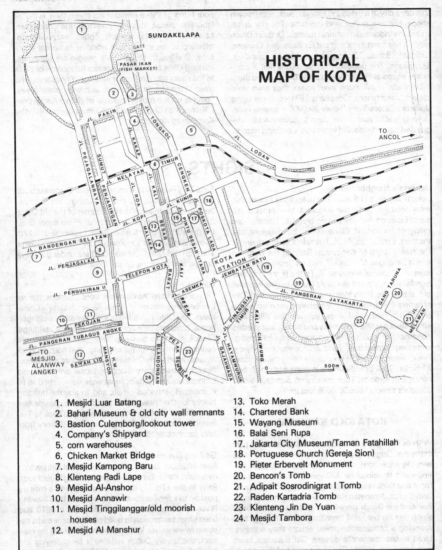

HISTORICAL MAP OF KOTA

SUNDAKELAPA

GATE

PASAR IKAN (FISH MARKET)

TO ANCOL →

JL. PAKIN
JL. TONGKOL
JL. NELAYAN
JL. KAKAP
JL. SUMUT PENJARINGAN
JL. PENGGAIANRAYA
JL. ROA
JL. KALI
JL. KOPI
JL. TIMUR CENGKEH
JL. KUNIR
JL. LODAN
JL. BANDENGAN SELATAN
JL. BESAR
JL. MALAKA
JL. PINTU BESAR UTARA
JL. POSKOTA LADA
JL. PENJAGALAN I
JL. TELEPON KOTA
JL. ASEMKA
KOTA STATION
JL. JEMBATAN BATU
JL. PENGUKIRAN II
JL. BESAR BARAT
JL. PINANGSIA TIMUR
JL. PANGERAN JAYAKARTA
KALI CILIWUNG
GANG TARUNA
JL. MELAWAN
JL. PEKOJAN
JL. PANGERAN TUBAGUS ANGKE
JL. H.M. MANSYOR
SAWAH LIO
JL. BLANDONGAN
JL. PETAK SEMBILAN
JL. HAYAMWURUK
JL. GAJAHMADA
← TO MESJID ALANWAY (ANGKE)
500 m

1. Mesjid Luar Batang
2. Bahari Museum & old city wall remnants
3. Bastion Culemborg/lookout tower
4. Company's Shipyard
5. corn warehouses
6. Chicken Market Bridge
7. Mesjid Kampong Baru
8. Klenteng Padi Lape
9. Mesjid Al-Anshor
10. Mesjid Annawir
11. Mesjid Tinggilanggar/old moorish houses
12. Mesjid Al Manshur
13. Toko Merah
14. Chartered Bank
15. Wayang Museum
16. Balai Seni Rupa
17. Jakarta City Museum/Taman Fatahillah
18. Portuguese Church (Gereja Sion)
19. Pieter Erbervelt Monument
20. Bencon's Tomb
21. Adipait Sosrodinigrat I Tomb
22. Raden Kartadria Tomb
23. Klenteng Jin De Yuan
24. Mesjid Tambora

house and meteorological station equipped with all the high-tech instruments of the day. Superb views from the roof. The Chinese inscriptions on the floor of the lookout are weight standards.

Museum Bahari

The Maritime or Naval Museum located near Sunda-

kelapa in lively Pasar Ikan (Jl. Pasar Ikan 1). Open Tues. to Thurs. 0900-1400, Fri. to 1100, Sat. to 1300, Sun. to 1500, closed Mon. (and any other time they feel like it). Museum Bahari consists of 2 restored Dutch East India Company warehouses (1652). Here the company stored its mountains of coffee, tea, pepper, cloth, spices, tin, and copper. One building now deals with spice trade memorabilia and the other with maritime history. In front of the museum is a wall and sentry box, last remnants of the wall which surrounded Old Batavia in the 17th and 18th centuries.

Company's Shipyard

Between Jl. Kakap and the Kali Besar canal was the VOC's wharf area used in the early 1700s for the repair of small ships. This unhealthy area once swarmed with ships' carpenters, smiths, coopers, rope- and chart-makers. The 2-story Company's Wharf (Timmerwerf der Compagnie) dates from the early 17th century. The fine balustrade facing the canal was added later. Because of abhorrent sanitary conditions, the government closed the shipyard in 1809 and rented it to Chinese shipwrights. Although in grave neglect today, these buildings are still very much in use.

Jalan Kali Besar Area

In the 18th C. this was a very swank residential neighborhood. Toko Merah is a venerable manor most likely constructed by van Imhoff, who later served as governor-general. Its name, meaning "Red Shop," derives from the building's unusual red brick exterior and its red-painted woodwork and furniture. Inside Toko Merah are fanlights, a fine wooden staircase, carved doors, inner courts and hallways, all in rich, dark mahogany. Toko Merah also has the distinction of having been the first Nautical Academy in the Orient, Academi de Marine (1743-1755). Later, widows of former governors-general de Klerk and Parra lived and died there. In the 1940s, Toko Merah was restored and taken over by the Bank voor Indie. South of Toko Merah is a building now occupied by the Chartered Bank; it was built in the 18th C. and restored in 1921. Visit the Kali Besar area to see the slums of Jakarta. Indonesians are ingenious with hiding their slums behind tall buildings, so tourists don't usually see them. But they are everywhere. Head due E of Taman Fatahillah, sticking to the canals and walking under bridges; here you'll see poverty as grinding and despairing as anywhere on earth.

Pasar Ikan

Wander around this area and absorb waterfront life, especially at dawn when the night's catch is auctioned off. Stinking fish lie in glistening heaps on slimy floors, or hang fly-covered to dry in the sun. Watch the fishmongers and customers haggle. Explore the multitude of small alleys, fish auction halls, fishermen's and sailors' *kampung,* stalls and shops selling stuffed exotic animals, seashells, and 19th C. fishing and nautical equipment. Pasar Ikan is a fascinating place — with few tourists and no hotels. The big commercial fish market is 3 km to the E at Muara Amke.

Sundakelapa

This 500-year-old harbor area is an easy walk from the Jakarta City Museum. Entrance Rp100; Rp500 for automobiles, Rp200 for motorcycles. The Ciliwung River — now a clogged and stinking canal — was a vital link to the markets of the outside world for the 15th C. kingdom of Pajajaran (near present-day Bogor). Since then this port has belonged to the Portuguese, Muslims, and Dutch. Though little remains of bustling old Sundakelapa except the name, the harbor is still one of the most important calls for sailing vessels from all over the archipelago — you could catch a ride to Palembang, Kalimantan, or S. Sulawesi. Local fishermen still set sail from here. See row upon row of handmade shallow-draft oceangoing Makassar-type schooners. For around Rp3000 boatmen will take you around the waterfront; see sailors cooking rice onboard and unload lumber as peddlers hawk souvenirs. These rustic seamen make miniature *prahu* which sell for around Rp15,000.

Gereja Sion

Also called the "Old Portuguese Church" or "Gereja Portugis," on Jl. Pangeran Jayakarta 1. Emerging from the the L side of the Stasiun Kota, walk down Jl. Batu to the bridge; it's on the corner. View the interior (guestbook, donation) Tues. to Sat. 0900-1500. Built in 1693, Gereja Sion is Jakarta's oldest standing house of worship. The Portuguese themselves never built a church in Jakarta, but they imported Portuguese-speaking Indian slaves. Their descendants — freed when they converted to Christianity — eventually became a prominent social class known as *Mardjikers* or "Black Portuguese," though they had only a drop of Portuguese blood. In 1695 the Dutch gave them this church to replace their outgrown shantytown one. A bell cast in Batavia in 1675 still hangs in the tower next to the church. Gereja Sion was restored in 1920, then again in 1978. The interior contains fine 17th C. carved wood pillars, a baroque pulpit, lavish ebony pews, and big copper chandeliers. Wooden shields lining the walls commemorate former governors-general and military men. Within the church graveyard many prominent people of Old Batavia were interred. The most beautiful tomb is Governor-General Zwaardecroon's; he asked to be buried here so that he might "sleep amongst the common folk."

Pieter Erbervelt Monument

Near Gereja Sion walking E on Jl. Pangeran Jayakarta is a monument built to commemorate a Eurasian who, in cooperation with a Javanese nobleman, planned an indigenous uprising to overthrow Dutch rule in 1721. Deep-rooted Dutch phobia of the possibility of Eurasians aiding native peoples against the Dutch is reflected in the inscription's severity. On top is a skull pierced by an iron spear as a sign of dishonor, and underneath a plaque: "In loathsome memory of the punished traitor Pieter Erbervelt, no one may build, carpenter, lay bricks, or plant on this place either now or on any further day. Batavia. April 14, 1722." The Japanese destroyed the original monument built on the site of Erbervelt's house; the original stone is now in the Jakarta City Museum.

Museum Taman Prasasti

Means "Park of the Memorial Stones." The large Tanah Abang Cemetery, which received Jakarta's dead for hundreds of years, was closed in 1976 and much of it leveled to make way for urban growth. Luckily, a small section of the old cemetery was spared and stones have been gathered from Tanah Abang and other demolished churchyards of Kota. Taman Prasasti has a wide range of tombstones reflecting the diverse ethnic, racial, and social backgrounds, as well as the historical periods, of 17th and 18th C. Batavia's citizens. People have been buried here since 1795, the internments reaching an all-time peak in the awful years of pestilence in the early 19th C. when the hearses from the local hospitals would bring piles of bodies to be laid in mass graves. The tombstones are romantic, gothic, baroque, and sinister, with touching and mysterious inscriptions. The museum is open daily 0800-1500, Fri. to 1100, Sat. to 1400, closed on Sundays.

TAMAN FATAHILLAH

In front of the Jakarta City Museum is a stone-paved square called Taman Fatahillah, once Batavia's main square. The fountain in the middle—faithfully reconstructed from a 1788 sketch—sits on the foundation of the original. Here the early inhabitants fetched—and later died from—their drinking water; nearby criminals were flogged or beheaded, and merry festivals and public markets took place. North of the fountain, the 16th C. Portuguese cannon goes by the honorific title of *Si Jagur* ("Mr. Sturdy"). Because of its phallic shape and its clenched fist (a symbol of fertility on Java), for many years women believed the cannon could cure infertility. Barren women used to offer it flowers, then sit on top of it (the Dutch attempted to end this practice by removing it to a museum for some years). *Si Jagur* was also thought to bring about prosperity and health to those who paid homage to it. Its Latin inscription, *"Ex me ipsa renata sum"* ("I am reborn from myself") alludes to the fact that the cannon was recast from an older one. In front of *Si Jagur* every day except Sun. from 0600-1400, there's a bustling thieves market.

Balai Seni Rupa

This Museum of Fine Arts (tel. 271062) is on the E side of Taman Fatahillah Square in a large building with a classical facade. Open daily from 0900-1400, closed Mon., Fri. to 1100, Sat. to 1300, Sun to 1500, entrance Rp200, children Rp100. Built in 1870, it was formerly the Court of Justice. Balai Seni Rupa houses a permanent exhibition of Indonesian paintings from the Raden Saleh era up to contemporary times, including a number of carved tree trunks. A Ceramics Museum, Museum Keramik, shares the same building. Also open daily 0900-1400 except Mon. and Fri.; tel. 177424. Some descriptions are in English.

JAKARTA CITY MUSEUM

Also known as Museum Kota, or "Fatahillah." Located on Jl. Taman Fatahillah 1 on the S side of Fatahillah Square right behind Stasiun Kota. Entrance Rp100, plus a Rp500 camera charge. Open daily 0900-1400, closed Mon., Fri to 1100, Sat. to 1300, Sun. 1500. Once the City Hall of Batavia (Stadhuis), this magnificent 2-story building is one of the finest examples of Dutch colonial architecture. Built in 1710, the whole building was converted in 1974 into a museum charting Jakarta's long and dramatic history. The interior is almost devoid of decoration, the floor plan pragmatically designed to serve the needs of bureaucrats and a populace who for 250 years flocked here for marriage licenses, to attend sermons, pay taxes, legalize contracts. After torture-exacted confessions, criminals were executed or severely flogged in the square while solemn judges looked down from the balcony. The basements in the wings contained the infamous "water prisons" where up to 300 unfortunates were chained in cells flooded with filthy water for weeks on end; see the strong double bars on the basement windows along Jl. Pintu Besar. A bell has been in the steeple since the end of the 18th C.; though older bells exist in Indonesia, none has played such a role in its history as this one, which chimed to mark momentous occasions. Most exhibits are annotated in Indonesian; no numbering system, catalog, or explanations in English. The building contains an amazingly rich collection of massive antique furniture and VOC memorabilia. Small 17th and 18th C. domestic utensils vividly bring colonial history to life. See the old oil portraits of past Dutch governors-general, from Pieter Botha to Tiarda; their hardset, heavy faces, staring out from the wall, give you an idea of the stern mentality of the times. The museum also has maps dating from 1619, a fine numismatic collection, archaeological exhibits, historical sketches, and blunderbusses of every variety.

MUSEUM WAYANG

A puppet museum is on Jl. Pintu Besar Utara 27 (tel. 279560). Open daily except Mon., on Tues., Wed., Thurs. and Sun. 0900-1400, Fri. to 1100, Sat. to 1300. Entrance Rp200 adults, Rp100 children, Rp500 for a camera, Rp1000 for a movie camera (postcards are for sale inside, Rp300). This long, narrow building (1912) and the building behind it (1939) were built to serve as "the Museum of Old Batavia." In 1975 all the collections were moved to the Jakarta City Museum and this building was turned into the Museum Wayang. Construction workers excavated gravestones dated as far back as 1650, when this site was the principal church graveyard for 18 Dutch governors-general and their families and other high officials—the Westminster Abbey of Dutch colonial times. This 2-story building has 9 rooms, each containing priceless collections of puppets from all over the world. Because seawater seeps into the ground floor, only the second floor is used for exhibits, sealed off and air-conditioned to reduce salty air, humidity, and dust. This makes the museum a welcome refuge from sticky Jakarta. Go on an "off day" such as a Tues. morning when you could find the museum almost empty. For specific questions, see the helpful director, Mr. Bambang Gunardjo.

A museum for lovers of *wayang*, dolls, and doll-making—all highly developed art forms in Indonesia. Along with Indonesian *wayang* forms, it contains puppetry from India, Thailand, China, Kampuchea, even a Punch and Judy troupe presented by the English ambassador. In the *wayang Melayu* from Malaysia, see how the figures metamorphosed during their migration from their source on Java. Also note regional Indonesian differences: as the forms spread into the Outer Islands, they become cruder. Notice how the puppets have been used to illustrate mythological, historical, social, religious, and political themes and characters, depicting for example guerillas fighting the Dutch, and John the Baptist. Also displayed are a number of experimental *wayang* forms which show how far this medium can go; old themes but extremely stylized shapes. The museum also contains a 1,500-volume library (Dutch, English, and German books) on the subject of *wayang*. **performances:** In back of the museum is a stage surrounded by *wayang beber* scrolls from Solo. At 1000 or 1100 every alternating Sun. there are *wayang kulit* and *wayang golek* performances accompanied by *gamelan*. *Dalang* of high repute, who usually perform for 3 million *rupiah* and up, may perform here just for the honor.

MEDAN MERDEKA

One-square-kilometer Medan Merdeka ("Freedom Square") is one of the largest city squares in the world. Once a muddy grazing field, in 1809 Governor-General Daendels turned it into a military parade ground. After the British occupation in 1818, the vast field was renamed King's Square or Koningsplein by the Dutch and all their state bureaucratic headquarters were built around it. The buildings still standing date from the early 19th century. This square now contains city government and national buildings, banks, hotels, and businesses. The modern Parliament building resembles the Sydney Opera House. The Ministry of Finance, NE of Lapangan Banteng, is a copy of Amsterdam's Sutick Palace. In the N part of the square is the Presidential Palace complex containing the Istana

Merdeka and the Istana Negara. To the E is a military police compound.

Istana Negara

This impressive white-fronted palace, on Jl. Medan Merdeka Utara facing Jl. Veteran, is one of 2 Presidential Palaces on Medan Merdeka. First a country house built by a wealthy Dutchman in the late 1700s, it once served as the governor-general's residence. View the front from Jl. Veteran; note the colonnaded porch, twin columns at the corners, and large gates. The lavishly appointed interior boasts Dutch Colonial furniture, a neo-classic dining hall, and ceiling decorations resembling Ambonese lace. For a tour, first get permission from the Chief of the Presidential Household, Istana Negara, Jakarta; give it 2 weeks. Dress, shirt, and tie are obligatory.

Istana Merdeka

Built nearly 100 years after Istana Negara by the Dutch to replace that aging palace, this stately edifice (inaugurated in 1879) was called Koningsplein Paleis. It has been occupied by 15 Dutch governors-general, 3 Dutch high military commanders, and 2 presidents of Republik Indonesia. In an emotion-filled ceremony, the Dutch flag atop it was hauled down forever on 27 December 1949. Eyewitnesses relate that when the Indonesian red and white *Dwikora* was raised above the building 100,000 people roared *"Merdeka! Merdeka!"* ("Freedom! Freedom!"), the culminating act of 3 centuries of Dutch colonial rule. The palace was renamed Istana Merdeka, or "Freedom Palace." The building is more a formal reception hall than a residence. The portico's marble steps lead up to enormous Corinthian pillars. From the terrace one first enters the so-called Credential Hall, where foreign dignitaries were received by the head of state; you can still see the bullet hole in one of the hall's 4 big mirrors put there by a MiG-17 fighter in an assassination attempt on Sukarno in 1960. Official rooms lead off the Credential Hall, and the president's private quarters were in the wings. In the back, a terrace looks out upon a tranquil garden.

Emmanuel Church

On Jl. Merdeka Timur 10 on the E side of the square opposite Gambir RR Station, this unique classicist Dutch Protestant church was erected between 1834 and 1839. The architect, J.H. Horst, incorporated elements from Greek temples, Renaissance theaters, and the Roman arena in its circular construction. The congregation surrounds the pulpit while the sun bathes the whole interior with an even, well-diffused light. Some precious articles in the Emmanuel Church were preserved after several Kota churches were demolished: silver and gilt dishes, boxes, and chalices, an elaborate baptismal font, and a baroque organ built in Holland in 1843 (only 2 others like it in the world). On Sun., the service in Dutch is at 1000, in Korean at 1115, and in English at 1700.

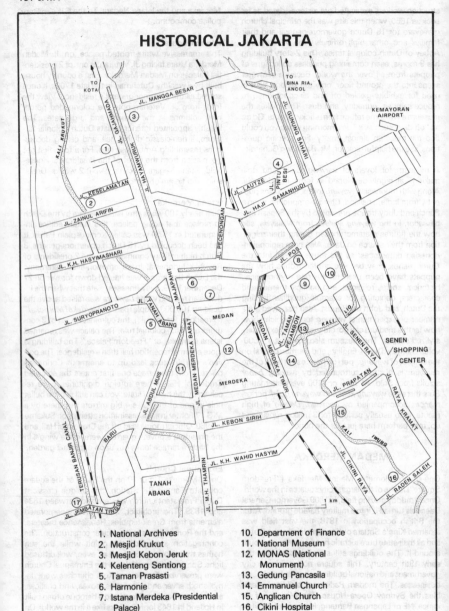

HISTORICAL JAKARTA

TO KOTA

JL. MANGGA BESAR

TO BINA RIA, ANCOL

KEMAYORAN AIRPORT

JL. GAJAHMADA

KALI KRUKUT

JL. KESELAMATAN

JL. HAYAMWURUK

JL. ZAINUL ARIFIN

JL. K.H. HASYIMASHARI

JL. GUNUNG SAHARI

JL. LAUTZE

JL. PINTU BESI

JL. HAJI SAMANHUDI

JL. PECENONGAN

JL. POS

JL. MAJAPAHIT

JL. TANAH ABANG

JL. SURYOPRANOTO

MEDAN

JL. TAMAN PEJAMBON

KALI

JL. SENEN RAYA

JL. LIO

SENEN SHOPPING CENTER

JL. MEDAN MERDEKA BARAT

JL. ABDUL MUIS

MEDAN MERDEKA TIMUR

MERDEKA

JL. KEBON SIRIH

JL. PRAPATAN

JL. RAYA KRAMAT

KALI IWUNG

JL. K.H. WAHID HASYIM

JL. M.H. THAMRIN

TANAH ABANG

JL. CIKINI RAYA

JL. RADEN SALEH

BARU

TERUSAN BANJIR CANAL

JL. JEMBATAN TINGGI

0   1 km

1. National Archives
2. Mesjid Krukut
3. Mesjid Kebon Jeruk
4. Kelenteng Sentiong
5. Taman Prasasti
6. Harmonie
7. Istana Merdeka (Presidential Palace)
8. Gedung Kesenian
9. Lapangan Banteng
10. Department of Finance
11. National Museum
12. MONAS (National Monument)
13. Gedung Pancasila
14. Emmanuel Church
15. Anglican Church
16. Cikini Hospital
17. Textile Museum

Istiqlal Mosque

In the NE corner of Merdeka Square, massive 6-level Istiqlal Mosque, with its minarets and grandiose lines, is Jakarta's most central and grandest place of Muslim worship. Its size is more impressive than its beauty: its huge white dome can be seen for 15 km and is easily identified from an aircraft far out over the Java Sea. On Fri., the mosque is crowded with thousands of worshippers, and after *Ramadan* up to 200,000 people crowd around Istiqlal. Reputed to be the largest mosque in SE Asia and the 2nd largest in the world, this was one of Sukarno's pet projects (this city still very much wears his mark). Seventeen years in the making, it was finely crafted from the best materials. English-speaking tours are offered for Rp1000; photos allowed. (See "Central Jakarta" map.)

The Harmonie

The oldest existing clubhouse in Asia. Located on the busy traffic junction of Jl. Pos and Jl. Hayamwuruk, it is now occupied by Sekretariat Negara. In 1810 Daendels—hoping to undermine the influence of Batavia's masonic lodges which he considered hotbeds of conspiracies—commissioned the construction of a clubhouse on the site of a strategic Dutch fort. In 1814 the clubhouse was finished by Raffles who also installed a scientific museum and a library in an annex. Though the building's exterior has been chopped back to widen a street, its interior is still in good condition and retains a relaxed, patrician air reminiscent of the days when colonial gentry spent long, idle evenings at the club sipping Bols gin, playing cards and billiards. Try to take yourself back to this golden age of colonialism whilst the heavy traffic snarls and spews around you.

THE NATIONAL MUSEUM

Also called the Museum Pusat (Central Museum), it's a 10-min. walk from the Jl. Jaksa area at Jl. Merdeka Barat 12 on the W side of Medan Merdeka. Open Tues. to Thurs. 0830-1400, Fri. to 1100, Sat. to 1300, Sun. to 1500, closed Mondays. Admission, Rp200; Rp500 for a camera. On Sun. at 0930 *gamelan* performances are open to the public. The building was erected between 1862 and 1868 by the Batavian Society for the Arts and Sciences—the oldest scientific institution in SE Asia (founded in 1778). Converted into a museum in 1947, it contains the richest collection of Indonesiana in the world, though its 85,000 items haven't been dusted since the Dutch left! Although poorly lit, you could spend a whole day in the prehistory and ethnographic sections, and its Hindu-Javanese antiquities exhibit rivals Leyden Museum's in Holland. It also houses one of the largest, rarest collections of Oriental ceramics outside China. (To help understand the huge ceramics room, buy Egbert Willem van Orsey de Flines' *Guide to the Ceramic Collection* for Rp5500 at the book counter.) Scale

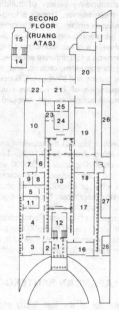

SECOND FLOOR (RUANG ATAS)

1. entrance hall
2. ticket windows
3. historical collection
4. exhibition room
5. numismatic collection

Library

6. lending service
7. reading room
8. administration of the library
9. librarian's office
10. book storage
11. book bindery

Archaeological Collection

12. rotunda
13. inner court (statuary)
14. treasure room (2nd floor)
15. bronze collection (2nd floor)
16. audio-visual room

Ethnographic Collection

17. Java and Sumatra
18. woodcarving
19. Bali, Kalimantan, and Sulawesi
20. Irian Barat, Maluku, and Nusatenggara
21. foreign ceramics
22. prehistory
23. manuscript collection
24. administrative offices
25. director
26. storage of archaeological objects
27. training center
28. bathrooms

models of traditional dwellings, villages, and *prahu* show the astounding variety of building styles throughout these islands. There's a king-size relief map (learn what mountains on Java to climb), each of Indonesia's geographic regions has its own display case, and there's a great ethnic map representing many of Indonesia's 450 different societies. The Gold Room, with its statuettes, crowns, and medallions, protected by guards and steel gates, is open only on Sun.; see examples of *kris* handles studded with rubies, emeralds, sapphires, and wrapped in beaten gold.

Services

Free art collection tours of the museum are given on Tues. and Wed. from 0930-1030. To use the museum's outstanding library (700,000 volumes on Indonesian and Asian subjects and ethnographica), you need a letter of introduction to obtain a card (Rp500). See the magnificent Krom monograph of b/w prints of the Borobudur reliefs taken in the 1920s. With the exception of the Gold Room, photos may be taken after buying a permit for Rp500 per camera. The use of a flash, however, is not allowed in the ethnographic rooms as strong light fades objects.

LAPANGAN BANTENG

As you stare out of the lush lobby of the Hotel Borobudur International onto Lapangan Banteng it's difficult to believe that in the mid-17th C. this whole area was a primitive swamp inhabited by crocodiles, tigers, and rhinoceros. During the 18th C., it became a vast military area with barracks, administrative buildings, and parade ground. By the 19th C., this small square had become the lively, genteel hub of Dutch social life.

Sights

Only 2 old buildings are left from that era: the neoclassical Supreme Court and the Empire-style Department of Finance. Built between 1809 and 1828, the Department of Finance was formerly the monumental palace Witte Huis "White House" which was Weltevreden's capital during the 19th C. — the nerve center for the whole VOC commercial empire. On Jl. Budi Utomo is a pharmacy now called Kimia Farma; this typical building was the 19th C. masonic lodge, De Ster in het Osten "The Star in the East," which the local people called Gedung Setan ("Devil's House") because of the unremitting secretiveness of its members. About 100 m farther on the corner of Jl. Pos and Jl. Gedung Kesesian is the Jakarta City Theatre or Gedung Kesenian. Built in typical Empire-style in 1821, this was formerly the Schouwburg Theatre. Lastly, the Roman Catholic cathedral, Jl. Kathedral 7 on the NW corner of Lapangan Banteng, was built in 1901 — a uniquely grotesque gothic style with 3 black spires.

Statuary

Indonesia's former president-for-life Sukarno left a good number of monuments to Jakarta. Symbols of Sukarno's megalomaniacal sense of nationalism, some of these monuments have been nicknamed by the residents. An example is the statue of a youth carrying the torch of development, the Youth Spirit Monument, *Patung Pemuda*, located on the roundabout at the entrance to Kebayoran where Jl. Jen. Sudirman meets Jl. Senopati. Since this figure seems to be holding a flaming dish, it's known locally as "the Mad Waiter." See also the statue of a man with outstretched arms atop a curving pedestal in the traffic circle of Jl. Gatot; the bronze figure of Prince Diponegoro astride his horse in the MONAS compound, Merdeka Square; the statue of Gajah Mada, the famous prime minister of the 15th C. Majapahit Kingdom, on the corner of Police Headquarters and Jl. Trunojoyo in Kebayoran. Kartini, the Javanese princess who first championed women's rights in Indonesia, is honored by a monument in front of the BAPPENAS building on Jl. Iman Bonjol. The statue of a woman giving rice to a peasant soldier stands in the square at Menteng Prapatan. The bronze figures of a young man and woman extending their arms in the circle in front of Hotel Indonesia was sculpted by Edi Sunarso of Yogya for the 4th Asian Games in 1962. The "Chainbreaker" statue, of a man breaking the chains of bondage, commemorates the "liberation" of West Irian from the Dutch — crude but unforgettable. Built in 1963, it towers over Lapangan Banteng.

1. Istana Merdeka and Istana Negara
2. Mandala office
3. Istiqlal Mosque
4. Paket Post (send parcels)
5. Hotel Borobudor Intercontinental
6. National Museum
7. Merdeka Monument
8. Gambir Train Station
9. Taman Ria
10. U.S. Embassy
11. Quantas
12. Natrabu Restaurant
13. Wisma Delima (Jl. Jaksa)
14. cheap losmen
15. Pondok Soedibjo
16. Wisma Ise
17. Jakarta Information Center/telephone office
18. Bali International Hotel
19. Sarinah Department Store
20. Australian Embassy
21. Burmese Embassy
22. Immigration Department
23. Jalan Surabaya (antiques)
24. Hotel Indonesia
25. British Embassy
26. Hotel Mandarin

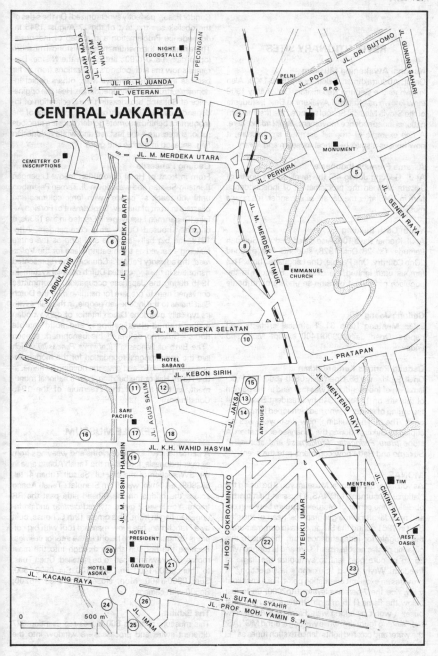

CENTRAL JAKARTA

JL. GAJAH MADA
JL. HAYAM WURUK
JL. IR. H. JUANDA
JL. PECONGAN
JL. VETERAN
JL. DR. SUTOMO
JL. GUNUNG SAHARI

NIGHT FOODSTALLS

PELNI
JL. POS
G.P.O.

(2)
(3)
(4)

MONUMENT

(5)

CEMETERY OF INSCRIPTIONS

JL. M. MERDEKA UTARA
(1)

JL. PERWIRA

JL. SENEN RAYA

JL. M. MERDEKA BARAT

JL. ABDUL MUIS

(6)
(7)
(8)

JL. M. MERDEKA TIMUR

EMMANUEL CHURCH

(9)

JL. M. MERDEKA SELATAN
(10)

JL. PRATAPAN

HOTEL SABANG

JL. KEBON SIRIH

JL. MENTENG RAYA

(11)
(12)
(15)
(13)
(14)

JL. JAKSA

SARI PACIFIC
(17)
(16)
JL. AGUS SALIM
(18)

ANTIQUES

JL. K.H. WAHID HASYIM

(19)

JL. HUSNI THAMRIN

JL. HOS. COKROAMINOTO

JL. CKINI RAYA

MENTENG
TIM

HOTEL PRESIDENT

GARUDA

(20)
(21)
(22)
(23)

JL. TEUKU UMAR

REST. OASIS

HOTEL ASOKA

JL. KACANG RAYA

(24)
(26)
(25)

JL. IMAM

JL. SUTAN SYAHIR
JL. PROF. MOH. YAMIN S. H.

0   500 m

REVOLUTIONARY SITES

National Awakening Museum
On Jl. Abdurrakhman Saleh, open 0900-1400. Also known as the Gedung Kebankitan. On 20 May 1908 (now known as "National Awakening Day"), students of the Stovia Medical School founded the first modern national independence movement, *Budi Utomo*, here. A fine example of tropical Jakartan architecture, it now houses a small historical museum and library.

Asrama Pemuda Indonesia
At Jl. Gedung Joang 45, the revolutionary youth of Jakarta planned the proclamation of independence here in 1945 after the Japanese surrender. It's now a museum.

Youth Oath Building
At Jl. Kramat Raya 106. Also called Gedung Sumpah Pemuda. On 28 Oct. 1928, students first pledged "One Country, One People, One Language" here. This famous oath ignited the desire for freedom in the populace of Java; it became an underground battle cry.

Gedung Joang '45
Jalan Menteng Raya 31. Historical artifacts and papers. Open daily 0900-1400 except Mon. and Friday.

Gedung Perintis Kemerdekaan
On Jl. Proklamasi 56. Open daily 0800-1600. The Proclamation of Independence was first read in the garden of this site on 17 Aug. 1945 by President Sukarno at the urging of students who had kidnapped him at gunpoint. The original building, now destroyed, was occupied by Sukarno during the Japanese occupation. A stone *(Batu Peringatan Proklamasi)* and statues of Sukarno and Hatta now commemorate the event.

MONAS
As you leave the National Museum you'll be facing the National Monument, MONAS, a Russian-built marble obelisk in the center of Merdeka Square between old and new Jakarta in the geographical heart of the city. Built in 1961 during the Sukarno era to commemorate the struggle for independence from the Dutch, this gigantic phallic needle rises 137 m and is topped with 35 kg of pure gold leaf to symbolize the flame of freedom. Wryly called "Sukarno's last erection," it provides an excellent orientation point. For a knockout view, ride the 7-person elevator (Rp2000) up to just below the flame (115 m high). If there are no tourist buses it won't be a long wait. From 0730-1000 view the "singing fountain" while walking around MONAS; the water and colored lights dance to such tunes as "El Condor Pasa," perfectly synchronized! On the sides of the obelisk see the text of the 17 August 1945 Independence Proclamation and a map of Indonesia. Three m under the monument is an historical museum (open daily 0800-1700); enter from the N side. Dioramas show the archipelago's civilizations from as far back as the prehistoric Java Man; others depict Indonesia's struggle for independence. Hear the original voice of Sukarno broadcasting the Declaration of Independence. Also jealously guarded in the base of the monument behind an ornate golden door is a precious national treasure — the first red and white Indonesian flag, encased in marble and glass.

Gedung Pancasila
From in front of Hotel Borobudor, follow Lapangan Banteng Selatan and walk down Jl. Taman Pejambon until you reach a "palace" with Ionic columns and pilasters in front of the new Department of Foreign Affairs (Departmen Luar Negeri). Erected in the 1830s, it originally housed Dutch army commanders. After 1918, the big hall — as wide and long as the entire building — served as the meeting place for the *Volksraad*, the advisory People's Council, who represented minorities in the segregated Dutch colonial system. In 1945 during the Japanese occupation, a committee convened here to prepare for handing over the Dutch East Indies to the Indonesian people. In this hall — with its typically overdone Dutch interior of dark wooden walls, stained-glass ceilings, and solid marble floors — Sukarno delivered his benchmark speech "The Birth of Pancasila" *(Lahirnya Pancasila)* which laid the constitutional foundation for the modern Indonesian Republic, and gave the building its name. In the Treaty Hall of the building, now a national monument, is the text of the Preamble of the 1945 Constitution.

TEXTILE MUSEUM

A permanent exhibition of cloths and weavings from all over Indonesia, located in the Tanah Abang area in the SW section of the city (Jl. Satsuit Tuban 4, tel. 593909), a 10-min. walk from Stanplatz Tanah Abang across the bridge on the R-hand side past the RR tracks. You'll see 2 giant, stylized *canting* and an Indonesian flag in front. This ornate 19th C. house, built by a Frenchman, has a low mansard roof with big columns rising to the same height as the interior ceilings. Because the hot sun shone through into the main rooms, large awnings had to be installed. Open Tues. to Thurs. 0900-1400, Fri. 0900-1100, Sat. 0900-1300, Sun. 0900-1400, Mon. closed. Entrance Rp200; Rp500 with camera.

The Exhibit
This museum contains 600 pieces representing 327 different styles and processes — a window into the

crafts of all Indonesian cultures. If you can't get to a real *batik* factory, see these exhibits instead. And if you're planning to spend serious money on fabrics, do some research here: peruse the books in the museum's library and study the pieces on display. Exhibits include: old weaving contraptions, a model of a Javanese *kain* being woven on a breast loom, all 9 processes of *batik* making, the different types of *canting* and *cap* used, plus all the various dyes. Emphasis is equally divided between textiles of Solo and Yogya, and those of the Outer Islands. Almost every *batik* center on Java is represented and also view the gorgeous woven arts of the Outer Islands, now very rare. One whole room is devoted to *ikat*. Outer Island specimens include Tapanuli *batik* of N. Sumatra, examples of the rare double-*ikat gringsing* cloths of Bali; some incredible Dayak *ikat* cloths. One exhibit depicts a Palembang loom with a partially completed weaving, with all of the equipment in place. Oddities include an example of "rubber *batik*" (*batik karet*) made from the product of the rubber tree, and some seldom seen bark cloths from Sulawesi. *Ikat colup* (a tie-dye process), and gold-interwoven cloths (*benang mas*) from Bali, Palembang, and Sumbawa are displayed. **note:** The lighting is terrible (the doors are kept closed to keep out the heat), so open the windows—sunlight brings out the vividness of the colors.

Information

One purpose of the Museum Tekstil is to collect historical data for research, thus photographs are one of this museum's best features. Some are in color, often showing the women of the area wearing the displayed fabric; some prints are very old, valuable in themselves. Captions are in Indonesian. A small collection of books on the textile arts is available for you to read in the small reading room. The museum also sells a few publications on looms and other textile-making implements, and a booklet in Indonesian describing the museum's contents. A diagrammatic floor plan codifies and explains the exhibits, and several of the ticket takers will give you a tour of the museum (also only in Indonesian).

ACCOMMODATIONS

The area for inexpensive accommodations in expensive Jakarta is the Jl. Jaksa/Kebon Sirih district, within walking distance of most of the city's attractions and services. Jalan Jaksa is getting very Kutaish, with Westernized bamboo restaurants serving up banal food and guys approaching you on the street pitching one *losmen* or the other as the best. Accommodations charge Rp4000-7000 and they fill up fast so you have your best chance of getting a room early in the morning. The majority have only double rooms with shared bathrooms (exceptions are noted below) and most charge the same price for s or d. At most places tea and/or drinking water are included in the price, but other extras must be paid for.

Budget

Best known is Jl. Jaksa 5, or **Wisma Delima**, which has the most traffic but has been sabotaged by its own success. Dormitory beds cost Rp2000 s (with YHA card Rp1750), Rp6000 d, Rp7500 t. Hasn't changed a bit in 10 years—bad lighting, stuffy, noisy, cramped; rooms upstairs are nicer. Very high turnover. All right for a few days. The rooms upstairs at **Nick's Hostel** (no. 16) are airier, cleaner, and roomier than Delima's; they even arrange transport to the airport. For even more comfort, head for **Hostel Noordwijk** (or Norbek), Jl. Jaksa 14 (tel. 330392) where you have a telephone, good security, outdoor lounge, multi-lingual friendly managers, free tea, laundry service, 20-cm-thick mattresses! Norbek charges Rp3000 for a/c dorm, Rp5000 s, Rp11,000 for a/c rooms. **Wim's Hostel**, Jl. Kebon Sirih Barat Dalam 1 (tel. 327723), is a spacious family home with about 6 extra rooms upstairs for guests. Clean and friendly—Vilhelm speaks Dutch and English. Higher-priced, Islamic-style **Karya Hotel**, Jl. Jaksa 36, has non-a/c Rp14,000 d rooms, including breakfast, fan, toilet, shower. You'd be lucky to get into **Djody Hostel**, Jl. Jaksa 27; Rp8500-10,500 s or d or Rp19,000 for a/c. There's a branch down the street (no. 270) with dorm beds, Rp2000. **Borneo Youth Hostel**, just around the corner and 75 m down a side street (Jl. Kebon Sirih Barat Dalam 35) is cool and comfortable; Rp2500 dorm (or Rp2000 for YH members), Rp7000-10,000 for room with bathroom and fan. **Bloemsteen**, Jl. Kebon Sirih Timur I/173, is a small, tight, hot, cheap place just off Jl. Jaksa; Rp4000-7000 s or d. An excellent place near Jl. Jaksa is **Pondok Soedibjo**, Jl. Kebon Sirih 23, only a 10-min. walk SW of the Chainbreaker statue. Go to the R of the travel agency (P.T. Bhayangkara) in the front, and walk to the rear where you'll find the *pondok* located around a pleasant inner courtyard. Small but adequate rooms, the downstairs ones with fan are Rp6000 s or d, upstairs are hotter (no fan); tea and bread for breakfast. Clean, good service, quiet and back from the road. The helpful proprietor will store luggage. Popular **Wisma Ise**, Jl. Wahid Hasyim 168, 3rd floor (tel. 333463) is reached by walking from Jl. Jaksa along Jl. Wahid Hasyim, then crossing Jl. Thamrin. They offer 20 newly remodeled rooms for Rp5500 s, Rp8800 d—a nice, quiet place with magnificent patio, only 5-min. walk E from Sarinah Dept. Store.

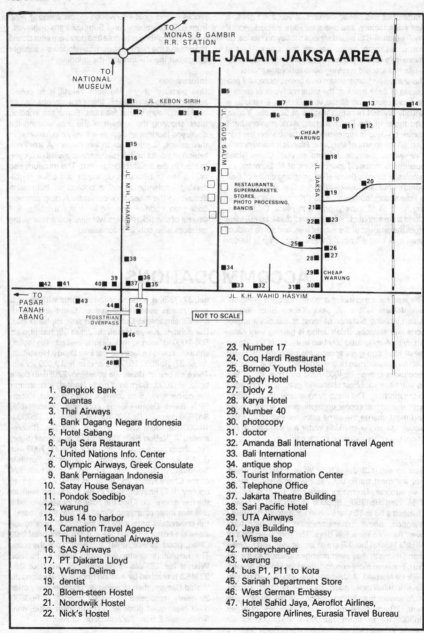

THE JALAN JAKSA AREA

TO
MONAS & GAMBIR
R.R. STATION

TO
NATIONAL
MUSEUM

JL. KEBON SIRIH

JL. AGUS SALIM

JL. M.H. THAMRIN

JL. JAKSA

CHEAP
WARUNG

RESTAURANTS,
SUPERMARKETS,
STORES,
PHOTO PROCESSING,
BANCIS

CHEAP
WARUNG

TO
PASAR
TANAH
ABANG

PEDESTRIAN
OVERPASS

JL. K.H. WAHID HASYIM

NOT TO SCALE

1. Bangkok Bank
2. Quantas
3. Thai Airways
4. Bank Dagang Negara Indonesia
5. Hotel Sabang
6. Puja Sera Restaurant
7. United Nations Info. Center
8. Olympic Airways, Greek Consulate
9. Bank Perniagaan Indonesia
10. Satay House Senayan
11. Pondok Soedibjo
12. warung
13. bus 14 to harbor
14. Carnation Travel Agency
15. Thai International Airways
16. SAS Airways
17. PT Djakarta Lloyd
18. Wisma Delima
19. dentist
20. Bloem-steen Hostel
21. Noordwijk Hostel
22. Nick's Hostel

23. Number 17
24. Coq Hardi Restaurant
25. Borneo Youth Hostel
26. Djody Hotel
27. Djody 2
28. Karya Hotel
29. Number 40
30. photocopy
31. doctor
32. Amanda Bali International Travel Agent
33. Bali International
34. antique shop
35. Tourist Information Center
36. Telephone Office
37. Jakarta Theatre Building
38. Sari Pacific Hotel
39. UTA Airways
40. Jaya Building
41. Wisma Ise
42. moneychanger
43. warung
44. bus P1, P11 to Kota
45. Sarinah Department Store
46. West German Embassy
47. Hotel Sahid Jaya, Aeroflot Airlines,
    Singapore Airlines, Eurasia Travel Bureau

Guesthouses

Wisma Petra (tel. 325149) is across the street from Bir Bintang on Jl. Wahid Hasyim, just down from Jl. Jaksa; Rp18,000 a/c rooms, Dutch- and English-speaking, Christian hosts. Mrs. Rugeprecht, Jl. Kamboja 6 (tel. 343903), also rents rooms for around US$12. Another homestyle guesthouse is run by the incomparable David Mussry, world traveler, fluent in 5 languages, and lord over a domain consisting of a travel agency, a cozy and seductive Japanese restaurant, and perhaps Jakarta's seediest nightclub. His comfortable a/c "family" rooms go for US$9-14 s or d. Inquire at Amanda Bali International Travel Agency, Jl. Wahid Hasyim 116 (tel. 325056).

Moderate

Sabang Hotel, Jl. Agus Salim 11 (tel. 354031/ 357621), at US$22-46 s or d, gives more bang for your buck than the international-style hotels. Clean, efficient, central, fully outfitted rooms with pool, restaurants, newsstand, business center. Another full-service, reasonable hotel is the **Marco Polo**, Rp29,000 (including tax and service). Patronized for the most part by small businessmen from all over Asia, it is one of the cheapest places to have an ice-cold draft beer (Rp800) and smorgasbord (Rp3500) in an a/c, fairly sophisticated environment. A Kodak film processing lab and one of Jakarta's best Japanese restaurants (the Kikugawa) are nearby, and the best *nasi goreng* in Indonesia are made across the street. The Marco Polo is just right for cleaning up and resting after some hard traveling.

International Class

In this class hotel you'll find essentially the same high standards as are found in any European or Asian capital city, but at US$20-30 less. Though you must add 10% tax and 11% service charge to room rates, business discounts of between 10-20% are sometimes given. Many of these leading hotels have nightclubs with floor shows hosting local and imported talent. **Hotel Indonesia**, recently completely revamped and modernized, was the first skyscraper built (in the 1960s) in Indonesia—the grandest structure put up by Indonesians since the erection of Borobudur 1,000 years earlier. The **Mandarin Hotel** (US$160 d) is probably the most elegant of Jakarta's top hotels nowadays; they welcome you with a bowl of exotic fruit with a diagram explaining how to eat each one! **Sari Pacific**, Jl. Thamrin, charges about US$120 d, and also gets good reports. Everybody still seems to like the atmosphere and the service at the venerable **Hotel Borobudur Intercontinental** (US$130 d) on Jl. Lapangan Banteng Selatan; in its restaurant read newspapers in every language. The largest hotel in Indonesia (1117 rooms), HBI also has tennis and squash courts, a large pool, and an outdoor cafe where a buffet brunch is served every Sunday. The garden-surrounded **Jakarta Hilton** shares a 32-acre site with several authentic Batak tribal houses (lugged all the way from N. Sumatra), a Balinese temple, and even a jogging path; this whole complex is a luxurious enclave (US$120 d), well insulated from the downtown bustle, with swimming pool, health club, tennis courts, bowling alley, shopping arcade, nursery, and an American restaurant that serves authentic hamburgers, fancy and expensive drinks, sundaes, pizza. Get in on its famous buffet-style *rijstaffel* on Fri. nights. The new **Aryaduta Hyatt**, Jl. Prapatan 44/46 (tel. 357631), is a luxurious hotel with pool and several high-class restaurants—another favorite among those who can afford it.

FOOD

Street Food

Keep your eyes peeled for mobile carts which could roll right by your door, offering all kinds of authentic Indonesian cuisines. Learn hawkers' cries such as "Tay, tay" which means *sate* (pronounced "sah-tay"). A soft tinkling of a spoon on an empty glass announces the *sekotang* man, while the cry "Wooo-deee, es!" is the signal of the Woody Woodpecker ice cream man. These carts can even dispense complete *nasi campur* with egg, vegetables, fish, meat, sauce, *sambal*, potato, tons of rice, for less than Rp1000. This same meal costs Rp2500 in a restaurant. The vendor pours tea from a kettle, provides you with a wash bucket, hand towel, and matches which you break in half to clean your teeth! Other meals on wheels include *martabak* (Indian-style pancake-omelette), *mie baso* (meatball and noodle soup), slices of fresh fruit, and such exotic items as ginger milk

wine tonic. And nowhere else in Indonesia is *gado-gado* served with such finesse as in Jakarta!

Warung

These informal foodstalls, which open around twilight and close around midnight, are found all over Jakarta. No matter where your hotel is, you're never more than a few hundred m from a delicious taste experience. Akin to the food markets of Singapore, a new phenomenon is the *pujasera*, an assembly of *warung* representing the entire spectrum of Indonesian cooking. One of the most popular is the cavernous basement of the Sarinah Jaya Dept. Store in Kebayoran Basu. *Warung* selling such Batavian dishes as *nasi uduk* and *bubur ayam* set up at night along Jl. Wahid Hasyim, just around the corner from Jl. Jaksa. For C. and E. Javanese food, *tahu pong* (fried beancake slices with egg and ketchup), the crispiest *babi kluyuk* (sweet-sour pork), and *lumpia semarang* go to: Jl. Pecenongan (near the big mosque); Jl. Biak; Jl. Roxy; Jl. Gereja Ayam; Jl. Mangga Besar; Pasar Baru; and Jl. Sawah Besar. For *nasi uduk betawi* (rice cooked in coconut milk with assorted fried delicacies), Jl. Saman Hudi is the place, opposite the Krekot Theatre, as well as Jl. Salemba Raya or Pasar Kenari. For Chinese food go to the *warung* on Jl. Pecenongan, Jl. Biak (Roxy), Jl. Mangga Besar, Jl. Sawah Besar, Jl. Gunung Sahari, and Taman Lokasari. For *sate kambing* (mutton *satel*), *gulai kambing* (mutton curry), and *sop kambing* try Jl. Kendal and Jl. Wahid Hasyim in the Pasar Tanah Abang area. For specialties like monkey, turtle *sate*, dog, snake, or iguana, head for Taman Lokasari and the Chinese quarter of Glodok in Kota.

Food Markets

Behind the National Museum are some excellent and friendly lunch *warung*. Along Jl. Mangga Besar, in northern Jakarta off Jl. Hayam Wuruk, foodstalls sell *nasi padang*, Indian, and Chinese cuisines. The market area on Jl. Taman Sari specializes in Chinese delicacies such as fried lizard and snake *sate*. Take a bus to Kota and get off at the Hayam Wuruk Plaza from where you can take a *bajai*. Jalan Pintu Besar Selatan, a continuation of Jl. Hayam Wuruk in Glodok, is crammed with Chinese restaurants and foodstalls; take a bus for Kota and get off at the Glodok Shopping Center. Directly N of the giant Monas statue, the Jl. Pecenongan market runs N to S between Jl. Batutulis and Jl. Juanda; specializes in Chinese food. Pasar Senen, one km E of Monas, has a comprehensive collection of foods: Chinese, *nasi padang*, Javanese. Closes at night. The Jl. Cikini Raya area blossoms into stalls in the early evening: follow your nose. These *warung* along Jl. Kendal serve the famous goat's foot soup *(sop kaki kambing)*, Makassarese broiled fish, and typical Batawi cooking. Bring Rp200 for strolling minstrels! Jalan Kendal runs parallel to the canal and RR tracks off Jl. Thamrin in Menteng. Take any bus S on Jl. Thamrin and get off after Hotel Mandarin. Walk S by the massage parlors on Jl. Blora. An open-air market forms every evening in the parking lot of the Sarinah Dept. Store. At the Menteng Theatre, *sop kaki kambing* costs at least Rp2000—a delicacy. Nearby on Jl. Haji Agus Salim behind Sarinah are many Padang and Chinese restaurants. At Blok M, a major shopping center in Kebayoran Baru, is a staggering array of stalls near the bus terminal, open from 0600-0100. The emphasis here is on C. and E. Javanese cuisines; also tasty snacks like coconut cakes and *es pokat*.

Indonesian Restaurants

Normal business hours: 1100-1500 and 1800-1100. Few restaurants are open for breakfast. *Rumah makan nasi padang* restaurants can be expensive. Jalan Agus Salim, just up the street from Jl. Jaksa, is a tatty, frenetic street filled with cassette tape stores,

haberdashers, *sate* carts, and fast-food restaurants. The **Natrabu**, Jl. Agus Salim 9A, is good but pricey. Many Indonesian restaurants are found on nearby Jl. Kebon Sirih. **Sari Bundo Padang**, Jl. Juanda 27 next to Sarinah Dept. Store, is one of the best in town. The **Roda**, Jl. Blora 11, is another highly recommended Padang-style restaurant. For Manadonese food, go to **RM Manado**, Jl. Gondangdia Lama (tel. 336430). Makassarese cooking (from S. Sulawesi) can be sampled at **Angin Mamiri**, Jl. K.H. Ashari, and at **Happy's**, Jl. Mangga Besar Raya 4C. From the shortage of Javanese restaurants one would think that the Javanese were outnumbered in their own capital city! For the good *gudeg*, try **Bu Citro's**, Jl. Cikanjang II, Kebayoran. For Madurese cooking, try the famous **RM Pak Ali** on Jl. Jen. Gatot Subroto, Mapeng *(sate, soto ayam*, and don't miss the *es kelapa kopyor.)* For *sate*, go to the good, inexpensive **Senayan Satay House**, Jl. Kebon Sirih 31-A, Kebayoran (on corner of Jl. Jaksa). Just as good is **Sate Blora Cirebon**, Jl. Pemuda 47. The best known Javanese-style fried chicken restaurants in Jakarta are: **Ayam Bulungan**, Jl. Bulungan 64, and **Ayam Goreng Mbok Berek**, Jl. P. Polim Raya 93.

Chinese Restaurants

Bakmi Gajah Mada, Jl. Gajah Mada 92 and another at Jl. Melawai IV/25 in Blok M, specializes in all kinds of delicious noodle dishes. Tasty noodle soups can be found in the *warung* and small restaurants in the Kota area. **Cahaya Kota**, Jl. Wahid Hasyim 9 (tel. 3533015), is one of Jakarta's finest Chinese-Indonesian restaurants, where the capital's rich and powerful go. It'll cost Rp10,000 pp for matchless Chinese food (the *best* frog legs!). **Istana Naga**, Jl. Jen. Gatot Subroto (Kav. 12 Case Bldg., tel. 511809), also has a good reputation. **Paramount**, Jl. Gondangdia Lama 35 (tel. 34311), open 7 days a week 1100-2100, is a family restaurant serving Cantonese-style food. The **Moon Palace**, Jl. Melawai VIII/15A (tel. 711765), Kebayoran, also has excellent Chinese food. The **Sky Room Permai**, Duta Merlin Shopping Centre 3-5 on Jl. Gajah Mada, features excellent *dim-sum* (Chinese breakfast or lunch). In Kota, the **Blue Ocean**, Jl. Hayam Wuruk 5 (tel. 366650), open daily 0700-1200, also serves up high quality *dim-sum*.

Seafood

In Glodok, the **Jun Nyan** on Jl. Batuceper 69 (off Jl. Hayam Wuruk), closed Mon. until 1800, is very possibly the best seafood restaurant in all SE Asia. Popular specialties include cracked crab with fantastic sauce, fried whole fish, boiled shrimp (Rp6000, serves 4), squid and frog legs in black sauce. Extremely fresh. Be sure to make a reservation (tel. 364063/364434). **Ratu Bahari**, Jl. Melawai VII/4 in Blok M (tel. 774115/370918), for sizzling Chinese seafood; another Ratu Bahari is on Jl. Batuceper 59 (tel. 370918).

Ethnic

Omar Khayam, Jl. Antara 5-7 across from GPO (tel. 356719), open 1200-1500/1830-2400, offers an extensive menu of Indian specialties. Buffet lunch every day (Rp4200). Jakarta's numerous Japanese restaurants are expensive, though less so than in the West. **Kikugawa,** Jl. Kebon Bintang III/13, Cikini (tel. 327198), near the Marco Polo Hotel, is very authentic, has beautiful surroundings, where you can eat superbly for Rp10,000 pp. Also check out the **Yoshiko,** Jl. Museum 1 (tel. 535479), and the **Okoh,** Horizon Hotel at Ancol (tel. 680008). For Korean food try the **Korean Tower,** Bank Bumi Daya Plaza (30th floor), Jl. Iman Bonjol, and the **Seoul House,** Jl. Telukbetung 38 (tel. 321817). Enjoy Thai food at the **Dijit Pochana,** Kompleks Kehutanan, Ground Floor, Jl. Jen. Gatot Subroto. To observe how the Colonel goes over in Indonesia, look in at the palatial **Kentucky Fried Chicken** on Jl. Agus Salim near Jl. Jaksa.

European Restaurants

Bavaria is a German restaurant in the Prince Centre Bldg. 3-4, Jl. Jen. Sudirman (tel. 586683). For inimitable Dutch colonial *rijstaffel,* try **Club Noordwijk,** Jl. Ir. H. Juanda 54 (tel. 353909); and **Art and Curio,** Jl. Kebon Binatang III/8A (near TIM), Cikini (tel. 322879). **George & Dragon** is an English pub a few minutes' walk from the Sheraton and the Kartika Plaza at Jl. Teluk Betung 32. Sip a Guinness while dining on cheese with pickles, or farmhouse liver pate. In Kebayoran, **Le Bistro,** Jl. Wahid Hasyim 75 (tel. 347475), serves excellent, expensive French food; live music. Enjoy Italian dishes at the **Rugantino,** Jl. Melawai Raya 28 (tel. 714727); and pizza at the several American **Pizza Huts** (in the Jakarta Theatre Bldg.), Jl. Thamrin 9, and at Jl. Lapangan Hijau 3 in Cilandak.

For an unbelievably wide-ranging breakfast, many of the hotels serve a morning all-you-can-eat buffet—a real pig out! Good ol' American hamburgers are available at **American Hamburger,** Jl. Melawai IV/17 inside Blok M in Kebayoran, open 1000-2000; their superburger costs Rp1200, cheeseburgers Rp1000. Burger urges can also be satisfied at the **American Embassy** if you have the right passport.

The Oasis

In a class of its own. This lavish restaurant, Jl. Raden Saleh 47, Kebayoran (tel. 347819), closed Sun., is decked out in true Casablanca style. A giant gong sounds your entrance as footmen dressed like Genghis Khan open the door. You are whisked into the grand dining rooms, where the service and surroundings make you feel like an honored diplomat at a state dinner! Originally the residence of a Dutch millionaire who died of starvation in a detention camp during the Japanese occupation. Fascinating photos in the main hall date from colonial times, and a fine collection of Irian Jaya artifacts lines the stairs by the door. An Italian garden with antique marble statues lies under stars and pine trees. Some Kalimantan carvings are for sale; Hendra paintings decorate the restaurant. Batak singers perform Tues., Thurs., and Sat. nights, providing unusual and delightful entertainment—a cross between black spirituals and flamenco music. The food is gourmet; flaming dishes prepared at your table are a house specialty. Reminiscent of pre-independence dinner clubs, 15-20 waiters and waitresses come up to your table in a long line, each with a different dish, ready to serve you as much as you want of anything. A *kampung ibu,* one of the best cooks in Jakarta, prepares the *rijstaffel* for which The Oasis is famous. Reservations recommended. Expect to spend US$20 pp.

ENTERTAINMENT

Jakarta has a full range of expensive and free, seductive and sedate, instructive and zany entertainments. Only in Jakarta can one attend a Batak tribal concert, a shadow puppet play, and an Irian Jaya dance performance all in the same week. Indonesian cultural events as well as Western-originated entertainments (except gambling) are well represented. Jakarta has at least 5 bowling alleys (more than in Amsterdam!). Near Jl. Jaksa is a bowling alley at Taman Ria Monas; another is at Ancol. Some Indonesians are expert bowlers; they have clubs and hold championships with prizes. Games cost about Rp1100 per, shoes Rp400 a pair. Marco Polo, Jl. Teuku Cik Ditiro 17-19 (only 5 min. SW of Taman Ismail Marzuki), has a pool open from 0700 to 1700 daily; entrance Rp500. Jai alai, the fastest game in the world, takes place at Ancol nightly at 1900.

Ancol

A mammoth 551-ha family park for round-the-clock entertainment. Probably the largest amusement complex in SE Asia, this shoreline resort lies 10 km from downtown on the bay between Jakarta and Tanjung Priok. If you're already in Kota, you could easily visit Ancol at the same time. From the stanplatz near Jembatan Dua, get an *oplet* for Rp300 to Ancol or take a bus from Tanjung Priok. Entrance Rp600 weekdays, Rp1000 on weekends. Avoid the park on weekends if you don't like crowds. Jakarta's only waterfront hotel, the expensive **Horizon,** is here. There's an exhausting array of diversions: a 40-lane bowling alley, huge swimming pool complexes (including a wave-making machine!) with 20-m-long fiberglass slides, SE Asia's only oceanarium where trained dolphins, sea lions, and penguins perform. Horseback riding, a drive-in theater, go-cart tracks, an 18-hole golf course and driving ranges are available, plus nightclubs and all classes of restaurants galore (superb fish dinners). In the oceanarium, take the canal ride through a mini zoo of different varieties of water birds, turtles, and crocodiles. Beyond Ancol by the sea is a haunting civilian graveyard, Ereveld ("Field of Honor"), for those killed during the Japanese occupation.

NIGHTLIFE

The best discos, where flashy young Indonesians flock on weekends, include the plush **Ebony Videoteque** at the Kuningan Plaza Bldg., Jl. Rasunsaid, but brace yourself for the Rp20,000 cover for their Sat. night floorshow! The latest is **The Parrots,** a 4-story restaurant and discoteque on Jl. Wahid Hasyim which caters to all ages (Rp5500 for 1st drink). Down the street is **Faces,** another videoteque which also has live performances. **My Place,** in the Panin Bldg. on Jl. Jen. Sudirman, has some of the most innovative programs (Rp8000 weekdays, Rp12,000 weekends). The venerable old **Jaya Pub,** behind the Jaya Bldg. roughly across from the Sarinah Dept. Store on Jl. Thamrin, is a nice piano bar featuring music and a relaxed atmosphere (usually no cover) where artists, writers, musicians, and filmmakers hang out. It claims to be the only pub in Jakarta where you can take your wife, girlfriend, or mother-in-law and still enjoy. Still popular with expats is the dimly lit 17-year-old **Tanamur,** Jl. Tanah Abang Timur 14; bouncing to good music nightly and always crowded (Rp5000-7000). A rowdy time can be had at the **George & Dragon Pub** on a side road (Jl. Telukbetung) off Jl. Thamrin, between Hotel Kartika and Hotel Indonesia. **Bina Ria,** a recreation area on Jakarta's N shore inside the great Ancol Complex, is frequented by young lovers. If you invite your girl to Bina Ria and she says yes, it's understood what's going to happen. Unlit tents rent for Rp2000. Prostitutes ply their trade here after 2000.

Banci

Jakarta's "sister boys"—female impersonators and transsexuals—are a phenomenon going back to at least 1947. Decked out in sleek dresses, they look like beautiful women. *Banci* hang out at Tamang Lawang near Kartika Plaza, and at Hotel Indonesia in the evenings. A neat thing to do is go and laugh and joke with the *banci* in the Taman Lawang (Menteng) area, then afterwards dine in special nearby *warung* on potent aphrodisiacal goats' testicles *(sate terpedo)* which will fortify you for another round with the *banci*. Other *banci* cruise Kebayoran, Jatinegara, and Slipi. The *banci* of Jatinegara and Slipi could be pickpockets. Transvestites also hang out in the Jl. Kendal area and around the foodstalls on Jl. Mangga Besar off Jl. Hayam Wuruk in N. Jakarta. Homosexuality here is forbidden by the government but a special bar is allowed: Discoteque Isabela on Jl. Hayam Wuruk, Rp3000 cover.

Amusement Parks

Taman Ria MONAS, on the SW corner of Merdeka Square within easy walking distance of Jl. Jaksa, features a playground, carnival rides (Rp500), several restaurants, band performances. Open Mon. to Sat. 1700-2300, Sun. and holidays 0900-2400. Entrance Rp500. Pretty tame, half empty even on weekends. Livelier is Takara Kiddy Land, Tomang Plaza, Jl. Kyai Tapa, a family recreational a/c park with over 100 "rides"—both places perfect for young kids. Fantasy Land is a 9.5-ha kids' entertainment park inside Ancol Dreamland.

PERFORMING ARTS

Try to catch the drama and music indigenous only to Jakarta: *kroncong* groups (Portuguese influence), *terbangan* (Islamic music adapted to Indonesian culture), and *Lenong,* a comic satirical play accompanied by the *gambeng kromong,* Jakarta's traditional *gamelan* orchestra. Traditional Sundanese folk theater performances are staged at the authentic **Teater Miss Tjihtjih,** Jl. Kapal (near Cempaka Putih). *Gamelan* performances are held at the **Wayang Museum,** Jl. Pintu Besar in Kota, on Sun. at 1000 for Rp500. Also catch the hilarious comedy shows at **Sri Mulat** in Taman Ria Remaja in Slipi—pure Javanese *Ketoprak*-style slapstick. At Ancol's **Pasar Seni** each evening, *gamelan,* punk concerts, and occasional cultural shows featuring dancers and musicians from throughout Indonesia are staged, Rp500. The **School of Folk Art** in the Faculty of Fine Arts, National University of Indonesia, is at Bakti Budaya, Jl. Bunga 5, Jatinegara near Jl. Matraman Raya; see teachers and students playing Cirebon-style *gamelan,* Sundanese traditional dancing, *suling* orchestras, and *wayang topeng, kulit* and *golek* puppet theater. Performances at 1100 every day except Sundays. Watch the newspapers for announcements and schedules. At **Taman Mini Indonesia** (open 0900-1700 each day) are dances and cultural performances on Sundays. This park is in Pondok Gede in E. Jakarta near Halim Airport; take a bus from downtown to Cililitan, then a *bemo* to Taman Mini. At the **National Museum** nearby are excellent Javanese *gamelan* concerts one or 2 Sun. mornings a month at 1000-1100; Rp300. At **Bharata Theatre,** (also called Gedung Bharata) Jl. Kali Lio, 15 near Pasar Senen. *Wayang Orang Bharata* (dance drama) shows are staged Tues., Wed., Fri., and Sat. 2000-2300. *Ketoprak* performances are put on Mon. and Thurs. tickets cost Rp2500 for front seats, Rp1200 for back seats. Packed with Javanese—abundant local color.

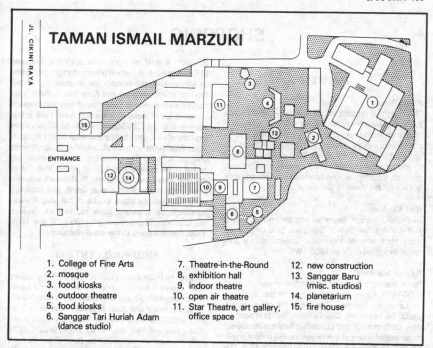

TAMAN ISMAIL MARZUKI

JL. CIKINI RAYA

ENTRANCE

1. College of Fine Arts
2. mosque
3. food kiosks
4. outdoor theatre
5. food kiosks
6. Sanggar Tari Huriah Adam (dance studio)
7. Theatre-in-the-Round
8. exhibition hall
9. indoor theatre
10. open air theatre
11. Star Theatre, art gallery, office space
12. new construction
13. Sanggar Baru (misc. studios)
14. planetarium
15. fire house

Taman Ismail Marzuki (TIM)

The Jakarta Arts Center. At Jl. Cikini Raya 73, this is Jakarta's "Lincoln Center"—a big complex of theaters, exhibition halls, and galleries, with performances almost every night of the year. Get TIM's monthly program from their box office, shops, travel agencies, Jakarta Visitor's Center, or from most large hotels or embassies. The cultural showcase of the nation, TIM sponsors an incredible variety of Indonesian and international cultural events: from avant-garde ballet to Australian rock bands, from harp concerts to Ibsen plays in Indonesian. Open daily from 0800-2000. Planetarium open Tues. to Sun. at 2000. Admission Rp100. Take a Manggarai bus from Lapangan Banteng; or catch this same bus from the Jl. Jaksa area as it heads down Jl. Merdeka Timur.

FOREIGN CULTURAL CENTERS

A number of developed nations maintain cultural centers in Jakarta, serving as showcases for the host country's arts, science, and literature. Most are open to the public (small fee) and feature well-stocked libraries (in the native language of the center), often with spacious reading rooms, plus snack bars, concert halls, art galleries. All publish monthly programs of upcoming cultural and educational events, offer language instruction, sporting activities, audio-visual and film showings, frequent art and cultural exhibitions. Go here to read newspapers and mags from home for free. Ask the Tourist Information Center for addresses of any cultural centers not given below. **addresses:** The old Dutch colonial days are back once you enter **Erasmus Huis,** the Dutch Cultural Center at Jl. Rasuna Said (next to the Dutch Embassy), tel. 352047. In fact, they never left. Disco, reading and film rooms, garden, fantastic art books collection. The **Indonesian-American Cultural Center,** Jl. Pramuka Kav. 30, Jakarta Timur (tel. 881241), offers a vast array of American-style activities and facilities. Watch a video of the American president addressing Congress. **Goethe Institut,** Jl. Mataram Raya 23, Jakarta Timur (tel. 882798), shows films by Fassbinder to exhibits from Dusseldorf; also German language lessons. **Centre Cultural Francais** is at Jl. Salemba Raya 25 (tel. 882284). The **British Council,** Widjoyo Building, Jl. Jen. Sudirman 56 (tel. 586749/587854), contains a comprehensive collection of films, cassettes, and audio-visual materials. The **Australian Cultural Centre,** in the Citibank Bldg. on Jl. Thamrin (tel. 884306), has extensive holdings in anthropology, history, and sociology of SE Asia; open Mon. to Thurs. 0900-1400, Fri. until 1200.

SHOPPING

MARKETS

Pasar Seni

This delightful outdoor art fair at Ancol, open 24 hours a day, is a permanent setting for working artists and craftsmen from every corner of the archipelago. Like art markets everywhere, some high-quality items but also a lot of junk. Good prices. Each stall is numbered so you can return to make purchases once you've seen them all. Excellent seafood restaurants abound; stick around for the evening live music concert.

Bird Markets

All the bird markets *(pasar burung)* are on Jl. Pramuka in the Matraman district. See birds (and other small pets) from all over Indonesia. Sellers usually only speak Indonesian. Open 0800-1800.

Flower Markets

Rawa Belong is Jakarta's largest flower market, open 0300-1600. A new one has opened on Sat. and Sun. on Lapangan Banteng. The place for photo enthusiasts. For bouquets, Cikini's Pasar Bunga is best. Indonesia Permai (Orchid Garden) in Slipi is a 35,000-sq-m garden with one of the largest orchid collections in SE Asia; take a bus to Grogol then down to Slipi. The Orchid Nursery in Cipete displays hundreds of different kinds of orchids. Buy orchid seedlings or whole flowering plants. In the mini laboratory see botanists cross-fertilize specimens. Open daily 0800-1800.

Fabrics, Clothes:

Tanah Abang, Jl. H. Fakhrudin, is the heart of Jakarta's textile operation. **Pasar Baru** is in a N. Indian neighborhood near the G.P.O., one of Jakarta's oldest and most popular markets, selling just about everything, but best for fabrics. *Batik* cloth and garments are sold in all the city's *pasar*, particularly in Blok M, Senen, and Glodok. The price depends on your bargaining skill. The *batik* in the **Batik Keris** shop in Sarinah is generally high quality; one of the largest selections in Indonesia. For boutiques and ready-to-wear garments, style and quality vary sharply and sizes seldom conform to U.S. standards. Avoid high-priced imported apparel. Boutiques usually offer alteration and custom tailoring; most accept credit cards. Many small clothing shops are on Jl. Agus Salim in Menteng, Blok M in Kebayoran, and on Jl. Pasar Baru in Kota. Visit the boutique of Iwan Tirta (Jl. Panarukan 25), Indonesia's foremost *batik* designer.

Miscellaneous

Cassette tapes used to be a real bargain, but since Soeharto signed an agreement with the European EEC and the U.S.A., which gives copyright protection to songwriters, the bottom has dropped out of this market. Many Jakartan and Kuta Beach shops have thrived selling pirated cassettes of pop and classical music at US$1 apiece, but since June 1988 prices have risen to the US$3-5 range. Blok M still has some big tape shops, and there are several others along Jl. Agus Salim (just up from Jl. Jaksa) with comprehensive collections. The classiest jewelry pieces are found in the hotel shops at high prices. Visit the Indonesia Jaya Crocodile Farm in Pluitt where you may buy goods made from snake, lizard, and crocodile skin. No quantity stock on hand but they'll make handbags, belts, wallets, vests, etc. to order. On Sun. the Crocodile Show is put on 1100-1300 and 1500-1700. Sample lizard in the small restaurant.

SHOPPING CENTERS

See all the Indonesian yuppies in action! Big department stores have fixed prices (a relief after a heavy day of bargaining!), but they also have a wide variety of goods under one roof. And they tend to be honest—you'll get what you pay for. The various municipal *pasar* and their *toko* (small shops) usually go by their city section name: Senen, Pasar Baru, Blok M, etc. Also check out the **Ratu Plaza**, Jl. Jen. Sudirman, **Griya Mataram**, Jl. Mataram Raya 46-48; **Hayam Wuruk Plaza**, Jl. Hayam Wuruk, and **Gajah Mada Plaza**, Jl. Gajah Mada. Great bargains in these a/c shopping complexes, and they are a welcome refuge from the heat. **Blok M** in the elite suburb Kebayoran Baru offers a myriad of shops selling everything under the tropical sun. The **Sarinah Jaya** complex here is the "new" Sarinah; also visit the 3-story a/c **Aldiron Plaza** on Jl. Melawai inside Blok M, next to the *pasar* (open 0900-2000)—a modern shopping center with an index on each floor above the escalators. **Pasar Senen** is a well-planned shopping complex near central Jakarta specializing in housewares and daily needs, going since 1733! Although the prices are generally quite reasonable, still haggle.

Glodok And Pasar Pagi

Jakarta's Chinatown. Good prices. The 6-story Glodok Shopping Centre, on Jl. Pinangsia, near the train station, is a clean, modern, multi-story shopping complex; open 0900-1200/1600-2000. Glodok Plaza, Jl. Pinangsia, is 5 stories of a/c shops. Pasar Pagi Shopping Centre, a km NE of Glodok Shopping Centre, offers mostly small wares and textiles which are generally cheaper than in other markets.

Sarinah

Near the Jl. Jaksa area on the corner of Jl. Thamrin and Jl. Wahid Hasyim, open daily 0900-1800 (tel. 351412/351421). Operated by the government, Sarinah was named after a valued maidservant of Sukarno's. Like an Indonesian Macy's, it has everything from Borneo *parang* and coral jewelry to *batik* slippers and Batak woodcarvings. A visit to this well-organized department store is sure to satisfy your shopping fantasies. Since it has the best selection of traditional-type goods available, Sarinah is a good place for the newcomer to acquaint himself with what is available, but at rather high, fixed prices. Hunt for bargains! Most clerks speak some English. Don't miss the Batik Center on the 4th floor with its special salesroom for *batik tulis,* very complete and fairly priced.

Bookstores

In Kebayoran, **Gramedia**, Jl. Gajah Mada 109 (tel. 274397), has Jakarta's best collection of English books and magazines. Other Gramedia Bookshops are at Jl. Melawai IX and at Jl. Pintu Air 72 in Pasar Baru. **Gunung Agung** is the largest bookstore chain in Indonesia. The huge Jakarta branch, Jl. Kwitang 8, near Pasar Senen and Monas (tel. 346069/344678), sells cassettes, magazines, maps, etc. The whole 4th floor of Pasar Senen, one km E of Monas, consists of bookshops. Some of the best bookstores are in Blok M shopping center in Kebayoran Baru. Foreign books and magazines are quite dear *(Herald Tribune, Rp2500l)* and newspapers arrive a few days late. Purchase them at most of the international-class hotels such as Hotel Borobudur and the Mandarin (which also have excellent sections of English books on Indonesia).

ARTS AND CRAFTS

Although Yogya's sidewalk vendors and shops are better and cheaper places to shop for crafts, Jakarta's outlets contain crafts from all over this 4,200-km-wide archipelago (though often at prices 5 times what they would be in their place of origin). Notable are the 30-40 boutiques of the Jakarta Hilton's Indonesian Bazaar, and the 200 kiosks of Ancol's Arts Market, Pasar Seni, where you can see artists at work. Because of the heat, shops close in the afternoon and reopen in the evening.

Art Galleries

Not only galleries but also hotels, banks, clubs, and restaurants exhibit and sell works of art; the artist could even be on hand to discuss special orders with you. Modern Indonesian painting exhibitions are usually on at Balai Budaya, Jl. Gereja Theresia, behind Sarinah Dept. Store; the free exhibitions change weekly. TIM, Jl. Cikini Raya 73, often displays modern In-

JAKARTA

(MAP ON NEXT PAGE)

1. Cipete Orchid Nursery
2. Blok M/bookstore
3. Blok M/bus terminal
4. Museum Abri Satriamandala
5. Jakarta Handicraft Center
6. Taman Ria Remaja
7. Ria Loka Istana Anggrek
8. Museum Tekstil
9. Hotel Indonesia
10. Sarinah Department Store
11. Jalan Surabaya (antiques)
12. Cikini Fruit Market
13. Oasis Restaurant
14. Gedung Pola
15. Manggarai Train Station
16. Taman Anggrek Ragunan
17. Taman Margasatwa Ragunan
18. Pasar Burung
19. Cililitan Bus Terminal
20. Kampung Melayu Bus Terminal
21. Jatinegara Train Station
22. Rawamangun Bus Terminal
23. Taman Anggrek
24. Kalideres Bus Terminal
25. Taman Buaya Indonesia Jaya
26. Museum Bahari
27. Sundakelapa/Pasar Ikan
28. Glodok Building Shopping Center
29. Glodok Plaza Shopping Center
30. Museum Wayang
31. Museum Jakarta
32. Kota Train Station
33. Balai Seni Rupa Jakarta
34. Kota Bus Terminal
35. Hayam Wuruk Plaza
36. Duta Merlin Shopping Arcade
37. Museum Nasional
38. Taman Ria
39. MONAS
40. Gambir Train Station
41. Pasar Baru
42. Lapangan Banten Bus Terminal
43. Borobudur Hotel
44. Senen Train Station
45. Senen Shopping Center
46. Gunung Agung Bookstore
47. Ancol, Pasar Seni
48. Tanjung Priok Train Station
49. Tanjung Priok Bus Terminal

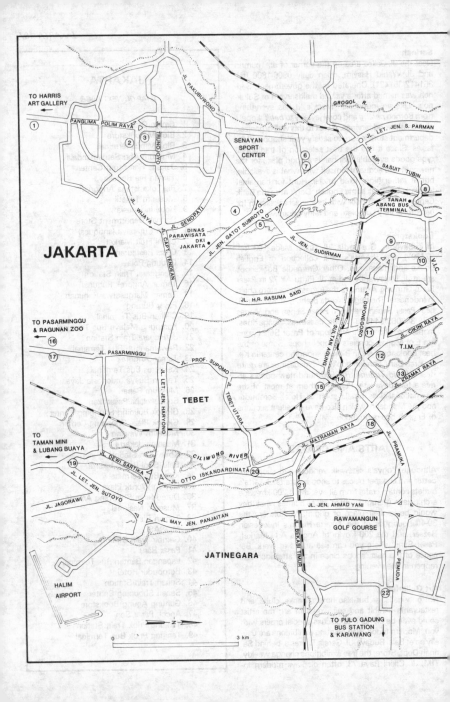

JAKARTA

TO HARRIS
ART GALLERY

① PANGLIMA POLIM RAYA

② ③ JL. TRUNOJOYO

JL. PAKUBUWONO

GROGOL R.

JL. LET. JEN. S. PARMAN

JL. AIP SASUIT TUBIN

SENAYAN
SPORT
CENTER

⑥
⑦

TANAH
ABANG BUS
TERMINAL

⑧

④

JL. WIJAYA

JL. CAPT. TENDEAN

JL. SENOPATI

DINAS
PARAWISATA
DKI JAKARTA

JL. JEN. GATOT SUBROTO

⑤

JL. JEN. SUDIRMAN

⑨

JL. DIPONEGORO

⑩ V.I.C.

JL. H.R. RASUMA SAID

JL. SULTAN AGUNG

JL. CIKINI RAYA

⑪

T.I.M.

⑫

JL. KRAMAT RAYA

⑬

TO PASARMINGGU
& RAGUNAN ZOO

⑯

⑰ JL. PASARMINGGU

JL. PROF. SUPOMO

JL. LET. JEN. HARYONO

TEBET

JL. TEBET UTARA

⑮ ⑭

JL. MATRAMAN RAYA

⑱

JL. PRAMUKA

TO
TAMAN MINI
& LUBANG BUAYA

JL. DEWI SARTIKA

⑲

CILIWUNG RIVER

JL. OTTO ISKANDARDINATA

⑳

JL. LET. JEN. SUTOYO

JL. JAGORAWI

㉑

JL. JEN. AHMAD YANI

RAWAMANGUN
GOLF COURSE

JL. MAY. JEN. PANJAITAN

JATINEGARA

JL. BEKASI TIMUR

JL. PEMUDA

HALIM
AIRPORT

㉒

TO PULO GADUNG
BUS STATION
& KARAWANG

N

0   3 km

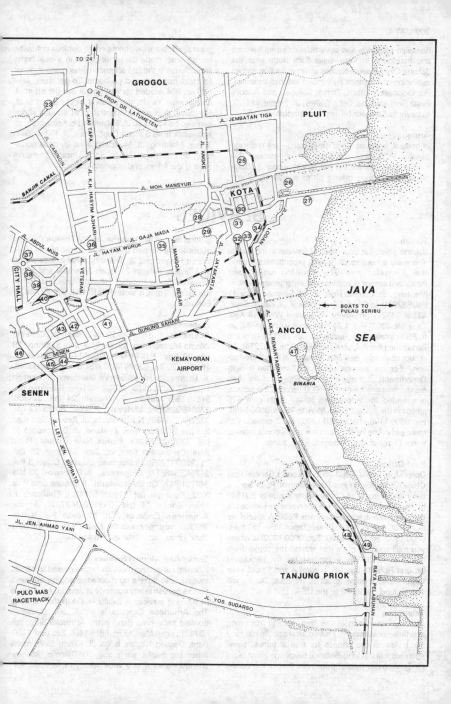

donesian paintings and advertises on street banners and handouts. In Kota, Balai Seni Rupa near the Jakarta City Museum houses an art collection and an exhibition of paintings by famous Indonesian artists. For Indonesian kitsch, Taman Suropati and Ancol's Pasar Seni are tops. Oet's Gallery, Jl. Palatehan 1/33, Kebayoran Baru, for brilliant contemporary work.

Antiques

In general, antiques—and other crafts—are really expensive in Jakarta. Jakarta's densely packed flea market stretches for several blocks along Jl. Surabaya. These shops offer a bit of everything. Some great finds, but many items are of dubious antiquity, having been made the week before in a local crafts shop. Arrive in the late afternoon when vendors want to make last sales and go home. To get there, take bus no. 804 headed for Manggarai and get off at Jl. Mohammed Yamin, then walk 4 blocks down to Jl. Surabaya. A pricier concentration of antique shops can also be found at: Jl. Palatehan I in Kebayoran, an easy walk from Sarinah Dept. Store; Jl. Kebon Sirih Timur, Menteng; Jl. Majapahit, Kota (antique porcelain); and Jl. Gajah Mada, Kota. Unearth treasures among the fakery and hopeless discards.

SERVICES

Health

Jakarta offers the best medical services in Indonesia. There are a number of general practitioners around the Jl. Jakasa area. The following *rumah sakit* (hospitals) accept outpatient and emergency cases: in Menteng, St. Carolus Hospital, Jl. Salemba Raya 41 (tel. 882981); in Cikini, Cikini Hospital, Jl. Raden Saleh 40 (tel. 349211); in Grogol, RS Sumber Waras, Jl. Kyai Tapa (tel. 396011). For 24-hour emergency service, go to RS Fatmawati, Jl. Fatmawati (tel. 760121-4); or the Pertamina Hospital, Jl. Kyai Maja 29 (tel. 707214). All accept cash only. See also "Health" in the "Introduction." For inoculations, the Dinas Kesehatan (Health Department), Jl. Kesehatan 10 in Grogol, offers cholera vaccinations for only Rp5000 because this service is intended for Indonesians (these shots cost $25 apiece in the States). Open Mon. to Thurs. 0800-1400, Fri. 0800-1100, Sat. 0800-1300, Sun. closed. Get there early. The Health Port near the airport's International Terminal also dispenses inoculations.

Post Offices

Open Mon. to Sat. 0800-1600, Jakarta's General Post Office (GPO), Kantor Pos Pusat, is on Jl. Pasar Baru, a 6-min. walk from the Chainbreaker statue or Rp1500 by *bajai* from Jl. Jaksa. Their *post restante* service is a bit disorganized; each letter costs Rp50. A special annex on Jl. Pos, called Pos Paket (open Mon. to Thurs. 0800-1300, Fri. 0800-1100, Sat. 0800-1300) is where you mail packages; it's just around the corner from the main GPO. Pay a modest fee for packaging (around Rp500—bargain, naturally) and fill out your forms (Rp400); allow about 30 minutes. Ten kg will cost around Rp28,900 to the USA.

Telephone

Although improving all the time, it's still frustrating and time-consuming to make a local call (Rp100 for 3 min.). Ask to use phones for free at hotels, travel agencies, bars. A long-distance telephone office (Kantor Telekommunikasi), open round the clock, is on the ground floor of the high-rise Jakarta Theatre Building opposite the Sarinah Dept. Store on the corner of Jl. Wahid Hasyim and Jl. Thamrin. Other offices are on Jl. Merdeka Selatan 21 (open 24 hours) and in the Jayakarta Tower Hotel, Jl. Hayam Wuruk 126. To call the States, 3 min. is around Rp13,650; slightly less for Europe.

Embassies

Australia, Jl. Thamrin 15 (tel. 359611); **Canada**, Wisma Metropolitan, 5th floor, Jl. Jen. Sudirman 29 Kav. 29, Box 52/JKT (tel. 510709/514022); **France**, Jl. Thamrin 20 (tel. 332807/332375); **United Kingdom**, Jl. Thamrin 75 (tel. 33094); **W. Germany**, Jl. Thamrin 1 (tel. 323908); **India**, Jl. Rasuna Said, Kuningan (tel. 518150/52); **Japan**, Jl. Thamrin 24 (tel. 324308/324948/325396); **Malaysia**, Jl. Iman Bonjol 17 (tel. 332170/336438); **Netherlands**, Jl. Rasuna Said Kav. S-3 (tel. 511515); **New Zealand**, Jl. Diponegoro 41 (tel. 330552/330620); **Papua New Guinea**, Panin Bank Centre, 6th floor, Jl. Jen. Sudirman 29 (tel. 711218/711225); **Philippines**, Jl. Iman Bonjol 9 (tel. 347942/348917); **Singapore**, Jl. Proklamasi 23 (tel. 348761/347783); **Switzerland**, Jl. Rasuna Said Blok X/32, Kuningan (tel. 516061/517451); **Thailand**, Jl. Iman Bonjol 74 (tel. 349180/343762). At the **American Embassy**, Jl. Merdeka Sel. 5 (tel. 360360), you may read the *Herald Tribune*, the *New York Times*, etc. in the a/c reading room.

Banks And Moneychangers

Indonesia is getting more and more geared to handle tourists, and there's no problem changing traveler's checks or cash in any currency in Jakarta. A full range of banking services is available. Go in the morning. The **American Express** is on Jl. Jen. Sudirman (toward Kebayoran Baru) in the Arthaloka Bldg. (tel. 587401); open Mon. to Fri. 0815-1400, Sat. until 1100. Bank Dagang Negara is on Jl. Kebon Sirih; many other big banks are along Jl. Thamrin. Moneychangers also offer a wide variety of services. P.T.

Ayumas Gunung Agung, Jl. Kwitang 24 (near Jl. Jaksa), consistently gives good rates. Also check P.T. Trisrikandi, Jl. Alaydrus 60 (tel. 362232/365428); and P.T. Sinar Iriawan, Jl. Irian 3-5 (tel. 345605/351115).

Photography

Jalan Agus Salim, 5 min.-walk up from Jl. Jaksa and parallel with Jl. Thamrin, has several well-stocked photo supply and film processing shops. Sakurafilm color prints cost around Rp200 apiece and take only an hour if they're not busy. For bulk slide processing, the central Kodak lab is in Blok M (any photo store knows where it is), but for small quantities the Kodak counter in the Hero Supermarket, Jl. Gondangdilama, Menteng (beside the Menteng Hotel) is quite adequate. Cost of Kodak processing, Rp2500; prints Rp200 each.

Immigration

The Directorate General of Immigration, Jl. Teuku Umar, Menteng 1 (tel. 349811/349812), is the head office for all of Indonesia—where the buck stops. Ironically, it's often easier to get a break here than in most *imigrasi* offices as you can see the right person (after perhaps a 1½-hour wait). Open Mon. to Thurs. 0800-1400, Fri. 0800-1200, Sat. 0800-1400; closed Sundays. To get processed relatively quickly, get there *early* in the day when the doors open.

Tourist Information

The Visitor Information Center (VIC) at Soekarno/Hatta Airport is open 0800-2000, closed Sunday. The city's big VIC is in the Jakarta Theater Bldg., opposite Sarinah Dept. Store on Jl. Wahid Hasyim (tel. 354094/364093); their info is limited to the Jakarta area. Open Mon. to Thurs. 0800-1500, Fri. 0800-1130, Sat. 0800-1400. They hand out free theme-oriented maps and train schedules, but you have to ask specifically for what you want. The Director General of Tourism carries helpful info on all of Indonesia; the office is way out on Jl. Kramet Raya 81; open Sun. to Thurs. 0800-1500, Fri. 0800-1130, Sat. 0800-1400. Get the Falk City Map of Jakarta (the best) for Rp9500 at any major hotel or bookstore.

TRANSPORTATION

GETTING THERE

By Air

Indonesia's principal gateway, Jakarta is served by 14 carriers direct from Europe, SE Asia, the Orient, the Indian subcontinent, the South Pacific, and a new direct service from Los Angeles. Jakarta is only an hour by air from Singapore and 4 hours from Hong Kong. **arriving:** At the new superdeluxe Soekarno/Hatta Airport porters in yellow shirts will want to carry your bags, but this is up to you. Grab a free baggage cart. A new toll road connects the airport, 13 km W of the city, to downtown. Although taxi drivers will approach you right away for a fare, blue-striped Damri buses with a/c and reclining seats leave regularly from right in front of the airport terminals for only Rp2000, 40 minutes. Running from 0300 to 2200, these fast comfortable buses take passengers to all major sections of Jakarta: Kemayoran, Rawamangun, Blok M, and Gambir (closest to the Jl. Jaksa hotels). From Soekarno/Hatta, taxi drivers want Rp15,000 (30 min.). If you want to avoid Jakarta altogether, take a Bluebird taxi all the way to Cililitan Station (about Rp20,000) where you can board a bus further to Bandung or Yogya and leave Jakarta behind you in about one hour flat.

By Sea

Pelni ships dock at Tanjung Priok (E of the city), Dock no. 1, which is 2 km from the Tanjung Priok Bus Sta-

tion from where you board bus no. 63 (Rp200) which runs the remaining 18 km into the center of the city. Or share a taxi with several people, Rp15,000; ask to go through Kota (Chinatown) on the way.

By Train And Bus

Five major train stations serve Jakarta. If arriving at Senen Station, walk up to the corner of Jl. Kramat Raya and Jl. Kwitang and take bus nos. 913 or 40 (Rp200) to the hotel area of Jl. Jaksa. Or, if overburdened, hire a *bajai* (Rp1500-2500) from the train station to your hotel. If arriving at Cililitan Bus Station, take a Patas 13 (Rp350) or Patas 3 bus to Sarinah Dept. Store, then walk down to Jl. Jaksa.

GETTING AROUND

Indonesia's premier city—sprawling, bustling, congested—is a bitch to get around in. It's 25 km N to S, hot and muggy, and hardly any non-Indonesian ever walks. And even if you charter an a/c sedan or hire a taxi, the traffic is horrendous and you crawl to your destination. Streets maddeningly change names every 2-3 blocks. Be patient. Buy Falk's *Street Directory of Jakarta* at any good bookshop or major hotel (Rp9500). Lay low from 1200 to 1600 or collapse from heat exhaustion.

By Bus

The city has at least 20 private bus companies which

all charge a Rp200 flat fare. All over Jakarta there are bus stations—Pintu Air (near the G.P.O. in Pasar Baru), Grogol, Tg. Priok, Kota, Blok M, etc.—from where you can take buses in every direction. Buses have signboards stating their ultimate destination, but it helps to know the city. Cheap and plentiful, these buses are also crowded, difficult to board or to see where you're going. Avoid travel during the peak commuting hours of 0700-0830 and 1600-1730. Watch for pickpockets and Jakarta's "bus gangs" of 6-7 youths who surround unwary travelers, slashing packs with razors and stealing everything of value—even moneybelts! Wisma Delima now posts a sign urging travelers to avoid bus nos. 70 and 700 from Sarinah to Kota/Pasar Ikan; they suggest taking the Rp350 Patas 1 or 11 instead. To avoid these rip-offs: 1) enter through the front door only; 2) sit or stand up front; 3) travel with at least one other person; 4) stand clear of groups of young men. **Patas:** These smaller buses have better security because they don't accept standing passengers and they stop where you want. If you want to get from say Kota to Grogol real fast, take a Patas bus and pay the little bit extra (Rp350 per ride) for the security and peace of mind.

Bajai, Becak

The *bajai* is Jakarta's motorized equivalent of the *becak,* costing about Rp500 per km. Split between 3 people, these gutsy, smelly rattletraps can be almost as inexpensive as city buses though much faster. Like agile ants, they weave and sputter in and out of traffic. *Bajai* can also be hired by the hour for around Rp3000—the poor man's taxi—but are prohibited on some main thoroughfares of the city such as Jl. Thamrin and Jl. Kuningan. Don't expect the drivers to speak English or to have change for large bills. *Always* bargain the fare in advance. For short hops, the *becak* (a 3-wheeled pedicab) offers inexpensive, convenient transport on the fringes of the city or inside *kampung.* Many main streets of the city are forbidden to *becak* during daylight hours.

Taxis, Rental Cars

The safest and most convenient form of transport. Though painfully expensive, licensed ones are usually metered and charge the standard fare (President Taxis don't use meters). Taxis can also be hired on an hourly basis (about Rp4000). Private taxis, such as in front of the Jakarta Theatre Building, can be hired for even less if you bargain. Both types of taxis can be hired from taxi stands, parking areas located throughout the city, major hotels, or flagged down on the street. Meter charges on taxis run Rp500 for the first km and about Rp300 for each additional ½ km or each 50 seconds of waiting time. Licensed radio cabs can also be summoned by telephone: **Bluebird,** Jl. H.O.S. Cokroaminoto (tel. 325607) is the most reli-

able; another good one is **President Taxi,** Jl. Jen. A. Yani (tel. 411354). **rental cars: Avis,** P.T. Multi Sri Service Corp., Jl. Diponegoro 25 (tel. 341964/ 349206/882014); **Hertz,** Jl. Thamrin (Hotel Mandarin), tel. 371208/321307; **National,** Hotel Kartika Plaza, ground floor, Jl. Thamrin 10 (tel. 332849/ 322006).

FROM JAKARTA BY BUS

Go to the bus station that's closest to your destination: if you're heading E (Yogya, Surabaya), get to the Pulo Gadung Terminal—the most easterly bus station. Likewise, buses to the S (Bogor, Bandung) leave from the southernmost station, Cililitan (Patas 3 or 13 buses from Jl. Thamrin). Kalideres which has westerly buses to Merak, Labuhan, Sumatra. Get to Kalideres by taking bus no. 913 from in front of Stasiun Gambir, Rp200. It's also possible to take a bus out to the Soekarno/Hatta Airport from Kalideres for only Rp200 but it takes 2 hours. All bus stations can be reached by local buses (Rp200) from around Gambir Station, and none of the city's stations is more than Rp10,000 by metered taxi from the Jl. Jaksa area. Long-distance buses leave Jakarta daily 1600-1800 for Semarang, Solo, and Yogya. **to Bogor:** Jakarta-Bogor costs Rp600 (40 min.), departing Cililitan Station about every 15 minutes. Another bus station has just been opened, Lebak Buluk, to relieve the congestion at Cililitan. Lebak Buluk has buses only to Bogor (via Parung). Trains for Bogor leave Gambir Station 25-minute walk from Jl. Jaksa); 1½ hours. **to Bandung:** Take the bus—better views than the train. However, buses to Bandung on Sun. and holidays because of heavy traffic don't go over the Puncak Pass but travel via Sukabumi. If leaving for Bandung in the morning, get seats on the R side of the bus (to avoid the sun), and if leaving in the afternoon sit on the left side. You get reclining DC-9 seats, snacks, and newspaper (in Indonesian). Buses leave for Bandung every 20 min. around the clock, and take 3½ hours; via Puncak, Rp2000; via Sukabumi, Rp2500. A faster, more comfortable but expensive way to get to nearby cities (such as Bandung) is to take a long-distance taxi or chartered minibus which will pick you up at your hotel and drop you at your destination. Call Media, Jl. Johar 15 (tel. 343643); Parahiyangan, Jl. K.H. Wahid Hasyim 13 (tel. 353434/ 350124); and "4848," Jl. Kramat Raya 23 (tel. 357656). These companies charge about Rp9000 to Bandung in a minibus (10 people). **to Yogya:** The best company is Raya (via Salatiga-Magelang), Jl. Alydrus 13 (tel. 372246), and Dewi Jaya, Jl. Sawah Besar 13 (tel. 6494916/6491973). Both charge Rp13,000 and leave at 1600-1700 every day. **to Surabaya:** Costs Rp7000-8000. Buses start from Pulo Gadung's night bus terminal.

Other Fares

Buses to C. and E. Java depart from the Pulo Gadung Station, located where Jl. Perintis Kemerdekaan meets Jl. Bekasi Timur Raya. To Cirebon, Rp3600; Semarang, Rp7000; Tasikmalaya via Sukabumi and Garut, Rp2800; Banjar, around Rp3200; Pekalongan, Rp3800. From Kalideres, buses to Merak and Banten, Rp1200; Labuhan, Rp1500; Cilegon, Rp1200; Rangkasbitung, Rp1100.

Night Buses

All express night bus *(bis malam kilat)* passengers leaving the city for the longer hauls can go to the bus company's office or wait for the next bus leaving from any of the terminals. It's best to reserve your seat in advance, although you can usually get a seat if you just show up. Prices depend on the company, the age of the bus, and the route. Some buses are a/c, most are direct, with 1-2 stops for food and a break. Travel time by *bis malam* and trains is about the same. For the latest best bus companies, the Jakarta Visitor's Center gives out good advice.

To Bali

There are special a/c buses to Denpasar. Buy your ticket at Continental Ekspres, Jl. Antara, Pasar Baru (5 min. walk from the G.P.O.); Lorena, Jl. Hasim Ashari. Costs Rp32,000; 32 hours. Passengers receive a *nasi padang* and a drink along the way. Buses leave at about 1630 from the Pulo Gadung Bus Station. Get there early to book a good front seat (even earlier on holidays).

To The West And Sumatra

Buses to Serang (Rp1500) and Merak (Rp2000) leave from Kalideres, Rp200 by bus no. 913 from Gambir Station. Buses (a/c with reclining seats) to both Padang and Bukittinggi cost Rp34,000 (36 hours), but it's cheaper to break your trip up: first to Merak, take ferry to Tanjungkarang, then catch another bus up to Bukittinggi. For ferry info to Sumatra, see "Merak." Best company for Sumatra: Bintang Kejora, Jl. K.H. Mas Mansyur 59 (behind Hotel Indonesia in the Tanah Abang area), tel. 336672/375662/358111).

FROM JAKARTA BY TRAIN

Jakarta's 5 major stations have trains departing for all points on Java and also S. Sumatra. Tickets may be bought on the morning of departure from the station's *loket*. Prices depend on the class, speed and/or comfort. Some travel agencies such as Carnation, Jl. Menteng Raya 24 (tel. 344027/356728); or P.T. Bhayangkara, Jl. Kebon Sirih 23 (tel. 327387), even closer to Jl. Jaksa. Both outfits handle reservations for such trains as the *Bima, Mutiara,* and *Parahiyangan.* Always get the name of the station

your train is departing from. Most trains leave for other Javanese cities from Gambir Station, centrally located on Jl. Merdeka Timur (within walking distance of Jl. Jaksa), and from Kota Station, Jl. Stasiun Kota 1 (allow plenty of time to get there during the rush hour). Student discounts are available for economy class only, but at the discretion of the station-master; this could take several hours and include the obligatory English lesson.

Points West

The train departs daily for Palembang, S. Sumatra (via Merak) at 0635 (from Kota) and at 1710 (from Tanah Abang). The morning train is better. Take the train to Merak, then board the ferry across the Sunda Strait to Srengsem, Tanjungkarang's port. The ferry in Merak waits for the train to arrive. If you travel by bus to Merak you might have to wait for the ferry, but only for as long as 3 hours. From Srengsem the train continues N 400 km to Palembang. However, most people prefer nowadays to take faster buses from Jakarta's Kalideres Station, leaving for Padang and Medan practically around the clock.

To Bogor And Bandung

Trains leave Kota every 20 min. until 2000; Rp500. All Bogor-bound trains stop at Gambir. For Bandung, trains depart Kota 4 times daily except on Sat. (5 times), all stopping at Gambir (close to Jl. Jaksa). The *Parahiyangan* ("Abode of the Gods") is more convenient but less scenic than the bus, getting you there in 3 hours. This well-maintained train has a good restaurant; other coaches are well-ventilated with large fans. Tickets, which cost around Rp6000 for ordinary class *(kelas rata rata)* may be picked up just one hour before departure. Second-class (a/c) tickets cost Rp8000.

To Yogya

Trains leave from Tanjung Priok and Kota stations once daily; from Gambir 4 times daily. The *Senja Utama Solo* costs Rp15,000 2nd class a/c, Rp11,000 2nd class non a/c, leaving Gambir at 1800, arriving in Yogya at 0615 (the same train departs Yogya at 1800 and arrives in Jakarta at 0615). Third-class fare is Rp8000. Buy meals on the train, or bring your own.

To Surabaya

At Rp10,000 the *GBM Selatan* is the cheapest, departing twice daily from Gambir Station. It takes 17 hours; the evening train arrives in Surabaya around 0500. Both the *Bima II* and the *Mutiara Utara* a/c night express trains to Surabaya are more comfortable and expensive. The advantages of express trains are speed, comfort, a better clientele (less worry about theft), good lighting (read and write after dark), and clean washrooms. The *Bima II* takes the southern route through Cirebon, Purwokerto, Yogya, Madiun, Kertosono, Surabaya. It leaves Kota Station at 1600; arrives Yogya 0140; arrives Surabaya's Gubeng Station at 0830. Serves a luxury dinner and breakfast. Economy class with fan costs Rp21,000 for reclining seats, 1st class Rp33,000 (for berths). Go to Kota Station at 1000 on departure day to reserve a berth, or buy your ticket (for an extra Rp2000) at Carnation Travel, Jl. Menteng Raya 24 (near Jl. Jaksa). Travel time from Jakarta to Yogya is 12 hours, from Yogya to Surabaya 6 hours. The *Mutiara Utara* takes the northern route from Kota Station via Cirebon, Tegal, Pekalongan, and Semarang—a journey of 15½ hours. The segment between Jakarta and Semarang takes 9½ hours and between Surabaya and Semarang about 6 hours. You get a comfortable reclining seat and footrest; no berths. It leaves at 1630, arrives in Surabaya's Pasar Turi Station at 0800, costs Rp25,000 (reclining seats, a/c, meals), one class only. The *Mutiara Utara* goes on to Banyuwangi and Denpasar (with bus connection).

FROM JAKARTA BY AIR

Jakarta offers some good discounts on airline tickets; shop around. Flights leave from Soekarno/Hatta Airport, 13 km W of the city. Take a Damri bus from Gambir, Rawamangun, Blok M, or Kemayoran, Rp2000; a taxi for Rp15,000; or a minibus service for Rp4000 offered by Wisma Delima, Jl. Jaksa 5. Domestic departure tax Rp2000, international departure tax Rp9000. At Soekarno/Hatta, luggage can be stored for Rp1000 per piece; inquire at the information counter.

To Singapore

A number of airlines, such as Garuda, UTA, and SIA, offer tickets. UTA is in the Jaya Bldg., on corner of Jl. Wahid Hasyim and Jl. Thamrin (tel. 323507), charges US$110. Singapore Airlines (SIA), Sahid Jaya Hotel, Jl. Jen. Sudirman 86 (tel. 584021/584041/584011/587441), charges US$140. Also try Thai International, BDN Bldg., Jl. Thamrin 5 (tel. 320607). The Garuda fare (Jl. Juanda 15, tel. 370709) is also US$110 OW, US$160 RT.

Other Destinations

One of the cheapest ways to get back to the States through the N. Pacific is with Korean Airlines via Bangkok with 6 stops along the way: Taiwan, Tokyo, Hawaii, etc. Also check out UTA flights every Mon. night to the States, stopping in Sydney and Papeete (French Polynesia) en route to Los Angeles or San Francisco. You hear UTA prices quoted as low as US$686 OW. If you add Auckland (New Zealand), it costs only US$30 extra! Travel agencies could have some bargain deals: Indosangrila, Jl. Gajah Mada 219G (tel. 632703), sells tickets to Europe for US$524; Seattle, US$617; Japan, US$414 (stops in Hong Kong). P.T. Tomaco, Jakarta Theatre Bldg., could

even be cheaper: Europe, US$500; Dallas, US$700; Japan, US$350.

International Airline Offices

Cathay Pacific, Qantas, and **Thai International** are all in the BDN Building on Jl. Thamrin. Other addresses: **British Airways,** Mandarin Hotel, 1st Floor, Jl. Thamrin (tel. 333207/333092/333198/333572); **China Airlines,** Jl. Gajah Mada 3-5, Complex Duta Merlin, Blok A No. 11 (tel. 353195/344489/361368); **Garuda,** Jl. Ir. H. Juanda 15 (tel. 370709); **Japan Airlines,** Wisma Nusantara Bldg., Jl. Thamrin (tel. 333909); **KLM,** Hotel Indonesia, Jl. Thamrin (tel. 320708); **Philippine Airlines,** Borobudur Inter-Continental Hotel, 3rd Floor, Jl. Lapangan Banteng Selatan (tel. 370108 ext. 2310, 2312, 2314, or 2336); **Korean Airlines,** Hotel Indonesia, Jl. Thamrin (tel. 320708/322034); **Singapore Airlines,** Sahid Jaya Hotel, Jl. Jen. Sudirman 86 (tel. 584021/584041/583711/583691); **UTA,** Gedung Jaya, Jl. Thamrin 12 (tel. 323507).

Domestic Airlines Offices

In the more remote areas, check out lesser-known airlines (which could be about 10% cheaper than Garuda) such as **Pelita,** Jl. Abdul Muis 52-54 (tel. 375908), or **Mandala Airlines,** Jl. Veteran 1/34 (tel. 368107). Also check with **Bouraq,** Jl. Angkasa 1-3, Kemayoran (tel. 6295150/6595179); **Merpati,** Jl. Angkasa 2, (tel. 413608/417404); **Sempati,** Jl. Merdeka Timur 7 (tel. 348760/363975). **Garuda's** main office is on Jl. Ir. H. Juanda 15 (tel. 370709); other branches are at Soekarno/Hatta Airport, in the Nusantara Bldg. on Jl. Thamrin (tel. 330464), and at Hotel Borobudur (tel. 370108 ext. 2241 and 2242). **travel agencies:** For tickets to anywhere in Indonesia with Garuda, Merpati, Bouraq, or any other domestic airlines, try convenient and friendly P.T. Tomaco Travels on the ground floor of the Jakarta Theatre Building (tel. 320087/320215), and Indosangrila, Jl. Gajah Mada 219G (tel. 632703). P.T. Amanda Bali International, Jl. Wahid Hasyim 116 (tel. 325056/325057), handles expensive tours but also provides useful tips for low-budget travelers.

Sample Domestic Fares

The following are all Garuda fares; other domestic airlines can be 10-20% cheaper: Yogya, Rp62,400; Denpasar, Rp106,500; Tg. Pinang (with Merpati), Rp106,500; Ujung Pandang, Rp159,000; Ambon, Rp225,200; Manado, Rp26,700; Padang, Rp115,000; Medan, Rp162,400; Banda Aceh, Rp212,200; Jambi, Rp84,000; Balikpapan, Rp150,000; Jayapura, Rp355,100; Biak, Rp320,400. Take note that Mandala charges only Rp136,000 to Medan, Rp189,300 to Ambon, Rp133,000 to Ujung Pandang. Garuda has "shuttle services" to Surabaya and Semarang; buy these tickets at the airport 30 min. before departure at 15% less than the "business class."

FROM JAKARTA BY SEA

To get to Tanjung Priok, 20 km NE of the city center, take Patas P14 (express) bus from Jl. Kebon Sirih near Jl. Jaksa; taxis cost Rp10,000-15,000 from Jl. Jaksa. Also check out the *syahbandar's* office in the small ships' harbor, Sundakelapa (near Pasar Ikan). For example, you could score a small cargo boat for Rp15,000 to Tg. Pinang, including OK food. Pelni, the state shipping line, has Indonesia's most extensive shipping network: 6 brand new ships built in W. Germany ply all corners of the archipelago. For the unbelievable price of only around Rp28,000 per day at sea you can stay in absolutely luxurious 1st class cabins (children's fares are about two-thirds of adult fares). Pelni's head office is at Jl. Pintu Air 1 (tel. 358398), near rail and bus terminals in Tanjung Priok. Kill time waiting for your ship by visiting some of the sights of W. or C. Java.

To Medan And N. Sumatra

Pelni hasn't sailed direct from Jakarta to Singapore since the days of *konfrontasi* in the early 1960s, but 3 of the new Pelni passenger ships sail to the N. Sumatran city of Medan: the MV *Kambuna* (leaves Tg. Priok on Sat. at 1300), MV *Rinjani* (leaves Tg. Priok every other Sat. at 1300), and the MV *Lawit* which stops in Dumai, Riau Daratan, from where you can go overland to Bukittinggi (via Pekanbaru). From Medan, take the cargo boat or the MAS flight over to Penang, W. Malaysia. Don't take the Medan-bound Pelni ship when all the Bataks are going home for Christmas; too crowded.

To Padang

The MV *Kerinci* makes this run in about 36 hours at a cost of Rp55,000 1st class, Rp24,500 economy class, plus agent's fee of about Rp500. This large, clean, and comfortable ship almost flies over the water nonstop. Leaving once monthly on Fri. at around 2100, buy your tickets Thurs. or early Fri. at the Jl. Bungur Besar 54 or Jl. Pintu Air offices before embarkation. The MV *Kerinci* arrives in Padang Sun. at 0700. Get ready for the cooler weather of Sumatra's W coast.

Other Destinations

For Ujung Pandang, the Pelni ship KM *Rinjani* departs on Wed. at 1700 for Surabaya (Rp28,000 Economy), then on to Ujung Pandang (Rp36,500), Bau-Bau (Rp45,500), Ambon (Rp60,250), and Sorong (Rp71,500) which it reaches on Mon. at 1000. Other Pelni fares from Tanjung Priok: Jambi, S. Sumatra, Rp36,000 1st class, Rp18,000 economy class; Manado, Rp120,000 1st class, Rp36,000 economy class; Ternate, Rp137,000 1st class, Rp17,000 economy class; Pontianak, Rp30,000 1st class, Rp15,500 economy class.

VICINITY OF JAKARTA

PULAU SERIBU

Pulau Seribu means "Thousand Islands" and refers to only 600 or so small islands situated in the shallow waters off Jakarta's coast. These tiny islands, the "Key West" of Java, can best be seen from a plane just after takeoff from Jakarta's Soekarno/Hatta Airport. Some islands are located as far N as the Java Sea. Only 7 of the islands are populated, the rest are covered with coconut palms, shrubs, and beautiful virgin beaches of white sand—difficult to believe that Jakarta is so close. As early as the 17th C., this popular island group was connected to Batavia by daily ferries, and is still a sought-after destination for both recreational and historical reasons.

Sights

A number of the islands have become private holiday havens, the more accessible ones just 10-15 km from Jakarta. Coral gardens abound off P. Putri, P. Genteng (Besar and Kecil), and P. Opak Besar—all excellent dive sites. On P. Untung Jawa, site of a Sun. market, are picnic facilities and a campground. Pulau Onrust and P. Air Besar are both accessible daytrips from Tanjung Priok. More remote uninhabited islands include Pabelokan, Sibaru Kecil, and Sibaru Besar: wooded islands with talcum powder beaches and coconut plantations. About 100 km N of Jakarta is a National Marine Park, set aside as a sea nature reserve.

Precautions

Exploring its coral shores is one of the great attractions of visiting Pulau Seribu: seashells and coral are found in an infinite variety of colors and shapes. Take snorkeling gear but exercise a few simple precautions: in the water always wear enclosed shoes or flippers which cover the whole foot—never walk barefoot on coral. When collecting wood or coconuts for a fire, beware of scorpions. On many islands (such as P. Melinjo and P. Kelor) are 1½-m-long black lizards which will fight with birds over your scraps but will not attack people. Bring mosquito repellent, a *kelambu* (mosquito net), hat, and sunscreen lotion. Don't try to swim to another island because it may be farther than it looks and the channel currents could be very powerful.

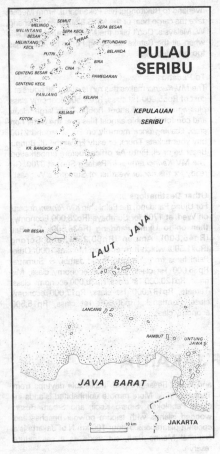

PULAU SERIBU

KEPULAUAN SERIBU

LAUT JAVA

JAVA BARAT

JAKARTA

0   10 km

Accommodations
The most developed island is P. Putri which features bungalows, a restaurant, even "entertainment." These bungalows compare in price favorably with standard international-class rates in Jakarta—weekday rates are less (though still not cheap). On weekends and during holiday periods a surcharge of 25% is common. Add to this boat fare, local taxes, food costs, and service tax (21%). Emergency walkie-talkie communications are maintained with the mainland. For more about P. Putri's accommodations and services see "Pulau Putri" below. Besides P. Putri, other islands have bungalows which aren't advertised but which you may rent. **food:** Restaurant (and bar) prices are expensive (except for fish dishes), especially on P. Putri. Bring your own food—kitchen equipment can be rented and fresh fish and shellfish can

usually be bought locally and cooked in pits on the beach. On the outer islands, you *must* supply your own food and drink.

Getting There
The islands can be reached on a Skyvan flight from Soekarno/Hatta Airport. Pulau Panjang, 64 km from Jakarta, is the only island with a landing strip. Plane fare includes the charge for a boat from P. Panjang to P. Putri. From P. Panjang take boats to other islands in the group. Any travel agent should be able to give you details and prices (don't believe them if they say that you must rent a bungalow first). **by boat:** Most of the main islands can be reached from Marina Jaya Ancol or from Muara Kamal N of Soekarno/Hatta Airport on the way to Tangerang. From Ancol ferries leave around 1000 (on Sat. also at 1400) for P. Bidadari (touristy), from where you can embark to the outlying islands. Day excursions are available, RT price is around US$50. Travel to the outlying islands only by private or hired boat—you'll feel like a temporary castaway. **note:** During the week you'll most likely be on your own; on weekends and public holidays the islands are packed.

Pulau Putri
The most developed island, only 20 min. by air from Soekarno/Hatta Airport or 40 min. by speedboat from Ancol. This high-priced resort has a restaurant and accommodations ranging from cottages to family bungalows. Furnishings are spartan but all rooms have electricity at night, Western plumbing, and ocean views. Book in advance through a travel agent or through Putri Pulau Seribu Paradise, Jl. Thamrin 9, Jakarta Theatre Bldg. (tel. 359333/4). The dive shop on the island rents equipment for skin and scuba diving and snorkeling; sailboats and sailboards are also available.

Pulau Melinjo
Cheaper and just as enjoyable as P. Putri is neighboring P. Melinjo. This enchanting island offers basic facilities for campers: drinking water, toilets, showers, barbecue, etc., plus an excellent swimming beach. Free transport to and from the airport is available.

Pulau Bidadari
Only 15 km from the mainland, P. Bidadari is fresh, natural, unspoiled, the real pearl of Pulau Seribu. On the highest point of the island are the remains of a mighty round fort, today held intact by the tentacle-like roots of trees and shrubbery. See the second floor entrance and the big gunpowder magazine. A leper hospital was built here in 1679 and another name for the island is *Pulau Sakit,* "Island of the Sick." All the gravestones were removed to P. Kelor when Bidadari was "developed into a paradise." Bidadari has electricity. A path runs along the coast, and the shallow sea is safe for even small children. At intervals along

the path are 10 bungalows for rent which include bath and toilet, for up to 4 people. Other bungalows *(pondok)* are built on stilts over the sea and reached via a small pier. Each has a large room, *mandi,* toilet, and small kitchenette. Lying in bed, look out over the water to see fish gliding over coral beds. An open-air restaurant provides varied fare at reasonable prices: fresh *kepitang,* roasted young goat, or *nasi goreng.*

Pulau Onrust

Accessible by motorboat from P. Bidadari, Onrust is between P. Bidadari and P. Khayangan. Historically, Onrust is the most important island of P. Seribu. Even before Batavia was established, this island served as a busy ship repair yard which careened, caulked, and renewed VOC vessels *(onrust* in Dutch means "restlessness, bustle"). Sawmills, ammunition depots, *godowns,* and cranes were built here. Ask the warden to show you around the historical remains: the port's ruined foundations and wharf, the foundations of a small church, and the ruins of a VOC fort. Also see the old graveyard with moss-covered tombstones (most without inscriptions), dating back to 1693. A bastion with an artillery battery was built in 1671 to protect the ships while they were being overhauled (see a model of this fortress in Museum Bahari, Jakarta). Captain Cook's ship, the *Endeavor,* put in for repairs here in 1770. In his journal Cook praised the ships' carpenters on Onrust as "the ablest in the East." The British burned the fortifications to the ground in 1800, 1806, and again in 1810. Later in the 19th C. the island was used as a quarantine for *Haji* returning from Mecca. Today cassava is cultivated. Ruins of old structures have been renovated to make very acceptable dormitories for vacationers. **vicinity of:** On P. Khayangan, see foundations of a big round fort and 4 old ships' cannons excavated nearby. The many walls were once part of a seamen's prison. The warden will show you the natural sweet-water well and the remains of a cell used for executions. On the neighbor-

ing island of Kelor are the ruins of a round fort with mighty walls; this bastion once protected the shipyard on P. Onrust.

Pulau Damar

Damar got its name ("torch") from an important lighthouse, now converted to a radar station which guides planes into Jakarta's airports. Renowned in the 18th C. as a resort for wealthy Batavians, only a few relics survive of a magnificent house erected here in 1685 by Governor-General Camphuijs (1634-1695). Built in Japanese style, on the grounds were a famous collection of rare plants and animals, and a Japanese garden. Prisoners serving forced labor terms worked in the island's ropery and sawmill. There were several uprisings and bloody repressions.

TAMAN MINI INDONESIA

This 120-ha open-air cultural/amusement park is a window into the cultural and environmental complexity of Indonesia. Pavilions built in traditional style exhibit artifacts, customs, and lifestyles of the peoples of each of Indonesia's 27 provinces. The exhibit of one province alone, such as Kalimantan Barat's, is as big as Sydney Town Hall. You could spend half a day in the Riau pavilion. It would take a week to see everything. In fact, Indonesians will proudly tell you that there will be no need to see the rest of Indonesia if you visit this park, which they compare to Disneyland. Apparently, Madame Suharto visited Disneyland in 1971 and became so enraptured that when she returned she immediately applied her almost embarrassing talent for fund-raising. The president's wife solicited "voluntary" contributions from businesses, bought up the surrounding smallholder farmlands at rock-bottom prices, and graced Taman Mini with the usual tourist schlock of a cement *anoa* and artificial waterfall. After years of development, the result is an

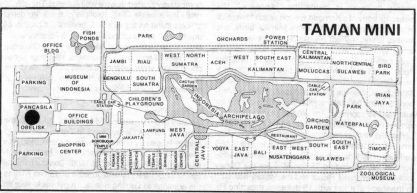

impressive, sprawling complex with open spaces well suited for leisurely strolling—an instant albeit superficial introduction to Indonesia. A number of souvenir stalls and Indonesian-style restaurants dot the grounds, plus there's a friendly *warung* complex. On Sun. there are dozens of outstanding, free traditional dance performances, films, and cultural shows. Get a calendar of events in any Garuda or VIC office, or hotel. Open daily 0900-1700, but most of the pavilions' hours are 0900-1600. They close the gates at around 2000. Entrance Rp300, children Rp150.

Exhibits

The cultural exhibits and the genuine Indonesian architecture are the most valuable aspects of this park. Many structures were dismantled then reconstructed here; replicas of houses, temples, mosques, and churches, represent every important ethnic group of Indonesia. Each pavilion has its own program of cultural performances, ceremonies, and dances, all noted in the monthly Taman Mini program. The bigger houses are showrooms for handicrafts, historical artifacts, ancient clothing, and dioramas of heroic events; there could also be exhibits of industrial, agricultural, and mineral products. In the smaller pavilions the making of local crafts is sometimes demonstrated. Near the park entrance, the **Indonesia Museum** is billed as the best-displayed collection of Indonesian artifacts and handicrafts in the country—one of the highlights of Taman Mini. Inside is a stunning exhibit of 35 mannequin couples dressed in distinctive local wedding costumes. The second floor features "Man and His Environment" with model houses, panoramas, exhibits of tools and cooking utensils. The third floor is all handicrafts. Open 0900-1700, admission Rp300. See the "Indonesia Indah II" show in the **Keong Mas Theatre**, which focuses on the children of Indonesia; Rp1500, with curved-screen shows every hour 1100 to 1600 Mon. to Thurs., Sun. 1000-1700. A wildlife and natural history museum is inside the "dinosaur," the awesome body of a Komodo dragon which towers 25 m above the ground! Indonesia's animals, birds, and reptiles (albeit stuffed) are exhibited here in realistic jungle settings. The **bird park** contains 650 species of birds native to Indonesia—a great spot to relax. For Rp300, walk through the 6-ha bird park with its 9 wire-domed aviaries to see birds of paradise (Irian Jaya), *cikukua* (Nusatenggara), pelicans (Ambon), *beleang* (W. Kalimantan). The park is divided by a stream to represent the Wallace Line, thus bird species are separated into those found in the eastern part of the country and those indigenous to the western half. A terraced orchid garden contains 3,000 varieties of orchids, some indigenous. The latest additions to ever-expanding Taman Mini are the Disney look-alike *Children's Palace* and the *Military Museum* in the shape of a fort with 19 dioramas depicting lib-

eration wars in Indonesia between the 7th and 19th centuries.

Getting There

Located 12 km S of the city on the highway to Bogor and Ciawi, the long bus trip through Jakarta's neighborhoods gives you a good overview of the size and diversity of this Asian megalopolis. From Jl. Thamrin (in front of Sarinah Dept. Store), take bus no. 408 or Patas bus no. 11 (Rp200) to Cililitan Station, then board a bus marked MINI INDONESIA (the whole trip takes 1½ hours). Leaving Taman Mini, get a *becak* out to the main highway for Rp300 (buses back to the city stop around 1700). Or walk out to the road and flag down a bus back to Cililitan where you can easily find another bus into Jakarta.

Getting Around

Tour buses make a complete loop of the park, Rp600. Take the bus tour first on the ring road to check out which area you like the most, then either walk back or take another tour to that area. A touring train (Rp400) also slowly circles Taman Mini, and 3 types of horse-drawn carts rent for Rp4000 per hour. Ride the 4-seat cable cars (Rp1000) high up over the park for a spectacular aerial overview. See earthen mounds shaped like Indonesia's islands, covered in grass and sculptured mountains, representing the whole archipelago in miniature, all laid out to scale on a huge 8-ha "sea"! Keep your ticket stubs for the return flight. Paddleboats take you around the artificial lake (loaded with fish), Rp1500.

LUBANG BUAYA

Means "Crocodile Hole." This massive monument commemorates 7 Indonesian officers who were tortured and killed on 30 Sept. 1965 during the alleged communist coup d'etat, their mutilated bodies ignominiously stuffed down a well *(lubang)*. The official name is *Pancasila Cakti*. Replicas of the 7 murdered officers stand on top of a wall. Ironically, a brother of one of the 6 senior officers (Lt. Jen. S. Parman) was a high-ranking communist ideologue. The Crocodile Hole itself is built upon a *pendopo;* take your shoes off as if you were entering a mosque. In front of the monument is a parade field where military ceremonies take place, honoring the ghastly event.

Getting There

Located in a rural setting 16 km SE of Jakarta in the village of Pondok Gede, 3 km E of Taman Mini. Get to Mini Indonesia by noon so you have a chance to also see Pancasila Cakti and get back in time for the coach tour around the park (ends at 1600). Board a minibus (Rp200) from the highway in front of Taman Mini to the entrance to Lubang Buaya. To get back, take an *oplet* (or a 1952 Austin!) to the entrance of Taman Mini and then either take a *becak* (Rp300) back into Taman Mini, or flag down an orange Metro Mini or *bemo* back to Cililitan.

RAGUNAN ZOO

The best and largest zoo in Indonesia. Situated in the suburb of Pasar Minggu, about 16 km S of Jakarta's city center. From downtown, take bus nos. 87 or 90, which go straight to the entrance of the zoo for Rp200. Or take a bus to Pasar Minggu, then get an *oplet* to the front or back entrances for Rp200. Open daily 0900-1800; entrance Rp300. Ragunan is less crowded than Surabaya's famous zoo, especially on a weekday, and is a shady refuge on a hot afternoon. It is as well a favorite place for children, picnickers, sweethearts. A large foodstall section serves Indonesian foods and iced drinks. The animals are kept in humane enclosures, not cages, maintained in conditions as near to their natural habitats as possible. Signs in English and Indonesian point the way to each of the animal groups' environs. The zoo also plays a direct role in conservation—several species of threatened fauna are bred here. See the botanical garden with a wide variety of Indonesian tropical trees and plants labeled with their Latin names, perhaps the best botanical garden in Indonesia excepting Bogor (W. Java) and Purwodadi (E. Java).

Exhibits
The zoo's collections are relatively small—but this is more than made up for by quality animal-keeping. See the rare species of lesser ape here, misnamed the Klossi gibbon, a sort of pygmy *siamang* monkey (only one other specimen in captivity). Also in their natural surroundings are Komodo dragons, several *anoa* (dwarf buffalo), the *babirusa* (wild pig), plus 2 specimens of the nearly extinct Java tiger. In the aviaries, besides the gorgeously plumed birds of paradise, the star attraction is the *maleo* fowl, a megapode which builds its own artificial incubation system. There's also a great number of reptiles and nocturnal animals. At the oceanarium trained dolphins perform, the only spectacle of its kind in all of SE Asia, drawing as many as 2,000 spectators daily. **note:** On the way back from the zoo, stop at the Rattan House on Jl. Bangka Raya where rattan weaving can be seen in the back.

the maleo: *Related to the pheasants, this is one of the most peculiar bird families in the world. Their English name is variously brush turkey, junglefowl, incubator bird, or the Dutch maleo. Their scientific name is Megapodiidae, from the Greek for "large feet". All megapodes have large tails, short wings and powerful claws. Confined to eastern Indonesia, Polynesia, New Guinea, and Australia, these ground-living birds never sit on their eggs but—like turtles— lay them in holes in the sand to be hatched by the heat of the sun. Some species lay their eggs in huge mounds of decaying forest litter to be incubated by the natural heat of fermentation. Another species digs nesting holes into the ground, where their eggs are heated from beneath by percolating volcanic steam. See them at Ragunan Zoo or in the wild near Luwuk, C. Sulawesi.*

WEST JAVA

Extending from Krakatoa volcano all the way to Cirebon, this province is a diverse and culturally rich region of beautiful mountains, deep-green tea plantations, rugged wildlife reserves, lush botanical gardens, fertile rice paddies, and beaches with magnificent coral formations. The name *Sunda*, meaning "white," refers to the white ash which covers the land after volcanic eruptions, rendering the soil rich and fecund. West Java's volcanos are exceedingly active: in 1982 Galunggung erupted, killing 20 people and causing an estimated $25 million in damage, and covering the villages of the area with mud and thick dust. Jakarta, capital of Indonesia, is located within the province, though the capital and cultural center of W. Java is the fresh mountain city of Bandung. Transportation here is well developed.

The People
Several racial groups are indigenous to this part of Java. The interior plateau of W. Java is called the Priangan, heartland of the Sundanese who make up the majority of the province's population. These people, of all the peoples of Java, are nearest to Malay, yet they have their own distinct, non-Javanese culture. Acclaimed for the beauty of their women, their dreamy melancholy music, and evocative poetic imagery, the Sundanese tend to be earthier and more lighthearted than the refined Javanese race of C. and E. Java. The Sundanese language has numerous levels of formal address, a legacy of the 8th-12th C. Hindu kingdoms which held sway here. *Wayang golek* (wooden stick puppets-in-the-round) are associated with this region. The Sundanese also have a rich tradition of performing arts and orchestras such as *angklung* (bamboo percussion instrument) and *kecapi suling* (flute music). They are also characterized by a strong devotion to Islam. In addition to this dominant racial group, the Badui people live in the remote mountainous region S of Rangkasbitung; some scholars believe ancestors of this tribe were the original inhabitants of the region.

UJUNG KULON RESERVE

This completely untamed wilderness lies on the far W tip of Java, connected to the rest of the island by a narrow boggy isthmus. Two separate national parks here total more than 420 sq km, one located on the Ujung Kulon Peninsula and the other on the island of Panaitan across a narrow strait. Established by the Dutch in 1921 as a refuge for the threatened Javan rhinoceros, the setup of this last large area of lowland forest on Java has since been credited with saving a number of rare life forms from extinction. Observation towers have been erected at Cigenter, and grazing fields are found at Cijungkulon on P. Peucang. Unspoiled beaches with beautiful coral formations off the S and W sides of P. Peucang and P. Panaitan make for spectacular diving, snorkeling, and swimming (but there are sharks on the Krakatoa side of the islands). Water sports are also not advised off the S or W beaches of the Ujung Kulon Peninsula due to rocky coastlines and exposure to rough open seas. Best time to visit is April-Aug. when the sea is calmer and the ground is not as marshy. For really detailed information on this reserve, refer to the large tome, *Ujung Kulon*, by the high-ranking Dutch naturalist, A. Hoogerwerf (E.J. Brill, Leiden, 1970).

Flora And Fauna
The reserve has open broad meadows, waterfalls, reedy swamps, estuarine shallows with crocodiles, steam rising from *alang-alang* grass, flocks of peacocks, rooting wild pigs, hornbills, gibbons, river otters, miniature deer, *sambur* stags with huge antlers, marine and coral life including several species of dolphin. There are also wild buffalos, tigers, panthers, and over 200 species of birds including herons and wild ducks. Now 45 protected rhinos remain. Similar to its Indian relative found now only in very small pockets in Assam and Nepal, the armor on this one-horned white rhino's back is divided into 4 sections. His little pig eyes don't see well, but he'll attack blind anyway. At a sandy beach at Nyuir these rare behemoths sometimes seek refuge (also on the peninsula portion to the SW); look out for fresh 3-toed hoofmarks, making sure that a tree is always nearby.

Permit And Supplies
You no longer need to get the entry permit *(surat jalan)* from the PPA office in Bogor; permits are available now from the very friendly Forestry Officer in Labuhan (2 km from town on road to Carita). It's free, and they help with everything including reservations for accommodations and you can even pay Rp2000 for a man to go to the market to stock up on provisions on your behalf. Another PPA office is at Carita Beach, a resort 7 km N of Labuhan. Pulau Handeleum and P. Peucang offer cooking facilities and water, bring food and beverages with you. The last place to shop for supplies is at either Labuhan or Carita Beach, N of Labuhan. Also bring food for the guide which you must hire for the day.

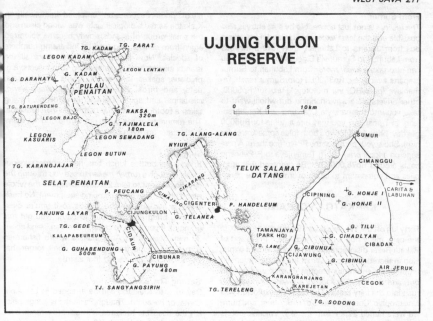

UJUNG KULON RESERVE

Accommodations

Before taking the trip into the park, you may want to spend the night at the **Carita Beach** or **Wisma Badui** (cheaper), 7 km N of Labuhan, or at **Losmen Dian Dukatu** (Rp1500) in Labuhan. In the park itself, you can stay on **P. Handeleum** (one hour by boat from park HQ at Tamanjaya) where the guesthouse (sleeps 8) has reasonably central access to the eastern park. About 20 km farther W on the far side of the peninsula, and also booked through Carita's PPA office, is **P. Peucang**, providing several large bungalows which sleep 16. All around these camps are fine beaches (even better beaches on the mainland). Bookings for these 2 islands must be confirmed and permits to enter the park will be rechecked at the PPA office or at the park headquarters at Tamanjaya. Both islands are posts for the park where guards and their families live. There's also a homestay on P. Peucang and it helps to get a letter from the forestry people in Labuhan in order to stay there.

Getting There

Best time to visit is the dry season (April-Oct.) when the rhinos make their way to clay pits to sun themselves. Get an entry permit first from the Forestry Office in Labuhan. You can charter a boat in Labuhan (plenty of offers) or even hire the PPA boat for around Rp250,000 RT. Jakartan travel agents also offer 4-day tours of Ujung Kulon at a cost of Rp125,000-150,000,

including accommodations in a guesthouse on P. Peucang, a photo safari with guide, all meals, and 2 nights at relaxing Carita Beach. Tours are often advertised in the *Indonesian Times*. The expense of your total package is determined to a large extent by the quality of the food you request. If you join a Jakarta tour group at Labuhan, it could cost as little as Rp50,000 pp.

By Land And Sea

By road from Serang there are 3 ways to get to Labuhan, from where you can take boats out to Ujung Kulon: the N route (70 km) via Cilegon (intersection for Merak) and Anyer is quickest; the central route (80 km) passes through Mandalawangi; and the S route (65 km) goes through the mountain village of Pandeglang. The PPA boat (called *Badak* or "Rhinoceros") from Labuhan to P. Peucang off Ujung Kulon takes 8-10 hours (90 km), depending on the weather; or share a *prahu*, much cheaper. (You can also hire boats out to the volcanic isle of Krakatoa from Labuhan.) Gasoline is not plentiful within the park so plan to bring your own if you wish to hire the PPA guard boat or a private boat to make daily trips from your island accommodations to the wildlife peninsula. Stick to the walking tracks; in the SE corner of the reserve are watchtowers where you may sleep. Bring lifevests, a medicine kit, and an ice chest full of cold drinks. A guide (who can show you the other side of P. Peucang, for example) will cost around Rp5000 per day.

From Sumur

The reserve is not just accessible by sea; entry is also possible and the least expensive by land. First take a bus from Jakarta to Labuhan, then take a minibus from Labuhan to Sumur via Cigeulis for Rp1500. You can also take a *kapal motor* from Labuhan to Sumur (departs every day, Rp3500). From Sumur reach Tamanjaya (park HQ) via motorcycle-taxi for Rp5000; other drivers are always hanging out who'll want to take you into the park via Cijawung and Karangranjang. In Tamanjaya you may hire a guide for Rp5000 per day; bring food for you both (plus some *kretek* for him). Show your permit at the PPA office there. A passage on a local *prahu* from Tamanjaya to P. Peucang costs around Rp75,000 OW. Be prepared with supplies and equipment to camp overnight in the park.

KRAKATOA VOLCANO

Forty km off the W. Java coast. Over a century ago, in the early misty hours of 27 Aug. 1883, the island of Rakata Besar disintegrated in the most violent explosion in recorded history. When the central mountain erupted, an enormous amount of rock was heaved out, and the island collapsed, allowing sea water to rush into the fiery crater. The resulting explosion was catastrophic. Countless tons of rocks, dust, and pumice were hurled 27 km into the sky. Volcanic debris landed on Madagascar on the other side of the Indian Ocean. The boom was heard in Brisbane over 4,000 km away. Atmospheric waves circled the globe 7 times. Tidal waves reached 30 m high, wiping out 163 villages along the coasts of western Java and southern Sumatra and rocking vessels as far away as the English Channel. A chain of explosions all but destroyed Rakata Besar, leveling its original crater and digging a submarine cavity 300 m below sea level. All remained calm in the middle of the demolished crater until 1927 when a thick plume of steam roared from the sea bed, and before long rocks and ash rose far enough to form a small cone. It still rumbles occasionally, and Anak Krakatoa ("Son of Krakatoa") has since risen 150 m above the sea. Renewed seismic activity was detected in 1979.

Fauna And Flora

Just 17 years after the island was blown to bits, Krakatoa was again astonishingly covered in plantlife, either carried by wind, birds, or sea. Although this awesome volcanic disaster killed an estimated 36,000 people, the eruption of Krakatoa became immensely instructive ecologically, a boon for biologists and geophysicists who study these islands' renascence for clues to Earth's evolution. After the eruption the Netherlands East Indies government, at the time entirely geared to maximizing agricultural returns, studied Krakatoa intensely. Thus, it was here that tropical soil science originated. The ecological principle of "primary succession" unfolded dramatically on Krakatoa as the biological slate was wiped clean and the small group of islands slowly became colonized again from surrounding land by increasing numbers of species. Now dense vegetation covers all the islands except Anak Rakata, along with insects, amphibians, snakes, land snails, lizards, spiders, rats, bats, and birds. Pine trees, bush, *alang-alang*, casuarina, and spinifex are all in evidence, having taken a foothold on the far corner of Anak Krakatoa. The remnants of the outer rim of the original mammoth crater are even covered in trees.

Supplies

Bring water bottles, lunch, tins, rice, or order take-out meals through a *rumah makan* to see you through the day. If you want to take 2-3 days to explore the whole island group, also bring camping equipment. No fresh water is available on the islands so if you're overnighting bring enough water to bathe (you get real grungy!). If you want to camp, there's an island about 30 min. away from Anak Rakata where fishermen sometimes spend the night. And don't forget that 24-mm wide-angle lens to fit it all in!

Getting There

Day trips to Krakatoa can be arranged in Labuhan, Carita, or Pasauran. Though Pasauran is geographically the closest to Krakatoa, it's easier to arrange boat transport from Labuhan (40 km and 4 hours from Krakatoa, if the sea is fine). Krakatoa is in most cases a one-day RT; leave before dawn to avoid too much sun. Also, the earlier you leave the more time you'll have on the island. (Stay the night before in either the Carita Beach Hotel or across the road in Wisma Badui Carita, or Losmen Caringin in Labuhan.) For boat rentals, the PPA staff in Labuhan can help you or any boy can lead you to the home of fishermen who make the trip. Once the word gets out you're after a boat, a number of middlemen will offer you vessels at varying prices, conditions, ages, and sizes. Rent a good boat; don't take any chances. Get one at least 12 m long that can handle itself in rough seas. The least expensive rental is with local fishermen for around Rp100,000 after bargaining; the highest can be upwards of Rp250,000 (between 5-6 people) from the Carita Beach Hotel. Approaching Krakatoa, have the captain do a slow tour around half the island (takes about 1½ hours), and upon exiting cover the other half of the island so you get your 360 degrees of photos. Bear in mind that the passage could be too hazardous in the monsoon season, Nov. to March. Even during Sept. winds and waves could make for a harrowing trip; starting in Oct. it gets difficult to find a captain willing to take you. The ideal time is April to September. But no matter what season, each time you go, the volcano is in a different mood. Surrounding waters could be 60 degrees C. Hot ash blackens your face, the roar is deafening, charcoal smoke

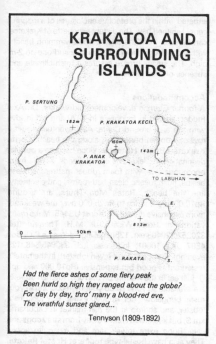

KRAKATOA AND SURROUNDING ISLANDS

P. SERTUNG

182 m P. KRAKATOA KECIL

150 m 143 m

P. ANAK KRAKATOA

TO LABUHAN →

N. E.

813 m

W. S.

0   5   10 km

P. RAKATA

Had the fierce ashes of some fiery peak
Been hurld so high they ranged about the globe?
For day by day, thro' many a blood-red eve,
The wrathful sunset glared...

Tennyson (1809-1892)

clouds the sky. If you're there during an active phase, see flaming boulders the size of basketballs tossed out like pebbles.

Exploring

Get an early start so you arrive at the island in the cool of the morning. The captain will anchor off a quiet, moonlike landscape where you jump overboard and wade ashore. Ascending the crater is a 30-min. climb at most. You'll need good walking shoes. Take water. An abundance of beauty surrounds you, the more spectacular the higher you climb. A primordial setting. At the summit, surrounded by rivers of lava, volcanic slag piles, and ravines, you see 2 peaks and a long ridgeline which you can follow over the top. The soles of your shoes will turn hot. The gaseous areas should be avoided as they can cause breathing difficulty, or worse. On the other side of the island is a long curving beach with bizarre driftwood; the swimming is not tempting. Incoming waves are laced with very fine black sand, but when they retreat the water is as lucid as you'd ever dream possible. Back on the boat the crew will be cooking their dinner, caught on the journey out; dine on delicious curried fish only 2 hours old served with hot tea.

Labuhan

Accessible by public bus (Rp1400, 160 km SW of

Grogol Station in Jakarta), Labuhan is a traditional fishing village. Stay at adequate **Losmen Dian Dukatu.** Gemas, the owner, will charge Rp1500 s or Rp2500 d, but can be bargained down if business is slow. Other options are **Sudimampur** (Rp1500) or the **Murawar** (Rp5000). Ask directions at the *stanplatz.* If you're going directly E from Labuhan to Rangkasbitung (and the Baduis), you usually have to do it in 2 segments: from Labuhan to Pandeglang, Rp750, then from Pandeglang to Rangkas (20 km). Get your permit for Ujung Kulon at Labuhan's PPA office, about 2 km from Labuhan towards Carita. The PPA staff has maps, brochures, and can arrange for boat transport. Go in the morning.

Anyer

In this coastal town, halfway between Labuhan and Merak, is an old lighthouse built by the Dutch in 1885, with a great view over the Sunda Strait. From Jakarta, the 3- to 4-hour drive (150 km) takes you through Tanggerang, Serang, and to Cilegon. From Serang onward, watch for signs directing you to the Anyer Beach Motel. A little N of Cilegon, the road forks: N to Merak and SE to Anyer. Anyer was the largest Dutch port on the coast of W. Java before being wiped out by *tsunami* from the eruption of Krakatoa in 1883. Anyer was also the start of the old Java Highway (Postweg) which commenced construction during the rule of Daendels (1762-1818), a Dutch colonial governor. You can still recognize fragments of this highway by the gnarly old tamarind trees by the side of the road right across Java! Hire a boat for Rp50,000 RT for the island of Sangiang (see below). **accommodations:** A modern, expensive Pertamina-owned motel complex **Anyer Beach Motel** has a/c beachfront units with hot water for Rp50,000 d plus 21% and service; restaurant and bar. For reservations, call Jakarta (tel. 510322).

SANGIANG ISLAND

Visible from the N portion of Java's W coast, about 1½ hours by *kapal motor* from Anyer Kidul, just S of Anyer. This uninhabited island is covered in 700 ha of jungle, completely surrounded by spectacular coral reefs. You have to take water, salt tablets, and other supplies and equipment — a trip for stout adventurers. The lagoon on the NW coast offers incredible diving and snorkeling — even octopus and a sunken wreck. Brown monkeys, delectable fruits, shells, coral, and lonely beaches abound. To menace shipping traffic through the channel, on a clifftop on the S peninsula of the island facing the Sunda Strait the Japanese built fortified shore batteries; a road leads from the barracks to the top where huge guns poke through creepers. Nearby are also remains of a harbor and airstrip, almost completely overgrown and inhabited by black gibbons and snakes.

Camping And Supplies

The best camping spots are on the SE part of the island on coral beaches under shady trees. Elsewhere the jungle is too dense, swampy, and mosquito infested. There are dangers from the heat, insects, coral, and small animals, so go prepared: take a first-aid kit, sunscreen, insect repellent, compass, extra food, tennis shoes for walking on treacherously sharp coral and as protection against stonefish. Count on about 5 liters per day pp just for drinking water. Don't go alone.

Getting There

Boat hire is much more reasonable from Anyer Kidul (around Rp50,000 RT) than from Merak. You could be escorted by a school of dolphins on the 1 ½-hour crossing of the Sunda Strait. Instruct your boatman to drop you off and then return in 3-5 days, depending upon how much you want to explore. If for some reason your boat doesn't return to collect you, other boats passing by can always be signaled to land.

KARANG BOLANG

A recreation spot and hotsprings facing the Sunda Strait, 6 km S of Anyer Kidul and 25 km N of Labuhan. Legend has it that the huge perforated boulder here was spewed out during Krakatoa's eruption. A nice, rarely used beach (except on weekends) meanders in and out of inlets lined with coconut trees. With a long, narrow slope, the surf is safe for children (though Dec.-Jan. it could get choppy). Admission Rp200— the complex also includes a swimming pool, playground, tennis courts, parking lot, small refreshment kiosks. Every Sun. there's a crowded market, but on weekdays it could be deserted.

Practicalities

The Batu Kuwung Recreation Complex has cabins; hot water is piped in from the hotsprings to the more expensive units. You may also stay with families for about Rp4000 per day; bargain! From the N minibuses go from town to town down this coast, so you have to do it in stages. From Cilegon to Sirit (Rp500), you pass by Anyer and its famous, photogenic lighthouse. Then from Sirit to Karang Bolang it's only 2 km (Rp100).

PANTAI CARITA

Down the whole W coast, from Merak to just S of Labuhan, are some of the most idyllic beaches on Java—shady, sandy, and a warm sea perfect for swimming, snorkeling, fishing, waterskiing, sailing, etc. Pantai Carita, only 3 hours by car from Jakarta, is a beautiful, 2-km-long, immaculate white-sand beach,

situated within the protective enclosures of a magnificent U-shaped bay. The distant silhouette of Krakatoa can be seen from the beach. The swimming beach, without rocks or undertow, has safe surf one- to 2-m high. The steady breeze assures a fresh climate and absence of mosquitos.

Accommodations

A former German development aid worker, Dr. Axel Ridder, arrived in Indonesia in 1970 and fell in love with the area around Carita. Axel eventually built a row of wooden bungalows along the beach. Carita Krakatau Beach Hotel has since become a popular destination for Jakartans on weekends. Simple bamboo bungalows, with foam rubber mattresses, wash basins, flush toilets, clean bathrooms, and electricity, line the beach. Rates Mon.-Thurs. are around Rp10,000 pp but rise to Rp25,000 over the weekend; more expensive deluxe units cost US$45. Make reservations at Hotel Wisata, Jl. M.H. Thamrin (tel. 320252/320408 ext. 125); mailing address is P.O. Box 4507 JKT 10001, Indonesia (tel. 330846/5483129 evening). European food (even lobster!) in the hotel's restaurant is good but expensive (Rp10,000 and up). Or just eat in the warung on the road. Kitchen utensils are available so you can do your own cooking in your rustic bungalows (for Rp5000 extra). Buy local fish, lobster, and shrimp at the fish market in Labuhan 7 km S, but keep food locked away from stray dogs and cats. Bring extra towels, ant and mosquito spray. They also have hostel-type rooms at Hostel Rakata, with paper-thin walls; Rp5000. Check out the display boards in the hotel lobby for newspaper and magazine clippings on Krakatoa, both in English and Indonesian, a good topo map of Krakatoa, other maps of the Badui area. Losmen- style Wisma Badui, on the other side of the road and 200 m from the beach (stay here if the waves keep you awake at night), also asks Rp25,000 on weekends but they're more willing to bargain. Here there is a wealth of information, photos, and maps on the Badui people—a very nice exhibit. Other hotels nearby, such as the Sambolo Beach Hotel and the Selat Sunda Wisata Seaside Cottages, charge about the same weekday and weekend prices as the Carita Krakatau Beach Hotel.

Getting There

By minibus 7 km N of Labuhan (Rp400), or 40 km S of Anyer (Rp1000). A bus also leaves every hour from Jakarta's Kalideres Bus Station for around Rp3500 (158 km); look for the sign JAKARTA-LABUHAN. If driving your own vehicle, it's a 3-hour drive, partly on a new superhighway, from Jakarta via Tanggerang and Serang. For a more scenic route, drive to Serang, then S in the direction of Pandeglang, W over the mountains to Batu Kuwung and Karang Bolong, then S along the coast to Carita (3-4 hours).

Tours

Walk 6 km over hills to the Gurug Gendeng Waterfalls and visit the nearby village of Sindanglaut where the tidal waves from the Krakatoa eruption are said to have reached. A giddy variety of contrived and high-priced weekend packages is offered at all the upscale hotels along this coast: the "Krakatoa Boat Trip" (Rp35,000 pp) in which 30 people or so climb up Anak Krakatoa all at once; the "Carita-Ujung Kulon Wildlife Boat Trip" (Rp75,000 pp); "Night Fishing at Carita" (Rp10,000); plus trips to the Pulau Dua bird sanctuary and Banten, roundtrips of Carita Bay, and trips to the Batu Kuwung hotsprings, etc. Masks, flippers, and snorkels can be rented from the hotel for Rp2000.

SERANG DISTRICT

Serang

Regular buses run from Jakarta's Kalideres station, 20 km out of town (Rp150 by *bis kota* from Jl. Jaksa) to Serang, Rp1500, 2 hours, 95 km. Or take the train; less money but fewer departures. Set out from this densely populated town to see regional attractions such as the Bird Islands, Banten, and the Merak area. A minibus from Serang to Merak costs Rp600, one hour. A revered tomb in the village of Katengahan, 5 km from Serang and 90 km W of Jakarta, is known locally as the burial place of the 17th C. Prince Jayawikarta. **accommodations:** The nondescript places along Jl. A. Yani, running from the Ciceri Bus Station to the *alun-alun,* are nothing to rave about. The best is probably **Peng. Bugis;** Rp5000. Also check out **Hotel Abadi** near the bus station, and **Hotel Serang,** Jl. Jen. A. Yani 5 (tel. 81641) at about the same price.

Events

The renowned *debus* "dancing" of this area is performed by religious ascetics known as *nayaga* who can control fear, pain, the heat of fire, the sharpness of weapons. This artform requires great confidence and devotion. Accompanied by traditional drums *(gendang, terbang),* recitation, and *almadab* music, 2 men enter the arena where they undergo torture, are pounded with iron stakes, burned or buried alive, cut, slashed, etc., and emerge unscathed. The players also show their invulnerability by eating glass fragments, cutting the tongue, rolling over barbed-wire. The play is watched over by a *pawang* who assures their safety and the success of the performance. *Debus* players don't perform regularly but do so before tourists on a for-hire basis. The local tourist office in Serang will arrange an "event," though more genuine peformances are those which spring up unannounced.

Pandeglang

The capital of Pandeglang Regency at the foot of G. Karang directly S of Serang. The road from Serang runs through the mountains; fantastic views. One of the neatest towns on Java. Held here at the great mosque each Idhul Fitri is a traditional drum competition, accompanied by Bantenese music, to celebrate the Islamic holiday. Batu Kuwung is a cave and hotsprings located between Pandeglang and Serang; from Serang catch a minibus for around Rp500. These are medicinal springs containing sulphur—but really hot water! There's also a small open-air public pool. Entrance Rp300. A small *losmen* is also located at Batu Kuwung.

BANTEN

Ten km N of Serang near the coast and 150 km and 2½ hours by car W of Jakarta, Banten is world renowned for its short-legged bantam hen, *ayam katik,* and known in Indonesia for its valuable historical remains that signify the advent of Islam to Java. Ruins of the once great Bantenese Islamic kingdom can still be viewed by visitors, and some portions of a palace have even been restored. A museum houses 200-year-old archaeological objects. Once a powerful and wealthy 16th C. trading center for the pepper trade between the Spice Islands and India, Banten figures largely in the history of W. Java. By 1545 a Portuguese trading station had been established here. The first haggard Dutchman set foot on Java at Banten in 1596, founding the first Dutch settlement on Java after a 14-month voyage in a fleet of 4 ships during which 250 men died. Their rivals, the British, set up a factory at Banten in 1603 but such enmity developed between them that the English was expelled in 1683. Along with the Mataram empire, Banten was one of Java's 2 dominant states in the 17th century. In 1684 the Dutch vanquished the sultan of Banten's forces and consolidated their power. Though it was so continuously rebellious toward Dutch rule that Banten became known as "The Aceh of Java," by the 19th C. its harbor had silted up and it became a backwater fishing village. But today the Banterese are still a proud and culturally distinct people. The small dusty village of Banten practices an orthodox form of Islam; there's an Islamic school nearby and you could run into hundreds of veiled schoolgirls in white. **note:** If you're here for just the day, leave your pack at the police post.

Pulau Krakatoa: When this volcano blew in 1883, it shot debris 27 km into the air. The whole of the northern and lower portions were blown away leaving a 300-m-deep, 41-sq-km submarine cavity. Waves catapulted boats in the Sunda Strait to the tops of mountains. Volcanic ash and dust shot up so high that dust clouds could be seen in S. America; amazing sunsets were seen all over the world for weeks. Tidal waves washed away all tall vegetation on the land facing the strait, and many nearby areas remain barren and lifeless. Scientists estimate that on P. Krakatoa and several neighboring volcanic islands, it will take a million years before animal and plant life regenerate fully.

WEST JAVA

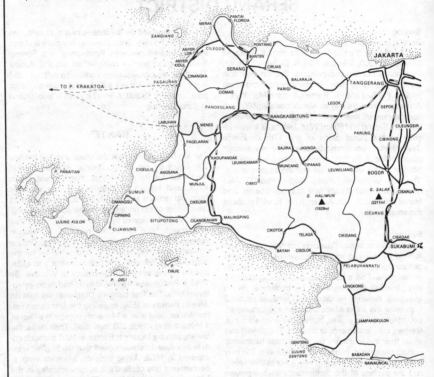

Badui people: Also known as the "Invisible Ones," this tribe lives in the wild jungle recluses of W. Java S of Rangkasbitung. Since the 15th C., they have built walls around their villages to maintain their isolation. Visitors may not enter the inner villages, though the outer Blue Badui villages can be contacted. The Baduis don't usually turn away a foreign tourist but strongly object to visits from government officials. Eating rice is forbidden and it's also taboo for the Badui to breed livestock. The Badui keep strictly to a simple forest diet and eat meat only 3 times a year on feast occasions. They earn their living from such crops as taro and tapioca. The men are sooth-sayers and cast spells, believe in the stars as signs, burn incense, recite chants. It's said that the Badui can converse with spirits and influence events. Family genealogies must be carefully kept. Each year the priests and leaders of the 3 inner clan villages gather to feast and meditate at Arcas Domas, a sacred grove of family trees in an area near the source of the Cilibon River. These trees have been planted to represent tribal leaders. The Badui can read in the condition of the branches the Message of the Trees, i.e., whatever good tidings or misfortune will befall the member of the family it represents.

Pulau Dua: Off the NW coast of W. Java near Banten. This island attracts migratory birds from as far as Australia, India, China, and many points in Asia. See flocks of white and orange cattle egrets, red night herons, snake birds, doves, ibises, spoonbills, storks, purple herons, and hated night herons ("gangster birds") which steal newly hatched birds from their nests. The whole bay is very shallow with long-legged birds wading in lines. The island's highest point is only 3 m above sea level.

TG. KARAWANG

SUNGAIBUNTU

SRENGSENG

BEKASI

CIKARANG WADAS SUKAMANDI

KARAWANG

KOSAMBI CIKAMPEK PAGADENBARU

PANGKALAN

JONGGOL

LAKE JATILUHUR PURWAKARTA SUBANG

PLERED

G. GEDE

CIPANAS PACET

CIANJUR CIMAHI BANDUNG

G. MALANG (1305m) GUNUNG HALU UJUNGBERUNG

SUKANAGARA CICALENGKA

LAUWIMANGGU BANJARAN

PAGELARAN PANGALENGAN

SANTOSA G. PAPANDAYAN (2622m) CIKURAY (2821m)

CISEWU KERTASARI

CIJARIAN SINDANGBARANG

CIKAROGOL CIPANDAK CIDAUN

BUNGBULANG

CIKELET

PAMEUNGPEUK

TG. GEDE

PAMANUKAN

BINOG KANDANGHAUR

INDRAMAYU

LOHBENER

KANDANGHAUR

JATIBARANG KARANGAMPEL

HAURGEULIS

JATITUJUH ARJAWINANGUN

KEDAWUNG CIREBON

CISALAK G. TAMPEMAS (1684m)

LEMBANG G. BUKITTUNGUL (2203m) CIEMAS

SUMEDANG KADIPATEN

MAJALENGKA LINGGARJATI SINDANGLAUT

G. CIREMAY (3078m) LOSARI

DARMARAJA KUNINGAN CILEDUG

NAGREK TELAGAKULON

G. GUNTUR (2244m) LELES CIBATU MALANGBONG PANJALA

CENTRAL JAVA

G. PATUNA (2434m) GARUT KAWALI

G. SAWAL (1784m) PURWOKERTO

TASIKMALAYA CIAMIS

CIKAJANG SINGAPARNA BANJAR TO YOGYA

DEUDEUL

SOREANG SALOPA

KARANGNUNGAL CIKATOMAS

PANGANDARAN

KALIPUCANG

KARANGANYAR KALALONG KALAPAGENEP CIJULANG TK. PENANJUNG

CIPATUJAH LEGOKJAWA

TG. INDRAMAYU

0 —— 50 km

Monuments and historical remains: West Java has few monuments and historical remains: a ruin dating from the very end of the Hindu-Javanese period on G. Cibodas mear Ciampea (Bogor), a single stone temple (Situ Cangkuang) near Garut, and prehistoric terraced sanctuaries and megaliths built in the hills around Bandung.

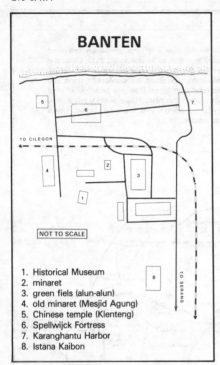

BANTEN

TO CILEGON

TO SERANG

NOT TO SCALE

1. Historical Museum
2. minaret
3. green fiels (alun-alun)
4. old minaret (Mesjid Agung)
5. Chinese temple (Klenteng)
6. Spellwijck Fortress
7. Karanghantu Harbor
8. Istana Kaibon

Sights

Guides are available (limited English) to the many well-preserved historical sites. The majestic Mesjid Agung, built in 1559 by the son of Sultan Hasanuddin in a flourishing, pagoda-like Chinese style, contains a small historical museum of weapons, kitchen utensils, terra-cotta wares, etc. It was designed by a Chinese Muslim. Visitors may also climb the spiral staircase of the nearby white *menara,* with a fine view over the coast. Graves of the royal family can be found in a neighboring building. North of the mosque, Spellwijck Fortress was constructed in 1682 and defended until the early 1800s. Though now in ruins, it's still a pleasant spot to wander in. A lichen-covered ancient graveyard lies behind the fort's eastern gate with some European tombstones. Climb the single remaining watchtower for another marvelous view. Klenteng is a newly renovated 200-year-old Chinese temple (one of the first in Indonesia), located NW of Spellwijck, a gift of the sultan to Banten's large Chinese community, given out of gratitude when the Chinese supplied medicine to curb a malaria epidemic. Here dozens of deities are enthroned, there's a sacred chair in a glass case, and a museum. Istana Kaibon (Royal Palace) is a heavily fortified compound with arch-

ways, a main gate, and massive 4-m-high crumbling walls built around what is now a completely pastoral setting. Originally constructed by a Dutch Muslim, Henrik Lucas Cardil, it is reminiscent of bastions found in Europe; see the ruins of Chinese temples and an old minaret inside the grounds. As a result of Dutch intrigue and manipulative politics, this *kraton* was destroyed by the son of the sultan, driven by the Dutch against his own father. The palace was burned down again by Dutch Governor-General Daendels. Inside the old walls excavations are still taking place and underground you can see evidence of a fire. A great many pieces of iron and bronze have been unearthed from workshops where armaments, ammunition, swords, and musical instruments were made.

Accommodations And Food

A surprising number of nationalities visit here: Japanese, American, Filipino, French, as well as the occasional Dutch scholar, though few stay overnight. Someone will take you first to a house where you'll be handed a 26-page guidebook, asked to see your passport, and tapped for a donation of Rp200—your introductory dues into Banten. If you want to stay the night, **Peng. Karanghantau Indah** has large clean rooms at about Rp5000. Eat in one of the *warung* in the *desa* nearby. An alternative is to base yourself in Serang, Merak, or Cilegon, where there are ample accommodations, and make Banten just a day trip.

Getting There

From Jakarta's Kalideres Station, board a bus to Merak but pay only Rp1000 to the Ciceri Bus Station in Serang. Next, take a *becak* to the Pasar Lama minibus station for Rp400, from where it's only 6 km and Rp500 by minibus to Banten. If driving your own vehicle, Banten is only about 150 km (2½ -3 hours) W of Jakarta; take the new, faster *jalan tol,* not very expensive and well worth the price, which ends just outside of Cilegon. Pack a picnic lunch.

Vicinity Of Banten

A great side trip is the old harbor of Karanghantu, only one km and Rp250 by *oplet* from Banten. This was the former international harbor of the 17th C. Banten kingdom. Good photo possibilities. Karanghantu is one of the main places in Java where Bugis *prahu* stop, and you can view the traditional life of a unique Bugis fishing village and market.

BIRD SANCTUARIES

Only 10 km on a rough road N of Serang and one km from Banten, off the NW coast of Java, are 3 sea-level islands—Dua, Semut, and Bokor—all within reach of Karanghantu Harbor. Designated as a small reserve, P. Dua shelters large breeding colonies of many bird species of great interest to ornithologists, amateur or otherwise. Although P. Semut, one hour from Karanghantu by motorized *prahu*, P. Panjang (has a *kampung)*, and P. Bokor (18 ha) are all visitable, only P. Dua is inhabited by large numbers of birds. The different bird colonies can be observed from observation towers, with nesting sites as close as 5 m away! Take care when walking under nesting places because birds will spew you with slimy vomit and jets of guano. Breeding season restrictions are enforced now and game wardens posted on the islands protect the birds against poachers.

Pulau Dua

Also called Pulau Burung ("Bird Island"). Along with Peru's guano islands and the Norwegian Bird Cliffs, P. Dua is one of the world's chief bird islands. It's 30 min. by *prahu* from Karanghantu Habor in Banten Bay. The police will arrange a boat for you. Cheapest *prahu* cost about Rp50,000 for a one- to 2-hour tour. Pulau Dua, a coral reef now covered by sand and mud, is beginning to form a peninsula in the direction of the mainland. During the breeding season *(Musim Burung)* March to July each year, its 8 ha are a favorite breeding ground for 40,000-50,000 migratory birds (even breeds of ice birds!) and waterfowl. Species from as far away as India and China, as well as those escaping the Australian winter, touch down on P. Dua. When the young are grown they return to their respective country of origin. Species include white and black ibis, egrets, snake birds, doves and teals, pelicans, cormorants, black-crowned night herons, coastal seabirds *(burung laut)*, parakeets, parrots, Indonesian *beos, burung buntul, bangau,* and *jepelins.* Even after the end of the breeding season in Sept., you can still see the white-bellied eagle, all the herons, and thousands of wading birds from the north. As P. Dua (the island with the shortest crossing time) is very popular with tour groups, especially on weekends, the island is unusually vulnerable to disturbance. It is important that visitors are kept to a minimum. No large parties, please.

Pulau Rambut

A 15-ha bird nesting site and nature sanctuary next to P. Untung Java, one hour by sea from Jakarta's Sundakelapa or Tanjung Priok harbors. A speedboat costs Rp150,000 per day. From watchtowers observe the coming and going of the seabirds and courtship rituals such as the dance of the egrets. The Forestry Service maintains a *pasanggrahan* on the island, plus there are bungalows (Rp30,000 pp); for booking, contact the Pulau Putri, Jakarta Theatre Bldg., Jl. Thamrin 9 (tel. 359333-4).

MERAK

A dirty port town on the western tip of Java, Rp1200 (140 km) by bus from Jakarta, from where you board the ferry to Sumatra. The bus and train stations are both quite near the ferry terminal. The big petroleum base here is run by Pertamina; the high tanker and truck traffic makes for a bumpy main street! On the N side of Merak all the foreign oil workers live in their estates surrounded by fences with their own golf courses, schools, community centers, and stores. A new container terminal opened in 1987.

Accommodations

Tends to be expensive because you're a captive. **Losmen Robinson**, Rp6000 for upstairs rooms, is spacious and each room has a fan. Resident ladies. **Penginapan Anda**, Jl. Florida 4 (pronounced "PLORi-da"), is Rp4000 s, Rp5000 d with fan; though not a whorehouse, it's noisy but comfortable enough. Eat down the street at Tabahati, very good *nasi rames*. **Losmen Kunia**, also on Jl. Florida, is cheaper still. **Hotel Indola** (Rp6000-8000 d) is about 1½ km southeast of town on the road to Grogol. On the way out to Pantai Suralaya (or Florida Beach) there's **Losmen Sitar Kali Mas**. **Losmen Florida**, on the way from Merak to Florida Beach, charges Rp10,000. Even more expensive is the **Merak Beach Hotel**, Jl. Raya Merak Banten (tel. 15 Merak), 3 km before Merak on a sandy beach; Rp25,000 s or d. It has individual beachfront and family units, restaurant, bar, watersport facilities. Very quiet during the week but packed with Jakarta high-rollers on the weekend.

From Merak

Buses to Jakarta on the new toll road operate from 0500 to 0300 and take only 2½ hours, Rp1500. Third Class tickets cost only Rp1500 on the train (departing 0630 and 1630) all the way from Merak to the Tanah Abang Station in Jakarta. Ferries from Merak to Serengsen and Bakauheni in Lampung Province of S. Sumatra leave at least every 3 hours from 0730 to 2300. The ferry to Serengsen, S of Telukbetung on the S tip of Sumatra, leaves at 1100 and 2300; prices range from Rp1500 Deck Class up to Rp3800 1st Class, 5-6 hours. Cars cost Rp21,000; motorcycles Rp5000. Ferries also embark for the much closer port of Bakauheni, a large new ferry terminal on the SE tip of S. Sumatra; Rp1200 3rd Class, Rp2000 1st Class. From Bakauheni, it's 85 km and 2 hours by minibus on a good road to Panjang; you can also board buses to all points on Sumatra from Bakauheni.

VICINITY OF MERAK

One of the centers of the steel industry in Indonesia, Cilegon is 15 km and Rp600 SE of Merak. The giant **Krakatoa Steelworks** here was an earlier Russian project, abandoned and left to rust after the coup in 1965, then taken over by Pertamina. This is the country's biggest steel mill and, with an estimated investment of US$2500 million, one of the largest industrial projects ever undertaken in Indonesia. Because of corruption, including a million-dollar home and personal helicoptor for the director, the project cost 3 times the price of a similar steelworks in Taiwan. It took 20 years (starting in 1960) to design and bring the massive complex on line. A modern 500-megawatt oil/gas-fired power station at Suralaya in NW Java supplies the electric furnaces at the steelworks. Pellets arrive by bulk carriers from Brazil. Cruel contrasts between the old men and women collecting cartloads of coral to burn in primitive furnaces and the sophisticated conveyors and thermal-powered furnaces at the mill. The **Krakatoa Guest House** here is expensive; better to board a bus to Merak and spend the night there.

Ranca Danau

A reserve, 15 km W of Serang, which provides the necessary water for the steelworks. This 3,715-ha nature reserve, with its 90-m-deep lake, is a protected sanctuary of freshwater swamps supporting unique species of swamp vegetation and birds. The lake, Ranca Danau, is 10 km long. There are no facilities, no boating, and guards watch over the area. Because of a proposed dam and local exploitation of the area, this reserve is endangered.

FLORIDA BEACH

On the NW tip of Java, this area offers several well-patronized stretches of clean white-sand beaches and protected bays. It costs Rp300 to travel the 5 km from Merak to Florida. During weekdays the village, located on a tiny bay, is quiet, but on Sun. it's swamped. Though it lacks the charm of Carita Beach farther S, for such a small port there's lots of activity with freighters, banana boats, outriggers, and *keelong* out in the bay, and old men walking up and down the beach net-fishing. Take in the life of a W. Javanese fishing village. Swim the 350 m or hire a motorboat (Rp5000) out to the small island in the bay called Pulau Rida. From Florida it's a 3-km walk to the village of Suralaya which has a beach, numerous *warung,* and *losmen.*

Accommodations And Food

Restaurant Florida wants Rp5000 for a decrepit room, no matter how many people stay in it, complete with mosquitos and a wooden platform for a bed. Try to bargain them down to a package deal—for example, 2 people for 3 days for Rp2000 pp per day. You could get an offer from a family to rent you a room in their house for less, but don't expect any privacy. Restaurant Florida sells a greasy *mie goreng* for Rp1000; there are many other kiosks to eat at. The fenced-in complex 2 km before Merak is the **Merak Beach Hotel** (also called the Ramayana Beach Hotel), with individual a/c units with beach front; expensive restaurant, bar. They want Rp25,000 s or d.

RANGKASBITUNG

From Jakarta it's 107 km southwest. It was in the vicinity of Rangkasbitung where Max Havelaar, the idealistic character in the famous 19th C. Dutch novel by the same name, actually lived and worked. From Labuhan to Rangkasbitung (or "Rangkas" for short), you usually have to take 2 minibuses, the first from Labuhan to Pandeglang (Rp1500), the second from Pandeglang to Rangkas (Rp500, 20 km). If driving from Bogor, the trim, meandering country road W from Bogor to Jasinga and then W to Rangkas is slow and difficult. If arriving late, stay at **Terminal Hotel,** Jl. S.N. Kalijaja 165; the cheapest rooms are Rp4000 s, Rp5000 d. Also try **Hotel Vijaya**, Rp5000 s or d.

From Rangkas

To Bogor by minibus you have to do it in 2 stages: first to Jasinga, 40 km, Rp1500, from there to Bogor, Rp1000. On the way from Rangkas to Jasinga you pass through many scenic rubber and coconut tree plantations over an undulating, narrow, cool mountain road (also broken pavement and severe bumps in many places). This is one of the prettiest roads on Java through a sparsely populated area—an immaculate little toy road of rickety bamboo fences, sedate villages, stone buildings, miniature telephone poles—a photographic wonderland. **to Pelabuhan Ratu:** For an adventurous drive S, head for the T-junction at the end of the main street, then take a left. This road, passable only by 4WD, takes you to Melingping from where you can head E over the coastal hills to Pelabuhanratu. If you take a R at the T-junction over the river crowded with bamboo rafts, it will take you to Pandeglang. From Pandeglang, keep L for Labuhan and the coast.

THE BADUI PEOPLE

This small tribe (2,000-4,000) of Sunda-speaking people—the mysterious "Amish of West Java"—lives in 25 villages in a 50-sq-km forest territory around G. Kendang, SE of Rangkasbitung. A visit to this area is not easy and would appeal only to dedicated students of isolated cultures. For 400 years the White Badui have maintained complete isolation from the outside world, preserving intact every aspect of their way of life. Despite study by anthropologists, little is known of the Badui except that they are reputed to have powerful mystic and clairvoyant powers. Held in awe by common Javanese and politicians, they predicted both world wars. Suharto safely ignores them. Now their isolation is beginning to break down with the increasing population pressures of the plains to the N of G. Kendang encroaching more and more on traditional Badui lands. New schools and low-cost housing are also drawing the Badui away from their traditional territory.

Badui Dalam

Badui villages are divided into Badui Dalam (the inner 3 villages of Cibeo, Cikartawana, and Cikeusik) and the Badui Luar (outer 22 villages). The inner or White Badui consist of 40 families *(Kajeroan),* or about 400 people, purest of Badui stock. This inner clan dresses only in coarse white cloth woven by themselves and follows rigorous rules of conduct which were first laid down by an ancestral divinity called Batatunggal. They are forbidden to kill, steal, lie, commit adultery, get drunk, eat food at night, take any form of conveyance, wear flowers or perfumes, accept gold or silver, touch money, cut their hair. Other taboos relate to rendering Badui lands unattractive to invaders: they may not grow *sawah,* use fertilizers, raise cash crops, use modern tools for working *ladang* soil, or keep large domestic animals. The Badui Dalam live in *tanah larangan* where no strangers are permitted to spend the night; travelers may enter only on a walk-in, walk-out basis. (This area is denoted by diagonal lines on adjacent map.) You are able to hear the drumbeats at night but you won't be allowed to approach the gathering which you can hear through the trees.

Badui Luar

Outside the "sacred inner circle" are the Outer Badui or Badui Luar *(Kaluaran).* This outer clan wears bluish-black turbans and all-black *sarung (loreng hitam),* lives less strictly, is permitted to sell crops and trade, and generally serves as go-between for the White Baduis and the rest of the world. This group oversees both the entry of strangers into Badui lands and the exit of Badui people. In the past no one was allowed to leave this jungle fastness, but now you sometimes see Badui men in the streets of Jakarta or even as far away as Bandung. But 2 things are certain: they have come on foot and have a good reason for being there.

History

Their origins are uncertain; Dr. B. van Tricht's expedition in 1928 to gather medical and anthropological data on the Badui was a complete failure. One theory maintains that the Badui could be the only surviving remnants of the aristocracy of the Sunda Kingdom of Pajajaran who lived near Batutulis in the hills around Bogor; their domestic architecture follows most closely traditional Sundanese architecture. Pakuwan, the capital of Pajajaran, was destroyed by invading Muslims in 1579. To preserve their basic animism (with Buddhist and Hindu overtones), Badui ancestors are thought to have fled to this mountain retreat. Badui still pay their respects to Siliwangi, the last of the Hindu kings. Another theory traces their origin to northern Banten; pockets of people in the northern

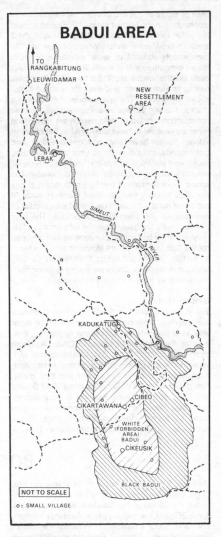

BADUI AREA

TO RANGKABITUNG
LEUWIDAMAR
NEW RESETTLEMENT AREA
LEBAK
SIMEUT
RIVER
KADUKATUG
CIBEO
CIKARTAWANA
WHITE (FORBIDDEN AREA) BADUI
CIKEUSIK
BLACK BADUI

NOT TO SCALE
o = SMALL VILLAGE

hills still speak the archaic dialect of Sunda that the Badui use today.

Crafts And Architecture

Badui crafts can be bought at the Carita Krakatoa Beach Hotel—at around Rp35,000-40,000 for one *sarung!* In Badui territory itself, they seldom sell their fabrics; most crafts are made only for their own use. Even cotton they produce themselves. The detail and style of Badui village architecture are very similar to architecture in the animist areas of S. Sumatra, most likely due to some cultural exchange between the 2 areas in pre-Muslim times. Village houses tend to form streets about 4 m wide, running E to west. House orientation is N to south. Rice barns (lumpung padi), like the houses, are timber framed, built on piles resting on river stones, and the floor is about 40 cm above the ground. The space under the house is a chicken run and storage area. Pegs are used in their construction instead of nails, which are taboo, and joints are wedged to make them rigid. In Badui Dalam villages houses have only one room, one door, and one veranda, though in Badui Luar villages houses could have additional rooms and verandas. The walls are made of bamboo mats woven diagonally. The springy floor is made of bamboo slats which allows the wind to blow through. Roof thatch is made of pandanus palm with peaks decorated with circular or heart-shaped ijuk (palm fiber) ornaments. The floor plan is simple: the hearth is in the far corner in a fire-resistant tinder box and smoke escapes through open gables. Salt and salt fish are stored nearby. One room is used for cooking and eating, the other for sleeping and receiving guests. Doors are always fastened from the outside as theft is virtually unknown.

Getting There

The rigid taboo system makes it difficult for tourists to visit the inner territory, but you can get to the outer villages of Leuwidamar, Lebak, and Kadukatug, then walk to the inner Badui village of Cibeo. Although both the Inner and Outer Badui resist contact with large numbers of people, they are known to be friendly to those who brave the journey into their midst. First get to the town of Rangkasbitung SE of Serang and E of Labuhan. Using Rangkas as your starting point into Badui lands, obtain written permission (surat ijin) from the local government office, Kantor Kabupaten, Jl. Alun-alun (the town square). This is a simple procedure: show your passport, sign the application, and surrender Rp3000 plus one photograph of yourself during regular office hours every day except Sunday.

The Walk In

This trip is for those who are physically fit, have planned and packed wisely, and can adjust to local living during the journey. Bring gifts and enough money to reciprocate overnighting in village homes; also take food to supplement village meals. It would also be appropriate to adopt quiet, attentive behavior during your stay with the Badui. The journey is probably best accomplished in groups no larger than 4-8 people. Ideal would be to find a Badui Luar guide in Rangkas who is going back home to one of the outer villages. It takes at least 4 days to walk over hills to the inner villages; no vehicular roads reach the Badui inner territory. The trek starts from Leuwidamar village, at the end of a fairly good road, about 20 km S of Rangkas. (You may also travel to Leuwidamar from Rangkas by minibus for Rp1000-1500.) Stay in the residence of the kepala polisi (police chief) in Leuwidamar. This kind man doesn't ask for money, but give a donation "for the food, snacks, and tea." From Cisimeut you cross the river and travel the next 30 km over about 12 hills to the Muslim village of Muncang by foot or motorcycle. Some travelers spend the night in Muncang before continuing on the next day at dawn (motorcycle must be left in Muncang) another 20 km to the outer Badui village of Kadukatug. Kadukatug is strikingly different physically as well as in atmosphere from typical Muslim villages of W. Java. From Kadukatug a Badui guide will take you the last 3-hour (15-km) hard climb on a jungle track to the village of Cibeo, the very heartland of the inner Badui. It takes in all 2 days of difficult walking from Leuwidamar to Cibeo. Travelers to Cibeo are sometimes able to get local food and accommodation.

BOGOR

Sixty km S and only 2 hours by bus from Jakarta, Bogor sprawls noisily and smokily among hills between the Ciliwung and Cisadane rivers. Its population is 250,000, the majority pegawi and their families. The name Bogor is taken from the name of an extinct species of palm, "Bagor." Founded over 500 years ago, Bogor is built around a huge, verdant botanical garden, one of the most magnificent in the world and one of Indonesia's major tourist attractions. A smog-filled crowded city of pretty villas, and banana, mimosa, and wild almond trees, one wonders how delightful a town this was before the advent of the petrol age. Check out the superb, fully restored Dutch Catholic school, Regina Pacis, opposite the Istana Bogor. A great variety of scenic valleys and mountain resort towns surround Bogor.

Climate

Being in the more exposed uplands (200-300 m), Bogor maintains a cooler and more refreshing climate than Jakarta. And with the amount of rainfall the city receives, it's no wonder that Indonesia's largest botanical garden is located here. Bogor probably leads the world in thunderstorms, which arrive precisely at 1600 two out of three days year round. It's a tradition here that if G. Salak to the SW of the city is clouded, then it will rain that day. If the peak is free of clouds, it will not.

ISTANA BOGOR

The road from Jakarta runs smack into this gleaming white former Dutch governor's mansion, a magnificent sight with its graceful colonnaded frontage and domed and mansard roof, complete with a spotted deer herd roaming over undulating lawns under big shady trees. The Bogor palace has not been used as a residence since Sukarno's time; the main building is used for official occasions, installations, and ceremonies. The R wing is used for heads-of-state or presidents, the L wing for guests of the ministerial or vice-presidential level. The palace interior covers an area of about 14,000 sq m, and the grounds cover an area of about 24 hectares. Inside the mansion are sumptuously appointed rooms, lavish reception chambers, and a fabulous international collection of fine art.

History
This was the official residence of the Dutch governors-general from 1870-1942. While Baron Gustaf Willem van Imhoff, governor-general for the Dutch East Indies Company, was making a duty tour of the upper interior territories, he was fascinated by the peaceful village of Bogor. In 1745 he had a small resthouse built here and named it *Buitenzorg* ("Without a Care"). Twisting uphill for 60 km from his residence in Batavia the road led right into the 20-ha resthouse yard. Used as a retreat from the busy social life and government responsibilities in Batavia, over time pleasant Bogor village eventually developed into the noisy city of today, and the humble country estate was enlarged into a splendid colonial palace. The ensuing years saw many changes and additions to the original building by a whole succession of Dutch governors-general. Huge glamorous parties were held here, the Dutch elite coming up from Batavia for riding, hunting, and dancing on the immaculately kept grounds. The deer were fattened by the Dutch to provide venison for their banquets. In 1950, after their victory against colonial domination, the palace was taken over by the Indonesian government. The present-day status of the building is "Palace of the President of the Republic of Indonesia," or simply Istana Bogor (Bogor Palace). Suharto, however, doesn't ever stay here because the ghost of Sukarno is said to haunt the corridors at night. Certainly his presence is still overwhelming.

The Collections
The Japanese in WW II looted all the Dutch treasures so what you see now are only what the late President Sukarno collected during his political career. Being half-Balinese, Sukarno fancied himself quite the art connoisseur: there are incredible paintings by some of Indonesia's most renowned painters, a few of which it is said he "improved" to suit his tastes. Among the 219 paintings and 136 sculptures are many voluptuous nudes representing every race. (Sukarno's private collection of erotic paintings and sculptures is locked in a special room.) In the L wing is a famous painting by Le Maire of his wife Ni Polok in 12 different aspects. See Sukarno's bedroom, the half-ton chandeliers from Czechoslovakia, and wander through the wonderful statuary in the palace garden.

Tours
The palace, not normally open to the public, may be visited by prior arrangement through tour agencies. Contact Dinas Pariwisata, Jl. Juanda 38A (tel. 21350), at least a week in advance. There must be a minimum of 10 people in a group, Rp6000 pp. It's also possible, by special arrangement, to dine in the palace. If you don't want to go through a tour agency, make a request by letter, including the name of each visitor, the date, and exact time you hope to view the palace. Send to: Head of Protocol, Istana Negara, Jl. Veteran, Jakarta. If alone, perhaps the Tourist Office can fit you in another group, but you may have to wait as long as 5-7 days.

KEBON RAYA

The Bogor Botanical Gardens, right behind the presidential palace, are an incredible 87-ha (275-acre) estate, one of the leading botanical institutions in the world as well as an important scientific research center. These gardens have been here for over 170 years; Bogor has risen up around them. The gardens boast hundreds of species of trees, an herbarium with 5,620 plant species, a cultivated park of paths, pools, glades, shrubs, lawns, open-air cactus gardens, great twisting foot-thick overhead vines, enormous waterlilies, with a river bubbling through it all. About 12,695 specimens of native plants have been collected not only from all over the Malay Archipelago but from many other tropical regions as well. Kebon Raya is also a favorite trysting place for lovers. Because of the great number of today's married couples who met here for the first time, the other name for the gardens is *Kebon Jodoh*, which means something like "Garden of Betrothal." There are so far 5 branches of the Kebon Raya Gardens: Sibolangit, 40 km SW of Medan, N. Sumatra; Sukarno/Hatta Reserve, 20 km E of Padang, W. Sumatra; Purwodadi, 30 km NE of Malang, E. Java; Cibodas, 45 km SE of Bogor; and Eka Karya, 30 km SE of Singaraja, N. Bali.

History
These world-famous gardens were the inspiration of the Dutch Governor-General Van der Capelan, who expanded the garden first put in during the Napoleonic Wars by the English governor-general of Indonesia, Sir Stamford Raffles, an avid botanist. Early Dutch

KEBON RAYA

JL. JEN. SUDIRMAN

GATE

BHINNEKA GARDEN & HOLY BANYAN TREE

MEDICINAL PLANTS

ORCHID HOUSE

JL. G. GEDE

PALACE GROUNDS

JL. MUSLIHAT

PALACE WALL

CLIMBERS

2nd. CANARIUM AVE.

ASTRID AVE.

SULAWESI

OIL PALMS

TEA HOUSE

DUTCH CEMETERY

1st. CANARIUM AVE.

LAKE

AUSTRALIA

WATER LILIES

BAMBOOS

PALMS

FOUNTAIN

PALMS

WATER PLANTS

FERNS

WILD CORNER

TOURIST OFFICE

RATTAN

TROPICAL RAINFOREST

JL. PALEDAN

CACTUS

SHRUBS

INSCRIBED STONE

JL. RAYA PAJAJARAN

S. GILIWUNG

PHPA

JL. SURYA KENCANA

JL. EMPANG

1. National Biological Institute (central office)
2. Bibliotheca Bogoriensis
3. Herbarium Bogoriensis
4. Presidential Palace
5. Teysmann Memorial
6. Olivia Raffles Memorial
7. nursery
8. entrance
9. office
10. Treub Laboratory
11. Museum Zoologieum Bogoriense

researchers used these gardens to develop cash crops in order to provide profits for the mother country during the so-called Forced Cultivation Period (1830-70) when all of Java was turned into one vast work camp. Today, one of the main tasks of the gardens still is to collect and maintain living plants, "with special interest in those which have economic potential." Among the many economic and ornamental plants that have been imported into the country for the purpose of widespread cultivation are cinchona, bougainvillea, cassava, cinnamon, cacao, coffee, conifers, shade and timber trees, cotton, kapok, mahogany, maize, beans, sugarcane, tea, tobacco, and vanilla. The rubber plant was introduced in 1876 and the very first specimen of oil palm introduced into Indonesia (in 1848) is still growing in the gardens. This is the ancestor of the high-grade oil palms now cultivated throughout Indonesia and Malaysia, and the crop is one of Indonesia's main exports.

Sights

See the memorial pavilion for Lady Raffles, wife of Sir Stamford. A beautifully restored Dutch graveyard is at the end of the Pasar Bogor entrance road, past the presidential guesthouse, in the middle of a bamboo grove. Also in the gardens is one of the world's leading orchid hothouse laboratories. The Orchid House has 4,522 registered hybrids, including Borneo's rare black orchid, the giant orchid *(Grammatophylum speciosum)* which can bear 3,000 flowers at one time; corpse plant *(Amorphophallus titanum)*, a stinky giant flower which is pictured on the Rp500 note. Unfortunately, the Orchid House is open only to specialists (apply in advance).

Practicalities

Open to the public 0800-1600 every day. Admission is Rp800, though on Sun. and holidays (when it's especially crowded) admission drops to only Rp200. To avoid crowds, visit Kebon Raya on a weekday; to avoid the rain, visit in the morning. Guides, some quite knowledgeable and entertaining, make themselves available in the park itself. To prevent misunderstanding, negotiate a fee in advance (about Rp3000 per hour).

Affiliated Institutes

Bogor is one of the most important scientific centers in Indonesia, and at least 17 affiliated institutes are scattered all over the city, most of them progeny of the gardens. Institut Pertanian Bogor (IPB), or Bogor Agricultural Institute, has 525 teachers and almost 3,000 students studying Indonesia's agricultural and forest ecosystems. Perhaps their greatest triumph in modern times was the Bimas program of the 1960s which achieved spectacular increases in rice output, and heralded the famous "Green Revolution." The Treub Laboratory was founded in 1884 with the primary aim of accommodating visiting scientists who wished to study Indonesian plants *in situ*. The main task of the Herbarium Bogoriense, established in 1844, is to study the flora of Melasia (Indonesia, Philippines, Malaysia, and PNG); its collection covers the whole plant kingdom from algae to fungi (more than 40,000 species) and it has a well-stocked biology library. Museum Zoologicum Bogoriense was founded in 1894 under the guidance of Dr. K.G. Koningsberger with the purpose of studying the fauna of the Indonesian archipelago. Admission Rp200 (Sun. Rp100). The entrance gate to the museum is just in front of the building at Jl. Ir. H. Juanda 3. The first book on Indonesian mammalia was published by the museum's staff. About 300,000 specimens of insects, molluscs, birds, mammals, reptiles, amphibians, fish, and other invertebrates have been collected. The majority of the stuffed specimens are in pretty bad shape. Nearly every year an expedition is undertaken by this institute to explore several insufficiently known areas of Indonesia and enrich the museum's collections. The results of these forays appear in its publication *Treubia*. Bibliotheca Bogoriensis is on Jl. Ir. H. Juanda; this scientific library welcomes visitors Mon. to Thurs. 0800-1200. Interested persons can obtain access to the library's several thousand books and hundreds of magazines by becoming members.

ACCOMMODATIONS

Being so close to Jakarta, there's a constant shortage of accommodations, and what's available may not be so pleasant. Most travelers either go on to Jakarta, or visit Bogor on a day excursion and stay at the hill stations SE of town (the Kopo Hostel in Cisarua, for example, is a great deal). **Penginapan Pasundan** is on Jl. Veteran 19 (tel. 28249), near Pasar De Fries, about 2 blocks SW of Bogor's main *bemo* station; Rp7500 s or d (doubles with *mandi*). Central but noisy, and kept in moral order by an *orang Islam*. Fruit, snacks, and meals *warung* are just outside. **Penginapan Damai** is also on the W side of town at Jl. May. Oking Jayaatmaja 29, only a few hundred m from the train station. It charges Rp6500 for a large drab double room and Rp3500 for a big drab single room. Comfortable **Wisma Karunia**, Jl. Sempur 35-37, is close to the gardens and charges only Rp8000-10,000 d; Rp6000 for dorm beds; good reports. **Wisma Teladan**, Jl. Sawojajar, is equally good value for Rp7,000-12,000 d.

Moving up in price, on the N side of town is guesthouse-style **Elsana Transit Hotel**, Jl. Sawojajar 36 (tel. 22552); 3 classes of rooms, the cheapest running about Rp17,500 d for 2nd Class rooms with pavilion, up to Rp22,000 for bigger rooms. Prices include breakfast, tax, service, fan, Indo-style bath, showers, towels, and soap. There's also a plush lob-

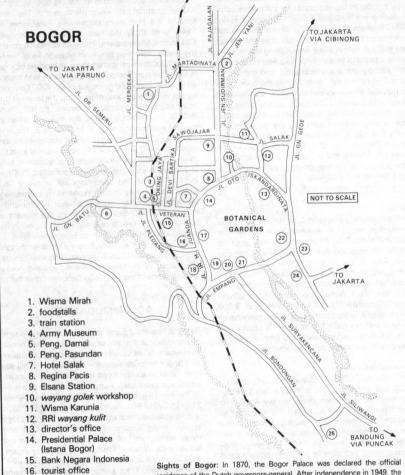

BOGOR

TO JAKARTA
VIA PARUNG

TO JAKARTA
VIA CIBINONG

BOTANICAL
GARDENS

NOT TO SCALE

TO
JAKARTA

TO
BANDUNG
VIA PUNCAK

1. Wisma Mirah
2. foodstalls
3. train station
4. Army Museum
5. Peng. Damai
6. Peng. Pasundan
7. Hotel Salak
8. Regina Pacis
9. Elsana Station
10. *wayang golek* workshop
11. Wisma Karunia
12. RRI *wayang kulit*
13. director's office
14. Presidential Palace
    (Istana Bogor)
15. Bank Negara Indonesia
16. tourist office
17. post office
18. police station
19. Zoological Museum
20. Treub Laboratory & PPA
21. main entrance to
    Kebon Raya
22. Orchid House
23. hospital
24. bus terminal
25. Batutulis

Sights of Bogor: In 1870, the Bogor Palace was declared the official residence of the Dutch governors-general. After independence in 1949, the palace became the home of President Sukarno. See gilded mirrors, Japanese paintings, giant banquet tables, big conference rooms, half-ton chandeliers from Czechoslovakia, Chinese ceramics, Jepara-carved furniture, Sukarno's personal library, a statue of Tito, Persian carpets, Italian lamps and crystal, the Hall of a Thousand Mirrors, Sukarno's bedroom, and the State Guest Room. Wander through the wonderful statuary in the palace garden. Also lying in the center of Bogor, next to the palace, are the world-renowned Bogor Botanical Gardens. established in 1817. From early on, the gardens helped develop cash crops for the burgeoning Dutch colonial plantations. Protein-poor cassava was even encouraged as a second food crop on Java to support an increasing agrarian population so as to increase productivity. There was famine in many parts of Java because rice was being exported to Australia and Europe in the early 19th century.

by, small kiosk, and quiet courtyard. Not very central; to get there, take a *daihatsu* no. 13 to the front of the palace, then no. 7 to Jl. Sawojajar. Elsana is just off Jl. Jen. Sudirman, one of the main approach roads into Bogor from the north. Spacious **Hotel Salak**, Jl. Ir. H. Juanda 8 (tel. 22091/22092/22093), is opposite Istana Bogor. Prices depend upon if you stay upstairs, downstairs, in the front, or in the newer building in the rear. Survey several rooms to get the one suited for your needs; they come with or without bath; Rp18,940 s and d, up to Rp23,175-32,250 including breakfast and a/c. These are enormous rooms but the whole place is fast going to seed. The atmosphere, like many of the older hotels of Indonesia, is reminiscent of old Dutch times. Very obliging staff, and the manager might be able to attach you to a group tour to see the Istana Bogor if you give him some notice. Hotel Salak has a restaurant; stick to the Indonesian dishes. Another *tempoe doeloe* remnant is the very nice **Wisma Parmata**, Jl. Raya Pajajaran 35 (tel. 23402), Rp30,000-55,000, with hot water, huge rooms and bathrooms, big beds, breakfast, and homestyle restaurant. **Bogor Inn**, Jl. Kumbang 12A (tel. 28134), Rp17,500-55,000 plus 21% taxes, gives as much as 50% discount for long-term stays.

FOOD

Sundanese Food

Unlike accommodations, restaurants are numerous. Sundanese food is a little drier and less spicy hot than *nasi padang,* and it also tends to be cheaper. One of the most popular Sundanese dishes is *asinan,* a mixture of fruit, vegetables, and peanuts in a hot peanut sauce. The best places to sample *asinan* are at **Asinan Bogor**, Jl. Kapt. Muslihat, and at **Asinan Segar**, Jl. Veteran, next to the barbershops. **Imah Kuring**, Jl. Tajur near Billiard Amusement, and **Pondok Nineung**, Jl. Dr. Semeru 6 (tel. 21785) both offer special Sundanese cooking; eat well for around Rp1500.

Street Food

Wagons and carts clog the streets; eat well for Rp500. The foodstall area beyond Dinas Pariwisata toward Hotel Salak has an unusually good *mie baso* (fishball soup). Pasar Bogor contains some inexpensive foodstalls, and Jl. Merdeka at night has numerous *sate ayam* and *sate kambing* wagons: 10 sticks for Rp700. Try the local *bandrek* and *bajigur* drinks—coconut milk boiled with ginger flour and stirred with coffee or chocolate. Bogor is famous as a fruit and vegetable center. All along Jl. Oto Iskandardinata and around the gate of Kebon Raya—especially on a Sunday—an immense variety of fruit and vegetables (even blackberries!) are sold. The Bogor area is known for its black radishes *(talas), salak,* ½-m-long horn-

shaped bananas *(pisang tanduk*—Rp250 each). Sweet, small pineapples cost Rp250-400. Pasar Bogor, a 2-min. walk SE of the botanical gardens, is the place to go for fresh fruit. The fruit market at Cibinong is very popular with home-bound Jakartans. Both sides of Jl. Parung in Parung (20 km NW of Bogor) host numerous fruit stands where you can sample virtually any fruit in season grown around Bogor and in the nearby districts.

Restaurants

The **Sari Bundo Restaurant** and the **Trio Jaya,** both near the bus terminal, offer decent, inexpensive meals for under Rp1500. Popular with Westerners are the **Ramayana Restaurant**, Jl. Dewi Sartika 45, and the **Bogor Permai**, Jl. Jen. Sudirman 15 (Chinese/Indo food upstairs, Western food downstairs). Very good also are the **Singosari** and **RM Cairo**, on Jl. Ir. H. Juanda 28 near the Ramayana Theatre (great *sate kambing).* The **Singosar** in Pasar Anyar specializes in take-out frog legs. The **Simpang Raya** on the corner of Jl. Kapt. Muslihat and Jl. May. Oking Jayaatmaja is a *nasi padang* restaurant which serves a very decent *soto ayam* for Rp600 (Rp200 extra for rice), *es papaya* for Rp500. **Terang Bulan**, Jl. Ir. H. Juanda 68, for Indo/Chinese; try **Mirah Steak House**, Jl. Kebon Jahe 2 (off Jl. Veteran one block behind Jl. Merdeka), and the **Lezat**, Jl. Siliwangi 12, for Indo/Chinese/Euro cooking. Also, many restaurants are located along the main Bogor/Jakarta road; the number of cars in front of each indicates its popularity. For example, **Restaurant Situ Lebak Wangi**, 2 km from Bogor on the district's main highway N, is built in the middle of a lake; it offers such Sundanese delicacies as golden carp and fresh vegetable salad. **bakeries: Deliceus**, Jl. Mawar 18, sells freshly baked bread which is ready about 1130 and sold out by 1300. The **Mirah Steak House & Restaurant**, Jl. Perintis Kemerdekaan (tel. 21192), sells bread, rolls, and Danish pastry, as well as European and Chinese food.

SHOPPING

Check out Pasar Bogor, on Jl. Suryakencana right on the *bemo* route, for folk crafts and implements (plus fruits and vegetables). Crafts include *kenari* shell, semi-precious and precious stones, buffalo horn, *wayang golek* puppets, pottery, and bamboo ornaments. Souvenir sellers also cluster around the gate of the botanic gardens and even infiltrate the gardens on foot selling framed butterflies, *wayang golek* carvings, jewelry, etc. Their prices aren't that bad either, as little as Rp10,000 for a whole case of butterflies or exotic lizards mounted under glass. Other vendors sell wood sculpture, Rp15,000 for a royal *prahu* which they claim they bought for Rp10,000 (don't fall for this line!). Bear in mind that there could be trouble at customs if you try to take back crafts made of feathers and other organic materials. Bogor's new shopping center, Internusa on Jl. Pajajaran (opposite the mayor's house, Rumah Balai Kota), has a big Gunung Agung Bookshop. The Java carpet works of P.P. Dobbe & Son is at Jl. Kantor Batu 19 (tel. 21421); arrange through Mrs. Dobbe (speaks English) to watch hand-made carpets under construction and you may order your own rug. Handbags, baskets, placemats, etc. are also for sale. Buy carpets and other products made from plant fibers (rami and mendong) at Parung just NW of Bogor. On the way out to Cipanas at the side of the road beautifully colored kites sell for Rp1200. Finally, Cibinong, at the crossroads between Bogor, Jakarta, and Citeureup, has been known since Dutch times for its souvenirs and fruits. Visit the curio shop Sweet Aminah on the industrial road to Jakarta past Cibinong which features many arts of Indonesia (especially from Bali).

Souvenir Outlets

Nusa Penida Souvenir & Art Shop, Jl. Ir. H. Juanda, is behind the Ramayana Cinema, a 5-min. walk from Kebon Raya's geteway. This shop's specialty is bamboo crafts: bamboo purses from Rp800-3000, Balinese woodcarvings, lamps for Rp4500; also beads, shells, pottery, etc. **Kenari Indah**, Jl. Bondongan Blok 30, is right in the Arab kampung of Lolongok. This family business specializes in kenari and white-silver handicrafts. Kenari (see many specimens in Kebon Raya) is used to make necklaces, belts, belt buckles, rings, bracelets, spoons. This shop's silver pieces (25% silver) start from only Rp800 and go up to Rp16,000. Also for sale is buffalo-horn work, from Rp800-Rp15,000; a whole carved horn will cost around Rp25,000 first price. There are also wayang topeng masks for Rp8000, wayang golek for Rp14,000. Butterflies from G. Salak, mounted in a case, sell for Rp11,000. Finally, check out Susanna Beauty Salon and Batik Shop, Jl. Sawojajar 27 (tel. 21115), near Elsana Transit Hotel. A glass factory is at Jl. Bondongan 55; see handblowing of lanterns and bottles. Children must be accompanied by an adult!

Batik Shops

Abundant fabrics are found in the pasar and specialty shops. All shops mentioned below sell batik cloth as well as ready-made batik shirts and dresses. **Mrs. Yati Malada**, Jl. Sempur Kaler 19 (tel. 22608), is open weekdays after 1400 and Sun. all day. There's also **Batik Keris**, Jl. Merdeka 6; **Wisma Batik Indah**, Jl. Oto Iskandardinata 51; Ibu Prawiro, Jl. Cikurai 42; and **Mrs. Stans Stolte**, Jl. Bincarung 19, who sells adult and children's clothes, as well as toys, dolls, and batik dolls' clothes.

Gongmaker

One of the few remaining gongsmiths on Java (or in the world, for that matter) is **Pak Sukarna's**, Jl. Pan-casan 17, ½ km from Istana Bogor down Jl. Empang near Bogor's town center. (The only other gong foundry on Java is in the Mangkunegaran Kraton in Solo.) Walk through town until you reach the large cinema, then take the road to the L (Jl. Empang) toward Muara and keep R at the next T-junction. Cross the river and 200 m up this narrow street you'll see carpenters working outside a house on the L, making frames for the gongs. The foundry is across the road; follow the sound of the hot metal being pounded into shape. The secret of gamelan making has always been closely guarded due to a certain amount of mysticism involved. Each instrument was made to order for the kraton or orchestra of a priyayi. Only the master craftsmen knew the whole process, and as these men die, the craft is becoming lost. The metal for the gong, a combination of copper and tin, is heated over a charcoal fire; when it has attained the required temperature and hue it's poured into a hollowed-out rock and allowed to cool slightly. The instrument is beaten into shape while hot then thrown hissing into a well of cold water. The artisans ritually wash their faces in this water. The pitch of the gong depends upon its size and the thickness of the metal. When buying a gong, listen for clear undulations in tone. The means of creating these undulations remains a secret. In the showroom they take special orders for gongs and other gamelan instruments.

Precious Stones

A semi-precious stone factory, Tiasky, is located before Cibulang. Owned by Mrs. Soekotjo, it's just before (turn L) the Ussu International Hotel, about a 30-min. drive from Bogor. Here they cut, shape, and polish batu cin cin, a decorative marble jewelry. Visitors may see stone and silver polishing. There's a sales room for jewelry and accessories. Write to Mrs. Soekotjo, Jl. Hankam 718 (Cipari-Cisarua), tel. 94063.

SERVICES

For specific questions about the sights of the city, go to the Bogor Dinas Pariwisata, SE of Kebon Raya, near the GPO at Jl. Ir. H. Juanda 38A (tel. 21350). Mr. Syafruddin will take care of you, and provide maps as well as information on places of interest and events in and around Bogor. On the same street (no. 9) is the headquarters for the Directorate of Conservation and Preservation of Natural Resources (PPA), the official body for the administration of Indonesia's wildlife reserves. This is the place to get information and permission to enter the reserves. The Red Cross Hospital, R.S. Umum P.M.I. (pronounced PAY EM EE), Jl. Raya Pajajaran (tel. 24080), near the Kebon Raya, is where victims of Puncak traffic accidents are usually brought for emergency treatment. Physicans are on duty in the hospital weekdays from 0800-1400.

TRANSPORTATION

Getting There

By bus from Jakarta via Cibinong takes 2 hours, Rp600, with frequent departures every day from Cililitan Station. The express buses take the smooth new Jagorawi Highway, which cuts at least an hour off the trip! From Bandung by bus takes 3 hours, Rp1750. Although buses are more comfortable than trains, the train takes only an hour and makes about 22 runs a day from Jakarta to Bogor. Bogor's train station lies in the center of the city. The drawbacks are that trains are hot and you sometimes have to stand. If driving your own vehicle to Bogor and the Puncak, take the Jagorawi (toll) Highway; entrance off Jl. Maj. J. Subroto.

Getting Around

Because of the massive gardens in its center, Bogor is very spread out. *Becak* are everywhere, but prohibited from the main drags. *Daihatsu* rides around town cost Rp100. Pasar Bogor and the Bemo Terminal on Jl. P. Muslihat opposite Toko Sinar Matahari are the central stands. Charter a *bajai* direct to your destination, or hire them by the hour (Rp3000). Bar-

gain and agree on a price before you get in the vehicle. *Delman* (horse-drawn buggy) stands may also be found at Pasar Bogor, near Pasar Anyar on Jl. M.A. Salmun (Jl. Pabrik Gas), and near the railroad station at Jl. May. Oking Jayaatmaja. A taxi stand is in front of Pasar Bogor next to the Forestry Institute; you have to bargain as they are unmetered.

From Bogor

The *terminal bis* is on Jl. Pajajaran SE of town; by bus to Jakarta's Cililitan Station the long way costs Rp500 via Parung, NW of Bogor, 2 hours. The other road from Bogor to Jakarta, Jl. Raya Pajajaran, goes through Cibinong (stops at the fruit market) and also ends up at Cililitan Station. Much faster than both of these routes is the freeway; ask for *jalan tol;* Rp600. From the train station in the center of town, the train to Jakarta costs Rp300 (3rd Class), but avoid the jammed commuter trains in the early morning and late afternoon. Rangkas is 52 km from Jasinga, and Jasinga is 41 km from Bogor, Rp750 by minibus. To the Puncak, take a *bajai* (Rp750) first to Stasiun Colt Baranang Siang, then a minibus up to the pass through one solid village, Rp700. Sukabumi is one hour and Rp700 from Bogor, or take one of the 3 daily trains (0630, 1130, and 1630). To Bandung by bus costs Rp1200, 4-4½ hours.

VICINITY OF BOGOR

Batutulis

Despite the fact that Bogor used to be the capital of the immensely powerful Hindu kingdom of Pajajaran from the 12th-16th C., and an historic rival of the central Javanese kingdoms, there is remarkably little to show for it. One of the few remaining physical traces which the all-conquering tropical climate has not claimed is Batutulis (meaning "Writing in Stone"), an ancient 9-lined inscription in old Sundanese Sanskrit etched on a conical-shaped stone (145 cm wide by 150 cm high). The purpose of the inscription is to attest to the supernatural powers of the king, and was a means of protecting the realm from its enemies. King Surawisesa (1521-1535) succeeded Sri Baduga Maharaja and decreed in 1533 that the message be written in stone. The site is housed in a small building nearly opposite the gate to Sukarno's former home (Hing Puri Bima Cakti), 3 km SE of Bogor's Ramayana Cinema. Open from 0700 until late at night, the *juru kunci* will take a small donation and let you in, shoeless. There will be children begging (people are thought to have larger hearts when they visit a holy place). The inscription here is still sacred to many people, and despite the whining *bemo* going by on the road outside, it's even got the feel of a holy place of

meditation and devotion. Inside the concrete building a ritual of some sort could be going on, with mats and incense burning, and both an Indonesian and a Sundanese flag on display. One set of footprints, which look like someone has stepped onto wet cement, is said to have been imprinted into the stone by the sheer magical strength and power of King Surawisesa. The monarch's knee marks are also there as further evidence.

Batutulis Ciampea

Another mysterious "written stone" is located in a riverbed in Ciampea, 15 km NW of Bogor. From in front of the Ramayana Cinema in Bogor, catch a *bemo* to Ciampea. This is the only reasonably good road out of Bogor heading to Java's W coast at Labuhan. If driving your own vehicle, leave Bogor on Jl. Veteran, cross the railroad tracks, and head for Jasinga, passing through a quiet countryside of boulder-strewn rivers. About 15 km out of Bogor the road bends L in Warungborang village and on the corner a track leads off to the R for 2½ km over *sawah* to the small farming *kampung* of Ciampea. Here you'll have to hire a young boy to show you the way to the river (actually about 30 will volunteer their services!). After one hour's pleasant walk you come to an enormous gorge which you have to scramble down to the large polished black boulder firmly embedded and half-submerged in the river. This 1,500-year-old inscribed stone, with the footprints of a Hindu king and those of his elephant, is one of the first written records of man on Java. The dedicated stone dates from the kingdom of Taruna, one of the earliest (6th-7th C.) Indianinfluenced kingdoms on Java. The inscription is in Old Palava script, the basis for modern Malay. The footprints represent those of Vishnu; the surface and carving is so immaculate and precise that they could have been carved yesterday. A little old man will struggle down the opposite bank and cross the river with the ubiquitous visitor's book balanced in his hands. Once signing it, he'll ask for Rp1000 but will accept the fairer donation of Rp200. Not many visitors make it to this ancient relic.

THE PUNCAK

Stretching under monsoon clouds from Bogor all the way to Cianjur, the Puncak is an invigorating mountain district and favorite W. Java domestic tourist area. The winding road passes lush rainforests, fog-enshrouded volcanos, mountain waterfalls and lakes, gaping valleys, endless stretches of tea plantations, and innumerable guesthouses and restaurants. All along the roadside are fruit, vegetable, and handicraft markets. On weekends, bumper-to-bumper traffic stretches all the way from Bandung to Jakarta. The foggy 1,200-m-high Puncak Pass (puncak means "summit") is the highest point over which you'll drive—truly awesome when not covered in cloud, rain, or traffic. Nights can be surprisingly cool (average 22 degrees C), so bring warm clothing. Fairy tale walks can be enjoyed out of Cisarua, Cibodas, and Cipanas.

Tea Cultivation

The best tea thrives on these high, cool mountain slopes (up to 800 m) because the cooler air slows growth and increases flavor. Constant pruning keeps plants short and bushy. Harvesters, mostly young girls earning only Rp850 per day, take only the young leaves and buds; they can pick up to 25 kg daily, enough to make 5 kg of dried tea. Two kinds of tea are processed: black tea is fermented; green tea is not. The roots of tea bushes are made into carvings which are sold alongside the road. About 6 km on the Puncak side of the Cianjur is the entrance to the Gunung Gedeh Tea Estate which leads you to many picnic places and beautiful views of the mountains. Another 8 km heading SE is the entrance to the Malaber Tea Estate, which allows visitors.

Accommodations And Food

The volcanic slopes of dominating G. Gede and G. Pangrango are dotted with expensive hotels and bungalows. On weekends it's difficult to find a hotel for less than Rp10,000. Mid-week prices frequently start at half of those charged on weekends when all accommodations—in every class—are packed. Seventy km from Jakarta, the **Kopo International Youth Hostel**, Jl. Raya 502 (tel. 0251-4296), has probably the cheapest rooms in the whole Puncak area (starting at Rp5000 pp) and dormitories (Rp1500 pp with youth hostel card). No mosquitos, cool fresh air, restaurants, supermarkets, and swimming pool all are nearby. Lots to see in the area. Ask directions to the waterfalls near Cisarua, and to the Cikopo Selatan One Tea Plantation which offers great views of surrounding mountains. If you advertise in Jakarta's newspapers, it's possible to find reasonable long-term rentals in the Puncak in exchange for English lessons. In Cisarua, 10 km SE of Bogor, are the best frog legs at **Jatiwangi,** and good and cheap food at **Dewi Sri** (opposite the Safari Hotel).

Cibulan

Hotel Cibulan, directly across from this small town's large kolam renang, is an old Dutch-era hotel built in art deco style; Rp12,000 d on weekdays. **Chalet Bali International,** Jl. Puncak Cisarua, has rooms for Rp12,000-15,000 and pristine, breath-stopping views from the rooms and front patio. They also hire out bungalows with bath and hot running water for Rp15,000 (but ask for the "student price"). Up the road from Hotel Cibulan is **Peng. Cibulan Indah,** which charges only Rp7500 d with private baths.

Telaga Warna

A small, unexpectedly pleasant pond of changing colors (red, green, or yellow), due to reflections caused by changing daylight. Coming from Bogor, Telaga Warna is ½ km before Puncak Pass and 25 km beyond the Sukabumi/Samudra turnoff. Just before the pass watch for the sign on the left. The lake is reached by a 5-min. walk on a path through the grounds of the Gunung Mas tea plantation, one of the largest and best known in all of Indonesia. The best time to see the lake is in the last hour of daylight when the clouds and mist swirl around and roll down the steep jungle slopes and across the calm water. Go on weekdays when it is most likely to be deserted.

Transport

The Puncak area is about 1½ hour and 34 km SE of Bogor by bus, 26 km NW of Cianjur, or about 110 km from Bandung. From Bogor's Stasiun Colt Cisarua, take a minibus for Rp500 all the way to the Cisarua Petrol Station (Pompa Bensin Cisarua) if you intend to stay at the (inexpensive) Kopo Hostel. If you want to go up or down the pass, just hop on any bus from Bandung or Bogor and pay for only the distance you travel. Going back (on the weekends), there's 24-hour bus service to both Bandung and Jakarta. If you're

VICINITY OF BOGOR

leaving Indonesia and don't want to stay in Jakarta, just catch a minibus to Bogor's train station, then a train every hour (Rp350) to Gambir Station, then by Damri bus to the airport (Rp2500).

CIPANAS

Located in the mountains on the other side of Puncak Pass about 5 km beyond the turnoff to Cibodas at the foot of G. Guntur and G. Putri. This area of recreational hotsprings is a pleasant place to break the journey between Bogor and Bandung, which is only 2 hours away by bus from here. Visit the picturesque market which sells cut flowers, plants, vegetables, and fruit. The hot sulphur baths here (Cipanas means "Hot River" in Javanese) are famous for their remedial powers; the water originates from natural springs on G. Guntur. See the top of G. Guntur, still bare from a 1889 eruption. Cipanas can be a bit hectic and unpretty at times, a traffic-snarled noisy town surrounding a single peaceful oasis—the president's holiday home. This elegant Victorian country house (built in 1750), called **Istana Cipanas**, is in a huge park with gardens, triple-canopy jungle and hotsprings. On the grounds is a bungalow where Sukarno composed some of his most famous speeches. Suharto seldom uses the 6 presidential retreats dotted all over Java, preferring to tend cattle on his gentleman's farm on the slopes of G. Gede. A

Catholic church near the Presidential Palace is presided over by an old Dutch priest, Father Vanderland.

Accommodations And Food
Lots of places to stay and eat in different classes and tastes, and crowded on weekends with Jakartans escaping the heat. Stay at **Sindanglaya Hotel** and **Hotel Sanggabuana**, Rp15,000 d. Eat at the Padang-style restaurants **Roda** or **Padang Sati**. More expensive places to stay include the **Bukit Raya**, with large swimming pool. The **Lembur Kuring**, S of Cipanas, has Sundanese-style bungalows, clean and sparsely furnished, with hot water from the springs. Bring your own towel, top sheet, and soap; serves plain Indonesian food.

Vicinity Of Cipanas
On the L after the turnoff to Cibodas Botanical Garden and several km before the town of Cipanas, see the small sign pointing up a dirt track to the R to **Santa Yusup Convent**. This nunnery is a simple and quiet retreat where it's possible to rent rooms if you book in advance. Of the 3 *vihara* in Cipanas, the one in town with all the electric lights is hilarious to look at, but the retreat in the hills is the nice one. Once you're in Cipanas, several signs indicate the walking path to the *vihara*, or close to the market catch a *bemo* out to it; ask for the *Gereja Buddhist*. All the *vihara* are under the same *bhikku*, one of Indonesia's leading Buddhist religious leaders, who lives in the one out of town. You are given a booklet which explains his philosophy, though it's also OK if you just want to practice your own method of meditation here. The monastery is in a really beautiful spot, and serves outstanding vegetarian food. What you pay for room and board is up to you; they never ask for money but you should give a daily donation of at least Rp2000. You need a good sleeping bag for the many 2-blanket nights. During the day it's sunny and you can look down the valley with mountain streams in the distance, a lovely and peaceful view. Visitors may also stay at the **Biara Catholic Camp**, next to Padang Sati restaurant, Rp8000 pp.

CIBODAS BOTANICAL GARDENS

A cool, high-altitude extension of the gardens at Bogor, about 10 km and Rp400 by *bemo* beyond Puncak Pass and 5 km S of Cibodas village. Open daily but don't go on Sunday. Cibodas is easily accessible by car and makes a fine day's outing from Jakarta (90 km), Bogor (46 km), or Bandung (70 km). The turnoff has been improved but you still need to look carefully for the small sign, KEBUN RAYA, on the L side in Cimacan. If driving, leave your car at the carpark about 5 km up this road, and walk up to the gardens.

The first botanic reserve in Indonesia, Cibodas was established in 1889, primarily to protect the region's unusually rich mountain flora. It is today the scene of important botanical research. Beautiful Cibodas Park covers about 80 ha and attracts 80,000 visitors a year. Admission Rp200. Attached to the garden is a forest reserve of more than 1,200 ha extending up to the summit of G. Pangrango (3,000 m) and the crater of G. Gede (2,950 m). Camp at the **Mandala Kitri Camping Ground** or stay in friendly and well-run **Pondok Pemuda Cibodas** (ask for directions at the PPA office); Rp5000 s, Rp10,000 d. Plenty of inexpensive *warung*.

The Collection

During the last century the Dutch planted mountain trees collected from Australia, Canary Islands, South Africa, and many other temperate areas. Alongside the original plantings was left the thick tropical jungle covering the slopes of G. Gede. Good paths run through the jungle, some stone-paved; names, both Latin and popular, are displayed on the trees. See 15-m-high tree ferns *(alsophila)*, beds of roses, begonias in full bloom, an "elfin" forest where moss-strewn ground and lichen-draped trees impart a fairyland look. Also check out the eucalyptus and lily collections, and the superb view of G. Gegerbentang from over the pond, covered in dense rainforest.

GUNUNG GEDE AND GUNUNG PANGRANGO

Apart from the scientific importance of the Cibodas Gardens, the reserve itself is scenically worthwhile with its beautiful forests, hotsprings, tumbling Cibeureum Waterfalls, and—for those sufficiently energetic to reach them—these bare windy mountaintops, a 5- to 7-hour hike starting from the parking lot of the Cibodas Gardens. As the area is a protected nature reserve, first get information and a free *surat jalan* at the Forestry Office (PPA) behind the parking lot. They hand out some brochures and a hiking map too; open Mon.-Thurs. 0800-1500, on Fri. until 1100, on Sat. until 1400, closed on Sun. and holidays. Guides can also be arranged.

The Climb

Wear warm clothing and good footwear; the best time to do this hike is May to Oct. The 10-km hike to the rim of G. Gede (2,958 m) takes at most 6-7 hours. Follow the trail up G. Gede from the parking lot. After an hour you pass a turnoff down to the waterfall (the sign says CIBEUREUM), then go over the (hot) waterfall to the ruined cottage. Ignore the L fork, 30 m before the ruins. Directly after the ruins, the trail forks again; take the R fork to the summit or the L fork to enter the crater. You'll get the most out of this experience by camping overnight near one of the hot-springs, reaching the top for sunrise. To camp overnight, follow the blue-painted stones along the crater lip and down into the valley. Or make the walk at night (starting at around 2000) during the full moon, timing your arrival at the top for the sunrise. The Kopo Hostel will help you prepare everything you need (they've gotten many people started on this climb). On the way up, stop for a free tour of the giant Gunung Mas Tea Estate on the slopes of G. Gede. From the Cibodas Gardens parking lot, the hike up to the perfect cone of G. Pangerango (3,019 m) takes at most 7-8 hours.

PELABUHANRATU

This isolated fishing village 90 km SE of Bogor and 150 km SW of Bandung is also the site of the large, international-class Samudra Beach Hotel, a popular weekend destination for Jakarta and Bandung residents. Visit the fish market next to the gas station in the early morning to shop for all manner of sea creatures. The beaches are splendid along this coastline, but don't venture too far out. Though the water has a serene appearance, it's best to take heed of all the posted warning signs (the Bulgarian ambassador drowned here about 10 years ago). Of course, all the swimming "accidents" and other strange happenings around Pelabuhanratu are invariably attributed to Nyai Loro Kidul, Goddess of the South Seas. In fact, the name Pelabuhanratu means "Queen's Harbor." Homage is paid to her every June when a garish thanksgiving festival, *Pesta Nelayan,* is celebrated all along this coast. Featured are lines of colorfully decorated fishing boats, *pencak silat* martial arts contests, *Ketuk Tilu* dances, and various sporting competitions such as rowing and swimming. Flowers are scattered on the water and a buffalo head is sacrificed to the sea.

Accommodations

This busy seaside holiday resort has high prices and sometimes substandard service. A number of seaside bungalows and motel-type accommodations lie along the 4-km stretch between the village market and the Samudra Beach Hotel. Doubles run Rp15,000-30,000, but on weekdays you can bargain the best rates. To camp, follow the shoreline road W from the village past one of the president's houses (not used now); after 2 km are nice camping sites under the palms next to the shore (busy weekends). **Sindang Laut** is one of the cheapest places in town, ½ km past the *pasar* on Jl. Kidang Kencana (tel. 38); rooms with balconies overlook the ocean for Rp8500 d, Rp12,500 t, 2 cottages go for Rp20,000-25,000. The one-km-long beach in front is said to be safer and more sheltered than the Samudra Beach Hotel's. No meals served, but a restaurant is within walking distance. **Pondok Dewata** (tel. 22, or in Bandung 772426), just

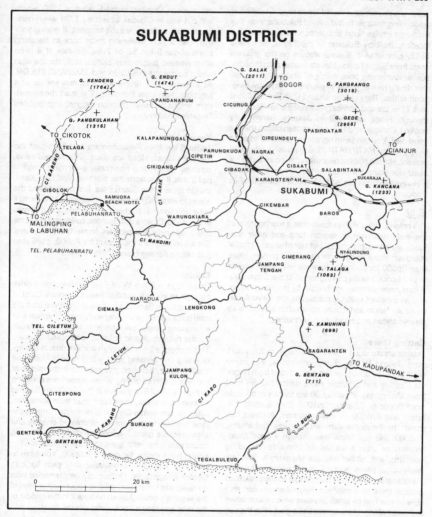

SUKABUMI DISTRICT

G. KENDENG (1764)

G. ENDUT (1474)

G. SALAK (2211)

TO BOGOR

G. PANGRANGO (3019)

OPANDANARUM

CICURUG

G. PANGKULAHAN (1315)

TO CIKOTOK

TELAGA

KALAPANUNGGAL

CIREUNDEU

OPASIRDATAR

G. GEDE (2958)

TO CIANJUR

CI BARENO

CISOLOK

CIKIDANG

PARUNGKUOA
CIPETIR

NAGRAK

CIBADAK

CISAAT

SALABINTANA

SUKARAJA

SAMUDRA BEACH HOTEL

PELABUHANRATU

CI TARIK

KARANGTENGAH

SUKABUMI

G. KANCANA (1233)

TO MALINGPING & LABUHAN

WARUNGKIARA

CIKEMBAR

BAROS

TEL. PELABUHANRATU

CI MANDIRI

CIMERANG

NYALINDUNG

JAMPANG TENGAH

G. TALAGA (1083)

KIARADUA

LENGKONG

G. KAMUNING (699)

CIEMAS

TEL. CILETUH

CI LETUH

SAGARANTEN

TO KADUPANDAK

CI KASO

JAMPANG KULON

G. BENTANG (711)

CITESPONG

CI KARANG

SURADE

CI BUNI

GENTENG

U. GENTENG

TEGALBULEUD

0   20 km

beyond the petrol station, is probably the best place for families as it has a safe beach and is reasonably priced (Rp30,000-Rp55,000). Dewata's set of Balinese-style a/c bungalows go for Rp18,000 (2 beds)—a good value if everything works. There's a pool, small restaurant, shady gardens. Bring your own stove for cooking; they also rent a fishing boat. **Penginapan Laut Kidul**, Jl. Siliwangi 140, about ⅓ km before the market on the R-hand side coming into town; no food. Rooms cost Rp6500 s or d. **Karangsari** is 200 m beyond Pondok Dewata on the R on a

hill overlooking the sea. At these cheaper, basic bungalows, be careful of security. Just beyond the Karangsari is a steep hill turning L to **Bayu Amirta** (tel. 31, or 50882 in Bandung), more commonly known as the Fish Restaurant or Hoffmann's, the name of the owner. Hangs right on the edge of a cliff; superb sunsets. Ask for the bungalow on the cliff; more expensive (Rp25,000) but delightful.

Samudra Beach Hotel (tel. 23) is 4 km past Pelabu-hanratu village, Rp350 from the market by minibus down a picturesque wooded shore road. Standing in astounding contrast to disheveled Palabuhanratu, this modern highrise hotel sits alone in a truly beautiful location. Built by Sukarno in the 1960s, he always heftily promoted it. Several statues on the grounds came from Bogor Palace. Has a/c rooms, private baths, suites, swimming pool, mini-golf and tennis, expensive dining rooms, *gamelan* playing in the lobby, ping-pong tables. They charge around US$35 s, US$45 d plus 21% tax and service; reservations can be made through Hotel Indonesia in Jakarta. Rarely fully booked. Compared to U.S. or European prices, this is a good deal. You can swim right in front of the hotel but heed the sign *HATI! HATI!* ("Dangerous!"). Lifeguard present. Horses stabled near the hotel are available for beachside riding at a moderate fee. A room at the hotel is always kept unoccupied for Nyai Loro Kidul, the Sea Goddess.

Food
The colorful *pasar ikan* in town does a roaring trade in the early mornings. In-season tuna and other sea-foods are incredibly cheap, but out-of-season lobster could run about Rp8000 per kilo! Don't pay any more than Rp500 for coconuts (tourists have been known to pay Rp5000 while playing tennis at the Samudra!). A *nasi padang* restaurant is right by the pier in town, and an excellent seafood restaurant, the **Bayu Amirta**, cooks fish to perfection; crowded on weekends so reserve ahead and bring your own wine.

Getting There
Pelabuhanratu is 2½ hours from Bogor or 3½ hours from Jakarta by car. Buses, minibuses, and *bemo* regularly head down here on a good road from Bogor via Cicurug and Cibadak; more difficult is the road from Malingping. It's about 30 km by bus or minibus from Bogor to Cibadak, Rp1000, then another 1½ hours and Rp1500 to Pelabuhanratu. A direct bus down to Pelabuhanratu also leaves Sukabumi, Rp2000; this ride takes you through a good cross-section of Java's varied countryside including ricefields, and rubber and tea plantations. The bus rarely stops; passengers are usually going all the way. You can also take a train from Bogor to Cibadak, then change there to a minibus. Pelabuhanratu can also now be reached by small Skyvans which touch down at Rawa Kalong—looks more like a goat farm than an airfield. Before a plane lands someone has to chase all the goats off the runway, and the terminal is a thatched roof over a table. Book through Jakarta's Tunas Indonesia (tel. 341085/355167/355168) or with Pelita Air Service, Jl. Abdul Muis 52 (tel. 275908), or at the reservations desk of any major international hotel.

From Pelabuhanratu
If you're down here just for a day, don't wait for the last minibus back to Bogor at around 1900; you might get stuck in Cibadak. Instead, leave at 1600, which will put you in Cibadak at around 1730 when mini-buses back to Bogor are still frequent. If driving your own car, a more intriguing route back to Bandung starts about 5 km SE of Pelabuhanratu at a large silver-painted suspension bridge; look for the sign which points to KIARADUA and JAMPANG KULON. At Kiaradua (2 oil drums and a banana vendor at a junction), turn L for Bandung. The road then meanders endlessly down through ragged, unpopulated limestone country.

Karang Hawu
About 5 km from Pelabuhanratu and 2 km past the Samudra Beach Hotel are giant cliffs, ragged reefs, crashing waves, and hazardous swimming. Legend has it that it was from this cliff that Nyai Loro Kidul, the Goddess of the South Seas, first plunged into the ocean to establish her watery kingdom. At this point a large lava flow has pushed over the beach and flowed into the sea. Explore the crevices, caves and pools for fossilized shells and pebbles frozen into rocky lava. Get a minibus from the market for Rp500; it will stop just before Karang Hawu ("the Rocks").

Cisolok
This village is 9 km W of Pelabuhanratu on a drive through lovely rice paddies near the ocean. Catch a *bemo* past the Samudra following the shore until the road turns inland a short way and stops in the center of a *kampung*. There, ask directions to the narrow path for the hotsprings and volcanic area called Cipanas. This is about a 2-km hike or motorbike ride. In this enchanting and relaxing spot, a tiny river bubbles and steams its way between grassy banks. In the middle of the river is a jet of boiling water, sometimes spouting as high as 10 m! Everywhere in the vicinity are fissures spraying out water, steam and mud from some vast subterranean kettle. Cisolok is renowned among the local population as a source of colored crystals and semi-precious gems. **accommodations:** One big house near here, with giant rooms and really old furniture, rents rooms for around Rp3500. You have to walk 1½ km down a beautiful river path back to Cisolok village to eat. On Sun. it's very crowded with domestic sightseers and children, but on other days of the week it's dead. Just sit on a rock in the middle of the river and read a book—and this on Java!

Cikotok
One of the only operating goldmines in Indonesia is W of Samudra Beach. Halfway between Karang Hawu and the Samudra Beach Hotel, a good road turns inland at the sign P.T. ANEKA TAMBANG. The road is impassable to sedans, but a 4WD, local bus, or *bemo* can make it all the way to the end (at least 4 hours OW) beyond the goldmine and through some spectacular scenery to Malingping and finally up to Rangkasbitung.

BANDUNG

Roughly 180 km SE of Jakarta, Bandung is Indonesia's 3rd largest city, with 1.7 million people. Lying in a high valley surrounded by mountains covered in tea plantations, the city is a bustling center of Sundanese cultural life. It is the site of at least 50 universities and colleges, many small academies, and such prestigious institutions as the Nuclear Research Center, and the Volcanologists Monitoring Center (VSI), and Indonesia's only aircraft industry (IPTN). Indonesia's elite army division, *Siliwangi*, is headquartered in Bandung, occupying the former command center of Netherlands Indies Army. Bandung is also a center for industry (textiles and food processing) and fine arts, luring musicians, dancers, and artists from all over Indonesia to study here. Once referred to as the "Paris of the East," the Dutch loved it here and their long occupation is seen in the somber middle-class architecture recalling early 20th C. Western European cities—an overabundance of ferro-concrete buildings. In spite of its tree-lined avenues, however, Bandung has unfortunately lost much of the charm and glamour it once had; nowadays it appears dilapidated, choked with exhaust fumes and dust, becoming horribly polluted with the rabbit-like multiplication of *bemo*, almost as bad as Jakarta's! Fortunately, the city government has provided parks, sports centers, and like amenities so that people have a few places where they can at least breathe. Though most travelers make Bandung a short stop between Yogya and Jakarta, Bandung is one of the least known and most underrated highland cities in all of SE Asia and gets only 50,000 foreign visitors per year.

Climate

Situated in the middle of a great tangle of high volcanic peaks, Bandung's center sits at 769 m above sea level, but new developments and crowded *kampung* already climb far into the hills up to 900 m. Because of its generally high altitude and many shady trees, Bandung has perfect weather with cool fresh air. Temperatures average 25 degrees C (77 F), with a mild humidity of 70-75%. Rainy season is Sept.-Feb. and the dry March-August. Annual rainfall is 1,884 mm. The rain, dramatic and unforgettable, usually only falls in the afternoons, all at once, like standing under a waterfall. Most mornings are sunny with blue skies.

History

In prehistoric times, an immense flow of solidified mud *(lahar)* 35 km long and up to 100 m thick erupted from the twin volcano Burangrang and blocked the river valleys, forming a huge high-mountain lake in the same valley where Bandung sprawls today. Another volcanic explosion created a rift in the basin of the lake, emptying it, and leaving behind rich alluvial soil which for hundreds of years nourished a successful farming community. Bandung was first written about in 1488 in connection with the Hindu kingdom of Pajajaran, which at the time reigned over all of W. Java. This thinly populated feudal kingdom deep in the Preanger Mountains enjoyed a peaceful, isolated existence until the arrival of the Dutch in the late 18th C., attracted to the region for its coffee-growing potential. The infamous Forced Cultivation System was first instituted in this region, and lasted 200 years. In 1810, the residence of the Regent of Bandung Province was moved from Dayeuhkolot to where the newly built Great Post Road (present-day Jl. Asia-Afrika) crossed the river Cikapundung—and the city of Bandung was born. Incorporated in 1811, Bandung quickly became one of the principal operating bases for the Dutch colonial government. In 1819, there were only 1,800 inhabitants; in 1884, the railway arrived. During WW II Bandung was the main defense position of the Dutch government; Allied headquarters here was captured by the Japanese on 7 March 1942. During the struggle for independence, Sukarno first emerged as a nationalist leader at the Bandung Institute of Technology, the "MIT of Indonesia." In 1955, Bandung was the site of the famous Asian-African Conference which launched the non-aligned movement—one of the greatest triumphs of Indonesian foreign policy efforts.

The People

Bandung is a cosmopolitan city with the usual Indonesian mix: Sundanese, Javanese, Balinese, Chinese, Arab, and a large European community. The city is split by the RR tracks: to the N are the richer neighborhoods, to the S the poorer. Because of the numerous universities and colleges housing some of Indonesia's brightest students, this is a youthful city, a haven for academics and intellectuals. Bandung's ITB student leaders pride themselves on being the most radical in all of Indonesia, claiming to be the catalyst for nationwide student protests and strikes. Youth groups are constantly agitating for social and political change, regularly disseminating their propaganda in vituperative underground print and broadcast media. In 1978, ITB students published the famous *White Book of the 1978 Students Struggle*, railing against corruption and cronyism in high places. Today, *crossboys udara* or "air cowboys" is the epithet given to the unlicensed radio transmitters of Bandung. The first Indonesian rock festival took place in Bandung (in 1975), featuring such groups as Voodoo Child, God Bless. In the post-WW II period Bandung was once a hotbed of fanatical fundamentalist Islamic movements such as the murderous Darul Islam group. An Islamic university, Universitas Islam Bandung (UNISBA), is at Jl. Tamansari 1.

SIGHTS

Gedung Merdeka

Also known as the Asia-Afrika Building, Gedung Merdeka is right in the center of the city on Jl. Asia-Afrika 65 (tel. 59503) on the corner of Jl. Braga, near the city's *alun-alun*. Built in 1895, it was renovated to its present form by Van Gallenlast and Wolf Shoemaker in 1926. Open 0800-1300 daily, Fri. to 1100, Sat. to 1200. In 1955, Indonesia's then-President Sukarno invited leaders of 29 developing non-aligned nations to a solidarity conference in this building. Bandung hit the headlines that year and nothing of like magnitude has happened since. Such figures as Nehru, Nasser, Ho Chi Minh, and Chou En Lai attended, with Sukarno acting as the Grand Dalang. It was said that he employed dozens of professional, specially trained prostitutes to spy on the delegates. In this building the first openly anti-colonialist conference took place, laying the groundwork for today's non-aligned movement. All nations attending had recently achieved independence and, with the exception of Japan, all were underdeveloped; all announced themselves independent according to "Ten Principles of Non-alignment for Peaceful Co-existence." In the building's Museum Konperensi Asia Afrika is a fine, well-annotated exhibit consisting of large black-and-white and color photos commemorating the conference. Now the powerful non-aligned movement comprises 66 members, mostly from the Third World. Attended by trade ministers and government officials, the last conference of non-aligned states was held in Harare, Zimbabwe, in 1985.

Museums

Sundanese Museum of Art and **Museum of W. Java,** Jl. Otista in SW of city; open daily 0800-1200 (closed Mon.), Rp200 entrance. The **Army Museum** (Museum Mandala Wangsit Siliwangi), on Jl. Lembong near the Istana Hotel, contains a collection of weapons used in the freedom struggle against the Dutch in the 1940s and graphic photos of the work of the Darul Islam movement. Open Mon. to Thurs. 0900-1200; free. **Geological Museum,** on Jl. Diponegoro 57 near Gedung Sate, has a huge floor space of fossils, minerals, models of volcanos and photos of eruptions, relief maps, etc. Open Mon. to Thurs. 0900-1400, Fri. 0900-1100, and Sat. 0900-1300; free. Buy geologic and topo maps of Indonesia in the museum's Publications Department. **Museum**

Post and Philateli, in the L wing of Gedung Sate, Jl. Cilaki 73, contains not only an extensive stamp collection but also a graphic history of Indonesia's postal services. Opened in 1931. Open Sun., Mon., and Thurs. 0900-1300.

Parks And Gardens

Kebun Bintang is Bandung's large park-like zoo, close to Babakan Siliwangi on Jl. Taman Sari, across from ITB. Discover a wide variety of unusual bird species from all over Indonesia and SE Asia, the usual Komodo dragons, and other protected species. Crowded on holidays and Sundays. Admission Rp400. Bandung's town square was created at the same time (1850) as Gedung Pakuan (the Regent's Residence) and the Great Mosque. Surrounded by shopping centers, offices, and cinemas. The **Traffic Garden** (Taman Lalu Lintas), Jl. Belitung, was established to give small children their first lessons in traffic regulations. There's a library, a mini-theater, small cars and trains, miniature roads with traffic signs. Visit the biggest recreation center (swimming pool, playground, etc.) in Bandung, **Karang Setra,** near IKIP.

Bandung Institute Of Technology

Premier among Bandung's many colleges and universities is the Bandung Institute of Technology, or ITB (pronounced EE-TAY-BAY), on the N side of the city; take a Dago-bound Honda and get off at Jl. Ganeca. This is the oldest, largest, and one of Indonesia's most prestigious technical universities. ITB was established in 1920 by a group of enterprising Dutch planters, merchants, and industrialists led by the Malabar planter H.A.R. Bosscha. Its curriculum, based on the famous Technical High School in Delft, was designed to provide training for native engineers and architects. Yearly, around 30,000 students attend 17 higher educational institutions on campus. ITB has produced many of Indonesia's foremost engineers and political personalities, including Sukarno (1920-1925). The studios and galleries of its well-regarded department of painting and plastic arts (textiles, weaving, etc.) may be visited. The student body is very active politically. Meet students (many of whom speak English) in the cafeteria of the student dorm, Asrama Mahasiswa, opposite the main gate. Afterwards, take a walk on the impressive grounds. The original buildings are very distinctive with their spectacular ship-prowed Minangkabau architecture. The whole 25-ha complex is a national treasure.

Architecture

Few of the city's buildings predate the 20th century. What exists today is a curious mixture of neglected dignified colonial structures, such as the venerable **Gedung Sate** on Jl. Diponegoro built in 1920, and modern, flashy, nondescript architecture. However, there are pre-1900 remnants: **Gedung Merdeka** ("The Freedom Building"), on Jl. Asia-Afrika, was once a lively Dutch social center; **Gedung Pakuan**, on Jl. Oto Iskandarinata, was the official house of the governor of W. Java; and **Gedung Papak**, on Jl. Wastukancana, was built in 1819 by order of Governor-General van der Capellan. One of the city's oldest buildings (1850) is the **Pendopo Kabupaten** on the N side of the *alun-alun* in the classical trilogy of palace-*alun-alun*-mosque-jail. With its pagoda-style tiled roof, Mataram influence is obvious (Bandung's regent was a vassal king under C. Java's Sultan Agung). The huge tree was planted to commemorate the birth of Queen Wilhelmina in 1880. Ask at Kantor Protokol for permission to enter. The 1920-40 period was Bandung's Golden Age of art deco/nouveau structures, a time when concrete was used with flair and grace. The **Savoy Homann Hotel** is probably this vigorous period's most superb specimen. One of Asia's grand hotels, all its rooms are mini-suites, with drivers' and servants' quarters, and even the furniture and fittings bespeak the art nouveau look. The dining room is a spectacular replica of one in a 1930s trans-Atlantic oceanliner. More glimpses of this era can be picked out along Jl. Braga, around Jl. Pasar Baru and Jl. Banceuy, and the amazing building on the corner of Jl. Braga and Jl. Naripan. Also check out the **IKIP Building** on Jl. Setiabudi, several private homes in the Dago area (especially the one on the corner of Jl. Sultan Agung). Criticized at the time for its remoteness from the central area of Bandung, the ITB campus is higher, cooler, drier, better drained, and better able to expand, than more central sites would have been. Graceful, soundly built, and functionally brilliant, ITB's original complex is one of the most architecturally important 20th C. buildings in Indonesia. For contemporary architecture, visit the **Government Office Building** on the football pitch next to Gedung Sate on Jl. Diponegoro. The tallest building of Bandung, with fantastic views, it looks like a water tower in disguise — a 4-story office block supported on 14-story slender concrete columns sweeping stylishly upward.

ACCOMMODATIONS

Around The Railroad Station

The cheap hotel area is around the train station. Students tend to commandeer the cheaper accommodations. **Hotel Malabar**, Jl. Kebon Jukut 3, is rock-bottom. Turn L after emerging from the RR station, walk over the overpass and you'll see it. Their cheapest, fairly clean, small rooms cost Rp5000 s or d, while bigger rooms run Rp6000-8250. Rooms in front are too noisy, in back too small and dark. Be ready for the blast from the mosque at 0430. **Hotel Sahara**, Jl. Oto Iskandardinata 3 (tel. 51684), is across from the governor's residence and only a 5-min. walk

from RR station. Go over the pedestrian overpass, then walk straight along the street perpendicular to the tracks; it's at the end of this street on your right. Charges Rp3500 s, Rp7500 d, with breakfast. Comfortable for the money, with your own veranda. **Penginapan Sakadarna**, Jl. Kebon Jati 34, is behind the train station down an alleyway, Gang Mesjid, right beside Hotel Melati. Walk down the *gang* and Sakadarna is the first *penginapan* you run into. Clean, Rp3500 s for smallish rooms, shared *mandi,* no meals but coffee served. Moving dramatically up in price, a favorite of the Javanese is **Hotel Melati II**, Jl. Kebonjati 27 (tel. 56409), Rp11,900 s, Rp17,300 d and up, all rooms with baths and breakfast included.

Low-priced

Losmen Mawar, Jl. Pangaran 14 (tel. 51934), is very good value; Rp4500 s, Rp5500 d, including breakfast from 0530-7000 (coffee with milk and bread). Located down a lane, it's reasonably quiet, clean, central (5 min. from Gedung Merdeka), with a small garden and very low-priced laundry service. If you want something a little more Westernized, just up the lane is the **Pangarang Sari Hotel**, Jl. Pangaran 3 (tel. 51205), Rp15,000 with *mandi.* Nice lounge area, skylight. Price includes breakfast.

Odds And Ends

Hotel Brajawijaya, Jl. Pungkur 28 (tel. 50673), charges Rp14,000 s or d for quite large, comfortable rooms with coffee or tea and breakfast. Close to the Kebon Kelapa Bus Station. Every room has a bath. Also on Jl. Pungkur (no. 97, tel. 56027) is the **Pacific Hotel**, with hot water and beautiful rooms (with living room) for Rp22,500 d; also cheaper rooms at Rp17,500 d. One of the best-value hotels for the businessman is **Hotel Harapan**, Jl. Kapatihan 14-16 (tel. 51212), Rp11,000-15,000 — cheap for a hotel of this class in the downtown, opposite King's Shopping Centre, yet set back from the street and quiet. In Chinatown is the **Trio**, Jl. Gardu Jati, Rp35,000 d, catering to guests from Taiwan and Singapore; many Chinese restaurants nearby. Out of town, many *penginapan,* guesthouses, and *wisma* are found on both sides of the road climbing up from Bandung to Lembang; most are in the 25,000-30,000 range (with full board) but often have a few Rp8000-10,000 rooms (without board).

Student Hostels

Wisma Remaja, Jl. Merdeka 64, is near the corner of Jl. Merdeka and Jl. Martadinata, Rp150 by *bemo* from the train station and about 2 km from city center. Take a Dago-bound *bemo* from the bus station or a Dago *oplet* from the RR station. If you can get one in the dorm (Rp3000), these are the cheapest beds in Bandung, though usually full during school term or when groups fill the place. Good place to meet Indonesian students, with reasonably priced restaurant, open 24 hours (but meals only served from 0800-1900). A focus of youth activities and conferences, anything could be happening at Wisma Remaja: a kung fu conference, an American accounting seminar, public relations training classes. Tends to lock up by 2230.

High-priced

Plentiful, pleasant, with all the modern conveniences. At Jl. Oto Iskandardinata 20 is the more expensive **Hotel Guntur;** Rp19,360 d, Rp22,385 for the suite. On Jl. Asia-Afrika is the high-priced **Savoy Homann Hotel** (no. 112, tel. 58091), designed in art deco-style with large rooms off a lovely inner garden; their cheapest "Superior" room runs US$31 d, while their "Moderate" ones cost US$35 d; add 21% tax and service. Mint condition for a hotel built in the 1930s! Has a Pacto office, and the Garuda office is right across the street. The **Kumala Hotel & Restaurant,** Jl. Asia-Afrika 140 (tel. 52141/2), is popular with ex-pats. **Istana Hotel,** Jl. Lembong 22/24 (tel. 57240/58240), has full a/c, hot water, TV, good Chinese restaurant; Rp60,000 s. More highly recommended is the annex across the street from the original hotel building. Book early as this hotel is popular with European tour groups. **Hotel Panghegar,** Jl. Merdeka 2 (tel. 57584), with rooms up to Rp30,000, is well maintained and managed, with modern a/c rooms with TV, convenient location, good food, swimming pool. Although the Istana Hotel is more expensive, Hotel Panghegar is Bandung's best hotel. From the hotel's revolving restaurant (Indonesia's first) in the evening see beautiful equatorial sunsets over the city.

FOOD

Do you salivate over luscious avocados and corn on the cob? Do you crave strawberries, blackberries, and other "temperate" treats? Well, due to the higher elevation, nearly every kind of fruit and vegetable is not only grown in Bandung but is available *in abundance.* What's more, they're very flavorful and cost next to nothing. Canned goods are imported from all over the world, but cost 2-3 times what they do in the U.S. or Australia. The best place for imported goods is **Hero Supermarket,** Jl. Alun-alun Timor; and **Galael Supermarket,** Jl. Dago.

Street Food

Clusters of nocturnal and daytime *warung* are found all over the city, specializing in their own dishes. Many are set up at night around the *alun-alun.* Some of the best coffee in Bandung is served just opposite the Tourist Info Office in a *warung* called **Bejo.** With milk and *roti bakar,* the bill comes to only Rp600. Downstairs in the same building is **PA Edeng's**

modest *warung* serving high-quality, cheap Sundanese meals. Opposite Hotel Guntur, Jl. Oto Iskandardinata, right around the corner from Peng. Malabar, is a whole alleyway full of small, cheap *warung.* For noodle dishes, the *gang* next to the Dian Cinema is the place. Fantastic *bakso tahu* (tofu and fishball soup—an Asian standby) can be had at several *warung* on Jl. Dalem Kaum just W of the *alun-alun.* The PLN complex sells delicious *martabak* and side dishes; for around Rp850 you can eat your fill. Many *warung* and night markets downtown serve a Bandung specialty, tasty *soto ayam.* Directly across Jl. Asia-Afrika on Jl. Cikapundung is a busy night market popular with Indonesians. And low-priced food, as always, can also be found around the RR station.

Restaurants

Bakmie Raos, Jl. Kepjaksaan 19, is a good *bakmie* noodle place; Rp850 for a bowl. Noodles, *nasi goreng,* and *pangsit* dishes are served, all with a Chinese accent. Always crowded, with a convivial *kampung* atmosphere. **Koja Sate House,** Jl. Pasir Koja 1, served on a hot plate, and **Pakarjan** Jl. Pasir Kaliki, are both very outstanding. **Sate Ponorogo,** Jl. Jen. Gatot Subroto, specializes in *sate;* one portion for 2 with noodle soup, rice cakes for dessert, and 7 cups of tea will put you back Rp3000. It has an open-air atmosphere like a garden; also tasty *sate* in the restaurants in front of the *stasiun kereta api;* try **Hudori,** the oldest. **Galaya Pub and Restaurant,** Jl. Asia-Afrika 113 (tel. 52642), has good food and service. On Jl. Braga, the exclusive **Braga Permai** is a sidewalk cafe featuring Chinese and European cuisine. Low-priced **Bandung Food Center,** near the

BANDUNG

1. Penginapan Sakadarna
2. Melati Hotel
3. Guntur Hotel
4. Hotel Malabar
5. Y.P.K. Theatre
6. Merpati office
7. Losmen International
8. Gedung Merdeka
9. Garuda office
10. Hotel Savoy Homann
11. Pangarang Sari Hotel
12. Losmen Mawar
13. Pairuhiyat (*wayang* maker)
14. Hotel Brajawijaya
15. Kebun Kelapa bus station
16. Pacific Hotel

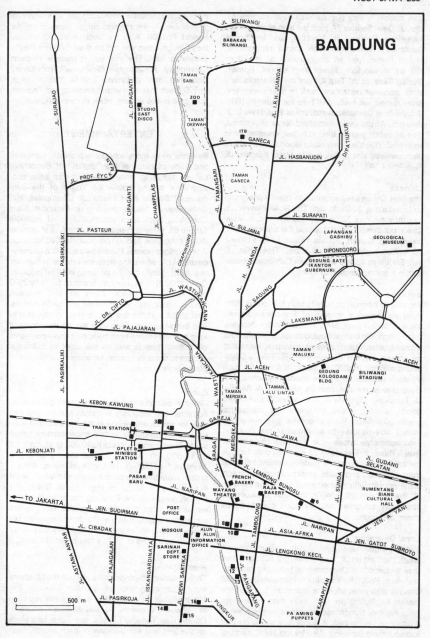

BANDUNG

train station, is very popular with travelers. **Pak M. Uju**, Jl. Dewi Saritika 7A (near the *alun-alun*), and the marvelous **Ponyo**, Jl. Malabar, are traditional Sundanese restaurants with sound reputations. At the Ponyo, you sit on cushions on the floor and are served fish chosen from a pool. **Rumah Gudeg Tera**, at Jl. Tera 4, near the RR tracks, is a small Javanese restaurant; stick to their *gudeg* and *pecel* dishes; eat really well here for under Rp1000. But the best Javanese restaurant is **Handayani**, Jl. Sukajadi. At the snake restaurant **Naya**, Jl. Pasteur, dine on cobra, python fried in butter, steamed, or in soup (Rp5000); also fresh snake blood. There's also a Japanese restaurant **Sakura**, in Hotel Kumala, Jl. Asia-Afrika 140.

Chinese

The best Chinese restaurants and open *warung* can be found along Jl. Gardo Jati. **The Rose Flower**, Jl. Jen. Ahmad Yani 32, is only 150 m from Jl. Asia-Afrika; outstanding food—sample the asparagus and cream soup. **Queen**, Jl. Dalam Kaum 53-A, is crowded on Sat. nights; moderate prices. **Tjoen Kie**, Jl. Jen. Sudirman 46, is a well-known Cantonese restaurant in a colorful section of town.

Bakeries

Because of its great popularity with Europeans, Bandung developed a number of first-class bakeries, some of which have been in business for decades. Jalan Braga, the main shopping street, is the place for sidewalk cafes, French pastries, marzipan, ice cream; try popular **French Bakery** (no. 18). Take a Dago-bound minibus (Rp300) to **Tizi's**, Jl. Dago, for such Western delights as T-bone steaks (fantastic), delicious breads, cookies, pastries, crackers. At **Rasa's**, Jl. Tamblong 15, enjoy all kinds of expensive baked goods—waffles, eclairs, chocolate cake, superb ice cream, 30 different kinds of cookies, plus everything from a fruit pancake to an American hot dog and Indonesian-style meals—for the wild plunge. The **Steak Rasa**, Jl. Tamblong 36, is a small shop famous for its desserts, especially puddings (more influence from Holland), and good steaks. Another dessert place, popular with Westerners, is the **Braga Permai**, Jl. Braga (open 0900-2400), for fresh strawberries, strawberry pancakes with whipped cream, or ice cream and such.

Local Delicacies

These include *sate, rujak, lotek, bajigur* (coconut juice), the best on Jl. Supratman near RRI, and *bandrek* (ginger drink). *Oncom* is fried beancake, peanuts, and yeast; Rp300 for a small one. *Peuyeum* is made of cassava with yeast added (a little sour); buy it at any market for Rp500 per kilo—more than enough for two. Another Sundanese favorite is *lalap-lalapan*, a mixture of vegies with a gooey soy sauce on top; known only in Bandung. Also try *roti bakar*, a sort of

Indonesian submarine sandwich filled with whatever is available. In the markets Bogor papayas sell for around Rp1000. Also try luscious *comro* sweets; they'll laugh when you ask for them because they're usually for kids. The best yogurt place is **Yoghurt Cisangkuy**, Jl. Cisangkuy (8-min. walk from Kantor Gubernur), serving Lychee Special Yogurt Juice, Rp900, fresh fruit, and yogurt desserts, etc. This outdoor cafe is also an easy place to meet students.

ENTERTAINMENT

By virtue of its many schools, rich artistic traditions, and pride of place as the "capital" of Sundanese culture, Bandung since the 1920s has been considered a cultural hub—"the Yogya of the Sundanese." **Studio East Disco**, Jl. Cihampelas, and **Galactica**, Jl. Maskumambang (in Pasundan Plaza Complex), both have entrance fees of Rp6000. **Studio 81**, in Hotel Preanger (Jl. Asia-Afrika) features dance hostesses, Rp5000 per hour, Rp2000 entrance. A very unique place is **Purwa Setra**, Jl. Oto Iskandardinata 541A, where the hostesses dance in Sundanese-*Jaipong*-style and the audience is asked to join in. Open 2100-0100 every night, entrance fee is Rp2000 plus Rp500 per dance. There are also frequent theater, music, dance and martial arts performances. First check in at the tourist office on the *alun-alun* to find out what's on. Keep your eye on the scores of long banners draped from trees, plus announcements on bulletin boards and on the sides of buildings. Tickets to these events can be bought in a number of places around town.

Banci

Along Jl. Sumatra and Jl. Jawa (a continuation of Jl. Sumatra), and especially in Taman Maluku, you can view (or participate in) one of the more colorful subcultures of Bandung—female impersonators called *banci*. Their company costs Rp10,000 or all night for Rp30,000 (or more). These ultra-glamorous "females," inhabiting the bodies of males, will approach male travelers on the street and ask if they'd like to "play." Many of them speak Dutch and English. In gay circles, Bandung has an international reputation, listed in all the gay guides. Gay hustlers sometimes approach you in the downtown area, basically cruising for money. For straight ladies, order through your hotel or go to a few private houses.

Ram Fighting

These exciting spectacles take place in the hill towns around Lembang such as Babakan Siliwangi and Maribaya, but they take place irregularly or you have to "charter" a match. At **Aki Bohon's** house in Cilimus near Terminal Ledeng, ram fights take place on the 2nd and 4th Sundays of each month, from

0900 to 1200. On the 1st and 3rd Sundays of each month, ram fights are held on Jl. Cibuntu (off Jl. Soekarno/Hatta). Admission to both is free. These matches are local, low-level competitions which lead to championship matches held annually on the first Sun. after 17 August (Independence Day), when hundreds of rams are brought to the Bandung area to battle for "the cup." The sport is closely tied in with breeders' efforts to upgrade the quality of their rams. Champion rams, which can weigh up to 60 kg and are adorned with names like "Bima" (a giant *wayang* hero) and "Si Kilat" ("Sir Lightning"), are quick to attack and cunning in evasion. A contest usually consists of around 50 "strokes" (ferocious head-on collisions) at distances of 20 to 30 m. The Sundanese are orthodox Muslims and are forbidden to gamble. Thus, almost unbelievably, no money changes hands at these contests; they are staged purely for the pleasure of the handlers and breeders!

THE PERFORMING ARTS

SMKI And ASTI

Bandung's **Music Conservatory** (Konservatori Karawitan), Jl. Buah Batu 212, consists of 2 parts: ASTI (academic, professional level), and SMKI (for high school students). Ask at the **Tourist Information Office** on the *alun-alun* (tel. 56644) about performances. Take a *bemo* from the Kebun Kelapa Bus Station or a bus from Perapatan Lima, E of the *alun-alun* on Jl. Asia-Afrika. **ASTI**, the Institute of Fine Arts, often stages performances by its students. Listen to a traditional Sundanese orchestra, the *kecapi suling* with its soft-toned flutes and the long vibrating notes of the *kecapi*, or an ensemble of *angklung*, bamboo instruments used in olden times to create excitement while marching into battle or to announce the arrival of a ruler. Visit any time to see students practice and to ask the lecturers any specific questions.

Gedung Kesenian

West Java is the home of *wayang golek*, which any Sundanese would rather see than the shadow play. Plots are taken from W. Javanese folktales or from the Indian epics, the *Ramayana* and *Mahabharata*. Since no curtain separates the puppets from the spectators, you can enjoy the puppets as both characters in a story and as sculptural creations. Sundanese music is provided by a *gamelan* orchestra, dulcet *suling* flutes, and *kecapi*. The *wayang golek* shows on Fri. and Sat. nights at Gedung Kesenian are attended mostly by the Sundanese themselves. They last all night (1830-0400) so you are able to make early morning trains leaving Bandung the next day (deposit your pack at the station the evening before the show). Other types of art performances take place from

2000-2300; keep your ear out. Go to the *konservatori* in the mornings; students are very receptive and might show you how to play the *kecapi*.

Rumentang Siang

This theater hall is on Jl. Baranang Siang 1 (Pasar Kosambi area); take a city bus toward Cicaheum. Theater, music, or dances are held every Fri. night and sometimes other nights of the week: *wayang golek, calung* dance dramas, special film presentations, *wayang orang*, Western theater productions, ballet, drama, *reyog*, even Sundanese country music *(musik keroncang)*. Entrance Rp1000. Check first at the tourist office.

Yayasan Pusat Kebudayaan (YPK)

At Jl. Naripan 7 off Jl. Braga; take the first R as you walk up Jl. Braga from the Asia-Afrika Building on Jl. Asia-Afrika. Very informal *wayang golek* performances take place here every Sat. (2100-0500). Admission Rp1000 (Rp1500 if it's a famous *dalang*). Other entertainment (most often weeknights) might include *wayang orang* or *gamelan* which usually last from 2100 to midnight. The YPK also teaches Sundanese dance and music as well as *pencak silat* (martial arts). Practice sessions, held almost any afternoon or evening, may be viewed; donations are in order.

Others

Sundanese cultural performances are staged every Wed. night at 2000 at the **Pasundan Restaurant** of Hotel Panghegar, Jl. Merdeka 2 (tel. 432286). Free entrance but drinks cost Rp2000-4000. Show includes traditional music and dance, *wayang golek, debus* magicians, *angklung*. Sit on the floor for the best view. Also call **Pak Ujo's**, Jl. Padasuka 118 (tel. 71714) in the middle of a genuine Javanese *kampung* on the outer fringe of Bandung, for "tourist" performances of *wayang golek* or *angklung*. Or first ask at the tourist office if anything is on. Admission Rp3000, or go down a small *gang* and watch over the fence with the neighborhood kids for free. Very popular with the Dutch, it's really a sight to see high-spirited old Dutch ladies kicking up their heels with whirling Indonesian children dressed in traditional Javanese attire.

SHOPPING AND CRAFTS

As the capital city of W. Java Province, Bandung's shops are filled with the products of this far-flung archipelago as well as imported goods. For the visitor, souvenirs abound. While prices are somewhat higher and choices less wide-ranging than in the products' home regions, shopping in Bandung is fast, simple, and extensive. West Java accounts for 60% of Indonesia's commercial textile production, mostly concentrated in Bandung. For back-street exploring, cruise Pasar Baru and the streets around Jl. ABC (electronics), Jl. Oto Iskandardinata (gold shops), Kosambi Blok (everything); Pasar Jatayu (flea market), on Jl. Arjuna behind the motorbike parts shop, is a great place to find antiques and second-hand junk.

Shops And Workshops

Shops in the *pasar* are normally open until 2100; others are open 0830-1400 and 1700-2030. Except for those in markets, shops are closed on Sun. and public holidays. The nearest Bandung gets to Paris is Jl. Braga, the city's Champs Elysees. Many shops are also found on Jl. Asia-Afrika: handicrafts, souvenirs, leather, antiques, art, *batik,* high-quality leather shoes, and ornately dressed wooden *wayang golek.* Recommended souvenir and craft ships: **Aneka Lukisan**, Jl. Cihampelas 96, for paintings, textiles, *batik;* **Batik Semar Solo**, Jl. Dalam Kaum 40, for *suling* and ceramics; **Cupu Manik Handicraft Center**, Jl. Kebon Kawung, **Gang Umar 2**, for *suling,* puppetry, ceramics; **Karya Nusantara**, Jl. Asia-Africa 94, for paintings and textiles; **Lumayan**, Jl. Cicendo 5, for paintings, lacework, basketry; **Luwes Art Shop**, Jl. Braga 46, for paintings, ceramics, sculpture, *angklung;* **Mayang Sari**, Gang Madurasa 275, for *gamelan* instruments. **Cupu Manik** on Gang Haji Umar (off Jl. Kebon Kawung), only 500 m from the Sakadana Losmen, is a small *wayang golek* factory. **Pak Ruhiyat**, on Jl. Pangarang, is another fine *wayang golek* craftsman working out of his home. **Sarinah**, Jl. Braga 10 (tel. 52798) sells new *wayang golek* at very good prices (Rp2200-6875), depending on the size. **Pritico**, Jl. Braga 72, for *batik* and paintings; **Saung Angklung**, Jl. Padasuka 118, for *wayang* and *angklung;* **Sin Sin**, Jl. Braga, for antiques. **The Leather Palace**, Jl. Braga 67, sells well-made, inexpensive shoes and all manner of other contemporary leather goods—all crafted locally. Leather shoes start at Rp20,000; boots at Rp50,000. For snakeskin articles, **Banowati**, Jl. Geger Kalong Hilir: shoes, bags, belts, etc.

Ceramics

The **Ceramics Research Institute** (Balai Penelitian Keramik), Jl. A. Yani 318 near Pasar Cicadas, is a government-sponsored research and test center for the ceramics industry. The institute itself does not market the products but concerns itself with each facet of the operation of turning clay into practical and beautiful objects. Here you'll see raw clay, much of it from the nearby Gunung Gurun region, being mixed electrically with kaolin, feldspar, and quartz, in large wooden vats. After being thrown and molded into the requisite shapes, the pieces are hand-painted and glazed, then fired in kilns at 160 degrees C. The range of finishes and techniques is amazing. The institute turns out everything from small coarsely finished eggcup-size plant pots and miniature ornamental

horses to exquisite copies of classic Chinese vases. The **Technical Institute of Bandung** is also becoming well known for its ceramic products, notably convincing copies of Chinese porcelain, curios, ornamental pots, and figurines. They use a variety of glazes and high-temperature firing. On Jl. Sukapura in Kiara Condong, one km from Balai Penelitian Keramik, is a Kasongan-type ceramics center which sells lampshades, wall decorations, etc.; located in an alleyway. Farther afield, **Plered** is an active traditional ceramics center SW of Purwakarta (70 km NE of Bandung), and the site of an experimental station of the Bandung Ceramics Research Institute.

Textiles, Plaiting, Bamboo

Both modern and traditional *batik* designs in cotton, silk, and synthetic fabrics are widely available in Bandung. At the **Textile Research Institute**, Jl. Jen. A. Yani next to the Ceramics Research Center, watch *kapok* processing and hand weaving. Free tours are offered, particularly interesting for children. Cane, bamboo, and rattan handicrafts, furniture, lampshades, curtains, fruit baskets, and chairs from W. Java are reputed to be some of the best in Indonesia. Traditional woven crafts can be found in the excellent **Craftworks Shop** on Jl. Tirtaywasa, about a 3-km walk from the main *alun-alun*—very fine quality but reasonable prices. One of the renowned products of W. Java is the bamboo *angklung.* Each one, cut from different lengths of bamboo, produces a different tone when shaken. Mini "souvenir" sizes of this instrument can be bought in almost every souvenir shop in Bandung or from vendors on the street and around hotels. Other works of bamboo art, such as sailing ships, interior home furnishings, carpets, etc., can be bought at the **Gallery 16**, Jl. Raya Cibeureum 16. Out of town handicraft centers are at **Kopki**, W of Bandung; in Peuyeum Ketan (household goods and utensils). In Rajamandala, 8 km from Bandung, is **Art Shop Susilowati** (antiques and paintings). **Cipacing**, 17 km to the E of Bandung, sells blowpipes, rifles, shell paintings, and other handicrafts.

Painting And Sculpture

Bandung has many commercial landscape painters and now and then hosts art fairs. Local painters use every conceivable media, which gives the art-fancier a wide choice—from world-class works of recognized masters to *batik*-painting and mass-produced schlock. A number of shops and art galleries deal exclusively in painting, styles mostly leaning toward the Western genres. Also, street vendors will set up paintings and sculptures on the sidewalks (also near the Kantor Pos)—one of Bandung's charms. For high quality, visit **Decenta**, Jl. Dipatjukur 99 (expensive, ITB's best artists); **Tatarah's**, Jl. Braga 51C, and **Naini's Fine Arts**, Jl. Tamblong 26. Check both these streets out for displays of not only paintings, but graphic arts, reliefs, and sculptures.

Miscellaneous

Many name brands of foreign cosmetics, perfume, toiletries, stationery, and electrical equipment are seen in abundance in many shops in the city. Tapes and film are easily available and quite cheap. For film and photo equipment, go to **Niaga Photo Supply** or **P.T. Modern Photo Film Co.**, Jl. Braga. For wooden shoes (Rp10,000), try **Kelom Geulis** on the corner of Jl. Pacinan Lama and Jl. Banceuy. Two jewelry shops, **Runa Jewelry**, Jl. Gegerkalong Hilir 64, and **Timur Studio**, Jl. Ranggamalela 4, offer a variety of cut stones and locally fashioned jewelry. A candle factory is at Jl. Aksan 18.

SERVICES AND INFORMATION

Shop around for the best exchange rate; hit first **Bank Negara Indonesia 1946** and **Bank Dagang Negara** on Jl. Asia-Afrika. The main **Immigration Office** is located on Jl. Suci. There are 12 hospitals in Bandung. An outstanding one is the **Seventh-day Adventists Hospital**, Jl. Cihampelas 135 (tel. 82091), with English-speaking missionary staff. Bandung's **Boromius Hospital**, Jl. Ir. H. Juanda 80 (tel. 81011), has a very fine outpatient clinic. Most of the local doctors and dentists speak English, and hold clinic/office hours during the early evening. Most brand-name drugs are available from the city's pharmacies.

Tourist Information

The **Bandung Tourist Information Office** is in the NE corner of the *alun-alun;* open Mon.-Thurs. 0800-2000, Fri. 0800-1100, Sat. 0800-1400. Staffed for the most part by well-informed volunteers, they hand out basic city maps, and give sound verbal information and updates on cultural happenings. They also dispense advice on other points of interest on Java and Bali, itinerary planning, and can even make hotel reservations for you in Yogya when you arrive there at 0200! The **West Java Provincial Tourist Office** (Diparda Jawa Barat) is in the Jl. Gedung Merdeka Building; go early.

Direktorat Volkanologi

An organization at Jl. Diponegoro 57 (in the same building as the Geological Museum), made up of about 70 geologists, geophysicists, engineers, and chemists, who have taken on the monumental and heroic task of monitoring the seismic activity and recording the physical changes in Indonesia's active volcanos. The nation's volcanos are not tucked away in isolated regions like Mt. St. Helens in the U.S., and this "early warning" network attempts to save the lives and property of millions of islanders living around Indonesia's angry summits. Understaffed, underfunded, and underequipped, VSI maintains observatories on only 26 of Indonesia's 125 active volcanos.

TRANSPORT

Arriving

Although the airport lies only 4 km from town in the NW of the city; taxi drivers want Rp4000 to take you into town. Instead, just walk out the gate, turn R, and walk down to the main road and take a *microlet* into town for Rp100. From Bandung's Kebon Kalapa Bus Station, board one of the Sukajati *bemo* for the 1½-km ride to the *alun-alun.* Buses arriving from the E end up at Cicaheum Bus Station. *Bemo* drivers will drop you off near the central train station, where many cheap hotels are located. Several hotels are around the bus station too, but they tend to be more expensive. **from Bogor:** The bus costs Rp1500 and takes 4 hours, 129 km; or take a minibus from Bogor to Bandung for around Rp1500. However, on Sat. and Sun., buses and minibuses don't pass over Puncak Pass.

Getting There

From Cirebon, a bus costs Rp1500, 4 hours, 130 km. **from Jakarta:** The *Parahiyangan* (1st and 2nd Class only) costs Rp8000 and Rp6000 respectively, 3½ hours, but some *ekonomi* trains cost as little as Rp3000 3rd Class, 4 hours. By Patas bus from Cililitan Station costs Rp3500, 5 hours. By shared taxi from Jakarta, Rp7500, 4 hours, straight to your hotel. The scenic overland routes differ little in distance or time. One route goes through the Puncak, another is by way of Lake Jatiluhur, outside Purwakarta, and a third through Sukabumi. Bandung is also served by air (Garuda, Merpati, and Bouraq) from Jakarta on a 30-min. flight; planes land at Husen Sastranegara Airport. **from Yogya:** Three trains serve Yogya and Bandung daily: the *Ekspres Siang* costs Rp4800 (2nd Class); Rp3500 (3rd Class); takes 6 hours. By a/c *bis malam* costs Rp6000, 12 hours, 486 km. Bouraq also connects Bandung-Yogya by air, one flight daily, Rp43,300. **from Pangandaran:** The "4848" Bus Co. takes 8 hours, Rp6000, by bus from Banjar, N of Pangandaran.

Getting Around

Public transport is complicated, so always ask first. The only major E-W connecting street (Jl. Asia-Afrika) is at the southern end of the city. Get around town easiest on mini-pickup trucks (called Hondas or Daihatsus), *bemo*, and city buses. All *bemo* and *oplet* rides within the city cost just Rp150 but often don't go through the center. Hondas and *bemo* depart from Kebun Kelapa Station, 4 blocks S of the central *alun-alun.* Angkutan Kota (minibuses) carry passengers within the city and to outskirts such as Lembang, Ciumbuleuit, and Dago, the fare depending on distance. An alternative is to buy a bicycle (new or used) at the Jl. ABC bicycle market. **taxis:** Usually private cars, taxis are available near the Tourist Info Office, not by hailing them on the street; Rp3500 per hour. Taxis are also available to out of town, for example to Ciwedey, Rp35,000. Guide fees Rp6000 pp, min. 2 persons. *bis kota:* Bandung's pollution is so bad that the air barely supports life anymore, and their badly maintained Indian-built *bis kota* system is just as foul, inside and out. Nevertheless, these suffocatingly crowded city buses (Rp125 any trip) offer useful and regular service on the E-W route along Jl. Asia-Afrika and Jl. A. Yani, and also travel from N to south. Patas buses are quicker and cost Rp250.

FROM BANDUNG

Tour Guides

Few of Bandung's travel agencies are run by native Sundanese but are branches of Jakarta-based agencies and only give the tours — such as long shopping weekends in Singapore or Hong Kong — that the Jakarta head office wants them to do. Two examples of Sundanese firms are **Interlink** (near Balai Kota) and **Surya Budaya** on Jl. A. Yani. They publish tours of Bandung and vicinity in their pamphlets but only operate if there're enough people (10 or more). For more individualized touring, **Soehardhie Yogantara** (or "Yoga" for short) or **Mamun Rustina** can be contacted at the Tourist Info Office (tel. 56644) on the *alun-alun.* Very flexible, willing to make any arrangements to suit individual needs. Yoga, who speaks excellent English, takes tourists on overnight trips out to rustic villages, staying in traditional houses to view Sundanese circumcision ceremonies, weddings, etc.

By Long-distance Bus

Bandung has 2 bus terminals: Cicaheum for buses going E (Yogya) and Kebun Kelapa for buses going W (Bogor, Jakarta). Kebun Kelapa Station is quite central, but Cicaheum Station is 45 min. (Rp350) by *bemo* out of town. *Bis malam* companies offer the best long-distance services; to get the best seats, go the day before to the bus company's terminal/office where passengers converge at departure time. The best companies for Yogya are the **Bandung Express**, Jl. Dr. Cipto 5; **Muncul**, Jl. Cendana; the **Yogya Express**, Jl. Sunda 54 (tel. 52507), not far from the intersection with Jl. Asia-Afrika; **Apollo Express**, Jl. Lengkong Besar; **Maju Makmur**, Jl. Martadinata (tel. 58854). Sample fares: Cianjur, Rp700; Cirebon, Rp1500; Ciwedey, Rp3500; Semarang, Rp5000; Solo, Rp2000; Sumedang, Rp500; Sukabumi, Rp1100; Purwokerto, Rp3500. **to Jakarta:** Buses leave all day long from the bus offices, Rp6000, arriving at Jakarta's Cililitan Station; from there take a no. 401 bus to Jl. Cikini Raya (close to the Jl. Jaksa hotel area). An alternative is to take the bus to Bogor, stay overnight, then board a bus early the next morning on

to Jakarta for another Rp600. If you wish to leave Indonesia directly from Bandung and skip Jakarta, take the train from Bandung which ends up at Jakarta's Gambir Station from where you can get a Damri bus direct to the airport, Rp2000. **to Bogor:** By bus Rp1500 and 3½ hours (129 km). Just going over the beautiful Puncak Pass makes this trip worth it (but buses take a different, less crowded route on Sat. and Sunday). **to Pangandaran:** Bandung's Terminal Bis Cicaheum on Jl. A. Yani has buses every hour to Banjar, Rp6000, 4-5 hours. For example, "4848" Co. has buses departing for Banjar at 1400, arriving at 1900. From Banjar take a bus (Rp800) or minibus (Rp1500) down to Pangandaran. **to Yogya:** Most *bis malam* leave at around 1900, arriving in Yogya at around 0600. They charge about Rp6000, with a/c and snacks.

Long-distance Trains

To Jakarta, at least 7 daily express trains run in each direction (3 hours). The *Cepat* departs at 0500 and 1330, arriving at 0825 and 1450; Rp3500 3rd Class. The *Parahyangan I* departs 0505, arrives 0817; Rp6250 1st Class, Rp4750 2nd Class. A number of other *Parahyangan* trains leave throughout the day, with the same fares. **to Surabaya:** The *Ekspres Siang* leaves each day (via Madiun and Solo) at 0520, arriving 2215, costing Rp8000 2nd Class; the night express *Mutiara Selatan* leaves at 1720, arriving at 0945, costing Rp9750 2nd Class, Rp14,000 1st Class. **to Yogya:** It's preferable to take the train to Yogya rather than to endure 18 miserable hours on the bus. Three trains depart at 0510, 0720, and 1730, arriving at 1415, 1735, and 0159; Rp4800-12,000. Departure times are posted at the Bandung Train Station. Get up at least an hour before the 0510 train departs; tickets are often sold out by as early as 0445. Better to make a reservation before noon the day before. The 0510 train arrives in Yogya around 1425, which is more desirable than arriving at 1735 on the 0720 train. If you miss both trains, just get on any train leaving for Surabaya. Nice scenery along the way, but lousy food. Thankfully, the train passes through a number of stations, such as Kutoardjo, where you can hop off to get a quick bite. **alternative route:** Consider breaking the long Bandung-Yogya train journey into 2 segments by first taking the train from Bandung to Banjar, go down to the Pangandaran beach resort, then resume your journey to Yogya. For Banjar, trains leave Bandung at 0730 and 1130 (Rp2000). By minibus from Banjar to Pangandaran costs only Rp1800, a good value for the superb scenery.

By Air

The airport lies 4 km from the city center; taxis near the Tourist Info Office want Rp4000 to take you into town. Sample fares: Jakarta (one Bouraq flight daily), Rp25,900; Semarang (one Merpati flight daily), Rp47,600; Yogya (Merpati flights 3 times weekly),

Rp43,300; Surabaya (one Merpati flight each day), Rp52,500; Denpasar (Merpati, every day except Tues., at 0700), Rp88,600; Palembang (Merpati, every day), Rp72,800; Waingapu (Merpati, Wed., Thurs., and Sun.), Rp152,600. Airline offices: Bouraq, Grand Hotel Preanger, Jl. Asia-Afrika 81 (tel. 431631/437896); Merpati, Jl. Veteran 46 (tel. 437893/439742); Garuda, Jl. Asia-Afrika 73 (tel. 51497/56986).

VICINITY OF BANDUNG

The real joy of Bandung is the surrounding countryside. The whole regency is situated in the beautiful Parahiangan Highlands which soar up to 2,500 m, boasting spectacular and unbelievably varied landscapes. Here you can really get away from the congestion of urban Java. Wildflowers grow in great profusion, bamboo and pines compete for space, and everywhere you look are meticulously groomed tea plantations. The area is also Jakarta's market garden and in these hills grow cauliflowers, carrots, and many other imported high-altitude vegetables. You'll also encounter vast expanses of cinchona estates; the bark from these trees goes to make quinine. The first quinine factory in the world was opened in Bandung in 1905 and today the area still produces more than 80% of the world's supply. Boarding houses, holiday hotels, park and garden resorts crowd the hilly outskirts of the city. In all these upland villages canopied horsecarts *(sado, delman,* and *dokar)* are available for rent; the drivers wear *peci* and their boney horses colorful pompoms. Hill villages nestle at high altitudes, so be sure to take a jacket or sweater and raincoat.

Dago Tea House

The northern third of Bandung lies on the slopes of a series of hills rising eventually to the volcano Tangkuban Prahu. Flag down a N-bound *oplet* on Jl. Merdeka, then from the Jl. Siliwangi traffic light walk about 2 km uphill, turn L for 250 m to the Dago Tea House (760 m). Or simply take a minibus from the RR station, telling the driver you want to get off at the tea house. It's built on a grassy mound surrounded by lawns, pathways, wooden benches. A modest fee is charged for entry into the grounds. The whole city can be viewed from here—great sunsets, and at night it's a marvelous festival of lights. The weather is cool even on the hottest days of the dry season. The teahouse, run by ITB students, serves well-prepared, inexpensive, though limited, food. In the evenings you can see scores of students here, and on weekends there's barely standing room.

Vicinity Of Dago

The **Curug Dago Waterfalls,** used to generate hydro power, is just one km from the teahouse. Nearby also is an excellent Sundanese restaurant called **Babakan Siliwangi.** The **Dago Golf Course** is at the top of Jl. Dago. A rough track leads down from the Dago Golf Course to the **Hero's Cemetery** (Taman Pahlawan). Before you reach the course, look for a road to the L,

Jl. Pakar, which heads for Pakar village. Walk through the village, turn L toward the lake among pine trees. This is the start of a fantastic walk up the gorge of the Cikapundung River to Maribaya. Just as the road bends L (at the Spanish-style house), take the track straight down the hill. At the bottom are tunnels carved out by the Japanese during WW II for ammunition storage; one goes right through the hill.

The Cimahi Hills

The road to Jakarta W of Bandung follows a line of small hills straddling the flat plain just S of Cimahi. This area contains the enormous Citarum Cataracts, the Balinese temple of Cimahi, hiking paths, and unique exploring possibilities. The town of Cimahi itself, 7 km NW of Bandung, has its own distinctive character. At the traffic lights on the Bandung side of Cimahi's center, turn L and you'll enter an idyllically laid-out residential section, now largely occupied by the army, but still retaining a pre-war Dutch country town atmosphere. Many old Dutch houses have their original letterboxes in front, beautifully cast in iron with a crown on top, surely one of the only places in Indonesia where these can still be found. **the Balinese temple:** This surprisingly large temple complex, the only one in the Bandung area, will probably be locked when you arrive so you'll have to find the *juru kunci.* The temple is easy to find; in Cimahi turn L, walk about ½ km and turn R, then after 400 m turn left. Follow this straight road until you see the walls of the temple compound on your L just before the railroad line.

The Citarum Cataracts were first recorded by the German explorer Franz Junghuhn in the 1850s. The Citarum River flows along the southern side of the Bandung Plain, lazily at first, gradually creating a classic set of oxbow lakes. As it reaches the Cimahi Hills, S of town, it flows over hard lava and drops more than 25 m into a 150-m-deep gorge in the lower plain SE of Batujajar. To get there, before crossing the bridge (about 15 km S of Cimahi) over the Citarum River, take the path to the R through the bamboo which leads after 200 m to brick-making tunnels and after 800 m to the cataracts. This is probably the largest waterfall on Java, though not the highest. Walk to a rocky promontory just above the falls from where you can climb down through the trees to the rocks below to experience a tremendously noisy, densely humid world, with rainbows arcing through the thick spray.

Ciwidey

Thirty km SW of Bandung, on the road to G. Putuha (2,434 m). Here ironsmiths create an unending number of hand-forged daggers, *cangkul*, and agricultural tools with beautifully carved sheaths and wooden handles—a thriving cottage industry. This is the last area in W. Java where traditional ironworking is still practiced, the final remnants of an art stretching back to Hindu times. Today scrap iron is used, but in the hills around Bandung and Dago traces of siliceous iron slag are still found. From Bandung's train station, first take a 3-wheeled *bemo* for Rp150 to Terminal Bis Kebon Kelapa. Then take a bus (Putra Setia) for Rp400 to Ciwidey. The ironworks center is a few km out of town, although a number of smithies work in town too. As you enter Ciwidey, take the turn to the L toward the *pasar*. On this bend take the other road straight ahead for approximately 2 km. After the bridge, take the L track to the *kampung* where every house has a forge, each making a different iron product. Ask the village *lurah* to show you around. Afterward, eat fish wrapped in banana leaves, roasted fried chicken, raw greens, and other typical Sundanese specialties at **Sindang Peret**; also has bungalows and sells souvenir knives and other iron goods.

Situ Patenggang

South of Ciwedy, this is a high (1,600 m) circular mountain lake surrounded by forests, tea plantations, and swirling mists. The water source is G. Patuha (2,434 m) above the lake. With its nearby steam craters and hotsprings, this area is quiet, blessed with cool gentle breezes and attractive landscapes. From Ciwedy, grab a minibus to Rancabali, Rp600, then walk or take a *dokar* to the lake. Visitors can fish, rent boats, and swim (although the water is cold). Hire a rowboat out to the island in the middle; see the old Buddha statue beneath the cliff. The lake tends to get crowded on Sun. with domestic tourists, but it's easy to get away on the many trails in the vicinity. It takes about 1½ hours to walk the path around the lake. Keep a lookout for the "Monster of Patenggang Lake," which resembles a giant black fish with golden fins. Sighted intermittently since Dutch colonial times, this mysterious creature only appears at dusk when it's quiet. Fishermen still make offerings to the "monster" before going out fishing each day. There's one **penginapan** at Situ Patenggang, only Rp6000 s with cheap meals. A **guesthouse** overlooks the lake near the parking lot. Visitors may stay here as guests of the tea estate but speak to the estate manager to make reservations.

Rancabali Tea Factory

One of the most modern in all of Indonesia, an easy walk from the Situ Patenggang Lake. To use the delightful hot-bath house you must first get permission from the friendly management. Southwest of the lake is the rocky road leading to the older Cibuni Tea Factory; beyond the factory a footpath leads after 3 km to little-known Kawah Cibuni, which offers hot-water bathing via bamboo pipes and an active solfatara field. Pemandian Air Panas Cimanggu, a small *kampung* and hotsprings in the forest, is just 2 km before Situ Patenggang.

Malabar Tea Estate

A government-controlled tea plantation at the base of G. Malabar in the hills around Pangalengan, S of Bandung. With wide vistas over the valleys below, immaculate buildings, splendid roads and cultivated fields, this vast estate is an unending delight to the eye. In 1896 K.A.R. Bosscha pioneered its development, and it quickly became famous for its beauty, efficiency, and top-quality tea. Bosscha was an eminent philanthropist and member of the Dutch governing body Volksraad in Batavia. His name lives on in the Bosscha Observatory, just outside of Lembang, N of Bandung. Bosscha's memorial (he died in 1928), together with the beautiful house that was once his home, are fastidiously maintained. **accommodations:** Guesthouse Malabar is high on the slopes of G. Malabar (2,321 m) in the middle of the Malabar Tea Plantation. Very quiet, relaxing, and cold. At night it could get as low as zero degrees; a heater is put in the room overnight. Reservations recommended.

KAWAH PAPANDAYAN

A mighty 2,622-m-high crater and nature reserve 65 km SE of Bandung, towering 1,950 m above the Garut Plateau. Papandayan forms the southernmost cone in one long row of volcanos. Of Java's 100 volcanos, about 35 are still active; Papandayan is one of 7 kept under constant surveillance by volcanologists. Visiting this fiery crater is a more primeval experience than the over-touristed Tangkuban Prahu outside of Lembang (N of Bandung), and even more otherworldly than G. Bromo of E. Java. It's frightening to stare into the seething heart of these 6 craters, which cover an area of 25 ha. Accompanied by a guide, you can walk between the bubbling lava pools, sulphur pillars, and solfataras, amid the deafening noise of the fumaroles, hissing hot vapors, and mud volcanos. Numerous geysers, which reach 10 m high and roar like jet engines, are found in the active crater—an astonishing sight! Not many visitors are drawn here because of its remoteness and lack of publicity. **history:** Originally, a large mountain here was estimated to have consisted of more than a cubic mile of rock which exploded sideways across the Garut Plateau during the night of 11 August 1772. This catastrophe killed 2,957 people and completely devastated 40 villages. It left a gaping V-shaped notch in the side of the crater which can still be seen, with pale green lowlands stretching away far below. During the 1920s there was so much activity—explo-

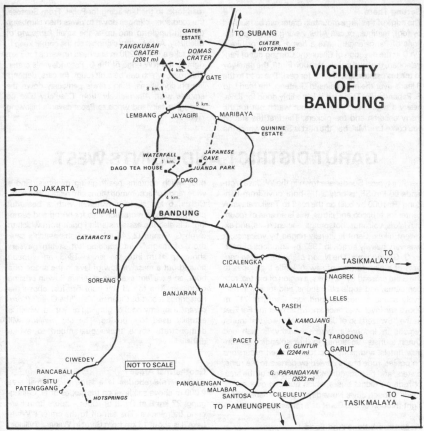

VICINITY OF BANDUNG

NOT TO SCALE

sions, rock blasts, earth tremors, *lahar* flows, etc.—that the crater was virtually unapproachable.

Sights

Four big craters make up the Papandayan complex, among which Kawah Alun-Alun alone possesses the classic volcanic shape. Kawah Papandayan is the youngest, still showing indications of last century's eruptions, and still-active fumeroles. The road emerges onto an inactive part of the crater, overgrown with scrub. Then the road leads to the active crater, Kawah Mas or "Golden Crater," named because its most active part is a gigantic dome of sulphur. This astonishing crater boils with lava and rolls with the sound of thunder. Under high pressure, steam is emitted from its many fissures. The sulphur condenses first as a pool of dark brown liquid at a temperature of about 200 degrees C, then changes to

pale yellow as it cools to 110 degrees and crystallizes. Wonderfully fragile crystals form around the jet holes, mud boils up, streams flow with milky blue water, and pillars of mud and rocks of fantastic colors have piled up. Trace the source of the boiling stream, a steaming blue pool encrusted with sparkling white deposits. Early in the morning, before the crater is covered with mist or cloud, enjoy the view over the city of Garut; if you mount the summit itself you might be able to see the Indian Ocean. **note:** Kawah Mas can be a very dangerous place. Take precautions. You could scald your feet in boiling mud, or be poisoned by gases. Mummified bodies of animals are still occasionally found in the gas-filled valleys. No one will stop you from entering the active area but if you want to get up real close be sure to have a guide. Camping can be unbelievably cold so bring warm clothing, sleeping bag, and tent.

Getting There

The edge of this large mountain crater can be reached by foot, minibus, or car. After visiting the tea plantations of Pangalengan, take a *bemo, oplet,* or hire a 4WD in the direction of Cileuleuy. Coming out of Pangalengan, the road passes through Pintu, the gateway to the tea estates (last chance for gas). The road to the R leads over the mountains to Genteng, the road L to G. Papandayan. This road is incredibly good for Java, nearly a high-speed highway, but watch out for the many children and tea pickers. The first tea station you come to is Malabar, the next is Santosa where the road forks to the L heading for Pacet. From Santosa, the road soon plunges down to rivers then climbs up through jungle to end up at the small *kampung* of Cileuleuy. At the white signpost on the corner keep L, then take a R after 200 m and head upwards for 7 km right to the NW edge of the G. Papandayan's crater. This road, which can be a bit rough for cars, depending on conditions, then crawls perilously down the crater's wall. Alternatively, from Cileuleuy hike up through a fairyland wood to Papandayan's billowing crater.

GARUT DISTRICT AND POINTS WEST

Garut, a typical Sundanese town in the W. Java highlands 60 km SE, is only a 1½-hour drive from Bandung (Rp1000 by bus) on the road to Tasikmalaya. A center for tobacco and citrus, this is an area of mountain lakes, volcanos, hotsprings, ancient ruins, and excellent hikes. Garut is literally ringed by volcanos; it was very heavily struck in 1982 by eruptions of nearby G. Galunggung. The N part of the *kabupaten* consists of a plateau area of *sawah,* while the slopes to the S are crossed by 12 rivers, a region of big tea, rubber, citrus, and apple plantations, and forests in relatively sound ecological condition. Garut, at 717 m above sea level, was once known all over the Far East as the "Switzerland of Java," one of the oldest tourist regions in Indonesia, where wealthy English and Dutch tourists vacationed in their splendid, fashionable hotels, and signed up for packaged excursions on ponies, rode chairs carried by porters to the ruins, craters, and picturesque manicured lakes of the area, or rode on tourist buses which bumped over scenic roads through Java. Nowadays travelers usually pass right through or use Garut as a refreshment stop.

Accommodations And Food

Stay in one of the many *penginapan* (Rp5000-7000) in town; there are plenty of budding English speakers also anxious to put you up. **Penginapan Gelora Intan,** Jl. Karacak 4, Rp7000 d, is very comfortable, with friendly people; serves coffee and tea, sometimes bananas. Other places to try are: **Hotel Nasonal,** Jl. Kenanga 19; **Pribumi,** Jl. Raya 105; **Biasa,** Jl. Cigong 57; **Famili,** Jl. Ranggalawe 66; **Pusaka Wanaraja,** Jl. Papandayan 21; and **Hotel Mulia,** Jl. Kenanga 17. Garut's specialty is sweetcakes, *dodol Garut,* found in many shops in town and in surrounding villages. This delicacy is made from flour, brown palm sugar, sticky rice, and sometimes jelly.

Vicinity Of Garut

Tarogong, 5 km N, has a hotsprings (Cipanas) and pool which contains health-giving minerals. Find a wide range of accommodations and restaurants here. **Cititis,** 6 km N, is a waterfall with a beautiful panorama and a recreation area for hiking and camping; it is also the easiest starting point from which to climb G. Guntur (2,244 m), a veritable witch's cauldron of magnificent scalding-hot steam geysers shooting 30 m into the air. In 1843, an eruption poured out a massive flow of lava in the shape of a boot, an excellent example of a lava flow in pristine condition. The toe of the boot lies just above the hotsprings resort of Cipanas. Visit "the Oven" *(Komporan),* a steamy pool of gurgling gray mud, which is actually used for cooking. The old *penjaga* will demonstrate some tricks guaranteed to evoke disbelief.

Geothermal Areas

Kawah Talagabodas is a large geothermal area 2,000 m above sea level on the slopes of G. Galunggung, 27 km E of Garut or about 4 hours from Bandung by minibus. The turnoff to the crater ("White Lake") is about 13 km from Garut in Wanaraja village, and though the track is bad, it's accessible by automobile and definitely worth it. This steamy sulphur lake, about 215 m in diameter, is a pale greenish-white. It gets its color from the sulphur and alum at the bottom; its surface is disturbed only by the constant noisy bubbling caused by escaping gases. **Kawah Kamojang** is a large geothermal site on the top of a mountain range, accessible from Tarogong, 5 km N of Garut. This whole bubbling, hissing area contains steam geysers, sulphur springs, and fantastic boiling mud pools. Since Dutch times, engineers have drilled for steam in this crater; in fact, the first hole the Dutch drilled is still going strong! Holes have been drilled as deep as 2,000 m to tap a regular supply of geothermal steam which drives turbines in a 30-megawatt power station on top of the mountain.

SITU CANGKUANG

About 17 km N of Garut, this is one of the oldest temples in Indonesia and the largest temple in W. Java. According to archaeological evidence, this 9th C. *candi* even predates Prambanan and Borobudur of C. Java. In comparison with those classical monuments, however, this structure is no larger than a shrine. About 40% of the building is original, the remainder having been carved over the course of a very successful reconstruction process which was completed in 1976. Candi Cangkuang is the only ancient building of its type in W. Java, although others certainly existed. The *kampung* in the vicinity of Desa Cangkuang make large pots by means of primitive methods.

History

In 1893, a Dutch archaeologist, Vorderman, noted that at Desa Cangkuang was an ancient tomb (Arif Muhamad's) and a deformed stone statue. On the basis of that information, in 1966 an Indonesian archaeologist led an expedition which discovered not only the tomb and statue but also the remains of a classical Hindu temple, Candi Cangkuang. Further explorations and excavations have now established that the Cangkuang location in the Leles Valley must have been for hundreds of years the center for a number of Neolithic, megalithic, Hindu, and Muslim cultures. The more animist aspects of Java-Hinduism still linger today: near the *candi* is a watchman's hut complete with a place for religious ceremonies, *Desapulo*.

Getting There

From Leles, 15 km N of Garut, follow the small road to Desa Cangkuang. At the large grass *alun-alun* next to the *mesjid* in the center of town turn L down a good rock road and continue for about 3 km. Near the village of Cangkuang the hills form a peninsula jutting out into the lake where you'll see the temple among a group of trees. Cross the lake to the island on small boats or on unusual bamboo rafts with seats, or walk around on a small road for 2 km to reach the temple.

PAMEUNGPEUK

Immaculate beaches can be found all along the coast S of Garut, but the swimming is dangerous (the South Sea Goddess' appetite is insatiable). From Garut, follow a good mountain road via Cikajang over teetering bridges down to the white sands and rolling waves of beautiful Pameungpeuk (Pam-MUNG-perk) Bay. Along the way watch men make charcoal from forest timber (100 million people in Indonesia cook on

charcoal). Grapes and citrus grow wild. You pass by constantly changing vistas, rocky cliffs, huge jungle trees, rushing rivers, swarms of butterflies. Though it looks close, it's too far for a one-day trip from either Garut or Bandung. The small Sundanese village of Pameungpeuk contains 2 *losmen* and one balconied hotel with goats and chickens decorating the stairs. It's also possible to camp out along the coast several km from town. Explore the old harbor built by the Dutch with its collapsed jetty and broken rusty bridge. Walk along the rocky peninsula built of reef limestone taken from the sea. In this area are lagoons, good fishing, and shell-collecting places. To get to the harbor you must go around an army rocket-testing area.

Vicinity Of Pameungpeuk

The roads around Pameungpeuk are good for walkers, but not cars. Hike along the coast, crossing big rivers like the Cikandang, Cilayu, and the Cipandak, for Sindangbarang. Stay in the *kampung* of Cikelet and Cidaun along the way. East of Pameungpeuk and close to Miramare Plantation is **Leuweung Sancang**, about 118 km S of Garut and 147 km SE of Bandung. This 2,157-ha coastal nature reserve and wildlife refuge contains thousands of species of flora, among which is a tree called *Kayu Kaboa*, found nowhere else. Founded in 1941, the reserve has dunes, sea grass, mangroves, 1,300 ha of swamp, sub-montane meadow vegetation, lowland forest, as well as *banteng*, small deer, squirrels, gibbons, wild pigs, crocodiles, iguanas, monitor lizards, snakes, and jungle fowl and peacocks. Get permission first from the PPA officer before exploring.

TASIKMALAYA

A rattan weaving center 57 km E of Garut and 116 km SE of Bandung (Rp2500 by bus) on the road to Yogya; take a train from either city. A volcanic area, Tasikmalaya is surrounded by curative hotsprings. Change money at Bank Rakyat Indonesia, Jl. Kalektoran; or at Bank Bumi Daya, Jl. Oto Iskandarinata. The post office is on Jl. Oto Iskandarinata. The public hospital, RS Umum, is on Jl. Rumah Sakit; RS Bersalin Bhakti Kartini is on Jl. Oto Iskandarinata. From Tasik, 2 trains a day leave for Yogya, an express at 0830, a slow one at 1026, and another one at 2010; all cost around Rp2500 3rd Class, 8 hours.

Accommodations

On the lower end (Rp2000-4000) are **Sentosa**, Jl. Guning Sabeulah 43 (tel. 807); **Pustaka**, Jl. Yudanegara 32; and **Mulia Budi Rasa**, Jl. Stasiun 20 (tel. 527). **Merdeka**, Jl. Siliwangi 54, is a 4-min. walk from the train station, Rp4000 s or d. Also good value is **Kencana**, Jl. Yudanegara 5B (tel. 858). **Tasik**, Jl.

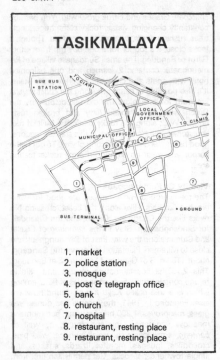

TASIKMALAYA

1. market
2. police station
3. mosque
4. post & telegraph office
5. bank
6. church
7. hospital
8. restaurant, resting place
9. restaurant, resting place

Komalasari 18 (a back street) is clean; Rp5000-6000 per room with *mandi*. Clean and central **Selamat**, Jl. Empang 26, charges Rp3500 s, Rp5000 d. Also try **Pribadi**, Jl. Gg. Negarawangi 19; **Kalimantan**, Jl. Pasarwetan 17; and **Mekar**, Jl. Kebontiwu 1/25 (tel. 815).

Food

Many tasty *warung* on Jl. Pemuda, while the restaurants are found along Jl. Dr. Sukarjo. **Garuda**, Jl. Dr. Sukarjo 19, for Indonesian food. For Indonesian and Sundanese food, try **Cahaya**, Jl. Dr. Sukarjo 15, and **Priangan**, Jl. Mesjid 16. For Padang food, go to the **Simpang Raya**, Jl. Yudanegara 14. **Banda Pulai**, Jl. Yudanegara 14, right across the street from Hotel Kencana, also features *nasi padang*. **Rumah Makan Sederhana**, Jl. Mesjid 16, has *gado-gado, gule, mie telor, sop buntut*, etc. — all well prepared. **Resmi**, next door, is good too. At **Tasik**, Jl. Mustafa 35, see live pythons in the kitchen; excellent snake soup.

Crafts

Tasikmalaya is a center for woven rattan (*rotan*) and pandanus (screw palm or *pandan*) woven articles such as baskets, sandals, hats, handbags, floormats,

medong, etc., all attractively plaited in artistic patterns. High-quality wares from Tasik are seen all over Java and exported around the world. Beautiful canvas and wooden umbrellas, each hand-painted and stitched with colored cotton, are also sold ridiculously cheap. Also, lovely lamp covers and other bamboo decorations, as well as wooden, ornamented shoes, are crafted here. **craft shops:** Shops usually carry a variety of goods, but specialties are noted: Agung, Jl. Paseh, Gg. Ciparaga I/9 (wooden thongs); Aquarius, Jl. Raya Rajapolah 118; Alas, Jl. Galuh 11/4 (caps, garments); Enjo Karo, Jl. H.Z. Mustofa 262 blk (embroideries); Panyombo, Jl. Pasar Wetan 65 (knittings); KUD Mukti, Jl. Rajapolah 2 (bamboo and pandanus pieces); Motekar, Jl. Cicariang (embroideries). The Kusumah Art Shop, on Jl. R.E. Martadinata 216, is one of the town's main crafts shop, particularly for baskets.

Batik Tasik

A special high-quality cloth found only in the Tasikmalaya area. This style uses local motifs (mostly detailed floral patterns) and colors (mostly red backgrounds). Tasik's *batik* designs even vary quite a bit from those of nearby Cirebon, Garut, and Ciamis. At any of the crafts shops listed below, ask someone to take you to see *batik tulis* being made; different processes take place in different home workshops. Embroidered *batik* is also available.

Shops And Workshops

For generally cheaper prices and a more unusual selection try Rajapolah village 12 km N where the weavers, and some *batikers*, actually work. The rattan furniture and pandanus weaving industries, and some *batik*, are also centered in and around this village. If driving, don't try to get back to Bandung via Rajapolan — bad road. In Tasik itself, shop for *batik* articles at **Batik Bordir Kota Resik**, Jl. Seladarma 96 (tel. 41385); **Batik Kartika**, Jl. R. E. Martadinata 127; **Kabinangkitan**, Jl. Sutisna Senjaya 20 (tel. 41548); **Mitara Batik**, Jl. R.E. Martadinata 81 (tel. 21253/21322); and the *batik* cooperative **Kopinka Ciamis** on Jl. Raya Timur.

PANGANDARAN

A favorite beauty spot 88 km SE of Ciamis and 223 km SE of Bandung on the S coast near the border of C. Java, this small fishing village at the entrance of a small peninsula is almost completely surrounded by the Indian Ocean. At the isthmus' narrowest point, the shores are just 300 m apart. The whole peninsula, Cagar Alam Pananjung, has been turned into a wildlife reserve. Stretch your stiff legs by hiking along its long white-sand beaches, swim in the gentle surf, dive on coral reefs, or enjoy other watersports here. Pangandaran has accommodations, restaurants, souvenir shops, recreational facilities — a good place to unwind. Domestic tourists swamp the place during weekends and holidays. After a hard day's bus ride you might be just settling down when suddenly a whole Indonesian extended family moves in and takes over the *losmen!* One idea is to stay at Pangandaran only on the weekdays and take off on the weekends. Becoming increasingly better known by the traveling community, it is slowly developing a scruffiness typical of many beach resorts. Shades of Kuta (Bali) are evident: the motorized *prahu* are a rip-off, and prostitutes talk their stuff while gliding by on *becak.* Necklaces of local shells and attractively painted canvas umbrellas are sold on the beach by vendors, Kuta-style; and the craft shops Sari and Iti Kurih (Jl. Pananjung 9), as well as many others, carry all the usual Kuta-style craft products.

Beaches

No matter which hotel you stay in you can hear waves breaking on either side of the peninsula. See the sun set on the W beach and the moon rise on the E beach. The E coast of Pananjung Peninsula is reserved for fishermen, W for visitors. The beach on the eastern side has rough, dangerous surf but the beach on the W is safe (sheltered by coral reefs) and clean. This beach slopes and the water isn't muddy; there's no seaweed, coral, or jellyfish—one of the safest swimming beaches on Java's entire S coast. Because the western beach is so broad, sharks do not enter these waters. Good snorkeling off Pasir Putih (White Beach), an excellent coral beach for sunbathing on the W side of the peninsula; you can either walk there in 15 min. from the village or take a *prahu* for Rp3000. It costs Rp5000 to get out on the reefs by sailboat; beware of boatmen who agree to take you out to see the *kebon laut* (coral reefs) for a certain amount, then demand twice as much once you're out to sea! Visit the small island 10 min. offshore where turtles and monitor lizards sun themselves.

Accommodations

The standards and cleanliness of the 40 or so *losmen,* hotels, and bungalows are rising all the time. Rooms for Rp3500-5000 are uncomfortable: tiny, no electricity after 2100, lots of mosquitos. Might as well live it up and spend Rp8000 on a nicer room. Try for a cheaper rate if you stay any longer than 3 days. Be prepared for no vacancies in the *wisma*-class accommodations as many of the hotels of Pangandaran cater to big groups coming down from Bandung. And during the crowded *Lebaran* holidays, rates can go up to as much as Rp35,000, paid for *in advance* by rich Bandung Chinese. The **Laut Bira,** near the end of the main road on the R, is the best *losmen,* with nicely furnished rooms—a clean, inexpensive (Rp3500 s, Rp5000 d) place near the beach. **Mini Losmen I,** near the Sipia Hotel, is also popular with travelers. Avoid their dumpy little rooms; try for one of their modern ones with *mandi,* at Rp8000 d, one of the best deals in Indonesia. **Mini Losmen II** is an upbeat version of Mini Losmen I; go out of Mini Losmen I, take a R, then a L and walk

down the lane and it's on the R side. Clean, friendly, free coffee, Rp3000 a night per double bed! More upscale places, such as **Wisma Pelangi** (tel. 81531 Bandung), have bungalows with full kitchen facilities in the Rp20,000-30,000 range. **Hotel Bumi Nusantara** is near the beach and tourist info office; Rp5000 s or d, Rp15,000 for bungalows. The **Panorama Hotel,** also overlooking the beach, has nicely appointed rooms costing Rp8000-15,000 s or d.

Food

Almost at the end of the main road leading through town is a whole nest of greasy-spoon *warung* on your L—a wonderful place to sit and watch village life while sipping *Orang Tua* with ice. The standard eatery hangout, serving Indo-Western food, is **Elly's Warung** right in the center of the small tourist *kampung* near the market where many of the *losmen* are concentrated. Westerners and Indonesians both eat here, one of the best places in town. **Cafe Sympathy,** on the main street near the *warung* on the R, is also very popular, good-value, and cheap. An (expensive) Chinese restaurant is near Losmen Mini. **Rumah Makan Sumedang** specializes in Sundanese food, the only one in Pangandaran. Good *sate* place next door. **Restaurant Cilacap** also serves delectable food. Other *rumah makan* can be found all along Jl. Pantai Pananjung. For dessert, mouth-watering mangosteens go for Rp50 apiece.

Getting There

First get to Banjar, 63 km N, on the provincial border, a RR junction and crossroads for Tasikmalaya (42 km W). Banjar is the last place to change money if you're heading for Pangandaran. If driving your own vehicle, Pangandaran is at least a 5-hour drive from Bandung (223 km). Expect bad road conditions and bridges down. From Bandung, take the early train *(Ekspres Siang),* leaving at 0730 to Banjar (normal 3rd-Class price is Rp2500, but if you show your International Student Card to the stationmaster you might get a ticket for Rp1600 plus a reserved seat); not that crowded. This slow train is an all-day trip: 5-6 hours to Banjar, then 2-2½ hours by minibus (Rp1000) to Pangandaran. There are also buses from Bandung to Banjar, Rp1800, 12 hours. **from Yogya:** It's 7 hours on the *Ekspres Siang* to Banjar, Rp3000. Buses also make the trip Yogya-Banjar in 8 hours. An alternative route to Pangandaran from Yogya is to take the train W to Kroya (Rp1900), bus or minibus to Cilacap, *prahu* to Kalipucang, (Rp825) then a minibus (Rp400-500) to Pangandaran. **from Banjar:** As soon as you come out of the train station in Banjar, the minibus drivers will be on you. To Pangandaran, minibuses cost Rp1000, 2 hours. The last minibus or bus will let you off at the market. Your pack will be pulled off the roof and thrown to a group of unruly, gross *becak* drivers, the strongest of which will get your fare. They get commissions from the *losmen* owners, so you can talk

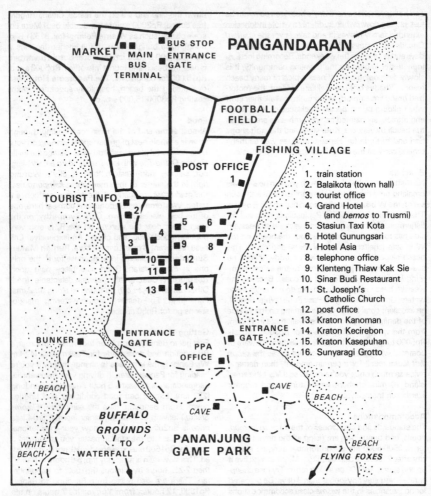

PANGANDARAN

1. train station
2. Balaikota (town hall)
3. tourist office
4. Grand Hotel
   (and *bemos* to Trusmi)
5. Stasiun Taxi Kota
6. Hotel Gunungsari
7. Hotel Asia
8. telephone office
9. Klenteng Thiaw Kak Sie
10. Sinar Budi Restaurant
11. St. Joseph's
    Catholic Church
12. post office
13. Kraton Kanoman
14. Kraton Kecirebon
15. Kraton Kasepuhan
16. Sunyaragi Grotto

them down in price (Rp200?) to get into town. To avoid all this, just walk the 2 km to the *losmen* area.

Getting Around

Rent a bicycle for Rp850 for 4 hours, or for Rp1500 per day. The bike rental place is off the main road on a side road down to the western beach, only about a block from Elly's Warung. At the gate near where the mini-bus drops you they charge you Rp300 to get into the town. At the entrance to Cagar Alam Pananjung Reserve it costs another Rp300.

PANANJUNG PANGANDARAN

This 530-ha *cagar alam* (nature reserve) is S of the village of Pangandaran and takes up a whole 3-km peninsula. Highest altitude is 100 m. Entrance, Rp300. Stuffed and mounted animals, poached from the wildlife reserve, are for sale in *warung* before entering the park; live squirrels and civet cats are also for sale. At the PPA office maps are available which show all the different paths through the park, and which animals are where. An intriguing place. Some segments of the beach are right out of *Robinson Crusoe;* you can really get away from it all. Many parts of the reserve are difficult to reach, which helps preserve the animals. Study the map carefully to find a path which will take you into the heart, tag along with a walking tour group, or hitch a jeep. If you take the beach path, it's a 10-km walk around the entire peninsula at low tide. By motorboat the same circuit can be done in 1½ hours for Rp25,000; 15 to a boat. They'll ask Rp4000-5000/hour for a motorless *prahu* and it's hard to budge them.

Sights

Within its relatively confined area, the park seems to have everything: stalactite and stalagmite caves to crawl into, teak forests, shady banyan trees, grazing fields, scrub areas, mytho-historical remains, seashore, WWII Japanese pillboxes, abundant wildlife such as black monkeys, tapir, tame deer, porcupine, peafowls, lumbering hornbills, even 10-m-long pythons draping from trees. Watch enormous wild *banteng* emerge to graze on the grassy clearings in the late afternoon (climb the observation towers to get a better look), and a *taman laut* (coral garden) is on the S tip of the preserve. Most of the peninsula is limestone so a visit should be made to the spectacular caves. Ask at the entrance for the short path leading to the *gua,* or use one of the local guides. The charming Mr. Taha, who can be contacted through the Losmen Mini I, is an older, more experienced guide who has more respect for the reserve than the younger ones. His tour fee is Rp2000 pp.

FROM PANGANDARAN

To Banjar a *bemo* or minibus costs Rp800-900. Bus Banjar-Bandung, 5 hours, Rp1800-2000; bus Banjar-Cililitan Station (Jakarta), Rp5000. A fantastic way to leave Pangandaran, much nicer than via Banjar, is by river. First take a *bemo* at 0600 to Kalipucang, Rp500, 17 km N of Pangandaran. From Kalipucang get the ferry at 0730, 0830, 1030 (or, if you wish, catch the same ferry from Majungklak to the S). The minibus terminal in Kalipucang is only 200 m from the ferry so you don't need a *becak*. It costs Rp825 by this government ferry, 3-4 hours to Cilacap—via segara Anakan, Klaces, Mutean, Candi—through an incredible Disneyland jungle of stilted villages, men fishing out of dugouts, and endless species of birds. You'll hear the constant calls of the maribou storks in these swampy wilds. Excellent photo opportunities. At Cilica's wharf it's a few km to the bus station on the other side of town; bargain the horsecarts down to Rp800. From Cilacap take a bus NE to Kroya, Rp500, 2 hours. Only one train daily (at 0430) runs from Cilacap to Kroya (change at Kroya for many points). From Kroya board a train which leaves for Yogya at 1400 or 1500 for

BOAT TRIP FROM KALIPUCANG

TO PURWOKERTO

CENTRAL JAVA

S. CITANDUY

← TO PAGANDARAN

KALIPUCANG

KESUGIHAN

TO KROYA

MAJUNGKLAK

KR. ANYAR

SEGARA ANAKAN

MUTEAN

CANDI

CILICAP

KLACES

NUSA KAMBANGAN

NOT TO SCALE

INDIAN OCEAN

around Rp1800. If you get on the 0730 ferry from Kalipucang you shouldn't have any trouble making all the connections. This entire "alternative" and very picturesque route takes 12 hours to Yogya. Direct buses also depart from Cilacap to Yogya for Rp2000. Yet another option: if you want to visit the Dieng Plateau before going to Yogya, from Cilacap take the local rattletrap bus up to Wonosobo which leaves at around 1330 each day. If you get the 0830 ferry from Kalipucang, to make this bus you really have to hustle from Cilacap's docks.

Vicinity Of Pangandaran

Three coastal villages are fairly easy to reach from Pangandaran. Start walking W early to reach the first village before it gets hot. The headman will put you up. Visit Karang Tirta, a campground near an estuary. Along this coast are many less accessible but quieter beaches than Pangandaran's: Batu Hiu, Parigi, and Batu Karas, get a minibus from Pangandaran to Cijulang, Rp1500 (40km), then walk down to the beach. **Batu Hiu:** A picturesque rocky area 18 km W of Pangandaran where a dramatic sea cliff drops right down into a sea of huge violent waves right on the edge of the Java Trench; mystic forces at work. This part of W. Java's long curving coast is visited often, especially during holidays, because of its great natural beauty. Retake the famous photograph from the cliff with a single palm tree in the foreground. The name *Batu Hiu* ("Shark Rock") is derived from the shark-shaped boulder. During the colonial era a beautiful park was laid out here and there are still remains of some old buildings. Hire a bike in Pangandaran for Rp1500 per day and ride to Batu Hiu. Good exercise, level the whole way. Ride down a dirt road, through a palm grove, then you reach a grassy plateau, with Batu Hiu's cliff beyond. Also accessible by car.

*"Sir Lightning"
Ram-fighting is
unique to the hills
around Bandung.*

NORTH OF BANDUNG

LEMBANG

A cool upland (elev. 1,400 m) village 16 km N of Bandung, nestled into the wooded lower slopes of Tangkuban Prahu volcano. From in front of Bandung's train station, get a minibus to Lembang via Ledeng; Rp450 and (45 min.). An agricultural community, Lembang has since Dutch times been a favorite destination for domestic and foreign tourists. Its houses and villas are built in the style of a past era, with masses of flowers and neatly tended gardens strangely at odds with the tropical landscape. The surrounding mist-shrouded peaks, lush pastureland, and rolling lower hills heavy with fruit and vegetables make sections of this mountain town a place of peace and beauty. Enjoy sweeping views of Bandung, especially at night. The town is also situated at a crossroads to many attractions in the area such as thermal spas and highland walks.

Sights
The fruit market (open 7 days) is on Jl. Raya Lembang in the town center, where vendors sell a wondrous variety of produce. Try mouth-watering corn on the cob (*jagung bakar*), refreshing *bajigur* drink, and the best avocados. Sometimes at night a small circus is held at the market with dancing dogs. P.T. Baru Adjak, on the same side of the road as the Grand Hotel, runs the largest dairy farm in the area, with fresh milk available daily, and where European-type vegetables are for sale. Another outlet for vegetables is the nunnery, down a small track almost opposite the entrance to the Grand Hotel; walk in at the KARMEL GEREJA KATOLOK sign. Several piggeries in the outskirts of town supply pork for Bandung's Chinese. Visit the cattle-breeding and artificial insemination station where 2-ton Brahman bulls graze through luxuriously thick, high grass. For crafts, the Lembang Art Shop (Jl. Raya 264) sells long flutes, Rp1500; small *wayang golek*, Rp6500 (a modest collection); handmade baskets, Rp2500-3500.

Accommodations And Food
Cheaper *losmen* and *penginapan* are down the mountain between Lembang and Ledeng, charging Rp3500-8000 (less if you bargain or if it's mid-week or off-season). Some are brothels. **Penginapan Cemara** is at the km 12 mark on the road from Bandung; Lembang is 4 km farther up. Keep a careful eye out as the sign is small. Also try the **Setiwan** on the L-hand side, and the **Sayuli,** closer to Ledeng. The **Biara Karmel** is off to the L of the main road before the center of Lembang, charging Rp5000 pp with breakfast. **The Grand Hotel,** Jl. Raya 228 (tel. 82393), is in a class of its own. A spacious complex spread out amongst pine trees, flowers, and gardens, the Grand exudes old colonial charm. Opened for business in 1926, a number of different classes of rooms are all spread out inside a giant shaded yard. The family units consist of 2 bedrooms, European *mandi*, sitting room, and a servant's room—like the good old days: Rp15,000-38,000 s or d. Breakfast is served 0700-1000, and in the evenings full-course *rijstaffles* are put on for Rp7500. There's also a bar, restaurant, pool, and asphalt tennis courts. The principal clientele are domestic tourists, for the most part Chinese—the only ones who can afford it! Freshly boiled or grilled corn-on-the-cob goes for Rp100-150. Also sample toasted *ketan,* a type of rice cake, with a spicy sauce. Down the street from (and cheaper than) the Grand is **RM Marantina,** Jl. Raya 234. Other restaurants are farther up the road. One is

Puspcha Minang, a *nasi padang* place. Restaurant Erna serves European and Asian food; try Restaurant Pulau Laut for Indonesian and Chinese.

Desa Taruna

About 15 min. out of Lembang, take the road which leads to the 10 similar houses on the same hill as the Bosscha Observatory. Founded in Austria at the end of WW II, similar "children's villages" (SOS-Kinderdorf) eventually opened all over the world. In traditional orphanages, children often live in groups of 20 or more without adequate adult guidance. The approach at children's villages is to find older children willing to act as "parents" to small, family-like groups of younger kids. At Desa Taruna 80-100 children live harmoniously together with a "mother" in "families" of 5-9 persons. The complex contains an elementary school; a number of Kinderdorf residents also travel to the SMP (secondary school) in Lembang. In the administration room you may leave a donation and make the difficult choice from all the photos of one child you'd like to correspond with and sponsor for a small monthly stipend.

TANGKUBAN PRAHU

This smoldering, 2,081-m-high volcano, distinguished by its low, flat top, lies 13 km N of Lembang, or 29 km N of Bandung. Tangkuban Prahu's crater (actually 10 craters) is the remnant of a gigantic collapsed volcano which also formed the huge crater-like depression between it and the jagged peak of G. Burangrang (2,064) to the west. Tangkuban Prahu last erupted in 1969, filling the area with black clouds, ash, and mud flows. The name Tangkuban Prahu stems from the Sundanese legend of a mother who drowned her son in order to prevent him from marrying her. Queen Dayang had a quarrel with her son, Prince Sangkuriang, and he left the palace. Years passed and the prince prospered. One day he met and fell in love with a beautiful girl—Queen Dayang, of course—who had lost none of her youth and beauty. Discovering in horror that her lover was her son, she promised to marry him if, between sunrise and sunset, he could dam the Citarum River so that the Bandung Plateau would become a lake. The son, with the gods' assistance, managed the herculean task, flooding the whole plateau, but his mother caused the waters to quickly subside, overturning her son's canoe and drowning him. She then took her own life and to this day the volcano, in the shape of an overturned boat *(Tangkuban Prahu)*, bears this name to commemorate this agonizing Oedipal tragedy. The lake is now the city of Bandung.

The Craters

Go early in the morning before the clouds roll in. Entrance Rp250. This highly commercialized volcano is visited by tourists from all over the world, being one of the few live craters in Indonesia that can be reached by car. As soon as you arrive the vendors descend upon you, with postcards, rocks, peanuts, etc. Around the spacious parking lot are restaurants and souvenir shops selling crystallized sulphur and tree-fern sculptures. It's cold until you go down into the steaming craters. The main and most accessible crater, Kawah Ratu ("Queen's Crater") is not so active now and looks like a big muddy gray pancake. Other craters and geothermal areas farther down—such as Kawah Jurig ("Devil's Crater"), Kawah Upas, and Kawah Domas—are still going strong. You have to walk for about 20 min. around the edge of the first crater before the others come into view. If allowed, descend into the depths and walk around in sulphur fumes, thick yellow crusts, and bubbling mud, all betraying the cauldron beneath the mountain. Gas emits continuously through fissures in the clefts at the bottom of the crater; nearby shrubs and trees are bleached snow white. A seismic station (Pos Pengawasan), to the W of Kawah Upas, monitors the volcano's moods constantly. Plan a 3- to 4-hour rugged hike to explore all the craters, hotsprings, and sulphur holes. Don't try to go to the very bottom of the craters as several years ago 3 young boys died doing so. Wear sturdy shoes and take a sweater. Guides want Rp5000 to accompany you down into the craters, but you can do it yourself quite easily; it's not very dangerous if you watch your step.

Getting There

Get a Subang-bound minibus from Lembang's market, Rp600 (9 km), to the volcano turnoff. From the entrance gate, it's a 4-km (one-hour) walk uphill through an exotic wood to the top, or take another minibus to the top for Rp400. On weekends minibuses from Lembang's market run straight up to the crater. If taking your own vehicle, a km beyond Lembang's market turn L toward the volcano or continue straight several km, then take the L fork up to the volcano (4½ km). The right fork goes to Ciater hotsprings (7 km). Another approach is to get off the minibus in Jayagiri village, then walk 8 km up to the crater. taxis: A taxi will take you all the way from Bandung's train station for Rp25,000-35,000; from Lembang, it costs about Rp6000 (after rigorous bargaining).

CIATER

These well-managed Roman-style baths (both public and private) at the foot of Tangkuban Prahu are 7 km from the volcano's crater, 15 km NE of Lembang, and 32 km from Bandung. Just go back down the main road from Tangkuban Prahu, turn L at the tollgate, and Ciater is 7 km farther on. Minibuses also run direct from Lembang to Ciater. At 1,100 m, the hotsprings (Rp500 entrance) command a panoramic view of the surrounding paddyfields, tea plantations, and on a clear day Kawah Domas above. The area enjoys a mild climate with an average temperature of 18-25 degrees C. Ciater is an old Dutch resort which is now being enlarged and improved, becoming more touristy each year — popular with Japanese and Europeans. There's a large picnic area, cafeteria, tennis courts, bungalows, children's boat and pony rides, horses are for hire, a night disco, and even a helipad. Native-style bungalows with woven walls can be rented for about Rp12,000 d. Get the newer ones, not the older cement ones. An assembly hall stages cultural performances such as *ketuk tilu* (Sundanese communal dance) and *Gotong Singa* (in which a lion statue is carried in procession).

The Hotsprings

Hot swimming pools and private baths are on the slope of a hill; probably the best in the Bandung area. The mineral water, which comes from Tangkuban Prahu and contains sulphur and radioactive salts, is said to possess remedial powers against rheumatism, poliomyelitis, asthma, and several skin diseases. One pool has warm water for novices, the other scalding water where it's not advisable to remain more than 15 minutes. They cost in all about Rp2000 pp; of several to choose from, the cheaper ones are lower down the hill. Sari Ater resort is one of the cleanest and best-run spas in SE Asia. There's also a small hotsprings creek (free).

Ciater Tea Estate

From the gate at the base of the Tangkuban Prahu, take a minibus (Rp400) to the tea factory (ask for *pabrik teh*). This famous estate in the cool hills outside of Ciater extends as far as Subang in the N, former headquarters of these once British-owned estates. Travel along a road through ricefields which gradually give way to forested terrain: *kapok*, breadfruit, tall eucalyptus, thick copses of fir. The twisting road passes an electricity substation, then an aqueduct carrying water from the mountains down to Bandung. As you climb higher, take in glorious views of distant peaks and densely forested valleys. Then, at about 1,000 m, everything suddenly turns dark green. Across hills that roll in all directions, like an enormous petrified ocean, undulate tens of thousands of healthy tea bushes in closely packed rows, separated in places by grassy tracks the width of a car. The total planted area of the estate is 757 ha (1,870 acres); another 1,633 ha (4,035 acres) is used for other purposes and as reserve land. Most of the plantation lies on a single massive lava flow from Tangkuban Prahu, resulting in some of the highest yields of tea on Java. The pickers — smiling Sundanese girls in bright dresses and wide sunhats, most around 15 or 16 — gingerly hoist loaded wicker baskets and sacks. Proceed to the factory and the magnificent vista from the lookout tower, with clouds scudding *below* the enormous plantation, then walk through the blackened gateposts and take a tour of the efficient processing sheds, weighing station, machine crushers, fermentation area, then the sorting, grading, and testing areas. Visitors may taste a sample and purchase packets of the "No. 1 Export Blend."

MARIBAYA

An attractive park and hotsprings in a steep-walled valley 5 km E of Lembang. Worth visiting (Rp200) but never on Sunday! Bathe in colored volcanic water which is said to contain natural healing agents; bring a *sarung* as it's a bit chilly. Although Maribaya itself is too commercialized to be inspiring, its gardens are well manicured with paths, pools, a children's playground, magnificent waterfalls, tall evergreens. Horses rent for Rp2500; it's a 30-min. bareback ride to the top of the mountain. Several open-air pools and changing rooms have spring-fed running hot sulphur water from Tangkuban Prahu. Superb country for walking all around Maribaya; just follow the paths up the hills or deep into the valleys.

Accommodations And Food

One chalet-style *penginapan* near the falls right over the river costs Rp15,000, but only has 4 rooms. A *pasanggrahan* here has 8 rooms. A restaurant serves European, Chinese, and Indonesian meals. Small refreshment *warung* sell *nasi goreng*, *mie baso*, and *gado-gado*. Other *warung* are found out by the river in the parking lot. There are also the usual sellers of crafts, buffalo horn, etc.

Getting There

Take a minibus from Lembang (Rp600) or Tangkuban Prahu, or from Dago Tea House it's a 2-hour walk for the fit with lovely views and friendly locals. Another way to walk to Maribaya is from a parking place almost 4 km from the Tangkuban Prahu crossroads just before the road descends steeply into the valley. Start on the track near the small restaurant. The R-hand trail follows the ridge to Lembang, the L-hand trail to the hilltop above Maribaya. At the point where the road takes a sharp R turn, walk directly into the pine trees toward the panorama which towers 300 m above a gorge with jagged cliffs — one of the best sights around Bandung. If you keep walking to the R and follow the track downhill, in an hour you'll arrive at the Dago Tea House near the power station. It's also possible, but quite arduous, to descend straight down to Maribaya from the top of this gorge.

From Maribaya

Minibuses are available straight through to Lembang and then down to Bandung. Ram fights are held in Sukarandeg, one km from Maribaya. For a splendid walk to the Dago Tea House, follow the path through the Maribaya gardens to a bridge which crosses over a thunderous 25-m-high waterfall. Two rivers join together at this juncture and flow down to Bandung through a deep forested gorge. The path over the bridge continues along a rocky track down to a bamboo bridge over the second river (the Cikapundung) and from here it's a good trail straight to the tea house from where you can get a minibus to Bandung. Another track, after crossing the bamboo bridge, takes you up to the top of the ridge, then down until you reach Dago. Allow 2 hours (6 km) from Maribaya to Dago.

CIREBON

Located on Java's northern coast, midway between Jakarta and Semarang, 125 km NE of Bandung. Cirebon (pronounced chirry-BON) is not on the popular tourist routes of Java. It boasts no golden sandy beaches or trendy travelers' restaurants or hotels, but it's a clean, well-run town, well worth a diversion—especially for its rich variety of arts and crafts and historical attractions. Lying between the sea and the mountains, Cirebon's hot temperatures are often buffeted by cool mountain breezes. An ancient precolonial port town on the border of W. and C. Java, Cirebon is the meeting point of the Sundanese and Javanese cultures, and its local dialect is a blending of the two (the city's name derives from the Javanese *caruban*, or "mixture"). The sultanate here was split into 2 main houses, Kanoman and Kesepuhan, both of whose palaces are open to visitors, occasionally hosting court dances and *gamelan* recitals. The interiors and furnishings manifest a fantastic conglomeration of Sundanese, Javanese, Islamic, Chinese, and Dutch civilizations.

History

Wedged between the warring kingdoms of Banten to the W and Mataram in the interior, and caught between Javanese and Sundanese power politics, Cirebon has always had a turbulent history. In 1375, Islam established its first foothold on Java at Gresik in E. Java. One of the *Wali Sanga*, 9 saints credited with bringing the new religion to Java's shores, eventually set up Cirebon as a religious and artistic center. He took the title Sunan Gunung Jati ("Sultan of Teak Mountain") after Cirebon had become one of the first Islamic bases in the territory of the older Hindu-Buddhist kingdom of Pajajaran. (Sunan Gunung Jati's gravesite, 6 km N of Cirebon on the road to Indramayu, is still a highly revered spot, drawing pilgrims from all over Java.) The sultanate came under the domination of the Dutch East Indies Co. in the 17th C., and by the early 18th C., the administration of native affairs was the joint responsibility of 3 courts which rivaled in extravagance and wealth even those of C. Java. Through Cirebon's fine harbor vast quantities of rice, sugar, pepper, and wood were exported. In the 18th C., the Dutch created a monopoly in the imports of cotton and opium.

Economy

Cirebon today is still a principal N coast port, a major import-export point for all of W. Java, as well as a port from which pilgrims set sail for Mecca. Cirebon is also known as the "Shrimp City" *(Kota Udang)*, and the air around the harbor reeks of drying shrimp. In the daytime be sure to visit Cirebon's harbor, Pelabuhan Laut Tanjung Emas (no photography allowed), to see old Dutch *godong*, and Bugis sailing *prahu* and Japanese freighters offloading. A town of 350,000, Cirebon is made up of merchants, small businessmen, office workers, *pegawai,* harbor laborers, and others who make their living from the sea, with the agricultural segment not very much in evidence: unlike the majority of Java's cities, rice *sawah* do not surround the city.

CIREBON'S *KRATON*

No less than 7 *kraton* have existed in Cirebon. Four are extant; the other 3 are either in ruins or else have been absorbed by surrounding *kampung*. The largest, Kraton Kasepuhan and Kraton Kanoman (which may be toured), were both constructed around 1678 when the sultanate split. The court for the older prince, Kasepuhan, was erected on the site of a 15th C. palace called Pakungwati, the *kraton* of Cirebon's earlier Hindu-Java regents. Kanoman was raised for the younger prince; it's smaller and less elaborate. These native courts, quite distinct from the reserved and stately courts of C. Java, reflect the many cultural influences which have invaded this busy port city through the centuries: the Chinese legacy is embodied in the elaborate phoenixes, cranes, and peonies, while memories of the Dutch era are seen in the inlaid decorative tiles. The Muslims have made their mark in such architectural details as the dark brown woodcarving, while the *kraton's* terra-cotta stepped walls invoke Hindu rule. Kraton Kasepuhan even adopted for its crest the white tiger that once guarded Siliwangi, a venerated Hindu ruler, linking the new Islamic court with its Hindu ancestors. Since Indonesian independence, the royal status of all the different *kraton* have gradually evaporated.

Kraton Kacirebonan

An offshoot of Kraton Kanoman, Kraton Kacirebonan lies close to Jl. Pulosaren W of Kraton Kasepuhan; on its *alun-alun* a bicycle market is held. This *kraton* has been less touched by Dutch and Western ways than Cirebon's more famous palaces.

Kraton Kasepuhan

In 1478, Kraton Pakungwati surrendered to Sunan Gunung Jati. In that same year, the city of Cirebon proclaimed itself an Islamic principality and work began immediately on Kraton Kasepuhan. The palace grew decrepit over the centuries until 1928 when it was restored by a Dutch archaeologist. Located today in the SE corner of the city, W of the *alun-alun* and next to the graceful tiered-roof mosque, Mesjid Kasepuhan. Take a *becak* (Rp400) from Hotel Asia. From Lapangan Kasepuhan, walk directly down the lane leading to the palace. Find it yourself; don't let one of the crafty old men around the *kraton* "guide" you. Walk through the split red-brick *candi bentar* into the *kraton;* ornate Chinese carved tigers guard the *kraton's* front gateway. Domestic tourists come in the morning; by afternoon it's usually deserted because of the heat, so you might have the place to yourself. Photos may be taken inside the museum, but not in the *kraton* itself. The neatly restored complex comprises 25 ha of beautiful garden surroundings. A comatose place very much smelling its age, the sultanate has long since been deposed and the sultan is now a banker. Open every day 0700-1700. **the museum:** A small edifice on the R-hand side as you enter the compound. In the main poorly lit display room is a *gamelan degung* set (1426), a legacy of Demak's royal house it's played only on Mohammed's Birthday. A *gamelan slendro* dates from 1748. The museum also displays a collection of ancient Cirebon *batik,* old *wayang,* and *topeng* masks quite different from the usual Javanese styles, a whole set of gold-plated *kris,* Chinese ceramics, old Delft ware, and some exquisite Balinese-style carved panels (some quite naughty); one depicts the story of Adam.

Kraton Kanoman

Walk straight through the market, Pasar Kanoman, to this palace built by Pangeran Cakrabuana in the 17th C. on the edge of what was then the small village of Witana. Woodcarvings on the main door of the hall symbolize the opening date (the Javanese date of 1510 translates to A.D. 1670). Istana Kanoman has a restful courtyard of shady banyan trees and kids flying kites — the remnants of the old Javanese *priyayi* world lie decaying in overgrown plazas and *pendopo.* **Gedung Musium:** In the museum are *pustaka* and objects of historical interest similar to what's found in Kraton Kasepuhan's museum. Like a medieval torture chamber, sets of *Seni Debus* stakes decorate the walls; these were driven into men on Mohammed's Birthday each year, a mystical sort of self-injury in the Prophet's honor. Other exhibits include carvings, weapons, royal souvenirs from different regencies of Indonesia as well as from abroad; small admission charge. **Kareta Paksi Naga Liman:** Find the man with the key to the Gedung Pusaka ("Heirloom Building") inside the *kraton* compound to see this in-

credible coach, the prize attraction of Kanoman. The 3 creatures depicted on this royal carriage are symbols of earthly and metaphysical powers: the *Paksi* or great mythical *garuda* bird represents the realm of the air; the *naga* (snake bird) represents sea; and the *Liman* or *gajah* represents land. All of them are combined in one Pegasus-like creation called the *Paksi Naga Liman.* These fused symbols — each considered by the Javanese the strongest creatures of their elements — represent, respectively, the Indonesian air force, navy, and army. This extravagant carriage, built by Pangeran Losari, was used only during occasions of great royal festivals. See also a coach on which the queen sat in the middle of her woodcarved "cloud puff."

OTHER SIGHTS

Have a look at Cirebon's architecture to appreciate the city's history. Side by side you'll find Javanese *adat* houses, mosques and minarets, Chinese temples, neat white-walled villas with red-tiled roofs, and ornate civic structures built by the Dutch. To the W of Desa Panjunan, in the building of the Sekolah Dasar, is kept an ancient relic, Pedati Gede, the Giant Cart. This huge wheel — possibly inspired by the iron wheels of steam locomotives — originally belonged to Kraton Kasepuhan. If you enter the city from the N (from Indramayu), you run into the old house of the Dutch Resident from the times of the VOC. One of the landmarks of Cirebon is the fine old Pabrik Rokok B.A.T. (British-American Tobacco Manufacturers Ltd.) building on Jl. Pabean which was completed in 1924.

Mosques, Temples, Churches

A few hundred m S of Desa Panjunan on Jl. R. A. Kartini, in front of Kantor Kab. Cirebon, is the city's oldest mosque, **Mesjid Jalagrahan.** About 100 m farther to the S, in Desa Panjunan, is the second oldest mosque, built by a Baghdad merchant in the 14th century. Adjacent to Kraton Kasepuhan in the southern part of the city is **Mesjid Agung** (built around 1500), one of the oldest extant Islamic structures on Java. Its 2-tiered *meru*-style roof (an architectural device now found mostly on Bali) is supported by an intricate wooden substructure and elaborate sandstone doorways. Inside, there's a *kala*-head pulpit of pure *jati.* **Klinteng Thiaw Kak Sie:** In the harbor's immediate vicinity, on Jl. Kantor to the L of Bank Dagang Negara, is one of the most beautiful Chinese temples on Java as well as one of Indonesia's oldest. Its history can be traced back to 1658 when it was built by followers of Buddha. A number of well-preserved wall frescoes are inside. From Hotel Asia, get there by *becak* (Rp400). **Klinteng Dewi Welas Asih:** A few hundred m to the S of Jl. Benteng lies Cirebon's oldest Chinese temple. In the back room is an old iron anchor, the object of worship for scores of pilgrims each week. The Chinese believe that the anchor once

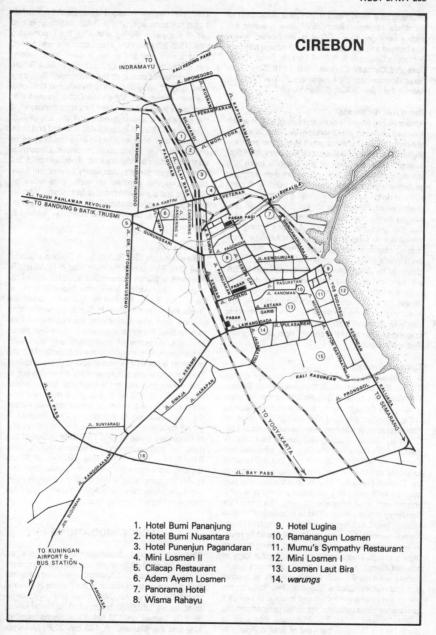

CIREBON

TO INDRAMAYU

KALI KEDUNG PANE

JL. DIPONEGORO

JL. KUSNAN

JL. PENAMPARAN

JL. SILIWANGI

JL. KAPTEN SAMADIKUN

JL. MOH TOHA

JL. OLAH RAGA

JL. PASUARAN

JL. DR. WAHIDIN SUDIRO HUSODO

JL. R.A. KARTINI

JL. VETERAN

KALI SUKALILA

JL. TUJUH PAHLAWAN REVOLUSI
TO BANDUNG & BATIK TRUSMI

JL. GUNUNGSARI

JL. CANGKRING I

JL. CANGKRING II

JL. SUKA

JL. S. TUBUN

PASAR PAGI

JL. SONOMANGGALA

JL. PAGONGAN

JL. KENDURUAN

JL. DR. CIPTOMANGUNKUSOMO

JL. PANJUNAN

JL. KEBON CAI

PASUKETAN

JL. KANOMAN

JL. SEBRAR

JL. GUDANG

JL. ASTANA GARIB

JL. YOS SUDARSO

JL. MESTIKA

JL. MAYOR SASTRATMAJA

JL. KESUNEAN

JL. PULASAREN

PASAR

JL. LAWANGGADA

JL. JAGASATRU

KALI KASUNEAN

JL. PRONGGOL

TO SEMARANG

KALIJAGA

JL. KESAMBI

JL. SIMAJA

JL. HARAPAN

TO YOGYAKARTA

JL. BAY PASS

JL. SUNYARAGI

JL. BAY PASS

JL. KANGGRAKSAN

JEN SUDIRMAN

TO KUNINGAN
AIRPORT &
BUS STATION

JL. ANGKASA

1. Hotel Bumi Pananjung
2. Hotel Bumi Nusantara
3. Hotel Punenjun Pagandaran
4. Mini Losmen II
5. Cilacap Restaurant
6. Adem Ayem Losmen
7. Panorama Hotel
8. Wisma Rahayu
9. Hotel Lugina
10. Ramanangun Losmen
11. Mumu's Sympathy Restaurant
12. Mini Losmen I
13. Losmen Laut Bira
14. *warungs*

belonged to a sailing ship from China. According to the official Javanese history of W. Java, however, the anchor belonged to a VOC ship, the *Leiden,* which was burned and sunk in 1835 by Indonesian freedom fighters in Cirebon's harbor of Tanjung Emas. **Saint Joseph's Catholic Church:** Built in 1878 by Theodores Gauntsoltez, it's located on Jl. Yos Sudarso. Ask for the "Gareja Katolik San Yusuf."

Town Hall (Balaikota)

A magnificent example of an architectural style which flowered between the 2 world wars. This is a town hall probably like no other you'll ever come across—eligible for a Ripley's Believe It Or Not entry. It's full of shrimps! Over the door of the mayor's room is a stained-glass window with a pink curled-up shrimp in its center. And high on top of the building 8 giant stone shrimps seem to be clinging to the 2 square towers which flank the entrance. Once painted contrasting colors, one could not mistake, even from afar, that this was the town hall of "Kota Udang"—a monument to Cirebon's status as an important processing center for this popular shellfish. Ask to see the mayor's office where many of the original chairs (designed by Jiskoot) remain, now renovated in dark red fabric and equipped with castors. Other details include the relief sculptures of sugarcane, larger than lifesize, on both sides of the covered entrance. And when you enter the immense hall, the first object to rivet your attention is an imposing stained-glass lamp suspended high from the ceiling, right over a green-tiled water basin.

Taman Sunyaragi

A grotesque 3-story red brick and concrete grotto, 4½ km SW of town on Jl. Sunyaragi. From Stasiun Taxi Kota, take minibus G10, Rp300. Taman Sunyaragi has gone through several transformations since its initial construction in 1703 during the reign of Pangeran Arya. It was originally the resthouse of 14th C. royalty: Sunan Gunung Jati used it as a country palace for his Chinese bride, Ong Tien, who died just 3 years after arriving on Java. It is, in fact, still referred to locally as "the *Taman Sari* (Pleasure Gardens) of the Chinese Princess." At that time the building was adorned with cascading waterfalls and the area landscaped with small lakes and gardens. The name Gua Sunyaragi actually means "Place of Isolation" *(sunya* means "zero" and *ragi* means "soul"). In Java-Hindu history, remote sites were traditionally used by royalty for seeking inner knowledge and strength, or as testing places where adherents practiced a form of spiritual discipline. In these secret chambers practitioners were taught such ascetic pursuits as meditation and military science. Sunyaragi later became the site of a weapons workshop and armory, as well as the conference place between the civilian *adipati* and the military *prajurit.* After S.S. Matangaji was shot to death by the Dutch in the yard of Mesjid Agung in

1787, the complex remained unoccupied. Legend has it that partisans against the Dutch regime operated out of Sunyaragi during and after the Diponegoro War (1825-30) when the whole structure was turned into a guerilla post and weapons warehouse. Spears, *kris,* and swords were forged on the premises. Before the Dutch could attack, all the weapons of Sunyaragi were spirited away to the countryside and the building was abandoned. When the Dutch learned that their plans were foiled, in their fury they destroyed all the decorations and statues. Under the rule of S.S. Adiwijaya in 1853, Sunyaragi was restored and redesigned by a Chinese architect in a curious Chinese architectural style. Restoration continues. Discernible on the structure are decorations of not only brick but stone from coral reefs; also sentry towers, old fountains, gargoyles perched on walls, plus other ornaments and plates which derive from China. Wander through secret chambers, narrow gates, caves, miniature doors, corridors and staircases leading to nowhere.

Gunung Jati

Take a *taxi kota* (GG, Rp300) from Cirebon's Stasiun Taxi Kota 7 km down the main road N to Jakarta to this tomb of Sunan Gunung Jati (d. 1570), one of the original missionaries *(wali)* who brought Islam to Java. This 9th C. spiritual conquistador ruined the Hindu Pajajaran Kingdom in Sunda by overcoming Jakarta, then after subjugating the kingdom of Cirebon, he died. His tomb is still one of the holiest places on Java. A series of courtyards are filled with gravestones, all surrounding the holy tomb. This site is visited by both Indonesian and Chinese pilgrims. Take off your shoes before entering. If you're going to give money, give only to the *juru kunci.* Empty bottles are sold for Rp100 so that pilgrims may take holy water away for sickness or to give to relatives. Across the road, walk up to the small hilltop covered in graves for a nice view of the sea. Among this cluster of graves are those of Ong Tien, wife of Sunan Gunung Jati, and the grave of the Sunan's *mullah*, Sheik Datu Kahfi. **note:** The inner sanctum of Sunan Gunung Jati's grave is closed to the public. Best time to visit the complex is on *Jumat Kliwon* (Holy Fridays) in the Javanese calendar, when the complex is filled with worshippers burning incense.

ACCOMMODATIONS

Cirebon is curiously expensive. For those on a real budget (Rp4500-6000 range), a whole row of inexpensive hotels is along Jl. Siliwangi: right down the street from Cirebon's train station is the **Palapa Hotel** and **Hotel Famili** (no. 76), both clean and quiet; **Sidodadi**, no. 84 (tel. 2305); **Islam**, no. 116; **Hotel Islam**, no. 116; **Damai**, no. 122 (tel. 3045); **Semarang**, no. 124; and the **Slamet**, no. 183 (tel. 3296). A campground, **Kebon Pelok,** is 3 km S of Cirebon. **Hotel Asia** is a Chinese-run hotel—the best-value *losmen*-style accommodation in Cirebon. Located in an old Dutch home, the whole building itself is an antique. Quite centrally located down a quiet street facing a canal at Jl. Kalibaru Selatan 15 (tel. 2182), its rooms range from Rp6500 d up to Rp15,000 for mini-suites. All rooms are clean with white-washed walls and old-style wooden furniture, mosquito nets, good lighting. The higher-priced rooms have fans, inside toilets, and wardrobes. *Nasi gudeg* vendors come around the courtyard in the mornings. A masseuse also works on the premises (Rp2500). The English-speaking manager can answer any specific questions.

Other Inexpensive Hotels
Hotel Gunungsari is at Jl. Gunungsari 49; rooms go for Rp5000 s, Rp6500 d—about the cheapest in Cirebon and the nicest for the price. Extremely central, the bus station is just down the noisy street. The sparsely furnished rooms have fans. Right in front of the hotel is a very reasonable *warung;* next door is a more expensive eating place. **Hotel Nusantara** is right around the corner from Hotel Gunungsari at Jl. Gunungsari 39/41 (tel. 3941), close to *stasiun oplet* facing the *stanplatz.* A clean place with good service, Rp4500-6500 s. Giant inner courtyard. Its restaurant serves tasty Indonesian food; fast laundry and taxi service. **Hotel Sentosa,** Jl. Gunungsari 61, opposite Pangkalan Taxi Kota, Rp5000 s or d. **Hotel Fatimah,** Jl. Gunungsari 21, has 23 rooms (Rp5000) with inside *mandi;* quiet. **Hotel Tidar Jaya I,** Jl. Cemara 19, has rooms for Rp4000-6500 with *kamar mandi* inside and big double beds. Depressing, dirty, but cheap. A branch of **Tidar Jaya** is on Jl. Jen. Sudirman, Ciperna, Rp4500.

High-priced
Cirebon Plaza Hotel, Jl. Kartini 54 (tel. 2061/2), is a clean, modern hotel on the road from Bandung coming into town; Rp30,000 s or d for a/c rooms with *mandi;* coffee shop and restaurant. **Omega Motel,** Jl. Tuparev 20 (Box 23, tel. 3072/3073/5023), is comfortable with 60 a/c rooms. **Grand Hotel** has all the amenities, plus great service and style. This old colonial hotel, Jl. Siliwangi 98 (tel. 2014/2015), offers a multitude of large rooms in every price range: from Rp12,000 on up to the "President's Suite" for Rp90,000 with refrigerator and guestroom. The hotel restaurant has a long menu with Indonesian, Cantonese, and some unusual dishes. Splendid veranda, coffee shop, and bar (open until 2400).

FOOD

Specialties
Nasi lengko, made of rice, *tempe, tahu, sambal,* lemon, cucumber, sprouts, fried crispy onions, and meat. *Nasi jamblang* consists of sour fish, beef jerky, dried lung of cow, vegetables, and *tahu goreng,* served with a specially prepared rice. This dish is made in the village of Jamblang, 16 km from Cirebon; vendors come all the way into Cirebon to sell it. Try some at Hotel Asia around 0900 when the vendors arrive. Eat it with the fingers off a *jati* leaf, Rp600. Westerners love it. You can also buy it at the harbor and bus station. Another place to try local dishes is **Pasar Pagi,** open until 2100. **Warung Nasi Gunungsari,** near Hotel Asia, has good Cirebon-style *nasi-campur,* Rp800, and *nasi goreng* with lots of vegetables, Rp850. **Pasar Kanoman** is another colorful, noisy market selling fruit, *tahu,* crab—or whatever. For all kinds of baked goods and crackly *krupuk,* head for **Toko Famili,** Jl. Siliwangi 96.

Restaurants
A number of inexpensive restaurants serve Chinese and Indonesian food in the center of town on Jl. Karanggetas. For excellent Padang-style food, delicious ice juices (Rp600-800), and stereo music, hit **Sinar Budi,** Jl. Karanggetas 22. Right across the street (no. 9) is **Restaurant Kopyor;** their famous *es kopyor* goes for Rp1100, and tasty meals such as *udang saos* and *mie baso,* Rp1000-2000; open 0800-1030. Other good restaurants on this street are: **RM Kecil,** no. 14, and the **Jatibarang,** no. 1. For Sundanese cuisine, go to **Kencana,** Jl. Karang Kencana, or the **Lembur Kuring** farther out of town on Jl. Bay Pass. Most higher-priced hotels have restaurant/coffee shops and bars too; most noteworthy is the reasonably priced Chinese food at the **Patra Jasa Cirebon.**

Seafood
Cirebon's specialty is shellfish; the pungent odor of drying fish is ubiquitous. The best seafood restaurant in Cirebon is **Maxim's,** Jl. Bahagia 45-47 (tel. 2679). Open 1000-2300 every day, Maxim's has over 50 items to choose from on their menu, the best deals being the freshly caught crab and shrimp dishes. Fried shrimp with butter sauce is Rp4000; sour vegetables *(sayur asam kuah kakap),* Rp3000; *angsio gurami* fish has a different price each day; crab soup with dove eggs *(telor puyuh),* Rp3500. Check out the old black-and-white photographs in the front lobby, taken by the grandfather of the present owner, which illustrate the history of Cirebon's *kraton.* Other high-quality seafood restaurants include the **Corner Restaurant,** Jl. Pasuketan 31A; and **Restaurant Canton,** Jl. Pagongan 8A (tel. 2967), Rp500 by *becak* from Hotel Asia. At the S end of Jl. Bahagia, a Chinese *pasar malam* sets up each evening at around 1800; prices are slightly lower than the restaurants.

ARTS AND CRAFTS

Since the 15th C., Cirebon's well-established Chinese community has influenced the city's unique arts, their stamp seen both in motifs (megamendung, or "rock and clouds") and in lacquer techniques. Cirebon also uses stylized rocks, clouds, etc., to decorate monochromatic carved door panels, and carves wooden wayang puppets especially for wall decorations. The principal wood used is that of the sawo fruit tree. Chinese characteristics are also evident in stone, jade, and ivory carvings. A Jepara woodcarving (ukiran jepara) shop is on Jl. Bahagia 53. Also look up Kardita, a becak lukisan (becak painter). Cirebon is a very active bamboo furniture center, manufacturing many different styles of chairs, stools, and tables. Out of town W, near Weru, stalls sell economical rotan furniture. In Sura Nanggala Lor, 12 km from Cirebon, see a wayang topeng carver at work; also specimens are for sale cheaper than in Bandung.

Batik

Stylistic nuances and the bright accents of Cirebon batik—an art which is a composite of so many incoming cultures and religions—are found nowhere else on Java. Traditionally, the motifs most associated with Cirebon batik are Chinese in origin. Glorious mythological animals such as dragons, tigers, lions, and elephants, and of course "rocks and clouds" (likened to weather patterns), are executed in light to dark coloring. Sealife, so vital to the economic well-being of the city, is also frequently portrayed. Since the artists' guilds decreed that only men may work in batik, Cirebon became one of the few locales on Java where females did not draw and paint the cloth. This has infused the batik of this area with bold, masculine designs, a minimum of busy detail, and large, drama-

tic portions of free space, quite distinct from other N coastal or central Java areas. View the zenith of this art form in Cirebon's kraton museums, though all the finest pieces have been sold and only small collections are left. See once again the kraton state carriage and the gates of the sultan's palace—but this time woven in dark brown and blue on batik kain and sarung.

Batik Outlets

Batik cap sarung cost Rp6000-8000. Batik kain in the shops start at Rp10,000. The more expensive batik tulis goes for Rp40,000 (first price); don't expect lively bargaining as most shops adhere to a harga pesti (fixed price). Being too expensive for the local market (Rp40,000-90,000), most of the traditional "rock and clouds" batik is sent to Jakarta, then marked up fivefold. Around Pasar Pagi on Jl. Karanggetas, one of Cirebon's main streets, are numerous batik shops: Taman Batik Asri, for example, is in the middle of the bustling market street, Pasar Pagi 9. Note, however, that the Pasar Pagi area has a lot of batik from Solo, Pekalongan, and other cities but little asli Cirebon batik. You'll also find many examples of the Indramayu batik style (more involved red and blue patterns). Batik cap, the stamped variety, sells for Rp20,000-25,000, still quite pricey but unique. Also, try Pasar Balong until 1600. Toko Batik Permana, Jl. Karanggetas 18; and Toko Batik Saudara, Jl. Karanggetas 46, are also worth checking. Finally, check out the GKBI (Batik Cooperative) at Jl. Pekarungan 33 which sells a wider selection of Cirebon batik than any other outlet. Walk easily to GKBI from Hotel Asia, or take a becak. Open Mon.-Fri. 0800-1200, Sat. 0800-1230.

Trusmi

Some of Cirebon's finest batik is made in Trusmi near the town of Weru, 6 km W of Cirebon; take a becak first to Stasiun Kota Taxi on Jl. Gunungsari, then a

Motifs such as clouds, the phoenix, butterflies, and flowers done in vivid chemical dyes reveal Chinese influence in Cirebon batik. Chinese porcelain designs can be recognized on many N coast batik pieces, such as Cirebon's incredibly hypnotic megamendung or "stormy clouds." Purchase this famous batik in Trusmi batik village, 7 km W of Cirebon (2 connections, Rp400).

taxi kota (G4) to Plered. At the SUMBER 6 KM sign, walk one km to Trusmi down a narrow country lane full of color-rich batik waving and drying in the sun. Although the batik is actually made here, it's not necessarily cheaper—you just have more of a selection. They still want Rp40,000-90,000 for the fine pieces. Visit H. Mohammed Masina's workshop in the long one-story white building opposite a grass clearing. Mr. Masina and his wife have rejuvenated some of the old Cirebon court designs, using mostly traditional creams and browns against tan backgrounds, as well as superb Chinese reds and blues depicting birds and oversized lions. Family workshops such as the Masina's proliferated during the 1920s and '30s, and their extraordinary hand-drawn technique is a throwback to that golden age. Many of the best pieces are destined for the GKBI Institute in Jakarta, so their prices depend upon how low their stock is. Another workshop, one of Trusmi's largest, is Budhi Tesna's, particularly noted for batik printing. Numerous other workshops are found both here and in the neighboring village of Kalitengah.

PRACTICALITIES

Services

Change money at the banks along Jl. Yos Sudarso. Bank Dagang Negara is on Jl. Kantor near the harbor, while Bank Bumi Daya is on Jl. Siliwangi; open Mon.-Fri. 0800-1400, Sat. until 1200. The main post office is on Jl. Yos Sudarso near the harbor. The telephone office is on Jl. Pagongan. The Tourist Office (Dinas Pariwisata) which dispenses a local map and whose staff speaks fragmentary English, is at Jl. Siliwangi 88, a few buildings up from Hotel Grand. One reader reports that they tried to charge him Rp2500 just for asking directions! Sightseeing information is also available at Kantor Kotyamadya. For books, stationery supplies, etc., go to P.D. Equator, Jl. Bahagia 41.

Getting There

Reached by road or rail. The quickest way to cover the 266 km from Jakarta is by the daily Gunung Jati train which leaves Jakarta's Kota Station at 0700 (4½ hours); Rp4200 2nd Class, Rp3000 3rd Class. You may also board the more upscale Bima with a/c sleepers for Rp24,500. From Yogya, the train costs Rp6000 3rd Class, or Rp25,500 on the Bima. From Semarang, fares range from Rp5200 3rd Class up to Rp19,500 on the Mutiara Ekspres; approximately 3½ hours. By long-distance bus from Jakarta, Rp3500, 6-7 hours. If driving your own vehicle from Jakarta, the N coast road via Bekasi, Cikampek, and Jatibarang is rather flat and boring but much faster (5-6 hours) than the scenic route via the Puncak and Bandung. From Bandung, Cirebon is 2½ hours by car, the

road twisting down to Sumedang, then emerging onto the plain at Kadipaten from where it heads straight into Cirebon. Or take the bus 130 km from Bandung, Rp2500, 4 hours.

Getting Around

Any place of interest in this small city can be reached by minibus (taxi kota), bemo, or becak. Stasiun Taxi Kota (also called the stanplatz) is right on Jl. Gunungsari and has taxi kota going out in all directions; within the city costs Rp200, to the outskirts Rp300. The becak drivers of Cirebon tie bundles of metal discs and iron gears under their pedicab seats (which sound like sleigh bells); no fixed rates. Try to negotiate one for a full hour for around Rp3000. Becak are banned in certain parts of the city, like around the large hotels. Strike a private deal and rent a taxi for around Rp4000/hour within the city or Rp5000 outside the city, minimum 3 hours. The manager at Hotel Asia will arrange this for you by telephone if you wish.

From Cirebon

Stasiun Taxi Kota on Jl. Gunungsari is the minibus station for all of Cirebon. Get minibuses to the Sunyaragi Grotto from here; also to Linggarjati, Rp500; Sumedang, Rp1000; Tegal, Rp1200; Bandung, Rp2500. bus station: Take minibuses G7 or G9 to the stasiun bis, 5 km SW of town on the road to Kuningan. To Pekalongan or Semarang, it's better to take the bus. Sample fares: Tegal, 73 km, Rp1000; Indramaya, 56 km, Rp750; Kuningan, 90 min., Rp650; Tasikmalaya, 118 km, Rp1200; Bandung, 127 km, 4 hours, Rp2500; Yogya, 365 km, 6 hours, Rp4500; Pekalongan, 90 min., Rp1500; Semarang, 237 km, 5 hours, Rp6500 (a/c); Jakarta, 257 km, 5-6 hours, Rp3600; Surabaya, Rp6500. The offices of the reputable "4848" Bus Co. are at Jl. Karanggetas 7 offering buses to Semarang, Yogya, Bandung, etc.

By Train

Luckily, the train to Jakarta takes only 3-4 hours, whereas the bus could take as long as 5-6 hours and is more tiring. The Gunung Jati trains depart for Jakarta 3 times daily early in the morning and cost anywhere from Rp3500 3rd Class and Rp5000-6000 2nd Class direct to Jakarta. Sometimes you can buy the ticket a day before for an additional fee of Rp250. There are also trains E along the N coast to Semarang (tracks could be flooded in the monsoon) and to Yogya. by air: Pelabuhan Udar Penggung Airport is 5 km from the city toward Kuningan. To Jakarta, twice daily, Rp30,000 with Garuda; another Garuda flight leaves for Ujungpandang, Balikpapan, Pekanbaru, and Palembang at 0830.

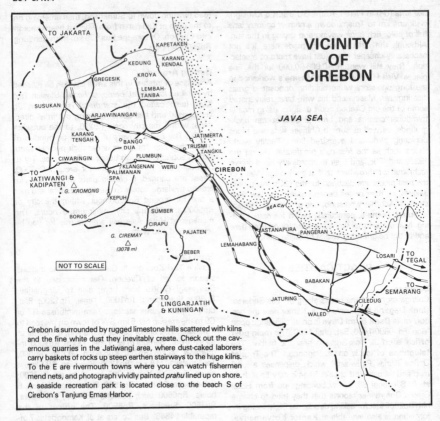

VICINITY OF CIREBON

Cirebon is surrounded by rugged limestone hills scattered with kilns and the fine white dust they inevitably create. Check out the cavernous quarries in the Jatiwangi area, where dust-caked laborers carry baskets of rocks up steep earthen stairways to the huge kilns. To the E are rivermouth towns where you can watch fishermen mend nets, and photograph vividly painted *prahu* lined up on shore. A seaside recreation park is located close to the beach S of Cirebon's Tanjung Emas Harbor.

VICINITY OF CIREBON

Indramayu
Fifty-four km NW of Cirebon, Rp500 by minibus from Cirebon's bus station. This area has developed its own style of *batik*, characterized by subdued *mengkuku* red (terra cotta or Turkish red) and various shades of traditional indigo. The dramatic and continued use of blue and red in the Indramayu area is thought to have been a result of the long Chinese presence in the area: blue is their symbol for mourning and melancholy, while red symbolizes happiness, fertility, and good fortune. Indramayu *batikers* also distinguish their designs by filling all the background with tiny dots which, over time, became so involved that the dramatic central motifs gradually lose their impact. For the best *batik*, visit the village of Pamuan, only a Rp500

becak ride from Indramayu's minibus station. *Batik tulis* pieces cost Rp50,000-75,000 on the average.

Linggarjati
This 300-m-high resort, 13 km N of Kuningan and 22 SW of Cirebon, is a clean, cool village with beautiful panoramas (even Cirebon's beach is visible!). Take a minibus from Kuningan's terminal (Rp600), or drive from Bandung via Majalengka. Perched on G. Ciremay, with hills and green *sawah* all around, this is where the people of Cirebon go to relax. The resort has bungalows, hotels, good walks, and gardens. Most travelers just come up for the day from Cirebon. Linggarjati is famous as the venue of negotiations between the Dutch and the "rebel" government of Indonesia in 1947. With Lord Killearn of England presiding as mediator, the Indonesians' de facto authority over Java and Sumatra was first recognized at this conference. In the

talks, however, the West Irian question was left unresolved, an issue that exploded in armed conflict 15 years later. The building where the conference was held has been fully restored and turned into a museum. Nearby are relics from prehistoric diggings around Cigugur and other excavations at Cipari village in Kuningan District. People have dwelt at the foot of G. Ciremay (3,078 m) for thousands of years; remains and stone tools found are said to span the New Stone Age to the Megalithic Age (2500-1500 B.C.). There are no *losmen;* hotels cost anywhere from Rp6000 to Rp35,000. **Hotel Linggarjati**, Rp12,000-25,000, has a swimming pool, tennis courts, and full resort amenities. **Linggarjati Cilimus** is situated in a nice setting with dining room, tennis courts, swimming pool, some bungalows, and is only 2 km to the hot-water mineral baths.

Air Panas Kedung Bunder

With its restful panoramas, this spa lies in Desa Paliaman (Kec. Paliaman), 17 km from the main Cirebon-Bandung highway. The water from the underground well feeding the hotsprings is so hot that it has to be held in a reservoir for a time before it is released into the actual swimming pool. **Gunung Kromong** is the source of the sulphur-rich water, which is ideal for treating skin diseases.

Gunung Ciremay

At 3,078 m, G. Ciremay is the highest mountain in the region. Lying SW of Cirebon, it's greatly loved by naturalists and domestic tourists for its vistas and beautiful surroundings (though it's often covered in mists). The best climbing route is from the village of Linggarjati; you should have a guide.

rice: In most of Indonesia, life revolves around rice. Four out of 5 Indonesians work ricefields. Religious festivals and marriages are scheduled to fit in with planting and harvesting. Rice stalks are often cut with tiny, hidden knives so that the spirits in the fields won't be offended. Government employees are paid partly in rice, and the price of rice is known as the "Mother Price," as it affects prices of all other commodities. Rice is so important that Bahasa Indonesia has 3 words for it: when it's growing it's called *padi*, when the grains are removed from the stalk it's called *beras*, and when it has been cooked it is *nasi*. In fact, the word *nasi* is frequently used as a synonym for food in general. Just a mound of cold boiled rice with chilis and a little fish is enough to keep most Indonesians going. The rigid organization, labor, and control required of *sawah* (wet-rice) cultivation have given rise to a long tradition of despotic rule in Asia, with kingships having absolute power over the waters, the earth, the crops, the life, and death of the people.

CENTRAL JAVA

Central Java, which contains the special autonomous region (Daerah Istimewa) of Yogyakarta, is the cultural, geographic, and historic heartland of the island. Lofty mountains march down the entire central portion of this province, on the cool slopes of which are numerous resorts such as Colo, Kopeng, Bandungan, and Kaliurang. A predominantly volcanic region, G. Slamet in the Banyumas area and G. Merapi near Magelang are still active. Central Java is also extremely rich in archaeological sites: ancient Hindu temples (Dieng, Prambanan, Sewu, Plaosan); Buddhist remains (Borobudur and Mendut); primitive remains (Sukuh and Ceta); ancient mosques (Demak and Kudus); ruined Portuguese fortresses (Jepara and Cilegon); and sultans' palaces (Yogya and Solo). Big industry can be found at Cilacap (cement), Solo and Kudus (handmade *kretek* cigarettes), and Tegal and Semarang (boatbuilding). Moderate industries are *jamu*, food and soft-drink production, and *batik*. Semarang on the N coast and Cilacap on the S are the province's 2 important harbors. The island's most crowded province, of C. Java's 25.5 million people, only about 10% live in cities, the rest in villages. The population density is about 690 people per sq km over a total area of 34,205 sq km. The rainy season is Oct. through April, dry the rest of the year.

Crafts

Cottage industries are found all over the region, but the towns most noted for their handicrafts are Solo, Pekalongan, Lasem, and Banyumas for *batik*; Jepara and Sukoharjo for carvings; Semarang, Kudus, Solo, Batang, Pemalang, Tegal, Salatiga, and Secang for textiles. Also, a number of "pottery villages" produce whimsical but fragile animals from red clay. The Seketan Fair in Yogya and Solo 11 days before Mohammed's birthday is an ideal place to see the best examples of Indonesian folk ceramics.

PEKALONGAN

Pronounced "Pek-HALLO-ang." Population around 125,000. It lies on the N coast 101 km W of Semarang on the road to Jakarta. Known as *Kota Batik* ("Batik City"), Pekalongan is an important textile center famed for colorful hand-waxed, machine-printed *batik* using distinct motifs. Pekalongan even has a Batik Museum near the *pasar buahan* on Jl. Pasar Ratu; open 0900-1300, closed Sundays. Pekalongan has always been a fortress and trade city; visible to this day are the remains of a VOC fort built in 1753, later turned into a prison by the Dutch. On 7 Oct. 1945, the Pekalongan residency became the first in Indonesia to free itself of Japanese rule, touching off a violent social revolution which became known in this part of Java as the "Tiga Daerah Movement."

Batik Pekalongan

Pekalongan has always played a leading role in the development of modern *batik* designs and techniques (see Java's "Introduction" for the history of *batik*). The town has numerous *batik* factories and shops; as in Yogya, peddlers with their bundles of *batik* approach you on the street, come up to restaurant tables, and hang around the hotel lobbies. Coming directly from the *kampung* where the *batik* is made, these pieces are generally cheaper than in the shops on main streets Jl. Hayam Wuruk and Jl. Hasanudin. For *batik cap*, the price is around Rp6000-8000, for *batik tulis* anywhere from Rp15,000-35,000. The whole town is involved in *batik*. Wander through the streets and look through doorways. If you see the bamboo drying racks it means one of hundreds of *batik* factories in town. Recognizable by usually red and blue birds and flowers on white or pink backgrounds, Pekalongan *batik* is some of the most *alus* on the island; you could easily pay Rp200,000 for a fine piece.

Buying *Batik*

The nationwide cooperative GKBI on Jl. H.A. Salim 39 (tel. 183811) represents more than 500 local *batik* producers, selling original Pekalongan *batik* in various designs and qualities; closed Fridays. Shop at Tobal Batik, Jl. Teratai 7A; tell the *becak* driver to go to Klego (a suburb of Pekalongan). This warehouse is almost exclusively wholesale. B.L. Pekalongan, Jl. K.H. Mansyur 87 (tel. 1358/589), is one of the largest *batik* shops; open 0800-1700. For lower prices, buy directly from the factories: P.T. Rimbung Djaya Company, Jl. Jen Urip Soemoroharjo 20, is right opposite Kantor Perdangan, 2 km from the city; open 0800-1600. Pandawa Graha Company, run by Suryanto Tri, Jl. Jawa 24 (tel. 1499). For really superb work, visit the Leonardo of *batik*, Pak Oey Tjoen, at Jl. Raya 104 in Kedungwuni, 9 km from Pekalongan. Unbelievably intricate designs, using 8-9 colors on one piece! A number of other factories here also charge as much: at Krapyak Desa, about 4 km from Pekalongan; Kampung Sampangan off Jl. Hasanudin, about one km from the city; and Kampung Pesindon (see Mr. Yahya).

Accommodations

A good number of *losmen* here; the more expensive hotels include breakfast in the price. Three convenient cheap accommodations are opposite the train station on Jl. Gajah Mada: **Hotel Gajah Mada** (no. 11A, tel. 41185) is more personable and cheery than the others; Rp5000 s, Rp6000 d. **Damai** (Rp5000 d) is a businessmen's hotel. **Losmen Ramayana** has a noisy billiard hall; also Rp5000 d. **Losmen Sari Dewi**, Jl. Hayam Wuruk 1, is clean and comfortable; Rp8000 d. **Hotel Murni**, Jl. Mansyur 4, is a friendly flophouse at Rp2500 s, Rp3000 d, Rp5000 t. **Losmen Asia**, Jl. Wahid Hasyim 49 (tel. 41125), is popular with travelers; Rp6000 s, Rp8000 d with *mandi* and continental breakfast. Moving up in price, **Hotel Hayam Wuruk**, Jl. Hayam Wuruk 152-158, has a wide selection of

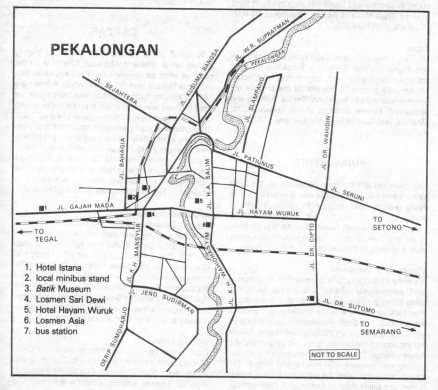

PEKALONGAN

JL. W.R. SUPRATMAN

S. PEKALONGAN

JL. KUSUMA BANGSA

JL. SEJAHTERA

JL. SLAMPANG

JL. DR. WAHIDIN

JL. PATIUNUS

JL. BAHAGIA

JL. H.A. SALIM

JL. SERUNI

JL. GAJAH MADA

JL. HAYAM WURUK

JL. DR. CIPTO

TO SETONO

← TO TEGAL

JL. K.H. MANSYUR

JL. K.H. WAHIDIN

JL. WAHID HASYIM

JL. JEND. SUDIRMAN

JL. DR. SUTOMO

TO SEMARANG

OERIP SUMOHARJO

1. Hotel Istana
2. local minibus stand
3. *Batik* Museum
4. Losmen Sari Dewi
5. Hotel Hayam Wuruk
6. Losmen Asia
7. bus station

NOT TO SCALE

rooms at Rp8,000 to Rp15,000. **Hotel Istana**, Jl. Gajah Mada 23-25 (tel. 61581), is just down the street from the train station; go out and turn L; Rp12,000-15,000 s or d, Rp20,000-25,000 s or d with a/c.

Food
Sample such typical Pekalongan delicacies as *jangen asam (sayur asum), semur, sambal tempe,* etc., at the night market stalls which spring up around Pasar Buahan at night. **Pekalongan Remaja**, Jl. Dr. Cipto 20, serves good value Chinese meals. **Restaurant Siti** on Jl. Gajah Mada also specializes in Chinese food. **RM Oen** and **RM Saiyo** are across the street from Hotel Istana.

From Pekalongan
The local minibus station is behind the Pertamina petrol station on Jl. Hayam Wuruk. Pekalongan's bus station is 2 km from the town center, Rp500 by *becak* or Rp200 by minibus. By bus to Cirebon, Rp2000 (136 km); Jakarta, Rp4500 (402 km); Semarang, Rp1500 (2 hours); Bandung, Rp2500. In the early mornings, buses to Cirebon and Semarang stop briefly in front of Hotel Gajah Mada to pick up passengers. By train to Jakarta, Rp4200-5500.

Tegal
On the N coast of C. Java, Tegal is the province's second largest city after Semarang. Bargain at roadside stalls for brassware and handcrafted red ochre earthenware pottery. A number of comfortable accommodations, including **Hotel Karlita** (with bar and restaurant), **Hotels Susana, Maya, Gajah Mada, Urumba**, and **Sari**, all have average rates of Rp2500-Rp10,000.

PURWOKERTO

This town lies 204 km from Semarang on the *Bima* train's route between Jakarta and Surabaya. Stay in **Peng. Asli** in front of the train station, or one of several *losmen*, or in a number of hotels along the main drag. The largest, **Hotel Santosa**, is in the heart of the city. Specialties to dine on include *sate ayam, soto*, and *tahu*. In the daytime eat at Pasar Wage.

Vicinity Of Purwokerto
A variety of handicrafts is produced in **Sukaraja** (7 km E) where artists paint on canvas, glass, walls, etc., using techniques passed down through generations. Also look for flatware, brass implements, ceramics, *wayang kulit*, and *batik*. **Pemandian Kalibacin** is 25 km S of Purwokerto via Patikraja and Notog, following the edge of the Serayu River, just before reaching Rawalo village. This hotspring contains minerals said to cure skin diseases, bad nerves, and fatigue. The springs are named after the sulphur odor (*kali* means "river" and *bacin* means "bad smell"). Accommoda-

tions are available. Twenty-five km W of Purwokerto at **Ajibarang** is another bathing place, Pemandian Pancasan, reached from Purwokerto by *bemo*. Southeast of Purwokerto, the small town of **Banyumas** has wide streets and white 19th C. buildings. Banyumas has its own particular *batik* design. The surrounding region has *sawah*, mountains, *ladang* fields, and residential areas.

Gunung Slamet
The climb up this live 3,428-m-high volcano, 15 km N of Purwokerto, is through resin forests, dense jungle, vegetable gardens, steep riverbanks, and treacherous ravines. Wild forest pig are found in this mountainous region. **Baturaden** is a mountain retreat on the slopes of G. Slamet, 14 km N of Purwokerto, with a beautiful camping reserve and nice panoramas. The climate is cool, the trees tall, and the earth fertile. The area of the actual reserve is 1.5 ha, covered in a green carpet of grass, pines, and resinous *kaliandon*. The area's thick green forest is surrounded by mountains (Candilana, Buandur, and Sendangpitu), all lying at the foot of G. Slamet.

CILACAP

Fifty km S of Purwokerto and 216 W of Yogya, known for its cliffs and wild seas, Cilacap is on the coast of what Indonesians call the Indonesian Sea (which is like the Irish calling the whole Atlantic the Irish Sea!). The natural harbor here, which can be used by large sea-going ships, is protected by a long island, Nusakambangan. Enjoy views of Pantai Teluk Penyu. Seashell crafts are sold in souvenir stalls; there are many billiard halls for the sailors, and a children's park. Benteng Pendem is an old, partly buried Portuguese fort one km S of Pantai Teluk Penyu. From here you get a panorama over the iron deposits along the "iron beach" E of Cilacap; this iron is exported to Japan via a special harbor near Benteng Pendem.

Accommodations
Losmen Bahagia and **Losmen Lima** are both on Jl. Sudirman near the Sleko jetty from where you get the ferry to Pangandaran. **Hotel Peni Wijaya**, Jl. Suprapto 4 (tel. 256), in the center of the city, has special Cilacap cuisine, and prices within reach. Many other hotels charge the usual tariffs (Rp6000-15,000); check out **Losmen Tiga**, Jl. Mayor Sutoyo 61, at Rp4000 s, Rp6000 d. Try also the **Sarawati Motel** not far from Jl. Raya Gumilir before you enter Cilacap. At night go dancing at **Bar and Restaurant Serayu**.

Getting There
From Yogya, take the 0650 train to Kroya for Rp3200 (5 hours), then a minibus (one hour) to Cilacap. Or take a bus direct from Yogya to Cilacap via Purworejo (Rp4500, 5 hours). Another popular way to reach Cila-

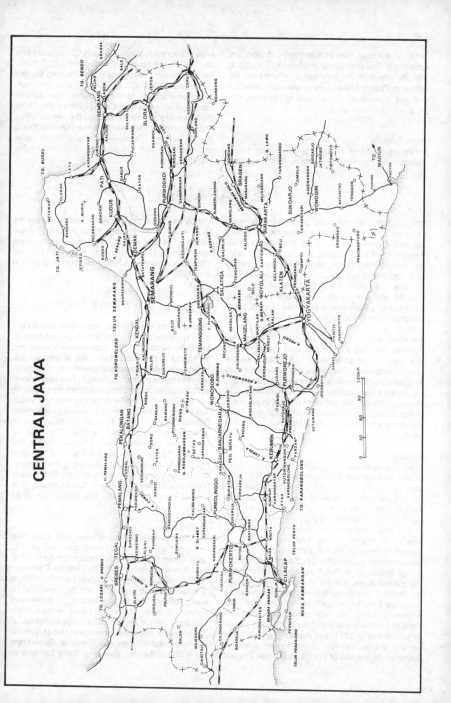

CENTRAL JAVA

cap is on the boat from Pangandaran (W. Java) via Kalipucang. The boat docks at Cilacap's Sleko dock area. Arriving from Pangandaran, minibuses will be waiting at Cilacap's Sleko jetty to take you all the way to Yogya, Rp4500. For more details on this route, see the section on "Pangandaran."

From Cilacap
If heading E, many travelers prefer to visit Dieng Plateau before arriving in Yogya so that they don't have to backtrack. Minibuses leave Cilacap and travel the 150 km in 6 hours to Wonosobo (Rp3000-4000); from Wonosobo, minibuses leave all during the day for the plateau (Rp1000, 1 ½ hours). Get an early start. **Nusakambangan:** While in Cilacap, take the car/passenger ferry over to this island off the coast. Pantai Permisan lies on the S side of the island, offers clusters of rocks, fresh sea air, and a resthouse facing the sea. Remains of a Dutch fort which once served as an important military outpost are also found on this island.

SEMARANG

The administrative capital of C. Java, on the northcentral coast 120 km N of Yogya. Quite unlike the gentle, age-mellowed *kraton* cities of Yogya and Solo, Semarang is a busy harbor city, a government, trading, and industrial center, as well as a major fishing port. The population is 1.2 million, of which 40% is Chinese. The mainly residential Candi section is behind the city up in the cooler hills, with the markets, restaurants, government offices, harbor, and transportation terminals in the lower section. Semarang is in many ways a more orderly city than Java's other important ports, Jakarta and Surabaya. It offers lively nightlife, with many clubs and massage parlors. In fact, there's so much business traffic that hotels are often overbooked. Although more a commercial center than a city for tourists, Semarang is a good starting point for many holiday resorts in the mountains to the south. It's the only port open to large ships on this stretch of coast, and cruise ships often call here. From Semarang you can easily visit Borobudur, Dieng, and nearby hill stations.

History
The silting up of this harbor in the 17th C. might have been a factor in the shifting of power from C. to E. Java by cutting off the ruler's income through sea trade. Even today, because of the shallowness of its harbor, ships must anchor out in the estuary of the Kali Baru River, their cargos and passengers unloaded at sea and transferred to shore by launch. Great wealth has always passed through this city: agricultural produce going out, industrial raw materials and processed goods coming in. Semarang once held a huge population of Dutch traders and officials during colonial times, and the city is still crowded with old Dutch churches, warehouses, and administrative buildings. Long known as "The Red City," center of socialist activity in the archipelago, the Communist Party of Indonesia was born here in 1920 (introduced by a Dutchman in 1914), and eventually grew into the world's largest, outside of communist-controlled countries. At the end of WW II, Indonesian irregular troops frantically tried to wrest weapons from the Japanese in order to oppose the landing of Allied forces intent upon retaking Java. In Semarang, these guerilla bands fought a pitched battle from 14-19 Oct. 1945 against garrisoned Japanese crack troops, and lost 2,000 men.

SIGHTS

Because of its large Chinese community, the city has been a center of *jamu* production for hundreds of years: the factories of Cap Jago, Nonya Meneer, and Borobudur are all based here, and all are visitable. **Makam Pandan Arang** (also called Makam Bergota) is an old cemetery and pilgrimage place once known as Pulau Tirang; because of silting over the years a hill has formed in the middle of the city with nice views. The old Dutch section along Jl. Suprapto is wonderfully photogenic. The **THR**, on Jl. Sriwijaya, puts on various presentations and exhibits. The most famous—and underrated—is the Snake Garden. Semarang's 400-ha **Tegalwareng Zoo** on Jl. Sriwijaya has comical chimpanzees and *wayang* and *ketropak* dramas, as well as rock bands and exhibits of traditional arts. **Universitas Islam Sultan Agung** is in front of Terminal Bis Terboyo (also called Terminal Bis Induk).

Architecture
The modern **Mesjid Baiturahman**, NW of Simpang Lima, is the largest and most elegant mosque of C. Java. Distinctive colonial architecture can be found all over downtown; go on foot. The **Catholic Church** on Jl. Karanganyar recites its liturgy to *gamelan* music on Sunday. **Gereja Blenduk**, Jl. Jen. Suprapto S of Tawang Railway Station, was built in 1753 (*blendoek* means "to swell," given this name because of the building's unique dome roof). **Gereja Bangkon**, Jl. Mataram 908, about the same age as Gereja Blenduk, has been beautifully restored. The oldest Chinese temple (1772) in the city, **Klenteng Gang Lombok** on

Gang Lombok, is right in the heart of Chinatown; to the Chinese this temple is better known as Thay Kak Sie. This is a well-maintained, *living* temple, used by Buddhists, Confucianists, and Taoists. The amazing **Lawang Sewu**, which used to house the Dutch Railway Authority or NIS (Nederlandisch Indische Spoorweg Maatscahappij), can easily be picked out amongst all the buildings surrounding the Tugu Muda roundabout. Its name means "One Thousand Doors." Now occupied by the army, it's a hassle to photograph this remarkable structure; you must get permission from the military commander at Bintaldam IV Dina Sejarah on the other side of the traffic circle.

Museums
Museum Jamu Nyouya Meneer, in the *jamu* factory of P.T. Nyouya Meneer, Jl. Raya Kaligawe Km 4 (tel. 285732), is Indonesia's first facility dedicated to the country's traditional herbal medicine: old photographs, tools, spices used as ingredients, etc. Open Mon. to Fri. 1000-1530. **Museum Jawa Tengah**, Jl. Abdul Rahman (one km from Semarang's Ahmad Yani Airport) has fossils, Java-Hindu reliefs and statues, *wayang*. Free entrance. A military museum, **Museum Perjuangan Mandala Bhakti**, is S of the Tugu Muda monument.

Tugu Muda Monument
In the center of the city, this monument commemorates the 5-day battle by Indonesian partisan troops against elite Japanese soldiers at the end of WW II. In the form of a candle, the monument symbolizes the memory and spirit of the struggle for independence. Murals on the base of the obelisk show the sufferings of the people under both Dutch and Japanese domination, and the events during the famous struggle, painted communally by one of the oldest artists' organizations in Indonesia. On 14 Oct. each year, the *Pertempuran Lima Hari* ceremony is held around this monument to honor the ragtag but disciplined and fearless Indonesian youths and students who participated in the battle.

Sam Poo Kong Temple
Also known as *Gedung Batu* ("Stone Building"), this great cave-temple is on the main road to Kendal in the western part of the city. Take a Daihatsu direct from Terminal Senow (or Terminal Daihatsu), Rp150, on Jl. Suari. One of the largest and most honored Chinese temple complexes in Indonesia, Gedung Batu houses the spirit of a Ming Dynasty Chinese admiral who landed on Java in 1406 with a fleet of 62 vessels and 27,000 sailors. Twice a month, on *Jum'at Kliwon* (Friday) and on *Selasa Kliwon* (Tuesday) of the Javanese calendar, multitudes of pilgrims arrive. Since Sam Poo Kong helped carry the Islamic religion to Java, Gedung Batu is a rare "double sanctuary," sacred to both Buddhists and Muslims. Seeing Indonesians

wearing *peci* in the temple's interior, carrying incense sticks in their hands, praying in a Chinese temple to a Chinese admiral gives one hope that these two races will one day live in harmony. Free entrance; no photography permitted inside the altar areas.

ACCOMMODATIONS

Inexpensive
Losmen Sinar, Jl. K.P. Pandan Sari 397 (off Jl. Gendingan), wins the cheapest award (Rp1000) but be sure to bring a mosquito coil. **Losmen Tentrum** in the Kauman (Arab Quarter) is only Rp2000. **Losmen Martanova**, Jl. Gendingan 11, has definitely low-grade rooms without fan for Rp3000 s. Several dozen small, inexpensive *losmen* are concentrated along Jl. Imam Bonjol. Curiously, some of the smaller accommodations don't accept foreign guests, or else seem full. If you are unable or don't wish to stay in Semarang, hotels and guesthouses are also found up in the hills S of the city (Candi). **Losmen Singapore**, Jl. Imam Bonjol 12 (across the street from Hotel Oewa-Asia), charges Rp4000 s, Rp6000 d, including breakfast. No fan, pretty dingy; get a room in back. Basic, clean accommodations are offered at **Losmen Rahayu**, Jl. Imam Bonjol 35-37 (tel. 22532); Rp8000 s or d, breakfast included. The higher-priced rooms have *kamar mandi;* the rest share a bathroom. The cheapest rooms at **Hotel Losmen Surya**, Jl. Imam Bonjol 58, run Rp3000 s; other rooms go for Rp5000-7000 d, Rp6500-11,000 t. Away from the street, these quiet rooms are clean, most with inside bath. Centrally located but drab **Losmen Poncol**, Jl. Imam Bonjol 60 (near the Poncol RR Station), asks Rp4500 s, Rp6000 d, Rp8000 t; bring mosquito coils. **Losmen Bahagia**, Jl. Pemuda 16-18, right opposite the Dibya Puri, is very central; Rp7000 s or d for small rooms with fan—OK for one night. Big, breezy **Hotel Jaya** (Rp5000 d with breakfast), about one km S of the bus station at Jl. M.T. Haryono 87 (tel. 23604); Rp8000 for large, fairly clean s or d rooms with inside *mandi*. They also have Rp5000 rooms. Secure; gate closes at night—one of the best cheap hotels in Semarang.

Moderate
The old Dutch colonial **Hotel Oewa-Asia** (pronounced WAH-Asia), is on Jl. Imam Bonjol right in the noisy center of the city. Rooms in a quieter part of the hotel are Rp8000 with wall fan and 2 beds, but kind of dingy. In the front building rooms run Rp14,500-15,500, with *mandi*, toilet, but are still noisy even with the a/c on. The ice water is a nice touch, but the prostitutes in the back degrade the place. A better deal is the well-run **Losmen Djelita**, Jl. M.T. Haryono 32-36 (tel. 23891); Rp3500 s rooms, but often full. Their Rp15,000 a/c rooms are a better value, good lighting, clean and neat, and nice cool inner courtyard.

High-priced

The **Metro Grand Park**, Jl. H.A. Salim 2-4 (tel. 27371, ext. 7), is one of Semarang's premier hotels where rooms run Rp45,000 s, Rp52,500 d; deluxe rooms Rp52,500 s, Rp57,500 d, and with balconies Rp55,000 s and 62,000 d. Just across the street from the central market, this full a/c hotel has it all: beauty parlor and barber shop, restaurants, lounge, a disco, coffee shop, boutiques. Be sure to add the 21% government tax and service charge. Popular with domestic businessmen. Also rather steep is the central **Queen Hotel**, Jl. Gajah Mada 44-52 (tel. 27063), with cheapest a/c rooms at Rp30,000, all the way up to Rp47,500. Rooms are clean, but not really worth the price. The older, colonial-style, centrally located **Hotel Dibya Puri**, Jl. Pemuda 11 (tel. 27821), charges from Rp24,000 for Standard A rooms with a/c facing quiet courtyard, up to Rp51,000 s or d for the Semi Suite. Huge B Class rooms cost only Rp10,000 with balcony facing the street, but are noisy and have no fan. The hotel's glory days have passed; even with its attempt at modernity and efficiency it's one of the saddest hotels in Indonesia. **Siranda Hotel**, Jl. Diponegoro 1 (tel. 313271), is high up on a hill on the way to Candi. Beautiful views at night, but restaurant is not as good as Hotel Telomuryo. No lift, so you'll get a lot of exercise. Rooms (a/c) start out at Rp31,600 s and Rp39,400 d on first floor, but descend in price as you ascend in height (Rp23,300 s, Rp31,200 d). Amex and Visa cards are accepted, and prices already include tax and service. Take a taxi into the city or take a Daihatsu, Rp125. Built in 1974 for Indonesia's first PATA conference, today the Siranda is getting a little frayed at the edges, but still a good value. The **Telomoyo**, Jl. Gajah Mada 138 (tel. 20926/25436/27037), is central, with 67 a/c rooms and large open courtyard. Takes Amex, Visa, and Diners Club cards. Nice lobby and has a homey feeling. Popular with Dutch package tourists and Japanese businessmen, it's higher-priced rooms (Rp23,000-42,200) are better value; tax and breakfast included in the price. Its restaurant features European food. **Hotel Santika**, Jl. A. Yani 189 (tel. 314491), has Standard rooms for Rp26,000 and Moderate rooms for Rp31,500; a/c, telephone, in-house video, restaurant. This hotel is opposite Es Teler, one of the best *bakso* restaurants on Java.

Candi

If you want a knockout view, try some of the plush hotels up on Candi Baru in the hills overlooking the city. The exorbitant **Patra Jasa**, Jl. Sisingamangaraja (tel. 314441), sits lordly above the city with beautiful rooms complete with a/c, refrigerator, and TV for US$42-49 s, US$48-52 d plus 21% service and government tax. Takes Amex, Visa, and Diners Club. Facilities include restaurant, coffee shop, bowling alley, tennis courts, swimming pool, billiards, travel bureau,

drugstore, bank, and more—the best tourist hotel in Semarang. The **Sky Garden Motel**, Jl. Setia Budi (tel.312733/4) is a/c with full facilities; Rp26,500 for "motel" rooms and Rp21,150 s for "hotel" rooms. There's a perpetual 30% discount in force. Rates include breakfast and 21% service and government tax. **Hotel & Motel Fanny Cottage**, Jl. Setya Budi 34 (tel. 312704), is across the road from the Sky Garden and about the same price, but is better managed and has a restaurant and bar. Also check out the comfortable **Green Guest House**, Jl. Kesambi 7 (tel. 312642).

FOOD

Street Food

Scores of eating tents serve food and drink—from *soto ayam* to *tahu pong*—at all hours on Jl. Depok, Jl. Pringgading, and along Jl. M.T. Haryono. These tents offer some of the best eating in Semarang. Try the *bolong baling*, a big puff donut. A great cheap place to eat is **Pasar Yalik** (open at night) near **Pasar Johar** (open in the daytime) for special Semarang dishes such as *sate kerang* (oyster *sate*). For inexpensive foodstalls serving *martabak, sate*, soups, Indonesian and Chinese food, head for **Komplek Yaik Permai**, near Metro Grand Park Hotel. Along Gang Lombok, off Jl. Pekojan near Klenteng Gang Lombok, are a string of Chinese *warung* and restaurants; open 0800-1300. **Es Teler**, Jl. Jen. A. Yani 178, is always crowded; their *bakso* is only Rp750.

Restaurants

Mbok Berek, Jl. Siliwangi 376, serves a special *ayam goreng*. For Chinese and European food, and plenty of baked goods and ice cream, try **Toko Oen**, Jl. Pemuda 52 (open 0900-2130), the longest-existing eating establishment in Semarang. The number one Padang-style restaurant is **RM Sari Medan**, Jl. Pemuda (just past Toko Oen), where even the high and mighty dine; clean and complete menu. **RM Istana**, Jl. M.T. Haryono (near Gereja Bangkon), serves Indonesian, Japanese, and European food in the Rp3000-5000 range. For Chinese dishes like *djawn-lo, hie pio, kim ci bak, yongkee*, **Phien Tjawn Hiang**, Jl. Gang Pinggir 86, is the place. **Kit Wan Kie**, Gang Pinggir 23-25, is also highly recommended. Of the many Chinese restaurants along Jl. Gajah Mada, **RM Gajah Mada** (no. 43) is best known for its seafood—a bit pricey, but worth it. The city's very best seafood, however, is found in **Restoran Soen**, Jl. A. Yani 164 (tel. 024-316174), and fast service too. **RM Santai Ria**, Jl. Gajah Mada 112, open 0700-1500/1700-2200, serves Indonesian and Chinese food. **Happy**, right across the street, has similar high standards. **Pringgading**, Jl. Pringgading 4 (tel. 288973), is considered a top-class Chinese restaurant.

SEMARANG

JL. SIMONGAN

TO AIRPORT, JAKARTA

JL. SILIWANGI

JL. PUSPONJOLO

JL. INDRAPRASTA

LAUT JAVA

JL. SUTOMO

JL. IMAM BONJOL

NOT TO SCALE

JL. KYAI SALEH

JL. PANDANARAN

JL. TENDEAN

JL. VETERAN

JL. THAMRIN

JL. PEMUDA

JL. IMAM BONJOL

JL. GAJAH MADA

JL. TAHIR

JL. YOS SUDARSO

JL. PAHLAWAN

BATIK KERIS

JL. WAHID HASYIM

JL. SRIWIJAYA

JL. SUTOYO SISW.

JL. PANJAHITAN

JL. H.A. SALIM

JL. SUPRAPTO

HARBOR

JL. JAGALAN

JL. USMAN JANATIN

TO PURWODADI

JL. A. YANI

TO SOLO

MATARAM

JL. M.T. HARYONO

TO SURABAYA

1. Sam Poo Kong Temple
2. hospital
3. Pandanaran grave
4. Bulu Market
5. C. Java Tourist Office
6. Tugu Muda
7. Kantor Bupati's (mayor's)
8. Restoran Gajah Mada
9. Klenteng Temple
10. Hotel Oewa-Asia
11. shopping centers Johar/Yaik
12. Metro Grand Park Hotel
13. post office
14. Tanjung Mas Recreation Center
15. Tawang Railway Station
16. Gereja Blenduk
17. Induk (Terboyo) Bus Station
18. Taman Hiburan Diponegoro
19. Gang Lombok and Klenteng Gang Lombok
20. Stadium Diponegoro
21. Restaurant Soen
22. Hotel Santika
23. Municipality Tourist Office
24. Shopping Center Gedung Ohlaraga
25. Mesjid Baiturahman
26. Simpang Lima
27. Kantor Gubernor
28. Metro Grand Park Hotel

On Gang Lombok, off Jl. Pekojan in Chinatown, are also outstanding small Chinese seafood restaurants at moderate prices. Also excellent Chinese restaurants adjacent to Sam Poo Kong Temple (or Gedung Batu) in the western part of the city.

ENTERTAINMENT AND SERVICES

Tirta Ria, with its water sports, is located at the harbor. **Tanjung Mas Rekreasi**, N of the harbor area, is Semarang's Ancol; it's about 40% completed. Target date: 1990. **Taman Hiburan Diponegoro**, Jl. H. Agus Salim, features movies, *joget,* and a children's amusement park. **Simpang Lima** (the big traffic circle) is jumping on Sat. night when all the middle-class kids ride around in their motorbikes and cars—just like in Akron, Ohio! A sports hall (basketball, volleyball, badminton, boxing, kungfu, etc.) is near Simpang Lima and Mesjid Baiturahman; watch the banners hung around town to see what's on. Semarang also has at least 25 cinemas.

Ngesti Pandowo, Jl. Pemuda 116, puts on rather pallid performances of Solonese-style *wayang orang* in a theater with wall-to-wall mosquitos and a primitive bathroom. Of higher quality are the performances staged occasionally at **Wisma Pancasila** (in the same building as the tourist office) on the second Sat. of each month. *Wayang kulit* performances start at 2100 and last until early morning; tickets cost Rp1500, Rp2500, and Rp5000. Also, each late Mon. morning *gamelan* rehearsals take place in this building's ground floor. *Wayang* productions, *jaran kepang,* and *reyog,* are staged at the city's **THR** on Jl. Sriwijaya. Also check out the **Wahyu Budoyo**, Kompleks Tegal Wareng, Jl. Sriwijaya, for performances every night. Regional folk dances include *kuda lumping* (dancers riding on bamboo horses), the *reyog,* and the *gambang semarang.*

Discos And Nightclubs

Being a business center, there's no shortage of nightclubs, massage parlors, and discos, some of which "rent" out hostesses for polite conversation at Rp5000 per hour. **Canasta**, Jl. Kenari 3-5; **Disco Den**, Metro Grand Park Hotel, Jl. H.A. Salim; **Crazy Horse**, Sky Garden Hotel, Jl. Setiabudi; and the **Spider**, Complex Shopping Center Johar, 2nd Floor. **Disco INAC**, in back of the Metro Grand Park Hotel in SC Johar (3rd Floor), has billiards, a disco, bar, and massage parlor; the busiest night is Sat. night. Plus there are massage parlors: the **Nirwana** on Jl. Jagalan, **Shinta Sauna** in the Complex Shopping Centre Johar, 3rd Floor, and the **Rama**, Jl. Pekojan 89 (tel. 21398). At a "special house" at Jl. Kartini 54, around 15 high-priced ladies entertain for Rp40,000 or Rp80,000 all night.

Events

Dugderan is a traditional bazaar and carnival which takes place yearly in front of Mesjid Agung for 3 consecutive days starting the first day of the fasting month, *Bulan Puasa. Dugderan* is essentially a huge night market which draws vendors from the countryside and other cities. This is the time to sample numerous regional specialities. Besides the New Year, the Chinese of Semarang hold a traditional religious festival called *Jaran Sam Poo* in honor of Sam Poo Kong's historic arrival in the 15th century. The highlight of this event is the procession *(Pek Kong),* which leaves the Klenteng Gang Lombok Temple, bearing a statue of Sam Poo Kong, and proceeds all the way to the *klenteng* at Sam Poo Kong. Many penitents participate, and only those with strong stomachs should view the parade. One of the most incredible sights you'll ever see in Indonesia.

Shopping

Semarang has about 20 markets and shopping centers selling everyday necessities to luxury goods. The main shopping centers for textiles, earthenware, and leatherwork are around Pasar Johar just off Jl. Pemuda, Jl. Gajah Mada next to the main square, and on Jl. Bojong. Pasar Yaik, next to Pasar Johar, is open from 1700-2300. Another public market is at Gang Baru, open only from 0600-1200, where you can buy almost anything at *the best* prices. Neon-lit **Mickey Mouse Dept. Store** is the big shopping center; also visit **Supermarket Metro & Movie Theatre** on Jl. M.T. Haryono. For *batik,* go to **Batik Danar Hadi**, Jl. Gajahmada 186 (tel. 25999); **Batik Keris**, Complex Pertokoan, Gajahmada Plaza; and **Batik Cendrawasih**, Jl. Pemuda 46 (tel. 25985). (Both Danar Hadi and Batik Keris are within 5 min. walking distance of Dinas Pariwisata.) For more textile shops, head for Jl. Gang Pinggir. For food products, Jl. Benteng is the place. Jalan Mataram is a long street lined with shops selling household and electronic goods and motorcycles. Jalan Kranggan Timur has numerous shops filled with shops selling jewelry, gold, and precious stones. Silver items, leather puppets, ceramics, and other Javanese crafts are available at **Panjang**, Jl. Widohargo 31A. A bird market, **Pasar Burung**, is on Jl. Kartini (one km from the tourist office) which is open all day. Antique shops include: **Mustika**, Jl. Pemuda 56-58 (tel. 21959); **Topaz**, Jl. Gajahmada (near the Queen Hotel). Statues, woodcarvings, and *batik* are sold at **Kertaniaga**, Jl. Mangunsarkoro 1 (tel. 20901).

Services

The **Municipality Tourist Office** (Dinas Pariwisata) is in Wisma Pancasila on Jl. Simpang Lima (tel. 288690); open Mon. to Thurs. 0800-1400; Fri. 0800-1100; Sat. 0800-1330. The **Central Java Tourist Office** is at Jl. Pemuda 171; take a *bis kota*

(Rp150) from Pasar Johar or a Daihatsu (Rp150). They give out brochures, maps, calendar of events. **Kantor Imigrasi** is 7 km out of town, beyond the airport on the road to Krapyak; get there by city bus from Pasar Johar, or take a Daihatsu from Terminal Sendowo on Jl. Suari. The **GPO** is near Pasar Johar, right beside the telephone office. Buy film and camera supplies around Jl. Pemuda, Gajahmada and on Jl. M.T. Haryono. A major bookseller is **Gramedia**, Jl. Pandanaran (behind Baiturahman Mosque). Change money at **Bank Rakyat Indonesia**, Jl. A. Yani (5 min. walk from the Municipality Tourist Office). **RS Telogorejo** is on Jl. Ahmad Dahlan (tel. 25571), only 200 m from the Municipality Tourist Office. But the best hospital, with English-speaking doctors, is **RS St. Elizabeth**, up in Candi (take city bus from Jl. Pemuda) at Jl. Kawi 1 (tel. 315).

TRANSPORT

Getting There

The entire N coast road—in either direction—is suitable for an ordinary car. **by bus:** From: Yogya (Rp1200, 3½ hours) or minibus (Rp2000); Jakarta, Rp7500 (or Rp9500 a/c); Surabaya, Rp5000; Pekalongan, Rp1500; Solo, Rp1200. By yellow taxi from Semarang's Terminal Bis Induk to Tawang Train Station, Rp2500. **by train:** From: Solo, Rp1200; 4 hours; Surabaya, Rp2500-4000; Cirebon or Jakarta (Rp22,000 First Class (on the *Mutiara*, and Rp9500 2nd Class, and Rp5800 3rd Class on the *Senja* "dusk" train. The *Mutiara Utara* a/c express train departs Jakarta's Kota Station at around 1630, arriving in Semarang at 0110. All trains pull into Semarang's central and historic Tawang Train Station. **by air:** From Jakarta on Garuda, Merpati, and Bouraq it takes 45-60 min. and costs Rp35,000-55,500. Fly from Bandung with Merpati, Rp40,000; or from Surabaya with Garuda, Rp33,400 (about 35 min.). A taxi from the A. Yani Airport into the city (8 km) costs Rp4500. A new toll road from the airport to Jl. Banyumaniki was completed in Aug. 1987. Alternatively, one can get a *bemo* from outside the airport, but it's a 15 min. walk to where you catch the *bemo*. If you don't want to stop in Semarang at all, catch a taxi from the airport all the way to Terminal Bis Induk for Rp4500. **by sea:** Semarang is a port of call for excursion ships whose passengers embark for Borobudur and other sights of C. Java; a taxi from the harbor into town costs Rp2000. Only *transmigrasi* ships leave from this port, but you may inquire about Pelni services out of the much larger ports of Jakarta or Surabaya at their office at Jl. Tantular 25 (tel. 20488).

Getting Around

The main city conveyance are bright orange Daihatsus, small Japanese microlets which run like ants all over town at a fixed price of Rp100. Flag one going in your direction, or go to Terminal Sendowo (or Stasiun Angkotan Kota), centrally located on Jl. Suari, only a 5-min. walk from the Metro Grand Park Hotel (Pasar Johar) and near Gereja Blenduk. From this station, Daihatsus spew forth in these directions: W to Pasar Karang Ayu, Ahmad Yani Airport, and Krapyak; E to Peterongan, THR (Tegalwareng Zoo), and Jomblang; S to Gombel and Banyumanik. Terminal Bis Induk, Semarang's main bus station (it means "Mother" Bus Station), is about 6 km from Pasar Johar; get there by Daihatsu from Jl. Suari (Rp150) or by blue city bus from in front of Hotel Oewa-Asia. If your hotel calls a taxi for you, it's more expensive. Just walk to the taxi stand at Johar Baru in front of Supermarket Metro; another smaller stand is behind Metro Grand Park Hotel. Hourly rate: Rp4000, or Rp4500 with a/c.

FROM SEMARANG

By Air

Ahmad Yani Airport is 8 km W of Semarang. Catch or call a taxi to the airport from Pasar Johar or behind the Metro Grand Park Hotel for Rp4500, or anywhere on the street flag down an orange Daihatsu to the airport for only Rp3000-4000. Or take a city bus from in front of Hotel Dibya Puri in the direction of Mangang, get off at the roundabout on the road to the airport, then walk 1.5 km to the airport on Jl. Kali Banteng. Garuda (Jl. Gajahmada 11, tel. 20178) has a handy shuttle service every hour (0720-1620) for only Rp55,000 to Jakarta or Rp35,100 to Surabaya; buy ticket at cash window. Merpati (Jl. Gajahmada 23, in front of Queen Hotel, tel. 23027) flies to Jakarta (Rp35,000), Ketapang (Rp73,150), and Pangkalanbun in C. Kalimantan (Rp53,800). Fly Bouraq (Jl. Pemuda 40A, tel. 23779) to Banjarmasin once daily for Rp81,700 and Bandung (via Jakarta), Rp47,600. Mandala, Jl. Pemuda (next to Bouraq), has a flight to Jakarta at 0700 each day for Rp37,000. **by bus:** Terminal Bis Induk (or Terminal Bis Terboyo) is 6 km from the city center, Rp150 by Daihatsu from Terminal Sendowo on Jl. Suari, or Rp4000 by taxi. To: Boyolali, Rp785; Blitar, Rp3860; Demak, Rp520; Kudus, Rp600; Malang, Rp5000; Pati, Rp810; Salatiga, Rp510; Yogya or Solo, Rp1200; Jakarta, Rp7500 (or Rp9500 by a/c night bus, 7 hours); Kediri, Rp3210; Pekalongan, Rp1500; Surabaya, Rp5000. **by train:** To Solo by fast train *(Cepat)*, Rp1200; or by slow train only Rp700. To Jakarta by *Senja Ekonomi*, Rp5800, departs 2050, arrives 0500; by *Senja Utama*, Rp9500, departs 2000, arrives 0400; by the *Mutiara*, Rp22,000, departs 2200, arrives 0600. From Semarang to Surabaya by *Gayabaru Malam I*, Rp4000, departs 2300, arrives 0500; by *KA Cepat*, Rp2500, departs 0530, arrives 1140. **travel agents:** These can help with tours, reservations, ticketing, and travel documents. Recommended is **Satura**, Complex Supermarket Simpang Lima (tel. 314161). Closer to downtown is the **Royal Java Tour & Travel**, Jl. Pemuda 11 (tel. 25870) in the Dibya Puri Hotel.

Vicinity Of Semarang
One km SW of Semarang's Ahmad Yani Airport is an immaculate **Dutch Cemetery** for civilians who died in Japanese detention camps during WW II. **Taman Lele** is a 6-ha park made up of 30% lowland plain and 70% high river and valley country. Also the site of a reptile exhibit, over 100 different kinds of snakes include Javanese pythons, as well as dead-but-alive crocodiles. **Gombel** is a cool, quiet recreation area in the hills S of Semarang. At 270 m above sea level, the park provides veiws of all of Semarang including ships anchored offshore. Lots of restaurants, plus a children's playground. **Gua Kreo** is another natural area S of Semarang which has been designed for day excursions with a cave, waterfall, and a multitude of stray monkeys. Near **Weleri**, 40 km W of Semarang on the road to Pekalongan, are some of Java's only surviving teakwood forests; they're up in the mountains at Banuputih, and more at Plelen. Twelve km N of Weleri is **Sendang Sikucing Beach**, where traditional fishermen put to sea. Heading W from Weleri, you start going over some big hills, the air gets cooler, the vegetation thicker—what Java used to look like. Quite refreshing if traveling on a day bus.

SOUTH OF SEMARANG

Ambarawa
A small mountain town (elev. 474 m) 40 km S or one hour by bus (Rp500) from Semarang. Or take a bus from Yogya (90 km, 2½ hours) via Magelang; Rp1000. A pivotal clash took place in Ambarawa between the Dutch and revolutionaries in 1949; a huge ugly statue in Ambarawa commemorates this famous action. **The Railway Museum** (Museum Kereta Api) is nearby the old Ambarawa train station complex where locomotives built from 1891 to 1927 in Germany, Holland, and elsewhere are exhibited. Used to pull former trains in Indonesia, all 25 or so iron beasts were collected from other museums on Java. Free admission. **accommodations: Peng. Sederhana** is close to the Railway Museum. **Hotel Aman**, Jl. Pemuda 14, is a 5-min. walk up the street. Their cheapest rooms are Rp3500 s, Rp5000 d. Right in front of the hotel there's a place to eat.

Cog Railway
The only operating cog railway on Java can be experienced on the **Railway Mountain Tour** from Ambarawa to the villages of Jambu and Bedono, 15 km distance uphill. Ride in antique coaches, remodeled according to the original designs, and hauled by a 1903 steam locomotive. The cogwheel is still running, its beautifully working engine in prime shape. All working parts are original. The engineer starts burning fuel wood and coal in the locomotive around 0400 and by 0900 the engine is ready for the climb. In the middle of the climb the cogwheel stops and the passengers hop down, take pictures, rest, have a picnic. To sign up for this special tourist attraction, inquire at the PJKA office, Jl. Thamrin 3, Semarang, or at the Municipality Tourist Office (Dinas Pariwisata) in Wisma Pancasila on Jl. Simpang Lima (tel. 288690).

Bandungan
This popular 981-m-high resort is always crowded, especially during the holidays. It's remarkable that this remote and traditional area is only one hour's drive from Semarang! First take a minibus from Semarang to Ambarawa, then turn NW off the main road and follow the small road for about 7 km. Or from Ungaran, travel about 3 km out of town to the turnoff. Bandungan produces abundant vegetables, fruits, and decorative flowers; there are even flower *warung!* The locals hire out horses to explore the surrounding countryside. On these mountain roads the women dress in colorful turbans and *sarung kebaya*. **accommodations and food:** Numerous hotels and *penginapan* rent rooms from Rp4000-35,000 s. Check out **Peng. Sri Rejeki** and the nearby **Riani I** which charge Rp4000-12,000 s or d. Even cheaper hotels, such as the **Santosa** and **Parahita**, are found lower down the mountain. The **Wisma Kereta Api**, run by the PJKA (Railway Authority), was built in classical 1930s' art-deco architecture; picturesque bungalows rent for Rp8,000-Rp20,000. The *wisma* overlooks the swimming pool and the plains of C. Java. Avoid the restaurant which serves terrible food. The 40-room **Hotel Wina** (Rp8000-35,000 d), higher up the mountain, has sweeping views. Places out of town also with exquisite views include the **Rawa Pening Hotel** (Rp15,800 s) and the **Pojok Sari** (Rp8000 s). Camping spots can be found among pine trees at Gedung Songo, 15 km distance. Lots of *warung* in town. Shop for fruit in the *pasar pagi* near the intersection to Gedung Songo.

Gedung Songo
This archaeological park, whose name means "Nine Temples," is located 7 km from Bandungan on the slopes of a small valley on the southern side of G. Ungaran. This group (actually 7 temples) was built in the 8th century (730 to 780). The complex, approx. 15 km from Ambarawa, can be reached from hilly Bandungan. Take a bus first from Semarang to Am-

barawa (Rp800), then change to a minibus to Bandungan (Rp350). Or take a bus from Semarang to Ungaran, then 3 km from town hop on the back of a motorcycle up the mountain for Rp500 (worth it). Though vehicles can drive to the first temple up an incredibly steep road, even better is to walk to Gedung Songo from Bandungan through a region of vegetable patches, roses, and pine trees. Rent horses up to the top for about Rp4000 an hour. These *candi*, at around 900 m altitude, are at probably the most beautiful temple location on Java. Although most of the main shrines of each group were dedicated to Shiva, one temple was set aside for Vishnu, a Hindu god rarely worshipped on Java. See Temple II with its well-preserved *kala-makara* relief on the portal; this site was chosen with great care for its magnificent views that take in G. Ungaran (2,050 m), Danau Rawapening, G. Merbabu (3,142 m), and even hazy G. Merapi (2,914 m). Walk the ancient pilgrims' trails; allow about one hour to visit all the sites.

Lake Rawapening

The largest lake in C. Java, surrounded by mountains and green hills, has an unusual marsh of floating rice paddies caused by released gases from the lake's floor. From Ambarawa, if you walk along the edge of the lake to the E you run into Muncul village with its crystal-clear swimming pool. The *warung* around the pool serve fried goldfish and *nasi pecel*.
Banyubiru: Beyond Muncul is Banyubiru on the shore of Lake Rawapening, NW of Salatiga. Banyubiru was the site of a women's concentration camp during the Japanese occupation; it still holds political prisoners (mostly male). Indonesia stands in history as probably the first country ever to accept concentration camps from its occupying power (also bequeathed was the notorious Boven Digul camp at Tanah Merah, Irian Jaya).

Kopeng

A 1,400-m-high resort about 15 km from Salatiga, on the slopes of G. Merbabu, easy to reach from Salatiga by minibus. Enjoy the bracing cold air, mountain walks and scenery, horse rides, and dips in the deep swimming pool. The town has a pleasant old hotel with a restaurant and its many bungalows and *pasanggrahan* range from Rp4500-35,000 s or d. **Hotel Victoria** costs Rp6000; restaurant next door.

Magelang

The cool city of Magelang (pop. 115,000) is a crossroads town connecting 3 big C. Javanese cities: Yogya (42 km SE), Semarang, and Purworejo. On the way from Yogya to Magelang, you pass the turnoff to Borobudur to the west. Magelang is a town of heroes. During the Java War (1825-1830), the guerilla leader Diponegoro was tricked into negotiating with the Dutch and captured here. Visit the room where this nobleman was taken prisoner and see some artifacts. Diponegoro was sent into exile in Makassar for the remaining 25 years of his life. Later, the town's residents fought bravely in the revolution (1945-1950) and on the town's crest 2 bamboo spears symbolize their struggle against the Dutch. In keeping with its bellicose traditions, Magelang is today the location of the national military academy, AKABRI. **Musium Akabri,** one km from the city's center on the AKABRI campus, features displays explaining the training of the cadets at the academy and some historical artifacts. Also see **Musium Soedirman,** Jl. Badaan, Blok C-F. Out of town is **Ambarawa,** a remarkable Dutch colonial rectangular stone security fortress surrounded by diamond-shaped blockhouses.

KUDUS

Kudus lies 54 NE of Semarang, Rp650 by bus, or 20 km E of Demak. The name Kudus has its origins in the founding of a mosque here in 1546 by Sunan Kudus, one of Java's *wali* (holy men). Though a staunch Islamic town (censoring looks if you wear shorts), some old Hindu customs prevail: cows may not be slaughtered within the city limits and schoolboys still spend a night at the shrine of Sunan Muria (at Colo, 18 km N) to improve their chances in exams. Kudus is a rich clove town, famed as a center for the clove cigarette industry (nearly 25% of Indonesia's annual output). The *Kiajis* of Kudus (in the Old Town) have a reputation as healers. It's easy getting around town, either walking or by *becak* which are really cheap in this town, as low as Rp2000 per hour! The *becak* drivers are very polite, tilting the *becak* forward so you can climb in easier and then lifting it up again when you want to climb out — rarely found *becak* etiquette!

Sights

One km beyond the *alun-alun* in the Kauman (Old Town) is ancient **Al Manar Mosque** containing a famous minaret. First built by Sunan Kudus in 1546, this mosque has undergone numerous improvements and modifications. The 20-m-high, red-brick minaret in front, built around 1685, closely resembles the temple-building style of E. Java. Combining both Hindu and Islamic architecture, it actually looks like a Javanese Hindu temple. This *menara* is so radically different from the traditional Muslim minarets in Saudi Arabia or Egypt that it is really just a modified *kulkul* tower (watchtower) which was added to fortified temples during Hindu times to warn rice farmers of danger. It's now used to announce the Islamic daily prayers and you may climb the wooden ladder inside for a view over the city. Malam Dandang takes place annually during Ramadan; this traditional ceremony is connected with the opening of the Al Manar Mosque.

KUDUS

NOT TO SCALE

1. *menara* (minaret)
2. Hotel Duta Wisata
3. Arry Art
4. market
5. bank
6. Hotel Slamet
7. police station
8. post office
9. Garuda Restaurant
10. mosque
11. Kembang Express
12. Hotel Notosari
13. Djarum Kretek Factory
14. bank
15. train station
16. bus terminal
17. RM Hijau

In the rear of the complex is the elaborately carved and inlaid mausoleum of Sunan Kudus. Wander the narrow streets of the staunchly Islamic *Kauman;* ask directions to the ruins of the Hindu-period **Mesjid Bubar.**

Kretek Factories

Clove cigarettes were invented in the 1920s by an entrepreneur who claimed the smoke ameliorated his asthma. Indonesians now smoke over 36,000 tons of cloves a year, outstripping domestic supplies and even importing cloves from Madagascar and Zanzibar. Take free tours at the factories of Djarum, Noryorono, Seokun, Jambu Boh, etc. Chinese-owned Djarum, established in 1952, is now the biggest, having made spectacular ground on Gudang Garam over the past several years. Djarum's 17 factory buildings each produces a million hand-rolled *kretek* cigarettes per day. Five hundred people work in the rolling shed; some roll up to 5,000 a day. In the packaging building 2,000 women work like ants, all dressed so fine in dainty *kebaya* and jewelry. Visit Djarum's modern offices on Jl. Jen. A. Yani and take part in a free tour.

Accommodations

About 10 *penginapan* and hotels range from Rp2500 to Rp6500. Homey **Losmen Dewi Tungal,** Jl. Kenari 2, is quite central and close to the *bis malam* offices; Rp2500 pp. **Losmen Amin,** Jl. Manur 448, is cheap and adequate. **Peng. Sederhana,** in Desa Rendang at the end of Jl. Jen. Sudirman, is near Pasar Kliwon. Also on Jl. Jen. Sudirman (no. 63) is **Losmen Slamat;** Rp2500 s, Rp4500 d; the Flamingo Cafe is at the same address. Their menu is in Indonesian, so it's the real thing. **Hotel Duta Wisata**, Jl. Sunan Muria-Barongan 194 (tel. 694), is a poor-man's plush hotel. Their cheapest rooms are Rp6000 d, not including a 10% service charge and 10% tax. It's a quiet place on a back street. Moving up in price, the town's premier hotel is **Notosari**, Jl. Kepodang 17 (tel. 21245). Within walking distance of the bus station, rooms start at around Rp12,000 with breakfast and go up to Rp21,500 with a/c. Friendly people, clean, quiet, and good service.

Food

A *pasar malam* springs up around the *alun-alun* each evening. Kudus is known for a few specialty dishes, among which are *soto ayam* and porridge; sample at the bus terminal *warung* or at **Simpang Tujuh** in front of Kantor Kabupaten. The people of Kudus are for the most part prohibited from eating beef, but buffalo meat, chicken, goat, and fish are all available. Try the specialty *jenang kudus*, made of glutinous rice, brown sugar, and coconut. Another specialty is chicken soup *(soto kudus);* experience it in the Kudus Bus Terminal. **The Garuda Restaurant**, Jl. Jen. Sudirman 1, offers Javanese, European, and Chinese dishes in the Rp2500-3500 range.

From Kudus

The minibus station is right behind the bus station. Sample fares: Demak, Rp500 (25 km); Semarang, Rp650 (55 km, 1 hour); Surabaya, Rp6000 (286 km); Jakarta, Rp7500; Jepara, Rp500 (38 km); Rembang, Rp500; Mayong, Rp500; Solo, Rp2000 (2 hours). Kembang Express, Jl. Jen. A. Yani 90 (tel. 282), has night and morning buses to Yogya, Rp2000 (2 hours).

Vicinity Of Kudus

Colo, 18 km N at the foot of G. Muria (750 m), is a recreational spot with cool, healthy, cloudy weather. Catch a minibus from Simpang Lima and ride up the mountain; stay at the *penginapan*. About 1 ½ km N of Colo is **Montel Falls**. West of the resort, climb the thousand steps to the grave of Sunan Muria. Colo's specialties are *nasi pecel pakis* and *ayam panggang* which can be bought at many of the *warung*. **Mayong:** The birthplace of Kartini is in Mayong, 12 km NW of Kudus or 25 km S of Jepara on the way to Kudus. The house is 50 m from the highway. The daughter of a Javanese civil servant in the Dutch colonial government, Raden Ajeng Kartini (1879-1904) wrote the most important Indonesian literary work of this century—in Dutch! Titled originally *Through Darkness to Light* in 1911, the letters have been reissued by the University Press of America in 1985 under the title *Letters of a Javanese Princess.* The *Letters* providing a fascinating picture of the life and spirit of the times. Although she died in childbirth at only age 24, Kartini posthumously became a spokesperson for liberation and education of women and an advocate for Indonesian nationalist aspirations.

Pilgrimages are still made to her grave near Rembang every April 21 to celebrate Kartini Day. In Rembang's Kantor Kabupaten is the **Kartini Museum. P. Seprapat:** In the estuary of the Silugonggo River, 12 km from Pati, see wild monkeys and the fairytale tomb of Ki Ludang.

the Demak mosque

Demak

Twenty-five km NE of Semarang on the road to Surabaya, Demak was once the capital of the first Islamic kingdom on Java. Although it was a prosperous seaport up until the 16th century, because of the heavy silting of its harbor Demak is now 3 km inland. In 1428, the Islamic ruler Raden Patah built Demak's wooden mosque, **Mesjid Agung**. This is the oldest mosque on Java, considered so holy that 7 pilgrimages to it are the equivalent of one pilgrimage to Mecca. The structure is a prime example of the joint architectural influences of the Java-Hindu and Islamic cultures. Legend has it that the great mosque, with its 3-tiered roof and open hall, was built in a single night. Four of the nine *wali* erected the 4 main pillars; the pillars of the outer hall were said to have been taken from the court of Majapahit after its fall in 1518. Symbolism abounds. The 3 tiers of the roof, for example, are said to symbolize the 3 main levels of religious consciousness, while the 5 doorways the 5 fundamentals of Islamic teaching. Newly refurbished and renovated, President Suharto himself officiated at the rededication ceremonies in April 1987. Inside are many relics. Behind the mosque, visit the venerated grave of the founder of the Demak kingdom, Raden Patah. Sunan Kalijaga's mausoleum is found at Kadilangu, 2 km S of Demak. On Besar 10 of the Javanese calendar, tens of thousands gather here to celebrate Idhul Adha Day.

JEPARA

A small town 90 km NE (Rp950 by bus) of Semarang on the N coast, or Rp500 (38 km) from Kudus' Terminal Bis. Jepara was the main port of the mighty 8th C. Hindu Mataram empire, playing an important role in rice export. Now it's a scruffy country town, noteworthy as the center of some of the best traditional carvers on Java. Jepara's other name is Kota Ukir, "the carving town." Except for the hinges, no nails, screws, or metal joinery are used. The wood comes from Blora and Cepu (E. Java)—teakwood mostly, but also mahogany, *kayu meranti*, and *sono* wood. Coming into town you start to see shops with bedstands, furniture, tables, chairs, couches, cabinets piled high inside and out. Paid by the meter, men come in from the surrounding villages to carve in the shops. To see them in action, visit the nearby villages of Tahunan, Mantingan, and Blakanggunung. Purchase furniture, jewelery boxes, wooden buttons (Rp2000 for 12). Many shops are concentrated along Jl. Pemuda. Learn carving? S.T.N. (Bagian Ukir) offers a 3-year course in both modern and traditional styles. An old Dutch VOC fort and graveyard lie in the vicinity of Jepara.

Accommodations And Food

Right next to the noisy bus station on Jl. Kol. Sugiono is **Hotel Terminal**; rooms with European toilet cost Rp15,000 d with a/c. They also have rooms for Rp3500 with just a sink inside, no fan, but good lighting. Many rooms face a garden, and there's a restaurant attached. Try also **Losmen Asia**, Jl. Kartini 36, or **Losmen Jakarta**, Jl. Pemuda 16—both are in the Rp5000-6500 range. At the Terminal Bis, eat at **RM Rahayu**. The Ritz of Jepara is the **Memo Jaya Inn**, Jl. Diponegoro 40/B (tel. 143); Rp6000-12,000 d.

Vicinity Of Jepara

Kartini Beach is 2 km from town. Rent a *prahu* and visit nearby Pulau Mandalika; nice swimming. Seven km E of Jepara is Pantai Bandengan, one of the few beaches in all of C. Java which is clean with clear water; also a camping area here. A Portuguese fortress lies on the on the steep coast in Desa Kelet E of Jepara; get a *bemo* first to Keling, then on to Kelet for Rp550, then by foot to the fort. At **Mantingan** (locally known as Makam Sunan), 8 km from Jepara or 20 km S of Rembang, are remains of an old mosque (1559) and cemetery. Charter a minibus for Rp3000, or by *andong* down a lovely country lane, Rp1500. Examine the Hindu-style medallions on the tomb of Ratu Kalinjamat, a warrior-queen of Jepara who attacked the Portuguese fortress in Melaka twice in the 1500s. Though they appear as leaf decorations, when viewed from a distance you can make out the figure of a monkey. Although Islamic religious laws forbade representing living creatures, the desire to draw people and animals was so strong that the sculptors composed them of leaves and flowers.

DIENG PLATEAU

The oldest temples of Java lie at 2,093 m altitude on this pear-shaped plateau, 26 km NW of Wonosobo. A sacred spot since early times, this enchanting highland offers lovely mountain scenery, a cool climate, fascinating volcanic fissures, and ancient Hindu temples named after the heros of the *wayang*. Dieng was once a huge volcano which erupted; the remaining caldera, after thousands of years of weathering, has become the present soggy plateau. Under the powerful Saliendra Dynasty, small Indian-style temples were built beginning in the 9th century. Archaeologists first believed present-day remains indicated that Dieng was a ruined city, but realized later that Dieng was just a flourishing temple complex of hermitages housing priests, attendants, servants, and visiting pilgrims. The name Dieng comes from *Di Hyang* meaning "Abode of the Gods." At that time Dieng was reached by 2 huge stairways, one of which was reputed to have had 4,000 steps! An elaborate system of irrigation ditches kept the ground dry and level, but after 1000 years of neglect Dieng has reverted to swamp. Dieng is still an extremely active geothermal area and one can walk right up to the rims of boiling, smoking, odorous cauldrons! In June 1979, poisonous gases rose from underground passages and from several lakes, killing 150 villagers. A geothermal power plant has been established near Kawah Sikidang.

One can spend days just hiking around; sturdy footwear is recommended as the ground is often waterlogged. The energetic can walk to many sites within minutes, including Sembungan, the highest (2,160 m) village on Java. Like G. Bromo's crater in E. Java, at night in the dry season Dieng's temperature could drop to freezing, so dress accordingly. Get there in the morning because by early afternoon a thick silvery mist creeps down the wooded slopes and wraps the whole plateau in a chilly white blanket. The cold watery mists make an excellent environment for the rich green grasses and dozens of species of flowers—dahlias and marigolds, lupines and roses—which enhance the strange beauty of the plateau. Around the lakes reeds grow as tall as 2.5 m! Bring paints, charcoal, or crayons; this eerie plateau has always been a favorite artists' subject. At the entrance road to Dieng, pay Rp300 at the tollgate where a man sells hand-colored Dieng Plateau maps for Rp200.

Kawah Sileri And Sikidang

Among the many natural wonders are Kawah Siki-

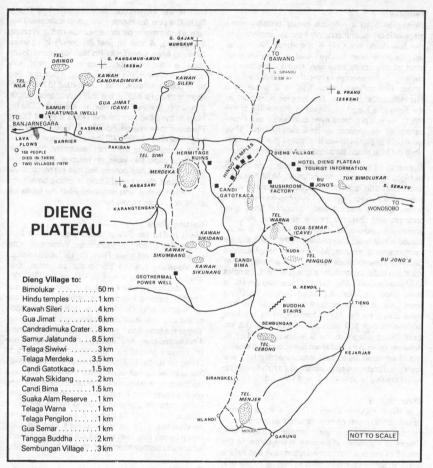

Dieng Village to:

Bimolukar	50 m
Hindu temples	1 km
Kawah Sileri	4 km
Gua Jimat	6 km
Candradimuka Crater	8 km
Samur Jalatunda	8.5 km
Telaga Siwiwi	3 km
Telaga Merdeka	3.5 km
Candi Gatotkaca	1.5 km
Kawah Sikidang	2 km
Candi Bima	1.5 km
Suaka Alam Reserve	1 km
Telaga Warna	1 km
Telaga Pengilon	1 km
Gua Semar	1 km
Tangga Buddha	2 km
Sembungan Village	3 km

dang and Kawah Sileri, as well as a number of other crater lakes, each sparkling with strange shimmering colors, boiling with sulphur mud, while whitish smoke hovers over their surfaces. To the sides of the craters the crystals of bright yellow sulphur outcroppings glitter in the sunlight. Kawah Sileri ("Hot Lake") looks very hot, with smoke and vapors rising out of it, and a strong sulphur smell, but it's a magical area. Walking around it can be dangerous: if you step on a weak spot in the caked mud you'll boil your feet.

Gua Semar

Several small caves are situated on a peninsula between the lakes Tel. Warna and Tel. Pengilen. Gua Semar is popularly believed to be the dwelling place of the clown-god Semar. In this famous cave many Indonesians go to meditate; Suharto has been known to spend the night here when things are piling up. The fate of Portuguese Timor may have been sealed in this cave when Suharto and the then-Australian Prime Minister Whitlam confered within its dank walls in 1974; in April 1975 the Indonesian army invaded the former Portuguese colony. There's a whole ritual to go through to visit it. Bathe first at Bimolukar (gives you "a pliable heart" and "a swift mind"), then walk into the cave where flowers are laid and incense burns. The cave is said to be the exact physical center of Java. Nice camping along Tel. Warna but stay away from the sulphur fumes bubbling out of part of the lake.

Temples

Dieng has been a religious center possibly since megalithic times, and certainly from the beginning of the Java-Hindu era. Only 8 of perhaps 200 original temples have been restored over a 10-sq-km area; most of the others have only their foundations remaining. In the swampy center of the plateau, a crater whose rim collapsed eons ago, is a group of 5 Hindu-Buddhist temples. The temples were built by the Saliendra Kingdom, begun in the middle of the 8th C., which pre-dates even Borobudur and Prambanan. All monuments are dedicated to Shiva. They were built as places of worship, not to glorify kings as were the later Hindu-Buddhist monuments of C. Java.

The *candi* are each very compactly built, none over 15 m high, with sparse ornamentation. Most have the same basic shape: a square, squat base with a vestibule in front and projections for niches on the other 3 sides. Strong vertical and horizontal lines give strength and character to the structures, most of which are two-storied. Over the entrance is often placed a *kala*-head; also peculiar to the Dieng site are sinister animal mounts. Many of the temples share uncanny resemblances with temple architecture of southern India, in particular a group of 7th C. temples at Mamallapuram. After 10 centuries, they are still in fairly good condition. All extant temples on Dieng were given their names (after members of the Pandava clan from the *Mahabharata* epic) by the local population over 100 years ago. Candi Bima (1.5 km from Dieng village) to the S is unique in all of Indonesia: faces in its roof seem like spectators looking out of windows. Its elegant lines, pyramidal roof, and lovely sculpture are reminiscent of its more sophisticated ancestors: Prambanan and Mendut.

Other Sights

Gua Jimat ("Death Valley") Cave, a volcanic vent, pours out so much carbon dioxide that animals cannot live here; this is a world-famous ecological site. Traces of a palace can be seen in the center of the plain E of the Gua Semar meditation cave and Arjuna Temple. Stone staircases used to lead up to this site, and you can still see remains of a complicated underground tunnel system which once drained the crater floor. Along a rocky woodland path 2 km S of the lakes is a pool of hot bubbling mud where geysers and sulphur fumes shoot from the earth. About 10 km E of Dieng village is a Trappist monastery. A guesthouse is set aside for visitors, but women aren't allowed to enter the monastery itself.

Accommodations And Food

Consider sleeping in a tent under those brilliant stars, but bring a good sleeping bag or shiver. About 8 *losmen* are located in or around Dieng village. Some have wooden balconies overlooking it all, some provide quilts. One of the best places to stay is comfortable **Bu Jono's**, the small *losmen* with the little old

man at the intersection as you come into Dieng; Rp3500 s or d for rooms up a steep staircase. They have a spare menu; better fare can be had at **Warung Sederhana**. A little bit past Bu Jono's is **Losmen Gunung Mas**, which asks Rp3500 for rooms downstairs, a little more for rooms upstairs: dirty, rundown, no water in the toilets—avoid if possible. Better is **Losmen Sederhana** on the road to the mushroom factory; Rp3000 d, but they may accept Rp2000 if business is slow. Very basic, no electricity. The big hotel in the village on the main road is **Hotel Dieng Plateau**; they charge Rp8000 d, though you can negotiate down to Rp5000 in the off-season. They offer a *mandi* inside the room, electricity, hot water, blankets, paper-thin walls, no balcony. *Warung* here serve the usual *nasi goreng* and *mie goreng* and one of the great pleasures of Dieng is eating back-home cornbread, beans, and potatoes; what the locals eat since rice doesn't grow here.

Getting There

Dieng is 119 km SW of Semarang, 110 km from Yogya, and 26 km N of Wonosobo. Wonosobo is the usual jumping off point. From Yogya, take a minibus to Magelang (visiting Borobudur en route), then another minibus or *bemo* to Wonosobo (Rp1000). From Wonosobo take a minibus or *bemo* up to Dieng (Rp950), passing tobacco plantations, rugged steep landscapes with clouds below the road, bamboo aqueducts, pale eucalyptus, sleeping volcanos. From Yogya the total direct trip to Wonosobo takes almost 4 hours and costs Rp2500-3000. It's easier to join one of Yogya's myriad tour groups which do tours to Dieng for Rp7500-10,000; inquire at your hotel desk. Yet another access route is from Java's north coast via Bawang; it takes about 4 hours to travel to Dieng on this route from Pekalongan. If coming from Bandung, consider stopping at Dieng before arriving in Yogya. Take the 0510 train to Kroya, then a minibus to Wonosobo. Or go to Bandung's Terminal Cicaheum by city bus, then take a local bus to Purwokerto where you change to another minibus for Wonosobo.

From Dieng

Buses and *bemo* leave Dieng every 5 min. or so down to Wonosobo (Rp900, one hour). A unique exit from the Dieng Plateau is the 13-km walk N down to Bawang, leaving the plateau by G. Sipandau. This walk requires good shoes with traction as the path is often slippery. Pass through villages which have seldom seen foreigners. Steps are cut into the path; you lose all that altitude in just 4 hours. From Bawang take a regular bus or *bemo* to Pekalongan, Rp600. If you start early, you'll be in Pekalongan by that afternoon.

Via Garung

Leaving Dieng about 0630, first head for Telaga Cebong which sits right at the edge of a cliff going down into a valley. Just before you reach the village

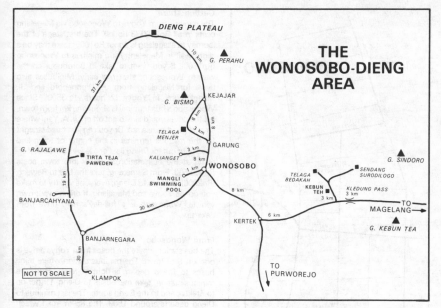

THE
WONOSOBO-DIENG
AREA

DIENG PLATEAU

G. PERAHU

G. BISMO

KEJAJAR

TELAGA MENJER

GARUNG

G. RAJALAWE

TIRTA TEJA PAWEDEN

KALIANGET

WONOSOBO

G. SINDORO

MANGLI SWIMMING POOL

TELAGA BEDAKAH

SENDANG SURODILOGO

KEBUN TEH

KLEDUNG PASS

TO MAGELANG

BANJARCAHYANA

KERTEK

G. KEBUN TEA

BANJARNEGARA

TO PURWOREJO

NOT TO SCALE

KLAMPOK

of Sembungan, a path leads off to the R down into a very steep valley. The only path into the valley at this point, it's quite noticeable (if you take the wrong path you end up in a cabbage patch). Find your way down the side of the valley along a cliffside path. About halfway between Telaga Cebong and Sirangkel (it's difficult to imagine a more beautiful site for a village), there's a water slide over rock which falls about 75 m. From Sirangkel, you must walk to the road that connects Wonosobo and Dieng village. Beyond Sirangkel you walk through a small village on the L-hand side; this is a shortcut to Menjer. You could also walk to the village of Mlandi and get transportation all the way to Garung, then from Garung hop a *bemo* farther to Wonosobo. From Dieng to Mlandi it takes 3 hours; it's so steep you move right along. Then it's maybe another hour's walk from Mlandi to Garung. Paths also lead from Mlandi all the way to Wonosobo.

WONOSOBO DISTRICT

The district's largest town, Wonosobo is a busy country town and favorite stopping-off point while *en route* to Dieng. In this mountainous area (elev. 772 m), rain falls about half the days of the year; average temperature is 20-25 degrees Celsius. Wonosobo is surrounded by G. Sindoro, G. Sumbing, the Kulon Mountains, the Dieng Plateau, and G. Perahu. The district produces an abundance of vegetables, tobac-

co, *klembak, cayuputi, pyrethum* and *kecang babi.* For detailed information about Wonosobo and environs, the **Tourist Information Center** is in the Gedung Sasana Bhakti 45, Jl. Pemuda 1 (tel. 194), on the S side of the *alun-alun.* Souvenir shops: **Dendeng Favorit**, Jl. A. Yani 3 (tel. 163) and **Wisma Galar**, Jl. Dieng 254. Two banks, **BNI** and **BRI**, are on Jl. A. Yani.

Accommodations

Hotel Petra, Jl. Jen. Yani 81, is easy to reach since it's near the terminal and the main shopping center; Rp3500 s. **Losmen Widuri**, Jl. Tanggung 20, is not bad; Rp3500. **Losmen Surya**, on the corner of Jl. A. Yani and Jl. Penjara, asks Rp3000 s. **Hotel Nirwana**, Jl. Tanggung 18, is comfortable and more expensive at Rp6000-10,000; offers afternoon tea and full breakfast with double room. **Hotel Merdeka**, Jl. Sindoro 2 (tel. 53), is clean, but offers little in the way of food or service. The new **Hotel Bima**, Jl. Achmad Yani 5, has clean, Western-style *mandi* with hot water; Rp25,000 d including breakfast.

Food

Wonosobo's food is vastly superior to the fare up on the Dieng Plateau; might be a good idea to bring some snacks up the mountain. The specialty of Wonosobo is *kacang babi* and *dendeng gepuk* (crushed spiced dry meat), sold in many shops. Recommended eateries are: **Dieng Restaurant**, Jl.

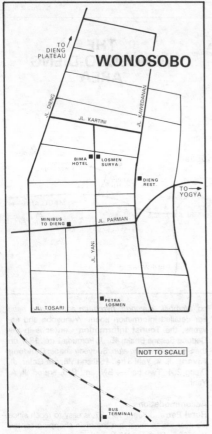

Getting There
The minibus from Yogya to Wonosobo via Magelang costs in all Rp2500 (3 hours). The first stage of the journey to Magelang is about Rp1000; there may be a slight wait in Magelang for a minibus to Wonosobo (Rp1500). If you want to take in Borobudur on the way to Wonosobo, start *real* early. Minibuses also leave for Magelang from Jl. Diponegoro and Jl. Mangkubumi in Yogya (2 hours, Rp3500). Since Wonosobo's bus terminal is about one km from town, tell the driver you'd like to get off on Jl. A. Yani where several good hotels are. Or you can just head straight for the minibus terminal in the center of town and head right out for Dieng (last one leaves at 1800). If arriving at the bus station, a *dokar* into town costs Rp400-500. From Semarang, take the bus to Bawang (Rp2000), then up to Dieng; everyone will try to make you go via Yogya and Magelang. If driving your own vehicle, Wonosobo is a full-day's hard drive from Jakarta.

From Wonosobo
The bus station where the buses from Yogya arrive is one km S of town. The minibus station where minibuses to Dieng depart is right in town. From the minibus station, take minibuses to Dieng, farther on to Krakan, and to the E and south. The last minibus to Dieng departs around 1800. The 85-km road which links Wonosobo and Banyumas runs beside a foaming, rocky river called Kali Serayu; enjoy green valleys on both sides of the river. To Cilacap, buses leave Wonosobo early morning and mid-morning; Rp2000, 6 hours. If you intend to take the ferry from Cilacap to Pangandaran, take the Purwokerto bus at 0530 (Rp1500, 3 hours), then from Purwokerto to Cilacap (Rp1000, 3 hours); the minibus arrives in time to meet the ferry to Pangandaran. To Semarang, buses depart early in the morning and travel via Secang and Ambarawa; Rp2000 (4 hours). For Jakarta, Remaja Travel (Jl. A. Yani 83) has *bis malam* departing at 1600; Rp7500, 14 hours.

Vicinity Of Wonosobo
Kalianget is a hot-water sulphur spring 3 km N of Wonosobo on the road to Dieng. The water is said to cure skin disease, stiff aching muscles, and the weariness of a long, tiring journey. **Telaga Menjer**, a 1,200-m-high cool mountain lake, 45-m-deep with an area of 70 ha, is 12 km N of Wonosobo, reachable in 30 min. by minibus for Rp500. **Kebun Tea** plantation is 17 km E of Wonosobo; **Lake Telaga Bedakah** is 3 km N and springs at **Sendang Surodilogo** are 4 km east. **Tirta Teja Paweden** is a swimming pool and playground 19 km N of Banjarnegara, 50 km W of Wonosobo. **Klampok** is a ceramics center 30 km S of Banjarnegara.

Kawedanan 23, which has excellent food, including a number of dishes with (straight) mushrooms from the factory up on the plateau; the average meal costs Rp1500 *(mie goreng* with mushrooms), Rp900 for mushroom soup. The managers, L. Agus Tjugianto and his wife, are nice, soft-spoken, helpful, and informative. **Anda Bar & Restaurant**, Jl. Kawedanan 25, serves tasty Chinese food at reasonable prices. For baked goods, **Toko Roti ABC** is the best. **Asia Restaurant**, Jl. Kawedanan 35 (tel. 165), is run by a whole family of benevolent Chinese albinos! Amazing cooking at fair prices—especially the fried fish with sweet and sour sauce, the Asia fried chicken, and the Hong Kong fried spring rolls. Out of town, **Restaurant Kledung Pass** is a popular roadside restaurant on the way up to Dieng.

YOGYAKARTA

One of the largest villages in the world, Yogyakarta (usually shortened to "Yogya"—pronounced "JOAG-jah") is Java's cultural capital and an important center for higher learning—Java's Kyoto. For centuries a royal city and major trade center, the Yogya *kraton* is the highest-ranking court in Indonesia and "Special Region Yogyakarta" (pop. 3 million) is still responsible directly to the central government in Jakarta and not to the provincial head of C. Java. From 1946-1950, Yogya was the grassroots capital of Indonesia and the headquarters of the revolutionary forces. Today, with its rich culture, economy hotels and restaurants, it's a city streamlined for travelers. Well-known as the "main door to traditional Javanese culture," the city draws thousands of talented people from around the world. There are numerous music and dance schools; brilliant choreographers; drama and poetry workshops; folk theater and *wayang* troupes; and its artists excel in the plastic arts. It's also one of the best places to shop in SE Asia, if you know where to look. Along with Solo, Yogya is a major *batik*-producing center and because of increased tourist awareness this art is developing even higher standards. The painters and sculptors here are Indonesia's elite, strongly individualistic but increasingly commercialized.

History

Yogya lies in the center of Java's "Realm of the Dead," a city surrounded by ancient ruins. Only an hour away is the great Buddhist temple of Borobudur and the stately Hindu temple Prambanan, built in the 8th and 9th centuries respectively. The Mataram Empire of C. Java fell apart under Dutch pressure and formed the states of Surakarta (Solo) and Yogyakarta in 1755. Yogya is still governed by an ancient line of sultans and, in fact, it's the only functioning sultanate remaining in Indonesia. The layout of the city still reflects the traditional formal relationship between the sultan, marketplace, and the mosque. For the Javanese, Yogya has always been a symbol of nationalistic passion and resistance to alien rule. A stubborn

center of the guerilla struggle against the Dutch, during Indonesia's War of Independence it was the first capital of the infant Republic. During the Dutch occupation, the sultan locked himself in his *kraton* and when he finally consented to negotiate with the Dutch it was from the top of his palace wall looking down on them, with all his people watching. A 3-nation committee tried to bring the Dutch and Indonesians together here, but they could only agree on minor points. Finally, in 1948, the Dutch launched an all-out attack on the city, dropping 900 paratroopers, heavy bombs, and rocket fire while U.S.- and British-built planes strafed the streets. With all the Republican leaders captured and its ministries closed down, the rebel forces retired from Yogya to the countryside and carried out a people's war. The U.S. Senate, whose Marshall Plan money appeared to be supporting Holland's fight against the Republican army, threatened to withdraw support. Finally, in Dec. 1949, Holland formally recognized the new Republic. With the Javanese now in command, Solo's sultanate which had sided with the Dutch was summarily and unceremoniously dissolved, while Yogya's was rewarded its own status as a Special Region. The territory was allowed to govern itself and its sultan appointed as its first governor—a lifetime position—as well as Indonesia's first Vice President.

SIGHTS

Taman Sari (Water Palace)

A pleasure park built in feudal splendor between the years 1758 and 1765 for the sultan and his family. Like the Hanging Gardens of Babylon, Taman Sari once had lighted underwater corridors, cool subterranean mosques, meditation platforms in the middle of lily ponds, *gamelan* towers, and galleries for dancing, all in mock Spanish architecture. Princesses bathed in flower-strewn pools, streams flowed above covered passageways, and boats drifted in man-made lakes.

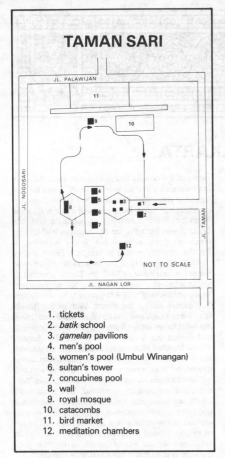

TAMAN SARI

JL. PALAWIJAN

JL. NOGOSARI

JL. TAMAN

NOT TO SCALE

JL. NAGAN LOR

1. tickets
2. *batik* school
3. *gamelan* pavilions
4. men's pool
5. women's pool (Umbul Winangan)
6. sultan's tower
7. concubines pool
8. wall
9. royal mosque
10. catacombs
11. bird market
12. meditation chambers

Today 60% of these "Fragrant Gardens" are still in ruins. Go on foot between 0800-1700; Rp150 admission. See the men's and women's bathing pools (where the harem was kept), and the underground mosque. Though sections of the ruins are being renovated, the ornate swimming pools and crumbling walls rebuilt, and many of the gates replastered, the gardens on the whole are in a decrepit and charming state of disrepair. Students will volunteer to work as guides to show you the most secret places. But the "living ruins" are much more interesting. The area of narrow dusty lanes and small houses behind the Water Palace is a center of the *batik* industry, where many painters work in bamboo studios. Guides could lead you into certain shops because they get a com-

mission on all sales from that shop. Also visit the Batik School. Pasar Ngasem, the grotty, cacophonous bird market N of Taman Sari, has parrots, orioles, roosters, and singing turtle doves *(perkutut)* in 9-m-high ornamental cages, plus such pet animals as squirrels, rabbits, and guinea pigs.

The *Kraton*

Built in 1757, this is the palace compound of the sultans of Yogyakarta—classical Javanese palace-court architecture at its finest. It costs Rp400, including a guide, to get into the front portion of the *kraton*, called *Pagelaran*, and another Rp400 to get into the *di dalam* portion (the inner sanctum). Open Sun. to Thurs. 0830-1230; Fri. to 1100, Sat. to 1230. Dress conservatively (men should wear long trousers). The population of this small city-within-a-city is about 25,000 (including jesters and 100 elderly, aloof court attendants). The *kraton* has *batik* and silver workshops, mosques, schools, markets, offices, and 2 museums, all enclosed by 3-m-thick white walls, one km long, their construction imitating European fortifications. Interiors especially remind one of pre-war Dutch bourgeois mansions. During the war of independence, guerilla commander Suharto (now President Suharto) dressed as a barefoot peasant and peddled vegetables at the rear of the *kraton* in order to confer with the sultan on guerilla tactics to use against the Dutch. See ornate and heavily gilded Bangsal Kencono (Golden Pavilion), with its carved solid teak pillars. The Glass Pavilion combines Hindu motifs, Buddhist lotus flowers, stylized opening words from the *Koran*, marble floors, and vortex ceilings. The sultan's collection is made up of *wayang* puppets, royal carriages, Raden Saleh portraits, and life-sized costumed figures (except for the sultan). A museum displays trappings of the sultanate, including a saddle made with gold and silver thread, royal heirlooms exuding an odor of sanctity (at the Proboyekso), huge 600-year-old brass gongs, a *gamelan* that was inaugurated during the Majapahit Empire—and much more. At the souvenir concession, buy copies of old photographic prints for Rp300 apiece—a good selection. The *batik* factory in the *kraton* is run by one of the sultan's sons, and is well worth a visit since the process is still completely unmechanized. His prices are pretty reasonable too, and he carries the full range of traditional court designs. To visit *all* parts of this palace, first put in an application at the Kraton Office. To videotape, permission is required from the tourist office.

Kraton Performances

The inner court, with male and female steps to the entrance, has 2 small museums and a pavilion where you may see a classical dance rehearsal each Sun. between 1030 and 1200. Also on Mon. and Wed. from 1030 to 1200, traditional *gamelan* rehearsals (without dancing) are staged. Both performances are included in the price of admission. The standards of the performance here are highest in the country. The Yogya dance style, created by Sultan Hamango Kubowono I (1755-1772) in time of war, reflects an almost military discipline of mind and body. Dancers are awesomely distant and withdrawn with all their pauses, silences, meditative poses, and motions arrested in space. In the dances put on by this court, even the jangle of bells is considered coarse; anklets are used only for monkey and animal roles played by men.

The Pakualaman

On Jl. Sultan Agung, this is the other *kraton* of Yogya, a princedom founded within the sultanate of Yogya by Paku Alam I in 1813. Having intermarried considerably, the Pakualam royalty has many connections with the *kraton* family in Solo. This court also receives visitors. *Gamelan* concerts are held here about once every 5th Sunday. Open 0800-1300; donation requested. Yet another fine example of Javanese *kraton* architecture is the Ambarrukmo palace built by Hamengkubuwono VII in the 1890s.

Museums

Musium Biologi, Jl. Sultan Agung 22, displays a collection of plants and stuffed animals from the entire archipelago, Rp 100 entrance, open 0800-1300 (on Fri. until 1100). The **Army Museum,** Jl. Bintaran Wetan, is in the S part of the city near the Biology Museum. Although it's supposed to open in the mornings (closed Fri.), you'll find it is often closed for one reason or another. This museum records the Indonesian revolution: documents, photos, historical articles, homemade weapons, uniforms and equipment from the 1945-49 struggle—especially as they relate to the military career of the Commander of the Revolutionary Forces, General Sudirman. The house in which Sudirman lived, **Sasmita Loka Jendral Sudirman** on Jl. B. Harun, is also open in the mornings to the public everyday but Monday.

Sonobudoyo Museum

Located on Alun-alun Utara (the square N of the *kraton),* this building was constructed in the classical Javanese *kraton* style. Open Tues. to Thurs. 0800-1300; Fri. to 1100, and Sun. 0800-1300. A first-rate collection of Javanese, Madurese, and Balinese arts and crafts, particularly C. Javanese artifacts; excellent exhibits of *batik* cloth, musical instruments, palace furnishings, archaeological objects such as an 18 carat gold Buddha and another Buddha with gold lips, ancient Chinese spearheads, plus a big library. Best displays are the *wayang golek* puppets, woodcarvings including marvelous sculptural screens and figures, two very old *gamelan*, models of *prahu*, and a renowned collection of the Reni *wayang topeng*

masks from Malang. The weapons room displays many varieties of *kris*. Give a contribution (Rp100) as you enter.

Monumen Diponegoro

A reconstruction of Diponegoro's residence, which was destroyed by the Dutch in 1825. Located 4 km W of Yogya at Tegalrejo, only a 15-min. bicycle ride from town, by *becak* Rp1000 OW, or take bus no. 1 from Jl. H.O.S. Cokroaminoto straight to the museum, Rp150. This museum is dedicated to Prince Diponegoro (1785-1855) who led partisans during the Java War (1825-1830). His *kris* are hung with flowers in glass cases, there are photos of his other sacred possessions, as well as a large commemorative *pendopo.* See the hole through which he and his followers escaped to go into hiding at Gua Selarong near Parangtritis 8 km SE of Yogya. After 5 years of bloody war this nobleman was at last cunningly tricked into negotiations at Magelang and arrested, then sent into exile to Sulawesi the remaining 25 years of his life. Diponegoro's grave in Ujung Pandang is still highly venerated. At Magelang you can still see the room in which he was captured and the wooden chair scratched by his nails as he tried to control his fury.

Gajah Mada University

A famous prime minister of the 13th C. Majapahit Empire, Gajah Mada has been commemorated in the naming of Yogya's university. Located in the northern part of the city, G. Merapi volcano smokes behind the complex. With 17,000 students, this is the largest tertiary-level institute in Indonesia. Opened in Dec. 1949 with a total student body of 483, many part-time guerilla fighters among them. Since there was no campus or any other facilities, from 1949 to 1973 the northern courtyards of the Yogya *kraton* were utilized as university lecture halls; its first medical faculty was set up on the *pendopo* of the crown prince's palace and the *gamelan* store was turned into the university dispensary. An informal place to meet students is the main building in the middle of the campus called Gedung Induk, and in the Balai Budaya (the art and cultural exhibits building).

Mosques And Churches

Best to visit mosques during the non-praying time between sunrise and noon. Dress straight. Two-hundred-year-old *Mesjid Agung* is on the western side of Alun-alun Lor. This is where the *kraton's* royal *gamelan* are kept during *Seketan* week and where the famous *Gunungan* procession terminates. *Mesjid Soko Tunggal,* opposite the main gate (Pintu Gerbang) of Taman Sari, was built in the *kraton* pavilion style; it has stories from the *Koran* carved on its pillars. Ethereal Batak hymn-singing vibrates form the **Huria Kristen Batak Protestant Church,** Jl.

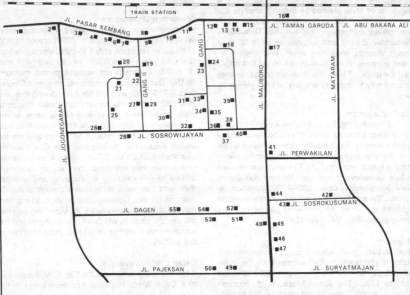

CENTRAL YOGYA

TRAIN STATION

JL. PASAR KEMBANG

JL. TAMAN GARUDA · JL. ABU BAKARA ALI

JL. GANG I · JL. GANG II · JL. MALIOBORO · JL. MATARAM

JL. JOGONEGARAN

JL. SOSROWIJAYAN

JL. PERWAKILAN

JL. SOSROKUSUMAN

JL. DAGEN

JL. PAJEKSAN

JL. SURYATMAJAN

1. Wisma Perdana	29. Gandhi Losmen
2. Hotel Kota	30. Dewi Homestay
3. Hotel Mataram	31. Eka Restaurant
4. Hotel Nusantara	32. Hotel Rama
5. Tugu Hotel	33. Hotel Jogya
6. Hotel Mendut	34. Hotel Rama
7. Hotel Satria	35. bus system
8. Mama's Restaurant	36. Kartika Hotel
9. Batak Palace Hotel	37. Indonesia Hotel
10. Asia-Africa Hotel	38. Hotel Aziatic
11. Ratnu Hotel	39. French Grill Lima
12. Losmen Rencana	40. Hotel Jogya
13. Asia-Africa	41. Legian Garden Restaurant
14. Candi Losmen	42. Hotel Zamrud
15. Wahyu Losmen	43. Hotel Intan
16. basketware, antiques	44. Helen's Restaurant
17. Hotel Garuda	45. Mutiara Hotel
18. Lucy Losmen	46. Mutiara New Hotel
19. Bagus Hotel	47. tourist information
20. Losmen Setia	48. Shinta Restaurant
21. Utar Pension	49. Losmen Bahagia
22. Anna Restaurant	50. Tiong San Restaurant
23. Beta Losmen	51. Sri Wibowa Hotel
24. Superman Restaurant	52. Litik G.H.
25. Wisma Wijaya	53. Petimar G.H.
26. post office	54. Blue Saphir
27. Heru Jaya Losmen	55. Wisma Nendra
28. Wisma Gembira	

Nyoman Oka 22, Kota Baru, early Sun. mornings. Visit the Indonesian-style Catholic Mass in the oldest church in Yogya, **St. Francis Xavier**, Jl. P. Senopati (near the GPO); masses are held Sat. at 1730 and Sun. at 0530 and 0700.

ACCOMMODATIONS

Although inflation over the past few years has diminished Yogya's reputation as Indonesia's *losmen* mecca, it still has remarkably good values. During the Ramayana Ballet (4 days only, each May, June, July, and Aug.), Yogya's hotels are packed.

Pasar Kembang Area
The area between the 2 parallel streets Jl. Pasar Kembang and Jl. Sosrowijayan is the cheapest; it's so close to the train station that it sounds like little toy trains are running all night. Most of the *losmen* here charge Rp2000-2500 s, Rp2000-3000 d. On the small lane, Gang I, running between Jl. Pasar Kembang and Jl. Sosrowijayan are a number of small *losmen*. Go down Jl. Pasar Kembang from the RR station until you run into Ratnu Hotel; about 5 doors past this hotel take a R down Gang I, a small lane marked with a sign—keep your eyes peeled. Most of these *losmen* have rules that don't allow you to come in later than 2330 or 2400. Take care with the super bargains on this lane; make sure your room is secure or you may find yourself minus your backpack or camera. **Beta Losmen**, with its own *kampung*, is one of the largest; Rp1250 s, Rp2000 d—clean, friendly, secure, and usually full in July and August. **Home Sweet Home**, opposite Superman's, has rooms for Rp2000 s—not the most comfortable environment, but cheap. Cute little Eko Restaurant, just around the corner, is open 0600-2100 for breakfast. **Hotel Jogya** has only double rooms for Rp3000; relaxing, clean *kamar mandi*, central—a pretty good value. **Losmen Bu Purwo**, the oldest, is on the little walkway right next to Superman's; the 6 rooms here go for Rp1000 s, Rp1500 d; quite small rooms but the security is excellent (there's always a *penjaga* even if you come in at 2 or 3 in the morning). The other small *gang*, Gang II, which runs between Jl. Pasar Kembang and Jl. Sosrowijayan, offers comparable values. For example, **Bagus Hotel** charges Rp1750 s, Rp2500 d (with fans). More *bagus* than Bagus is the **Ghandi Losmen**, also on Gang II, one of the cheapest (Rp1750 s, Rp 2500 d) and best accommodations going. Family very friendly, helpful, free tea, laundry—a secure place with beautiful garden to sit in.

Jalan Pasar Kembang
Slightly flashy **Ratnu Hotel**, no. 17A, is set back from the road and quiet; Rp10,000-15,000 d, including private *mandi* and toilet, also Rp6000 rooms with outside *mandi*. They also offer local tours, starting at Rp6500. Farther down is **Hotel Mataram**, no. 41;

Rp3500 d with private *mandi* and toilet. **Hotel Nusantara**, no. 59 (Rp6000 s or d); the **Rachamat**, and the **Shinta** at no. 49A, have rooms in the Rp3500 range. At the end of Jl. Pasar Kembang is **Hotel Kota**, still one of Yogya's better places; Rp5000 d rooms, plus others for Rp8500. Beautiful spacious rooms, nicely laid out, showers, leafy gardens, tea, boiled water. Drawbacks are that front rooms are noisy, it's run like a boarding school, and that they require a deposit of Rp7500 pp. **Asia-Africa Hotel**, no. 25 (tel. 4489), has rooms with private patio. The smallish, dark, and damp rooms in back go for Rp3500, while rooms in front are much better at Rp7500 s or d with private *mandi*. For a Western motel experience, **Hotel Mendut** (opposite Mama's Restaurant) has a/c rooms for Rp26,000-29,000, room service, and a nice cold pool.

Jalan Sosrowijayan
Just around the corner from Gang I is the Arab-owned **Hotel Aziatic**, Jl. Sosrowijayan 6. They offer super security with doors locked up tight at night and stout bars on the windows. The Aziatic (Rp4000 s, Rp5000 d) is clean, comfortable, and has large beds in big rooms, but they're too stingy to buy fans. **Indonesia Hotel**, across the road at no. 9, has rooms for Rp2000 s in the back; Rp6000 d rooms have a bath and shower or only Rp3000 rooms with fan and outside *mandi*. This big hotel consists of a maze of 28 rooms surrounding garden courtyard. Pleasant environment, good laundry facilities.

Jalan Sosrokusuman
This street is right after Helen's if you're heading down Jl. Malioboro towards the *kraton*. Of the 5 guesthouses on this street, **The Puri** gets the most tourists; Rp4000 s, Rp5000 d. If you have kids, get the one large room with TV, fan, refrigerator, and 2 extra beds—less expensive than 2 regular rooms. The **Intan Hotel**, no. 1/16, offers rooms for Rp3750 s with fan, Rp3500 without; Rp5250 d with fan, Rp5000 without. Extremely central (quiet for being so) and clean. Mostly Indonesians stay here. Comfortable **Prambanan Guesthouse**, no. 18-20 (tel. 3303), charges Rp5000 s or Rp5500-6000 d with bath.

Jalan Prawirotaman
A European yuppie enclave just 10 min. by *becak* S of the *kraton* area; ask directions. Fifteen small guesthouses and private homes on this street rent out the majority of their rooms to European package tourists. A quiet and peaceful neighborhood, these guesthouses are much better value than accommodations near the train station. They all differ in their interiors, services offered, and number and classes of rooms, but they all seem to be about the same price: Rp10,000-15,000 s, Rp13,000-19,000 d, with a/c rooms Rp3000-4000 more. Most also have economy rooms in the Rp7500-10,000 range, which are the best deals going in Yogya! Usually included in the

price is a breakfast, tea, juice, and snacks. Often built around attractive gardens, these guesthouses are very comfortable with Western toilets and offer postal, laundry, taxi, and ticketing services. Nearly all take credit cards. They are also close to the best *batik* galleries in Yogya (on the street just opposite), good restaurants, and to the buses for Borobudur and Prambanan, while the train station is only Rp600 away by *becak*. Management can arrange taxis for a tour of the temple sites for Rp15,000-Rp20,000, 3-4 hours, 4-5 people. To be competitive, most of the guesthouses are now trying to put in swimming pools (right now the best pool is at the Rose). During the high season, July-Aug., it's best to call first to see if they have a vacancy. The **French Grill** at the Perwita Sari has the best restaurant; the **Garden Restaurant** is very beautiful. At **Airlangga Guesthouse**, no. 4 (tel. 3344), you may pay in US dollars or in *rupiah;* US$11-14 s, US$14-17 (a/c) plus 20% tax and service. The **Sriwijaya Guesthouse**, Jl. Prawirotaman 7 (tel. 55153), has 26 rooms in all, each with private bath. Except for the color TV, the Sriwijawa is simple and plain, more in the Indonesian style, no hot water, but a safe place to store valuables. Book in advance, especially during the holiday season. Rates: Rp9000 s (fan), Rp 15,000 (a/c). **Wisma Indah Guesthouse**, no. 12 (tel. 88021), is a family-run Indonesian-style hotel with private bath, shower, fan, complimentary snacks and tea; Rp 9000 s, Rp12,000 d, taxes included. See Anto who knows all about Yogya, especially archaeological sites. **Duta Guest House**, no. 20, is very relaxing with showers and Western-style toilets, electric fan, a lovely courtyard, refreshing swimming pool; Rp11,000 s, Rp14,000 d. The Duta bills itself as having the most Javanese atmosphere. Another outstanding value is **Metro Guesthouse**, no. 7/71; Rp10,000 d (Rp16,000 a/c) free tea, swimming pool, clean, friendly service, with a fair-priced restaurant.

Others

Hotel Garuda, Jl. Malioboro 72 (86353), is a high-priced colonial-style hotel in the center of town; Rp67,795 s, Rp82,837 (a/c) d for commodious suites. Built in 1911, rooms have been completely restored and modernized, with a new 7-story annex added in the rear. **Mutiara Hotel**, Jl. Malioboro 18 (tel.4531/5173), has an excellent downtown location; Rp20,000 s, Rp35,000 d, includes breakfast, a/c, all taxes, Western baths and shower, 24-hour room service, bar and restaurant, pool. The Mutiara has a new annex just up the street beside the Tourist Info Center; Rp71,225 s, Rp81,312 d with bigger deluxe rooms, TV, in-house video. Along with the Garuda, this is one of Yogya's most modern downtown hotels. The **Puri Artha**, Jl. Cendrawasih 9 (just off Jl. Solo near Pasar Baru), must be one of the best small hotels in the world. It is well-run, attractive, has a good restaurant, swimming pool, and costs only about US$30 pp. A *gamelan* plays in the evening, and

each Thurs. and Sun. the staff will even take you to play tennis! Book well in advance as the Puri Artha is often full up with package tourists from Holland. Within easy walking distance of the Ambarrukmo is the **Sriwedari**, Jl. Adisucipto (tel. 88288), and the **Sri Manganti**, Jl. Urip Sumoharjo (tel. 2881), both supercomfortable with refreshing pools, and similar prices as the Puri Artha. The **Gajah Mada Guesthouse**, Jl. Bulaksumur, Kampus Universitas Gajah Mada (tel. 88461/88688, ext. 625), charges Rp25,000 d; add 20% for tax and service. All 20 a/c rooms have wall-to-wall carpeting, private bath and shower, telephone service, and continental breakfast included in price.

Homestays

If you'd like to stay with a Dutch or English-speaking family, and enjoy home-cooked meals in a family atmosphere, use **Indraloka Homestay Service**, Jl. Cik Ditiro 14 (tel. 3614/0274); see Mrs. Moerdiyono. Expect to pay around Rp22,000 d, plus 21% service and tax, but including breakfast. Mrs. Moerdiyono also arranges excursions to tourist sites near Yogya, and is plugged into a network of homestays in other Javanese cities.

International-class

The **Ambarrukmo** is about 7 km down the road (Jl. Solo) to Prambanan it's a gas to see this environment. They charge US$65 for the cheapest single room, US$350 for the presidential suite. Swimming pool for non-guests, Rp1500. Expensive restaurants with little variety. Javanese *gamelan* concerts are put on every day 1000-1200 and 1700-1800 in the lobby, traditional dances at night, and each Wed. (2030-2200) a puppet show, usually *wayang kulit,* is staged. *Ramayana* and *wayang orang* performances are also held from 2000 to 2100 on the 7th floor in the Borobudur Restaurant. Don't even touch the handles on the doors to the shops in the arcade here—ridiculous prices. There's also a small post office and a bank. Another splendid 4-star hotel nearby is the **Saihd Garden**, Jl. Babar Sari (500 m E of the Ambarrukmo) with swimming pool, a/c, and Rp50,000 rooms.

Long-term

The Jl. Pasar Kembang is very colorful, but not the place to settle in Yogya for awhile. Scan or put an ad in the town rag, *Kedaulatan Rakyat,* Jl. Magkubumi 42, to find a small house, flat, or room with a family. Or ask your hotel proprietor if he can arrange for accommodations in a private home, usually 4-5 km from the city center, Rp20,000-30,000 per month (room only), depending. One possible long-term place, an excellent Indonesian-style hotel—and very good value—is the **Ghandi Losmen**, about 100 m down Gang II which is opposite Mama's *warung.* They charge Rp2000-3500 s or d for fairly big rooms (some 2 to a bed). Coffee or tea served in the mornings, but no food. It's quiet, central, clean, and friendly.

Another good long-term place for those studying music or one of the arts, or teaching English, is **Salonfifani**, Gergen 13; Rp150,000 per month, but they like you to stay for 6 months.

FOOD

Specialties

Yogya is godsent for vegetarians: bean cakes, *rempeyek* (peanut cookies), and vegetable soups galore. The *makan asli* of Yogya, *gudeg*, is jackfruit cooked in coconut milk with a mixture of eggs, tofu, chicken, and spicy sauce. Served in Indonesian-style restaurants all over town, find the best *gudeg* at **Bu Citro's** on Jl. Adisucipto near the entrance to the airport, and at **Juminten**, Jl. Asem Gede 22, Kranggan 69, N of Jl. Diponegoro. One of the best *warung* deals in town is *nasi rames* —a very healthy, tasty meal with 4-5 different vegetables. Also try tasty Javanese *opor ayam*, slices of chicken simmered in coconut milk; and sumptuous *mbok berek*, one whole fried chicken for Rp4000 — Colonel Sanders can't hold a candle to it. The best *mbok berek* restaurant is the famous **Suharti Mbok Berek**, Jl. Solo (between Ambarrukmo Hotel and Prambanan, 7 km E of Yogya) where one can also take orders out in baskets.

Street Food

Jalan Malioboro is particularly popular as "restaurant row"; but even the best of these Chinese restaurants are inconsistent, overpriced for the size of their servings, and not recommended. Eat instead at *warung,* where the people eat. Right at the end of the lane where Gang I joins Jl. Pasar Kembang (towards the train station) is a *nasi rames* and *nasi pecel warung*. After 2100 on Jl. Malioboro vendors sell delicious chicken, rice and vegie dishes, and even deep fried dove *(burung dara goreng)*, *nasi gudeg* —tasty meals for Rp800-1000. Eat from banana-leaf fronds on mats spread on the sidewalk and watch the street life while tolerating just a few beggars. Stands on Jl. Alun Utara sell Arabian pancakes *(martabak)* for around Rp800; open till midnight.

Nasi Padang

All the genuine Indonesian cooking is found N of the RR tracks; all the Western-style restaurants are generally S of the tracks. Some outstanding *nasi padang* places are just across the tracks on Jl. Mangkubumi (where Jl. Malioboro changes its name). On the R-hand side are *sate* and soup tents serving *sate, kambing, sop kaki sapi* (buffalo-feet soup), etc. The **Sinar Budi**, Jl. Mangkubumi 41, about 500 m N of the RR tracks on the L (across from the movie theater), is the oldest *nasi padang* restaurant in Yogya. Try their inimitable *otak sapi* (calves brain) and classic *rendang*.

Travelers' Eateries

In many of these popular hangouts, livened up by resident Indonesian hipsters, Westerners sit sardined with other Westerners, playing Western music, eating Kuta Beach-style food. The current hot place is **Bu Sis**, Gang I (the lane parallel to Jl. Malioboro), which serves up a huge variety of inexpensive and well-prepared meals, desserts, and drinks. Best fried chicken in Indonesia, and the fish dinner is a world travel bargain! It's packed at night during Happy Hour (Bintangs, Rp1350) between 1700 and 1900, so get there early. **Superman's**, on the lane between Jl. Pasar Kembang and Jl. Sosrowijayan, is one of the best breakfast places; it's also a buoyant social center in the evenings, opening promptly at 0700, closing at 2100. On the next lane over, Gang II, **Anna's** serves good tourist fare. The quality at long-running **Mama's** on Jl. Pasar Kembang, has unfortunately fallen, though even late at night these Jl. Pasar Kembang eateries are still going strong. **Restaurant Malioboro**, Jl. Mangkubumi (in front of the Garuda office), is a cheerful place with bargain dishes. It's open 0630-2000. On Jl. Malioboro, the **Colombo Restaurant**, no. 25, is primarily an ice juice place with prices in the Rp600-1000 range. Though their *es juice* portions have shrunk over the years, they still serve a superb *es jus zirzak, es jus apokat* and *es juice apel*. Their meals tend to be too high priced. A hardcore tourist hangout is **Helen's**. At Jl. Malioboro 57, the **Shinta** has a full menu and delicious drinks (including *es kopyor* for only Rp750). **Legian Restaurant**, on the corner of Jl. Perwakilan and Jl. Malioboro, is slightly more expensive but has excellent meals at roof-top level.

Restaurants

A reliably good Javanese restaurant is **Warung Makan Sederhana**, Jl. Mangkubumi 61-B: *nasi rames, gado-gado, es jus, soto babar.* The **Legian Garden Restaurant**, Jl. Perwakilin 9 (where Jl. Malioboro meets Jl. Suryatmajan), specializes in such expensive Western dishes as pork chops, steaks, and avocado seafood salads. At Jl. Mangkubumi 48 in the Arjuna Plaza Hotel is a surprisingly good French restaurant, the **French Grill**, where Yogya's French community takes its guests, so it *has* to be good. The **Gita Buana**, on Jl. Diponegoro 52A (from the Rugu Monument walk W about 1 ½ km), is a small restaurant charging reasonable prices for international and Chinese dishes. Lethal a/c, so bring a sweater. **Lejong's Restaurant** is on Jl. Brig. Jen. Katamso; from the GPO follow Jl. Senopati E to the traffic light, then turn due S—it's on the E side of the road. Lejong's specializes in seafoods, especially crab soup. On the other side of the *kraton* on the "guesthouse street," Jl. Prawirotaman, is the unusual garden restaurant, **Hanoman's Forest**. For the Rp1000 cover charge you may enjoy local *wayang, gamelan,* and the traditional dances of Java. Their menu offers a full range of delicious and moderately priced lunches and dinners. Anton, the owner, and his staff are very friendly. The **Sintawang Restaurant** is a peerless seafood place and probably the city's best Chinese restaurant. First go up to the Tugu Monument, then keep heading west. At Jl. Magelang, turn R, then N, and it's immediately on your left.

Fruits, Desserts, Drinks
A plethora of fruits are found on Jl. Malioboro under the covered portion of the sidewalk. Inside **Beringharjo** market is a feast for the senses: women in colorful *batik sarung*, a delightful melange of earthy aromas, great crimson mounds of fresh chilies, grains, and beans bulging in handwoven baskets. **Tip Top Ice Cream Parlor**, Jl. Mangkubumi 28 (tel. 3682), sells excellent creamy ice cream in many flavors, including *durian*, mocha, and tutti frutti; open 0900-1330 and 1700-2100. For more pastries and ice cream, next to the President Movie Theater is **Chitty Chitty Bang Bang** and the **Holland Bakery**. Yogya's wide variety of street stalls serve many special Javanese beverages: *es strop* with *kelapa* on top, delicious *tapi*, *coklat* with *cingkong* and *kelapa* (this one has a mocha-vanilla-butterscotch flavor — a delicious dessert). For black rice pudding (the perfect breakfast, Rp200), vendors pad down the Gang I and Gang II in the Pasar Kembang area between 0730 and 0900.

THE PERFORMING ARTS

Wayang and dance dramas are put on for tourists and Javanese. Tourists' performances are usually shortened, with just the highlights of the epic versions, but others such as the plays held at **Sasono Hinggil** (S of the *alun-alun)* are marathons which start at 2100 and last for 9 hours without a break. Tourist performances are not necessarily inferior to the genuine article; often they are better funded and have more lavish props and costuming than an authentic *kampung* production. You will not be able to understand the words but the magical scenes will fascinate and hold your attention for at least several hours. Go to the tourist office, Jl. Malioboro 16, for the latest venues and a schedule of performances. The following is only a partial list. note: *Gamelan* and dance rehearsals at the palace don't take place during *Ramadan* or the week following.

Wayang **And** *Gamelan*
The **Agastya Art Institute**, Gedongkiwo MD III/237, is a training school for *dalang.* Shadow plays are staged here from 1500 to 1700 (except Sat.). It's off Jl. Buntul over the railroad tracks, about 3 km from the city in a small *kampung.* Entrance: Rp1500. Also

trains *wayang golek dalang;* every Sat. 1500-1700 you may see one in action for Rp1500. **Nitour,** Jl. Dahlan 71, stages almost paralytic, poor quality *wayang golek* performances every day 1100-1300 except Sun.; Rp1500 admission. At the **THR** on Jl. Brig. Jen. Katamso, nightly performances are held of *wayang orang* performances with the Ramayana plot; Rp2500. *Wayang kulit* takes place at **Ambar Budaya** in the Yogya Karta Crafts Center, opposite the Ambarrukmo on Jl. Adisucipto, every Mon., Wed., and Sat. from 2130 to 2230; Rp1500. It's a long walk from the

YOGYA

1. bus stop Pingit (to Borobudur)
2. Gunung Agung Bookstore
3. Merpati office
4. Bank Niaga
5. Terminal Terban
6. Bouraq office
7. Garuda office
8. Arjuna Plaza Hotel
9. telephone office
10. soccer stadium
11. Tip Top Ice Cream
12. railway station
13. Hotel Kota
14. Mama's
15. Superman's
16. Hotel Aziatic
17. Maliobo Restaurant
18. Mutiara Hotel
19. Tourist Information Center
20. Happy Restaurant
21. Pasar Beringharjo
22. Vredburg Museum
23. minibus stand (shopping)
24. *Batik* Research Institute
25. Nitour Puppet Show
26. Bank Negara Indonesia
27. post office
28. Sasono Hinggil
29. THR (Sasanasuka Ramayana)
30. Pasar Ngasem
31. *batik* painters' colony
32. Moejosoehardjo
33. Dalem Pujokuseman Ramayana
34. minibuses to Imogiri
35. Swastigita
36. Agastya Art Institute
37. Tirtodipuran *batik* factories
38. Wisma Gajah
39. Duta Guest House
40. Rose Guest House

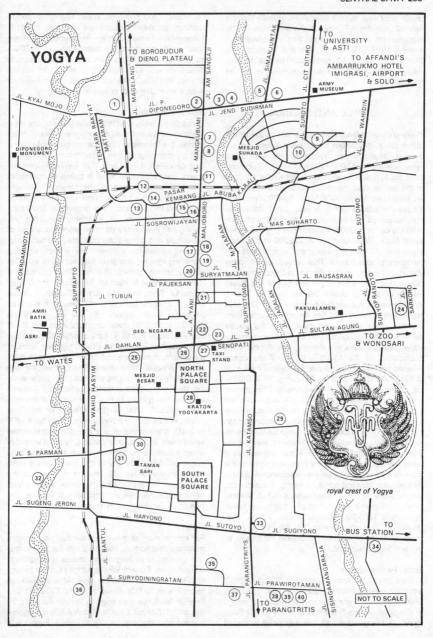

YOGYA

TO BOROBUDUR & DIENG PLATEAU

TO UNIVERSITY & ASTI

TO AFFANDI'S AMBARRUKMO HOTEL IMIGRASI, AIRPORT & SOLO

JL. KYAI MOJO

JL. MAGELANG

JL. P. DIPONEGORO

JL. AM SANGAJI

JL. SIMANJUNTAK

JL. CIT DITIRO

JL. JEND. SUDIRMAN

JL. SUROTO

JL. DR. WAHIDIN

ARMY MUSEUM

DIPONEGORO MONUMENT

JL. TENTARA RAKYAT MATARAM

JL. MANGKUBUMI

MESJID SUHADA

JL. DR. SUTOMO

JL. COKROAMINOTO

JL. SUPRAPTO

JL. ABUBAKARALI

PASAR KEMBANG

JL. MAS SUHARTO

JL. SOSROWIJAYAN

JL. MALIOBORO

JL. MATARAM

JL. SURYATMAJAN

JL. BAUSASRAN

JL. PAJEKSAN

JL. TUBUN

JL. A. YANI

JL. SURYOTOMO

JL. JAGALAN

PAKUALAMAN

JL. SURYOPRANOTO

JL. SARKORO

AMRI BATIK

ASRI

GED. NEGARA

JL. DAHLAN

JL. SULTAN AGUNG

TO ZOO & WONOSARI

TO WATES

SENOPATI TAXI STAND

JL. WAHID HASYIM

MESJID BESAR

NORTH PALACE SQUARE

KRATON YOGYAKARTA

JL. KATAMSO

JL. S. PARMAN

TAMAN SARI

SOUTH PALACE SQUARE

royal crest of Yogya

JL. SUGENG JERONI

JL. HARYONO

JL. SUTOYO

JL. SUGIYONO

TO BUS STATION

JL. BANTUL

JL. PARANGTRITIS

JL. SISINGAMANGARAJA

JL. SURYODININGRATAN

JL. PRAWIROTAMAN

TO PARANGTRITIS

NOT TO SCALE

cheap hotel area, so take a *becak*. **Habiranda Dalang School**, on the NE side of the *alun-alun* in the Pracimasono pavilion, puts on free rehearsals each evening 1900-2000, except Sun. and Thursdays. At **Sentolo**, 20 km W of Yogya (Rp250 by bus), famous *dalang* can be hired out for *wayang* performances; fee negotiable.

DANCE AND DRAMA

There are many dance companies. Ask at the tourist office on Jl. Malioboro about exact times and addresses. At the *kraton,* Yogyanese classical dance rehearsals are held 1000-1200 on Sunday. Ask directions on Jl. Rotowijayan. Tickets are sold at the door of the palace. Also, *gamelan* rehearsals are held here on Mon. and Wed., 1030-1200; Rp400. **Grhadika Yogya Pariwisata** (GYP), Jl. Brig. Jen. Katamso 45, puts on almost nightly tourist performances of Javanese dance for Rp3000. *Wayang orang* is performed every Mon., Wed., and Fri. 2000-2200 in the Kasatriyan Hall in Dalem Pujokusuman Sultan's Palace by members of this school. This prestigious company also stages such classical dances as the *Serimpi* and the *Bedaya* in both the Yogya and Solo styles. **Krido Beksa Wirama** in Dalem Tejokusuman on Jl. K.H. Wahid Hasyim, has packed classes—watch Old Java come alive in the story of *Ken Angrok,* episodes from the *Ramayana,* and ancient mask plays. Rehearsals are from 2000-2100 on Sun. on the Tejakusuman *pendopo.* Classical Javanese dancing was the exclusive prerogative of the courts until the Krida Bekso Wirama school opened outside the walls of the *kraton* in 1918. **ASTI:** This Dance Academy, on Jl. Colombo, is one of only 5 in all of Indonesia. This government school attracts some of the most talented young contemporary dancers from C. Java. **Prambanan:** Each Sat. at 0900 the *Kuda Kepang* (horse trance dance) is performed near Candi Sewu in Prambanan village—the whole bit: whinnying, eating grass and hay, slurping water from a pail. Sometimes it takes the leader *(pamong)* a whole hour to bring the dancers out of trance. **dance teachers:** A superb dancer and choreographer, Bagong Kussudiardjo, whose studio is on Jl. Singosaren 9 (off Jl. Wates), teaches his own interpretation of modern jazz ballet. Rehearsals 1600-2000 except Friday. Vishnu Wardhana, Jl. Suryodiningratan 13, teaches a whole range of dance styles, from traditional Indonesian to modern improvisational.

Hotel Performances

In the lobby of the **Ambarrukmo** on Jl. Adisucipto a small *gamelan* performs each day 1030-1230 and 1600-1800; free. There are also nightly cultural shows at this hotel. At the **French Grill** in the Arjuna Plaza Hotel, Jl. Mangkubumi 48, *wayang golek* is staged

each Sat. 1900-2100; on Tues. 1900-2100 performances of *wayang kulit* are put on; Rp2000. **Hanoman's Forest Garden Restaurant**, Jl. Prawirotaman 9b (by *andong* between 4 people, Rp2000), stages nightly (1900) modern and classical Javanese dance, as well as *wayang kulit* and *golek* puppet shows; Rp1500. There could even be an Italian or Australian rock group, or jazz or pop singing!

Ramayana Ballet

These de Mille-like spectacles take place on the enormous stone stage of the Lorojonggrang open-air theater near the Prambanan Temple complex on 4 successive full-moon nights in each month from June to Oct. (but cancelled if it rains). This 6-episode contemporary *sendratari*-style ballet is based on traditional *wayang orang* dancing of the classical Javanese theater. The plot is a modernized, dramatized version of the Indian epic poem, the *Ramayana*. The Prambanan temple panels are, in effect, re-enacted live. Taking part is an entire *gamelan* orchestra, scores of beautifully and grotesquely costumed dancers, singers and musicians, with monkey armies, strutting menacing *rawana*, acrobatic miracles, giant kings on stilts, clashing battles, *real* fire. The Tourist Info Center and Hotel Mutiara (Jl. Malioboro); the Ambarrukmo (Jl. Solo); Nitour (Jl. Ahmad Dahlan 71); Intras (Jl. Malioboro, in front of Hotel Garuda); and almost any other travel agency can sell you RT tickets (Rp5000 to Rp7000, depending on the seating). It's of course cheaper just to go early and take the local bus by yourself to Prambanan village, sightsee some of the temples, have a rest and a cold drink, and be there when the ticket office opens. This way you can see the temple in the daylight, at sunset, and in the evening, the Shiva temple as floodlit backdrop. If you wait until the last minute to buy your tickets at the window, probably only the 2nd Class and 3rd Class tickets will be left. The performance lasts from 1900 to 2100. Bring cushions or a sleeping bag to soften stone seats. If taking your camera, listen to your conscience because the flash is distracting to many in the audience. Don't buy any of the books or the postcards at the ballet site; they're cheaper in the bookstores in the city. After the show, a whole herd of minibuses will take you right back to Terminal Terban on Jl. Simanjuntak in Yogya.

Others

For events such as traditional dances, pop groups, musical performances, keep your eye out for information banners stretching across streets and buildings around town. Current Western movies could be running too—always look in the paper. Movie tickets sell for as low as Rp750; a/c seats run Rp1750-2500. The **French Institute**, Lembaga Indonesia Perancis, Jl. Sagan 1/1 (behind Cinema Rahayu) offers frequent cultural presentations, usually in French. Everyone is

WAYANG, DANCING, AND GAMELAN VENUES

TYPE	PLACE	DAY	TIME	COST
Yogyanese Classical Dance Rehearsals	Sunday	1030-1200	Rp400	
Traditional *Gamelan* Rehearsal	Sultan's Kraton	Mon. and Wed.	1030-1200	Rp400
Wayang Kulit	Agastya Art Institute, Jl. Gedongkiwo MD. III/237	daily	1500-1700	Rp1500
	Ambar Dudaya (Yogya Craft Center), Jl. Adisucipto	Mon., Wed., Sat.	2130-2230	1500
	Arjuna Plaza Hotel, Jl. Mangkubumi 48	Tues.	1900-2100	Rp2000
Wayang Golek	Agastya Art Institute, Jl. Gedongkiwo MD. III/237	Sat.	1500-1700	Rp1500
	Arjuna Plaza Hotel Jl. Mangkubumi 48	Sat.	1900-2100	Rp2000
	Nitour, Inc. Jl. Ahmad Dalan	daily except Sun.	1100-1300	Rp1500
Ramayana Ballet	Arjuna Plaza Hotel, Jl. Mangkubumi 48	Thurs.	1900-2100	Rp2000
	Dalem Pujokusuman, Jl. Katamso 45	Mon., Wed., Fri.	2000-2200	Rp3000
	Sasanasuka, Jl. Katamso	daily	2000-2200	Rp2500

welcome. The Institute teaches French every day and organizes all sorts of events—local artists, European astronomers, chamber music. Their library is open 1000-1900. The Germans (Jl. Jend. Sudirman 18, in front of Hotel Merdaka) and the Dutch also have cultural institutes in Yogya where they too present cultural shows. **Karta Pustaka**, the Dutch club, on Jl. Jend. Sudirman 46, has a big theater which regularly hosts lectures, guitar concerts, films, etc.

FESTIVALS AND EVENTS

Most center on the *kraton*. In the past their purpose was to reinforce the prestige of the reigning sultan and his court. Even today the bathwater of the sultan of Yogya is considered holy and his fingernail clippings are kept for their latent power. However, the current sultan is reformed and democratic, so Yogya's festivals aren't nearly as grandiose as they once were; they are now more like folk festivals. The *Garebeg* procession, held 3 times within the Islamic year, was at one time a cultic pre-Muslim charity feast that was carried over and grafted onto the Islamic feast days of *Maulud* and *Idul Fitri*. In fact, there is such an admixture of animism, Hinduism, and Islam in the rites of Yogya's festivals that no one really knows the origins of many, or what all the symbols mean. All is buried under centuries of custom. The following are the more important events (refer to an Islamic calendar for dates).

Sekaten
Also called *Garebeg Maulud*, a ceremony to commemorate the birth of the Prophet Mohammed. This great festival centers around the *kraton* and the Royal Mosque, Mesjid Agung. A big fair is held on the great open square N of the *kraton* while continuous prayer is held in the mosque compound. The ceremony begins at midnight with a procession of the palace guards; 2 sets of sacred *gamelan* are brought from the palace to the Royal Mosque. The climax is the great procession carrying the beehive-shaped *Gunungan* ("Rice Mountains") on bamboo frames from the *kraton* to Mesjid Agung on the N square. These "Mountains of Food," representing the tree-of-life symbol (like the Christmas tree), are escorted by 800 palace guards *(prajurit)*, all dressed in zany uniforms with zebra-striped shirts, slipper shoes, Napoleonic and top hats, armed with bows and arrows, spears, swords, and rifles, parading in 100 platoons while firing blanks into the air. Accompanying the *gamelan*, bulky female *kraton* guards march with *kris* in their sashes, and dignified *kraton* officials in white turbans and flowing white robes sit on thick cushions. Vendors sell sweets, balloons, pinwheels, etc., and the fair includes night markets and folk theater presentations such as *Ketoprak*.

Garebeg Besar
In this religious festival, mass prayers are held in mosques and public squares, then goats, sheep, lambs, cows, and buffalos are ceremonially slaughtered to commemorate Abraham's willingness to sacrifice his own son to God. The meat is then distributed to the poor. The sultan, with a retinue of nobility, court dignitaries, and large floats of *gunungan*, takes part in a procession from the *kraton* to Mesjid Agung. A big bamboo theater is set up in the northern *alun-alun*.

Labuhan
Means "offering." Held yearly the day after the sultan's birthday. At 0800 offerings are taken from the *kraton* to Punden Krendowahono on the S coast of the Indian Ocean. Here the sultan's old clothes are dedicated to the Queen of the South Seas, Loro Kidul, and put out to sea on a raft. Other offerings (nail clippings and hair trimmings) are buried in the sand. Each *Juma'at*, every 35 days, Chinese women come and offer sacrifices as well. Once every 8 years, similar offerings are sent to the volcanos Merapi and Lawu and to the village of Dlepih near Wonogiri.

Sendangsano Pilgrimage
During May a religious ceremony is observed by Catholic devotees at Sendangsano, 32 km NW of Yogya, where a statue of the Virgin Mary stands in a cave on the slopes of the Menorah mountain range. Sendangsano is the Javanese Lourdes; the well water here is considered holy. On the way you pass through Boro, a Catholic village where people have names like Josuf, Petrus, and Maria.

Waicak
A solemn festival commemorating the birth, enlightenment, death, and final ascension of Buddha. *Waicak* takes place at the 1,100-year-old Borobudur and Mendut temples, 41 km NW of Yogya. For details, see "Borobudur."

CRAFTS AND SHOPPING

Spend several days in Yogya before buying so you can learn the good values and the right prices at the right places. In almost all instances, be prepared to bargain—with grace. To get acquainted with the full range of crafts offered, visit first the **Yogyakarta Crafts Center**, Jl. Adisucipto (across from the Ambarrukmo Hotel), a government-sponsored crafts cooperative. A visit should also be made to **Pasar Beringharjo**, a giant market off the southern end of Jl. Malioboro. Swarming with brazen rats, here a maze of over one km of market stalls sells everything from macrame to mutton and mangos. Beware that the people selling textiles and old *batik* in this municipal *pasar* lie like snakes. Anyone who goes in there without doing their homework first will be robbed blind. Leathergoods and an endless assortment of food, baskets, dry goods, and everyday craft items are also sold at reasonable prices in front of and around the market.

Wayang

For the most part, Yogya's *wayang kulit* puppets are made from goat skin, not buffalo hide; the best cost at least Rp20,000. *Wayang* puppets can be found all over town, but the best place is **Pak Ledjar** on Jl. Mataram DN I/370; from Helen's on Jl. Malioboro walk E down the alley to Jl. Mataram, then turn left. Another good place is **Toko Jawa**, Jl. Malioboro (opp. Mutiara Hotel), which also sells musical instruments and *Ramayana* ballet costumes. *Wayang golek* puppets are made at master **Pak Warno's** on Jl. Bantul, 8 km S of Yogya. High-quality *wayang kulit* puppets are made at **Moejosoehardjo's**, Jl. S. Parman Sari 37B (tel. 2873), W of the Winingo River; he specializes in large *gonongan* screens. Of the many shops along Jl. Malioboro, **Toko Setia** (at nos. 79 and 165) carries the best quality *wayang* puppets. The *wayang kulit* schools are also good-value places to shop for puppets: **Swasthigita**, Jl. Ngadinegaran MD 7/50 (tel. 4346), is on a small alley to the L at the beginning of Jl. Panjaitan S of the *kraton*.

Antiques

The **Jul Shop**, Jl. T. Mangkubumi 29 (tel. 2157), specializes in really old stuff, and not many people make it here. **Toko Asia**, Jl. Malioboro opposite Garuda Hotel, sells an outstanding collection of old *kris*. Several other small shops are close by, on the same side of the street. **Madiyono**, Jl. Tirtodipuran 36 (open 0900-2100), has a full range of art antiques. Also worth checking out is the group of antique shops in the vicinity of the Ambarrukmo, plus about 4 shops on Jl. Prawirotaman. The majority of *batik* factories (listed below) also sell antiques. Jalan Taman Garuda is another good hunting ground: try **Seni Jaya** (no. 11), and **Pusaka** (no. 22), plus several more. But probably the most soulful antiques in Yogya, at exorbitant prices, are found at **Ardianto**, Jl. Magelang (Km 7).

Leather

You seldom see leather work as inexpensive as this: fully embossed buff-colored suitcases, Rp5000-15,000; shoulder bags, Rp3000-5000; briefcases, overnight bags, money belts, and pouches. Make sure the leather is thick, and it's treated after you buy it. Sometimes the handtooling is lousy, or a layer of cardboard is glued between 2 thin layers of leather to make it thick and stiff. Note carefully how the buckles are fastened; they tend to break off first. In Indonesia you can still sit down with a craftsman and decide together on a design, what hide will be chosen, reinforced stitching, etc.—it's a creative process between you and the artisan. You can have a pair of high boots made to order for about Rp20,000 that would cost you US$250 in Italy. On Jl. Malioboro's sidewalks and shops are cheerful leather lampshades (Rp3500-10,000) with *wayang* characters stenciled out, glinting with color from the backlighting. Genuine leather sandals on Jl. Malioboro go for as low as Rp7000, though shops along Jl. Pasar Kembang tend to be cheaper. To name just a few of the many leather outlets: **Aries Handicraft**, Jl. Kauman 14; **B.S. Store**, Jl. Ngasem 10; **Kusuma**, Jl. Kauman 50; **Budi Murni**, Jl. Muju Muju; **Balai Penelitian Kulit**, Jl. Sokonandi 3; **Amie**, Jl. Kemasan, in Kota Gede.

Silver

Kota Gede, a village 2 km SE of Yogya (Rp150 by bus), is the hub of Yogya's silver industry with dozens of large and small shops; see "Vicinity of Yogya." You needn't confine yourself to only those items you see on display. Though it may take them as long as a week, almost any workshop is able to produce special-order pieces. Make a sketch, supply a photograph or a specimen, and they'll skillfully produce a facsimile, charged usually by the weight and grade of silver used. Outlets in town: **Tan Jam An**, Jl. Mas Sangaji (go past Tugu Monument several streets and it's on the R-hand side); **Tjokrosuharto**, Jl. Panembahan 58; **Sri Moeljo's**, Jl. Mentri Supeno UH XII/1 (tel. 88042).

Miscellaneous

At **Tjokrosuharto**, Jl. Panembahan 58, buy *angklung* for Rp5000; they also sell medium-quality *wayang kulit* puppets for Rp3000-4000, superior to the ones on the street, though not as good as in the fancy souvenir shops. You can also buy individual notes for your *angklung* set for only Rp1500; inquire at some of the wickerware shops down from Mama's. *Kebaya* (filmy lace jackets) are now out of style in the West so there are plenty around. Older Chinese *kebaya* are sold at **Busana Dewi**, Jl. Dr. Sutomo 9/B, but are cheaper from the sidewalk sellers and in the shops along Jl. Malioboro; Rp8000-10,000 for the better ones. **Tan Jam An**, Jl. Mas Sangaji, carries (in addition to silverware) a fine collection of old Chinese *sarung*, definitely worth looking at. (The ones in Pasar Beringharjo have been picked over and are ratty). Have fine embroidery done on pants and shirts at some clothing shops for Rp3000-4000. Genuine Javanese *petani* hats *(caping)* on Jl. Malioboro cost Rp750 (tourist price). Custom-made rubber stamps cost only Rp2000 with hand-carved personal logo, weird emblems, family crest, address, or whatever—a real steal. The best shops for cassette tapes are **Podomoro** and **Atlantic** on Jl. Malioboro, as well as many shops on Jl. Solo. They only last a year, but what do you want for US$1.75? On Jl. Taman Garuda on the L-hand side coming from Jl. Pasar Kembang, basketware and mats are for sale; large baskets sell for Rp1500-Rp2000. Delightful singing tops are sold on Jl. Malioboro by several vendors for Rp750 (after bargaining). **Agastya Art Institute,** Jl. Gedongkiwo MDIII/237, is the only place that you'll find paintings done on canvas (not *batik* paintings).

Out-of-Town Crafts

For woodcarvings, visit Moyudan village, NW of Yogya. Ceramics enthusiasts should visit Kasongan (7 km from Yogya) to view piggy banks being modeled, fired, and painted by hand; see "Vicinity of Yogya." *Kuda Kepang* (flat hobby-horses made from plaited bamboo) are crafted near Candi Sewu in the Prambanan temple complex. Bamboo whistling tops— great gifts for kids—can be bought at the Prambanan and Borobudur temple complexes. **Supowiyono,** son of the late Empu Supowinangun, has re-established the once-vanished art of *kris*-making at his residence in Jitar/Moyudan, about one hour by *bemo* W of Yogya.

Affandi

On Jl. Adisucipto, at the large bridge before the river. Indonesia's best-known contemporary artist, Affandi was born in 1908 in Cirebon. When the Japanese asked him to paint a poster to help recruit more Javanese forced labor for Burma, he submitted a canvas showing starving men slaving in a hellhole jungle. This vital, genial old man now lives in an airy, bizarre studio house where you could possibly meet him in the late afternoon. Ask to see his private collection; some amazing self-portraits from the '30s and '40s. View his paintings best from a distance because he's farsighted. Affandi finishes his paintings on the spot, most of them within 30 min. to an hour. The starting price is 1 ½ million *rupiah*. He also exhibits the works of promising young artists in his gallery and one section exhibits the work of his daughter, Kartika, a fine artist in her own right.

Amri Yahya

For modern *batik* paintings, visit this dynamic, internationally known Sumatran artist. A permanent oil and *batik* painting exhibition is on display at his large gallery located at Jl. Gampingan 67, next to ASKI (just 75 m from Jl. Wates up a little hill). Be prepared: these slick top-of-the-line paintings sell for as much as US$1000. See artists at work on the premises. In 1987, Amri completed a lecture series at Ohio State University.

ASRI

The School of Fine Arts on Jl. Gampingan. With 78 faculty and 1500-2000 students, this is one of the top art academies in Indonesia. Sculpture, painting, graphics, commercial and industrial arts, primitive, symbolic, and decorative paintings (even nude drawing) are all taught here. ASRI is rediscovering the lost Javanese art of stone sculpture, and the school has a huge interior design department with excellent facilities. A big art carnival is held in the second half of Jan.

each year and a permanent exhibition of paintings are always on sale. It's obvious that ASRI's students go to Bali for their artistic inspiration.

BATIK

Not even including the markets and sidewalk vendors along Jl. Malioboro, there are literally hundreds of *batik* outlets in Yogya. Most shops selling *batik* open in the mornings, close from 1300 to 1630, then open again at 2000. There's a big difference in quality of *batik tulis;* not just anyone can do it well. Some artists just draw the outline and have teams of girls fill in the intricate details—assembly-line fashion. Look around the galleries before you buy. High-quality *batik* paintings, cheaper than oils, run US$100-250 average, but it's worth paying a bit more if it helps to improve the art. When shopping, avoid being led into the galleries—you'll end up paying the guide's commission, an arrangement which almost amounts to an extortion racket. These "guides" can get quite pushy with the shop and gallery owners. Better to deal directly with the outlets themselves. When buying *batik,* you should appreciate the price in human servitude. The 14- to 16-year-old girls who work in the *batik* factories earn only Rp15,000 a month, work 12 hours a day, sleep on a mat on the floor, are given 2 meals a day plus free tea, and when business is slow they are forced to return to their village.

Batik Painting

You could search the factories and shops for a full day and find nothing original, just kitsch. Realism means an arm sticking out of a face. Many young "artists" approach tourists on the street asking them to see their exhibition, which they say will only be in town for another day before moving on to Jakarta or Singapore. Don't buy this line, or the one about a portion of the cost of the paintings going to the Ministry of Culture & Education. Pay only as much as you would to any other artist.

Factories

Of the 25 *batik* factories on Jl. Tirtodipuran and on Jl. Parangtritis S of the *kraton*, most can be toured. The majority produce soulless junk. There are lots of classy salerooms, but generally they are not the place to buy *tulis* (handmade) work as most of the pieces are made by the *cap* method. On Jl. Tirtodipuran, peek in at **Plentong,** no. 28 (Chinese-style *batik); ***Batik Srimpi,** no. 22 (Batik Solo). **Winotosastro,** no. 34, has an excellent selection, including some fine *tulis* pieces and some ready-made clothing. **Raradtaonggrang,** no. 6A, displays paintings by at least 15 artists, plus ready-made *batik* fashions. Another large factory is **Suryakencana,** Jl. Ngadinegaran (on the same *gang* as Swasthigita), with a wide selection in its showroom.

Terang Bulan

Yogya's *batik* supermarket, Jl. Jen. A. Yani 76, opposite Happy Restaurant. This shop is especially rewarding if you don't know anything about *batik*. Has a fine selection from a Rp2500 *sarung* up to a Rp275,000 *batik tulis alus* from Solo. Also, all kinds of material at fixed, honest prices gives you an idea of what you should be paying; browse and learn. Terang Bulan also sells fine locally made *lurik-batik* material, 3 m for Rp2650-3650. One other *batik* store with fixed prices, **Juwita**, is on the same side of the street down a little ways towards the *pasar*.

Studios And Galleries

F. Agus Mudjono, Mergangsan Kidul, Mg. III/102, creates traditional *batik* paintings going for Rp10,000-Rp350,000. Agus has exhibited his work all over the world. **Tjokrosuharto**, Jl. Panembahan 58, is a large fixed-price shop with a variety of crafts including *batik*. **Siti Astana Bilai-Batik**, Jl. K.H. Dahlan 29, features *batik tulis;* workshop nearby. **Gallery Yogya**, Jl. Gampingan 42 (behind ASRI), is an excellent source for *lurik*, the Javanese homespun. If the color you'd like is not in stock, it can be ordered; view the weaving process in the rear. **Ardiyanto Batik**, Jl. Taman Garuda, adopts traditional designs for fabric in cotton and silk for dresses, blouses, pillows, and pictures. Has a limited selection of good-quality *batik* at fixed prices. **Saptohudoyo Gallery**, Jl. Adisucipto (near airport), exhibits works of a variety of artists. **Lod Gallery**, in Taman Sari, sells highly original work by younger artists. The Water Palace area has the best bargains for *batik* paintings (as low as Rp1500), but much of it is amateurish. Also check out for possible bargains by top-of-the-line artists: **Amri Gallery**, Jl. Gampingan 67 (tel. 5135), and **Bagong Kussudiardjo**, Jl. Singosaren 9.

LEARNING *BATIK*

Batik is a lot more technical than you might imagine; without the technique, artistic development is impossible. *Batik* courses range from Rp4000 to Rp60,000 per week including materials (cotton, wax, *canting*, dyes), and sometimes even meals and accommodations. Courses teach the history of *batik;* the traditional designs, formulas for various waxes, how to prepare and use both chemical and natural dyes, how to hold, use, and clean the *canting* (wax pen) and *jegul* (brush); how to apply wax in fine and thick lines, how to remove wax from cloth. Most tourists who study *batik* in Yogya are quite satisfied with some of the low-standard courses offered because they are able to actually produce something—a moon rising over ricefields, a peasant's hut, cane stalks, a soaring *garuda*—or other such tourist drivel. The one-week courses offered down in the Water Palace area are generally not good value because the artists are too young and inexperienced, most of them just learning the trade themselves. Also beware of courses taught by the "world masters"; students are supposed to get a charge out of studying under such prestigious names, but you learn zero. The teacher doesn't teach but employs assistants (who sometimes don't speak English) to teach you.

Tops

Right around the corner from Superman's. For beginners, Tops teaches *batik* for as low as Rp4000 per week, including materials. Can't get any cheaper. An intensive study course with skilled artisans. Ask questions constantly. Open 6 days from 0830 to 1530; closed Sundays.

Bagong Kussudiardjo

This 7-day course, run by the dance choreographer Kussudiardjo, costs Rp23,000. Bagong practices an abstract, splashy style. He's located down a little side alley from Jl. Wates. Go over the RR tracks, down the hill, over the bridge, up the hill, and it's on the R-hand side. Look for a large black sign that points into the alley; the address is Jl. Laksamana Martadinata 9. The school only provides the wax and dyes; the student must supply his own *canting*, pencils, brushes, and cloth. Count on 3 m of thick cotton per day because you produce a lot of *batik*.

Tulus Warsito

Opposite a Chinese restaurant on Jl. Wates 31, this *batik* workshop offers courses for one day (Rp4000), 3 days (Rp11,500), 6 days (Rp23,000), 10 days (Rp37,000), and 3 weeks (Rp60,000). Open Mon.-Sat. 1000-1500. Instruction is in English by the internationally known artist Tulus Warsito.

Hadjir's

At the main entrance to the Water Castle, Taman Kp. 3/177. Hadjir, a graduate of IKIP Institute, has 12 years experience teaching *batik* to Westerners. The course is from 1400 to 1800, 3 to 5 days per week, and costs from Rp11,500 to Rp23,000.

Trihono's

At Tarate Gallery, Jl. Ngasem 75. Good training in *batik* as well as traditional and contemporary *batik* painting—Javanese and Balinese subjects. Always open and he welcomes visitors. He has some interesting work and occasionally puts on a show.

Batik Research Center

The most thorough course with the best facilities is Balai Penelitian Batik Kerayinan (Batik Research

Sri Sultan Hamengkubuwono XI: A thunderbolt came from a blue sky when this sultan of Yogya voted against the Dutch. Since then, he's shown himself to be one of the more enlightened leaders, a man of the people, a sort of aristocratic republican. When Gadjah Mada University sprang up during the war of independence, the sultan allowed students to sit for lectures in his throne room, and he gave the palace grounds over to the people for recreation. For more than 20 years the sultan has been a minister in several national governments, and he was Indonesia's vice-president until he stepped down in 1978. Hamengkubuwono is the last of Indonesia's hereditary rulers to retain royal status and his bathwater and fingernails are considered holy. Although his father died young, he has 31 brothers.

pendopo: The Yogya *kraton* is famous for its *pendopo* (open-sided pavilions with marble floors) incorporating both European and Indonesian court design, with combined Hindu, Buddhist, and Islamic motifs. All its pavilions are ornately gilded with painted rafters and panels, platforms supported by finely carved wooden beams, and cast-iron columns. Check out the carved solid teak pillars on the Bengsal Kencono, once famed for its grand *wayang wong* performances in the 1930s when all the royal courts of Java were competing for distinction in artistic pomp and skill. See also the small bandstand pavilion, and the Glass Pavilion with its vortex ceilings and red beams with carving all over them, the main pavilion for ceremonies and occasional banquets. The *kraton's* small museum contains paintings and photos of the royal lineage of sultans and their families, as well as gifts from foreign diplomats.

structure: The *kraton* is one km-square with walls 4 m high and 3 m thick, a walled fortress town 4.83 km in circumference. Its external walls were imitations of European castles' glacis, parapets, moats, bastions, and drawbridges (now vanished). Visitors must enter through a little side portal. On the *alun-alun* (large plazas) to the N and S of the palace complex grow the sacred *waringin* trees which still receive offerings. These *alun-alun* also serve as sportsfields and grounds for large annual fairs, parades, and religious celebrations. Mosques are usually located on a Javanese *kraton's* eastern side, facing W toward Mecca.

gateways: There are 5 gateways. Notice the cryptic symbols over the main ceremonial gate on the northern wall: 2 great snakes facing in opposite directions with their tails intertwined carved on a wooden lintel. According to ancient Javanese numerology: the number assigned to the snakes is 8, but to entwine is 4; therefore 2 snakes entwined as one translates as 2861. If this is read backwards it becomes 1682, the Javanese equivalent to our 1757, the year the *kraton* was built.

staff: Court attendants and *gamelan* musicians of the *kraton* wear special court costumes of *batik* and dark blue *pranarkan* (close-fitting, high-necked coats) with a *destar* headcloth (a neat Javanese turban) and bun in the back. *Kraton* women wear high-collared black *batik kebaya* dresses with special *gelung* hairdos. In the great *Garebeg* procession, 800 palace guards fire rifles in the air while they accompany mountains of food (*gunungan*) which are afterwards distributed to the poor. Soldiers use whips to keep the crowds back. These volunteer guardsmen are drawn from every class: workers, students, noblemen, farmers.

the interior: The ultimate in 18th C. palatial decor. Peacocks strut around the dusty yards. Extensive renovations were done in the 1920s by the sultan of that time. The *kraton* contains an extraordinary potpourri of gifts and furnishings from Europe: Italianate bronzes, carvings, stained glass, gilded mirrors, crystal chandeliers, Murano glasswork. See sacred *kris* in shrines with lamps burning before them, wooden palanquins and sedan chairs, horse-drawn carriages, venerable antique *gamelan* instruments. On Tues. and Fri. hundreds of *wayang* puppets—some of the nation's finest—are taken out from their boxes for an airing.

The Yogya *kraton*: Entrance fee: Rp400. This royal palace of the sultan is the archetype of classical court architecture on Java in which old-fashioned ideals of courtesy and etiquette are still practiced. The *kraton* has always been a center for artistic creation and many rituals and activities still take place. *Gamelan* and dance rehearsals are open to the public and guided tours are offered. A classical dance school teaches classical Yogyanese dance; for a schedule see chart on p. 295

Center), Jl. Kusumanegara 2 (tel. 3753), about 3 km E of the center of town. Open every day 0800-1330, Fri. until 1130, Sat. until 1230. The Institute (est. 1951) provides facilities, laboratories, and also carries out research, surveys, scientific investigation, and gives assistance and guidance on all the technical problems faced by artisans, home industries, and government agencies involved in *batik*. The Center offers 3-month courses, 6 days a week, 0900-1200, 3 people per class. Call for information on fees. The emphasis here is more on the industrial approach. The Research Center isn't the usual tourist circus but a real piece of Javanese culture. The exhibition room opens at 0800, and the factory at 0900, so you have an hour to look around the well-executed display on all the *batik* processes, even samples of the roots and fruits which are used to make various organic dyes. Buy *batik* here with the wax still smelling hot; not a huge selection but representative. Visitors may also tour the center's workshops and take photographs (with a flash) of all the processes. For the free tour by an English-speaking guide, check in at the front desk first.

THE YOGYA KRATON

1. Alun-alun Lor (Northern Square)
2. Tratag Pagelaran
3. Bangsal Pangrawit (Pangrawit Pavilion)
4. Tratag Sitinggil
5. Bangsal Manguntur Tangkil
6. Bangsal Witono
7. Kemandungan Utara (Keben Courtyard)
8. Bangsal Ponconiti
9. Bangsal Srimanganti
10. Bangsal Trajumas
11. Gedong Perworetno (Office of Sultan's Private Secretary)
12. Gedong Kuning (Yellow House, sultan's living quarters
13. Living quarters for the sultan's family
14. Bangsal Proboyekso
15. Bangsal Kencono (Golden Pavilion)
16. Bangsal Manis (Sweet Pavilion)
17. Tratag Bangsal Kencono
18. Bangsal Kemagangan
19. Kemagangan
20. Bangsal Kemandungan Kidul (Southern Kemandungan Pavilion)
21. Bangsal Sitinggil Kidul (Southern Sitinggil Pavilion
22. Alun-alun Kidul (Southern Square)
23. Gedong Kopo (Museum)
24. Bangsal Kesatriyan

SERVICES

Tourist Information Center
Stop here first, at Jl. Malioboro 16 (tel. 2812, ext. 30). From Jl. Pasar Kembang the office is halfway down Jl. Malioboro toward the GPO; open Mon.-Sat. from 0800 until the unusually late hour of 2100. An extremely helpful staff, they have a town plan, regional maps, calendar of events, etc., and complete train and bus schedules are posted on bulletin boards.

Public Services
The **GPO** is in an historic building on the corner of Jl. Senopati and Jl. Jen. A. Yani. They have a small philatelist department. The Pos Paket is in a side room. First they'll inspect your parcel, then give it to a *tukang bungkus* outside who will wrap it up securely in nylon for only Rp750. The **Immigration Office** is open Mon.-Thurs. 0730-1330; Fri. 0730-1100, and Sat. 0900-1230. Located 8 km out of town on Jl. Adisucipto on the road to Solo and the airport. The *bemo* drivers will let you off right in front.

Change Money
Better rates of exchange in Bali or Jakarta. Shop around for the best rate. **Bank Niaga** (Jl. Sudirman) usually gives the best rate; open 0800-1400, Sat. until 1300. Compare their rate with **Bank Bumi Daya** (on Jl. Sudirman beside the Merpati office). **Bank Negara 46,** adjacent to the GPO, also should be tried; go in the foreign exchange door. On holidays change cash or Amex cheques with the moneychangers who have a counter at Hotel Garuda.

Medical
Yogya on the whole has good medical and emergency treatment because Gajah Mada University is such an important center for medical studies. **RS Bethesda,** Jl. Jen. Sudirman 70 (tel. 2281) is the local hospital, (open 0900-1400); they usually just turn a mob of incompetent interns on you. Better just to go to a private doctor, 90% of whom speak English. Recommended are **Dr. Gandha,** Jl. Pringgodusuman 1, and **Dr. Sukadis,** Jl. Dagen.

Miscellaneous
The largest bookshop in Yoyga is **Agung Agung,** corner of Jl. Mangkubumi and Jl. Diponegoro; open 0900-2000 every day except Sunday. A real library, **Perpustakaan Negara,** is on Jl. Malioboro opposite the police headquarters—more books in the card catalogs than in the stacks. Old women (up to 95!) give massages (Rp3500 per hour) on the lane off Jl. Sosrowijaya. One of the most competent is **Panti Pijat** a blind man living at Jl. Gondongan Kidul 6 (beside Pramitha Hotel); ask for Tuna Netra. Another *pijat* (masseuse) works in the back of Losmen Jaya,

Gang II off Jl. Sosrowijayan. **P.T. Modern Photo Film Co.**, Jl. Malioboro 159 (very close to Jl. Sosrowijayan), charges only Rp195 per glossy print and takes only 25 minutes (if there's no line).

GETTING THERE

From Gambir Station in Jakarta, trains leave 9 times daily; 7½-12 hours, Rp4500-17,000 (depending on the train). The express night train, *Bima*, has 1st Class (Rp17,000) tickets which entitle you to a sleeping compartment. It leaves Jakarta's Gambir Station at 1600 and arrives in Yogya a bit after 2130; you can make arrangements with international-class hotels like Mutiara and Garuda to have someone pick you up at the station. By train from Surabaya is Rp3800-17,000, 7 hours, 6 trains daily. Three trains run daily from Bandung, Rp3800 3rd Class on the *Cepat,*, Rp13,500 2nd Class (8 hours) on the *Mutiara*. Once at Yogya's only train station, walk out the back entrance onto Jl. Pasar Kembang, closer to "hotel row" than going up to the main street and turning back. If arriving very early in the morning, Hotel Asia-Afrika or Hotel Mendut, very near the train station, are always open.

Night buses between Jakarta and Yogya cost around Rp8500 (Rp11,000 with a/c), 14 hours, 585 km. By night bus from Bandung is also Rp8500 (Rp10,000 with a/c), 6-7 hours. From Surabaya by night bus, Rp8500 (Rp10,000 with a/c), 8½ hours. From Semarang, Rp1350, 3 hours; Rp2700 by minibus, 2½ hours. By bus from Solo, Rp750, 2½ hours, or by minibus Rp1250, 2 hours.

Flights between Jakarta's Soekarno/Hatta Airport and Yogya (Rp60,100 on Garuda, Rp51,100 on Bouraq) are heavily booked; confirm reservations and be at the airport at least an hour early for check-in. At Yogya's Adisucipto Airport, catch a minibus into town on the highway which runs 300 m in front of the terminal. It costs Rp300 to Terminal Terban, then from there get a *becak* to the Jl. Kembang area for Rp500. Taxis to or from Yogya's airport charge Rp5500.

GETTING AROUND

The best way to see the city is to walk or ride a bicycle, like everyone else. The streets are filled with friendly hellos and the jangle of bicycle bells. Getting around town is easy: Jl. Malioboro is the main drag with the railroad station at the N end and the *kraton* at the S; all the inexpensive places to stay are just off this street. The main bus station, Terminal Umbulharjo, is in the SE of town, Rp150 by minibus.

Bikes And Motorcycles

At about Rp750-1000 per day, bikes are much cheaper than taking *becak*. To get the best rate, rent one for a week for around Rp4000-5000. Hotel Bagus on Gang II, Hotel Aziatic (Jl. Sosrowijayan 6), and Hotel Kartika all rent bikes. Get to these bike rental places before 0900-1000, otherwise all the good bikes are gone. Check your bike out carefully, and read the fine print. Always lock your bike where you can keep your eye on it. At the main market, GPO, and cinemas, watchmen guard your bike for Rp100. Return the bicycle and report the needed repairs to the manager. You pay for flats, Rp200, but if you bring it back to the rental place they'll do it. Motorcycles can be rented at Yogya Rental, Ana Rental, Java Rental, and Indonesia Rental (all on Jl. Pasar Kembang) for Rp7500 per day; negotiate cheaper weekly rates. **note:** Buy a bicycle or motorcycle at Pasar Sepeda on Jl. Haryono where there are hundreds of them, row on row. Good used 100 cc motorbikes run about Rp450,000, bicycles Rp6000-15,000 (new ones cost Rp60,000).

Becak, Andong, Bis

Becak here are extremely reasonable, costing only around Rp400 per km, or Rp1000 by the hour. There's no shortage of them, so if you don't get this rate or near it, just walk away and give your business to the competition. Many *becak* drivers approach you proposing Rp300-500 per hour, but their intention is to take you on a shopping tour. If you're interested, this is an excellent way to shop around, though you have to pay the cost of their commissions from the shopowners if you buy anything. Horsedrawn *andong* (capacity 3 people) are another delightful way to get out to places like Kota Gede (Rp3000 RT) or Kasongan (Rp5000 RT). *Andong* hang around Jl. Senopati to the E of the GPO, behind Pasar Beringharjo (Jl. Suryotomo), and down the small streets on the edge of town. Orange *bis kota*, which run only from 0600 to 1900 cost Rp150, as do the much smaller minibuses which circulate constantly on set routes around the city. The tourist office, Jl. Malioboro 16, will sketch out a quick *bis kota* route map for you. From Jl. Malioboro, board a bus (no. 1 or 4) to the Terminal Bis Umbulharjo, passing Kota Gede en route (you have to walk 300 m). Catch minibuses to Prambanan (Rp400) from Terminal Terban, Jl Simanjuntak. Local *kobutri* (yellow) minibuses also depart from the terminal beside the Jl. Senopati shopping center for all points in the city.

Taxis, Rented Cars

Hire taxis from Jl. Senopati beside the main GPO or from in front of big hotels like Garuda and Mutiara. Taxi fare from the airport is Rp5500. Within the city, Rp4500 per hour (min. 2 hours), or from say Jl. Malioboro to the airport or to the Ambarrukmo Hotel, Rp5000. To make arrangements to charter taxis or minibuses, go through your hotel or go to the taxi stand beside the GPO on Jl. Senopati. Out-of-town taxi trips have fixed rates: Prambanan, Rp15,000 (32 km RT); Borobudur, Rp25,000 (84 km RT); Solo, Rp40,000 (130 km RT); Dieng Plateau, Rp80,000 (650 km RT), etc. Taxis (up to 4 people) and minibuses (8-9) can be chartered for approx. Rp60,000 per day within the city, Rp80,000 per day outside the city.

FROM YOGYA

Local Buses And Minibuses
The main bus station, Umbulharjo, is 5 km from Yogya's center in the SE corner of the city near Kota Gede, on Jl. Veteran and Jl. Menteri Supeno. Buses leave from here 0330-1900, every 10-15 min. for all the towns in the immediate area: Magelang, Rp475; Muntilan, Rp400; Parangtritis, Rp400; Klaten, Rp450; Wates, Rp450; Kaliurang, Rp450 (or catch a minibus from Terminal Terban on Jl. Senopati); Kartosuro, Rp600; Samas, Rp350. **to Borobudur:** Buses N to Magelang and Borobudur depart from either Terminal Umbulharjo or from Terminal Pingit (Jl. Magelang), which is only a 10-min. walk N of the Jl. Pasar Kembang area. Bus from Yogya to Muntilan is Rp400, then change buses at Muntilan for Borobudur, Rp250. Be very careful of pickpockets on local buses out to Borobudur. They're particularly deft at cutting shoulder bags with razors and extracting valuables without you even knowing it.

Long-distance Buses/Minibuses
Many bus offices are on the Jl. Mangkubumi/Jl. Malioboro extension, just up the street from the train station, while ticket agencies conveniently line Jl. Sosrowijayan (where express buses also pick you up). Learn from other travelers or the tourist office about the latest best buses and fares. Long-distance buses usually leave from between 1500 and 1930 from in front of their offices, and travel straight through the cool night; get there at least 30 min. before departure. To Bandung, **Bandung Express,** Jl. Diponegoro 116; Rp8500 (10,000 a/c), 13 hours. To Bogor, **Bogor Jaya Co.,** Jl. Mangkubumi 79; Rp9000, 15 hours. To Malang, **Agung** or **Pemudi,** Jl. Mangkubumi 15; Rp8500 (11,000 a/c), 10 hours. To Surabaya, **Agung Express,** Jl. Mangkubumi 15 (tel. 2157), or **Kembang,** Jl. Diponegoro 116; Rp8500 (Rp11,000 a/c), 10 hours. Many companies do the run to Jakarta — **Agung, Limex, Muncul** (with offices all along Jl. Mangkubumi). Check fares, seating, routes, and photos of buses at the numerous ticket agents along Jl. Sosrowijayan; could save you a lot of time visiting individual company offices. For Cilicap (where you board the ferry to Pangandaran), buses leave early in the morning from Jl. Sosrowijaya; Rp65000.

To Bali
Buses leave for Denpasar from 1600 to 1800, and get in at 0630-0830. They charge from Rp13,000 (Rp17,000 for deluxe a/c bus) including ferry trip, serve tasteless meals, and no standing passengers are allowed. Companies with good night buses to Bali are **Cakrawala** and **Puspasari,** but they all drive like madmen. Buy tickets at **Terminal Umbulharjo** or at Jl. Sosrowijayan where there are dozens of agents. It's cheaper to do it step by step: train to Surabaya, another train to Banyuwangi, minibus to ferry at Ketapang, ferry to Gilimanuk, then local minibuses to Denpasar or Lovina Beach.

By Train
The railroad station is right in the middle of town just off Jl. Mangkubumi. Trains to W. Java are generally uncomfortable and more expensive than buses, but trains to E. Java are cleaner, faster, and less expensive. Except on the more expensive trains like the *Bima* or *Mutiara,* students are sometimes able to get a 25% discount. For the *Bima,* buy your ticket at least 2-3 days in advance. For the *Senja* (dusk) trains, get in line early on the day of departure to buy your ticket. *Mutiara* tickets are sold only one hour before departure. Buy snacks for the train from the *warung* and shops along Jl. Pasar Kembang. **to Jakarta:** Nine trains daily, 12 hours, from Rp4500 on the *Cepat* to Rp17,000 on the *Bima.* Catch the late *Senja* trains and roll in early in the morning. The *Cepat* departs at 0650, arrives at 2100; the *Senja V* departs 1700, arrives 0500; the *Senja Ekonomi* departs 1826, arrives 0630; the *Gaya Baru Malam* departs 2025, arrives 0830; the *Bima* departs 2140, arrives 0900. **to Bandung:** Three trains per day, from as low Rp3500 3rd Class on the *Cepat* up to Rp13,500 on the *Mutiara.* The *Cepat* departs 0820, arrives 1800; the *Ekspres Siang* departs 1140, arrives 2100; the *Mutiara* departs at 2339, arrives 0800. **to Mt. Bromo:** A train leaves at 0635 (3rd Class only) and arrives in Probolinggo at around 1700 which leaves plenty of time to get to Ngadisari by nightfall to rest up for the Bromo climb the next morning. **to Surabaya:** Six trains daily, from Rp2900 on the *Argopuro* up to Rp17,000 1st Class on the *Bima.* The *Gaya Baru Malam* departs 2238, arrives 0500; the *Bima* departs 0120 and arrives 0800. **to Bali:** Take a Surabaya train, with further connections to Banyuwangi, then ferry and bus to Denpasar. If you catch the *Ekspres Siang* at 1420 from Yogya, it gets you in Surabaya at 2030, time enough to catch the *Mutiara Timur* which leaves Surabaya at 2200 for Banyuwangi.

By Air
Garuda, Jl. Mangkubumi 56 (tel. 4400, closes at 1600); **Merpati,** Jl. Sudirman 9-11 (tel. 4272, closes at 1500) in Hotel Merdeka; **Bouraq,** Jl. Sudirman 37 (tel. 86664, closes at 1700). Airport tax, Rp1400. For the airport, take the bus to Solo and get off in front of the terminal, a 300-m walk. Garuda sample fares: Jakarta, 4 flights daily, Rp60,100; Denpasar, 3 flights daily, Rp56,200; Palembang, one flight per day, Rp116,700.

Merpati has a wide range of flights from Yogya to the eastern half of the archipelago. Sample fares: Surabaya, daily at 0700, Rp29,300; Samarinda, daily at 1400, Rp130,400; Denpasar, Tues. and Sat. at 0700, Rp143,600; Ampenan (Lombok), 5 days weekly at 1240, Rp65,600; Kupang (Timor), 5 days weekly at 0700, Rp143,600. Also check out Bouraq flights; they have one to Tarakan (E. Kalimantan) each day at 0835 for Rp178,700.

Tours

If you're a little short on time or would like to get a quick introduction into a specific site, dozens of small tour companies and/or hotels offer 4- to 8-hour tours around the city and to surrounding areas. The early-morning tours organized by the travel agents and hotels (Aziatic, Asia-Afrika, Kota, etc.) in the Jl. Kembang and Jl. Sosrowijayan areas are the cheapest. In these, as many as 15 travelers, or as few at 4, go along in one bus; if they don't make the minimum, they don't leave. Examples: "Borobudur Sunrise Tour"

(Rp8500, 4 hours); "Merapi Volcano Close-up Tour," starting at 2230, Rp65,000 (4 people); and tours to the Dieng Plateau, Rp9000 pp (a bit steep), min. 6 people, departing at 0700. The "City Arts and Craft Tour" (3 hours) takes you around to silversmiths, *wayang* plays, a *batik* factory and an art gallery; Rp8000. If you want to spend longer at certain sites, one idea is to take, for example, Hotel Indonesia's Rp6000 tour to Dieng (which visits Borobudur en route), then just stay overnight at Dieng and catch the same tour company going back the next day.

Ask the tourist office, Jl. Malioboro 16, about other, higher-priced special-interest tours. The travel agent **Sri Rama** in Hotel LPP (Jl. Demangan Baru 8) sells luxury-class a/c tours for Rp12,500-30,000. **Intan Pelangi**, Jl. Malioboro 18 (tel. 3644), offers daily cultural tours of Yogya by bus, Rp12,000. For organized tours such as to Imogiri (US$15), Borobudur (US$18), also inquire at **Pacto**, Jl. Mangkubumi (tel. 2740), and **Nitour Inc.**, Jl. K.H.A. Dahlan 71 (tel. 3165/2114, ext. 4).

VICINITY OF YOGYA

Kasongan is a potters' village 45 min. (Rp200) by minibus from the corner of Jl. Bantul and Jl. Haryono, or take a delightful ride in a 4-wheeled horsedrawn carriage *(andong)*. Well known for its decorative, brightly painted children's moneyboxes resembling roosters, lions, elephants, dragons, *garuda;* Rp1000-4000. Ceramics such as large pots, vases, and bowls are also for sale. Walk around to see the potters bisquing pieces in big blazing straw fires. In front of each is a display showcase. Customers—tourists, villagers, purchasing agents from curio shops—choose the articles they want and haggle over the price (half what they go for in Yogya's Pasar Ngasem). Pieces can also be special-ordered (allow 10 days).

Pak Warno's

High-quality *wayang golek* and carved leather screens are made at Pak Warno's in a village near Kasongan, near Suharto's birthplace. Start walking from Kasongan on the road back to Yogya but turn L at the 6.5-km marker where the sugarcane train tracks cross the road, then follow this side road for about 10 min.; villagers will point the way. The delicacy of this brilliant man's work is extraordinary. Some sell for as little as Rp6000, though if it's done in gold leaf, it's twice as much. Put these beautiful *wayang* in a window to show them off, display them on a framed textile background, or tie them on a string and let them dangle so that the light leaks through.

KOTA GEDE

Pronounced "GEE-day." Six km SE of Yogya's city center, Kota Gede (founded in 1579) was once the capital of the old Mataram kingdom and is older than Yogya itself. The grave of Prince Senopati, founder of the Mataram kingdom, is only ½ km from the *pasar.* Coming from Tom's Silver, take the first L after the market and enter the mossy burial ground (donation), shady courtyards, and ancient mosque. Dress conservatively. Only go to the graveyard on Mon. 0930-1200 and Fri. 1330-1600 when there's activity; otherwise there's nothing to see but sacred turtles in a dirty pool. Many other royal personalities, under ornamental parasols, are entombed in Makam Senopati, less than one km beyond. Visit the village's country market which sells all kinds of fruits, clothes, implements. Not many tourists—too bad there's no accommodation in this village.

Silverworking

The many busy, clanging silverware shops here consume some 50 tons of silver annually! You're free to wander around through big workshops full of men and boys hammering on anvils, filing, polishing, heating, and soldering on strips of bright silver, using the simplest of handtools. There are 2 grades of silver: 92.5% sterling, and 80%. For sale in display rooms is a huge variety of pieces. Pay anything from Rp3000 for a ring set with a semi-precious stone, up to Rp3,725,000 for complete silver dinner service for 12. Most of the silver shops inventory the same items, seldom deviating from the sure sellers, but all will make anything to order. Visit **Tom's Silver**, Jl. Kota Gede 3-1 A (tel. 3070/2818), the largest and most established workshop, with a large showroom (they bargain only if you buy wholesale). Their workmanship is better, but their prices are also higher. If you spend enough, they might even lay a Tom's Silver T-shirt on you. At **MD Silver** down the street (on Jl. Keboan), jewelry sells for less; here you may also see *wayang kulit* being made from *kerbau* hide. Their showroom is open 0800-2000 (until 1700 on Sun.); workshop open 0800-1700. Numerous other shops line the streets of Kota Gede, many selling not only silver but tortoise shell and horn handicrafts, curios such as small stuffed turtles (Rp15,000), and fake antiques.

Getting There
Pedal the back way down Jl. Gembira Loka through the countryside. Travel first straight down the road past the zoo until you come to a bend to the L, then head straight until you reach a paved road. Turn R at the sign KOTA GEDE 3 KM. Costs around Rp3000 for a chartered *andong* or Rp1500 for a *becak* for 2 from Yogya.

IMOGIRI

A cemetery for the royal houses of Yogya and Solo since the early kings of Mataram, Imogiri lies 20 km SE of Yogya, a 30-min. (Rp450) minibus ride. Climb barefoot up the 345 warm stone steps to the sacred burial ground at the top. A great sun-dappled stairway, like a ladder leaning up against the sky, begins a short walk from where the minibus drops you off. The mighty Sultan Agung was the first Javanese king to be interred here, his tomb built in the mid-17th C. on a small rocky promontory. Since then, nearly every king—*susuhunan* and sultan alike—have found their final resting place side by side on this highly venerated hill. As you walk up the shady stairs, get some of the best views of the surroundings and sea. Allow several hours, but it's worth the effort.

Sights
This is not a place where crowds of tourists come on buses; you have to make an effort to get here. You may very well be the only Westerner present, but it could be one of the highlights of your visit to Yogya. Hardly anyone speaks English. Pay the entrance fee (Rp200) and sign the visitors book. An important pilgrimage site of ancestor worship, you must wear formal Javanese dress to enter. On the premises men

palace guard, prajurit warengan

may rent a *sarung* and women a *kain* and *kebaya* for a modest fee. Three major courtyards are laid out at the top of the stairway: to the L are buried the *susuhunan* of Solo, to the R the sultans of Yogya, and in the center are the Mataram kings. Each big courtyard contains smaller forecourts, inner courts, and tombs; some graves are over 400 years old. The Royal Tombs are only open Mon. 1030-1200, and Fri. 1330-1600; the tomb of Sultan Agung is open around 1430 on Fri., the best day to visit. The graves are closed during *Ramadan* and no photography is permitted in the graveyards themselves.

Vicinity Of Imogiri
At one end of the front courtyard a path takes you up to the silent, windswept summit that takes in magnificent views of green *sawah* and brown *tegalan* below to the W, while G. Merapi broods darkly under clouds to the N and the tempestuous Indian Ocean can be made out through the haze to the south. It takes 10 min. to walk the path completely around the burial complex.

PARANGTRITIS

The place to go if you want to take a break from Yogya, Parangtritis is 27 km S on the Indian Ocean. This is the most popular and accessible of the beaches S of Yogya—a beautiful, isolated seaside

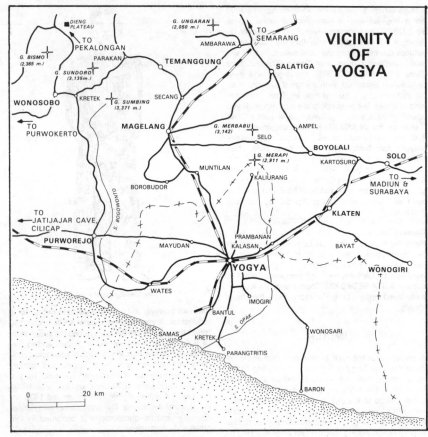

VICINITY OF YOGYA

0 _____ 20 km

spot with wild seas, dangerous riptides, a good swimming pool, and friendly people. Just take your books, *sarung*, and a musical instrument. Accommodations are inexpensive, and food is cheap and plentiful. During the week, life is simple here and very quiet; on holidays and weekends the place swarms with thousands of local tourists. Fortunately, most visitors stay only for a few hours. Meet Dahalan, the witchdoctor who sells snakes, stones, bracelets, and gives massages. Magic mushrooms can be bought from little old ladies or from kids on bikes ("Hello, Mushroom!"); freshest in the afternoons. Take them to a *warung* and have them cooked up for you in a soup or omelette. Visit the excellent *pemandian*, a freshwater swimming pool and *mandi* (Rp200 entrance). A superstitious, lonely place; when the village is half-deserted it feels like a ghost town, pitch black at night under a million stars. The surrounding area is

dramatic too, with many jagged cliffs and beaches of meadow-like gray sand dunes and eerie moonscapes stretching for kilometers.

Nyai Loro Kidul

Parangtritis is the domain of Nyai Loro Kidul, the legendary Queen of the South Seas. Like Neptune, her hair is green and full of shells and seaweed; she holds court over sea nymphs and creatures of the deep. Venerated and feared by the Javanese, Loro Kidul is summoned by a gong on the evening of the Muslim day of rest (Thurs.), when a bamboo tray of rice, bananas, jasmine flowers, cosmetics, and coconuts is offered to the eternally youthful goddess. Don't wear green; that's *her* color, and she has been known to yank people into the sea for the transgression! Parangkusumo, one km down the beach, is where Sultan Senopati lived for some months with

Nyai Loro Kidul in the 17th century. The sacred spot of their rendezvous is enclosed by a fence, contains a symbolic tree, a lamp, and remains of flowers and incense offerings from Javanese (including the mayor of Jakarta) who come to ask direction and aid from Nyai Loro Kidul. Visitors may enter this enclosure; the *juru kunci;* will offer your questions to the queen for Rp200, plus take your offerings.

Accommodations And Food
About 15 *losmen* line the main road down to the beach. Facilities are similar, a bit limited and unhygienic (the nickname for Parangtritis is "meningitis"). Cheaper places tend to have no electricity. Rooms rent from Rp2000 to Rp3500, but it could be cheaper off-season or during the week. Right at the entrance is **Suharjo's,** the cheapest *warung* and the place to socialize. One of the best and coolest *losmen,* with good food, is **Widodo's;** Rp2000 s, Rp3000 d. **Peng. Parang Endong** is a little beyond the village; Rp2000-4000 s or d, with a well-maintained freshwater *kolam renang* (swimming pool).

Getting There
Catch a minibus on the corner of Jl. Kol Sugiyono and Jl. Parangtritis in Yogya all the way to Parangtritis for Rp600; poor road but good ride. If the river at Kretek is swollen during the wet season, a *sampan* charges Rp300 to take you to the other side. At other side of the river either walk 4 km to Parangtritis (recommended), or take another minibus (Rp200). You can also ride on the back of a motorcycle into Parangtritis (Rp500), for the experience! *Dokar* are used to asking (and getting) exorbitant prices as if they were swank carriages in New York's Central Park! Alternatively, rent a bicycle in Yogya and bike, ferry, and walk—depending on the season—all the way to Parangtritis. The last minibuses return to Yogya around 1800.

Vicinity Of Parangtritis
One km before the village is the hotspring **Parang Wedang,** entrance Rp200. Take nice walks up into the hills of this weirdly beautiful and menacing area. An odd plant here "wilts" when you touch it. Watch men gather the ingredients for Chinese birds-nest soup on elastic-like bamboo scaffolding over steep cliffs. The soup isn't actually made from the whole nest but from the saliva which the birds use to glue their nests together. During the war for independence, caves in the vicinity were used as hideouts by General Sudirman and his band of guerillas. Follow the marked route of the guerillas toward the top, then turn R where a rock points to **Gua Langse.** The walk to this cave is through undergrowth; rough getting there but upon your arrival they may have a pot of tea waiting. Ceremonies are often held here—strange Javanese arts of witchcraft. Swim in the pools (Rp350) fed by spring water flowing through bamboo pipes. Another path eventually leads to cliffs with

superb views down the coast and out to sea.

Other Beaches
Samas Beach is 30 km S, Rp1000 by minibus from Yogya via Bantul: violent surf, hot black sand, lagoons, eerie landscapes, steel-colored dunes, several *warung.* **Baron Beach** is 55 km SE of Yogya. First take a minibus to Wonosari (Rp1200, 40 km), then catch another one to Baron. Relatively isolated, a long narrow beach, with shallow water and safe swimming, stretches along a sheltered cove. **Kukup** is yet another white-sand beach E of Baron, with several caves and limestone shallows. The Kukup turn-off is one km before Baron; take the road all the way. Though safer than Parangtritis, be careful of currents while swimming.

GUNUNG MERAPI

Its name means "Fire Mountain." More or less continuously erupting, this 2,950-m-high mountain 25 km N of Yogya is one of the most destructive volcanos in the world. Merapi needs 6 volcanologists' posts high on its slopes to keep an eye on it, plus a crew of up to 1,000 men on call to keep a rein on the volcano's destructive force. When G. Merapi erupted in 1006, it covered Borobudur 48 km away and devastated the land around the monument to such an extent that it remained uninhabitable for generations. Merapi has killed nearly 1,500 people in 25 eruptions since 1930. The mountain erupts about once every 5½ years. Its last major eruption was in 1969, when boiling volcanic mud smothered and burned more than 300 houses, 18 bridges, and hundreds of hectares of cropland. That only 3 people died was a tribute to the early-warning system the government initiated in earnest in 1961. Today more than 40 checkdams and dikes protect the populace, and large areas beneath the volcano are "forbidden zones."

From Selo
Merapi can be climbed easiest from Selo; from Kaliurang it's much more challenging. First get to Selo (about 1,000 m above sea level), a small village near Boyolali. From Yogya to Boyolali it's Rp400 by minibus, then from Boyolali to Selo, Rp350. Once in Selo, register at the police station. Stay overnight in the dormitory (Rp2000) or perhaps on a bamboo bed in the house of the guide you've already hired. Look around for a good guide so you don't walk to your death; he must have experience with the mountain. A recommendation from the police helps. When the minibus stops, a guide should present himself. He charges depending on the size of the group, about Rp15,000 pp during the day and up to Rp20,000 for a night climb, maybe cheaper if you bargain. To make the sunrise, leave at 0100 and it's a 4-5 hour climb to the top. The guide leads the way up through steep

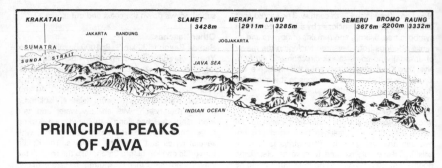

PRINCIPAL PEAKS OF JAVA

mountain forest tracks to the 2,950-m peak, puffing away on cigarettes he's bummed from you. **organized tours:** Travel agencies and hotels along Jl. Sosrowijayan in Yogya also organize climbs up G. Merapi, charging anywhere from Rp50,000-60,000 for 4-6 people. This price includes transport, breakfast, snacks, drinks. You start by van from Yogya at 2100, arriving in Selo at 2300. After resting in a small *kampung* house, you start the climb at 0130, arriving at the top by 0530 or 0600.

The Climb
Take a sleeping bag, waterproof clothing, food, water, and wear good boots. The very steep climb first takes you through a countryside of *lantana* flowers and misty ridges, then up through raspberry country to the barren peak. The view before the sunrise is unbelievable—the whole Milky Way! It's possible to go down into the crater where the sulphur burns your throat. It takes 4-5 hours to go up, but only 2 hours to get back down. Little lava stones, acting like ball bearings underfoot, help your descent immeasurably. If you want to see the gates of hell, go up while Merapi is erupting at night to see huge red globs of molten rock glowing in the darkness. It could be extremely dangerous to do this night climb without a guide who knows the mountain intimately, not just somebody who tells you he does. It's about a 10-min. walk from the summit to the gas jets which at night glare red hot, with rivulets of orange-red molten lava and sparks spilling over the rim, black acrid smoke, and enormous clouds of steam. During this hot lava stage, Yogya's normally tranquil river is turned into a cocoa-colored torrent.

From Kaliurang To G. Plawangan
Two gates (Rp200 each), the W. Gate and the E. Gate, and 2 trails lead up to the seismological station on G. Plawangan (1,260 m), but from there neither leads to the summit. It takes less than 1½ hours to climb to this volcanologist observatory where you can observe activity on G. Merapi. Friendly guys here—their only

instruments are seismographs and binoculars. See their photos of the big 1954 eruption. The *warung* near the observatory sells drinks, fruits, and biscuits (if there are too many tourists, prices are high). You can't see the crater from this post; there's a difference of 1,636 m between this observatory and the top.

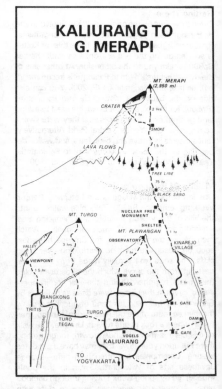

KALIURANG TO G. MERAPI

From Kaliurang To G. Merapi

The beginning of one path up the mountain, the S. Gate, is at the end of the road where the bus stops. Follow an easy, well-trod footpath with log steps to the NE; you can't really lose your way. Walk about an hour from Kaliurang to the small village of Kinarejo on the NE side of G. Plawangan, and from there make your ascent to Merapi's peak, (2,950 m) via a special route—a long way. This is not something tourists would normally undertake as it's a very strenuous but rewarding 6-7 hour climb in all from Kaliurang. Refer to map; times given are from either the E. or S. gates.

KALIURANG

A 900-m-high mountain resort, 26 km N of Yogya on G. Merapi's southern slope, with guesthouses, restaurants, snack bars, tennis courts, swimming pool, waterfalls, fantastic montane hiking. Merapi is usually visible around 0600-0700 but becomes cloud-covered the rest of the day. If you want to just while away some time, head up here. Kaliurang is the closest resort to the city, but is only busy on weekends. Go up during the week when it's cheaper. Minibuses leave every 15 min. from Jl. Mataram in Yogya, Rp600 (Rp500 return). From Yogya you can also take a bus (Rp300) leaving 4 times daily—board them at the bus station or at the intersection of Jl. Simantunjak and Jl. Sudirman (northern part of the city).

Accommodations And Food

Vogels Homestay gets high marks from travelers—it ranks right up there with the Cave Lodge in northern Thailand. Charging only Rp1500 dorm and Rp3000 d, they also serve good food. But its best feature is the amount of information on Indonesia posted on the wall and in visitors' books, and in the enthusiasm shown visitors by your Christian host. You'll see Vogels as soon as you get off the bus. Comfortable old **Hotel Kaliurang** is on the R just before you reach the top of the hill. Good location and nice garden; Rp3000 s, Rp4000 d, but can be bargained down, particularly on weekdays. During the weekend most hotels charge steeper rates (Rp6000-8000); if you stay a week, maybe less. Many cheap *warung* are in the vicinity of the market and the parking lot.

THE PRAMBANAN PLAIN

It took a staggering agricultural productivity to enable pompous feudal monarchs to erect temples to their own glorification. Thus the rich Prambanan Plain, 17 km NE of Yogya (Rp400 by minibus) on the road to Solo, has the most extensive Hindu temple ruins in all of Indonesia. There's no telling how many more are still under the earth. Lying today among villages and green ricefields with the sharp peak of G. Merapi in the background, most of these temple complexes were built between the 8th and 10th centuries. They were abandoned when the Hindu-Javanese kings moved from C. to E. Java in the 13th century. Around 1600, all extant temples were toppled by an earthquake. In the 19th C., their blocks were carried off to pave roads, build sugar mills, bridges, and railroads. The Dutch finally started restoration work in the late 1930s.

Getting There

Only Rp400 by minibus from Yogya's Jl. Solo, or a flat, easy bike ride from Yogya on a special bicycle lane to Prambanan village. Or you can sling your rented bike on top of the minibus, then use it to tour the temples. Just 1½ km before Prambanan is a restaurant which serves special *mbok berek* chicken for Rp4000-5000, enough for 4; other *mbok berek* restaurants are found close to the Prambanan's minibus terminal. **from Solo:** Take a minibus (Rp1000) from the minibus station near Cilingin Terminal to Prambanan village. On this road to Yogya, about 5 km outside of Klaten, is a side road to Candi Merak, 5 km from the highway.

PRAMBANAN TEMPLE COMPLEX

The largest temple complex on Java, Prambanan's central courtyard contains 3 large structures: a main temple dedicated to Shiva flanked by those of Brahma (to the S) and Vishnu (to the N). Besides these, the complex originally contained 244 minor temples *(candi perwara)*, all arranged in 4 rows. Only 2-3 of these have been restored. The 2 small *candi* at the side of the main terrace were probably the treasuries where the jewels and gold were kept. There's a Rp100 admission to the main complex. Open 0600-1800; go early. See the Ramayana Ballet performed here, illuminated by generator-powered spotlights, during full moon nights from June to Oct. (see Yogya's "Events" for details).

Shiva Temple

This large central temple was dedicated to Shiva the Destroyer. It was built to contain the remains of the Mataram King Balitung who reigned in the middle of the 9th C. and claimed himself to be a reincarnation of Shiva. Much of the structure had collapsed by the last century and not until 1937 was reconstruction begun.

Now a wonder of restoration, this tall, elegant temple is a synthesis of both N. and S. Indian architectural styles. Almost 50 m high, for 1,000 years it was the tallest building on Java. Its lavish decorations, panels, motifs, statues, details of architecture all show an outstanding sense of composition. The whole structure is perfectly balanced and fit together; while walking around its 20 sides, it never seems to change. See it late in the day when the crowds thin out and the angle of the sun turns it gold.

Reliefs

Candi Prambanan's relief sculptures, realistic and humorous at the same time, are among the finest in all of Indonesian art. With the renovation of the Brahma temple (finished in March 1987), the panels are now complete. Four stairways lead up to the walk-around gallery that takes you entirely around the temple, facing the 4 points of the compass. The body of the terrace is decorated with the unique "Prambanan motifs." Steps are lined with part-fish, part-elephants, and little niches of smiling dancers, with trees-of-heaven on each side. On the lower foundations are seated deities flanked by attendants. On the outer walls are 62 panels of dynamic dancing figures and celestial musicians taken from the ancient *Manual of the Indian Art of Dancing;* see the beautiful, haunting, cosmic dance of Shiva. In order to follow the story, go up the E stairway first, down to the L after the gallery, then slowly around the temple proper. On the inner wall gallery are *Ramayana* scenes even more dramatic, expressive and down to earth than Borobudur's. *Rama* stories, of an unknown version, were first depicted in Indonesia on this temple in the 9th century. Sprinkled throughout are trees-of-heaven surrounded by animals, pots of money, half-women and half-birds *(kannara);* also rams, deer, cats, monkeys, geese, and comic hares with oversized ears. Trees, rocks, and water are more stylized, more earthy and responsive than Borobudur's, with monkeys frolicing in fruit trees and busy kitchen scenes. Here and there on the reliefs you can even see traces of Buddhism (many *stupa).* In the office at Candi Prambanan, ask to see the erotic bas-relief.

Sculpture

A 3-m-high statue of the 4-armed god Shiva in royal dress is enshrined in the main eastern chamber; there are also minor rooms for the Divine Teacher, Ganesha, and in the northern cell the goddess Durga kills a demon-bull. The Prambanan temple is often called Candi Lorojonggrang after the statue of the "slender cursed virgin" in the N room, her nose missing and her breasts worn shiny smooth by adoring hands over hundreds of years. Legend has it that this cursed virgin was turned to stone when she refused to wed a *raksasa.* In the courtyard in the small shrine opposite Shiva's great temple is a statue of Shiva's bull, Nandi,

the only free-standing stone statue of an animal in ancient Indonesian art, sculpted in a simple, powerful, yet natural style.

OUTLYING TEMPLES

Numerous other temple complexes are found along the 17-km road between Yogya and Solo. Keep a sharp lookout for the small signs posted by the Archaeological Service. Temples Sambisari, Kalasan, and Sari lie between the airport and the town of Prambanan. Temples Lumbung, Bubrah, Sewu, and Candi Plaosan are all more or less N along the same side of the road from the Prambanan complex. To start, follow road signs pointing towards Candi Lumbung. To visit these outlying temples, *andong* can be hired near Prambanan's minibus terminal at about Rp1000 per hour but it's more enjoyable walking (in the cool of the morning) the network of trails over hills and through fields or take a bicycle (perfect). Only Kalasan and Prambanan ask for money (Rp200 each) to enter; none but the Shiva Temple (also called Candi Lorojonggrang) charge for photography (Rp200).

Candi Sewu

The "Thousand Temples," one km N of Prambanan: take the road behind Candi Lorojonggrang. Dating from the first half of the 9th C., today Sewu is largely in ruins, scattered in piles of stone blocks. It consisted once of a large central temple and 250 minor temples and shrines with 2 rows of side chapels. To assist pilgrims in their meditations, the whole complex was built in the shape of a *mandala.* Many niches, dark passageways, and 2-m-tall *dwarapala* (Sanskrit for "gate guard") demons lean on one knee, armed with swords and clubs, guard the entrances. The main temple has been completely dismantled and removed for restoration with only a slab in the shape of a Greek cross remaining to mark its position.

Candi Plaosan

To the NE of Candi Sewu 2½ km, this Buddhist temple complex consists of 3 groups of principal temples in a row. Attributed to a 9th C. Saliendra princess, Plaosan combines the function of both temple and monastery. Statues of pilgrims and well-preserved reliefs show groups of devout pilgrims in procession with downcast eyes. An image of Raksasa Dwarapala was made out of a single block of stone. Although the outside is still rough, the *kala-*heads over the windows inside are in mint condition. Both Hindu and Buddhist religious symbols and ornamentation exist here side by side, indicative of peaceful coexistence of the 2 religions at that time on Java.

Candi Lumbung

Five hundred m NE of Candi Lorojonggrang, this

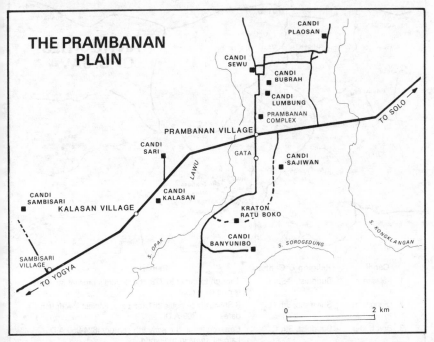

THE PRAMBANAN PLAIN

CANDI PLAOSAN

CANDI SEWU

CANDI BUBRAH

CANDI LUMBUNG

PRAMBANAN COMPLEX

PRAMBANAN VILLAGE

TO SOLO

CANDI SARI

LAWU

GATA

CANDI SAJIWAN

CANDI SAMBISARI

KALASAN VILLAGE

CANDI KALASAN

KRATON RATU BOKO

SAMBISARI VILLAGE

TO YOGYA

S. OPAK

CANDI BANYUNIBO

S. SOROGEDUNG

S. KONGKLANGAN

0   2 km

Buddhist-style temple.consists of one main temple surrounded by 16 smaller ones.

Candi Sari
Near Kalasan village, 200 m N of the "14.4-KM" signpost from Yogya, in the middle of coconut and banana groves. Its design is woven together superbly, like a basket. The 2nd floor served as a priests' dormitory. The famous decorations on the panels between the windows, with 36 large semi-divine beings dancing and playing instruments, are similar in style to Candi Kalasan's reliefs.

Candi Kalasan
On the L bank of the Opak River just 50 m from the Yogya-Solo highway at the "14 KM" marker, it's one of the easiest of the outlying group to visit. Kalasan is the oldest Mahayana Buddhist temple in Indonesia to which a date can be set: A.D. 778. The present exterior was done much later. In fact, there are actually 3 Candi Kalasans: the present one, still standing, turned out to be the 3rd building erected on top of and around the second one, within which are the remains of the first. This Buddhist royal mausoleum is set in a lush garden landscape. Once completely covered in multicolored shining stucco, unique niche decora-

tions and probably the most beautiful *kala*-head in C. Javanese art are surrounded by heavenly musicians. Beautiful craftsmanship. The exquisite moss-covered interior is bathed in light.

Candi Sajiwan
Two km SE of the Prambanan temple complex near the village of Sajiwan. Turn S at the sign on the eastern outskirts of Prambanan village and walk about 2 km. At the foot of this Buddhist temple are reliefs depicting the Tantric tales with the main theme being education; the base and staircase are decorated with animal fables, the *Jatakas.*

Ratu Boko
Also called King Boko's Temple. A few km S of Prambanan village on the road to Piyungan. Coming from Yogya, turn R at the large triangular intersection in Prambanan village, then walk 2½ km down the road. It's a steep, rocky 15-min. ascent from the '18 KM" signpost. Keep looking for the sign DINAS PURBAKALA—RATU BOKO. Ratu Boko lies on the ridge of Gunung Sewu ("Thousand Hills"). Once the site of a huge fortified 9th C. *kraton,* it overlooks luxuriant rolling green fields, bamboo groves, and the feathery palms of Prambanan Plain. With its beautiful views,

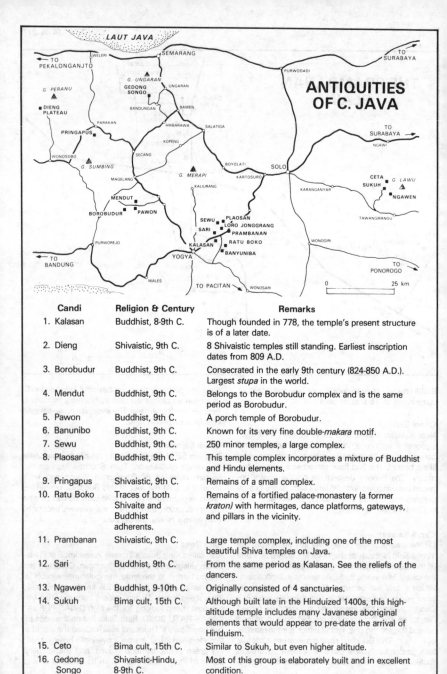

ANTIQUITIES OF C. JAVA

Candi	Religion & Century	Remarks
1. Kalasan	Buddhist, 8-9th C.	Though founded in 778, the temple's present structure is of a later date.
2. Dieng	Shivaistic, 9th C.	8 Shivaistic temples still standing. Earliest inscription dates from 809 A.D.
3. Borobudur	Buddhist, 9th C.	Consecrated in the early 9th century (824-850 A.D.). Largest *stupa* in the world.
4. Mendut	Buddhist, 9th C.	Belongs to the Borobudur complex and is the same period as Borobudur.
5. Pawon	Buddhist, 9th C.	A porch temple of Borobudur.
6. Banunibo	Buddhist, 9th C.	Known for its very fine double-*makara* motif.
7. Sewu	Buddhist, 9th C.	250 minor temples, a large complex.
8. Plaosan	Buddhist, 9th C.	This temple complex incorporates a mixture of Buddhist and Hindu elements.
9. Pringapus	Shivaistic, 9th C.	Remains of a small complex.
10. Ratu Boko	Traces of both Shivaite and Buddhist adherents.	Remains of a fortified palace-monastery (a former *kraton*) with hermitages, dance platforms, gateways, and pillars in the vicinity.
11. Prambanan	Shivaistic, 9th C.	Large temple complex, including one of the most beautiful Shiva temples on Java.
12. Sari	Buddhist, 9th C.	From the same period as Kalasan. See the reliefs of the dancers.
13. Ngawen	Buddhist, 9-10th C.	Originally consisted of 4 sanctuaries.
14. Sukuh	Bima cult, 15th C.	Although built late in the Hinduized 1400s, this high-altitude temple includes many Javanese aboriginal elements that would appear to pre-date the arrival of Hinduism.
15. Ceto	Bima cult, 15th C.	Similar to Sukuh, but even higher altitude.
16. Gedong Songo	Shivaistic-Hindu, 8-9th C.	Most of this group is elaborately built and in excellent condition.

it's well worth an early morning walk up here. This entire plateau is full of ruins, a few bathing pools (still used by villagers), waterspouts, and gateways are still in good shape. Some sites have not yet been completely excavated. Once a retreat for royal hermits, a stone discovered here had an inscription on it which showed that a Saliendra princess who ruled in Java between the 8th and 9th C. was related to a reigning dynasty of ancient Sri Lanka. Sinhalese monks lived in a fortress monastery here more than 1,000 years ago. Don't pay "admission" to the guys working on restoration.

Candi Banyunibo

After Ratu Boko, turn L (SE) and walk one km. This temple is near a small village on the other side of a gully. A beautifully carved double *makara*-motif is above the niche which frames a seated female deity. Three stone oxen stand in a row. See the spaces where the most important sculptures have been lifted. A statue of a goddess points to Java's ancient links with Ceylon, some believe, in its strong facial and bodily form, very reminiscent of South Asia. An almost duplicate goddess can be found in a niche above the entrance

of the House of Pilgrims behind the Temple of the Tooth in Kandy, Sri Lanka. Other scanty temple remains on this ridgeline are reached by crossing the river beyond Candi Banyunibo and climbing the hill: *candi* Ijo, Mtring, Tinjong.

Candi Sambisari

Two km from the village of Sambisari, at the end of a country lane (see the giant sign). If driving, turn in at the "10.2 KM" signpost and drive for about 2 km. This 8th-9th C. Shiva temple was discovered in 1966 when a farmer broke the blade of his plow against a stone. Unearthed from underneath 5 m of volcanic ash, Sambisari could be part of a larger complex. The ornamentation on the outer walls is in low relief. See stone images of Durga and Ganesha, a lovely tree-of-heaven motif, and a *makara*-ornamented doorway. Sambisari can be studied in a perfectly preserved state, unmarred by plunderers or the elements. The lintels are roughly cut but *kala*-heads have hardly changed from what they looked like on the day they were chiseled. About 90% of the restoration is new stone.

Greek and Indian Influences in Indonesian art: The invasion of Alexander the Great from the W into India had 2 effects on Indonesia. Many Sumatran rulers henceforth claimed that they were descended from "Iskander" or Alexander. The brief invasion also brought Greco-Buddhist art, which allowed deities to be represented in sculpture. Sculptures of Indian sages with typical classical folds of the robe began to appear. The stupa, which used to be just a mound containing relics of Buddha, became elaborate with stone hemispheres. Indianized Malays carried the image of the elephant-headed god, Ganesha, to New Guinea where it lingers on today in carved figures with grotesquely elongated noses. But the farther you move W from New Guinea, the more detailed the trunk becomes until you find statues of Ganesha on Java and Bali identical to those found in India. In this sprawling mass of islands which had no individual artistic expression, Indonesian artists have created in almost 40 years since independence a modern national art that assimilates every idea that comes its way. Indonesians will absorb the European influences now taking place in painting, sculpture, and dance just as they did with Greek, Hindu, Chinese, and Arabian forms—coming up with artforms all their own.

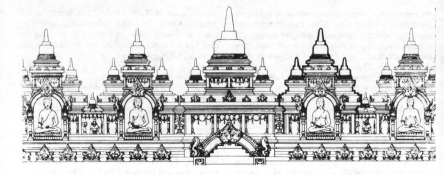

BOROBUDUR

This colossal, cosmic mountain is one of the most imposing creations of mankind—nothing else like it exists! Erected 200 years before the Notre Dame and Chartres cathedrals, it also predates the Buddhist temple of Angkor Wat in Cambodia by 3 centuries. Built with more than 2 million cubic feet of stone, it's the world's largest *stupa* and largest ancient monument in the Southern Hemisphere. See it on a rainy day when water spews out of the mouths of its gargoyles. Guides and booklets in English, such as *Glimpses of the Borobudur* and *The Borobudur and The Lara Jonggrang Temples* are for sale at the park. Also read the relevant sections of Claire Holt's *Art in Indonesia.*

All the garish souvenir stalls have been moved, thankfully, about one km from the monument to where the minibuses and tourist buses park. Go very early in the cool of the morning to avoid the large crowds (admission: Rp200). Although there are quite a number of tourists, the immediate surrounds are well-kept and attractive. Walk up to the top of the hill (4 hours, bring water) behind Borobudur for a splendid birds-eye view of the monument and rolling plains beyond. Other antiquities in the immediate area—Mendut, Pawon, Banon, etc.—are all within walking distance. Or just hop on a minibus back to Muntilan and ask to be dropped off at the temples on the way.

History

Its name is probably derived from the Sanskrit *Vihara Buddha Uhr. Vihara* means monastery, *Uhr* means high; thus "Buddhist monastery on a high place." Artisans and specialists from India undoubtedly visited the site; Borobudur is related to both the Indian monuments of NW India (the terraced bases of Indian *stupas)* and the terraced sanctuaries of prehistoric Indonesian architecture. Although the structure has many characteristics of the C. Javanese style (A.D.

700-950), it has little else in common with other Buddhist temples in SE Asia. Persian, Babylonian, and Greek influences have also been incorporated in Borobudur's art and architecture. Planned by men with a profound knowledge of Buddhist philosophy, on it Buddha and Shiva are spiritually the same being. Used for veneration, worship, and meditation, this giant monument was an achievement of the Vajrayana sect of the Tantric School of Buddhism which found acceptance in Indonesia around A.D. 700. The feudal Saliendra princes—not elite savages but highly advanced technicians—erected it with peasant labor between 778 and 850. No one knows how this great structure was built at a time when modern engineering techniques were yet to be developed. No nation or group of men could possibly build it today. Thousands of laborers, slaves, carvers, sculptors, carriers, and expert supervisors worked for decades rolling logs, working ropes, levers, hammers, mallets, and chisels, using only their hands and arms. The monument took perhaps 10,000 men a century to build. Records indicate that the population of the countryside of C. Java was drastically reduced after the completion of Borobudur in the 9th C.; it exhausted 5 generations! The Saliendras were finally overthrown by Hindus on Java in 856, and Borobudur was abandoned soon after completion. It might have started to collapse just when the sculptors were putting on the finishing touches; there's evidence of work initiated to reinforce the base, and some panels were found to have trace marks begun on them. The monument was buried under a thousand years of volcanic eruptions and tropical growth until discovered by an English colonel during the British occupation of Indonesia in 1814. Though buried, it was not unknown; a 19th C. Javanese historical work mentions that a Yogya prince went out to visit "the 1,000 statues standing on a natural hill, and a holy man in a cave." In 1855,

Borobudur was cleared, and the long process of restoration began.

Location

Borobudur was built on the confluence of 2 rivers, always considered a holy spot in India. It's a magic place, one of the most magical in Indonesia. When you stand on the top it feels like you're floating between all the mountains, greenery, volcanos, and fantastic landscapes. According to tradition, the architect who designed the monument was Gunadharma, whose face you can see to the R of the largest pinnacle in the Menorah Mountains just behind the monument. Kenari trees were planted around Borobudur in 1840. At the foot of the E stairway once stood a sacred fig tree descended from the original *Bodhi*-tree under which the Buddha attained enlightenment. This particular tree had been brought to Borobudur in 1928, a shoot of the holy tree in Ceylon which was itself a shoot of the original tree brought from India in the 3rd century B.C. It was chopped down to get the crane in for the restoration work! Later, in the early 1980s, hundreds of families were evicted—with meager compensation or none at all—to make way for the archaeological park.

Shape

Borobudur's famous silhouette, in the form of a giant Buddhist prayer symbol *(mandala)*, can only be appreciated when viewed from the air. It's an unspectacular, almost impassive shape, like something carved out of solid rock or like a bursting fruit. The structure was constructed to look like the holy Mt. Meru of India, a mythological model of the universe. You can't enter the *stupa* because it consists of just terraces built over the top of a hill. Greek columns and Gothic cathedrals of Europe have a vertical structure, but in Asia the pattern is horizontal. Temples are laid out in square or rectangular enclosures and they rise up to a gently culminating pyramid. This massive, perfectly symmetrical *stupa* is only one of 84,000 all over Asia, many said to contain the remains or essence of Buddha. But Borobudur is a *stupa* with a difference. This unique building combines symbols of the circle (heaven), of the square (Earth), and of a *stupa* into one coherent whole. Many projections, make in all 36 corners. The foot is 122 sq m and the temple goes up tier by tier. Turn L upon entering to pay tribute to the gods. The widest and lowest terraces are used for processions, while the 5 galleries above have but one internal and one external wall. There are 10 terraces from the base to the main topmost *stupa*, each representing the individual stages toward perfection in a man's life. The pilgrim's walk takes you around the temple 9 times before reaching the top. The E side's third gallery has the best-preserved and most beautiful gateway. Visitors are swallowed up symbolically by the *kala*-monster upon entering, then given new spiritual life.

Reliefs

One of the largest and most complete ensembles of Buddhist reliefs in existence, amounting to a virtual textbook of Mahayana Buddhist doctrine in stone. There are 1,500 pictorial relief panels of Buddha's teachings, plus 1,212 purely ornamental panels. Once glistening with bright purple, crimson, green, blue, and yellow paint, over 8,235 sq m of stone surface are carved in high relief, telling scholars much about the material culture of 8th-9th C. Java. There are lessons on history, religion, art, morality, literature, clothing styles, family life, architecture, agriculture, shipping, fighting arts, dancing—the whole Buddhist cosmos. Sculptors trained in the best tradition of Indian classical temple building poured their abundant talents into the most delicate, intricate detail. The distance through all the galleries to the summit is a walk of over 5 km, a labyrinth of narrow corridors. To read all the reliefs from the beginning of the story, go through the door on the E side. Because of so many right-angle corners, you are able to see only a few steps ahead. This was designed to force you to take in each phase of the story a frame at a time—like 9th century TV!

Terraces

The 5-storied pyramid is subdivided vertically into 3 spheres of Buddhism, symbolizing religious microcosms: the base, *kamadhatu,* means "world of passion," with reliefs illustrating worldly life and toil; *rupadhatu,* above the base, consists of 4 terraces with beautiful reliefs depicting Buddha's life; and *Arupadhatu,* the 3 circular terraces, means "world of form-

temple guardian, Borobudur

BOROBUDUR

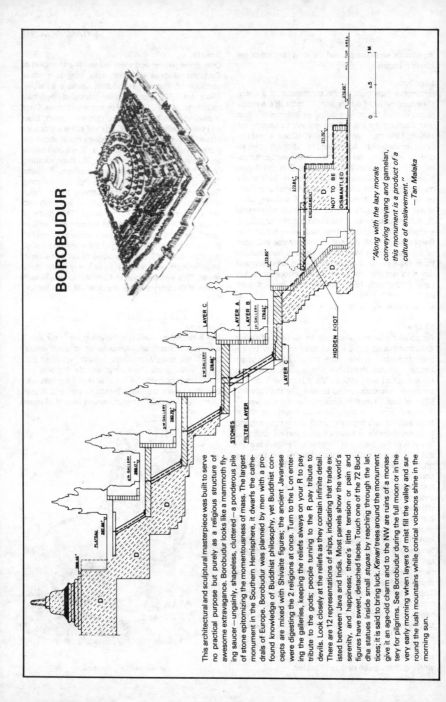

This architectural and sculptural masterpiece was built to serve no practical purpose but purely as a religious structure of awesome extravagance. Borobudur looks like a mammoth flying saucer — ungainly, shapeless, cluttered — a ponderous pile of stone epitomizing the momentousness of mass. The largest monument in the Southern Hemisphere, it dwarfs the cathedrals of Europe. Borobudur was planned by men with a profound knowledge of Buddhist philosophy, yet Buddhist concepts are mixed with Shivaite figures; the ancient Javanese were digesting the 2 religions at once. Turn to the L on entering the galleries, keeping the reliefs always on your R to pay tribute to the gods; people turning to the R pay tribute to devils. Look closely at the reliefs as they contain infinite detail. There are 12 representations of ships, indicating that trade existed between Java and India. Most panels show the world's serenity, and happiness; there's little tension or pain and figures have sweet, detached faces. Touch one of the 72 Buddha statues inside small *stupas* by reaching through the lattices; it is said to bring luck. *Kenari* trees around the monument give it an age-old charm and to the NW are ruins of a monastery for pilgrims. See Borobudur during the full moon or in the very early morning when layers of mist fill the valley and surround the lush mountains while conical volcanos shine in the morning sun.

"Along with the lazy morals conveying wayang and gamelan, this monument is a product of a culture of enslavement."
— Tan Malaka

lessness." Lower, richly adorned square terraces are for the senses, the round top terraces are for the soul. The base-terrace or "hidden foot" wasn't discovered until 1885. It contains a series of reliefs showing man shackled to greed, a world dominated by desire, lust, and death. The lower terraces are full of scenes of *karma* and earthly existence, woe and desire, good and evil deeds, rewards and punishments—all the *samsara* of the world. But as you climb to the higher levels, reliefs become more heavenly. By the time you emerge on the square terraces nearer the top, man has eliminated desire, though he is still tied to the world of the senses. Man finally attains perfection and is released from all his earthly bonds when he reaches the round terraces. Each sphere shows striking differences, from the richly decorated squares to the round terraces devoid of all decoration. The top is more spacious and simple: the topmost central *stupa* (15 m diameter) is the symbol of heaven, where all suffering ends. This pinnacle was once 10 m higher than it is now, seen from kilometers away to guide the pilgrim.

Buddha *Stupas*
On the upper round terraces are over 72 *stupas* which look like inverted lotus blossoms, each formerly containing a sitting statue of an athletic young Buddha sculpted in the round. Through the apertures the Buddha could be seen half in sunlight, half in shadows, each statue only partly visible—calculated to bring home to the visitor both the formless and the absolute reality—the two faces of god. In each, Buddha's hands are held in different positions to represent various *mudra*, or symbols, for Buddha's different actions, e.g. teaching, blessing, preaching, etc. Reaching in through the lattices and touching Buddha's hands brings good luck. There are subtle differences between the latticed bells of the first and second rows and those of the third. Most of the heads are missing, knocked off or destroyed by Muslim vandals. You can find them today in museums in Bangkok, Holland, Paris, London, and Boston. In the niches above the galleries are statues of reincarnated Buddhas, each pointing to a different compass direction.

Restoration
Over the last 12 centuries, Borobudur gracefully survived the ravages of moss and lichen, heavy tropical downpours, and devastating stone cancers. It took almost 100 years (1814-1911) to uncover the monument and bring it back to life. Under the supervision of Theodor van Erp, a major scientific 4-year restoration project was launched in 1907; van Erp's photographs (see the magnificent Krom monograph in Jakarta's National Museum) proved invaluable during later restoration efforts, But over the following decades the monument continued to deteriorate rapidly. By the 1960s Borobudur's foundation was so badly weakened that the whole structure was in danger of collapse. Finally, in 1973, the restoration of

Borobudur began in earnest, financed by funds from the Indonesian government, donor countries, private organizations, and member states of UNESCO. No other archaeological rescue of such magnitude had been attempted since the raising of the Egyptian temple of Abu Simbel in 1966 to protect it from the floodwaters of the Aswam Dam. A technique (used at Angkor Wat) was employed which called for the ruin being taken apart stone by stone, the stones and blocks numbered, then all of the pieces cleaned and chemically treated, then put back together again like a maddeningly complex jigsaw puzzle. The foundation also had to be reinforced and the lower galleries completely dismantled section by section and rebuilt on a solid foundation with adequate drainage. For years the whole restoration project fell prey to bureaucratic neptitude, corruption, and financial mismanagement, but the work was at last completed in 1983 at a cost of over US$25 million. President Suharto himself presided over the formal opening ceremony in March 1983. In January 1985, nine bombs destroyed parts of the *stupa,* causing extensive damage; the government blamed either Muslim extremists or local people who were evicted from their homes to make way for the archaeological park. This massive *stupa* is still in an almost continual state of reconstruction.

Getting There
The ruins of this 1,200-year-old temple lie 42 km NW of Yogya and 17 km SW of Magelang. From Yogya, buses N to Muntilan and farther to Borobudur depart either Terminal Umbulharjo or from Terminal Pingit on Jl. Magelang (only a 10 min. walk from the Jl. Pasar Kembang area). Minibuses from Yogya to Muntilan (31 km) depart as early as 0500 and cost Rp400, then change buses from Muntilan to Borobudur (Rp250). The whole trip takes 1 ½ hours OW. Beware of pickpockets *(tukang copet)* on these buses. Hotels in Yogya such as Beta and Indonesia, as well as many tour agencies, also conduct early morning minibus or taxi tours out to Borobudur (Rp8500-12,000, 4 hours), or you can charter a taxi for Rp25,000 RT. If using your own vehicle, the drive from Yogya takes one hour.

MENDUT

Take the beautiful walk to Candi Pawon (2 km), then on to Mendut (3 km E of Borobudur). Or, after making the L-hand turn to the W beyond Muntilan, the first temple you run into is Mendut which stands quietly alone in the middle of a grassy traffic circle. Mendut is a genuine 9th C. temple of worship, not a *candi* to the dead. It faces Saranath, where Buddha spoke his first words of deliverance. Originally over 27 m tall, Mendut was only a mound of rubble with cows grazing on top until 1836 when it was first cleared. Complete restoration by the Dutch took place between 1897 and 1904. The temple dates from A.D. 850, about the same time as Borobudur. The temple has extensive galleries, terraces, and a *stupa* on top. Its roof is pyramid-shaped. A very sophisticated knowledge of Buddhist and Shivaistic texts, Indian inconography, symbolism, and monumental architecture was crucial to build it. Its builders no doubt visited the Indian holy land. Admission: Rp100.

Relief Panels

Mendut's 30 relief panels are among the finest and largest compositions of Hindu-Javanese art. The stories are drawn from the Jataka Tales, old Buddhist folk myths about Buddha's previous incarnations. There are trees-of-heaven at the entrance to the antechamber and folktale decorations on the stairs. The stone images in the temple interior are very well preserved. A 2½-m-high Buddha relaxes between 2 of his Bodhisattvas: The Congregation between The Law. These colossal statues weren't ripped off, simply because of their sheer weight. Buddha's feet rest upon a stylized lotus blossom and his hand is held in the gesture of a preacher. Architects put a shaft on one side of the chamber to let in moon and sunrays to illuminate the main Buddha image. Buddha's back support is flanked by an elephant, lion, and *makara*. What was once holy to the ancestors of the Javanese is still holy; there might be fresh offerings of flowers and food in the laps of the statues and incense smoking at Buddha's feet. A profound air of tranquility inside.

Vicinity Of Mendut

The temples which belong to the Borobudur complex—Mendut, Borobudur, and Pawon—fall along a straight E-W axis which connects them all to the Deer Park in Saranath in India. Pilgrims had to pass each temple to reach the main monument of Borobudur. **Candi Pawon** is located about 2 km E of Borobudur (or 1.5 km NE of Mendut) and only about 100 m from the road; see the turnoff and a sign showing the way.

Pawon probably served as a porch temple of Borobudur dedicated to Kuvera, God of Riches, a little jewel of a temple with tiny windows and dwarves pouring riches from bags above the door. Exquisite body decoration. The space inside the temple is empty. Free entrance. Also walking distance from the Borobudur/Mendut complex near the village of Muntilan is **Candi Ngawen**. The corners of its base are decorated with lions. Candi Ngawen is actually a collection of 4 temples in a row, about 3 m apart, but only one temple has been restored. On a plateau just S of Muntilan (ask directions), the temple remains of Gunung Wukir could date from as early as the 8th C., making it the oldest identified Shiva sanctuary on Java. Only foundation stones remain.

Waicak Day

An annual Buddhist ceremony which commemorates Buddha's birth, death, and the day he received enlightenment under the Bodhi Tree in Bodh Gaya, India, 500 years before Jesus. This event usually falls during the full moon on the most auspicious day in May. Since 1959 *Waicak* has taken place at Borobudur, attended each year by Indonesian Buddhists and also by a great many from abroad, especially Theravada Buddhists from Sri Lanka. The festival actually begins at Candi Mendut with the bearing of holy water which is brought in a procession to Borobudur. The climax comes at 0400 when all the worshippers converge on the monument. Each carrying a lighted candle, thousands of followers in saffron robes (for men) and white saris (for women) move barefoot in a slow, solemn procession up the stairs of Borobudur while chanting and praying. Then they circle the temple clockwise toward the main *stupa* at the top, where they wait for the moon to appear on the horizon—the legendary time of Buddha's birth. The highlight of the ceremony is when the participants carry the call of the Buddha, welcoming the audience with the song "Maha Manggala Suta."

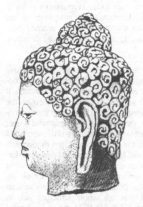

Buddha head, Borobudur: Initially, there were 500 Buddha heads on the monument. Their oval-shaped faces, eyes like lotus petals, eyebrows curved like a bow, and lips with the fullness of a mango give these remarkable sculptures a combination of sensuality and remoteness. Based on Indian prototypes of the 5th and 6th C., the Javanese examples are distinguished by larger, flatter curls, rounder faces, and softer features. The coarse volcanic stone abundant in C. Java lent itself to this soft, generalized sculptural style.

SOLO

The cultural linchpin of Java, 102 km S of Semarang and 64 km NE of Yogya. Also called Surakarta, it's often spelled Sala but still pronounced "Solo." Solo's population of 500,000 is larger than Yogya's, its sister city. Java's oldest cultural center, considered the island's least Westernized (or most Javanese) city, Solo is a *priyayi* stronghold. In the hearts of its people, Solo is the traditional, original capital of the Javanese kingdom—not Yogya. Solo is not as inundated by tourists as Yogya, not so commercialized. It's the only Javanese city where you see the Javanese written language widely used on buildings, signs, pamphlets, etc. It's a very livable place, the streets are cleaned daily. In fact, Solo has everything Yogya has but without all the tourists: art galleries, theaters, mystical fraternities, dance and music academies, extensive markets and traditional crafts, Chinese temples, inexpensive *losmen,* good restaurants, and a frivolous nightlife (the girls of Solo are said "to walk like hungry tigers"). Here you can learn *batik, gamelan,* dancing, *wayang,* and even meditation techniques! The city never sleeps; people roam the streets 24 hours a day. There are 2 *kraton,* one even larger and more venerable than Yogya's. Religion is soft and flowing here, not the more orthodox form of Islam practiced on the N coast and in W. Java. With a tradition of religious tolerance, you could even find a mosque and a church in the same courtyard. Yet the Solonese are not found lacking in devotion; real live *muezzins* and *mushollas* (prayer rooms) are found in even the smallest hotels. But change is overtaking this ancient capital. Traffic lights are found on all the major intersections now. The modern Purwosari shopping center, E of town on Jl. Slamet Riyadi, was Solo's first slick shopping center which introduced a consumer mentality into what was basically an urban market economy. As if one wasn't enough, a huge new Singosaren Plaza shopping center was put in downtown in 1987, replacing the venerable old household market Pasar Singosaren.

History

Once just a village in the middle of a forest, founded by the legendary Kyai Sala, Solo became the seat of the Mataram kingdom in the mid-18th C. when the previous capital at Kartosuro (12 km W) was reduced to rubble during a war with the Dutch. An auspicious site near the Solo River was chosen by the sultan and the palace was completed in 1745. In one magnificent procession, the entire *kraton* moved from Kartosuro to the new palace, called Kraton Surakarta Hadiningrat. This dynasty lasted only 10 years, until the realm was partitioned in 1755 after the death of Sultan Pakubuwono II. The *susuhunan's* uncle, claim-

ing Yogya to the W as his territory, shifted out and became the first sultan of that royal city. The reigning *susuhunan* of Solo, in spite of his diminished authority, was permitted by the Dutch to continue receiving income from his holdings. This vast revenue went toward the promotion of the arts: music, dance, and *wayang* all flowered under the early *susuhunans'* royal patronage. During the Diponegoro revolt (1825-1830), most of Yogya's *priyayi* families supported Diponegoro, while those of Solo remained loyal to the Dutch. Over 120 years later when the Dutch occupied Solo in the Second Police Action during the fight for independence, the *susuhunan* of Solo even held a reception for them in his *kraton.* This was all remembered in 1950 once Indonesia became a republic, and the *susuhunan* lost all his authority. Yogya's sultanate, however, remained semiautonomous because its sultan had played such an active part in the independence movement. In the 1960s Solo was one of the focal points for the Communist Party in C. Java where the PKI had consolidated some of their most tenacious support.

KRATON HADININGRAT

Also called Istana Kasuhunan, or the Susuhunan's Palace, located SE of the city center. Susuhunan means "royal foot placed on the head of vassals paying homage"—a title dating from the conquering King Agung of Mataram who reigned in the 1600s. The present palace was originally built in 1745 by Pakubuwono II. Before the fire of 1985, gaudy vulgarity was the dominant theme. All the gold vessels, gilded furniture, mirrors, and flamboyant hangings all seemed like stage props in the home of a colossal profiteer. Rumors about the raja's womanizing and extravagances were rampant. Living in Jakarta, he neglected the upkeep of the palace and failed to propitiate the hidden powers that be. Finally, during the night of 1 January 1985, catastrophe struck when the main core of the *kraton,* the Dalem Gede—with all its priceless wood architecture and furniture—caught fire. What followed was a comic tragedy. Fire engines, which could have easily doused the fire, responded quickly but couldn't fit through the main gate. Since this gate was sacred, a powerful symbol of authority, the firemen refused to smash it down and consequently 60% of the palace burned to the ground. The official cause of the fire was a faulty electrical circuit, but it is the local belief that the real reason was that the king no longer deserved the protection of the palace spirits which, as the Javanese say, "went back home." An elaborate ceremony of appeasement was performed, in which the head of a tiger, a buffalo, a deer, and a snake were buried, and 30 truckloads of ashes were returned to the Southern Sea, the domain of Nyai Loro Kidul, from whence they came. Presently, the living quarters, the main *pendopo*, and various rooms of the palace are being rebuilt and the raja has moved back to Surakarta and begun to mend his ways. One antique building of great interest which survived the fire is the multi-storied minaret, Panggung Songgo Buwono, seen over the wall in the NE corner of the courtyard. According to an ancient legend, it was used by the rajas of Surakarta as a trysting place with Nyai Loro Kidul. The servants' quarters, the women's quarters, and (luckily) the priceless library of *lontar* manuscripts also survived the fateful holocaust.

The Art Gallery

Next to the *kraton* is this museum, open 0900-1230, closed Friday. Buy your ticket on the NE corner of the *kraton*, Rp400 (Rp300 for students). At the ticket office, guides are available to explain, in English or Indonesian, the functions and history of the objects in the museum. The main portions of the palace are closed for restoration. The museum contains a lavish collection of regal pomp: a model of a *dalang* and his puppets, an odd international assortment of statues, valuable collections of old Hindu-Javanese bronzes, ancient Chinese porcelain, a diorama of Prince Diponegoro fighting the Dutch. But the carriages are the

highlight: superb 18th C. European royal coaches with plush interiors. One given the name of Kyai Grudo (another like it is in Lisbon) is especially resplendent. This extravagant gift was presented by the Dutch under the reign of Pakubuwono II for the occasion of the moving of the capital from Kartosuro to Solo on 17 March 1745. Four companies of Dutch soldiers accompanied this royal procession and the *raja* was even chauffeured by Dutchmen. Also see large, demonic gargoyle figureheads which once graced splendid royal barges that journeyed down the Solo River to Gresik in the 18th century. The Art Gallery museum is full of surprises; too bad it's poorly lit.

Dance And Music

Although the Sasono Mulyo, the royal dance pavilion, survived the 1985 fire, the *kraton's* troupe of dancers moved to the ASKI (Academy of Fine Arts) building—a more academic, sterile environment out of town. The Sasono Mulyo pavilion now stands hauntingly empty. In its day, however, this court was the origin of many lyrical dances such as *Golek* and *Bondan* ("mother tending her baby"), a fusion of professional *(taledek)* and classical Solo dance styles. Body movements of Solonese dancers are more liquid than Yogya's rigid discipline in which dancers move like wooden puppets. In fact, most of the Ramayana Ballet dancers of Yogya come from the Solo area. The zenith of the refined court dance forms is practiced at the *kraton* dance school; here you can see the emphasis the Javanese place on composure and perfection.

MANGKUNEGARAN PALACE

Open to tourists only since 1969. Mangkunegaran, N of Jl. Slamet Riyadi, is not actually a *kraton* but a 200-year-old Javanese aristocrat's home built on an extra large and splendid scale. This is the palace of the junior line of the royal family, a princedom, as opposed to the *susuhunan's* palace which is the seat of a kingdom. Still, this impressive palace complex contains a number of carved, gilded teak pavilions amidst a tropical garden, an excellent museum, souvenir shop, and one of Java's finest *gamelan* orchestras. And, since the fire in 1985 consumed the *susuhunan's* main pavilion, the Mangkunegaran has taken pride of place amongst Solo's tourist attractions. This smaller court hires its own artisans and dancing masters, and even has its own *gamelan* factory. The Mangkunegaran has equally extravagant architecture and furnishings as the *susuhunan's* palace had, but it's just a scaled-down version, occupying an area of "only" 10,000 sq m. Various parts and functions of the palace are explained in English by available guides. There's also a library of old Dutch books and works of the late Mangkunegoros written in ancient Javanese characters. In the souvenir shop are some good buys, such as *wayang kulit* made in the palace

entranceway and minaret, Kraton Handiningrat

workshops, but be selective. Entrance fee is Rp500 (Rp300 for students); report first to the registration office. Dress conservatively. Open Mon. to Sat. 0900-1230, closes Fri. at 1100, closed Sundays. **note:** If you go on Wed., you can see the dancing for free.

History

During the "Mataram Division" in 1755 when the Mataram Dynasty split into rival houses, the cousin of the reigning *susuhunan,* Mangkunegoro I, established another small court inside Surakarta's domain. The Mangkunegaran palace was built by Mangkunegaran II at the end of the 18th C., and was completed in 1866. After WW II, the royalty business in Indonesia underwent a marked decline. In the early 1970s, to make ends meet, the Mangkunegaran royal family was even forced to establish an adjoining hotel, accepting up to 10 paying guests complete with kneeling maid service. The young prince of the line died in an auto accident in 1979; the queen "followed her son," literally dying of grief and complications about a month later. After Suharto's ascension to power in the late 1960s, however, the fortunes of this royal house—to which Madame Tien Suharto is related—began to take a dramatic upswing. With presidential patronage, its financial dealings soon proved extraordinarily successful and members of this "pedigree family" *(keluarga trah)* were suddenly catapulted into key governmental and judiciary positions. All this good fortune seemed to confirm accusations of feudalism leveled against Suharto by his critics. The palace is presently the official residence of Mangkunegoro VII and his family.

Dalem

The grounds contain classical Javanese architecture, the entire palace built of solid *jati* (teakwood) with no nails used in its construction. There are 2 main parts, the huge front *pendopo* (reception/dance hall) and behind the *pendopo* the *Dalem* (ceremonial hall), flanked by the family's living quarters. A front room in the *Dalem* called the *Pringgitan* is where the family receives official guests, and is used as a stage for *wayang kulit* performances. Taking photos in the *Dalem,* the palace proper, and the prince's private house, is now allowed. Visitors may wander around portions of the royal residence containing dusty bric a brac, art deco mementos, family photographs, even the *mandi!*

The *Puro*

The giant *pendopo* (or *puro),* with its zany painted ceiling of Zodiac designs, is one of the finest examples of stately Javanese wood architecture in existence. The decoration on the *pendopo's* ceiling, painted in 1937, is thought to have been inspired by the prince's collection of old Javanese miniatures. The main motif is the ancient *Batik Mhodang* (flame) design, one of the most popular Javanese patterns. On the edge of the decoration you can see the

Javanese version of the Zodiac and the points of the compass, ornamented with *makara* heads. In the center are the 8 mystical colors. In 1925 the *pendopo* was covered with copper at the same time the Italian marble floor was laid. The roof is nearly 17 m high.

The Museum

Open Mon. to Sat. 0900-1200, Fri. until 1100, closed Sun.; Rp500 admission (Rp150 for Indonesians). See relics from the Java-Hindu era, displays of 14th C. jewelry, dance costumes, a solid gold chastity belt, silver *sate* skewers, old portraits of haughty sultans, a bridal bed, and a matchless collection of *wayang topeng* masks from different regions of Java and Madura, one of the most complete in Indonesia. Picture scrolls *(wayang beber)* relate stories from the *Panji Cycle;* leather and wooden puppets of different types and periods are displayed, along with rare gold and bronze articles from the Hindu, Majapahit, and Mataram periods.

Gamelan

This Javanese orchestra, which plays in the SW corner of the *pendopo,* has been given the honorific name *Kyai Kanyut Mesem* ("Drifting in Smiles"). Originally from Demak and dating back to 1778, it's one of the finest on Java and older than the palace itself. On Wed. mornings the *pustaka gamelan* is played, and dance rehearsals begin at 1000 on the *puro,* lasting for about 2 hours. Free entrance. Swallows dip and dive amongst the rafters as the *gamelan* plays, as if enraptured by the music.

OTHER SIGHTS

Neighborhoods

Solo's real flavor can only be experienced by exploring the small alleyways in the central part of town near the 2 *kraton*—with their whitewashed walls and fences, balconies, and families hanging out on the doorsteps. The Buddhist community is found in Prawit in the northern fringe of town. A Confucian group in Chinatown gathers each Sun. at the main temple, Lithang, on Jl. Jagalan. The Catholic church at Purbayan is built in the old cathedral style. A small Hindu *pura* is at Kentingan (Komplex UNS); a new Protestant church lies on the eastern end of the city's main street, Jl. Slamet Riyadi. The Arab quarter is around Pasar Kliwon. Imposing merchants' houses are found in the Lawiyan neighborhood, surrounded often by high walls which protect the compounds from the dusty roads crowded with oxcarts, laden donkeys, and bicycle cabs. A small museum of *kris* and other artifacts is at Jl. Kratonan 101, W of the palace, the home of Hardjonagoro. See Mesjid Besar (The Great Mosque), W of the *alun,* with its front verandah *(pendopo)* and minaret, a combination of Javanese and Muslim styles.

THR Sriwedari

Located on the western end of Jl. Slamet Riyadi, this amusement park is open daily to the public (only during special events is there an admittance charge). It offers an uncrowded, park-like atmosphere with children's playground (Rp200), and its zoo has the widest selection of animals in C. Java. Buy souvenirs in the art shops around and inside the park. On Mon. evenings or when it's raining the park could be near empty; in this case, treat yourself to a Bintang Beer at one of the good cheap *warung*. At night, take in one of the musical extravanganzas which are always going on: rock groups, female vocalists, string quartets, etc. Also from 2000-2400 view a variety of Javanese dramas for only Rp350-600. The Sriwedari *wayang orang* troupe is considered Indonesia's finest; Sukarno used to fly the whole troupe to Jakarta for the evening. Watch part of the *wayang orang* performance through the wire mesh along the side of the theater, or pay a few hundred *rupiah* to see some of the best performers on Java. Every fasting month a giant night market, *Maleman Sriwedari*, is set up in this people's park.

Radyapustoko Museum

Founded in 1890 by the Dutch, the Institute of Javanese Culture is the oldest such organization in Indonesia. The first task of the institute was to build a museum, create a library, and to publish a monthly magazine. The institute developed rapidly, well known in the world of scholarship, with many foreign cultural historians and oriental culture experts contributing to its archives over the years. The present aims of the institute are to standardize the Javanese alphabet, to offer courses in *Kawi* (Old Javanese), as well as painting, sculpture, *kris*- and *batik*-making, and training in puppetry. Located right next to the Sriwedari Amusement Park, it contains a miscellaneous but fascinating collection of royal paraphernalia, mementos from C. Java's past, as well as an excellent display of Javanese crafts. One room is filled with European tableware, vases from China, and pots. Perhaps the most unique display in the museum is its collection of exquisite *kris*. Classical period Java-Hindu statues of Shiva and Durga are displayed on the porch. Open daily (except Mon.) 0900-1230; Fri. until 1100. Admission: Rp100. The **City Library** right next door is open 0900-1300, on Fri. only until 1100.

ACCOMMODATIONS

Inexpensive

In the area between Jl. Ahmad Dahlan and the little lane Gang Keprabon (off Jl. Slamet Riyadi) are the cheapest and most convenient accommodations, only a 6-min. walk from the GPO; also a number of good places to eat in this area. On Jl. Achmad Dahlan are several places in the same price range. **Hotel Cen-**

DOWNTOWN SOLO

1. Ramayana Restaurant
2. Pak Dul's
3. Hotel Central
4. Peng. Timor
5. Hotel Keprabon
6. American Donut
7. movie house
8. Dr. Amien Romas
9. Sate Ayam Pak Dul
10. The Westerners
11. Toko Santoso
12. Bakso Taman Sari

tral, no. 32 (tel. 2842); Rp3000 s, Rp3500 d. Clean, good lighting. Next door, **Hotel Keprabon**, no. 14 (tel. 2811), is low-priced, clean, and quiet. Cheapest rooms are Rp3000 s, Rp3500 d, Rp5000-6000 with *mandi*. No meals but right down the street is RM Laris and right across the street is Pak Parto's. **Peng. Timur**, Gang Keprabon Wetan 1/5 (down the alleyway to the L of Hotel Central), is a small Javanese traders' hostel. Ask for the quieter row of rooms. Timur charges Rp2000 s, Rp2500 d for dark and close rooms with no windows; bathrooms are ill-lit and decrepit, but it's cheap! **Hotel Wigati**, Keprabon Wetan IV/4, right down the lane from Peng. Timur, charges Rp2500 s or Rp2500 d for the small rooms (often full), Rp5000 for the big rooms (but without fans). For this class of hotel it's a good deal. Vendors sell *nasi liwet* out front in the mornings. **Hotel Kota**, Jl. Slamet Riyadi 113, is also only a stone's throw from downtown. Although reasonable and convenient, it's smelly and has a worn-out appearance; Rp3500 and up. If you want to stay in Solo just one night and get right out the next morning, the **Solo Indah** is right by Gilingan Bus Station.

Homestays

A delightful homestay, and very good value, is Laura Tjokrodipo's place in Gajahan RT9/I no. 16, 5 of the Benteng Kraton, called **Joyokusuman**, a big traditional Javanese house *(kanjengan)* which once belonged to a *kraton* prince. Accommodations cost Rp2500 s, Rp3500 d with common kitchen; Rp3000 s, Rp4000 d with private bathroom, kitchen, and inner garden. You may also rent these rooms by the month (Rp50,000-60,000), or rent small apartments (Rp85,000 per month) or big apartments (Rp100,000 per month). For body massages (Rp1000), ask for Mbok Sumi. The best feature is the quiet one-hectare-large garden, full of birds and old mango trees and the old *pendopo;* some tourists who enter this former nobleman's home think it's Solo's main *kraton!* More central, but offering the same rates, is **The West-erners'**, Kemlayan Kidul 11 (tel. 3106). Since it may be difficult to find because the name is so strange for the local people, ask instead for **Pak Mawardi's Homestay** (see map). Except for the screeching birds in the morning and the almost compulsive sweeping, let nothing untoward be said about this delightful family-style accommodations; Rp2500 s, Rp3500 d for small but adequate rooms (plus several "private rooms" attached to the house for Rp6000). There's a kitchen (with utensils), cold water on hand 0600-1000, telephone, laundry area, bicycles for rent (Rp900 daily), and a Rp1000 breakfast (egg, toast, coffee). Relax in open-air sitting areas with flowering plants—an island of peace in the center of the city, where—just like the name says— only Westerners are allowed to stay.

Train Station Vicinity
Handily located near Balapan Train Station, though a bit far from town center, is clean, well-organized **Hotel Gajah Mada**, Jl. Gajah Mada 54; Rp4000 s and d. Get a room surrounding the large inner courtyard and fountain as the rooms facing Jl. Gajah Mada are too noisy and expensive. Quiet **Hotel Wismantara**, Jl. R.M. Said 53, is Rp5000 s or d with *kamar mandi.* Right down the street toward the city is friendly *losmen*-style **Hotel Kondang Asri**, Jl. R.M. Said; Rp3500 s or d. A number of other cheap basic hotels very close to the RR station charge Rp3500-8000 without *kamar mandi,* Rp5000-9,000 with. **San Francisco** is the best bet, cleaner and more spacious with restaurant attached (but also likely to be full); Rp3500 s, Rp5000 d. Opposite San Francisco is **Hotel Sinar Dadi** which offers small rooms (like a Salvation Army depot in Los Angeles) for Rp3500 s, but is poorly lit and cramped. In the same lane is **Hotel Marga Jaya;** Rp3200. **Hotel Soeboer,** Jl. Gajah Mada 172B, 3-min. walk SW of the RR station, is clean and each room has a bath; Rp3500 s or Rp5000 d.

Intermediate
One of the best deals in this price range is the homestyle **Ramayana Guest House,** Jl. Dr. Wahidin 15 (tel. 2841); Rp13,500 s to Rp22,000 d for large a/c rooms, including breakfast (0700-2100), tea, and evening snack. Nearby also check out the **Putri Ayu Hotel,** Jl. Slamet Riyadi 293 (tel. 6154), for commodious, quiet, extremely clean rooms—a much better deal than the downtown hotels for the same price. Though about 2.5 km out of town on the road to Yogya, a *bis kota* passes by night out front (Rp150) or take a *becak* for Rp500. Closer is the **Indah Jaya,** only a few min. from the train station, with large a/c rooms and adjoining Indonesian-style *mandi;* Rp15,500 s. Clean and comfortable. Chinese-owned **Hotel Trio,** opposite Pasar Gede, is good value; ask for the rooms in the back for Rp12,000 s.

Deluxe
The 100-room **Mangkunegaran Palace Hotel** (Jl. Mangkunegaran, tel. 5683/2226) and the 50-room **Kusuma Sahid Prince** (Jl. Sugiyopranoto 22, tel. 6356/7022) are considered the top hotels in town. On estates formerly owned by members of the royal family, both have pools and charge from US$33 up to US$1000 for the luxurious suite at the Kusuma. If you feel heatstroke coming on, pay Rp1500 to plunge into the Kusuma Sahid Prince's Olympic-size pool. Rising out of the ruins of a princely court built in 1909, the Kusuma Sahid Prince sits on 5 acres of landscaped gardens and lawns set back only 500 m from Jl. Slamet Riyadi. Bar (Rp4650 for a large Bintang!), coffee shop, credit cards accepted, and *gamelan* music every night 1700-2000. When Queen Juliana of the Netherlands (1982) and Prince Sihanouk (1984) came to town, this is where they stayed. Small **Hotel Cakra,** Jl. Slamet Riyadi 171 (tel. 5847/7000), in the Rp30,000 price range, has a restaurant, good central location, and is the only hotel with a business center. The plush **Hotel Sahid Sala,** Jl. Gajah Mada 104, has rooms for around US$21-25 (a/c, private baths), and suites and cottages from US$27-59. All the above are close to "international-class" standard, though only the Kusuma Sahid Prince is a 4-star hotel. A contender for the 4-star rating is the new **Persada Bengawan Motel** out of town 4 km in Jurug with a/c cottages overlooking the Solo River; Rp30,000-50,000.

FOOD

Street Food
A venerable old custom in Solo is snacking *(jajan)* at all hours of the day or night: cassava cakes, sticky rice *(jadal)*, *mie bakso*, hot tea, etc. For the cheapest food, learn the different trademark sounds of the barefoot vendors. The city's *warung* which are cheap and have lousy food look the same as those which are cheap and have superb food—you have to know the *warung.* In Kampung Purwosari, many small *warung* specialize in Solonese dishes, each dish served with rice and each using completely different condiments and sauces. Several *warung* on Jl. Widuran (beyond Pasar Gede) sell *ayam bakar* and other good quality

foods and snacks. A specialty of Solo is delicious *nasi liwet,* rice served with chicken and vegetables in coconut cream sauce. Try it at the *nasi gudeg* places on Jl. Teuku Umar: Rp750-900 for everything, including meat, vegetables, sauce, and boiled egg. **Ibu Mary's,** on Jl. Gatot Subroto in Pasar Singosaren, is another *warung nasi gudeg* open 1900-0500. A specialized *nasi liwet* place is **Nasi Liwet Lampu Ijo** on Jl. Purasari.

Another famous Solonese dish is *gampol plered;* try this one at **Restaurant Wijaya's,** where even the mayor of Solo eats. *Gampol,* made from rice flour, coconut milk, and spices, is served in a bowl, and is sort of salty. The best is sold by vendors who go around the different *kampung* with a *tenggok* (basket). In restaurants it costs Rp1000 and in the *kampung,* Rp500. Right across the street from Hotel Keprabon on Jl. Achmad Dahlan is **Nasi Gudeg Pak Parto,** a lively, cheap and crowded hole-in-the-wall. Opposite the lane down to Losmen Timur (on the same street as Hotel Keprabon) is a *gado-gado* restaurant called **Warung Baru.** Cheap eating places also cluster around the train station for such Solonese specialties as *nasi liwet, nasi rawon, nasi langgi* and *nasi tumpang;* another row of *warung* is on Jl. Diponegoro near the entrance to Pasar Triwindu. For Solonese chicken rice soup *(nasi timlo),* go to **RM Timlo Solo,** Jl. Jen. Urip Sumoharjo/Mesen 106. **Pak Dul's,** on corner of Jl. Iman Bonjol and Jl. Ronggowarsito, is an eating tent serving tasty "100% halal" rice dishes; order cold beer from the **Ramayana Restaurant** across the street. Another, huge *mie* place is **Mie Pancoran,** Jl. Pasar Kembang.

Jalan Teuku Umar
To reach Jl. Teuku Umar go up from Hotel Keprabon to Jl. Slamet Riyadi and take a R; it's the next street on the right. Also called Jalan Susu. Here, on tents with *NASI GUDEG* blazoned across them, sample Solo's filling specialty consisting of a whole egg, beans, *nasi,* coconut sauce, vegetables—a great deal for Rp700. Other Indonesian cuisines available: *wedang ronde* (soup); *telur puyum* (quail eggs); *sosis* (meat dish). On this same street hot milk tents also open up at night, cozy meeting places where *becak* drivers, businessmen, Chinese laborers, schoolchildren, and travelers all eat together; Rp300 for milk with honey, Rp600 for *Susu Itb,* a male virility tonic that gives new strength.

Sate
Several *sate ayam* places are about a 5-min. walk from Hotel Central. **Sate Ayam Madura** also offers *nasi soto* and *nasi rames,* though **Sate Ayam Pak Dul,** Jl. Nonongan 73, is better known. A good *sate kambing* place is on the corner of Jl. Nonongan and Jl. Slamet Riyadi, plus many others around: 10 sticks of chicken sate costs Rp700; *es teh* (they go well together) is Rp200.

Restaurants
Restaurant Sari, Jl. Slamet Riyadi 351 (tel. 2776), about 2.5 km from the tourist office, features such specials as sausages and smoked ham, as well as the best restaurant versions of Solonese dishes. **RM Populair,** Jl. Achmad Dahlan 70 (down the street from Hotel Keprabon), serves very good Chinese-style meals; their *cap cai* (Rp1500) is hard to beat—enough for two. Open 1000-1400, 1600-2000. Another Chinese restaurant is the excellent **RM Centrum,** Jl. Kratonan 151 (tel. 2826), serving seafood dishes in the Rp3000-4000 range (other dishes not good value); it's near the Westerners'. Open 1030-1500, 1730-2100. The **Ramayana Restaurant,** on the intersection of Jl. Imam Bonjol and Jl. Ronggowarsito, is a cozy little place with well-prepared Chinese cuisine, *sate,* and cold beer. **The Orient,** Jl. Slamet Riyadi 337A (near the Sari), is the top Chinese restaurant in Solo, with dishes costing between Rp3000-4000; the **Diamond** down the street toward town, with neon facade, serves the same quality food at higher prices (which explains why it's usually empty). Probably the best *nasi padang* restaurant in town is **Pasar Pon,** Jl. Slamet Riyadi (near Bioskop Dhady). For something cheaper, **Bakso Taman Sari,** Jl. Gatot Subroto 42C, has tasty dishes and competent ice drinks; count on about Rp1500 for a meal. Open 0800-1500/1700-2100. Finally, **Madukoro Restaurant,** 6 km W of Solo on the road to Yogya in the little town of Kartosuro, serves the best *burung dara* and *seger ayam* around; sample also their special *"madukoro* drink."

Desserts
At night on the sidewalks try the local sweet, *serabi,* rice custard on a cripsy pancake served out of carts in the Pasar Pon area. Best served hot with sprinkled chocolate shavings, pineapple, or *pisang* slices on top. Also give *jenang gulo* (sweet, sticky rice cakes) a try. At Jl. Slamet Riyadi 76 is the **New Holland Modern Bakery** which peddles delights like cheese danish (Rp500), hamburgers (Rp2000) with the works, chocolate jimmies, *kelapa muda* pastry, all kinds of cakes, confections, and very good ice cream. Nearby, and also on Jl. Slamet Riyadi, flashy **American Donut** has the best selection of baked goods. **Orion,** Jl. Urip Sumoharjo, is another outstanding bakery. Ice cream carts are everywhere; taste coconut ice cream, an overwhelming bowl for Rp300! Superlative ice juices are mixed at the **Tentrem Ice Cream,** Jl. Urip Sumoharjo. In **Pasar Gede** and **Pasar Sinjosaren** select from a mouth-watering cornucopia of local and imported fruits.

ENTERTAINMENT

Solo has always occupied a prominent place in the development of *wayang. Wayang* themes surround you everywhere in this city—in the inlaid work, carvings, paintings, court dances, and it is said there are 1,000 *wayang kulit dalang* working in the Solo area. Performances of *wayang kulit* and *wayang orang* are put on for the populace and not just for tourists as in Yogya. As for court dancing, the *Bedaya* and *Serimpi* are the last vestiges of the old ceremonial dances of the C. Javanese palace compounds of the 13th and 14th centuries. At **Mangkunegaran Kraton** every Wed. at 1000 you can see these traditional dances practiced for 2 hours free. In Kraton Susuhunan, only one very old woman still teaches the traditional *Serimpi*, paid by ASKI only Rp3500 per lesson! An American university has taken a videotape of her instruction method and copies made so that her great art and skill will not be lost.

Others

Pop concerts in Solo occur at least once a month; most groups seem to try to emulate The Talking Heads. Pubs are presently the rage: **Sasmaya**, Jl. Dr. Rajimani (same road as Danar Hadi, near the Singosaren Plaza); **Dinasti** on Jl. Honggowongso; and the **Dew Drop Inn** (behind the stadium). These are the places to go if you get tired of *nasi gudeg*, where you can enjoy some Western food (steak and ice cream) while listening to small bands play some new Indonesian pop music. No dancing, free entrance, and they open at 1200. If feeling hot and tired, take a dip for Rp1500 in the swimming pools at the **Mangkunegaran Hotel** and the **Kusuman Sahid Prince Hotel**. Both have very pleasant surroundings with nice gardens, changing rooms, showers, and are open in the evenings. Or join Mangkunegaran's swimming club for only Rp10,000 per month and have unlimited use of the pool. Sentimental melodramatic Indian films and violent kung fu movies play at the **Trisakti Theatre**, Jl. Kratonan, and at the **Solo Theater** in the Sriwedari Park. Try to see a traditional Solonese wedding *(temu)* in *Bulan Besar* in which the groom crushes an egg with his foot and the bride then washes the foot in flowery water. Before *Puasa*, Solonese make pilgrimages to graves and visit bathing places (at Cokrotulung and Pengging) to take ceremonial baths *(padusan)*. Occasionally, horseraces take place at the Manahan Sportsfield with visitors pouring in from surrounding cities.

ASKI

Solo's music conservatory, next door to the Law Department at Pagelaran Alun Utara. Over 60 years ago this prestigious academy devised a system of ciphers to mark traditional Javanese *gamelan* notes so that songs and music were able to be preserved. Before this, musicians learned the songs and meters by heart. Some of the royal *gamelan* musicians and dancers rehearse and teach here every morning (except Sundays) at around 0900 and last until around 1400. There's also a museum. Here you may see *wayang kulit* free of charge, Malaysian or Balinese dances, art exhibits, etc.

Sriwedari Theater

The Sriwedari Recreation Park, in the middle of town on Jl. Slamet Riyadi, is home base for the celebrated Wayang Orang Sriwedari. Because performances are put on every night except Sun., this park is one of the easiest places to see versions of not only the Hindu epics but also more popularized productions such as *Ketoprak* (historical dramas), and *wayang orang*. Tickets range from Rp350 to Rp400, or stand for free at the side of the building and look through the wire mesh with the kids. Starts at 2000, over by 2300. They use realistically painted stage props such as a palace hall, a dense wild forest, ricefields, or mountains. The dance style is sometimes learned 2nd- and 3rd-hand from the court masters down the street in the *kraton* dance schools. Saturday night shows are the most popular, so buy your ticket in advance. While waiting, wander around the park and snack at the small restaurants.

Radio Republic Indonesia

Wayang shows are put on at the RRI Bldg. near the RR station, Rp500 by *becak* from city center. Broadcast live all over C. Java, *wayang orang* performances (Rp400-750) are staged approx. 2 times per month on every other Wed., and *wayang kulit* (Rp500-1000) every third Sat. of each month. Keep your eyes and ears open and always check with the tourist office about these excellent performances; don't believe anybody else. At RRI's entrance the month's upcoming events are posted. Performances at the RRI are at least as good as those put on in Taman Sriwedari, better acoustics, and the dancers are generally younger.

SHOPPING AND CRAFTS

Jalan Secoyudan is Solo's shopping street, known for its dozens of goldsmith shops. For one of the largest collections of ancient *kris* in Indonesia, visit **Hardjonegoro** (or Raden Tumenggung), Jl. Kratonan 101. He has some quite famous *kris;* only in Solo do you find painted *kris* scabbards. Expect to pay anywhere from Rp100,000 up to 5 million *rupiah*. To see an *empu* (*kris* smithie) in action, go to **Pauzan**, Jl. Yosoroto 28/82; a craftsman of *kris* scabbards is **R. Ng. Prodjotjendono**, Jl. Nirbitan RT 16, No. 3. For the princely sum of Rp2500, select from a vast variety of prerecorded cassette tapes—Javanese and Western classical, *gamelan* music, *ketoprak*, new wave, hard rock—at dozens of audio shops around town. A bird market, **Pasar Depok**, is at the NW end of Jl. Tirtoyoso near Balemkambang Sports Center. Solo's newest addition to the consumer economy is the **Purwosari Plaza**, a good place for Western items like shampoo, soap, biscuits. Also many boutiques, gold and shoe shops, fabrics, and a big supermarket.

Others

For clicking, clacking handmade toys, some cut from scrap metal, go to the toy shops in Sriwedari Park. Also you can find 19th C. dollhouse furniture, small painted tea sets, orange clay dolls, cardboard *wayang kulit* puppets, plus miniature *gamelan* sets with silver xylophone keys and painted wooden frames, perfectly tuned to *slendro* key! Ceramics are not so common on Java as bamboo receptacles obviate the need for pots; **Slametho W.S. Karagan 291,** Panularan, sells extremely ornate pottery at reasonable prices. The *batiked* pots are Rp3000; ones made in the shape of geese, Rp4000. The biggest pots, about one m high, go for Rp5000-6000. **Glasscutter Hosanna,** Jl. Kerinci 10, Manahan, makes elaborate mirrors which look like cut crystal; Rp100,000 to 1 million.

Metallurgy

Sinar Kerajinan Logam, Jl. Gading Kidul 68 (tel. 5768), open Mon. to Sat. 0800-1600. This craftsman, Ko Kiem Han, will mount your logo, coat of arms, emblem, trophy, family crest, motto, genealogical or astrological sign, or whatever other motif or design you would like on plaques which are handmade from *kayu sono.* It takes a month for him to turn out a plaque.

Pasar Triwindu

Off Jl. Diponegoro, just N of Jl. Slamet, an easy walk from Kraton Mangkunegaran. In this flea market you'll find (at prices often cheaper than Yogya or Jakarta) bric-a-brac of every description. Some prize items but a lot of worthless junk as well, many mass-produced in Yogya. Ask to see more refined *(alus)* items often kept under or inside the stalls. Bargain hot and heavy for everything, even I Ching coins! The cheapest vendors are in back of the market (first price Rp5000-10,000 for the better quality *wayang golek).* Some may invite you to their home to view their private collections.

Antique Shops

The best are **Eka Hartono,** Jl. Dawung Tengah 11/38; **Toko Parto Art,** Jl. Slamet Riyadi 103 (the actual workshop is at Kusumoyudan Timur RT 3B); **Toko Singowidoyo,** Jl. Urip Sumoharjo (heaven for the lapidarist). On display in these dusty shops is a fascinating assortment of relics and curios of Dutch colonialism such as Delft ware, silverware, bronzes. Other shops along Jl. Slamet Riyadi sell extremely convincing reproductions of 17th and 18th C. Javanese furniture: herb chests, cabinets, and chairs that look so antique that you better get written verification that they're not (to avoid problems at the customs gate!). Noteworthy also for very fine reproductions is **Mirah Delima,** Jl. Kemasan RT XI.

Wayang

For good quality *wayang kulit,* expect to pay about Rp15,000 for small ones and Rp20,000 for larger

---

SOLO

1. Jebires Train Station
2. minibus to Candi Sukuh
3. cheap hotels
4. SMKI
5. RM Timlo
6. Solo Kota Train Station
7. Pasar Gede (bird market)
8. telegram office
9. Bank Negara Indonesia 1946
10. telephone office
11. *gamelan* store
12. Alun-Alun Utara
13. Pasar Kelwar Antique Market
14. Great Mosque
15. police station
16. post office
17. Dinas Kesehaten (health dept.)
18. Garuda Office
19. Struggle 1945 Monument
20. Pasir Legi
21. Sahid Jaya Hotel
22. Hotel Islam
23. Bank Bumi Daya
24. minibuses to Yogya, Semarang
25. Triwindu Antique Market
26. Batik Semar
27. Hotel Kota
28. Batik Keris
29. The Westerners
30. Hardjonegoro's
31. taxi stand
32. Pasar Singosaren
33. Batik Danar Hadi
34. Dinasti Pub
35. Cakra Hotel
36. police station
37. Sanggar Theosophi Sala
38. RRI
39. Balapan Train Station
40. minibus terminal
41. Gilingan Bus Station
42. Batik Semar
43. Toko Bedoyo Serimpi
44. Radyapustoko Museum
45. tourist office
46. Sriwedari Park
47. Slamet
48. hospital
49. police station
50. THR Amusement Center
51. Pasar Depok (bird market)
52. minibuses to Yogya, Semarang

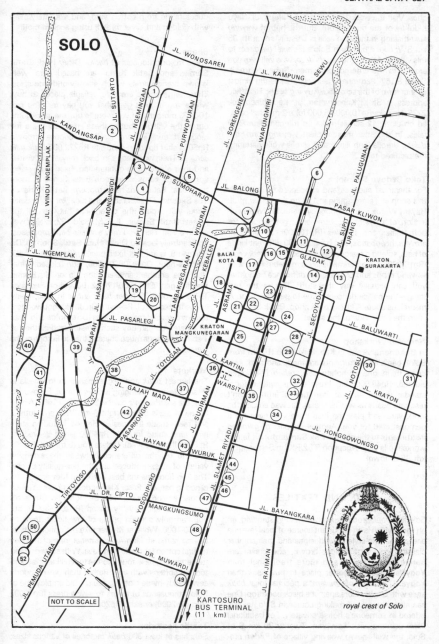

royal crest of Solo

ones. Visit the workshop of **Usaha Pelajar**, Jl. Nayu Kidul (N of the bus station). But the hub of *wayang kulit*-making in the Solo area is **Desa Manyaran**, 35 km SW; take a bus from Solo's *terminal bis* direct to this village. Ask for the *kepala desa*, who will take you around to the different craftsmen. **Subandono**, Jl. Sawu 8/162, Perumnas Palur, still makes the almost extinct form of the scroll-like *wayang beber*. His office address is SMKI Konservatori, Jl. Kepathihan, tel. 2225. He asks Rp10,000-15,000 for a 2-m scroll painted on cloth; 12 scrolls make up the complete *Panji* tales. In this, the most ancient *wayang* form, the *dalang* unrolls long illustrated scrolls while narrating the pictured tales.

Toko Bedoyo Serimpi

For theatrical supplies and dancers' costumes visit this shop at Temenggungan 116 on the corner of Jl. Hayam Wuruk and Jl. Ronggowarsito. A diverse collection of *wayang* accoutrements: gilt slippers for both males and females (Rp10,000), all kinds of armlets, headbands, and bangles, 800 different kinds of hats, splendid maroon belts (Rp5000), glittery vests (Rp10,000). Toko Serimpi is like a museum filled with *wayang* props and baubles, the difference being that you can actually buy the stuff! This is the real thing—the palace dancers come to get their gear. A marvelous shop. A classy *batik* shop, **Batik Serimpi**, is on the other side of the street.

Gamelan Workshop

In **Bekonang** village in Kab. Sukoharjo (10 km from Solo), gamelan instruments are made and sold: *kencong* (5 in one complete set); *rebab* (2-stringed zithers), Rp40,000; big brass gongs with dragon-stands; whole sets of iron gongs (iron doesn't resonate nearly as well as brass). Browse around the work yard and play the instruments or have them demonstrated for you. Another supplier of *gamelan* instruments to the court is **Pak Sarwanto**; his family workshop is at Jl. Ngepung RT 2/RK I in Semanggi (2 km SE of town).

BATIK AND TEXTILES

Solo is a *batik*-producing center of long standing, an art form which is an important source of local revenue and pride. Solo-style *batik* designs and their somber classical colors of indigo, brown, and cream are noticeably different and more traditional than Yogya's. Solo is a better place to buy *batik* than Yogya. Look for *Solo malam*, a peculiar local *batik* style with bright colors against a black backdrop. One can also take a *batik*-making course in Solo, usually offered in someone's house privately. For traditional *batik* painting, visit **Lawiyan**. Twenty 20 km S of Solo, the well-known weaving village of **Pedan** produces fabric from cotton yarn, and silk interwoven with golden and silver thread, using ancient motifs.

Shops

Three major producers of *batik*—**Dinar Hadi**, **Batik Semar**, and **Batik Keris**—are based here, well-known brand names which enjoy worldwide sales. These large shops are safe, reliable places to buy, where you at least get what you pay for. You pay 10-20% more than if you were to buy the same items out in the villages, but at these shops there's a full range of quality from which to choose—from a Rp5000 shirt up to an exquisite Rp222,000 *batik tulis sarung*. Their workshops in back may all be visited and their shops have outstanding, fixed-price selections (credit cards accepted). Batik Semar is more traditional, Batik Keris more modern. **Batik Keris**, Jl. Yos Sudarso 37, sells fabric and nice *ikat* work. Sales clerks will explain the differences between all the pieces. **Batik Semar**, Jl. R.M. Said 132, is also well worth a visit. Here you may also see *batik* processes. The centrally located **Dinar Hadi Batik Shop**, Jl. Dr. Rajiman 8, is another fixed-price outlet; see the *batik* process here. Open 0800-1600, Sun. closed. Dinar Hadi has another, smaller shop up on Jl. Slamet Riyadi, open 0900-1500/1700-2100 and on Sundays. There are over 70 other *batik* shops in Solo, many concentrated on Jl. Rajiman. On Jl. Honggowongso, there are several fashion shops (**Britannica** and **Topsi**) where you can buy such Westernized clothes as T-shirts and jeans much cheaper than in Europe or the states.

Markets

The largest *batik* and textile market in Indonesia is **Pasar Klewer** ("Hanging Market") on Jl. Secoyudan near the *susuhunan's* palace; open 0800-1600. A mad bustle of stalls offers bright *batik*, Western clothes, and ready-made Indonesian clothes, including stunning *lurik* shirts for only Rp4000 (short-sleeved) or Rp6000 (long-sleeved). Unless you're trained, it's difficult to tell the difference between the extensive variety of mass-produced and the fine-quality pieces. The 2nd floor has the best *batik*, but they are less inclined to bargain. Pasar Klewar doesn't have as much rubbish as Yogya's big Pasar Beringhardjo. Children's clothes are unbelievably cheap (Rp2000-3000), but you can only bargain prices of low ticket items by Rp500-1000. While at Klewer take the opportunity of buying some striking *lurik* material, one of the few natural cotton fabrics left on Java. With striped, colorful patterns, *lurik* is rough to the touch like Indian cotton but softens with age. Rather than buying poorly sewn ready-made clothes, you should employ one of Solo's thousands of tailors to sew a dress (Rp3000), shirt (Rp2000) or skirt (Rp2000).

Textile Factories

Solo has at least 300 *batik* factories of various sizes:

Garuda, Arjuna, etc. Most are scattered around the S part of the city; many others are out along Jl. Adisucipto, and several more are on Jl. Gremet. Though in the factories you can see the process of making *batik* and bold-patterned *ikat,* none sell material or *sarung* for a *rupiah* less than in the shops. For outstanding, elegant, and expensive *batik tulis,* visit the studio of Ibu Hartini (behind Pasar Klewer), one of the most famous *batik* designers on Java.

SERVICES

Do your official business early in Solo as most offices close between 1400 and 1700. The **Surakarta Municipality Tourist Office** is at Jl. Slamet Riyadi 235 (tel. 6508), between THR Sriwedari and the museum; open everyday 0800-1700; Sun. closed. With a staff of 100, they give out free maps and leaflets, and can help you find any type of information on events and sites or arrange for any type of tour. The **central p.o.** is on Jl. Sudirman. The best bookstore in town is **Sekawan,** with 2 branches: Jl. Slamet Riyadi and Jl. Kartini.

For changing money, banks are within 10 min. walking distance from the inexpensive hotels in the Jl. A. Dahlan area. **Bank Bumi Daya,** Jl. Slamet Riyadi 18 (tel. 5008); **Bank Negara Indonesia 1946,** Jl. Jen. Sudirman 19, tel. 2668 (probably the best rate); and **Bank Niaga,** Jl. Slamet Riyadi 8, tel. 7955.

The **telephone office** is located downtown on Jl. May. Kusmanto (tel. 108), open 24 hours. It takes just 5 minutes to make an international direct call, but takes too long to try to call collect.

City Photo, Jl. Slamet Riyadi 78A (open 0800-2100), does 1-hour Fuji film processing and printing.

Imigrasi is located on Jl. Adisucipto, 10 km out of the city on the way to the airport. Take a *bis kota* from Jl. Ronggowarsito.

Health

Dr. Benny Tahapari (an Ambonese who speaks Dutch and English), on Jl. Ir. Sutami in Jebres, 3 km W of the center. Nearer to the Westerners' is **Dr. Amien Romas** in Kauman Sememen; also speaks English well. The government health service, *Dinas Kesehatan,* is on Jl. Kampung Baru opposite Warung Sate Pak Jaman; see Dr. Johan Vandenberg. Solo has a wide reputation for traditional, natural healing. The city is a center for *jamu* processing, with the large *jamu* manufacturer Air Mancur based here. A traditional medicine store on Jl. Socoyudan, **Jamu Akar Sari,** is within easy walk of the Westerners'; here they'll concoct a made-to-order *jamu* to be drunk right on the spot. Chinese medicine is also a developed science here. At **Toko Sin She,** behind Pasar Gudeg on Jl. Ketan Dan, mime your illness (like diar-

rhea) and they'll subscribe the right medicine, herb, or elixer for you. Acupuncturists here charge only Rp2000 per session; ask at Toko Sin She for some names. Also some of the best Tai Chi teachers around. **massages:** Just the ticket after returning with aching bones from the G. Merapi climb. Massages are done by *tukang pijet,* many of them old ladies. Your hotel will order for you the one living closest; they ask Rp1500-3000 per session. Other, less common masseuses (called *tukang ururt*) do therapeutic massage, put you right back together. For yoga, see Mr. Anda Suyono, Jl. Ronggowarsito.

MEDITATION COURSES

Sanggar Theosofi Sala

Solo is a center for spiritual and occult groups. The **Theosophical Society** is at Jl. Gajah Mada 102, opposite Kantor Kesehatan and up the street from Hotel Sahid right at the beginning of Jl. Gajah Mada by the roundabout; the sign just says THEOSOPHIC. Theosophie is the science of metaphysics, the study of the cosmos as it applies to Man and Earth. There is no worship, but every Sun. meetings are held at the center when members discuss theory, read texts, and lecture.

Sumarah

A white-magic mystical fraternity founded by a bank clerk in 1937. Its name is an acronym for *Sujud Marang Allah,* which means "devotion, dedication, and surrender to God." With 10,000 followers worldwide, the organization accepts aspirants from all creeds. Sumarah is founded on the concept that every religion, at least in its original form, believed all paths lead to one god, all spiritual development was for the good of everyone. Every religion merges, and Sumarah does not hesitate to take wisdom from other religious sources that they believe is now a part of the world's heritage. Students try to maintain contact with the world, and be aware of what's outside their perception of the world. As in the Zen concept of "such-ness" of things, one must realize man's essence, his individuality. Javanese/Buddhist terminology is used to describe points on the body the soul has reached *(chakra),* from the genitals to the crown of the head. Each *pamong* (teacher) uses a different technique; for example, Pak Hardjanto is a follower of a mixture of Hinduism, Javaism, and Bali Hindu religions. None practice levitation or other spectacular public demonstrations of their faith, believing that any outward manifestation of God's favor is irrelevant. The idea is to maintain the spirit of humility and self-surrender and to constantly worship God, while at the same time to live at peace within society.

Studying *Sumarah*

Many resident Europeans study under the tutelage of a *pamong*. Meditation sessions usually last 2-3 hours, held in *pamongs'* or students' homes. First visit the Joyokusuman Guesthouse and ask for Laura (Gajahan RT 9/I no. 16) only between 0900 and 1000; buy the introductory booklet (Rp500). To further familiarize yourself with metaphysical thought, Pak Sujono (Jl. Bonggowarsito 60) has an outstanding library which you may visit and read volumes there. There's no registration fee now, and admission into a meditation group is by invitation only (usually not difficult). Go along to a meeting or two to see how you like it. Comfortable rooms for rent (from Rp60,000 per month) for long-term meditation students are available at Joyokusuman Guesthouse, Gajahan. To make ends meet, most of the meditators teach English in language schools or give private English tutorship at about Rp7500 per hour.

TRANSPORT

Touristically speaking, while Yogya is so well-organized that you can "do" it in 3 days, Solo is a complex, multi-layered community that doesn't give up its secrets as easily. Compounding the problem, the city's residents habitually mix so many Javanese words into their speech that it's difficult to be understood and to understand *Bahasa Indonesia* here. You can't do Solo fast; you need a week. Solo is ideal as a traveler's destination, being centrally located in the center of Java, roughly between Jakarta and Bali. Mountain resorts and forest wilds are within easy reach. Everything closes up for several hours in the afternoons, and none of the public buildings open up again until the evening, so get your business over with early.

Getting There

Minibuses (Rp1500) leave constantly (0700 to 1700) from a Terminal Terban (W of the Tugu Monument), or climb on a bus or minibus anywhere on Yogya's Jl. Sudirman or Jl. Solo (same street) to Solo. A shared taxi (Rp2500 pp) from Yogya's Kantor Pos is the easiest way to reach Solo. From Semarang, Solo is Rp1500 by bus or Rp2000 by minibus. From Surabaya, Rp4000 by bus, 6 hours. In front of Solo's Gilingan Bus Station, just N of the train station on Jl. A. Yani, stand by the roundabout to catch a *bemo* 3 km into town (Rp150) or take a *becak* (Rp750). **by train:** Trains from Yogya (one hour) run as cheap as Rp500; Solo is only an hour farther down the line on most trains. From Jakarta, the overnight (12 hours) 1st Class *Bima* goes via Yogya (about Rp28,500); there are also slower, much less expensive 2nd- and 3rd-Class non-a/c trains. Reverse the routes in "from Solo" below for other fares and destinations. Arriving at Solo's train station on Jl. Balapan in the N side of town, it's Rp600 by *becak* or Rp5000 by taxi to the hotel area off Jl. Slamet Riyadi. **flights:** The airport is 9 km W of town. Garuda has 2 flights (one hour) daily from Jakarta, Rp48,000; from Surabaya, Rp31,000; from Denpasar, Rp52,500 (via Surabaya).

Getting Around

Solo is definitely a city for walking. Pedicabs are ubiquitous, Rp300-400 and *andong* can take one-4 persons anywhere in Solo for Rp2500 per km. Pak Mawardi at the Westerners' (Kemalayan Kidul 11) has about 20 bikes for Rp900 per day (cheaper by the week). Joyokusuman Guesthouse, Gajahan, also rents bikes at Rp600 per day. The minibus station is by Hadiningrat Kraton opposite Pasar Klewar, or flag them down along the main streets. For longer distances, like out to Kartosuro, it costs Rp300 from the minibus station. Double decker *bis kota* run continually from W to E down Solo's main street, Jl. Slamet Riyadi, then circle around and head W up Jl. Secoyudan; Rp100 fixed fare. **tours:** If you're lucky enough to meet up with Abdul, who comes around the Westerners occasionally, he'll take you on a wild bicycle tour of Solo for only Rp1000 pp per day (plus Rp1000 for the bicycle). You'll cross the Solo River S of town, look at *batik* selections and a *gamelan* workshop, sample fruits and fried snake, visit the Arab quarter and a weaving village, then he'll take you to his friend's place for lunch. Speaks excellent English.

FROM SOLO

Buses

The big Gilingan Bus Station (or Terminal Tirtonadi) is 3 km N of central Solo on Jl. Tagore, Rp700 by *becak*. Approximate bus fares: Salatiga, 54 km, Rp1210 (a/c); Semarang, 102 km, Rp1485 or Rp2260 a/c; Purwokerta, 250 km, Rp3660 or Rp5485 a/c; Mojokerto, 230 km, Rp3385 or Rp5085 a/c; Surabaya, 276 km, Rp4035 or Rp6060 with a/c and reclining seats; Jakarta, Rp8785, Rp13,210 (a/c); Yogya, 65 km, Rp1635 or Rp2460 a/c. Many long-distance bus companies are found at Terminal Cilingin. **to Malang:** Day buses do this 298-km, 9-hour run via Surabaya, but for day travel it's more comfortable to travel from Solo to Surabaya by train, then take a minibus or even another train down to Malang. A night bus runs directly from Solo to Malang, 6 hours; Rp7000. **to Bali:** Damri, Agung Ekspres, and Mira all have offices at Terminal Cilingin, charging about Rp12,000 (a/c) and taking about 12 hours to Denpasar. **to Sukuh and Ceto:** From Cilingin, take a bus to Karangpandan (Rp250), then charter a minibus to both temples for Rp10,000. Much cheaper and slower local public transport is also available.

By Minibus/Taxis

Because buses are so crowded, many prefer to use

VICINITY OF SOLO

the countryside to Kartosuro (towards Yogya), then a horsecart, *delman* or *becak* (Rp200) from there. Garuda fares: Jakarta, every day (0855 and 1555), Rp61,600; Surabaya, every day at 0715, Rp28,200; Ujung Pandang, every day at 0715, Rp122,700. For Denpasar, you must change planes in Surabaya.

SANGIRAN

This region is well known mainly in scientific circles for its extraordinary finds in the fields of paleontology, anthropology, and geology. Since 1936, when a Dutch professor found the skull of Java Man *(Pithecanthropus erectus,* but now called *Homo erectus),* this area 15 km N of Solo has been the focus of intense research. Many prehistoric fossils—human and animal—have been unearthed here. Most of the fossilized remains have been buried under layers of fallow earth, laden with lime which has helped preserve them. The whole area is depressed with much of the terrain washed away or eroded, with gaping holes 3-4 m deep where earlier excavations took place. After heavy rains, especially, the fossils turn up in landslides. All the early hominid finds have laid the foundations for theories of the earliest human life on Java 250,000 years ago.

Plestosen Sangiran Museum
Entrance: Rp100. All the tags are in Latin and *Bahasa Indonesia.* This small, unique, and well-organized museum exhibits extinct elephant tusks; teeth and horns from extinct giant deer, antelope and other small animals; fragmented jawbones and vertebrae; fossilized molluscs; remnants of stegodon, ox, rhinocerous, crocodiles, pigs, apes. There are models of *Homo erectus* craniums (the originals are at Gajah Mada University in Yogya and the Geological Office in Bogor). The original owners of these skulls were avid meat-eaters—many of the museum's bones derive from the carcasses that this upright ancient creature brought down! Although the ape men in the diorama have Indonesian faces, in reality the men of that time were a completely different race. Books in the small library may be read on the premises; of special interest is the *Quaternery Geology of the Hominid Bearing Formation in Java.* It's illegal to collect or remove fossils, especially human ones: besides, the locals are much better at it than you and certainly discourage you. Before you even reach the museum, someone will approach you selling very clever stone-carved imitations of coral or ancient teeth for Rp7000 first price but will go down to Rp5000 if you bargain. Vendors also sell *batu aki* (semi-precious stones) Rp3500-5000. There's a small *bakso* (Rp250) and ice drink (Rp400) cart in the parking lot, and visitors can overnight in rooms on the grounds of the old museum up the road; Rp7000. Very nice setting.

faster vans which hold only 8-10 persons and leave every half hour or so and head straight to your address in Yogya (Rp1500), Semarang (Rp2500), Malang, etc. Catch these at the special minibus station near Cilingin Terminal. Seats can be reserved so be sure to get a seat away from the sun (to Semarang get a seat on the R side if it's early in the day, L side if it's late in the day). Also, on the *alun-alun,* in front of the Great Mosque, board tiny minivans W to Kartosuro, E to Karanganyar, and S to Sukoharjo. From the taxi stand on Jl. Gatot Subroto, catch taxis (private cars) to: Semarang, Rp10,000; Yogya, Rp7500; or anywhere else.

By Train
Five trains per day connect Yogya (Rp500-1200). To Semarang, one train daily at 0600; Rp6500. For longer hauls, book at least a day in advance. To Surabaya, trains depart at 0300, 0245, 0327, and 0818, 1244, and 1552. The 0818 departure time is the most popular one for travelers. This train, the *Argopuro* (Rp2000 3rd Class, Rp2800 2nd Class, Rp3700 1st Class) travels on to Probolinggo for the Mt. Bromo climb. The train to Malang leaves at 0145; Rp5000 3rd Class, Rp7300 1st Class. To Semarang, the train departs at 0600; Rp6500 3rd Class.

By Air
The Garuda office is in the forecourt of the Kusuma Said Hotel, Jl. Sugiopranoto, open every day 0700-1600, Sat. 0700-1300, Sun. and holidays 0900-1200. Solo's airport is 9 km, 25 min. and Rp5000 by taxi from the city; taxis are available at the private stand on Jl. Gatot Subroto. A tidy, relaxing little airport with a coffee *warung* across the parking lot. But the best way out to the airport is to take a *bis kota* from Jl. Secoyudan or Pasar Nongko for a nice ride through

Getting There

Located in Krikilan village, 15 km N of Solo on the highway toward Purwodadi via Kalioso. From Solo, take either a minibus from the minibus station near the *kraton,* or a Purwodadi-bound bus (cheaper) directly from Balapan Train Station, Rp250 to the turnoff at Kalijambi (one km beyond Kalioso), then it's an easy 3.5-km, ½-hour walk from the intersection to the museum, or flag down a motorcycle and ride on the back (Rp500). Returning, try to hitch a ride to the turnoff, or perhaps all the way back to your door in Solo!

Pithecanthropus erectus: *Along the Solo River in C. Java was one of the first places on earth where man lived. For decades paleontologists have dug out mastodon tusks, saber-toothed tiger teeth, and giant ox vertebrae fossils along its banks. To the R is pictured the remains of the skull of* Pithecanthropus erectus, *so-called "Java Man," one of the greatest fossil finds ever made. Belonging to one of the earliest known hominids, the discovery by Dubois of these skull fragments and a leg bone at* Sangiran on the Solo River in 1891 made all existing theories of man's evolution obsolete. Java Man was an upright creature weighing approximately 70 kg; his bones closely resemble Peking Man as well as species living in Africa, Europe, and Asia a quarter to a half million years ago. With a cranial capacity of 855 cubic centimeters, he would have made an excellent candidate for modern man's immediate ancestor. Below is an approximation by scientists of how the whole skull might have appeared.

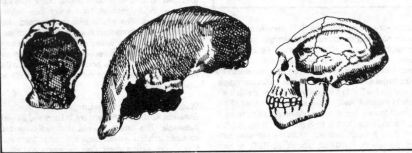

EAST JAVA

The island's least tourished province. Except for a brief stay in Surabaya, travelers usually pass straight through on the Yogya-Bali stretch. A heavily populated area of 30 million, E. Java abounds with bursting cities, towns, and *kampung* along roads which run through ceaselessly nurtured rice- and canefields. Mountain slopes are patched with fruit, coffee and tea plantations. This pastoral region was the site of the last powerful Hindu kingdom, the Majapahit. The province is more traditional and religious than C. Java; it falls short of plush tourist amenities, accommodation is relatively more expensive, and it's more difficult and time-consuming to travel in. But for those with time and transportation, the area's far-flung attractions can provide some unusual side trips through magnificent countryside. East Java is to C. Java as Mississippi is to Virginia: deep, deep Java, considerably more rural and less touched by the West. Rattletrap buses, *becak*, carts, bicycles, and *wong* (pedestrians) predominate. Surprisingly, along with all the towns, networks of roads, ricefields, sugarcane, and extensive teak plantations, wild forests still survive relatively undisturbed; E. Java has 7 wilderness reserves (including Meru Betiri, probably the last habitat of the Java tiger). For *batik* lovers, virtually every textile center in E. Java—Sidoharjo, Madura, Tulungagung, Trenggalak and Tuban—uses its own motifs and styles.

ANCIENT EAST JAVANESE ART

Bas-reliefs

Numerous differences exist between the *candi* of C. and E. Java. In C. Javanese art, mastery is shown in the handling and modifying of Hindu styles. But characteristic Indonesian elements are much more dominant in E. Javanese ruins. The nationalistic E. Javanese Majapahit Kingdom, which lasted the lifetime of one man, Gajah Mada, was the only ancient indigenous empire which controlled nearly all of Indonesia. When it arose in the 14th C., there was a sudden Javanisation of styles, a return to a flatter, highly stylized method of carving in which the figures resemble shadow puppets used in *wayang* shows today. Expressions are more subtle and human than anywhere else in ancient Indonesian art, and often there are magical or supernatural settings. The figures' bodies, sculpted delicately with scant clothing and *wayang* puppet caps, are seen from the front while the head and feet are turned sideways. This sculptural technique has been given the name "wayang-style," which is often used to describe E. Javanese bas-reliefs. Central Javanese bas-reliefs are deeply hollowed, whereas in E. Java they are much shallower.

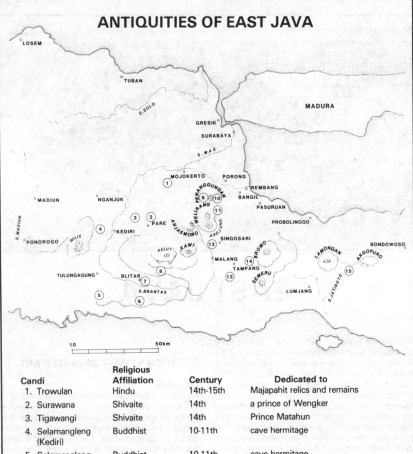

ANTIQUITIES OF EAST JAVA

Candi	Religious Affiliation	Century	Dedicated to
1. Trowulan	Hindu	14th-15th	Majapahit relics and remains
2. Surawana	Shivaite	14th	a prince of Wengker
3. Tigawangi	Shivaite	14th	Prince Matahun
4. Selamangleng (Kediri)	Buddhist	10-11th	cave hermitage
5. Selamangleng	Buddhist	10-11th	cave hermitage
6. Sumberjati	Shivaite	14th	King Martarajasa, first king of Majapahit
7. Bara	Shivaite	13th	a giant image of Ganesha
8. Panataran	Shivaite	14th	possibly the state temple of Majapahit
9. Jalatunda	Shivaite	10th	bathing place
10. Belahan	Vishnuite	11th	King Airlangga
11. Jawi	Shivaite-Buddhist	13-14th	King Kartanagara, last king of Singosari
12. Singosari	Shivaite-Buddhist	13-14th	King Kartanagara, last king of Singosari
13. Kidal	Shivaite	13th	King Anushapati, second king of Singosari
14. Jago	Buddhist	13th	King Vishnuvardhana, fourth king of Singosari
15. Kedaton	Shivaite	14th	

Architecture And Sculpture

The E. Javanese architectural style is likewise more slender: temples have narrower bases, are less symmetrical and smaller than the complexes of C. Java. East Javanese temple art was less religious, and syncretism went so far as to show both Buddhist and Hindu symbols on the same building. At *candi* Kedatan, Panataran, and Surawana, you can best see the *wayang*-style; on large-scale *candi* Jago, Singosari, and on the smaller Kidal the unusual blending of Buddhism and Hinduism is most evident. Humans and animal statues were also modeled more freely and show more movement in E. Java. The fierce guardian images in the *alun-alun* W of Singosari are done in a typical naturalistic E. Javanese style, while the C. Javanese guardians at Prambanan and at Kalasan have a more peaceful appearance.

TAWANGMANGU

Although Tawangmangu is technically in C. Java, it's covered here because it lies so near the provincial border. Tawangmangu is a pretty retreat on the slopes of G. Lawu, 42 km and Rp500 by bus from Solo via Karangpandan. This 1,000-m-high hill resort can be enjoyed for its variety of natural beauty, fresh breezes, clear streams, refreshing weather (2-blanket nights), and hilly woodland walks to historical remains and pilgrimage places. It has delicious drinking water, *pasanggrahan, wisma,* guesthouses, villas, hotels, and a campground—a nice place to get away to. Crowded with vacationers on holidays. There's a Kantor Telpon here, as well as a post office, and a Catholic church.

Sights

You've never seen such flowers as are found at **Kebun Hortikultura**— a botanist's delight! It's a herbal laboratory and horticultural experimental garden (elev. 1,050 m), with flowers of every description; the garden also produces ingredients used in traditional *jamu* folk medicine. Located on the L about 1½ km up the hill from the bus station; turn in at 2 white posts. Find a shady spot and relax, with only the wind for company. Two km from *stasiun bis* toward Sarangan is a bathing place, Rp100 entrance. As an alternative to walking around town, take the occasional *bemo* that labors up and down the town's main street, Jl. Lawu (or Jl. Raya); Rp150 flat rate. Or rent a horse from the villagers, Rp2000-3500/hour.

Accommodations

Most hotels and guesthouses here are in the Rp4000-8000 range, although it's possible to find a few for as low as Rp3500. **Pak Amat's** is the most convenient hotel and restaurant, only about 50 km from *stasiun bis* on the R-hand side toward the mountain; all individual units with verandahs are separated from the main building by a nice garden. Expect to pay around Rp6000-8000, but bargain! Right on the main street—watch the world go by. **Losmen Pondok Garuda**, on Jl. Lawu, ½ km up the hill from the bus station, has quite attractive rooms. **Wisma Yanti**, Jl. Lawu; good facilities, nice grounds, very quiet. No meals here but they have coffee and tea. The rooms at **Pasanggrahan Mali'jawan**, about 1½ km from the bus station on the R going toward Sarangan, aren't in the best shape (the Garuda is much better) but it has a huge *rumah makan,* open 0700-2300. Across the street is **Pondok Indah** at Rp8000 s, and they won't come down. Of several camping places in Tawangmangu, **Camping Tawangmangu Baru**, 4 km from *stasiun bis,* comes complete with tents, camping equipment, electricity, a cafeteria, sportsfield, swimming pool, and tennis courts.

Food

A specialty of Tawangmangu is *sate kelinci* (rabbit shish-kebab). Buy vegetables and fruit at roadside stands along Jl. Lawu and make your own picnic salad. Many eating stalls are around *stasiun bis.* Opposite the horticultural gardens is a cheap *warung* serving *nasi* dishes, drinks, and fruit. From Pasanggrahan Mali'jawan, turn L and go back 200 m toward Tawangmangu Bus Station; see the sign AYAM GORENG. This *rumah makan,* called **Sapto Argo**, offers *nasi gudek, nasi opor,* and *nasi rames.* Try their *es soda gembira* (a blend of soda, syrup, milk), a delicious drink. Other delicious restaurants along Jl. Balai Kambang are the **Bangun Trisno** and the **Puas Siti Sari.**

From Tawangmangu

It's 14 km to Sarangan, 10 km to Cemoro Sewu, and 42 km to Solo. Take very crowded minibuses over the top to Sarangan, Rp600. Or it's a cool, 5-hour walk on a precipitous road that climbs over 1,800 m, one of the highest roads on Java. Quite an unspoiled area. Also, climb the trail up to G. Lawu from Blumbang village. On top is the tomb of Sunan Lawu, a much visited pilgrimage spot (see "Sarangan" for more info on this climb). Because of its isolation and height (3,265 m), G. Lawu can be seen from as far away as Solo and Madiun. For Candi Sukuh, get the bus out of Tawangmangu W to Karangpandan from where it's only 11 km and Rp300 farther by *bemo.* Or, even better, take the easy, scenic path to the temple which leads from Tawangmangu's Grojogan Sewu Falls; 3-5 hours.

Vicinity Of Tawangmangu

The waterfall **Grojogan Sewu** is only ½ km from Tawangmangu. Get there on a small road from Kebon Hortikultura, or take the path nearly opposite Hotel Mali'jawan. Grojogan Sewu lies in the middle of pine forest with lovely natural panoramas (though there's trash everywhere). Descend to the bottom of the falls to the swimming pool (Rp150 entrance). In the forests

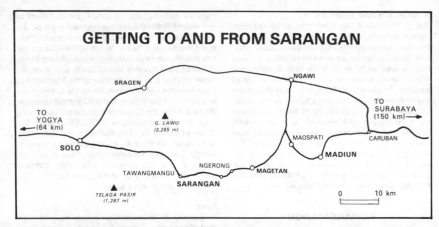

GETTING TO AND FROM SARANGAN

around Tawangmangu live many wild monkeys. A Hindu temple, **Reca Menggung**, lies in Desa Kelurahan Nglurah, a 30-min., 1½-km walk from Tawangmangu's bus station. Hotspring **Sumber Air Panas** is 5 km from Tawangmangu. At **Pablengan**, 17 km from Tawangmangu, are carbon dioxide and natural gas holes, oxygen vents, saltwater holes, hotsprings.

SARANGAN

This picturesque hill station (elev. 1,287 m) between Solo and Madiun makes a restful and enjoyable overnight stop on the way from Yogya to Surabaya. Situated W of Madiun on the slope of G. Lawu, the shape of the mammoth volcano looms forever above the town. A small, placid crater lake sits right in the middle of the Sarangan, with *losmen*, guesthouses, and hotels dotting the banks. A beautiful area, ideal for boating, swimming, fishing, tennis, horseback riding, and mountain climbing. Cabbages are grown up and down the hills, right outside your hotel doorstep! Friendly mountain people live here; very little stealing as it's bad for tourism. Not many budget-minded tourists visit Sarangan, but in the tourist season—July, Aug., and Sept.—a great many elderly Dutch tourists arrive, and every Sun. Indonesian day-trippers from Madiun and surroundings descend in droves. Sarangan is also popular with wealthy Chinese, and during holiday seasons, when all prices double, they're about the only ones who can afford to stay here! Tourists are approached on the street for ladies' company: Chinese girl, Rp40,000; Indonesian girl, Rp20,000. There's a *pasar* next to the police station.

Accommodations

Expensive! The most basic *losmen* want at least Rp5000; most others go for at least Rp10,000 and up,

and are quite unwilling to budge, especially during the tourist season. Most hotels have dining rooms and offer meals included in the room rate (if you wish), plus free tea and coffee. The most expensive place is **Villa Bentul**, a small complex on the lake with suites at Rp46,000 s per day! On the other end, there's **Losmen Baru** at Rp4000 d with a small sitting-room and no view of the lake. It's right at the intersection just before town where the road from Madiun to Tawangmangu turns into Sarangan. As with most inexpensive hotels here, Baru's 6 rooms with *mandi* are often booked. **Wisma Cemara**, cheapest on the hill, charges Rp6000 s with *mandi*, Rp8000 with fireplaces. The **Nusa Indah** is quite reasonable at Rp6500 s, Rp8500 d; they also offer a modern small apartment for Rp10,000 with breakfast (or Rp15,000 full board). European toilet, good lighting, porch, clean. The proprietor, Sugimani, is very knowledgeable about the G. Lawu climb. **Losmen Kartika**, up the hill 30 m from Nusa Indah, has 12 rooms around a courtyard; Rp5000 s, Rp8000 d, Rp12,000 t. **Losmen Lestair, Peng. Tentrem**, and **Peng. Purnama Jaya**, all a 5-min. walk from the lake, are in the Rp6000-8000 range. **Hotel Lawu**, the last one going up the hill, wants Rp5000 for room with annex. **Hotel Sarangan** is spacious with a terrific view, garage, parking area, children's playground, restaurant. English and Dutch spoken. Rooms (Rp10,000-35,000 s, Rp20,000-45,000 d) have porches high over the lake, bedroom and sitting room, fireplace, inside hotwater *mandi*, room service. For cheaper accommodation than Sarangan, try the *losmen* and guesthouses in the villages of Ngerong and Magetan lower down the mountain.

Food

On the lanes and streets are *bakso mie* vendors, and women who sell boiled eggs, still hot, 5 for Rp500!

RM Sari Rasa, right up the street from Nusa Indah, is popular with the Chinese. Asia Restaurant and RM Shinta both sell low-cost Indonesian food. Near the bemo terminal are 10 depots in a row serving Indonesian cuisine. A saberjet sits in front of them all. Warung Sederhana is the best and one of the cheapest—try her nasi goreng—fantastic at Rp800! Everyone eats with their fingers and they're tickled if you join in.

Getting To And From Sarangan

From Solo it costs Rp600 to Tawangmangu, then board a bemo (Rp500) over the mountain to Sarangan. From Sarangan, it's another Rp500 to Madiun. With the influx of visitors, many more minibuses shuttle between Tawangmangu and Sarangan on Sun-

days. From the bus terminal, bemo or minibuses don't even start for Tawangmangu until around 0800, so if you're in a hurry wait at the intersection of the road into town and try to hitchhike a passing truck. Or charter a minibus from Sarangan to Tawangmangu for Rp20,000, but expect at least 3 "helpers," frequent stops for "cousins" along the way, and your "chartered" minibus will be chock full by the time it reaches Tawangmangu. The twisting mountain road to the summit is so steep that many cars can't make it over the top and your vehicle might have to let half the passengers off at every other bend—a dramatic, spooky climb. If there are no bemo from Sarangan to Tawangmangu and you want to get to Solo, take a minibus for Rp1000 to Maospati, then a bus the long way to Solo via Ngawi, Rp1200.

GUNUNG LAWU AND VICINITY

Heavily forested G. Lawu (3,265 m) is an ancient, eroded volcano which has retained its symmetrical shape. The trail to the top is used by local people who make pilgrimages to the Hindu-Buddhist temple near the summit where offerings of food and baskets of flowers are left at a shrine. On the way up are remnants of old temples and terracing, and Majapahit graves. Stay overnight for giddy views and incredible photos of the sunrise. **guides:** Hire a guide at Blumbang village near the top, halfway between Tawangmangu and Sarangan; Rp9000 RT or Rp15,000 for 2 days and one night. If you get a guide in more touristy Sarangan, he'll charge Rp15,000-20,000 for one day and night. You can also rent horses for the ascent.

Climbing It

From Sarangan to the peak of G. Lawu (Puncak Lawu) takes 6 hours; to the crater (Kawah Lawu) only 3½ hours. The climb begins 300 m NW of Cemoro Sewu (5 km from Sarangan and 7 km from Tawangmangu) where you'll see several radio/TV towers. Just beyond the bridge, near Pos 1, is the start of the well-maintained and heavily used trail. Water is available at several points as the trail winds up the mountain; the final ascent is actually from the northeast. There are several huts plus emergency shelters on the way up: the first hut is at 2,400 m, the second at 2,850 m, the third at 3,100 m. If it's a full moon, it's possible to climb up and back in one day and night. Leave Sarangan at 0400, reach the peak at 0900, spend 2 hours at the top, then take only 2 hours to get back down to Sarangan. If you spend the night on the summit, expect frigid temperatures, but there's ample firewood. The rainiest season is Nov.-May, but the hike can be made all year.

CANDI SUKUH

This Hindu temple on the slopes of G. Lawu was built in the 15th C., late in the Hindu period just as Islam was penetrating coastal Java. The temple was approached in ancient times from the plains by a long flight of steps. The terraced pyramids at Sukuh and nearby Ceto have been compared with the ruins of ancient Mexico and Egypt. Both are dedicated to Bima, the giant warrior god of the Mahabharata. Often referred to as Java's only erotic temple, Sukuh has a highly distinctive character; it has elements not found in any other temple in Indonesia. Scholars have conjectured that Sukuh was the temple of worship for a family or clan cult, and might have been used for sex education. At 910 m above sea level, the sites were chosen with great care: these temples overlook the whole C. Javanese plain, an unforgettable location. From the upper terraces are sweeping panoramas of the wide Solo River Valley: purple mountains, lakes, rolling foothills, shimmering terraced sawah, trees in every shade of lush greenery.

Beside the stupendous views, another delightful aspect of Sukuh is that it's off the tourist track. Except for a would-be guide who tries to hit you up for another Rp500 admission, no one tries to sell you batik or souvenirs. Before the children start to collect, you could even have the grounds to yourself—a tranquil place with singing birds, grazing horses, and rustling pine trees. People laugh and smile at you on the way up, children run away and shriek, and the "minta uang's" ("Give me money!") seem half-hearted, even frivolous. Offerings are placed on this site by the Sultan of Yogya each year, and the temple still receives regular visits by Javanese pilgrims.

The Complex

The architecture alone sets Sukuh apart. The shape of Candi Sukuh, with its flight of steps leading to the upper part of the temple, is strikingly similar to the Mayan temples of Yucatan and Guatemala, which were being built at the same time! Walk up 3 grassy pyramids, passing through 3 gateways, each atop a flight of stairs, until you come to the main structure, a large stepped pyramid of roughhewn stone. The gate to the temple is next to the *kantor* where you register and show the tickets you've bought in Nglorok. After registering, walk back down to the bottom of the temple so you can climb up through the gateways. Stay in the *pondok* (no electricity) to the R as you're facing the temple; Rp2500 s plus food. A *kampung* nearby has excellent goats' milk; the watchman will take you there. Trails behind the *pondok* lead up to the misty heights of G. Lawu.

Sculpture

Though tame in comparison to India's Konarak or Khajuraho, Sukuh is one of the only explicitly erotic temples in all of Java. On the stone floor at the top of a steep stone tunnel leading into the complex, a large realistic penis faces a lovingly sculpted, swollen-in-excitement vagina carved in relief. Devotees still leave flower petals here. Other symbols of love or references to procreation are found in and around this temple, all executed in an exuberant and unabashed style. Facing the main temple, most of the standing carved figures are placed on a concrete slab to your left. The sculptures encompass an almost inexplicable hodgepodge of sculptural styles, eras, and themes. Three huge tortoises stand guard on the stone courtyard, a *garuda* is poised for flight on one side of an obelisk. See guardians holding their clubs in one hand and their penises in the other; statues of Bima; pylons decorated with the story of Garuda.

Bas-reliefs

Because of the scarcity of available light, bring a tripod or flash to capture the high quality of the reliefs here—strongly carved, intriguing figures executed in the crude, flat "*wayang*-puppet style." The first representation of a *kris* in Indonesian art is shown in one panel: Bima forging one with his bare hands while using his knee as an anvil. The clowns of the *wayang* plays are carved in a heavy and gross style compared with the grace and delicacy evident on C. Javanese Hindu temples. Also see carvings of crabs, lizards, tortoises, bats, and nasty underworld creatures. *Yoni* and phalluses are found in reliefs that depict sexual acts and growth in the womb before birth.

Getting There

Sukuh is just an hour's drive from Solo or 3 hours' drive from Semarang. From Solo take the road to Tawangmangu, but get off at Karangpandan, 29 km E (Rp500 and one hour by bus, or Rp750 by minibus) of Solo, where you'll see a sign at an intersection pointing to Candi Sukuh. As soon as you get into Karangpandan's *bemo* station, the drivers will ask you if you want to charter; if you can't afford it, just ignore them. From Karangpandan take a *bemo* or minibus 5 km to Nglorok, the beginning of the road leading up to the *candi,* and where you buy your ticket (don't throw it away as you'll need it to see the temple). Keep your pack at the *loket.* Everybody will point the way. It takes an hour of hard, steep slogging on a surfaced road to get up to the top (but only about a 20-min. descent, or try hitching). Walking back down, children will sing you songs as they carry 25-kilo baskets of pine cones on their backs to sell at market for cooking fuel. If driving your own vehicle, the road distance from Semarang to Sukuh, via Salatiga and Solo, is about 140 km; from Solo to Sukuh, 43 km. You can also approach just as easily from Madiun via Sarangan and Tawangmangu. **from Candi Sukuh:** Take the path which leads to Tawangmangu (3-4 hours) through villages with incredible and varied views. The path comes out at the Grojogan Sewu Waterfalls just below Tawangmangu's Kebon Hortikultura. Ask people along the way for directions.

Makam Suharto

Near Kapending (not far from Karangpandan), on the way to Candi Ceto, this is a nice place to spend the afternoon. Like the pharaohs of Egypt, President Suharto has built an enormous *pendopo* with huge gilded columns to serve as a final resting place for himself and his family. One would have thought that Suharto were trying to rival the memorial to Sukarno—a man under whose shadow he has always been walking—but Suharto's mausoleum was finished long before the government ever thought of building a memorial to Sukarno in Blitar. The construction of this lavish memorial upon a hill preserved for royal graves was completed in 1977 and immediately became the center of controversy; it even sparked a student riot in Jakarta. Details of the extravagant structure were circulated widely, and one student leader was quoted as saying: "While the people starve, the boss builds his grave." To further exacerbate the delicate situation, a Suharto business associate inadroitly answered charges that the mausoleum had cost US$10 million by saying it had cost "only" US$1 million! It is strictly forbidden to enter the *pendopo* or to take photos of it, but since it's so big, it's not at all difficult to see from a distance. From Solo take a bus or minibus heading for Tawangmangu, but get off at Karangpandan. From there take the road to Candi Sukuh, but go past the turnoff until you see the *pen-*

dopo in the foothills. For a closer look, enter Makam Mangkunegaran (the royal graveyard), which is open to the public, and then walk down the road going downhill to a point from where you can see the huge pendopo.

CANDI CETO

Built around the same time as Candi Sukuh, this terraced temple lies 28 km from Karanganyar, S of Jenawi, and near the small village of Kadipeso. At 1,500 m elevation, Ceto is 600 m higher and more northerly than Sukuh. Not as fascinating or lavishly decorated, the Ceto ruins are smaller and in poorer condition, without the statues and monuments that Sukuh has. You must be content with viewing terraces, broken guardian figures, *lingga,* and some relief frames, but overlooking spectacular views. Two main narrow terraces make up the complex. The highest terrace, which is stranger and more mysterious, formerly contained a stone floor and a wooden staircase, traces of which can still be seen. At least some portions of this complex were built in the 15th C., at the very end of the Majapahit era (Borobudur was constructed possibly 7 centuries earlier). Animal themes and figures play an important role at Ceto, particularly on the higher terraces. As at Sukuh, the Hindu religion was given only nominal obeisance, and it's supposed that this site was not just a temple but also a site for fertili-

ty rituals. Many of the symbols (such as the Bima statues) present on Sukuh are also found here, so both temples likely served the same purpose, whatever it was.

Getting There
When you come into Nglorok, the pot-holed road to Candi Ceto is to the L and the road to Candi Sukuh is to the right. The minibus travels from Nglorok 2 km further to Kemuning (3 km from Ceto), then on to Kadipeso, where it turns N to Jenawi and Sragen. Candi Ceto is only about one km up from Kadipeso. In the vicinity is Gumeng Waterfall and Cokrokembang Cave; ask in Kadipeso for directions.

MADIUN

Madiun is a pretty town 118 km E of Solo with abundant vegetation, although very dry, hazy, and dusty in summer. An abortive revolt in Madiun in Sept. 1948 was the first serious attempt by Indonesian communists to seize power by force. This rebellion was crushed in surprisingly short time by loyal troops of the Siliwangi Division. Although 17 years apart, there were many parallels between this rebellion and the Sept. 1965 alleged communist coup: a common prelude of rising political tensions and minor clashes, a common technique of power seizure including the abduction of opponents, the close cooperation between progressive revolutionary officers and communists; the premature opening of both revolts, the hopes of a popular uprising throughout Indonesia, the quick suppression of the rebellions by staunch anti-communist troops; the mass killings between communists and anti-communists (mainly Islamic and nationalist groups) at the end of both rebellions. The Indonesian Communist Party (PKI) was routed at Madiun and its leader forced into exile. But the political openness of the 1950s was used to rebuild the PKI's influence through mass organization.

Sights
The most respected *pesantren* (a religious boarding school for Muslims) in Indonesia, **Pondok Gontor,** is in Madiun. Also check out the 19th C. locomotives in the railyards of Balai Yasa P.J. Keretapi. To get to the yards, go out of Hotel Merdeka, turn L on Jl. Pahlawan, and follow it up about one km. See some of the oldest locomotives still running on Java, a few commissioned as early as 1881! Slip and slide over the tar puddles of the railyard trying to get good photographs. Take your children; they'll be enthralled. The last of the coalburners have been taken off the main line and are now just country trains; several woodburning locomotives are still in operation between Madiun and Kediri. If you're a steamrail enthusiast, Indonesia's railway stock is said to be the most diverse

and archaic anywhere in the world. But see the yard sooner rather than later; over the next 5 years steam engines are being phased out all over Java.

Accommodations And Food
Cheap hotels are clustered around the E end of town. **Hotel Madiun** charges Rp3000 d; cheaper is **Hotel 7777**. The best is central **Hotel Merdeka** on the main street, Jl. Pahlawan 42 (tel. 2547); Rp3500 s. A giant complex, bright and organized, with nice gardens. Across the street is **RM Ramayana** with standard prices. Also check out large Dutch-style **Losmen Pussat**, Jl. Dr. Sutomo 66; Rp3500 s. Comfortable, breezy, with nice front porch. **Hotel Tedjo**, Jl. Dr. Sutomo 55 (opposite Losmen Pussat), is a clean family-run place; Rp3500 s. Try the local specialty *babat,* a little cake filled with *kelapa muda.*

From Madiun
From Terminal Sleko to Ponorogo it's Rp600 by minibus; to Surabaya, Rp3000. Minibuses for Sarangan leave from Terminal Sleko infrequently; the drivers press you to charter one for Rp30,000! *(Jangan harga gila!)* If frustrated just hop on a minibus and do it in stages up to Sarangan, working your way by minibus up the mountain: first to Magetan, then Plaosan, Ngerong, then to Sarangan. To Solo or Yogya from Madiun, the train is the most direct; on the way to Yogya you'll pass the Prambanan temple complex so if it's early in the day, getting off and seeing it will save you having to double back the 20 km between Yogya and Prambanan village.

PACITAN

A fair-sized but easygoing village, 100 km SE of Solo on the southern coast. Splendid beaches stretch along a huge bay to either side of Pacitan. Bring good books, snacks, and a lover—the place is all your own. If you're coming from Solo, the road leads S to Wonogiri, then passes through Girimoyo, on the provincial border. Next comes the really bizarre section: a landscape made up of rows and rows of cone-shaped barren limestone hills containing dozens of caves, many of which can be visited. After these hills the road winds gently down through teak forests until the wide expanse of Pacitan Bay comes into view. Fishing *prahu* sway gently on the sheltered waters; behind the pier and storehouse is the marketplace for the day's catch. A small park (with a swimming pool) is an ideal place to sit back and drink in the view—all the way to the craggy summits of the distant Kidul Mountains.

Accommodations And Food
The cheapest place in town is **Losmen Remaja**; Rp3000 s, Rp4000 d. Real basic **Losmen Sido-**

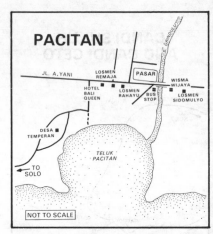

mulyo, Jl. A. Yani, is Rp3500 s, Rp5000 d. Next door is **Wisma Wijaya**. Across the street is an *es campur* place. On the other side of the minibus station, **Restaurant Adem Ayem** dishes out *nasi campur, nasi rames, gule,* and *sate.* Behind Losmen Sidomulyo, *sate* is sold at night. The **Bali Queen** is the town's big hotel; Rp10,000. The beach is 7 km from town on the large bay.

From Pacitan
Numerous buses depart for both Ponorogo and Solo. To Solo, Rp1500 (100 km, 4 hours), with buses via Wonogiri departing 0400-1400. To Ponorogo, the road climbs up through a scenic valley and gorge to a pass, then winds down onto plains; Rp1000 (4 hours). **vicinity of:** Visit **Desa Temperan**, a little cove 5 km out of Pacitan down the coast that offers some of the area's best swimming. A *warung* in the nearby *desa* serves rice, fish and vegetables. The *dokar* ride out to Desa Temperan and back (Rp2000) is a joy. On the way you pass a classical Greek mortuary temple. On the road to Solo, 9 km from Pacitan, is a monument to Sudirman and Slamet Riyadi and an overlook of the coast; nice spot for a picnic. Two other beaches in the area: Watu Karung (22 km) and Latiroco Lorok (41 km).

Gua Tubuhan And Vicinity
Punung is 30 km NW of Pacitan, Rp750 by bus. Four km and Rp100 by minibus beyond Punung village is **Gua Tabuhan**, the "Musical Cave" (Rp200). This giant limestone cavern is alleged to have been a hideaway for Prince Diponegoro in the 19th C.; the guerilla leader General Sudirman also made his headquarters here in the struggle against the Dutch. Follow the signposts down a dirt track to the cave; boys will guide you for Rp1000 through slippery

50-m-high caverns. In the main chamber an old man and assistants present an amazing reproduction of a *gamelan* orchestra. Played by striking rocks against stalactites, each in perfect pitch, the 3-toned melody vibrates and echoes at each blow. They ask Rp2000 for the performance. Cut and polished agate stones and rings sell from Rp850-15,000; have the silver- and goldsmiths on Bali set raw stones for you. Cave enthusiasts may also make a detour to **Gua Gombaksari** to see some beautiful white calcite formations; no admission fee. In nearby Danaraja village lives one of the last *dalang wayang beber* on Java, Pak Sarnen, who performs and reads using the 16th C. scrolls. **Kalak Caves** are 12 km S of Punung, near the S coast, which some say are the finest caves on Java; only accessible on foot. **Baksoka River Valley**, 4 km from Punung toward Pacitan, has petrified wood; many Neolithic stone tools have been found here.

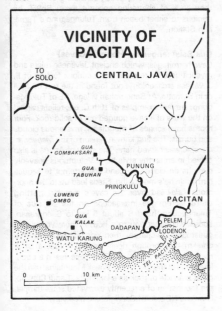

PARE

Twenty-four km and Rp500 by minibus NE of Kediri, and just over 100 km from Madiun, Pare is best known as a base from which to visit the nearby temples of Surawana and Tingawangi. The town has cooler, nicer weather than Kediri, and the people are friendly and helpful. Pare was where well-known anthropologist Clifford Geertz studied social change in Java in the 1950s. Geertz's classic work, *The Religion of Java,* is still a highly readable, fascinating account of the cross-currents of beliefs and customs that exist in Java.

Accommodations

Of Pare's 2 good *losmen,* the cheaper is **Peng. Sederhana** with electricity, bathrooms in the back, no meals, but coffee and tea; Rp3500 s, Rp5000 d. **Hotel Selamet,** Jl. Kandangan 1, is a poor-man's 5-star hotel—quiet and secure. The best rooms are the 4 in a separate building; large ones in the main building are a little more expensive. The proprietor can tell you all about surrounding areas and can arrange transportation; in a nearby forest see *kalong* (flying foxes) at night when they come to eat fruit. From Hotel Selamet it's a short walk up an alley to the town's main street where all the shops and conveniences are found. Other accommodations include **Losmen Centrum** and **Losmen Surakarta,** both Rp2500 s for smaller rooms. **food:** Several *depot* are on Jl. Kandangan, some of Pare's best Javanese/Indonesian food. Always crowded.

From Pare

Minibuses from Pare to Jombong cost Rp750; from Jombong board another minibus to the Trowulan ruins or Mojokerto. For Malang, take the rough 75-km-long road heading E through a kaleidoscope of landscapes: *sawah,* forested wilds, mountainous passes, apple orchards, wobbly bridges. **Pemanang:** Also called Memang, this site 15 km from Pare was the supposed capital of the 13th C. Kediri kingdom of the "Oracle King," Jayabaya, whose prophecies have all been fulfilled without exception. There's a small commemorative stone here and Jayabaya's restored *pendopo.* Many pilgrims arrive here to pray.

Candi Surawana

Located in Desa Canggu, about 6 km from Pare. In front of Hotel Selamet on Jl. Kandangan, negotiate for a 30-min. *becak* ride out to this temple for Rp2000 RT. If you have the time, though, it's better to walk. When you arrive at Canggu, hunt for the *juru kunci* to let you into the compound. Candi Surawana sits under a banyan tree in the midst of a beautiful tropical garden. All that's left of the 15th C. *Candi* is its gigantic unfinished base; on the grounds are scattered thousands of carved blocks, which are at least as intriguing as the temple itself. Architecturally, Surawana belongs to the *wayang*-style, its reliefs resembling the Balinese puppets of today. The depiction of nature in these reliefs is some of the most exciting in E. Javanese temple art. Panels illustrate humorous animal stories, erotic scenes; dwarves decorate the corners. By Indonesian standards, these ruins have been superbly kept up. A bathing place near the *candi* dates from the same era; ask the villagers where it is. A half km beyond the temple is the opening to an underground river which once was a tunnel which connected Tigawangi and Surawana.

Candi Tigawangi

Seven km and Rp350 by minibus to Tigawangi village or hire a *sepeda motor* from Pare. You may also meet someone at Surawana Temple and get a ride over on a motorbike. Travel about 2 km along the road to Kediri to a "Y"; the L fork goes to Kediri, the R to Desa Tigawangi. It's only about 4 km from the fork to a small school and a dirt-road turnoff to the right. Go up this dirt road for about one km and you'll come to the fenced-off temple. An unfinished Shivaistic complex built in the latter half of the 14th C., Tigawangi is not as intact as Surawana. The temple's N face has not been carved, and part of one of the corners has caved in. The carvings are not quite as accomplished. There are scenes of people delivered from dangers and spells, comical stories from the *Sundamala* epic, and exquisite landscapes. Scenes go around the corners without a break.

TULUNGAGUNG

Thirty km S of Kediri. Known as Kota Banjar, or "flood city," because the Brantas River overflows in April or Oct. every year and partially inundates the city. About 30 Hindu-Buddhist statues are in the Halaman Kabupaten on Jl. Kartini. For recreation, walk around the *alun-alun* in the cool of the early evening; there's often a soccer game going on. Antiques are sold in Pasar Wage, and on Jl. Wakhid Hasyim. For unique *batik tulungagung* check out Kalangbret, 6 km by minibus from Pasar Wage on Jl. Kapt. Kasinhin. *Tiban* is a whip fight festival popular in the Tulungagung area.

Accommodations And Food

Cheaper than Blitar. **Losmen Centrum**, Jl. Yani Barat 37, is the best; 3 sets of rooms, bathrooms outside, very secure. At night down the street is a cheerful little place where you can enjoy hot ginger drinks and Arabian-style coffee. Hang out with the boys. In the morning, very cheap *nasi pecel.* **Losmen Indonesia** is on a little lane off Jl. Kapt. Kisinhin in Kampung Plandaan; Rp2500 s, Rp4000 d. No meals, but you can eat at **Depot Arumdalu** nearby which serves good *nasi* dishes. **Losmen Rahayu** (Rp2500 s, Rp3000 d one bed, Rp3500 d for 2 beds) is near the train station; eat at **Warung Sederhana** nearby. Out of town 6 km is higher-altitude and more expensive **Pasanggrahan Argo Wilis** at Rp5000 a night. The best restaurant in town is the **Sumber Rasa**, Jl. Teuku Umar 58, filled with stuffed teddy bears. There's a *sate gule* place, Jl. Diponegoro 57, and a *sate kambing* and *nasi gule* place at Jl. Diponegoro

45. Try also **Depot Apollo**, Jl. Wahid Hasyim 7. **Es Djus Segar**, Jl. Teuku Umar, for iced juices.

From Tulungagung

It's Rp300 from Losmen Centrum by *becak* to Tamanan, the minibus and bus terminal near the Pertamina gas station. To Kediri, Rp600 by bus; Trenggalek (32 km), Rp300. For Pacitan, go first to Trenggalek by minibus (Rp600), then ride through the hills for another Rp600 to Ponorogo, then to Pacitan it's Rp1200 by minibus. To Blitar, 35 km E of Tulungagung, it's Rp550 by bus or Rp600 by minibus. **vicinity of:** A clove plantation at Trenggalek is owned by the local people. Two beaches lie S of Tulungagung: **Pantai Popoh,** 20 km, has comfortable hotels and bungalows. Visit 900-m-long **Trowongan Air,** not far from Popoh, and the marble factory, **Pabrik Marmar Tulungagung.** Twenty-five km S of Tulungagung at Parigi is a 10-km-long beach consisting of hills and thousands of chattering coconut trees; Rp950 by minibus to either beach from Tulungagung's Tamanan Station.

Gua Selamangeleng (Hermit's Caves)

Cave hermitages, which ancient Javanese rulers and mystics used as retreats, are a curious feature of E. Javanese archaeology, not found in the rest of Java or in Sumatra. At Sanggrahan village, SE of Tulungagung, are rare examples of 10th C. bas-reliefs carved on the walls of a cave gouged out of solid rock. Four rooms have scenes of mountains, mysterious clouds and burials. The first known version of the *Mahabharata* epic was carved here. The story of Arjuna is also carved in an earthy style here. Voluptuous heavenly nymphs on clouds descend and attempt to seduce him while he's meditating. Steps lead up to the enormous *kala*-head over the cave's mouth. **getting there:** From the intersection on the SE side of Tulungagung, head S about 5 km to Sanggrahan. Locals will direct you to a house where you sign a guestbook (no charge), then kids will take you on a one-km trail through ricefields and across a small river. Signs show the way. This cave lies in a populated area at the foot of the Wajak Mountains; use the great pinnacle of rock as a landmark. Candi Cunkup, the foundation of a recently excavated small temple, is on the NE side of Sanggrahan; nice view.

Gua Pasir

Gua Pasir, 4 km beyond the first cave, also has scenes of Arjuna being tempted, though not as well executed. These scenes show the love life of the comic dwarves, the *panakawan.* Unfortunately, Gua Pasir's carvings have been rendered nearly invisible due to graffiti. The walk out to Gua Pasir through rural E. Java is as rich an experience as the cave itself. The area around Boyolinggo village is a black- and white-

TULUNGAGUNG AND BLITAR AREAS

KAB. KEDIRI

G. WILIS
(2563m)

TO KEDIRI

NGADILUWIH

S. BRANTAS

KAB. TRENGGALEK

KALANGBRET

PANATARAN TEMPLE COMPLEX

TRENGGALEK

TO MALANG

TULUNGAGUNG

NGUNU

BLITAR

DURENAU

KADEMANGAN

D. WLINGGI

BANDUNG

CAMPURDARAT

GUA SELAMANGELENG

LADAYO

BESUKI

S. BRANTAS

GAMBIRAN

PERIGI

POPOH

TEL. POPOH

SERANG

INDIAN OCEAN

NOT TO SCALE

magic center. In Balairejo, call in on the most renowned magician *(orang sakti)* of them all, Gipowikromo.

BLITAR

A typical middle-sized Javanese community 50 km SE of Kediri, 200 km SW of Surabaya, or 80 km E of Malang (Rp1500 by minibus, 2 hours). Blitar is the birthplace of Sukarno, Indonesia's first president. Blitar is also known as "Kota Lahar." *Lahar* is a river of lava, water, and ash that gushes out of a volcano, in this case, G. Kelud. This small town, with just one main street, Jl. Merdeka, is a useful place from which to make tours of the surrounding countryside's sights and temples.

Accommodations And Food

The cheapest is one of the 3 small, low-standard *penginapan* down an alleyway inside a *kampung* off Blitar's fruit-selling street, Jl. Anggrek, only 5-min. walk from the post office or a Rp300 *becak* ride from *terminal minibus*. But you get what you pay for. **Peng. Arjuna** takes in foreign guests but the other *losmen* down this lane such as **Peng. Tentrum** seem reluctant. More central and comfortable is **Hotel Sri Lestari** on the main street (Jl. Merdeka 123, tel. 81766). They have rooms in the main building for Rp8000 d or Rp10,000 with *mandi;* also some a/c rooms with hot and cold water in the Rp20,000 range. The Sri Lestari's cheapest rooms behind the water-tower run Rp4000-6000 s or d. The moderately priced **Mandala Plaza**, Jl. Slamet Riyadi 37 (tel. 81810), has rooms with private bath and refrigerator but no a/c.

Peng. Aman, Jl. Merdeka 130, is a clean, Chinese-run hotel with spacious rooms (Rp5000 d) and a peaceful courtyard. The drawback is that they might insist upon a police permit. It's easier, though more expensive, just to stay at the Sri Lestari across the street.

Blitar is known for its *sambal pecel,* which is even exported to Holland. Hotel Sri Lestari serves up outstanding Javanese country home cooking; in the courtyard of the same hotel is a *warung* which serves Indonesian food and a few European dishes. The big **Ramayana Restaurant,** Jl. Merdeka 45-47, is like a Chinese delicatessen with a little bit of everything thrown in. At the bus terminal are a number of *warung* serving delicious chicken dishes. Jalan Anggrek is the best place to buy fruit and vegies.

From Blitar
Make an offer to the minibus drivers at the terminal to see all the temple complexes in the area — Panataran, Sewentar, Gadusari, Wlingi, Gado. Start at Rp25,000 for it will take a full day. Ask the owner of Hotel Sri Lestari if you can rent a motorscooter or motorcycle. Several trains go to Malang. By bus to Surabaya is 4 hours and Rp2500. Buses to Solo leave early in the morning, take 6 hours, and cost at least Rp4000 (370 km); Rp6000 a/c. Damri Bus Co., Jl. Mayang 92, has buses to Jakarta via Kediri and Solo at 0700, arriving 0500 (if you want to go to Yogya, get off in Solo and take a minibus). Their buses also leave for Banyuwangi via Malang at around 1800, arriving 0600. Purchase your ticket the night before. **vicinity of:** A cattle market *(pasar hewan)* is held at Sananwetan, about 2 km from Blitar's center. Pantai Tambak Beach is 20 km SE of Blitar; get there by minibus from Pasarpon. For more seascapes and shining beaches, Pantai Serang is 60 km S of Blitar; take a minibus to Ladayo, another to Bangunrejo, then one more to Serang — a 3-hour ride in all. Krisik is a quiet retreat 15 km NE of Blitar, Rp600 by minibus. The Blitar area is known for its export-quality coffee; at least 7 coffee plantations are within 30 km of town.

Sentul
On the way out to the Panataran complex is Sentul, Sukarno's elaborate grave. Open daily 0800-1700; no entrance fee. The site is also called *Makam Proklamator,* or "the Grave of the Declarer of Indonesia's Independence." For 8 years after his death in 1970, Sukarno's body lay in a plain unmarked grave beside that of his Balinese mother in Blitar's small cemetery for war veterans — as he explicitly desired in his will. But in order to counter the growing power of the Muslims and to recapture the loyalty of young intellectuals, Suharto in 1978 revived Sukarnoism. To this end, Sukarno's grave was lavishly refurbished. Sentul, a marble monument for Sukarno's remains, is now a *big* tourist attraction. There are restaurants, souvenir stands, and vendors even hawk T-shirts and poster portraits of the country's first president. Sukarno's black marble headstone is in the middle of an elaborate *pendopo* enclosed in glass which you are not allowed to enter; instead walk around the inner courtyard and gaze. His parents' graves are found to either side. A footnote: Sukarno was actually born in Surabaya, but lived with his parents from time to time in a house on Jl. Sultan Agung Gebang, Blitar.

Holy Gong Of Ladayo
An artifact of the Mataram kingdom, at Ladayo, 12 km and Rp650 from Blitar. The proper name of the gong is *Kayai Prada.* The structure containing the gong is right next to the Pembantu Bupati Building on the *alun-alun,* opposite Pasar Ladayo. The gong is taken out and sounded only twice a year, on *Hari Raya* and Mohammed's Birthday. As is the case with visiting many sacred objects on Java, it is the traveling that is the most memorable. The whole trip is a study in the melange of Javanese traditional behavior: village hospitality, customs, bureaucracy, hierarchal social systems, and religious syncretic beliefs. You might have to meet as many as 3 officials to get in to see *Kayai Prada.* After a moment of silence, you sign the guestbook and then they uncover the gong. It's swathed in a saffron cloth and surrounded by white textiles to keep it warm and holy. The whole atmosphere is filled with quiet, loving and expectant reverence.

PANATARAN

Ten km N of Blitar and 80 km SW of Malang, this is the largest and most imposing complex of ruins in E. Java, and one of the largest temple sanctuaries in all of Indonesia. The Panataran temple group took 250 years to build, starting in about 1197, during the Singosari Dynasty. Three gradually rising walled courtyards are laid out on a long field; see dance-play platforms, terraces, shrines, and the same *gapura* gateways found in almost every village in E. Java today. Temple reliefs show the transition from 3-dimensional to 2-dimensional representations: figures tend to take second place to the decorations. One of the most striking structures is the **Naga Temple,** on the second terrace. Once used to store sacred objects, all around it are colossal carvings of protective coiled serpents carried by priests — a sight which would make any medieval thief shudder. On its base are reliefs of animal tales. The whole complex is very well maintained. If you get here real early, you have the place all to yourself.

The Main Temple
Just the substructure remains of what was once the main sanctuary, located in the back of the complex

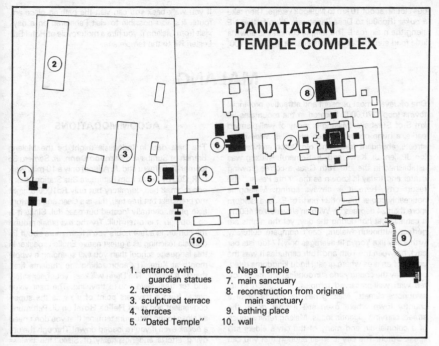

PANATARAN TEMPLE COMPLEX

1. entrance with guardian statues
2. terraces
3. sculptured terrace
4. terraces
5. "Dated Temple"
6. Naga Temple
7. main sanctuary
8. reconstruction from original main sanctuary
9. bathing place
10. wall

nearest the mountain. On its bas-reliefs the Monkey-General Hanuman leads his army through the air past the flying wounded, clouds of fighting monsters, battles, and monkeys building a dam across the sea. Different ornamentation is found on all 3 terraces of the main temple. On the first terrace scenes from the *Ramayana* are carved in *wayang*-style. These figures are permeated with supernaturalism—animals or spooky beings camouflaged in intricate motifs—so that the atmosphere seems charged with a life of its own. Along the second terrace, in a much more naturalistic style, are fables from the *Krishnayana*—the adventures of Krishna as he abducts the princess Rukmini just before she is betrothed to another suitor. Winged monsters gaze menacingly out from the third terrace.

medallion, Panataran

The "Dated Temple"

So called because of the date "1291" (A.D. 1369) over the entrance. A fine example of E. Javanese *candi* architecture, this temple is richly decorated with exuberant detail. Carvings show a test between a vegetarian and a corpulent meat-eater, the left and the right paths of a yogi, the corpulent Bubukshah and the thin Gagang Aking. The bands in the roof are filled with carved animals.

Bathing Places

Southeast of the main temple. Panataran was built more for the taste of the commoner than for the Brahman, and this bathing place built in 1415 shows flying tortoises, the bull and the crocodile fable, winged snakes, and a lion plowing a field. Reliefs also depict the Indian *Tantric Tales,* the Eastern equivalent of *Aesop's Fables.* Another bathing place is on the road between Ngelok and Panataran. Go through the village toward the complex and around the corner on the L by a river, just before the bridge, is a bathing temple with live spouts. Villagers still use this 16th C. structure for washing clothes and bathing.

Getting There

From Blitar take a *bemo* or minibus from Pasarpon

bus station about 10 km to Nglegok village. Then take a *dokar* (Rp500) to Desa Panataran, 2 km farther NE along the main road. The temple complex is down a little road surrounded by ricefields. Open 0600-1700.

If you walk back you can visit the bathing place en route. It's also possible to visit Panataran on a day visit from Malang if you hire a motorcycle at Hotel Sri Lestari RT to the temple site.

MALANG

One of Java's most pleasant and attractive provincial towns (pop. 270,000). Located in the mountains 90 km S of Surabaya, Malang is a city of well-planned parks, a huge central market, big villas, wide clean streets, abundant trees, and old Dutch architecture (on Jl. Ijen, Jl. Kawi, and Jl. Semeru). Malang was established in the late 18th C. as a coffee-growing center and today is known as the "Kota Pesiar," the resort city. Here it is always spring: Malang is noticeably cooler than other parts of E. Java (seldom more than 24 degrees C). With an elevation of 450 m, it can still get hot during the day, yet the nights are perfect. Although Malang can't compare culturally with a city like Yogya (it averages only 17 tourists per day), between the 10th and 15th centuries it was the center of an area where great Hindu kingdoms ruled, and today the countryside surrounding Malang is dotted with well-preserved temples. In addition to its salubrious climate, Malang has the casual air of a country town where oxen still lumber down the streets carrying gigantic loads. Malang retains much of a colonial air, and many of the city's elders still speak Dutch. The city is small enough that you can walk anywhere within its limits worth going to; *becak* are also cheap and plentiful.

Sights
Visit **Pasar Besar**, where tobacco traders haggle and where cigarettes from all over Indonesia are sold. Relax in a *becak* and enjoy the characters in the street and everyday life of this charming city. The **Brawijaya Army Museum** (Musium Brawijaya), on the W end of Jl. Ijen (no. 25, tel. 2394), houses weapons, photos, historical papers, and other military mementos documenting the role that the Brawijaya Army Division played in the revolutionary struggle. Open every day from 0800-1200. Jalan Raya Ijen is known for its many *Koningpalm* or "raja" palm trees. **Monumen Perjoangan "45,"** the Freedom Monument, is 150 m to the E of Tugu Pahlawan (Jl. Tugu) and W of the train station; on it are depicted the heroic deeds of the freedom fighters. The **Djamek Mosque** and the **Protestant Church**, beside one another on Jl. Merdeka Barat, are both said to have been founded in the early 1800s. A well-known Chinese temple, **En An Kiong**, is worth visiting; it's near Pasar Besar. A Balinese temple, **Pura Hindu Bali**, is out of town in Desa Lesanpuro Kedungkandang.

ACCOMMODATIONS

The best deal in Indonesia might be the Malang Branch of Surabaya's **Bamboo Denn**, Jl. Semeru 35 (corner Jl. Semeru and Jl. Arjuno) only a 10-min. walk or Rp300 by *becak* from Pattimura Bus Station. Just a one-room, 8-bed dormitory but only Rp1000 a night (no breakfast but free tea), this is a clean and comfortable place, centrally located but peaceful. Since it is so popular, it is often full. Try the *martabak* around the corner. In a few hours you'll learn more about Indonesia teaching as a guest native English speaker in this language school than you will spending a whole month at Kuta. Try approaching the students first, they're a bit shy. The Denn will keep your gear safely and for free while you're traveling. The best value place, from a travelers point of view, is the superconvenient and quiet **Helios Hotel** on Jl. Pattimura, so close to the Pattimura terminal that you don't need a *becak* even if you're loaded down! Through the undying efforts and hospitality of Sisilo, the tireless houseboy, this hotel is a travelers' haven kept immaculately clean; Rp5000 s or d with free breakfast (coffee and bread), big color TV, good laundry service. If you want to go to the temples near Blimbing its just a 5-min. walk to the bus station! Good info dispensed here too.

Hotel Simpang Tiga, Jl. Arief Margono, is a well-run hotel and usually heavily booked. On the SW edge of town, it's far from the bus station but close to the Sawahan Minibus Station, Rp100 by *bemo* from the *alun-alun*. A little noisy, but the rooms are quite clean and comfortable. **Hotel Santosa**, Jl. H. Agus Salim 24 (tel. 3889), asks Rp3500 s, Rp4700 d, Rp6000 t; some rooms with *kamar mandi*. Fairly close to the town square, it has 40 rooms in 2 houses. Not a bad deal for the money. **Losmen Asia**, Jl. Gajah Mada 4, is another favorite of travelers, and will sometimes come down to Rp6000 s or d, but it's a bit dirty and a house of ill-repute to boot. **Hotels Garuda, Mudah** and **Jakarta** (the classiest of the 3) also house prostitutes, so they are looser and noisier. **Hotel Semarang**, across the street from Hotel Tosari, is on the bus route across from the town square, an old, going-to-pot place, but quite reasonable at Rp2500 s,

Rp3500 d, Rp4500 t. No meals, but there's a Chinese *lumpia* (eggroll) restaurant and *martabak* are sold up the street toward the *alun-alun*. **Hotel Pajajaran**, Jl. Pajajaran 17, (tel. 23306), costs Rp7500 s or d for small rooms, Rp10,000 for large room, both with bath—not a bad deal for the money but has prostitutes. Just a 5-min. walk to the bus station! Right next door is a travel agency, P.T. Tomaco, where bus tickets for onward travel can be ordered. Also on Jl. Pajajaran (no. 5, tel. 22871) is **Hotel/Losmen Menara;** very nice rooms Rp7000-8500. Family-style, nice sitting areas, secure.

For a splash (each room has hot and cold water) try the **Splendid Inn**, a two-star hotel at Jl. Majapahit 4 (tel. 23860); it has standard room Rp20,000 s, Rp26,000 d, and VIP rooms Rp26,000 s, Rp32,000 d. No credit cards accepted. A large well-run hotel patronized by the Java/European business class, the Inn has profuse flowering plants, a library, restaurant, and good tourist info; feels more like a guesthouse. European breakfast is included in the rates, lunch or dinner run US$3.60. The tattered though still elegant **Hotel Aloha**, Jl. Gajah Mada 7, charges Rp12,500 s for clean standard rooms, Rp15,000 for standard downstairs rooms, and up to Rp25,000 d for the enormous *swit,* all prices including breakfast. It's on a quiet back street opposite Losmen Asia. **Hotel Pelangi**, Jl. Merdeka Selatan 3 (tel. 27456/27457), the biggest of Malang's hotels, is centrally located and offers a/c rooms with TV; Rp10,000 d downstairs rooms, comfortable enough, Rp25,000 d for downstairs rooms with fan, Rp35,000 for downstairs rooms with a/c. Full facilities, 24-hour room service, taxi service, and very central (on the *alun-alun*). If a big shot comes to Malang, he stays here. Originally known as the Palace Hotel in Dutch times (1915), on the walls of the restaurant (open 0600-2100) are unique tiles depicting famous Dutch landmarks—a must-see for a Hollander. The restaurant is the only part of the original building which hasn't been completely rebuilt.

FOOD

Street Food

A cornucopia of fruits and vegetables are available in this city: apples from Batu, grapes, citrus (Rp2000 per kg for big oranges, Rp1500 for small), giant Indonesian watermelons, locally grown avocados, papayas, tomatoes. There are also good eating *warung* at Stasiun Sawahan, and the Pattimura Bus Station stalls also offer decent, low-priced meals. **Ibu Pranoto's** is the best for down-home Javanese cooking, and travel snacks like *krupuk* and *rempeyak*. Most of these *warung* are open from 1700-1900 to catch the *bis malam* business. Another cheap, colorful place to eat at night is **Pasar Senggol** (where Jl. Majapahit meets

Jl. Gareja, by the Brantas River) which opens up around 1800. At this night market, don't miss the *terang bulan,* a sort of pancake stuffed with margarine, fresh pineapple jam, chocolate, and sweet milk (Rp350). The flower market nearby is also a must! Pasar Besar's *warung* are open until 2000; buy fruit here during the day.

Restaurants

The **Minang Jaya**, Jl. Besuki Rachmat 111 (tel. 5707), specializes in W. Sumatran cuisine. Open 24 hours a day, they put in front of you 20 different combinations of food—a real adventure in eating! Taste some *gulai kilkil* (buffalo feet curry). Better than the food you'll find out in the villages, order a packaged lunch if you're going out to the temples for a day trip. **Restaurant Cinta**, Jl. Sukarjo, is usually crowded with diners—a good sign. **Miramar Restaurant**, Jl. Pasar Besar 117, is pretty classy, the only restaurant in Malang with a neon sign. **Ayam Goreng Coffee House**, Jl. Pattimura 1 (just before bridge) is a special fried chicken restaurant only 5 min. walk from the Helios Hotel. **Cafeteria Aneka Rasa** next door to Toko Oen, has inexpensive food. The **New Hong Kong**, Jl. A.R. Hakim (near the *alun-alun*), is the best Chinese restaurant in Malang. For something different, the Arabian restaurant **RM Cairo**, Jl. Jagalna 1, is furnished with large, wooden, no-nonsense tables—they are here to *feed* you! The Cairo specializes in Indonesian food with a Middle-Eastern accent. **RM Marhaen**, Jl. S. Wiryo Branoto, is the place to sample Javanese and Arabian food combined.

Toko Oen

Its name means "castrated donkey." Just off the square near Hotel Pelangi, Toko Oen serves high-quality Western, Chinese, and Indonesian food, as well as iced drinks and great ice cream. Like an old-fashioned Dutch coffee shop, this is a real oasis with an authentic colonial atmosphere. Try their crisp vegetable salad, a meal in itself. The place even serves such anachronistic standbys as *uitsmijter* (Dutch sandwiches), *kaasstengels* (cheese sticks), *droptoffee* (licorice toffee), *kroket* (meat snacks), and *haagsehopjes* (Dutch mocha candies). Clean, spacious, good service. Open 0900-2030, Mon. closed. Next door is a bakery that sells all kinds of bread.

ENTERTAINMENT, SHOPPING, SERVICES

Performances

Gedung Cendrawasih, Jl. Tanimbar, irregularly stages *wayang orang, ketoprak, tari yeg oyeg,* etc. cultural performances. Watch dancers rehearse on the weekends at Sanggar Senaputra on Jl. Rumah Sakit. The art center at **Vina Seni Rupa**, Jl. K.H.

Hasyim, in front of Hotel Jakarta, is where painters, dancers, and carvers work. At night stroll by the **Katolik Sasono Budoyo** (Catholic Church, erected in 1934) on Jl. Gareja to hear *gamelan* music and see medieval Javanese dances during church services. Malang has long been a center of *topeng* culture and is host to a number of troupes. *Wayang topeng* is practiced all over the Malang area to celebrate marriages, circumcisions, and village festivities; it's not difficult to see one of these masked dances, especially in the Pakisaji in the Kepanjen area (SE of the city) or in the clove-growing Senggreng area, 7 km SE of Kepanjen. To learn *wayang topeng*, see Pak Karimun in Pakisaji.

Shopping

Visit the many *pasar* of Malang, at their liveliest from 0600-0630. Though not much of a place for crafts, some unique pottery is for sale on the street. From vendors on the sidewalks or in the *pasar* you can choose from nearly 50 different kinds of bamboo flutes *(suling)*. For fabrics, second-hand wares, good copper and bronze goods—indeed, all Asia under one roof—go to **Pasar Besar**, 2 blocks SE of the *alun-alun* on both sides of wide Jl. Kyai Tamin and Jl. Pasar Besar. Pasar Besar opens at 0800 and goes full blast until 1600, spilling over into the side streets. If you're quick you can get good photographs. A Saturday night clothes market is nearby, and Malang's antique shops are behind the *pasar* on Jl. Pasar Besar. A wonderful selection of flower stalls and shops are found on Jl. Majapahit. **Pasar Burung**, the bird market, is on Jl. Tjembaran. The best bookshop in town is **Gramedia** in front of Sarinah Supermarket on Jl. Basuki Rachmat, and **Toko Buku Siswa** on Jl. Agus Salim in the shopping center opposite Gereja Katolik. Wisma Batik (Danar Hadi) is on Jl. Basuki Rachmat. **shopping centers: Mitra Shopping Center,** Jl. Agus Salim 10-16 (same block as the post office), has Westernized food, coffee, cheese—a delicatessan-type enviornment. **Gajah Mada Plaza** and **Malang Plaza** are also on Jl. Agus Salim. The all-alit **Sarinah Supermarket** is not cheap.

Services

The **City Tourist Office** (Baparda) is beside the Balai Kota on Jl. Tugu; open 0700 until 1400, Fri. and Sat. until 1100. See Mr. Tontowi. Moderately informative. The **GPO**, on the S side of *alun-alun*, is open 0800-1400. **Bank Bumi Daya** accepts only U.S. and Australian dollars. The **Eskim Bank** accepts only U.S. dollars and Lloyd's of London traveler's cheques, but the Bank Bumi Daya is faster. **Kantor Imigrasi** is at Jl. Raung 2. A big public library on Jl. Ijen is in front of Museum Brawijaya. At least 10 medical specialists (skin specialist, gynecologist, pediatrician) practice at Jl. Kawi 13. Consultation hours: 1700-1900.

TRANSPORT

Getting There

Trains run between Surabaya and Malang at least 6 times daily. From Surabaya's Kota Station, a train leaves at 0715, while another one leaves Gubeng Station at 0723—both cost Rp1000 and take 2½ hours. Buses leave for Malang from Joyoboyo Station in Surabaya constantly, Rp1000, 1½ hours. In front of

MALANG

1. to Museum Brawijaya
2. minibuses to Batu & Selecta
3. Pemandian Senaputra & Sanggar Senaputra
4. Helios Hotel
5. Bhima Sakti Transport
6. Pattimura Bus Station
7. Hotel Losmen Menara
8. Splendid Inn
9. Bank Central Asia
10. RM Minang Jaya
11. fruit stands
12. Bamboo Denn Transito Inn
13. antique shop
14. Montana Hotel
15. *pasar malam*
16. Balai Kota Malang (town hall)
17. tourist office
18. Hotel Aloha
19. Losmen Asia
20. PT Sinar Express Apollo
21. Pasar Senggol *(pasar malam)*
22. telephone office
23. Toko Buku Gramedia
24. Richie Hotel
25. Sarinah Supermarket
26. New Hong Kong Restaurant
27. Djamek Mosque & Protestant Church
28. Bank Bumi Daya
29. Hotel Pelangi
30. PT Sinar Express Apollo
31. Hotel Santosa
32. RM Marhaen
33. Bis Malam Anugurah
34. Pasar Besar
35. En An Kiong Temple
36. RM Cairo
37. Sawahan Bemo Station
38. Gedung Cendrawasih
39. Hotel Simpang Tiga

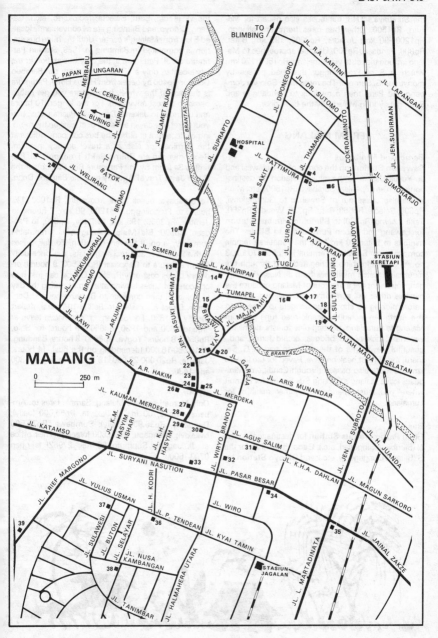

TO
BLIMBING

MALANG

0   250 m

the Surabaya's THR, minibuses also depart for Malang, Rp1500. Other bus fares from: Probolinggo, Rp1200, 90 km; Jember, Rp3000, 195 km; Blitar, Rp800; Pandaan, Rp500. Unusual approaches to Malang include the route via Lumajang (Rp1500, 120 km) which is S of Probolinggo; this road passes by monstrous G. Semeru. The route from Solo via Jombang and Pare, then a minibus to Kandangan and Batu, gets you in Malang by the back door.

FROM MALANG

Bemo And Minibuses
Sawahan Station, on the corner of Jl. Sulawesi and Jl. Yulius Usman, is the minibus station for destinations such as Kepanjen, Surabaya (Rp1500), etc. Minibuses also cruise out of Sawahan to Gunungkawi, Rp800; Selecta, Rp550; Batu, Rp350; Wendit, Rp350. Take a *bemo* (Rp200) to **Blimbing Minibus Station** for Lawang and Kebon Purwodadi. **to Blitar:** The minibus to Blitar (10 km from the Panataran temple complex) from Sawahan Terminal is Rp650 (70 km, 3 hours) on a refreshing, variegated road through the mountains. Catch minibuses from Jl. Nusa Kembangan; you might get a free tour of Malang because the minibus driver will sometimes drive all over the city before picking up enough passengers to depart. **to the east:** An incredibly scenic road runs SE from Malang to Lumajang, passing pine forests, ricefields, waterfalls, rickety old bridges, orchid farms, and beautiful viewpoints of the southern part of G. Semeru, the highest peak on Java. Paved for the first 35 km, the route also passes through Candipuro. Minibuses leave Malang's Gadang Bus Station for Dampit where you must change to another minibus for Lumajang.

Buses
Go to **Pattimura Bus Station** for destinations to the N (Blimbing, Singosari, etc.); **Gadang Station** for the S (Blitar, Tulungagung, etc.); and **Dinoyo Station** for the W (Kediri, Batu, Selecta, Mojokerto, etc.). Gadang, Dinoyo, and Blimbing are all conveniently located 5 km from Malang's center. Until the huge bus station is completed in Blimbing in 1989, Stasiun Pattimura on Jl. Pattimura is the only bus station in the city's center, only a 15 min. walk from the Bamboo Denn or Rp400 by *becak* from Helios Hotel. Pattimura is the hub of the wheel, from where you get public *bemo* to almost anywhere. For the longer (10 hours and up) rides to Jakarta, Denpasar, Pacitan, etc., buy your ticket one day in advance or at least on the morning of departure at either the bus company offices at the terminals or else at a travel agency in town. Recommended are **Bhima Sakti Transport**, Jl. Pattimura 34 (right by the Pattimura Bus Station); or the **Putra Jaya Travel Agency** near the Bamboo Denn.

To Surabaya, buses leave frequently, Rp1000, 1½ hours; to Probolinggo, Rp1200, 90 km, 2 hours; to Jember, Rp3000, 195 km; to Blitar, Rp800; to Pandaan, Rp500. **Bis Malam Anugurah**, a reputable company, is on Jl Suryani Nasution. To Bali, buses with toilets, a/c, and reclining seats, run once daily from Pattimura to Denpasar (Rp10,500, 9 hours); ordinary buses cost only Rp8500. Or you can just hop on scores of buses leaving at all times during the day to points E, then continue to Banyuwangi and Denpasar. Direct *bis malam* to Bali (9-10 hours), depart usually at 1830. For Semarang, *bis malam* leave at around 1800 and 1930, Rp8500, 9 hours; for Solo, Rp8500, 8 hours; Yogya, Rp8500, 9 hours; Bandung, Rp15,000-16,000 (depending on the bus), 14 hours; Jakarta, Rp20,000-22,000, 18 hours, leaving at 1300 and 1430.

By Air
Only Merpati services Malang. Sample fares to: Ampenan, Rp47,700 (daily); Jakarta, Rp65,000 (daily); Denpasar, Rp36,900 (daily); Sumbawa, Rp72,500 (weekly); Waingapu, Rp93,500 (weekly). Their office at Jl. Jagung Suprapto 50 (tel. 27962) is open 0700-1500.

VICINITY OF MALANG

Gunung Kawi

A pilgrimage place 40 km SW of Malang on the southern slopes of G. Kawi where a revered 19th C. spiritual leader, Mbah Yugo (d. 1871), is buried. The actual site is called Pesarean Mbah Sujono, which means "the grave of grandfather Sujono," another Muslim pioneer who is also interred here. Crowds, sometimes numbering in the thousands, continuously worship Mbah Yugo's and Mbah Sujono's graves. All faiths, including non-Muslim Chinese, visit G. Kawi from E. Java and from all over Indonesia seeking healing, fertility, a blessing for the mother of the paddyfields, success in exams, or just plain good luck. Stalls go all night selling everything from stuffed alligators to hair-growth stimulant. People are really friendly to the point of being tiresome. Mats are provided for the thousands of devotees staying the night. If you sleep in the public dorm, you'll be stared at like you just fell from the moon—your every action, every gesture followed by at least 20 pairs of eyes. Alternatively, there are some *losmen.* The site is accessible by minibus (Rp1000) from Malang's Stasiun Sawahan via Kebanjen. Thursday evenings minibuses frequently leave for G. Kawi, returning Fri. morning after the passengers have spent the night worshipping and watching 3-4 puppet shows.

Pantai Ngliyep

A magnificent rocky beach, 60 km S of Malang, with dense coastal forests, beautiful seascapes, and giant waves. Take a minibus (Rp1500) or bus (Rp1000) toward Blitar and transfer at Kepanjen, 18 km S of Malang. On holidays, if you like crowds, go from Sawahan Station in Malang straight to Ngliyep. Stay in **Peng. Ngliyep**, with outside *mandi.* A campground near the beach is usually crowded with young campers. Buy souvenirs made from coral here. The beaches are cleaner NW of Ngliyep. Balekambang Beach can be reached on foot from Sujono village, 6 km away; this white sand beach has a coral reef which stretches 250 m out to sea. **events:** Since 1913, Ngliyep has celebrated the annual *Labuhan* religious holiday with a procession to G. Kembang where an offering of a goat's head is thrown into the sea. For 5 days preceding the ceremony there are *wayang kulit* shows dedicated to Nyai Loro Kidul, the Goddess of the South Seas.

GUNUNG SEMERU

Also called *Mahameru,* or "Great Mountain." South of G. Bromo and E of Malang, Semeru is one of the world's most beautiful peaks, and at 3,676 m the highest mountain on Java. The Bromo-Semeru massif covers about 800 sq km, the biggest of all the volcanic regions of E. Java. It sits above a sparsely populated region of volcanic highlands, wooded hills, and picturesque crater lakes which offer excellent camping and trekking opportunities. Take the scenic 50-km highway from Dampit to Lumajang which skirts along the mountain's southern flanks with excellent views (more verdant in the wet season). Gunung Semeru, which means "One Mountain," is named after the Indian World Mountain—Meru. According to legend, all the other mountains of Java fell away from G. Semeru on its mythological journey from the Himalayas. Semeru is still quite active, on occasion spewing out hot ash and solidified chunks of lava, but usually contenting itself with a huge belch of smoke every 15 minutes. Eruptions in modern times include one in 1911 which destroyed 200 houses; and in 1946 6 people were killed and 81 houses destroyed. At night hot lava and dancing red lights shower down the volcano's steep sides, disappearing in the dark forests below. Inside the crater you walk in white sand up to your knees, and you could be chased from the summit by thundering explosions of gases and globs of red ash. The sunrise is spectacular over the crater's eastern rim, with all the mountains of E. Java visible if the weather is clear. Ideally, you should allow about 3 days for the climb.

Flora And Fauna

An abundance of wild animals are found in the area, including *rusa, muncak,* wild pigs, snakes, and leopards (rarely-seen). Flying squirrels are common in the forests, and ducks are often seen on the lakes. Finches and thrushes frequent even the highest screes where they feed on the purple berries of the *Vaccinium* bushes. Quite a few rare or endemic plants grow here: the dwarf shrub *Styphelia javanica* grows in cushions and has sharp-tipped narrow leaves and fragrant white flowers; it's only found in the mountains of E. Java and its only relatives are Australian. Outside the sand sea are casuarinas, Sunda island oaks, and the large-leaved *Homolanthus* trees.

Climate:

Climb G. Semeru only in the dry season. All of E. Java has a marked dry season. May-Oct., but high mountains such as G. Semeru collect moisture during the SE monsoon and thus there are pockets of fine wet forests on G. Semeru's southern slopes. It's warm in the villages in the Kobokan Gully, but at night and early morning temperatures near the peak can be freezing and it's always cloudy in the afternoon.

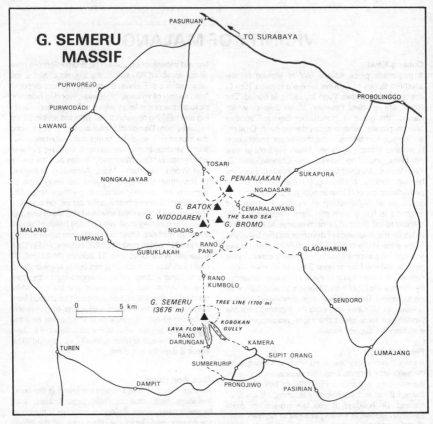

The Lakes

South of the immense Tengger crater are the lakes **Rano Pani** and **Rano Regulo** on a 2,200-m-high plateau which rises gently toward the peak of G. Semeru. Set in open pasture and *cemera* woodlands, these lakes make attractive camping places and a favorite starting point for the G. Semeru climb. This rolling, beautiful countryside is kept clear by annual fires set by the Tenggerese to promote new grass growth. Rano Pani village, on the lake of the same name, has a small 4-bed resthouse (no bedding, no food, no charges), for the most part used by youth groups climbing G. Semeru.

Climbing It

Though all of the approaches to G. Semeru are strenuous and only for the fit, the mountain is a far easier climb than G. Merapi and Sumatra's Sinabung

(which is simple but steep). The difficulty with G. Semeru is that you have to walk great distances from your last possible transport to the base of the cone (6-7 hours), and only then do you really start the steep part of the climb up to the summit (4 hours). If you're spending a night on the summit, bring a friend, a tent, flashlights, sleeping bags, warm clothing (especially a wind-breaker), campstove, food, and at least one liter of water per day per person. Horses are easily hired and are a great help too. Semeru's sand can be troublesome to hike on; you climb up 2 steps and fall back one. At the top there are explosions every 15 min., and you can also see stones thrown up out of the other peak, but you need oxygen for that one. The 2 peaks are only about 300 m apart. Get off the summit *no later than* 1200 because the wind sometimes shifts from S to N and carries with it poisonous sulphur, plus by that time visibility is nil.

From Malang/Tumpang

From Malang it costs Rp800 by bus or Rp1000 by minibus or *bemo* to Gubuklakah. From there take a minibus (if available) from Gubuklakah to Ngadas, then walk 6-7 hours up the steep, stony road from Ngadas to Rano Pani village (9 km). Stay in the uninhabited climbers' house in Rano Pani. Next day, hire a guide in Rano Pani for around Rp12,000-20,000 to make the ascent over the 2,800-m-high pass of G. Ayek Ayek to Rano Kumbolo, where you can replenish your water. The foot of G. Semeru is a hard 6-hour climb, including rest stops, from Rano Kumbolo. Camp overnight at the base. It will turn very cold with freezing rains, and ash and sand will fall after each eruption, extinguishing the fire that you build. Very early the next morning (0500), climb 3½ hours to reach G. Semeru's top. Remember to time your arrival at the summit between 0800 and 1000, because of the release of deadly volcanic gases. The air might become thick with ash but this is no problem if you breathe through a handkerchief. Also, electronic SLRs might not work even if you warm up the batteries. Sliding back down the mountain takes an exhilarating 30 minutes! You arrive back at Rano Pani around 1600 or 1700 that evening.

LAWANG

Eighteen km N of Malang. Except for the Purwodadi Gardens, there's nothing much to see here. Unless you plan to spend a good bit of time at the gardens, it's more convenient just to stay in Malang. The most noteworthy of Lawang's tourist attractions is a hotel, the **Niagara**. Located on the town's main street (Jl. Sutomo 63, tel. 106), this grand, 5-story art-nouveau former mansion was built by a Brazilian architect in 1918. Economy rooms without bathrooms—almost as nice as the suites—cost Rp12,500 s, Rp15,500 d. Restaurant attached. Although nothing but the best materials were used in this hotel's construction (stained glass everywhere, and the woodwork is spectacular), it's now rundown and lonely, stripped of all its splendor. Climb up to the roof for a new look at G. Arjuna. With the Surabaya-Malang highway running right through the town, Lawang has plenty of restaurants. **RM Kertoso**, with the blinking neon sign, is right on the main road and serves E. Javanese cuisine. Roadside stands at the entrance of Kebon Purwodadi, 5 km N of Lawang, sell *rojak, nasi campur,* drinks, and various snacks.

Kebon Raya Purwodadi

Founded in 1914 as a branch of the Botanical Gardens of Bogor, Purwodadi lies 23 km N of Malang on the lower slopes of G. Arjuna (elev. 300 m). These 85-ha gardens were established for the purpose of studying tropical high-elevation plants growing in a dry climate. More remote and less well known, this attractive botanic park tends to be less crowded than the Bogor Gardens, particularly on weekdays. As the staff is very helpful and friendly, perhaps an Indonesian student who works there will show you around. The park is especially invigorating in the early morning when everything is hosed down and smells fresh. Don't miss the tropical cacti, dozens of rare palms, the small, well-organized orchid house (contains 400 varieties!), and the waterfall, Loban Buang, over Sungai Welang in the rear of the gardens. Open daily 0700-1000; entrance Rp100. From Purwodadi you can also take one of the back ways up G. Arjuna. **getting there:** Purwodadi is Rp650 by minibus or Rp450 by bus from Malang, or Rp850 by minibus from Surabaya.

TEMPLES IN THE VICINITY OF MALANG

Malang is the best base for visiting the astonishingly rich Hindu ruins of E. Java. Allow at least a week. Chronologically, the sequence is: Candi Badut (9th C.), 3 km W of Malang; Candi Gunung Gangsir (10th C.), about 64 km NE; Candi Kidal (13th C.), about 20 km SE; Candi Jago (13th C.), 16 km SE; Candi Jawi (14th C.), 40 km N; and Candi Singosari (14th C.), 10 km north. **transport:** Your own vehicle or motorcycle would be ideal. If you go by *bemo* or minibus, allow more time. Catch a *bemo* from the Pattimura Bus Station, 5 min. walk from Helios Hotel, to Blimbing, a northern suburb of Malang and the focal point for *bemo* and minibuses whose routes pass by the various temple sites. Or just stand out on Jl. Basuki Rachmat and tell the *bemo* driver you want to go to Blimbing.

Suggested Routing

The following itinerary can be done easily in a day from Malang: first head for Blimbing, then catch a minibus N to Singosari, then backtrack to Blimbing. Next, take another minibus via Wendit to Tumpang (near Candi Jago), then head SE to Candi Kidal, then circle back to Malang via Tajinan. A separate outing must be made to Candi Badut from Malang; take a *bemo* (Rp200) from the Pattimura Bus Station to the Dinoyo Station (5 km NW of Malang), then a *becak* out to the village of Sumbersawi near Dinoyo. From Sumbersawi, walk about 30 min. to the temple remains. Nearby is an old graveyard.

Candi Singosari

Ten km N of Malang in the town of Singosari (halfway between Malang and Lawang). Local name is Candi Linggo. Dating from the 13th C., this Shiva shrine is the most imposing monument left of the murderous Singosari Dynasty. It was built to honor a king and all his priests who were killed in a palace revolt. This

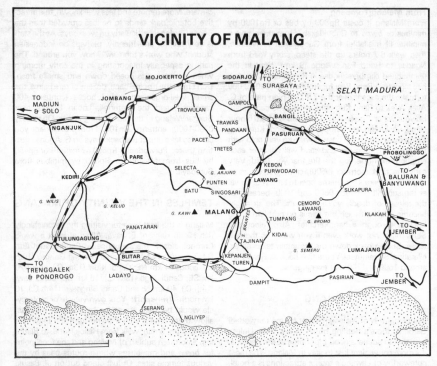

VICINITY OF MALANG

TO MADIUN & SOLO

MOJOKERTO

JOMBANG

SIDOARJO

TO SURABAYA

SELAT MADURA

NGANJUK

TROWULAN

GAMPOL

BANGIL

TRAWAS

PANDAAN

PASURUAN

PACET

TRETES

PROBOLINGGO

PARE

KEDIRI

SELECTA

G. ARJUNO

KEBON PURWODADI

LAWANG

TO BALURAN & BANYUWANGI

G. WILIS

PUNTEN

BATU

SINGOSARI

G. KELUD

G. KAWI

MALANG

SUKAPURA

CEMORO LAWANG

G. BROMO

KLAKAH

TO JEMBER

PANATARAN

TUMPANG

KIDAL

TAJINAN

G. SEMERU

LUMAJANG

TULUNGAGUNG

BLITAR

KEPANJEN

TUREN

TO TRENGGALEK & PONOROGO

LADAYO

DAMPIT

PASIRIAN

TO JEMBER

SERANG

NGLIYEP

0   20 km

monarch, King Kartanegara, is the same fellow who mortified Kublai Khan's emissaries by cutting off their noses and tattooing "NO!" across their foreheads, an act which precipitated the launching of 1,000 Mongol troop ships against Java in 1293. Candi Singosari's unique feature is its base, which is at the same time the central *cella* (inner sanctum) of the temple. Thus it's called a "cellar-temple" or "tower-temple" by archaeologists. Only the top of Singosari has ornamentation. Because of time, finance, or civil catastrophe, ornamentation wasn't completed on the remainder. Carving was always begun at the top of a *candi* and worked downwards so as not to damage lower, finished sculptures with falling pieces. Most of the statues originally at Singosari now form the backbone of the world-famous Hindu-Javanese collection at Leiden Musuem in Holland, including the renowned Prajnaparamita image. A statue of Shiva's guru, Agastya, is found in the yard, and 2 magnificent 3.8-m-tall *raksasa* guardian statues, one partly buried, stand 200 m away where a gate may have once stood. Note the necklaces—snakes and skull! **getting there:** Take a minibus for Rp300 from Malang to Blimbing, then pay another Rp200 for a minibus to Singosari village. At the intersection in the northern

fringe of town, near where the *bemo* stops, turn W down Jl. Kartenegara (next to Bioskop Garuda); the temple is about 600 m down the road on the right. Ask directions.

Candi Sumberawan

From Candi Singosari, go toward the guardian statues, then turn R down a country road and head NW for 6 km until you reach Sumberawan village. Ask for the gate key if you want to go right up to the *stupa*, which is about a km further on a trail through rice paddies. This bell-shaped *stupa* is one of only 2 in all of E. Java (the other is Borobudur).

Candi Jago

Eighteen km E of Malang, Candi Jago was a memorial to another Singosari king, Vishnuvardhana. Although the roof and body have caved in, it's still one of the most attractive and remarkable temples of the period. Candi Jago dates from 1268, yet it has distinct connections with the prehistoric monuments and terraced sanctuaries found in Java's mountains. The monument incorporates Buddhist sculptures, Krishna reliefs, Arjuna's fretful night in his hermitage, earthy scenes from everyday life, and some of the earliest and most grotesque *panakawan* carvings. Also see reliefs of the Pandavas going into exile, set in a frame of cloudy sky and rocky earth; the *Jataka* animal fables; the *Mahabharata* story decorates the side panels. See clearly the shift toward 2-dimensional figures that took place during this tumultuous dynasty. *Wayang*-like "moving picture" sculptures are placed right next to one another like figures in stiff parade; the action unfolds counter-clockwise. Temple reliefs are bolder, more vigorous than any earlier style—definitely a change was taking place. Jago's gatekeeper will provide a xerox copy of all the reliefs with explanations in English. The Sumberwringin watering place is nearby. **getting there:** From Malang first get to Blimbing, Rp200, then catch a minibus or a *bemo* (Rp300, 15 km) to Tumpang (24 km from Malang). About 100 m before Tumpang's *pasar,* 150 m down a side road to the L, is Candi Jago. Look for signpost.

Candi Kidal

This small but lovely sanctuary is an architectural jewel, one of the most perfect examples of Singosari temple art. Next to a papaya grove, the richly carved 13 C. *candi*—a 12.5-m-tall burial temple honoring a Singosari king—is presently being renovated (completion date 1989). The structure appears quite slender since the base towers up so high, the temple tapering at the top to form a pyramid. To the L of the steps are well-crafted episodes of Garuda carrying the nectar of immortality. Kidal also has elaborate carvings of medallions and *kala*-heads on the main body, while statues of Garuda guard its base. There used to be a tunnel beneath the temple leading all the way to Candi Singosari. **getting there:** The village of Kidal is 5 km SW of Tumpang. At Tumpang's market rent a *dokar* to the temple and back for Rp1500, or possibly catch a minibus straight to Desa Kidal, Rp200. The

road is pockmarked, passing by villages, fields of corn, *sawah,* and cabbages. On the far side of Desa Kidal, you'll see the sign for the temple. Pronounce it with an accent on the second syllable, so people will know where you're headed. From Desa Kidal all the way back to Malang, Rp500, 24 km.

BATU

Seventeen km NW of Malang, this 1,200-m-high mountain hill station is a sort of a poor man's resort. Batu is a better deal than Tretes, not as crowded or built up—a small, quiet town with few other travelers. On the slopes of a volcano, Batu offers hotsprings, a variety of sports, rest and relaxation, surrounded by a fantastic vegetable growing area. See the market next to the minibus terminal on Jl. Dewi Sartika, selling everything from dried fish to soldering irons. The town can also be very cold, especially June to Nov., but at least it's not damp. Because of its high, bracing climate on the slopes of G. Arjuna, Batu has since Dutch times been a TB center and a recuperative resort. Many of the hotels have a curative *air panas* and swimming pool. Take a minibus, Rp500, from Malang's Terminal Pattimura.

Accommodations And Food

Although many rich Chinese frequent Batu, it's still possible to get a nice room for Rp4000 or less. **Losmen Kawi,** Jl. Panglima Sudirman 19 (tel. Batu 139), is a cheerful place and quite central, with 17 large rooms for Rp4000 s, Rp6000-8000 d. Eat in the *rumah makan* next door to save money. Also check out the **Mustika,** Jl. Budiono 2; **Hotel Perdanan Wisma,** Jl. Trunojoyo 102; and **Hotel Batu**—all clean and reasonable. Other hotels have dining rooms and some include meals in their room rates. **Hotel**

East Javanese Art: From the 12th C. to the 15th, E. Java rejected the classicism of Indian traditions and went back to native ideas. Temple art became earthier, more realistic, and decorative, with wild flaming motifs, spirals, leaves, flowers, animals, and lively scenes from everyday life. The revitalized folk tradition has made it much more difficult to understand the symbols in the temple art of E. Java, as compared to C. Java, where the iconographic and religious symbols, though modified, are well known from the study of Indian art. As exemplified in such monuments as Candi Kidal and Candi Jago, on E. Javanese ruins it's often impossible to distinguish between Buddhist and Hindu elements. All you need to visit the temples of the Malang area is an early start each day, a pocketful of change, and a good dose of enthusiasm. Bemo drivers or passengers will see that you get dropped off at all the right places.

Asida, Jl. Panglima Sudirman 99, offers a swimming pool and tennis court. Better values are the **Palem Hotel**, Jl. Trunojoyo 26 (tel. Batu 177), with 22 family rooms with bath; the **Arumdalu** (tel. Batu 266) with full resort facilities; the **Batu Hotel and Village**, Jl. Hasannudin 4 (tel. 2340), with rooms and villas; and **Hotel Selecta**, Jl. Tulungrejo (Box 30, tel. Batu 25), with rooms and bungalows with private *mandi*.

Batu is well known for its delicious fruits and vegetables, especially apples, citrus, onions, potatoes, and cabbage. Near the *alun-alun* is a lively *pasar malam*. For excellent Chinese food at low prices, go to **Restaurant Kenangan** beside the market.

Vicinity Of Batu

Coban Rondo Falls is 9 km from Batu. For Rp200, take a minibus to Sebalo (Pandesari) village, a little *desa* about 6 km from Batu. Turn down the signposted trail by the memorial to the cows and walk 5 km to this 65-m-high waterfall at the foot of G. Panderman (3,037 m). Back out on the main road, continue through mountainous countryside to Pare and Kediri. On the way at Pujon, 9 km from Batu, is a bathing pool called **Dewi Sri**; an experimental agricultural project is underway here. If heading back down from Batu to Malang, stop in Junrejo and visit the **Buddhist Dharma Putra Asramam Temple** on the R side; you'll see the *stupa*. Take a minibus from Batu to Dinoyo (Rp300), then a *bajai* from Dinoyo to Terminal Pattimura (Rp150).

Songgoriti

From Batu walk 4 km, ride on the back of a motorbike (Rp500), or take a minibus (Rp200) up to these hotsprings. Songgoriti is a popular recreation area with a large swimming pool, surrounded by restaurants, gardens, casuarina trees, ricefields. Of the 2 classes of hotsprings offered, the better bargain is the public bath—the only one in E. Java. Entrance fee: Rp150, then going in the bath costs Rp600 for ½ hour. It's an ordinary bathroom (rusty); nothing special. A hotel and cheap *losmen* are right next to each other, plus restaurant, children's playground. Superb views.

Selecta

Only 6½ km NW of Batu and 23 km (45 min.) NW of Malang. First take a minibus to Batu (Rp500), then catch another (Rp250) or walk up to Selecta. Nestled on the side of G. Arjuna, Selecta is a fine resort surrounded by gorgeous mountain scenery, landscaped flower gardens, vegetable patches, and apple orchards. Enjoy the rock garden and swimming pool "Selecta Pemadian" (admission: Rp150) with its clear, fresh water. Several fine restaurants and souvenir stands. **accommodations**: **Hotel Santosa II**, Jl. Selecta-Tulungrejo (tel. Batu 66), charges only Rp6000 s including food. **Hotel Selecta** has 33 rooms and 3 bungalows; Rp8500-11,000 without

food; another plan includes food with the price. Good service and food, but their restaurant is quite pricey. Request hot water for baths, and plenty of blankets! It costs Rp800 to enter and use the pool. Also try the **Purnama Hotel**, Jl. Raya Selecta (Box 18, tel. Batu 195), an excellent hotel in the US$30 range, with very friendly and attractive waitresses, tennis courts. **Kartika Wijaya** has full facilities, fitness center, billiards, swimming pool, a pub, good views, and rooms costing up to Rp80,000 (but standard ones are Rp55,000).

Vicinity Of Selecta

Cheaper *losmen* are found in the towns of Punten (3 km from Selecta) and Tulungrejo, down the mountain from Selecta on the road back to Malang. **Losmen Punten** and **Peng. Pondok** ask Rp3000 s or d. North of Selecta, visit the little mountain town of Sumber Brantas, the source of the Brantas River. Selecta also makes a good base from which to climb the tropical volcanos to the north. From Junggo, hike 3-4 hours to the top of G. Anjasmoro (2,277 m), G. Welirang (3,156 m), or G. Arjuno (3,340 m). These mountains are in a clump; hit all 3 by hiking along the ridges connecting them. For the famous Trowulan ruins, take a minibus NW to Kandangan, then continue in the direction of Mojokerto. Be sure to tell the driver to let you off at the Trowulan Museum right on the highway.

PANDAAN

A cool and exhilarating mountain resort an hour's drive 45 km S of Surabaya on the road to Malang. The **Taman Candrawilwatikta** amphitheater here (capacity 2,000) sits at the base of the distant volcanos G. Arjuno, G. Welirang, and G. Anjasmoro. On the first and third Sat. of the month from May to Oct., E. Javanese classical dances, dramas, and temple rituals dating back to the 8th and 9th centuries are staged here. There's no dialog, so concentrate on the music and dancing as costumed players mime shortened versions of the *Ramayana* ballet in the *sendratari* school style. Performances are held against the flawless cone of G. Penanggungan.

Candi Jawi

Two and a half km from Pandaan Bus Station on the R-hand side of the road up to Tretes (or 7 km downhill from Tretes). An early 14th C. gem of masonry, built on a terrace of river rocks and formerly surrounded by a moat, this Shivaite *candi* was built in the shape of the mythical bird Garuda, dedicated to the murdered King Kertanegara (d. 1292). After the great earthquake of 1331, a Buddhist *stupa* was added to its base of red bricks. The structure would be quite beautiful if it weren't for the fact that most of its blocks were hauled off to build bridges, houses, dams. Unidentified reliefs are carved all around the temple, a

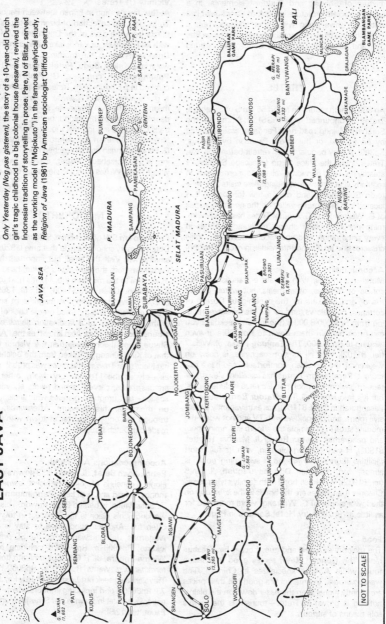

EAST JAVA

East Java Literary History: The Redjosari Sugar Estate near Madiun was the setting for an old Indies family tale. Maria Dermout's *Only Yesterday (Nog pas gisteren)*, the story of a 10-year-old Dutch girl's tragic childhood in a big colonial house *(besaran)*, revived the Indonesian tradition of storytelling in prose. Pare, N of Blitar, served as the working model ("Mojokuto") in the famous analytical study, *Religion of Java* (1961) by American sociologist Clifford Geertz.

NOT TO SCALE

mixture of Shivaite and Buddhist elements. In a barred concrete structure in back of Candi Jawi is a statue of Shiva along with other artifacts. Take a Tretes-bound minibus from the Pandaan Minibus Station and ask to be let off at Candi Jawi (around Rp300).

TRETES

An 850-m-high mountain resort 55 km S of Surabaya, Tretes (pronounced tray-TESS) is 9 km off the Surabaya-Malang road near Pandaan, easily reached by *bemo*, taxi, or bus (from Pandaan by minibus, Rp300). A very popular Dutch retreat before the war, Tretes is still the place to go to escape Surabaya's steamy heat and humidity—all the tour groups which regularly visit it notwithstanding. Also visited by well-to-do Surabayans, and only a few foreigners, it is located in a high green valley on the northern slopes of G. Welirang and G. Arjuno. Tretes has good swimming pools, souvenir shops, restaurants, hotels in every price range, and spectacular views with trails crisscrossing up the mountainsides in every direction.

Accommodations

Motel-style hotels, with private entrances and balconies or terraces, offer meals, hot water, private *mandi*, and blankets for the cool nights. Dozens of cottages, bungalows, and rooms are available, ranging from Rp6,000-8,000 s (though on weekdays you can often bargain them down to Rp5300 s or even less) up to Rp30,000. The **Tanjung Plaza**, Jl. Wilis 7 (tel. 81102), with all its slot machines, is noisy on weekends, though clean, comfortable, and has a restaurant. **Pemandian Tretes** has excellent views, restaurant, swimming pool; non a/c rates include meals, but it's frequently full. The **Natour Bath House**, Jl. Pasanggrahan 2 (tel. 81161), has extravagantly expensive rooms and bungalows with TV and not worth the money; stroll in to sample the superb swimming pool and panoramas. **Tretes Raya**, Jl. Malabar 166 (tel. 81902), is very comfortable and, with its full resort facilities (bungalows around a swimming pool), is almost worth the price. **Dirgahayu Indah**, Jl. Ijen 5 (tel. 81932), is a small hotel with family-style rooms. Cheaper than Tretes are the hotels in the *kampung* on the lower slopes of G. Welirang where rooms go for as little as Rp2500; try **Hotel Semeru** in Prigen.

Food

The majority of hotels and guesthouses have restaurants. The **Gunung Kawi** serves good Indonesian food, while **Abadis** specializes in Chinese. The *warung* around the market are good but their prices are slightly higher than the *pasar* down on the plains; nothing is grown in Tretes—tourism is the town's sole means of support.

Vicinity Of Tretes

At **Ibu Jaya's** shop in Prigen (between Pandaan and Tretes) is a big collection of bizarre antiques and artifacts from the days of the Dutch and even before, with lots of kitsch junk too; take a *bemo* from Tretes. Open everyday in the mornings. Visit the nearby waterfalls **Kakek Budo, Putuk Truno**, and the **Air Pasanggrahan** complex. **G. Welirang** can be climbed in 5-6 hours from Tretes. No problem finding a guide who speaks *Bahasa Indonesia*. Welirang means "sulphur" in Javanese, so just fall in behind people looking for the sulphur baths. There are many trails to explore around this mountain resort. The old temples of **Belahan** and **Jalatunda** on the slopes of G. Penanggungan can be reached from Tretes by hiking or on horseback. **Pacet**, a small high-altitude village to the W, has stunning views and cool, crisp air.

MOJOKERTO

Forty-two km SW of Surabaya. Sukarno attended the Dutch primary school here, at that time (1920s) a very small town. Visit the small but important Museum Purbakala; from the *alun-alun's* S side, head E along Jl. A. Yani to the museum (no. 14); it's next to Kantor Kabupaten. Open 0700-1400, Fri. til 1300, Sun. closed. Leave a donation. A magnificent sculptural group of Vishnu being carried on the back of Garuda is the centerpiece of a fascinating series of reliefs around the main room. Also known as the "Airlangga Statue," one theory holds that the Vishnu figure is that of King Airlangga. Taken from the Belahan Bathing Place near Trawas, this piece was probably carved as early as the 11th century. Many other life-like statues, relics, carved stoned reliefs showing daily scenes—and umpteen plaques with ancient writing on them—fill this museum. Afterwards, wander through the original quarter of town with its finely made old Dutch houses.

Accommodations And Food

Penginapan Barat, Jl. Kartini II/93 down a quiet path along a canal, is Mojokerto's nicest *losmen* for the money—clean and well kept. **Penginapan Mutiara**, Jl. Setia Mulio, is behind Pasar Kriwon. This cheerful workingman's place is the cheapest in town, so it's often full. Another good place to stay is **Losmen Nagamas**, Jl. Pahlawan 23, on the SE side of Mojokerto; Rp4000 s, Rp6000 d including breakfast. **Wisma Tenera**, Jl. H.O.S. Cokrominato (toward the *terminal bis*), wants Rp5000 s, Rp8000-12,000 d. Travelers also seek out **Losmen Merdeka**, Jl. Pamuji 73; Rp6000 s or d including light breakfast. The most expensive hotel in town is the **Sriwijaya** on Jl. Desa Pacot (tel. 12/9).

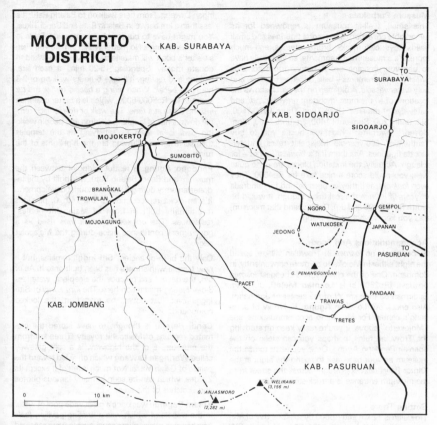

MOJOKERTO DISTRICT

KAB. SURABAYA

TO SURABAYA

KAB. SIDOARJO

SIDOARJO

MOJOKERTO

SUMOBITO

BRANGKAL

TROWULAN

NGORO

GEMPOL

MOJOAGUNG

WATUKOSEK

JAPANAN

JEDONG

TO PASURUAN

G. PENANGGUNGAN

PACET

PANDAAN

KAB. JOMBANG

TRAWAS

TRETES

KAB. PASURUAN

G. WELIRANG (3,156 m)

0   10 km

G. ANJASMORO (2,282 m)

Bright and cheerful **Depot Murni,** Jl. Majapahit 72, offers a *loo mie,* a type of beef-noodle stew, and *nasi bumbu rujak,* a spicy-hot chicken dish, plus a myriad of snacks. **Rumah Makan Anda,** near Stasiun Kereta Api, is a Chinese-style eating room. **Depot Endah,** Jl. Bhanyangkara 26, is right next to the train *stasiun.* At the bus station itself are also several eating places. At night **Pasar Kliwon** metamorphoses into a convivial eating place where gas lamps glow over dozens of small *warung.*

From Mojokerto

Two bus stations are here, one on Jl. Majapahit and the other on Jl. Pahlawan. From the Jl. Pahlawan station, buses depart for Madiun and Surabaya, Rp2000. There are no buses at night from the Jl. Majapahit station, so you have to rely on minibuses. If you're going to Trowulan, right after Pasar Kliwon take a L on Jl. Achmad Dahlan and catch a *bemo* or minibuses for

Rp600 (also to Surabaya or Jombang). For Malang, take a minibus to Jombang, then catch another through the hills SE to Malang.

TROWULAN

This small agricultural community was once the capital of the mighty Majapahit Empire (1292-1389) which, under the ruthless and efficient Gajah Mada, controlled most of the islands of the archipelago in the 14th century. This ancient capital and major trade center was once completely surrounded by a high brick wall enclosing pools, palaces, playing fields, plazas, and temples. Today, remains lie scattered over a 15-sq-km area. Impressively, all the temples were made from brick, with no stonework, granite, or sandstone. Over time, all the temples have lost their centerpieces — either to thieves or museums.

Museum Purbakala

This small, well-lit museum is renowned for its remarkable collection of terracotta figurines and small heads, toys, clay masks, bronze statues, and much more. It's a museum of fragments, so you really have to use your imagination. A bronze room contains priestly accoutrements — bells, incense burners, and holy water vessels. A big map on the porch shows the locations of all the most important graves, *candi,* and gateways of the area. Open Tues.-Thurs. 0700-1400, Sat. until 1200, Sun. until 1400, Fri. until 1100, Mon. closed. **warning:** Kids will hustle you to buy "authentic" 600-year-old Majapahit relics and terracotta figurines. Ask them if it's *"imitasi"* or not — for a laugh. Actually, the imitation pieces are done quite well; you could score a nice fake for Rp4000. They even *look* old, as if they've been around for hundreds of years (if it were the real thing though, it would be worth Rp100,000 and up). Don't spend that much unless you know what you're doing.

Accommodations And Food

Since there's no *losmen* in Trowulan village, spend the night either in Mojokerto or, more conveniently, in Jombang. One of the cleanest and cheapest *losmen* on Java (Rp2500 s) is **Losmen Melati,** Jl. Pang. Sudirman 63 (one km W of the center of Jombang). Also check out **Losmen Agung,** ½ km W of Jombang's center. For Mojokerto accommodations, see "Mojokerto" above. If you're really keen on studying the Trowulan ruins, perhaps you can sleep on the open-air Pendopo Agung. Or, if you want to use the museum as your base, ask to spend the night at the Kantor Polisi next door. Right across the street from the museum entrance is a truck-stop *warung.*

Getting There

Trowulan is 12 km and Rp600 by minibus SW of Mojokerto, and a 1½-hour (Rp2000, 60 km) bus ride SW of Surabaya. Take a bus from Surabaya's Joyoboyo Station heading for Mojokerto and Jombang. Ask to get off at the split gateway on the highway right in front of Museum Purbakala (the bus passes right in front of it). Keep your eyes peeled and don't let the driver fly on past. If coming from Jombang, go to Mojoagung first, then take a minibus (Rp200) to Trowulan. Start your tour from the museum.

TEMPLE SITES AROUND TROWULAN

You need only good footwear and an adventurous spirit. Allow one day. Leave your pack in the souvenir shop (guard's house) at the museum. Follow the museum's table-top map for directions. It's more fun to walk than to take a *becak.* A sensible route would be to go from the museum up to Candi Siti Inggil, back to Candi Berahu, then NE down the highway to War-

ingan Lawang. From here walk on to Bajang Ratu; it's less than a km between Bajang Ratu and Candi Tikus. You might have to cut (carefully) across ricefields in your meanderings. No matter which temple you visit, a visitor's book will materialize and you'll be asked to donate money. Spending 15-20 min. at each site, looking and resting, it'll take 6 hours walking or 2-3 hours by *becak.* When hiring a *becak,* try for the *tur komplet* for Rp5000-6000, which is a better deal than visiting a site at a time. The walk or ride to each temple down lanes of laughing children and people working *padi* is at least as satisfying as the temples themselves. The following are the highlights of the ruins:

Pendopo Agung, a restful midpoint between the museum and Candi Bajang Ratu, was built by the Indonesian army during a wave of tourist development. It's an exact reproduction of the 14th C. pavilions traditionally built in front of Majapahit nobles' residences. The original structure was used as a government conference place during the Majapahit reign.

Only the base of ancient **Siti Inggil** remains, but a new temple with shrines has been built onto it. As of old, the devout still practice the sleepless, waterless 3-day fasting meditation here. The *juru kunci* of Sitti Inggil lives just down the road from the locked compound.

Candi Berahu is thought to have stored the cremated remains of Majapahit royalty. Three km from the museum, E of the highway, is a split gateway called **Waringan Lawang** which once led toward the palace of Gajah Mada. Not much is left of it except its 2 sides, which can be seen in many famous photos and sketches of this area.

Kolam Segaran was once a great wide pool of water in the middle of which was a floating pavilion *(bale kambang),* a place where royal guests were received by Majapahit officials.

The brick monolith **Bajang Ratu** hardly looks like a temple; it is well maintained and looks new after almost 6 centuries. The ride out to it is really nice. Though the best preserved of all the temples, all that's left of Bajang Ratu's compound is a doorway with remains of the outer walls. Glowering *kala*-heads on all 4 sides add veracity to the curse thought to linger over the ancient doorway — anyone who walks through it will never marry.

Candi Tikus, 500 m SE of Bajang Ratu, was wistfully named the "Mouse Temple" by present-day farmers wishing to rid themselves of field mice. Candi Tikus was once a splendid bathing place with terraces, turrets, and spouts along the walls of the now-dry basin.

Two km S of the museum, the cemetery of **Makam Troloyo** contains possibly the oldest Muslim grave on Java, dating from 1376. Though members of the

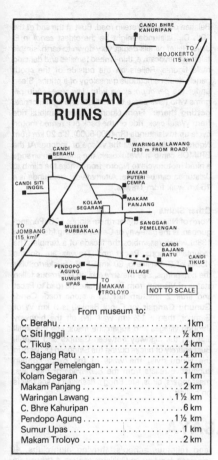

TROWULAN RUINS

CANDI BHRE KAHURIPAN

TO MOJOKERTO (15 km)

CANDI BERAHU

WARINGAN LAWANG (200 m FROM ROAD)

CANDI SITI INGGIL

MAKAM PUTERI CEMPA

KOLAM SEGARAN

MAKAM PANJANG

TO JOMBANG (15 km)

MUSEUM PURBAKALA

SANGGAR PEMELENGAN

CANDI BAJANG RATU

CANDI TIKUS

PENDOPO AGUNG

SUMUR UPAS

VILLAGE

TO MAKAM TROLOYO

NOT TO SCALE

From museum to:

C. Berahu	1 km
C. Siti Inggil	½ km
C. Tikus	4 km
C. Bajang Ratu	4 km
Sanggar Pemelengan	2 km
Kolam Segaran	1 km
Makam Panjang	2 km
Waringan Lawang	1½ km
C. Bhre Kahuripan	6 km
Pendopo Agung	1½ km
Sumur Upas	1 km
Makam Troloyo	2 km

royal family buried here had already become Muslims, some of their graves are decorated with the 6-point Sun of Majapahit. Another grave is that of a Champa princess from Cambodia (d. 1448).

An old waterpool, **Kolam Segaran**, is surrounded by a 1½-m wall. Crops are now being raised inside. Walk down into it by using the paths farmers use to get to their fields.

From Trowulan

To get back to Surabaya or Mojokerto, just flag down a returning bus or hitchhike. To Malang, take the road via Jombang and Batu, a nicer route than via Mojokerto and Surabaya. Another beautiful sylvan road leads from Trowulan to Pacet, then through to Tretes. Occasionally this road is out, so make inquiries first.

Pacet is a recreational resort in the mountains with cool weather and beautiful surroundings.

GUNUNG PENANGGUNGAN

A revered 9-peaked mountain 35 km SE of Mojokerto, shaped like the mythical Mt. Meru of India. In 1935, 81 monuments, sacred bathing places, meditation grottos, and ruined sanctuaries were discovered under dense jungle grass and rainforests covering G. Penanggungan's slopes. These ruins, dating from A.D. 977-1511, encompass many different and peculiar E. Javanese styles. Most are found on the northern and western slopes from 750 to 1,500 m in altitude. The *juru kunci* at Jalatunda will guide you to some of the more accessible sites. Though green with moss, most are still in excellent condition. All of the statues have either been stolen or removed to museums.

Transport

To get to G. Penanggungan, head N from Malang toward Gampol, then take the highway just before Gampol toward Mojokerto. After 4 km is the Pabrik Korek Kejapanan on your L; Watukosek is 2 km farther. Or take a minibus 35 km SE of Mojokerto (Rp800). As you approach, at least 5 of Penanggungang's peaks (there are 9 in all) are visible from the road. No *losmen* in Watukosek; the closet place to stay is in Pandaan. Alternately, stay at Mojokerto and do this whole outing in a day. The easiest way to get to both temples from Watukosek or Ngoro is by rented motorcycle. The paths are very narrow and steep; a car wouldn't make it. A guide might make himself available to take you on foot, but his first price up to both Belahan and Jalatunda might be as high as Rp25,000! These temples get very few tourists, and those that come only hike to Belahan. Leave your pack safely at the police post (BRIMOB).

Belahan

This bathing place, dating from A.D. 1049 and still being used, is in a quiet clearing in the jungle on the W side of G. Penanggungan. This could be King Airlangga's burial monument. There are two 4-armed spout figures of the goddesses Lakshmi and Shri, Vishnu's wives. The water trickling from their nipples is looked upon as nectar from the gods by the locals who call this place *Sumbergambar*, literally "the spring from the sculptures." These statues once flanked the splendid statue of Vishnu carried by Garuda which you can now see totally out of context in Mojokerto's museum. **getting there:** In Watukosek, where you make arrangements for your climb, report to the BRIMOB police complex first. The friendly police can arrange for motorcycle rental (Rp5000-6000) to see both Belahan (via Kandangan)

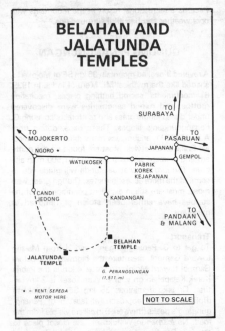

BELAHAN AND JALATUNDA TEMPLES

TO SURABAYA

TO MOJOKERTO

NGORO •

WATUKOSEK

JAPANAN

TO PASARUAN

GEMPOL

PABRIK KOREK KEJAPANAN

CANDI JEDONG

KANDANGAN

TO PANDAAN & MALANG

BELAHAN TEMPLE

JALATUNDA TEMPLE

▲ G. PENANGGUNGAN (1,511 m)

• = RENT *SEPEDA MOTOR* HERE

NOT TO SCALE

Belahan on a rough steep road. Built at the end of the 10th C., Jalatunda might be the oldest *candi* in E. Java. Relief panels depict very down-to-earth, simple tales with evocative, thin-limbed females and dancing male figures. Reliefs on the outside of the spout panels depict a fictitious genealogy of a prince. Sleep under the *pendopo* along with Javanese-Hindu pilgrims who have come to meditate and light incense. **getting there:** From Ngoro, a short minibus ride from Watukosek, ride on the back of a rented motorcycle up to Jalatunda (Rp4000-5000). It's 20 km from Ngoro to Jalatunda via the village of Jedong. At the BRIMOB camp in Watukosek, the police can arrange a hired motorcycle to Ngoro, from where the climb to Jalatunda can be made. Alternatively, Jalatunda is a 15-km walk from Trawas.

Other Sights

North of Ngoro, on the northern slopes of G. Penanggungan, is the gateway of **Candi Jedong** (dates from 1385) which resembles the facade of a temple. The mountain resorts **Pacet** and **Trawas** are on the slopes of G. Welirang, 30 km SE of Mojokerto; visit the hotsprings. See the *arca laki*, an enormous fallen statue of Vishnu; from Trawas take the road to Pacet and after 2 km turn left up a stone road. **Candi Gunung Gangsir** (or Candi Bankal) is 9 km W of Gampol, then a 1½-km walk (N) off the highway through villages and sugarcane fields; see the small sign on the highway between Gampol and Bangil. Built entirely of bricks during the Singosari Dynasty in the Hindu style, the walls of the *candi* contain superlative reliefs from the *Ramayana* of monkeys, messengers, birds, etc. Bring a flashlight to see reliefs on ceiling.

and Jalatunda (via Jedong). The road up to Belahan starts about 500 m before the police post.

Jalatunda

Also on the W side of the mountain, 4 km higher than

SURABAYA

Its melodious name belies the true nature of this city—a hot, dirty, and noisy industrial hub on Java's swampy NE coast, E. Java's biggest metropolis as well as its provincial capital. With an area extending over 300 sq km supporting a population of 3.6 million, Surabaya is in fact the second largest city in the country, a modern center for manufacturing, agriculture, and trade—its bustle and din a sharp contrast to the serene agrarian countryside around it. On the outskirts of the city are huge steel refineries, and sugar, plywood, and cement processing plants. Travelers use Surabaya as a stopover on their way E to Bali or W to Yogya or Jakarta, or as a place to hang around waiting for a ship or a plane. The pace here is less frantic than Jakarta, and it's generally cheaper. The city has broad, busy streets, red-tiled houses with neat little gardens, a 6-lane boulevard, horrendous traffic jams, quiet cul-de-sacs, technical universities

and religious schools, thriving nightclubs, 40 cinemas, bowling and billiards centers, 4 railway stations, at least 30,000 *becak*, a splendid zoo, and multistory shopping complexes with speed lifts and freezing airconditioning. Tunjungan, Surabaya's shopping district, could even have better bargains than Singapore. The city is the main base for the Indonesian navy and for hundreds of years it has been one of Indonesia's most important ports, its facilities second only to Jakarta's. This is also an active city for theater and E. Javanese dance forms such as the mesmerizing horse trance dance, *Kuda Kepang*.

Climate

Very hot and humid with an average humidity of 75%, annual rainfall of 152 cm, and an average temperature of 27.3 C (81 degrees F). The rainy season begins in Nov. and ends around April when

the Handelsstraat, Surabaya, circa 1920

street flooding is a recurrent problem. The rest of the year, particularly from June to Oct., is drier. Dust and pollution make Surabaya uncomfortable for people with asthma or allergies.

History

Alleged to have been founded on the spot where a legendary battle between a shark *(sura)* and a crocodile *(buaya)* took place, Surabaya has been the commercial center and chief harbor of E. Java since the fall of the 14th C. Majapahit Kingdom. Formerly, it consisted of islands and swamps where King Wijaya of Majapahit battled Kublai Khan's army in 1293. In the 16th C., its inhabitants converted to Islam and fought long and bitterly against the onslaught of the Mataram armies. Surabaya became the largest and most important seaport of the Dutch East Indies, exporting rubber, tobacco, teak, kapok, and sugar. In 1940, its population was 340,000, of whom 39,000 were Europeans. After WW II, Surabaya became a "City of Heros," where the first major battle in the revolution took place. Frustrated by fierce resistance, the British on 10 Nov. 1945 began a merciless aerial and artillery bombardment of this defenseless city which lasted for 3 days and nights. The Battle of Surabaya was a turning point in the struggle for Indonesian independence. Although independence took another 5 years to achieve, the battle demonstrated to the British and the world the grass roots nature of the struggle and the willingness of the masses to sacrifice their lives. The Tugu Pahlawan monument in the main city square commemorates this intense resistance against the Dutch and their allies. During the political upheavals of 1965-66 there were street executions, bodies clogged up under the bridges, and Surabaya's canals ran red for months. Outside the city near the airport thousands of "communists" were massacred by villagers cranked up on *Jihad.* The captives were led to believe that they were being driven to the airport to be deported but were murdered along the way.

The People

Surabaya's present population of 3.5 million (1984) is about 90% Muslim (primarily Javanese and Madurese), 7% Christian, and 3% Hindu. The several thousand making up the foreign community are either missionaries or involved in development projects. The people are super-friendly, but there are plenty of unfriendly ones as well — including probably the boldest purse-snatchers in all of Indonesia. Avoid street thefts by taking a few simple precautions: leave your valuables back at your hotel, secure with the desk or in your room; always walk with your purse or daypack held tightly under the arm which faces away from the street. Also beware of fast-talkers and con-men posing as students or artists whose intent it is to steal your money. If male travelers want the pimps around town to stop pestering them (prostitution is a big Surabayan industry), tell them you're a priest — *"Saya pendeta."* This is also a good way to keep down fares on *becak,* taxis, etc., as priests in this town are famous for their poverty.

SIGHTS

Historical Sights

The **Rakhmat** and **Sunan Bungkul** mosques, built in 1836, are the oldest in Surabaya and contain the tombs of the first Islamic settlers in E. Java. **Ngampel**, near Semut Station to the E of Jl. K.H. Mas Mansyur, is the tomb of the first carrier of Islam to E. Java, Sunan Ampel. Surabaya has several Dutch Reformed and Roman Catholic churches; the priest in the one near the U.S. Embassy speaks English. This church, **Gereja Katolik** (Santa Maria), is tucked away in a quiet side road (Jl. Soetomo). The oldest Chinese shrine in Surabaya is 18th C. **Hok An Kiong**, dedicated to the Chinese patron saint of sailors (Ma Co), is on Jl. Selompretan across from Jl. Kembang Jepun. Nearby to the W is the famous *Jembatan Merah* (Red Bridge), once the throbbing center of the old Dutch commercial district. Today it's surrounded by run-down Dutch warehouses and turn-of-the-century office buildings. **Grahadi**, the former residence of the Dutch governors, is located on one of the city's principal roads, Jl. Pemuda. With its huge flagpole on the lawn and cannons facing the road, it functions nowadays as the official residence of East Java's governor. Another historic building is the **Majapahit Hotel**, which was known as the "Oranji Hotel" during Dutch times and the "Yamato Hotel" during the Japanese occupation.

In the heart of the hotel district is the Buddhist stone statue, **Joko Dolog** (nicknamed "Fat Boy"), a remnant of the Singosari Dynasty. Joko Dolog depicts the great King Kartanegara seated on a pedestal inscribed 1289. The statue was transferred to this spot from its site near Malang by the Dutch about 300 years ago. This magic place lies in Taman Apsari, behind Suryo Monument. Bring flowers and a few *rupiah*. On Jl. Pahlawan Surabaya is the towering **Heros' Monument** (Tugu Pahlawan) which commemorates the victims of the terrible bombing of 10 November 1945.

Museums

North of the zoo, on Jl. Taman Mayangkera 6, is the small historical and archaeological museum **MPU Tantular**; open daily 0700-0200, Fri. to 1100, Sat. to 1230, Mon. closed. This ethnographic museum opposite the zoo houses mesolithic farming tools, stone statuary from the Majapahit period, Koranic manuscripts, ceremonial beds, *wayang*, photos of old Surabaya, a very good paper money collection, and early 20th C. technology including a Daimler steam-driven motorcycle! English texts. There's also the inevitable army museum, **Museum Angkatan '45**, containing relics from the war of independence, but it's a long way out on Jl. May. Jen. Sungkono (before the TVRI studio). It might interest Dutch visitors to visit the **Peneleh** and **Kembangkuning** cemeteries where many of their fellow countrymen have been laid to rest.

Neighborhoods

The Jarak and Bangunrejo redlight districts are world renowned, superb sociological studies in the dynamics of poverty sharing. Take a "W" *bemo* from the Joko Dolog station, Rp200. Jarak is like a huge honky-tonk Mexican border town in the Orient. It's best to take a mate along—more fun and safer. In row upon row of gaudy little dollhouse shanties, 15,000 girls and women (of all sizes, shapes, ages, races, humors, prices) work and live. Lanterns are strung out in the night, muddy streets are clogged with *becak*, lines of gas-lit carts sell antibiotics, while groups of men, hustlers, beggars, and even roving minstrel groups or *ronggeng* (street dancers who sing and dance for small change) rove the streets. No pimps needed, just go straight into the houses. Tandes is another entertainment district; take a *becak* all the way from the Bamboo Denn to Tandes to avoid the aggravation from the Jembatan Merah *becak* drivers. Hell, it's a night out, right? Taking the driver's own shortcuts, it's a fascinating ride through market and

---

SURABAYA

1. Tanjung Perak (ferries to Madura)
2. Mesjid Ampel
3. Jembatan Merah Station
4. Kempung Pecinan (Jl. Kembang Jepum)
5. grave of W.R. Supratman
6. Central Post Office
7. Heros' Monument (Tugu Pahlawan)
8. Pelni Office
9. Kantor Gubenor
10. grave of Dr. Soetomo
11. Wijaya Shopping Center
12. Baluran Night Market
13. Tanjungan Shopping Center
14. Kantor Bupati
15. telephone and telegraph office
16. statue of Joko Dolog
17. RRI (Jl. Pemuda)
18. flower market
19. antique shops
20. Pasar Keputran
21. post office (Jl. Darmo)
22. Catholic Cathedral (Gereja Katolik)
23. French Consulate
24. Musium MPU Tantular
25. Delby Restaurant
26. Taman Tirta Swimming Pool

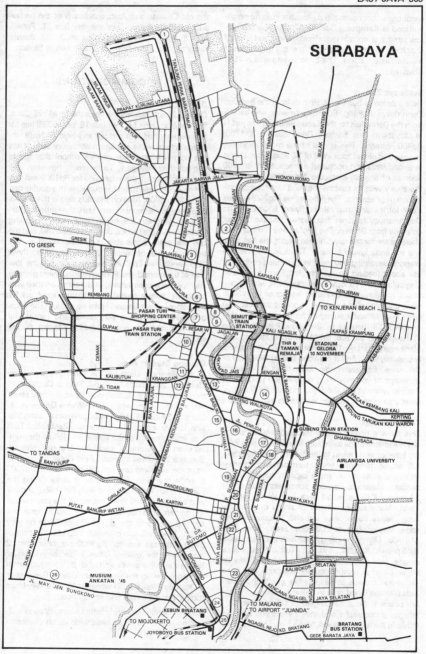

SURABAYA

canal areas that never sleep. Another colorful neighborhood is **Kampung Sasak**. With its winding narrow streets, women in lace shawls, and crumbling old Dutch warehouses, this area offers up a good dash of Middle Eastern flavor. The Simolawang area is 75% Madurese.

Surabaya Zoo

Take a *bemo* or bus (no. 2, Rp200) from the Bamboo Denn down Jl. Pang. Sudirman or walk one hour S from the Denn. Ask for the Kebun Binatang; it's just N of Joyoboyo Bus Station. Open daily 0730-1700; Rp400 entrance. This is one of the most complete, largest, and oldest zoos in all of SE Asia. Specializing in exotic birds and nocturnal animals, there are 500 species of animals including Mongolian bears. See the aviary with its cassowaries and outstanding collection of pheasants. The Nocturama (Rp200) houses slow lorries and marvelous flying squirrels. The Dolphinarium features freshwater Mahakam River dolphins from Borneo. The hoofed and ruminant enclosures are for the rare Chinese *wapiti*, the *babirusa*, and the *anoa* (dwarf buffalo). There are 18 Komodo dragons devouring raw meat in a sandbed enclosure; ask about feeding times. The Reptilium is home to king cobras. The canopy dwellers exhibit, with its proboscis monkeys, black-crested macaques from Sulawesi, and pig-tailed monkeys, is one of the best. The city's best saltwater aquarium for tropical fish is also here (Rp200); there's a smaller one at Pasar Bunga on Jl. Kayoon. In the zoo, Sri Mulat performances take place every night (Rp1500), starting at 1900. Extremely popular, you'll find it crowded almost every day of the week. Eat *gado-gado* under trees of swinging monkeys, or you may meet crazy Anton who knows the zoo well and will show you around. On Sundays, feast your eyes on women in dazzling native dress.

Tanjung Perak

This thriving harbor area in the northern part of the city is a unique place to explore (the big port area W of the lighthouse is closed to the public). Visit the grand, full a/c, 2-story passenger terminal with moneychangers, restaurants, and a capacity for 3,000 passengers. Motorless wooden schooners dock at the 2-km-long Kalimas wharf area just W of Tanjung Perak. Many different types of *prahu* drop anchor here, mainly Bugis *pinisi* but also Madurese types, some displacing over 200 tons. *Prahu* from Palu, Manado, Ujung Pandang, Sumbawa, Banjarmasin, Balikpapan, Kendiri, and Toli Toli offload copra, *cingke*, *lada* (pepper), *laso*, and *sombi* and take on sugar, bicycles, motor scooters, cars, rice, and soap. No tourist crowds at Kalimas like you'll find at the Sundakelapa wharf area in Jakarta. Promise the harbor police at the entrance gate to Kalimas that you'll take no photographs and they'll wave you through. While in the neighborhood, take a *bemo* or *bis kota* to

the old Chinese and Arab quarters S of the harbor area. **getting there:** Take the city bus "T. Perak" from in front of Bank Bumi Daya on Jl. Jen. Basuki Rachmat or a *bemo* from Jembatan Merah Station.

ACCOMMODATIONS

Bamboo Denn

Once a vibrant travelers' nerve center for all of E. Java, the Bamboo Denn (Jl. Pemuda 18, tel. 40333) has today degenerated into a close and fetid 2nd-rate language school with a sideline in dormitory beds. It has put so much attention into its school that it has neglected its hostelery. To its credit, however, it is undeniably cheap: dorm beds go for Rp1000 and you get a whole single room to yourself with a double bed for only Rp3000. Also on the plus side is the Denn's proximity to restaurants, the THR, the Gubeng Train Station, *imigrasi*, the huge Delta Plaza Shopping Center, while the harbor, Joyoboyo Terminal, and the zoo are easily accessible. You'll be asked to talk before a class of mostly Chinese students; these "Conversational English" classes subsidize the low cost of the rooms here. Perhaps a convenient place to stay for those overnighting in Surabaya on their way to Yogya, Jakarta, or Bali. If you're on a *becak*, ask for the better-known Garden Hotel next door. The Bamboo Denn also runs a very similar and very useful language school/dormitory setup in Malang, 60 km south.

Gubeng Station Area

If the Bamboo Denn is full (unlikely), try **Hotel Gubeng**, Jl. Sumatra 18; Rp6000 s or d. Come out of the station and turn L, then walk down the road about 300 m; look for the white sign. **Wisma Ganesha**, Jl. Sumatra 34 (tel. 45182), only 500 m from Gubeng Station, is very comfortable and an excellent value. Turn L as you come out of the station and follow the numbers on Jl. Sumatra carefully; it's opposite Jl. Sumatra 33 behind a beautiful old Dutch house. The front row of rooms cost Rp5000 s, Rp6000 d, Rp7000 t, while the nicer, bigger ones in back facing the garden fetch Rp8000 s or d with fan, toilet, shower *plus* breakfast. Very quiet except for the creatures of the garden. Some items on the menu are fictional, but the taxi service to the airport (Rp6500) can be very handy. Kayat will also drive you around in his unstoppable rattletrap van for Rp3000 per hour (min. 2 hours) and the owner, Chamdi (distant relative of Raden Kartini) is gentle and kind. By contrast, **Hotel Kayoon**, just up the street from Wisma Ganesha at Jl. Kayoon 5 (tel. 63522) wants Rp4000 for very basic rooms, but it's an old and scuzzy hotel.

About an 8-min *becak* ride from Gubeng Station is Jl. Embong Kenongo which has a wide variety of accommodations, from Rp4000 to Rp22,000. It's quiet and the good value, restful open-air nighttime eatery **Pasar Kayoon** is just down the street. **Hotel Santosa** (no. 40, tel. 43306) is the cheapest at Rp4000-Rp6000 s or d. The front row of rooms, facing a small garden, is better, tolerably clean, and not a bad deal for a major city. Communal *mandi*. **Bina Dirga Angkasa** (no. 52, tel. 42687) charges Rp9000 for their cheapest rooms; very secure (a family-run hotel) with a travel agent in front. The **Remaja Hotel** (no. 12, tel. 41359) is in the Rp17,000-Rp20,500 range plus 21% tax and service—a small, efficient businessman's hotel. But the best deal on the street is guesthouse-style **Wisma Mawarani** (no. 73, tel. 44839), very clean and well organized, with quiet rooms upstairs going for Rp12,500 s (Rp20,000 a/c) with *mandi*, telephone, laundry service, restaurant (Rp2000 for lunch and dinner).

Odds And Ends

If you want to be right in the middle of it, the **Olympic Hotel** (Jl. Urip Sumoharjo 65, below the ARDATH overpass) is the place—Rp4000 Standard, Rp13,000 a/c with *mandi*. Located on a busy extension of Jl. Pang. Sudirman, this old hotel couldn't be more central. *Bemo* stop just 50 m S, Nitour and Garuda offices are nearby, eat at Wiena Restaurant right on nearby corner. **Hotel Stasiun**, Jl. Stasiun Kota 1, is right down the street from Stasiun Semut. A secure hotel with few other travelers, located in a lively neighborhood with good bus connections, they ask Rp4500 s, Rp5750 d. The **Merdeka 1**, Jl. Bongkaran 6 (near Kota Station), has rooms for Rp2500 s or Rp4500 d. For **Losmen Sono Kembang**, Jl. Sono Kembang 2 (just off Jl. Sudirman), take a city bus from Joyoboyo and get off at Bioskop Bayu and ask for directions. The **Pavilyun**, an old centrally located Dutch-style hotel (Jl. Genteng Besar 98), asks Rp6000 s, Rp12,000 d.

Kampung Sasak

For something different, a number of cheap hotels lie along Jl. K.H.M. Mansyur in the middle of the orthodox Arab Quarter (Kampung Sasak), a busy warehouse and market neighborhood. Try **Hotel Indah** (no. 86), but avoid the rather decrepit **Hotel Islam** (no. 84-86). Although **Hotel Kemajuan** (no. 96, tel. 26232) charges only Rp3300-4500 s or d, it's a fleabag. It's located in the old Al-Arsjad School, built in 1924. The best deal going in Kampung Sasak is on the other side of the Kalimas canal: **Hotel Kalimantan**, Jl. Pegirian 202-A, charges Rp8000 non a/c, Rp12,000 a/c. It is secure and has a garden, travel agency, and restaurant in front which gives room service. Next door, at Jl. Pegirian 202 (tel. 311846), is **Peng. Gajah Mada**; Rp3000-4000 rooms but no a/c. Both these hotels are within walking distance of Jembatan Merah, the historic Mesjid Sunan Ampel; the Kalimas wharf area is only 2 km away.

Expensive

Most are in the business/entertainment district. The **Majapahit**, Jl. Tunjungan 65 (tel. 69501), with a/c, balcony, refrigerator, bar, restaurant, parking, etc., is a fully equipped and historic hotel where in 1949 the Dutch flag was ripped down and the Indonesian flag raised in its place, an incident which helped precipitate the "Battle of Surabaya." **Mirama Hotel**, Jl. Raya Darmo 68-72 (tel. 69501-9), offers a/c rooms with TV and refrigerator, restaurant, bar; US$60-65 s and d. **Garden Hotel**, centrally located at Jl. Pemuda 21 (tel. 47000), has a/c, swimming pool, good Chinese restaurant, bar—one of the best values in this price range (US$31-39). The plush **Ramayana**, Jl. Jen. Basuki Rakhmat 67-69 (tel. 46321), is US$42-60. Also in this category is the **New Grand Park**, Jl. Samudra 3-7 (tel. 270004-8), with a/c rooms (US$45-55) in a downtown location—eat at the excellent Kiet Wan Kie seafood restaurant across the street. The **Elmi Hotel** (Jl. P. Sudirman 42-44, tel. 47157) and the **Simpang Hotel** (Jl. Pemuda 1-3, tel. 42219/42220-5) have rooms in the US$80-98 range. The elegant 4-star **Hyatt Bumi**, Jl. Basuki Rachmat 124-128 (tel. 470875/470503), with its beautiful decor and service, is one of the best high-class hotels in Indonesia: Rp75,000 s. Has all the facilities—video movies, health club, businessmen's center, nightclub. Here you get to use your American Express or Visa. The **Garden Palace Hotel**, the city's newest international-class hotel on Jl. Yos Sudarso 11 (tel. 479251), charges US$55 s, US$65 d for spacious, a/c rooms with video, bar, TV, pub, ballroom, 24-hour coffee shop and restaurant. In all these first-class hotels, be prepared to pay 21% extra for tax and service.

FOOD

Night Markets And *Warung*

Pasar Kayoon, right along the banks of the scenic Kalimas on Jl. Kayoon, is a superb night market with scores of open-air foodstalls. Less than one kilometer from the Bamboo Denn and Wisma Ganesha (walk down the street and over the bridge and you'll see it). Open 0900-2300, this night market is a very cheap, picturesque, and convenient place to eat. Nearby, in front of Gubeng Station at night, stalls also offer inexpensive meals. On the side streets near the THR, vendors sell tasty snacks such as *terang bulan* ("full moon")—hot pancakes with chocolate, peanuts, and sweetened milk. At night go out of the THR and turn L, walk about 500 m, and there you'll find a cluster of *martabak* stands. On Jl. Tegalsari, about 100 m up on the R-hand side, is a pretty good *soto madura asli*, a *soto ayam* open-air restaurant, a Chinese wok place, and coffee and drink vendors. For *soto madura*, head for the *warung* at Stasiun Gubeng and the THR Complex. For *ayam goreng*, walk along Jl. Embong Malang, Jl. Pemuda, and Jl. Kapasari. The best place for *sate kambing* and *sate lomba* is at Bangil on the way to Probolinggo.

Specialties

Sample not only fine Indonesian food (plus Korean, Japanese, and Chinese) but also E. Javanese regional specialties such as *kilkil* (a hearty soup made from the hooves of goats and cows) which can be tried in **Kombes Duryat** behind Bioskop Ria. **Pasar Balauran Baru** (near Wijaya Shopping Center) is another place to experience E. Javanese food. East Java is also famous for its *krupuk;* buy kilos wholesale in the Sidoarjo District, the number one *krupuk* center for Java. In Pasar Genteng, or on Jl. P. Sudirman near Hotel Tanjung, myriad kinds of *krupuk* are offered for sale. Other Indonesians who pass through Surabaya always stock up on not only *krupuk* but also *bandeng* (a smoked river fish) to take back home. Also try *soto madura* (Madura-style soup), *bakwan* (soup with pork balls and wonton), *semanggi* (small boiled leaves eaten with peanut sauce), and *bumbu rujak* (chicken in chili sauce). For E. Javanese cuisine go to **Restaurant Jawa Timur** (Aloha Restaurant) on the way to the airport. **Finna Restaurant**, Jl. Sawo Tratap (next to the Aloha), is a well-known seafood restaurant.

Indonesian

Restoran Aquarius in the zoo (to the L after entering) is surprisingly good. Also check out the **Antika** on Jl. Kranggan, the **Wiena** on Jl. Urip Sumoharjo, and the **Beringin Jaya** on Jl. Darmo. **Koca LCC**, Jl. Tunjungan 73-75, is also very popular as is the Indonesian restaurant **Handayani** out by Airlangga University. The **Delta**, on Jl. Sawo Tratap near the airport, is also very good. Excellent Indonesian food is served at the **Tirta Indah Garden**, Jl. Majen Sungkono 47-A.

Near The Bamboo Denn

Near the intersection of Jl. Pemuda and Jl. Pang. Sudirman are some good eating places. Take a L on Jl. Pang. Sudirman toward the city. The full a/c **Chez Rose** at no. 12 is just 350 m from the Denn; for European, Japanese, and Chinese food as well as imported beef, great pastries, etc. Next door is cheaper **Depot Banyuwangi** for *nasi pecel* and *nasi tumpeng*. **RM Panglima Sudirman**, serving Chinese food, is still there and still crowded in the evenings. You're assured good big servings for reasonable prices plus a/c, fine service, music. The **Taman Sari Indah**, Jl. Taman Apsari 5, is next to the GPO; also try the **Bibi & Baba**, Jl. Tunjungan 76. For dessert, **Cafeteria Michiko**, Jl. Pang. Sudirman 10 (nearly opposite the Surabaya Post Bldg., just 4 min. walk from the Denn) sells delicious yogurt/fruit/ice drinks, quite thick, the real thing; their food is good too.

Chinese

Kit Wan Kie, Jl. Kembang Jepun 51, offers superb Cantonese cuisine. **Agung**, Jl. Baliwerti 1, is famous for its fried pigeon and other delicacies—almost worth the price! The **Oriental**, Jl. A.I.S. Nasution 37, has great but expensive seafood; their lobster is especially tasty. A fine Chinese/Indonesian restaurant on top of the Garden Hotel next to the Bamboo Denn dishes out smallish portions of good Hong Kong-style food. The **Bima Garden**, Jl Pahwalan 8 next to the Surabaya Movie Theater, is noticeably cheaper than the Kit Wan Kie but nearly as good. Other Chinese restaurants along Jl. Pasar Besar are even more reasonably priced. Well-prepared Chinese/Indonesian *pangsit goreng* can be had at **Koca LCC** (and billiard/bar), Jl. Tunjungan 73-75.

Miscellaneous

Want to get away from *nasi?* The Bumi Hyatt's **Hugo's Restaurant** charges Rp15,000 for a European meal. But the best-for-the-price European food is found in the old Dutch restaurant, the **Delby;** superb steak and mushrooms with delicious potatoes and vegies for only Rp4700. Also very good pastry and ice cream. This fine restaurant, superior even to the Simpang and the Chez Rose, is located at Jl. Raya Darmo 145 (tel. 66641), near the zoo. High marks (and high prices) for Japanese food go to the **Gandy Steak House & Bakery**, Jl. Swatra (just down the street from Jl. Sumatra's Wisma Ganesha). The restaurant at the Mirama Hotel serves Korean and Japanese dishes.

Sweets And Drinks

The best ice cream and other goodies in Surabaya are at **Hoenkwe's**, Jl. Tunjungan 98, laid out in full Dutch colonial splendor. Also, right around the corner from the Bamboo Denn is the **Zangrandi Ice Cream Parlor** for high-quality ice cream. Another top ice cream place is **Puri Ice Cream**, Jl. Embong Trengguli (one street over from Jl. Pemuda). The **Granada Modern Bakery**, opposite the Bamboo Denn, sells Danish pastry, donuts, small cakes, pies. Surabaya also makes fantastic deep-fried treats like puffy *cemblem* (jam donuts), as well as biscuits. The oldest *jamu* shop in E. Java is on Jl. Kedung Doro; handbeaten fresh drinks served in coconut cups. Lemon drinks like *es limon, es juruk*, are a real luxury item in drier E. Java, fetching as high as Rp1000.

ENTERTAINMENT

THR

On Jl. Kusuma Bangsa, N of Gubeng Train Station. Pronounced TAY-HAH-AIR. For purely mindless entertainment, this is one of the best Taman Hiburan Rakyat parks in Indonesia and not that crowded; open daily 1800-2400. There are actually 2 parks here: the one on the L as you're facing the main entrance is the THR park, while the one to your R is the children's

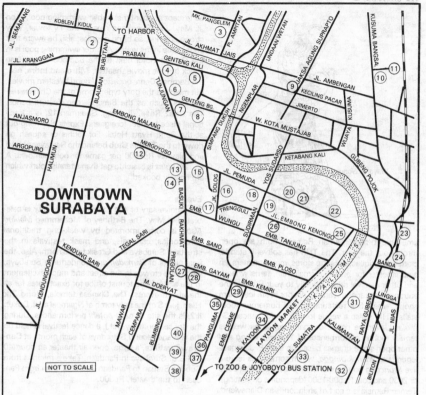

DOWNTOWN SURABAYA

NOT TO SCALE

1. Kembang Express Bus Co.
2. Wijaya Shopping Center
3. old Dutch cemetery
4. Sarinah Department Store
5. Taman Budaya
6. city buses for harbor
7. Hotel Majapahit
8. Pavilyun Hotel
9. Cafe Venezia
10. THR (People's Amusement Park)
11. Sriwedari Theatre
12. telephone office
13. city buses for harbor
14. Tanjungan Shopping Center
15. post office
16. post office (branch)
17. Joko Dolog Statue
18. Bank Negara Indonesia
19. Granada Modern Bakery
20. Bamboo Denn
21. Garden Hotel
22. Delta Plaza
23. Gubeng Train Station
24. Sahid Bhima Sakti Hotel
25. tourist office
26. Remaja Hotel
27. bus ticket offices
28. Hotel Ramayana
29. Max's Restaurant
30. Wisma Ganesha
31. Eiteha Bus Co.
32. Bon Cafe Restaurant
33. Vijaya Tour & Travel
34. telephone office
35. Hotel Elmi
36. Bouraq Office
37. Firma Faith & Co.
38. Merpati Office
39. Bank Rakyat Indonesia
40. Bumi Hyatt Hotel

Wayang Wong
dancer

amusement park, Taman Remaja. Both are open throughout the year. The THR has souvenir stands, clothes boutiques, cassette stores, movie theaters, an amphitheater for bands, a small train, ferris wheels, and other carnival rides. Directly to your R inside the entrance are various *warung*; deeper in are ice cream shops, small, fine restaurants, and numerous food-stalls. THR is also a venue for folk performances: *Sri Mulat* (Javanese comic drama), *Ludruk*, as well as regular nightly performances of *Wayang Wong* and other open-stage dramas based on such E. Javanese legends as *Menak Jinggo*, which sometimes feature live *Kroncong* pop-bands. Most shows begin at 2000 or 2030 and cost Rp500-1500 (depending on seating). Taman Remaja is a sort of an Indonesian Disneyland. Space cars float amongst trees, there's a ghost house, merry-go-rounds, popcorn, American fried chicken stands. Notice in the bumper car arena that polite Javanese kids seldom collide into each other as kids do in the West; that competitiveness and aggressiveness isn't bred in them.

Taman Budaya

Students at this Performing Arts Center can be seen in the mornings rehearsing dances like *Negremo* and *Gandrung*. Located at Jl. Geteng Kali 85, only Rp300 by *becak* from the Jl. Pemuda Tourist Office. Also bamboo *kolintang* music rehearsals, *Ketoprak*, classes in Javanese singing accompanied by *gamelan*, as well as *janur* (young coconut leaf arrangement), Chinese historical dramas, and old Javanese legends like *Aryopenangsang* and *Angreni Larung*. Tickets run Rp1000 for 2nd Class, Rp1500 for 1st Class, Rp2500 for VIP. Shows start at 2000 until 2400. Lots of snack carts outside.

Others

Pemandian Taman Tirta, an Olympic-sized, crowd-

ed (except at noontime) public swimming pool, is on Jl. May. Jen. Sungkono next to the TV tower. Very strong chlorine, so bring goggles; also be aware that people pee in the water. Another swimming pool is in the Garden Hotel next to the Bamboo Denn. Also check out the movie theaters, **Mitro** and **Indra**, near the Bamboo Denn; occasional good Western movies, but most are the gory type. Some of the Chinese restaurants, such as the Bima Garden, feature bands. The **Chez Rose**, Jl. Pang. Sudirman 12, is a traditional place to meet foreigners. Expats also hang out at the Bumi Hyatt Hotel. For tennis or squash go down to the **Tennis Club** behind the Ramayana Hotel and play for Rp2000 per game for non-members. A squash court is easier to get than a tennis court which are heavily booked.

Events

The anniversary of the founding of the city is celebrated in May. The Birthday of Mohammed *Maulud Nabi*, is commemorated by week-long traditional ceremonies, carnivals, and mask festivals in the streets of Surabaya and Gresik to the north. Also, the final nights of *Ramadan* are wonderful in Surabaya, with huge crowds in the street and much excitement in the air. Ask the tourist office for exact dates for all the above events. The Chinese temple, **Hong Tik Hian**, just S of the holy tomb of Ngampel at Jl. Dukuh II/2, is the site of daily *potehi* performances. During the dry season (May-Oct.), a dance festival is held on the first and second Saturdays of each month at **Candrawilwatikta**, a large, open-air theater an hour (40 km) S of Surabaya in Pandaan. Take a minibus from Gubeng Station to Pandaan (Rp1000), then from Pandaan to the theater, Rp300.

SHOPPING

Textiles

Surabaya is not known as a source for original *batik;* Gresik, Sidoarjo, Madura, and other coastal towns have always produced *batik* for the Surabaya market. The city is known, however, for its Chinese and Javanese tailors who can cut you a pair of made-to-measure trousers in an hour or so for only Rp6000! Visit the "Street of a Thousand Tailors" (Jl. Embong Malang); the *becak* drivers know where it is. **Batik Semar** is at Jl. Raya Gubeng 41 at Toko Metro; **Batik Keris** is in Toko Sarinah at Jl. Tunjungan 7; and **Rumah Batik Danar Hadi** (Jl. Pemuda 1) is near the Simpang Hotel. Besides these big chains, Indonesian fabrics and *batik* (as well as fine jewelry and Javanese artifacts) are displayed at **P.T. Santi Art Shop**, Jl. Sumatera 52, and **Mirota**, Jl. Sulawesi 24. At **Pasar Tunjungan Surya**, 3rd Floor (in front of Majapahit Hotel) on Jl. Tunjungan, is the place to go for East Javanese handicrafts. The government runs a show room **Dinas Perindustrian Jatim** on Jl. Kedungdoro

86-90; reasonable prices. There are crafts exhibits at least once a month at the **Balai Pemuda** (near Mitro Cinema) when stalls set up representing nearly every district of E. Java. The **GKBI** *(batik* cooperative) at Jl Kranggan 102 also shouldn't be missed. Some outstanding Indian textile shops are along Jl. Panggung and Jl. Sasak in the Arab Quarter around Mesjid Ampel.

Antiques

A whole row of small antique and curio shops lies near the Bumi Hyatt on Jl. Basuki Rachmat and along Jl. Urip Sumohardjo (5-6 tucked away). On Jl. Raya Darmo is the **Rokhim** (no. 27) and the **Whisnu** (no. 68-74). If you know what you're looking for and know how to bargain, you can still find some good buys (better values than Jakarta at any rate, mostly because Surabaya hasn't as many tourists). Good hunting also along Jl. Tunjungan; try **Sarinah** (no. 7) for paintings, silver and brassworks, etc.; and **Kundandas** (no. 97, tel. 43927), for statues, embroidery, shell handicrafts. The **Bali Art Shop**, Jl. Basuki Rachmat 143 (tel. 45933) opposite the Bumi Hyatt, has a large selection of Chinese porcelain and uncut agate. **Rais Art Shop** at no. 16 on the same street, near the Bumi Hyatt Hotel, has other unique antiques.

Tunjungan

The city's premier shopping center, Surabaya's Ginza strip. Walk down its main street Jl. Tunjungan, an extension of Jl. Basuki Rachmat, and follow the bright lights. This is a pretty colorful area which doesn't start to shut down until around 2100 or even 2200. The area is especially strong on consumer goods such as cameras, sound systems, cassette recorders, and other electronic goods. Though good prices for Indonesia, rivaling even those of Singapore, their starting prices are so high that you don't even feel like bargaining. But you can get anything here, if you're willing to pay. Tapes—hot jazz, classics, hillbilly, rock, Javanese *gamelan*, Balinese dance music—are a real bargain. Always listen to the cassette first, to hear if it's defective. Or try to get them made up on superior Maxell tapes (extra charge). Also the best of the city's bookstores are here.

Shopping Centers

In the Tunjungan District, check out the **Wijaya**, **Siola**, **Romano**, and **Aurora** shopping centers and the big art shop **Sarinah** (Jl. Tunjungan 7). Tunjungan's newest shopping center is the mammoth **Tunjungan Plaza**, Jl. Basuki Rachmat. As extravagant as anything you'll find in Dallas or Singapore, with giant, ice-cold a/c blowers (you'll freeze in a T-shirt), cylindrical glass-enclosed elevators, escalators everywhere, marble floors that you can see your face in, shops selling pieces of gold jewelry for Rp600,000. One of the largest shopping complexes in SE Asia is the 7-story **Delta Plaza** on Jl. Pemuda:

shops, supermarket, restaurants, theaters, 18 elevators, children's playground, 5 lifts—located strategically right in front of the Jl. Pemuda Tourist Info Office.

Goldsmiths

Dozens of goldsmiths are located on Jl. Baluran, walking distance from the Bamboo Denn; take the street between Jl. Tunjungan and Bank Bumi Daya. Jewelry sellers are found in the 1st Floor of the Wijaya Shopping Center and on Jl. Kapasan, and in *kampung* Gipo and Nyamplungan.

Markets

A down-to-earth black market is behind the zoo near the Terminal Joyoboyo selling shoes, jeans, T-shirts, and other cheap goods. **Pasar Keputran**, Surabaya's main night market, livens up around 1900, positively chaotic by 2300. The walk to Pasar Keputran is very enjoyable: get to the next main junction of Jl. Pemuda and Jl. Kayoon and walk one km south. As it's extremely crowded, watch for pickpockets and Surabaya's renowned watch-snatchers—who needs to tell time in this place anyway? Another big market is **Pasar Pabean**, a dirty, sprawling place in Chinatown. Worth a walk-through for the color and clamor and bustle. **Kayoon Flower Market**, along Jl. Kayoon on the banks of Kalimas River, is known as a park for strollers and lovers—guaranteed to charm your eyes. Sprouting spontaneously after flower hawkers were thrown off public roads for littering in 1960, you'll now find not only flowers here, but also a variety of tropical shrubs and trees, and fresh- and saltwater fish for home aquariums. At night this flower market turns into an open-air food hawkers market. Another Flower (and Bird) Market is near Terminal Bratang on Jl. Barat Jaya.

SERVICES

If the banks are closed (hours Mon.-Fri. 0800-1200/ 1300-1600, Sat. 0800-1300), change money at the moneychanger **Firma Fath and Co.**, Jl. Gentengkali 101. The **Central Post Office**, Jl. Kebon Rojo (next to Tugu Pahlawan), is open weekdays 0800-1600, Sat. 0800-1230, Sun. closed; several telex booths here may be rented. A branch more convenient to accommodations is located on Jl. Pemuda, just before the Joko Dolok statue. The **Telephone Office** (Kantor Telpon) is on Jl. Diponegoro on the corner of Jl. Kapuas; it offers direct dialing to all key cities in Indonesia and the world. **Kantor Imigrasi**, Jl. Kayoon 50 (tel. 472503), is only a 10-min. walk from the Gubeng Train Station. Open Mon. to Thurs. 0800-1400, Fri. 0830-1030, Sat. 0800-1200.

Information

The **E. Java Regional Tourist Information Office**

(Kantor Penerangan Pariwisata), Jl. Pemuda 118 (tel. 472503), is just up the street from the Bamboo Denn. Very helpful, get maps, brochures, and ask for their booklet *Events of E. Java.* Inquire if there are any current Madura bullraces. Check out the huge *reyog* mask from Ponorogo in this office, which is open Mon. to Thurs. 0730-1400, Fri. 0730-1100, Sat. 0730-1230, closed Sunday. Read books, magazines, and newspapers at **Perhimpunan Persahabatan Indonesia-Amerika**, Jl. Dr. Sutomo 110; lectures and films are sometimes held here, and they have a small lending library. Open Mon. to Fri. 0800-1300/ 1600-2000, Sat. 0800-1200. The **U.S. Consulate** is at Jl. Sutomo 33 (tel. 67545/68037). **UK Consulate** is at Jl. Dr. Sutomo 46 (tel. 66773), near Marmoyo Petrol Station. **Goethe Institute**, the German Cultural Center, faces the Bambu Runcing Monument, Oriental Restaurant, and the *Surabaya Post* offices. **Public libraries** are at Jl. Walikota Mustajab 68 (tel. 42707), at Jl. Pemuda 15, and at Airlangga University. Major booksellers are **Toko Buku Sari Agung**, Jl. Tunjungan 5; and **Gramedia**, Jl. Basuki Rachmat 95.

Health

At least 6 traditional medicine *(jamu)* shops are on Jl. Kedungdoro; the old Chinese lady at no. 239 really knows her stuff. For vaccinations and immunizations, or for a new International Health Certificate, go to **RS Dr. Sutomo** (Karangmenjangan), Jl. Dharmahusada 6-9, or to **Dinas Kesehatan Pelabuhan** (Health Department), Jl. Perak Timur 514-516. If you need medical help, **William Booth Hospital** is one of the best in Indonesia; it runs a reasonably priced outpatient clinic on Jl. Diponegoro, employing Western doctors and nurses (they won't take emergencies though). Pharmaceuticals are widely available; many *apotek* are around the corner where Jl. Kaliasen meets Jl. Tunjungan. A good place to have eyeglasses made or repaired are the opticians *(tukang kacamata)* along Jl. Tunjungan, Jl. Balauran, and in nearly every shopping center. A new pair of glasses costs Rp50,000-70,000 Many optometrists here speak English.

TRANSPORT

Getting There

In a sedan, Surabaya is a one-day (800 km, 12 hours) drive E of Jakarta; follow one of the well-marked routes via Yogya or Semarang. **by bus:** From Jakarta by night bus, Rp15,000, 15 hours; from Bali, Rp9000, 10 hours; from Yogya, Rp6500, 8 hours. For a/c buses, add at least Rp1000-2000 to these fares. **by air:** Flying into the city, G. Semeru glows red and the brown Kalimas River snakes below. There's a tourist information booth and an authorized moneychanger at Juanda. From Jakarta, Garuda flies a shuttle every 2 hours to Surabaya, Rp100,000 (one hour); no reser-

vations required. It's almost as easy to fly to Surabaya from Sulawesi, Kalimantan, or Maluku, as Surabaya is a major air link for the eastern islands. **by train:** One of the principal railheads of Java. If arriving by train, the Gubeng Train Station is closest to the best hotels. The *Bima* and *Mutiara* a/c express trains leave Jakarta daily in the late afternoon for the 18-hour (Rp22,500 1st Class, Rp27,000 for berths) trip to Surabaya. Make reservations at least 2 days beforehand through **Carnation Tours**, Jl. Menteng Raya 24 (tel. 344027), Jakarta. From Yogya, take the *Ekspres Siang* (Rp5000 2nd Class, Rp3800 3rd Class, 6½ hours), the *Mutiara Selatan* (Rp13,500 1st Class, Rp9000 2nd Class, 6 hours), or the *Bima* (Rp17,000 1st Class, Rp21,000 with sleeper).

Arriving By Bus

When arriving by bus at Terminal Joyoboyo, you can charter a *bemo* for Rp5000 (can bargain them down to Rp2000) to the Garden Hotel near the Bamboo Denn. But it's cheaper just to walk 200 m out to the main street (Jl. Joyoboyo) and take a public *bemo* or a *bis kota* for Rp200 which heads N to Jl. Pemuda.

Arriving By Air

Surabaya's Juanda Airport is 15 km S of town and taxis want Rp7500 to take you into the city. Alternatively, you can walk out of the terminal one km and board a *bis kota* to Jl. Pemuda (Rp200). Faster would be to hitch or take a taxi (Rp3000) to Terminal Aloha, 6½ km from the airport, then take a Patas bus (Rp250) or *bemo* (Rp200) direct to Joyoboyo Bus Station in the middle of Surabaya, Rp200. Or skip going into Surabaya altogether by getting dropped off on the road S of Aloha Terminal, then flagging down a bus (Rp1000) or minibus (Rp1500) and head straight down to Malang (though you get a better seat from Joyoboyo). Some people claim that Malang makes a better base for exploring E. Java anyway. Or you can take a bus from Terminal Aloha straight to Probolinggo (Rp1500, 2 hours) for the Mt. Bromo climb. Yet another alternative is to simply charter a taxi straight to the Trowulan ruins S of Mojokerto (Rp20,000), Malang (Rp25,000), Probolinggo (Rp79,500), or even to Denpasar on Bali (Rp160,000). A huge map is in front of the Juanda Air Terminal so you can see the relationships.

Getting Around

Very good city transport system. The main streets of Surabaya are Jl. Jen. Basuki Rachmat/Jl. Tunjungan which run roughly N to S, changing its name every km or so in order to honor all of Indonesia's heros. Car wrecks, along with warning signs, are on permanent display at major intersections. **by bemo:** Charging a flat rate of Rp200 within city limits, there's quite a good *bemo* system with routes all over the city. The Tourist Info Office on Jl. Pemuda has a complete list of *bemo* itineraries. Learn which letters—A, B, K, M,

V, etc.—go where. The 2 biggest *bemo* stations in Surabaya are at Wonokromo (near Joyoboyo, just past the zoo) and at Jembatan Merah, both accessible by "V" *bemo* from Jl. Pemuda and "M" *bemo* from Jl. Kayoon. ***bis kota:*** Also cheap are city buses which travel 3 main routes: from Aloha N to Tanjung Perak, from Jl. Demak to Kutisari, and from Wonokromo to the Jembatan Merah Station, for a flat rate of Rp200. ***becak:*** About Rp400 per km. The blue ones *(becak siang)* are for daytime use, while the white ones *(becak malam)* are for night. Ask the *becak* drivers to wend their way around the back streets, often the most fascinating way to go, as Indonesian life can seldom be seen at such close range and so anonymously. **taxis:** Unmetered taxis, charging about Rp3000/hour (min. 2 hours), are available at stands, hotels, the airport, or call the most reliable company, **Taxi Cab Surya**, Jl. Kranggan 100 (tel. 471340), which actually *uses* its meters (Rp225 per km). There's also a taxi stand at Gubeng Train Station where you can rent taxis or all species of private cars. Traffic is appalling, but ring roads, lateral highways, and even toll roads (such as one 4 km from the airport all the way to Tanjung Perak) are being built to relieve the pressure. The parking fee for cars is Rp200 but only pay if there's a ticket!

FROM SURABAYA

Intercity Buses

Surabaya has 3 main intercity bus terminals: Joyoboyo, Jembatan Merah, and Bratang; plus several others serving the peripheral areas of the city like Tanjung Perak and Aloha (6½ km from the airport). Surabaya's main bus station, Joyoboyo, is on the city's S edge near the zoo; from Jl. Pemuda take *bemo* "M" or "V" from Jl. Kayoon. From Joyoboyo (which regularly floods in the wet season), buses head S to: Mojokerto, Rp500; Madiun, Rp1685; Solo, Rp2885; Probolinggo, Rp1000; Jember, Rp2000; Bondowoso, Rp2500; Banyuwangi, Rp3235; Malang, Rp1000; Blitar, Rp1810; Kediri, Rp1335; Pare, Rp1060; Ponorogo; Rp2010. From Jembatan Merah, buses head generally to cities on Java's north coast: Gresik, Rp210; Lamongan, Rp510; Babat, Rp810; Tuban, Rp1135; Lasem, Rp1985; Rembang, Rp2135; Pati, Rp2485; Demak, Rp3035; Semarang, Rp3285. At either the Joyoboyo or Jembatan Merah stations, there's usually a row of buses with their engines running, ready to pull out. If the front bus is full, just climb on the one behind and it'll be ready to leave within minutes. **note:** An alternative to the buses are unofficial, impromptu minibus terminals around the city. For example, minibuses leave from in front of Surabaya's THR, drive along Jl. Gubeng looking for more passengers, then head right to your door in Malang for Rp1250.

For Madura

Take a *bis kota* (Rp200) from in front of Hotel Bumi Hyatt on Jl. Basuki Rachmat to the Madura Ferry Terminal at Ujung Baru in the Tanjung Perak area, then the ferry (Rp250) over to Kamal on Madura; there are also direct buses from Terminal Joyoboyo to Kamal, Rp515; Bangkalan, Rp700; Ketapang, Rp1365; Sumenep, Rp2250; Kalianget, Rp2350; Pamekasan (Rp2000).

For Mt. Bromo

To make the Bromo climb, it's Rp600 from Surabaya's Joyoboyo (in the daytime) or Bratang (at night) terminals to Pasuruan, then on to Tosari. Another approach is to take an early morning bus from Joyoboyo to Probolinggo; Rp1000 (98 km). This gets you into Probolinggo with plenty of time to spare before afternoon minibuses leave up to Ngadisari. From Probolinggo's bus station to the Mt. Bromo minibus station it's Rp300 by *becak*, then another Rp2000 by minibus up to Ngadisari.

Long-distance Buses

Terminal Bratang on the SE corner of the city is the principal express-bus terminal. From in front of Gubeng Train Station catch an "N" *bemo* S to Terminal Bratang. These express night buses are more expensive than day buses. Dozens of night bus companies have representatives at Terminal Bratang; go there in the afternoon to reserve your seat and return in the late afternoon to depart. If you get into Surabaya early and want to depart that night, buy your ticket at Bratang and leave all your luggage at the night bus company offices for the day. These long-distance buses leave almost non-stop until around 2100. VIP seating means a/c, reclining seats, toilets, snacks. Most bus companies represented at Bratang are reliable with a number of different grade buses at different prices. Recommended for Bali is Bali Cepat Co.; for the W (Yogya), Jawa Indah Co., Mirah Co.; for the N (Tuban, Semarang, Rembang), Lorena Co., Raseko Co., Continental Co.—all have good reputations. Sample fares: Jakarta, Rp19,000 VIP, Rp11,500 regular; Bandung, Rp15,000 VIP, Rp11,000 regular; Denpasar, Rp11,000 VIP, Rp10,000 regular; Semarang, Rp8000 VIP, Rp6000 regular; Yogya, Rp8000 VIP, Rp6000 regular.

By Train

Surabaya has 3 train stations: Pasar Turi serves trains which run along Java's N coast to Semarang and Cirebon, while Gubeng and Semut trains head S and SW (Malang, Yogya) and E (Banyuwangi and Denpasar). **to Banyuwangi:** Trains depart at 1000 and 2200, arriving at 1720 and 0530 respectively, Rp3500 2nd Class, Rp2800 3rd Class. **to Bandung:** The *Mutiara Selatan* departs at 1730 (Rp12,000 2nd Class, Rp17,500 1st Class), while the *Ekspres Siang* departs at 0515 (Rp6100 3rd Class, Rp8500 2nd Class). **to Jakarta:** The *GBM Selatan* (which takes the longer route via Yogya) departs at 1300, arrives at 0600, Rp7700; the *GBM Utara* departs 1745, arrives in Jakarta 0940, same price. **to Malang:** The *Katumapel* departs Gubeng Station at 0620, arrives 0850 (3 other departures); Rp1200 (but the bus is faster). **to Semarang:** The *GBM Utara* departs at 1745, arrives 2333, costs Rp4200. **to Bali:** To Denpasar the *Mutiara Timor* departs at 1000 and 2000 (Rp5900 2nd Class, Rp5200 3rd Class) from Gubeng Station. The ticket office is open 1-2 hours before. It's a 370-km, 16-hour run to the Bali Ferry Terminal at Ketapang (train fares include ferry crossing and onward bus to Denpasar). The train is more comfortable than the gruelling bus ride and it is very possibly the only train that runs *on time* in Indonesia. **to Yogya:** Three daily services: Rp2900 on the *Purbaya* and the *Argopura,* up to Rp17,000 1st Class on the *Bima* which departs at 1600. The *Purbaya* is the best (and cheapest), departing at 0815, because traveling the morning hours is cooler and you get to Yogya around 1455. The later trains for Yogya take longer and it gets very stuffy and hot on the last part of the journey; you may reach Yogya late in the afternoon in a foul mood. The best views are from the seats in the dining cars; horrendous food so buy fruit and *nasi campur* along the way. Solo is about an hour before Yogya if you want to jump off there.

By Ship

Surabaya is a major port and at least 15 ships a day take passengers to virtually all Outer Island and international ports. For Singapore or to other countries you must have clearances from *imigrasi* and the harbormaster. Tramp the docks and check around the dozens of shipping offices in Surabaya and see what they have going out. Inquire at the ticket agent **C.V. Usaha Bersama** (Jl. Pahlawan 7) near the Pelni office at Jl. Pahlawan 5. **Dwidjaya,** Jl. Slompretan 31, has ships to Balikpapan and Samarinda (Kalimantan). Also check the shipping news sections *(Berita Kapal)* in the daily *Surabaya Post* and *Jawa Post,* but the departure times are always changing. You might actually have better luck taking a smaller ship to Ujung Pandang or Kalimantan from Kaliangat on the eastern tip of Madura.

Pelni

With **Pelni's** new line of ships, it's hardly worth shopping around the other companies for inter-island travel. Their office is at Jl. Pahlawan 20 (tel. 21041) near the GPO (Jl. Rojo); from Jl. Pemuda take *bemo* "M" and get dropped off by Tugu Pahlawan. Open Mon. to Fri. 0800-1200/1300-1600, Sat. 0800-1300. Pelni has modern, comfortable ships circling the archipelago at all times: Kalimantan every 3 days; Sulawesi every week; Irian Jaya (and Maluku) every 15 days; also to Nusatenggara. Sample fares: the *Rinjani*

departs at 1800 each Thurs. for Ujung Pandang, arriving Fri. at 1800, Rp24,000 Deck Class; to Bau Bau, Rp31,500; Ambon, Rp45,500, Sorong, Rp63,500. For Nusatenggara, use the Pelni ship KM *Kelimutu* which departs Surabaya every other Tues. at 1800 for Semarang (Rp28,400 Economy) and Banjarmasin (Rp23,000 Economy). Returning to Surabaya, it then leaves for Padangbai, E. Bali (Rp16,700 Economy); Ujung Pandang (Rp21,000 Economy); Bima on Sumbawa (Rp24,000 Economy); Waingapu on Sumba (Rp42,500 Economy); Ende on Flores (Rp47,800 Economy); Kupang on Timor (Rp53,200 Economy).

Kapal Layar And Kapal Motor

While Jamrud (in Tanjung Perak) is the harbor for the bigger inter-island ships, Kalimas, just behind the port Authority Building in Tanjung Perak, is the *kapal layar* and *kapal motor* harbor which charge less than the bigger ships. Register with the harbor police (can't take photos) before entering the Kalimas area. The *syahbandar,* Jl. Kalimas Baru 194, will know of any scheduled departures. A *kapal motor* to Balikpapan, E. Kalimantan, leaves at least once weekly and takes 4 days; Ujung Pandang, at least one boat weekly; Ambon, one boat weekly.

Flights

Surabaya's airport is an important domestic air link to the whole eastern half of Indonesia and one of the busiest international airports and cargo terminals in Indonesia. It lies 15 km S of the city, Rp7500 by taxi; call **Taxi Cab Surya,** Jl. Kranggan 100 (tel. 471340) or go to Gubeng Station and hire a private car for less. Airlines offices: **Garuda,** Jl. Tunjungan 29 (tel. 44082); **Merpati,** Jl. Urip Sumoharjo 68 (tel. 406481/470568); **Mandala,** Jl. Raya Darmo 109 (tel. 66861); **Bouraq,** Jl. P. Sudirman 70-72 (tel. 46428/42383). Sample Merpati fares: Jakarta (at 1430), Rp64,300; Bandung (at 1500), Rp61,000; Yogya (at 1540), Rp31,600. Garuda's shuttle service to Jakarta (Rp88,500) leaves at 0705, 0805, 0905, etc. until 2005. Bouraq specializes in flights to Kalimantan: Banjar, Rp61,000 (once daily); Balikpapan, Rp95,000 (daily); Manado, Rp167,000 (daily). For RT tickets, 15% discount. Mandala offers a daily 0815 flight to Ujung Pandang for only Rp80,000, while Garuda flies to the same destination for Rp101,000!

Tour Agencies

Discover E. Java with one of Surabaya's 38 official tour companies; contact the head office of the **E. Java Dept. of Tourism** (Dinas Pariwisata), Jl. Darmokali 35 (tel. 65448/65449), for some recommendations. **P.T. Aneka Kartika,** Jl. Stasiun Kota Pusat Perniagaan Semut Indah, Blok D-28, tel. (031) 20981, offers a 3-hour Surabaya City Tour for 2 for US$12 pp; a 10-hour Malang and Nearby Temples Tour for 2 for US$66.70 pp, and a 5-hour Madura Bull Races Tour for 2 for US$85.20 pp. **Vaya Tours,** Jl. Pang.

Sudirman 11, near the Bamboo Denn, is another possibility. For something really different, take a cruise on a customized traditional Bugis sailing vessel (*pinisi*) to Flores, Lombok, Kalimantan, or Maluku.

P.T. Wisata Bahari Indah, Jl. Tanjung Priok 6, tel. (031) 291633/293313, has 16- to 35-day luxury *pinisi* cruises from US$295-777.

VICINITY OF SURABAYA

On the hilly northern outskirts of the city, huge factories loom up everywhere—over 3 million people live in the 20- to 30-sq km area along the Brantas River. Besides Madura, there are other islands off Surabaya. The tiny island of Bawean, N of Surabaya, is the only home for the very rare Bawean deer, a subspecies of the Indonesian *rusa*. Check out the small herds in the zoos of Jakarta and Surabaya, otherwise you'll never see them (unless you take a fishing boat from Gresik's harbor out to P. Bawean).

Beaches
Visit the beaches E of town, which are actually beachparks (Rp200 entrance), packed with people, beautifully dressed young women, *prahu* pulling right up on the beach to take people for rides. **Pantai Kenjeran** (an 8-km *bemo* ride from Jembatan Merah) is one such recreational beach, where *lis-alis* can be hired, especially on a Sunday. Not as scenic, white, or as distant as **Pasir Putih** (4 hours by bus), but you can enjoy yourself. Or take the ferry over to Madura for closer beaches, such as **Camplong**. To get down to **Puger Beach** on the S coast, get a minibus first to Gumukmas for Rp1500, then from Gumukmas to Puger it's another Rp800 by minibus.

Sidoarjo
This whole area 23 km S of Surabaya is known for its wide fishponds, mainly *bandeng*, a seafish raised in brackish water. Sidoarjo is also known for its *batik kenongo* (factory at Buduran) and fish and shrimp *krupuk petis* (congealed fish paste) processing. The biggest airport in E. Java, Lapangan Terbang Juanda, is also in this district. Every year in Sidoarjo's *alun-alun*, during birthday celebrations for the Prophet Mohammed, there is a public auction of a milk fish (*bandeng*) as big as a baby, one fish sometimes fetching as high as 6 million *rupiah*.

GRESIK

This old seaport, 25 km from Surabaya on the road to Semarang, was where the first Islamic traders from India landed and eventually overthrew Java's native Java-Hindu religion, setting up the first Islamic outpost on the island. Quite a few minibuses (Rp500) go to and from Gresik from Terminal Jembatan Merah until 2000. It'll take a long time to get from the outskirts of Gresik into the center because there's so much industry. There's an ancient cemetery 2 km S of Gresik where Muslim heros are buried; reverently interred here is one of Java's 9 early Islamic missionaries (*wali*). The town was also the first on Java to be visited by a European: the Portuguese discoverer of Maluku, Antonio d'Abreu, stopped here in 1511 and found a thriving seaport where many foreign mer-

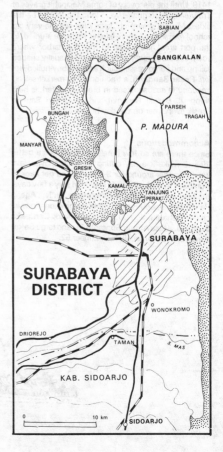

SURABAYA DISTRICT

chants had settled. With its strong Islamic traditions, Gresik survived as a sacred, tax-exempt enclave *(Desa Perdikan)* until finally subjugated by Mataram in 1680 — one of the last strongholds in northern Java to fall. In recent times, Gresik has become an important industrial estate. The biggest woodworking complex in SE Asia is here, processing the razed forests of Kalimantan; 80% of the factory's products are exported.

Sights

Wander the old **Arab Quarter's** narrow streets where women glide by in white shawls and veils. In Desa Candipuro, visit **Makam Maulana Malik Ibrahim**, the grave of one of the pioneers of Islam. His tomb and those of his wife and children are dated 1419. Until the discovery of some Majapahit graves at Trowulan, these graves were long thought to be the oldest Muslim graves on Java. Also see the very old school *(pesantren)* where Islamic texts are studied. In the port area, hire a boat to tour the harbor where you'll see some really amazing and unusually shaped sailing and cargo vessels such as the tubby-hulled *leti-leti*. **Pasar Bandeng**, a traditional fish market selling *bandeng* (a seafish raised in brackish water), is held along Jl. Basuki Rachmat and Jl. Raden Satri in Gresik every year on the day before *Idhul Fitri.*

Accommodations

Since there are so few hotels in Gresik, it's a better idea to make it a day outing from Surabaya. Have lunch, wander around for 3-4 hours, and get back to Surabaya by dark. If you *do* decide to stay a few days, the best *losmen* is **Putra Bengawan**, Jl. Ny. Ageng Penati 166; Rp6000s or d. Other accommodations include: **Bahagia**, Jl. H.O.S. Cokrominoto; **Cempaka Putih**, Jl. Jaksa Agung Suprapto 11; and large **Sekar Kedator** (16 rooms), Jl. K.H. Zubaer 52.

Crafts

A traditional *batik* center, hidden away in Gresik's back streets are many small textile cottage industries making *songket* from gold or silver thread with simple backgrounds and colorful designs of floating leaves. The quality of the weave is outstanding. Just wander through and you'll be invited to view a selection; also *sarung kembang* and raw silk are for sale. Check out Pasar Gresik along Jl. Basuki Rachmat. Gresik is also known as a center for copper implements, woven mats, and Muslim caps *(kopiah* and *songkok).*

Giri

Just 2 km S of town in Giri is **Makam Sunan Giri**, the grave of one of the most famous of Java's *wali.* Get a minibus from Terminal Gresik (Rp200) to Giri, then walk. This revered hill, which draws pilgrims from all over Java, is guarded by 2 Hindu mythological creatures. Many steps lead up to the bathing place of the *wali*, men who (it is said) were able to fly and work miracles. The mystic saint's shrine is appointed with fine lace, Persian tapestries, and Chinese carvings. A yearly religious festival, *Khol Sunan Giri*, commemorates the death of Sunan Giri; at this time the "flying jacket" is brought out: if you wear it, you can fly. Makam Panjang, another holy Islamic gravesite in Manyar, 8 km NW of Gresik, is known for its unusual mix of Buddhist and Islamic elements.

Vicinity Of Gresik

For centuries Gresik has been noteworthy for its production of salt; in the hot season see the salt pans being worked along the road S to Surabaya. Among the most impoverished groups in Indonesia are the fishermen who eke out an existence along the fished-out shores of northern Java, where fish are contaminated by the Gresik petrochemical industry. Java's longest and biggest river, the Bengawan Solo, disembogues in the district around this town. In other words, this area is one of Java's main sewerpipes.

Kerapan Sapi

MADURA

One of Indonesia's undiscovered gems, this large rugged island (160 km long by 30 km at its widest) lies off the NE coast of Java across a narrow strait from Surabaya. This beautiful but arid island is usually included in the statistics of E. Java, and is one of the poorest parts of the province. Yet it is blessed with numerous fine white-sand beaches, unpeopled countryside, inexpensive and uncrowded *losmen,* and unique cuisine. Although only 30 min. from Surabaya by ferry, Madura is almost totally free of tourists. As a traveler, you may be surrounded by hundreds of people at one time. You could spend a week here and not see another Westerner. The best day to visit Madura is Sunday, market day. Madura is famous for 3 things: its women, its salt, and its bullraces. Some of the best stockbreeders in Indonesia live here and these crowded farmers' festivals, held frequently in special arenas all over the island, attract visitors from around the world. note: Madura is worth more than just a day trip out of Surabaya and the only way to really see the island is to travel from Kamal on the highway which runs all around the coast. The direction of travel in our coverage is from Kamal-Sampang-Pamekasan-Sotabar-Ambunten-Ketapang-Arasbaya-Bangkalan-Kamal.

The Land
Madura belongs geographically and geologically to E. Java; the strait between the 2 islands flooded over only during the last ice age. Madura is a generally flat, dry island of treeless, infertile, rocky limestone slopes. The coast around Ambunten in the N has high dunes and strong waves; the island's lovely southern beaches are more suitable for small children. There are rambling fruit gardens and endless tobacco estates.

Bougainvillea bushes overhang the roads and brighten lanes, fishing villages stretch along the whole southern coastline, and the island's cemeteries with their mossy gravestones and craggy trees are the best haunted graveyards in Indonesia—excellent horror movie sets.

Economy
Central to Madura's economy are salt, tobacco, cattle, fishing, poultry, and goats. Since the days when the Dutch colonial government held a monopoly on salt, Madura has produced much of Indonesia's domestic supply of the product—its arid climate is perfect for it. Tides wash in the seawater where the salt collects and evaporates in marsh pools, notably at Manbakor and around Kalianget. Madura is still a center for the spice trade, and superb *jamu* are made here. In contrast to the volcanic plains of Java, Madura's permeable soil does not lend itself to rice cultivation. With its large areas of grassland, however, the island is ideally suited to animal husbandry. Cattle exporting is big business with some 1,600 studbulls bred a year for export to Java and overseas. Immaculately groomed cattle with long eyelashes and sheeny brown coats are driven along the roads in braces of four. One of the purposes of the frequent bullraces is to find the best bulls in order to improve the stock.

The rest of Madura is arable land covered in tobacco; in the Pakong area the hills are painstakingly irrigated by hand. High-quality papery Madurese tobacco, wrapped in cured banana leaf, costs only Rp1000 per kilo. There are also a few pineapple plantations, patches of *pohon ketela* (cassava plants) are everywhere, and in the NE portion *talas* (taro) is grown. The Madurese are one of Indonesia's most active seafaring peoples; their cargo boats take whole forests of timber out of Sumatra. In the fishing villages along the S coast such as Tanjung, double-outrigger canoes equipped with huge triangular sails are used.

The People

Cut off from the mainland, the Madurese are more traditional than the Javanese. Glimpse a bygone rural life, extinct in many other parts of Java. The younger Madurese wear the *peci* but the older ones still tend to wear the *destar* (headcovering). Even though tens of thousands of Madurese have moved to Java, they still retain their own distinct language. The Madurese relish their reputation for tenacity—a people of independent spirit. They are also well known for their energy, thrift, and hot-temperedness. The men are black-moustachioed with high cheekbones and narrow faces; the mere sight of one is enough to strike fear in the hearts of effete Surabayans. They are thought to all carry knives and practice a mystic form of *pencak silat* which has no sporting application; it's used only in seriousness—to kill. This hardly seems likely, though, as the peasants are ultra-cool, even aloof. The women of the island are small and dark with very fine features. They walk with a sensual grace, carrying most everything on their heads in enamel wash basins or trays. Madurese women are renowned all over Indonesia for a special style of movement and massage during lovemaking, called *goyang madura*.

Crafts

Madurese craftsmen were inspired by Chinese and European imports, and the island is perhaps best known for its fine beds, screens, chests, and cupboards. Also look for *tempet kue*, 3-legged bamboo containers used to store cakes; buy one in the morning *pasar*, Rp1200. Unusual, pre-Malayan pottery is made at **Sodar** in the mountains NW of Sumenep. Basketry and other articles are woven in **Satubaru** near the N coast. Madura's *batik* uses rich, bold *mengkudu* red, red-brown, or indigo coloring, incorporating vigorous winged *naga*-snakes, crocodiles, sharks, airborne horses with fish tails, and other strange animal representations associated with the ocean. Visit the *batik*-making center, **Tanjung Bumi**, about 5 km from Bangkalan. In **Telaga Biru**, a shipbuilding village (pop. 2,500) 15 km W of Ketapang, women draw *batik* designs on cotton cloth loomed at home; their husbands sell the pieces on their sea voyages. Fantastically gnarled, lucky seaweed (black coral) bracelets are also fashioned on Madura. Worn to ward off sickness, it's said these amulets can actually cure rheumatism.

Food

Conditions are not conducive to cultivating rice so corn (introduced by the Portuguese in 1625) has replaced that grain as a staple in Madurese cuisine. Don't miss the island's *perkedel jagung*, or corn-and-shrimp fritters. The best *salak* grow here, and a whole basket of 20 *jambu* (guava) costs only Rp200 in season. Try the regional beverage, the nutritious *la'ang*. *Blaken*, a fish paste used in *nasi goreng*, *sambal*, and sauce for *gado-gado*, costs Rp1500; comes in old handmade jars of rough glass. Madura's chicken and other kinds of *sate*, as well as *soto madura* (a rich, spicy soup) are famous and prepared all over Indonesia. For sweets, yam taffy is made from a pulverized tuber; Rp500 for packets or Rp25 apiece.

TRANSPORT

Getting There

From Tanjung Perak, Surabaya's port, it's only 30 min. by ferry (passenger, Rp250; cars, Rp1500) across the narrow strait to the harbor town of Kamal on the SW tip of Madura. The ferry leaves every half hour from 0630 to 2000. Also, several LSTs make continuous but unscheduled trips from a nearby dock; ask directions. On the ferry itself you might meet a minibus driver who will invite you to climb aboard for the ride from Kamal to Pamekasan (100 km, 2 hours, Rp1400) or Sumenep (160 km). You can also board a bus from Surabaya's Joyoboyo Bus Station from 0700 till dusk for Pamekasan (Rp2000), Bangkalan (Rp700), Kalianget (Rp2400), and other towns. Or you can take a bus from Joyoboyo as far as Kamal (Rp515), and from there catch a minibus, *oplet*, or hire a taxi. An alternative approach is from Panarukan, W of Situbondo; ferries leave daily at 1300 (Rp1200, 4 hours) for Kalianget in eastern Madura, returning to Panarukan at 0700 the next day. *Bemo* leave Kalianget for Sumenep (11 km) from where you can take buses to all over the island. Flights are also possible from Surabaya's airport to the Trunojoyo Airstrip near Sumenep. Returning, the first ferry leaves Kamal for Surabaya at 0530, the last at 1650. These ferries don't operate at low tide so don't miss the last one. **note:** If you're heading to Madura during bullrace season in your own vehicle, be sure to make car ferry reservations the day before and be at the ferry no less than 30 min. before departure time.

Getting Around

The island's transportation system is outstanding; minibuses travel to practically everywhere on the island worth going to, and there's even a train which departs Kamal each day for Pamekasan (a slow 6 hours). Careening *oplet* or *bemo* crammed with people run frequently along the main highway that encircles the island. For example, it's a 2-hour *bemo* trip from Kamal to Pamekasan, 100 km E, with nice scenery along the way. Probably the best way to really see Madura is to rent a motorcycle in Surabaya and take it

MADURA ISLAND

Map of Madura Island showing towns including Tanjungbumi, Sepulu, Arasbaya, Air Mata, Bangkalan, Kamal, Tanahmerah, Baliga, Kwanyar, Modeng, Sereseh, Durenbarat, Telaga Baru, Ketapang, Robatal, Pagantenan, Torjun, Sampang, Camplong, Tanjung, Padelegan, Pamekasan, Sokabana, Sotabar, Waru, Pakong, Gulukguluk, Talang, Prenduan, Bungbungan, Pasongsongan, Ambunten, Dasuk, Sumenep, Kalianget, Panggulan, Sergong, Bulutimur, Lombang, Dungket. Scale 0–20 km.

across. The roads have very few cars, so hitchhiking can be slow. Since Madura is such a poor island, *becak* rides are quite cheap—if you bargain. It's possible to catch freighters from Kalianget back to Bangkalan or Sampang or even to Kalimantan and Sulawesi (with *syahbandar* clearance).

KERAPAN SAPI RACES

Like a scene out of *Ben Hur*, these thrilling, high-speed spectacles of sleek racing bulls take place 2 Sundays each month at Bangkalan's stadium, usually coinciding with the arrival of tourist cruise ships. The word *kerapan* stems from an old Madurese word "to work the soil." The idea to race bulls caught on from racing plowing teams. The island's small, sturdy breed of cattle is descended from the wild *banteng* that once roamed freely over all of western Indonesia. Only the strongest, handsomest bulls are chosen for competition. For details on where and when upcoming races will be held, contact one of the E. Java Tourist offices in Surabaya (either Jl. Pemuda 18 or Jl. Darmokali 35).

Provincial Races
The first rounds are small, friendly village events *(Kerapan Desa)*, with no requirements as to the size, color, and strength of the bulls or the skill of the handlers. Next are the subdistrict races, usually held under government supervision. The winner takes part in the district races and that winner becomes eligible for the more important regency races *(Kerapan Kabupaten)*, sponsored by the government after harvest time. The first heats usually begin in April, the runoffs in May, the finals in late October.

Kerapan Besar
This is the grand finale, the all-Madura championship race held at the end of the dry season (Oct.) in the stadium at Pamekasan. The championship cup is

sometimes handed over by President Suharto himself. During the week prior to *Kerapan Besar*, traditional games, ceremonies, parades of decorated bulls, *gamelan* orchestras, and night bazaars take place in all the towns. Each day the bulls are given herbs, raw eggs (as many as 50 a day), honey, even beer. The night before the big race, cattle-raisers sing their best bulls to sleep. The next morning the champions are bathed, brushed, and tenderly massaged. At race time the bulls are decorated with gilt and tinsel leather bibs, flower-tassled horn sheaths, silver-studded head harnesses, and bells which jangle from the high, enameled yokes that couple the 2 bulls of each team. Thus adorned, the teams are paraded through the town under ceremonial parasols to the accompaniment of drums, gongs, flutes, and bells before the rostrums filled with wild spectators. Dances accompanied by Madurese *gamelan* are often performed before the races.

The Race
Held on a grassy straightaway 120 m long, 24 pairs of racing bulls are matched up, their ornaments stripped off, and the beasts lined up with their brightly dressed jockeys. Each is given a generous tote of *arak* from a bamboo tube, then *gamelan* music is played to excite the bulls. The 3-man judging panel takes its place. Dead silence before the race begins. The bulls look heavy and awkward, but watch. The starter drops his flag and the teams lunge forward, the riders straddling skids slung between the yoked bulls, the rear of the skids dragging along the ground. Jockeys prod and flog the animals mercilessly with thorns and spiked rods. With snorting nostrils and mud flying, the bulls look determined to trample over the crowd. They can cover 100 m in 9 seconds flat (about 45 km/h), faster than the world's human track record. The winners' front legs, not noses or heads, must cross the finish line first. The triumphant teams are raced again with each other and the losers also race, so in the end there will be 2 winners—the winner of

the winners and the winner of the losers. The winning teams then parade around the stadium. That night, the bulls are rubbed down and soothed with quiet *gamelan*. The owners of the fastest bulls are held in high esteem in their villages, the respect of the community considered more of a reward than the prizes received. Later, the bulls with the finest performances are used as stud.

PAMEKASAN

Even though it's Madura's capital, Pamekasan (100 km E of Kamal) is a slow-moving city with relatively few cars, just motorcycles, *becak*, pedestrians, cyclists. Very easygoing, quiet, undeveloped. The town center is lined with casuarina trees. Getting around Pamekasan is easy as the *becak* rides are cheaper than you'll find in even rural areas of Java. These guys bust their ass carrying 2 people, with packs, for Rp500 from the downtown area to the bus station, or to any of the hotels from the bus station, Rp300. *Bemo* also cruise Pamekasan's main streets. The *Kerapan Sapi* are held in a field about one km from city center.

Accommodations And Food

Hotel Garuda, on Jl. Mesigit 1 (tel. 81589), is a large complex opposite the town park—about the best for your money, very central, near the shopping district, theaters, and eating places; Rp4500 s, Rp8000 d, up to Rp15,000 with *mandi*. **Losmen Bahagia**, Jl. Trunojoyo 47, is Chinese-run, the rooms are stuffy, the security is a bit weak, the bathrooms dirty; in short, it's the worst but cheapest in town at Rp3500 s, Rp6000 d. A Chinese restaurant, **Depot Bahagia**, is attached. **Hotel Trunojoyo** (tel. 81181) is on a small *gang* off Jl. Trunojoyo; from Rp5000 s (including breakfast) up to Rp18,000 for a/c rooms with *mandi*. The **Government Guest House** is on the S coast (between Sampang and Pamekasan) on a nice shallow beach. Eat in the numerous *rumah makan* surrounding Pamekasan's *alun-alun*.

Crafts

Textiles are quite reasonable here: a 2.5-m piece of Madurese fabric bought in Pamekasan for Rp15,000 sells for up to Rp100,000 in Jakarta. For special Madurese-style *batik*, an Arabian family, Keluarga Muhammed, on Jl. T.H. Agus Salim 16A, has a wide selection, from Rp6000 *sarung* and *kain* to the more expensive Rp15,000 *(prisma)*. For rocking chairs *(kursi goyang)*, go to Jl. Segara 10. The village of Kardulak is a center for Madurese arts and crafts, from furniture to toy sailboats.

From Pamekasan

By bus or *bemo* to Omben, 20 km; Pagantenan, 16 km; Palengaan, 15 km; Pakong, 21 km (near Pakong at Pujung there's a beautiful panorama); Kalianget, 65 km; Kamal, 112 km; Bangkalan, 94 km; Sampang, 31 km. It's Rp1000 by minibus over the mountains right up the center of the island to Temberu, then it costs another Rp1000 by minibus from Temberu to Arasbaya (80 km). Another route leads up the center to Sotabar, where it intersects the N coast road; from this village it's 51 km to Sumenep and 23 km to Ambunten. Facial features and physiques of the people in the central region are quite distinct from those of the island's coastal peoples, with more of a Mongoloid appearance, slanting eyes, high cheekbones, slender bony frames, knotty hands—a mountain folk. Virtually every male wears the traditional *peci*. On the Pakong side of the central mountains area, forests are more numerous than on the Pamekasan side. On the road N from Pamekasan to Sotabar, stop at Puncak (or Poncu), the highest point on the island, where tobacco fields seem to stretch to the horizon. At night see clearly the thousands of lights of Pamekasan and the lamps the fishermen use for night fishing along the S coast.

Vicinity Of Pamekasan

The "Eternal Fire" *(Api Abadi)* is W of the city on the road to Kamal. Located in a natural gas field, fire spouts out of the earth. Legend has it that it comes from the mouth of a giant, sentenced thus by the gods. Turn in at the sign: TAK KUNJUNG PADAM, meaning "it will never go out." The site lies 800 m from the highway, surrounded by a metal fence. Try to see it on a moonlit night. Rain or dirt can put the fire out but it can be lit again immediately. You could even cook *sate* over it. This is the "male" one; about one km from here toward the city is the "female" one. Other gas vents in the vicinity burst into flames when lit. The tomb of Pangeran Jimat and other old graves are in a cemetery near Kalpajung Laur, N of Pamekasan. On the way E to Sumenep, stop at the lively country market at **Prenduan**.

Sampang

On the way from Kamal to Pamekasan you pass through this coastal town from where you can catch a *bemo* N to Ketapang. From Ketapang, your options are to go around the NW coast via Arasbaya or turn E and approach Sumenep from the N via Ambunten, avoiding Pamekasan altogether. In Sampang, stay at **Losmen Setia**, Jl. Iman Bonjol 63; or **Puri Trunojoyo**, Jl. K.H. Wakhid Hasyim. Both of these hotels may be full. **Gua Lebar** is an extensive cave complex with stalagmites and stalactites on top of a mountain near Sampang. Pleasant swimming and sunbathing at **Camplong**, with its long row of casuarinas and views of E. Java's volcanos across the Madura Strait. Rent a rowing outrigger or sampan from fishermen (Rp3000-4000 per hour) to see the reef.

SUMENEP

Compared to Sumenep, Pamekasan is like Surabaya. Sumenep, 53 km NE of Pamekasan, is sleepy, rural, almost a village, but definitely a more interesting place to base yourself after dull Pamekasan. It has more history, it's more remote and traditional. In the 13th C., Sumenep was an established regency of the Singosari Kingdom; its first governor was crowned by King Kertanegara himself. This makes Sumenep the oldest *kabupaten* on Madura, and one of the oldest in Indonesia. Sumenep derives a large share of its revenues from fruit, tobacco, and salt (salt-panning factories at nearby Kalianget). Bullraces are held at Sumenep's Giling Stadium; catch a local meet on this 750-m track, usually from 0900-1300 each Saturday.

Sights

The *alun-alun* is in the center of town, surrounded by the *kraton*, main mosque, government buildings, and markets. The 18th C. mosque, **Mesjid Jamik**, is the religious center for the people of Sumenep who are nearly 100% Islamic. It has a Javanese Hindu-style gate, 3-tiered Balinese-style *meru* roof, and is very cool inside. The *juru kunci* isn't pushy about asking for donations. Excellent morning market nearby. See the old columned houses which look like Roman funerary temples, and visit the great *pasar pagi* near the mosque.

Although very old, the condition of **Kraton Sumenep** is excellent. A remnant of Majapahit-style architecture, the royal compound is completely surrounded by a high white masonry wall. The *pendopo*, with carved pillars, dates back to 1763. The structure is filled with ancient *pusaka* and artifacts, and a fortune in 19th C. Dutch brass lamps in all sizes and shapes (converted now to take electricity). Ask to visit the mysterious Islamic praying room, the *Kamar Tempat Ibadah*, inside the *kraton*. *Gambu* and *Dalang Topeng* dances are occasionally held on the porch of the palace. A pool and well-kept flower garden area (Taman Sari) with benches, canopied rotunda — perfect for relaxing — is off to the side. Also inside the complex is the museum which contains precious old mementos, heirlooms, and artifacts: Chinese porcelain and earthenware, weapons, sculptures, old *wayang kulit* and *wayang golek*, *lontar* manuscripts, and other memorabilia. Donation: Rp300. The Royal Carriage House, formerly a garage for the raja's coaches is opposite the *kraton*. It houses a magnificent 300-year-old Chinese marriage bed and the throne of Queen Tirtonegoro.

Accommodations

Chinese-run **Hotel Wijaya I**, Jl. Trunojoyo 45-47 (tel. 233), is near the *stasiun bis* on the S side of the highway. Has all the conveniences, kitchen, clean bathrooms. At Rp8000 s, Rp12,000 d, this is a good deal considering all you get. A little kiosk sells cookies, snacks, *krupuk*, cigarettes, and their restaurant serves good cheap food. **Hotel Wijaya II** is nearby, charging about the same. Centrally located **Losmen Damai**, Jl. Jen. Sudirman 39, is an old Dutch-style hotel on one of the main streets with reasonable prices. **Losmen Matahari**, just down the street from Losmen Damai at Jl. Jen. Sudirman 42, is another possibility, but these 2 hotels might be "closed" to Westerners.

Food

Generally quite cheap. **RM 17 Augustus** on Jl. Diponegoro (5 min. walk from the *alun-alun*) serves delicious *ayam* dishes, tasty *nasi goreng*, *nasi campur*, and good drinks — a popular place at night. Other restaurants in Sumenep: **RM Mojo** also on Jl. Diponegoro, **RM Sederhana**, **Candra Restaurant**, **Osaka Restaurant**, and the **Wijaya Restaurant** in Hotel Wijaya. The best Chinese food is probably at the **Mawar**, Jl. Diponegoro 47A. The original *soto madura*, a rich, coconut milk soup found all over Indonesia, can't be had in the restaurants but only on the street. A group of eating stalls opens in the evening N of the *alun-alun*, selling *soto madura* and *sate*. The **Nasi Burung**, on Jl. Trunojoyo next to Station PIKNJ in front of Jiwita, is a breakfast place which the locals rate highly.

Crafts

Mustika Kempang, Jl. Trunojoyo 78, specializes in Maduurese-style *batik*. Delftware, old Chinese pottery, furniture, *kris*, and all manner of antique jewelry, is on display at the **A. Ba'bud Shop**, Jl. A. Yani; run by an Arab who specializes in *batik*. Eddy, the proprietor of RM 17 Augustus, sells old Madurese *batik* and *wayang topeng* masks.

From Sumenep

The *terminal bis* for W-bound (including Surabaya) buses is on the S edge of town, while minibuses for easterly destinations depart from the terminal near the Giling Stadium (only a Rp300 *becak* ride from the *alun-alun*). To Ambunten by *bemo*, Rp500. From Sumenep's Terminal Bis, it's Rp2250 by bus to Surabaya, or Rp1000 by minibus to Pamekasan (54 km). Or take a direct minibus from Sumenep to Surabaya through **Travel & Pikat Kilat**, Jl. Jen. Sudirman 43; Rp3000, departing at 0400. To reach Arasbaya in the W part of the island, allow plenty of time because the stretch of road in the NW is really rough. To Panarukan, E. Java, ferries depart Sumenep's port of Kalianget at 0700 each day (4 hours passage).

Vicinity Of Sumenep

The royal graves, **Asta Tinggi**, are only 2 km W of Sumenep. Once a resthouse for the rajas and queens of Sumenep, the main building was constructed in the 17th century. Here on a hilltop is where the sultan and his ancestors are interred. Sumenep's export harbor of **Kalianget**, 10 km SE of town, is not very deep as it has silted up over the centuries. Ships must anchor 11 km from the landing and people are ferried in by launch. There's also a salt factory here. At **Batang Batang**, located on a highway which rises into the mountains, is a superb view over the Sumenep area; the road is difficult to negotiate by taxi, car or *bemo*, so drive the 25-30 km on a motorcycle. On the N coast are the glistening white sands of **Dasuk** between the seacoast towns of Ambunten (20 N of Sumenep) and Sergong. **Lombang**, on the island's far NE coast, has one of the most scenic and isolated beaches on Madura; get a minibus from Sumenep's terminal minibus (Rp600 in all).

Offshore Islands

Catch a *kapal motor* from Kalianget to **P. Sapudi** off the E end of Madura. This pretty island is well known for its superior cattle, both for beef and as competitors in the bullraces. Visit the picturesque fishing village of **Tlaga** on the N coast, 18 km from Gayam. Far to the E of Sumenep, but still included in the Regency of Sumenep, is **P. Kangean** which is known for a bird species, *ayam bekisar,* and for its beautiful panoramas. Coral reefs encircle the whole island; visit the **Mamburit** sea gardens and natural aquarium. Get to P. Kangean by ship once weekly from Kalianget harbor; Rp5000-6000, 12 hours.

THE NORTH COAST

Madura's northern road, Jl. Udara, is more picturesque than the southern road. In the N, agriculture, not fishing, is the principal cash earner; farmland comes right up to within 3-4 m of the sea. The earth is redder than on the S coast, and here you start seeing banyan trees, cactus, rubbly volcanic rock, dense coconut groves, rolling dunes, sandy yellow beaches, with more vegetation and varied crops. The trees lining the road *(pohon asam)* bear sour berries used in cooking *galok, rojak,* and other sour-tasting dishes. Around **Arasbaya** in the NW corner are cornfields and haystacks. The N coast is more isolated and underpopulated than the S; the people of this region have retained more of their traditional customs and gained less benefit from government: one out of every ten kids seems to have a bad eye. You'll see more oxcarts and *dokar,* and few hotels. The women all wear colorful traditional *sarung kebaya* and turbans. In fact, it's like being in another century up here, difficult to grasp that this N coast area is only a few short hours from Surabaya. **Pasongsongan** and **Pasean** are small fishing villages with rows of *prahu,* dazzling beaches and sandhills to slide and run down.

Slopeng Beach

At Slopeng, 20 km (Rp600, 30 min. by *bemo)* N of Sumenep near Ambunten, are giant dunes, Gunung Pasir ("mountains of sand") that stretch for 3 km. Along this coastline grow graceful fan palm trees *(pohon siwalan).* The reefs go out much farther than those on the southern coasts; ask a fisherman to take you out in his uniquely carved *prahu.* You can see the reefs' turquoise water, and the blue of the ocean beyond. No hotels in Slopeng, only a decrepit little whorehouse on the W part of the beach, called the "special place" *(tempat istimewa).* By *bemo* from Slopeng to Ambunten, Rp400.

Ambunten

A large, traditional Madurese fishing village 13 km NE of Sumenep and an excellent day outing from Sumenep, costing about Rp1000 RT. The people are extremely friendly—too friendly; it's another Pied Piper scene with hundreds of kids following you all the way to the sea. Boats are packed together in a sheltered bay, with the fishermen working on them and mending sails. Occasionally, thunderous bullraces are held under the coconut trees out of town. There's no *penginapan;* some travelers have reported sleeping on the beach down the coast a bit with a sleeping bag and tent. One of the most beautiful spots on the whole island is the rolling yellow dunes here. The big salt factory is the only one of its kind in Indonesia. As it is such an important fishing center, get *prahu* rides to all over from Ambunten (to Kalianget for only Rp2500).

Ketapang

Fifty km from Ambunten and 28 km W of Sotabar by the northern road. Just before crossing the bridge into town on the L-hand side is a rocky graveyard. The cemeteries of Madura, with their small Islamic tombstones blackened with age and rain, seem to always be located between the tobacco fields and the house. Legions of dead inhabit this island! Just after the bridge a road leads 3 km to a waterfall. At Ketapang's minibus station is a little *warung* serving fruit and drinks. A *pasanggrahan* here charges Rp4000 d; you'll probably be the first Westerner for weeks who has stayed there.

AIR MATA

The oldest and most beautiful cemetery on Madura is located on a hill in the NW of the island near Arasbaya, only 11 km NE of Bangkalan or 27 km N of

Kamal. Its name means "Water of the Eye," or tears. Coming from Ketapang, right after the bridge when you first enter Arasbaya, take a L-hand turn. The minibus driver will drop you off here, or might turn in. About 2 km down the road is an intersection where you board another minibus which takes you to a little *desa* called Tampegan. If you get into Tampegan in the morning, there are *dokar* for people going to the market; they will take you down to Air Mata for Rp300. But walking is recommended. About ½ km from Tampegan is the entrance: see the sign AIR MATA and a long staircase leading up to another walkway lined with a chorus of chirping beggars. Within the actual burial compound, you'll be stunned by the vast complex of very old graves. There's one group of graves of family and relatives of the Cakraningrat royal line. Ask the *juru kunci* to show you the involved genealogical chart showing the connection between Mataram's rulers buried at Imogiri in C. Java and those royal personages resting at Air Mata. All of Sultan Agung's crowd are on the chart. You can easily spend an hour at Air Mata, worth the entrance fee for the peacefulness alone. Leave a donation.

Gunungan Ratu Ibu

The *piece de resistance* of this complex, the grave in the back of the cemetery on the highest terrace, is that of Ratu Ibu (1546-1569), a descendant of Sunan Giri, the great E. Javanese saint. Knockout view over a cultivated river valley; you can see why this spot has been chosen as a holy burial place. This 16th C. gravesite was consecrated at a time when the doctrines of Islam were just gaining strength and influence. Though it was prohibited by Islam to depict the human face or body or even animals, you can see how the carvers got around this. They couldn't resist the temptation to embellish their carving, so living forms are represented within very stylistic flower motifs. Ratu Ibu's family is buried to either side of her.

BANGKALAN

Bangkalan surrounds the usual *alun-alun* of stately old jacaranda trees. At one end of the *alun-alun* the *becak* drivers gather, and opposite Pasar Bangkalan is the minibus station and a line of shops. The bullracing arena is one km from downtown; a tall white wall surrounds the stadium and *sawah* grows to all sides. From Bangkalan, it's 18 km and Rp450 by minibus to Kamal, then Rp250 from the ferry depot to Surabaya. It costs Rp2000 by *bemo* to Sumenep, and to Pamekasan Rp1500.

Accommodations And Food

Since most domestic and foreign tourists only come over to Bangkalan as package tourists for racing day, there's a scarcity of accommodations. **Losmen Purnama**, Jl. Karinino 12 (right off Jl. Kartini opposite Bioskop Purnama), is the town's only *losmen*. It's set back from the street, about 20 m from Jl. Kartini. Its 12 rooms are plain and dark, but pretty good security. There's also a government guesthouse near the *lapangan* where rooms are available if not occupied, but forget it if it's during *Kerapan Sapi Besar* or when the tourist ships are in port. This *pasanggrahan* caters mostly to government personnel. In front of Losmen Purnama is a small *warung* serving *nasi goreng*. Down the street are small, cheap Madurese *warung* serving all kinds of *nasi* dishes. Opposite the *pasar* building in the minibus and *bemo* station is **RM Manalagi**, Jl. A. Yani 5, specializing in *soto madura* and *nasi krengsengan*, a *kambing* dish in a rich sauce. Many other *warung* can be found near Pasar Bangkalan, such as **Warung Amboina** at the end of the Terminal Minibus beyond the roundabout; reasonable prices and giant *krupuk*.

cakap-cakap

THE TENGGER HIGHLANDS

A mountain people with almost Tibetan features, numbering 300,000, who live in some 40 villages ranging from 1,500 m to 2,745 m elevation around G. Bromo. Their highlands comprise a rich variety of spectacular countryside. Speaking an archaic dialect of Javanese, the Tengger (or Tenggerese) of these volcanic slopes are esteemed by other Javanese as intelligent, unquarrelsome, hard-working, possessing high moral values and a history of opposition to foreign influences. Guests are invited deep inside Tengger houses next to the hearths because traditionally visitors must be kept warm to combat the cold outside. Tengger brick hearths burn perpetually to warm the kitchens and dry the vegetables which hang from the rafters. Food crops include onions, leeks, potatoes, carrots, maize, cabbage, and cauliflower, which are distributed all over E. Java. Vegetables are grown in expertly cultivated gardens on the steep mountain slopes which surround every village in these highlands. Rivaling even the Baguio ricefield builders of the Philippines, these climbing terraces are amazing feats of engineering.

Religion

When armed conflict broke out between the rebellious Islamicized coastal districts and the Majapahit Empire of E. Java at the end of the 1300s, the nobles, priests, and artisans fled to Bali, but the ordinary people withdrew to the Tengger Highlands to keep their Hindu faith. Today, the Tengger are the only people in all of E. Java who practice the Hindu religion openly. The Tenggerese call their religion Buddha Mahayana, though their belief system is more a mixture of Buddhism and Hinduism. The Tengger don't believe in reincarnation, but their caste system and calendar are similar to those of the Balinese. Although they have their own priests, there are no temples; an altar is maintained in each home instead. A communal place of worship, usually located on a hill overlooking the village, consists of a smooth, flat rock or a neatly fenced area of one or two large overhanging trees, sometimes strewn with flowers and crowded with people uttering prayers and performing other religious duties. The Bromo crater has also been, since Majapahit times, a Tengger center for the worship of Brahma.

GUNUNG BROMO

A convenient stop for travelers between Bali and Surabaya, and the most popular of all of E. Java's travel destinations, this active 2,392-m-high volcano lies 112 km (3 hours) SE of Surabaya. The caldera is like a vast, arid amphitheater measuring 10 km from N to S, enclosed by perpendicular walls 350 m high. This awesome, 2,200-m-high "sand sea" has 3 mountains within it: Widodaren (Bride), Batok (Cup), and Bromo (Fire), which are really craters within one huge crater—the Bromo-Semeru Massif. There are also 3 small crater lakes inside the larger crater, with waterfowl and excellent hiking. The ideal time to visit is in the dry season (April-Nov.) when you have a better chance of seeing a blood-red sunrise; in the wet season, you might as well sleep late and stroll across the sand sea during the warmer part of the day, after the heavy fog has blown away. The temperature on top of Bromo is around 5 degrees C; in July it could drop to zero, so dress warmly. Also, 3 times a year the site is overrun by tourists: in Feb. when an annual festival takes place; over Christmas; and during July and August. So plan your visit for another time if you don't like crowds. From Bromo's peak are stunning views of active G. Semeru, Java's highest mountain. Although Bromo can still vent steam and ash, smoke profusely, and occasionally boom from the central crater, lava has not been ejected in historical times.

The Legends

The whole crater is said to have been dug out by an ogre with a half a coconut shell in a single night to win the hand of a princess. When the king feared the ogre would succeed, he ordered all his servants to pound rice, at which time the cocks started crowing, thinking that dawn had broken. The ogre couldn't finish the job and died of grief and exhaustion. Inside Widodaren in the Bromo crater complex are buried the legendary ancestors of the Tengger, Roro Ateng (wife) and Joko Seger (husband). They were childless and prayed to the gods for offspring, vowing to sacrifice one of their children to the gods if their prayers were granted. The couple went on to produce 25 children, but never lived up to their end of the bargain. Joko Seger was finally reminded of his debt when pestilence and death swept through the village, claiming many lives. Finally, the sacred couple had to take their last child, Kusuma, into the sand sea to appease the gods. Immediately, a volcano erupted and G. Bromo was born. Roro Ateng and Joko Seger still live in a cave on Widodaren, Gua Adam, where the Tenggerese go to say their prayers and are granted wishes. The name "Tengger" is said to derive from the last syllables of their names—AnTENG and SeGER.

Kasada Festival

Also called the "Karo Feast," this a Tenggerese All

Souls' Day and a New Year's feast combined. It's held in the Bromo crater once a year, at midnight, on the 14th day of *Kasada*, the 12th month of the Teng- gerese year (usually in Feb.—the Surabaya Tourist Of- fice will know the exact date). The folk origin of this annual ceremony to commemorate deceased ances- tors and relatives (see "The Legends" above) goes back to Majapahit times. Offerings are carried, some on bamboo poles, by thousands of worshippers who hold oil torches and climb to the top of G. Bromo by foot and horseback. Hundreds of people at a time perch all along the razor-thin edge over roaring jets of steam 200 m below. Those who wish to ask special favors of the Bromo fire god bow their heads in front of their village priest and make their wishes known to him. The priest then utters a prayer, and the people throw their offerings of paddy, fruits, flowers, and vegetables into the crater. Local villagers also sacrifice goats and chickens. There's a fantastic air of unreality, like a Black Mass, until the sun comes up, dispelling the magic and fear.

GETTING TO G. BROMO

SURABAYA (93 km from PROBOLINGGO, 30 km from PASARUAN)

PASURUAN — TONGAS — PROBOLINGGO

TO BALI AND BANYUWANGI (195 km)

41 km   27 km   31 km

TOSARI   SUKAPURA

15 km   14 km

PENANJAKAN   3 km   NGADISARI

CEMORO LAWANG

G. BATOK

TO MALANG

G. BROMO   4 km

SURABAYA - PROBOLINGGO	98 km
SURABAYA - MALANG	89 km
SURABAYA - BANYUWANGI	245 km

Getting There

From Surabaya's Joyoboyo Bus Station board a bus or minibus 2½-3 hours (Rp1000, 93 km) to Probol- inggo. Leave Surabaya early, so you can make it to Ngadisari, below Bromo, the same day. From Probol- inggo to Ngadisari it costs Rp1000 by minibus, 2 hours, leaving every hour or so until 1900. On your way from Probolinggo to Ngadisari, you might have to change buses at Sukapura. The turnoff to Ngadi- sari is 4 km W of Probolinggo on the main highway between Surabaya and Banyuwangi. In the dry sea- son (April-Nov.), this road is passable all the way to Ngadisari. In the rainy season, you might only get as far as Sukapura and have to continue on vegetable trucks which come through at around 1500. Dis- tances: Probolinggo to Sukapura, 31 km; Sukapura to Ngadisari, 14 km; Ngadisari to Cemoro Lawang, 3 km; Cemoro Lawang to Bromo Crater, 4 km. From Ngadi-

sari to Cemoro Lawang, walk or take a horse (Rp5000) either the day before or start out very early on the morning of your climb. Prefer to hitch? Stand at the Ngadisari turnoff 4 km W of Probolinggo, or at another turnoff at Tongas, 12 km from Probolinggo, and travel up a tree-lined road of acacia forests to Sukapura.

Sukapura

The first big Tengger town from Probolinggo. With good views and a bracing climate, this is a more com- fortable and scenic place to stay than Probolinggo or Ngadisari. Try to find a *bemo* or minibus at least up to Sukapura the same day you arrive in Probolinggo. Stay in the only guesthouse in Sukapura—a grand and spacious establishment for such a little town! There's a big lounge/dining room area with a number of tables and chairs, a nice place to sit, read and relax. Big rooms cost only Rp3000 with 2 large double beds. Across the road there's a small *rumah makan* with reasonable, tasty meals. **from Sukapura:** Watch the sun come up early in the morning, have breakfast, then head up to Ngadisari. Hitch a ride on a vegetable truck or with a tourist, or hassle the minibus drivers down to the proper fare. Minibuses run up to Ngadisari fairly frequently from 0600 on, but on this steep 14-km stretch drivers aren't very enthused about making it as the evening wears on unless they have a full load.

Ngadisari

A friendly mountain village of shiny tin roofs, fish- ponds, and misty mornings. Flies can be bad. Visitors must report to the helpful *Pos Hansip* (village homeguard) who will charge Rp200 to get into the Bromo crater, will ask you to sign the visitors' book, and if it's late they'll suggest a place to stay. If you get into Ngadisari early enough (2 hours before darkness), continue the final steep 3-km (one-hour) ascent up to Cemoro Lawang or Lawang Sair on the crater's rim where you can also find accommodation. If you stay the night in Ngadisari, early the next morning walk up to Cemoro Lawang. It's also possible to arrange the night before for a horse from Ngadisari to the Bromo crater, Rp3000-4000. **from Ngadisari:** Minibuses head down to Probolinggo (via Sukapura) starting around 0600 but they don't leave until they fit in a record-breaking 21 people! A booking office in Ngadi- sari gets you on a bus leaving Probolinggo for Bali at 0830, arriving in Denpasar by 2130 that night. The supposedly a/c bus is so stuffed with people you can hardly breathe, but shows a movie en route, and at least you only have to shift your luggage once.

Accommodations And Food

Stay with villagers whose homes cluster around Nga- disari's town square, a whole row of quite modern, well-constructed, bungalow-type houses with Rp2500-5000 s or d rooms. Several nameless *losmen* offer 4-5 rooms just big enough to hold a bed each—like sleeping in a cupboard with a 10-watt lightbulb, definitely for one night only! Bargain vigorously! Watch for theft. Several *warung* serve coffee and *nasi goreng*—reasonable food but not wonderful. Spend a warm evening in the kitchen practicing your Indonesian with the family. After climbing G. Bromo, get back down to Ngadisari again around 0700 for breakfast (tea and buns are often included in the price of your room).

Cemoro Lawang

Three km higher than Ngadisari and only an hour's walk from G. Bromo. The road up is now cobblestoned but you'll still need good shoes. From Cemoro Lawang, it's only a 20-min. descent down into the crater. **Motel Bromo Permai**, just 30 m from the crater's edge, is similar to a youth hostel, but for all classes and ages. Cozy gatherings at night in the restaurant. Since there's nowhere else you can go, they charge inflated prices. Some dark, tiny, and dingy rooms facing the crater go as high as Rp8500, quite decrepit with dirty *mandi* water and odorous kero lamps. Their "upgraded" rooms go for Rp11,500, with cockroaches scampering across white sheets as you open the door. The situation is worse during the tourist season when rooms are often full or else all reserved. They'll still take your money, though, and put you in the staff's or kitchen-boys' quarters. The only alternative is to pitch a tent on the edge of the crater, or if you have a warm sleeping bag, sleep outside. In the village of Lawang Sair 100 m or so below the motel, rooms are also available; these villagers offer you lower prices than the motel and will even kick their kids out of their rooms to make room for you. A *warung* here has very reasonable prices and excellent food like fresh, delicious *pisang goreng* for only Rp100 each.

The Climb

No matter how much you've heard about it, you won't be prepared for this ethereal, unforgettable spectacle. Bromo—which looks like a hollowed-out shell of a decayed molar—is actually 3 craters within one vast crater. The ascent to the Bromo crater from Cemoro Lawang takes about 2 hours by foot or 1 ½ hours by horseback. For the sunrise, walk down the wall of the big crater so as to arrive on Bromo's narrow rim by daybreak. Take a flashlight. For this early morning hike, the best thing against the cold is a blanket borrowed from the motel. They'll wake you up at 0300; you'll hear all the commotion and the horses whinnying outside. Although guides can be arranged in Ngadisari, it's really easy to walk to Bromo without one by just falling in behind the tourists. It costs about Rp3000 RT to hire a guide and a horse rents for Rp5000; book your horse the night or day before. Under clear skies sparkling with stars, with the wind whistling, follow the guides and the sure-

footed pack horses across the crater floor straight up through the corridor of white-painted rocks which lead between Cemoro Lawang and G. Bromo. Stay behind the person with the torch or you may fall into a steep ditch. By the time you've crossed the lava plain and started up G. Bromo, it will have started to get light. At the top of a rise you'll see a steep 256-step concrete staircase up to the rim. It's possible to walk all the way around the rim (one hour), but it's precarious in places and very dusty, like fine flour. If you've got a real crazy streak in you, climb right down inside Bromo's crater—but if you fall into its maw, that's *it*. Travel light—this is a hard, cold, and dusty climb. Volcanic dust is very fine and will really do a job on your camera, getting inside the lens, causing damage, and making it difficult to focus. **note:** If you don't feel like taking the walk early in the morning, some consider that the sunrise from the motel is even more sweeping. Sit on the bench and take it in while drinking your coffee.

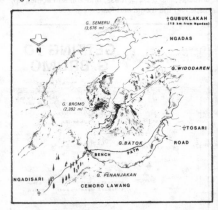

Gunung Batok

Another extinct volcano, G. Batok, sits behind Bromo, ridged from top to base like a giant lemon squeezer, as if somebody just took a giant knife and scarred lines up and down it. You can walk around G. Batok also, and if you feel really energetic you can climb it, which is just as rewarding a climb as Bromo. From the top see G. Semeru shooting up clouds of gas every 15 minutes. It's difficult to find the path, though, which is only visible during daylight.

OTHER APPROACHES

From Tosari

Another approach to G. Bromo is from the W via Tosari—a unique way to go. First take a bus from Pasuruan to Tosari. Tosari is 41 km from the main highway connecting Malang and Surabaya, and 19 km from Bromo. Pasuruan's minibus stop is a *becak* ride across town from the bus stop. Minibuses leave infrequently from Pasuruan to Tosari, so you might have to wait until one fills up—about once an hour. Once above the flatlands, the road is very steep, curvy, and narrow. The small hill resort of Tosari extends along a hillside. The main part of town by the market is a really nice area with terraces, pretty homes, guesthouses, and vegetable gardens. There's a stairway up to the market from where the minibus stops. About 5 m beyond that stairway is a house on the L where travelers stay for Rp3500 s. The walk from Tosari to the rim of the crater takes about 2 hours; it's not at all steep going this way. Do it in the early morning when the sun is not high enough to hit you in the face and you'll still be underneath the cool shade of the trees. If you start from Tosari at around 0300 or 0400, you can catch the sunrise over Bromo. You could also hire a horse, Rp5000, or catch a ride. From Bromo's rim, take the road along the rim all the way to Cemoro Lawang (see map), or zig-zag down the face of the crater where the track turns to undulating waves of sand. Your horse could become skittish on entering the caldera.

From Malang/Ngadas

Only to be attempted in the dry season; in the wet, dangerous mudslides block roads and could sweep you away. If up early enough, get a minibus or *bemo* from Malang to Tumpang, then another *bemo* to Gubuklakah (12 km). From Gubuklakah a very steep 16-km-long road leads up to Ngadas. One hell of a hill! The Tengger village of Ngadas is is built upon a great slope; this *desa* sees hardly any Western visitors at all. Incredible views of G. Semeru and all over the valley from here. Stay with one of the villagers; the *kepala desa* can arrange accommodations. From Ngadas it's about 3 km (30 min.) uphill to the crater lip. The track then branches S to G. Semeru, then over to Ngadisari, about a 3½-hour (15 km) steady walk. Or it takes about 3 hours in all to walk from Ngadas to G. Bromo, quite an ordeal but really worthwhile. This 15-km track is easy to follow through the grasslands around the S and E parts of the crater. Rows of stones mark the shortest path across the sands at the E end. (For maximum effect, however, it's more dramatic to cross the crater E to W, rather than W to east.) Gradually the vegetation disappears as you enter the great sand sea. You might fall in behind Tengger carrying bananas or produce on horseback all the way across the crater from Ngadas to Ngadisari.

PASIR PUTIH

The principal resort on E. Java's N coast, 175 km E of Surabaya on the road to Bali. Minibuses and *bemo* run from Probolinggo (Rp1000), or take a bus direct from Surabaya's Joyoboyo Station or from Banyuwangi (Rp2000, 4½ hours). Pasir Putih has a fine beach with surf, graceful painted outriggers lined up on shore, a few coconut palms, and easily accessible coral sea gardens. Admission: Rp200. Although the name means "white beach," the sand is really dark gray, but clean. This is a favorite beach resort for Indonesian families, offering shallow and calm swimming (ideal for children). Go during the week to avoid the crowds; on weekends it's elbow to elbow with tourists from Surabaya and Malang. A souvenir market has many stalls and restaurants, and occasional pigeon or chicken races. Swim and sunbathe, or negotiate a *prahu* out to the reef and dive. In the tourist season, boatmen will ask Rp10,000-15,000 for *prahu*-hire to the reef and back, but in the off-season you can get them as low as Rp6000 per hour for up to 5 persons. When you get ready to head for Bali, just go out on the road to Banyuwangi and flag down a minibus.

Accommodations And Food

A dozen hotels and guesthouses, of varying prices, lie between the highway and the sea. Could be a lot of noise from the road (overnight buses) and from hotel generators. Accommodations want Rp9000 to Rp12,000, though you may find a few as low as Rp5000. One of the cheapest is the **Sidho Muncul** (tel. 2273, Panarukan) on the E end; Rp4500 s, Rp8000 d. Check out also the **Wisma Bhayangkara**, Rp4000 for tight double rooms facing the highway; other more expensive rooms facing the beach. **Pasir Putih Inn**, the large complex near the restaurant on the W end, charges Rp6500 s for a room on the beach. Other rooms are Rp5000 d, without breakfast. The brothel in the hotel just up the road from Pasir Putih Inn towards Surabaya hires rooms on an hourly basis. Attached to the Pasir Putih Inn is a Westernized restaurant serving average-priced meals, its menu written in English and Indonesian. Some hotels feature charcoal-broiled fish, but the best seafood of all is available in the several beach *warung*. Also well-stocked fruit stands.

THE BONDOWOSO AREA

Situbondo

About 194 km from Surabaya. On the main street is **Hotel Asia**, Rp3500 d. **Losmen Baru**, on the Pasir Putih side of town charges only Rp2500; across the road is **Losmen Mustika**. Also try **Losmen Sarworini** near the *stasiun kereta api*— all reasonably priced. **vicinity of:** Prajikan, 12 km S of Situbondo or 24 km N of Bondowoso, is a pilgrimage spot—the holy grave of Kiai Emas Atmari. Kayumanis is a plantation area (coffee and apples) 29 km from Situbondo; before Asembagus, turn R and travel 14 km.

Bondowoso
Coffee plantations are found all over the valley floor surrounding Bondowoso, 196 km SE of Surabaya. Bondowoso and **Situbondo** are both renowned for their bullfighting contests (bull against bull). *Aduan Sapi,* the run-off for the winning bulls, is a popular annual event of the district. For months, sets of bulls are pitted against each other in separate heats, fighting their way up to regional *kecamatan* level, *kabupaten* level, then to "residency" level championships. You might catch one; inquire at Bondowoso's Kantor Kabupaten. Also visit the big livestock market at **Wonosari** where cattle, sheep, and goats are haggled over; in the *pasar* a wide range of traditional farming implements are for sale. The Bondowoso area is also known for its numerous ancient stone sarcophagi *(sacraphaag* in Indonesian). **Sumberwringin** is a cool resort in the foothills of the sulphurous, mountainous Yang Plateau.

Nusa Barung
An uninhabited island 12 km off Puger on the S coast of Java, which has been designated a nature reserve. The collection of edible swiftlet nests in cliffs on the wind-hammered southern shore, and of green turtle eggs on the island's beaches, are concessions granted by the local government. The structure of this 6,000 ha island is limestone which forms handsome undercut sea cliffs on the N side; crevices in the rocks are full of crabs, limpets, and snails. Along this same coast, egrets and blue and white reef herons are commonly seen. Small, deep bays at the NW end make good anchorages where local fishermen from Puger often shelter overnight. Hitch a ride with them, though their fishing schedules are erratic. Camp on the sandy beaches, but watch the sandflies. Allow at least 2 days to explore the island.

PROBOLINGGO

On the N coast of E. Java, Rp1000 (2½ hours) from Surabaya's Joyoboyo Bus Station, Rp2500 (6 hours) by bus from Banyuwangi, or Rp1000 (2 hours) by bus from Malang. Besides being famous for its mangos *(arun manis)* and grapes, and the starting point for the climb to G. Bromo, Probolinggo has few other charms. Beware of some thieving *becak* drivers at the railway station, and Probolinggo also known for its obnoxiously persistent crowds of gawkers, hecklers, and harassers who attack more quickly than flies on feces the moment you step off the bus.

Accommodations And Food
Most hotels are on the main road on the Bromo end of town. **Hotel Victoria,** at the crossroads of Jl. Pang. Sudirman and Jl. Suroyo 1-3, is the nicest hotel for the money. Rooms run from Rp3500-Rp17,000 (with *mandi* and a/c; its restaurant serves Chinese and Indonesian food, and it's close to the minibus station. Victoria is on the highway to either Banyuwangi or Surabaya, so you can flag down a bus in front. **Hotel Kemayoran,** Jl. Pang. Sudirman 75 (Rp3500 s, Rp6000 d), is above the restaurant of the same name, very convenient; on the other side of the street is a good Chinese restaurant. Also recommended, at Jl. Pang. Sudirman 94 (only Rp400 by *becak* from the bus station), is **Hotel Ratna**; Rp8500 d—quiet, central, comfortable beds, real furniture, TV, big fan, shower, flush toilet, big breakfast, good service. Inex-

pensive **Hotel Bromo Permai II** is opposite the bus station—an excellent source of info on Bromo. Many good *rumah makan* are found along Jl. Pang. Sudir-

man and there's a *pasar malam* near the minibus station. **RM Malang**, Jl. Sudirman 104, is just up the street from Hotel Victoria. Several cheap *warung* are in the back of the *terminal bis*, and **RM Sudi Mampir** is a competent eatery nearby.

From Probolinggo
The minibus station is only a 5-min. walk (300 m W) of the bus station. By bus to Pasir Putih, Rp1000; Banyuwangi, Rp2500 (5 hours). To Yogya, *bis malam* start running at 2000; Rp8500, 8½ hours. **to Mt. Bromo:** Minibuses to Ngadisari (via Sukapura) on Mt. Bromo's rim cost Rp1000 (1½-2 hours) and leave at least every hour from 0700 to 1900. Probolinggo to Ngadisari is 41 km; Ngadisari to Mt. Bromo is 7 km.

for Bali: No problem. From the bus terminal in the eastern end of town, catch buses all the way to Bali for Rp6500. Buses depart every hour from 1900 to 2300; arriving in Denpasar around 0300-0400. The best is an expensive (Rp8500, 8 hours) express night bus that leaves Probolinggo at 1900. Also see the manager at Hotel Bromo Permai II (opposite the bus station) for express minibuses to Denpasar for Rp6500, leaving at around 2100 (min. 5 persons). **by train:** The train station is 2½ km from Hotel Bromo Permai II. To Surabaya, Rp2000 3rd Class; Rp2800 2nd Class. To Banyuwangi, Rp2200 3rd Class. To Denpasar, Rp2800 3rd Class (although bus travel is faster). Ask about student discounts on trains (up to 35% off!).

BANYUWANGI

Not quite 300 km (10 hours by bus) from Surabaya on the far E coast of Java. Banyuwangi means "nice fragrance." Known as the "Kota Jajag" (from the verb *mejalaja*, which means "to traverse, to explore"), this is the jumping-off point for Bali and the eastern islands beyond. The ferry terminal to and from Bali is at Ketapang, 8 km north. See Banyuwangi's elegant mosque, **Mesjid Baiturrachman,** and the city's **Taman Sritanjung,** a botanical garden containing 35 kinds of tropical plants (open 0700-1800)—both are downtown. For exotic textiles, visit the fabric shops on Jl. Suit Ubun—like an Indian bazaar! The **THR** amusement park is the most cacophonous you've ever experienced: take your average THR, then double it! Not very good for relaxation or food either. Get there by *becak* or walk ½ km from Hotel Banyuwangi past some old Dutch warehouses along the seawall, cross over a bridge, and there it is.

Accommodations And Food
Over 30 *losmen* and hotels. One of the nicest, safest, and cheapest places, usually quiet but often full, is **Wisma Blambangan,** Jl. Dr. Wahidin 3 (tel. 21598), opposite one corner of the public square; Rp3500-9500 s and d. Next door **Hotel Banyuwangi,** Jl. Dr. Wahidin 10 (tel. 41178), offers expensive a/c rooms with private bath. Both Hotel Blambangan and Banyuwangi face the town *lapangan*. **Hotel AA** (only Rp3000 s), is 2 doors down from Hotel Blambangan, across the street from the post office, and near the mosque; Rp3000 d—but a lot of mosquitos and cockroaches. **Hotel Berlin Barat,** Jl. Pattimura 50 (tel. 21323), is dirty and noisy and their 20 rooms surround a courtyard where buses and trucks are repaired. In-

teresting neighborhood, though—Banyuwangi's Chinatown. Very popular with travelers, **Hotel Baru,** Jl. Pattimura 82-84 (tel. 21369), has 42 spacious, airy rooms going for Rp3500 s, Rp6000 d. **Hotel Selamat,** Jl. K.H.W. Hasyim 96 (tel. 41359); Rp3500 s, Rp3500 d. The best thing about this hotel is that the train station is only 100 m away. **Hotel Bhakti,** Jl. Jen. Sudirman 117 (tel. 21129); Rp3500 s, Rp6000 d. Clean, only about 100 m from the *mesjid*, and good value. **Hotel Manyar,** just one km S of Ketapang ferry (Jl. Situbondo, tel. 41741), is plush but too pricey; conveniently located though if you're traveling to Bali the next morning.

Eat at the *pasar malam* on Jl. Pattimura at night: *sate gule, kaldu, soto madura* and *kambing* dishes. Packed with Indonesians at dinner time. A *soto madura* place is next door. Opposite Hotel Baru, **Warung Baru** serves cheap good food. Near Hotel Selamat is **Depot Aida** (with a Coca Cola sign in front), and **RM Selamat,** a *bakso* joint.

Services
The **Tourist Office,** Jl. Diponegoro 2 (tel. 41761), is near hotels Blambangan and Banyuwangi, almost opposite Kantor Telpon and Kantor Pos. See these people for not only information, a map, and leaflets, but for booking any hotel in the area, and for arranging tours, chartered vehicles, etc. To get into the Baluran Park, the surfing area of Blambangan, or to any other government reserve area in E. Java, get your permit first at Banyuwangi's **PPA Office,** Jl. A. Yani 108 (tel. 41119). Bring a xerox copy of the front pages of your passport and Indonesian entry stamp. If you're in a

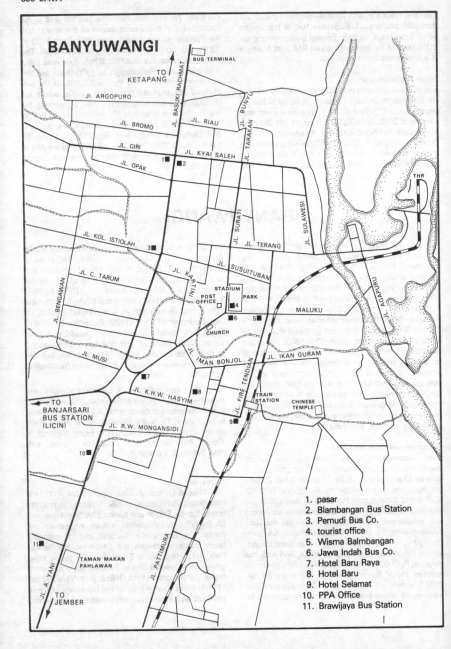

BANYUWANGI

TO
KETAPANG

BUS TERMINAL

JL. ARGOPURO

JL. BROMO   JL. RIAU

JL. BASUKI RACHMAT

JL. BUNYU

JL. GIRI   JL. KYAI SALEH

JL. OPAK   1■ ■2

JL. TARAKAN

JL. SURATI

JL. SULAWESI

THR

JL. KOL. ISTIQLAH   3■   JL. TERANG

JL. C. TARUM

JL. BENGAWAN

JL. KARTINI

JL. SUSUITUBAN

POST
OFFICE

STADIUM
PARK   ■4

MALUKU

■6   ■5

CHURCH

JL. MUSI

JL. IMAN BONJOL

JL. FIRE TENDIAN

JL. IKAN GURAM

JL. AGAPURU

7■

8■

JL. K.H.W. HASYIM

TRAIN
STATION

CHINESE
TEMPLE

TO
BANJARSARI
BUS STATION
(LICIN)

9■

JL. R.W. MONGANSIDI

10■

11■

TAMAN MAKAN
PAHLAWAN

JL. A. YANI

JL. PATTIMURA

TO
JEMBER

1. pasar
2. Blambangan Bus Station
3. Pemudi Bus Co.
4. tourist office
5. Wisma Balmbangan
6. Jawa Indah Bus Co.
7. Hotel Baru Raya
8. Hotel Baru
9. Hotel Selamat
10. PPA Office
11. Brawijaya Bus Station

group, only the group leader must have a *surat ijin.* Open Mon.-Thurs. 0700 to 1400, Fri. until 1200, Sat. until 1300.

Getting There

The only consistently dependable road follows the N coast from Surabaya, but during the dry season, experience rural E. Java by cutting S at Probolinggo and travel on small country roads via Jember or Besuki. This is a longer (375 km vs. 300 km) and slower, yet more attractive route. By train from Surabaya, the *Mutiara Timor* arrives in Banyuwangi at 0545. Another fast train arrives here from Yogya at 1910. When arriving at Banyuwangi's train station, don't hire a *bemo* to the hotels. Just walk; it's only about 600 m, for example, to Hotel Banyuwangi.

From Banyuwangi

The city's has 3 bus stations. **Terminal Brawijaya,** in the southern outskirts, has buses to points S such as Rogojampi, Muncar, Grajagan (Blambangan Peninsula), and Sukamade Beach in the Meru Betiri Reserve. A different way to get to Surabaya is via the plantation district of Jember, Rp1000 and 2 hours by bus from Banyuwangi, then board another bus to Surabaya for another Rp2000. From Terminal Banjarsari, take minibuses (Rp400) up to Licin on the slopes of the Ijen Plateau. **Terminal Blambangan** is N of town on the road to Ketapang (the ferry port to Bali). From here you take minibuses to Ketapang (Rp400), Kaliklatak (Rp850), Baluran (Rp750, 30 min.), Pasir Putih (Rp1000, 2 hours), Probolinggo (Rp2500, 4 hours), and Surabaya (Rp3000, 8 hours). Catch *bis malam* also from this station; for example, to Surabaya (Rp5000), leaving around 2100 and arriving 0300; to Malang (Rp8500, 8 hours). Reliable nightbus companies are Pemudi, Jl. Kapten Ilyas 6; and Jawah Indah, Jl. Dr. Sutomo 86.

If you're heading for Bali, catch ferries from Ketapang, 8 km N and Rp400 by minibus from town. The first ferry terminal you come to from Banyuwangi is the cheaper one; Rp300 by LCMs. The other, main terminal is farther down the road. Ferries cross to Gilimanuk (port on Bali side) 12 times a day; Rp400, 30 minutes, then it's 3 more hours by bus from Gilimanuk to Denpasar. Car and passenger ferries cross frequently until 2100. If you have your own vehicle, waiting in line, loading and unloading takes about 2 hours, Rp1500. Motorbikes, Rp750. If you're alone and miss the regular ferry, walk down the beach 250 m to the LCM depot and catch one of the converted WW II landing crafts which leave for Bali quite often until 2000.

Kaliklatak

This government agricultural co-op in high-altitude Kaliklatak, 20 km NW of Banyuwangi, grows such crops as coffee, cacao, rubber, citrus, cloves, and

marakisah, on the slopes of G. Merapi. Accessible by *bemo* or bus from Banyuwangi's *terminal bis.* Stay as a paying guest of the plantation in nice bungalows. **Wisata Irdjen** (tel. 323/41896), no a/c, has a restaurant; Rp9500 s or d. Take a free tour of the rubber and coffee processing plants which ready the crops for export.

BALURAN

The entrance to this 250-sq-km reserve in the NE corner of Java is at Batangan, just N of Wonorejo, 37 km N of Banyuwangi. The park headquarters at Bekol is 12 km from the main Surabaya-Banyuwangi coastal road. A reserve since Dutch times, created as a national park only in 1980, Baluran is one of Indonesia's most accessible game reserves. Little-known Baluran is unusual for Java in that it encompasses a mountainous area which gives way to open forests and scrubland to white-sand beaches washed by the Bali Straits. Baluran has coastal marshes, open rolling savannah, swampy groves, crab-eating monkeys, and grasslands with huge wild oxen. For Java, the game-watching conditions are unique. This is Java's one bit of Africa. Baluran even has poachers at the height of the dry season!

The Land

The whole park is dominated by the towering volcanic cone of G. Baluran (1,247 m). Though not as high as most E. Javan mountains, G. Baluran's solitary mound occupies the whole NE corner of Java. Park lands completely surround the cone and the open-sided crater, and are themselves bound on 3 sides by the sea. The NE corner of Java is exceptionally dry with little rain between April and October. Thus the N side of Baluran has extensive savannah grasslands threaded by stone-bedded streams *(curah)* which dry out completely May to October. In such open land, *rusa, banteng,* and feral buffalos graze. South and W of G. Baluran the monsoon forest is largely secondary, but splendid for birdwatchers. Nearly all species typical of such dry monsoon forests are found here; peafowl are particularly common. The park's western boundary has been encroached on by teak and turi plantations.

Preparations

Wear good shoes, bring food, binoculars, and a flashlight for viewing the animals at night. The time to see wildlife is at dawn or dusk during the drier months (April-Oct.), when the herds move to the waterholes. Just sit in the watchtower and observe; let the game come to you. When there's plenty of water (in the beginnning of July, for example), you have to go out to look for the animals. In the wet season bring a mosquito net; in the dry season the usually bloodthirsty mosquitos aren't as bad. **permit:** Either get your per-

wild rusa, Baluran

mit at the PPA (Pengawas Pelindungan Alam) Kepala Seksi in Banyuwangi (Jl. A Yani 108, tel. 41119), or at the PPA Office in Wonorejo, only 2 km from the main road which bounds the reserve. At the Banyuwangi PPA office, they hand out a sketch map of the park and you're able to book accommodation. The forestry officer in Wonorejo, the only one there who speaks English, will have you fill out some forms and issue you a permit for Rp2000.

Sights

Baluran is the best place on Java to see the widest variety of wild animals. With its high grasses, flat-topped acacias, dried-out water courses, and herds of animals grazing peacefully, this reserve is strikingly similar to the famous game parks of East Africa. Climb up through the mahogany and teakwood forests or tramp across the open grasslands bordering the Madura Strait. You can get as close as 50 m to herds of wild buffalos. These ponderous, mud-caked *banteng,* the bulls with black and white markings and their female consorts a golden brown, can be found in herds of 20 or more. There are also wild dogs, deer (groups of 30 or more are common), leopards, civet cats, squirrels, fruit bats, macaques, some leaf monkeys in the upland forests, and monitor lizards. See wild pigs thunder across savannahs of acacia trees, and a plethora of birds such as green jungle fowl *(ayam hutan),* prancing peacocks *(burung merak),* drongos, kingfishers, and peafowl which often roost in the low trees near the guesthouse at Bekol. It's not wise to get out of the jeep or off well-trodden tracks.

The guesthouse sits on a little raised area; behind it there's a hill with a path 500 m up to an old game observation tower (9 m high) which looks out over the plains. There's a telescope for viewing the animals. To the R is G. Baluran, with swamp forests and open savannah all around, cleared to create a grazing area for the *banteng* (wild oxen). It's a real joy to watch the sun rise and set from this tower.

From Bekol take the 2.5-km-long path through the savannah to the beach at Kelor. If driving, it's accessible only by 4-WD and only in the dry season. Though not a very pleasant beach and unsuitable for swimming, its marine environment boasts crab-eating macaques (who can swim) and a shore nursery of milkfish *(nener).* The small guesthouse here, **Bamma Guesthouse,** has no electricity, just gaslights; it might be all locked up so book in advance at the PPA office in Banyuwangi. At low tide the beach turns to mudflats which stretch for 400-500 m out to sea, a long way to go from the shore through the slush to the water, down a very gradual slope. This shoreline is generally broken and rocky, interspersed with small coves and mangroves where fishermen construct pond traps. East Javanese fishermen have traditionally visited this coastline. The spawning grounds for milkfish lie between Baluran and Madura and in season the shallow waters are thick with them. Whales and dolphins can sometimes be seen out in the Madura Strait.

Accommodations And Food

There's a campground near the entrance to the park. At the foot of the hill in Bekol is a comfortable, modest *pasanggrahan* belonging to the PPA (Forest Service); capacity 10 persons. It's best to make prior arrangements to stay here (Rp4000) through the PPA office either in Banyuwangi (Jl. A Yani 108, tel. 41119) or in Wonorejo. No electricity, just lamps and candles. This *pasanggrahan* is well run, and the staff friendly. There's a guard at all times, so your gear is safe. In the early morning you'll be awakened by the strident calls of nearby peafowl and jungle fowl. There's plenty of water, and cooking facilities, but no meals available. The guys who work at the park don't like to sell you food because they don't have that much for themselves. Some *warung* near the park entrance sell a take-away *nasi campur* in banana leaves. Better to buy fruit, tins of European-type food, and bread in Wonorejo so you can stay a few days and keep yourself fairly well nourished.

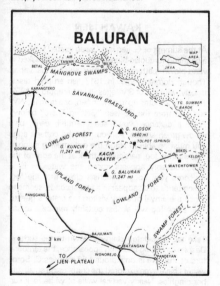

Getting There

Just 5 hours (Rp2500) and 264 km by bus from Surabaya on the road to Banyuwangi, and only about 18 km N of the Java-Bali ferry crossing at Ketapang (Rp600 by *bemo*), the entrance to Baluran is quite easy to reach. You may also take a bus from the Joyoboyo Station in Surabaya to Situbondo (4-5 hours), then a minibus to Batangan, the entrance to the park just before Wonorejo. Report to the guardpost, open 0700-1700. Mr. Sukri might lead you into the park; be sure to tip him. These forestry people might want to see your passport just for drill or out of curiosity. It's possible to stash your heavy luggage safely at the guardpost for 1-3 days. You don't need a guide; just head down the all-weather dirt road which leads from the S into the reserve. It's 12 km to the guesthouse in the center of the park, where there's a watchtower and a water reservoir. Carry water in—it could get really hot. The road is hard going because it's rocky, thus tiring on your feet and ankles. Supplies have to be trucked in but traffic is scarce and you'd be lucky to hitch a ride (for a price). Don't count on it. Once at Bekol, expect to pay about Rp4000-5000 for a guide.

From Baluran

The road out of the park is so rough it might take 3 hours to walk back to the guardpost at Batangan on the main highway, N of Wonorejo village, where you can easily flag down onward transport. From Wonorejo to Pasir Putih is an inexpensive minibus ride, and it's only 18 km S (Rp600 by minibus) to Ketapang where you can catch the ferry to Bali. About 100 km SE on Java's southern coast is another wildlife park and nature reserve, Meru Betiri. Quite distinct from Baluran, it has lush vegetation, tumbling mountain streams, and steep forested ridges; see below for details. Visit the long white beach between Ketapang and Menang, both N of Banyuwangi, where there's a holy stone (Watu Dodol) and nearby, the grave of an unknown hermit. This coastline facing Bali is rich copra country with kilometers upon kilometers of jungle slopes covered in coconut trees.

THE IJEN PLATEAU

Containing no less than 6 volcanic peaks 1,200-3,050 m high, the whole eastern end of Java is dominated by the high and seldom-visited Ijen Plateau. In particular, the volcanic cones of G. Ijen and its neighbor G. Merapi (2,800 m) loom over the landscape. This plateau offers savannah landscapes, ruggedly beautiful panoramas, cool weather, grand hiking, dormant volcanos, and a placid, bright yellow crater lake. The area's peaks are surrounded by villages (at least up to the highest waterholes), home to 7,500 people who make their living either working the coffee plantations or the sulphur mines high on the slopes. Tourists haven't made it up here yet and it's still quite primitive, but that's part of the appeal.

Sights

From the crater rim of Ijen, its barren screes colonized by the low, tenacious *Vaccinium* bushes and their long trailing roots, long ridges lead down toward Baluran in the northeast. This NE slope, called **Maelang**, with its wild rolling country (good deer habitat), was a former hunting reserve. Tracks lead from **Bajulmati** through old coffee and teak plantations on the lower slopes and up into the hills. To the W is the Ijen Plateau, its dry grassy plains frequently burned to obtain young growth. This is all high country, easy to walk in, but the only water here is from the Banyupahit ("Bitter River"), the source of which is Kawah Ijen's acid yellow-green crater lake. Sumatran pines and coffee plantations occupy the W end of the plateau. Just beyond Blawan is the small **Jeding Nature Reserve**, where the Banyupahit River plunges 30 m through deep limestone gorges. Because of so much settlement, disturbance, and fire, Ijen is not an outstanding wildlife area. *Rusa*, leopards, pigs, peafowl, and jungle fowl are found in Maelang; civet cats, *muncak*, pigs, and quite tame silverleaf monkeys inhabit the moist forests.

Preparations

Officially you're supposed to apply to the Forestry Service (PPA) in Banyuwangi for a permit, although most travelers are never questioned. Up on the plateau, State Forestry Corp. (Perum Perhutani) officers are available for assistance and advice. **Jampit**, which can be reached by bus, jeeps, or small trucks, has shops to replenish your supplies but it's best to buy food beforehand in Situbondo or Bondowoso. Also, take warm clothes; the higher the altitude, the wetter and colder it can be. The rainiest season is Nov.-March; the driest April-October.

Accommodations And Food

Pondok Kawah Ijen, a former Dutch resthouse near Ijen's crater, is in bad shape with only one room left, its windows broken, and no toilet. The **Jampit**, **Ungkup-Ungkup**, and **Blawan** guesthouses are controlled by the local forestry officers (need permission to stay); and the big old *pasanggrahan* at Sempol is no longer in use. In Sempol, however, you may stay at the **Asrama Polisi** (Police Mess). At Sumberwringen, or "Fig Tree Spring," a very pleasant old *pasanggrahan* provides food and accommodations in the old Dutch style; worth a visit if you're in the area.

KAWAH IJEN

At the summit of G. Ijen is a *kawah* (crater) filled with a haunting turquoise-blue lake, its surface streaked in wind-blown patterns of yellow sulphurous vapor. Though dormant now, in 1817 Ijen erupted disastrously, wiping out 3 villages. It last erupted in 1952. There are 2 routes up to Kawah Ijen, one from the NW and one from the SE (see "Getting There" below). From a distance, you'll see beautiful, eerie, pale yellow-green smoke. As you near the crater's edge you must be able to stand the evil-smelling sulphur. This strange fog, particularly thick at the edge of the lake, suddenly appears above the water as if to welcome you. Local folklorists claim that the fog, which tends to disappear in a few seconds, seems to sense the arrival of every visitor, the crater's guests. This same fog will almost certainly reappear to say good-bye.

Take the dilapidated stairway down to the surface. Despite its boiling-cauldron appearance, the temperature of the lake is only around 50 degrees C. Some visitors have even explored the crater using small rubber dinghies. Nearly vertical walls of white rock surround the lake, except where the wall has collapsed in the northwest. A dam has been built to regulate the flow of water into the Banyupahit River; the lake has been known to boil over when volcanic activity increases. From a tunnel dug through the crater rim on the S side, the lake can be watched for any unseemly activity, and the volcanology post at Ungkup-Ungkup (one km from the nearby mining cabin) is manned year round. Don't shout, or you'll disturb the sensitive seismographic monitor at this station. The best camping is around this station; there are other good spots as well. The seismologists will advise.

Gunung Raung erupting

Getting There

Kawah Ijen is about 44 km from Banyuwangi. First get a minibus 17 km from Banyuwangi to Jambu (the sulphur factory), then to Licin (27 km from Banyuwangi), passing en route coffee, rubber, and chocolate plantations. Sometimes trucks make the drive from Licin up to Sodong, but you had better expect to hire a guide (Rp4000-5000) or a horse (Rp8000) for the ascent. Climbing steeply through the undergrowth you eventually reach the P.T. Licin and Sriwulong coffee plantations. Beyond, you come to a huge forest managed by P.T. Perhutani and a short distance thereafter you pass through a treeless burned area. This is at 2,300 m, and the temperature is frigid. About 3 km from the crater is a cabin with 5 wooden beds for visitors who want to spend a night or two exploring. Finally, after 6 hours, you reach Ungkup-Ungkup (the location of the volcanologist's post), then it's another hour's climb to Kawah Ijen's rim (17 km in all from Licin) to view the crater.

For those who want to return the same day, leave around noon. Keep track of the time. It takes 6-7 hours to walk back out of the crater to Sondong, then to Licin. Bring a flashlight; it gets dark fast. Riding a horse makes the descent much easier, as the horse knows the way well. Or take the track W across the plateau from Ungkup-Ungkup to Macan, Turah and Jampit (6-7 hours). From Jampit, take a *bemo* or shared taxi to Sempol, then to Wonosari and Bondowoso.

Other Approaches

Climbing Kawah Ijen is less strenuous from the Bondowoso side than from the Banyuwangi side. First get to Wonosari or to Bondowoso; arrive the night before so you'll be ready for an early start. The bumpy road from Wonosari, which begins 2 km N of town, leads all the way to Sempol (48 km, 3 hours, Rp2500 by *bemo*). In Sempol, a village in the middle of a coffee estate, stay in the *pasanggrahan*. The police also put up travelers at the Police Mess, 200 m beyond the gateway to the estate. At Sempol, hire a guide (the police or the estate officers will suggest someone) for Rp5000 and start on the most used footpath to Jampit-Turah-Macan (4 hours), walking over plank bridges and jagged ravines. From Macan to the volcanologist's post at Ungkup-Ungkup takes another 2 hours, then it's only one km (one hour) farther to Kawah Ijen. As a variation, a guesthouse run by the estate in Jampit can be rented for the night. From Kawah Ijen, you may choose to exit via Sodong-Licin-Jambu-Banyuwangi (see above). Sometimes trucks are available on the Sodong-Licin segment, and *bemo* depart at least every hour from Licin down to Banyuwangi on the coast.

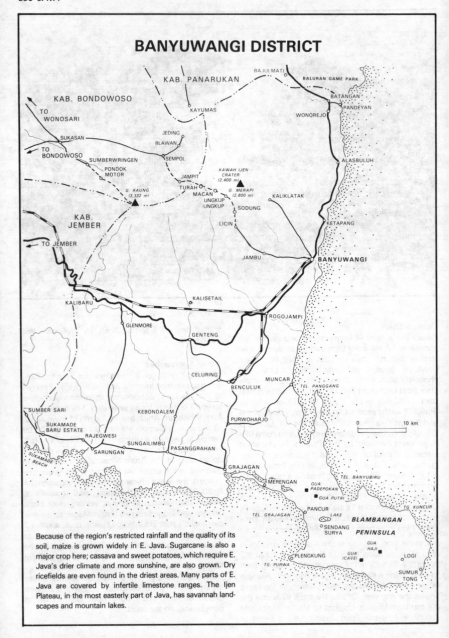

BANYUWANGI DISTRICT

KAB. PANARUKAN

BAJULMATI

BALURAN GAME PARK

KAB. BONDOWOSO

TO WONOSARI

KAYUMAS

BATANGAN
PANDEYAN

WONOREJO

SUKASAN

JEDING
BLAWAN

TO BONDOWOSO

SUMBERWRINGEN

SEMPOL

ALASBULUH

PONDOK MOTOR

JAMPIT

KAWAH IJEN CRATER (2,400 m)

G. RAUNG (3,332 m)

TURAH
MACAN

G. MERAPI (2,800 m)

KALIKLATAK

KAB. JEMBER

UNGKUP UNGKUP

SODUNG

KETAPANG

TO JEMBER

LICIN

JAMBU

BANYUWANGI

KALIBARU

KALISETAIL

ROGOJAMPI

GLENMORE

GENTENG

CELURING

MUNCAR

TEL. PANGGANG

BENCULUK

SUMBER SARI

KEBONDALEM

PURWOHARJO

0   10 km

SUKAMADE BARU ESTATE

RAJEGWESI

SUNGAILIMBU

PASANGGRAHAN

SARUNGAN

SUKAMADE BEACH

GRAJAGAN

MERENGAN

GUA PADEPOKAN

TEL. BANYUBIRU

GUA PUTRI

PANCUR

LAKE

TEL. GRAJAGAN

SENDANG SURYA

BLAMBANGAN

TG. KUNCUR

PLENGKUNG

GUA HAJI

PENINSULA

LOGI

TG. PURWA

GUA (CAVE)

SUMUR TONG

Because of the region's restricted rainfall and the quality of its soil, maize is grown widely in E. Java. Sugarcane is also a major crop here; cassava and sweet potatoes, which require E. Java's drier climate and more sunshine, are also grown. Dry ricefields are even found in the driest areas. Many parts of E. Java are covered by infertile limestone ranges. The Ijen Plateau, in the most easterly part of Java, has savannah landscapes and mountain lakes.

BLAMBANGAN PENINSULA

A remote peninsula on the far SE corner of Java, this region was the last stronghold of institutionalized Hinduism on Java, the legendary 17th century kingdom of Menak Jinggo. Battles for control of Blambangan were waged back and forth until Sultan Agung marched to the coast in 1639 and even conquered the western portion of Bali. Balinese troops rallied and fought the Muslim Mataram troops into the sea and the peninsula was controlled by Balinese kingdoms until 1768. Today, Blambangan is a relatively unexplored wildlife reserve called the **Banyuwangi Selatan Reserve**, a secluded archaeological region. The whole of **Teluk Grajagan** is a very popular swimming, boating, and recreation area, particularly for surfing which is fantastic, though expensive. Foreign surfers claim that **Plengkung** has the best surf in Indonesia: waves are up to 4 m high at 5 min. intervals and 3 km long. If there are no waves at other places on Java and Bali, there *will* be waves at Plengkung. The surfing season is May to July. It costs around Rp10,000 pp per day to stay at the surfers' camp at Plengkung where bamboo bungalows have been constructed. Only *warung* food is available so stock up on Bali and take along a cooking stove. It might be possible to stay on the boat you arrived on, or pitch a tent on the sand.

The Land

In general, the peninsula is dry and thickety, with the driest months April-October. Teak plantations have encroached on the landward side of the peninsula; its dry climate is ideal. Where plantations have not made inroads, mixed monsoon forests still exist. Blambangan is outstanding for 2 reasons: its turtle-nesting beaches (unfortunately much raided by Balinese turtle hunters), and as perhaps the last area in Indonesia where the *ajak*, the handsome, rufous, bushy-tailed wild dog (a sub-species of the Indian *dhole*) still thrive. Only on Blambangan are they safe from ruthless persecution. Packs of *ajak*, once common all over Java, have always been blamed for livestock losses, but on Blambangan their natural prey is deer, pig, and the *muncak*, not domestic animals. Besides these wild dogs, jungle fowl, macaques, leaf monkeys, some *banteng*, *muncak*, *rusa*, leopards, and pigs also inhabit Hutan Purwo, Blambangan's forest reserve.

Sights

Muncar, 41 km S of Banyuwangi, is the largest fishing *kampung* in E. Java. Watch the fishermen work along the beach and visit the fish market. **Sitihinggil** is a historical site near Muncar, a hill on which grow extra large and leafy banyan trees. At **Pancur**, 80 km S of Banyuwangi, stone pedestals are the only remnants of the kingdom of Menak Jinggo. A good swimming beach is found here, as well as a clean freshwater spring. Nearby, at **Desa Kedungrejo**, 90 km S of Banyuwangi, are scattered very large stone blocks which once formed the foundation of a palace, Umpak Songo. Other ancient archaeological sites are accessible on foot: at **Logi** are the remains of a building built by the Dutch in 1811; at **Sumur Tong**, an old well; at **Gua Haji**, a statue honoring a famous *haj*.

Getting There

From Banyuwangi's Terminal Brawijaya, get a minibus all the way to Benculuk, then a *bemo* or minibus on a rough road to Grajagan, a fishing village where the road ends and from where you embark for Plengkung by local fishing boat (Rp5000-6000) to Plengkung on the westerly corner of the Blambangan Peninsula. Total distances: from Banyuwangi to Grajagan is 52 km and from Grajagan to Plengkung is 25 km. The passage to the surfing locale is easy but coming back you have to go against the wind and tackle the waves. Other approaches: walk 2 days along the bay from Grajagan to Plengkung, find occasional boats to Grajagan from Benoa (S. Bali), charter a boat from Benoa, use the surfing camp's expensive diesel cruiser direct from Bali. Plengkung can also be reached by minibus from Banyuwangi to Trianggulasi (76 km), then from Trianggulasi to Plengkung along the shore's edge for 12 km. Before setting out for Blambangan, obtain a permit from the PPA office in Banyuwangi (Jl. A. Yani 108, tel. 41119).

THE MERU BETIRI RESERVE

From a conservation point of view, this is one of the most important reserves on Java. Established in 1972, this 50,000-ha game park lies on Java's rugged SE coast where thickly wooded hills rise steeply to an altitude of over 1,000 m. The reserve's highest point is G. Betiri (1,223 m). The World Wildlife Fund has assisted Indonesia's Forestry Service in drawing up a management plan for the relatively new reserve. Though best known as the last refuge of the Javan tiger, Meru Betiri is also of considerable botanical importance as one of the few remaining areas of relatively undisturbed primal montane forest on Java. It is the only known habitat of 2 of the island's endemic plant species, the *Rafflesia zollingeriana* and *Balanphora fungosa*. The reserve's 2 highest peaks, G. Betiri (1,223 m) and G. Tajem, catch the rain and create a sort of rain pocket; this makes the reserve often wetter than surrounding areas and accounts for the unbelievably thick jungles. There are even enclaves of true natural rainforests—almost the last on Java—ranging in elevation from 0-1,223 m.

Fauna

The steep, densely wooded hills provide a final stronghold for the indigenous Javan tiger *(harimau macan jawa)* which inhabits the hilly eastern boundary of the estate. Its numbers are so low that its future is very doubtful. Human interference is the major reason: plantations have taken over the tigers' traditional valley habitat. Lack of prey species has also contributed to the predators' decline. PPA guards now patrol the reserve to protect the remaining tigers. In 1978 an intensive study revealed that only 5-6 still survive. Sleek long-bodied panthers *(macan tutul)*, pigs, *muncak*, rabbits, squirrels, civets, some leopards, black and silverleaf monkeys, and the long-tailed macaque also inhabit the reserve. Birds of the sea and shore are common, though unlike Ujung Kulon, there are few migrants. Two species of hornbills (wreathed and the smaller pied hornbill) and egrets and terns are the most often seen. Most of the government's conservation efforts are concentrated on the sea turtle nesting beaches where, in the right season, 5 species of turtle (green, loggerhead, hawksbill, Pacific Ridley, and the leatherback) arrive to lay their leathery, golf-ball-sized eggs.

Accommodations

A comfortable PPA resthouse (sleeps 4-6), **Taman Rekreasi**, provides food and lodging at Rajegwesi, a small fishing village on a bay within the reserve, about 2 hours by road from the Sukamade Baru Estate. Meals can be ordered in advance. Another resthouse, closer to the turtle nesting beach, is **Wisma Sukamade** in the Sukamade Baru Estate itself (see below); Rp8000 s or d (about 25 beds). This large plantation sometimes hires out its jeep, if available. To explore the reserve, you must be accompanied by a PPA officer or local guide. A newly built observation tower has been raised in a cleared savannah.

SUKAMADE BARU ESTATE

Founded by Dutch planters in 1927, this bustling plantation comprises 1,200 ha in rubber, coffee, and coconut palms. The plantation is surrounded by dense jungles and a breathless expanse of coastline. The estate's *pasanggrahan* is extremely comfortable, with giant home-style meals served; its 5 rooms hold up to 25 people.

Sukamade Beach

Also called "Turtle Bay" or Pantai Penu, this famous 3-km-long beach lies at the E end of the reserve, about 90 km SE of Jember. Dark forested hills descend to the shoreline which is pounded by the deep green surf of the Indian Ocean. This long blinding beach, most of the time empty, is one of the few locales on Java where you can still observe huge sea turtles (up to 200 kg!) laying their eggs in the sand. From the Sukamade Baru Estate it's a 45-min. walk to this protected area. Platforms have been constructed at the beach for campers. Villagers might also be willing put you up. The best time for catching sight of the laying turtles is from 2100-0200 every night Nov.-March; take a flashlight and look for their notched tracks in the sand. To see these magnificent reptiles emerging from the surf on moonlit nights to dig their deep nesting pits is a rare experience. Turtle eggs are a popular delicacy on Java and most of the eggs are collected by the plantation workers for themselves or for market.

Vicinity Of Sukamade

A small cove called **Teluk Hijau**, or "Green Bay," has deep green surf; the 20-min. walk from the narrow track down to the beach leads through some fine primary jungle. The smaller sandy beaches of **Nanggalen, Sekar, Permisan,** and **Pisang** to the W are worth visiting. Only one truck daily, at around 0600, leaves the estate and travels to Rajegwesi. If you're sleeping on the beach, get up early and take the shortcut out to the main road to intercept the truck. **Rajegwesi** is a fishing village close to the southern sea, a spectacular environment of seascapes and steep-sloped mountains, *sawah,* and sailing *prahu.*

Getting There

The streams, rivers, and rough mountain trails make the trip a real adventure. The Sukamade Baru Estate lies about 100 km SW of Banyuwangi, about 67 km from Genteng, and 70 km S of Glenmore (both on the Jember-Banyuwangi road). The fastest access is from Glenmore. Another approach is by bus or *bemo* from Banyuwangi to Rogojampi, then a local bus to Benculuk, then a *bemo* via Celuring to Kebondalem, then another *bemo* on a dirt road to Sarungan via Pasanggrahan. Get a permit and information from the PPA offices in either Banyuwangi or Sarungan. From Sarungan a truck departs each day at around 1300 for Rajegwesi (or sometimes farther to the Sukamade Baru Estate). Once you reach Rajegwesi, the reserve is W about 2 hours on a rough road through coffee and rubber plantations. Allow at least 2 days for this trip as the section from Rogojampi to Rajegwesi alone takes half a day. There is no scheduled public transport so if time is a factor take your own vehicle, or charter a minibus (Rp20,000-25,000 per day from Banyuwangi). Don't attempt this trip in the rainy season as the road sometimes degenerates into a washed-out track or is rendered impassable by bridgeless river crossings: from Grajagan, there are 7 river crossings to Sukamade. The largest river is at Sumberjambi. August would be one of the best months to undertake this journey. On the way, stay at the **Muktisari** on Jl. Station in Rogojampi; and at the **Ramayana** (Jl. Jember 80) or the **Agung** (Jl. Gambiran) in Genteng.

BALI

This tiny island of nearly 3 million Hindus, sur-rounded by a sea of 160 million Muslims, is just 2 km from the far eastern tip of Java. When the first Dutch war-yacht pulled into Bali in the late 16th C., the whole crew immediately jumped ship—it was heaven on earth. It took the captain 2 years to round up his men before he could set sail back to Holland. Bali was really put on the map back in the 1930s when several popular documentaries were made about this paradise-like island. Then the world knew, and Bali has been degenerating into a tourist colony for well-nigh 50 years now—an Isle of Capri of the western Pacific. The number of tourists and earnings from tourism have doubled each year since 1970, and the industry is now aiming at one million tourists a year—one visitor for every 3 Balinese.

INTRODUCTION

Known as "Anthropology's Shakespeare," at last Bali's unbelievably complex social and religious fabric is breaking down under the onslaught: now you see signs like "Cremation! Rp5000! Book here!" and revered Hindu priests wear graffiti art T-shirts. When groups of men go to pray, some wear a hibiscus in their ear, a clean bright *sarung,* and their crisply pressed, soulfully faded Levi's jacket. Big-business tourism is now being foisted upon the Balinese by the Javanese and international consortiums, and hotels are built without the consent or consultation of local residents. Most of the money earned from the swank hotels doesn't remain on Bali to benefit the people but is siphoned back to Java or overseas. Tourism has brought corruption, crime, and disease as well. You used to be able to leave your bag in the open anywhere on the island for 3 days and nothing would move it but the wind. Not anymore. Thefts of tourists' belongings are now a regular occurrence, and the first AIDS death, a Dutchman, occurred on Bali in March 1987. Prices are getting higher, vendors in the tourist ghettos like Sanur, Kuta, and Denpasar hassle you, the sound of motorbikes is constant, quality of painting and carving is declining, etc.—you've heard it all before. With the revaluation of the Indonesian *rupiah* and the outstanding discounts Balinese hotels offer European travel agents and tour groups, there was an unprecedented surge of tourism to Bali in 1987; in 1988 tourism to the island is expected to expand exponentially. Even retired people are now making the 16-hour flight direct from Europe to Bali. More and more of the remote corners of the island are being penetrated: some tour companies specialize in highly mobile 4WD jimmys with just 3 passengers and their guide going out to villages where there are no cold drinks, no *losmen,* not even police. And these villages are starting to learn that money can be made in other ways than selling *lontong* in the market. But travelers and tourists haven't caused one-eighth of the cultural pollution that VCRs and the movie houses in Denpasar have, showing films which are so misleading and poisonous (e.g., all white women are insatiably promiscuous). People who were there during the '30s—or even the '60s—can't bear to go back now; it's too painful to see. How much more tourism can the island take? How much more traffic? How many more craft shops? How many more Kutas? How many more airplanes? The answer is that it never stops, the roads are widened, the hotels multiply, the direct flights to Bali increase.

What is left? The law which prohibits building any structures higher than a palm tree has saved the island, otherwise the developers would have taken over completely by this time. Bali has known innumerable visitors—Chinese, Javanese, Polynesians, Japanese, Europeans, and now travelers and tourists—assimilating them for hundreds of years. Although the island is only 144 km long by 80 km at its widest, you can still get as lost as you want on it. There are hundreds of villages which haven't changed in 50 years. You don't need directions; just head for the hills. The best things are still free: orange and gold tropical sunsets, an astoundingly rich culture, the dynamite smiles of the children, the sound of the palms, the talcum-powder beaches and coral dive sites. You can still get into hundreds of temple dances free, and live well for US$6 a day or less.

The Land

Bali is like one big sculpture. Every earthen step is manicured and polished, every field and niche is carved by hand. Once a geographic extension of Java, Bali still resembles it, mountains and all, sharing much the same climate, flora, and fauna as its mother island. There are few flat areas; hills and mountains are everywhere. The surface of the island is marked by deep ravines, fast-flowing rivers and in northern Bali, a W-to-E volcanic chain (1,500-3,000 m high), an extension of Java's central range. In the southern part of the island you see ricefields exquisitely carved out of hills and valleys, sparkling with water or vividly green. All seasons are one: in fields side by side there is rice that has just been planted, rice that is still growing, and rice that has ripened. Terracing and irrigation practices are even more elaborate and sophisticated than on Java, with remarkable systems of aqueducts, small dams, underground canals, and water carried by tunnels through solid rock hillsides. A village organization, the *subak,* controls the distribution of water coming from a reservoir or main pipeline. In S. Bali, besides rice (grown extensively up to 700 m), there are crops of tea, cacao, groundnuts, and tropical fruits. As you leave the southern plains and head N, the landscape changes from tiers of ricefields to gardens of onions, cabbages, and papaya which grow better in the cooler climate. Thatched palm huts change to sturdy cottages made of wood, tile, stone, and volcanic rock to withstand heavy rains. There's alpine country with mountain streams, moss, prehistoric ferns, wildflowers, creepers, orchids, leeches, butterflies, birds, and screaming monkeys. The western tip, known as Pulaki, is the unspoiled, uninhabited wilderness of Bali. Legend has it that Bali's first inhabitants had their origins here in a lost, invisible city.

Climate

Bali lies only 8 degrees S of the equator and has an eternal summer, warm sea breezes, high humidity. Don't worry if it rains because tropical showers can quickly give way to blinding sunshine. Rainfall, which usually is not heavy and continuous, arrives mainly in the late afternoon and night. From Nov. to April the rains really come; the wettest days are in Dec. and January. The dry season is May to October. From June to the end of Sept. is very pleasant.

History

Historically speaking, Bali is a fossilized Java, a living museum of the old Indo-Javanese civilization. Over 400 years ago all of E. Java was like Bali is today. Prior to 1815 Bali had a greater population density than Java, suggesting that its Bali-Hindu civilization was even more successful than Java's. Indian culture was present on Bali as early as the 9th C. and the Balinese language is derived from the Palava script of southern India. Bali today provides scholars with clues about India's past religious life in old sacred texts that have long ago vanished in India itself. When Gajah Mada of Java's Majapahit Empire conquered Bali in the mid-14th C., East Javanese influences spread from the purely religious and cultural spheres into fine art, dancing, sculpture, and architecture. When that empire fell in the 15th C. under pressure from the military and economic invasion of Islam, there was a mass migration of the cream of Java's Majapahit's scholars, dancers, and rulers to Bali. Priests took with them all their sacred books and historical records, and on Bali they found refuge and developed unique Bali-Hindu customs and institutions. But Hinduism is only the veneer. The Hindu practices of the new masters were merely superimposed on the deeply rooted aboriginal animism of the Balinese natives, who hold beliefs dating back to the Bronze Age and even earlier. In the early 19th C., Bali's sole export was its highly prized slaves; its imports were gold, rubies, and opium. The island remained obscure for so long because of its lack of spices and ivory, its steep cliffs rising from the sea, deep straits, and treacherous tidal currents and reefs which encircle it. Surprisingly, the incredibly fertile lava-rich lowlands of Bali were among the last areas to be occupied by the Dutch and only came under their colonial rule following prolonged resistance. When a wrecked cargo ship off the S coast was looted by the Balinese at the turn of this century (a traditional practice of island peoples), the Dutch used the incident as a pretense to implement their control over the island. One sunny morning in 1908 in Puputan Square, Denpasar, Hindu princes and their families, wearing splendid ceremonial costumes and waving priceless *kris* at the invaders, charged deliberately into Dutch rifles. This mass suicide *(puputan)* resulted in the annihilation of the entire royal family.

THE PEOPLE

The Balinese are small, handsome people with round, delicate features, long sweeping eyelashes, heart-shaped lips. Extraordinarily creative people who practice a highly theatrical culture, Bali's cults, customs, and worship of god and nature are animist, their music warm-blooded, their art as extravagant as their nature. Culturally, the Javanese lean more toward refinement, keeping themselves in check in life and art, whereas the Balinese prefer the flash sensations—laughs, terrors, spicier and sweeter foods. They're more lavish in their colors and decorations; they like explosive music and fast jerky dancing. Today there's still a distinction made between the *wong majapahit* (descendants of 15th C. migrants of E. Java's fallen Majapahit Empire) and the Bali Aga, the secluded original inhabitants of the island who retreated into the mountains where they are found to

bale: *This basic model of Balinese construction is very sturdy, even in high winds, and lasts more than 50 years. Roofs are made of ½-m-thick galang grass which keeps the structure cool; long ribs of coconut leaves are interwoven like shingles and lashed to the bamboo skeleton with strong cords of sugar palm fiber. The roof is combed with a special rake and all edges are trimmed with a knife. The end nearest where the roots were in the tree must correspond to the bottom part of the posts. Engraved beams (tiang) holding the roof are fitted together with pegs of coconut wood; no nails are used. Not built with any master plan, the builder has the design and the scale already worked out, as the Balinese say, "in his belly." On domestic bale platforms are low wooden beds with bamboo springs on which the family sits cross-legged to eat, sleep, work, play, rest, read, talk. The rural Balinese kitchen has a simpler roof of coarse thatch supported by 4 posts with a bamboo platform at one end (the kitchen table) and a mud stove at the other. The dirt floor keeps food inside the clay pots hot for hours, and is easy to clean and smooth.*

this day, indifferent to outsiders. Caste is indicated by name with the classical Hindu division into 3 main classes: the Brahmans with the title *Ida,* the Kshatriyas with the title *Deva,* and the Vaishyas with the title *Gusti.* The Bali Aga are *sudra* or casteless, though none is untouchable. Ninety percent of Bali's population practice Bali-Hinduism. There is also a sprinkling of Muslims in the coastal towns, Buddhists in the mountains, and Christians everywhere (Belimbingsari is a small Christian village in the far western part of Bali). About 500 Arabs and Indians, many dealers in textiles, live in Denpasar. Ten thousand Chinese are found in the main trading centers of Denpasar, Singaraja, and Amlapura, running the majority of the businesses.

Women And Family Life

Women often have independent incomes and are in charge of cultivating the fields, as well as all the landmarks in their family's life considered important or magic: birth, the first cutting of nails and hair, filing of teeth, piercing of earlobes, marriage, and death. Women carry loads of up to 30 kg and 1½ m tall on their heads, while men take up the rear cradling just their *parang.* A young Balinese girl can train herself to carry up to 40 coconuts, stacks of fruit, or great water jars on her head without even using her hands, all this while riding her bicycle down a bumpy country road. Women delousing each other and their children is a great social pastime and reaffirms familial love. Women wear bras like European women wear bikini tops. Unmarried girls often have a loose lock of hair hanging down the back over one shoulder with a *gonjer* (flower) dangling in it. As in many Indonesian societies, women are sent out of their homes while menstruating to board in a special house or compound set aside for that purpose. A Balinese man believes that if menstrual blood ever touches his scalp he will become impotent for the rest of his life and

follow his wife around like a dog. The birth of boy and girl twins is a calamity in a village, an evil omen. It's thought that the twins had committed incest in the womb and rigorous purification ceremonies must be carried out. If a child is sick too often its name is simply changed. The Balinese believe that each part of the house corresponds to a part of the human anatomy: the arms are the bedrooms and the social parlor, the navel is the courtyard, sexual organs are the gates, the anus is the garbage pit in the backyard, legs and feet are the kitchen and granary, and the head is the family shrine.

The *Banjar*

The community extension of the house and family. Each Balinese village is like a little republic, self-contained and independently run by the *banjar,* a sort of town council. More than any other factor, this village organization has kept intact the Balinese way of life after the decline of the local *adat* princes and chieftains. Each family pays a subscription fee and when a man marries, membership is compulsory; otherwise he's considered morally and spiritually dead. Attendance of all household heads is required at regular meetings; absentees are fined. The *banjar* runs its own communal bank from which villagers may borrow to buy farm equipment, cattle, or other necessary purchases. The *banjar* supports and maintains village temples and ditches, owns a *gamelan,* handles taxation, cockfighting, divorces, duck herding, helps to arrange and finance weddings, family celebrations, temple festivals, cremations, community feasts. The *banjar* advises villagers on matters of religion, marriage and morals, which are all regulated carefully by its elected members. Each *banjar* has its own meeting house for getting together in the evenings to sip *tuak,* talk, and gamble. Everyone takes turns acting as cooks and waiters. The leader of the *banjar* is elected by its members and approved by the gods through a medium. No other political system has yet broken through the patriarchal shield of the banjar, though recently its cohesiveness is being weakened by consumerism and the "modern" lifestyles of the growing towns and the travel industry. Many members now send a monetary contribution in lieu of their presence.

RELIGION

Bali-Hinduism

Bali is the largest Hindu outpost in the world outside of India. Although Hinduism originated in India, on Bali it has developed along lines all its own. And the way the Balinese practice their island form of frontier Hinduism is still their greatest art. Hinduism is at least 3,000 years old and dates from the writing of the Upanishads. The religion doesn't have a single founder or prophet, but instead a whole pantheon of gods. The Balinese call their own religion Agama Tirtal ("Science of the Holy Water"), an interpretation of religious ideas from China, India, and Java. It's much closer to the earth and more animist than Hinduism proper; the 2 sects are as different from each other as Ethiopian Christianity is from Episcopalian Christianity or from the Catholicism practiced by the Irish and the Catholicism practiced by American Indians. If a Hindu from Benares ever visited Bali, he'd think them savages. Although the Hindu epics are well known and form the basis of their favorite dances, the deities of the Hindu pantheon (Vishnu, Shiva, Brahma) worshipped in India are here considered too aloof and aristocratic. Often Balinese don't even know their names. The Balinese have their own corresponding trinity of supreme gods, a deity in itself called "The Shrine of the Three Forces." Because of the caste system, 200 million people are shunned in India. On Bali, though, only the older people still believe in the caste system; the young ignore it. In India a Hindu must be cremated at once in order to enter into heaven, but because of the expense, on Bali sometimes a whole village will temporarily bury its dead and then stage a mass cremation. In India widows must not remarry but on Bali they do again and again, and even high priests marry. In India, worship at home is all-important but on Bali group worship is preferred.

Balinese Animism

The Balinese are scared witless of ghosts, goblins and the like, which disguise themselves as black cats, a naked woman, crows. Spirits dominate everything they do and their lives are constantly taken up with offering fruit and flowers to appease angry deities. If put in our society, a Balinese would show all the classic symptoms of paranoid and neurotic disorders, but on Bali these traits are ritualized and institutionalized.

There are sun gods, totemic gods, deer gods, secretaries to the gods, mythical turtles, market deities. Clay figures of the animist fire god are put over kitchen hearths, and bank clerks place pandanus leaf offering trays on their desks. Ngedjot are seen in the courtyards of every house for the spirits which haunt that house; these house offerings consist of little squares of banana leaves with a few grains of rice, a flower, salt, and a pinch of chili pepper. No one eats before these ngedjot are placed in front of each house every morning. Though the mangy dogs follow and eat the offering as soon as it touches the ground, the essence has already been consumed by the spirits. Gods and goddesses, which protect or threaten every act performed by a person during his lifetime, inhabit stone thrones and statues or are simply in the air. Gods are often invited down to visit Earth and are gorged with offerings and entertained with music, but eventually must go back home because they are too expensive to maintain. The Balinese always try to stay on the good side of all the forces, and if the spirits are kept happy, they can relax and even be lighthearted. Children carry flowers to shrines and learn to dance at an early age to please the gods. Feasts mark special periods in the infant's first year: 3 days after birth, 42 days after the first bath, 105 days after birth, and finally 210 days after birth—his first birthday celebration. At each stage of the agricultural cycle ceremonies are held, offerings are made, and holy texts chanted. Even cockfighting was originally a temple ritual, blood spilled for the gods. During the 1965 political bloodletting in which 50,000 people died on Bali, victims and suspects would dress up in spotless white ceremonial attire before being led away to be executed. Devils were believed to live in the communists or their sympathizers and their deaths were necessary in order to cleanse the island of evil. Heaven? The Balinese believe that heaven will be exactly like Bali!

Dualism

The Balinese religion divides most concepts into polarities: heaven and earth, sun and moon, day and night, gods and demons, man and woman, clean and unclean, strong and weak, hot and cold. The interaction of all these contrasting pairs works in harmony with each other, runs the world, and determines one's fate. Thus the Balinese witch, Rangda, who symbolizes evil, plays her useful role guarding the temples. In Balinese folk medicine, headaches are cured by spraying the head with a mixture of crushed ginger and mashed bedbugs—a heated or irritated condition is cured with a cooling medicine. It's said that the Balinese are one of the few island peoples who don't turn their eyes toward the sea, but upwards towards the mountains. The Balinese believe that everything high such as mountains is good, powerfully magic, and healthy, while the ocean below

Balinese Festivals: For a week to pass without several celebrations or ceremonies happening in different villages is very unlikely. Njepi is an annual Balinese festival held to purify the whole island, a time when demons and evil spirts are driven out of the villages. All work stops for the procession to the coast. The Evil Ones are lured to great offerings set up at crossroads and then expelled by curses of the high priests (pedandas). The unclean earth is purified by the spilling of cock's blood and at sunset the villagers, especially the children, bang sticks together and beat on gongs or tin cans to frighten away any evil spirits who are still lingering. The Saraswati Festival is held annually in honor of the Hindu goddess of learning, science, and literature. Literary manuscripts receive offerings. No one may read on this day.

is sinister, filled with poisonous fish, sea snakes, and sharks. Their sacred mountains are "north" and the sea "south"; these are the cardinal points so their villages are aligned in these directions.

Festivals

There's an unending chain of festivals, over 60 religious holidays a year. The basic tenet of the Balinese religion is the belief that the island is owned by the supreme god *Sanghyang Widhi*, and that it has been handed down to the people in sacred trust. For this trust the people show their gratitude by filling their lives with symbolic activities and worship. Balinese seem to devote most of their waking hours to an endless series of offerings, purifications, temple festivities, processions, dances, cremations, and dozens of other religious rites. Festivals are dedicated to the art of woodcarving, to the birth of a goddess, to percussion instruments; there are temple festivals, fasting and retreat ceremonies, parades to the sea to cleanse villages, celebrations of wealth and learning. Get a Balinese calendar; besides being faithful pictorial representations of simple, realistic folk scenes, they show all the most propitious days for religious activities.

Cremation

On this extravagant occasion you'll see most of Bali's popular art and all of the more important religious symbols. Cremation is meant to liberate the soul of the dead, allowing it to journey to heaven to rejoin the Hindu cycle of reincarnation. Bodies are often buried twice on Bali: once at death, and then the villagers wait for a mass cremation to be held where the vast

expenses can be shared. These funerals are a time of tipsy hilarity, gossip, offerings, and dances, all brightened by continuous *gamelan* music. First the deceased is "re-awakened," the grave opened, and the remains put on a decorated wood and bamboo tower, a fantastic creation of tinsel, paper, flowers, mirrors, silk, and white cloth. Because of pervasive power lines all over the island, the really tall towers of the past are seldom used today. The corpse is then taken from the home in a noisy procession to the cremation grounds. On the way it is spun around on top of men's shoulders so as to confuse the soul, to prevent it from finding its way back to its house where it might cause mischief to the living. While tourists trip over themselves taking pictures, the splendid tower, offerings, and coffin are then set ablaze. As matches are considered unclean, blow torches blast both the cranium and feet, which also enables cremations to take place even when it rains. After the blaze subsides, the eldest son rakes the ashes to make sure all the flesh is burned. To free the soul, the ashes are then carried out to sea and scattered.

Temples

At least 20,000 on Bali; if you see *pura* in front of a word, it means temple *(puri,* on the other hand, means palace). You must wear a sash to enter and menstruating women are not allowed in. Notice the exuberant ornamentation; carvings on them are like the flowers and the trees. Bring binoculars to observe the extreme detail on some, such as the Gerta Gosa in Klungkung and the bronze drum of Pejeng. There are temples everywhere—in houses, courtyards, marketplaces, cemeteries, rice paddies, beaches, on barren rocks offshore, on deserted hilltops and mountain heights, deep inside caves, within tangled roots of *banyan* trees. At most intersections and other dangerous places temples are erected to prevent mishap. Even in the middle of jungle crossroads, incense burns at little shrines. There are simple domestic temples, island temples, and even some social groups have temples of their own. The Mother Temple of Bali, Besakih, is the state temple. It lies on the slopes of Gunung Agung, the "Navel of the World," the holiest mountain on Bali, where all the gods and goddesses live. **note:** It is common to sign a guestbook and be asked for a donation when entering a temple complex. Beware of guestbooks in which zeros have been added to all the preceeding figures, making it appear that donations have been substantial (Rp2000!). This deception is practiced at Besakih, Tanah Lot, and Tirta Empul.

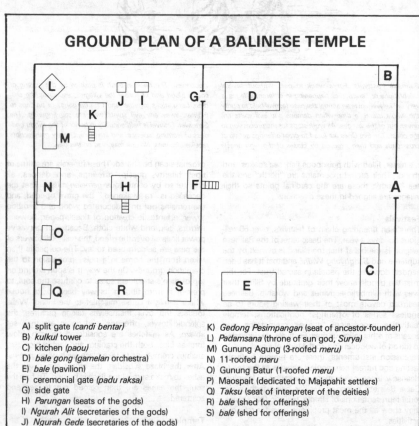

GROUND PLAN OF A BALINESE TEMPLE

A) split gate *(candi bentar)*
B) *kulkul* tower
C) kitchen *(paou)*
D) *bale gong* (gamelan orchestra)
E) *bale* (pavilion)
F) ceremonial gate *(padu raksa)*
G) side gate
H) *Parungan* (seats of the gods)
I) *Ngurah Alit* (secretaries of the gods)
J) *Ngurah Gede* (secretaries of the gods)
K) *Gedong Pesimpangan* (seat of ancestor-founder)
L) *Padamsana* (throne of sun god, *Surya)*
M) Gunung Agung (3-roofed *meru)*
N) 11-roofed *meru*
O) Gunung Batur (1-roofed *meru)*
P) Maospait (dedicated to Majapahit settlers)
Q) *Taksu* (seat of interpreter of the deities)
R) *bale* (shed for offerings)
S) *bale* (shed for offerings)

THE ARTS OF BALI

The island's very well-organized cultivation system and its astounding fertility have given the Balinese the leisure to develop their arts for centuries. It's incredible that so many people on such a small area of the Earth's surface (3,200 sq km) pour so much energy into creating beautiful things. Their worship of life and the gods encompasses a wide range of art forms, making an art out of even the very simple necessities of everyday life. Influenced by incoming European artists, modern Balinese art only began about 1927, when for the first time artists dated and signed their paintings. Before that, all art was for God. If the painting or sculpture was too innovative, it might not have qualified in the service of God and the artist was considered a failure. There is still no word in their language for "art" or "artist." A sculptor is a "carver," a painter is known as a "picture maker," a dancer goes by the name of the dance she performs. The Balinese have never allowed artistic knowledge to become centralized in a special intellectual class. Everyone on Bali is an artist. The simplest peasant and most slow-witted worker create something, or are aesthetically conscious as critical spectators. A field laborer will chide a clumsy instrument maker for a job poorly done. Even *dagang*, young girls who run small foodstalls, are skillful practitioners of Bali's classical dances. But Bali's art is living on borrowed time. Communities are becoming unwilling to subsidize the high cost involved in the sumptuous ceremonies, music and dance troupes, new costumes and masks for actors, etc., preferring the more desirable comforts of Western technology. The Balinese are very susceptible to fads: fashions, themes for theater, new painting styles and dance forms often sweep the island. They are unabashed and uncanny copyists and some of their stone temple carvings, such as a holdup or a plane crash, are copied right out of magazines. Stonecarvings and paintings show pregnant women, boys playing, beer drinking, seductions, even atomic bombs going off in heaven.

Lamak And *Wayang*

The purest and oldest example of Balinese art is the ancient mosaic-like *lamak* which last only for a day. Woven by women for Balinese feasts, *lamak* are made from strips of a palm leaf, bamboo, and yellow blades of sugar or coconut palm pinned or folded together to form fancy borders, rosettes, and diminutive tree designs. There are hundreds of different *lamak* designs. After hanging a unit on an altar or rice granary, they're wilted by night. Other of their perishable arts include 5-layered stacks of edible temple offerings, outrageous adornment on cremation towers, cones of fruits and cakes, long rectangular panels of sculptural tapestry hung on temples and shrines. Hourglass-shaped palm-leaf fertility figures of *cili* (girls) with round breasts and long thin arms start to appear when rice seeds first sprout about 3 months after planting. The Balinese form of *wayang kulit* has the same repertory as on Java but puppets are smaller and more realistic than the Javanese variety, which were more stylistic because Islam forbade portrayal of the human form. On Bali, *wayang* shows are performed in the open air and the men aren't separated from the women as on Java. In addition, Balinese theater forms aren't as strongly influenced by the two-dimensional shadow play as the Javanese are. On Java *wayang topeng* is a dying art, but on Bali it's still going strong. More expressive and typical of the characters than the *topeng* masks of Java, these performances act out deeds of local kings and warriors in Balinese history, with usually 2-3 players impersonating the heroes of the stories in pantomime.

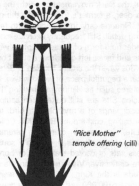

"Rice Mother"
temple offering (cili)

Sculpture

The Balinese sculpt with natural media such as wood, stone, bone, horn, and even deadwood or gnarled tree roots. For the most part, purely a souvenir variety of woodcarving is turned out now with successful creations often assembly-line produced. There are only half a dozen places at most in Mas, the main woodcarving center, that sell high-quality carvings and they want as much as US$200 for one. Using very simple tools, top-class woodcarvers are paid only Rp5000 a day. Often Balinese woodcarving is grotesque, almost psychotic, expressing so vividly their fear of the supernatural. The features of a subject are distorted to heighten its special character—a frog's

The Dutch painter, Rudolph Bonnet, working in the studio of his Balinese house. With Walter Spies, Bonnet was instrumental in creating in 1935 the painters' cooperative Pita Maha. Member painters brought their paintings to the cooperative where they were judged for their marketability by Spies and Bonnet, who exerted a profound influence over their painting styles. Pita Maha staged exhibitions on Java and in Europe and a number of painters received international awards and recognition. The majority of the magnificent paintings and statues in Ubud's museum, Puri Lukisan, were gathered in the 1930s by Rudolph Bonnet.

eyes, the sleek movement of a fish, the graceful legs of a deer, a farmer's toiling back, the prancing of a bird. Figurine carving is unique, with faces in painstaking detail. Still frequently seen are examples of the slender fluid form of figure sculpture with elongated arms and faces, left over from a style born one day in the '30s when the artist I Tegelan of Belaluan refused to cut a beautiful piece of wood in two. Mythological creatures such as Hanuman wrestling the serpent or dancing Sita are still quite often sculpted. Painted woodcarvings of a mythological bird, to hang from your ceiling, cost around Rp20,000. Called "The Bird of Life," it's used in cremation ceremonies as the bearer of the deceased person's soul to heaven. Chess sets of carved teakwood or bone pieces are quite distinctive; Vishnu riding on the shoulders of Garuda is the King. On Kuta the starting price is around Rp100,000, but they'll come down to half that or less; in Celuk, they could be even cheaper. For something different, the woodcarvings of the Bali Aga (aboriginal Balinese) villages in the uplands are more ancestral and have more of a primitive feeling than those produced in the Hinduized portions of the island. Stonecarving belongs to the craft of woodworking and, since soft volcanic rock is used, the technique is very much the same. Because they believe that constant maintenance of their stone temples is a moral obligation, stone sculpture survives today as the only Balinese art with a religious function. And stonecarving is relatively unaffected by tourist consumerism because it's too expensive to ship.

PAINTING

Painting virtually died out on Java when the last Hindu civilization there fled to Bali in the 15th C., but on Bali it has been practiced continuously for the last 400 years. For centuries Java was the "Mother Country" and this is reflected even today in the subject matter of traditional Balinese art. Now most Balinese artists work solely for money, reasoning that it's senseless to go to the trouble of making a good painting when a bad painting will sell for just as much, just as fast. Try to visit the home of the artist (which you can find after persistent inquiry), and save yourself a percentage of the painting which otherwise goes to the guide, driver, agent, or shop. The exact same paintings which sell for US$2500 in the art shops on the main road of Ubud, the artist himself sells for US$200 just down the path in the *kampung*. The cost of high-standard paintings, if you can find them, is roughly US$200-400 per sq meter. You'll often find that when you get back to Australia, the U.S., or Europe, *the frame* will cost more than the painting did (so be sure to buy your frame in Bali too!).

Traditional Painting

Religious narrative paintings derive from the 14th and 15th C., when the Hindu population of E. Java fled to Bali. They are characterized by a flat, stiff, formal style, painted according to a very strict traditional formula which lacks all emotion. Figures of Hindu gods, demons, and princesses in limewater colors are placed row on row in high state in the realm of the gods. Each god is distinguished by details of dress which set him or her apart. Shading to indicate perspective is traditionally not used. These paintings are read like a comic strip, the characters and events represented in separate cells, the scenes all taking place in a divine cosmic world. Cloud and wind patterns and flame and mountain motifs separate the scenes. Sometimes up to 15 m wide and 4 m long, these paintings are hung along temple eves as festive decoration. Modern examples of these cloth paintings are still turned out, especially around Klungkung (in Kamasen village). Although much influenced by Western art, Balinese painters have retained many traditional features in their art which stem from their Javanese cultural ancestors. Balinese painting is still limited in subject matter, treatment, symbolism, and especially in the colors used: blue, yellow, black, white, and Chinese red, with dull browns and greens mixed from the pigments.

Modern Painting

The period between the World Wars brought heavy changes. Balinese artists stopped painting according to rules and started to recreate their own visual experience. During the years 1933-39, such European artists as Walter Spies and Rudolph Bonnet (among others) demonstrated to Balinese artists that painters can be free of set formulas or a single stylistic convention, encouraging them to unfold individually. These Europeans also taught them the concept of the third dimension. You can still see Rousseau, who influenced Spies greatly, evident in Balinese painting. Artists are now working mostly for a European market, and the tourist's demand for paintings "suitable for framing" has again changed the technique and content of their painting style. Full-face representations are rare and profiles rarer still. Balinese painters are filled with stories and myths from childhood and never lack a theme to paint about. Sometimes dozens of stories are happening all at once in many of their paintings. In their paintings of jungle scenes there's elaborate, riotous decoration of leaves, flowers, and animals, with every leaf carefully outlined. Mindful of Persian miniatures or of the English artist Beardsley, tiny blades of grass and insects are found in the furthest corners of their paintings. Lately, birds and banana leaf panels have become the rage—more decoration than art.

Art Galleries And Museums

To familiarize yourself with high-quality historical works, visit the disintegrating collection of paintings at the Puri Lukisan Museum of Ubud. Many of Bali's finest painters live in and around this village. To understand contemporary Balinese painting, visit the

Neka Galley in Ubud, the Neka Museum N of Campuan (one km W of Ubud), and the superb Agung Rai Galley in Peliatan (one km E of Ubud). Also visit the Abiankapas complex in Denpasar with its permanent exhibition of Balinese painting (open 0800-1700, tel. 22776).

CRAFTS

Due to the extravagant sums package tourists pay for Balinese artifacts, prices have become ludicrously high, and the Balinese have developed a pathetically inflated notion of the true value of their crafts. Clothing, woodcarvings, bonework, and batik are cheaper in India and other Asian countries, and often of equal quality. Although Bali's silversmiths are more inventive, silverwork is usually cheaper in Yogya, C. Java. On Bali, the first asking price in a local market or by a peddler is not necessarily lower than that of the exclusive shop—they both start out at equally escalated prices. Clothes can no longer be traded for crafts; they now just want money. French tourists start raining down around mid-year and Australians and domestic tourists overrun the island at Christmas, but from March-June, crafts are about ¼ to ½ the usual price. The bargains are still extraordinary. There are mass-produced handicrafts all over the island now so if you don't like it or can't afford it, say vehemently, *"Sing ngeleh pipis!"* (Balinese for "I'm dead broke!"). If you let a guide take you into a crafts shop, he gets a commission of 10-20% or more; that's what you have to pay extra on your total purchase. North Bali (Singaraja) has cheaper crafts than the more touristy south.

Jewelry

Balinese silver is often only 60-70% pure and they cut it as thin as a razor. Sample prices: silver bracelets start at about US$120 with gold, US$60 without gold; silver necklaces, US$17; rings set with semiprecious stones, US$50. They will often come down 20-30%. Many of the jewelry shops also sell paintings, woodcarvings, and other souvenirs. Go in the back to watch them make silver articles. Buy gold cheaply in Bangkok and have it reworked into rings, brooches, and necklaces on Bali. Or trade silver for jewelry or give high-content silver coins and get back handmade jewelry. Artisans usually want a little cash-in-hand, too. Also bring stones for setting; very striking backgrounds. There are dozens of Westerners selling their own personalized jewelry around Kuta. Want to learn silversmithing? Some losmen owners do silversmithing on the side, or ask around Celuk. Find a kampung craftsman whose workshop is just a dirt floor and work with him directly.

Textiles

Take advantage of the inexpensive pants and shirts

that are available in shops and from the beach peddlers—Kuta and Sanur are the designer clothes capitals of Asia. It costs only Rp3000-5000 and 4 days to have a perfect fit made to order in a tailor shop, so you shouldn't ever pay a peddler more than that amount. Balinese *batik* garments are plentiful everywhere. Keep a lookout for *kain prada* fabrics woven of silk or cotton and decorated with silver or gold threads or gold leaf. These very colorful kerchiefs are worn during festivals by temple girls. A ceremonial 2-m-long cloth could take 3 weeks to a month to weave, depending on the intricacy of the design. Not washable; clean by dusting, then let it air in the sun.

Shells And Trinkets

Two-hundred-year-old perforated Chinese coins *(kepeng)* with Chinese characters on one side ("Year of the Corn," "Year of the Snake," etc.) and the Pali script on the other are used in casting I Ching. Find them at river-mouths and graveyards, or kick them up as you walk along the beach. On Kuta, you pay 10 times the price you get inland. *Puka* shells are small, round, white (sometimes dotted with brown) shells found only in Hawaii (where they're almost cleaned out), the Philippines, and Bali. The best ones are the small necklaces with all uniform-size shells. Again, pay premium prices on Kuta for a small necklace, but out at the surfers' hangout in Ulu Watu's souvenir *warung* you can find really long chains much cheaper. Turtle Island has the most gorgeous seashells. Conical-shaped straw hats used by fieldworkers cut out the sun's rays exactly below the eyes and also make good umbrellas, around Rp2500.

For handicrafts at their cheapest, and for the widest range, go to the following villages:

Babat: Sandstone carvings; silver and goldwork.

Bangli and Tampaksiring: Coconut, cattle-bone, and buckhorn carvings.

Batuan: Woven goods. Known for traditional woven cloth and carved and decorated painted wooden panels. Also some painting.

Batubulan: Stone sculpture center. Lining the roadsides are fantastic stone figures and statues of divinities and demons sold as protective figures for family shrines, crossroads, or temples. Also stone bas-reliefs of mythological heroes. Watch the stonecarvers and their apprentices at work without obligation to buy anything. They've got packing and shipping agents here as well.

Blaju and Gianyar Weaving. Where most of the good *sarung* come from. An excellent place to shop for textiles.

Bona: Near Gianyar. A center of the plaiting industry. Baskets, hats, sandals, bags, fans. They also build bamboo chairs, tables, birds, and flowers.

Bratan and Celuk: Weaving, gold and silverwork. In Celuk the tourist buses disgorge the hordes on the main road shops, but the back lanes are where it's all happening. More than 25

silver shops in Celuk. If you find the right shop, have your personal designs made up for you really inexpensively: ornaments, rings, bracelets, pendants, brooches made to order. Must leave a deposit.

Gua Gadjah: Baskets, shell carvings, and other curios. Cheaper than Denpasar.

Klungkung: Wood and horn handicrafts, bone carvings, fine woven silk. Also several antique shops sell Chinese porcelain, ornamental gold and silver jewelry, and some old Gelgel Dynasty relics.

Mas, Peliatan, and Ubud: Carving and painting centers. Some of the best-known Balinese carvers live in Mas, old masters who are still working and teaching apprentices. Visit Ida Bagus Nyana, Rodja, and Ida Bagus Glodok, noted for his carved wooden masks. Visit the home of Ida Bagus Tilum and his museum of carvings and panels.

Puaya: Near the village of Sukawati. Puppets are made from old Chinese coins. Leather puppets are also made here.

THE PERFORMING ARTS

Music

Enormously loved by the people. The sound of echoing xylophones, drums, and clashing cymbals are heard all hours of the night and day throughout the island. Bathers sing in the rivers, rattles clack in the fields, looms tingle with bells, kites vibrate in the wind, little boys walk along lanes imitating the sound of gongs, and flocks of pigeons circle overhead with whistles attached to their feet. Among the finest *gamelan* are made on Bali and cost up to US$4000. Every village has its orchestra, each given such names as "Sea of Honey," or "Snapping Crocodiles," and all its members are unpaid amateurs. Anyone may play and a musician might hand over his *gendang* to a spectator during a performance. The Balinese *gamelan* is played more vigorously and passionately than the slower, more aimless and haunting Javanese *gamelan*. The Balinese like their music electrifying and very loud, with sharp changes in tempo and volume. Similar instruments are tuned slightly out of pitch with each other to make the sound shimmer. Perfect music for spells and animist rites. Old men play flutes in the background, dogs prance across the dance floor, infants suckle, children play in the audience, the musicians oblivious to it all. Many village *gamelan* orchestras practice in the evenings, when entry is free. Listen for *genggong,* the Balinese jew's harp, a short thin strip cut from the rib of the sugar-palm leaf in which a tongue is cut. Tugging a string causes the instrument to vibrate; you "breathe" the tune. There's a whole repertoire of jew's harp pieces played by orchestras of up to 24 *genggong* players: "Crow Steals Eggs," "Frog Song" (which sounds like the blissful rhythms of frogs' breeding chorus). These instruments can bleat, trill, croak, laugh, or lull you to sleep. Another unique instrument of Bali is the *rejog:*

2 deep gongs fastened to hang vertically at each end of a stick.

Dancing

Balinese dance will probably be the most impressive sight you'll see and remember. With over 2,000 dance troupes on the island, dance is at the very center of Balinese life. On Java dance is in large part the prerogative of the courts, but on Bali it's most active in the ordinary villages. The Balinese consider Javanese dancing boring and the Javanese think that Balinese dancing is noisy and vulgar. Dancers on Bali perform for the pleasure of the gods, prestige, the entertainment of friends and family, and for tourists for money. Many performances are staged especially for tourists (Rp2000-4500) and many dances have been shortened to please the fickle foreigners. Instead, try to see performances connected with a temple festival or other local ritual events which are much cheaper or free. On any night of the week within a radius of just a few kilometers, you could see a number of different dance dramas and ballets to honor a local temple god, dedicate a new temple, exorcize evil, or celebrate a wedding, a tooth-filing ceremony, or a cremation. The stage could be an open dusty courtyard in front of a temple gate or at a crossroads with the open starry sky and the towering palm trees as the roof. The dance area will be encircled by hundreds of squatting, sitting, standing people of all ages. The mood is electric. Balinese dance is generally easy to understand; all you need is the thread of the story.

Dance Choreography

In their classical dance all movements and limbs speak—the joints, facial features, fingers, wrists, neck, eyes, hips, knees, feet, ankles. Balinese dance styles stem from the work they do; they are simply working gracefully and wearing beautiful clothes when they dance. Men climb coconut trees with prehensile toes which you also see utilized in some dance steps. *Pikulan*-carrying is excellent training for male dancers, the work giving them rhythm and a breathing sense, allowing them to rise and fall in dance almost without noticing them. Women carry burdens on their heads, flicking their eyes in the same way as in dance to greet each other and to watch where they step. Their fingers, trained from childhood to make small things, thus can flutter with agility in dance, expressing feelings. Women's dance is pure form. Only in the men's dancing is the content open to interpretation. The Balinese don't dance upwards and away from the earth, but move along its surface in slow, zig-zagging circles. Female postures are characterized by an outcurved spine and buttocks pushed back with the shoulders off-center. In both female and male dancing the limbs form angles with elbows pointing upwards with the head sinking down so far that the neck almost disappears. Sudden changes of direction and precise jerky steps are

marked features of Balinese choreography. They dance with a mesmerizing intensity like they're always being startled. The only exceptions to this intensity are the comic or grotesque characters who show shocked surprise or fear. Violence is shown on stage during a dance where it's not permitted in real life. You must have *fire* to dance, and it must come from the eyes. The complete lack of emotional expression of other facial features can be likened only to a trance state. It's said that experts can tell immediately who a dancer's teacher is by the style in which she dances, and a good Balinese *Legong* dancer can be judged solely by the complexity and suppleness of the girl's little finger. There are over 200 different kinds of dances, many religious, each a composite of not only dance, but also drama, music, spoken poetry, ballet. Here are some of the more popular.

Gambuh

The oldest dance practiced on Bali (over 1,000 years old), from which all the other dances descended. Its mysterious music and slow, stylized form are unique.

Pendet

The welcoming or offering dance, performed by young girls, before all dance performances. The basic female dance.

Kecak

This dramatic pre-Hindu dance is said to derive from the choral element of the trance dance, *Sangyang Dedari*. Also called the "Monkey Dance" because of the savage ape sounds the performers make, 100 or more seated men all shake, clap, and shout as one being. *Kecak* takes place in a big shadow-filled area at night with only burning torches around the all-male choir. No *gamelan* accompanies it, just the massed voices chattering in perfect unison, compassionate or fearful, or all voicing shock, despair, or panic. Fierce eerie hissing and moaning, bellows, and other weird, other-worldly primeval sounds pierce the night air. All bodies appear as black, throwing their arms out at once in the night and shaking their fingers wildly. *Kecak* has borrowed some typical

Kuntao movements, a secret fighting art imported from China. The plot is taken from the *Ramayana* and concerns Rama, his brother, and Sita, exiled in the dark forests of Sri Lanka (Ceylon). The monkey armies of Hanuman and Sugriwa later help rescue Sita.

Barong

Also called the "Kris Dance." A dance pantomime of a fantastic dragon-like holy animal, the Barong, pitched in battle against the machinations of a witch, Rangda. This is the most violent of Balinese dances and is often used as an exorcism. The open-air Barong Dance is usually held in the middle of the road. Rangda is Queen of the *Layak* (witches), her sawdust-filled breasts sagging and her tongue lolling wickedly. She is the Female Principal, a ruthless child-eater and black magician belonging to the "left" side, The Night, bringing sickness and death. Rangda's mask is painted white with a horrible expression of round bulging eyes and tusks protruding from the mouth, with long hairy pieces of rope hanging to the ground. A white cloth is her only weapon. She runs away but never dies. Some scholars say her origin is Shiva's wife Durga in her evil aspect. Barong, a hairy, eerie, mythical lion, sides with human beings against Rangda to thwart her evil plans. Without him, humanity would be lost. He is The Day, The Light, The Sun, the Male Principal, the "right" side, the force that overcomes evil. The huge and frightening Barong has a beard of human hair decorated with flowers, long hair, feathers and bells all over his body. Strength is concentrated in the beard. The Barong is manipulated by 2 men who take it through comic yet very complex dance movements that make people laugh — but not *too* loud. At its conclusion, Rangda turns the humans' power against them and you see men trying to willfully impale themselves on sharp *kris*. After the dance is over and when they come out of the trance, there is no trace of injury, bruising, or bleeding.

Legong

Considered the most dazzling of all Balinese dance. Swathed in cocoons of gold-plaited fabrics, with their hands palpitating and their eyes flashing, these dancers perform an interpretation of a literary classic. A pair of young girls is chosen for their good looks and for their supple physiques. If they can be found to look alike, all the better. They are chosen before they

Baris *dancer*

begin menstruation because only then are they considered pure and limber enough to perform all the necessary movements. Training begins at ages 4 or 5; they retire at about age 13. *Legong* dancers were once a Balinese prince's private property. Extraordinary muscular control and great physical endurance are required in this dance. Dancers are first dressed in gorgeous costumes: head to toe in silk and gold leaf with a headdress of frangipani and earplugs of gold. Their bodies are tightly girdled from chest to hips with many meters of heavy cloth and covered with rich beautiful silks decorated with gold. This clothing helps to support their backs and gives them a graceful line. They both have heavily powdered faces with a white dot *(priasan)* on their foreheads, a symbol of beauty in dancers. Their eyebrows are shaved and given a new line with black paint. These young nubile girls dance to rapid staccato rhythms with wide-open eyes, hips shifting and backs arched, all of their movements executed in perfect unison. Enacting the story of *Malat*, the Balinese "Thousand and One Nights," this is a drama of a princess kidnapped by a despised suitor.

Baris

A stately, un-Javanized native war dance performed on occasion of festivals and ritual feasts. Very typical of the most masculine aspects of Balinese life. The 10-12 men who perform dress in all white, black, or checkered clothes. Could also be performed by 8- or 9-year-olds who wear triangular headdresses of flowers. Featuring heroic poses, expressive faces, sham battles, duels, and violent music, the *Baris* is the basic male dance which goes through all the emotions: passion, pleasure, rage, tenderness, love.

Tari Tenun

A typical example of contemporary dance that portrays a woman making a *sarung*.

Sangyang Dedari

Held only in time of trouble to alleviate sickness or misfortune in a village, this celebrated shamanistic dance is a way of contacting the gods. The "Virgin" or "Trance Dances" offered by tour agents are not the *Sangyang Dedari*, but laughable shams of it. The real article is often closed to tourists, so you'd be fortunate to see it. The dance steps are the same as in the *Legong*. Two auto-hypnotized little girls become possessed by the spirit of a god and dance on the top of men's shoulders. They never open their eyes, yet their performances coincide perfectly. The girls have never had formal dance lessons, and once awake they don't remember any of the performance. When the performance is over the dancers are revived by priests who bring them out of the trance by means of incense, chants, and rhythmical movements.

Kebyar

An interpretive dance of man's many moods. Performed from the squatting position with only the knees changing position. The audience's attention is forced to focus on movements of the torso, arms, hands, and facial expression. Darting glances, gentle swaying. Many different styles.

Janger

A modern dance performed in a large square with 2 rows of young men and women opposite one another. The story tells of a prince's search for a magic arrow. Led by a man, those at the side accompany the dance with rhythmical movements, tinkling music, and singing.

Joget

A popular Balinese dance. Each girl who performs chooses a partner from the audience by tapping him with her fan. Partners are changed every 5 minutes. Especially hysterical when a French clerk or an Australian crayfisherman is tapped on the shoulder, with all his mates egging him on.

Dance Study

Watch or study *gamelan* and dance at KOLKAR, the Conservatory of Instrumental Arts and Dance in Batubulan, a suburb of Denpasar. There's also an ASTI (Akademi Seni Tari Indonesia-Bali) on Jl. Nusa Indah in Denpasar. Though at this dance college you may sit in on classes held many times a day, to seriously study Balinese classical dance you need a permit from LIPI in Jakarta as a "guest student." You can't really get that involved with dance within the length of time allotted on an ordinary tourist pass. An average course lasts one-2 years; they'll ask around Rp5000 an hour for tutoring but it's highly negotiable. For short term, it's more rewarding to go up to Ubud or out to a village to study dance informally. Stay for several weeks; they're glad to have you. When you leave, give a donation to the *gamelan* orchestra. Many of Bali's dance teachers are elderly women; they are the only ones who know the complete repertoire of the dances. It's a great pleasure to watch these masters teach their young students out in the villages; the interpersonal dynamics between teacher and pupil are truly captivating.

PRACTICALITIES

ACCOMMODATIONS

You used to be able to stay as a guest in a Balinese house anywhere on the island, but now families are no longer permitted to put you up as long as there's a hotel or *losmen* in the same village. And they're furiously building hotels in all the towns and villages now to the extent that at times it feels like you're vacationing on a building site. Homestays or *losmen* are the finer experience and preferable to hotels. You live right inside the family compound and participate in the life of the family. Learn how to make *lamak* from the grandmother, flutes from the father, kites from the small ones, or *bebek tutu* (smoked duck) from the mother. The grandfather will take you to the next cockfight and the daughter will show you the shortest way to the market or how to sew a *sarung* into a skirt. Your *losmen* owner can also find you the best dance, painting, or *wayang kulit* teachers, take you to a wedding, a special ceremony, etc. Your gear is usually quite safe in the family compound where someone is always home.

The low-season is Jan.-May when even Bali's expensive hotels will give as much as 50% off. But during the high season (June, July, Aug., and Dec.), accommodations are booked solid nearly all over the island. During this time, they don't need your business to survive. If the hotel has a swimming pool, they charge US$35 and up, but other comparable accommodations can be just as comfortable and cost only US$20. No matter what the price, breakfast (coffee or tea, toast, fruit salad, and egg) is almost always thrown in free. Some Westerners even take out a 10-year lease,

at around US$110 per month, make improvements on the property, then hand it all over to the Balinese family at the end of the lease. Also popular is renting out "under contract" a room or a section of a house for several months while studying dance, music, painting, or puppetry.

Kuta and Legian don't have a monopoly on the best homestays. Some excellent ones can be found in the villages of Ubud, Peliatan, and Penestanan (near Ubud), also in the vicinity of Amlapura, in Singaraja, and even in Denpasar itself. Quite often around Kuta and Legian you'll be approached by locals with offers of a room. These could be good, newly opened and eager to please. Some of the *losmen* and "Beach Inns" remind you of old peoples' homes the way the rooms are all set in a row; tourists have no choice but to sit and have breakfast together. Coffee, tea, and bananas are often included in the room price. Balinese-style accommodations, using *bale* with *atap* roofs, are now becoming the rage. The *atap* keeps your room cool all day.

FOOD

Balinese food is very spicy and peppery. Often it's served cold. Grated coconut meat *(nyuh)* is an essential ingredient in their cooking. Thick rich coconut cream, made by squeezing grated coconut over and over, is used in many native dishes; it doesn't keep so it must be used the same day. *Sate* is often kneaded into the cream. Frying is done in coconut oil. Such Indonesian national dishes as *mie goreng* and *gado gado* are also widely available.

Markets in most villages take place every 3 days; here you can find a cornucopia of grains, beans, greens, and fruit. Tropical fruits include *zirzak, salak* (best from Rendang), *nangka, jeruk* (pink are better), *durian, blimbing* (starfruit), breadfruit, mangosteens, passion fruit (from Kintamani), white mangos (melt in your mouth). Also you'll come across such exotic vegetables as acacia leaves *(twi),* greens *(kankang),* edible ferns *(paku),* tapioca leaves *(ketela poton),* etc., which go into many of the roadside *warung* dishes, which can cost as little as Rp400-600. Sweet potatoes *(ubi)* with coconut, palm sugar, and ketchup, are found at nearly every *warung.*

Most of Indonesia is Muslim but on Bali pigs are bred and cooked magnificently. Don't miss Bali's famous delicacy, *babi guling,* suckling pig roasted on a spit and stuffed with red chili, garlic, turmeric, *jahe,* ginger, aromatic leaves, peppercorn. The flesh is juicy and tender, the skin crisp and covered with a golden-brown glaze. Serves 4 or 5. Roast duck, an equally famous delicacy of Bali, serves 2 or 3. Order these specialty items at least 24 hours in advance, or you can try *babi guling* in the market. The very best is served in 2 *warung* in Pasar Gianyar, for only Rp750!

Balinese also eat worms, frogs, flying foxes, snakes, porcupines, anteaters, lizards, wild boars, centipedes, grubs, birds (bones and all), and ricefield eels which look like baby snakes. A Balinese kid will take you out dragonfly catching using a long thin pole with a sticky end. Take the wings off, fry the bodies in coconut oil until crisp and eat with spices and vegetables. Also sample some very mellow homemade native brews: *arak* (distilled rice brandy), *tuak* (sweet palm beer), and *brem* (rice wine). *Brem* is available by the bottle (Rp1200) or by the glass (Rp500). The *brem tua* ("old *brem")* is more expensive than the *brem manis* ("sweet *brem").*

MISCELLANEOUS

Sports
One of the world's top 50 golf courses, designed by course architect Peter Thomson and Associates, is on the grounds of the Bali Handara Kosaido Country Club in Pancasari (1,142 m above sea level) near Lake Bratan. Judged 5th in the world for technical design and 5th for service, this 18-hole championship course features tall trees and flowers in riotous colors separating the fairways. Bali is also a scuba and snorkeling center, famous among divers for its marine life, superb visibility, and sensational drop-offs. It was on Bali that drift diving was made popular because certain techniques had to be developed to accommodate the deep ocean currents surrounding the island. Gloria Maris, on the road between Kuta and the Ngurah Rai Airport, offers gear, tanks, wetsuits, lunch, transport, experienced dive master, excellent

Balinese-style accommodations, and even porters to and from the beach—all for around US$25-30 per day, depending upon the destination.

Cockfighting
Fights are now illegal, but still take place on the sly in almost every village, usually in the mornings. You'll hear of them. They may also take place at festivals, after the *banjar* first obtains permission. You only see men at the cockfights, though women may enter the tourist ones. Fighting cocks are given the greatest loving care, being massaged, bathed, and trained every day. Their feathers, combs, earlobes, and wattles are trimmed so that none provides a beak-hold for the opponent bird. The owner concentrates on the bird's diet so that it becomes lean and tireless. Pet, mascot, child, dreams, income, the bird is always carried with him around his courtyard and to the *warung* or *banjar* clubhouse, taking up as much attention as a new wife. Their bell-shaped cages are placed at roadsides so the cocks may be amused by the passersby and not get lonely. A village will put up as much as a million *rupiah* on its favorite cock. Two cocks eager to fight must be decided upon, then equal or unequal bets are placed. Then the fight is blessed. Evil spirits receive an offering which hopefully satisfies them and also assures a good harvest. Brokers squabble, the birds are teased by their handlers, tails pulled, feathers ruffled, and palm wine sometimes spit down their throats, all intended to arouse the fighting spirit. Razors are then strapped to their spurs. The fight is often finished in 15-20 seconds. The cocks display an amazing ferocity even when crippled with wounds. If both refuse to continue the fight they're put inside an upside-down basket, then one almost always kills the other. Often a badly wounded cock can be revived by artificial respiration or by special massages, then fight again, and win. The devotion, gesticulating, and hysteria of the audience are fascinating to watch.

Bullraces
At Negara, W. Bali, regional bullraces are held between July and October. Trained bulls are dressed up in silk banners with painted horns and big wooden bells. Each team is judged by speed and style. Like Roman charioteers they come thundering down to the finish line, whipping, shouting, and mud flying. Jockeys twist the bulls' tails to gain speed. Much gambling. This festival is staged to please the god of harvest.

Jail
Go straight to jail and do not collect for: overstaying your visa, shameful nudity (the Javanese, who administer Bali, can't handle it), or dope busts. As any intelligent person knows, cannabis causes blindness, insanity, satyriasis, and ultimate death. You could get up to 30 days and fined as much as A$100 for possession (of a little or a lot) of the noxious weed. Police

don't bust you out of any moral compunction or even to do their duty. They bust you to make money out of users; beware of narc cunning and stealth (trained by Aussies). Sellers are treated more harshly: in 1987 an Australian was sentenced to life imprisonment after being convicted of possessing 26.7 pounds of marijuana. Jails, euphemistically called "detention centers," are found in Denpasar and Singaraja. Jail need not be so bleak; they treat you humanely. If you can pay, get cigarettes or *batik* equipment. Visitors only on Sun. afternoons.

GETTING THERE

Just 3 international airlines have direct flights to Bali: Garuda (Indonesia's national carrier), Continental (U.S.A.), and Qantas (Australia). All other airlines first fly to Jakarta, then transfer on to Bali. **from Europe:** London bucket shops sell Garuda tickets London-Denpasar for around UK550 RT, UK300 OW. **from Australia:** Fly direct from Sydney, Melbourne, Perth, Darwin, or Port Hedland. Take advantage of the APEX RT fares which you must buy 21 days before departure; high season is Dec.-January. From Sydney, the fare is A$500 OW, A$750 RT in the high season; A$400 OW, A$625 RT in the low season. A unique way to reach Bali is via Kupang. From Darwin it costs A$320 RT (or US$202 OW) with Garuda all the way to Denpasar via Kupang on an Apex fare. **from U.S.A.:** From San Francisco, pay as low as US$440 OW plus tax. The Garuda Orient Tour packages (with accommodations) include several in the US$1100-1200 range; from L.A. it's a 23-hour flight. Buy tickets at the Garuda and Indonesian Consulate offices on Wilshire Blvd. in Los Angeles. Inquire also about the special student rate (around US$800, without accommodations). For details on international flights into Indonesia, see "Getting There" in the main "Introduction." **from within Indonesia:** To Denpasar from Bandung (via Surabaya), Rp88,600; Bima (via Mataram), Rp66,900; Kupang (via Waingapu), Rp95,800; Ende, Rp105,100; Malang, Rp42,400; Yogya, Rp47,800; Surabaya, Rp36,800; and Jakarta, Rp88,600.

Arriving By Air
In the airport lobby, go past all the people who want you to stay in their hotels and get a taxi to either Denpasar (Rp6000) or Kuta (Rp3000). If going to Ubud, get a taxi just to Denpasar's Kereneng Station, then a minibus up to Ubud (Rp400). Alternatively, if you want to avoid taking a taxi from the airport, walk 150 m out to the main road outside the airport where cheaper buses or *bemo* go by until 2200. Or just walk; as you emerge from the terminal, turn L, then walk down to the beach and turn right. It's about 3 km to Kuta village.

By Road
Board the ferry at Ketapang on E. Java's tip; Rp250 2nd Class, Rp450 1st Class, Rp600 for motorcycles, Rp5000 for a car. If you take the last ferry across you arrive in Bali at first light to see the whole island come to life: mists lifting over tiered pagodas, ducks off to the fields under flags of herders, women yawning in doorways, pots boiling on early morning fires, lines of shadowy people going off to market. If you're late for the ferry, just go down the beach to the LCM depot. From the ferry depot on the Bali side in Gilimanuk on the NW corner, take a *dokar* or *bemo* to the terminal where you can board a bus (Rp2000) or a minibus (Rp2500) for Denpasar, Bali's capital. Or walk to the edge of town and start hitching. If you want to go to Lovina Beach (near Singaraja) instead and avoid the more touristed south, the distance is 87 km, Rp1000 by bus, Rp1200 by minibus.

From Bali
Denspasar via Kupang on an APEX fare. **From U.S.A.:** From San Francisco, pay as low as US$440 OW plus For example, the Simpatik Bus Co. has overnight buses with free meals, cold water, a/c, video (violent Chinese samurai movies) to Malang, E. Java; Rp10,500. Other, non-a/c buses to Malang cost only Rp4500. They all leave at 1830, arriving at 0400. The Helios Hotel, 5-min. walk from Malang's bus station, will be open. For Jakarta, a/c buses cost Rp22,000 and take at least 26 hours.

GETTING AROUND

The best way to see Bali is to just start walking. In S-central Bali, take half-hidden narrow pathways at roadsides and follow them inland sometimes 15 km. You'll reach places about as outlandish as you want to be in, with no cold drinks, police, shops, or transport connections. Children pop up and yell out a singsong "HELLOW!" or you could come across infants who start screaming at the sight of you.

Vehicles-For-Rent
There are hundreds of hotels, restaurants, and travel agencies where you can rent 4-wheeled vehicles, priced according to the type of vehicle. Kuta Beach has the largest selection of rental places. Jimmys and VW convertibles, called Safaris, normally rent for Rp20,000-25,000 per day. Called "The Thing," the safari convertible came and left America within a year and now they're all here. They have a reputation for breakdowns, but you can sometimes rent them for as low as Rp15,000 per day. Huge chauffeured American cars (Rp20,000 per day), a/c Landcruisers (Rp75,000 per day), Japanese compacts like Mazda sedans (Rp30,000 per day), and Suzuki 4-wheel drives (Rp30,000) are also widely available. **gas:** Pertamina

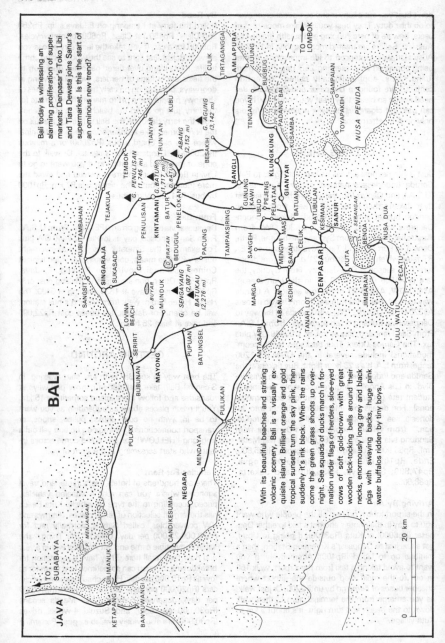

BALI

Bali today is witnessing an alarming proliferation of supermarkets: Denpasar's Toko Libi and Tiara Dewata joins Sanur's supermarket. Is this the start of an ominous new trend?

With its beautiful beaches and striking volcanic scenery, Bali is a visually exquisite island. Brilliant orange and gold tropical sunsets turn the sky pink, then suddenly it's ink black. When the rains come the green grass shoots up overnight. See squads of ducks march in formation under flags of herders, sloe-eyed cows of soft gold-brown with great wooden tick-tocking bells around their necks, enormously long grey and black pigs with swaying backs, huge pink water buffalos ridden by tiny boys.

TO LOMBOK

JAVA

TO SURABAYA

0   20 km

stations, found on all the main roads of the island, charge around Rp400 per liter. Roadside vendors, recognizable by the signs SOLAR (diesel) and PREMIUM (gas), charge only Rp250 per liter, but they water down the gas which causes your engine to sputter.

Boats

Benoa is Bali's main port where foreign yachts call; take a canoe out and ask around for a ride. Also check out the northern port of Celukan Bawang for Bugis schooners heading for Sulawesi or E. Kalimantan. For the eastern islands, ferries leave the E. Bali port of Padangbai for Lembar on Lombok. Sailfish-shaped *prahu (Gadjah-Mina)* look like a sort of elephant-fish with a long double trunk and big bloodshot eyes that can see you through the night. Sail it along the shore; it takes 2 people to handle.

Bicycles

If you ride a bicycle around Bali, you have much more contact with the villagers than if you were on a speeding, smelly, noisy motorbike. Bicycles rent for only Rp1000-1200 per day, cheaper by the week or month. The fewer the bikes they have left, the higher the rental fees. Or buy a bike from a *toko sepeda* in Denpasar, then arrange to have them buy it back from you after you use it for several weeks. Because the seats are hard and uncomfortable, buy a cushioned saddle and a seat post to heighten your seat for long-distance riding. To get to the highlands of Bali take your bike on a *bemo*, minibus, or bus, then when you get ready to come back it's just 2 days downhill, coasting all the way. It'll usually cost you an extra passenger's fare to put your bike on a *bemo* roof. Be sure to bring your bike inside your *losmen* at night; there are a lot of rip-offs and you could pay up to Rp25,000-50,000 for a lost rented bicycle.

Buses, *Bemo*, And Minibuses

Cheapest motorized transport on Bali are buses. To anywhere on the island, Rp100-2000. The local buses such as the one from Gilimanuk or Amlapura to Denpasar are often unbelievably slow (48 stops in one hour) but excellent for drinking in Balinese native life. Minibuses are more expensive but much faster. The *bemo* and bus system on Bali is now so extensive that you can go virtually anywhere worth going on daytrips from Denpasar, Ubud, or Singaraja. If there's no direct express service, do it in stages. For example, if you want to go from Ubud to Gianyar, get to the Sakah intersection first, then flag down another *bemo* for the rest of the way. Charter a whole *bemo* for about Rp25,000 per day between 5 or 6 people. Or just stand out on the roads and hitchhike whatever comes by. Hitching on Bali is the best in all of Indonesia, getting rides with tourists, mail trucks, or on the back of motorcycles. The Balinese have a hard time understanding the concept of a Westerner (i.e., a

rich man) asking for a free ride, but don't let their curious stares discourage you. **warning:** *Bemo* robberies of travelers on Bali are now a regular thing. Once confined only to Denpasar, now robber *bemo* cruise the roads looking for unwary travelers. Once onboard, the traveler is pickpocketed and/or manhandled out of his money by a group of young men who crowd around and intimidate and confuse the traveler.

Motorbikes

Motorbikes may appear the best but they often prove more trouble and expense than they're worth. Intrusiveness in quiet villages, pollution, breakdowns, and injuries all go against them. Even experienced bikies get shattered nerves after just a week of riding on Bali where trucks drive right down the center of the roads, and chickens, dogs, and children are everywhere. Driving at night is especially hazardous; lots of insects and very dark. You have to worry about petrol (Rp400 a liter), oil money, as well as parking fees at nearly every tourist site. Basic rules for driving a motorcycle on Bali: always wear a helmet, and goggles or glasses; don't drive too fast; never stop on sand or loose gravel; slow down on curves (because vehicles drive in the center of the road); always toot your horn when approaching people or animals on the road; carry a windbreaker at higher elevations; and stop driving before sundown when the insects come out.

Off-season rates are Rp3500-5000 per day, or from Rp14,000-28,000 per week. The more powerful and new the machine, the higher the daily rate; the longer the rental period, the lower the rate. Rental charges rise when the Europeans or Australians arrive in numbers in Aug., Dec., and January. On Kuta, you'll constantly be approached by guys offering to rent you bikes. Be wary of being overcharged for faulty equipment, bad tires, etc. The bike repair shops on the road from Kuta into Denpasar, just before town, have bikes-for-rent in much better condition than private rentals. In most cases, a helmet comes with the bike. More difficult to find but easier to drive are fully automatic motorbikes with automatic starting and shifting; just insist upon one and one will show up sooner or later.

Driver's License And Insurance

Also factor in the time it will take you (a whole morning!) to get a Balinese driver's license. If you don't have one, you could be fined heftily at police roadblocks set up occasionally. Your *losmen* owner or the man who finds you a motorcycle can usually arrange everything, assembly-line fashion. The license costs Rp11,000 plus you need a certified guide to accompany you (Rp5000), then you pay for insurance (Rp14,000), so it costs Rp33,000 to be able to legally drive on Bali. If you get your bike on Kuta, your guide first stops in a place a third of the way to Denpasar for some paperwork, then takes you to another place two-thirds of the way into Denpasar where you have your picture taken, then you practice driving at another place, then finally he takes you to the police station (Komdak XV, Jl. Supratman, Denpasar) for the actual driver's test (a figure 8, then pay another Rp2500 for the forms). The answers to the written test (BCBCBA) are even whispered along the bench. Wear long pants. Insurance is priced according to engine size and length of rental time, e.g. Rp14,000 for a 110-125 cc for one week; Rp17,500 for 135-200 cc for one week, etc. Insurance for jimmys is Rp25,000, but you need an International Driver's License to drive a car on Bali.

BADUNG DISTRICT

DENPASAR

Capital of Bali and the largest, busiest city on the island. The local name is Badung. This typical middle-sized Indonesian community is still small (pop. around 100,000 but growing). It's like Luna Park 24 hours a day, a hot dirty smelly noisy dusty city that gives you a headache when you visit it for a morning from Kuta Beach. Unless you've got business here, the city has few charms.

Sights

On Jl. Wisnu off Puputan Square, **Bali Museum** contains a survey of Balinese art from prehistoric times to the early 20th C.: masks, woodcarvings, cages for fighting crickets, Neolithic stone implements, scale models of ceremonial events. This museum's architecture combines the 2 principal edifices of Bali, the temple and the palace, a blending of building styles of N., E., and W. Bali. Open every morning; Rp200 admission. Wear long pants. Next door to the museum is a Hindu temple, **Pura Jaganatha**; see the golden statue of Ida Batara Sang Hyang Widi Wasa. Visit **Puri Pemecutan** near the central bus station on the corner of Jl. Thamrin and Jl. Hasanudin. Above the **St. Joseph Catholic Church**, Jl. Kepundung 2 (off Jl. Melati), are angels dressed like *Legong* dancers, and in a stone bas-relief of Christ, Pilate studies the scrolls by electric light and a motorbike sits in the background. The University Library near the Central Hospital contains a collection of masterpieces of illustrative art and calligraphy, called *lontar*. These palm-leaf "books"—along with the *candi* of Java—are the only record of ancient Indonesian culture, history, and literature.

Accommodations

Very cheap is **Losmen Puri**, Jl. Arjuna 10, at Rp3000 pp; only 30 m from Jl. Gajah Mada. **Wisma Taruna Inn**, Jl. Gadung 31 (tel. 26913), on a quiet, rubbly back street, 2 km from the city center (Rp200 by *bemo)* or a 20-min. walk. Walk up Jl. Hayamwuruk and turn in at the Arya Hotel, then it's only a short walk from there. Costs Rp3500 pp with a YHA card or Rp2000 s without. Rent motorcycles and bicycles here. Also laundry service, beverages and food available. This hostel is only a 10-min. walk from the Kereneng Bus Terminal, which provides transport to all of eastern Bali. Sumertha Centre, which holds performances of the *Kecak, Ramayana,* and *Legong* dances is also nearby. **Two Brothers Inn** is on the main road to Kuta Beach; go down the lane to the R of

1. Adi Yasa
2. telephone office
3. *Bali Post* Newspaper
4. Hotel Ami
5. Garuda Airlines
6. Merpati office
7. Kodak office (for driver's license)
8. Wisma Taruna (YHA)
9. Babi Guling Gianyar
10. Restaurant Atoom Baru
11. *bemos* to Sanur and Ubud
12. Kumbasari Night Market
13. catch *dokars*
14. Restaurant Gajah Mada
15. RM Beringin Jaya
16. Bank Negara Indonesia
17. Restaurant Puri Selera
18. Bali Hotel
19. Denpasar Tourist office (IM)
20. telegraph office
21. Badung Tourist Office (LP)
22. Bouraq Airlines
23. Kereneng bus station
24. Art Center Kesimon
25. Puri Pemecutan Palace Hotel
26. Suci terminal
27. Tegol bus station
28. Two Brothers Losmen
29. Hotel Denpasar
30. Hotel Arta
31. immigration office
32. Dinas Pariwisata for Bali
33. governor's office

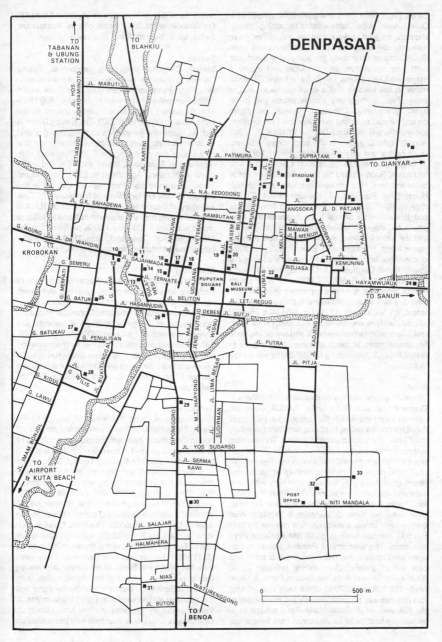

DENPASAR

TO
TABANAN
& UBUNG
STATION

TO
BLAHKIU

TO GIANYAR

TO KROBOKAN

TO SANUR

TO AIRPORT
& KUTA BEACH

TO BENOA

JL. MARUTI

JL. HOS TJOKROAMINOTO

JL. SETIABUDI

JL. KARTINI

JL. YUDISTIRA

JL. NANGKA

JL. SERUNI

JL. PATIMURA

JL. SUPRATAM

JL. RATNA

JL. G.K. SAHADEWA

JL. N.A. KEDODONG

JL. TERATAI

STADIUM

JL. DR. WAHIDIN

JL. RAMBUTAN

JL. BELIMBING

JL. KEPUNDUNG

ANGSOKA

JL. D. PATJAR

JL. MELATI

JL. ARDJUNA

JL. VETERAN

JL. KALASEM

MAWAR
MENUH

JL. KAMBODJA

JL. PALAWA

G. AGUNG

G. SEMERU

GAJAHMADA

JL. SULS. WISN

JL. TERNATE

JL. UDAJANA

PUPUTAN
SQUARE

JL. KEMUNING

JL. RIDJASA

G. MERPATI

G. BATUR

G. KAWI

JL. BELITON

BALI
MUSEUM

JL. KAJUMAS

JL. HAYAMWURUK

G. BATUKAU

JL. HASANNUDIN

JL. LET. REGUG

G. PENULISAN

JL. DEBES

JL. SUTJI

JL. WISNU

JL. PUTRA

JL. MAJ

JL. BUKITUNGGAL

G. KIDUL

G. WILIS

JL. PITJA

JL. SUTOJO

G. LAWU

JL. DIPONEGORO

JL. M.T. HARYONO

JL. LIMA BESAR

JL. SUDIRMAN

JL. YOS SUDARSO

JL. IMAM BONDJOL

JL. SERMA
KAWI

POST
OFFICE

JL. NITI MANDALA

JL. SALAJAR

JL. HALMAHERA

JL. NIAS

JL. BUTON

JL. WATURENGGONG

0   500 m

Banjar Tegal Gede. They charge Rp5000 s, Rp6000 d. Quiet, clean, safe, with electricity, sitting toilets, showers, fragrant flowers, free tea and coffee. From here you can easily walk or take a *bemo* into town (Rp250) or just stroll down the lane in your swim gear with your towel over your shoulder and thumb a *bemo* (Rp300) to Kuta Beach for a swim. Try local meals in the *warung* and a small restaurant 200 m away. Two Brothers will always inform you of an event going on in Denpasar—funeral, cockfight, dance, ceremony, or the like. Near the Two Brothers toward the city is **Hotel Darma Wisata**, Jl. Imam Bonjol; Rp5000 with *mandi*—cool, clean, efficient. Quite central and very reasonable is **Hotel Adi Yasa**, Jl. Nakula 23 (tel. 22679); Rp5000 s, Rp7500 d with bathroom. Rooms could be kind of close and hot at times (no fan). Nice environment and fairly central. **Hotel Elim**, Puri Oka, Jl. Kaliasem 3 (tel. 22165), charges Rp7500 s, Rp25,000 d for a/c front rooms, and is even more central (right opposite the Telephone & Telegraph office). Small breakfast, free tea and ice water included. Another reasonable place to stay is **Peng. Martapura**, Jl. Belimbing 22; Rp7500 s or d without fan. A little noisy because it's facing the street. **Hotel Denpasar**, Jl. Diponegoro 103, wants Rp6000-15,000 s, Rp8000-18,000 d for rooms with private bathroom; the more expensive ones have a/c. Centrally located at Jl. Veteran 5 is the venerable **Bali Hotel**. It's expensive—US$27 s, US$34 d (more if a/c), full facilities and breakfast included. Offers a bar, restaurant (with famous *rijstafel*), and swimming pool. For longer stays at much cheaper rates, inquire at **Hotel Ami**, Jl. Kepundung 58 (tel. 2976); ask for Ibu Wartawan.

Food

There are a large number of foodstalls everywhere in Denpasar; eat your fill for under Rp1000. Go to the open-air **night market** in Kumbasari after 1600 (until 2000) for noodle soups, fried rice, excellent *martabak*, roast pork, and good chocolate donuts. Try steaming *kue putu* smothered in coconut shavings. A splendid place to visit at night with thousands of milling people of all ages, races, and nations; fresh-killed goats hang above grills, boys play Balinese checkers with beercaps and stones on the sidewalk. Another night market, **Pasar Kamboja**, is in the Kereneng Terminal. Near Hotel Adi Yasa, Jl. Judistira, is **Warung Wardani**, which serves a delicious *nasi campur* for only Rp1500. For *nasi padang*, go to **RM Beringin Jaya** (see map). The specialty of **Pondok Selera** (on an open pavilion near the telephone office) is turtle *sate* plus lots of good chicken dishes; see sign SOTO AYAM. For Chinese food, the **Atoom Baru**, Jl. Gajah Mada 106-108 (tel. 22794), offers tasty *nasi goreng*, Rp1750, *cap cai*, Rp2500; also try the **Hongkong** or the **Ria**, also on Jl. Gajah Mada. For a splurge or to escape the heat, head for **Restoran Puri Selera**, op-posite Bank Rakyat Indonesia on Jl. Gajah Mada 16. For Indonesian food, a good one is **Restaurant Betty**, on Jl. Sumatra (near BNI 1946).

Events

Even in Denpasar, teeth-filing ceremonies, *Barong* Dances, cremations, and weddings take place regularly. Keep your eyes and ears open. The *Kecak* is held at the Sumertha Centre each night from 1800-1900. The *Ramayana* Ballet is sometimes staged at the Hyatt Hotel on Wed. 1900-2000. The *Barong* Dance is put on especially for tourists (but high quality and dynamic) at Batubulan, a suburb of Denpasar, on one of 3 stages every morning 0900-1000; jammed with hundreds of Europeans, buses and cars, and suffocated with sellers. Admission Rp2500. For cheaper, longer, and more traditional dances, get out to the villages to view celebrations and festivities. The Conservatory of Instrumental Arts and Dance (**KOLKAR**) is in Batubulan; here you may watch or study Balinese music and dance. *Wayang kulit* is performed at the Mars Hotel, Sun., Tues. and Thurs. 1800-1900. Many other "tourist" dance venues in the city.

Shopping

Visit the arts complex of **Abiankapas** on the E side of Denpasar for exhibits of modern painting and woodcarvings, plus regularly scheduled dances. **Sanggraha Kriya Asta Handicrafts Centre**, at Tophati in the suburbs of Denpasar, exhibits all aspects and styles of Balinese crafts. Open 0800-1300, 1700-2000. This center will give you a good feel for the prices you should be paying as it is government-run and all prices are fixed. See a weaving factory? **Pertenunan Carma** ("Cap Bajera"), Jl. Letda Suci 2 just S of the Bali Museum.

Services

For information about the island of Bali go to the **Dinas Pariwisata**, a 10-min. walk behind the post office in Denpasar's new administrative complex S of town; present yourself at the reception desk and fill in the request form. The **Badung Tourist Office** in on Jl. Surapati, a 5-min. walk from the Bali Museum. Ask them about any events taking place in the countryside. Open each day 0700-1400, Fri. until 1100, Sat. until 1200. The Telephone office is now on Jl. Veteran, near the Badung Tourist Office. Phone Jakarta for 3 min., Rp5000. The **DHL Courier Service**, Jl. Tanjung Bungkak 92, will send your envelope to Europe, Australia, or the States in 24 hours for US$10-15. The best bank to have your telegraphic transfers sent to is **Bank Bumi Daya**, Jl. Veteran; they also cash most kinds of travelers cheques. Both **BDN** and Bank Bumi Daya are near the Bali Hotel and the guardian statue, where Jl. Gajah Mada meets Jl. Veteran. Also try the rates at other banks along Jl. Gajah Mada. Don't have your mail sent *poste restante* to Denpasar's **post office** as it's too out of the way and a hassle to get to; have mail sent to either the Kuta or Ubud post offices instead. However, Denpasar's P.O. is one of the best places to have parcels sent as the clerks only charge Rp2000 per box for packaging. For packaging and sending your bulk shipments overseas, **Elteha's** head office is at Jl. Hasanudin 6.

FROM DENPASAR

Dokar charge at least Rp500; the Japanese are very fond of them, and groups often hire one for around Rp2000 per hour. The average *bemo* or minibus fare to anywhere in Denpasar is Rp200. Always ask the fare before you get in—it's around Rp150 for short distances, Rp250 for longer distances and between stations. There are 2 *bemo* stations, on Jl. Kartini and on Jl. Kamboja (Pasar Baru). Some *bemo*/minibus fares: **to C. Bali:** Leaving from Kereneng Station, Jl. Hayamwuruk: Sanur, Rp300; Ubud, Rp500; Bangli, Rp600; Padangbai (where ferries leave for Lombok), Rp1000; Klungkung, Rp600; Amlapura, Rp1500; Gianyar, Rp400; Kintamani, Rp1000. **to W. Bali:** From Stasiun Ubung, Jl. Cokroaminoto: Mengwi, Rp400; Sangeh, Rp400; Gilimanuk, Rp1500; Singaraja, Rp1500. **to Benoa:** From Stasiun Suci, Rp250. **to Kuta:** From Stasiun Tegal, on the road to Kuta, Rp300; Legian, Rp350.

Inter-island Buses

No bus fare to any town on the island is more than Rp2000 from any of Denpasar's 4 bus stations. Inter-island buses leave from Stasiun Suci for Surabaya, Yogya, Jakarta, Semarang. About 12 bus companies are on Jl. Hasanudin; go there the day before to book a good seat. There are a number of bus ticketing agencies at the Ubung Bus Station: just pick one with a convenient departure time. Also dozens of agents in Kuta, Legian, and Ubud where you can buy a ticket in advance, otherwise seats get booked out. If there are more than 3 people, the bus will pick you up at Kuta. **to Surabaya:** At least 10 buses per day but try to leave in the cool of the evening (last bus at 2100). Costs Rp11,000, including a meal halfway through the 11-hour trip. **to Yogya:** This 12-hour ride is Rp18,000, including 2 meals *(nasi campur* and drinks); bus leaves at 1530 and arrives at aroun 0700. **to Jakarta:** From Ubung the bus leaves at 0630, arrives at Jakarta's Pulau Gadung at 0930 the next day; Rp32,000.

By Air

From Stasiun Tegal, take a *bemo* to the airport, Rp250. During Dec., Jan., and Feb. flights out of Denpasar can be booked solid. Airport tax is Rp2300 for domestic flights, Rp9000 for international flights.

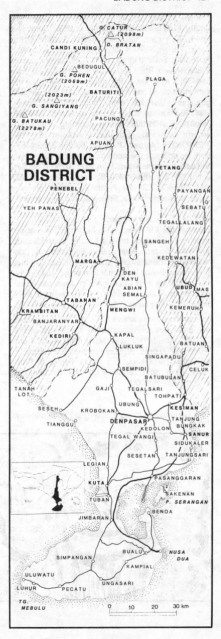

Sample airfares, including airport tax: Ampenan, Rp20,100, 6 flights daily starting at 0630; Surabaya, Rp44,700; Yogya, Rp47,800; Jakarta, Rp106,500; Kupang (Timor), Rp108,700; Waingapu (Sumbawa), Rp45,900; Ende (Flores), Rp107,300 (every day at 0750); Ruteng, Rp99,400 (every day at 0750). For Asia and Australia, shop for discount tickets at the numerous travel agencies around Kuta; for example: Singapore, US$120; Hong Kong, US$350; Darwin, US$205. Garuda offers flights to Guam, US$180; Jakarta, Rp104,000; Ujung Pandang, Rp73,100. **airline offices:** Garuda, Jl. Melati 61 (tel. 2028/27825); Merpati, Jl. Melati 59 (tel. 2159/4457). Both are opposite the stadium, are near to each other, and have the same hours: Mon. to Fri. 0700-1600, Sat. until 1300, Sun. 0900-1300. Bouraq, Jl. Kamboja 45D (tel. 23564/22252), for flights at very competitive prices to Nusatenggara, Sulawesi, and Kalimantan.

By Boat To Nusatenggara

Pelni has the KM *Kelimutu* to Kupang, Timor, about once every 2 weeks; takes 4-10 days depending on how many ports the boat calls on along the way. Contact Pelni in the small port of Benoa, SE Bali. Try hustling around Benoa Harbor for a lift on a private yacht; there could be a lot of competition from other travelers. Benoa is also the place to find a variety of small *prahu,* including some that bring turtles to Bali.

For Lombok, from where you can island-hop east, take a minibus to Padangbai on the E coast of Bali (Rp1000); the ferry leaves twice daily at 0930 and 1400; Rp2800 deck, Rp3325 economy Class, Rp4500 1st Class. Takes about 3½ hours. Ferries to Sumbawa leave from Labuhan Lombok (Lombok) at around 0900, Rp5000.

Mengwi

From Denpasar's Ubung Station, Rp400 by minibus.

Visit the nearly comatose **art center** and the small **art museum.** Also see the second largest temple complex on Bali here, the state temple of **Pura Taman Ayun,** the original structure dating from 1634. Located on high ground, a wide moat surrounds this impressive temple which is only ½ km E of the main highway. Feels like you're in the middle of a lake. Very beautifully crafted stone gate; small wooden doors of the shrines are masterfully carved as well. Its *candi bentar* has a half *kala*-face on each side of the gate. Give a donation. Eat lunch at the **Water Palace Restaurant.** At nearby Marga stands a monument honoring a regiment of guerilla fighters killed by Dutch aerial bombardment in the Battle of Marga in 1946. In all there are 94 small *stupa*-shaped headstones. The leader of this futile last stand, Lt. Col. I Gusti Ngurah Rai, now has Denpasar's airport named after him. A strange feeling to this place.

Sangeh

Twenty km N of Denpasar, Rp300 by *bemo,* is this Holy Monkey Forest with towering 30-m-tall trees and hundreds of monkeys crawling over lichen-covered **Bukit Sari Temple.** There are 10 ha of *pala* (nutmeg) trees here, a species which is not native to Bali and whose presence has never been explained, thus contributing to the mystery and holiness of the place. Buy a bag of peanuts and watch for the King of the Monkeys; also watch out for their claws and teeth. Hang on to your glasses, cameras, hats, and for god's sake don't have money sticking out of your pockets. The monkeys will grab at anything protruding and won't return them unless you divert them with peanuts or a banana. The peddlers pestering you can be even worse. Walk down a pathway by the river gorge in back. From Sangeh, take a rocky side road that crosses over to Mengwi.

Barong *mask*

Barong *Dance Mask: Because of their power to exorcise evil spirits, the Rangda and Barong dance masks are considered sacred (sakti). A purification ceremony with extravagant offerings and prayers is always held to initiate a new mask. When not in use, they're wrapped in a magic cloth and kept in a special bale surrounded by mountains of fruit and flowers. Sacrifices are presented before the masks and priests keep a close eye on them lest they "escape." Whenever they leave the temple, the masks are followed by colorful processions of hundreds of people.*

KUTA

Ten km S of Denpasar, Rp300 by *bemo*. Once a sleepy fishing village, tens of thousands of travelers and package tourists have over the years turned Kuta into a gigantic First World yuppie resort like France's St.-Tropez (but without the wine!). The massive tourist influx has transformed Kuta from Bali's poorest district in the early 1960s to one of the most prosperous in all of Indonesia. In the back lanes of Kuta at night you could meet pimps and Javanese hookers, bearded bicycle riders off to the beach, middle-aged Swiss couples on their way to Poppies, white children going home with flashlights, bronzed Japanese surfies, whole Australian families with Whoopie Goldberg hairdos, lone night walkers, Balinese and Javanese roaring by on their motorcycles, village fishermen setting off, farmers going home. You might meet the guy who started the *sarung* craze in Southern California, or your ex-husband. There's also a sprinkling of adventurous senior tourists thrown in. At least 4 out of 10 visitors here are free-spending Australians, especially during their peak vacation time of Dec. and January. (When you have restaurants that serve Vegemite sandwiches and a pub called Koala Blu, you know Australia can't be far away.) It gets really hectic as the Aug. holiday season nears with increasing numbers of French and German charter flights. At this time of year you can see the prices go up by the week.

The crass commercialism shows. Kuta is thick with hustlers wanting to sell you something or take you somewhere for money. Gaudy signs and souvenir shops lend a tawdry air to the main roads, even reaching back into some of the village's narrow dirt lanes. Peddlers pester sunbathers on the beach; boys in dark glasses on motorcycles hustle tourists to buy dope (and almost always cheat). Kuta is also one of the few places in the world where men are for sale: Western women could be propositioned 6 or 7 times while walking home at night. And if you don't want to take them back to your hotel, then they'll try to sell you a silver ring instead. There are chic boutiques, French restaurants, bookshops, beauty parlors, and Balinese with mohawks selling tapes in cassette shops. Everything is bargainable. Don't buy anything during your first few days until you can talk to people and learn the prices: first offers are ridiculous (such as Rp10,000 for a massage or a chartered *bemo* into Denpasar). Find a very secure and guarded room as the stealing can get bad (the Balinese say "It's the Javanese."). Walk down to the beach, which is longer than Sanur's, arching out of sight. Although rubbishy and increasingly crowded, the tropical sunsets are still splendid. Despite all its flaws, Kuta is one of the best-value travelers' enclaves in the world and the liveliest and naughtiest spot on the island.

ACCOMMODATIONS

Hotels have existed in Kuta since the 1930s, such as Miss Mank's with its little thatched houses, brick patios, small household temples and statues, and child servants in gay *sarung*. Today there are hundreds of *losmen*, hotels, bungalows, and more are constantly being built. Each lane is actually a little neighborhood in itself, with its own *warung*, shops, hotels, and a strip of beach where the neighborhood gathers at sunset. The cheapest category of rooms is in the Rp3000 range, though most ask Rp6000-8000; in the low season, March-June, prices tend to drop. Proprietors are always inclined to give a discount for stays of 2 or more days, so the inevitable first question is: "How many nights?" There is also a tremendous range in prices. At **Kuku Bu Bungalows** you get your own Balinese-style bungalow for Rp23,000 s or d, but right around the corner is **Adhi Ayu's** with rooms for Rp3000 — basically the same accommodations with toilet, shower, veranda, free tea, etc. So look around. In fact, the best thing to do when you blow into Kuta (if you intend to be here for awhile) is to just grab any old place for the night and spend an hour or so the next morning hunting for a superior place. The very least that could happen is that your first *losmen* will offer you a bigger/cheaper/nicer/cleaner/better room. There are so many places now and such intense competition that they'll do anything to keep you. Some *losmen* even offer rewards to their European boarders for each new customer they bring in. Lots of times you're waylaid at the airport or along the road by Balinese and brought to a *losmen;* these leads can turn out well.

The nicest places are down lanes on the wings of Kuta, where it starts to get quiet and shady again. These also tend to be lower priced, more relaxing, with fewer sellers bothering you. In general, the smaller, family-run homestays of 4-5 rooms or bungalows are more of a quality experience than the impersonal larger hotels which are run more like businesses. In the smaller places, you get to mix more with the family and you are under the wing of an *ibu* ("lady of the house"). Travelers also choose their *losmen* for the services and extras offered, e.g. if the family teaches dancing or *Bahasa Indonesia,* lends bicycles, offers a bigger and better breakfast, or an outstanding paperback library. There are too many accommodations to list. Below is just a sampling:

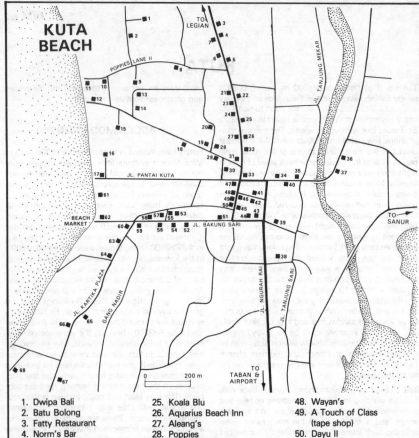

KUTA BEACH

1. Dwipa Bali
2. Batu Bolong
3. Fatty Restaurant
4. Norm's Bar
5. Puri Rama Cottages
6. Sari Club
7. Lenny's Garden Restaurant
8. Poppies Cottages
9. Barong Cottages
10. Maharani Hotel
11. Kuta Seaview Cottage
12. East & West Hotel
13. Arena Bungalows
14. Adhi Ayu's
15. Kubu Ku Bungalows
16. Yasa Samudra Bungalows
17. Made's Yogi Pub
18. Lasi Erawati's
19. TJ's
20. Ayu's Bungalows
21. Kuda Kayu Restaurant
22. Kuda postal agent
23. Twice Bar & Bakery
24. Mini Restaurant

25. Koala Blu
26. Aquarius Beach Inn
27. Aleang's
28. Poppies
29. Poppies Cottages
30. Made's Warung
31. Perama
32. Eldorado Coffee Shop
33. Quick Steak House
34. *bemo* station
35. telephone office
36. petrol station
37. supermarkets and
    Kentucky Fried Chicken
38. post office
39. police
40. Bali Photo Center
41. Kintamani (Asia) Restaurant
42. Garden Restaurant
43. Bank Negara Indonesia
44. Bank Rakyat Indonesia
45. Casa Blanca
46. Sweet Corner Restaurant
47. Bali Indah Restaurant

48. Wayan's
49. A Touch of Class
    (tape shop)
50. Dayu II
51. Pub Bagus
52. Yan's Tour & Travel
    Service
53. Lasi Bar
54. Kuta Beach Club
55. Puspa Beach Inn
56. Ramayana Bar &
    Restaurant
57. Dayu I
58. Nagasari
59. Rama Bistro (seafood)
60. Pasar Seni
61. Tom Dooley Bar
62. Blue Ocean Restaurant
63. Melasti Beach Bungalows
64. Kerti Inn
65. Kugu Villas
66. Kartika Plaza
67. Bali Bagus Cottages
68. Palm Beach Cottage

Budget

The bottom rung is probably **Tamansari Cottages**, Jl. Legian 2E (Poppies Lane), which honors youth hostel cardholders with dorm beds going for only Rp1800. Other Rp2500 places on Poppies Lane are on the grungy side, both inside and out. One of the best cheap places is **Taman Meka**, Poppies Lane II; 11 rooms with fan for Rp6000 s or d. Nice guys run this place, quiet, yet in the middle of it all. **Puspa Beach Inn**, Jl. Bakung Sari (tel. 51988) has rooms with fan, private bathroom, shower, secure inner courtyard—a good deal in the heart of Kuta for only Rp3000 s, Rp5000 d. **Dewa Baratha** wants Rp6000 d, Rp7000 with *mandi*, showers and swimming pool; also a set of Rp5000 rooms but smaller and no bathroom or free breakfast. The large 31-room outfit, Ketut Wisada's **Dwipa Bali**, asks Rp8000 s, Rp10,000 d, which includes breakfast. Features safety deposit box and jimmy and motorcycle rentals; Ketut holds to the same prices throughout the year. For a long-range stay, check out **Arena's Cottages**, close to the beach on a lane off Poppies Lane—small bungalows, clean, well-run, really quiet, all to yourself, only Rp5000 per day. If you walk to the R past TJ's Restaurant through a grass clearing for about 50 m, you'll reach **Ayu's Bungalows** with huge bright and airy rooms, white tile floors, flush toilet, new beds, high ceilings; Rp10,000 d. The new **Kuta Suci** is off Poppies Lane II (near Silver Fox Restaurant), Rp10,000 per room, lights over bed, quiet—a good value. They also have 2 bright, clean cottages at around Rp25,000.

South Side Of Kuta

The area around Kartika Plaza is more relaxed than busy Kuta village. **Kartika Plaza** rents immaculate traditional bungalows with thatch roofs going for US$34 (with garden view) and US$36 (with ocean view). Well suited for families—springbeds, private bath with hot and cold water, a/c, color TV, telephone. Add 15% for service and taxes. View the sunset from their Ocean View restaurant, open 24 hours. Leafy and cool **Puspa Ayu** asks Rp8000 per night, cheaper if you stay longer. Just around the corner is the **Pendawa Inn** with restaurant at similar prices but a prettier and breezier yard. **Bunut Gardens** (nice *ibu*) charges Rp6000 s, Rp9000 d. At the end of the lane is **Kubu Villas**, asking Rp30,000 but will bargain.

Higher Priced

Popular **Barong Cottages** has a/c rooms for Rp25,000 s or d (be sure to bargain), including breakfast and swimming pool. **Poppies Cottages**, in the center of the village on Poppies Lane, rents delightful bungalows. The front ones are US$17; others go for US$24 s and US$26 d, featuring refrigerator, swimming pool, the works. For something even more posh, **Yasa Samudra's** is close to the beach at the end of Jl. Pantai Kuta. Prime location. Good value for what you get, including big breakfast and delicious

nasi goreng. Other beachfront bungalows with twin bedrooms and all facilities can be found for US$20-25—unreal splendor. Many of these more expensive places deal only in dollars and may even find it difficult to figure out *rupiah* amounts. **Kuta Seaview Cottage** is right on the beach (tel. 51961/51962) with a Chinese/European restaurant. **Melasti Beach Bungalows**, next to Pasar Seni near the end of Jl. Bakung Sari, charges US$13 s, US$15 d for traditional-style accommodations; very near the beach, private *mandi*, swimming pool. **East and West Hotel**, a quiet, relaxing place right on the beach, also rents out bungalows. **Aquarius Beach Inn**, Jl. Legian, charges Rp25,000 d (breakfast included); the back units are very nice.

FOOD

Easily as many restaurants and *warung* as there are *losmen*, all within walking distance of the Jl. Pantai Kuta and Jl. Legian intersection. The small back-lane restaurants and *warung* are the best for the money, heaps of food for under Rp2000. If you get misty for home, some places offer toast and Vegemite or peanut butter-and-honey sandwiches. There's even a supermarket on the road to Denpasar with a Kentucky Fried Chicken, the **A.C.C.** on Jl. Legian. Such exotic hippie trail items as fruit-flavored *lasi* go for Rp1100, and in Kuta's pubs beer is served in frosted glasses. Some dishes, like "vegetable pie," somehow get lost in the translation; it could end up as just a pancake with vegies inside. On the beach ladies sell pineapples for Rp150, beautifully cut up. Several places prepare magic mushroom soups and omelettes, available in a variety of strengths and prices, depending on how altered you want to get.

The in place for breakfast is **Made's Warung**; also the very best jaffles (baked filled sandwiches), chili, yogurt, and an absolutely top-class *nasi campur*—a lively, cheap, crowded place and one of the best locations (right on Jl. Pantai Kuta) for people-watching. **The Treehouse**, down Poppies Lane, is another superb breakfast place. **Kempu Taman Ayu** has delectable vegetarian health food, good curries (Rp1200), and nice salads (Rp700), plus meat dishes. Another old favorite is **Lenny's**, an exceptionally good seafood restaurant near the beach, but not for the impecunious: Rp4000-5000 for a fish, while prawns run Rp5000-6000. Good service without them falling all over you. At very popular **Mini Restaurant**, opposite the post office on Jl. Legian, watch them cook the fish you picked out, about Rp5000 for a big one that feeds 2-3. Also delicious crabs, lobster (Rp25,000), and incomparable sweet and sour shrimp with rice, Rp1500; hamburgers, Rp1200 with all the trimmings. It's packed at night, so get there early. The best restaurant food is at **Poppies**, the premier yuppie hangout which even serves fish chowder

(Rp2000); also try the fish and chips, and the Mexican dishes like bean tacos are excellent. A delightful setting with meals about ⅓ more expensive (averages Rp2000-3000 and up) than most other restaurants, Poppies plays the Ritz of Kuta (it's worth going in just to try the toilet!). Another place for very passable Mexican food is **TJ's** (the former Kubu Krishnas), farther down Poppies Lane, especially for tacos, chips and salsa. The **Indah Sari**, Jl. Legian, is a fine Chinese restaurant with a truly international menu; specializes in seafood and barbecue dishes. A nice open-air place to eat (if you can get service) and watch tourists and other characters is the **Golden Snack** Chinese & Seafood Restaurant at the end of Jl. Bakung Sari inside the Pasar Seni (nice natural fruit drinks). Another place to look at all the craziness is the **Twice Bar & Bakery** from the second floor of the building opposite the Koala Blu.

ENTERTAINMENT

The new drug is alcohol, which is served in copious quantities in no less than 10 discos in Kuta, Legian and Seminyak, each with an atmosphere of its own. Most charge Rp3000-3500 entrance (usually with one free, watered-down drink) and close at 0400 (officially at 0200). Get ready for a real scene. The cool thing to do now is to start out the evening at Made's Warung and sip cappuccino until around 2100, then repair to one of the discos to dance the night away listening to live or recorded music. Another crowd likes to hang out at Goa's (outstanding vegetable curry and samosas) in Legian. The in place changes every month or so when a few key people start patronizing a new restaurant or bar, then the whole crowd along with accompanying motorcycle parking attendants gradually shifts to the new place. Each nationality seems to have its own favorite. The Americans and Europeans like the **Brunei Club, Gado Gado** or **Kayu Api**, with more traditional Balinese atmospheres. The Gado Gado, open only on Tues., Thurs. and Sat. nights, is a relaxing open-air disco close to the ocean, and the Kayu Api even has live music (The Police and Mick Jagger have both played here). The convivial **Koala Blu**, on Jl. Kuta, is the preference of Australians. This bar competes with another music club across the lane and the duel lasts into the night. **Rivoli** ("For Serious Night Lifers") and **Peanuts**, featuring Top-40 music, and numerous other bars around Peanuts, all cater to pub-crawling Australians. The **Sari Club** on Jl. Legian is a popular open-air place to take in the evening sights. See the classical Balinese dance, the *Legong*, every Sat. and Tues. from 1900 to 2000 at **Banjar Tegal Kuta**; buy tickets at the Perama Tourist Service, Jl. Legian 20 (tel. 51551/51170/51875).

Balinese boys began venturing into the surf around 1972. Each year there's a surfing contest at Kuta Beach, and each year more professional surfers arrive to test themselves on Bali's famous tubular waves.

Surfing

Though waves seldom get over 2 m high, Kuta boasts excellent bodysurfing with crystal-clear water and top to bottom tubes. The best months are during the Australian winter, March-July. During the summer, the weather is changeable, from glass to cyclone and then back to glass in 5 hours. Watch out for sneaky undertows and cross-currents and heed the danger signs posted on the beach. Take a *prahu* (Rp5000 out and back) to the reef where the surf is safer. There's a wide range of boards for rent (Rp2500 per day, Rp10,000 per week) and for sale leaning up against *losmen* walls. Buy wax for your board at **Sunshine Surfboard Shop** on Jl. Legian near Legian. There are many loud, arrogant Aussie surfies acting like they never left Manly or Ceduna, even down to the Aussie manhood thing of throwing girls in the water. A breed of hip young Balinese surfers has also evolved, wearing neck pendants, talking about their boards, and calling you "Mate" or "Hey, Spunky."

SHOPPING

Kuta and Legian are the fashion capitals of SE Asia with Indonesian, Italian, American, and French designers turning out highly original clothes and exporting them worldwide. Generally, those places which take American Express have classier lines (and higher, fixed prices!). No particular clothing shop can be recommended, but if you bargain vigorously it's cheaper to buy in the shops than from the vendors on the beach. It's potluck as some shops sell clothes that fall apart or are not colorfast, so examine their goods carefully. A great concentration of shops, most with OK prices, is found in **Pasar Seni** at the end of Jl. Bakung Sari. Some stunningly designed shirts can be bought for Rp15,500-17,500; jackets, Rp25,000; trousers, Rp22,000; dresses, Rp15,000; T-shirts, Rp2000-2500; *ikat* purses, Rp2000; *sarung*, Rp5000-6000. Antiquities are ridiculously expensive, with starting prices so high that you don't even feel like bargaining: Sumba blankets, Rp450,000; Dayak baby carriers with handmade brass bells and colored beads, Rp250,000-350,000 (in Kalimantan, Rp100,000). Browse in the **Cobra Shop**, Br. Temacun, run by Nyoman Sarung, which is really strong on wood sculptures; also check the shops in Sanur for antiques. The best (US$3-5) tape cassette shops are in the Kuta/Legian area; the clerks at **Mahogany**, Jl. Legian, really know their music. Some tape shops give a free tape if you buy 10. Buying marijuana on the beach is risky; you almost always get burned. Don't be deceived by the wrappings, sellers make it look convincingly like authentic Buddha weed. Penalties for possession are severe, and raids and busts do occur. If you get arrested, it's going to cost you money. Settle it with a payoff as early as possible and don't let it ever reach the court system.

SERVICES

Kuta has it all—banks, moneychangers, physicians, post offices, ticket agencies, photo processing shops, supermarkets. The **postal agent** on Jl. Legian sells stamps, aerograms, plus offers registered post, cable, and *post restante* service (address letters "Kuta Postal Agent, Jl. Legian, Kuta"). They also sell dictionaries, postcards, stationery supplies. Their parcel rates are the same as official government rates but they charge rip-off prices for packaging: Rp5000 for one- to 3-kg parcels, Rp7000 for 3-5 kg, Rp10,000 for 5-10 kg. Better yet, hire a *bemo* or minibus (Rp5000) into Denpasar's main post office's *paket pos* which charges only Rp2000 per box for packaging (separate from postal charges). Kuta's main **Kantor Pos**, where you may also have *post restante* letters sent (Rp50 per letter), is near the *pasar malam* and cinema. **Moneychangers** along Jl. Legian give good rates and faster service than Kuta's banks (located on the road to the airport); try cordial and efficient **C.V. Dirgahayu** near the crossroads of Jl. Legian and Jl. Pantai Kuta. Other moneychangers are found right after the traffic island on the L as you're coming into Kuta down Jl. Pantai Kuta. It's difficult using your American Express card in Kuta; clerks often claim they are fresh out of Amex sales slips. A **Super Foto** one-hour Kodak processing outlet is on Jl. Legian, not far from the *bemo* stop. **massage:** Platoons of licensed masseuses, all with conical hats and yellow T-shirts, cruise the beach. Go in the morning to get the best price; don't pay more than Rp2000-2500 for a 40-min. massage. Try several until you find one you really like.

TRANSPORT

Getting Around

Rent bicycles for about Rp1200 per day or motorcycles for Rp4000-5000 per day (depending upon the size and condition) from your *losmen*, hotel, or from anyone else you might meet. Many *losmen* buy a motorbike or a jimmy because there could be more money in renting them out than they get for renting rooms. See Bali's "Introduction" for information on procedures, licenses, and other fees. There's a path running parallel to Jl. Legian that starts from just beside TJ's on Poppies Lane, leading all the way through ricefields and *kampung* to Legian.

From

The *bemo* from Denpasar's Stasiun Tegal (Rp300) stop at the *bemo* stand near the intersection of Jl. Legian and Jl. Pantai Kuta, from where they travel farther down traffic-snarled Jl. Legian to Legian. These carnivores insist on Rp3000 to charter a *bemo* from Kuta to Legian, but will eventually come down to Rp1000. Or you can wait for one to depart once it fills up for only Rp500 to Legian. Scalpers charge at least Rp1500 to ride on the back of a motorcycle from Kuta to Legian. From Kuta to Ngurai Rai Bali Airport, minibus and *bemo* drivers first ask Rp10,000. Just laugh at them—the going charter rate is Rp1500-2000. Unlicensed *bemo* can't enter the airport and will drop you off at the gate from where you have to walk 60 m or so to the terminal. During the day just flag down a public minibus on the airport road, Rp200. For northern (Ubud, Singaraja, etc.) and eastern (Sanur, Karangasem, etc.) destinations, take a *bemo* first to, respectively, Denpasar's Kereneng and Suci *bemo* stations.

Tours

Tour companies offer minibus tours of the island.

Sample tours: on the **Singaraja Tour** (8 hours) you visit Bedugal, Lake Bratan Temple, Gitgit, Singaraja, Sangsit, Kubutambahan, Air Sanih, etc. On the **Besakih Tour** (8 hours), visit Batubulan, Celuk, Batuan, Mas, Gianyar, Klungkung, Gerta Gosa, Bukit Jambul, Pura Besakih. Tours start as low as Rp7000 (non a/c, 8-10 people) all the way up to Rp25,000 (a/c, fewer people). Everybody and his brother offer tours and sandwich boards advertise tours everywhere you turn.

LEGIAN

Kuta has expanded toward Legian, a village to the NW, to the point that Legian is now just an extension of Kuta. From Denpasar, Legian is Rp600 (2 connections) by *bemo*, or a 2-km walk N of Kuta Beach on a rather busy road. Rent a bicycle in Legian to make Kuta and villages to the N more accessible. A couple of notches less hectic than speedy Kuta, Legian is suited for people who want to stay for several weeks or months. This dusty seaside village is really being pushed by trendy fun-in-the-sun Australian travel agents, a playground for young surfies and suburbanites. It has good music, outstandingly cheap food, 3 bicycle repair shops, sophisticated fashion shops, a bank, 2 laundries, and dances at least every other day: *Arja* (opera), *Barong, Kecak,* and the *Ramayana*. Asse Baik Baik (tel. 0361-51622), next to Kayu Api, is one of the most original clothes designers on Bali. Legian also has a bad reputation for stealing. Thieves will steal gear from under your very bed while you sleep, so lock your windows and doors at night. If there are bars on the windows move all valuables out of reach. Ripoffs could be inside jobs or tip-offs by the guys who work in the *losmen*. They may wait right up to the night before you plan to leave when it's too much hassle for you to complain or try to track your goods down, so don't tell your *losmen* when you're leaving.

Accommodations

There are scores of *losmen* in and around Legian, some in unique, tucked-away places. **Pension Chandra**, off Jl. Padma, is quiet and pleasant enough for one night before finding someplace better; Rp3000 s, Rp5000 d. **Mirabo** is a central yet hidden *losmen*, off the main road and down a small path. Surrounded by jungle, you just hear the birds, insects, and geckos. Your things are quite safe here; constantly guarded. The **Janji Inn**, off Gang Uluwatu, is buried deep in a coconut grove; 7 rooms with *mandi* for Rp2500 s, Rp3500 d, plus a nicer big room for Rp5000. Good security and no dogs. For something closer to the beach, quiet **Sri Beach Inn** has 7 rooms for Rp3000 s, Rp5000 d, light breakfast included. Run by Wayang Tampa, who speaks good English, this *losmen* is in the middle of a beautiful and extensive orchid garden. **Villa Inn**, behind Kayu Api, is a bit farther from the

beach, but peaceful. Play volleyball with the boys each afternoon at the beginning of the lane. On Jl. Padma, the popular **Three Sisters** is a bargain at Rp7000. Just S of Jl. Melasti, try the peaceful **Legian Mas Inn**, Rp5000 d. Toward the beach from there, the **Baruna Beach Inn** has rooms for Rp7000-9000 s, Rp9000-12,000 d. Also larger rooms with veranda and bathrooms for about Rp15,000. On the same lane is **Senin Beach Inn** with rooms ranging from Rp2500-3500 d. Has an excellent, inexpensive restaurant run by a friendly family, serving brown rice, fruit drinks, black rice pudding, and huge fruit salads for Rp800. Next door to the Kuta Palace Hotel in the N of town, the relaxing **Orchid Garden Cottage** wants Rp8000 s and d, with attached bathrooms and breakfast. **Three Brothers**, with its excellent location, also gets high marks. There are yet more *losmen* N of Legian that are more remote and charge standard prices; spend a morning searching them out. The last *losmen* and some new bungalows are in Petitinget, one-hour's walk from Legian; an unreal area.

For something richer, the **Legian Beach Hotel** has luxurious facilities; US$38 s, US$42 d. Nearer the beach, the **Bali Mandira** (tel. 51381) charges US$30-35 s, US$35-40 d (plus 15%), with all the amenities: pool, a/c, sound system, tennis and squash courts, lush gardens, bar, restaurant.

Food

Many of Legian's fancier restaurants sell expensive rip-off food, especially Western dishes. Better value are the *warung* serving *babi guling*, rice cakes, and other goodies which are set up outside the dance hall on Jl. Legian on Mon. and Thurs. evenings; pay the people's prices. For those who pine after Indonesia, there's the *nasi padang* restaurant, **Densiko**, near Depot Dora. **Depot Viva** serves very good Indonesian and Chinese food at a fair price. Just up the road, get German food at the **Swiss Restaurant**. The cheapest place to drink beer and watch the crowds is the **Loji II** open-air cafe and market (opposite the Swiss Restaurant); Rp1500 for a large, cold *bir bintang*. Next to the Swiss Restaurant, **Made's Restaurant** offers steaks, and farther up, **Agung's Juice Park** right on the main road has a nice garden setting and incomparable iced juices (especially carrot). **Happy's** has high-quality food but caters mostly to Australian package tourists and gives shitty service to others. Aussies also flock to **Bali Aussie** on Jl. Melasti for their "Special Aussie Night" every Mon. at 1900; Rp5000 for an Aussie/Bali-style smorgasbord. Cheap beer at the **Dew Drop Inn**; their pepper steak with garlic and potatoes is cooked to perfection. Eat after midnight? **Pirata**, near Rivoli, closes at 0500; after the nightclubs close everyone heads here hungry for beer. **Goa Restaurant**, just beyond Legian on the R toward Seminyak, is a popular restaurant with well-prepared Indian dishes, but most peo-

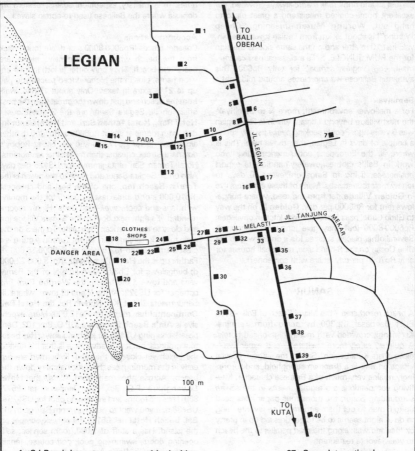

LEGIAN

TO BALI OBERAI

JL. PADA

JL. LEGIAN

JL. TANJUNG MEKAR

JL. MELASTI

CLOTHES SHOPS

DANGER AREA

0   100 m

TO KUTA

1. Sri Beach Inn
2. Scottie's Bar
3. Three Brothers Bungalows
4. push bikes for rent
5. Lobis Restaurant (seafood)
6. Gecko Quality Leather Clothing
7. Janji Inn
8. Masagung (moneychanger)
9. Norman Garden Restaurant
10. Happy Restaurant
11. Puri Damai Cottages
12. The Surf Shop
13. Pension Chandra

14. Joni Inn
15. Bali Mandira Cottages
16. Dew Drop Inn
17. Ned's Place
18. Legian Mas Beach Inn
19. Bali Wetan Cottages
20. Candra Ayu
21. Bruna
22. moneychanger
23. Bali Bamboo Restaurant
24. Sorga Beach Inn
25. postal service
26. Legian Garden Restaurant

27. Surya International
28. Bali Aussie Restaurant
29. Orchid Garden Restaurant
30. Legian Mas Beach Inn
31. Sayang Beach Lodging
32. Hotel Pasir Putih
33. Legian Music Centre
34. Kayu Api
35. Made's Restaurant
36. Bali Bilabong
37. Depot Viva
38. Pink Panther Club
39. Bali Bilabong
40. Adam Beer Garden

ple just sit and drink *tuak madu;* always crowded. For excellent home-cooked meals and a great place to hang out, **Warung Murah** (meaning "Cheap Warung") is about ½ km from Legian toward Seminyak, just 10 m after and on the same side as the sign for the RUM JUNGLE. Sells a classical *nasi campur:* meat, egg, vegies, *sambal,* for only Rp600. This authentic Balinese *warung* closes around midnight.

Seminyak

For a mellower environment, move N to Seminyak, the next village beyond Legian, which is like Legian was 5 years ago. People seeking peace usually spend a couple of days in Legian, then move here. This is where all the Europeans and Americans live who work in Bali's clothes/jewelery/handicrafts export businesses, flying to Singapore every 60 days to renew their tourist visas. Many of these exporters live in **Golden Village,** far from the road, where bungalows rent for Rp8000 per day. **Golden II,** on the way to Gado Gado, has nice rooms with kitchen privileges; Rp6000-8000 (but they give long-term discounts). Several other places, such as **Ida's** on the way to the Blue Ocean on the R-hand side, rent small houses for only Rp7000 per day (share with someone?).

SANUR

A beach resort area—the Miami Beach of Bali—9 km E of Denpasar (Rp300 by *bemo* from Terminal Kereneng), crowded with mostly high-priced hotels. A quieter, safer, more sheltered—and expensive—place than Kuta/Legian. Sanur, the largest coastal village on Bali, is a Brahman stronghold, and surprisingly retains very much of a Balinese character. Kite-flying competitions are regular events in the *sawah* surrounding Sanur; the monstrous paper kites need up to 6 men to get them airborne! The favorite thing to do at night seems to be to get dressed up in pretty clothes and walk along the road parallel to the beach to your favorite restaurant.

Sights

This area is known for its shrines carved in white coral, its painters, orchestras, and operas. Visit the former home-turned-museum of Le Mayeur, the Belgian artist who lived in Sanur from 1932 to 1958. Next to the Bali Beach Hotel, it's now run by the government; open 0900-1700. Sanur has a really fine lagoon, its coral reef stretching hundreds of meters out to sea with tidepools and swaths of sand. At low tide, wade out to the reef or rent a *prahu jukung,* Rp5000 (first price). Windsurfers rent for Rp10,000-15,000 from Beach Market Sanur; paraflying equipment can be rented too from here. At Blanjjong, past Hotel Sanur, is an inscribed stone pillar erected by King Sri Kesari Varma in A.D. 914. Only partially deciphered, its inscription refers to a military expedition against eastern Indonesia where the Balinese used to obtain slaves.

Accommodations

Cheaper places (Rp5000-8000 s or d) are found back from the beach while more expensive places are nearer the beach. They only differ (a lot!) in their environments, plus in the higher-priced places you pay up to 21% extra in taxes. Only about 15-min. walk from the beach and just down the street from the post office on Jl. Segara Sanur are the 3 guesthouses **Hotel Rani, Hotel Taman Sari,** and **Hotel Sanur Indah,** with rooms at about Rp6000 s, Rp7000 d; other a/c rooms go for Rp17,500 and up. Eat at Robby's down the street, cheaper than most other restaurants. Hotel Taman Sari rents jimmys for US$25 per day. Also on Jl. Segara Sanur and close to the beach is the **Tourist Beach Inn,** one of the best and cheapest (Rp10,000 s or d, breakfast included) for the money, with fans and cool *kapok*-filled beds. Highly recommended, it's right next door to the Segara Village Inn and close to the American Consulate. To the S on the main road, Jl. Tanjung Sari, **Hotel Taman Agung** is a pleasant place and reasonable at Rp9000-18,000 d. Farther up is the **Hotel Ramayana,** Rp18,000-22,000 d; bungalows for Rp30,000. A little N of the Ramayana and toward the beach, the **Werdha Pura** has cottages for US$22. At the N end of town, where Jl. Sanur meets Jl. Let. Kol. Ngurah Rai, the **Hotel Bali Continental** has rooms for Rp12,000. More expensive is **Alit's Beach Bungalows** (P.O. Box 102, Denpasar), charging US$35 for a/c bungalows. Has beautiful grounds, but its big advantage is that it's next to the beach yet close to the road. Fishermen are out early in the morning; see the turtle hatchery down the beach. Across the road from Alit's, the **Hotel Diwanghara** (P.O. Box 120, Denpasar, tel. 8577/8591) has a/c rooms and swimming pool for US$25 s, US$38 d. If you want to get away from Bali, go to the **Bali Beach Hotel** (tel. 8511), the only skyscraper on the island. Has a staff of 1,000, room service, self-opening doors, swimming pool, golf course, tennis courts, nightclub. Bali's American Express office, as well as the Garuda and Qantas offices, are all here. Sterilized units, US$65-75 s, US$70-80 d. No buildings were allowed to exceed the height of a palm tree after this 20-story building was put up in 1962 during the Sukarno regime. The **Bali Hyatt** (P.O. Box 392, Denpasar, tel. 8271/8277) has US$70-90 bungalows gracing landscaped grounds and boasts the most popular disco in Sanur, the Matahari.

Food

The Sanur area is known for its delicious rice. Naturally, the resort's hotel snack bars and restaurants are the most expensive. Near the 3 guesthouses (Rani, Taman Sari, and Sanur Indah) on Jl. Sindhu is a *warung* which serves *babi guling* (Rp500) and *nasi ayam*

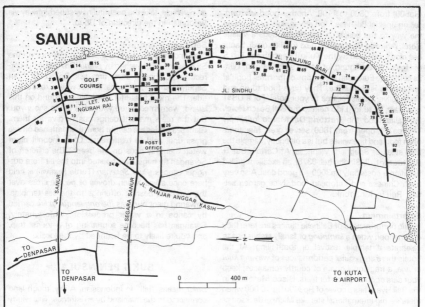

SANUR

1. Alit's Beach Bungalows	28. Pondok State Sitinggi
2. Ananda Restaurant	29. telephone office
3. Mira's Corner	30. U.S. Consular office
4. Watering Hole	31. Carlo Bar & Restaurant
5. S. Pino (seafood)	32. Tourist Beach Inn
6. Mars Bungalow	33. Bali Garments
7. Bali Sanur Bungalows-	34. Segara Village Hotel
Hotel Puri Dalem	35. Baruna Beach Inn
8. Indah Karya Nursery	36. Hello Bali Hello Disco
9. Trattoria da Marco	37. Sindhu Beach Hotel
10. Bali Continental	38. Sindhu Restaurant
11. Oasis Restaurant	39. Queen Bali Hotel
12. Mars Hotel	40. Bali Moon Restaurant &
13. Hotel Oiwangkara	Pizzeria
14. Le Mayeur Museum	41. Pasar Seni
15. Bali Beach Hotel	42. Swastika I Restaurant
16. Bali Beach Hotel Cottages	43. White Sands
17. Swiss Restoran	44. Raoul's Dragon Restaurant
18. Lenny's Restaurant	45. La Taverna
19. Robby's	46. Kuri Putim Restaurant
20. Hotel Rani	47. Gazebo Hotel
21. Hotel Taman Sari	48. Tanjung Sari Hotel
22. Hotel Sanur Indah	49. Sanur Photo Center
23. Temple Pemusan	50. Bali Sanur Bungalows
24. Temple Ma Pahit	(Besakih)
25. Coconut Grove Hotel	51. Santrian Beach Hotel
26. Kuba Restaurant	52. Werdha Pura
27. Bhinneka Restaurant	53. Arena Restaurant
	54. Kita Restaurant

55. Swastika II Restaurant
56. Hotel Ramayana
57. Number One Bar
58. Hotel Taman Agung
59. Penjor Restaurant
60. Restaurant Karya II
61. Kul Kul Restaurant
62. Karya Bar & Restaurant
63. Logmawa Beach Inn
64. Blue Diamond Restaurant
65. Villa Batu Jimar
66. Bali Sanur Bungalows
67. Peneeda View
68. Bali Hyatt Hotel
69. Restaurant Telaga Naga
70. Paon Restaurant
71. Leong Restaurant
72. Ronny's Pub
73. Whitesands Tavern
74. Ada Restaurant
75. Kesumasari Restaurant
76. Wisma Bahari
77. Kesumabar Restaurant
78. Balita Restaurant
79. Alita Garden Restaurant
80. Cemara Beach Restaurant
81. Sanur Beach Hotel
82. Surya Beach Hotel

(Rp500) from 0800 to 1100. Another good *warung,* selling special Balinese food at very low prices, is on the way to the beach on the R near Segara Village Hotel. **Ananda Restaurant** next to Alit's on Jl. Sanur has nice food. Also try the **Kulkul Restaurant,** just S of Hotel Taman Agung, or Lenny's for seafood. With its complete European menu, one of the most popular restaurants is **Swastika.** They have food to go and even deliver meals for free to your hotel. For a US$1 breakfast, head for **Lido** next to the Bali Beach Hotel. For Italian food, the **Trattoria Del Marco** (or simply "Marco's"), open from 1800, serves great Mediterranean food and fine wines but is a bit pricey; sample the fillet steak or Spaghetti Viennese. At **Carlo's Bar &** **Restaurant,** Jl. Sindhu (tel. 8375), an excellent grilled fish dinner costs only Rp3000 — a good deal. Also very fresh Chinese and European food. Nice garden setting. Run by Mr. Pronk.

Entertainment

Public performances of Balinese dances are rare; they only happen when a *kampung* or family stages one to celebrate a temple festival or tooth-filing. At the hotels there are regular performances of *wayang kulit* or *arja,* a traditional opera of courtly romances; keep your ears open and look for fliers. **Disco Matahari,** in the Bali Hyatt, has a cover of Rp3000 (Rp10,000 when there's a big international star like Michael Jackson or Lionel Ritchie). A lively time can also be had at **Sobek Disco** on Jl. Batujimat (near the Sanur Beach and Kulkul Restaurant). Lots of singles.

Services

All tourist services are available. Besides moneychangers, travel agencies, major airline offices, and telephone and telex services, Sanur has the largest concentration of packing and shipping companies to send home all those souvenirs. An **Australian Consulate** is at Jl. Sanur 146 (tel. 25997), and an **American Consulate** is on Jl. Segara Sanur; Margaret is very helpful and has a good attitude. For health problems, see English-speaking **Dr. Kt. Rina** on Jl. Bypass.

Transport

From Kuta to Sanur, take a *bemo* first to Terminal Tegal (Rp300), then another to Sanur (Rp300). From the airport to Sanur the official fare is Rp8000. In Sanur, bikes may be rented from Taman Sari Rent A Car, Jl. Segara Sanur (tel. 8187) in front of Hotel Taman Sari, at Rp1200 per day; see Agus. Also many other rental places, renting Suzuki jimmys, minibuses, safari convertibles, etc., for about US$20 per day. Try first to strike a good deal with your hotel manager. **from:** From 0400 to 2100 every day get *bemo* on Jl. Segara Sanur in front of the guesthouses, Rp300 into Denpasar. Or board a *bemo* from Prapatan (by the *waringan* tree) to Denpasar, Rp300. If you have your own vehicle, take the beautiful new superhighway via Batubulan in the direction of Ubud.

Serangan Island

Also known as Turtle Island. A short distance off the SE coast of Bali, reached by *prahu* (Rp7500 is the correct price, though they first ask Rp25,000) from Sanur, Nusa Dua, or Benoa. Or just walk across at low tide. The most beautiful seashells are found on this island; women come up with trays full to show you. But the reefs make it dangerous to dive for them. Giant sea turtles are caught here, then fattened on sea grass until sold to restaurants. On a moonlit night watch them lay eggs on the beach. The children of Serangan fly huge kites hoisted into the air from outrigger canoes. *Pura Sekenan* (Turtle Festival) is held here once a year when droves of people cross over the sandbars bearing offerings to the sea temples. Towering giant puppets *(barong landung)* are carried by canoe in a water procession. Unfortunately, Serangan has become something of a tourist trap, and you're likely to be hounded by the locals.

BUKIT PENINSULA

Bukit means "hill" in Indonesian. A dry, rough land connected to the mainland by an isthmus. This windy tableland of stunted bush and cactus was once at the bottom of the sea but is now 100-200 m above sea level, its sides rising straight up. Kilometers of open beach and volcanic caves; inland are quarries where blocks of stone are mined for building. On some clifftops are remains of ancient sea temples. Although hilly, it's possible to ride a bicycle around the pot-holed roads which crisscross the peninsula.

Ulu Watu

On the S coast of Bali there's a whole series of sea temples: Tanah Lot, Pura Sekenan, Pura Rambut Siwi, Pura Petitenget, and Pura Ulu Watu. All pay homage to the guardian spirits of the sea, but none is more spectacular than Ulu Watu. The road leads right by it. An unbelievable temple on a cliff overhanging the Indian Ocean 90 m below, fishermen come here to pray to the sea goddess for a good catch. Legend says that this temple is actually a ship turned to stone. Best time to be here is at sunset. Watch sea turtles swim below in a hundred shades of churning blue/green sea water.

Surfing

From Ulu Watu, isolated and lovely beaches are a 45-min. descent down cliffs; run naked in the sun. The surf under Ulu Watu sometimes reaches 8 m in height, purportedly one of the best left-handers in the world and the most challenging surf on the island. Though totally out of the mainstream, there's a full-service *warung* here called the Indra. Follow the sign just before Ulu Watu's parking lot, pointing to Sulubun Beach. Near the bottom is a motorcycle parking area from where you walk the rest of the way to the surfing beach. Go one km past Ulu Watu and ask farm boys, *"Dimana gua?"* and they'll show you where the caves are.

Nusa Dua

Bemo leave Kuta for Nusa Dua (Rp300) from the intersection of Jl. Pantai Kuta and the airport road. Courtesy of Hilton Hotels, there's a smart new highway running from S of the airport almost to Nusa Dua. This resort area has just as nice a beach as Kuta's but no *losmen* yet. The rock outcrop S along the beach produces spectacular water spouts even in a moderate swell (watch out for your camera). From Nusa Dua to Benoa it's 8 km; cross over to the fisheries and the Pelni office side by boat, then on to Denpasar. Taxi from Nusa Dua to the airport is a standard Rp8000. **accommodations:** The government is building a giant tourist project here consisting of international-class hotels. So safe are the confines of this tourist compound that Nusa Dua was chosen to host the 1986 ASEAN conference, where leaders of Indonesia, Malaysia, Philippines, Singapore, Thailand, and Brunei met to discuss economic and security ties. Although Mrs. Reagan made a game try at Balinese dancing, the Reagans never left Nusa Dua during their visit to Bali. Among the expensive tourist ghettos already erected are: the **Bali Nusa Dua Hotel**, the **Nusa Dua Beach Hotel** (where the Reagans stayed), the **Bali Sol Hotel**, Club Med's **Bali Holiday Village**. Cheapest rooms go for around US$65, with all the modern conveniences, but always expect that 21% tax and service charge.

BANGLI DISTRICT

BANGLI

Ten km N of Sidan in the cool, rich farmlands of central Bali. This capital of an ancient kingdom has great views of volcanic G. Batur. Bangli has a history dating back to A.D. 1204; a document tells of a feast being held in that year at the great state temple, Pura Kehen. It's claimed that Bangli, halfway between Denpasar and Penelokan on the slopes of G. Batur, has the most temperate climate in Bali. You can't change money here; the nearest bank is in Gianyar, 13 km and Rp250 by *bemo* to the southwest. A friendly place, temple ceremonies, dances, and *wayang kulit* are sometimes staged. Tourist dances—the Fire Dance, *Kecak,* and a ballet—are performed in Bona, 13 km from Bangli. Buy tickets 15 min. before showtime (1800).

Sights

One of the biggest *gamelan* on Bali is in Bangli. The Dutch captured it from the Klungkung Dynasty when the two went to war, then gave it to Bangli's raja. Art Center Wisata Budaya, one of the largest cultural complexes on Bali, is about 2½ km from the town center, just around the corner from Pura Kehen; theater performances *(Kecak, wayang* forms) and art exhibits are put on here. **Pura Kehen:** Thousands visit this terraced temple N of town at the foot of a hill. One of the finest examples of its kind on Bali, this big temple consists of 3 parts. At the foot of the long flight of steps is a museum. Its splendid closed gateway is called "the great exit" and above are the splayed hands and hideous face of a *kala-makara* demon, whose function is to prevent evil spirits from entering the temple grounds. *Wayang kulit*-like statues line the first terrace. The first courtyard is shadowed by a giant *banyan* tree and its walls are inlaid with (chipped) Chinese porcelain. Ornamentation on the highest temple is so overdone and uncontrolled that it's even rare for Bali. The inner sanctuary has a shrine of 11 tapering *meru* roofs, the highest honor that can be offered, resting places for the visiting gods.

Accommodations And Food

Homestay Darmaputra, up the road ½ km from the bus station toward Penelokan on Jl. Brahmaputra 1, Rp1250 s, Rp1750 d. A disorderly place with mediocre, expensive food, most of its drab rooms are occupied by women and children. Maybe okay for one night. Much better is the marvelous **Artha Sastra Inn**, an original raja's palace with very reasonable prices: Rp5000 d for outside rooms in front with *mandi.* Another set of larger rooms in traditional Balinese *bale*-style, Rp8000 d with breakfast, are in the back. Ideal location opposite the bus station and *alun-alun.* Eat at the *pasar malam* in front of the Artha Sastra, or at several *warung* around the bus station. This is also the town's premier tourist restaurant, full menu plus drinks; open until 2100.

From Bangli

Catch minibuses and *bemo* opposite the Artha Sastra Inn. *Bemo* to Penelokan, 26 km N (Rp300); Kintamani, 33 km (Rp400); Seribatu, 15 km; Tampaksiring, 22 km (take *bemo* to Gianyar first); Rendang, 12 km; Denpasar, 40 km (Rp800); Gianyar, 13 km (Rp250); Klungkung, 19 km (Rp450). Besakih (21 km) is also within easy reach (see "Karangasem District").

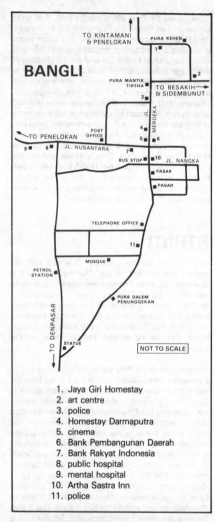

BANGLI

TO KINTAMANI
& PENELOKAN

PURA KEHEN

1■

■2

PURA MANTIK
TIRTHA

TO BESAKIH
& SIDEMBUNUT

3■

4■

5■ ■6

POST
OFFICE

JL. MERDEKA

TO PENELOKAN

9■ ■8

JL. NUSANTARA

7■ ■10 JL. NANGKA

BUS STOP

PASAR

PASAR

TELEPHONE OFFICE ■

11■

MOSQUE ■

PETROL
STATION ■

PURA DALEM
PENUNGGEKAN ■

TO DENPASAR

STATUE ■

NOT TO SCALE

1. Jaya Giri Homestay
2. art centre
3. police
4. Homestay Darmaputra
5. cinema
6. Bank Pembangunan Daerah
7. Bank Rakyat Indonesia
8. public hospital
9. mental hospital
10. Artha Sastra Inn
11. police

Vicinity Of Bangli

One half km S of Bangli towards Gianyar on the R is Pura Dalem Penunggekan, a temple of the dead where panels depict scene after scene of grotesque and vivid punishments heaped upon evildoers. **Sidembunut:** It's a nice walk to this village where you'll find the *kampung* of I Ketut Lebah, the only man on Bali who does cassowary egg carvings; he also carves ivory, bone, and wood. For any work, place an order.

Bukit Demulih: A one-hour walk W along the road from the post office toward Tampaksiring. Or from Bangli take a *bemo* 3 km toward Tampaksiring and you'll see the hill on the S side of the road. From the top of Bukit Demulih you can see the "Balinese Pyrenees," a range of 9 mountains to the W named after the nipple-like *trompang* percussion plates in the *gamelan* orchestra. Also visible is Pura Kehen under a *banyan* tree N of Bangli, the whole Bukit Peninsula to the S, and the ugly box of the Bali Beach Hotel along the E coast. Don't bathe under the sacred waterfall on the way to Demulih Hill; an Australian lost Rp600,000 after he failed to heed warnings. **Apuan village:** A 5-km walk from Bukit Demulih, or take a *bemo* from Bangli, Rp300. The house of the *kepala desa*, with its gold-leaf decoration, is as beautiful as a king's palace. **Bukit Jati:** Another scenic hill S of Bangli. Take a *bemo* first to Guliang, then walk 500 m to the top of the hill.

PENELOKAN

The name means "Place to Look." From Denpasar's Kereneng Station, Rp1500 by *bemo*. At 1,450-m altitude this cool village perches under the sacred, smoking G. Batur volcano. In the mornings you can see G. Agung and sometimes even beyond to G. Rinjani on Lombok from here. Penelokan used to be located at the base of the volcano, which erupted in 1917, 1926, and again in 1963 when the villagers finally decided it would be advisable to move to the higher cliffs overlooking the lake. Penelokan has a high, fresh climate, the *losmen* are cheap, there are some good walks across the mountains, and along the road the views of Lake Batur are unequalled. Sometimes the colors of the crater lake below change from glassy blue to platinum, a perfect mirror of the sky and mountains. At right see the moon sail over the volcano. People here tend to be very money-hungry and aggressive. At least down in Kuta you can laugh and joke a little, but not here. Being very isolated and thus inbred, they are likewise not very pretty to look at. In fact, they scare the hell out of you. Must be what living under a live volcano does to you.

Accommodations

From Penelokan's *losmen*, perched as they are on the crater rim, you'll discover that the most pleasant activity in this town is just to sit and look at the mountain and the lake. **Lakeview Homestay** (Rp5000 s or d, bungalows for Rp10,000) has been left to decay, with damp and smelly rooms and awful food. For better food, sleep, and a more hassle-free location, **Losmen Gunawan** is farther N (¼ km past the road down to Kedisan) on its own promontory. A row of rooms with bath directly over the volcano run Rp4000 s, Rp5000 d; also Rp3000 rooms but not with good

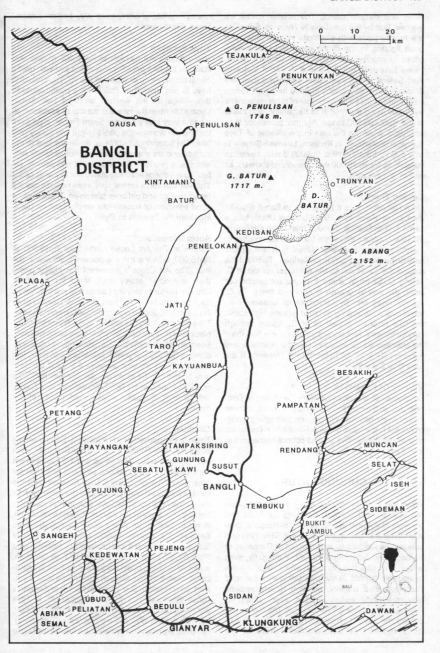

views and outside *mandi*. The smaller rooms are warmer. Run by the inimitable Ni Nyoman, Gunawan is a homey place with electricity in each room, and good lighting in the dining room for writing aerograms or reading. Also check out **Caldera Batur,** below Lakeview; Rp5000 s or d. Meals at **Volcano Puri Selera Restaurant,** one km up the road, are delicious but costly, about Rp5000 for lunch; rooms are for rent in the back. A number of other restaurants are found along the road N to Kintamani, with meals in the Rp6000-8000 range. Another possibility is to stay right down on the lake in the villages of Toya Bungkah or Kedisan. In Kedisan, **Losmen Segara** is only 500 m from the lake; Rp5000 d with *mandi,* or bungalows for Rp10,000 with *mandi* and showers, as well as a restaurant.

Getting There

From Denpasar, take a *bemo* first to Bangli (Rp800) then on to Penelokan (Rp400). From Ubud, take a *bemo* first to Gianyar (Rp500), then on to Penelokan (Rp400); there are also some backroad approaches to Penelokan from Ubud (see "Ubud"). **from:** To Kintamani by *bemo,* Rp200; to Kedisan, Rp500. Hike around the crater rim to the rainforest on top of G. Abang (2152 m) in about 5 hours; eat raspberries along the way to quench hunger and thirst. For G. Agung, head first by motorbike to Kedisan, then travel over a fascinating dirt road running high above the lake across the foothills of G. Agung through remote villages. Not many tourists on this bad road; the Balinese are surprised to see you. A little before Rendang (14 km S of Penelokan) at Menanga is the turnoff to Besakih.

Vicinity Of Penelokan

Southwest of and downhill from Penelokan is Taro, near Jati on the road to Peliatan (SE of Ubud). In these mountaineer Bali Aga villages, the *bale agung* (council house) is the heart of the political and religious life of the community. The longest council house on Bali is in Taro.

GUNUNG BATUR

When this 1,717-m-high volcano is erupting, it glows red at night and bellows, throwing out rocks and showers of volcanic debris. When this happens, drop everything and get up here to see it. This mountain area can be reached by highway out of Denpasar, or by back road from Ubud through Pujung. Or, even wilder, from Ubud via Payangan with a 100cc or more motorcycle (carries 2) through the deep interior of Bali: variegated scenery, bamboo forests, remote, hilly, pre-Hindu walled villages. From Ubud via Payangan, it's about a 12-hour walk. The higher you ascend the more it changes. The natives of the G. Batur region look different from those of the coasts—darker, shorter, more wiry bodies, pinched faces, direct gazes.

Toya Bungkah

Bemo drivers ask as high as Rp15,000 to take you down to the lake from Penelokan but just wait until a *bemo* comes along or until one fills up. You shouldn't have to pay more than Rp500 for a public *bemo* to this village on the western shore of Lake Batur. Located right on the lake and the site of a hotsprings, it has a very lovely setting. Swim Finnish-style from the shallow warm-water pool straight into the icy cold lake. The hotsprings bubble up under the lake to the surface and are not really that hot. Sutan Takdir Alisjahbana, a pre-1945 Sumatran poet and painter, established a dance academy above the *air panas* called **The Art Center,** a serene spot. Here new dances are being created and old ones preserved. There's also a good selection of books—the emphasis is on painting, from the Fauvists to Dyer!

Accommodations

Rooms at The Art Center range from Rp12,000 to Rp15,000, with the more expensive units nearer the lake. The Art Center's restaurant has higher prices than any other eatery (fruit salad for Rp1000!). Cheaper places to stay are **Losmen Mountain View,** back from the beach just past Balai Seri Toyabungkah Art Center; Rp3500 d but small rooms and no shower. Take the path from the *losmen* to the N crossing over black lava rocks; newer lava flows are along the way. **Losmen Wayan Matra,** just above the hotsprings, charges Rp5000 s or d with breakfast; also has a fine restaurant over the lake. **Amerta Accommodation,** only 10 m from the *air panas,* also charges Rp5000 s or d, or bungalows for Rp10,000 with shower and inside *mandi.* Beautiful views, and good, cheap restaurant.

Climbing It

There are 2 approaches to climbing G. Batur from the lakeside—from Purajati or from Toya Bungkah. From both points it takes 2 hours up and 1½ hours to get back down, so climb up one way and go down another way. The climb from Toya Bungkah and the climb from Purjati end up in exactly the same spot. Of the 2, the hike up from Toya Bungkah is the most popular. For a warm up, start at Penelokan and walk down to Kedisan (or take a *bemo* for Rp500). From Kedisan, it's another Rp200 *bemo* ride to Toya Bungkah, like riding a roller coaster! Or take the boat (Rp5000, 4-5 people) from Kedisan to Toya Bungkah, walk up the volcano, get back down to Toya Bungkah again, then back to Kedisan—all in one day if you start early enough. Buy your boat ticket at Kedisan's police station so you don't get ripped off. In Toya Bungkah, people will offer to guide you for Rp6000, but you don't really need a guide. From Toya Bungkah there are many, many trails, and they all lead up to

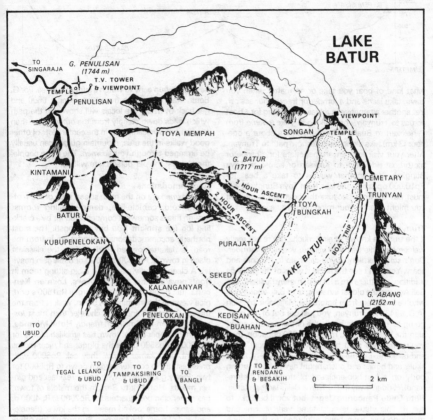

LAKE BATUR

TO SINGARAJA

G. PENULISAN (1744 m)
T.V. TOWER & VIEWPOINT
TEMPLE
PENULISAN

TOYA MEMPAH

VIEWPOINT

SONGAN
TEMPLE

KINTAMANI

G. BATUR (1717 m)

3 HOUR ASCENT

CEMETARY
TRUNYAN

BATUR

2 HOUR ASCENT

TOYA BUNGKAH

KUBUPENELOKAN

PURAJATI

LAKE BATUR

BOAT TRIP

SEKED

KALANGANYAR

G. ABANG (2152 m)

PENELOKAN

KEDISAN
BUAHAN

TO UBUD

TO TEGAL LELANG & UBUD

TO TAMPAKSIRING & UBUD

TO BANGLI

TO RENDANG & BESAKIH

0   2 km

the same place. Just pick a trail that's going straight up. The way is well trodden and well maintained. If you do get lost, don't expect anyone to show you the way without exacting payment. If you decide to hire a guide, you'll need a *young* boy because it's an arduous ascent. Start out at least by 0600 before it gets hot, and when the locals are still sleepy; not as many hassles. There are even cold drink (Rp500) stands on the way up the mountain, at one-third of the way up, at the halfway mark, and even on the top itself! Or choose to climb while it's overcast. Sit on the top for awhile. Sweeping view of the lake and inside the crater; you can't see G. Agung because it's behind the tall ridge of the lake. Look for the relatively recent lava flows, all black, and walk around the crater. When you come back down to Toya Bungkah and Purajati, bathe in the cool lake—it'll be just what you need. **note:** An alternative is to start at around 0230 to make it to G. Batur's peak in time for the sunrise when

you see the sun slowly lighting the whole lake and beautiful views of G. Rinjani on Lombok in the distance.

LAKE BATUR

The Lake Trip
Buy your boat tickets at the fixed-price ticket office in Kedisan, where the boats leave, and beware of scalpers. From Penelokan down to Kedisan on the crater floor, get a lift on a *bemo* (Rp500), or walk this corkscrew road in 45 minutes. Five people can hire a motorboat (about Rp20,000) for the 2½- to 3-hour tour of Trunyan, the cemetery, *air panas,* and back to Kedisan. If you get an offer to take you around the lake for under Rp20,000, it's probably in a canoe, even though they might claim it's a motorboat. This cheaper 5-hour canoe trip is an alternative. No matter

what kind of boat you take or no matter when you leave, take jeans and a jumper or freeze your ass off. Yet another alternative involves no hassling for a boat across to Trunyan—by walking it! Take a *bemo* from Penelokan to Buahan. From there, it's about a one-hour (3 km) hike along the lakeshore path to Trunyan. After your visit to Trunyan, negotiate for a canoe or motorboat ride back to Kedisan or across to Toya Bungkah. Yet another way is to take a boat for Rp10,000 pp across the lake from Toya Bungkah; you must pay up front because the boatmen know that you might change your mind once you see it.

Trunyan

If the truth be known, it ain't much. You're not really welcome in this Bali Aga village; you're an intruder. Don't stay overnight if you can help it; it's cold and scary. You don't see the ancient ways of the Bali Aga tradition, and there are a lot of of money hustlers. The Bali Aga are the oldest inhabitants of Bali, aboriginals who've lived here from before the Majapahit invasion (A.D. 1343). At Trunyan, you just get out of the boat, go up to a temple which you're not allowed to enter, sign the Visitors Book, make a Rp200 donation, then you're marched right back down to the boat again and taken next to the cemetery. The cemetery, full of skulls and bones and bush, might have a fresh rotting body on a bamboo-enclosed platform (eat beforehand). Hidden away in Trunyan is Bali's largest statue, **Ratu Gede Pancering Jaget**, but you'll be lucky to see it. This statue is considered very ancient and magic powers have been attributed to it. Though Trunyan isn't worth it, the setting is spectacular.

KINTAMANI

A windblown little town spread out along the top of G. Batur's crater rim, Rp200 by *bemo* N of Penelokan. There's a big market along the highway every 3 days when mountain people come in from all the surrounding villages; go early. In this damp climate, a variety of vegetables and fruits (try the passion fruit and abundant citrus) not found elsewhere on the island are grown. In Kintamani, *Sangyang* Trance Dances, seldom seen in other parts of Bali, are practiced, but are often barred to tourists. Kintamani has more angry dogs per sq m than any other place on Bali. Yet many travelers prefer to stay in Kintamani instead of Penelokan. There are fewer annoyances from the locals; you're treated more like a human being. The people up here will remind you of the Nepalese in the way they dress and stare, and they're always carrying their

parang. Get up early to watch a superb sunrise. For G. Batur, start your climb from Kintamani at 0600 and get back by 1200; the locals will show you the path which leads down steeply from the outer crater, then climbs up the volcanic plus in the center. Lots of other good walks in the area; mountain guides can usually be arranged through your *losmen*. The more people, the cheaper the per person rate will be.

Accommodations

Most *losmen* are on the main street, each of them offering cold, cubicle-like, damp-smelling rooms, though this is somewhat compensated for by a crackling log fire at night (*you* buy the logs!). The most northerly accommodations, a quarter km in from the road, is Jakartan-owned **Puri Astina**, the classiest place in town at Rp6000-16,000 s or d (bargain heavily). A clean, friendly place with a big sitting room in front, private baths, beautiful views. **Losmen Kencana**, just below Puri Astina, charges Rp1500 s or d; nice views in the mornings. A 5-min. walk N from the market, Losmen Kencana is cheerier than most *losmen* in Kintamani. Small and friendly **Hotel Miranda**, also in the upper end of town, has smallish rooms for Rp2000 s, Rp3500 d. For the bigger and nicer rooms in front, with *kamar mandi*, they ask Rp6000 with breakfast; try to counter-bargain down to Rp5000 for two. Pretty good meals, with both breakfast and dinner menus. **Hotel Batu Sari**, in the middle of town, has rather cramped quarters for Rp2000 s, Rp4000 d, and serves homecooked meals. In the lower (Penelokan) end of town, the **Losmen Supermen Inn** offers small rooms with breakfast Rp3000 d with **mandi**, Rp4000 for bigger double rooms. This *losmen*, run by the hippest, youngest *losmen*-owner (I Made Rubin), is the best place in Kintamani to eat cheap: omelettes, pancakes, etc.

Penulisan

Means "Place of Writing." Eight km N of Kintamani at a bend in the road. Take a gigantic broken stairway covered in green mold up a hill to lonely **Pura Sukawana** temple at the top. This is the highest (1,744 m) and perhaps the oldest temple on Bali and one of Bali's 5 holiest. Not visited by a European until 1885, for years outsiders were forcibly stopped from entering by armed natives. The site is being restored constantly since the sculptures and statues are in a pretty decrepit state. Most sculptures are from the 11th C., but there are pagan phallic symbols that date even older. Surrounded by mountains, with a nice breeze on top, on a clear day you can see half the island all the way to the Java Sea.

Gunung Kawi Temple Complex

GIANYAR DISTRICT

Batubulan
Heading NE out of Denpasar up the "tourist corridor," Batubulan is only 5 km from Denpasar (virtually a suburb) and 17 km before Gianyar. Renowned for its stonecarving, this village's creations are found in temples and at crossroads all over the island. Visit the many workshops along the road where young artisans chip away at stone blocks to liberate the heroes, gods, and demons of Bali's rich mythology. On the gate of **Pura Puseh**, only 150 m from the highway, are Hindu deities next to a meditating Buddha with Balinese facial features. This temple is dedicated to the village founder who is worshipped with the gods who own the ground. Also in Batubulan is Kolkar (The Conservatory of Instrumental Arts and Dance) where you can watch or study Balinese dance.

Celuk
A silverworking center. Sample prices: earrings with red coral inset, Rp5000; beaten silver necklaces, Rp30,000; large silver tray with embossing, Rp80,000. **Rama Sitha** and **Widiartha Art Shop** have pretty good prices, but it's difficult to recommend any one place because there are at least 25 other silver and crafts shops along the roadway, most with a wide variety of goods including paintings, woodcarvings (for example, Rp12,000 for small ebony statue), and a variety of souvenirs. Prices are usually given in US dollars, which reveals who their

clientele are. For the most part, package tourists on buses pull in, inundate a shop owned by the brother-in-law of the driver, then just as suddenly as they came they're gone again in a cloud of dust.

Batuan
A woodcarving and painting village SW of Gianyar. Many shops line the highway selling *patung* (statuary): demons, US$45-75; *pandil* (carved wooden screens and reliefs), US$75-150. Also based here (in Banjar Dentiyis) is Wayan Darmawan, a young painter who is not only very talented but is also a nice, generous person. Wayan paints in various styles but is especially effective in the traditional style. Sukawati village, nearby, is the windchime-making capital of Bali.

Blahbatuh
Seven km W of Gianyar. The remarkable **Pura Gaduh** here was destroyed by the 1917 earthquake and rebuilt. Its massive head is a portrait of the fearsome mythical giant, Kebo Yuwo. Though it dates from the 14th C., the statue doesn't resemble Hindu-Javanese iconography of that time; it might be a native Balinese creation. There are numerous carvings inside the gate on the main stairway. **vicinity of:** Opposite the *pura* is the road leading straight to Kutri and Bedulu. Take the steep path through a *banyan* tree forest up to a sanctuary on top of a hill sheltering the worn but

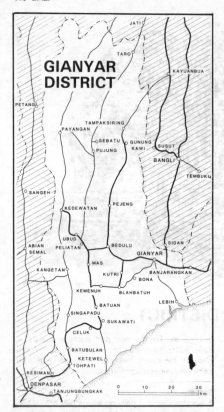

GIANYAR
DISTRICT

arresting statue of King Airlangga's mother, Guna-priadarmapatni, who came to Bali to rule until her death in A.D. 1006. In the shape of the goddesss of death (Durga), this famous widow cursed and plagued her own son's kingdom. Scholars speculate that she could be the historical origin of the witch-queen Rangda seen in the *Barong* dance. Bona, only 3 km NE of Blahbatuh, is the original home of a *Kecak* dance (put on every week, Rp3500), as well as a basket-weaving center.

Gianyar

From Denpasar's Kereneng Station, Rp600 by *bemo*. Shop for your textiles and *sarung* here. On the R just before entering town from Denpasar are a number of textile shops and factories. Quite cheap prices for *sarung* (Rp7000), with quantity discounts, plus you can go in the back to view the weaving processes (it takes about 6 hours to complete a *sarung*). Colorfully decorated T-shirts go cheap, but the selection is often

picked clean by the hordes dumped out by tourist buses. At **Pertenunan Popular** the clerks can come down 15% automatically; anything more than that they have to ask the boss. The textile factories here pay the scores of young girls and boys in back only Rp15,000 per month (they work 0700-1500); all these female workers are too poor themselves to wear any of the *sarung* they make—they wear cheap dresses instead. Also take a look in at **Meru**, Jl. Kesatria 5, **Cap Togog**, **Cap Bakti**, and **Cap Putri**. An old palace, visible through a gate, is in the middle of town. Eat in the *warung* near the Balaibudaya and the tennis courts. Probably the very best *babi guling* (Rp750) in Bali can be experienced in several *warung* in Pasar Gianyar. **vicinity of:** There are exceptionally beautiful temples in this area. In the whole area between Kutri and Klungkung are lush river gorges, valleys of farming villages, and country tracks down to the sea. **Pura Dalem** is a small but exquisitely carved temple in Sidan, 3 km N of Gianyar on the road to Kintamani. A fine example of a Pura Dalem (Temple of the Dead), the *kulkul* tower has reliefs showing tormented evildoers being punished by devil giants. Gates are flanked by deities of death and the witch-queen Rangda.

Mas

A woodcarving center with craft shops lining both sides of the road. Bali's most famous mask-makers work in Mas; their shops are in the back lanes of the village. These are actually wall-hangings, not true masks; Balinese would never buy them for use in performances. Prices ranges from US$1-50, depending upon the mask's size and complexity. Wander from workshop to workshop; each shop specializes in different kinds of masks. Take your time and bargain while sipping coconut juice. Get better prices later in the day. Some carvers teach mask carving for around Rp2000 per day. I Wayan Muka is a highly original and skilled carver. He might act out the character depicted in the mask (waking up, laughing, crying, etc.).

Tampaksiring

The source of the Pakrisan River, 36 km from Denpasar. From Denpasar, take a *bemo* first to Gianyar (Rp400), then change to another to Tampaksiring, Rp300. Stay at **Tampaksiring Inn** or the **Bali Inn**, about Rp3000 s or d. **Tampaksiring Restaurant** (pricey) is a good place to eat, or eat in the *warung* in front of Tirta Empul. **Pura Bukit** is on a hill (take the L fork) coming into Tampaksiring—a grand location. **Tirta Empul:** People journey from all over Bali to bathe in the sacred cleansing spring of Tampaksiring. Bring a temple scarf or you must rent one, Rp500. This spring was created by Indra, who pierced the Earth to tap *amerta,* the elixir of immortality. For more than 1,000 years villagers have worshipped a holy stone here on a precise day each year without ever knowing

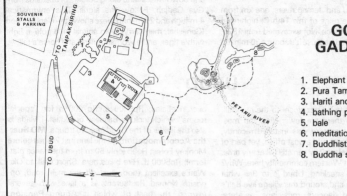

GOA GADJAH

1. Elephant Cave
2. Pura Taman
3. Hariti and other statues
4. bathing place
5. bale
6. meditation niche
7. Buddhist antiquities
8. Buddha statues

SOUVENIR STALLS & PARKING

TO TAMPAKSIRING

TO UBUD

PETANU RIVER

the origin or the whyfor, only that it was *adat*. It wasn't just a coincidence that in 1954 Sukarno built his secret retreat on the hill overlooking this Balinese "Fountain of Eternal Youth," a splendid twin palace connected by a footbridge. The Soviet premier Krushchev once watched a *Kecak* dance on these palace grounds at a time (1965) when Sukarno's government had incurred debts of US$2477 million, half of that on loans for purchases of war material from Russia. The palace is now a government resthouse. In the parking lot are 400 m of stalls selling everything from bone and ivory carvings to coconut shell ornaments and chess sets—a major hawker area.

Gunung Kawi

One and a half km from Tampaksiring towards Denpasar. One of the more impressive historical sites on Bali, in this green watery canyon are 2 rows of ancient blackened tombs hewn from solid rock. These very well-preserved 11th C. temples, carved into niches on 2 cliffs facing each other with a river running in between, are royal memorials for a king and his wife, son, concubines, and his son's concubines. A legendary giant carved out all the tombs in one night with his fingernails. Historically, the tombs probably have some connection with King Anak Wungsu (1050-1078). Across the gorge is also a hermitage for the keepers of the tombs. The elephant cave, Gua Gadjah, and the Gunung Kawi temples, are the earliest monuments of Balinese art.

THE PEJENG AREA

The town of Pejeng, not far from Tampaksiring, is the location of the government archaeological offices. Hanging in a pavilion in the temple of Pura Panataran Sasih is a superb example of Bronze Age art, the monumental bronze drum known as the "Moon of Pejeng." Considered a masterpiece in the art of bronze-casting, this is thought to be the largest kettledrum in

the world cast in a single piece. Legend says that it fell from the sky (a meteorite?) and landed in a tree. Because it was so bright it stopped the work of a thief, so he urinated on it and it exploded (thus the crack). A highly revered object, the drum even *looks* like a legend with its supernaturally charged moonstruck faces. Dates from 300 B.C., the beginning of the Bronze Age in Indonesia, though no one is sure if it originated in Bali or came from overseas. Bring binoculars because it's so high up you can hardly see it.

Visit the **Museum Arkeologi** on the R coming from the road junction at Bedulu. Over 40 old temples are in this area. South of Pejeng is **Pura Kebo Edan**, the "Mad Buffalo Temple." Small but significant, it features a 4-m-high masked image of Bima fighting a buffalo. Nearby is the larger **Pura Puser Ing Jagat** (A.D. 1329) with unique reliefs. There's a rock temple at Kalebutan, near Tatiapi, W of Pejeng Timor. **Gua Garba**, "The Womb" (an old hermit's cave), is W of Pejeng on the bank of a river. Another 6-m-high rock temple is at Krobokan (12th C.) N of Gua Garba at the meeting of the 2 rivers near Cemadik village.

Gua Gadjah

Means "Elephant Cave." West of Bedulu on the road to Gianyar. A former Buddhist monastery similar to the hermits' cells of E. Java, this antiquity dates from the 11th century. Admission Rp200. Carvings on the cave's exterior depict forests, waves, animals, and people running in panic. An enormous demon above the entrance splits the rock apart with its hands. A boy holding a candle or flashlight will take you inside to see T-shaped niches which probably served as monks' meditation chambers or sleeping compartments for ascetics. Deep silence. In front are 2 square bathing pools presided over by 6 carved nymphs holding gushing waterspouts. Clamber down rocks and rice terraces to see fragments of a fallen cliff face with broken bas-reliefs and a small cavern containing 2 ancient Buddha statues.

Yeh Pulu
Between the Petanu and Jurang rivers, one km from Gua Gadjah, are the ruins of this 14th C. high-relief carving on a low cliff face. Not excavated until 1925, this site is rarely visited because it's about a 30-min. up and down walk inland along borders of ricefields from Gua Gadjah. Follow the signs. This enigmatical 4-m-high and 25-m-long frieze shows the elephant god (Ganesha), men carrying an animal on a pole, a fight with a tiger, and a woman pulling at a horse's tail.

UBUD

Go to Ubud, not Kuta, to get closer to the *real* Bali. Higher and cooler, there are fewer flies and mosquitos. A telephone system was installed recently, there's a moneychanger and a post office, yet part of its charm is that the electricity can still fail at any time. There's a permanent Western community here. Why? Because, culturally speaking, Ubud is to Bali what Yogya is to Java. In and around this village live Bali's most accomplished dancers, musicians, painters, weavers, and carvers. There's a dance school here, plus you can learn how to make a bamboo jew's harp, study painting, mask-making, or study the art of the *dalang*. With its many art galleries, studios, souvenir shops, new 2-story market, and congested main road, the town first strikes you as one big commercial scene. But you can take a walk down any one of the village's many lanes to easily get away from this. The sellers can be a bit much but just tell them you're not interested and the next time they see you they'll leave you alone. Take care with security here; the stealing is worst on the Monkey Forest Road. Ubud is very centrally located: Candidasa is as close as Denpasar, the airport is only an hour's drive, and beautiful landscapes—at Gunungkawi, Tampaksiring, Yeh Pulu, Pujung, etc.—are nearby. Scores of scenic nature walks can be enjoyed around the village.

ACCOMMODATIONS

Walk along the back lanes of Ubud's various *kampung* as here are where all of Ubud's best *losmen* and homestays are located. Always work out a special per day rate for long-term stays. No matter what class of hotel, breakfast is included in the price. The following is only a sampling of the 100 or so unique accommodations in this village—hunt them out! **note:** You'll need a flashlight to wend your way at night along the rutted, muddy back lanes of Ubud!

Inexpensive
In Padangteal, on the way into Ubud from Peliatan, is **Weda Accommodations** in its own family *kampung;* Rp3000 s, Rp5000 d. **Matahari Pension,** more uptown, is on the same lane. Stay with a painter? Homestay **Gerhana Sari;** Rp3000 d. Turn off the main road and walk 400 m up a dirt road, then see his sign. Another painter is **I Made Sadia** in Kampung Sari who runs a real good homestay with a view over ricefields; Rp5000 s, Rp7000 d for "special rooms" which include Balinese breakfast. I Made is also the leader of the Ubud *Legong* troupe. **MD Suartha Accommodation,** on the lane just 2 lanes before Monkey Forest Road (only 50 m from the dance platform); Rp5000 d. Hire bikes here. Short walk to Oka Wati's excellent food. Just off the main road, opposite Nomad Restaurant, is a lane with several *losmen,* the best of which is **Agung Pension;** Rp2500-3500 d, with breakfast in a serene, beautifully landscaped setting. **Happy Inn** is a quiet family homestay with 6 double rooms (monster beds, fan, and private outdoor *mandi* with shower and toilet); Rp5000-6000 d. **Hotel Menara,** in the middle of town, charges only Rp4000 s, Rp7000 d—a good deal because the rooms look out over ricefields. Learn *gamelan* and dance here (only Rp2000 per lesson), plus they have a very complete arts library (one of the best things about staying here). **Homestay Geria Taman Sari** is on a little hill above the main road; 5 rooms, some with mosquito nets, Rp2500 and up. **Artini Accommodation** wants Rp3000 s for rooms with their own *mandi,* sizeable veranda, magnificent garden, and an award-winning breakfast. **Pondok Indah,** on L-hand side as you go down to the bridge crossing over to Campuan, is a small, quiet (no dogs), family-run hotel just 2 m from bright green ricefields; Rp3000 s, Rp5000 d with *mandi* and huge breakfast. Annie takes good care of you.

Monkey Forest Road
Tjanderi's is a very central, lively, long-established *losmen;* Rp3000 s, Rp4000 d, with bath and toilet, plus *bale*-style rooms in the back of the *kampung* for Rp6000 s, Rp8000 d with inside *mandi.* Banana sweets in the morning and you can arrange for motorbike rental here. Down from Tjanderi's toward the Monkey Forest is **Ibu Rai's,** Rp3000 s, Rp4500 d. Just across the soccerfield is **Wahyu** with only 4 rooms (often full) at Rp3000 s, Rp5000 d. No dogs; can really kick back here. One of the cheapest places on the Monkey Forest Road is friendly **Nani House** with a row of rooms, *mandi* and shower, at Rp4000. Also new edition 2nd floor rooms for Rp8000; really nice people. **Warsi** has upstairs rooms overlooking the family compound and the soccerfield for Rp6000 d with large breakfast. The perfect Balinese place to stay. Right by the ricefields is **I Gusti Karyawan,** Rp6000 s with *mandi,* shower; also much bigger

rooms for Rp15,000 s or d with fantastic breakfast. Among the dozen or so other *losmen* on Monkey Forest Road is **Frog Pond Inn**, a great place to stay for Rp5000 d with breakfast. Though small (4 rooms), the new **Jaya Losmen** gets high marks; Rp3000 s, Rp4000 d, and their breakfast is out of this world. Lots of freebies. In the center is a fishpond. At the bottom of the road on the R-hand side just before the Monkey Forest is the charming **Monkey Forest Hideaway** with spacious, airy rooms right over the forest, Rp10,000 s, Rp12,000 d. Eat breakfast in the small, cozy adjoining restaurant. Peaceful. Even has a swimming hole where the local children come for a dip in the afternoons.

Higher Priced

In this price range are a number of hotels off Ubud's main road which have the layout of a Brahman palace *(puri)*, with individual *bale* converted to Western tastes with full bathrooms and front verandas. Usually running US$20-30, these traditional-style hotels have great personality and charm. Foremost among these is the **Hotel Puri Saren Agung**, the oldest hotel in Ubud which existed even in Dutch times; US$18 s, US$24 d plus 15% tax and service. You should at least peek in on this old remodeled raja's palace even if you don't intend to stay here. **Oka Kartini's** is opposite the big Gerudug Art Gallery in Padangtegal, just as you're entering Ubud from Peliatan. Her restful, Balinese-style bungalows, surrounded by gardens, are in the US$10-30 range with hot/cold showers; also be sure to see the VIP *bale*. Out of the busy center of Ubud with all its traffic and sellers, Oka Kartini's is at the same time close to a moneychanger, the post office, and good restaurants. Oka Kartini's is often fully booked with European or Australian groups during June, July, and August. Oka worked for 6 years as a guide in the Puri Lukisan Art Museum and is well-informed about painting. She will give you good, honest prices on paintings, store your luggage while you're traveling around, find you a dance teacher, and is inclined to give out free treats to patrons whom she — and her small army of handsome sons — treat like honored guests. **Puri Saraswati**, right on the main road, has rooms for US$25 s, US$30 d, but a better deal are the bungalows (US$12 s, US$15 d, but no hot water). In the shape of a nobleman's house, this hotel is similar in layout to the Hotel Puri Saren Agung but not as venerable. On the Monkey Forest Road is **Oka Wati's Art Bungalows**, Rp23,000 s or d for quiet rooms upstairs over beautiful *sawah*, with fan, big bathroom, balcony. Downstairs rooms cost Rp19,500 s or d. Pricey but beautifully appointed is the **Ubud Inn** also on the Monkey Forest Road; US$20 for double rooms, US$30 for rooms with veranda. Hot water, room service, nicely landscaped, with paintings, carvings, and flowers in every room. **Kampung Aman Homestay** is down a path to the L heading toward Campuan

(turn in at the SAN MIGUEL sign). Rooms cost Rp14,000 s, Rp20,000 d, with pricey restaurant, bar over ricefields, and a wide selection of foreign reading material.

FOOD

Several foodstalls by the market serve the cheapest food. In the late afternoons and evenings, get *pisang goreng* from the vendor in front of the movie theater — said to be the best on Bali. In Ubud you pick your restaurants by their specialties. For Japanese food you go to the Ubud Raya, for barbecue go to Griya, for grilled fish to Murni's, etc. **Oka Kartini** arranges special buffets, min. 10 people (Rp5000 pp, with drinks Rp7000 pp). For pure entertainment, *brem* is the real bargain around here. Don't pay the Rp800 a glass at the Lotus or Nomad, instead buy a whole bottle for Rp2000 and order a big bowl of ice, then get fairly plastered for fairly cheap while watching the street go by. The only "bar" in town is the **Puri Restaurant** in front of the market; open until the wee hours on Sat. night if people are still drinking.

Ubud is so far from the sea that seafood is not the town's strong point. But **Murni's** (by the bridge) and Lotus have fresh seafood specials 2-3 times a week, but you never know when and for how long. The only reason you don't go to **Cafe Lotus** is that you don't want to see your friends. This pricey restaurant, on the main road near the tourist office, is an elegant experience. Recline on pillows sipping infused coffee in the gazebo on the edge of a lotus pond, jazz music in the background. Excellent homemade bread and baked goods, daily specials, fresh carrot juice, Bali smoked salmon (Rp2300), very rich cheesecake. Outstanding food, clean, friendly and good service, but they close too early (2100). Toward Padangtegal on the R, **Nomad Restaurant** stays open until 2030, serving very cheap and good food like spicy guacamole with *krupuk*, Rp1000. Also in Padangtegal is the very tasteful **Ubud Raya**, run by a Javanese/Japanese couple who put a lot of energy into their food; the winners are their yogurt ice cream (Rp850), fried chicken (Rp2200), and superb coffee. **Tjanderi's** lays out delicious and abundant meals. Her vegetable tacos and banana coconut tacos are acclaimed. Gregarious gatherings in the evenings. Farther down, the **Ubud Restaurant** is the number one place for Balinese food — *sate, lawar,* sometimes *babi guling* and smoked duck. **Griya Restaurant**, near the lane next to the SMP school, is the place to go for barbecued chicken, pork, and beef.

Oka Wati's *warung*, a little out of the town center, has evolved into a full-fledged restaurant out in the rice paddies. Opposite the soccer field on Monkey Forest Road is **Bendi's** which specializes in simple and delicious Balinese village food such as ferns and grated coconut, chicken, vegetables, and an admirable *nasi campur* for only Rp900. The hottest new place is **Cafe Wayan**, on the Monkey Forest Road, with inimitable chicken sate (Rp2000) and coconut pie. Farther afield, **Jati Homestay**, run by the painter Mahardika (also the best *Kebyar* dancer around), is 1½ km from Ubud in Pengosekan. Nice gallery set among beautiful surroundings; delicious fish steamed in banana leaves with spices, great fried crispy noodles, and well-made rice wine. For cakes and ice cream, yogurt and other desserts, Murni's by the bridge is the best, with knockout service.

SHOPPING

Ubud is in the middle of the surrounding villages of Penestanan, Padangtegal, Peliatan, and Campuan, which have all more or less grown together. In these craft villages live and work literally hundreds of painters, dancers, carvers, and musicians, who offer wares to be sold in the galleries, art shops, and boutiques. Always buy handicrafts in the workshops rather than in the shops. Ubud's main street is lined with shops and kiosks selling carvings, basketry, antiques, clothes, *batik*, and of course, paintings. In front of and around Pasar Ubud, right on the main road in the middle of town, there's a crowded market every 3 days. An excellent tape shop, **Ubud Music**, is opposite Cafe Lotus. Near the Monkey Forest is **Kubu**

Ku Windchimes, the place for unusual and elegant noisemakers.

Painting

Ubud is noted for its painters; each works in his own distinct style. Ask locals where they all live. Always try to buy from the painter direct because you could save up to 35%. If the painter puts his work in a gallery, a sizeable commission is tacked onto the price. Also if you allow yourself to be led around to the numerous art shops of Ubud, your driver will get 10% and your guide up to 15% of the amount you pay for a painting. This means you could actually be paying 25% more than you need to. It's sometimes 1,000% (or more) cheaper if you seek out the artists yourself, avoiding business with the galleries.

Studios

Visit the studios of A.A. Gd. Sobart, Gusti Ketut Kobot (in Pengosekan), I.B. Made Poleng, Mujawan, Sudiarto, I Bagus Nadra—all fine artists, men to learn from. Many talented painters live in the Padangtegal area. I Bagus Made, in Tebasiya near Padangtegal, doesn't care about money. He states a deliberately high price so his paintings won't sell (like Rp6 million!), then gets angry when they do! Eighteen of them were stolen in 1986; some ended up in museums later. This eccentric Brahmin only sells paintings when his village needs money for a religious festival. Fine painters of the second rank include Meja in

---

UBUD

1. Sayan Terrace Cottages	24. Griga Barbeque	47. Hotel Ubud
2. Chaya Dewata Villas	25. Okawati's Warung	48. Hotel Tjampuhan
3. Kupu Kupu Barang Cottages	26. Hotel Menara	49. Nomad Restaurant
& Restaurant	27. Puri Saraswati	50. Agung Pension
4. Iny Goram Cottages	28. Cafe Lotus	51. Banjar Padang Tegal (dance)
5. Sadia Homestay	29. Ary's Warung	52. M.D. Suartha Accommodation
6. Manut Bungalows	30. community hall	53. Artini Accommodation
7. Pugig Homestay	(Balai Banjar dance)	54. Jati Homestay
8. Sadri & Rasman	31. Okawati's Bungalows	55. Kebun Indah
9. Kardi	32. Bendi's Restaurant	56. Bali Breeze Bungalows
10. Blanco's House	33. Warsi	57. Oku Homestay
11. Murni's Warung	34. Karyawan	58. Geria Taman San
12. Arjuna Inn Restaurant	35. Agus Pension	59. Weda Accommodations
13. Bridge Inn Restaurant	36. Jaya Losmen	60. Agung Pension
14. Beggar's Bush Restaurant	37. Monkey Forest Hideaway	61. Oka Kartini (shadow puppet)
15. Hotel Tjampuhan	38. Madri Pension	62. Puri Dalem Puri (dance)
16. Homestay Purna	39. Ubud Inn	63. Mudita Inn
17. Sika Garden Cottages	40. Frog Pond Inn	64. Puri Kaleron Peliatan Dance
18. Wisata Losmen	41. Gerhana Sari	(Taman Sari)
19. Ananda Cottages	42. Wahya	65. Mandala Bungalows
20. Jepun Homestay	43. Wahyu Accommodation	66. Puri Agung Homestay
21. Ulun Ubud Cottages	44. Ibu Rai	67. Ibu Arsa Homestay
22. Kampung Aman Homestay	45. Tjanderi	68. Mandala Homestay
23. I Made Sadia Homestay	46. Puri Saren Agung (dance)	69. Homestay Lantu

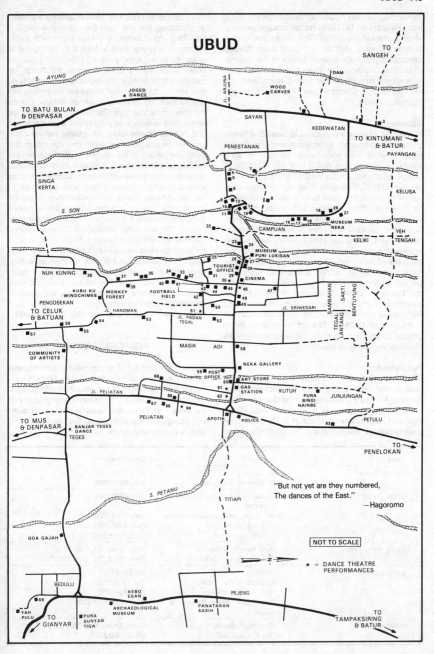

UBUD

TO SANGEH

S. AYUNG

★ JOGED DANCE

DAM

WOOD CARVER

TO BATU BULAN & DENPASAR

JL. ARJUNA

SAYAN

KEDEWATAN

TO KINTUMANI & BATUR

PENESTANAN

PAYANGAN

SINGA KERTA

S. SON

KELUSA

CAMPUAN

KELIKI

YEH TENGAH

MUSEUM NEKA

MUSEUM PURI LUKISAN

NUH KUNING

KUBU KU WINDCHIMES

MONKEY FOREST

TOURIST OFFICE

CINEMA

PENGOSEKAN

FOOTBALL FIELD

TO CELUK & BATUAN

JL. HANOMAN

JL. PADAN TEGAL

JL. SRIWEDARI

SAMBAHAN

TEGAL LANTANG SAKTI

BENTUYUNG

MASIK ADI

COMMUNITY OF ARTISTS

NEKA GALLERY

POST OFFICE

ART STORE

JL. PELIATAN

GAS STATION

KUTUH

PURA BINGI NAINBE

JUNJUNGAN

TO MUS & DENPASAR

BANJAR TEGES DANCE TEGES

PELIATAN

APOTIK

POLICE

PETULU

TO PENELOKAN

S. PETANU

TITIAPI

"But not yet are they numbered,
The dances of the East."

—Hagoromo

NOT TO SCALE

★ = DANCE THEATRE PERFORMANCES

GOA GAJAH

BEDULU

KEBO EDAN

ARCHAEOLOGICAL MUSEUM

PEJENG

PANATARAN SASIH

YAH PULU

TO GIANYAR

PURA SUNYAN TIGA

TO TAMPAKSIRING & BATUR

Taman near Nomad Restaurant; turn to the R coming from Peliatan. At US$2000 for an average painting, Meja is already expensive. Guru Mirsa and Gugul, both in Tebasiya, also do very good work *(Barong* dances). Sadia in Panestanen paints in the Bonnet-style. There's a small European and Australian artist colony here as well: Donald Friend, Hans Snell, and the Catalan artist Bianco whose thing is erotic art and illustrated poetry.

Galleries

In most of Ubud's art galleries at least 5 different styles are represented. Most galleries charge Rp200 or so to enter their showrooms. Be sure to shop around: a painting that would cost you US$5000 in Gallery Agung Rai, in Oka Kartini's Gallery you could pay only US$1000. In spite of its high prices, a must gallery to visit is the Neka Gallery. Neka established his gallery in 1966 in Peliatan, and in 1982 the Neka Museum N of Campuan was formally opened. Affandi, Sujono, Lempad, and other famous artists are exhibited here. Whereas Puri Lukisan (see below) represents only Balinese artists, the Neka Galley and the Neka Museum exhibit painters from all over Indonesia as well as foreign artists who lived and worked on Bali like Theo Meier, Hofker, Hans Snell, etc. The Neka Gallery on the eastern edge of Ubud consists of 5 different buildings, all at different levels. Price ranges from US$10 to US$10,000 (often can get a discount of 10-25%). The art students of Bali's Udayan University must study the works in the Neka Museum in order to graduate.

Puri Lukisan

Ubud's Art Museum. Situated in a garden with rice paddies and water buffalos out the back windows. Entrance fee Rp200. This museum houses one of the island's finest selections of modern paintings, drawings, and sculptures (Bali Museum in Denpasar specializes mainly in traditional art). The establishment of this museum in 1956 was the first deliberate attempt at separating the arts from the communal religious life. Thus Puri Lukisan is a monument or a tomb, whichever way you want to look at it. During the 10 years of frenzied activity in the 1930s, young painters broke away from the old Balinese traditional formalistic paintings of mythological scenes and Hindu epic stories. It was in Ubud where Balinese artists first started painting subjects such as village scenes, funerals, and landscapes. The old style was combined with a new realism, many rigid rules were discarded, and natural figures were set against natural backgrounds (in sculpture as well). This naturalism has been maintained to the present. In Puri Lukisan see sculptures and paintings exhibited in chronological order, covering the whole modern movement and the evolution into modern idiom with paintings of dances, temples, feasts, and rice harvests. Some artists include Hondas and transistor radios in scenes along jungle paths. Puri Lukisan was also designed to record for posterity untarnished, unvulgarized Balinese art before the tourist industry finished it off for good. Use this museum as a standard when shopping in the galleries and studios on the road below. Unfortunately, since Bonnet's and Cikorde's death the museum has fallen into serious disrepair. And, because of the lack of air conditioning, the paintings are literally disintegrating before your eyes, with green fungus under the glass *eating* the canvases!

PERFORMANCES

Below is a partial list of all the cultural performances held in Ubud and surrounding villages. Something is happening every night of the week. Get info from the tourist office, or ask any of the locals selling tickets on the street near the market. Seats for performances are not numbered; it's first come, first served. Photo flashes disturb spectators.

Type	Location	Days/Times
Barong Dance	Batubulan	daily 0900-1000
	Br. Abasan, Singapadu	daily 0900-1000
Kecak Dance	Ayoda Pura, Tanjung Bungkak, Denpasar	daily 1800-1900
	Art Center, Abiankapas, Denpasar	daily 1800-1900
	Br. Pengabetan, Kuta	daily 1800-1900
	Padangtegal, Ubud	Sun., Wed. 1800-1900
Kecak & Fire Dance	Bone Kangin, Blahbatuh	Mon., Wed., Fri. 1800-1930
	Bonesari, Bone, Gianyar	Mon., Wed., Fri., Sun. 1800-1900
Legong Dance	Peliatan	Fri. 1800-1900
	Pura Dalem Puri, Peliatan	Sat. 1830-1930
	Puri Agung, Peliatan	Sat 1830-1930
	Rest. Beach Market, Sanur (plus Kecak)	Wed., Sat. 1930-2100
Wayang Kulit	Mars Hotel, Sanur	Tues., Thurs., Sun. 1800-1900
	Oka Kartini, Ubud	Wed. 1900-2030

Dalang: *The* wayang *puppeteer. A man of extraordinary physical endurance, he must stand the strain of working many characters (up to 6 rods with his 10 fingers) in a cross-legged position under a burning lamp from sundown to sunrise. He is highly skilled in ventriloquism, dramatization, storytelling, stage direction, and production. His voice can create any mood in the audience—contentment or chaos, tragedy or danger, grief, mystery, magic, or inner voices. The leading performer, he must know by heart all the ancient legends and have a deep understanding of the Balinese (or Javanese) mystique and attitudes, interjecting his own comments as the tale unfolds. He has wit and repartee, often using crude village humor which* contrasts hilariously against the snobby airs of kings. He has spiritual and metaphysical knowledge, magical powers, and many practice the art of semadi. The dalang is responsible for buying and maintaining his huge cast of puppets, must organize the erection of the special covered stage for each village performance, and hire the gamelan for orchestral accompaniment. During a performance, traditional ways are used to cue his musicians. These signals (sasmita) are expressed by the dalang either musically, visually, or verbally: puppets hit their chests, raise their arms in the air, or utter verbal cues. Even his requests for drinks, cigarettes, and betelnut are made indirectly through the mouths of the* wayang *puppets.*

OTHER PRACTICALITIES

Services

Sudharsana Bungalows has a telephone. A tourist information booth is right opposite Cafe Lotus. A great place to find out what's going on, they post dance schedules, notice of ceremonies, etc. Invaluable. The best moneychanger in Ubud is next to the Ubud Raya Restaurant in Padangtegal. A *post restante* service is available at Ubud's post office in Padangtegal. There's also a *paket pos* here; first have your parcel inspected, then have it wrapped by the *tukang bungkus* outside for Rp400-10,000, depending upon the size of the parcel and the material used (Rp10,000 for wooden box filled with protective foam). Hotel Menara has a very sizeable lending library—some trashy English novels but also many fine cultural books on SE Asia. The fee is Rp200 per book per week, plus deposit of Rp2000. The more valuable volumes in cases behind glass must be read on the premises.

Transport

Surya International, opposite the Puri Lukisan, confirms tickets on Garuda, Qantas, JAL, MAS, etc.

flights for only Rp1000. They make reservations in hotels also (only necessary in the high seasons), but charge a fee. Call tel. 51673/51786. Also offers daily sightseeing tours. A bike rental place is right opposite Nyoman Swasta Antiques; Rp1500 for 24 hours. They have big bikes for European frames and many to choose from. For car or motorcycle rentals, your hotel or *losmen* can almost always arrange this for you. **Tino Drug Store,** next to the tape shop across from Cafe Lotus, is the source for jimmys at Rp20,000 daily with a/c, cassette player, etc. Most of the hotels go to Tino for their jimmys. Oka Kartini's has 2 jimmys at Rp25,000 per day.

Tours

Many hotels offer coach tours all over the island. For example, the **Kintamani Volcano Tour** includes Gua Gadjah, Pejeng, Tampaksiring, Penelokan, Bangli, Gianyar, Rp6000 pp; **Besakih Tour,** Rp6000 pp; **Karangasem/East Bali Tour,** Rp6000 pp. Most also take in a lot of sites along the way. Minimum number of persons 4-6, depending on the tour.

Bemo From Ubud

Fares: Blahbatuh, Rp300; Campuan, Rp100; Denpasar, Rp450; Mas, Rp200; Peliatan, Rp100. For many destinations, you first have to go to the crossroads village of Sakah, 6 km down the road, then take another *bemo*. For example, for Klungkung (22 km), go to Sakah first (Rp200), then take another *bemo* to Klungkung, Rp600. Distances from Sakah: Singaraja, 102 km; Amlapura, 60 km; Gianyar, 10 km; Tampaksiring, 19 km; Peliatan, 5 km; Mas, 2 km.

Walks From Ubud

All around this spread-out village are deep river gorges, lush vegetation, Tarzan pools, and even a Monkey Forest. If it rains the night before, take the path to Pejeng and pick mushrooms; the bluish ones are the best. Various homestays will cook them up "in secret" into a tasty dish for you. Walk to the Monkey Forest, where a donation is requested to enter. Buy *kacang* for the monkeys, Rp100. Beware: if you touch their young they might savage you. Refresh yourself in the *warung* beyond, Rp500 per iced drink. From the Monkey Forest walk on to Pengosekan, Peliatan, and back to Ubud; takes 2 hours. Or walk through the Monkey Forest to Nyuhkuning-Penestanan-Campuan-Ubud; 5 hours. **for Kintamani:** If you leave Ubud at 0500 and go through Payangan, you reach Kintamani around 1700 or 1800. Another way, a bit longer, is from Ubud through Taman and Sibatu to Kintamani via Penelokan; most of C. Bali's principal mountains can be seen on this beautiful walk. On the way up to Penelokan by way of Sibatu, stay on one of the village platforms when it starts to get dark. It's a big event in the village when a car drives by, when a plane flies over, and when you arrive. From Ubud to Penelokan it's a 7-hour walk, steadily uphill. **to Petulu:** A scenic area 6 km from Ubud. Time your arrival for the late afternoon (1600-1800) to see all the white herons come in to roost in the trees. North of Petulu are a few souvenir shops and a traditional bathing place divided into men's and women's sections, and a carved temple with water coming out of stone animal mouths. Stay in the Mudita Inn, a 2-story house with 4 rooms, showers, flush toilets; Rp10,000 d (bargain if slow season). **to Pejeng:** Surpassing views on this walk. From Ubud walk straight E to Titiapi (30 min.) where they make the best *arak*. Swim in the river under a waterfall; it's difficult to find, so have local boys in Titiapi lead you. Farther on after the river, in Pejeng Timor E of the *kepala desa's* office, you pass a temple with 2 amazing reliefs with very deep dimension and almost animated carvings with fish leaping from the panel! From Pejeng, most walk on to Yeh Pulu. **Pujung:** A woodcarving village 14 km from Ubud. Dynamite panoramas. **Sibatu:** A village high on a ridge with a miniature temple complex like Gunung Kawi, high quality *gamelan*, lovely scenery, and a bathing place separated into men's and women's sections.

PELIATAN

One and a half km before Ubud in the direction of Denpasar, Peliatan and its neighboring hamlets are known among the Balinese for their famous dance troupes and fine *gamelan* orchestras. In the early 1950s, the Peliatan *Legong* troupe was the first Balinese dance company to perform abroad. They were feted in Paris, London, and New York, and in Hollywood they co-starred with Bing Crosby, Bob Hope, and Dorothy Lamour in *Road to Bali*. Peliatan is a popular place for Westerners to study music, dance, and *Bahasa Indonesia* because there aren't that many tourists around and the isolation is conducive for studying. Peliatan is also a center for carving and painting; young boys have no worries in life, they just carve. Art galleries line the main street of the village. Two moneychangers in Peliatan: **Bakti Art Shop** and **Diana Express**. Rent pushbikes (Rp1000 per day) from **Mudita Inn** or from the place opposite Agung Rai Gallery.

Accommodations And Food

Cheapest is **Negara Homestay**, down a long lane at the Denpasar end of town; has 6 rooms in a quiet family compound; Rp1500 s, Rp3000 d. Ketut will take you to temple festivals and lays on free afternoon snacks and breakfast. Some rooms better than others. **Homestay Puri Agung**, has Balinese-style bungalows with their own pavilion; Rp5000-6000 s or Rp10,000-12,000 d. So bright, clean, spacious and peaceful that people stay for months on end. Cockatoos and parrots cackle in the attractive courtyard. Anom teaches dance; she will tell you of the time in the 1950s when her dance troupe toured the world. **Mudita Inn**, also on Jl. Peliatan, around a family compound with rooms without *mandi*, Rp3000 s or d, and rooms with *mandi* and showers for Rp5000 s or d. Central. (Mudita Inn also has a branch in the ricefields of Petulu, about 3 km N of Peliatan.) They prepare lunch and dinner with 2 hours notice; smoked duck must be ordered 24 hours in advance. Your host, Mudita, is a guide and speaks excellent English. **Mandala Homestay** (Rp3000 s, Rp5000 d) is a quiet little back-lane place, 5-min. walk from the main road. **Mandala Bungalows** charges Rp8000 s, Rp10,000 d, for bungalows with fan, hot water, showers, inside *mandi*. Their restaurant is only open in the "high" season when more rooms magically come on line. Eat also at **Ibu Arsa's Homestay** under the *banyan* tree on the main road; some *bubur* and *lawar* stalls nearby. Mudita Inn, Peng. Beringin, and Puri Agung each have small restaurants.

Dance

At the village *puri* dance is taught to 5-year-olds and up. Usually on Sun., there's a dance rehearsal beginning around 0900 at the *balai banjar*. *Legong* is staged each Fri. night at 1830 in the *banjar* (with the big BENTOEL sign over it), halfway between the T-junction to Ubud and the *banyan* tree on Jl. Peliatan. Other performances are held at **Puri Kaleran** on Fri. at 1830 by the Tirta Sari group; Rp3500. Learn dancing at **Homestay Puri Agung** (see A.A. Anom); Tutur from Petulu also comes into town to teach *Baris*.

Agung Rai Gallery

One of the best galleries on Bali, a mammoth art complex of *atap*-roofed *balai*, each housing a different school of Balinese art—house after house of dazzling paintings! Established in 1978 by Agung Rai who got his start in the art business by flogging his paintings to tourists on the hot sands of Kuta Beach in the early 1970s. More of an educational experience than even Ubud's Puri Lukisan, here you get a real clear view of the scope and development of modern Balinese painting. See the room with marble floor filled with US$1500-2000 pieces but some priced as high as US$12,500. In the private collection in back are the haunting works of pre-war Dutch, German, and Austrian artists who lived and worked on Bali.

Pengosekan

In this artists' center one km from Peliatan is an accommodation of exceeding beauty, **Oka Homestay**, perched on the edge of a small river valley. Managed by I Dewa Made Oka, who will always try to foist his paintings on you. Rooms have no electricity (gas lanterns) but shower and bathrooms; Rp5000 s, Rp7000 d. Meals available with the family. **Jati Homestay**, Jl. Hanoman, has beautiful rooms right on the rice paddies; Rp6000 s, Rp8000 d; also one upstairs for Rp10,000 s or d. Can't beat this location, but you need a bicycle or a motorbike.

CAMPUAN

One km W of Ubud. Walk down the road between huge green embankments with fireflies and dripping water, then cross the bridge over the river. Ever since Walter Spies in the 1930s took up residence on the grounds of the present Hotel Tjampuan, this village has been popular with long-term residents of Ubud. Both Spies and Rudolph Bonnet gave canvas, paints, and much coaching to Balinese artists and made important contributions to modern Balinese painting. **The Neka Museum**, about one km N of Campuan on the R side of the road, exhibits and sells some of the highest quality contemporary paintings found anywhere in Bali; all the greats—Lempad, Blanco, Spies, etc.—are represented. Admission Rp200.

Accommodations

Many of the more picturesque accommodations in Campuan are often "under contract" for months at a time. Take a stroll through **Hotel Tjampuan**, the former home of Walter Spies; US$18 s, US$26 d for standard rooms; US$25 s, US$38 d for standard rooms with full board; US$39 s, US$50 d for suite rooms with full board. All rates subject to 15% tax and service. Swimming pool, tennis court, and lots of exquisite privacy and luxury. The staff serves an unreal Indonesian lunch and dinner, and will pack you a lunch for the day if you're traveling around the island. Just up the street is **Sika Garden Cottages** in the US$10-15 range. **Homestay Purna**, also up from Hotel Tjampuan on the R, has over-the-ricefields rooms at very reasonable long-term prices but usually full. Ask for Gusti. Uphill ¼ km from the main road is **Munut Bungalows** with nice surrounding gardens; Rp8000 s or d, but often full. **Arjuna Inn**, across the road, is cheaper and more likely to have vacant rooms. **Sadri & Rasman**, up on a hillock off the roadway, has Balinese-style houses with big pavilions. Tea or coffee in the mornings, or *komplet* breakfast (eggs, bread, fruit salad). High up in the ricefields, the panorama is magnificent with G. Agung looming up in the distance.

Food

Murni's Warung, just before the bridge on the L walking from Ubud down to Campuan, is number one: yogurt, chili con carne, sweet and sour pork, grilled fish, great french fries, ice-cold beer, and very *jegeag* (pretty) waitresses. Across the road, the Beggar's Bush and the Bridge Inn also offer delicious food.

VICINITY OF CAMPUAN

Penestanan

From Campuan, turn in at the sign. Around Penestanan, only a 1½-km walk from the main road, are a number of family-run *losmen* on the edge of ricefields; try **Pugig Homestay, Pagur Londa, Iny Goram Cottages**, etc. The largest *banyan* tree in Bali, 100 m across, is in Bonangkas near Sayan. Ask permission as it's on private property.

Kedewatan

A small village about 7 km from Ubud on the road to Kintamani via Payangan. Stay in scenic **Cahaya Dewata Bungalows** atop a deep ravine; US$35 d in nicely appointed 2-story bungalows with veranda, solar-heated showers, kitchen, refrigerator, swimming pool. Eat in the **Kupu Kupu Restaurant** nearby, expensive but almost worth it if you consider the surroundings.

KLUNGKUNG DISTRICT

KLUNGKUNG

Thirty-nine km from Denpasar by bus, Rp600. An old royal cultural center for music, drama, and fine arts, it was the seat of the old Gelgel Dynasty which ruled Bali for more than 300 years before it was vanquished by the Dutch. Most of the Balinese nobility draws its descent from the royal family that settled here, and even today the raja of Klungkung is regarded as the most exalted prince among the Balinese aristocracy. Klungkung's minibus station (or *stanplatz)* is an important transport hub for *bemo* and minibuses en route to Besakih, Padangbai, Amlapura, and Candidasa.

Accommodations And Food

Very central **Hotel Wisnu**, Jl. Rinjani 4, is just a 3-min. walk from Stasiun Klungkung and back from the main road; Rp2000 s or Rp3500 d. Rooms upstairs are nicer and breezier, with a hotel balcony over the street. This is the cleaner of the town's 2 *losmen*. Ex-losmen **Sudihati**, Jl. Diponegoro 125, is an 8-min. walk from the *stasiun;* Rp2000 s, Rp3000 d. Grubby

but cheap. Down the road is the best place in town, the **Ramayana Palace Hotel & Restaurant**; Rp3000 s, Rp5000 d, but only 5 rooms. Eat at the Ramayana, or at the **Sumber Rasa** across from the *stanplatz.* Many *warung* at Pasar Malam Singol (open 1400-2100) or at Stasiun Klungkung.

Crafts

In the Klungkung area many of the old crafts are still produced. Visit the marketplace for handicrafts. Right by Pasar Klungkung are some antique shops and along Jl. Diponegoro are shops selling Kamasan-style paintings. Or go direct to **Kamasan village** (4 km S of Klungkung) for traditional *wayang*-style paintings — the oldest school of painting still practiced on Bali. In the parking lot opposite the Gerta Gosa vendors sell reproductions of Court of Justice paintings for Rp25,000 (first price).

Gerta Gosa

This royal Court of Justice, right at the start of the town center on the R, was constructed in the late 18th century. Once the high court of the land, terrifying episodes and scenes of the horrors a defendant would meet after his death are depicted on the walls

KLUNGKUNG

TO BESAKIH

TO AMLAPURA

DAM

POLICE POST

BANK

JL. G. RINJANI

HOTEL WISNU

MOSQUE

HANDICRAFT PROMOTION CENTER & TICKET BOOTH

MINI BUS

BANK

HOTEL SUDIHAT

POLICE

GERTA GOSA

JL. DIPONEGORO

CINEMA

POST OFFICE

PALACE

TELEPHONE

PASAR

REST. BALI INDAH

REST. SUMBER RASA

RAMAYANA PALACE & REST.

CINEMA

TO DENPASAR

TO KAMASAN & GELGEL

NOT TO SCALE

and ceilings as a warning to evildoers and the guilty: thieves boiling in oil, decapitated whores walking a plank over fires, liars being clawed by tigers, women who have aborted themselves having their breasts gnawed away by rats, and on and on. Bring binoculars for more detailed study. Above hell's miseries and agonies, the beauty of heaven and the joys of marriage are seen. The highest panels show the rewards of heaven when good souls are attended by councils of divinities. Also visit the adjoining **Bale Kambang** or "Floating Pavilion." Admission Rp200. For an exhaustive pictorial survey, and discussion of each of the Gerta Gosa panels, refer to *The Epic of Life* by Idanna Pucci (Alfred Van Der Marck Editions, New York, 1985).

Vicinity Of Klungkung

Tihingan is a gong-making town near Klungkung. On the way from Denpasar, it's about 2 km before Takmung, which is about 10 km from Klungkung. They forge the gongs on Sundays, and work at filing and polishing them the rest of the week. Few travelers pass through here; very friendly people. Wander through the countryside around Klungkung, lots of brickmaking; artisans will show you how they make and bake the bricks. Four km S is the village of **Gelgel**, the early capital of the old kingdom which was moved to Klungkung in 1710. In Gelgel see megalithic stone seats under *waringan* trees. On the road from Klungkung to Kusamba, pass one of the many lava flows which are seen throughout Karangasem District. Where there were once iridescent ricefields, rivers, villages, now is just a wide strip of volcanic rubble down to the sea. Lines of fruit trees rising out of the ash once lined a village street and tops of old crumbling brick temples and shrines protrude from rocky, barren stretches. At **Bukit Jambul**, 8 km N of Klungkung, take in a wide unbroken view of Klungkung Valley and of Nusa Penida Island.

Gua Lawah

A bat cave just N of Kusamba, the roof of which is carpeted with tens of thousands of fluttering, squeaking, vibrating bats—an awesome sight. This cave is said to extend all the way to the base of G. Agung. In 1904 the kings of Bali held an historic conference in this cave to plan action against the encroaching Dutch armies. Today it's a real tourist trap. After alighting from the minibus, platoons of postcard sellers will be upon you and around the cave itself are scores of pushy souvenir sellers. The only place on Bali where they actually grab at you and *punch* you if you don't buy something! A lot of anger. Watch out for the young girls who throw shell necklaces to you as "welcome gifts," then demand payment before you leave. Sea salt is produced all along this coast in "salt factories" where salt-saturated wet sea sand is first spread and dried along the beach, then dumped

in long bins. Salt water is drained through the sands, then poured into briny bamboo troughs so that the water can evaporate, leaving a pure sea salt residue. Across the road from Gua Lawah, they'll ask for money just to peer into one of the briny troughs, so go farther up the coast to observe this natural saltmaking process.

NUSA PENIDA

Nusa Penida (pop. 42,000), clearly visible from Sanur Beach, was once the Siberia of Bali, a penitentiary "demon" isle of banishment for criminals and undesirable subjects from the Kingdom of Klungkung. In Balinese mythology, the island is the home of the fanged giant Jero Gede Mecaling and is the origin of all plagues, famines, and invasions of rats. The strait between Bali and Nusa Penida roughly marks the division between Asia and Oceania. As the Balinese say, "Here the tigers end." In great contrast to Bali, Nusa Penida is a dry, hostile land of arid hills, big cacti, low trees, patches of green, small flowers, thorny bush, no surface water, where a few marsupials live—or rather, survive. Offshore a multitude of coral gardens and white sand beaches are found along the coasts; many houses are made of jagged sea stones. There's not really any native vegetation, and the few uncultivated patches are mostly imported weeds such as lantana. White cockatoos swarm in the trees and the island is the indigenous home of the exceedingly rare Rothchild's mynah. Lacking rice lands, the people live on corn and cassava. The island's mountain folk are even worse off than the coastal villagers, who can at least fish. The majority of the people don't even speak or understand Indonesian, and many beg whenever they see a white person. The government is trying to resettle Nusa Penida's inhabitants in S. Sulawesi, and in an attempt at irrigation, rain catchment tanks have been financed and built by an overseas aid program.

Sights

From Toyapekeh, ride on a tree-lined road along the sea to **Pura Ped**, a temple complex consisting of a garden pond with a miniature island and a shrine in the middle of it. In Toyapekeh, stay with the *kepala desa*. About one km N of Sewana is a big limestone cave, **Gua Karangsari**. Descend through a small traplike opening down into tremendously deep, vaulted halls with stalactites; so still and silent it's like being inside a hollow mountain. To the S of Sewana are several pagoda-like temples; **Pura Batakuning** is on the beach. There are also villages in the mountains. **Tanglad** is a rocky mountain village of steep-roofed stone houses sprawling across the hills. See the throne for the sun-god Surya supported by a huge stone woman; reminiscent of the style of E. Java's

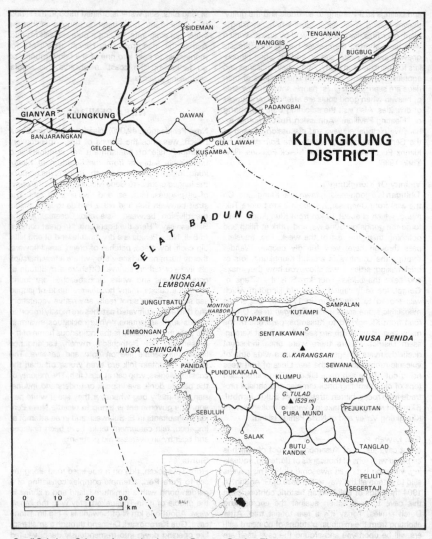

SIDEMAN

MANGGIS

TENGANAN

BUGBUG

PADANGBAI

GIANYAR KLUNGKUNG

DAWAN

KLUNGKUNG DISTRICT

BANJARANGKAN

GELGEL

GUA LAWAH

KUSAMBA

SELAT BADUNG

NUSA LEMBONGAN

JUNGUTBATU

MONTIGI HARBOR

KUTAMPI

SAMPALAN

TOYAPAKEH

SENTAIKAWAN

NUSA PENIDA

LEMBONGAN

NUSA CENINGAN

G. KARANGSARI

PANIDA

PUNDUKAKAJA

KLUMPU

SEWANA

KARANGSARI

G. TULAD
▲ (529 m)
PURA MUNDI

PEJUKUTAN

SEBULUH

SALAK

BUTU KANDIK

TANGLAD

PELILIT

SEGERTAJI

0 10 20 30
km

BALI

Candi Sukuh on G. Lawu. Across the plateau at **Batu-kandik** are shrines, one "male" and the other "female." This unique temple has a prehistoric stone altar: a woman with enormous breasts supports a stone throne on her head with 2 roosters standing on her shoulders. The **Holy Forest of Sahab** hides a temple, the exit of a mythical tunnel connecting Bali with Nusa Penida; it apparently starts from a hole in Pejeng. In the village **Salak**, on the S coast, stand on a yellowish rock cliff and watch the dazzling green sea 200 m below.

Getting There

You can see the island looming offshore from Kusamba, a fishing village on the SE coast of Bali, only a 7-km *bemo* ride from Klungkung. From the market of this small Muslim coastal village take a *kapal motor* or *kapal layar* over to Nusa Penida. The road down to Kusamba's market is by the *waringin* tree. Depending on the season, fishermen carry peanuts, fruit, and rice to the island. A boat leaves at least once daily, in the mornings, as soon as there are enough passengers. Most boats arrive in Sampalan, the island's principal harbor on the NE coast, about a 2-hour passage (Rp1800) from Kusamba. If you arrive in Montigi Harbor on the other side of the island, sign the police report book, then take a minibus (Rp500) to Toyapekeh. You can also sail to Nusa Penida from Benoa, around Rp7000 pp (if they offer Rp15,000, just wait for more passengers which improves your bargaining position). *Prahu* also leave from Sanur Beach very early in the morning, but less frequently. On the island itself, *bemo* run between the main villages, but because of the shortage of vehicles in the out areas, the best way to travel is by horse or foot.

NUSA LEMBONGAN

A protected island, only 4 km by ½ km, off Nusa Penida's NW coast. The island's economy centers on seaweed cultivation; see the seaweed gardens at low tide (big difference between the 2 tides) which look like a gigantic underwater botanic gardens. Most of the island's 4,000 people are into seaweed and the air is even permeated with its smell. The seaweed, which is processed into crackers and other products, is sold to France, Japan, and Singapore. Visited for the most part by a mixture of travelers and surfies, life here is very relaxing, with no *bemo*, no traffic, and best of all, no one trying to sell you anything! There's even a bamboo Aussie surfie restaurant with TV, video, and good loud music! Since the seaweed gardens must be protected from petrol-based pollutants, hotel motorboats are not allowed in these waters, and development on the island itself is kept in check because of lack of land. Only a bamboo culture, thank god, is permitted.

Sights

Observe the island's birdlife. There's a little kids' karate club, and during each full moon a festival takes place with cockfights. From the island are beautiful views of G. Agung; at night lights twinkle all along the SE coast of Bali from Sanur's Bali Beach Hotel to the airport. But Nusa Lembongan is best known for its superb snorkeling; package tours sold in Kuta Beach take divers and surfers out to the island. Pay only Rp4000 pp all day for a *prahu* and snorkeling gear. Since there are such good connections with Sanur, you can also rent surfboards, scuba equipment, masks, flippers—the works. In Lembongan ask for

Ketut, who speaks good English. When the tide is low walk out to see the reef animals, colored fish—amazingly clear water, much cleaner than Kuta's.

Accommodations And Food

Accommodations, restaurants, and *warung* are in the little village of Lembongan on the southern shore of the island. The *losmen* are on an unpaved street with beach beyond. **Losmen Wayan**, near the restaurant, wants Rp1000 pp with mosquito nets, new toilets, plus several cabin bungalows for Rp7000—a good deal. The other *losmen*, **Johnny's**, also charges Rp1000 but they try to rip you off, are unhelpful, and the service stinks, so nobody stays here. Where the Sanur boats pull in, *warung* have been set up, and it's only about 100 m to Johnny's Losmen. Losmen Wayan has its own restaurant; good vegetable soup. Or eat in the huge bamboo restaurant with sand floor and luxurious oversize furniture. Aussie-oriented (jaffles, etc.) and Euro breakfasts are served, delicious ice drinks, *gado-gado*, salads, yogurt, etc.—the normal Kuta menu. The best are the lobster and fish curry; suckling pig can be ordered in advance. More *losmen* are being built all the time.

Getting There

From Sanur, get a *kapal motor* for Rp3000 if there are a lot of passengers. Or wait until a few people collect to charter a motorized outrigger for as low as Rp7000 pp (minimum: 2); ask for Captain Coconut. The boatmen always want the money in advance "to buy petrol." Take care that the boat is not heading for Sampalan on Nusa Penida; you'll still have to pay if it does arrive there. Occasional *prahu* also depart from Benoa, but the cheapest way to reach Nusa Lembongan is to take a *prahu* for Rp1500 from Kusamba to an offshore island, then another boat to Nusa Lembongan for Rp1000. Returning from Lembongan could be more expensive; there are only 2 boats daily, one in the early morning and the other around 1400.

Vicinity Of Nusa Lembongan

It's a nice walk to the local village; take the stairs at one end of the beach which leads up into the hills. Smaller, neighboring **Nusa Geningan** can be reached by walking out to it from Nusa Lembongan at low tide. It has great surfing, lazuli and cobalt-blue coral pools for diving, starfish, and infinite other small sealife.

KARANGASEM DISTRICT

Besakih

Bali's most austere yet impressive temple group, 60 km NE of Denpasar on the slopes of G. Agung. Take a *bemo* directly from Klungkung (Rp500), or take one first to Menanga (Rp350), then another up the steep 6-km climb (Rp250) to the temple parking lot from where you must walk about one km through souvenir stalls selling the usual tourist crap (or ride on the back of a motorcycle, Rp1000). Bring your change purse as it's a very money-oriented tourist site. First they sting you for parking (Rp50), then ask for an inflated donation, *then* they hit you for the ticket itself (Rp200)! Students will then volunteer their guide services, also for a donation. You're not allowed to enter the central inner courtyards. Why? Besakih is the "Mother Temple" of Bali and the island's most important religious shrine. Every district on the island maintains its own temple within this complex. Pura Besakih dates from before the 14th C. invasion of Hinduism and was built on a site where animist rites, ceremonies, and feasts once took place. It is a very complex architectural structure incorporating the holy triad of temples venerating the Hindu trinity. Long stone steps lead up through 7 rising terraces to a godly view from the top, over 1,000 m high. **accommodations:** The **Arca Valley Inn** is 5 km below Besakih and offers rooms at Rp6000 d, or inquire about accommodations at the *warung* in the parking area.

Gunung Agung

It's a 10-km climb to G. Agung's peak (at 3,142 m, usually cloudy) behind Besakih from where you can see Singaraja and the whole N coast. Not an easy day's hike as it gets very steep the higher you ascend. Start your climb (the path begins to the R of the temple) by at least 0600 and you'll get back down before dark (10 hours in all). You don't need a guide (which cost around Rp15,000 RT) as the path is easy to follow, but bring a flashlight, warm clothes, and trail food. This mountain is to the Balinese what Mt. Olympus was to the ancient Greeks. The Balinese call it "the navel of the world." East of Klungkung the countryside is still blackened by the lava streams of Agung's massive 1963 eruption in which 1,600 people died and 86,000 left homeless. One quarter of Bali was covered in lava. Hot choking dust was scattered all over the island for a week and also clouded up the whole of E. Java. Besakih's temples were covered with ash, stone, and ruin. Hindu priests rushed into the lava, hoping to appease the angry gods. This eruption occurred at the time of the greatest of Balinese sacrifices, *Eka Dasa Rudra,* which takes place only once every 100 years. It was the first time this sacred volcano had blown since A.D. 1350. The Balinese don't take such coincidences lightly.

Padangbai

A perfect pearl-shaped bay and tiny Muslim port of transit for the neighboring island of Lombok and beyond. No place to change travelers' checks, so be sure to bring enough *rupiah* cash. As many as 20-30 tourists stay in this small port village at all times, only half of whom are either leaving for or arriving from Lombok. Listen to travelers' tales from Nusatenggara, the Southeast Islands. Holland American Lines' cruise ships stop in Padangbai about every 3 weeks. When these ships call, the streets of this small port instantly fill with strings of gaudy, noisy souvenir stalls which bark their wares to the wandering passengers. If you're facing the bay, there's a sandy beach with palm trees over the hill to the right. People seldom go there; very quiet. Pulau Kambing, off the coast of

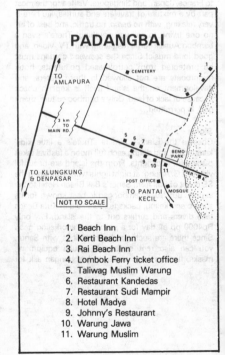

PADANGBAI

TO AMLAPURA

CEMETERY

3 km TO MAIN RD.

TO KLUNGKUNG & DENPASAR

BEMO PARK

POST OFFICE

TO PANTAI KECIL

PIER

MOSQUE

NOT TO SCALE

1. Beach Inn
2. Kerti Beach Inn
3. Rai Beach Inn
4. Lombok Ferry ticket office
5. Taliwag Muslim Warung
6. Restaurant Kandedas
7. Restaurant Sudi Mampir
8. Hotel Madya
9. Johnny's Restaurant
10. Warung Jawa
11. Warung Muslim

Padangbai, has magnificent reefs, but only go with experienced divers such as the Gloria Maris diving club of Kuta. **accommodations and food: Hotel Madya,** in the center of town, wants Rp2000 s, Rp3000 d. But much more relaxing are the several bungalow complexes N of town; the nearest one (**Rai Beach Inn**) consists of 5 high quality bungalows at only Rp5000 s or d. At **Kerti Beach Inn,** each bungalow has 2 rooms and is situated under the shade of palm trees with nice seaviews. Several *warung* in town serve the best meals, and **Restaurant Sudi Mampir** across the street from Hotel Madya specializes in *nasi goreng* and fried fish.

From Pandangbai

The ferry ticket office is right on the main street. Many *kapal laut* shuttle between Padangbai and Lembar (on Lombok), a 4-hour crossing. Lembar is 22 km S and Rp1000 by *bemo* from Lombok's Ampenan. The KM *Lembar* sails daily at 0900 and 1400. Economy Class is Rp3500, 1st Class Rp4500. Smaller boats generally cost less, but take the larger boats if you're prone to seasickness. Pay extra to take bicycles, motorbikes, or cars. From Padangbai to Sumbawa Besar (on P. Sumbawa) catch a boat on Sat., 12 hours, about Rp5500; arrives Sun. morning.

Balina Beach

About 5 km beyong the turnoff to Padangbai and 5 km before Candidasa is this beach resort known for its diving excursions in a marine reserve off the coast of E. Bali. Snorkeling and scuba diving rates, which include land and sea transport, all equipment, a guide, soft drink, porterage, tax, and services, depend upon location. Sample: US$5 pp (up to 4 persons) to Blue Lagoon, but US$30 pp to Tulamben (a shipwreck 40 km from Balina). **accommodations:** Balinese-style bungalows amidst ricefields, right at a point where a stream meets the sea. Bungalows range in size from small, 2-bed units (US$10), US$20 for 3-person units, up to US$35 for family units (with the best views). Similar to "Beach Inn" complexes found on Nusa Dua and Kuta, the difference here being that the Balina Beach resort is *all by itself!* Although it has brilliant weather and nice views the food is terrible and the service poor; ideal for the sports-minded. Join in the volleyball game outside the admin office each evening.

TENGANAN

An original Balinese settlement (like Trunyan), long a stronghold of native Bali Aga traditions, with its own culture and way of life. There's not a lot of hard selling of souvenirs to tourists; people are quieter, friendlier, more dignified, and they even invite you in to have tea and take photos of the rhythmical backstrap weavers or musicians playing the *calung.* The most striking feature about this walled-in isolationist town is its layout, totally different from any other community on Bali. There are 2 parallel streets lined with walled living compounds, all nearly identical. These wide, stone-paved streets rise up so the rain flows down, providing drainage. One gate is so narrow that a fat person could never get through it. Very mellow. Water buffalo graze peacefully on lovely spacious lawns gracing the village. On the widest avenue is the administrative building, meetinghall, school, playing field, and rice barns. At one end of the street is a big square (the *banjar*) where all the important village events take place. Many of the village's oldest structures are labeled in Indonesian: the mill house, storage sheds, etc. The only sign of the 20th century is the TV antennas piercing rooftops. Only 180 families, about 400 people, live in Tenganan. Seldom do the young people marry outside the village, which has resulted in Tengenan almost achieving zero population growth.

Events

A special ceremony is held once a year around June or July when one of the area's 5 crude ferris wheels are erected. The women sit on chairs and the contraption is revolved for hours on end. At the same time there's also a trance procession. *Kawin pandan* is also practiced here once yearly: a young man throws a flower over the wall and whoever catches it (even a one-eyed girl), he must marry. The *gamelan selunding,* a sacred archaic orchestra heard in Tenganan at least once monthly, is peculiar only to these ancient cloistered conservative villages of E. Bali. *Rejeng* is a formal ritual offering dance originally performed by virgin boys and girls. Also see the boy-meets-girl mating dance, *Abuang.* For many years even the *joget* was forbidden here.

Crafts

Tenganan is the only place in all of Indonesia where double-*ikat* cloths are woven. In this technique, both the warp and weft are played into the weaving design. Very loosely woven, this so-called "flaming cloth" (*kamben gringsing*) is said to immunize the wearer against illness. Reddish or dark brown backgrounds are used to show up whitish and yellow designs. These cloths are used now for ceremonial purposes: weddings, teeth-filings, covering the dead, or for a child's first haircut. You can't buy the "perfect ones" anymore, which have just the right tones. Only about 6 families still know all the double-*ikat* processes (coloring, tying, dyeing, etc.), and only about 30 people still weave *gringsing* on small makeshift breastlooms. A few specimens are found in Jakarta's Textile Museum. Threads were once dyed in human blood.

You get a better price for crafts in the morning than in the afternoons when tour buses start arriving and prices skyrocket. The craft shops on the outside of

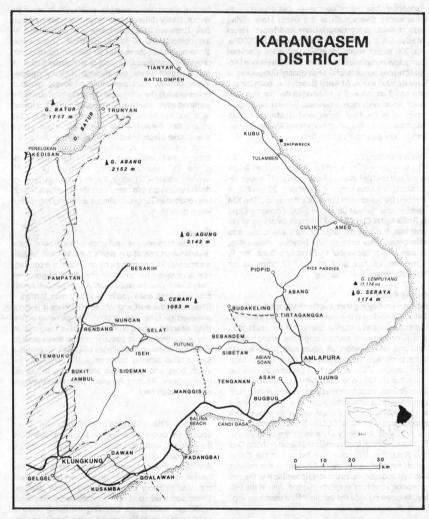

KARANGASEM DISTRICT

the entrance gate don't sell true *gringsing*, but carry woven fabrics, handsome tassled shawls, *ata* baskets, betelnut containers, woven reeds, and numerous textiles from the eastern isles (Sumba, Flores, etc.). Gagaron is right inside the entrance gate. The owner, I Nyoman Suarna, sells smallish *gringsing* (US$200-500), *kain* from Sumbawa, Sumba, Timor, plus palm leaf books and beautiful bamboo xylophonic instruments called *calung* (Rp25,000, but check the notes which may not ring true). Several other shops also sell *gringsing*, at about the same

price. As if to prove the authenticity of his wares, Mr. Sudarma's shop has a collection of books on *gringsing*. A guide (who will ask for a donation) might volunteer his services to show you the village. He might lead you to the house of I Wayang Muditadnana who makes 5-page *lontar* books (about Rp20,000). You may find them cheaper in Tenganan's craft shops (Rp7000-10,000), but they may not be as high quality. I Made Pasek is another *lontar* carver right at the start of the village. It could take him a month to carve Ramayana scenes in his palm leaf books.

Getting There

Tenganan is 3 km off the main road between Gianyar and Amlapura. Catch a *bemo* from Denpasar or Gianyar to the Tenganan turnoff (just before Candidasa), then mount the back of one of the 30 or so motorcycles (Rp300). Or stay in Candidasa, then early in the morning walk 3 km from the main road up a small, pleasant tree-shaded country road to the village. Or hitch a minibus, *oplet*, a truck, or anything that's going along the way. Where the road ends is the entrance gate to this traditional village.

CANDIDASA

From Denpasar, Klungkung, or Pandangbai, take a *bemo* headed for Amlapura and get off about one km past the turnoff to Tenganan, where you start to see *losmen* signs popping up everywhere. Though this is the fastest-growing beach resort area on Bali, unfortunately the beach itself is not big enough to accommodate all the people they hope to bring in during the next few years. The rhythm and attitude of the locals is noticeably more downbeat than Kuta, though there are signs of creeping Kuta-ism. Consisting basically of *losmen* and restaurants, and the businesses that service them, the locals have moved out to the edge as the resort takes over the central strip. Outsiders from Amlapura and Ubud are starting up all the businesses. Only one business, the Kelapa Mas, is owned by a native of the area. Local color can be found in the wings of Candidasa, however, in the form of a few *warung*. Still, Candidasa is a nice relatively unspoiled getaway if you want white sand, gentle waves, fine dining, few sellers, and nothing to do but soak up the sun by day and lull yourself to sleep with the sound of crickets and crashing surf by night. It's the type of place where you think you'll stay 2 days but end up staying 6!

Sights

Nice views of Nusa Penida and Lombok. Because of the scarcity of exposed sand at high tide, sunbathing is best on the seawall several meters above. The tide, when it comes in, chases beachcombers up above the seawall. On calm days you can swim out past where the waves break, about ¼ km, to see loads of psychedelic fish and coral, though not so spectacular as those at Lovina or the Outer Islands. Shops rent masks and flippers and you see signs in hotels offering snorkeling outings from 0800 to 1500, Rp5000 pp. Balinese from Amlapura and nearby inland areas come to this beach to bathe in the sea for special ceremonies. A small temple looks out over a spring-fed lotus pond which empties into the sea. This beautiful lagoon, with its tepid water, is also the village bath. A must is to see the sunset from the fishing village beyond, reached by walking around the

headland when the tide is out (after 1300). In the mornings, *sampan* with their brightly colored sails drift in bearing the night's catch. A few small fish or a medium-sized one brings satisfaction and food for the family or *warung* and may be sold in Klungkung or Amlapura, but no big-time commercial fishing here. These fishing families seem a bit leery of the recent influx of Western travelers who prance across their beach wearing next to nothing. Past the village, a wide, black-sand beach has perfect swimming for children.

Accommodations

This small village, a couple of years ago only a few thatched huts and one private homestay, now boasts over 40 *losmen*, with some sprouting up monthly. They're practically the only buildings around, on both sides of the road, so just take your pick. The owners are friendly and eager to please, most still naive about the tourist industry — a refreshing change. The accommodations on the other side of the road tend to be cheaper than those closer and/or facing the sea. Prices and conditions of accommodations are comparable, and most include the same simple breakfast of one hardboiled egg, bananas, and coffee or tea. In August prices — which normally average Rp4000-6000 s or d for beachside bungalows — go up at least 25%.

Homestay Lilaberata is one of the best deals, a ways in from the road with all the bungalows facing the beach just meters away; Rp4000 s, Rp5000 d with private *mandi*, cheaper without. The homestay has a small *warung* and one of the owners, Pak Lila, speaks good English and often organizes Sunday tours to Amlapura, Tirtagangga, Ujung, temple ceremonies, or wherever else people are interested in going. **Candidasa Beach Inn** is also popular and near the beach, Rp3500 d. Avoid **Homestay Sasra Baru** because it's too close to the Tropical Beer Garden. Better value is **Homestay Purwa**, with small individual bungalows for Rp4000 s or d, with flush toilets. **Wiratha Bungalows** is Rp7000 s, Rp8000 d, and is comfortable, as are the **Puri Putuk Losmen** and **Bendi's Homestay** next door. **Gringsing** is one of the most luxurious, with 2 of the ornate bungalows facing the beach (Rp4000 s), while others are set back, Rp3000 s. **Sri Arta Inn**, facing the road, is set in a coconut and banana grove, and has a good view of the sea; Rp3500 d.

Another option is to stay out of town a bit. On the road to Denpasar are **Pelangi** (5 rooms) and **Taruna** with their very own beach. Taruna has bungalows out on their own, very quiet and good value; Rp5000 s, Rp8000 d. The manager, Nyoman Gelgel, is a real character. On the Amlapura side of town are a few out-of-the-way and inexpensive lodgings: the **Sidhu Brata**, **Rama Bungalows**, and **Srikandi Bungalows**. The Sidhu Barta's bungalows go for Rp10,000 (but can bargain down to Rp9000); incredible bathtub

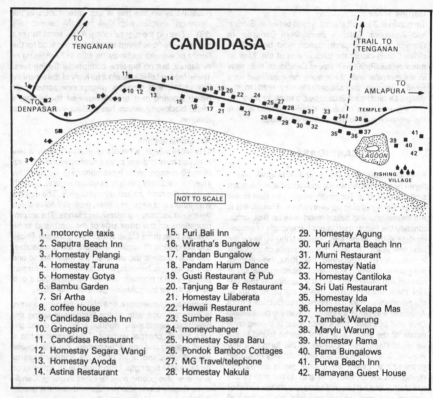

CANDIDASA

TO TENGANAN

TRAIL TO TENGANAN

TO DENPASAR

TO AMLAPURA →

TEMPLE

LAGOON

NOT TO SCALE

FISHING VILLAGE

1. motorcycle taxis
2. Saputra Beach Inn
3. Homestay Pelangi
4. Homestay Taruna
5. Homestay Gotya
6. Bambu Garden
7. Sri Artha
8. coffee house
9. Candidasa Beach Inn
10. Gringsing
11. Candidasa Restaurant
12. Homestay Segara Wangi
13. Homestay Ayoda
14. Astina Restaurant
15. Puri Bali Inn
16. Wiratha's Bungalow
17. Pandan Bungalow
18. Pandam Harum Dance
19. Gusti Restaurant & Pub
20. Tanjung Bar & Restaurant
21. Homestay Lilaberata
22. Hawaii Restaurant
23. Sumber Rasa
24. moneychanger
25. Homestay Sasra Baru
26. Pondok Bamboo Cottages
27. MG Travel/telephone
28. Homestay Nakula
29. Homestay Agung
30. Puri Amarta Beach Inn
31. Murni Restaurant
32. Homestay Natia
33. Homestay Cantiloka
34. Sri Uati Restaurant
35. Homestay Ida
36. Homestay Kelapa Mas
37. Tambak Warung
38. Marylu Warung
39. Homestay Rama
40. Rama Bungalows
41. Purwa Beach Inn
42. Ramayana Guest House

and flush toilet all in burgundy. No fan though, so a bit hot at night. Larger bungalows, Rp15,000.

Food

Dinner is the big social event around here. Candidasa's imposing eateries, many set back from the road on big pavilions amongst the palms, present the usual Kuta/Legian formula menus. Some, with their fancy decor and high prices, seem out of place in this area—Rp500 for fruit juices! There's even an Italian restaurant (Rp7000 pp for a pasta dinner) at the Denpasar-end of the village. The hottest places to eat right now are **Candra Warung** and **Wiratha's**, but the family-run *warung* with makeshift tables are the best bet, serving the tastiest and cheapest food with the most atmosphere by far. Stroll by on the street outside to see which is the liveliest. One of the longest established is **Warung Ibu Rasmini**, next to the temple. Try her delicious fresh fish with spicy tomato sauce, vegetables and fried potatoes for Rp900. Also *nasi campur, nasi goreng, mie kuah,* banana pancakes, fruit salads, and shots of *arak* at

Rp50 each. The attractive and gentle family here will win your heart. The **Sumber Rasa** Chinese restaurant, in front of the Lilaberata, employs competent chefs. Opposite the Lilaberata is **Candra Warung** which features cheap but unusually good traditional Balinese food (the best peanut sauce in Indonesia?). It fills up quickly because it has its regulars. The standout among breakfast places is the **Sidhu Barta**, which seems to change its menu *daily,* and offers fruit salad, pancakes, etc. Stay up late (sometimes until 0100) drinking and listening to music at the **Tropical Beer Garden.**

Services

With its hundreds of European yuppie tourists, Candidasa has come of age. It has travel agencies, tour operators, a library, a Tel/Tel office (at the Nakula), a doctor, *Barong* dances (Rp2000, at Pandam Harum), a moneychanger (Tri Ayu Graha, but at least 6 points lower than Kuta), bike rental places (Rp1000 per day), and even a massage service. The generator comes on promptly at 1700. MG Travel can confirm flight tickets (Rp2000), rents VW jeeps for Rp25,000 daily (including insurance), arranges minibus tours, airport transfers (Rp25,000, 6 people with luggage), and they are the proud proprietors of the only telephone (0361-27969) in Candidasa; see Harijanto. Dr. Suryono's office, near MG Travel, is only open 1400-1600, Sun. closed.

Transport

From 0500 to 1900 *bemo* and minibuses travel up and down the road through town to: Amlapura, Rp250; Goa Lawah, Rp300; Klungkung, Rp500; Sakah (turnoff for Ubud), Rp800; Denpasar, Rp1000.

AMLAPURA

Today the capital of Karangasem District. Its old name is Karangasem. The name was changed to mislead evil spirits from burying the town again under a volcanic eruption. Can't change money at Amlapura's Bank Rakyat Indonesia; nearest moneychanger is at Candidasa (but lousy rate). See Puri Kanginan, the last raja's famous palace built early this century. Attached to the main building is Bale London, a combination of European, Chinese, and Balinese architecture and interior design; it was given this name because its furniture was decorated with English royal emblems. Puri Kanginan is an enormous complex, though the fountains have stopped spouting; dragons and serpents sit stonily with wide-open mouths. Still in good shape are the tiered gate and carved panels on the outside of the main structure. Sometimes the *puri* accepts guests (Rp10,000-12,000); guests are also let in on palace feasts, if any are scheduled.

Accommodations And Food

Most travelers prefer to stay at more idyllic Tirtagangga or Abian Soan, both about 5 km from town. If you must stay in Amlapura, friendly **Lahar Mas Inn**, on the L just as you're entering town, has rooms for Rp6000 d with breakfast. Clean and efficient **Homestay Sidya Karya**, on the R at the beginning of Jl. Hasanudin, is Rp4000 d. Coffee, tea, and bananas are served in the mornings. The *pasar* and the bus, *bemo*, and minibus stations are all about a one-km walk from this *losmen*. Many *warung* are set up around the *stasiun bis*, serving Javanese- and Balinese-style *nasi campur* on banana leaves. Also try **Lenny's**, about the only restaurant around, which has a complete Chinese menu.

From Amlapura

For Denpasar, take minibuses or *bemo* for Rp2000, 2½ hours; buses cost Rp1500 but are painfully slow (about 2 hours). Red *bemo* travel all the way to Singaraja along the E coast via Culik and Tianyar over a paved road with unusual scenery; they start at 0400 and leave all day long until around 1700; takes 3

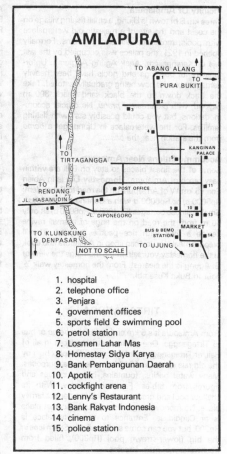

AMLAPURA

1. hospital
2. telephone office
3. Penjara
4. government offices
5. sports field & swimming pool
6. petrol station
7. Losmen Lahar Mas
8. Homestay Sidya Karya
9. Bank Pembangunan Daerah
10. Apotik
11. cockfight arena
12. Lenny's Restaurant
13. Bank Rakyat Indonesia
14. cinema
15. police station

hours, Rp2100. Bicyclists without low gears may want to take the bus up the big hill between Culik and Amlapura. Spectacular volcanic washouts along the way. From Amlapura's terminal, take a bus to Sibetan and Iseh, or straight to Rendang. Magnificent views on this road. Between Selat and Rendang you travel over a scenic paved road which winds right through a section of *sawah* which looks like a natural amphitheatre. East Bali is the home of the sweet-sour *salak*, the snake-skinned fruit that grows on the stunted palms in plantations on G. Agung's slopes around the village of Sibetan. The markets which rotate between the towns of Rendang, Selat, and Bebandem are a colorful sight, full of fresh produce. Every 3 days in Bebandem there's a cattle market.

Vicinity Of Amplapura

Three km S of town is Ujung, a small fishing village on the coast and the site of a majestic old waterpalace with pools, moats, canals, and fountains. Formally opened in 1921, the palace was occupied by the last raja of Karangasem, Anak Agung Anglurah. Unfortunately its buildings and pools have been heavily damaged, but are now being gradually restored. Take the track down to the black sand beach 300 m beyond, with picturesque *prahu*. No official accommodations, but you could possibly stay with fishing families. For the waterpalace in Ujung, get a *bemo* from the station near the *pasar*.

Accommodations Near Amlapura

Some of the finest places to stay on Bali are within easy reach of Amlapura. **Homestay Lila** is in Abian Soan 5 km W of Amlapura on the road to Bebandem; Rp5000 s, or Rp6000 d with a Continental breakfast. Small Balinese cottages (Rp4000 s, Rp6000 d) sit only 50 m from the road on the edge of a small ravine beside a river with rice paddies beyond. They'll prepare meals, or you can shop in Amlapura and cook at the homestay yourself. In the mornings the view of G. Agung is the clearest. From the homestay walk ½ hour to Bukit Kusambi.

TIRTAGANGGA

From Amlapura it's 5 km and Rp300 by *bemo* or bus to Tirtagangga. One of the prettiest places in all of Bali, at Tirtagangga is another water complex built by the old raja as late as 1947 for recreational purposes. Many water basins, fountains, bizarre statues and figures from fables. Fantastic scenery. With its shallow pool and great beauty, this is a perfect family place. No moneychanger here though; nearest place is at Candidasa. Entrance to the waterpalace is Rp200, but you can come and go all day. Swim laps in the big flower-strewn pool (Rp300), filled from freshwater mountain streams.

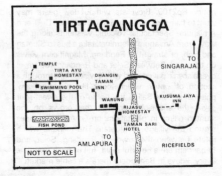

Accommodations And Food

Five *losmen*. **Dhangin Taman Inn** charges Rp3000 s, Rp4000 d; other rooms cost Rp5000 d, with better views. Sunlight streams through the windows, and all rooms have baths inside. The robust owner speaks good English. Another "unofficial" *losmen* with 4 rooms, **Tirta Ayu Homestay**, is right inside the waterpalace. Owned by a king's son, it overlooks the whole area and costs only Rp6000 (includes free admission to the bathing pool). Outside the waterpalace complex, across the road from the *warung*, are several more *losmen:* **Taman Sari Hotel** (Rp5000 s, Rp6000 d) has 15 lovely rooms overlooking a vast expanse of ricefields with the sea beyond. Lower-priced rooms (Rp3000 s, Rp4000 d) in the back. Next door to Taman Sari is **Homestay Rijasu;** Rp2000 s, Rp3000 d. A short walk up steps beyond the waterpalace is the **Kusuma Jaya Inn;** Rp2500-3000 d; with superb views from the hill. All of Tirtagangga's accommodations have restaurants, serving fresh fish taken right from the pools (Rp1500), and you may special-order Balinese food. Eating stalls at the start of the road to the waterpalace are cheaper and have surprisingly good *nasi campur* (Rp350), plus cold drinks, peanuts, fruits, snacks. **Gede's Warung**, opposite the T-junction, gets high marks.

From Tirtagangga

It's easy to get *bemo* from the main road into Amlapura (Rp300), running up until 1700. For Singaraja, buses pass right in front of Dhangin Inn starting at 0900, doing the 92-km trip for Rp1200. *Bemo* also pass by all day long, from 0300 up to around 1600 — at least 10 per day, Rp2100. If you want to visit Kintamani from here, just take the *bemo* to Kubutambahan (Rp1500, 2 hours), then from there to Kintamani (Rp1000, one hour).

Vicinity Of Tirtagannga

Climb the hill in the back and walk 1½ km up to the village where there are occasional (secret) cockfights. Come back by way of the road which winds through the valley; coconut palms, brilliant ricefields, the sea in the distance, and the biggest mountain on Bali towering above you. Take more extended walks in mountain areas. Budakeling, NW of Tirtagangga, is a Mahayana Buddhist colony on the slopes of G. Agung. Here live 2 different castes of Buddhists who have retained prehistoric feasting traditions.

Tulemben

Bali's NE coastal road is one of the few stretches on Bali where village life is largely unaffected by tourism. On this incredible drive, you pass by villages with people waving, temple festivals, banana and coconut plantations, and subsistence farmers eking out a living gathering seasalt and coral. Breathtaking slopes of tiered ricefields alternate with massive black rivers of volcanic ash and boulders, the ravages of the 1963 eruption of G. Agung. Between Tirtagangga and Kubutambahan, lava has cut across the road in at least 7 places. At Tulumben, along a hot, dry, and barren coast, is a dive *losmen*, the **Paradise Palm Beach Bungalows**, with only 4 rooms at Rp7000 s or d (bargain if not full). Their restaurant serves *cap cay* (Rp750), *ayam goreng*, *ikan laut* (about Rp2000, according to size of fish). No electricity. Most people just happen upon this place but end up staying *for*

days because of the amazing fish life (but not much coral) in the ocean right out in front of the *losmen*. Rent snorkeling gear for Rp1500 per day. Another, larger coral outcropping is 100 m away to the east. A sunken American Liberty ship, which was torpedoed by the Japanese in 1942 and later abandoned, can also be dived on; it's about 1 ½ km away to the east. One diver reports seeing a human skeleton among the wreck.

BULELENG DISTRICT

The Dutch invaded Buleleng in 1845, 1848, and finally conquered the region in 1849. Although the Balinese were extraordinarily brave, they were no match for repeating rifles and modern howitzers. The Dutch occupied N. Bali and ended the feudal rule of the local rajas a full 60 years prior to their colonization of the south. Thus N. Bali still has more of a European air, the class system isn't as strictly adhered to, and the social order centers more on the individual family than in the more communalized agricultural *banjar* of the south. Today it's a main cattle export center and a coffee-growing district. Since the climate in this area is drier than the south, Indian corn and oranges are also grown. Singaraja, the capital, has been an important educational and cultural center since Dutch times and the education faculty of Denpasar's Udayana University is housed here. Not as culturally rich as the classicist Bali-Hindu, rice-oriented southern half of the island, travelers are attracted to the N mostly because of the stretch of quiet beaches dotted with very reasonable accommodations, and the shallow reefs offshore which offer some of the best snorkeling on the island.

Temple Art
South Bali has small shrines and *meru* towers with classical lines, but the soft pink sandstone quarried near Singaraja in the N allows sculptors more exuberance. Tall gates have a dynamic flowing style covered with spiky, flame-like shapes. Steep flights of narrow steps lead up to airy thrones and shrines. Painted temples seethe with baroque figures, and the scale is more exaggerated. On bas-reliefs see plump Dutchmen cramped into a motorcar, people copulating in the bushes, and a man riding a bicycle composed of leaves and flowers.

SINGARAJA

Take a minibus (Rp1000) from Kintamani or from Stasiun Suci in Denpasar (Rp1500). Go through a mountain pass, descend from a point 1,200 m above sea level, and there it is. Holland fought powerful rajas at a

fierce battle in the village of Jagaraga and finally took control of the northern Buleleng region in 1849. Singaraja was the Dutch capital and a major transshipping point for Nusatenggara during colonial times. Women here wore the Malay blouse first "in order to protect the morals of the Dutch soldiers." In the harbor area, a monument commemorates the raising of the Indonesian flag when Holland handed over the island to the republic in 1949. With a present population of around 16,000, Singaraja today has a cosmopolitan air with many ethnic and religious groups living here: Islamic, European, Chinese, Buddhists, Hindu, Arab, and Christians, all existing in harmony. A city of tree-lined avenues, a wide market street, a square with rows of Chinese shops, and still much 19th C. colonial architecture around. Horse-drawn *dokar* are everywhere; it's prettier, quieter, and cleaner than Denpasar. Delicate orchids are sold in the market, also the island's best, richest, stinkiest *durian*. It's amazing the way the prices go down the farther you move north, the central mountain range seeming to block those bad influences from the south. For example, a package of Commodore cigarettes here costs half what you pay on Kuta! Doctor Kwari Dermawan, Jl. A. Yani 58 (opp. the Nitour/Garuda office) has a good reputation; open 0630-1900, 1600-1900.

Sights
View *lontar* books, miniature pictures and texts incised on palm leaves and framed by ornamental wooden panels, at **Gedong Kirtya** (open 0800 to 1200) just down the street from Hotel Singaraja. First collected by the Dutch, the 3,000-odd *lontar* in this historical library record the literature, mythology, medical science, and history of N. Bali. See also examples of *prasastis*, metal plates inscribed in the Balinese language, among the earliest written documents found on the island. Many imposing residences of European design still stand, one of the most noticeable being **Hotel Singaraja**. Loftily overlooking the whole city, it was once the seat of the Dutch government. Beautiful sunsets can be enjoyed over the old harbor area with its fishing and cargo

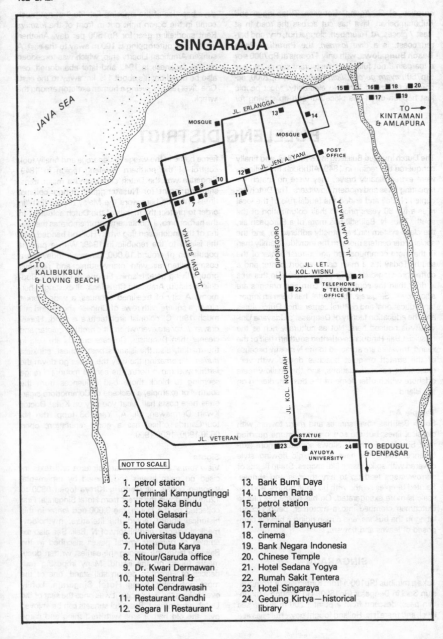

SINGARAJA

JAVA SEA

TO KINTAMANI & AMLAPURA

JL. ERLANGGA

MOSQUE

MOSQUE

POST OFFICE

JL. JEN. A. YANI

TO KALIBUKBUK & LOVING BEACH

JL. DEWI SARTIKA

JL. DIPONEGORO

JL. GAJAH MADA

JL. LET. KOL. WISNU

TELEPHONE & TELEGRAPH OFFICE

JL. KOL. NGURAH

JL. VETERAN

STATUE

AYUDYA UNIVERSITY

TO BEDUGUL & DENPASAR

NOT TO SCALE

1. petrol station
2. Terminal Kampungtinggi
3. Hotel Saka Bindu
4. Hotel Gelasari
5. Hotel Garuda
6. Universitas Udayana
7. Hotel Duta Karya
8. Nitour/Garuda office
9. Dr. Kwari Dermawan
10. Hotel Sentral & Hotel Cendrawasih
11. Restaurant Gandhi
12. Segara II Restaurant
13. Bank Bumi Daya
14. Losmen Ratna
15. petrol station
16. bank
17. Terminal Banyusari
18. cinema
19. Bank Negara Indonesia
20. Chinese Temple
21. Hotel Sedana Yogya
22. Rumah Sakit Tentera
23. Hotel Singaraya
24. Gedung Kirtya—historical library

prahu. The new harbor of **Celukan Bawang**, 40 km to the W of Singaraja, is now Bali's principal import and export harbor.

Crafts
Puri Agung on Jl. Veteran sells distinctive hand-woven *sarung* or *kain*. In this *kampung*, there's a loom in practically every home. Also try the **Sari Busana**, Jl. Veteran 20, right up the street from Hotel Singaraja; enter next to Gedong Kirtya. Have a look in the factory to see the *kain tenun*, a typical Balinese weave, being produced. In the southern *kampung* of **Bera-tan** many silversmiths work.

Accommodations
It's more pleasant to stay out at Lovina Beach (11 km W) than in the city itself. Most of Singaraja's hotels are conveniently located on Jl. A. Yani, heading W out of town towards Lovina and Gilimanuk. **Hotel Garuda**, no. 76, is Rp5000-7000 with *kamar mandi* inside; larger rooms are more expensive. **Hotel Duta Karya**, right next to the Nitour/Garuda agent's office, charges Rp8500 for a bit fancier room with fans and sinks but the **Hotel Gelasari**, no. 87 (tel. 21495), at Rp3000 s and Rp5000 d *(mandi* outside) is a better deal; clean, cool, and close to Lovina side of town. The **Saka Bindu**, nearly across the street, wants Rp5000 but is not that much better value. More central **Hotel Sentral**, no. 48, is Rp5200 d with inside *mandi* but no fan. Next door is **Hotel Cendrawasih**; Rp3500 d. For those who like a city scene, the inexpensive **Losmen Ratna**, Jl. Iman Bonjol 102 (near the mosque), asks Rp4000 s or d; plain but clean and plenty of eating places nearby. Finally, there's the **Sedana Yoga** on Jl. Gajah Mada at start of town; Rp6000 s, Rp9000 d. Clean, fan, inside *mandi*.

Food
Numerous good eating places can be found around the bus station and near Pasar Mumbul on Jl. A. Yani. Highly recommended is the popular **Restaurant Gandhi** for Chinese dishes: *mie*, prawns, lobster, pigeon. Rather expensive, but the best restaurant in Singaraja. Other Chinese eateries nearby.

From Singaraja
Bemo anywhere in town cost Rp150. From **Stasiun Banyusari**, a little E of Singaraja after the bridge, catch buses, minibuses or *oplet* to: Denpasar's Ubung Station, Rp1500; Gilimanuk, Rp1650; Kin-tamani, Rp1250; Karangasem, Rp2500; Klungkung, Rp2000. From **Stasiun Kampungtinggi**, on the Lovina-side of town, catch *oplet* for points east: Amlapura, Rp1800; Denpasar (via Bedugal), Rp1500 (leaving every ½ hour from 0600 to 1600); Lovina, Rp300; Tejakula, Rp600; Kintamani, Rp1000; Gili-manuk, Rp1800. Inquire also about buses direct to Surabaya, E. Java, which obviates going down to Denpasar or Kuta. Lots of *bakwan* carts. The

horse baths, Tejakula

Nitour Garuda agent on Jl. A. Yani cannot reliably confirm booking on flights out of Bali's airport; do this only at the main Garuda Airlines office in Denpasar.

Vicinity Of Singaraja
At Tejakula, 35 km E of Singaraja (Rp600 by *bemo)* on the way to Amlapura, see the famous horse bath, even more elaborate than the baths for people. There's a nice view of the seacoast farther on at Culik. **Sawan:** In this small village SE of Singaraja is the small temple of Jagaraga. Bas-reliefs show 2 corpulent Europeans in a Model-T Ford held up by an armed bandit, aircraft falling from the sky into the sea, Dutch steamers being attacked by sea monsters. Also incredibly flamboyant statues of Rangda the witch, and of a dazed mother buried under a pile of children. The temple is surrounded by big trees. Gongs are made at Sawan village where there's also a bamboo *angklung* orchestra.

Sangsit
Seven km E of Singaraja. See the brilliant **Pura Beji**, dedicated to the goddess of agriculture, Dewi Sri. A perfect example of the northern baroque-style of temple carving, stone vegetation grows in and out of the carvings. Strange off-angle symmetry. There's a spell-

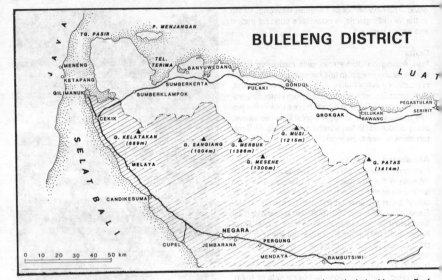

BULELENG DISTRICT

binding gateway of *naga*-snakes and imaginary beasts, devils, demon guardians, wooden statues, and a throne of the sun god. Kids follow you around and show you features, give flowers, etc. Extraordinarily different. Donation.

Kubutambahan

From Amlapura, Rp1500 by *bemo*. Visit the unusual **Pura Medruwe Karang,** the "Temple of the Owner of the Land," worshipped to ensure success of crops grown on unirrigated land. Carvings show ghouls, home scenes, lovers, noblemen, an official riding a bicycle with flowered spokes, a riot of leaves and tendrils, all on top of an almost *stupa*-like structure. Donation. Next to this temple is a small *warung* that sells black rice pudding Rp50, very possibly the best on Bali (this dessert at Poppies on Kuta for Rp800 can't compare with it).

Yeh Sanih

Local name is Air Sanih. Deserted beaches and sea temples are found all along the northern coast of Bali. Catch an *oplet* from Singaraja's Terminal Banyusari

and travel down a road sentineled with trees E of Singaraja to this shady seaside spot with its big enclosed natural swimming pool of clear, fresh water fed from underground springs, Rp250 to enter. Also a beautiful, well-cared-for botanical gardens, including *pink* frangipani. Sometimes this retreat is stampeded by 150 screeching school children and at other times it's virtually empty 3 days in a row. Mostly visited by locals. Nice swimming in the sea. From Yeh Sanih, a good paved road S along the NE coast leads to Amlapura; this is one of the most spellbinding journeys on Bali. **accommodations and food:** Next to the pool is the expensive **Bungalow Puri Sanih,** Rp8000-10,000 d with fan and mosquito nets, and fresh flowers with breakfast. **Hotel Ginza Beach Inn** has nice cottages with giant private baths under trees facing the ocean and overlooking lily ponds. Quite a good deal for Rp6000 per "house." No disturbances, just the birds. A cheaper *losmen* with foam rubber beds is located on the L-hand side just before the pool coming from Amlapura. A restaurant overlooks the pool but very slow service, expensive, and not good value.

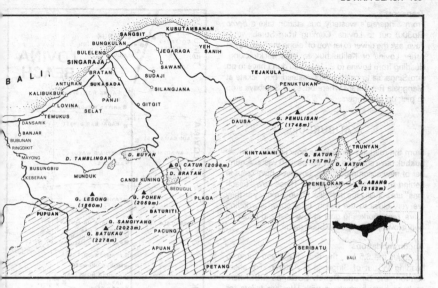

LOVINA BEACH

Eleven km W of Singaraja on the road to Seririt. Catch a *bemo* (Rp300) anywhere on Jl. A. Yani which turns into Jl. Seririt heading W out of Singaraja. Actually, "Lovina Beach," the original seaside resort that sprang up about 12 years ago, is now the generic term for a number of small villages, beaches and accommodations strung out for 8 km along the coast W of Singaraja: Anturan, Happy Beach, Kalikbubuk, Lovina, Temukas. Generally, starting about the 6 km mark, all the restaurants, stores and services are on the S side of the road, while the accommodations are on the N side. The Lovina Beach "strip" is not Bali, but for pure relaxation, this is the place. Though not as scenic as the southern coastline, most people who arrive here are refugees from Kuta Beach wanting to get away from all the frenzy and the ripoffs and get back to nature. They pick a place as far away and as completely opposite Kuta and Sanur as they can find—no flash menus, no surfies, few motorbikes, little music, few dogs—and quite cheap. However, pushy sellers are starting to turn up at the beach in increasing numbers, along with kids trying to practice their English. You can easily live on about US$6 a day here; a tourist economy hasn't set in yet. But it's growing. There's a bit of a pub scene, with the nightlifers gathering at Jacky's Restaurant in Kalikbubuk to look at the pretty girls and listen to live electric guitar, but it's not nearly as self-conscious as in the south. Social events revolve around food. In order to draw customers, all the competing restaurants put on a big buffet or an all-you-can-eat fish fry for Rp2000-3000 with curries, grilled meats, salads, etc., then starting after dinner at around 2000 throw a "free" *rejog* or *legong* dance into the bargain. Enjoying the beautiful sunsets simply involves, in most cases, just walking out on your veranda. At the 2 moneychangers, rates are about 10-15 *rupiah* lower than in Denpasar or Kuta.

Marine Sports

At night the whole fishing fleet of this coastal village goes night fishing, with lanterns glowing all along the ocean front. There's good swimming inside the bay where the sea just laps lazily at the black-sand shore, quite safe and tame compared to the volatile southern coasts. Yet the snorkeling and diving is surprisingly brilliant for a reef so close to the beach. The shallowness of the water makes this coast ideal for beginners and young divers. Rent an outrigger (Rp2000-4000 pp) to take you out the sloping reef where you can view the reef fauna for several hours right from the boat by just sticking your head underwater. It's like being inside an aquarium with moray eels, tropical fish, pastel corals, etc. The boatmen often provide snorkeling gear, or rent gear from the hotels (Rp2000 for 2-3 hours) if you take out your own *prahu* or simply swim out to the reef.

Transport

From Singaraja's westerly bus station take a *bemo* (Rp300) out to Lovina. Coming from Surabaya, E. Java, ask the driver to let you off along the highway at either Lovina or Kalibukbuk to save backtracking. Heading from Lovina to E. Java, you don't have to go into Singaraja to catch a bus. Instead, buy tickets at Manggala Restaurant where buses to Surabaya stop to pick up passengers.

KALIBUKBUK

From the road, it's remarkable how little Lovina/Kalibukbuk have changed over the past 10 years. A number of new accommodations, however, have crept in behind the roadside homestays. These new "beach inns" are actually the best deal for your money as they are very close to the beach, offer cheap snorkeling tours, rent snorkeling gear at low cost and beautiful bungalows in the Rp6000-8000 range.

Accommodations

At about the 6.5 km, the first village you come to heading W out of Singaraja is Anturan. For sheer comfort, the **Baruna Beach Cottages** (BBC) here can't be beat: bungalows with Western toilets for Rp8000 very near the beach, price including Continental breakfast. Made's a good cook; fried chicken, Rp2500; *nasi campur,* Rp1000. Also in Anturan, the **Lila Cita Beach Inn** has rooms going for Rp3000-4000 d (including breakfast), plus other rooms upstairs. Nice staff, good atmosphere, and superb snorkeling out front. Their restaurant has average food. **Homestay Agung** is another Anturan accommation, with resident masseuse, that travelers like (Rp3000 s, Rp6000 d).

About one km before Kalibukbuk proper is the small, homey, well-organized **Janur Dive Inn** with 6 rooms going for Rp3000-5000 s or d. John (Made Janur) is a good cook, an expert guide to the G. Batur area, and he also takes groups out to dive on the reef only 800 m out in front of his *losmen.* John's Australian wife provides the cordial, nice little touches. **Banyualit,** just up from Janur's, also gets high marks; Rp7000 s, Rp8500 d including breakfast in both concrete and traditional bungalows with nice rooms, fan, and *mandi.* Quiet, all by itself within sight of the ocean. An established place run by an old *ibu* is **Ayodya Accommodations,** within its own enclosed compound (good security); Rp2000 s, Rp3000 d. **Ayoda Inn II** (or Astina's) is right on the beach away from everything but only a 500-m walk to everything; Rp7000 d for your own bungalow with breakfast (soggy toast!), sink, toilet, shower, with woodcarved furniture, swept 10 times daily, extraordinary security. Don't dispute the bill or the manager and deputy manager will threaten you with a machete (as was perpetrated

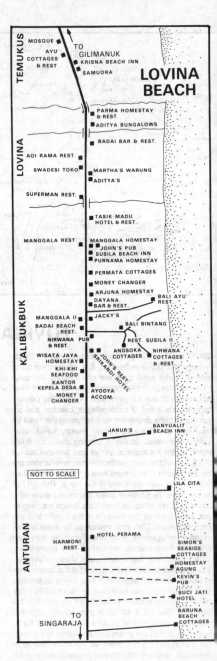

on 2 guests in 1986). Less risky and highly recommended is **Nirwana's Cottages**; Rp5000-8000 s or d, Rp10,000 for bungalows (also a cheap set of bungalows for Rp4000) with a breakfast of salad and tea or coffee; good service and also has a restaurant. An old favorite, with a "downtown" location, is **Manggala Homestay**: Rp2000 s (without shower), Rp3500-4000 for bungalows with *mandi*. Excellent security, and it's opposite a very good restaurant. They also offer snorkeling gear (Rp2000 pp for 2 hours) and the beach is right out front.

Food

The **Harmoni Restaurant** in Anturan has fantastic fresh lobster (Rp7000), *babi guling* (Rp3000), and tuna steak dinners (Rp2000). Although food served at **Badai Restaurant** is tasty, quick, and cheap, it's often too crowded. The fare at **Nirwana's** is also overrated. Much better than both is the **Khi Khi** where dishes are more expensive but you'll see why. Khi Khi serves wonderful food, particularly the fresh seafood: lobster; Rp8500-10,000; crab with choice of 7 sauces; grilled fish, etc., plus free *krupuk*. A 30-min. dance in the evening is free and includes a complimentary dessert of rice cakes. Managed by Made, whom you can see through the open kitchen. Travelers also rave about the smorgasbord *(sate, gado-gado, ayam kari, nasi goreng,* etc.) at **Tony's Place** for only Rp2000—an evening of fun and good food. **Perama** also has a very experienced chef (all dishes are nice), a friendly place for dinner. **Banyualit Beach Restaurant** specializes in seafood and Indonesian food with a Chinese flavor.

LOVINA VILLAGE

Accommodations

Tasik Madu ("Sea of Honey") is one of the cheapest with rooms going for Rp1500 s, Rp2000 d, plus 3 beachfront bungalows for only Rp2000 s, Rp3000 d (almost always full). Two cabinets of interesting books and magazines are available to guests. A good location but rundown with inactive restaurant (changing owners). **Aditya Bungalows** (P.O. Box 35, Singaraja 81101, tel. 0362-21781); Rp10,000 s or d for bungalows with *mandi*, literally 7 m from the beach. No breakfast, just tea or coffee; also runs a popular restaurant and pub. The **Samudra Beach Cottages & Restaurant** is the most expensive place on this coastline, located in a nice setting ½ km W of Aditya on road to Gilimanuk; Rp25,000 for a/c rooms with hot water, just 10 m from the beach. Continental breakfast, in their breezy restaurant, included in price. Next door is Mr. Tisna's **Krisna Beach Inn**, about 13 km W of Singaraja, with rather drab rooms for Rp3500-5000 s or d, but very near the ocean. Has a restaurant and coral reef right out front. Cheaper set of rooms with outside *kamar mandi*.

Food

Several good restaurants are along the beach. **Marta's Warung**, near the bridge and exactly opposite the mosque, is famous for its jaffles—21 different flavors! Also serves tasty *nasi campur* and *pisang goreng;* the smiles and the playfulness are free.

Vicinity Of Lovina

Walk to Singaraja along the beach, crossing about 6 small rivers, in a couple of hours. For the waterfalls, take a *bemo* for Temukus, 3 km from Lovina toward Seririt. Or walk it in 45 min. from the bridge in Lovina village, a one-km walk from Temukus. Turn in at the sign SINGSING AIR TERJUN. Good eating stalls along the way. Boys will show you the way to the falls where you can swim while cool fresh water cascades over you. There's another bigger, better, and more isolated waterfall up a path to the left (E) which is also swimmable.

Buddhist Monastery

Go first to Dansarik village, about 18 km W of Singaraja. From the highway where the *bemo* lets you off, walk 2 km and then turn in at the road going uphill just before Banjar's market. Climb another 2 km to this gleaming orange storybook monastery high on a hill with Buddha statues, *raksasa* guardians, and exuberant woodcarvings. Or take a *honda ojek* all the way up the hill, Rp500. A breathing technique *(prana-yama)* and a "slow walking technique" are practiced here, the aim being to produce clear comprehension and mindfulness. Resident *bhikku* (Buddhist teachers) guide you on your way to equanimity. The course is 14 days but stay as long as you want. Quite comfortable with plenty of *mandi* water and good vegetarian food. Unsurpassed views on all sides. At night in these highlands of Bali, stars reflect in the rice paddies, and in between, fireflies fill the air. The road continues past the monastery and up the mountain.

Air Panas

A hotspring is only about an hour's walk away from the monastery, 1½ km beyond Banjar's market; look for the AIR PANAS sign and follow the dirt track to the motorcycle parking area. While 8 dragons' heads spit out lukewarm water, lay back in one of 2 lovingly warm pools of green-yellow sulphur water and feel like a million. Entrance: Rp1000. Toilets and changing rooms are clean, and a fairly good restaurant overlooks the pool.

Pulau Menjangan

A new national park off the NW coast of Bali which boasts the premier scuba diving and snorkeling spot on the whole island, frequented by fish of every size, shape, and color. If going alone, pay Rp500 at the PPA post at entrance to the park. *Prahu* to P. Menjangan cost around Rp5000 plus another Rp5000 for a one- to 2-hour guided tour. One-day excursions can also be arranged from Kuta or Denpasar. Tours start at 0800, arrive 2 hours later, return at 1700, and cost around US$40 pp. The well-known **Gloria Maris Diving Club**, on the airport road in Kuta, organizes tours to not only P. Menjangan Is. but also P. Lomongan,

Tulamben, etc. They will arrange everything, including the PPA permit. On the way to P. Menjangan from Lovina, stop at **Pulaki** 53 km W of Singaraja to see the dramatic monkey temple only 25 m from the beach with cliffs towering up behind it.

TABANAN DISTRICT

BEDUGAL

A small lakeside village in the middle of the central highlands E of G. Batur, as near to paradise as you can get. At 1,500 m above sea level, Bedugal is nearly as cool as Kintamani. Lake Bratan fills the crater of G. Bratan (2,020 m), which overlooks the lake. Children fish for minnows, and canoes cross the lake carrying firewood to villages on the far side. Take lakeshore walks through pine forests with shrines along the shore. Overcast skies or rain cause the area to become severely cold, so bring a sweater. Chilly swimming. Just below Bedugal is the market of **Bukit Mungsu** where live and stuffed birds (parrots and cuckoos), rabbits, beautiful wild orchids, such vegetables as carrots and potatoes, pomegranates,

and corn on the cob are sold. Many species of orchids and dark, heavy-coated monkeys are seen in the area of Lila Graha. Visit the botanic gardens and orchid collection **Kebon Raya**, near the market; Rp200 entrance.

Accommodations
Hotel Bedugal, on a little hill above the lake, charges Rp10,000 d; also cottages for Rp20,000. Here you can also rent a boat (Rp1500 pp). **Hadi Rahajo**, at the junction of the road to the lake, is Rp6000 with breakfast. **Lila Graha**, also above the lake, has rooms for Rp10,000 s, Rp15,000 d. **Bali Handara Country Club** (P.O. Box 324, Denpasar, tel. 0361-28866), is an international-class hotel with tennis court, a good restaurant, snack bar, and a world-class 18-hole championship golf course designed by Peter Thomson and Associates. Balinese-style bungalows, with fireplaces, rent from US$44 to US$165 (luxury suite) per day. All credit cards accepted. Extravagant isolation; the hotel bar overlooks the whole of Lake Bratan.

Vicinity Of Bedugal
Two km N is the Muslim village of **Candi Kuning** where, on a small promontory above the lake, is the peaceful half-Hindu, half-Buddhist **Uludanu Temple.** Dewi Danau, the water goddess, is worshipped here. With flowers everywhere, this temple is a 50 times better experience than Tanah Lot (see below). Walk from Candi Kuning all the way to Munduk via the 2 other tranquil lakes inside these mountains, D. Buyan and D. Tamblingan. You can cover the 27 km in 6-8 hours. At **Gitgit**, 10 km N of Bedugal, is a sweeping panorama over the coast and the Madura Strait. Also a waterfall in this area. It's also possible to walk to the 3 lakes, D. Bratan, D. Tamblingan, and D. Buyan, from Gitgit. Another retreat is **Baturiti**, 4 km S of Bedugal, where a market takes place every 3 days. Eat at **Green Valley Restaurant** in the N part of town; fantastic views. At the DENPASAR 40 KM sign at Baturiti, a dirt back road will take you to just before Mengwi. But it's so full of boulders that it'll shake the guts out of you. No fun.

Getting There
A good road runs from Singaraja to Bedugal, Rp1000 by *bemo* or minibus. Or, if you're going to Singaraja,

THE BEDUGAL AREA

TO PANCASARI

GUNUNG CATUR (2089m) △

ULUDANU TEMPLE

MESJID

PASAR KANTUNG

LAKE

BRATAN

GUA JEPANG (JAPANESE CAVE)

DOCK

SUMMIT

WARUNG

TO BATURITI

1. Raksa Gangga
2. Sindu Srama
3. *pasanggrahan*
4. Wisma Lila Graha
5. Peng. Hadiraharjo

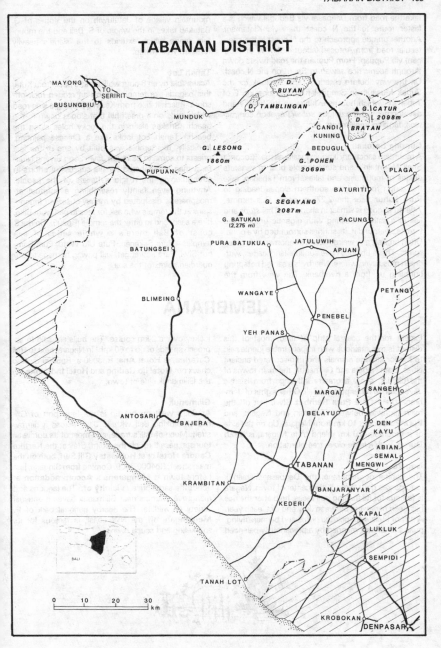

TABANAN DISTRICT

MAYONG
TO SERIRIT
BUSUNGBIU
MUNDUK

D. BUYAN
D. TAMBLINGAN

G. CATUR
2098m
D. BRATAN
CANDI KUNING
BEDUGUL

G. LESONG
1860m

G. POHEN
2069m

PLAGA

PUPUAN

BATURITI

G. SEGAYANG
2087m

G. BATUKAU
(2,275 m)

PACUNG

PURA BATUKUA
JATULUWIH
APUAN

BATUNGSEI

PETANG

WANGAYE

BLIMEING

PENEBEL

YEH PANAS

MARGA

SANGEH

ANTOSARI
BAJERA

BELAYU

DEN KAYU

ABIAN SEMAL
MENGWI

TABANAN

KRAMBITAN

BANJARANYAR

KEDERI

KAPAL

LUKLUK

SEMPIDI

TANAH LOT

BALI

0   10   20   30
km

KROBOKAN
DENPASAR

take the road from Denpasar via Bedugal which is a faster route to the N coast than via Kintamani. Another unique approach to the N coast is the spectacular road from Antosari (about 42 km W of Tabanan) via Pupuan. From Pupuan the road twists down through scenic rice *sawah* to Seririt on the N coast. On the way, before entering Tabanan, look for the Subak Museum in Sanggulan village (one km E of Tabanan), which houses exhibits on the history and development of the unique *subak* irrigation committees, farming implements, etc.

Gunung Batukau

A mountain sanctuary (known locally as the "Coconut Shell Mountain") and state temple built to venerate deities of mountains and lakes. From Tabanan, take the rough road up the southern slopes leading to **Pura Luhur** near the 2,275-m peak. This remote, 7-tiered pagoda is similar in shape to a Thai *stupa* and lies in a solitary clearing with gigantic uninhabited forests all around it, its shrines surrounded by a pond. Often on Bali, any weird natural phenomenon is given spirits. These uplands have sublime landscapes, with green moss everywhere. Nearby is a sacred hotspring bubbling up from a riverbank. The view from the mountain village of Jatuluwih on the slopes of G. Batukau takes in the whole of S. Bali and the mountain range which extends to the island's heavily forested western tip.

Tanah Lot

Accessible by an 8-hour walk up and back from Kuta, this pagoda-like temple sits on an eroded rock offshore. Reach it also from Kediri by taking a side road which ends on a green hill that slopes down to the beach. (Snakes sleep in the rocky holes along the beach.) Tanah Lot looks like a Chinese painting. Ironically, this temple was built by one of the last priests to come to Bali from Java, Sang Hiyang Nirarta, a man remembered for his successful efforts in strengthening the religious beliefs of the people. Anything even faintly resembling a spiritual atmosphere is dissipated by money-obsessed Indonesians at the temple who ask for fees to park your bike, hire a sash, and to enter the temple (Rp200). On the S coast of Bali there's a whole series of sea temples — Pura Sekenan, Pura Ulu Watu, Pura Rambut Siwi, Pura Petitenget — all paying homage to the guardian spirits of the sea.

JEMBRANA

Except for the coastal strip of land, most of this district is mountainous with impenetrable jungle said to harbor strange animals and undiscovered ancient cities. Both Negara and Gilimanuk, the main towns of the district, show a greater influence from Islamic Java than do other parts of Bali. Other sights of Jembrana District are **Pura Rambut Siwi**, just off the main highway between Tabanan and Negara, and **Pura Purancak**, 10 km from Negara. Up on the side of a mountain, 20 km inland from Negara, is **Asah Duren**, with a large clove tree plantation.

Negara

The capital of Jembrana, the Denpasar-Gilimanuk road passes right through the center of town. Negara is famous for its thrilling bull races, held after the rice has been harvested between July and Oct. each year. A pair of bulls, with painted horns and banners flying, pulls a small cart manned by a precariously balanced jockey over a 2-km course. The bulls are said to approach speeds of up to 60 kph! In Negara, next to **RM Caterina**, is **Hotel Ana**; Rp3000 s, Rp5000 d. Also check out **Hotel Ijo Gading** and **Hotel Indraloka** on the Gilimanuk side of town.

Gilimanuk

At Bali's westernmost tip is the ferry port of Gilimanuk, linking Bali with E. Java across a narrow strait. Much of Bali's trade, and most of its domestic tourists, pass through this point. Stay at the **Kartika Candra Hotel** or at **Homestay Gili Sari**, both on the main street; Rp4000-6000. Coming from Singaraja, just before town is **Mangarana's Accommodation** at about the same price. **vicinity of:** The lagoons and mangrove swamps near Gilimanuk have an unusual variety of wildlife. The nearby national park of **P. Menjangan**, off the NW coast, is famous for its snorkeling and scuba diving.

SUMATRA

*T*his gigantic island—fifth largest in the world—is 1,760 km long and up to 400 km wide. It accounts for a full 25% of the total Indonesian land area. In just about every way—economically, politically, and strategically—Sumatra is Indonesia's most important island. With its grass huts, lake tribes, wildlife reserves, steamy jungles, swampy lowlands, swift clear rivers, spectacular waterfalls, crater lakes, and immense forests full of tropical 30-m-high trees, Sumatra has become the third most popular tourist destination in Indonesia. Called the "Isle of Hope" or the "Isle of Gold," this island's natural wealth is fabulous. Sumatra is like the Africa of SE Asia.

INTRODUCTION

You'll feel a vast difference between Sumatra and neighboring Java. Sumatra is far wilder, more rugged, and more difficult to get around on. Unlike Java, enormous communication problems exist. Islam entered some coastal regions of Sumatra more than 300 years before it touched Java. Unlike Java's feudalistic rule and caste system, on Sumatra free election of local chiefs has been the age-old custom. Sumatrans are generally less educated and poorer than the Javanese, and their culture is not as refined. People are shorter, darker, more wiry—a jungle people. You are apt to find more *kasar* personalities on Sumatra, which—after Java—is sometimes refreshing. Compared to Java, this island has a grand beauty, and the distances and space are enormous.

The Land
Sumatra's name is a modified version of the Latin term meaning "black earth" *(suma tera)*. This name referred to the dark, fertile soil which produced a high crop yield that impressed the first European planters. About the same size and population as California, almost one-third of the island is continuous lowland and saltwater swamp with nipa palms and mangrove trees extending 1,370 km down the whole E coast. The rivers are shallow and winding as drainage is poor and flooding is common; it's difficult to find nice beaches on the E coast because of these rivers that empty into the sea. Fine white-sand beaches are found only on the W coast and its offshore islands.

An unbroken mountain wall ranging from 1,575 to 3,805 m marches down the entire western aspect of the island. Called Bukit Barisan ("Parade of Mountains"), this range includes 93 volcanic peaks, 15 of them still active. On its western side the mountains plunge steeply into the sea, while on its eastern side they slope gently down to the plains and swamps. The island's forest areas are estimated to be about 60-70% of Sumatra's total land area, including forest land already exploited. All the major ecosystems are well represented in reserves found throughout the island with the exception of lowland rainforests, always the first kind to come under the axe. The NW and SW regions are still quite inaccessible and wild. There's a chain of islands off the west coast—Nias, Mentawai, and Enggano—with rocky, reef-enclosed coasts.

Climate
The equator cuts this island in 2 equal halves. Heaviest rains N of the equator occur Oct.-Apr., while the dry season is May-September. South of the equator, the rainy season is Dec.-Feb., sometimes making the southern roads nearly impassable. Because clouds coming in from the ocean are blocked by the Bukit Barisan range, the climate W of the range is often rainy and hot. The ideal time to travel through Sumatra is Sept.-Oct., when the rains have started—they're not so torrential that the roads are out, and unlike in the dry season, the dust isn't that prevalent.

Fauna
Sumatra has always been famous for its animals. It has a greater variety of wildlife than any other island in Indonesia: 176 different mammals, 194 reptiles, 62 amphibians, and 150 birds. The jungle is near at hand and the island's wild creatures have always played a great part in its myth and folklore. Observe the many thousands of tigers, mythical birds and other beasts painted on *becak* and signboards all over Sumatra. Since the island's flora and fauna is largely shared with Malaysia, Kalimantan, and Java, few species are endemic. Elephants, Sumatran rhinoceros, and large free-ranging populations of Sumatran orangutans are Sumatra's best known fauna. Orangutans, rhinos, and wild pigs are only found in the N, while the tapir

and certain species of monkeys are found only in the south.

A cousin to the Javanese tiger, Sumatran tigers occasionally venture into Sumatra's more remote villages to take a pig or calf. It is customary to call a tiger "grandfather" (and when crossing rivers, be sure to address a crocodile as "grandmother"). Tigers' claws are a powerful good luck charm, and their whiskers grated in alcohol will make one man as strong as 10. Other species of cat include the elusive Sumatran clouded leopard, civet cat, and a small, striped predator called the *macan akar*. A tree hunter, the *macan akar* can be seen in some areas with a flashlight in branches at night.

Tapirs, 2-horned rhinoceros, wild dogs, bearded pigs, sun bears, flying foxes, squirrels, wild oxen, the Sumatran hare, and barking and mouse deer, also live here. Other unique mammals include the slow lori *(nycticebus)*, the subalpine gray shrew, and the rare goat antelope *(serow)*, which lives at above 1,500-m-altitude. Honeybears *(Helarctos malayanus)* have footprints similar to man's and can walk upright on their hind legs—characteristics which generated many stories and even search parties in the early

1900s. There are also numerous species of monkeys, such as the pigtailed macaque and the fox-nosed monkey *(tarsius)*. The flying lemur *(culogos)* and the proboscis monkey are found in the island's mangrove swamps. One species of orangutan lives on Sumatra, a rare primate found only in the most remote parts of the island. Don't be deceived by look-alikes such as red-leaf monkeys, which are orange, hairy, and swing and crash through treetops. To be certain, just look for a tail, as great apes such as orangutans are tailless; also orangutans do not hoot, as do red-leaf monkeys. Orangutans may be observed in a semi-wild state in the Bukitlawang Rehabilitation Center at Bohorok in northern Sumatra. Another huge reserve, where many of Sumatra's species are found, is the G. Leuser National Park in N. Sumatra

Sumatra is also the home of Indonesia's grandest animal, the Indian elephant. Moving in herds of 20-30, an estimated 2,000 survive. The Sumatran species has small ears and isn't as hairy or as large as the African variety—it stands only 3-m-high, a pygmy pachyderm! Sumatra's wide variety of birdlife (150 species at least) includes dazzling parrots and cockatoos, hornbills, the Great Argus pheasant, the crested partridge, the rose-crested bee-eater,

subadult orangutan

orangutan ("Man of the Woods"): Latin name is *Pongo pygamaeus*. Found only in N. Sumatra and on Borneo. About 1½ m tall with a 1½-m armspan and weighing as much as 130 kilos. Has glinting reddish-gold fur, beard, and moustache, and its long powerful arms reach down to its feet. Orangutans have been known to live up to 55 years in captivity. Wild orangutans are mild tempered and retiring and usually won't bite unless provoked. Adult males are always solitary. The primate's young bear a startling resemblance to the human baby. A slow-motion acrobat while feeding, the orangutan lives most of the time in tall trees and builds an elevated sleeping platform by weaving plant fibers together. They can travel long distances on the ground, foraging as long as 6 hours, and even take naps on the ground. Females forage together with a sub-

adult male. Orangutans never eat meat, though they themselves are often eaten by predators. They enjoy eating fruits, young plants, and leaves. Since orangutans sell for as much as US$25,000 to zoos around the world, hunters shoot the mother down from trees, then catch the young as they fall. Besides this slaughter by poachers, their habitat is being destroyed by logging and land-clearing agricultural operations. The Indonesian government is only now beginning to enforce a long-standing law against keeping orangutans as pets or hunting them. Orangutan Rehabilitation Centers have been set up in Kalimantan and North Sumatra to prepare confiscated young orangutans for the wild. At these centers you can see them come bounding out of the rainforest at feeding times.

woodpeckers, and nearly all the pigeons of Indonesia. Sumatra is also famed for its endemic species of insects, including a submarine diving grasshopper, a very rare olive-and-black moth *(E. battaka)*, which has a wingspan of over 10 cm. There's even a cave-dwelling cricket with antennae over 20 cm long!

Flora

In the rainforests are trees such as the *ketapang* which soar over 60 m high, supported by 6-m-high buttress roots. In N. Sumatra is the single indigenous pine, *Pinus merkusii*, now being extensively used in reforestation schemes on Java and elsewhere in SE Asia. Vines called "wait-a-minute" are tipped with spines that often snare people on jungle tracks. Strangler figs send long tendril roots to the ground from branches of tall trees, gradually suffocating its host tree. The corpse plant, a huge, foul plant that smells like putrifying animal flesh, consists of a central spike over 2 m high which rises from a bowl of giant leaves. Its stench attracts beetles and other insects which help it pollinate.

The extraordinary *rafflesia* grows up to one meter in diameter — the largest bloom in the world. Found on the island's west coast, this fascinating plant rises from the fungus-like, litter-filled forest floor. A bud develops which grows and reaches the size of a large cabbage, brown in color. Nine months later (usually in Aug. or Sept.) the flower opens, spreading out brilliant white-spotted orange petals. Finally it rots to a spongy mess on the mossy, damp ground, the plant's large sticky seeds carried to new soil by animals that eat or brush against it.

History

In mythical times, Sinbad the Sailor is said to have landed on an "extremely fertile island of abundance" off Sumatra where he met the "Old Man of the Sea." In the 1st C., a Chinese emperor dispatched an expedition to Sumatra to procure a rhinoceros for the Imperial Zoo. By the 7th C., Sumatra was the most important island in the archipelago and the cultural heart of SE Asia. Two seagoing, piratical, mercantile empires were based near present-day Palembang and at Jambi. The Sriwijaya Kingdom was an 11th C. Buddhist offshoot of the Hindu Saliendra cult of *devaraj* (God Kings). Sriwijaya had no agricultural lands to speak of but, guarding one of the main waterways of the ancient world (the Straits of Melaka), this mercantile empire at its height controlled an area which included Sumatra, the western end of Java, and the E coast of Malaysia. Its commercial and political influence extended as far as ancient Formosa and Hainan. A Sriwijayan prince even became ruler of Cambodia. In the 13th C., the empire finally broke up into city states, mainly on coasts and mouths of rivers.

Sumatra has a long history of foreign contact. Accounts of Indonesia's first Islamic community, Perlak (present-day Aceh), were brought back to Europe by Marco Polo, who had visited the northern tip of Sumatra in the 13th century. He also recorded that Sumatra was "Java the Less," though the island is 3 times larger than Java. Portuguese influence on Sumatra is apparent in some of the island names. On the E. coast of Sumatra the island of "Enggano" was probably named after a Portuguese navigational error. "Engano" is the Portuguese equivalent to the English word "mistake." By the 17th C., the Dutch had become a major controlling power in Sumatra — and the archipelago — by first establishing the Dutch East India Company. In 1602, when the Company went bankrupt, the Dutch government took over all their holdings. From 1811-1816, the English established fortified factories on the W. coast of Sumatra, trading in pepper and other spices, but abandoned this effort by treaty with the Dutch in 1824. The Japanese launched the invasion of Sumatra up the Musi River in February 1942, capturing the oilfields around Palembang, one of the richest prizes of the Pacific War.

Economy

With all its untold mineral wealth and cash crops, the Dutch used to refer to Sumatra as the "Isle of the Future." World War II abruptly and permanently interrupted their development plans. Now the Javanese are the chief exploiters of the island's wealth. Sumatra is today the mainstay of the Java-centered Indonesian economy. Profitable plantations of oil palm and rubber fill most of the lowland areas; big cities sit at important river junctions; oil wells dot the eastern coastal regions. Sumatra supplies a full 50% of Indonesia's gross import earnings — more than half of its oil, ¾ of its rubber and palm oil, a major portion of its coffee, and the total output of the country's tin, as well substantial quantities of coal, bauxite, aluminum and gold. Thirty percent of Indonesian exports — oil, natural gas, rubber, palm oil, tea, sisal, and tobacco — originate from N. Sumatra alone. On the other hand, Sumatra has only 9% of Indonesia's limited industry and only 18% of the people live in the towns. Shipping, trading, and fishing in the coastal areas traditionally form the mainstays of the island's local subsistence economy.

Oil is Sumatra's big money earner, accounting for nearly 40% of Indonesia's petroleum revenues. Earth oil was valued in ancient times by the Chinese as a medicine for skin diseases, rheumatism and other ailments. During Sriwijayan times, jars of the curious substance were brought from S. Sumatra to Peking for the Emperor of China in 971. In the 1500s, naval warriors of N. Sumatra poured oil on the waters of bays to keep intruding ships out of their ports. In 1866, American Alvin S. Bickmore was given a bottle of crude oil by a local raja on a trip to Palembang, where the first oil in S. Sumatra was discovered by the West in 1896—a herald of the great Talang Akar oilfields 48 km N of Palembang. Sumatra now produces about three quarters of Indonesia's crude oil and many refined petrochemical products—kerosene, gasoline, urea, and plastics. Until the oil price slump of 1986, this created an economic boom in the large coastal cities of Pekanbaru, Jambi, Medan, and Palembang.

The People

With its great diversity of tribes *(puak)*, and numerous megalithic, aboriginal, and matriarchal societies, Sumatra is one of the richest cultural areas of SE Asia—an ethnological goldmine. During the mesolithic era, while Java and Bali were still connected to mainland SE Asia, groups of proto-Malay peoples drifted S from China and Burma. Since then, wave after wave of Chinese, Indians, Arabians and Javanese have made Sumatra their home. Although Sumatra has the highest birthrate in the nation, the island is today underpopulated with only 25,723,000 people, a mere 15% of Indonesia's total. While Sumatra has about 30 persons per sq km, Java has over 800. On Java you see people everywhere you look, but on this island you can often travel for 20 km or more without seeing a soul.

Numerous ethnic groups *(suku bangsa)* are found in Sumatra, among them some of the most ancient cultures of Indonesia. Besides the main groups (Acehnese, Batak, Minangkabau, Lampungese, etc.) are isolated aborigines such as the Sakai in Riau Daratan, the Kubu in S. Sumatra, and the Sakkudai of the Mentawais—all descendants of the original inhabitants of the archipelago. Most of the aboriginal inhabitants of the islands of Nias, Mentawai, and Enggano off the W coast have been bypassed by the mainstreams of the 20th century. Coastal Malays are another long-settled group who live in Sumatra's southern and eastern parts, and have probably populated the island as hardy seafarers for several millenia. The majority of Sumatra's population does not, however, live along the coasts. In the mountain regions of N. Sumatra live the Christian Batak, and the high uplands of W. Sumatra around Bukittinggi are the home of the matriarchal Minangkabau. Both the Batak and the Minangkabau live as traders and as successful cultivators of the land. Peripheral groups such as the "Sea Gypsies" (or *Orang Laut*) still fish and trade in small, unsturdy boats along the swampy shores of eastern Sumatra and in the hundreds of islands of the Riau Archipelago. In northernmost Aceh Province live the staunchest Muslims who, from the late 16th C. onward, ruled the coasts of Sumatra from their river-based Islamic trading kingdoms.

Transmigrasi

Java, being Indonesia's most crowded island, has launched an ambitious program relocating 65 percent of its transmigrants to southern Sumatra. Sumatra's provinces of Bengkulu, South Sumatra, and Lampung have received more than their fair share. The government's new 5-year plan—2½ million people between 1985 and 1990—is on a scale reminiscent of post-bellum Europe's movement of masses of refugees. Each wearing a numbered red and white tag, the transmigrants comprise old people as well as babies and young children. Coming from the poorest families and leaving nothing behind, they start their new life with a mixture of worry and hope. The government pays for their passage to their new homesites in Sumatra and each family is given 2 hectare of land. These agricultural pioneers must to laboriously beat back the forest before they can start to plant. A lot of promises are made, but oftentimes families lack seed to plant; seed and tools are sold to the highest bidder by officials whose duty it is to distribute them. The *transmigrasi* program is ironic because Sumatra's most successful citizens move to Java, where they can make a better living. It is generally conceded that the transmigration scheme hasn't made much of a dent in Java's overpopulation, because the high birthrate far exceeds any migration.

ARTS AND CRAFTS

Music

Sumatra's pervasive Islamic influence is reflected in its musical instruments. A primitive type of oboe *(serunai)* is almost identical to the *surnai*, originally from Persia. A tamborine-like drum *(rebana)*, bamboo flute, and various forms of lutes and string instruments found throughout the island are also common in other Islamic areas of the world. The gong and drum of southern Sumatra show a strong Javanese influence. The various musical structures and differently tuned instruments also indicate Chinese, Indian, Arabic, and Portuguese input.

Dance

It is said that there's a different dance for every one of Sumatra's 100 districts, and as many dancers as it has single girls. Married women do not dance. When a woman dances at her wedding ceremony, it's for the last time. Sumatran dancers, known for their *gaya* (grace), are masters of smooth, soft, willowy movements. Candledances *(tari lilin* or *tari piring)*, in one form or the other, are performed all over the island. In the Handkerchief Dance, men and women each hold one end of a large white square cloth. They perform a kind of Maypole dance, winding in and out and turning around, tying the handkerchiefs in a series of knots. At the conclusion, they can untangle the cloth immediately and faultlessly.

Textiles

Sumata produces 2 types of cloth: dye-resist *ikat* on a backstrap loom, and *songket,* a discontinuous supplementary weft-technique, which often incorporates metallic threads of silver or gold into the weave. The dye-resist and supplementary weft *ikat* techniques are associated with areas — such as Batakland or Lampung — where proto-Malayans first migrated to Sumatra. The Neolithic and Dongson-style patterns commonly found on them reflect the little contact these areas have had with later cultural influences such as Islam. The *songket,* on the other hand, found in locales such as the Minang highlands, has had a considerable amount of outside cultural and mercantile influence. Today, the *songket* is produced on a self-standing frame loom employing chemical dyes and gold-foil covered thread. Used mainly for wedding ceremonies, the clothing made from this *songket* is extremely elaborate, the finest examples found in the Palembang area where until very recently pure gold and silver thread were used.

Architecture

The traditional architecture, especially of north and west Sumatra, is magnificent. Large rectangular buildings on wooden pilings are built 1-2 meters off the ground with swooping saddle-shaped roofs and high gables at both ends which rise to a point. Structures are often adorned with geometric designs and buffalo horns, and carvings grace the gable-ends. So impressive are these structures that they have served as the model after which the "national" architectural style is patterned (as exemplified on the ITB campus, Bandung). By contrast, houses along the rivers, swamps, and jungles of east and south Sumatra are simple pole cottages with ladders (tigers can't climb ladders!). As for classical monuments, since Sumatra's great Sriwijaya was more concerned with international trade and its control over the Straits of Melaka than in controlling the interior, no great monument complexes were produced, as on Java. The few temples and stupas that do exist (such as at Padang-lawas, Muaro Takus, and Kota Cina) are in such a state of ruin that they don't grab you like Java's finely crafted and preserved monuments.

GETTING TO SUMATRA

Visas And Money

An entry permit, issued on the spot, is the only requirement needed to get into Indonesia at the main international entry point of Medan in northern Sumatra. However, the 2 months you receive upon entry cannot be extended and after 60 days you must leave the country. Many travelers get around this by traveling from Penang (Malaysia) to Medan by air or by boat, spend 1-2 months in Sumatra, catch a riverboat from Palembang to the Riau Islands and farther to Singapore, then come in again via Jakarta for another 2-month stay through Java or Bali. Another way to get from Sumatra to Singapore is to catch a flight from Pekanbaru to Singapore for US$78. The currency exchange rates in Medan are as good as anywhere on Java, but the rates in interior Sumatra are unfavorable. For all your currency needs on Sumatra, change in Jakarta or Medan.

Approaches

Sumatra can be approached by air, sea, and land from many different directions. Most travelers choose to get it over with quickly and board the 20-min. flight from Penang, Malaysia to Medan, N. Sumatra, then start their journey down (N to S) through the island. One can break up this journey by taking a reasonably priced, fast, modern ship from Padang, W. Sumatra, straight to Jakarta, W. Java. Or one may experience the flatter southern part of the island by traveling from Padang to Palembang, then exiting on the ferry out of Bakauheni or Panjang in far southern Sumatra to Merak on Java's NW coast. One may also approach from the S by taking a riverboat from Tg. Pinang, in the Riau Islands, and sailing up the Batanghari to Pekanbaru, E. Sumatra, and from there heading SE for Bukittinggi, capital of the culture-rich Minang highlands. There are also regular flights from Kuala Lumpur, capital of Malaysia, to Medan for around US$88.

From Merak, West Java

Trains for Merak, on the NE tip of Java, depart at 0615 and 1700 from Jakarta's Tanah Abang station; Rp1600-2500. Take the morning train with its through connection on the faster daytime ferry for Panjang, S of Telukbetung in S. Sumatra. The Merak ferry terminal is within walking distance of the train station. Buses for Merak depart Jakarta's Grogol Station about every 10 min. from 0300 to 2400, 3½ hours, Rp2500. The ferry takes 5-6 hours, departing at 1100 and 2300, passing within 20 km of Krakatoa in the Sunda Strait. Above this still-active volcano you can see (in good weather) puffs of smoke drifting off like artillery ordinance.

There are 3 classes on the ferry: 1st, Rp4000; 2nd, Rp3000; and 3rd, Rp1500. The railway ferry's RoRo-coaches roll off at the Strengsem Terminal (5 km E of Panjang), while the regular passenger ferries dock at Panjang, 10 km S of Telukbetung. Scores of local and long-distance buses at Panjang and at Strengsem are

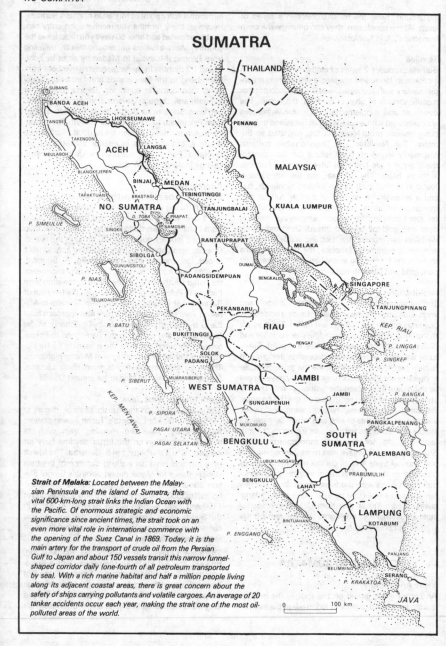

SUMATRA

THAILAND

SUBANG
BANDA ACEH
TANGSE
TAKENGON
MEULABOH
BLANGKEJEREN
TAPAKTUAN
SINGKIL
LHOKSEUMAWE
LANGSA
ACEH
BINJAI
MEDAN
BRASTAGI
TEBINGTINGGI
NO. SUMATRA
TANJUNGBALAI
D. TOBA
PRAPAT
SAMOSIR

PENANG

MALAYSIA

KUALA LUMPUR

MELAKA

P. SIMEULUE

SIBOLGA
GUNUNGSITOLI
RANTAUPRAPAT

P. NIAS

TELUKDALEM
PADANGSIDEMPUAN
DUMAI
BENGKALIS

SINGAPORE

TANJUNGPINANG

P. BATU
PEKANBARU
RIAU
KEP. RIAU
P. LINGGA

BUKITTINGGI
RENGAT
P. SINGKEP

SOLOK
PADANG
MUARASIBERUT

P. SIBERUT
WEST SUMATRA
JAMBI
JAMBI
P. BANGKA

KEP. MENTAWAI
SUNGAIPENUH

P. SIPORA
MUKOMUKO
PANGKALPENANG

PAGAI UTARA
BENGKULU
SOUTH
SUMATRA
PALEMBANG

PAGAI SELATAN
LUBUKLINGGAU
PRABUMULIH

BENGKULU
LAHAT

P. ENGGANO
LAMPUNG
KOTABUMI

BINTUAHAN
PANJANG
BELIMBING
SERANG
P. KRAKATOA
JAVA

Strait of Melaka: Located between the Malaysian Peninsula and the island of Sumatra, this vital 600-km-long strait links the Indian Ocean with the Pacific. Of enormous strategic and economic significance since ancient times, the strait took on an even more vital role in international commerce with the opening of the Suez Canal in 1869. Today, it is the main artery for the transport of crude oil from the Persian Gulf to Japan and about 150 vessels transit this narrow funnel-shaped corridor daily (one-fourth of all petroleum transported by sea). With a rich marine habitat and half a million people living along its adjacent coastal areas, there is great concern about the safety of ships carrying pollutants and volatile cargoes. An average of 20 tanker accidents occur each year, making the strait one of the most oil-polluted areas of the world.

0   100 km

ready to roll—if you desire—all the way to Bukittinggi and Medan.

From Merak, ferries also sail for Bakauheni on the easternmost tip of Sumatra at least 5 times daily; Rp2000 1st Class, Rp1800 2nd Class, and Rp1000 3rd Class. From Bakauheni take a bus (2 hours) to Tanjungkarang's Terminal Rajabasa, from where you may catch other buses up to Palembang and points north. One also has the option of purchasing a OW through ticket from Jakarta to virtually any point on Sumatra.

From Jakarta

To avoid the experience of your life riding up through the fetid swamplands of S. Sumatra, simply fly Merpati from Jakarta to: Padang (the main gateway to W. Sumatra) for Rp85,000; Pekanbaru, Rp91,400; Jambi, Rp50,400; and Palembang, Rp46,300. Also at least one Merpati flight goes daily from Jakarta to Medan, Rp118,000.

Slower and more pleasant is the Pelni ship KM *Rinjani* which departs Jakarta at 1340 (be there at 1130). It costs Rp38,000 for Economy Class (under cover and a/c), but you'll need to rent a mattress if you don't have one with you. Take munchies. The passage takes 36 hours, *not* stopping in Tg. Pinang, arriving in Medan on Monday morning. Real good cruising on a beautiful new boat with nice showers. Fourth Class goes for Rp48,000, 1st Class Rp110,000.

Jakarta to Padang, W. Sumatra (and vice versa) on the weekly Pelni ship KM *Kerinci* is popular with those who want to avoid the grueling but memorable bus trip or the expensive Jakarta-Padang flight (Garuda, Rp100,000; Merpati, Rp85,000). This modern deluxe ship departs Jakarta's port of Tg. Priok every Sat. at around 2100. The passage takes about 33 hours, arriving in Padang on Mon. morning at 0600: Ekonomi Class, Rp22,500; 4th Class, Rp26,100; 3rd Class, Rp30,200; 2nd Class, Rp37,800; and 1st Class, Rp46,900. Three meals are served per day, and there are luxurious hot showers, restaurants, etc. If you're going deck class, take along extra goodies to break up the monotony of the almost pure rice diet. From Padang, the ship returns to Jakarta on Tuesday. Buy your ticket at Pelni's Jakarta office: Jl. Angkasa 18 (tel. 417569/415428).

From Malaysia

The shortest, quickest way into Sumatra—and Indonesia—is to fly from Penang, Malaysia, to Medan, N. Sumatra. Flying this route takes you into what is probably Sumatra's most attractive region, home to the island's richest natural and human geography. You can most likely purchase this ticket cheaper in Malaysia than you can in the US or Australia. The inexpensive Penang/Medan-Medan/Penang hops are the ones most often chosen to fulfill the Indonesian requirement that all visitors possess a ticket not only into but also out of Indonesia. From the Prangin Road Bus Station in Penang, take a bus every hour from 0700 to 1000 for M\$1.20 out to Penang's airport (allow 1 hour). The MAS flight leaves at 1030 daily and takes just 20 min. to Medan (M\$105 OW, M\$150 RT).

A regular ferry, the *Gadis Langkasuka*, also sails from Penang to Medan's port of Belawan on Mon. and Wednesdays. The easiest is to buy tickets at Penang's Tourist Association Office on Jl. Syed Barakhbah, at the shipping company itself (Sanren Delta Marine on Jl. Leboh Ferquhar, tel. 379325), or at a number of travel agencies and hotels along Chulia Street. Tickets cost M\$55 2nd Class, M\$65 1st Class (berths in 4-person staterooms). The ferry departs from near Penang's Port Commission at 1830, arriving in Medan at 0800. Before you get your boarding pass, you must pay a compulsory M\$6 seaport tax plus M\$5 for transportation from Belawan to Medan's bus station. Guys who meet the boat at Belawan offer to take you on the bus to the bank first, then on to Medan. Also investigate the Monday ferry service between Kuala Lumpur's Port Kelang and Dumai in E. Sumatra which costs about M\$125.

FROM SINGAPORE

To P. Batam

From Singapore first take a launch (S\$20 or S\$37 RT) 20 min. down to P. Batam where you go through customs and get your passport stamped; make sure you have your ticket out of Indonesia before arriving. Launches leave Mon. through Fri. from Singapore's Finger Pier at 0800 and 1430, but only one on Sat. and Sunday. Be sure to get the fast boat (Ekspres), more comfortable (with videos) than the slow boat. Yet another alternative is the hydrofoil which connects Singapore and P. Batam, but costs Rp20,000-22,500, with a/c and deluxe amenities. Buy tickets for all the above at Finger Pier, Singapore. From P. Batam to Tg. Pinang, it costs Rp5000 by local *kapal motor*, 4 hours, leaving often.

From Tg. Pinang To Pekanbaru

In the following connections you move along quickly, the boats leaving as soon as there's enough people. From P. Batam's dock where the Singapore launch comes in, take a taxi to Kabil (Rp7000 for 2; bargain because their first price is Rp10,000!). From Kabil, take a fishing boat (fits 20 people) to Tanjung Uban (Rp1800, 45 min.), then from Tg. Uban to Tg. Pinang take a minibus (Rp1800, 2 hours). Leave the bus station in Tg. Pinang and turn to the R, then ask where the boat is. Everyone works on a commission so they'll all want to lead you. The truth is that no one really knows when boats sail, they could leave anytime. So go hang out at the pier where you see a lot of people assembling—that means a boat is ready to go. Don't buy a ticket from anyone, buy only when you get on the boat: Rp12,500 Deck Class, Rp17,000 for cabin including food (rice and fish). As there are only 2 rice-based meals a day, bring food, tea, and coffee. The deck is best because it's empty at night, but no mattresses, just bunks. Evenings are splendid with stars, fireflies upriver, monkeys and fishing eagles in the trees. Your first stop is **Moro** (for 2 hours), then after 5 hours another harbor, then you pass some more islands, oil platforms, police boats, till you finally you enter the Siak River, which leads straight to Pekanbaru, arriving at around 0800. From Pekanbaru's harbor area, get to Pasar Pusat by minibus (Rp100, watch your bags!), then another minibus (Rp150) to the Pasar Nangka Bus Station. Or just charter a minibus (Rp3000 for 4 people with bags) direct to the bus station on Jl. Nangka.

There's also a boat from Singapore directly to Tg. Pinang (S$65, 4 hours), a port town on P. Bintan in the Riau Archipelago, as well as a boat from P. Batam straight to Tg. Pinang (Rp20,000). In order to avoid spending 2 days on the boat from P. Batam to Pekanbaru (described above), take a boat (S$20) from Singapore's Finger Pier to P. Batam's port, then take a taxi (no buses) to the airport (Rp6000-8000, 30 min.), then the Merpati flight (Rp47,000) to Pekanbaru. From Tg. Pinang, regular Garuda flights go to such Sumatran destinations as: Palembang, 4 days weekly; Padang, 3 days weekly; and Pekanbaru every day at 1000 and 1110. If it's a weekend, change money before departure in Singapore as you can't change TCs anywhere on Batam on Sat. or Sunday.

GETTING AROUND

Since the weather has such an effect on the condition of the roads of Sumatra, it is important to plan your itinerary to avoid road and bridge washouts and swollen river crossings. The equator splits the island into 2 equal halves. The wet season in the north part of the island is Oct.-Apr., while that of the south is Oct.-January. Between May and Sept. is the best (driest) time to visit the island.

It's advisable not to travel toward the end of *Ramadan* in the Islamic calendar. At this time millions of Indonesians are on the move, and the buses get very crowded. Also—if you can get a seat at all—you may have to pay double the usual bus fare. This state of affairs lasts about 2 weeks when it seems half of Sumatra goes by bus to see the other half. Even ships, such as the Pelni ship connecting Medan and Jakarta, change their schedules during this difficult travel period. Feeding oneself during daylight hours of *Ramadan* isn't a problem as most restaurants remain open in Lampung, S. Sumatra, and Bengkulu provinces (though in orthodox W. Sumatra and Aceh, most restaurants are closed during the day).

BY BUS

The chief interest in Sumatra is the journey through it. If you want to experience the true art of riding a Sumatran bus, take the bus trip N from Tanjungkarang to Medan. Don't be put off by the tales you hear of this journey; the country in between more than makes up for the suffering. The lengthwise journey through Sumatra is one of the last modern adventures on Earth. Because of the lack of vehicles on this huge island, Sumatran buses are generally more crowded than on Java and Bali. You could travel on a bus with gunny-sacked pigs, casks of coconut wine, goats pissing on your foot, and occupied coffins resting on the shoulders of relatives. Whereas delays of an hour or so are normal on Java and Bali, delays in Sumatra can vary by days. Here you'll have a guaranteed breakdown at least once, and a comic repair show. You'll get bogged down in mud, driven over log-strewn cow paddocks, with your head beaten against the ceiling (if you're over 5 feet tall), and your buttocks resting on spikes. You'll spend more time airborne than on the seat, like being inside a cement mixer. Sometimes a rope is strung out in front of you to lean on for relief or to sleep on, if you can. Bus sickness is rampant and companies thoughtfully dispense plastic bags, which Indonesian passengers take frequent advantage of. Endless Indonesian music is played right above your head at full distorted volume. And latest addition to the Sumatran bus ride is the VCR. Often on the longer journeys, movies will be shown without pause. *Kung Fu* may be played in English, followed by a tearjerker in Indonesian.

A stoker usually accompanies the driver to do running repairs, errands, and collect fares. The driver eats 5 times a day at Padang-style restaurants along the way, with untold stops for drinks and snacks. On some N. Sumatran runs, the drivers even race each other, the passengers unwilling spectators. Unlike Java, trucks are seldom seen on Sumatra's roads since most goods are transported by bus. Up on the roof is a crawl space provided for the crew between the goods covered by a tarpaulin. Try to wrangle a place up here—it's like riding a wild bronco, but the air is much better and there's much more to look at. Bus fares are extremely economical; for example, Pekanbaru-Bukittinggi is less than Rp5000.

The Machine

On Java big Mercedes buses are the favorite, but on Sumatra smaller Mercedes buses are the rule, since the long luxury chassis can't take the hairpin turns and all the punishment meted out on the island's more difficult stretches. Sumatra's old boxy buses of the '70s are being replaced with a new generation of sleek Mercedes on the long-distance runs, and Mitsubishis on short ones. These latest arrivals are still painted extravagantly. The private "chicken-catcher" buses must be inspired by the same muse that created the jeepneys in Manila: they are vividly colored, sometimes with a high gloss, and the painting on them has to be competitive. Given such macho names as *Guntar* ("Thunderbolt") and *Kilat* ("Lightning"), some of these beauties also have the most incredible horn systems you can imagine, complete with a full set of keys capable of playing such tunes as "We Are the World." The driver will come down full throttle on an intersection or have a car turn in front of him, and instead of honking will render these great soaring crescendos.

The Road

During Dutch times 60 years ago they used to hold car rallies that would take 10 days from the S all the way up to Aceh. It took a leisurely week to travel by motorcar from Panjang to Medan, overnighting in comfortable motor lodges along the way. But history has wrought heavy changes. The many bridges destroyed during the Japanese invasion and the 1958 Sumatran rebellion are steadily being replaced. Today, the magnificent 2,500-km Trans-Sumatran Highway runs right up through the center of Sumatra from Tanjungkarang to Banda Aceh. This highway is still being built, or actually built and rebuilt time and again. Though it has been vastly improved, it will never really be finished because it is constantly washed away or blocked by landslides, particularly in the wetter south. The road S of Padang is generally worse than north. The only consistently sealed segment is from Sungaidareh to Bukittinggi. Surolangun, as well as the section between Muara Amin and Baturaja in the south, may be trouble spots. It's possible to cross the whole distance from Lubuklinggau to Bukittinggi in 2 days. And you can do the whole highway in the dry season in 3-4 days if you meet all your connections. If you don't want to rupture your spleen, however, at least one week should be allowed.

Most other roads, with the exception of the Padang-Bukittinggi and those in Lake Toba region, will be in poor condition, particularly in the wet season. About 60% of all roads are single lane. One can never really predict what conditions will be like. In April toward the end of the rainy season, whole stretches of the road may have disappeared under devastating landslides. At night you could just come upon a gigantic hole in the ground; pray that the driver sees it. If a road runs along the river, a flood might have eroded it so much that the bus cannot pass, or is forced to go through a swamp-like area for 200-300 m. Expect it. The crew will sometimes lay lumber on the mud and drive over it, or attach a winch to a tree. Some buses without winches could be hung up in one place for as long as a week, its passengers camping in and around

the bus and on the roof. Whole caravans could get trapped, stranded in the mud for days. You see buses which have just made some journeys *completely* covered in mud. In the wet season river levels at ferry crossings might be swollen too high for vehicles to board the unwieldy rope-bound wooden rafts which are used as ferries. These rafts are hauled across the river along a steel hawser slung between the 2 banks. If bridges are out in S. Sumatra you can often catch a barge downriver (a bona fide adventure!) to a town where you can wait more comfortably for another bus. Swim in the rivers while waiting (up to 2 days) for your bus to cross.

Tips

If you're coming up from the S by bus, consider breaking your journey up and taking 1-3 day rest stops. This way you can appreciate S. Sumatra and not have your journey associated only with pain. The first leg might be Tanjungkarang to Palembang, then Palembang to Bengkulu, then Bengkulu to Padang, then the last segment Padang to Lake Toba or Medan. Take the train when you can, especially in the rainy season because nothing can stop it. The train is secure, comfortable, you can move around in it, stand or sit, and eat. Board the train, for example, from Palembang to Lubuklinggau, spend the night there (Peng. Damai), then the next morning get the ALS Mercedes bus N to Bukittinggi (24 hours).

There are many private bus companies. ALS, with a wideranging network throughout the island, is about the most reliable, but their seats may be horribly narrow for big Western buttocks. Next best is ANS. For less wear and tear on your big buttocks, it's imperative that you get a seat in front of the back axle of the bus. A good idea is to buy a pillow or foam for cushioning, or use your sleeping bag. Also your luggage is safe from theft up front where the whole bus can keep an eye on it. Try to book as far ahead as possible for a seat in the first 2 rows. Even if you get a seat in the front, you're still fed up after 20 hours (such as the Bukittinggi-Lubuklinggau marathon). Book immediately on your bus out as soon as you get in a town, even if it doesn't leave until the next day. During the rainy season, choose a bus with a winch; these can pull themselves out of the mud more easily. Also make sure your window closes completely! Beware of pickpockets who are thick on the buses of Sumatra. To get around quickly, always pick the fullest bus in your direction at bus stations.

Bus Fares

On Bali and Java the prices vary only by Rp100-200, but in Sumatra prices could vary by thousands of *rupiah*, especially in S. Sumatra. Fares are deregulated: it's an entrepreneureal free-for-all. Always ask the local people or other travelers what the correct fare is before buying your ticket. On long bus journeys you could pay as much as Rp4000 over the usual fare. One traveler, who traveled from the S to the middle of the island to Padang, tells of starting off bargaining at Rp20,000 for a 2-day bus ride and it took him 2 days to bargain the seller down to the right fare. The smaller local buses and *oplet* will pick up all the locals even if the bus is already full, whereas the express Mercedes buses don't pick up many extra passengers. The big Mercedes also have better suspension, slightly roomier seating, and tickets which cost Rp2000-4000 more.

OTHER MODES OF TRANSPORT

By Train

The island's rail system is concentrated in the south. A line starts in Tanjungkarang, and heads N to Prabumulih, E to Palembang, and W to Lubuklinggau. Don't reserve seats on a train that hasn't arrived yet because the seats are already full and people won't move; only reserve seats on a train which originates from the station you're standing in. If you want to stretch out, buy tickets for 2 seats. Vendors working the aisles of the train sell all kinds of fruit, drinks, rice combos, etc. The dining car is always a relaxing place to hang out because it has more breathing space and the windows are bigger; a middling *nasi goreng* goes for Rp1500. When the train stops, it fills suddenly with humid jungle air. If you're lucky, you might witness onboard these trains one of the greatest migrations in modern history—the *orang transmigrasi*—a heart-rending Javanese program which has been termed an exercise in cultural genocide. With their sewing machines, fences, chickens, sacks of seed, and bicycles cramming the aisles and fastened to racks over their heads, these are the poorest of Java's poor. Since so many are being moved, you have a good chance of finding 2-3 cars filled with transmigrants, each wearing a numbered red-and-white tag.

By Air

There's a fairly extensive air network within the island, and using planes will definitely save much time and hassles. Garuda sample fares: Palembang-Jambi, Rp35,000; Palembang-Padang, Rp72,300; Palembang-Bengkulu, Rp42,500; Bengkulu-Jambi, Rp72,300; Jambi-Bengkulu, Rp71,200; Medan-Palembang, Rp115,000; Medan-Padang, Rp72,500; and Medan-Banda-Aceh, Rp59,300. Also be sure to check Mandala's and Merpati's prices, as they often fly identical routes at cheaper prices. SMAC is an extremely useful airlines flying in Aceh Province, and has a flight every day from Medan to Gunungsitoli, northern Nias. For people who don't have a lot of time, but do have money.

LAMPUNG PROVINCE

A wild, forested, underpopulated district known for its pepper, stunning *tapi* fabrics, and ambitious *transmigrasi* projects. Sumatra's southernmost province has a long coastline with innumerable bays, a rugged mountain interior with game reserves and sealevel swamplands, and some densely populated rural areas that appear to be lifted straight out of Java. It also shares beautiful Lake Ranau with S. Sumatra Province. The highest mountain is G. Pesagi (2,231 m), followed by G. Tanggamas (2102 m), G. Seminung (1881 m), G. Sekincau (1718 m), and G. Raya (1645 m)—all dormant volcanos. Pulau Krakatoa, just 30 km from Lampung's S shore, exploded violently in 1883, killing 36,000 people and darkening the sky for months. Coastal villages were washed away by tidal waves but the seamatter, minerals, and volcanic ash and debris enriched the soil. Boats can be chartered from Canti village, near Kalianda, to visit Krakatoa (although the sea journey is not as rough if taken from Java's W coast). Not only pepper, but cloves, coffee, and copra are now all grown extensively along the rich southern coast. Inland, rice, coffee, maize, cassava, and rubber are cultivated. Bakauheni, on the SE tip of Lampung, is the main gateway to Sumatra for

overland travelers from Java (see Sumatra's "Intro" for more detail).

History

According to folklore, the first people to settle this area came from Batakland. Prior to Islam the Lampungese practiced a syncretic Buddhist-Hindu ancestor cult; menhirs and other archaeological remains of this Buddhist heritage are found on stone inscriptions scattered around the province. To cultivate the valuable pepper spice for sale to European and Asian traders, the sultans of Banten centuries ago sent the first transmigrants to Lampung to carve villages and farms out of the jungle and spread Islam. The arrival of the Dutch began a long period of isolation for Lampung while the colonial masters monopolized all trade. Raden Intan II (1830-1889) was a Lampungese hero who battled against Dutch hegemony. He built a fortress in Kalianda and another on nearby G. Rajabasa. Today, his grave, built on an earth mound remaining from his Kalianda fort, is an object of pilgrimage. In WW II the Japanese drove out the Dutch and established a base in Kalianda to guard the vital Sunda Strait.

LAMPUNG PROVINCE

The People

The province's 4,624,785 (1980) population is divided into 3 groups. The Lampung Pemanggir live in the coastal areas from Lake Ranau in the W to Labuhan Meringgai in the east. The interior Lampung Pepadun are subdivided into northern and central groups. Traditional native Lampungese villages can be recognized by their well-constructed wooden houses raised 2 m above ground on pillars, many with a balcony. Often these "balcony houses" will have decora- tive latticework under the eaves or around the outside edges. The third group is the *transmigrasi* people from Java who have arrived in such numbers now that they are becoming a major part of the human geography of the region.

The Dutch first created *transmigrasi* settlements here to cut down on Java's overpopulation in 1932. Since then, large numbers of settlers have arrived. In N. Lampung, 10% of the population are Javanese trans- migrants, in S. Lampung 60%, Central Lampung about 75%. Huge land-clearing equipment has leveled the age-old forests to make way for the transmigrants. Each family is then given 2 hectares, a substantial holding for mostly landless peasants. But coupled with an uncertain future, it is a wrenching experience for a Javanese or Balinese to leave his home island. Gradually, the same overpopulation and work-sharing problems have emerged, though without Java's corresponding high fertility of soils, efficient drainage, and water control. These Javanese have brought with them their *sawah* cultivation techniques, their *gamelan* and *wayang*, and even their hometown names such as Labuhanratu, Banyuwangi and Jepara. Balinese *transmigrasi* colonies are found at Pematang Panggang near Martapura, and around the Kotabumi and Kota Gajah areas.

Textiles

At one time the pepper wealth enabled the Lampung groups to costume themselves in cloths known all over the archipelago for their extravagance. Now you see these grand old fabrics only in museums or amongst family *pusaka*. Holland is host to some of the finest and largest collections of Lampungese cloth. Two types of cloth were once widespread in the district. The **tampan,** found especially in the Krui region, is made by the floating weft technique with brown and blue designs. This fabric covered dishes, gifts, and sacrificial offerings. Equally elaborate are the plain cotton *sarung* called **tapi,** covered with layers of designs interwoven with gold thread, complicated embroidery, even bits of mirror. *Sarung tapi* are made by women for ritual occasions and display ancient designs of people, horses, elephants, and other land and water animals. But the principal motif was the Ship of the Dead. This so-called "ship cloth" survives from an earlier people who believed that the souls of the dead journeyed to the Land of Souls by ship. Big pieces of ship-cloth were used in circumcision ceremonies and at weddings; for important conferences they were hung up on the wall to spread good vibes. Sadly, because of the influx of synthetic modern textiles, the Lampungese stopped making this traditional cloth at least 10 years ago. Now they are only passed down in certain families as wedding gifts. Beg a family to break out their heirlooms so you can have a look at one of these exquisite textiles. Old *tapi* can be seen and new *tapi* purchased in Blambangan Pagar village 20 km E of Kotabumi.

SOUTH LAMPUNG

Kalianda

A small port town on Lampung Bay, 53 km SE of Telukbetung and 33 km NW of Bakauheni. From Bakauheni, take a bus to the junction 3 km outside town, then walk or get local transportation into Kalianda. Attractions of the Kalianda area include hotsprings,

pretty coastal scenery, hiking on 1,281-m-high G. Rajabasa, beaches, and trips to offshore islands. Kalianda has had its share of misfortune. It was the site of bitter struggles against the Dutch in the late 1800s. Krakatoa's 1883 eruption caused a giant tidal wave, destroying the town. WW II brought fierce fighting between Japanese and Australian forces. Today, Kalianda is small, quiet, and easy. Most of the town's population are Muslim, but a small Chinese community maintains a temple. Visit the fish market near the harbor to see catches of fish, sharks, and rays auctioned off. The grave and fort of Raden Intan II, a local nationalist hero, is near town; ask directions. **Peng. Beringin,** Jl. Kesuma Bangsa 55 (near the cinemas), is clean and spacious; Rp4000 s, Rp5000 d with breakfast. Several restaurants and many *warung* in town.

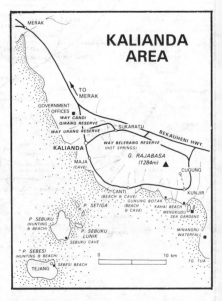

Weary travelers may revitalize in the sulphurous hot-spring baths, **Way Belerang,** 2 km from town. Take the street beside Peng. Beringin uphill toward the mountain, G. Rajabasa. Constructed by the Dutch, 3 pools each have different mineral content; Rp250 admission; refreshments available. **G. Rajabasa,** an inactive volcano, is most easily climbed from its S side; take a minibus first to Cugung, then climb several hours to the summit. Get an early start.

Fishing is the traditional occupation of the resident Lampung Peminggir people. *Cengkeh* (clove) trees are a profitable source of income for the district; the lower, highly fertile slopes of G. Rajabasa are covered with them. Cloves, drying on mats by the roadside, give local villages a sweet spicy scent.

Of the many offshore islands, **P. Sebesi** is the easiest to visit. It has a village (Tejang), plus beaches, coral reefs, and good hiking. Boats (small *kapal motor*) leave most days from Canti (SE of Kalianda) and cost Rp3500. From Canti boats can also be chartered to visit **Krakatoa**, Rp175,000 for up to 10 people.

Panjang

A port town 9 km SE of Telukbetung; it has a hotel, and frequent minibuses to town. Also the train departs here for Palembang, usually mornings and evenings. If arriving on the ferry, travelers usually go up to Tanjungkarang and take trains and buses N out of there. If you have to overnight in Panjang, stay at **Losmen Kastari**. Several bigger express busses leave from Panjang's terminal for the north at 1900; all the way to Bukittinggi might take 65 hours. ALS and ANS are several of the best bus companies. Another alternative is to take the train to Palembang and Lubuklinggau; from Lubuklinggau take a bus to Bukittinggi (see "Tanjungkarang" for transport details to points north). From Panjang, ferries depart twice daily (at 1100 and 2300, 6 hours) for Merak, W. Java. But usually it's faster to take a bus to Bakauheni, 2 hours, then board the 1½-hour ferry from there. From Merak, it's another three hours (Rp1000) by bus to Jakarta.

Pulau Tegal, 2 hours from Panjang, is where many Lampungese seek recreation; take an *oplet* to Lampasing, then rent a boat for Rp10,000-15,000 out to P. Tegal. It's also possible to visit several other islands but P. Tegal is preferred because of its nice beaches, good swimming, and lovely coconut trees. **Batumenyan**, on the W side of Teluk Lampung, is another recreation spot with a nice beach. In olden times pirates and bandit gangs hid out in the coves around **Batu Serampok** *(serampok* means "robbery"). The infuriated Dutch could never find their hideouts.

TELUKBETUNG

The twin cities Telukbetung and Tanjungkarang are located at the N end of Lampung Bay. Telukbetung, only a 30-min. flight from Jakarta, is a port town and capital of Lampung Province. A 100-year-old ship's buoy lies right opposite the Brimob police station in Telukbetung on a hill under a *pohon ambon* tree. It overlooks the same bay from which it was originally catapulted on a giant Krakatoa *tsunami*. Because of its shape, the buoy goes locally by the name of *bom* ("bomb") or *bel* ("bell"). It's now used as a distance marker. The tourist office (Diparda) for the twin cities on Jl. Selat Gaspar 39 is fairly hopeless. But one of its

staff, Yaman Aziz (who runs a homestay), is knowledgeable on Lampung's attractions and can help arrange guided trips. Kantor Imigrasi is on Jl. Diponegoro. Tanjungkarang, 5 km N, is the rail and road transport center. Minibuses (Rp200) travel the main streets within and between Telukbetung and Tanjungkarang. *Becak* are plentiful in the downtown areas.

Accommodations

Cheapest are **Losmen Bahagia Raya**, Jl. Bawal 72, and **Losmen Tirta**, across the street. Both are Rp4500 s and d with small, dark rooms. Also check out **Malaya Losmen**, Jl. Tongkol 25 (tel. 41581); **Kenanga International**, Jl. Kenanga 4 (tel. 41888), Rp11,500 s, Rp14,000 d; **Wijaya Kesuma Hotel**, Jl. Serayu 12 (tel. 52163); **New Jakarta Hotel**, Jl. Belanak 28 (tel. 41048); and the **Sriwijaya Hotel**, Jl. Kalimantan 30 (tel. 41046). Yaman Aziz of the tourist office runs a homestay off Jl. W.R. Supratman on Gang Cendrawasih, Kampung Pengajaran, RT/1 (tel. 41059). The city's top-of-the-line accommodation, the **Marcopolo Hotel**, Jl. Dr. Susilo 4 (tel. 41511), features TV, refrigerator, bellmen, laundry—the whole shot for Rp25,500 s, Rp35,000 d. Get a room facing S for a truly magnificent view of the bay, islands and mountains beyond. The Marcopolo also has an expensive restaurant, Garuda Airlines office, taxi stand, etc. Train tickets can be arranged at the front desk: a very helpful and informed staff.

Transportation

The Panjang ferry terminal is 9 km SE of Telukbetung. Other ferries from W. Java come in at the terminal at Bakauheni, 87 km (2 hours) by bus from Telukbetung on a good but hilly road. Up to 30-40 buses are waiting at both terminals to take passengers onward to Sumatran destinations. To Padang, for example, it might cost around Rp25,000 and take 60 hours. It's also easy to take your own vehicle onboard the ferries in either direction across the Sunda Strait. By air, Garuda has 5 daily 30-min. flights from Jakarta to Telukbetung, Rp30,500. Merpati flies from Palembang everyday; Rp33,500. Branti Airport is 30 km N of Tanjungkarang, Rp6500 by taxi. Daily trains arrive in Tanjungkarang from Lubuklinggau and Palembang. Most Sumatran cities have at least daily bus services to Tanjungkarang.

Taxis can be hired at the Marcopolo and Sriwijaya Hotels in Telukbetung. As in most of Sumatra, vehicles may be hired based on either a time period or distance. Fixed prices apply, usually Rp4500 per hour for a minimum of 2 hours. Sample fares: Kalianda, Rp26,000, 5 hours; Pasir Putih, Rp19,000, 3 hours; Lempasing, Rp19,000, 3 hours; Metro, Rp27,500, 5 hours; Kotaagung, Rp31,000, 5 hours; Kotabumi, Rp31,000, 5 hours. Most trips within town cost Rp4000; to Branti Airport Rp6500. The "4545 Special

Ferry Transport," operated by Yudha Sakti, Jl. Raden Intan 47 (tel. 53068), specializes in the trip to Bakauheni; Rp3500/person.

Vicinity Of Telukbetung

At **Kotaagung**, 125 km W of Telukbetung on the coast, is a Pertamina Depot, a waterfall, and public accommodation. Around Kotaagung live the South Lampungese people, the Lampung Pemanggir, who speak their own language and have a quite distinct culture from the Lampungese of the interior. These hilly coastal areas are ideal country for the clove plantations which dot the area, organized into government collectives. **Krui**, S. Lampung, can be reached by bus from Telukbetung; Rp5000 (12 hours).

TANJUNGKARANG

Five km N of Telukbetung, this town is a starting point for the journey north. Catch *oplet* on the main street, use *becak* for local transport. Outside of Tanjungkarang are popular beaches, islands, and mountains. With the bus and train terminals situated in town, Tanjungkarang has a greater number of places to stay than Telukbetung. If you walk straight out the train station and along Jl. Kota Raja, the first place you come to is **Losmen Gunungsari** (no. 21), Rp5000 s, Rp6000 d; then **Peng. Berkah** (no. 19), Rp2500 s, Rp3000 d. Next is **Peng. Renny** (no. 7), Rp2500 s, Rp3500 d. Across from the end of this street is **Hotel Ria**, Jl. Dwiwarna, Rp8500 s and d with fan or Rp15,000 s and d with a/c. Take a local taxi S on Jl. Medan to the **Intan Hotel**, Jl. Raden Intan 45 (tel. 52289). Farther is **Losmen Kurnia II**, Jl. Raden Intan 75 (tel. 52905), Rp9000 s, Rp11,000 d; and **Losmen Kurnia I** (no. 114, tel. 52875), Rp3500 s, Rp4500 d. A block farther is **Hotel Nusa Indah** (no. 132, tel. 53029), Rp15,000 s, Rp19,000 d. Past the Nusa Indah and R at the corner is the **BNW Hotel**, Jl. J.A. Yani 6 (tel. 53624), Rp9500 s, Rp12,500 d with fan or Rp15,000 s and d with a/c. There are two bakeries and a supermarket on Jl. Medan in downtown Tanjungkarang. This area is especially busy at night with many stalls selling food and merchandise.

From Tanjungkarang

Most minibuses and buses originate from terminals on the N side of town. Just ask where the terminal is for your destination. Towns in Lampung Province are served by minibuses and a few old brightly painted Chevrolet Apaches, relics from the postwar years. Large buses leave from Tanjungkarang's Terminal Rajabasa, where bus companies such as Damri, ANS, and ALS (best reputation) have their offices. A network of roads reaches N into the main cities of Sumatra as well as S to destinations on Java. Sample

fares: Lahat, Rp8,000, 16 hours; Jambi, Rp17,000, 30 hours; Padang, Rp21,200, 36 hours; Bukittinggi, Rp24,000, 38 hours; Sibolga, Rp26,500, 48 hours; Banda Aceh, Rp38,500, 72 hours.

The direct bus service to Medan (Rp27,500) takes 3 days and 2 nights and is reserved only for masochists and fugitives. For this long haul N, the first 390 km are over a reasonable dirt road (only about 50 km are really bad), then 290 km on the Trans-Sumatra Highway. Get a front seat on the bus. Sometimes the bridge is out at Lubuklinggau where you might have to change buses. Bengkulu, on Sumatra's SW coast, is connected to Tanjunkarang by daily buses.

From Tanjungkarang's depot on the N side of town, 2 daily trains depart for Palembang with connections beyond to Lubuklinggau. The day train, *Rajabasa*, departs 0800 and arrives in Pelembang 1700; *Ekonomi* seats, Rp3800; 1st Class, Rp4700. The nighttime train, *Sriwijaya Ekspres*, departs 2030 and arrives in Palembang at 0500; only 1st Class seats are available at Rp8000. Trains commonly run an hour or so late; the day trains are less crowded. From Tanjungkarang northward on a trans-Sumatra journey, you have several strategies. One is to train up to Palembang and Lubuklinggau where you take a bus to Bukittinggi. If you don't want to stop in Palembang, only pay to Prabumulih (an hour short of Palembang) and wait 3 hours or so for the train which comes back from Palembang at around 2000 that night, arriving in Lubuklinggau at 0500. But don't get stuck in Prabumulih, it's a real hole. After arriving in Lubuklinggau, if you're still not totally whacked, there could be a place on a bus leaving for Bukittinggi at around 0700, or on to Padang. Or go from Lubuklinggau by bus to Bengkulu (4 hours, one change), then from Bengkulu take a boat or bus up to Padang. This is a more time-consuming way to get up to Padang, but Bengkulu is worth a stop.

Garuda connects Jakarta 5 times daily and Merpati connects Palembang each day. The Garuda office is in the Marcopolo Hotel, Jl. Dr. Susilo 4. Merpati is on Jl. Simba 20 (tel. 42325). The airport is 30 km N at Branti, not far from the main road. Take a local bus from Tanjungkarang, then walk in. A taxi would cost Rp6500.

Vicinity Of Tanjungkarang

Two km W of Tanjungkarang is **Sumur Puteri**, a hiking and camping area. Six km SW of Telukbetung, on the W side of Lampung Bay, is **Nusa Indah Permai Beach**. From nearby Lempasing, catch charter speedboats (Rp10,000?) to P. Tegal, an island with good beaches and swimming. Past Lampasing to the SW are more beaches and coastal scenery. On the E side of this bay are several beaches at **Pasir Putih**, 11 km SE of Telukbetung. Offshore are the small islands Dewi, Cendong, and Tengah, reached by *spet-bot*. Bargain hard.

Another campground is at **Gedongtataan**, 20 km W of Tanjungkarang. Twenty km SE of Tanjungkarang are beautiful land and seascapes at **Tarahan**. At **Padangcermin**, 65 km SW of Tanjungkarang, are nice landscapes and a beach resort. At **Putih Doh**, a

2-hour 100-km journey from Tanjungkarang, is a 200-year-old traditional gateway, dolmen and other prehistoric relics. Two hours from Tanjungkarang by bus there's a lake resort and small reserve called **Way Jepara**. Fifty-four km NW of Tanjunkarang is **Bekri**, a lake resort and recreation spot.

CENTRAL AND EAST LAMPUNG

Metro

The capital of Lampung Tengah (Central Lampung), 50 km NE of Tanjungkarang. The number of Javanese transmigrants settled in this area make Metro nothing less than a transplanted Javanese country town. Surrounding the *kampung* are irrigation canals and extensive *padi* fields. But it is not pure *asli* Javanese—there is more space and more discretionary income here than in a corresponding crowded Javanese town. Javanese settlers have built a dam nearby and an artificial lake at Way Jepara. Native Lampungese villages in the area can be distinguished by their solid-looking wood houses on pillars, often with a front porch. Balinese villages are fewer in number but have the unmistakable Hindu temples (visit the Balinese *transmigrasi* colony at Ramanutara). A small number of people in this area have transmigrated from Lombok.

Near the bus terminal on Jl. Soekarso are **Losmen Hasdalifa**, Rp4500 s and d; **Losmen Familie II**, Rp5500 s and d; and **Peng. Nusantara**, Rp4500 s and d. On the main street, Jl. J. Sudirman near the big mosque is **Losmen Serayu**, Rp3000 s, Rp5000 d. There are many *warung*. For Chinese/Indonesian meals, try **RM Modern**, Jl. J. Sudirman.

Taman Purbakala

An antiquities park near the Javanese village of Pugung, 50 km E of Tanjungkarang or 50 km SE of Metro. In a beautifully landscaped setting is a ring of dolmen (stone tables) and menhir (vertical stone slabs). In the center of the ring is an erect 2-m-high stone phallus. Nearby is a giant *punden*, an earth and rock mound; smaller *punden* are in the vicinity. Picnic shelters and a spring-fed swimming hole have been built for visitors (crowded on Sun. only). Stone pathways connect all the sites so it's easy to find your way around the 25-ha park.

In the nearby village of Pugung is a small museum housed in a funny-looking wooden building. People in an office next door will open the museum for you. Inside is an unusual 1-m-high stone statue of a man, described as a "Polynesian" art style. Another statue, quite different, is a Bodhisattva of the E. Java Ma-

japahit Kingdom excavated near Pugung. Pottery fragments, diagrams, photos, and maps are also on exhibit. A small library contains books and papers on archaeology studies carried out in the area. There's no *losmen*.

The direct route from Tanjungkarang is along the highway from Panjang. The road climbs up from the coast to a gently rolling plateau of vast rubber and oil palm plantations. Twenty km before Sribawono, turn L at the crossroads, then travel 2 km N to Pugung. The park is 1 km east. Few commercial vehicles travel this route, however; it might be easier to approach via Metro using public transportation. From Metro, the road passes through the many villages, gardens, and *sawah* of the Lampungese, Javanese, and Balinese.

Gedung Wani is a Lampungese village 10 km N of Pugung with a 200-year-old wooden gate covered with intricate carvings. The gate was a gift from the Banten Kingdom of W. Java. Look for a small building near the road. Peer through the windows or ask the man in the house behind to open the building for a better look.

The Road To Jepara

Jepara is a country town probably named after the village of the same name in C. Java. The scenic road from Telukbetung to Jepara via Sukadana passes by date palms, coconut, pepper and rubber plantations, and flowers in profusion. In **Natar**, toy windmills are sold, some pumped by mechanical little men, all fashioned from wood and painted decoratively. After Natar the road crosses a bridge built by the Dutch in 1932 over the Sekumpung River; on the R side the irrigation canal you see was built with slave labor by the Japanese during the war. For some kilometers the road then follows the canal which is crossed by little bamboo foot-bridges. The antlers mounted on the houses in the **Gununghadji** area indicate of the number of stags *(sambur)* inhabiting the forests of this region. **Sukadana** is an old native Lampungese (not *transmigrasi*) town of about 100 *asli* families, surrounded by *transmigrasi* settlements. Here you can see genuine *rumah adat*, the original Lampung-style traditional dwellings. After Sukadana are many cassava gardens; see mounds of cassava in baskets on the back of bicycles along the highway. Refresh yourself at roadside stalls where whole bunches of bananas sell for Rp100 and pineapples for Rp200.

Way Kambas

A wildlife reserve (est. 1973), covering 130,000 ha on the E coast of the province. With a maximum elevation of 225 m, most of the reserve's forest has been logged or burned, leaving open grasslands and marsh (excellent birdwatching!). Way Kambas is probably the best place in Sumatra to see elephants in the wild (around 30 have been sighted). Tigers, monkeys, tapirs, *sambur, muncak*, otters, and wild pigs also live in this low-lying terrain.

The PPA (Forestry Office), Gedong Meneng, Tanjungkarang, can provide information and issue permits to visit the reserve. Roads are paved to within 12 km of the reserve. Labuhanmaringgai, a Lampungese village on the reserve's SE border, can be reached on the road from Panjang or via Metro; from here boats take 4 hours to the Kambas River estuary. Depending on their size, boats can go up to 25 km upstream. And in the Nov.-March rainy season, canoes can be used to explore normally inaccessible marshlands. Boats can also travel on Way Penet along the southern border, Way Sukadana on the western, and Way Pegadungan on the northwestern borders *(way* means "river" or "water" in Lampungese). Guides cost Rp20,000-30,000 per day.

SOUTH SUMATRA PROVINCE

The Bukit Barisan Range, on the western border of this province, is the source of large, sluggish rivers which flow through highland plateaus and rift valleys before dropping onto lowland plains and a belt of brackish coastal marshes along the island's whole SE coast. These "green deserts" of S. Sumatra are up to 250 km wide, some of the largest swamps in the world. Much of the rest of the province, both in the mountains and lowlands, is covered by dark green jungle. More volcanos are found in Sumatra's southern half than the northern. Volcanic G. Dempo (3159 m), on the border with Bengkulu Province to the W, is the highest, followed by G. Seminung (1881 m).

The giant Musi River is joined in its lower reaches by other big rivers: the Lematang, Ogan, and Komering. Ships up to 10,000 tons can travel the Musi upstream as far as Palembang. Smaller *kapal motor* sputter for hundreds of km upstream into the interior. For travelers, the cool highlands hold the greatest attractions: vast primary forests, the breathtaking panoramas of Lake Ranau, a giant mountain lake; the mountain town of Pagar Alam surrounded by megalithic sites; an 80-m-high waterfall in Sugiwaras; and hotsprings near Tanjung Sakti. On the islands of Bangka and Belitung, off the province's E coast, are found some of the most beautiful beaches in Asia.

The province's climate is equatorial. The temperature in mountain areas averages a fresh 25 degrees C, and Palembang's days are a hot 30-32 degrees C, though nighttime brings are pleasant breezes. The rainy season lasts Sept.-March and the dry season April-August.

History

For students of history and archaeology, this province offers a rich storehouse of statues, old inscriptions, sultans' graveyards, and a large number of prehistoric carved stones (particularly in the Lahat area) covered in carved animals and strange shapes of people. In its heyday before the 14th C., the mighty Buddhist kingdom of Sriwijaya based around Palembang received tribute and homage from rulers as far afield as Madagascar and Japan. The Sriwijaya kings were so powerful they could install vassal kings as far away as Cambodia. The empire was finally toppled by a S. Indian kingdom that launched a mammoth seaborne force, fought its way up the Musi River, and conquered the Sriwijayan capital.

This feat was nearly duplicated more than 500 years later during WW II, when the Japanese launched an invasion of the whole Dutch East Indies up the Musi River in February of 1942. As 700 paratroopers dropped over Palembang, a Japanese infantry division in small river craft battled upriver toward the important river port. The outflanked and outgunned defenders desperately tried to turn back the attack by pouring oil on the river and setting it afire. The wall of fire engulfed hundreds of Japanese troops but the weight of their numbers finally turned the tide, and Palembang fell the next day, along with half the oil reserves of the Indies.

The People

The population is about 5 million (around 700,000 live in the Palembang area), a blending of Javanese, Malay, and Minangkabau races and cultures—though human geography doesn't offer the variety or cultural level of Java. You don't often see anybody reading a book in S. Sumatra, and the children are much more likely to go naked here, even little girls. In the eastern part of the province, not much is traditional or unusual in the folk lifestyles except for the province's 17,000 or so isolated tribespeople who have yet to be "assimilated" by the government; eventually they will

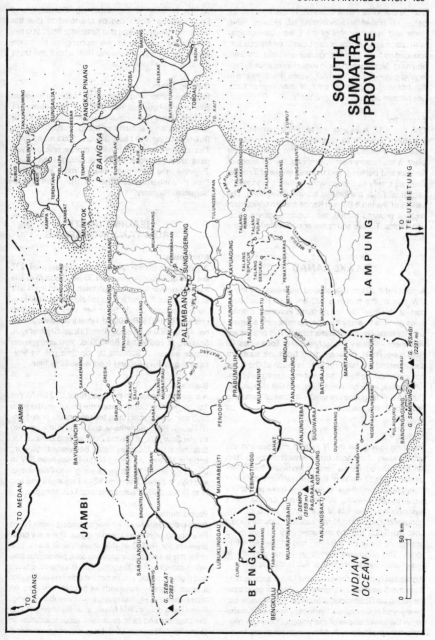

also be put in settlement centers where they can be better controlled and indoctrinated. Houses along rivers and in the jungles of the E are pole cottages with ladders (which tigers can't climb) on hilltops surrounded by hens, skinny dogs, banana trees, children, and mud. Not much to eat in these hinterlands except *pisang goreng* (fried bananas). Nearer the cities and in the *transmigrasi* projects are row upon row of tract-like houses on stilts with zinc roofs.

Economy

Only about 15 years ago, this province changed from a trading province to one with a strong industrial base: the Pertamina oil refinery, the Pusri fertilizer plant, a tire factory near Palembang, the tin mines of Bangka and Belitung, and the coal mines of Tanjung Enim all testify to this growth. Some of Indonesia's largest oil fields are located around Palembang. The valleys of the Bukit Barisan Range are rich agricultural regions growing coffee, tea, tobacco, cloves, rice, vegetables. Timber and rattan are harvested from the jungle.

LAKE RANAU

A giant (40 X 29 km) oval-shaped mountain lake in the SW part of the province 330 km from Palembang, part of this lake lies in Lampung Province. Indonesians go here to enjoy the cool climate, nice scenery, sulphur hotsprings, and water sports. This pristine environment—like an untouched Lake Toba—has G. Seminung (1881 m) soaring up from the southern shore behind the lake. Here, as in much of the Bukit Barisan range, coffee is the most important cash crop, with cloves, tobacco, vegetables, and rice also grown. Culture and language are similar to coastal Lampung Province to the south.

Sights

Bandingagung, on the N side of the lake and the largest town of the area, offers several places to stay. All the "Danau Ranau" buses terminate here. Bandingagung is 12 km W of the main highway; turn in at Simpangsender village. Quieter and more restful is a small lakeside resort, **Wisma Putri,** on the lake's eastern shore. Turn in at the sign, 8 km S of Simpangsender, or 7 km N of Kotabatu. Double rooms cost Rp15,000 but the manager may let you camp outside or sleep on a folding bed in the recreation room. The restaurant serves generous portions at reasonable prices; freshwater fish is their specialty.

Kotabatu is the first town on the lake if approaching from the S and has a *penginapan*. This is a good base for hiking up G. Seminung. Sulphurous hot water can be enjoyed at **Gemuhak Springs,** 3 km from Kotabatu on the lower slopes of the volcano. Offshore nearby is the small island, **P. Mariza.** Beaches are found

on the N coast at Bandingagung, Surabaya, and Senangkalang. Boats can be chartered to tour the lake from Bandingagung and Kotabatu; Rp20,000 per day. Boating is best in the morning as afternoon winds really stir up the waves. Rent a boat and cross the lake to the hotsprings.

Getting There

From Palembang and other points N, this picturesque lake is an 8-hour bus ride (Rp7500) over dozens of bridges. From Tanjungkarang and other points S, take a bus on a sometimes bumpy, paved road via Bukitkemuning and Liwa, 8 hours, 299 km, Rp7500. The southern approach is hillier, more scenic, and you pass through more traditional villages en route. Together, the two roads make a more interesting, though longer, alternative to the main Trans-Sumatran Highway.

HEADING NORTH FROM TANJUNGKARANG

Martapura

A small town on the railway line and main road, 237 km NW of Tanjungkarang and 35 SE of Baturaja. The Komering River flows through town. A road leads SW to Muara Dua (54 km) and on to Lake Ranau (108 km). Hotel Sentosa, Jl. J. Sudirman (the main street) charges Rp4000 s, Rp6000 d; Hotel Indonesia, Jl. Kartini, is Rp2500 s, Rp5000 d; and Hotel Sejahtera, Jl. Stasiun, is Rp2500 s, Rp4500 d. You really know you've arrived in Sumatra by the time you hit Martapura; only fiery Padang food is available here.

Baturaja

A large transit town on the Ogan River, 272 km NW of Tanjungkarang. South across the bridge on the main highway (Jl. Kemala Raya) are reasonably priced Hotel Pesagi, Peng. Sederhana, and Hotel Purnama. Also try the Sriwijaya, Jl. Serma Zakaria; Tiga Dara, Jl. Dr. Sutomo; Bali, Jl. Durian Pasar; Belawan, Jl. Stasion; and the Malaya, Jl. Saung Naga. Buses head SW to Danau Ranau, SE to Tanjungkarang; N to Palembang; and NW to Lahat. Trains go SE to Tanjungkarang and N to Prabumulih, Palembang, and Lubuklinggau.

Prabumulih

A rail-crossroads town for trains heading either NE to Palembang or NW to Lubuklinggau. There are great showers for Rp300 at this small transit town, and since this is a pineapple growing area, pineapples also sell cheap (only Rp100 each!). This is a one-stop town and if you're stuck, you're not the only one looking for a place to stay—thousands of people stay here on trips between Tanjungkarang amd Palembang. Peng. Surya (next door to RM Musi), at Jl. Rambang 611, is the cleanest and best organized accommodation in town; Rp4500 s, Rp6000 d. Long row of *kamar mandi* in the back, and flowered balconies. Losmen Kenangan, right behind RM Musi, is a real dump. Also try Akor I, Jl. Rambang 96; Rosmala, Jl. Stasion; and Akor II, or Sederhana, both on Jl. Veteran II; and the Damai on Jl. Veteran. Get good cheap meals in the dozen or so restaurants. RM Musi sells *martabak* (Rp600). RM Jayaya has the only cold drinks in town. Their *sop ayam, udang saus tomat,* and *mie goreng* are all good.

The 3rd Class train is Rp4500 with student's card from Prabumulih to Lubuklinggau, leaving at 1000 or after, arriving about 11 hours later; the seats are horrible. Since the train starts in Palembang, it may already be full by the time it arrives in Prabumulih, so just buy a 3rd Class ticket; standing up isn't any more comfortable with a 2nd Class ticket in your pocket! In front of the **Pagi Sore Restaurant** on the main street, Jl. Rambang, tickets for the various bus lines are sold: the Jaya Ekspres, ANS, Tambamaya, all Mercedes buses.

The Road to Lahat

It's 3 hours by bus from Prabumulih to Lahat. The road twists and winds in and out of the RR line, and for a good distance it parallels the Lematang River. This is an area of raw, unexploited natural wealth. The livelihood of the people comes from logging and lumber milling; you'll also come across many natural gas flares with their high-shooting orange flames. *Durian* are stacked up beside the road in season. Also, in the right season, every km or so in certain sections of the road *warung* sell pineapples for Rp100 apiece. And always the burning of *ladang* fields where rice, cloves, coconuts, pineapples, bananas, and tapioca are grown — subsistence mixed-farming in the hopes that at least one or two of their crops will pull through.

In **Muaraenim**, stay in either Hotel Ambah or Hotel Muara Enim, Jl. Jen. Sudirman. After Muaraenim, the road bridges a number of rivers and tributaries. Women carry goods in a basket attached to a strap around the forehead, a sight not to be seen since mountain Java, or Torajaland. At Tanjungenim, 13 km S of Muaraenim, is an open coal mine; stay in Hotel Kita, Jl. Teduh 118, charging Rp3500; Hotel Ambarsari, Rp3500; and beds also at Mess "Taba." There's an 80-m-high waterfall, **Curup Tenang**, in Sugiwaras village; it can be seen on the road between Tanjungenim and Pagar Alam.

Lahat

This large town on the Lematang River is a rest stop on the long trip through Sumatra, and a jumping-off point for visiting the many 7-13th C. megalithic sites between Lahat and Pagaralam. Lahat is 226 km and 5 hours by bus from Palembang; also reachable by train from Palembang (Rp6500). Near the train terminal on Jl. Stasiun are 4 basic places: Peng. Horas,

Peng. Baru, Peng. Sederhana, and Peng. Surakarta — all in the Rp3500-6000 s range. Much better are the 2 hotels around the corner on the main street, Jl. Mayor Ruslan: Hotel Permata, Rp5500 s, Rp7000 d with fan or Rp19,000 s, Rp22,500 d with a/c, TV, and *mandi*; and Losmen Simpang, across from the bus station, Rp4500 s, Rp6000 d and up. RM Mutiarabaru, on Jl. Mayor Ruslan, is bright and clean and has good Padang food. Many other restaurants and *warung* serve Indonesian, Padang, or Palembang dishes. Grocery stores are well stocked with drinks, biscuits, imported canned food, etc.

The bus station is in center of town on Jl. Mayor Ruslan. Sample fares: Tanjungkarang is 10 hours, 428 km, Rp9500; Prabumulih is 3 hours, 131 km, Rp4500; Palembang is 5 hours, 226 km, Rp6000; Bukittinggi is 20 hours, Rp14,000; Pagaralam is 1½ hours, 67 km, Rp3500; Bengkulu is 8 hours, 242 km (via Pagaralam), Rp8500. Trains go N to Lubuklinggau, E to Prabumulih, then on to Palembang before returning to Prabumulih and heading SE to Tanjungkarang.

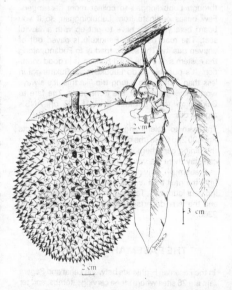

the durian: A 30- to 40-m-tall rainforest tree (Durio zibethinus) with subglobose fruits up to 30 cm long covered with hard, sharp, conical spines. Ripe durian on sale in the pasar or on a streetcorner need no other advertising than their overpowering, unforgettable odor. The fruit has been described as having an odor of onions, garlic, Limburger cheese, and the smell of the beach at low tide. The fruit's 12 or so large seeds are chestnut-like and edible after roasting. The great naturalist Russel Wallace remarked that it's worth a trip to the Orient just to eat a durian.

Lubuklinggau

Another transit town at the very end of the rail line. Take the real slow morning train (Rp6500 2nd Class) from Tanjungkarang all the way N to Lubuklinggau; most buses from Palembang to Bengkulu also pass through this town. Other buses travel via the mountain town of Pagaralam. See the old Dutch bridge in town. There's no bank so it's troublesome to change money.

Stay at **Peng. Damai** (Rp4000 s) above the Nurdin family's 2 stores. Come out of the RR station, turn R, and it's only 50 m down the road—nice rooms, nice people. Passable **Losmen Subur**, Jl. Jambi 154 (near the RR station on the main street), charges Rp2500. Many other inexpensive *losmen:* the **Jakarta** and **Merdeka** on Jl. Jen. Sudirman; the **Bahagia** on Jl. Jambi; the **Sempurna, Fajar, Setia, Lubes Jaya, Ridan Jaya,** and **Lintas Sumatera** on Jl. Yos Sudarso. Most cost Rp3000-5000 d. *Nasi padang* and *sate* places are everywhere.

Most buses start from Tanjungkarang and pass through Lubuklinggau to collect more passengers. Few buses originate from Lubuklinggau, so if you board here you may have to put up with an awful seat. The road down to Bengkulu is paved but of uneven quality. The scenic road N to Padang, along the eastern side of the Bukit Barisan, is in good condition. It's possible to do Lubuklinggau-Bukittinggi in less than 3 days. On a long trip like this, it's always worth paying extra for the front seats. The fare to Bukittinggi (and Jakarta) is Rp15,000 on ANS's regular bus.

The train to Palembang leaves at 2300, and costs Rp6500 2nd Class (the only class offered). Hang out in the dining car where it's the least crowded and you can stay there the whole trip. This train travels as far as Prabumulih, arriving at 0530; then you wait 6 hours until the next train arrives from Palembang. Continuing your journey S, Tanjungkarang is reached by 1030 and the ferry departs for Merak (W. Java) at around 2300.

THE PASEMAH HIGHLANDS

In the Pasemah Highlands between Lahat and Pagaralam are 26 sites where stone carvings, tombs, and terraced sanctuaries have been documented. These remains, which date as far back as A.D. 100, are said to be the most concentrated collection of monumental symbolic culture in Indonesia. Huge queerly shaped stones are carved into fantastic figures and groups of figures: warriors mounted on elephants, men wrestling a huge snake, animals copulating, frogs, a footprint, a waterwheel, even ocean waves. A great number of these extraordinary carvings, menhirs, dolmens, stone cist graves, and terraced sanctuaries

were erected at a time when metals were already known in the area; figures carry swords, wear helmets, rings, anklets, and men hold giant bronze kettledrums—artifacts and implements which all belong to the Bronze Age. Many of the figures appear at first to be 3-dimensional but they are in fact bas-reliefs, the illusion created by the skillful use of the curved surface of the boulders. The modern-day Pasemahans still use some statuary as vow-redemption shrines, calling upon their ancestors to bestow blessings and to stave off ill-fortune.

Most sites are found in the subdistricts of Kec. Pulau Pinang, Kotaagung, and Pagaralam. Some are easily visited but most are well off the main road. The more accessible sites are described below, but serious seekers need their own vehicle. The PDK office in the Bupati's office, 2 km NE of Lahat, can give directions, detailed information, and even has photographs of some stones and sites. Ask to see the English translation of a book documenting the ramblings of an eccentric Dutch archaeologist in the area in the early 1930s.

Vicinity Of Pagaralam

A stone elephant *(batu gajah)* is found in **Belumai** village; turn SW off the main road at the E edge of Pagaralam. In **Tegurwangi** village are several carved human figures in a complex plus the ruins of a tomb; pillars are decorated with men riding elephants, faces have thick negroid lips. From the Lahat-Pagaralam junction, walk 4 km toward Tanjungsakti then turn left 2 km to Tegurwangi village. Or it costs around Rp20,000 to charter a jeep on the bad road out to Tegurwangi. A hotsprings in **Pungar Bunga** village near Tanjungsakti, 34 km from Pagaralam. Local vehicles make the trip from Pagaralam for Rp2500.

Pagaralam To Bengkuku

This scenic 175-km route is paved but at about halfway mark the potholes begin to achieve a complete and utter victory. These highlands comprise one continuous village of wooden houses on 2-m-high stilts, in which live farmers, timbermen, carpenters, and river fishermen. Cords of firewood are stacked up alongside tools and lumber under the rickety houses. After crossing the Musi River, a road branches R to Tebingtinggi in the lowlands, 77 km N of Lahat. The condition of the pavement improves upon entering Bengkulu Province. Kepahiang is a small crossroads town with a *losmen*. Turn L here and travel 60 km for Bengkulu city, go straight 25 km for Curup, or 75 km to Danau Tes. The road to Bengkulu crosses the Musi River, then climbs 8 km to a pass covered in magnificent jungle forest. The giant (up to 1-m-across) *rafflesia Arnoldy* flower is found in season in these forests; ask in Kepahiang or in Tabah Penanjung. Tebingbinjai is 42 km before Bengkulu. The road then starts winding down the mountain. Bukit Barisan Coffee House is at the 48-km mark, a place where drivers most always make a stop for a good *nasi padang*, drinks or snacks; in the morning there's a clear view out over the 30-km-wide coastal plane on which Bengkulu city is located below. If you start from Lahat for Bengkulu early in the morning, you should roll in at the coffee house around 1700. Coming into Bengkulu the sunsets are very soft. You know you're close when the TV antennas start to appear.

Gunung Dempo

At 3,159 m, this is one of Sumatra's mightier cones. The diameter of Dempo's largest crater is estimated at about 1,150 m across. Start your climb from the tea plantation (Perkebunan Teh), 11 km from Pagaralam on the volcano's E slope. In fact, the plantation comes right up to the edge of Dempo's crater and lava flows are evident around the tea plantation; a motor vehicle can negotiate the road to around 1,665 m. From the plantation it's a 7- to 10-hour hard climb to the sum-mit. The climb isn't attempted that often because the footpath to the top is poorly maintained. Up until 2,700 m, the forests are thick; nearer the top the woods are less dense and consist of smaller, twisted, gnarly trees. The best camping spot is on the flat plain between the 2 peaks at 3,000 m—a fresh spring and the remains of an old crater; on a steep bank on the E side is spread-out lava. G. Dempo's last serious eruption was in Sept. 1976, killing 8 people.

The easiest approach to G. Dempo is from Lahat, 67 km from Pagaralam on a good road. Other approaches are: from Bengkulu via Kepahiang, 175 km, on a paved road with some rough sections; from Bengkulu via Manna and Tanjungsakti, 235 km (the 60 km section from Manna to Tanjungsakti is very rough); from Lubuklinggau via Curup on a paved road with some rough sections, 205 km; and from Tebingtinggi (midway between Lahat and Lubuklinggau) on a fairly good paved road.

PALEMBANG

The main market and oil export center of S. Sumatra Province, located on both sides of the Musi River only 80 km upstream from the sea, Palembang is (after Medan) Sumarta's 2nd most populous city (pop. 700,000). For over 1300 years, the basis of Palembang's economy has been river and ocean commerce. If you come into Palembang by train, notice the many rubber and coffee plantations and factories; this area is also known for its oil wells and forest products. One-third of the total Indonesian government revenue comes from this oil province alone. Pertamina, the government oil company, has donated to the city a large sports stadium, TV station, town clock, and a handsome minaret for its mosque. As is typical of an outlying provincial capital, this staunchly Islamic city practices its own dances, songs, customs, and cuisines. Much of the city is built on piles over tidal mudflats; the weather could get very sticky and hot. The Musi River divides the city into 2 sections: the southern half, Ulu, and the northern half, Ilir. The symbol of Palembang is the Ampera Bridge, built in the 1960s. You see paintings of the bridge everywhere; a floating trading society lives on either side of its gigantic steel spans.

An excursion up or downriver by speedboat or ferry is mandatory. Rent one of the many other water-going contraptions from in front of the *benteng* for Rp5000-10,000 per hour. Be cautious with the boatmen down on the Musi; you hear stories of people being taken out in the middle of the river and pressured for more money. Always go with a friend. A sampan ride across the river costs Rp400.

History

By tradition an ancient Oriental trading center, for 500 years up to the 13th C. Palembang was one of the principal ports of the world. The city was born on pepper, raised on tin, and grew rich on oil. Palembang was once the capital of the Sriwijaya Empire (7th-12th centuries), whom scholars have called "The Phoenicians of the East." The first tangible signs in the whole archipelago of the arrival of Mahayana Buddhism appeared in the vicinity in the early 600s. A full 100 years later traces of this religion show up in inscriptions of Candi Kalasan in C. Java. On his way to India in 671, a Chinese Buddhist pilgrim, I Tsing, arrived at the university in Palembang and stayed 4 years, writing memoirs and handing down a valuable description of the city. He described a huge marketplace where Tamil, Persian, Arabic, Greek, Cambodian, Siamese, Chinese, and Burmese were all spoken. A thousand ships laid at anchor, and Sriwijaya sent its mercenaries as far as Mesopotamia to do battle. Thousands of monks learned Buddhist teachings and translated Sanskrit texts here. The city reached its zenith in the beginning of the 11th century. Then in A.D. 1028 it was brutally attacked by a jealous Chola king from S. India and it never recovered. By the end of the 14th C., Sriwijaya had splintered into 8 smaller princedoms, the largest of which, Melayu, was centered around Jambi and became a strong maritime power. Finally, with the rise of Melaka in the 14th C., Sriwijaya became a remote backwater. On 17 June 1983, Palembang celebrated its 1300th birthday!

Sriwijaya's origins have lately been disputed. Some

researchers claim that the empire originated near Chaiya, Thailand, and not in the Palembang area. One indication of this theory is that, except for the artifacts in the city's museums, little physical evidence remains of Palembang's past splendor. The region around Palembang still produces fine woven fabrics and performs unique Hindu-influenced dances. S. Sumatran dancers wear elaborate tree-like headdresses with glittering pendants and festoons or crowns, and carry gold-gilt fans. Wedding costumes are still patterned after the royal courts of the old medieval empire with a flap on the groom's headdress preventing him from looking at the bride.

SIGHTS

The **Mesjid Raya** (Grand Mosque) near the bridge greets you as you come into town; it was built by Sultan Mahmud Badaruddin in the 18th century. Go for a ride along the road heading upstream beside the Musi River where whole residential areas are built out over the water and see some good examples of traditional architecture. During the springtime rainy season and floods, this broad river becomes a lake and all the residences built on rafts rise and fall with the water. Palembang's old fort, with its tall whitewashed walls, is on Jl. Benteng just back from the river in the center of the city. It was built in 1780 during the reign of the Sultan Ahmad Najamudin II. **Benteng** is now occupied by the army, so permission to enter and tour it must be acquired from the fort commander.

The area in front of the *benteng* and to the sides of the Ampera Bridge is one of Palembang's most unique attractions. Here ships of 10,000 tons lie amidst small, bobbing rowboats and sailboats, as motorized *prahu* dart back and forth across the river. Houseboats are moored along the riverbank, functioning not only as dwellings but as floating *warung*. It was this river life that gave Palembang its prewar nickname, "The Venice of the Far East." Even today the scene is reminiscent of Hong Kong, but with more Third World flavor thrown in. Palembang's famous "floating markets" are in the Pasar 16 Ilir area, 2 km downstream from the bridge. This crowded quarter consists of 2 km of funky markets selling anything and everything. Just like the *klongs* of Bangkok, boats going to market have to travel down these canals. Locals will tell you to be careful walking in this area because of the "many gangsters." (Tangga Buntungis in Ulu is another rough section where one shouldn't walk alone at night).

Rumah Bari Museum

Located on Jl. Rumah Bari, the main building is a traditional Palembang *rumah adat* (called here *rumah limas*), a solid wooden building made of *kayu*

Ampera Bridge, Palembang's famous landmark

tembesu. The Dutch moved it from the countryside to this location piece by piece. Since 1931 it has served as a museum. A large portion of the collection has been shipped down to Jakarta's Mini Indonesia at the behest of the President-for-Life's wife, Madame Tien Suharto. Still, it is an important museum, with the best sculptures from the Pasemah Plateau (near Tegurwangi). See implements from the Mesolithic (15,000-30,000 B.C.), Chinese, Sriwijaya, Portuguese, and Dutch periods. Your guide replies *Jaman Dulu* ("from times past") each time you ask "What is it?" See the picture of Palembang in 1659 when it was a fortified plantation; you can make out the present *benteng* and even several camels. But the high point is out on the front lawn: crude Pasemeh-style *ganesha*, elephants, horses, *lingga,* and a 9-m-long wooden paddle which propelled the royal barge up and down the Musi 200 years ago. Open daily (except Fri.) 0800-1300, give a donation.

Rumah Hasim Ning, 23 Ilir, is another traditional Palembang *rumah limas* N of Rumah Bari; open 0800-1500 when the family is in. **Rumah Adat Bayumi** in the Jl. Mayor Ruslan area by a golf course is over 100 years old. Moved from a village some years ago and rebuilt here; the downstairs is a residence, but tourists may go upstairs to see antiques, lavish carpets, and furnishings. There's no charge to enter but get permission at Kantor Rambang, Jl. Mayor Ruslan.

Chinese Temples

Klenteng Kwa Sam Yo, between the river and Jl. Sungai Lapangan Hatal, is remarkable for its hundreds of fascinating murals and wall paintings, which depict the story of the great Kublai Khan and other Mongolian heros. Ask to see the vicious-looking self-torture chair, a means by which to gain spiritual knowledge through pain and suffering *(prihatin,* or in Chinese, *songkong)*. Another pain-inflicting activity was the immersion of the penitent's hands in boiling oil; see the color photos of the old Chinese whose unscarred hands were so honored! Another Chinese temple is on P. Kemarau downriver at the junction of the Musi, Komering and Ogan rivers. Hire a motorized sampan in front of the *benteng* for the 15-min., 2-km, Rp4500, ride. This temple is also a *kramat* (holy place) to Muslims. Sites like this sacred to both religions are known as "double sanctuaries"; the only other ones that exist in Indonesia are in Ancol (Klenteng Ancol) in Jakarta and in Semarang (Gedung Batu), C. Java.

PRACTICALITIES

Accommodations

Economy-class **Hotel Segaran**, Jl. Segaran 207, is a basic hotel on a very busy street. At Rp3500 s, Rp5500 d, it's divey but friendly. No windows and poor lighting in most of the rooms, boiled water available. **Hotel Aman**, up the street on Jl. Lematang, charges Rp4000 s, Rp7500 d—a huge dingy hotel with 35 rooms, but in this price range you can't complain. Plenty of places to eat in nearby *warung*. **Hotel Asiana**, Jl. Jen. Sudirman 45, charges Rp5000 s; an easy walk from the bus station. The **Lusyana**, also reasonable, is just around the corner. **Hotel Sintera**, Jl. Jen. Sudirman 30-38, is central but you get a lot of street noise. Their cheapest rooms run Rp5000 s plus Rp400 for some mysterious tax, doubles run Rp8500 (with a fan Rp12,000, a/c Rp15,500). Right around the corner is a small alleyway with many noodle and Padang-style restaurants.

The **Swarna Dwipa**, Jl. Tasik 2 (tel. 22322), is one of Sumatra's best hotels. The old building, built during colonial times, has large rooms for Rp12,500, but is rather rundown and stuffy. The cheerier newer building offers modern motel-like rooms (Rp25,500) overlooking a neighborhood of red-tiled roofs and quiet streets. Everything—telephone, lights, bells, buzzers, swimming pool, and the central a/c—seems to work. Good taxi and *becak* service in front. Swarna Dwipa's best feature is that it's located in a quiet neighborhood, across the street from a park. Yet the Rumah Bari Museum is only a 10-min. walk. Several comfortable Chinese-run guesthouses are also in the neighborhood. The centrally located **Sanjaya Hotel**, Jl. Kapt. A. Rivai (tel. 20272), is more expensive than the Swarna Dwipa (Rp35,000 and up). They have a good Chinese restaurant and bar.

Food

The restaurant streets of Palembang are Jl. Jen. Sudirman and Jl. Veteran. The higher-priced hotels listed have excellent restaurants, with dishes are in the Rp2000-3000 range. **Maxim's**, Jl. Jen Sudirman 87 (tel. 26635), features steaks and delicious Maxim Fried Chicken, served with the honorable chicken's head peering up at you. Try **City Bar & Restaurant**, Jl. Jen. Sudirman 589, Makmur Store, 3rd floor (tel. 26710), for Indonesian, Chinese and European dishes. The **Miranda Steak House** on Jl. Veteran imports its beef from New Zealand and specializes in steak dinners. Nicely decorated, clean, a bit expensive. The **Marga Ria** is both a nightclub and restaurant serving Chinese food. **Grand Park Restaurant**, Jl. Veteran, offers Chinese food even better than Maxim's. Try the **Mandala**, Jl. Veteran 86-88 (tel. 23614), for Indonesian, Chinese, Japanese, and European food. **Pagi Sore** is a *nasi padang* place on the intersection of Jl. Sudirman and Jl. Veteran, right down the street from Hotel Sanjaya.

Entertainment

Palembang has 3 swimming pools, one bowling alley (at Sungai Gerong), and 8 billiard halls. The city's 20 cinemas (most with a/c) are a godsend for those who like Shaw Brothers extravaganzas, Italian spaghetti westerns, kung fu movies, and bad old American films like "Silver Streak." Ask the *becak* drivers to take you to one of the city's safe nightclubs. Many of the girls who work in these late-night spots are just dance hostesses, not for hire for continuing companionship.

Events

Palembang's traditional **wedding ritual** dates back to the 7th C. Hindu Sriwijaya era. Weddings and receptions are usually held on Sun. mornings every week. The busiest wedding season is the time of the *haj,* when many Sumatrans embark on a pilgrimage to Mecca. Tradition dictates that the bride must propose to the husband and pay him a dowry commensurate with his social and economic stature in the community; this arrangement gives her added clout in the marriage as she figuratively "pays for him." On Java, weddings often take place in the mosque but here the custom is that engagement parties and weddings are held at the home of the bride. In the wedding's egg-breaking ceremony, the groom crushes an egg beneath his bare foot, which the bride then cleanses, symbolizing fertility. Finally, with all the pomp of a sultan's court, the bride and groom sit in state on a white-satin couch blanketed in flowers and fanned by young handmaidens.

Except for the wedding ceremony, the *Gending*

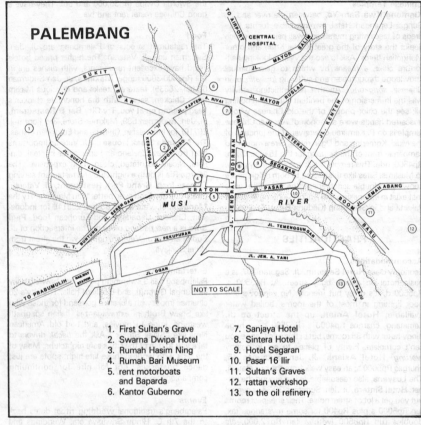

PALEMBANG

1. First Sultan's Grave
2. Swarna Dwipa Hotel
3. Rumah Hasim Ning
4. Rumah Bari Museum
5. rent motorboats
   and Baparda
6. Kantor Gubernor
7. Sanjaya Hotel
8. Sintera Hotel
9. Hotel Segaran
10. Pasar 16 Ilir
11. Sultan's Graves
12. rattan workshop
13. to the oil refinery

NOT TO SCALE

Sriwijaya dance is the only other remnant of the Sriwijaya kingdom. A welcome dance which traditionally greets a VIP arriving in the city, it's also put on at weddings. Seven girls kneel before the guests, never looking them full in the face. Elaborate headdresses are worn with slivers of gold, the dancers' bodices draped in thick multi-colored brocades. Fingertips have long arching gold fingernails from which trinkets dangle. In the days of the sultanate the dance used to take place with more regularity, but the political power of the region's royalty has long since been abolished.

The anniversary of the founding of Palembang is commemorated every 17 June. The occasion is celebrated with sports events, community projects, and performances of music and dance on an open-air stage. *Bidar* (canoe) races are held at noon a day or two after the Independence Day celebrations on 17

August. The *bidar*, shaped like animals, are manned by up to 40 rowers. This event is very popular among Palembang's citizens.

Arts And Crafts

Influenced by centuries of foreign trade, the weavers of S. Sumatra have been deeply affected by diverse cultures. The Palembang *songket*, considered symbols of a family's wealth, is usually made of silk, then given an overlaid design of gold or silver. The *kain songket,* a traditional cloth woven with gilt thread, is sold in the Sumatra Shopping Center and Pasar Ilir. Visiting the weaveries is even more interesting; the tourist office can suggest a few. Go in the mornings; the weavers tend to take the afternoons off. In Rumah Bari, see the small diorama of weavers, traditional textiles, some spinning wheels, and an exhibit of the whole 9-phase process.

Palembang's *plangi* is unbelievably involved and colorful. *Plangi* ("tie-dye") comes from the word *pelangi,* meaning "rainbow." Traditional Palembang *plangi* is rarely made; even old pieces are quite difficult to get ahold of. These cloths are now only seen at weddings, draped around the bride's shoulders after the cleansing ceremony. Ask a family to drag out some of their old *plangi* cloths and take them out to the sunlight.

Services

The tourist office (Baparda) is beside the governor's office on Jl. Kapt. Rivai; open 0730-1400 Mon.-Thurs., Fri. until 1130, Sat. until 1300, closed Sunday. Change money upstairs in **Bank Bumi Daya**. At **Apotik Dempo**, Jl. Dempo 6, open 0800-2000 Mon.-Sat., the pharmicist speaks English. Palembang's best hospital, where expats and Pertamina employees go when they're sick, is the *rumah sakit* in the Plaju Oil Refinery complex. If it's not that serious, there's **RM Charitas**, a Catholic public hospital just across the steet from Hotel Senjaya. A good doctor is **Dr. Hardi**, tel. 23173, whose office is on Jl. Lt. Sayuti off Jl. Sudirman; Hardi specializes in tropical diseases. **Dr. Handoyono**, Jl. Ratna 27, is another English-speaking GP who even makes housecalls. Travel agents: **Tunas Jaya**, Jl. Mayor Safria Rahman 1; and **Elteha**, Jl. Jen. Sudirman.

TRANSPORT

Getting There

All roads, rivers, and railways in S. Sumatra end up eventually in Palembang; even 10,000-ton ships can voyage this far upriver from the Bangka Straits. To reach Palembang by train, get to Merak (W. Java), then board the overnight ferry to Bakauheni on the SE tip of Sumatra. At 0800 take either the *Rajabasa* (Rp4000 2nd Class) or the *Sriwijaya Ekspres* (Rp7500 2nd Class) trains up to Palembang, arriving at 1600 or 1800. Palembang's *stasiun kerata api*, called Kertapi, is on the other side of the river in the Ulu section of the city; taxi drivers will take you the 8 km into Palembang for Rp4500-5000, or take a *bemo* (Rp300). Alternatively, take the bus to Palembang from: Padang, Rp14,500 (48 hours); Medan, Rp22,000 (72 hours). There are also regularly scheduled daily flights from Jakarta (Merpati Rp46,500, Garuda, Rp55,000, both 1 hour), as well as from Medan and Singapore. The Talang Betutu Airport is 17 km N of Palembang, Rp4500 for two into town.

Getting Around

Palembang's distinctive vehicle, the *kejang,* looks like a small armored personnel carrier; also rampant is a jeep-like *oplet* with a square back, painted the usual rainbow. Buses, *becak, oplet,* and taxis go all over, ex-

cept for some restricted areas. The big *oplet/kejang* station, Stasiun Ampera, is right next to the market beside the bridge; fares run Rp200-300. All the Ilirs (neighborhoods) are preceded by their numbers: if you want to go to Hotel Swarna Dwipa, look for drivers and their assistants at Stasiun Ampera holding up four fingers meaning "Ilir 4." Charter an *oplet* or a *kejang* for half the price of hiring private cars. Most taxi (sedans) rides within the city cost Rp2500-3000, but it will cost only Rp200 if you're on one of the regular fixed-fare routes, or only Rp1000-2000 if you want to charter a *kejang*. To charter a motorboat RT to destinations such as the refinery at Sungai Gerong costs Rp20,000-30,000.

FROM PALEMBANG

By Bus

From Palembang's Terminal Bis Tujuluh, public buses go to Jambi, Padang, Medan, and other points north. Buses (Rp7000) connect Palembang with Bakauheni, the ferry terminal to Java, then on to Jakarta for Rp20,000 in all. It's about 6 hours, 380 km, and Rp9,500 to Lubuklinggau. To Bukittinggi takes 20 hours, costs Rp14,000, with one stop in Prabumulih and other dinner stops. To Padang is a 48- to 72-hour journey (depending on the season); Rp14,500 to 17,500 (in the wet). A few Mercedes ALS buses make this trip, a faster and more comfortable way to go. Changing money is difficult between Palembang and Padang. To Jambi is Rp9,000 and 36 hours through a flat, ghostly country of oil derricks, dry tufted grass, rolling meadows of yellow flowers and swamps, and more swamps.

By Train

Take a *bemo* (Rp300) to the Kertapi Train Station, about 8 km out of Palembang on a tributary of the Musi. Watch for pickpockets here. Try for a discount with your International Student Card. One option, instead of the grueling Padang bus ride, is to take the 10-hour Rp6500 train trip from Palembang to Lubuklinggau, then bus it from there (Rp8000) to Padang in about 24 hours—still hard traveling. For Jakarta, the train leaves at 0900, 2030, and 2200. The 2030 train travels nonstop for Rp9500 1st Class; 12 hours to Panjang, 4 hours on the ferry across the strait to Merak (W. Java), then another 3 hours to Jakarta (ticket includes the cost of the ferry to Java). This night train is much cooler and not as crowded as day trains.

By Boat

Since Palembang is S. Sumatra's principal port, many ships take passengers both down and upriver. Every day an overnight riverboat (Rp12,000) cruises down Palembang's ancient highway to Muntok, a harbor city on the W side of the tin island of Bangka. Passengers depart from Palembang's Boom Baru Harbor, 2 km from the city center and 80 km from the sea. Government-run boat services travel up the Musi, as far as one-day's distance from Palembang, making stops in villages along the way. Just ask for the *kapal biru* ("Blue Boat"), which are also available for group charter. One place to catch the *kapal biru* is at Tangga Buntungis.

An adventuresome way to reach Jambi to the N is on a ferry for the small town of Bayunglincir, 60 km S of Jambi. The ferry leaves at around 1400 on Mon., Wed., and Sat., and costs Rp8500. The boat first enters the delta area, then heads up a smaller tributary of the Musi to Bayunglincir. The water is yellow and heavy with mud; navigation is cautious. You pass through dense riverine jungles with fireflies, flying foxes and lemurs, basking crocodiles, exotic birds, plenty of monkeys—an Amazon-like, untraveled region. The piloting takes places mostly at night, arriving at Bayunglincir the next morning at 0500. Awaiting *bemo* take you into Jambi for around Rp1500 (3-4 hours).

By Air

Talang Betutu Airport, 17 km N of Palembang, is Rp4500 by taxi or Rp2500 by hired *kejang*. Air tickets can be bought at: Garuda, Jl. Kapt. Rivai 20 (tel. 22933/22029); Merpati, also on Jl. Kapt. Rivai (tel. 21604/26051); or at Hotel Segaran. At least 5 Garuda flights per day connect Jakarta for Rp55,000. Merpati flights also depart for: Pangkalpinang on P. Bangka, Rp22,400; Surabaya, Rp110,300; Dumai, Rp76,500; Tanjung Pinang in Riau, Rp53,800; Telukbetung, Rp33,500. On the Padang flight (Rp62,500), the plane climbs steeply from the flat lowlands in order to clear the 3000-m mountain peaks, a dramatic experience.

VICINITY OF PALEMBANG

One of the largest oil refineries in Asia is Rp300 by *kejang* from Palembang. See them at night when they're all lit up like Cape Canaveral. The monstrous Sungei Gerong Refinery has a daily capacity of 75,000 barrels. Adjacent is the US$200 million petrochemical complex of Plaju. Virtual cities within a city, there are office buildings, bowling alleys, a swimming pool, clubs, and row upon row of housing areas for employees (in contrast, notice the squatter villages outside the refineries' gates). On the other side of Sungei Gerong is the loading harbor where you can see the big ships lined up to take on oil.

The huge **Pusri** urea complex, also downriver from Palembang, produces 1.6 million tons of fertilizer annually. Because of the enormous amount of power it consumes, the plant (reputedly one of the largest in the world) was sited close to the oilfields. The workers are well cared for: mosque, recreation halls, swimming pools, a hospital, movie theaters, golf course, bus station, canteens. The plant has a perpetual white cloud hanging over it. Go at night when the mosque is backdropped by the glowing lights of the superstructure, an eerie sight.

River Trips

Rent speedboats *(spetbot)* for Rp10,000-15,000 per hour from the busy waterfront in front of the *benteng* and Stasiun Ampera near the bridge. Allow Rp60,000-Rp100,000 for a meaningful river trip. A *spetbot* is a narrow 8-m-long boat which rises out of the river at full speed, spraying water over the passengers on the choppier, wider sections of the river near the city. Boats can fit up to 8 people (though that's a bit crowded). Traditional stilt houses start up right away after leaving Palembang, as you enter a more industrialized area. Farther downstream, the riverbanks become less populated and the water becomes calmer; you're in the country sooner than you expect. The boatman adroitly swerves to avoid wakes of other boats, as well as pieces of trees, clumps of palm, stumps, etc. He stops every km or so to lift the motor out of the water and clean his propeller of debris. Then you come upon stilt villages that contain few articles of the Western world. Women wash clothes on the shores, villagers fish with bamboo poles. Later, when it turns dark the trees glow and sparkle with fireflies, like candle-lit Christmas trees all along the river banks. The boatman uses their light to navigate down the black river. The spluttering motor drowns out the piercing calls of birds. Riverine Sumatra.

THE KUBU PEOPLE

Remnants of a pygmy race of nomadic Negrito peoples, the Kubu live in small bands of 20-30 along the swamps and dense jungles of the eastern coast of south and central Sumatra. A pure branch of the first inhabitants of the archipelago who began to migrate in about 3000 B.C., the arrival of the Kubus even precedes that of the proto-Malayan Bataks of N. Sumatra and the Torajans of S. Sulawesi. So primitive that they learned of the bow and arrow from *later* migrations, the Kubu are quite distinct from the Mongoloid races. Wild members of this tribe don't practice agriculture, nor do their children enter the school system. They use spears, stones, and digging sticks in search for food. Considered savages by the present inhabitants of their areas, these naked aboriginals occasionally come out of the forest and stop the bus between Jambi and Palembang to beg for money and food. Now, because their traditional forest habitats are being destroyed by timber cutting and oil exploration, the government has set up a number of resettlement camps on the edge of the jungle. The hope is that the Kubu will eventually give up their migratory ways and voluntarily choose a more settled lifestyle in villages equipped with schools, a *kepala desa,* and small out-patient clinics.

Getting There
To meet the Kubu, trek into the jungle in the vicinity of Sekayu about 150 km and Rp4000 by bus NW of Palembang. Wait patiently in small villages where they come to trade simple woven products in exchange for food. Some of the villages are accessible by car or truck, some are not. You might have to go by government vehicle on a forest road *(jalan hutan).* The area around Sekayu produces rubber and other forest products. Sekayu is also a hunting area for tigers, bears, pigs, and other wild animals. Stay at **Tanggonang,** Jl. Merdeka 12; **DMS,** Jl. Kantor; try also **Losmen Rangonang** and **Losmen Senang** which cost Rp4000 s.

BENGKULU

Only a few travelers ever visit this wild, sparsely populated, historic province (pop. approx. 1 million). In the E rise majestic G. Dempo (3,159 m), Sumatra's third largest volcano, and jungle-covered G. Ulupalik, source of the giant Musi River. The Bukit Barisan mountain range bisects Bengkulu; there is a rich reserve of natural forests, particularly in the N where rainforests come right down to deserted shorelines with cliffs up to 30 m high. The province's southern portion is highly fertile thanks to the Krakatoa explosion, and its extensive forests are rich in plant and animal life. Indian Ocean murky surf crashes everywhere along Bengkulu's western boundary. Bengkulu is divided into 4 districts: the provincial capital of Bengkulu on the coast; Rejang Lebong, with Curup as its main town, located in the mountainous E; South Bengkulu with Manna the main town; and North Bengkulu, with Arga Makmur its district capital. The roads and air transport have improved recently and undiscovered Bengkulu can easily be included in a trip through Sumatra.

Climate
Coastal temperatures average 26-29 degrees C, often with a sea breeze. In the mountain valleys the average temperature is 22-26 degrees C. Humidity is high. It rains most days of the year, usually in the afternoon or evenings. The W monsoon (Oct.-Feb.) has heavier rainfall, but downpours can be devastating any time of year. In May 1987 rivers overflowed, swept through coastal villages, and carried at least 37 people downriver to their deaths in the Indian Ocean.

Flora And Fauna
Much of the province is covered by jungle forests. The giant *rafflesia Arnoldy,* the world's biggest flower at nearly 1 meter across, is found in the mountainous terrain. *Vanda hookeriana,* a water orchid with tiny flowers, can be seen at Lake Dendam Tak Sudah near Bengkulu city. Wild orchids are rampant. Monkeys, elephants, crocodiles, bears, pigs, buffalo, and tigers inhabit the forests. Wild pigs are considered pests because they eat farmers' crops; the pigs are hunted not for food but to keep their numbers down. All other animals are protected by the government and their hunting (without a permit) is forbidden. Bengkulu has been overlooked by tourists because of the decrepit condition of its roads and the consequent difficulty of access. But the hunters have found it. Bengkulu is Sumatra's "Hunting State." The tourist office can help with guides and permits for gamewatching and hunting. It takes just 1 day's travel to get to almost any area of the province by rented Land Rover or jeep.

People
Of the million people, 98% are Muslim. Large numbers of transmigrant settlers have settled in the province, at the yearly rate of around 12,000 since 1979. Settlements are scattered around the province, but most transmigrants have settled around Arga Makmur and Tais (80 km N and 60 km S of Bengkulu city respectively). Balinese transmigrants have established the villages of Sumber Agung and Rama Agung, both near Arga Makmur.

Most of the natives and transmigrants are farmers who grow coffee, cloves, pepper, tobacco, coconut, fruit, rice, and vegetables. Three major ethnic groups and many minor ones, each speaking a different dialect, are native to the province. The largest groups are: the Bengkulunese of Bengkulu city; the Rejang of the Curup and Arga Makmur areas; and the Serawai of S. Bengkulu district. Smaller clans *(suku)* include: the Lembak (between Curup and Lubuklinggau); Mukomuko (far N with a culture similar to the Minangkabau of neighboring W. Sumatra Province); Pekal (Ketaun, Seblat, and Ipuh areas on the N coast); Pasemah (in the mountains of S. Bengkulu District);

and the Engganese (on P. Enggano, 114 km offshore to the SW). As a result of the long English occupation, many English words have crept into the Bengkulu dialects; "cupbod," "poket," and "try." Try to get invited to a wedding in this province. A local band is hired and they call people up from the audience to sing, a great way to make friends quickly. Just sing whatever you want in English, French, Spanish, Serbo-Croation, Indonesian. If you can sing in *Bahasa Bengkulu,* the crowd will go wild.

BENGKULU CITY

Formerly known as Bencoolen, this old city of 70,000 on the SW coast of Sumatra is the capital of Bengkulu Province. A famous 18th and 19th C. British trading settlement, Bengkulu is rich in history. In 1973 it had only 10 motorcycles, 10 cars, one restaurant, several small *warung;* the first traffic light was installed in 1979. Today development is accelerating with paved roads, more regular flights, a new port for larger ships, and a population increase. Still, Bengkulu is a small, peaceful town and a pleasure to visit. Sea breezes cool the town and a long sandy beach lines the coast. There isn't much to do at night except take in a movie at one of the 4 cinemas, or play dominos. No nightclubs or open prostitution permitted by the town fathers; it's very quiet. Long neglected by the tourism industry, mostly because of its isolation, travelers are recently beginning to discover Bengkulu. Hotels are generally well run and clean, there are good restaurants, and the local people are friendly and easy going. Bengkulu gets rain almost every day (300-400 mm per year), usually starting after 1200. Temperature ranges from 25.5 degrees C to 29 degrees C.

History

The British, driven from their last stronghold in W. Java at Banten, built several fortresses in Bengkulu and stayed 150 years. The British East India Company chose Bengkulu as a "factory" (the old word for settlement) site because Banten was a major importer of Bengkulu pepper, at the time a fabulous cash earner. Their intention was to try to achieve a larger market share of the pepper trade, which up until this time was controlled almost solely by the Dutch. After striking a deal with the local raja for the exclusive rights to purchase the pepper crop, the first English factory, York, was built in 1685 about 3 km N of present Fort Marlborough. Malaria and other diseases killed off so many British that it was said that "two monsoons were the life of a man." At one point in the 17th C., slaves were even brought in from Madagascar to man the fort. Due to the lack of European women, it was common for the British to take native women; by the end of the 18th C. Eurasians rose to high posts in the service of the British East Indies Company. This original fort was finally abandoned, and another built where Fort Marlborough is today.

Unwilling or unable to pay the natives enough for their pepper, the British had to resort to coercive and repressive measures to maintain production. By March 1719 relations had so deteriorated that the Bengkulunese stormed and burned the fort, and forced the British to flee in their ships for Batavia and later to India. The British did not return until 1724, when they reoccupied the fort. In the early 19th C., British administrator Parr was murdered, and bitter reprisals followed. British fortunes in W. Sumatra went from bad to worse.

Sir Stamford Raffles, the founder of Singapore, arrived in Bengkulu in 1818 to revive the failing pepper trade. Raffles preferred Java over Sumatra. "I would not give one Java for a thousand such islands," he said. But this brilliant and ambitious 30-year-old ex-lieutenant governor of the Indies was charged with building a prosperous new colony for Britain and edging out the Dutch by taking over Sumatra's W coast. Over the next several years the great Englishman freed the slaves, pacified the pepper chiefs, and healed the old wounds.

After Raffles' recall to Britain in 1820, British rule in W. Sumatra was doomed. The Dutch undercut the productivity of Bengkulu's yields, glutting the market and underselling in Europe. This finally culminated in the British handing over the W coast plantations to the Dutch in return for control over Melaka and its straits, a waterway critical to the English company's lucrative China trade. Thus, the English era in W. Sumatra came to an end and Bengkulu was returned to the Dutch in 1824.

The greatest sea disaster in history took place during the war in 1942 off Bengkulu's coast when a Japanese ship with 7,000 POWs was sunk by British submarines with a loss of over 5,000 souls.

SIGHTS

The tourist office on Jl. Sukarno-Hatta has little printed info but can help arrange guided jungle excursions to see wildlife or to hunt for the *rafflesia* flower. Travelers are attracted to **Kampung Cina** (Chinatown), the old part of town and its row of traditional buildings with red-tiled roofs, where most of the hotels, restaurants, and attractions are concentrated. Ask the tourist office how to get to **Makam Sentot Alisbasja**, the memorial grave of an exiled national hero who died in Bengkulu during the occupation of the Dutch. Often visited by pilgrims.

The Parr Monument, a dome supported by columns, is a memorial to an early 1800s English governor of Bengkulu. This courageous but headstrong administrator, who preceded Raffles, was immensely unpopular. He forced the natives to cultivate coffee; worse, he attempted to disband the Bugis officer corps at Fort Marlborough. Worst, Parr would not double his guard or take warning. On the night of 27 Sept. 1807 he was overpowered as he slept, stabbed to death, and decapitated, most likely by the Bugis officers whose economic interests were threatened by Parr's policies. Soon after the tragedy, his wife and children sailed for England and the ship was wrecked and all aboard were lost. The Parr Monument, said to have been built by Raffles, overlooks Kampung Cina. A simple obelisk to yet another English officer, Hamilton, is 1½ km S of Kampung Cina at the intersection of Jl. Sentoso and Jl. Hasan. A cement monument to the monstrous *rafflesia* flower is in Jembatan Kecil in the middle of an intersection on the road to the airport N of town.

Sukarno's House

Sukarno, who distinguished himself early in his political career by his vocal opposition to colonial rule, was arrested by the Dutch on Java in 1933, brought to Bengkulu, and put under house arrest for 9 years. Later, when the Japanese occupied Sumatra he was captured again. The first Indonesian President's former house is quite small; it's off Jl. Sukarno-Hatta near the tourist office, the one with the flag in front of it. You may see it in the mornings after getting permission from the people who live in it. Sukarno was an engineer by trade, trained at the famous Bandung Institute of Technology in the 1920s; he designed Mesjid Jamik during his exile here. The mosque is at the intersection of Jl. Jen. Sudirman and Jl. Suprapio.

Fort Marlborough

Built from 1709 to 1719 by the British East India Co., Fort Marlborough is named after the same British duke whose name was given to Yogya's main street, Malioboro. This is the most formidable fort ever built by the British in the Orient, occupied now, as usual, by the Indonesian army. The whole structure is presently being refinished in cement, which really lessens its historic drama. The well-preserved castle-like parapets around the courtyard contain the original tracks on which the cannons were wielded to fire in different directions. From its high walls are excellent views of the sleepy harbor, the *pasar*, Kampung Cina, oxcarts, and whirling kites. The back of the fort has been left in its original state; take a walk along the high and windy battlements that overlook the ruins of a rear drawbridge. Two jutting seawalls stretch out past the beach. The old prison with its original bars is now used as a bicycle room for army personnel; inside the compound stand old English gravestones with inscriptions. No entrance fee. Just sign your name in the guestbook a soldier keeps near the entrance.

The English Governor's Building

This dramatic ruin overlooks the harbor in Kampung Cina, a 5-min. walk from Fort Marlborough. The whole structure, though still standing, is slowly being engulfed by banyan tree roots which crawl through its windows and make a mockery of its nearly meter-thick walls. In its day this building was the center of political and social life in the old city of Bencoolen, a well-constructed edifice with metalwork throughout. Now, devoured by sinewy tendrils, it seems haunted.

PRACTICALITIES

Accommodations

For the cheapies, go to Kampung Cina. **Peng. Aman**, Jl. Pendakian, has rooms that are reasonably clean but can be hot and noisy; Rp3500 s, Rp6000 d. Nearby, across from the fort, is **Peng. Samudera**, Jl. Benteng, Rp4000 s, Rp7000 d (not as good as Peng. Aman). The other 2 cheap places are near Pasar Minggu on Jl. K.Z. Abidin: **Peng. Surya** and **Peng. Damai**, both Rp3500 s, Rp6000 d.

At Jl. Jen. A. Yani 922B (tel. 31901), **Hotel Asia's** double rooms are Rp12,500 with fan and Rp25,000 with a/c and TV. **Wisma Rafflesia**, Jl. Jen. A. Yani 924 (tel. 31650) is Rp8500 d. Guesthouse-style **Wisma Kenanga**, Jl. Sentosa 1007 (tel. 390), charges Rp12,500 for doubles with fan; right opposite a small park. **Wisma Melati**, near the Protestant church on Jl. Veteran 35 (tel. 31186), is Rp8500 s, Rp10,500 d (room only) or Rp12,500 s, Rp25,000 d (including 3 meals) **Wisma Malabero**, Jl. Dr. Hazairin 1 (tel. 31004) has doubles for Rp15,000 with fan and Rp25,000 with a/c. **Wisma Balai Buntar**, Jl. Khadijah 122, is Rp25,000 s, Rp32,000 with a/c.

Offering surf and sand at your doorstep, the best place in town is **Pantai Nala Samudra Hotel**. Located 20 min. from the airport and a 5-min. drive from downtown on Jl. Pantai Nala (no. 142, tel. 31722), they charge Rp20,000 (1-3 persons, extra bed is Rp3500) per room, and have 40 a/c rooms with private bath and shower, TV, and telephone. Transfers from airport available. There's also a restaurant and showroom for traditional handicrafts, tennis courts, and a mini golf course. Next door is the similarly priced **Nala Beach Cottages & Restaurant**.

Make reservations at Jl. P. Jayakarta 68, Block C-21 (tel. 632511/632630/6597483), Jakarta.

Food

The **Ragil Kuning Restaurant**, Jl. Kenanga, has excellent food at reasonable prices. At the **Ragil Kuning Nala Cafeteria**, Jl. P. Nala, enjoy your meal while looking out over the ocean. Street *warung* are set up at night in many places, such as across the street from the fort. Buy groceries and drinks in one of the numerous Chinese shops along Jl. Panjaitan in Kampung Cina, or at **Pintu Batu Supermarket** on Jl. Jen. Sudirman. Pasar Minggu is Bengkulu's biggest market and the place for vegies and fruit; delightful to wander around, easy to reach, and all the local taxis terminate here. **Pasar Ikan**, on the W side of Kampung Cina, is the place for fresh fish.

Events

The **Tabot Carnival** is Bengkulu's Mardi Gras. Some say Gurkahs from Nepal, English mercenaries, started this tradition; since some of them were Muslims themselves, they married Bengkulu women. It commemorates the heroism of Hassan and Hussin, grandsons of the Prophet Mohammed, in their struggle for Islam. In the festival about 50 colorful towers *(tabot)* made of bamboo and decorated with colored paper, each built in the shape of an Islamic minaret, are carried in procession around town, then are heaved into the ocean. The *tabot* may be carried only by hereditary Tabot families, descendants of the Gurkah and Bengkulunese marriages. Huge prayer-drums *(beduk)*, made from the slats of coconut and breadfruit trees and covered with goat or cowskin, are beaten continuously throughout the ceremonies. No special costumes are worn, just beautiful clothes. The festival lasts 10 days, from the 1st to the 10th of Muharram of the Muslim calendar each year. The climax is on the 10th day with the closing Ceremony of Exile. Practiced only in Bengkulu and Pariaman (W. Sumatra), Bengkulu overflows with visitors from all over Sumatra who have come to participate in this authentic and much-loved folk event.

Shopping

Gold is about the only precious commodity you can buy at a reasonble price in this province. In fact, gold is all they have—native cloth, no folk arts of any sort. Buy gold for about Rp8000 per gram, plus Rp500 for some phantom fee. A fair gold store is **Toko Linda**, which sells clean 24-karat gold mined in the area. Many Chinese *toko mas* are also in the Kampung Cina area. Offered for sale also are fetching semi-precious stones such as agate, moon opals *(baiduri)*, for setting in rings.

Services

Change money at Bank Bumi Daya, around the corner from the post office; they could give a lousy rate because they must "pay the cost of the transaction in Jakarta," whatever that means. Rates are slightly less than in Jakarta. The post and telegraph offices are across from the domed Parr Monument. Swadaya Tours, Jl. J. Suprapto 67 (tel. 31331), can help with travel arrangements.

TRANSPORT

Getting There

Most buses on the Trans-Sumatran Hwy. take the paved 142-km Lubuklinggau-Curup-Bengkulu road; others take the 242-km Lahat-Pagar Alam-Bengkulu route, which is very rough in its middle section. Several bus companies run direct daily bus services to Bengkulu from the other Sumatran cities. From the N, Damri offers daily buses on the rough coastal road from Padang, 560 km, 20 hours, Rp9000. Access from the S is more difficult, but improving. A rough 60-km road connects Tanjung Sakti (just across the border in S. Sumatra Province) with Manna (S. Bengkulu District). From Danau Ranau or Krui would require some hiking or sea travel if crossing directly into S. Bengkulu. An economy-class train leaves every evening (2010) from Palembang, arriving the next morning (0600) at Lubuklinggau; from Lubuklinggau take the Curup bus, then from Curup take another bus down to Bengkulu.

A new port at Pulau Baai, 14 km S, handles larger boats. Cargo boats sail from Padang and Jakarta to Bengkulu and sometimes the regular Pelni Jakarta-Padang-Jakarta ship stops here. Check with the Pelni office and at the harbormaster's office next to the fort for sailing schedules and prices. Smaller *kapal motor* may call at P. Enggano on their way to or from Jakarta.

Garuda has daily flights from Jakarta, Rp66,500; from Palembang, Rp41,600. Merpati flies from: Padang (on Mon. and Wed.), Rp52,500; Jakarta (4 days weekly), Rp56,400; Palembang, Rp31,200; Telukbetung, Rp45,900; Muko-Muko, Rp24,000.

Getting Around

Bemo travel the main streets from their terminal in Pasar Minggu, Rp200. Or negotiate a ride in a horse cart. Across from Hotel Asia is a taxi company, Koperasi Jasa Angkutan Umum, Jl. Jen. A. Yani 329B (tel. 31901). Trips within town are Rp5000. To the airport or Pulai Baai (both 14 km from town), Rp6000. Bicycling, if you can borrow or rent one, is pleasant around Bengkulu, out to Lake Dendam Tak Sudah, or to the beach.

From Bengkulu

Small trucks and buses serve provincial towns from

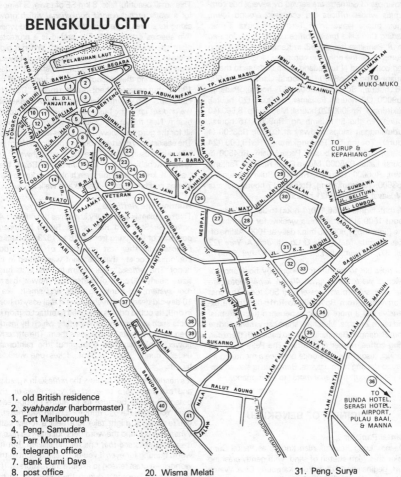

BENGKULU CITY

1. old British residence
2. *syahbandar* (harbormaster)
3. Fort Marlborough
4. Peng. Samudera
5. Parr Monument
6. telegraph office
7. Bank Bumi Daya
8. post office
9. police
10. Gading Cempaka Bus Co.
11. Hotel Aman
12. Pasar Ikan
13. Protestant church
14. Wisma Malabero
15. Gedung Daerah
16. RM Asia
17. Hotel Asia
18. Garuda Airlines
19. Wisma Rafflesia
20. Wisma Melati
21. Wisma Kenanga
22. Wisma Balai Buntar
23. RM Mirasa
24. Taxi Koperasi Jasa Angkutan Umum
25. Kiki Coffee Shop
26. RM Gembira
27. Pintu Batu Supermarket
28. Mesjid Djamik
29. Makam Sentot Alibasjah
30. Niaga Hotel
31. Peng. Surya
32. Peng. Damai
33. Pasar Minggu and local bus terminal
34. Balai Kota
35. Dena Hotel
36. Merpati Airlines
37. Hamilton Monument
38. Sukarno's House
39. tourist office
40. Pantai Panjang
41. Nala Beach Cottage

Terminal Lingka Timur, 9 km from town. The other provinces of Sumatra are served by several bus companies whose offices are scattered around town. Their buses leave from Terminal Lingka Timur. Gading Cempaka has an office conveniently located on Jl. Panjaitan (tel. 31993) in Kampung Cina. Damri seems to be the only bus company tackling the rugged coast road N to Padang. Sample fares to the N: Muara Bungo, Rp8500 (15 hours); Jambi, Rp12,500 (16 hours); Solok, Rp9000 (17 hours); Padang, Rp9000 (20 hours); Pariaman, Rp9000 (20 hours); Bukittinggi, Rp9000 (20 hours); Medan, Rp18,500 (40 hours). To the E: Palembang, Rp9000 (15 hours); Lubuklinggau (stops midway at Curup), Rp3500 (4 hours). To the S: Tanjungkarang, Rp10,000 (24 hours). Other daily buses: Pagar Alam, Rp4500 (6 hours); Lahat, Rp5000; Muara Enim, Rp5500; Tanjung Enim, Rp6000; Baturaja, Rp8000; Bukit Kemuning, Rp8500; Tanjungkarang, Rp9000 (17 hours); Jakarta (W. Java), Rp13,500 (21 hours).

Merpati flights (Rp56,400, 1 hour) to Jakarta leave at about 1500 at least 4 times weekly; for Palembang, one flight (Rp31,500, 45 min.) daily at 1000. Airline offices: Garuda, M.J. Assik & Co., Jl. Jen. A. Yani 922 (tel. 87); Merpati, Jl. Let. Suprapto 67 (tel. 31331).

It's possible to get up to Padang by boat once or twice a week. Only small 40-ton *kapal motor* are available, seldom any vessel over 500 tons. The cost is anywhere from Rp10,000 to Rp15,000 (more expensive but a more exotic experience than the bus) and takes 2 nights. Merchant ships carry merchandise from Padang to Bengkulu; you go back with them carrying coffee, rubber and rattan. The Pelni ship, KM *Kerinci*, also stops here once or twice a month on its way to Padang from Jakarta. Bengkulu is also an embarkation point for *kapal motor* to P. Enggano.

VICINITY OF BENGKULU

Pantai Panjang

Means "Long Beach." Also known as Pantai Cempaka, this 7-km stretch of sand, with gently crashing surf, begins just 1½ km from Kampung Cina. Watch fishing *prahu* go out at dusk. Food and drink are available from *warung* in a grove of beautiful native casuarina trees at the S end of Jl. Putri Gading Cempaka, 3 km from Kampung Cina. The small boat harbor is right in front of a crumbling English residence; just walk down the little lane to the L of the *warung* which leads to the ocean. **Pulau Tikus** ("Rat Island") is a small coral island 4 km W of Bengkulu's small boat harbor. Only 60 m x 100 m, it is inhabited by harmless gray snakes. Good swimming and snorkeling. Hire a boat for the day (Rp15,000) from the harbor. Bring food and drinking water.

Danau Dendam Tak Sudah

This small beautiful lake, 8 km SE of town, is famous for a water orchid *(vanda hookeriana)* which grows along its shores—the only place in the world where this species grows wild. The orchid is a protected plant species and may not be picked! When it blossoms in June/July and Oct., the lake is completely surrounded in brilliant pink! The English started to dam the lake during their occupation in the first half of the 19th C., but never finished; its name means "Dam Not Finished." No tourist facilities except makeshift *warung* set up in the busy seasons when the orchids bloom. Near the lake are cabanas where visitors may sit for the gorgeous view. Two routes lead to the lake. The easiest is by chartered taxi or a public taxi from the village of Dusun Besar. Take the main highway 7 km toward Kepahiang, turn L on Jl. Dusun Besar, then walk 1½ km. Or take the main highway 5 km toward Manna and turn L on Jl. Danau and walk 2½ km.

Hunting The *Rafflesia*

This rare plant is universally known as the *rafflesia Arnoldy*. Sir Stamford Raffles, the British lieutenant-governor of Bengkulu from 1818 to 1823, worked so tirelessly as the first president of the London Zoological Society that the plant was named in his honor. The *rafflesia's* main claim to fame is its huge size—nearly 100 cm in diameter. This "flower" has no root system, no trunk, no leafs, and smells like a 10-day-old dead rat (which makes it real easy to hone in on!). Its putrid odor is designed to attract carrion insects such as bees and unwary flies which fly inside, then the plant "eats" and digests them. The attractive flower, which spreads throughout the rainforests usually during Aug. or Sept., takes one week to bloom.

It's nearly impossible to grow the *rafflesia* in a garden, and extremely rare to ever set your eyes on this botanical classic because its locations change each year. You really have to hunt for it (with your nose). If you're lucky, it might take root near a forest path. When one is found the word gets out and you hike to it—the tourists see *that* one for the season. But it's worth hunting for even if you don't catch sight of this wonder—a great reason to explore the rainforest. The giant flower blossoms during the monsoon, so the morning when it's clear and cool is the best time to set out; it could be raining in the afternoon. The rain always starts in the mountains and works its way down to Bengkulu. One hint: the plant generally prefers to take hold below banyan trees.

The *rafflesia* has been known to grow in the areas of Pagar Gunung (Kepahiang), Lubuk Tapi, Tabah Penanjung, Bukittinggi in W. Sumatra and on Mt. Kinabalu in E. Malaysia. It's also found around Tebing Binjai, 45 km and Rp1500 from Bengkulu and 15 km SW of Kepahiang, deep in spectacular rainforest only 2 km up the mountain from the Tabah Penanjung restaurant. The only house between Tabah Penanjung and Kepahiang is at Tebing Binjai. Depart Bengkulu 0600, and arrive at Tebing Binjai at around 0730. Go down into a high-canopied primary rainforest of *meranti* trees with splayed trunks, strangler tendrils, wait-a-minute vines, giant ferns, termite mounds like giant cow-droppings, gigantic leaves 75 cm wide, and sniff the air. You should be able to smell it at 25 meters.

Tabah Penanjung is the official *rafflesia* reserve, protected by the government. A plaque here, found off the road, informs the hiker that the *rafflesia* is 4.2 km down one path and 3 km up another. A guide might be needed to show the way up and down hills through sections of *alang* and prickly grass as birds cry and wild pigs bolt away. Wear boots and long pants.

Curup

The district's main town and capital, 85 km NE of Bengkulu (Rp4000, 3 hours) on a spectacular 85-km paved road which climbs up through virgin primary forest to a high pass in the mighty Bukit Barisan Range. At some points along the way are glimpses of Bengkulu city and the Indian Ocean. One of the best views is from Tabah Penanjung restaurant, about 37 km from town. The road descends from the pass to Kepahiang, then follows the Musi River valley upstream to Curup. Stay at Wisma Bukit Kaba on Jl. Sukowati. Cheap vegetables are available and tea is grown nearby.

The **Suban Air Panas** thermal springs area, only 5 km N of town, can be reached by public bus or minibus. Stand under bamboo pipes which lead down from a mountain. The few hot water swimming pools here aren't too clean but people use them anyway. A 75-m-high waterfall is 6 km from Curup; ask for the *air terjun*. Near the bottom of the falls is an *air panas*. Sixteen km from Curup is **Pematang Danau**, a recreation area in the foothills on the highway between Bengkulu and Lubuklinggau. **Danau Tes**, a 7-km-long by 1 ½ -km-wide lake with a mountain panorama surrounded by traditional villages, is 50 km from Curup by public bus.

Bukit Kaba

Nineteen km from Curup, Bukit Kaba is an extensive sulphuric volcanic crater — an astonishing sight. At least 10 deadly eruptions have taken place since the mid-1800s. To climb it, depart from Curup and head for Kampung Bukit Kaba. Overnight in Sumber Urip, the remnants of an old plantation called Pematang Danau (on the N side of the mountain). From there, climbing to the top takes about 4 hours. Because there's no road, only schoolboys and scouts make this difficult climb through rattan and leeches. At the top, climb down into the volcano's 3 big craters.

NORTH BENGKULU

This district, stretching N from Bengkulu city to W. Sumatra Province, and mostly covered in tropical jungle, also boasts extremes of cold mountainous climes and luxurious, virtually unspoiled beaches. Dense forests extend from the high mountains clear down to the coast in many places. Villages, usually situated on a river, are often far apart. **Arga Makmur**, 80 km N of Bengkulu, is a center for the nearby *transmigrasi* communities and the district's main town. There is a *losmen*.

Ketaun

Two river trips can be made from Ketaun, 85 km N of Bengkulu. Take a motorized canoe 4 hours up Air Langi (a tributary of the lower Ketaun River) to Tanjung Dalam village. The **Lubuk Ismael** falls is 5 km farther. **Napal Putih** is 2-3 hours up the Ketaun River itself, Rp3500. From there a small railroad leaves about 0900 each day for **Lebong Tandai**, a gold mining area. The Aussies may let you take their train, a 2-hour trip. From Lebong Tandai it's possible to walk to **Muara Aman** and continue by road to **Lake Tes** and **Curup**. Guides will probably be needed for the walk.

Coastal Road To Padang

To see some of N. Bengkulu's deserted beaches and vast jungles, try this adventurous trip. It's about 300 km from Bengkulu city to the province's northern border, then another 250 km to Padang. Allow anywhere from 14 to 48 hours. Damri is the only regular bus company doing the whole run but local buses, Land Rovers, and trucks also carry paying passengers. The rainy season (Oct.-Feb.) could cause delays or close sections of the road; ask the bus drivers about conditions. Once you reach Mukomuko, frequent buses head N to Tapan and Padang.

Traveling N from Bengkulu, you can see the culture gradually change from Bengkulunese to Minangkabau. No *losmen* are on this route within the province but restaurants often put travelers up or you can stay in the Mess Pemda (accommodations normally kept for visiting government officials) in Lais. Ketaun, Ipuh, and Mukomuko. Most of the road is within sound of the surf but usually the ocean is separated by a grove of casuarina trees. Beautiful lonesome seascapes of beaches stretch to the horizon or low cliffs drop straight into the surf.

The following distances are from Bengkulu city: 28 km to **Kerkam**; the road for Arga Makmur turns off here. **Lais** is 49 km; at 56 km the asphalt runs out. From here on villages are often separated by long stretches of jungle, but you can still find Padang-style restaurants about every 40 km. **Pasar Desa I Ketaun** (80 km) is a Javanese village and market. In the logging town of **Ketaun** (85 km), at the mouth of the large Ketaun River, live the Pekal-Ketaun people. Javanese transmigrants are hacking at the jungle to build new farms and villages in the area.

Continuing on the coastal road, **Seblat** (124 km) is a large village on the Seblat River. **Air Rami** (148 km) has a long sweeping beach and a restaurant S of the village. **Ipuh** (161 km) is a small administrative town in two parts: Pasar Ipuh near the coast and Medan Jaya on the main road. Still heading N, the road turns inland, rejoining the coast about 20 km S of Mukomuko. Mukomuko (271 km) is a small town with an airstrip. Upriver on the Selagan River from Mukomuko are small riverine villages. From Mukomuko, by Damri bus to Padang, 10 hours, Rp5000; back to Bengkulu, 10 hours, Rp5500. **Lubuk Pinang** (307 km) is a small market village on the Menyut River and the last village before crossing into W. Sumatra Province. **Tapan** is 40 km beyond Lubuk Pinang.

ENGGANO ISLAND

Largest of a group of 6 islands in the Indian Ocean 274 km S of the Mentawais and 114 km off the SW coast of Sumatra, a subdistrict of N. Bengkulu District. Enggano is 29 km long by nearly 18 km wide, and the total area of the subdistrict, including its nearby islets, is 443 sq. km. It's made up of low, rolling hill country covered in secondary rainforest, while the coasts are swampy. In the center is the island's highest hill, Bua Bua (281 m). Buffalos, pigs, *banteng,* and many species of birds are found in the wild. The western monsoon lasts from Jan. to June, the southern monsoon from July to December.

Since 1961, Enggano has been a rehabilitation center for juvenile delinquents from Java. The island's chief commodity is Chinese-owned copra, exporting about 20 tons to Telukbetung each month. Coffee, pepper, and cloves are also cultivated. Good swimming along pristine coastline, with numerous coral sea gardens. There is no *losmen,* so stay with the police, local inhabitants, or on the ship.

History
Enganno's name means "disappointment" or "mistake" in Portuguese, probably referring to some ancient blunder in navigation. The island's Engganese name is *Soloppo,* or simply "the land," and its indigenous inhabitants call themselves *etaka,* or "human beings." Having been completely cut off from the outside world, the origins of the Engganese

BUSES FROM BENGKULU CITY

Town	Time	Fare
to the North:		
Muara Bungo	15 hours	Rp8500
Jambi	16 hours	Rp12,500
Solok	17 hours	Rp9000
Padang Panjang	18 hours	Rp9000
Padang	20 hours	Rp9000
Pariaman	20 hours	Rp9000
Bukittinggi	20 hours	Rp9000
Medan	40 hours	Rp18,500
to the East:		
Palembang	15 hours	Rp9000
Lubuklinggau, (stops midway at Curup)	4 hours	Rp3500
to the South:		
Tanjungkarang	24 hours	Rp10,000
Garuda Dempo's daily buses:		
Pagar Alam	6 hours	Rp4500
Lahat		Rp5000
Muara Enim		Rp5500
Tanjung Enim		Rp6000
Palembang	10 hours	Rp7500
Baturaja		Rp8000
Bukit Kemuning		Rp8500
Tanjungkarang	17 hours	Rp9000
Jakarta (W. Java)	21 hours	Rp13,500

BENGKULU

Rejang Lebong District: *An active volcano, hotsprings, waterfalls, lakes, and gold are found in this mountainous area around Curup (NE of Bengkulu City). Known for its long traditions of music, dancing, and poetry, the Rejang Lebong district has some 180,000 speakers of the Rejang dialect. Their poetry, written in the so-called ka-ga-nga script, is actually Old Malay (Melayu Purbo), derived from the court language of the medieval kingdom of Melayu. Rejang traditional literature includes love songs, incantations, spells, proverbs, maxims, and clan histories written on bamboo cylinders, barkcloth, buffalo horn, and rattan sticks. By 1962, there were only around 400 people who could still read this ancient script; today there are under ten.*

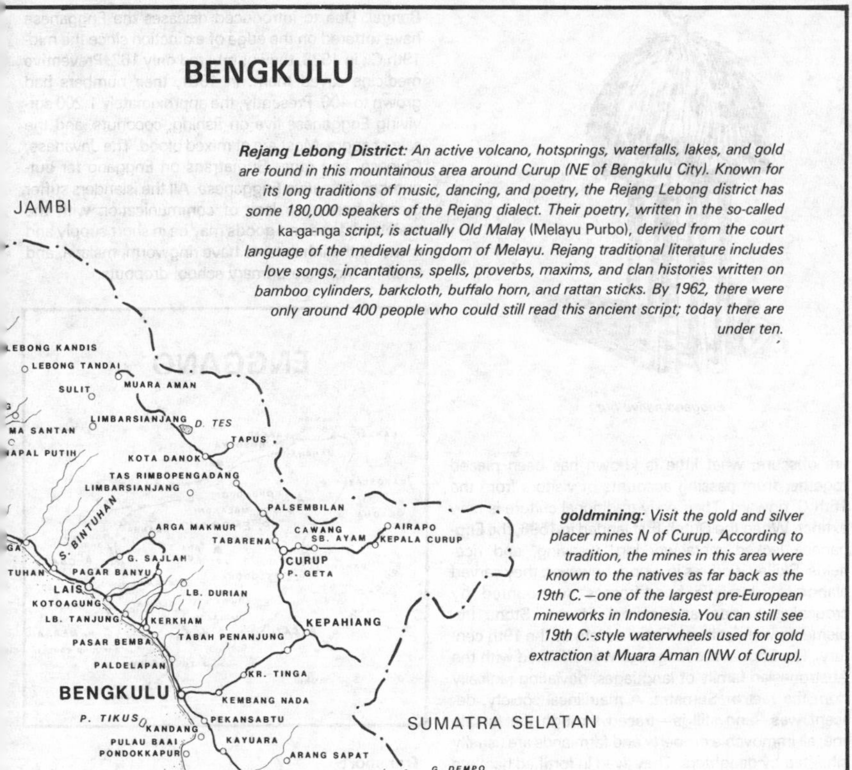

goldmining: *Visit the gold and silver placer mines N of Curup. According to tradition, the mines in this area were known to the natives as far back as the 19th C.—one of the largest pre-European mineworks in Indonesia. You can still see 19th C.-style waterwheels used for gold extraction at Muara Aman (NW of Curup).*

South Bengkulu District: *The Pasar Tala area, about 80 km S of Bengkulu city, is known for its weaving arts. Manna, another 80 km S and the district capital of S. Bengkulu, is served by regular bus (7 hours over a washboard road from Bengkulu). Stay at Wisma Amiko, Jl. Jen. Sudirman. A rich area for megaliths is the cool-altitude district of Pagaralam on the way E to Palembang. Farther S near Lampung and S. Sumatra Provinces is the beautiful 40-km-long Lake Ranau.*

JAMBI

LEBONG KANDIS
LEBONG TANDAI
MUARA AMAN
SULIT
LIMBARSIANJANG D. TES
MA SANTAN
APAL PUTIH
TAPUS
KOTA DANOK
TAS RIMBOPENGADANG
LIMBARSIANJANG
S. BINTUHAN
ARGA MAKMUR
G. SAJLAH
TABARENA
PALSEMBILAN
CAWANG
SB. AYAM
AIRAPO
KEPALA CURUP
TUHAN
PAGAR BANYU
LAIS
KOTOAGUNG
LB. DURIAN
CURUP
P. GETA
LB. TANJUNG
KERKHAM
PASAR BEMBA
TABAH PENANJUNG
KEPAHIANG
PALDELAPAN
KR. TINGA
BENGKULU
KEMBANG NADA
P. TIKUS KANDANG
PEKANSABTU
PULAU BAAI
KAYUARA
PONDOKKAPUR
ARANG SAPAT
SUMATRA SELATAN
G. DEMPO
TAIS
TUMBUHAN
NGALAM
PENANDINGAN
INDIAN OCEAN
KUNDURAN
AIR TERUS
PASAR SELUMA
PASAR TALA
LB. TAP
PASARALAS
SELATI
MASAT
GLUMBANG
MANNA
GN. KAYAT
GN. KAYAT
TAL. PADANG
PADANG GUCI
TG. ALAM
TG. KEMUNING
AWAL MATA
BENUARATU
SUKAMARINOU
BINTUHAN
TG. AGUNG
BARULANGUN
TEBING RAMBUTAN

0   40 km

Enggano native hut

Bengal. Due to introduced diseases the Engganese have tottered on the edge of extinction since the mid-19th C.; in 1928, they numbered only 162. Preventive medicine saved them. In 1961, their numbers had grown to 400. Presently, the approximately 1,200 surviving Engganese live on fishing, coconuts, and the sale of copra. Most are of mixed blood. The Javanese, Chinese, and other Sumatrans on Enggano far outnumber the native Engganese. All the islanders suffer greatly from their lack of communication with the mainland; food and goods may be in short supply and many of the inhabitants have ringworm, malaria, and anemia. Most are primary school dropouts.

are obscure; what little is known has been pieced together from passing accounts of visitors from the 16th C. onward. Their early traditional culture is now extinct. When the Dutch first landed in 1596, the Engganese lacked metal-working, weaving, and ricefields. Skilled workers in wood, however, they carved elaborate women's headdresses surmounted by crouching human and animal figures. Stone implements were still used here as late as the 19th century. The Engganese language was affiliated with the Austronesian family of languages, deviating radically from the rest of Sumatra. A matrilineal society, descent was — and still is — traced through the female line; all immovable property and farmlands are usually inherited by daughters. They lived in fortified hamlets of circular beehive houses raised on piles. The entrance to each house was an elliptical hole in the wall just large enough for a man to crawl through. Villages used to dot the coast. Now only 15 remain, most concentrated on the narrow plains near the sea.

People

Engganese are thought to be a mixture of the Veddoid race of S. India and Proto-Malays from mainland Sumatra. One theory is that they descended from aboriginal Sumatrans who fled when Malaysian peoples began to arrive on the mainland; this helps explain the slight Hindu influence in their culture. Also, a striking physical similarity corresponds to the Nicobarese of the Nicobar Islands in the Bay of

Transport

Catch a *kapal motor* or ship from Bengkulu or Bintuhan to Malakoni, Enggano's largest town and harbor. Boats out to Enggano are not that frequent and you could end up waiting up to a week. The 500-ton *Bragasena* sails once monthly from Bengkulu; Rp17,500, 1 night. Unfortunately, this ship returns the very next day. Of course, another option is to stay a month until the next time the *Bragasena* calls, giving you a chance to really study the *adat*. The villages of Enggano — Meok and Kaanna on the E coast, Pahanuma in the W, Banjar Sari in the N, and Malakoni in the S — are all connected by dirt tracks first cleared by the Japanese in WW II. There are few vehicles and walking or by bicycle are the principal means of getting around.

JAMBI

This E coast province (pop. 1.3 million) faces the Straits of Melaka. The province's highest peak, G. Kerinci (3,800 m), is the source of Sumatra's longest river, the Batanghari. As a result of the river and *transmigrasi* schemes, many racial groups have settled in the region. In the western part of the province are large oil survey camps managed by Caltex, Jambi Oil Co., and Japex; mineral exploration and production, plus rubber and timber, bring in the principal revenues.

Fauna
Here is one of your best chances to see Sumatran wildlife; take a week just to concentrate on game watching. The hundreds of elephants of eastern Sumatra are the world's smallest, more related to the Indian elephant than to the African. Tigers sometimes even wander in from the lush jungle nearby and carry off domestic animals and careless children. Jambi Province is the region of the "Tiger Man" (or *cigau*) who changes into a tiger at night and becomes a man-eater. There have also been reported "sightings" in the western regions of the mysterious *orang pendek* (a hairy, very strong 1.5-m hominid), and strange *kuda liar* or wild horses, both of which terrify the populace. If you're going to do some jungle trekking, get hold of a *stanis stia* (stainless steel ring) to keep the tigers away.

JAMBI

Capital city of the province, Jambi is a thriving river port on the Batanghari River about 200 km N of Palembang. Its population (165,000) is ethnically very mixed: Minangkabau, Chinese, Sundanese, Javanese, Batak, Arab, Indian, Pakistani, Japanese, Malaysian, Kubu. Jambi is a connecting point for ships and *prahu*, usually carrying timber, traveling down the Batanghari to Jakarta and the Outer Islands. This small city has a very high rainfall.

Sights
Jambi has an unusual mosque with stained-glass windows. There's also a university and library: Universitas Negeri Jambi, on Jl. Diponegoro 16. A trip on the Batanghari River in a motorized dugout canoe or any other weird rivercraft is a fascinating experience. Walk along the waterfront; take a narrow sampan across the river to visit the orthodox Muslim village on the other side, Olak Kemang. See the Sriwijaya

dance, and a local "maypole" version in which colored ribbons are wound together by dancers who then untangle them perfectly; sometimes dances are held at Jambi's Gedung Nasional.

Practicalities
Hotels average Rp2500. **The Mustika**, Jl. Sultan Agung 31 (tel. 24672), is 2 km from the bus terminal on the W side of town; big beds but small rooms. In the town's center, the **Sumatera** and the **Jelita** are cheaper but reputed to be unfriendly. **Ambassador Hotel** (Rp15,000 s) is also central; just ask the taxi drivers where it is. **Hotel Makmur**, Jl. Cut Nyak Dien 14 (tel. 22324), charges Rp3000-4000 d. **The Wisata Hotel** asks Rp15,000 s; some rooms are a/c and breakfast is included in the room rate, no dining facilities, comfortable beds, clean. **Hotel Rinang**, Jl. Dr. Sutomo 9, is another a/c hotel. **Hotel Makassar** on the road in from the airport, has a/c. The **Governor's Guest House** is the best place to stay in Jambi, with several clean, a/c rooms, and excellent Indonesian food. Plenty of Padang-style food in the *rumah makan* and a couple of Chinese coffee shops in the downtown shopping area. The **Pagi Sore Restaurant** has good Indonesian food. Go to the **Terkenal Restaurant** for Chinese food.

Garuda and Merpati fly from Jakarta in one hour, plus Palembang, Medan, etc. Jambi is accessible by a long bus ride from Palembang and even on riverboats (see p. 498).

FROM JAMBI

By Air
Airlines offices: Garuda, Jl. Dr. Wahidin (tel. Otomat 220/22041/22303); Merpati, Jl. Damar 55 (tel. 22184). Sample fares: Jakarta, Rp75,000; Padang, Rp65,250; Palembang, Rp35,500. Also check out the SMAC and the Pertamina airline, Pelita, which offers charter flights (Singapore, etc.).

By Bus
Frequent bus service to Palembang, Padang, and Bukittinggi. Daily buses to Palembang cost Rp4500-5000, including river ferries. On this run sometimes you have to get out and walk a km or so while the bus is pulled by winches, or help repair the bridge planking so that the bus can cross. Another way to get to Palembang is take a *bemo* to Bayunglincir for Rp1500, then from there a riverboat for Rp7500 down

to Palembang. For Bukittinggi or Padang, take ANS for Rp6500. For Lake Kerinci, take a bus first to Bangko (Rp5000), then another night bus across the mountainous jungles of southcentral Sumatra to Sungaipenuh for Rp4000.

By Boat

Catch a riverboat or motorized dugout up the Batanghari, all the way to Sungaidaerah; expect to pay Rp7000-10,000 for this slow hot trip; more boats are available for this downstream trip in the wet season. At Jambi's riverfront you can also find boats to Jakarta, Singapore, and Banten. Other sample river bus fares from Jambi: to Nipah Panjang (160 km), Rp5000; Kuala Simpang (90 km), Rp2500; Sei Puding (101 km), Rp3000; Kp. Laut (187 km), Rp5000.

Bayunglincir-Palembang River Trip

An adventuresome way to get to Palembang from Jambi is by ferry. First, take the Rp1500 bus ride S to Bayunglincir. The boat is supposed to leave once or twice a week, so you might have to wait in Bayunglincir up to three days (this is when your bookbag comes in handy). There is no *losmen* in this drab place so either stay in the *warung* closest to the river or you might be able to sleep on the boat. The river on which you journey goes out to the sea and then winds its way upriver to Palembang, taking two nights and one day (30 hours) in a 10-m-long boat, Rp7000, with three meals a day (often fresh crayfish at Rp1000 per kilo). The water is yellow and heavy with mud; navigation must be cautious because of the ever-changing banks. Go past river whorehouses on stilts, monkeys swinging in trees, giant hornbills flapping up from the bush like B-29 bombers. Shine your torch at night into the swamps and you might see the glowing red eyes of crocodiles. The trip itself is not very comfortable because the boat rocks, you're squeezed in with all the cargo, and the benches are too hard. The experience is unforgettable — once it's over.

LAKE KERINCI

Situated in a 70-km-long mountain valley with several hundred villages scattered around the principal town, Sungaipenuh; this is Jambi's tourist area, with volcanos, hotsprings, cinnamon trees, and the lake (no swimming). The scenery is beautiful, especially around the crater lake of G. Tujuh (1,996 m). To the NE G. Kerinci (3,800 m) is a spectacular volcanic cone and the highest mountain in the whole Greater Sunda Is. chain.

The surrounding mountains, especially in the west, collect rain throughout the year, and the highest peaks are often cloud-covered except in the morning. The valley around Sungaipenuh — in spite of its name, "Full River" — has a dry climate, lying in the rain shadow of the mountains both to the E and the west. However it gets pretty wet from Oct. to Dec. and in April, when road travel can be difficult.

Getting There

Lake Kerinci can be reached faster from Padang than from Jambi; the Kerinci District goes by the name SUNGAIPENUH on bus signs. Sungaipenuh, the main town in this area, lies about 60 km up in the mountains from Tapan which is about halfway (150 km plus) between Padang and Bengkulu. ALS does the trip, but Habeko is recommended. They use real buses (Mercedes) which have glass windows, and rarely stop en route. Buses depart each direction at 0800 or 0900 (Rp7500). From Padang to Sungaipenuh takes 12-14 hours, departing 0900 and 1500, a scenic drive on a good road along the coast and through small villages. **from Jambi:** First get a direct bus (several times daily) to Bangko, Rp6000, driving part way on the constantly improving Trans-Sumatran Highway. In Bangko, the best place to eat is at Restaurant Minang Soto. From Bangko, take the night bus to Sungaipenuh (Rp3500), departing 1700-1900 for a chilly 6-hour journey over the mountains. There are also flights from Jambi to Sungaipenuh twice a week on SMAC Britten-Norman 9-seater planes.

SUNGAIPENUH

This small dirty town sits in the middle of a broad, lush valley of rich green rice paddies surrounded by a ring of mountains, tea plantations, and small farms growing cinnamon, cloves, coffee (Rp1500 per kg in town), and tobacco. Sungaipenuh is as yet undeveloped for Western tourists. In town there's a large *mesjid* constructed in the pagoda-style; a mosque has been occupying this site, legend has it, since the 16th century. Inside are large carved wood beams and Dutch Delft tiles.

Accommodations And Food

You might have to report to the police station if the hotel owner asks you to. The proprietors of **Hotel Jaya** and **Hotel Anak Gunung**, each Rp2500 s, Rp3500 d, speak English and Dutch and can help you get around. **Hotel Mata Han** is nicer at Rp4000-5000. There are good restaurants along the L side going up the main street (the one with the center divider). Try the specialty of the area, smoked grilled steak *(dending batokok),* the Kerinci form of *satay.*

Vicinity Of Sungaipenuh

Check out the possibility of renting a bicycle or motorbike to the lake, otherwise take a bus or *oplet* to Sanggaranagung, walk some, then flag another back to town. Or take a minibus tour around the entire lake.

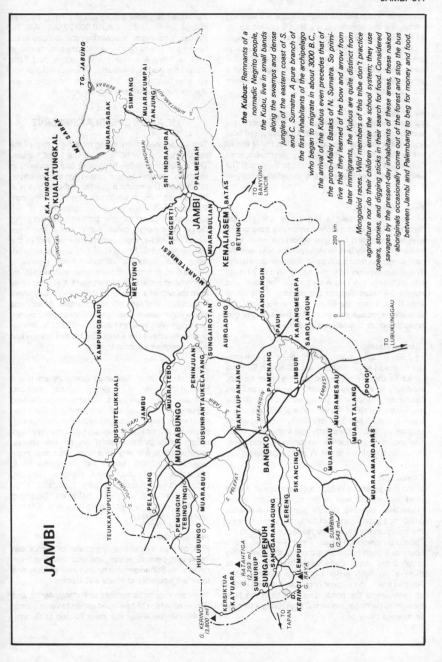

JAMBI

the Kubus: Remnants of a nomadic Negrito people, the Kubu, live in small bands along the swamps and dense jungles of the eastern coast of S. and C. Sumatra. A pure branch of the first inhabitants of the archipelago who began to migrate in about 3000 B.C., the arrival of the Kubus even precedes that of the proto-Malay Bataks of N. Sumatra. So primitive that they learned of the bow and arrow from later immigrants, the Kubus are quite distinct from Mongoloid races. Wild members of this tribe don't practice agriculture nor do their children enter the school system; they use spears, stones, and digging sticks in their search for food. Considered savages by the present-day inhabitants of these areas, these naked aboriginals occasionally come out of the forest and stop the bus between Jambi and Palembang to beg for money and food.

0   200 km

Nearby at Dusun Sungai Tetung village is a weaving center. To the hotsprings it's Rp200 or less for an 11-km ride past Sumurup to the AIR PANAS sign, then walk in the last km. The public bath is free; huge private room is Rp200. Boil eggs or bananas in the central pool, which is too hot for bathing, and eat a pineapple for only Rp200 (the locals think pineapples are low class).

Kayo Aro

Near the hotsprings, the Kayo Aro Tea Plantation is well worth visiting for a tour of its factory; see how your daily beverage is produced. It's at the N end of the valley, 42 km (Rp1000) by jeep/*oplet* from Sungaipenuh on the beautiful road to Kersiktua. The entire product of this estate is exported directly to Europe.

From Sungaipenuh

In good weather take a real jungle ride 160 km (Rp4000, Rp4750 for a more comfortable front seat) E over the mountains (low gear almost the whole way) to Bangko. A daily bus service operates now, and the narrow asphalt road is a once-in-a-lifetime experience. The diesel minibus does the trip in about 12 hours, not including the uncounted stops for food and maybe 3-4 hours sleep at the roadside if the driver feels like it. Watch the 15-cm-long mantis catch flies at roadside restaurants. From Bangko, take the bus on to Jambi, or S down to Lubuklinggau.

Gunung Kerinci

At 3,800 m, this volcano is the highest on Sumatra, the source of innumerable rivers. Although Sumatra is not as densely populated as Java, near Kerinci, especially on the N and S sides, are heavily populated farmlands. The cone is young and bare, while the main crater lies NE of the remnants of the Berapi/Elok crater system (3,649-3,655 m). Kerinci's crater, which erupted in 1934, is filled with yellowish-green water. The mountain is squeezed in between even older mountain complexes to the W and to the east.

Climbing It

In the first ascent in 1878, it took van Hasselt a solid week to hack his way to the top and back again. Nowadays, climbers usually start from Kersiktua (1500 m), a small village S of the peak, 5 km farther up the mountain from Koya Aru tea factory, right on the Padang-Sungaipenuh road. From Kersiktua it's 8 hours to a bush hut, then 4 more to the summit—a tough 2-day climb. Carry water from Kersiktua as there is no fresh water higher up the mountain. Another trail to the summit originates from the village of Timbulan to the north. This hike from the N is thought to be longer, perhaps 3 days. Bring a tent for an overnight stay on G. Kerinci.

Kersiktua has guides to take you to the top, but they charge anything from Rp10,000-20,000. Ask for Paiman, who seems trustworthy; you can stay in his house too. If you don't want to pay that much, go back to Koya Aru, visit the tea factory, and hang around the market. Eventually, someone will pick you up who might guide you up the mountain in exchange for goodwill and English practice.

THE KERINCI-SEBLAT RESERVE

This big reserve covers a lengthy 345-km strip of the mountainous spine of Sumatra, the Bukit Barisan. The enclave spans the borders of four provinces in southern Sumatra (which makes for administrative difficulties). The northern quarter of the reserve is in W. Sumatra through which you pass on the ride from Padang to Sungaipenuh. Sungaipenuh is the jumping-off point for the high-altitude marsh of Danau Bentu (also called Sangir Hulu), and from which the wilder, more remote southern half of the reserve around G. Seblat (2,363 m) can be explored, using local footpaths. Altitude of the reserve is 50-3,800 m, but most of the reserve is above 400 m, welcome after the heat of the coasts. If you get away from the settled areas around the Kerinci Valley, there is excellent lowland, hill and montane forest, and alpine vegetation on the highest slopes, with a correspondingly wide variety of animal and bird life. The extensive forests of the Kerinci-Seblat area are the last such in southern Sumatra.

Fauna

Most of the larger Sumatran mammals are found here: rhino, tiger, tapir, *serow, sambar,* elephant, clouded leopard, sun bears, *siamang,* long-tailed and pig-tailed macaque, as well as the endemic Sumatran short-eared rabbit, *Nesolagus netscheri,* a burrowing, nocturnal animal hardly ever seen and the only lagomorph native to Indonesia. There are also cobras, monitor lizards, and very large toads—but no orangutans. Birds of the reserve include egrets, kites, pheasants, junglefowl, doves, pigeons, cuckoos, coucals, owls, bulbuls, barbets, broadbills, kingfishers, fantails, wagtails, babblers, laughing thrushes, crows, orioles, drongos, and 5 different species of hornbill!

Practicalities

PPA officials in Padang, Bengkulu, or Jambi can assist with permits, advice, and local traveling information. In Sungaipenuh one can hire guides, and there are a number of hotels and *losmen.*

There are regular air services to Padang, Jambi, and Bengkulu, which all have road access to various parts of the reserve. Buses run from Padang to Sungaipenuh via Painan and Tapan, a scenic route along the W coast, or via the inland highland route from Bangko. From Bengkulu and Curup (S of the reserve), roads branch W of the reserve to Tambang Sawah (tracks from here to G. Seblat) and E of the reserve via Lubuklinggau N to Trawas and Bangko. From Jambi, it is also possible to fly to Sungaipenuh. See "Kerinci Lake" above for further info.

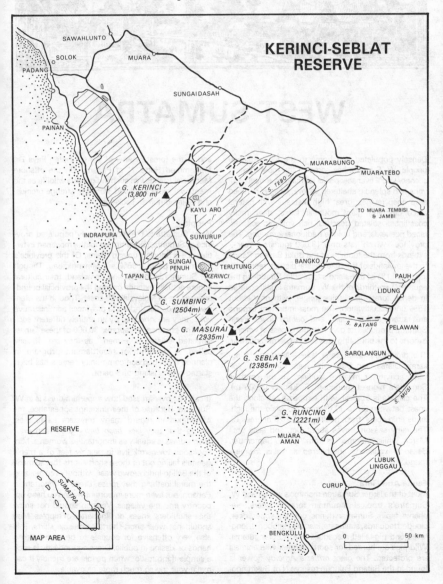

KERINCI-SEBLAT RESERVE

WEST SUMATRA

Densely populated and home to the Minangkabau people, W. Sumatra has some of the most exciting scenery you'll ever see: peaks looming over deep canyons and splendid sheltered valleys, villages perched atop deep ravines, great high plateaus with natural air-conditioning, giant mountain lakes, steep rocky coastlines, isolated beaches, rich volcanic soil, terraced ricefields, and unique traditional *kampung*. The province—which gets only 18,000 tourists a year—extends from the foothills of the Bukit Barisan Range to the lowlands of the Riau coastal district, representing only 11% of the island's total area. Straddling the equator, two-thirds of the W. Sumatra is still covered in dense forests and thick jungle, with only about 15% under cultivation. The most important exports are rattan, timber, resin, and *gambir* (dye). West Sumatra produces its own rice, the excess of which it exports to the bordering provinces of Jambi and Riau.

The province's deep crater lakes—Maninjau, Singkarak, Diatas, and Dibawah—were formed by volcanic activity or massive faulting. To the south is Sumatra's highest mountain, G. Kerinci (3,805 m). The climate is tropical, with temperatures along the coast between 28 to 30 degrees C., while the highlands enjoy cool, fresh healthy air (22-26 degrees C). The rainy season arrives about Oct. and lasts until March, while "summer" is from April to September. Seasonal variations are blurred as rains fall year round.

Fauna And Flora

Most of the larger Sumatran mammals still inhabit W. Sumatra's tropical mountain forests: tigers, elephants, tapirs, Sumatran rhinos, goat antelopes, deer, clouded leopards, sun bears, *siamang* (gibbons), long-tailed and pig-tailed macaques (but no orangutans). Wild pigs are hunted for sport; all other wild animals are protected. The giant *rafflesia Arnoldy* flower is found in the Batang Palupuh reserve N of Bukittinggi

and in the forest reserve of Taman Hutan Raya Dr. Mohammed Hatta, N of Padang. On the offshore Mentawai Islands live such indigenous wildlife as the Mentawai monkey, dwarf *siamang,* strange orchids, and isolated human societies.

People

West Sumatra is the most densely populated province of Sumatra, concentrated for the most part in fertile, rice-producing upland plains. Of this province's 3.7 million people, 95% are Minangkabau. Though W. Sumatra is the Minang homeland, their cultural sphere actually extends beyond the provincial boundaries, as far as Malaysia's W coast. Though the Mentawai Islands fall under the provinces administrative yoke, they are inhabited by an entirely different society. The province has approx. 30,000 of these "unassimilated isolated tribesmen," as they are officially called. A government resettlement program in planned multi-purpose community centers has been started on the island of Siberut.

It can't be overstressed how important dress is in W. Sumatra. Because of their unkempt appearance, the Minangkabau regard many travelers as hippies, saying that they lack *baso basi* "good manners." Men's dress is equally as important as women's. Minangkabau townsfolk live in deathly fear of a man's genitals falling out of those short-shorts that so many of the Bali-to-India crowd wear, without even realizing the moral loathing they rouse. Dress is important in Padang, but even more important when you head upcountry into the villages. Women should not show their shoulders, knees, or silhouettes of nipples. Men should not wear short-shorts or muscle shirts. It is also very offensive for couples to be seen holding hands or kissing in public. Dressing modestly is such a simple thing to do; when people are friendly it can make your trip so much more enjoyable.

THE MINANGKABAU

Adjacent to Batak territory in W. Sumatra is the land of the Minangkabau people, remarkable for their unique matrilineal society. The Minangkabau have a level of political and social equality unique in SE Asia. Although sometimes called *Orang Padang*, they are an interior, not a coastal, people. West Sumatra is almost entirely ethnic Minangkabau, who comprise about ¼ of Sumatra's total population of 14 million and are the 4th largest ethnic group in Indonesia. The traveler sees their influence most visibly in the spicy cuisine served at Padang restaurants everywhere. Most Minang are farmers who live in small independent villages. The rest are skilled traders who live in or near the towns. Due to the rich soil of the ricefields, their villages are prosperous. They are easy-going, peaceful, self-confident, hard working, and shrewd commercially—the only ethnic group that can compete successfully with the Chinese in Jakarta. Fervent Muslims, they are one of the best educated and most vigorous peoples in the whole country; many of the nation's intellectuals and leading authors are Minangkabau.

Adat

This ethnic group is famous for its matrilineal and matrilocal social system. Minangkabau queens are still celebrated in many old legends such as *Kaba Cinda Mata* (the formal narration of which can take 17 evenings). Even afterlife beliefs are mother-oriented, reflected in the saying "Heaven is below the sole of mother's foot" (i.e., you won't get to heaven if you mistreat your mother). All decisions are made in a democratic manner. Little squabbling occurs in the Minang way of life as everything is ruled by strict *adat*, with consensus the basic principle. The culture of the coastal towns of W. Sumatra, such as Pariaman and Painan, although bearing the stamp of Minangkabau *adat*, has always followed a strongly modified form of the *adat* practiced in the interior. Their traditional cultures tend to be more male-oriented and aristocratic, and less democratic.

Descent And Inheritance

In this strong matrilineal society, probably the largest in the world, titles, inherited property, and family names are handed down through the same female line generation after generation. Here a man's children are not his heirs. Instead, he is bound to leave his possessions to the children of his eldest sister. His nephews and nieces are therefore his *kamanakan*, "those who inherit." The grandmother is the grand matriarch, though her eldest brother or first son is now considered the family representative. Relatives

from the mother's side hold the weight in family politics. Houses are very much the domain of women. Daughters usually inherit the property which is worked collectively, and own the shops. All inherited property through the mother's line belongs to her children. The matrilineage persists through generations.

Clans

Like the Batak, there are clans *(kaum)* in Minangkabau society such as Tanjung, Melayu, Chaniago, Jambak, etc. All the children bear the clan name of their mother. Membership in a clan, the right to use its land, and the right to be given a clan title, is transmitted by the mother's or grandmother's brother. The family consists of a *saparuik* ("people of the same womb")—mothers, their offspring, and their brothers. Descendants of an ancestral mother live together in one house; in the highlands, up to 30 members can still be found living under a single roof. Each clan has a chief, called *penghulu* or *datuk*, who is chosen among the brothers of certain families. The *penghulu* settles clan disagreements or quarrels before it goes to the civil courts. When a *penghulu* dies or is too old to lead his people, the title passes to his first nephew or one of his brothers.

Marriage

The woman's family generally initiates the marriage proposal, though if a man has his eye on someone, his family may propose also. The only restriction is that the spouse is from a different *suku* or clan. In rural and coastal areas there may even be a groom price. The bride doesn't leave home at all: the husband moves in with her. After the wedding, the bridegroom is escorted to the home of his bride, proudly taking with him all his possessions or his workshop to prove that he is a man of substance. After marriage, the man will spend most of his time at his sister's house, working and eating there, returning to his wife's house only at night. Men seen loitering around their in-law's place are considered lazy. Today, the men assume more responsibility for their own families. Much of the old ways are changing now; in the big towns, married couples spend a symbolic few nights at the mother's house and then go live in their own.

Uncles

Once, it would seem, men were used mainly for procreation, ceremony, and labor. In the past, when a boy was about 10 years old, he would move out of his mother's house and into a *surua* (prayer house) to live and study cooking, martial arts, and the Koran. The mother's brother would then become the father figure for her children. A child is regarded as a member of the mother's family group; the father's group regards the child as purely a blood relative without any rights of inheritance. Thus, the important male figure in the family is not the father but the mother's brother. This doesn't mean that male privileges are non-existent or that a man is free from his responsibilities toward his own family, however; his guidance and wisdom is very much sought. A Minang proverb sums it up: *Anak dipangku, kemanakan dibimbing.* ("Put your own children on your lap, but give guidance to your nephews and nieces.") The mother's brothers are refered to as *minik namak,* and the eldest among them is called *tungganai.* The *minik namak* is responsible for the harmony and welfare of the brothers and sisters, nephews and nieces as well as for the safety of family property. The real father stays out of family affairs and the *mamak* replaces the father and gives advice on business deals and marrying off the children. The *mamak* is also responsible for the education of his sister's children, while his wife's brother is responsible for the education of his own children.

Merantau

The central area of the Minangkabau culture, a group of fertile valleys surrounding 3 imposing volcanos (G. Merapi, G. Sago, and G. Singgalang), is known as the *darek.* Because of rapid population growth, this central homeland area has expanded along the W coast around Padang and into much of the swampy lowlands extending toward the E coast. These areas outside the *darek* are called *rantau,* originally meaning "outer reaches or frontier" but now referring to any area where one goes out in the world to seek his fortune. Thus the word *merantau* today means "to go abroad"—a vital part of Minangkabau custom. From time immemorial Minangkabau men have had to leave the *darek* to do business, for scholastic study, or to seek more land or opportunities.

There's really not that much to keep a man down on the farm except to wait politely until a girl or her family asks for his hand in marriage through an intermediary. Then, all he looks forward to is a life of working on his mother-in-law's farm under the watchful scrutiny of his *mamak* (brother-in-law). With so little industrial development and population pressure constantly increasing, half the Minangkabau males are driven from the Man's World of Java. In the past, men would leave the village for 3-12 months, returning to their families with money and commodities—and worldly tales of fame, fortune, and adventure. But since the 1950s more and more are settling permanently elsewhere, and today men often take their families with them. This spontaneous mass migration has resulted in the Minangkabau population of Jakarta being greater today than that of

Padang itself. Minangkabaus are found in pockets throughout this whole island nation, as well as in Malaysia and Singapore. Most still retain their *adat* and many Minang men have achieved high status as national figures. An important segment of the leadership of modern Indonesia today is ethnically Minangkabau.

Spirits And Magic

Although strong believers in Allah, many spirits are indigenous to this area: *Urang Jadi-jadian* can become tigers; *cindaku* are human-appearing monsters like Dracula who suck people's blood and eat naughty children; *cindai* are beautiful women with long flowing hair who laugh eerily; *palasik* make children sickly and weak. Crystalized elephant sperm is an especially powerful ingredient for use in love potions. On the side of good, *dukun* specialize in massage, muscular disorders, and organ displacement, using a wide range of medicinal herbs and foods. Visit Bukittinggi's market (Wed. and Sat.) which has probably the weirdest collection of magicians, charlatans, electrotherapists, acupuncturists, drugsellers, chanting Muslim holymen, and snake oil merchants in the whole of Indonesia!

HISTORY

The Legends

The Minang attribute their origin to Adam's youngest son, who married a nymph from paradise and begat Iskander Zulkarnain (reported in some versions to be Alexander the Great). His 3rd son, Maharaj Diraja, sailed to G. Merapi when the rest of Sumatra was still submerged in water. There he started the first matrilineal clan. As the water receded, the people spread out into what is now the interior of W. Sumatra. Some say the word Minangkabau derives simply from *pinang kabhu* meaning "original home,"—their earliest homeland. Another legend has it that their name means "Victorious Buffalo" *(minang* and *kerbau),* alluding to a legendary fight with the Javanese. The chiefs of the Javanese and Minangs decided to settle the issue with a fight between 2 *kerbau.* The Minangs cunningly starved a calf for 10 days, bound a sharp iron spike to its nose, and set it free to run enthusiastically for the belly of the Javanese buffalo whom it thought was its mother. The starving calf, frantically trying to suckle, gorged its adversary to death. To this day, roofs of houses and some women's headdresses are shaped like buffalo horns. Another key myth of this matriarchal society is the legend of *Kaba Cinda Mato,* a sort of apologia for a woman ruler, Bundo Kanduang, and defines Minangkabau rules of behavior and society. Mother-oriented legends abound: *Sabai Nan Aluih* is a popular story of a young heroine who shoots her father's murderer when her brother refuses out of cowardice.

Hinduism

The Hindu-Malay Kingdom of Minangkabau rose in the 12th-14th centuries after the decay of the Sriwijaya Empire to the E, when Indian cultural influences began to spread into the highlands. The imprint of this Brahmanic Indian civilization is still evident in a wide range of present-day features: a multitude of Hindu loan words, Indian-style script, agricultural skills, methods of political organization, even remains of Hindu-Buddhist monuments. The royal court sat at Pagarruyung; the first royal village was Pariangan. These kings had no strong authority except to settle disputes; they were more symbolic unifiers of the *Alam Minangkabau* ("Minangkabau World"). They also organized extensive trade and commerce with the outside world. Tin and pepper were major exports. The Minangkabau have also had a long history of brassworking, plus mining, smelting, processing and forging weapons and farm tools out of iron and steel. They used cannons and bored matchlocks long before Europeans arrived.

Advent Of Islam

Eventually, small Muslim states ruled by sultans became powerful in Sumatra, gradually forcing the Minang Kingdom into the central regions where it hung onto its independence and culture until 1825. By the time the first Europeans landed, the area was entirely under Islamic influence. Between 1820-1837 a violent struggle in Minangkabau regions raged, with the Dutch and the traditional *adat* chiefs and the Minangkabau royal family on one side, and the Padris on the other. The Padris were ultra-orthodox religious extremists who tried to purify the Islam of the area by eliminating such widespread pre-Islamic customs as gambling and drinking. In this prolonged and bloody rebellion, the Padris annihilated virtually the entire royal bloodline. A religious and political leader, Tuanku Iman Bonjol, along with his Padri defenders held out until the last fortress fell at Bonjol and the Padris' power was at last checked. Songs, poems, and books have been written about this folk hero. Since the fall of the Padris, Islam has grown—like the Hinduism of Bali—into a fervent community religion.

Today, the Minangkabau ardently embrace both Islam and their female-oriented *adat,* and have tried to synchronize the two. The area is one of the most staunchly Islamicized regions in Indonesia—most of the people actually *do* pray 3-5 times a day. But at the same time, these people are known for their very strict adherence to local customs, a system which would appear in direct opposition to Islamic law. For example, it's rare that a Minangkabau husband will have more than one wife even though Islam allows him up to four. And even though women have a strong voice they still remain modestly dressed. Being Islamic and matrilineal may seem contradic-

tory, but it is this blend that makes the culture so intriguing.

ARCHITECTURE

Minangkabau architecture is some of the most magnificent in all of Indonesia. As seen on new government offices and public buildings on Java, this unique architecture has even had a great influence on modern Indonesian architecture. The peaked, swooping roofs of many Minang buildings are reminiscent of the curved horns of the revered water buffalo and of the women's ceremonial headdress. Traditional houses are disappearing now, replaced with brick and iron-roofed structures; aside from hotels and government buildings, few of the expensive thatch-roof *rumah adat* are being built nowadays.

Rumah Gadang

Means "big house," the traditional Minang dwelling. Each cluster of houses in a village is often the locale of one matrilineage, with a communal *surau* nearby where the men and boys hang out. Bedrooms are set aside for daughters of the household and their husbands, and there's a long common room for living and dining. The back half of the house is divided into small rooms where the married and marriageable women sleep. The maternal uncle, responsible for adding on to a house or building a new one, makes sure that each marriageable woman has a room of her own. An annex may be added for each daughter who comes of age, and that structure is home for her lifetime. You can often tell how many husbands and children a family's daughters have by the number of "horn" extensions on the *rumah gadang,* curving skyward and adorned with swinging ridgepoles. In front of the *rumah gadang* is a long veranda used for dining, meetings, and as a sleeping area for children, elders, and guests. Raised up to 3½ m off the ground on wooden pillars with small livestock kept underneath, one must climb up and down *rumah gadang* on a single piece of notched timber that's pulled up quickly in case of enemies, tigers, or snakes. The traditional house is thatched with thick layers of blackened palm. Exterior wooden walls are often carved painstakingly with scrolls and flowers, each geometric pattern colored in lavender, orange, and other pastels.

Outside of each *rumah gadang* are 2-3 granaries, called *rangkiang* or *gudang*. In addition to storing rice, these serve a social function. The paddy stored in one rice barn is put aside for ceremonies and festivals, another for widows and orphans, a third is for visitors or men returning from *merantau.* Whenever wanderers return or guests arrive, they can always be assured of a bowl of rice.

Mosques

Drums in many Minang villages are beaten to announce the time of prayer, public announcements, or to give the alarm in case of emergency; because of dense foilage, a muezzin's voice would never carry. Each mosque's drum has its own distinct tone. In the Tanah Datar region, instead of shiny galvanized iron roofs, mosques are divided into 4-5 pagoda-like roofs which mirror lingering Hindu-Buddhist influences (the old mosque of Lima Kaum has 5 stories, symbolizing the 5 villages of the district).

ARTS AND CRAFTS

Pencak Silat

A technique of self-defense originating in W. Sumatra. Although found in different forms throughout the country, the Minang regional version is feared and admired all over Indonesia. In fact, the art is accorded the ultimate honor: it is taught in the national military. A young man is not considered ready to enter manhood until he has mastered the martial arts (and learned to recite the Koran.) Pencak silat must be executed with elegance; Minang dance styles, such as the Randai, are patterned after it, and many basic movements are rich with ornamental gestures. When performed, most of the wide variety of styles are accompanied by drums and flutes. Women also study this dramatic art. The fighting style Mudo is performed by 2 men. This very technical and potentially deadly mock combat dance, with dramatic pauses after each stance, is called off just before it becomes violent. And well it should: Minangkabau men can kill fish in the water with lightning blows of their feet. In the Painan area (S coast), a form of pencak silat has been inspired by a tiger's stalking and killing methods. Called silatharimau, it's the most violent, dangerous, and kasar form of all Minang silat. Every Wed. and Sat. night, starting at 2000, pencak silat can be seen at Tarok Ujung Bukit, 1 km from Bukittinggi.

Literature

The Minangkabau, both men and women, have one of the highest literacy levels in Indonesia, partially due to strong family support. Their traditional literature is oral, and was written down only in the 16th C. when Arabic script was first introduced in the area. These traditional forms are still in use in everyday life such as kaba (narrative poems), pepatah-petitih (wise sayings), and the Malay-like pantun (rhymed couplets). The Minangkabau are also very fond of oratory. Whenever any customary ceremony takes place, such as at a wedding party, the maternal uncle opens with an obligatory and formal speech of welcome and gratitude called panitahan, which can last up to 4 hours! Minangkabau men love to argue at

length in their mosques, coffee houses, and at formal meeting places in the community. The Minangkabau also excel in modern literature. Although they make up only 4% of the Indonesian population, there are more Minangkabau among 20th C. Indonesian writers than any other ethnic group. And they are, after all, practically writing in their native tongue; the Indonesian language was derived in part from W. Sumatra. In the 50 years of modern Indonesian literature, such important pre-war writers as Rusli (Sitti Nurabaya), Muis (Salah Asuhan), Pustaka, Iskander, Pane, Anwar, Idrus, and the first noteworthy female novelist, Selasih (If Fortune Does Not Favor), all have come out of this region. These novels in their time were controversial, and some were shattering. One can even go as far as to state that the modern Indonesian novel is virtually a product of the collision between matriarchal Minang adat, the patriarchal Muslim religion in place for over 350 years, and the temptations and pressures of the more dynamic Western culture. Rusli's Sitti Nurabaya and Iskandar's Salah Pilih (1922) are examples of the tensions created by this collision.

The first important modern Indonesian poet, who employed Western poetic devices and concepts, was Muhammed Yamin (1903). One of the earliest and best known of his poems is Tanah Air ("My Fatherland"), published in 1920. In it, Yamin stands on the hills of his native Minangkabau country, singing of its beauty. His efforts revealed the potential of verse written in the Indonesian language. Rustam Effendi (1903) is another outstanding poet of W. Sumatra.

Dance

In the graceful Tari Piring or "Dish Dance," entranced dancers hold plates alit with candles, deftly twisting and turning without extinguishing the flame. Also known as Tari Lilin. Your only chance of seeing a performance is to charter one for 2 hours for around Rp150,000. Tari Payung, or "Umbrella Dance," portrays a young man's loving protection of his girlfriend. A combination of literature, sport, song, and drama, Randai is derived from pencak silat, the oldest dance in the Minang repertoire. Most often held outdoors at night, 9-20 young men in a circle are accompanied only by sharp cries from the audience. The dance is performed under the supervision of the Gurutuo Silek (dance and martial arts coach) and the Gurutuo Gurindam (rhyme and song coach). The dress is colorful and the dialog captivating. The dance consists of a succession of slow and then rapid steps, depicting the story of a wicked woman driven from her village. Annual Randai competitions are held both at the kabupaten and provincial levels, and this dance form is so popular that over 300 Randai troupes are now found in these highlands, each with its own name (example: Randai Ikan Sakti, the "Randai Troupe of the

Sacred Fish"). *Randai* is performed best in the Paguruyung area, the traditional seat of Minangkabau royalty. Minangkabau also perform one dance demonstrating how a *beruk* monkey climbs a coconut tree and picks choice coconuts for its owner. While under a religiously induced trance, men in the *Dabuih* ceremony stick themselves with steel awls, a Hindu-style show of faith.

The Minangkabau *gamelan*-style folk orchestra consists of the following: *rebab* (a stringed instrument), *talempong* (like a xylophone), *puput* (a straw flute), *gandang* (tambourine), drums, and many different kinds of bamboo flutes *(salung),* some of which are known to put love spells on women.

The white Sumatran beruk monkey is put on a long leash and trained to climb palm trees to pick ripe select coconuts for its owner. It's customary to hire the services of the beruk and its owner who takes cash payment, a portion of the harvest, or both.

Handicrafts
Each Minangkabau village is known for its specialty: woven sugarcane and reed purses (Payakumbuh), gold jewelry (Bukittinggi), silver filigree (Kota Gadang), weaving (Pandai Sikat and Silungkang), embroidery (Pariangan), pottery (Sungai Janiah), metallurgy (Sungaipuar). Artisans in other villages turn out bamboo carving, landscape paintings, wooden models of Minangkabau traditional houses, etc. Antiques galore can be bought in the antique shops of Padang or Bukittinggi.

A very active cottage industry is the handlooming of silk *kain songket,* woven with a supplementary weft of foil thread, which creates a gleaming metallic design. Formerly, these cloths were woven with pure gold and silver threads (very expensive), but now synthetic yarns are most often used. As old *kain songket* decay, the valuable threads are picked out and recycled. The women's traditional headdress is a turban with sharp conical points called *tanduk* (horns) which resemble those of water buffalo or cows. Minang bridal gowns, perhaps inspired by 17th C. European suits, are magnificent pieces of embroidery often framed in pictures or simply admired on a wall.

Very light necklaces, pendants, bracelets, and hair ornaments are crafted here, small pieces attached to a string of light metal and then dipped in gold or silver. Intended only for ceremonial use, this jewelry is quite fragile. Don't be deceived by the low price found in many of the small shops of Bukittinggi when these delicate necklaces and bracelets are placed on unreliable scales and sold by weight. More important is to ascertain the gold's or silver's quality. Remember, the Minangkabaus are shrewd traders; the true carat may not actually be what is stamped on the back of the piece.

EVENTS

Transitional Events
If you're lucky you'll see a Minang procession on the road. These could celebrate, for example, that a man has just become an uncle—an even more significant transition than when a man becomes a father! Another traditional ceremony, *Batagak Panghulu,* is held to replace a village headman. This 2-day event is enlivened with a debating session. Dress nicely on a Sunday and you may find a wedding to go to; wedding processions could very well take place on roads in Padang, Solok, and Bukittinggi. Usually Minang weddings start at 0700 and last all day and all night, especially on the last Sundays before *Ramadan* begins. Weddings display a curious blend of old and new customs. The bride might wear the traditional Minangkabau wedding attire with a magnificent gaudy golden headdress, while her ladies-in-waiting cover their heads discreetly in Muslim scarves.

Racing

When it's time to prepare the ricefields for planting, many villages hold a *pacu sapi* or bull race. Cattle compete by racing down a muddy field pulling rice plows behind them. Duck-racing *(pacu itik)* is held only in the tiny village of Limbukan near Payakumbuh; the winner of this race is the first duck which flutters over the finish line! Ask about the riotous bareback horse races *(pacu kuda)* held at least once every 3 months in each of the following towns: Padang, Solok, Padangpanjang, Bukittinggi, Batusangkar, Pariaman, Payakumbuh. They are a major, well-organized event, with vividly dressed jockeys. The Minangkabau also race dogs.

Bullfights

Also called *Lagu Minang,* this exciting event pits bull against bull. Bullfights are usually held at least once a week in the vicinity of Kotobaru, 10 km S of Bukittinggi; fights are also held in Pasarrebo, Kotolawas, and Pincuran Tujuh. Ask around Bukittinggi's hotels or *bemo* drivers for times and locales. These events are the province of village men; few women attend. There are 2 types: *adu kerbau* (a pair of water buffalo) and *adu sapi* or *adu lembu* (a pair of cattle bulls). They don't actually fight to the death; this humane contest, which takes place in a muddy field, is more a test of stamina and strength than of ferocity. Ostensibly staged to celebrate the rice harvest, most of the fun is watching the animated locals make their bets (up to Rp200,000 on a single wager!). Buyers from the livestock markets look over the potential stud bulls: a good fighter is a good breeder. The owner, beaming proudly, might get a very good price for the victor bull. Quite popular, there could be as many as 1,000 spectators (rainy days cut down on the attendance and the dust). A bullfight could last for a minute or an hour: one bull could just tire out, one could get bored with the proceedings and wander off, or run away. Sometimes the bulls are knocked unconscious in their first impact; see blood and mud flare and blow from their nostrils and dirt fly as their horns lock, grinding and butting. Sometimes the 2 bulls chase each other

around and the onlookers scatter in every direction, having the time of their lives! Magic is also invoked to make the bulls win. The trainers stand by each of their beasts and blow into a length of frayed rope. This is called *main angin,* supposed to breathe strength into their animals. This ol' rope trick really works powerful magic, too. Loud cheering from the crowd further encourages the combatants. Admission: Rp300.

Pig-hunting

The quintessential male activity in the Minangkabau Highlands. Males of all ages, titles, and classes take part in this collective, violent, and exciting sport. There are hunt associations with elected chairmen in nearly every village; from bus windows you often see men with their hunting dogs on every roadside. Locations and times of the hunt are often posted in the town *lepau* (coffee shop), snack house, or *toko.* Armed with hatchets, knives, spears and a few old rifles, as many as 50-100 men participate. The hunters pile into a chartered bus early Sun. morning, and head for a wilderness area known for its abundance of pigs. The dogs, snapping and barking, strain at their leashes. Once a pig is flushed out or a fresh trail discovered, the hunt leader *(Muncak Rajo)* gives the word to release the dogs. When the pig has been run down, the dogs start tearing at its carcass. Dogs are prized for their courage, keen sense of smell, and loud, distinctive bay which its owner will recognize while giving chase. Owners take great pride in the number of wounds their dog receives from pigs as a sign of its courage, and dogs could be sold for as much as Rp600,000. Not only is it a traditional sport, but pig-hunting also helps to protect crops. It's believed that embodied in the pig—a religiously taboo animal—is the soul of an evil human sorcerer or magician who is being punished by Allah. The activity is also an asocial release from the rigid constraints and formalities of Minang society and its customary laws; it's a time when ordinarily refined and correct members of the community become—for one day—rowdy, roughly dressed, noisy marauders.

PADANG

The main gateway of the W coast, a center of commerce, and thriving capital city of W. Sumatra Province. This seaport, only 2-4 m above sea level, is situated almost midway on Sumatra's north/south axis. Padang has one of the heaviest rainfalls in the world (310 cm per annum) and is dreadfully hot (even at 0800 in the morning!). Although 3rd largest city in Sumatra, Padang still has the feel of a small town with its low buildings, bright *sarung,* countless bicycles, whining Japanese motorbikes, and friendly people.

Though the cultural focus of the Minang people is inland at Bukittinggi, over 90% of Padang's half million people are ethnically Minangkabau. Most travelers consider the Minangkabau countryside a better experience than Padang, so most just do their business, go for a walk along the seawall, and move on.

On the flight from Java to Padang, the stark differences between Sumatrans and Javanese become immediately clear. Twice the winner of "Indonesia's Cleanest City," Padang's orderliness is also unlike

Java, and its economy is unusual for Indonesia: it's a city of native, not Chinese, merchants. There is more Indian blood in these W. Sumatrans; the Minangkabau have very direct, even piercing, gazes. Padangese didn't change from colonialism as much as the Javanese. It's also a very strict Muslim town and a woman could be stopped on the street for not wearing a bra, or an unmarried couple denied a hotel room. Conservative dress is *very* important; the more appropriately you dress, the friendlier the people and the closer you'll get to the culture. The Minangkabau language is very close to Indonesian; you'll make progress here. To the point of being downright aggressive, everyone wants to practice their English on you.

Sights

See the lovely old homes set back from wide, tree-lined streets in **Pandang Baru**, and old Dutch homes along Jl. Sudirman and Jl. Proklamasi. Chinese temples are in **Kampung Cina** (Chinatown). **Adityawarman Museum** is housed in a huge traditional-style house *(rumah gadang)*, with its rice barn and walls fully carved and painted), this museum lies on the corner of Jl. Diponegoro and Jl. Gereja; open 0800-1800, Fri. until 1100, closed Monday. Inside are antiques, textiles, and other objects of historical and cultural interest from all parts of Sumatra, but a poor display. Check out the happenings at the **Institute of Minangkabau Studies** (SSMR) in Cengke. The Arts Center, **Taman Budaya**, just across from the museum, has regular dancing and *pencak silat* performances; open 0900-1400. Padang's university, **Universitas Andalas**, is out in Air Tawar. From the top of **Kantor Gubernor**, view all of Padang, the sea beyond, and offshore islands. Off Padang's **seawall** is a veritable sea aquarium with rainbows of fish. But don't go swimming—they'll nibble at you. Nice sunsets can also be seen from here, a place where the local population promenades in the late afternoon and twilight. Although Padang's old harbor of Muara is swimmable, its not too appetizing. Take a stroll along the beach instead and watch the fishermen and fishmongers along Jl. Muara and Jl. Samudera.

Accommodations

Right across the street from the bus station are 2 convenient cheap hotels. The **Tiga Tiga**, Jl. Pemuda 31 (tel. 22635), has a nice tropical garden, is very helpful at the desk, and a *penjaga* is usually asleep outside if you arrive early in the morning on the bus. At Rp3000 s, Rp6800 d, most travelers gravitate to the Tiga Tiga, but right next door, the newly renovated **Hotel Candrawasih**, Jl. Pemuda 27 (tel. 22894), charges only Rp2000-3000 more. Don't get the Tiga Tiga confused with the other, newer Tiga Tiga on Jl. Veteran 33 (tel. 22173) which costs Rp15,000 including breakfast, fan, and hot water.

If you are staying more than one night in Padang, you see more of the city staying in a downtown hotel. Most have cheap rooms along with the expensive ones, and are more than willing to show you each type. **Machudum's Hotel**, Jl. Hiligoo 45 (tel. 22333/23997), is a centrally located old Dutch hotel between the museum and *oplet* station/market. A double "transit room" here costs Rp10,000 with fan and *mandi*. Executive rooms with a/c, wall-to-wall, and hot water run Rp18,000; tax included. The not-so **Grand Hotel** at Jl. Pondok 84 (tel. 22088), has character and is friendly, Rp11,500 s (with fan), Rp21,500 (a/c). **Hotel Aldilla**, Jl. Damar 1, has Rp15,000 (fan) and Rp20,000 (a/c) rooms, nice dining room, and excellent Chinese food; they also give a 10% discount. The seawall is just down the street. **Hotel Hang Tuah**, Jl. Pemuda (tel. 26556), charges Rp8000 for Economy, Rp11,000-Rp12,000 for VIP. The Hang Tuah is convenient (nearly opposite the bus terminal) and rooms are clean, spacious, and well-lighted. Restaurant downstairs serves Continental breakfast (included in the room price). A Merpati and Garuda office is just next door.

Luxury-class hotels include the **Mariani International**, Jl. Bundo Kandung 35 (tel. 25466), Standard Rp25,000 a/c, 1st Class Rp30,000 a/c. The Mariani has a very helpful travel office (arranges tours) and secure, tropical surroundings; also takes AMEX, VISA, and MasterCard. **Muara Hotel**, on Jl. Gereja 34 (tel. 25600/25078) opposite the museum, has new motel-style rooms for Rp24,000, huge open lobby and travel agency. Padang's top hotel is **Pangeran's**, Jl. Dobi 3-5 (tel. 26233), within walking distance of Kampung Cina and the central business district. Standard Rp20,000, 1st Class Rp29,000 (only difference is a fridge and better a/c). Prices include tax and service; AMEX, VISA, and MasterCard accepted. Squeaky clean.

Food

If you haven't been eating spicy food up to this point, now is the time to start. The famous *nasi padang* cuisine is a flavorful blend of fresh spices and coconut cream. The best way is to let them serve you in the traditional manner in which a waiter carries up to 20 saucers of food on one arm. Choose what you want at the table and only pay for what you eat. A huge meal should cost Rp1500-2000. Or you can choose a one-dish meal, a *nasi ramas*, and eat for a lot less. The local brand of *gado-gado* is usually under Rp600.

A good *nasi padang* restaurant is the central **Simpang Raya** at Jl. Prof. Yamin 125. Other places to try this cuisine are **Serba Nikmat**, Jl. Agus Salim 20; **Tanpa Nama**, Jl. Rohana Kudus 87; **Bopet Buyan**, Jl. Brig. Aziz Chan (near the post office), and the excellent **Roda Baru**, Jl. Pasar Raya 6. **Wisma Baru**, a fine eating place on Jl. Hiligoo, has noodles, rice, *gado-gado,* and *soto* for about Rp550 each. On the cheaper side, the large Pasar Raya has foodstalls with a tasty meal for around Rp250. Many *warung* open up around the *oplet* station in the mornings selling pancakes and small, delicious coconut-rice flapjacks.

If you'd rather go Chinese, try the various stalls and small restaurants in Kampung Cina (Jl. Pondok area): **Phoenix, Chan's,** etc. The **RiRi** on Jl. Pondok specializes in Javanese food. The most famous and expensive Chinese restaurant in town is the **King's** at Jl. Pondok 86, where a superb meal and beer for 3 people will cost around Rp20,000. If you'd rather go American, the ritzy **Pangeran Hotel,** Jl. Dobi 3-5, has steaks and milkshakes but it's cold inside (multi-air-conditioners) and expensive. Enjoy European food also at **Hotel Muara,** a 10-min. walk from the Pangeran. For sweets, head for **Dallas Restoran & Cake Shop,** Jl. Pondok.

Entertainment
Across the street from the museum, same side as the Tiga Tiga, is the **Cultural Center** (Taman Budaya); on Sun. you might see students taking lessons in *pencak silat* or Sumatran dance. Several moviehouses are located in Padang's Chinatown, tickets Rp600-800. **Chan's Ice Cream,** Jl. Pondok, is the naughtiest place in town and it isn't even a nightclub, just a restaurant. There is only one nightclub (a disco called **Luki** near Hotel Muara) since this is a strong, puritanical Muslim area and the town elders close them down soon after they open. Another measure of Padang's orthodoxy is the fervor with which they adhere to the Islamic fasting month, *Ramadan,* when all of Padang's sidewalks are rolled up, its streets empty, its shops shuttered. People are either home or at the mosque; you'll never see an Indonesian city so dead.

Shopping
The main market, **Pasar Raya,** next to the Balai Kota, has *songket* cloth, richly decorated with fake gold and silver thread, plus acres of fruit, vegetable hawkers, *dukun,* and blind musicians. Some very cheap machine-printed *kain batik* can be bought in Padang's shops, even as low as Rp2000, though the quality is poor. A new 3-floor department store, **Ramanda,** is on Jl. Iman Bonjol; also try **Matahari** on the same street. For textiles, try **Toko Batik Arjuna,** Jl. Pasar Raya (tel. 23253); **Batik Semar,** Jl. Hiligoo (tel. 21215), and **Silungkang** (also paintings, carvings, embroideries and baskets), Jl. Iman Bonjol 6A (tel. 26426). Also check **Panay,** Jl. Iman Bonjol 5/IV (tel. 21259), for Minang *songket* textiles, embroidery, paintings, carvings, basket and silverwork, bamboo crafts, and more. Under the same owner is the **Abunawas Souvenir Shop** at Tabing Airport as well as another shop at the Mariani Hotel. Many fine antique and local artifact shops: **Toko Sartika,** Jl. Jen.

Sudirman 5 (tel. 22101) and **Sonket Silungkang,** Jl. Iman Bonjol. For nice *kebaya,* Rp6000 is the starting price.

Services
Get all your business done early, it gets hot! The **tourist office** for W. Sumatra and Riau is Kanwil Postel, way out on Jl. Khatib Sulaiman (tel. 22118/ 28231). They mostly just hand out pamphlets; open 0730-1400, except Sat. 0730-1300. The **Padang Tourist Office** (Dinas Parawisata) is on Jl. Semudra. The Regional Tourist Office (Dinas Parawisata Sumatra Barat) is at Jl. Sudirman A3. Of all 3, you'll probably get the best info at the Kanwil Postel. More information about local sights is available at the various commercial tourist agencies in town. **Tunas Indonesia,** Jl. Pondok 86C, is very helpful, as is **Pac-to,** Jl. Pemuda 1 (tel. 27780) and **Nitour,** Jl. Pemuda 20 (tel. 22175).

The **Immigration Office,** Jl. Pahlawan (tel. 21294), is N of town in Padang Baru. Change money at **Bank Negara Indonesia,** Jl. Dobi 1. Better rates than the banks are given at the moneychanger **C.V. Eka Jasa Utama,** Jl. Niaga. The **post office** is at Jl. Bgd. Aziz Chan 7. You don't need a permit for Harau Canyon or even to Siberut I. anymore, but the **Forestry Office** (PPA) is at Jl. Raden Saleh 8A, Padang Baru. For P. Mentawai, get a *surat jalan* at the main police station on Jl. Prof. M. Yamin. A **public library** is on Jl. Ghairil Anwar, behind the museum. The best and biggest bookstore in town is **Budi Jaya,** Jl. Prof. M. Yamin,

---

PADANG

1. Pacto Tours Ltd.
2. Hang Tuah Hotel
3. central bus terminal
4. Hotel Dahlia
5. souvenir shop
6. *pasar*
7. Hotel Mariani
8. Grand Hotel
9. Tepi Pasang
10. immigration office
11. Garuda Airlines
12. Bank Negara Indonesia
13. Impor Ekspor Bank
14. museum
15. ferry (Rp200) to Air Manis
16. Hotel Muara, Natour office
17. Candrawasih Hotel
18. Tiga Tiga Hotel
19. Pangeran's Hotel
20. Panay souvenir shop

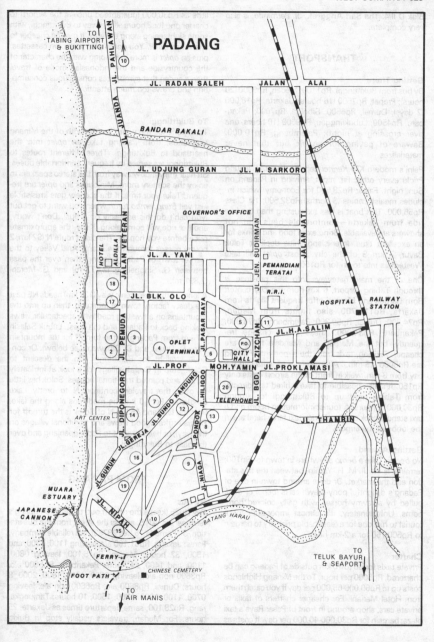

PADANG

TO TABING AIRPORT & BUKITTINGI

JL. PAHLAWAN

JL. JUANDA

JL. RADEN SALEH

JALAN ALAI

BANDAR BAKALI

JL. UDJUNG GURAN

JL. M. SARKORO

GOVERNOR'S OFFICE

JALAN VETERAN

HOTEL ALDILLA

JL. A. YANI

JL. BLK. OLO

JL. PEMUDA

JL. PASAR RAYA

JL. JEN. SUDIRMAN

JALAN JATI

PEMANDIAN TERATAI

R.R.I.

HOSPITAL

RAILWAY STATION

OPLET TERMINAL

P.O.

CITY HALL

JL. AZIZCHAN

JL. H.A. SALIM

JL. PROF. MOH. YAMIN

JL. PROKLAMASI

JL. DIPONEGORO

JL. BUNDO KANDUNG

JL. HILIGO

JL. BGD.

TELEPHONE

ART CENTER

JL. GEREJA

JL. GURUN

JL. PONDOK

JL. NIAGA

JL. THAMRIN

MUARA ESTUARY

JAPANESE CANNON

JL. NIPAH

BATANG HARAU

FERRY

CHINESE CEMETERY

FOOT PATH

TO AIR MANIS

TO TELUK BAYUR & SEAPORT

Blok D II/4. The **Sari Anggrek**, Jl. Permindo, is also very complete.

TRANSPORT

Getting There

By bus from Bukittinggi, Rp1100; Medan, Rp9000 (20 hours); Prapat, Rp7500 (16 hours); Jakarta, Rp18,000 (2 days); Dumai, Rp6500; Sibolga, Rp7000; Pekanbaru, Rp4500; Lubuklinggau, Rp9500 (10 hours, one river crossing at night); Palembang, Rp10,000. Beware of paying for an a/c bus that never materializes.

Pelni's modern KM *Kerinci* departs Jakarta (Tanjung Priok) every other Fri. night, arriving in Padang on Sun. night. Fares: Rp28,500 for Economy (which includes meals); cabins (6 berths) Rp32,500; 1st Class Rp55,000. This boat is less exhausting than the bus ride from Jakarta—comfortable beds and hot showers are available. Bring extra food and drinks for an excellent time. Inter-island ships dock at Teluk Bayur, 7 km S of the city. Most *oplet* will take Westerners into town for Rp150.

One of the main gateways into this province is through Tabing Airport, 6 km from the city center. Both Garuda and Merpati offer frequent flights from Jakarta, Rp116,700, also flights from Medan, Rp74,800; Dumai, Rp50,300; Palembang, Rp78,000; Pekanbaru, Rp34,000. These prices change frequently, but the Merpati and Mandala flights are cheaper. Arriving, taxis from the airport into Padang are Rp5000 (15 min.). Alternately, a *bis kota* into the city from 3-min. walk in front of the airport costs only Rp150. It's also possible to take a hired taxi directly from Tabing right up to Bukittinggi for around Rp30,000, 2 hours. A tourist information booth and a taxi stand (check out fixed-price taxi fares here) are in the lobby of the airport.

Getting Around

No *becak*. Take a *bemo* anywhere in town for Rp100; terminal is off Jl. M. H. Yamin, between the bus station and the market. Or drive around town in one of Padang's delightful pony-drawn carts *(bendi* or *dos)*, pulled by scrawny horses with gaily colored pompoms. Unfortunately, it's almost impossible for a tourist to hire one for a reasonable price (try to bargain to Rp500-750 for a 2-km ride).

Charter

Private taxis for up to 10 km outside of Padang can be chartered, Rp5000 per hour. To the Minang Highlands costs up to Rp60,000-65,000 per day if you catch them from Hotel Mariani. For cheaper charters of taxis or private cars, shop around in front of Pasar Raya's taxi plaza; bargain for Rp30,000-40,000 per day. It costs as little as Rp30,000 (guaranteed price at the airport) to charter one for 3 hours all the way to Bukittinggi, with some sightseeing along the way. It may be cheaper to charter an *oplet.* You get to play your own cassettes, plus an *oplet* is more in keeping with the character of the countryside and the Indonesian mode of travel than a sedan that symbolizes conspicuous consumption and draws too much attention.

To Bukittinggi

To experience the width and breadth of the Minang Highlands, from Padang take an *oplet* into the heartland to Bukittinggi. Three different routes to Bukittinggi are served by frequent comfortable buses. Sit near the window away from the stereo speakers to enjoy the scenery more. Minibuses and *oplet* are frequent. Take your time; if the scenery gets irresistible just yell *Bung, ambo turun* when you want to get out (you can't do this as easily on a bus). Don't worry; another ride will come along. Know the approximate price before you hop on. The direct route N (92 km, 2 hours) passes through the scenic Anai Valley to the market town of Padangpanjang, then over the pass between G. Singgalang (2,877 m) and G. Merapi (2,891 m).

A longer but more scenic way (137 km) heads NE past the dusty factory town of Indarung, then up into the mountains on a twisting road with spectacular views looking back to Padang and the coast. Lubuk Selasih (37 km from Padang) is the turnoff for the mountain lakes D. Diatas and D. Dibawah (see below). Or continue straight for Bukittinggi. On the descent to Solok, stop in **Cupak** village for a look at intricately carved and painted traditional houses. Solok has little to offer the traveler; continue N to pretty Lake Singkarak. For 10 km the road runs along the lake. Past the lake and 45 km N of Solok is the turnoff for **Batusangkar** (good views and traditional villages on the way), or head straight to Padangpanjang and over the pass to Bukittinggi.

FROM PADANG

By Bus

Pay Rp25 (keeps the riff-raff out) to get into Padang's *terminal bis.* **ANS**, across the street from the bus station, Jl. Pemuda 15 (tel. 23793), is a reliable company. Fares: Jakarta, Rp31,100 a/c, leaving 1100, 1300, and 1500, 32 hours; Medan, Rp15,100, leaving 0800, 1100, and 1400, 24 hours; Pekanbaru, Rp5600 a/c, Rp3600 non a/c, leaving 0800, 0900, 1900, 2000, 8 hours; Dumai, Rp8600 a/c, Rp6600 non a/c, leaving 0700, 1100, 1200, 1300, 1500, 10 hours; Tanjungkarang, Rp28,100, same departure times as Jakarta, 25 hours. For Medan, travelers usually stop in Bukit-

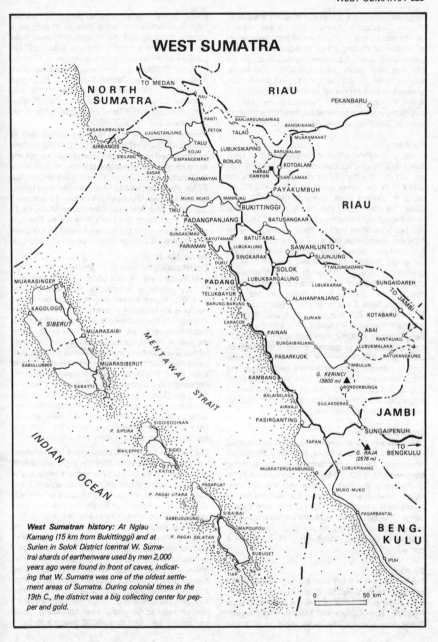

WEST SUMATRA

West Sumatran history: At Nglau Kamang (15 km from Bukittinggi) and at Surien in Solok District (central W. Sumatra) shards of earthenware used by men 2,000 years ago were found in front of caves, indicating that W. Sumatra was one of the oldest settlement areas of Sumatra. During colonial times in the 19th C., the district was a big collecting center for pepper and gold.

0   50 km

tinggi en route—one of the richest culture areas of Indonesia. Overland to Jakarta is cheaper than the ship and far less serene. Stock up on an incredible variety of snacks at Padang's bus station for the unforgettable trip south. Roads are impassable during the Dec.-Feb. rainy season. It takes 30-40 sleepless hours; you can break up your marathon trip in Lubuklinggau (where there are rooms for around Rp2500-3000), or spend a couple of days in Palembang. Bengkulu Indah Bus Co., in the *terminal bis,* has buses down to coast to Bengkulu, around Rp15,000, 12 hours.

By Boat

Check at the **Pelni** office at Padang's port of Teluk Bayur S of the city; it's located at Jl. Tanjung Priok 32 (tel. 121127). For the 30-hour passage to Jakarta, the ship KM *Kerinci* leaves every other Sun. at 2400, arriving in Jakarta Tues. morning, Rp32,400 Deck Class, 1st Class Rp63,700. Ships tend to be less crowded out of Padang than they are out of Jakarta. If you buy your ticket from an agent in town it will be 10% more expensive, but you'll save a trip to the harbor, Rp150 by *bemo*. Other shipping lines also have some old buckets sailing down the W coast of Sumatra, stopping in Bengkulu or the Mentawais; check the small boat harbor, too. The Perintis Lines' ship, KM *Baruna Artha,* for example, runs every fortnight from Teluk Bayur to Sikakap (Pagai Utara) and Bengkulu (Rp6170), then on to Enggano, Bintuhan (southern Bengkulu Province), Krui (northern Lampung Province, Rp8390), then back again. Takes 10½ days altogether. You spend 1-2 nights in Bengkulu, which is perfect. Technically, the passage excludes food, but since *orang asing* are rare (and those taking the *pulang-pergi komplet* RT rarer still), you'll probably be fed by the crew. Perintis Lines also has the *Niaga XIII,* which does Sibolga-Aceh (and P. Sabang) via 3-4 other ports-of-call along the way.

Small Boat Harbor

Check the small boat harbor, Muara, at the mouth of the Arau River at Teluk Bayur, Rp100 by *bemo* from downtown. *Kapal motor* sometimes cruise to the Mentawais, Rp2500 to Siberut or Sipora. Check in the afternoons at the harbor police near the exit from Muara; boats intending to leave the next day for the Mentawai Is. often report their intention here. Expect delays. The *syahbandar* at Muara could be unwilling to issue you a *surat ijin,* so you might find yourself obliged to go small boat-hunting at Teluk Bayur instead.

By Air

Tabing Airport is 6 km from the city's center. Take an orange *bis kota* (Rp150, 20 min.) out to the airport from Padang, or order a taxi through your hotel (Rp5000). Both Garuda and Merpati offer frequent flights from Padang (for fares, refer to "Getting

There" above). The last flight to Jakarta in the afternoon is sometimes cancelled because of rain; get a morning flight instead. An interesting Merpati flight (Rp17,500) is the one from Padang to Rokot on P. Pagai from where you can take an outrigger to Muarasiberaut on P. Sipora (see the Mentawais section). Also available is a direct Garuda flight from Padang to Singapore, US$98. Airlines offices: **Garuda,** Jl. Jen. Sudirman 2 (tel. 23823/23224), opens at 0700; **Merpati,** Jl. Pemuda 45 E (tel. 27908/25367); **Mandala,** Jl. Pemuda 29A (tel. 22350/21979).

Another spectacular route is on the coastal road via Pariaman, Tiku, and Lake Maninjau. This 193-km-long and little-used route involves several bus changes and some rough road. First, travel N by bus or train 50 km to Pariaman, a historic port town. Take another bus 37 km along the coast to Tiku, then inland via Lubukbasung to Muko Muko on the W shore of the magnificent crater lake, Maninjau. From Muko Muko, it's 16 km by road along the lake's N shore to Maninjau village. Buses climb the 44 switchbacks up the crater wall, then wind through scenic valleys to Bukittinggi.

To Air Manis

The hike along the coast to Air Manis, a fishing village S of Padang with a nice beach, huge waves, and friendly people, is spectacular. First take a *bemo* (Rp100) to Muara, the estuary just S of the city. Muara Harbor is a lively scene of smaller vessels connecting Padang with the Mentawai Is. and other regional destinations. A canoe will ferry you to the other side of the river. A huge Japanese cannon still in its concrete bunker sits near the river mouth. Follow the wide path over hills covered in clove trees, with excellent views. Walk the 3 km in about 45 minutes. All over the slopes of this mountain, called G. Monyet ("Monkey Hill"), are Chinese graves, plus a few monkeys. Here also is the grave of Sitti Nurabaya. A novel of the same name by Murah Rusli, one of the first novels ever written in the Indonesian language, relates the Minangkabau counterpart of the Romeo and Juliet legend.

The beach at Air Manis is not so good for swimming, but there's a great view. Stay the night with one of the villagers. Papa Cili Cili's Homestay is famous; give Rp1500 for the big bed with a curtain around it and not much privacy. Villagers will probably only be able to speak a smattering of English so this is a good place to pick up some Indonesian. Food is basic: fish, rice, vegetables, coconut. Go out night-fishing; the fishermen return with fish you'll have that night. Walk on the path (30 min.) over the next hill S for a panorama over the harbor of Teluk Bayur, then walk down and catch the KM *Kerinci* to Jakarta. During low-tide in the mornings wade out to P. Pisang Ketek ("Small Banana Island"), but be sure to return before high tide. Pulau Pisang Gadang ("Big Banana Island") can be reached by *prahu* after bargaining. Small bungalows there rent for Rp5000. Beach is rocky.

VICINITY OF PADANG

The coastline is very rugged and scenic for the first 100 km S of Padang, with pulse-stopping views from the highway as it twists over rocky ridges and curves and along sandy coves. Mountains drop straight into the ocean, forming countless bays and peaceful beaches. Fishermen can take you out to visit small islands with white-sand beaches. A number of white-sand beaches are also within easy reach of Padang; the farther away from Padang, the cleaner the swimming and the fewer the people. **Pasir Jambak** is a quiet, out-of-the-way stretch of open palm-lined seashore, quite calm and shallow, about 20 km N of Padang. Take a minibus first to Muara Panjalinan, then walk 6 km down to the beach. Good bodysurfing.

Bungus Bay
A natural bay 23 km S of Padang with a virgin crescent-shaped beach fringed with coconut-palms and exquisite sunsets, Rp400 (1 hour) by *oplet*. This is a memorable ride; try to get on one of the 1950 Chevrolet *oplet*, painted about 25 different colors with chickens, vegetables, and goats sticking out the windows. Because of its depth, Teluk Bayur and not Bungus Bay was chosen as Padang's harbor. Bungus Bay is a perfect place to relax, sunbathe, swim, or beachcomb. The shallow ocean here is almost too warm—like a bathtub. This is the reason you come to Indonesia; to be in a place like this. Borrow a canoe or rent one for Rp1000-1500, or hire a *prahu* (Rp3000) out to small nearby islands in the bay. Swim in the waterfall 2 km up the side of a nearby mountain. Don't wear scanty clothing as this is a conservative area. Stay at **Carolina Guesthouse**, 10 rooms at

Rp6000-10,000. The locals also run some homestays such as **Pak Thamrin's** (around Rp1500 for spare rooms), or pitch a tent right on the beach. If you are just visiting Bungus for the day, remember that the last *oplet* back to Padang leaves soon after it starts to get dark.

South To Painan
A large fishing village 77 km S of Padang. The principal town of the southern coast, the Dutch established their first W coast trading center here. By the 18th C., Padang had eclipsed it as a commercial center. The long sweeping beach has hundreds of fishing boats pulled up on it. At night their lights sparkle out in the bay. Stay at clean and pleasant **Hotel Andhika**, Jl. Pemuda 23-25 (several blocks off the main road); Rp3500 s, Rp6000 d. Meals are available if arranged in advance. Nearer the bus station in an old large house is **Hotel Mustika**; Rp4000 s or d. A market and several Padang-style restaurants are found at the bus station. Continuing S from Painan, the mountains recede a bit after 100 km from Padang and the road follows a sandy coastal plain. The pavement runs out at the 150 km mark S of Padang.

Tapan is a junction town in the far S of the province, 213 km from Padang. Not many visitors—if you drop into a *warung* for a meal, the whole populace turns out to watch. No regular place to stay but a *warung* might let you sleep inside. From Tapan, a paved road turns inland 64 km to Sungaipenuh and Lake Kerinci of Jambi Province. A rough road continues S from Tapan into wild Bengkulu Province—347 km of jungle and nearly deserted beaches to Bengkulu, the main city. Towns and villages are often widely separated. Damri has daily buses on this adventurous route.

NORTH OF PADANG

Solok And Vicinity
The 64-km bus ride (Rp900) from Padang to Solok right over the Bukit Barisan Range is fantastic. Approaching from Bukittinggi, the bus costs Rp950. Solok (388 m) is an attractive *adat* town in the middle of a broad, rich plain. The area is known for its extensive *sawah*, tasty white rice, wealthy landowners, numerous *rumah adat*, and traditional clothing: women here wear ceremonial headdresses that look like cow horns. Quite different from other W. Sumatran districts, their clothing shows influences from Jambi and Palembang areas. In Solok, stay in the **Ully Hotel** or **Peng. Sinar Timbulan I** (Jl. Merdeka 24), both near the bus station. Don't accept *bemo* rides from the bus station across the street to the hotel!

Sinar Timbulan II, Jl. Bundo Kandung, is also worth checking out.

Cupak is in the hills 19 km S of Solok and 45 km NE of Padang. With its beautifully carved and painted exterior woodwork, this traditional village has perhaps the best Minang traditional-style houses in W. Sumatra, either newly built or really old. Some houses still have thatched roofs made from black sugar-palm fiber. Unfortunately, the town's water-wheel ricemills have given way to the petrol age, and are now getting mossy and moldy. **Silungkang**, 21 km E of Solok on the way to Sijunjung and Sawahlunto, is renowned for its *kain songket* and other textiles. Nearly every household has a simple loom from which fabrics of the highest quality are made. See the biggest *rumah* *gadang* in the region, near the mosque at Sulit Air (Rp400 from Solok).

LAKE SINGKARAK

This large (8- by 20-km, 396-m-high) mountain lake is 23 km SE of Padangpanjang and 31 km NW of Solok. Take a bus from Solok, Rp400; Padang, Rp600; Bukittinggi, Rp900. This lake is the "back way" to get to Bukittinggi from Padang. Make sure you get dropped off at the town of Singkarak (not at Umbilan) if you want to eat. From Singkarak village, hitchhike 3 km up to the accommodations. The highway and railway from Solok to Padangpanjang run 18 km along the shore of the lake, and the wide-open view is superb. The shore is gently sloping and clean, with excellent freshwater swimming, boating, fishing, waterskiing. As big and beautiful as more popular Lake Maninjau to the N, Singkarak's placid water feeds into the Umbilan River (though some white water surges through Umbilan village). The area is dotted with motels, restaurants, and other recreational facilities. Hire a *prahu* in Umbilan for a tour of the lake or ask about motorized touring boats. A ferry from Singkarak cruises lengthwise (NW direction) across the lake to Batu Beragung on the northern shore. P.T. Parindo (Jl. A. Yani 99, Bukittinggi) offers a tour (Rp10,000) to Malalo, opposite Umbilan, where traditional dances are staged in the evenings.

Sights

Umbilan, on the E shore, is the lake's largest town, where the rushing Umbilan River begins. Take a bus (Rp500) from Umbilan which follows the river (with water wheels and rice culture economy) to Batusangkar, from where you catch a bus farther to Bukittinggi (Rp450). Less scenic is the bus ride to Padangpanjang (Rp500) from where you catch another bus to Bukittinggi (Rp450).

Sulitair is a nice village on a rough road which climbs into the hills, 14 km NE from Singkarak village. Since this village is located on top of a hill, water is rare; its name means "Difficult Water." Sulitair has some of the most beautiful examples of Minangkabau houses seen in these highlands, including 70-m-long houses with 20 families all living in one huge room. No regular place to stay. Get a bus from Bukittinggi in the direction of Solok and get off at the turnoff, then hitch up to Sulitair, the whole way for around Rp1000 at most. The best time to go is on market day when transportation is more plentiful. Sulitair is easy to reach from Padang with Sulitair Bus Co. which makes a daily RT. The last bus back to the main road leaves at 1500, or you'll have to walk the 14 km.

Accommodations And Food

Singkarak village on the S shore (15 km N of Solok)

has the only inexpensive place to stay. **Villa Merpati** (no sign) is right on the lake beside a small park. Simple, pleasant rooms go for Rp2500 s, Rp5000 d. Three km N of Umbilan right on the lake is **Hotel Jayakarta**; Rp6000 with *mandi*. However, being next to the highway and railroad tracks tends to spoil the tranquility. A *rumah makan* is right next door. The **Minang Hotel** in Batytebak, 4 km N of Umbilan, is also on the lake but away from the road—a beautiful and peaceful spot. Go ½ km N of Hotel Jayakarta and turn L ½ km through the gateway. Doubles begin at Rp12,500 s; they also have cottages for around Rp35,000. Food at the Minang is good but expensive; breakfast (Rp2500) is served in silver pots, tea mugs, real decadence! Lunch or dinner: Rp5000. The beach here is pebbly and littered, but speedboats and waterskis are available for rent.

In Umbilan are several quite good *nasi padang* restaurants (but no place to stay); another *nasi padang* is in Singkarak village. Being a pit stop for *bemo* and buses passing through, many other restaurants are along the lake: the **Lintas Sumatra** has a patio right on the lake and offers *nasi padang*. In Umbilan, stop and buy snacks and fruit (oranges at Rp1000 per kg).

PADANGPANJANG

A busy, rainy market town known for its *sate* and cool (773 m elev.) climate, Padangpanjang lies on a crossroads 72 km NE of Padang, 54 km NW of Solok, and 20 km S of Bukittinggi. Hop on any bus or *bemo* heading for Padang from Bukittinggi (Rp600, 30 min.). The market is worth sauntering through to try local foods and see the array of produce; Thurs. is the biggest market day. See Lake Singkarak from the Rantai Lookout point.

Accommodations And Food

Two basic places to stay are near the market on the main street, Jl. H.A. Dahlan: **Hotel Minang,** no. 18, and the really scuzzy **Hotel Mamur** at no. 34. Both are Rp3000 s, noisy, with a nice collection of creepy men. The Minang is marginally cleaner and a little less seedy. On the main road from Bukittinggi, coming down to the market, is **Wisma Singgara Indah;** since they bill themselves as an "international hotel" they charge Rp22,000-32,000, though it looks more like a middle-class house. *Rumah makan* and countless *warung sate* are nearby. Better to stay in Bukittinggi and make it a day trip.

ASKI

Located just N of town, this is The Conservatory of Minangkabau Dance and Music, an organization dedicated to preserving traditional instruments, music, and dance. Dance rehearsals are held most weekday mornings and afternoons until 1400. Possibly see the

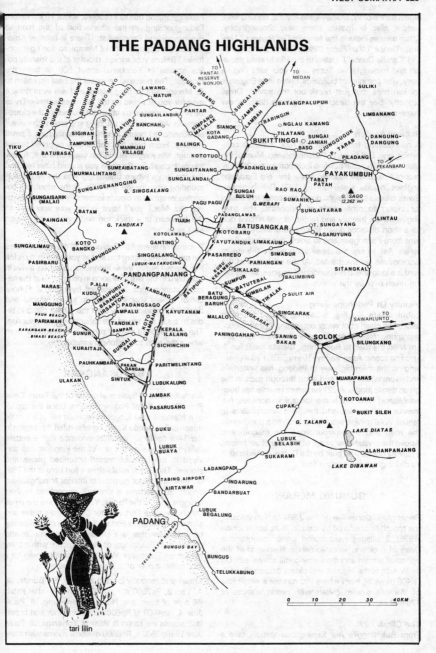

THE PADANG HIGHLANDS

tari lilin

0   10   20   30   40KM

oldest dance of W. Sumatra, the *Randai*, derived from *pencak silat*, or maybe some new choreography. Other dances include the famous *Tari Payung* ("Umbrella Dance"), *Tari Piring* ("Plate Dance"), and *Tari Lilin* ("Candle Dance"). Listen to the Hindu-style *gamelan* and minangkabau flutes until your ears ring. A busy, vital complex of buildings, only a little English is spoken here, but just break out the smiles. Dress properly. See the director to charter a dance show (expensive).

Railway Station

A coal-burning freight train still runs from the coal-mining area E of Solok to Padangpanjang. Most of the area's surviving coal-burning locomotives are 20-plus-year-old Japanese models, but a few old European engines include a still-running 1921 British model. Swiss diesels take freight down the coast to Padang for export to other parts of Indonesia. The train engineers are friendly and might let you hitch a ride for a short distance down to Kotobaru. Another train runs from Padangpanjang to Solok, but its 'schedule' varies. Ask to see the repair shop where the steam locomotives are overhauled. At the other end of the yard is a long lineup of abandoned engines, slowly being taken over by the weeds.

Vicinity Of Padangpanjang

Lubuk Mata Kucing, a bathing spot 3 km from town, has clear, cool water originating from a mountain spring. **Nagari Air Angat** is a hotwater springs 6 km N on the road to Bukittinggi, then to the R for ½ km. The scenic **Anai Valley**, 10 km SE of Padangpanjang on the main highway to Padang, has waterfalls and rivers which twist and wind through gaps in the green dense jungle. A 221-ha nature reserve has been established here, the home for tapirs, monkeys, numerous bird species, and the giant Amorphallus titanum. A 40-m-high waterfall drops into a pool beside the road and the surroundings are magnificent. Above the crystal clear water of the Anai River below, a railway bridge was built by the Dutch, considered in its day a great engineering feat.

GUNUNG MERAPI

Bright green slopes rise up this 2,891-m-high volcano, the top often obscured by clouds. In its last eruption (1979), 3 villages were buried under mountainous rivers of rock and volcanic debris. Remnants of the upheaval remain and the volcano still spews ash. On its W side is the highest and oldest caldera, Bancah (1,400 m wide), from where you can see a whole row of Merapi's smaller craters with circumferences of 175-600 m.

The Climb

From Bukittinggi's Aur Kuning bus station, take a Padangpanjang bus to Kotobaru, about 10 km before Padangpanjang, at the intersection of the road to Bukittinggi and Pandaisikat. (There is another Kotobaru on the opposite side of Merapi, so don't get confused.) Before your ascent, register at the friendly police station in Kotobaru, about 500 m from the mosque. The police will suggest the best approach to G. Merapi (and G. Singgalang) and will even draw a map for you. It's cold up top, so dress warmly. Try to be on your way up by at least 0700 before the clouds come in. After an hour climbing you reach "the villa," an abandoned house in which a family runs a small *warung*. From here the trail is easy (a green tunnel through the jungle) but when you come out, follow the path carefully. By noon you should have reached the top, from where Bukittinggi and the whole surrounding countryside is visible. If the mountain becomes wrapped in clouds (especially in the rainy season Oct.-Mar.), you'll have to find your way back to the trailhead in a thick fog and moonscape, which ain't easy.

If you climb Merapi on Sat. night, all the local climbers are making the ascent too and all you have to do is follow them. Usually these Indonesian climbers arrive in Kotobaru in the late afternoon in order to be at the forestry station *(pos kehutanan)* by nightfall (1-hour climb), where shops are set up selling snacks and drinks. At midnight they start the 4-hour climb in order to be at the top of the mountain for the sunrise. The best place to meet climbers is in Kotobaru, from where the path to the forestry station begins.

BATUSANGKAR

A small town and traditional center of the Tanah Datar Plain, 20 km NE of Padangpanjang. Once the capital of a Minangkabau kingdom, legends tell of a female queen called Bundo Kandung who ruled this region in the 14th century. Historical evidence that a certain Adityawarman was the raja of the kingdom has survived in the form of *prasati* (inscribed plates and stones). The Dutch established a fort here in the 19th C., their first major garrison in interior Minangkabau, which later became a strategic stronghold in their struggle against the Padris. You can still see the small Dutch *benteng*, Fort van der Capelen, a smaller version of Bukittinggi's Fort de Kock (now the police station). Batusangkar is a pleasant place, smaller and quieter than Bukittinggi or Payakumbuh, with a busy market on Thursdays. Walk to the back of town for a nice lookout over both sides of the valley.

Cheap and centrally located is **Peng. Sri Bunda**, Jl. A. Yani 3, Rp2500 s, Rp4000 d. On the Tabat Patah (N) side of town are: **Hotel Pagaruyung**, Jl. Parak Juar 4, Rp4000 s/ Rp6000 d with *mandi* and breakfast; across the street is **Wisma Yoherma**, Jl. Parak Juar 15 (Rp3500 s, Rp6000 d), some rooms with *man-*

di. Several restaurants, *warung,* and nightstalls will feed you.

Vicinity Of Batusangkar

The surrounding area is quite traditional—with nice views of the countryside and *rumah gadang* with their palm-fiber roofs intact. Most of these villages have maintained all of their most important social institutions and structures right up to the present day, and you see many of the old customs still carried out. One such village is **Balimbing**, between Umbilin and Batusangkar, where travelers may stay in a big *adat* house for around Rp1500. Get *oplet* from Batusangkar 3 times daily, Rp300.

Limakaum

Five km W of Batusangkar. An old mosque here was constructed with 5 stories, symbolizing the 5 villages of the district. Also see a large, very old *rumah adat* with original mountain *atap* roofing. The "Stabbed Stones" and the unexplained "Written Stone" are located in a small park on the N side of the highway near Limakaum. According to existing records, these "Stabbed Stones" *(Batu Batikam)* are a vow of unity between Datuk Perpatih, founder of the Pilang clan, and Datuk Katumanggugan, founder of the Bodi Caniago clan. This set of ancient inscribed stones is near the only hotel in the area, **Mess Kiambang**, charging Rp2500 s, Rp4000 d, tea included.

Pariangan

An ancient royal village on the slopes of G. Merapi, close to the main road between Padangpanjang and Batusangkar. For a trip into the past, take a stroll through this living Minangkabau museum where *adat* houses and waterwheel-run gristmills abound, with people relaxing on front steps as the volcano fumes above! See the community house *(balai)*, mosque, and *padi* storage sheds. According to Minangkabau folk history, ancestors of present-day Minangkabaus first settled in the vicinity of this *desa.* Back on the main road and another 10 km is one of the last surviving traditional Minangkabau-style mosques at **Lubuk Alung**. Over 100 years old, it has a multi-peaked roof, each peak symbolizing one of the original clans that settled the area. Adjoining it is a *surau* where the men and the boys gather.

Pagaruyung

From Batusangkar, either walk 1½ hours or take a *bendi* (Rp500 correct price). Pagaruyung is the former site of the raja's court, heart of the old Minangkabau kingdom. The other towns of the area also had traditional importance: Buo, Limakaum, and Sungaitarab, each site of a high-ranking advisor or minister of the raja. One of the finest man-made objects in Indonesia is the "big house" *(rumah gadang)* called **Istano Pagaruyung**, in the middle of nowhere beyond Pagaruyung. The magnificent building (note the 10-point roof) has been built on the original location of another structure which burned down in 1976. Still being renovated, plans exist for opening a museum inside. Lots of tour buses bring hordes of day trippers to the site. Also in the vicinity are rajas' tombs, still maintained as sacred sites.

Tabat Patah

A sweeping view from the ridge of Tapat Patah takes in the entire plain of Lima Puluh Kota to the N: rice terraces, the Payakumbuh area, the Harau Canyon, and on a clear day even distant mountains 50 km away. The viewpoint is located at the pass N of Batusangkar, 1 km off the main road. If traveling by bus, be sure and ask to be dropped off at the entrance or you'll miss it. Tours often include a stop here. Admission: Rp200. The village itself, and neighboring Rao Rao, are both picturesque *adat* villages. But be prepared for the onslaught of local kids! **Rao Rao**, between Batusangkar and Tabat Patah, is noted for its unusual mosque. The unique structure is built in a 3-story pagoda-style and has a smaller version of Bukittinggi's clock tower in front. Like many of the area's mosques, a pond beside it is used as a bathing place by men and a swimming pool for children.

PAYAKUMBUH

Thirty-three km E of Bukittinggi, Payakumbuh is a market town and government center for the Lima Puluh Kota District ("50 Cities") as well as a transfer point to the Harau Canyon. Take a minibus from Bukittinggi for Rp500 (45 min.). In the center of a large rice plain, Payakumbuh has a different character than Bukittinggi, which lies in the middle of hill country. The *adat* traditions of the rice plain emphasize chiefly perogatives with a strict social hierarchy, while the social structure around Bukittinggi is characterized by merchant and artisan family traditions. Tourist literature is fond of calling this area the "District of 50 Cities," but "District of 50 Villages" is more accurate. Payakumbuh is a good base for visiting surrounding villages, there are plenty of places to stay and eat, and it has a large market (best day is Sun.).

Accommodations And Food

Koli Vera, Jl. Pendidikan 54, is the best place to stay (Rp6000 s or d), located outside of town on the road to Air Tabit. **Wisma Flamboyant**, Jl. Ade Irma Suryani 73 (on the Pekanbaru side of town), isn't really flamboyant but it's OK value for the money (Rp4000 s, Rp7000 with *mandi).* Rooms are large and clean, and it's in a quiet location. **Wisma Sari**, Jl. Jen. Sudirman KB47 (the main road), charges Rp6000 s and d—clean but no inside bathrooms. Scattered around the market are several basic, noisy accommodations, costing around Rp2500 s, Rp4000 d: **Losmen Harau**, Jl. Cempaka (near the market); **Asia Baru Losmen**

and *rumah makan*, Jl. Sudirman 1. Nightstalls and *nasi padang* restaurants line Jl. Sudirman, the main street; **RM Sari Bunda** is a good one. For *martabak*, fried chicken, and ice juices go to **RM Minangasli**, Jl. Sudirman (toward Bukittinggi). *Warung* are located around the market. Try the local *kalamai* cakes (like *dodol*).

Crafts

A well-known crafts center specializing in pandanus and rattan basketware, cotton mattresses, and bird cages. At **Widjaya**, Jl. A. Yani 83, the embroidery arts are practiced by dozens of young girls. More embroidery can be seen in Payakumbuh's market; also native *kain songket* with imitation gold thread (Rp7500) at Kubung. Payakumbuh weaving is characterized by no designs, just plain rattan interwoven intricately in a sort of herringbone design. Bamboo crafts are the strong point of the market. *Takrow* (rattan balls) sell for Rp1000; shoulder bags go for Rp2500. Visit the handicraft village of Andaleh, 11 km from town, where rattan-woven wares such as schoolbags, picnic baskets, dinner hampers, and all manner of basketry are made and sold at **Jolita**. Beyond Andaleh is the beautiful **Taram Valley** and Taram village with its *rumah adat*.

THE HARAU CANYON

A green fertile valley surrounded by sheer granite mountain walls 100-150 m high with waterfalls—an astonishing sight. In the Harau Valley is also a 315-ha nature and game reserve, Cagar Alam Harau, with butterflies, monkeys, tiger footprints, steamy rainforests, and meadows on top of a canyon. Each month only about 600 people visit this remote nature reserve, an average of 20 or so a day, though on weekends a group as big as 250 could suddenly roll in on 3 buses! Most Indonesians visit to picnic or to buy exotic orchids at the nursery—some very unusual species. This is an excellent recreation area for mountain climbing, nature hiking, and the surroundings are rich in wildlife. The tigers of the area are protected but the bears are not because of the damage they cause to the fields. Once a week hunters from the surrounding districts gather here to hunt bear, assisted by a special breed of hunting dog. These valuable dogs can be seen in the marketplace, waiting for someone to hire them out to hunt bear. No place to stay near the ranger station but you can camp in the area. Bring food. The ranger may be able to help arrange for you to stay overnight in the nearby hamlets, or in Harau village about 3 km beyond the ranger station.

Sights

Sign your name in a book and, if he's around or not busy, an Indonesian forest ranger will open the small **museum** (Rp200) of stuffed animals near the entrance and answer questions. Two brochures in Indonesian (Rp500 apiece) inform about the natural phenomena of the area: tigers, *macan dahan* (Sumatran leopard), *macan kambung* (Sumatran panther), *kucing hutan* (forest cat), tapir, deer, *serow*, wild pig, honey bear, monkeys, and more than 30 varieties of forest birds live in the jungle hills up above the cliffs. The monkeys often descend to gawk at the tourists. This is also a butterfly collector's paradise—they are as thick as confetti. After buying your ticket, bear L for 750 m to **Air Terjun Akar Berayun**, a high cascade dropping down to a cold swimming pool. Drinks and snacks are on sale here, and swim trunks can be rented (Rp200).

For a good view of the valley, climb the steps to the observation point. Trails also lead up the side of the canyon. From the ranger station, the road continues 9 km to Desa Harau in a wide valley with ricefields. For the **Lulus**, **Bunta**, and **Murai** waterfalls, take the other road just inside the entrance gate and follow the cliffs around for 1 km. More isolated canyon walls can be seen by following the valley road outside the park to the NW or from the Payakumbuh-Pekanbaru highway to the east. The cliffs get steeper as you drive deeper into the park.

Getting There

The Harau Canyon is 37 km from Bukittinggi, 35 km from Batusangkar, and 14 km N of Payakumbuh. From Payakumbuh, take a minibus or *bisdaerah* 11 km (Rp400) toward Pekanbaru and get off at the gateway in Sari Lamak village. Unless you hire a *bendi* or hitch here, you'll probably have to walk the 3 km on a narrow paved road into the park. Keep R at the junction with another paved road. Past a small village the road finally turns to dirt, then you come to the ticket office and a small refreshment stand. This is the reserve, located in the middle of a steep gorge. Minibuses can also be hired from Sari Lamak to Harau for Rp4000-5000. A good idea is to take a minibus from Payakumbuh (Rp250) on Sari Lamak's market day (Sat.), then you can easily get a ride to Harau village, passing through the canyon en route. **guided tours:** Both long and short tours are given by the park ranger, Chairuddin Amin, for around Rp3000 pp; leave Bukittinggi by 0700 and you'll get at Harau in time for a complete 3-4 hour walk. The guy who owns the nursery will point out all the plants.

BUKITTINGGI

The administrative, cultural, and educational center for the Minangkabau people, Bukittinggi is one of the loveliest, friendliest, most relaxed towns in all Sumatra—a real oasis after bouncing your buttocks raw on long Sumatran bus rides. Nestled in mountains (910-930 m), its name means "High Place" just S of the equator, it's cool and sunny. This small university town has the oldest teacher's college in the country and many other schools. There are musical taxis, pompadoured horsecarts, streetsweepers, veiled schoolgirls, regal women walking sedately under parasols, banks of flowers, good restaurants, and a wide selection of reasonable accommodation. Bukittinggi even has sidewalks. The town is very compact, with many tourist services and bus pickups concentrated along Jl. A. Yani. Providing you are dressed properly, the women are friendly and the men are not cheeky. Most of the businesses are owned by women and run by men. You don't have to bargain so vehemently here as the Minangkabau start out with a realistic first price. For gifts/souvenirs, you can get 10-20% off, but for food in the market and at restaurants you can't bargain—it's already low. This area is worth at least a week.

SIGHTS

In the center of town and overlooking the market is a venerable clocktower constructed by the Dutch in 1827. The "Big Ben" of Bukittinggi, residents call the clock *Kota Jam Gadang*—a Dutch idea and Minangkabau design. Nearby is the botanical gardens (where locals may ask to take your picture). For good info, go to Parindo Tourist Service next to Yany Hotel. Visit the cattle market, **Pasar Ternak**, a short walk from Bukittinggi on the road to Sungai Tanang. See livestock still sold in the traditional way, the would-be buyer and owner bargaining under a piece of cloth using their fingers instead of words. If no agreement is reached, they part as gentlemen.

The Zoo

The zoo is the highest point in town; just behind the museum, both lie within the confines of Taman Bundo Kanduang Park (Minang for "Kind-Hearted Mother"). Walk around on Sun., when all the women parade around in their best Minang apparel. The zoo (usually Rp200 entrance) specializes in Sumatran wildlife. The animals are not always kept under the best conditions but the hilltop setting is pleasant. Clouded leopards, forest cats, tapirs, goat antelopes

(serow), deer, honey bears, crocodiles, gibbons, macaques, argus pheasants, hornbills, owls, and pigeons can also be seen. The zoo is especially strong on birds, with at least 150 species.

In the center of the park is a traditional Minangkabau building flanked by 2 rice barns with fine woodcarving. Opened in 1844, this is the oldest museum in W. Sumatra (Rp250). Specializing in local history and culture, inside are resplendent traditional wedding costumes, headdresses, musical instruments, architectural models of current and obsolete village buildings, old specimens of matchlock rifles (no rifling process used!). A billboard lists biweekly shows at the museum amphitheater where you could see 8-year-old boys do traditional fighting—with knives!

Ngarai Canyon

Also called "Buffalo Hole." On the SE edge of town lies this 4-km-long chasm with sheer rocky walls plunging 100-120 m down to the riverbed below. This canyon, which borders Bukittinggi in the S and W and separates it from the foothills of G. Singgalang, is the pride of W. Sumatra. Ngarai is sometimes even billed as "The Grand Canyon of Indonesia" (though Harau Canyon more deserves this title). Viewed from Panorama Park, it's quite a sight, particularly in the mornings when a veil of mist hangs over the valley. Gunung Singgalang (2,877 m) rises in the background. A 2-km trail leads down through the layers of faulted volcanic ash, across the river on a small bridge, then up the other side to the rim and on to **Kota Gadang**, the "silversmith" village. Underneath Panorama Park are Japanese tunnels built in WW II; with the help of a guide, one can tour these caves for hundreds of meters.

The hike to Kota Gadang takes about an hour. Follow the concrete sidewalk past Mesjid Panorama (next to the park) over the canyon rim and down a long flight of steps to the road. More Japanese tunnels are cut into the cliffs along this road. Walk downhill on the road and take a distinct trail on the L just after a sharp switchback. The trail descends to a bridge and then on up to Kota Gadang, to the far side of the canyon—in all a 5-km walk. To return to Bukittinggi by road, continue S one km to Koto Tuo on the Bukittinggi-Maninjau highway and take an *oplet* the 4 km into town (but walking back via the canyon would be faster). Walking *in* the gorge can be a day's trip in itself—a fascinating geologic area. It's possible to walk even farther along tracks made by water buffalo as far as a bamboo bridge 12 km upriver.

Army Museum

Across from Panorama Park. A WW II vintage plane stands in front. Inside are weapon displays dating as far back as the Padri Wars of the 1830s, radios and other military equipment, paintings of battle scenes and national heros, and photos of the kangaroo courts of the late '60s trying communists. See Sumatra independence money issued in 1958 and arms (supplied by the CIA) to help in their effort to join Malaysia. Admission: Rp250. Open 7 days a week.

Fort de Kock

The Dutch built a fort on this promontory in 1825 during the Padri Wars. Dutch forts, like Fort de Kock, eventually became towns. Now the site is a small park and viewpoint where old cannon and a moat overlook Bukittinggi, valleys, and surrounding hills. Arrive in time for the sunset. At dusk the giant fruit bats come out, looking like birds without tails (the bats nest in trees in the canyon below Kota Gadang).

ACCOMMODATIONS

Jalan A. Yani

The tourist belt of Bukittinggi and the center for cheap lodging. Centrally located in a little valley separating the zoo and Fort de Kock, several "coffee houses" are also along this street. Be forewarned, however, that you are awakened each morning by the sounds of motorcycles, cars, and buses—the noise level could be ferocious! Try to get one of the back rooms. But at night it's quiet with only the sounds of horses' hoofs on the street outside. All the following prices include tax. Walking down Jl. A. Yani from the clocktower the best are: the **Gangga Hotel**, no. 70, Rp2500 s, Rp3000 d, up to Rp7500 with *mandi*; central with nice sitting areas, ticketing and taxi service, a big rambling building. **Wisma Tigo Balai**, no. 100, Rp2500 s, Rp5000 d; a bit dingy but one of the few that will open at 0300! **Grand Hotel**, no. 99, Rp2500 s, Rp3500 d and up (in the new building). **Yany Hotel** (also has a travel agency), no. 101, Rp4000 s, Rp7500 d with *mandi*, hot water, and breakfast. **Hotel Singgalang**, no. 130, Rp1500 s, Rp3000 d; clean, quiet, good breakfast, nice sitting area, friendly, and good atmosphere. **Hotel Murni**, at the bottom of Jl. A. Yani, is clean, popular, and geared toward travelers (even has a place to wash your clothes); Rp1500 s, Rp3000 d. See Japang for answers to your questions, tours, and tickets. Watch the peepholes! Next door, the small clean **Hotel Nirwana** charges Rp2500 s and Rp5000 d with free tea.

Jalan Benteng Area

To beat the noise, and for a generally nicer neighborhood, go up the path on the R just off the bottom of Jl. Tengku Umar (road to the canyon); it comes out

near Hotel Benteng. **Suwarni's Guesthouse**, along with the **Mountain View**, are the best deals in their class. Both guesthouses are beautifully located; out one window the zoo is visible, out the other G. Merapi, and at the end of the road is Fort de Kock. **Hotel Benteng** (tel. 22596/21115), Rp10,000 s or d for Economy rooms, outside *mandi*, hot water, terrific service, reliably clean, spacious lobby with bar, good security. Their higher-priced rooms have balconies (Rp20,000 and up) and the hotel restaurant serves expensive European, Chinese, and Indonesian food (better just to eat in the Roda Group).

Suwarni's Guesthouse, Jl. Benteng 2, is a basic homestay-type place but a quiet location, dorm Rp1750 or room Rp4000-5000 d. This guesthouse offers a family atmosphere. The landlady cooks really great food (order in the morning, 4-person min.), and can help you out with transportation info. The man of

BUKITTINGGI

1. hospital
2. Denai Hotel
3. Lima's Hotel
4. Zakiah Hotel
5. Murni Hotel
6. Nirwana Hotel
7. Tourist Information Center
8. Three Tables Coffee House
9. Hotel Singgalangi
10. Yany Hotel
11. Grand Hotel
12. Fort de Kock
13. Famili Restaurant
14. Mountain View Hotel
15. Suwarni's Guesthouse
16. Hotel Benteng
17. sports hall
18. youth center
19. Sovia Theater
20. Army Museum
21. Minang Hotel
22. Jogja Hotel
23. Bank Negara Indonesia 1946
24. Roda Group Restaurant
25. *camat's* office
26. souvenir shops
27. Mona Lisa Restaurant
28. Roda Barn
29. bus & *oplet* station
30. telephone/telegraph office
31. post office
32. Dymen's Hotel
33. police

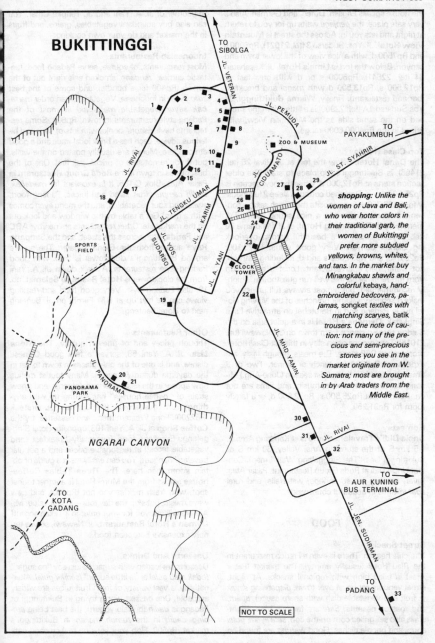

BUKITTINGGI

TO SIBOLGA

JL. VETERAN

JL. PEMUDA

TO PAYAKUMBUH

JL. RIVAI

JL. ST. SYAHRIR

ZOO & MUSEUM

JL. TENGKU UMAR

JL. A. KARIM

JL. CIDUAMATO

JL. YOS SUDARSO

JL. A. YANI

SPORTS FIELD

CLOCK TOWER

PANORAMA PARK

JL. PANORAMA

JL. MHD YAMIN

NGARAI CANYON

TO KOTA GADANG

JL. RIVAI

TO AUR KUNING BUS TERMINAL

JL. JEN SUDIRMAN

TO PADANG

NOT TO SCALE

shopping: Unlike the women of Java and Bali, who wear hotter colors in their traditional garb, the women of Bukittinggi prefer more subdued yellows, browns, whites, and tans. In the market buy Minangkabau shawls and colorful kebaya, hand-embroidered bedcovers, pajamas, songket textiles with matching scarves, batik trousers. One note of caution: not many of the precious and semi-precious stones you see in the market originate from W. Sumatra; most are brought in by Arab traders from the Middle East.

the house speaks English, Dutch, and German. Also a very safe place: the *penjaga* waits up for you to return at night and lets you in. Across the street is **Mountain View Hotel**, Jl. Yos. Sudarso 3 (tel. 21621), Rp6000 s and Rp7500 d, with a nice view of the lower town and canyon. Below the fort is **Lima's Hotel**, Jl. Kesehatan 34 (tel. 22641), Rp6000 s or d with breakfast or Rp12,500 s, Rp13,500 d with *mandi* and breakfast (bar and restaurant). Finally, **Wisma Bukittinggi**, Jl. Yos Sudarso 1A (tel. 22900) is a little down the street and on the same side as the Mountain View, with prices in the Rp4000-6000 range.

Top-Class Hotels

The **Denai Hotel**, below the fort at Jl. Rivai 26 (tel. 21466), is Bukittinggi's top place to stay. The older section starts at Rp12,000 d, while the new section is Rp25,500 s or d. Detached cottages sleep 2 luxuriously for Rp26,750. It lies opposite the *rumah sakit,* a convenient location, and has a nice sitting room, TV, friendly staff. The **Minang Hotel**, at Jl. Panorama 20 (tel. 21120), is set in a beautiful garden overlooking Sianok Canyon. Very good value: Rp23,100, Rp28,875, and Rp34,650 s and d, including bathtub, hot water, bar, and restaurant. Located only 1 km from the *terminal bis* this well-run guesthouse is highly recommended, but almost always full unless you make reservations. Other branches of the Minang Hotel are in Padang and in Batutebal on attractive Lake Singkarak. **Dymens's Hotel** is in a quiet area on the S edge some distance from town on Jl. Nawawi (tel. 21015). Tour groups often stay in this 1st-Class hotel, pronounced DEE-mens. The meals, though tasty, are expensive: Rp6200 for lunch or dinner. Two or 3 times per month in the tourist season (June-Aug.) Minang dance performances, music, and films are put on. Rooms cost Rp25,500 s, Rp32,500 d, or a family room for Rp91,250.

Homestay

Uncle Didi's Travelers Home is at Kandang Ampat, 1.5 km S of the stunning Anai Valley, 30 km S of Bukittinggi (see "The Singgalang Walk" map). Contact Uncle Didi at Roda Group Restaurant, Pasar Atas. River, monkey forest, springs, waterfalls, and rural *adat* villages in beautiful countryside.

FOOD

Street Snacks

Munchie heaven. There is even a French restaurant in the Riau Hotel (usually empty). The market (Pasar Atas) is piled high with regional snacks. At night, street vendors set up all over town, dispensing *sayak* (a fruit and vegetable dish with sharp sauce), *apam,* and roasted peanuts. *Sate* are famous here. Nightstalls also sell grilled corn-on-the-cob, *sate ayam, gulai* soup, and noodle dishes. Good *warung* are found on

the corner of Jl. A. Yani and Jl. Tengku Umar. You can also buy abundant vegetables, grains, and fruits in the market and do your own cooking.

Indonesian Restaurants

Most restaurants, of course, serve Padang food: fantastic curries, *rendang,* smoked eels right out of the *sawah* (Rp400 for a bundle), and some of the best *soto ayam* in Indonesia. Vegetarians can order *martabak sayur* (vegetable *martabak)* at most of the Padang-style restaurants in town, Rp600. Some restaurants have visitors' books with lots of sage and hilarious advice. Each has a brisk local trade and a good atmosphere. Menus are usually posted on the walls, but if you're not sure of prices, ask first. One of the best places in town is the **Roda Group Restaurant** in Pasar Atas, Blok C-155. It is excellent for *martabak, dadih campur,* fruit salad and juices, Padang food, sweet and sour vegetables, and the menu even comes with a map! Get a table by the window and look out on the market life. Other restaurants are nearby: **ABC** and **Farida,** both across the street, and the **Simpang Raya** across from the Gloria Theater. The square around Bukittinggi's clocktower is thick with good Padang-style restaurants. A walk down Jl. A. Yani from the clocktower is **Hotel Restoran Selamat**, no. 19, also Padang-style. Very good food and relaxing views can be had up at **RM Famili** on Jl. Benteng next to Hotel Benteng.

Other Restaurants

Though pricey and of uneven quality, **The Mona Lisa,** Jl. A. Yani 58, serves a few good Chinese dishes, and is one of the only places in town to eat in the daytime during *Ramadan.* Many tourist menus now appear in the *nasi padang* restaurants, and a new strain of "coffee houses" has sprung up with anything from guacamole (Rp500) to peppersteak (Rp2200). For a Western menu and cassettes, try the **Coffee Shop** at Jl. A. Yani 103, opposite Hotel Singgalang. Excellent food (especially breakfast, and vegetable tacos!) at reasonable prices and a popular travelers' hangout. You can easily meet a guide or obtain information here. The **Three Tables Coffeehouse** across from the Murni Hotel is another tourist spot, with fresh milk served hot (Rp400), and new wave music, but skip the day tour—a poor value. Mr. Adlibra will ask you for your order in a Texan accent! **Dymen's Hotel Restaurant,** Jl. Nawawi, serves terribly expensive European food.

Desserts And Drinks

Desserts are loaded with sugar, so just say "no sugar" *(tidak mau gula)* or "a little sugar" *(sedikit gula).* Alternatively, a vast variety of fresh fruit juices are widely available. One dessert worth trying in Bukittinggi or Padang is *dadih* (buffalo yogurt), the best being *amping dadih* in the *rumah makan* in Bukittinggi's market, Rp500. Flop your jaws on real crushed oats with avocado, bananas, coconut, topped with cane syrup and grated coconut. Afterwards, it feels like you've swallowed a boulder. **Roda Group Restaurant** in Pasar Atas is popular with sweet-toothed travelers. The only good bakery in town is opposite the Yany Hotel. Also try **Warung Noni** on the corner at the bottom of Jl. A. Yani (evenings) for flawless *pisang goreng*.

CRAFTS AND SHOPPING

Being a tourist center, Bukittinggi boasts a multitude of craft, souvenir, jewelry, and antique shops. Many are found along Jl. Minangkabau, especially near Bioskop Gloria. Some items are even cheaper than in the village where they were actually made. The shops have fixed prices but you may still bargain a little. There's a great variety of quality goods, with a sprinkling of poor-quality merchandise. **Aishachalik**, Jl. Cindur Mato 94 (an extension of Jl. Minangkabau past the Gloria Theater walking from the market), probably has the best variety and the best (fixed) prices. Also try the following along Jl. Minangkabau: **H. Muchtar Is**, no. 90; Souvenir Shop Juni, a tiny shop in front of the clocktower, selling men's *telok belanga* and women's blouses, Rp6000, **Nuraini**, no. 25. Basrida, Jl. Yos. Sudarso 2, has carvings, embroidery, and *batik*. The **Aladdin Art & Antique Shop**, Jl. A. Yani 14, sells outstanding handwoven articles.

Jewelry

The Bukittinggi area is a center for skilled gold and silver artisans. Both the jewelry itself and the interior of the jewelry shops, done in intricately inlaid wood, are fine examples of Minangkabau expertise. Stones from all over the world are imported and set by craftsmen in their mothers' shops. Also see stones dug from various local mountains, set in brass (Rp2000 and up) and hawked in the market, along with colored uncut gems the size of golfballs, and delicate earrings and bracelets hammered out in nearby villages.

Market

A market happens daily, but Wed. and Sat. host the biggest. During market days Bukittinggi is flooded with thousands of Minangkabau coming in from every nook and corner of these highlands. The sprawling market, which literally covers a whole hill, lasts from about 0700 to 1700 and contains everything from antiques and local crafts to produce and spices—a profusion of overpowering smells, colors, and sounds. Get up to it by either climbing the 300-step stairway or use the twisting cart lanes. There's a sweeping view over the town from the top. The two levels, Upper Market *(Pasar Atas)* and Lower Market *(Pasar Bawah)*, are connected by a number of stairways. It is cheaper near the stairs, and below the

main market, but there are fewer crafts and souvenirs in these areas. The huge market area is divided into sections: a row of barbers, a row of cigarette-lighter repairmen, rows of crunchy-munchy snacks and sweets stalls, *warung*, a fish market, a meat market with piles of red meat and intestines, and countless rows of produce: piles of cabbage, *durian*, cauliflowers, and 50 kinds of rice! In this magical and colossal bazaar is perhaps the strangest assemblage of snakeoil merchants and buskers in all of Indonesia. A must is to have lunch in one of the market *warung*. Sit down and one of the ladies will give you a plate of rice heaped with all kinds of Padang-style vegies and whatever other side dishes you point out. Thankfully, no tourist menus—a great experience and very reasonable.

Craft Villages

Many other "craft villages" lie within an hour's *oplet* ride from Bukittinggi. **Desa Sunga**, on the slopes of G. Merapi near Kotobaru and 17 km from Bukittinggi, is a center for brasswork, especially dishes and *sirih* cases. **Kotobaru** produces handwoven gold-threaded weaving, Rp70,000 for a *sarung*. **Ampek Angkek**, on the edge of Bukittinggi, is known for its *kain sulaman*, embroidery and crochet work. **Sungaipuar** is best known for blacksmithing (from candelabra to plows), **Kota Gadang** for spiderweb-like silversmithing, **Guguk Tabek-Sarojo** for goldsmithing, and **Pandaisikat** (near Padangpanjang on the main highway from Bukittinggi to Padang) for woodcarving, embroidery work, and loom weaving. Visit **Silungkang** village for woodcarving, bright handwoven gold-threaded *sarung*, scarves and headwear (though overpriced).

OTHER PRACTICALITIES

Entertainment

The **Pelita Hotel**, Jl. A. Yani 17, has a poolhall. Traditional dancing *(randai)* is staged at 1230 every Wed., Sat., and Sun. at the zoo; art performances are also held in front of the clocktower or near the Gloria Theater at 2000. *Pencak silat* peformances are staged every Wed. and Sat. night (2000) at Tarok Ujung Bukit, 1 km from Bukittinggi. Another thing to do at night is get a massage. For a real blast, go to a bullfight, which usually take place on Tues. near Kotobaru (S of Bukittinggi) at 1700, Rp250 admission. So much waiting for so little fighting!

Services

The **tourist office**, in the Pasar Atas (tel. 22403) across from the clocktower, is helpful and has a few maps and brochures, but for the best brochure they'll charge you Rp500! The manager, Ar, conducts private 8-hour tours of Bukittinggi and vicinity on which you can see and learn more than if you were on your own; you're in good hands. The tourist office is supposed to be open weekdays 0800-1400, Fri. until 1130, and Sat. until 1100. Free maps of the area are also dispensed from various hotels and restaurants (menus sometimes come with a map). One of the best places to get all your questions answered is at **Hotel Yany's Travel Agency** or at the **Coffee Shop** next door. Bukittinggi's bookstore, **Jaya Agency**, is across from the clocktower on Jl. Minang Kabau; it stocks some books in English. **RS Uman Pusat**, Jl. Sudiman, has English-speaking doctors. Bukittinggi's banks are renowned for giving terrible exchange rates. Better is to change in Padang (Bank Negara Indonesia, Jl. Dobi 1) before coming up to the highlands. **Dhany Laundry Service** is next to Suwarni's Guesthouse up on the hill down from the fort.

Transport

Get to Bukittinggi by bus to experience the beauty of the countryside. Good roads. The drive up from Padang (Rp1100, 2 hours) is spectacular. The Aur Kuning bus station is 3 km from Jl. A. Yani, which is the center for accommodations. Rail service from Padang is only for freight. When arriving at 0300 from Prapat on the bus, ask to be let off at the start of the hotel street, Jl. A. Yani, instead of wasting time and money going all the way to the bus station and having to pay Rp1000 pp on a *bendi* to get back!

Getting Around

Bukittinggi's sights can easily be reached by walking. Horsecarts provide a leisurely alternative, Rp750 for the average 1- to 2-km ride. These horsedrawn carts *(bendi)* decked out with huge white plumes, scarlet frills, and bells, are always available. Minang horses are famous and some of the best looked-after in Indonesia. It's difficult to bargain with the drivers, however, who consistently overcharge tourists. There are some *becak*, but the town's hills are so steep that pedicabs can only be used on the straightaways. Motorcycles can sometimes be rented privately through your hotel for Rp5000 and up per day.

FROM BUKITTINGGI

Villages and most scenic areas outside of town can be reached from the *oplet* station at Aur Kuning, 3 km from downtown Bukittinggi, where minibuses, trucks, and old Chevrolet station wagons provide a cheap but uncomfortable out-of-town service. Fairly good roads connect with all parts of the island. Sample destinations and fares: Payakumbuh, Rp650; Padangpanjang, Rp300; Solok, Rp1000; Batusangkar, Rp1000; Lake Maninjau, Rp650; Panti, Rp1500.

Taxis

Taxis can be hired from travel agencies and at the ma-

jor hotels. Sample destinations and fares: Padang, Rp40,000 OW or Rp65,000 RT; Padang (via Solok), Rp65,000 OW, full-day tour, Rp65,000; Lake Maninjau, Rp30,000 OW or Rp50,000 RT; Batusangkar or Harau Canyon, Rp45,000 RT; Payakumbuh, Rp50,000 RT; Batang Palupuh *(rafflesia)*, Rp20,000 RT. Taxis can also be chartered for longer-distance trips. Some OW fares: Pekanbaru, Rp75,000 (or Rp12,000 per person on share basis); Sibolga, Rp100,000 OW; Prapat, Rp175,000; and Medan, Rp230,000. Parindo Tourist Service Inc., Jl. A. Yani (tel. 21133), can arrange everything.

By Bus

Aur Kuning *terminal bis* is 3 km SE of town. Buses to Padang (Rp1100, 2 hours) cruise Jl. A. Yani for passengers between 0500 and 0600; after that (up to 1900) you have to go to the Aur Kuning Station for buses. Most of the major companies—ALS, ANS, Enggano, etc.—have offices at the *terminal bis*. The **Yany Hotel** (Jl. A. Yani 101) travel agency and some other hotels and travel agencies sell bus tickets; check out the **Maju Indo Sari Travel Bureau** on Jl. Sudirman between the clock and market. Avoid buying tickets from mendacious scalpers who haunt travelers' hangouts, and be careful buying tickets for a/c buses because they seldom arrive. Sample travel times and fares north: Sibolga, 15 hours, Rp6500; Prapat, 18 hours, Rp7500; Medan, 24 hours, Rp15,000 a/c, Rp9000 without. Eager to test the limits of your endurance? Bus from Parapet right on up to Banda Aceh at the N end of Sumatra. East: Pekanbaru, 6 hours, Rp3500; Rengat, 23-24 hours, Rp5000; Jambi, 22 hours, Rp12,000 with a/c, Rp10,000 without. South: Padang, 2 hours, Rp1100; Lubuklinggau, 12 hours, Rp11,000; Bengkulu (via Lubuklinggau) 15 hours, Rp12,000; Jakarta, 36 hours, Rp25,500 (or with a/c, Rp33,500).

Tours

Six- to 8-hour tours are often organized by hotels, travel agencies, and even restaurants to such destinations as Lake Maninjau, Lake Singkarak, Harau Canyon, Kamang Cave, Batusangkar, the *rafflesia* site, cinnamon plantations, traditional waterwheels, rivers for swimming, woodcarving villages, and so forth. Licensed guides are usually better informed than unlicensed ones. Tours can be a good deal—on your own you'll have long waits for public transport. Most tours cost Rp7000, use private cars and vans, and start by 0830; often refreshments and entrance fees are included. They'll leave if there's enough people (min. 6) and if it's not raining. These small tour outfits can also organize special-interest outings: to see butterflies, study biology, archaeology, architecture, even the Kubus and the Sakai.

Hotel Yany's travel agency, **Parindo Tourist Service**, offers minibus tours, leaving on Sun., Tues., and Thurs., for Rp7000 per head with enough people. **Hotel Singgalang**, Jl. A. Yani 130, also does tours. The **Coffee Shop** (See Bujang; speaks smatterings of French, English, and Dutch) also conducts high-quality tours. Another idea is to get a group together and just hire an *oplet* for the day for about Rp60,000 (which includes gas). Meet friendly Uncle Didi at the Roda Group Restaurant and get him to take you on beautiful walks of the area. He prefers sincere people to money. He also has a good repertoire of card and cigarette tricks, and be sure to ask to see his photo album.

KOTA GADANG

A quiet village well known for its fine hand-embroidered shawls, weaving, and silver filigree work. Here you may also view the silversmithing process. This one tiny village produced a steady stream of competent colonial bureaucrats in the early 1900s, and since independence it has been the birthplace of a remarkable number of Indonesian professors, cabinet ministers, prime ministers, diplomats, etc. Schoolchildren have to traverse a rugged, grueling footpath, twice a day every day, to Bukittinggi, year after year until graduation; only those with an intense desire to learn stick with it. Dutch influence is still very much in evidence here, but the women's names on the houses are 100% Minangkabau. Many of the older people of this village still speak Dutch. Kota Gadang can be seen from Panorama Park in Bukittinggi.

Crafts
Visit Denny and Daisy at **Silverwork**. They ask Rp3500 for filigree-like brocades and rings (without precious stones), tiny silver Minangkabau houses, etc. They always have a cup of tea ready for you and might even serve fruit while you bargain like mad and chickens cackle out the windows. The selection is wider and the prices less expensive at **Kerajinan Amai Setia** Souvenir Center on the other side of the village; signs show the way. Housed in a traditional structure built in 1915, the Souvenir Center is open everyday 0900-1730. Their collection of embroidery, lacework, handkerchiefs, *sarung*, and Minangkabau bridal headdresses is especially good, though difficult to bargain down. There are miniature Minang houses, rings, and *kris*—all claimed to be 90% silver. If lighting is poor, take items outside to have a good look at them. Order embroidery here as well, such as a *kebaya* (the Minang version differs from the shorter Javanese version). The lady will dress you up in a complete Minang bride's costume—blouse, headdress, *kain*, spangled jacket, dress, everything—for Rp3000, so you can play bride for photographs.

Getting There
This "silversmith" village is a 2-hour walk up to the other side of the gorge from Bukittinggi. Take a *mandi* in the river on the way; in fact, you can spend the whole morning in the gorge—somewhat grandiloquently dubbed the "Grand Canyon of Indonesia." A number of *warung* are strung along the walk. The sides of the valleys in the Minangkabau highlands are so steep that the buffalos which feed on the grasslands above the valleys often unconsciously venture too close and are killed by the high fall. Thus the Dutch nickname for Bukittinggi's Ngarai Canyon: "Buffalo Hole." The path ends at 100 giant steps leading up to Kota Gadang. To reach the start of the footpath, first walk or catch a *bendi* (Rp1000) down the twisting road which begins below Panorama Park; enter the path on the L after the little *warung*. Notice all the deep ammunition caves gouged out by the Japanese during WW II; some actually reach underneath Panorama Park. Or take an *oplet* or bus by paved road 5 km from Bukittinggi Rp250. To get back, you can either take the minibus or walk 7 km to Sianok village where you can descend on steep dirt steps back down into the canyon.

WEST SUMATRA HIGHLANDS

Bukittinggi is the usual choice as a base for exploring the highlands, but the towns of Payakumbuh and Batusangkar also have acceptable accommodations and transport. Your own vehicle would be ideal for touring the beautiful countryside and traditional villages, but slower *oplet* go almost everywhere and cheaply, too. There is superb mountain and valley scenery on the road to the border with N. Sumatra Province. About 20 km N of Nglau Kamang on the main road to Medan is Bonjol, right on the equator.

After crossing into N. Sumatra Province, you'll see a change in the architecture of village houses and will start hearing the familiar *Horas!* greeting from the Mandailing Batak people.

Batangpalupuh
The giant flower *rafflesia Arnoldi* grows in a reserve 12 km N of Bukittinggi. The fare is Rp300 by *oplet* or minibus (30 min.). The *rafflesia* is about 1 ½ km from the main road; follow the sign down the path which leads you to the edge of the forest to a gate. Guides to this botanic classic ask Rp2000-3000, or find kids to lead you for less. The *rafflesia* often blooms after a heavy rain. Some say in January, others say in June—no one seems to really know. It's as rare as a tiger print to see. If the giant flower isn't in bloom when you go, you'll have to content yourself with a 30-min. walk, and a view of the bulb only (the size of a softball), or the disintegrating mass. All the gates into the reserve may be locked up so get the key in the village first.

Bonjol

Formerly the headquarters of the religious and military leader, Iman Bonjol, this town is 56 km N of Bukittinggi on the Trans-Sumatran Highway. Iman Bonjol was one of Indonesia's first nationalist folk heroes who fought bravely against Dutch colonial "pacification" during the Padri Wars (1803-1837). Old Dutch cannons and Bonjol's prayer house are still found in this village, the center of intense guerilla resistance. Betrayed to the Dutch by another religious figure, Bonjol was finally captured in 1837 and sent into exile to Ambon and then to Manado, N. Sulawesi, where he died. Bonjol is right on the equator; a large globe in the rice paddy to the side of the road marks the spot. Pause for a few moments to notice that you've lost your shadow. Following closely like a child all your life, growing from short to long, it suddenly and alarmingly vanishes. Also at this point, the island of Sumatra is at its widest (362 km).

Panti Hot Springs

Located 105 km N of Bukittinggi in the 2,830-ha Rimbo Panti Nature Reserve. The highway goes right through the middle; the springs are about 50 m E of it. A 2-m-deep pool of muddy water boils up and feeds a small stream. The water is too hot for swimming but hard-boil your eggs! Wildlife includes tigers, tapirs, deer, *serow*, monkeys, and birds. At the town of Panti, just N of the reserve, a partially paved road leads to the coastal towns of Sasak, 94 km, and Air Bangis, 148 km, the northernmost town in W. Sumatra Province, on the fringe of the Minangkabau culture.

Sungai Janiah

About 15 km E of Bukittinggi on the road to Payakumbuh. From Bukittinggi's bus station get an *oplet*, Rp500. Or get a ride to Baso, then walk inland 4 km to this "Place of the Holy Fish." A pond near the mosque is full of big tame carp, believed sacred by the locals, contrary to orthodox Islamic law. There are so many carp it looks like a fish-breeding pond. Throw a *krupuk* in and the water churns as if piranhas were devouring a goat carcass. The legend maintains that a mother placed her 2 children in a small pit for safekeeping while she worked nearby *ladang* fields. When she returned to the hole, she found the children gone, the hole filled with water, and a pair of tame fish swimming in it. Her children were never seen again. The 1,200 inhabitants of Sungai Janiah are very proud of their high-standard *randai* dance troupe, named after the sacred fish: *Randai Ikan Sakti*. **Bukit Tanjua**, a lofty, craggy peak, towers above the sacred pool. It takes about 45 min. to climb to the top. map 23

The Singgalang Walk

This loop, one of the finest things you can do from Bukittinggi, starts at Padanglawas and ends at Sing-

THE SINGGALANG WALK

NOT TO SCALE

galang, a 12-km tour from Padanglawas. The walk, which skirts along the base of G. Singgalang, goes through a countryside of abundance and beauty; you'll see several traditional agricultural implements not used in the West for over 100 years! First get a *bemo* from Bukittinggi to Padang Giring-Giring, 8 km. Walk in to Padanglawas, not far from the highway, then across beautiful ricefields to Kototinggi, the next village. Trudge in to Luhung, a high village on the slopes of G. Singgalang, then down to Tanjung. Notice that almost every other house has a loom in it. Weavers ask around Rp40,000 for a traditional *sarung tenun pandai sikat*. On the paved road up from **Tanjung** village is a mill where blindfolded *kerbau* on a turnwheel compress sugarcane to pulp—a unique traditional factory. Inside the boiling room observe the cane juice boil down to a syrup which is then made into round cakes; ask to try some, still warm. Walk over the hill from Tanjung to Pagu Pagu, then over to **Pinjuran Tujuh**. Just before this village is an *asli* rice mill by a small waterfall. Keep hiking to Kandang Guguk, Ganting, and E to Singgalang. From Singgalang to Padangpanjang is about 4 km. About 3 km after Singgalang is **Lubuk Mata Kucing**, an artesian swimming pool (Rp250 entrance), with cold healthy water. The road finally comes out at Padangpanjang, from where you can board a bus back to Bukittinggi. Allow 5-6 hours.

Kotobaru

A dirty, nondescript town at the pass between G. Singgalang and G. Merapi, 30 km (Rp200 by bus) S of Bukittinggi. Combine a visit here with a visit to the weaving village of Pandaisikat (see below). Check out Kotobaru's market with embroidered scarves and *sarung songket*. On Tues. afternoons (be there at 1600, they begin at 1700) bullfights are usually held in one of the nearby villages. Fall in behind other people heading there along a picturesque path through the rice paddies. Bulls create pandemonium as they run through the crowded spectators surrounding the unfenced ring—Indonesia's own Pamplona! Kotobaru is also the starting point for the G. Merapi climb; best to go on Sat. night when local climbers are making the climb and just fall in behind them (see p. 530).

If you'd like a short walk in this area, take a bus (Rp200) to Pasarrebo, then walk about 15-20 min. on a beautiful footpath to **Kotolawas**. Or take a bus (Rp200) to Kotobaru, then catch another bus to Kotolawas via Pandaisikat, Rp100. Leaving Kotolawas, walk downhill out to the main road, then flag down a bus or *oplet* back to Bukittinggi. Sometimes bullfights are held in Kotolawas, too.

Pandaisikat

A lovely village 12 km S of Bukittinggi (Rp250 by bus), off the road to Padangpanjang on the cool slopes of G. Singgalang. Take an *oplet* to Kotobaru (Rp200), then walk (delightful) or take another *oplet* the remaining 2 km. It seems that every man in this village is a carver and every woman a weaver; a native ironsmith also makes axes for a living. Pandaisikat is noted for the excellent quality and variety of its red- and gold-decorated woodcarvings, copperwork, and cloths richly interwoven with gold and silver threads *(songket)*. See the traditional embroidery process (Rp40,000-50,000 for a *songket)* on simple wooden frames; there are about 1,000 looms in the village. Local carvers also make house roof eaves, murals, panels, furniture. They work every day, including Sunday; morning is the best time to see them. Visit the *Wali Negeri's* (headman's) house. **Pusako Weaving House**, which sells *songket,* is a traditional Minang house with carvings on the inside and out—a new house beautifully made and landscaped. Foreigners stay here to learn weaving. Good hiking around this area.

LAKE MANINJAU

Known for its culture, remoteness, and beauty, this huge crater lake 38 km E of Bukittinggi is a retreat for famous poets and philosophers. The height of the edge of the crater of this dead volcano, from where you descend, is 1,097 m. The lake itself is 470 m above sea level. The 610 m drop down to the lake is a spectacular drive or walk. The crater holding the lake is one of the largest in the world—a wonder in itself. Even the crater inside the Tengger Mountains (E. Java) in which G. Bromo sits is an infant compared to Maninjau! The deep blue water of the lake is always calm. There are facilities for waterskiing, swimming, fishing, and boating (both motorboats and canoes). Lake Maninjau abounds with fish and in the restaurant on the shore you may order a freshwater fish dinner cooked to taste. If you're coming from Bukittinggi on a day trip, start early. There's lots to see.

The ride out to Lake Maninjau and back on the bus or *oplet* is incredibly scenic. From Bukittinggi's *stasiun bis* it only takes 1½ hours (Rp650) to get there. **Embun Pagi** ("Morning Cloud") is a small *desa* and lookout (1,097 m), 30 km from Bukittinggi, just before the descent down to the lake. It's so high you can see clouds inside the crater beneath you. Children will approach you selling wonderful straw purses and pandanus palm bags in an infinite variety of shapes, sizes, colors, uses, prices; stalls sell refreshments. You can also spend the night at this admiring viewpoint. **Embun Pagi Cottages** charges Rp20,000 d and Rp40,000 for cottages (4 persons). Breakfast is Rp3000, lunch or dinner, Rp5000.

From Embun Pagi, it's a 2-hour walk with 44 sharp switchbacks to the bottom of the crater. The mountains slope right down to the lake, the green reflecting in the shining blue water, like the picture of a fantasy world in a child's storybook. On the way down you can hear siamang apes hooting in the trees; other monkeys with the young gripping the mother's belly scurry along the road. When it's raining the mist lays over the lake but often it blows away and the weather is bright and clear.

The Lawang Top

Take this alternate route to Lake Maninjau, and enjoy all the beauty of the area. Puncak Lawang is 1,400 m above sea level and about 1,000 m above the level of Lake Maninjau. From Bukittinggi, take the bus (Rp600) all the way to Lawang (5 km from Matur), then walk (1 hour) or take a *bemo* 5 km past Lawang to the lookout. Friday is best because it's market day. Then walk for 2 hours (17 km) down a steep, beautiful trail to the lake past houses and cultivated fields com-

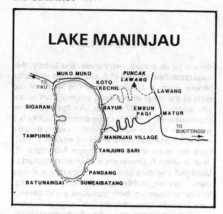

LAKE MANINJAU

ing out at the village of Bayur (lots of monkeys). From Bayur walk 2 km to Maninjau Village, passing some warm springs on the way. Or you can go right from Matur straight on the roadway down to the lake via Embun Pagi.

Maninjau Village

A noisy lakeside village at the bottom of the descent from Embun Pagi. Visit the warmsprings, 500 m down the road from the bus stop and a short walk in. It would be perfect if bicycles were for rent, but it's not so easy to find them. The best place to stay is simply called the **Guesthouse** (Rp3000-5000), right around the corner of the market, a 125-year-old Dutch house with high ceilings, a library of old Dutch books, and a friendly proprietor who gives out a map of all the "tourist objects" and dispenses a map and good information. There could be other homestays; ask around. From the porch of one of **Hotel Maninjau's** 30 rooms, you can literally jump into the lake (Rp 8500-30,000 d). The hotel restaurant specializes in fresh lake fish. Speedboats can be rented for sightseeing or waterskiing (Rp6500 per hour). On the N side of town is the quieter **Pasir Panjang Permai Hotel**, Rp19,500 s, Rp23,000 d, including hot water and breakfast. Eat at the 3 really simple restaurants serving Padang food, or at the Guesthouse on a magnificent veranda (unfortunately, uncreative food).

From Maninjau

The last bus from Maninjau village to Bukittinggi leaves at around 1500 (but check!) and tends to be

very crowded. On market day, buses leave as late as 1700. If you miss the bus, and don't want to stay over, you'll have to charter a *bemo*. A worthwhile trip if you have the time is to walk the scenic 16-km road following the N shore of the lake from Maninjau to Muko Muko on the other side (this road actually continues for 139 km all the way to Padang via Tiku and Pariaman). The trip around the S shore to Muko Muko is much more difficult. A complete circle around the lake is 70 km; takes 2-3 days. Small ferry boats leave from the docks beside Hotel Maninjau to lakeside *kampung*. Or just rent a canoe from someone and go fishing. When visiting the outlying villages, stay either at the *kepala kampung's* house or with other villagers.

Bayur is 3 km N of Maninjau, a little *desa* from where you can take a footpath through the jungle up to Puncak Lawang. From here a road leads to Matur and on to Bukittinggi. For entomologists, *buprestidae* butterflies can be found in this area; ask the children. Bayur is the setting for Frederick K. Errington's brilliantly written and illustrated book on the Minangkabau, *Manners and Meaning in West Sumatra*, Yale University Press, 1984, the first analysis in English of how Minangs interpret their own customs and etiquette.

Muko Muko

Steep jungle-covered crater walls tower above this village on the W shore of Lake Maninjau, 17 km from Maninjau village; catch the occasional bus for Rp300. In Muko Muko a river cuts through the crater wall at its weakest and thinnest point, draining the lake. A major hydroelectric project is based here. The **Alamada hotsprings** are nearby. Speedboats are available. During the day loud calls from siamang apes can be heard booming out of the forest. Walk to the river an hour before dusk to watch birds and monkeys coming down for a drink.

Stay in the villa on the small island offshore (ask at the hydroelectric office) or ask to sleep in one of the *warung* along the road. Kedai Kopi Sultan Malano may have some rooms. Try *ikan kecap*; meals average Rp2000 pp. If it's *durian* season, stock up here. Whole truckloads are exported to other parts of the province. A lakeside *rumah makan*, 1 km before Muko Muko, is popular for Minang-style fresh lake fish (Rp2000), but closes at 1800. Many people from Bukittinggi come out to Muko Muko on the weekends just to eat here. Very charming people run the place.

THE MENTAWAIS

The Mentawais are made up of 4 islands parallel to and about 100 km off Sumatra's W coast. These islands are actually the tops of a submerged mountain range, which also forms the islands of the Simulue, Nias, and Batu groups. The peaks of this long continuous ridge became separated from the mainland by a deep submarine trench sometime during the mid-Pleistocene Age, perhaps 500,000 years ago. This isolation accounts for their completely separate evolution from Sumatra. Throughout the Mentawais dwell many endemic animals and plants of Indo-Malay origin which have been left to their own distribution and evolution. The islands—Siberut, Sipora, N. and S. Pagai—are generally flat, with marshy coastlines of mangrove swamps, and only a few gray sandy beaches. Dense tropical vegetation covers 65% of the islands' interiors. The heaviest rainfall is in April and Oct., and often causes serious floods. February and June are relatively dry. Because of the bureaucratic hassles involved, the islands receive only about 20 visitors per year. Take your malaria pills 2 weeks before going. Also, have a look at Mr. Pane's amazing photos of Siberut; he's the manager of Padang's Pacto office, Jl. Pemuda 1 (tel. 27780).

History
Long locked in its own time and space zone, isolated from the rest of the archipelago, these people lacked weaving, rice, pottery, stonework, even betelnut chewing right up until the early 1900s. The German enthnologist Maass published in 1902 a landmark travelogue, *Among the Gentle Savages,* a sympathetic portrait of the Mentawai natives which first attracted the interest of scholars. Large-scale conversion to Christianity didn't take place until the 1950s. Today, German Christian missionaries claim the allegiance of perhaps half the inhabitants, while the other half are animists with a veneer of Christianity. All schools on all the islands are run by missionaries, and there are now about 80 Protestant churches throughout the Mentawais.

THE PEOPLE

The people of the Mentawais, whose total population is only around 30,000, actually consist of 3 different ethnic groups: the inhabitants of the Pagai Is., P. Sipora, and P. Siberut. All are of Mongoloid blood, with some Veddoid characteristics, and are closely related to, though less developed than, the Dayaks of Borneo and the Torajas of S. Sulawesi—all belonging to the Ancient Peoples of Indonesia (see "Introduc-

tion"). These shy, disarming people, formerly a proud, self-assured democratic community practicing hunting and gathering, can be picked out right away from the coastal townspeople as "outsiders." You can still see a few traces today of their rich traditional culture. Sometimes their black hair is twisted into topknots.

On older people, traditional tattoos of blue lines can be seen on faces or peek out from under clothes. The Mentawaians also exhibit a certain alertness and agility missing in the coastal townspeople. Unfortunately, Western civilization is having its usual effects: disease, dislocation, poverty, despair.

Traditional Villages
Most Mentawai islanders have traditionally settled inland along the banks in the upper reaches of rivers. In the past, when head-hunting raids were an ever-present threat, villages attempted to remain as inconspicuous as possible, separated from the rivers by a wall of seemingly impenetrable tropical forests. Today, one need travel only a short distance inland before the forest canopy opens on extensive, sunlit gardens. In the center is the village, a vast clearing

Mentawai islanders, 19th century

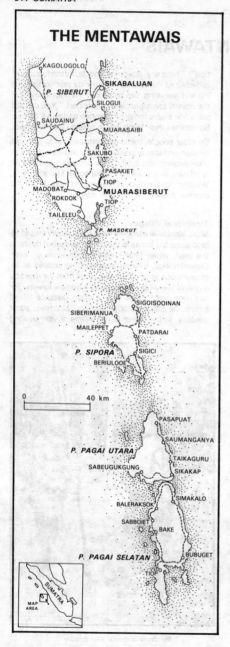

THE MENTAWAIS

KAGOGOLGOL

SIKABALUAN

P. SIBERUT

SILOGUI

SAUDAINU

MUARASAIBI

SAKUBO

PASAKIET

TIOP

MADOBAT

MUARASIBERUT

ROKDOK

TIOP

TAILELEU

P. MASOKUT

SIGOISOOINAN

SIBERIMANUA

MAILEPPET

PATDARAI

P. SIPORA

SIGICI

BERIULOOE

0   40 km

PASAPUAT

SAUMANGANYA

P. PAGAI UTARA

TAIKAGURU

SABEUGUKGUNG

SIKAKAP

SIMAKALO

BALERAKSOK

SABBOIET

BAKE

P. PAGAI SELATAN

BUBUGET

TIOP

SUMATRA

MAP AREA

---

dominated by many thatch-roofed houses. These compact villages may accommodate several hundred people: patrilineal clans made up of 5-10 families each occupying their own section of the village. Each has their own *uma* or clan house, a beautifully constructed, massive structure, and the focus of Mentawaian social and ceremonial life. Today, as in the past, Mentawaian family dwellings are rectangular with palm-wood floors raised on posts to give protection from seasonal flooding. The walls intersect with the crossbeams of gabled roofs, which are covered by layers of intricately woven palm thatch. An open platform extends beyond the overhang of the roof, and at least one notched tree trunk rests against the platform.

PRACTICALITIES

Accommodations And Food
No hotels or homestays, but there's a PPA guesthouse in Muarasiberut. In the interior, ask the assistance of the *wali negari* (chief) of the village. If you stay with a family, be sure to give a donation. Expect to eat coconuts, *mie, nasi,* vegetables, and fish. The inland Siberutese eat sago and bananas, while the Siporese and Pagaiese prefer taro and bananas, barely subsistence diets. There are also cassava, sweet potato and other root vegetables, pepper, *durian,* mango, and pineapple.

Getting There
You first need to obtain permission at Padang's police station (Jl. Prof. M. Yamin). Without their *surat ijin,* you may not be allowed to travel into the interior. Siberut's reserve may not be visited without a *surat jalan* from Padang's PPA office on Jl. Raden Saleh. Take along tobacco (Gudang Garam filters), plenty of *rupiah* (no banks or moneychangers), gifts anti-malaria pills, and extra food. All the islands are serviced by supply ships that take some passengers. Some of these cargo boats depart from Telukdalam (N. Nias) around 2000, arriving at Sipora by 0700. Ferries also leave (Rp5000) from Padang's Teluk Bayur Harbor to P. Siberut. *Kapal motor* leave even more frequently from Padang's small boat harbor (Muara), but it could be tough to get on one. The larger ships from Padang cost only Rp5000-7500 and take 12 hours to reach P. Siberut. Local steamers also call in at N. and S. Pagai Islands, 20 hours. Another option is to charter a speedboat from Padang's Muara Harbor, Rp100,000 per day. There is only one airstrip in the group, called Rokot, located on P. Sipora and accessible by motorized outrigger (pay in cigarettes) from Sioban and Muarasiberut. Each Mon. a Merpati flight leaves Padang for Rokot (Rp15,500) and returns the same day, so you must stay a week.

Getting Around

After you clear with the military police in Muarasiberut, and leave your passport at their headquarters, arrange for inter-island transport with the *camat*, missionaries, or the *wali negari* of each village. A guide (about Rp5000 daily) is important here. Officials will tell you that you'll need twice as much food and gas than is necessary, and you must bargain continually. Give small gifts to the police as you go. The people of the coastal villages—Minangkabaus from mainland Sumatra, Javanese immigrants, and the tribal people—are all very helpful. Bring some pencils and sweets for the kids. Everytime anyone sees you beyond the towns, they want tobacco. If it's a small river town, you could get stuck waiting for a boat for as long as a week.

PULAU SIBERUT

The largest of the Mentawais, this 86-km-long island lies 150 km off the coast of Sumatra opposite Padang. Pulau Siberut has its own subculture, quite different from that of the Batu Is. to the N and P. Sipora and P. Enggano to the south. Ringed by untouched coral reefs, 60% of the island is still covered in tropical rainforest. The island's main towns are **Sikabaluan** in the N and **Muarasiberut** on the SE tip, inhabited for the most part by Minangkabaus, Javanese *pegawi*, Bataks, and Chinese shopkeepers. The principal economy of the towns is the export of timber and rattan. There's no public transport, no hotels, no restaurants. Use speedboats or canoes for around Rp100,000 per day. From Muarasiberut, you can only walk to Sakelot (1 km), Maileppet (3 km), and Pasakiet (6 km). Only Sakelot has longhouses, while the others are new government settlements. A 50,000-ha reserve (0-384-m-altitude) is located in the western portion of the island, but it's area is steadily being eroded by the timber companies which bulldoze large muddy tracks through the reserve to fell patches of primary rainforest.

Sights

Up the rivers of P. Siberut you can still visit many primitive villages with loinclothed men, women wearing beads and brass rings on their arms and toes, naked children, and traditional dwellings *(lalep)* on stilts. Toyon, or some other self-appointed guide, will come around the PPA guesthouse in Muarasiberut; he can arrange everything. An easy trip is to **Tiop**, SE of Muarasiberut, accessible by river boat in just 2 hours. More ambitious is **Rokdok**, a longhouse village 6 hours RT upriver. **Madobat**, about 12 hours RT, is deep into Sakkudai territory. The police will want you to use guides and motorized canoes because they feel you would not be safe otherwise.

THE SAKKUDAI

The 5,000 or so native inhabitants of interior P. Siberut, the Sakkudai, have evolved a unique and fascinating belief system. Their belief in magic is still prevalent and they still practice ritual taboos, sometimes for months on end. However, their way of life is now being threatened by the intrusion of missionaries, government, and the timber concessions. Japanese trawlers, working off P. Siberut, have spawned a business in prostitution which has added even more to the cultural corruption of the traditional life of the island.

Religion

The old religion, though forbidden by the government, still persists. Their brand of animism is based on the belief that everything, everywhere, is alive and possesses a soul, including states of nature such as floods, rainbows, phases of the moon, and even "non-living" objects. No object is ever thrown away while it's still functioning for its soul would be greatly offended. It's an insult to ask someone to hurry—*moile moile* ("slowly, slowly") is one of their most common calls. Souls and the bodies they inhabit are interdependent, so that what happens to the soul happens equally to the body, and vice versa. Too much "soul stress" is the primary explanation for illness and death among the Sakkudai, as well as accidents, long periods of fruitless hunting, and even the withering of plants.

The Taboo System

Taboos *(punen)* exist because the Sakkudai believe that every human enterprise interferes with the environment. When misfortune strikes, the Sakkudai attribute it to something they have done to upset their extraordinary harmony with the supernatural or with one another. They search for the fault within themselves. Harmony is restored by deliberately changing behavior, abstaining from certain activities. Or, the occasion of these holy periods of abstinence and taboos could be in anticipation of violating harmony: building a new house or boat, clearing a field, felling a coconut tree, etc. Taboos might prohibit certain foods, or close the village to all outsiders. If the violation is really big, the peoples' daily lives could come to a complete standstill. In the same spirit, they beg forgiveness of the animals they slaughter. Fish are killed with poisoned arrows which paralyze them, causing less pain. Under missionary and government pressure, the enforcement of *punen* periods have almost disappeared, being only observed on Sundays.

RIAU

A portion of this province, called *Riau Daratan* (Mainland Riau), is located on the island of Sumatra. The other part consists of thousands of islands, large and small, stretching from the E coast of Sumatra N to Malaysia and E toward Kalimantan. This portion of the province is called *Kepulauan Riau*, or Insular Riau. Both "Riaus" share the same capital: Pekanbaru on mainland Sumatra, gateway to some of the largest oilfields in Asia. Riau Province is a rich area for natural phenomena, historical sites and ruins, architecture, crafts, as well as a popular pilgrimage area because of its old mosques, reconstructed palaces, and tombs interring venerated saints. Eight generations of sultans have ruled in the area.

INSULAR RIAU

Insular Riau comprises 1,176,530 sq km, while its land territory is 94,561 sq km. It is made up of a vast expanse of sea bordered on the N by Singapore, in the W by mainland Sumatra, and in the E by Borneo. Of its 3,214 large and small islands, about 1,000 are occupied, and only 743 named; total land area is about 800,000 ha, with a sea area over 17 million ha. The Riau Islands 300 years ago were the heart of Malay civilization. Little evidence of this remains today as the islands are quiet and peaceful, a fantastic explorers' territory. Like Joseph Conrad, you can easily get lost in the South China Sea (Natuna Is.), go diving off the wild coasts of P. Mantang or P. Abang, or simply search for the ultimate beach—which you'll probably find. If you happen to have a cabin cruiser along, this is a quiet and safe paradise to roam around in. The Riau Islands are also a rich ethnographic area inhabited by many varied cultures. The best primeval forest and wilderness hiking is found on P. Lingga.

Climate

The islands have an equatorial climate with a maximum temperature of 31 degrees C and an average min. temperature of 20 degrees C. The rainy season is from Oct. to Feb.; humidity hovers around 80-90%. Rainfall averages 250 mm/month between Oct. and Feb., and 150 mm/month between March and September. It can be quite cool during Dec. and Jan., even though most islands are near the equator. If you're planning to visit the eastern islands (such as the Natunas), don't travel during the "winter" monsoon season (Nov. through March). The South China Sea is notorious for typhoons and hurricanes.

Fauna And Flora

Food crops consist of rice, corn, cassava, chilis, soybeans, peanuts, vegetables, fruit, etc.; trading crops are rubber (especially on Lingga Is.), cloves, coconuts, coffee, *gambir,* sago, oil palm. The islands' primary forests yield various timbers, benzoin, palm-leaves, resin, rubber, beeswax, honey, etc. You see remarkable flowers everywhere, including the *Nusa Indah* (yields a hallucinogenic drug), and the big red flowers of the bayam plant (a species of amaranthus; also gives edible leaves).

The fauna is not very different from mainland Sumatra's: domesticated livestock such as cows, buffalo, and goats, and in the jungle wild boar, monkeys, deer (particularly on P. Penuba), and birdlife in abundance. The principal fauna reserves are the 200-ha P. Burung, set aside for the protection of turtles and seabirds; and the far NE island of P. Laut (400 ha). The seas around Riau are generally shallow; *keelong* have been built out over the water for catching fish. In these seas are stingrays, hammerhead sharks, marlin, coral fish, and poisonous seasnakes (take care while diving).

History

The earliest known residents of these islands were the Wedoide tribes, thought to have migrated from Southern India. The years 2500-1500 B.C. saw the rise of the proto-Malays, followed in 300 B.C. by the deutero-Malays. Around A.D. 1000 several island-states rose into prominence. The emergence of P. Bintan as a separate kingdom can be traced back to this time; the kingdom was ruled by a king known as Asyar Aya. A queen, later dubbed the "Queen of Bintan", gave birth to a daughter, Wan Seri Beni, who married Sang Nila Utama (son of the King of Palembang), who built a capital in Temasik (now Singapore). Between 1300-1328, the Kingdom of Temasik held sway over P. Bintan. But by 1500, the Kingdom of Melayu, at Melaka, had not only conquered P. Bintan but also the Riau islands of Kundur, Jemaja, Bunguran, Tambelan, and Lingga. Over the next several centuries, Riau's fate was tied to the fortunes of the great seaport of Melaka. The fall of

Melaka in 1511 began the short 18-year era of Portuguese control over Riau. The departure of the Portuguese marked the beginning of Riau's Golden Age: from about 1530 to nearly the end of the 18th C., the Riau archipelago became the nucleus of the Malay civilization. Its main centers of power were P. Penyenget and P. Lingga, but its capital was moved several times to avoid the attacks of ferocious *Orang Laut* (sea pirates).

In 1685, Sultan Mahmud Syah II was forced to sign a cooperative agreement with an increasingly powerful emerging force, the Dutch. Over the next century the raja's authority was greatly eroded. From 1721 until the death of the last sultan in 1911, the kingdom was split into 2 centers of government. On one side, the Melayu sultan, known as Yang Dipertuan Besar, moved from P. Bintan to P. Lingga. His sphere of authority was known as *Lingga-Riau*. His brother-in-law (Yang Dipertuan Muda) moved his government to P. Penyenget; his kingdom was called *Riau-Lingga*. Finally, in 1784, Raja Haji Yang Dipertama Muda Riau IV was killed in a war against the Dutch. (You can visit his remains, or at least the earth covering them, on P.

Penyenget.) From 1784 on, the Dutch exercised absolute control, though the rajas had residual authority in the sphere of *adat* law. Opposition to the Dutch went underground, surfacing in the early 1900s, with the establishment of the Rusydiah Club. This club was founded by Sultan Abdurrachman Muazan Syah (1883-1911), the last sultan of Riau-Lingga. Syah realized he couldn't confront the Dutch openly, so the club was ostensibly formed as a cultural and literary organization. (You can still see the remains of its headquarters on P. Penyenget.) While active in the cultural and economic spheres, the Rusydiah Club secretly organized as a para-military group. It later joined forces with the famous nationalist organization *Sarikat Islam,* and its efforts greatly assisted in the struggle for Indonesian independence.

Economy

Considerable wealth is found on some islands in the form of minerals: oil on Batam, granite on Karimun, tin on Bangka, Singkep, and Kundur. The tin mines on P. Bangka are some of Indonesia's oldest (early 1700s). On P. Billiton, the first mine was started in 1861, and on P. Singkep in 1887. Indonesia is today

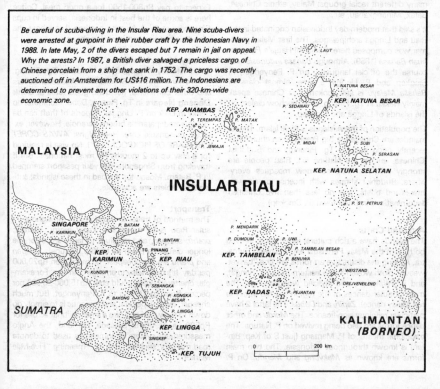

Be careful of scuba-diving in the Insular Riau area. Nine scuba-divers were arrested at gunpoint in their rubber craft by the Indonesian Navy in 1988. In late May, 2 of the divers escaped but 7 remain in jail on appeal. Why the arrests? In 1987, a British diver salvaged a priceless cargo of Chinese porcelain from a ship that sank in 1752. The cargo was recently auctioned off in Amsterdam for US$16 million. The Indonesians are determined to prevent any other violations of their 320-km-wide economic zone.

MALAYSIA

SINGAPORE

KEP. ANAMBAS
P. TEREMPAS P. MATAK

P. LAUT

P. NATUNA BESAR

KEP. NATUNA BESAR
P. SEDANAU

P. JEMAJA

P. MIDAI

P. SUBI

P. SERASAN

INSULAR RIAU

KEP. NATUNA SELATAN

P. BATAM
P. KARIMUN

P. BINTAN

TG. PINANG

KEP.
KARIMUN

KEP. RIAU

P. KUNDUR

P. SEBANGKA

P. BAKONG

P. KONGKA
BESAR

P. LINGGA

KEP. LINGGA

P. SINGKEP

KEP. TUJUH

P. MENDARIK
P. DUMDUM

P. UWI

P. TAMBLAN BESAR
P. BENUWA

KEP. TAMBELAN

KEP. DADAS

P. PEJANTAN

P. ST. PETRUS

P. WEISTAND

P. OREJVENEILEND

**KALIMANTAN
(BORNEO)**

SUMATRA

0   200 km

the world's 4th largest producer of tin, which is second only to petroleum as the principal foreign currency-earning mineral. Thanks to all this mineral wealth, Insular Riau is one of the richest parts of Indonesia. Tg. Pinang is nearly as clean a city as Singapore, a great contrast to Jakarta. New buildings are going up at every turn, there's a new sports stadium, and roads in most towns through the islands are neatly lined with parks and gardens. Even the poorest houses have TV antennas now. Of course it doesn't do any harm being so close to commodity-rich Singapore; Riau has always had close economic ties with that island-republic and even used Singapore currency right up to Sukarno's militant 1964-65 *konfrontasi* campaign.

The People
The main population group of the Riau Islands is of pure Malay stock. Several indigenous population groupings include the *Orang Laut* (sea gypsies) from the Natuna Is. and Sulawesi, as well as the *akit* tribes of the Bengkalis District, the Mantang people of P. Penuba and P. Kelumu (in Kec. Lingga), and the Baruk people of Sungeibuluh, P. Singkep. On P. Bintan live many different racial groups: Malay, ethnic Chinese, Batak, Minangkabau, etc.

It's said that modern-day Indonesian originated in the Riau and Lingga archipelagos. The first Malay grammar was composed here: Radja Ali Hadja's *Pengetahuan Bahasa* (1859). Although *Bahasa Indonesia* is of course the official language, on P. Penyenget, P. Singkep and P. Lingga, a pure, almost classical *Bahasa Melayu* is still spoken. The Chinese speak mainly Hakka in Tg. Pinang, and Teuchow dialect on the islands of Lingga and Singkep.

The population of these islands is 90% Islam. The remainder are Christian (a big Presbyterian church has recently been built in Tg. Pinang), and Buddhist (Chinese, animist on Natuna Is.). Riau people are strongly religious. You see new mosques everywhere, Buddhist shrines with incense burning on inter-island boats, and no less than five Christian denominations in Dabo town (P. Singkep).

Arts And Crafts
The islands have a rich cultural inheritance, derived both from the Malay Peninsula and mainland Sumatra. Among the distinctive art forms are fine "basket-weave" cloth woven in the eastern Riaus, P. Rengat, and P. Pelalawan, and stylized woodcarvings. The most popular dances of the region are the *Joget* (a fun Malay dance), *Zapin*, and *Dabus*. The latter 2 have particular religious significance. The *Merdu* and other dance forms are also being revived on P. Natuna. The traditional theater of P. Mantang (just S of Kep. Bintan) is known throughout Indonesia. The two main forms are known as *Makyong* and *Mendu*. On P.

Singkep, traditional Malay theater is very much alive.

The main type of traditional house in the Riau Islands is the *Rumah Lipat Kijang*, or "hairpin-bend" house (named after the shape of the roof-apex). This style of building, long neglected, is currently experiencing a revival. The decorative carving on each house has its own significance, though it's difficult to tell how much meaning is traditionally symbolic and how much is fanciful speculation. Flowers symbolize prosperity and happiness for the visitor, birds signify the only true God, decorations such as wings on each corner of the house mean the ability to survive anywhere, while the 4 pillars symbolize the ability to live happily in any of the 4 corners of the earth. You also see different styles of woodcarving on the friezes surrounding the section of the roof overhanging the veranda.

PRACTICALITIES

Food
Fish and rice are staples. On P. Penuba, deer meat is eaten. In the bigger towns, Chinese food is available. Otherwise, food is generally prepared Padang-style. Expect to pay Rp800-1500 for a good meal. Coffee here is some of the best in Indonesia, served in cups Singapore-style. A favorite pastime throughout the islands is hanging out in coffee shops.

Money, Visas, Health
Oriki Money Changer, Jl. Merdeka, Tg. Pinang, gives a good rate for U.S. dollars. For Australian dollars and other currencies, get quite good rates at **Bank Dagang Negara** in Tg. Pinang, Dabo, etc. (note: no banks in Daik on P. Lingga). Reports of theft can be exaggerated: paranoia breeds paranoia. However, exercise reasonable care. Heed signs: *AWAS COPET* ("BEWARE OF PICKPOCKETS"). No visa is required for a stay up to 2 months for most nationals. But if traveling from Singapore, get your passport stamped in P. Batam. Mosquitos are bad in these islands; anti-malarial tablets are advisable.

Transport
The method of travel and exploration throughout Insular Riau is by *kapal laut, kapal motor, spetbot, prahu, sampan,* and medium to large ships for the longer distances (such as to Kep. Natuna). *Sampan* and *prahu* are the cheapest, no more than Rp20,000 per day. It's quite easy to arrange boat-hire. For example, chartered boats could cost Rp15,000-20,000 per person from Tg. Pinang to P. Penyenget. But much cheaper, more expedient and romantic is to simply go down to the wharf and hire a small sailboat across for Rp500—a delightful passage. On land, the Anglo measurement system is sometimes used to denote road markers, such as "Batu V," meaning "Five-Mile Marker."

TANJUNG PINANG

Bintan is the largest island in the Riau Archipelago (1,075 sq km), containing the towns of Tg. Pinang (capital of the *kabupaten)* and Tanjung Uban. It's generally flat except for several "mountains": G. Bintan Besar (334 m) and G. Kijang. The airport (Kijang) is at the SE tip of the island. Besides its bauxite mines, P. Bintan's most notable assets are its deserted, lovely, white-sand beaches. Good diving possibilities include hulls from ships sunk during WW II off P. Mapor and Tg. Brakit.

Tg. Pinang is a small Malay-Chinese trading center and the principal town of Insular Riau, located only 80 km S and 4 hours by launch (S$60) from Singapore. This relaxing and clean city is a good place to watch people come and go from the length and breadth of SE Asia. Tanjung Pinang is developing fast with new buildings going up all over town, and new facilities along the waterfront. The harbor is filled with all imaginable craft. Tg. Pinang serves as an important commercial shopping center for such cities as Medan, Jambi, Jakarta, Palembang, and even Padang, so lots of goods are around, though not cheap. The main shopping street is Jl. Merdeka, leading to the markets. Everyone seems to own a TV set: 2 Malaysian, 2 Singaporean, and one Indonesian channel are all received crystal clear. People watch Australian, American, and Chinese movies. The main nightlife for non-TV-inclined Westerners is just walking around.

History
Situated on the important commercial sea lanes, P. Bintan has always held strategic importance. The sultan of Tg. Pinang, Hussein, once held power over Johore, the southern islands of Kep. Lingga, and his influence even extended as far as Tembilahan on the E. coast of Sumatra. Learning the use of gunpowder from the Turks and Portuguese, he reigned by virtue of a powerful sea fleet. It was from Hussein that Raffles obtained his license to establish a trading post on Singapore Island. The sultan of Tg. Pinang actually chose to set up his kingdom on P. Penyenget, a small island opposite Tg. Pinang; the royal residence was built there in 1803. Before WW II, the capital of Riau Province was Tg. Pinang; now the capital is at Pekanbaru.

Sights
A new sports stadium is in the center of the city. Also visit the old Chinese temple. The wharves are worth a look—especially the old harbor of Pejantan II with its wooden houses along a wooden street leading out to the pier. Climb the hill behind town for a fantastic

view. Also walk down by the harbor at sunset—very peaceful. Out of town a bit, have a look at the **Regional Houses of Parliament** at Batu V, a complex of buildings in the traditional Riau architectural style. **Riau Kandil Museum**, Jl. Bakarbatu 2 km out of town on the road to Kijang (Rp300 by *ojek*), contains most of the surviving *pusaka* of the old Riau kingdoms. Amazing collection of old *kris*, guns, ships, ceramic plates, manuscripts, charts, antique brassware, etc., mostly still uncatalogued. Musty smell of history. The genealogical chart is fascinating. Go any time—Raja Razak, an enthused and dedicated curator, will open up the museum for you no matter when you call.

Accommodations
Tg. Pinang is a busy transit town with people passing through from all over, most seeking out the cheap rooms. Cheapest of all is to stay with families. Be careful of which house you stay in: thefts of foreigners' gear have been reported. Ask Indonesians in the street and touts on the quay; they know who take tourists. Most of these private rooms go for Rp1500-2000 per person. For budget accommodations, look for the sign **PENGINAPAN**; the term *losmen* is not widely used here. Try the following hotels: **Hotel Tanjung Pinang**, Jl. Pasar Ikan, rents good economy class rooms for Rp6500 s; get your bearings on a large relief map of Riau upstairs. **Johnny's Guesthouse** offers rooms for Rp2500 s and has fine snooker tables. **Hotel Surya**, Rp8500 s, isn't bad and there are a couple of homestays on the same street. **Wisma Riau**, Jl. Yusuf Kahar, opposite Peng. Sempurna Jaya International, Rp12,500 and up for two. **Hotel Sondang**, Jl. Yusuf Kahar, also Rp12,500 and up for 2, Rp14,500 t (ask Sal if he has room at his house about 4 km from town; he charges about Rp2000 per night). Luxury **Peng. Sempurna Jaya International** has luxury prices: Rp17,500 s, Rp19,500 d. **Sempurna Inn**, Jl. Yusuf Kahar, opp. the Merpati office, starts at Rp9000 s. A new no-name *losmen* is about 300 m from the wharf; ask for Rommell on the wharf. Several more *penginapan* are found between Bank Dagang Negara and the Chinese temple.

Food
Twice as expensive as on Java. It costs Rp1500 for a *nasi goreng* and Rp1000 for a *nasi campur*, *Gado2* and *soto ayam* are the cheapest meals going. Good cheap Padang food is available at the small *warung* on the corner of Jl. Rimbajaya and Jl. Bakarbatu. But the best eats by far are at the *pasar malam* (night market), close to the Tanjung Pinang Hotel. The whole town converges here at night, a great people-watching place (sip from a bottle of *arak*, Rp1200, or Rp450 for black coffee, Rp650 with milk). The sea-

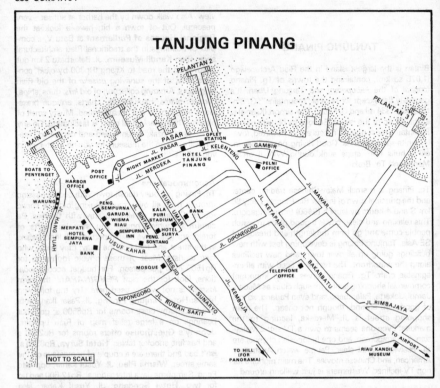

TANJUNG PINANG

food stands serve the best value; try *makan hakau,* or *kepitang cinkong goreng tepung* (crab claws) fried in light crispy batter and only Rp2500! According to connoisseurs, Tg. Pinang still has the best coffee on earth.

Services

The post office is on Jl. Merdeka near the harbor. To change currency, go to the moneychangers, or just ask in the shops; some will refuse, others will offer you Rp1100 or more per U.S. dollar. The **Kantor Imigrasi** here is an outpost on the edge of Indonesia. Since they are less monitored, they will give you more slack, with no further "fees" if you've missed your boat, if it's run aground, or if there's no boat out the next day. The nearest tourist office is in Pekanbaru on the mainland. If you're contemplating an extended visit to the islands, write 4 weeks ahead to: Baparda, Kantor Gubernor Riau, TK I, Pekanbaru, Riau, Indonesia. The best map of Riau is at the Kandil Riau Museum; other maps are difficult to find. In Tg. Pinang, **Netra Service Jaya,** located down on the harbor, is most helpful; ask to see their wall map of

Tg. Pinang. For employment, Westerners could teach English here, a language in high demand because of the proximity to Singapore.

Getting There

From Singapore, first get to P. Batam (port: Sekupang) by fast launch (S$20 OW or S$27 RT), leaving Mon. to Fri. at 0815, 1015, 1215, 1415, and 1615. Don't forget to have your passport stamped. From P. Batam, board another launch to Tg. Pinang (Rp5000, 4 hours), leaving often. Buy your ticket at Singapore's Finger Pier at the end of Prince Edward Road. A cheaper way, and better if you want to see more, is bus from Sekupang to Nagoya (Rp500) on P. Batam. Then from Nagoya take a taxi to Kabil (Rp8000, but cheaper if you share). From Kabil, boats leave about every 20 min. throughout the day to Tanjung Uban on P. Bintan (Rp2000). From Tanjung Uban take a bus to Tg. Pinang (Rp1850). P. Batam is 1 hour ahead of Singapore time. A launch from Singapore goes directly to Tg. Pinang (S$65, 4 hours), though cheaper in the other direction (Rp33,000). From Pekanbaru, the 48-hour trip up the Siak River costs Rp12,500 Deck

Class, Rp17,000 for a cabin. Can be rough traveling. Stop at riverside villages to buy food along the way. From Dabo, P. Singkep, the KM *Hentry* does this run, a nice new ship, Rp15,000 including a meal. Leaves Dabo about noon on Tues., Thurs., and Saturday. By air, daily Merpati flights from Pekanbaru to Tg. Pinang for Rp47,000. Garuda also flies from Palembang to Tg. Pinang 4 days weekly, from Padang 3 days weekly. You may also fly from Jakarta to Pangkalpinang (P. Bangka) daily at 1005 (20 min.), from where you can get boats to Tg. Pinang. From P. Bintan's Kijang Airport (TNJ), it's 17 km (Rp6000 by taxi or Rp2000 by *ojek)* into Tg. Pinang.

Getting Around
The universal means of transport is the *ojek* (public motorcycle), discernable by a small yellow reflector on the front left-hand side. The fare is Rp200 to anywhere in the inner city, Rp300 to anywhere in the suburbs. Also, *oplet* are available at the standard fare of Rp200.

FROM TG. PINANG

Everyone in Tg. Pinang seems to work for a travel agency and is dying to sell you tickets. This can be a real pain. If you're told no more seating is available on a trip, go down to the harbor where a ticket can suddenly become available. It is customary to hand your passport over to the agent who sells you your ticket, but make sure the exchange takes place in a bona fide shipping office and not out on the docks with a stranger. Tg. Pinang is a jumping-off point for P. Penyenget, one of the main cradles of Malay history, as well as P. Singkep, P. Lingga, P. Kundur, and many outlying islands to the east. Intriguing palace ruins are located on nearby and farther out islands. Travel companies won't conduct tours to these sites as they are difficult to organize and lack appeal to the ordinary tourist. So you have to get out to the more remote islands by local ferries. A twice-weekly ferry goes to Tg. Batu on P. Kundur (Rp5000), and Daik on P. Lingga twice weekly (allow 3 days RT).

For Singapore
The "slow" boat back to Singapore stops at P. Batam (no new visa required) on the way and costs up to Rp22,500. Or buy a ticket at Tg. Pinang's wharf for P Batam (departing 1000) for Rp5000. The launch leaves Sekupang on P. Batam for Singapore (45 min., Rp15,500). The direct launch from Tg. Pinang to Singapore departs daily at 1400, arriving approximately 1900; costs Rp33,000. A hydrofoil also does the trip from Sekupang on P. Batam to Singapore for Rp38,500.

For Sumatra
A slow but enjoyable way to Sumatra, is the boat from Tg. Pinang to Pekanbaru; costs Rp12,500 deck class. Some "fast" boats could charge more. This unique trip takes about 48 hours. At least one boat departs daily, sometimes 2 or 3. Most leave around 1400, depending on the cargo. The boats usually travel at night, spending much of the day at several ports, as long as 12 hours; get off and walk around towns with no cars, trucks—just bicycles, motorbikes, and trishaws. At Siak Sri Indrapura, take in the palace. Sleep on deck and pray for good weather; a bunk in the cabin costs Rp5000 extra but may be worth it if it looks like rain or if the deck is too crowded. Guard your belongings! Bring snacks.

By Ship
For larger ships sailing to the eastern islands, try Perintis Lines' RT ticket out of Tg. Pinang every 12 days. Allow yourself at least a month. Their schedule is: Tg. Pinang-Letung-Tarempa-Sedanau-Midai-Serasan-Sintete-Serasan-Sedanau-Midai-Tambelan-Tg. Pinang. Other freighters visit the islands in the South China Sea with varying schedules and prices; ask around the shipping offices. Sample fares: Batam, Rp6500, daily; Selatpanjang, Rp18,500, daily; Tanjungbalai, Rp12,500; Moro, Rp6000, weekly, Dabo, Rp11,500, Fri. and Tuesdays. Farther afield, check out the big blackboard at the Pelni office at Jl. Temiang 190: for example, to Singkawang (N of Pontianak, W. Kalimantan) costs Rp24,500. For Jakarta, the good ship KM *Pokoworto* stops at Tg. Pinang to pick up Jakarta-bound passengers. Get out to Kijang, Rp1500 shared taxi or Rp5000 chartered taxi, to board the ship. The fare is Rp24,5000 deck class (the crew will rent you a bunk for about Rp1500), or Rp49,500 with cabin. The agent will take your passport and your ticket will materialize surprisingly just before you board. The passage takes 3 days. Stops at Muntok on the way. Watch out for theft—cameras have been ripped off. You reach Jakarta at around 0700.

Flights
A Merpati flight leaves every day at 1140 for Pekanbaru, Rp47,500 (arriving 1250). A taxi from Tg. Pinang's *stanplatz* on Jl. Gambir out to Kijang Airport costs Rp6000 (12 km). Sempati Airlines offers the widest range of destinations out of Tg. Pinang: Jakarta, Rp80,500, daily; Medan, Rp82,500, Wed. and Sat.; Tanjungbalai, Rp31,750, Fri. (SMAC); Pekanbaru, Rp45,000, daily; Dabo (P. Singkep), Rp45,000, Fri.; Palembang, Rp50,500, daily; Pangkalpinang (P. Bangka), Rp48,500, Friday.

VICINITY OF TG. PINANG

Males will be approached in Tg. Pinang by Indonesians wanting to escort them to the renowned "villages of joy": **Batu Duabelas** and **Batu**

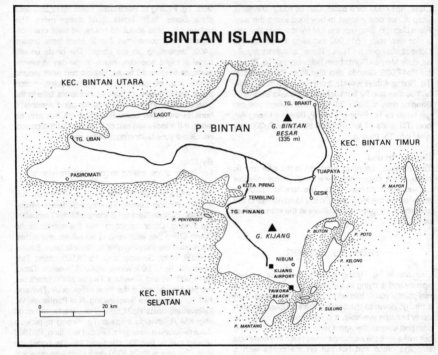

BINTAN ISLAND

KEC. BINTAN UTARA

TG. BRAKIT

LAGOT

G. BINTAN
BESAR
(335 m)

P. BINTAN

KEC. BINTAN TIMUR

TG. UBAN

PASIROMATI

P. MAPOR

TUAPAYA

KOTA PIRING

GESIK

TEMBILING

P. PENYENGET

TG. PINANG

G. KIJANG

P. BUTON

P. POTO

NIBUM

P. KELONG

KIJANG
AIRPORT

KEC. BINTAN
SELATAN

TRIKORA
BEACH

0   20 km

P. SULUNG

P. MANTANG

Enambelas, where young men may meet young women on an informal basis. These villages are located out of Tg. Pinang in the direction of Kawal, Rp2000 by shared taxi. **Kota Piring,** "City of Plates," is reachable by *spetbot* (30 min.) or taxi (Rp8000 RT). The ruined palace in this village was built by the 4th viceroy of Riau, Raja Haji. Its walls are embedded with ceramic plates. **Senggarang** is a Chinese *kampung* accessible by sampan (Rp500-600), which depart from the landing near Hotel Tanjung Pinang. You'll travel up the Snake River, through mangrove swamps—a mysterious atmosphere. The Chinese *klenteng* complex in this village is over 150 years old.

Beaches

Pantai Brakit is on the NE coast of P. Bintan at Tg. Brakit. Reached by bus, Rp500 (30 min.), or by boat (Rp3500 RT, 6 hours) from Tg. Pinang's harbor. Deserted beach and excellent diving in glass-clear water in coral reefs during the summer months. **Pantai Trikora** is another beautiful pristine beach (connected to several other lonely beaches), 50 km S of Tg. Pinang. Its white sands and coral reef are ideal for swimming, diving, and picnicking. There's now a new road, only Rp5000 by taxi. Occasionally, *bemo* also

make the trip, or rent a motorcycle (Rp10,000 daily) and take the road to Kijang. At Batu Sepuluh (10-Mile Stone), turn L at the fork after the *mesjid* and follow the road to Kawal for 18 km. At Kawal, take a R and follow this road another 9 km to Trikora Beach. Stay in the cottage-style *penginapan.*

G. Bintan Besar

At 335 m, the highest mountain on P. Bintan. Stay the night with the *kepala kampung* in Sekuning at its base, then next morning rise very early and climb 2-3 hours up through jungle to the top from where you can see all the surrounding islands. To get to Sekuning, rent a *spetbot* or *prahu* across the bay and up a small jungle river to the *kampung.* Another way is to rent a taxi for Rp25,000 to travel the 80 km to Sekuning. Or take a ferry (Rp5000) for Tg. Uban (leaves each day at 1400), then on to the *kampung* for an additional Rp2500 by *ojek.* Though it's also possible to take an *ojek* to Tg. Uban, the road is sometimes in too rough a shape to take a car.

Pulau Penyenget

A tiny island (2½ sq km) off Tg. Pinang, inhabited by 2,000 Malay fishermen. A sampan from Tg. Pinang's wharf costs Rp400-500. Go early in the morning when it's cool. It is possible to stay with a family at modest cost; ask Kampung Ladi. The island, which you can walk completely around in several hours, boasts a history and hosts visitors way out of proportion to its size. Everywhere you go are ruins and old graveyards; many pilgrims arrive to pay homage to the notables in these royal graves. Tradition has it that the island was given to Sultan Yang Dipertuan Riau-Lingga VI in 1805 as a wedding present by his brother-in-law, Sultan Yang Dipertuan Lingga-Riau IV. Pure Melayu is spoken here.

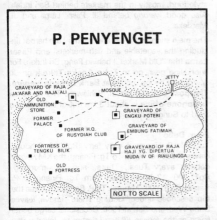

P. PENYENGET

NOT TO SCALE

Once on P. Penyenget, turn R and walk along the "main road" (no vehicles or motorbikes on the island). The principal points of interest are at the NW end of the island. Don't miss the magnificent yellow mosque, built in 1818 by Yang Dipertuan VII. With its pillars, minarets and domes, this unusual structure is like something out of Disneyland. Inside is a famous **library** with hundreds of books on history, religion, culture, law and languages, as well as 5 ancient handscripted copies of the *Koran*. Nearby is the **graveyard** of Raja Jaafar and Raja Ali, and the ruins of the former palace of Raja Ali. Beyond the graveyard is a 180-year-old ruined palace, the **Kerajaan Melayu**, the banyan trees pulling it down. This old palace was made by using millions of egg whites for mortar; nearby is a finely crafted well and bathing place. Other extensive ruins are along wide, quiet paths under lush groves. Also royal bathing places, ornate watchtowers, and burial pavilions (the men have penis-shaped tombstones, the women's are shaped accordingly), some quite well maintained. All significant sites are marked with small plaques and inscriptions. Raja Sulaiman will show you his mementos and photo album; he knows well the genealogy of the local aristocracy.

Sunken Wrecks

Pulau Mantang has a stunning coral reef and a 15,000-ton British freighter sunk by the Japanese; it lies 28 m below the water. Also excellent fishing. Uninhabited P. Pompong is only 35 km from the equator; there are 3 wrecks here, all about 18 m underwater: the *Kurala, Tunkuang,* and *Kuangwo*, all sunk trying to escape from Singapore during the Japanese attack in WW II. Favorable conditions for underwater photography here. At the southern end of the unpeopled island of P. Abang is a large freighter that still contains some of its cargo, also bombed and sunk during The Big One. This is a good dive site, the depth ranging from 6-18 m. All around the island are coral reefs and many small coves and beaches.

Pulau Batam

A 466-sq-km island directly W of P. Bintan. Opposite Singapore, its N shore borders the Singapore Strait. Batam is a free port so look around for good buys on electronic goods. Because of its proximity to Singapore and duty-free status, P. Batam is expensive. Short transit visas are available for 1-day visits from Singapore; apply at Wisma Indonesia in Singapore. Big plans are afoot to develop P. Batam as an industrial hub, with swank hotels and manufacturing enclaves along the NE shore. The main town, Sekupang, consists of not much more than customs and immigration offices. Nagoya is a new city on reclaimed land, built in the last 6 years. **Hotel Batamjaya** is expensive, but good cheap accommodations are on Jl. Tenku Umar, about 2 km out of town near the post office. Four *penginapan* right next to each other charge Rp6500. **Peng. Sederhana** or **Peng. Sempura** charge Rp10,000-11,000. There are also

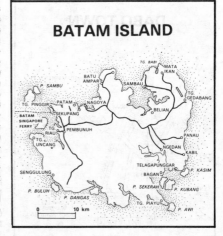

BATAM ISLAND

0   10 km

more expensive resort hotels. Nongsa is a good beach at the N of the island. From Telagapunggar (Batam) catch small boats to Pulau Ngenang. On the eastern side of P. Ngenang are fine deserted beaches. P. Batam can be reached from Singapore's Finger Pier and from Tg. Pinang by a 2½ hour ferry ride (S$20 OW, S$27 RT); the jetfoil takes only a half an hour. There are direct flights from P. Batam to Jakarta. From Sekupang, hop a local ferry to either P. Sambu (with the oil tanks) or P. Belakangpadang. Both islands offer spectacular night views of the bright lights of Singapore and have expensive (Rp8500-15,000) poor-value hotels. The ferry from P. Sambu to Tg. Pinang departs daily at 1030 for Rp4500; nice trip.

DABO

Pulau Singkep is in the Lingga Archipelago, SW of P. Lingga, separated from the E coast of Sumatra by the Berhala Strait. Though the 3rd largest island in Insular Riau, P. Singkep is only visited by the few travelers on the Singapore-Tg. Pinang-Dabo-Pangkalpinang-Palembang (or Jakarta) route. Numerous white-sand beaches. Dabo is the main town, the headquarters of the Riau Tin and Timah Mining companies. Half a dozen main roads converge on a beautiful central park. Dabo has a friendly population of only about 20,000 people but offers most of the services you'd find in a big city. There's a particularly large concentration of Chinese, long ago indentured to work the tin mines on the island; the rest are of pure Malay stock.

See the big mosque in the center of Dabo town. Every Sat. night delightful performances of classical Malay

drama are staged at **Taman Seni;** just Rp200 admission. Elaborate customs and stylized acting. There's a bar in Wisma Timah, and 2 movie theaters. Pantai Batu Bedaun is a pretty white-sand beach lined with palm trees, only 3½ km out of town; other nearby beaches are Sergant and Jago. Walk up the hill past the residential area of Bukit Asem for good views.

Wisma Timah is Rp22,500 per room. Recommended is the **Sari Indah,** Jl. Perusahaan; Rp6000 d, Rp9,000 t. Very clean, with a comfortable sitting room, you may use the kitchen, and it's only a 10-min. walk from the harbor. Dabo offers mainly expensive Padang-style food, mostly in the markets behind Sari Indah. Also good *warung* behind Jl. Pasar Lama and Jl. Merdeka.

The main shopping areas are down by the harbor (including the vegetable and fish markets) and **Pasar Lama** (the "Old Market") behind Peng. Sri Indah. For snorkeling gear, go to **Toko Aneka Teknik** on Jl. Merdeka. Change money at **Bank Dagang Negara.** The **post office** is on Jl. Pahlawan. The overseas **telephone office** is about 3 km out of town on the road to Sungeibuluh.

From Dabo
To Daik, P. Lingga, a daily ferry (Rp5000, 3 hours) leaves at 0900 or 1000. To Tg. Pinang, the KM *Hentry* departs every Tues., Thurs., and Sat. morning, Rp11,500, 12 hours (then from Tg. Pinang to P. Batam, Rp10,000, 7 hours). To P. Bangka, reverse the trip described under "Getting There" above; leaves Dabo Wed. and Sat. at 1500. Occasional cargo boats (such as the *Intisari III)* carry timber to Jakarta; you might be lucky enough to get aboard. Sempati has a flight to Jakarta every Wed. and Sat. for Rp70,500; to Tg. Pinang, every Tues. and Sat. at 1240 for Rp41,500; and to Tg. Balai, every Thurs. at 1315.

Vicinity Of Dabo
Sungeibuluh, a port town on Singkep's N coast (36 km from Dabo), is port of call for the KM *Bhaito V* from Tg. Balai, P. Karimun. Get to Sungeibuluh by bus from Dabo, Rp3000-4000, depending upon how hard you bargain. About 5 km before you reach Sungeibuluh are the remains of the old jetty, and a little harbor still used by small craft. At the N end of this harbor is a fine white-sand surfing beach.

Getting There
From Tg. Pinang, take the KM *Hentry,* a well-built ship made entirely of teak. This is an enjoyable trip of 11-12 hours through some of the loveliest islands you'll ever see. Costing Rp11,500 including a meal, it leaves Tg. Pinang on Mon., Wed., and Fri.; try Agent **P.T. Cuaca Teran,** Jl. Lorong Merdeka IV (tel. 21906) in Tg. Pinang (in Dabo, their office is at Jl. Pramuka 63). It's also possible to take cargo boats to Dabo from Jambi, SE Sumatra; Rp12,500, 18 hours. **from Belinyu, P. Bangka:** Board the *Batam Baru* on Wed.

DABO TOWN

TO AIRPORT

JL. MERDEKA

JL. PAHLAWAN

TO SUNGEIBULUH

JL. PERUSALAAN

PENG. SRI INDAH

JL. PELABUHAN

HARBORMASTER'S OFFICE

VEGETABLE MARKET

FISH MARKET

JL. PASAR

JL. PASAR LAMA

MOSQUE

TO BUKIT ASEM

CHURCH

PLAYING FIELD

WISMA TIMAH

CENTRAL PARK

TAMAN SENI

CHINESE WARUNG & RESTAURANTS

NOT TO SCALE

and Sat. at 1100. The trip is free (courtesy Riau Tin), but you must first register at the Riau Tin Co. office or you won't be allowed onboard. Their office is in Pangkalpinang; ask for Mr. Bompie. The boat stops at the small island of Cebia where you're served an elaborate meal (again free), then board a fast launch to Dabo. Don't abuse the privilege please. **by air:** From Tg. Pinang, Sempati has a flight to Dabo each Fri. for about Rp45,500, or from Jakarta to Dabo every Wed. and Sat. at 0700 and 0800 (Rp74,500). SMAC has a flight Tues. and Fri. (Rp36,000) and also flies from Tg. Balai (P. Karimun) on Thurs. at 1200. **Dabo Singkep Airport** (SIQ), modern and clean with a small cafeteria, is 5 km from town center.

Pulau Penuba isn't the easiest of islands to get to, but the warm reception and beautiful scenery more than make up for difficulties of the passage. Nothing much to do but swim, walk around, and relax. On the northern side of P. Penuba is the settlement of Tanjung Dua with some fine nearby beaches. For those into hunting, the island abounds in deer and wild pigs. **Penuba** is a small village on a little bay on the SE side of the island. Just 10 min. to your L around the point are nice beaches and coconut palms. The whole place looks like it's been laid out by a landscape contractor. See the **Attaqwa Mosque** in the center of the village. Stay at **Peng. Desa Penuba** above a billiards saloon; Rp6500 d. Eat at the *warung kopi* several doors away. To get to this island, take a bus from Dabo (P. Singkep) to Sungeibuluh, from where you get a launch (30 min.). Bargain with the boat owner, or wait until he has enough passengers to make up a full load.

DAIK

Three hundred years ago, the rajas of Lingga-Riau held sway over a vast area. Now only overgrown ruins reflect this former glory. In fact, when you first glance at P. Lingga you might think there's nothing there at all—strictly an island for nature lovers and history nuts. To get to this island take the daily ferry (Rp5000) from Dabo, P. Singkep, at 0900 or 1000. The boat *Sabar Menanti* plies infrequently between Tg. Pinang and Daik, Lingga's main town. It's only a small boat, so it's not recommended in the rainy season. The small, nondescript town of Daik lies about 5 km inland, along a muddy river. There's a little narrow street, cargo wharves, about a dozen Chinese shops—that's it. Farther inland lie the Malay *kampung* and administrative headquarters for the island, a little better laid out. Only 2 motor vehicles operate on the entire island; one of them is a 1945 truck still in daily use. No bank.

Report to the *polisi* when you arrive; they'll arrange a

place for you to stay for free. Local people are reserved but friendly. Eat at **Warung Kopi Pak Tani** (Pak Ahmadi) which serves very good food. There are several pool rooms, but since Muslims here are prohibited from playing pool that leaves all the racks for degenerate Western tourists. From Daik you can travel back to Dabo (P. Singkep) daily at about 1000. Alternatively, you might be able to get a ride on one of the many cargo boats from Pekanbaru, Jambi, etc. that stop here to load rubber and other commodities.

Vicinity Of Daik
The main item of interest near Daik (2-hour walk) is the former palace of Sultan Suleiman, the last sultan

THE SOUTHERN RIAU ISLANDS

of Lingga-Riau. You'll have to get someone to show you the way along a maze of nearly overgrown forest paths. Beautiful scenery. Nearer to Daik are the graveyards of Sultan Mahmud (1832-1841), Sultan Abdurrachman (1812-1831), and second-to-the-last sultan, Raja Mohammed Yusuf Yang Dipertuan Besar

Lingga-Riau Yang Ke V. The graveyard of Sultan Mahmud has the ruins of an old mosque in the middle, with lovely lattice-work carved out of volcanic stone. Inland a little farther lies **G. Daik** (1,163 m) with its 3 main peaks. Because it's too steep, the center

peak is said never to have been climbed (here's a challenge to some lunatic!). It's also possible to walk right across the entire island, from Daik via Restum and Duara to **Sekanak** on the N coast, camping out along the way.

RIAU DARATAN

The Land

Riau Daratan is the E coast mainland portion (9½ million ha) of Riau Province. An equatorial area of huge forests with high rainfall, east-central Sumatra is a region of swampy lowlands crossed by large meandering rivers—extremely important to the communications, transportation, and economy of Riau—are the Siak, Indragiri, Kampar, and Rokan; all drain into the Straits of Melaka. The shallow, coastal estuarine mudflats created by these E. Sumatran rivers cover an astonishing 155,000 sq km, or more than one-third of the island's entire land area! So shallow that even small fishing vessels must keep hundreds of meters offshore so they won't run aground, these endless marshlands stink of hydrogen sulphide, the putrid rotten-egg smell of decay.

Flora And Fauna

Most of eastern Sumatra's swamps are densely overgrown with plantlife, especially mangrove, while the open tidal flats literally bubble and seethe with crawling things. Inland, the soil is not really suitable to agriculture and even rice is difficult to grow. Most vegetables and fruit must be imported, but do try the delicious and cheap local pineapples. Although much of Riau Daratan's land area is Caltex oil country, this region is still one of the least contaminated Indonesian wilderness. Even as late as the 1960s, if you took the bus from Pekanbaru to Dumai you could still see tigers running across the road. Though this happens very rarely now, the jungle still isn't that far away. Tigers ravage villages occasionally, carrying off cattle, dogs, and people, all found in pieces afterwards. Small hairy rhinos are found in the Buatan area, a swamp near Pelalawan (E of Pekanbaru), in the muddy river country to Tenajan Ulu, and in the Kampar River region. These sullen-faced behemoths love to take mud baths; *durian* is their favorite dessert. To make up for its poor eyesight, the rhinoceros' sense of smell and hearing is keen, so keep alert: big round tracks in soft mud show clear impressions of the rhino's hoofs. Herds of 40 or more elephants move around the Pekanbaru timbering areas. Hear the black *beo* bird's crazy laughter, croaking 30-cm-high frogs, and honking hornbills. Animals such as wild pigs, black monkeys, etc., can often be seen from early-morning buses traveling to and from Pekanbaru. In

Riau Daratan are also occasional deer, wild boar, tapir, bear, explosively colored butterflies, brilliant tropical birds. All kinds of snakes are commonly seen: king and spitting cobras, and other lethal varieties. So, unless you're an *Orang Sakai,* don't just go walking off into the jungle.

History

In the lowlands of eastern Sumatra, Indian acculturation can be traced back to at least the 5th C.; the Buddhist ruins at Muara Takus (near Bangkinang) testify to a developed Buddhist culture in the 9th and 10th centuries. But the area's history goes back even earlier. Today you can still see 3-m-high piles of shells remaining where Middle Stone Age people lived. These hunter-gatherers, who migrated with their dogs from Indochina to Indonesia around 2000-600 B.C. left these shell piles behind, sometimes with their dead buried inside. Since the shortest sailing route between India and China is through the Straits of Melaka, farsighted rulers have always tried to establish their authority on land to both sides of this all-important strait. Consequently, the E coast of Sumatra has had a turbulent history and many kingdoms and powers—Indians, Arabs, Portuguese, Dutch, and British—have come and gone. The strait took on even more economic and strategic importance in 1869 with the opening of the Suez Canal, and since 1950 it has been the main lifeline for tankers transporting crude oil to Japan.

Economy

While tin and timber comprise the riches of Insular Riau, the economy of Riau Daratan is concentrated mainly in oil. Caltex Pacific Indonesia's (CPI) administrative base is at Duri, several hours' drive N of the provincial capital of Pekanbaru. Indonesia produces about 1.5 million barrels of oil per day in its approx. 50 fields, and the share of that which goes to Caltex is 750,000-780,000 per day! After oil, the secondary industry is logging. Loggers usually wait until the oil companies build roads, then they go in. Caltex has built and maintains all the roads in the region. Once they no longer use them, they become government property. Dumai is the export harbor and freight terminal for the timber and petroleum. Fishing is a mainstay of mainland Riau's economy—more

RIAU DARATAN

than one-third of Indonesia's motorized vessels work out of Pekanbaru and Bagansiapiapi. Other commercial products of the area include rattan and crocodile leather.

The People

Islam is the predominant religion of Riau (2,000,000 out of 2,688,944 people). This province is a very rich ethnographic area. From Pekanbaru all the way down the E coast to Palembang are descendants of the original deutero-Malay race, referred to as *Orang Melayu*. As authentic a race as the Batak, Minangkabau, and other Sumatran peoples, the Melayu on both sides of the strait between Sumatra and Malaysia share the same ethnicity, though it is not known for sure which arrived first; they dress in the same manner too. Downriver from Pekanbaru you can still see the old-style roofs, with crossbeams extending beyond the level of the roof, for which Riau Daratan is known. The land portion of Riau Province is also under much cultural influence from the Minangkabaus of W. Sumatra. Inhabiting remote regions of the province are also numerous proto-Malayan and even pre-Malayan tribes. One of the most visible of these pre-industrial groups is the nomadic aboriginal tribe, the *Orang Sakai,* who trade forest products—rattan, camphor, and wild rubber—for salt and tobacco at nearby villages. These animists also earn money posing for tourists on the Rumbai-Duri road. The government and oil companies have tried to settle the Sakai in communities with schools and clinics near the oilfields to assure a steady supply of labor, but very few have taken root (outside of Duri is a settlement). In some E. Sumatran coastal districts beach nomads, *Orang Laut,* use 2-m-long, ½-m-wide mudboards (curved in front like a surfboard) to cross over swamps by pushing swiftly with hands and feet for hours on end. In the oil centers of Rumbai, Duri, and Dumai, slightly over 100 foreigners live and work.

Transport

In W. Sumatra rivers are only navigable for short distances, but the large rivers of E. Sumatra—their waters darkened to a deep brown by tannic acid oozing from millions of swamp trees—are an important means of transport. The muddy Siak is the province's main river, a busy throughfare of ocean-going ships, barges, fishing boats, hand- and motor-powered sampans. Riau Daratan doesn't boast that many all-weather roads; they cut back building roads here once helicopters started transporting equipment. Now the road system on mainland Riau connects only Dumai, Pekanbaru, Bukittinggi, and Padang; another good road leads from Pekanbaru to Rengat, eventually joining the Trans-Sumatran Highway. To travel by air N or S from E. Sumatra, fly from Pekanbaru's Simpang Tiga Aerodrome. There's also an airstrip on P. Batam, 20 km S of Singapore, and commercial flights connect Jakarta with Tg. Pinang, P. Batam, Dumai, and Pekanbaru.

PEKANBARU

Capital of Riau Province (pop. approx. 210,000) and the main city of oil-rich Riau Daratan, Pekanbaru is a clean, well laid-out town located on the Siak River. It's also the gateway to the largest and richest oil fields of SE Asia, an important and rapidly developing area of Sumatra. A crazy mixture of races — but with a strong Melayu element — has converged on this busy, hot lowland city. Pekanbaru is not what you'd imagine an oil-city to be like: it's unexpectedly friendly. The oil companies have made significant contributions to the city's health, communications, agriculture, recreation, power, education, transportation, and maintenance projects. Pekanbaru is a modern town with wide and spacious tree-lined streets, impressive and unusual government buildings, a modern airport, and a large volume of traffic in proportion to its small size.

From a tourist's point of view, however, it's a singularly unappealing city to visit. Most travelers who visit this river port do so for the same reason: to take the ferry up the river to Tg. Pinang, and farther to Singapore. Pekanbaru is also a useful transit point between Insular Riau and the beautiful highlands surrounding Bukittinggi to the southwest. Oil wealth has also driven up the prices and Pekanbaru can be expensive. Jalan Jen. Sudirman, the main street, runs north to south. The Siak River forms the northern boundary; shops, hotels, banks, and the port are in the N half of the city, while government offices and the main bus station are in the S part of town. Flat and surrounded by swamps, Pekanbaru suffers from an oppressively hot and humid climate.

History

Pekanbaru, which means "New Market," was founded in 1784 at a point as far upstream on the Siak River as big ships could conveniently navigate. Hang Tuah was a legendary guerilla in the war of independence who raided Dutch outposts on the Siak and in the Straits of Melaka in colonial times. This saboteur fought from a swift little sailboat, which always eluded the Dutch; a town street and many shops are now named in his honor. In 1944-45, the Japanese had Allied POWs and Javanese *romusha* build a rail link between Pekanbaru and Muara (W of Sawahlunto) in an attempt to get coal from W. Sumatra to the E coast. Fifteen thousand men died in the process; the first train ran just days before the end of WW II. Prior to the discovery of oil in the 1950s, Pekanbaru served as the main port for exporting rubber, cloves, indigo, gold, and tin from inland C. Sumatra and for importing cloth, machinery, foodstuffs, and other articles. The city has increased eightfold since 1958. Now commercial jets to and from Jakarta and Singapore zoom in and out of its airport daily.

Sights

See the Grand Mosque (*an Nur*, "The Light") on Jl. Sheikh Burhanudin, with its bright onion dome. This mosque and Pekanbaru's church face each other. Stroll around the fruit and fish markets, open daily. Visit the sleazy harbor area. In front of the DPRD building is a monument to revolutionary heros. Furniture-makers and other cottage industries are along Jl. H.O.S. Cokrominoto heading toward Terminal Kodim. For *rumah adat*, go to Jl. Diponegoro in front of the Riau Hotel, or to Jl. Setiabudhi near P.T Agung Concern. Bookstores and gold shops are all along Jl. Jen. Sudirman. Caltex built a swimming pool and stadium in Pekanbaru and has left them to the city.

Accommodations

Tends to be expensive with few singles available. A fan or a/c is worthwhile if you can afford it. Always ask if all taxes are included in the price (sometimes are, sometimes aren't). *Losmen* crowd the vicinity of the bus terminal on Jl. Nangka; try **Hotel Linda**, Jl. Nangka 133, Rp7500 s and Rp10,000 d — good value for Pekanbaru. Near the harbor on Jl. M. Yatim are several divey hotels such as the **Nirmala**, Jl. Pasar Bawah (tel. 21314), a handy place to stay if you're taking a boat out, and the cheapest (Rp4000) place in town. Quite ordinary **Hotel Dharma Utama**, Jl. Sisingamangaraja 10, is centrally located just off Jl. Sudirman. They charge Rp5000 s, Rp6000 d; with *mandi* and a/c Rp15,000 s and d. **Hotel Anom** is 1 block N of Hotel Dharma Utama on Jl. Gatot Subroto 3 (tel. 22636/25188); from Rp12,000 to Rp20,500 d a/c. Rooms are small but clean. Nice garden courtyard and one of Pekanbaru's best Chinese restaurants, **Restoran Anom**, is just off the lobby. Big TV screen. **Asian Hotel**, Jl. Sudirman, is noisy with prostitutes.

Pekanbaru's hotels in the Rp20,000 range are remarkable for their drab sameness. The guys at the airport taxi desk push the **Badarussamsi Hotel**, Jl. Sisingamangaraja 71 (tel. 22475) but for Rp22,000 stan-

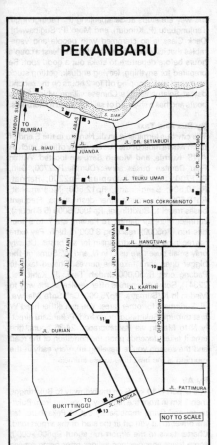

PEKANBARU

NOT TO SCALE

1. Stasiun Bombaru
2. RM Asia (buy boat tickets to Tg. Pinang)
3. Wisma Nirmala
4. Hotel Sri Indrayani
5. Pasar Kokim
6. Pasar Pusat
7. Hotel Anom, Restaurant Anom
8. Indrapura Hotel
9. Dharma Utama Hotel
10. RSUP
11. Kantor Gubernor
12. Terminal Bis Jalan Nangka
13. Hotel Linda

dard rooms, it's a bit run down. **Afri Hotel,** Jl. Dr. Setiabudhi 5, and **Bukit Zaitum Hotel,** Jl. Dr. Setiabudhi 83, and even the **Riau Hotel,** Jl. Diponegoro 26, are all very plain. For the same money, you might as well stay in the town's top hotel, **The Indrapura,** in the back of town at Jl. Sutomo 86, only Rp18,500 s and bordering on the luxurious. Of similar high standards is the more central **Sri Indrayani Hotel,** Jl. N. Bangka (tel. 21870/23461), in a more happening neighborhood, and only Rp18,500 s. These last 2 should rightfully put the other "luxury" hotels out of business.

Food
A multitude of restaurants and *kedai kopi* serves up Indonesian, Padang, and Chinese dishes. Fish is plentiful and cheap. Try such regional dishes as *asam pedas* at **Pelita Pantai,** Jl. Jen. Sudirman Ujung, 1 km from downtown. Another specialty of this city is smoked fish *(ikan salai);* sample it in the downtown market, Pasar Pusat. The number-one Indonesian restaurant, serving *nasi padang,* is the **Buana Baru,** Jl. H.O.S. Cokrominoto 16 (known simply as Jl. Cokro), near Pasar Pusat. Also at Pasar Pusat's Chinese section are several excellent Chinese restaurants: **Restoran Medan,** Jl. Juanda 28, and **Restoran Glas Mas,** at corner of Jl. Ir. H. Juanda and Jl. Dago. Not far away from the Buana Baru, on Jl. Jen. Sudirman, is the very good **RM Roda.** Also try **Medan Eskrim,** Jl. Juanda, for Chinese food. The **Prahiyangan,** Jl. Cempaka, specializes in Sudanese cooking.

For snacks, **Mitra Sari,** Jl. Sisingamangaraja, offers very good *sate, bakso, soto,* etc. In front of the Anom Hotel buy delicious *jagung bakar, sorbat,* and *bakso*—cheap! For dessert, sample the local sweets *buah melako* and *tepung gomok* in a *kedai kopi.* The **New Holland Bakery,** Jl. Sudirman 135, is the place for ice cream, fresh bread, and other baked goods. Also, very sweet pineapples are available in the Pekanbaru (Pasar Nangka) and Palembang regions for Rp100-300.

Services
After 45 min. and 20 signatures, change money at **Bank Negara Indonesia 1946,** Jl. Jen. Sudirman 63. Many other banks (**Bank Bumi Daya, BRI, BPD,** etc.) are along Jl. Jen. Sudirman. The main **post office,** the telegram and telex offices, police station, and *kantor imigrasi* are also all on Jl. Jen. Sudirman. The **Public Library** is on Jl. Diponegoro 18. The main hospital, **RS Umum Pekanbaru,** is at Jl. Diponegoro 2. Internist **Andi Zainal,** Jl. A. Yani (tel. 23111) is more expensive than American-trained **Dr. Tabrani Rab,** Jl. Sudirman (tel. 21972). The **tourist office** (Baparda) is in the building to the L of Kantor Gubernur, Jl. Jen. Sudirman 344; ask for the helpful Indonesian-speaking Mr. Zulkifli, who will hand out

several tourist brochures (in Indonesian) on Riau Province (but no map of Pekanbaru).

GETTING THERE

At 18 m deep, the Siak River is deepest of all E Sumatra rivers, though it still isn't wide enough for the really big ocean-going ships and tankers, which have to dock at Dumai. Thus, only small slow *kapal motor* do the run between Tg. Pinang and Pekanbaru. The cost is Rp12,500 Deck Class, Rp17,000 Cabin Class, but some boats charge up to Rp25,000 (just one class). Boats depart at least 3 days a week (never on Sun.) and the trip takes about 36 hours (1 day and 2 nights) with 4 simple meals provided. Approaching from the sea via the Straits of Melaka, intermediate stops are made at Moro, Tg. Batu, and Selatpanjang.

By bus from Bukittinggi is around Rp5000. On the road from Payakumbuh to Pekanbaru, most of the bridges are quite new and well-constructed. You go through a tunnel built by the Dutch in 1929, smelling wonderfully of the mountain which surrounds it. The last 30 km into Pekanbaru are on a very flat, straight road, so you make much better time. If you want to break your trip in Bangkinang, stay in the *penginapan*-style **Wisma Langdini**, or **Losmen Arqon**, Jl. A. Yamin. Eat at **Restoran Cahaya Buana**.

The Garuda flight from Singapore to Pekanbaru is US$78, departing every day. The **Simpang Tiga Airport** is 10 km from Pekanbaru, Rp7000 by taxi, or Rp3500 by shared taxi (2 persons). If you hang around the taxi desk, it's fairly easy to find someone to go in with.

Getting Around

Charter taxis through your hotel, Rp5000 per hour within the city. *Microlets* (small vans) travel constantly up and down Jl. Sudirman and back and forth between Kodim and Loket stations, Rp100 for an average ride. The easiest way to get around town quickly is to charter one of the orange ladybug-like *bajai,* Rp1000 for average ride. Find them at Pasar Pusat.

FROM PEKANBARU

By Boat

A popular trip for travelers is the cheap, slow cargo boat to Tg. Pinang from Pekanbaru's harbor. As soon as the *microlet* from town drops you off in the harbor area, they'll call you over to RM Asia, Jl. Salieh Abas 22, just before the gate to the *pelabuhan*. Buy tickets here for Rp12,450 Deck Class. Boats depart only 3 times weekly: Mon., Wed., and Saturday at 1700. For a cabin with a bed, Rp17,000. If you go through a travel agent, it'll be Rp1500 more expensive. Along

the way are stops at Selatpanjang (P. Tebingtinggi), Tanjungbatu (P. Kundur), and Moro (P. Sugibawah). Deck Class is so crammed with people and vegetables that its wise to be at the docks at least a couple hours before departure to stake out a good spot. Be prepared for anything: leaving at dusk, getting stuck on a coral reef, stopping off for 2 hours on the second day at Selatpanjang, a Chinese village which builds boats and has a shipyard of sailboats and motorboats.

By Bus And Taxi

The city bus terminal is on Jl. Nangka in the S end of town where most of the bus company offices, such as **ANS, Kurnia,** and **Merah Sari,** are located. Within Riau Daratan buses serve: Dumai, Rp2700; Duri, Rp1700; Siak Sri Indrapura, Rp2200; Rengat, Rp10,500; Bangkinang, Rp12,500; Muaramahat, Rp19,500; plus many other destinations. Frequent buses travel to Bukittinggi, Rp4000-5000 (5-6 hours); connect there for Jambi. To Padang is a 7- to 8-hour bus trip (Rp5000), reaching 3,000 m high. Pay extra for reclining seats, extra again for a/c buses. Usually only small buses are used in N. and W. Sumatra; the bigger ones can't take the curves. Shared taxis to Padang cost Rp50,000 (**Indah Taxi**, Jl. Karet, tel. 22341). Some companies offer service all the way to Medan in N. Sumatra, Rp75,000. Call **Safa Marwa,** Jl. Sudirman, for other fares. You can either head W first through Bukittinggi or go from Pekanbaru directly N to Medan via Rantauprapat, 24-36 hours, (the time it takes depends upon the condition of the road and the season you're traveling in). Very early in the morning is the best time to see animals.

By Air

The airport is 10 km S on the highway to Bukittinggi, then 1 km in from the highway. If coming from Bukittinggi and flying immediately out of Pekanbaru, tell the driver to let you off at the start of the airport road. Charter taxis to the airport run about Rp5000-6000; some travel agencies and airlines offer *bemo* service for around Rp1500. Garuda has daily morning (0920) and afternoon (1615) flights to Jakarta (Rp118,500) and daily flights (1350) to Medan (Rp67,500) and Singapore. Also flights 4 times weekly to Palembang (Rp124,800) and flights on Mon., Wed., and Fri. to Padang (Rp34,000). Merpati has daily flights at 1200 to Tg. Pinang (Rp55,500) and every day to Jakarta (Rp95,500). Sempati has Fri., Sun., and Tues. flights to Tg. Pinang (Rp55,500) and Jakarta (Rp95,500). SMAC has regional scheduled flights to: Tg. Pinang (Rp55,400); Jambi (Rp54,700); Singkep (Rp82,800); Rengat (Rp33,400); Medan (Rp56,000); Batam (Rp59,600).

Merpati is at Jl. H.O.S. Cokrominoto 18 (tel. 23558); Garuda, Jl. Jen. Sudirman 207 (tel. 21026/21575); SMAC, Jl. Jen. Sudirman 25 (tel. 23922). Sempati flights can be booked at Jl. Sisingamangaraja 2, or at a travel agency like **P.T. Centrawasih Kencana Tours & Travel**, Jl. Iman Bonjol 32 (tel. 22286) or at **P.T. Kota Piring Kencana**, Jl. Sisingamangaraja (tel. 21382/21040) near the Sempati office.

VICINITY OF PEKANBARU

Candi Muara Takus

A topless *candi* (actually a brick stupa) found among a number of other ruins at a remote 9th and 10th C. Buddhist complex about 130 km W of Pekanbaru. This site, possibly related to the Padanglawas ruins 100 km N, is located in the foothills of the upper Kampar River near the provincial border between W. Riau and W. Sumatra, only 26 km from the main Pekanbaru-Bukittinggi Highway. The rivers in this area NW of Bangkinang are very clear, unlike those around Pekanbaru which are the color of Coca Cola.

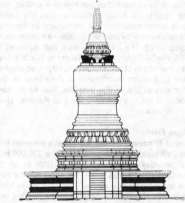

Candi Malagai: This slender, graceful stupa has a rectangular foundation measuring 9.1 by 10.62 m. On the N side is a flight of steps. The stupa's body rests on a double lotus cushion. The 36-sided crown is related to the 36 nat spirits of the Burmese pantheon.

This place of worship for followers of a Mahayana Buddhist sect, is thought to have been built by Sriwijaya Empire temple builders around A.D. 900-1000. The major feature is a large stupa-form temple called **Candi Malagai**, one of the few stupas ever recovered in Indonesia. The outer walls of this structure surround an earlier building which has been not been possible to describe or date. The only known parallel to this style of stupa is in Villagaam in Sri Lanka. An inscribed gold plate found in one of the ruins dates from the 12th C.; it is conjectured that the complex was used only for a short period and there is a legend of a Batak attack on the site. The whole complex is in a state of partial excavation and renovation.

The *pasanggrahan* outside of Muaramahat is called **Arga Sonya**, or you can ask a family in Desa Pongkai (2 km from the temple site) to put you up. At Muaramahat, 97 km SE of Pekanbaru (125 km from Bukittinggi), change to a minibus and then proceed (for Rp2000) on a gravel road for 26 km (one ferry crossing) to Desa Pongkai. Local vehicles travel to Desa Pongkai irregularly, so don't count on that minibus waiting for you when you step from the bus. Get an early start as the roads are bad, particularly in the rainy season.

Siak Sri Indrapura

Located on the Siak River 160 km E of Pekanbaru, this impressive *istana* (palace), which some say is reminiscent of Versailles, was formerly used by the Siak sultans. Before Indonesia achieved independence in 1949, Sumatra was made up of kingdoms ruled by sultans. **Istana Asserayah Hasyimiah** was built in 1889 by Sultan Assaidi Syarif Hasim Abdul Jalil Saifuddin, the 11th Siak sultan, who controlled the region from Langkat (N. Sumatra) nearly all the way to Jambi. His son, Sultan Syarief Kasim II, (educated in Amsterdam) lost power in 1946 when the sultanate was taken over by the republican government. Unlike many sultans during the war of independence who willingly collaborated with the Dutch, the Sultan of Siak openly sided with the Republicans and was much admired for his courage. Istana Asserayah Hasyimiah was abandoned after the revolution and, with no maintenance carried out on it, soon began to fall apart. Caltex has contributed substantially to its reconstruction and renovation; now the local government pays for the upkeep. Some members of this royal family are still alive; the Widow (Syarifah Fadlon) of the last sultan occasionally visits the house behind the palace called Istana Praduan, and is very talkative and friendly.

A small museum inside the palace contains many of the sultan's possessions: old furniture, Chinaware and other ceramic pieces, odd historical objects, a still-working 19th C. European gramophone (crank it up and listen to old records), and the former sultan's gold-plated throne. On the grounds are a mosque, a burial complex for the Siak royal family, and the High Court Building, in which criminal cases and other lawsuits were tried on behalf of the populace of the sultanate. Old people can tell you stories of the kingdom.

To get there, take a bus (150 km, 2 hours, Rp2500) from Pekanbaru to the small town of Siak Sri Indrapura. Regular river ferries also run from Pekanbaru, traveling downstream to Siak Sri Indrapura in 6 hours for Rp1500. Not far from the palace, near the pier, is **Peng. Sraiwangi**, Rp5000 pp. Eat in the restaurant in the *pasar*, 300 m from the *penginapan*. Alternatives are to stay as a paying guest with a family or to ask to stay on the boat you arrived on. The town is located on both sides of the river, take a *sampan* (Rp200) to the other side and watch the river life.

CALTEX PACIFIC INDONESIA (CPI)

Besides its wide swamps and forests, another of Riau Province's unique assets is oil. One can see these wells operating along the road from Pekanbaru to Minas, Duri, and Dumai. With a total oil production of more than US$4 billion per year, the central part of Sumatra is by far the biggest oil producing area in Indonesia, which is itself one of the world's 10 largest producers. CPI (owned by Chevron and Texaco) accounts for half of Indonesia's total production; Pertamina, Arco, Mobil, City Service, and others produce the remainder. The contract between CPI and the government, as is the case with most of the big oil companies working Indonesian fields, calls for a production-sharing in which 88% goes to the government and 12% to the company.

History

Located NE of the Barisan Mountain range, this rich mineral area borders Lake Toba in the N and the Kuantan and Indragiri rivers in the south. Explorations were started by Chevron in 1924. Caltex arrived in 1936, then evacuated at the outset of the Japanese invasion in 1942. Since the 1930s, CPI has built a road network totaling more than 2,000 km crisscrossing the often remote and inhospitable swamps of E Sumatra. In 1968 CPI opened a new page in petroleum exploration history with the use of helicoptors. Now, with production equipment and personnel also moved in by helicoptors, the need for building any additional costly (Rp250,000 per km) roads is eliminated. Presently, more than 6,000 Indonesians, over 10,000 other subcontractors, and slightly over 100 foreigners work for CPI. Because big oil tankers cannot negotiate the heavily silted Siak River, 2 pipelines now extend from Minas to Dumai and from Bangko to Dumai, 2 power plants have been installed at Duri and Minas, plus there are 1,300 km of power transmission and distribution lines and a central shop complex in Duri. A huge installation.

Sights

Since the highway from Pekanbaru to Dumai is a public road, tourists may pass through the facilities. For an official tour, however, go through the trade desk at your embassy. There are 4 camps: Rumbai, Minas, Duri, and Dumai. To visit the various outlying installations, you must drive on slippery roads which have been sprayed with waxy oil residue. If you get out of your car and try to walk, you'll fall. Trucks use snow chains which dig into the waxy tar and mud for their traction. These roads get even more slippery when wet, which occurs about eight days a week—

like riding on the wet surface of a candle. These roads, in fact, have been called "the longest candle in the world."

Rumbai

With its neat square streets, Rumbai is a supply base and residential area for CPI personnel. It has an 18-hole golf course, 6 tennis courts, club, restaurant, dining hall, and commissary (employees only). The Rumbai guesthouse is only available for company guests. The town has its own power and water system, and TV from Jakarta comes in loud and clear. In the Kalimantan oilfields the Indonesians and foreigners are strictly segregated, but here they mix. Reminiscent of a California suburb, each house has a neat little name plate in front: Parker, Sudarso, etc. Indonesians, who comprise 98% of CPI personnel, seem to enjoy doing all the same things that any ordinary suburban American family enjoys. They eat hamburgers, go to the country club, and the housewives all try to make their gardens look prettier than their neighbor's. A well-manicured, park-like, rather sterile community. See the monument to the one-billionth barrel of oil reached in 1969—a monument to a drop of oil. The 2-billionth mark was achieved in 1973, the 3-billionth in 1985. To get to Rumbai, first get a *microlet* to Stasiun Kodim (Rp100), then another 2 km to Stasium Bombaru N of Pekanbaru on the other side of the bridge over the Siak River, then another 5 km to the gate leading to Rumbai. Then hitch or walk.

Minas Fields

Around Minas are the biggest oilfields between Iran and California, 300 wells producing over 330,000 barrels per day. Minas produces a fifth of all of Indonesia's oil. "Minas crude" has a low sulphur content and a high waxy residue. Though it's very high-quality, the drawback is that after all the gasoline and kerosene are refined, what is left (50%) is very waxy residue. So Minas crude is run through special refineries, such as in Dumai, which remove most of the wax. This residue has its industrial uses: for example all the roads leading through CPI lease holdings are covered with it. Three km N on the main road to Duri is the area's very first well, opened in March 1941. "Old Number One" had to be abandoned in 1942; the Japanese army repaired it and commenced pumping in 1944. Number One is not the original structure, but the well itself still pumps up about 70 barrels of oil a day, as it has done for the last 48 years. All the data is on the plaque.

Duri

Another field like Minas, since 1957 the center of CPI field operations with many major oilfields nearby. Duri, 115 km and 2 hours N of Rumbai, is the real hub of the operation—where you go to see a rig in action.

THE SAKAI

From Rumbai out to the Minas fields you pass wooden dwellings on stilts, set back from the highway. These are homes of the Sakai, a dispossessed people. The *Orang Sakai* live throughout the alluvial coastal plains of eastern Sumatra and in scattered small mountain pockets on Peninsular Malaysia. The exact origins of these short-statured, wavy-haired people is puzzling; they are thought to be linked to the Veddoid race of Sri Lanka, remnants of an ancient people that once extended from India to Australia. They share the same physical type: long narrow heads, light skin color, broad flat forehead, dark deep-set eyes, hairless bodies. They might also be related to the all but vanished Toala of Central Sulawesi. Their own language is quasi-Dravidian with some Mon-Khmer influences, but they also speak a Malay dialect similar to Indonesian. They are a shy, chain-smoking people who actually do not like to be called "Sakai" (which originally meant "slave"), prefering to call themselves *Orang Batin,* which means "the inner people," borrowed from the Malay and assumed by a group of Sakai nobles.

Culture

To our way of thinking, it's difficult to imagine how a people can live with so few possessions as the Sakai; they seem to be content owning nothing. Even as late as the mid '60s members of this animist group were still wearing bark clothing, though now they dress the same as any rural Indonesian. Though some Sakai still live out in the forest and haven't "come in" yet, when the road which connects Rumbai and Duri was built right through their territory, they chose to construct their dwellings alongside it. They walk on top the big oil pipeline when the road is very slippery, and even dry their clothes on the hot pipe. Some of their children go to school in Minas now. When CPI employs them, it's only for clearing scrub or forest.

Nominally, some are Christian, some Islamic, but like all the isolated aboriginal peoples of Indonesia, the Sakai have a very strong belief in magic, evil spirits, and animism. Storms are caused by spirits of the dead which are driven away by a bonfire made of bad-smelling herbs. Taboos—such as burning bugs on the hearth, teasing domestic pets, imitating certain birds or insects—abound. Except for fashioning ingenious traditional technology such as traps and spears, they practice no craft.

Subsistence

The Sakai traditionally supported themselves by hunting, trapping, and fishing; their favorite food is monkey meat. They never eat any animal they raise (though they trade them to be eaten). Unlike Muslim Indonesians, dogs are friends and assist hunters. These tribes as a rule did not practice agriculture. However, some Sakai now own land on which they garden brush products and lay hillside fields, growing tapioca, sweet potatoes, bananas, rice, etc. After 3-4 harvests when the soil no longer yields, they move on and start the process all over again in another part of the forest, which is all shared property. The more settled groups maintain gardens and fences to keep out deer and other wild animals. On the drive from Rumbai N

to Duri, you cross several rivers around which cluster Sakai villages. The Sakai fish these rivers, using either hooks and line or long funnel-shaped basket fish traps; they also set traps along the banks to catch pigs. Though ordinarily a timid people, when you see them with a wild pig which they've just speared slung over their shoulder they glow with a fierce pride. A forager/hunter carries a basket by a head strap, water in a gourd. Hip pouches contain tobacco, matches, tools. When hunting, the Sakai make temporary leaf shelters. Bamboo springtraps and slip-noose traps are favored; others consist of powerful levers that hurl spears across a trail when a line is tripped. The Sakai tote their spear and *parang* in the jungle in a manner that is best able to protect them instantly if attacked. Tigers are well-known for attacking from behind, so the Sakai carry spears with the blade pointing back over his shoulder. When a tiger attacks, he falls down on his knees and rams the spear (hopefully) through the tiger's throat. He also carries his *parang* cradled in his arms ready for action. Usually the *parang's* handle is rounded at the end so it can be more easily pushed into the prey's body.

Dwellings

Before WW II, Sakai houses were built of tree bark with bamboo walls and thatch roofs. The houses you see along the road nowadays are more permanent structures, although straw and bamboo are still used extensively. Dwellings consist of just one room, used mainly for cooking and sleeping. Because of snakes, wild pigs, and tigers, the Sakai always build their houses off the ground on piles with their chickens and fish plus a miscellany of traps, baskets, and digging sticks hanging underneath. To keep wild animals from climbing into their homes and to signal a desire for privacy, at night when they retire The Sakai push the ladder down; the next morning they pull it back up with rattan twine. If you come upon one of their houses and the ladder is leaning against the door, after a greeting you may enter the house. But if the ladder is down from the door, it means stay away. This custom might have its origins from the time the Sakai were purely nomadic hunters who erected dwellings in the forest, opening their dwellings to offer food, water, and shelter to strangers.

Photographing

The Sakai want Rp2000 for a photo, posing beside their dogs and native huts. If you try to take their photograph without paying, they become hostile: mothers will yank their children from doorways or they might beat their chests, growl, make faces—acting it up to mock you. Starting with Caltex oil people about 12 years ago, so many people have gone up and down this road peering at them that they are tired of being treated as curiosities and not getting anything out of it. Being captured on film might also be against their beliefs. Sometimes it might be possible to pay for a photo with water, which can be in short supply, or cigarettes. But leaving your camera behind is best of all; then they are quite hospitable, talkative, and you can even get invited inside their huts.

In 1924, Standard Oil Company sent 4 American geologists to the Dutch East Indies to evaluate sedimentary basins for possible oil exploration. This was the earliest effort in the Eastern Hemisphere by what was to become the future Caltex Pacific enterprise. In 1935, Standard of California was offered 600,000 hectares in little explored central Sumatra. Though the area was not regarded as very promising, oil was discovered there in 1940 and in 1941 other wells were drilled at Duri. Subsequent drilling in the area led to the development of the giant Minas oilfield, the largest between Iran and California with a total capacity of 330,000 barrels per day. Above is a hand-counterflush drill rig at work in C. Sumatra (1939).

Take a public bus from Pekanbaru, Rp1700. In 1956 oil was first struck here (shallower wells than Minas). Since then more than 700 wells have been drilled, most so small that they only pump 4-5 barrels a day. Duri is a complete community with employee housing, water-sprinkled lawns, 4 movie houses, golf course, churches, mosques, schools, repair shops, a power plant, and numerous maintenance buildings — all in the middle of nowhere. Meat is flown in from Singapore, vegetables come from Bukittinggi. Visit the Indonesian community beyond Duri, Simpang Padang, where most of the people work for Caltex. Several shops here sell furniture, woodcarving, driftwood, etc. Kandes is a Sakai village located on the main highway between Km 70 and 80 going back from Duri to Rumbai, about 25 km S of Duri.

Dumai
Dumai is some 180 km NE of Pekanbaru (Rp3500 by bus) and 61 km NE of Duri. The refinery here produces 100,000 barrels of oil per day. Dumai has the largest and busiest harbor in Indonesia in terms of the volume of cargo movement. In fact, this is one of the major oil ports of the world, with a capacity of 1,200,000 barrels of oil daily. Support facilities presently consist of 4 wharves which serve 70 ocean tankers a month. In addition, fishermen working out of this Caltex port catch 50 tons a month. The best joint in town is **Tasia Internasional**, Jl. Sultan Syarif Kasim 65 (tel. 21397/21077), on a small street off Jl. Jen. Sudirman. Also try **Hotel International**, Jl. Jen. Sudirman 63 (tel 21169). At the **Taman Sari** beer garden and restaurant, you could meet sailors from all over the world. Taking you for a sailor, the *becak* drivers in Dumai will try to charge Rp4000 to go from one end of town to the other (1½ km) when you should only be paying Rp500! Local *bemo, oplet,* and minibuses depart from Dumai's *pasar* on Jl. Jen. Sudirman for Pekanbaru, (1 change en route) or by direct bus for Rp2700. A very fast ferry service leaves for Melaka (Peninsular Malaysia) every Tues. and Thurs. at 1200; 2½ hours, Rp15,000 plus Rp1500 "harbor tax." This is a very comfortable, large boat with nice seats, snacks, electronic entertainment.

NORTH SUMATRA

North Sumatra covers an area of 70,687 sq. km, stretching from the boundaries of Aceh in the N to W. Sumatra and Riau provinces in the south—a land of volcanos, high plateaus, waterfalls, lakes, and plantations. Lake Toba, the gigantic crater lake in the center of the province, is so large it has been referred to as an inland sea. Isolated from the outside world until recent times, these upland plateaus of the Bukit Barisan Range are homeland to the Batak people who are divided into 6 tribes. In addition, coastal Malays along the Melaka Straits and Niah islanders on the island of Nias off the W coast also contribute to the province's population of 8.5 million. North Sumatra offers some unique experiences for the visitor. Samosir Island in Lake Toba has become one of Indonesia's major travel destinations, so relaxing that many travelers spend weeks here. From Brastagi one can visit traditional villages and climb 2 active volcanos. Orangutans can be seen in a rehabilitation center at Bukit Lawang; here injured animals and former pets are trained to live in the forest again. Hindu ruins are found on a plain in the S near Padangsidempuan. Nias Island off the W coast is famous for its monumental megalithic sculpture, traditional villages, "stone-jumpers," and surf. **note:** You'll see SUMUT on many signs in the province: the government's abbreviation for "Sumatra Utara" (North Sumatra).

History

Thanks to the silt deposits of rivers, a long strip of land near the eastern coast of the province contains soil of extraordinary fertility. Plantations growing tobacco and other cash crops were established here by the Dutch over 100 years ago, each a microcosm of the colonial capitalist effort. The Dutch government summarily took over all the unused arable land, reducing the small slash-and-burn farmers of the area to subsistence laborers. The Dutch invited the sultan of Deli to lease land to plantation overseers, and in time both parties became immensely wealthy. The sultan was able to build the fabulous rococo Maimoon Palace in Medan, and commodity trading houses sprang up all over the city. Chinese coolies, as well as Batak, Indian, and Javanese workers, were brought in to work the plantations, many of them dying of diseases and maltreatment under the appalling conditions. Those workers who ran off were caught by Bengali watchmen and executed. In the early part of the 20th C., basic humanitarian reforms were finally instituted. By 1930 the plantations of N. Sumatra—which constituted one of the most intense and successful foreign agricultural enterprises in the Third World—were generating 200 million *guilders* annually. The quality of tobacco produced in this *cultuurgebied* ("plantation belt") gained world notoriety as "Deli Tobacco." After independence from the Dutch, most of the estates were either divided among smallholders or nationalized. In 1965 foreign investors were again allowed to invest in cashcrop enterprises.

Economy

Though the region is rugged, it is definitely not undeveloped. North Sumatra is one of Indonesia's richest provinces, accounting for the largest share of the country's agricultural production and more than one-quarter of its agricultural exports (out of the port of Belawan, 26 km E of Medan). It is completely self-sufficient in food. The traveler will see kilometer after kilometer of rubber estates with neat rows of trees, well laid-out palm oil plantations, vast tobacco, clove, cacao, and tea estates, terraced ricefields, vegetable and flower gardens. The first priority of the provincial economy has always been farming, with industrialization and tourism second and third. Agricultural wealth is in the hands of private estates, hundreds of smallholders (about 10% of the total area), and about 50 government plantations totaling over 1,000 sq. km, all of which grow and sell their own produce. Multinational corporations such as Goodyear, Uniroyal, Harrison & Crossfield all have substantial investments and facilities here. With the establishment of processing and canning plants, even the province's industrial base is farm-oriented. In the mining sector, there are also proven deposits of iron, coal, gold, copper, bauxite, quartz and kaolin.

THE PADANGLAWAS RUINS

An archaeologist's dream is found near the little village of Portibi, 23 km SE of Gunungtua. This is a haunting area, even for non-archaeologists. Because of the area's isolation in the middle of the Sumatran jungle, this collection of ruined 11th and 12th C. Hindu monuments remained virtually unknown to the outside world until quite recently. It wasn't until about 1970 that the government attempted to to enclose the shattered ruins, appointing Portibi's *kepala kampung* to double as caretaker and guide. And only since 1976 have the artifacts here received any professional treatment to preserve them. Little by little,

Padanglawas is awakening archaeological interest in visiting scholars and travelers. This region lies on a dry plain on the eastern fringe of the Barisan range, precisely at the starting point to the easiest pass over the range. Through here (*Padanglawas* means "Broad Plain"), the ancients could reach the W coast.

History

Two large east-flowing rivers, the Baruman and the Panai, spring from sources in the plain. Despite its favorable location on transport routes, the Padanglawas Plain is unlikely to have supported a large sedentary population. Scorching winds from the W coast are able to climb through the pass and sweep down with blistering intensity, creating an extremely dry and inhospitable landscape. The forbidding and gloomy aspect of the site is completely in keeping with the nature of the rituals once performed in at least some of the numerous temples on the plain, including human sacrifices. The sculptures and inscriptions from some monuments show that they were funerary sites and sanctuaries reserved for devotees of a form of Tantric Buddhism. A survey conducted in 1976 yielded no indication of early habitation remains, which supports the hypothesis that the Padanglawas complexes were established, like the Dieng Plateau in C. Java, in a special region reserved for ceremonial activity.

The earliest dated object from Padanglawas is a bronze statue inscribed 1024. Other inscriptions found in the region give dates of 1179, 1245, and 1372. In addition, a bronze female image from the Bahal I temple may be of S. Indian origin, evidence of continued contact between N. Sumatra and S. India. Communication routes may have passed this way during the classical period (13th C.), accounting for the variety of Javanese and Indian-derived characteristics on some of the temples. The statuary and stoneware (but not the bricks) are thought to have come from India, transported to this site on barges all the way from the E coast of Sumatra during Java-Hindu times. The Baruman River passes by here and empties into the Melaka Straits. It's used to this day by river barges trading between S. Tapanuli and the E coast town of Labuhanbilik.

The Site

About 1,500 sq. km of the plain contain at least 26 ruined brick temples and temple complexes, with numerous associated remains. Out of the 26 temple ruins, 5 broken-down but beautiful Hindu temples still stand. The best preserved and least visited are the 2 temples S of the river across the plain (if it's hot, take water!). You have to cross the river by the pulley raft; friendly Muslim villagers here at Kampung Bahal. The main vaults of the temples remain—the walls are decorated with dancing *raksasa* swinging swords and clubs, lions, with many warriors and guardians. The

other temple sites are but mounds of bricks. In addition, untold numbers of scattered and broken Hindu statues, carvings, and ancient artifacts lying around have only recently been enumerated and cared for.

Bahal I

This 13-m-tall temple is in the best shape, and it has the strangest iconography; demonic scenes of tyrannical anger and revenge with thunderbolts and skulls and hideous laughter. Some traits, including its asymmetric ground plan, are connected with E. Java architecturally, though a distinct type of Buddhism was practiced by these ancient Batak peoples, a Tibetan-like Tantric cult full of weird magic. The statuary includes one of the handful of known images of the Tantric deity Heruka, plus a *lingga* on a lotus cushion associated with bodhisattvas in the ruins of Si Joreng Belangah. This "Buddhistic *lingga*" is characteristic of the blending of various external traits with local Batak culture to produce a unique system of mystical symbols. On Batak soil, intensive changes and transformations of the religion have obviously taken place.

Getting There

Since there are no direct buses from Padangsidempuan to Portibi village, you must first get to Gunungtua, 70 km E of Padangsidempuan. As many as 5 buses daily leave for Gunungtua, Rp2500. From Gunungtua, it's easy to get an *oplet* to the turnoff for the ruins just past the little bridge after Portibi village. Allow a full day as the ruins are spread out and the weather could be incredibly hot; leave Padangsidempuan by 0730 at the latest. Once in Portibi, Raja Usin Harahap, the caretaker, will show you around the site. Be sure to tip him for his trouble. Catch a bus back to Padangsidempuan from Gunungtua before dusk.

From Gunungtua

Instead of backtracking to Padangsidempuan, consider taking the road to the NE via Longgapayung to visit the hard-to-get-to Batak village of **Hutagodang** in Labuhan Batu. From Gunungtua, take a bus to Longgapayung (Rp1000, 45 km). Or take a train or bus from Medan to Rantauprapat, then another bus to Longgapayung. Hutagodang is another 12 km away from the junction near Longgapayung. There's no transport from the road except *hondas* that charge Rp5000 (first price) or Rp4000 (2nd price). In Hutagodang, see still-intact thick dark-thatched traditional houses. Visit in particular the ceremonial house which holds sacred heirlooms. All the buildings are old, worn, dark, harsh. Ceremonial drums are beaten while suspended from the railings of high platforms supported by posts blackened with age. In Batakland, drum music is called by different names according to the sound of the rhythm played—"Rolling Boulders," "Thundering Storm," etc.

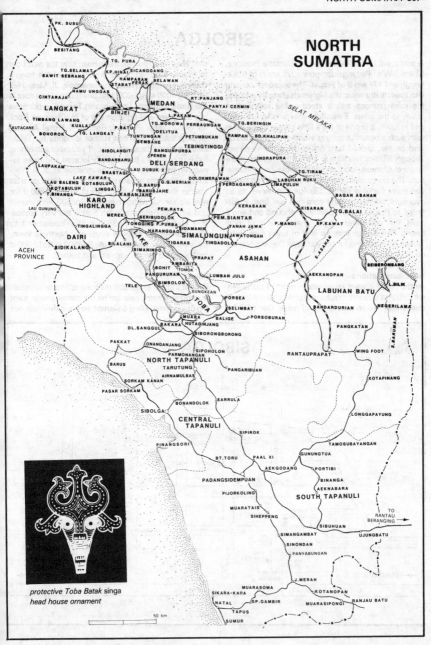

NORTH SUMATRA

protective Toba Batak singa
head house ornament

50 km

SIBOLGA

A port town on the W coast of N. Sumatra Province, 88 km NW of Padangsidempuan, 378 km N of Bukittinggi, and 174 km S of Prapat. The approach coming into town is dramatic: the highlands abruptly end and the road plunges into a steep-walled valley, then down to the coast. Beautiful sunsets from this road and in town. It is one of life's little ironies that a town with such a beautiful setting, whether approached by land or sea, should turn out to be so uninspiring. Though Sibolga has little to attract the traveler, there is good Chinese food and reasonable accommodation. The port's main claim to fame is as an embarcation point for Nias Island. Sibolga also serves as an overnight pit-stop on the hard bus run from Bukittinggi to Prapat. "Hello Mister's" abound and you'll meet the odd sleazy type, characteristic of port towns. The *Kantor Imigrasi* is N of town near Hotel Taman Nauli. Change money at Bank Dagang Negara on Jl. A. Yani.

Accommodations

All the *becak* drivers know where most of the hotels are. Sibolga's accommodations tend to have a lack of cleanliness and an abundance of noise. Don't fall for the "Nias trick," where the *losmen* says the next boat to Nias will go "in a few days." One of the town's cheapest hotels is **Hotel Sudimampir**, Jl. Mesjid 98; Rp3500-4000 s, Rp6000 d for tiny rooms. Next door is the **Roda Minang**. The **Bintang Terang** is primitive but adequate and right on top of the Baringin Dock for Gunungsitoli (P. Nias); Rp5500 d. **Hotel Anwar**, Jl. Suprapto, in Sambas Harbor is handy for Telukdalam intendents; same price. If you want something more upscale, try the centrally located and more expensive **Indah Sari** near the mosque at Jl. A. Yani 27-29 which has private baths and a/c. Although a bit cleaner than other hotels, they charge Rp6500 d for non a/c rooms without *mandi*, Rp8500 with *mandi* and a/c. Opposite the Indah Sari is the very reasonable **Hotel Maturi**, Rp3500 s. Well-heeled or into Maugham-esque colonial nostalgia? North of town, try quiet **Hotel Taman Nauli**, Rp8500 s, Rp12,000 d for balconied rooms with a/c and bath.

Food

Decent though expensive restaurants and an unusually good ice cream cafe are on the corner across from the big cinema. **Bing Selamat** serves a delicious hot

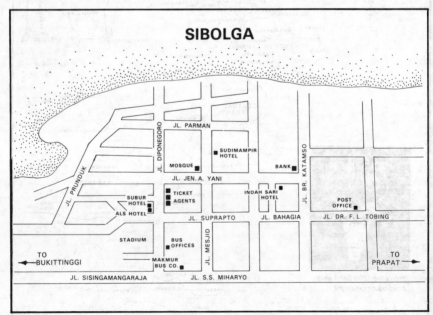

SIBOLGA

rice specialty. Chinese restaurant **Telok Indah**, Jl. Jen. A. Yani 63-65, has excellent *funjunghai*. **Teluk Indah** is OK, but the other Chinese restaurants on the corner closer to the Indah Sari are as good and cheaper; also foodstalls outside. **RM Slamet**, clean and expensive, on Jl. Katamso 30, also has quite good food.

From Sibolga

A new bus terminal on Jl. Sisingamangaraja is where most of the *ekspres* bus companies have their offices. Regional buses leave for Padangsidempuan, Balige, and Barus, Rp1500. For longer distances: Bukittinggi, Rp6000, 10 hours; Padang, Rp8000, 18 hours; Prapat, Rp3500. Buses leave irregularly; get on the one that's already full if you want to leave quickly. If you want a better seat, however, reserve a place the day before at the bus station.

To Nias

Self-appointed guides will appear at the bus station, in your hotel, at restaurants, or in the street to arrange every detail of transport to Nias; for a small fee, they could save a lot of time and trouble. It's better to get a boat to the southern port of Telukdalam rather than to the northern port of Gunungsitoli. Culturally, the south has a lot more going for it than the north. Ask the harbormaster where the wharfie hangout is.

Kapal leave every day but Sun. from the Sambas end of the harbor for Telukdalam, S. Nias (Rp6000-7000, 12-14 hours). Departure time is around 2100, arriving in Telukdalam at 0900 the next day. Sambas is 3 km from Sibolga, Rp200 by *bemo*. On both sides of the road leading to the harbor are shipping offices; ask at CV Damai Sambas, and P.T. Perlani (Jl. Letjen 57),

both of which operate several regular boats. Boats leave every evening from Sibolga's Baringin Harbor to Gunungsitoli (N. Nias); Rp6000, 10-12 hours. Inquire at Baringin Lloyd. Perintis Lines services Nias; every 2 weeks the *Blekok* departs from Padang to Nias, then sails to Sibolga and back to Padang. The *Duran* sails Padang to Sibolga, then on to Banda Aceh and back every 2 weeks.

From Sibolga to Nias, only the larger 2-decker boats may carry passengers; it's the regulation. At least 5 other companies service Nias, along with a number of other destinations up and down the coast of W. Sumatra. Pick a big, fast boat rather than a small, crowded one. In the event of rain, undercover accommodation on the smaller boats is cramped and very unpleasant. Take a *tikar* (mat), foodstuffs and fruit onboard.

Vicinity of Sibolga

Eleven km S of Sibolga on the road to Padangsidempuan is a white sandy beach at Pandan with magnificent views of the Indian Ocean, fishing *prahu*, restaurants specializing in fresh *ikan bakar*, and souvenir shops selling seashells, coral, ringstones, etc. **Barus** is an ancient trading port 65 km N of Sibolga on the coast road, exactly in the middle of Tapanuli. Its name means "camphor," a commodity once produced in great quantity in this area. Hundreds of years ago Islam was introduced to the people of the Tampanuli area by Arab merchants. Later, the Portuguese arrived and their fortifications can still be seen. The Dutch also maintained a remote factory here. See the ancient burial place at Barus with old 7th C. Chinese gravestones.

NIAS

The island of Nias is located off the W coast of Sumatra, 125 km SE of the city of Sibolga. With its famous megalithic stone altars and furniture, spectacular traditional architecture, and complex religious rites, a trip to this fascinating island is a journey into the past. The N. Nias culture was annihilated by the missionaries; in S. Nias the monumental culture is also dead, though relatively extant. The major city and capital of this subdistrict (which, administratively, falls under W. Sumatra Province), is Gunungsitoli on the NE coast, while the main port of the island is Telukdalam on the SE tip. Not far from Telukdalam is the surfie's hangout of Jamborai village, which boasts some of the best right-handers in Indonesia. Nias can easily be reached by regular ferry from Sibolga, N. Sumatra, or by air from Medan. Exchange rates are poor, so bring

plenty of cash. Gunungsitoli is the only town on the island where you can cash travelers cheques in banks. There are no banks in Telukdalam but Chinese stores will cash travelers cheques.

The Land

Off Sumatra's W coast 100 km are a series of islands: the Simeulue, Nias, Batu, and Mentawai groups, plus the lone island of Enggano. These are all actually peaks of a massive undersea ridge which runs parallel with the coast, separated from the mainland by a deep undersea gully. Isolated for at least 500,000 years, the human populations of these islands have evolved extraordinary cultures. Nias is the largest (100 km long by 50 km wide) and best known of this string of islands. This ancient island, just N of the equator,

Niasers hauling an 8-ton megalith 4 km uphill to the village of Bawamataluo in April of 1914. The large stone was first roughed out in a quarry 4 km from the village, then placed on a V-shaped sled (owo'owo, or "ship") of 2 logs. A series of brackets (golu) were socketed into the stone and around the stone. Massive ropes fastened the stone to the sled. Two holes were then gouged into the logs at the front of the sled, and long heavy ropes tied to it for pulling. A path was cleared between the quarry and Bawamataluo and logs were laid down for the "ship" to roll over. On steep uphill sections logs were held in place with stakes pounded into the ground. Big wooden levers forced the ship forward and kept it from moving sideways or backwards. It took 325 men 3 days to drag the rude megalith to the paved village square in front of the deceased chief's house, that of Saonigeho, the last traditional ruler of South Nias.

has rolling, mountainous terrain, gorges, ravines, rivers, and is subject to earthquakes. Badly maintained roads make the going arduous and time-consuming.

History

A magnificent megalithic heroic culture flourished on Nias well into the 20th century. Claire Holt was filming traditional group dances here in the 1920s and a Dutchman, Edwin Loeb, reported that head-hunting and human sacrifices were still practiced on Nias as late as 1935. A travel diary written in A.D. 851 by Persian merchant Sulayman is the first literary record of Nias; he described the head-hunters and slavers of "Niang." In the S part of the island during the 1800s Acehnese slave raiders regularly went on the rampage. A situation existed much like in Africa in the 1700s; chiefs would carry off captives from neighboring villages and sell them for gold to seamen. Today this same gold is used for bride prices at weddings and adorns headdresses of Niah dancers. The Dutch first gained a foothold in N. Nias in the 17th C.; the first missionaries arrived in 1865. After repeated military expeditions, the Dutch finally gained control over S. Nias in 1914. The Dutch controlled Nias by working through the traditional hierarchy and even restored some decadent Niah political institutions. A German Protestant mission was established on Nias in 1912 and the Catholic mission began work in 1937. The Protestants today are still in the majority, the professed faith of about 80% of the population.

The Economy

Traditionally, the Niah economy was based on agriculture and pig-raising; to supplement their diet, Niasers also fished and hunted. Today, most of the 500,000 people of Nias and Batu Is. are rice growers; other main food crops include taro, maize, sweet potatoes. In swampy areas, wet rice is grown, and in south Nias dryfield rice cultivation is practiced. But due to population pressure, available cultivatable land is shrinking. The island exports copra, pigs, rubber, and *nilam* (a fragrant oil used in perfumes and medicine, is known as pachouli oil in English).

Pigs are not only an important ritual food but also a source of wealth and prestige. Pig-raising is a profitable and secure business, requiring capital that few men can acquire. Historically, there has always been a division in Niah society between the aristocratic farmers and pig-raisers who loan money, pork, and other commodities to commoners, in effect turning them into permanent debtors. Pork is expensive, usually eaten only once a week. Market day is pig-slaughtering day, when pork is often served for both lunch and dinner.

Since the early 1970s when travelers first started arriving, tourism has become an increasingly important source of income. It's supported by the local chiefs who desire to raise cash to send their children off to technical schools and universities in Medan and Jakarta. (Educated offspring are the new symbol of prestige.) Tourism is seen as the way to enter the mainstream economy, a dubious achievement attained by such mainland tourist areas as Lake Toba and Bukittinggi.

THE PEOPLE

The native name for the island is *Tano Niha*, "Land of the People." The word *niha* was converted by the Dutch into Nias. Ethnically, the Niah (who call themselves the *Ono Niah*) are a mixed population of deutero-Malays imposed on a basic stock of Veddoid and proto-Malay. Their exact origin is misty. Many features of their culture and practices are all their own. Niasers speak a language most closely related to Malagasy, yet their sculpture shows uncanny similarities to the woodcarvings made by the Nagas of Assam in the high Himalayas. Because of the similarities of physical type, language, and customs between the two peoples, the Niah are thought to have derived from the Bataks. This would trace their ancestry to the hilltribes of Burma; they are thus related to the Dayak of Borneo and the Naga of Assam in NE India. It is thought that the ancestors of the present-day Niah migrated to the island between 3000 and 5000 B.C. Since their arrival, they have been strongly influenced by the Bronze Age Dongson culture of North Vietnam, as well as by contacts with Chinese, Hindu, and Muslim traders.

Traditional Culture

When the first visitors arrived in the late 18th C., they found the island divided into 50 territorial-genealogical federations. In these former times, each village and district traced its descent from a number of original clans which first settled the island. All local authority was invested in the village chief *(siulu)*; above him were paramount district chiefs. Elders sat in council to prescribe punishment for taboo breakers, and decide questions of boundaries, *adat*, and civil disputes. The population in the S was sharply divided into 3 classes: aristocrats *(siulu)*, commoners *(si'ila)*, and slaves *(sawuyu)*. Their separation was rigidly enforced. The relationship between the first two was roughly one between creditors and debtors. Slaves were acquired through war or indebtedness; they spent their whole lives toiling in the fields or in the homes of the chiefs, and were symbols of rank and prestige.

Wars were started to exact revenge, to capture slaves, or to acquire heads to plant under the posts of new *rumah adat*. In order to acquire full rank and title, "feasts of merit" were staged in which human sacrifices were made and stone memorials (menhir) erected. Most chiefly ceremonies—birth, naming, and circumcision—included mock battles, ritual chanting, animal sacrifice, trance-dancing, and offerings made to funerary figures. In the S, young men had to perform bride service in the house of his future bride. The perfect marriage was with the boy's mother's brother's daughter; a man would also marry the wife of his deceased father. Marriage involved a complex exchange of feasts and gifts which included a heavy bride-price *(bowo,* usually pigs and gold), the amount set according to the rank of the bride. Today, the bride price is up to one million *rupiah* in the south, up to 3 million in the center and north. Real estate is still handed down through the sons.

Religion

Owing to German Lutheran missionaries proselytizing here for more than 100 years, about 95% of the island's population has been converted to nominal Christianity, the people now gentle and obedient to authority. Islam (5% of the population) has made the most progress in the port towns, especially Gunungsitoli. Instead of hunting heads, today Niasers sing hymns; instead of waging war and keeping slaves, today they barter copra and pigs for bicycles and ghetto boxes, and put on diluted war dances for tourists. Children go to government elementary and missionary schools. Yet vestiges of the old culture still survive: the village architecture, staged war dances, performances of masculine strength, and inherited social offices. The old religion is now completely dead, the new religion followed with a fundamentalist fervor. The few supersitions that have survived are infused with Christian symbols and practices which carry more prestige. Strict Sabbath prohibitions are practiced—no work on Sundays, not even picking a coconut!

North Vs. South

In the past, north Nias was vastly different from south Nias. Poor communications contributed to their mutual isolation, and the inhabitants of each region speak their own dialect. The north was conquered early by the Dutch, but tribes of the south resisted to the bitter end in fortified hillside villages. In contrast to the megalithic culture and rigid class structure of the south, the culture of north Nias became modern Indonesian/quasi-European with little class distinctions. Today, however, this stereotypical picture of the south being traditional and the north totally acculturated just isn't true anymore. Visually, the south is much more traditional with the best villages and stonework, while the only indigenous physical features left in the north are the distinct oval-shaped huts with curved sides. For this reason, south Nias is more appealing for travelers than other parts of the island. But the famed traditional kinship network still at work in the south is at least as strong in other parts of the island (e.g. in Sirumbu, west Nias) with a higher bride-price. In the south traditional obligations have been moderated as a deliberate official policy, hence the south's greater prosperity.

THE ARTS

Crafts

Genuine Niah antiquities? Forget it. When the first German Protestant missionaries arrived on the island at the turn of the century, the statues, effigies, and ancestor figures *(adu)* that weren't destroyed were taken back to Europe. Now the best Niah artifacts and sculptures, including whole huts and entire wardrobes, are in Germany at the famous Rautenstrauch-Joest Museum of Cologne, and in other private Continental collections. In the villages, the people will show you a whole array of traditional gear, such as *kalabubu* (necklaces), *sialu* (earrings), *gare* (swords), *oroba* (crocodile skin armor), and old photos. Seldom are these heirlooms for sale.

Niah mortuary figurine

As for musical instruments, enormous skin drums occasionally reach almost 3 m long. Niasers also play a bamboo "buzzer"—a hollow bamboo cane with 2 holes, the hand acting as resonator. Two buzzers of different notes can be played simultaneously. Versions of this instrument are also found in N. Sumatra, Kalimantan, and Sumbawa. The buzzer exists only in S. Nias; in N. Nias buzzers have been replaced with trumpets to accompany European Christian hymns.

Dance

Warlike S. Niah dances are the only ones in Indonesia which specialize in high acrobatic jumps. In the *Tulo-Tulo* dance, performers in warrior costume hold hands and move in a ring counterclockwise, all chanting together, the circle shrinking and expanding as if breathing. Then the tempo accelerates and the men begin to shout rhythmically, leaping frog-like high into the air and performing mock fights and armed combat dances brandishing their spears. Then the "battlefield" dissolves in utter confusion, just like after a *real*

battle. The Headhunter's Dance is an eerie dance-song with its rattling hypnotizing sound of shields. With their horned helmets, flaring shoulder plates, face masks with long boar tusks protruding, and double-edged swords and spears barbed like harpoons, the dancers' battle dress understandably struck terror in the hearts of an enemy.

Niah female dancing—if you're lucky enough to see it at a wedding—is unbelievably slow by Western standards: 5 seconds for a foot to touch the pavement each time. Two files of women move with downcast eyes and completely immobile faces. The colors of their costumes—red, yellow, gold, and black—seen against expanses of gray stone or sand make a fantastic total effect. Wearing long scarves and ear ornaments that look more like bracelets, the older women are the most accomplished dancers. See the Dance of the Hawk with its skipping, rotating, hovering movements. Then the women dance as cats, coiling and springing and clawing at each other.

Stone-jumping

Vestiges of the earlier monumental Niah culture survive not only in their dances but in the sport of stone-jumping *(fahombe)*. This frightening sport requires great acrobatic skill, particularly when it's executed with sword in hand! A solid stone column over 2 m high and ½ m broad stands in the great "runway" of the village between the rows of dwellings. In front of the column is a smaller stone about ½ m high. The young man runs from a distance of 20 m for the smaller stone and from it launches himself feet-first high into the air over the column. Much like jumping the high horse in gymnastics, jumpers gyrate around in midair to alight on their feet on rough heavy paving stones facing the column. In olden times stones were covered with sharp spikes and pointed bamboo sticks: *fahombe* was used to train young loinclothed warriors to clear walls of enemy villages at night with a torch in one hand and a sword in the other. *Fahombe* also proved a young man's fitness to take a wife. Now, dressed as athletes, stone-jumping takes place only at Bawomataluo, and costs Rp150,000 for a private showing. Another traditional Niah sport is a football game in which players keep a rattan ball suspended in the air in order to "keep the sun from setting."

Stone Sculpture

There were two phases in the history of Niah classical sculpture, the stonework of the proto-Malayan Ancient Peoples and the woodcrafts of the 1400s. Though it would be difficult to find a single stonecutter on Nias today, much remains of their megalithic culture, which was of a standard found nowhere else in SE Asia. Missionaries who first penetrated into the interior of the island in the 1930s came across abandoned villages in the mountains with their entire inventory of stone sculptures still intact, ripping them off by the hundreds. The finest collections of Niah stone sculpture today are in Germany.

These islanders once utilized stone as the most important material of civilization—for tools, utensils, pillows, even money. On this island whole villages are paved with great flat stone tiles, and in some cases long stone staircases lead up to hilltop villages. Master masons constructed throne-like chairs twisting with serpents, ornamental tables, bathing places, monolithic stelae and obelisks, elaborate seats for chiefs in the shape of hornbills, chests, or drums, and horizontal slabs erected as memorials to the dead—all very primitive yet very strong. Stone slabs were carved here similar in shape to those found everywhere in the early history of the planet, from Stonehenge to Easter Island. Hauled from distant riverbed quarries, Niah carvings were executed in light grayish stone with imagination and superb precision. The villagers themselves are ignorant of where the megaliths originated, who carved them or when (some are believed to be as old as 800 years). They've also long forgotten the meaning of the magical symbols and rosettes adorning stone pyramids and terraces in front of chiefs' houses and in ceremonial places in south Niah villages, at one time the center of sacrifices.

Wood Sculpture

The old religion is portrayed vividly in these Easter Island-like armless statues of ancestral beings distinguished by their tall Niah-style headgear, elaborate earrings, sharp features (but no chin), elongated torsos, large male organs, heads with small stuck-on beards and right ears with distended lobes. Note the bold, aggressive stance of the Niah *adu* (ancestor figure); at the funerals of chiefs, this wooden image was required so that the ghost of the deceased could transfer into it. Wooden statues were also used to propitiate spirits in case of family illness. Well-executed wooden statues (heavy to ship) start at Rp200,000, but the seller may come down as low as Rp45,000. Smaller ones go for Rp7500-10,000.

Architecture

Southern villages, constructed during the time of internecine warfare, are deceptive fortresses. Bars guarded windows, and trapdoors opened out to roofs. Structures were erected so close together that inside connecting doors made it possible for residents to walk the whole length of the village (sometimes over 300 m) without ever touching the ground; many structures had just a trapdoor in the floor, with no other exits or entrances. The most imposing houses belong to the aristocracy; on them, steeply pitched roofs soar over 15 m high, with overhanging gables which create a hooded appearance. Rectangular in shape, these chiefly structures rest on a substructure of stone and massive wooden beams, resisting trem-

ors that often shake the island. The older houses are made of handhewn polished timbers, ingeniously joined without pegs or nails, and panels and moldings are decoratively carved.

The oldest *adat* houses are still untouched in remote areas of the island; in the more Westernized villages Niasers prefer standard Indonesian construction. Now more and more *rumah adat* are replacing thatch with corrugated steel roofs; within a few years construction techniques will have vanished and the whole silhouette of the typical Niah village will be forever altered. To preserve what is left, in at least one case (Hilimondegaraya), a chief's *adat* house was completely dismantled piece by piece by a Danish professor and shipped back to Europe. In north Nias, traditional houses are less spectacular and more varied; the oval shape is predominant.

PRACTICALITIES

Accommodations

There are a number of comfortable *losmen* and hotels in Telukdalam and Gunungsitoli, but most visitors prefer to stay in one of the sleepy seacoast villages on Lagundi Bay (either in Lagundi or Jamborai) or with the people in southern hilltop villages where most anyone will take you in for around Rp1000-1500. There are even a few places on Lagundi Beach that will let you stay free if you eat there. Bring a thick wad of Rp100 notes as nobody can change a big note.

Food

The principal foods of Niasers are rice and pork. Besides its nutritional value, the pig is important as a status symbol and sacrificial animal. For great cultic festivities, large numbers are slaughtered, and pigs, along with money and perhaps gold and silver, are paid as a dowry for a bride. In the north, fish is the main staple of the diet. All cooking is done with coconut milk. Bananas and rice are grown in Nias, but vegetables are imported from Sibolga. Vegetables the missionaries taught the Niah to grow, such as *ubi* leaves, are fed exclusively to the pigs. Therefore, you see many illnesses here: curved and diseased bones, swollen and crossed eyes, infected feet covered in scars.

Health

It's important to get a cholera shot before arriving as there are still seasonal outbreaks. Malaria also occurs on Nias, so take your pills. The strains that have evolved here are resistent to choloroquine-based preventatives, so a pyrimethane-sulfadoxine alternative, such as Faladar, Methipox, and Antemal, is suggested. Be sure to take mosquito repellent and—if you're on a low-budget and need to stay in low-cost *losmen*—a mosquito net.

Conduct

Some of the people on Nias who are involved with tourism come on strong and pushy, and misinform tourists about prices, routes, *losmen*, etc. There are many cheats and thieves. Don't let anyone try to charge you a "tourist tax"; you've already paid for your visa, show them that! Also, if you do get anything stolen, go to the police to retrieve it. You might have to "buy" it back in the form of a tip.

Kids, such as those found in Hilisimaetano, can be downright vicious. Children will inevitably yell "HELLO MISTE-R-R-R-R!!" and "HELLO MISS!!" to which you should simply reply "YAHO'WU! (the traditional Niah greeting, meaning "Strength!"). This usually stops them cold, watching wide-eyed as you pass by, figuring that if you can greet them you can also possibly understand them. In the non-touristed areas, such as Orahili, people are usually very helpful and kind. In the remote areas, you could suddenly come across threatening-looking hunters with their spears and dogs. In these instances, you have surprise on your side and they are so dumfounded that you are long gone before they have time to react.

The behavior of visitors can go a long way in cutting down on the number of negative experiences. Always visit the headman's house first to pay your respects, and to ask permission to photograph or enter someone's house. If the headman is in the *sawah*, go through a subordinate or a lesser chief. There is usually no charge to see traditional houses; the best are sometimes unoccupied, the former occupants living in a more contemporary and less-visited structure. Most important of all: dress ultra-modest. On Lagundi Beach and at nearby Jamborae, the atmosphere is casual: shorts, swimsuits, no shirts (for males) are the rule. But upon leaving the beach area, women should wear long pants or a long skirt, a short-sleeved blouse, and a bra. Women should never wear just a *sarung* tied under their arms; that is what Indonesians wear to bathe, not to visit or saunter. Men should wear shirts. To dress otherwise will offend the morals of the local people. Travelers who dress in shorts, singlets, or without bras often have stones thrown at them by children. Such children should be reported to the local *kepala desa*, and not yelled at.

TRANSPORT

Getting There

The quickest way is to fly from Medan to Gunungsitoli; Merpati offers at least 3 flights (Rp52,500 OW) weekly. A SMAC flight (Rp55,000 OW) departs Medan at 0800; their office is at Jl. Imam Bonjol 59 (tel. 515934/516617) in Medan. Arriving, Gunungsitoli's Binaka Airport is 19 km from town; the *bemo*

costs Rp3000. The airport is small: only 7-seat Cessna Islanders can land here.

By sea is another way. First drive or take a bus from Medan to Sibolga (SW of Lake Toba), either stopping on the way at Lake Toba (Prapat), or travel the whole way in one day (12 hours, Rp9000). The road from Lake Toba to Sibolga is spectacular—narrow and mountainous. Sibolga is the usual port of embarkation to Gunungsitoli (Rp6000, 10-12 hours) and to Telukdalam (Rp7000, 17-24 hours). Twice a month there are also boats from Padang's port of Teluk Bayur to Telukdalam, Rp7000 (48 hours). Inclement weather may cancel ferry departures; during these times Nias runs out of fuel as its supply lines are cut.

The 2 places to purchase tickets in Sibolga are at the Pelabuhan Lama and Pelabuhan Baru ("Old" and "New" harbors, respectively). The ticket office at P. Lama has info and tickets to Telukdalam, the P. Baru office to Gunungsitoli. Some local character will probably latch on to you and help you out for a fee. Ferries to Gunungsitoli depart P. Baru twice daily (except Sunday), in the morning and evening, while the daily ferry to Telukdalam costs Rp5000. One ship is the *Sumber Makmur* which travels to Gunungsitoli. Another, older ship, the eternal *Agape* (a gift from the German Protestant church to the missionaries) is a slower and less comfortable bigger boat. Departures are not always a sure thing. Besides the regular ferries, several cheaper cargo boats do the passage, carrying salt, rice, and cement to Nias; these leave about every 4 days and cost as little as Rp4000 to Gunungsitoli. A few stop in Pulau Tello (1 day only), then Telukdalam, then on to Gunungsitoli.

The passage can either be grueling or pleasant. The regular ferries are usually more comfortable; the cargo boats *(kapal motor)* are definitely grittier. Seas are usually glassy, with a bit of rain around midnight. On the smaller boats it could be crowded: sometimes there is only ⅓ m of freeboard between you and the water, and you might spend much of your passage vomiting over the side. If it rains get under canvas (which isn't waterproof) with perhaps 30 or more other people; if somebody moves their leg then 30 other people have to move their legs too. Pray that it doesn't rain hard because then you can stay on deck and it turns into a much nicer passage. The larger boats such as the *Sumber Makmur* (an immaculate boat with superb toilets) are clean and dry. A foam sleeping pad would be helpful.

Getting Around

Even as late as the 1950s a fairly reliable road system was in use on the island, one route going completely around Nias. But since independence many roads have been swallowed up by the jungle and torrential

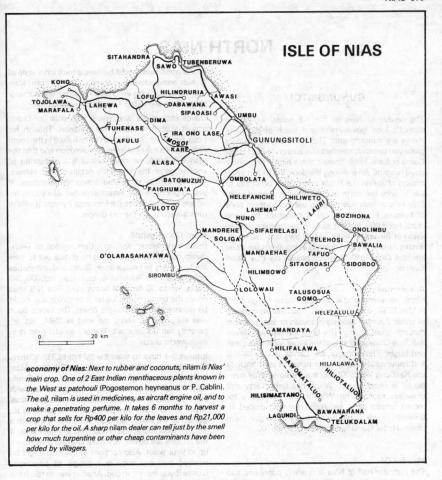

ISLE OF NIAS

SITAHANDRA
SAWÓ
TUBENBERUWA
KOHO
HILINDRURIA
LOFU
AWASI
TOJOLAWA
LAHEWA
DABAWANA
MARAFALA
SIPAOASI
DIMA
UMBU
TUHENASE
IRA ONO LASE
GUNUNGSITOLI
AFULU
MOSOI
KARE
ALASA
BATOMUZUI
OMBOLATA
FAIGHUMA'A
HELEFANICHE
HILIWETO
FULOTO
LAHEMA
HUNO
I. LAURI
BOZIHONA
MANDREHE
SIFAERELASI
ONOLIMBU
SOLIGA
TELEHOSI
BAWALIA
O'OLARASAHAYAWA
MANDAEHAE
TAFUO
SIDORDO
SITAOROASI
SIROMBU
HILIMBOWO
LOLOWAU
TALUSOSUA
GOMO
HELEZALULU
AMANDAYA
HILIFALAWA
HILIALAWA
BAWOMATALUO
HILIOTALUO
HILISIMAETANO
BAWANAHANA
LAGUNDI
TELUKDALAM

0   20 km

economy of Nias: Next to rubber and coconuts, nilam is Nias'
main crop. One of 2 East Indian menthaceous plants known in
the West as patchouli (Pogostemon heyneanus or P. Cablin).
The oil, nilam is used in medicines, as aircraft engine oil, and to
make a penetrating perfume. It takes 6 months to harvest a
crop that sells for Rp400 per kilo for the leaves and Rp21,000
per kilo for the oil. A sharp nilam dealer can tell just by the smell
how much turpentine or other cheap contaminants have been
added by villagers.

tropical downpours keep most that now exist in deplorable condition. Buses, trucks, *bemo,* and jeeps
run tortuously along existing main roads, but in the
remote areas walking is your only option. All over the
island are forest tracks leading from village to village.
In the S many of these paths are paved with stones!
Locals will offer to give you a lift on the back of their
motorcycles and motorbikes (a method of transport
called *honda sikap).* It's also possible, in the tourist
villages of the S, to rent bicycles. The influx of tourists
has made some *bemo* and other drivers greedy; they
will try to get you to charter and are not inclined to

barter. Also, be home before 1600 when their prices
go up 1,000%!

A bus now departs at 0900 each day from Gunungsitoli in the N for Telukdalam in the S; Rp4000, 10-16
hours—except for the first hour, shaking all the way.
As an alternative, from Gunungsitoli travelers can occasionally take a *kapal motor* to Telukdalam for
Rp5000—a scenic trip with thick jungle the whole
way down the coast. Take along a *nasi campur* as the
trip takes up to 8 hours.

NORTH NIAS

GUNUNGSITOLI

The capital of Nias on the NE coast, where the district's local government and much of the commerce are concentrated. This small city is the only place you can cash travelers cheques on Nias: at Hotel Gomo or Bank 1946. There's also a high school and a good hospital. After exiting the dock, the tourist information office on the R has information on sights to see in both the north and south, plus a good map. Stay here at least overnight to see the northern style of houses. From Medan to Gunungsitoli by plane costs Rp65,000, leaving early in the morning and arriving at Binaka at 0800. SMAC also flies this route. Binaka Airport is 19 km from Gunungsitoli; take a bus into the city (Rp1000) which passes right by Hotel Ketilang.

Accommodations

Highly recommended is the new Wisma Soliga (built in May 1987), 6 km from town. You have your choice of either 2 *rumah adat*-style houses or very pleasant modern guest rooms. The hotel's restaurant serves delicious Chinese food, and the larger rooms are clean and bright. The manager, Mr. Ganda, is very helpful and knowledgeable. Cheaper hotels in town include the **Ketilang** (Rp2500) and the **Tenang**. Way overpriced is Hotel Gomo, which has rather dirty and cheerless rooms. The **Wisata** asks Rp8000 s for rooms, private bath, and restaurant with limited Indonesian menu. Could be noisy; try to bargain them down. **Hotel Gunungsitoli** charges Rp6000.

Vicinity Of

The northern half of Nias is sparsely populated and has large swampy areas. There are nice walks around the Gunungsitoli area, which is known for its few

oval-shaped *rumah adat* houses, a traditional style of N. Nias architecture. See some up the hill from Hilimbawedesolo, 13 km and Rp600 by bus from Gunungsitoli. More are found 4 km S of Gunungsitoli.

Dance enthusiasts who speak Indonesian or Dutch should visit Amarojama, the historian. Though his book *Fondroko Ono Niha* isn't much liked in the south (they say it's full of incorrect information and that the man is biased), he nevertheless is a wellspring of knowledge on the nitty-gritty details of Niah culture. Ask Mr. Ganda at Wisma Soliga for directions. If you've got Rp75,000, Amarojama can take you to his village to see a dance performance by young village men trained to do the old dances.

From Gunungsitoli

Boats very seldom sail from Gunungsitoli to Telukdalam nowadays so you have no choice but to take the bus, or try to hitch a truck. Buses and sometimes *oplet* depart for Telukdalam each day, Rp5000, 3-9 hours (up to 30 hours if heavy rain). The N-S road down the center of the island is potholed and could be washed out with bridges down. The World Bank was supposed to finish the road in 1984, but apparently ran out of cash. The old coastal road is in even worse shape.

It takes 3-4 days to walk the 80 km to Telukdalam. First take a bus from Gunungsitoli to Soliga or Mandrehe. Then walk to Hilismaetano, then bus to Telukdalam. Stay in true *asli* villages along the way, with either families or the *kepala desa*. En route are 2 sites where stone stelae and pyramids were gathered together by the missionaries 30 years ago; it's about a 1 ½ day walk to the first group. This is a hard walk. If the bridges are down, you have to cross 3 big rivers up to your waist. Also sections of the road might be washed out, and there is a danger of poisonous snakes if you leave the road. Another way to reach the S is by light motorcycle, but you or your driver might have to carry the motorcycle over river crossings.

SOUTH NIAS

The 30 or so traditional fortress villages of S. Nias are the most spectacular inhabited sites on the whole island. Villages were either built on naturally fortified sites or on top of hills, a practice which stems from the days of clan warfare in the not-so-distant past. These hilltop fortresses were made almost impregnable; the paths leading up to them are full of switchbacks and are built deliberately narrow. Stairways

were always cut into the steepest side of the hill, with moss-covered slippery stones rising nearly perpendicular past razor grass, elephant ferns, and other heavy jungle. Some villages were further protected by stone walls. Village ground plans are rectangular with an open central square—a "highway" of paving stones—and 2 long rows of houses on pilings in between. Formerly, a temple *(bale)* was situated in the middle; it held the skulls of heads taken for ritual burials, and the sacred stone weights for weighing pigs and gold. Each house is inhabited by one or more extended families. The furniture is very basic: sleeping mats and crude wooden tables. Nowadays more and more Niasers choose not to rebuild the traditional raised houses of their ancestors and instead erect conventional Indonesian-style houses on the ground, with sheet metal replacing the thatch roofs.

Telukdalam

Second largest town on Nias on its far SE tip and the main port of entry for southern Nias. If arriving from Sibolga, you pull into a small palm-fringed bay with the town extending into the surrounding hills. A red church is one of the town's principal landmarks. If the ferry is crowded, it might be a good idea to make a dash to one of the several *losmen* on the waterfront: **Sabar Menanti** and the concrete **Wisma Jamburae**, both Rp4000s; and the **Effendi**, Rp8000 s. The Sabar Menanti is in a large 2-story building with big double rooms above a store. This combination hotel and restaurant might also have bicycles for hire at Rp1000 per day (if you bargain). Though a filthy dump, it has the big attraction of possessing a truly amazing fridge which cools beer to a temperature fit for Australian consumption in 3½ min. flat. A few good restaurants in town serve Padang food and noodle dishes.

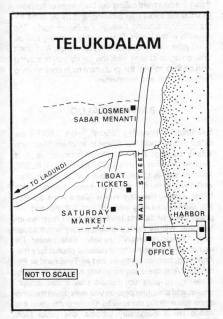

From Telukdalam

Buses run to the following S. Nias villages: Botohili, Lagundi, Hilisimaetano, Bawamataluo. Motorbikes can sometimes be hired; ask the shipping agents. The road from Telukdalam to the N gets bad after only a few km. The ferry to Sibolga runs twice weekly, Rp5000. Occasional ships (about twice monthly) sail for Padang (Rp6000-7000, 48 hours), saving you the 12-hour bus ride from Sibolga up to Padang. But since the boat to Padang is unreliable, in the long run it might be faster just to get a boat to Sibolga and then bus to Padang.

LAGUNDI BAY

Twelve km from Telukdalam, this horseshoe-shaped bay consists of 2 villages: Muslim Lagundi, and at the far end of the bay Christian Jamborai (or "Surf City"). Together, these fishing villages are the Kuta and Legian of Nias, discovered by Australian and American surfers in the mid-'70s. Lagundi Bay used to be the main port of S. Nias but the Krakatoa eruption in 1883 wiped it out and the port was moved to Telukdalam (which means "Port of Peace"), leaving Lagundi to sleep on. Join the local soccer games on Sunday afternoons. Take enough money because you get a lousy exchange rate in Lagundi; to live reasonably comfortably you'll need about Rp4000-5000 per day. Watch your stuff; theft has become a problem.

The beach at Jamborai is 1 km (a 20-min. walk) down the beach from Lagundi village, on the point at the W opening of the bay. This village is a renowned surfer's mecca. The waves are much better for surfing than Bali's Kuta Beach and it offers safer swimming too (but no snorkeling). The surf here can reach over 3 m high and travels sometimes 200 m. Out in the wide bay there's a reef, then white sand, then another coral reef over 50 m wide—an unreal world, like a dream. The best surf is a 15-min. walk to the point, where all the right-handers peel off, with wild sea turtles in the water! And there's seldom any more than a dozen people on the beach—a few fishermen out in their canoes, a few Australian surfers, a few French and Italians. Top of the season there could be all of 20 surfers, some of whom have been here for a month or so. Surfboards can be rented on the beach for Rp1000 per day. Because of the size of the waves and the coral, this surf is not really for learners. Bring lots of reading material.

Accommodations

The 12 or so *losmen* in Jamburai village on the point toward the W opening of the bay—Sea Breeze, Ama Soni, Rufus, Friendly's, Jamburai, Immanuel, etc.—average Rp1000-1500 in price. Check the places out *personally*. Make the best choice. Consider good security (bars on windows, good *penjaga*); most places have mosquito nets, are only 40 m through coconut trees to the beach, and you can hear the surf. One of the best accommodations is **Ama Yanti's** Losmen across the river. Marvelous Mr. Yanti is related to the royal line of Bawamataluo families and has many evenings' worth of information in store for you on Niah magic, culture, arts, language, etc. A real find! Ina Yanti, his wife, is a superb cook and can help with learning Niah as well. The kids of the family are quiet and fun-loving. Aman Dolyn, the manager of Aman Losmen (Rp1500-2000), is also a nice guy. At **Ama Soni** they really look after you too, but rooms will probably be occupied.

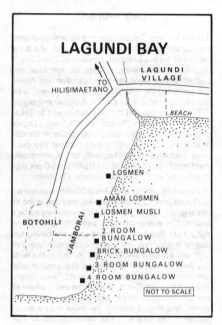

LAGUNDI BAY

TO HILISIMAETANO

LAGUNDI VILLAGE

BEACH

LOSMEN

AMAN LOSMEN

LOSMEN MUSLI

BOTOHILI

JAMBORAI

2 ROOM BUNGALOW

BRICK BUNGALOW

3 ROOM BUNGALOW

4 ROOM BUNGALOW

NOT TO SCALE

Food

Most of the *losmen* provide at least evening meals at Rp600-1000 extra. Meals tend to be monotonous, the same ol' *mie goreng, nasi goreng, gado-gado,* omelettes, etc., so take extra vittles to liven the fare up (peanut butter is like gold!). A few *warung* snackbars have opened up. **Ama Yanti's** has far and away the best food; Manuel's is also good. Great seafood; crayfish and lobster can be bought on the beach for only Rp1000, fish for Rp300-500, *kelapa* for Rp200. Use your boy scout skills and make tea, coffee, roast fish and lobster dinners on the beach.

Transport

The Lagundi turn-off is 6 km W of Telukdalam, a dirt

road which leads 6 km farther down to Lagundi village. Lagundi Bay can be reached by irregular *oplet* (Rp600), bus (Rp500), or you can hitch a ride *(ojek)* on the back of a motorbike (Rp1500) right to Jamborai village outside the row of *losmen*. Truck-buses only on Sat. to and from Telukdalam for market. Leaving Lagundi for the mainland, allow several days as something might go wrong. Sometimes if you arrive on the afternoon bus in Telukdalam, you can go straight to the harbor and climb on a boat to Sibolga (Rp5000, 12 hours) right away. Beware of David and his friend Martin's shady boat-ticket deals; they tend to hang around the *losmen*. Don't pay in advance.

Vicinity Of

Botohili is only a 3-km walk or a short bus ride from Lagundi, the end of the road for vehicles. This is the place to go if you don't want to surf but want to experience Niah village life. Two rows of houses are separated by a courtyard of big stone squares. All of the *rumah adat* have doors between them that occupants of each house are forbidden to shut; this would mean that they have something to hide. If you stay in one of the *adat* houses, you'll sleep in one big room with 30 family members. When you want to be left alone at night, just say *Bolehkah saya tidur?* ("May I sleep now please?"). Young men of the village might play the guitar and talk until midnight. At 0300 sharp the head fisherman starts walking up and down the courtyard calling out the names of his crew. At 0500 the cocks start crowing, and by 0600 the entire family is running through the house again. The *mandi* is in the jungle down muddy stepping stones. Don't miss this whole humble experience. And don't miss going to church with the family you're staying with on Sun. to hear the exuberant male choir singing hymns in Niah and Indonesian.

BAWAMATALUO

Bawamataluo (meaning "Sunhill," pop. 3,600) is the oldest extant traditional village in southern Nias, with suberb carvings and high-roofed architecture. It is reached by minibus from Telukdalam, 14 km, Rp500. Another way is to take the bus just to Orahili, then walk 1 km up the 480 steep stone steps leading to this hilltop village. Bawamataluo is Nias's most accessible, popular, touristy *adat* village; Suharto and the police chief of Jakarta have even been here! Its inhabitants will try to flog contemporary wood sculpture, "precious family" *pusaka,* kids pester for money, and villagers offer to pose for photos for a fee. Annoying, but not nearly as bad as Torajaland or Penelokan. And this is too important a village, culturally speaking, to pass up. People play chess, sculpt, weave, and slaughter pigs as you walk down the long street laid with big stone slabs. On the outskirts of the village are 3 elementary schools, one junior high

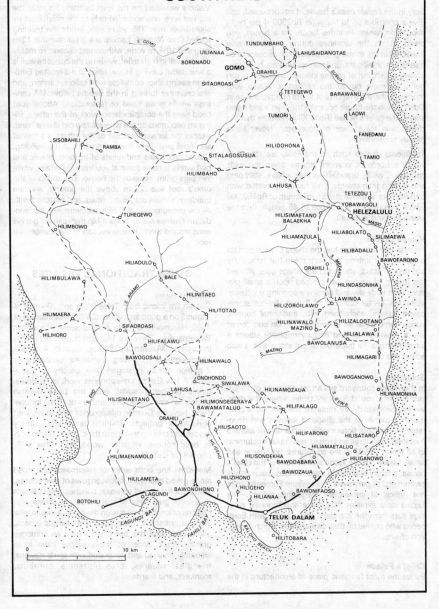

SOUTH NIAS

TUNDUMBAHO
UILIANAA
BORONADU
GOMO
S. GOMO
LAHUSAIDANOTAE
ORAHILI
SITAOROASI
TETEGEWO
BARAWANU
SITALAGOSUSUA
TUMORI
LAOWI
S. SUSUA
HILIDOHONA
FANEDANU
HILIMBAHO
TAMIO
LAHUSA
SISOBAHILI
RAMBA
TETEZOU
YOBAWAGOLI
HELEZALULU
HILISIMAETANO
BALAEKHA
S. MASIO
HILIABOLATO
SILIMAEWA
TUHEGEWO
HILIAMAZULA
HILIBADALU
BAWOFARONO
HILIMBOWO
ORAHILI
S. MEZAVIA
HILINDASONIHA
HILIADULO
BALE
LAWINDA
HILINITAEO
HILIZOROILAWO
HILIMBULAWA
HILITOTAO
HILINAWALO
MAZINO
HILIZALOOTANO
HILIMAERA
S. ARAMO
SIFAOROASI
HILIALAWA
HILIHORO
HILIFALAWU
BAWOLANUSA
S. MAZINO
HILIMAGARI
HILINAWALO
BAWOGOSALI
ONOHONDO
SIWALAWA
BAWOGANOWO
S. ENO
LAHUSA
HILINAMOZAUA
HILINAMONIHA
HILISIMAETANO
HILIMONDEGERAYA
BAWAMATALUO
S. CEWA
ORAHILI
HILIFALAGO
HILISAOTO
HILIFARONO
HILISATARO
S. HILIGEHO
HILIAMAETALUO
HILIMAENAMOLO
HILISONDEKHA
BAWODABARA
HILIGANOWO
HILILAMETA
HILIZIHONO
BAWOZAUA
BOTOHILI
LAGUNDI
BAWONOHONO
HILIGEHO
BAWONIFAOSO
HILIANAA
LAGUNDI BAY
FAHILI BAY
S. RATOMO
TELUK DALAM
RATOMO BEACH
HILITOBARA

0   10 km

school, and a Protestant and a Catholic church. Visit the other villages of the area. Few roads here; most of the time you have to walk on narrow paths through banana orchards and ricefields.

Stay in the *kepala desa's* house, if not occupied, and give a contribution to his wife; Rp2500 d per night should do, which includes lunch. As a bonus, you could sit on the sidelines during a village *rapat* (meeting) in the evening. The headman appears to be a sensitive, intelligent, and perceptive man; he speaks some English, but of course Indonesian speakers can get a lot more out of the exchange. Watch your money as there are reports of thefts of travelers' gear. Don't stay in the house opposite the chief's and if you stay in the chief's house (Rp1500) make sure that the chief's son stays clear of your gear. Never leave money unguarded.

Traditional dances such as the *Foalo* are staged in which a horde of warriors storms down the wide courtyard, wildly brandishing their spears, stamping and rattling their shields, their heads decorated with bird feathers. A dance costs a minimum of Rp150,000 which includes the full dance of 46 people (but the stone-jumping is extra!).

Village Layout
From the air the village has the shape of an imperfect cross. After climbing the very steep but beautifully laid tiers of stairs, you reach the village gate; you get the feeling of having just climbed upon a small plateau, with wide sky and sunshine opening up. Bawamataluo's center consists of 2 well laid-out stone-paved streets, each lined with traditional houses, which come together to form a "T." On one corner sits a meeting hall and directly opposite stands a jumping stone—a trapezoid of cut stone with a slab across the top.

Sculpture
In the village courtyard sits an arrangement of 18-ton stone chairs, round funerary tables where the dead were once left to decay, menhirs, obelisks, stone ceremonial benches in the shape of animals and decorated with simple floral motifs, and a disc of stone a foot thick, very large and round, resting on 4 columns. In all there are 287 stone sculptures, both large and small. Check out the stone slab in front of the chief's house: a figure chained in irons, whales, young boys swimming, all portrayed in a realistic European style not typical of an ancient megalithic culture. The *kepala desa* explains that these anachronistic carvings date from the islanders' first contact with Europeans who arrived on their sailing ships, which carried iron chains.

Chief's Palace
By far the most fantastic piece of architecture in the

whole village, and the finest and largest of its kind in all of Nias, is the 16-m-high chief's "palace." It is built on wooden pillars nearly one meter thick, with a stepped floor constructed of heavy wooden planks. Visitors would sit on the level befitting his rank; the highest level was accorded only to the chief. Built by slave labor over 185 years ago, inside the building (called *Omo Namada Laowa*) is a great chamber 12 m long and 10½ m wide, with carved decorative motifs on one wall in high relief, while on the opposite wall is a wonderful carving in low relief of a 2-masted European sailing ship, complete with sailors, cannon, and sea creatures lurking in the depths below. (All carvings are in great need of restoration.) Above your head rises the complex latticework of the rafters, filling an enormous space where a few old drums hang. Across the forward section of the rafters is a row of sacrificial pigs' jaws the entire width of the building. Carved crocodiles and reliefs of bosoms, phallic and bird symbols stare down at you from the rafters, while live pigs grunt beneath the house. The spikes of the *omo's* roof soar 23 m above the ground, and the buildings's walls are joined, fitted, and matched with all the consummate skill of a cabinetmaker. Its foundation timbers are so huge a big man cannot get his arms around them. Its one eyesore is the sheet metal roof.

OTHER TRADITIONAL VILLAGES

Hilisimaetano
Sixteen km inland from Telukdalam and 20 km N of Lagundi on a good asphalt road. With a population of 4500, Hilisimaetano is a larger and newer village than Bawamataluo. There are 140 *adat* houses here. Stay in *Losmen Mawan*; Rp2500 pp, capacity 4 people. Stone-jumping by young unmarried jumpers over 2 m-high stones is staged here, usually on Saturdays. A few German missionaries work in Hilisimaetano's 120-bed hospital, once run by a German church but since taken over and run down by Indonesians. Now the German missionaries tend to work on agricultural projects; children leave the primary grades and take up training at the project to learn how to build houses, irrigation works, and other skills needed for daily life.

Megaliths line both sides of Hilisimaetano's broad stone-paved courtyard, between rows of *adat* houses. There are flat-tipped obelisks, benches and dolmens of smooth gray slabs of stone, treasure chests with designs of keys and pistols on the sides, a throne with stone armrests and a crocodile embracing the back, and a chair that has been hewn from an immense granite block. Most of these pieces have been smoothly finished and decorated with spiral designs, triangles, squares, lotus blossoms, hornbills, monkeys, and lizards.

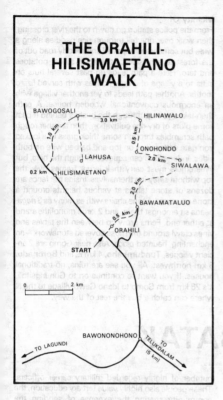

THE ORAHILI-HILISIMAETANO WALK

BAWOGOSALI
HILINAWALO
3.0 km
1.0 km
0.5 km
ONOHONDO
LAHUSA
2.0 km
SIWALAWA
0.2 km
HILISIMAETANO
2.0 km
BAWAMATALUO
0.5 km
ORAHILI
START
0   2 km

BAWONONOHONO
TO LAGUNDI
TO TELUKDALAM
(5 km)

The Orahili-Hilisimaetano Walk

An outstanding 2-day walk via a back path which passes through a number of traditional villages. Nearly every village has stone seats, memorial benches, stairs of honor. People are very friendly, especially once you get past Bawamataluo. Orahili is the nicest village because of the relative absence of *Allo Turis!* Bawatamaluo is the best for tribal houses. Siwalawa is rather rundown. Onohondo is a decent, friendly place. Onohondo has a *losmen* (Jirman Handra, Rp1000), a swimmimg pool, and a waterfall ½ km east. Hilinawalo is the most traditional village, over 700 years old, the village from which Bawamataluo and the present noble line originate. It has a beautifully laid central stone walk with stone benches and a pair of thrones. Bawogosali is a pleasant, picturesque village. Hilisimaetano is the worst for rascally kids.

On this easy 15-km walk, all you have to do is follow the stone path which connects all the villages. The way could be tricky if you're wearing big European boots. Take mosquito repellent. It's possible to stay overnight in the houses of the *kepala desa*. If you want to do it on your own, ask directions in each village; otherwise, you shouldn't have any trouble finding a guide for around Rp4000-5000 per day. It's a day trip from Bawamataluo NE to Siwalawa, a difficult segment. Your guide will probably know all the people along the way and will go to all the high hats of each village; your hosts will probably serve soup or tea or chop up a coconut for you. From Hilisimaetano at the end of the walk, ride back to Telukdalam by bus or *oplet*.

GOMO

This village near the Gomo River, roughly halfway between Telukdalam and Gunungsitoli, has been called the cradle of Niah culture. It is claimed that the ancestors of the present-day *Ono Niah* originated from this area, and it is thus looked upon as sacred. From the town's center, it's 1 km to the Gomo police station where you must show your passport and enter your name in the tourist register. Notice the register records only about 30 tourists a year, which explains why people are friendly (but not overly so). Children still hide in the bushes or pick up their screaming baby siblings and dive into their houses when they see you. Stay with the *kepala desa* in a fine, 3-generations-old king's house.

Getting There

From Telukdalam, boats leave for the market town of Helezalulu fairly regularly, 3 hours, Rp4000. The boat anchors in a small bay; you get dropped on the beach after a 5-min. Rp500 *prahu* ride. If the boat arrives late, sleep at the *stasiun polisi,* at one of the *warung* around the marketplace (marketday is Wed.), or on the boat. The hike to Gomo from Helezalulu, over difficult but fascinating terrain, takes about 2 days. The track passes through a gorge, then follows a river for some distance passing small villages with occasional *adat* houses. At a point where the road meets the river, a stone stairway rises to a village on the L and a muddy track adjacent to a wide strong river straight ahead. Cross the river here. The water level varies with the rain and could be knee deep on the trip out but waist deep on the return; the current could be strong enough to sweep you off your feet.

From the other side of the river, the track is all stone except for some very muddy sections that will ruin any pair of shoes. After about 3 hours and the crossing of another shallower river, a stone path on the R leads from the main road, and rises through a village with some stone tables and *naga*-head chairs. If you pass through a gap between 2 not-very-high and thickly vegetated rises, you've gone too far. People walk along this road with bundles of firewood and sacks of rice on their heads, so if in doubt just inquire, though they will not, most likely, speak Indonesian. From the village on the hill the road leads down to a wide river which must be crossed, then passes alongside some rice paddies. There are 2 more small creeks to cross before a stone stairway leads up through the trees on the R to the village of Gomo. Another way to get to Gomo from Telukdalam is by motorbike, but it will cost around Rp25,000 as the driver has to carry his bike across rivers.

Sights

Gomo is an important site for stone seats, menhirs, phallic stones. Representing symbols of authority, replicas of these megaliths now stand in the yard of the Kantor Bupati in Gunungsitoli, the district capital. There are only 6 *rumah adat* here; the others burned down years ago. In the old chief's house, notice the single- and double-tailed lizard motifs on the building's front, including a larger-than-lifesize monkey's- head carving descending from the forward rafters (another one is outside) and an arm coming out from the wall in a Nazi salute. Out front sits a series of round stone tables *(gouk)* and a couple of *naga* chairs, one high atop a monolith with small stepping blocks sticking out at intervals to either side. This monolith, called a *behu,* is about 4 m tall.

Vicinity Of

From the police station go down to the river crossing, then walk over one hill through rice paddies along a wide but sometimes unpaved and muddy road out of the forest to a hillside cultivated in sweet potatoes and taro. Here a path leads up past several huts on stilts to a village of 3 *adat* houses with carved lizard motifs. Another path leads to yet another village with an enormous conventional wooden house. A path then takes you up through the bushes behind it past some plots of dry-rice cultivation, then another rough path scrambles through some thick grass to a locked iron gate with spikes on top and barbed wire on both sides. Indonesians can squeeze through the bars, but Westerners must carry their larger frames over the top without *satey*-ing themselves. Inside the fence are dozens of stone tables at various heights around a stone courtyard. Stone chairs with as many as 3 *naga*-heads sit amongst them, and 2 large monoliths stand at either end. Ferns grow up between the tables and vines crawl around the moss-covered stonework—an enchanting, haunted place. Also near Gomo are 2 ancient villages, **Tundumbaho,** 4 km E, and **Boronadu,** 8 km northwest. All you see are ruins, no traditional houses. If you want to continue on to Gunungsitoli, it's 28 km from Gomo to Idano Gawo village to the N where can catch a bus the rest of the way.

THE BATAK

Some scholars believe that the word *batak,* already in use in the 17th C., was originally a derogatory Old Malay term for "robber"; other translations give it as "pig eaters." Yet another theory insists that the word originates from Bataha, the name of a Karen village in the Burma/Siam area from where the Batak people originate. These sturdy rice-growing people (the saying goes, "The Batak are workers, not thinkers") live in fertile mountainous valleys extending up to 200 km N and 300 km S of Lake Toba (a total of 1,700 sq. km) in the narrowest stretch of the island's upper neck. The Batak are shorter and heavier than the Minangkabau; they have kept their racial stock pure having lived inland and developed an early reputation for ferocity and cannibalism.

Because of mass migrations of Batak seeking a better life in the lowland regions and Jakarta, modernization in the Batak homeland is slow. Their society is stubbornly traditional in structure, the majority living in small, independent, self-sufficient, tightly knit villages. Many of the tribes' (particularly the Toba Batak) traditional agriculture and land-tenure practices—thus their way of life—remain almost unchanged. Well-known for their warlike traditions, the Batak have provided modern-day Indonesia with a

number of highly regarded military career officers. These people also highly value tertiary education, the community sharing the expense of sending the brightest boys in the village off to school in Medan or Jakarta. Many Batak are thus well placed in government, academia, and business circles. Batak are very able musicians and chorus singers, members of nationally popular bands. They are also some of the best chess players in the East. Learned from age 10 or 11, every village has its master. A barefoot peasant once stalemated the Dutch World Champion in the Grand Hotel in Medan in 1939, a major event in Batak history!

Tribes

The Batak are divided into a number of related ethnolinguistic groups: Karo (N of Lake Toba in the area around Brastagi and Kabanjahe); Pakpak (W of Lake Toba around Sidikalang); Simelungun (E of Lake Toba); Toba Batak (Samosir Island and S of Lake Toba); Mandailing (far S of N. Sumatra Province in Tapanuli District); and the Angkola (southcentral N. Sumatra Province). Though many of their customs are different, they all share the same cultural patterns. Perceived differences between the subgroups have

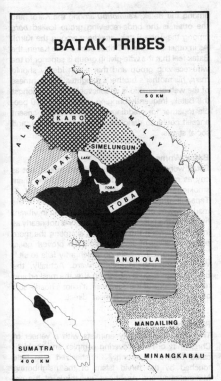

BATAK TRIBES

KARO
MALAY
ALAS
SIMELUNGUN
PAKPAK
LAKE
TOBA
TOBA
50 KM

ANGKOLA

MANDAILING

SUMATRA
400 KM

MINANGKABAU

Karen. Over 1,500 years ago, this tribe was forced to migrate due to overcrowding from the southward movement of expanding Mongolian and Siamese tribes. Some came to Barus on the W coast of Sumatra, then moved inland to become the Gayo, Alas, and Pakpak peoples. Others came down the E coast, then trekked up the Wampu and Belawan rivers to become the Karo people. The ancestors of the Toba traveled from the E coast up the Asahan River to Lake Toba.

On their travels the Karen people came in contact with Tamils from S. India who were trading in Sumatra. The Karen picked up aspects of Hindu religion and Tamil culture. It is thought that some Tamils also migrated to the interior. Numerous cultural, linguistic, and physical indications of early Hindu contact can be traced in the way the Batak cultivate rice by irrigation, plow with the water buffalo, their distinctive style of dwellings, the spinning wheel and cotton, Hindu vocabulary, chess, religious ideas, and script. Also, certain Karo tribes have darker skin, evidence of the S. Indian blood.

The Batak tribes retained their own way of life and isolation right up to the middle of the 19th C., when Dutch and Rheinische German missionaries discovered and began to convert them. Although some Batak groups were united under one raja, by the arrival of the Dutch they were just beginning to evolve into a number of petty states. Their last king, Sisingamangaraja, died in battle against the Dutch in 1907. Today the Batak are still very conservative by nature; foreign elements have only been accepted when they could be worked in with their original cosmic views. Samosir Island was the last bastion of the Toba Batak, conquered by tourists in the early '70s.

Cannibalism

The only human-flesh eaters on the island, the Batak were the infamous "headhunters of Sumatra" in tales of yore. Cannibalism was most prevalent among the Pakpak, although usually only token bits of flesh were eaten for ceremonial occasions, to obtain the attributes, luck, or courage of the victim. Herodotus, the Greek historian, first recorded the practice; Marco Polo in 1292 reported that the Batak ate their parents when they got too old to work. Marsden, in 1783, wrote the first accurate account of cannibalism; when it was published it shocked the so-called civilized world.

Cases were reported of flesh torn from human carcasses with the teeth, and of human flesh sold in markets. Those judged guilty of incest, murder, thievery, or adultery were condemned to be eaten by their fellow villagers, the most degrading of all punishments. An old Batak curse went, "I pick the flesh of your relatives from between my teeth!" In these punitive feasts the victims were not passionately or vengefully killed, but devoured according to fixed ethical rules. Raffles reports in the 19th C.: "For

been exacerbated by artificial administrative boundaries created by the Dutch, and by religious differences (Islam and Christianity). The Toba Batak is the only clan which strongly identifies with the name Batak; the other tribes seem ashamed to be known as such. The word definitely has an unsavory stigma amongst other Indonesians, to whom it is almost a synonym for barbarism, since the Batak once practiced cannibalism and they still eat dog (cooked in its own blood), a practice repugnant to 90% of Indonesians, who are Islamic.

HISTORY

Racially, the Batak are cousins to such "First Wave" tribes as the Igorots of the Philippines, the Dayaks of Kalimantan, and the Torajans of S. Sulawesi. Unlike the majority of Indonesia's advanced states which arose in coastal valleys with rich soil and accessible to trade, the Batak established their kingdom deep in the mountains. The proto-Malayan Batak are actually descendants of wandering clans of Neolithic mountain-dwellers from northern Thailand and Burma, the

certain crimes, a criminal would be eaten alive. The flesh was sometimes eaten raw, or grilled and eaten with lime, salt, pepper, and a little rice. Human blood was drunk out of bamboo containers. Palms of the hands and soles of the feet were delicacies of the epicures." Though this ghastly practice largely ceased when the Batak converted to Islam and Christianity, there have been incidences of the Batak indulging in cannibalism up until quite recent times.

Traditional Culture

Their traditional society was divided into 3 classes: nobles, peasants, and slaves. Villages were once hostile to one another, and you can still find remnants of old bamboo and earth fortifications at Nanggar and Lumban Garaga (22 and 30 km from Prapat, respectively); fortified heirarchal earthenworks can also be seen in the museum villages of Simanindo and Pematang Purba. Ramparts were surrounded by a ring of hidden traps, tunnel-like entrances, and prickly bamboo stakes able to inflict puncture wounds which took months to heal. Scouts were constantly on watch on towers from where they could fire muskets, blowpipes, arrows, and spears. Slavery of war captives and debtors was widespread, and enemies were eaten so that they should be utterly obliterated. Their dead were buried in boat-shaped stone coffins, a prime example being the tomb of King Sidobutar in Tomok on Samosir Island. Old customs of tattooing, tooth filing and blackening have almost completely died out.

MODERN CULTURE

Genealogy

Batak social organization is more similar to that of the slash-and-burn tribes of mainland SE Asia than to the irrigated heirarchal rice societies of insular SE Asia. The Batak are a patrilineal society, considered to have the most clearly defined patrilineal structure in Indonesia. They live in communities (huta), consisting of small clusters of multi-family households. A larger unit (marga) is made up of a number of huta, each tracing their descent from a single male ancestor. The headman of the clan, the marga-raja, has the responsibility to see that each individual in a group has land to work. The bride must move into the husband's settlement and land is passed down the male line. Some of their patrilineages extend back 500 years.

The ideal family size of a Batak is 17 sons and 16 daughters, and good wishes are expressed with the gesture of hagabeon, which means "have as many offspring as possible." Genealogies are followed intensely. When Batak meet, they rigorously ertutur, cross-examine each other as to their lineages and clan. All clan members must marry outside the clan (infant weddings were once commonplace). One marga is the bride-providing group (called hula hula

among the Batak, kalimbubu among the Karo), and the other is the bride-receiving group (called boru among the Toba Batak, anakberu among the Karo). As in other SE Asian hilltribes such as the Karen, the Batak feel that the wife-giving group is superior to the wife-receiving group and that a son ideally should marry his mother's brother's daughter. The tightness of the web of kinship is unbelievably strong amongst the Batak, frequently bringing more than 1,000 people together for weddings and funerals. To absent oneself could be dangerous to health, welfare, and social status.

Batak Women

Batak women are strong-spirited and robust, not as coy as many of their Indonesian sisters. See them smoking foot-long stogies in the ricefields of S. Tapanuli, dress their husbands up like dolls in the market towns of Lake Toba, and break out in vibrant hymns on the buses. Premarital purity is not nearly as important among the Batak as it is among the more puritan Muslims of Java. An old Batak proverb goes, "There is no dainty cake on which a fly fails to sit." Women are unbelievably forward. Actually, the Batak's aggression is refreshing after the masked and refined feelings of the Javanese; it's not a hostile sort of aggression but open, honest, direct.

Religion

The Batak are basically animists with a veneer of Christianity or Islam covering complex and sophisticated beliefs. A strongly Christianized area little touched by the fervid Islam of the neighboring Minangkabau and Acehnese, two-thirds of the approximately 1.5 million Batak are Christian. The Muslim Batak, mostly the Mandailing group, live in southern Batak territory (Tapanuli). Christianized Batak are both Catholic and Protestant. The Protestants, who belong to a branch of the Protestant church called Huriah Kristen Batak Protestan, form the largest Christian community in Indonesia. Churches are divided into 3 sections, one each for the men, mothers, and daughters.

The Batak were first converted by a fearless German missionary, Nommensen, who arrived in 1861 with only a Bible and a violin. Many of the older people to this day have German evangelical names such as Luther, Bismark, and Wilhelm, since nearly all the missionaries in those early days were German. Nommensen delivered the death sentence on the old religion when he persuaded the Dutch government to prohibit the collective sacrificial celebrations (bius) and playing Batak musical instruments, wiping out in one blow their whole "pagan" world. This founder of the Batak church is now buried in Balige, 30 km from Prapat, where there's a memorial marker, and you can often see his portrait hanging in Batak churches.

figurehead of a Ship of the Dead from the Sembiring Batak district of North Sumatra

Regardless of their nominal faith, half the population today still believes in spirits of dead ancestors, sacred trees, stones, and places, and in a Hindu-like pantheon of higher deities *(begu)*. All Batak trace their descent from one Si Radja Batak, an ancestor-hero of supernatural origin who was born on a holy mountain near Lake Toba. This god-man gave the Batak their sacred laws; his offspring founded the first patrilineal clan *(marga)*. The Batak recognize an Upper-, Middle-, and Lower-world, the seats of the gods, men, and dragon respectively. *Mula Jati* is the creator and Lord of the Universe, linking the 3 worlds. This lord has a dual nature, bringing both good and evil, with both male and female aspects. Decisions must be inspired and sanctioned by ancestors, so elders sit on ancestral stone chairs for communal meetings, transmitting the wisdom of the ages. Male priests and wizards *(datu)*, skilled in sorcery and the use of natural poisons, are also specialists in occult knowledge and divination, using Hindu zodiac and magical tables.

Death And Burial

Tondi (soul stuff) determines contentment, temporal wealth, and power; at death it departs to dwell in another organism. Spirits of the dead are contacted ritually through female mediums *(sibaso)*. Only in the 1920s could the Dutch compel the Batak to bury their dead. They once kept corpses for days under their houses until, at final rites, they drained the decaying body with bamboo runners. The remnants were then placed in large stone sarcophagi (like big stone boxes), which you can still see close to the villages. If you're lucky, you'll see a funeral—Christian Batak funerals have brass bands!

Events

There is a rich variety of male-oriented ceremonies, feasts, and rituals. Even numbers are traditionally considered ill-omened and dangerous, so no feasts or celebrations are ever held on even-numbered days. Odd numbers are more auspicious, especially 7, the number of the original Batak tribes. At Batak weddings literally thousands gather at a ritual feast of buffalo and pig. Traditionally, the bridegroom's family gives the bride-giver family a substantial dowry of livestock, land, and money.

THE ARTS

Architecture

Older settlements have a distinctive type of house found nowhere else in Indonesia. Raised on piles soaked in mud for years, these houses are so sturdy that they often last 100 years. With not a single nail used, just rope and wooden pegs, the gable ends of these dynamic structures are richly ornamented with mosaics and woodcarvings of serpents, double spirals, snail lines, lizards, life-giving female breasts, and elongated dark-colored monsters' heads with bulging eyes *(singa)*. The walls are made from heavy planks and the roof rises high, often sloping inward toward the center. Some of these steep, saddle-shaped roofs are made of palm thatch *atap*, others of bright new galvanized iron. The building maintains a cool indoor temperature even during the hottest part of the day.

In each house live up to 10-12 families, each in an apartment *(bilik)* along the 2 outer sides. The space between is used as a public corridor where children play, men work, women cook, and people visit. The family's rooms are occupied according to rank in this strongly patriarchal society—the head of the house, the son-in-law, etc., right down through the 18-m-long house. A village communal hall *(sopo* or *bale)* serves as council hall, trophy room, and sleeping place for boys and unmarried men.

Language And Literature

All of the Bataks' different dialects are intelligible to one another. Their own language is most closely affiliated to Aceh's Gayo. Esoteric idioms are sometimes uttered by priests and female mourners. In Batak, "thank you" is *Maulitate,* and *Tayo-tay* means "Shit on you!" When ordering tea in Batak country, call it *tes* and not *teh* because *teh* means feces in their language! Most homeland Batak speak an almost remedial form of *Bahasa Indonesia.*

Although there is a native writing system *(Surat Batak)*, no chronicles have been found written in that script. The only "books" which exist deal mostly with spells and divination by priests *(guru)* on bark, bamboo and, nowadays, paper. Batak script, transmitted orally down through the generations, is used only as part of the decorative motif on handicrafts, and has little application in everyday life. Scholarship in linguistic studies is scanty. The most important linguistic event in recent years has been the publication of H. Neubronner van der Turk's remarkable *Toba Batak Dictionary, Comprehensive Grammar and Reader.*

Music

Village men make their own music. A *gondang* band is made up of cloth-covered metal gongs of different sizes, clarinet-type instruments, and 2-stringed lutes made of palm fibers. The Toba Batak play a whole row of drums tuned to different pitches. Beaten with sticks, they make a zany sound to Western ears. The Batak are renowned for their powerfully expressive, ethereal hymn singing.

Dance

Batak women's traditional dancing is ritualistic and slow-moving. Toba Batak wear turbans and long shawls across one shoulder, bobbing up and down with only the hands expressing; it is very confined dancing, repetitious, almost solemn. Somehow overlooked by the church, a few animist features remain in their dancing, like snapping fingers. But the only truly traditional folk dance left is their trance-dancing. Similar to Balinese trance dances, the big difference is that on Bali it's still a part of their religion. Dance festivals take place on certain dates fixed each year by the priest-doctors of the old religion. In one, a pony is tied to a stake in the middle of the road and male dancers form a circle around it, trance-dancing to gongs and drums. This ritual dates from the time a sacred breed of horse was regularly sacrificed. Offerings of *slendang* (dance scarves) are made nowadays.

Si Gale Gale

The main protagonist in this dance drama is an almost life-sized human puppet *(si gale gale)*. This dance is restricted to the island of Samosir and to the village on the S shore of Lake Toba. When a childless Batak dies, in order that they may enter the realm of the dead and not haunt the living, musicians play for the *si gale gale*, which is jerked to life. With its moveable palm-wood head, eyeballs, and hands, the marionette goes through grotesque sudden movements while dancing with the villagers. Tears are produced from sponges set behind the eyes. Each movement of the puppet is controlled by hidden strings. The strings lead into a box on which the puppet is mounted and small wheels are attached to it so that it can be wheeled about. A man sits at the other end of the box, his hands concealed, manipulating the strings. Its face is carved in the image of the deceased, and the *si gale gale* is wheeled from villager to villager, embracing friends and relatives in its hard wooden arms as tears roll down its cheeks. Unforgettable! You will be

Si Gale Gale
mask

hard put to find a genuine *si gale gale* performance on Samosir or even in a museum (an excellent specimen is in Jakarta's Wayang Museum). Tourist performances of the dance are staged at Tomok and Simanindo once weekly (usually); ask the tourist office and hotels for details.

Crafts

The art of the Batak is an expression of their religious ideas, deeply concerned with magic. The Batak are skilled and sophisticated in the arts of metalworking, tie-dying, woodcarving, boat-making, and also in bone, shell, and bark fabrication, which all show a mixture of Dongson and Indian influences. In the area around Lake Toba, black and white straw is utilized for a profusion of craft items. Buffalo or mountain goat "powder horns," used as containers for magical substances, are artistically made.

Making massive silver earrings, shell armbands, copper-wire neck rings, ½-kg long-stemmed copper pipes, bejeweled swords and sheaths are all dying or dead arts now. Tourists can pay up to Rp150,000 for a Batak sword, but you also hear starting prices of Rp40,000 for genuine metal antiques. Buy carefully. Of dubious quality, new ones are being turned out for tourist consumption.

Batak *ikat* comes in traditional blue, black, or maroon cloth called *ulos.* This cloth, still important in marriage, birth, and funeral ceremonies, has a central dark panel where the *ikat* is dyed; 2 white smaller sections top and bottom have woven patterns of darker thread woven in.

Batak woodcarving incorporates magic signs and fertility symbols into the decorations. Figureheads of carved hornbills adorn boats, and sorcerer's wooden staffs have weird figures climbing up the whole length, like grotesque, miniature totem-poles. *Pustaha,* Batak magic augury books made from bark or bamboo, contain esoteric idioms spoken by priests and female mourners. They record the Batak "sciences" of magic staves, magic preparations, and divinations. These *pustaha* form the most important part of Batak written literature. Old ones cost up to Rp200,000 in the tourist shops of Medan and Prapat.

LAKE TOBA

Lake Toba is the largest lake in SE Asia (1,707 sq. km), and one of the deepest (450 m) and highest (900 m) in the world. The mythical homeland of all the Batak people, Lake Toba was formed as a result of a gigantic volcanic explosion. Surrounded on all sides by pine-covered beaches, steep mountain slopes and cliffs, with Samosir Island sitting right in the middle, it has a spellbinding setting. Besides its beauty, this area is also celebrated for its traditional villages, *adat* houses, and rich Batak culture. Although several huge hydro-electric dams on the Asahan River are a cheap and abundant power source, they are fed by Lake Toba; the lake's water level has been slowly but steadily declining. The power stations have caused the lake to sink 2½ m, so much so that the Samosir ferries can't even dock anymore at the Tigaraja terminal in Prapat!

Toba Batak

The best known Batak clan. One million strong, they are considered the most aggressive, direct, and flamboyant of all Batak groups, and proud of it. The original tribe, the Toba Batak have the purest lineages and speak the most uncorrupted dialect. They can trace their family lines back 10 generations or so, to a time when any stranger who stared upon them was killed and eaten (this fate probably befell the first missionaries in the area and continued to occur as late as the 1920s). Most Toba Batak live around Lake Toba. Eighty percent are Christian, but their religion is mixed strongly with ancestor worship. Many isolated Toba Batak tribes, who live on the far side of the lake opposite Prapat, still haven't had much contact with the outside.

Getting There

Coming up from the S, your first view of Lake Toba will be from the hills above Balige, off the SE shore of the lake 114 km N of Sibolga; Prapat is another 60 km on a good road. Prapat, on the E shore, is the most popular and commercialized of the lake's resort areas and has the best ferry connections to Samosir Island. Travelers usually head straight for Tuk Tuk village on the island, where accommodations are widely available at good prices and the atmosphere is relaxed. Government *pasanggrahan* are found at Prapat, Ajibata, Tongging, and Pangururan, where you can also stay. From Medan the direct route through Tebingtinggi and Siantar takes only 5 hours (176 km) to Prapat. A longer but more interesting route (about 260 km) goes via Brastagi, Sipisopiso Waterfall, Pematang Purba (location of a raja's palace), and Simarjarunjung Lookout (1,760 m). A look at the map will reveal other approaches—for example, roads from Aceh Province, or you could come in from the W at Tele and cross over the bridge to Pangururan in western Samosir Island. Local buses do most of these routes.

Transport

Many lakeside villages have market days; by using market ferries you can hop from village to village. People are glad to see you and they may come up with someone who can speak basic English, though it's much easier if you know Indonesian. Some of the *losmen* on Samosir Island charter excursion boats and do RT tours of lakeside villages for around Rp4000 pp, usually leaving Ambarita for Tomok (to pick up more people), then out to the hotsprings near Pangururan, then back to Ambarita via Tomok.

PRAPAT

A lakeside resort on a small bay on the E side of the lake, this is the main town on Lake Toba and the principal embarcation point for ferries to P. Samosir in the middle of Lake Toba. Sukarno, together with Sjahrir and Hadji Agus Salim, were exiled to a house in Prapat during the war for independence (1948-49). The revolutionaries were kept under house arrest (now Pasanggrahan Negara) on the shore of Lake Toba, guarded by Dutch soldiers. Twice guerilla bands tried to free them, unsuccessfully. Today, Prapat has grown into a busy tourist resort, with a cool, dry climate, pine-covered beaches, and spectacular views. Most of the upscale tourists are Indonesians and Chinese from Medan and Singapore, while the international influx is made up of the post-hippie budget set. Thus Prapat is a destination where the affluent visitors are brown-skinned nationals while the Caucasians congregate in the cheapies. Most of the higher-priced hotels (some Rp40,000 and up) line the lakefront, while lower-priced ones are found along the main highway coming into town. Cheapest of all is to stay on P. Samosir. Evenings are pleasant, whether sitting on a balcony or else walking back from the cinema. One can always hear singing on the night air from a small child down the street or a group of Batak gathered in a *kedai kopi*.

A tourist office is in the arched entrance to Prapat. Drop in at the Batak Cultural Center, Jl. Josep Sinaga 19, to see what's brewing; dances and music performances are usually held on Sat. night, Rp1250 entrance. Clean beaches are in Ajibata village, 1 km S of Prapat down a small road. Turn off the highway onto

Jl. Bangun Dolok and walk 1 km to the campground on the hill behind town. Tents can be rented for Rp3500 or pitch your own for free. Best view in town. A golf course is 2 km S of town in a superb setting; pony rides also available.

Accommodations

Prapat accommodations are handy if you arrive late or are leaving early, otherwise just head straight for Samosir. Most hotels in Prapat cater to holiday-makers from Medan, Singapore, and Malaysia on higher budgets who like to stay as close to the lakeshore as possible. Many have bars, restaurants, room service, private baths, nice furnishings, but hot water might be available only part of the day. The wide choice of lakeside hotels and guest bungalows tend to be more expensive. Most have access to their own beach. But you have an excellent chance to bargain if it's off-season, a weekday, or if for some other reason they're not as busy.

Bedsitter-type hotels line the main road, Jl. Sisinga-mangaraja. The ones above restaurants and/or travel agencies, are cheapest. P.T. Andilo Nancy is the only one on the water. Be aware that all of these accommodations overlook a segment of the Trans-Sumatran Highway, with buses and trucks rolling along all night long honking their horns, so avoid noisy front rooms over the street. From the gateway, it's about a 30-min. (1½-km) walk to the ferry landing over the hill, or take a *bemo* (Rp150). Restaurants are nearby. On the Medan end of town, try **Motel Samosir**, Rp6000 s, Rp12,000 d; and **P.T. Andilo Nancy Service**, Rp2500 s, Rp4000 d, both on the main highway. You can purchase bus tickets at P.T. Andilo Nancy and they offer dusty but OK rooms. Walk through the building down to the water's edge, where ferries leave for Samosir (Rp500). On the Balige end of town are **Hotel Singgalang** (with good restaurant), Rp3000 s, Rp5000 d, and **Hotel Saudara**, Rp3000 s, Rp5000 d. Well-managed **P.T. Dolok Silau Tour & Travel Service**, Jl. Balige 113 (tel. 41444), is one of the best deals with clean rooms, *mandi*, and free tea. Musician-proprietor June speaks good English.

The old travelers' standby **Pago Pago Inn**, along the street between Hotel Prapat and the Tigaraja Ferry Terminal, wants Rp4000 s, Rp6000 d. The nearby **Soloh Jaya** has terrific views of the lake. They charge Rp6000-12,000 for rooms with bath (Rp3000 without bath)—a big hotel with spacious verandas high over the lake.

Higher-priced accommodations include breakfast and full bath (sometimes with hot water): **Aurora**, Jl. Josep Sinaga, and **Wisma Samosir**, both want Rp12,000 s and d. The **Sinar Baru** asks Rp9500 s, Rp15,000 d. Others include: the Mimpin Tua, Rp8500 s, Rp12,500 d; Rp20,000 with a/c and hot water; **Peng. "I and You"** (overlooks the water near TV tower), Rp10,000 s and d; **Wisma Gurning** (on lakeshore just past market), Rp7000 s and d; **Wisma Danau Toba**, Rp15,000 s, Rp17,500 d; **Tarabunga Hotel**, Rp16,500 s, Rp17,500 d (quite basic rooms for the price); and the **Atsari Hotel**, Rp15,000 s, Rp17,500 d. The **Budi Mulya**, Jl. Pulau Samosir 17 (tel. 41216/41485), is a comfortable middle-of-the-road hotel that's empty on weekdays in the off season. Willing to bargain down to Rp15,000 for huge double room, hot/cold water, *mandi* on top of building.

Of the first-class, 3-star hotels, Wisma Danau Toba and Hotel Prapat, the latter is the better value. Hotel Prapat is a gracious old Dutch hotel with a *Tempoe doeloe*-style lobby and big lovely rooms looking over the lake. It's clean, comfortable, with hot water, private baths, and great Indonesian/Chinese food. Lowest cost rooms are Rp37,500; most are in the Rp40,000 range. On occasion enthusiastic Batak singers and other forms of entertainment are featured, and on weekends the work of local artists is exhibited in the lobby. The Danau Toba International charges Rp22,000 s, Rp25,000 d. The newest hotel is the Toba Hotel, right on the lake (only 50 m from tourist info office). The most expensive and isolated is the Patra Jasa Hotel, 4 km N of town and perched 300 m above the lake. Facilities of this stunning self-contained resort include swimming pool, tennis court, 9-hole golf course, and billiards. Rooms are Rp35,000 and Rp45,000. In a class of its own, a tourist ghetto.

Food

If on a tight budget, eat where the locals, not the tourists, eat. Cheapest are the cluster of Indonesian *rumah makan* on the main highway (Jl. Sisinga-mangaraja) where one can eat for Rp1500-2500. Padang-style or **Indonesian food** is found at Gumarang, Bundo Kandung, and Rachmat Minang next to P.T. Andillo Nancy. Tarabunga Hotel, Jl. Pulau Samosir, serves high-standard Western, Indonesian and Chinese meals, but at inflated prices. **Chinese food** can be enjoyed at the following restaurants: Brastagi, Asia, City, Paten, Sehat, etc. The Asia charges the same prices but is superior; one dish will almost feed two. Between Hotel Prapat and the Tigaraja ferry dock is a line of at least 5 Chinese restaurants; Hong Kong is best. Go to the market by Tigaraja ferry dock or on Trans-Sumatra Highway (Jl. Sisingamangaraja) for a wide selection of oranges, *marquisa*, mangosteen, *rambutan*, mangos, bananas, etc.

Services

On the main road (Jl. Sisingamangaraja) is a post and telegraph office. Bring sufficient cash with you. Changing money is easy but expensive. The nearest bank is 44 km away in Pematang Siantar. Travel agencies (P.T. Andilo Nancy, next to the market) and a few

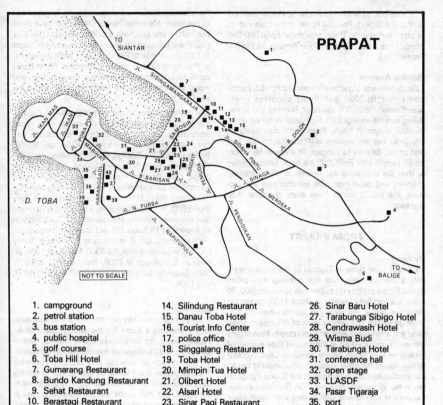

PRAPAT

TO SIANTAR

TO BALIGE

D. TOBA

NOT TO SCALE

1. campground
2. petrol station
3. bus station
4. public hospital
5. golf course
6. Toba Hill Hotel
7. Gumarang Restaurant
8. Bundo Kandung Restaurant
9. Sehat Restaurant
10. Berastagi Restaurant
11. Paten Restaurant
12. Asia Restaurant
13. post office

14. Silindung Restaurant
15. Danau Toba Hotel
16. Tourist Info Center
17. police office
18. Singgalang Restaurant
19. Toba Hotel
20. Mimpin Tua Hotel
21. Olibert Hotel
22. Alsari Hotel
23. Sinar Pagi Restaurant
24. Budi Mulia Hotel
25. Danau Toba International Hotel

26. Sinar Baru Hotel
27. Tarabunga Sibigo Hotel
28. Cendrawasih Hotel
29. Wisma Budi
30. Tarabunga Hotel
31. conference hall
32. open stage
33. LLASDF
34. Pasar Tigaraja
35. port
36. Hong Kong Restaurant
37. Bali Restaurant
38. Soloh Jaya Hotel

hotels in Prapat and in Tuk Tuk (on P. Samosir) will change money but at a poor rate (about Rp1550 for US$1). A public clinic *(puskesmas)* is on the main road just after the bridge.

Shopping

Saturday has the biggest market, when Prapat's market swarms with Batak from outlying villages. Not to be missed. To get there, walk around the main waterfront past the expensive tourist hotels; the *pasar* is by the Tigaraja ferry dock. Old coins, curiosity items, and the usual tourist fare such as *batik*, carvings, and antique jewlery are on sale at relatively high prices. Many souvenir shops line the main highway (Jl. Sisingamangaraja) selling a great variety of over-priced handicrafts: leather goods, clothing, *batik*;

striking *kain ulor* (usually given as a wedding gift or spread over someone who is ill), woodcarving, and other Batak crafts. Many souvenir stalls are also on P. Samosir, at Tomok and Ambarita.

Getting There

From Brastagi, you may have to change buses in Kabanjahe and Pematang Siantar (which is a good place to stop and have lunch anyway). From Sibolga, frequent buses make the trip (5-6 hours); ANS has 4 buses per day, Rp4000. From Bukittinggi, it's about 20-24 hours; ANS has 3 buses per day, Rp6000. From Medan, frequent buses do the 4- to 5-hour trip via Tebingtinggi; ANS (right across the street from Mesjid Raya on Jl. Sisingamangaraja) has 5 buses per day; Rp2500. The bus from Medan usually stops in front of

P.T. Andilo's. In Medan hire-taxis to Prapat are available at the airport, Polomia Hotel, at the train station, or other taxi stands. The cost is about Rp50,000 OW. Merpati has a Sat. flight to Sibisa Airstrip, 16 km S of Prapat.

Getting Around:

Take *bemo* rides anywhere in town for Rp150. Paddle boats run Rp2000 per hour; scooters (mini-speedboats), Rp20,000 per hour. Boating and water-skiing can be arranged through your hotel on an individual or group basis. Speedboats can easily be chartered but are expensive (Rp20,000 to Tuk Tuk, first price). Be sure to bargain. Or a whole ferry boat for 50 people only Rp25,000 per hour. Loaded down as they are with bananas, women in bright scarves, children, and piled high with merchandise and produce, the public ferries have more character than charters.

FROM PRAPAT

By Ferry

The main boat dock is Tigaraja in the market area, only a 30-min. walk from the archway into town. About 5 trips per day go to Samosir Island (Rp500, 30 min.), the last ferry leaving at about 1730; no regular departure times, the ferry just leaves when it's full. Most go to Tuk Tuk, where most of the accommodations are, then on to Ambarita or Tomok. Passengers are usually dropped off at the dock of their *losmen* of choice; be sure to ask before boarding. Less frequent ferries depart for other villages: Simanindo in the N, Nainggolan and Onan Runggu in the S, and Panguruan in the W (usually on Wed.). On Sat., market day, the dock is wall-to-wall with ferries, with continuous departures at half price until 1300. Nearer the entrance gate to Prapat, behind P.T. Andilo, is a dock used by tourist boats (Rp500) with less frequent departures; they usually go to Tomok, Ambarita, and Simanindo. **Note:** Though the blue-green waters of the lake are normally calm, winds can whip up waves like a stormy ocean. Morning is the best time for lake travel as waves often appear in the afternoon. Rough waters are most likely from June to September.

By Bus

If you take local buses, expect hour-long stops to load sacks of rice, 30-min.-long meal stops, and no telling how many stops for fixing flat tires or tying elastic bands around broken water pumps, and so forth. For the distant villages off the main roads, be ready for spine-jarring, gut-twisting, teeth-chattering, bone-knocking, eye-popping, pot-holed mountain roads. Try out this experience on the "back way" to Medan, via Tele.

For more comfort on the longer trips, try to get on one of the newer Mercedes buses. Clarify that it is a direct bus before you purchase a ticket (although that's no guarantee!). Except for the express bus which leaves at 1300, a bus ride to Brastagi could entail 2 changes, at Pematang Siantar and at Kabanjahe. Night buses could be cold so take a sweater, sleeping bag, and warm socks to keep your feet from turning a whiter shade of pale.

The travel agencies on the main highway (Jl. Sisingamangaraja) in Prapat sell bus tickets for most major destinations in Sumatra. Sample destinations and fares (ALS buses) from Prapat to: P. Siantar, Rp750; Brastagi, Rp2500; Sibolga, Rp4000; Padang, Rp9500; Palembang, Rp23,500; and Jakarta, Rp35,000 (express). Long-distance buses leave at least every hour up until the early afternoon. Two buses daily leave for Pekanbaru (Rp12,000); to Jambi at least once daily (Rp16,500). For Bukittinggi, ALS now has an express that bypasses Sibolga and makes it to Bukittinggi in an incredible 15 hours flat. No standing passengers, reclining seats, fan. Buy tickets at P.T. Andilo Nancy on Jl. Sisingamangaraja, Rp 8500. Leaves at 1300, arrives in Bukittinggi at 0500, then Padang at 0700. Other buses for Bukittinggi leave at 0700, 0900, 1000, and 1200.

Bookings

A lot of nightmare stories circulate about misbookings—receiving a ticket for the wrong bus, missed buses, paying for an *ekspres* but ending up with a local, etc. The likelihood of this happening can possibly be cut back by booking your seats on buses for faraway places like Padang or Bukittinggi at least 3 days in advance. P.T. Andilo Nancy is a reliable booking agent, but also check out the travel agencies at the Balige end of town on Prapat's main highway: P.T. Dolok Silau and Trident Tour Service. If you want to cancel, give your *losmen* owner a note and he'll take it to your travel agent when he goes over to shop in Prapat. Cancel at least 1 day before or lose 25% of the ticket price. During holidays such as Hari Raya, it's even more critical to book a seat. Or don't book at all and get a series of more frequently departing local buses to your destination; just set out—a ticket to adventure!

If someone in Prapat or Samosir tells you he can get a confirmed booking on a flight from Medan to Penang if you buy a ticket on his bus, don't believe him. Neither do confirmed telephone bookings direct to the airline office in Medan always work out. The only way to get a definite booking is to deal face to face with the MAS or Merpati offices, or book 3 days in advance at P.T. Andilo Nancy and get confirmation next day (you have to pay Rp1000 for the phone call). The 0500 bus from Prapat usually reaches Medan in time to connect with the MAS flight to Penang which leaves at 1125.

By Taxi

Time-saving long-distance taxis (5 passengers) and combi-vans (8 foreigners or 12 Indonesians) can be chartered through Prapat's travel agents. OW fares: Medan, Rp40,000 by taxi, Rp60,000 by combi; Sibolga, Rp45,000 by taxi, Rp60,000 by combi; Padangsidempuan, Rp75,000 by taxi, Rp90,000 by combi; Bukittinggi, Rp175,000 by taxi, Rp200,000 by combi.

Siguragura Falls

Northeast of the southern shore of Lake Toba, upriver from Balige and 30 km from Porsea, is this impressive waterfall on the Asahan River—the only one of several rivers in these highlands with its source in Lake Toba. At 200 m high, Siguragura is one of the highest natural falls in SE Asia. But it's now off limits because of the massive Japanese-built hydroelectric plant, largest in Sumatra, being built here here. You have to have a *surat ijin* from Inalum Co., Jl. Palang Merah (4th floor), Medan, to see it. Harimau Waterfall, which appears to flow right out of a mountain, is 10 km from Siguragura. For both falls, take the road along the lake to Porsea where signs point to the falls. Follow a spectacular road with lookout points along the way.

Balige

An attractive market town on the SE shore of Lake Toba, 60 km S of Prapat. The buildings in the market have high sweeping traditional-style roofs. Balige is also known for its Batak cloth, available in the market. Stay at Laut Tawar, Losmen Selamat, or Losmen Lora, or in the Hotel Gelora (Rp8000-Rp12,000 s or d). Traditional Batak food is served at RM Elektra, while Chinese food is served at Restoran Sakura, all on the main street. Friday is market day. The Batak king **Raja Sisingamangaraja**, who died in battle (1907) opposing the Dutch and became a national hero, is buried just outside of town—a tomb of great veneration. To get there, go 2½ km toward Sibolga, then ½ km down a lane. This raja's former palace is in Bakara to the SW of Balige, and is now being restored. The woodcarving village of **Hepata**, in Laguboti district 10 km from Balige on the road to Prapat, employs invalid artisans; run by the Protestants. The hills around Balige and southwards have impressively large tombs; often life-sized figures of the deceased are mounted on top.

Asahan Project

This hydroelectric-power dam and SE Asia's largest aluminum smelter was built by Japan in 1975 at a cost of nearly US$2 billion, a gigantic venture harnessing the Asahan River which flows from Lake Toba into the Straits of Melaka. Asahan is Indonesia's showcase example of Suharto's great leap into the industrial age, helping to earn him the title of "Father of Development." The scheme, involving 3 dams and 2 power stations, generates 500 megawatts and enables the smelter to produce 225,000 tons of aluminum yearly. The supply of Asahan aluminum is vital to the Japanese industry and the cost of producing the power is one-tenth of what it would be in Japan. Besides improving Jakarta's foreign-exchange budget, the benefit to Indonesia is less evident. Indonesia has the right to reserve part of the aluminum production for its own use, but it lacks the industry to utilize much of it. The project has provided jobs for 3,000 Indonesians (with 30 Japanese supervisors) and small-scale aluminum industries producing pipes and kitchen utensils have sprung up downstream. But due to the 1985-86 downswing in world aluminum prices, the plant is now in financial straits and needs a capital injection of around US$200 million to keep it running. Unable to come up with its share in this joint venture, the cash-strapped Indonesian government may have to let the Japanese bail them out, though it throws the ideals of this flagship project for regional development right out the window.

NORTH OF PRAPAT

Haranggaol

This small picturesque village and market town is before Tongging on the NE edge of Lake Toba. A stupendous view above the town and over the lake is just before the road from Kabanjahe begins its twists and turns down to the lake's shore. A Catholic church and some typical Simalungun-style *rumah adat* can be seen. Its strategic location prompts one of the largest bulk markets in the area (Mon.): Karo Batak from the highlands, other Batak tribes from all the surrounding area, and shoppers arrive from as far as Pematangsiantar. *Ulos* fabrics here cost approx. half what they do in Tomok village: starting price Rp75,000 for an old *ulos* blanket (called *sadum sipirok);* for the newer ones the price starts at Rp40,000 (these are not as good quality, however). Watch for slit thieves. The market people will say that your camera gives them a headache, a nice way of asking you not to take their picture.

Haranggaol has several *losmen* and a good selection of *rumah makan.* **Peng. Meliala** charges Rp4000 s or d. **RM Bahagia** has inexpensive food such as *mie goreng;* good view over the lake. Buses arrive every day from Medan (140 km), Pematangsiantar (68 km), and Kabanjahe (51 km). The turnoff for Haranggaol is 5 km S of Seribudolok, then it's 10 km down to the lake. On Mon. and Thurs. (smaller market), market ferries leave for Haranggaol early in the morning from Ambarita, Pangururan, Tigaras, Simanindo, and other lakeside villages. The same ferries start to leave Haranggaol for the return trip in the mid-afternoon and stop around 1800. The ferry takes about 2-3 hours to, for example, Ambarita, because there are a number of stops along the way. Other days, transport could be difficult.

Sipisopiso Waterfall

Located at the northern end of Lake Toba just above the village of Tongging, between Kabanjahe and Pematang Purba, 24 km from Kabanjahe. From the 120-m-high lookout point above this beautiful falls is a

360-degree panorama of the waterfall, the precipitous valley below, Tongging, Lake Toba with Samosir Island, and mountains—an unforgettable sight! From Brastagi take a *bemo* to Kabanjahe, then on to Merek on the road to Haranggaol. Get off at the junction for the road to Tongging, 1 km E of Merek. Walk 3 km (one hour) toward Tongging and turn R to the viewpoint. Small admission charge. Another approach is to take the boat to Haranggaol from Samosir Island, then walk or take a *bemo* to Tongging. Refreshments are available and you could camp here (bring food).

SAMOSIR ISLAND

The original home of the Toba Batak, Samosir Island offers a cool, sunny climate, royal tombs, dramatic Batak architecture, stone carvings, superb hiking, swimming, accommodations and food! Batak culture lives on in traditional villages (S side), megaliths, and cemeteries; most Toba Batak live either on Samosir Island or S of Lake Toba. Samosir is very relaxing (only about 30 cars), and costs are low. If you plan to stay awhile, bring some good books. Also take cash; exchange rates on this island are bad (only Rp1500 for US$1 at Carolinas). Watch your gear, there have been thefts. During the rainy season the mosquitos are vicious. Yell *"Horas!"* and see the smiles; it means "Long life!" or "God protect you!" No matter what your religion, go to church on Samosir; the ardor with which they worship and sing in praise of Christ is a sight to see.

The Land

Wherever you stand on the shore of Lake Toba, you see this 630-sq.-km island in the middle of it. Samosir may once have been a piece of the plateau at the same elevation as the cliffs surrounding Lake Toba. But in what was probably the greatest single cataclysm known to have occurred on Earth, a volcanic eruption blew a 30- by 90-km depression in the earth, collapsing the piece of crust that is now the island. It didn't come straight down, however; the surface slopes gently into the waters on the W side while the E edge forms 500-m-high cliffs. Some volcanologists believe that the incandescent ash generated by this terrible eruption may have blotted out the sun and helped plunge the planet into the last great ice age.

Samosir "Island" is technically a peninsula, connected by a narrow isthmus at the foot of G. Belirang opposite Pangururan. In 1906, the Dutch dug a canal so boats could circle the island. Since then, this channel has silted up and only the smallest boats can make it through today.

Rumah Adat

Samosir has many of these traditional houses; some can be rented by visitors for as little as Rp1500-3000 per day. The houses are mounted on posts to better catch the breezes and provide space underneath for firewood and livestock. The swinging curves, sloping sides, and sweeping upturned roofs are reminiscent of sailing ships. The swayback roof sheds water quickly, though now nearly all are of corrugated metal instead of the traditional thatch. Decorations in the roof gables represent faces of residents looking down in respect to all visitors; conversely, doors are low, forcing guests to bow in respect as they enter. Half a dozen families may share the interior, with no walls, screens, nothing to give privacy (believed to have helped develop the Batak's frank and open character). The house is fitted together with notches and pins; no nails are used. The structures can last easily 100 years. Very few new ones are being built now.

Events

A musically gifted tribe, a feast of music is continuous, either on cassettes or from young Batak playing flutes, guitars, xylophones, drums. You could see musicians playing on the 2nd floor of a Batak house, with men and women circle-dancing below. See the "opera" which takes place continuously but in different parts of the island (regularly held in Ambarita every two weeks). These melodramas feature crooning male vocalists, slapstick skits, painted girls singing traditional village love songs *(ture ture)*, all cackly, loud and really comic, similar to a great, big nighttime Punch 'n Judy puppet show with fireworks. If the girl is a good vocalist, walk over to the stage and give her Rp500 like the Batak do. Also, because of its ardent Christian population, Samosir could be the best place in Indonesia to spend Christmas (except perhaps Manado, N. Sulawesi).

Old Graves And Tombs

Toba Batak have interred their dead in stone urns and

a sepulchral stone monument of the Toba Batak

3-m-long stone sarcophagi carved in the shape of squatting gargoyles whose faces are astoundingly similar to Easter Island statues. Elaborately carved stone heads *(singa)* with 3 horns and huge round devil eyes are also seen (especially fine ones at Tomok, Huta Pangalohan, and Huta Pansur). These skull-caskets *(parholian)* contain the skulls of high-ranking Batak dead, which were dug up one year after death. More recent are the Batak tribal mausoleums, solid mudbrick mounds with polished bones inside topped with rough-cut wooden crosses. Contemporary tombs are sometimes found in the form of a brightly colored Batak house or a statue of the deceased. See the Soldier's Grave between Tuk Tuk and Ambarita. The present-day Batak do not know who carved in stone all the old tombs, plus chairs, tables, benches, and shaped thrones, but they are dotted all over Samosir Island.

Accommodations

The shore of hilly Tuk Tuk peninsula is dotted with places to stay, as are Tomok (5 km S), and Ambarita (3 km N). But scores of other "accommodations" are also sprinkled in between. Most places on Samosir are basic: no wall-to-wall, no telephone, no TV, no *mandi* (use the lake). But it's easy to find laundry service, at about Rp3000 for 15 pieces. Try to get a window that looks out onto the lake. The standard cost for basic living is Rp1500 s, Rp1500-2000 d, but you could spend as little as Rp1000 pp or even Rp500 in the off-season, making Samosir one of the cheapest travelers' recluses in the world. It's also possible to rent a whole *adat* house from a family for as little as Rp3000 per day, but these are popular and you must wait your turn. Ask around. Or take a tent which is ideal for Samosir because the island is a walker's paradise, and safe. Nearly every place has electricity now.

Of the higher-standard places (with inside *mandi*, patios, dining rooms, etc.), **Carolina's** has long been popular and a very good deal (at Rp3000 s, Rp6000 d) and is still improving. Located on its own peninsula, Carolina has a telephone (0664/41920) so reservations can be made from Prapat or Medan. A short walk from Carolina's toward Tomok is **Dumasari;** Rp17,000-30,000 s and d. The fanciest place of all is Toledo Hotel on the NE tip of Tuk Tuk. Rooms are Rp3000-19,500 s, Rp5000-25,000 d. All but the cheapest rooms include breakfast and the boat ride from Prapat. You can rent a sailboat here (Rp4000 per hour), one of the few on this large body of water. When tour groups are staying here, there are dance performances. Toledo booking office: Jl. Ikan Porapora, Prapat (tel. 41101). The closest thing to a travel agent on the island is Toledo's (and Carolina's) ability to phone Prapat and book advance seats on buses.

Food

Though overpriced and repetitious, eating out is a big event on Samosir. You can run into wonderfully fresh vegetable soup and fruit salads, but there tends to be too many carbohydrates in Samosir cooking, with lots of *gado-gado*, vegie dishes, rice, and packaged noodles. The menus are tiresome and Western-oriented and when you ask about many items, you get *"sudah habis!"* ("out of it") — it just looked good on the menu! If you're starting to feel protein-starved, restaurants serve fish dinners, Chinese pork, imaginative chicken, or beef dishes. Passionfruit and bananas grow on the island. Some restaurants attached to hotels give "credit"; accounts are kept in a book and paid up when you leave. Best cheap restaurants on the island: Pepy's (near Carolina) and Bernard's (Tuk Tuk Pulo). It's reported that Pepy's serves magic mushrooms, Rp6000 (also the island's best guacamole).

TRANSPORT

Getting There

Five or more ferries leave Prapat for Samosir between 0930 and 1730, 50 min., Rp500 OW. Some of the hotels also have ferries, free for their guests; paying passengers are also welcome. Ferries and speedboats can also be chartered for around Rp25,000 per hour. Samosir can also be reached any day by taking a bus from P. Siantar to Tigaras, then a ferry over to Simanindo, then a bus S to Tuk Tuk. A unique approach is from the N at Haranggaol: ferries return on Mon. and Thurs. after Haranggaol's afternoon market to Ambarita on Samosir. You can also drive or take buses by following the road to Tele (W of Lake Toba), descend to the isthmus, and cross a bridge to Pangururan. A road follows the shore of Samosir around the N to Simanindo and on to Ambarita.

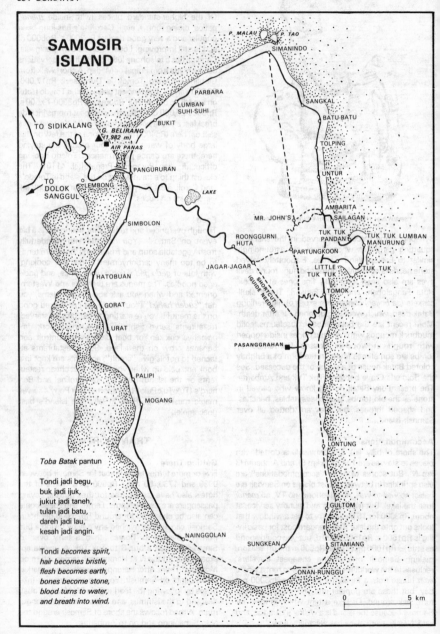

SAMOSIR ISLAND

TO SIDIKALANG

G. BELIRANG
(1,982 m)
AIR PANAS

TO DOLOK SANGGUL

LEMBONG

PANGURURAN

SIMBOLON

HATOBUAN

GORAT

URAT

PALIPI

MOGANG

NAINGGOLAN

P. MALAU   P. TAO

SIMANINDO

PARBARA

LUMBAN
SUHI-SUHI

BUKIT

SANGKAL

BATU-BATU

TOLPING

UNTUR

AMBARITA
SAILAGAN

MR. JOHN'S

ROONGGURNI
HUTA

TUK TUK
PANDAN

TUK TUK LUMBAN
MANURUNG

PARTUNGKOON

JAGAR-JAGAR

LITTLE
TUK TUK

TUK TUK

TOMOK

SHORTCUT
(GUIDE NEEDED)

PASANGGRAHAN

LAKE

LONTUNG

GULTOM

SUNGKEAN

SITAMIANG

ONAN-RUNGGU

0   5 km

Toba Batak pantun

Tondi jadi begu,
buk jadi ijuk,
jukut jadi taneh,
tulan jadi batu,
dareh jadi lau,
kesah jadi angin.

Tondi *becomes spirit,*
hair becomes bristle,
flesh becomes earth,
bones become stone,
blood turns to water,
and breath into wind.

Getting Around

A bumpy paved road goes about ¾ around Samosir. Most of the way S of Tomok for 30 km to Sigaol is a rough track. Out of superstition, the road between Naingolan and Sungkean was never built. You can walk it in a long day. Another 30-km trail climbs up from Ambarita and crosses the island to Pangururan. An easier way is the daily bus leaving Tomok about 1000 and going around the N to Pangururan (1½ hours, Rp2000), with stops at Ambarita, Simanindo, and other villages. Note that this bus travels between Tomok and Ambarita on the road atop the Tuk Tuk peninsula; you must walk from Tuk Tuk up to this road to catch it. From Pangururan a bus heads W to Sidikalang, where you can connect to Brastagi, Medan, or even up the W coast of Aceh Province. From Pangururan a bus continues around Samosir to Nainggolan in the S, or to Simanindo. Another bus even runs at 0600 from the highland town of Roongurni Huta to Pangururan (Rp900).

If walking, take the coastal path between the towns, more picturesque than the road. The children make the best guides for island walks. Start walks early—in the afternoon it gets too hot. Motorcycles and bicycles are rented by some of the Tuk Tuk hotels, such as Carolina's, for a standard price of Rp10,000 per day, plus Rp3000 for gas *(minyak)*. Some ask Rp15,000, so bargain. Ride your motorbike to Siminando or Pangururan. No license required.

Cross-island Walk

Strongly recommended. Paths start from both Tomok and Ambarita. The 1,600-m-high climb from Tomok to the top of the mountain in the center of the island is a mud scramble over logs and tangled tree roots. There are 2 paths, one a zigzag and the other a straight-up. The zigzag path has wooden steps scarred into the earth. Stay overnight in the village of Roongurni Huta on top; about 50 people live in 9 houses. The view is outrageous up here, and it's quiet—a wonderful change from the track around the island where all the kids scream "Hello! Money!" at you. Simple food is available; give a donation of Rp1000 or a gift. Or stay at Nadeak's or Love Happy, accommodation and breakfast for only Rp1500 pp. Nadeak is the grandson of a Batak chief. Do not ignore his directions on how to get back down to Ambarita, or on to Pangururan, or you'll get lost. Believe it or not, the children of this village walk down and up this mountain every day to attend school.

Allow 2 days from Tomok to Pangururan on the other side. It's 13 km (6 hours) from Tomok to the southernmost *pasanggrahan*; from here Roongurni Huta is another 16 km. Alternatively, there's a *pasanggrahan* about 16 N of Ambarita, then another 6 km into Roongurni Huta. (Another name for *pasanggrahan* is *rumah kehutanan*.) Or just ask any of the villagers along the

way if they'll put you up and feed you—about Rp1500 sleep, Rp1000 food, but always agree on price first. Friendly people will always point the way if you get lost. From Roongurni Huta it's a 17-km walk downhill to Pangururan, or take the daily bus at 0600 (Rp1000). **Note:** This hike is easier if approached from the Pangururan side because then you avoid the very steep climb.

Lake Cruises

On Sun. and Wed. pleasure cruises depart Tuk Tuk, then Ambarita, for a trip to the other side of Samosir. The major destination is the hotsprings across from Pangururan. Stops are also made at Simanindo to see the traditional village and chief's house, and at the resort on Tao Island. The enjoyable all-day trip, which could boast non-stop music and a floating restaurant, costs Rp4000. Because the canal is silted up, the boat can't cruise completely around Samosir (which would take a very long day, even if possible), so it just does the N side. John comes around the different *losmen* to see if anyone wants to go. One can also rent, from a few *losmen*, a mahogany dugout canoe for Rp6000 and tour the island; ask around.

TOMOK

The main day-tourist entry point, a traditional village noted for its old stone coffins, Tomok is 9 km and 50 min. across the water from Prapat. The man who runs Golden Tourist Information Center speaks English. It's a must to attend church on Sunday; watch the whole Christian population turn out in their Sunday's best. Hellfire preaching, praise to *Kristus*, and floating on the air the sound of rich Batak voices singing in full volume strains from Handel's "Hallelujah!"

At the intersection of the main road and the dock road in Tomok, climb the steps to the top of a small hill. A huge *hariam* tree houses the spirit of Raja Sidabutar, pre-Christian head of the first tribe to migrate to this lake in the 4th century—at that time one of the most remote parts of Sumatra. The *hariam* tree was planted close to his tomb on the anniversary of his death 180 years ago. His stone coffin has carvings on the front and on the cover. The carved statue of a woman with a coconut shell on her head was Sidabutar's queen. Mysteriously, the 3rd tomb has a woman's face and is covered with large crimson splotches. The story goes that this was Sidabutar's lover, whom the king left orders to be killed on the same day that he died, so that they could enter the afterlife together. His orders were followed and she was given her own tomb in the royal cemetery, but her tomb was smeared with her blood, the stains becoming permanent. Nearby are more eloquent statues and stone chairs. Taking the path inland past dozens of souvenir stands is the Museum of King Soributnu Sidabutar, in a traditional house. Farther inland is another graveyard with stone coffins and old trees. No admission charge to see the coffins but donations are appreciated.

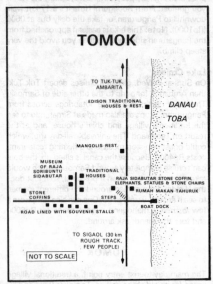

TOMOK

TO TUK-TUK, AMBARITA

EDISON TRADITIONAL HOUSES & REST.

DANAU TOBA

MANGOLIS REST.

MUSEUM OF RAJA SORIBUNTU SIDABUTAR

TRADITIONAL HOUSES

RAJA SIDABUTAR STONE COFFIN, ELEPHANTS, STATUES & STONE CHAIRS

STONE COFFINS

RUMAH MAKAN TAHURUK

STEPS

ROAD LINED WITH SOUVENIR STALLS

BOAT DOCK

TO SIGAOL (30 km ROUGH TRACK, FEW PEOPLE)

NOT TO SCALE

Accommodations And Food

Just S of Tomok's boat dock is **Silalahi Accommodation & Restaurant**. The pictures hanging on the wall are of all the travelers who've stayed here. North 200 m is **Edison's**. Motel-like **Toba Beach Hotel** is expensive but has good Indonesian food; it is more cocooned from the island's life, whereas at Silalahi's you live right with the family. A few *warung* have limited menus such as **Tahuruk** and **Mangolois Restaurant**, in addition to the *losmen* restaurants. Small market here too. **Note:** Tuk Tuk (5 km) has more of a variety of accommodations and restaurants than Tomok.

Crafts

Over 200 "antique" stands sell artifacts, cloth, clothing, and "antiques" made while you wait. Prices go up when the tourist boats disgorge their cargo. Bargain intensely. Watch young girls or old grannies weave *ulos* cloths by their booths: Rp3000-15,000. Buy new, cheap *ulos* blankets for as little as Rp8000, though most run Rp20,000-40,000. For the older color-fast ones you have haggle and do the walkaway to get a good price. There are also Batak calendars, magic medicine staffs, *pustaha*-augury books (Rp10,000), whole carved doors (Rp150,000), 2-stringed mandolins, etc.

TUK TUK

Tuk Tuk is on the tip of a small peninsula, a 5-km, 1-hour stroll from Tomok. The island's best selection of low-priced lodging and restaurants is scattered on this small peninsula. Although it's getting touristy, Tuk Tuk is quieter and more private than Tomok, yet has frequent ferry connections. Rent a motorbike from Carolina or one of the local teenagers, but expect to pay up to Rp10,000 per day; bicycles are also for rent. Beware of theft from rooms all over Tuk Tuk/Ambarita. If you go to bed early, you'll miss some of the best music of your life, especially on Sat. nights—buy a bottle of *arak bangkilo* and join the outdoor groups. For a splendid view, climb up on the grassy plateau behind the village, between Tuk Tuk and the mountain. Sweeping view, perfect meditation venue, weird trees.

Accommodations

A cluster of cheap and expensive hotels and dormitory-type *losmen* stretch from the Matahari (Rp1500) on the waterfront to the Toledo (Rp15,000) on top of the hill. In the cheaper places, the lake is your *mandi*. **Sibayak**, on the Ambarita side, gets very good reports: quiet, private beach, free canoe, and good food. **Karidin's Hotel** offers comfortable rooms in traditional Batak houses, delicious meals, plus a sandy and secluded beach nearby; Rp2000 s, Rp3000 d—one of the best *losmen* in Tuk Tuk. **Rosita's Batak Houses** are right over the water, with a good restaurant. **Bernard's** is low-priced and offers rooms overlooking one of the nicest beaches on the island. **Pepy's** is on the road to Carolina; Rp2000 s, Rp3000 d; good location, outstanding restaurant. Get in on the smorgasbord if there are enough people (Rp2500 pp).

In a class of its own is **Carolina** with 9 individual mock-Batak bungalows on the slopes of a small hill overlooking the whole lake, with bathrooms, showers, electricity, and motorbikes for hire. Plus there are truly luxurious motel-type accommodations with hot water for as little as Rp7500-Rp10,000 per day! Get a room with big windows overlooking the lake. The food is reasonable (fresh bread baked daily) and imaginative. Carolina has its own pier, a private swimming cove with a diving board and clean beach. Extremely busy July-Aug. when it might be full. Make reservations by phone (0664/41920) or letter.

Judita, a short walk from Toledo Hotel, has quiet Batak houses and extra rooms, a charming family, free canoe, and complete menu serving delicious food. Plain rooms with little furniture: Rp1500 d. **Dumasari** and **Silintong** are both new expensive hotels, of the same standard as the Toledo—comfor-

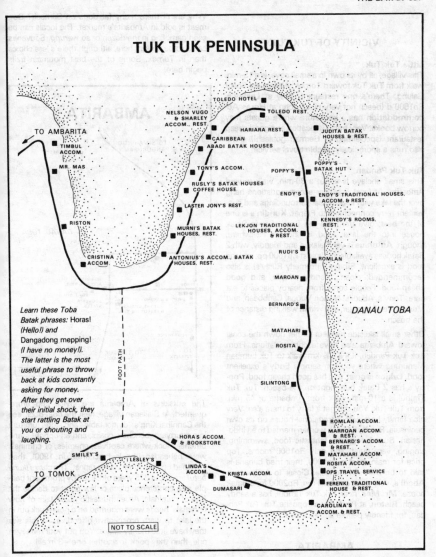

TUK TUK PENINSULA

TO AMBARITA

TIMBUL ACCOM.

MR. MAS

RISTON

CRISTINA ACCOM.

NELSON VUGO & SHARLEY ACCOM. REST.

CARIBBEAN

ABADI BATAK HOUSES

TONY'S ACCOM.

RUSLY'S BATAK HOUSES COFFEE HOUSE

LASTER JONY'S REST.

MURNI'S BATAK HOUSES, REST.

ANTONIUS'S ACCOM., BATAK HOUSES, REST.

TOLEDO HOTEL

TOLEDO REST.

HARIARA REST.

JUDITA BATAK HOUSES & REST.

POPPY'S

POPPY'S BATAK HUT

ENDY'S

ENDY'S TRADITIONAL HOUSES, ACCOM. & REST.

LEKJON TRADITIONAL HOUSES, ACCOM. & REST.

KENNEDY'S ROOMS, REST.

RUDI'S

ROMLAN

MAROAN

BERNARD'S

MATAHARI

ROSITA

SILINTONG

DANAU TOBA

Learn these Toba Batak phrases: Horas! (Hello!) and Dangadong mepping! (I have no money!). The latter is the most useful phrase to throw back at kids constantly asking for money. After they get over their initial shock, they start rattling Batak at you or shouting and laughing.

FOOT PATH

SMILEY'S

LESLEY'S

TO TOMOK

HORAS ACCOM. & BOOKSTORE

LINDA'S ACCOM.

KRISTA ACCOM.

DUMASARI

ROMLAN ACCOM.

MARROAN ACCOM. & REST.

BERNARD'S ACCOM. & REST.

MATAHARI ACCOM.

ROSITA ACCOM.

OPS TRAVEL SERVICE

FERNKI TRADITIONAL HOUSE & REST.

CAROLINA'S ACCOM. & REST.

NOT TO SCALE

---

table, modern, private bath, hot water, electricity, nice garden. The **Toledo Hotel**, beyond Carolina's, features hot water, nice beach, paddleboats for rent. The barbed wire is an eyesore, but the comfort level is top class for Samosir. They charge Rp20,000 for 1st-Class d, Rp15,000 2nd-Class d. Free ferry service to

Ambarita in the morning. The proprietress, Mrs. Tobing, is the niece of the Batak national hero, Sisingamangaraja, after whom streets are named all over Indonesia. Sisingamangaraja was shot by Dutch soldiers on 17 June 1907, forevermore known as "the day the Dutch shot the king."

VICINITY OF TUK TUK

Little Tuk Tuk
This village, all by its own in a small cove, is a 15-min. walk from Tuk Tuk toward Tomok. Also called Sosor Galung. There's one restaurant. Stay at **Lesley's,** Rp1500 d (beach not very nice). John at **Horas Accommodation** has a bookstore where guests may borrow books. Very tranquil location and good cheap restaurant (specializing in German goulash!). John also runs a sporadically reliable travel service.

Tuk Tuk Pandan
This small enclave is about a 30-min. walk toward Ambarita. At least 5 similar accommodations hang over the lake with spectacular surroundings and convenient ferry connections to Prapat. **Kuridin's** is one of the best; dive from the top floor of your Batak house into the lake; food is cheaper elsewhere, though. **Antonius** is very relaxed and friendly, with 2 Batak houses available; beds cost Rp1500 pp, and the food is excellent. **Sibayak** (formerly Rusly's) is also recommended; clean, friendly people, and good cheap food. People come from nearby places to eat here. Tony's, Abadi's, Nelson Vugos, Caribbean, and Murni's are all popular, and within walking distance of the beach.

Other small lakeside hamlets farther down the coast toward Ambarita also have accommodations. From Tuk Tuk Pandan, it's a 1 ½-km walk to Tuk Lumban Manurung where you can sample **Endy's** excellent food. **Lekjon** is quiet, and has good cheap food. **Poppy's** has 2 Batak huts right on the beach. Tuk Tuk Timbul is a 10-min. walk from Ambarita or 45 min. from Tuk Tuk. You can get a ferry to there also. Very nice family here with a traditional house on its own peninsula. Run by a Dutch woman married to an Indonesian. Superb location, fantastic food, swimming, singing, very quiet, and only Rp1500 rooms. Top price for main meal is Rp1000; their fried banana is said to be best in Indonesia. Closer to Ambarita is **Abadi's,** very quiet and well-run; Rp2000 for a Batak house. **Mr. Mas,** near Tuk Tuk Timbul, has a sandy beach. **Riston,** at Pinda Raya opposite Tuk Tuk Pandan, for friendly people and nice beach.

AMBARITA

A lovely village with flowered coves and old Batak houses, 13 nautical km from Prapat or a dramatic 45-min. walk around the Tuk Tuk peninsula from Tomok. Even with several ferries a day from Prapat, Ambarita has considerably fewer Westerners. Samosir's largest settlement, there is a post office, small hospital, and market near the boat dock on Tuesdays.

Why aren't there many fat dogs on Samosir? Dog meat is sold in Ambarita's market. The locals can be seen gambling in the dozen or so *warung*. Souvenirs can also be bought here, although there's less choice than in Tomok. Some of the best mountain trails begin here.

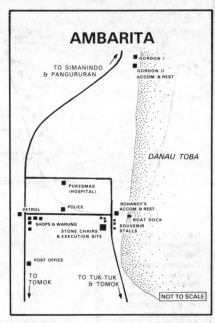

The outskirts of Ambarita are idyllic and unfrequented. At Siallagan village, near the boat dock, see the Cannibal King's "dinner table" and stone furniture in a courtyard: benches, chairs, and an upright stone butcher block where captives, enemies, or criminals were beheaded (the last occurred in 1900), then chopped up for a ritual village repast. The chairs *(kursi batu)* are about 275 years old, used by prominent people as a conference place or law court to decide the fate of criminals. An enthusiastic guide tells of how criminals' heads were mounted on a pole stuck out in the lake to warn prospective offenders. At this site they have little money boxes. You put your money in one, then they point to another one—3 in all!

Accommodations
Rohandy's Accommodation (Rp1500 d) is right on its own peninsula. Quiet, and you can spit in the water from the veranda. The Rohandys are wonderful and the food is delicious. Share smallish, dormitory-type rooms in their Batak house—one of the nicest locations in Ambarita. **Gordon II** is a lakeside *losmen* in

Unjur, on the edge of the village, with cheap rooms (Rp1500-2000 pp). This is a nice area, quiet, but 4 km toward Tuk Tuk from Ambarita's dock—no joke with a heavy rucksack. The food is well-prepared (especially vegetable and fruit tacos), and it's clean and comfortable. Average beach. **Sopo Toba Hotel** has a nice garden and sandy beach, but it's Rp25,000 s.

From Ambarita

It's a 30-min. walk from Ambarita to Tuk Tuk if you take the shortcut, or 45 min. on the coastal path. From Ambarita to Simanindo, it's a 7-hour walk. On Sat. morning many boats pick up people at Rohandy's, heading for the Prapat market. On Sun., Wed., and Fri. a boat goes around to the hotsprings near Pangururan; Rp2000 OW. Then you can walk from Pangururan back to Ambarita in 1½ days, either along the coast path or over the mountain via Roongurni Huta. Villagers along the way will put you up; expect to give about Rp3000 pp room and board.

On Mon. and Thurs. a market boat (Rp1500) leaves Ambarita at 0600 or 0700 for Haranggaol on the NE shore of Lake Toba, arriving around 1000. Haranggaol is a beautiful and untouristed village with a superb view of P. Samosir and Prapat on the far side. At 1500 (approx.), the boat returns to Ambarita. Or from Haranggaol you can board a bus for Brastagi (Rp2000), departing at around 1300—a unique way to leave the lake.

SIMANINDO

A traditional village on the N tip of Samosir, 16 km by road from Ambarita toward Pangururan along the coast from Tomok. The entrance gate of this fortress-like Toba Batak village used to be locked up during the night to prevent hostile intruders from entering. Market day is Saturday. There are once-weekly tourist performances of the life-sized wooden puppet *si gale gale*. The oldest part of the village, Huta Bolon Simanindo, is now a museum. Surrounding the living compound is a 2-m-high earthen wall planted with bamboo. The only entrance is through a stone tunnel just wide enough for the horns of a large water buffalo and just high enough for a woman with a basket on her head. Outside the gate is a long canoe and some tombs. Admission is Rp400, which includes a guidebook in English. Inside are *adat* houses and rice barns.

All over the island are superb examples of beautiful Batak houses, but the former king's house here is by the far the most outstanding. This large earthquake-proof structure has elaborate carvings on the front. The 10 sets of buffalo horns on the outside represent the 10 generations of the dynasty. Inside is a collection of household utensils: large Dutch and Chinese platters, spears, *kris* and other weapons, carvings,

witch doctor charms, and *huda-huda* (imitation horse), formerly used in a dance before going off to battle. The last king to live in this palace was Raja Simalungun. After the Japanese occupation, armed youths ran riot throughout Batakland, killing aristocrats and ransacking their palaces because they had collaborated with the Dutch. Simalungun was assassinated in March 1946.

Practicalities

Simanindo can be reached on foot (½ day from Tomok), by bicycle, bus, or on the RT lake cruises from Tuk Tuk and Ambarita. There are also road connections from Pangururan and Sidikalang to Simanindo. Opposite the museum is a small family homestay, **Boloboloni's**. Villagers or a *warung* might also put you up. Tao Island just offshore has expensive cottages. *Warung* are near the old dock.

The Ambarita-Haranggaol ferry (Rp1500) stops here on Mon. and Thurs.; from Haranggaol you can board the bus up to Brastagi via Seribudolok and Kabanjahe. About 4 ferries a day go across from Simanindo to Tigaras where you can catch further buses to Pematangsiantar.

Tao Island

A small resort island offshore from Simanindo, perfect for privacy and relaxation. Its only residents are the service workers. The restaurant is good and moderately priced, but rooms are Rp15,000 s, Rp20,000 d. You're right in the middle of the lake so you can see Samosir, the lake shore, and the mountains all around. There is no beach but an area of shallow water is nice for swimming and waterskiing equipment and motorboats are available for rent. It is easy to charter a speedboat here to Simanindo, Tigaras (Rp25,000), and Prapat (Rp60,000).

OVER THE MOUNTAIN

Follow the accompanying map from Ambarita till you reach the top of the mountain. Mr. John's Accommodation is a ½-hour walk past a nice forest, Rp1500 per night in a hut—quite comfortable and nice view. Or stay with the Gelbok family. From Mr. John's go through the village, take a L, walk down a valley, and go up again. Then go straight on through a deep forest. This is easier than taking the path on the map which leads directly north. North of the tree farm is the Fern Valley, but if you go into the forest you might lose your way; you can find your way back but not forward. Although there is a path, you must have a guide in order to venture N from the Fern Valley—the path is too difficult to find. The Fern Valley has horses and wild buffalo (could be dangerous, keep your distance) and is worth seeing, but then go back. Next, you

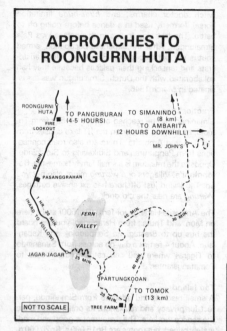

APPROACHES TO ROONGURNI HUTA

ROONGURNI HUTA — TO PANGURURAN (4-5 HOURS) TO SIMANINDO (8 km)
FIRE LOOKOUT
TO AMBARITA (2 HOURS DOWNHILL)
MR. JOHN'S
50 MIN.
PASANGGRAHAN
1 HR. 30 MIN.
(HARD TO FOLLOW)
FERN VALLEY
40 MIN.
30 MIN.
JAGAR-JAGAR 25 MIN.
40 MIN.
PARTUNGKOOAN
20 MIN.
TO TOMOK (13 km)
TREE FARM
NOT TO SCALE

reach the *rumah kehutanan* (forest hut or *pasang-grahan* in Indonesian), but bear in mind that these rooms are only open to visitors in the tourist season (June-Aug., Dec.-March). The forest dwellers here may overcharge (Rp1000 for a plate of rice!), but lodging is only Rp2500 d. Beyond the *rumah kehutanan* is Roonggurni Huta.

Roongurni Huta

You'll have no trouble finding a place to stay in this village; the locals are friendly and really make you feel welcome. Just ask the first English-speaking person you find about accommodations and food, all at Tuk Tuk prices. Love Happy Accommodation & Restaurant has inexpensive and appetizing cooking with large portions. Located only 10 m from the main road, it's a secure and relaxing place. Prices start at Rp1500, meals between Rp750 and Rp1500. Proprietor T. R. Sinaga can guide travelers to the more remote villages such as Jagar-Jagar (a bamboo-fortified jungle village), R. Nihuta, and Jinlakkosa. His English is also good. Nadeak's is another place to stay.

The overgrown Lorry Road ot Roongurni Huta is blocked by growth after a few km, which is a real letdown because it looks so good at the start. From Love Happy, it's 300 m for magnificent views, 600 m to a clean water swimming pool, 1,000 m to the waterfall. Also check out the government plantation nearby. One km out of town on the R just before a stream, up

above the track beside a white tomb surrounded by a brick wall, is a giant pre-Christian burial urn (with a lid) carved out of solid rock.

PANGURURAN

On the W coast of Samosir near the isthmus to the mainland, 16 km byond Simanindo. The area's major attraction is nearby G. Belirang with hotsprings bathing, hiking, and views. A stone bridge here over a canal connects the island to the mainland. In this village you could see dogs roasted whole upon fires, ungutted with their tongues hanging out, like the aborigines cook a kangaroo. Dog is done when the flesh separates easily and when the meat falls away from the bone. Don't miss your chance to see this.

Kedai Kopi Barat, near the bus stop and wharf, has rooms above a shop with a great balcony; Rp1500 pp. The toilet is downstairs, no washing facilities though. Proprietor Richard Barat speaks English, knows the area, draws maps, cashes TCs—caters to Western-

TRANSPORT FROM PANGURURAN

From Pangururan: By Bus To:	Cost	Times
Medan	Rp2500	0700, 0800, 0900
Brastagi	Rp2000	0700, 0800, 0900
Tarutung	Rp1750	0800, 0900
Sibolga	Rp3000	0800, 0900
Sidikalang	Rp1250	0700, 0800, 0900, 1200
Simanindo	Rp1000	8 departures 0730-1130
Ambarita	Rp1500	0730
Tuk Tuk	Rp1500	0730
Tomok	Rp1800	0730
Limbong	Rp1000	0800
Nainggolan	Rp1100	0800
By Boat To	Cost	Times
Balige	Rp1500	0900, Sun. and Thurs.
Tomok, Tuk Tuk	Rp2000	1400 daily
Nainggolan	Rp1250	0900 Mon.
Tulas, Simanindo	Rp1500	1000 daily
Harranggoal	Rp1500	0730, 0800 Mon. and Thurs.

ers. He also makes delicious *mie goreng, nasi goreng* dinners.

Getting There

There are a number of ways. The bus from Brastagi crosses the mountains from the direction of Sidikalang, then runs over Pangururan's short stone bridge. Daily buses also leave from Tomok, 41 km, 1½ hours, Rp2500. This same buses passes through Simanindo.

From Simanindo, it takes 45 min. to Pangururan but the road is so bad many prefer the boat. Or hike from Simanindo, which takes about 7 hours. Boats make the trip to Pangururan from Tuk Tuk or Prapat. From Tuk Tuk an excursion boat on Sun., Wed., and Fri. does a tour to Pangururan; it costs Rp4000 RT with a stop in the hotsprings on the way.

Vicinity Of Pangururan

Gunung Belirang volcano to the W has hotsprings on its lower slopes and great views from its 1,982-m-high top. Cross Pangururan's bridge to the mainland, take a R, then walk 1 hour (3½ km) halfway up the summit to just over 1,000 m above the lake's surface. Hot water comes out of 2 small valleys amidst sulphur deposits and steam. Bathe lower down where the cascading water has cooled sufficiently, in either the men's or women's separate bathing places. The sulphuric water is said to have a healing effect. Below are some mud pools for wallowing. Then cool off in the lake's clear brisk water. Refresh yourself in several *warung* here.

Nainggolan

A large village 34 km S of Pangururan, on the SW tip of Samosir Island. From Nainggolan, buses travel to Tomok (87 km) via the W coast only; there's also a daily ferry to Prapat. Accommodation is available in several old traditional houses, or at a simple *losmen* near the harbor. Market day is Monday. Sigaol is the end of the road, 15 km beyond Nainggolan. From here it's 30 km to Tomok on a rough track.

THE KARO

A strong patrilineal society living between Medan and Lake Toba, the Karo are the youngest Batak tribe and are remarkable because so much of their close-knit traditional life is still intact. While the lowlands are more influenced by the Malay culture, *adat* is very strong in these highlands. The Karo dress like the Karen of Thailand in heavy broad turbans and tightly wrapped dark clothing. Many of the women wear traditional wide-brimmed tasseled headdresses *(tudung)*. The Karo are legendary for their warmness and speak a very *alus* (soft) dialect, which sounds almost as musical as Italian. Theft is an appalling offense in Karoland—the police take it *personally*. Of all the *puak* of Sumatra, other Sumatrans consider the Karo Tribe to be the most preoccupied with witchcraft and spells. Their literature consists mostly of books dealing with magic, medicine, and divination. Chess is widely played by the Karo. In a recent Asian chess tournament, 3 of the 5-man Indonesian team were Karonese.

Some Karo greetings: *Majuwajuah* means the same as *Horas!* around Lake Toba; it roughly translates as "Good luck!" "Thank you" is *bujour* (like *bonjour* but no "n"). And *Kai-berita* is "How do you do?"; the answer is *Majuwajuah*.

Karoland

The 5 Karo Batak clans and 83 subclans inhabit a high plateau of mountain slopes, rich volcanic valleys, and deep ravines N and W of Lake Toba. *Tanah Karo* is approx. 5,000 sq. km, divided into 2 main areas, the highlands (700-1,400 m) and the lowlands (40-200 m). The 7 highest mountains, several still active, range from 1,815 m to 2,417 m—Sibayak (2,070 m) and G. Sinabung (2,417 m). Roughly speaking, the 1st half of the year in the highlands is dry and the 2nd half is wet. Possessing a temperate climate and little seasonal variation, the highlands cover an area of 1,640 sq km with more than 247 villages inhabited by approx. 250,000 people. Most villages are named after either a geographical feature, a flower, or some other natural wonder of the locale. Eleven villages in subdistricts Juhar and Kutabuluh are still so isolated they can't be reached by motor vehicle. *Kuala* preceding a name means that the village is near a river estuary or the meeting of 2 rivers.

Economy

The high altitude and cool climate of Karoland make for a plentiful garden area, and the Karo run a prosperous cash-crop economy of dry rice and *sawah* areas, rolling cornfields, and extensive vegetable patches. The Dutch began experimental gardens here in 1911; a scientist, Botje, demonstrated first that tomatoes grown under scientific methods could flourish here. Botje also showed that European vegetables grown in these highlands were in great demand in Medan, only 68 km from Karoland, which has contributed largely to the economic development of the area. The 2 most important cash crops today are vegetables and coffee. Brastagi even markets its vegetables as far away as Penang and Singapore.

Kinship

Islam never made deep inroads here. Under Dutch rule for only 40 years, Dutch Christian missionaries started work in these highlands as late as 1902. During the political upheavals and slaughter of the 1965-66 period there were mass conversions to Christianity to avoid being suspected of atheism. Now 60% are either Islamic or Christian. Though unofficial, the strongest and most widely practiced Karonese religion is actually kinship. Almost all the inhabitants of a traditional Karo village are related in one way or the other to members of the ruling class of the village. All faiths are bound by kinship and *adat* obligations, and if the lineage has been offended, illness, drought and crop failures could result.

Marriage creates totally new relationships among many people. There's almost a spiritual relationship with the wife's family, who are called "the gods that can be seen" *(kalimbubu)*. When a Karo woman marries, her father and brother become her husband's *kalimbubu*, who are higher in status. The husband's status, in turn, is inferior *(anakberu)*. Anakberu serve *kalimbubu;* they do all the work at *adat* ceremonies such as weddings, feasts, etc. They must address them very politely, offer them cigarettes, cook for them, act as legal spokesmen, never bathe in their presence. The exchange of favors and obligations, however, is mutual; the *kalimbubu* side also has heavy financial commitments to give presents and land to *anakberu* relatives. Since it often brings about tension and conflict, the rigidity of this system is now breaking down, especially among the younger generation.

An unmarried man without sons is grievously pitied and called *bangkaren* (old bamboo); his social obligations and mission in life were never fulfilled. Couples sometimes have 3-5 children before they're ceremonially married, at which time the groom's family fulfills its obligation to the bridegroom's family. Karo women obey orders and work for their fathers or brothers in an almost formal relationship; joking or affection is seldom shown.

Architecture

There is a rough-hewn primitive energy in the form and plan of a Karo village. The old mossy black sugar palm fiber *(ijuk),* sprouting ferns along the eave lines, as well as the buffalo horns on the gable ends poking toward the sky all give off this energy. Karo houses are raised off the ground on heavy posts. Their wide front verandas are used for working, bathing, playing, cooking, and socializing. Nowadays, as with the Toba Batak, the Karo are moving out of these 8- to 10-family *rumah adat* into single-family houses. They're cheaper, and few big trees are left with which to build the imposing traditional structures. Even boys as young as 15 move into their own house, sharing the rent with others.

Crafts

Their crafts indicate a strong connection with the

Balkans. The spiral heart ornaments found in Croatia are almost identical to the huge ear pendants you see Karo wear. Ear pendants *(padung)* are made of silver rods coiled in a flat double spiral. Weighing almost one kilo, they often stretch the earlobes of Karo women. Some specimens measure up to 20 cm long and are the size of a baseball! You still see such earlobes on the older women.

EVENTS

The Karo attend about 60 ceremonial occasions a year. Obligations to attend feasts and ceremonies in their clan brotherhood are very strong. Various rituals, such as *Curka Dudu* and *Belah Purnama Raya,* aim at warding off evil spirits. If you're really interested, they are proud to take you around to the different functions for free. Pelawi, the proprietor of Wisma Sibayak in Brastagi, will take you to a Karo wedding if one is happening in the area. For these formal ceremonial occasions, the attire is *paken adat* (customary). Men wear a black velvet cap *(songkok)* and coat. Besides a *sarung* and *kebaya,* and long clothes covering their *sarung,* woman wear stoles *(uis)* which they drape over their shoulder, and sometimes a folded, heavy, colorful cloth headdress *(tudung* or *uis nipes),* gold bracelets and necklaces *(sertali).*

Kerja Tahun

This is the Karonese New Year. Only at this time can you see all the *adat* at play and eat special Karonese cake, *cimpa, Teritis,* and *cipera.* Ritualized offerings are often made to dead ancestors.

Funerals

There's dancing to the music of the *gendang* (traditional Karo orchestra), accompanied by minor-keyed singing. Betel leaves, cigarettes, and money are often placed in the coffin. When a child dies, it's laid out in the center of the house and symbolically "married"; with a dead boy the *dukun* enfolds warm bamboo around his penis, and a girl has a banana inserted into the vagina to symbolize intercourse. This is performed before the burial so that the spirit *(begu)* of the frustrated deceased child will not come to disturb the living kinsmen of the village.

Others

Nurun-nurun is a ritual in which the bones of ancestors are washed and reburied. *Erpangir* is a group hair-washing ceremony which even Christian Karo attend. The *Ngerires Festival* petitions God for a good harvest. It's held at the village of Batukarang near Brastagi at the beginning of the year. In July, *Mejuah-juah* gives thanks for a good harvest. It features reading Karo scripts, communal pounding of paddy to music, violin playing, dancing.

KAROLAND

KABANJAHE AND VICINITY

Kabanjahe

Though Kabanjahe is a sizable, modern town, the capital city of the Karo Highlands and the administrative seat for the government, Brastagi is more scenic, more central, and has superior accommodations. Kabanjahe, surrounded by rich plantation country, is 11 km S by public bus (Rp150) or minibus (Rp200) from Brastagi. Through buses from Prapat and Sidakalang also stop here, or you can take to ferry from Simanindo on P. Samosir to Haranggaol, then grab a northbound bus to Kabanjahe. Kabanjahe's big market day is Monday—a sea of Karonese headdresses! The Tugu Abdi Dharma monument is dedicated to the courageous Karonese of the revolution.

Hotel Penlingdung (Rp3000 d) has clean rooms. Or check out the **Segar** or **Pinjowan** (same price, best of the 3). From the market, take a minibus to any one of them for Rp100. Lots of street *warung* in Kabanjahe. The National Building frequently serves as the venue for folk ceremonies, funerals, weddings, the Karonese New Year, harvest festivals, and other traditional performances. Change money at fairly decent rates at Bank 1946 on Jl. Kapt. Pula Bangun (1 km from bus station). From Kabanjahe, take minibuses to Brastagi, Rp200; Haranggaol. Rp500; P. Siantar, Rp1000; Balige, Rp2500.

Lingga

North of Kabanjahe 4½ km (Rp200 by minibus), on the same road as Lake Kawar. This touristy village, which bills itself as "typical," is easier to get to than Barusjahe (below). Lingga is a complete Karonese village of 32 large, painted, and decorated communal Batak longhouses where people work and live practically in the dark. The village architecture is fascinating, but too many hassles go along with it. Kids pester travelers, and some of the adults want money for everything. Entrance: Rp200. Stay with the *kepala kampung*. Go here only if you're pressed for time; otherwise visit Bintang Mariach or Barusjahe.

Barusjahe

A very old, uniquely laid-out village with *adat* houses, about 15 km (Rp300 by public bus) from Kabanjahe, 10 km from Tongkoh village, or 72 km from Medan. Here live a cross-section of all Karo peoples. Its well-preserved, monumental buildings *(geriten)* were used for storing skulls and bones of dead Karonese nobility; a few are more than 250 years old. Not a single nail was used in their construction, only rope and wooden pegs, yet they are still sound and strong. Villagers may take you around on motorcycles. The village school kids might prove bothersome. It's possible to stay in one of the longhouses.

BRASTAGI

A township and popular resort town in a mountain forest region 11 km N of Kabanjahe. It's like taking an elevator up to these highlands, almost 1,400 m above sea level. With its cool healthy climate and fine plantations, a market center for the open and friendly Karo people, Brastagi is one of the highlights of the journey through Sumatra. Starting in 1920, the Dutch built access roads, bungalows, administration buildings, and clinics in Brastagi, and Dutch merchants used to retire here after prosperous careers in Medan. This whole region is still a rich area for European vegetables (including beets, red cabbage, and lima beans!), fragrant flowers, and fruits, which are even exported to Penang and Singapore. Plump ripe avocados are grown here, and carrots are so plentiful that they're fed to horses. Flies in this market town, due to the manure used, are most numerous; make sure that your room has a screen. Surrounding the town are several live volcanos, G. Sibayak and G. Sinabung. **Note:** Bring sufficient cash as there are no banks in Brastagi. The nearest one is in Kabanjahe, 11 km away. Money can be changed (at about Rp1550 = US$1) in Brastagi at the Rudang Hotel, Bukit Kubu Hotel, and even Wisma Sibayak (up to US$100).

Sights

On entering the town, the visitor will first come across Tugu Perjuangan, a memorial to the courage of the Karo people who took part in the '45 revolution against the Dutch, against vastly superior firepower and technology. The Kolam Renang (swimming pool), with its picture-postcard lawn, charges Rp200 entrance on Sun. when it's crowded; it's free every other day. On Tues. and Sat. (market days), the pool is dead quiet. Another attractive swimming pool is at the Rudang Hotel (2 km from Wisma Sibayak), Rp1000 entrance. A German missionary boarding school for teenage girls is about 200 m up the road from Wisma Sibayak. The girls spend about 4 months learning modern domestic arts at the school — the best-looking and best-kept complex of buildings in town.

Crafts And Shopping

Visit the Karo Batak market on Tues. and Fri. where fake, attractive Balinese *ikat* as well as a surprising abundance of fruits and vegetables are sold. For handicrafts from all over Indonesia, try **Modesty Souvenir Shop**, Jl. Veteran 85 (tel. 65); Batak ornaments, antiques, stones, postcards. Practically right across the street near the Asia Restaurant is **Namaken Souvenir Shop**. Also check out **Tannta**, Jl. Petran 76. **Sinulingga**, 50 m across the street from Wisma Sibayak, has the most original antiques, but prices are expensive.

Accommodations

Starting with the cheapest, **Losmen Gunung** (Jl. Veteran 48C, across from Cinema Ria) asks only Rp1500 s, Rp2500 d. Because it's right opposite the movie house, you'll want a room in the back. A cluster of hotels surrounds the monument in the town center: **Lingga Inn & Restaurant**, Jl. Veteran 48C (Rp6000 s or d); **Ginsata Hotel**, Jl. Veteran 79 (Rp3000 s, Rp4000 d); **Timur Hotel**, Jl. Veteran 82 (Rp2500 s, Rp4000 d); **Torong Inn & RM Umar**, Jl. Veteran 4 (Rp4000 s, Rp5000 d).

Most travelers head for well-run and friendly **Wisma Sibayak** on the Kabanjahe side of town: Rp2500 s, Rp4000 d, or Rp2000 for a bed in the dorm. All the "extras" are free and make this an unusual and worthwhile place to stay. But the best feature of this family-run guesthouse is the owner, Pelawi. He speaks good English and is a local expert on Karo culture and history. If Wisma Sibayak is full, head for nearby **Wisma Dieng**, Jl. Udara 27, Rp3500 s, Rp4500 d and Rp5000 s and d. Nice quiet rooms, free tea, and sitting room. **Bukit Tongging Hotel & Restaurant**, Jl. Veteran 48G, offers big and clean rooms with clean *mandi* at fair prices: Rp2500 s,

Rp3500 d, and Rp4500 t. Attached is a coffee shop and a restaurant which serves a variety of quite good Chinese dishes.

Brastagi also has a large number of medium-priced bungalows. The following are all on Jl. Jaranguda on the hill overlooking town, 1½-2 km outside of town: **Karo Hill**, Rp8500; **Papirpir**, Rp9000; **Gema**, Rp14,000; **Latersia**, Rp9000; and **Kaliaga**, Rp14,000. **Harapan**, Jl. Surya (turn in next to Jl. Veteran 49), though a bit damp is on its own promontory; Rp4500 s and d. **Brastagi Cottage** is on Jl. Gundaling, 2 km from town; Rp14,000 s or d. **Rose Garden Hotel**, with bar and restaurant, wants Rp15,000 s, Rp25,000 d with hot water, *mandi*, and breakfast — the only 3-Star Hotel in Brastagi.

High-priced hotels are found on the edge of town on the road to Medan. You'll feel like a Dutch colonialist at the gracious **Bukit Kubu Hotel**, Jl. Sempurna 2 (1 km before town); Rp15,000-25,000 s, Rp17,500-27,000 d (all prices include breakfast). Built in 1939, this is one of the most faithfully preserved colonial-style hotels in Indonesia with complete and original Dutch furnishings, bar, restaurant, and a fire at night in the lounge. The vast and immaculate lawn surrounding the hotel is a golf course (green fees, Rp3000 pp). Tour groups usually stay at **Rudang Hotel**, Jl. Sempurna (tel. 43); Rp15,500 s, Rp17,500 d to Rp38,000 s or d. Has bar, restaurant, and souvenir shop. At either of these expensive hotels one can hire horses (and hope that they don't throw you off!).

If you're willing to shoo a few flies away, you can eat some wonderfully fresh vegetable soups in small places with rough tables and bare concrete floors that would get rave reviews in any San Francisco gourmet restaurant. Local dishes include yogurt *(minyak susu)* made from buffalo milk, and for breakfast carts on the street sell bean porridge *(bubur kecang ijo)* (Rp250). Other local meals can be had for as little as Rp400 in open-air *warung* around town. *Tritis* is a ceremonial food made with not fully digested grass from a cow's first stomach; thus the Dutch used to say "the Karo eat cowshit." *Cipera* is made of corn powder with chicken soup, *santen*, and spices. Another specialty of some Brastagi's restaurants is stewed dog meat. They'll take you into the kitchen where a large white enameled pot, containing a dark brown stew, will be simmering away over a low flame. Leering at you, the cook will dare you to try it.

If heading for Medan or Toba, take fruit along from Brastagi's open-air market off Jl. Veteran. Fruits and vegetables here — including passionfruit, persimmons, and pomegranates — are much cheaper and there's a bigger variety. A specialty is the vitamin-rich *marquisa* fruit, grown only here and on Sulawesi; makes a delicious drink. The sour black *marquisa* are

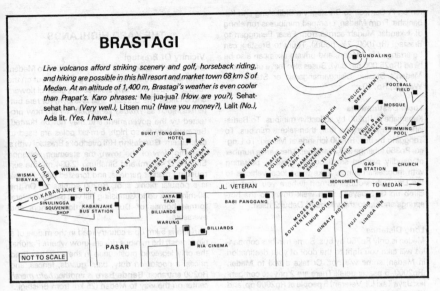

BRASTAGI

Live volcanos afford striking scenery and golf, horseback riding, and hiking are possible in this hill resort and market town 68 km S of Medan. At an altitude of 1,400 m, Brastagi's weather is even cooler than Prapat's. Karo phrases: Me jua-jua? (How are you?), Sehat-sehat han. (Very well.), Litsen mu? (Have you money?), Lalit (No.), Ada lit. (Yes, I have.).

NOT TO SCALE

the best; the sweet green/yellow variety are the same price, around Rp500 per kg. Or buy a bottle of the refreshing *marquisa* concentrate. Also try an exotic "Brastagi apple," a cross between a persimmon and peach (closest description). Vegetables include a profusion of immense carrots and cabbages.

The Karo, a Christian minority in a Muslim country, go for pork in a big way, with the result that Brastagi sports 3 kinds of restaurants: Karo, Islamic, and Chinese. *Babi panggang*, a traditional Karonese meal of roast pork, rice, and blood sauce (Rp650) can be sampled in the market *warung*, plus several places on Jl. Veteran (look for the sign) and around the market-place. **Piara Babi Panggang**, specializing in this dish, is on the road to Kabanjahe, opposite the junction to Rumah Brastagi Village, only 200 m from Wisma Sibayak.

Bukit Kubu Restaurant offers beautiful scenery from their dining room and quite good, high-priced Indonesian food. **Brastagi Cottage Bar & Restaurant** has expensive Indonesian, Chinese, and European food (excellent shark-fin soup). By contrast, one of the best street restaurants in SE Asia is the one without a name featuring Losmen Gunung and the Billiard Hall (dish no. 58 is outstanding); look for the sign: CHINESE AND WESTERN FOOD. **RM Terang**, on the main street at Jl. Veteran 369, serves good, inexpensive Chinese food: noodle dishes, sweet and sour fish, *babi kecap, nasi goreng*. A larger Chinese menu and also larger prices can be found in **RM Asia**, Jl. Veteran 9.

Hot spiced ginger milk *(bandrek)* may be enjoyed by night at Warung Buyun on Jl. Veteran near the public health center. And for coffee fans, Northern Sumatra is one of the numerous locales in Indonesia where really high-quality coffee can be had. Many of the local *kedai kopi* (cafes) around town serve *tuak* and *bandrek*. By day meeting places for the men where they sip coffee, smoke *kretek*, and gossip, by night they ring with guitar music, lusty singing, and heated debate, a convivial place to go and hoist a few. Some even have their own vocal groups! *Tuak*, wine made from glutinous rice which looks like milk, is served in a water glass, and costs Rp150. Some believe the first sip is promising, the second doubtful, the third insipid, and the rest revolting—some can't finish the glass. If you do like it, be careful! It's potent. If you dislike *tuak*, then try Anggur Vigour (40% alcohol). *Anggur* means "grape" and is marketed as a health builder, an ol'-time patent Karo medicine. It looks like Coca Cola, comes in a Coke-sized bottle, costs Rp300, and tastes like nothing on Earth. Sample it at the Ora et Labora coffee shop on the main street.

TRANSPORT

Getting There

Direct buses run from Prapat to Brastagi (Rp2000, 5 hours), or on Mon. and Thurs. you can take the ferry from Simanindo on P. Samosir to Haranggaol for Rp1500, then from Haranggaol to Brastagi via Seribu-dolok it's another Rp1000. Buses also leave Pangururan on P. Samosir to Brastagi via Sidikalang and Kabanjahe. From Medan, cramped minibuses run along Jl. Iskandar Mudah across from Pasar Peringgan to Brastagi (Rp1000, 2½ hours). Tours to Brastagi can be arranged in Medan, and private taxis can also be hired (Rp25,000 per day). Buses also leave often from Medan's Stasiun Sisingamangaraja or Stasiun Sei Wampu; Rp750.

Local Destinations

Kabanjahe is Rp200 by collective minibus. To Barusjahe, go to Kabanjahe first, then take a minibus. To Tongging by bus, Rp500 (change at Merek). To Lingga, Rp350 (change at Kabanjahe). There are a number of gaudily painted small buses *(sudaku)*, pulsating with Indonesian songs. Take these local vehicles to the Lau Dubuk-dubuk turnoff (where you start the climb up G. Sibayak), then walk down to the hotsprings and up to the village of Debuk2 itself.

Long-Distance

Medan is only Rp750 by bus. Some minibus companies will take you right to the door of your destination in Medan, some will not. Or take a taxi to Medan (Rp2000, 5 passengers). There are 2 private companies: Jaya Taxi (Jl. Veteran) 5 people at Rp2000 pp, and Hiba Taxi (Jl. Veteran, Channel 2) Rp1500 p, 8 people. Jaya's taxis leave at 0800 and 0900, Hiba from 0600 to 1300 (every 30 min.). Both companies will drop off anywhere in the city you want to go, but reserve the day before! To P. Siantar by bus is Rp850 (from P. Siantar to Brastagi it's only Rp750). A unique and breath-taking way to get to P. Samosir from Brastagi is to take the bus on Mon. or Thurs. (market days) to Haranggaol, then board a ferry and cross the lake to Tomok, Tuk Tuk, or Ambarita. To get to Prapat take a minibus to Kabanjahe's terminal (Rp150), then another to P. Siantar, then switch to a bus to Prapat (Rp500). Alternatively, you can travel to Haranggaol (see above) on Mon. or Thurs., then catch 2 boats across the lake. To Kutacane, take bus to Kabanjahe (11 km), then change to Kutacane (Rp2000). From Kutacane, get another bus to Ketembe (Leuser National Park) for Rp500. For more info on the trip to Kutacane and Ketembe, see the end of the Aceh chapter.

Private Taxis

It's easy to hire a private taxi in Brastagi (5 people can fit in one). Some approximate starting prices to: Prapat, Rp50,000; Barusjahe, Rp15,000; Tongging, Rp25,000; Lingga, a ridiculous Rp10,000. Or hire a minibus for Rp15,000-20,000 per day for local sightseeing. Bargain vigorously. If you're hiring a taxi to Prapat, or have your own vehicle, go via Simarjarunjung for one of the most awesome views over Lake Toba. Buses normally bypass this giddy road. Other popular stops on the way to the Lake Toba resort are the Sipisopiso falls and viewpoint, and P. Purba (Batak raja's house).

THE KARO HIGHLANDS

Vicinity Of Brastagi

Behind the Rudang Hotel (2 km on the road to Medan) is the maze cave **Kamar Bingung**. Farther out on the road to Medan are many stalls selling colorful flowers and orchids. The Brastagi area is known for rare butterflies, such as *Troides vandepolli;* all are now protected by the government and may not be hunted. Because they fly so high, 5-m-tall poles are used to catch them. **Gundaling Hill** overlooks Brastagi with a fantastic view of the town, the steaming volcanos Sibayak (2,451 m) and Sinabung (2,094 m), the surrounding market gardens, and forested hills. The hill is a popular picnic spot; Rp200 admission. On the 30-min. walk up to Gundaling Hill you pass by several former homes of Dutch plantation owners and overseers.

Perloha is 5 km up a country road in the middle of a pine forest; the minibus drivers know where. Perloha, the only legalized prostitution in the area, has fixed prices, a doctor on duty, bars, guards, fences, and Rp200 entrance. **Banda Baru** is another *batu merah* center on the way to Medan (25 km from Brastagi).

Lake Kawar

A small pretty lake at the base of G. Sinabung. The road burrows deep into the mountains, 30 km E and 1 hour by bus from Brastagi. The deeper you penetrate, the wilder the forest, until all signs of human occupancy vanish except for the road itself. Go fishing, canoeing, or take a jungle walk. The forest reaches down to water's edge, so the lake has no real beach except for a cleared space where picnics are held. Heed the sign DANGERS! DON'T JUMPING HERE. Charter a minibus for Rp15,000 but during market days (Tues. and Fri.), catch a bus from Brastagi after 1200. The same bus waits at the lake for 30 min. before returning. Last bus from the lake to Brastagi is at 1700. Ask the Lake Kawar village chief *(pengulu)* for accommodation (Rp2000 plus Rp1000 for food per day).

To Bukit Lawang

It's possible to trek to Bukit Lawang, the orangutan rehabilitation center near Bohorok. However, you will need local guidance for this minimum 3-day jungle walk (with monkeys, snakes, and plenty of leeches) through hilly jungle on a narrow path. The first overnight is in a village (Pamah Sumelir) about 8 hours down the trail. The guide from Brastagi charges Rp127,500 for 3 people, including food, transport costs, accommodations, and permit to enter the G. Leuser Park. Ask Pelawi, who has done the trip, for details and to make arrangements; also see Binjei section. Without a guide, only ex-Green Berets who want to relive their Vietnam recon experiences should do this walk alone (with a compass). Otherwise at least 2

Batak magic wands (tungkat malaikat): *The most decorative and imaginative form of Batak art. Like miniature totem poles from 1- to 2-m long with figures of snakes, horses, buffalos, dogs, lizards, elephants, chameleons, naga snakes, and copulating couples twisting down the pole. Tungkat malaikat are used by a Batak datu (medicine man) in healing, rainmaking, blessing a marriage, to induce illness and death, and as protection in battle. Antique ones cost Rp500,000; newer ones, Rp10,000.*

people should make the walk (with compass). The Karo say that if you get lost, take a long piece of vine and put the two ends together. If you step through, you'll find your way out again.

Traditional Villages

Mr. Pelawi of Wisma Sibayak can help plan trips to traditional villages, mountain climbing ventures, river trips in Aceh, jungle walks from Brastagi to Bukit Lawang, and walks to nearby villages of the region where you may stay at the courtesy of the *pengulu*. Don't miss your chance of seeing animist ceremonies or a traditional Karonese wedding. Stay the night in Pelawi's own family house in **Ajijahe** (10 km from Brastagi), a large longhouse with carving inside, the beams and the rafters black with soot and smoke. They are fundamentalist Christians. In Wisma Sibayak, maps, hiking info, and notices are tacked up everywhere and the *wisma's* guestbook has some fascinating stories of adventures and misadventures by previous travelers.

Note that if you visit a village in Karoland, the host family should fill out a government regstration form called Surat Tanda Melaporkan, or be subject to a heavy fine and/or imprisonment. Your hotel in Brastagi should have the forms (also called Form PP No. 45). After your host family fills it out, bring it back to Brastagi so your hotel proprietor can take it to the police.

To visit the really untouched Karo villages, befriend a native in Brastagi and go home with him. If you bust by yourself into one of these conservative villages, it's like walking into someone's living room uninvited. Still strict in their adherence to Karo customs are Tiga Binanga, Kuta Gambar, and Liren. The villages of Kuta Gambar and Liren lie in mountainous terrain on the slope of G. Deleng Kambawa (650 m). By foot from Tiga Binanga to Kuta Gambar is 12 km, 3 hours; from Kotabuluh to Kuta Gambar is 8 km, 2 hours. On the way from Tiga Binanga to Kuta Gambar, you have to walk over a mountain. These villages are dependent upon shifting cultivation. More than two-thirds of the people live in *adat* houses and believe strongly in the traditional religion. In this area you can still find spirit mediums (*guru si baso*) and medicine men (*guru*).

GUNUNG SIBAYAK AND VICINITY

The 2,451 summit of this volcano dominates Brastagi's skyline N of town. From Semangat Gunung (Radja Berne) at the base, it's a 1½- to 2-hour climb to the top. Start early (by 0700 from Brastagi), before it clouds over. Wisma Sibayak and the Ginsata Hotel sell a map to G. Sibayak for Rp500. For the climb, be sure to bring something to drink, a warm jumper, and wear good shoes as the trail up is treacherously slippery almost year round. But the spectacular view from the summit is worth the effort.

There are 2 routes to the base. From Brastagi a trail goes over the ridge separating the town from the volcano. You'll need a guide to lead you over the dark jungle paths (Rp4000 to Semangat Gunung village or Rp6000 all the way to the summit). The alternative is to take a road going around the ridge; get on a bus to Daulu Junction (Simpang Daulu), 9 km down the road toward Medan. Buses leave Brastagi for Medan every 15 min. starting at 0530. From Daulu Junction, walk 3 km to Semangat Gunung, keeping to the L at road junctions and passing Daulu I about halfway. Perhaps the best way to and from the volcano is to take the bus and walk the road in the morning, then return by the direct path over the ridge to Brastagi in the afternoon. There will be people around in the afternoon to ask directions on the trail to Brastagi. This way you get to enjoy the attractive valley walk past Daulu I. To take the trail from Brastagi over the ridge, climb G. Sibayak, and take the trail back to Brastagi is only for the very fit. Alternatively, since it's tiring to climb down G. Sibayak's steps, take the old timber road (NW of the volcano) back to Brastagi, a 2½-hour walk.

The Climb

At Semangat Gunung there may be a small entrance fee (Rp200). You don't need a guide from here as the trail is easy to follow. The village has teashops and *warung* selling snacks. If you want to spend the night

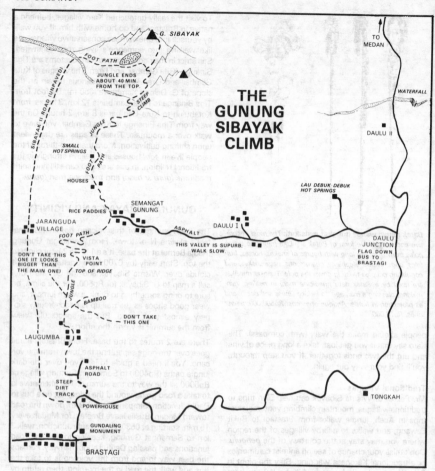

THE GUNUNG SIBAYAK CLIMB

here, get a letter of introduction from your Brastagi accommodations and be sure to bring Form PP No. 45! Note the communal rice pounding shed on the R past the teashops. The people of Semangat Gunung alternate between growing rice and vegetables. They credit the area's hotsprings for their fertile soils. Pay your homage to *Nini* before starting your early-morning climb.

After walking through the village, look for a well-trod trail to the right. The path climbs up through the terraced fields, passes between 2 small houses (note small hotsprings here), then enters a forest. Keep R at a trail junction. The L branch goes to a sulphur-processing site. Workers in the crater dig out solidified sulphur, carry it to the peak overlooking this site, then drop it down a long wooden chute. On the way

up you'll hear loud booming calls from gibbons *(siamang)* in the trees. The trail is in good shape and even has steps, though it does become quite steep. Be warned that on weekends and school holidays (May-June), hundreds or even a thousand climbers will be scampering up Sibayak.

Sights

The broken crater, still belching sulphurous fumes, is fascinating. There is a turquoise-colored lake at the bottom (boiling in spots), hundreds of fumaroles depositing gleaming yellow sulphur crystals, and several peaks to climb. Be cautious around the fumaroles; they can be very hot and gases could be poisonous—don't go to the bottom of the crater on a windless day. H_2S is in less-than-lethal quantities, but definite-

CABBAGE PATCH

CHAIR UNDER LARGE TREE

MINOR PATH

JUNGLE

VERY EASY TO MISS THIS TURN

DENSE UNDERGROWTH

SEVERAL PATHS HERE. KEEP LEFT MOST OF THE TIME.

SCRUB

G. SINABUNG

THE TOP (2-3 HOURS WALK, USUALLY SHROUDED IN EVIL SMELLING FOG. THE VIEW STRETCHES FOR METERS AROUND)

TO KABANJAHE

SPECIAL WHITE MAN'S HUT (VERY BASIC)

SIGARANGGALANG

HUT

MAIN PATH

MOSQUE

BUS STOP

GUNUNG SINABUNG CLIMB

CABBAGE PATCH

KASO VILLAGE

TOMATO & CHILI PLANTATION

CAFE

BUNGALOWS

NOT TO SCALE

LAKE KAWAR

ly almost enough to induce vomiting/nausea.

Nini Kertah Ernala ("Grandmother of the Gleaming Sulphur") is the mountain's spirit. Be polite to her (excuse yourself if you have to urinate), or suffer the consequences. Locals go through an incense-burning and betelnut-chewing ritual before the climb (all the trappings for the ceremony cost around Rp200). Instances of disrespect might include throwing stones from the top, defiling the mountain by defecating on it, or cursing the spirit. Sample punishments might include getting sick, collapsing, or becoming wracked with pain. On the trail you'll often see cigarette butts stuck on forked sticks—if the cigarette burned evenly and regularly, the climber proceeded; if not, he should have waited until another day.

After your climb, soak your aching feet and thighs in **Lau Debuk2** medicinal hot sulphur springs which have been developed into a large swimming pool (admission Rp200). The turquoise-colored water is more warm than hot. Chinese Buddhists place offerings of flowers and incense here. The springs are 500 m from the Brastagi-Medan highway. Get off at the Daulu Junction, 9 km from Brastagi.

Pertekteken is a sacred place near G. Sibayak, about 1 km NW of Daulu I. Farmers will point the way across fields. Strangely shaped twisted trees and sulphurous gases add an eerie feeling to the site. There are 2 pools here (thought to contain the spirits of 2 daughters,) one bubbling but cold, the other still but hot.

Sikulikap Waterfall is near the highway to Medan, about 12 km from Brastagi. An alternate way of getting here is to take a bus to the Daulu junction, walk 500 m to Lau Debuk2 Hotsprings, then 2 km farther to the falls. Or take a Medan-bound bus (Rp250) 4 km past Daulu turnoff, then go down path on the R by wooden fruit stalls to the waterfall. Don't miss the beautiful panorama, Penatapen, about 200 m before the road to the waterfall on the right from where you can see the jungle and lowlands as far as Medan!

GUNUNG SINABUNG

Although the view from the top of G. Sinabung isn't as sweeping as it is from the summit of G. Sibayak, this active volcano is well worth the climb. It is unlikely there will be other climbers. Most climbers spend one night in the village at the base of the mountain, Singaranggalang; places to stay can be recommended by Pelawi of Brastagi's Wisma Sibayak. Guides are advisable as there are many crucial R and L turns in the first 30 min. of the climb; in other places the track disappears into dense jungle. From Singaranggalang, the climb to the top takes 3 hours; the descent is 2-3 hours. Pick a cloudless day. Start the climb early, around 0530; this is the coolest time, also the summit will not yet be obscured by clouds. The track—once you find it—is an unremittingly steep climb.

Getting There

Take a minibus from Brastagi to Kabanjahe, Rp200, then another from Kabanjahe to Singaranggalang, Rp500. There's no accommodation or restaurants in Singaranggalang, so bring your own food. Stay in the house of the guide, or the villagers will let you sleep in the government's office. Depending upon how many are in your party, a guide will cost Rp5000-10,000. To get one, just hang around the village and eventually someone will ask you if you want a guide.

MEDAN

Medan is Sumatra's largest city (at 2 million, Indonesia's 4th largest) and a dominant port. Capital of N. Sumatra Province, the city is notorious among travelers for being noisy, dirty, crowded—yet it's a necessary traveler's departure point for Malaysia or points inland like Prapat and Brastagi. With its congested rubble-stewn streets and choking carbon-monoxide fumes, Medan really has little to recommend it. It's one of the worst places to arrive in on your first trip to Indonesia, so first-time visitors should immediately head out to Lake Toba and fit in Medan later when you're more inured to travel in Indonesia.

Rising out of the swamps around 1682, this former old and graceful trading center lies slightly N of the equator. If you get beyond the crazy and ugly parts of the city, there's a fantastic confluence of cultures concentrated here—even more of a plural society than the average Indonesian metropolis. Medan is big enough to be cosmopolitan with all the conveniences, yet small enough to get around easily and recognize your friends on the street. Medan's expatriate community of 200 (including 97 Americans, 15 Dutch) is composed of diplomats and businesspeople, with its own fully accredited International School. The huge Toyota dealership on the road W out of town testifies to the strong Japanese presence here. The city is also the site of the University of N. Sumatra (Universitas Sumatera Utara). Only 25-m above sea level, Medan's climate is generally hot and humid. The heaviest rains are in late Sept., Oct., and early November. By 1100 the whole city is one blue smoggy haze, as bad as Athens!

History

The first rulers of Medan, according to local sources, were generals from Delhi, India (where the name Deli Plain, on which Medan sits, derives). This area used to be a regular battle site in wars between the sultans of Deli and Aceh; *Medan* means "Battleground." The city was founded in the 17th C. by Sultan Mahmud Perdasa Alam, who lived in his palace at Labuhan Deli, 10 km away. It grew out of a tiny group of *kampung* in a marshy lowland. Because of the hot climate and immense fertility of this narrow swamp-belt which faced a major shipping route of the Orient, by 1860 the NE Deli coastal area had become a highly productive plantation district. The Dutch colonial government decided to make it the capital of the N. Sumatra region in 1866. With the success of Deli Tobacco as a premium cigar wrapper (the firm outerwrapping leaf of a good cigar), the city kept growing; it was finally incorporated as a municipality in 1909.

Much of the city's dignified stone buildings and wide tree-lined streets date from the early 20th century. A small town 90 years ago, in 1910 the population was 17,500; now it is over 2 million.

Economy

More a business than cultural city, Medan has 15 foreign consulates and many foreign business houses. Also a leading industrial city, next to Jakarta Medan is the largest banking and commercial community in Indonesia. Although it's known as one of Indonesia's dirtiest cities, it's also one of the richest—handling a staggering 65% of Indonesia's exports, and has a higher standard of living than most other major Indonesian cities. Rubber is the staple industry of the area, Indonesia being the world's 2nd largest producer. Coffee, cacao, and some of the finest tobacco are still grown here. In addition, most of Indonesia's annual production of palm oil comes from the huge estates on the Deli Plain. All of the area's petroleum, tobacco, and plantation products are exported from the port of Belawan, 26 km N of Medan on the coast, while such unrecorded trade as cigarettes, *ganja*, medicines, electronics, and stolen dismantled motor vehicles centers around Teluknibung and L. Bilik which, since colonial times, have operated as Chinese-controlled smuggling ports. About 31% of big businesses, 55% of middle-sized businesses, and 67% of small businesses are owned by Chinese entrepreneurs, although this ethnic group comprises only 8% of Medan's total population!

The People

Because of its location and the frenetic level of its commerce, all of the region's races have converged on Medan. The Javanese came to work on its thriving plantations. Riau people flocked here because the city is the economic center of Sumatra. There are also communities of Sikhs, Acehnese, Arabians, as well as very strong Chinese, Indian, Minangkabau, Melayu, Islamic, and Christian Batak elements. Ethnologically, the city is the hub of the Batak people. Because of its large Batak Christian and Chinese populations, 40% of the city's population is non-Muslim.

SIGHTS

Medan is basically a well laid-out city with big parks and wide shady streets. Though the traffic is Asian, many downtown buildings are Western. Visit the stately residential area of **Polonia**, Medan's old quarter with elegant government buildings, parks, and large peaked tile-roof houses built by the colonials. Now most are occupied by government and commercial elites and foreign residents. Most of the city's population, however, live in a multitude of teeming *kampung* where housing and other facilities have not kept pace with the arrival of masses of unemployed rural youths who come in search of a niche in the city's cash economy. Most remain underemployed. **Chinatown** is a busy, crowded section of town—all the Chinese characters above the store fronts were removed in the 1960s by government decree. Goods here may be twice as expensive as in Penang or Singapore. Look for *klenteng* (temples).

Mosques, Temples, Churches

The largest mosque in Sumatra, elegant **Mesjid Raya** (The Great Mosque) was built in the pre-war Moroccon style in 1906. On Jl. Sisingamangaraja (the road to Tebingtinggi), this edifice is beautifully and richly decorated, set off by bright stained-glass windows. **Gang Bengkok Mosque** is the oldest mosque in Medan, built by Datuk of Kesawan in the 17th C.; it was partly constructed of square-hewn granite stones taken from Hindu and Buddhist temples.

Chinese, Hindu, and Sikh temples, which may be visited with permission of the attendant in charge, are scattered throughout the city. Some are off-limits on Fri. and to women on certain days; shoes are always removed before entering and photography isn't permitted. The first Chinese temple built in Medan (1870) is on Jl. Pandu; an even older one is in Labuhan Deli. **Vihara Gunung Timur** on Jl. Cik Ditiro, Indonesia's largest Chinese temple, is visited by Medan's Buddhist and Taoist Chinese community. **Vihara Borobudur**, adjacent to the Danau Toba Hotel, is a Buddhist temple frequented by Javanese. **Candi Hindu** is an Indian temple off Jl. Arifin, the spiritual hub for Medan's considerable Indian population. The **Roman Catholic church** on Jl. Pemuda was built in 1929; it holds services in Indonesian, Batak, and Chinese. The oldest **Protestant church**, the art deco Immanuel on Jl. Diponegoro, was built in 1921.

Colonial Architecture

Former Dutch planters' large villas can be found along wide flowering avenues such as Jl. Jen. Sudirman in the Polonia area near the airport, on the W side of Medan across the Deli River, and along Jl. Iman Bonjol and Jl. Balai Kota. Rococo, art deco, and art nouveau architectural styles are very much in evidence. Clusters of other old colonial buildings can be seen along Jl. Jen. A. Yani, and around Lapangan Merdeka, the old esplanade in Dutch times. **Deli Maatschappij** (now PTP Tobacco Co.) was the first European building, built by Nienhuys as his plantations office in 1869 (the first Dutch tobacco planter arrived in 1865). A fountain commemorating Nienhuys now stands in front of the post office. The **White Society Club** (present Bank Negara Building) was the first European whites-only club in Medan, opened in 1879. **Hotel de Boer** (now Hotel Dharma Deli) is in front of the old post office; it was built 1880-1887. Hotel de Boer is to Medan what the Raffles Hotel is to Singapore. The **Grand Hotel Medan** (now a bank), the former high-class hotel for Europeans, was built in 1887. The **Kesawan Shopping Center** was originally an office building opened in 1874 to provide Dutch tobacco planters with an outlet. On Jl. Jen. A. Yani is the beautifully decorated Chinese mansion of the late Chinese millionaire Chong A. Fie; it is not actually open to the public but be cheeky and just walk up and ask if you may see the place. Fie died of starvation in a POW camp during WW II; his mausoleum is in the Pulau Brayan cemetery.

Next to the British Consulate on Jl. Imam Bonjol is the **Harrison-Crossfield's** building, now P.T. London Sumatra Indonesia. Until 1970, this was the tallest building in Sumatra and represents the oldest British influence in N. Sumatra—that of a British rubber exporting company. The **City Hall** on Jl. Balai Kota was built in 1908 for the first mayor of Medan, Baron Mackay. Go inside the **General Post Office** (opposite Hotel Dharma Deli) which also served as the old Dutch post office; notice the artful interior with messenger pigeons in tile up on the walls with the gold bugle, the Dutch postal emblem. The old **Dutch Church**, on the same street but an extension of Jl. Jen. A. Yani, is now called the Gareja Katedral. **Gubernoran**, Jl. Jen. Sudirman 41, is the imposing mansion of the former Dutch governor. This mansion is presently the residence of the Indonesian governor of Sumatera Utara. To see inside, contact Dinas Pariwisata, Jl. Parang Merah 66.

In 1942, the Japanese occupation army built a Shinto/Buddhist Temple, now the private **Medan Club** (750 members) on Jl. Kartini. Constructed without any nails or screws (notice the beams hewn by hand), sumo wrestling matches used to be staged here on Sat. evenings. Some current members were subjugated by the Japanese as slave laborers. The emphasis today is on sports; matches and socials are held frequently.

Medan Garnizoen

On Jl. Kapt. M. Lubis, this was Medan's first Dutch Colonial army fort, built in 1873 during the Sunggal War. Cannons point upriver and there's an old bridge in front. Now a military police garrison occupies it. At Delitua, within the city limits, is the remains of another old fort, built by the celebrated Princess Putri Hijau. It was repeatedly attacked and finally destroyed by an Acehnese invasion in the late 16th century.

Museums

The **Bukit Barisan Museum**, Jl. H. Zainal. Arifin 8, opposite Bank Pembangunan Daerah, features a patriotic and military display in the main building. See mementos from the wartime resistance movement as well as the 1958 Sumatran rebellion; replicas of traditional houses and tribal cultural exhibits are in the backyard. Open Mon. to Fri. 0800-1230; free admission.

Margasatwa Zoo

A so-so zoo 4 km from the City Hall down Jl. Katamso (the Medan-Delitua road), about 20 min. from Polonia by *bemo* (Rp300) which you catch along Jl. Sisingamangaraja. Open only mornings and late afternoons, the zoo cages a variety of SE Asian species: civet cats, gibbons, orangutans, (great antics!), *kancil*, cassowaries, toucans, crocodiles, etc. The animals are fed around 1600. Also visit the crocodile farm near Pam Sunggal 6 km from Medan where 1,500 Sumatran crocs (considered the most dangerous of all) are bred for their skins. The reptiles are fed at 1630, Rp300 entrance, open 0900-1700. Take a minibus from Sambu Station, Rp200.

Istana Sultan Deli

The historic Sultan of Deli's Palace, also called the Maimoon Palace, is an ornate building at Jl. Katamso 66 on the SE fringe of the city on the road to Tebingtinggi. The palace is open all day. For a private visit, apply to the sultan's aide, tel. 22123. Tours can also be arranged. A small donation toward the restoration project is requested.

Designed by an Italian architect in 1888, this splendid palace is 75 m long, 14 m high, with 3 domes and 3 summits. The highest technology of the day was used in its construction, incorporating an astounding mixture of Oriental, Middle Eastern, and Western architectural styles. Some elements derive from the Weimar Palace in Vienna, yet all the elaborate pillars, porches, arches, and colonades reflect Arab art. Sit out on the front porch to get the feel of the palace. The sultanate, in existence since the 16th C., was terminated by the central government after the War of Independence. Though the sultan has been pensioned off by the government, he and his family still live in the palace. It is continually undergoing much-needed renovation. For further information on the sultan and his genealogy see Mr. T. Luckman Sinar (Jl. Abdullah Lubis 42, tel. 20092) who speaks Dutch and English, serves as an archivist for the court, and specializes in writing about the customs of the people of the Deli area.

The well-preserved interior, with walls like a *batik* painting, is now completely open to tourists. To the R of the main hall is a room for the sultan's male and female attendants. The walls of the main meeting hall are embellished with regal chandeliers, mirrors, paintings, and photographs of the previous Sultans of Deli, photogravures, and some haunting b/w photographic portraits. Also notice the 3-dimensional paintings of Goethe, Schiller, and Beethoven. See the main dais where the sultan sits in all his pomp. The back hall was formerly used for weddings and banquets. The prison for the sultan's subjects who had broken Koranic law was in the basement of the main building.

DOWNTOWN MEDAN

1. Glugur Station
2. Hotel Angkasa
3. Nitour
4. Hotel Dharma Deli
5. Bank Indonesia
6. Balai Kota (city hall)
7. railway station
8. Perintis Lines
9. post office
10. Radio Republik Indonesia
11. Pasar Pusat (central market)
12. *batik* shops
13. Indonesian Arts Shop
14. Bali Plaza Nightclub
15. ABC Indonesian Arts
16. Toko Seni Souvenirs
17. Tip Top Restaurant
18. Medan Tourist office
19. Hotel Irama
20. Hotel Danau Toba
21. Hotel Dirgasurya
22. Casablanca Nightclub
23. U.S. Consulate
24. Museum Bukit Barisan
25. British Consulate
26. Hotel Danau Toba
27. MAS Airlines
28. Catholic Church
29. Bank Negara Indonesia
30. Pelni Office
31. Tropicana Nightclub
32. Garuda Airlines
33. Siguragura Hotel & Travel Service
34. Chinese *warung* (after 6 p.m.)
35. Padang food
36. Merpati Airlines
37. Seulawah Airlines
38. MAS Airlines
39. Malaysian Consulate
40. St. Elisabeth Hospital
41. Maimoon Palace
42. Mesjid Raya
43. Hotel Garuda
44. Hotel Sumatra
45. Hotel Melat

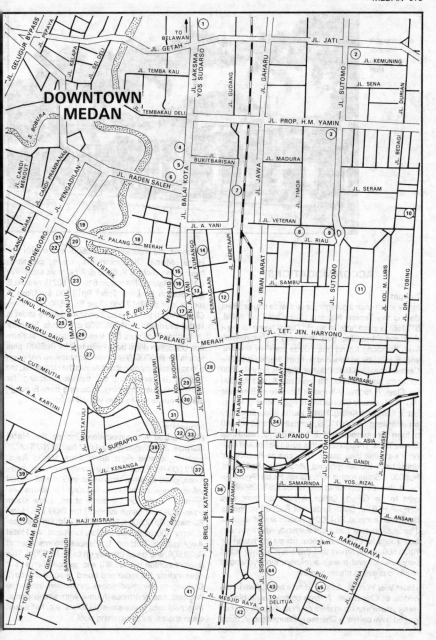

the venerable Hotel de Boer, circa 1935

ACCOMMODATIONS

Budget

In the lower-priced category, not a wide choice. Best deal is the **Tapian Nabaru**, Jl. Haing Tuah 6 (tel. 512155), a clean hotel in an old Dutch home facing a river and a tree-filled park. It is only a 10-min. walk from Kampong Keling (the "Ginza strip" of Medan), and 5 min. by *mesin becak* from the airport. The German-speaking Batak owner charges only Rp2500 for dorm beds, Rp8500 for big Class A, and Rp6500 for Class B rooms. All rooms have fans. Breakfast (Rp1000) consists of bread, jam, egg, coffee or tea, or eat at Kampung Keling. **Hotel Irama** is in a little alley off Jl. Palang Merah 112-S, centrally located only 50 m from the intersection of Jl. Imam Bonjol, near Hotel Danau Toba. Though its rooms could be hot and stuffy, it's cleaner than many. They charge Rp2000 for dorm beds (claustrophobic), Rp3000 s, Rp4000 d, Rp6000 t. Some rooms with *mandi*. **Hotel Siguragura**, Jl. Jen. Let. Suprapto 2/K (tel. 323991/325686), is next to the Garuda Office. A sign out front says CHEAP HOTEL. Dorm beds cost Rp2000 pp (better dorm than Irama's), Rp4000 d. Rooms are rather drab. The Siguragura is also a travel agency where you can buy tickets for airlines and boat tickets to Penang for Rp38,500 (some report that this travel agency is not very reliable), and there's a resident moneychanger. Numerous eating places nearby.

Hotel Wai Wat, Jl. Asia 44, is on a busy street in the middle of Chinatown. A large complex with blaring music, there's an open inner courtyard where you can sit and have coffee; a Chinese restaurant too. A maze of rooms, the cheapest cost Rp6000 s or d with fan. **Hotel Mona**, Jl. Sukamulia — clean, pleasant, basic — also charges Rp6000 d. A bit more expensive is **Hotel Melati**, Jl. Amaluin 6 (tel. 516021), near ALS Bus Station (to Lake Toba) Rp15,000 for Class A rooms (s or d), Rp12,500 Class B: Rp5000 Economy Class. Watch the Peeping Toms. Across the street is **Hotel Waringin**, Rp4000-7000 d. **Wisma Sibayak** Jl. Kapitan Pattimura 627 (near intersection of Kampus USU), has dorm beds (with fan) for Rp3000, plus rooms for Rp6000. Very clean, light meals. Although a long 25 min. by *daihatsu* ride into the city center, the Sibayak is convenient for travelers heading for Brastagi the next morning. If coming from Brastagi, ask the bus driver to drop you off in front.

Moderate

Higher-priced accommodations include the **Hotel Garuda**, Jl. Sisingamangaraja 27 (tel. 22760/51203), centrally located right down from Mesjid Raya; Rp12,000-Rp25,000 for clean rooms with fan, bathroom, good lighting, Indonesian-style *mandi* — good value. A reasonably priced restaurant is downstairs. Friendly people. On the same street, a few doors down at Jl. Sisingamangaraja 21 (tel. 24973), is **Hotel Sumatra**: Rp12,500 s, Rp17,500 d, with fan and *mandi*, only 400 m to bus station to Prapat. At **Hotel Angkasa**, Jl. Sutomo 1, cheapest rooms *start* at Rp28,500, and go all the way up to Rp 50,000 d. This doesn't include tax, (20%!) and service charge, but does include full room and board (3 squares a day). Catering to the middle-class Indonesian trade, the Angkasa has enormous rooms with sitting parlor, mosquito nets, European-style toilets, a/c, hot water, clean sheets, and swimming pool.

Hotel Dharma Deli is an old colonial-style hotel, the former Dutch de Boer Hotel, Jl. Balai Kota 2 (tel. 327011); Rp18,250 s, Rp25,250 d. The hotel's famous gardens have now been turned into private suites. Superb hot water, a/c rooms, and a great a/c lobby, bar, and a couple of *batik* shops. Right across the street is the historic old post office, and the taxi stand is just across the *alun-alun*. The hotel swimming pool is always crowded with Chinese, the only ones who can afford the entrance fee. Avoid the breakfast (Rp4500). Read the funniest hotel rules in all of Indonesia. **Hotel Dirgasurya**, Jl. Imam Bonjol 6 (tel. 323433), near the American Consulate, is older, some a/c rooms, showers, clean, fair food, but rather noisy. Rooms range from Rp20,000 up to Rp30,500 d. The **Garuda Plaza Hotel**, Jl. Sisingamangaraja 18 (tel. 326255/51300), specializes in catering to domestic businessmen. Standard rooms are Rp45,000, with excellent Indonesian restaurant downstairs.

Expensive

Among the international-class accommodations is the **Tiara Medan**, Jl. Cut Mutiah (tel. 516000), Medan's leading hotel with full facilities and outstanding service. Its elegant, lavishly appointed rooms are expensive. Has 2 international restaurants, bars, coffee shop, taxi service, pool and health club. Ideal for businesspeople as the commerical district is nearby. **Danau Toba International**, Jl. Imam Bonjol 17 (tel. 327000), is a large, well-established, high-priced hotel with a/c rooms, bar, restaurant, pool, bowling alley. This modern hotel has a/c rooms with high balcony views looking out over the city, swimming pool and tennis court; Rp45,000-55,000 s, Rp50,000-60,000 d. But try to avoid the hotel's restaurants: the food is either fiendishly expensive or demonically dreadful. **Polonia Hotel**, Jl. Jen. Sudirman 14 (tel. 325300), asks Rp32,250 s, Rp35,500 d, Rp78,500 for a suite. Located on "Embassy Row," one of the nicest sections of Medan; this is where embassy people stay when they are on assignment or while they're looking for long-term accommodations. Centrally located with very good service and in-room video, swimming pool, health center, reputable Chinese restaurant. **Pardede International Hotel**, Jl. Ir. H. Juanda 14 (tel. 323866) near the airport, offers 1st Class a/c rooms, private baths, garden views, bar, restaurant and nightclub; Rp35,000 s, Rp45,000 d.

FOOD AND ENTERTAINMENT

The **Tip Top Restaurant**, on the shopping street Jl. Jen. A. Yani 92/A, specializes in Western food and in *nasi padang*. Quite good fish and meat dishes. For dessert, sample their delicious ice cream, ice cream cake, etc. This attractive sidewalk cafe is a nice place to sit day or night and take in the street life. If the

fumes get too much, sit inside in a/c comfort. **Lyn's Bar & Restaurant** on Jl. Jen. A. Yani next door to Tip Top, has probably the city's best Western meat dishes. Lyn's serves such pretentious Western dishes as Chateaubriand steaks, Spaghetti Bolognaise, and no one should pass through Medan without having Melaka Straits lobster at Lyn's; it's marvelous. The **Garuda Plaza Hotel**, Jl. Sisingamangaraja 18, offers very good scrambled eggs and raisin pancakes. Complete American breakfast is Rp3500.

For Indonesian cuisine, **RM Garuda**, Jl. Pemuda 20C-D (tel. 327692), has very good Padang food (*nasi Lampur* costs about Rp1200). Their fruit juices are especially knockout. Other good places are **Family Restoran**, Jl. S.M. Raji 21B (Minang food); **Gembira Restoran**, Jl. Raja 4BC. **Jenar Restaurant**, Jl. Gatot Suprapto across from Taman Ria, features Javanese cuisine. **Bukit Kubu**, Jl. Padang Bulang, is a famous restaurant 7 km from Medan, with bar, swimming pool, floor show every Sun.; serves delicious Indonesian, Chinese, and Western food at average prices.

Chinese

Crowded Chinese shops serving breakfast noodle soup early in the morning are found along Jl. Surabaya; Rp600 per bowl. For Chinese banquet-style cuisine at its best, go to the **Bali Plaza Restaurant**, Jl. Kumango 1A (tel. 515505/14852)—remarkable cooking and very fast service. Only the best ingredients are used, very fresh vegies. You are treated like royalty: hostesses light your cigarettes, continually fill your glass with beer, ladle soup for you. Try the shrimp hot plate, fried chicken, soups, and desserts (outrageous Shanghai Pancake which 3 people have trouble finishing!). Upstairs there's a restaurant where hostesses can be rented out as dancing partners. The **Polonia Restaurant**, Polonia Hotel, Jl. Sudirman, is an outstanding dining experience where meals are served even up to 2200-2300. Stick to their Chinese menu; prices are moderate to expensive. Other unusually good Chinese restaurants: **Seafood Wonderland**, Jl. Airlangga (near Kampong Keling); **Mandarin Restaurant**, Jl. Kol. Sugiono 16-C; **Micado**, Jl. Prof. H.M. Yamin 236H (Chinese-Indonesian and European dishes, reasonable prices).

Ethnic And Vegetarian

Ethnic restaurants include the **Toshiba**, Jl. Palang Merah, and the **Fuji** in the Danau Toba International, both serving Japanese food. **Alor Star**, Jl. Mesjid, has reasonable and tasty Indian food (try the *nasi briyani*). **Chopsticks Restaurant**, Jl. Sugiono 7C, specializes in Korean barbecue.

Medan is blessed with an incredibly good vegetarian restaurant, **Restaurant Vegetarian Indonesia** which is located at Jl. Gandhi 63A (beside Bioskop

Benteng), tel. 526812. Next door to a Buddhist temple, it's run by people from the temple. They speak no English and have no English menu but have lots of photographs of the varied, delicious food. Gluten is used to make meat and fish substitute dishes.

For Chinese, Indian, and Indonesian food at night, visit **Jalan Selat Panjang**, between Jl. Nusantara and Jl. Pundu, about a 5-min. walk from Jl. Jen. A. Yani. Delicious food and beer at good prices. Many open-air foodstalls, which serve snake, frog, goat's testicles, etc., from around 1800 until 0100. All *becak* drivers know where the Selat Panjang night market is. *Warung* also blossom at night at **Taman Ria**, Jl. Jen. Gatot Subroto. Another popular *pasar malam* is **Kampong Keling**, Jl. Zainal Arifin, with many small alleyways filled with stalls selling Indonesian, Chinese, Indian, and European food. **Pasar Hong Kong's** Chinese stalls (on Jl. Cirebon) sell dumplings and steamed bread.

Fruit and Gourmet

For fruit lovers, Medan is known for its *durian;* when it's in season in Aug. and Sept., stalls everywhere offer this unique aromatic fruit at low prices. Start on the road to P. Siantar; at the 12-km mark they sell watermelons (Rp400 per kg) and *nangka.* Binjei, 22 km from Medan, is renowned for its *rambutan.*

Holland Bakery, Jl. Taruma, has outstanding baked goods and ice cream delights. Another good ice cream place is **Batik Cafe**, Jl. Pemuda 14C. **Toko Roti**, Jl. Zainal Arifin, stocks imported cheese, salamis, ground beef, and other meats. Delicious whole wheat bread *(roti merah)* is sold at the **Indian Bakery** at Jl. Thamrin 9. For more baked goods, check out **Tahiti Modern Bakery & Cake Shop**, Jl. Taruma 66; the **Medan Bakery**, Jl. Zainal Arifin; and **Tip Top Bakery**, Jl. Jen. A. Yani 92/A.

Entertainment

Most of Medan's dozens of a/c movie theaters are located in the city's new shopping plazas (Medan, Plaza, Olympia, Deli). Though rarely offering English-language films, the **Deli Plaza cinemas** on Jl. Perdana specializes in Western films dubbed in Indonesian. These are the nicest cinemas in town; easy parking, a/c, crowded on weekends. When Medan's heat, dust and fumes are getting you down, take a dip in one of the hotel swimming pools (Rp1250 entrance): Hotel Dharma Deli, Jl. Balai Kota; Danau Toba International, Jl. Iman Bonjol; Tiara Hotel, Jl. Cutmutiah; Angkasa, Jl. Sutomo. **Taman Ria Amusement Park** on Jl. Gatot Suprapto, houses permanent cultural, agricultural, and industrial exhibits. The park is also the site of the Medan Fair from March to May (40 days) when there are sports contests, *adat* houses open for inspection, and exhibitions relating to trade, industry, and agriculture.

The city has many nightclubs and discotheques such as **Casablanca** in the Dirgasurya Hotel, Jl. Iman Bonjol; and **Bali Plaza**, Jl. Kumango 1A (the best known). For a more low-brow environment, visit the disco attached to the Motel Danau Toba near the corner of Jl. Hayamwuruk and Iskandar Muda—a throbbing den of iniquity. There are also several pool halls in town like at **Medan Plaza**, where hostesses rack the balls and play with you for Rp3000-5000. Another expat hangout, filled with fortyish Australians, Americans, and Europeans, is **Lyn's Bar & Restaurant**, Jl. Jen. A. Yani near the Tip Top—the only place in Medan you can sit in a *real* bar. Good draft beer! The private **Medan Club**, Jl. Kartini, is another focal point for expatriate social life with tennis, squash, golf, badminton, bowling, swimming, and horseback riding (also available at many of the city's upscale hotels). Bring basic sports equipment with you.

Cultural performances take place twice weekly at the **Bina Budaya**, Jl. Perintis Kemerdekaan (opposite the Angkasa Hotel); free admission. Also check out the **RRI** (Radio Republik Indonesia) auditorium, Jl. Let. Kol. Martinus Lubis near the Central Market, where public concerts, lectures, and cultural shows take place. No a/c but comfortable most of the time. The **Tapian Daya Cultural Center**, Jl. Binjei at Km 2, is one of the biggest art campuses in Indonesia.

OTHER PRACTICALITIES

Events

Medan takes its religious and dance festivals seriously, and due to its polyglot, multi-racial community there are many. One of the most exciting is the Indian community's **Tabut Kaling**, highlighted by a colorful *tabut*-procession around the city. *Leberan* is also lavishly celebrated here. On the Islamic holy day of **Idul Fitri**, hundreds of devotees and well-wishers converge on the Maimoon Palace in traditional dress. Malay ladies wear the *baju panjang* and a gold woven *songket*, while men are dressed in the long-sleeved *teluk belang* and *tengkuluk* headdress. This is the best time to visit the palace. **Marahhalim**, an annual soccer tournament (April-May), attracts top Indonesian and foreign teams. Medan's anniversary takes place on 1 July; sports events and cultural entertainment celebrate the founding of N. Sumatra's capital.

Shopping

The **Central Market** (Pasar Pusat), off Jl. Sutomo near downtown, is one of the largest in SE Asia. It was the very largest in Asia until half of it was destroyed by a fire in 1971. Very old, colorful. Opens at dawn. Crowded. Rows of huge 2-story warehouses. Hang on to your belongings and beware of pickpockets. Wear thongs as it's muddy. In this area there are actually a number of markets: Pasar Ramas, Pasar Kampung Keling, Pasar Hong Kong, plus the most modern shopping complex in Sumatra, the

Olympia Plaza. You can buy almost anything in these markets; electronic consumer goods jam the shops. In Pasar Ramai, off Jl. Thamrin, Boutique Cornelia is filled with treasures and unique shopping buys from all over Indonesia; also check out the other small but loaded shops of this market. Here's where you can blow your remaining *rupiah* before leaving the country. Good hunting!

Go to Pasar Ikan Lama (Old Fish Market) on Jl. Perniagaan, between Jl. Jen. A. Yani and the RR tracks, to buy men's and women's ready-to-wear, *batik*, and Indian goods, but bargain. Indonesians themselves shop in this neighborhood so prices are extremely reasonable, and the stock is large. The shops on the main street sell wholesale only, so shop inside the market for the smaller pieces of gingham, nylon net, cotton, *batik cap*, and an endless selection of men's shirts and children's clothing. The shop with probably the best selection of inexpensive sun dresses is Feminina near Pasar Ikan Lama.

For souvenirs and antiques, Jl. Jen. A. Yani is the main shopping street of Medan, where genuine Batak antiques are very rare, reproductions very convincing. Ersatz buffalo "powder horns," swirling with Neolithic carvings, go for Rp45,000. Toba Batak calendars are also reproduced en masse. Bamboo weaving, woven blankets *(ulos)*, and woodcarvings are probably the best values; but bargain intensely. Toko Selatan, no. 44, has a gigantic variety, a little on the pricey side. Indonesia Art Shop, no. 1A, sells a real potpourri of junky arts with a few fine-quality antiques. Borobudor Art Shop, no. 32, specializes in Batak artifacts, Karo primitive carvings, textiles, Chinese porcelain, and old Niah funereal carvings.

The best bookshop in Medan is Toko Buku Deli, Jl. Jen. A. Yani 1. The Gramedia, Jl. Gajah Mada 23, is also well-stocked. All local papers are in Indonesian, although the English-language *Singapore Straits Times, Jakarta Times,* plus Asian editions of *Time* and *Newsweek,* and even *USA Today* (Rp3000!) are all available.

Services

For brochures, maps, and general information on Medan and North Sumatra Province, visit the North Sumatran Tourist Office *(Dinas Pariwisata),* Jl. Palang Merah 66 (tel. 511101/512300 ps46). There's also an "information booth" out at Polonia Airport which seems more interested in changing your money than in dispensing its few meager handouts. Another tourist office is Kantor Wilayah I Sumatera Utara-Aceh, Jl. Alpalah 22 (tel. 322838), which also can inform about Aceh Province. Good-quality information can also be had from travel agencies such as Nitour, Jl. Prof. H. M. Yamin 21E (tel. 23191).

Make sure you change your money in Medan if you're

venturing by road inland where banks are few and far between. Bank Negara Indonesia, Jl. Pemuda 12 (tel. 22333), gives the best rates. Also try the Bali Bank, Jl. Balai Kota. The worst rates are at the airport. The *imigrasi* office is at Jl. Jen. A. Yani 74. Medan's GPO is a historic structure on Jl. Bukit Barisan (tel. 23612/25945) on Merdeka Square (the *alun-alun);* this full-service p.o. will take parcels *(paket post)* as well as ordinary mail. There's another post office at Polonia Airport, but it won't accept parcels.

Hospitals And Clinics

For a quick fix, Clinic Bunda, Jl. Sisisingamangaraja (opposite the Garuda Plaza), runs a health service open 24-hours daily; Rp2000-5000 for an average consultation. Medan's Rumah Sakit (General Hospital) is on the corner of Jl. Prof. M. Yamin and Jl. Thamrin (tel. 23332). RM St. Elizabeth, Jl. Imam Bonjol 38 (tel.322455), is a private hospital run by expat nuns with very good X-ray facilities. RM Herna, Jl. Majapahit 118 (tel. 510766), is another private hospital with an intensive-care unit.

TRANSPORT

Getting There

Sample bus fares from: Padang, Rp9500 (26 hours); Prapat, Rp2500 (5 hours); Banda Aceh, Rp6500 (buses arrive at station on Jl. K. W. Hasyim in the northern part of the city); Bukittinggi, Rp8500 (22-24 hours); Pekanbaru, Rp11,000; Jakarta, Rp35,000 (a/c), Rp29,000 (ordinary). A regular ferry makes the Penang-Medan, Medan-Penang crossing. Buy tickets at Penang's Tourist Assoc. office on Jl. Syed Barakhbah, at the shipping company itself (Sanren, Delta Marine on Jl. Leboh Ferquhar), or at numerous travel agencies and hotels along Chulia Street, Penang. Second Class costs M$55, 1st Class M$55 (berths in 4-person staterooms). Departs only on Mon. and Wed. from near Penang's Port Commission at 1830, arriving in Belawan (26 km N of Medan) at 0800. From Jakarta, the weekly Pelni ship KM *Rinjani* sails every Sat. at around 1800 and docks in Belawan on Mon. morning; Rp38,000 Economy Class. Real good cruising, beautiful new boat, nice showers. First Class (Rp110,000) is absolutely luxurious. From Belawan, take a bus 26 km into the city, Rp1000. Medan is the western air gateway to Indonesia, only 35-min. flying time across the narrow Melaka Strait from Penang, Malaysia. MAS flights leave at 1030 daily (M$105 OW, M$150 RT). Take the bus from Jl. Prangin in Penang every hour 0700-1000 for M$1.20 (45 min.) to Penang's airport. Garuda, Merpati, Seulawah, and Pelita all connect Jakarta and Medan in 1½ hours. From Singapore to Medan, about S$275 (1 hour).

THE MEDAN AREA

1. bus terminal
2. Taman Ria and Medan Fair
3. Glugar bus station
4. General Hospital
5. railway station
6. central market (pasar pusat)
7. German Consulate
8. Tapian Nabaru Hotel
9. Medan Club
10. Sei Wampu bus station
11. French Consulate
12. Grundaling Tours
13. Netherlands Consulate
14. buses to Padang
15. Sisingamangaraja bus station
16. Bus Terminal Teladini
17. Polonia Airport

Arriving

Medan's Polonia Airport has no luggage storage. Emerging from Customs, a mob of porters in yellow jumpsuits will descend upon you to carry your gear. Motorized super-powered *mesin becak* are available from the airport to anywhere in the city; Rp2000-3000. Taxis are the most expensive (Rp5000), and the drivers really press themselves on you. Get around this by sharing a taxi, or going through the airport's taxi desk (Rp5000), or just walking past them and getting a *becak*. *Becak* are not allowed in the airport area: walk 300 m to the outside gate and get a *becak* for Rp1500 to your hotel. Or, if you're not burdened down, walk all the way into the city (2 km).

Getting Around

Medan's traffic is noisy and chaotic with swarms of fume-spewing motorized *becak,* motorcycles, bicycles, new Japanese cars, buses, trucks, and jaywalking pedestrians. A OW street system has helped city traffic, but for the newcomer it makes the city a puzzle to navigate. Its acrid fumes can be worse than Bangkok's. The most convenient inner-city conveyance is the *becak*. Four-wheeled *Sudaco,* filled to overflowing, whizz down streets at incredible speeds. Travel established routes in town and in the suburbs (watch the pickpockets!). Stasiun Sambu is the big minibus station from where you can get *Sudaco* to points all over the city. *Mesin becak,* with motorbike engines alongside powering them, charge Rp1000-1500 for distances within the city. Double-decker *bis damri* (Rp200) run mostly on the outskirts of town.

Taxis are licensed but not metered; rates are high so bargain first. Service within the city costs Rp2000-

3000, but Rp5000 from the airport. Taxi stands are located at Polonia Airport, Danau Toba International Hotel, the Polonia Hotel. Illegal ones (the cheapest) are found at the *stasiun kereta api* (train station). These private taxis, usually in the form of unmarked sedans, are frequently used for travel outside the city. Rates are high. For example, to Prapat it costs Rp100,000 for 2 days, though this includes all operating expenses. Legitimate taxi companies: Bali, Jl. S.M. Raja 81 (tel. 322111); Bengawan, Jl. S.M. Raja 79 (tel. 327788/29327).

FROM MEDAN

By Bus

Buses are the principal means of public transportation around Sumatra. Trips are long, road conditions vary from not bad to unbelievable, and non-express buses are very crowded. But if you don't have a private car and if plane fares are outside your budget, it's the only way. Medan has many bus stations. Generally, go to the one that is on the way to where you want to travel: Sei Wampu Station has transport to the N, Sisingamangaraja Station has transport to the S (Prapat). Buses for points S also cruise from bus company offices along Jl. Iskandar Muda toward the Grand Mosque and past it, picking up passengers as they go. To get out to Sisingamangaraja, hop a minibus on Jl. Sisingamangaraja. Sambu is the busiest and noisiest transportation clearing house for Medan.

Leaving Medan, the 2 largest and best bus companies are ALS (Jl. Amuliun 2A) and ATS (Jl. Bintang), which operate Mercedes on scheduled routes. Many other bus company offices (such as Medan Raya Express) are along Jl. Sisingamangaraja and down side streets. Reserve a seat 2 days in advance if you want the more comfortable front seats. Other (ALS) bus fares: Sibolga, Rp5000; Bukittinggi, Rp9500; Jakarta, Rp37,000; Jambi, Rp16,500.

To Lake Toba

From Sisingamangaraja Station it's Rp2000 (4 hours) to Prapat on wildly painted Chevy buses, or Rp2500 on direct buses. Buses start to roll at 0600 right up until around 1700. Prapat and Brastagi buses also cruise along the main roads out of Medan, such as Jl. Sisingamangaraja and Jl. Iskandar Muda. Alternatively, one can take a bus first to Pematangsiantar (Rp1500), then it's another Rp500 to Prapat. The longer drive via Brastagi (69 km from Medan) to Prapat is more scenic. Or catch a *mesin becak* from in front of the Siguragura Hotel (Rp500) to Sambu Station from where minibuses leave almost constantly for Prapat, Rp3000. To Haranggaol on Lake Toba, you must go to Kabanjahe first; take a bus direct from Sei Wampu.

By Ship

From Stasiun Sei Wampu, Jl. Sei Wampu, get a bus (Rp500) or a *bemo* (Rp900) to Belawan 26 km N (1 hour). From Belawan, a boat service now operates between Medan and Penang, Malaysia, departing Medan each Tues. and Thurs. at 1800. Buy tickets (Rp 75,000 Deck, Rp 80,000 Cabin) at Siguragura Travel Agency on Jl. Jen Suprapto 2/K or at PT Eka Sukma, Jl. Brig. Jen. Katamso 62A. Boats arrive in Penang at around 0600 or 0700. Price includes transport costs to Belawan and insurance. Check in by 1600.

Pelni's office is at Jl. Sugiono 5 (tel. 25100/25190), or on Jl. Palang Merah in Medan's port of Belawan. Pelni's KM *Rinjani* embarks for Tg. Pinang (Rp30,000), from where one can board a launch up to Singapore (Rp10,000). Or take a Pelni ship straight from Medan to Jakarta for around Rp38,000 Economy. From Belawan, a number of other cargo lines carry passengers to Melaka, Singapore, etc. at approx. one-third the cost of flying; inquire at **Oriental Lines,** Jl. Kol. Sugiono 10G (tel. 20802/26729/26510), and **Perintis Lines,** Jl. Veteran 16E (tel. 20375).

By Air

Medan's Polonia Airport is 2 km from downtown. If you take a *becak* out to the airport, you have to get off outside the gate and walk 300 m the rest of the way. If in a hurry or burdened down, take a minibus to the terminal for an inflated Rp1000. From Polonia, one can make domestic Merpati connections to Gunungsitoli (Nias) for around Rp52,700 (departs 0700, arrives 0820), as well as to: Padang, Rp54,800; Pekanbaru, Rp48,600; Palembang, Rp89,300; Sibolga, Rp24,000. International flights are available to Penang, Kuala Lumpur, and Singapore. Make sure that you get confirmed booking through your airline office itself as there are many stories of reserved seats not materializing. This situation worsens on weekends when Malaysians and Indonesians want to swap sides. If you miss a booking get out to the airport and onto the waiting list; seats are always available at the last minute. Airlines offices: Garuda, Jl. Lt. Jen. Suprapto 2 (tel. 25703); Merpati, Jl. Brig. Jen. Katamso 37 (tel. 516617); MAS (Malaysia), in the Hotel Danau Toba International, Jl. Imam Bonjol 17 (tel. 519333); Singapore Airlines (SIA), Jl. Imam Bonjol 16; SMAC, Jl. Imam Bonjol 59, and at the airport.

VICINITY OF MEDAN

PEMATANG SIANTAR

Southeast of Medan 128 km, or a 48-km (Rp1000) bus ride from Prapat, located in one of the richest tea and tobacco growing districts in Sumatra. Pematang Siantar is the 2nd largest city in N. Sumatra, a smaller, cooler version of Medan and just as noisy. This city is the capital and largest town of the Simalungun Batak tribe, though there are many non-Simalungun people here: Chinese, Indians, Karo, and Toba Batak. Also site of Universitas Simalungan, N of town. Pasar Horas, Siantar Plaza, and Pantoan are the town's new, glitzy shopping centers. Pematang Siantar is the nearest city to Prapat for visa matters, and a major transport hub for the whole Simalungun area. Take motorized *becak* anywhere in town, Rp400-500.

Simalungun Batak

A branch of the Batak people; the tribal name means "he that is lonely, quiet, or sad." The Simalungun are a gentle, soft-mannered people who have many sad, nostalgic songs, and speak with a slow, lilting intonation. These people were beginning to evolve from sedentary *ladang* cultivators into a feudal society when the Dutch first arrived; they weren't conquered until 1910. Half the Simalungun are animist, the other half Islamic or Christian, though all attend animist ceremonies such as the "group hair-washing ritual" (*Erpangir*). Dance is particularly popular in the Simalungun district. The most macabre is a mask-dance performed at funerals while the dead body is being washed. The happiest is the Marriage Dance (*Sitalasari*) in which the bride and bridesmaid hold flowers in one hand and slap their hips with the other while gliding across the floor doing Suzy-Qs. The

Farewell Dance *(Tading Maham Na Tading)* is put on by all the young girls of the village when a man leaves, warning him "Don't marry anybody abroad, just come back to us." A number of Simalungun festivals and events are held in early Dec. at the royal museum village of Pematang Purba, W of Pematangsiantar. To really understand the Simalungun culture, a visit should be paid to this village.

lizard relief over doorway in Sitorang

Sights

Museum Simalungun on Jl. Sudirman houses a special exhibit of the Simalungun Batak clan. Open every day 0800-1200 and 1400-1700; closed on Sun. (although Mr. Purba might open it for you if he's around). Check out the sculpture in the front yard dating from Portuguese times, a purely animist, powerfully carved seated woman cradling children. An enormous lizard on the door looks like a crocodile, though it's really a *cikcak* (small lizard). The Simalungun keep this over their doors because the *cikcak* animal lives in the home and thus offers protection against the house being robbed. Inside are manuscripts in Batak script, spears, gongs, masks, artwork, *pustaha* divination books, 300-year-old iron tools, opium pipes, old Portuguese guns, bygone children's games. All labels are in Indonesian but Mr. Purba will answer all your questions (in German, Dutch, Indonesian, or English) and will relate some vivid tiger and cannibal stories from his boyhood days.

A large but sparsely populated **zoo** with peacocks and Sumatran fauna is behind the museum. Also visit the zoological museum, archaeological displays, and children's park on the grounds. Bah Sorma Swimming Pool is another recreation spot (with restaurants) in town.

Accommodations And Food

A small clump of hotels in the middle of town is only a 5-min. walk from the museum or a 10-min. walk from the bus station. **Hotel Garuda**, Jl. Merdeka 33, asks Rp8500-12,500, but you can sometimes bargain them down. Rooms aren't particularly clean and no inside *mandi*; rooms in the back are quiet but have no windows. **Hotel Bali**, near Hotel Garuda at Jl. Merdeka 52, charges Rp5500 d. **Hotel Dagang**, across the street from the Bali, is the same price. **Hotel Delima**, Jl. Thamrin 131, is on the other end of town near the

bus station; Rp2500 pp. **Hotel Segar**, Jl. Merdeka 234, Rp4500 pp; noisy, unclean sheets, but their rooftop overlooks a *pasar* neighborhood. **Siantar Hotel**, Jl. W.R. Supratman, is the only high-standard accommodation. At Rp16,850 s, this is the best Siantar has to offer: private bath, hot water, breakfast, plus the privilege of paying government tax. The Siantar also has a small but select library, nice garden, souvenir shop, billiards, restaurant with European and Indonesian food—a nicely maintained colonial-style hotel with excellent service.

Numerous Chinese shops sell fresh baked goods along the town's main street. Good *mie* places as well. Hotel Siantar's restaurant is reasonably priced, though uninspiring. **Miramar Restaurant** has tasty Indonesian food, but the best Indonesian restaurant for *nasi padang* is **Asmara Murni** on Jl. Sutomo; around Rp2000 for a flawless meal.

Crafts

Batak and Karo tribal artifacts are for sale in Pasar Besar: average-quality homespun *kain ulos* cost Rp35,000-40,000. Made by the *ikat* method and up to 2 m long, these fabrics are used for wedding gifts or are spread over an ill person. Though each tribe uses different colors and patterns, *ulos* generally have vertical stripes with horizontal ends and blue backgrounds with red and white designs. *Ulos* are still regularly produced because when a Simalungun Batak marries he must give these blankets to his in-laws. The best *ulos* now cost up to Rp125,000. First go the Simalungun Museum (near the zoo); the proprietor will tell you what to look for, how each type should be worn, inform about comparative prices, show you some specimens, and suggest vendors. Go out to the *kampung* itself to order one (takes one month); the best are always ordered. You can also buy *ragidup* fabrics in Pasar Besar.

Transport

There are 2 bus stations: Stasiun Sentral on the Medan end of town and Parlusan Station 2 km from town. Stasiun Sentral is just another creepy bus station, but the only way to avoid it is to get a through-bus. Catch minibuses to Medan, Rp1500; Haranggaol, Rp2500. From Parlusan Station, catch buses to Haranggaol for Rp1000; Brastagi, Rp1800; Kabanjahe, Rp1500, (via Brastagi in the Karo Highlands); Prapat (on Lake Toba), Rp1000, 4 hours; Sibolga, Rp6000 (on this 8-hour ride you pass Balige with its riotously colorful fruit market); Bukittinggi, Rp9000.

PEMATANG PURBA

A 200-year-old village of Simalungun tribal chiefs, 65 km W of P. Siantar, 140 km S of Medan, and 62 km (1 hour) SE of Kabanjahe. Pematang Purba used to be the site of an old "execution tree" under which men were judged to death and subsequently ritually eaten by the villagers. The tree was cut down by Dutch soldiers, one of the measures the Dutch took to put an end to cannibalistic practices. The village's former entrance tunnel and some earthworks can still be seen.

Within the complex are the ancient courthouse, carved pillars, rice barns, rice mortars, and raja's palace (Rumah Bolon). This beautiful 150-year-old palace longhouse was inhabited by Batak royalty until 1945. Inside are fireplaces for the many wives (the last raja had 12!) and attendants. The king signaled his desire to sleep with a certain wife by having his eunoch *(wadam)* take a betelnut offering to the chosen wife. Today, the coat of paint on the palace is just a little too fresh. Busloads of tourists pass through in the mornings. A guide hits you up for a donation and tries to sell you souvenirs; when you give only Rp200 he is clearly disappointed. It's sad to see descendants of kings begging. A living village, like in the Tiga Gambar hinterlands of Karoland, would be more interesting.

The longhouse complex is the site of a number of events in early December. The *Rondang Bintang* ("full moon") festival is highlighted by a variety of arts performances by the Simalungun such as *Tortor balang sahua, Sitalasari, Bunyut mangan sihala,* and others. The young men and women recite *pantun* (quatrain poetry). There are also traditional sporting events such as *marjalengkat, margala,* and *marsampak hotang.*

Transport
This museum village is 200 m S of the highway, about midway between P. Siantar and Kabanjahe, and Rp750 by bus from Haranggaol. From P. Purba, the scenic, bumpy road eventually leads to Kabanjahe. Also, there's an ancient path from P. Purba all the way down to Lake Toba.

BINJEI
Binjei, known as "Rambutan City," is a large unremarkable town 22 km W of Medan on the road to Banda Aceh, Rp450 by minibus from Medan's Central Market area, or share a taxi for Rp1500 from the Juwita Shopping Center on Jl. Surabaya. A normally quiet town except in the *rambutan* season July-Aug., when its many trees start bearing fruit. Every yard has a *rambutan* tree and at that time small *warung* selling the aromatic fruit are set up every few meters along the road. A sizeable Chinese community lives downtown; **Tepekong,** their large, well-kept Buddhist temple, is on the R side of the road just after crossing a bridge when coming into town from Medan. **Tugu Perjuangan,** at the start of Binjei, is a monument honoring heros who fought the Japanese in 1942.

From this town there is easy access to Brastagi, and the Orangutan Rehabilitation Center at Bukitlawang.

Practicalities
There are 2 *losmen,* one on Jl. Irian and one on Jl. Cokroaminoto. But the best place to stay is the Doeky family's homestay, **Cafe de Malioboro,** Jl. Ksatria 1 (tel. 21987). Relax in this comfortable old creaking wooden Dutch house with large rooms for Rp2500 s, Rp4000 d, Continental breakfast included. Be sure to ask Mr. Doeky for a mosquito coil before retiring. Set back from the road, and insulated from it by towering shade trees, there's a menagerie of pets, a garden, and a well in the backyard for your ablutions. Food is reasonable and very good but must be ordered in advance, or walk across the street to a Padang-style restaurant. Also check out the **Phoenix,** Jl. Sutomo 51-53, a full a/c Chinese restaurant.

BUKITLAWANG

A relaxing village of a few hundred people, 76 km W of Medan and 15 km W of Bohorok on the edge of 8000-sq.-km G. Leuser Reserve, deep in N. Sumatra's backcountry. The most memorable part of a visit here is the ride out to the reserve through tropical rainforests and rubber plantations. Try to arrive on weekdays to avoid hundreds of day-trippers from Medan on boisterous Sunday outings; also, come in the mornings to miss domestic tour groups that descend after noontime. Most travelers venture this far for one reason only, to see the Orangutan Rehabilitation Center located nearby within the Leuser Reserve. The great apes are very different in their natural habitat than when seen in a zoo. They still can be very playful but are prone to throw sticks and piss on you. From the government's *pasanggrahan* (forest guesthouse), it's an easy 20-min. walk to the boat crossing and entrance to the reserve. The canoe across the river is free going but Rp300 coming back. Three-day permits are also obtainable for Rp2000 from the PPA in Medan, Jl. Sisingamangaraja, Km 55. Only 1-day permits are issued in Bukitlawang, also Rp2000. Food served.

Swim in the Bohorok River. In the nearby village visit the rubber-processing factory; the manager will show you around. Go at 2000 to see the rubber being pressed, dried, packed. During the day, up to 600 plantation workers bring in 15 liters of latex they've collected from the trees. The village chief will tell you fascinating facts about the social system of the rubber workers.

The Center
Since the orangutan *(mawas)* are now headed for extinction (only about 1,000 left in Sumatran jungles),

this center and others like it in Sumatra and Borneo were created to preserve wild *mawas* from slaughter and capture, and to rehabilitate confiscated specimens. At the center, called *Pusat Rehabilitasi Mawas,* one may observe orangutans being trained to return to their original habitat—a rare opportunity. Another rehabilitation center is located in Central Kalimantan for the Bornean sub-species of this endangered ape; both the Sumatran and Bornean species are quite distinct. The 2 centers are a joint project of the World Wildlife Fund and the Indonesian Nature Conservation Service, financed largely by the Frankfurt Zoological Society and private donations.

The center is a 45-min. walk from Bukitlawang at the end of a river trail on top of a steep hill. A canoe on a cable is provided for crossing the river, where visitors are met by a ranger who accompanies you on the strenuous hike up the mountain to watch the feeding of the semi-wild orangutans (on your way back down, take a bath in the river). The rangers will ask for a donation of Rp1000.

Officially, only 50 tourists are allowed into the center each day, but in reality up to 500 tourists visit it each week because the government is really pushing it as a tourist attraction. Hordes of domestic tourists drive out from Medan in their jeeps and Land Rovers, teasing the animals and leaving their garbage on the trails; luckily the center is well-maintained with an understanding staff. Rules and regulations are followed and the animals get the care and attention they need without being harassed. Furthermore, the rehabilitation station has great propaganda value. "Animals belong in their natural habitat and not in cages" is the message, and that message is worth transmitting. So if you have a great love of nature, are silent, and will only stay for half an hour or so, you'll be a little bit welcome at the center.

The Orangutan

One of the great apes, the vegetarian, tailless *mawas* is the Oriental equivalent of Africa's gorilla and chimpanzee. They are the most arboreal of all the great apes. Their name, in Indonesian, means "Man of the Forest." Orangutans make trees sway in order to reach another tree, and sometimes even use a forked tree branch as a tool to get at fruit. The simian has few natural enemies except clouded leopards which seize youngsters occasionally. Orangutans are loners and don't go around in large families. Their wiry hair offers protection from the rain, or they could use a big leaf with which to cover themselves. Before you go to Bukitlawang, read the Oct. 1975 *National Geographic* article "Orangutans: Indonesia's People of the Forest."

Acquiring Specimens

The *mawas* at this center were illegally captured and kept as pets in Indonesian homes. Even "responsible"

senior government officials in Medan still domesticate them, a legacy from Dutch times when to own a gentle, shaggy orangutan was the perogative of a colonial gentleman. As *mawas* grow older, however, they cease being cute bundles of wispy orange fur and become large, powerful 90-kg adults which bite, defecate all over the place, and finally have to be kept in a cage. The orangutans at the center have either been voluntarily donated by former owners, confiscated by the PPA, or captured from poachers.

The Weaning Process

Acting as a sort of halfway house for orangutans, it is the task of the rehab station to retrain about 20 animals at a time to live in the wild again. But the conditions in which they have usually been kept and the age at which they were originally captured (usually by shooting the mother) mean that most of the animals have to spend many months at the station relearning essential forest skills.

The tame and semi-tame orangutans are also studied, measured, tested for disease by the scientists; much is learned about orangutan behavior in a setting that is more natural than any zoo. Orangutans are susceptible to most human diseases and some arrive at the center in pitiful condition, traumatized, their fur gone from scabies, or suffering from lungworm picked up by walking on the forest floor. After a 1-month quarantine period and anti-polio and anti-tuberculosis innoculations, the orangutans are released from cages, but are still fed daily (between 1500 and 1600) when they come bounding and crashing through the trees.

At first the orphans are fed bananas and milk, but gradually their food supply is decreased, forcing them to forage for themselves. It is a very good sign if one of them shows up late for a feeding session! Giving the animals monotonous but nutritious bananas encourages them to search for more palatable food during their long hours in the rainforest. They must also learn how to climb and build nests in the trees and how to camouflage themselves with leaves for protection against tigers and panthers. Most difficult, however, is learning to become wary of human beings. Although magnificently strong, the vulnerable orangutan is an utter pacifist and never attacks. Its most aggressive gesture is hurling branches down at woodcutters below.

The Release

When their dependence on human care has lessened to the point when they seem able to fend for themselves, they are taken across a river (orangutans don't swim) or flown by helicoptor to a distant part of the reserve and released. Like a child's first day at preschool, orangutans are sometimes reluctant to leave their cages and venture into the unknown. Released specimens do not carry a radio transmitter which would be impossible to follow on foot, and the orangutan will not wear the larger variety of radio transmitter that an aircraft can track.

In modern nature conservation practice, much emphasis is placed on the conservation of entire ecosystems, including trees and plants, soil stability, and climatic factors. It is impossible to preserve orangutan populations in the wild without giving just as much attention to the preservation of the closed canopy of rainforest which provides the orangutans' lines of communication, their sources of food, and their safe resting places. The bulldozers and chain saws are the enemies of the forest. In the so-called G. Leuser "reserve," they carry out logging operations with the tacit approval of the Indonesian authorities; more than 4,000 ha have already been logged. This is why in the long run the timbering operations in the G. Leuser reserve pose the greatest danger of all to the survival of the released *mawas*. On the brighter side, a permit to extend the logging area to the reserve's full 8,000 ha was turned down in 1986, so at least there's restraint in their madness.

Accommodations

Bukitlawang village itself is very small with spartan accommodation in the **PPA guesthouse**; Rp2500 pp plus Rp1000 for a very plain dinner. The PPA guesthouse, which sleeps 8, is the last house beyond the village, directly across from the river. Swim and bathe in the clear, rushing Bohorok River right out the front door. Another PPA guesthouse, which sleeps 5, is outside the reserve and also charges Rp2500 s, but the food is exorbitant. **Wisma Sibayak** is next to the river; friendly people and good food (their fruit salad has to be seen to be believed). Mr. Burhan runs **Wisma Leuser Guest House**; Rp5000 with mosquito net (Rp4000 without), Rp2000 for the dorm, Rp1500 for the floor. Mr. Burhan can help arrange the jungle trek to Brastagi.

Food

Bring snacks as food available on this trip isn't the greatest. Eat in the *warung* of the nearby village (5 min. away on foot) rather than the guesthouse — too expensive. People are very friendly and some speak quite good English. Another place to eat is in several restaurants and a few *kedai kopi* in the village of Gotong Royong, 1 km back through the rubber trees in the direction of Binjei. Here the food is noticeably superior and cheaper than at Bukitlawang.

Getting There

The direct bus from Medan departs each day between 1300-1500 from Stasiun Sei Wampu on Jl. Sei Wampu, Rp200 (Rp1500 coming back), 3-4 hours. Or leave earlier by taking a bus to Binjei, then another to Bukitlawang. Buses depart for Binjei (22 km W of Medan) all day long; the last bus departs Binjei at about 1400, and you bump into Bukitlawang at dusk.

pangolin: Malayan for "one who rolls up." This nocturnal anteater has a narrow head which it tucks inside its tail, winding it so tightly around its body that you can't get your fingers between the tip of the tail and the body. The pangolin can be lifted and carried like a bowling ball without the finger holes. With a long scaly tail and sharp digging claws, the upper part of its body is protected by hard overlapping scales. The pangolin digs its way into ant or termite heaps, licking the insects up with its long sticky tongue. It has no teeth though its digestive track has miniature ones which chew up its food. Sometimes it plays dead on an anthead, with its tongue sticking out, letting the ants crawl over it, then eats them. Ants will also crawl underneath the pangolin's scales; it later drowns them in the river, then swallows them when they float to the surface. To harm one is to ask for 40 days of bad luck.

Buses for Bukitlawang can also be boarded along Jl. Veteran in Brastagi, Rp2500, departing in the morning. A more reliable, less crowded alternative than the bus is for a group of people to charter a Land Rover from a tour service in Medan such as Nitour, Jl. H.M. Yamin 21 or Worta Holiday, Jl. Brig. Katamso 32E, for around Rp95,000.

Hiking

Tracks lead into the dense forests of the G. Leuser Reserve where you have a good chance of seeing such wild animals as forest goat, squirrels, the *owa, beruk,* and jet-black monkeys *(dutung),* macaques, and *siamang* lurching through trees, as well as much birdlife, and superb botanical specimens including rainforest trees up to 50 m high. If you want to walk upriver even deeper into the rainforest, ask the forestry people or the Rehab Center (usually Europeans work here) where you can find *orang melayu* (forest guides). A permit issued by the PPA office in Medan (Jl. Sisingamangaraja Km 55) is needed for jungle hiking. For more information on exploring this reserve, see "G. Leuser National Park" in the Aceh Province chapter.

To Brastagi

Pay Rp50,000 pp per day for a guide all the way to Brastagi (2-3 days), which includes food (salt, plain rice, dried fish, *sambal).* Mudjeni has the best reputation. But whichever guide you choose they bring the food. You also get to sleep in a different village each night and each day take a *mandi* in the river. Tobacco juice is used to ward off leeches. Bring warm clothes because it's bloody cold at night.

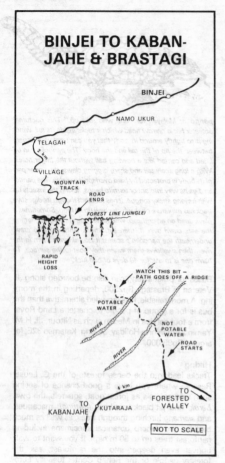

BINJEI TO KABAN- JAHE & BRASTAGI

BINJEI

NAMO UKUR

TELAGAH

2 km

VILLAGE

MOUNTAIN TRACK

ROAD ENDS

FOREST LINE (JUNGLE)

RAPID HEIGHT LOSS

WATCH THIS BIT — PATH GOES OFF A RIDGE

POTABLE WATER

RIVER

NOT POTABLE WATER

RIVER

ROAD STARTS

4 km

TO KUTARAJA

TO KABANJAHE

TO FORESTED VALLEY

NOT TO SCALE

Another shorter trip through the jungle (with monkeys and snakes) can be made from Binjei. First get a *bemo* (Rp250) from Binjei's *terminal bis* to Namo Ukur, where you can have breakfast if you've gotten a real early start. From Namo Ukur board another *bemo* (Rp500) to Telagah. The track starts ½ km from Telagah and finally leads to an unpaved road to Kutaraja 6-10 hours later. You should only attempt this hike alone if you're experienced and have a compass; if not experienced, 2 people should make the hike (with a compass!). Be careful of patches where trees have uprooted. Take your time, keep calm, and make sure you find the right path if lost (e.g. always stick to the most worn path in the right direction). From Kutaraja, take a bus to Kabanjahe (Rp500), then a minibus to Brastagi (Rp200, 11 km N).

NORTH OF MEDAN

Villagers of Kota Cina have found 23 granite Buddha statues, one of which is very similar to a 13th C. South Indian image. One intact *linggam* of polished granite and a fragment of another have also been found. These pieces of religious imagery suggest that the people of Kota Cina probably had at least 2 religious communities. About a ton of potsherds have been recovered here, two-thirds of which are earthenware, most probably made locally, while the remaining third are imported procelain and stoneware, mostly of Chinese manufacture from the Tang, Ming, and Sung dynasties. No other habitation site in SE Asia yet excavated has yielded so much high-quality procelain. Some of the potsherds possibly orignate from West Asia, perhaps near the Persian Gulf. Seven coins found on site originate from Sri Lanka, struck during the reign of Sahasa Malla (1200-1202), and the many glass fragments found in the debris probably came to rest here via South Indian or Sri Lankan ports. Several thousand copper coins minted in China plus numerous procelain and stoneware fragments indicate that direct commerce flourished between this site and China.

Belawan

The largest and busiest port outside of Java, and the third largest in Indonesia, 26 km N of Medan on Sumatra's NE coast. Notice all the industrial development along the highway approaching the port; before the year 2000 Medan and Belawan may well touch. After Dumai, Belawan is the second largest oil terminal and installation of Pertamina (the state oil company) in Sumatra. A large portion of N. Sumatra's commodities, such as palm oil, are exported from Belawan to every corner of Earth, and the port is presently being expanded to handle even more trade. The visitor can see long stretches of palm oil tanks from the main port of town out to the terminal, with a steady stream of trucks bringing in more. Rent a small boat to Pulau Monyet, a 30-min. ride across the terminal: monkeys, beach, and swimming.

Hotel Belawan, Jl. Indrapura 6-12B, is in a quiet area of town, expensive, friendly, pretty gardens, a/c rooms, no service charge, good food. Belawan is known for its seafood restaurants. Clean R.M. Malaysia, Jl. Sumatra 19/20, serves reasonably priced Indonesian food. Expensive Sinar Asia, Jl. Sumatra 36, a/c specializes in Chinese-style seafood. The Sudi Mampir Restaurant Jl. Veteran 172, also features seafood and Chinese; try their delicious crab. Restaurant Metro, Jl. Veteran 158, boasts an international menu including crab and lobster.

Port watering spots include the Hotel New Belawan's Aquarium Bar, part of the restaurant. The dimly lit and expensive Amethyst Bar and the Blue Diamond Bar are in the Passenger Terminal. The Seahorse Bar, also in the terminal, features a disco each evening; big dance floor, a/c.

Toko Bintang Souvenir Shop, Jl. Sumatra 64, has a wide range of souvenirs. The souvenir shop in the Passenger Terminal sells woodcarvings, *batik*, rattan ware, ready-made clothing. They will bargain.

Tanjung Pura

About 50 km N of Medan. Look for Mesjid Azizi, an impressive Moorish-style mosque. The downtown area has long rows of nearly identical shophouses and many Chinese inhabitants. North of town are many roadside stalls selling *dodol*, a fruit preserve.

Pangkalan Brandan

Northwest of Medan 82 km. At the Pertamina Complex, get permission to see the burned-out Oil Well Monument; you might have to see the HUMAS officer. Oil was discovered in Sumatra in 1880 by a Dutch tobacco planter, A.J. Zijlker, who was given a lease to drill by the Sultan of Langkat, striking oil in 1885 at 21 m. The Pangkalan Brandan well was the forerunner of the giant Royal Dutch Shell Oil Co., which started out as just an exporter of exotic seashells from the East Indies to Holland. The structure of Pangkalan Brandan is the first physically extant equipment of Pertamina, Indonesia's first national oil company which started operations in the 1950s with just a heap of scrap iron, a few old wells seeping oil, some rusted pumps, one leaky pipeline, and this first refinery. The monument has been bombed and burned by invasions, scorched-earth fighters, and Dutch "police actions"—a testament to Indonesia's tumultuous history. Destroyed and rebuilt 3 times, the plaque reads "No reason exists to be overproud,

as this ruin proves." Just outside of town is a monument of a freedom fighter standing on a giant drill bit. Heading N, just outside of Pangkalan Brandan, you'll see your first natural gas flare, the start of the gigantic natural gas field which centers on Lhokseumawe on the eastern coast of Aceh Province.

The Road To Aceh

At least 3 buses leave for Banda Aceh in far northern Sumatra each day for Rp6000. The border of Aceh Province is about 118 km N of Medan; a fairly good highway continues to the provincial capital, Banda Aceh, 488 km farther. The road may be flooded in places, so allow as much as 14 hours for this trip (6 hours just to get to Lhokseumawe). Catch buses to Banda Aceh from Jl. Rupat or from Jl. Japaris, near Stasiun Sei Wampu. (There is no longer a train running up to Banda Aceh.) The road is almost perfectly straight and very flat at first. River after river intersects the road, and all the bridges are OW. Pickup trucks are a principal means of local transportation, carrying as many as 25 people. Farther N are rubber and oil palm plantations. At Tanjungpura, about 200 km S of Lhokseumawe, you are not able to buy beer anymore; you have entered orthodox Aceh Province. The women in the Bireuen region dress very much the same as the women on Java, with *sarung kebaya*, but hotter colors. After Sigli (see the town and sea beyond through the trees), the road veers inland and passes through some high country with mountains to the R and the L, and rolling country in between. Meadows and pastures, interrupted by occasional trees and clumps of shrubs, are fenced off with barbed wire. In these pastures you'll see beef cattle, an unusual sight for SE Asia. The road then begins to descend, farms and people begin to appear, and Banda Aceh is less than an hour away.

ACEH

The northernmost province of Sumatra and westernmost province of Indonesia, Aceh seems a nation apart from the rest of the island and the country; it could indeed support itself very well from its natural gas revenues alone. Few travelers make it up this far because of Aceh's reputation for religious extremism (mostly unfounded); the province received only 1,721 foreign visitors in 1986, 650 of whom went to the scientific research station at Ketembe. If you don't wear shorts and braless jerseys, and you speak some Indonesian, you may find this the friendliest, most civilized province in Indonesia. Its hospitable people, historic architecture and remains, rugged mountains, superlative beaches, and picturesque rural areas will

make the trip long remembered afterwards. Two points to keep in mind: beer is largely forbidden to Aceh residents; foreigners can buy it in the hotels and restaurants. And *do not carry marijuana,* despite the fact locals sometimes grow it. The police search likely looking foreigners and throw them behind bars for a few (or many) months if anything is found.

The Land

Sumatra's highest peak, still-active G. Leuser (3,500 m) is in the S of Aceh Province, part of one of Indonesia's largest and least explored wildlife reserves. G. Bandahara (3,012 m) is another of the province's formidable peaks; fumeroles are still being created by both these volcanos. Aceh's lowland rainforests are immensely tall with hundreds of different species of trees, some up to 60 m high. The pristine coastlines have clear water and unpolluted beaches; the W coast is generally more scenic than the E coast: 2-3 hours from Banda Aceh down the Indian Ocean side is some of the best scenery northern Sumatra has to offer. The central region is mostly sparsely populated mountain wasteland, except for a few fertile districts such as the Takengon area where the Gayo people cultivate coffee plantations.

Fauna
When Marco Polo landed in Aceh Province in 1292, he claimed he saw a unicorn; it was most likely the 1-horned hairy Sumatran rhinoceros, restricted now to the G. Leuser Reserve N of Kotacane and in pockets along SE Sumatra. Gunung Leuser, one of the largest natural reserves in the world, harbors most of Sumatra's representative fauna. Tigers and elephants are concentrated in the more remote central and western parts of the province. A *matsun* is one who communicates with tigers, usually a woman much feared in the village; a *pawang* (medicine men) is able to cast a spell over crocodiles. The province has about 600 wild elephants. In 1985, 55 "killer elephants" went on a rampage, smashing homes, chasing villagers, and trampling crops in their attempt to reach the sea for badly needed salt. With the aid of a helicoptor and 350 beaters, they were driven back into the G. Leuser National Park, but by mid-1986 they were trickling back down their corridor to the sea.

HISTORY

Lying almost 1,700 km NW of Jakarta, Aceh is historically and culturally quite distinct from the rest of Indonesia. Contrary to its recent image as an "isolated" Indonesian province, the ethnic state of Aceh has been trading with Malaya, China, India, Sri Lanka, and the Red Sea for well over 1,000 years. During most of its history this state, which possessed a high culture and excelled in statecraft, has been an independent kingdom. But because of its critical location at the head of the Straits of Melaka, its territories were always fought over by colonial powers. It was through this northernmost tip of Sumatra where, traditionally, the outside "Western" world first touched Indonesia.

Early Islamic Sultanates
The 5th C. *Liang* annals of China mention the Buddhist state of Poli where Aceh is now. In the 7th and 8th centuries, Indian traders introduced Hinduism, and by the 9th C. Islam had made its first inroads into Indonesia at present-day Lhokseumawe. When Marco Polo visited Aceh on his return journey from China

in 1292, he wrote an account of the first well-established Islamic sultanate in SE Asia (it had already been Islamic for more than 300 years!). The small sultanates in regions such as Perlak, Bonua, Lingga, and Pidie were all gradually consolidated under one sultanate with its capital in Great Aceh (where Banda Aceh is today). In 1507 began a long line of sultanates which lasted until the final sultan, Tuanku Muhamat Dawot, capitulated to the Dutch in 1903. The kingdom fought the Portuguese almost continually after the Portuguese conquered Melaka in 1511. Fatahillah, the prince who founded Jakarta, is believed to have come from Pasai in Aceh Province, and local legend claims that Jakarta was settled from Pasai. Sunan Gunung Jati, the Sultan of Cirebon, and one of the 9 Islamic saints *(wali)* who brought Islam to Java, is also thought to have come originally from Aceh.

Golden Age
During the 16th and 17th centuries the capital, Banda Aceh, was a major international trading center that attracted settlements of such diversified ethnic groups as Indians, Chinese, Arabs, Persians, and Turks. In the 17th C., under the great ruler Sultan Iskandar Muda, Aceh reached the height of its political and economic power. During this Golden Age (1604-1637) the Acehnese had a representative in Istanbul, and even in the court of St. James in England. Its navy once held sway over virtually all of the Straits of Melaka as well as large tracts of the Malayan Peninsula and the Riau Archipelago, including Singapore. The tolls levied on shipping brought untold wealth into the state's coffers.

Colonial Resistance
Aceh was fiercely rebellious during Dutch colonial times. The maritime power of the Dutch East Indies Co. broke Aceh's economic control of the pepper trade, but when a Dutch expedition was sent to pacify Aceh in 1873, it was driven into the sea. The Dutch declared war on Aceh that April, which was in essence a declaration of war on a sovereign state. A bitter "holy war" *(perang sabi)* then broke out, which pitted the Acehnese against approx. 10,000 colonial army troops and the ablest field commanders the Dutch could muster. Aceh's civilian cabinet was reorganized as a war cabinet. At last when the *kraton* of Aceh fell in 1878, it had cost the lives of thousands of Dutch regular troops, including several generals. Decades of guerilla warfare and skirmishing ensued; smuggled British arms were financed in large part by trade in the rebel-controlled inland areas. Many cultural heros rose to fame during this period. In one of the many rebellions against the Dutch (1896), a guerilla band under the fearless Teuku Umar "defected" to the Dutch side, then escaped with a whole company of men, rifles, and ammunition. For over 40 years this rabid holy war dragged on, costing hundreds of thousands of lives. Muslim priests and

The Acehnese have always been known for their fierce resistence to outside control. Above is an old photo of General van Heutsz with his staff at the battle of Bate Ilie in 1901. During the colonial power's bloody 40-year struggle against the Acehnese, members of the K.N.I. (Koninkljk Nederlands Indisch Leger or Royal Netherlands Indies Army) assisted the Dutch. These soldiers consisted mostly of Ambonese, the gurkhas of the Dutch East Indies empire.

religious teachers (mullah) were military leaders. In desperation the Dutch employed counterinsurgency measures, arming their Ambonese troops with modern firearms and deadly klewang sabres. This tactic soon brought partial success, and the Dutch were able to build a railroad along the coast from Medan all the way up to Banda Aceh. But the colonial army was virtually barricaded in the coastal towns of Bireuen, Sigli, and Langsa. The turning point finally came when a famous Islamic scholar, Snouch Hurgronje (d. 1938), advised the Dutch on how to neutralize the ulama's authority over the people, and to break the bond between the ulama and the traditional chieftains, thé uleebalang. By the early 1900s this new policy enabled the Dutch to maintain an uneasy peace in the province. But the Acehnese were never conquered, they were just held better in hand. Dutch troops had to be stationed in Banda Aceh right up to the eve of the Japanese invasion in 1942.

Meet The New Boss

Under their new oppresssors, the Japanese, the Acehnese were forced every morning to face to the E toward Tokyo, exactly the opposite of praying to the W toward Mecca. This made the Japanese even more hated than the Dutch. In June 1944, the British carrier Illustrious and its escort Atheling raided Sabang in the Indian Ocean off Aceh. During the Indonesian war for independence (1945-49), the region was ruled by Daud Beureueh, the leader of an Islamic modernist movement. Even during their "Police Actions" of 1947-48, the Dutch seemed to have learned their lesson and pointedly left Aceh alone. During the struggle for independence, only remained republican

territory while the rest of the archipelago fell again to the Dutch. The Acehnese even managed to buy an airplane for the republic by selling national bonds to its citizens for gold (the bonds were never able to be redeemed for cash, still a sore point with the Acehnese). It was also during this period that most of the uleebalang (hereditary royalty), who served as administrative officials under the Dutch, were wiped out.

In the early years of the new republic the Darul Islam terrorist movement, based in W. Java, attempted to establish a theocratic state in Indonesia. The Acehnese joined the rebellion and it took from 1953 to 1961 for them to reach a compromise with the central government. Today it is still a very tender area politically. Jakarta wisely treats the Acehnese with kid gloves and has declared Aceh a "Special Autonomous Territory" (Daerah Istimewa) where Islamic Law applies.

Politics

During the war of independence with the Dutch, the Acehnese always remained loyal to the revolutionary government but they were never given reciprocal respect after the revolution. The Acehnese contributed the first airplane to the revolutionary cause in 1945, and financed fighting against the Dutch in Medan. In the 1953 Civil War in N. Sumatra, Kalimantan, and N. Sulawesi, although it remained independent, Aceh never raised its sword against the central government. During the N. Sumatra uprisings in 1965, Aceh continued to side with Jakarta. Recently, however, when the Acehnese wanted to hold a ceremony commemorating the 100-year-war against the Dutch, the

Javanese military commander forbade it for fear that it would rekindle the flame of regionalism. And today all the religious scholars *(ulama)* in Aceh must be members of a kind of spiritual trade union called *Majelis Alim Ulama,* enabling the government to better keep its eye on them.

Aceh Merdeka's *coat of arms*

Today, Aceh has all the advantages of centralization, that is—none. The Acehnese certainly resist and resent the fact that the Javanese centralists are taking out more than they put back. The Javanese don't really ly understand the Acehnese, and there is little historic, political, cultural, economic, or geographic relationship between the two peoples. Indeed, the Javanese attitude seems to be "Why should we develop the savages?" As a result of off-handed political and social injustice, military forays were mounted in the name of the Acehnese independence movement, *Aceh Merdeka* ("Freedom for Aceh"). In 1977, all the passengers on a bus were told to empty out and the bus was fired Freedom Rider-style. And in 1977 there was a brief but bloody attack on foreign contractors working the huge LNG field at Arun. Even as late as December 1980, Indonesian security forces claimed they had shot and killed the leader of the Acehnese Freedom Fighters, Hasan Tiro, in the jungle. Rumor has it, however, that this was a government fabrication, and that the shadowy leader of the movement is still alive in New York. In the face of sustained counterattacks by Indonesian troops, *Aceh Merdeka's* back was broken by the early 1980s with the death of 5 of the movement's 10 "cabinet ministers." Though now the consensus among the Acehnese is to stay within Indonesia, the feeling among these people is for more consultation and compensation for the wealth which Jakarta is gouging from the region. The money earned from 10 tankers of natural gas could alone open up new tertiary educational institutes in the province. Although run aground, the *Aceh Merdeka* movement (ASNLF) is remembered: the graves of all the leaders who fought the Dutch are still meticulously maintained (they don't show you the

graves until you've been around for awhile). The purpose in this is not only to honor them but also to make sure that the pride of the *Aceh Merdeka* movement is transmitted and sustained. The kids speak Acehnese until they are 3, and are taught legends and traditions; then they start learning *Bahasa Indonesian*. The governor is also a native son; even Jakarta wouldn't dare install a Javanese governor here. Aceh was the only province to defeat the army-backed Golkar Party in the 1987 parliamentary elections.

Economy
Aceh Province is one of the most productive and prosperous regions of Indonesia, exporting rubber, palm oil, pepper, cloves, timber, and coffee. Essentially agriculturalists, an old Acehnese saying goes: "Good government means good judgement and accurate weights and measures." The Acehnese cannot sell their commodities to the export markets directly—all goods must be sold through Jakarta. The US$400 million natural gas project at Arun is the biggest in all of Asia, expected to net Jakarta US$10 billion over the next 20 years. Formerly, Aceh was one of the archipelago's main producers of rubber, but the onslaught of synthetics over the past 20 years has lessened the incentive to plant more trees. A privately owned goldmine is located on the W coast at Tutut near Meloboh, and there's also a whole mountain of quartz in the area. Cattle breeding is another important source of income. About 70% of the region consists of forests, of which very little has been logged. Aceh has a surplus of rice and meat, and large quantities of fish are caught off its coasts. There is not the crushing population and shortage of land as is found on Java, and the per capita income of Aceh, not including oil or natural gas which "belong" to the central government, is above the national average. You'll notice the *batik* the people wear aren't as faded as in other parts of Indonesia.

THE PEOPLE

The 3 million native inhabitants of northernmost Sumatra are divided into earlier proto-Malayan hill peoples, the Gayo and the Alas, and the more recent lowland, coastal people who are a product of centuries of inbreeding with the Batak, Dravidians, North Indians, Javanese, Arabs, Chinese, and Niasans. The heterogeneous coastal Acehnese are taller, stouter, and darker than most other Sumatrans, an indication of their Arabian, Indian, and Portuguese descent. You can see all this by simply looking at their faces. The Malay- and Chinese-looking types are just as Acehnese as everyone else. As the Acehnese say, the word A-C-E-H stands for Arabic, Chinese, European, and Hindu. The older Gayo don't incorporate as much of the Indian and Arab admixtures. And they are not fighters like the Acehnese. There are even traces of small forest pygmies, called Orang Mante, deep in Leuser National Park, survivors of an aboriginal race. The Chinese minority handles most of the retail businesses, and they do most of the construction work. The students still regularly riot against the Chinese (the last a 2-day riot in Oct. of 1981), so the Chinese of Aceh are gradually converting to Islam and intermarrying in order to simply survive. At one time the Acehnese in some areas were not friendly to foreigners, especially the Dutch. But they have historically received bad press. In truth, the Acehnese treat you with the utmost warmth. Their hospitality, indeed, is almost equivalent to an abduction.

Language

The Acehnese have their own language (5 dialects), modified from Arabic, with some similarities to the Cham languages of Indochina. People's names, such as Cut Nyak Dhien, have obvious Indochinese origins. Until recently, there was no written Acehnese language, but now Acehnese is written in Latin script. Acehnese, though distinct from Indonesian, has many similar words, and *Bahasa Indonesia* is spoken by nearly everyone. Formerly, most Acehnese could read and write Arabic; the marriage law and the statute books are written in Arabic. The Acehnese often pray in Arabic and are still more likely to understand Arabic than other ethnic groups in Indonesia. The Gayonese language is closer to Karonese (a highland Batak tribe of N. Sumatra) than to Acehnese.

Village Life

Acehnese are very attached to their villages and invitations out to someone's home in a village occur frequently. Village dwellings, which are well cared-for, neat and clean, are built of bamboo with a thatched roofs. Multi-family structures, separate quarters are provided for males and females, marrieds and unmarrieds. The *kepala desa* and other village men meet at centrally located *meunasah* communal halls (open-air, pile-raised platforms), structures not often seen in other areas of Sumatra. Members of a council of elders in a village are consulted on questions of inheritance and marriage laws. *Meunasah* are also used as schools, sleeping places for young men, guest quarters, prayer sites, and for public ceremonies. It is common in this province for relatives and loved ones to be buried in the front yard of the family house right under the deceased's favorite tree. Sometimes only a small mound serves as the marker.

Marriage

Marriage is basically a contract between the father of the bride and the bridegroom. In return for the bride-price, the bride's parents support their daughter and her children. This sometimes includes the purchase of

a house. Characteristic of Acehnese weddings are elaborate costumes: the bride is dressed in all the finery of a Balinese *Legong* dancer. In rural areas for a certain period after the wedding the bride and bride-groom are not allowed to remain alone in one room with the door locked, and they are forbidden to have sex. To ensure this, their hands and nails are painted red and the bride's body is examined each morning by the mother to make sure that she has not been touched — all of which only encourages very subtle and contortionist acrobatics. After the wedding, the bride and groom won't usually move in together until they can give a big party.

Family Life

Strangely, in this male-dominated society, the family is matriarchal (although this is a relatively recent development). The woman and her sisters, particularly in Pidie District, often own the home and inherit the land. The word for wife is *nyang po rumoh*, "the one who owns the house." In Aceh Besar, the bride often receives a house as a dowry from her parents, or the couples may take up residence in the home of the bride's parents, though today many young couples set up their own households soon after marriage. Husbands are nearly powerless in the home, playing a minor role in raising children and maintaining the house. The Acehnese are primarily farmers, fisher-men, laborers, and businessmen. Like most people in Sumatra, men leave the village for long periods to take care of business, coming back during the fasting month of *Ramadan*. The wife manages the fields and household with the help of the cash provided by the husband (or her parents if the bride-price had been high enough). Wives are called "brides" until the birth of their first child. After birth rural women can't leave the house for 44 days and there are also many dietary restrictions. Her body is sometimes "roasted" over hot bricks which will make her trim and healthy again.

Religion

Aceh, along with Yogya and Jakarta, is designated a "Special Autonomous Territory" *(Propinsi Daerah Istimewa Aceh)* where Islamic Law is in force. Islam is incorporated into the Acehnese constitution, and it has served as inspiration for Aceh's literature. The Acehnese are socially conservative but religiously radical. Known as the "verandah of Mecca," Aceh was the first part of the archipelago to be converted. Today it is a rockbed of Islam, where — outwardly at least — the faith is practiced with unusual intensity and severity for Indonesia. Their traditions and daily lifestyles strictly follow Islam's "Five Pillars of Faith": the *shahadat*, declaration of faith; *shalat*, prayer; *zakat* the charity tithe; *puasa* (fasting month); and the *haj* to Mecca. Rich men are not respected unless they give to Islamic causes, and the poor have a right to expect what the rich have a duty to give. Even their games have a religious function.

But zealotry is relative, and if you compare Aceh with Iran or Saudi Arabia, the Acehnese would be flaming liberals. Compared with the rest of Indonesia, however, they are ultra conservatives. Banda Aceh, the capital, tends to be quite liberal in comparison with the countryside or areas down the coast. The Sigli area, for example, is much more conservative than Banda Aceh; in Sigli, you don't drink beer *at all;* and in many *kampung* traditional houses are built facing Mecca. Along with the village headman, the local religious leader is also very influential in village life. Knowledgeable in the Islamic religious code *(teungku meunasah)*, he conducts public prayer meetings and supervises the religious boarding school *(pesantren)*, the administration of which is not a village function. An example of the application of Islamic Law was the recent incident of the breaking of a thief's arm for stealing an old banged-up US$35 tape recorder. Cruel and unusual punishment? Perhaps, but stealing in this province is seldom heard of and there is no juvenile delinquency problem.

Yet, with all their strict adherence to the precepts of Islam, it is surprising that the Acehnese still give great credence to heretical, almost pantheistic practices. The Islamic judicial system *(hukom)* is the law of the land as long as it does not interfere with *adat* which remains very strong. Ritual offerings are still employed when planting and harvesting, and the interpretation of dreams and omens is widespread. Like so many other places in Indonesia, the religion has been adapted to fit local needs.

Prayer

It's believed that prayer turns man into a rational being and distinguishes him from an animal or a child. One's sacred duty is to try to pray with great precision and humility with full prostrations, touching the forehead to the ground while pronouncing Arabic prayers perfectly. Central to the Acehnese belief system is the separation between "earthly desire," which has a negative stigma, and "the faculty of knowing," epitomized by prayer. In religious schools beginning at age 6, young boys learn to chant prayers, read the Koran, and practice writing Arabic daily from 0600. At age 8 a boy is circumcised and he begins to wear pants. The society believes he reaches maturity when he has his first wet dream. It's because of this early training and emphasis on prayer that the Acehnese walk and stand so erectly. The Acehnese even evaluate a stranger by the way he prays, as they themselves truly surrender (the true meaning of "Islam") during prayer. Observe the Acehnese praying in public places: they give no indication of knowing where they are or what happens around them.

Christianity Vs. Acehnese Islam

Not only Westernization and colonization but also Christianity were all furiously resisted by the Aceh-

nese. Historically, the Christians have not had the most benign influence on the Acehnese. All foreigners who have come to conquer Aceh have carried flags with crosses on them—the Portuguese, the Dutch, the Batak—all killing for Christ. The Dutch and the Portuguese first came as traders, then their priests came, then the *soldiers* came. Many of the Indonesian troops who fought against the Acehnese on the side of the Dutch, such as the Ambonese and Batak, were also Christian. The Batak are traditional enemies of the Acehnese; in 1979, there was fighting and churches burned in southern Aceh in the border area of N. Sumatra Province. Ten people were "officially" killed but more likely it was as many as 50. The Christian Bible may not be translated into the phonetic, Latin-script Acehnese language, nor may cassette tapes of the Bible be sold here. But churches are found in Banda Aceh, even a Catholic church with a resident Italian Father on P. Weh off the coast. If you don't go to church on Sunday, you will probably be asked why not.

Conduct

Considering its religious orthodoxy and this society's highly structured moral code, Aceh's moral climate is not what you'd expect. Nobody is going to throw stones at you if you do nothing to offend the community. The Acehnese people are open, warm, friendly, and gracious. Just respect their culture, their religion, and their women—not so much to ask. And here, more than anywhere else in Indonesia, you should dress respectfully—no shorts or see-through blouses. *Sarung* are not that popular and the majority of the girls wear short skirts. Women always show their faces and you'll never see the full veils in the towns; it's more common in the *kampung*. A woman need not worry at night, she can go anywhere. However, the Acehnese are very quick to take offense if you don't respect their customs. If you get fresh with their women, just fervently hope that the police arrive in time to protect you from the people. If you tell the local people their society is too strict, they might ask you how many women are hurt or killed in rape attempts where you come from. Their statistics are undoubtably far, far better than yours. The rule is that if you want sex, you get married. Foreigners and local girls date, but they are strictly chaperoned. Though in Banda Aceh young couples are often seen together, it's not a good idea to hold hands with the opposite sex on the street, even if you're married. Be careful about photographing women; ask permission first. Dancing isn't acceptable, due to their over-protectiveness of women. A woman wearing a bathing suit isn't welcome either (women here wade in their dresses). Drinking by and large is not sanctioned behavior: when you go to a restaurant with your Acehnese friend, you will have a beer, he will have a coke. Movies are censored in Aceh *after* they are censored by the Indonesian government; so when you go to a 2-hour movie and it takes only 45 min., you'll know why. During *Ramadan* no one may smoke on the street during the day; if you do citizens will come up and ask you not to. All restaurants and *warung* will be closed during the day.

The Future

Acehnese society is going through traumatic changes. Men who once left the *kampung* on *merantau* to earn wealth to support their families now tend to stay away permanently and marry others. The influx of foreign investments, Javanese temporary workers, and transmigrants have created problems and frictions completely alien to the Acehnese. A schism between the generations is looming, perhaps overdue. The youth hear contemporary music, watch rock videos, meet foreigners, see movie stars, and when they start to ape this behavior, it's a real heartbreak for the parents. The split will occur all the sooner among the city university students who tend to be much more worldly and Jakarta-ized, than the rural youth who are more traditional in their customs and in their practice of Islam. The elders and parents must find a way to make some compromises, otherwise they will alienate their young people who are taking more and more to modern ways.

Arts And Crafts

The best markets are those at the mouths of navigable rivers, having better access to the interior where traditional technology still survives: sewing, metalwork, filigree, weapons—all disappearing with the introduction of synthetic goods. And the lack of tourism hastens their disappearance. Once renowned for its fine unglazed earthenware pottery, this craft is still practiced on a small scale in Aceh's backcountry. The pots are dried in the sun before being fired in a homemade kiln, then taken to market on bicycles in fiber baskets. Acehnese metalworking is superlative; lamps are ornamented with large bird figures, copper bowls are intricately engraved, and brocades are elaborate. Their finely crafted weaponry, an art developed over decades of holy war, includes shields with Moorish designs, and blades *(peudeung)* of swords and *rencong* with mystic Arabic markings, very attractive and unique—if you can still find them.

Gold and silver is worked extensively; gold jewelry is on the increase now that it is being minted again on the W coast of the province. The Acehnese identified very early with U.S. (New England) traders arriving here in the early 1800s: if you go into the goldshops today you can still find imitations of early American gold coinage. *Pinto Aceh* ("Gate of Aceh") is a form of traditional gold jewelry (Rp75,000-Rp125,000, depending on size), always wrought in traditional patterns in the form of necklace pendants, pins, or brocades. Gold here is sold by weight and you pay nothing for the exquisite work. Gold jewelry is occa-

sionally treated with acid to give it a reddish tint, considered more appealing than its true yellow color!

Still an active craft, Acehnese cotton and silk fabrics, embroidered clothes, and gold-threaded *songket* are imaginative and high quality. Pieces take several months to complete and you have to order them. The traditional Acehnese loom is made simply of bamboo with one end tied around the weaver's waist and the other end around a post. Silk weaving is done especially for weddings in the area around Banda Aceh. Embroidered pillow coverings (Rp10,000-Rp12,500) are popular all over the province (such as in Garot near Sigli) as wedding gifts. Acehnese also fashion fans. The Indian/Arab influence is seen clearly in female dress. For example, a version of the Indian sari worn here is much longer and doesn't show the midrif. *Sarung* are worn on formal occasions as a sort of corset on the outside to flatten the contour and add to the shapeliness of the woman.

Traditional dancing is now being revived. The *seudati* folk dance, popular in Banda Aceh, Pidi and N. Aceh areas, is put on during important village and family rituals, public holidays, and harvest times. It is performed by 10 men dressed in white trousers, long white shirts, red folded hats *(tengkuluk)* and wearing Acehnese daggers *(rencong)*. Some *seudati* groups enjoy widespread provincial and national notoriety. This complex art—a combination of dance, storytelling, and poetic recitation—is led by a *syech*, stage director and choreographer. The dancers stand in 2 rows facing each other. The *syech* then leads the group in a chorus of narrative songs, rhymes and spells, while the dancers move rhythmically with varying tempos, occasionally beating their chests and snapping their fingers. The stories revolve around local historical events, but can also convey criticism of members of the community or the consequences of neglecting religious studies. The government uses the *seudati* to instruct the people on birth control and health matters. In some of the more orthodox villages the dance is not allowed because it is considered too worldly and it lasts too long into the night. To hire a group of *seudati* dancers, it might cost Rp350,000-500,000. The *Laweut*, performed in the Tangse area, is an Acehnese war dance which features dancers in brocaded costumes accompanied by a sweet, solemn song, characterized by graceful dips and swirls. Only at the houses of foreigners do you find modern dancing. Special instruments played in Aceh are the 3-stringed bamboo zither, a vase-shaped drum with a single drumhead, types of tambourines *(geudrang)*, and the flute *(seurne kale)*.

Food

In the villages you can't buy *mie goreng* or *cap cai*, although you might come across a *nasi goreng*. The inland Gayo and Alas highlanders eat dried fish and venison; cattle are bred but their flesh, and that of buffalo, goat, and sheep, is eaten only during celebrations and *puasa*. Acehnese youths have been known to beat Chinese restaurateurs and wreck Chinese shops because they serve pork during *Ramadan*, and at other times *babi* is almost an underground commodity. The best restaurants for regional dishes are the **Braden**, 8 km SW, and the seafood restaurant with no name at Ujung Batec, 16 km S of Banda Aceh. Watch for polluted water; some of the *warung* don't practice the best sanitation. In the summer of 1983 there was a big cholera epidemic in Aceh which hospitalized 500 people and killed 30.

TRANSPORT

Getting There

Garuda flies out of Medan twice daily to the provincial capital of Banda Aceh in the far N for Rp61,900; from Jakarta, Rp209,900; from P. Batam (S of Singapore), Rp130,500. The Merpati fare is Rp155,100 from Jakarta. Access by bus is now also fast and easy from Medan via the 604-km fully paved E coast highway, 10-12 hours in modern buses, Rp8500 (Rp9500 a/c). Scenery tends to be dull: wide, flat coastal plain most of the way. More adventurous is to take the mountainous W coast road via Sidikalang, Tapaktuan, and Meulaboh, but this route takes twice as long. Most adventurous of all is the road through the rugged center via Kutacane, Blangkejeren, and Takengeon. There's no telling how long this trip may take. You may have to walk part of the way!

Getting Around

The 3 main ports of Aceh are Langsa, Lhokseumawe, and Kreung Raya. Smaller ports are at Tapaktuan and Melaboh on the W coast. During the Dutch occupation all these ports were active and well-functioning: now the Acehnese must bring their goods into Belawan near Medan and truck them north. The roads in the interior are ill-maintained; when the Dutch fought to occupy the territory, they established their military camps in the coastal areas and built roads all along the coasts, but neglected roadbuilding in the inland areas. Minibuses, open-bed pickup trucks, and *bemo* are used in the southern part of the province; elsewhere *bemo* and minibuses are used. Bicycles are everywhere. Merpati flies over to northerly P. Sabang Rp19,900; Meulaboh for Rp36,200.

The Road To Banda Aceh

Traveling N from Medan the ocean is never far from the highway, but it is seldom glimpsed. Extensive ricefields, oil palms, and rubber plantations have all but replaced coastal forest. Nipa palms thrive in the low, swampy areas. Traditional houses are sometimes seen sitting on 2-m-high posts with very low 2-gable roofs. With walls made of bamboo or the ribs of *sago* leaves, their ground plan is rectangular. Old narrow-gauge railroad tracks parallel the road much of the way N, but all train service ended long ago. Rubber and oil palm plantations 118 km N of Medan mark the entrance to Aceh. Kuala Simpang is the first town, 13 km N of the border and 474 km from Banda Aceh. Stay in **Losmen Mini**, Jl. May J. Sutoyo 45, Rp3500-4500. **Losmen Kuala Simpang**, Jl. Let. S. Parman 4 (tel. 31376), is the same standard and prices. So is **Losmen Teduh**, Jl. Jen. A Yani 17. **Losmen Mori**, Jl. Iskandarmuda 25 (tel. 31155) is the town's upmarket place; Rp5000-7500. Nearby gas flares light the night sky. Langsa is a large town, with market, 14 *losmen* and hotels, and *rumah makan* 33 km N of Kuala Simpang. Idi is a small market town 66 km N of Langsa.

HEADING NORTH FROM MEDAN

Lhokseumawe

This unspellable, unpronounceable town is located on the Straits of Melaka about halfway between Medan and Banda Aceh near one of the largest liquified natural gasfields in the world. Rounding a lazy corner, this boomtown is an astounding sight to run smack into after traveling for hours on a peaceful tropical road. From Medan, buses to Lhokseumawe take 6 hours, Rp5000. From Banda Aceh, 6½ hours, Rp5000; buses with a/c cost about Rp1000 more. The town center is a few km off the main highway. Enter Jl. Merdeka, pass the old RR station on the R, then turn R on Jl. Sukarami or Jl. Perdagangan (good restaurants on both of these streets) to the bus station.

Across from the bus station on Jl. Perdangangan stay at **Losmen Nasional**, no. 18, Rp4000-7500 s or d, or at Losmen Warga, no. 9 (set back from the road and quieter); Rp6000-9000. Follow signs for **Losmen Kuta Karang Baru**, Jl. Panglateh 8 (tel. 22492), Rp7000-17,500. Also check out **Wisma Kuta Karang** Rp5000 s, Rp16,000 d with fan and *mandi;* and **Hotel Mawar Baru**, Jl. Malikul Saleh 17, Rp4000-6000. On the way into town from the highway, follow the signs for **Hotel Dewi Plaza** with full a/c and restaurant; Rp12,000-Rp36,000. This hotel is disintegrating quickly, so hurry. The new 3-star **Hotel Lido Graha**, Jl. Medan, charges Rp35,000 for Standard rooms and up to Rp45,000 for Superior, with restaurant and full facilities.

Fresh fruit and snacks are sold near the bus station. Nearby on Jl. Sukarami are **Restoran Maju** (Padang and Indonesian) and the **Bali Restaurant**, the latter

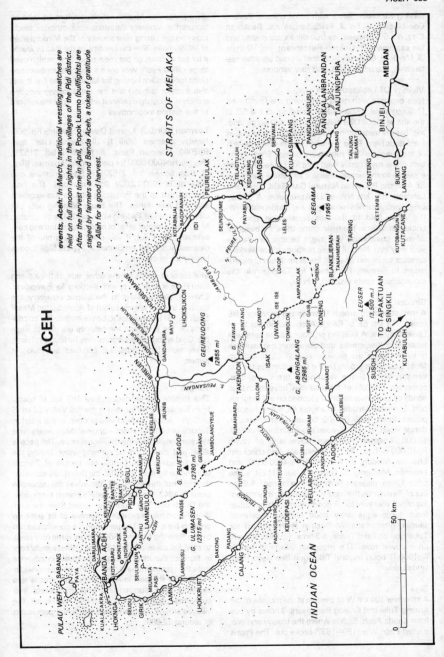

ACEH

events. Aceh: In March, traditional wrestling matches are held on full moon nights in the villages of the Pidi district. After the harvest time in April, Popok Leumo (bullfights) are staged by farmers around Banda Aceh, a token of gratitude to Allah for a good harvest.

serving ice cream floats with some unusual flavors. One block over on Jl. Perdagangan are: **Restoran City**, no. 50 (Chinese, ice fruit drinks, ice cream) and the expensive a/c **Golden Restaurant**, no. 1D (near Jl. Merdeka; Chinese). Scattered around are other restaurants, *martabak* stalls, and *sate* vendors.

Vicinity Of Lhokseumawe

Nice beaches with good swimming are found near Lhokseumawe. **Lhok Sukon Landing**, to the SE, is the site of Mobil Oil's helicoptor pad and barge landing; barges transporting equipment for the Arun Gas Field dock here. **Pase** is a small village where several of the queens of the sultans are buried. Some members of the royal family lived here for a time. The main entrance to the largest reservoir of natural gas in the SE Asia, the **P.T. Arun Natural Gas Field**, is at Blang Lancang, 8½ km NW of Lhokseumawe. A 32-km-long pipeline carries natural gas and condensate from the Arun field to the gas liquefaction plant in Lhokseumawe. In the main camp there's a beautiful 28-room guesthouse you might be able to wrangle your way into. Helpful public relations office workers conduct tours and give out literature. From Lhokseumawe to Bireuen, the turnoff for Takengon in the mountains, it costs Rp2500, 1 hour.

Bireuen

A market and crossroads town on the province's NE coast, 218 km SE of Banda Aceh and 56 km W of Lhokseumawe. A bustling produce market here sells tobacco, coffee, cloves, and cinnamon; it is especially lively during the tobacco season (June-August) Most tobacco is grown by the Gayo living in the Takengon area. Since Acehnese firms are non-corporate, one kilo of tobacco may have to change hands up to 6 times before it's loaded on a ship for export. **Losmen Garuda**, J. Langgar 48, is the cheapest place in town; Rp2500-3000. **Losmen Sari Murni**, Jl. Banda Aceh, is near Bireuen's bus station; Rp6500-10,000. **Losmen Purnama Raya** is E of town; Rp10,000 with fan, Rp20,150 with a/c. Also check out **Losmen Medan**, Jl. Andalas 1, Rp4000-5500; and **Losmen Mutiara**, Jl. Gayo 56 (tel. 21125), same price. Clean, pleasant **Norma's Restaurant**, 1.6 km out of Bireuen on the road to Takengon, is worth going out of your way for. A good variety of tasty, cheap food: turtle eggs, very good chicken, Acehnese sauces, giant crabs. At Bireuen is the turnoff for Takengon on Lake Tawar, a 3-hour, Rp1500 bus ride on a paved road. The mountain village of Isak is Rp1000 (1 hour) beyond Takengon (see Gayo Highlands below).

Sigli

A little over 100 km W of Bireuen at the mouths of the Krueng Tuka and Krueng Baru rivers, 3 hours by bus from Banda Aceh. Sigli is where the bloody and protracted Padri War (1804-1837) broke out. The Padris were puritanical Muslim religious reformers who attempted to violently introduce their othodox teachings into the strong *adat* society of the Minangkabau of W. Sumatra. See the remains of the Padri's *kraton* a bit out of town on the main road. Sigli, which used to be called Padri, was once a principal embarcation point for Muslims leaving for Mecca on the *haj*. It was also a major railhead and the old decaying wooden station is a nostalgic colonial edifice. Tour the railyard to see rusting locomotives.

Losmen Bakti, Jl. Kramat Dalam 19, wants Rp2500. Nearby **Losmen Mali II**, Jl. Kramat Luar, asks Rp2000. **Losmen Paris**, Jl. Melati 1 (tel. 21521), charges Rp4000-6000 for clean rooms. **Losmen Riza**, Jl. Blok Sawah (tel. 21527), is Sigli's number one hotel at Rp6000-12,000 (for a/c room). The little *warung* next to the Pertamina Station has excellent *sate* and *mie* dishes. The **Sinar Minang** puts out quite a spread of Padang-style food. The proprietor, M. Yunus, a former seller of medicine, is kind and considerate. The toilet, if you need one, is one of the cleanest and finest on Sumatra. Typical Sigli food is known for its curries.

In a coconut grove on the other side of the Krueng Baru River is a cemetery with sections for Europeans, Chinese, and Muslims; in the Islamic cemetery, the tomb of the first Islamic sultan of Aceh, Sultan Maarif Syah (d. 1511) continues to be venerated. The inscriptions on the European tombstones are almost illegible. Gold embroidered articles may be found in Garot, 8 km from Sigli; pots and ceramics are made in Klibeit.

Tangse

This remote rice-producing area 188 km (7 hours) from Banda Aceh is located in the Pidi Valley 52 km S of Sigli. A cool, upland village deep in the interior, Tangse is virtually intact—*original* Aceh where you still see people wearing traditional attire. The pace is slow, and there's still no running water. During the struggle against the Dutch, the people of Tangse were fierce fighters. By 1918, the Dutch had extended their control this far inland, but when the Japanese came in 1942, the Tangse people helped them drive the Dutch out. The Indonesian-based Save the Children Foundation operates a number of its self-help projects here. The "Tangse Hilton," a guesthouse run by the Save the Children Foundation, is the only place to stay. Eat cakes and bread in the Chinese *kedai kopi* in front of the market, but order meals in advance from the restaurant next door. Many people consider Tangse rice the best in Aceh; Robusto coffee is also available. The surrounding area of forests and cultivated paddyfields is ideal for walks; all the villages around Tangse have a combined population of around 12,000.

THE GAYO HIGHLANDS

The Gayo and Alas people are the dominant ethnic groups of the isolated lake plains and river valleys of Central Aceh District, around and to the SE of Danau Tawar. Isolated from contact with Westerners until the early 20th century, they live in a mountainous range with some peaks over 3,000 m, bounded on the W, E, and N by the Achenese, and to the S by Batak highlanders. These proto-Malay agriculturalists, closely related to the Batak, carry out wet rice and swidden cultivation (tobacco, maize, tuber crops), their irrigation water obtained from rivers. Having converted to Islam at a later date than the coastal Acehnese (in the 17th C.), the Gayo and Alas have their own patrilineal culture, language, and traditional arts. In 1904 the ruthless Dutch General van Daalen first penetrated these upland regions to subdue these tribes. Wiping out whole villages as he went, van Daalen meticulously recorded his macabre conquests. Since most of their area today is surrounded by the Acehnese, the Gayo and Alas have borrowed heavily from their neighbors; consequently, their customs are almost the same as those of the Acehnese, except for some groups deep in the mountains *(Orang Lingga)*, who still practice a syncretic 19th C. Islam/animist religion, believing strongly in local spirits, transmigration of souls, and omens. The Gayo are noted for their *didong* choral circle groups, frequently staged by local governments in order to raise funds for community projects.

TAKENGON

The "capital" of the Gayo and principal town of Central Aceh (Aceh Tengah), deep in the hinterlands (331 km from Banda Aceh). This sizeable mountain town, located on beautiful and placid Lake Tawar, is surrounded by coffee plantations. Some of the best coffee in Indonesia grows in this fertile region — the main producing area for N. Sumatra. Being so remote, the town gets just over 100 visitors a year — it's a quiet back-water with no souvenir stands or Western menus. You'll be continually surrounded by a sea of chirpy school children in brown and tan uniforms.

Takengon is renowned for its *didong* choral group; see Pak Armas. Traditional Gayo/Alas clothes, pillows, and tapestry are made in this area. Your hotel staff can put you in touch with the right people. Explore the market where sets of ornately engraved pottery *(keunire)* are for sale. And swim in the lake. If you have the time, visit the 2 Swiss guys in jail for possession of *ganja;* bring them reading material. Cannabis, some of the most potent in SE Asia, grows well in the

Aceh Tengah and Aceh Tenggara regions, though its cultivation is gradually being eradicated. Under no circumstances should you buy marijuana or even smoke it. And don't make friends with policemen in this town. Reports have been circulating that they will invite you to join them for a joint, then arrest you. There are even police searches on the way back down into N. Sumatra Province through Kutacane via Blankejeran. Don't go near the stuff.

Accommodations And Food

Cheapest is **Losmen Purnama Ujung Reje,** but it's a dump; they want Rp2000 for very plain rooms. Signing in at this *losmen* is no casual formality either: the form is more like a job application, and you'll be required to fill out 6 copies, one of which will shortly find its way across the police sergeant's desk. The **Losmen Danau Laut Tawar** is much better, with a friendly and competent staff, but they want Rp10,000-15,000. Here you only need to fill in the hotel register. Other choices are: **Losmen Batang Ruang,** Jl. Batang Ruang 5 (tel. 104 ST), Rp5000-7500; **Losmen Fajar,** Jl. Mahkamah 92, Rp5000. Although there're at least 6 other *losmen* to choose from, the best deal for the money by far is the 2-star **Hotel Renggali,** Jl. Bintang (tel. 244/245), right on the edge of the water with fantastic views over the quiet, unspoiled lake. The Renggali has tennis courts, patios, a beautiful lobby, mammoth bathrooms, and interesting people run it. Standard rooms are Rp25,000, Deluxe Rp34,000, Family Rp55,000. As for food, the whole town closes down at about 2000 except for several *rumah makan* in the downtown area where travelers usually hang out; *martabak* and *nasi goreng* are especially good. Another *rumah makan* over near the big market has better food, but it closes earlier.

Getting There

Takengon is about 100 km off the main coastal highway. From Bireuen S to Takengon takes 3 hours (Rp1500), sitting sardine fashion in a Mitsubishi minibus. This curving road has breathtaking scenery, and coming into town — with Takengon's crater lake and the surrounding cultivated fields, mountains, and forests — is a glorious sight. Another approach is by bus from Banda Aceh (Rp5000, 7-8 hours) or from Blangkejeren, NW of Kutacane. There are also direct *ekspres* buses to Takengon from Medan, 10 hours (Rp6000) on a real good road with the only bad patch in the lower section.

Vicinity Of Takengon

Lake Tawar is a big peaceful 25-km-long crater lake —

smooth as glass—surrounded by forests and plantations, a ½-km walk from Takengon's center. Because of local superstitions and abundant seaweed and algae growing in it, the locals refuse to swim in its cool water. A famous protein-rich fish called *depik* (in Latin, *Respora rectosona*) is harvested from this lake, one of Central Aceh's best-known delicacies. Rent one of the fishing boats and paddle around the lake. Bathe in the hotsprings and public baths at **Kampong Balik**. Take the local boat across the lake to **Bintang** village on the other side. **Isak**, 34 km S of Takengon, is Rp1500 (1 hour) by bus up in the mountains. Most of the people here speak only Gayo. Call on the anthropologist who speaks the local dialect and Acehnese. Another traditional Gayo village, only 20 km from Takengon, is **Angkub**; ask about local woven mats *(tikar)* with riveting designs. For volcano-climbing, get a minibus to the villages of Pondok Baru or Angkup from where you can climb G. Geureudong (2855 m) and G. Telong (with moss forest and rare orchids).

The Road To Blangkejeren

A minibus runs once daily (but not very reliable) from Takengon to Blangkejeren (and on to Lake Toba) on a track built by *romusha* (slave laborers) during WW II. This is a rugged ride through Aceh's mountainous center past seldom-visited Gayo villages with their long, low communal houses. *Do not carry marijuana on this trip.* The police search you! Tigers are considered a great danger in some areas along this route, and if you get off the road you can see their tracks.

The beasts come down from the forests at their "dinner time," about 1500-1900. Check with locals before going on an early-morning or late-afternoon walk! From Takengon and Lake Tawar, first travel S for 34 km to **Isak**, then on to Ise Ise by bus (Rp4000). At Ise Ise, buses depart S toward Blangkejeren, Rp5000. There could be a wait of one day or more. Or walk 30 km through forests (no villages but there are huts) over a mountain to **Panamban** village and 12 km more to **Rigit Gaib**. In In Blangkejeren, a minibus leaves everyday to Blangkejeren, 20 km. In Blangkejeren, stay at **Losmen Nusantara** (Rp2000-3000), or at **Losmen Juli**, Jl. Kong Buri 12, Rp2000. **Losmen Mardhatillah**, Jl. Besar 15, is the town's best hotel at Rp6000. Buy color-rich traditional woven Gayo fabrics in Blangkejeren's market. From Blangkejeren, buses leave for Kutacane each day, 4-5 hours, Rp3500. Kabanjahe is another 4 hours by bus, Rp2500.

GUNUNG LEUSER NATIONAL PARK

The largest national park in SE Asia, and the most important in Indonesia, the massive G. Leuser National Park (8,000 sq km) NW of Medan remains largely un-explored. Formerly a group of reserves surrounding the well-populated Alas Valley of northern Sumatra, G. Leuser became a national park in 1980. The World Wildlife Fund, whose representatives are in Bogor and Kutacane, assist with the park's management. Increasing population pressures in the valley continue to be the biggest management problem, particularly since the Gayo, Alas, and Batak immigrants are hardly phased by the rules and regulations emanating from Jakarta. These proto-Malays by tradition practice shifting cultivation, which is now illegal. Furthermore, the construction of a new highway along the steep Alas Valley has succeeded in cutting the park in two. November is the coolest and rainiest time of year to visit.

The Land

The park lies for the most part in Aceh Province, though a finger projects into N. Sumatra Province almost as far as Brastagi. A wild and beautiful area made up of full and submontane primary rainforest, lowland and swamp forest (in Kluet), and moss forest above 1,600 m. Plant species include orchids, dipterocarps, and 50-m-high hardwood trees. Most of the reserve is rough and mountainous, part of the Bukit Barisan Range, with G. Leuser the highest point at 3,500 m. The only lowland areas are the Alas Valley, and the lower Kluet River Valley which slopes down to the W coast of Sumatra at Kandang. Natural salt licks are found in several places; they attract all the herbivores, from elephants to mouse deer, and probably orangutan and some carnivores as well. The park is a paradise for primatologists: orangutans, *siamang* (black apes), gibbons, leaf monkeys, and macaques. Its colorful tropical birds include hornbills, argus pheasant, and many other species common to SE Asia.

Practicalities

First take a bus from Medan to Ketembe via Brastagi and Kabanjahe, 120 km and 6 full hours. The road climbs up and over the Karo Highlands, then down into the heart of the rich, rice-growing Alas Valley. Alternatively, Kutacane is a 3-hour ride from Brastagi. This journey, a graphic lesson in conflicting land use, offers some spectacular views. The reserve's rainforest areas are only accessible by mounting an expedition. Obtain a permit (Rp1000) to enter the park at the PPA office in **Tanah Merah** ("Red Earth"), 2 km N of Kutacane. Hours: Sun.-Thurs. 0730-1430, Fri. 0730-1200, Sat. 0730-1400. Before heading for Tanah Merah, get 3 copies of the front page of your passport and 3 of your entry stamp/visa at the copy shop in Kutacane (main road, easy to find). Be sure to get trail maps handed out by the PPA, and ask about the mattress situation in Ketembe, where there's comfortable accommodation (with sometimes only 6 mattress available). The park warden will help with advice, guide arrangements, transport, porters, etc.

Kutacane

A heavy Muslim market town right in the middle of the G. Leuser National Park, surrounded by steep mountains. In contrast to the slash-and-burn agriculture practiced by the Batak and Gayo in the park, wet-rice cultivation is practiced around Kutacane. English is rarely spoken here. In the town's restaurants, try *cicang anjing* (curried dog) served with *tuak* (palm toddy). If you have to stay the night in this town (a hassle especially for women), cheap accommodations are along Jl. Jen. A. Yani: Losmen Aceh Tenggara, no. 1; Losmen Lawe Mamas, no. 8; Losmen Murni, no. 14; Losmen Lawe Bulan, no. 77, Rp6500; and Losmen Kutatjane, no. 94—all in the Rp2000-7500 range. The best place for the money is Wisma Sari Alga with dorm beds for Rp2000 and rooms for Rp3000 d. If you have to wait for a bus in Kutacane, take refuge in the stationmaster's office away from the crowds.

Ketembe

A scientific research station on the Alas River N of of Kutacane. There are usually 3-4 scientific projects in progress at all times in either the Ketembe Station or at Bukitlawang near Bohorok, the site of N. Sumatra's Orangutan Rehabilitation Center. These efforts draw much local and overseas attention. Stay in the guesthouse next to the rushing Alas River (good swimming; Rp2500 (no electricity, so take candles). The rangers will cook food for you; guests may not use the kitchen. Also free camping area nearby with raised concrete platforms for tents. Eat in the basic *rumah makan* (Rp800 for *nasi goreng)* near the entrance to the guesthouse. Walk alone in the jungle on trails. Guides cost Rp10,000 per day and 2-, 3-, and 4-day treks are offered. You see more animals if you walk alone slowly, stopping frequently and sitting quietly. Concoct tobacco juice to fight the leeches; you see horrible bites on people who come out of this park.

In Ketembe, you'll find out quickly who deserves your friendliness. Don't give any cigarettes to the minibus boys—they're the worst hasslers, especially the one with the spotted face. They hang around your veranda, devouring the girls with their eyes for hours on end. Don't bathe nude, there are lots of sexually frustrated Muslim boys hiding in the jungle—some of them even with binoculars. Be extremely careful with *ganja.* You hear horror stories about the dope dealers and police working together; there are also checks on the border of Aceh-Sumatra Utara.

The Alas River

The Alas slices right through the center of the G. Leuser Reserve, dropping 10 times steeper than the Colorado River through the Grand Canyon. Starting from the northern face of G. Leuser, plunging through 320 km of the reserve, this dramatic yet delicate river

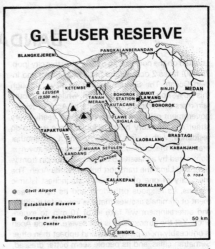

drains at last into the Indian Ocean. The lower part of the Alas is easily navigable, and a journey downriver by canoe or raft is a once-in-a-lifetime experience—a wild ride combining adventure, wildlife study, photography, cultural and natural history. Start your trip through the reserve from the village of Lawe Sigala, traveling all the way to the southern border of G. Leuser Reserve on the Bengkong River. There are exciting and beautiful river scenes with gorges as high as cathedrals, a relaxing and enjoyable introduction to life of a primary rainforest. The rapids here are not that dangerous: once the strong river current takes the craft, it's just a matter of steering through minor whitewater by day and camping on riverbanks at night. The middle portion of the journey has a few villages; later the river turns into paradise with steep limestone gorges giving the surroundings an unearthly quiet. In this section sidetrips can be taken to follow the animal trails through the forest and to visit elephant salt licks.

Long dugout canoes manned by up to 5 men are for hire at **Lawe Sigala**. Another approach is to take a boat from **Muara Setulen** at the junction of the Alas and Renun rivers to the Bengkong River; allow 10 days for this trip. Each canoe can carry up to 3 passengers and their gear. You'll need a permit first from the PPA office in Medan or at the Head Office, Jl. Juanda 9, Bogor, then make arrangements at park headquarters in Tanah Merah. A very professional tour group specializing in river journeys is the inimitable Sobek Expeditions, c/o Pacto Travel, Jl. Palah Merah 29F, Medan. They offer 4- to 5-day river rafting trips between Ketembe and Gelombang. Be sure to see Sobek's video, "River of the Red Ape," which documents the first expedition mounted on the wild Alas.

BANDA ACEH

Located on the northern tip of Sumatra, this city (pop. 75,000) faces 2 oceans: the Straits of Melaka and Indian Ocean. The Sungai Aceh River flows through this busy, noisy, shophouse town, while a big mountain rears up behind it. The capital of Aceh Province, government offices are everywhere; on nearly every street a single-story building looks like a well-to-do residence, with a sign that proclaims it yet another branch of the bureaucracy. The center of town is dominated by a massive 5-domed mosque; in front is Simpang Lima, the transport hub of Banda Aceh. The main city of one of Indonesia's staunchest Islamic regions, its religious orthodoxy and its harsh treatment of criminals assures that it is very safe; nightlife and entertainment will take all of 10 min. to experience. Yet the atmosphere is not severe. Banda Aceh is noticeably more prosperous and upbeat than other Sumatran cities, and its people seem better dressed, friendlier, more respectful to outsiders. You don't see that many *peci* and not as many veils as in other parts of Indonesia; girls in Levis ride motorscooters and couples walk affectionately down the street. Everyone prays in Aceh, if only to keep up appearances. One's first impression is its neatness, orderliness, and lack of masses of people in the streets. It got its first traffic light in 1978!

History

In the Middle Ages, this city was a huge multi-ethnic metropolis with giant international markets and compounds of Indians, Arabs, Turks, Chinese, Abyssinians, and Persians. At that time Banda Aceh was known as the "Doorway to Mecca," a stopping-off place for pilgrims journeying by ship to the Holy City. Great teachers, poets, and philosophers taught here; schools were everywhere. During the 17th C., under Sultan Iskander Muda, Aceh reached its height of political power, wealth, and cosmopolitanism. In Aceh's struggle to gain total supremacy over the NW archipelago, it engaged in great sea battles with the Portuguese (1629) and almost succeeded in capturing Melaka, though its fleet was destroyed in the process. Banda Aceh was one of the centers of fierce resistance during the 19th and 20th centuries, when the Acehnese launched a 40-year guerilla war against the Dutch, whom they fought almost singlehandedly. The wealthy group of aristocrats (*uleebalang*) which were ousted by the Dutch in 1872 when they invaded, and then suffered persecution and murder during the social revolution of the 1950s, today forms the elite ruling class in the Acehnese community.

SIGHTS

Kher Khoff

Cared for meticulously, almost affectionately, this Dutch cemetery on Jl. Iskandar Muda contains an estimated 2,200 graves of Dutch soldiers who died during the Acehnese resistance movement throughout the 2nd half of the 19th century. Nicknamed by the Acehnese "the former Dutch neighborhood," this is one of Aceh's main tourist attractions. Open usually from 0800-1200 and 1400-1700, visitors should first report to the office. Like a 19th C. Dutch "Vietnam Memorial," the names of the thousands of Dutchmen who died have been engraved on the commemorative wall of the wrought-iron art nouveau entranceway. The lanes of this good-sized cemetery are named after Dutch officers. The first grave you come to when you walk in is that of General Kohler, the first major officer killed while storming the mosque in the very first expedition against Aceh in 1873. Walk through stubbly grass between row upon row of ornate Christian stone markers and tombstones; there's even a section in the rear for Banda Aceh's Jewish community. Every 3 months, Rp250,000 is dispatched from Holland which is put toward the upkeep of the cemetery; the Dutch still send out an official once a year to see that the grounds are properly cared for. The caretaker, Mayor Bustamam, will proudly point out to you all the more interesting inscriptions. On the gravestones you'll see the names of not only Dutch who were killed but also names of German and Indonesian mercenaries (mostly Ambonese) who fought for the Dutch. Also some local Acehnese, considered traitors, were buried here amongst the enemy in disgrace.

Aceh State Museum

Called **Muzium Negeri Aceh**, this large 3-story museum on Jl. S.A. Mahmudsyah displays local artifacts, a great range of handicrafts, and ceremonial clothing (but with no exhibit descriptions). Free admission. In the same museum complex is **Rumah Aceh**, an *adat* a model of a former home of an Acehnese *uleebalang* (aristocrats) built in 1914 in Semarang. Open 0800-1300, until 1100 on Fri., until 1200 on Sunday. A giant cast-iron Chinese bell, *Cakra Donya*, sits in front of the building; it's said to have been a gift from a 1st C. Chinese emperor. Nearby are some old cannons and the gracious old *pendopo*

BANDA ACEH

In spite of Aceh's extreme religious orthodoxy, there are several churches in town; Gareja Katolik on Jl. Pante Pirak and a Methodist church on Jl. Pucut Baren. A good number of churches are also found in the transmigrasi areas to the S near the border of N. Sumatra Province. Take care with your conduct: in 1977 an Australian and an Acehnese girl were decapitated at one of the beaches near Banda Aceh. They were adulterers.

1. Garuda Airlines
2. Bank Negara Indonesia
3. swimming pool
4. Bank Bumi Daya
5. Bank Dagang Negara Indonesia
6. PT Krueng Waya Travel Agency
7. Hotel Sultan
8. Pusat Promosi Industri Kecil
9. post office
10. Governor's Office
11. police station
12. General Hospital
13. Mesjid Baturrachman
14. Taman Sari
15. city hall
16. Museum of Aceh
17. Governor's House
18. Anjung Monmata Conference Hall
19. war graves
20. Kher Khoff
21. Gunongan
22. Bus Station Setu

where the Dutch governors once lived, now the residence of the Acehnese governor. On both sides of the governor's house are the former billets for the Dutch military. All these sites were once inside a palace compound destroyed and rebuilt by the Dutch; now only remnants of a wall are left. About 100 m from the museum on Jl. S.A. Mahmudsyah to the S of the museum are some Islamic graves of Acehnese rulers, including that of Sultan Iskandar Muda; the tree there was planted at the time of the first burial. Another group of royal tombs, dating from the 15th and 16th centuries, is on Jl. Kraton. On Jl. Panglima Merah (Komplek Neusu) row upon row of former Dutch military barracks have survived, occupied, right up until WW II; they are now used by military families.

Mesjid Baturrachman

This unusual mosque (with marble interior) is a beehive of religious activity. Built in 1879 by the Dutch occupiers as a peace offering to the Acehnese, it failed in its purpose: all through the 1880s and 1890s Dutchmen were still dying. The structure replaces a grand mosque which the Dutch destroyed, along with the sultan's palace and fortress. The elaborate multi-arched facade is a mixture of styles from Arabia, India, and Malaysia. Behind the mosque is the minaret, higher than the highest dome, and in front is an expanse of gardens and pathways. The gardens have benches, which seem available to anyone who feels reflective or maybe just wants to take a load off his feet. The *mesjid* may be visited by non-Muslims during non-praying times: 0700-1100/1330-1600. Rules: veiled dress, take off shoes, get the guard's permission (at N gate), and women must not be in menses.

Gunongan

The baths and pleasure gardens of the former sultan's ladies, on the banks of the river on Jl. Teuku Umar. As you come through the front gate of the yard, ask for the key in the building facing you. The story goes that this "Walking Palace" was built for a Malay princess who married one of the sultans of Aceh. It enabled her to take an evening walk, not permitted women at that time. Some also speculate that this stark white structure served as an astronomical observatory reminiscent of one in Jaipur, India, built in the mid-17th century. From the top of Gunongan you can see a small white structure, the sultan's bathing place, on the other side of the road close to the river. It's also locked, so get the key first.

PRACTICALITIES

Accommodations

Very reasonable and good value. A 10% tax is often added to hotel rooms (and to restaurant bills), even in quite modest establishments. In town, **Hotel Lading,** Jl. Cut Meutia 9 (on L past police station coming from mosque) is an old colonial building set back from the street (tel. 21359). Rooms range Rp4000-12,250 with a/c; rather run-down. For less-expensive accommodations, also try **Wisma Sari,** Jl. Merduati 12 (tel. 22919), Rp4000 s, Rp8000 d with fan, Rp12,250 with a/c. Homestay-style **Losmen Lampriet,** Jl. T. Nyak Arif 7 (tel. 23995), is on the road to the tourist office; Rp6500-7000. **Losmen Kiyah,** Jl. Merduati 2, Rp1500 s, wins Aceh's rock-bottom award—no coffee, no meals, just sleep and *mandi.* Barely liveable.

A cluster of "medium-priced" hotels is along Jl. A. Yani, in Penayong (Chinatown). **Losman International,** no. 19 (tel. 21834), Rp400 by *bemo* from the town center, charges Rp4500-6500 s or d; comfortable with good restaurants nearby. **Hotel Medan,** no. 15 (tel. 21501), asks Rp9000 d with fan and *mandi;* clean but simple a/c rooms with color TV, hot water, Western-style toilets, run Rp18,000-22,000. **Hotel Prapat,** no. 17 (tel. 22159), next door to Hotel Medan, is Rp7500 d, or Rp20,000 s or d with a/c. Chinese-run, clean rooms, courtyard full of life, verandahs, good eating nearby. In the same neighborhood, try **Peng. Palembang,** Jl. Chairil Anwar 51 (Rp4500) and **Losmen Ganda Cendana** (same price)—both are dumpy (not that much better than the Kiyah).

Higher-priced hotels include the **Aceh Hotel,** Jl. Moh. Jam 1 (tel. 21345), right on the main square to one side of the Grand Mosque Baturrachman. An old colonial hotel built in ornate, gingerbread style, the Aceh Hotel is still trying to pretend that it is the prestigious 1st-class Dutch Hotel that it ceased to be about 40 years ago. With its stained ceilings, peeling walls, dripping faucets, it even *smells* old. Worth a walk through to try to imagine what it once was like, but don't stay there. At **Losmen Yusri,** Jl. K.H.A. Dahlan 74 (tel. 23543), Rp12,500 s or d will get you a mattress fit to be slept on and a/c in the bargain. **Hotel Seulwah,** Jl. Nyak Adam Kamil IV 1 (tel. 21749), charges from Rp17,000 s Rp22,500 d. All a/c rooms, hot/cold water, fridge, etc. Very nice people. Located right opposite a sportsfield, the Seulwah is quiet and has nice gardens. Near Simpang Lima is one of the best deals going in Aceh, the new **Hotel Sultan,** Jl. T.P. Polem (tel. 22581/23663) with superb service, restaurant, clean, working a/c rooms, and only Rp20,000 s or Rp30,000 d for Standard rooms (also the only place in town that accepts VISA and AMEX). **Hotel Rasa Sayang,** Jl. Teuku Umar 439, is a tattier version of the Sultan. The city's premier hotel is the 3-star **Kuala Trip,** Jl. Mesjid Raya 24 (tel. 21879/21455), with deluxe spacious rooms, full facilities, opposite a green park and only a 7-min. walk from Mesjid Raya.

Food

Acehnese food is as hot or hotter than *nasi padang.* They serve rice with everything, even with rice! Curried mutton *(gule kambing)* and *ayam goreng* are special dishes, and their dried beef jerky *(dendeng aceh)* is pretty good too, like a dry *rendang Minang.*

The best *gule kambing* is found at the **Samahani**, Kilometer 17 on the main road to Sigli—the locals love it. There's also a lot of dried fish. Other common dishes are: *ikan panggang* (fish), *sayur bayam* (spinach and eggs), and black twice-cooked rice dessert *(pulot hitam dua masak)*. Cannabis is common in Aceh and the Karolands to the S; it's traditional to cook with *ganja*, as in some of the Acehnese curries; very hot, spicy, and potent. The *ganja* base used in curry is a light golden green, dry, and only the flowers are used.

Fruit and vegetable markets are on Jl. Kartini, Jl. A. Yani, Jl. Cut Nyak Dhien, and Jl. Sibolga. Vegetables come from Takengon, Medan, or Brastagi. Aceh also has coffee (on the bitter side), Rp200 for a small glass; ask for *kopi tok* (always without sugar). For some of the best eating in Aceh go out the airport gate, and turn R at the WELCOME TO ACEH sign. Two stalls feature superb curried chicken and *kambing*, genuine Acehnese medium-hot curry, very filling and rich. A plate of rice and one bowl of this *kari* should do you very nicely. Bananas for dessert. An excellent way to kill time if your plane is late.

The *warung (mie sop)* opposite the Gadjah Theatre is open until late at night. Also at night along Jl. Tgk. Syik Ditiro are *warung* serving *nasi goreng, nasi padang*, etc.—a pleasant place to relax, enjoy delectable national Indonesian dishes, and take in the local crowd, only a 5-min. walk from the mosque. In Penayong (Chinatown), stalls, tables, and chairs are set up around the square (called, locally, Rec), facing Hotel Prapat on Jl. A. Yani. This is a lively and inexpensive night market: ice juices, *martabak, sate, nasi goreng, mie goreng, kerang* (clams) etc. Padang restaurants also face this square. Wonderful, cheap food.

For tasty Acehnese-style cuisine, go to Asia Baru on Jl. Cut Nyak Dhien; on Fri. try their yellow rice dish *(nasi briyani)* and *gule plik u*, a vegetable dish. The best Padang restaurants are the **Minang Surya** on the other side of the river opposite Hotel Medan and the **Dian** on Jl. A. Yani. Also check out the **Aroma Restaurant**, Jl. Cut Nyak Dhien, for well-prepared Chinese and Indonesian dishes. **Tropicana Restaurant**, Jl. A. Yani 56 in Chinatown, serves delicious Chinese food including fresh seafood purchased daily in the market. Their crabmeat is worth raving about, and the sharksfin soup is as good as anywhere in the world. **Braden**, 9 km from the city on the road to Lhoknga, surrounded by ricefields, specializes in Acehnese cooking like *ikan lele* (swamp fish), *ikan gabus* and *sia reuboh*. On the road to Kreung Raya in the fishing village of Ujung Batee, 16 km S of Banda Aceh, is a restaurant specializing in seafood—probably the best restaurant in Sumatra if not Indonesia. Only open 1130-1400. Fabulous fresh crab, squid, giant tiger prawns, and whole fish (Rp3000-5000).

Entertainment

At the stadium, bullfights and kite-flying competitions

are sometimes staged. At Krueng Aceh is canoe racing on Independence Day (17 Aug). The Gadjah Movie Theatre and the Merpati feature very tame love and *kung fu* movies, but these theaters are being put out of business by VCRs (prevalent in Banda Aceh). Coffee shops routinely show tapes at night, with everyone facing one way. Your hotel reception desk will probably be very helpful with advising about local sights and events.

Crafts And Shopping

Special crafts to look for in Banda Aceh include *rencong* (traditional Acehnese daggers), delicate gold filigree jewelry, and embroidered cloths and clothing. The best place to shop for *rencong* is at **H. Kevchik Leumiek**, Jl. Perdagangan 115 (tel. 23313); ivory ones cost Rp60,000-150,000. Souvenir models go for Rp4000-10,000 (Rp9,000-12,000 at the airport!). Mr. Harun also offers Acehnese, Chinese, and Dutch antiques—the largest collection in Banda Aceh. High-quality cotton and silk embroideries, wedding accessories, *opo adat, kain adat* and rattan and pandanus purses and handbags are sold at the excellent **Pusat Promosi Industri Kecil**, Jl. S.R. Safiatuddin 54. Several gold shops are located on Jl. Perdagangan, where you may observe craftsmen designing and hammering out their wares. Look for the distinctive *Pinto Aceh* design. The largest bookshop in Banda Aceh is **Toko Buku Muhammad**, Jl. Perdagangan. Near the roundabout in front of the mosque is a little row of shops where you can buy such rare delicacies as Skippy Peanut Butter.

Services

Change money at **BBDN, Bank Dagang Negara,** or **Bank Bumi Daya,** all on the main square across from the mosque. They give decent rates for being so far away from Jakarta. Open Mon. to Thurs. 0800-1130, Fri. and Sat. 0800-1030. The Government Tourist Office, **Dinas Pariwisata** at Jl. Teuku Nyak Arief (tel. 2241/23692), hands out well-researched brochures and maps. This is one of the best organized tourist offices in Indonesia. Hop on a *labi labi* from Simpang Lima (Rp200), or just take one of the numerous blue "DARUSALAM" buses from in front of Bank Dagang Negara (in front of the mosque), Rp50. A **public library** is at Jl. Darusalam (near the UNSIA Campus). **RS Zanoel Abidan Umum** is on Jl. T. Nyak Arief 6A (tel. 22616). **Post office** is on Jl. T. Angkasah.

TRANSPORT

Getting There

Linked by air and road from Medan, N. Sumatra (there has been no rail connection since 1968), well-built, modern and comfortable a/c buses with reclining seats, videos, fans do this run frequently in 12-14 hours, Rp10,000-12,000 OW. Try **Melati, ALS, ATS,** or **Kurnia.** Most a/c buses depart in the afternoon

(1600); non-a/c buses depart anytime. Book a day or 2 in advance to get a good window seat. The road has been improved by the oil companies (you used to see youngsters swimming in potholes up to their chests). Also 2 minibus companies—**Widuri** (Jl. Asia Simpang Bakaran Batu, tel 515734) and **Flamboyan** (Jl. St. Subroto 104, tel. 514363)—charge Rp12,000, 10 hours, leaving 2000 and arriving 0600.

Garuda has 2 flights every day from Medan, Rp65,000, 1 hour. Merpati flies from Medan 5 times weekly, Rp63,600 OW. The flights could differ in their routes, but you eventually arrive in Banda Aceh. There are also flights from Jakarta via Medan for around Rp211,600. From Pekanbaru, Rp68,100. Blang Bintang Airport is 17 km from the city, Rp6000-7000 by taxi. The drivers want Rp10,000 at first, so try to hitch a ride into the city with one of the passengers whom you've befriended on the plane. No moneychanger at the airport and the info booth is usually closed. Someone, perhaps Lukman, will meet you in the terminal and escort you to a hotel. Airline offices: **Garuda**, Jl. Merduati, (tel. 21305); for **Merpati** tickets, go to P.T. Kreung Wayla, Jl. S.R. Safiatuddin.

Getting Around

Roads are narrow, with uneven pavement, undisciplined drivers, and dangerous traffic. Traffic is all motorized, with motorscooters predominating. There is little congestion, fumes, or din, but the town isn't somnolent either. The best way to get around is to use *labi labi* (means "turtle"), small passenger vans holding 12 people, costing Rp200 and running everywhere in town. *Mesin becak* are cheaper than Medan. Borrow a bicycle; this flat city is easy to bike around in. *Becak* are Rp400-600; more for longer distances. Taxis (Rp4000 per hour, min. 2 hours) and motorcycle rentals are available for sightseeing though the hotels. Boats (capacity 40 persons) cost around Rp160,000-180,000 per day to charter; smaller boats are also available.

From Banda Aceh

Terminal Jl. **Teuku Umar** (in front of Rasa Sayang Hotel) is the long-distance bus station: Sigli, Rp2000; Takengon, Rp5000; Bireuen, Rp3500; Lhokseumawe, Rp4400; Idi, Rp7500; Kuala Simpang, Rp5500; Medan, Rp12,500; Langsa, Rp7000; Meulaboh, Rp5000 (9 hours, paved road); Tapaktuan, Rp7500 (15 hours, paved road). Buy tickets for the W coast at **Aceh Barat**, Jl. Moh. Jam 22 in the old town *(kramet)*. Most of these long-distance buses start at 0600-0700, but there are departures throughout the day too. Short-distance buses—for example, to Sigli and Lhokseumawe—depart from **Stasiun Kota** near the big mosque right in the center of town. From Stasiun Kereta Api, get a *labi labi* to the airport for Rp300 (or charter one for Rp4000). From Jl. Diponegoro, also near the mosque, board a bus 4 km to the old harbor area of Uleelheue, Rp300. To Krueng Raya, the new

harbor, it's Rp600 (35 km). Hiring a private taxi for use outside Banda Aceh costs an expensive Rp90,000 per day. Taxis to Blang Bintang Airport, 17 km from the city, Rp3000 pp (shared), Rp7000 (charter).

Fly with Garuda to Medan every day (Rp65,000) at 0805 and 1445; also Garuda flights to Jakarta for about Rp209,900. Very useful is SMAC, a specialized, efficient airlines with twice-weekly service to the W coast: Meulaboh, Rp43,900; Tapaktuan, Rp53,000; Sinabang (P. Simeulue), Rp78,000; Medan (daily), Rp68,000, plus flights within interior Aceh. Buy SMAC tickets at the agent's office, Jl. Cut Nyak Dhien 93 (tel. 21626). Instead of driving to Meulaboh for 14 hours on a bus, SMAC does it in 50 min. in a 9-seater Islander. A travel agency, **P.T. Krueng Wayla Ltd.** Jl. S.R. Safiatuddin 3 (tel. 22066), is most helpful; see Mr. Kumar. For ticketing, go to **P.T. Nustra Agung**, Jl. Diponegoro (tel. 22026). They give out sound advice and can not only sell air tickets, but book tours and help in chartering.

To P. Weh

Boats leave at 1400 each day from the sleepy old harbor Uleelheue for P. Weh (Sabang); Rp2500 (2½ hours). Faster boats depart for Sabang at 1000 every day from the new port of Krueng Raya; Rp2300 Economy, Rp3300 1st Class (1½ hours). Get the morning bus (Rp800) from Jl. Diponegoro (in front of Bank Bumi Daya) to Krueng Raya or you'll miss the ferry. SMAC flies to P. Weh from Blang Bintang Airport for Rp25,250 OW, but only Wed. and Saturday.

VICINITY OF BANDA ACEH

There's some picturesque hill country around Kab. Aceh Besar, the capital district where Banda Aceh is located, with mountains up to 3,660 m; you'll see much more of the local culture out in these hinterland regions. Very few examples of *Rumah Adat Aceh* are found in Banda Aceh. Besides the Museum Rumah Aceh, another *rumah adat*, **Cut Nyak Dhien Museum**, is 8 km SW of the city, a mammoth reconstructed many-roomed house with old photos and a few family heirlooms on display. In the old harbor area of **Uleelheue**, 3 km from town, visit Pasar Ikan when boats unload their catches; arrive before 0800 when you'll see the most activity. Probably the most remote private library in the world is at **Tanoe Abee** near Seulimeuu, a town SE of Banda Aceh, about Rp1000 from Jl. Diponegoro Station. Owned by Tengku Shaikh Abdel-wahhab, it contains rare 17th C. Arabic commentaries on *al-Quran al-Karim*. Climb G. Seulawah (1806 m) from the high, cool town of Saree, 1½ km S of Banda Aceh on the road to Sigli. The police near the market can help you find a guide; the steep climb takes 5 hours, 3 hours down.

Universitas Darusalam

Located in the direction of Krueng Raya, catch one of

the many blue "Darusalam" buses for only Rp50 in front of Bank Dagang Negara (near Simpang Lima). Cross several rivers to a wide, flat plain 7 km from the city. The modernization of Aceh begins at this university, which works very closely with the government in programs of change. *Darusalam* means "Peace," a name bestowed on this school once the heavy fighting with the Dutch ceased. Many of the students speak fairly good English, which they are eager to practice. Universitas Darusalam is 160 ha, has 13,000 students and 574 lecturers. About 30 Australians and Americans teach English and science here on contract. Also on campus is an Institute of Islamic Studies (I.A.I.N.). **Krueng Raya** is an old harbor, originally a Dutch fortification, with several bunkers and other emplacements remaining. It's around 30 km from the junction where you turn off to Universitas Darusalam, in all 33 km from Banda Aceh.

Beaches

Lhoknga, 15 km SW of Banda Aceh, is the city's nearest beach. From the Setui Terminal Bis get an *oplet* or in front of the Bumi Daya Bank a PML bus (Rp400). Lhoknga is the most scenic spot on the N. Aceh coast. Since Muslims can't show their bodies there will be no swimmers, but foreigners may swim wearing *modest* bathing attire. Watch the lethal undertow off this coast. The most popular part of the beach is 2 km beyond Lhokna village right opposite a coconut grove which echoes with the regurgitations of a giant cement factory, Semen Andalas Indonesia. Don't pay the beach "fee" without receiving a ticket in return. On Sun., as in any recreation spot in Indonesia, it's very crowded with citified Acehnese taking their ease under the row of palms nearer the village. Several *warung* serve meals, snacks, coffee. Stay with the villagers at the homestay near the golf course. Rent a *prahu* for skindiving and snorkeling, and to explore the coastline of the area. To an island offshore it might cost Rp8000 for a chartered boat, which should be arranged through your hotel at least a day before.

Ujong Batee Beach is 17 km E of Banda Aceh on the road to Krueng Raya; more beach areas are farther east. About 5 times more scenic than Bali's Kuta, **Lam Puuk Beach,** 17 km from Aceh, is a gorgeous white-sand shoreline which can be reached by PML buses from Jl. Tgk. Syik Ditiro to Pasar Lam Puuk, then walk 2 km to the beach. Breathtaking sunsets and you can stay the night in a small fishing *kampung* here.

THE WEST COAST

For P. Simeulue

Take a bus first to Meulaboh, 9 hours from Banda Aceh, then take a boat out to P. Simeulue (130 people crammed for 16 hours in a 30-m-long boat). Another approach is by bus first to Takengon, then walk over the Pusat Gayo Range down to Tapaktuan on the coast. From Tapaktuan, take a boat out to Sinabang on P. Simeulue, an area of vast *cengke* and coconut plantations. Friendly people. Food is basic. From P. Simeulue, supply and fishing boats sail farther down to Gunungsitoli, Nias, and to the port of Sibolga, N. Sumatra.

To Meulaboh

Between Lhoknga and the old Dutch lookout (68 km from Banda Aceh) is one of the prettiest roads in the world; it begins just 1 hour W of Aceh on this coast road. This is one of the most untouched areas of Indonesia, where tigers come down from the mountains to steal livestock. Visit the giant Green Cave at **Lhoknga,** and quite a number of bat species roost in Lhoknga's Quarry Cave. There's a waterfall at **Sarah,** 42 km from Banda Aceh, with nice swimming beneath it. At **Calang,** halfway between Banda Aceh and Meulaboh, is a real beautiful beach, an Australian holiday camp, and a deserted graveyard. **Meulaboh** is 8 hours and 246 km by bus from Banda Aceh; the contrast of ocean, jungle, and rocky shores presents nature at her wildest. Or take the Merpati flight (Rp36,200) from Banda Aceh to the airport, 16 km S of Meulaboh. Do something exciting? When the Seunagan River is in flood, go down to the beach to see it hit the sea.

In Meulaboh, stay at the reasonably clean **Losmen Mutiara Ie;** Rp6000, Rp20,000 for a/c. Good service, they'll do anything for you. Other places to stay: **Losmen Bandung,** Jl. Merdeka 83, Rp2500-3000; **Losmen Erna,** Jl. Singgah Mata 98-A; **Losmen Harapaan/Wisma,** Jl. Merdeka 27; **Losmen Kenangan,** Jl. Cut Nyak Dhien 3; and **Losmen Merdeka,** Jl. Merdeka—all in the Rp2000-5000 range. Eat at Restoran Tropicana on Jl. Merdeka. Swimming is safe at **Lhok Bubon,** 16 km from Meulaboh on the road to Banda Aceh; other beaches could be dangerous. Drive to **Tutut,** 60 km N of Meulaboh, the site of an abandoned Australian gold mine which ceased operations in 1945.

To Tapaktuan

The road between Meulaboh and Tapaktuan is very good, about the same distance as between Banda Aceh and Meulaboh. This west coast road is dusty and bumpy, but the scenery is exuberant—some of the nicest this province has to offer. The road passes over mountains as spectacular as Java's. **Tapaktuan** can also be reached from Medan, the bus using 2 rafts en route. Tapaktuan is friendly and has 6 simple *losmen:* **Gunung Tuan, Jambu, Panorama** (the best, with a/c). **Losmen Rahmat,** Jl. Supratman 61, is a homestay. Eat outstanding *mie goreng* in the restaurant without a name at the upper end of the main street; you'll probably see 2 attractive women with blue eyes standing by the door. South of Tapaktuan is Singkil in Aceh Selatan, the jumping-off point for the fabulous **Pulau Banyak** ("Many Islands") group, only 3-5 hours by boat (Rp4000). The inhabitants of these 99 islands (only 3 inhabited) dive for pearl, collect and dry fish, squid, and giant clam meat, exporting their products to the mainland. Another, even easier place to catch a boat is from Barus, just over the border in N. Sumatra Province.

WEH ISLAND

A delightful discovery. This small 154-sq -km island is the westernmost tip of the world's largest archipelago (actually uninhabited P. Rondo is more westerly), the other side of which extends 4,000 km all the way to New Guinea in Melanesia. The first settlers of Weh were thought to have come from P. Nias. Today the population is mixed, with Acehnese, Javanese, Batak, Minangkabau, and Chinese. Islam is the main religion but there is also a church and a Chinese temple. Tourists are welcome, and many come—one at a time. If you're up as far as Banda Aceh, it would be a shame not to take the ferry (1 ½ hours) or plane (15 min.) over. The town of Sabang is a sleepy port (pop. 25,000) which comes to life only in the evenings. Visitors may enjoy the island's white-sand beaches, as well as snorkeling, swimming, fishing, and hiking. Narrow twisting roads weave through spice groves and coconut plantations past scenic coves and small villages. With its good hotels and restaurants, P. Weh is also cheaper than Banda Aceh. Few natives speak English so you'll really learn Indonesian here. Though Sabang is administered as a part of Aceh Province, its atmosphere is more akin to a Caribbean or Indian Ocean port, or like an unspoiled Penang I. in W. Malaysia. It is, in fact, a sort of escape valve from Acehnese social and religious orthodoxy. The *rumah sakit* is above the town on Jl. Diponegoro. Change money in **Bank Negara Indonesia** on Jl. Perdagangan.

History

Sabang has a glamorous history. Though now only one ship arrives per week, before WW II the port was bigger than Singapore's. Most of the facilities are still there, decaying. Sabang is strategically located at the northern entrance to the Straits of Melaka, one of the world's busiest waterways, right on the main trade artery between Singapore, Melaka, Penang, and Calcutta—why there's so much military walking around. Sabang is also a symbol for *Indonesia Raya* (Greater Indonesia), used in the resounding patriotic phrase "Dari Sabang ke Merauke," the Indonesian equivalent of America's jingoistic "From sea to shining sea."

In 1900 it was a tiny fishing village, with an excellent harbor and climate. A coal depot was soon established by the Dutch here. The harbor was deepened, land was reclaimed, wharves capable of storing 25,000 tons of coal were built. Foreign steamships used to stop here regularly to collect coal, and water

from Sabang's huge freshwater lake, Anak Laut. There was a drydock for repairing ships, and a large oil storage depot. It is said that the Russian fleet took refuge here and coaled during the Russo-Japanese War, and the Germans used this island as a base during WW I. After Singapore gained ascendency and diesel ships came in, Sabang's importance as a port diminished. After WW II, the first Dutch commandos in postwar Indonesia landed here in Aug. 1945, liberating a small group of Dutchmen incarcerated by the Japanese. In the 1960s, during the confrontation between Malaysia and Indonesia, P. Weh was turned into a fortress. Today there is an overgrown, bygone air to this island.

Economy

In 1970, to improve the island's economy, the port was made a duty-free zone. In 1978, in an attempt to attract more tourist dollars, there was discussion about opening parts of Sabang for gambling, drinking, and nightclubs, like a little Monaco. Everybody agreed that it would bring in a lot of money for the island. Everybody also agreed that it would be better not to have the money. Instead, a decision was made to develop Sabang in other ways, such as installing cold storage facilities, opening the island up to industry, providing shipping facilities, and generally creating an attractive investment climate. In this way the culture could be maintained and island life would not affect Banda Aceh adversely. Luckily, none of these alternative economic plans have been implemented, and even its duty-free status was eliminated in 1986. Sabang slumbers on, of little economic importance nowadays. Copra and cloves are now the main products of the island, plus there's a fish- and shrimp-processing factory here.

Pulau Weh's great attraction is its natural beauty, rocky coves, Lake Anak Laut, hillside lookouts, the harbor views, and its marvelous beaches. The water off P. Weh is so clear that the seabed is visible from 15 m, with colorful tropical fish and bright coral reefs. **Losmen Holiday,** Jl. Perdagangan Balakang (tel. 21131), runs tours around the island and to offshore islands; see Dodant, the tour manager. M. Amin is another self-appointed guide you may hire to show you around the island for US$5 per day. Sabang has 3 tennis courts, and you are welcomed as a guest player without having to pay charges. The **Golf Club** has a 9-hole course near the airstrip. Don't go around photographing military and coastal installations or the airport; the police might confiscate your film.

Sabang

See the northernmost Chinese temple in Indonesia, **Tua Peh Kong Bio.** In front of the Sabang Hotel is a monument marking Sabang as the NW extremity of Indonesia. Merauke, a town in the far SE corner of the

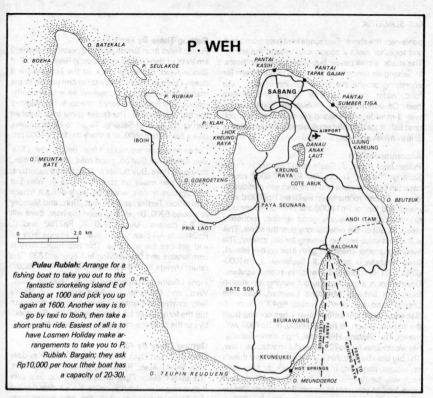

P. WEH

O. BATEKALA
O. BOEHA
P. SEULAKOE
P. RUBIAH
PANTAI KASIH
PANTAI TAPAK GAJAH
SABANG
PANTAI SUMBER TIGA
P. KLAH
LHOK KREUNG RAYA
AIRPORT
DANAU ANAK LAUT
UJUNG KAREUNG
IBOIH
O. MEUNTA BATE
O. GOEROETENG
KREUNG RAYA
COTE ABUK
O. BEUTEUK
PAYA SEUNARA
ANOI ITAM
PRIA LAOT
BALOHAN
O. PIC
BATE SOK
FERRY TO OLEELHEUE
FERRY TO KRUENG RAYA
BEURAWANG
KEUNEUKEI
HOT SPRINGS
O. TEUPIN REUDUENG
O. MEUNDOEROE

0 — 2.0 km

Pulau Rubiah: Arrange for a fishing boat to take you out to this fantastic snorkeling island E of Sabang at 1000 and pick you up again at 1600. Another way is to go by taxi to Iboih, then take a short prahu ride. Easiest of all is to have Losmen Holiday make arrangements to take you to P. Rubiah. Bargain; they ask Rp10,000 per hour (their boat has a capacity of 20-30).

country, has a similar monument. Tour the old port area with its lines of abandoned buildings, factories, warehouses, all the piers now disused and in shambles. The cannons are still there from the various militarizations of the island, covered with canvas, well-greased and ready for action. Many of the old Japanese fortifications have houses built over them. The harbor is the place for beautiful sunsets. About 2 km from Sabang, go past the old, disused swimming pool and continue a bit farther to a large pretty lake, **Danau Anak Laut** (Child of the Sea). This freshwater lake lies in a minor crater. Beyond the lake the road climbs to a good vantage point over the Sabang's harbor, the bay, and offshore islands.

The Coast Road
The nearest beach is **Pantai Kasih** (Love Beach), a 2-km stroll under palm trees along a peninsula. On the way are many gun emplacements; some are wrecked, others only lack the ammo. Following the coast 2 km farther is **Pantai Tapak Gajah** (Elephant Walk Beach). There's a grassy area here where you can lie down and have a picnic practically undisturbed. From Tapak Gajah, take a shortcut back to Sabang over the peninsula or continue along the coast 3 km to **Pantai Sumber Tiga** (Well Number Three Beach), the

island's best. Turn in at the big concrete gun emplacement and walk down the trail. The fresh sweetwater well by the beach is *sumber tiga*, where nearby villagers get their water. The beach, one of the most scenic in Indonesia, is a great place to swim and snorkel with crystal-clear water, coral, and the whitest, softest sand. Yet it is nearly deserted, even on weekends. From Sabang, a taxi can take you here for Rp5000 OW and will fetch you at an appointed time. Pay the driver upon his return to make sure he'll be there (it's a long walk back to town!).

The rocky coastline near **Ujung Kareung**, 2 km beyond Pantai Sumur Tiga, has small beaches, plenty of brain coral, goats wandering the beach, and good fishing from the rocks. Hunt for starfish in the crevices near the shore. A trail from here climbs up to the airport and main road. The narrow coast road continues S past Anoi Itam, then turns inland and abruptly ends 10 km beyond Ujung Kareung. From the road's end you can walk straight ahead 1 km on a footpath which drops sharply to the coast near Balohan, the island's harbor 12 km S of Sabang. **Keuneukei Hot Springs** is about 20 km S of Sabang. Take a minibus from Sabang for Rp1000, but it's easy to hitch back to Sabang. People of this village have built small bathing pools near the shore. Two roads lead here from town and together make a scenic loop around the island. The roads are all paved but expect some potholes. In Sabang equipment can be rented or purchased for snorkeling around the small outlying islands. Take food, water, insect repellent, fishing and cooking gear. On unpopulated P. Rubiah are coral gardens with 1-m-wide pearl-shaped clams and tropical colored fish. It's a beautiful small island with remnants of British mines and a big house in ruins.

Accommodations

Pulau Jaya Hotel, Jl. Seulawah 17 (across from the Sabang Theatre), is popular; Rp4000-6000 rooms have fan but thin walls and only a screen partition at the top. Quieter rooms (solid walls) are Rp7000 d with *mandi* and fan, or Rp14,000 a/c. Bathrooms are outside the rooms, no meals, good lighting, spotlessly clean. Sit out on the nice balcony over the street. This is the best-value hotel in Sabang for the money. The friendly manager speaks English (rare on this island). **Irma Losmen** is nearby, Jl. Seulawah 3, Rp4000-6000 with fan (but thin walls) in rooms upstairs. Downstairs is a good restaurant serving Indonesian food. The **Sabang Merauke Losmen**, near Irma Losmen and the cinema, costs Rp4000 s or d. **Sabang Hotel**, just before town when coming from the ferry or airport, is Rp4000-8000, or Rp7000 with *mandi*. The **Sabang Hill Hotel**, high above Sabang, has a/c doubles for Rp20,000, and a spectacular view. The big drawback is that it's out of town and there's no regular transport; it's a long walk, or take taxis each way for Rp2500. Also the Sabang Hill doesn't serve food so you have to go into town to eat. Also try **Raja Wali Losmen** in town center, Rp4000 s, Rp6000 d.

Food

Out on the street at night *gado-gado, sate*, and *martabak* are sold. Delicious and reasonable spicy-hot Padang-style food can be enjoyed at **RM Minang** (next to Sabang Merauke Losmen). **Restaurant Irma** is good for a variety of Indonesian foods. **Restaurant Selecta** on the main street offers Chinese-style dishes. The best place for Chinese is at **Ten Sun's Restaurant**, inside his house down a little side lane off the main street (Jl. Perdagangan), between the Selecta and Toko Majatex. Open 1200-2300 every day, the restaurant is run by Ten Sun, an old Chinese who speaks little English. There's no menu but he will tell you what's on hand. Ask Ten Sun if you may see his old photos and rare wide-angle postcards showing Sabang in its heyday. This town used to have elegant nightclubs, fine restaurants, and private clubs. One photo of Sabang's harbor before the Great War shows 16 major-sized steamers. Another has a Dutch ship that had just arrived with all the passengers coming down the gangplank wearing pith helmets and white shorts; German cruisers are in the background. It appears as if that era would never end.

Getting There By Ferry

Ferries leave from Banda Aceh's 2 ports, Uleelheue, 9 km W of Banda Aceh, and Krueng Raya, 35 km E of Banda Aceh. Sit in the back of the boat where it doesn't rock as much. It only takes one person to get *mabuk* before other Indonesians have a sympathy *mabuk*, which they are very prone to. In fine weather the trip is enjoyable. The ferries come in at Balohan Harbor, 12 km S of Sabang. To get to Sabang town, take a *bemo* for Rp500, or a share-taxi for Rp4000 pp.

Get an early-morning minibus from Banda Aceh's Stasiun Kereta Api Station, good road, Rp800, 30 min., to Kreung Raya. Buy tickets an hour before departure. Bicycles can easily be taken along to P. Weh but motorcycles or cars would be more difficult (check with office). Ferries leave Fri., Sat., Sun., and Monday at around 0900. Depending upon the boat, there will be 2-3 classes: AA, Rp3300; A, Rp2750; and C, Rp2400. In AA class you sit in an a/c lounge with TV and get free tea or coffee. This twin-hulled ferry is comfortable and fast, arriving in 1 hour at 1830. The return voyage from Balohan (P. Sabang) is at 0800.

From Uleelheue, departures are at 1400 on Tues., Wed., and Thursday. The ferry arrives in P. Weh's ferry terminal at Balohan 3 hours later. On the return trip the ferry leaves for Uleelheue at 0700. Say goodbye to the tip of the longest island chain in the world.

Getting There By Air

SMAC (Jl. Cut Nyak Dhien 93, tel. 21626) flies daily from Banda Aceh, Rp25,000, an exhilarating flight. The small 8-seater Piper takes off and you soar over the very tip of northern Sumatra. If it's a clear day the visibility is almost unlimited. The pilot circles lazily over the eastern portion of P. Weh, really close to the coast with turquoise shorelines and secret beaches that you can only climb down to. Just before the plane lands at Sabang Airport, a guy goes out on a bicycle and chases all the goats, water buffalos, and cows off the grass runway. By taxi it costs Rp5000 pp into the city, right to the Sabang Hill Hotel if desired. The plane stays in Sabang 45 minutes. There's also a SMAC office in Sabang. Merpati also does this flight for Rp19,100.

Getting Around

Vehicles meet boats and planes, and Holden Specials (Rp7000 per day) and minibuses (Rp500 for 10 km ride) travel the roads of the island frequently. To enjoy the views and fresh air, walking is the best; some of the beaches and sights are easily reached on foot. Bicycles are only used around town and along the E coast road because of very hilly terrain elsewhere. So if you bring your own 10-speed, you're all set. Ask your hotel proprietor about motorcycle rental. Taxis could be handy for exploring the island: Pantai Tapak Gajah, Rp2500-3000; Pantai Sumber Tiga, Rp5000; Balohan Harbor, Rp8000, etc. A taxi stand is right on Sabang's Jl. Perdagangan.

NUSATENGGARA

A fascinating experience for the hardy traveler, Nusatenggara is home to hundreds of ethnic groups who speak scores of different languages and dialects and hold widespread beliefs in magic. Flores and Sumba produce some of the most exquisite handwoven ikat of Indonesia. Another of the area's striking cultural characteristics is the great variety of adat architecture: the Balinese-style temples of Lombok, the shaggy, elliptical thatch houses of Timor, and the Sumbanese native houses which resemble a gigantic straw hat. On Sumbawa megaliths are carved in cryptic reliefs, and on Sumba massive stone-slab tombs sit in front yards of houses. Astounding natural wonders include Komodo's 3-m-long monitor lizards, the colored volcanic lakes of Keli Mutu, superlative snorkeling with 100-m drop-offs on Flores, seashell collecting on Gili Trawangan off NW Lombok, the virgin game reserve of P. Moyo on Flores, and the huge rocks of Amanuban in W. Timor, which look like the ruins of ancient castles. The area is also rich in dances, fighting arts, animist ceremonies, and unique religious holidays.

Varanus komodensis

INTRODUCTION

Stretching 1,500 km E from Java, the Lesser Sundas include the 6 major islands of Bali, Lombok, Sumbawa, Sumba, Flores, and Timor, as well as hundreds of smaller islands and islets. The northern string of islands is a continuation of the volcanic belt that runs through Sumatra and Java as far E as Banda, while Sumba, Sawu, Roti, and Timor, forming the "Outer Arc" of the Lesser Sundas, are non-volcanic. This entire region is known as Nusatenggara, meaning "Southeastern Islands." Administratively, the islands are further divided into Nusatenggara Barat (or NTB, including Lombok and Sumbawa), Nusatenggara Timur (NTT, comprising Sumba, Flores, and W. Timor), with provincial capitals at Mataram (Lombok) and Kupang (W. Timor), respectively. These divisions exclude Bali, which has been a separate province since 1951, and the province of E. Timor, which is closed to travelers.

Nusatenggara also includes some of the country's poorest, least productive and developed areas. Though the government in recent years has greatly improved communications, transportation, education, and tourism facilities, Nusatenggara's infrastructure is still in its developing stages. Tourism in the region was given a tremendous boost in 1986 with

the inauguration of Merpati's Thurs. and Sat. Darwin-Kupang flight (for only A$175), bringing thousands of travelers into Nusatenggara each year and spawning a mini travel industry in Timor and neighboring islands. Now there are flights to such outlying islands as Roti, Sawu, Lembata, and Alor. Ships loop regularly around this small archipelago, and ferries connect all the main islands. Travel here can be inexpensive; 2 months could cost you only US$500 for all food, accommodations, and transport.

The Land And Climate

Nusatenggara comprises less than 4% of Indonesia's total land area. Unlike Bali and Java, these islands are typically steep and mountainous, with narrow coastal plains and little arable land, and are surrounded by deep seas and fierce currents. Forests are much less widespread than elsewhere in Indonesia; instead, most of the land is covered with dry savannah, scrub and open grassland, eucalyptus groves and monsoon forest. The region is characterized by prolonged dry seasons interrupted by often heavy rains. Dry months are Aug. and Sept., though droughts sometimes last months and even *years*—especially on Sumba and Timor, which are raked by hot winds blowing N from the Australian deserts. The wet season is Nov. to

June, when the arid landscapes turn a lush green, dry riverbeds roar with floodwaters, and dirt roads become impassable quagmires. Timor and the nearby islands are the only region in Indonesia hit by tropical cyclones, at a rate of 3-5 per year.

Flora And Fauna

About 120 million years ago, melting ice caps cleaved Bali and Lombok apart, creating the 48-km-wide, 600-m-deep Lombok Strait, the archipelago's deepest. The strait marks the so-called "Wallace Line," named after the great naturalist Sir Alfred Wallace. Sir Alfred observed, after years of zoological and botanical research, that on all the islands W of Lombok are found tropical vegetation, monkeys, elephants, tigers, wild cattle, and straight-haired Asiatics, while on the islands E of Bali are thorny arid plants, cockatoos, parrots, giant lizards, marsupials, and frizzy-haired Papuans—all lifeforms typical of Australia. The more advanced placental animals and flora which were beginning to evolve at that time in Asia proper could not cross the turbulent strait between the 2 islands. Thus, zoological Model-T Fords such as kangaroos and echidnas were allowed to proliferate on the islands E of Bali and Australia because of the absence of predatory mammals.

On the easternmost islands of the chain reside the spectacular New Guinea parrots plus a few Australian species like the cockatoos and honeyeaters which braved the 480-km hop across the Timor Sea. Other than these, Nusatenggara is remarkable for the scarcity of its bird species. Whereas Java and Bali have nearly 200 breeding species of Asiatic birds, across the Lombok Strait on Lombok there are 68 less. Beyond Lombok is the Alas Strait and the island of Sumbawa, with 10 fewer species still. By P. Wetar at the end of the island chain, 122 species have been stopped by these ancient ocean gaps. Other classes of animals, such as the Asiatic fishes, were nearly cut off altogether.

The People

Population is estimated at close to 10 million, a highly diverse and fragmented cultural conglomeration with hundreds of ethnic and linguistic distinctions. Racial types are very complex, especially on Flores and Timor, where not only Malays and mixed-blood Portuguese are found, but also descendants of even earlier Veddoids, Negritos, archaic Melanesians, and Australoids. Many of these peoples still exhibit the rudiments of ancient cultures, with beliefs in spirits, ancestor cults, and magic prevalent. For the most part, the people are friendly (except for the crazies). But you should know beforehand that you'll cause a great stir when you venture into the interior of the islands where Westerners are such a rarity. In some outlying villages, a hundred people may crowd around you, wanting to touch the hair on your white skin. It's amusing at first, but can grow annoying in a hurry. Just try to grin and bear your unwanted notoriety. On the other hand, in certain areas, such as parts of Flores, isolated villagers may be quite hostile to outsiders, so be wary. And in predominantly Muslim territory like E. Lombok and Sumbawa, respect the conservative codes of dress and behavior lest you incur local disfavor, which can even result in fruit and rock throwing. To some groups, travelers represent a cultural threat, and people have been stoned for dressing "indecently." Women should wear bras, long pants, or skirts, and full shirts or blouses. Unfortunately, women who travel alone through the heavily Islamicized islands should expect to get hassled.

Religion

Already by 1577, the Portuguese claimed there were 50,000 Catholics in the Lesser Sundas. Having been converted over the last 4 centuries by Portuguese and Dutch missionaries, most of the population of NTT is today at least nominally Catholic or Protestant. Muslims are the majority on Lombok and Sumbawa, but Lombok also has a sizeable faction of Hindu Balinese. On Timor, it's about half and half, yet the neighboring island of Roti (off W. Timor) is almost all Christian. Despite the veneer of Christianity or Islam, animism is still pervasive, kept alive by numerous tribal groups scattered throughout the region. Some religious prayers and services, including the Portuguese-influenced Good Friday Procession in Larantuka (E. Flores), have been observed unchanged since the 16th century.

Economy

Nusatenggara has no modern industry. Most goods must be imported from Java and paid for with exported cattle and horses, coffee, beans, copra, and fish. Besides limited deposits of sulphur, and oil in E. Timor, the region has few mineral resources. Though the government employs some people in the provincial capitals, the great majority eke a livelihood from fishing or subsistence agriculture. In the interior of Sumba and Timor, primitive *ladang* is still used in cultivating taro and yams. The staple crops are corn and sago; little rice can be grown with such dry weather and generally poor land dessicated by the rainless eastern monsoon season. On Lembata and Solor, whaling with harpoons is still practiced by the last 2 whaling communities in Indonesia. And on Roti and Sawu, the economy is based on the almost total exploitation of the sap from the *lontar* palm. Horses have been raised for export in Sumba since the 1840s, and Balinese cattle have been bred for export on Timor since 1910. Although tourism remains in its infancy, with generally unreliable transportation, few facilities, and little government support, it was given a big shot in the arm by the start of the twice-weekly Darwin (northern Australia) to Kupang (W. Timor) flight in 1986.

Crafts

Weaving and plaiting are practiced throughout Nusatenggara. Though they are strictly cottage industries at best, weaving — particularly *ikat* style — has reached its most sublime expressions in these backwater islands, especially on Sumba, Flores, and Timor. Their colors and motifs are as yet undiluted by the tourist trade, and they sell at a fraction of the price you'd pay on Java or Bali. Plenty of fine porcelain is found on Sumba. Visit Flores for fine old ivory and silverwork. The tiny island of Ndao, W of Timor, is noted for its silversmiths.

History

For over 800 years, Chinese and Arab traders have called at the remote ports of Nusatenggara to exchange textiles, metal weapons, and porcelain for cinnamon, tortoiseshell, sandalwood, hardwoods, and other forest products. The 14th C. Majapahit Empire claimed the whole of Nusatenggara as part of its domain, though theirs was more a mercantile relationship with the islands rather than direct rule, as there is little evidence today of Hinduization in the area. Via Ternate and later from Makassar, Islam started to make inroads in the 15th and 16th centuries. During this period, slaves and ponies became major export items. The Portuguese explorer Antonio de Abreu reconnoitered the coast of Flores in 1512, giving the island its present name. From that time on, Portuguese ships stopped frequently along the island chain to replenish their supplies of fresh water and food, and to trade for sandalwood. A Portuguese priest was converting souls on Timor and Solor as early as 1522. With alms from Macao, a fortress was constructed in Solor and a seminary in Larantuka (E. Flores) in 1566.

Except for the sandalwood-producing islands of Flores and Timor, there were few resources in Nusatenggara to interest the Dutch, and the VOC did not become active in the area until the 17th century. In 1613, the Dutch, allied with Muslim groups, conquered the fort of Solor, and the Portuguese fled to Flores. The Dutch took Kupang in 1653, but for over 100 years competed with the Portuguese for the control of the sandalwood trade on Timor. Finally, a Portuguese-speaking Christian mestizo group, the "black Portuguese," attacked Kupang in 1749 but were soundly defeated. This ended the stalemate and the Portuguese retreated to E. Timor, leaving the western end of the island in the hands of the Dutch. In 1859, Portugal signed a treaty with Holland renouncing all its rights in eastern Flores.

Sawu was forced open in 1860, and within 9 years 50% of the population died from a European-borne smallpox epidemic. In 1843, the Balinese lords of W. Lombok succumbed to Dutch sovereignty, but it wasn't until 1891, when a Sasak rebellion in E. Lombok broke out, that the Dutch found a pretext to intervene and rule the island directly. A Dutch regiment invaded in 1894 but were nearly massacred by a Balinese counterattack and reinforcements had to be sent. With the sudden and horrific end of Balinese independence in the *puputan* of 1906 on Bali, the Dutch began to consolidate their hold on the islands to the east. Using slave-trading and the natives' looting of shipwrecks as the justification, expeditions had been launched against Flores in 1838 and 1846, but that island, and the remainder of Nusatenggara, was not brought under effective control until the first decade of the 20th century. Ruling through tribal chieftains (rajas), the Dutch governed Nusatenggara until the Japanese invasion of 1942 rudely shook the region out of its lethargy and political isolation.

Getting There

Nusatenggara need no longer be an out-and-back trip from Bali. Merpati flies Bima-Ujung Pandang (Rp67,000) twice weekly, as well as daily Kupang-Maumere-Ujung Pandang-Balikpapan-Tarakan. Bali is still the logical and least expensive jumping-off point. From Padangbai (E. Bali), there are daily ferries (4-5 hours) to Lombok, and regular Merpati flights from Denpasar to Lombok (Rp19,400), Sumbawa (Rp38,400), Flores (Rp91,400), and Timor (Rp83,300). Garuda flies from Jakarta to Kupang (Rp209,300) and to Mataram (Rp119,000). Merpati flights also depart Darwin, northern Australia, for Denpasar each Thurs. and Sat. at 0930. This marvelous connection, costing only A$175 OW (2 hours to Kupang), allows for up to 7 stops: Darwin-Kupang-Maumere-Ruteng-Labuhanbajo-Bima-Ampenan-Denpasar. The sleek Pelni ship MV *Kelimutu* sails every 2 weeks from Semarang to Banjarmasin-Surabaya-Padangbai-Lembar (Lombok)-Ujung Pandang-Bima-Waingapu-Ende-Kupang, then back to Semarang. If you've got the time, Perintis ships also sail between Java, Bali, Lombok, Sumbawa, Sumba, Sawu, Roti, and Timor.

GETTING AROUND

General intra-island and inter-island transport is now so much better than it used to be — almost seems like a cop-out going to Nusatenggara these days! Zamrud has finally gone out of business so you'll miss the thrill of meeting a real dinosaur. The gap has been filled by Merpati, and to a lesser extent Bouraq, which have fairly reliable flights connecting all the major towns on circle routes from Bali, Lombok, Sumbawa Besar, Kupang via Waingapu and/or Ende and Mataram. No flights on Sundays. Using small DC-3s and F-27s, new routes (such as to Roti and Sawu from Kupang) are being added all the time. Flights are so frequent now that booking usually isn't necessary. No air service, however, links Lombok to Sumba or Timor

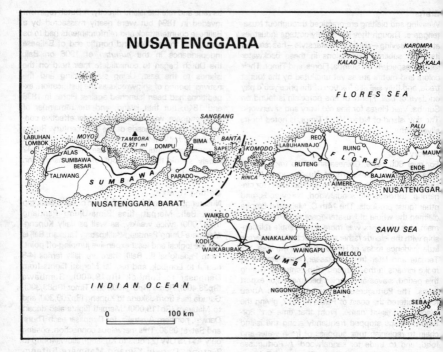

NUSATENGGARA

FLORES SEA

SANGEANG

KAROMPA
KALAO
KALA

PALU

LABUHAN
LOMBOK
MOYO
TAMBORA
(2,821 m)
DOMPU
BIMA
BANTA
SAPE
KOMODO
LABUHANBAJO
REO
RUING
MAUM
ALAS
SUMBAWA
BESAR
TALIWANG
SUMBAWA
PARADO
RINCA
RUTENG
F L O R E S
ENDE
BAJAWA
AIMERE
NUSATENGGAR

NUSATENGGARA BARAT

WAIKELO

SAWU SEA

KODI
WAIKABUBAK
ANAKALANG
WAINGAPU
MELOLO
S U M B A

INDIAN OCEAN

NGGONGI
BAING

SEBA
SA

0   100 km

(which doesn't really matter), or links Sumba with Flores (which does matter).

Departure Points

It's worth noting where flights do and don't exist. Flights depart Bali to anywhere in Nusatenggara; from Lombok only to Sumbawa, western Flores (not to Sumba, Timor, Maumere). From Sumbawa, it depends where you are: from Bima you can fly anywhere, but from Sumbawa Besar only to Lombok, Bali, and Java. From Sumba, flights go only to Bima (Rp42,400), Denpasar (Rp74,600), and Kupang (Rp54,200), but not to Flores or Lombok. From Flores, it depends where you are: Labuhanbajo now has an airport, making Komodo a little bit more accessible for the jet set; direct flights only to Bima, Denpasar, Ruteng. From Ruteng or Ende, you can fly to almost anywhere. Maumere has almost daily Merpati flights to Bali (and on to Java) for Rp80,200, and daily flights to Kupang (Rp31,600). Larantuka now has an airport from where you can fly to Kupang (Rp42,400) if you really want to.

By Sea

Motorized and sailing vessels ply the coasts and travel between islands; in the Solor and Alor archi-

pelagos E of Flores, these are about your only inter-island options. Also, good passenger ferry services link Bali-Lombok-Sumbawa-Komodo-Flores-Adonara. These frequent ferries are run by Angkutan Sungei Danau dan Penyeberangan (ASDP), which tends to be even more reliable than Pelni. Once a week there's ferry service from E. Sumbawa to W. Flores which stops at Komodo Island on the way, or you can simply charter a *kapal motor* from Labuhanbajo (W. Flores) to Komodo and back for Rp125,000. Another service likely to be used by travelers is the Pelni boat between Ende and Waingapu (no air service Ende-Waingapu these days). It's an overnight trip, costs Rp12,000, and supposedly runs once a week. The shipping offices and harbormasters in the various ports can tell you about other connections. In Ende, it's fairly easy to get on a boat for Kupang (perhaps 35 hours, so choose a big one). Other boats? If you hang around Maumere or Bima long enough, you'll find boats going to Singaraja and Surabaya. Better fly if you can't wait forever. For the right price, small boats, motorized outriggers, and canoes can be chartered from any port to visit outlying islands and reefs.

Road System

The larger islands have buses, canopied trucks with

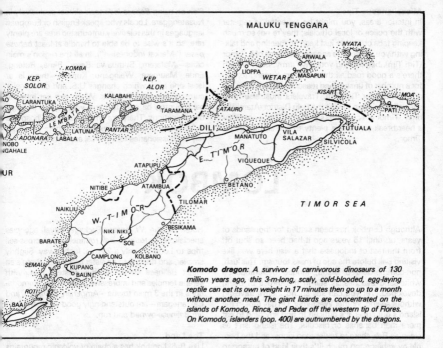

Komodo dragon: A survivor of carnivorous dinosaurs of 130 million years ago, this 3-m-long, scaly, cold-blooded, egg-laying reptile can eat its own weight in 17 minutes then go up to a month without another meal. The giant lizards are concentrated on the islands of Komodo, Rinca, and Padar off the western tip of Flores. On Komodo, islanders (pop. 400) are outnumbered by the dragons.

benches, *bemo, dokar,* minibuses, etc., and you can often hitch a ride (for a fee) with a passing transport truck or motorcycle. With asphalted roads all over Lombok and Sumbawa, it's easy to get around. Move on to Flores and roads are generally wretched to nonexistent, and land travel is a bone-cracking ordeal in the dry season; in the wet, it could take a week to slog 100 km through the mud. On Timor, the Indonesian army has built a well-surfaced road from Kupang to Dili to move its war materiel to subjugate the eastern half of the island. The best rule in Nusatenggara Timor is not to plan your schedule too tightly or you'll just wind up frustrated and angry. Relax, read, practice your Indonesian, and expect boats, planes, *bemo,* horses, whatever, to be late—or not materialize at all. One way to get around the transport problem is to bring a motorcycle, which you can take aboard (for as little as Rp3500) all the ferries connecting the string of islands. Bicycles are another alternative, but it would be best to bring your own. A used, fairly sturdy, black-painted bike—nothing less than a 2-wheeled tank—can be bought on Bali, Lombok, or Sumba for Rp20,000-25,000.

Tours

A number of specialized tourist agencies have sprung up in Nusatenggara in the last several years. On Lombok, **Losmen Srikandi,** Jl. Kebudayaan, Cakranegara (tel. 22747), offers a 3-day, 2-night package tour of Lombok including accommodations, homecooked buffet dinners, and a dance performance, at only US$50 pp. **PT Sao Wisata** sells all-inclusive tours to the superb dive sites off Waiara (10 km from Maumere, C. Flores). This first-class resort complex charges US$60 pp per day in fancy little bungalows. That price includes all dive equipment, meals, transport, and 2-3 dives per day. Book or get further information from PT Sao Wisata, Borobudur Office Bldg., 2nd Floor, Room 6B, Jl. Lapangan Banteng Selatan, Jakarta Pusat, tel. 360209 (ext. 78222/78227), or phone them in Maumere (tel. 342). In Kupang, the popular Darwin-Kupang air connection has spawned a number of tour services—both official and unofficial. Try **PT Pitoby Travel Service,** Jl. Siliwangi 65 (tel. 21222/21333). They have tours to, for example, Komodo (5 days, US$148 1 person, US$120 2 persons), Keli Mutu (4 days, US$163 1 person, US$109 2 persons), Sumba (5 days, US$181 1 person, US$150 2 persons), 1-day local tours of Kupang (US$50 1 person, US$25 2 persons); also tours to Roti, W. Timor, and Flores' dive sites.

Miscellaneous Tips

In interior areas, you might be expected to register with the police or local officials; they're not so much keeping tabs on you as just keen on meeting and talking with you. To see the annexed province of E. Timor (Tim Tim), better bring your own army. Even though there's a good road all the way from Kupang to Dili, for a number of unspecified reasons tourist passes are not granted for Tim Tim. Travelers must also have special permission to visit the Belu District (Atambua) of W. Timor which borders E. Timor. This is not really a heartbreak as there is plenty to see and do in W. Timor.

Plan on using *Bahasa Indonesia* almost exclusively in Nusatenggara. Locals who speak English or European languages in this relatively untouristed area are plenty rare, so it's wise to be able to handle at least *bahasa pasar* ("Market Indonesian"). In all the region's main cities—Mataram, Sumbawa Besar, Bima, Ruteng, Ende, Maumere, Waingapu, Kupang—there is at least one bank which changes U.S. and other major currency travelers cheques. When you get into the backcountry, be sure to carry your *rupiah* in small denominations. There are small missionary hospitals in Mataram, Ende, and Kupang; elsewhere you must rely on missionaries for medical assistance.

LOMBOK

Although Lombok has been settled for thousands of years, up until 15 years ago it had been so shut off from the rest of Indonesia that a visit here was like visiting Bali before the age of mass tourism. This lush, non-commercialized island, fringed by untouched white-sand beaches, is still in the throes of being developed. Yet you can still spend 2 days traveling without seeing another Westerner. On day trips in the island's out areas, it's difficult to find anything to eat more than bananas or biscuits. The island isn't as clean as Bali, there're fewer road signs, and the people overcharge too much (it's their kind of humor: to make you angry is funny), particularly in E. Lombok. It's a poor island, subject to famines; children in remote interior villages are covered in open infections and sores. One of the biggest annoyances on Lombok is that, being such a curiosity, people stop and stare at you wherever you go; sometimes whole villages of kids trail after you. It takes some getting used to, and moments alone are exquisitely delicious.

Lombok was first put on the map back in 1979 when the German *Geo* magazine (now defunct) published a photo article on G. Rinjani. Featured was a color spread on the imposing volcano, and for months thereafter hundreds of Germans arrived to climb it. Then, with the publication of Lonely Planet's *Bali & Lombok*, more and more tourists and travelers began discovering it. There's a surprising lack of reliable information about Lombok: the Balinese will tell you that there're only rice and bananas to eat, no roads, no places to stay, that Lombok people are skilled at knife-fighting and are easily provoked—all quite untrue. The Balinese, who want to keep the tourist business all to themselves, don't want you to come here. The national government would like to discourage Kuta-type visitors in favor of "quality" tourists exemplified by the patrons of the new Senggigi Beach

Hotel on the W coast. Package travel agencies specializing in tours to Bali routinely try to cross-sell trips to Lombok, only a 20-min. flight away. Slightly smaller, and drier, than its sister island Bali, there's an intact Balinese culture in the western part, with serene temples and impressive palaces. Accommodations in the 3 main towns—Ampenan, Mataram, and Cakranegara—are outstandingly good value; the best are Balinese-owned and run.

The Land

Like Bali, Lombok has a chain of volcanic mountains in the northern half. The island's land mass, some 4,595 sq km in area, is dominated by G. Rinjani, rising 3,726 m above a high plateau. Segara Anak Lake fills most of Rinjani's crater. Lombok has similar climate and soil as Bali's for growing coffee, tobacco, market vegetables, rice, and other crops. Lombok has long been an exporter of rice and coffee. The island's central area is chronically dry; the government calls it "the critical area," with crops frequently wiped out by mice, insects, too much rain, or too little rain! In 1966, 50,000 people starved to death during a famine on the island. It's a very hard life, which is why the government steadily transmigrates the inhabitants of Lombok's central area to Indonesia's Outer Islands. In the W are fertile alluvial plains (a continuation of the mountain slopes), with picturesque, finely crafted rice terraces. In the extreme S are scrubby barren hills, quite dry and strikingly different from the rest of the island.

Fauna

As in the rest of the Lesser Sundas, there are *rusa*, barking deer, wild pig, long-tailed macaques, and civets; the wild deer, boar, and other wildlife proliferate in the SW and NW of the island. Like parts of

Java, Lombok has wild buffalos. It's also noteworthy as the most westernmost island where the sulphur-crested cockatoo is found; there are also honeyeaters and bee eaters (an Australian species, *Merops ornatus*), and a mound-builder *(Megapodius reinwardti)*. Ducks, so far unidentified, frequent Lake Segara Anak on G. Rinjani. Whales are often spotted off the S coast, where there's also turtle fishing, especially at Kuta Beach.

History
In the 14th C., Lombok was settled by Hindu-Javanese under the auspices of the powerful Majapahit Empire of E. Java. The Islamic religion was brought to Lombok between 1506 and 1545 by Sunan Prapen, the son of Sunan Ratu Giri from Demak (N. Java). In the 17th C., the island was divided into a number of petty princedoms. In return for Balinese support in their struggle against the raja of Sumbawa in the early 18th C., the Sasaks allowed the Balinese to settle in the W part of their island. The Balinese king of Karangasem, exploiting the disunity of the feuding princes, conquered Lombok in the mid-17th C., enslaving the Islamic Sasaks in the western part of the island. At the same time, Islamic Makassarese traders from Sumbawa colonized Lombok's eastern half, converting the Sasak to Islam. Though the Makassarese were expelled by a joint Balinese/Sasak force in 1677, the Sasaks soon found themselves oppressed by the newcomers from Bali. Over the next several hundred years, they became second-class citizens on their own island.

The Dutch colonialists used the conflict between the 2 groups to their advantage. In the late 19th C., the Sasaks sought assistance from the Dutch, who had occupied northern Bali in 1882. In 1894, the Dutch mounted an elaborate military expedition to Lombok and demanded a war indemnity of one million guilders to be paid by the old raja. The raja accepted but the princes rose up and attacked the main Dutch encampment in Cakranegara. After 3 days of fierce rifle fire, merciless tomtoms, and ear-splitting Balinese war cries, the Dutch retreated toward the sea, leaving nearly 300 wounded and 100 dead (including a Dutch general). When news of the defeat reached Java and Holland, the press flared up against the "sinister treachery" of the Balinese. Large reinforcements of men and heavy artillery were mustered and sent from Java. After a bitter month-long campaign of destruction, with the Dutch razing Balinese villages and the Sasaks looting them, the Balinese stronghold at Cakranegara was finally taken. The crown prince, Anak Agung Ketut, a bitter enemy of the Dutch, was murdered; the old raja was captured and sent into exile. Soon after, Lombok formally became a part of the Dutch East Indies. Strained feelings still exist between the Sasaks and the Balinese.

THE PEOPLE

Lombok's 1.7 million people are a mixture of Islamic Sasak (80%) and Hindu Balinese (10%). The poorer Sasaks live in the eastern part of the island, while the Balinese live mainly in the towns and villages of the western central plain. The Balinese believe that G. Rinjani and G. Agung are man and wife, and G. Semeru on Java completes the trinity of peaks on which all the gods live. If you want a Bali without the all-prevading intense culture, religion, and arts, go straight to Lombok. Yet here are found Balinese food, customs, traditional walled villages with *kulkul* towers, *banjar* irrigation systems, even all the Balinese festivals such as *Galungan* are celebrated at full throttle. Most of Lombok's Chinese were killed off in 1965-66 purges; together with Arabs they now comprise only 5% of the population. The aboriginals of Lombok, called the Bodhas, live in the isolated SE corner—what's left of them.

The Sasaks
An Islamic hill tribe of atypical racial stock with dark skin, long heads, wavy hair, and more Caucasian facial features. These attributes are a result of migration streams at an earlier time than most Indonesian ethnic groups. The Sasaks are thought to have come overland from NW India or Burma to Java, then migrated across the Lombok Strait to Lombok. The Sasaks are divided into 2 groups, the secular **Waktu Telu** ("Three Prayer Islam") and the more orthodox **Waktu Lima** ("Five Prayer Islam"). The Waktu Telu, comprising about 30% of the Sasaks, celebrate only 3 different occasions: the Prophet's Birthday, the holy day of Friday, and *Leberan.* Instead of praying 5 times a day like conservative Muslims, they pray only 3 times daily. Reminiscent of the worship of *lingga* by the Hindu Balinese, the Waktu Telu also revere monoliths set in the ground. Only a few still eat pork and drink alcohol. The Waktu Telu live mostly in the S-central region—**Puyung, Sengkol, Rambitan**—in villages with traditional round thatched huts supported by rough beams.

Customs
The quickest way to tell the difference between Sasaks and Balinese is that the latter don't mind being photographed. Both the Waktu Telu and Waktu Lima show their Hindu roots by having adopted a watered-down caste system and using linguistic codes in addressing commoners and noblemen. Though Muslim, Sasak boys are carried in a Hindu-style circumcision ceremony borrowed from the Balinese. The boy rides on a lion with a tail of palm fronds. No anesthetic is used: each boy is expected to

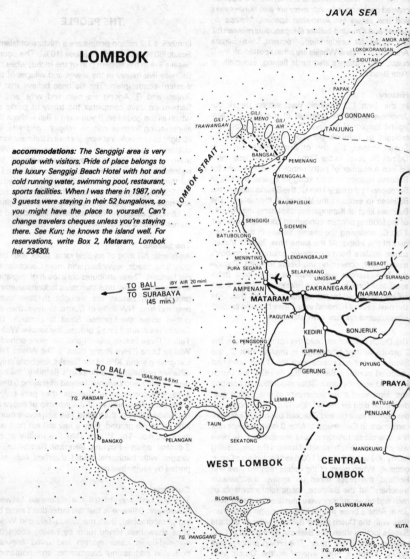

LOMBOK

JAVA SEA

AMOR AMO
LOKOKORANGAN
SIDUTAN
PAPAK

GILI
MENO
GILI
TRAWANGAN
GILI
AIR

GONDANG
TANJUNG

BANGSAL

PEMENANG

MENGGALA

BAUMPUSUK

SENGGIGI

SIDEMEN

BATUBOLONG

LENDANGBAJUR

MENINTING

PURA SEGARA

SELAPARANG

LINGSAR

SESAOT

SURANAD

accommodations: *The Senggigi area is very popular with visitors. Pride of place belongs to the luxury Senggigi Beach Hotel with hot and cold running water, swimming pool, restaurant, sports facilities. When I was there in 1987, only 3 guests were staying in their 52 bungalows, so you might have the place to yourself. Can't change travelers cheques unless you're staying there. See Kun; he knows the island well. For reservations, write Box 2, Mataram, Lombok (tel. 23430).*

TO BALI (BY AIR 20 min.)
TO SURABAYA (45 min.)

AMPENAN
MATARAM
CAKRANEGARA
NARMADA

PAGUTAN

KEDIRI
BONJERUK

G. PENGSONG
KURIPAN
PUYUNG

GERUNG

TO BALI (SAILING 4-5 hr.)

TG. PANDAN

PRAYA

BATUJAI
PENUJAK

LEMBAR

TAUN

BANGKO
PELANGAN

SEKATONG
MANGKUNG

WEST LOMBOK

**CENTRAL
LOMBOK**

BLONGAS
SILUNGBLANAK

KUTA

TG. PANGGANG

TG. TAMPA

0   10 km

INDIAN OCEAN

LOMBOK STRAIT

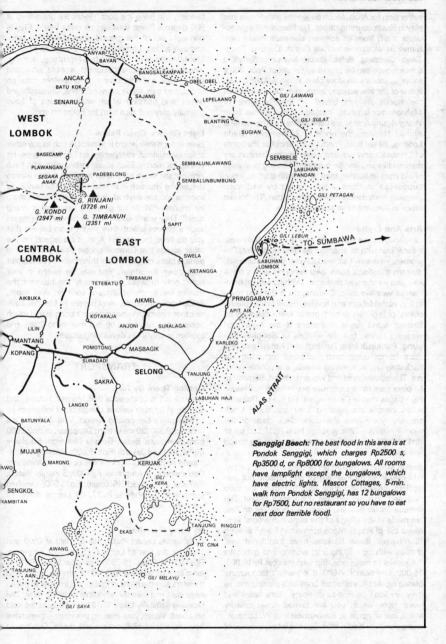

WEST LOMBOK

CENTRAL LOMBOK

EAST LOMBOK

ANYAR
BAYAN
ANCAK
BATU KOK
SENARU
BANGSALKAMPAR
OBEL OBEL
SAJANG
LEPELAANG
GILI LAWANG
BLANTING
GILI SULAT
SUGIAN
SEMBELIE
LABUHAN PANDAN
BASECAMP
PLAWANGAN
SEGARA ANAK
PADEBELONG
SEMBALUNLAWANG
SEMBALUNBUMBUNG
GILI PETAGAN
G. KONDO (2947 m)
G. RINJANI (3726 m)
G. TIMBANUH (2351 m)
SAPIT
GILI LEBUR
TO SUMBAWA
SWELA
KETANGGA
LABUHAN LOMBOK
TIMBANUH
TETEBATU
AIKBUKA
AIKMEL
PRINGGABAYA
KOTARAJA
APIT AIK
ANJONI
SURALAGA
LILIN
MANTANG
POMOTONG
MASBAGIK
KARLEKO
KOPANG
SURADADI
SELONG
TANJUNG
LABUHAN HAJI
SAKRA
LANGKO
BATUNYALA
ALAS STRAIT
MUJUR
MARONG
KERUAK
GILI KERA
SENGKOL
RAMBITAN
EKAS
TANJUNG RINGGIT
TG. CINA
AWANG
TANJUNG AAN
GILI MELAYU
GILI SAYA

Senggigi Beach: The best food in this area is at Pondok Senggigi, which charges Rp2500 s, Rp3500 d, or Rp8000 for bungalows. All rooms have lamplight except the bungalows, which have electric lights. Mascot Cottages, 5-min. walk from Pondok Senggigi, has 12 bungalows for Rp7500, but no restaurant so you have to eat next door (terrible food).

suffer pain for Allah. Much pageantry also comes into play in Sasak courting rituals. Traditionally, if a girl accepts a gift from an admirer, she must marry him. Native Sasak dances include *Cupuk, Cepung, Tawa-Tawa, Gendang, Belek, Rudat, Kroncang Sampi;* a dance troupe can be chartered for about Rp50,000 a show. Lombok's shadow play, *Wayang Kulit Sasak,* is one of the few *wayang* forms in Indonesia in which the stories are not based on the *Ramayana* or *Mahabharata* legends. Instead, Islamic stories from *Wong Agung Menak* are used (Menak's other name is Ahmad Hamzah, the uncle of Mohammed). **Sada Loteng,** 20 km from Praya (C. Lombok), is the home of Lombok's only *wayang orang* troupe. Dancers are dressed like and imitate puppets. Wearing costumes of old cracked leather, they dance with startled, jerky, puppet-like motions. Accompanied by traditional *gamelan,* each dancer recites his own part. The tourist office in Ampenan can arrange a show.

Arts And Crafts

Gorgeous fabrics are woven on this island. Men wear a *batik kain* with an attached *ikat (sapuk)* border. The women, who aren't allowed to wear gold ornaments, don the traditional black *baju lambung* with a black *kain* and a red shawl *(beberut).* With its several commercial weaving mills, Cakranegara is the best town to buy native fabrics and textiles, usually with splashy colors, plus glittery tinsel types of *kain*—definitely an Eastern Island flavor. **Sukarare** is the main rural weaving center, but the villages of **Sengkol, Puyung, Punjuruk** (near Puyung), and **Ketap** also produce fabrics using such traditional technology as backstrap looms, spinning wheels, and bobbin winders. Threads are dyed and woven by hand. Surprisingly, pieces are more expensive out in the actual weaving villages than in Cakranegara! Go out on Thursday when people are wearing their traditional black blouses; you'll hear the clack clack clack of the women weaving. Prices range from Rp15,000 up to Rp150,000 for a *songket,* depending upon the thread and material used.

Basket weaving in traditional colors (black, yellow, and red) is found everywhere on Lombok, but particularly around Kotaraja and Suradadi (bamboo basketry); also see samples at **Sweta's** market. The famous Belaka baskets, selling like hotcakes on Bali, are made in the village of the same name outside of Mujur (SE of Praya). Made from rattan from Taliwang (Sumbawa), these baskets have traditional oval shapes with tight-fitting lids; women and girls take 1-4 weeks to make one. Big baskets cost Rp10,000-15,000; tiny ones Rp1500. If it weren't for tourism, plastic would have killed off Lombok's plaiting arts, as they wouldn't be able to compete. Giant vases and water pots, which you see carried down country roads, are all made at **Banyumolok** in W. Lombok, and around the **Kediri** area. See the whole process of building and firing the pots. Pieces are grass-fired at 900 degrees F and thus can be quite brittle. Clay is dug right out of the ground, then chemicals, sand, and ash added. Lombok is also a treasure trove of Third World toys—all kinds of pushing, turning, wheeling contraptions that clatter, wobble, whirl, and spin. There are little cars with propellors, cars on sticks, and cars made of wood, cans, tin, cardboard boxes, and bamboo which whole groups of boys gleefully play and race with for hours on end!

Light Fingers, Open Palms

Even though their island is in parts as rich as any other Indonesian island, everywhere on Lombok people hit you up for money. Even young strong guys who have jobs put the touch on you for a handout. One way to defuse the situation is to beat them to the punch; as soon as you see anybody hovering around, ask *them* for money: *"Minta uang, minta uang untuk orang turis!"* They won't know how to handle it. Being on such a remote island, they might even believe that you do need the money! Also, it's a legend on the other islands that Lombok people use a sort of *guna guna,* a black magic, to steal things while you sleep or walk down the street. You may be asleep in your hotel, only to wake up suddenly the moment the thieves leave, after putting a spell on your room. Aside from agriculture, most people on Lombok have no other income. Weaving doesn't bring in that much because one *kain* takes up to 2 months to finish, and tourism is only in its developing stages.

TRANSPORT

Getting There By Air

Lombok is 1 hour ahead of Bali. Merpati, Bouraq, and Garuda all fly from various cities around Indonesia into Mataram's Selaparang Airport. With Merpati, it's only Rp19,300 (20 min.) from Denpasar, or Rp25,000 from Sumbawa Besar. Garuda flies from Surabaya (Rp54,900) and Jakarta (Rp119,000). Arriving at Selaparang Airport, a taxi price list is posted: to Mataram, Cakranegara, or Ampenan, Rp4000; Senggigi Beach, Rp7500; Kuta Beach (S coast), Rp25,000; Labuhan Lombok (to Sumbawa), Rp27,500. Longer distances are better value.

By Ferry From Bali

Daily ferries depart Padangbai (E. Bali) at 0900 and 1400 for the port of Lembar, 25 km S of Ampenan; Rp4500 1st Class, Rp3500 Economy Class; Rp1000 extra for a bicycle and Rp3500 for a motorcycle. Most travelers stay the night at Padangbai in order to get an early start and take the smoother morning ferry. The crossing generally takes 4½-5 hours; snacks are sold on board. Watch your gear on this route—there have been reports of pickpockets and thefts. Don't trust *anyone* to look after your things. The *kelas ekonomi* is as good as *kelas utara,* which is darker (since the doors are kept closed to keep the a/c in). Best is to go up 1 flight to the breezy classless deck where the pilot's room is. Arriving at Lembar in W. Lombok, mobs of minibuses wait to take you the 25-30 km (Rp1500) straight to your address in either Ampenan, Mataram, or Cakranegara. Transport may be scarce or higher-priced if the 1400 ferry arrives late; tickets are available on board. Ferries also depart Alas (W. Sumbawa) for Labuhan Lombok (E. Lombok) daily at 0900; Rp2000, 3 hours.

Getting Around

Transport is improving all the time and the roads are not that congested. Horsedrawn *cidomo (dokar)* are the main means of transport in the towns. Quite cheap, charter one for Rp5000 per day, a slow and earthy way to explore the towns or the countryside. *Bemo* run between Ampenan, Mataram, and Cakranegara (Rp250) and farther east. Some acceptable roads run around Lombok, but the only good one stretches between Ampenan and Labuhan Lombok. Along this central highway are a number of crossroad towns—Narmada, Mantang, Pomotong, Magbagik, etc.—from where you take *bemo* or *dokar* to the island's main tourist attractions. Clusters of waiting *dokar, bemo,* a little marketplace, children playing, and one-story buildings mark each of these highway towns. Lombok isn't a large island and the long, narrow, fertile corridor between the E and W coasts can be traversed in only 2 hours at most by bus.

Lying right on the main cross-island road, Cakranegara's Sweta Terminal in W. Lombok is the focal point for transportation to all over Lombok. A good many of the temples, palaces, traditional villages, and historical sites worth going to are within 20 km of Cakra. From the airport into town by taxi is Rp4000. You can see an awful lot of the sights of W. Lombok by rented taxi for only Rp4000 per hour (with driver) and save yourself a lot of time and hassle. Or charter a *bemo* or an old car for about Rp35,000 per day with driver. Motorcycles rent for Rp4000-6000 (cheaper rates for longer rental periods) per day from the owners who hang out on the street near Losmen Srikandi in Cakranegara. Take these machines around the block several times first to check out brakes, lights, gears, etc. Flat tires should only cost Rp400 to

repair but Sasak mechanics often charge tourists Rp1000. For cyclists, bring your rented or purchased bicycle over from Bali because there's some really superb riding country here (one loop is from Mataram, Suranadi, Lingsar, and then back to Cakranegara). Put your bike on top of a *bemo* if you get tired. **to Senggigi:** From Ampenan's *bemo* stand, take a *bemo* all the way to Senggigi Beach (Rp400-500), stopping briefly in Rembiga and Ledengbajur en route.

From Lombok To Bali

Ferries depart from the port of Lembar for Padangbai (E. Bali) at 0900 and 1400. First Class, Rp4500; Economy Class, Rp3500; car, Rp35,000; bicycle, Rp1000. The passage takes 4-5 hours. Catch minibuses (Rp1500) to Lembar from Terminal Sweta (Rp150 from Ampenan); leave by 0800 to catch the 1400 ferry. Sometimes minibuses come into the hotel yards or cruise the main road linking Ampenan, Mataram, and Cakra seeking passengers. Minibuses drop you off right in front of the ticket office in Lembar. If you don't like Deck Class, pay your way into the upper classes. Lots of trucks onboard so it's easy to hitch a ride into Denpasar.

From Lombok To Komodo Island

Get first to Labuhan Lombok (E. Lombok) from where you take a regular ferry to W. Sumbawa (Rp1500, 3 hours, 76 km). Board the ferry in Labuhan Lombok at 0800, 0900, and 1000 to Alas Harbor (Sumbawa), across Sumbawa to Sape, then get another ferry to Komodo. Since the accommodations are so poor in Labuhan Lombok, it's advisable to stay the night in Ampenan or Cakranegara and take a bus across the island the next morning at 0500, arriving in time to catch the Sumbawa-bound ferry. Your hotel can help arrange bus pick-up in Ampenan or Cakra on the morning of departure.

From Lombok By Air

From Mataram's Selaparang Airport, Merpati flies to: Denpasar (Rp19,300) and Jakarta (Rp103,000) once daily. Their flight to Denpasar is nothing less than a shuttle service from 0810 up to 1600 (7 flights daily). Garuda flies to Surabaya once daily at 1215 for Rp56,400; to Banjarmasin (via Surabaya) for Rp129,200. Beautiful mountain views from Mataram's airport.

WEST LOMBOK

AMPENAN

Formerly Lombok's main seaport but now a crumbling shadow of its former self. Of the 3 large towns—Ampenan, Mataram, and Cakra—Ampenan is the most colorful with more native dress and much harbor and market activity. From Ampenan, the W coast beaches and resorts are readily accessible, and plentiful transport makes it easy to sightsee around the island's S-central tourist area. The town has a market, a shopping center, movie theaters, travel agents, some handy travelers' accommodations, and the food served in several of its Chinese restaurants would make the seafood dinners of Kuta Beach (Bali) execrable by comparison. *Dokar* cost Rp400 to anywhere in town. A **museum** is on Jl. Banjar Tiler Negara, S of Jl. Langko. The **Regional Tourist Office**, opposite the main post office at Jl. Langko 70 (tel. 21866/21730), employs a very helpful staff of 20 but has little literature available (except a map). See Mr. Putupriatna or Mr. Mahid. Open Mon.-Fri. 0700-1400, Fri. until 1100, Sat. until 1300. Another tourist office for all of West Nusatenggara (NTB) is on Jl. Bung Hatta.

Across the road, the **post office** is open 0800-1400 and on Fri. 0800-1100; for *post restante*, go to Mataram's post office. The **Merpati** office (tel. 22226) in the Selaparang Hotel, **Garuda** (tel. 23762) near the tourist office, as well as several travel agencies that can arrange tours are all located on Jl. Langko. Change money (US$ only) at **Bank Umum Nasional**, Jl. Pabean 47-49 (tel. 21626); for U.S. and other currencies go to **Bank Negara Indonesia** on Jl. Langko in Mataram (Rp200 by *bemo* down the road). Also while in Ampenan, to visit the copra factory near Losmen Pabean (toward the harbor).

Accommodations

There's a whole string of typically overpriced businessmen's hotels like the Mataram, Granada, Zahir, Selaparang. Better values are the cheaper hotels. If you like a city scene, **Hotel Tigamas** in Kampung Melayu Tengah (tel. 23211), just off Jl. Pabean near the waterfront, is cheap at Rp2500 pp, but has 2 competing mosque loudspeakers and a school behind it that teaches chanting starting at 0400! Just N is the superior, Chinese-owned and well-run **Losmen Pabean**, Jl. Yos Sudarso 146 (tel. 21758), a popular travelers' *losmen* with laundry facilities and lots of mosquitos; Rp2500 s, Rp3500 d. Toast, bana-

na, and coffee for breakfast. *Rumah makan* and excellent Chinese restaurants are down the street. Several other hotels and *losmen* are along Jl. Koperasi. At no. 12 is **Hotel Zahir** (tel. 22403), run by nice people, has a breezy garden, but tends to be dirty; Rp3500s to Rp5000 d. At no. 65, **Losmen Horas** (tel. 21695) has the same prices but is a bit cramped and too close to a mosque.

Wisma Triguna (tel. 21705), farther up on Jl. Koperasi toward the airport, is more comfy and very good value at Rp2500 s, Rp3500 d. This is very possibly the best cheap hotel on the island, with showers, *teh panas,* a flower and bush-filled yard, plus full travel information and services. Each spacious room has private bathroom; Rp2500 s, Rp3500 d, Rp5000 t; breakfast is Rp1000. Only Westerners stay here. Eddy Barubara, the proprietor, can take you on tours of the island, arrange motorcycle rental, help you climb and camp on G. Rinjani, give information on Gili Air, Komodo, etc., and will help you call home collect from the *wisma.* **Wisma Melati**, Jl. Langko 80 (tel. 23780) beside the Garuda office, is considered the best city hotel; very comfortable a/c rooms (Rp25,000-35,000) with telephone, restaurant, bar.

Food

At night the street stalls open up, as well as rolling *apam* and *kolak* wagons. *Kolak* is made from *ubi* with steamed bananas mixed with red sugar—a Third World treat! Two very good Chinese restaurants side by side on Jl. Yos Sudarso are the **RM Pabean** and **RM Tjirebon**, with complete, well-priced menus; Rp2000 for crab, steak, chicken, or big river fish. They're strong on seafood, but also feature such Western combos as steak, chips, and salad (only Rp2000). For Indo-style meals, go to **RM Setia, RM Mulia**, or **RM Arafat**, all within close walking distance of downtown Ampenan.

Shops

At **Toko Buku Rinjani** in front of the RS Umum in Mataram, buy the stunning coffee-table book, *Lombok: Just Beyond Bali* (1984, PT Indira), for around Rp20,000. **Toko Buku Titian**, Jl. Pabean, sells postcards and is the best bookshop in Ampenan. Also visit the antique shop, **Sudirman's**, Jl. Pabean 16A, several hundred meters down a narrow lane off Jl. Pabean opposite the *stasiun bemo*. This is a wonderful, tasteful shop run by a real gentleman who serves you tea and ginger cookies. Both new stuff and old, not overpriced, like big traditional *tenun lombok* weaving (US$80), old *kris* handles *(bengku),* carved figurines, and other intriguing pieces. Although the shop is well arranged, you gotta dig for the treasures. Two other good antique shops are **Haji Zohdi's** (Jl. Koperasi) and **Musdah Antique Shop** (Jl. Saleh Sungkar).

From Ampenan
Sweta, 2 km E of Cakranegara, is the main transport terminal for all of Lombok; head there for minibuses and *bemo* out to Lingsar, Narmada, Tetebatu, etc. If you're in a hurry to get to Sumbawa and Komodo, have the bus pick you up right outside your hotel in Ampenan at about 0500, then it's Rp1500 (80 km) to Labuhan Lombok, arriving at 0700.

Vicinity Of Ampenan
Along the coast N of Ampenan are temples, holy places, beach resorts. **Pura Segara** is a Balinese temple 3 km N of Ampenan; see the Muslim and Chinese cemeteries nearby. From in front of Hotel Horas, catch a *bemo* (Rp300) to Sasaka Beach Hotel (tel. 22711), 5 km N of Ampenan. Since its auspicious establishment 10 years ago, the Sasaka has lately turned dumpy. Nothing's been taken care of, yet they still want US$25 plus 21% tax and service for bungalows. They'll take US$15 because nobody's there; the Senggigi Beach Hotel (10 km N of Ampenan) has stolen the spotlight.

A fine beach nearby is at **Meninting,** an easy walk, bicycle, or *dokar* ride (amazing seeing the horses wade or swim the river!). **Batubolong,** 8 km N of Ampenan, is worth a visit for the scenic views of Bali from the cliff that juts out over a quiet beach. The "Hollow Stone" temple underneath was built by the Balinese from the sea; they wanted a temple that overlooked Lombok with Bali's G. Agung visible. Best approached from the beach, or about Rp500 by public *bemo* from Ampenan. Go at sunset. **Pantai Pemenang** is N of Meninting, with coral diving and a multitude of tropical fish; more pristine marine gardens can be found offshore on Gili Air, Gili Trawangan, and Gili Meno (see "Offshore Islands" below).

MATARAM

Administrative center of Nusatenggara Barat as well as the capital of W. Lombok, Mataram has spread out into the towns of Cakranegara and Ampenan. Now it's just one continuous strip of government offices, banks, *bioskop,* pre-fab homes, and many soldiers. Right in the center of Mataram is the **Kantor Gubernor** where 1,000 people work, a prime example of the featherbedded Indonesian bureaucracy. Visas and other bureaucratic needs can usually be sorted out here. **Kantor Imigrasi** is on Jl. Udayana, about 1 km N of town (near Bank Indonesia) on the road to the airport. The impressive main **post office,** the only one on Lombok with *post restante* service, is S of town on

Jl. Ismail Marzuki; get a *dokar* from Hotel Kamboja, Rp500. **Bank Negara Indonesia 1946,** Jl. Langko (tel. 21046) just W of Jl. Udayana, is the best place on the island to change money and all-currency travelers cheques.

Accommodations And Food
A wonderful Balinese-run *losmen,* **Wisma Tresna Yana,** Jl. Menjangan 15 (tel. 22454), is clean, inexpensive (Rp3,500 s, plus Rp2000 for a good breakfast and dinner), and relatively quiet. But best of all are Made and his family, who make you feel most welcome. The family is helpful, kind, and most of them speak English. Arrange to sightsee in their private *bemo* or jeep. This *wisma* may be difficult to find, so if you have any problem give them a call. **Losmen Rinjani,** Jl. Panca Warga 18, is one of the cheapest and not a bad deal for Rp2000 s, Rp3000 d with *mandi* inside rooms, free tea all day. Close to the governor's house, RM Garden House, and post office. At Jl. Supratman 10 is **Hotel Kamboja** (tel. 22211). Though friendly, clean, and reasonable (Rp3000 s or d), it's on a main intersection and the TV is kept on all night! *Dokar* conveniently park out front. **Wisma Paradiso,** Jl. Angsoka 3 (tel. 22074), has VIP rooms with a/c, hot water, but ugly bathroom and cockroaches, for Rp17,500. The lower-class rooms (Rp2500 s), with bath and facing a garden, are a better deal.

Pricier are **Hotel Selaparang** (Rp10,000 pp) and **Hotel Mataram** (Rp15,000 pp) on the main street. Hotel Mataram has 3 classes of rooms, the cheapest being Rp14,000; nothing special but it's clean. **Granada Hotel,** Jl. Bung Karno (tel. 22275/23138), has standard rooms for Rp21,000 s, VIP for Rp25,000 s, and bungalows for Rp35,000 s (all rates include tax, service, and breakfast). Facilities include full a/c, telephone, swimming pool, hot and cold water, TV, refrigerator, and a small zoo. Don't miss the *ayam pelicing* (hot curried chicken) at **RM Taliwang** on Jl. Pejanggik. The **Garden House** specializes in Chinese, European, and Indonesian cuisine, but is a bit more expensive.

CAKRANEGARA

The shopping and market center of Lombok, Cakranegara is a relatively wealthy city where many Chinese, Balinese, and Arabs live. Balinese women wearing beautiful *sarung* and *kebaya* walk down the main street at sunset with offerings on their heads— just like on Bali! It's also a bustling crafts center, well known for basketware, bought up by the Balinese and sold to the tourists on Bali at ridiculous prices. Visit the public market to see silver- and goldsmiths at work; here you may also come across clay animal figurines and elegant ceramics. The center of town

AMPENAN/MATARAM/CAKRANEGARA

AIRPORT

0 ——— 1 km

JL. SUDIRMAN

JL. ADI SUCIPTO

TO SENGGIGI
BEACH

JL.
DUYUNG

TO SENGGIGI BEACH,
GILI TRAWANGAN &
MT. RINJANI

AMPENAN

JL. UDAYANA

JL. COKROAMINOTO

MATARAM

JL. HASANUDIN

TO
LINGSAR
TEMPLE

JL. GORA

JL. LANGKO

JL. PENDIDIKAN

JL. AIRLANGGA

JL. HAKIM

CAKRANEGARA

TO
NARMADA

JL. MAYASARI

JL. SRIWIJAYA

TO LEMBAR HARBOR
& KUTA BEACH

1. Chinese cemetry
2. Segara Temple
3. Tjirabou and Pabean Restaurants
4. cinema
5. Zahir Hotel
6. Horas Losmen
7. Wisma Triguna
8. Sudirman Antiques
9. Ampenan *Bemo* Station
10. Merpati Office
11. Wisma Helati
12. Garuda Office
13. post office
14. police
15. museum
16. tourist office
17. Immigration
18. Bank Indonesia
19. Bank Ragkat Indonesia
20. General Post Office
21. Kambodja Hotel
22. Governor's Office
23. Governor's House
24. Garden Restaurant
25. Rinjani Hotel
26. Kertayaoga Hotel
27. petrol
28. Granada Hotel
29. Selaparang Hotel
30. Mataram Hotel
31. Sekawan Restaurant
32. Losmen Srikandi
33. motorcycle rental
34. Cakra Plaza Shopping Center
35. Pusaka Hotel
36. market
37. Selamat Riady Weaving Center
38. Mayura Water Palace
39. Meru Temple
40. petrol
41. cattle market
42. Sweta Bus Terminal
43. market

has all that you'll need within walking distance: bank, branch post office, telephone office, shopping center, cinema. Get around town by *bemo*, Rp125.

Sights

Only in Aceh Province and on Lombok has a Dutch general been killed in battle; see the grave of General Van Ham, second in command of the Dutch expeditionary force during the Lombok War of 1894, in **Karang Jangkong** between Cakra and Ampenan (near the petrol station). The well-kept **Mayura Water Palace** (Puri Mayura), Jl. Selaparang, is a huge ceremonial pond built in 1744 during the Balin-

ese occupation. In the 18th C., Cakra was the center of the Balinese royal court; the floating pavilion *(Bale Kambang)*, behind the garden and surrounded by a moat, served as a meeting hall and court of justice for the island's Hindu overlords. Now a museum, the hall is filled with old photographs and Dutch colonial memorabilia. See cockfights nearby. The surrounding park, crisscrossed by footpaths, contains fountains and shrines—a pleasant place to stroll around, though you may be wading through kids. Across the street is **Pura Meru**, one of Lombok's main Hindu temples and the largest Balinese temple on Lombok. Built in 1720 by the Balinese Prince Anak Agung

Made Karang, it was meant to symbolize the unity of all the small kingdoms on Lombok. The *puri* is constructed with the usual 3 separate courtyards with 34 *meru*-roofed shrines. Pura Meru is often locked up and you get the usual runaround with the key. Nine km S of Cakranegara is another unique temple perched atop rocky **G. Pengsong**; it's quiet with a beautiful panorama of the towns below.

Accommodations

Losmen Srikandi, Jl. Kebudayaan 2 (tel. 22747), is in the heart of Cakra. It has rooms from Rp5000-8000 with tiled bathrooms, fans, showers; also has a restaurant, attractive gardens, and is close to P.O. and motorcycle rental stand. Take a *bemo* right out front for Terminal Sweta (Rp150). Also central is **Losmen Merpati** at Jl. Hasanuddin 17 (about 50 m from the *stanplatz*); Rp3500 pp with bath. Just up the street, at no. 23, is **Hotel Pusaka** (tel. 23119); Rp4000-10,000 for nice, cool rooms, Rp6500 with private *kamar mandi* and fan. Opposite Bank Bumi Daya (where you can change money), this is a central hotel with peaceful courtyard and a good breakfast. **Losmen Cakra Jaya**, Jl. Okir Kawi (a side street off Jl. Hasanuddin), wants Rp4600 s, Rp6000 d, both classes of rooms with *mandi* inside. Okay, but the Pusaka across the street is better. **Hotel Ratih**, Jl. Selaparang 71 (tel. 21096), charges Rp3000-5000 s, Rp4000-8000 d. **Selaparang Hotel**, Jl. Pejanggik 40-42 (tel. 22670/23235), is a rather overpriced businessmen's hotel: Rp10,500 s, Rp12,500 d, up to Rp22,500 s, Rp26,000 d with restaurant, bar, and Merpati office next door. On the same street is **Hotel Mataram**, Rp7000 s for standard, up to Rp15,000 for a/c rooms. Prices include breakfast.

Food

Plenty of *warung* around Cakranegara serve real *asli* eating such as spicy-hot buffalo curry. For *sate kambing*, try **Warung Istimewa** on Jl. Selaparang. **RM Asia** is just down the street from Hotel Ratih, a little hole in the wall but the food's good and cheap. For Indonesian food, on Jl. Hasanuddin is **RM Madya** and **Restaurant Minang**. For local food, go to **RM Taliwang**, Jl. Rajawali; fried chicken is their specialty. Sample mouth-watering Arabic *kambing* dishes *(sate, gule,* etc.), W. Lombok's specialty, in open-air Pasar Gili near the *bioskop*. Most everyone can cook in Indonesia and a number of the hotels have very good restaurants. Losmen Srikandi serves delicious local, Indonesian and Chinese food. When there are 10 guests or more, Marty, the Balinese owner, puts on all-you-can-eat buffets at Rp1500 pp. Right beside Srikandi is **RM Jasmin**, Jl. Kebudayaan 3, serving a combination of Javanese, Sasak, and Minang food.

Shopping

Unique fabrics and striking *sarung* and *selendang*

woven with gold thread are available in Cakra, but go to the weaving factories where they are actually made. Try **Slamet Riady** at Jl. Ukir Kawi 10, or **Giri Kusuma** (Jl. Selaparang). The shops inside the factories display high-quality authentic weaving, tie-dye (white splotches on linen) pieces, as well as color-rich embroidered wall hangings. Pieces are usually cheaper in Cakranegara than in the outlying villages. Tour the workshops to see the actual weaving processes. For antiques, **Wayan Wika Antique Shop**, Jl. Bangau 12 (in the western part of Cakra), is second only to Sudirman's (in Ampenan) as the best souvenir shop on Lombok. Nice porcelain collection at excellent prices. Sindu village near Cakra makes all the walking sticks you see on Bali. Dozens of *warung* and drink stands surround Terminal Sweta (2 km E of Cakranegara), plus there's a giant covered wholesale market alongside it, biggest on Lombok, selling everything and open everyday. Although nothing like Yogya's, see the bird market with good cockfights and bicycles with up to 60 chickens loaded on them!

From Cakranegara

The only place to rent bikes on Lombok (other than through your hotel) is on the corner of Jl. Kabudayaan, about a 1-min. walk from Losmen Srikandi. These guys want Rp4500 for 12 hours, Rp5500 for 24 hours. Don't just take any machine; stick to your guns until you get a bike that's in reasonably good shape. One will show up eventually. **Sweta**, 2 km E of Cakra (7 km from Ampenan), is the transport hub of Lombok, spewing forth buses, minibuses, and *bemo* to all over the island. For Senggigi, first take a *bemo* to Ampenan (Rp125) then another (Rp300) up to Senggigi. Other sample fares: Tanjung, Rp500; Pemenang (Rp500); Narmada, Rp150; Suranadi, Rp300; Selong and Tansor, Rp750; Kotaraja, Rp750; Bayan, Rp1200; Sengkol (first to Praya, Rp400, then from Praya to Sengkol, Rp300); Lembar (ferry to Bali), Rp1500 or just to the terminal, Rp750. Buses also run to Labuhan Lombok every 30 min. or when they're full. Or arrange for minibuses to pick you up at your hotel at 0530 and see the whole island wake up, arriving in time for the Sumbawa ferry at 1000. If driving a motorcycle to Tetebatu, 5 km before Masbagik take a L on the road to Kotaraja.

OTHER SIGHTS IN WEST LOMBOK

Gunung Pengsong

About 5 km S of Mataram, and 9 km from Cakranegara, a series of temples has been built on a rocky promontory. Climb the long flight of steps up to the shrines for a magnificent view. Pengsong is Lombok's equivalent of Bali's G. Agung. Go early in the morning for a clear view of both Agung and Rinjani. Take a *bemo* first to Pagesangan (Rp150), then another *bemo* to Prampuan (Rp150), then get a *dokar* the rest of the way to G. Pengsong (Rp200).

Pagutan Village

About 5 km SE of Ampenan. One of Lombok's most historic temples, this was where the ancient *Nagarakertagama* manuscript was kept. Written in about 1365 by Prapanca, it's one of Java's *Kawi* classics. Only after the 1894 Dutch invasion and occupation of the raja's palace in Cakranegara did this precious *lontar* chronicle become known to the West. Now stored in the National Museum in Jakarta, the *Nagarakertagama* is one of the main sources of information on the ancient E. Javanese Majapahit Empire.

Narmada

Ten km E of Cakranegara, or Rp300 and 7 km from Sweta by *bemo*. From Narmada's *bemo* stop, cross the road and walk down a side street to the entrance (Rp100). In 1801, a raja's summer palace was built here upon an artificial plateau. From a hidden place above a restful 3-tiered swimming pool, the old raja used to make his selection from the village lovelies. Built by the king of Karangasem (E. Bali), the large complex encompasses a mixture of Balinese, Islamic, and Sasak architecture. The overall design is typically Balinese, the series of compounds laid out as a miniature replica of the summit of G. Rinjani and its crater lake, Segara Anak. Since the king in his old age could no longer make the ascent up to the volcano to lay his offerings, he had this palace constructed to fulfill his spiritual obligations. Worth a couple of hours walking around and swimming (Rp100). The lakeside park is surrounded by somewhat unkempt gardens, which abruptly slope in tiers down to a river valley below. Several *warung* are inside the complex (and plenty more in town). Crowded on weekends. Just before the town of Narmada, see village handicrafts, clothing, and food in the market, one of the largest on Lombok. Opposite the *bemo* station, walk down to the peaceful, clean river fed by cold mountain water.

Suranadi

A small temple and gardens, one of the oldest on Lombok, 7 km and Rp300 by *bemo* N of Narmada and 22 km from Mataram in the cooler hills. See the rebuilt baths of kings carved in the Balinese style and icy clean water bubbling up from natural springs; the pool is said to have been built in exactly the same shape as Lake Segara Anak. At the Temple of the Holy Eels, eels swim out of conduits if you drop an egg in the water. For a little self-indulgence, stay at the former colonial Hotel Suranadi (tel. 23686). Reputed to be the finest hotel on Lombok, offered are all classes of rooms from Rp10,000 to Rp40,000 (cottages with a/c), plus a pool, restaurant, bar, tennis courts—the works. Service and rooms, clean and well kept up, are not bad value and the location is fantastic. Meals are rather expensive (breakfast is a rip-

off), but out in front of the hotel several friendly *warung* serve *gado-gado*, snacks, and genuine Balinese food (vegetables dishes are cheapest). Take a *bemo* (Rp300) up the river 5 km through farming villages to Sesaot, with *bemo* station, market, and forest nearby. The deeper you go, the more proud and *asli* the people become. See people carrying 40-kg loads of firewood on their heads which they've trudged in from the rainforest, selling the load for only Rp3000 in the market.

Lingsar

Three km to the W, back towards Cakranegara, is another sacred eel pool and a large, old Balinese temple complex—holiest on the island—which combines Hindu and Islamic motifs. This worn and faded temple and its pretty courtyard, believed to have been built in 1714, have more of a feeling of an Indian *puri* than anything on Bali; the colors are even more flamboyant than in India! The Waktu Telu Muslims and Balinese worship together here, using different levels of the temple. The Hindu *pura* in the northern part of the complex has 4 shrines, each dedicated to the gods and god-kings of Bali and Lombok. The Waktu Telu temple, in the southern part of the complex, contains an eel pond dedicated to Vishnu. On all-night festivals (during the full moon), sleep in the temple on mats. Lingsar is a highlight of Lombok, an extremely enjoyable experience. Buy eggs for the slug-like holy eels in the *warung*, Rp200 each. In the countryside between Suranadi and Lingsar is **Tragtag**, a pure Balinese village on a small hill, and many other traditional Balinese villages. Take a *bemo* close to Cakranegara's mosque direct to Lingsar (Rp300), or by *dokar* (Rp1000). You can also take a *bemo* from Terminal Sweta to Narmada (Rp200), then board another for Lingsar (Rp200). From Lingsar's *bemo* stop, it's only a 5-min. walk to the temple complex.

Meninting

The whole of NW Lombok is popular with sunbathers, skin divers, and snorkelers. The Meninting area, 3 km N of Ampenan, is one base from which to travel each day out to kilometers of unspoiled, virtually empty beaches such as Sira, Pemenang, and Senggigi, as well as the 3 islands off Bangsal. Further up the coast, the beaches turn white. The rather run-down **Sasaka Beach Hotel** starts at US$25 s, on up to US$29 d for bungalows in a garden setting. Very easy to bargain down to US$10, (cheaper for longer stays), especially if they're half empty. See a regatta of colorful sailing vessels float by in the mornings; Bali's G. Agung is in the distance through the clouds. Don't go strolling naked on the beach—very provocative, rude, and possibly dangerous for travelers who follow you. To get to Meninting, take a *bemo* from near the cinema in Ampenan. The Chinese cemeteries climbing the hills near Meninting were created by popular demand in 1965-67. **Batubulong** is only 1 km N of Meninting; approach this cave temple from the beach.

Senggigi Beach

The coral and snorkeling at this popular beach area, 6 km and a 1½-hours' walk N of Ampenan, is fantastic—4 straight kilometers of pure white sand, blue-green sea, and no crowds. From Ampenan, take a *bemo* for Rp400-500 via Rembiga and Ledengbajur to Senggigi; some drivers take you halfway and demand another Rp1000 or you have to walk! Four *losmen* are near the beach. **Pondok Senggigi** is run by an Australian women who married a Sasak. Only 30 m from the beach, it has 10 bungalows renting for Rp8000 d each. Other possibilities are the **Holiday Inn** (Rp17,000 per room), the Mascot (Rp7000-8000), and the much higher-priced 52-room **Senggigi Beach Hotel**, on the junction of 2 white sandy beaches, looking out across the sea to Bali and G. Agung. The hotel has combined modern-day comforts with traditional bungalow-style Lombok materials (thatch roofs, bamboo mat walls, wooden floors); there's a restaurant open 24 hours, room service, laundry service, telephones, refrigerators, TV, tennis, badminton, and volleyball courts, windsurfing, snorkeling, and outrigger canoes for hire. Standard rooms cost US$43 s, US$53 d; superior rooms US$48 s, US$58 d (prices including government tax and service). You would not be able to tell by its occupancy rate that this is Lombok's most luxurious hotel.

Various *warung* near the beach sell bananas, snacks, *ikan laut* and other meals. There's a *warung* serving *mie* and *nasi campur* only 50 m from Pondok Senggigi on the R going toward the Senggigi Beach Hotel. Drink coconuts to your heart's content. Lots of good walks in the area through coconut groves and unfrequented villages. Travel up and down this coast by just walking out to the road and flagging down a *dokar*, motorcyclist, minibus, *bemo*, or anything else that comes along.

OFFSHORE ISLANDS

The 3 tiny islands of Gili Air, Gili Meno, and Gili Trawangan are off Lombok's NW coast, seen far off on your L as you're flying in from Denpasar or Surabaya. The islands are magnificent, unpopulated (except for 15 houses on Gili Trawangan!), and completely unspoiled. There're about 20 or so accommodations, mostly basic thatch bungalows with wooden floors, small rooms, outside toilet and *mandi*, and meals in the family common room or on the verandah. Gili Meno, the middle island, has only 1 *losmen*. If you're heading for any of the "Gilis," bring extra food, snacks, alcohol, smokes, amusements, paperbacks, and mosquito net because there're no shops. Great quantities of squid *(cumi-cumi)* are caught around these islands, especially in June when

the water is very cool. Brilliant marinelife and coral for snorkeling and skin diving, plus exquisite seashells. The island accommodations rent snorkels, masks, and fins. No roads or vehicles, but you can charter a fishing boat for Rp4000-5000/hour and some *losmen* owners, like Pak Majid, arrange day trips to surrounding islets.

Gili Trawangan

Gili Trawangan has the best snorkeling, with a nice beach, and the locals don't bother you. Great sunsets and views of Bali and G. Rinjani from a hill. Walk completely around this 340-ha island in a leisurely 4 hours. Three *losmen* here, the rates averaging around Rp4500 pp, which includes 3 basic meals a day. The best *losmen* is **Pak Majid's** (good food), a single traveler's haven with room for 20-25 plus people. The managers are really special and enjoy travelers; the beach is only a 20-min. walk away. Other accommodations on Trawangan, such as **Danau Hijau Bungalows** between Pak Majid's and Homestay Makmur, have private, out-of-the-way bungalows for Rp10,000 d, including excellent homecooked meals.

Gili Air

The "tourist" island, the nearest one to the mainland. The coral reef near the boat landing is dying or already dead. Many *losmen* on Gili Air: Rp4500-5000 s, Rp7500-8000 d for most places, which includes meals (food is generally better than on Trawangan). The island's best accommodation is **Gili Indah**, which also has a good restaurant. **Losmen Hanarek** and *Losmen Paradiso* are also recommended. Also many good *warung*. Somewhat overcrowded; if you want peace and quiet, go to Trawangan.

Getting There

First take an overcrowded bus (from 0700-1700) or *bemo* from Terminal Sweta to Pemenang (Rp600, 26 km, 45 min.). Get on a full bus in Sweta if you want to get there fast. Or catch a *bemo* or minibus from in front of Wisma Triguna to Pemenang (Rp500). Once in Pemenang, catch a *cidomo (dokar)* (Rp150) or a *bemo* (Rp100, 1½ km) to the dock at Bangsal. For the closest island, Gili Air, there are many boats per day from 0600-1700 (Rp500, 25 min.). But for Gili Trawangan, you must be at the dock before 1200 because there's only one boat per day. Loaded with travelers, women, and market supplies, this public boat costs Rp1500 pp (1 hour). Or you can charter one for Rp10,000, but freeloaders will also hop onboard.

On the bus N from Sweta you first stop at Lendangbajur (local village market), then Sidemen (see black sugar being made), then Baumpusuk (nice view). From Sidemen climb through wild forests, then from Baumpusuk start descending for 5 km to Pemenang. You could also rent a motorized sampan to Bangsal from Ampenan's Wisma Triguna (1½ hours); ask for Eddy.

CENTRAL LOMBOK

Aikbuka

This resort consists of one large guesthouse (Rp8000-12,000 s or d) overlooking a swimming pool. Surrounded by *sawah*, with a mountain rearing up behind, flower gardens, and godawful loud Indonesian radio music. Meals served. Located in Lombok's central highlands, take a *bemo* from Sweta to Pancardao (Rp400), then another to Aikbuka (Rp200). Or from Mantang, it's Rp600 by *bemo*. If coming from Praya in the S, the road runs right into Mantang, then take a L and travel up to Pancardao, then NE to Aikbuka.

Sukarare

An Islamic weaving center 25 km SE of Mataram and only about 1½ km from Puyung turnoff. From Sweta, first go to Puyung by minibus (Rp350), then hire a *dokar* (Rp200) or walk the 2 km to Sukarare. Nearly everyone in this village is involved with making intricate traditional fabrics such as *songket* (Rp15,000) and *lambung* (black blouses), as well as *sarung* (Rp12,500) and *selendang* (shawls). Bobbin winders, cleverly designed examples of industrial technology, sell for Rp3000 apiece. You have to bargain half the afternoon to get the price for a set down to a realistic level. Also tablecloths, Sasak woven belts, and poor-quality *kris* (Rp25,000 first price!) are sold. The *kepala desa* will show you around and put you up. Tourists have had a negative impact on this place, as seen by the prices asked and the behavior of some money-grubbing individuals. Go early in the mornings when you have a better chance of seeing handloom weaving.

The Kotaraja Area

Kotaraja, 32 km and several *bemo* rides from Terminal Sweta, is a center for woven bamboo basketry, mats, and other plaited ware. Balinese take woven goods back to Bali and sell them as Balinese goods at Balinese prices! An inexpensive homestay, **Sikar Bajang**, charges Rp5000; ask directions. Take a *dokar* up a rocky road straight up to Tetebatu through beautiful countryside (or walk it in 3 hours). The village of **Loyok**, 3 km from Kotaraja, is another bamboo-plaiting center; take a *dokar* from Kotaraja or Paokmotong. Also visit the weaving looms and iron smithies of **Lendangnangka**, a small traditional Sasak *kampung* 4 km from Kotaraja. Get a *bemo* from Sweta to Masbagik, then take a *dokar* (Rp1000, 4 km) up to Lendangnangka. Stay at Radiah's Homestay; Rp6000 s, Rp8500 d including all meals and beverages—an authentic Sasak experience. Radiah is the English-speaking village schoolteacher who, in

the afternoons, is free to take you on tours of the surrounding area. **Jojang**, reputed to be the largest *mata air* on Lombok, is 2 km from Ledangnangka. Sasak weavers work in **Pringgasela**, also 2 km distant. **Labuhan Haji**, 17 km away on the coast, has a nice nearby beach.

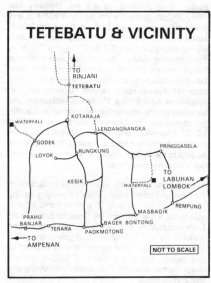

TETEBATU & VICINITY

NOT TO SCALE

Tetebatu

Fifty km E of Mataram and 7 km N of Kotaraja on the cool slopes of G. Rinjani. From Terminal Sweta the minibus drops you off at Paokmotong (Rp700), the turnoff up to Tetebatu. From Paokmotong, take another minibus (Rp600) or a *dokar* all the way to Tetebatu (Rp1500) up through good rich earth and rice and cornfields. Set in a garden and surrounded by fruit orchards, **Wisma Soejono** is an old colonial-style house with spring-fed, ice-cold swimming pools. Actually located 2 km beyond the village of Tetebatu (means "stone bridge"), it was formerly the house of a rich country doctor from Java. The *wisma's* bungalows on the hill, equipped with Western-style toilets and hot and cold showers, cost Rp10,000-12,000 d per night with breakfast. A cheaper set of out-of-the-way bungalows, down the hill near a stream, are only Rp5000 including breakfast. The proprietress fixes excellent homecooked suppers (Dutch, Indonesian, or Javanese) and makes delicious bread, though meals are not included in room price. Cheaper is to eat in the local *warung*. Two springs are near the hotel. You can't reach the summit of G. Rinjani from Tetebatu, but walk for a while up into the thick jungle full of butterflies (use the *wisma's* net scoop) and screaming black monkeys swinging in the trees. Spectacular forest views.

GUNUNG RINJANI

Famed for its great beauty and eerie isolation, G. Rinjani is the third highest mountain in Indonesia, towering over every corner of Lombok. At 3,726 m, Rinjani is even higher than Java's G. Semeru, though well under the snowcapped mountains of Irian Jaya. Its name comes from an old Chinese word meaning "place where the child was born." Shrouded in mists throughout most of the day, the enormous crater of this semi-active volcano is nearly filled with the bright emerald-green water of Lake Segara Anak. Virtually this whole mountain complex, its steep slopes covered in dense forests, has been declared a national reserve. One shudders to think that the government is planning to build a road up to this magnificent natural wonder.

If you ever catch an unimpeded view of G. Rinjani, you are truly blessed. Morning is your best chance (0600?). Photographers often must wait a full week on its rim for a clear shot of the caldera, before it clouds over again in 5 minutes! The mountain is sacred to both the Balinese and the Muslim Sasaks on Lombok. Balinese make a twice-yearly pilgrimage to the top to throw ritual rice and goldfish into the lake, a Hindu offering to the goddess of the mountain. The Sasaks may tramp up the mountain several times a year, especially during the full moon when the caldera could be invaded by groups of noisy *pemuda*.

The Caldera

The volcanos which make up the complex are considered quite young: **G. Barujari** (2,375 m) and **G. Rombongan** in the NW have risen in the caldera only during the last century or two. Barujari still smokes but its last known eruptions were in 1884 and 1901 (a rain of ash). There have also been explosions (1906), thick smoke, and lava flows (1915), cloudy smoke on G. Rinjani's peak (1944), and thundering noise and bellowing thick smoke (1951). Puncak Rinjani itself, highest and steepest point on the edge of the caldera, is 3,726 m high, while the caldera itself is at 1,998 m, and oval in shape. The crescent-shaped **Lake Segara Anak** within the caldera measures 2,400 by 2,800 m, while its depth is 230 m. No fish inhabit its waters, though waterfowl can be seen. Water flows out at a point on the NNE shore called **Kokok Putih**; here are also hotwater springs fed by underground tunnels. It has been estimated that the force necessary to create

G. Rombongan and Barujari, as well as form the lake inside the caldera, was equal to 274 Hiroshima-type atomic bombs.

Climate

Definitely a place to visit in the dry season (April-Oct.), preferably June-Aug., as it's too dangerous in the wet. Streams at the higher altitudes do not dry up and the paths, steep and slippery at the best of times, are much safer and views are better than in the wet season. The steep descent to Segara Anak can be particularly hazardous. However, G. Rinjani itself will most likely be cloud-capped (except in the early morning) most of the year. Pay attention to the altitude! The crater rim, very exposed at any season, can be quite cold. In the mornings the heavy mists gather on your tent like rain.

Preparations

You'll need a tent, ground sheet, cooking gear, matches, flashlight, sleeping bag, warm clothes, stout shoes with good traction, and water for at least 3 days. Buy food in Ampenan, or you must get it all from a *kepala desa* en route. Buy enough food for your guide too, and he'll do the cooking. The guide sometimes provides a pot and water jug. Don't climb it alone. Ideally, 3 people should make the climb because one can care for the injured or sick while the other goes for help. Eddy Batubara at the Wisma Triguna (Jl. Koperasi, Ampenan) can arrange the climb for you, as well as rent you complete camping equipment for around Rp17,500. Other hotels, such as Losmen Kamboja, also render this service.

Climbing It

This is one of Indonesia's unique experiences, and certainly the most brilliant thing to do on Lombok. Unless you're a serious mountain climber, your destination is not actually G. Rinjani, but the beautiful lake inside the caldera. It's an arduous climb, so be in shape. The favorite — and easiest — approaches are from Senaru in the N or Sapit to the E, but actually many routes lead to Segara Anak. Guides and porters can be hired from the Senaru and Sapit departure points; more difficult from the other approaches. The tracks marked on the map are well used, either by pilgrims, by people visiting the hotsprings for medicinal purposes, or for the collection of forest products. Good camping areas are found on the shores of the lake. Inside the crater is often completely deserted — just you, your guide, and your maker.

From Senaru

The shortest and easiest way to climb G. Rinjani, making maximum use of motorized transport. First board the 0900 bus (Rp1500, 70 km, 2 hours) from Terminal Sweta to Ancak near the N coast of the island. Some buses go all the way from Sweta to Bayan, an isolated,

GUNUNG RINJANI APPROACHES

FLORES SEA

TO AMPENAN

ANYAR
ANCAK
LILOAN

BAYAN

BATU KOK

SENARU

WATERFALL

2 HRS.

POS 1 (920 m)

SAJANG

3 HRS.

POS 2 (1,550 m)

3 HRS.

BASE CAMP (2,100 m)

2 HRS

HOTSPRINGS

PADEBELONG

D. SEGARA

PLAWANGAN II

4 HRS

6 HRS

SEMBALUNLAWANG

G. RINJANI
(3,726 m)

SEMBALUNBUMBUNG

PLAWANGAN I

NOT TO SCALE

TO PRINGGABAYA

SAPIT

traditional Muslim village where Hindu-style dances are still practiced. Anthropologists have for years been fascinated by the customs of the complex societies living in sparsely populated northern Lombok, the source of the Waktu Telu religion. Stay with Bayan's *kepala desa*; Rp5000 with 2 meals, and pick up last-minute supplies. From Bayan, walk or catch an occasional truck 5 km to the village of Batu Kok, where the schoolteacher, Mr. Kertabakti, can arrange accommodations in the Sekolah Dasar for Rp3500 (goes to school fund), including a meal. Ask for the *kepala sekolah* (headmaster). Mr. Kertabakti can also arrange a guide (about Rp15,000 RT). It's wise to hire a guide/porter, as it's easy to lose your way on the innumerable paths up the mountain. Guides can also help you cook, carry gear, and fetch water. See the spectacular **Sindanggila Waterfall** near Batu Kok, only an hour's walk up the mountain. From Batu Kok, follow the trail 1 km to the traditional Sasak village of Senaru with its 2 rows of 20 thatched wooden huts. Trucks collect firewood in Senaru, and you could catch a ride with them (though irregular). From Senaru start at 0600 on the 6 + -hour climb to the base camp (water available) just below the crater rim (2,100 m).

The Descent
From the basecamp, start the 2-hour climb up to the lip of the caldera (2,900 m) early the next morning. On the barren rim it's cool and breezy. If it's clear, you may be able see as far as Bali's G. Agung, the whole coastline, and the neighboring island of Sumbawa to the east. Inside the crater, stands of pine dot the slopes, and the otherworldly green expanse of Segara Anak spreads before you. From only 2 points, **Plawangan I** on the N side and **Plawangan II** on the E side, can you make the dizzy descent down the precipitous crater wall to the lake. Taking 6 hours and with scary sections of loose rubble, this is not for the weak at heart. Camp by the lake (water available), enjoy views of new lava flows and puffing G. Barujari, walk to Kokok Putih, and soak your aching bones in the delightful hotsprings nearby (reputed to aid skin ailments). Count on 10-12 hours to hike back to Batu Kok, so start at daybreak. If you return to Ancak by 1530, you'll make the last bus which departs for Terminal Sweta at around 1600. The last bus departs Bayan for Sweta around 1800. If you don't make it, spend the night at the schoolhouse in Batu Kok.

From Sapit
More difficult than the northern approach from Bayan. First take a bus (Rp1500, 2 hours) from Sweta on the main highway across the island to Pringgabaya, then catch a *bemo* (Rp500) N to Swela. At Swela (elev. 500 m) is a neglected colonial-style guesthouse (with icecold *mandi*) only 100 m from the road on top of a hill (views of Sumbawa), surrounded by a huge garden; 3 rooms (Rp3000 d) with big iron beds and Dutch embroidered bedsheets. Good meals for Rp1500. Visitors are so rare that children wait at the guesthouse gate for hours just to catch a glimpse of you. Swela is 100% Muslim: the minaret's loudspeaker is going from early morning to late evening. From Swela, take a *bemo* down a jungle road to Sapit. In Sapit (or Swela) hire a guide—so many paths go up G. Rinjani that you can't tell the main one from the others. Horses are also for hire. For 3-4 hour after Sapit, catch views (only between 0800 and 0900) on the L through paddyfields of G. Rinjani. Walk through unspoiled villages, practically the whole population following you for 2 km after you leave each village. The climb is very gradual, not difficult, but you must cross frequent rivers and the trail could be muddy.

From Sapit, continue walking N 5 hours to **Sembalunbumbung**, then it's another 5 km to **Sembalunlawang**, where you can stay the night with the *kepala desa* and also hire a guide. This Sasak village, in a cold, picturesque valley, is quite friendly and a pleasant base from which to explore the surrounding countryside. From Sembalunlawang, it's about a 12-hour hike to Rinjani's rim. There are some shelters on the way up, the lower portion for sheep and goats, the upper

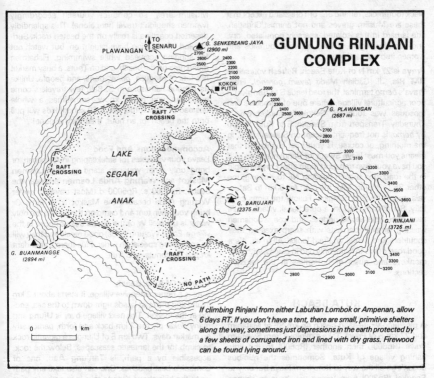

GUNUNG RINJANI COMPLEX

TO SENARU

PLAWANGAN

G. SENKEREANG JAYA (2900 m)
2700
2600
2500
2400
2300
2200
2100
2000

KOKOK PUTIH

2000
2100
2200
2300
2400
2500 2600

G. PLAWANGAN (2687 m)

2700
2800
2900

3000
3100
3200
3300
3400
3500
3600

RAFT CROSSING

LAKE

SEGARA

ANAK

RAFT CROSSING

G. BARUJARI (2375 m)

G. RINJANI (3726 m)

G. BUANMANGGE (2894 m)

RAFT CROSSING

3400
3300
3200

NO PATH

2800   2900   3000   3100   3200

0   1 km

If climbing Rinjani from either Labuhan Lombok or Ampenan, allow 6 days RT. If you don't have a tent, there are small, primitive shelters along the way, sometimes just depressions in the earth protected by a few sheets of corrugated iron and lined with dry grass. Firewood can be found lying around.

platform for people, as well as some mountain hamlets such as **Padebelong**; for help, contact the *mangku,* the local name for head of the clan. About 10 km from Sembalunlawang is the mountain village of **Raga,** where you may spend the night in the home of a farm family (give a donation). From Raga straight up to the rim is 4 km. Or spend the night in the basecamp (elev. 2,100 m) below the rim, then very early the next morning climb up and over the rim at Plawangan II down into the crater. Go out via Bayan so you don't have to backtrack.

Other Approaches
From Sembalunlawang, take one day to traverse the

rim of the whole complex via **Sajang** and **Liloan** to Bayan and start your climb from there. From Bayan, you may also walk to Torean, then make your way along the edge of Sungai Kokok Putih (which drains Lake Segara Anak) straight to the floor of the crater. This severe route takes one day.

From Sesaot
Sesaot, 5 km NW of Suranadi and SW of the Rinjani complex, is another approach but you have to spend 2 nights in the slippery jungle. This long, challenging hike, which should only be attempted in the dry season, will not treat the hiker with beautiful views as the path leads through a thick forest. Guide needed.

SOUTH LOMBOK

The trip to the S coast of the island is a journey through time. All of Lombok was once like Lombok Selatan. You'll pass by whole villages of thatched houses built on hilltops to defend against human predators. Surrounding these Sasak villages are cul-

tivated fields of *ubi kayu, ubi jalar* (types of sweet potato), and other crops which support the subsistence economy. March is rice-harvesting time when you see women in the fields cutting and men carrying. Hilltop graveyards of tiny upright stones, like gnarly black toothpicks, remind one of Torajaland except that these are Muslim graves and not animist/Christian. Life is hard in this isolated, sparsely populated, dry, and scrubby region, a land of water buffalos and women in black clothing.

Praya is 27 km N of Kuta Beach. Refresh yourself at **RM Ria**, Jl. Gadjah Mada *(ayam goreng)*. From Praya's *bemo* terminal, the road leads S to **Sengkol**, a poor agricultural village, where one of Lombok's first mosques was founded. Sengkol's market day is Thursday. Transport from Sengkol S to Kuta, Rp600 by *bemo*, is not frequent (except on Sunday). During the morning, of course, is your best chance, so that means you must leave Sweta for Sengkol real early. If you have your own transport, right after Praya is a split in the road, one branch heading NE to Kopang, the other SE to Mujur. Take the road for 6 km to Batun-yala, then turn S to Sengkol. Follow the signs carefully. South of Rambitan, a pure Sasak village, you'll pass over little stone bridges and see woodsmen wearing lantana-fiber hats with sharp axes on their shoulders and fierce, unafraid looks. All in all, it's a good road down to Kuta, only bad in places, with wild monkeys and gusts of butterflies in the forested sections.

KUTA BEACH

A gleaming white-sand beach 45 km SE of Mataram and 27 km S of Praya. Take a minibus from Sweta to Praya (Rp600), then another (Rp600) to the little fishing village of Kuta. Sometimes the minibus doesn't go all the way to Kuta from Praya but only to Sengkol (Rp300) from where you have to change minibuses again to Kuta (Rp300). Kuta is a strong

Muslim area, so conduct yourself accordingly (women shouldn't travel here alone). This splendidly deserted coastline is really off the beaten track. Surfing and windsurfing have caught on, but watch out for stinging seaweed while swimming. Fishermen mend nets on the beach, and on Thurs. a busy market has lots of produce, *dokar*, dogs, and people. Unlike its famous namesake in S. Bali, few travelers come here. But you never know; sometimes a whole busload of French tourists or 50 school kids will pull onto the beach for an hour, then they're gone!

Accommodations And Food

Leave your valuables for safekeeping in Ampenan, or bring only what you can stand to lose. **Losmen Maskot** and **Warung Anda Losmen** are near the beach; Rp4000 s, Rp5000 d. Most travelers prefer Warung Anda because the Maskot is so dirty. Or bring your own tent and camp on the beach; the only water is the well W of the *kepala desa's* house in the village. Eat at Warung Anda; good meals and they will fix something special on order. Plus there's abundant *krupuk*, coconuts, and fruit.

Vicinity Of Kuta Beach

Kuta is a rather extensive village; it starts about 2 km inland and the road heads right down to the sea, ending at the market. The next village over is **Ujung**, and many *dokar* ply the 2 km back and forth, particularly on market days. Two km E of Ujung is a gigantic rock to climb for the fantastic seascapes. Below the rock, accessible by a path, is **Tanjung Aan**, one of Lombok's best beaches. One can also take any path up to the hills above Kuta to take in superb views of the ocean, mountains, and the thin line of beaches.

EAST LOMBOK

On the road E across Lombok, catch intermittent views of G. Rinjani looming above you. The dry eastern half of Lombok has much less contact with tourists than the western half. Kids shout "Jerman! Jerman!" to nearly every traveler, and when you take out your camera it's "Kodak! Kodak!" Instead of asking for money when photographed, the people *thank you!* Like the Javanese, the women wear the typical *sarung kebaya*. The field workers wear large conical-shaped straw hats and live in straw and bamboo huts, just as are found in Lombok Selatan. An older race, their faces are longer, with higher cheekbones, and more Mongolian features. Chinese are noticeably absent from E. Lombok; the people will tell you that they fled long ago and their houses were burned to the ground.

Labuhan Lombok

A poor Muslim town on the NE coast, from Sweta by bus, Rp1500, 3-4 hours. Located on a beautiful bay with fine views of G. Rinjani, but kind of run-down, with scraggly dogs in the street, uneducated, strictly Islamic people (nearest Christian church is in Selong). Not much to entertain yourself with, but some of Lombok's finest blankets are produced in the area. **Losmen Mawar**, about ½ km from the harbor, charges Rp3000 s, Rp5000 d. The only place near the harbor is a stinking, vile *losmen* called the **Sudimampir**. On Jl. Kajangan, all the way through town to the harbor, about a 10- min. walk from the *bemo* station, it consists of 12 tatty rooms at Rp2500 s, Rp3500 d. Electricity is irregular. Tickets for the boat to Sumbawa are sold at the boat office in the harbor. *Warung* and several *rumah makan* are around the *bemo* station/market selling basic but edible meals and beverages. Try the popular vegetable soup called *bayam*.

From Labuhan Lombok

If you're headed for Sumbawa, it may be preferable to spend your last night in Ampenan or Cakranegara rather than in Labuhan Lombok. But be on a big bus heading out no later than 0500 or 0530 to catch the Sumbawa ferry; most hostelers in Ampenan and Cakra will arrange ticket purchase and pickup. Ferries to Alas Harbor depart Labuhan Lombok daily around 0800 and 0900; Rp2500 (one class only), motorcycles Rp3000; 3-4 hours. The 0800 boat arrives in Alas at around 1300. The dock area is 2 km from town on the road past the *bemo* stand and *pasar*, Rp500 by *dokar*.

Vicinity Of Labuhan Lombok

Something to do in East Lombok? Climb **G. Kayangan** (elev. 500 m) on the path which starts near the harbor; takes only 30 minutes. Good view of Selat Alas from the top, with *prahu* slicing through the strait to Sumbawa. Heading 4 km N towards Labuhan Pandan is **Kampung Nelayan**, a fishermen's *kampung* (can easily see it from G. Kayangan). At **Timbanuh**, an old Dutch resort N of Pringgasela, is a resthouse and a rather broken-down swimming pool. **Labuhan Haji**, 30 km S of Labuhan Lombok, is an old port which in former times was a disembarkation point for pilgrims *(haji)* sailing to Mecca, thus its name. From the small beach beyond the market boats embark for Alas (2½ hours, Rp2500), though less frequently (0900 and in the afternoon sometime) than from Labuhan Lombok. Wait on the beach with all the other passengers. At the market buy 15-20 giant shrimp for Rp1000! On the way to Labuhan Haji, only 1½ km from **Tanjung**, is a bathing place called Kembang Kuning. At **Tanjung Ringgit**, 110 km S of Labuhan Lombok, are large caves where, it's said, a legendary *raksasa* lives. First get a *bemo* S to Keruak, then another *bemo* to Senange, then walk one day to the fishing village of Tanjung Ringgit.

SUMBAWA

An extension of the volcanic mountain chain extending E from Java all the way to the Alor Archipelago, 15,600-sq-km Sumbawa is made up of rolling uplands, eroded foothills, volcanic ridges, and ancient crater walls. Wildlife here is abundant, and although flora and fauna are predominantly Asian in origin, Australian climatic influence is also obvious: spiny bush, acacia, thorn, cactus, and extensive savannah. Sumbawa's S coast is lined with extinct volcanic peaks that plunge straight into the Indian Ocean. For the most part, the N coast consists of plains and river basins, except for the jagged peak of **G. Tambora** (elev. 2,820 m) on Teluk Saleh, towering 915 m above any other point in Sumbawa's mountainous spine. Fertile valleys with bright green ricefields surrounding the towns occur mainly along the rivers on the northern coast and in river valleys in the central uplands. As you travel E on the island's single paved highway, much of the land is covered with a park-like landscape of large, open tracts of countryside alleviated only by small clusters of trees and shrubs, brown hills, and a mountainous coast with picturesque bays and harbors. The island's rainy season is usually Nov. to April, with little daily variation in temperature.

History

Certain areas, particularly in the E, are known for their megaliths and sacrophagi which date from Sumbawa's Neolithic era over 2,000 years ago. The Java-nese epic, *Nagarakertagama*, written on *lontar* leaf in 1365, mentions 4 principalities on Sumbawa as dependencies of the great Majapahit Empire of E. Java; the names of these early princes indicate Hindu influence. The earliest known indigenous kingdoms in W. Nusatenggara were the comparatively small states of the Sasaks in Lombok, the Sumbawans in W. Sumbawa, and the Bimans and Dompuese in E. Sumbawa. For several centuries the Makassarese of southern Celebes indulged in pillage and slaving raids along Sumbawa's N coast, using the concept of "holy war" to justify conquest. It was they who first brought Islam to Sumbawa. The Kingdom of Goa in S. Celebes subjugated Bima in 1616, and established many small sultanates. Even today, the political system, the descent of the royal sultanate families of the N coast, and the world view derive from that Makassarese kingdom near Ujung Pandang. The palaces of the old sultans still exist; Bima's palace is now a college and the stilted, barn-like palace of Sumbawa Besar was also restored in the early 1980s. The Dutch first landed in 1605, but since the island had little commercial value, they maintained only representatives there and did not rule effectively until the start of this century. The most violent event in Sumbawa's history was the awesome 1815 eruption of G. Tambora; its suffocating rain of ash either directly killed or eventually starved to death 90,000 people, most of the island's and neighboring islands' population at the time. Although the size of the volcano was reduced from nearly 4,000 m to a puny 2,821 m, it's still the world's largest volcanic cone.

Economy

As early as the 14th C., Sumbawa had become very wealthy through its natural resources of timber and horses. Along with Timor, this island was the source of the fragrant woods *sapan* and sandalwood, valuable commodities which Asian and later European trading powers exported for over 300 years. The island's exports today are almost completely agricultural: rice, coconuts, corn, tobacco, cotton, peanuts, and beans. Cattle and some of the country's best-bred horses are also exported; the Sumbawa horse is in high demand all over Indonesia as a draft animal for pulling *dokar* and *andong* (called here *benhur*). Many of the island's forests are virgin, and raw timber has recently become a major export commodity, the result of a joint venture with Filipino companies. The denuding of Sumbawa's forests is causing the usual ecological devastation. About 90% of the Sumbawanese farm for a living, growing mainly rice, and those inland even hunt for their protein. During the dry season, but just before the rains, much of the farming populace migrates from their permanent villages to flimsy makeshift huts in their fields in the mountains. When the plowing and planting begin they stay and guard the fields against wild boar, deer, monkeys, birds, rodents, wild cattle, and insects until the harvest is in. Sumbawa is well known for its honey, which is believed to increase sexual potency.

The People

This island, as big as Lombok and Bali together, has about 800,000 inhabitants. Lying at a transitional point between the Indianized "high" cultures of western Indonesia and the traditional pagan cultures of eastern Indonesia, Sumbawa is a fascinating ethnographic area. From prehistoric times, Sumbawa has been inhabited by 2 linguistic groups who for centuries couldn't understand each other: the Sumbawa-speaking states to the W and the Bima-speaking clans of the east. The western Sumbawans and Lombok's Sasaks share similar customs and language. The Bimans, on the other hand, are shorter, darker-complexioned, more fiery tempered, and earthier than the Sumbawans, and speak a language resembling that of Sumba and Flores. Today, *Bahasa Indonesia* bridges the linguistic gap. There has never been any Christian missionary activity on the island and both groups are today strict Muslims; there is, however, a powerful undercurrent of animist beliefs and adherence to *adat*. The Biman-speaking Dou Donggo people, living in the mountains of the Donggo area W of Teluk Bima, are the descendants of the island's aboriginals and number around 20,000. Yet another small, linguistically separate group, the Dou Tarlawi, inhabit the mountains E of Teluk Bima.

Sumbawa is heavily Islamic: many of the women still cover their faces, and the eastern districts send proportionally more *haji* to Mecca than any other region of Indonesia. The western part is a mixture of cultures and customs. Mountaineer rustics live in the interior villages of the western peninsula's foothills; see them come down to the more prosperous urban lowlands to trade their horseloads of woven mats and baskets. These upland Sumbawans often carry large machete-like knives *(berang)*, ornamented with carved dragons. The Dompu area is well known for its cloth worked with silver thread. Eastern Sumbawa is a rocky, dusty, parched country of stubbly growth and bamboo villages on stilts.

Events

Especially during Ramadan, the loudspeakers from the mosques in both Sumbawa Besar and Bima keep you up into the wee hours. But people in the eastern end, at least in Bima, are not that fanatical and food is available all day during this religious holiday. Mock battles, with men wearing Arabic rolled turbans, can be seen on this island. On holidays, at festivals, and harvest times, you might see traditional Sumbawan boxing matches (see them in E. Bali too). With palms bound with sharp rice stalks, which can inflict ugly cuts, this nearly bare-fisted boxing (called *berempah*) usually ends in a draw. Sumbawan men are skilled archers and still hold contests occasionally, firing their arrows into targets which move along a high wire. Water buffalo races also take place at festival times. A few indigenous dances survive; one is the *barapan kebo*, which depicts the *kerbau* race. Sumbawan orchestras, made up of drums and flutes, sound like bagpipes. *Kulkus* (long hollow drums) are still used for sending messages, and fine violins are also crafted by hand on this island.

Getting There

Heading into Nusatenggara Barat from Bali, put your watch ahead an hour. Merpati flies between Denpasar and Sumbawa Besar via Ampenan (Lombok) for around Rp45,000. Every Fri. Merpati also flies from Denpasar to Bima, continuing on to Labuhanbajo and Ruteng on Flores the same day. Ferries connect E. Lombok with Alas; see "Labuhan Lombok" in the Lombok chapter. Buses wait at Alas Harbor to take you direct to: Sumbawa Besar, Taliwang, or Bima. More frequent buses depart from the bus station in Alas, 2 km from the harbor.

Getting Around

No problem. Pony carts (called here *benhur* or *bendi* but not *dokar*) are widely used, and *bemo* and minibuses for local transport are plentiful. Besides the good, paved road—the only one—traversing Sumbawa from W to E (Jareweh to Sape), the island is crisscrossed by foot tracks. If you get off the main road, get ready for a spleen-splitting ride with many stops for cargo, passengers, or to retie goats on the roof. A twisting bumpy trail follows Sumbawa's N coast, but the southern coast is difficult to reach. During the wet months (Nov.-April), there are many washed out, rotted bridges. Occasional floods between late Nov. and Feb. can carry shacks, fences, and cattle down to the ocean. From Sumbawa, Merpati services inter-island connections such as Sumbawa Besar to Denpasar (Rp48,400), with same-day connectons to Jakarta and Surabaya. Flights from Bima to Denpasar cost Rp68,200, with onward connections to Surabaya and Jakarta. Merpati also offers a number of connections from Bima to other towns of Nusatenggara: Labuhanbajo, Rp39,700; Malang, Rp94,400; Ruteng, Rp52,600; Ende, Rp49,700; Kupang, Rp101,400; Waingapu, Rp55,400.

ALAS

A W coast port where the ferry from Lombok docks. Besides the Makassarese fishing village on stilts out in the bay, nothing much to see. Kids are pesky and the streets unpretty. Stay in **Losmen Salemat** (Rp5000 s), 1 km out of town on the road to the harbor at Jl. Pahlawan 7 (tel. 26); another rather basic *losmen* near the *stasiun polisi* charges Rp3500 s. Get to the harbor from town by *benhur* (Rp200) and buy your ticket for Lombok at the pier. Daily ferries for Labuhan Lombok depart Alas at 0800 or 0900 and perhaps—if the weather is good—another at 1000. The fare is Rp2075 pp, Rp3500 for motorcycles. Arriving in Labuhan Lombok, buses wait to take passengers across the island.

From Alas

Arriving in Alas from Lombok, at the pier you are greeted by hordes of agents, all trying to get you into their direct bus or minibus to: Sumbawa Besar, Rp1500 (65 km, 1½-2 hours); Bima, Rp6000 (9-10 hours). For Taliwang to the S, take a *benhur* to the Alas bus terminal (Rp400 for 2) from where numerous buses leave; Rp1500 (1½ hours). If heading all the way across the island, it's less grueling to break the journey up at Sumbawa Besar. On the way you pass over forested mountains; in the villages of **Utan** and **Ree** trees come right down to serene beaches. Some buses meeting the boat in Alas *do* go all the way to Sape (yes, in a single day—you arrive in Sape about 2300, totally whacked).

TALIWANG

In spite of a long, indented coastline and deep bays, Sumbawa's population is not oriented to the sea and

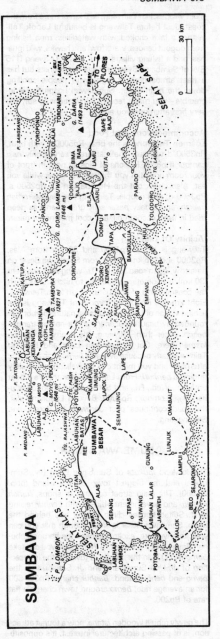

most villages, like Taliwang, lie 5 km or more from the coast. Just before Taliwang is beautiful **Lebok Taliwang,** a lake choked with waterlilies, men fishing from dugout canoes, waterfowl and hawks, wild iguanas, and a fishing village. Dirty, dusty Taliwang (115 SW of Sumbawa Besar) attracts few tourists but has a neat atmosphere at night with people strolling down the main street. Sumbawan hospitality is incredible—you might receive 6 invitations to stay the very first afternoon you arrive.

Accommodations And Food
Losmen Tubalong is the best; Rp5000 d with bath, Rp3500 d without. The restaurant serves only *nasi campur* (Rp850). Millions of kids sit right in front of your room or watch you through windows while you eat. Also check out the **Hamba Inn** for Rp2500 s, Rp3500 d; nice people. Taliwang has several *rumah makan,* and a daily *pasar* sells green bananas deep fried in fresh coconut oil, and cool melons for thirst.

Vicinity Of Taliwang
Taliwang is about Rp1500 and 30 km from Alas, Rp2000 and 115 km by bus from Sumbawa Besar on a narrow, good road. On the Taliwang-Alas segment (30 km), it's sometimes possible to hitch trucks. Visit the coastal resort of Potobatu, 15 km from Taliwang. Eight km and Rp300 by *bemo* S of Taliwang is the fishing village of **Labuhan Lalar,** a natural harbor surrounded by beautiful scenery and a nearby tranquil beach. Nicer than Taliwang, it's a pity there's no *losmen* here. Get to Labuhan Lalar and back to Taliwang early because available *bemo* drop off in the afternoon and you might end up walking (or possibly finding a *benhur)*. From Labuhan Lalar there's a boat on Mon., Wed., Fri., and Sat. at about noon to Labuhan Haji, Lombok, Rp2000. Beyond Labuhan Lalar, the road continues past Jareweh to Berete and Sekongkang.

SUMBAWA BESAR

The lowland *ibukota* of Sumbawa Barat (W. Sumbawa) and the biggest town on the island (pop. 32,000). The main street consists of shops, *rumah makan,* and government offices, with *benhur* raising dust. Stilted houses climb up the hills behind the town. Sumbawa Besar is small enough that you can walk to anywhere, except perhaps the harbor (Labuhan Batas) past the airport, in which case you can take *bemo* (Rp300). In the middle of town, at the intersection of Jl. Urip Sumoharjo and Jl. Setiabudi, is the *bemo* and *benhur* stand. *Benhur* charge Rp300-500 for an average ride; *bemo* around town charge a flat rate of Rp200.

The newly rebuilt wooden *istana,* now a tourist attraction, is of passing architectural interest. It's opposite

the mosque and only a 10-min. walk from the *bemo* and *benhur* station on Jl. Setiabudi. This old, barn-like former sultan's palace (built in 1932), with its rusty cannon, is called the **Dalem Loka**. It is a solid timber structure raised high off the ground on hardwood logs. Up until the mid-1970s, a wrinkled 100-year-old woman with snow-white hair, Sultan Jalaluddin III's fourth and only surviving wife, still lived in this building of creaking carved doors, carpets full of dust, a huge wall with a row of nuptial couches on either side. There's talk of opening up a portion of it as a museum containing *pusaka* and historical objects. Also visit the **Pura Agung Girinatha** Bali-style Hindu temple, near the intersection of Jl. Setiabudi and Jl. Yos Sudarso.

Accommodations And Food
Many good *losmen* are within easy walking distance from the *stasiun bis,* surrounding the mosque on Jl. Hasanuddin and all in the Rp2500-3500 s, Rp4000-6000 d range. Though too close to the mosque to be restful, **Losmen Saudara** (tel. 21528) is clean, central, and friendly. If Losmen Saudara is full, try clean **Losmen Succi,** Jl. Hasanuddin 57 (tel. 21589), with nice courtyard and garden (Rp5000 d with private bath). The *penjaga* will cheerfully arrange bus tickets for you (he gets a commission from the bus company). Right next door to Losmen Succi is basic **Losmen Tunas**. **Losmen Indra** (tel. 21878) is also near the bus station. Also try **Losmen Asia,** Jl. Dr. Sutomo 4, or **Losmen Baru,** Jl. Wahidin 45. Forget divey **Losmen Bahagia**. Sumbawa's top hotel is the **Hotel Tambora** (tel. 21555), a Rp200 ride from *stasiun bis* (or only a 15-min. walk). Rp7500 s, Rp8500 d with private *mandi*. Also more expensive rooms with fans (Rp9500) and a/c Rp16,500-18,500. Check out the splendid wall map of Sumbawa!

Eat in the *warung* that line Jl. Wahiddin near the intersection of Jl. Merdeka at night. Decent Chinese-style meals are served at **RM Anda** (Jl. Wahiddin) or down the street at the cheaper **RM Taliwang** try the *nasi campur*. For the best *nasi goreng* in town, go to **RM Surabaya,** only 2-min. walk from the *stasiun bis*. For Chinese food, **Aneka Rasa Jaya** is the place. Directly opposite the Dalem Loka is a Padang restaurant, **RM Minang Jaya**. **Hotel Tambora** has a nice garden restaurant.

Services
The **post office** is way out past the airport; take one of the *bemo* which cruise Jl. Hasanuddin (Rp200). Change money at **Bank Negara Indonesia,** Jl. Kartini 10 (tel. 21936). Open Mon. to Sat. 0730-1130, it's easy to change the better-known travelers cheques and cash all the major currencies, but they will balk at anything wierd like Citibank TCs or Spanish pesos. The **PPA office** is on Jl. Garuda on the way to the airport. The main shopping street is Jl. Kartini, but be

sure to check out **Kantor Departmen Perindustrian Kabupaten Sumbawa** on Jl. Garuda (opposite the PPA office), where some native handicrafts are on display.

From Sumbawa Besar

Merpati (Jl. Hasanuddin 80) has flights to Ampenan (Rp34,500) and Denpasar (Rp48,500). The bus station is in the center of town on Jl. Diponegoro; most passengers are local, traveling only for short distances. All fares are posted: Taliwang, 115 km, Rp2000; Empang, 93 km, Rp2800; Bima, 250 km, Rp5000; Alas, 69 km, Rp1500. Buses to Dompu leave about 0900 (Rp5000, 9 hours). Buses to Bima, on a well-surfaced road with spectacular scenery, depart at 0900 and 1400. Buy tickets at the bus station yourself or your *losmen* will send a boy; minibuses come by the *losmen* to pick passengers up. Avoid getting a seat over the rear axle and don't ride on top because branches could sweep you off.

For boats to Lombok and beyond, check with the *syahbandar* in Sumbawa Besar's port of **Labuhan Batas,** accessible by public *bemo* for around Rp300. Or charter a *bemo* straight to the harbor for Rp2000–3000. Ferries sail irregularly to Ampenan (Lombok), then on to Padangbai (Bali) for around Rp7500. Try the *Kuda Putih,* which might leave Labuhan Batas on Sun. at 1600 and arrive in Padangbai on Mon. at 0300; no food onboard. For Labuhan Lombok, buy tickets at Losmen Saudara. Start out from Sumbawa Besar by bus at 0530 for Alas so you'll have plenty of time to reach the boat which leaves at 0900.

Vicinity Of Sumbawa Besar

Saliperate is a sandy beach with coconut trees 5 km and Rp400 by *benhur.* At **Semongkat** is a swimming pool in the cool mountains, by *bemo* 17 km. Visit the dark caves of **Liang Petang,** where magic stones resemble women's breasts; 25 km by bus and foot. **Tepas** is a traditional Sumbawan village on the slopes of the Batu Lante Mountains, 60 km by *bemo* and horseback from Sumbawa Besar. In **Berang Rea,** 30 km, is an interesting geological phenomenon: if you put a stick in a pool called Aik Kawat, the water solidifies around it. On the beach at **Lampui,** 80 km S on the S coast, are turtle nesting sites; take a bus as far as you can, then walk or take a horse.

In the foothills SE of Sumbawa Besar are a number of megaliths dating from Neolithic times. A particularly rich archaeological area is around the village of **Batu Tering** (near Semamung), Rp600 and 14 km by *bemo* from Sumbawa Besar. Hire a guide for Rp5000 for the complete 2-hour tour to massive sarcophagi with human and crocodile figures carved in low relief. Scholars belief that these were the tombs of tribal chieftains who lived over 2,000 years ago. Other archaeological sites are **Punik,** 35 km from Sumbawa

Besar, a cryptic stone pillar depicting a man, a dog, and a hen; and **Aik Renung** (a Neolithic sarcophagus), 25 km from Sumbawa Besar.

Pulau Moyo

An island 3 km off the N coast of Sumbawa, ⅔ of which is a virgin game reserve. Moyo's central plateau, with its grassy savannahs and intermittent monsoonal forest, is ideal country for *rusa* deer as well as the feral cattle that have been released here. Wildlife is easy to see; even as you're approaching on the boat you see deer running wild! Hunting requires a permit from the police; you can bag a deer in 5 minutes. There are also wild boar, abundant birds (orioles, drongos, koels, coucals, sunbirds), as well as megapodes and shore birds. There are also good beaches with fine coral sand, and a splendid coral reef at the S end of the island. From P. Moyo, there are magnificent views of G. Tambora to the east. All the human settlements (21 villages) are concentrated at the N end of the island; the main town is **Sebaru.** To get there, take a boat from Labuhan Batas, or from Sumbawa Besar take a minibus to **Limung,** 20 km NE of Sumbawa, then by *prahu* across the 3-km strait to Tg. Pasir on Moyo's S coast. The PPA office (Jl. Garuda) in Sumbawa Besar can be of assistance; their motorboat occasionally visits Moyo, so inquire. Plan your trip for the dry season (April-Oct.) and if camping bring supplies, food, and water as there are no facilities on the island.

GUNUNG TAMBORA

The massive 1815 eruption of G. Tambora, one of the most destructive and powerful in human history, started on 5 April 1815. For several years prior to the blast, dark thick smoke poured out of the cone, the rumblings and thundering growing more and more powerful. Finally, on 5 April, the volcano exploded with a boom that could be heard as far away as Ternate (1,400 km). In Batavia, 1,250 km from the blast, the sounds of the eruption resembled distant cannon fire and prompted the English governor-general, Sir Stamford Raffles, to march troops into the city to defend it against rebel attack. The volcanic paroxysm reached its greatest magnitude between 10-12 April, when the whole mountain turned into a body of liquid fire, blowing 100 cubic km of debris into the sky. The thunder could be heard 1,775 km away at Bengkulu on Sumatra. Tremors were felt in Surabaya (600 km), and stones as large as 2 fists were catapulted 40 km from the demolished peak. The ejecta which circled the globe caused temperatures to drop almost 2 degrees F below normal for a whole year, resulting in the famous "year without summer" of 1816. Volcanic dust sent into the stratosphere also acted as a giant filter, creating spectacular orange sunsets around the world which some theorize inspired the moody lighting in paintings by the great British artist J.M.W. Turner.

On and around Sumbawa, a thick blanket of ash settled over an area of 2½ million sq km, darkening the whole region for 3 days, while the sea around the island was clogged with thousands of uprooted trees and huge islands of floating pumice. Earthquakes, whirlwinds, and tidal waves caused by the collapse of the peak killed 12,000 people outright, while another 78,000 died of cholera, overexposure, and starvation during the ensuing drought and crop failure throughout the whole of Nusatenggara. All the arable land on Sumbawa was rendered infertile, its surface covered in ½ m of ash and mud, making it impossible to plant rice for several years. The monster having spent itself, 2 years of minor activity followed, but even as late as Aug. 1819 one could still hear strong thunder, feel the earth move, and fire could be seen glistening on the mountain. It was not until 1847, that the first scientific expedition (headed by the Swiss, Zollinger) was dispatched to study G. Tambora. Only then did there emerge a clear understanding of what had happened, and all the strange phenomena which had visited the earth decades earlier at last understood.

The Crater
Prior to 1815, Tambora consisted of 2 giant soaring peaks each over 4,000 m high, its majestic cone visible from 30 km away at sea. The gigantic eruptions of 1815 reduced the volcano to a jagged 2,821-m-high crater, **Doro Afi Toi,** which is today made up of 4 cones: Tahe (877 m), Molo (602 m), Kadiendinae, and Kubah (1,648 m). Beautiful forests cover its western slopes, for the most part *Duabanga molluccana* trees up to 60 m high. Tambor's enormous caldera measures 6 km wide with a depth of 600-700 m. The crater floor to the NW is higher than other areas in the crater, the highest area being to the N covered in grass and underbrush. The lowest area of the crater floor is to the E where there's a small colored lake. A small volcanic plug to the SW has a diameter of 100 m and height of 60 m. A tongue of lava flows to the NE for 350 m, probably a result of the most recent eruption (1913). Close to the S crater wall are the remains of a secondary crater.

Climbing It
The usual way is from **Labuhan Kenanga** to the NW. First take a *prahu* from Labuhan Batas to **Sebaru** on the N coast of P. Moyo, then charter a *prahu* to Labuhan Kenanga. Or charter a *prahu* direct to Labuhan Kenanga from Labuhan Batas. From Labuhan Kenanga, hike or take a horse first 15 km to the coffee estate, **Perkebunan Kopi Tambora.** The climb from the plantation to the top takes 4-5 days. Another approach is from **Dompu** in eastern Sumbawa; a part of the way to the village of Doro Kempo can be driven by 4WD vehicles (charter from Bima). From the top of G. Tambora are spectacular views over Teluk Saleh, the rest of Sumbawa to the E, and W past P. Moyo to Lombok and G. Rinjani. **Pulau Satonda,** just off G. Tambora's NW coast and surrounded by a fine coral reef, is itself an old volcanic cone, its crater now submerged. Try to stop at Satonda's coral reefs on the way to P. Moyo.

EAST SUMBAWA

Greater racial and cultural diversity is found among the darker-skinned Biman-speaking people of E. Sumbawa than among the W. Sumbawans. In the E live lowland people, descendants of 18th C. sultanates, as well as the hill-dwelling Dou Donggo, and descendants of earlier Makassarese, Kalimantan, and Javanese immigrants. The Biman language is related to Savunese and Manggarai of Flores. Local folklore claims that the realm grew from a line of 52 princes, the tenth of whom founded the independent kingdoms of Bima and Dompu, which eventually ruled over Sumba, parts of Flores, to Timor. The Goa Kingdom of S. Celebes subjugated Bima in 1616, and the 38th sultan of Bima was converted to Islam in 1640. When the Dutch conquered Makassar in 1667, Bima was liberated from Goa but strong cultural influence from the N continued even under VOC rule. The Bima area has mellowed since its days as a notoriously fanatic Islamic stronghold. Darul Islam, a group which wanted Indonesia to become a theocratic state, conducted a terrorist guerilla campaign in W.

Java from 1949-62 which amounted to open rebellion. In 1957, 3 fanatics from Bima tried to assassinate President Sukarno at Cikini School in Jakarta, but only managed to kill 13 schoolgirls with grenade fragments instead.

Dompu
A tolerable place, 129 E of Sumbawa Besar, to break up the long bus ride from Sumbawa Besar to Bima. Dating back to the Hindu-Javanese period, Dompu was once the center of a sultanate probably founded by a palace nobleman *(datu)* immigrating from the Kingdom of Goa in Makassar in the early 17th century. Ask around to see the town's *pusaka:* fine, hand-woven silver-brocaded cloth; decayed spears, helmets, chain mail armor, and rusted swords bequeathed by the Dutch to the old sultan generations ago. Stay at **Wisma Praja** (Rp5500 d for a big room); they'll take you to report to the police. This same service is provided at **Losmen Anda** across the street. Both are on Jl. Jen. A. Yani, close to the bus station.

The only other accommodation is **Wisma Karya Jawa**, farther out on Jl. Jen. Sudirman. All 3 are much the same, each with its own *rumah makan* — nothing special. Better to just eat in the *warung*. Lots of buses, starting at about 0630 and running late into the night to Bima (Rp1200, 2 hours). On the way to Dompu from Sumbawa Besar, you pass P. Rakit on your L, an island rich in wildlife; charter a motorized *prahu* (Rp25,000) from Jamu on the N coast.

BIMA

Sumbawa's main port (pop. 40,000) in the eastern end of the island. A strongly Muslim town, take care on Fridays with your dress and demeanor. Bima is a handy pit-stop on your trip across the island to Komodo, but has little else to recommend it. Many travelers go straight on to Sape. Experience the town first by *benhur*. The only tourist sight is the restored former sultan's palace which houses *pusaka* such as a royal crown and *kris* with gem-studded gold and ivory hilts. To see them, find someone with access to a key or contact the city government. A universty of sorts is headquartered in the palace. Stroll around the *pasar malam*, especially the area set up for *warung* where the food is great. The **post office** is on Jl. Kampung Salama, out beyond the palace, Rp300 by *benhur*; open Mon. to Thurs. 0800-1200, Fri. 0800-1100, Sat. 0800-1200, closed Sundays. Change major currencies at **Bank Negara Indonesia**.

Accommodations

Lots of places of varying standards are concentrated in the town's center near the old sultan's palace. You may try several places, only to be told that they are full and that you should "try the Lila Graha." Bima's best for the money, **Losmen Lila Graha**, Jl. Belakang Bioskop (tel. 740), is run by a cheerful, moustachioed Balinese sergeant-major and his guitar-strumming nephew; Rp4000 s, Rp6000-7000 d with fan and *mandi*. It's spotlessly clean, very safe, central (only 10 min. from bus station), and offers a breakfast of boiled eggs and bright-colored bread. Government-run **Losmen Komodo**, next to the *istana*, charges Rp2500 s, Rp4500 d; all rooms are enormous with 3-5 beds and your own bathroom. The manager can be overbearing if you don't speak Indonesian, swaggering about his sexual exploits with Western women, which the townspeople just lap up. Opposite Wisma Komodo is **Hotel Sangiang**, supposedly the town's swankiest but nothing works and mosquitos have taken over; a/c rooms go for Rp15,000 s or d; others with fans cost Rp5000 s (bargain!). Each room has a broken-down *mandi*, showers, Western toilets, plus an open-air restaurant. **Losmen Vivi**, on the corner of Jl. Hasanuddin and Jl. Sukarno/Hatta (tel. 411), is a dirty rathole; not recommended. **Hotel Bima**, behind the palace, is more expensive — a network of cool ver-

andahs with food served by *bancis* in skin-tight jeans, makeup immaculate even at 0500 (polite, they won't bother you). **Losmen Kartini**, Jl. Sultan Kaharuddin, is another hotel near the palace with basic Rp4000-7000 rooms.

Food

Stroll in the market at night for *sate, nasi goreng*, desserts, etc., and there are also a number of good *warung* around town. **RM Nirwana** and **RM Anda**, near the town center, are both good value. The Nirwana (Jl. Belakang Bioskop near Losmen Lila Graha) offers more privacy from the hordes of kids, but the Anda has better food (Chinese-Indonesian style). A Padang-style restaurant, predictably named **RM Minang**, is just around the corner from Losmen Vivi on Jl. Martadinata; quite good but slightly expensive. Ice-cold beer is available at **Losmen Lila Graha**.

FROM BIMA

By Bus

The long-distance bus station is a 10-min. walk from town, or Rp200 by *benhur*. (If arriving from Sumbawa Besar, the bus stops at another terminal 8 km from town; take a *bemo* for Rp200 into Bima.) Express bus fares: Dompu, Rp1100; Sumbawa Besar, Rp5500; Alas, Rp6000; Denpasar, Rp21,500, 22 hours (Damai Indah Bus Co.); Surabaya, Rp25,400, 30 hours (try Hotel Sangiang's Wisata Komodo Bus Co.). Night buses to Sumbawa Besar and/or Alas leave every evening at 1700 or 1800. For Sape, stay the night in Bima and get up early for the first bus, which connects with the ferry to Komodo. First get a *bemo* (Rp300) from Jl. Hasanuddin in Bima to Raba's Kumbe Station (3 km inland from Bima), then take a bus for Rp1050 to Sape, 1-2 hours. Buses leave Raba for Sape approximately every hour (but not before 0700) and run late into the night. Chartering a *bemo* from Bima to Sape will cost around Rp20,000 after bargaining. Don't risk this winding mountain road after dark as this is one of the worst stretches of road on Sumbawa (at least it's sealed); heavier rainfall makes it even more treacherous.

For Flores

It's fairly easy to get a boat from Bima's harbor to Labuhanbajo or Reo, Flores, but most don't stop at Komodo (except by charter). Bargain with the captain; a fair price to Labuhanbajo is Rp7000-8000. Sometimes a Pelni ship sails from Bima to Kupang, and a Perintis ship (the KM *Elang*) sails twice-monthly Ujung Pandang-Bima-Labuhanbajo-Reo-Maumere-Larantuka-Kupang, then back to Ujung Pandang; buy your ticket (Rp5000 from Bima to Labuhanbajo) and find out when it's next in port at the Pelni office, Jl. Pelabuhan 27, tel. 224, in Bima's port, Rp300 by *benhur* from the town's center. There are also boats from Bima to Lombok's port of Lembar (Rp8000), but they could take up to 8 days. At least 3 ships per week sail from Bima to Surabaya carrying cattle, copra, rice, sometimes passengers. Also, motorized *prahu* ply regularly from Bima to Ujung Pandang, Rp9500, 36 hours (try C.V. Suasana Baru, Jl. Pelabuhan); and to Banjarmasin, S. Kalimantan.

By Air
Merpati (Jl. Belakang Bioskop 17) has flights to: Ampenan, Rp45,000; Jakarta, Rp145,800; Denpasar, Rp68,000; Ende, Rp45,000; Kupang, Rp90,000; Labuhanbajo (once weekly), Rp40,000; Ruteng, Rp53,000; Tambolaka, Rp46,000; Ujung Pandang, Rp77,000. Bima's airport is 15 km from town, Rp300 by *bemo*.

VICINITY OF BIMA

Several Muslim pilgrimage spots are near Bima, the most important located in the village of **Tololalai**, the grave of the first sultan to embrace Islam. In **Dara** village, 2 km from Bima, is the precious *kris* of Bima Sakti and other heirlooms of an ancient Biman kingdom, as well as the text of an old treaty which was renewed for the last time 100 years ago. For swimming and relaxing, **Pantai Lawata** is 4 km and Rp600 by pony cart (the bus terminal is on the way) or Rp200 be *bemo* (if one comes along). Another sandy beach is at **Lewa Mori**, 35 km; take a bus first to Sila, then take a *bemo*. In the hills at **Wawo** is a swimming pool built by the Dutch over 65 years ago; take a bus in the direction of Sape, it's 17 km from Bima.

The Donggo Area
A traditional mountain area W of Teluk Bima, the home of 20,000 swidden-farmers called the **Dou Donggo** (literally "Mountain People"). Speaking an archaic form of Bimanese, they live in patrilineal clans *(london)* in 6 villages. Though the Dou Donggo share many cultural traits with Biman lowlanders, they have preserved a unique ethnic identity, wear distinctive black clothing, observe their own hierarchical order, and build traditional houses called *uma leme*. These rectangular high-gabled *adat* dwellings, raised on piles and located next to steep cliffs high on mountain ridges, represent probably the original E. Sumbawanese house form, once prevalent all over the region. The darker-skinned Dou Donggo, believed to be descendants of the island's indigenous peoples, until recent times practiced an animist religion, the only non-Muslims on the island. They adopted Christianity or Islam only in the last 20 years and practice those faiths with varying degrees of orthodoxy. This mountain tribe also weaves outstanding cloth on breastlooms. Ask to see the sacred places *(ntsala)*, marked by *lingga*, where the gods are said to gather to copulate. To the Donggo area, about 40 km from Bima, first catch a bus from Daru to Bajo, then walk uphill to Donggo, Kala, then into Mbawa. Near

Donggo, see the stone inscription and the graves of the 2 folk heroes. **Mbawa** (pop. 3,000) is the only village where the black clothing and *uma leme* can be seen in everyday use. Another way is to walk in from Sila, which you must pass on the bus on the Sumbawa Besar-Bima trip. If you get an early enough start, it's possible to get to Donggo and return to Bima in the same day.

SAPE

A harbor town on Sumbawa's E coast, the departure point for Komodo Island and/or Labuhanbajo, of Flores. Take a bus from Raba's Kumbe Station (4 km SE of Bima) to Sape, 2 hours, Rp850. The earliest buses leave around 0730, or earlier on Mon., Wed., and Sat. to connect with the ferry. If arriving late on the bus, Sape looks like a ghost town. Very friendly people in Sape—a million "Hello Misters!"—and even the police are friendly. (Sape might be a hassle, however, for lone female travelers.) There is a **post office** but no bank. The **PPA office** (closes at 1400), where you get your permit to visit Komodo, is in the green house just past the *kantor polisi* on the N side of Jl. Pelabuhan, a 5-min. walk from Sape's only *losmen*. These gentlemen can also handle inquiries about transport, chartering, etc.; the permit to visit Komodo's reserve you get on P. Komodo itself. If heading directly to Komodo, Sape is your last chance to stock up on supplies.

Accommodations
Losmen Give is the only place to stay; tiny rooms with thin walls (some without glass in the windows), but nice back garden. Charges Rp2500 s, Rp5000 d. Free tea, evening meals for Rp850. Try asking the bus to drop you off here (they won't do it for everyone), or take a *benhur* from the bus station, Rp200. Several *rumah makan* are near the cinema, the **Kawan** and the **Kitamemorable**, neither very clean. Better is to eat in the *losmen* at night; their *mie telur goreng* is laudable, and sometimes fish and chicken are available.

From Sape To Komodo
The ferry to Komodo and Flores leaves from Sape's harbor, called simply *pelabuhan*, about Rp500 (3½ km) by *benhur* from Sape. The regular ferry service between Sape-Komodo-Labuhanbajo costs Rp7500 pp (bicycles, motorcycles, and cars are extra) either to Komodo or Labuhanbajo (or Rp3500 from Komodo to Labuhanbajo). Sape's harbor tax is Rp100, and the sampan ride out to the ferry should be only Rp200 or so (but they'll try to charge you Rp500). Also be prepared for another Rp200 for another sampan ride in Labuhanbajo, as the ferry doesn't always let you off at the port's rock pier.

The ferry leaves from Sape to Komodo (and on to Flores) only on Sat. at 0800 (5 hours) or from Sape to Labuhanbajo on Mon. and Wed., 0900, 7 hours. The

Sape Strait during the wet season is notorious for its dangerous whirlpools, high waves, powerful currents, and riptides, thus the crossing to Komodo is only possible April-September. At any other time, the ferry service could be closed and you'll have to take one of the many other Bugis boats making the direct crossing to Flores for around the same price. Avoid chartering a boat to Komodo from Sape (Rp 150,000-200,000; 2 days); it is substantially cheaper in Labuhanbajo. Motorized outriggers from Sape are only Rp50,000, but not as seaworthy.

Vicinity Of Sape

If you're bored, wander W of town to admire the irrigation system; the surrounding countryside is quite photogenic. The Bugis harbor, about 3½ km from Sape on a rocky road, consists of a row of houses on stilts and a shipyard where you can see the building of all types of hand-carved ships. Check out the catamaran *(bagan)* fleet which fishes at night using bright parafin pressure lamps to attract fish. Once the fish have collected underwater, the net is raised and they're hauled aboard. More a fixed fishing contraption than a boat, the square, twin-sailed *bagan* are equipped with a platform up to 18 m long on which sits a small hut where the crew rests during the day. Other *bagan* are motorized, and some even have an ingenious electric generator running off the engine which lights the powerful fishing lanterns at night. Sape's harbor can be just a day trip from Bima. North of Sape about 25 km is the fishing village of **Toronaru**, with white-sand beaches, coconut palms, and good coral reefs just out of town.

Gili Banta is a small islet off Sape, where giant turtles swim in a jade lagoon. On the ferry to Labuhanbajo, you'll pass this island on the L after 3 hours. Gili Banta has a secluded cove protected on 3 sides, very calm, with a fine sandy beach and tall stone cliffs—a pirate's hideout! Utter solitude; makes you wish you had your own boat. At the foot of the high cliffs are incredibly craggy perforated rocks. From the clifftops you can just make out Komodo. Get to Gili Banta by chartered *prahu* from Sape; giant turtles will splash away as you glide into the cove. From Gili Banta, go by *prahu* around the N coast of Komodo and enter Selat Lintah on its eastern side.

KOMODO ISLAND

One of the great wildlife regions of the world, this small archipelago nestled between Sumbawa and Flores is home of the Komodo dragon, (native name: *ora),* the sole survivor of carnivorous dinosaurs that thrived in tropical Asia 130 million years ago. The giant monitor lizards—largest on Earth—were only a myth until the turn of this century when a few pearl fishermen were forced to land here one night in a storm. Today, isolated by the strong, unpredictable currents in the straits which separate them, these dry and barren islands draw thousands of travelers from all over the world who endure 4-5 days of hard land travel from Bali to view the lizards in their natural habitat. The reserve also has become a popular stop for tour boats from Bali. Komodo, as well as the neighboring islands of Padar and Rinca, were made a national park in 1980. The entire island of Komodo, world's largest undisturbed habitat of the Komodo dragon, is run by the PPA (Forestry Authority) which keeps tight control over tourists. If they find you not playing by the rules, they could have you deported from the island.

The Land

Thirty-six km long by 16 km at its widest, 500 km E of Bali, P. Komodo lies in one of the driest regions in Indonesia. The highly permeable soil is shallow and poor. Above 500 m are dense, cool, shady, moist cloud forests. The highest mountain is G. Ara (elev. 730 m). The S portion of the island, little frequented by visitors, has wild mountain landscapes and empty seashores. One fishing village hugs the E coast on Teluk Slawi; 2-3 other temporary fishing encampments are maintained as long as the water supply lasts after the rains. Prior to the wet season, the 300 or so islanders burn off much of the island's grassland to improve the fresh growth of new grass for grazing. These conditions all maintain Komodo as a tropical savannah with dramatic landscapes of hills covered mostly in high, coarse, golden-green grass, scattered fire-resistant thickets, stunted scrub growth, thorny zizyphus trees, and tall, fan-leafed *lontar* palms breaking the horizon like exploding artillery flak. Volcanic in origin, the island is composed of pyroclastic-like ash which has solidified into arid tuffstone hillsides. The whole E coast is an eroded cliff that plunges straight into the sea, with alluvial fans, occasional coastal mangroves, rocky streambeds, valley floors, and great black ravines gouged out of the cliffs. Perfect dragon country!

Climate

The wet season is from Nov. to April, heaviest during the monsoon months (Dec.-March), but the rain lasts just a few hours. Rain squalls during this period may prevent or delay sea travel and make land travel on adjacent islands hard. Between June and Sept., rainfall is very low, with no June monsoon. The dry

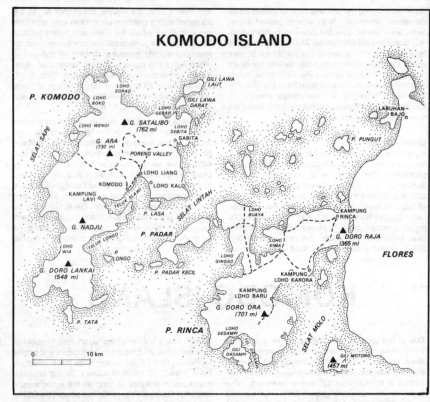

KOMODO ISLAND

season here can last 8-10 months, and standing water is even rare during the wet. Komodo, in fact, receives the least rainfall of any of the surrounding islands. From April through the rest of the year, it's scorching hot, when searing winds from Australia desiccate the land. In the rainy season coarse green grass covers the island, but in the dry season (July-Oct.) it turns yellowish-brown. May is a good time to visit; water is more plentiful, grass is green, and temperatures agreeable.

Flora And Fauna

Only *lontar* palms and zizyphus trees (typical vegetation of the lesser Sundas) can survive Komodo's barren land during the dry spell. Riots of endemic orchids droop pellmell over the trails, and high grass covers the hills. Herds of wild deer, wild hogs, water buffalo, and cattle share the upland valleys of the island with the Komodo reserve, all serving as prey for the dragons. Cave bats *(kelelewar)* hover around black hollowed cliffs and the island swarms with snakes.

The strong yellow plastic-like webs of *Nephilia,* a 15-cm-long spider, stretch for as long as 6 m across walking tracks. Birds includes the sulfur-crested cockatoo which shrieks hysterically, equally noisy friar birds, stunning yellow-breasted sun birds, black-naped orioles, masked cuckoo shrikes, spangled drongos, bee eaters, and a great number of sea and shore birds. Mound-building megapodes nest on southern Komodo and P. Rinca, their mounds often raided by the dragons for eggs. Dolphins, whales, and sea turtles are often seen in the straits.

History

Fossil remains indicate that the Komodo monitor genus has a considerable evolutionary history. Although the monitor is able to traverse marine barriers by swimming over open sea, chromosomal studies have indicated that it most likely did not swim all the way from Australia via Timor, Sumba, and Flores as is popularly theorized. In the prehistoric past, the creature probably lived throughout the entire region.

Only later did water separate all the different islands, then the area's isolation and strong ocean currents assured the monitor's survival. Although Chinese traders had been visiting the island and taking dragon skins as early as the 12th C., the skins on the whole were considered too scarred for commercial use. The decorative granular skin was, however, formerly much prized for native drums. *Ora* were also procured for medicinal value, their tail fat boiled down and applied to burns; also, because the animals are such remarkable swimmers, body fluids also provided the Chinese with "swimming medicine."

Named by a Dutch scientist, P.A. Ouwens, who first published a description of them, the dragons have been luring expeditions since they were "discovered" in 1912. The *ora* came under legislative protection by the sultan of Bima in 1915, a mere 3 years later! Yet hunting continued until 1937, when the Dutch finally put a stop to it. About 600 *ora* have been trapped, shot, or embalmed for museums in the past 60 years. Now the Wildlife Management Office in Bogor has set a limit of only 5 per year, for strictly scientific purposes.

THE KOMODO DRAGON

The Komodo dragon *(Varanus komodoensis)* belongs to the group know as monitor lizards (from the ancient belief that it warns of the presence of crocodiles) found throughout Asia, Africa, and Australia (this species being the largest). The natives call it *ora* or *buaya darat* ("land crocodile"). Fossils strikingly similar to this lizard have been unearthed from chalk deposits dating back 130 million years, about the end of the great Age of Dinosaurs. This creature has been extinct everywhere else but here since the Jurassic Age. Its great bulk and weight are its most unique characteristics; even hatchlings, averaging 50 cm long, are dramatically longer than adults of most lizard species. Without any serious competing scavengers or predators, this solitary carnivore has achieved optimal size. Weighing up to 150 kg, the *ora* has a barrel-like, battle-scarred body up to 3 m long, enormous, rough, fearsome-looking jaws, sharp claws and muscular legs, to support the heavy body. But it can move like a weasel, eat like a crocodile, stuff food into its mouth like a pelican, and its forked tongue is like a snake's!

The fiercest lizard known, *ora* can down a deer, goat, or wild pig, ripping them apart with saw-like teeth. These highly specialized slicing teeth, as well as its predatory habits, are unique among reptiles. Also, unlike other reptiles, the monitor's internal body temperature remains uniform throughout the day and night, a metabolism that emulates large mammalian predators. A truly spectacular creature, it can run swiftly, jump, walk on 2 feet, and is a splendid climber, swimmer, diver, and digger. Coming toward you, an *ora* raises its head up out of the grass like a periscope, then disappears down rocky holes without a trace. Its tongue, which protrudes up to ½ m, is an organ of both touch and smell. Historians believe that the Chinese dragon was modeled after this creature because its long, forked, yellow-orange tongue was thought to be fire. It has uncanny senses of smell and touch, and is one of the world's most intelligent reptiles. In captivity, they have the ability to recognize and obey only certain zookeepers. Barely a dozen specimens of this rare species are found in the world's zoos outside of Indonesia, and if kept in captivity for long periods, *ora* grow fat and phlegmatic, and usually die within a few years of amoebic parasites. In Indonesia, specimens can be found in Jakarta, Yogya, and Surabaya.

Habitat
Varanus komodoensis has the smallest permanent habitat range (about 1,000 sq km) of any of the world's large carnivores, being confined to Komodo, Padar, and P. Rinca; the favorite destination for expeditions is Loho Buaja on the N coast. On Flores *ora* are dense only in the wide valleys on the far W end, restricted to the Beliling Range in the center and Cerumba in the S, but with sightings as far E as Ngondo. A small permanent colony is found along Flores' SW coast and sections of the N coast (near Dampek and Pota). But the single largest *ora* habitat is P. Komodo, with an average density of 17 per sq km. The total population is estimated at 5,000-7,000. Burning practices, planting of gardens by the villagers, livestock grazing, introduction of feral animals such as the pig and dog, and poaching of their primary food source (deer) all pose serious threats. However, since they are protected by water barriers, the lizards' chances for survival are excellent. Increased tourism protects the animals even more. This is fortunate because the Indonesian government simply does not have the financial resources to enforce conservation measures, keep poachers away, control fires, etc.

PRACTICALITIES

Kampung Komodo Village
The native fishing families on Komodo today are descendants of convicts banished to the island from Flores in the early 16th century. These colonists and their women, petrified on this arid island crawling with 4-legged monsters, and built their *kampung* on posts

continued on page 685

VARANUS KOMODOENSIS: VITAL STATISTICS

For the most thorough, definitive study of the Komodo dragon yet published, get *The Behavioral Ecology of the Komodo Monitor* by Walter Auffenberg (1981). Costing US$45, it's available from University Presses of Florida, 15 Northwest 15th St., Gainesville, FL 32603. With grateful acknowledgements, the following notes are a synopsis of that outstanding book. One of the world's largest living reptiles, the local name for the Komodo dragon is *ora*, a cognate of the Indonesian word for "snake" *(ular)*. A highly predatory species of the family *Varanidae*, it possesses a number of traits unique among terrestrial reptiles.

Distribution/Population

The varanid lizard has the smallest permanent habitat range of any of the world's great carnivores. Confined to P. Komodo, P. Padar, P. Rinca, Uwada Sami (off P. Rinca), Gili Motong (off the SW tip of Flores), and western Flores, their total area comprises just under 1,000 sq km. Pulau Komodo is the largest single undisturbed *ora* habitat in the world. The total number of lizards is estimated at 5,000-7,000. Population density averages 17 lizards per sq km on P. Komodo, 6-7 per sq km on P. Padar, P. Rinca, and western Flores.

Body Form

The longest specimen ever recorded was a male in the St. Louis Zoo which measured 3.13 m from tail to snout. Villagers in the Lenteng area of Flores swear that a 3.5-m-long *ora* lives in the vicinity, and through the years there have been absurd, unsubstantiated reports by downed airmen and fishermen of dragons up to 14.5 m long. Most full-grown specimens are 1.7-1.8 m long, and average 35-55 kg in weight, their bodies tending to be proportionally flatter than smaller ones. The tail is the adult's most dangerous weapon and best defense. An adult runs through the grass with its tail lifted off the ground, lashing it about, or can wind it like a snake and deliver mighty blows. Its thick, strong front legs and huge claws enable it to climb hilly terrain, and hold down carrion while ripping and tearing. Varanids are superlative diggers, able to excavate a 1-m-deep hole in less than an hour, and when trapped in stockades can easily dig under the walls to escape. Hind legs and tails are long in juveniles (for scrambling and for balance on tree limbs), stouter and shorter in older ones. Starting in Feb., varanids shed their skins; the sloughing is completed by the end of the month.

Coloration

Coloration changes from speckled, multihued, greenish-yellow subadults to the standard dappled gray adults; larger male specimens have yellowish-green spots on their snouts. The clay color camouflages the mature *ora* as they wait in ambush, while the young's coloration protects them while scampering through leafy trees.

Gender

It's nearly impossible to tell the sex of a lizard from a distance. The only way to determine the gender is to examine the scales. On males they are arranged in 2 rosette-shaped clusters; females do not possess these. Also, females attain only two-thirds the size of the average male. The sex ratio is 3½ males to 1 female, which guarantees that every breeding female will have a mate and that the birth rate will be maintained.

Subadults

The young are slender with long necks, limbs, and tails; they are also more agile and lightweight than the adults. Lizards smaller than 1.5 m can be subdued simply by lifting them off the ground and holding them by the neck and tail (be sure to also hold the mouth shut). Young dragons are the most unpredictable, the speediest, and most skillful tree climbers; sometimes you see them perched in trees preying on monkeys. Pursued by voracious larger lizards, they often spend up to 2 days in the lower branches of trees, and even live in hollow trees. Like dogs, the young roll themselves in rotting carrion to mask their own scent to keep from being eaten by older *ora*.

Locomotion

Combined with serpentine undulations of body and tail, *ora* walk with the typical quadrupedal gait of lizards. They can lift up their heavy tails and bellies to sprint at 8-18 km per hour, but only for short distances. When running, they sound somewhat like muffled machine-gun fire. Dragons also enter the sea and swim, sometimes against strong tidal currents, up to 1,000 m to offshore islets. They can plunge to depths of up to 4 m, easily swimming 100 m while still submerged.

Senses

Komodo monitors are in large part scent-oriented and only use their eyes to observe movement in thickets and on the horizon when they can't use their sense of smell. They have good sight up to 5-6 m; visual signals also pick up impending attack or breeding displays. In spite of the popular belief that they are stone deaf, dragons hear moderately well. They just choose not to pay attention to noise, unless it pertains to food (a zookeeper's approach) or danger (shouting or clapping in the bush). Much information is passed from lizard to lizard through scent alone: highly odoriferous fresh fecal pellets of the larger dragons are often "read" by the smaller ones who stop along the tracks and carry out exhaustive olfactory examinations. By flicking its tongue and touching the droppings, it's thought that smaller lizards can tell the size and age of the departed *ora*, as well as how long ago they deposited the droppings. If very fresh, they retreat; if less fresh, they continue with caution; if completely dry, they proceed unafraid. Evidence indicates that even information on sex and maturity may be conveyed via fecal matter. Dragons also locate carrion by smell: a ripe, putrifying carcass can draw a dragon from 11 km away! *Ora* can also track the spoor of a deer in the wild as well as any hunting dog. The reptile's long tongue, forked and protrusible like a snake's, is both an organ of smell and taste, flicking out and taking scent "samples" of rotten meat before eating. These carnivores also use their all-important sense of smell to recognize territorial boundaries.

Burrows

Komodo monitors have a preference for naturally made burrows along the banks of dry riverbeds, or on the steep slopes of open hills, usually behind overhanging vegetation, big rocks, or tree roots. Kampung Komodo villagers know of the best sites. The dragons seek refuge in these holes during the really hot days of the dry season (June-Nov.); they are seldom used during the wet (Dec.-Feb.). Burrows serve as a heat sink at high temperatures, conserving the panting lizard's body water, as well as an insulated chamber when night temperatures drop. Being large, cold-blooded reptiles, the dragons don't as a rule come out of their holes until after 0800-0900 when the air starts to get hot. Being diurnal, they retire into their burrows by 1930 and are very deep sleepers. Having been commandeered from rodents or porcupines, the length of the burrow averages only 1.5 m, so the reptile's head and shoulders often protrude from the entrance; inside the burrow their tails are bent like a hairpin. Sometimes several dragons use the same burrow, which also may be inhabited by a multitude of insects, snails, even wild boars. There could be as many as 18 burrows to a burrow cluster.

Hunting

Komodo dragons ambush deer and wild boars along their victims' accustomed trails by hiding to the side and waiting, or cunningly creep up to within striking distance of their victim while it's sleeping in tangled thickets. Because of the lack of cover, *ora* seldom hunt on open slopes. Dragons have also been known to come into a village in broad daylight to steal goats. Although almost exclusively active only during the day, occasionally *ora* raid the village at night for goats or fish kept under the houses. Dragons assume the attack posture when they hold their heads low, slightly cocked to one side, crouching low to the ground. Large ones often strike their prey with their tail, then grasp it by the throat and head and jerk it violently from side to side. It's a popular myth that varanids inflict poisonous bites; in fact, a great number of bitten deer who escape do eventually die of massive infection. Dragons scavenge and forage up to 10 km per day from sea level to 500 m, to offshore islets, mangrove swamps, grass thickets, even over reefs and bars, following the year—the largest foraging area of any other lizard. They feed erratically—it's feast or famine. In 1985, a Swiss tourist was taken as he went out for a hike alone and apparently fell asleep by a tree. All they found was his hat, camera case, and knapsack. Local women and children have also been reported missing.

Diet

Newly hatched *ora* feed on small lizards and insects. Subadults prey on shellfish, rodents, eels, geckos, sea turtle eggs, bird eggs, and birds (swallowed live). Adults feed on roe deer, crab-eating macaques, feral dogs, boars, small game, even game larger than themselves which they seize along trails. Large dragons can kill water buffalo 10-15 times their weight. Dragons will eat virtually anything that they can catch or kill—including other dragons. A live goat the Komodo lizard can kill in 2-4 minutes; the goat will try to remain on its feet and is unexpectedly quiet while it is being eviscerated. The carnivores show a marked preference for pregnant hoofed animals, and are able to distinguish these females by scent. On Flores and P. Rinca, dragons wait beneath a foaling mare so that it can eat the newborn; the straining mare can only try to kick the lizard as she gives birth. Not only are they fond of fetuses and afterbirth, but their harassment of the female so distresses and worries her that it often causes a miscarriage, which then leaves her virtually incapacitated and more open to attack herself.

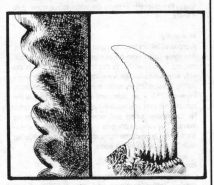

close-up of ora *tooth*   ora *tooth*

Feeding

With the only exception of large snakes, varanids consume prey faster (about 2.5 kg per minute) than any other large predator, including lions and crocodiles. They are equipped with lateral rows of jagged teeth, serrated and curved with sharp tips and wide bases—like curved scalpel blades—superlatively designed for cutting through flesh somewhat like the action of a plow. Their digestive juices are so strong that not only animal flesh and other animal products are eaten, but maggots, grass, and leaves sticking to the carcass are also ingested, along with soil and pebbles (which may help in digestion). If driven by hunger, dragons will even swallow horns, hooves, antlers, hair, bones—everything. They plunge their heads first into the bellies of carcasses to rip out the intestines and stomach (not eaten). The only reptiles that cut their prey into sections before swallowing it, varanids rock back and forth as they bite, bolting down each chunk after it is "sawed" off the body. A 40-kg *ora* can eat a 30-kg wild boar, swallowing the hindquarters whole. It takes several lizards 3-5 days to devour a 1,200-kg water buffalo, and a calf's head, fawn, or a whole hog are sometimes swallowed whole without chewing. Profuse salivation aids in swallowing such large hunks. With articulate jaws like a snake's, the moveable joints enable it to maneuver such odd shapes as horned heads and pelvic sections into their stomachs. The dragon's powerful front legs, sharp claws, and thick back legs are vital for holding down carrion, tearing off rotted hide, ripping open underbellies, and digging out megapode nests and rodent burrows. In comparison with the world's other large carnivores, Komodos have the fewest competitors for carrion. Only with flies, wild dogs, beetles, crows, and kites is this magnificent scavenger-predator willing to share its carrion. But even the largest dragons can be driven from a kill on a hot day by a belligerent and persistent boar. Varanids can go up to 1½ months without water; when drinking water they plunge their heads in up to their eyes, gulp water, then raise their heads like chickens to allow the water to run down their throats.

Hierarchy

A group of 3-4 *ora* feeding together on carrion is common, and there could even be as many as 20 at the banquet, ranging from juveniles to the largest adults. This is the only time when smaller varanids are tolerated. Behavior during feeding is very antagonistic, with a definite pecking order. The larger, dominant male takes his pick of the carcass, the best position around it, and most of the food. He determines when and where the carcass is to be moved. The younger *ora* may help snap off ligaments and tendons which prevent the dominant male from swallowing really large chunks of the body.

Reproduction

Courting males exhibit themselves to the females by dancing, calling, posturing, and other conspicuous and curious visual behavior. Females behave likewise, with push-ups, back-arching, and head-bobbing. Courtship takes place through nearly the entire year. Actual copulation often occurs near carrion and is usually preceded by tongue flicks over the female's back or by the male grasping the female's neck skin with his jaws. When the male mounts, you can often hear his claws dragging over scales on the female's back from as far as 30-40 m, and his hisses quite audibly. Males and females copulate for as long as 12 minutes. Females are very aggressive during courtship, biting the male trying to mount her, sometimes severely injuring or even killing him. A male must completely overpower the female in order to copulate successfully. Eggs are layed approximately 2 weeks after breeding. With her front claws, the female digs out a ½-m-deep hole in the sand under a living shrub or on a hillside, then lays the soft, smooth, leathery, golfball-size eggs. The incubation period is about 8 months, usually hatching out in April or May. Occasionally, the male and female will eat some or all of a brood of eggs, perhaps the only lizard which uses this method of controlling overpopulation.

Fighting

Unlike other lizard species, males often display scars from slash wounds they've received while fighting each other. When fighting, Komodo lizards attack and parry with their open jaws. Zoologists call this "jaw fencing," a habit common among lizards. They also bite, tear, paw, and shake their opponent, sometimes causing death. When high-ranking *ora* approach carrion, younger generation low-ranking individuals often scatter headlong into the underbrush. Smaller Komodos also go through elaborate appeasement displays in front of larger dragons to keep from being attacked. And for good reason: few vertebrates show such a disparity in size between young and adult. The larger the *ora*, the more likely he is to attack and kill others.

Mortality

The lifespan of varanids in the wild is about 50 years maximum, while in captivity about half that. Size is directly related to the age of the reptile. Rats, dogs, cats, sea eagles, brahminy kites, osprey, and snakes prey on *ora* under 1 m in length, while *kerbau*, desert vipers, and wild boar are able to kill larger specimens. Others die from burrow collapse, getting trapped in land depressions, lack of water, starvation, poaching. Man and dogs are the lizard's major competitors; dogs hunt deer and piglets in packs, and even compete for carrion, including dragon corpses, while men living in the dragons' habitat illegally poach about 150 deer yearly.

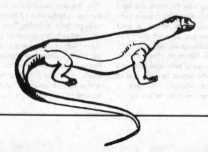

as near to the sea as possible. Later, settlers from Flores, Sumbawa, as well as the ubiquitous Bugis, arrived, and now they are all just *Bangsa Komodo*. Their dialect, *Bahasa Komodo*, is close to Biman, the language of eastern Sumbawa. Because of the dry, unyielding climate, rice cultivation is impossible, so the islanders fish at night by using *bagan*, grow a few meager subsistence crops, and trade by transporting copra between Sumbawa and Flores. Tourists usually disembark at the PPA camp, but boats may also pull onto the piers of this Islamic village, the island's only settlement. With a strictly controlled population of around 500, Kampung Komodo consists of a few rows of bamboo houses on stilts. Pay your respects first to the *kepala kampung*. You may not stay here though; all tourists are required to use the visitors' accommodations in the PPA park headquarters in Loho Liang, a half-hour's walk (2 km N) or Rp1000 by boat from Kampung Komodo. You may also hire a boat (Rp3000) out to P. Lasa opposite the village to snorkel and swim. Komodo villagers make a cash income from acting as guides.

Permits

As Komodo is a national park, you need a permit (Rp1000) to visit it. Maximum stay is 7 days. Although some PPA offices (such as at Sape) insist you obtain your permit in advance, it's possible to get one upon arrival in the PPA camp at Loho Liang. The PPA office in Bogor, W. Java (Jl. Juanda 9), Denpasar (Jl. Sawung 40), as well as at Mataram, Raba, Sape, Labuhanbajo, Ruteng, and Kupang, can dispense advice; some hand out information sheets.

Preparations

You'll need insect spray, suntan lotion, food supplies, etc.; also take a telephoto lens (80 mm will do, 200 mm is better). For baiting the extremely shy lizards, the PPA officials on P. Komodo require that your group take a dead goat to the dragon-viewing site. If you're hunting *ora* on the other islands, a dead dog, stinky goat heads, chicken feet, entrails, etc. will also suffice to capture their olfactory attention. As many as 24 dragons may show up to feast on a single goat. Buy a goat either from the Komodo villagers (Rp20,000-35,000, depending upon the size) or cheaper (Rp20,000) in Labuhanbajo (the *losmen* might arrange it for you) or on P. Papagaran on the way. Young *ora* wander around the PPA visitors' center in Loho Liang, so bringing a putrifying goat with you is no longer sensible; neither will a heap of stinking fish make you popular with the PPA. Further costs include the Rp1000 pp entrance fee to the park, which includes the 7-day permit. For cameras, Rp1000 each; movie cameras, Rp4000; tape recorders, Rp1500. The guides are superb and cost only Rp2000 per group; usually there are a couple who speak pretty good English.

LOHO LIANG

At the N part of Teluk Slawi on the SE coast of the island, Loho Liang is an area of open grasslands, riverbeds, old *ladang*, savannahs, and a small mangrove swamp on the bay's W end near the coast. It's also the location of the well-kept PPA camp, 2 km (30-min. walk) N of Kampung Komodo. Villagers maintain some gardens at Loho Liang as there's year-round water. Tourists may only stay in the PPA camp's visitor accommodations—several large, low-budget bungalows costing Rp3000 pp in the dorm or Rp5000 for a 2-bed room you can lock up; also higher-priced bungalows with toilet, *mandi*, and balcony. You could get lucky and have a whole cabin to yourself. Generator-produced electricity only operates from 1800-2000.

Drool over the pictures in the Time-Life books in the PPA library. Cooking facilities aren't much, so you'll probably go hungry or end up paying heavily if you don't bring your own food to the camp (ant-proof your food!). The only food regularly available is boiled or fried rice (occasionally they have fish or eggs), so stock up in Labuhanbajo or Bima (not much available in Sape) with noodles, fruit, vegetables, tins, cheese, tea, and snacks) and have your own cooking gear. The staff will charge perhaps Rp2000-3000 per day to cook your food. A soda costs Rp11,000 and their canned beef looks like dog food! Eggs, fish, and chickens (Rp4000 each!) can be bought in Kampung Komodo.

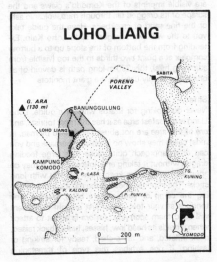

LOHO LIANG

G. ARA
(130 m)

SABITA

PORENG
VALLEY

BANUNGGULUNG

LOHO LIANG

KAMPUNG
KOMODO

P. LASA

TG.
KUNING

P. KALONG

P. PUNYA

0   200 m

KOMODO

Dragon Watching

Best time is May-September. Early in the morning the PPA guide takes your group from the camp to the dragon-watching site at **Banunggulung**. One guide (Rp2000) is required for every 3 people, plus another guide to take the goat (also Rp2000). Try being nice to the guides; they seem to get more than their fair share of abuse from tourists. The old dry riverbed site is about a 30 to 40-min. walk (2 km) from Loho Liang, split-level, so you can safely view the dragons from above. Some of the area is protected by a fence. The guide does all the work, slitting the goat's throat and hanging it on a tree that overhangs the ravine. Red clothes are forbidden; Komodos might mistake your clothing for blood and attack you. The *ora* are well trained already; unless you really want to see action while they feed, the goat really isn't necessary. Even without food they are quite active, not lethargic as they are in zoos. Enough tourists always visit the island with meat to bait the lizards anyway, and since the lizards seldom move far from their feeding grounds, you're almost sure to find them there even without bait. Anyone who wants to see how the lizards devour the goats must be quick, as the feast is over in no time. You'll hear them hissing before you see them. The whole outing takes about an hour.

It must be a much tamer experience than it was years ago: the same several dozen or so dragons come to the feeding site regularly, so they've forgotten how to hunt. If someone else has visited the site in the last several days, they might be overfed and not interested in the dead goat. But that still leaves 2,000-plus lizards on the island which can hunt. Follow the spoor trails left by the creatures searching for carrion; these are visible imprints of the Komodo's claws and the scrape of its dragged tail through mud, volcanic ash, or the fine sand of creekbeds. Have the guide take you to the well-worn dragon trail in **Loho Kalo**. Extending from the bottom of the slope up to a burrow complex at a point two-thirds to the top (visible from adjoining hills), this 300-m-long path is devoid of all brush and is only used by the giant monitors.

Safety

Never go looking for lizards without a guide. Loho Liang is the safest area as it has the most tourists, and *ora* of this area are not abused and killed by man. In most cases they show no interest in humans and you can often approach quite close to a large feeding dragon without it taking any notice of you. If they do approach, the guides keep them off you with long sticks. The younger ones are the most curious, entering the camp or your camera blind, flicking their tongues at your feet. Often just a slight movement will send them scurrying. An *ora* is about to attack when it holds its head low, hisses, has its back raised, neck inflated, and tail arched, ready for striking or lashing. If one exhibits this type of threatening

behavior, just hit him in the snout with a stick, tripod, or throw a handful of pebbles. The infection caused by a bite could be very dangerous. Very few will attack humans unprovoked and most attacks occur in self-defense. Like people, some *ora* are meaner than others; all should be watched carefully. You may want to use an observation blind—an A-frame with a palm mat and woven bamboo front is the easiest to construct and carry. Leave the ends of the A-frame open (because of the heat) and cut holes in the sides through which to observe and poke camera lenses. Suspend the bait by a rope from the branch of a large tree in front of the blind, raising and lowering the rope from within the blind.

observation blind with slaughtered goat

GETTING THERE

Seeing these lizards is no easy task. If traveling overland from Bali, at least 6 days should be allowed for the trip (each way). The usual embarkation point, the port of Labuhanbajo on the W coast of Flores, has an airfield, hotels, and restaurants. The fastest possible land route is to take the daily ferry on Thurs. from Padangbai (E. Bali) over to Lembar on Lombok. From Lombok's Sweta's station early Fri. morning take a minibus direct to Labuhan Lombok (E. Lombok), then the 0900 ferry across to Alas on Sumbawa where a connecting bus will be waiting to take you across Sumbawa to Bima-Raba, arriving late Fri. night. On Sat., take a *bemo* down to Sape's harbor for the ferry to P. Komodo which departs at 0800.

Regular Ferries

These ferries have few passengers; most run at a heavy loss. The ferry from Sape in E. Sumbawa departs for Labuhanbajo Mon., Wed., and Sat., but only stops at Komodo on Saturday. Leaving at 0800, the latter ferry arrives in Komodo at 1300 and at 1400 continues to Labuhanbajo. From Labuhanbajo in W. Flores, the ferry leaves for Sape at 0700 or 0800 on Tues., Thurs., and Sun., calling at Komodo only on Sun. at around 1100. Schedules are always changing. Komodo's harbor, on the eastern side of the island, is much closer to Labuhanbajo than to Sape. The fares reflect this: from Sape to either Labuhanbajo or Komodo it's Rp7500 Economy Class (or Rp6000 Deck Class if you enjoy sunburn); from Labuhanbajo to Komodo, Rp3500. Practice your Indonesian watching the video on the ferry. The ferry is too big to come to shore at Komodo; instead, you are shuttled in on a small fishing *prahu*. Mind your luggage at this stage lest it end up on the bottom of the sea. The *prahu* costs Rp200 pp from the ferry to either Loho Liang or Kampung Komodo. Loho Liang is about 1-hour's punting from Kampung Komodo, Rp500. If you think that's a lot for a short boat ride, just remember that it's the only time Komodo villagers make any money at all out of you (unless you buy a goat from them). You may also be able to get a lift to Komodo on the PPA's twice-monthly staff boat from Labuhanbajo; about Rp8500 RT, inquire at their office for details. Also, on days besides Sat. and Sun., it's possible to pay the captain extra to stop at P. Komodo on the Sape-Labuhanbajo or Labuhanbajo-Sape crossings. Pelni or Perintis vessels also call at Komodo, though irregularly; look into their schedule and prices in Surabaya, Bima, or Reo (N coast of W. Flores).

Tours

Expensive package tours using small yachts or combination yacht and planes can be arranged in Jakarta, Denpasar, and Lombok. Depending upon the number of add-ons, the size and class of the boat, and the size of your group, these tours could cost US$400-500 pp. Ask Jakarta's or Denpasar's tourist office to give you the names of travel agencies specializing in Komodo tours. Agaphos Tours & Travel (Jl. Gajah Mada 16, tel. 359659/351331, Jakarta) includes Komodo on their 6-day Minor Sunda Islands program, but most tours average 3 days and 2 nights. Garuda's Spice Island Cruises (P.O. Box 98/MT, Jakarta Pusat, Indonesia 12910, tel. 593401/593402) has a 14-day Bali-to-Ambon cruise on their luxurious *Island Explorer* which stops at Komodo.

Charters

If you use the regular ferries, you can stay on Komodo for one night only (which is rushing things), or stay for about 4 days (too long, especially if you didn't bring enough food). So chartering is best. From Sape a charter is too expensive, perhaps Rp250,000. Instead, charter a boat OW from Labuhanbajo, the PPA office there says Rp125,000 is a fair price. Ask your *losmen* owner to suggest a boat owner. Captain Leo will

come down to Rp100,000 if you speak Indonesian, but his little boat takes nearly 6 hours. Make it clear if you only want a OW charter; he asks Rp150,000 if his boat waits on Komodo to bring you back to Labuhanbajo. A few boat owners in Labuhanbajo, such as 14-year-old Herman, ask Rp100,000 OW for a group of 5. On Herman's boat, if you leave at 1500, you get to the PPA camp at Loho Liang at 2000. Always try to charter the whole boat, no matter how many additional people show up to share the cost. The PPA also occasionally charters their boat, around Rp100,000 OW. After arriving on Komodo by ferry, it's possible to charter a boat from there, but you have less bargaining power than in Labuhanbajo.

Negotiating the narrow Selat Lintah, weaving in and out of about 30 haunting islands, Komodo is difficult to reach by boat. The locals use land points to navigate. There are some very treacherous currents, whirlpools, and tides in the area, which you can see from the boat. The whirlpools are large enough to pull a small outrigger down. If the boat owner wants to leave Labuhanbajo at 0400, don't argue—he knows when the seas are safest. August, even though in the middle of the dry season, can have quite rough seas; in Feb. and March, the seas are nearly impossible for boats. Also, make sure you charter from someone who knows where he's going. In 1986, a group of Australians left Komodo for Sape on a chartered boat, got lost, and ended up in Sumba. It finally took 10 days for them to reach Sape and they nearly perished at sea. It turned out the captain had never been to Sape before.

Air, Land, Sea

Another popular route is to fly Denpasar-Ende (Flores) with Merpati (Rp91,400), visit the Keli Mutu volcano and lakes, overnight in Ende, then proceed the next morning by land to Labuhanbajo and then by sea to Komodo. You may also fly on Fri. from Denpasar to Bima (Sumbawa), then take a minibus straight to Sape for the Komodo ferry the next morning at 0800.

KOMODO ISLAND SIGHTS AND NEARBY ISLANDS

Loho Liang Bay

Explore this small, semi-circular bay, a pristine area of white sulfur-crested cockatoos, mound-building jungle fowls, bush turkeys, *wili wili* birds, bellowing Timor deer, and snorting boars crashing through the grass. When walking from Loho Liang to Kampung Komodo, there are many rocks, so go at low tide and without your pack; by boat it's Rp500. Above the coastal hills are green-forested highlands. Follow only the marked trails to the Poreng Valley. The rules are that every time you leave the PPA camp, a guide (Rp2000 per day) must accompany you. When walking, always wear long pants and shoes to protect against snakes and poisonous insects. Other isolated bays in the northern part of the island are **Loho Boko** and **Loho Sorao** with thick woods, rocky lava cliffs, unspoiled coral gardens. *Ora* are larger here than on the village side of the island.

Gunung Ara

A beautiful dormant conical volcano (elev. 730 m) surging right out of the sea. With clouds enveloping its top, this mountain is covered in bamboo woods, monkeys, wild buffalo. Many natives will not climb it for fear it's possessed by evil spirits and their reptile companions, the *naga*. The legend goes that a handful of Arabs once tried to settle Komodo, and relics of their settlement remain on this mountain; the wild buffalo found on Komodo are descended from the Arabs' cattle. Climb to the top through the well-trampled tracks made by wild pigs and deer; a path starts from behind Kampung Komodo. Count on it taking all day: 3 hours up, 2 hours' rest at the top (it's hot!), and 2 hours down. You'll need strong shoes and about Rp6000 for a guide. Tickly, head-high *alang-alang* grass hides rubble and blocks of lava, so watch out. Marvelous savannah landscapes can be seen from the summit, with chains of valleys and bays in the distance; bring binoculars. **Gunung Satalibo** is a taller peak to the NE, not as easy to get to, but on top are dense, cool, shady, moist cloud-forests.

Water Sports

Komodo is also a marine reserve with fine mangroves and coral reefs rich in diverse marine fauna (such as the *caranx* species) and shellfish. **Teluk Slawi** even has a resident population of baleen whales. After you're through viewing dragons, spend the rest of the afternoon snorkeling on the reef. PPA can advise you on the best spots, and can arrange boats and canoes. Snorkeling is particularly good off the N coast of the island, teeming with more than 180 species of fish. An outrigger costs Rp5000-10,000 per day; the PPA may have snorkeling equipment for hire, but to be safe bring your own. Local fishermen say the sharks are harmless; still, only snorkel in calm water close to the beach. More treacherous than sharks are the 4- to

5-knot currents in the straits between the islands. Komodo's numerous sheltered coves offer more safety.

Pulau Rinca

Pronounced RIN-cha. A 195-sq-km island SE of Komodo, also a habitat of the *ora*. Flores is only 2 km away across a strait which, although very narrow, is not as treacherous as Selat Lintah and Selat Sape. Several villages are on P. Rinca; tracks leading into the interior start at Kampung Rinca. Northern Rinca is open, undulating country; the only high hills are just W and S of Kampung Rinca. The grassy plains support many buffalo and horses gone wild from domestic stock: it's said that the horses were placed on the island by decree of the sultan of Bima. Though small, they are fine, sturdy animals. The horses and wild pigs are preyed upon by the Rincan lizards. The favorite destination for expeditions is Loho Buaya off the N coast of P. Rinca where there's a small guesthouse, shelters, and viewing tower. Dense forests climb the slopes of Doro Ora ("Dragon Mountain"), while island-sheltered Teluk Dasampi provides good anchorage for exploring the southern part of the island, home to brush turkeys and megapode birds. There are few paths; watch out for stinging wasps.

Pulau Padar

Separated from Komodo by the powerful Selat Lintah, 20-sq-km Padar is drier than Komodo except in the rainy season. The currents and whirlpools that swirl around this tiny island can be extremely dangerous. Padar has some of the most spectacular scenery in the archipelago: pink beaches contrast with orange coral and a vividly ultramarine sea. There's only one source of water, on the NW coast, so bring your own. Numerous campsites are found along attractive beaches. There's little wildlife: competing with *ora* for food, packs of wild dogs bring down roe deer. For dragon viewing, the W side of the island is the most accessible observation locale, but lizards range all over the island from its coastal mangrove swamps to its highest elevations. On small islands off southern Padar, edible birdnests are harvested from cliffs.

FLORES

A mostly Christian island which few travelers visit, mountainous Flores could very well be the highlight of your visit to Nusatenggara. Considered by many one of Indonesia's most beautiful islands, Flores has grandiose volcanos, high mountain lakes, stretches of savannah, and tropical deciduous forests. One of Indonesia's most fascinating ethnological regions, the island has intact tribes practicing their own brand of animism, as well as cultural and artistic traditions little known outside of obscure missionary journals. Flores is particularly interesting as a foil for Bali; in the contrast is a clear glimpse of the action of human culture upon a landscape to create a symbiosis. The island offers similar natural conditions as Bali—a constant source of water from the mountains, sufficient rain for 2 and even 3 yearly rice crops, but the land remains undeveloped and resources are little used. Traditionally, the Florinese practice slash-and-burn agriculture.

Although reasonable accommodations exist in the main towns all along the main W-E trunk road, Flores food is generally pretty bland, a combination of local, pseudo-Western, and tinned foods. Women should not travel alone through any of the villages. And everyone should stay away from **Lekluo** on the E end, where travelers have reported that the children stone strangers. Bring some antibiotic drying power: in this region wounds are easily infected and medicine could be difficult to find. If you get sick or injured, go to the Catholic hospital in Maumere, the best on the island. Money can be changed only in Labuhanbajo, Ende, and Maumere.

The Land And Climate

About 360 km long, the island averages 60 km wide (72 km at its widest). Frequently shaken by earthquakes and volcanic eruptions, Flores is riven with deep ravines and rugged valleys, which accounts for the difficulty of travel and the island's distinctive cultures. One spectacular ridge of very weathered mountains runs down the middle with 15 lazily smoking volcanos which fall softly into the sea on both sides. The peaks of this range are all over 2,100 m and the highest, in the island's western end, is 2,600 m. Flores' interior and eastern parts are covered in heavy tropical forests. The S coast (known as the "male sea") has rougher seas than the N coast (the "female" sea).

The wet season is Nov.-April. Rainfall can be irregular, so sometimes serious water shortages occur. Then when it does rain, roads frequently wash out and there are fuel shortages. Temperatures in the rainy season are slightly lower than in the mid-dry season when they reach 30 degrees C (and seem higher due to lack of water). The dry season is April-Oct.; eastern Flores is generally drier than western Flores. Near Ruteng, it can be decidedly cool at elevations over 1,500-2,000 m.

Flora And Fauna

Above 500-700 m, quasi-cloud forest harbors many endemic species of flora: rattan, bamboo groves, mosses, and many species of high-elevation trees. Near sea level, monsoon forests dominated by thorny bamboo are widespread. Except for coconut plantations, *ladang* areas are generally used in rotation every 5-15 years. When these gardens are abandoned, they become covered with shrubs, low trees, and grasses. One spectacular species of grass (*Rottoehia escalbata*) reaches 3½ m in height during the course of one wet season. An unbroken fringe of tangled, buttress-like roots has formed an almost impenetrable barrier along some of the island's coasts. Behind this tidal zone are thickets inhabited by wild boar. Flores is also well known for its large numbers of domestic horses: small but sturdy, standing only 1.2 m high at the shoulder, and weighing an average of 250 kg.

History

Giant bats, reptiles, stegosaurs, and one species of elephant once roamed this island. Over thousands of years, waves of migrants have passed through Flores, including early Veddoids, and later Hindus from India. Melanesian types are also found. Scholars also theorize, because of the similarity of musical instruments, that in about 800 B.C. migrants arrived from the Balkan area. Other scholars connect ancient Flores with Easter Island in the Pacific. With its rich stores of sandalwood, textiles, and slaves, the island in the 14th C. fell under the economic and political aegis of the Majapahit Empire, which established coastal states. Seeing the eastern cape covered in blooming flamboyants, the Portuguese explorer S.M. Cabot christened the island *Cabo de Flores* or "Cape of Flowers" in 1544. Ironically, Flores has few flowers and was known to Javanese sailors as "Stone Island."

The Portuguese, who arrived in the mid-16th C., included Flores as a stop on their way to the Spice

Islands, establishing several trading bases. In 1566 they built a fort on P. Solor to the E of Flores to guard their trading interests on Timor. Dominican priests were subsequently sent to the eastern part of Flores and founded missions at Larantuka, Paga, and Sikka, from where they began converting the island's inhabitants to Catholicism. Today the people of these areas have Portuguese names, practice old Portuguese customs and dances, and even *look* Portuguese. In the coastal towns, Florinese began converting to Islam in the 15th and 16th centuries; in the 1660s Gowanese Muslims from S. Celebes invaded Ende; their influence in that area remains evident to this day. In 1859, the Dutch took over Flores from the Portuguese. Under their administration their own Jesuit and Franciscan priests were brought in, and entry to all other Christian denominations refused. The Dutch crushed a native rebellion against their rule in 1907-08, but it was not until 1936 that they considered the island safe enough to be transferred from military to civil control.

The People

With 1,350,000 people, Flores is Nusatenggara's most populous island. The island has an amazing racial mix, consisting mostly of Bimanese, Sumbawanese, Makassarese, Bugis, Solorese, and Sumbanese. Flores is in fact a sort of transition point for both the Papuan and Malay races; thus you find both types here in abundance. Many of its inhabitants, particularly in the east and interior, look more Papuan than Indonesian, with dark brown to almost black skin, heavy brows, wide flat noses, stocky builds, and black, often curly hair. They don't mention Portuguese, but they don't have to—you can see it. Along coastal areas and in the W live the ethnic Malays. Many people describe themselves as *campur* ("mixed"), naming different island ethnicities—Sikka, Lio, etc.—as well as Bugis, Makassarese, Malay—in their paternities. Life in the interior is simple; most Florinese live by fishing, hunting, and simple agriculture revolving around palm and taro cultivation. A man's daily routine is devoted to planting, harvesting, and protecting his crops from rodents, while his animals forage for themselves. These indigenous peoples of the deep inland areas can still be defensively hostile.

Agriculture

Rice has been grown on this island only since the 1920s, from strains introduced by the Dutch from Vietnam. Before this, the Florinese were strictly hunters of small game and swidden farmers growing bananas and cassava. Even today these protein-deficient crops are still widely grown and account for many health problems among the Florinese. The main farming method, slash and burn, exacerbates the island's erosion problem. Rice is raised in the lowlands; maize and coffee are grown in the hilly districts, and coconuts along the coasts. Though the terrain is quite fertile, the markets in western Flores are impoverished because of the ineffective use of resources, unreliable rainfall, and crop-destructive pests. Water can be as scarce as it is on Timor; each year the people are near to famine because the food from last year's harvest is almost gone and the new crop isn't yet ready.

Religion

At least 85% of the population are Catholic, 11% are Muslim, and the remainder are animists. Christianity was brought to Flores by the Portuguese, who first established bases in Maumere and Sikka which remain church administrative centers to this day. Today, Florinese traditions closely adhere to the Portuguese Catholic heritage. Catholicism has flourished—Flores has the largest Roman Catholic community in Indonesia. Through funding by church donations from the country of origin, the church has improved daily living conditions, initiated agricultural projects, and established health clinics. From the central towns to the most remote villages you find large, beautifully appointed concrete churches with lofty spires. One of the best shows in town is church on Sunday morning when people come by boat, minibus, bicycles, and *bemo*, all dressed in their best ornaments. But don't be deceived; not all Florinese wholeheartedly accept Western religion. Totemism and animism are widespread, and the island is steeped in witchcraft. Meet the *roh*, local shaman and healer, often an old woman. Megalithic cultures, animist belief systems, and ancestor spirit cults still persist in remote areas. Next to Nias Island (off NW Sumatra), Flores has the greatest collection of contemporary megaliths in Indonesia. In round grass areas surrounded by stones, villagers dance for weddings, burials, and to celebrate planting and harvesting. Peculiar organic arrangements like scarecrows of dried branches and leaves are placed at certain sites to keep away evil spirits. Outside the village, stone pillars are set up to receive offerings to the gods and to perpetuate the power of those who erected them; in E. Flores an altar or totem pole is found in the village's largest traditional-style wooden hut *(kada)*, in which idols and spirits are worshipped. You can still find Stonehenge-like tombs throughout Flores.

The Missionaries

The missionaries are remarkable and unusual people who have to deal with bureaucrats, speak several dialects, meet payrolls, and accommodate local conditions. How you're treated in a given area depends a lot on how the local pastor is regarded. For example, at Moni the father is a kind and simple man who talks to everyone (even though he's been in Australia for 10 years). In Ende, on the other hand, the missions are divided into different factions and the locals are almost rude to you. The missions are quite strong and

Ikat *cloths still make up part of the bride's dowry on Flores. See traditional patterns woven on looms such as the one pictured at right in the Jopu area of east-central Flores.*

rich on Flores (everybody seems to work for them), and you may have to depend on them for transportation and accommodations in some areas. The missionaries are an excellent source of information too, and can be turned to for health problems. At nearly every mission is at least a makeshift clinic, and in many cases the priest doubles as a medic.

Music
Musically, Flores is especially rich. The people love to sing hymns, dirges, working songs, satirical songs, and *pantun*. In the districts of Ende and Reo harvest songs are popular, the people of Manggarai (W. Flores) yodel, and in E. Flores folksongs originating from 17th C. Portugal are still preserved. Percussion-type instruments are dominant with bamboo slit drums, small gongs, simple xylophones; hand-played drums are made from parchment stretched over the end of a hollow piece of coconut trunk. Florinese orchestras are particularly strong on flutes; other instruments include an end-blown bamboo instrument which plays deep thumping notes, a primitive 1-stringed lute played with a bow, and idiochords (bamboo drum zithers) which sound like banjos. Earlier this century, Jaap Kunst, the Dutch musicologist, counted 54 types of musical instruments on Flores.

Dances
War-like dances are still practiced, and women perform graceful "round dances." A solo dancer, man or woman, holds out a long scarf and dances with shuffling steps around a stone-edged grass area, hands fluttering and body gyrating while advancing, retreating, and encircling other dancers. Large groups also dance in a circle with arms linked, revolving counter-clockwise. In the *caci* whip duel, 2 dancers enter an open area, each with leather shields and painted wooden helmets tufted with horsehair which protect the face like an uplifted welder's

mask. They tie *sarung* over their pants, attach bells to their ankles, and wind towels around their arms to protect their skin from the blows. To the accompaniment of whistling, gongs, and drum beats, the dancers circle each other like cats, their snapping rawhide whips hissing through the air. Although they seldom show any sign of pain, each whips the other mercilessly. At intervals the men trade off weapons. *Caci* is now performed only at festivals in W. Flores.

Crafts And Antiques
Exquisite cloths are made on Flores, but are becoming increasingly rare. Machine-spun imported cotton and synthetic dyes have made deep inroads, but locally grown cotton and organic dyes are still used in the hinterlands. Before spinning, small, hand-operated gins remove the seeds from the raw cotton. Using the highly developed, demanding, labor-intensive warp *ikat* method, the spun cotton is then bundled, tightly tied, and the pattern dyed into the warp threads before being wound onto the breastloom. Monochromatic, unpatterned threads, mostly store-bought and brightly colored, are then used to finish the textile. In the eastern part of the island (and on P. Solor), intricately worked, fantastically ornamented and colored fabrics, *sarung*, and scarves are still woven. Portuguese influences from the 16th and 17th C. are still in evidence: see peacocks and European architecture in the fabric designs. One can tell which clan did the weaving by the way the blue, reddish-brown, and yellow designs are arranged.

If you go to Sikka, word will spread through the village that you're looking for cloths. You'll be seated in front of a house and all the women will come up and sit before you. You'll be shown *ikat* after *ikat;* all that beauty could be a traumatic experience! A better place to buy cloth, with a greater selection and cheaper prices, is in the market of almost any village. Buses run to really out-of-the-way villages, such as

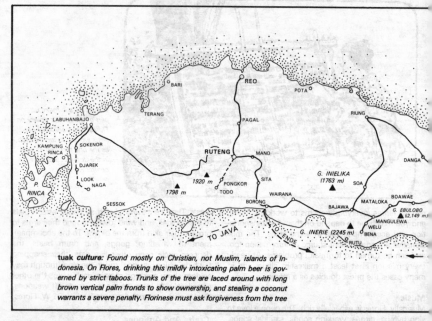

tuak *culture: Found mostly on Christian, not Muslim, islands of Indonesia. On Flores, drinking this mildly intoxicating palm beer is governed by strict taboos. Trunks of the tree are laced around with long brown vertical palm fronds to show ownership, and stealing a coconut warrants a severe penalty. Florinese must ask forgiveness from the tree*

Wolonjita, only on market day. Markets are more amenable to bargaining. In many places — such as in the **Jopu** and **Sikka** areas — the cloths are sold open-ended so you can finish the piece yourself. In most other places, *ikat* cloths are made into *sarung*. Blankets show up occasionally, such as in **Maumere's** *pasar*. Don't try to wash organically dyed *ikat:* the indigo dye will turn your washbasin purple. Antiques include old Venetian beads, probably brought by Arab traders, which are coveted by the people. Elephant tusks cost Rp500,000 in E. Flores. Orange or serrated red and blue Indian beads, from Hindu migrations centuries ago, are very rare and valuable. The Florinese believe they were given as gifts by mountaintop spirits *(nitu)*.

GETTING THERE

By Air

Denpasar is the usual jumping-off point for flights to: Ende, Rp91,400; Maumere, Rp80,200; Ruteng, Rp86,400. Scheduled Merpati flights also depart Sumbawa, Timor, Sumba, Sawu, and Sulawesi to one or several of the 6 airstrips on the island: Labuhanbajo, Ruteng, Bajawa, Ende, Maumere, and Larantuka. Now with the Darwin-Kupang connection established, flights for Kupang to Larantuka, Rp42,400, Maumere, Rp31,600, and Ruteng, Rp57,300, have be-

come especially popular. To avoid the ferry crossing from Sumbawa to Labuhanbajo, take the Merpati flight from Bima to: Labuhanbajo, Rp39,700; Ruteng, Rp52,500; Bajawa, Rp60,400; Maumere, Rp48,500; Ende, Rp39,700. Bouraq, serving only Maumere, flies from Denpasar, Rp90,500; and from Surabaya (via Denpasar), Rp118,400. There is no taxi service to and from Maumere's Waioti Airport (2½ km from Maumere) or Ende's Ipi Airport (½ km), but minibuses or station wagons transfer passengers (Rp1000 pp OW), and some of the hotels have representatives at the airports to pick up prospective guests. Merpati and Bouraq maintain offices in Maumere and the former also in Ende.

By Boat

From Sape, on Sumbawa, ferries depart on Sat. (with a stop in Komodo), Mon., and Wed. mornings for Labuhanbajo, W. Flores. Also, regular Pelni and Perintis cargo ships call at Labuhanbajo, Reo, Borong, Ende, Maumere, and Larantuka. Pretty rough-looking ships! Ende is the island's biggest port.

GETTING AROUND

Flores has the worst road system in Nusatenggara. The 667-km Trans-Flores Highway between Labuhanbajo in the W and Waiklibang in the extreme NE was

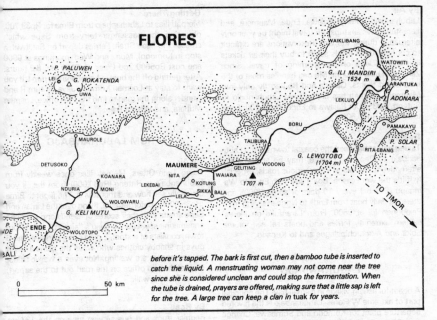

FLORES

before it's tapped. The bark is first cut, then a bamboo tube is inserted to catch the liquid. A menstruating woman may not come near the tree since she is considered unclean and could stop the fermentation. When the tube is drained, prayers are offered, making sure that a little sap is left for the tree. A large tree can keep a clan in tuak for years.

supposed to have been completed in 1926, but you'd never know it. A number of conditions conspire to slow down your travel. Only a section of road between Ende to Maumere is partially paved; the rest has just about disintegrated due to the island's impossible (but incredibly scenic) topography. During the rainy season (Nov.-April), the cross-island road can become an unbelievable mire. Except for the Ende-Maumere segment, buses seldom run at night (and a good thing too). During the wet, ships are unable to unload cargo on such S coast ports as Borong, which causes widespread fuel shortages. Though the road system is improving, the roads W of Ende are even worse than the roads east. In spite of all this, there's regular transport from one end of the island to the other now, albeit slow and uncomfortable, with ample accommodations in the major towns along the way. Under the best conditions, it takes about 5-6 days to cross Flores overland.

Labuhanbajo To Ruteng: This shitty road is even worse than the Trans-Sulawesi Highway, with long mud patches (you didn't expect asphalt, did you?); you'll never want to ride a roller coaster again. Sometimes all the passengers must pile out to let the driver negotiate a particularly dangerous stretch alone—even in the middle of the dry season! Sometimes departing as infrequently as twice weekly, this trip takes 8-9 hours and costs Rp3500 (137 km). One open-windowed bus leaves at 0800, another at 1700 (connects with the ferry from Sape, but travels at night);

others depart in between. The 0800 bus stops for a lunch break, but it's strictly bring-your-own. Similar times if going in the other direction.

Ruteng To Bajawa: Trucks (with hardwood benches, not seats) drive around town from 0700-0900 looking for passengers, so just wait at your *losmen*. Several trucks make the journey at the same time; about 8 hours, 138 km, Rp3500, lousy roads. Sometimes there are only 2 buses weekly. Bring your own food and water; or maybe the truck will stop at a *rumah makan* in Aimere. Feeling more ambitious? Real masochists can do the 258-km Ruteng to Ende run in a single bus ride.

Bajawa to Ende: At least a real bus is used on this section, but they tint the windows just to spoil the view. Boarding and departure times similar to Ruteng. A very dusty ride, 5-6 hours, 125 km, Rp3500. Buy snacks at a small roadside market on the way.

Ende to Moni: Frequent *bemo*, no problem.

Moni to Wolowaru: About 10 buses and *bemo* per day, most between 0900 and noon, plus 2 in the evening which don't always seem to arrive, so watch for them; Rp250, 13 km.

Ende/Moni/Wolowaru to Maumere: About 10 buses daily; Rp2000 from Wolowaru.

Maumere to Larantuka: Several buses each morning; count on about 7 hours.

By Air

Labuhanbajo Ruteng, Bajawa, Ende, Maumere, and Larantuka have airstrips. Air travel might be your only alternative during the wet. Reservations are difficult to confirm; most locals seem to buy their air tickets like train tickets on the morning of travel. Since Zamrud is now defunct, Merpati handles most of the intra-island flights. Garuda and Bouraq fly only into Maumere. Merpati has flights from Labuhanbajo to Ruteng, Rp35,500; Bajawa to Ende, Rp35,100; Ende to Ruteng, Rp40,500.

By Ship

Taking a boat between the coastal towns, from Labuhanbajo to Reo for example, may be an attractive alternative to the island's horrendous roads, especially if it's the wet season. Boats sail from Ende to Waingapu (Sumba) every 10 days or so (Rp9900), and there's a daily boat from Ende to Nggela, sailing from Pelabuhan Ipi at 0800. From Larantuka on Flores' eastern extremity ferries and boats set sail for the Solor and Alor archipelagos and to Kupang.

LABUHANBAJO

A beautiful fishing village in a small bay. The principal port of extreme W Flores, Labuhanbajo is the favored departure point for Komodo and Sumbawa. Change your TCs at **Bank Rakyat Indonesia**. If you're traveling on to P. Komodo, get your visitor's permit, brochures, and the latest information at the PPA office only several minutes' walk N of Wisma Bajo; go in the morning. Really nice skin diving in this area, and there's a big cultured pearl farm off Labuhanbajo.

Accommodations And Food

Chinese-run **Wisma Bajo** has electricity and clean sit-down Western toilets. Cheapest rooms are Rp6000 pp including breakfast which is too expensive. Nothing special about the meals. Across the road at Jl. Pelabuhan 31, **Losmen Mutiara** (formerly Leo's Losmen; it changes its name every few years), captained by Leonardo Kati, is basic but adequate; Rp2500-4000 s without food, up to Rp6000 which includes 3 fantastic meals per day (fish and chicken dishes with nice sauces and rice). The restaurant is not bad (cold drinks), although there's not a great variety. Leo rents vehicles but will try to squeeze every *rupiah* out of you; he cuts in on every deal. The town's most upmarket place is **Losmen Ora**, opposite Losmen Mutiara; Rp10,000 s, Rp12,000 d; meals cost Rp2500; free tea. Near the ferry dock, a good deal is **Losmen Komodo Jaya**; bunkbed accommodation in 5 rooms costs Rp3500 pp, Rp5000 with meals. Although a bit hard to find, it's clean, friendly, and the food is better than average. A few grotty *warung* in town; fresh fruit and cheaper meals in the morning market.

Getting There

Merpati flies to Labuhanbajo from Bima for Rp39,700, obviating the passenger ferry from Sape which crosses the Sape Strait. Ferries depart on Sat. (with a stop in Komodo), Mon., and Wed. mornings at 0900 and cost Rp5600 2nd Class, Rp7100 1st; 8-9 hours. After getting off the boat in Labuhanbajo, turn L if you want to stay at Losmen Komodo Jaya, or turn R and wander along the road to find the PPA office, Losmen Mutiara, and Wisma Bajo.

FROM LABUHANBAJO

By Air

Using Twin Otters, Merpati flies once weekly from Labuhanbajo to Ruteng (Rp30,000); from the air you can really see how arid this area is. The flight to Bima (Rp35,000) is unforgettable, flying over the Lintah and Sape straits and the deep aquamarine sea. Labuhanbajo's "airport," 3 km from town, consists of a stool, 2 ping-pong paddles, and 6 guys in shabby clothes who wave the plane away if no passengers are waiting. Not even a walkie-talkie! Merpati has an office on the road out to the airport, about 30 min. walk.

By Road

Regular truck and bus service runs on the 137-km ungraveled nerve-wracking track between Labuhanbajo and Ruteng; Rp3500. Leaving in the early morning (when and if there are enough passengers), this trip is made on a rattling truck, slipping and sliding over muddy roads. Flores trucks are canopied, with plank seats suspended across the bed, filled with chickens, goats, and people. Bridges, with numerous planks missing, span 80-m-high ravines—so beautiful but you're too scared to look. It should take 8-9 hours in the dry season; in the wet it could take from 16-48 hours (so bring food) or you might have to forget road travel and take the local coaster to Reo, and then down to Ruteng. Day trucks from Labuhanbajo to Reo leave about every 3 days, Rp5000, if there are enough passengers and if the weather is good.

By Boat

Regular overnight boats connect Reo (Rp4000). These *kapal motor* are more suitable for ponds than for the open sea; if they lose their way in the dark, it could take as long as 16 hours; pray for calm weather and a safe arrival. From Labuhanbajo are also occasional boats to Bari, Ende, Maumere, and even to Waingapu, Sumba (Rp12,000-15,000). For small boat departures and arrivals, ask at Kantor Syahbandar near the ferry jetty where they also sell boat tickets.

Ferries depart for Sape (E. Sumbawa) every Tues. and Thurs. at 0900; Rp5600 2nd Class, Rp7100 1st Class. Ferries depart for Komodo (and on to Sape) on Sun.

and sometimes on Sat. at 0800. On this passage there are very strong currents, especially between P. Padar and P. Rinca. You pass hundreds of beautiful islands and may even see migrating whales. Approaching Komodo, see the Sataliso volcano rising out of the sea. The Labuhanbajo ferry terminal is only a few minutes' walk from Wisma Bajo. To charter a boat for P. Komodo it'll cost around Rp125,000 between 4-5 people, 36 hours RT; always bargain directly with the boat captains as the *losmen* owners and even the *syahbandar* tack on too high a commission (Rp10,000-20,000!). Check the PPA office to see if one of their boats is heading to Komodo (only around Rp5000 pp!) or if they could recommend someone. As you might be able to find more people to go in on the cost, settle on one price for the whole boat, regardless of how many people show up.

VICINITY OF LABUHANBAJO

Visit the small harbor filled with native and Bugis *prahu*. Stilted Bajo fishermen's houses are built out over the water, dugout canoes tied underneath. There is particularly good snorkeling and some nice shells in the sea gardens out in the bay. You can usually charter a small catamaran for Rp4000 (and up) pp for 3 hours out to P. Badadari; snorkeling and diving equipment can also be rented in Labuhanbajo. Forget about doing any snorkeling around the village as sewage, trash, etc. kill the coral reefs. From Labuhanbajo, walk up the hill behind town for the sunset over the village and harbor. Also some caves with bats, stalagmites, and stalactites, just 1 km past the airstrip; local kids will show you where. A petrified prehistoric forest is 5 km S of town, where stone tree trunks lie in tangled broken heaps. People use the fossilized chunks of wood for stepping stones to their houses and for building walls.

Reo
Located 2 km from a rivermouth on the NW coast, Reo has grown around a large Catholic mission. Not much to do in this little town, though there's a lovely beach 5 km from town. Stay at **Losmen Teluk Bayur**, Jl. Mesjit (tel. 17); Rp3000 s, Rp6000 d; the rooms on the second floor are more secluded. Eat at **RM Selera Anda** near the Gereja Katolik, the only restaurant in town. If arriving by boat from Labuhanbajo or Maumere, a truck or bus might be waiting at the docks to take you to Ruteng; 4 hours (if weather permits), Rp5000. From Reo, buses or trucks leave at least every 3 days for Ruteng. The road twists and climbs through the refreshing cool air of the highlands, over clouded mountains, past giant ferns, creepers, and huge bamboo thrusting up in thick growths — a wild country. This partially paved road, superior to the section from Labuhanbajo to Ruteng, is being improved all the time. For boats to Labuhanbajo (Rp4000, 8-10 hours) and along the N coast to Maumere (Rp6000) and beyond, head 5 km from Reo to the cattle-exporting port of Kendini (Rp300 by *bemo*).

RUTENG

A cool, neat town set amidst the scenic hills (if not cloudy) of the Manggarai District, with tree-shaded streets and photogenic churches. Reachable by 5 flights weekly from Denpasar (Rp86,400). This village is so high (1,100 m) it could *snow;* you'll definitely need to don warm clothing by the late afternoon. Embroidered *sarung* are available in the *pasar*. The **post office** is on Jl. Baruk 6; open 0800-1400, Fri. until 1100, Sat. until 1230. Cash U.S. and Australian travelers' cheques at **Bank Rakyat Indonesia**; open Mon.-Fri. 0730-1200, Fri. and Sat. until 1100. They may not know the exchange rate and there might not be any connection with Ende by telephone; the mission might kindly change a US$50 cheque. On a commanding height over the town sits the HQ of the **Society of the Divine Word**, a German mission where Florinese are taught math, history, home economics, health care, and vocational skills like carpentry, blacksmithing, and masonry. The society, which started missionary activity on Flores in 1913, is also responsible for elementary and secondary schools throughout the island. They also try to teach the people more efficient agricultural methods to increase their productivity and improve their lives. This is a large market area; all around Ruteng are the productive farms of the mission which supply dairy products and meat. Go for walks out of the city — excellent views of beautiful lush green paddyfields, hills, mountains, and valleys.

Accommodations And Food
Good value is the well-run, extremely clean **Wisma Agung II** (Rp5000 s, Rp6000 d, Rp8000 t), Jl. Wae Cos 10, which has its own cab from the airport. Located about 1 km (15-min. walk) from the town center in a nice location in ricefields. The owner, a graduate in engineering and economics, spent 8 years in Canada and is a great guy to talk to. He has his hand in every type of business from a family-owned bakery to a road construction company. If he asks you to go fishing, he's not talking about some adventurous lake in the mountains. He's talking about his aquaculture pond made from a converted swimming pool where you can catch a fish in less than 2 minutes! Smelly blankets are provided against the cold night. Another Wisma Agung, **Wisma Agung I**, is in the city. **Losmen Karya**, also downtown, has 5 rooms at Rp4000 pp, but doesn't seem to welcome tourists. **Wisma Sindha** on Jl. Yos Sudarso asks an exorbitant Rp8500 pp; restaurant attached. Or eat at **RM Agung**, which serves decent Chinese food; since

the same people own Wisma Agung II, they might give you a lift. There's also a *restoran Minang*, about halfway between Wisma Agung II and town. A number of other *rumah makan* and small *warung* are at the bus terminal and in the nearby market.

FROM RUTENG

Catch buses and trucks early in the morning (0630) at the bus station next to the market, or buy your ticket at **Toko Orion** in town (commission: Rp500). Frequent buses take you to Reo (Rp5000, 4 hours). Trucks also head for Labuhanbajo (8-9 hours to 2 days). In 1987, a Swiss guy on his bicycle left Ruteng the same time the truck did and beat it to Labuhanbajo by an hour! Alternatively, the Merpati flight (Rp35,500) takes 15 minutes! Daily trucks to Wairana and on to Bajawa; Rp3500, 7-8 hours, 138 km. Also daily buses all the way to Ende cost Rp7000, taking 14 hours (258 km) in the dry season. Buses and trucks will pick you up at your *losmen*. Merpati (Jl. Pertiwi 15, tel. 147) flies to Ende (Rp41,000), Bima (Rp52,000), Kupang (Rp57,000), Denpasar (Rp96,000); they also provide a bus to the airport (Rp2000).

The Manggarai

A Malayan-Indonesian people who live in the western third of Flores, a land of mountains cut by deep valleys where rivers wend their way down to the N and S coasts. The Bimanese kingdom of E. Sumbawa dominated the Manggarai region during the 17th C., establishing a principality in Cibal in the center of W. Flores. But the catastrophic eruption of Sumbawa's G. Tambora (1814) so debilitated the kingdom that the Manggarai revolted in 1815. Backed by the Dutch, the Bimanese regained control over the Manggarai in 1851, only to be superseded by the Dutch in 1907. Catholic missionaries entered the area in 1913. Today the region is self-sufficient in rice (introduced in 1920) and maize, and exports high-quality coffee, sturdy horses, and beef cattle. The Manggarai speak a language unintelligible to the E. Florinese.

Only in **Todo** and **Pongkor**, the former seats of 2 rajas, can you find the celebrated cone-like traditional round houses of the Manggarai, built on piles 1 m off the ground with no walls; a thatched roof and a central pillar rise 6 m. At one time all the villages of the Manggarai had round houses but the Dutch discouraged their construction in favor of smaller, rectangular houses. Like the houses, villages are also circular, with a central square and a large ceremonial "drum house" *(mbaru gendang)* occupied by a patrilineal clan and presided over by the *tuan tanah* ("lord of the land"). In an open arena in the middle of the village stands a sacred tree surrounded by flat rocks *(kota)*, where buffalo sacrifices used to take place. The Manggarai also cultivated round fields in which each clan received a pie-shaped section. Now most of the round houses, round villages, and round fields have disappeared. From Ruteng, get a minibus as far as **Sokenor,** then hire small, sturdy, sure-footed horses up steep trails, across river valleys and grassy uplands SW towards the coast. High on your R will be Todo and lower on your L across the valley is Pongkor.

Borong

On the S coast, 6 hours by truck or mission jeep from Ruteng. Market here on Tuesdays. The Polish priest will help you find lodging in the village; expect around Rp2000 for bed and meals. Buy tickets (fixed price) for one of 4 boats returning to Ende on Wednesday. Leave at sunrise for the beach, a 30-min. walk from the *kampung,* to stake out a good place on the boat, which departs around 0800; beautiful views all along the S coast. Arrives approximately 2000.

Wairana

Fifty km SE of Ruteng by road, Wairana is a little paradise in a small valley with streams running through it. Houses are built in Swiss-chalet style. The priest, Rene Daen, arrived in 1960 and built his house on a swamp where a man had been murdered. They say Rene's house shook for years. People here are friendly because the missionary is so kind and good-natured. Market day is Saturday. No official accommodations yet, but the local townspeople put up travelers; ask around. Superb hikes in this area; use Wairana as a base. The Dutch have established an irrigation project in the area. A bus regularly leaves Wairana around noon for Bajawa (Rp2500), or wait and see what else blows through. Buses to Ende are about Rp3500.

BAJAWA

From Ruteng to Bajawa is a spectacular though grueling ride. Like Ruteng, this hill town is scenic but cold. Be sure to see Bajawa's ancestral poles; there's one at the end of Jl. Satsuitubu, and a whole group of them on the edge of town on the road to Ende. Called locally *ngebu* for men and *bhaga* for women, these totems protect the town and the fields against bad spirits *(polo)* or are raised in honor of the gods of clouds and mists *(noca)* and good spirits *(ngebu)*. Boxing matches are popular at festivals in this area: just the middle knuckle of a semi-clenched fist is used and partners steer their fighter from behind like puppeteers. Another important event is the Catholic Maha Kudus Mass in which a boisterous band of villagers leads a procession around town carrying the holy cross. Bajawa makes a good base for excursions into surrounding villages such as Soa and Bena. Climb G. Inielika (elev. 1,763 m) in 5 hours via its western slope from Kampung Menge, 13 km from Bajawa.

Accommodations And Food

Try comfortable **Losmen Dani** on Jl. Gereja (near the church); Rp4000-5000 s; Rp7000-8000 d. Wisma Mawar, Jl. Berhagia 139 (close to the market) charges Rp5000 s, Rp7500 d for large rooms; **Losmen Kembang**, more adequate, has rooms for Rp8500 d. Avoid damp, noisome, and distinctly unfriendly **Wisma Johnni** on Jl. Jen. A. Yani, a last resort at Rp3500 pp without breakfast. All the above hotels are close to the bus station, but in different directions. Food at **RM Beringin**, Jl. Besuki Rachmat, is nothing special; better is **RM Kasih** on Jl. A. Yani, close to the market. Like everywhere, there's also a Padang restaurant. Or try the *warung* near the market; the local specialty is dog meat. Stands also sell fresh fruit.

From Bajawa

Using Twin Otters, Merpati has 3 flights a week to Ende; also flights (not Twin Otters!) to Bima, Rp49,700; Denpasar, Rp101,400; Kupang, Rp65,300; and Waingapu (Sumba), Rp41,500. Buy tickets in the shop opposite the *terminal bis*. Early in the morning 2-3 trucks leave on the long, exhausting ride to Ruteng; Rp3500 (10-12 hours, or 2 days in the rainy season). Numerous minibuses depart daily for Ende, Rp3500; takes 5-6 hours on a fairly good road. On the way you'll pass huge **G. Ebulobo** which can be climbed from **Boawae** (elev. 522 m). Walking S, you'll eventually reach Rega, then on to Laja, Numu Pie, and at last Kampung Mulakoli (elev. 900 m), where it's a good idea to spend the night before the final 3-hour assault on the 2,149-m-high peak the next morning.

THE BAJAWA HIGHLANDS

One of the most traditional areas of Flores, and one of great natural beauty, the Bajawa Highlands is home to the Ngada people. Known in early Dutch literature as the Rokka (named after the old name for the region's principal peak, 2,245-m-high G. Inerie), this mixed Malay/Melanesian race, who believe they originated from Java, settled this region during the 17th century. They were pacified by the Dutch in 1907, and Christian missionaries began converting them around 1920. The Ngada occupy the S coast around G. Inerie, and inland on the high Bajawa Plateau to Riung in the north. The Bajawa Highlands is mostly covered in reedlike *alang-alang* grass. In the highest villages the temperatures could drop in the rainy season (Dec. to April) to freezing. Coconut, areca, *lontar* palms, tamarind, bamboo, citrus trees, bananas, breadfruit, and mangos grow wild. The Ngada have domesticated the buffalo and horse, and they keep pigs, chickens, goats. They hunt from horses using bamboo spears and iron-tipped war lances. The Ngada practice ironsmithing, pottery, and dye cloth to make traditional *sarung* with yellow embroidery.

Ngada villages consist of 2 rows of up to 50 closely spaced houses facing a small square. Some of their villages have stone walls, stone pillars, stone megaliths, and ritual poles where buffalo sacrifices once took place. Their traditional raised wooden houses consist of living quarters with a thatched, gabled roof and a veranda. Though small, each dwelling may house up to 20 people. There are a number of traditional villages surrounding Bajawa where *ngebu* totems and *rumah adat* can be seen. It's polite to always check in with the *kepala desa* before visiting sacred stones or taking photos. One village is about a 15-min. drive on the road to Soa. Another, **Bolozi**, is an hour's walk in the direction of Boawae; after passing Bajawa's *ngebu* on the R, continue straight but take a L at the fork. **Langka**, at the foot of G. Inerie, is 7 km by *bemo* from Bajawa; about 3 km down the road to Ende take a right. The *adat* village of Borado is 3 km farther.

Bena

A traditional village 21 km SE of Bajawa at the foot of the Inerie volcano, with stone totem figures and megaliths in the town square, surrounded by traditional Ngadanese bamboo dwellings and ritual houses. The *kepala desa* will ask for a donation; Rp500 is fair, or perhaps Rp1000 if you have a camera. First take a minibus from Bajawa to Mangulewa (10 km, Rp500), then another to **Welu** (6 km, Rp400), then ride a motorbike or walk 5 km to Bena. In **Mengulewa**, a wooden post is carved with the face of the Buffalo Man, a feature of ancestor worship.

Soa

A subdistrict where the society of the Soa live, numbering about 6,000. In the not-so-distant past, yearly ritual deer hunts used to take place in this district, at which time the teeth of pubescent girls were filed and blackened and boys were circumcised. After the deer was slain, the young girls would smear themselves with its blood to increase their fertility. Many trucks travel up from Bajawa (Rp1000, 18 km, 30 min.) taking people to Soa's big market on Sunday. Soa village is built around a huge amphitheater with tiers of great megaliths forming walls at different levels. Needle-like stones, with flatter stones on top serving as altars, have also been placed around the amphitheater. In the center stands a *peo* totem pole shaped like a doll. Visit the nearby *air panas*.

ENDE

Once an important port, administrative seat of the eastern archipelago, and the domain of a raja, Ende is now the capital of Flores. Though the aristocratic families of this area trace their ancestry back to the Majapahit Empire, today Ende is a miserable place

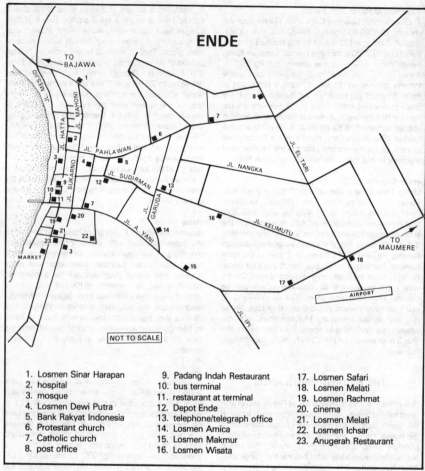

ENDE

TO
BAJAWA

JL. MESJID
JL. MAHONI
JL. HATTA
JL. PAHLAWAN
JL. SUKARNO
JL. SUDIRMAN
JL. NANGKA
JL. EL TARI
JL. GARUDA
JL. KELIMUTU
JL. A. YANI
MARKET
JL. IPI
NOT TO SCALE
TO
MAUMERE
AIRPORT

1. Losmen Sinar Harapan
2. hospital
3. mosque
4. Losmen Dewi Putra
5. Bank Rakyat Indonesia
6. Protestant church
7. Catholic church
8. post office
9. Padang Indah Restaurant
10. bus terminal
11. restaurant at terminal
12. Depot Ende
13. telephone/telegraph office
14. Losmen Amica
15. Losmen Makmur
16. Losmen Wisata
17. Losmen Safari
18. Losmen Melati
19. Losmen Rachmat
20. cinema
21. Losmen Melati
22. Losmen Ichsar
23. Anugerah Restaurant

with a garbage-strewn beach and goats grazing the trash piles. Wander the paths between the main roads to see people with *betel*-stained mouths, broken-down bamboo shacks, hungry children. From a traveler's point of view, Ende is principally a pitstop on the road to Keli Mutu volcano and the *ikat*-weaving villages of Jopu and Nggela. Also, a lot of *sarung* weaving and dyeing goes on close to the market. Change only U.S. and Aussie TCs and cash at **Bank Rakyat Indonesia**, Jl. Jen. Sudirman. The **post office** is a 5-min. walk from Flores University in the western part of town. The **telephone office** is on Jl. Keli Mutu (open Mon.-Thurs. 0800-1200, until 1000

on Fri. and Sat.). A *bemo* will take you anywhere in town for Rp200.

Sights
Visit the house where Sukarno lived when he was exiled to Flores by the Dutch in 1933; it's now a national shrine. At the mission talk to the priests for info about the surrounding area; they know the customs and laws of the island well. This large, noisy fishing village is also the place to catch a glimpse of boat-building techniques. Not to be missed are the remarkable stemless boats at Ende's Pelabuhan Ipi, 2 km and Rp200 by *bemo* from town. Described by Noote-

boom 50 years ago, they are still being built today by Bugis immigrants who join together planks on both sides where they meet at the end of the boat. Used all over Flores, they are now called *sope;* if the stem is decorated, they are called *jukut.* These boats have 12 ribs, just like the human body, and are usually constructed from the base of a dugout canoe. Many use the old Dutch spritsail rig.

Accommodations

Generally low standard and noisy, most falling in the Rp2500-6000 range. **Losmen Ikhlas** is on Jl. Wolowaru (on a hill on the way out to the airport); get one of the 2 good rooms with windows but be sure to close them when you're off your guard (someone stole my change purse when I turned to shoo away a *sarung* peddler; probably were in cahoots!). If you don't like Losmen Ikhlas, go down the street to upmarket **Wisma Safari** (N side of town near airport) which is twice the price. **Losmen Solafide**, Jl. Anekere 2 (out of town a bit), is clean and quiet; Rp5000 s, Rp8500 d with private, tiled *mandi* and sit-down toilets. You can take a *bemo* into town, and the owner's jeep can be rented (expensive) for the ascent of Keli Mutu or for going to the airstrip (Rp2000). **Wisma Flores**, Jl. Jen. Sudirman 18, is pretty grotty. On Jl. Wolowaru is **Losmen Makmur**, next to the mosque but it's clean with mosquito nets. On Jl. Kelimutu (no. 68, tel. 368) is **Wisma Wisata**; Rp10,000 s, Rp15,000 d—though comfortable, it's pretentious and poor value. Try instead **Losmen Ihsaar** on a road off Jl. Katedral; quite adequate at Rp6000 pp. Near Detusoko, 35 km NE of Ende (3 km from the "Lourdes" statue of Flores), a Catholic seminary retreat run by sisters charges Rp7500 pp including great meals.

Food

Go at night to the market when many *warung* serve *nasi campur, sate,* etc. In the day, eat (in order of quality) at **Depot Ende, Terminal Restoran** (next to bus station), **RM Anugrah** (near harbor), and **Minang Restoran.** Depot Ende (Jl. Jen. Sudirman 6) has wonderful *markisa* (passion fruit) and other juices, plus ice cream. Nice fellow who runs it. A fruit and vegetable market, **Pasar Potulando**, is on the road to the airport (Jl. Kelimutu).

Crafts

Check the *pasar pagi* near the waterfront for *sarung* and *ikat* from the Lio (NE) and Jopu (E) areas of Ende; thin, stark black and yellow, with triangular motifs made up of continuous lines like a maze. Prices asked are from Rp15,000 to Rp25,000. In Manokwari, Irian Jaya, where they're used as a bride price, *lio* cloths fetch up to Rp250,000. Prices are lower and quality is higher for *ikat* fabric in the villages of Jopu, Nduria, Wolonjita, and Nggela (see "Vicinity Of Wolowaru" below).

From Ende

The bus and *bemo* terminal is right across from the *lapangan fotbol.* Regular buses leave daily to Moni (Rp1200, 52 km), Maumere (Rp3500, 7 hours), Bajawa (Rp3500, 6 hours, 125 km), Wolowaru (Rp1500), Ruteng (Rp6500, 16 hours, 286 km), leaving twice weekly. Remember that road conditions change quickly on Flores—earthquakes, landslides, erosion, flooding, etc.—so travel times are uncertain. Get an early start as bus departures really slow down in the afternoon. The 148-km trip by road to Maumere is spectacular. G. Keli Mutu with its 3 colored crater lakes is almost halfway between Ende and Maumere. Moni is a good base for expeditions up the mountain. Coming from Ende, the 14-km road up to Keli Mutu starts about 1½ km before Moni on the right. Buses from Ende to Moni usually leave between 0800 and 0900; night buses between 1600 and 1700. Groups may also charter a minibus straight to the volcano for around Rp75,000 per day (allow 2 days). A *bemo* could be cheaper (Rp50,000?). Ask around the *bemo* station.

Terrifying landings at Ende's paved, well-equipped but windy airstrip. Wind whips across the bottleneck of a promontory formed by a small outlying volcano; you can see the palm heads toss as you come down. For the Merpati office, get a *bemo* (Rp200) to the intersection to the airport, then it's only a 10-min. walk. Merpati flies to Larantuka (via Kupang), Rp36,700; Bima (daily, Rp29,000), Kupang (Rp57,000, 4 times weekly), Surabaya (Rp103,700), Waingapu (Rp32,800, weekly). The inter-island flight back to Bali (Rp101,400, 4 times weekly) takes just 2 hours over a distance which may have taken you 2 weeks on the outward journey! Flying out of Ende you may get a glimpse of the volcano near Ende which blew 2 years ago; half of the volcano is gone and smoke and sulfuric gases are still being emitted. Only Java and Sumatra have more active volcanos than Flores (which has 15).

Boats dock at Ende's port, Pelabuhan Ipi, 2 km (Rp200) by *bemo* from town, down Jl. Wolowaru. Three times monthly, catch a Perintis ship (Rp8000-10,000) to either Kupang or Waingapu, Sumba (the actual route is Kupang-Roti-Savu-Ende-Sumba-Kupang). Pelni's MV *Kelimutu* also calls in at Ende about every 2 weeks on its loops from Semarang-Padangbai and Kupang; Pelni's office is on Jl. Pabean. Take a launch for Rp1000 out to the larger ships in the harbor. *Kapal motor* depart for Labuhanbajo and Waingapu. Inquire for boats at the *syahbandar's* office at Pelabuhan Ipi. There's a daily boat from Ende to Nggela, leaving the harbor at 0800.

KELI MUTU

Northeast of Ende, Keli Mutu volcano is one of the

more otherworldly sights in all of Indonesia. Much visited since Dutch times, the 3 lakes atop this extinct volcano, separated by low ridges, have different colored waters. Legend has it that Keli Mutu is an abode of the dead: in the maroon lake live the souls of sinners; in the green lake the souls of young men, virgins, and the pure of heart; while in the blue lake dwell the souls of the elderly. Actually, the colors are in constant flux as their waters leach minerals from the earth, which dissolve and color the water. From the viewpoint, you can see the complex's highest peak (to the W), 1,613 m, and the even higher Keli Bara (1,731 m) to the south. Rather dangerous trails run along the crater rims. Below the lakes are the remains of the old Dutch *pasanggrahan*. Keli Mutu gets only about 300 foreign tourists per year, about 100 of them in July and Aug.; any other time of the year it can be eerily quiet. The dry season is April-October.

To get there fast, fly into Maumere's well-equipped airport (96 km, 5 hours by bus from Moni), or the paved, windswept landing strip at Ende (66 km from Moni, 3 hours by bus). Coastal vessels also call at Ende and Maumere. From Ende or Maumere, take the bus to Moni from where you climb the volcano. If you're in a super hurry, coming from Ende, ask the bus driver to let you off on the road up to Keli Mutu about 1½ km before Moni, then walk or hitch up to the complex. Park your gear at the seismologist's post on the way up. It's possible to do Keli Mutu and get back to Ende the same day (pray for a sunny day). On Sundays, busloads of local tourists assault the mountain, most of them direct from Ende. You might get a ride, but they often don't get to the top until around 1100, by which time the mountain has clouded over and there isn't much to see. Or follow Pak Harto's example and go by helicopter; a landing pad has been cleared near the top specially for a visit he made 5 years ago.

Moni

A small village 14 km N of G. Keli Mutu on the Ende-Maumere road, 66 km from Ende (Rp1500 by bus, 2 hours, morning departures). The constant sound of running water through ricefields, fantastic views of surrounding volcanos, and in the far distance the ocean, all give this village a tranquil feeling. Moni's busy market day is Tues., with a good selection of *sarung* and *selandang*. Stay at the Catholic mission's guesthouse, **Wisma Keli Mutu**, between the *gereja* and the rectory (cross the *pasar* and the open soccer field to reach it). Clean and orderly, it costs Rp3500 s plus Rp1000 for bland, pseudo-Western meals. The constant sound of a running stream makes it very peaceful. There's another *losmen* on the main road straight across from the *pasar* next to a store; Rp2000. Run by an English teacher who seems ever ready to separate you from your *rupiah*, the food is OK (Rp1000 per meal), but the place is rat-infested. Some

private houses around the bus station also put up travelers for the same price. After climbing Keli Mutu, catch a bus in the late morning on to Maumere, Rp2000, 148 km, 3-4 hours; or back to Ende, Rp1500, 2 hours, 66 km. This is a pulse-pounding ride along high cliffs over a river valley, amazing as you come down into Ende.

The Climb

It's important to go up the volcano early, before clouds roll in. To view these colored lakes under the best light, get up at 0200 and walk the whole 14 km to the top. Start about 1½ km (15-min. walk) out of Moni toward Ende; a square pole arches over the start of the road. The climb will take about 3½-4 hours, so carry water, snacks, and you'll definitely need a flashlight (it's pitch dark!). Gorgeous stars (if no moon); follow the Southern Cross up to the crater. People in this region keep lamps burning in their houses at night to frighten the spirits (and to calm themselves). The mountain is steep, but the ascent isn't. Walking along the asphalted road is not difficult even in the dark. About halfway up the mountain (7 km) is the PPA checkpoint (they'll charge Rp200 pp on your way back down). From the checkpoint it's about another 7 to the top. Alternatively, there is a shortcut *(jalan potong)* from Moni to the checkpoint; ask about this at the checkpoint, the guys there don't always volunteer the information. Kids in Moni will happily show you where to get on to the path which begins about halfway between Moni and the road up. This way saves a lot of time, but is steep, slippery, and involves walking through a small gorge, 3 small *kampung*, with several river and bamboo-bridge crossings. If starting before sunrise, you might feel more comfortable sticking to the main road *(jalan raya)*. You'll reach the top around 0600, then wait for a break in the clouds.

A jeep can also be chartered from Wisma Keli Mutu in Moni—Rp15,000-20,000 for 2 people, or maybe Rp25,000 for larger groups (can hold 6-8). These guys are patient, allowing you to spend as much time as you want at the top, watching the light change on the lakes. From Ende, a *bemo* (ask at *bemo* terminal near waterfront) costs around Rp50,000 RT. You could also pay someone in Moni to give you a lift on the back of their motorbike (Rp6000-7000 RT). Jerky and uncomfortable ponies, hired in the villages on the way up, don't seem worth the effort and walk no faster than a human. Don't take a horse unless you want a sore ass for a week because it's a 4-hour bareback climb! Horses have no saddles and cost Rp5000 with guide (when you get tired, *he* can ride it). Guides are totally unnecessary. Heading back, take the trail down near the PPA office which leads through a village and comes out on the road by a nice waterfall just 1 km from Moni. An *air panas* is just 450 m away.

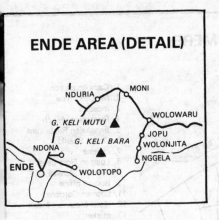

ENDE AREA (DETAIL)

THE WOLOWARU AREA

Wolowaru

Twelve km E of Moni on the road to Maumere. As you're coming into town, see the cluster of old-style *rumah adat* with their high, steeply pitched roofs. Stay in **Losmen Setia** (Rp2500 s), a nice place with limited electricity and hundreds of kids filling every window and doorway. Good food. No other *losmen* but the **RM Selera Kita** has beds available if you ask. **RM Jawa Timur** has decent food. **RM Betania**, though very pleasant, is hopelessly disorganized; one wonders if they'll be in business much longer. Buy blankets at Wolowaru's market on Sat., plus 2 other days per week.

Visit the traditional village of **Lekebai**, NE of Wolowaru. Daily buses depart in the mornings from Wolowaru to Ende (Rp1500) and Maumere (Rp2500); book tickets at **RM Jawa Timur**, where all the *bemo* stop to eat. Or flag down a bus or truck to the E or W out on the main road. Wolowaru is the start of the road S to Jopu, Wolonjita, and Nggela. Jopu is an easy walk (5 km) or hitch from Wolowaru. Minibuses run direct to Jopu from Ende (Rp1500), but no regular departures. Wolonjita is 4 km beyond Jopu, and Nggela is another 5 km (1-hour walk) S of Wolonjita. The entire 20-km-RT walking tour from Wolowaru down to Nggela can be done handily in one day. Trucks run Wolowaru-Wolonjita on Sat. market day. Yet another alternative is to take the daily 0800 boat from Ende's Pelabuhan Ipi to Nggela (Rp2000, 2 hours), then walk up through Wolonjita and Jopu to Wolowaru.

Jopu

An old-style Florinese village with steep-roofed *adat* houses and a distinctive Flemish-looking church, secluded in a valley with magnificent volcanos on all sides. Also a small hospital here. Some of the best weaving in C. Flores comes from Jopu and the surrounding 6 coastal villages. Beautiful, tapestry-like *sarung ikat* and other richly dyed fabrics; all you have to do is unthread the seam and you have a wall-hanging. *Selandang* shawls for carrying *barang*, for warmth, and at one time for wrapping the dead, are also for sale. The going rate for a reasonable quality shawl is Rp20,000-25,000, but for the *ikat* they ask as high as Rp130,000! Jopu has one *rumah makan,* but no *penginapan.*

Vicinity Of Jopu

An interesting hilly part of Flores. *Ikat* cloths, with unique motifs, are also fashioned in the neighboring villages of Nduria, Wolonjita, and Nggela. **Nggela,** which has traditional dwellings and practices weaving styles different from Jopu's, sits on a high cliff with stupendous views over the Savu Sea. The best *lio* cloths come from Leo. Reasonable prices for high-quality *sarung* are Rp17,000-20,000. But you can pay as high as Rp25,000-30,000 for an excellent one. First asking prices range from Rp35,000 to Rp50,000. Keli Mutu can be climbed from Nggela (or from Jopu), but it's a much longer and steeper climb than tackling it from Moni. The volcano Keli Baru (1,459 m), NW of Nggela, erupted in 1969, covering nearly all of western Flores in a blanket of ash over 30 cm deep. Crops and plants were crushed under the weight of the ash, and the wildlife of the area stumbled about and died wholesale for lack of food and water.

MAUMERE

A port town 148 km E of Ende (by bus, Rp3500, 5-6 hours) on the narrow eastern stretch of the island. Built like a Spanish town with a main square and market occupying its center, Maumere's principal attraction is its large Catholic church just down from Losmen Bogor on Jl. Slamet Riyadi in the W side of town. Inside are paintings of the Twelve Stations of the Cross executed by a local artist with all Indonesian characters. The church usually is locked up, but you can get the key from the priest; visit also the old musty cemetery in the rear. A center of Catholic enterprise, the local mission finances and manages a copra and coffee export business. The Catholic hospital (Western-trained staff) is the place to go if you get sick on Flores. The market, though untidy, is really nice. Buy thick, distinctive Maumere blankets for about Rp16,000-22,000 (Rp150,000 on Bali); also see ivory (from Sumatra) jewelry being carved by local craftsmen. Change U.S. and Aussie TCs and currency at **Bank Rakyat Indonesia.** The **tourist office,** Jl. A. Yani 44 (tel. 181), dispenses several pamphlets and gives out good advice. The **post office,** in the E. part

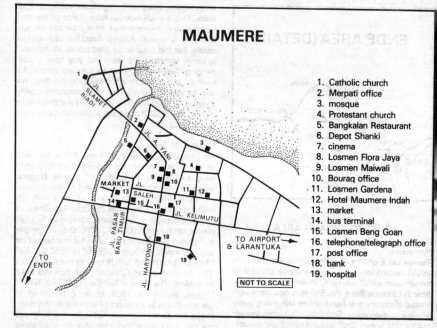

MAUMERE

1. Catholic church
2. Merpati office
3. mosque
4. Protestant church
5. Bangkalan Restaurant
6. Depot Shanki
7. cinema
8. Losmen Flora Jaya
9. Losmen Maiwali
10. Bouraq office
11. Losmen Gardena
12. Hotel Maumere Indah
13. market
14. bus terminal
15. Losmen Beng Goan
16. telephone/telegraph office
17. post office
18. bank
19. hospital

TO AIRPORT →
& LARANTUKA

NOT TO SCALE

of town, is open Mon.-Thurs. 0800-1400, Fri. until 1100, and Sat. until 1230.

Not much else to do, but if you're stuck for a few days try getting out to the **Sea World Diving Club** in Waiara 12 km E, where you can rent snorkeling gear (also at Sao Wisata) at Rp600 per day including fins (see "Vicinity Of Maumere"). Also visit Maumere's copra-exporting harbor to observe the unusual stemless *sope*, a remnant of 17th C. Portuguese shipbuilding techniques. Note that the planks don't meet along the center line at the bow and stern, but alternating planks join their partners first on one side then the other. The harbor is due N of Losmen Beng Goan.

Accommodations And Food

Losmen Bogor asks Rp4000 for tiny rooms; it's on Jl. Slamet Riyadi out of the main center. Although the plumbing isn't that swift (toilet paper blocks the pipes), it's still a good deal. Also not too bad is noisy but clean **Losmen Beng Goan**, Jl. Pasar Baru (right across from the *pasar*, tel. 247), which charges Rp3500 for B Class singles, Rp4500 with morning and evening tea. Or eat meals separately; for example, Rp1000 for breakfast. Laundry service is available and beds have mosquito nets. Also 2 places on Jl. Pasar Baru Timur. One is **Wisma Flora Jaya**, 2 blocks back from the market; Rp6000-12,000 for rooms without *mandi* plus Rp5000 per day for meals. Has a friendly

atmosphere and excellent food; you'll have a great time with Mama Jo. The other is **Losmen Maiwali**; large rooms for Rp5000 s, Rp7500 d. The most expensive accommodations is Sea World Club in Waiara 12 km E; bungalows run Rp35,000, including meals. Maumere has several *rumah makan* on Jl. Pasar Baru Barat. The Padang restaurant **RM Surya Judah** near the market is the best of the bunch; the only chance in Indonesia to eat tasty Padang-style food that isn't hot! Other restaurants near the market are strong on Muslim-style goat *sate* and *gulai*. Delicious avocados, *zirzak*, papaya, etc. are sold in the market.

From Maumere

Daily early-morning bus departures from Maumere's market for Wolowaru (Rp2500, 3½ hours), Ende (Rp3500, 5-6 hours), and Larantuka (Rp3500, 5-6 hours, 127 km). The road to Ende is good year-round, but in the wet season the bus fare to Larantuka can increase to Rp6000 and can take to 3 days for this trip. For G. Keli Mutu, buses to Moni (14 km N of the volcano) cost Rp3000 and leave around 0730; they are not hard to catch as they circle around the market for 15 min. before departure. This is a 3 to 4-hour ride but the beautiful, rugged scenery, plus the variety of architecture, horticulture, and cultures, makes it worth every minute. The bus will stop in Wolowaru, one of the main roadstops with *rumah makan* and market; as you leave Wolowaru on the way to Moni

(30-min. drive), you can see *rumah adat* with their thatched, sloping roofs. It's also possible to charter a *bemo* from Maumere straight to the top of G. Keli Mutu for Rp100,000-Rp125,000 RT, returning the next day.

Maumere has good air connections, better than Ende's, with connecting flights to Timor, Sumbawa, Bali, etc. Merpati's office (tel. 242) is on Jl. A. Yani, about a 15-min. walk from Losmen Beng Goan. Sample Merpati fares to: Kupang, Rp31,600; Bima, Rp48,500; Denpasar, Rp80,200; Ende, Rp20,200; Larantuka, Rp26,600. Fly Bouraq (Jl. Madawat, tel. 167) to: Denpasar (direct) Rp92,200; Jakarta (via Denpasar and Surabaya), Rp176,300; Kupang (direct), Rp36,300. Try to book in advance as flights are sometimes full. Charter a *bemo* out to the Wai Oti Airport, 3 km from town, for Rp1500; or take a public one (Rp200) on the road to Geliting to the airport turnoff, then walk in ½ km.

Boats often call at this N coast port. Check the Pelni office, on Jl. Slamet Riyadi opposite Losmen Bogor, for ships to Sulawesi, Surabaya, Sumbawa, Timor, and the islands E of Flores. The MV *Kelimutu* calls in at Ende, 6 hours down the road, every 2 weeks on its way from Semarang to Kupang. Ask the *syahbandar* about *kapal motor* heading for Reo, Labuhanbajo, Bima, and Ujung Pandang.

Vicinity Of Maumere

Maumere is surrounded by coconut plantations; racks drying copra are everywhere. There's a beach close to town. Charter a *prahu* (1 day, 1 night) out to G. Rokatenda, a volcano on P. Puluweh. NW of Maumere. In 1928, emissions caused tidal waves which killed 266 people. Climb Rokatenda's peak in 3 hours from the *kampung* of **Uwa** on the SE coast. The large Catholic seminary (300 hopefuls) in **Ladelero**, 24 km SW (Rp500, 30 min.) of Maumere, has a museum which exhibits swords, shields, statues, Chinese porcelain, anthropological artifacts, and rare *ikat* textiles (from Sikka and Jopu) and other weavings from pre-Dutch times which reflect Flores' rich mosaic of ethnic groups. Presided over by Father Peter, a Florinese priest, the trick is catching him there. Leave a donation. The seminary has a wonderful view of the N bay area. Some students speak a little English and are very helpful in showing you around. Stay and have dinner! Another Catholic mission is in **Watublapi**; from this village, walk to the *kampung* of **Ohe** from where you can see both the N and S coasts of Flores.

PT Sao Wisata

Reputed to contain some of the finest diving sites in the world, the whole marine area within 1 hour by boat of Maumere comprises numerous detached coral reefs forming strings near the shores and around or near several islands (**Besar, Babi,** and **Pamana**). Dive

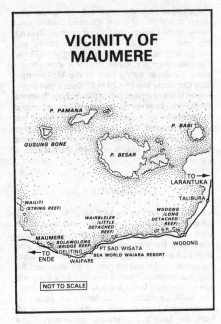

VICINITY OF MAUMERE

NOT TO SCALE

sites range from 200-2,000 m deep and feature a great diversity of marine life, shallow areas of seagrass (off P. Besar), spectacular world-class drop-offs with ultimate visibility of 50 m or more, and an average water temperature of 30 degrees Celsius. The total lack of swells and currents makes diving very comfortable (but no diving in rainy season Dec.-Feb.). What makes this area particularly attractive are the first-class dive resorts: **Sea World Resort** and **PT Sao Wisata** (tel. 342) at Waiara, 10 km E of Maumere. The latter charges US$60 pp per day in fancy little bungalows. That price includes all dive equipment, meals, transport, and 2-3 dives per day. Both resorts are accessible by *bemo* (Rp300) from Maumere. Book or get further information from PT Sao Wisata, Borobudur Office Bldg., 2nd Floor, Room 6B, Jl. Lapangan Banteng Selatan, Jakarta Pusat, tel. 360209 (ext. 78222/78227).

Sikka

An important weaving center, Rp500 (1 hour) by minibus S of Maumere. Watch the old women weave heavy *ikat*, spinning homegrown cotton thread using a device operated with their feet. Practically every house owns a primitive loom consisting of just threads stretched between stakes stuck in the ground. Warp threads are tied tightly with grass fibers and then dyed with native indigo, red, and a yellow dye made from cudrania wood. In the Sikka

District, *sarung* are often accented with narrow warp stripes of a shade of green the exact color of plant leaves! (Unfortunately, the brighter synthetic dyes are now making inroads.) Motifs include plants, and animals such as lizards—a fertility symbol on Flores. Sikkanese dress and songs still show strong Portuguese influences dating back to the 16th century. After Christmas Mass on 26 or 27 Dec., a play is performed in the courtyard before the local raja. Neither a native Portuguese nor the people of Sikka understand the words as the original Portuguese language has been so corrupted. **Lela**, **Nita**, and **Kotung** are other villages in the area that faithfully preserve Portuguese traditions. A lovely palm-lined beach, **Pantai Lela**, is 4 km from Sikka.

LARANTUKA

A picturesque port on the far E tip of the island, 667 km from Labuhanbajo; also an embarkation point for boats to the islands E of Flores. Larantuka has a long-established Eurasian colony and since Portuguese times (starting in the 16th C.) has been the administrative center for the eastern neck of the island and the islands to the east. Travelers embark for the Solor and Alor archipelagos from Larantuka by crossing the narrow Selat Lewotobi. Larantuka's main street, Jl. Niaga, which contains most of the government offices, the town's 2 churches, and many of the businesses, runs along the waterfront. The Muslim section of town is to the northeast. The **post office** is a bit out of town on Jl. Pasar, past the *pasar pusat* (take a *bemo*, Rp200); open Mon.-Thurs. 0800-1400; Fri. until 1100; Sat. until 1230. Change money at **Bank Rakyat Indonesia** on Jl. Niaga. The *bemo* station is opposite the main pier on Jl. Niaga, Rp200 flat rate.

For centuries a Portuguese trading center (Larantuka's seminary was built in 1516), traces of the Portuguese era are still evident in the old stone and stucco houses, in the large-boned, Latin-featured inhabitants, in family names such as Monteiros and da Silva, and even in the place names in town such as *posto* (the town's center). With its prayers, ceremonies, Christmas and Good Friday processions, and Iberian church architecture, the Catholic religious life of Larantuka follows Portuguese traditions. Many of the prayers are recited in broken Portuguese, and during religious processions men carry a bier which symbolically contains the body of Jesus. They wear long white cloaks with high pointed hoods, costumes resembling those donned in Portugal during the Middle Ages. Old relics from the 1500s and 1600s are still preserved in bamboo chapels as village *pustaka*—vestments, devotional clothes, ivory crucifixes, silver chalices. A statue of a black Virgin Mary, claimed to have been washed ashore in a man's dream, is vener-

ated. An old Portuguese bell hangs outside the **Church of Kepala Maria**, a bit out of town on the road to Maumere. In the corner of the bishop's garden *(Peca da Penha)* is the Portuguese font where hundreds of Larantuka's ancestors were baptised.

Accommodations And Food

Highly recommended is **Losmen Rullis** on Jl. Yos Sudarso; 8 rooms at Rp6000-7000 pp. On the same street are **Hotel Tresna** (Rp5000-6000) and **Wisma Kartika**, Rp3500 pp, though a bit noisy. Also try **Losmen Kurnia**, Rp3500 pp. The culinary possibilities are limited. **Depot Nirwana**, on the main street, is a surprisingly good little restaurant, plus there are a number of *warung* and fruit and vegetables in the market.

Portuguese cannon, Larantuka

Getting There

Leaving Maumere for the 137-km trip (Rp3500, 5 hours) to Larantuka, the road suddenly drops from the mountains to the coast where Larantuka sits. You plunge from a region of tall, broad-leafed trees into luxuriant jungle and grassland—spectacular scenery. From Larantuka you can see the vague shapes of the islands of the Solor Archipelago in the distance. Larantuka faces P. Adonara, only 2 km across the narrow Flores Strait, and just beyond, P. Solor almost blocks the view of the Savu Sea. If arriving by boat from the E, buses wait near the wharf to take you to Maumere (Rp3500, 5 hours, 137 km) and other points west.

From Larantuka

Larantuka is an important harbor for the easterly islands; boats depart daily for Lembata, Adonara,

Solor, Latuna, and Alor, and at least twice weekly departures for Kupang, Rp10,000-12,000. Boats leave daily for Waiwerang (P. Adonara), Rp1000, 2½ hours, and about 3 times weekly for Lewoleba on P. Lembata (Rp2500, 4-5 hours). For details, check with the *syahbandar*'s office on Jl. Niaga; boats disembark from the wharf nearby. Inquire also at the Pelni office (Jl. Niaga) for Perintis ships which leave about every 10 days for Kupang (Rp12,000, 3 days) via Waiwerang (P. Adonara), Lewoleba (P. Lomblem), and Kalabahi (P. Alor). **flights:** Taxis cost Rp2000 pp for the 10-km ride to the airport. The Merpati office is opposite the big church, one street down from Jl. Niaga: 3 flights weekly to Kupang; Maumere, Rp36,600; Ruteng, Rp63,500; Lewoleba, Rp33,800.

SOLOR AND ALOR ARCHIPELAGOS

Separated by swift, narrow straits, this small string of islands is off the E coast of Flores. The people of the extreme eastern end of Flores, as well as the off-lying islands of Solor, Adonara, and Lembata, are referred to as Solorese. These peoples, a mixture of Malay and Melanesian, share strong cultural traits, speak the same language, and have experienced the same history. With a sword in one hand and a Bible in the other, the Portuguese Dominican missionaries controlled the area from the 16th-19th centuries. Dutch Jesuits and Franciscans arrived between 1860 and 1880. As a result of all this proselytizing, the majority of the population is Christian, although in the ports there are sizable Islamic communities. For hundreds of years, the islands E of Flores were known as the "Isles of Murderers." Two clans, the Demons and the Padzis (like the American Hatfields and McCoys), carried on a deadly feud believed by anthropologists to have been started by 2 brothers back in the 1500s. No one was able to stop the fighting or discover its ringleaders, for often the old men behind the killings appointed young men to confess and go to prison in their place. The parties have now been pacified.

Getting There

Larantuka is the starting point for scheduled ferries across the Flores Strait to Adonara, Solor, and Lembata. Departing Larantuka daily at 0800, they stop at Waiwerang on the S coast of P. Adonara before reaching Lewoleba on P. Lembata at around 1300; Rp750-1000 OW. From P. Lembata boats sail farther to P. Pantar and P. Alor. Ships also leave Kupang for Waiwerang and Larantuka and back for Rp12,000-15,000. Merpati flies from Kupang 4 times weekly to both Lewoleba (P. Lembata) and Kalabahi (P. Alor), both flights Rp41,200. On the islands themselves, stay either with the local Catholic priest or the *kepala kampung*.

ADONARA

This island is separated from eastern Flores by a narrow strait. Soaring above P. Adonara is a 1,650-m-high peak to the SE, Ili Boleng. Most Adonara people speak Solorese. Although a Catholic island with Portuguese-style religious practices, beneath the veneer of Christianity many inhabitants worship reptiles and other creatures. Nearly every village, particularly inland, has an altar or totem to the spirits thought to live in large trees, rocks, on mountaintops, and near the graves of ancestors. Men brandishing spears and wearing war paint and palm fronds as battle camouflage still stage full-dress war dances once or twice a year. Many make their living from pearl diving.

The main town of P. Adonara is **Waiwerang**. Market day is Thursday. Catch the daily boat from Larantuka (Flores) for Waiwerang at 0800; takes about 2 hours, Rp1000. Wairwerang is also accessible from the other direction: boats leave every Wed. and Thurs. from Lamalera (P. Lembata), Rp1500. Another ship runs twice a week from Kupang to Larantuka, stopping in Waiwerang on the way. Stay at **Losmen Taufik**, Rp2500 pp.

Vure

This village has a similar religious structure and practices to Larantuka. In fact, the bell in the church, inscribed with the date "10 December 1714," originally came from the Catholic church in Larantuka. Wander through the bamboo chapels with sand floors; many Portuguese and *adat* artifacts, some from Melaka and Goa (S. Sulawesi). Prayers are uttered in almost indecipherable Portuguese.

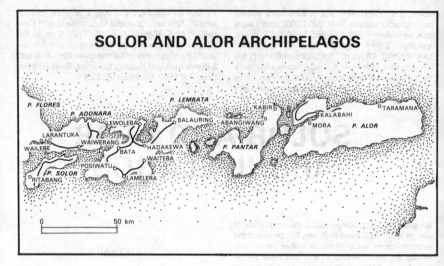

SOLOR AND ALOR ARCHIPELAGOS

P. FLORES
P. ADONARA
P. LEMBATA
KABIR
TARAMANA
KALABAHI
LEWOLEBA
BALAURING
ABANGIWANG
MORA
P. ALOR
LARANTUKA
WAIWERANG
WAILEBE
HADAKEWA
P. PANTAR
BATA
WAITEBA
P. SOLOR
POSIWATU
LAMELERA
RITABANG

0   50 km

SOLOR

For many years the rendezvous point for Portuguese sandalwood traders, 2,100-sq-km P. Solor nestles between Flores, Adonara, and Lembata. Get a boat from Waiwerang to Lawajong, Rp1000. In 1566, Dominican monks built the stone fortress of Henrique on the N coast near the present-day village of **Lahajong**, a well-chosen spot which provided good anchorage. Although the fortress itself lies in ruins, its massively thick walls (2 m wide by 4 m high) still stand, and some rusty cannons remain in the courtyard. The small village of **Lamalera** on the E side is 1 of only 2 whaling villages in Indonesia. Being a volcanic island where only a few scanty crops are raised from the stony soil on the coast, the women of Lamalera must tramp up to the mountain villages to barter whale meat and oil for maize, rice, and cassava. To reach P. Solor, boats depart Larantuka each morning for Lahajong (Rp1500) as well as to **Pamakajo** on the N coast; Rp1000. From Pamakajo, boats hop across to Waiwerang.

LEMBATA ISLAND

Also known as Lomblem, this is a dry island due to hot, parching winds blowing up from Australia, creating expanses of scrub grasslands, inland stands of eucalyptus trees, and open savannahs. Wildlife is plentiful. Every district on the island has its own dialect, customs, and brand of animism; a famous village in the S still practices a primitive form of whaling. The quality of Lembata's fine homespun *ikat* weaving and fabrics is commensurate with Sumba's. Two districts worth visiting are in the N, Iliape and Kedang, where villages are scattered along the coast under the shadow of volcanos. The best *sarung* are made in **Iliape District**, but you won't find them easily as they're mainly for ceremonial use and cost up to Rp75,000. In **Kedang District** is a lot of porcelain, even in the inland villages, plus ivory (including whole tusks) from Sumatra. Expect to do a lot of walking.

The People

Most inhabitants practice slash-and-burn agriculture and are Melanesian-looking; some have Portuguese features, while others are unmistakably Papuan. A superstitious people with spooky beliefs and practices, some interior villagers still display the skulls of their ancestors in full view; in others no one goes out at night. The people are difficult to get to know beyond the initial meeting, though the men are fond of drinking *tuak* and often ask travelers to stop and drink with them along the trails: it's believed that if a stranger shares *tuak*, then he is not an enemy. Islanders often call you "father" because most of the Westerners they meet are priests. The missionaries maintain a strong presence on the island but tribalism and mysticism are still pervasive. Ask about the community houses *(kokay)* where you can observe all the rituals taking place right under the missionaries' noses.

Getting There And Around

Catch the daily 0800 boat from Larantuka to Waiwerang (Rp2000), then the same boat or another

(Rp2000) from Waiwerang to Lewolaba on the W coast of P. Lembata. The complete journey takes about 5-6 hours. Boats ply the coastline between Lamalera, Lewolaba, and Balauring, and a bad road encircles the whole island. Merpati flies to the landing strip near Lewoleba twice weekly, Rp44,000. The only land transport on Lembata is by foot, horseback, or trucks that carry goods between the coastal towns. At the missions scattered around the island, you can find food and accommodation, and the priests, *losmen* owner, or *kepala desa* can often arrange for horse rental or guides. While walking, stay comfortably in the home of the *kepala desa* in each village, or he'll find a place for you. Register with the police at each post.

Lewolaba

The island's main town—a small, lazy village where boats from Larantuka dock (leaving at 0800, Rp2000). Change money at **Bank Rakyat Indonesia.** Stay at **Peng. Rejeki** in the *pasar* (15-min. walk from the pier), run by a nice Chinese family; Rp2500 pp, Rp3500 d. Meals often include roast fish, corn and fishball soup, squid and other delicacies. They feed you royally for Rp2000 and will even make you a meal to go wrapped in banana leaf. Some *warung* are also around but Rejeki's food is unbeatable. Losmen's Rejeki's manager can arrange a guide for island walks. For Larantuka, boats leave each day (except Mon.) at 0700 and at 1400; Rp2000-2500 (4 ½ hours), stopping at Waiwerang en route.

Balauring

Reach this village by boat from Lewoleba (on Tues., Rp3000, 5 hours), by truck twice weekly (3 hours), or walk the 80 km in 3 days through fabulous country of tall grass, big green hills, swampy lowlands, and volcanos. In Balauring, stay in the unofficial *losmen* or with the *kepala desa*. Walk out of town to a back trail up through cornfields and high above the cliffs, then drop down to the villages along the shore. Eastern Lembata is very rocky and quite beautiful. From Balauring, continue on to Pantar or Alor by *prahu* or motorboat.

LAMALERA

A whaling village (pop. 3,000) on the S coast, one of only 2 in all Indonesia (the other is on Solor). Few other villages on P. Lembata are so dependent on fishing and so poor agriculturally as Lamalera. Made up of settlers from the Kais, C. Maluku, Ceram, and Flores, each clan has its own boat and boathouse. Their boats (*pledang*) are painted, named, and decorated on the bow and sides with slogans in *Bahasa Indonesia* or Latin. Built completely without nails (only wooden pegs and rattan are used), the

planks are cut with the necessary curve instead of being artificially bent. To keep the flow of life force, plank ends from the base of the tree always lie toward the bow of the boat. A feast takes place when all the largest planks of a new boat have been fitted, and pigs' blood is smeared on the tools. When a manta ray is caught, they "feed" its brain to the boat. Though the population is Catholic, animist temples are still placed around the village. Stay with the padre or ask the *kepala kampung* about accommodations.

The whaling season is from about May, when the rains end and the seas are calmer, until Nov. when the rains return. Villagers also hunt sea cows, manta rays, turtles, and porpoises, but always prefer to go after a whale. Boats are manned by 7-14 helmsmen, oarsmen, and harpooners. After spotting a whale and before they go in for the kill, the whole crew urinates, pulls down the sails, and all say a communal *Pater Noster*. From a platform extending forward from the bow, the harpooner leaps *with* his 3-m-long harpoon to give it extra thrust, sometimes landing on the back of the whale like Captain Ahab! If the whale spouts bright crimson, it's a fatal wound. Sometimes a boat is pulled all the way to Timor by a maddened, runaway whale. The villagers take about 20 whales a year, mostly sperm whales, and place their skulls at the village gate.

Getting There

Twice a week regularly scheduled boats sail for Lamalera from Lewoleba. Also, from Waiwerang, a boat departs each Wed. for Lamalera. Or take the twice-weekly truck from Lewoleba. Yet another way is to hike from Lewoleba down to Lamalera via Namaweke in 10-12 hours; ask Peng. Rejeki to assist you in finding a suitable guide. Take water; villagers along the way are friendly. You can also hitch the occasional trucks which drive along the coastal road, or ride on the back of a motorcycle which you can charter in Lewoleba.

ALOR

For centuries cut off from the cultural and historical changes taking place around it, the island of Alor (80 km by 50 km) lies approximately 60 km N of Timor. In 1908, rajas were installed by the Dutch in the principal coastal communities. Starting in the 1940s, Protestants opened missions and schools in the interior and began the systematic abolition of spirit-worship throughout the island. The population today is sharply divided between Islamic peoples—for the most part immigrants from Flores, Timor, and Kisar—living in the relatively narrow lowlands, and an extraordinary number of indigenous ethno-linguistic groups living in the extremely mountainous interior. These Christian/animist mountain dwellers speak some 70 dialects, most of them unintelligible to anyone living more than 20 km away; a number of Papuan languages linger as well. The isolated villages, which sit like fortresses on hilltops, have little contact with each other. Maize is the staple crop, grown on swiddens; secondary crops are rice (ceremonial), millet, beans, and tubers. The diet is supplemented by wild pig, hunted with bow and arrow during the dry season. In spite of the heavy Catholic presence, the people aren't fooled; the *naga*-snake cult persists, with sacrifices of meat and rice made to this protective deity. In the villages, carved wooden *naga* on posts, often surrounded by piles of stones, are endowed with magic properties. Women spend much of their time making baskets and weaving fine *ikat*-style cloth. Small islands off the coast of Alor still don't use Indonesian currency but rely on the barter system, trading fish for maize and tapioca. With a population of 120,000, **Kalabahi** is the main town. It sits at the end of a 16-km-long bay which is more like an estuary because the current reverses violently as the tide turns. Stay at **Adhi Dharma**, the town's only accommodation; 10 rooms (5 with private bath) for about Rp4500 pp.

Moko Drums

Among the most fascinating enigmas in Nusatenggara, these small cast-bronze kettle drums *(moko)* are

found nowhere else in Indonesia in such incredible numbers. The drums are usually about ½ m high and ½-⅓ m in diameter, tapered in the middle like an hourglass with 4 ear-shaped grips around their circumferences, open at one end and closed at the other. All are decorated with Hindu motifs and have a rich, dark patina. Imported originally by Indians, Makassarese and Chinese traders on their way to Timor (to trade its sandalwood), the origin of the drums was probably N. Vietnam, seat of the Dongson Culture, whose bronze-casting skills reached Indonesia around 500 years before Christ and spread as far as New Guinea. The Alorese have never had any expertise in working bronze and there is no copper (for the making of bronze) on the island.

On Alor, *moko* were used until quite recently as ceremonial objects and are still central to an elaborate pattern of exchange. A symbol of status and wealth, drums are used as currency to buy land (and once human heads). The exchange of *moko* (and gongs) still unofficially serves as a means of population control. When a man wants to marry, he is required by custom to give a *moko* to his in-laws. But since there's a limited number of the drums left, and new ones aren't made or imported, there aren't enough to go around and often the unlucky couple must leave the island to wed. Valued as high as US$3500, outsiders can't buy *moko* for any amount of money. Hun-

bamboo: *A whole civilization is seen through this towering 30-m-high weed. Bamboo has uncounted uses: toothpicks, whisks, flutes, blowguns, xylophones, mats, animal cages, boxes, furniture, ladders, sunhats, multi-purpose baskets, chopsticks, arrows, quivers, needles, dolls, kites, sandals, pens, fishing rods, water pipes, scaffolding, ships, sails, windmills; for cooking, tying, thatching, carrying and storing liquids, decoration, bridges. Bamboo has the strength of steel and the qualities of the lightest wood. The plant can be woven into light, movable screens, and plaited bamboo walls of houses last 10 years if they are coated annually with a lime wash. Poison can be made out of new leaves, shoots are good to eat, while other parts are used for medicines. With its amazing versatility, ease in working with simple tools, and striking beauty, bamboo has played a longer and more varied role in human cultural evolution than any other plant on earth.*

dreds, perhaps thousands, are said to be still buried under the earth.

Transport

Get to Kalabahi by a fairly regular 6-seater mission plane from Kupang; Rp30,000. Merpati also flies to Kalabahi from Kupang at least 3 times weekly. Or take a motorboat twice weekly from Kupang harbor; 18 hours, Rp12,000. Land-and-sea travel entails first boarding a boat from Larantuka to Lewoleba (P. Lembata), then another boat or truck to Balauring, then a *prahu* or *kapal motor* to Kalabahi. Also, 3 times monthly a Perintis ship leaves Larantuka for Kupang,

calling at Waiwerang, Lewoleba, and Kalabahi en route. For P. Pantar, take a boat from Larantuka to Lewoleba, then another one to Kabir on the N coast of Pantar. Travel in the interior of Alor is greatly affected by torrential rains during the winter months, when many of the tracks are impassable even on foot. The wet season (Nov.-March) is followed by a hot dry season which lasts through September. In the interior the mountains are so steep that even horses are useless. A number of inland villages have never been visited by white men. Luckily, most of the people have learned *Bahasa Indonesia* in the mission schools.

THE TIMOR ARCHIPELAGO

The easternmost islands of the Nusatenggara group, between the Savu Sea on the W and the Timor Sea on the E, the Timor archipelago (including the "Outer Arc" islands of Roti, Ndao, and Savu) is the largest of the Lesser Sunda island groups. Its capital, Kupang, is only a short flight from Darwin, northern Australia, or just 1½ hours from Denpasar, Bali. The population of the main island (480 m long x 80 km wide) is 1.2 million. Formerly divided between the Dutch in the W and the Portuguese in the E, when Indonesia gained its independence in 1950 the whole western portion of the island went to the Republic while the eastern remained with the Portuguese. But after a military coup toppled the dictatorship in Portugal in April 1974, the Portuguese sought to rid themselves of all their former colonial possessions. In 1975, the Portuguese-controlled eastern half was thus granted complete independence by Lisbon. Fearing that separatism would inspire revolt in other parts of Indonesia and that the new government would fall under the influence of communists, the Indonesian military brutally invaded in 1975 and then annexed that territory in July 1976.

Now the whole island of Timor, divided into Timor Barat (W. Timor) and Timor Timor (or "Tim Tim" or E. Timor), belongs to Indonesia. Prior to annexation, the eastern half was a popular stop between Australia and Singapore, but after Indonesia's occupation its borders were closed. Today, isolated fighting in E. Timor continues and it's still a very sensitive area politically. Travelers must have special permission to visit the eastern territory (which is never given); Tim Tim is effectively closed to anyone but church officials, aid workers, and diplomats. Its services and accommodations are undeveloped and expensive, and the infrequent visitor encounters numerous bureaucratic restrictions. However, a steady stream of travelers now enters Timor Barat via Kupang from

Darwin. They spend an enjoyable holiday snorkeling and sightseeing around Kupang, then island-hop westward to Bali and Java, or just fly directly to Bali for around US$45. A visa is no longer required to enter Kupang; a 60-day entry stamp is issued at the airport upon arrival. The inauguration of this important Darwin-Kupang flight has resulted in a sort of fast-developing mini tourist boom for the western half of the island.

The Land

Timor's landforms are markedly different from the rest of Indonesia. The western half is mountainous, with much of the land consisting of rugged, rocky hills, high plateaus cut by deep valleys, and loose-soiled, grassy terrain. A central mountain range marches down Timor Barat, culminating in 3,000-m high G. Tata Mai, with many other peaks exceeding 2,500 m. Aromatic sandalwood has been Timor's "tree of destiny." By the 16th C. the Hindu-Javanese traders had discovered it, and by the end of the 19th C. nearly all the sandalwood stands had been cut down, leaving behind large areas of rugged savannah grasslands. One of the most characteristic features of the island's landscape are acacia trees, with their solitary flat-topped crowns and wide branches. Lantana palms cover 25-50% of the total land area of Timor Barat. Only deep in the mountains of this highly eroded island are traces of primary forests, especially in Tim Tim. Higher up are patches of original evergreen forest. Timor's flora and fauna resemble both Asia's and Australia's.

Climate

Timor is a transition point between humid, tropical Indonesia and more temperate Australia. The island's main climatic problem is rain—too little or too much. Heavy rains fall Nov.-March, while throughout the remainder of the year the island is one of the driest in all

Indonesia. Much more rain falls in the N than in the S and west. During the dry season (May- Sept.), the Timorese make salt, fell trees, collect beeswax, build houses, relax, feast, and dance. Landscapes during the dry are similar to the Australian bush—parched and brown, leaves fall, rivers and wells dry up, drought sets in, the hot winds blow all day long. Later in the season dust and smoke from grass fires fill the air. The first rains in Nov. turn the savannah into a vast garden: dust disappears, skies clear—Timor at its best. At the beginning of the wet season the rural people move out to the *ladang* and live in shelters; villages are practically deserted except for old people and children. When the rains really set in, the island becomes impassable. The end of the rainy season is the high season in western Timor, when the maize is harvested, and all the *pasar* are alive with news and gossip. People travel, visitors pass through, there are more marriages, kids go to school, and new houses are started.

HISTORY

Little is known of Timorese history prior to 1500 except that the territory was split into dozens of independent, warring kingdoms. Starting in the 14th C., the aboriginal inhabitants, the Atoni, were displaced from their lands by invaders from S. Celebes and E. Flores. These newcomers, known in history as the Tetum (or Belu) peoples, brought rice and maize, and the federation they established in the eastern regions of Timor Barat lasted for hundreds of years. The sandalwood and beeswax of Timor attracted traders from Java and Malaya long before European contact, and there is considerable evidence of early Hindu influence. Native princedoms were also mentioned in early Chinese accounts. The first Europeans to reach Timor were the Portuguese who arrived from Melaka at the turn of the 16th century. The Dutch captured Melaka in 1641 and, after a prolonged struggle, eventually gained control of Kupang and western Timor. An expedition sent out by the Dutch in 1821 in search of the legendary *Noil Noni* ("River of Gold") failed but 8 years later, with an escort of 1,200 men, they penetrated the interior, finally opening up W. Timor to the outside world. The heated and long-standing territorial dispute between the Dutch and Portuguese over the sandalwood trade continued until 1904 when the 2 European powers finally carved up the island. The Portuguese were assigned the eastern half and the small enclave of Ocussi in the W, and the Dutch the remainder. But with few remaining resources left to exploit, Timor remained in the backwaters of colonialism. In E. Timor, the Portuguese ruled indirectly through local chiefs *(liurai)*, mercilessly crushing popular rebellions. And in the W, the

Dutch territory was administered at an economic loss until Indonesia's independence.

Decolonization
During WW II, fighting by Australian, Dutch, and Japanese troops dragged E. Timor headlong into the war, and the island was eventually occupied by the Japanese. Australian commandos resisted for over a year, crediting their success—and many of their lives—to the wholehearted support they received from the Timorese. During the war the island's few towns and many villages were destroyed or badly damaged by Allied bombing, and over 50,000 Timorese civilians were killed outright or died in famines caused by food shortages. It is cruelly ironic that after WW II, the victorious Allies favored independence for Indonesia under Sukarno and others who collaborated with the Japanese, yet remained unopposed to the recolonization of E. Timor by Portugal. After the Indonesian revolution in the 1950s, Indonesia took control of the Dutch possessions but refrained from meddling with the Portuguese half. On 25 April 1974, however, military officers overthrew the government in Portugal, and the new regime resolutely began dismantling the Portuguese colonial empire, including E. Timor.

Indonesia Invades
Historically, E. Timor has had little to do with Java; it has never been within the boundaries of colonial or post-colonial Indonesia, and the mountain people of the region have always wanted freedom. Thus when Portugal announced that it would grant E. Timor independence in April 1974, the E. Timorese zealously formed 2 main political parties. The more popular was Fretilin, whose programs of social development and literacy campaigns appealed to more than 60% of the population. The party had strong links with the common people in the Timorese hinterlands; it could be described as a moderate, reformist, nationalist front calling for gradual steps toward complete independence, agrarian reform, educational programs, controlled foreign aid and investment, and a foreign policy of non-alignment. Fretilin, an acronym which translates "Revolutionary Front for the Independence of East Timor" was an unfortunate choice of name for it signalled to the Indonesians an alleged communist identity. Several months of civil war ensued, during which political parties of the right and left made bids for power in the political vacuum created by the sudden Portuguese departure. Despite its moderate, progressive stance, Fretilin members were labeled by the Indonesians as "Marxist terrorists," bent on totalitarianism. Under pretense of restoring order, Indonesian attacks along the border escalated until, on 7 Dec. 1975, only hours after a visit by then U.S. Secretary of State Henry Kissinger, Indonesia

launched a full-scale invasion. In the weeks that followed, Fretilin forces faded into the hills to wage protracted and bloody guerilla warfare.

Aftermath

At first the ambushes, raids, and sniping by Fretilin irregulars severely tested the Indonesian armed forces; over 1,800 Indonesian troops were killed and Jakarta's hospitals filled up with 7,000 wounded in the first 4 years of fighting. In 1977, after a split in the party, Fretilin's fortunes began to decline. Well armed with U.S.-supplied attack helicoptors and other Vietnam-surplus weapons, Indonesian troops during the next 2 years conducted a ruthless "pacification" campaign. Amnesty International has documented widespread use of torture, extra-judicial executions, and systematic intimidation of E. Timorese civilians. Starvation and disease, in the wake of large-scale military operations, have been devastating: since the start of the civil war in Aug. 1975, an estimated 100,000 people—*one-sixth* of E. Timor's total population—have died. This is a clear, brutal case of genocide—the most massive since Kampuchea's Pol Pot regime—yet the international press and world community have remained inexplicably silent. Guerillas continue to fight for liberation from Indonesia, but E. Timor today remains broken, dominated, and virtually forgotten, under the yoke of yet another colonial power. In July 1976, Indonesia formally annexed E. Timor as the country's 27th province. In 1978 Australia, New Zealand, the U.S., and most Islamic countries formally recognized the Indonesian integration of E. Timor, but in Dec. 1978 the UN passed another resolution calling for the withdrawal of Indonesian troops from the territory. With E. Timor alongside a deep-sea trench vital to the U.S. as a route for its nuclear-powered submarines, it appears that U.S. strategic interests are taking primacy over the rights of the E. Timorese. Since the passage of the resolution, Indonesia has doggedly tried to enlist the support of the world community for their territorial claim. One important success of this effort was Mr. Hawke's Australian government extending recognition of Indonesian sovereignty over E. Timor in 1986.

THE ECONOMY

The Timorese make a living from farming or the sea. Life inland on the parched land is very hard; the rapid spread of a cash economy in the postwar period has not greatly affected the subsistence patterns of the majority of the indigenous population. Soil is generally poor and thin; where rainfall and soil conditions permit, wet rice agriculture and gardening are practiced, the villagers relying most of the year on such crops as corn, dry rice, sweet potatoes, cassava, and some

millet, all grown in swidden gardens, as well as the cultivation of coconuts. Different locales grow different crops: the lowland villages of the central plain center their economy on corn, while the upland people of the N grow rice. West Timorese have never accepted the plow and fields are still tilled by driving herds of water buffalo over the wet ground until it turns into a smooth sea of mud.

The population exerts great pressure on the land's resources; severe famine and drought are facts of life here. A 2 to 3-month period each year, when food supplies are depleted and the new harvest is not yet gathered, is known as the *lapar biasa,* the "ordinary period of hunger." In recent decades these periods have increased in length and severity, now having become known as *lapar luar biasa* ("extraordinary hunger period") and even *lapar betul* ("true famine"). The open rainy grasslands of the island's western half make natural grazing regions, and the local economy is heavily tied to cattle raising. Bali cattle were introduced in Timor Barat by the Dutch on a large scale in the 1930s and distributed among the rajas. Raised for the export market, cattle are now twice as numerous as humans. Rain leaching the soil in the wet, together with the herds which run in the thousands, have resulted in serious overgrazing and erosion. The whole island is now experiencing progressive and irreversible ecological deterioration.

In the mid-1970s, the economy and agriculture of E. Timor were initially totally disrupted because of guerilla warfare. But gradually the economy has improved under Indonesia's administration, with positive developments in health and education. Jill Joliffe reported in the *Christian Science Monitor* that in Aug. 1986 a Portuguese parliamentarian visited E. Timor, the first visit by a Portuguese official since the 1975 invasion. Allowed the freedom to travel where he wished, Anacoreta Correia was able to talk directly with many people who still speak Portuguese. He reported that, although he was impressed with the prosperity, the general population is unhappy with the Indonesian occupation, especially those aspects of the Indonesian administration identified with the army and security. She wrote that in some country villages you can still feel the atmosphere of fear and intimidation reminiscent of the "strategic hamlets" of the Vietnam War. The island of Atauro off the N coast functions as a detention center for over 130 soldiers and political detainees suspected of guerilla links.

THE PEOPLE AND CULTURE

The Atoni

Timor is racially divided into 2 main groups: the Atoni, the old indigenous Melanesian element, and the Belunese and Rotinese, who arrived at a later date and pushed the Atoni into the eroded mountains of the interior where they try to eke out a living in the inhospitable environment to this day. The patrilineal Atoni are short, with dark brown skin and frizzy hair like Papuans; Negrito types are commonly seen in the west. The native Atoni belong to 10 traditional princedoms *(swapradja)*, now administrative districts, and speak an extraordinary number of different Malayo-Polynesian languages. Their hamlets, containing a church and school, are usually found along ridges or slopes. Traditional Atoni dwellings *(ume)*, with mud floors and bamboo frames, are characteristically beehive-shaped with high conical thatched roofs which extend downward almost to the ground; the different parts of the house are arranged according to cosmological beliefs. Although the Indonesian government has depoliticized the native headmen (rajas), some are still quite powerful and control the allotment of village agricultural lands.

Other Groups

The Helong are remnants of a group which once inhabited all of SW Timor; by the 17th C., expanding native Atoni states had confined them to a small coastal strip in far western Timor; still later they migrated to the offshore island of Semau. The dwindling Helong today live in one village near the port of Tenau in W. Timor, and in several villages on Semau where they grow dryfield rice and maize. The people of Roti and Savu trace their lineages back to the Majapahit Empire of E. Java and practice traditional cultures quite distinct from mainland Timor. *Lontar*-palm tapping, to obtain the main ingredient in the alcoholic beverage *sopo*, is widespread. All ethnic groups in the archipelago chew *sirih* after meals and especially on ceremonial occasions. An adult chews 15 betelnut seeds a day; children start chewing at ages 7 or 8. Some natives of the deep interior still hunt with blowpipes; clubs *(gada)* with stone heads like tomahawks are used in places, and boomerangs are still employed along the SE coastal regions.

Religion

Half the Timorese are animist, 25% Protestant, 20% Catholic, and about 5% Muslim. Christianity arrived in 1624, but wholesale conversions didn't take place until 1920 when the Dutch scholar-missionary Middelkoop began proselytizing. In spite of the Timorese's professed religion, however, traditional beliefs and rituals are widely practiced. They believe that in the afterlife exist all the same occupations, worries, and necessities of this earthly life. Like the snake on Flores, reptiles play a vital role in the religion of the native Timorese, particularly in the central and eastern districts. Known as a fertility god, the most sacred reptile of all is the crocodile. The Atoni prohibit hunting crocodiles; if one is killed in self-defense, it must be accorded all the privileges of a human burial.

Reports as late as the early 19th C. claim that virgins were sacrificed on the shore to hungry crocodiles. Crocodiles are still found frequently in Timorese weaving motifs.

Music

The Timorese use music in their everyday lives, but to hear it you must seek it out—they aren't showy. There is no *gamelan*, but one of the most unusual instruments of the Indonesian archipelago is the *sasando* plucked bamboo tube zither of Roti, Timor, and surrounding islands. On display in the Kupang tourist office, the *sasando* has up to 22 strings made from a civet cat's gut, stretched over pyramidal bridges between 2 ends of a deep, boat-shaped body fashioned from dried *lontar* leaf. High in the mountains people call each other with the *hoholo*, an instrument with a deep and penetrating voice made from buffalo horn. The *farafara*, which makes a harsh, vulgar sound, is used to scare wild pigs from the crops. The *queuqueuquepere* (both a string and percussion instrument) is played by witch doctors to diagnose influences causing illness or misfortune. "Songs of Death," Timor's *Iliad*, tell of prehistoric migrations woven around the lives of ancestors. Some fetching melodies are Western in origin, but their rhythmical structure is Timorese—much wilder than Western renditions.

Crafts

Traditional weaving, plaiting, and basketry are still widely practiced inland. Atoni women decorate betelnut baskets *(oko)* with elaborate and vivid patterns. The weaving arts, such as the tapestry weaving *(kelim)* and the embroidered warp technique *(sungkit)*, are highly developed, among the most intricate in Indonesia. Both men and women wear traditional *kain, sarung,* and ornamental *selendang* (scarves), all symbols of wealth and often given as gifts. All these cotton fabrics have naturalistic, ceremonial designs: bright geometric patterns, crocodiles, lizards, geckos, elongated ghost figures, sometimes mounted riders. Patterns worn indicate the princedom a person belongs to, and a strict etiquette governs wearing them. Using natural dyes, colors range from solid black (Amfoan and Isana areas), shades of brown and black (Roti), to red, black, and white (Soba District).

Very expensive in the shops of Kupang, the women's *lau* garment can take 6 weeks of continuous work; cloths are sometimes buried to deepen the colors. In the central highlands, beautiful homemade *sarung* have narrow warp-wise stripes of orange, yellow, red, or other bright colors, and incorporate designs which can be traced back to the Dongson period of influence in Indonesia over 2,000 years ago. Intricate and finely woven cloth is still made in the Isana region. Timor has one of the largest reserves of an-

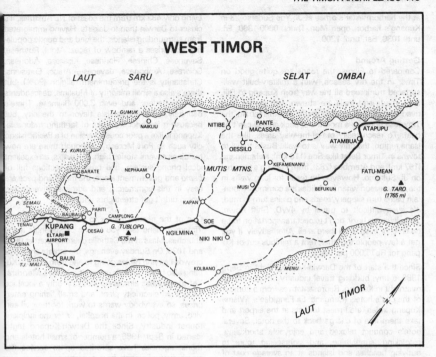

WEST TIMOR

LAUT SARU

SELAT OMBAI

TJ. GUMUK

NAIKLIU

NITIBE

PANTE MACASSAR

ATAPUPU

ATAMBUA

TJ. KURUS

OESSILO

KEFAMENANU

FATU-MEAN

BARATE

NEPHAAM

MUTIS MTNS.

MUSI

BEFUKUN

G. TARO (1765 m)

P. SEMAU

PARITI

CAMPLONG

KAPAN

TEL. KUPANG

BAUBAU

TENAU

OESAU

G. TUBLOPO (575 m)

SOE

KUPANG

ELTARI AIRPORT

NGILMINA

NIKI NIKI

ASINA

BAUN

KOLBANO

TJ. MENU

TIMOR

TJ. MALI

LAUT

N

tique ivory in the world. Originally brought by the sandalwood merchants from Flores, and before that from Sumatra, ivory is still used as part of the dowry price. A whole antique tusk costs Rp500,000 and an old bracelet around Rp50,000. Aged ivory is like a dark, polished wood, taking years to turn brown from the oil in your skin. But don't get caught taking ivory out; the police will confiscate it. There's no stone or metal work, but the gold and silver ornaments produced by the roving Ndaonese (from a small island W of Roti) are highly prized.

PRACTICALITIES

Getting There

Kupang is accessible from many points in the archipelago on Garuda, Merpati, or Bouraq flights. Garuda charges, for example, Rp106,500 from Denpasar (2 daily flights) and Rp209,300 from Jakarta, using Fokker 28s. Bouraq charges Rp36,300 from Maumere (Flores) and Rp62,300 from Waingapu (Sumba). Other Merpati fares to Kupang from: Denpasar, Rp105,600; Jakarta, Rp195,000; Larantuka, Rp52,500; Maumere, Rp41,600; Ruteng, Rp67,700; Samarinda, Rp195,000; Surabaya, Rp125,600; Ujung

Pandang, Rp86,600; Waingapu, Rp64,500; Lewoleba, 51,300; Tambaloka (Sumba), Rp86,200; Yogyakarta, Rp152,500. Flights to Dili leave from Jakarta (Rp186,600) and Kupang (Rp45,700). From Kupang's El Tari Airport it costs Rp4000 (12 km) by taxi into town (pay the driver, not the taxi desk).

Merpati aircraft also depart Darwin, Australia, for Kupang each Tues. and Fri. at 0930; A$105 OW (2 hours) or A$196 RT. This is a cheaper way to get from Darwin to Bali; you save more than A$80. At least 3 travel agencies in Darwin—San Michele, All Points Travel, and Natrabu—sell these tickets on 44-seater Fokker 27s (though roomier F28s will start flying soon). No visa required, as Kupang is now an official entry point.

Kupang's Tenau Harbor, 7 km from the *bemo* terminal (Rp500), is home base for 2 Pelni pioneer ships: the MV *Kelimutu* which follows a regular schedule to ports in other islands in E. and W. Nusatenggara and beyond, and the KM *Baruna Fajar* which sails to Savu (Rp6000) and Sumba (Rp12,000) about every 2 weeks. For schedules and fares, check with the Pelni office, Jl. Pahlawan 5, Kupang (tel. 21977). From Kupang, there are also regular boats to Roti, Savu, Sumba, the Solor and Alor groups, and Flores. Inquire at the harbormaster's office at Jl. Yos Sudarso 23 in Kupang's harbor, open Mon.-Thurs. 0800-1300, Fri. until 1030, Sat. until 1200.

Getting Around

Compared to Flores, the roads are quite good on Timor in the dry season, with a military-built well-surfaced trunk road all the way from Kupang to Dili. Back roads and trails are strewn with stones, and riverbeds are even used for traffic. For this terrain, the Timorese horse as a mount and pack animal can't be beat. To reach really out-of-the-way areas, like the Isana region, the only way is to walk. Buses travel to towns in Timor Barat like Soe (110 km), Kefamenanu (197 km), and Atambua (283), from Kupang's terminal on Jl. Sukarno. However, be ready for long waits in the rainy season when landslides are common, mountain paths turn slippery, roads and plains turn to mud; it's even difficult to travel by 4WD. Shift down. Schedules are hazy: don't expect transportation to be on time, or even to be there at all. Alternatively, if you get a few people together, rent a minibus out of Kupang for Rp75,000 per day.

Since the start of the Darwin-Kupang flight in Sept. 1986, a tiny, budding travel industry has sprung up overnight in Kupang. Representatives from a number of the city's hotels (Cendana, Eli Fangidae's, Wisma Kupang Indah, etc.) meet tourists at the airport and take them free of charge back to the hotel. Several hotels conduct relaxed and enjoyable snorkeling, picnicking, sunbathing, and sightseeing tours to outlying beaches and islands at an average cost of around Rp10,000 pp per day (see Kupang's "Transport" section for details).

While roaming around the countryside, you'll notice how friendly the Timorese are. They wave from their fields, some bow, others will give you a sharp military salute (a holdover from the Japanese occupation). Hunters on horseback with bows and arrows may gallop alongside your vehicle, or you may wake up from a nap with 100 people staring down at you. A **travel permit** *(surat jalan)* is officially required to visit W. Timor's most easterly district, Kabupaten Belu (the Atambua area) bordering E. Timor. Upon arrival in Kupang, check into the Militer Resort, Jl. Dr. Moh. Hatta, for your *surat jalan* and advice on road conditions. Travelers have made it without a permit to Atambua on the bus which leaves every other day from Kupang (Rp6000, 8 hours), but be prepared to be put right back on the bus to Kupang. In this area the police can be tight on cameras, too.

KUPANG

Kupang is the largest urban center (pop. 120,000) in Nusatenggara and capital of Indonesia's south-easternmost islands (Nusatenggara Timor or NTT).

Lying only 483 km from the coast of NE Australia, it's closer to Darwin than to Jakarta. Having immigrated from surrounding islands, the kind and gentle population comprises a rainbow of races: Atoni, Rotinese, Savunese, Chinese, Florinese, Kisarese, Adonese, Solorese, Ambonese, Javanese, Arabs, Eurasians. Christianity is the predominant religion (90%), but there's also a small minority of Muslims, descendants of Arab traders, and even 3,000 Balinese. There's definitely a Melanesian-isle flavor to the city, but because it is under the yoke of far-flung Indonesia, Kupang is like a poor cousin version of a Pacific island city such as Port Moresby. Although there are now buildings several stories high, sidewalks, an excellent local phone system, and busy intersections full of *bemo* and government jeeps, the mood and pace are easy in this commercial and administrative center, which didn't get streetlights until 1971.

One of the neatest things to do here is to have a Timorese friend take you to one of Kupang's many churches. Mass at the Catholic churches start at 0830 and 1030. On Sunday evenings, the streets are full of crowds carrying Bibles going to and from church. Kupang also has a Catholic university, **Widya Mandira.** Yet the city has almost no industry, only a local ice factory, an electricity plant, and small fishing enterprises, so everybody wants to work for the civil service, army, police, in the hospital, or for the incipient tourist industry. Since the Darwin-Kupang flight started in Sept. 1986, a number of small hotels and tourist agencies have sprouted up to service the steady flow of arrivals from Australia.

History

Early in the 17th C., the Dutch established a trading post here; in 1653 they took possession of the town and then for more than a century they struggled against the Portuguese for control of the island. The Dutch were almost repulsed from Timor in 1749 when a "Black Portuguese" raja from the northern Portuguese enclave of Ocussi threatened Kupang with a band of 200 angry men, but were thrown back and the town saved. Finally, in 1859, the boundary between the Dutch and the Portuguese was formally drawn. In 1791, the irascible Capt. Bligh ended his epic 6,500-mile journey in Kupang after the mutiny on his ship, the HMS *Bounty*. In the first half of the 19th C., Kupang was a port of call for English and American whalers. Somerset Maugham's stories of Timor are set here. After independence in 1945, Kupang experienced a boom and the government bureaucracy and population expanded exponentially. Today, Kupang is well connected by air and sea to other parts of Indonesia and serves as the principal land transport center for Timor Barat. The present, native-born governor of Timor Barat, Governor Benboy, is an astute and friendly man.

Accommodations

Overnighting in any of Kupang's 12 hostelries is no bargain—most range Rp7000-8000 s, Rp15,000-20,000 d (including tax and service). Quiet **Wisma Cendana**, Jl. Raya El Tari 15, is one of the best places for the traveler. Rooms are Rp5000 s with *mandi*, Rp10,000 s with all meals; also a/c rooms with meals for Rp15,000 s, Rp25,000 d. Although it's a bit out of town, they more than make up for it by providing a free ride in from the airport (worth Rp4000, with a small tour en route!) and a free ride out to the airport when leaving. The hotel *bemo* is available for hire at Rp4000 per hour. The man of the house is a doctor, and the very helpful and friendly staff come from Roti, Savu, Flores, and other surrounding islands. Leo, the Batak Simalungun with the purple shoes, is a fantastic guide. Call 21541 or 21127 for reservations.

Eli Fangidae's Homestay, Jl. Pahlawan 65 (tel. 22580), charges Rp5000 s with breakfast, coffee and tea all day, or Rp8500 s including meals. Located 2 km from town and right across from a beach, the proprietor Eli is an ex-soldier-minister who speaks good English and is very helpful without being overbearing. The director of PT Ausindo Tours & Travel, Eli can also arrange for vehicle charter, sightseeing tours, or almost anything. Overlooking the sea, efficiently run **Wisma Susi** at Jl. Sumatera 37 (tel. 22172) isn't bad; Rp7000 s (2 rooms only), other rooms at Rp8500 s, on up to Rp22,500 with TV, a/c, beachfront. All rooms are big and have fan and *mandi*. Lunch and dinner are both Rp2500 pp.

Losmen Astiti, Jl. Jen. Sudirman 96 (tel. 21810), is good value. Although it has no restaurant and isn't that strategically located (4 km from the bus terminal and no view), it's well run by its Balinese owner. Its 21 rooms go for Rp15,000 s, Rp20,000 d. The plain but honest **Laguna Inn**, Jl. Gn. Kelimutu 7A (tel. 21571), is 1 km from the bus terminal. Very small rooms go for Rp5000, all the way up to Rp15,500. All tax and service charges included. Their restaurant serves Indo-Javanese food. This is the "city" hotel of Kupang, only 200 m from the shops. **Wisma Kupang Indah**, Jl. Gn. Kelimutu 21A (tel. 21919/22638), asks Rp4000 with fan, Rp5000 (bigger and better rooms), Rp11,000 for very nice a/c rooms with Indonesian breakfast. You're made to feel like one of the family. Free pick-ups and drop-offs at the airport. The Kuta-style Rp5000 rooms are on a high balcony above the town, with the ocean visible—couldn't be better!

Kupang's most expensive hotel is the spacious **Flobamor**, Jl. Sudirman 21 (in city center): A$25 s, A$30 d for clean full a/c rooms with private baths and balconies, TV, video, fridge, hot and cold water. This is where all the foreign project workers, such as Australians building a cattle ranch, live. Their restaurant serves Chinese food, plus disco dancing and bar, gift shop, convenient Merpati office next door. The city's

top business hotel, make reservations by calling 21346/22688/21963.

Hotel Sasando, Jl. Perintis Kemerdekaan (tel. 22224), is a luxury 3-star international standard hotel on a parched, windy hilltop 6 km N of town. Rates: Rp22,500 s, Rp31,000 d (subject to 10% service charge). All rooms face the ocean from where you can see the sunset each evening.

Facilities include telex, tennis courts, swimming pool, terrible restaurant (on second floor), and a Pitoby Travel Service office. Must take taxi into town (Rp4000 OW) or hop on a *bemo* from Jl. Raya, 1 hot kilometer away. Free delivery to and from the airport. With a capacity rate of only 60%, this rather out-of-place hotel seems to cater to a type of tourist—high-rolling businessmen and tourists—who simply don't come here. Kupang isn't Bali!

Food

Around the bus station at night buy the potato chip of Timor, *ubi* (called *klipik*), only Rp100 per small bag. *Tuak, es stroop, daging se'i* (smoked beef), apples in season twice a year, and honey from Amfoan (Rp2000 per bottle) are also available on the street. A small eatery is next to Wisma Nusantara on Jl. Tim Tim; other *rumah makan* are found up the street. You'll also find good eating places along the waterfront. **Pantai Laut**, Jl. Ikan Tongkol 3, specializes in seafood with a Chinese slant—the best restaurant in Kupang, with dishes running Rp2500-3500. Open 0800-1500/1800-2230. The bar next door is owned by an Australian woman who married a Chinese. The **Istana Garden** on Jl. Tim Tim (the road to airport) has a bar, disco, and live music. For *nasi padang*, go to **Beringin Jaya**, Jl. Garuda 30 (tel. 22123). Another good Indonesian restaurant is **RM Lima Jaya**, Jl. Cendrawasih. **RM Rotterdam**, Jl. Harimau, has Indonesian, Chinese, and Western food including good beefsteak and chicken steak. (Beef, the animal protein of choice over chicken, is plentiful in Kupang.) Very nice garden setting. Several Chinese restaurants are on Jl. Siliwangi: the **Karang Mas** (no. 84/88) specializes in *kangrung tumis* (vegetable salad), Rp1000, and Chinese dishes. Sit on a balcony jutting out over the sea and boys swimming naked in the water, with the ports of Barate and Pariti visible across Kupang's bay. Flobamor Hotel's restaurant, on Jl. Sudirman, has a wide vareity of Indo and Western food at reasonable prices.

Entertainment

Kupang has 3 cinemas with shows at 1700 and 1900. The city's main expat nightspot is **Teddy's Bar** on the waterfront next to RM Pantai Laut on Jl. Ikan Tongkol; sometimes closes at 0200! The **Laguna Inn**, Jl. Gn. Kelimutu, is the red-light hotel of Kupang. **Kampung Tenau**, over Kupang's port 9 km from town,

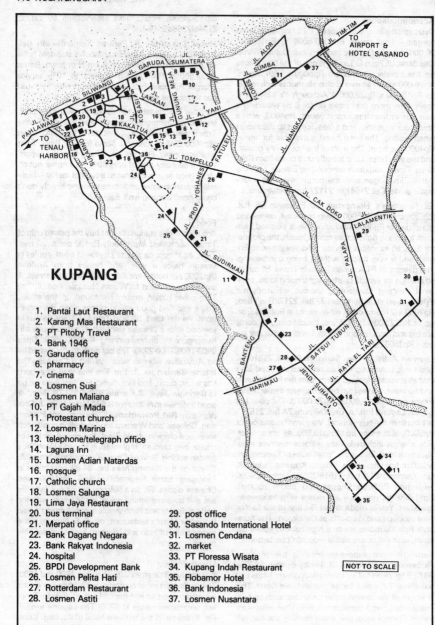

KUPANG

1. Pantai Laut Restaurant
2. Karang Mas Restaurant
3. PT Pitoby Travel
4. Bank 1946
5. Garuda office
6. pharmacy
7. cinema
8. Losmen Susi
9. Losmen Maliana
10. PT Gajah Mada
11. Protestant church
12. Losmen Marina
13. telephone/telegraph office
14. Laguna Inn
15. Losmen Adian Natardas
16. mosque
17. Catholic church
18. Losmen Salunga
19. Lima Jaya Restaurant
20. bus terminal
21. Merpati office
22. Bank Dagang Negara
23. Bank Rakyat Indonesia
24. hospital
25. BPDI Development Bank
26. Losmen Pelita Hati
27. Rotterdam Restaurant
28. Losmen Astiti
29. post office
30. Sasando International Hotel
31. Losmen Cendana
32. market
33. PT Floressa Wisata
34. Kupang Indah Restaurant
35. Flobamor Hotel
36. Bank Indonesia
37. Losmen Nusantara

NOT TO SCALE

also has hostesses. A crossroads of dozens of different cultures, Kupang has 10 different dance and music troupes; arrange performances through your hotel. **Pak Edupa** is a masterful musician on the Timorese *sasando*. Hear him in his home at Laisiana Beach (12 km from town); he sits cross-legged and holds the head of this bamboo zither in his L hand while plucking the gut strings with his R fingernails. The *sasando* has a boat-shaped body made of dried *lontar* leaves; buy one at Wisma Marina (near the stadium) for around Rp20,000. Electrically amplified ones cost Rp120,000 and up.

Shopping

Visit the large daily market, 3 km from town, where you can see all the peoples of eastern Nusatenggara in microcosm: work-hardened rustics from the mountain districts and natives from the neighboring islands of Roti, Savu, and Flores wandering through wearing resplendent woven garments. **Toko Dharma Bakti**, Jl. Sumba (near Rumah Bupati), is the largest souvenir/crafts shop in Kupang: aromatic sandalwood oil, Rp10,000 per bottle; sandalwood ashtrays and canes; decorative fans (Rp4000) and other *lontar*-leaf weavings; flamboyant Rotinese hats; *sarung* and *ikat* from all over NTT; ornamental bamboo *sirih* boxes; old statues (Rp50,000-90,000) and silver rings, etc. Also try **Toko Padang Sari**, Jl. Suharto 57 (tel. 21538), and **Toko Sinar Baru**, Jl. Siliwangi 22 (tel. 22056). **Yayasan Ie Rai** is the Sabu Ikat Weavers Cooperative located on Jl. Hati Suci (tel. 22692). Set up in 1984 by the Unitarian Service Committee of Canada and Oxfam, the goal of this non-government, non-profit organization is to preserve and encourage *ikat* weaving on the remote island of Savu, 257 km W of Timor. In their showroom are displayed *ikat* articles, from small purses (Rp3500) to blankets and bedspreads (Rp145,000).

Services

The tourist office (Diparda NTT) is at Jl. Basuki Rahmat 1 (tel. 21540) in Gubernoran Lama (the old governor's complex); see Mr. Sylvester or Mr. Lake and get their latest brochures on NTT. On display are traditional garments, *ikat* weavings, Rotinese hats, paintings, and a *sasando*. For photographic supplies, film processing and printing: **Prima Photo**, Jl. Siliwangi; **Tari Photo**, Jl. Sudirman 51; and **Sinar Baru**, Jl. Siliwangi 22. No slide film processing, but Prima and Tati can process slides outside of Kupang within 7 days. If you want to travel E to the Atambua area (Kab. Belu), get a *surat jalan* from the Militer Resort office on Jl. Dr. Moh. Hatta, a short walk from the junction of Jl. Jen. Urip Sumahardjo and Jl. Sukarno. For a number of unspecified reasons, permits to destinations such as Ocussi and Dili are not issued.

Change TCs and cash at **Bank Dagang Negara**, near the waterfront, or **Bank Rakyat Indonesia** — both on Jl. Sukarno and both open Mon.-Fri. 0700-1230, Sat. until 1130. The **post** office is opposite the latter, but have your *post restante* mail addressed to the main post office, **Kantor Pos Besar** on Jl. Palapa (2 km from town, open 0700-1400 daily). Another branch post office is on Jl. Suharto. The **telephone and telegraph** office is on Jl. Urip Sumoharjo (open 0700-1430/1700-1800 daily); the city prefix is 0391. Only the banks and Sasando Hotel have telex services. The city hospital, **RS Umum**, is on Jl. Moh. Hatta (near the BPD bank and in front of RM Surabaya). For medicines, go to **Apotik Kota**, Jl. Garuda 31 (tel. 21303), or **Apotik Sonbai**, Jl. Sudirman 93 (tel. 21073).

Transport

Arriving by air, taxis into town from El Tari Airport cost Rp4000 OW, or walk 100 m to the main road and wait for one into the city, Rp300. Kupang is too sprawling to explore on foot, so take Philippine *jeepney*-like *bemo*. Painted and bedecked with lights and elaborate facades, they cruise all the main streets at Rp150 per ride while Indonesian-language Christian pop music blares at full volume overhead. *Bemo* can be found at the main terminal on the corner of Jl. Siliwangi and Jl. Sukarno. In front of RM Beringin Jaya is a *bemo* stop for destinations outside the city (Rp200 per ride). Sedans (Rp4000 per hour) and motorbikes (Rp12,500 per day) can also be rented; inquire through your hotel. Whole *bemo* or taxis cost Rp25,000 per day to charter.

FROM KUPANG

By Road

Kupang is a major communications and transport hub for the region, with buses heading out to points in W. and E. Timor, as well as air and sea connections to destinations within Nusatenggara and other parts of Indonesia. A whole string of towns — Soe, Kefamenanu, Atambua — are connected via a road that winds its way E into the interior to Dili, former capital of Portuguese Timor and now the provincial capital of Timor Timur. This trunk road, having been upgraded by the military to move war materiel, is well surfaced and scenic. Because of the periodic fighting in Tim Tim, you're supposed to obtain a *surat jalan* from the military command (Komando Militer Resort, Jl. Dr. Moh. Hatta) in Kupang for travel to Timor Barat's most easterly district (Kab. Belu) which borders Timor Timor. Kupang's main *terminal bis/bemo* is near the waterfront, in the square where Jl. Siliwangi meets Jl. Sukarno. Buses start leaving at around 0500 for points E; buy tickets at the photo store opposite the station. Bus fares: Tenau (Kupang's harbor), Rp200 (9 km); El Tari Airport, Rp300 (12 km); Baumata, Rp300 (15 km); Tarus, Rp500 (17 km); Oesao, Rp500 (28 km); Camplong, Rp800 (47 km); Soe, Rp3000 (110 km, 3 hours); Baun, Rp500 (25 km); Oekabiti, Rp700 (40 km); Takari, Rp1200 (71 km); Buraen, Rp900 (52 km); Kefamenanu, Rp3500 (197 km); Atambua, Rp6000 (287 km, 9 hours); Niki Niki, Rp2500 (138 km).

By Sea

Check at the *syahbandar*'s office (Jl. Yos Sudarso 23) in Kupang's Tenau Harbor; open Mon.-Thurs. 0800-1300, Fri. until 1030, Sat. until 1200. **Pelni** (Jl. Pahlawan 5, near Asrama Benteng Tentara) for ships to most of the principal ports of Nusatenggara. A **Perintis** ship sails every 10 days to Ende (Rp9000) and Waingapu (Rp11,000) via Savu (Rp9000) or Roti (Rp6000); see Pelni for Perintis tickets. Pelni operates a line between Semarang and Nusatenggara, calling at several ports en route, including Kupang. Their boat, the MV *Kelimutu*, arrives in Kupang's harbor every second Sun., sailing on to Ende, Waingapu, Bima, Ujung Pandang, Lembar, Padangbai, Surabaya, Banjarmasin, and Semarang (its home port). Pelni's KM *Baruna Fajar* embarks for Savu (Rp7500) and Waingapu (Rp12,500) about every 2 weeks.

Every Mon. and Thurs., ferries leave at 1500 from Kupang to Larantuka at the eastern end of Flores (Rp8250, 14 hours). On the way to Larantuka, this ferry stops at Waiwerang on P. Adonara. About every 3 days a ferry departs for Ende; Rp13,500 pp, 18 hours. Another ferry (tel. 21140) leaves for the island of Roti every Wed. and Sat. at 0900; Rp3200. Get onboard these ferries at least 2 hours before sailing to stake your claim for space. The *pelabuhan* is 9 km and Rp300 by blue *bemo* (leaving 0600-2100) from Kupang's *terminal bis*.

By Air

Air transport is improving all the time; Merpati seems to be adding new routes every month (10 years ago there was only MAF). Now Merpati Twin Otters do 6 flights per week to Alor, 3 times weekly to Savu, daily flights to Ende and Ruteng (Flores). However, no airlines will sell you tickets to Timor Timor or Ocussi (in Timor Barat) unless you have a *surat jalan*. If you're flying W, sit on the R side of the plane to see Flores, Komodo, Sumba, and Sumbawa, flying over volcano after cloud-wreathed volcano—a beautiful sight! **Merpati** fares from Kupang to: Denpasar, Rp97,500; Jakarta, Rp179,600; Larantuka, Rp42,400; Maumere, Rp31,600; Roti, Rp20,700; Ruteng, Rp57,300; Savu, Rp36,700; Surabaya, Rp130,000; Waingapu, Rp54,200; Lewoleba, Rp41,200. **Garuda** fares to: Denpasar, Rp106,500; Dili, Rp46,900; Jakarta, Rp209,300; Surabaya, Rp142,600. **Bouraq** fares: Banjarmasin, daily at 0800, Rp186,800; Denpasar, daily at 0800, Rp95,800; Jakarta, daily at 0800, Rp177,900; Maumere, 4 times weekly, Rp36,300;

Surabaya, daily at 0800, Rp128,300; Waingapu, 3 times weekly at 0800, Rp62,300.

The **Garuda** office is at Jl. Kosasi 2 (tel. 22088); see map. Garuda has an agent (PT Gajah Mada Travel Service) at Wisma Susi, Jl. Sumatera 37. The **Merpati** office is beside Hotel Flobamor, Jl. Jen. Sudirman 21 (tel. 21346/22668/21963). **Bouraq** office is at Jl. Jen. A. Yani 21 (tel. 21392). A Garuda and Bouraq agent is near Restaurant Karang Mas on Jl. Siliwangi, just up from the *terminal bis*. Both Garuda and Quantas do the Darwin-Kupang flight for around Rp125,000 OW (2 hours); be sure to get an Australian visa in Jakarta first! A *bemo* to or from the airport (15 km) is Rp300; a taxi costs Rp4000. Also inquire at **Mission Aviation Fellowship** (MAF) for regional flights; their office is at the airport terminal. Eat reasonably and well at the airport restaurant.

Tours

Since the popular Darwin-Kupang air connection began in 1986, a number of tour services—both official and unofficial—have sprung up in Kupang. The city has 3 legitimate travel agencies, while others are connected with hotels. For example, Hassan at **Wisma Kupang Indah** puts on a tour out to Semau Island (15 km from Kupang), which has a nice sandy beach, waving palm trees, small villages, and walks in the hills. The price (Rp10,000 pp) includes all transport (an 8-m-long village dugout), barbecued whole fish and chicken plus beer and coke for lunch. Apparently, Hassan's is a better deal than Teddy's Bar which offers basically the same tour but charges Rp15,000. Of Kupang's 3 travel agencies, **PT Gajah Mada Travel Service**, Jl. Sumatera 37 (tel. 22522/22622), and **PT Floressa Wisata**, Jl. Mawar 15, tel. 22594 (off Jl. Basuki Rahmat) are just for ticketing. **PT Pitoby Travel Service**, Jl. Siliwangi 65 (tel. 21222/21333), quite near RM Karang Mas, is the only agent that has tours. Sample fares: to Komodo (5 days, US$148 1 person, US$120 2 persons), Keli Mutu (4 days, US$163 1 person, US$109 2 persons), Sumba (5 days, US$181 1 person, US$150 2 persons), 1-day local tours of Kupang (US$50 1 person, US$25 2 persons); also tours to Roti, W. Timor, and Flores' ginclear dive sites. Pitoby has a branch office at the Sasando Hotel (tel. 22224, ext. 405); see George Repie.

VICINITY OF KUPANG

All of the following fares and distances are from Kupang's *terminal bis*. At **Kelapa Lima** on the road to the airport is a demolished shore battery, a remnant of WW II fighting with the Japanese. Visit the sacred royal family grave of Taebenu in **Mantasi** (Rp150 by *bemo)*, a traditional village just outside of Kupang. At **Bakunasa** (3 km) is a sandalwood oil processing factory. **Baumata** (18 km, Rp250 by *bemo*) is a popular picnic spot with a large spring-fed swimming pool (Rp100 entrance); nearby is a big underground cave with impressive stalactites and stalagmites (Kero lambs can be hired for Rp300). **Pantai Laisiana** is a nice white-sand beach with grass huts, 12 km N of Kupang (Rp300 by *bemo*). The beach is 1 km from the main road. On weekends, 50 people stand around and watch you drink beer, so go on a weekday instead.

Oesau, 28 km E of Kupang (Rp500 by *bemo*) across the Noilbaki River, is where a battle between the Australians and Japanese took place on 20 Feb. 1942; try to arrive on market day. More hand-to-hand combat took place at **Tanah Merah** ("Red Earth") near Noilbaki. **Camplong** is a quiet little market town 45 km E of Kupang (Rp1000 by *bemo*), with a man-made lake and small forest. The Australians have established an agricultural and irrigation project here. If you have a chance, visit the Christian preschools. The Australians are also building clay water-storage reservoirs in **Basipai**, SE of Camplong. Thatched huts can be seen in the village of Takari (Rp1200, 71 km).

Ikat Weaving

The variety of *ikat* available on Timor is beyond belief; visit the shops in Kupang or tour the nearby weaving villages such as **Baun** (18 km), with a weekly market, Dutch colonial architecture, and traditional Timorese houses. At 600 m elevation, Baun affords panoramic views of the rolling landscapes all the way to the sea. From the old Dutch *pasanggrahan* is a view of the beach on which Japanese troops landed in 1942. The traditional villagers of **Kotabes** (40 km) practice the Amarasi-style of *ikat* weaving. Farther afield, another weaving village is **Desa Sonraen**, Rp3000 by *bemo*. **Oelolok** is a traditional weaving center of the Isana area.

Soe and Vicinity

This cool mountain town is 110 km E of Kupang in the Protestant half of W. Timor. *Bemo* depart Kupang for Soe all day from 0700 to 1700; Rp3000, 3 hours. Soe is a typical Dutch government settlement built along the trunk highway in the 1930s, its layout and population makeup different from any other Timorese town. Stay at **Losmen Bahagia** on Jl. Diponegoro (Rp3000 s, Rp6000 d) or at **Losmen Anda** on Jl. Kartini (Rp2500 s, Rp5000 d). Hotel Bahagia has a restaurant and several *warung* are near the hotels.

Visit the women's textile cooperative at **Molo** (24 km and Rp500 by *bemo*) where students are taught the arts of embroidery, lace-making, and the weaving of unique Timorese designs on fabrics. This cooperative enables women to maintain their family's clothing, and the surplus is sold to shops in Kupang or traded for goods. Also an orange, apple, and huge grapefruit (*jeruk bali*) growing area. North of Soe are the Mutis Mountains, W. Timor's highest—the "Rockies of W. Timor"—a region much wetter than the coasts or plains. You still see the native beehive-shaped huts in such higher-elevation places as the **Miumafo** area. In the mountain village of **Lamaknen**, dwellings have roofs which reach right down to the ground. These shaggy, elliptical thatched houses are pitch black inside, not a ray of light.

Niki Niki, near Soe, has some old royal graves. The natives of this area have remarkably strong teeth and use biting tactics when fighting, going for the neck and throat—combatants are able to tear off chunks from wood planking with their teeth. Beehive huts are found around Niki Niki; see the raja's big royal storehouse and ceremonial meeting place (*lopo*). Around **Amanuban** and **Amanatun** is very rugged terrain with gigantic rocks rising suddenly hundreds of meters above the surrounding countryside, looking like enormous antheaps or the ruins of ancient castles. Timorese mountain folk call them *fatu*, and have woven myths around them, believing that souls of the dead gather there and that the rocks are where the first marriages took place.

Kefamenanu

Some of the finest rugs in Timor are sold in Kefamenanu, a reststop town on the highway about halfway between Kupang and Atambua (197 km, Rp3500 and 4 hours by bus from Kupang). Stay at the town's best hotel, **Losmen Ariesta**, Jl. Basuki Rahmat; 13 rooms for Rp6500 s, Rp11,000 d; clean and good service. **Losmen Sederhana**, Jl. Pattimura (tel. 69), has 8 rooms for Rp3500 s, Rp5000 d; simple but still comfortable. **Losmen Soko Windu**, Jl. Kartini; Rp3500 s, Rp6500 d. Visit the traditional village of **Namasi**, 5 km from Kefamenanu.

Atambua

The main town of the Belu Plain, 7 hours and Rp6000 by bus from Kupang, location of the old border crossing between Timor Barat and Portuguese Timor. Stay at **Wisma Sahabat**, Jl. Merdeka 7; Rp5500 s, Rp7500 d. Meals are served for around Rp1200 pp, or eat at the nearby *warung*. **ABC Losmen** and **Wisma Liurai** are alternatives. The only good restaurant in town is **RM Sinar Kasih**, especially for their fish dishes. **PT Pitoby** has an express night bus leaving for Kupang at around 2000, taking about 8 hours; buy tickets at RM Roda Baru, Jl. Merdeka 73. Visit the hot mudpools near Atambua. Travelers are not permitted to go beyond Atambua E into Tim Tim without permits, which are not issued.

Atapupu

Twenty-five km N of Atambua, on a narrow bay extending far inland, this is one of Timor's busiest cattle ports. Unbelievably, this town was included on Riberiro's map as far back in 1529. From Atapupu make ship and boat connections to Kupang, Roti, Savu, Flores, Sumbawa, Lombok, Bali, and Java. To the S of Atapupu is the Belu Plain, one of the most fertile regions of Timor where the missions have poured in substantial aid to promote the cultivation of a wide variety of crops: maize, sorghum, tobacco, rice, onions, cassava, cotton, and fruit trees such as papaya, banana, coconut. From Kupang, both Pelni and Perintis have ships to Atapupu for around Rp5000 about once every 2 weeks, leaving at 1700, arriving at 0600. Or take a bus from Atambua, Rp750.

THE OUTER ARC

Three rarely visited islands SW of Timor—Roti, Ndao, and Savu—are known as the Outer Arc islands. Actually island kingdoms, the 3 are still ruled by royal lineages which trace their origins back to the E. Javanese Majapahit Dynasty. Because of their isolation and inaccessibility, these islands practice a rich traditional culture with distinctive textile arts, dances, and music. The outside world intrudes only in the form of cruise ships which visit Savu 3 times a year to watch traditional welcoming dances for one afternoon and then are gone. It's thought that these dry, hot isles, more vulnerable to erosion than Sumba and Timor, became infertile hundreds of years ago. Gradually, the inhabitants were forced to learn to use the tens of thousands of palms which colonized their soil-depleted environment. Today the people depend to an extraordinary degree on the cultivation of lontar, a palm which is "harvested" twice yearly. Providing all the necessities of life, the near total exploitation of this palm blesses the islands with a complex, successful, and diverse economy. After the trees are tapped, the menfolk of Roti, Ndao, and Savu have ample leisure to engage in such pursuits as semipermanent gardening, offshore fishing, pig-, goat- and sheep-rearing, seaweed- and honey-gathering, and trading. Rotinese men, in fact, have so much time on their hands to devote to non-agricultural, non-subsistence activities that they have a reputation as the most vigorous entrepreneurs of eastern Nusatenggara.

THE LONTAR CULTURE

On these islands grow a drought-resistant, solitary-stemmed, separately sexed species (Borassus) of the lontar palm. Attaining a height of up to 30 m and a width of nearly ¾ m, this magnificent palm is the tree-of-life for the peoples of the Outer Arc. At the beginning and end of the dry season (April-Nov.), when the palm blossoms, a sweet juice is extracted by breeching its huge leaves which droop fan-like from the palm's crown. These islanders are highly skilled palm tappers, taking only 15-20 min. to climb and tap a tree, servicing up to 15 trees per day. The tapper climbs by using a rope made of lontar leaf stalks; on his belt are the arit tool to cut the spadix and a lontar-leaf basket to collect the juice. But fatality awaits the inexperienced; you often hear of someone's death caused by "a fall from a tree."

Food Source
The lontar is one of the earth's most efficient sugar-producing plants and the islanders' guarantee against famine. After the juice is gathered by climbers, it may be drunk as is; during the tapping season the Roti-nese and Savunese sustain themselves solely from the yield of these trees. What juice is not drunk is cooked over clay earth ovens, producing a brown syrup which can be stored in vats for long periods and, if diluted with water, provides nutrition during the off-season. The syrup can be crystallized to form thick, dark sugar squares, or fermented to make alcoholic toddy. The Rotinese distill a fine sweet gin from the mash, and newborn babies are even fed lontar sugar mixed with water. The froth from the boiling juice and the sago-mash from the soaked wood is fed to the pigs, directly converting the palm into protein. Because of the year-round availability of lontar food products, the advanced food gatherers of Roti and Savu are the only islands in eastern Nusatenggara that do not experience the annual period of hunger (lapar biasa). Their population densities way outstrip those on neighboring Timor and Sumba, and in some areas are comparable to the spectacular densities of the wet-rice cultivation regions of Java and Bali. Yields are very high; a single full-grown palm can produce over 100 liters of juice per month (which can be boiled down to about 15 liters of syrup), and a whole family can support itself from several palms' yields through an entire season. Tens of thousands of palms, all oozing sugary sap from their crowns, have created huge populations of bees, and since the time of Dutch East Indies honey has been a valuable export of Roti and Savu.

Crafts And Implements
Life is surrounded by this tree's products: lontar leaves and stalks can be bent, shaped, sliced, whittled, and tied to make furniture, umbrellas, hats, knife sheaths, sandals, belts, toys, cigarette papers, clothing, sailcloth, musical instruments, bucket-like

containers, saddlebags, and an mindboggling number of other household articles including sacks, baskets, furniture, fans, mats, and rope. The fan leaves are used for thatching for house roofs and walls, and the fibrous leafstalks twined to fashion durable harnesses, bridles, and straps, or interlocked to build fences. The wood is used for building planks, while the hollow trunks are made into feeding troughs. A blanket of *lontar* leaves is spread over gardens and then burned to create excellent fertilizer. At the end of their lives the Rotinese are even buried in a *lontar* coffin, and the majority of Savunese are interred wrapped in a *lontar*-mat shroud!

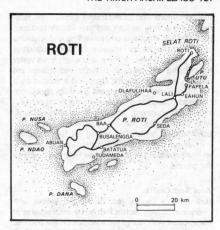

ROTI

Off the SW tip of Timor, Roti is the southernmost island of the Indonesian archipelago. Geologically and climatically similar to Timor, Roti is a dry island with flat areas of cultivation, bare rolling hills, palm and acacia savannahs, patches of secondary forests, and almost no remaining primary forests. There are 2 distinct climactic seasons: the east monsoon (April-Oct.) brings dry, gusty, hot winds, while the west monsoon (Nov.-April) brings sporadic rain. Roti's economy is also palm-centered. Because of their spectacularly successful exploitation of the island's superabundance of *lontar* palms, Roti is a surprisingly densely populated island whose overflow have migrated to Kupang (where Rotinese form one-third of the population). Wet ricefields, irrigated by laboriously built channels and diverted rivers, are cultivated in the N and E areas of the island, while the *lontar* palm is harvested most intensively in the W, which has a proportionally higher population. The Rotinese (along with the Savunese) also keep large herds of sheep and goats, and water buffalos are prized as bridewealth and as a means of plowing wet ricefields. Driven in circles through fields, turning the ground into a muddy mire, the animals are not used as a plow animal but as the plow itself. The small, arid town of Baa, on the central N coast, serves as the government and trading center for the island. For accommodations, go directly to the *kepala desa* in each village. Be sure to try the famous sweet *tuak*, also *sopi, gula air, gula lempeng,* and *laru*—all drinks concocted from *lontar* palm juice. Some Rotinese men drink an average of 10 bottles of *tuak* daily.

History

Myths of the present inhabitants of Roti claim that their ancestors migrated via Timor from "the north." Portuguese Dominicans founded a mission on the island in the late 16th C., but by 1662 most of the autonomous states of Roti had signed treaties with the VOC. The Rotinese were close allies with the Dutch; VOC archival records indicate that they ac-

cepted Christianity as early as the 18th C. and were active in the Dutch colonial service. The Rotinese, like the Ambonese, even fought some battles for the Dutch against rebellious natives on other islands. As early as 1679 an extensive system of native schools, assisted by first the Dutch Missionary Society and later by the Dutch colonial government, was established for the purpose of teaching Malay. By 1871 no less than 34 local schools had been established on the island. Thus the Rotinese very early had a distinct educational advantage in eastern Indonesia, and upon independence their transition to the use of *Bahasa Indonesia* was almost effortless. Working as merchants, rice growers, *lontar* tappers, and civil servants, large numbers of Rotinese have migrated to NE Timor, Kupang and the island of Semau, Sumba, and Flores. They participate in all levels of the Indonesian economy and national life.

The People

Roti is divided into 18 autonomous domains, each under its own "lord" *(manek),* and each adhering to its own dress, *adat,* and dialect. Malay in appearance, the Rotinese are characterized by their broad, sombrero-like *lontar*-leaf hats. These short, light-skinned, lightly built people have had longer contact with western Indonesia and are, in general, agriculturally, educationally, and politically more sophisticated than the Timorese. Christian Rotinese claim to be the oldest Protestants of the whole Timor area; the island's ruling families were the first to convert to Christianity in 1729. But their Dutch Reformed Protestantism is interwoven with strong customary beliefs centering on ancestral spirts. Major ceremonies are held at marriage and death; minor rituals are held at the seventh month of pregnancy, at first hair-cutting, baptism, naming, and at specific times during the agricultural and palm-tapping cycles. The Rotinese have a long written and oral literary tradition, placing great emphasis on storytelling and speaking well. Most villages are located in and about stands of *lontar* palms, wherever there is enough fresh water for drinking and gardening. Wells and springs are usually owned by specific clans and managed by a "lord of the earth" *(dae langak)*. Swidden agriculture has nearly disappeared; nowadays the Rotinese cultivate semipermanent, fertilized household gardens, with some limited wet-rice cultivation. Their traditional houses, which resemble great furry hunched animals, are rectangular with gabled ends covered by an immense stack of *lontar* leaves reaching nearly to the ground.

Arts And Crafts

Roti cloth is usually red, black, and yellow with designs of flower rosettes formed by small squares of color, often with elongated triangles on the borders, all of which give their cloths a mosaic-like effect. Textiles play an integral role in burial ceremonies, and certain heirloom weavings are used to pass on oral legends and stories through the generations. Each of Roti's 18 kingdoms once had its own textile motifs so it was immediately apparent to which kingdom the wearer belonged; nowadays, with districts borrowing motifs from each other, these distinctions have become blurred. Today, men dress up in a store-bought white shirt and plaid cotton *sarung,* but with a homespun *selimut* draped over one shoulder. The Rotinese musical instrument, the *sasando,* is like a bamboo zither with 22 civet cat gut or copper strings and a hemispheric resonator made from a full, boat-shaped leaf of the *lontar* palm. Decorated antique axes with cast handles and blades are products of the Bronze Age, though the date of their origin on Roti is unknown. The Rotinese make at least 8 styles of hats fashioned from *lontar* leaves. Patterned after 16th and 17th C. Portuguese helmets, the bright-colored hats feature a jaunty cock feather or single woven "horn" curling up in front. Each hat has its own use in everyday life: to store tobacco in, work in, dance in, and so forth (some specimens in Kupang's tourist office). Also check out *lontar*-leaf baskets, plaited protective spirit figures *(maik* or *ola),* and heavy burlap-like clothing made from *lontar* leaf and still worn by laborers.

Getting There

Roti is separated from Timor by the 10-km-wide Roti Strait which, because of monsoonal turbulence July-Aug., has been called "the Grave of the Rotinese." Ferries (call 21140) leave Kupang's Tenau Harbor every Wed. and Sat. at 0900 (Rp5000) for Terminal Oelaba near Baa on Roti. Other ferries dock at Papela on Roti's N coast (Rp3000). Get onboard 2 hours early to stake a place; the harbor is 9 km and Rp300 by blue

bemo from Kupang's *terminal bis.* Selat Roti is also navigable by *prahu layar* from Kupang in 2-3 hours. Also, every 10 days a Perintis ship stops at Terminal Oelaba en route to Kupang from Ende and Waingapu. Merpati flies to Baa 3 times weekly from Kupang, Rp25,600.

Ndao

A lonely, rocky, eroded island (pop. about 3,000) 12 km off Roti's NW coast. Since the signing of a treaty with the Dutch in 1756, Ndao has been considered an autonomous domain of Roti and traditionally Roti has absorbed the excess population of Ndao. Like the Rotinese and Savunese, the Ndaonese are *lontar*-tappers; they speak a dialect of Savunese, drink palm juice *tuak,* and wear distinctive *ikat*-dyed cloths and Rotinese-style *lontar* hats. Nearly all the men of the island supplement their *lontar*-based incomes by fashioning traditional silver and gold articles and selling their native woven *ikat* cloths and pandanus mats. Having had long contacts with Javanese artisans, their jewelry is however less elaborate and adorned than Yogyanese or Kendari work. At the beginning of each dry season, these smiths wander throughout the Timor area making anklets, bracelets, and other finished jewelry; they also take advances on orders for work to be delivered the following dry season. In most cases the customer supplies the precious metal in the form of old coins or jewelry to be reworked, and the jewelers are paid in foodstuffs or small livestock. Most of the itinerant craftsmen return to Ndao by Nov., in time to tap their palms during the peak harvest season. Because of the intensive cultivation of Ndao's overabundance of *lontar* palms, this tiny speck of an island (9 sq km) has a population density of around 235 per sq km, which is even higher than Roti and Savu. Between Roti and Ndao is yet another smaller island, P. Nuse, which has a small Ndaonese settlement. Take a local *prahu* from Baa on Roti.

SAVU

An isolated island group 100 km NW of Roti and 257 km W of Timor, about midway between Sumba and Timor. The largest island of the group, which has a population of about 60,000, is P. Savu (697 sq km, 16 x 24 km) on which sits the main town, Seba: one street, a few *toko,* daily market, 3-4 motor vehicles, and no electricity. No official accommodations are on the island. In Seba, there are 3 homestays: the home of Ongko Kido Dena, a Chinese married to a Savunese, is only 15 m from the harbor; Madu Buky, 5 m from Kido Dena; Octo Djonaga, a member of the regional DPR and director of the high school (SMA), 1½ km from harbor. Travelers must rely on village heads *(temugu)* to make sleeping arrangements.

This bare, stony island, uplifted on an ancient bed of

lontar palm: This species (Borassus flabellifer L.) of fan-palm can endure long dry periods and grows very slowly. Once it starts producing juice, it remains productive for 70-100 years, yielding an average of 600 liters of juice yearly. Besides providing palm juice, sweet syrup, and myriad other products, the eastern islands have a rich literature mostly in the form of old legends inscribed on lontar leaf. Small masterpieces of the engraver's art, these documents record old Indonesian myths and histories. They have been made out of this palm leaf for centuries, the text and illustrations engraved with a fine stylus, then darkened by rubbing the soot of burned palm-leaf spines into the grooves. The individual palm leaves are next cut into strips and sandwiched between slats of ornamented wood. These 2.5-cm-wide "books" fit neatly into narrow wooden boxes carved and decorated with animal heads or made completely in the shape of animals. Each box or "volume" holds several books. This whole procedure is still used by lontar copyists today (such as in the E. Balinese village of Tenganan). It's thought that the curli-cue appearance of many ancient Asian scripts came into being because scribes were forced to inscribe curved lines on the ribbed surface of lontar palm strips so as not to split them.

a Roti hat made from lontar *palm* leaf

coral limestone, has to endure up to 10 months of parching heat and scorching wind each dry season (April-Oct.), while the west monsoon (Nov.-March) is a period of scant, spotty rain. The island's N and E portions are wetter than the SW, and water is scarce all over Savu. No forests remain, and the island's highest elevation is 240 m (in the S). Despite this seemingly inhospitable environment, the Savunese are among the most cultured people of the Outer Arc islands and their *ikat* weavings are among Indonesia's finest. Villages *(rae)* are often surrounded by stone walls, and each village is composed of members of one clan *(udu)*. The island kingdom is ruled by a full-figured queen *(mone weto)* whom you can see attending important ceremonies.

Take the main track inland from Seba, crossing rice paddies and palm plantations, to **Namata** on a hill where you'll find a circle of huge lens-shaped boulders. Known to the local people as the "Oracle Stones," each weighs 6 tons and are thought to be over 3,000 years old. On the summit of the hill is a small stone depicting on one side an early 4-masted schooner under full sail and on the other side an inscription in English: "Stranded 1418." Tradition has it that a ship ran aground here, the crew staying on to mix with the local women.

History

Savu has strong historical ties with Hindu Java and the people believe they are descended from a nobleman of the 15th C. Majapahit Empire. The Portuguese were the first Europeans to land on Savu, establishing several missions in the 16th century. The Dutch signed a treaty with the island's rulers in 1756, and united the separate kingdoms under a single raja *(douae)* in 1918. Savu is today divided into 5 native states (the tiny, offshore island of Raijua forms a sixth), all recognized as administrative units by the Republic, each with its own complex priesthood, ritual events based on the lunar calendar, and established agricultural and *lontar* palm boundaries. Sizable Savunese colonies are also found on Sumba, Timor, and Flores.

The Land And Economy

In contrast to the neighboring islands of Sumba and Timor, the basis of the Savunese economy is the cultivation and harvesting of the island's tens of thousands of *lontar* palms. Individual palm enclosures are fenced in, owned, worked, and harvested by households; the best-kept, family-worked *lontar* enclosures are found in **Liae** on the S coast and **Mesara** in the west. Some irrigated *sawah* are found in coastal areas, the fields worked to mud by water buffalos, and some pepper is grown. A seagrub (*nyale*), which appears in huge quantities off the S coast at about the same time each year, is harvested and then pickled in *lontar* vinegar. *Nyale* are considered a great delicacy. The Savunese also live by fishing, selling copra, and raising water buffalo, sheep, and fine, spirited, sturdy horses, one of the islanders' most prized exports.

Events

In spite of missionary efforts, Savu remains an animist stronghold where important collective rituals are still regularly staged. In the 18th and 19th centuries, fierce warfare between the native island domains was endemic, and feuding continues to this day. This warlike tradition can best be seen in Savunese dances. Like the nearby Sumbanese, the Savunese raise a small, stout breed of horse which plays a central role in their ceremonies; the *Perhere Jara* dance depicts the story of how horses saved the island from grasshopper plagues each rainy season. In the *Pedoa* harvest dance, staged under the full moon between March and May, baskets of unhusked rice or dried peas are tied to the dancers' ankles; when shaken, they provide the dance's rhythmic accompaniment. In a blessing ritual *(dabba)*, a sort of Savunese *bar mitzvah*, parents anoint a child's head with flowers and betelnut in the hopes of a good life. Savunese mortuary ceremonies are unbelievably complex. Cockfights between rival villages are popular as well as being ritually important such as when employed to cast omens. The Savunese are also proud of their musical traditions.

Crafts

The Savunese weave exquisite *ikat* out of native cotton, typically with narrow design strips in somber blue, black, and white, with touches of beige, rust, brown, and red. Weaving designs, their significance long since forgotten, are unaltered from the time when the clans came into existence over 20 generations ago. Delicate floral and geometric motifs still serve as a system of clan identification. Some motifs have obviously been inspired by Portuguese and Dutch patterns: crocheted roses, grape vines, Western-style birds, lions from old Dutch coins, cherubs. Women weave during the day, and animals are penned at night, in the man-tall space underneath the raised, palm-thatched house. Other traditional technology practiced is the plaiting of basketry, ropes, and harnesses.

Transport

A Pelni ship, the KM *Baruna Fajar,* sails from Kupang to Waingapu (Sumba) via Savu every 2 weeks; the fare from Kupang to Savu is Rp9200 and from Waingapu to Savu around Rp12,000. Or take a motorized *prahu* at least 3 times weekly from Kupang to Savu (Rp5000, 1 night). Or fly with Merpati 3 times weekly from Kupang; Rp45,800. Big cruise ships visit Savu 3 times a year. Motorized *prahu* depart Seba for Kupang at least every 3 days; Rp5000, 24-36 hours. Take one of the island's 4 *bemo* from Seba to Savu Timor (the eastern district) for Rp750. No buses, but a few trucks run on the island. It takes just 2 days to walk completely around Savu on the coastal path.

SUMBA

Outlying, dry, mostly barren Sumba is one of the most fascinating islands of Nusatenggara. A principal island of the E. Nusatenggara group, situated S of Flores and midway between Sumbawa and Timor, Sumba is known as the source of some of the most handsome *ikat* fabrics in Indonesia, the breeding ground for the country's strongest horses, for its ritual tribal life, flawlessly built high-peaked thatch-roofed villages, and mammoth sculptured stone tombs. Here you find an authentic ancient culture with none of the layers of Hinduism, Islam, or Christianity found elsewhere in Indonesia. About 300 km long by 80 km wide, oval-shaped Sumba's 11,180-sq-km area and its total population of 382,000 is divided into E and W regencies, with significant topographic, climatic, cultural, linguistic, and historical differences between the 2 halves. The island's chief air- and seaport is **Waingapu** on the N coast, which is also the capital of the

eastern *kabupaten;* **Waikabubak** is the principal town for the western half. Being so much out of the mainstream, neither the food nor the accommodations are up to the standards found on other islands of Indonesia. But prices are cheap: an egg costs Rp100, a chicken Rp1000. Very good *tuak* is available.

The Land And Economy

Lying outside the volcanic belt that runs through the length of the archipelago, much of interior Sumba consists of extensive plateaus with scattered, irregular hills, especially in the western part of the island. The climate is hot and dry, particularly in the E where widespread eucalpytus savannahs and large tracts of flat grasslands and steppe-like landscapes provide good grazing for cattle and support small-scale agriculture. The rainy season is Nov.-March. West Sumba receives a higher rainfall of 1,826 mm, while E. Sumba has a low annual rainfall of 846 mm. East Sumba's soil is generally thin and nonvolcanic; small unnavigable rivers which supply the only irrigation tend to be dry up to 8 months of the year. At the approach of the rainy season the rivers are thick with spawning sea fish.

The 250,000 people of more verdant W. Sumba (Sumba Barat) are mainly farmers, while the 132,000 or so E. Sumbanese (Sumba Timor) raise horses, cattle, buffalo, and other livestock. Sumba practices mostly subsistence agriculture: rice, tobacco, and maize are the main crops; coffee and coconuts (copra) are secondary. An archaic method of plowing is still used here (as elsewhere in Nusatengarra) in which 20-30 buffalo are driven across flooded fields, trampling them to a muddy consistency. Sumba's famous breed of sturdy "sandalwood" horses, symbols of wealth and status on the island, are some of Indonesia's finest, exported to Java and other islands for drawing carts. The island's forests yield cinnamon and sandalwood. Greed over the centuries has forced the government to forbid cutting down those few stands of sandalwood that remain; now you need a special license to export the fragrant wood from Indonesia.

History

Documented history begins with a reference to Sumba in 14th C. East Javanese chronicles as a dependency of the Majapahit Empire. During the 17th C. Sumba fell under the dominance of the Bima rajadom of E. Sumbawa, and later the entire island was subordinated to the powerful Goanese kingdom of S. Celebes. Right up until the 19th C., Bugis *prahu* regularly raided Sumba for slaves, transporting 20-30 boatloads each year for sale in S. Celebes, Lombok, and Bali. In 1756, a contract was signed between the Dutch VOC and a coalition of Sumbanese rajas. Although Dutch civil officers were later assigned to Sumba as "political observers," it wasn't until around 1900 that the Netherlands began to actively intervene in Sumbanese internal affairs. As elsewhere in Indonesia, the Dutch governed the Sumbanese under a policy of indirect rule. Native rulers were appointed to administer the 2 regencies, E. and W. Sumba, an administrative division maintained by the Republic of Indonesia to this day. In WW II, Waingapu was bombed by the Japanese and 3,000 Sumbanese were killed. At the end of the war when independence was declared by Sukarno on 17 Aug. 1945, it took 6 months for the news to reach Waingapu.

The People

A harsh climate and difficult natural surroundings have forged a hard people predominantly proto-Malay in appearance, but with some Melanesian features. The men are farmers with weather-beaten faces who ride horses bareback, drape color-rich handwoven fabrics around their shoulders, and carry long knives with buffalo-horn hilts stuck in their waistbands. The eastern part of the island constitutes a relatively homogeneous ethno-linguistic entity, while the western half is more mixed. Minorities include immigrants from Savu, Timor, and Flores, plus Chinese merchants in the coastal towns. Formerly, there were 3 castes in native Sumbanese society: *maramba* were nobility, the *kabisu* were free commoners, while *ata* were ex-slaves and their descendants (slave trade was abolished here in 1901). Although upon independence the new Indonesian Republic refused to recognize the authority of the native princedoms, some elements of this caste system are still in evidence; members of the nobility continue to hold the highest positions in the native civil service and exert strong influence. The Sumbanese variety of *Bahasa Indonesia* is spoken with an almost Italian-sounding accent; in addition, over a dozen native dialects are in use; Sumba Barat alone has 2 languages divided into 8 dialects.

Religion

Because it was sparsely populated and poor in resources, Sumba escaped the proselytizing zeal of Muslims and Christians who concentrated their efforts in higher-yield places. Though the majority of Sumbanese today are nominally Protestant, with colonies of Catholics and Muslims, the Sumbanese largely practice animism—one of the last strongholds of pre-Hindu and pre-Islamic religions. The greatest concentration of those who worship ancestral and land spirits is found in Sumba Barat, where some ⅔ of the population hold on to the traditional religion *(marapu)*. Unofficial, traditional ceremonies, complex burial rites, and gift-exchange rituals are widespread. Forgiveness will be asked of ancestral spirits if a harvest has failed or if someone has fallen from a tree or been thrown by a horse. Even megalithic cultures are still extant in the outlying areas, particularly in Sumba Barat where you find large numbers of huge stone tombs and dolmens along roads, amid lush hilltop vegetation, around villages, and even in the front yards of houses! Anthropologists study these isolated Sumbanese societies to learn about similar cultures now dead or dying.

Village Life

The bulk of the population lives on the interior plateaus in fortified hilltop villages *(paraing)* where large clan houses face a central square containing the stone slab tombs of semi-divine ancestors. Traditional Sumbanese houses (such as in **Mani** village on the N coast and at **Rende** on the SE coast), which resemble gigantic straw hats, consist of a big platform raised on piles with low walls, the thatched roofs sloping gently upward from all 4 sides, then rising sharply toward the center to characteristically high gables. Just as in Tanatoraja (S. Sulawesi), some are also adorned with sacrificed buffalo horns and pigs' jawbones. Inside, massive center posts hold up the roof and high in the rafters are stored precious ceremonial textiles and sacred objects of the deified ancestors who founded the clan. Sumbanese women as well as men chew betelnut, and the people are quite fond of coconut toddy and gin. Puberty for boys is marked by a token circumcision, while girls who come of age are tattooed and their teeth filed, and cross-cousin marriages were once strictly adhered to. Though these traditional customs are now dying out, you still see older married women with blue horses and monkeys tattooed on their arms.

Events

Family heads make great efforts to accumulate wealth (buffalos, horses, textiles, and jewelry) which are sacrificed or displayed at religious and funeral rites which they sponsor. In the *pasola* traditional battle of W. Sumba, hundreds of horsemen fling spears at each other. Dances, along with bloody sacrifices and traditional boxing matches *(pajura),* are frequently staged during harvest festivals July to October. Prior to a boxing match, the fists of the combatants are wrapped in wild grass leaf, the barbed edges of which can produce vicious wounds. Swipes across the eyes are highly prized—blood flowing from such wounds blinds the opponent, usually bringing about his defeat. While carrying shields and swords and letting out blood-tingling war cries, performers in tribal war dances perform energetic and rhythmic leaps. These expressive dances are not that far from reality as clans still fight over land rights. The dancing of the girls of E. Sumba, derived from weaving and spinning thread, feature many hand and shoulder movements but limited movements of the feet. Other women watching the lively dances let out a sort of excited, shrill warble called the *karakul.* These "vibrated shriek" songs of the women of Sumba were once used ritually to welcome their husbands back from headhunting expeditions. The dances of western Sumba are, in contrast, slow and sedate. Visit the Kepala Seksi Kebudayaan in Waikabubak (W. Sumba) for information on current cultural events; these genial officials can also help with hiring guides.

Death And Funerals

If you have a chance to attend a funeral for a deceased member of the nobility, don't miss it. As well as occasions for gaining immense social prestige, royal funerals are a major focus of Sumbanese culture and thus prime opportunities to witness the lavish display and destruction of family wealth. Funerals take place at the time of the second burial, which is more or less the re-interment of a dug-up mummified corpse. Multitudes of buffalos, pigs, dogs, and horses (and formerly slaves and captives) are slaughtered, and a massive memorial stone tomb is sometimes erected. Dutch officials at the turn of the century reported attending funerals where dazzling textile wealth and

valuables, after propitiary sacrifices, were interred with the dead chief. Although not as widespread, this practice continues with textiles, gold, porcelain, and antiques interred to feed, transport, and make life in the afterworld comfortable for the deceased. Your heart aches as magnificent *ikat* specimens are lowered into mother earth, tens of thousands of dollars worth left to moulder and decay! And the tombs are not built in a remote graveyard outside the village where thieves can work quietly, but right in the front of the house with all the extended family coming and going. The people *live* with their dead. First a hole is dug in the ground and cement poured into it with a room formed to place the bones and the valuables. Then on each corner are rolled big, heavy stones, then another giant slab with perhaps images of a man and a woman placed on top. The gigantic stone slabs and troughs—some weighing up to 30 tons—may require the labor of 40 men 2 years to cut, and 1,000 men to drag by means of ropes and rollers from quarry to hilltop village. Great prestige attaches to the enormity of the stone and the distance covered.

IKAT SUMBA

Ikat is a very ancient tie-dye method of decorating rugs, shawls, and blankets. Each completed fabric represents a colossal amount of human labor and only isolated, feudal, agricultural societies like Sumba's still produce these handwoven textiles. Although *ikat* fabrics are also woven on nearby islands such as Flores and Roti, the craft here has reached an unusually high level. Woven from locally grown cotton, the cloths figure prominently in the ceremonial and social life of the island. Each region has its own distinctive designs and shades. Some heirloom pieces are considered so priceless and magically powerful that they cannot be viewed in safety but must be kept in sealed baskets high up among the roofbeams. The really fine blankets, family *pusaka,* you cannot buy. Families already have 1,000 buffalos, so why should they sell a blanket? It's easy to find more cattle, but difficult to find more blankets.

Types Of *Ikat*

Worn only by men, large, rectangular cloths, called *hinggi*—with horizontal rows of involved human and animal motifs—are usually made and sold in pairs. One is used as a shoulder cloth and the other to wrap around the hips; they also do duty as attractive wall decorations or door curtains. In addition, there are 4 classes of single-piece blankets *(selimut sumba)* which are traditionally used only in festivities or as burial shrouds. East Sumbanese *sarung,* called *lau,* have light figures standing out on dark backgrounds; W. Sumbanese *ikat* are more abstract, with blue the dominant color.

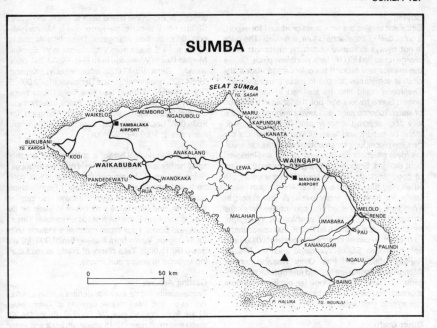

SUMBA

The Process

Under nearly every E. Sumba stilted house is a primitive loom. While sway-backed pigs grunt nearby and babies crawl across their laps to nurse, women weave these elaborate and beautiful works of art that can sell for upwards of US$2000 in Chicago or Sydney. Either the warp or the weft threads (rarely both) are tied up and and then dipped into a natural dye. The parts of the thread that have been tied remain untreated, while the untied areas take up the dye. When the next color is applied, the already dyed parts are bound up and the parts left blank receive the required coloring. This process is repeated as often as required by the design and the number of colors; some pieces can take up to 2 years to complete. Sumba fabrics are often woven together unevenly and inexactly, which gives the cloths a strange, shimmering, 3-dimensional effect.

Colors

The age-old colors for *hinggi* are blue and white, or red and white and black. Dyes are usually made of natural ingredients, but artificial dyes are creeping into use. In E. Sumba the rust-colored bark of the *kombu* tree is used; in W. Sumba the color from the blue indigo plant *(wora)* is preferred. Red is obtained by crushing and soaking the root and bark of certain trees. The weaver must sometimes wait for one particular week in the year when a certain berry comes out to make a particular natural dye. Many different shades can be derived from just 2 colors, depending upon how often the fabric is dipped into the dye bath. For example, dark brown is the result of consecutive immersions in red and blue dyes. Often, to achieve the correct intensity of color, several immersions are needed. After the fibers have been painstakingly dyed, they are woven on a loom consisting simply of 4 bamboo sticks stuck in the ground, with a band behind the woman's hips to maintain tension.

Motifs

Designs differ greatly, but all reflect the life, culture, and history of the island. The most frequent motifs are of tiny men (on foot or armed on horseback), horses, Dutch lions, stags, chickens, dogs, monkeys, birds, snakes, crocodiles, turtles, lizards, Chinese dragons, crayfish, crabs, even octopus. The blurred outline of the "Tree-of-Life" is a recurrent pattern. The common "skull-tree" motif dates from headhunting days when captured heads were hung in celebration on the bare, blood-soaked limbs of a tree in the village center. *Mana* or life-essence was imbued in the heads, thus the skull-tree ensured fertility and was the main religious object of the village.

Buying

Since *ikat* textiles are now mass-produced for export, a great deal of substandard junk is around. The price is not always indicative of quality; merchants could charge up to Rp150,000 for a worthless piece. Sellers use many, many tricks: if the colors are too faded, the cloth is sometimes painted to make it more vibrant. The fabric could also be starched to make it feel newer. Some traders also boil the fabric in a solution of water, tobacco juice, and *kayu kuning* to give it the look of great age. *Caveat emptor.* Don't buy immediately; be patient and learn all you can first. On the genuine pieces look for smooth, sharp lines, clean colors (dyes must not run into each other), and intricate, tight designs. Smoothly curving lines is another sign of good work, as well as how clean the colors are when they run into other colors. And bargain relentlessly, for each and every piece. At the airport in Waingapu you're greeted with confetti-like *ikat* cloths strung out along lines like washing. In Waingapu, merchants want as much as Rp250,000 apiece (natural dyes); they can be bought cheaper (Rp100,000 and up) in villages SE of Waingapu such as Melolo, Rende, Kaliuda, and Pau. Other weaving centers (Mangili and Prailiu) are located just outside of Waingapu. You won't have to look far; armies of vendors approach you on foot or on bicycles with *hinggi* wrapped around their arms, shoulders, and handlebars.

Other Crafts

Sumba boxes, made from *lontar* palm, come in all sizes; used for betelnut, storage, etc. Much of Indonesia's precious Chinese porcelain originates in Sumba, dug up from old graves. Since the most valuable possessions of the deceased (gold, ivory, china, fabrics, and coins) were buried with the corpse, there are vast hoards of porcelain still under the earth. They could search you at the airport but some people manage (illegally) to get away with a few plates stuck down their pants or skirts.

TRANSPORT

Getting There

Most travelers visit Sumba in transit to and from other islands. Lying so far off the main track, it could be a difficult or expensive island both to reach and leave. Sumba has 2 airports; the larger one is Mauhau Airport, 6 km outside Waingapu. Tambolaka Airport is 42 km and 1 ½ hours from Waikabubak in W. Sumba. Merpati flies to Waingapu from Ende (Rp33,000, once weekly); Bima (Rp42,000, once weekly), Kupang (Rp54,000, once weekly); and Denpasar (Rp80,000, 5 flights weekly). Merpati also flies Twin Otters twice weekly from Bali to Tambolaka. Twice weekly there are flights between Tambolaka and Waingapu for Rp34,000. Bouraq flies from Surabaya to Waingapu every day at 1000 (Rp102,400).

The island's principal harbor is at Waingapu; another small harbor is at Waikelo, 50 km NW of Waikabubak. Ships and small, freight-carrying boats call at both ports and take deck passengers. Larger Perintis ships on their passage to and from Surabaya also stop at the ports; one calls twice a month at Waikelo on its way to and from Ende (with stops en route at Timor, Roti, and Savu). Four times monthly a Perintis ship for Waingapu leaves from Kupang (Rp20,000 pp) via Sawu (Rp15,000). Take plenty of books to read during layovers in sleepy port towns.

Getting Around

Twice-weekly flights connect Sumba's main towns, Waingapu and Waikabubak (arriving at Tambolaka, 42 km from Waikabubak, W. Sumba). Buses (24-30 seats) and minibuses (12-15 seats) run back and forth down the 137-km paved road connecting Waingapu and Waikabubak; Rp4000 OW, 5 hours. Buses fill up quickly. Passenger trucks can take you to the remotest corners of the island, but some of Sumba's limited outlying road network is in bad shape. Buses (Rp75,000 per day) and minibuses (Rp50,000 per day) can be chartered. *Bemo* operate regularly in and around most traditional villages, weaving centers, megalithic sites, and other tourist attractions. Otherwise, hitch a lift on a jeep, walk, or ride a horse. In the E, herds of wild horses are exploited as mounts (and for export); you see horses everywhere, on their own, with a rider, in small groups, and on the *ikat*. These "sandalwood" horses can be hired out; riding experience is essential as they can be quite temperamental, plus the hilly, rocky terrain (especially in the W) can be trying.

EAST SUMBA

East Sumba is characterized by flat, barren plateaus and canyons, and dramatic, world-class *ikat* weavings. A common language and elements of shared culture are found throughout this region of Sumba, which has received the lion's share of attention from anthropologists. East Sumba's most traditional villages are located near Melolo (60 km SE of Waingapu), and along the SE coastline from Melolo to Baing. All are accessible by *bemo* from Melolo, but be sure to get an early start each day.

WAINGAPU

The district capital (pop. 23,000) of E. Sumba, the island's main town and seaport, and from 1906-49 a Dutch administrative and trading center. Immediately upon arrival at the harbor or at Waingapu's Mauhau Airport, *ikat* traders descend upon you, pushing their wares. Waingapu sells the widest range of Sumba fabrics, but you can do better price-wise by heading for the textile-producing villages such as Prailiu, just 4 km from Waingapu, and others SE of the capital. Change U.S. and Australian cash and TCs at **Bank Rakyat Indonesia**. *Bemo* run up and down the main streets of town, and in the hotel area you can walk to most anywhere. The market is in the harbor area. Waingapu makes a good base from which to explore traditional villages to the southeast (Rende, Kaliuda, Umabara, etc.). **Kuta Beach** is 12 km from Waingapu; charter a *bemo* for Rp4000.

Accommodations And Food
Quiet, Chinese-run **Elim Hotel**, Jl. A. Yani 35 (tel. 32/162), has 18 rooms from Rp4000 to Rp10,000; meals served. **Losmen Lima Saudara**, Jl. Wanggametti 2 (tel. 83); Rp4000-8500 pp. Some rooms have a *mandi* and food is served. **Surabaya Hotel**, Jl. Eltari 2 (tel. 125), near the *mesjid*, is a little steeper at Rp6000 s, Rp12,000 d. Number one is **Hotel Sandalwood**, Jl. Matawai (tel. 117), the town's best and cleanest; Rp8000 for real basic rooms, Rp12,000-17,500 with *mandi*, and Rp20,000-25,000 d for a/c rooms. Most of the hotels have restaurants, plus there are 3 other restaurants in town: **RM Feni**, Jl. Tribrata; **RM Jakarta**, Jl. A. Yani, and the **Rajawali**. Good meals can also be had in the various *warung* around town.

From Waingapu
At least 4 buses per day leave for Waikabubak via Anakalang (Rp3000, 5-6 hours); most buses pick you

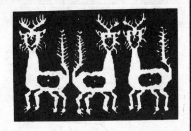

ikat: *A tie-dye method of ornamenting fabrics. Threads are stretched out on simple looms and women hand-dye them each with natural colors (A). Either the warp or weft threads (rarely both) are tied up, then dipped into a dye. The tied parts of the thread remain untreated (B, C, and D). When the next color is applied the already dyed parts are bound up and the parts left blank receive the coloring. The process is repeated as often as is required by the design and the number or colors desired (E). Nusatenggara has many regional and island differences.*

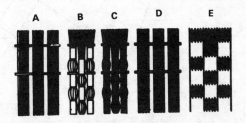

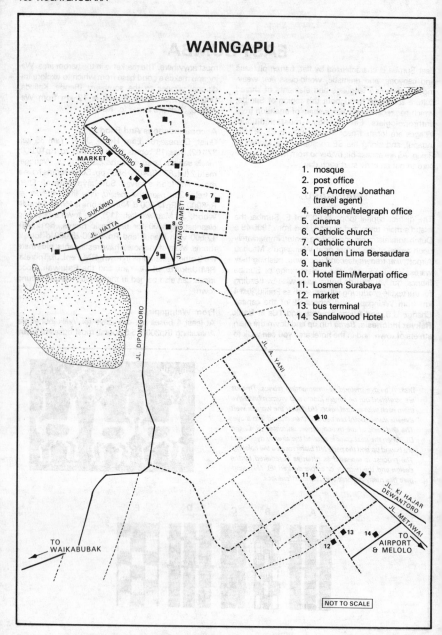

WAINGAPU

MARKET

JL. YOS SUDARSO

JL. SUKARNO

JL. HATTA

JL. WANGGAMETI

JL. DIPONEGORO

JL. A. YANI

JL. KI HAJAR DEWANTORO

JL. METAWAI

TO WAIKABUBAK

TO AIRPORT & MELOLO

1. mosque
2. post office
3. PT Andrew Jonathan (travel agent)
4. telephone/telegraph office
5. cinema
6. Catholic church
7. Catholic church
8. Losmen Lima Bersaudara
9. bank
10. Hotel Elim/Merpati office
11. Losmen Surabaya
12. market
13. bus terminal
14. Sandalwood Hotel

NOT TO SCALE

up at your hotel and depart in the mornings, but book in advance. *Bemo* charge Rp300 to Waingapu's port, and Rp200 (6 km) out to Mahau Airport (or charter a *bemo* or a minibus for Rp3000-4000). Merpati flies from Waingapu to Ende (Rp33,000, once weekly); Bima (Rp42,000, once weekly), Kupang (Rp54,000, once weekly); and Denpasar (Rp80,000, 5 weekly). Twice weekly Merpati flights (Rp36,000) leave Waingapu for Tambolaka, 42 km from Waikabubak, the main town of W. Sumba. Bouraq flights leave 3 times weekly for: Bandung, Rp152,600; Denpasar, Rp85,800; Jakarta, Rp174,400; Kupang, Rp62,300; Surabaya, Rp102,400. The **Merpati** office is at Jl. Matawai 20 (tel. 180); a booking agent is in Hotel Elim, Jl. A. Yani 55. **Bouraq** is at Jl. Yos Sudarso 49 (tel. 36). The Pelni ship, KM *Baruna Fajar*, calls at Waingapu's port about every 2 weeks on its passage from Kupang, and 4 times monthly a Perintis ship embarks from Waingapu for Kupang (Rp20,000 pp) via Sawu (Rp15,000). The Pelni office is in the port area. Small boats heading to and from Flores also call at Waingapu's port.

VICINITY OF WAINGAPU

Maru

On the coast about 20 km NW of Waingapu, this village sits at the foot of a former hilltop priestly capital. Different clans, including a warrior clan, once clustered around the king's residence. Now this royal walled village is deserted, the populace having moved down to the Maru River valley. In Maru are several traditional high-peaked houses. Major ceremonies take place in and around these houses, and inside treasures sacred to the deities from the old capital are stored. During the *Ratu* Festival, prayers, sacrifices, and myth narration open the planting season. Along this coast live the Kupundak people, subsistence farmers among whom divisions by class are still hereditary. The Kupundak divide themselves into patrilineal clans, each claiming descent from a single founder *(marapu)*. Bride prices are exceptionally high, a method of maintaining loyalty and class rigidity. There are many villages in the Kupundak area, and the king is a nice fellow. Get to the main village of Kupundak by minibus from Waingapu, Rp3000. Or rent a motorbike in Waingapu in the morning, and you'll get

to Kupundak by around 1500. Even faster is by *kapal motor* from Waingapu's harbor (to Karoku), but they'll ask Rp150,000 RT (2 days and 1 night).

The Melolo Area

A small town 60 km SE of Waingapu at the end of a savannah-like plain pitted with deep craters and muddy pools, the bus twists and lurches the whole way (Rp2500, 62 km, 2 hours). Travelers may stay in the *kantor polisi*, one of the last houses on the main street. You could also, if invited, overnight in the raja's house. Melolo has its own diesel generator. At 2200 the electricity is abruptly shut off, followed by the deafening cackle of cocks. The whole area around Melolo is still quite traditional and untouched, and the people are hospitable to visitors. It's possible to continue farther down the coast from here: the *ikat*-weaving centers of **Ngalu** and **Kaliuda** can be reached by local *bemo* from Melolo (or by an early bus leaving Waingapu and returning that afternoon). Farther down the coast is **Baing**, famous for its *hinggi kombu* scarves. Five km from Baing, at **Kalala**, is a great surfing beach; waves are best Dec.-May.

Rende

Seven km S of Melolo, Rende contains traditional clan houses and a row of huge 375-year-old carved megalithic stone tombs; Rp500 admission. Get a 0700 minibus from Waingapu direct (Rp3000, 69 km, 2 hours), or board a bus just to Melolo (Rp2500, 62 km), then take a *bemo* or walk to Rende. On the way pass women in front of their houses dyeing yarn and weaving *ikat*.

Pau

A nice 6-km walk from Melolo is the Kingdom of Pau (65 km SE of Waingapu). On the way is the village of Umabara (30 min. and 3 km SW of Melolo) which contains stone tombs and *adat* houses; take a minibus part of the way. In Pau, sign the visitor's book and ask the local raja if you may see his outstanding collection of exceptionally beautiful *ikat* blankets and *sarung*; many are embroidered with shells and red and gold coral. Other pieces are offered for sale. Traditional houses are also found in this village. The king, an impressive figure with long, white beard and white headscarf, is very knowledgeable about the different *ikat* styles.

WEST SUMBA

An area of gently sloping hills and savannahs and green forests, agriculturally-based West Sumba is known for its giant megalithic stone memorial tablets, traditional villages, conical-shaped, thatch-roofed, high-peaked clan houses, and the *pasola*, a tribal war-game ritual held during April or March. Events of Sumba Barat include *pajura* (traditional boxing), festivals of the lunar New Year (Oct. and Nov.), Independence Day (17 Aug.), horse races, and the building of *adat* houses and burials (July-Oct.). The isolated **Bukambero** in the Kodi subdistrict in the extreme W, numbering about 6,000, still practice their ancient ways and are considered a culture apart.

Less dry, cooler, more fertile, hillier, and greener than Sumba Timor, vegetables grow well in Sumba Barat. Many villages are located on a hilltop, a circle of tall houses around the ancestral graves; some villages are still walled and fortified. Houses typically have an open ground floor with chickens and pigs, where the weaving loom might be set up, sheltered from the hot sun. About 1 m above is a bamboo floor, the actual living quarters. A veranda is often built on at least one side of the house. Large table-like slabs in the center of each *kampung* serve as a drying rack for roots, rice, buffalo dung for heating, chalk for *sirih*, or where

newly woven baskets are placed or childen play or old men sun themselves. Pegs-and-pebble gameboards are sometimes carved into the stone.

The *Pasola*

A ritual tribal war which takes place in different villages Feb. and March of each year, beginning several days after the full moon and coinciding with the ritual harvesting of a strange, multihued seaworm. Essentially a jousting match between horsemen carrying long wooden spears and shields, riders are frequently injured and, just as in an American football or boxing match, occasionally killed. The government allows the ritual to take place, but spears must be blunted. Famed as rugged, skilled horsemen, hundreds of Sumbanese combatants charge along circular runways tangent to each other. When their courses intersect they fling spears at each other or try to club opponents from their mounts with the butt end of their spears. Women are the chief observers and supporters of these mock combats, each cheering loudly for her favorites. Big thatch houses, grass-floor shelters, and foodstalls are set up in the spectator area for people streaming in from all over the island. The governor of Sumba and officials from

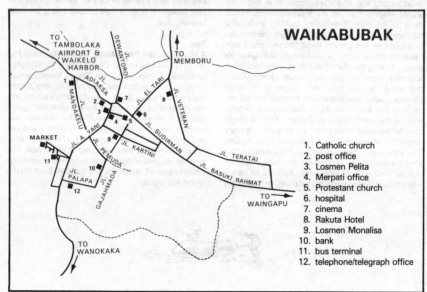

WAIKABUBAK

TO TAMBOLAKA AIRPORT & WAIKELO HARBOR

TO MEMBORU

JL. DEWANTORO
JL. ADIAKSA
JL. EL TARI
JL. VETERAN
JL. MANDAKELU
JL. A. YANI
JL. SUDIRMAN
JL. KARTINI
JL. PEMUDA
JL. TERATAI
JL. GAJAHMADA
JL. PALAPA
JL. BASUKI RAHMAT

MARKET

TO WAINGAPU

TO WANOKAKA

1. Catholic church
2. post office
3. Losmen Pelita
4. Merpati office
5. Protestant church
6. hospital
7. cinema
8. Rakuta Hotel
9. Losmen Monalisa
10. bank
11. bus terminal
12. telephone/telegraph office

Jakarta might even show up. Before setting out, find out in Waingapu exactly when the *pasola* takes place. From Waingapu get a bus to Waikabubak (Rp3000, 5-6 hours), or take a flight to Tambolaka, the small airstrip 42 km from Waikabubak. During Feb., the ceremony takes place in **Kodi** and **Lamboya**. Lamboya is 20 km SW of Waikabubak, Rp1000 by *bemo* or Rp35,000-40,000 RT by chartered *bemo*. In March, the mock battle is staged in **Gaura** and **Wanokaka** (18 km from Waikabubak). In any of these villages, you may stay overnight with the local raja.

WAIKABUBAK

Waikabubak (pop. 8000) is the *Kota Kabupaten* (capital) of Sumba Barat and can be reached from Waingapu by bus for Rp3000 in 5-6 hours— bad road all the way. Right in Waikabubak itself are several megalithic tombs— **Kadung Tana, Watu Karagata, Bulu Peka Mila**—as well as old high-peaked clan houses. For information or a reliable guide, contact Pak Mude, the *kepala seksi* of **Kantor Kebudayaan** (Cultural Office). He may have a schedule of the many fascinating events and festivals in the villages of the area (Anakalang, Prai Bokul, Tarung, etc.). The **Merpati** agent is on Jl. A. Yani, only a 10-min. walk from Rakuta Hotel. The town's airstrip is at Tambolaka, 42 km and Rp3000 pp by Merpati taxi.

Accommodations And Food
Losmen Pelita, Jl. Udayana (only ½ km from the bus terminal), is no-frills, but reasonable at Rp3500 pp, Rp6000 d; meals are Rp2000-3000 extra. All 14 rooms have 2-4 beds, but no inside *mandi*. This hotel can arrange transportation to the *pasola* villages of Lamboya and Wanokaka. **Wisma Pemuda** is definitely a step up; Rp5000-8000 pp for rooms with clean toilets; meals available for around Rp2000 pp. Comfortable **Rakuta Hotel**, Jl. Veteran, is by far the best hotel in town; Rp8500 s, Rp16,000 d for large rooms with *mandi* and toilet attached. Also has room and board arrangements, for around Rp20,000 per day. The manager, Heroe Nugroho, speaks good English; ask to see his photo album. Of **Wisma Pemda's** 5 rooms, 2 have clean, modern bathrooms/toilets. The better rooms cost Rp6000; the others which share a bath/toilet cost Rp3500. If all the hotels in Waikabubak are full, the government *pasanggrahan* might assist you. Eat at your hotel, or in the one good restaurant in town, **RM Bandung**.

VICINITY OF WAIKABUBAK

Most traditional villages surrounding Waikabubak are accessible by *bemo;* best visited during their colorful weekly open-air markets. Some are as close as ½ km; others, like **Pandedewatu** to the S, are 4-hours' walk. Ask villagers along the way where the big stones, elaborate megaliths, and nice carvings are. Different villages bury their dead in different ways, each with unusual carvings and arrangements of the stones. The Christian cross is found on more recent graves, alongside such traditional ornaments as buffalo heads (symbolizing power and strength), the horse (a safe trip to heaven), and the dog (faithfulness).

The closest is **Tarung**, a small hilltop *desa* and ceremonial center *(paraing)* with several tombs. Tarung is just ½ km to the W and within easy walking distance of Waikabubak. The front of the *adat* houses here are embellished with sets of water buffalo horns, trophies of past sacrifices. If you're waiting for some ritual to take place or just want to relax, swim off the white-sand beach at **Rua**, 21 km S of town. Or try the natural freshwater pools at **Waikelo Sawah**, 10 km W of the city. *Bemo* will take you to both places.

South of Waikabubak 18 km in the district of Wanokaka is the traditional village of **Prai Goli**, believed to contain the oldest megalith (called Watu Kajiwa) on Sumba. Located 25 km SW of Waikabubak and just a few km from Lamboya is **Sodan**, another traditional village. An important lunar New Year ceremony takes place here in October. The village has a sacred drum whose playing surface is covered in human skin from an enemy flayed long ago; it's used to call ancestor spirits.

Anakalang
Twenty-two km and Rp1000 by *bemo* E of Waikabubak on the main road to Waingapu, the focal point of this village is its massive graveyard. Sumbanese believe that the present world is just an antechamber to the palace of the next world and that death is the most important event in life. Note the beautifully built thatch homes here with their high, conical roofs, plus a concentration of old burial stones with strong carvings. Every 2 years a mass marriage ceremony, *Purung Takadonga*, is held in Anakalang in the early summer. Check out the nearby village of **Pasunga** where 50 years ago the last great ruler of the Anakalang Kingdom, Umbu Dongga, was buried in a unique tomb called Resi Moni. Resembling a giant's footstool, the huge 30-ton stone slab (now broken) sat on 6 short columns. It took 2 years to carve out from a quarry, then thousands of men took 2 months to drag the stone to its present site in the village square in 1939. The funeral feast lasted a week and 250 water buffalos and scores of horses, pigs, and chickens were slaughtered to honor the departed chief (the sacrifice of slaves died out centuries ago). Another vertical tomb, carved in 1926, has figures of a man and a woman. Houses in Pasunga stand in 2 rows like gigantic brown straw hats. The traditional village of **Lai Tarung**, nearby, has numerous old graves.

Prai Bokul

In this village an hour's walk N of Anakalang (the path starts opposite the *tempat makam),* the heaviest single megalith on Sumba sits like a fallen meteor. This 70-ton sepulcher, known as **Umbu Sawola,** was erected by one of the richest rajas on the island, who hired 2,000 workers to chisel and haul it out of a remote mountain. The slab measures 5 m long and 4 m wide and rests on short columns. It took 3 years and 3 lives to transport it. When the rope broke and killed men it was not considered an accident; the men were but sacrifices to provide the necesssa y spiritual guardianship for the grave. Ten tons of rice were consumed and 250 buffalo sacrificed in the ritual accompanying the dragging, with priests egging the men on with invocations and chants, all in the belief that the stone would ensure the owner's entrance into heaven. The whole project cost US$50,000 to complete, a sum which present-day relatives are trying implacably to recoup by charging tourists Rp5000 per photo!

horse sacrifice: The Sumbanese believe that if their ancestors are provided for, then they in turn will provide for the present generation. This rare photo, from the archives of the Tropical Institute in Amsterdam, shows the ritual slaughter of a horse during the stone-laying ceremony at the tomb of the deceased Raja of Helolo (East Sumba) in Kampung Tambatra in 1909. Funeral rites for deceased members of the nobility are still prime occasions for the display and destruction of vast family wealth; if there were no tax on slaughtered animals, there would be even more slaughter on Sumba. Funeral rites may be extended over several years until sufficient capital can be accumulated for a second burial, accompanied by the slaughter of scores of water buffalo, pigs, and horses and the erection of massive stone slabs and troughs. The deceased's riding horse (ndjara kalitina) must follow its master in death to serve him in the afterlife. Livestock can be slaughtered only if certain rituals are carried out. Before its head is pulled up and its carotoid artery slashed, the animal must be told the occasion for its slaughter; if there isn't a good reason it can be dangerous, as "animals seek revenge." In Sumbanese society, a man of high social rank is obliged to give feasts and it's very unflattering to say of a man "nda napara'a pongukingge natarana" ("he never lets blood flow on the village square, he never slaughters, he never gives a feast"). If a nobleman never gives a feast, he will never be spoken of in ceremonial speech and thus his zunga tamu dendo ngara ("the renown of one's name, the celebration of one's fame") will never spread.

KALIMANTAN

*K*alimantan comprises roughly the southern three-quarters of the equatorial island of Borneo—the third largest island in the world after Greenland and New Guinea. Despite exploration and development, many areas of Kalimantan are almost untouched by the Western world. Joseph Conrad visited E. Kalimantan on several occasions. In Heart of Darkness, the character Marlowe remembers being mesmerized as a child by a map showing vast, uncharted jungle with a river running through it: "It fascinated me as a snake would a bird—a silly little bird." Maps of Kalimantan's river-laced interior still excite the imagination. On the political map, the Malaysian states of Sarawak and Sabah and the sultanate of Brunei lie to the north, occupying the top one-quarter of the island. The territory makes a unique travel experience for the more rough and ready traveler.

INTRODUCTION

Tourist facilities are relatively undeveloped in Kalimantan, and visitors are few. Those Westerners you do meet are leftovers from the oil and wood booms of the 1970s, their jobs gradually being taken over by Indonesians. Good roads are found only in oil and timbering centers and around big coastal cities. Travel is restricted in some areas, as are border crossings into Malaysia. Although travelers may arrive here to visit interior Dayak villages and wildlife reserves, most natives will take you for an expat worker. Expect to encounter officialdom wherever there are navigable rivers, airstrips, and roads (though most roads shown on maps don't exist). Good roads run between Banjarmasin and Samarinda and around Pontianak, but rivers are the main transportation arteries. There are airports in major cities, and airstrips throughout the interior serviced by Merpati and missionary aircraft.

Demographics

Kalimantan is divided into 4 provinces (East, South, Central, and West), 24 regencies, and 346 subdistricts. The territory totals 539,500 sq km, roughly 28% of Indonesia's land area, but has only 4.5% of its population (7 million), or about 12 people per sq km. An exact census is impossible, but the native Dayak make up over 40% of the population, the Chinese 20%; Indian, Javanese, and other Indonesian settlers and transmigrants account for the remainder. Kalimantan's most populous areas are the major cities in coastal areas: Banjarmasin, Balikpapan, Pontianak, Samarinda, and Tarakan. Most towns and villages in the vast interior (home of the Dayaks) and along the coast make little impression on the jungles and swamps.

THE LAND

No volcanic activity here, unlike most of Indonesia, though major eruptions took place in Kalimantan's interior over 50,000 years ago. Half of the territory's land area is under 150 m in elevation, especially near the coasts, with forested peaks, craggy ridges, and river valleys extending into the interior. The island's central mountain ranges—heavily eroded over thousands of years—appear like the spokes of a wheel, separated by broad river valleys. Kalimantan's highest peak is G. Murut (2,438 m), in the Iran Range, in the NE near the Sabah/Sarawak border. Kalimantan is crisscrossed by giant rivers, including the Mahakam, Barito, Sampit, and Kapuas. River deltas and much of the southern coastal areas are swampy. Eighty percent of the territory is jungle, though the lush native vegetation doesn't mean fertile soil. As is the case in temperate forests, the rainforest's soil minerals and life energy never accumulate as humus. Nutrients are perpetually "stored" in the diverse plantlife, with the help of an extremely efficient recycling system: bacteria, fungi, insects, and animals. Soil avalanches are common on jungle slopes after heavy rains, even in areas undisturbed by human toil. Rain percolates into the deep subsoil beneath the tangle of roots and accumulates, then entire hillsides break away and slide—trees, vines, soil, and all—in one mass into the valley below, leaving behind scars of raw, exposed earth. In large swampland areas of S. Kalimantan the land is usually flooded, making cultivation impossible during the wet season; rice is transplanted as seedlings from floating seedbeds after the waters recede.

A naturalist with jungle experience recently traveled through the deep interior for 26 days without coming into open sunlight or encountering any sign of cultivation. Resource development makes a lasting impression, however—at major cost to the environment. Many areas have been devastated by logging, mining, and oil and natural gas drilling—activities which destroy the jungle's delicate balance of plant and animal life. Conserving rainforests—necessarily a long-term effort—unfortunately collides with this nation's immediate political goals and economic imperatives.

Climate

Hot and humid. The temperature never falls below 21 degrees C, and can be much higher. Rainfall averages 381 cm per year. Monsoons herald the arrival of the rainy season; Oct.-March (most violent storms occur Nov.- May). July and Aug. are drier. Rainstorms in the jungle can be torrential, a gentle rustling in the forest canopy quickly becoming a dark, gloomy curtain of rain in a primeval cathedral.

Flora

Kalimantan has a wide variety of montane and lowland forests, each an important genetic resource and wildlife habitat, but none adequately protected by Indonesia's reserves—which too often exist in name only. Fewer than half the endemic species of rainforest plants and animals are known to science. More than half the known species of dipterocarps, a family of hardwood trees valued for timber, are found only in Borneo's lowland rainforests below 500-m elevation. The aerial roots of the tree fern or *tapang* cascade down from the forest canopy, buttressing the massive trunk. Indonesian teak trees take 80 years to reach maturity. Pines are broadleafs here, since they don't need to conserve water. These lowland forests are also rich in wild fruit and nut trees, a significant food source for people, primates, and other animals. Coastal swamp forests host *nipa* palms and a variety of valuable timber trees. The ironwood—immune to insect attacks and used for railway ties and roofing shingles—fringes the island's swampland.

Climbing rattan palms, vines, orchids, ferns, and insectivorous pitcher plants are also common. Kalimantan's Veiled Lady is a toxic fungus which shoots up out of the spongy earth in only 24 hours; its disgusting odor attracts scavenger flies and bees which spread its spores. Epiphytes and mosses are found in sandy heath forests. There are 800 known types of orchids in Kalimantan—the most beautiful hidden away in the high treetops—and 1,100 identified species of ferns. In heavily logged, cultivated, or soil-avalanche areas, bracken, giant sharp-stemmed ferns up to 2½ m high, quickly form stable but unnatural plant communities which the jungle cannot reclaim for hundreds of years. Other specialized forest environments include *kerangas,* peat forests where the water runs red, and along the low-lying coasts and river deltas are endless mangrove swamps.

Fauna

The region's wildlife is unusually diverse. Wherever you go in Kalimantan's forests, animal sounds follow. With luck, you may see some of the noisy (and not-so-noisy) creatures: monkeys, gibbons, bearded wild pigs, deer, wild ox, civets, wildcats, flying lemur, martins, weasels, badgers, otters, porcupines, mongooses, anteaters, 32 species of squirrels, 41 types of bats.

Freshwater Irrawaddy dolphins, found elsewhere only in the rivers and inland lakes of S. America and Asia, thrive in the Mahakam River, and playfully follow river traffic. The elusive and endangered orangutan, "man of the woods," lives here and in N. Sumatra. Standing 1½ m tall with an even greater arm span, and weighing as much as 130 kg, this primate is a mild-tempered vegetarian tree-dweller which builds sleeping platforms by weaving plant fibers together. Its young bear a striking resemblance to human babies. Other primates include macaque monkeys, various species of leaf monkeys, and Bornean gibbons. The rare Sumatran rhinoceros is found only near Banamuda, N of the Kutai Reserve in E. Kalimantan. Wild elephants (probably introduced) are occasionally spotted near the E. Malaysian border. Some animals are endemic. Borneo's sun bear *(beruang,* meaning "has money"), has a large white circle on its chest. The handsome silver and red *bakantan* or proboscis monkey can still be observed in the wild; males have very long, pendulous noses, while females and young also have prominent, but upturned, noses. The clouded leopard is a jungle-camouflaged predator; indistinct splotches of black, brown, and yellowish gray blend ingeniously with the forest canopy.

Symbolically, the most important creature in Kalimantan forests is the black hornbill, the Dayaks' soul carrier. The hornbill's barking call disturbs the peace as it glides slowly and rhythmically; interconnected air pouches beneath the skin act as resonators. Prized by hunters for its feathers and beak and once nearly extinct, its numbers are now increasing. Hundreds of other exotic birds include parrots, parakeets, argus and crested fireback pheasants, *bul-buls,* flycatchers, quail, black partridges, and pigeons. Herons, egrets, and storks are common in Kalimantan's watery southern areas.

Also inhabiting the island are 134 kinds of snakes, including one which can flatten out and "fly." Pythons and monitor lizards frequent riverbanks. A venomous rear-fanged colubrid *(ular cincin mas)* or gold-ringed snake—prized by reptile fanciers for its glittering coloration and reasonable disposition—is found along the coast and inland. The *koele* (panther snake), *apoei* (fire snake), and *ata-bla* (red water snake) are all as bad as they sound, but you can usually see them coming. Borneo has 89 species of frogs: one species has webs of skin between its toes enabling it to glide from branch to branch; another species never touches ground, laying eggs in rain pools which collect on leaves. A flying lizard swoops between trees on leathery membranes attached between its limbs and trunk. Crocodiles inhabit swamp areas and river tributaries.

Kalimantan is host to beautiful metallic green and blue butterflies, as well as hundreds of species of

PRIMATES OF BORNEO

Twenty-one species of primates are represented on Borneo. All have adapted to tree life and, like man, have developed large forward-facing eyes which give them binocular vision to judge distances when leaping through trees. The spectacular tarsier derives from the Tertiary Era of 70 million years ago and stands at the crossroads on the evolutionary chart where man and ape branch off from one another. Scarcely larger than a rat with ghostly globular eyes, the native Dayaks believe that the souls of dead ancestors are reincarnated in its tiny body. Macaque monkeys will follow and abuse you as they move along the other bank while you walk along a river. Gibbons keep together in families and live up in the trees. Skilled gymnasts, they make terrifying piercing sounds which carry long distances through the jungle. Their pouch and throat swell up like a balloon which gives their call a booming quality. You can easily hear their movements through the trees, but you can't see them.

tarsier

proboscis monkey

The proboscis monkey (bekantan) is the Yeti of Borneo. He has an uncanny resemblance to man. Though only 1½ m tall, Dayak tribes believe that the bekantan is not an animal but a hairy man who lives in the jungle and eats fruit. The skunk monkey, no bigger than an alley cat, has a horrible stench.

gibbon

orangutan

metallic beetles. There are queer insects — poisonous polypods, brightly colored millipedes, giant walking sticks, and walking leaves. The island's version of a praying mantis looks like a miniature bright green banana leaf; the main "stem" is the body, the ribs and veins are the legs, and the stalk is the insect's head. Mosquitos and leeches abound, but bees can be more dangerous. If disturbed (bees often live in *tabang* trees), hundreds may swarm and sting an intruder.

HISTORY

Prehistory

Borneo was a cultural crossroads in ancient times, a trade center on the much-traveled route between the Javanese Majapahit Kingdom, the Philippines, and China. Migrants moving S from China brought technology and cultural artifacts from the Sino-Vietnamese Dongson culture and China during the Neolithic period; Chou Dynasty-style porcelain and bronze objects have been found in Kalimantan. In the 2nd C., the Greco-Roman geographer Ptolemy published an atlas containing an uncannily accurate description of Borneo; Indian traders traveling in merchant fleets of large, sea-going junks no doubt passed on the information. Roman and Marco Polo-vintage Chinese beads have also been found here, as well as Hindu-Javanese relics from around A.D. 400, and the Chinese may have traded with coastal Borneo, especially in the NW, as early as the 7th C. during the Tang Dynasty. In the Kutai area on E. Kalimantan's Mahakam River, the oldest historic artifacts yet found in Indonesia have been uncovered: 3 rough plinths dating from the beginning of the 5th C. record, in South Indian Palawa script, "a gift to a Brahmin priest." The inscriptions are 50 years older than the most ancient inscribed stones found at Batutulis in W. Java. These stone poles *(yupas)*, which once stood upright, are thought to have been used for animal sacrifices. The S. Kalimantan heartland, the early kingdoms of Negara Dipa and Negara Daha, has been an important agricultural region for hundreds of years.

Early History

From prehistoric times, human immigration has always been centered along the coasts and along the major waterways. By A.D. 1000, Chinese trading posts had sprung up along the NW coast where Pontianak is today. Such rainforest riches as sandalwood, beeswax, camphor, hornbill ivory, decorative feathers, edible bird's nests, rhinoceros horn, and precious metals were traded for glass beads, coins, and giant ceramic pots. Chinese mining communities, extracting gold and diamonds, also appeared on the island's S and W coasts. These coastal areas gradually became Islamicized during the 15th and 16th C.,

developing into small independent sultanates at Sambas, Kutai, and Banjarmasin; each had strong mercantile ties to the Islamic northern ports of Java. Borneo's history also centers on the Brunei sultanate to the N; the sultan and his powerful maritime kingdom spread their influence over most of the island. Royal descendants still live in the E. Kalimantan river ports of Tenggarong and Berau — small kingdoms deprived of political power when the Indonesian Republic gained real independence in 1950.

Arrival Of Europeans

The first fully documented European arrival did not occur until 1521, when one of Magellan's ships pulled into the harbor of Brunei on the N coast. The word "Borneo," in fact, is the anglicized word for Brunei, an ancient kingdom (independent since 1984) named after the *berunai* fruit, and still used as the geographic designation for the entire island. Because of the island's interminable and inhospitable interior and its few natural harbors, the Europeans had difficulty establishing control. Finally, in 1839, the British gained a foothold in the N of the island, establishing the legendary dynasty of the White Rajas who ruled over Sarawak for more than 100 years. The British eventually took control of the northern part of the island, and during the second half of the 19th C. the Dutch concluded treaties with the E coast sultans and assumed autocratic administration of the southern three-quarters, bringing Borneo into the economic orbit of the Dutch East Indies empire. Except for minor disruptions such as the Banjarmasin War (1859-64, basically a succession dispute), Kalimantan remained in Dutch hands until the Japanese invaded in 1942.

World War II

The Japanese occupied the island from 1942 to 1945, their ruthless policies of repression resulting in the deaths of as many as 20,000 intellectuals, missionaries, businessmen, and aristocrats. During its occupation, the island supplied Japan with almost half its wartime fuel oil. Though both Australia and Britain thought that taking the island was of dubious value, the U.S. invasion of the Philippines suddenly separated Borneo, its oil, and 30,000 defenders from Japan. Early in 1945, General Douglas MacArthur decided to liberate Borneo and establish an Allied airbase and Pacific port for the British navy. The British declined to participate in the invasion, and the Australian army commander, General Blamey, was reluctant to risk his troops. But MacArthur won out. There were subsequently 3 separate Allied landings on Borneo, all preceded by intense bombardments. Tarakan Island was shelled for 4 days and captured on 1 May; its airfield, one of MacArthur's objectives, was so heavily damaged it was useless to the Allies. Brunei Bay was bombed even longer, then captured on 10 June. MacArthur's third target, Balikpapan, was leveled by 20 days of ceaseless bombing. When Australian troops came ashore on 1 July in WW II's last major amphibious landing, they found only 10 live defenders; most Japanese had died in the firestorm of bombed and burning oil tanks, the rest fled to nearby hills. With Indonesian independence after WW II, the Javanese gave the territory its new name, *Kaliman-tan,* meaning "Rivers of Precious Stones"—an apt term to describe the many regions of the island known for their rich deposits of gold, diamonds, amethysts, agates, sapphires, and emeralds.

ECONOMY

Kalimantan was for many years an economic burden on both the Dutch East Indies Company and the new Indonesian Republic. Then, in the 1950s, her natural resources of oil, gas, and timber were finally tapped. Kalimantan is still not very developed, even less so than Sumatra. Most of the territory's wealth comes from E. Kalimantan, which produced in 1978 nearly 25% of Indonesia's total export earnings. Mineral resources are rich. Coal, petroleum, and natural gas production are big business here (around 25% of the country's total). So is the forest products industry: timber, rubber, copra, resin, gum, and camphor. Kalimantan is Indonesia's richest area for gems. Diamond mining and processing are important in S. Kalimantan. Agate, amethyst, citrine, tiger eye, and topaz are plentiful. Gold and iron are also mined. Because of its boom economy, transport to E. Kalimantan is convenient, though accommodations and food are quite pricey.

The Timber Industry

Between 1968 and 1978, E. Kalimantan alone exported around 50% of Indonesia's timber, mostly from the Mahakam River and its tributaries. Huge, rugged tracts of primary rainforest are being wantonly plundered by more than 100 overseas and domestic timber companies, with little concern for the ecological and social consequences. Over 30 million ha of Kalimantan's tropical jungle have been earmarked for clearcutting of its valuable tropical hardwoods, while unregulated transmigration settlements have turned marginal agricultural areas into a wasteland of *alang alang* grass. As an indirect result of overlogging, one of the largest forest fires in recorded history took place in E. Kalimantan in 1982-83, wiping out 20% of the province's rainforests and eradicating forever a number of species of plants and animals. The "Great Fire" severely damaged the island's ecology and contributed immensely to soil erosion. Extra forest reserves were set aside to compensate for those lost in the fire, but tree-felling continues unabated. Reforestation efforts are minimal.

PEOPLE

Most of Kalimantan's population lives near coastal areas, with Chinese and Malays predominating. Javanese, Buginese, and other Indonesians come here to find work, competing with other Indonesians and even other nationalities for skilled jobs. Urban dwellers of Kalimantan's coastal cities live not by agriculture but by trading or working in service or manufacturing industries. Because of the island's vast coastal swamplands, cultivation is difficult, so food must be imported from Singapore and Java. Under Indonesia's massive *transmigrasi* program, tens of thousands of Javanese and Balinese families have been brought in to settle the island's hinterlands. These resettlement schemes began in 1921 when the Dutch moved 250 families from C. Java to Barabai, 140 km N of Banjarmasin; this project was terminated because of the inhospitable land and rampant malaria. In 1938, they tried again, this time successfully: 86 people were moved from E. Java to Jambayan in the Kutai area. After WW II, *transmigrasi* moved into high gear. Between 1957 and 1980, around 50,000 Javanese were sent to E. Kalimantan alone. A large number of projects have failed because of unsuitable land, lack of marketing opportunities, cultural and social conflicts, an ill-prepared resettlement infrastructure, or as a result of the poor farming skills of the transmigrants.

Most of the native Dayak peoples, almost half the territory's population, still live deeper inland along the banks of major rivers and tributaries. Recent exposure to the forces of modernization is changing many aspects of traditional life. The Indonesian government is abolishing multiple-family longhouses and replacing them with modern, single-family dwellings—a drastic change in village life. Tattooing, mastery of traditional crafts, and the custom of wearing huge bunches of metal earrings to elongate earlobes are all disappearing. Few Dayaks hunt with blowguns and poison darts or spears these days, preferring instead homemade Daniel Boone-style flintlocks. Though there are occasional unexplained decapitations in remote regions, the traditional practice of headhunting has officially ended. Increasingly, young Dayaks leave their villages to hire on with timber and oil companies or take menial jobs in Kalimantan's boom towns. Children of wealthy Dayaks study engineering, forestry, and other subjects in Indonesian and European universities.

The Punan

The Punan tribespeople are the original inhabitants of Borneo, preceding even the Dayaks. With successive waves of migration over the centuries, the Punan gradually moved inland from the coast to continue their way of life; about 10,000 are left in isolated, scattered pockets in the upper Mahakam and in the Apo Kayan. The government has encouraged the Punan to settle in villages and cultivate rice, though most are not that interested. Wizards in jungle craft and masters of the terrain, the Punan tribes don't traditionally eat rice, living instead off fruit, wild berries, and game. They hunt with blowpipes (and rarely miss), using packs of hunting dogs to track wild pigs. The Punan may live in a village for a few weeks or months, then abandon it to become nomadic hunter-gatherers once again. You might see them in villages bartering their boar-tusk necklaces, panther teeth and skins, bear claws, deer horns, monkey gallbladders, snake stones, orangutan skulls, and other items for salt and tobacco. They smoke like locomotives. Arrange to go with a government party if in search of the fearless Punan, as they can be defensively hostile. One group, the Stone Punan, still lives a mesolithic existence in a stone cave.

THE DAYAK CULTURE

"Dayak" is a collective name for over 200 different tribes, the island's native people, who live throughout the interior of Borneo. Each *sukuh* (tribe) has its own tribal name and speaks its own dialect. Contrary to myth, the Dayak race is light-skinned (resembling Chinese) with rounded, well-featured faces and slightly slanted eyes. Mountain Dayak tribes are physically imposing, taller than most Asians, heavily muscled, and weighing 75 kg or more. Numbering in the millions, Dayaks have traditionally lived upriver in hill areas, thriving as hunters, gatherers, and more recently, as slash-and-burn hill rice growers. Only one crop a year is grown, planted in Aug. and harvested in Jan. and February. Vegetables and the common Indonesian fruits are also grown. *Kerbau*, cows, pigs, chickens, ducks, and a few goats are kept. Since the 1970s, the government has encouraged the Dayak to take up wet rice cultivation and to produce such cash crops as rubber, pepper, and cloves.

Other Indonesians call the Dayak villagers *orang bodoh* ("stupid men"), considering them backward because of headhunting and other animist customs. The truth is that they practice responsible local government with elected members, maintain their own political boundaries, and even have a capital city (Palangkayara). Dayak people are scrupulously honest by nature, though exposure to Christianity and modern values has muted this trait. Since theft is unimaginable, in remote interior areas valuables are still left unlocked and unguarded. Traditional villages have few modern problems, but the people suffer from curable diseases: malaria, dysentery, infections. Don't take advantage of Dayak village hospitality; returning generosity by giving useful gifts is a traditional gesture.

Dayak girl from the upper Tingar River region. Note the earlobes stretched to shoulder length.

History

Since at least 5000 B.C., Dayak tribes have lived in splendid isolation throughout Kalimantan. Though flights now touch down on jungle airstrips hundreds of kilometers inland, Dayak territory is still some of the most inaccessible on Earth. Historians and ethnologists have always given the Dayak a bum rap, characterizing their culture as primitive, but by the late Neolithic period (1800 to 500 B.C.), when Europeans were wearing deerskins and throwing spears, Borneo people already had a highly advanced culture, fashioning polished stone tools, earthenware pottery, bone ornaments, *pandan* mats, bamboo caskets, wooden coffins, and cotton textiles. They buried their dead with great ceremony, believed in a cult of "death ships" which carried their loved ones to the afterworld, and practiced elaborate spirit rituals. When the Malays began to arrive in coastal areas, the native Dayaks retreated farther inland, not wanting to become part of a religion and culture which prohibited their favorite food, pork. Throughout the 1800s when the Dutch began to settle and trade in the interior, the magnificent traditional culture of the Dayak began to decline.

Dayak Society

A man seeks a wife outside his own village; the new couple may set up housekeeping in either the wife's or husband's village. Women and men share the work equally, including child care, though women don't hunt, and men usually cook only when women aren't present. A child traces both its mother's and father's lineage; dependence on each is sometimes symbolized during the ear-piercing ritual: one ear is pierced by a relative of the mother, the other by paternal kin. Parents and children make up the basic family unit, with adopted children usually sharing equal rights and privileges. The spirit of mutual help and cooperation among relatives and between longhouse members is very strong. Old women look after the children and do domestic chores, while old men sit, gossip, smoke, and repair traditional implements. Children play on the covered longhouse veranda or in the nearby river. The longhouse leader, responsible for handling internal and external village affairs, usually lives in the center of the longhouse. Even in Christianized villages, shamans, medicine women (some men), are responsible for the mental, physical, and spiritual health of the people. The only commonly held village property is the graveyard. Village social organization varies. The Kenyah and Kayan tribes of E. Kalimantan practiced slavery until recent times; these villages are ruled by an indigenous aristocracy. The Iban of W. Kalimantan are cheerful, cooperative, liberal, and highly democratic, with elected longhouse representatives (men and women) serving at the pleasure of village elders.

Village Life

Mostly older people, husbands, women, and children live in villages now; young men go downriver to seek work. Dayak villages swarm with hunting dogs, cats, hens, crowing cocks, pigs rooting under houses. Women are the first to rise, to light cooking fires, fetch water, and bathe in the river. Rice is then boiled, and for those who will work in the fields portions are wrapped in banana leaves. Next, the men rise and go down to the river to bathe, light up their first cigarette of the day and then eat breakfast. The women and children eat after the men. At evening meals you sit around the hearth eating with your fingers: rice is heaped on tin plates, along with either fresh or dried fish, sauces and spices, corn, green vegetables, forest fruits, and tapioca. Pork is only eaten on special occasions. The Dayaks also like to party hearty. In remote villages, where young children have never seen white people, your arrival will turn into an all-out festival. Rice harvest celebrations can go on for 72 hours nonstop. If you pass out, they just prop you up and pour more rice wine down your throat. Dogs are numerous in Dayak villages and must be the best fed in Asia; also the most valuable, since they are necessary for pig hunting. Pork is the favorite meat, and a good hunting dog can fetch Rp150,000, or half the price of a *kerbau*.

Life Events

Death is the major event of Dayak life (see "Ship of the Dead" below), while birth and marriage are comparatively inconsequential. When a child is born, the celebration consists of offering a sacrifice of rice and chicken or pig blood to the river in which the midwife first bathes the child. *Ba'*, traditional, often elaborately decorated woven rattan baby carriers, are handed down as family heirlooms; they protect infants' spirits against death and disease. No fertility rites exist among the Dayak; marriage becomes official at the birth of the first child. Modern marriages may be simple, Christian affairs, with both bride and groom dressed in Western clothes. For traditional animist ceremonies, the best time to visit is July and Aug., after the harvest.

Religion

All Dayak groups recognize a principal deity who is responsible for creating the world; other powerful deities include those in charge of weather cycles and agricultural yields. Belare, the thunder ghost, goes by the same name all over Borneo. He rides with the storm clouds, and every time he opens his mouth thunder roars; lightning flashes whenever he winks an eye. Belare shatters trees and houses with his claws. *Siram*, a water-dripping ceremony, takes place during rice harvest, when the rain ghosts pour water from the sky so river ghosts can float home. Legendary spirit heroes and supernatural beings usually comprise both the male and female aspects, and traditionally there was very little anguish about dying or one's destiny after death. The river, presided over by the spirits, is an all-important element in Dayak life—the provider of water, food, and transport.

Animals and birds often have religious significance. For example, the hornbill is sacred to the Dayak and associated with the world's creation. Hearing or spotting certain birds and mammals reveal good or evil omens. Ritual sacrifices of animals (and at one time—people) appease the spirits and create magic. Before slaughtering village creatures, Dayaks explain the necessity and beg their forgiveness. Beginning about 400 years ago, Chinese traders sold Dayak tribes huge porcelain jars decorated with dragons; the people believed the dragons' spirits lived inside. Many Dayak ideas of good and evil are based on the noises of the jungle. Before a cloudburst, the jungle becomes deathly silent, but when the rains stop it all begins again—the cicadas, the frogs, the birds, the monkeys, the people, the gods.

Placed outside villages, elaborately decorated *belawang* poles are hung with rotten eggs and other smelly matter to signify *katang*, an annual casting-out of spirits accompanied by ritual dancing. Roads and paths leading to the village are blocked off for 2-3 days. Leaving the village is fine, since you'll take the spirits with you, but no one is allowed to enter until all the various rites are completed, for fear the spirits will sneak back into town.

Christianity

White Rheinische evangelists began work in south Borneo in 1835 by first converting the village medicine women, who in turn converted the people, either actively or by example. Throughout the 1800s, Christian birth and marriage rituals began to take hold, undermining the native death rites and other religious ceremonies. Longhouses were gradually abandoned in favor of Malay-type dwellings, and Malay dress was adopted. Villagers quickly embraced Christianity because it tolerated their ideas about reincarnation; they also got to eat pork and keep their dogs. The Christian faith also freed families from the financial burden of *Kaharingan,* traditional funeral rites, which required expensive preparations. Christian missionaries used the Dayak language and the Bible was translated into the native language. The Christians also set up schools, which changed the Dayaks' value system and attitudes. A common sight in Kalimantan now is young children holding satchels of books wending their way along muddy jungle trails to missionary schools. Sometimes pupils walk 2 hours to reach school and often there are boarding houses *(asrama)* established to house pupils from distant areas. Though Protestantism and Catholicism have made deep inroads, elaborate Dayak mythology, ritual order, and ancient animist spirit cults still persist in a number of places, such as the Barong Tongkok area and the Apo Kayan.

Vanishing Customs

Many Dayak customs have gone the way of the razed forests and eroded hillsides of the island's interior. For example, Dayak people believe that only jungle beasts and dogs should have white teeth. So if betel-nut chewing didn't sufficiently darken their teeth, they once varnished them black. They also bored holes in their teeth.

Women's sexual pleasure is important. Sometimes *palang* or penis rings which function like French ticklers are worn. Also, small, ornately carved wooden pins adorned with feathers on each end — worn much like a pierced earring, inserted through a small hole in the fleshy head of the penis — were *not* decorative. Men without "penis pins" were not considered marriage material, and were rejected by women.

Traditional Dayak people wear charms all over their bodies: anklets, necklaces, bracelets, headdresses, earrings. Though men and women now often wear Western clothes, loincloths and animal-skin vests were once common attire for men, bark-cloth wraps for women. Perforated, elongated earlobes were once considered a sign of beauty. Sometimes only 3 days after a baby girl's birth, holes were pierced in her ears with sharp bamboo and a silver, gold, or brass ring

added. This first earring was followed by many more over the years, until a heavy, jangling bunch of rings hung down to her shoulders or breasts. Young girls would have to hold the rings when they ran to keep their earlobes from tearing. Older women can still be seen wearing these elaborate sets of earrings, though young women are *malu* (embarrassed) by them. The modern style is wearing no rings in public, though holes in earlobes are permanent, large, and quite apparent. Men, too, have ornamentally pierced ears. In bygone days, headhunters' upper ears were pierced to display trophies.

Headhunting

Officially, headhunting doesn't exist in Kalimantan, though isolated jungle beheadings are still reported. Despite distaste for such practices, the British encouraged Dayak people to hunt Japanese heads during World War II. In former times, men would awaken the spirit of courage, *Bali Akang,* for assistance during headhunting expeditions. After decapitating the enemy, great homecoming celebrations awaited warriors returning with trophies. The brains were carefully extracted through the nostrils, then fresh *ulu* (heads) were placed in plaited rattan nets and smoke-cured over fires. Dried skulls were the most powerful magic in the world, vital transfusions of energy for villages. As a symbol par excellence of the procreative power of nature, a good head could save a village from plague, produce rain, ward off evil spirits, or triple rice yields. The great *Mamat Ulu* feast was celebrated by blessing freshly taken heads. Dayak people believed that a man's spirit continued to inhabit his head after death. Surrounded by palm leaves, heads were offered food and cigarettes — already lit for smoking — so their spirits would forgive, forget, and feel welcome in their new home. New heads increased the prestige of their owner, and impressed sweethearts; they were an initiation into manhood. In some tribes, a head's powers increased over time; cherished ones were handed down from generation to generation. In other tribes, a skull's magic faded with age, so fresh heads were always needed. Villages without *ulu* were spiritually weak, easy prey for enemies, poison darts, *mandau* knives, and pestilence. In remote villages of Kalimantan, travelers still come across skulls — gratefully not fresh ones.

Sumpit

Dayak tribes once commonly used blowguns both in hunting pigs and warfare. *Sumpit,* 2- to 3-m-long narrow tubes made of hardwood or bamboo fitted with iron sights, shot darts with deadly accuracy for distances of 100 m or more. The small arrows are made of leaf ribs or bark of palm trees, the sharp tips dipped in toxic tree sap, then dried until hard and brittle. The arrow shaft falls away on impact, the deadly tip firmly embedded in the prey's flesh. Paralysis occurs instant-

Ship of the Dead: A Dayak coffin, Kalimantan. The Ship of the Dead cult persists in Sulawesi in the form of chants and rites, while on Sumatra you can see it live on in rare textiles, particularly in the Lampung District.

ly, followed by death in 3 minutes or less. Though most Dayak tribes have forsaken both the blowgun and spear for homemade rifles, the aboriginal Punan still use *sumpit* for hunting. Making blowguns is a painstaking process. An iron rod is pushed and twisted through a length of ironwood, boring a rough passage. To scrape and sand it smooth, a long, notched iron rod is inserted, then rotated until splinters no longer come out the other end.

Ship Of The Dead

It is believed that the dead will continue to live in the Land of the Dead, but they need a *prahu* to get there. At ceremonial funerals, lavishly carved and decorated burial canoes containing the deceased are launched, drifting downriver to the sea. It takes 3 days to get to heaven, to which the Dayaks even have *maps!* These boat-shaped coffins are modeled after the water snake for men, the hornbill for women. On the eve of the "final sailing," men wear animal masks and grass cloaks and dance around the coffin. The dead are given painted hats for their trip to the afterworld. Funeral rites have now been modified in most tribes: decorative, canoe-like coffins may still be used, but the dead set sail from village graveyards. Elaborate funerals are now held only for tribal leaders, and Christian burials are the rule.

Lamin

A special feature of Dayak life is the longhouse *(lamin* or *betang.)* Built along riverbanks, these ridge-roofed structures can be up to 180 m long and 9-18 m wide. Several longhouses, each with 50 or more families and as many as 200 doors, may make up a Dayak village. Villagers, working cooperatively, can erect a new one in less than a week. Due to rapid tropical decomposition, however, longhouses don't usually last longer than 15 years. Considerable variation exists throughout Kalimantan in longhouse size, method of construction, and interior arrangement. Most are raised one-3 m off the ground on wooden piles—easier to replace than rotting floorboards. The current of air below reduces vermin and prevents dry rot. Pigs and chickens are kept underneath. Stilt construction also provides protection against snakes, floods, and enemies; longhouses evolved in a time of constant intertribal warfare. One or 2 logs with notched steps, or rough, flexible ladders, are pulled up at night.

In some areas, Dayak architecture and craftsmanship are magnificent, with many parts of the longhouse—door frames, galleries, posts—decoratively carved. Teakwood railings are carved into dragons, snakes, demons, or birds, showing detail down to scales and feathers, even lessons in sex education. A covered veranda, the communal living area, runs the full length of the building, usually facing the river. The veranda is used for loafing, child care, visiting with neighbors, repairing implements, and hanging fish traps, boat paddles, weapons, and other articles of daily use. Clothes (and in past times, heads) are also hung out to dry here. One narrow longhouse door faces E, in recognition of sunrise and its association with life. Interior partitions separate family groups; distant relatives may live at the other end of the building. A loft upstairs is used for storing rice, baskets, stacks of woven mats, fishing nets, and firewood. The longhouse is sometimes infested with fleas.

If invited to visit a *lamin* (always ask permission or wait for an invitation), remove your shoes and socks as a courtesy. Gratefully accept the welcoming food or drink offered you, with both hands; one outstretched hand could be construed as a threat or challenge. Take useful items into the interior with you as gifts for your hosts; immediately reciprocate any kindness offered. Show respect for the lowly village animals—the dogs, chickens, pigs, etc., since the people believe that mistreating them will cause various natural disasters. Don't wait too long to visit a *lamin*—they're disappearing. The government thinks the longhouse concept is too communistic. With help from the government and Christian missionaries, the extended communal family structure is breaking down. Only a small percentage of Dayak young people follow the old ways, such as marrying and then moving into their parents' longhouses.

Medicine Women

Shamans *(wadian* or *dajung),* in most cases older women, are a strong tradition here. These priestesses are the *dalang* of Dayak society. People will travel for days to see a famous *wadian* in action, lining village streets or crowding into hot, stuffy rooms. Many skills are required of her. She is a magician-healer who must seek out the cause of sickness or evil-doing, a mistress of the ceremonial chanting which accompanies many ceremonies, and she is also the local social historian. The village *wadian,* with uncoiled hair and huge jangling bracelets, is a hypnotic entertainer capable of performing ritual dances for days on end. In order to communicate directly with the spirits, a *wadian* must drop into a trance state, believed to be "the door of the spirit world." These witch doctors have been known to yank out toenails without anesthesia, i.e., treating shock with shock. If someone comes down with fever or is possessed by demons, a *wadian* hired by the family may go out into the jungle with a basket, imploring the devilish spirit to drop the wayward soul into the basket so she can return it. Everyday magic includes various handcrafted amulets—considered "divine gifts," a collaboration between tribespeople and the deities—and an amazing array of herbal potions.

DAYAK ARTS AND CRAFTS

Each tribe specializes in its own handicrafts. Most craft products are utilitarian—for use in agriculture, daily village life, hunting, or fishing. Agriculturalists construct traps and snares to catch pigs, deer, monkeys. Borneo people are also accomplished at devising cast nets, flat nets, scoop nets, and the Ngaju of the Upper Kahayan build a remarkable 50-m-long bamboo and rattan fish trap *(mihing)* shaped like a slide. Beautiful, high-quality bamboo receptacles of all sizes and shapes are fashioned. Thin bamboo containers hold fire-making gear, jewelry, tobacco, sewing implements, yarn; thicker ones store darts for blow-guns. Bamboo containers are often covered completely with intricate designs: yellowish-red floral decorations, spiral or triangular motifs, S-lines curving around in opposite directions, sometimes battle scenes.

Men generally do the woodcarving and metallurgy; women do the tattooing, weaving, basketry, beadwork, embroidery, and sewing. Patterns and designs are inherited, and decorations are often more ornate and detailed than in nature itself. Tangled, effusive S-patterns and curlicues are typical Dayak motifs, a mirror of their jungle environment. The highly sophisticated Late Chou style from China penetrated this island as nowhere else in Indonesia. Characterized by more typically Chinese motifs than the Dongson culture common throughout the remainder of the archipelago, Chou influence is apparent in the complex animal motifs, decorative designs, and mythological afterlife themes used in Dayak art, especially among the Iban people in the northwest. Hindu-Java inspiration includes exuberant arabesques, the *naga* (snake), and the *harimau* (tiger) motif (though tigers aren't found on Borneo).

Traditional Dances

Social dancing is more typical in the Malay coastal areas, while Dayak tribal and ritualistic dance is common up the rivers of the interior. But the two are much intermingled. The Indonesian national social dance, *joged,* is performed in the Ma'anjan area of S. Kalimantan when a Banjar orchestra visits the area by boat. Ritual dances, very popular in the interior, mark the transitional stages of life and important village events: the coming of age, marriage, death, banishing illness, fighting and finishing wars, rice planting and harvests. Usually held at night, Dayak dances are exciting spectacles with screaming, tom-tomming dancers wearing animal skins and plumes of feathers. In mock battle dances, attackers noisily invade the village, then start dancing to the jugband equivalent of a *gamelan.* The Dayaks are also renowned for their solo sword dances: the *Ngejiak* shows the skill of a young man using a sharp *mandau.* The *Kancet Papatai* is a mock fight between 2 men, also wielding *mandau.* Accompanied by bronze gongs, hoop drums, and rattles, Dayak dancers use staffs, bracelets, scarves, and black and white *engang* (hornbill) feathers in their ceremonies and religious rites. Animal-like demon masks with fangs, big noses, and bulging eyes are worn by some tribes. Dancing is sometimes associated with other events such as cockfighting, the Dayak national sport. Roosters' spurs are sometimes coated with fast-acting poisons; death occurs in seconds once a wound is inflicted. Men scratched by clawing roosters have also died.

Music

Some Dayak tribes still play a curious musical instrument, the *kledi,* a mouth organ like a bagpipe, with 6 or 8 narrow strips of bamboo cane protruding from a hollow oval gourd. Found on 9th C. Borobudur bas-reliefs, the *kledi*—known in Indonesia since the Bronze Age—survives only in Kalimantan's interior. Also played are goblet-shaped drums made from heavy, hollowed-out tree trunks. In the northern regions, magnificent dragon gongs are played. Another unusual instrument found among some tribes is the *sampe,* a large flat lute with rattan strings which resonate over a painted wooden box.

Tattooing

Dayak tribes' outstanding aesthetic sense is apparent in incredibly fine tattoo designs combining snake, bird, and plant motifs—an art practiced by all tribes. Woodcuts are usually made first, then colored with charcoal. The woodcut design is then stamped on the skin, which is punctured with brass needles dipped in dye. The most intricate tattooing may require months of hard work—and torture. Tattooing is not just decorative; elaborate tattoos denote tribe, family, and social standing or recognize acts of bravery. With Christianity and government prohibition, however, tattooing has become a lost art, though you can still see fine examples on older tribespeople in remote

Dayak tattoo motifs: Flowers, hornbills, dogs, dragons, bamboo trees, and hibiscus designs tell at once the tribe, family, and station in life of a Dayak. Tales of long journeys, headhunts, and feats of bravery are also documented on the skin. Dayak tattoos show amazing delicacy, such as precise parallel blue lines running around ankles. Woodcuts are usually made first with charcoal of the fragrant dammar wood applied to it, then stamped on the skin. The skin is punctured with brass needles hammered with a stick. Some designs take months of hard work and torture. The Kayans of the NE have the most attractive and complicated tattoo patterns.

villages; the Kenyah and Kayan tribes of the NE have the most attractive and complicated tattoo patterns. Male tattoos were meant to beautify a man for heaven. Boys get their first tattoos at the age of 12. As they grow to manhood, journeys, skirmishes, and spiritual events are all recorded. At death, a historical and biological map of a man's life is tattooed on his shoulders, chest, and legs. Tattoos on certain parts of the female anatomy are related to rank; in some tribes, only wives and daughters of chiefs may tattoo their thighs. Differences in social status are also shown by the number of lines in a design.

Plaiting

Both S. and E. Kalimantan are famous throughout Indonesia for their fine-quality mats and baskets, as durable as they are beautiful. Traditional Dayak plaited mats are almost indistinguishable from some ancient Croatian weaving, suggesting links between the peoples of the Balkans and Borneo—probably during the so-called Pontianak Migration which spread E across Europe to Asia and into the Tonkin area, giving rise to the Dongson culture. Baskets for carrying rice and large objects, called *bambok* in W. Kalimantan, are made of natural yellow rattan, sometimes dyed or decorated in black and red. The Kantu' make high-quality split bamboo mats, sought after by other Upper Kapuas people; the Kapuas Punan and the Ot Danum are also known for their excellent mats and basketmaking. Woven mats may feature the Ship of the Dead design. Food containers are also plaited, usually made from strips of pandanus, leaves. Among any family's most prized possessions are *ba'*, baby carriers made of wood or rattan. Passed down from generation to generation, and believed to magically protect infants' spirits, *ba'* are elaborately beaded, carved, painted, or hung with ribbons, pieces of ivory, and coins.

Weaving

Many Dayak tribes are known for their colorful fabrics, woven by women on simple horizontal looms. Along with the Sumbanese, Iban Dayak women weave exquisite *ikat* cloth. Dayak cloth is less stiff and formal, more multicolored and lively, than the *ikat* of Sumba. Large pieces of *ikat* are still used to mark sacred spots but seldom worn; they were once used to carry fresh heads. On festivals and other special occasions you may see traditional Dayak woven costumes: kerchiefs, loincloths, decorated poncho-like coats *(jawat),* and a girdle of bark cloth wrapped around the waist, then passed through the legs. *Belet* are hundreds of fiber garters clipped around the legs at knee level. Women still wear *sholang*-shell skirts or bright applique cloth skirts, an ancient technique in which black human figures and dogs are sewn onto light-colored fabrics. These traditional costumes are fast disappearing, worn now only in remote parts of E. Kalimantan.

Beadwork

With their marvelous sense of color, Dayak women work with glass beads—including ancient Chinese beads from the days of Marco Polo—much more than other Indonesian ethnic groups. Tobacco and betelnut containers, sword cases, baby carriers, bracelets, necklaces, basket lids, men's caps, headbands, and skirt hems are traditionally decorated with tassels and colorful beaded embroidery. The Kelabit, Kayan, and Maloh are particularly adept at beadwork; Kenyah (E. Kalimantan) beadwork usually features black designs against yellow backgrounds.

Sculpture

Dayak carving technique is unique. A small knife with a long handle is clamped tightly under the armpit, and the object being carved is moved, not the knife. Such everyday objects as plates, bowls, spoons, seats, and foot-stools are carved and decorated, but most carvings are of guardian figures—village spirits, water spirits, forest spirits. Carving these figures may be a religious function. Each Dayak has his own personal spirit, about 12 cm tall; most are standing, but ancestral figures or *balian* (hereditary priest) figures may sit or crouch. Lifesize village guardians are made of ironwood and placed at the community's entrance or where an accident happened, to prevent it from happening again. Figures with monkeys on their heads or hips are forest guardians. Tall, skinny wooden statues (always male) can be seen at burial grounds, with open arms, tusks, swords, and erect penises—because devils hate to see sexual excitement. *Hampatong* figures represent the live slave which once accompanied the Soul of the Dead to the afterworld, intended to provide protection against evil; they have deformed faces, tongues sticking out, and tigers sitting on the tops of their heads. *Hudog* (masks) are carved from single pieces of wood, *bukung* (black) or *bukong* (white), are often bearded, and have 2 eye teeth. Some tribes fashion one-m-high to lifesize sacrificial hardwood columns *(temadu)*, with male and female figures representing the dead. Kayan, Kenyah, and Berawan are accomplished woodcarvers. Surreal, dynamic sculpture in the round is seen most frequently among the Ot-Danum, Ngaju, and Dasan groups of SE Borneo. Central poles in meeting houses of E. Kalimantan may be quite intricate, with carvings of flowing water, *mandau*, hornbills, and other creatures.

Metallurgy

The Dayak even surpassed the Javanese and Malays in the making of iron products. Dayaks once forged axes, knives, and adzes out of their own iron, but this art has all but been forgotten—the mines, ancient forges, and smelters since reclaimed by the jungle. Only a few specimens of this traditional art can be found, the prize of any museum curator. The brasswork done by the braziers of Negara, SE Kalimantan, still reflect Javanese-Hindu influence. The Maloh of W. Kalimantan are particularly skilled in the manufacture of brass and silver earrings, belts, bracelets, armlets, leg-rings, and anklets. The most important Dayak weapon is the *mandau* or sword, once worn in battle but now used mostly for decoration or magic. Known for their pliancy and strength, special battle swords have superb inlay work, and those made from rust-free Mantikai iron with carved staghorn hilts are masterpieces. Kenyah *ukir mandau* are the finest; some very old and rare specimens are set with precious stones. In E. Kalimantan, knives are forged today from recycled steel chainsaw blades.

Dayak Crafts Of East Kalimantan

Visit Tering and Keliwai for Dayak Bahal crafts:

a typical Dayak motif engraved on a bamboo case

baskets, woven rattan mats, spears, and shields. Old Chinese stone trading beads can be bought in Tering and Melak. For a long chain of big blue-green stones *(malik)*, Rp10,000-plus; these are getting rarer now that tourists have been buying them up. Females of Tanjung and Benuaq (Bentian tribe) still wear *ta-ah*, bark and tree-root clothing. *Kelbit* (shields) and Dayak *hudog* (carved masks) make striking wall ornaments, as do lances made of *kayu besi*. *Sumpit* (blowpipes) are made of *ulin* wood. Dayak *biru*-leaf hats *(seraung)* are priced from Rp1500; *anjar* traveling bags last for years. Each tribe has its own style of painted mats. In Sabintulung village, Muara Kaman, women still make *purun* mats out of long swamp grass. *Ba'* baby and child carriers are covered in antique beads but very expensive—if you can even find them. Totem poles *(belongtong)* are still seen in many villages; you may be able to get smaller souvenir versions. The Bahau and Kenyah groups deep in the interior are masters of detailed ornamental woodcarving: handles, daggers, sheaths, also bone and horn engravings. For Kenyah crafts, Muara Ancalong village is best.

GETTING THERE

By Air

Flying to Kalimantan is easy, but expensive. Bouraq, Merpati, and Garuda all fly into the territory's major cities from other Indonesian islands, and have regular flights connecting Kalimantan airports. Bouraq and Merpati are generally less expensive than Garuda. All 3 carriers connect Balikpapan from Ujung Pandang (S. Sulawesi), Surabaya (E. Java), Jakarta, and Manado (N. Sulawesi). Balikpapan is the main destination for Garuda flights originating from Jakarta (Rp147,400; 4-5 times daily), and from Surabaya (Rp103,000; twice daily). From Jakarta, Merpati also flies to Pontianak (Rp69,200). And from Jakarta, Bouraq flies to Banjarmasin (Rp97,800; twice daily) and Balikpapan (Rp125,300; 3 times daily). Bouraq even flies 3 times weekly from Denpasar (Bali) to Banjarmasin (Rp94,500).

Overland treks between E. Malaysia (Sabah and Sarawak) and Kalimantan are out, though people manage it now and again. Also, going from one country to the other without a visa gets you jailed or deported. But you can fly. Tawau in Sabah, is a busy Chinese commercial city. A little-known connection between Malaysia and Indonesia is the Tawau-Tarakan Bali Air flight (M$100; 4 times weekly). It's sometimes full (or cancelled) so allow a few extra days before your visa expires. You'll need an Indonesian visa as Tarakan is not among the official entry points into Indonesia. Indonesia has consulates in Kucing (Sarawak) and Kota Kinabalu (Sabah). Unless you have a letter from Kota Kinabalu's main consular offices, Tawau's Wisma Indonesia won't issue visas to non-Malaysians; they just read newspapers. The Bali Air agent is Merdata Travel Service, 41 Dunlop St. (tel. 72531), Tawau. The Hong Kong and Shanghai Bank gives fairly good rates. On the other side of the island, Merpati has flights from Kucing, Sarawak, to Pontianak, W. Kalimantan, for Rp97,700. The land border between Sarawak and W. Kalimantan has been closed since 1975.

By Boat

Pelni and other companies connect Kalimantan (mostly E coast) with Java and Sulawesi. Take Pelni, for example, from Surabaya (E. Java) to Balikpapan for Rp32,000 Deck Class (shared cabins slightly more). Other passenger ships depart Surabaya for Banjarmasin twice weekly. From Jakarta (Tanjung Priok) a Pelni ship sails for Balikpapan for Rp36,000 (deck) via Surabaya and Ujung Pandang. Pelni also offers a Jakarta-Pontianak trip, 2 days, Rp37,000-plus with food (deck only). From Pare Pare or Ujung Padang (S. Sulawesi), take a frequent *kapal motor* to the E. Kalimantan coast.

Going by ship or boat from Palawan Island in the southern Philippines is more trouble than it's worth; you have all the usual official hassles plus the risk of piracy. But you can fly from Zamboanga to Tawau, then on to Tarakan, but you'll need an Indonesian visa first (get one in Manila, Singapore, or Kota Kinabalu). Boats sail from Tawau (Sabah) to Nunukan (E. Kalimantan) every Mon., Wed., and Fri. at 1400, departing from Tawau's customs pier. The cost is M$25 (2 hours). From Nunukan (E. Kalimantan) each day at 0500 a somewhat larger boat leaves for Tarakan; Rp8000 (8½ hours). In Tarakan, stay at **Losmen Zakarto**; Rp2500 s. From Tarakan the big Pelni ship MV *Kerinci* sails to Balikpapan in 3 days.

GETTING AROUND

No railways. The territory's 4 limited road systems—in Pontianak, Balikpapan/Samarinda, Banjarmasin, and from Banjarmasin to Samarinda—are fairly reliable, questionable only during the wet season. A widely used method of transport all over Kalimantan is on the back of a motorcycle as a paying passenger. As soon as you get off a bus in Banjarmasin, Balikpapan, or Samarinda, there'll be a gaggle of motorcycles there waiting to take you to your next destination for Rp400-500 per 2 km; these drivers are recognizable by the extra helmet hanging from the bike's handlebars.

Kalimantan's rivers are the island's main thoroughfares, traveled by *sampan* and motorized canoes *(ketinting)*, canopied rivercraft *(klotok)*, speedboats or longboats *(longbots)*, and ferries. Sea-going ships travel up the large rivers; daily ferries connect Banjarmasin and Palangkaraya; longboats run from Tarakan to both Berau and Nunukan. Airlines (Bouraq, Garuda, Merpati) fly regularly into the interior. MAF (Missionary Aviation Fellowship) has bases throughout Kalimantan; if space is available you can fly MAF into the most remote interior areas, and then from airstrip to airstrip. Pilots working for MAF and other missionary airlines are also their own mechanics. DAS (Dirgantara Air Service) has many interior flights. See "By Air" below.

Visas

If you plan to enter Indonesia through Kalimantan, first get an Indonesian visa; Kalimantan entry points don't issue 60-day tourist entry stamps on arrival. *Imigrasi* offices are only at Tarakan, Samarinda, Balikpapan, Banjarmasin, and Pontianak. In E. Malaysia, Indonesian consulates are at Kucing and Kota Kinabalu in Sarawak, and at Tawau in Sabah. If you run out of time while traveling in the interior, ask the local police to write you a covering letter.

Tours

If you have more money than time, **Sobek Expeditions** (Angels Camp, CA 95222, USA) offers a month-long "Indonesian Highlights" tour, which includes river trips in Kalimantan, Torajaland in S. Sulawesi, G. Bromo, plus visits to Bali, Sumatra, and Jakarta. Not cheap (US$3100). One of the most experienced domestic tour companies giving tours to E. Kalimantan is **P.T. Tomaco**, Jakarta Theatre Bldg., Jl. M.H. Thamrin 9, Jakarta (tel. 347453/354551/320087). Sample tours include the 3-day "Banuaq Package" to Tenggarong and Tanjung Isui, the 6-day "Enggang Package" to Muara Ancalong, plus helicoptor tours and customized special interest and/or adventure tours. They use local 20-m-long boats and provide basic facilities such as toilets, mattresses, and blankets. P.T. Tomaco has a branch office at Hotel Benakutai, Jl. P. Antasari, Balikpapan (tel. 21747/22747). Prices are around US$499 (4-7 persons), US$468 (8-12 persons), US$452 (13-16 persons).

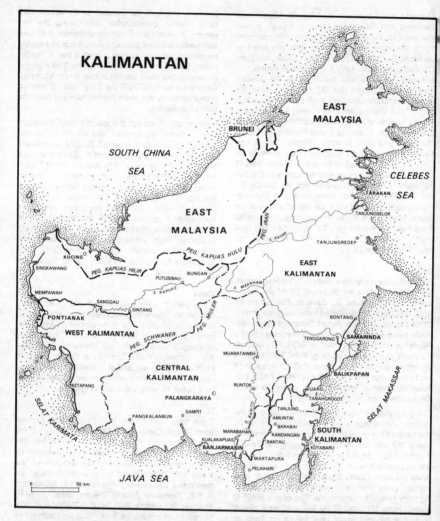

KALIMANTAN

SOUTH CHINA SEA

BRUNEI

EAST MALAYSIA

CELEBES SEA

TARAKAN

TANJUNGSELOR

EAST MALAYSIA

TANJUNGREDEP

EAST KALIMANTAN

KUCING

SINGKAWANG

PEG. KAPUAS HULU

MEMPAWAH

SANGGAU

PUTUSIBAU

BUNGAN

S. KAPUAS

PEG. KAPUAS HILIR

PEG. IRAN

S. KAYAN

S. MAKAHAM

BONTANG

SINTANG

PONTIANAK

WEST KALIMANTAN

PEG. SCHWANER

PEG. MULER

TENGGARONG

SAMARINDA

MUARATAWEH

KETAPANG

CENTRAL KALIMANTAN

BUNTOK

KUARO

BALIKPAPAN

TANAHGROGOT

PALANGKARAYA

S. BARITO

TANJUNG

AMUNTAI

SELAT MAKASSAR

PANGKALANBUN

SAMPIT

BARABAI

KANDANGAN

SOUTH KALIMANTAN

MARABAHAN

RANTAU

KUALAKAPUAS

BANJARMASIN

KOTABARU

MARTAPURA

PELAIHARI

JAVA SEA

SELAT KARIMATA

0   50 km

THE INTERIOR

Everyone going to Kalimantan is well advised to learn at least some rudimentary Indonesian. Also, anti-malarial pills should always be taken everywhere in Kalimantan (start 2 weeks before your arrival); it's best to take chloroquine (such as Resochin) *and* the non-chloroquine-type (Fansidar). Be sure to take all the *rupiah* you'll need; no banks or moneychangers can

be found in the interior. In Dayak country, the kindness and hospitality may be overwhelming. The head of the longhouse would love things like sunglasses or all your clothes; pencils and paper go over big with the kids.

Jungle Officialdom

Make contact through the handing-on of addresses ("I know somebody in a department..."). Maybe you can arrange to go upriver with a government party or on a police boat. Check in at the local police post or Kantor Camat (local government office) at each river stop, as sometimes you need their permission to travel. Officials in E. Kalimantan, especially in remote areas, are unusually helpful—even willing to help you find accommodations and food. Elsewhere (W. Kalimantan is a politically touchy area), they can be overbearing and officious at times, asking for your passport and surat jalan, and even searching you for weapons. Travel on until you find friendly ones; their sponsorship is valuable. Be aboveboard.

River Travel

Some stretches of Kalimantan's rivers are so long and wide that amphibious aircraft can land on them. Traveling the interior is cheapest by boat on major rivers like the Kapuas, Barito, and Mahakam, and their large tributaries. West to E is best (and cheaper), because you can often float downriver, avoiding fuel costs. For going beyond cities and trading villages you'll need specially designed rivercraft. Possibilities include a klotok or stempel (dangerous for night travel), a ketingting (small motorized canoes suitable for shallow water), or a longbot. Many boats are decorated with painted bloodshot eyes to guide them safely through treacherous waters. Skippers steer by using mangrove trees, mudbanks, stumps, and other natural features as markers. Upriver areas are closed to larger craft because currents and courses are unpredictable. Seasonal flooding could be lethal; during heavy rains, rivers may double in size within hours. The farther inland you travel, the less it costs to live.

By Air

Of all commercial airlines operating within Kalimantan, Bouraq offers the cheapest fares and the most extensive interior flight network. Also check with Merpati. If there's room, MAF and other missionary air services will gladly take paying passengers; if you make advance arrangements, MAF (Box 82, Samarinda; Box 18, Tarakan) will even pick you up at remote interior villages. Due to uneven demand, MAF flights out of the interior are half the price of the same trip in. Plan your trip accordingly. If you're into skyhitching, try to get rides on aircraft leaving Balikpapan's airport, one of the busiest in all Indonesia. There are missionary and mining planes, timber and oil company cargo carriers, Bell and Sikorsky choppers, Skyvans, Lear jets, DC-3s and DC-4s, Garuda jet carriers, even

private aircraft. From here, you can easily fly into the interior—or to virtually anywhere in Indonesia and SE Asia.

A popular thing to do now in E. Kalimantan is to fly with Merpati from Samarinda to Datah Dawai (200 m from Long Lunuk on the Upper Mahakam River; Rp30,000, leaving Mon. and Thurs. at 1000 or 1100. Then take a river bus downstream from Long Nunuk to Long Apari, Long Pahangai, then all the way to Rukun Damai at a cost of only Rp70,000 (for one, 3, or 20 people). (But if you want to head upstream (many waterfalls) from Rukun Damai to Long Lunuk, it'll cost you Rp175,000 and up.)

Trans-Borneo Treks

Rarely done—very rarely, in fact. Of the few successful coast-to-coast treks across Borneo's vast interior that have been made, the first was in 1897 by a Dutch group with 110 porters and bodyguards. In 1858 Robert Burns, the poet's grandson, tried. He lost his head while exploring the island's northern reaches. Two completed trips were announced in the mid-1980s. Four California adventurers, loaded down with the latest in high-tech Western wilderness gear and sponsored by the R.J. Reynolds Tobacco Company ("Camel Expeditions"), set out to cross Kalimantan from W to E (Pontianak to Tarakan) in July 1983. The team leader contracted typhoid and was airlifted out of the interior by a missionary pilot, but the remaining 3 finished the trip in 43 days—after wisely declining to run the formidable Embun rapids on E. Kalimantan's Kayan River. Their trip, launched in the tradition of intrepid exploration, was widely hailed as the first known expedition across the island. But another Californian, Eric Hansen, made an unpublicized roundtrip trans-Borneo trek just the year before. He took no sleeping bag, camping equipment, water, food, or medicine except anti-malarials, traveling alone—without government permission—from Malaysia S into Kalimantan. "If you travel like the native people, you don't have to bring anything," Hansen said later. "And you don't destroy the culture." He got along well with the remote Dayak tribes he encountered. "The key to getting along with these people is making a complete fool out of yourself," including dancing dressed only in a loincloth, feather headdress, and bearskin vest. "If you can do that, they trust you."

EAST KALIMANTAN

With an area of 211,500 sq km, E. Kalimantan is 1½ times the size of Java. Most rain falls between Nov. and May in this land laced by rivers, swamps, and rainforests. Hundreds of different orchid varieties grow here, including the rare black orchid; exotic animals include orangutans, proboscis monkeys, barking deer, bearded wild pigs, freshwater river dolphins, pythons. About 800,000 people live in the province (roughly 1% of Java's population), giving it an average density of 4 persons per sq km. Most live in coastal cities and major river towns.

It was on the Mahakam River that Hindu culture first arrived in Indonesia, in around A.D. 400. Traditional culture and animist beliefs are practiced in isolated areas, but many tribes are thoroughly Christianized. Joseph Conrad visited Berau and Tanjungredeb 4 times, using "that Settlement hidden in the heart of the forest-land, up that sombre stream" as the setting for his first 2 novels, *Almayer's Folly* and *An Outcast of the Islands,* as well as the second part of *Lord Jim.*

Economy

East Kalimantan is prized in modern times as a major oil and natural gas producing area; its timber exports are also critical to the Indonesian economy. Between 1968 and 1978, the province produced 25% of the country's total export earnings, the value of its exports outstripping those of the other 3 Kalimantan provinces combined. Balikpapan is the province's

petroleum industry capital, while Samarinda is its timber capital. These dynamic, relatively wealthy urban centers are surrounded by rural native settlements, their economies based on subsistence *ladang* cultivation. Crops include coconuts, rubber, coffee, pepper, and cloves; Dayak tribes customarily grow hill rice. The forests of E. Kalimantan have been ruthlessly logged, with more than 20 million ha of concessions granted by 1982. Logging trails gouged by bulldozers now push deep into the virgin forests, the timber concessions widening their paths of destruction, with no end in sight.

The Great Fire

Through late 1982 and the first quarter of 1983, the forests of E. Kalimantan suffered a grievous blow when millions of hectares of forests were destroyed. Ranking as one of the worst man-made ecological catastrophes in history, the "Great Fire" destroyed more than 20% of the province's rainforests. For months on end, ships off Balikpapan had to drop anchor because of poor visibility, the midday sun over much of the province was just a pale yellow orb in the sky, and at Singapore's airport 1,400 km to the W flights were cancelled because of the grey-brown haze which hung over that city. In all, 3½ million ha of forest were destroyed, equal to an area the size of Holland, and dozens of species of plants and animals were wiped off the face of the planet. Experts have attributed the Great Fire to a pattern of unrestrained commercial logging activities. Logging debris on the forest floor served to kindle the flames, and because of widespread forest destruction, the remaining forests could no longer supply the moisture necessary to subdue the effects of the fire. As evidence of this, the primeval Kutai National Park escaped destruction even though the logged area surrounding it was completely engulfed in flames.

Getting There

One of Indonesia's busiest airports is 8 km W of Balikpapan at Sepinggan. Hitch into town with an oil company car or bus; taxis cost about Rp3000-4000 pp, or walk 2 km to the main road and take a local taxi *kijang* (Rp500). The airport has a bank (good rates), snack bar, post office counter, and offices for Garuda, Merpati, Air Fast, Bali Air, and Pertamina. Merpati has flights connecting Ujung Pandang, Rp89,200; Surabaya, Rp80,200; Jakarta, Rp115,400; and Manado, Rp97,800; Gorontalo (N. Sulawesi), Rp80,900. Bouraq flies into another airport, Rp2500 by taxi from downtown Balikpapan, from: Palu (C. Sulawesi), Rp52,900;

Semarang, Rp111,900; and Yogya, Rp106,700. Garuda has more expensive connections from Palangkaraya (every day), Rp60,800; Pontianak, Rp109,900; Surabaya, Rp105,100, and Jakarta, Rp149,500.

From Banjarmasin in S. Kalimantan, buses and other vehicles make the 12-hour (Rp13,000) trip to Penajam, across the bay from Balikpapan. Speedboats cross frequently to Kampung Baru in Balikpapan (Rp1200 pp). From Samarinda, cross the Mahakam River at Pasar Pagi by ferry, then take a bus to Rapak Station in Balikpapan (2 hours, Rp2000).

Boats leave for Nunukan, E. Kalimantan, from Tawau (Sabah, E. Malaysia) on Mon., Wed., and Fri., costing M$25 (2 hours). However, since Nunukan is not an official entry point you need an Indonesian visa. From Nunukan to Tarakan costs Rp10,000 (8-9 hours). From Tarakan, take the plane to Balikpapan for Rp62,500. Boats, mostly wood-hulled *kapal motor*, also cross every 2-3 days from Pare Pare (S. Sulawesi) to Balikpapan. Pelni *(Kambuna* and the *Kerinci)*, as well as other shipping companies, provides less frequent service from Surabaya and other Indonesian ports.

BALIKPAPAN

Once a tiny fishing village fringed by tropical forest, Balikpapan is now a booming oil town and port city — the major economic transport center of E. Kalimantan. The people of Balikpapan are ultra friendly and helpful. The discovery of coastal oil and gas here in the late 1960s quickly transformed traditional village life in the area. Many American, European, and Australian oil and timber company employees ("oilies" and "chippies") work here or in nearby Badak, where there are gas liquefaction and fertilizer production plants. Foreign workers live either in modern pre-fab camps or in housing provided by Pertamina; most of the remainder of the population of the area are less indulged. Stay one-2 days to see the combined effects of the oil boom and Indonesian cultural mixing: once-feared Dayaks serve cocktails to expatriates in air-conditioned bars and nightclubs ("Tornado") on hills overlooking fishing *kampung*. The city has no central district; it just sprawls. New, expensive buildings are surrounded by trash piles and sewage ditches. All the main public buildings — mayor's office, a number of big banks, police station, immigration office, etc. — are on Jl. Jen. A. Yani which runs along the Makassar Strait to the south. Americans, Australians, Europeans, and high-placed Indonesians live on hills overlooking the town. The oil companies have recreation facilities, but only for employees. Walk up Pasir Ridge to the Union Oil Complex to see this "other world" of manicured lawns and trees, swimming pools, and modern suburban homes. Below are

crowded *kampung,* and Pertamina's oil refinery complex — a landscape of gas flares, pipes, tanks, and girders.

Sights

Taman Hiburan Tunas Remaja is Balikpapan's zoo and botanical gardens. You get the best view of Balikpapan from **Tanki I,** Gunung Dubbs. To the N of the oil refinery is a whole neighborhood of houses on stilts connected by wooden walkways over a muddy estuary. In a row of houses down on the harbor, women are for sale on a temporary basis; this service was set up for Muslims who'd come far from home to work at the refineries or on the rigs but now provides short-term "wives" for oilies and chippies. These teenage women, mostly Javanese, do washing, cooking, and other wifely tasks, receiving a hefty bonus when their "husbands" leave.

There's an enormous, highly organized brothel called Lembah Harapan ("Valley of Hope") in an army camp: a long row of whitewashed huts, with about 300 rather worn-out Surabayan prostitutes per hut. Kids cover up your license plate numbers so no one can spot you, and even clean your car while you're taking care of business. Closed on Thurs. for "housecleaning" (seeing the doctor) and resting up for the big weekend. The favorite sport at the Hotel Balikpapan is staring at women on display behind the glass wall, like watching a fishbowl. More relaxing is having a

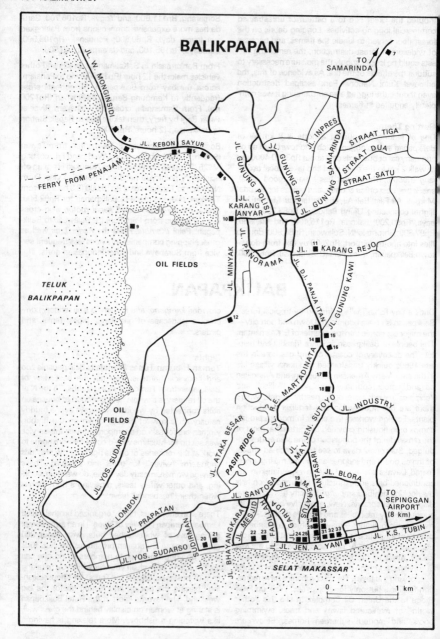

BALIKPAPAN

TO SAMARINDA

JL. W. MONGINSIDI

JL. KEBON SAYUR

FERRY FROM PENAJAM

TELUK BALIKPAPAN

OIL FIELDS

OIL FIELDS

JL. GUNUNG POLISI

JL. KARANG ANYAR

JL. MINYAK

JL. PANORAMA

JL. INPRES

JL. GUNUNG PIPA

JL. GUNUNG SAMARINDA

STRAAT TIGA

STRAAT DUA

STRAAT SATU

JL. KARANG REJO

JL. D.I. PANJA ITAN

JL. GUNUNG KAWI

JL. R.E. MARTADINATA

JL. INDUSTRY

JL. MAY. JEN. SUTOYO

JL. ATAKA BESAR

PASIR RIDGE

JL. YOS. SUDARSO

JL. LOMBOK

JL. PRAPATAN

JL. YOS. SUDARSO

JL. SUDIRMAN

JL. BHAYANGKARA

JL. MESJID

JL. FADILLAH

JL. SANTOSA

JL. GARUDA

JL. MERATUS

JL. P. ANTASARI

JL. BLORA

TO SEPINGGAN AIRPORT (8 km)

JL. JEN. A. YANI

JL. K.S. TUBIN

SELAT MAKASSAR

0   1 km

drink in the bars (not whorehouses) such as the Blue Sky Hotel which has pool tables, pinball, and massage.

PRACTICALITIES

Accommodations

Look for foreign faces; maybe someone can put you up. As in all boom towns, expect to pay more for accommodations; most are in the middle price range (Rp9000-18,000). About the cheapest you'll find is family-run **Peng. Lumayan**, Jl. Panjaitan 49; Rp6000 s, Rp10,000 d for small but clean rooms with fan. In Kampung Baru, try **Hotel Kal Tim**, Jl. J. Suprapto 6, Rp6000 s or d (Rp13,000 s or d with a/c), or the **Hotel**

BALIKPAPAN

1. Bina Bersara
2. Hotel Kam Tim
3. Pasar Baru
4. 169 Hotel
5. Hotel Pandan Sari
6. Susila Art Shop
7. bus station to Samarinda
8. Hotel Blue Sky
9. Pompa Air Asin
10. Pasir Kebun Sayur
11. Cinema Nusantara
12. Wisma Parta
13. Tirta Plaza
14. Wisma Aida
15. Pasar Senang
16. Hotel Murni
17. public hospital
18. Warung Segeri *(ikan bakar)*
19. Sweet Sixteen Nightclub
20. Kantor Imigrasi
21. post office
22. Pasar Klandasan
    & Mesjid Jami Attagwo
23. Hotel Sederhana
24. police
25. Bank Negara Indonesia 1946
26. Garuda office
27. Grand Park Hotel
28. Atomic Restaurant
29. Bank Dagang Negara
30. Hotel Benakutai
31. moneychanger
32. Kentucky Fried Chicken
33. Hotel Royal
34. Pasar Baru bus stop

Bina Bersama, fairly clean with a balcony over the harbor. At Jl. Panjaitan 31 is **Peng. Murni**, Rp6500 s, Rp12,000 d for small, drab rooms with *mandi*; located on a noisy street corner right over a *nasi padang* restaurant.

With a fancy front but unprepossessing interior, **Wisma Aida**, Jl. D.I. Penjaitan 50 (tel. 21006), wants Rp8000-10,000 s, Rp12,000-15,000 d, deluxe Rp17,500 s, Rp20,000 d (in the back). Low-priced rooms are small but clean, with fan. The **Tirta Plaza**, Jl. D.I. Panjaitan 51-52 (tel. 22324/22132), is an American-style hotel with swimming pool; Rp10,000 s, 15,000 d for non-a/c with bath, or Rp19,000 s, Rp24,000 d with a/c. Bungalows, Rp30,000. To all prices add 21% tax and service. Cheaper rates on the weekends. Between Pasar Baru and the post office, in the S part of town, are: very central and rather plain **Hotel Sederhana**, Jl. A. Yani 290 (next to Bioskop Gelora); Rp21,175-24,000 up to Rp30,250 d for a/c rooms. Cheaper rooms in the *penginapan* of the same name in the same building; Rp7,260-10,285 s or d. **Hotel Puri Kencana**, Jl. Gajah Mada 11, Rp10,500 s, Rp13,500 d with bath (Rp15,500 s, Rp18,000 d with a/c). Also check out the **Hotel Djelita** on the same street.

The **Mirama Hotel**, Jl. May. Jen. Sutoyo (across the street from a baked seafood place), has a nice a/c lobby; Rp25,000 s or Rp32,500 1st Class—both classes include breakfast. On a N extension of Jl. Antasari is the **Noor Hotel**, Jl. Gunung Sari Ilir IX 5; Rp10,000 s, Rp15,000 d with *mandi*. The **Grand Park Hotel** on Jl. P. Antasari (tel. 22942) has full a/c (Rp18,000 s, 19,000 d) plus 21% tax. Also on Jl. P. Antasari (near the Benakutai and opposite the Garuda office) is the spacious **Hotel Budiman**; Rp23,000-25,000 for a/c rooms—good downtown location. The newest of Balikpapan's international-class hotels is the 5-star 216-room **Benakutai Hotel** (the big 11-story building you see when flying into Balikpapan), Jl. P. Antasari (tel. 21804/21813). Managed by the very capable Herman Diener, these are luxury digs catering to oilies, chippies, and tourists (cheapest rooms are US$90 plus 21% tax!).

Food

Most food is brought in from Sulawesi and Java, so prices are high. The city's diverse Indonesian population is reflected in the selection—*martabak*, noodle dishes, and specialties of Palembang, Banjar, Padang, Sunda, Java, and China. *Warung* are scattered throughout the town, busiest at night. For fancier eating, Jl. P. Antasari is an excellent place to look for restaurants. Splurge at the **Seafood Restaurant** at Hotel Benakutai; the cost is high (about Rp3500 per course) but food and service are superb. Try the grill downstairs for hamburgers and other foreign exotica. The **Atomic** is a highly overrated Chinese restaurant (many foreigners eat here) at Jl. P. Antasari 8, but has delicious chili crayfish.

The **Rainbow Coffee Shop and Restaurant** in the Blue Sky Hotel, Jl. Suprapto 1 (tel. 22267/22268), is expensive but popular with expatriates, serving incomparable seafood, especially the abalone. If you're hungry for very reasonably priced sirloin, try the **Barunawati** near the harbor—the best steakhouse in town. For Padang-style food, eat well and reasonably at **Minang Saiyo**, Jl. Gajah Mada 45, and similar places nearby. For Indonesian, Chinese, and European fare, head for the **Mirama**, in Hotel Mirama, Jl. Let. Soetoyo (tel. 561/562). Modern **Holland Bakery**, Jl. Gunungsari 3, has baked goods, hot dogs, ice cream, and 15 types of sundaes. Great *rambutan* in January.

Services And Information
The post office on Jl. J. Yani (S side of town) will hold *poste restante* mail for travelers. **Banks** and one moneychanger are on Jl. P. Antasari near intersection of Jl. Gajah Mada. Be sure to get all the *rupiah* you could possibly need before heading into the interior, where there are *no* banks. Banks in Balikpapan give the best rates in E. Kalimantan, but rates vary so shop around. (Exchange rates in Samarinda and Tarakan are only slightly lower.) Travelers cheques give the best return at banks, but don't cash them with a moneychanger.

Crafts
Susila Art Shop, Jl. Let. Suprapto 7 RT 17 RW 6 (tel. 24586), past the Blue Sky Hotel, is a marvelous, very representative craft shop specializing in E. Kalimantan (Dayak) and C. Kalimantan handicrafts, as well as Chinese porcelain. A wide range of rattan ware, weavings, beads, statuary, huge Ming Dynasty vases, *mandau*, etc., at good prices. Another more touristy souvenir shop closer to town is the **Syahda Mestika**, Jl. S. Parman RT VIII/147, and yet another shop is in Hotel Benakutai, both with higher prices. A real good buy in Balikpapan are 200- to 400-year-old Ming and Ching dynasty ceramics originally from the kingdom of Kutai to the N; small plates cost only Rp12,000-15,000.

TRANSPORT

Arriving
Taxis from Sepinggan Airport to your hotel in Balikpapan cost Rp7000, or you can walk or hitch out to the highway (3 km), then catch a *kijang* into town for only Rp400. From the airport you can also charter a taxi direct to Samarinda, Rp35,000 (but only Rp20,000 from Balikpapan); Tenggarong, Rp40,000; Pasar Baru (where you board minibuses for Penajam and then down to Banjarmasin), Rp25,000.

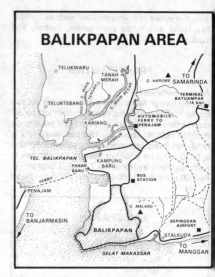

BALIKPAPAN AREA

Getting Around
Balikpapan is too spread out to walk everywhere, but hundreds of *kijang* (which look like armored personnel carriers) are the best all-round transport, running frequently along the main streets and costing Rp200-400. Let the driver know when you want to get out by simply yelling "Stop!"—no Indonesian required! Local *kijang* transport helps in finding addresses, which can be difficult as names for the same street change every few blocks. Major *kijang* terminals are **Pasar Baru** in the S, **Terminal Penajam** across Teluk Balikpapan, and **Terminal Batuampar** on the road to Samarinda in the north. Catch taxis at large hotels and minibus terminals. Anywhere in town one can also ride piggyback on a motorcycle. For example, a *honda ojek* ride from Jl. Panorama to Terminal Batuampar should cost around Rp500 (first price: Rp1000). There's no need to rent a *kijang* to see Balikpapan, but if you're so inclined they rent for only Rp2000-3000 per hour (regular taxis Rp4000-5000 per hour, minimum 2 hours).

Tours
See P.T. Tomaco (tel. 21747/22747) in the Hotel Benakutai on Jl. P. Antasari for E. Kalimantan river tours. Their head office is in the Jakarta Theatre Bldg., Jl. M.H. Thamrin 9, tel. 347453/354551/320087. Mahakam River trips are offered to such places as Tanjung Isui, Data Bilang, Rukun Dami, and Tering; cost is about US$100 pp per day, depending on group size. If time is short and money long, this agency can also arrange a helicopter day trip to Tanjung Isui from the hotel's rooftop helipad.

FROM BALIKPAPAN

Flights

From Pasar Baru to Sepinggan Airport it's 15 km, Rp5000 by *kijang* or Rp7000 by taxi. Bouraq and Merpati both fly to Banjarmasin for around Rp47,000. Garuda to Banjarmasin is Rp55,200. Other Garuda fares to: Pontianak, every day except Sun., Rp107,900; Jakarta, 4 times daily, Rp147,400; Surabaya, 2 flights daily, Rp103,000. Sample Bouraq fares to: Pontianak, Rp91,600; Ujung Pandang, Rp102,600; Yogya, Rp125,500; Ternate (N. Maluku), Rp179,600; Manado, Rp135,000. Bouraq also flies to: Samarinda, Rp31,500; Tarakan, Rp72,000; Ternate, Rp177,300.

Bali Air and Fast Air fly Islanders and other small planes on charter. Flights from Balikpapan include Rp300 insurance fee and Rp1500 tax. Bali Air flies to Samarinda (Rp23,300) and also has scheduled Balikpapan-Samarinda-Tarakan and Tarakan-Tawau (Sabah, Malaysia) flights. Bouraq is across the parking lot of the Hotel Benakutai, and the main Garuda office is just down the street in front of Hotel Budiman; open Mon.-Thurs. 0700-1400, Fri. and Sat. 0700-1300, Sun. 0900-1200. For other flights connecting other Indonesian cities, see "Getting There" above.

For the Philippines, either fly first to Tawau (E. Malaysia) with Bali Air for Rp40,000, then fly with MAS from Tawau to Kota Kinabalu for M$80 and on to Manila. Or else fly with Bouraq to Tarakan for Rp72,000 (one hour), then from Tarakan to Zamboanga, Mindanao. Other possibilities include Pertamina's Pelita flights to Bontong (oil base), Tanjung Santan, Tarakan, and to the Bunju Islands. The Pelita office is at the airport.

Other Departures

Board *kijang* to Terminal Batuampar (Kilo Empat) from where it's only 2½ hours and 113 km (Rp1500) by bus to Samarinda on the new paved road. Another way to Samarinda is to take a *kijang* to Pasar Baru (Rp450), then board a *spetbot* along the coast and then upriver to Samarinda (60 km). This trip takes 5 hours, and the price has come down due to competition with the new road.

From Terminal Batuampar, take a *kijang* (Rp450) to Kampung Baru, then get a *spetbot* (Rp500) over to Penajam. Chartered taxis and buses also depart Penajam to Banjarmasin and other points south. For Pare Pare (2 days, Rp14,000) and other Sulawesi destinations, check the boat offices near the Kampung Baru piers. All major Indonesian shipping companies have boats arriving and departing Balikpapan Harbor. For example, Pelni's KM *Kerinci* and KM *Kambuna* call every 2 weeks.

You can find yourself deep in the interior of Kalimantan quite suddenly by air. Missionary Aviation Fellowship (MAF) pilots take passengers in small Cessnas to Long Nawang and other mission stations on a space-available basis; government officials fly in missionary planes because there's little other transport so deep into Borneo. MAF has many interior airstrips; planes are based at Samarinda, Long Bai, and Tarakan. (See "Samarinda" chapter.)

VICINITY OF BALIKPAPAN

Get on the Union Oil boat just past Banana Town and take it out to very pretty Lawi Lawi Beach. Twenty km S of Balikpapan is **Panggar** (Rp300-500 from Pasar Baru), a quiet black-sand beach (crowded on Sun.). Visit the oil rigs if you can go as a guest of one of the oil companies; after flying over miles of jungle and landing on helicopter pads, you'll discover in amazement that the rigs are manned by men who look (and sound) like sheriffs from Texas. Many of the helicopter pilots are Vietnam vets who have never gone home, drifting instead around SE Asia since the war. Look for experimental reforestation stations, where Caribbean pine, Indonesian albizzia, and eucalyptus have been planted.

Penajam

A small town on the W side of Teluk Balikpapan and the starting point on the road S to Banjarmasin. From Penajam the road winds slowly through scenic mountain country before dropping to the S. Kalimantan plains. Kuaro is a junction town on the road between Penajam, 114 km N, and Banjarmasin, 362 km south. Stay at Peng. Isniba, Rp3000/5000; several *warung*. The road is rough gravel near the S. Kalimantan border; paving work and bridge upgrading are an unremitting fact of life here.

From Penajam, Balikpapan is 15 min. by small ferry (Rp500), leaving frequently. Can be a wet ride, so keep a poncho handy to cover yourself and your gear. Harapan Indah buses leave for Banjarmasin from 1100 to 1400; Damri buses leave about 1600. More expensive than buses, station wagons and cars leave for Banjarmasin or intermediate towns at any time, day or night. Bus prices and travel times from Penajam: Tanahgrogot, Rp 3500 (3 hours); Tanjung, Rp9000 (6 hours); Amuntai, Rp10,500 (7 hours); Barabai, Rp10,500 (8 hours); Kandangan, Rp11,000 (9 hours); and Banjarmasin, Rp12,000 (12 hours).

Tanahgrogot

Capital of the Pasir Regency and starting point on the river trip to the site of the old kingdom of Pasir Belengkong, 28 km SE of Kuaro. A branch of Sungai Kandilo (or Kendillo) flows through town, clogged with small boat traffic. The mixed population is

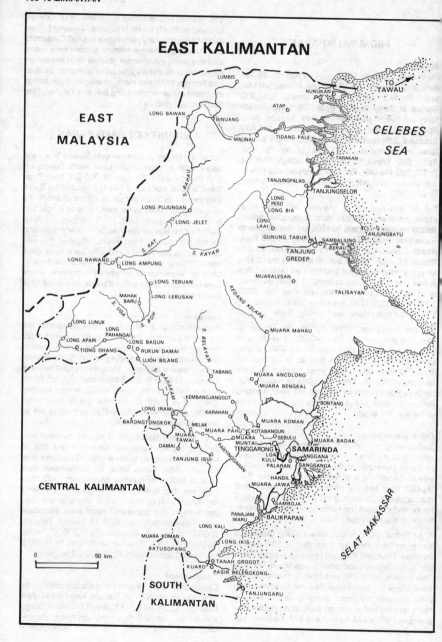

EAST KALIMANTAN

EAST MALAYSIA

CELEBES SEA

TO TAWAU

NUNUKAN

LUMBIS

LONG BAWAN

ATAP

BINUANG

TIDANG PALE

MALINAU

TARAKAN

TANJUNGPALAS

S. BAHAU

TANJUNGSELOR

LONG PESO

LONG PUJUNGAN

LONG BIA

LONG JELET

LONG LAAI

GUNUNG TABUR

SAMBALIUNG

TANJUNGBATU

S. KAT

S. KAYAN

TANJUNG GREDEP

S. BERAU

LONG NAWANG

LONG AMPUNG

MUARALESAN

LONG TEBUAN

KEDANG KELAPA

TALISAYAN

MAHAK BARU

LONG LEBUSAN

S. UGA

S. BOH

LONG LUNUK

LONG PAHANGAI

MUARA MAHAU

LONG APARI

TIONG OHANG

LONG BAGUN

S. BELAYAN

RUKUN DAMAI

UJOH BILANG

TABANG

MUARA ANCOLONG

MUARA BENGKAL

S. MAHAKAM

KEMBANGJANGGUT

BONTANG

LONG IRAM

KARAHAN

MUARA KOMAN

BARONGTONGKOK

MELAK

MUARA PAHU

KOTABANGUN

MUARA BADAK

MUARA TAWAI

SEBULU

DAMAI

PANYINGGAHAN

MUARA MUNTAI

TENGGARONG

SAMARINDA

TANJUNG ISUI

LOA KULU

ANGGANA

PALARAN

SANGSANGA

CENTRAL KALIMANTAN

HANDIL

MUARA JAWA

SAMBOJA

PANAJAM

WARU

BALIKPAPAN

LONG KALI

SELAT MAKASSAR

MUARA KOMAN

LONG IKIS

BATUSOPANG

0   50 km

KUARO

TANAH GROGOT

PASIR BELENGKONG

SOUTH KALIMANTAN

TANJUNGARU

predominantly Muslim, of the Bugis and Banjar groups. Inland are a few Dayak including the Basap, Benuaq, and Buroq Moto tribes. The Buroq or "Mata Putih" are noted for their unusually light-colored eyes. Industries of the Pasir regency are farming, fishing, lumbering, rattan harvesting, some nickel mining. In Tanahgrogot, stay at **Peng. Sederhana** or **Peng. Sabar**, both central; Rp2500 s, Rp5000 d. Better and more expensive are **Wisma Rindang** on Jl. Kartini and **Wisma Ilham** on Jl. Pasar Pagi. Small *warung* are scattered around town. Market days Mon. and Thursdays.

For Tanahgrogot, take frequent minibuses from Penajam (Balikpapan), 3 hours, Rp4000, and from Kuaro, 45 min., Rp1500. Heading S from Tanahgrogot involves changing vehicles in Kuaro (buses and cars are often full) or going all the way back to Penajam.

Pasir Belengkong Kingdom

A place long forgotten by the outside world. But the people of Belengkong village remember and carefully maintain the former sultan's palace, small museum, and mosque. The kingdom, founded in 1565, was known as Sadurangas. The Dutch "purchased" Pasir Kingdom in 1906 from Sultan Ibrahim. The "sale" didn't go over well with the local aristocracy, but the Dutch quickly put down their rebellion and exiled the sultan, ending the kingdom. The old palace is architecturally unusual, with beautiful floral woodcarvings, Koranic inscriptions, a pair of baroque figures (half-human, half-flying horse), and latticework. Now a museum, the building houses a small collection of Chinese dragon jars, locally made pottery, old Dayak carvings, gongs, and small cannon. These old relics are still considered magical and sacred by the local people; the cannon are wrapped in cloths and draped with strands of flowers, and small offerings may be burning nearby. The sultan's mosque, still used by the village, is next door.

Pasir Belengkong is 45 min. by boat downriver from Tanahgrogot. The river trip is great fun; as you cruise past tropical greenery and the river people's small wood houses, look for riverside platforms where sago palm workers tread the pulp and wash out the flour. Easiest and cheapest is to go on Pasir Belengkong's market days (Sun. and Wed.), with boats leaving Tanahgrogot around sunrise and returning midday, Rp750 each way. Other days, negotiate for a boat ride or charter a *ketingting* for around Rp8000.

SAMARINDA

Sixty km upstream from the mouth of the Mahakam River, Samarinda is the capital of E. Kalimantan, half the size of Balikpapan. You can see the giant silver-domed Mesjid Raya gleaming in the sun as you approach this city of countless government offices, busy ports, and sawmills lining the river. A trading town established in 1730, Samarinda is cheaper and more easygoing than Balikpapan. Be wary of snatch thieves on the street. Its location on the northern bank of the Mahakam with low hills in the background as you come upriver is lovely. At this point, the Mahakam is up to 5 km wide at high water and deep enough to accommodate sea-going ships. Logs, often tied together into timber rafts, float everywhere, and modern hand sawmills line the river's banks. All manner of watercraft chug back and forth on the river. Taxiboats depart frequently for upstream destinations, making Samarinda the natural starting point for trips to Dayak villages.

Shopping And Sights

Sellers of gold, and precious and semi-precious stones are found in the market along Jl. P. Batur (try Toko Intan Jaya); several souvenir shops selling Dayak handicrafts are also found along this street. Hotel Sukarni sells Bugis *sarung*. Sebarang, just across the Mahakam, is known for its finely woven *sarung*. Bugis women use a simple loom called the *gedokan;* at least 150 weavers work in Samarinda. Traditionally, *sutera* (silk) thread is used for *sarung samarinda*, woven in many designs and colors and made to last 100 years. Prices start at Rp25,000 but can be reduced a bit by bargaining. Many shops sell these fabrics, but there are also many imitation *sarung* going for the same price. Pasar Pagi is Samarinda's biggest market; other markets are Pasar Sungai Dama over the bridge S of town, and Pasar Segiri in the north.

Mulawarman University has several campuses scattered around town, with the main campus to the far north; ask for Jailani at the university, a fluent English-speaker and extremely knowledgeable and useful, who understands Westerners' needs. Samarinda's red-light district is Air Biru, which charges admission and is closed Thurs.; another one is at Kilo 10 (get an *ojek* from Sebarang). Rent a motorbike and drive along the road from Sebarang to Tenggarong; lumber mills line both sides of the river, hungrily contributing to the ecological carnage of E. Kalimantan. Climb the hills NE of Samarinda to get a look at countryside ravaged by the timber concessions.

Accommodations

Losmen Hidayah, Jl. Abdul Hasan, wants Rp5500 s, Rp8000 for double beds, up to Rp15,000 for inside *mandi*. Upstairs rooms, with outside *mandi*, are

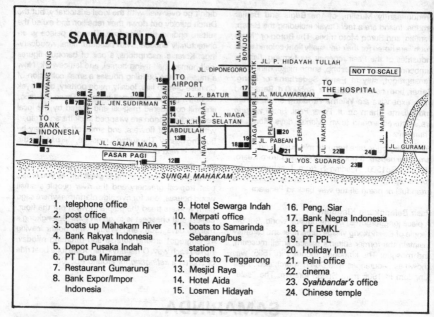

SAMARINDA

NOT TO SCALE

TO AIRPORT

TO THE HOSPITAL

TO BANK INDONESIA

PASAR PAGI

SUNGAI MAHAKAM

1. telephone office
2. post office
3. boats up Mahakam River
4. Bank Rakyat Indonesia
5. Depot Pusaka Indah
6. PT Duta Miramar
7. Restaurant Gumarung
8. Bank Expor/Impor Indonesia
9. Hotel Sewarga Indah
10. Merpati office
11. boats to Samarinda Sebarang/bus station
12. boats to Tenggarong
13. Mesjid Raya
14. Hotel Aida
15. Losmen Hidayah
16. Peng. Siar
17. Bank Negra Indonesia
18. PT EMKL
19. PT PPL
20. Holiday Inn
21. Pelni office
22. cinema
23. *Syahbandar's* office
24. Chinese temple

cheaper. Lots of travelers stay here. For the money, their Rp5500 rooms are the nicest in town. Be sure to ask for a fan. For other cheapies, continue N up the same street: **Peng. Siar**, no. 213, Rp3500 s, Rp6000 d; the fancier **Hotel Rahayu**, no. 17, asks Rp5000 s, Rp9000 d, and Rp12,000 s, Rp15,000 d with *mandi*; 21% tax and service must be added. No a/c but fans, spacious, clean though dark, and central; eat at Depot Mirasa across the street. **Hotel Andika**, Jl. A. Salim 37 (tel. 22358), Rp9000 s, Rp15,000 d (Rp11,500 s, Rp18,500 d with *mandi)*, is much cleaner. **Gelora Hotel**, Jl. Niaga Selatan 34 (tel. 22024), Rp14,000 for economy (upstairs) rooms up to Rp25,000 for VIP (a/c) rooms. All rooms have *mandi*. Close to the harbor and bars, many sailors stay here. Friendly front desk. Across the river in Sebarang, stay in quieter **Losmen Loupathy** down a lane (Gang 8) off of Jl. Antasari.

Downtown, medium-priced hotels include: **Hotel Jakarta**, Jl. Jen. Sudirman 57 (tel. 22624), Rp6000 s or d; **Hotel Diana Mas**, Jl. Petran 3/8 (tel.21882), Rp5,500 s, Rp9000 d; and **Hotel Hayani**, Jl. Pirus 17 (tel. 22653), Rp9,500 s, Rp12,800 d with *mandi* and breakfast. Near the port is the **Holiday Inn** (not part of the chain), Jl. Pelabuhan 29 (tel. 21185). **Hotel Sukarni**, Jl. P. Batur 154, has all classes of rooms from Rp7500-20,000 d; looks out over Pasar Kaltim which is also a minibus station and where you can eat at night. No a/c rooms, all have fans.

Higher-priced hotels include the **Hotel Sewarga**, Jl. Sudirman 43 (tel. 22066), with room service, bar, coffee shop, steakhouse, gift shop, travel service, central a/c, etc.; Rp15,000 s, Rp18,000 d, up to Rp26,000 s, Rp29,000 d for standard rooms. Their Rp15,000 room is a pretty good deal for Samarinda. Top-of-the-line **Hotel Mesra** on a hilltop at Jl. Pahlawan 1 (tel. 21011) has full luxury facilities with tennis court, swimming pool, golf course, full a/c, restaurants, nice location; Rp20,000 s for economy rooms, up to Rp45,000 d for deluxe-class doubles (plus 21% tax and service charge). For a small fee, visitors may use the pool. Nearby is another expensive hotel, the **Lamin Indah** at Jl. Bayangkara 57.

Food
Jalan Abdul Hasan gets real busy at night with stalls selling *sate, martabak,* and various *soto.* Fruit *(nangka, salak,* bananas, pineapples, etc.) can be found in stalls around **Terminal Kaltim** and along Jl. Adbul Hasan. At **Holiday Inn** (Jl. Pelabuhan), **Ramayana Restaurant** (Jl. Yos. Sudarso), and at **Lamin Indah** (Jl. Bayangkara 57) are hostesses. There's an abundance of freshwater and saltwater fish in Samarinda; a specialty is *udang galah* (giant river shrimp). The best Kalimantan-style river fish is found at **Restoran Haur Gading**, Rp5000 for an average meal. More expensive restaurants include: the **Sari Bundo**, Jl. P. Batur; Chinese food at **Lezat**

Baru, Jl. Mulawarman 34, and **Lamin Indah**, Jl. Bayangkara 57. Expensive hotels such as Mesra also offer Western food. Excellent Indonesian food at **RM Gumarang**, right next to the travel agency P.T. Duta Miramar on Jl. Jen. Sudirman, and branches on Jl. Sulawesi and Jl. Veteran. Just around the corner at Jl. Veteran 63, there's a great *soto ayam* (Rp1400) place, **Depot Pusaka Indah**.

Services And Information

Visit the E. Kalimantan **tourist office** in Gedung Nasional on Jl. P. Batur, the building with the Dayak shields outside. They have maps and brochures and will try to answer questions. The **post office** is on the corner of Jl. Awanglong and Jl. Gajah Mada. *Imigrasi* is at Jl. A. Yamin (near RRI). The **public library** is at Jl. Sutoyo Kompleks Prefab Segiri. Change money at **Bank Expor Impor Indonesia**, next to the Sewarga Indah Hotel. **Bank Negara Indonesia**, is on the corner of Jl. P. Batur and Jl. Sebatik; their hours are Mon.-Thurs. 0800-1230, until 1130 on Fri. and Saturday. Take plenty of *rupiah* if heading upriver. **P.T. Duta Miramar**, Jl. Jen. Sudirman 20 (tel. 23385), sells Garuda, Bouraq, and Merpati tickets, and offers tours up the Mahakam River.

Getting There And Around

Bouraq flies to Samarinda from: Balikpapan 3 times daily, Rp31,500; Bajarmasin, twice daily, Rp63,100; Ujung Pandang, once daily, Rp114,100. Merpati flies from: Ujung Pandang, Rp99,200; Long Ampung, Rp30,000. At the airport desk, hire a taxi into town (Rp5000) or walk 5 min. down Jl. Pipit to Jl. Serindit and hop a minibus (Rp400). By road from Balikpapan's Batuampar Station to Samarinda is Rp1500 (2½ hours) by bus. This bus usually stops just before the bridge into Samarinda where motorcyclists are ready to take you across the bridge into the city, or you may continue to the bus station in Sebarang. From the dock across the street, it's a short ferry ride (Rp100) across the Mahakam. The speedboat from Balikpapan's Kampung Baru to Samarinda takes one hour. Or go by *kapal motor* from Surabaya (E. Java), or Pare Pare, Palu, Pantoloan or Donggala in Sulawesi. To get around Samarinda, minibus taxis (Rp200) cruise major streets but not on fixed routes. Stop one and give your destination/street name to see if it's going there, but make it clear that you don't want to charter. The main minibus taxi terminal is at Pasar Pagi; another terminal is at Pasar Kaltim. Or hire a sedan taxi from in front of Hotel Sewarga Indah, Rp4000 per hour.

FROM SAMARINDA

By Air

Timindung Airport, on the N side of town, is used only by small aircraft (12-person capacity). For long-distance flights, you must fly to Balikpapan and transfer to larger planes. Bali Air and Merpati fly to Balikpapan, Rp31,500. Merpati also flies from Samarinda to Datah Dawai on the Mahakam River every Mon. and Thurs. at 1300 for Rp37,200. Bali Air also flies to Berau (Rp62,600) and Tarakan (Rp63,600). Buy tickets at **P.T. Duta Miramar**, Jl. Jen. Sudirman 20 (tel. 23385). Other sample Merpati fare: Surabaya, daily, Rp102,900; Jakarta, Tues. and Sun., Rp154,200; Yogya, daily, Rp132,500; Maumere, daily, Rp182,900; Kupang, daily, Rp204,000.

To The Interior

A travel agent will ask Rp1,800,000 to take you from Samarinda to the headwaters of the Mahakam at Long Lunuk and back. MAF flights are a better deal. The main purpose of MAF is to assist church and mission work in the interior, though travelers are welcome to fly if there's extra space. MAF flights are very useful for getting to the remote Apo Kayan region, since going by river and walking could take weeks (see "Apo Kayan" below). MAF also flies to villages on the upper tributaries of the Mahakam River. Check with the pilot to see if you can go to unscheduled destinations where there are MAF strips; if planning to fly out of the interior, be sure to arrange it in advance with the pilot. Return trips cost only about ½ of the trip in. The pilot based here lives in a brown residence on a hill near the main campus of the Mulawarman University in N. Samarinda, or write MAF, Box 82, Samarinda (cable: MISSAVIA), to see if he can take you where you want to go.

MAF fares to Mahakam River tributaries, paid in *rupiah* equivalent: Miau Baru (Wahau River), 185 km, US$83; Long Segar (Kedang Kepala River), 145 km, US$70; Long Lees (Kelinjau River), 161 km, US$75; Sentosa (Kelinjau River), 161 km, US$75; Makar Baru (Kelinjau River), 169 km, US$78. MAF also flies to the following villages of the Apo Kayan: Mahak Baru, 300 km, US$158; Long Sule, 300 km, US$160; Long Nawang, 360 km, US$185; Data Dian, 360 km, US$185; Sungai Barang, 340 km, US$175; Long Ampung, 355 km, US$180. TAD, a joint W. German-Indonesian development organization, has an Islander that flies to strips along Mahakam River tributaries; its office is on Jl. Kesuma Bangsa. Check with Merpati to see if they offer any interior flights such as to Long Ampung.

By Bus And Boat

The new road from Samarinda to Tenggarong runs across the bridge and then along the S bank of the Mahakam; midway between Samarinda and Loa Kulu it branches off S to Balikpapan. Quickest to Tenggarong from Terminal Sebarang is the minibus for Rp1000 (one hour). You may also charter a minibus from Sebarang; Rp6000-8000 (up to 4 persons). If returning to Balikpapan, the last minibuses from

Sebarang go back around 1900, and after that they'll want Rp15,000 for charter.

The taxiboat from Pasar Pagi in Samarinda to Tenggarong, 2-3 hours, is more enjoyable than taking the road. Destinations, distances, and fares for riverbuses up the Mahakam from Samarinda: Tenggarong, 44 km, Rp550; Muara Kaman, 133 km, Rp1500; Kota Bangun, 161 km, Rp1700; Maura Muntai, 201 km, Rp2000; Muara Pahu, 169 km, Rp2500; Melak, 325 km, Rp3000; Long Iram, 404 km, Rp4500; Muara Angalong, 313 km, Rp3000; Muara Bengkai, 323 km, Rp3200. For long-distance ships from Samarinda, check Pelni and other shipping offices in the port area (see city map). Ships depart for Tanjungredeb (Berau), (Rp15,000, 48 hours), from where boats sail farther up to Tarakan and Tawau (Sabah). For Pare Pare (S. Sulawesi), inquire at P.T. Harapanku Mekar, Jl. Abdullah Marisi 7 (across from the Great Mosque), tel. 22689.

TENGGARONG

Capital of the Kutai Regency and site of the former Kutai Kingdom, 39 km upriver from Samarinda on the Mahakam River. Though the new road has banished much of the town's charm, the people here are still friendly and there's no officialdom to contend with. Visit the **tourist office**, Jl. P. Diponegoro 2 (open Mon. to Thurs. 0800-1430, Fri. 0800-1100, and Sat. 0800-1530) for information and advice on traveling in the Mahakam River basin. A souvenir shop below sells mostly new Dayak Kenyah crafts. Near the Sporting and Cultural Complex is an unusual mosque built during the reign of Haji Aji Pangeran Sosro Negoro (1926-35), the minaret constructed in 1965. Inside you'll find what is surely the only Indonesian public library housed in a minaret! Doctor Achmad Thantawi, Jl. Cut Nyak Dihn, practices acupuncture and is open every day (1800-2000) except Sunday.

History

The Kutai Kingdom has its roots in the old Hindu kingdom of Martapura (Mulawarman), founded upriver at Muara Kaman around A.D. 400. In the 14th C. a Muslim kingdom, Kartanegara, was founded downstream nearer the coast at Pamarangan. The 2 kingdoms waged war until the Muslims won, but then Kartanegara was plagued by Philippine pirate raids. In 1782 the sultanate moved to a safer spot upstream, Tepian Padang, the site of present-day Tenggarong. The Chinese—impressed with the kingdom which once included the Samarinda and Balikpapan areas as well as part of the Dayak territory—called it "Ku-Tai" ("Big Kingdom"). The original sultan's palace was reached by a long flight of steps from the river. The Buginese people gave it the name Tenggarong, from *tangga* ("steps") and *arung* ("palace"). The last sultan, the 18th in succession, was Aji Sultan Muhamad Parikesit, who lost power when his kingdom was abolished in 1960 by the Indonesian government. He donated his palace to the people as a museum, and the government presented him with a new house in exchange. The sultan, who was in his 70s and had 20 wives, died in 1982. The Kutai will have no more sacred kings.

Mulawarman Museum Complex

This imposing white palace is the town's top attraction. An earlier wooden palace was torn down and this one built in its place in 1936. Designed by a Dutch architect, this large, solid structure is built in classical 1930s' futurist style—what a Dutchman considered suitable for an Indonesian sultan. Some exhibits are similar to those in other famous Indonesian *kraton*: regal throne rooms, *gamelan*, *kris*, royal clothing. Over the years, Dayak tribes presented gifts to the sultan in recognition of his sovereignty, and these are all on display: hollowed-out canoes, huge dragon gongs, etc. China's long contact with the Kutai and Dayak people can be seen in the ceramic collection, which includes Ming china. The bedroom is fantastic: the bridal bed is decorated with elaborate beadwork, and there are chairs made from deer antlers. See the startling representation of a *Lembu Suana*, a mythological animal with an elephant's trunk, tusks, and cow's legs, which originated in Burma in the 1800s. There are some inscribed stones and 3 not-so-refined Hindu sculptures from Gua Kombeng of the old Muara Kaman Kingdom (hundreds of others remain in the cave). Museum labeling is hit-or-miss, but many items are described in English. Good luck understanding the English-speaking guide!

In front of the museum is a massive *belawang* pole, a Dayak-carved wood pillar topped by a hornbill bird. Around to the side is a garden of wood statues: beautifully carved Dayak coffins suspended above the earth and dozens of *blontang* carvings and *nguga tahuh* (obelisks made of ironwood) crafted by Benuaq and Tunjung tribesmen. Beyond this fascinating collection of animist art is the royal cemetery where you can see Muslim headstones and posts intricately carved from wood with floral designs, geometric patterns, and Koranic inscriptions. Sultan Muslidhuddin, the founder of Tenggarong in 1782, is buried here, along with his royal descendants. The large weathered wood pillars nearby are said to be from the previous *kraton* structure. Walk up one of the 3 trunk ladders leaning against the Dayak *lamin* (longhouse) and notice the rice-pounding platform. Colonial-style Mesjid Jami Hasanuddin is behind the *kraton* area. Behind the museum is the *taman anggrek* (orchid gardens). The Kutai region has 33 indigenous orchid varieties, many of them grown here, along with coconut, hibiscus, mango, *emau, jambu, jambu biji, ramania, rambutan,* and *jambu agung* trees.

TENGGARONG

- 1. hospital
- 2. Mesjid Raya
- 3. post office
- 4. telephone office
- 5. police
- 6. Mesjid Jami Hassanuddin
- 7. Pasar Pagi
- 8. museum
- 9. Dayak wood sculpture
- 10. police
- 11. Kantor Camat
- 12. Kantor Bupati
- 13. minibus terminal
- 14. *dermaga*
- 15. "Karyah Indah" art shop
- 16. tourist office
- 17. Peng. Zaranah
- 18. Peng. Anda I
- 19. Garuda/Bouraq office
- 20. Pasar Tepian Pandang
- 21. Pasar Ikan
- 22. Peng. Anda II
- 23. Peng. Diana
- 24. RM Padan

Accommodations And Food

For **Peng. Zaranah** (Rp2500 s, Rp5000 d) and **Peng. Anda I**, (Rp3000 s, Rp6000 d), turn L from the *dermaga* (boat landing) and go down Jl. Diponegoro ½ block; they're right over the water and very conveniently located. For **Peng. Anda II**, walk past Anda I and turn L after the bridge, then walk 40 m on the right to Jl. Jen. Sudirman 129. The Anda II is in 2 parts, a front building with Rp3000 s, Rp6000 d rooms; larger, more expensive rooms in the rear go for Rp11,000 s or d. This clean and friendly family-style hotel on stilts juts out on a pier, the waters of the Mahakam whispering below. The best hotel in town is the **Payoeng Asri**, Jl. A. Yani (tel. 289); Rp7,500 s, Rp10,000 d. Quiet and faces a garden. Both afternoon and evening meals cost Rp6000, extra bed Rp4000. The Darongke family, who run the place, are nice people. Jimmy can advise on river travel; his Banjarese wife comes from Long Iram.

Cafeteria 17 on the *dermaga* is not really a cafeteria but offers some of the fanciest eating in town: Indonesian, Chinese, and Western dishes, plus ice drinks. For Padang food try **RM Padang**, Jl. Jen. Sudirman. **RM Tepian Pandan**, behind the Karya Indah Art Shop, offers *sate rusa* (venison *sate*) and very good *sate ayam*, curries, etc. At night, stalls for *sate, martabak, mie goreng*, etc. are set up around Pasar Pagi. Magnificent, wild *durian*, with orange insides, are sold in Pasar Pagi. During the *durian* season, try *tempuyak*, a famous dish made of preserved *durian*. Or try *gangan terong*, cassava soup with sour eggplant, hot chilies, and fish paste.

Shopping

Pasar Pagi is Tenggarong's main market. Dayak crafts can be seen here, but better selection at **Karya Indah Art Shop** near the *dermaga*. This shop is an excellent introduction to the variety of old and new crafts from the interior: baskets, old stone necklaces, masks, *mandau*, woodcarvings, and much more. A souvenir shop below Kantor Baparda (tourist office) also sells Dayak Kenyah crafts (mostly new). Crafts can be purchased more cheaply in the villages, but you won't see the variety you'll see in Tenggarong.

Events

Every 3 years, during the last week in Sept., Tenggarong celebrates the anniversary of its founding. This cultural festival at the Taman Puskora (Cultural and Sports Center) includes traditional sports, rattan-lashing and blowpipe competitions, and a motorcycle race from Loa Janan to Tenggarong. Don't miss performances of traditional dances, such as the *belian* and *timbak*, with dancers chanting and accompanied by gongs; the male and female *nguwai*, with drums and gongs; the *ngibau*, a young man and girl wearing hornbill feathers dancing to *sampe* accompaniment. You may even see the mass *gantar* dance, homage to the rice-planting time. The party can last as long as 5 days!

Transport

From Samarinda the quickest way to Tenggarong is by shared taxi (5 persons) from across the river at Samarinda Sebarang, or by minibus (one hour, Rp1000) from the same station. From Balikpapan, change to a Tenggarong-bound minibus or taxiboat at Loa Janan. More leisurely, and far better for seeing the sights, is a taxiboat from Samarinda's Pasar Pagi, 2-3 hours. Pass little villages with ramshackle old buildings while slowly crisscrossing the river, the boat stopping at *kampung* and timber-loading stages along the way. The old wooden town of Tenggarong is at its best early in the morning, when the river mists transform the weathered pastel wood houses into a magic land.

Tenggarong is so small you can walk everywhere. At the *dermaga* (boat landing) negotiate rides with one of the many *becak* (Rp2000 per hour) or motor-cyclists. Minibuses for Samarinda (Rp1000) and Balik-papan (Rp1750) stop at the *dermaga*, but most leave from Terminal Tepian Pandan, the last ones heading back to Samarinda Sebarang around 2000 or earlier.

The travel agency, **P.T. Mahakam Kutai Permai**, Jl. Diponegoro (right opposite Terminal Tepian Pandan), sells Garuda and Bouraq tickets. For views, climb Bukit Biru, a hill 7 km outside town. If it's been raining, there are waterfalls. Travel 5 km on the road to Samarinda Sebarang and turn R at the group of Dayak statues, walking 2 km to Bukit Biru. Continue another 5 km inland to Hasfarm, a joint American-Indonesian cacao plantation. A *transmigrasi* settlement is here too.

Dayaks attacked by an orangutan: This is only one illustration from a classic 19th C. study of Indonesian flora and fauna, The Malay Archipelago, The Land of the Orangutan and The Bird of Paradise written by Sir Alfred Russel Wallace (1823-1913), the great naturalist, explorer, and author. A friend of Charles Darwin and the namesake of the so-called Wallace Line, Wallace observed how shallow the seas between Java, Sumatra, and the Asian mainland were in contrast to depths farther E around the Moluccus and New Guinea, concluding that elephants, big cats and apes were geologically marooned on one side and marsupials on the other. Charged with the task of collecting exotic specimens for wealthy amateur scientists of Victorian England, Wallace traveled for 8 years (1854-62) throughout Borneo, Java, Celebes, Maluku, the Arus, New Guinea, and Singapore. His paper, On the Law Which Has Regulated the Introduction of New Species, written on Borneo, was probably the most important contribution to evolutionary theory until the publication of Darwin's The Origin of Species. In 1856, Wallace wrote "I excited terror alike in man and beast wherever I went, dogs barked, children screamed, women ran away, and men stared as though I was some strange and terrible cannibal monster." This is much the same reaction travelers provoke today in many remote parts of Indonesia.

THE MAHAKAM RIVER

This giant muddy river, up to 5 km wide at some points, is the highway to the interior. Ocean-going ships reach as far as Samarinda, 60 km upstream from its mouth, to load huge logs which have been floated down to the port. There are about 96 lakes near the river, 14 larger than 1,000 ha; Danau Jempang is the largest. The lower half of the river valley is populated by Muslim Malay groups, including the native Kutai. Dayak tribes, rejecting a religion prohibiting their favorite food (pork), originally moved away from the coasts to settle the many Mahakam tributaries and the uppermost reaches of the river itself. Since WW II, however, they have begun to move into the downstream river towns to avail themselves of education, jobs, and opportunity. Also, don't expect to see longhouses lining the banks as you chug up the Mahakam; Western-style dwellings are steadily replacing them, and motorcycles and lumber trucks have appeared in the towns. Neither will your journey take you through impenetrable tropical forests, with large trees and dense undergrowth draped in giant orchids, mangrove flowers, lianas, and pythons. Instead, you'll notice that much of the jungle is secondary growth or has been clearcut by Weyerhauser. To see Dayak life, head up the river's tributaries, walk inland, or travel far upriver *(ulo)* to the Apo Kayan/Krayan regions. You'll see the unusual freshwater dolphin which enjoys the Mahakam's waters. Crocodiles live in swamps and small tributaries of the lower Mahakam but not in the river itself. Though hunting them is now illegal, they're still killed for their meat and hides.

River Travel

Most of the Mahakam is navigable year-round. Best to travel up the smaller tributaries from Sept. to Dec., when they're most passable. If they're too shallow, paddle canoes are the only option. When the water is swift and high, you may have to walk along riverbanks and carry your canoe over boulders or through jungle. In a hard rain, you may have to wait 2-3 days for the waters to recede; about all you can do is try to stay dry and sleep. Water levels in the upper reaches of the Mahakam can change dramatically in a short time, so don't camp by riverbanks. In the wet season, it could take 3 months to get to Long Pahangai. Though now attracting only about 1,000 tourists per year, tourism in the region is growing. Most tourists visit only Tanjung Isui or Long Iram, seldom venturing N of Long Bagun. When they do, it's usually in expensive guided tours of 30 or more. The key to doing this whole river cheaply is *time*, along with plenty of luck. Food in the Mahakam region isn't that good, and

what there is is more expensive than Java. Don't expect your cargo boat to stop for breakfast, lunch, and dinner! Plenty of water is available.

Transport

Samarinda is the usual starting point for trips up the Mahakam, which has been open to travelers for well over a decade now. Taxiboats provide frequent, leisurely service at low cost, traveling both day and night. Except in the more remote regions, paddle canoes are used only for transport over short distance. Most rivercraft, including taxiboats, are long, wood hulled and roofed, powered by small 2- or 3-cylinder diesel engines. These can go as far upriver as Long Bagun. People travel by longboats (fast outboard-powered canoes) and *ketingting* (small canoes powered by engines on swivel mounts). Check out different boats as travel on the hard seats can be rough; double-decker boats are more comfortable and you can see more scenery. In 1987 I met 2 Germans who had bought a motorless canoe in Long Bagun for Rp80,000; they intended to travel slowly downriver to Kota Bangun. According to them, the rowing wasn't that difficult and they were often taken alongside a *ketingting.* They were having a great time, and all for little money.

To go upstream to Long Pahangai and Long Apari, only longboats have the oomph to get up the many rapids. Longboats are extremely expensive due to fuel cost. Outboard fuel costs Rp600/liter and these boats can use 30-40 liters/hour, so chartering a longboat might run you Rp200,000 per day. *Ketingting* (or, as the upriver people say, *ces),* are cheaper (Rp25,000 per day), but slower. A small taxiboat (8-10 passengers) could cost Rp95,000 per day including fuel. Taxiboats make frequent stops for passengers at floating docks along the riverbanks; these docks sometimes have *warung* and even *losmen* on them. There are no regular river taxis from Long Lunuk to downriver. Regular taxis only begin from Long Iram to Samarinda or Tenggarong (Rp5000, Rp6000 with a bed).

Reaching Long Iram, about halfway up the Mahakam, takes 2 days and one night. Long Bagun is 3 days farther. Beyond Long Bagun, river craft are infrequent and can be very expensive. Upriver from Long Bagun is a major fork where the Boh River comes in from the east. Longboats and *ketingting* travel up the Boh to the Benahan River. A 2-day walk takes you to Mahak Baru in the Apo Kayan. A travel agent will ask Rp1,800,000 for a tour from Samarinda to near the Mahakam's headwaters at Long Lunuk and back. If you want to go to the upper-Mahakam, you'll probab-

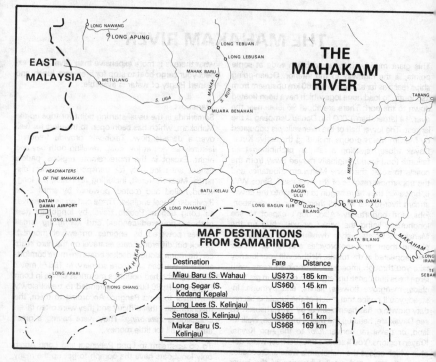

THE MAHAKAM RIVER

EAST MALAYSIA

LONG NAWANG
LONG APUNG
LONG TEBUAN
LONG LEBUSAN
METULANG
MAHAK BARU
S. UGA
MUARA BENAHAN
TABANG
HEADWATERS OF THE MAHAKAM
BATU KELAU
LONG BAGUN ULU
S. MERAH
RUKUN DAMAI
DATAH DAWAI AIRPORT
LONG LUNUK
LONG PAHANGAI
LONG BAGUN ILIR
UJOH BILANG
DATA BILANG
S. MAHAKAM
LONG APARI
S. MAHAKAM
TIONG OHANG

MAF DESTINATIONS FROM SAMARINDA

Destination	Fare	Distance
Miau Baru (S. Wahau)	US$73	185 km
Long Segar (S. Kedang Kepala)	US$60	145 km
Long Lees (S. Kelinjau)	US$65	161 km
Sentosa (S. Kelinjau)	US$65	161 km
Makar Baru (S. Kelinjau)	US$68	169 km

ly have to fly. There are not that many boats, even in the dry season. Several drownings occur each year in the rapids up from Long Bagun.

LOWER RIVER AND TRIBUTARY TOWNS

The best maps of the lower Mahakam are those from TAD, the big German development program, with its headquarters in Kota Bagun; even the smaller walking paths are drawn in. The lower river no longer has any jungle; all the land is cleared. The first longhouse up the Mahakam is at Tanjung Isui, but there's no *losmen*. Longhouses are also found at Tanjung Disur, past Muara Muntai. Tering is the first completely ethnic Dayak village you come to. A church here has an American pastor and a *losmen*. Look for orangutans in the Binulung Daerah area, Kecamatan Muara Kaman; stay with the *kepala desa* and ask him where they are (about 10 km away). Going upriver you still occasionally see huge timber-carrying rafts made of logs lashed together with rattan. In the middle of the raft is a palm hut for the crew, and at the stern is a steersman. Pulled by motorboat, several rafts linked together form a tow about 75 m long; it can take the entourage 3 weeks to reach Samarinda.

Muara Kaman And Vicinity

Formerly the sight of the Hindu Mulawarman Kingdom, now a Muslim town. A few ruins of the old kingdom can still be seen: old entrenchments, stone rice mortars, pig head monuments. By boat to Muara Kaman is 5-6 hours from Tenggarong, or 2 hours downstream from Kota Bagun. Get off here to take boats up the Kedang Kepala River for Gua Kombeng and to visit Dayak villages.

Muara Ancalong is a Muslim Kutai and Kenyah Dayak town up the Kedang Kepala River from Muara Kaman. Taxiboats take 16 hours from Tenggarong, 11 hours from Muara Kaman. If the water is high, river taxis can take you as far as **Muara Wahau;** otherwise, travel by longboat or *ketinting*. MAF sometimes flies to airstrips at Makar Baru (downstream from Long Puh), Sentosa, and Long Le'es. Kenyah villages are found upstream to the NW on the tributary Sungai Kelinjau. The Kenyah are migrants from remote Apo Kayan seeking new land and better access to the outside world. Makar Baru people, for example, came from Mahak in Kec. Kayan Hulu. Muara Wahau is a town farther up the Kedang Kepala. Gua Kombeng and fascinating Kenyah villages are here.

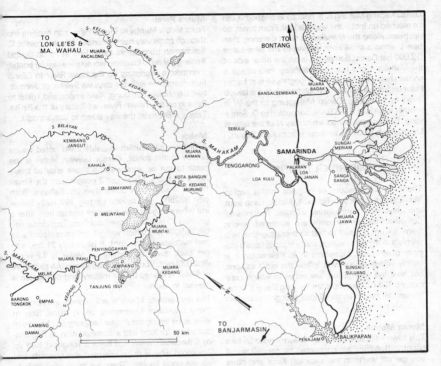

Gua Kombeng is a mountain cave with 5 statues from the old Hindu kingdom once based at Muara Kaman. Images of Brahma, Vishnu, and other gods are kept in the 50-m-high rooms. The statues were brought here to safeguard them from the spread of Islam in Borneo. Stalagmites are closing in fast, so be sure to see them. Be prepared to spend the night. Flat land surrounds this peak just E of Muara Wahau. There are 2 ways to reach the cave: from Jakluay downstream from Muara Wahau, walk E 8 hours; or starting from Slahbing, a lumber camp ½ hour upstream from Muara Wahau, take a company vehicle E, then walk ½ hour. There's a longhouse in Muara Kenyak, a ½-hour walk from Muara Marah (downstream from Muara Wahau). There are other Kenyah villages between Muara Ancalong and Muara Wahau. MAF airstrips are located between these towns at Merah (Batu) and Long Segar; Miau Baru, N of Muara Wahau, also has an MAF strip. People here are Kayan and come from Data Dian in Kec. Kayan Hilir.

Tabang

Kenyah village on Sungai Belayan, a tributary of the Mahakam which enters the river NW of Kota Bagun. From the Mahakam, Tabang can be reached in 2 days by longboat if water levels are high enough. *Keting-ting* take 3-5 days (Rp35,000 per day chartered) and can go in shallow water. Tabang also has an MAF airstrip. Trails through the mountain jungles to the Apo Kayan exist; people may be willing to work as guides—essential, since the trek involves river travel and rugged hiking. From Tabang, walk 2 days around the river rapids, paddle up Sungai Tabang for 3 days, then walk 2 days through the mountains to the Punan settlement of Long Suleh (see "Apo Kayan").

Kota Bagun

A Muslim town in a swampy region with about 10,000 people and several large lakes. Reach Kota Bagun by an 84-km-long dirt road, 2 hours from Tenggarong by motorbike or truck, or about 8 hours from Tenggarong by taxiboat (Rp3000). From here upstream, Melak is 12 hours; Long Iram takes 21 hours. The TAD office for joint W. German-Indonesian projects is in Kota Bagun; TAD also has an airstrip. Stay at **Peng. Marini**, Rp4000 s, Rp5000 d; **Peng. Mekar**, Rp3000 s, Rp5000 d; or **Peng. Mu'jizat**, Rp1500 s, Rp3000 d. Small *rumah makan* and a movie theater are nearby.

Danau Kedang Murung is ½ hour by *ketinting;* it can be reached on foot if the water is low. From town, go upstream along the Mahakam a short distance, then turn L along a small river leading to the lake. Large (13,000 ha) Danau Semayang is on the other side of the Mahakam, one hour by *ketinting.* Pela village is on the shore near the outlet. A longhouse is at Lamin Pulut on Sungai Berambi, which flows into the lake, 5 hours by *ketinting.* Danau Melingtang to the W is another large lake (11,000 ha), connected to D. Semayang. Longhouses are on a tributary N of the lake at Enggelam, 5 hours by *ketinting* from Kota Bagun.

MID-RIVER TOWNS

There's a smorgasbord of religions in this region: Muslims live in Barong Tongkok, Melak, Long Iram, and Javanese *transmigrasi* villages; Protestants, Catholics, and Pentecostals are scattered among them. It's not unusual to find all these together with animists in the same village; many villages have a majority of animists. Elsewhere in E. Kalimantan it is mostly village elders who follow the old traditions, but here the young, too, are active in village ceremonies. The native people are Tanjung Dayaks. Longhouses still exist in some villages, though this custom is slowly dying out.

Muara Muntai

This town—flat as a pancake—is surrounded by lake country. Buildings are connected by gangplanks; if you get off you're in the swamps! Kutai and other Muslim people live here. To get to Muara Muntai, take a taxiboat from Tenggarong (10 hours), or from Kota Bagun, 3 hours (Rp4000). For Tanjung Isui and Danau Jempang, take a taxiboat or *ketinting,* 3 hours. If water is low, only *ketinting* can make the trip.

Tanjung Isui

Muara Muntai is a good jumping-off point for **Tanjung Isui,** a beautiful Benuaq Dayak village on the S shore of the giant Danau Jempang (15,000 ha), 184 km upstream from Tenggarong. From Muara Muntai, there are 2 bigger boats weekly to Tanjung Isui, but smaller ones leave early in the morning each day; a nice 3½-hour trip (Rp3000). Tanjung Isui is a popular place to view longhouses and traditional Dayak life. See *air tawar* (freshwater dolphins), birds feeding on fish, soft sunsets. There's one *losmen* (Rp2500) but you can sleep for the same price in the old longhouse. There are 2 longhouses, one in the center, not very remarkable, only for touristy dance performances. The "old" longhouse is nicer, some handicrafts inside, and lots of *patong* around the courtyard. From Tanjung Isui walk 8 km to Mancong with a not-too-impressive longhouse, but 4 km from Mancong by chartered boat are 3 villages with better longhouses.

Muara Pahu

From Muara Muntai to Muara Pahu is an exciting trip through some very narrow canals. You can cross to C. Kalimantan from Muara Pahu. First travel up Sungai Kedang Pahau to Lambing (sometimes-regular boats), then take a *ketinting* up the Lawa River to Dilang Puti. From here walk 3-4 days via Swakong, Jelmusibak, Sembulan, Sambung, Randampas, and Tokuk to Payeng on the Teweh River, a tributary of the Barito. Take the Barito all the way down to Banjarmasin.

Melak

A picturesque Muslim riverside town noted for its nearby orchid forest, **Kersik Luway.** Melak is the place to put on your walking shoes after all those hours on boats. Melak has 2 *penginapan;* the **Flamboyan** is somewhat better than the **Bahaya.** Both cost Rp2500. Also several *warung.* Not really knowing where to go, many travelers end up here after a grueling 29 hours on a riverboat from Samarinda; pay the Rp5000 fare which will get you an enclosed area and mattress, but no light. It takes only 21 hours to get back down to Samarinda. Melak is 12 hours (Rp3000) by taxiboat from Kota Bagun. An airstrip W of Melak is owned by the military, and permission is needed to use it.

The area around Melak is still strongly animist with many traditional ceremonies taking place. Stay in villages by asking the *kepala kampung* and be sure to contribute for food and accommodation. In Samarinda II (between Melak and Barong Tongkok), look up Agusnoto who is quite informed about events and speaks good English. There are many easy trails to villages in the surrounding hills and plains, commonly used by bicycles and motorbikes. A good gravel road goes to Barong Tongkok (18 km), and another road S to the orchid reserve (Kersik Luway) on the Tanjung Plateau (16 km). The road NW to Tering Sebarang (cross the Mahakam) is 43 km; to Long Iram, 51 km. If you get tired of walking, get a lift on the back of a motorbike (Rp4000 from Melak-Barong Tongkok) or wait for irregular trucks (small charge).

BARONG TONGKOK

An administrative center in an area of villages, rolling hills, small streams, waterfalls, and gardens—a lovely *kampung* to stay at for a while. **Wisma Tamu Anggrek,** a small house with a mattress on the floor, is maintained for visitors (Rp2500 pp). Ask a neighbor or at the *camat's* office for the key. Wash up at the *mandi* area down past the mosque. Behind Wisma Tamu Anggrek in the market area are several small *warung.* On Mon. people come to buy and sell local produce here. The friendly staff at the *camat's* office can give tips on area travel; they also have statistics on population, land area, and religion for each *desa.* It's possible to stay in the villages; ask the *kepala kampung.* Camp-

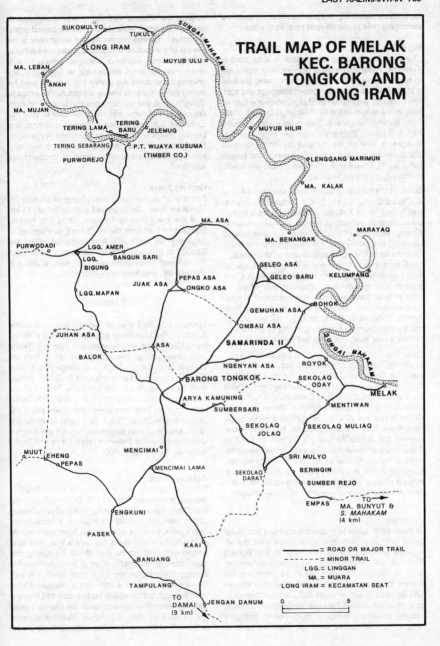

TRAIL MAP OF MELAK KEC. BARONG TONGKOK, AND LONG IRAM

SUNGAI MAHAKAM

SUKOMULYO
TUKUL
LONG IRAM
MUYUB ULU
MA. LEBAN
ANAH
MA. MUJAN
TERING LAMA
TERING BARU
JELEMUG
TERING SEBARANG
P.T. WIJAYA KUSUMA (TIMBER CO.)
PURWOREJO
MUYUB HILIR
OLENGGANG MARIMUN
MA. KALAK
MARAYAQ
MA. ASA
MA. BENANGAK
PURWODADI
LGG. AMER
BANGUN SARI
LGG. BIGUNG
JUAK ASA
PEPAS ASA
ONGKO ASA
LGG. MAPAN
GELEO ASA
GELEO BARU
KELUMPANG
BOHOK
GEMUHAN ASA
JUHAN ASA
OMBAU ASA
SAMARINDA II
BALOK
ASA
NGENYAN ASA
ROYOK
SEKOLAQ ODAY
BARONG TONGKOK
MENTIWAN
ARYA KAMUNING
SUMBERSARI
SEKOLAQ MULIAQ
MUUT
EHENG
PEPAS
MENCIMAI
SEKOLAQ JOLAQ
MENCIMAI LAMA
SRI MULYO
BERINGIN
SUMBER REJO
SEKOLAQ DARAT
ENGKUNI
EMPAS
TO MA. BUNYUT & S. MAHAKAM (4 km)
PASEK
KAAI
BANUANG
TAMPULANG
TO DAMAI (9 km)
JENGAN DANUM
MELAK
SUNGAI MAHAKAM

= ROAD OR MAJOR TRAIL
------- = MINOR TRAIL
LGG. = LINGGAN
MA. = MUARA
LONG IRAM = KECAMATAN SEAT

0   5

ing is also a possibility, but ask first. There is usually a swimming hole or *mandi* spot near each village.

Walks

There are many hiking possibilities in Kec. Barong Tongkok. The terrain is flat or gently rolling; trails pass through groves of bamboo or small trees, gardens and ricefields, areas of overgrown clearings and scattered houses. *Babi hutan* (wild pig) and deer are abundant in the woods to the W of Barong Tongkok. Walk from Barong Tongkok to Tering on a very pleasant trail in 6 hours. Blacksmith sites are often found in villages: a fire pit surrounded by hand-powered bamboo-tube blowers, a trough of water, and simple hand tools. Knives and other steel tools are made, reworked, tempered, repaired.

Some of the best longhouses you'll see can be found in **Pepas/Eheng**, 17 km SW, a village 75% animist and noted for its *kuburan* (cemetery). Hire a motorcycle driver to get you to the big, dark longhouse in **Eheng**, with lots of people living in it (see basket-weaving) and *patong* (for catching ghosts) out front. On the way to Eheng, be sure to stop in **Mencimai**, 7 km S (on the road from Barong Tongkok to Engkuni) with a small longhouse with old people living in it, and several *patong.*. Between Engkuni and Eheng is another small longhouse with some primitive totems. Furthermore, you can walk most of the way from Barong Tongkok to Damai (only for the last part do you have to charter a *ketinting*, Rp8000); on the way there's a very long, still-inhabited longhouse.

Other fine longhouses are found at **Engkuni**, 12 km S of Barong Tongkok; and at **Geleo Baru**, 13 km northeast. For Geleo Baru, head E on the road to Melak, turn L after 2½ km onto a wide trail (no sign). After 9 km the road forks; bear R to Geleo Baru, which has a longhouse with 5 animist families. **Geleo Asa** (Old Geleo) is one km W and has ruins of a much larger longhouse. The massive posts in the center once marked the *kepala kampung's* section. In front of Geleo Asa's community hall is a carved wooden post used to tie up *kerbau* to be sacrificed. Purwodadi, Linggang Amer, and Rejo Basuki are Javanese *transmigrasi* villages with *sawah* in contrast to the dominant *ladang* traditionally worked by native villagers.

Animism

In most other parts of Indonesia animism has faded under pressure from the government and the influence of missionaries, but not in the Barong Tongkok area. Many villages are dominantly animist, with longhouses occupied mostly by traditional believers. Keep an eye out for animist sites in villages and along trails: carved posts and statues, offerings of rice in small plaited baskets, rough-hewn offering tables, streamers hanging from poles, strangely shaped structures, bird carvings. Visit the *kuburan*

outside the villages. Animist graves have unusual markers like small painted wood boxes, carved posts, or statues. Carved human figures commonly show the sex of the deceased. Christian crosses are either in a separate area nearby or scattered among animist grave markers. Also, ask around to find out if any animist ceremonies are planned. These are held for curing sick people, to assure successful rice crops or drought relief, and for marriages and funerals. Visitors are usually welcome, and might be able to take pictures (but ask first). Dancing, singing, chanting, and beating gongs and drums can take place day or night. For the funeral of an important person, a *kerbau* is killed; in other ceremonies, pigs or chickens are sacrificed.

Getting There

Only a small part of Kec. Barong Tongkok borders the Mahakam River. Taxiboats will stop at Bohok, 14 km E of the town Barong Tongkok. Or get to Borong Tongkok by road from Melak, 18 km E, or from Tering Sebarang, 25 km north. A motorcyclist might ask Rp4000 to give you a lift for either trip. Sometimes trucks travel these roads and cost less. Walking is cheaper still, and more enjoyable.

TERING

Tering is actually 3 villages. Tering Sebarang is on the S side of the Mahakam; across the river are Tering Lama (Old Tering) and, downstream a ways, is Tering Baru (New Tering). Most people in Tering Baru are Catholic and Bahau Dayak; the village has a large Catholic church and a *rumah sakit* (hospital). Across from Tering Baru is a timber company. Tering Lama, a 1½-km walk from Long Iram, has a few posts (some with carvings) from long-gone longhouses but is still almost totally Dayak. The Tering Lama longhouse is only used for special occasions, but it's still worth a visit. Cross the river between Tering Lama and Tering Sebarang by canoe, Rp500.

Getting There

From Tenggarong to Tering by river taxi is Rp5000, leaving nearly every day at 1100. Or a rough dirt road leads from Barong Tongkok to Tering, an easy 6-hour, 25-km walk (or Rp3000 on back of a motorcycle). Don't believe people who say you'll get lost because of the many turns; there are only a few, and local people will point out the way. When it's raining, this track could be covered in ½ m of mud. Just outside Barong Tongkok on the main road make a R turn (there might even be a sign). It's a pleasant 15-km walk through gently rolling countryside to Linggang Bigung, which has *warung*. Look for Mapan Waterfall, 11 km from Barong Tongkok. (Another waterfall is 5 km S of Barong Tongkok, near Sekolaq Darat.)

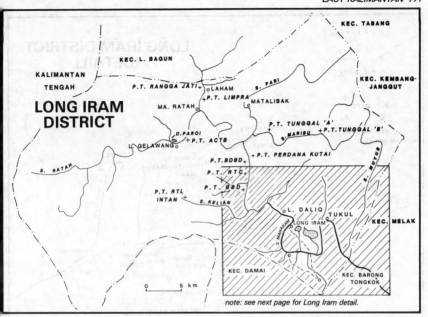

LONG IRAM DISTRICT

note: see next page for Long Iram detail.

After passing through Linggang, Bigung, turn R at the "T" intersection. Just past the "8-KM" roadpost look for an animist site on the L (7.8 km S of Tering Sebarang), where 2 large carved poles stand near the road. Back in the forest 30 m find many small poles with carved human figures on top and plaited baskets holding rice offerings. Just before Tering Sebarang is the *transmigrasi* village of Purworejo, inhabited by people from Blitar in E. Java.

LONG IRAM

From Tering, it's an easy 1½-hour, 7-km walk past a lake and over a level terrain of gardens and jungles to Long Iram. Also, at least 8 taxiboats a week arrive at Long Iram from Samarinda, 33 hours; from Tenggarong, 30 hours (Rp5000); from Kota Bagun, 21 hours; and from Melak, 8-9 hours. Long Iram is a friendly town on the equator, though you won't see many Dayaks here. This is the last place you can count on for finding ice for your beer, *nasi goreng*, large *toko*, a *kantor pos*, etc. People arriving here from downriver won't be impressed, but this is the Big City if you're coming from upriver. The village is about 50% Muslim, with 4 mosques. The native Bahau Dayak people are mostly Catholic. Five km E is the village of Tukul and lakes. It's 3 km N to Sukomulyo (the *camat's* office is here); more lakes to the south.

Accommodations And Food

Long Iram is a one-street town. From the taxiboat dock, walk up the riverbank and turn R for places to stay. **Penginapan Wahyu** (Rp3500 s, Rp5500 d) is on the L a short distance. **Losmen Sukarasa** (no sign) is 70 m farther on the R across from a church; Rp3500 s, Rp5500 d. Or sleep on the river at **Peng. Merante** (no sign), Rp2500 s, Rp3500 d, by walking ½ km farther and turning R across from the "Merante Broadcasting Sistim." If you reach a Kuburan Muslimin, you've gone too far. Follow the plank path down to the floating dock; drinks and simple meals are available. **RM Jawa Timor,** near the ferry dock path, is a clean restaurant serving Javanese-style *mie, nasi goreng,* and curries—the best place to eat in town. Other *warung* offer light meals, drinks and snacks.

Boat Travel

Boats of all varieties leave Long Iram often; from here you can get a ride to almost anywhere on the Mahakam. Keep in mind that boats run on *jam karet.* From Long Iram taxiboats head downstream for Samarinda at 0730 and 1200 on Wed., Thurs. (sometimes), and Sat. (at least 2 boats departing); Rp5000 lower deck, Rp6000 upper. The best boat is the *Karya Utama 77C.* If you're traveling upriver from Long Iram, Data Bilang is 6 hours, Rp2500; boats leave on Sat., Sun., Tues., and Thursdays. The one which leaves Long Iram on Tues. goes all the way to Long Bagun, returning on

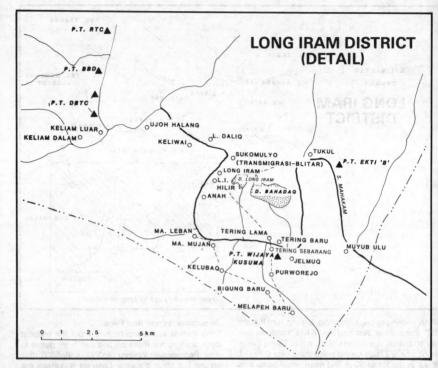

LONG IRAM DISTRICT (DETAIL)

P.T. RTC ▲

P.T. BBD ▲

,P.T. DBTC ▲

KELIAM LUAR ○
KELIAM DALAM ○

○ UJOH HALANG
KELIWAI ○

○ L. DALIQ

○ SUKOMULYO (TRANSMIGRASI-BLITAR)

○ TUKUL

▲ P.T. EKTI 'B'

LONG IRAM ―
○ L.I. ● D. LONG IRAM
HILIR
○ ANAH

D. BAHADAQ

S. MAHAKAM

MA. LEBAN ○
MA. MUJAN ○

TERING LAMA ○

○ TERING BARU
○ TERING SEBARANG

MUYUB ULU ●

P.T. WIJAYA ▲
KUSUMA

○ JELMUQ

KELUBAQ ○

○ PURWOREJO

. BIGUNG BARU ○

MELAPEH BARU ○

0   1   2.5   5 km

Thurs. (relevant for overnighting in Rukun Damai, another Kenyah village). There's another riverboat to Long Iram, but it's on an irregular schedule and isn't very fast.

To reach Rukun Damai takes 1½-2 days; Ujoh Bilang and Long Bagun, 2-3 days. (A *longbot* from Long Iram can zip up in just 7 hours but is very expensive.) Riverboats are less inclined to travel at night above Long Iram due to swifter currents and irregular channels. Rapids above Long Bagun are impassable for larger craft; only longboats and *ketingting* are used. Floating *toko* make slow runs upstream, stopping often to buy locally mined gold and selling everything from nails to biscuits. Lumber company boats, mining boats, and government boats are other possibilities.

DATA BILANG

Apo Kayan people founded this large Protestant 100% Dayak village in recent years, leaving their isolated homelands in the upper Mahakam for new opportunities and a new life. Traditional longhouses have been forsaken for modern single-family dwell-

ings. Noisy rice-milling machines have replaced the sounds of hand-pounding that once echoed through the old villages. But other facets of life are much the same. You'll see woven baskets full of rice carried in from the fields; rice is stored in traditional barns supported by tall wood posts. Intricately beaded backpacks are used to carry babies. Older women, some with bunches of large metal rings dangling from their earlobes, sport elaborate leg and arm tattoos. Untouristed dances are held in one of the intricately carved and painted longhouses every Sun. evening. In this village there are no *losmen,* not even a *warung.* Sleep in one of the *toko,* or in the Blf-Acquitaine camp one km downriver: nice room, good meals, all for free.

Sights

Be sure to see the 2 large modern meeting halls overlooking the river. They are full of wild, curlicued Apo Kayan paintings and woodcarvings—colorful combinations of human and abstract forms. The halls are supported by one-m-high wood posts carved into human figures, no two alike. Outside is a 30-m-long canoe with 30 seats, painted with traditional designs. Another piece of local art is near the school soccer field: an angry carved dragon clinging to a massive post, with worried human figures on the other side. Ask if a *pesta kawan* (wedding) or other ceremonies are planned. Apo Kayan people are famous for making attractive baskets, both large backpacks and small shoulder bags. Their impeccable sense of design and color is apparent in the beadwork on containers, ceremonial clothing, baby carriers. Ask about buying crafts, but don't expect to find anyone willing to part with a baby carrier; they are family heirlooms.

Getting There

A weekly taxiboat "through" service to and from Samarinda takes 2-plus days each way, though it's more comfortable to do the trip in stages. Boats from Long Iram are sporadic, 6 hours, Rp3000. MAF sometimes flies to an airstrip near Data Bilang from the Apo Kayan or Samarinda. If flying out of the Apo Kayan, this is a good place to be dropped off for a Mahakam River trip.

UPPER RIVER TOWNS

Rukun Damai

Four hours upstream from Data Bilang. If you take the weekly boat from Long Iram to Long Bagun, spend the night in Rukun Damai and then board the same boat coming back. Wishing to be less isolated, this village was established about 12 years ago by the Kenyahs from the mountains in the backland. It is today a thriving community with 2 longhouses, one 150 m long. A handsome people, some stretched earlobes, a few traditional baby carriers, dances in the longhouse on Sun. evenings, but no big wooden images. One hour by *ketinting* downstream and up a side river from Data Bilang is Matalibag, a Bahau Dayak village with a 200-year-old *lamin*. Not often visited, very shy people, and the longhouse is in disuse. The village headman can tell you some stories about old *patong*, the carved doors, and the skulls of former opponents which have all been sold. He'll explain that they are all good Catholics now and don't need that old stuff anymore.

Ujoh Bilang

Administrative center for the large Kec. Long Bagun. The main trail through Ujoh Bilang even has streetlights. A Kantor Camat, police station, small clinic, school, and several small *toko* are here, but no *losmen*. Travelers passing through are expected to report to the police (upstream end of village), who are friendly, helpful, and happy to find you a place to stay, perhaps with the *Kepala Kampung*. No special sights; the longhouses have all been torn down. The population is a mixture of Dayak groups, including Bahau, Kenyah, Modang, and a handful of coastal people. Nearly all 600 inhabitants are Catholic due to the work

of Dutch missionaries who came up the Mahakam in the 1920s. Only some older people remain solidly animist. Ujoh Bilang and other upriver villages on the Mahakam have small mosques despite the very few Muslims.

Three boats arrive here from Long Iram weekly, Rp4000. The small diesel-powered boat takes 3 days up, 1½ days down. *Longbots* from Long Iram are speedy but cost a bundle—Rp300,000 per day!

LONG BAGUN

A series of 3 *Ulu* villages stretched out in a line, total pop. 400, where you'll probably see your first Dayak with long earlobes and tattoos. Long Bagun Hulu (upstream village) is the original of the 3. Uma Waj and other groups live here; see the 1½-m-tall carved animist post erected for a sick person. In Long Bagun Tengah, the central village, live Punan and others who moved downstream from Batu Kelau. Long Bagun Hilir has been settled by a group of Penihing people who have moved from Tiong Ohang. See the large house of the *kepala adat*. The veranda has carved posts, roof beams, and trim; a 2-m-long drum is suspended from the ceiling. A good trail links the 3 villages, which are predominantly Catholic though some elders are still animist. Except for an odd pole still standing here and there, the longhouses have long since disappeared. A half-finished mosque sits sadly abandoned in an overgrown field. There are no regular accommodations; one of the *kepala kampung* will find you lodging and food. There are several small *toko*. Across the river from Long Bagun is a joint Indonesian-Japanese logging venture; other logging projects are underway both upriver and down.

Getting There

The villages are so close together you'd expect a good trail between Ujoh Bilang and Long Bagun. There is one, but these boat-oriented people don't use it so it's overgrown and hard to follow. Some boats from Long Iram continue to Long Bagun, about 5 km past Ujoh Bilang. If not, wait for someone heading there in a *ketinting* or charter one for around Rp10,000. Between Ujoh Bilang and Long Bagun look for a large grave on the L bank (to the west). If "you can't take it with you" when you die, this man from Long Bagun made a good effort: his packed suitcase was placed next to his coffin!

From Long Bagun

The border of C. Kalimantan is just W of Long Bagun. To get there, head 5 min. up the Mahakam by *ketingting* to Muara Sebunut, then 2 hours up Sungai Sebunut to the trailhead. Walk one day over the divide to **Tupus**. From here you can go downstream on the Sungai Murung, a tributary of the Barito. Getting to Banjarmasin is the hard part; it's a long way downstream.

To The Apo Kayan

The easiest overland trips N to the Apo Kayan are from Long Bagun. A longboat can go up the Mahakam and Boh rivers to Muara Benahan in 2 days. Charter cost might be Rp450,000 (the trip takes 220 liters of outboard fuel) and the boat can carry about 8 passengers. Some regular traffic of people and goods goes to the Apo Kayan. Rattan is harvested along the Boh River (stay in temporary shelters used by the rattan workers; there are no villages), so there's a chance of going fairly cheap. Unfortunately, rapids make it impossible to take the Boh all the way. Instead, take a boat up the Benahan River (or walk, with great difficulty, along the banks) to Muara Tanit, then walk 2 days to Mahak Baru (see "Apo Kayan" for details). Or turn up the Uga River from the Boh and continue to Long Metulang and the Apo Kayan village. Trails lead from here to Long Ampung and Long Nawang on the Kayan River. Check with the timber company across the river from Long Bagun; ask about the logging trail that eventually will reach the Boh River and the Muara Benahan trail to Mahak Baru.

To Long Pahangai

Several different tribes live in this scenic but hard-to-reach area, including the Bahau, Modang, and Penihing. There are orangutans here, tall trees with giant trunks, true Dayak *adat* life. Most people are Catholic, some are animists. Ask to stay at the Catholic mission. Between Long Bagun and Long Pahangai are about 13 rapids, 7 major. Only longboats can make it up, taking 2 days (but back down takes only a day). Long Pahangai is the administrative village for

Kec. Long Pahangai; report to officials if passing by. There are only a few small rapids beyond this town.

Tiong Ohang

Penihing and other tribes live here, the administrative center for Kec. Long Apari. Be sure to report to officialdom here, too. From Tiong Ohang, you can reach W. Kalimantan. First, travel by boat to Sungai Huvung, one day upstream from the Tiong Ohang, then go up Sungai Huvung. Walk to the border, then down to a tributary of the Kapuas River. Gold is mined in these mountains.

Long Apari

Penihing, Bahau, and other tribes live in this area. Nearly everyone sports tattoos and wears *mandau;* ask the old people about the headhunting days. It's possible to continue upriver to the headwaters of the Mahakam (3 days or more), then hike E to Long Metulang (another 3 days) in the Apo Kayan. With a guide, it's also possible to cross into Sarawak, E. Malaysia (Iban Dayak tribe), from the Mahakam's headwaters. But unless you have advance permission from both countries (not easy), you will most likely get deported from Malaysia. This is especially true while the Swiss Bruno Masur, mastermind of an ecological monkey wrench band of Punans, remains at large.

Long Lunuk is the uppermost village on the Mahakam River, the end of the line, about Rp350,000 by longboat from Long Bagun. It's a nice trip down from Long Lunuk to Long Apari (5 waterfalls), from Long Apari to Long Pahangai (5 waterfalls), and from Long Pahangai to Rukun Damai (3 waterfalls). There's a Merpati connection from Long Lunuk to Samarinda on a 20-seat Fokker.

THE APO KAYAN

The Apo Kayan area includes all of the Kayan River and tributaries above the great rapids *(brem-brem),* as well as the upper Boh River and its tributaries. On the N are the Iran Mountains, the natural and political border between E. Kalimantan and Sarawak, E. Malaysia. The Apo Kayan is divided into Kec. Kayan Hilir and Kec. Kayan Hulu. Most of the population live in Kec. Kayan Hulu, the uppermost Kayan River area. Of the 3 groups of people here, the largest is the Kenyah. Kayan people once controlled nearly the entire region but have now moved downstream to the lower Kayan River. Of the Apo Kayan villages once populated by the Kayan, only Data Dian remains. Several groups of Punan, formerly nomadic hunter-gatherers, have settled in the Apo Kayan, taking up longhouse construction, rice growing, and the language of their Kenyah neighbors.

The Land And Climate

The Apo Kayan jungles are among the most fascinating places on Earth. No commercial logging is yet taking place. The villages make little impression on the vastness of the interior; the population density of the Apo Kayan is about one person per sq km. Except for short trips, it's best to have local guides; don't count on being able to walk or raft out if lost. (Also, the belief in spirits persists and if you hike with the local people you avoid being mistaken for one.) Mountain ranges are irregular, some river sections are impassable, and animal trails may lead nowhere. Even if rescue aircraft were looking for you (unlikely), the search could take many hours of flying.

The climate in the Apo Kayan is nearly ideal. There are pronounced wet and dry seasons. During Aug. and

Sept., the dry months, felled jungle is burned to make new *ladang* fields. Even then some rain falls. South toward Samarinda, the dry season is more pronounced and there may be weeks with no rain at all. Most rainfall comes at night, handy for travelers. When it has been raining, river travel is faster and easier but leeches on jungle trails are friskier. Romantic Victorian explorers and authors of modern-day guidebooks have delighted in describing the "steaming jungles" of the tropics. But barring fires or geothermal activity, Kalimantan jungles never get that hot (except in cleared *ladang*). The jungle of the Apo Kayan has fairly even temperatures, cool to warm during the day and cooling a bit at night. The jungle *is* perpetually humid, though, and the sweat pours off your skin while hiking. The jungle doesn't steam; you do!

Fauna

Leeches, gnats, and mosquitos are plentiful. Most leeches are brown, bustling around on the ground in search of a fresh source of blood and grabbing onto the first warm body to pass by. Another variety is green and drops down out of the trees on its victims. Insect repellent applied to the tops of shoes, socks, shoe eyelets, and other clothing openings will turn them back — but river trekking and rain will wash repellent away. Expect at least a few leeches to get through (a firmly attached leech will come off with a drop of insect repellent, salt, or a hot match.) Termites, which look like ants with ringed abdomens, are the most hungry and industrious creatures in the jungle. Marching in parallel lines across the jungle floor, up and down trees, they look like cars on a California freeway during rush hour. Fallen timber doesn't last long, nor do buildings. Ants are as long as 3 cm but rarely bite. Beetles come in an infinite variety of colors, shapes, and sizes. Some have a brilliant blue or green metallic sheen. Cicadas keep up a din in the forest and fly away if approached, but at night they are attracted to bright lights and are easily caught; they are a favorite toy of forest children. Butterflies are seen in a great variety of colors and patterns, often perched on stream banks and glittering in the sun. Birds are very hard to see, though you can hear the vibrating wingbeats of the slowly cruising hornbill overhead. The best bird-watching is from a canoe while quietly paddling. Some birds are quite musical, singing bits of familiar tunes. (For the mammals, see Kalimantan's "Introduction").

Flora

The jungle has hundreds of kinds of fruits. Some are edible and some not; local people can tell the difference. *Durian* fanciers will want to keep a nose up for the wild *durian merah*, which is bright orange inside and out. One minor hazard of hiking through the bush is the "wait-a-minute" vine; little hooks snag your clothing and skin. Look for insect-eating pitcher plants on rotting logs, especially at higher elevations. Homesick Westerners will be happy to see familiar

plantlife of Borneo: An illustration of one of Borneo's strange forest trees, the tree fern (polyalthea), taken from Wallace's The Malay Archipelago. *Notice the outline of a man in the lower L-hand corner. There are other giant trees such as the extremely hard, durable ironwood which is immune to insect attack and is so heavy it can't float, and the monstrous teak, which takes 80 years to mature. Borneo's flora is very complex, nature's way of protecting the seeds from scavenging animals. Spiky shoot branches are found below ferns lined with thorns. Because the soil is so poor at the bottom of the sunless jungles, certain other plants become insect eaters and parasites. The insect-eating pitcher plant hangs a 45-cm-long trap whose fiery red lips emit a sweet odor, attracting insects. Insects drop through slippery hairs to the bottom of the pitcher where they're dissolved by pepsins. Sometimes this plant has an insect living in it to help chew up and digest victims in a mellow symbiosis. Borneo's botanical riches remain far from fully explored; only around 100,000 specimens have been collected.*

oak and eucalyptus-like trees. Pine trees have familiar cones and sticky sap, but broad leaves instead of needles to catch scant sunlight.

History

One of the first Europeans to visit this region was the Dutchman Nieuwenhuis, who started for the Apo Kayan in May 1900 with a photographer, 2 other Europeans, 3 Javanese collectors of flora and fauna, and a group of "Bahaus." Nieuwenhuis worked to make peace in the area and to settle the long-standing feud between the Kenyah and the Sarawak Ibans, who had lost a number of heads to Apo Kayan raiding parties. To promote stability, the Dutch named the Lepo Tau leader as chief of all Apo Kayan. The Dutch days were generally peaceful; inter-tribal warfare ceased and most headhunting was abolished. A Dutch post was built at Long Nawang in 1907. A school was established there in 1927, and trails to other villages were constructed. At the large rapids, which made travel to the coast difficult, the Dutch constructed a portage route with warehouses at each end. Supplies for the Dutch garrison and Chinese shopkeepers at Long Nawang were transported by canoe from the coast to the lower warehouse, portaged to the upper one, then canoed to Long Nawang—a 3-month trip in the days before motorboats. The Kenyah, highly skilled in canoeing, were often hired for this work; some even assisted in the exploration of New Guinea. All this ended with the arrival of Japanese troops at Long Nawang during WW II. The garrison, taken by surprise, quickly surrendered; the Japanese executed 109 men, women, and children, including missionaries and British refugees from Sarawak. Missionaries returned after the war, but the Dutch never reestablished a garrison.

The Apo Kayan people were first exposed to Christianity by trading, traveling to the coast where they were influenced by missionaries. In 1929 George Fiske, an American with the Christian Missionary Alliance (CMA), arrived at the coastal island of Tarakan, E. Kalimantan. He later moved his work to Tanjungselor on the lower Kayan River. By 1938 one village, Nahakramo, was over half Christian. In 1940, Fiske attempted the first flight into the Apo Kayan, making a daring landing at Data Dian in a floatplane. At first, Christianity and the *adat kama* (the old religion) coexisted peacefully, with Christian and *adat lama* longhouses in the same village. But in the early 1950s villages started breaking apart. At Long Nawang, the *adat lama* people moved across the river and founded Nawang Baru. The Kenyah knew that spirits cannot cross water and so lived peacefully.

Because the Apo Kayan borders a Malaysian territory, Indonesian troops were stationed here in 1963-65 during Sukarno's war against that country. Their presence affected many aspects of Kenyah life. Pagan beliefs of the *adat lama* and the short-lived Bungan cult were actively discouraged. With the Indonesian troops came Lt. Herman, a Roman Catholic from Ambon (Maluku). Holding up a Bible and a bullet, Herman went around to animist villages reminding people that Indonesia is based on the 5 *Pancasila* beliefs, including the belief in God. Herman's message: adopt a "true religion," not animism, or be considered communist sympathizers. Despite this heavy-handed approach, few Kenyah reverted back to *adat lama* or to the Bungan cult after the army left. Another result of *konfrontasi* was the removal of Chinese traders and foreign missionaries from the interior. Village and regional leadership also changed. The leader of all Apo Kayan, the *Paran Bio,* was deposed by Indonesian authorities; his replacement was elected under Indonesian military "guidance." Since *konfrontasi,* native church leaders do nearly all mission work in the Apo Kayan, though resident foreign missionaries have taught at the church school at Long Bia near Tanjungselor. In 1972 the first Apo Kayan airstrips were completed at Long Nawang and Data Dian, dramatically ending the area's extreme isolation.

The Economy

Kenyah life is dependent on rice, and so centers on it. Villages may be nearly empty when people are working in their *ladang* fields, returning only on weekends for church. Land is cleared of jungle growth and then used for growing rice for up to 3 years. No irrigation is normally needed. Soils are poor; only one crop is harvested each year. Fields are commonly one or more hours' walk away from the village, so field houses are built for eating, sleeping, and rice storage. Planting usually begins in Oct., after the village chief has determined the proper date, and takes one or 2 weeks. Weeding is done a month later with small hoes. The harvest, in Feb. and March, is a happy time when the people can eat fresh rice again. Thirsty harvesters sometimes take jugs of *borak* (rice wine) into the fields. Rice stalks are cut with small knives, then threshed by people treading on a special mat on a platform. Then the rice is winnowed by fanning. It is stored in woven baskets in rice barns, tiny houses mounted on 2-m-high poles. Curved boards atop the poles discourage hungry mice. Feasts, weddings, and a few animist rites follow the harvest. In the old days men celebrated with *mamat* ceremonies, by going out and collecting fresh heads. Now a less heady thanksgiving dinner is held.

Besides all-important rice, other crops include cassava, sugarcane, squash, corn, beans, small tomatoes, hot peppers, and green leafy vegetables. Pineapple, papaya, coconut, banana, tangerines, *durian,* and coffee are also grown. *Durian,* of course, is the favorite fruit. Sago palms are harvested by some Kenyah; others won't touch them. Many of the jungle's native fruits and plants are edible: *paku* ferns are harvested along riverbanks, immature wild grapes are used to spice up greens, and *petai* seed pods are collected in the jungle (and give urine a pungent odor, a source of jokes).

Workers also gather rattan from the forest, tie it into giant bundles, then drift it downstream. Rattan rafts spend as much time stuck on rocks as floating. For example, the trip from Muara Benahan to Long Bagun could take more than a week. Cane poles, nets, fish traps, and spears are all used for fishing; spearfishing underwater or from canoes is common. Sometimes the *tuba* root is used for mass fish kills—producing many dead mature fish but also killing off the next generation. Hunting is a favorite sport of the men. Dogs are usually used in pursuit of wild pigs, deer, and small animals. Guns are the favored weapons, but both ammunition and guns are scarce and expensive. More often spears are used. Blowpipes are considered too dangerous by the Apo Kayan Kenyah, reasoning that if a man is scratched by a poison dart he dies, but if by a bullet he may live. The Punan do use blowpipes.

THE PEOPLE

The Kenyah

Before the Dutch arrived, the Kenyah lived near the headwaters of the Kayan River, N across the divide (now Sarawak), and near the headwaters of the Rejang and Baram rivers. Since 1900, thousands have migrated from the upper Kayan E to the lower Kayan and S to the Mahakam River and its tributaries. Many Kenyah people have moved to Sarawak in the Balui (tributary of the Rejang) and upper Baram rivers. In all of E. Kalimantan there are about 30,000 Kenyah, plus 8,000 in Sarawak. Superficially, the Kenyah are similar to their neighbors, the Kayan—and there are intermarriages—but customs and languages are quite different. The Kenyah consider the headwaters of the Iwan River, a tributary of the Kayan, their historic homeland. Nomadic hunter-gatherers who originally learned rice cultivation in the Iwan headwaters, the Kenyah's post-agriculture population increase led to overcropping, which resulted in migrations during the past 8-10 generations across to Sarawak and downstream on the Iwan to the Kayan. Large areas of *alang-alang* grass, indicating overcropping, remain in the Iwan River area to this day. Once populous, that area is now nearly deserted.

All Kenyah groups can trace their migration, village-site by village-site, back to the headwaters of the Iwan River. Names of the 40 Kenyah subgroups are based on the original longhouse locations in the Iwan headwaters. The Kenyah were able to migrate into the upper Kayan as the native Kayan people moved out. Of the many Kenyah subgroups, the Lepo Tau rose to prominence as the oldest, most culturally pure aris-

tocracy. The Lepo Tau village, Long Nawang, is the main administrative center for the Apo Kayan.

Village Longhouse Life

Villages are almost always on a river. The preferred spot is a place where a small stream joins a large one—the reason so many village names are preceded by *long,* meaning "confluence." Drinking water can be obtained from the clean stream, while the larger river is used for travel. Villages don't have much in the way of plumbing, indoor or outdoor, so people go down to the river (at night they open a crack in the floorboards). Upstream is thus preferred for washing and bathing! Longhouses *(lamin)* are used by most Kenyah and accommodate 11 or 12 households on the average. Stories tell of the glorious old days when longhouses held over 100 families, and when other buildings were as high as 3 stories. But longhouses must be torn down and rebuilt often, due to wood rot and insects. In Long Nawang, they are rebuilt every 10-15 years. By gathering timber in advance, the people can rebuild a longhouse in only 4 days.

Kenyah longhouses have a covered area across the front, for both working and socializing, and a safe place for children to play. The buildings are elevated 1-2 m and reached by logs with notched steps. Inside, barriers separating the different family sections rarely reach to the roof; close families may have a door in their shared wall. Parts of the longhouse roof may be higher, for the *kepala kampung's* section. Padlocks are rare here. Valuables such as mats, gongs, old Chinese jars, and baby carriers are stored in rice barns, which are often unlocked and unguarded. Your gear is safe too, but don't leave things lying around. Kids might be tempted to borrow something. Cooking is done in a small room attached to the back of each section or house, though traditionally the kitchen was inside the main room. Each house has a *paran uma* who represents his longhouse at village meetings. Single-family homes are a new development in the Apo Kayan and still somewhat experimental. Longhouses are cooler, afford easier and more casual visits between neighbors, and provide a place for the children to play out of the mud. Kenyah villages tend to be larger than those in neighboring areas; life is busier and considered more fun. As you approach, every dog in the village will spontaneously join in a howling concert.

Traditional Customs

In the old days men wore a simple loincloth of cotton or bark cloth 25-30 cm wide and 2 m long. Women wore rectangular cotton or bark cloth about 65 by 90 cm. Both men and women had their ears pierced to hold heavy rings of silver or brass. Men also punched a one-cm hole in their upper ears. The men's ears were lengthened only a few cm, but women added

Dayak chief

more rings until their earlobes reached down to their chests. Body hair was distasteful; beards, moustaches, and even eyebrows and eyelashes were plucked. The Kenyah had 3 social classes: *panyin lamin* (slaves, war captives, and their offspring); *panyin* (commoners); and *paran* (aristocrats).

Marriage is mostly a Christian ceremony now, complete with pastor, best man, and maid of honor. The bride usually wears traditional clothing and decorations, the man a suit and tie. Traditionally the bride and groom aren't allowed to become lonely on their wedding night, but are kept company by several of the bride's friends and siblings. It may be days or weeks before a husband talks his wife into sending home the "guests."

At death, a burial house *(liang)* was once used for all Kenyah, but now only for chiefs and others of high social standing. The *liang* is a small, roofed structure one m off the ground and supported by posts. It is decorated with paintings, ornate scroll-like carvings, and carved tigers, hornbills, or men. Ordinary buried graves may have a roof and carved, painted decorations. Gravesites are not maintained; grass and weeds grow quickly and the carvings slowly disintegrate.

Arts And Crafts

Metik (tattooing) was for both men and women, as decoration and as a sign of social status. Usually women did the tattooing, which could take months or even years to complete. Men had small tattoos on their arms, chests, legs, back, and sometimes the front of the neck. Associated with the taking of heads, tattooing on males all but disappeared with the end of headhunting. Women of the *paran* class had exclusive designs tattooed on their arms, and their legs

from thigh to toe. The geometric designs and animal motifs were so finely detailed that from a distance they looked like solid colors. Women who endured the intense, prolonged pain of tattooing were considered strong, to be respected. Now the government has banned tattooing for health reasons, and the art is found only on older women.

Often villages have a roofed shelter with anvil, air blowers, and a water trough where blacksmiths work. Long, flat chainsaw blades are a popular source of steel and are cut and shaped into knife blades. A Kenyah *mandau* (bushknife) makes a good souvenir.

Large baskets are for carrying rice from the fields and storing it. The smaller, more flexible shoulder bags are for personal use. These have attractive designs of black on natural cane, the dye added after weaving; only the rough side of the cane strips (turned outward in the preferred design) absorbs the dye. A baby carrier *(ba')*, which may show family status, is prepared for every child in Kenyah society. This traditional carrier also protects the child's spirit, as loss of the soul is believed to be the prime reason for infant mortality. The symbols on the *ba'* remain important despite the waning of their power due to Christian influence and modernization.

PRACTICALITIES

Jungle Travel

Long pants are best for hiking: some plants and vines are mildly poisonous and tough ferns will cut your legs. Boots should be sturdy, lightweight, and non-skid to navigate the slippery logs and rocks you'll be walking on; old or untreated leather shoes may fall apart in the humid jungle. Foot powder is recommended. Bring antiseptic for scratches and to prevent infections after being bitten, and also skin cream to relieve rashes caused by contact with poison plants. Iodine purification tablets are a good idea; the Kenyah boil their water but it tastes like last night's fish stew. A tent is useful for extended trips but must be very lightweight, well-ventilated, and insect-proof. The Kenyah make simple lean-tos and cover them with thatch or a plastic sheet, then scratch their mosquito bites all night. Leeches and gnats will also be looking for you; not particularly numerous, but they can still be annoying.

Large villages have small general stores *(toko)* which carry just a few shelves of the basics: soap, salt, men's underwear, sugar, pots and pans, "D" flashlight batteries, sewing thread, etc. The only foods are usually biscuits, noodles, and tinned sardines. Prices are 3 times those on the coast, so bring in all your necessities. Don't forget anti-malarial pills and insect repellent. Items such as suntan lotion, ChapStick, toilet paper, and insect repellent are unheard of.

Jungle Photography

Nature photographers will have an opportunity of a lifetime. Bring extra film and batteries; none are available locally. A macro lens, close-up lens, or extension rings will enable you to photograph strange insects and unusual flowers. The jungle is surprisingly dark, even at midday. Higher speed film is easier to use but not necessary; a flash is often needed for close-ups, even with high-speed film. A lightweight tripod is handy for those misty early morning shots, and others in natural light. Most people are happy to be photographed and will probably be ecstatic if given a photo from an instant camera. Women with tattoos and dangling earlobes are *malu* (shy) but may consent.

GETTING THERE

There is one easy way to get to the Apo Kayan, and many hard ways. The easiest is to fly, in just an hour or two, in an MAF missionary plane to one of the territory's 7 airstrips. Smoke in the air can cause delays or closures at interior strips in the Apo Kayan and at MAF bases elsewhere. The air can be smoky anytime but more likely in the Aug.-Sept. field-burning season. The jungle looks quite different from the air. Just take the first airplane seat available; it doesn't really matter which strip you fly into, since trails connect them all. If planning to fly out later, make advance arrangements with the pilot.

MAF

MAF has 3 bases in E. Kalimantan: at Samarinda, Long Bia (reachable by boat from Tarakan), and Tarakan all with planes to or near the Apo Kayan. The Samarinda pilot usually flies to the southern Apo Kayan, the Long Bia pilot to N areas, and the Tarakan pilot to the Krayan (NE of Apo Kayan). Planes are single-engine Cessna 185s which can carry 5 passengers (if baggage is light). It's sometimes possible to charter a plane or be dropped off at a different destination; talk to the pilot. Keep a loose schedule: planes break down, pilots get sick or go on vacation, and bad weather or emergencies can mean delays. But waiting a few extra days beats slogging through leech-infested jungles and running dangerous river rapids for 2 months, unless you're into that kind of thing (see below). From Samarinda, Merpati offers flights to Long Bawan and Long Ampung (Rp30,000).

Overland

This is the hard way, and there are at least 5 overland trips to the Apo Kayan. All involve extensive boat travel in longboats, *ketinting*, or canoe, as well as jungle hiking, and all approaches require a guide. There are also several routes across from Sarawak, but unauthorized border crossings are frowned upon

From	To	Fare	Km
Samarinda	Mahak Baru	$128	300
	Long Sule	$128	300
	Long Nawang	$155	360
	Data Dian	$155	360
	Sungai Barang	$145	360
	Long Ampung	$151	355
Long Bia	Data Dian	$72	210
	Long Nawang	$80	235
	Mahak Baru	$80	235
	Long Lebusan	$80	235
	Long Sule	$63	185
	Sungai Barang	$74	220
Tarakan	Data Dian	$110	320
	Long Nawang	$118	345
	Mahak Baru	$116	340
	Long Lebusan	$116	340
Long Nawang	Samarinda	$62	360
	Long Bia	$40	235
	Tarakan	$60	345
	Miau Baru	$41	240

note: flights among the Apo Kayan strips $12-26

by both countries; only native people are allowed across the border with minimal formalities. The easiest Indonesian route is from Long Bagun on the Mahakam River; go by longboat or *ketinting* to Muara Benahan on the Boh River (a trip of 2 days), then hike 2 days to Mahak Baru. Or head up the Uga River to the NW from the Boh to Metulang, then N several days to Long Nawang by foot and canoe (see "Long Nawang" section). More difficult is taking rivers and trails from Tabang on the Belayan River, a tributary of the Mahakam; it's several days from the Mahakam to Tabang, then 7 days to the Punan village of Long Suleh. (See "Tabang" in the Mahakam River chapter).

Approaching up the Kayan River from Tanjungselor seems a good way to reach the Apo Kayan, but its midsection has many rapids and impassable waterfalls. Bypass these by turning up the Bahau River when coming up the lower Kayan from the coast. Boats are left behind for the several-day hike over the mountains to either the Kat or Iwan rivers, both tributaries of the Kayan River *above* the big rapids. The route to Mahak Baru via the Boh is easiest to arrange, as people from Tanjungselor make the trip about once weekly. Finally, from Long Pujungan in Kec. Pujungan take a *ketinting* or canoe up the Pujungan River to Long Jelet, ½ to one day. Walk 2 days over the pass to the Kat River, then canoe to Data Dian or Long Nawang, 3 days.

Guides

Necessary for any long hike. There are no topographic maps available; maps in this book are about the best you'll find for hiking, though they're not good enough for navigation. The jungle has many trails but confusing branches, some leading only to a favorite pig wallow. There are no trail signs, no tourist offices, no park rangers to help you. Local people are usually happy to guide you for anywhere from Rp5000 to Rp10,000 per day. On a long trip at least 2 guides are needed, and you are expected to pay for their return trip, unless they're already heading for your destination. Guides can supply rice and canoes for the journey, but always ask if there are extra costs. The Kenyah are honest, so don't worry about being cheated. But talk things over to be sure there are no misunderstandings. There are no villages on long sections of the overland routes; the fishing is fantastic. If your guides have dogs, count on fresh pork. All the people in the interior are good swimmers; if you aren't, bring a life jacket for canoe trips. You'll be speaking in *Bahasa Indonesia,* so study a phrasebook and bring a dictionary if your Indonesian is rudimentary.

VILLAGES AND HIKES IN THE APO KAYAN

Long Nawang

Home of the Lepo Tau Kenyah, oldest aristocracy in the Apo Kayan. Today Long Nawang, near the Sarawak border, is the government administrative center with an airstrip (a short distance downstream), clinic, police station, military post, Kantor Camat, school, 2 tiny *toko,* and several longhouses. This is one of the largest and richest *kampung* in the Apo Kayan, with a large number of *paran bui* (noblemen), thought to be direct descendants of the first people in Borneo—the deepest black eyes you've ever seen! The people of Long Nawang set fashion standards for the rest of E. and C. Kalimantan. Drop in at the *camat's* office to say hello and let them know you're here. The police, in the same building, will want to register you. People in the office can help with any questions about the area and will know if a group is about to head off to a distant village. If the radio's working, they have contact with the outside world.

See examples of curlicue Kenyah paintings on some rice barns in this town. Three-dimensional wood sculptures decorate graves near the airstrip and on the trail to Nawang Baru. Outside the village are some *sawah,* a rarity in the Apo Kayan. Watch for women working a sugarcane crusher: they rock a giant log back and forth over stalks of sugarcane. Longhouses are in the S part of the village (upstream), government offices in the north. Across from the village are single-family homes used by civil servants and the military. If you can swim, cross the rickety suspension bridge.

All villages in the Apo Kayan are fascinating to visit. For exploring the jungle and seeing *ladang* cultivation, day hikes can be made from any of them.

Nawang Baru

A large village in a pretty setting along the Nawang River. *Adat lama* people split off from Long Nawang in the 1950s and formed this village to get away from the Christians. Now, though, you see churches in the hills above town. It's only a ½-hour walk to Nawang Baru. Cross the suspension bridge at Long Nawang, then take either of the 2 trails to the left. The first follows the riverbanks, going upstream on the Kayan and Nawang rivers. The other goes straight up the hill (good views). After the trails rejoin there's a *kuburan* (gravesite) on the R with decorative paintings and woodcarvings.

Long Ampung

A large village of Ma'Jalan Kenyah upstream (SE) on the Kayan from Long Nawang. One of the longhouses is exceptionally long. There's a small clinic, and across the river is an airstrip suitable for Merpati's commercial twin-engine planes such as Islanders and Twin Otters. Long Ampung can be reached by *keting-ting* or canoe from Long Nawang, or walk it in 5 hours. Take the trail upstream along the bank. Soon after fording shallow Tepayan River, take the trail's R fork. Continue through forest and *ladang* fields to the Anye River, later crossing the suspension bridge over the Kayan to Long Ampung. A guide is recommended but not essential on the Long Nawang-Long Sungai Barang trails which lead to Long Ampung.

Long Uro

A Lepo Tau village 2½ hours by foot from Long Ampung. The small trail is easy to follow through the forest and *ladang.* Take the trail going upstream from Long Ampung; don't cross the suspension bridge. Another suspension bridge is at Long Uro. Lidung Payau is a Lepo Tau village just ½ hour on a good trail upstream from Long Uro.

Long Sungai Barang

A Lepo Tukung village ringed by hills. Sungai Barang means "River Things." The *kepala kampung's* section of the longhouse has a higher roof, bigger veranda, and massive support timbers, with Kenyah artwork on the front. From Lidung Payau, the trail to Long Sungai Barang climbs into the hills, passing many mountain streams in the jungle. For some distance, there are 2 trails; the higher one (L fork coming from Lidung Payau) is better. *Ladang* fields are near the villages, with forest in between.

From Long Sungai Barang

The good jungle forests in the area have attracted graduate students doing forestry or agricultural proj-

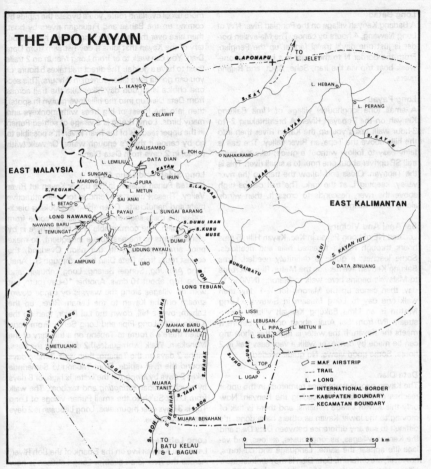

ects, and there may be an *orang putih* here. A suspension bridge across the Kayan connects the 2 parts of the village. The airstrip is a ½-hour walk. From Sungai Barang, 2 trails lead S across the divide to Mahak Baru and Long Lebusan on tributaries of the Mahakam. Both routes involve hiking, then river travel. The preferred way is to hike to the pass, then down to the Kubu Muse streambed to the Dumu Iran River in one day, then canoe to the Boh and on to Long Lissi (abandoned) or Long Lebusan, 1 ½ days more. Mahak Baru is then 2½-3 hours by trail. The other route from Sungai Barang is a 2½-day hike over mountains, then ½ day by canoe down the Mahak River to Mahak Baru. Guides and canoes are needed for either

journey. Scenically, these trips are unbelievable: jungles of giant trees, clear streams full of fish, monkeys climbing overhead, birds flying back and forth across the river. The real Borneo! Apo Kayan people, given a choice, prefer long river trips to long jungle hikes, so most go via the Boh River.

Metulang

By continuing past Nawang Baru up the Nawang and following a trail over the mountain pass 3-4 days S you can reach this Uma Bakung Kenyah village. From Metulang it's possible to head downstream by boat to the Uga then Boh rivers, then on to the Mahakam.

Long Betao

A Badang Kenyah village on the Pengian River NW of Long Nawang, 4 hours by canoe. The Malaysian border is just one day's travel farther up the Pengian. From the border N to the coast is a hazardous one-week boat trip via the Iran, Sahe, Aput, and Rajang rivers.

Long Payau

A small (one longhouse) village of Uma Bakung Kenyah on the Tepayan River. A breathtaking 2- to 3-hour walk takes you up the Kayan River then into the hills above the Tepayan River valley. The trail is fairly easy to follow without a guide; take the main trail SE upriver about one hour to a small river. This is the Tepayan. Cross and follow the trail up the river valley, keeping L at the fork. The trail climbs high above the river, descends to cross it, then winds along to the village.

Sai Anai And Vicinity

Located NE of Long Payau in Kec. Kayan Hilir, 5-plus hours through rolling forested hills and ricefields. Some leeches; a guide is definitely needed. Uma Bakung Kenyah live here on the Metun River. A route to Malaysia begins here: walk to Marong (NW) in ½ day, then canoe up the Marong for ½-1 day, then walk one day to Long Musam in Sarawak. **Long Metun** is an Uma Bakung Kenyah village downstream (N) from Sai Anai, about one km before it meets the Kayan. If the water is high, this short trip can be made by canoe; or walk a very easy trail in 2 hours. Some good views. No guide needed.

Data Dian

The Kayan people were once numerous in the upper reaches of the Kayan, preceding the Kenyah. Now only this Kayan village remains, and there is talk of moving to the lower Kayan as others have done. It's difficult to see any difference between Data Dian and the Kenyah villages as longhouses, canoes, and village life appear the same. Language and customs, however, are different. Data Dian is the administrative village of the vast Kayan Hilir wilderness: 80,000 sq km with only 5 villages. A *camat* office (check in) and a handful of civil and military officials here. To the E, the Kayan River enters Giram Deku and Giram Ambun, the first of many major rapids.

From Data Dian

Data Dian's airstrip is 1½ km downstream on the N bank of the Kayan; canoes are used to reach it. From the other airstrips in the Apo Kayan, Data Dian can be reached in 15-30 minutes. From Long Nawang to Data Dian by canoe takes one day, but going back takes 2½ days. Coming up from the coast on the Kayan River takes a little longer; allow a month if going by *ketingting*, 3 months if paddling. If you take the

more usual overland route, you'll bypass the rapids by coming up the Bahau and Pujungan rivers by boat, then hike over the mountain range to the Kat, a tributary of the Kayan that joins it downstream from Data Dian. You can walk to or from Long Metun on 2 trails (best to have a guide). The direct trail takes 5 hours; or you can go via Pura (abandoned) in 9 hours. This second choice is a good day hike; take the trail across from Data Dian up into the hills (overgrown in spots), then into the forest of big trees with monkeys and many birds. **Long Ikang** is a village of settled Punan in the upper reaches of the Iwan River. It's possible to go by canoe if there's enough water. Or walk (with guide) in 2 days from Data Dian.

Long Suleh And Long Pipa

Isolated Punan villages in the upper Kayan Iut River Valley. These Punan are famous for their attractive mats and handicrafts. Often the good-looking black-and-white mats seen in Kenyah villages come from Long Suleh. The comfortable way to get here is by plane. Flights to the airstrip are infrequent, so make prior arrangements with the pilot. Overland, the easiest route from Data Dian loops through Sai Anai, Long Ampung, Sungai Barang, Long Lebusan, and Long Top, about 10 days. Another 10-day route, but with no villages along the way, is by canoe downstream on the Kayan to the Laham River, up the Laham, over a hill, down the Lui River, then up the Kayan Iut to Long Pipa and Long Suleh. From Long Suleh there's a route to Tabang on a tributary of the Mahakam. Walk (with guides!) 2 days over the pass, canoe 2 days on the Tabang, then walk 2 more days around the river rapids. From Tabang to Samarinda takes 2 days by *longbot* if the water is high, or 8 days by much cheaper *ketinting* and taxiboat. The walk from Long Suleh to the small Punan village of Long Top is 3 days over mountains. Long Lebusan is 2 days farther by canoe.

Long Lebusan

Lepo Tau Kenyah live on the E bank of the Boh River. Across the river is an airstrip. Long Lebusan is now the only village on this river; upstream are the abandoned village sites of Long Lissi (the people moved to Mahak Baru in 1983), Long Tebuan, and Dumu. Most of the people in Long Lebusan are Catholic, converted by missionaries coming up from the Mahakam. There are also some Catholics in Long Sungai Barang and Mahak Baru. Other villages in the Apo Kayan are solidly Protestant.

Long Top

A small Punan village on the Uho River, a tributary of the Boh. Long Top can be reached in 1½ days by canoe from Long Lebusan. Another approach is from the Punan village of Long Suleh (has an airstrip) by hiking 3 days through the jungle.

MAJOR DAYAK GROUPS OF EAST KALIMANTAN

Group	Location/Remarks
Kenyah	Their homeland is the remote Apo Kayan of the upper Kayan River. Many have migrated out during this century, founding villages to the S on the Boh, Tabang, Kelinjau, and Kedang Kepala—all tributaries of the Mahakam. They have also migrated N to Sarawak in E. Malaysia and E to the lower Kayan. Almost 100% are Protestant. In the upper Kayan and Boh rivers nearly all live in longhouses. They are known for their handicrafts. Intermarriage is common among the Kenyah and Kayan.
Kayan	The Kayan's homeland is the Apo Kayan but most have now moved down the lower Kayan and its tributaries. Data Dian, the only Kayan village remaining in the Apo Kayan, may eventually move downstream too. Outwardly, they are similar to the Kenyah and sometimes live together in the same village, but language and customs are different. Like the Kenyah, they possess a hierarchial social order of aristocrats and commoners.
Bahau	Live in the upper Mahakam in Long Iram, Long Bagun, Long Pahangai, and Long Apari areas. Mostly Catholic. Not to be confused with the Bahau tributary of the Kayan River.
Modang	An offshoot of the Kenyah-Kayan complex, the Modang have moved from the heartland to the upper Mahakam basin in the Long Iram, Long Bagun, and Long Pahangai areas, as well as the upper parts of the Kelinjau and Kedang Kepala valleys. Most are Catholic.
Tanjung	Found near the middle Mahakam inland in the Melak and Barong Tongkok areas. Mixed Catholic, Protestant, animist.
Benuaq	Live near the middle Mahakam in Muara Pahu, Damai, Muara Lawa, and Tanjung Isui. Most are Catholic. They weave *ikat* dresses and vests in a snake-scale pattern.
Bentian	Bentian Besar area in the upper Kedang River. Catholic.
Penihing	Long Apari area and Long Bagun.
Murut	Bulungan District, including Long Bawan and Malinau areas. Nearly 100% Protestant. They have largely abandoned old ways. Only a few longhouses remain.
Punan	Scattered in small groups throughout the interior, the Punan are nomadic hunter-gatherers who use *sumpit* (blowpipes), spears, and dogs in pursuit of wild pigs and other game. Most have not learned to grow rice. Punan build only simple shelters; villages move frequently. Some have settled and taken up rice-growing, longhouse construction, even languages of neighboring tribes. In the Apo Kayan, settlements are found at Long Ikang, Long Pipa, Long Sule, and Long Top. Other Punan live in the Balungan and Berau districts.

Mahak Baru

A large Uma Bakung Kenyah village on the Mahak River, a tributary of the Boh. An airstrip is just down-river. Mahak Baru and Dumu Mahak, shown as separate villages on some maps, are at the same site. Many inhabitants are recent arrivals from other villages, including Long Lissi and Long Payau. A school, clinic, and several small *toko* are here. From Mahak Baru, Long Lebusan is an easy 3-hour walk. To Sungai Barang on the Kayan is a 4-day trip by either of 2 routes: canoe one day up the Mahak, then hike 3 days over mountains; or walk to Long Lebusan and take a canoe up the Boh to the Kubu Muse River in 3 days, then hike one day.

FROM THE APO KAYAN

To The Mahakam River

Looking at maps, one would expect to be able to zip on down the Mahak and Boh rivers from Mahak Baru to the Mahakam, but it isn't that easy. The Boh has impassable rapids between the junctions of the Uho and Benahan rivers, and because of a river gorge at this point, there's no portage route. To bypass the rapids it's necessary to hike W from Mahak Baru 1 ½ days to Muara Tanit on the Benahan. Then take to the water again to Muara Benahan and on down the Boh to Long Bagun on the Mahakam. No villages are on this route, but rattan workers often live at Muara Benahan and other camps. Locals often hike from Mahak Baru to Muara Tanit in one day, but 1 ½ or 2 days are more comfortable. A guide is needed; it would be wise to have someone carry your pack on this rugged trail. Large roofed shelters are 5 hours W of Mahak Baru and at Muara Tanit. After the first shelter there is a 2- to 3-hour section of ridge trail with no water until the Tanit River. From Muara Tanit downstream to Muara Benahan is 1 ½ hours by canoe, or walk along the riverbanks (it isn't easy) in 4-5 hours.

From Muara Benahan to Long Bagun direct by *long-bot* takes only one day. There's no telling what the trip might cost. It depends on how well you hit it off with the skipper, who else wants to go along, how long you're willing to wait, etc. The trip could be free or it might cost Rp250,000. *Ketinting* would be cheaper to charter. Some small-scale trading takes place between the Mahakam and the Apo Kayan, with manufactured items going in and chickens coming out. Catholic church workers do the trip too. A possible option is taking a lumber company road, on which you can reach Long Bagun from the Boh River in one day.

The Journey

Below Muara Benahan are some fascinating rapids *(giram)* on the Boh River trip: about 3 hours below Muara Uga the river is full of giant red quartzite boulders, Giram Batu Merah. Downstream, Giram Hulu is the biggest rapid on this section of river. It's navigable by experienced boatmen but passengers may be asked to walk the trail on the W bank. Below, Giram Burung causes concern in high water; otherwise you'll never know it's there. In the lower Boh, the river enters a scenic gorge. The Boh and Mahakam rivers are about the same size when they meet. Then more gorge sections; look for burial markers on the cliffs. Giram Udang on the Mahakam is navigable but passengers may need to walk around via the trail on the N bank. From Long Bagun riverboats head downstream at least every few days.

Overland Routes

Four overland market routes connect the Apo Kayan to: Belaga, Malaysia, via the Aput River; to Belaga via the Item River; to Samarinda via the Boh and Mahakam rivers; and to Tanjungselor via the Kayan River. The shortest trips are those to Sarawak and Samarinda (15-plus days); getting to Tanjungselor may take more than a month. All involve long and dangerous river travel. The Kenyah once used 12- to 15-m-long cargo canoes to make these trips. The 27-km section of waterfalls on the Kayan River below the Apo Kayan is impassable, and the trail past the falls is too rough for carrying canoes. All the trees at the lower end of the falls were cut to make canoes; this route is rarely used today. An alternative is to head up the Iwan River for a day, leave the canoe, go overland to the headwaters of the Bahau, then canoe down the Kayan River below the falls. Another bypass involves descending the Kayan to Nahakeramo (abandoned) just above the falls, then canoeing up the Kat for a day. Leave the canoe and walk over the mountains to Long Jelet, then canoe to the Bahau River and down to the lower Kayan. Only on the routes to Malaysia is it possible to drag canoes over the pass. Travel to the Mahakam River involves a 1- to 3-day hike over the divide between the upper Kayan and upper Boh rivers, a canoe trip to Long Lebusan or Mahak Baru (1-2 days), a hike around the Boh's impassable rapids (1-2 days), then canoeing from Muara Tanit to Long Bagun—a long river trip via the Boh and Mahakam rivers.

BERAU DISTRICT

Tanjungredeb

The capital of Berau Regency is Tanjungredeb, a secondary harbor since WW II. With a population of 32,000, this waterfront of 2-story buildings is 59 km from the mouth of the Berau River. Eight boats monthly arrive here from Samarinda or Balikpapan. The only road (10 km long) is between Tanjungredeb and Teluk Bayur. The autonomous kingdom of Berau, dating back to the 14th C., was divided in 1883, with the Berau River a natural boundary between new capitals established at Sambaliung and Gunung Tabur. In 1960 both kingdoms were abolished by Indonesian parliamentary decree. The 2 palaces still have small private museums. Take a canoe (Rp300) from Tanjungredeb across the river to see Istana Sambaliung. Stay at **Losmen Sempurna** or **Losmen Sederhana**. Food is expensive.

From Tanjungredeb, it's Rp9500 (possibly less with student discount) by fast, custom-built *longbot* to Tarakan, 55 km and 9 hours north. Boats leave at least every other day. Up the unfrequented Kelai and Segan rivers, find the Dayak Basap, Kenyah Tumbit, and Lebu tribes. Upriver by boat is 2 hours and 40 liters of fuel—and that's just the *first* stage of the trip.

The Land

The regency's upper Bahau area, bordering Malaysia and the catchment areas of the Tubu and Malinau rivers to the E and S, is one of few remaining areas of undisturbed lowland forest in Kalimantan. These forests are of immense ecological importance. The area is quite beautiful, with crystal waters—very rare, now that modern mechanical logging has penetrated so far inland. The ridges between the 3 rivers, rarely over 800-m altitude, are very steep and well forested, having been disturbed little by the shifting, small-scale cultivation sites of local tribes. The forest here is rich in edible fruit trees, tropical oaks, and ironwoods. Local paths cross the watershed into the upper tributaries of the Tubu and upper Bahau at Long Berini. The Tubu has many more rapids than the gentle Malinau, but the river is generally navigable downstream from Long Tete. Above Long Tua, the Bahau is not navigable; local trails continue to Long Berang and from here to Sarawak, as they do from the Kelabit Highlands farther N and from Long Nawang in the Apo Kayan. Traditional village and *ladang* hospitality.

The Krayan

The Krayan is tucked into the N corner of E. Kalimantan, bordering Sabah and Sarawak. This region is very difficult to reach overland from Tarakan but an easy hour by plane. The first missionaries here, the Dutch, arrived in 1927. Now the Krayan's Dayaks are quite modern; they've dropped most old customs. Nearly 100% are members of the Kemah Injil Gereja Masehi (KINGMI) Protestant church. *Bahasa Indonesia* is spoken by all but the oldest villagers; in some families the native Krayan language is secondary. Soil here is poor and many people have moved into Malaysia or E to the lowlands around the Malinau River for better land and more economic opportunities. The government encourages people to stay in their homeland by establishing clinics, schools, social programs, and regular Merpati flights to Long Bawan.

Krayan people, also known as Muruts, live on both sides of the Indonesian-Malaysian border. There is much foot traffic across the border between the villages. Tourists, however, are not allowed to cross without advance permission from both countries—almost impossible to obtain! No *imigrasi* or departure taxes here yet, though that may change. This is one of the easiest overland crossings between the 2 countries: on foot it takes only half a day from Long Bawan, the main town of the Krayan, to Bakalalan in Sarawak. People walk there and back in the same day. Indonesians often work in Malaysia and bring goods and money back home.

Village Life

Western contacts and gradual preference for a modern lifestyle have erased most of the old ways. Old men and women with traditional tattoos and elongated earlobes are still seen, but the heavy earrings are now gone. Longhouses are nearly gone, too, but do exist in some villages. Kurid has longhouses with up to 5 families; they are like tunnels, with no interior walls. Five kitchens are lined up on one side; the other side is used for working, eating, and sleeping. There is no outside veranda as in other Dayak villages. To see traditional longhouse life, dances, and crafts, it's better to visit the Apo Kayan, Punjungan, or upper Mahakam areas.

Until recently the church prohibited alcohol and tobacco. Now church rules have eased and many men are hooked on tobacco and spend large sums of money on beer. Sodium cyclamate is being pushed by Indonesian chemical companies, sometimes under the brand name "Tiga Tebu" (Three Sugar Canes). Local people think this is a new, improved sugar, and leave their own natural sugarcane in the fields while consuming doses of this highly potent synthetic, banned in the U.S. because it is carcinogenic.

Tall poles with firewood stacked around them are

commonly seen in Krayan villages. If the wood is stacked to the top and a banner waves from a pole, a wedding or other ceremony is about to take place. After the wedding the bride's family gets the wood. If looking for a Krayan bride, be sure to have 3 *kerbau* handy for the bride price—and consider that a bargain. In the old days, it would have cost 20!

LONG BAWAN

The main town of Kec. Krayan. The Krayan River, also known as the Bawan, is the region's main river. Long Bawan, some distance away, is sometimes referred to as Long Bawan Darat ("Far From River"). There's no *losmen* in Long Bawan but people are friendly and someone will help you find a place. Be sure to leave a contribution for your stay, even though it's not likely they'll ask. Guinness Stout drinkers will be pleased to find their favorite brew here; also Coca-Cola, coffee, tea, and simple meals. But don't expect ice or refrigeration. The town's *toko* are reasonably well stocked with the basic groceries. Rice is the most important food for the Krayan people; the favorite method of serving it is wrapped in leaves, *nasi bungkus*. Join in soccer, volleyball, or rattan ball games. Videos and movies are shown in the evenings, Rp400.

Some reminders of Sukarno's efforts to grab E. Malaysia can be seen near Long Bawan's airstrip at the end nearest town. A small graveyard has been erected for Indonesian soldiers killed while fighting British Gurkha troops in the nearby border area. Wreckage of a large transport plane shot down by Indonesian gunners is nearby. Unfortunately, it was an Indonesian plane. The crew and about 100 soldiers parachuted to safety.

Transport

This area is the easiest place to reach in interior E. Kalimantan; there are 2 Merpati Twin Otter flights (Rp60,000) a week and several MAF flights. MAF also flies frequently from Long Bawan to Malinau (take the regular boat to Tarakan) and (less frequently) to the Apo Kayan. MAF is more expensive than Merpati flying into the Krayan, but cheaper flying out. MAF fares (payable in *rupiah* equivalent) are: Tarakan to Long Bawan, US$100; Long Bawan to Malinau, US$45; Long Bawan to Tarakan, US$67. There's a radio (and an MAF operator) in Long Bawan, so it's possible to know when planes are expected. If making just a day trip to the Krayan with MAF, the pilot may charge only the fare in. The Krayan area can be reached overland from the Apo Kayan (Long Nawang) by first traveling N to the headwaters of the Bahau, then walking across the divide to Pa' Ibang, Pa' Upan, and Long Bawan; allow 2 weeks. Overland travel to and from Tarakan is almost unknown these days, but it's possible for the determined (see "Hikes" below).

HIKES FROM LONG BAWAN

Many walks can be made from Long Bawan, ranging from very easy to extremely difficult. (Or fly among the 8 Krayan airstrips with MAF at about $12 per trip—if the pilot is going there.) Little-used trails also lead S to the Long Punjungan area and E toward Malinau. The mountain trails (marked by a cross on map) can be difficult to follow. A guide is a wise investment. A trip N to Bukit Harun, at an elevation of 2,160 m the highest mountain in the area, takes 3 days. Wind and rain often force climbers to turn back. Between Long Padi and Long Rian, it's possible to canoe 7 hours upstream or 5 hours downstream.

On these hikes don't expect dense tropical jungle. Soil is poor, and where land surrounding Long Bawan has been cleared, only shrubs and scrub trees have regrown. Up in the mountains are 30-m-tall trees, flowers, waterfalls, spiraling vines, sparkling streams, butterflies—and leeches. First get oriented by climbing Buduk Yuvai Samarin, a 45-min. walk E of Long Bawan; from the top you can see surrounding villages, *padi*, and mountains. Find good forests on trails from Long Bawan to Pa' Padi, Pa' Padi to Kurid, Kurid to Lembudud, and many others.

Head SE on the trail to Terang Baru. After crossing the small stream Pa' Lutut, note the *kuburan* on the R: graves are covered by shiny sheet-metal roofs. Pass through a *kerbau* gate, then angle off to the L on a small track. Cross a small streambed, follow the Pa' Lutut a short way, then take the trail straight up the

HIKES FROM LONG BAWAN

To	Direction	Duration
Kampung Baru	N	30 min.
Long Umung	N	4 hours
Terang Baru	SE	1 hour
Long Rian	SE	1½ hours
Binuang	SE	1½ days
Kuala Belawit	SW	15 min.
Brian Baru	SW	1½ hours
Tanjung Karya	SW	2½ hours
Long Api	W	1 hour
Long Midang	W	2 hours
Pa' Padi	S	6 hours
Harapan Karya	S	2 days
Pa' Upan	S	2½ days
Long Rungan	S	3 days

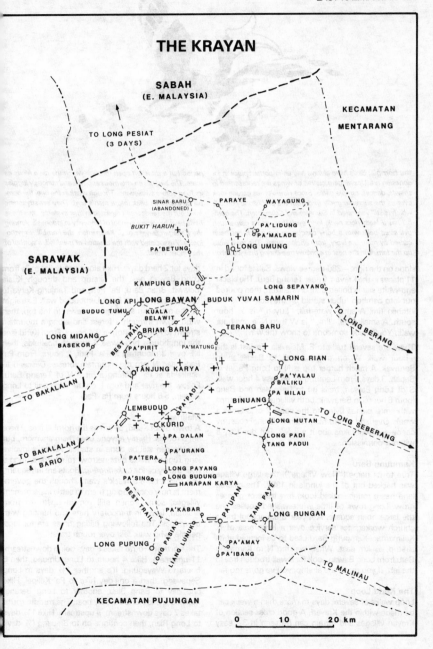

THE KRAYAN

SABAH
(E. MALAYSIA)

TO LONG PESIAT
(3 DAYS)

**KECAMATAN
MENTARANG**

SARAWAK
(E. MALAYSIA)

SINAR BARU
(ABANDONED)

PARAYE   WAYAGUNG

BUKIT HARUH   PA'LIDUNG
PA'MALADE
PA'BETUNG   LONG UMUNG

KAMPUNG BARU   LONG SEPAYANG
TO LONG BERANG

LONG API LONG BAWAN   BUDUK YUVAI SAMARIN

BUDUC TUMU   KUALA
BELAWIT
BRIAN BARU   TERANG BARU
LONG MIDANG   PA'PIRIT   PA'MATUNG
BASEKOR
LONG RIAN
TANJUNG KARYA   PA'YALAU
BALIKU
PA MILAU
TO BAKALALAN   PA'PADI   BINUANG   TO LONG SEBERANG
LEMBUDUD
KURID   LONG MUTAN
PA DALAN
LONG PADI
TO BAKALALAN   PA'URANG   TANG PADUI
& BARIO   PA'TERA
LONG PAYANG
PA'SINGO   LONG BUDUG
HARAPAN KARYA
PA'KABAR   PA'UPAN   LONG RUNGAN
BEST TRAIL
LONG PUPUNG   PA'AMAY
PA'IBANG   TO MALINAU

KECAMATAN PUJUNGAN

0   10   20 km

the hornbill: *Birds have always had an important place in Indonesian art. Upswinging curves of wings are represented in shawls, dances, temple gates. Since Hindu times garuda took over as the supreme godly bird from the prehistoric hornbill, which is still venerated in Sumatra and Kalimantan. The hornbill has a featherless neck, long eyelashes, and a gargantuan oversized beak with a bony casque on top which has been carved by man, like ivory, from ancient times. The male walls up the female in the nest in a hollow tree during the incubation period but a slit is left open through which the male feeds its mate. The bird has an enormous appetite and curiously juggles its food before swallowing. Though weak in the bite, the hornbill can drive its beak into a man's arm. They eat strychnine fruits but the seeds aren't digested in their systems, thus these birds have become a symbol of longevity in Indonesia. Among the Katingan Dayaks of S. Kalimantan, the hornbill is mythologically associated with the creation of mankind, a symbol of the Upper World.*

slope on the right — 360-degree views. Salt is found in 11 places in the Krayan, 6 near Terang Baru. The black-and-white salt is boiled until crystallized, then poured out into bamboo tubes stored on the rack above the kitchen fire. A small waterfall, "Luyan," is ½ hour south. A small cave, "Iluk," is W then N, a one-hour walk. You'll need someone to show the way.

There are several trails to E. Malaysia. Easiest is the 4-hour walk W on a good trail to Bakalalan in Sarawak. A much harder trip is N to Long Pesiat in Sabah, 3 days. From Lembudud, an easy 4-hour walk S of Long Bawan, trails go to Bakalalan and Bario (both 6 hours) in Sarawak; both villages have airstrips with small planes flying to the coast 2 or 3 times a week. Overland to the Malaysian or Brunei coast by canoe and trail takes about a week. But don't try it without permission.

Kampung Baru

True to its name ("New Village"), this large village was hacked out of the jungle in 1982. The cleared land has a rough, naked look; few trees or grasses grow. Long rows of little whitewashed houses line the large open square. A 4-year Bible school trains church workers for service over a large area of E. Kalimantan. Kampung Baru used to be located at its airstrip, ½ km east. When walking N to Kampung Baru from Long Bawan, look for a well-trodden trail to the left. If you reach the airstrip, you've gone too far.

The Kurid Loop

Loop walks of several days to more than a week can be made within the Krayan. A good cross-section of Krayan villages and terrain can be seen in 3-4 easy days (or 2 hard days). Hike along nearly flat trails from Long Bawan past the airstrip and through Kuala Belawit, Brian Baru, Pa' Pirit, and Tanjung Karya to Lembudud, 4 hours. From Lembudud walk E straight up the mountain slope (good views) to the top, then wind down through a forest and along a mountain stream to Kurid in another 3-4 hours. From Kurid (see the longhouses here) walk E through ricefields, then NE over a mountain to Pa' Padi, 2 hours. From Pa' Padi head N into the mountain forests. Descend to ricefields at Pa' Matung a bit SW of Terang Baru. Follow the river and turn L on the wide trail to Long Bawan, 5-6 hours from Pa' Padi.

Malinau

A town SE of Kurid, 50 km as the hornbill flies. There are 3 routes. Hardly anyone uses them anymore, but the trip can still be done in stages. All trails involve long rugged walks over narrow, rough trails, then a river trip by canoe or *ketinting*. Boats are infrequent; you might have a week's wait. Though the government is now encouraging them to settle in permanent villages, some Punan still remain upstream from Malinau, living in temporary huts and hunting with blowpipes. The following hiking times are for local people, who walk *fast* over rough trails:

The **northern route** takes 8 days going downstream, 11 upstream. Hike 4 hours to Long Umung, then 6 hours to Wayagung. It's another 1½ days to Long Sepayang, then a one-day hike to Pa' Kelipal. Hike one day to Bang Biau, another to Long Berang. Malinau is another 2 days by boat. The **middle route** takes 7 days downstream, 9 upstream. Hike 1½ days to Long Rian, then continue on to Binuang (½ day).

Continue on to Lepo Pupung, Long Semamu, and Long Seberang (one day each). From Long Seberang, Malinau is 2 days by boat. The **southern route** takes 7½ days downstream, 9 upstream. Hike to Pa' Padi, then on to Long Rungan, Pa' Sebangar, Bang Lan, and Long Sibiling (one day each). From there it's 1½ days by boat to Malinau.

Long Punjungan

A Kenyah area on the Punjungan River where it joins the Bahau, about 2 weeks S via Lembudud, Pa' Upan, Pa' Ibang, and the Bahau River. There are airstrips along the river at Apau Ping and Long Aran (½ hour by *ketinting*, one hour by canoe). Other airstrips are at Long Bena and Apau Ping. A longboat departs Long Punjungan about once weekly to Long Bia on the Kayan, 2 days (Rp55,000). A boat from Long Bia to Tanjungselor takes 6-8 hours, Rp9500, and continues on to the coastal island of Tarakan, 2½ hours, Rp6900.

People of the Long Punjungan area live in large longhouses and are nearly all Christian. A series of tombs here are built like miniature houses, supported by dwarfed pilings. Their roofs are adorned with *lukir*, carved and painted wooden dragons. If you're lucky you'll see some Krayan dancing; dance platforms are set up in many villages. See masked Krayan men and women take part in rice-sowing festivities. Masks of evil spirits and demons carved of wood have big round eyes made of mirrors, grotesquely large ears, and teeth and lower jaws that "speak."

Long Bia And Beyond

One of MAF's 3 East Kalimantan bases is here. Beyond Long Bia is the notorious Giram Raya (Grand Rapids) on the Kayan River—a 275-m-long, 55-m-wide gorge with rocky whirlpools and studded with treacherous chunks of granite. The boat must head straight up through the central channel or else it'll capsize on the foaming cliffs. Passengers are often told to take the path along the banks. From Long Bia, the following fares are paid in *rupiah* equivalent: Data Dian, 210 km, US$95; Long Nawang, 235 km, US$105; Mahak Baru, 235 km, US$110; Long Lebusan, 235 km, US$105; Long Sule, 185 km, US$85; Sungai Barang, 220 km, US$95.

TARAKAN

Trading and supply town for NE Kalimantan, located on an island off the coast near the border to Sabah. A short-lived though major battle took place here between the Japanese and Australians during WW II, and a number of Japanese bunkers and blockhouses are still standing. The taking of Tarakan I. in Feb. 1945 cost the Australian 26th Brigade 225 men—all killed for a worthless objective. Minesweepers first swept the approach channels clean of mines, then Australian sappers, using demolition charges, had to clear a path through several arcs of lethal steel barriers studded with booby traps and barbed wire. Infantrymen next fought a series of ugly pitched battles against a fanatical 2,500-man Japanese garrison which resisted the invasion so desperately that at one point they charged the exhausted Australians with bayonets fixed on the ends of bamboo poles. The objective of the assault, the island's airfield, was so heavily pockmarked by American bombing that it was of no use to the Allies as a base from which to support other Borneo operations.

Tarakan has an oilfield but production is declining. The low hills overlooking the port are capped by oil tanks. Most of the population (60%) are Chinese; the rest include Bugis, Banjar, Javanese, and Dayaks. No special sights but the markets have a wealth of produce and seafood. The best is Pasar Lingkas; the fish section is on a pier out over the water. Find other markets near the traffic circle and on a side street in Kampung Bugis.

Accommodations

Kampung Bugis has the best selection of cheap and medium hotels, all on Jl. Jen. Sudirman: **Losmen Herlina**, no. 126, Rp4500 s, Rp5000 d; **Barito Hotel** (tel. 435), no. 133, Rp5500 s, Rp7500 d; **Hotel Orchid**, no. 171, Rp6000 s, Rp11,000 d; **Hotel Wisata** (tel. 21245), no. 46 (near junction to Jl. Mulawarman), Rp7000 s, Rp10,000 d; and **Losmen Jakarta**, no. 112 (tel. 21919), Rp2500 s, Rp4000 d. Near Pasar Lingkas on Jl. Yos Sudarso: **Peng. Taufig**, no. 5, Rp4000 s or d; nearby **Peng. Alam Indah**, Rp7000 s, Rp10,000 d; and top-of-the-line **Hotel Tarakan Plaza**, Jl. Yos Sudarso (tel. 501/502), with a/c, private bath, bar, and restaurant, Rp32,000 s, Rp40,000 d. Oilmen stay at the **Oriental Hotel** (with a/c and restaurant), Jl. Sulawesi, Rp9000-21,000; or **Hotel Bahtera**, across the street at Jl. Sulawesi (tel. 298), with a/c, bar, restaurant, disco. The best hotel in town is the **Tarakan Plaza**, Jl. Yos Sudarso (Rp35,000 s, Rp45,000 d), full a/c, bar, restaurant.

Food And Entertainment

RM Cahaya on Jl. Jen. Sudirman (in Kampung Bugis, opposite Losmen Jakarta) has delicious Chinese and seafood dishes for Rp3000-5000. On Jl. Jen. Sudirman near the traffic circle are several *ikan bakar* restaurants specializing in grilled fish, Rp2500-3500 each. Many small, inexpensive *warung* are scattered around town; try those at the intersection of Jl. Jen. Sudirman and Jl. Sudarso. Citrus fruits and apples are

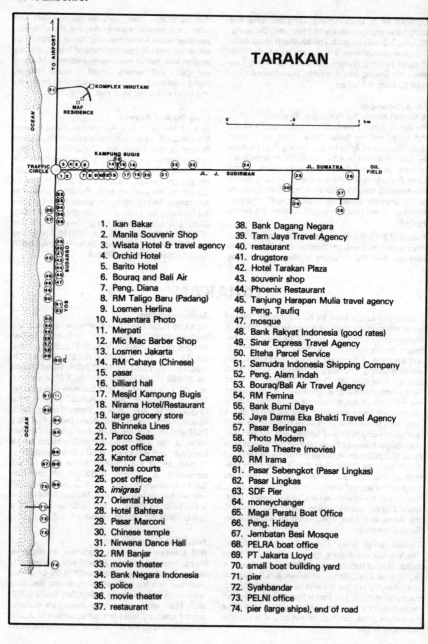

TARAKAN

0 .5 1 km

KOMPLEK INHUTANI

MAF RESIDENCE

OCEAN

TO AIRPORT

KAMPUNG BUGIS

TRAFFIC CIRCLE

JL. J. SUDIRMAN

JL. SUMATRA

OIL FIELD

JL. SUDARBO

JL. YOS

OCEAN

1. Ikan Bakar
2. Manila Souvenir Shop
3. Wisata Hotel & travel agency
4. Orchid Hotel
5. Barito Hotel
6. Bouraq and Bali Air
7. Peng. Diana
8. RM Taligo Baru (Padang)
9. Losmen Herlina
10. Nusantara Photo
11. Merpati
12. Mic Mac Barber Shop
13. Losmen Jakarta
14. RM Cahaya (Chinese)
15. pasar
16. billiard hall
17. Mesjid Kampung Bugis
18. Nirama Hotel/Restaurant
19. large grocery store
20. Bhinneka Lines
21. Parco Seas
22. post office
23. Kantor Camat
24. tennis courts
25. post office
26. *imigrasi*
27. Oriental Hotel
28. Hotel Bahtera
29. Pasar Marconi
30. Chinese temple
31. Nirwana Dance Hall
32. RM Banjar
33. movie theater
34. Bank Negara Indonesia
35. police
36. movie theater
37. restaurant
38. Bank Dagang Negara
39. Tam Jaya Travel Agency
40. restaurant
41. drugstore
42. Hotel Tarakan Plaza
43. souvenir shop
44. Phoenix Restaurant
45. Tanjung Harapan Mulia travel agency
46. Peng. Taufiq
47. mosque
48. Bank Rakyat Indonesia (good rates)
49. Sinar Express Travel Agency
50. Elteha Parcel Service
51. Samudra Indonesia Shipping Company
52. Peng. Alam Indah
53. Bouraq/Bali Air Travel Agency
54. RM Femina
55. Bank Bumi Daya
56. Jaya Darma Eka Bhakti Travel Agency
57. Pasar Beringan
58. Photo Modern
59. Jelita Theatre (movies)
60. RM Irama
61. Pasar Sebengkot (Pasar Lingkas)
62. Pasar Lingkas
63. SDF Pier
64. moneychanger
65. Maga Peratu Boat Office
66. Peng. Hidaya
67. Jembatan Besi Mosque
68. PELRA boat office
69. PT Jakarta Lloyd
70. small boat building yard
71. pier
72. Syahbandar
73. PELNI office
74. pier (large ships), end of road

imported and cost over Rp3000 per kilo! The **Nirwana Dance Hall Coffee House**, on the road to the airport, has music, dancing, drinks, and food in the evenings. Three movie theaters, S of the traffic circle, offer the usual violence and sex. Two billiard halls are across from Mesjid Kampung Bugis.

Services

Two km E of the traffic circle is *imigrasi*, on an extension of Jl. Jen. Sudirman. Elteha shipping service is one km S of the traffic circle. Four banks, which will change US, Singapore, and Malaysian cash as well as US travelers cheques, are scattered along Jl. Yos Sudarso; rates vary, but try Bank Rakyat Indonesia and Bank Dagang Negara. If heading upriver be sure to carry enough *rupiah*—no banks in the interior. A moneychanger is 200 m S of Pasar Lingkas and open 7 days a week, but good only for cash (US, Malaysian, and Singapore dollars). Rates for travelers cheques are terrible.

Transport

Bouraq has twice-daily flights (0830 and 1230) to and from Balikpapan, Rp72,000. It's easy to fly MAF from Long Bawan to Malinau, then take a regular boat to Tarakan. MAF flies to Tarakan from the following villages (fares payable in *rupiah*): Long Bia, US$58; Malinau, US$56; Long Bawan, US$60; Long Nawang, US$80; Data Dian, US$75; Tanjungselor, US$42. MAF planes can sometimes be diverted or chartered, at a cost of about US$1/km.

The airport is only 2½ km N of town. The taxi desk wants Rp4000, but walk ½ km to the main road and take a minibus taxi into the city (10 min.) for Rp400, or just keep walking the rest of the way in. At the traffic circle, turn L for Jl. Jen. Sudirman, Kampung Bugis (cheap hotels), and *imigrasi*. Straight ahead are Jl. Yos Sudarso, Pasar Lingkas, and the port. Tarakan is a cluster of *kampung* grown into a town; it has no real center. Minibus taxis run frequently on the 2 main roads, charging Rp200-500 depending on distance. Small boats are available for charter at the SDF pier. Pelni's office (tel. 202) is in the port; take a minibus for Rp200 from the city center all the way to the end of Jl. Yos Sudarso.

From Tarakan

Bali Air (the charter arm of Bouraq) flies small planes S every day to Berau (Rp41,000), and on to Samarinda (Rp62,000). They also make the *only* permitted connection for foreigners to Sabah from Kalimantan. Depending on passengers, there are 4 flights a week: Mon., Wed., Thurs., and Saturday. If planning on returning to Tarakan, it may be cheaper to buy this ticket in Tarakan rather than Tawau; the flight is overpriced at Rp70,000 for the 100-km hop. The agent for Bouraq and Bali Air is at Jl. Yos Sudarso 9B (tel.

21248/21987). Sample Bouraq fares to: Balikpapan, twice daily, Rp72,000; Banjarmasin, daily, Rp107,500; Manado, daily, Rp204,400; Ternate, daily, Rp249,300; Yogya, daily, Rp178,700. Merpati, Jl. Jen. Yos Sudarso 48 (tel. 568), flies to Long Bawan on Tues. and Fri., Rp66,000, but only 10 kg of baggage is free.

MAF flies to many places in the interior; a pilot and plane are based here. There's a flight to the Krayan (Long Bawan area) almost daily, less frequently to the Punjungan and Apo Kayan strips. Ask or write the pilot (MAF, Box 18, Tarakan) to see if he can take you where you want to go. The pilot's residence is a brown house on the hill between the airport and the town; take the road up to Komplex Inhutani, Peningri. Another MAF pilot is based in Long Bia on the lower Kayan River, above Tanjungselor. Boats depart for Long Bia, from which MAF has frequent flights to the Apo Kayan. Sample MAF interior fares, payable in *rupiah* equivalent: Malinau, 105 km, US$56; Long Bawan, 217 km, US$95; Data Dian, 322 km, US$125; Long Bai, 113 km, US$60; Long Nawang, 345 km, US$130; Mahak/Long Lebusan, 338 km, US$132; Long Aran, 109 km, US$95; Tanjungselor, 64 km, US$45; Batu Putih, 242 km, US$105.

Other Destinations

Long, roofed boats, powered by as many as 4 large outboards, leave on regular schedules to nearby islands and towns; inquire at C.V. Tam Bersaudara, opposite Pasar Sebangkol. For Tanjungselor (2½ hours, Rp4900), boats leave at 0900 every day from SDF pier near Pasar Lingkas (buy your ticket at 0700). For Bhayangkara, take a boat from Tanjungselor, Rp4500. Long Bai (or Long Peso): take a boat from Tanjungselor, Rp6500, 7 hours. For Palau Bunju (oil island N of Tarakan), Rp5500 every day from SDF pier. For Malinau (Rp9000), a boat leaves every 3 days at 0800, arriving 1800; buy ticket at 0700 at SDF pier. Cargo boats to other parts of Indonesia, Japan, S. Korea, etc. are a possibility (check with shipping companies).

Travel up to Tawau may be restricted. At times, only Indonesians and Malaysians can make this trip. Foreigners sometimes must take the overpriced plane (see above), so check with Tarakan *imigrasi* for the latest word. You might need permission from them just to go to the Indonesian oil island of Nunukan near the border (see below). Samarinda *imigrasi* may say you can get to Tawau, travel agents may think you can, even people at the docks may think you can, but you can't unless Tarakan *imigrasi* permits it. For Nunukan a boat leaves every day (Rp9500); buy ticket at Pasar Lingkas.

Nunukan

A timber town on a small island, the last town heading N before you reach the busy Chinese commercial city of Tawau. In Nunukan, you've never seen so many moneychangers per capita in your life. **Hotel Sebar Menanti** is reasonable, or share a bed at **Losmen Arena**. Dayak tribes can be reached in the area around Pembelingan, 64 km up the Sebuku River. See the timber people P.T. Jamaker and get a

letter first in order to stay at the E. Malaysia Camp or the Mukah Sawmill Camp, both in Indonesian territory. Their office is in Tanjungselor in the "old town," one km from Nunukan. They might even give you a free lift to the camp.

EAST KALIMANTAN GLOSSARY

(D) connotes a Dayak word; others are *Bahasa Indonesia*. An apostrophe (') indicates a glottal stop.

asa—old (D)

ba'—baby carrier backpack, covered in colorful beadwork (D)

baru—new, as in Kota Baru ("New Town"). It's common for villages to move to a new site when the surrounding land is exhausted by *ladang* agriculture.

buduk—mountain (D); *bukit* is the Malaysian and Indonesian word

burung enggang—rhinoceros hornbill bird

Camat—(pronounced CHA'mat) local government leader of the *kecamatan* or subdistrict who represents the national government

darat—land far from the river

hilir (or *ilir*)—downstream

hulu (or *ulu*)—upstream

konfrontasi—Indonesia's war of aggression against Malaysia in the early 1960s

ladang—hill ricefields (no irrigation), the traditional Dayak cultivation method

lamin—longhouse (D)

lama—old. Tering Lama, for example, is the oldest of the 3 Tering villages.

liang—a grave

long—confluence of 2 rivers (D); same meaning as *muara*. Long Nawang village, for example, is the site where the Nawang joins the larger Krayan River.

mandau—a large bush knife often made in village forges from scrap steel; a smaller knife or *pue* is kept behind the large sheath.

metik—tattoo (D)

muara—confluence of 2 rivers

payau—large deer of the elk family

pue—small knife usually tied to the *mandau* sheath (D)

sampe'—large, flat lute, often with 3 strings (D)

saop—large bush knife; same as *mandau* (D)

sumpit—blowpipe made from *ulin* wood

sungai—river, large or small

tela'o—barking deer (D)

temator—rhinoceros (D)

tuhan—a respected person; also if capitalized as in *Tuhan* it means "Lord" in reference to Jesus

ubi kayu—cassava root

uma—ricefield (D)

SOUTH KALIMANTAN

This southern province is predominantly flat swampland and comprises a total land area of 37,600 sq km. Straddling the equator, temperatures range from 18-36 degrees C in the lowlands, but lower in the mountains to the east. Mangrove forests and orchids are abundant; proboscis monkeys *(bakantan)* can be seen on the Barito River. Modern roads link some cities and villages, but rivers are still the primary communication network. The province's population density (100 persons per sq km) is high for Kalimantan. Ninety percent of the population embrace Islam; there are also minute numbers of Christians, Buddhists, and other faiths. The Trans-Kalimantan Hwy. starts at Batakan, S of Banjarmasin, and extends all the way to Bontong (N of Samarinda) in E. Kalimantan. When construction is completed in the late 1980s, this highway will stretch all the way to Tarakan. The timber industry (plywood) is the number one money-earner in S. Kalimantan, followed by rattan products (furniture, carpets).

South Kalimantan, with its distinctive and colorful Banjarese culture, deserves more tourists than it gets. Banjarmasin, the capital city, is famous for its floating houses and markets. The Banjarese are friendly and the bureaucrats non-threatening. However, tourism development is really an uphill battle in this province. The banks don't accept traveler's cheques, high standard hotels charge Rp40,000 instead of the usual Rp30,000, and guides charge commissions at craft shops — all conspiring to drive prices up. Young Swiss and Swedish tourists now make up the largest propor-

tion of visitors to the province; groups of as many as 40 people arrive 4 times a year to take part in tours organized by P.T. Adi Angkasa Travel in Banjarmasin.

History

The Javanese Majapahit Kingdom took control of this region during the second half of the 14th C.; today you can still recognize Java's influence in men's clothing styles, in some aspects of the region's *wayang kulit* forms, and even in Banjarese dance dramas. The area was ruled by the sultan of Banjarmasin until the mid-1800s. Dutch colonialists tried to enthrone the unpopular son of the former ruler in 1857, but a joint uprising by Prince Pangeran Antasari and peasants challenged the usurper's rule in 1859. The rebellion was crushed, but with heavy Dutch losses, and it took more than 50 years to completely pacify the province. Once strictly the domain of the *Orang Banjar*, S. Kalimantan's mangrove-sheltered coastline was unsafe due to piracy until the 1950s. Today, one of the economic staples of the province is diamond mining, an industry which employs over 30,000.

BANJARMASIN

More than 450 years old, the city is renowned for its floating houses and its network of crisscrossing rivers, streams, and canals. Banjarmasin is below sea level, and the water level rises and falls with the tides. Situated on the banks of the Martapura River where it enters the Barito River, 22 km upriver from the sea, this is a convenient jumping-off point for both C. and E. Kalimantan. Banjarmasin is the largest city in Kalimantan, with over 350,000 people (80% Muslim, 15% Christian, 5% Buddhist/Hindu). Banjarmasin was once populated by pirates, now turned Islamic conservatives. The Banjarese practice a decidedly more orthodox form of Islam than other Muslim groups on Indonesia's western islands. Thousands make the pilgrimage to Mecca each year; during *Ramadan,* piercing sirens announce the beginning and end of each day's fast, and cigarettes could be snatched from your mouth as you walk the streets. Women should be accompanied by a male. Modernity is fast approaching, and with it traffic jams, a thriving precious stones market, craft shops, fine ethnic restaurants, and other signs of wealth. If you want to hang out for a time in S. Kalimantan, Martapura, Barabai, and Palangkaraya are cheaper, but they lack the charms and idiosyncrasies of this "Venice of the East."

History

Banjarmasin has a long history of intrigue and murder. The Dutch arrived first for the pepper; in 1603 they began to trade with the sultan of Banjarmasin. Four years later, however, a Dutch East Indies vessel was attacked, and its crew massacred—provoking a punitive assault which razed the entire town. The sultan fled to Martapura. The Dutch were granted a pepper monopoly in 1635, but disgruntled growers murdered all 64 residents of the Dutch trading post; another 40 Dutch were slaughtered at Kotawaringin. After further reprisals, the Dutch and the sultan drew up another monopoly agreement in 1658. But when the English undermined the world market, the Dutch finally withdrew in 1669. They returned in 1733, building a settlement at Banjarmasin and Fort Tatas at Tabanio, where they hung on until the 1800s. Many Portuguese merchants also set up shop here following the discovery of the southern route to the Moluccas.

Sights

The city should be seen from the Barito River, which flows red, the color of the spongy peat bogs upriver; take a boat 4 km to **Tamban,** the "Venice of Kalimantan." Thousands of houses here are built on log floats, connected by an intricate system of canals. The well-known **Kuin Market,** one of many similar floating markets, isn't far from **Trisakti Harbor.** The market, a gaggle of boats, is visited by shoppers and traders paddling *jukung,* simple dugout canoes. Market day begins soon after sunrise and lasts only until 0900 or so; vendors wear the traditional straw *tanggui* hats to protect them from the tropical sun. River traders ply the waters of Banjarmasin, selling fish, vegetables, fruits, and household necessities door-to-door. Near the center of the city on Jl. Lambung Mangkurat,

across from the Islamic University, is the **Mesjid Raya Sabilal Muhtadin** ("The Road Unto God's Blessings"). Built on the former site of the old Dutch fort, this massive mosque covers 100,000 sq m, with an area of 3,250 sq m set aside for religious practice. The main minaret is 45 m high; the 4 smaller ones stand up to 21 m. This modern-art mosque has a copper-colored dome shaped like an alien space vehicle. In the more secular realm, there are hundreds of brothels here (take a *sampan* or *becak* to **Bagau)** and about a dozen cinemas.

If you're here on Independence Day, be sure to take in the canoe (*prahu dayung)* races. The Ramadan Cake Fair starts 30 days before *Hari Raya,* from 1400-1800 all during *puasa,* a time in which *asli* super-sweet cakes are sold. These cakes, eaten to break the fast *(buka puasa)* each day, are prepared by rich people who are doing good deeds *(bikin amal)* and sold for Rp1000-2000 (small size). March is the traditional month for marriage, so arrive then to see a Banjar wedding.

Accommodations

There are many *losmen,* though getting into one can be a challenge. Even when you see noticeboards with unoccupied room numbers, most places will insist they're booked up for the duration of your visit. They either shun Westerners, don't want to bother with the extra paperwork, tire of giving the police *uang rokok* ("cigarette money"), or all three!

Losmen Noormas, Jl. Baru 120 (tel. 2014), is in the market area; Rp2500 s or d—a dive but cheap. **Hotel Beauty,** Jl. Haryono M.T. 176 (tel. 4493), is one of the best for the money and they'll take foreigners. Rooms have fans, bathrooms are outside the rooms, and, *warung* are close by, reasonably central. **Hotel Mestika,** next door, is of the same standard and price (Rp4000), but usually full. **Hotel Kalimantan,** Jl. Haryono M.T. 256 (just down the street), also seems full all the time, but since it's 5 m from a particularly vociferous mosque, no big loss. **Losmen Abang Amat** at Jl. Penatu 17 (Rp4000 s or d) is central and fairly quiet but usually full. At Jl. A. Yani 9 is the **Hotel Rachmat** (Rp4000 s, Rp7000 d), with friendly and informative staff. Close by are the **Kuripan** and **Madiyati,** both Rp5000 s, Rp7500 d. Also decent is the **Hotel Sabrina** at Jl. Bank Rakyat 21, Rp7000 s, Rp8500 d (with fan).

Moving up in price, the **New River City Hotel,** Jl. Martadinata 3 (tel. 2983), wants Rp15,000 Ekonomi, Rp20,000 for VIP rooms. Foreigners stay here from time to time. Though the worse for wear, a fun place with a Suzy Wong feel to it (big cold Bintangs, Rp3600; Guinness Rp4250). All rooms have a/c, color TV, massage for Rp6500 per hour. Also in the Rp20,000 class is the **Kartika Hotel,** Jl. Bali, with a/c rooms—a better deal than the Perdana (below) but not as central.

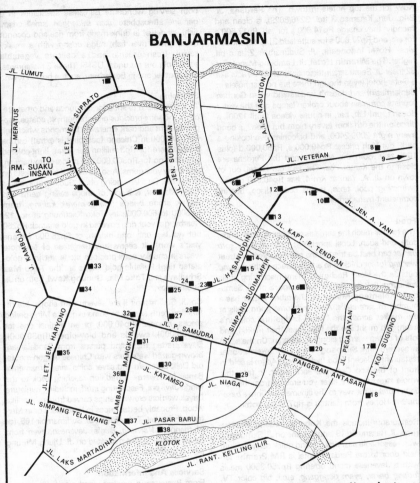

BANJARMASIN

1. Kartika Hotel
2. mosque
3. Rita City Hotel
4. Hotel Anda
5. Bank Negara Indonesia
6. Chinese temple
7. RM Simpang Tiga
8. International Restaurant
9. to Martapura and Barbai
10. Hotel Kuripan
11. Hotel Madiyati
12. Hotel Rahmat

13. Losmen Mawar
14. Restaurant Blue Ocean
15. Hotel Berkat
16. *spetbot* for Palangkaraya
17. Losmen Mess Kai Teng
18. Losmen Noor Arpiah
19. Losmen Peng. Tabalong
20. boat to Tamban
21. Sinar Amandit
22. Hotel Indonesia
23. PT Adi Angkasa Travel Ltd.
24. Garuda Airlines' Office
25. DAS Airlines

26. Losmen Abang Amat
27. Hotel Sabrina
28. Bank Rakyat Indonesia
29. Kelenteng Market
30. Losmen Noor Mas
31. Kantor Pos
32. Hotel Miramin
33. Hotel Benua
34. Hotel Perdana
35. Hotel Beauty
36. Bouraq Airlines
37. Bank Negara Indonesia
38. taxi air to Palangkaraya

Now for the top hotels in town. The **Perdana**, Jl. Brig. Jen. Katamso 3 (tel. 3276/8029), is clean and friendly; they charge Rp14,000 s for fan, Rp17,500 s for a/c, and Rp27,000 s for suite (add 21% tax and service). **Hotel Indonesia**, Jl. Sudimampir 2, is a bit higher. The **Miramin Hotel**, Jl. Lambung Mangkurat 32 (near Jl. Samudera intersection, tel. 8944) acts like a 5-star hotel (even though there are no star hotels in Banjarmasin) and doesn't understand when German tourists complain about broken lamps or if the water doesn't run! Lift, bar, in-house videos (until 1200), a disco on the 6th floor (every night but Mon.), a band every night 2000-2400, and balconies overlooking a park, but high prices: Rp40,000 s, Rp50,000 d (plus 10% tax). Both the Miramin and the Perdana are close to the Kantor Pos. The **Febiola Hotel**, out of town on Jl. A. Yani at Km 4, has Rp40,000 rooms, swimming pool, taxis, tennis court, disco, but incompetent management.

Food

The food is much the same as on Java: noodle soups, *sate*, and such. Local specialties such as spicy *soto banjar* can best be tried in the night markets or street *warung* (great chicken in a tasty sauce at the *warung* outside the Hotel Rachmat). Many fascinating stalls are along Jl. Pasar Baru and Jl. Niaga, S off Jl. Samudera. **Kelentang Market** in the fabric bazaar has a number of *sate* stalls. Also find some good stalls at the market across the "new" bridge (the chicken's fresh; you might see the fowl meet their maker), and lots of cheap *warung* along Jl. Veteran. On the same street are the **Simpang Tiga** and **International** restaurants, decent food fairly cheap. *Apam* is sold in front of Bioskop Cempaka each night. In fact, this whole street to the L after you emerge from the Perdana Hotel all the way to the cinema turns into a *pasar malam*. Honey from Rantau is Rp750 per bottle.

Restaurants include the **Kobana Padang Restaurant**, Jl. Hasanudin 19 (another one on Jl. Samudera), with reasonable *nasi padang* and quick service. Right next door to the Perdana Hotel is **RM Prambanan** with a Javanese menu offering Rp750-3500 meals (*udang bakar, ayam panggang*, etc.), big color TV, nice atmosphere. The **Blue Ocean**, up the street at no. 44, has delicious Chinese food (Rp3500-5000 average meal), or go to the **Phoenix**, Jl. A. Yani (near the state hospital, RM Ulin). The **Shinta**, Jl. Lambung Mangkurat, is the city's elite Chinese restaurant with dishes running as high as Rp8000. European and Indonesian food are also available at the **Miramin Hotel** and at **Banjar Permai Inn** in Banjarbaru (not cheap).

For Banjarese food such as *sop banjar* (Rp1000) and *sayur asem*, go to **RM Simpang Ampat**, Jl. Simpang Ampat. But the real culinary delights of Banjarmasin are the twin restaurants **Depot Makan Kaganangan** and **RM Cendrawasih**, both on Jl. Samudera and both serving wonderful Banjarese specialties in a genuine atmosphere: *ikan saluangan* (small crispy fish), *es dewet* (a drink made from rice and coconut milk), baked river fish, huge *udang* with a musky sauce, fresh greens, and a delicate vegetable soup—pig out for under US$5! These 2 restaurants, and another one in Banjarbaru, are the best in town.

Shopping

This is the place to shop for diamonds and other precious and semi-precious gems: amethyst, agates, sapphires, light and dark emeralds. Diamonds which sell for US$5000 in Chicago (polishing is extra!) can be bought here for Rp3 million per karat; light-colored emeralds go for Rp300,000. Be prepared to bargain, and *know* your gems. Also, beware of pickpockets on this street. On a lane going off Jl. Sudimampir, called Gang Malabar, is a row of shops selling gems and Dayak stone beads (*manik-manik kalung*, from Rp5000 to 500,000); try Toko Kecubung at no. 12. Nearby, get your ring covered in gold enamel: Rp250 but will last only one month, or Rp25,000 for one year's worth. It seems any Banjarese of any note wears a chunky semi-precious stone set in a gold-plated ring! Reliable gold shops are the **Toko Mas Sriwijaya** and **Toko Mas Gunung Kawi**, both on Jl. Sudimampir.

On Jl. Sudimampir II are several craft shops. **Ida** offers fine gems as well as some exquisite Ming-period pieces, *mandau* (Rp40,000, or an original one for Rp300,000), swords and blowpipes (Rp30,000), Dayak rattan mats and purses from Pandalaman, brown-glazed water jars with Chinese dragon motifs, old Delft porcelain and silver coins, even ornamental Banjar brassware—a tradition reaching back to the Hindu-Java era. Fascinating stuff, including miniature Dayak warriors crewing ships carved from rubber-like wood. Probably better prices in Pasar Baru or in Martapura's market. **Toko Batik**, Jl. Sudimampir 108, for all manner of *sarung*, Bugis, Javanese, even from Saudi Arabia! A bird market is on Jl. Ujung Murung (also a textile market).

Services And Information

From Banjarmasin you can send a telex or make a phone call to most major cities in Indonesia and overseas at the **Telephone Office**, Jl. P. Sudirman 92. Visit the **South Kalimantan Tourist Office**, Dinas Pariwisata Kalimantan Selatan, Jl. Panjaitan 31 (tel. 2982). Check out the **university** and its library at Jl. Lambung Mangkurat 3. The banks, such as **Bank Expor Impor Indonesia** on Jl. Lambung Mangkurat, only willingly accept U.S. dollar travelers checks or cash. If banks are closed or if you have other than US dollar TCs, **P.T. Adi Angkasa Travel** has been helping travelers and tourists change nearly any kind of foreign currency for 10 years now. If you get sick, **RM Suaka Insan**, Jl. Pembanguan, is under Philippine management and its doctors speak English well.

the canals of Banjarmasin

Getting There

Passenger ships from Surabaya arrive twice weekly; ships also arrive from numerous other ports. Or take the bus from Panajam near Balikpapan; takes 12 hours (be prepared for rough gravel roads near S. Kalimantan border), Rp12,000. Garuda has 2 daily flights to Banjarmasin from Surabaya, Rp68,800; Bouraq also flies from Surabaya 3 times daily for Rp58,500. Garuda also flies from Balikpapan, Rp53,100; Jakarta, Rp115,000; or Palembang, Rp168,800. **Syamsudin Noor Airport** is 26 km from Banjarmasin, about halfway to Martapura. Hitchhiking is difficult. From the terminal, walk to the Banjarmasin-Martapura highway, about 2½ km to the L when leaving the airport. From the highway (Jl. A. Yani), take a *bemo* into town for Rp500. Taxis from the airport's taxi counter are Rp7500, with no hope of bargaining.

Getting Around

Though the local dialect is Banjarese, *Bahasa Indonesia* is spoken everywhere. Lots of *becak,* but the drivers ask high prices and are difficult to bargain with. Take a yellow minicab *(taxi kuning)* anywhere around town for a flat rate of Rp150. For example, from Jl. Hasanuddin, take a minicab to Terminal Km 6, Banjarsari, Terminal Antasari—all for only Rp150. For local transport, everything starts and ends at Terminal Antasari, the central city terminal. *Taxi kuning* go to: Trisakti, Kayutangi (university complex), old harbor. Hire a *klotok* river craft to see this city from the water (a must); boatmen want about Rp3000 per hour. Inquire near the junction of Jl. Lambung Mangkurat and Jl. Pasar Baru.

FROM BANJARMASIN

If you're traveling anywhere *except* the Barito River and to P. Kembang, you need to have permission from the police or a copy of your police-stamped hotel registration from the first hotel you stayed in. Bring lots of copies of your passport, the number depending upon how far you're going.

Lots of roads in the area, not all good. The long-distance terminal is Terminal Km 6, where minibuses and buses leave frequently for Martapura, Banjarbaru, and other interior towns. Sample fares: Martapura, Rp650 (40 km); Binuang, Rp1400 (87 km); Kandangan, Rp2500 (138 km); Barabai, Rp3000 (168 km); Amuntai, Rp3500 (193 km); Tanjung, Rp4000 (235 km); Panajam, Rp10,000 (512 km, by bus only). The cheapest way to Balikpapan (and on to Samarinda) is by minibus, Rp12,000. The mountainous road via Rantau, Kandangan, Barabai, Amuntai, and Tanjung is in good condition. **Rantau** appears to have a mosque for every 5 people. Its main population are descendants of Malays who immigrated from Sumatra between the 4th and 10th C. and now live off fish, bananas, nuts, rice, and corn. From **Barabai**, there's excellent access to *adat* Dayak country (guides Rp4000-5000 or so per day). Buses from Barabai to Banjarmasin (Rp4500) leave between 1900 and 2000 and take one night. You can also go by road from Banjarmasin to **Buntok** in C. Kalimantan, but it's easier to take a riverboat or fly first to either Palangkaraya or Pangkalanbun.

By Water

The delta canal connections near Banjarmasin make it possible to travel inland by riverboat *(taxi air)*. Taxi air leave (when full) for Marabahan and take about 2 hours, Rp2000. Chartered speedboats are faster but cost Rp50,000. For C. Kalimantan, it's 240 km and 16 hours (Rp6000) from Banjarmasin by *taxi air* to Palangkaraya, the Dayak capital in C. Kalimantan. Jenamas, 250 km, Rp2500 (boat leaves at noon, arrives at 2000), is on the way to Buntok, Rp4500 (or by speedboat charter, Rp300,000); and Muarateweh (3 days), Rp7500 (Rp9500 for berth). From the *dermaga* in Banjarmasin by speedboat to Kualakapuas is Rp2500 (39 km). To Mandomai, take the boat from the *dermaga* to Palangkaraya (where sometimes you have to change boats), Rp7500, 2 days travel. Stay at the mission station and school (where they make furniture) at Mandomai; a Swiss family stays here. There's also a mission station at Tolong Laha, a very beautiful area. Orangutans are plentiful around Pundu.

From Trisakti Harbor, 1½ km away, large ships cruise up the S. Barito River as far as Muarateweh. Also, regular ships to Surabaya cost Rp15,000-20,000; buy your tickets across from the harbormaster's office. **Pelni**, Jl. Martadinata 192 (tel. 3171/3077), has vessels every 2 weeks to: Surabaya, Rp25,000 Deck (18 hours); Semarang, Rp26,000 Deck (19 hours).

By Air

Lots of flights from Banjarmasin's Syasmuddin Airport to coastal Kalimantan airports and major Indonesian cities. Be sure to get a copy of your registration from your hotel or the police will make it difficult for you to leave at the airport. They will also ask to see your passport. Any police station can now stamp this registration paper. Garuda (Jl. Hasanudin 11A, tel. 4023/3885) fares to: Jakarta, Rp117,000 (0730 and 1235); Surabaya, Rp70,900 (0840 and 1605); Balikpapan, Rp55,100 (Sun., Wed., and Fri. at 1400). Merpati (Jl. Suprapto 5A, tel. 4307/4433) fares to: Balikpapan, Rp47,500 (1100); Surabaya, Rp60,800 (1130 and 1430); Yogya, Rp91,000 (1430); Jakarta, Rp100,000 (1130); Tarakan, Rp109,400 (1130); Samarinda, Rp65,900 (1130); Palangkaraya, Rp36,000 (0900). DAS (tel. 2902, Jl. Hasanudin across from Garuda) fares to: Palangkaraya, Rp38,500 (0900 and 1400); Kotabaru, Rp46,000 (0700 and 1200); Sampit, Rp51,500 (0700, 0930 and 1130); Muaratewe, Rp60,000 (0700); Pangkalanbun, Rp61,000 (0930). DAS aircraft have a capacity of only 8-16 passengers. Bouraq (Jl. Lambung Mangkurat 40D, tel. 2445/3285) fares to: Sampit, Rp52,000 (twice daily); Kotabaru, Rp46,600 (every day); Palangkaraya, Rp38,600 (0830); Balikpapan, Rp47,400 (3 times daily); Semarang, Rp84,000 (1230); Yogya, Rp91,700 (1230).

Ask your airline if it offers pickup service to the airport. Or, if you're traveling light, take a motorbike (ask around Pasar Baru or the minibus station). Or take a *taxi kuning* to the terminal across the river, then a minibus in the direction of Martapura; get off at the airport road, then walk the 2½ km to the terminal. Airport tax is Rp1800.

Travel Agencies

Of the 12 that exist in Banjarmasin, only 6 sell tickets and do business with (mostly European) tourists. About half of that business is done by the very efficient **P.T. Adi Angkasa Travel**, Jl. Hasanudin HM27, which is open 0700-2200, 7 days a week, 365 days a year. Mr. B. Marioso and his friendly staff will change travelers checks (through the Trophy Money Changer), do hotel bookings, sell airline tickets (authorized agents of Garuda, Bouraq, and Merpati), and has 7 vehicles for charter. All credit cards accepted. Marioso, who speaks Dutch, conducts a 3-day floating market and diamond polishing tour, a 6-day tour to the Orangutan Project at Tanjung Puting near Sungai Sekonyer, and a 6-day tour to the Loksado Dayak area. Sample tour: South Kalimantan's diamond mines, the monkey island, and the cultural museum at Banjarbaru for US$113 pp, 3 days and 2 nights with all costs paid.

VICINITY OF BANJARMASIN

At **Alalak**, see an old-style native Banjar timbermill; take a taxi to Kuin, then a *sampan* across the river. The remains of a Hindu temple, **Candi Laras**, is near the town of Rantau, 100 km NE of Banjarmasin. There are few good beaches in S. Kalimantan; you have to fly to Kotabaru (by DAS or Bouraq, Rp46,600, with flights leaving twice daily) on the island of P. Laut. An annual *mapandre tasi* ceremony is celebrated in Pagatan (on the coast opposite P. Laut) in which fishermen give thanks for the catch and their safety with offerings, dancing, and feasts.

Pulau Kaget is just 12 km S of Banjarmasin by chartered riverboat (Rp40,000 RT). The S end of this tiny Barito River island preserve has become an ideal environment for the leaf-eating *bakantan* or proboscis monkey, which is found only on Borneo. These oddly attractive red and silver-gray primates have unusually long, vulnerable noses. You sometimes have to wait 2 days to see them, and then only from your chartered *klotok* with binoculars, 100 m away. Not far from P. Kaget is the delta island of P. Kembang with half-tame monkeys—some consenting to take peanuts. From Banjarmasin's *dermaga*, charter a *klotok* (Rp10,000 RT). Be careful with your glasses or they'll get snatched. The *Orang Banjar* believe being surrounded by monkeys brings good luck. An old Chinese temple is also on the island.

Banjarbaru

About ½ hour SE of Banjarmasin by minibus

SOUTH KALIMANTAN

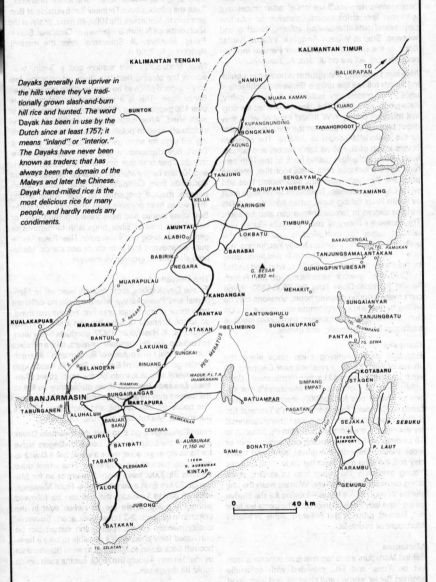

Dayaks generally live upriver in the hills where they've traditionally grown slash-and-burn hill rice and hunted. The word Dayak has been in use by the Dutch since at least 1757; it means "inland" or "interior." The Dayaks have never been known as traders; that has always been the domain of the Malays and later the Chinese. Dayak hand-milled rice is the most delicious rice for many people, and hardly needs any condiments.

KALIMANTAN TENGAH

KALIMANTAN TIMUR

TO BALIKPAPAN

NAMUN

MUARA KAMAN

KUARO

BUNTOK

KUPANGNUNDING

TANAHGROGOT

BONGKANG

AGUNG

TANJUNG

SENGAYAM

BARUPANYAMBERAN

TAMIANG

KELUA

PARINGIN

AMUNTAI

TIMBURU

ALABIO

LOKBATU

BAKAUCENGAL

TEL. PAMUKAN

BABIRIK

BARABAI

NEGARA

G. BESAR
(1,892 m)

TANJUNGSAMALANTAKAN

GUNUNGPINTUBESAR

MUARAPULAU

MEHAKIT

KANDANGAN

SUNGAIANYAR

TANJUNGBATU

KUALAKAPUAS

ORANTAU

CANTUNGHULU

TEL. KLUMPANG

MARABAHAN

TATAKAN

OBELIMBING

SUNGAIKUPANG

PANTAR

TG. DEWA

BANTUIL

LAKUANG

SUNGKAI

PEG. MERATUS

KOTABARU

BELANDEAN

BINUANG

WADUK P.L.T.A.
(RIAMKANANI)

SIMPANG EMPAT

STAGEN

S. BARITO

S. RIAMKIRI

BATUAMPAR

BANJARMASIN

SUNGAIRANGAS

S. NEGARA

MARTAPURA

S. RIAMKANAN

PAGATAN

SEJAKA

TABUNGANEN

ALUHALUH

STAGEN AIRPORT

P. SEBUKU

BANJAR BARU

KURAU

CEMPAKA

BONATI

P. LAUT

BATIBATI

G. AURBUNAK
(1,150 m)

SAMI

TABANIO

PLEIHARA

KARAMBU

: 150m

TALOK

KINTAP

G. AURBUNAK

GEMURU

JURONG

BATAKAN

0   40 km

TG. SELATAN

SELAT LAUT

(Rp1000) from Terminal Km 6, on the road from Banjarmasin to Martapura. This new administrative center has numerous modern Indonesian buildings. Banjarbaru's is usually cooler and less humid than Banjarmasin. Here you'll see lots of rattan processing, with raw fiber strips expertly transformed into fine carpets and mats after peeling, splitting, twisting, and weaving. Stay at **Wisma Anggrek, Wisma Banjar Baru,** or the upscale **Hotel Banjar Permai Inn** (but poor service). All are on Jl. Jen. A. Yani.

Musium Lambung Mangkurat is housed in a building which follows the unique Banjarese architectural style. The present-day collection is pretty paltry, dating only from 1967. The Japanese looted the original museum during WW II, and most of what they didn't take the Dutch got after the war. The rest went to the National Museum in Jakarta. The museum covers much of S. Kalimantan's history and culture, even Hindu antiquities dating back to the 14th century. Pottery includes terra cotta roof tiles, cooking pots, and 7-m-high water jars; also superb blue and white Chinese porcelain. Traditional technology such as Barito River fishing tools, rattan baskets, and *kris* handles carved in female shapes can also be seen. The museum's library of coconut shells (Banjar was without paper for centuries) is fascinating; the hollowed-out interiors contain Malay inscriptions. Adjacent is a gallery featuring portraits and landscapes by the Banjar painter Gusti Sholihin, who died on Bali in 1970—his artwork reminiscent of the French Fauvist tradition. Open Tues.-Fri. 0830-1400. If you can't make it during opening hours, someone may be willing to give you an impromptu tour (give a tip). On Sun. and holidays, the museum sometimes features traditional dancing, music, and games.

Cempaka

Extensive diamond-mining takes place along the shores of Riam Kanan, a reservoir near Cempaka, 10 km from Banjarbaru or 43 km from Banjarmasin. Get a public *bemo* to Cempaka from Martapura's bus station or charter one for Rp5000; there are also minibuses to Cempaka from Banjarmasin's Terminal Km 6. Using traditional tools, the miners (many Javanese) try their luck in the diamond pits. Men dig holes up to 10 m deep in the sour-smelling clay under a roof of loose thatch. They dig out gravel, sand, and heavy clay soil, handing it up from the pit in small baskets. Young girls carry the heavy load to sluicing areas along canals or the lake shore. Women wash the raw sludge through sluice boxes—looking for the elusive *galuh*, "the lady" (raw diamonds). The gems are later cut, faceted, ground, and polished, either in nearby Martapura or overseas.

Martapura

Behind Martapura's bus terminal is an enormous market on Tues. and Fri., crowded with colorfully adorned Banjar women and children, and with good prices on almost everything. High-quality diamonds are also sold in Martapura. South Kalimantan province is one of the major diamond-producing areas of Indonesia; *Kali* means "river," and *intan* "diamond." Take the minibus from Terminal Km 6 outside of Banjarmasin to Martapura (Rp1000, 45 min.), or travel the short distance N from Banjarbaru or Cempaka. Stay in **Peng. Mutiara,** Jl. Sukaramai (near the market); Rp5000 s, Rp7500 d.

Near Martapura's bus station and a 3-min. walk across the playing field is a diamond-polishing factory—a good place to buy gems, often cheaper than Banjarmasin. This is a traditional workshop where over 150 people, using 200-year-old methods, work in each shed. After cutting, giant wheels, belts, and sluices are used to polish the stones—a process taking 2-3 days for small gems, 30 days for large ones. Don't buy diamonds unless you know about diamonds. Take note that the mines are closed on Fri., and 10 days before *Idul Fitri.* Local people believe that diamonds from Cempaka and other nearby places possess magical properties, so local *dukun* selling their wares from portable stalls do a very brisk trade. Buy loose stones and have them mounted here, or bargain for gold or silver rings with birthstones or gems symbolizing one's character. Near Pasar Martapura are souvenir and gem shops and stands. Martapura also has an impressive mosque.

The Loksado Area

To see Dayak tribes, most tourists head off to Mandomai and Palangkaraya where people no different from those of the Banjar area live. For the real thing, go to the Loksado or Batu Benawa areas. **P.T. Adi Angkasa,** Jl. Hasanudin HM27, conducts 6-day tours to Loksado. For independent travelers, take a minibus from Terminal Km 6 outside of Banjarmasin 138 km to Kandangan, 30 km S of Barabai; Rp2500. Kandangan has several simple *losmen* on the main street **(Santosa, Loksado Inn),** but these places may be full as the owners may be afraid of dealing with Westerners. The police are also helpful, and might even offer to put you up. Market days are Tues. and Friday.

From Kandangan, go E to visit the mountain Dayak people of the Loksado area. Loksado villagers arrive for Kandangan's market twice a week; ask a Dayak to guide you back to his longhouse. Four-wheel drive vehicles (Rp3000) leave every 2 hours or so for Mawangi, 20 km E on a very bad road. From Mawangi, walk all day to Loksado; the trail can be followed without a guide. There are 29 *rumah adat* in the Loksado area, each 2-3 hours walk apart. Souvenir-quality *mandau* knives, spears, and *sumpit* can be purchased fairly cheaply. It's possible to take a bamboo raft back down to Mawangi (then to Banjarmasin by road) in only 4 hours (Rp7500), but the swift rapids could be dangerous.

CENTRAL KALIMANTAN

The province of C. Kalimantan is large (156,610 sq km), with vast areas of swampland and lowland terrain in the south. The Muller Mountains border the province in the far N, with the Schwaner Mountains to the W and northwest. Many rivers flow here, draining the highlands, including the Kahayan, Sumpit, Mendawai, upriver portions of the Barito, and one of Kalimantan's several Kapuas rivers. The population of 850,000 is predominantly Islamic (63%); the rest are native Dayak: 17% animist, 16% Protestant, 3% Catholic, while other faiths comprise just one percent.

The Barito River

Navigable up to 750 km upriver, the Barito is the most expedient and economical way to enter the province. Travel by land is difficult here (few highways); roads are expensive to build (stone must be imported) and to maintain, while river highways are already abundant. From Banjarmasin one can take the Barito River all the way to Muarateweh and beyond. The boat is always stopping to pick up and deliver both people and goods. Many Banjar settlements and agricultural areas are located along the river, wide and muddy in its lower courses, and flowing through rich marshy country. Towns here are Islamic, with the ornate domes and spires of mosques nestled away in the trees. Villagers live by fishing, rice-growing, and hand-sawing logs into planks. Traditionally, the people of Kalimantan decorate their homes with flowers. Along the Barito River grows the *pasak bumi*, the roots used in *Strong Pa* medicinal capsules for increasing men's sexual potency. Continuing N, you soon enter Dayak country and start to notice Christian churches.

PALANGKARAYA

A provincial capital not frequently visited by tourists and once intended as the Indonesian capital of the entire territory. In the 1950s when President Sukarno visited this town on the Kahayan River, then called Pahandut, he learned it was the mythical birthplace of the Dayak people—where the first human being descended to earth from the upper world. With his usual political astuteness, he ordered that the governor's residence have 8 doors and 17 windows, symbolizing 17 Aug.—the day Indonesia's Proclamation of Independence was signed in 1945. Concrete administrative buildings and asphalt roads suddenly appeared, and a military statue was erected in the center

of a great traffic rotary—all totally incongruous and inappropriate in such a remote, undeveloped area. Except for the fact that Palangkaraya is strategically located on the Kahayan River, this city hardly earns its title as the capital of such a large province.

Be sure to bring all the *rupiah* you'll need before arriving in C. Kalimantan. Except at **P.T. Adi Angkasa Travel**, Jl. A. Yani 11 in Palangkaraya, you can't change travelers cheques anywhere else in the province.

Sights

A surprising find in this small, backwater town is the striking local **Museum Balanga**, complete with classical white fluted pillars and the word "MUSEUM" proudly announced on top. Inside are Chinese ceramics, Kahayan Dayak *kayu besi* guardian figurines (10-12 cm tall), ferocious Dayak weaponry, farming and forestry implements, and all types of original Dayak handicrafts such as belts decorated with boars' teeth. Notice also the photographs of the *mihing*, great Dayak rattan fish traps traditionally used only in the Kahayan River area. It takes 3 months to construct these rectangular structures, open at one

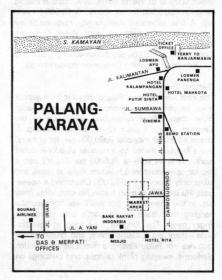

end and at the top, each 100 m long and 8 m wide. A trap is placed downstream, and while fish swim in on all 4 sides about 20 fishermen sit on the rattan fences and net the trapped fish. Behind the museum is a small zoo with a dirty pond of crocodiles; also monkeys, several deer, and a *kancil*. Take a walk in the gardens; the museum is on 5 ha of grounds and another 5 ha are reserved as a Taman Budaya ("cultural garden").

Buy some of the museum's featured crafts in the market, near the Pelabuhan *dermaga* (pier). The *pasar* has baskets made of rushes, the so-called Borneo bags of Kuta Beach, used for carrying food or babies on your back (actually made in the Kapuas River area). Also find gold and other precious metals here, and weird green-rubber Dayak figures (Rp2500). Lots of basketry, wicker fish traps, Dayak rattan goods, fake *mandau* swords and leather sheaths (expensive), even Chinese porcelain. Old Spanish and fake Dutch money or pottery can also be purchased here. The **public library** is at Jl. Ade Irma Suryani Nasution 3; also visit the University of Palangkaraya.

Accommodations And Food

A concentration of cheap *losmen* are found by the *dermaga* where the *longbot* and *taxi air* leave for and arrive from Banjarmasin. **Hotel Kalampangan**, Jl. Nias 17 (tel. 21746), charges Rp5000 s, Rp8000 d. Across the street is **Losmen Mahkota** (Rp5000 s or d) and down the road at no. 2 is **Losmen Putir Sinta**, with cheaper rooms. Higher priced is **Hotel Dandang Tingan** (the best, at Rp50,000), or the **Adidas** (Rp36,000 s or d). **Hotel Virgo**, Jl. A. Yani, is middle range at Rp20,500 for a/c rooms, Rp15,500 for non a/c. A few expensive *nasi padang* restaurants are within walking distance of Hotel Virgo. There are *warung* and foodstalls down at the docks and in the night markets, but you pay 2-3 times what you'd pay on Java (even speaking Indonesian doesn't help!).

Getting There

The best way to reach Palangkaraya is by riverboat from Banjarmasin's *dermaga* (pier) up the Barito River, then follow connecting canals up to the Kayahan. This is a great 12- to 13-hour river trip. A chartered *taxi air* may cost Rp90,000 per day or more, but a *longbot* shared by a number of people could work out to as little as Rp6000 pp. There's also a regular speedboat which leaves daily at noon and takes only 5 hours (Rp15,000). Chartering a speedboat (Rp350,000) is even faster. No crocodiles (they nap in the afternoons), but you'll see honeycombs hanging from trees as the boat's pilot avoids the angry bees. The *longbot* may stop at Kualakapuas—there are 2 *losmen* here, and crumb-rubber factories—or Pulau Pisang, a river town of wooden platforms, swaying plank bridges, and buildings on

stilts. At Palangkaraya, the walk from the docks to the center of town takes 20 min., or take one of the Suzuki *bemo* around town for a flat fee of Rp200. Or take one of the ubiquitous, hustling *becak*.

Garuda has one flight daily (at 0915) from Jakarta to Palangkaraya (Rp109,900) and one flight daily (at 1055) from Balikpapan (Rp58,700). From the airport to town is Rp5000 by taxi or Rp2000 by shared taxi.

From Palangkaraya

The Kahayan River begins in the Muller Mountains, emptying into the sea at Tanjung Tawas. You can travel upriver on the Kahayan past Palangkaraya to dozens of villages, then trek to more distant destinations. *Spetbot* to Banjarmasin cost Rp15,000 (5 hours); buy your ticket an hour before at the little office on the pier.

Merpati has an office on Jl. A. Yani; the Bouraq office is at Jl. A. Yani 6, tel. (0514) 21622. Sample Merpati fares to: Pangkalanbun, Rp42,100; Pangkalpinang, Rp23,800; Sampit, Rp29,800; Surabaya, Rp85,200. Or fly with Garuda (Jl. Sudirman 45, tel. 21121/21132) direct to Jakarta (Rp109,900) or Balikpapan (Rp58,700). For information and ticketing, contact Adi Angkasa Travel, Jl. A. Yani 11; they accept all credit cards.

Vicinity Of Palangkaraya

Tangkiling is only Rp1500 (if many people, less) and 30 min. from the *bemo* terminal on the western edge of Palangkaraya. This town is at the end of the province's only highway. As a propaganda ploy, the Russians built this road as far as 31 km, but suddenly found themselves unwelcome in Indonesia when the communists staged their alleged coup in 1965; Indonesians completed the last 3 km to nowhere. The road was supposed to reach Kasungan to the NE, but that plan has been abandoned. It is a beautiful well-built highway in the middle of the Kalimantan swamps and still nobody knows why it was ever constructed. Few vehicles use the road, and no crops grow alongside it because of the soil's acidity. Tangkiling's hill is known as Bukit Batu (stony hill), since there is a quarry there and a few bungalows. From Tangkiling's landing stage, it's 3 hours by *longbot* back to Palangkaraya, or about Rp1500 pp by shared taxi. Take the *air taxi* upriver 1½ hours (Rp4000) to **Bukitrawi**, river town of about 1,000 people. Boats leave 3-4 times a day when there's enough passengers, or hitch a motorcycle ride along the tracks by the river then inland. Bukitrawi is a Protestant village with 2 primary schools and a lower secondary school. Walk down the sandy lanes with children shrieking behind you. Pressed natural rubber sheets drape fences; there are 2 crumb-rubber factories downstream in Kualakapuas.

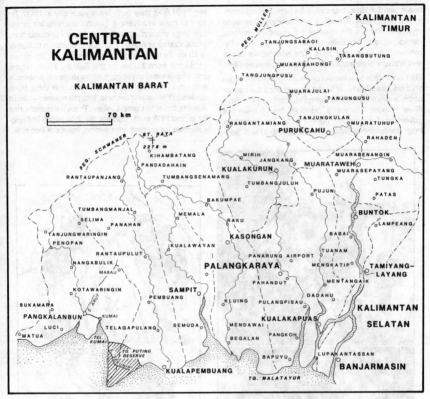

OTHER CENTRAL KALIMANTAN DESTINATIONS

Muarateweh

Fly from Banjarmasin to Muarateweh for Rp62,900 with DAS (they have a monopoly so book at least 5 days in advance). A trip by *klotok*, which holds 10 people, costs about Rp60,000 total, though speedboats, which hold only 3 people, could run upward of Rp350,000! In Muarateweh, there's **Losmen Gunung Sintuk**, charging Rp6000, plus 2 movie theaters, billiard halls, and *warung*. From Muarateweh go S on the Barito to Buntok and Lake Matur, then on to Banjarmasin. Or get a guide and trek E or NE to the Mahakam River area in E. Kalimantan.

Tanjung Puting Reserve

Established in 1936, this is one of the largest (305,000

ha) lowland reserves in Kalimantan. Tanjung Puting consists mostly of a freshwater swamp forest with extensive peat bogs, and nipa palm swamps nearer the coast. Dry forest lands are to the N, some *padang* to the east. The reserve covers most of Kotawaringan Sampit, or the cape of Tanjung Puting on the S coast of C. Kalimantan in the W between the Seruyan and Kumai rivers. Camp Leakey Station in the reserve specializes in orangutan research and rehabilitation. The only other orangutan rehabilitation center is in the Bohorok area of N. Sumatra.

There's a network of trails in the 3,500-ha study area, where orangutans are accustomed to people and fairly easy to observe. Swamp trekking involves wading (sometimes up to your chest) in the reddish waters, and clambering over tree roots. But you can tour the reserve by boat along the Sekunir River. Otters, false gavials, and occasional crocodiles, pythons, and monitor lizards can be spotted in the wetter areas. Where it's drier, look for gibbons, macaques, sun bears, *sambar* deer, *muncak,* wild pigs, and squirrels. In the bay, **Teluk Kumai,** a few *dugong* have been reported. Birds in the reserve are abundant: herons, storks, egrets, hornbills, pigeons, kingfishers, flycatchers, bulbuls, and *pitta.* The spectacular argus and fireback pheasants are rarer, but sometimes seen.

Plan on 4 days to a week for your trip. Kotawaringin on the Lamandau River to the W was once the capital of an ancient sultanate. **Pangkalanbun** on the Arut River is now the area's principal town; there's a government resthouse here. Fly to Pangkalanbun from Banjarmasin: DAS charges Rp60,000 and Bou-

raq Rp61,900; they both leave each day at 0900. Be sure to book in advance! Sea connections are possible; large ships ply the Arut as far as Pangkalanbun, and also stop at Kumai. From Pangkalanbun to Kumai is 15 km by road. To get to the reserve, go downriver by *klotok* from Kumai to the Sekunir River, where you'll have excellent opportunities to watch proboscis monkeys. Boat up the Sekunir, through thick trees covered in vines and orchids, into the reserve—about 3 hours travel to Camp Leakey. There's a guesthouse here, and PPA staff. Contact the PPA office in Pangkalanbun for current information, maybe a free ride.

A beautiful specimen of a tree orchid in bloom. Borneo's 72 genera of wild orchids range from microscopically small species to giant purple ones that drape clear to the ground from 15-m-high branches; also orchids in bush form, orchids twisting like gazelle horns, epiphytes clinging to tree trunks, orchids like the pure white Coelogyne shooting out of sodden mosses, and the fantastic comet-like "finger orchids." The most delicate and brilliantly colored specimens frequently grow in the thickest darkness. Hundreds more orchid genera have yet to be recognized and collected.

Remarkable beetles in Kalimantan, several with antennae up to 25 cm long. Many insect species have ingeniously disguised themselves as twigs, leaves or other insects to avoid being devoured by the jungle's birds, lizards, civet cats, toads, and insects. Some appear to grow out of the very leaf the insect feeds upon. Bright-colored insects give off evil-smelling, rank-tasting fluids; others fend off predators with poisonous stings or startle attacking birds by suddenly exposing their bright markings, giving the insect time to escape.

WEST KALIMANTAN

An immense, rugged, sparsely populated province where English is not that widely spoken and travel is slow and/or expensive. Government troops and communist guerrillas fought an intermittent war here for several years starting in 1968, the year Chinese insurgents moved their bases across the border from Sarawak in E. Malaysia. The region is still politically sensitive: when flying into Pontianak's airport there's an *imigrasi* checkpoint where you must sign in. If you want to travel beyond the capital, Pontianak, you must report to the police and get a *surat jalan,* plus you might even have to report to *Laksus* (military intelligence) as well as the *camat's* office. It'll take you hours just to file the paperwork—and you have to repeat the process at every town along the Kapuas River! Officials discourage you from going upriver alone; they'd rather you join a tour group (see "Travel Agencies," p. 811).

The Kapuas is the 1,100-km-long "mother river" of the province, connecting areas near Pontianak with Sanggau, Sintang, Putusibau, and even points near the E. Malaysian border. Life and work here are typical of riverine peoples: catching river fish and selling them at market; transporting jungle products such as rubber from the interior; and delivering goods from the city to upriver villages—a virtual flotilla of floating shops working the river. Pontianak is *the* point of arrival and departure for the province: hop a ferry across the massive Kapuas to Terminal Siantan on the other side, then take a series of minibuses N as far as Kartiasa (W of Sambas), S as far Supadio, and E as far as Sintang.

The Land And Climate

West Kalimantan's area totals 146,760 sq km, larger than the Indonesian islands of Java and Madura combined. The equator bisects Pontianak. The land is low and level near the coast, with extensive swampland. The Kapuas River, flowing NE to SW in the center of the province, dominates W. Kalimantan. The longest river in Indonesia, it is also wide and deep: sea-going ships can sail upriver as far as Putusibau. Its tributaries, which drain the island's entire western interior, include the Melawai, Sekayan, Mandai, and Ketungan rivers. There are also many natural interior lakes, most good for fishing. Higher and hillier areas surround the Kapuas River basin. To the N along the Sarawak border are the Kapuas Hilir and Kapuas Hulu ranges, while the Muller Mtns. fringe the province to the E and the Schwaner Mtns. to the southeast. Soil in W. Kalimantan is generally poor and acidic, so *ladang* cultivation is

widespread. Wet ricefields are found N of Pamangkat. The province has a hot and humid tropical climate, with an average daily temperature of 29 degrees C. The annual rainfall averages 300 cm, with about 170 rainy days annually. Seasons here are indistinct: Dec.-April is the wet season, May-June the dry.

Flora And Fauna

Vegetation zones include a variety of swamp and lowland forests, jungle areas still pristine with abundant orchids and liana, and montane vegetation at higher elevations. Numerous snakes, including pythons, and primates such as leaf monkeys, the white-handed gibbon, the red-furred *kelasi,* and the *simpai* are found here. In certain areas, monkeys are heavily hunted because they damage the coconut crop. Other wild mammals include sun bears, *sambar* and mouse deer, *muncak,* bearded pigs, porcupines, and fruit bats. Bird species include chattering parrots, rare long-tailed parakeets, pheasants, rhinoceros and helmeted hornbills, and *pitta.*

History

During the 17th C., the most important states of W. Kalimantan were Sukadana, S of Pontianak, and Sambas to the north. The Dutch tried to trade these 2 areas for diamonds. When the British attempted to colonize Sukadana, the Dutch stepped in to support the Banjarese pirates who held the area. In 1778, the Dutch installed an Arab as sultan of Pontianak, but pulled out altogether 3 years later due to lack of men, guns, and money. During the entire colonial period, right up until the Japanese occupation in WW II, there were only 2 Dutch Residents—the total government of Borneo—stationed in Banjarmasin and Pontianak, and an Assistant-Resident at Sambas. If you *really* want to get into the history of the province, Toko Buku Menara (Jl. Asahan 4, Pontianak) sells a thick book on just the dynastic history and culture of Kalimantan Barat: *Sejarah Kebudayan dan Istiradat* (Rp10,000).

Of all the Kalimantan provinces, W. Kalimantan in particular felt the full brunt of the Japanese occupation (1942-45). Between Oct. 1943 and July 1944, thousands of Indonesian intellectuals, members of the Islamic aristocracy, and prominent Chinese were rounded up, brought to secret places, and executed. After the war, mass graves were uncovered, the largest at Mandor (1,000 victims). Estimates of the exact number of victims of this "Sungkup Affair" *(sunkup* is sail-cloth; those arrested were taken away in trucks covered by sail-cloth) ranges from 3,000 to 20,000. Starting in 1945, the guerilla group *Majang Desa,* comprised of Dayaks, Malays, and Chinese, emerged. Dayak warriors often attacked during forest-clearing operations, taking numerous Japanese heads and hanging them on poles for all to see. As one sees tipsy groups of free-spending Japanese timbermen dining in Pontianak's expensive seafood restaurants, it's difficult to believe that the deep scars of the war have healed over so completely.

Economy And Handicrafts

West Kalimantan is a major source of Indonesian rubber, second only to N. Sumatra. But the most rapidly expanding industry is plywood processing, with mills concentrated in the Pontianak and Ketapang areas. In 1967, the forested area of Kalbar covered 9.3 million ha. Over the next 15 years, commercial logging operations savaged over 5 million ha. Sadly, there is no large-scale, integrated, and sustained program for reforestation: in 1979-80 forestry officials targeted 50,000 ha of land to be reforested, but actually achieved only 9,960 ha. Most people live by farming, trading, harbor work, and in construction or some provincial industry such as timber processing. Agricultural development schemes and cash crop agriculture have also contributed to economic growth. Traditional ceramics are produced in Singkawang and Pontianak. Folk crafts include basketry, weaving, ceramics, and woodcarving. Available are Sejangkung hats, Sambas *kain,* Singkawang *songket,* and Iban Dayak weavings with traditional motifs. Miniature equator monuments, Dayak *mandau,* and shields are sold in Pontianak's *pasar,* and at souvenir shops along Jl. Tanjungpura.

The People

The population of W. Kalimantan is about 2.2 million, giving the province an average density of 19 people per sq km. The most densely populated areas are near Singkawang and Pontianak. *Orang melayu* (many brought in on *transmigrasi* schemes) make up 39% of the total population, Dayaks 41%, Chinese 15%, and the remaining 5% are Bugis, Madurese, Minangkabau. Initially brought in to mine gold ore by the sultan of Sambas in the 18th C., the Chinese today live for the most part in the cities of Pontianak and Singkawang and in the towns. Though they have gradually moved closer to the coasts to find jobs and education, the Dayak people have traditionally lived along the rivers. The Iban Dayaks live primarily N of the Kapuas, many in Sarawak where their culture is generally more intact than is the case in Kalimantan Barat. Whereas in Kalimantan Barat river travel is expensive and fraught with bureaucratic hassels, in Sarawak it's fairly easy to travel alone and experience much more of the animist longhouse culture. On the Indonesian side of the border a larger proportion of the Dayaks have taken to Christianity and have as-similated to a large extent with the Indonesian culture. To study the near-vanished, remote native cultures of this province, visit the enthnographic collections of Museum Negeri Propinsi in Pontianak, plus small local museums in Sintang (400 km E of Pontianak) and in Putusibau in the Upper Kapuas.

Getting There

Supadio Airport, 20 km from Pontianak, is the main gateway into W. Kalimantan, with 3 Garuda flights (Rp95,700 OW) from Jakarta each day, taking 55 min. by F-28 or 1½ hours on an F-27. Merpati and Sempati also fly from Jakarta (when they're busy they charge more, when they're slow they charge less). Merpati also flies to Pontianak from Kucing in Sarawak (E. Malaysia); Rp97,000. MAS doesn't have a Kucing-Pontianak flight, and there isn't even a Garuda office in Kucing. Garuda, however, does have a flight from Balikpapan (Rp110,000 OW). note: Pontianak is only 200 km S of Sarawak. The border area—declared an anti-communist "operations area"—has been closed since Jan. 1975. Indonesia is afraid the undesirables they pushed over the border into Sarawak in the 1960s are going to return, so the entire area N of the Kapuas River resembles a military occupation zone. Foreigners cross the border only by air.

Getting Around

From Pontianak, DAS and Deraya fly to Sintang, Nanga Pinoh, Putusibau, and other remote airstrips. MAF also takes passengers to the interior if space is available. Riverboats reach Sintang, Putusibau, and other towns along the Kapuas River. While traveling, expect to be stopped frequently and asked for your papers, receive a stamp *(cap),* and maybe even searched for weapons in tense areas. Before leaving Pontianak for upriver, get a *surat jalan* from the Kantor Polisi on Jl. Zainuddin, Pontianak. Taking a guide, joining a tour group, and making advance reservations is often required for upriver travel.

PONTIANAK

A bustling, sprawling town (pop. 350,000) on the equator, Pontianak is also known as *Kota Khatulistiwa* ("Equator City") or the "Floating Town." Founded in 1771 by Syarif Abdur, an Arab, Pontianak is W. Kalimantan's center of government, trade, banking, and culture. Hot and humid, its annual rainfall averages 320 cm. This overgrown village's name literally means "vampire ghosts of women dead in childbirth," and refers to a baleful Indonesian spirit who lures young men into cemeteries. Located strategically where the river Kapuas Kecil meets the Landak, Pontianak is Borneo's largest city and the province's rubber and plywood capital. Few tourists arrive here and the only foreigners are Japanese and Koreans working in the plywood industry; if flying in

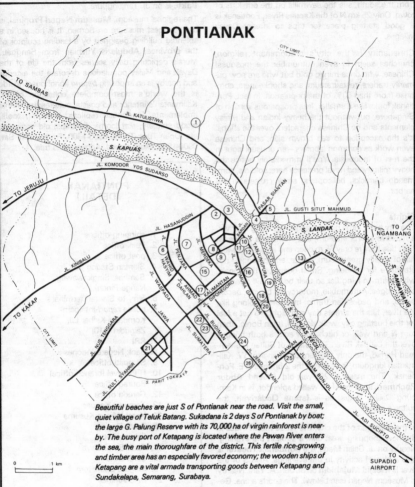

PONTIANAK

TO SAMBAS

S. KAPUAS

JL. KATULISTIWA

JL. KOMODOR YOS SUDARSO

TO JERUJU

TO KAKAP

CITY LIMIT

JL. KINIBALU

JL. HASANUDDIN

JL. WASPADA

JL. PERIJAYA

JL. AHMAD DAHLAN

JL. KALIMANTAN

JL. MERDEKA

JL. HASYIM

JL. PATTIMURA GAJAMADA

JL. TANJUNGNURA

JL. DIPONEGORO

JL. JAWA

JL. BUDIMAN

JL. SUMATERA

JL. NUS TENGGARA

JL. SULT SYAHRIR

S. PARIT TOKRAYA

JL. JEND A. YANI

JL. PAHLAWAN

JL. IMAM BONJOL

JL. ADI SUCIPTO

PASAR SIANTAN

JL. GUSTI SITUT MAHMUD

S. LANDAK

JL. TANJUNG RAYA

S. KAPUAS KECIL

S. AMBAWANG

CITY LIMIT

TO NGAMBANG

TO SUPADIO AIRPORT

Beautiful beaches are just S of Pontianak near the road. Visit the small, quiet village of Teluk Batang. Sukadana is 2 days S of Pontianak by boat; the large G. Palung Reserve with its 70,000 ha of virgin rainforest is nearby. The busy port of Ketapang is located where the Pawan River enters the sea, the main thoroughfare of the district. This fertile rice-growing and timber area has an especially favored economy; the wooden ships of Ketapang are a vital armada transporting goods between Ketapang and Sundakelapa, Semarang, Surabaya.

0   1 km

1. Tugu Khatulistiwa
2. Pontianak City Hotel
3. Pelabuhan Divicora Pontianak
4. River bus (Jl. Bardan) or Bardan ferry
5. Santian bus station
6. Mini Hotel
7. Arena Remaja
8. Friendship Inn
9. Bouraq Office
10. Bank Negara Indonesia 1946
11. Pontianak Theater
12. Pasar Pontianak
13. Masjid Sultan Abdur Rachman
14. Istana Quadariyah
15. Polisi Resort Pontianak
16. Komando Distrik Militer (Kodim)
17. Kantor Walikotamadaya Pontianak
18. Equator Guesthouse
19. Orient Hotel
20. Hotel Kapuas Permai
21. governor's mansion
22. Kantor imigrasi
23. Police Mess "Bhayang Kava"
24. Stasion TVRI
25. MAF (Mission Avation Fellowship)
26. Museum Neger

from the south, see the sawmills on the outskirts of town. Only 25 km N of the Kapuas River, Pontianak is a good starting place for trips to interior Dayak villages.

Christianity is the city's predominant religion; churches seem to even outnumber the mosques! Chinese, who once mined gold but who are now primarily traders, restaurateurs, and shopkeepers, comprise more than 60% of the population. In fact, Pontianak looks like a smaller, less prosperous version of Singapore, but without the heavy Indian and Malay elements and no Chinese characters over the shops. It's the exception to see brown skin, and Chinese even work as common laborers—an unusual sight in the rest of Indonesia. You'll immediately notice the heavy military and naval presence here: soldiers, commando barracks, helicopters, small cruisers in the harbor.

Sights
The city has 2 large girder bridges spanning the river, a massive sports stadium, and numerous canals: at high tide they're only ⅔ m deep and about 6 m wide, full of smelly green scum, waste, and garbage—not attractive for canoeing. Small boats ply the canals, with boatmen lying flat so their bodies will clear low city bridges. Automobile, motorcycle, bicycle, *becak, bemo,* and pedestrian traffic, meandering along like the river, fills the streets day and night. To get a feel for this bustling city, walk along Jl. Iman Bonjol, then turn N and walk or hitch *oplet* across both bridges over the Landak River. The *kraton* of Sultan Muhammad Hamid, the only remnant of an ancient W. Kalimantan kingdom, is between the 2 bridges in E. Pontianak. The massive 250-year-old **Mesjid Abdur Rachman,** in all its white-walled splendor, is in Kampung Dalam Bugis, as is **Istana Qadariyah,** the sultan's palace.

In the main part of the city, **the Nusa Indah Plaza** is the new shopping area; take a stroll in the evening. Nearby on Jl. Gajah Mada, the **Pontianak Theater** is also of activity in the evenings. Also S of the river is **Mesjid Mujahidin** on Jl. Jen. A. Yani. Nearby is Museum Negeri (see below). The sports arena, **Gedung Arena Remaja,** is S of the city on Jl. Sultan Abdur Rachman, within walking distance of the governor's mansion. See **Sekolah Santo Paulus** and the **Gereja Katolik** for Dutch-style architecture. Traditional handicrafts, paintings, ceramics, and carvings are sold in a half dozen shops along Jl. Tanjungpura (try the **Fazalally,** no. 59, and **H. Ahmadali,** no. 49) and in the markets. Pontianak Harbor, the center for both foreign and domestic trade, exports such products as rubber and timber. In the evening after it rains, thousands of sparrows swarm along the waterfront. A Chinese temple, **Yayasan Kelenteng DW Darma**

Bakti, is on Jl. Tanjungpura.

The regional museum, **Museum Negeri Propinsi,** is the youngest museum on Borneo. It is housed in a splendid building designed by a leading sculptor of the province, Abdulazis Yusnian from Sanggau. Murals depicting daily scenes from the life of the Dayak and Malay populations decorate the exterior and nearby is an imposing *betang* (longhouse). Inside is the world's most complete collection of W. Kalimantan's interior and coastal cultures: traditional implements, longhouse replicas, tattooing tools, wood statuary, *ikat* looms, fishtraps, old ceramics, etc. Open Tues.-Thurs. 0900-1300, Fri. to 1100, Sat. 0900-1300, Mon. closed. Admission is free.

PONTIANAK
(DETAIL)

1. shipping offices
2. Pelni office
3. post office
4. Siantan Station (to Samhas, Singkawawag, Nanga Pinoh)
5. ferry to Siantan terminal
6. police *report*-Intelpam-Komdakyi-Kalbar (Jl. Zainudin 2/10)
7. RRI
8. Bank Negara Indonesia
9. Sempati office
10. ITT Travel (branch office)
11. Bouraq office
12. Garuda office
13. Terminal Kapuas
14. Hotel Wijaya Kusuma
15. Pasar Daging
16. fish market
17. Bank Bumi Daya
18. Bank Duta
19. Menara Bookstore
20. DAS Airlines
21. Bank Dagang Negara
22. Hawaii Restoran
23. *Bis air* dock-waterbus dock (boats for Sanggau, Sintang)
24. boat dock for Saipan
25. Abadi Plaza
26. PT Bank Umum Nasional
27. ITT Travel
28. RM Barita

PONTIANAK (DETAIL)

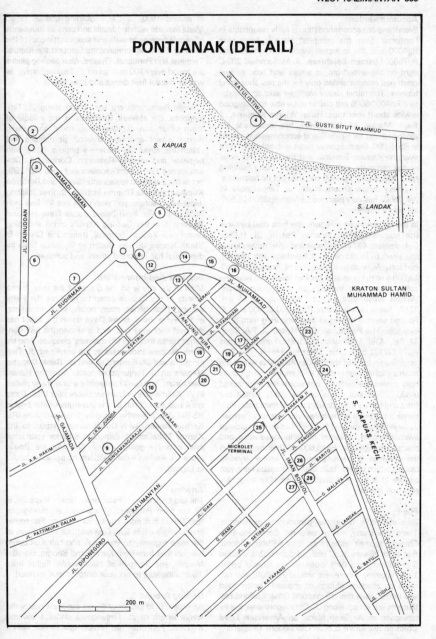

Accommodations

Everything *but* accommodation is fairly reasonable in Pontianak. Even the dumpiest place in town asks Rp4000 and the cheapest livable room is at least Rp7500. **Losmen Sejahtera**, Jl. Mohammed 209-C right on the waterfront, is a dark and fetid sailors' crash pad recommended only for the real shoestring traveler. The rather sleazy manager asks an exhorbitant Rp4000-6000 but claims to be able to give good advice about river trips. **Hotel Wijaya Kusuma**, Jl. Kapt. Marsan 51 (tel. 2547), has *sederhana* (ordinary) rooms for Rp7500 and economy-class rooms at Rp15,000. Get the corner room with balconies right over the Kapuas Terminal and the river. This hotel comes complete with resident *banci*, has a "singing hall" downstairs; Rp3000 entrance but no hostesses. The very central **Orient Hotel**, Jl. Tanjungpura 45 (tel. 2650), has very plain rooms from Rp8500-16,500; it's also a brothel.

In the higher-priced category, the best deal by far is the homestay-style **Wisma Patria**, Jl. H.O.S. Cokrominoto 497 (most *becak* and *oplet* drivers know this street by its old name, Jl. Merdeka) with 18 large, comfortable, well-furnished rooms from Rp16,000-18,000 s or d. Located in back of town, this *wisma* is quiet, clean, and well-run by a gracious family. **Wisma Nusantara**, Jl. Lt. Jen. Subroto 14 (tel. 4217), has a nice location; Rp22,000-27,000 s or d. Foreign sawmill managers live here; long term rents available. The **Pontianak City Hotel**, Jl. Pak Kasih 44 (tel. 438), very near the harbor area, charges Rp19,500-21,500. The **Dharma Hotel**, Jl. Tanjungpura (in front of the Kapuas Permai) is where the town's slightly higher-class hookers hang out, but its tatty rooms are certainly not worth the price asked (Rp25,000-30,000). Taxis can be easily rented out front and there's a nightclub, bar, and restaurant. Pontianak's top hotel is the full-service **Kapuas Permai**, Jl. Gajah Mada (tel. 4374), which has an Olympic-size swimming pool, big lobby, disco, in-house video, and charges Rp39,440 s, Rp46,600 d. Their best deal is the cottages in back, popular as lovers' trysting places, which go for Rp25,000. No tourists here, just people in the ever-expanding, insatiably voracious plywood industry.

Food

Pontianak is a wonderful gastronomc experience. There are many, many excellent Cantonese-style Chinese open-air restaurants, most without a menu, that serve up very good seafood dishes. One is about 5 m behind Toko Bata (opposite the temple) on Jl. Tanjungkarang where, for around Rp5000, you can make an absolute glutton of yourself—better food and better value than Singapore! Other seafood restaurants are set up along Jl. Diponegoro near the intersection of Jl. Gajah Mada; an **American Fried Chicken** restaurant is at Jl. Diponegoro 19. Starting at around 1800, Jl. Tanjungkarang and Jl. Gajah Mada explode with foodstalls and carts as thousands of people emerge to walk and snack in the cool of the evening. Stalls are concentrated around the Kapuas Terminal and Pontianak Theatre. *Nasi padang* places are found every 100 m or so on Jl. Tanjungkarang, as well as natural fruit drinks and cake shops.

Chinese restaurants are also found along Jl. Tanjungpura: the **Hawaii Restoran** in the middle of town offers *sop kepitang* (crab soup) and *udang angsio* (sweet and sour shrimp); sit upstairs and watch the street life below—a popular place with *pegawai* and expats. **Restoran Corina**, Jl. Tanjungkarang 124, serves excellent *mie baso* (Rp1250), but in the 2 seafood restaurants (**Segar** and **Bamboo Kuning**) opposite Dharma Hotel, with their feasting Japanese clientele, you won't get out for less than Rp5000 pp. For fresh baked goods **New Holland Bakery** is in the Gedung Kapuas Indah shopping center near Kapuas Terminal. **Italian Ice Cream & Steak House**, Jl. Jen. Sudirman (opposite Nusa Indah Plaza) has imported steaks and sundaes.

Services And Information

Most of the city is on the S side of the river. In the vicinity of the Kapuas *bemo* terminal are the **Pelni** airlines office, banks, many hotels, several markets, and *warung*. **Bank Bumi Daya** down the street has the best exchange rate, and is among the few Pontianak banks that take US travelers' cheques. Also try **Bank Negara Indonesia** at the corner of Jl. Tanjungpura and Jl. Bardan, as well as **Bank Dagang Negara** on Jl. Tanjungpura across from the Hawaii Restaurant. You can't use credit cards at many places in W. Kalimantan; only a few places take Visa. There are 4 hospitals, 3 run by the government (the best is **RS Sui Jawi**); another is run by the missionaries (**RS Karitas Bhakti**) with Dutch nurses. Report to the **Kantor Polisi** on Jl. Zainuddin 8-10 for your *surat jalan* if you're going upriver. The **Menara Bookstore**, Jl. Asahan 4 (tel. 493), has maps, some books in English.

Arriving

The laid-back airport, **Pelabuhan Udara Supadio**, is 20 km from Pontianak. Taxis want an outrageous Rp6000 (30-min. ride), but it's fairly easy to find someone to share a ride with (just ask!). Or walk down to the main highway to Pontianak and catch an *oplet*. Merpati flies here from Kucing and Bouraq, Garuda, Merpati, and Sempati all have regular flights from Jakarta (be sure to set your watch ahead an hour).

Getting Around

An easy city to get around; you can walk nearly the whole length of Jl. Tanjungpura under a covered walkway. Pontianak has reliable taxi service with a stand at the Dharma Hotel (Rp7000 for 2 hours). *Becak* abound; the drivers may overcharge, but you can bargain. For a flat rate of Rp100, minibuses (here called *oplet)* run on established "lines": Panjara, Kota Baru, Gajah Mada, and Merdeka, plus there are *bis kota* which run up and down Jl. Tanjungpura (Rp200). The main *bemo*/minibus terminals are on Jl. Sisingamangaraja and the Kapuas Terminal (just off Jl. Tanjungpura). From the ferry terminal just off Jl. Ramadi Usman, a 24-hour ferry (Rp200) runs to the other side of the river to Terminal Siantan, the city's long-distance bus station.

FROM PONTIANAK

By Boat

Riverboats *(bis air)* head into the interior to Sintang and even farther to Putusibau. The boat *Bandung* leaves once weekly and costs around Rp26,000 to Putusibau; see the Chinese Johnny in Paret Pekong (near bridge at end of Jl. Serayu). Boats also head for many destinations near Pontianak: Tayan, 160 km, Rp3200; Sanggau, 256 km, Rp5100; Sekadau, 331 km, Rp6600; Sungai Ayak, 357 km, Rp7150; Nangasepuak, 380 km, Rp7600; Sintang, 458 km, Rp9160; Putusibau, 870 km, Rp17,410. From Pontianak, the riverbus to Nanga Pinoh turns up the Melawai River at Sintang, 578 km, Rp11,560. The Pelni ship *Lawit* sails twice monthly to: Ketapang (Rp12,000 Ekonomi, Rp28,400 1st Class); Tg. Priok (Rp28,200 Ekonomi, Rp69,800 1st Class); Dumai (Rp58,300 Ekonomi, Rp153,100 1st Class); Belawan (Rp64,500 Ekonomi, Rp183,000 1st Class); and Lhokseumawe (Rp71,400 Ekonomi Rp201,800 1st Class).

By Road

Many areas are accessible by road from the Siantan Terminal, which can be reached by motorboat from the dock near the Kapuas *bemo* terminal. From Siantan, minibuses head N for Sungei Duri, Rp1525, 91 km, 1½ hours; Singkawang, Rp2510, 3 hours; Pemangkat, Rp3010, 175 km, 4 hours; Tebas, Rp3360, 196 km, 4½ hours; Sambas, Rp3835, 225 km, 5 hours; Kartiasa, Rp3910, 229 km, 5 hours—the end of the line north. You can also reach Pahuaman and Mandor (Rp1500, 1½ hours) by bus, as well as river towns along the Kapuas such as Sanggau (Rp8000, 5 hours) and Sintang (Rp13,000, 10 hours on a bad road, departing at 0800).

By Air

From Terminal Sisingamangaraja, take a minibus to the airport (you have to walk in a bit); an *imigrasi* officer may or may not be there to sign you out. Merpati has flights to Kucing (Rp97,700). Bouraq flies twice weekly to Balikpapan (Rp110,000). Most airlines fly regularly to Jakarta, some to Singapore. Garuda has 3

flights daily to: Jakarta, Rp95,700; Balikpapan, Rp110,000; Batam, Rp82,000; Medan, Rp173,600; Singapore, Rp175,000. Sempati flies to Jakarta for Rp81,000 (Merpati and Bouraq charge about the same).

For internal flights, DAS flies to Ketapang every day at 0800, arriving 0900, Rp47,900; to Sintang every day at 0815, arriving 0925, Rp53,700; to Putusibau every day at 0805, arriving 1010, Rp79,600; to Nanga Pinoh at 0805 (only 5 days a week), arriving 0935, Rp70,500; to Pangkalanbun at 0805 on Mon., Thurs., and Sat., arriving 1010, Rp64,700. Also check out Deraya flights to some places, generally cheaper by at least Rp10,000. Airline offices: **Merpati**, Jl. Ir. H. Juanda 50A (tel. 2332); **Bouraq**, Jl. Gajah Mada, near Orient Hotel, (tel. 2683); **DAS**, Jl. Gajah Mada 67 (tel. 4383); **Deraya**, Jl. Sisingamangaraja (tel. 4840); **MAF**, Jl. Jen. Urip (tel. 2757); **Garuda**, Jl. Ramadi Usman 8A (tel. 4986); **Sempati**, Jl. Gaja Mada (tel. 4350). For Merpati, book flights at either ITT Travel or P.T. Asia Tour and Travel. (see below).

To the interior, DAS and Deraya are the quickest; buy tickets for both these airlines through ITT. For Putusibau, DAS charges Rp79,600, departs daily at 0800, carries 8 people. Deraya charges Rp66,500, departs Mon., Wed., and Sat. also at 0800, carrying 16 people. MAF flies to about 50 remote interior airstrips such as Ketapang, Sintang, Pangkalan, and Putusibau. MAF's primary business is transporting church personnel and sometimes government officials, but they'll take paying passengers on a space available basis.

Travel Agencies

Instead of running all over town to the various airline offices, it's easier just to go through a travel agency such as the highly efficient and central **ITT Travel**, Jl. Tanjungpura 149 AB (tel. 4257/2841/6349). Any and all air tickets can be bought here, and they accept Visa cards. Mr. Joseph Lee is very helpful, interested, and speaks good English. ITT also conducts 8- and 16-day (US$800) adventure tours down the Kapuas River, flying first to Putusibau, then returning to Pontianak on the *Bandung* riverboat, passing through river towns the whole way. They telex Baparda (the government tourist office) ahead of time to arrange for dances and meals, and to ensure a safe, smooth journey, ITT has a branch office at Jl. Ir. H. Juanda 50 (tel. 4707/4266). Merpati, DAS, and Garuda tickets can also be bought through P.T. Asia, Jl. Mahakam II 1 (tel. 620).

NORTH OF PONTIANAK

Across the river in Pontianak Utara (reach it by ferry from just off Jl. Ramadi Usman) there is the large

Siantan Bus Station and about 4 km from the station on Jl. Khatulistiwa is a small, oft-photographed monument marking the precise location of the equator; nearby is an Italian sawmill. Traveling N from here on the road to Sambas, you'll pass many privately owned coconut and a few rubber plantations. Visit the fish market at **Jungkat** on the way. Locals go N from Pontianak to the beaches near Singkawang, sometimes taking a side trip to Mandor where there's a war memorial and a small botanical reserve. Sambas is famous for its beautiful gold-threaded cloth (expensive). Farther N is a reserve area, Hutan Sambas, bordering Sarawak; with official permission, you may be able to visit turtle nesting beaches.

Mandor

About 40 km N of Pontianak. An easy day trip, take the bus or *bemo* N from Pontianak on the coast road to Singkawang, then turn R at Sungai Pinyuh. Mandor's war memorial, completed in 1977 and partly funded by the United Nations, commemorates a mass burial grave. In the first year following the invasion from Kucing, the Japanese rounded up around 5,000 intellectuals, business people, and government employees from Pontianak, Singkawang, and other towns. They shot them, then buried most of them still alive. Near town are beautiful, extensive orchid gardens in the small, 2,000-ha **Mandor Nature Reserve**. This reserve attracts plenty of locals and tends to be crowded on Sun. and holidays. You'll find scores of orchid varieties, peat and heath forests, the red *pinang* palm, some birds. You also won't starve; there's plenty of food and soft drinks stands.

Singkawang

A clean, pleasant, well-built town 145 km NW of Pontianak, accessible by minibus (Rp2510, 3 hours) on a picturesque drive N of Pontianak's Siantan Terminal. On the way up, stop at **Pulau Kijang**, a coastal rest stop just before Sungaiduri. Singkawang's climate is cool, much like Bandung. A friendly, very Chinese place, the town has a beautiful lake and pavilion in the center of town, Chinese temples, and unique traditional pottery is made here.

Though less pricey than Pontianak, hotels in Singkawang still aren't cheap. Small *penginapan* have rooms for Rp5000-8000. Right opposite the bus station in the S end of town is **Hotel Sahuri**. Also check out **Wisma Batu Payung, Losmen Pelita,** and **Losmen Khatulistiwa** (Jl. Selamat Karman 17, tel. 205). **Losmen Bandung**, Jl. Pasar Tengah, is an 8-min. walk from the bus station; Rp4000 s, Rp7000 d. Splurge at the **Palapa Hotel**, Jl. Ismail Tahir 152, Rp10,000-18,000, and **Hotel Kalimantan Barat** on Jl. Kepol Mahmud, about Rp15,000. No shortage of inexpensive *rumah makan* and fantastic fruits, and delicious orange drinks.

The town's major attraction is its nearby beaches. **Batu Payung** is a lovely half-deserted beach where bungalows rent for Rp6000. Very popular with the locals, there're also a *losmen* and outdoor restaurants. Hire a *sampan* from the fishermen. More remote (15 km away) is **Pasir Panjang**, a 5-km-long beach with golden sand—nicer than Bali's Kuta Beach! The *camat* in Singkawang rents out his big concrete beachhouse here at quite reasonable rates. Or bring camping gear and food. From Singkawang, get minibuses S to Pontianak (Rp2500), N to Pamangkat (Rp500), and to Sambas (Rp1500). **Pamangkat** is famous for its fish production and natural swimming holes.

Sambas

North of Pontianak 250 km, or 55 km N of Singkawang. Many of the houses here are built on stilts along the river and above the water where the air is cool and fresh. The friendly people of the town go about their lives in the same quiet rhythm as the Sambas River which flows nearby. Sambas is an old city, part of an ancient kingdom established over 400 years ago. Walk among the ruins of an old abandoned diamond mine. Outside the *camat's* office and on the palace grounds are old cannons. The sultan's palace was built in 1812, during Sir Stamford Raffles' time. Most of the servants left the service of the present-day sultan to work in Pontianak's mills. Next door to the palace is the oldest mosque in Sambas, built in the 1890s. The Sambas Regency capital was moved from Sambas to Singkawang in 1954, turning this town into a secondary cultural center. Stay in **Losmen Ujung Pandang** and sample the renowned Siamese citrus *(jeruk manis Siam)*. From Sambas, try to arrange cheap boat passage to Tanjung Pinang, in Riau.

Some of Indonesia's most beautiful cloth is produced in villages near Sambas; ask about the superb *kain sambas*. This expensive cloth is hand-stitched with gold thread in unique native motifs, taking months to weave. Iban Dayak people in the area make the finest *ikat* fabrics, fashioned into reddish-brown skirts, jackets, kerchiefs, and blankets decorated with human figures; ask around nearby *kampung*.

Hutan Sambas Reserve is a proposed forest reserve adjacent to Sarawak's Samunsan Reserve along the coast N of Paloh. These joint "transfrontier" reserves are meant to protect mutual water catchment areas, provide large genetic reservoirs of rainforest plant species, and protect arboreal animal habitat. Wildlife is abundant here; the turtle nesting beaches are well worth a visit if authorities will allow it. Political sensitivities make this a potentially dangerous place, so check with the police, military, or PPA officials before you go.

WEST KALIMANTAN

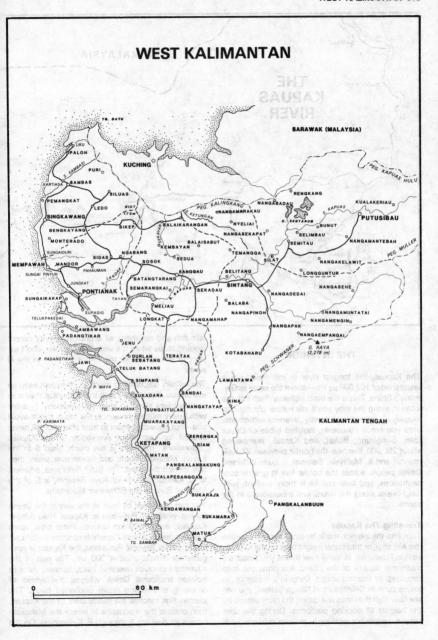

SARAWAK (MALAYSIA)

0   60 km

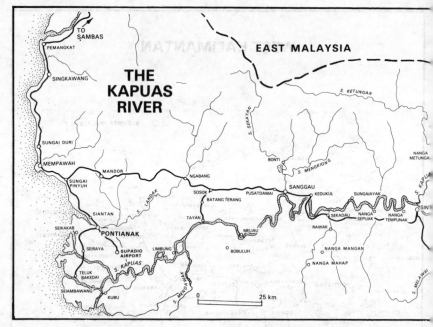

THE INTERIOR

The Kapuas, the longest river in Indonesia, has a watershed of 102,000 sq km—about the same as Germany's Rhine. This is the main highway deep into the interior; along the way you'll see rubber plantations, logging operations, and mostly Javanese settlements until you reach Putusibau. Isolated tribes of Dayak Iban, Sungkung, Bukat, and Kantuk, numbering about 250,000, live near the border between W. Kalimantan and E. Malaysia. Sarawak is quite different; Dayak people across the border live in greater concentrations, and their culture is more evident, with longhouses along the rivers, and tribespeople in the towns.

Traveling The Kapuas

Trips into the interior, made by small aircraft, riverbus (bis air), ship, or traditional freight boat up the Kapuas, start in Pontianak. In many river towns you'll notice a traditional feature of the inland economy, the toko terapung, or floating shops. Deep in the interior, in towns such as Selimbau and Nanga Suhaid, you can see how high the rivers rise during the rainy season by the heights of docking platforms. During the drier season, people not working in modern industry catch lake fish and sell them; all economic activity except logging stops when it's wet. Once upriver, don't expect to see much but the towns, at least in the N areas.

The military has nothing much to do except keep an eye on you. If you take a walk in the country, they may send soldiers along to keep you company. In areas with heavy military presence, the locals might avoid you—not knowing whom to trust after years of being abused by just about everybody. If the Kapuas "operations" mentality is too much, head S to the Kayan, Melawai, Pinoh, and Sayan river areas, then SW toward the coast. The Bukit Baka area, adjacent to C. Kalimantan's Bukit Raya Reserve, is S of the Melawai River in the Schwaner Mountains.

You can also travel by boat all the way to the Dayak fishing village of Putisibau in Kapuas Hulu (Upper Kapuas), nearly 900 km upriver. From here, some travelers head E across the whole continent—difficult but possible. Beyond Putusibau, the Kapuas is navigable for almost another 300 km. The rest of the adventure involves overland treks, leeches, visits to isolated traditional Dayak villages, and weeks of canoeing and rafting down uncharted rivers. The journey first reaches the headwaters of the Kapuas, then crosses the mountains to where the Mahakam begins its descent S through E. Kalimantan. On the

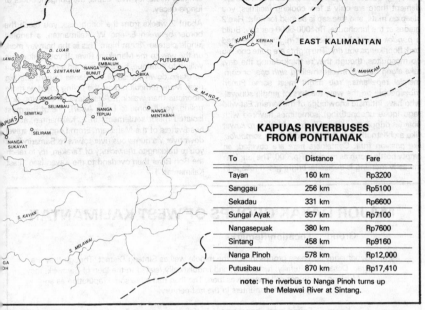

KAPUAS RIVERBUSES FROM PONTIANAK

To	Distance	Fare
Tayan	160 km	Rp3200
Sanggau	256 km	Rp5100
Sekadau	331 km	Rp6600
Sungai Ayak	357 km	Rp7100
Nangasepuak	380 km	Rp7600
Sintang	458 km	Rp9160
Nanga Pinoh	578 km	Rp12,000
Putusibau	870 km	Rp17,410

note: The riverbus to Nanga Pinoh turns up the Melawai River at Sintang.

Mahakam, you can reach the coast near Samarinda; or continue on to Tarakan via the Boh and Kayan rivers.

Sanggau

There's a big pineapple and *durian* plantation at **Tayan** on the way to Sanggau—all the free *rambutan* you can eat. Slogging through all the officials here and elsewhere to get the required paperwork can be tough going, but necessary if you're going upriver. Get to Sanggau from Pontianak by riverbus (16-18 hours), cheaper than the bus. The trip upriver is tiring, mostly night travel, so rest awhile in Tayan. There are 2 small hotels in Sanggau; **Peng. Kitono** is the best. Eat in the restaurant across from the Kitono, in the few *nasi padang* places, or at a place called **Melati's** (good Chinese food).

To Putusibau

The easiest way to get here is flying with Deraya (Rp66,500, 3 times weekly) or DAS (Rp79,600, daily) from Pontianak. River travel is another option. From Pontianak, the ship *Bandung* sails all the way up; other boat connections are possible. About 4 days upriver from Pontianak is **Simitau,** then you pass through several more river towns on stilts, such as **Selimbau** (see the *mesjid*) and **Nangabunut**. Just N of Selimbau is a large area of freshwater lakes (the

Bekuan, Genali, Luar, Sentarum, and Seriang) proposed for nature reserve status. Another very large reserve area takes in W. Kalimantan's entire Kapuas Hulu range, including the headwaters and upper reaches of the Kapuas River and E to the E. Kalimantan boundary. After a hot 14-day journey, you arrive in Putusibau. Rest at the mission here, presided over by the Dutch pastor van Fleuten, who's been here for over 25 years.

To East Kalimantan

The Kapuas and Mahakam rivers are the largest on Borneo, together forming an inverted "V," the tip of which is near Putusibau in the watershed highlands of the interior. From Putusibau, get to Bungan. To get there you need about 200 liters of gas (at Rp600 per liter) for the power boat, and the boatman will charge about Rp5000-8000 per day. Upriver there are raging rapids and whirlpools; the river might be swollen by rains, and is particularly dangerous where tributaries converge. You'll see dugouts seating up to 12 people wearing huge circular hats made of palm leaves. Eventually the river becomes quieter and calmer, with giant trees hugging the banks. About 3 days above Bungan, the overland trek begins.

The first stage is through mountain forests, dense jungles with giant trees, and *ladang* ricefields. The first longhouse is 2 days by foot and canoe. In this settlement there are only a few cooking facilities; you sleep on mats, and tree sap is burned for light. Hire 2 guides at the longhouse, Rp4000-5000 per day. Build a *pondok* (lean-to) for shelter at night; an elevated bark floor keeps you dry. The nights are quite cool, so no mosquitos, though they're thick during the day; take along netting, sweet-smelling *sirih olie*, or commercial repellents. You might meet some Punan tribespeople on the way, masters of jungle survival, who have intimate knowledge of the terrain. Eat wild sago (quite unappetizing), sometimes flavored with boar fat drippings; speared lizards with rice; *to kawat* (like a chestnut); *soar*, a bitter red fruit; or *somboloc*, like passion fruit. Containers here are coveted, an empty bottle worth as much as Rp2000. The jungle in the early morning is exquisite: bright green foliage in clinging mists, icy river baths, the pungent odors of jungle decay.

About 2 weeks from the longhouse, you reach the border between E. and W. Kalimantan, a tangled jungle plateau 780 m high. This is the halfway mark on the way to the Mahakam River. If your guides are willing to continue, have them build a raft which you can take down the small tributaries toward the big river. Many difficult rapids; the poling could be more laborious than walking. After days of trudging and poling, you'll come to **Long Apari**, one of the most isolated major settlements in E. Kalimantan, at the headwaters of the Mahakam. From Longapari, travel downriver via numerous river towns to Samarinda. If you're trekking to the vicinity of Tarakan, try to reach the Boh River then overland to the Kayan (see "East Kalimantan").

MAJOR DAYAK GROUPS OF WEST KALIMANTAN

Group	Location/Remarks
Kantu', Seberuang, Bugau, Desa, Mualang	These groups inhabit the middle well as Sintang District. Though they are culturally, historically, and linquistically related to the Iban of Sarawak, they do not call themselves Iban. The Iban had a fearsome reputation as aggressive headhunters in the last century.
Kayan	Found for the most part in E. Kalimantan, a small pocket of Kayans inhabit the Mendalam River in the Upper Kapuas. As in E. Kalimantan, they practice a stratified social order.
Maloh	Comprising 3 subgroups (Taman, Embaloh, and Kalis), the Maloh live deep in the interior of W. Kalimantan. Skilled in metalwork, beadwork, woodworking, painting.
Land Dayak	Upstream on the Sanggau and Sekayam rivers in the lower basin of the Kapuas River. They form a diverse number of subgroups which are all linguistically related. In former times the Land Dayak constructed a "head house," a separate building in the village where the heads of slain enemies were kept.
Selaka, Kendayan	Sambas region N to the Lundu District of Sarawak and E of Pontianak in the lower reaches of the Kapuas. Their language is closely related to Malay. Christian.
Pinoh Dayak, Desa, Lebang	Lower and middle sections of the Melawai River. Language closely related to Malay, but their exact ethnic and cultural affiliations are unclear.

SULAWESI

*T*he world's most peculiarly shaped island, Sulawesi resembles anything from an open-jawed crocodile to a
spastic letter "K." Lying between huge Kalimantan and
the Maluku Islands, Sulawesi is Indonesia's 3rd largest island,
with an area of 172,000 sq km (about the size of Kansas). The
population of multi-racial Sulawesi is almost 11 million. An
amazing diversity of societies exists here, with a distinct separation of old and new, traditional and modern within the many
cultures themselves. There are the fiercely Islamic Bugis and
Makassarese of the S, the animist-Christian Torajans in the
south-central region, and the prosperous Christian Minahasans
of the north. This variety, along with some spectacular mountains, coastline, lakes and plains, makes Sulawesi a highly
visited island, 3rd highest in the country in numbers of tourists,
who remain largely concentrated in the southern leg and
especially in the Tanatoraja culture region. However, Sulawesi
also contains some of the most remote jungle areas in Indonesia,
with unusual flora and fauna and nearly unknown tribes, and is
a unique place to explore. Transportation has improved greatly
and a road now connects the whole way between Ujung Pandang in the S and Manado in the far north.

INTRODUCTION

Sit and stare at a large wall map of Sulawesi for awhile, and you'll see dragons, giraffes, spiders, orchids, even a headless octopus. Four long, narrow peninsulas, separated by 3 great gulfs, are joined in the mountainous heart of Sulawesi. The island's rivers are of little importance, not nearly as life-giving as those on Kalimantan. The main land mass is 1,300 km long, although only 56-200 km wide. Except for some narrow plains near the coast and in the mountain ranges, almost the whole of Sulawesi consists of mountains—the most mountainous of any of Indonesia's large islands. From N to S stretches a volcanic range, a part of the same chain which Australia, New Zealand, and Polynesia all share. Covered mostly in rainforests and high, uninhabited, unarable wasteland, there are 1,800- to 3,000-m mountains everywhere with unspoiled, pollution-free, spectacular tropical scenery. Sulawesi is surrounded by very deep seas. Selat Makassar is 2,000-2,500 m deep, while the southern part is 4,500-5,140 m. Monsoons heave big surf onto beaches along beautiful but treacherous coasts with hills rising abruptly up to 500 m. Few areas are more than 40 km from the sea. Lakes are widespread in the center. Sulawesi enjoys a constant temperature of around 72-86 degrees F the year round. Rainfall is much heavier in the S around Ujung Pandang than in Palu (C. Sulawesi) or Manado (N. Sulawesi).

Fauna And Flora

Separated from any land connection to either Asia or Australia since before the last great Ice Age, Sulawesi harbors fauna and flora found nowhere else on Earth. The 4 distinct peninsulas led to a mammalian evolution in isolation—nearly 40% of the birds and a remarkable 90% of Sulawesi's 59 species of mammals are endemic. This island is home to such extraordinary beasts as the *babirusa,* a pig-like creature with upward curving tusks and 3 species of *anoa,* a rare, fierce pygmy buffalo that resembles an antelope. Also dwelling here are 4 primitive forms of black macaques (misnamed "black-crested baboon"), a genus of heavily built monkeys, as well as saucer-eyed tarsiers and cuscus. Over 220 known species of birds are found on Sulawesi; on Lokan volcano (N. Sulawesi), *maleo* (bush turkeys) dig nesting holes in ground heated by volcanic steam. The Togian Is. in Teluk Tomini are nesting grounds for giant sea turtles. A

the unusual fauna of Sulawesi: Two unique animals found on Sulawesi and nearby islands are the babirusa (Babyrousa babyrussa, *or literally "pig deer"*), a very rare 100-kg boar with ornately curved tusks like the horns of a stag. Good swimmers in both salt and fresh water, the babirusa *is found only in swampy forests. The upper canines of the male grow through the skin and bone of the upper jaw. Another rarity is the* anoa *or Bubalus depressicornis. The smallest of the wild oxen and one of the oldest forms of all living oxen, the anoa is known also as the dwarf buffalo. This shy hoofed animal, which has developed similar to an antelope, is confined to remote mountainous forests and is very seldom seen. They stand only about 1 m high at the shoulder and weigh around 200 kg.*

true paradise for lepidopterists, 86 species of butterflies and over 200 species of beetles inhabit Sulawesi, and its spiders can measure 15 cm long. The reptilian family is represented by 60 species of snakes, 40 different lizards, 22 kinds of frogs; a Dutch doctor recorded in 1985 one of the few documented cases of a man-eating snake, a 6-m-long python in northern C. Sulawesi. The island's flora consists of sago palms, wine palms, and a palm whose stem is like a snake's, growing corkscrew fashion, shooting out green sprouts at each half circle. Ferns here grow in geometric shapes. The best places for observing natural phenomena are in the island's reserves: Morowali, Tanjung Api, and Lore Lindu in C. Sulawesi; Bone-Dumoga, G. Dua Saudara and Panua in N. Sulawesi.

History

On the W coast on the lower course of the Karama River at Maros (35 km NE of Ujung Pandang), a Neolithic settlement and prehistoric remains have been discovered; small 4,000-year-old hollow-based stone arrowheads, known as Maros points, have also been found in cave deposits in other S. Sulawesi locales. South Sulawesi ports were an important stop on international spice trading routes for more than 1,000 years. Buddhist images found at Sampaga on the SW coast belong to the Indian Amarawati school of art which flourished in the 2nd C., indicating that Hinayana Buddhism existed on Sulawesi prior to the 5th century A.D. The famous bronze "Sulawesi Buddha," now in Jakarta's National Museum, shows many stylistic similarities with Indian sculpture, such as the treatment of the open eyes, bare right shoulder, and incised lines on the robe showing the folds. Mysterious megaliths, sarcophagi, and other prehistoric artifacts can be seen in the remote Besoa and Bada valleys of C. Sulawesi (Lore Lindu Reserve, SE of Palu), and in N. Sulawesi carved stone sarcophagi are scattered over a wide area of Minahasa—remnants of vanished cultures. For centuries, Sulawesi was a refuge for pirates who hid out in its deserted coastal mangrove swamps. As new waves of migration inhabited the coasts, the island's indigenous peoples fled into the mountainous interior. Until the Spanish brought horses in the 17th C., the only mode of transport inland was on foot. When the missionaries penetrated the mountains in the 19th C., they found ancient peoples like the Toala and Torajans who had been living in almost total isolation.

The peoples of Sulawesi were among the very last to be converted to Islam; the Makassarese came under the sway of emerging Muslim kingdoms on Java's N coast only in 1605. They in turn forced Islam on the Bugis of S. Sulawesi. In 1580, during his historic circumnavigation of the globe, Sir Francis Drake's ship *The Golden Hind* ran aground in C. Sulawesi. The bloodthirsty Portuguese arrived soon after their conquest of Melaka in 1511. These seafarers believed the 4 tentacle-like arms of Sulawesi to be separate islands. They called the island *"Ponto dos Celebres"* (Cape of the Infamous Ones), their name for the cape N of Minahasa which had caused them so many shipwrecks; from this name was derived the English word for the island, Celebes. Also in the 16th C., Spanish missionaries began colonizing northern Sulawesi from their base in the Philippines. After the departure of the Spanish in the late 16th C., the spice sultanates of Ternate in the northern Moluccas exerted their authority over northern and eastern Sulawesi.

The Dutch gained complete control over the docile Minahasans in the N in the 17th C., but they had a long, bloody struggle to control the independent Muslim tribes of the south. The rebellious Bugis and Makassarese were finally conquered — but not completely subjugated — by a Dutch fleet in 1666-67. Although the Dutch imposed a maritime monopoly on spice trading in the southern part of the island, wars between the Dutch and the Islamic states of Goa and Bone continued throughout the 19th century. And it was not until 1905-06 that the Dutch achieved political control over the Toraja highlands.

The Japanese occupied the island for 3½ years starting in 1942; their overriding concern was the maintenance of law and order, the establishment of land defenses (see numerous ammunition and supply caves in Minahasa, N. Sulawesi), and the efficient extraction of resources needed for the war effort. Although independence was declared in August 1945, there followed 5 years of guerilla warfare against the Dutch in which thousands of suspected anti-Dutch rebels were either killed or executed. During the chaotic period of Indonesia's civil war, in March 1957 the commander of the East Indonesia military region based in Ujung Pandang issued the so-called Permesta charter, demanding greater regional autonomy from the central government and a larger share of national revenues for local development. With the declaration of an autonomous state in North Sulawesi in June of 1957, the dissension soon developed into a full-fledged separatist movement.

The bombing of Manado and the landing of troops on Minahasa by the central government in 1958 neutralized the Permesta revolt, though it was not completely suppressed until 1961.

The People
Most of the populaton is concentrated in the island's southern and northern peninsulas, where relatively flat plains allow for large settlements. The people of the interior are still isolated, with resulting tighter ethnic customs and traditions. There are 4 major ethnic groups. The Islamic Makassarese and Buginese, inhabiting the southwestern peninsula, each have their own language (one with a modified Arabic script, the other with a modified Sanskrit writing system); well-known as traders and seafarers, large numbers have migrated all over eastern Indonesia. The Torajans, once feared as headhunters, live in the highlands of S-central Sulawesi. A self-sufficient people, the Torajans practice dry rice and shifting cultivation. Although a Christian people, the cult of death is all-pervasive: the Torajans carry out bloody animal sacrifices and bury their dead in trees and in tombs cut into rock walls. The Christian Minahasans of the northern peninsula have been more influenced by Dutch colonial culture and education than any other group in Indonesia.

Getting There
Ujung Pandang (formerly Makassar) on the tip of the SW peninsula is the major port of call and gateway to Sulawesi. Take a ship from Surabaya (2 days), or fly there from just about anywhere in Indonesia. Garuda, Merpati, Bouraq, and Mandala all offer flights to Ujung Pandang (Garuda fares: Rp156,700 from Jakarta, Rp114,500 from Manado; Rp301,000 from Medan; Rp98,700 from Surabaya). Manado/Bitung on the northern tip is another possibility to fly or float to. From Java, most travelers fly out of Surabaya (the cheapest, flights twice daily), but also consider flying from Denpasar straight to Ujung Pandang (Merpati, Rp54,100). Garuda flies daily from Denpasar or Jakarta to Manado, N. Sulawesi, for Rp178,300. Yet another aerial approach is from Kalimantan in the W; Bouraq hops across the Makassar Strait from Balikpapan to Ujung Pandang for Rp96,900; from Banjarmasin to Palu for Rp98,000; from Tarakan to Manado for Rp204,000. Popular with travelers is the loop flying from Surabaya to Ujung Pandang, traveling overland and across lakes up through C. Sulawesi to Manado, then flying to Ternate and Ambon, then back to Surabaya by ship or plane. Bouraq flies 4 days weekly (at 1400) from Manado to Ternate, N. Maluku (Rp44,900).

The new Pelni ships MV *Kambuna* and MV *Kerinci* stop at Ujung Pandang regularly en route from the big northern coastal ports of Java, and Sumatra and Kalimantan. From Ujung Pandang, the *Kambuna* sails to Bitung (Manado's port) for Rp37,500 Economy, with

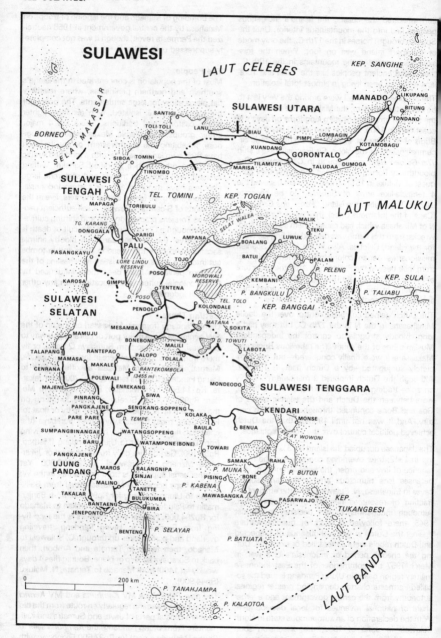

SULAWESI

LAUT CELEBES

KEP. SANGIHE

SULAWESI UTARA

MANADO
LIKUPANG
BITUNG
TONDANO

BORNEO

SELAT MAKASSAR

SANTIGI
TOLI-TOLI
LANU
BIAU
LOMBAGIN
PIMPI
KOTAMOBAGU
KUANDANG
GORONTALO
TILAMUTA
TALUDAA
DUMOGA
MARISA

SIBOA
TOMINI
TINOMBO

SULAWESI
TENGAH

MAPAGA
TORIBULU

TG. KARANG
DONGGALA
PARIGI

PASANGKAYU

PALU

LORE LINDU
RESERVE
POSO

GIMPU

KAROSA

TENTENA

TEL. TOMINI
KEP. TOGIAN

SELAT WALEA

AMPANA

TOJO

D. POSO

MOROWALI
RESERVE

MALIK
TEKU
LUWUK
BOALANG
BATUI

LAUT MALUKU

PALAM
P. PELENG

KEMBANI
P. BANGKULU

TEL. TOLO

KEP. SULA

P. TALIABU

SULAWESI
SELATAN

MAMUJU

TALAPANG
MAMASA
CENRANA

MAJENE

PINRANG
PANGKAJENE
PARE PARE

SUMPANGBINANGAE

BARU

PANGKAJENE

UJUNG
PANDANG

TAKALAR

MALINO

MAROS
BALANGNIPA
SINJAI
TANETTE
BULUKUMBA
BIRA

BANTAENG

JENEPONTO

RANTEPAO
MAKALE
POLEWALI
ENREKANG

SENGKANG SOPPENG
WATANSOPPENG
WATAMPONE (BONE)

D. TEMPE

SIWA

MESAMBA
BONEBONE
PALOPO
TOLALA

G. RANTEKOMBOLA
(3455 m)

PENDOLO

KOLONDALE

D. MATANA
SOKITA
D. TOWUTI
LABOTA

MALILI

MONDEODO

KOLAKA
BAULA
BENUA

TOWARI

SAMAK
P. MUNA
PISING
BONE
P. KABENA
MAWASANGKA

SULAWESI TENGGARA

KENDARI
MONSE

SELAT WOWONI

RAHA
P. BUTON

PASARWAJO

SELAYAR

BENTENG

P. SELAYAR

0   200 km

P. TANAHJAMPA

P. BATUATA

SAMAK
P. KABENA

KEP.
TUKANGBESI

LAUT BANDA

P. KALAOTOA

stops in between at Balikpapan and Pantoloan. Once every 2 weeks, Pelni's MV *Rinjani* sails Tg. Priok-Surabaya-Ujung Pandang-Bau Bau-Ambon-Sorong-Ambon-Bau Bau-Ujung Pandang-Surabaya-Tg. Priok-Belawan-Tg. Priok. Inquire at your nearest Pelni office for the latest schedules and prices. There's also the possibility of catching a ride on a Makassarese *pinisi* out of Surabaya's Kalimas to Ujung Pandang for around Rp15,000. It's fairly easy to get to Sulawesi ports such as Pare Pare, Donggala, and Palu from Balikpapan and Tarakan in Kalimantan, and regular *kapal motor* link Ternate (N. Maluku) and Bitung, N. Sulawesi.

Getting Around

The SW peninsula (S. Sulawesi) and the northern peninsula (Minahasa region) have the best road systems on the island. Typical of the Outer Islands, the remainder is criss-crossed by poorly surfaced roads, which turn into quagmires during the monsoons. One can now, however, travel the whole length of the island (Ujung Pandang to Manado) by road. In C. Sulawesi and SE Sulawesi provinces, a more expedient way to travel is by coasters or flying. Pelni ships embark from Ujung Pandang up the W coast of Sulawesi to Pantoloan (Palu's port), Toli Toli, Kwandang, and Bitung; inquire at U.P.'s Pelni office. In C.

Sulawesi, fleets are clustered in Palu and Poso. From Palu, boats work the western coast of the northern peninsula, stopping at such small ports as Toli Toli and Kwandang. From Poso, ships cross Teluk Tomini to Gorontalo, calling at the Togian Is. on the way. Using *kapal motor* saves you the arduous road journey between C. Sulawesi and N. Sulawesi.

But flying is the easiest (and most expensive) of all: Bouraq and Merpati are the principal carriers for internal flights around Sulawesi. Bouraq offers such tremendously time-saving flights as: Ujung Pandang to Manado, 4 times weekly at 0800, Rp108,800; Ujung Pandang to Gorontalo, 4 times weekly at 0800, Rp106,600; and Palu to Gorontalo, 10 times weekly, Rp50,000; Palu to Manado, 10 times weekly, Rp93,000. Merpati flies from Ujung Pandang to Kendari (Rp38,300), the capital of the SE peninsula, and to such outliers as P. Buton off the SE coast in the Banda Sea (Rp63,800) and P. Selayar (Rp32,500) in the Flores Sea. Also check out little-known Mandala Airlines (Jl. Irian 2F, tel. 21289/4288/3326, Ujung Pandang; and Jl. Sarapung 17, tel. 51743/51324/51824/52086, Manado) for such interesting flights as Ujung Pandang to Ambon (Rp98,800, daily at 1145).

Everyone going to Sulawesi is well advised to have at least a working knowledge of *Bahasa Indonesia.*

SOUTH SULAWESI

This remarkable province offers spectacular limestone mountains; an almost endless coastline with large ocean harbors and romantic fishing ports; huge shallow lakes; hotsprings, caves and waterfalls; rare and exotic flora and fauna; ancient and distinctive Islamic mosques and graves; Dutch fortress ruins; age-old *prahu* building; and diverse and fascinating cultures with unequaled ceremonies and festivals. The province comprises 85,061 sq km, with a population of just over 6.5 million. The 3 major cultures of the region are Bugis, Makassarese, and Torajan. The Muslim Bugis and Makassarese, who live in the S and along the coast, are renowned for their handbuilt wooden schooners and for their seamanship. The Christian Torajas of the N keep old customs; their ceremonies and architecture are the primary reason that this province attracts so many tourists. Ujung Pandang is the capital, main port, and gateway to all of S. Sulawesi. The people have a stereotyped reputation, especially among other Indonesians, for being *kasar* (rough and coarse), but in fact the manners of the Bugis and Makassarese differ little from the Javanese. Locals are generally curious and friendly to

Western visitors. But travelers in S. Sulawesi should avoid extremes of dress and behavior, especially women (no provocative shorts!). As elsewhere in Indonesia, bureaucrats love abbreviations and acronyms. You'll see SULSEL for Sulawesi Selatan, POLMAS for Polewali-Mamasa Regency, and TATOR for Tanatoraja. Note: SULSEL is one hour ahead of Java and Bali.

The Land

A mountain range runs down the spine of this Florida-like peninsula, which is cut in half in the middle by a narrow, Z-shaped plain. The mountains range in altitude from 500-1,000 m. There is only one volcano in this region, G. Lompobatang (2,871 m), or Bonthain Peak, which is now extinct; it contains a large crater. Many caves of stalagmites and stalactites are found in S. Sulawesi, the most famous of which are ancient caves of the vanished Toala people near Maros (Leang-Leang Cave), as well as Mampu Cave near Watampone, and others at Sinjai. There are lakes everywhere. The biggest are in the central valley of the province—Danau Sidenreng and Danau Tempe.

These lakes, part of the sea itself in prehistoric times, are very shallow (only 1-2 m), and contain commercial fish *(ikan mas* and *ikan sepat)*. Waterfalls are found in many regions. Most beaches are white because they lie near coral deposits—these can be found along the S and W shores of the peninsula. Barombang Beach S of Ujung Pandang has black sand because it's close to the mouth of the Jeneberang River. There are great coral reefs to the W of Ujung Pandang in the Makassar Straits as well as to the E in Teluk Bone.

Climate

South Sulawesi's mountain range creates 2 different rainy seasons. The *Musim Timor* (East Monsoon) blows April-September. The *Musim Barat* (West Monsoon) blows on the W side of the mountains Sept.-April and brings rain all along the W coast. It rains heaviest in Dec. and Jan., when the whole countryside is verdant. As a result, S. Sulawesi harvests twice a year and seldom experiences famine. The average temperature in Ujung Pandang is 25-29 degrees C (75-85 degrees F), but with a humidity of 72-89%! During June, July, and Aug., the "high" tourist season, it is very hot in this province. In the mountainous areas the temperature is pleasant, but above 1,000 m it can be unexpectedly cold.

Fauna And Flora

South Sulawesi is a transition zone between Asian and Australian-type species of animals and birds, a locale for special breeds found nowhere else in Indonesia or the world. There is, for example, the *anoa,* a small, hoofed animal like an antelope, which lives wild in the forest. The *babirusa* appears to be a cross between the pig and the deer; its legs are long like a deer's but its snout is short and flat. There are also unique species of monkeys, such as the almost tailless "black ape," which is actually a macaque. All of these are protected by the government. Not only rice and corn are cultivated, but also rubber, coffee, sugarcane, coconut, tobacco, and cloves. Also found in this province are *alang-alang, durian, duku, pandanus, kayu hitam* (ebony), rattan, mangrove swamps, nipa palms, and a great variety of beautiful forest orchids.

History

In the middle of this province an area of Pleistocene vertebrate fossils has been discovered, which resembles similar fossil fields in the Philippines. The stone implements found here are similar to those unearthed in C. Java and give a picture of life 400,000-500,000 years ago. Later the Toala people (their name means "Forest People") arrived, possibly from India, and there is some trace of Philippine Negritos (from about 10,000 B.C.). The Negritos lived in the lime mountain caves in Maros, Sinjai, Bone, and Soppeng, in which paintings of *babirusa* and hands have been found on walls, as well as stone tools.

Western influences began during the era of the European spice trade with Maluku. At this time, S. Sulawesi had many small kingdoms which were all dominated by 3 large ruling elites: Luwu, Gowa (Makassar), and Bone. During this period of intensive trade there was much rivalry between the English, Portuguese, and Dutch. The Portuguese worked very closely with the regent of Makassar in the 16th C., but were defeated by the Dutch in the early 1600s. There was constant war between the raja of Makassar and the Dutch, who were aggressively seeking a monopoly over the Mollucan spice trade at the time. The Dutch enlisted the assistance of Aru Palakka from Bone, a Bugis prince, and together they defeated the Makassarese in 1667. After this victory, the Dutch and Gowans went on to defeat the Mataram and Bantanese armies, which brought about the opening of Java itself for Dutch colonialism. Although more and more S. Sulawesi lands came under the control of the Dutch, this did not mean that the Bugis and Makassar submitted passively. Rebellions continued for over 200 years of Dutch domination, and it wasn't until 1905 that the Dutch finally achieved relative "peace" in the southern part of the island. Sporadic armed struggle continued even later in the northern mountains of the province (Luwu, Tanatoraja, Mamasa), ending in 1916 in Luwu and Torajaland, and not until 1932 in Mamasa.

After the war, the Dutch were determined to re-occupy the province but met fierce resistance from Republican youths trained by the Japanese on Java. The Dutch committed many atrocities, including (Feb. 1947) an infamous campaign commanded by Captain "Turk" Westerling which employed a policy of arbitrary terror. Although it was claimed that upwards of 40,000 local people were killed, a figure of 3,000 seems closer to the truth. As elsewhere in Indonesia, there are many remnants of Dutch colonialism: Fort Rotterdam in Ujung Pandang, and Dutch homes in Soppeng, Rantepao, and Mamasa. Numerous monuments commemorating the struggle against the Dutch can be seen on a "Freedom Struggle" tour offered by Ujung Pandang tour companies. After the Dutch, the military of the new Republic ruled with an iron fist from 1950 to 1965, until most rebellious groups were suppressed.

Economy

Irrigated *sawah* is the predominant agriculture; other crops include sugarcane, cotton, corn, all of which provide the principal revenues for S. Sulawesi. There are also plantations of coconuts, coffee, and rubber for export. In the S part, in the wide and fertile Jeneponto district, salt is produced and cotton, tobacco, and citrus are grown. In Bone, sugarcane is cultivated, and in Luwu, cloves and palm oil. With its extensive grass plains, S. Sulawesi is able to support herds of cattle, and is the second largest exporter of

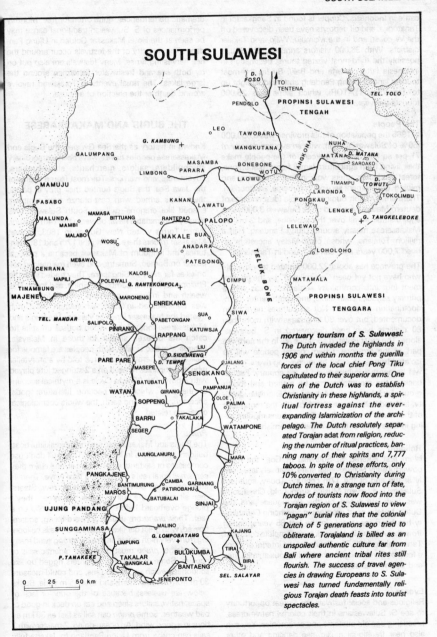

SOUTH SULAWESI

mortuary tourism of S. Sulawesi:
The Dutch invaded the highlands in
1906 and within months the guerilla
forces of the local chief Pong Tiku
capitulated to their superior arms. One
aim of the Dutch was to establish
Christianity in these highlands, a spiritual fortress against the ever-
expanding Islamicization of the archipelago. The Dutch resolutely separated Torajan adat from religion, reducing the number of ritual practices, banning many of their spirits and 7,777
taboos. In spite of these efforts, only
10% converted to Christianity in
Dutch times. In a strange turn of fate,
hordes of tourists now flood into the
Torajan region of S. Sulawesi to view
"pagan" burial rites that the colonial
Dutch of 5 generations ago tried to
obliterate. Torajaland is billed as an
unspoiled authentic culture far from
Bali where ancient tribal rites still
flourish. The success of travel agencies in drawing Europeans to S. Sulawesi has turned fundamentally religious Torajan death feasts into tourist
spectacles.

cattle in Indonesia. Copper is found in Sangkarapi in Tanatoraja, and oil deposits have been discovered off the W coast, and in the Mamuju, Wajo, and Takalar districts. With 36,000 visitors annually, SULSEL is possibly the third-most visited tourist destination in Indonesia (after Jakarta and Bali). By far the most tourists land at Ujung Pandang and head straight up to Tanatoraja (TATOR), which alone gets 25,000 tourists per year.

The People

In 1985 the population of this province was 6,650,000 (60% of Sulawesi's total), with an average density of 71 per sq km. Seventy percent of the people make their living from agriculture (small farms, plantations, forest products); others work in fishing, industry and mining, government service, commerce, and tourism. There are 4 million Buginese people (descendants of deutero-Malays who lived on S. Sulawesi 3,000 years ago) distributed all over the province, and 2 million Makassarese mostly around Ujung Pandang. Half a million Torajans, whose proto-Malay ancestors arrived 7,000 years ago, can be found in Tanatoraja.

The province has about 22,000 isolated tribespeople who have not yet been "assimilated" by the government (put into community settlement areas with a primary school, health clinic, and youth center for indoctrination purposes). Not all cultures have been documented, but over 30 languages with more than 80 dialects have been discovered in S. Sulawesi alone. The most isolated societies are in the northern part of the province. Often coastal people will be isolated from each other by intervening rivers. Inland will be another culture living in hill country. Farther back in the mountains may be a third and fourth group. Each has its own cultural and linguistic identity. Isolated cultures are also found in the mountains of the south. One, the Tana Towa, shuns modern living in a way similar to the American Amish.

Religion

Islam first entered S. Sulawesi at Goa, the most powerful early Makassarese state, relatively late—only at the end of the 17th century. Today, southern Sulawesi is a fervent Muslim stronghold. Christianity was first introduced by the Portuguese and the Dutch, but the most progress in advancing Christianity has been made only in the last 85 years, dating from the year the Dutch took over complete control of Tanatoraja in 1905. The Torajas of the interior practice a form of Christianity in which numerous animist rites and ceremonies survive.

Events

Religious and social festivals are a great opportunity to see S. Sulawesians in their colorful native dress, practicing age-old customs and ceremonies. You can also hear traditional music, see dancing and other dramatic performances, quite often for free. Monthly performances of S. Sulwesian traditional dance may be seen at the Hotel Makassar Golden in Ujung Pandang. The majority of the festivals occur around the rice harvesting times. Many festivals are also put on by both sea and freshwater fishermen around the large lakes. The ritual events in Torajaland revolve around death or the erection of a house.

THE BUGIS AND MAKASSARESE

Known in history as the Sea Gypsies, the Bugis and Makassarese peoples have always been extraordinary shipbuilders, sailors, merchants, slave-runners, adventurers, and warriors. The most feared pirates of the Java Sea, the Bugis hunted their prey in packs, their ships armed with cast-bronze bow rammers shaped like dragons' gullets. South Sulawesi was already a formidable naval power in the 14th century. When Torres visited New Guinea in 1603, he met Makassar traders there. During the 17th and 18th centuries, the kingdom of Makassar became a political power on Borneo, Sumatra, and even maintained colonies as far away as Singapore. They traded with the Philippines, Burma, Cambodia, China, and India. This wealth and influence persisted until Dutch control was consolidated in 1905, whereupon the Dutch treated the Makassar kings as vassals. The Bugis and Makassarese today live in wood houses on stilts (to catch the breeze), similar to those in Malaysia. Language is also similar. Both peoples are famous for their chanted heroic epic poems told by a storyteller who accompanies himself on a 2-stringed lute played with a bow. The *I Caligo* Cycle is a mythical account of the past which has become literature: gods, ancestors, heaven and earth, the whole cosmological order are related.

Prahu

The Bugis and Makassarese are the most skillful boatbuilders and sailors in Indonesia. They still don't use compasses or sextants when they sail, and claim they can *smell* coral reefs or a coming tidal wave. There is little distinction between captain and crew. Steersmen sit outside the hull so if they fall asleep, they'll plunge overboard before they crash the *prahu* on a reef. Their *prahu* are usually forward-tilting, square-bowed, with great oar-like rudders and 7 sails ballooning from very high masts. In a really strong wind many of the larger *prahu* must drop their gigantic sails or capsize. Some of the cargo freighters rigged up like schooners weigh up to 250 tons, and could measure 30 m from stem to stern, and over 15 m wide. Bunks below are useless; because of the odor or lack of space, native sailors sleep and eat on deck in good or bad weather. Some *prahu* can sail as fast as 30 km an hour in a good wind. An ocean-going, 2-master with 7 sails can cruise from Ujung Pandang to Jakarta fully

Pinisi-building, Pasture Harbor, Ujung Pandang. Bugis pinisi are one of the major surviving sailing fleets of the world.

loaded with 4 tons of copra in only 5 days. Some 30-ton *prahu* carry loads that are even heavier than the ship's deadweight. Bugis *prahu* were used extensively in the war for independence, and flotillas are still employed as a part of the Indonesian naval force.

Types Of *Prahu*

Some designs *(palari),* with their giant rectangular sails, still reflect Portuguese influence. There are numerous other types: *pinisi* weigh 50-200 tons and have 2 sailing masts with different sizes and numbers of sails; the *lambo* is 25-50 tons with one sailing mast; the *sande* is a fast and agile *prahu* of only 2-3 tons which sails between S. Sulawesi and E. Kalimantan. Racing *prahu* have one or 2 outriggers whose width is twice the hull's length (8 m), and whose height is 20 times the beam. These very fast wildflying ½-m-wide boats can turn in just a few seconds with their outriggers clear out of the water. Under sail they have the grace of a bird. See a good cross-section of *prahu* at Paotare harbor, only a Rp400 *becak* ride from Ujung Pandang's downtown. For complete information on all types of *prahu*, get ahold of *The Prahu*, 2nd Ed., by Adrian Horridge (Oxford University Press, 1985).

Prahu Building

Bugis *prahu* are built virtually everywhere where there are Bugis people, which includes all of coastal Sulawesi, and parts of south Sumatra, east Kalimantan, and Maluku. Whole communities (such as in Bulukumba) of shipwrights, sailors, and carpenters are involved in their construction. Expert *prahu* builders don't use plans, but build from knowledge and experience. Watch a boat grow from a pile of teak logs into a highly seaworthy vessel, said to last 25-30 years. The work takes place on a palm-shaded beach and the shipwrights have about 8 tools between them—age-old equipment including iron scrapers, a giant wooden mallet, and wooden planes. The only modern tools used are metal augers and steel blades.

Long straight planks are first hewn out of solid teak logs (usually from Kalimantan). Boats are built in cradles of scaffolding with round wooden bottoms and big broad beams, ribbed like a whale. Little iron is used, the entire hull is planked and fastened by long ironwood pegs, then the frames are pegged to it. Deadeyes are carved from blocks of teak. Caulking consists of shreds of paper bark poked into the cracks. Bunks, tables, galleys, proper floorboards and cupboards are totally unfamiliar to the Bugis who design their *prahu* to carry copra, stinking dried fish, timber, and live turtles to Java, and sleep on mats under the stars at night. Sails are made of cotton cloth from India (about US$350 for the mainsail). Hundreds of *prahu* are built each year, adding to an already existing fleet of thousands.

UJUNG PANDANG

With a population of over 750,000, Ujung Pandang is the 5th largest city in Indonesia. Formerly known as Makassar, this bustling commercial, shipping, and government center constitutes a major air-sea crossroad between western and eastern Indonesia—the largest and busiest mercantile center in all of eastern Indonesia for almost 500 years. Also the capital of S. Sulawesi, the government buildings are in the center of town with traffic sputtering past areas of trees and lawns. The city's surrounding area—the SW coast of the SW peninsula—was once known as Jumpandang, or Pandan Point, for its abundant *pandan* (screw pine) trees. A fort was built here by an early sultan of Goa to protect the strategic harbor from pirate gangs; it now lies more or less in the center town. The old fort was subsequently reconstructed by the Portuguese and then the Dutch, who renamed it Fort Rotterdam. They also renamed the town Makassar, after the local people. In 1971, the name was changed to Ujung Pandang, closer to the original Jumpandang. Today, Ujung Pandang is one of the most colorful cities in Indonesia, a unique place to wander around in (but watch the holes in the sidewalks!). Makassar Bay teems with sailing *prahu* and hosts spectacularly beautiful sunsets. There are many florist shops, and you might even see deer grazing unafraid in grassy spots around the city. Ujung Pandang has a large Chinese population who run most of the businesses and operate numerous restaurants. People are friendly and, as expected, many are eager to practice English.

SIGHTS

In the downtown, a few blocks S of Fort Rotterdam on Jl. Mokhtar Lufthi 15A (tel. 22572), visit **Clara L. Bundt's** collection of over 200 varieties of seashells (including giant clams), along with her father's 50-year-old orchid nursery. Now with Bogor's orchid nursery closed, this is the largest orchid garden in Indonesia open to the public. You're greeted by 15 barking dachshunds, and admission is free. Orchid-fiber crafts such as baskets are also made here. Peak orchid-blooming times are March and September. Some shells and orchids can be purchased; orchids range from Rp1000 to Rp35,000 (for the Moon orchid). Another orchid garden is 7 km from here (Rp100 by *bemo*) in a natural setting.

Ibu Agung Bahari, Jl. Sulawesi 41, is the most ornate of several Chinese temples in the neighborhood. This 350-year-old Buddhist temple contains paintings, stonecarvings and woodcarvings—a riot of col-

or! Also see the old Dutch **governor's mansion**, now the Indonesian governor's residence, on Jl. Jen. Sudirman. A new university, **Universitas "45,"** opened in 1987 in Panaikang on the edge of the city. But the best show in town happens nightly, has unlimited seating capacity, only takes an hour, and is free: the magnificent sunsets over Makassar Bay. Claim some grass on the beachside boulevard; you won't be disappointed. The beach, however, along Jl. Penghiburis filthy.

Fort Rotterdam

This old fortress on Jl. Ujung Pandang, overlooking the harbor right in the heart of the city, is one of the principal attractions of Ujung Pandang. Enter from the ocean side. Some historians contend that on this site once stood a fortified outpost of the great Malay kingdoms, but most believe that the original fort stood adjacent to the palace of the King of Goa when the Portuguese gained control and undertook the first reconstruction in 1545. The fort was captured in 1608 by the Dutch, who added extensively to the fortifications. The once crumbling, blackened fort has been restored yet a 3rd time, and within are some of the best-preserved examples of 17th C. Dutch colonial fortress architecture in all of Indonesia. The shape of the fort resembles a turtle facing the city. The fort contains 13 buildings, 11 built by the Dutch, 2 by the Japanese during the war. Open 0700-1800, free.

The fort's big **La Galigo Museum** consists of 2 buildings, one covering ethnology and the other history. The ethnology museum has 2 floors of ceramics, old money, seals, musical instruments, weaving technology, miniature houses with extraordinary detail, and traditional tools and handicrafts. Top floor has weapons. Local guides are available. Open Tues. to Thurs. 0800-1400, Fri. 0800-1100, Sat. and Sun. 0800-1230, closed Mon. and holidays. Entrance Rp200. The gift shop sells Bugis pure silk *sarung* (Rp17,500-20,000) as well as 53 postcards! Across the yard in the NE corner of the complex is the historical museum (no sign) with fascinating photos of all the fort's main buildings before and after reconstruction, prehistoric tools and jewelry, the famous Sikendang statue of Buddha, stone pottery, a whole section devoted to the cultural heritage of the Goa Kingdom, old coins and money, national heros with their bios, and a Chinese and European porcelain collection. Admission Rp200.

In the center of Fort Rotterdam is the Conservatory of Dance and Music (**Taman Budaya**) where you may see children practice dance or recite Koranic passages in the mornings, and on Sat. at 2000 dances are often staged. In the SW corner request to see the gloomy but revered cell (no sign) where the rebel Prince Diponegoro was held for 26 years. The Historical & Archaeological Institute (see Wiwiek P. Yusuf), the National Archives, and the Art Development Services are also within the walls of the fort.

Diponegoro Monument

A few blocks W, in a small cemetery on Jl. Diponegoro, is Diponegoro's grave and genealogy chart. Indonesians still pay homage at this tomb. Diponegoro, considered Indonesia's first nationalist leader, skillfully fought the Dutch on Java for 5 years (1830-1835) until he was tricked into negotiations and arrested, then exiled to Ujung Pandang for the remaining 26 years of his life. The tomb of a Makassarese hero, **Sultan Hasanudin** (1629-1670), who fought the Dutch in the 17th C., is on the outskirts of Ujung Pandang; take a *bis kota* from the central bus station and ask the driver to let you off at the start of the street down to *Makam Hasanudin*, only a ½-km walk. Just 15 min. away is the historic **Katangka Mosque** and nearby cemetery with old engraved tombs of rajas. Other stone-engraved stone graves are found in Soppeng and Binamu (Kab. Jeneponto, S. Sulawesi).

Harbors

A row of sailing ships from Banjarmasin, Surabaya, Kendari, etc. moor in Soekarno Harbor unloading foodstuffs, consumer goods, rattan, etc. These laborers, who make only Rp2000 per day, come from the countryside in search of cash after the harvest. It's enjoyable to walk around this very busy harbor area and you may take photos. Sail all the way to Banjarmasin for Rp4500 if you first get *ijin* from the *syahbandar's* office. Eat a little farther along at **RM Parmato Bundo** (*nasi padang*), just before the entrance to Pelabuhan Makassar.

At Paotare Harbor (pronounced "putre") in the NW end of town, see handsome Bugis schooners (*pinisi*) whose designs haven't changed since Genghis Khan. You might even see water skiers here among the fishermen spreading their nets to dry, mending sails, or paddling dinghies across the harbor. Hire a boat to chase and photograph *prahu* in the harbor. Get to Paotare by *becak* or taxi, but take a *bemo* back to town. Ujung Pandang's harbor, also in the N part of town, is reachable by *bemo, becak,* or a long walk up Jl. Martadinata. Color photographers will enjoy themselves here, especially at sunset. Don't try to walk from the W along the coast, as military installations block the way. At the S end of town is the harbor for *prahu patorani* and fishing canoes.

Tours

City tours through a travel agency are expensive so just hire a *bemo* (Rp15,000) plus a guide from the tourist office for a 5- to 6-hour tour. One agency with a good reputation and a lot of experience is **Ramayana Travel**, Jl. Anuang 94A, Ujung Pandang; their French and German-speaking guides specialize in tours to not only U.P. but Tanatoraja and SE Sulawesi. Recommended is the guide Oetovianus Pasolang. **Pacto Ltd.**, Jl. Jen. Sudirman 56 (tel. 83208), is another Sulawesi specialist with tours to the megaliths of C. Sulawesi, an intriguing Sea Safari to SE Sulawesi, plus more localized tours to the Leang-Leang prehistoric caves, Bantimurung Waterfall, Makassar Bay islands, and Torajaland.

ACCOMMODATIONS

Inexpensive

Hotels in the cheapest category tend to be either full, double as brothels, or else turn away Westerners. Most are in the middle range of Rp6000-Rp20,000. If that's a little rich for your blood, the best low-cost hotel, popular with travelers, is the **Hotel Nusantara**, Jl. Sarappo 103 (tel. 3163), near Jl. Sulawesi; Rp3000 s, Rp5000 d. An Islamic traders' hotel close to the harbor, color TV and drinks in the lobby. The 2nd- and 3rd-floor balconies are the ticket for relaxing and looking over a busy market street below. The rooms are tiny but usually clean; windows don't close—lots of mosquitos for company. An automatic alarm system will have you up for predawn prayers at the mosque next door. Across the street from Hotel Nusantara at Jl. Sarappo 60 (tel. 3101) is basic but cheap **Hotel Murah**; Rp3000 s, Rp5000 d. Also popular with travelers is the tidy and clean **Hotel Oriental**, Jl. Monginsidi (S of Jl. Saddang), Rp6000 s or d which includes free tea, Continental breakfast, and good-eating *warung* nearby. Makassar Cottage (Jl. Dangko 50, tel. 83363/83559), about 15 min. by *becak* from town, features private Torajan-style houses (Rp7500 d) around a tranquil pond. Simple luxury; very comfortable and friendly people.

Mid-priced

Midtown places include: **Hotel Purnama**, Jl. Pattimura 3 (tel. 3830); Rp7500 s, Rp10,000 d (with breakfast) for *ekonomi* rooms; Rp10,000 s, Rp12,500 d for standard. Though centrally located just to the S of Fort Rotterdam, it's expensive for the drab rooms you get. On the W side near Losari Beach Inn is the rather rundown **Hotel Benteng**, Jl. Ujung Pandang 8; Rp7500 s, Rp11,000 d with *mandi*. Right on the waterfront, the **Losari Beach Inn**, Jl. Pasar Ikan 8 (tel. 4363/6303) asks Rp27,900 s, Rp30,960 d for rather overpriced rooms. Has a bar and restaurant, but its nicest feature is its location near the business and shopping districts. **Pasanggrahan Beach Hotel**, Jl.

Somba Opu 297 (tel. 84210); Rp12,000 s, Rp18,500 d with meals—front rooms have a beautiful view of the harbor.

To the E, on the way to the airport and just down the street from the Merpati office, is the **Ramayana Hotel**, Jl. Gunung Bawakaraeng (tel. 22165/4153); Rp9000 Economy Class s or d, Rp15,000 1st Class (a/c). Although you get a welcoming homemade marquisa drink upon arrival, many other of the hotel's policies (such as a 10% "tax" added to the already rip-off breakfast!) are designed to wheedle as much money out of you as possible. It's a shame that as many as 30% of all independent travelers stay here and that there is no viable alternative accommodations in the same price range in Ujung Pandang. On the same street (no. 120) is **Hotel Marlin**; Rp17,500 s, Rp25,000 d. Other recommended hotels are: **Hotel Widhana**, Jl. Botolempangan 53 (tel. 22499), Rp18,500 s, Rp25,000 d for large, quiet and comfortable rooms; and **Tiatira House**, Jl. Dr. Soetomo (tel. 28948), Rp14,500 s, Rp17,500 d. **Pondok Delta**, Jl. Hasanuddin 25 (tel. 22553), charges Rp16,500 s, Rp20,000 d (breakfast included). For a place to stay on the shopping street, try **Hotel Kenaripante**, Jl. Sombu Opu; Rp12,000 s. Near the airport, the **Afiat** is on the corner of the airport road and the main highway; Rp7500 s.

Expensive

The top hotel and one of the city's newest is the **Marannu City Hotel**, Jl. Sultan Hasanuddin 3, close by the post office, Garuda office, and shopping area. Charges are US$26 s, US$30 d (plus 21% tax and service) for big rooms with fridge, TV, video, and all the amenities including nice pool (Rp2000 for non-guests) and occasional buffets. The 3-star **Makassar Golden Hotel**, Jl. Pasar Ikan 52 (tel. 22208), has the best view of any large city hotel with commodious rooms, super magazine kiosk, disco, pool, a French restaurant with great service, and higher prices than even the Marannu City Hotel. Standard rooms cost US$45 s, US$52 d; also Toraja-style cottages at US$74 s, US$82 d right on the seaside. Add to all prices tax and service.

For something a little cheaper and more authentic, check out the old Dutch-style **Pondok Suada Indah**, Jl. Sultan Hasanuddin 14 (tel. 7179); a bit overpriced at Rp35,000 s, Rp40,000 d (plus 10% tax). With only 14 (enormous) rooms, it feels more like a guesthouse with a colonial air. Other possibilities are the **Raodah Hotel**, Jl. Khairil Anwar 28 (tel. 7055), Rp35,000 s, Rp45,000 d, with restaurant, bar, shops, swimming pool; **Victoria Hotel**, Jl. Jen. Sudirman 24 (tel. 21429); Rp24,800 s, Rp30,000 d—a small hotel with inside rooms and balconies overlooking a small, clean restaurant.

FOOD

The markets and restaurants of Ujung Pandang are renowned for their delicacies of the sea, but expect to spend Rp2500 and up for a restaurant meal. Barbecued fish *(ikan bakar)*—sea bass or red snapper grilled over a firepit—is a Bugis and Makassarese specialty. Another (in)famous regional specialty is *soto makassar*, a savory, super-nutritious soup made from buffalo guts which can be found in *warung* all over town.

UJUNG PANDANG

1. entrance to Pel. Makassar
2. immigration office
3. Jameson's Supermarket
4. Nusantara Hotel
5. RM Malabar
6. RM Parmato Bundo
7. Kantor Syahbandar
8. Pelni office
9. Setia Restaurant
10. PT Stras Raya
11. Bank Dagang Negara
12. King Barber Bath & Massage
13. *bemo* station
14. *bemo* station
15. Liman express bus
16. moneychanger
17. Modern Photo
18. PT Bhakti Toko Buku
19. taxi stand (Rp3500 per hour)
20. Garuda Airlines
21. Bank Pembangunan Indonesia
22. Governor's office
23. telephone & telegraph office
24. BPK Gunung Mulia
25. police
26. Bank Indonesia
27. Merpati Nusantara Airlines
28. Hotel Ramayana
29. Hotel Benteng
30. Losari Beach Inn
31. Kanebo Art Shop
32. Hotel Purnama
33. Losari Beach Restaurant
34. Pondok Suada Ondah
35. Marannu City Hotel
36. Rai Asia Baru
37. Clara L. Bundt's
38. moneychanger

UJUNG PANDANG

TO
AIRPORT &
TOURIST OFFICE

JL. SERAM UJUNG

JL. BUTUNG

JL. BANDA

JL. BURU

JL. SANGIR

JL. DIPONEGORO

JL. LEMBE

JL. K.H. HASYIM

JL. TIMOR

JL. K.H. RAMLI

JL. BALI

JL. SUMBA

JL. SERUI

CHINESE
TEMPLE

JL. RIBURANE

A. YANI

JL. MESJID RAYA

FORT
ROTTERDAM

POST
OFFICE

JL.
SUPRATMAN

JL. PATTIMURA

JL. KARTINI

JL. G. BAWAKARAENG

TO
PAOTARE HARBOR

JL. THAMRIN

JL. AMANAGAPPA

JL. INCE NURDIN

JL. SALAHUTU

JL. BAUMASEPE

JL. KHAIRIL ANWAR

JL. ALI MALAKA

JL. SAWER GADING

JL. MOKTHAR LUFTHI

JL. VETERAN

JL. DATUMUSENG

JL. EMMY SAELAN

SOEKARNO HARBOR

HATTA HARBOR

JL. NUSANTARA

JL. SULAWESI

JL. RACAN

JL. SARAPPO

JL. MARTADINATA

JL. UJUNG PANDANG

JL. SLAMET RYADI

BALAI KOTA

JL. KATAOLADINO

L.P. KAREBOSI

JL. JEND. SUDIRMAN

JL. H.O.S. COKROAMINOTO

JL. ANDALAS

JL. BULUL SERAUNG

JL. IRIAN

JL. TINUMBU

JL. SOMBA OPU

JL. PENGHIBUR

PANTAI LOSARI

JL. PASAR IKAN

JL. SAMI'UN

JL. HASANUDDIN

JL. DR. SOETOMO

JL. LATIMOJONG

CENTRAL
MARKET

Markets And Stores

The **Pasar Ikan** (Fish Market) is on the coast just S of the Losari Beach Inn, 1 km from Fort Rotterdam. A vast variety of fish, live or otherwise—eels, lobster, crab, squid, prawns—are laid out. Busiest at dawn and early afternoon. The **Central Market** (Pasar Pusat) is on Jl. Andalas near Diponegoro's grave and monument. Night markets take place from 1800 to 2300 near the THR and Jl. Sungai Poso—excellent sidewalk trolleys and stalls. A fruit market is at the intersection of Jl. Sulawesi and Jl. Timor, with all kinds of fruits and vegetables (6 different kinds of eggplant!). There are well-stocked grocery stores on Jl. Sulawesi selling 57 varieties of fresh-baked biscuits and cookies in glass jars, Australian cheese and wine, Dutch chocolates. Drop into **Jamesons Supermarket**, Jl. Irian, for milkshakes, imported groceries and a super selection of booze. Just down the street from the Ramayana Hotel is the **Harapan Supermarket** for baked goods, breakfast, fruit drinks, cold apples (Rp2250 per kg), sweets, cakes, donuts, and a multitude of other high-priced Western groceries. Open 0900-2200.

Warung

Numerous eating stalls set up between 1600 and 2400 on **Pantai Losari**, the seawall opposite Losari Beach Restaurant. This is the place to go to eat local foods including cakes, *soto makassar*, and terrific *ikan bakar* (Rp2000) complete with rice, cucumber, chili sauce and hot tea! At Jl. Sulawesi 185 (near RM Malabar) is a little Chinese place serving big portions of tasty *mie goreng*. Their *cap cai* soup is unbelievably good at Rp2500. Lots of other *warung* along Jl. Sulawesi. The **THR** (People's Amusement Park) is another center for *warung* serving fish dishes.

Restaurants

European food can be enjoyed at a number of restaurants: **Wisma Ria** on Jl. Pasar Ikan and **Happy** on Jl. Sulawesi, etc., but stay away from the hotel restaurants if you want reasonably priced meals. Although it's a bit touristy, the **Asia Baru**, Jl. Salahutu 2, serves expensive seafood, excellent grilled fish, and *sate* in a tacky but unforgettable atmosphere. Here you get real king prawns, the *big* ones. The price of a whole fish depends on the size but expect around Rp3500 for the average; sample *baronang* (very few bones), a big fat fish with a great taste. The *cumi cumi* (barbecued squid) is not too big a portion so you'll need something else. Also delicious is Makassar boiled fish in spiced sauce *(pulu mara)*. Prices are steep for the small servings. Better value is **RM Empang**, Jl. Siau 7, for outstanding traditional Makassarese food; baked fish *(ikan bakar)* is at its best here. For *martabak*, Indian curry and *roti* (Rp2000), go to **RM Malabar**, Jl. Sulawesi 290 near the Nusantara Hotel. **RM Mirama**, Jl. Bawakaraeng (same street as Ramayana Hotel), offers self-serve Indonesian food. The **Bamboo Denn**, next door, serves Chinese and European food.

Chinese

The city's large Chinese population ensures good Chinese restaurants. The **Steak House Depot**, Jl. Sulawesi 178, offers a peerless *fu hung hai* (Rp2500). **Hilman**, Jl. Jampea 2 (upstairs), serves delicious crab and egg soup, fried prawns, and fried *kaki kodok* (frog legs). Their menu is a mixture of Western, Chinese, and Indonesian food. **Surya/Supercrab**, Jl. Nusakambangan 16, offers probably the finest crab, fish and prawn dishes in S. Sulawesi; very clean, no a/c. Pretty tasty Chinese fare (Rp4000 for one) can also be experienced at the **Setia Restaurant**, Jl. Racan 1A (tel. 22679); open 1000-2000.

SHOPPING

Ujung Pandang is a busy metalcrafts center where exquisite Kendari-style filigree-like silver jewelry is made and sold. The Goanese are known for their brillant brasswork; brass bells, and candleholder from Kuningan look almost Tibetan. Bugis and Makassarese women bedeck themselves in jewelry and much of a family's worth is invested in women's adornments. The Bugis also produce some of the most attractive pottery in Indonesia, with the top half of the dishes and bowls engraved with flowers, leaves, human and animal motifs and figures. Other regional crafts for sale in U.P. include the most unusual baskets and boxes made out of orchid fibers from Bone on the E coast of S. Sulawesi; orchid fiber crafts are also sold at Clara L. Bundt's, Jl. Mokthar Lufthi 15A. Beautiful carved bamboo and wooden pieces made by the Torajans are another possibility. Street hawkers often sell mounted butterflies (including protected species) from the Bantimurung Waterfall area. At Paotare Harbor, get real woven and silk cloth bargains by buying straight from the ship's captain.

Jalan Somba Opu

All down this street, located S of Fort Rotterdam and E of the waterfront, are jewelry shops selling silver and gold Kendari-style crafts, along with Goa brasswork; Torajan crafts, woven items, Bugis flutes, bonecarvings, seashells, Chinese ceramics, and Sulawesi silk. Peep in at the following art shops: **Art Shop** (no. 199) for paintings, woodcarvings, plaited work; the **Mutiara** (no. 117A) for carvings, *sarung*, seashells; **Paleori** (no. 108) for paintings, Torajan crafts, and bamboo crafts; **Asdra** (no. 26) for paintings, china, seashells, silvercrafts; and **Toko Kerajina** (no. 20) for every imaginable souvenir. **Kanebo Art Shop**, on the corner of Jl. Pattimura 27 and Jl. Somba Opu, is a good introduction to the many fine crafts of

S. Sulawesi: mother-of-pearl broaches (Rp3500-4000), intricate silver bracelets (Rp5000-8000), clove artifacts (houses, ships, etc., around Rp15,000), shells, Bone *lontar* plaited articles (Rp2500-6000), Torajan and Bugis *sarung*, postcards (Rp135), and other crafts from all over eastern Indonesia.

Fabrics

The Central Market (Jl. Andalas, near Diponegoro's tomb) has a wide variety of colorful *ikat*-dyed silk and other cloth (65% of Indonesia's silk is produced in this province); silk *sarung* cost Rp12,000 first price, but they quickly come down to Rp10,000 in the shops. At **Pertenunan Sutera Alam Sulawesi**, Jl. Onta 408, (in the southern part of the city between Jl. Dr. Ratulangi and Jl. Veteran) the dyeing, spinning, and weaving processes can be seen; this silk factory produces *sarung* and other products made of silk from Mandar. Place special orders or buy your silk by the meter at fixed but reasonable prices.

Antiques

Antique Chinese porcelain is still available in Ujung Pandang. For genuine antiques (you can usually tell by the prices), stop in at **Cony Karya**, Jl. Pasar Ikan 26. Even if you don't intend to buy, you'll find museum-quality pieces here. Hawkers also come around to the hotels to flog "antique" Chinese porcelain and highly suspect "old" VOC coins; let the buyer beware.... The street vendors of Indonesia sell amazingly realistic reproductions. If you *do* buy, the law says you must obtain an official permit from the office in the old Dutch fort in order to remove porcelain from Ujung Pandang. Failure to do so may result in the confiscation of your pieces at the airport.

ENTERTAINMENT

Go to the **THR** (People's Amusement Park) for some inexpensive diversion and very reasonable *warung*. Visit the seamen's bars down on the waterfront; Bugis women, *Kupu Kupu Malam* ("Night Butterflies"), will keep you company all night for Rp25,000. **Queen Massage Parlor** is the most favored by expats who have been in Ujung Pandang for a few years. Pay Rp10,000 to the gent at the desk, negotiate further with the young lady herself inside (for health reasons, the Seaview Hotel is not recommended). The city's nightclubs feature, for example, the "Sweet Sisters" from Thailand, or Filipino duets. **Losari Beach Restaurant** opposite the Makassar Golden Hotel has a rollicking bar. For a nice view of the harbor at sunset, try the **Eva Ria** up the street, and **Kios Semarang**, both on Jl. Penghibur. Both have open-air 3rd-floor decks and serve snacks, chilled bottled drinks, coffee, and fruit-and-ice combinations.

Recreation

If you don't want to join the local people swimming at Pantai Losari, try the large **Taman Bahari** swimming pool near the fort; Rp250 admission, closed Mondays. Almost the only thing Indonesians enjoy more than playing chess with Westerners is beating them! It's easy to find tennis players at the tennis courts on Jl. Sam Ratulangi, or at the military police barracks. Or join volleyball and soccer games; soccer players often practice at **Karebosi Park**, and during the soccer season matches are played at the stadium. Learn to play *karambor*, a game with sliding discs on a chalked board. A billiard hall is on Jl. A. Yani. Makassar Golf Club is 16 km to the NE, near the airport.

SERVICES

Stella Maris Hospital is on Jl. Penghibur near Losari Beach; also **RM Dadi**, Jl. Daeng Pasewang, and **RM Labuang Baji**, Jl. Dr. Ratulangi. *Imigrasi* is at Jl. Seram Ujung 8-12, near the harbor. **Kantor Pos Besar** (on Jl. Slamet Riyadi (walking distance SE of the fort) on the corner of Jl. Supratman. The **Telephone & Telegraph Office**, Jl. Balai Kota 2, is open Mon.-Thurs. 0730-2300, Fri. 0730-1100 and 1400-2000, Sat. 0730-2000, Sun. 0900-1200. If you're starved for reading material, pay a call at **Toko Baru** on Jl. Balai Kota where they have a selection of secondhand books and magazines in English. Check different banks for different rates of exchange—there could be a big difference. Start out with **Bank Rakyat Indonesia** on Jl. Slamet Riyadi (E of fort); open Mon.-Thurs. 0800-1130 and 1330-1430, Fri. 0800-1130 and 1330-1430, Sat. 0800-1130. Or try other banks such as **Bank Indonesia** on Jl. Sudirman and **Bank Bumi Daya** on Jl. Nusantara, or any of the 5 or so moneychangers downtown.

Information

A tourist information booth might be open at the airport. The **tourist office** (Kantor Pariwisata) for S. Sulawesi is friendly, has maps, pamphlets, and spot-on information. They also double as a sort of travel agency, arranging for guides, car rentals, etc. Depending on what you want to do, if you have a letter of recommendation from them, it helps move it along. If there are 4 or 5 in your group, the tourist office can buy tickets for you. Open Mon. to Thurs. and Sat. 0700-1400, Fri. 0700-1100. Unfortunately, it's inconveniently located 4 km SE of the city center on Jl. Andi Pangerang Petta Rani (heads E off the airport road), a street lined with other government buildings. Their tel. number is 0411 or 7128. Take a *bemo* (Rp300) from the central *bemo* station that goes right by the office, or take a *bis kota* from the Central Market.

TRANSPORT

Getting There

Ujung Pandang is the main air gateway to Sulawesi as well as a connecting point for travel to and from the eastern islands of Indonesia. Garuda flies from: Denpasar (Bali), Rp73,100; Jakarta, Rp156,700; Manado, Rp114,500; Medan, Rp301,000; Solo, Rp121,200; and Surabaya, Rp98,700. Merpati also connects Surabaya to Ujung Pandang (Rp126,500); also flights from Manado, Rp72,900; Balikpapan, Rp99,100; and Gorontalo, Rp97,600. Mandala Airlines, the cheapest of all, has flights to U.P. from Jakarta (Rp133,100) and Surabaya (Rp73,000).

Arriving, Hasanuddin Airport is 23 km NE of the city at Mandai. From 0800-1700 the tourist info booth at the airport is open and a tourist officer and a rep or two from a tour company are usually in attendence. A taxi into the city costs Rp9000. Alternatively, you can simply walk (or take a *becak*, Rp200) the ½ km to the main road, then flag down a local bus (Rp300) or *bemo* (Rp500) all the way to the Central Market (Pasar Pusat). If heading up to Tanatoraja, get yourself out to the highway (½ km from airport) and flag down a passing bus (Rp7500 or an a/c bus with reclining seats, 8 hours). Your chances of finding an empty seat are best in the mornings.

Pelni docks at Pelabuhan Hatta, close to the city center. From Surabaya, one of the Pelni ships KM *Kambuna* and KM *Kerinci* leaves every 7-10 days, takes 40-plus hours, and charges Rp22,500 Economy Class or Rp40,000 2nd Class cabin. From Tg. Priok (Jakarta), these same Pelni ships charge Rp35,500 Economy, Rp65,000 2nd Class. Other cargo ships make the trip too. Ships also embark from Pelabuhan Hatta in many directions; see "From Ujung Pandang" below.

Getting Around

If you don't feel like walking, bargain with a *becak* driver, but the going rates are about twice that of Java. There are 2 main transport hubs, the *bemo* station at Central Market, and the Panaikang Bus Terminal, 4 km N of the city. From the *bemo* terminal along the N side of the central market at the end of Jl. Cokroaminoto, *bemo* travel to all corners of the city: N to Paotere Harbor, SE to the tourist office, and S to Sungguminasa Palace and Pabaeng Baeng market. Unfortunately, destinations are not labeled. Fares in town, Rp200-300. To Hasanuddin Airport (Rp500, 23 km), the *bemo* driver drops you off at the start of the road to the airport. Down the street from Hotel Nusantara near the harbor are station wagon "buses" leaving when full to all directions in Sulawesi (Majene, Palopo, Pare Pare, etc.), but no fixed prices and no fixed departure times.

Double-decker buses (Rp200 flat fare) pass in front of the main *bemo* station and down Jl. Cokroaminoto which changes farther S into Jl. Sudirman. All buses pass through the heart of the city and then head in only 3 directions: out Jl. Bawakaraeng to the airport, to the tourist office down Jl. A. Pangerang Petta Rani, and also to Sultan Hasanuddin's Tomb. A very useful service. In the city, stand at the bus stops just outside of downtown just flag it down.

Taxis are unmetered and prices should be negotiated. A convenient taxi stand is at the corner of Jl. Kataoladino and Jl. A. Yani, but they change all the time. Taxis to Hasanuddin Airport cost less (Rp6000 or even Rp5000) than taxis *from* the airport (Rp9000). Order your taxi in advance from one of the taxi stands in the city to meet you at your hotel at a certain time, or just have your hotel arrange it (Rp7500). If you pay extra for the toll road, you can get to the airport in 15 min. as opposed to 30 minutes. *Bemo* are cheaper to hire. Car rental can be provided through the tourist office (tel. 7128/21142/29220). Count on about Rp20,000 per day, capacity 5 persons (cheaper than *becak*, Rp1000). Or rent a car through a travel agent or through your hotel.

FROM UJUNG PANDANG

By Bus

Minibus and bus companies provide frequent and inexpensive service to the other cities and towns in S. Sulawesi. Hitching is fairly easy on the main roads, either as a paying passenger or for free. For Torajaland, a beautiful journey into the hills on a well-surfaced road, take Liman Express at Jl. Laiya no. 25 (only 100 m from the Central Market), tel. 5851. Buses take 10-12 hours, leaving 0700 and 1900; Rp7500, 328 km. Be ready by 0600 at the depot opposite Hotel Ramayana, where tickets may also be bought. Buy tickets a day in advance and try to get a seat in the front, or bounce around like iron filings in the back. Don't go on the night coach and miss the scenery. You'll go to the bus terminal first, then set off only at 0730. The route is through Pare Pare, then inland.

Even though Ujung Pandang's Ramayana Hotel employs a rather lackluster staff and their cheap rooms are dusty, close, and clouded with mosquitos, you can't deny the usefulness of the Hotel Ramayana-Wisma Maria connection. It's extremely convenient to be picked up at 0600 in front of Hotel Ramayana and then be let off in front of Rantepao's best *wisma* when you arrive in Tanatoraja at 1700. Then, when you're ready to go back to Ujung Pandang, you just climb on the morning bus which picks you up in front of Wisma Maria and are let off in front of Hotel Ramayana in Ujung Pandang at 0300.

Liman Ekspres also offers direct services to Enrekang, 0700 (5 hours), Rp3500; Pare Pare, 0700 (4 hours),

Rp2500; Mumuju, 1900 and passing en route Majene (Rp5000, 7 hours) on the coastal road. Another Liman bus leaves at 1900 for Soroako, Rp12,000, 16 hours, passing en route Malili, Rp9000; Palopo, Rp6000 (8 hours); Siwa, Rp4500 (6 hours). No Liman pickup at the Ramayana Hotel on any other bus but the TATOR bus. Work out your own itinerary so you see as much of S. Sulawesi's sights as possible on your route up to Tanatoraja. For example, hop your way up to Tanatoraja via Malino, Watampone, Sengkang-Soppeng, Siwa, and Palopo (just over the mountain from Rantepao). From Rantepao, you can always come back to U.P. via the easterly route Palopo-Sengkang-Watampone, or vice-versa.

Other Land Transport

Liman Ekspres is convenient, but gets its share of complaints. An alternative is to find *bemo* or minibuses heading up to Tanatoraja—same price as the buses, but less time, less people, and thus more comfortable. **CV Ningo Jaya**, Jl. Sarappo 100A (tel. 3367) offers minibuses to: Pare Pare for Rp3000; Pinrang, Rp3000; Watamapone (Bone), Rp3000. Similar service is offered by **CV Setia Jaya**, Jl. Seram (tel. 3422); **CV Haji Kalla**, Jl. Cokroaminoto 76 (tel. 4997); **CV Surya**, Jl. Kerung-Kerung 11 (tel. 5798). From Ujung Pandang's central *bemo* station catch frequently departing *bemo* to: Malino, Rp1500; Bantimurung, Rp1000 (one hour); Barombang, Rp1000; to the airport, Rp500.

By Air

Ujung Pandang has always been a busy transit point between Java and Maluku and Irian Jaya and it is served by a number of airlines. **Garuda**, Jl. Selamet Riyadi 5, tel. 22804/227005 (airport office, tel. 22573); open Mon.-Fri. 0700-1600, Sat. 0700-1300, Sun. 0900-1200. **Merpati**, Jl. G. Bawakaraeng 109 (tel. 4114/4118), very near Ramayana Hotel; **Mandala**, Jl. Irian 2F (tel. 21289/4288; airport office, 3326); **Bouraq**, Jl. Cokroaminoto 7C, tel. 22253. Some airlines pick you up at your hotel and drive you 23 km to the airport. Hasanuddin Airport is your last chance to buy high-quality *marquisha* syrup, native to only S. Sulawesi and N. Sumatra; Rp4600 for 2 bottles. Hasanuddin also has one of the nicest airport cafeterias in Indonesia; average meal Rp4000.

Sample Merpati fares to: Poso, Rp75,700 (0700 on Mon. and Fri.); Ambon, Rp93,100; Biak, Rp166,500; Bima, Rp71,700; Jakarta, Rp135,300; Pomalaa (Sulawesi Tenggara), Rp55,100 (takes off at 0900 on Wed. and Fri.); Kupang, Rp90,200 (leaving 5 days weekly at 1220); Soroako, Rp65,600; Surabaya, Rp86,000. Sample Bouraq fares: Manado, Rp116,800 (twice daily); Balikpapan, Rp104,900 (once daily at 0700); Tarakan, Rp176,900 (leaving at 0700 each day); Samarinda, Rp136,400; Ternate, Rp161,700.

Mandala has a flight to Ambon daily at 1145 (arrive 1445) for Rp90,800, and to Jakarta daily at 1045 (arrive 1350) for Rp133,100.

By Prahu

Visit some fine beaches and peaceful fishing villages on islands way out in Makassar Bay. On Sundays in the bay, scores of brightly painted craft with their wide sails look like flocks of butterflies on the wing. The nearer islands are reachable in just 15-20 min. by motorboat from the pier opposite Fort Rotterdam. **Pulau Kayangan**, an artificial island and holiday resort just 15-min. ride offshore, offers bungalows, restaurants, playground and beer garden, but nothing natural. Boats leave every hour (depending on demand); Rp1000 RT. Crowded on Sundays. **Pulau Samalona**, surrounded by reefs with clean, clear water, is another "floating bar" close by (also Rp1000 RT). There's a village here, so no privacy; also quite busy on Sundays. For swimming and snorkeling, it's better to go to half-deserted islands farther out, such as **Lai Lai**, a natural island seasonally inhabited by Makassar fishermen. There are no regular boats to P. Lai Lai, P. Barancadi, or other outer islands; inquire at the Pasar Ikan (fish market), one km S of Fort Rotterdam.

Travelers can also catch sailing *prahu* to just about anywhere in E. Indonesia from Paotare Harbor, 4 km N of the main square. The helpful guys in the customs office can advise about which vessels are leaving and to where. From Pare Pare, boats to E. Kalimantan are cheaper. *Kapal* also leave to Gorontalo and Bitung in N. Sulawesi, and to Surabaya.

By Ship

There are more than 25 shipping companies in this port town, most located in the crowded streets around the harbor in the NW corner of the city. Many shipping agents (which charge a commission but save chasing around) are also found on Jl. Martadinata and Jl. Nusantara near the harbor. The orange-colored Pelni office (Jl. Martadinata 38, tel. 7979) sells tickets to their own vessels which make regular calls at ports on Sulawesi, Java, and Kalimantan. Sample fares on the KM *Kambuna* to: Bitung, 2nd Class Rp75,500, Economy Rp36,200; Surabaya, 2nd Class Rp48,000, Economy Rp22,000; Jakarta, 2nd Class Rp79,000, Economy Rp36,300. On the KM *Kerinci* to: Jakarta, 2nd Class Rp65,000, Economy Class Rp36,500; Padang, 2nd Class Rp101,800, Economy Rp53,000. On the KM *Rinjani* to: Ambon, 2nd Class Rp49,500, Economy 27,500; Sorong, 2nd Class Rp69,000, Economy Rp39,700. While you're in the neighborhood, check out **PT Pelajaran Rakyat Indonesia** at Jl. Nusantara 32, and (for foreign SE Asian destinations) **PT Trikora Lloyd**, Jl. Martadinata 26.

NORTHEAST OF UJUNG PANDANG

Gua Leang-Leang

Also known as the Pattae Cave, this is the site of the oldest art in Indonesia, dating from the Mesolithic Era. These handprints and prehistoric paintings of ox and deer are believed to be 5,000-10,000 years old. Small fee to enter; ask the guide one question and he's off and running in Indonesian. Located in steep limestone hills 38 km NE of Ujung Pandang, the surroundings have been turned into a beautiful archaeological park with shrubbery and walkways. From Ujung Pandang's central station, take a *bemo* 30 km to Maros (Rp800), then another *bemo* 5 km E to the turnoff (2 km before the Bantimurung turnoff), then walk 3 km north. Or charter a *bemo* in Maros, Rp4000 +. There are no hotels in Maros, but bungalows are Rp3500 a night.

Malino And Cikorok

Cool hill resorts 71 km E of Ujung Pandang, about R1000 by minibus which depart most frequently in the mornings. Malino is 1,050 m above sea level on the side of G. Lompobatang (2871 m). See spectacular Takapala Waterfall in the middle of rice paddies, 4 km from Malino. On the road to Malino, you'll see imposing masses of firs and pines, planted about 50 years ago; today it's almost impossible to penetrate their dense greenery. The local people use the pine trunks to grow pepper vines. They also use the prickly leaves of the pandanus palm for plaiting hats and baskets — and if you think a cactus is prickly, it's nothing compared to a good, healthy pandanus, which has been likened to a tree-shaped porcupine!

Bantimurung Waterfall

Located 41 km NE of the city in a steep limestone valley with lush tropical vegetation. Entrance: Rp400. Cool off at the bottom of 15-m-high falls, then follow the trail upstream from the falls for 15 min. to a smaller waterfall and cave. Someone might have a lantern to show you through the cave, or bring a flashlight. This valley is famous for its swarms of colorful butterflies. The great naturalist Alfred Russel Wallace (1823-1913) collected specimens here in 1856. Early morning is the best viewing time, but it's crowded on Sat. and Sundays. *Kupu-kupu* (butterfly) specimens, mounted attractively on cardboard, are sold by little kids and at the *warung*. The forested hills hereabouts are riddled with caves, but be careful of the *daun gatal* (stinging nettles). Only one poor-value place to stay in Bantimurung, a *wisma* which charges Rp6000 s and d (might be closed in the rainy season). *Warung* serve simple meals near the parking area. To get to Bantimurung, take a *bemo* direct from Ujung Pandang's

BANTIMURUNG

central *bemo* station to Maros (Rp750, 50 min.), then another from Maros to Bantimurung (Rp400, 25 min.). The turnoff for Bantimurung is a few km past the one for Gua Leang-Leang. Returning, a *bemo* costs Rp600 (2 persons) to Maros, then from Maros to U.P., Rp1000 (2 persons).

SOUTH OF UJUNG PANDANG

Hasanuddin's Tomb

The tomb of Sultan Hasanuddin and tombs of other kings of Goa are located off the main road 9 km south. Take a bus (Rp300) from U.P.'s *stasiun bis* to the start of the road to the tombs (see the sign), then walk or take a *becak* the remaining 500 m. Hasanuddin (1629-1670) was the 12th and most famous of the Gowa kings, earning his place as a national hero by waging a long and vigorous war against the Dutch. Next to the cemetery is the Goa Kingdom's coronation stone, the *tomanurung*. The sultans of Gowa claimed to rule by divine right through their ancestor, the Tomanurung, who verily descended from heaven onto this stone. Elaborate coronations were held here. About 15 min. walk from the stone is the Katanga Mosque, originally built in 1603; check out the massive crypts in the nearby graveyard. Other ruins from the time of Sultan Hasanuddin can be found all over the Makassar district.

Sunggaminasa

Eleven km S of Ujung Pandang was the site of the Goa Kingdom. The old wooden palace, mounted on stilts, is now a museum, called Ballalompoa. Historical artifacts, royal costumes, and 7½ kilos of gold weapons are on display. By request it's also possible to see the 15.4-kg gold crown. To get to Sunggaminasa, take a *bemo* from U.P.'s *stasiun bemo* (Rp350, 30 min.). Open Mon.-Thurs. 0800-1300, Fri. 0800-1030, Sat. 0800-1200, closed on Sun. and holidays.

The Southern Seacoast

Barombang is a beach resort 20 km S of Ujung Pandang, but difficult connections, dirty black-sand beaches, and aggressive people make it anything but relaxing. **Palengo** is a small village built on stilts, 50 km S of U.P. by minibus, where you may see workmen making *prahu*. **Birta Ria** (Pleasure Beach) is 74 km S and offers cottages and swimming pools on high cliffs overlooking the ocean. The beach is reached by descending a bamboo ladder. **Bantaeng**, on the S coast 123 km by minibus from U.P., has beaches and traditional boatbuilding; stay at Ahrianas Hotel, Rp5000 s, Rp8000 d, or in 2 other hotels. Other boatyards lie along the coast road S of Pare Pare (N of Ujung Pandang).

Bulukumba

A small town (154 km by minibus from U.P.) of little 2-story shops with balconies. Bulukumba can also be reached from Watampone by minibus or bus, but you might have to change buses in Sinjai. Visit Bugis and Makassarese villages near Bulukumba to see houses on stilts, boatbuilding and repairing (take a minibus to Tana Beru), as well as preparations for fishing. Pleasant beaches are found outside town. Stay near the waterfront at **Peng. Sinar Fajar**, Jl. Sawerigading 4, Rp3000 s, Rp5000 d; or near the market at **Peng. Bawakaraeng**, Jl. Pahlawan, Rp3500 s, Rp5000 d. There's another *losmen* but they always say they're full because they don't want to deal with the police and there's thousands of mosquitos. Bulukumba's market has a wide selection of fish, local vegetables, and fruits.

The ferry for P. Salayar (Rp5000, 5 hours) leaves at a spot 2 km E of town. Ride in a *becak* (Rp800, but bargain!), or take a scenic walk along the beach for free. The shortest sea voyage to P. Salayar is from Bira, a small town E of Bulukumba. From Bira it's just 1½ hours to Pamatata Harbor on the N end of P. Salayar.

SALAYAR ISLAND

A long, narrow island (82 km long, 670 sq km) in the Flores Sea 17 km off the SW tip of Sulawesi. Salayar people live at a slower pace than those on the mainland. The 5 dialects spoken here are similar to Makassarese. Most of the population is Muslim but one Christian church is found in the main town of **Benteng** in the central part of the W coast. Chief crops are copra, hemp, tobacco, and cotton. Though the island has much to offer, it's quite undeveloped for visitors. Except for the market, P. Salayar is a quiet place, good for taking walks, observing village life, and watching wood-hulled ships being fashioned

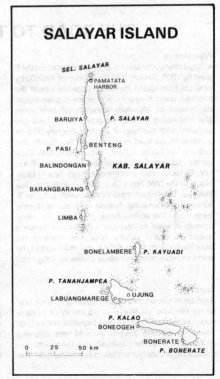

SALAYAR ISLAND

SEL. SALAYAR
PAMATATA HARBOR
BARUIYA
P. SALAYAR
P. PASI
BENTENG
BALINDONGAN
KAB. SALAYAR
BARANGBARANG
LIMBA
BONELAMBERE
P. KAYUADI
P. TANAHJAMPEA
LABUANGMAREGE
UJUNG
P. KALAO
BONEOGEH
BONERATE
P. BONERATE

0   25   50 km

with traditional tools. There are many ancient remains *(nekara)* here, tens of thousands of years old, in unusually good condition.

Benteng has 2 hotels, both with private *mandi:* new and clean **Hotel Berlian**, Rp5000 s, Rp6000 d; and older **Hotel Harmita**, Rp4000 s, Rp5000 d. On Benteng's main street are several *warung* and stalls.

Sights

Giant wood-hulled *prahu layar* (sailboats) and *kapal motor* can usually be seen under construction by walking along the beach several km S of Benteng. It may take 2 years for the small group of workmen to build a large boat. **Pulau Pasi** (or Gusong), across from Benteng, is most easily reached by boat from Padang, 10 km S of Benteng. Benteng's big *pasar,* the social and commercial center of the island, is busiest in the mornings when a cornucopia of produce and fish is sold. For a great view of the island, visit the *puncak* (mountain peak), 14 km NE of Benteng. Walk through inland villages or take a vehicle from the market. A bronze drum, *Nekara,* is kept near Benteng. It's about one meter across and is reputed to date from E. Java's Majapahit Kingdom. The drum is thought to have magic powers and is still used on important occasions, such as to bring rain during a drought.

Getting There And Around

Boats leave most days from 2 km E of Bulukumba for the 5-hour trip to Benteng. If you're prone to seasickness, a better bet would be to take a boat from Bira, E of Bulukumba, for just the 2-hour (17 km) passage to Pamatata Harbor in northern P. Salayar from where you can take a minibus on to Benteng. From Bulukumba, boats leave usually in the afternoon or at night. The fare to Benteng is Rp6000 and a Rp500 lighter fee is paid at each end of the trip (no wharves). Cabin space is Rp3000 extra and well worth it. The combined boat and minibus trip to Benteng from Bulukumba or Bira is about Rp7000. Perintis Lines has direct Ujung Pandang-Benteng service twice a month. Trucks and minibuses provide irregular transportation to the villages from Benteng's market. Ask drivers at the market about your destination. A bicycle would be handy to bring to the island.

THE ROAD TO TANATORAJA

Watampone

A Bugis town, also known as Bone, situated on the E coast Rp2000, 5 hours (180 km) by bus (or Rp2500 by minibus) from Ujung Pandang. Once the site of the powerful Bone Kingdom, former royal possessions are housed in **Museum Lapawawoi** near town (Dutch-speaking guide). The graves of the rajas can be found with the help of a guide. Brightly colored orchid roots are used in locally made woodcrafts and baskets. Minibuses connect Watampone with Bulukumba, 139 km S, Rp2000; and Sengkang, 69 km NW, Rp1500. From Watampone, travel first to Uloe, 34 km to the NW. From Uloe, take a minibus to **Gua Mampu**, the largest cave system (with bats) in S. Sulawesi. Resembling human and animal forms, these rock formations have given rise to many legends. A sugar refinery and a large cattle-breeding station are in the vicinity. Also from Watampone, *kapal motor* embark for Kolaka, the main port of the island's southeastern peninsula (Sulawesi Tenggara).

Soppeng

A center of silk production and weaving, 175 km N of Ujung Pandang via Maros, or 75 km W of Watampone. Silkworms are bred and beautiful silk *sarung,* woven in traditonal designs, are sold here. Weaving on handlooms can be observed with the results purchasable in private homes; ask to see *sutera* (silk). The 2-m lengths of silk cloth can take up to a month to produce. Soppeng has an attractive hilly backdrop, with flurries of bats in the tamarind trees, but is only a transit place with nowhere cheap to stay.

SENGKANG

A small Bugis town E of Pare Pare on the plains E of large Lake Tempe. The impressive, large, white **Mesjid Raya** lies on the E side of town; another large mosque is in the western part. There's a fine view over Sengkang, the surrounding area, and the lake from the *pasanggrahan.* **Danau Tempe** and nearby **Danau Sidenreng** are only 9 m above sea level and just 2 m deep; both lakes empty into Teluk Bone via the Cenranae River. Lake Tempe is quite shallow and varies in size with the seasons. Fields of sugarcane and peanuts surround the lake.

Brightly colored long canoes *(prahu)* cruise up and down the river through town. Fares for regular trips are Rp1000, or charter one at Rp4000 per hour. Boats equipped with outboard motors can travel upstream to Danau Tempe—bargain hard. Or you can walk on paths over bamboo suspension bridges across streams, and through Bugis fishing villages of stilt houses. If an old man at a bridge asks for money, he's not begging, but collecting the Rp100 bridge toll. Five km W of Sengkang is a *pabrik sutera* (silk factory) where women handspin and weave silk cloth. The 2-m-long and ½-m-wide lengths come in a wide variety of colors and designs. Starting price: Rp25,000.

Accommodations And Food

Near the *bemo*/bus station is **Hotel Al Salaam**, Jl. Sentosa 27; Rp3500 s, Rp4000 d. Going E toward Jl. Mesjid Raya: at Jl. Puangrimaggalatung 48 is **Wisma Danau Tempe**, Rp2500 s, Rp4000 d; no. 18 is **Wisma Ayuni**, Rp5000 s, Rp7000 d; and no. 3 is **Wisma Herawati**, Rp3500 s, Rp6000 d. On Jl. Mesjid Raya is rickety and old but not bad **Peng. Merdeka**, Rp3500 s, Rp5000 d — the manager is very friendly. Comfortable **Wisma Wahyuddin** charges Rp7000 s or d. *Ikan bakar* (grilled fish) and *ayam bakar* (grilled chicken) are local favorites served at *warung*. Stalls selling *martabak* and other Indonesian foods are scattered along the main street. **Warung Bara Muncul**, ½ km S on the street which runs parallel to the main road through town, has good *gado-gado* and *nasi campur*. A hundred m down the block from Peng. Merdeka is a tent serving coffee, tea and *sereba*, a hot, spicy drink made from palm sugar, coconut and pepper.

Transport

From Watampone, it's 69 km and Rp1500 to Sengkang; from Pare Pare, 90 km, 2 hours, Rp1800; from Palopo, 177 km, 6 hours, Rp3500. Most vehicles are passenger trucks. From Ujung Pandang, you can travel by *bemo* on the road to Enrekang to the junction (Rp1000), but it's almost certain you'll wait there awhile for a ride. It's advisable to make Sengkang (and especially Enrekang) a day trip from Pare Pare. Sengkang sits right in the middle of the southern peninsula and buses, *bemo*, and minibuses head out in all directions: N to Palopo, W to Pare Pare, SE to Watampone, and SW to Ujung Pandang.

PARE PARE

The second largest city and seaport of S. Sulawesi, 155 km N of Ujung Pandang, Pare Pare is much smaller and slower-paced than Ujung Pandang. Travelers often stop here on their way to Rantepao or Mamasa in Tanatoraja, and the town's port is a major embarkation point for cargo and passenger boats up to central and northern Sulawesi and over to E. Kalimantan — Pare Pare is located near areas which produce large quantities of such export commodities as rice, corn, cattle, rattan, coffee, oil, and resin. The city is divided into northern and southern commercial districts, with a quiet tree-lined government section in the center, and the waterfront is never far away. Many *toko mas* (gold shops) are on Jl. Lasinrang. The **Bangenge Museum of Ethnography**, which features *Bacu Kiki* art, is in Cappa Galung village, 2 km

before town. Three km S of Pare Pare, Rp400 by minibus, is **Lumpue Beach** with its white sand and black coral. See the Great Mosque (Mesjid Raya) with its white cupola surmounted by a silver spire.

Accommodations And Food

Hotel Siswa, Jl. Baso Dg. Patompo 30 (tel. 21374); Rp3500 s, Rp6000 d. In the quieter government area you'll find **Wisma Rio**, Jl. Pinggir Laut 10; Rp5500 s and d, with *mandi* Rp7000 s or d. Also very pleasant is **Hotel Jusida**, right on the waterfront at Jl. Pinggir Laut 3; Rp5000 s, Rp8000 with *mandi*. Inland one block is **Tantri Hotel**, Jl. Sultan Hasanuddin 5; Rp8000 s or d with *mandi*. In the southern commercial district is **Losmen Murni**, Jl. Bau Massepe 175; Rp3500 s, Rp6000 d — rather basic, has electricity (the old bulb-between-2-rooms number), and there's a cheap restaurant 100 m down the road. Near Losmen Murni are **Peng. Palanro** and **Peng. A M** (tel. 21801), with similar prices. For a place to park your Mercedes try the new **Nurlina Hotel**, Jl. Dg. Pawero 8; Rp25,000 s or d. More reasonable is nearby **Hotel Djuarana**, Jl. Andi Makkasau; Rp12,000 s, Rp16,000 d or Rp15,000 s, Rp20,000 d with a/c.

Kios Anging Mammiri, right over the sea at Jl. Pinggir Laut 1, is a pleasant seafood restaurant and popular lunch stop on the Ujung Pandang-Tanatoraja trip. Seafood dishes cost around Rp2500. Slightly more expensive are the seafood restaurants **Sempurna**, Jl. Bau Massepe, and **Asia Restaurant** across from the Roxy Hotel. Try the asparagus soup at any of these. Good *mie kua* places are on Jl. Lasingrang. On the same street is a fruit market.

Transport

From Ujung Pandang frequent minibuses make the trip to Pare Pare in 4 hours, Rp2500; the road passes through scenic rural villages and rice-paddy countryside with mountains rising in the east. From E. Kalimantan small boats leave frequently for Pare Pare from Balikpapan and Samarinda. From Pare Pare, frequent buses and minibuses head out in all directions such as N to Mamasa and Makale (via Rappang), SE to Sengkang and the lakes Sidenreng and Tempe, etc. Buy tickets at the bus station in the SE part of town (Rp200 by *bemo* from the Tantri Hotel). Sample bus fares: Sengkang, Rp1000, 2½ hours; Palopo (240 km NE), Rp5000, 7 hours; Rantepao (173 km NE), Rp3000, 6-7 hours; Polewali (97 km N), Rp3000, 2½ hours; Majene, Rp3500; Watampone, Rp1500.

Boats From Pare Pare

Frequent seagoing wood-hulled boats depart from docks in both northern and southern Pare Pare for the island's northern ports: Mamuju (Rp10,000, 1½ days), Toli Toli (Rp20,000, 3 days), Donggala (Rp20,000, 2 days), etc. The awful condition of the roads through C. Sulawesi makes taking a boat to the northern peninsula an attractive proposition. *Kapal motor* also depart regularly for the E coast of Kalimantan: Tarakan (Rp30,000, 3 days); Nunukan (Rp40,000, 4 days); Samarinda (Rp25,000, 3 days); and Balikpapan (Rp30,000, 4 days). Cabins cost Rp5,000-10,000 extra. Numerous shipping companies (such as **PT Nurlina**, Jl. Mawar Barat 50, **PT Tanjung Selamat**, Jl. Usahawan 73, tel. 21609, and **PT Cahaya Makkarannu** at Jl. Usahawan 58) and shipping agents **(Travel Biro)** line the waterfront on Jl. Usahawan. In the S several more agents are on Jl. Andicammi, including **CV Orde Baru** at no. 4 (tel. 21887). Other agents are scattered around town. Also inquire at **Pelni**, Jl. Andicammi 130, and the *syahbandar's* office further N on the L-hand side of the same street. As you inquire, you'll find out soon enough which company has the next boat sailing to where you want—you'll be pointed the right way. Not all agents will have every ship listed, so check several. You shouldn't have to wait more than a day for a boat. Some boats travel as far as Jambi, S. Sumatra. Before embarking for anywhere, sometimes you have to clear with the customs police, but all they actually want to do is meet you for their own entertainment (perhaps mutual).

A Reader's Experience

R.T. Whalen writes, "We took a boat to Nunukan (E. Kalimantan), the *Harampanku II.* This slave-ship does a regular run from Pare Pare to Tarakan-Nunukan. Conditions are appalling, a once-in-a-lifetime opportunity to find out what it was like to be a slave or a convict in the 18th and 19th centuries. There was not enough space for everyone to lie down at night. People sat on the railing all night long. I slept with my feet partway down the stairs. Sometimes as many as 3 people would be lying partly on top of me. There was no protection from the rain, no room to move even if it did rain. One toilet for 500 passengers plus 20 crew. Often people didn't bother waiting, just pissed against the back of the toilet room, where it all washed down into the kitchen just next door. It took me a month to get my digestive system back to normal. It took 3 days of sailing to get to Tarakan, 2 in port, and then another day from Tarakan to Nunukan...."

Polewali

A small Bugis port town on Teluk Mandar, 247 km N of Ujung Pandang. Polewali is divided into 2 sections: the southern part with market, port, and guesthouse; and the northern part comprising the administrative buildings of the Polewali Mamasa Regency (POLMAS). The best place in town to stay is **Guest House Melati**, across from the Protestant church; Rp4500 s, Rp7000 d. Nearby is cheaper but dirty **Wisma Anda**, Rp3000 s, Rp5000 d. A *penginapan* is beside the minibus station E of town. Eat at **RM Melati**, across from the guesthouse.

From Ujung Pandang, Polewali is 247 km, 5-6 hours, Rp4000; from Pare Pare, 92 km, 2½ hours, Rp3000. For those heading for Mamasa, Toyota Kijang, jeeps, and small trucks somehow negotiate the 92 km N over a twisting, scenic mountain road of ruts, sagging bridges, and landslides. Vehicles usually leave in the morning or early afternoon from the minibus station one km E of the port, as well as from various other points in town. Fares (Rp4000-6000) are expensive for the distance, the price depending on the vehicle and driver; the back of a truck is cheapest (and wettest if it rains). An alternative is to hike up to Mamasa from Polewali in 2-3 days. There's a *pasanggrahan* with a nice view at Tomongo (at the head of the valley) on the way. Or you can stay in the villages.

Majene

Majene (55 km SW, one hour, Rp2000) from Polewali, is a lovely little port with many white sailing ships, but visitors are so rare that dozens of children will follow you *everywhere*. Stay at **Peng. Mesra** beside the mosque, Rp4000. From Majene, bump N along the coast to **Mamuju** on a bad road, 5 hours, 141 km. Jeep drivers could ask up to Rp8500 for this trip. From Mamuju, walk inland to Mambi and Mamasa. Another trail from Mamuju leads NE to Galumpang, then E to Rongkong and Sabang on the far side of S. Sulawesi. The government plans to build a road to Galumpang but no doubt it will take years.

MAMASA

Mamasa is a clean, cool mountain town in a large valley. Churches stand like sentinels on surrounding hilltops. Muslims, Protestants, Catholics, and followers of the old religion *(Aluk Todolo)* live here. To say the road from Polewali to Mamasa is difficult would be the height of optimism—this is why Mamasa is the way it is, a quiet little town high in the mountains (1,130 m), quite cold when the evening mists set in. This area contains the second-highest mountain on Sulawesi, G. Quarles (3,107 m). The Mamasa region is sometimes called "West Toraja" because culture and language are similar to those of the better-known Torajans of Rantepao and Makale. However, the W. Torajan culture of the Mamasa district is considerably less exploited than the cultures found around Rantepao. The Mamasa region has far fewer *kerbau* (water buffalo) than Tanatoraja, and its funeral ceremonies lack the spectacle and bloody *kerbau* slaughter of the better known Torajans. Thus, with the crummy road and without the spectacular funerals, Mamasa has very few tourists. No banks in town so bring enough cash.

The area offers some wonderful walks among rolling hills, rice terraces, and villages. For getting around,

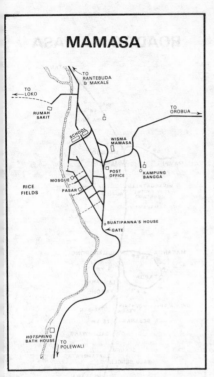

MAMASA

TO
RANTEBUDA
& MAKALE

TO
LOKO

RUMAH
SAKIT

TO
OROBUA

SCHOOL

WISMA
MAMASA

POST
OFFICE

KAMPUNG
BANGGA

MOSQUE

RICE
FIELDS

PASAR

BUATIPANNA'S HOUSE
GATE

HOTSPRING
BATH HOUSE

TO
POLEWALI

ings. *Kubur tua* (old graves) are small houses for the dead. Rarely seen now (one is located in a ricefield beside Rantebuda, NE of Mamasa), *kubur tua* have had no maintenance or paint and are slowly weathering away.

Accommodations And Food
Losmen Mini is clean and only Rp5000 s, Rp8500 d. It serves beer, soda, snacks, and meals. The manager, Daniel Sarrin, dispenses information on walks and outings to villages and is most helpful. Another place to stay is **Wisma Mamasa** on a nearby hill; Rp3000 s or d. With its wicker chairs and patio, great high ceilings and big rooms, you usually have the place all to yourself. Finally, **Guest House BPS** charges Rp3500 s.

For food, meals at Losmen Mini's **Restoran Mini** are the best bet—Rp2000 breakfast, Rp35000 lunch, Rp3500 dinner. Also simple meals, snacks and drinks can be had at the few *warung*. Eat delicious *nasi antur* (similar to *nasi campur*, but distinguished by buffalo meat) in the town restaurant near the police station. Avoid the other restaurants. The market is open every day, but Mon. and Thurs. are the busiest. Vegetables, fruit, *balok* (palm wine), tobacco, coffee, and brown palm sugar are brought in from the hills. Mounds of dried fish and salt are brought up from the coast.

walking is best as there are only 16 km of usable roads, but experienced motorcyclists can reach many of the area's villages. Numerous hotsprings surround Mamasa, though not all are suitable for bathing; the map in Wisma Mamasa shows their location. One km S of town is an indoor, concrete-pool hotspring, Rp1000 entrance, where there's a good chance you'll be an amusing attraction for the locals.

Architecture
There are significant differences between Mamasan architecture and that found in eastern Torajaland. In Mamasa, the overhang of the front roof on the *adat* houses is longer, and the rice barns usually have only 4 support posts (as opposed to the 6 or more in Torajaland). Three types of *adat* buildings are in use in Mamasa. The *rumah adat* are large buildings containing living quarters and kitchen; their roofs are much longer than the house and curve up at the ends. Exteriors are carved and painted with animal, human, and abstract designs. Rice barns, supported on 4 stout pillars, are small, windowless, and have just a tiny door. Some rice barns have carvings and paint-

detail of rumah adat, *Rantebuda (near Mamasa)*

Crafts

Colorful Sambu blankets are just the thing for Mamasa's cold nights. Cost depends on quality; count on around Rp75,000 for first grade, Rp50,000 for 2nd grade, Rp35,000 for 3rd grade. Some of these 8-m-long cloths take 7 years to complete on a loom consisting of just stakes stuck in the ground. Several W. Torajan clans use a bronze-casting technique called the lost wax process *(cire perdue)* which originated in SW Europe in the 8th and 9th centuries, then traveled through Central Asia and China by way of the Dongson empire. Copperwork is practiced by only a few specialized groups living N of Mamasa who make small human and animal figures, pendants, balls, coiled ornaments *(sanggori),* jewelry and bracelets. Deep in the interior, tribespeople still produce pottery by means of a Neolithic beating technique.

Getting There

There's only one road to Mamasa, the 92-km route heading N from Polewali. Toyota Kijang, jeeps, and small trucks slip and slide up this rough mountain road. Passengers may be asked to walk across a few of the worst bridges. Costing Rp4000-6000 (depending on road conditions), allow 5-7 hours for the trip. Distances between villages: Polewali-Pokko, 10 km; Pokko-Tomonga, 12 km; Tomonga-Messawa, 12 km; Messawa-Tabone, 15 km; Tabone-Sumarorong, 4 km; Sumarorong-Tamalantik, 12 km; Tamalantik-Malobo, 11 km; Malobo-Mamasa, 16 km. Or walk up from the Mamuju area on the W coast in 3 days; Mamuju is accessible from Majene, SW of Polewali. From Makale to the E, walk to Mamasa in 3 days (see "The Bittuang Walk" below).

Short Walks

Adat houses and scenic countryside can be seen on an easy walk SE to Sepang, 9 km. As people are living in these houses, it's polite to ask permission to go into the village and look around. **Tawalian,** 4 km on the trail to Sepang, has traditional houses and rice barns. One km SE of Mamasa on the Orobua road is a group of traditional houses at **Bangga.** Three km N of Mamasa is the traditional village of **Rantebuda,** which has fine *adat* houses, rice barns, and a decaying *kubur tua* (old grave) just outside the village on the edge of a ricefield. Also near Rantebuda are hotsprings. Continue N on this road to several more villages before a long climb through the forest toward Makale. Northwest of Mamasa, trails are narrow and winding. Cross the Mamasa River at the bridge N of town or wade across near the market. Many day-hike possibilities in the Mamasa valley. See map.

The Bittuang Walk

Bittuang, near Makale, is a scenic 3-day hike through

ROAD TO MAMASA

MAMASA
DENGEN
PINA
16 km
PINA PINA
30 km
MALOBO
MAMBI
BALABATU
11 km
MINANGATALLU
(TOP OF THE
MOUNTAIN)
RUPISIPI
TAMALANTIK
12 km
BUSSU
MATANGA
SUMARORONG
18 km
22 km
4 km
TAPUA
LAMBANAN
4 km
TABONE
OVER A SMALL MOUNTAIN
PASS
SIBAN
SEBANAWA
15 km
SALU AWANG
SEKUKU
BATAMEPATA
SALU DENGEN
MESSAWA
TAPANG
SALU KUPA
TALULADI
MAKUANG
POGDO SALA
PONDO SALA
12 km
TALANGBARO
PESAPPA
PARATEAN
TOMONGA
KELAPA DUA
12 km
LEKKE
CLIMB FROM POKO TO PESAPPA
POKKO
LEAVE VALLEY HERE
KUNYI
DARMA
KIRI KIRI
10 km
PASAR
POLISI
POLEWALI

SHORT WALKS FROM MAMASA

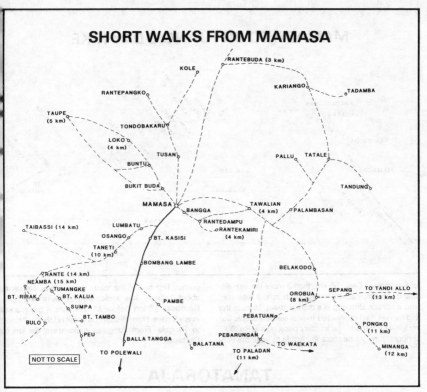

RANTEBUDA (3 km)

KOLE

KARIANGO

TADAMBA

RANTEPANGKO

TAUPE
(5 km)

TONDOBAKARU

LOKO
(4 km)

TUSAN

PALLU   TATALE

BUNTU

TANDUNG

BUKIT BUDA

MAMASA   BANGGA   TAWALIAN   PALAMBASAN
(4 km)

RANTEDAMPU

LUMBATU   RANTEKAMIRI
(4 km)

TAIBASSI (14 km)

OSANGO   BT. KASISI

TANETI
(10 km)

BOMBANG LAMBE

BELAKODO

RANTE (14 km)

NEAMBA (15 km)   TUMANGKE

BT. RIRAK   BT. KALUA

OROBUA   SEPANG   TO TANDI ALLO
(8 km)   (13 km)

SUMPA

PAMBE

BT. TAMBO   PEBATUAN

BULO   PONGKO
(11 km)

PEU   PEBARUNGAN

BALLA TANGGA   BALATANA   TO WAEKATA

MINANGA
(12 km)

TO PALADAN
(11 km)

TO POLEWALI

NOT TO SCALE

valleys and over 2 mountain passes. Hiking is of moderate difficulty as grades are mostly gentle. Wear good walking shoes as sections are rocky or muddy. Hiking is good in the rainy season too, but have an umbrella and pack cover for the afternoon rains.

Horses can be hired to carry your gear, about Rp7500 per day. Some people do this trip in just 2 days by traveling fast and light from dawn to dusk, but 3-4 days is more enjoyable. No *losmen* on the trail but the *kepala desa,* a schoolteacher, or any villager could put you up. **Timbaan** and **Ponding** are the most commonly used overnight stops. Try to arrive at a reasonable hour to allow time for washing up, cooking, and sleeping arrangements. Introduce yourself in *Bahasa Indonesia,* informing who you are, what you are doing, where you are from, and where you are going. Bring gifts of canned meat or fish, salt, soap, skin ointment, etc. Or give Rp1500 to the lady of the house in exchange for hospitality received. Food is usually just reddish-brown rice straight from the fields and some local vegetables. *Please* don't give little kids any

presents directly as the kids might pester the next visitors for gifts.

To get to Bittuang from Mamasa, follow the road N along the river past Rantebuda, 4 km; Lambanan, 7 km; and Pakkassasan, 10 km; from here the trail (once a Dutch-built vehicle road) climbs high up to a pass *(puncak)* through a beautiful forest of big trees and ferns. No place to stay on this 14-km mountain section so get an early start or have a tent with you. From the pass the trail winds down to **Timbaan** (24 km), then drops sharply to **Mawai** (28 km) on the Mawai River. This is the halfway point to Bittuang. The trail follows the Mawai River to the Masuppu River and then winds through the Masuppu Valley to a covered bridge (33 km). Cross the bridge and climb the steep trail to Ponding (37 km). Wash up in a small stream at a little covered bridge just before Ponding. From Ponding, continue climbing through rice terraces to Belau (a *rumah adat* here), 40 km; Paku, 44 km; Pasangtau, 49 km; and through a forest to the pass, 52 km; descend 3 km on a badly rutted trail to the rice terraces

MAMASA TO BITTUANG: 3 DAY HIKE

of Patongloan Desa, 55 km; then 3 more km into Bittuang, 58 km, passing a hilltop church, a reservoir, and a school. Bittuang is a market town (Mon. is the big market day) connected to Makale by a scenic but rough 41-km road. Trucks carry passengers, Rp3000, 3 hours. It might be more enjoyable to walk the very

bumpy first half of the road—good views. **Se'seng**, about halfway, has a nice natural swimming hole. **Rembon**, 12 km before Makale, has a big market every 6 days. From Bittuang is a trail N (36 km, 2 days) to Pangala. From Pangala, trucks travel 58 km to Rantepao.

TANATORAJA

Tanatoraja (TATOR, or Torajaland) means "Land of the Torajan People." These proto-Malay peoples are believed to have originated from the Kampuchean region of Indochina; to support this theory, their legends claim that their ancestors arrived in a storm from the northern seas, pulled their splintered boats ashore, and used them as roofs. Today, one of the principal attractions of Tanatoraja is its houses: shaped like ships, they all face N, the direction of their origin. Another draw for tourists is the Torajans' frequent and highly ritualistic religious ceremonies, including rites of birth, marriage, fertility, and the most famous, death. Finally, Tanatoraja is one of the country's most ruggedly magnificent regions—a high, mountain-bounded fertile plateau. The mountains have protected patterns of life and custom which have evolved and changed little over centuries. These same mountains have prevented easy access by tourists, who haven't yet entirely overrun the area. Yet. Start your sightseeing early in the day, especially for photo-taking; even in the dry season, it could rain by

1600. Makale and Rantepao are the 2 main towns of TATOR. Both are fascinating places, have busy, traditional markets, and make excellent bases for walks into the countryside. Makale is smaller but has the government offices. Rantepao is more central to the region's attractions and offers a greater selection of accommodations and food, though it's definitely more touristy.

The People

Before the Dutch arrived in 1905, the Torajans (called "mountain people" in the Bugis language) were one of the fiercest and most remote people in all of Indonesia. Their skill in using spears was uncanny, able to pin small animals and birds at 15 m, and impale a man at 30 m. They once lived in small walled fortress villages on top of hills, resembling European medieval fortifications (see some 400-year-old remains at Pangala' and Pontiko). There was much suspicion within Torajan communities between individual members. Villagers who were suspected of witchcraft or sorcery were tried by a cultic ordeal. Their fingers were forced into burning pitch; if the hand burned, they were guilty, then given over to other villagers for sacrificial beheading. When the Dutch moved them down into the valleys and introduced agriculture, taxes, Christianity and disease, the old family structure started to break down. Although buffalos have now replaced human heads as sacrifices and the old religion has been diluted, very strong *adat* continues to be practiced in Torajaland. Also, there still exist 3 classes of Torajans. *Tokapua* are the noblemen. They generally have longer hair, wear special turbans and loincloths, and employ servants. Although only about 5% of the population, the *Tokapua* still own most of the land. The *Tomokaka* are the middle-class tradesmen, 25% of Torajans. Finally, the *Tobuda* are the common people, farmers and sharecroppers, about 7 out of every 10 Torajans.

Religion

The old religion is called *Aluk Todolo* ("Worship of the Spirits of Ancestors"). In 1975, 50% of Torajans continued to practice it, but today it's estimated that only 30% do so, with 60% practicing Christianity and 10% the Islamic faith. *Aluk Todolo* divides the universe and the world of ritual in half: life and death. It is probable that, originally, equal attention was paid to both halves of the ritual world. Today, however, partly because the "life" side emphasized fertility, it was considered "pagan" by Christianity, and forbidden. The funeral, on the other hand, was always acceptable to the Church, and has assumed much greater importance than in the old equation. Still, many of the old ceremonies and animist rites can be observed carried over into the Christian domain—indeed, there's a fantastic mixing of the two religions. For example, buffalo are still sacrificed *(rambu)* at The Feast of the Dead; however, participants make sure they attend church that morning, too. The *Aluk Todolo* Torajans worshipped the buffalo as a fertility cult figure, and you still see the people wear headdresses of buffalo horns or use symbolic horns in their dances. Buffalos, which are the equivalent of a Torajan savings account, are sacrificed on 3 different occasions: at the end of a funeral, in gratitude for years of prosperity, and when a serf gains his freedom. *Tuka* is performed for housewarming and harvest ceremonies; also the *Maro* ritual is still staged in order to exorcise evil spells. The hereafter, called *Puya*, is where everyone will live under the same conditions as he or she did on Earth. This is why every Torajan tries to attain as much wealth as possible during his lifetime. Souls of animals will follow their masters into heaven, thus the animal sacrifices. In a very real way, Torajans *live* for death.

Funerals

Tanatoraja is famous for 2 things: its natural beauty and its funerals. The Torajans believe that when a person dies, the soul leaves the body, though not the general vicinity. It remains restless and dissatisfied until the burial ritual has been completed. The corpse itself, partially embalmed, lies in the back of the house (or in a temporary grave) for the weeks or months necessary to complete the expensive funeral arrangements and assemble far-flung relatives. A family's wealth is accumulated over a whole lifetime, then most of it is spent on staging the finest, most elaborate funeral they can afford, a strange blending of solemnity and celebration. The multi-phased ceremony used to be held in special fields *(rante)* where tall spires (monuments to ancestors) stand, and where temporary buildings were constructed, then burned afterwards. In olden times, freshly severed human heads were the required offerings at the final burial. After the funeral, the heads were hung in the *rumah adat* and in the houses of the closest kin. You can still find old heads in some houses. Today, buffalos and pigs are slaughtered, still a very gruesome sight.

rumah adat *dedication ceremony*

First the throat is slit, and it's the privilege of little boys to catch the arterial blood in bamboo tubes; they get covered in it. Then they jump on the animal to force the last blood out; the buffalo is alive and looking at you. Then they cut off the feet and tail, and wait for it to finally die. At this point the meat is divided according to rank and status: the largest cut to the highest station. Often there can be up to a thousand guests, each of whom must be fed; 100 buffalo could be slaughtered at a very wealthy family's funeral, which can easily last a week or two. Finally, a gong is sounded, and a cock which has been tied to a branch is released, signifying the departure of the soul. This is the beginning of the "Festival of the Dead," a happy, almost orgiastic occasion. The corpse, which has been embalmed and wrapped in so many shrouds it looks like a big striped pillow, is kept company by professional mourners so it won't become lonely during the celebratory feasting. Bamboo effigies are erected, long "hair" for women, short for men. Villagers participate in singing, dancing, palm wine drinking, watch cock and buffalo fights, and choreographed kick bouts.

The corpse is next carried down from the house and put inside a granary-shaped structure on a stretcher to be transported to its final resting place, *liang*. These sunken family graves in cliffs came into fashion after thieves from outside Tanatoraja began robbing the gold and jewels interred with the dead. For each *liang* there is a wooden effigy *(tau tau)* on a rock or platform carved into the cliff, as a representation of the spirit. Athletic pallbearers carry the tightly wrapped body bundle up 4-30 m by means of a simple, notched, nearly vertical bamboo ladder. Every face looks up, then the corpse is placed into the hole. Although the opening is small, the interiors of these cave-graves are able to contain entire families.

What You Might See
Ask in Indonesian for the *Pesta Mati,* the "Party for the Dead." The Torajan funeral ceremony varies according to the class and wealth of the deceased. *Tokapua,* the lords and rajas of Toraja, are buried in an elaborate 7- to 10-day ceremony of dances, feasting, and animal sacrifices. Twenty to more than 100 *kerbau* are killed, along with many pigs. Hundreds of guests attend, staying in shelters constructed for the occasion. *Tomokaka,* the middle class, are accorded a 3- to 6-day ceremony, with 4-10 *kerbau* and many pigs killed, depending on how much the family can afford. *Tobuda* are the lowest class and have a simple funeral ceremony lasting 1-2 days with one or 2 *kerbau* and a few pigs killed. The young of any class are buried with a simple ceremony; only one *kerbau* and some pigs are killed. For a baby, one pig might be killed. On Earth, the ceremony reinforces family ties, as most animals have been given by relatives who

themselves had received animals for funerals. Churches and government discourage large funeral sacrifices, but tradition is often stronger than their influence. There is a local tax imposed on ceremonies in which more than 2 *kerbau* are killed; the tax might be Rp70,000 per *kerbau* and Rp10,000 for each pig, paid directly to the *kepala desa.*

Other Ceremonies
Some fertility rites are still practiced by the older Torajans on occasion of the birth of a baby or a buffalo. Rice is the most important crop and has more than 10 ceremonies related to its planting, growth, and harvesting. Blessing houses requires a series of important ceremonies. A small one marks the beginning of construction, followed by others during stages of work. After completion, a major celebration is held which may include dancing. During the dance, relatives in the audience may dart among the dancers stuffing Rp10,000 notes into their headbands. Another ritual is the *Rambu Tuka* in which offerings are made to *Puang Matua* (God) to ward off epidemics and calamities, and to ensure a good harvest. The *Mabua* is a major ceremony taking place at 12-year intervals, a dance spiritually and ecologically invaluable to the Torajans. Months of work are involved in getting ready for this night-long ritual — preparing a ceremonial field, costumes, and miniature implements of everyday life. Featured are stately female singers, festival poles, war yells, and bonfires of exploding bamboo stalks, while priests wearing water buffalo headdresses rush about a sacred tree. *Mabua* concludes with a mock copulation with a buffalo.

Conduct
Make sure that ceremonies are in progress before venturing out to a specific site; you could end up spending the whole day watching preparations with nothing happening. Latch onto a local guide (for a reasonable fee of not more than Rp5000) who can keep you informed about what's going on during a ceremony, or ask around in the hotels and restaurants, or at Rantepao's tourist office, about current events before setting out. When attending a funeral find out who the host and village dignitaries are, then go up and shake their hands. If you give cigarettes perfume, soap, etc., it means that you share in their grief. At ceremonies, don't sit in any prepared or roped-off areas unless invited. Be discreet with your camera and dress. Men should wear shirts and pants, women full tops with sleeves, longish dresses or *sarung.* Don't take a non-local guide along as the Torajans interact easily and are happy to give explanations. Also, they are put more at ease if you're alone, guides tend to tell too many tall tales. Please don't give out candy *(gula-gula)* as it encourages both children and grownups to always ask for it.

When To Go

Torajaland's best months climate-wise are April through Oct.—the dry season. However, afternoon showers are not unusual. In July and Aug. (vacation time in Europe), Torajaland is flooded with French and Italian package tourists (not travelers) and it may be difficult to get a room in Rantepao or Makale. During this high season, as many as 1,000 Europeans may overrun Rantepao, sometimes staying just long enough to buy up all the woodcarvings and other handicrafts in town. For a handout, groups of little kids will even sing "Alouette" in perfect chorus. June, July, and Aug. are very hot. The time with the fewest tourists is May-July. After the harvest, between Sept. and Dec., is probably the best time; the people have sufficient funds and free time to spend on their ritual occasions such as funerals. The government is now encouraging the Torajans to space their death festivals throughout the year in order to attract more tourists.

TORAJAN ARTS AND CRAFTS

Architecture

Torajans are known for their remarkable dwellings, quite similar to the Batak buildings of N. Sumatra. These houses (tongkonan) are raised on wooden poles, built so they can be moved on runners from one place to another, and look as if they could make the journey by sea—their sweeping roofs appear like huge slope-prowed vessels riding in an ocean of tropical foliage. In some villages where the houses and granaries stand in rows, it feels like you're in the middle of a fleet of ships floating on the wind. Usually richly ornamented and built solely by the tongue-and-groove method of construction, a traditional house has a layered bamboo roof, and on its sides a maze of geometric ornamentation in black, red and white (representing aspects of the festivals of Aluk Todolo), and no metal nails. People are allowed to place only those designs on their houses which are appropriate to their caste. Horns of the buffalo—symbol of fertility, strength and protection from evil—decorate the gables of Torajan houses. Family status is shown by the number of horns at the entrance of the house. Villages are very simply designed: a row of residences with square columns facing another row of matching grain sheds with round pillars. All houses point north. Though tongkonan houses in each village are still the focus of religious activity, modern technology is replacing much of the traditional construction (zinc roofs instead of bamboo, and metal nails) and new buildings are now interspersed among the old. Government subsidy programs, however, encourage the use of the old techniques. Like a model "Wild West" town for a movie set, Pacto Tours and other travel agencies have begun constructing rumah adat especially for the tourist trade.

Dance

Torajan dances are slow-moving, rhythmical, even majestic, usually accompanied by taped music or the beat of a large drum. Dancers are dressed in long, colorful silk skirts and woven fabrics, adorning themselves in beaded corsets and capes, with gold jewelry draping from their necks and encircling their arms, while men wear spectacular kris in silver or gold scabbards. This regal pageantry can even be seen in tiny villages deep in the mountains of Torajaland. Dances are mostly ceremonial, though sometimes tourists are asked to join in circle-dances, and local dances are sometimes held in the Rantepao marketplace.

The Magellu dance is usually performed at a thanksgiving ceremony, after the harvest or the completion of a house. In this serene dance, 3-5 teenage girls wearing beaded costumes stretch out slender arms and flutter fingers while advancing towards and retreating from the audience to the rhythm of a drum. In the Manganda performance, a group of men wearing gigantic headdresses of silver coins, bulls' horns, and black velvet are accompanied by a bell and the voice of a leader. These headdresses are so heavy that the dance lasts only a few minutes. The Maro dance rite is held when a sick person must be purified. The Manimbong and Ma'bugi are harvest dance ceremonies. The Pa'daobulan is danced by a group of young people wearing long white dresses.

Games

Sisemba (kick fights) can be seen from late June to early Aug., a terrifying recreational sport where old and young men fly into the air, sometimes knocking each other unconscious. The hands may not be used in this mock combat in which either individuals or whole villages take part. Takro is a ball game using a rattan ball which is kicked and bounced (with only the head and legs) over a bamboo stick about one m high and fixed parallel to the ground. Played something like volleyball, but with only 2-3 players.

Music

The bamboo flute is the favorite Torajan instrument, played at funerals and harvests, and schoolboys and girls play lively flute music out of sheer joy. There are short transverse flutes as well as longer ones, all decorated in the old style with poker work, beautifully engraved and colored. Sometimes resonating cones, made out of buffalo horn, are used. Other instruments are fashioned from palm leaves and there are also Torajan jew's harps. Though their singing is monotonous and restricted to just a few notes, songs include chants, poetic love epics, mourners' dirges, etc.

tapa *clothing, Kageroa, C. Sulawesi*

Singers are frequently accompanied by one-stringed lutes played with a bow.

Crafts

Torajan crafts are very similar to Dayak art of Borneo, mostly 2-dimensional and not very dynamic, yet some crafts make striking wall ornaments and hangings. Different villages specialize in different crafts. Torajaland is very much a bamboo culture: roofs, water carriers, cooking vessels, and engraved and decorated cases are all made from bamboo. Lime cases and bamboo flutes are covered with intricate black designs burnt in with a hot iron. If you go out to the villages themselves

(such as Kete' Kesu), buy flutes for Rp1000-1500; bamboo necklaces, Rp1200; and carved murals, Rp5000-15,000. In the interiors, expert pottery is made. Torajans also produce attractive carved wooden panels with stylized lucky talismans of buffalos and leaves, embellished in subtle shades of blacks, whites, reds, mustards. These panels were copied from those decorating their houses and granaries. Now craftsmen are becoming aware that these decorative panels may be adapted to other uses, and are modifying them to make trays, plates, etc.

Textiles

Sa'dan is the weaving center, where local women have formed a cooperative. All the designs seen in Torajan houses are also seen in their fabrics. Human figures are so cleverly interwoven into strict geometric patterns that only an expert can pick out the figures from the lines. Much Torajan weaving is very similar to Guatemalan weaving in the texture, designs and in even the colors: red, white, yellow, and black. Some beautiful and expensive *sarung* (Rp3000-5000) can be bought in Rantepao's market. Expensive, organically dyed *ikat* blankets take up to 3 months to make; the best come from Makki, Rongkong and Seko, and cost Rp75,000-250,000! Reddish *ikat* weaving with black and blue patterns found in the shops of Rantepao are artificially dyed and cost Rp25,000-35,000. Artificially dyed ones in the villages are cheaper at Rp15,000-25,000. Torajan *ikat* cloths are most often handspun cotton funeral blankets with large geometric motifs in the traditional colors: rust, red, white, and black.

Bark-clothing *(tapa* or *fuyus)* of the Sulawesi-Moluccan areas reached a finesse unknown anywhere else in the world and was widespread in the hinterland until around the 1930s. With the shortage of fabrics brought on by the Japanese occupation of the island in WW II, there was a revival of this art in which fibrous inner tree bark is soaked in water for weeks, then beaten until soft and flexible. Small pieces are felted into large ones, eliminating the need for seams. You can find old examples in the interior, and bark cloth is still being produced using traditional implements in Kageroa, Bada, in C. Sulawesi. Some very rare *tapa* specimens can also be seen in the Jakarta's Textile Museum, Jl. Satsuit Tabun, Tanah Abang.

RANTEPAO

Rantepao is a cool, small, pleasant town with a big market, a focal point for tourists visiting Torajan villages and sites, right in the center of their traditional territory. A good place to base yourself, especially if you're walking, because most roads fan out from Rantepao. And despite all the tourists who inundate it, it's actually very mellow with lots of atmosphere. After the Bugis, it's refreshing to see proto-Malayan faces again—high cheekbones, dark skin, stocky, bony bodies. People are very helpful and friendly; except for souvenirs, you're charged the same prices the locals are charged. It's remarkable how little the town has changed over the past 10 years. Blood 'n' guts movies (tickets: Rp750) are shown at **Bioskop Apollo** near the market. See some skillful playing at the billiard hall across from the N side of the market, or hang out in the market's *tuak* stalls or nighttime *warung*, jamming in the evening with young guitarists and travelers. It only takes a couple of days to get to know your way around this small town. *Becak* ride up and down Jl. Mappanyuki looking for fares, but you can easily walk to anywhere in town worth going to.

Characteristic of the institutionalized rottenness widespread in Indonesia, an official comes around personally to collect the "tourist tax" (Rp1000 for foreigners, Rp500 for Indonesians). As it's collected right at the hotels, some travelers get hit, others avoid it. Be sure to get a receipt, even after being there 5 days. Do *not* pay Benjamin who says that he's a tourist officer and tries to collect a "new" tourist tax of Rp2000 pp.

Sights

Rantepao's fascinating market is the biggest in the region and offers an enormous variety of produce, merchandise, and handicrafts. It's open every day but the big market is every 6 days. You know it's happening when all the villagers come pouring into town. An exotic place to explore: bamboo flutes, decorated containers, model houses, swords, and the giant conical hats used in the ricefields can be purchased cheap—after bargaining strenuously, of course. At **Pasar Hewan** (livestock market), held on the big market days, you can pick up a *kerbau* or a squealing pig. The spotted water buffalo have great ceremonial value and a correspondingly high price—up to 2 million *rupiah!* They are rarely found outside of Tanatoraja. Black *kerbau* are also killed in ceremonies. Pink, albino *kerbau* may not be used for sacrifices. In the old days they were destroyed at birth, but now they are kept for plowing. By the river in the N of town

on the main road to Palawa, just walk up Jl. Pahlawan several blocks and turn R on Jl. Pasar Hewan and follow the squeals!

ACCOMMODATIONS

With 36 accommodations, Rantepao offers a wide selection of places to stay and prices are reasonable. During late July, Aug. and Sept., huge groups of Italians, French, Japanese, Dutch, and Germans flood into town on tour buses, sending prices skywards. At such times you'd be lucky to even get a bed and might have to go out into the countryside to find a place to sleep, be forced to stay in an expensive hotel, or go down to Makale to hunt for accommodation. The rest of the year hotels will be dying for customers. If staying for several days or more in the off season, be sure to ask for a discount. The hotels on the main street are most easily found, but quieter and more pleasant accommodations can be searched out down the side roads, often with their own private gardens alongside brilliant green ricefields.

Budget

Centrally located are: **Losmen Flora**, Jl. Sesean 25 (tel. 28), across from the mosque (W off Jl. Mappanyuki); Rp3500 s, Rp6000 d—OK, but not for light sleepers. This is the oldest *losmen* in Rantepao, now fallen into disrepute and doesn't get that many guests. **Hotel Marlin** is at Jl. Mappanyuki 75 (tel. 21215), right next to the Liman Express office. Balcony over noisy street. At first asking Rp12,000 d, Rp15,000 t, they will plunge dramatically in price if you bargain; your bargaining position is stronger if there are no other guests or hot water, which is frequently the case. **Guesthouse Sarla** and **Wisma Palawa** (both with 6 rooms) are also within walking distance; similar prices and conditions. A better deal than all of the above is the newer **Wisma Indo Grace**, Jl. Mappanyuki 72 (opp. Hotel Marlin); Rp5000 s, Rp6000 d. Other places along the main street: **Guest House Batutumonga** (no. 65), **Wisma Siporannu** (no. 71), **Losmen Onasis** (no. 79), all in the Rp3000-7500 range.

Pasar Hewan Area

Turn R on Jl. Abdul Gani, N of the intersection of Jl. Mappanyuki and Jl. Stappang, for 2 quiet (except on market days) *wisma*: **Wisma Linda**, no. 2, and Wisma irama, no. 16. **Wisma Irama** (tel. 21371) charges Rp6000 s, Rp7500 d. After Wisma Maria, this is the second best guesthouse in Rantepao with laundry service and nice rooms with baths and showers. Their minibus may be chartered for Rp25,000-30,000 per day. Breakfast costs Rp2500 (homemade *roti, telur,* fresh fruit juice, butter); lunch or dinner, Rp3500 (Torajan cuisine). Meals must be ordered in advance. **Wisma Nirmala,** same price, is back on the main street, Jl. Mappanyuki. Heading N, cross the bridge over the Sadan River for **Wisma Rosa;** Rp3500 s, Rp5000 d with *mandi,* plus free tea (must pay for coffee). Cheaper rooms in the rear, Rp3500 d. Located on the road to Sadan, the last *wisma* on the way out of town (on the R), quiet Wisma Rosa is surrounded by trees and a garden. Relax in the evenings on the nice front verandah and watch the local people walking back and forth between their villages and town. Eat in **RM Rima** down the road; Rp500 meals and English-speaking owners.

Wisma

Rantepao's *wisma,* family homes with guestrooms added, are nearly always clean, quiet, and very good value. Always ask if any tax or service charge will be added to the asking price. **Wisma Maria** is Rantepao's best *wisma,* isolated, quiet, nice lawn and garden, boiled water, good lighting and carpeting in rooms (Rp4000, Rp7500, and Rp12,000), American and Continental breakfasts (with delicious homemade bread!). Though the owners almost shun guests, Wisma Maria is very efficiently managed. The Liman Express *bis malam,* on its way down to Ujung Pandang, picks guests up here every evening at 1830 — a very convenient service. Other popular *wisma* include: **Wisma Monika,** Jl. Ratulangi 38; Rp2500 s, Rp3500 d with *mandi* and toilet. Wisma-style **Hotel Indra,** Jl. Landorundun 63 (tel. 21163), is built in traditional Torajan architecture with big restaurant (serving *pa'piong),* gardens, moneychanger. Clean rooms from Rp7500 s or d up to Rp12,500 (for suites with hot water). Nice people run this place; see Martina at front desk. Nearly adjacent is plain **Hotel Barita,** Jl. Pasar 55; Rp5000 s, Rp7500 d. **Wisma Martini,** Jl. Ratulangi 62, asks Rp5000 s or d. **Wisma Te Bass,** Jl. Tanah Lapang Bajkti 14, wants Rp8000 s or d. A new place in town receiving good reports is comfortable **Pia's Pension,** Jl. Pong Tikku 27A; Rp4800 s, Rp6400 d for clean rooms with breakfast. Located right over *sawah,* low-priced, homecooked meals are also available. Only 3 rooms.

Expensive

Two expensive hotels are outside of town. Their facilities include restaurant, bar, swimming pool, meeting facilities. Large, 2-star **Hotel Misiliana** (P.O. Box 1, tel. 21367), 2 km S on the road to Makale, is designed for package tourists; 62 rooms at Rp30,000-40,000 with balconies, TV, wall-to-wall, souvenir shop, courteous staff, transfer service, etc. Three-star **Toraja Cottages,** Jl. Paku Balasara (tel. 21268), is 4 km NE on the road to Palopo. Its 63 rooms go for US$27 s, US$30 d — the deluxe accommodations of Rantepao. Cottages are spread out over the side of a landscaped hill, with big restaurant and bar. Very popular with European clients of Insatra and Ramayana Tours.

RANTEPAO

1. Wisma Rosa
2. Wisma Nirmala
3. RM Rima
4. Wisma Irama
5. Liman Express
6. Hotel Marlin
7. Wisma Indo Grace
8. Agen bis "Merry"
9. Warung Murni
10. agent for buses
    to Bone and Batutumonga
11. Losmen Flora
12. RM Bayu
13. Hotel Victoria
14. Chez Dodeng
15. Toko Obat
16. RM Dodeng
17. Kios Gembira
18. souvenir shop "No. 21"
19. souvenir shop "No. 9"
20. Kios Mambo
21. Wisma Monika
22. Hotel Indra
23. Wisma Maria
24. Hotel Barita
25. Wira Agung, coffee dealer
26. Wisma Te Bass
27. Agen bis "Raden Jaya"
28. Agen bis "Erlin"
29. moneychanger
30. Restaurant Rachmat
31. Warung Anda
32. Bank Rakyat Indonesia
33. Pelni agent
34. Tangketasik photo studio
35. Wisma Nanggala
36. Kios Ramayana
37. Apotik Delta
38. RS ELIM
39. tourist office
    (Pusat Informasi Wisata)
40. Bupati's office

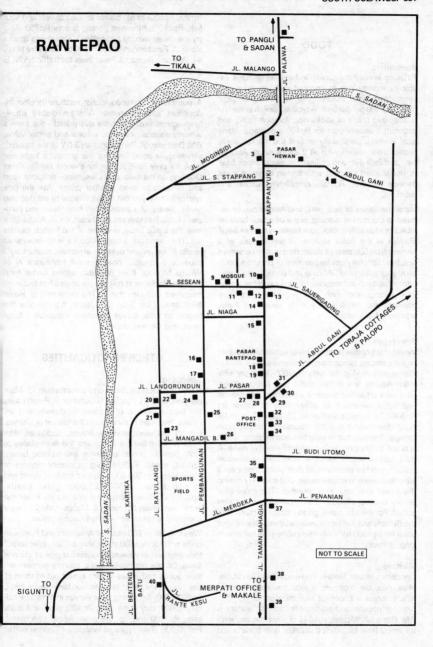

FOOD

Specialties

Pa'piong is anything cooked in bamboo sections. Examples include rice in coconut milk, or meat and vegetables *(daun bulunangko)* in buffalo or pigs' blood (Rp500 per portion). A typical Torajan breakfast is *songkolo* made of sticky rice, *lombok* (chili), and coconut; it usually sells for Rp100 a package. Many local *warung,* particularly around the market, serve *kerbau* meat dishes with all the trimmings. Also try *bale* and *lada* (fish and chilies), the sweet snack *baje'* or *dodol* (fried coconut with brown sugar, 4 small packets for only Rp100), completely natural and delicious.

Local specialties of fish, pork, and *kerbau* can be enjoyed in the market *warung,* some of which have no tables or chairs. First pick up a bamboo tube of *balok* (Rp750) in the *balok* section, or just a glass at a *warung* (Rp150), then sit down on a mat to be served rice, fried fish, fiery hot *kerbau* meat or pork to accompany your palm wine. *Warung* and portable stalls also offer standard Indonesian foods — *martabak, sate, nasi goreng,* etc. Fish and vegetables are very popular; also for sale is a wide variety of fruits, especially bananas.

Beverages

World-class coffee is grown here, especially in colder regions around Panggala and Pedamaran; it is sold in Rantepao's market for only Rp2500-3000 per kilo. **Wira Agung** is a coffee dealer (see Marcus Kapa) who sells attractive souvenir containers, pre-ground and vacuum-packed, of either type of coffee for Rp3000 (1st price); see map, no. 25. *Balok* (Torajan for *tuak,* palm wine) is often drunk at Torajan ceremonies. Transported in long bamboo sections, *balok* is drunk all day long out in the *padi* instead of water. A mild, mellow booze, the same milky color as Mexican *pulque,* you feel more stoned than drunk. There are 3 varieties: sweet, medium sweet, and sour. Try mixing the sweet and sour kind together. The more sour variety is always redder; it's had more coconut skin added. For the real *balok,* go to eastern Torajaland to the Batualu and Rantebua areas; all these little villages sell it for Rp1000 for a whole bamboo pipe full (one m long, 3 liters).

Warung

Opposite Losmen Flora is **Warung Murni** (on Jl. Sesean, near the mosque), a local travelers' hangout which serves a knockout *nasi campur* for Rp1000. Another popular and reasonable "tourist" eatery is **RM Rima** (Jl. Mappanyuki) N of town center, with full menu from breakfast (pancakes with banana and lemon, Rp500) to full-course dinners (sweet and sour fish, Rp2500); their *nasi goreng* is only Rp750. Also try the cheap *warung* and coffee stalls serving snacks along Jl. Pembangunan such as **Kios Gembira** at no. 44. **Warung Roma,** Jl. Pasar (near the traffic circle), is good value.

Restaurants

A number of Rantepao tourist restaurants offer Indonesian and Indonesian-Western dishes on 4-language menus. Most are overpriced — the town's *warung* generally have more color and better value. **RM Dodeng,** Jl. Pembangunan 3 (W of the market), serves quite good food for the money: a large *mie kuah* for only Rp750! Run by a warm family, **Chez Dodeng** on the main street is similar — delicious food and desserts at even cheaper prices. Ask the proprietor to take you out to the villages to eat dog and snake. **Sedia,** Jl. Irawan, offers Indonesian and European food. **Restaurant Rachmat,** on Jl. Abdul Gani near the traffic circle, is where all the French tourists eat. They hand out a map. Good ice lemonade *(air es jeruk).* If you protest over the expensive menu, they'll produce a cheaper one. A small restaurant N of Wisma Monika, **Kios Mamba,** serves better food than the Rachmat at half the price; also has better atmosphere and nice music. The restaurant at **Hotel Misiliana,** 2 km S on the road to Makale near the turnoff to Kete, serves expensive Indonesian, European, and Chinese dishes.

OTHER PRACTICALITIES

Shopping

A row of 4 souvenir shops on the main street (Jl. Mappanyuki, on the L heading N just after Jl. Pasar) offers the best selections of Torajan handicrafts and antiques. Prices are higher than in the market or villages, but for old woodcarvings, knives, necklaces, *ikat*-dyed cloth, these art shops are the best places to look. Sample prices: engraved and painted boxes, Rp1000 (small), Rp2000 (big); miniature replicas of *tongkanan,* Rp1500-3000; statues made of wood and *kerbau* bone, Rp5000-20,000; glass beads, Rp200-750. Some bargaining will usually lower the price. **Art Shop Marura,** Jl. Mappanyuki 21, has a complete range of items at reasonable prices.

Watch it: those 200-year-old American and European coins sold for Rp1500 in the shops ("for collections," they say) and in villages are clever copies of the real thing. On the big market days, country people with their goods and wears stream in and out of town all day long. In the *pasar,* buy bamboo basketware *(nasi),* Rp900-1200; flat sifting trays woven in attractive colors, Rp600; clay water pots, Rp400; work and dress hats, Rp2000 and up; old *pisau labok'* (machetes), Rp170,000. Two types of wonderful Torajan coffee are also sold in the market: *Robusta* (Rp2000 per liter) and *Arabika* (Rp3500 per liter). The ladies will even pack your coffee up in bamboo tubes for traveling!

Services
The **tourist office** (Pusat Informasi Wisata) on Jl. Taman Bahagia hands out a few brochures and a map. It lies opposite the largest church in Rantepao, Gereja Besar. Open 0800-1400 every day except Sun.; Fri. until 1100; and Sat. until 1330. Change money at the moneychanger's office (faster than the bank) near the traffic circle (intersection of Jl. Abdul Gani and Jl. Mappanyuki), or at Hotel Indra (Jl. Landorundun). **Bank Rakyat Indonesia**, 1 block S on Jl. Mappanyuki, gives poor rates for both cash or TCs; open Mon.-Fri. 0730-1200, Sat. 0730-1100. The **post office** (only small parcels of 3 kg or less accepted) and telephone office are 1 block S of the traffic circle on Jl. Taman Bahagia, right opp. Bank Rakyat Indonesia; open Mon.-Thurs. 0800-1400, Fri. 0800-1100, Sat. 0800-1230. Overseas telephone calls can now be made direct from Rantepao: Europe, Rp30,000, 3 min.; USA, Rp22,750, 3 min. (more expensive than Jakarta).

Getting There
Liman Express (Jl. Laiya, 100 m S of Central Market, tel. 5851, Ujung Pandang) buses leave Ujung Pandang for Rantepao at 0700 and 1900 every day; Rp5000. The night bus takes 10-12 hours, the day bus 8-9 hours. Book in advance. At 0630, Liman sometimes sends a minibus around to pick up passengers at the hotels for transfer to the terminal. Although Liman is one of the best companies operating to TATOR (express buses and large seats for European frames), 8 other bus companies in U.P. also do this run. In fact, buses for Tanatoraja leave all morning long; just go out to the *terminal bis* in Panaikang (4 km from city on the road to the airport) and board your bus.

The scenic route to Tanatoraja passes through lush agricultural land on the western coastal plain to Pare Pare, then climbs into spectacular limestone mountains and rich valleys. Don't miss the views by taking the night coach! The Southern Torajans, who grow high-altitude crops like corn and *ubi gayo*, wear *sarung*, ride horses, worship Allah, and are ethnically the same people as the Torajans. Stopping in these friendly roadside restaurants is one of the best parts of the trip up to TATOR. A number of companies (such as Falitah at the market, and Satra near the Restaurant Rachmat in Rantepao) also offer bus and minibus service to and from Tanatoraja at about the same prices as Liman; check the "From Ujung Pandang" section. Taking a minibus, though faster than a bus, is also more crowded. From Palopo on the E coast a road corkscrews high into the mountains then down to Rantepao, a 2-hour trip by minibus, Rp2500.

The alternative to the long bus trip is to fly Ujung Pandang-Rantepao with Merpati every Tues. at 0900, arriving 0955; Thurs. at 1030, arriving 1125; Sat. at 0900, arriving 1955. This very scenic, 50-min. flight costs Rp40,400 plus tax. It's not 100% reliable but is generally reckoned to run as advertised. You might have trouble locating the Rantepao agent at Jl. Pongtiku 11, tel. 38. Rantetayo Airport is 24 km from Rantepao, Rp10,000-15,000 by taxi.

FROM RANTEPAO

Local
If tired of walking out to nearby villages, take local minibuses or *bemo* heading your way—find them on Rantepao's main street near the traffic circle. Or just hop on a *bemo* heading down to Makale (17 km S, Rp300) and jump out when you see the LONDA (Rp150) and LEMO (Rp250) signs. Buses and minivans also leave frequently (until 1900) for Makale. All vehicles leave only when full; sometimes the drivers will cruise around town for half an hour looking for more passengers. You can get to the northern towns of Palawa, Pangli, and Sa'dan easier on Rantepao's big market day when jeeps and old trucks leave constantly for these northern villages, returning each hour until nightfall, charging Rp500 OW. Other local fares: Sa'dan Rp400; Tikala, Rp200; Lempo, Rp600; Nanggala, Rp300; turnoff for Tilanga, Rp200; Batutumonga, Rp2000. In the wet, the already poorly surfaced roads turn into mud pits; see "Trekking" below.

Long-distance Buses/Minibuses/Flights
Liman Express (Jl. A. Mappanyuki 77) has buses for Rp5000 pp departing mornings (around 0700) and evenings (around 1900) for Ujung Pandang with a stop in Pare Pare. Bus company offices (Falitah, Erlin, Virgo, etc.) are all clustered around the traffic circle (intersection of Jl. A. Mappanyuki and Jl. Abdul Gani). Starting at 0900 buses leave from near the traffic circle all day long heading over the mountain to the harbor town of Palopo, Rp2500. This road gets frequently washed out by landslides (one at the start of 1987 killed 6 people), in which case you either have to take the long way around via Siwa (Rp4000), or take a bus up to the point of the landslide, then walk to the other side, where transport will be waiting to take you the rest of the way down to Palopo. Other bus/minibus fares/durations: Watampone, Rp7000, 6-7 hours; Pare Pare, Rp3000, 3 hours; Sengkang, Rp4000; Enrekang, Rp2000; Masamba, Rp3000; Palu, Rp15,500, 30 hours; Saroako, Rp6000, 10 hours; Poso, Rp18,500, 20 hours. Merpati flights depart from TATOR's Rantetayo Airport (24 km from Rantepao) for Ujung Pandang on Tues. at 1015, arrive 1110; Thurs. at 1145, arrive 1125; Sat. at 1015, arrive 1110. Taxi to airport: Rp10,000-15,000.

Charters/Tour Groups

Motorcycles can occasionally be rented, if they're not broken, from the locals at Toko Buku Imanuel for Rp9,000-12,000 per day. Charter minibuses asking around at hotels or at the market; Misiliana Hotel and Wisma Irama, for example, have vehicles for rent. Daily costs start at around Rp20,000, so find a few other people to share. There are a lot of self-appointed local tour guides (about Rp10,000-20,000 per day) and English-speaking young people who can show you around; get invited back to their villages where you'll definitely receive a lot of attention. English-speaking guides ask more: Rp10,000-20,000 per day. Or a tour group operator, like one working for good ol' Pacto Tours, might be able to fit you into his group. They usually rent a whole minibus, which you might also consider doing, for Rp40,000 a day.

Trekking

Rantepao can still be touristy in the off season, but once you're just a km out of town, you're in a tropical Xanadu, peaceful and beautiful. People ask you in for coffee and cigarettes, invite you to attend their ceremonies, or you can even spend the night with them. Since the roads in Torajaland are so bone-jarring in vehicles, walking can be a great relief. But you'll need sturdy footwear for support through the mud and rocks. Walking is best in the late dry season when clouds protect you a little from the intense sun; it's always a good idea to take a water bottle as drinking spots are few and day-walking is very hot. Carry a flashlight in case you get caught walking at night. If you're going into the mountains, take salt, dried fish, sugar, cigarettes, and betelnut to the villages as friendly offerings. Please don't give out candy; it'll ruin it for the rest of us and the Torajans can hardly afford dental bills! Photos are in great demand; people love having their photos taken. Another hot item to take out to distant villages on the long walks is medicine—for them and for you—especially antibiotics for carbuncles and skin infections.

There are always people around to ask the way, provided you speak Indonesian; you're handicapped without it. To the most touristed sites, signs point the way and the distance. Or you can hire Indonesian-speaking guides in Rantepao for as little as Rp10,000 per day, plus expenses. Virtually anywhere in Torajaland you can spend the night in the *tongkonan* houses, or ask the *kepala kampung* for help with accommodations. Always give the lady of the house Rp1500-2000 per day for food. Although some *kampung* will on occasion slaughter a chicken for you, don't expect much more than brown rice straight from the *padi*, vegetables such as *jagung* (corn), *sayur labuk* (pumpkin), cucumber, and sometimes *daging babi* and *daging kerbau*, but more often dried fish. There are coffee and tea stands in most villages where you can get refreshments after walking. If

you're unlucky enough to be in one of the small *kampung* when swarms of European tourists overrun the place, don't despair. They'll be gone after several hours (but they buy up everything in sight, including all the beer and coke!).

SOUTH OF RANTEPAO

Many sites are reachable by just 1- or 2-hour walks from Rantepao, but these can be super-touristy and often thronged with kids asking for money and candy *("mintah uang, kasih gula")*. As a rule, children of Torajaland are very relaxed and talkative, except for those in the highly touristed villages near Rantepao. Try to get in with some of the locals who don't speak English; they'll take you around to lesser-known places that aren't in the guidebooks. The way to really do it right is to go off for 3-4 days and stay in more distant villages. **note:** Metric distances from Rantepao follow the town and place names below.

Karasbik

Just one km S of town on road to Makale. Constructed in 1983 for a funeral, this horseshoe-shaped row of *rumah adat* is arranged around a group of megaliths *(rante)*. Some dwellings are inhabited.

Londa

8 km. Go 6 km S on the road to Makale, then 2 km east. Take a Makale *bemo* and ask to be let off at the turnoff to Londa, then walk. Two natural burial caves under a cliff face are here, with interconnecting passages and impressive entrances. Inside are stacks of old wooden coffins arranged in family groups (the black painted ones are Christian), with skulls and bones strategically placed for show. The entrance was once guarded by a balcony of *tau-tau* effigies, which have now all disappeared. Guides with gas-lamps take *orang turis* through both caves for Rp1000, or just bring your own flashlight. Kids hold your hands until you give them something.

Pa'baisenan (Liang Pia)

8½ km. Located behind the Londa Caves. A big tree is used as a grave for infants who died under 7 months (before teething) so that their "body-soul" can grow with the tree. Although most Torajans today bury babies in the ground, some followers of the old *Aluk Todolo* religion still follow this custom.

Tilanga

12 km. Nine km S on the main road, then turn E for 3 km, or walk a 2½-km trail from Lemo. A really beautiful walk to this natural swimming pool with cool, crystal-clear water. By the time you get to Tilanga you're ready for it—a nice place to hang out all day, with few other people. On Sun., food and drinks are

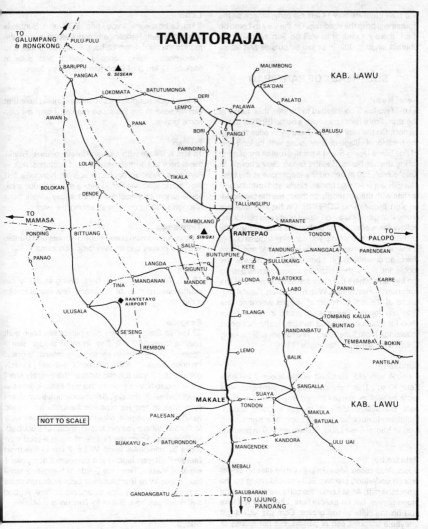

TANATORAJA

TO GALUMPANG & RONGKONG

PULU-PULU

BARUPPU

PANGALA

▲ G. SESEAN

LOKOMATA   BATUTUMONGA

DERI

LEMPO

MALIMBONG

SA'DAN

PALATO

KAB. LAWU

AWAN

PANA

BORI

PALAWA

PANGLI

BALUSU

PARINDING

LOLAI

TIKALA

BOLOKAN

DENDE

TALLUNGLIPU

TO MAMASA

TAMBOLANG

▲ G. SINGKI

MARANTE

RANTEPAO

TONDON

TO PALOPO

PONDING

BITTUANG

SALU

BUNTUPUNE

TANDUNG   NANGGALA

PARENDEAN

PANAO

LANGDA

SIGUNTU

KETE

SULLUKANG

TINA   MANDANAN

MANDOE

LONDA   PALATOKKE

LABO

PANIKI

KARRE

◆ RANTETAYO AIRPORT

ULUSALA

SE'SENG

TILANGA

TOMBANG KALUA

BUNTAO

RANDANBATU

TEMBAMBA   BOKIN'

REMBON

LEMO

BALIK

PANTILAN

MAKALE

SUAYA

SANGALLA

TONDON

MAKULA

KAB. LAWU

PALESAN

BATUALA

BUAKAYU   BATURONDON

KANDORA   ULU UAI

MANGENDEK

MEBALI

GANDANGBATU

SALUBARANI
TO UJUNG PANDANG

NOT TO SCALE

---

sold. A trail through *sawah* leads from Tilanga to Londa, but be sure to continually ask directions along the way.

Lemo

12 km. Twelve km S on the main road by *bemo,* then walk E for 2 km (15 minutes). Rows of *tau-tau* peer down from balconies jutting out from 30 funerary niches carved out of the cliffs. Only the upper classes had the luxury of a *tau-tau* watching over their graves (today their use is suppressed by Christianity). Standing like spectators, the wide-eyed doubles lean on the railings. These realistic puppets are protected by thick paint; their clothing, worn by sun, wind, and rain, is changed periodically. Some of the figures have traveling sacks for their trip to the Land of Souls. Numbering at one time over 60, this used to be the largest *tau-tau* group in all of Tanatoraja. Most have been stolen

and now there are only 14 left. Go early, otherwise the figures will be in the shadows. On the way to Lemo on the L there's a church to visit on Sun. morning; exuberant singing. Join in or just sit outside and listen.

SOUTHEAST OF RANTEPAO

Kete' Kesu'

5 km. Two km S on the road to Makale, then turn E at the sign. From Rantepao, take a *bemo* (Rp200) to the turnoff. On the way to Kete' Kesu', you pass through the traditional village of Buntupune with its long row of rice barns facing S and a parallel row of *tongkonan* facing the rice barns. See the *kepala desa's* house. In Kete' Kesu', 100 m behind the *tongkonan* at the base of a cliff are scattered bones, skulls, and rotted wood coffins with dragon motifs on them; see the big wooden sign proclaiming COFFINS. On the cliff face are *erong* (hanging graves) on wood posts and platforms. Follow the well-surfaced path at the base of the cliffs to the R to a cave where you can play Indiana Jones crawling over bones and skulls in the darkness. From there, go down through a bamboo grove, pass all the rubble and skulls, then climb up a steep narrow path to the big cave where the more favored members of the community were buried. Watch your step. Kete' Kesu' is one of the real commercial villages where no one lives any longer. Outrageous prices in the antique shop for woodcarvings and bamboo crafts (but good browsing). From Kete' Kesu' hike 15 min. to Sullukang (2 km) and farther to Pala'tokke (3 km).

Sullukang

6 km. A very old, secluded village about 2 km past Kete' Kesu'. This *kampung* has megaliths around a *rante* as well as statues seated in a rundown shack near the village (difficult to get a good photo). Sullukang is not often visited. Look for a sign on the road to Kantor Desa Labo. Statues are 100 m beyond.

Pala'tokke

9 km. Also called Mengke'pe'. While human bones crunch underfoot, see two 800-year-old *erong* on the limestone cliff. As at Lemo, the cliffs are also used for stone graves, but no *tau-tau* here. Little kids will take you up the cliffs to the graves. Give the kids a gift (maybe a ballpoint pen or pencils, but not money or candy!). For the adventurous, 2 trails reach this beautiful out-of-the-way site (consider hiring a guide). Turn S on a small rocky trail a short distance past Sullukang and wind past old traditional houses beside bright green rice *padi* to Pala'tokke. No signs, so keep asking the way. The other route is to continue on the road, keeping R at La'bo, to the Gareja Katolik (Catholic church) at Randanbatu (10 km), then walk 2 more km on the trail leading past the church.

La'bo

9 km. La'bo means "large knife" in Torajan. Buntao is straight ahead; Randanbatu and Makula are on the road to the right. From La'bo, the road continues S to Randanbatu, Balik, Sangalla, Suaya, and ends in Makale, 17 km S of Rantepao (Rp300 by *bemo*).

Randanbatu

10 km. Local people make tools and knives here that can be seen at the Rantepao market. There are also some graves.

Buntao

16 km. A village with a *patane* (grave house). Trucks travel here but sometimes the road is closed. Ask in Rantepao. Another approach is from Nanggala (off the Palopo road) via Paniki over a mountainous area, some jungle and leeches. It's a full day's walk from Nanggala. No signs so keep asking the way.

Tembamba

17 km. A mountain pass village 3 km beyond Buntao with old graves and an awesome panorama.

Bokin

18 km. A nice view from here, taking in the whole southeastern portion of Torajaland. Few tourists make it this far.

Sangalla

22 km. At Sangalla a very nice palace has been built upon a leveled-off hill. Bear in mind though that a "palace" in the Torajan sense really means "a grand bamboo house." Also children's graves, privately owned, but if you ask the woman there nicely she'll allow you to have a look. In this picturesque area see hawks wheel in the sky. *Bemo* sometimes run direct from Makale and Rantepao to Sangalla for around Rp500. From Sangalla, take the excellent 2-hour walk to Buntao, where you can find a minibus or truck back to Rantepao. From the N side of town a road traversed by minibuses leads W for 7 km to the main Makale-Rantepao highway: it comes out at a point 4 km N of Makale. From the S side of Sangalla a small road heads W to Buntukalando (*adat* buildings and a museum), and Suaya (*tau-tau* and old coffins). A good trail continues from Suaya to Tondon and Makale.

Suaya

25 km, or 2 km beyond Buntukalando. Make this village a morning excursion from Makale. See the row of coffins at the foot of a cliff with *tau-tau* statues above. Suaya is one of the best places to see *tau-tau*: in all there are 37 on 3 balconies, impressive because they're so cramped. A lovely church is here too.

Makula

25 km (or 20 km E of Makale). A fairly level hike. You

can spend the night at a *pasanggrahan* here (but sometimes the key is *"di Makale."*) In front is a concrete bathing pool (not too clean), fed by a steaming hotspring. From Makula the road continues on to Batualu and Ulu Uai with more good scenery.

SOUTHWEST OF RANTEPAO

Singki Hill
One km. From the southern edge of town, walk W across the river, then look on the R for the nearly overgrown trail going up the hill—a short but precipitous climb. Good views of Rantepao and surroundings from the top.

Siguntu'
6 km. A traditional village, 5 km beyond Singki, with views of the valley below. Continue walking past the Singki Hill turnoff to Singki village and beyond on a level road, then look for a road turning R up the hill. Ask to be sure it's the correct road. See the remarkable carving on the nobleman's house in Siguntu' village, filled with trichromatic symbolic forms. Handsome rice barns here too. Seldom visited. Continue past the Siguntu' turnoff, then turn R on the next road to **Mandoe**, a typical Torajan village 6 km from Rantepao.

Alang-Alang
7 km. From Mandoe, first cross the covered bridge to the Rantepao-Makale road. There's good fishing from the bridge. The other road, to the W, goes to Mandandan. To Londa caves, cross the bridge, turn L ½ km toward Rantepao, then after 2 km take a right.

Salu
15 km. Good places to swim near a bamboo bridge over the river flowing through this village.

Bittuang
This 6-day roundtrip through seldom-visited traditional villages and forest country can be made using a combination of walking and vehicle transport. The trip is easiest with a guide, but each day on the walk you'll come across villages and people to show you the way. Carry some food in case no extra is available in the villages.

Day 1: Rantepao to Batutumonga via Tikala and Pana. This 11-km walk takes about 5 hours.

Day 2: Batutumonga to Pulu-Pulu. Get an early start for a long day, 30 km, 10 hours.

Day 3: Pulu-Pulu to Baruppu. This 16-km walk takes 5 hours.

Day 4: Baruppu to Awan. This walk is 18 km and takes 6 hours. Stop for a swim at Sulutallang, about halfway.

Day 5: Awan to Bittuang. Walk is 18 km, 8 hours. A swimming spot is at Bolokan, about halfway.

Day 6: Return to Rantepao by truck and minibus, a 59-km drive (3½ hours).

EAST OF RANTEPAO

Marante
6 km. Located just off the road to Palopo. Marante is a mixture of traditional Torajan dwellings and wooden houses, with some coffins and *tau-tau*. The children are terrible. See the *kepala desa,* Lulung Manika.

Tandung
17 km. A spectacular area with pine forests, 18-m-high bamboo, and a gorgeous lake.

Nanggala
15 km. Off the road to Palopo, Rp300 direct from Rantepao by *bemo,* or only Rp300 to the turnoff then about a 2-km walk. In an area of pretty ricefields, Nanggala is a traditional Torajan village known for its large *tongkonan* and 14 rice barns—the best you'll see. Besides storing rice (on the 2nd floor), these structures are also used for ceremonies. Guests are received on the 1st floor, where they'll be asked for a donation.

From Nanggala, walk S on a dirt trail over mountains 10 km (3 hours) to Paniki, then on to the Buntao area (2 more hours), a full day's walk in all. **PT Toraco Jaya** is a Japanese-Indonesian coffee-growing and exporting company between Nanggala and Paniki. The fieldworkers earn Rp2000 a day while coffee beans sell for around Rp3000 per kilo. All over Tokyo, Torajan coffee is advertised and highly prized. If you pass through the plantation, you must stop and register at their office. From Buntao, return to Rantepao (15 km) by *bemo;* it's also possible to walk in 2 days to Palopo on the E coast via Tembamba (nice scenery), Bokin, and Pantilang.

NORTH OF RANTEPAO

Parinding
7 km. Walk N from Rantepao on Jl. Mappanyuki and cross the river, turn L at the intersection, and keep R at the Tikala road intersection. Easy, mostly level walking through ricefields. Infrequent vehicles on this route. Parinding is in 2 parts, both with handsome *tongkonan* and rice barns.

Bori
8 km. One of the best *rante* of the region. Many other

Rante, *Bori.* These stone menhirs dedicated to important ancestors ring a field reserved for Torajan funerals.

villages have *rante,* but here the stones are huge, some towering several meters high. A small trail near Bori climbs to **Deri,** passing many *tongkonan* on the way. Deri is on the road to Batutumonga and Pangala.

Pangli

8 km. Here a house grave with a stone statue has the likeness of a dead man, one Pong Massangka, carved on it. House graves are built when there are no cliff faces for carving out deep burial pockets; graves are instead dug into the earth and a small statue or *tongkonan* is built over the top. Each house grave contains members of an entire family, wrapped in shrouds and interred without coffins. Pangli is also the source of a famous *tuak;* peddlers can be seen carrying bamboo sections of this alcoholic drink into Rantepao on market day each week. The *tuak* foams up on the ends of each bamboo section.

Palawa

13 km (or 9 km by direct road), about 1 km N of Pangli, then 1 km W on a side road. This traditional village has numerous *tongkonan* and rice barns, fine examples of Torajan domestic architecture. Large numbers of *kerbau* horns are attached to the fronts of some *tongkonan.* Palawa is built on terraces which rise, and as you climb the soaring rooftops of the Torajan *rumah adat* remind you of the spires of Gothic cathedrals. Palawa's highest terrace has 7 big houses facing 7 big storehouses (in Toraja you don't stare out at other neighbors but you stare across upon your own family's wealth). Also visit Palawa's Stonehenge-like circle of stones.

Sa'dan

16 km, or 12 km by direct road (Rp600 by *bemo).* Hyped as the weaving center of Tanatoraja, the cultural significance of this place is greatly exag-

gerated. Most products, sold at fixed prices, are made to suit the package tourists' tastes and pocketbooks. Women demonstrate traditional weaving at a center near Sa'dan (turn L at the sign before crossing the bridge) where you may also bargain for old and new cloth. Sa'dan has the best distilleries of the strong palm toddy drink, *tuak sissing biang;* one bamboo full, Rp1500.

Lempo

25 km. Turn L onto the Pangala road at Pangli. This traditional village has a *tongkonan* with 100 sets of *kerbau* horns.

Batutumonga

30 km by road, but only 10 km by trail via Tikala and Pana. Direct *bemo* travel here from Rantepao (Rp1500). A trip to Batutumonga is worth it for the superb views over Rantepao and surrounding valleys. A schoolteacher maintains a room in his house for travelers. The trail climb is steep and should be done before the afternoon rains turn it into slippery mud. Near Batutumonga, visit the circle of 56 stones with 5 trees in their center. Most of the stones are 2-3 m high and the whole site looks down on *sawah* arranged amphitheater-fashion, an appropriate location for a stone altar. For even better views, climb G. Sesean early in the morning; a guide would be handy. You can see Rantepao in the distance, rock hillsides, and varied landscapes. From Batutumonga, walk uphill a ways to the turnoff S to Pana; the beautiful descent to Rantepao takes 3-4 hours.

Pana

About 31 km, or take the trail through Tikala. Near Pana is a very old set of cliff graves in a beautiful setting—some of the best *rante, liang,* and *tau-tau* in Toraja. From Rantepao, take a *bemo* direct to Pana

(Rp2000); the road runs out of pavement fast, and you could get stuck in the mud. From Batutumonga, it's a real easy walk down to Pana and farther to Rantepao. First walk W on the road 300 m, then turn L down a wide grassy path. After Pana look for a small trail up the bank to the left. If you pass a large school you've gone about 300 m too far. Coming up from Tikala, look for the small trail to the graves on your R, some 300 m after the school. Or you can take a *bemo* from Tikala to Pana (Rp200).

Lokomata

35 km. Take a *bemo* to Tikala (Rp1000), then walk up to Lokomata. A huge 4-story-tall boulder beside the road has about 60 cliff graves carved into 3 sides. Many other boulders with graves in this area. Some of the burials are recent, and you might even see a guy chipping away at a boulder. The walk from Batutumonga to Lokomata is level and has nearly continuous panoramas of rice terraces, mountains, and the valley below—considered some of the best trekking in Tanatoraja. Northeast of Lokomata is **G. Sesean**, highest mountain in Tanatoraja.

Pangala

58 km. A coffee-growing area (PT Torako Jaya). Also known for its dancers. Small trails lead S to Bittuang (36 km, 2-day walk) and N to Galumpang (6 days).

Galumpang

The trail to Galumpang, in the northermost reaches of S. Sulawesi, is difficult: long forest sections, lots of mud and mountains, big rivers, snakes, lizards, wild orchids. No *kampung*, only huts to stay in. Go well-prepared. Walk via Baruppu, Makki, then through either Seko or Rongkong. Another way is to start from Palopo, then on to Sabbang by jeep, Rp2000. From Sabbang, walk to Rongkong in 2 days, Seko in 3, then Galumpang in another two. From Galumpang, hike to Tamleo where you can catch a riverboat to Mamuju, then trek down to Mamasa. From Mamasa, minibuses and *bemo* head down to Polewali, then on to Pare Pare and Ujung Pandang. In all, the walk from Galumpang to Mamasa could take about 4 weeks. The aboriginal Toala people live in these mountains—superstitious and unpredictable. Galumpang and Rongkong are famous for very high-quality *ikat*-dyed cloth, each town possessing its own style. These clothes are used ceremonially to wrap around corpses. A bride's dowry must contain at least one piece, or they could also even be used as part payment for a contract murder.

MAKALE

Makale, an administrative center built by the Dutch in 1925, is the 2nd largest town of Tanatoraja. Located 17 km S of Rantepao, Makale overlooks a lotus lake and has a good bazaar. There are some fine walks in the area (though Rantepao is more centrally located for walking). The region's only tertiary level school, run by a Protestant church, is in Makale and offers a 3-year degree program. Few tourists stay in Makale, there's no tourist tax, it's cleaner than Rantepao, and there are no souvenir shops or "tourist restaurants." A tourist office is located in the Bupati Daerah building, 2½ km N of town. No tourist literature though, as the staff seem to do little more than keep their chairs warm. The entrance lobby of the Bupati Daerah building has a large, detailed relief map of Tanatoraja. The hospital, RS Fatimah, is at Jl. Pong Tiku 103. Makale's large market is worth a visit to see local produce and meet people from surrounding villages. The big market occurs every 6 days, in rotation with Rembon, Rantepao, Bittuang, and Sangalla—every day there's a market somewhere in Tanatoraja. See the slimy greenish eels from the *sawah* pools. Most fish are brought up from the coast. Tobacco is from Watampone and other Bugis areas to the south.

Accommodations And Food

Right in the center of town is very basic **Losmen Litha**, Jl. Nusantara; Rp3000-5000. Up the street toward Rantepao on Jl. Pahlawan is the popular **Losmen Merry**; Rp4000-7500 s or d. There's another, flashier **Losmen Merry** a little out on the Rantepao side of town. **Hotel Yani**, Jl. Pong Tiku 3 across the square, is in the Rp5000 + range. North ½ km on the road to Rantepao is pleasant family-run **Wisma Martha**, Jl. Pong Tiku 75; Rp3000-6000 with *mandi*. Modern **Hotel Batu** is 3½ km N; Rp8000 s, 10,000 d (meals Rp2000). **Losmen Indra**, Jl. Jen. Sudirman (tel. 43), just S of the *mesjid*, charges Rp4000-6000 s or d (best rooms are upstairs). The best accommodation in Makale is the 1-Star **Batupapan Hotel**; Rp5000 s, Rp10,000 d, Rp12,000 suite, with restaurant, bar, tennis court, in a quiet location up on a hill. **Hotel Kartika**, 2½ km N, is Rp12,000 s or d, their 9 rooms usually only for government people. Eat in one of the several *warung* on Jl. Pong Tiku (such as **Kios Asra** and **Kios Ermita**) which serve standard Indonesian food. At night portable stalls offer *sate* and *martabak*.

Transport

Minibuses arrive frequently from Rantepao (Rp400, ½ hour), Pare Pare, and Ujung Pandang. When there are enough passengers, Merpati flies Twin Otters from Ujung Pandang to an airstrip at Rantetayo, 12 km NW of Makale. From Makale, local trucks and minibuses travel W up into the mountains to Bit-

TANATORAJA GLOSSARY

alang: rice barn

aluk: animist religion or symbolic ritual

Aluk Todolo: traditional religion of Torajaland

Banua: house

Bombo: ghost

erong: grave for a coffin, supported by wood beams driven into a cliff face. Most have fallen down over the years. See them, for example, at Pala'tokke, Kete' Kesu', Alla', and Tambolang.

Kaunan: slave, dependent

katik: mythical animal resembling a snake; symbolizes nobility. *Katik:* are carved on the fronts of some *tongkonan*

kerusu mengat: Thank you

la'bo': large knife

lo'ko: cave

liang: grave

Ma'bua': an important smoke-rising ritual

Ma'nene': a ritual in honor of the ancestors

Menammu: harvest ritual

pa'piong: food cooked in bamboo tubes; *kerbau* blood is a common ingredient

pastor: Catholic church leader

patane: grave house

pemali: prohibition

pendeta: Protestant church leader

puang: owner, master; highest-ranking Torajan nobility

puya: Land of the Dead

rarabuku: family; lit. "blood bones"

sisemba': kick fight

tau-tau: effigies of the deceased, usually carved from wood and clothed. Sex but not likeness is shown, with a few exceptions

tedong bonga: spotted *kerbau*

tongkonan: traditional ancestral Torajan house, of tongue-and-groove construction. Divided into 3 rooms, all have symbolic carvings on the outside.

---

tuang, Rp2500, 3 hours; NE to Sangalla, Rp400, ½ hour; and SE to Kandora, Rp300, 15 minutes. Most minibuses leave from around Jl. Nusantara, for example to Palopo each morning for Rp2500. You arrive at Palopo's bus terminal from where it's a half-hour's walk (or Rp200 by *becak*) to the *losmen*. Buy long-distance bus tickets from agents along Jl. Nusantara and Jl. Pahlawan for about the same prices you'd pay in Rantepao. Liman Ekspres office: Jl. Ichwan 6.

WALKS FROM MAKALE

Some of the longer walks described below require communicating with villagers in *Bahasa Indonesia*. Buy a phrasebook and learn to use it! Horses can be rented to carry gear for many of these trips. Guides make travel and trailfinding easier; ask at the hotels. Most speak good English and can organize everything. Guides usually specialize in certain areas of Tanatoraja and have varied styles of travel. Some use horses and some travel only by foot. Cost for a guide in Rantepao runs Rp10,000 or more per day. For an 8-day trip, such as the **Simbuang Loop**, which passes through or near many traditional Torajan villages such as Makkodo and Paun, expect to spend about US$100-150 on everything. Create your own walks. In order of difficulty, some walks (with distances) from Makale include:

Tondon

½ km. Walk from the Makale market E on a small road. A row of *tau-tau* in the cliff overlooks cliff graves. Old caskets, bones, and skulls are found in small caves around the cliffs.

Suaya

6 km. Walk E from Tondon (or Makale) through spectacular, small limestone mountains, then along ricefields. Turn L 250 m to the village at the base of a limestone hill. In the cliff are a row of *tau-tau* and scattered cliff graves. On the ground is a row of old coffins full of bones. Some coffins have elaborate geometric designs, and several are carved in the shape of *kerbau*.

Buntukalando

8 km (5 hours). East on the R is a king's *tongkonan* and rice barns. The *tongkonan* is open as a "mini-museum" of royal possessions and Torajan household artifacts, Rp300 admission. One of the rice barns is unusually large and has 10 supporting pillars instead of the usual 6. A *rante* with huge strangely shaped stones is on the other side of the road.

Sangalla

9½ km. Turn L at Sangalla for roads and minibuses to Makale and Rantepao. Turn R for Makula. Trucks and minibuses travel this road regularly.

Makula

13 km. The *pasanggrahan* has hotspring baths inside and a swimming pool (not too clean) fed with hotspring water from the outside.

Rembon

12 km northwest. A market town with a large market every 6 days.

Se'seng

20 km. A good natural swimming hole here. From Se'seng the road winds for 21 km up into the moun-

tains to Bittuang. This walk would probably be more enjoyable than taking *bemo,* as the road is very bumpy.

Bittuang

41 km. A market town (Mon. is the big day). Trucks carry passengers and goods on the road to Makale, Rp2000, 3 hours. From Bittuang a trail goes N to Pangala, 36 km, 2 days. The 58-km trail to Mamasa in western Toraja can usually be walked in 3 days, with luscious scenery of valleys, mountains, villages, and rice terraces. (See "Bittuang" under "Southwest Of Rantepao" for hiking and overnight details.) The following distances are calculated from Bittuang: from Bittuang, walk through Patongloan Desa (3 km); descend 5 km to Pakun (14 km); descend 4 km to Belau (18 km); descend 3 km to Ponding (21 km); descend 4 km to a covered bridge over the Masuppu River (25 km); follow the Masuppu and Mawai rivers 5 km upstream to Mawai (30 km); climb 4 steep km to Timbaan (34 km); climb to a pass and descend through forest 14 km to Pakkassasan (48 km); level 3 km to Lambanan (51 km); level 3 km to Rantebuda (54

km); and a level 4 km to Mamasa (58 km). There are several other routes to Mamasa from the Makale area. See maps.

THE SIMBUANG LOOP

Day 1: Bittuang to Ponding (same route as to Mamasa)

Day 2: Ponding to Pana

Day 3: Pana to Nosu (Batupapan)

Day 4: Nosu to Simbuang

Day 5: Day hikes to surrounding villages of Sarangdena, Kanan, Paun, Rea, Simbuang, Tua, Buka and Pongbembe.

Day 6: Simbuang to Petarian

Day 7: Petarian to Sanik. Crocodiles live in the Masuppu River where it is crossed.

Day 8: Sanik to Malimbong (near Rembon). Walk 2 days more to either Bittuang (by the road), or to Rantepao (via Bittuang), or to Makale via Palesan. See route maps for details. Or just take a vehicle from Rembon.

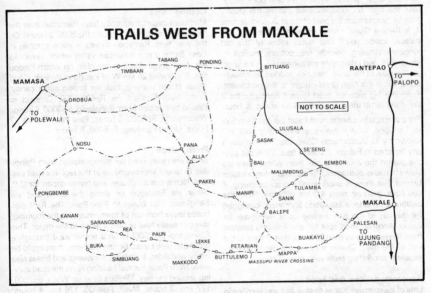

TRAILS WEST FROM MAKALE

NOT TO SCALE

MAMASA — TO POLEWALI

TABANG — PONDING — BITTUANG — RANTEPAO — TO PALOPO

TIMBAAN

OROBUA

NOSU — PANA — ALLA — SASAK — SE'SENG — ULUSALA

PONGBEMBE — PAKEN — BAU — REMBON — MALIMBONG

KANAN — MANIPI — TULAMBA

SARANGDENA — SANIK — BALEPE — MAKALE

REA — PAUN — PALESAN — TO UJUNG PANDANG

BUKA — LEKKE — BUAKAYU

SIMBUANG — MAKKODO — PETARIAN — MAPPA

BUTTULEMO — MASUPPU RIVER CROSSING

TO CENTRAL SULAWESI

PALOPO AND VICINITY

A small Muslim port, Palopo is the administrative capital of the Lawu regency. This district curves around the NW and W stretch of Teluk Bone. Before the Dutch, the Lawu Kingdom based here was a major power in the region. The old *kraton* is now a museum. Palopo also served as the port from which enchained Torajan slaves were sold and shipped out to Java and Siam. *Durian* grown in this region are famous for their flavor throughout Sulawesi; the whole of Lawu smells overripe during the Nov.-March *durian* season. The climate in Palopo is hot and humid. Lots of "Hello misters" from the friendly inhabitants.

The giant **Kris Memorial** in town, with its lethal bamboo-spear fencing, symbolizes and commemorates the fight for independence against the Dutch. Nearby, across from the post office at Jl. Andi Jemma 1, is **Batara Guru**, a small museum in the old Lawu palace. Inside you'll find dusty relics of the old kingdom: clothing, swords, *kris*, pottery, musical instruments, and other royal paraphernalia. For a spectacular view of the town, bay, rice paddies, and mountains, climb the high grassy ridge to the northwest. From the big mosque head toward Rantepao for 3 km, then climb the ridge to the R for about ½ hour.

For a swim, take a *bemo* from Pasar Sentral 3 km SW to Lattuppa, where there's a swimming pool still known by its Dutch name "Zwembat." There aren't any beaches in Palopo, just mud flats. Walk out over the sea on the 2-km-long pier from where there are views of native outriggers, Palopo, and the mountains behind. But there is snorkeling (and scuba diving, if you have gear) on reefs 4-5 km offshore. From the *pelabuhan*, charter a *ketingting* (motorized outrigger) for the day to the *batu karang* (coral reefs); ask for Basso. Another good spot for snorkeling is reached from Bassean. Go by road 37 km S, then 7 km E to the end of the road. Charter a *ketingting* (Rp20,000) for excellent snorkeling reefs with many fish.

Accommodations And Food

Lots of inexpensive places to stay, but you sacrifice in cleanliness what you save in *rupiah*. Cheapest are: **Peng. Lima** and **Peng. Muncul**, next door to each other off Jl. Kartini, both Rp3000 s, Rp4000 d. **Losmen Marlia**, Jl. Diponegoro 25, offers a room with private *mandi* for Rp3500 s, Rp5000 d. Nearer the harbor are: **Losmen Rismaria**, Jl. A. Jemma 14, Rp3000 s, Rp5000 d; and **Hotel Rio Rita**, Jl. A. Jem-

ma 10, Rp3500 s, Rp6000 d, both with *mandi* and *makan pagi*. **Hotel Palopo**, Jl. Kelapa 11 (tel. 209), is handy to the minibus and bus terminal; Rp4000 s, Rp7000 d with *mandi*. **Hotel Bumi Sawerigading** (Rp5000 d) is a Rp200 *becak* ride from the bus station. The best accommodation in town is **Hotel Adifati**, Jl. Patimura (behind a *Komando Militer* complex), Rp5000 s, Rp8000 d with *mandi* and fan, or Rp15,000 with a/c.

Seafood *(cumi cumi, ikan bakar*, etc.) is Palopo's savior. Most restaurants are on Jl. Diponegoro, or an extension of it. On this street enjoy Indonesian or Chinese meals at: **RM Segar, Victoria Restaurant, Kios Mini Indah**, or **Marannu Restaurant**; Padang food at **RM Bukittinggi**. The **Palopo Hotel** and **Hotel Rio Rita** also have restaurants. *Warung* are found around town and at Pasar Sentral.

Getting There

Minbuses depart frequently from Rantepao over the mountain road down to Palopo (Rp2500, 3 hours). On the way from Rantepao there's a *pasanggrahan* in Desa Battang in a mountain valley which overlooks the deep gorge down to the plain on which Palopo sits. It's located 25 km W of Palopo at Puncak. Good meals at the *warung;* look for brown sugar candy; exotic butterflies sell for Rp600-4000. Connect to Palopo by bus also from: Sengkang, Rp3000, 6 hours; Watampone, Rp5000, 6 hours; Pare Pare, Rp5000, 7 hours; Ujung Pandang, Rp6000, 8 hours.

From Palopo

Boats are rarely used for transportation from Palopo due to recent improvements in the region's road system. Numerous minibuses and buses depart for U.P. either via Rantepao or along the coast and via Sengkang; also buses to Pare Pare. The Rantepao buses leave from out of town, mostly in the morning; you can easily hike or take a *bemo* to the depot. This 62-km trip (Rp2500) is on a scenic road through a mountain pine forest. During the rains, there could be many landslides. In Palopo, minibuses and buses also leave from Pasar Sentral heading N up the road curving around the bay. Minibus fares to: Wotu, Rp2500, 127 km, 3 hours; Malili, Rp4000, 176 km, 4 hours; Saroako, Rp6000, 228 km, 5 hours.

For C. Sulawesi, take a bus direct to Mangkutana, leaving several times daily; Rp4000, 4 hours. There, minibuses meet buses for the 6-hour trip over a rough mountain road to Pendolo on the S shore of Lake Poso. The nearest airport to Palopo is at Masamba, 63 km N—just one flight weekly to Ujung Pandang.

Since there are no boats directly to Kolaka (SE Sulawesi) from Palopo, the usual approach is by road to Watampone, then by boat to Kolaka and by road to Kendari. Minibuses to Watampone cost Rp5000, departure 0900, 6 hours, 247 km. A very good road the first 120 km, but then it disintegrates.

Wotu

A small nondescript crossroads town 127 km NE of Palopo, Rp2500 and 3 hours by minibus. Traveling N

from Palopo, it's best to take the bus through Wotu (so as not to get stuck there) to Mangkutana, where you connect by *bemo* to Pendolo on the S shore of Lake Poso, C. Sulawesi. Eastbound, a minibus also runs from Palopo through Wotu another 50 km to Malili. If you have to stay in Wotu's drab hotel (Rp2500), kids stand under your room and look in peepholes.

Pantai Lemo Beach, near Wotu, has good snorkeling; take the road to the *pelabuhan,* 3 km from Wotu, then charter a *ketinting* for Rp6000-12,000. From

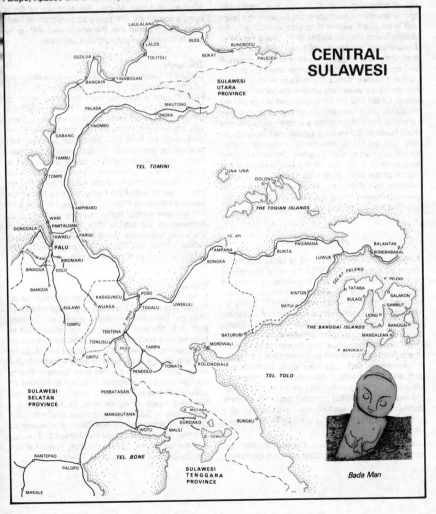

CENTRAL SULAWESI

Bada Man

Wotu, travel downriver to the coast, then turn R for 2-3 km, where you'll find a white-sand beach and pristine coral in inner and outer reefs.

Malili

On the NE shore of Teluk Bone, the mining company **PT Inco** built this port in 1972, complete with admin buildings, schools, a clinic, and Indonesian government customs station! Today Malili hosts Inco's Sulawesi headquarters. This is one of the only places in C. Sulawesi where the police are quite used to Europeans wandering around, though they might pay special attention if one happens to be wearing a beard and a backpack with a flute sticking out of it. An airstrip hosts Merpati flights from Ujung Pandang. Accommodations for Rp7500 can be found in the Bechtel camp in Malili, and in other satellite villages. If you don't make a friend amongst the Inco people, stay in **Losmen Satria** (Rp3500) or in other cheap *losmen* on the waterfront close to the harbor. Food is cheap. Or roll into the Inco camp and ask to pay for breakfast. Good food and a/c; you won't believe their cafeteria! From Malili, there are continual buses and truck-buses to Soroako on a good road (Rp3000, 52 km). Also, get lifts on Inco trucks or chartered planes by first negotiating with the crews. One of the Bechtel barges takes a run out to the islands around the mouth of the Malili River each Sunday: coral reefs, beaches, skin diving, etc. Book way in advance. Or you can charter a *ketinting*, Rp15,000-25,000 for the 1½-hour trip. No people live on these islands.

SAROAKO

A mining community, 52 km NE of Malili, which produces an extraordinary 8% of the world's supply of nickel. Saroako was a tiny impoverished village of several hundred people when Inco moved in and constructed a smelting works nearby in 1972. Inco's investment in the region represents one of the biggest non-oil investments in Indonesia (US$850 million). Inco built a tortuous 52-km all-weather road through thick, mountainous jungle from the port of Malili, hundreds of prefab houses for employees and managers, a hydroelectric dam, a power station, a satellite station, and a plant which incorporates some of the most advanced smelting technology in the world. Nickel-mining in this torrential monsoon region is a messy business. Mud is ubiquitous and the camp's sodden roads are negotiable only by great balloon-tire trucks called Manhauls.

The community is in in 2 parts. The original, tidier part is made up of company expat housing, a supermarket

stocking Australian and Singaporean goods, a recreation hall, and a social club. Because of the process of Indonesianization and current low world nickel prices, expat personnel are down to 40 people. Saroako village consists of a shanty growth around the *pasar*, built up by the influx of Indonesians who saw a *rupiah* or two in Inco's presence. Small native stores sell canned foods, plastic toys, electronics, plus there's a bevy of prostitutes to keep the 2,000 or so Indonesian workers company. In this village you could be addressed not only as Mister, Boss, *Tuan*, but also *Minjheer*, and even Master! But once you're down there a few times, you lose your attraction as fresh meat. On Christmas Eve, the whole town is lit up by candle lanterns, an unforgettable spectacle.

Transport

Saroako is 5 hours by minibus on an outstanding road which runs direct from Palopo, 228 km, Rp6000. Or for Rp6000 take a minibus from Rantepao direct to Saroako. The main Inco camp is a 15-min. walk from Saroako, via a creek and a buffalo paddock. In Saroako, it's best not to try hitching the Manhauls and trucks near the mine site. The drivers, however, will pick you up out of sight of plant security (for "payment," American or English cigarettes are popular). A temporary motorcycle permit from the Saroako police costs Rp3000 (just one photo and a current foreign licence, but no test). Each Friday, there's a flight from Saroako's airport to Poso in C. Sulawesi for Rp32,800; this will save a lot of bother traveling up through C. Sulawesi on the terrible Wotu-Pendolo section of road. Also twice-daily flights from Saroako to Ujung Pandang (Rp55,500, 325 km). You might also be able to hitch a lift on an American missionary plane.

Vicinity Of

In this region are 2 magnificent and very deep lakes, Towuti and Matana. Inco maintains elegant lakeside villas and there are recreational speedboats for Inco staff on **D. Matana**, the deepest non-volcanic lake in Indonesia—a body of water excellent for swimming, water skiing, or sailing. Or you could get boats to **Matana village** at the head of the lake and to **Nuha** village directly across the lake from Saroako. This is also an area of underground caves, repositories of spearheads and helmets, etc., and D. Matana even has burial caves. At 48 km wide, **D. Towuti** is the largest lake in Sulawesi, comparable in size to Lake Geneva. Besides the bus from Malili to Wawondula and then on to Timampu (on the shore of D. Towuti), Inco has the only vehicles to the lakes. Enquire about the possibility of a launch on D. Towuti.

SOUTHEAST SULAWESI

The lower right leg of this spider-shaped island, Sulawesi Tenggara is rugged and isolated. This heavily Islamicized province exports forest products, is famous for its fine silver crafts, and boasts a Japanese nickel project. Access is by boat or air. In Watampone, on the E coast of Sulawesi Selatan, take a *bemo* to Bajoe (harbor entrance: Rp100). Tickets for the boat cost Rp5000 Deck Class, Rp6500 2nd Class, and Rp8500 1st Class; prices include the *bemo* ride (3 km) to the pier where the ship lies. From the pier, boats cruise across Teluk Bone to Kolaka, a small port on the W coast of the SE peninsula. The ferry leaves at 2000 and arrives around 0800 the next morning. From Kolaka, a whole slew of minibuses are ready to take you for Rp3500 down the *jalan raya* to Kendari, capital city of the province on the E coast. From the minibus station, it's another 13 km and Rp300 into Kendari by *bemo*. There's also an airport 30 km out of Kendari, served by Merpati and Garuda.

Kolaka

A port on the W coast of the SE peninsula. In the center of town is **Peng. Mustika**, Rp2500 pp. **Wisma Beringing**, on a hill overlooking the bay, is run by the government; Rp4500 pp. Take *bemo* around town, Rp200 for all distances. From Kolaka take a minibus, 173 km, Rp4500, to Kendari; it stops at a terminal 13 km before Kendari from where you have to take another *bemo* into town. Ferries depart for Bajoe (Watampone), Rp5000 Deck Class; crews charge Rp5000 for use of their cabins during the passage.

KENDARI

This mining town lies on the E coast in a fertile plain at the base of 2 separate legs of the central mountain range. During WW II, the Japanese built an airfield (still remnants) which stopped dead at the foot of the mountains to prevent American strafing (only crosswise). Kendari has all the amenities: a few moderately priced to expensive *losmen*, good *warung*, a tourist office, a *pasar sentral*, and a bus station (by the harbor). Visit the PDK (provincial education) office to view a collection of local weapons, including 3-m-long spears.

Filigree-like silver crafts are made here. In this so-called *kendari*-style ware, you'll see some of the most intricate patterns imaginable, spun from cobweb-like silver threads, a technique learned centuries ago from the Chinese. See brooches, necklaces, lizards with emerald eyes, even large fruit bowls. Check out inexpensive goldwork too. *Kendari*-style ware is also produced in Ujung Pandang, where there's a much wider selection.

Accommodations And Food

In the western end of town on the main road is **Wisma Mutiara**; Rp4000 s, Rp6000-8000 d. Near the harbor is **Peng. Kendari**; Rp4000 s or d. Other cheap *losmen* are found around the *bioskop*. Also check out **Peng. Noer Indah** (Rp4000 pp), and **Wisma Nirwana** (on a hill, Rp5000 pp). Out of town, the first place you'll see when coming into Kendari from Kolaka is **Wisma Maiwali**. The best hotel in town (Rp18,000 full a/c rooms) is **Wisma Andika**. Along the waterfront (1 km from the harbor), *warung* open up at night serving *nasi campur* and *soto daging*; even cheaper (though dark and unclean) foodstalls are found around the *pasar*. Nothing under Rp2000 in the *rumah makan*.

From Kendari

As capital of SE Sulawesi, Kendari serves as an air hub for the region. Merpati (Jl. Sudirman 29, tel. 360/109) has flights to: Luwuk, Rp65,500; Namlea, Rp92,600; Raha, Rp29,400; Surabaya, Rp107,300; Ujung Pandang, Rp45,400. Also check the fares and flight schedules at Garuda's office (Jl. Diponegoro 59, tel. 21729) for flights to Ujung Pandang, Rp51,900; Jakarta (Rp198,000), Surabaya (Rp134,200). The airport is 30 km from town. At Kendari's harbor (1 km from the waterfront), inquire at Meratus Lines about ships to Surabaya, Rp23,000, 4 nights; about 2 ships per month. Also occasional boats to the Tukangbesi Group, and daily boats to Bau Bau on P. Buton to the south; Rp7500, 12 hours. Regular services between Ambon, Ujung Pandang, and (sometimes) Surabaya also stop at Bau Bau.

Vicinity Of

Huge Kendari Bay is enclosed, making it excellent for water sports. There's a recreation park a few km from Kendari toward the bay, and coastal villages of stilt houses. Visit the fine beach at **Desa Mata** (5 km from town), and **Desa Pongolaka** where there's a brick-making factory. There are also *sago* palm marshes in the vicinity — the people prefer *sago* over rice. The **Bajau** are a nomadic, boat-dwelling shore people usually living around Bugis settlements on the remote coasts of the eastern peninsula along Teluk Bone, the Straits

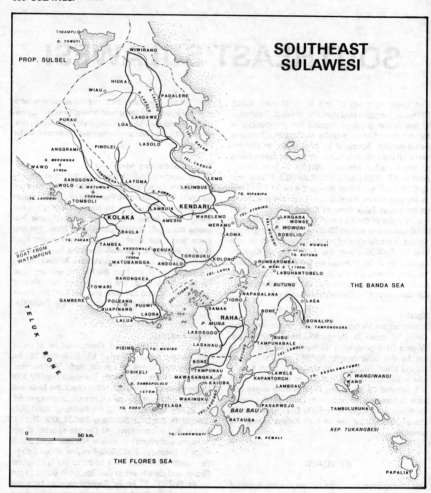

SOUTHEAST SULAWESI

of Tioro and Butung, the island of Wowoni, Kendari Bay, and the Salabangka Islands. Many supernatural abilities are attributed to these "sea gypsies." Outstanding swimmers, they are able to dive so deep that it's said they have gills like fish, and their children are thrown into the sea to make them drown-proof. The Bajau use trident harpoons and bamboo spears to hunt the giant stingray, sometimes employing its poisonous spine as a point for daggers. They are dead accurate with these weapons. The Bajau are masters of a cross-legged defensive art adapted to fighting on boats or in very cramped quarters.

Pulau Butung

A mountainous, colorful island (also called Buton), off the SW coast of SE Sulawesi. Formerly a center of piracy and slave trade, the Sultanate of Buton was ruled by an unbroken dynasty from the 14th C., its level of commerce rivaling that of Makassar and Melaka. The irrepressible Butonese stubbornly retained their independence, even successfully repelling an invasion by Dutch warships in 1740 with the help of Portuguese-made cannons fired from a European-style fortress overlooking the harbor of Bau Bau. The region came under Dutch control only in 1908.

Famous for their seamanship and boat-building, the Islamic Butonese have migrated all over Eastern Indonesia, particularly to Maluku. Pulau Butung is also inhabited by numerous Buginese. Maize, millet, and *ubi* are the staples in the hinterlands, and basket and mat weaving are the only crafts. **Bau Bau**, the old seat of the sultan, is the major town and port. Two-meter-high stone fortifications still encircle the hilltop *kraton*, which contains the oldest mosque in eastern Indonesia (15th C.). Marine tourism is growing in this pristine area. To get to Bau Bau, board a *kapal motor* from Kendari (Rp7000, 12 hours). From Bau Bau, catch

boats or *prahu layar* to Ujung Pandang (leaving every 10 days or so) and Kendari.

Wangi Wangi is a small island in the Tukangbesi Group off the W coast of P. Butung. A beautiful lagoon surrounds the *kampung* of **Wangi Wangi** with only a 5-m-wide, 2-m-deep entrance, though inside the lagoon itself it's 5 m deep. Just outside of town, enter a hole in the ground down through an underground cavern with a cool freshwater spring, the only one in the area. *Prahu* from Ujung Pandang frequently stop at Bau Bau and Wangi Wangi on their way to Ambon.

CENTRAL SULAWESI

The province of mountainous Sulawesi Tengah (area 88,561 sq km; population around 1.5 million) offers beautiful scenery, primitive tribes, ancient megaliths, sleepy port towns, vast stretches of coastline, fantastic diving on coral reefs, unusual natural phenomena. Until recently, this province was isolated, but now, with the Trans-Sulawesi highway completed, there is access from the far northern (Manado) and southern (Ujung Pandang) tips of the island to and through C. Sulawesi. Even so, you might roam for weeks without meeting another traveler. Palu, the province's capital, has a tourist office, tourist hotel, cultural museum, but no tourists. Yet adventurous trips can be made more easily and cheaply here than in Irian Jaya or Kalimantan. The *rumah makan* of C. Sulawesi are exceptionally poor value; stick to the *warung*.

One can reach C. Sulawesi by flying into Mutiara Airport near Palu; for example, the Bouraq flight from Ujung Pandang leaves each day at 0700 and costs Rp56,000. Also check Merpati. The majority of visitors, however, head E by minibus from Rantepao, then NE via Palopo, Wotu, Mangkutana and then into C. Sulawesi. This chapter follows that route, which takes in all 24-36 hours. The section of road from Wotu to Pendolo (on the S shore of Lake Poso) is horrible with ditches in the middle of the road and long muddy stretches. This road was originally built by Japanese *romusha* (Indonesian slave laborers) during WW II at a great cost in lives. There is a monument to the *romusha* at **Perbatasan**, the highest point on the road from Wotu to Pendolo.

Mangkutana is a tiny, pleasant town with a market 3 times a week. This is the jumping-off spot for the minibus ride over the mountains to C. Sulawesi. No regular *losmen*, but you can stay at either of the 2 *warung* (for free if you eat there), or at the barracks of

the drivers for Pendolo. From Mangkutana, minibuses make stops at *warung* on their way north. Expect to get stuck at least once, plus one breakdown and one flat tire. (By contrast, the road from Tentena to Poso is well-surfaced.) From Pendolo, large, barge-shaped motorized canoes equipped with small cabins cross D. Poso to Tentena on the lake's northern shore. Yet another option is to take a minibus from Rantepao to Saroako (Rp6000), timing your arrival to catch the once weekly (on Fri.) Merpati flight from Saroako to Tentena. Alternatively, you might be able to hitch a lift on a missionary plane to Tentena, or retrace your steps to Ujung Pandang and fly over C. Sulawesi to Manado (Rp108,800 with Bouraq, Rp114,500 with Garuda).

Pendolo

A village on the S shore of D. Poso. This lake is still remarkably clean, clear, and beautiful. Help to keep it that way. Watch locals speed by in outrigger canoes. For swimming, go down to the pier, then turn right. Accommodations are all on the lakeshore and charge about Rp2500 s, Rp4000 d. Try **Peng. Sederhana** and across the street **Peng. Danau Poso**. Eat at **RM Makan Cahaya**, or in inexpensive *warung* along Jl. Pelabuhan. Outriggers usually leave Pendolo for Tentena between 0700 and 0800; 3 hours, Rp5000. A rough road through the mountains along the eastern shore of the lake (via Taripa and Pondo) connects Pendolo with Tentena by minibus, 4-5 hours, Rp6000.

TENTENA

Tentena is a small Christian town in a lovely location on the N shore of D. Poso, a beautiful deep lake ringed by high forested mountains, with some white-sand beaches. Coffee, vegetables, and *cengkih* (clove

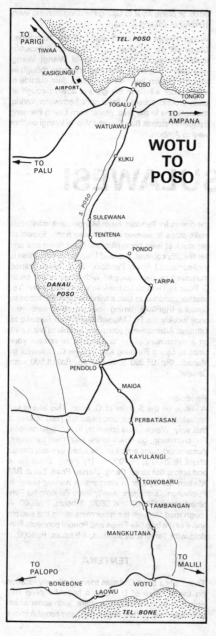

trees) are grown on the hills surrounding Tentena. Rice is the main food, grown in irrigated *padi*. Catch a movie at the **Beringin Theatre** (Rp400-500), 1½ km N from the boat docks. **Balai Buku**, ½ km N of the docks, has books in *Bahasa Indonesia* about early missionary work in Sulawesi. A half-decent road runs between Poso and Tentena with fairly frequent minibuses (Rp2000, 2-3 hours).

Accommodations And Food

Peng. Wisata Remaja is near the boat landing, very convenient for the boat S across the lake. Run by a Pakistani from Medan, it costs Rp2500-4000 pp for large, spotlessly clean doubles with your own *mandi*. A 1-km walk farther on the road to Poso is church-run **Wisma Tiberias**, Rp4000-6000 with *mandi*. Same price is the **Hotel Puse Lemba**, which also has a restaurant. **Hotel Panorama** is 2 km from the boat docks and high up on the hillside. Ask where the trail is, or continue to the hotel road and turn right. Rooms are pleasant, a bit expensive (Rp8000), but what a view over the lake! The local cuisine is fiery hot. That isn't tomato sauce on your *ikan mas;* it's chopped chili peppers. Eat at the few *warung* or at Peng. Wisata Remaja. Wisma Tiberias and Hotel Panorama also serve meals if arranged in advance.

Transport

From Pendolo on the S shore of Lake Poso, motorized outriggers cross Lake Poso to Tentena once a day (and return). Or it's 5 hours by road to Tentena from Pendolo. From the N, minibuses connect from Poso, 59 km, 2 hours, Rp2000. From Tentena, boats across the lake (Rp2500) to Pendolo could leave anytime, depending on the weather. The weather is no joke; 11 people died in 1986 when a boat overturned. When the waves get a little heavy, the skipper sometimes pulls onto the shore for the night. Arriving in Pendolo, 4WD vehicles immediately head S to Mangkutana and beyond. The price is highly negotiable; anything from Rp6000-13,000. Periodically, you stop to clear the road. South of Mangkutana, the road is sealed so transport prices plummet (Rp2500 to Palopo). Missionary Aviation Fellowship (MAF) has a branch in Tentena. Most flights leave on Mon., and one other day of the week. It's a 5-seater, flown by an American pilot from Alaska. Don't depend on it: the plane may be full, in the shop, or under the weather. From Tentena, a good all-weather road leads N to Poso on the southern shore of Teluk Tomini.

Vicinity of Tentena

Gua Pomona is a natural limestone cave near Tentena, a great place to explore. The cave was once used for burials, and old human bones remain. Birds and bats live inside. Bring a flashlight. The cave is at the start of the Poso River on the W bank, just across the river from the boat dock. From the dock, cross the

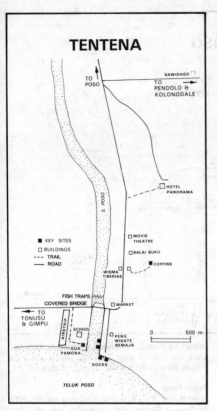

TENTENA

SAWIDAGO

TO POSO

TO PENDOLO & KOLONODALE

S. POSO

HOTEL PANORAMA

■ KEY SITES
□ BUILDINGS
--- TRAIL
— ROAD

□ MOVIE THEATRE

□ BALAI BUKU

■ COFFINS

WISMA TIBERIAS

FISH TRAPS
COVERED BRIDGE

□ MARKET

TO TONUSU & GIMPU

AIRSTRIP

□ SCHOOL

0   500 m

□ PENG WISATE REMAJA

GUA PAMONA

DOCKS

TELUK POSO

long covered bridge (note the elaborate fish traps downstream), turn L before the airstrip, then L again after the school. Other, smaller caves are also found in the limestone hills to the north of town. Old wooden coffins filled with bones are found under a ledge 300 m E of the Balai Buku in Tentena; ask for Peti Mayat. Farther afield, **Kolonodale** is on Tolo Bay on the SE coast of C. Sulawesi. Home for the Mori people, famous for their dancing. From Tentena, vehicles travel the 178-km road in 6 hours. Local boats (try Perintis Lines) depart from Kolonodale for Baturubi and the Morowali Nature Reserve (see details below).

Lake Poso

This lake is the main attraction of the area. Sailing outriggers, canoes, or *prahu motor* can be chartered for trips on the lake and to lakeside villages. Start out early; the afternoon winds make travel rough. *Ikan mas* (carp) from the lake make good eating. The Poso River, however, is not suitable for boating. The

Pamona people who live around Lake Poso are distant relatives of the Torajans of central S. Sulawesi. However, eastern Torajan culture is now extinct around Lake Poso. Dutch missionaries first arrived in the 1880s; now 90% of the populace are Protestant. In the old days, for funeral ceremonies the Pamona made *pemia* masks with handles and a bag of cleaned bones attached. Today, it's not easy to find a *pemia* mask. In fact—except for the enigmatic monoliths near Gintu and one burial cave in Tentena near the *lapangan*—little remains in C. Sulawesi of pre-Christian artifacts.

For Bada Valley

See giant 4½-m stone statues *(patung)* and other huge, free-standing stone megaliths such as 1-m-wide washbasins and some very large wells. Take a *bemo* 12 km W to Tonusu (Rp600), then try to find people walking to Bada. There's a rough road the next 60 km to Gintu; minibuses or jeeps can do it in the dry season for around Rp10,000. Otherwise, this is a beautiful 2- to 3-day walk. Though overgrown in some places, the trail is clearly visible at all times. Watch out for poisonous snakes, giant centipedes, and *anoa*—they attack when encountered! There are no *losmen* or *warung,* so bring a tent and food, or sleep under bridges. (There's one bridgeless river to cross.) Or stay with the *kepala desa.* No English speakers, and except for occasional groups of Germans arriving with a guide from Palu, no tourists. You're completely dependent on the locals for anything you don't have, including information about locating the megaliths, which are deep in the forest or in remote fields. No one knows who constructed them, or why; they were there when the local people arrived. From Bada, follow the same trail 42 km to Tompi, where transportation is available to Palu, Rp6000. Or catch the MAF plane if it's in Tompi, Rp20,000.

POSO

A main port town on the southern shore of Teluk Tomini, with big trees, fragrant flowers, and much greenery. A small military outpost in Dutch times, Poso today serves mostly as a transit point for travelers heading W to Palu or sailing N to Gorontalo in N. Sulawesi Province. Muslim, Catholic, and Protestant people live here. Although fairly spread out, all important places are within walking distance. Change money at **Bank Negara Indonesia** on Jl. Yos Sudarso, about a 30-min. walk N of Peng. Sederhana. The **Telegraph & Telephone office** and **post office,** are 1 block inland from Jl. Sultan Hasanuddin which runs along the harbor. The Poso River is on the W side of town; small outriggers cross the river (Rp200) to the big *pasar* on the other side.

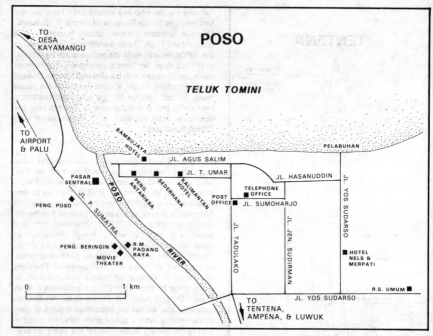

POSO

TELUK TOMINI

TO DESA KAYAMANGU

TO AIRPORT & PALU

PASAR SENTRAL

PENG. POSO

PENG. BERINGIN

MOVIE THEATER

BAMBUJAYA HOTEL

PENG. ANTARIKSA

SEDERHANA

KALIMANTAN HOTEL

POST OFFICE

R.M. PADANG RAYA

JL. P. SUMATRA

POSO RIVER

JL. AGUS SALIM

JL. T. UMAR

JL. HASANUDDIN

TELEPHONE OFFICE

JL. SUMOHARJO

JL. TADULAKO

JL. JEN. SUDIRMAN

JL. YOS SUDARSO

PELABUHAN

HOTEL NELS & MERPATI

JL. YOS SUDARSO

R.S. UMUM

0   1 km

TO TENTENA, AMPENA, & LUWUK

Accommodations And Food

The cheapest places to stay are near the central market (Pasar Sentral) in the western part of town: **Peng. Poso** (Rp2500-4000) and **Peng. Beringin** (Rp3000-5000) are both on Jl. P. Sumatra. Many *warung* also in the area. The town's best hotel is **Bambujaya**, Jl. Agus Salim 101 (Rp6000 Standard, Rp12,5000 a/c), right on the bay and has a restaurant. The street one block inland has 3 places to stay, all with private *mandi* and including meals: **Hotel Kalimantan**, no. 18, Rp5000-10,000; **Sederhana**, no. 32, Rp5000-9000; and **Antariksa**, no. 40, Rp5000-10,000. Also check out **Peng. Sulawesi** (corner of Jl. Imam Bonjol and Jl. Agus Salim) and **Peng. Delie**, both Rp2500 s. Very comfortable is **Hotel Nels**, Jl. Yos Sudarso 9, Rp7000-13,000 (which includes *mandi* and meals). For Padang food, head for **RM Padang Raya** across from **Peng. Beringin**. Other places to eat include **RM Makan Mekar** on Jl. Iman Bonjol and **Warung Lamayan** on Jl. Teluk Umar on the left N of the traffic circle.

Getting There

A good road connects Tentena to Poso, 57 km, 2 hours, Rp2500 by minibus. From Gorontalo, on the S shore of Sulawesi's northern peninsula, *kapal motor*

depart for Poso 2-3 mornings each week, Rp18,500 Deck Class, 2-2½ days. This ship pays a call at the Togian Island's main town, Dolong, en route.

From Poso

Northbound, it's a 6- to 7-hour minibus ride (Rp7500) to Besusu Station, Palu, departing regularly; buy tickets at the *stasiun bis,* agency offices around Pasar Sentral, or at the Merrennu Express office in Peng. Sulawesi. Along parts of this fairly well-surfaced road you might think you're in Bali. Bamboo pole streamers wave over rice *padi,* offerings are laid out on small stands for the gods, and brightly painted temple statues decorate the landscape. These are Balinese *transmigrasi* villages. Poso is also the gateway to the isolated E end of C. Sulawesi. Bus companies at the station sell tickets to: Ampana, 6 hours, Rp8000, along the coast road. Luwuk is 18 hours farther, another Rp22,000. However, the fords at Sungai Bongka (before Ampana) and Sungai Bunto (after Ampana) can be impassable at times, forcing vehicles to wait long hours while the water subsides. Kolonodale is Rp12,500. Southbound, Tentena on Lake Poso is a 2-hour (57 km) minibus ride, Rp2500. From Tentena, motorized outriggers start crossing D. Poso at about 0900 for Pendolo on the S shore of the lake; Rp2500. From Pendolo, ride 4WD vehicles or minibuses via Palopo to Rantepao in Tanatoraja for around Rp16,000.

The major shipping offices and harbor are in the northern part of town. A Pelni vessel (office: on Jl. Pattimura) calls at Poso about every 2 weeks, with stops at Gorontalo, Parigi, Poso, Ampana, Una-Una (Togian Is.), Banggai, Luwuk, Kolonodale, and back again. This one's cheap, but conditions are over-crowded and primitive. Generally, the boat arrives at each port-of-call in the morning, then leaves in the evening. For this and other boats, check several times a day at the pier and at the Syahbandar's office, Jl. Pattimura 3 (tel. 444/446). A good plan is to take the boat to Parigi, then the road to Palu.

Only Merpati (Jl. Yos Sudarso, tel. 368) serves Poso with flights to many points on Sulawesi, as well as Surabaya and Jakarta. Sample fares: Palu, Rp40,800; Saroako, Rp42,800; Ujung Pandang, Rp90,900. Poso's airport is 13 km W at Kasiguncu; Merpati pro-vides a taxi or minibus.

Vicinity Of Poso

Beaches in Poso town are badly trashed; head outside for swimming. Visit the fishing village of Kaya-manya, NW from the market. Good snorkeling is found on reefs off Polande, a 2-hour drive west. Charter a *ketingting* (outboard-powered outrigger) for the ½-hour trip offshore.

Ampana

Ampana is the embarkation point for exploring the Togian Is., which offer good beaches, snorkeling, sea turtles, fishing, and some of the best coral reefs in In-donesia. Pulau Unauna is a small island (pop. 7,500) which was first settled by Bugis people. It has an ac-tive volcano. Ask the local rangers to take you there in 30 min. in their motorized canoe; cheap and they pro-vide lots of info. On the coast between Uwekuli and Ampana live colonies of the amazing megapode birds. South of Ampana in the mountains live the isolated Ta people; this province still has 12,000 unassimilated, isolated tribespeople who have yet to come in to government relocation centers. At Tan-jung Api (means "Fire Cape"), a flame is fed by underground natural gas, a magical spot to the locals. Many Sulawesi macaques can be seen here, as well as deer, pigs, pythons and *babirusa*. Reach the flame by canoe (30-45 min.) from Ampana. It's a beautiful 6-hour drive (by regular minibus) from Ampana along the coast to Luwuk.

Luwuk

A small port on the Peleng Strait on the E end of C. Sulawesi. Good diving in this area. A road SW along the coast passes Hanga-Hanga Waterfall and ends after 1 hour at Batui, where wildlife, including *burung*

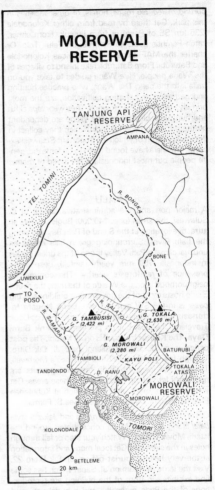

maleo (megapode birds which use natural heat sources to incubate their eggs) can be observed. Con-nected to Luwuk just 3 hours by boat are the Banggai Is. (wonderful beaches, nature walks, snorkeling, fishing) as well as Baturubi (Morowali Nature Reserve).

Morowali Nature Reserve

A 100,000-ha wilderness area, home of the famous Ranu Lakes (or "Moon Lakes"). Five rivers flow through the reserve, 3 of them into long, narrow Tomori Bay. Look for the shy *anoa*, *babirusa*, and burung maleo. No roads, hotels, or other facilities in this park. Get there by road from either Kolonodale (235 km SE of Poso) or from Luwuk. From either, catch Perentis boats to Baturubi on Teluk Tolo. Or charter the MAF plane, which services Kolonodale and Baturubi. From Baturubi, hike inland to villages of the Wana people. Hire Wana guides to take you on trails into the park. The Wana, who practice hunting and gathering and shifting cultivation, are the most primitive people of the province. They wear *tapa* cloth and hunt with blowpipes. The Wana are dependent on the rattan and agathis resin which they collect in the interior, both of which are important Sulawesi exports. Travelers have found them to be fantastic, gentle people but most Indonesians are afraid of them.

PALU

A major port and the administrative capital of C. Sulawesi, this small (pop. 140,000) Bugis city has an attractive location at the S end of Palu Bay and along the Palu River. Surrounding green hills create an unusual climate; Palu Valley is one of the driest places in Indonesia (700 mm yearly rainfall), despite the presence of rainforests nearby. The commercial neighborhood is on the W side of the river; the river's E side hosts most of the government buildings. A big *pasar* is in the SW part of town. **Bank Negara Indonesia** will probably refuse to change Thomas Cook Travelers Cheques, but no problem at **Bank Bumi Daya**. The **Kantor Imigrasi** is on Jl. Kartini. The **post office** is on Jl. Sam Ratulangi near Jl. Cik Ditro. Though few travelers visit this province's Morowali, Tanjung Api, or Lore Lindu reserves, permits are necessary for touring most parts of these areas. Get your *surat ijin*, maps, and information at Kehutanan Propinsi, Kantor Dinas, Jl. Letjen. See S. Parma.

Get around town by catching *bemo* and Jakarta-style *bajai* along Jl. Gajah Mada concentrated around the Istana Movie Theater. Watch your step or fall through holes in the sidewalk. Get local maps and information at the very helpful **tourist office**, Jl. Cik Ditiro 22. Visit the large museum on Jl. Sapiri which has some fine exhibits—in front of the building are reproductions of the Bada megaliths and a burial vat—and houses an impressive library of books in Dutch, English, and Indonesian on the anthropology and archaeology of C. Sulawesi. See Kaili costumes and jewelry, and photos of Easter Island-like stone sculptures and dolmens. The **Gedung Olah Seni** (GONI) building contains exhibits of local arts, dances, and musical instruments. Inquire if any performances are planned.

Accommodations

On Jl. Gajah Mada, the cheapest is **Peng. Latimodjong**, at Rp2500-3500; also try clean and friendly **Hotel Pasifik**, Jl. Gajah Mada 130; Rp3000 s, Rp5000 d, with fan Rp4000, with bath Rp8500.**Peng. Arafah**, just off the main street on Jl. S. Wuno (close to Hotel Pasifik), is Rp3000-5000. On Jl. Imam Bonjol, there's **Peng. Palopo**; Rp1500-3000. Across the river is quiet **Peng. Karsam**, Jl. Dr. Suharso, Rp3000-5000. **Hotel Taurus**, Jl. Hasanuddin (tel. 21567) asks Rp4000 s, Rp6000 d for its small but clean rooms. For a splash, try the **Palu Beach Hotel** right on Jl. S. Parman (10 min. walk from the GPO), tel. 21326/21426. Absolutely 1st Class by Sulawesi standards. They ask Rp28,000 s and Rp30,000 d for their 60 a/c rooms, pool, and restaurant (if working); few guests though, and the beach is too dirty for swimming. Their taxi service takes you to the airport for Rp3000.

Food

No problem locating good eats. Many stalls are set up nightly on Jl. Gajah Mada, and other *warung* and *rumah makan* are found all over town, especially along Jl. S. Aldjufrie and Jl. Wahidin. *Martabak* sellers roll in at night near the bridge along Jl. Hasanuddin. **RM Malabar** (related to the one in Ujung Pandang), Jl. Imam Bonjol 171, offers *martabak, sate,* and curry dishes. **Rainbow Restaurant,** Jl. Hasanuddin 19, features Chinese cuisine. For Padang food, go to **Padang Raya**, Jl. Imam Bonjol 55. Buy imported goodies at a/c **ADA Supermarket,** Jl. Hasanuddin 58.

Entertainment

Cool off during the day in the pool at the Palu Beach Hotel, Rp500, if it has water! Cool off in the evening in the a/c Istana Movie Theatre. Or heat up at night in **Tondo Village,** 4 km N toward Pantoloan, on the left. This officially sponsored nightspot features a bar, music and 300 working girls—Rp8000, negotiable. The Palu Beach Hotel, right on Palu Bay, also has a disco.

Getting There

To reach Palu by road, follow the "From Palu, By Road" section below in reverse. Bouraq makes the long-distance connections to Palu from: Manado, Rp93,000; Ujung Pandang, Rp56,600; Balikpapan, Rp52,900; Jakarta, Rp189,800. Merpati charges Rp59,100 (once daily) from Luwuk or Rp49,200 (twice weekly) from Ujung Pandang. Taxis ask Rp3000 from the airport 7 km into town. Or hitch a ride—the highway is visible.

FROM PALU

By Road

Palu is a major transport hub for C. Sulawesi. Take minibuses from Besusu Station (Jl. Dr. Wahidin) to Parigi and other points N such as Gorontalo and

Manado, to Poso and other points S such as Tentena, Pendolo, Wotu, and Rantepao, also a rough road SE to Wuasa and Sidaunta, a 34-km road NW to Donggala, and a 24-km road to Tawaeli. The road N to Manado (around Rp20,000, 2 days) is especially trying; buy tickets at **PT Popula** near the corner of Jl. Hasanuddin and Jl. Sudirman. A corkscrew highway joins Palu with the Trans-Sulawesi highway at Parigi, 84 km east. In places, this road bears a remarkable resemblance to a walking track, and is quite useless in the wet season. For Poso, buy tickets at **Marrennu Express**, Jl. Hasanuddin 46 (tel. 21868) or PO Sabar Jaya, Jl. Gajah Mada 69 (Rp7500); vehicles depart every day at approximately 1000, arriving even more approximately 6-7 hours later. For Rantepao, buy tickets at **CV Alpit Jaya**, Jl. Gajah Mada 130 (tel. 21168), Rp25,000, 2 days.

By Ship

From the ports of Donggala, Wani, or Pantaloan (all reachable by minibus in under an hour from Palu), you can board *kapal motor* to Toli Toli in N. Sulawesi, Pare Pare in S. Sulawesi, and even to Balikpapan or Tawau in E. Kalimantan. Pantaloan is 25 km, Rp600 (30 min.) by minibus from Jl. Gajah Mada (near Bank Bumi Daya). The small boat harbor of Wani is 2 km beyond Pantaloan. Donggala is 34 km N of Palu on a nice road (Rp1000); catch minibuses on Jl. Imam Bonjol near Bioskop Istana. For more details on the shipping services from each of these harbors, see below. Shipping offices to check in Palu: **PT Surya**, Jl. Gajah Mada 71; **Pelni**, Jl. Gajah Mada 86 (tel. 528), upstairs.

By Air

Bouraq (Jl. Mawar 5 (tel. 21195/22995) flies to: Balikpapan, every day at 0905 and at 0955, Rp52,900; Banjarmasin, every day at 0905, Rp189,100; Gorontalo, each day at 0905 and 0955, Rp98,000; Jakarta, twice daily, Rp189,800; Manado, 10 times weekly, Rp93,000; Surabaya, every day at 0905, Rp164,800; Ternate, every day at 1105, Rp137,900; Ujung Pandang, 10 times weekly, Rp56,600. **Garuda** (Jl. S. Aldjufrie, tel. 21095) also flies to: Jakarta, Rp223,300; Surabaya, Rp144,900; Ujung Pandang, Rp66,600. **Merpati** (Jl. Hasanuddin 33, tel. 21295) does the short hops (Poso, Rp35,900, twice weekly; Luwuk, at the eastern tip of the province, Rp62,400). MAF also flies to their base in Tentena (Lake Poso) once a week. Airport tax, Rp1000. The Mutiara Airport is 7 km SE of Palu, reachable by *bemo* if you get an early enough start. More reliable is to charter a *bajai* or *bemo*, around Rp2000 after brisk bargaining.

VICINITY OF PALU

Pantaloan

The main port for Palu to the NE, a small (pop. 6,000) picturesque town with just 2 *rumah makan*. Allow 10 min. to walk through it. Board a minibus for Pantaloan near Palu's Bioskop Istana for the 30-min., Rp600 *bemo* ride. For ships to E. Kalimantan, inquire at shipping offices like Pelni's and at Kantor Syahbandar along Pantaloan's harborfront. Pelni's sleek KM *Kambuna* calls at Pantaloan en route to ports on Sulawesi and Kalimantan. Sample Deck Class fares: Toli Toli, Rp13,000; Tarakan, Rp17,500; Balikpapan, Rp15,000; Ujung Pandang, Rp18,500; Surabaya, Rp33,500.

Wani Harbor (means "bees" in the local Kaili dialect) is a small port 2 km beyond Pantaloan; Rp600 (40 min.) by minibus from Palu. See fat-hulled Bugis *prahu* being built here. Wani's shipwrights can finish the job in 2-3 months, some living in nothing but thatch huts on the beach. There's no *losmen*, but you can stay as a paying guest with a family. From Wani, catch a minibus to Pantaloan, Rp200. Small *kapal layar* depart regularly for Donggala across the bay (Rp1000, 3 hours). Daily motorboats to: Balaesong (S of Sabang on the N coast), Rp10,000, 6 hours; Toli Toli (Rp15,000); Kwandang (Rp20,500) and Manado (Rp25,000) in N. Sulawesi; Samarinda (Rp17,500) in E. Kalimantan. For other boat departures, inquire in the offices of **CV Sumber Indah** or **CV Selamat Bahari**; everyone knows where they are.

Lore Lindu

This park SE of Palu, the biggest in Sulawesi, consists of a large beautiful highland lake and heavily forested mountains. Get info at the PPA office on Jl. S. Parman in Palu. For Lake Lindu, you can approach from the E by traveling 3 hours by road from Palu to Wuasa on the eastern boundary of the park. Or from Palu take a minibus S by road S to **Sidaunta** (just N of Toro). Then walk 4 hours E on a good trail to the lake; no permit needed. Outstanding campsites along the rivers, but don't go swimming or drink untreated water because this lake is one of the only places in SE Asia with the blood fluke disease bilharzia. A *pondok* shelter (roof and raised floor) is at **Ranorano**; ask permission at the PPA's Palu office. It can get chilly, so bring blankets or a sleeping bag. **Gunung Nokilalaki** (elev. 2,355 m) is near the lake; climbing permit needed. For the starting point and guides, ask at Desa Rachmat on Jl. Japon. The climb takes 12 hours up and 5 down; no trail to the summit. The usual method is to climb up 1 day and camp. Next morning make the summit—eerie moss forests near the top—then return to the road. Head S for the **Marena Hotsprings**, and a World Wildlife Fund resthouse (walk 10 min. E from the road S of Toro). It's possible to walk across the park from Sidaunta to Wuasa via D. Lindu in about 3 days. At the southern end of the park are the Besoa and Bada valleys where ancient water cisterns and megaliths are found; see also "Vicinity of Tentena."

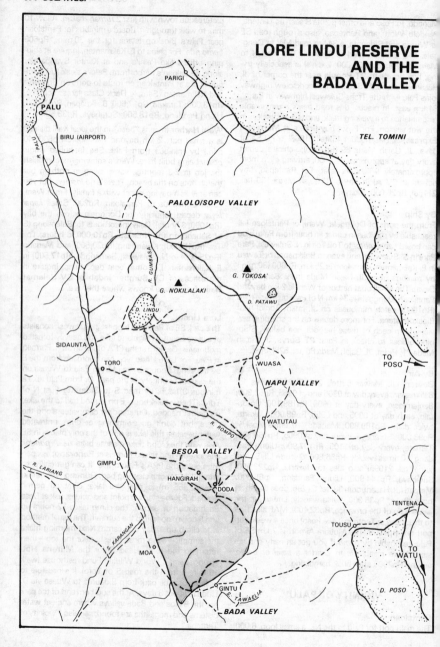

LORE LINDU RESERVE AND THE BADA VALLEY

PALU

R. PALU

BIRU (AIRPORT)

PARIGI

TEL. TOMINI

PALOLO/SOPU VALLEY

R. GUMBASA

G. TOKOSA

G. NOKILALAKI

D. PATAWU

D. LINDU

SIDAUNTA

TORO

WUASA

TO POSO

NAPU VALLEY

WATUTAU

R. ROMPO

BESOA VALLEY

GIMPU

HANGIRAH

DODA

R. LARIANG

TENTENA

TOUSU

TO WATU

MOA

S. KARANGAN

GINTU

S. TAWAELIA

D. POSO

BADA VALLEY

The Besoa Wells And Bada Man
On this trip, see giant stone statues and other huge free-standing stone megaliths. Indulge your fantasy of being an amateur archaeologist! First travel 5 hours by minibus 99 km S of Palu to Gimpu, the end of the road. Gimpu's *kepala desa* will arrange a guestroom for the night. The next day, negotiate for a guide and perhaps a packhorse with a bark saddle. From Gimpu, the Besoa Valley is 1 day's walk to the east. This valley is famed for its 10 strange monuments which look like wells but are not deep enough to have held water. They are made of gray stone, though there is no trace of rock anywhere. The largest is over 1 m high and 1.5 m deep; a few have covers nearly 2 m wide. Real archaeologists have speculated that the wells of Besoa were actually treasuries or tombs.

Another route from Gimpu leads S to Moa and on to Gintu in the Bada Valley. In the morning, the trail leads through a magic land of forests, stately trees, and giant tropical ferns. In the afternoon, the trail narrows and climbs up the side of a mountain, following the course of the mighty Karanganan River below. By evening you arrive in Moa, with its thatched houses, bright poinsettias, coffee and fruit gardens, and steepled church. The *kepala desa* will put you up; bathe in the river. This is an area where men still hunt wild pigs with spears, women pound rice in hollow tree trunk mortars, and bark clothing is still worn. Early the next morning, walk hard another day over a mountain to the Bada Valley with its sleepy villages, irrigation canals, and wobbly suspension bridges. After crossing an unpopulated plateau, you reach the village of Gintu, site of the cryptic Bada Man. Children will lead you across the Tawaelia River on a bamboo raft; on the other side you'll catch the outline of the giant stone sculpture in a meadow surrounded by hills like a natural amphitheater. The impact of the legless megalith is derived from its simplicity, size, and symbols—upright penis, faint slit mouth, flared nose, round stone eyes, high forehead, topknot.

Another approach is to drive from Palu to Wuasa, then walk 2 days S to Gintu. Organized groups visit Bada, Besoa, and Lake Poso from Palu; for details see Budi Tumewu, owner of Hotel Viscana, Jl. Pattimura 57, Palu (tel. 21375). **Pacto Ltd.** does a "Megaliths of Central Sulawesi" tour (6 days, 5 nights) for around US$700 (2 people), US$529 (3 people), US$434 (4-6 people); inquire at their office at Jl. Jen. Sudirman 56 (tel. 83208), Ujung Pandang. The Bada Valley can also be approached from Tentena; see "Vicinity of Tentena."

DONGGALA

This sleepy port was once the largest and most important settlement in C. Sulawesi. A *kraton* and Dutch residency house here were destroyed by Japanese bombers in WW II. In the 1950s, the surrounding hills were used by guerrillas fighting Indonesian government soldiers. Over the years, Donggala's harbor silted up so only small boats could use the port; most shipping switched to Pantaloan Harbor on the other side of the bay, and Palu became the provincial capital. Donggala is small and friendly, a pleasant place to spend a few days. Most travelers come here to catch boats to the southern or northern ports of Sulawesi.

Accommodations And Food
Penginapan Anda, though central (movie house down the street), is very basic; Rp2500 s. You fall through the floorboards, and kids peer up at you from under the building. Nearby is **Wisma Bakti** (Rp3000-4000), clean and quiet, Chinese-run. Or try **Peng. Bruri** just after the bridge into town from Palu, go L (about 1½ km from the harbor); Rp2500 s. A clean, comfortable, family-run place is **Wisma Donggala**, Rp3500 d, Rp4000 t, meals extra. For its size, the fruit and vegetable market is incredibly well stocked; open every day. Superkitsch **Toko 39** has lots of everything—try their hot Quaker Oats drink. For Chinese food, head for **RM Gembira** or **RM Dinda** where one *cap cai kua* is enough for two. Papaya, jackfruit, bananas in the market.

Transport
Minibuses for Donggala leave Palu often from along Jl. Imam Bonjol (near Bioskop Istana); Rp850 for the 34-km *bemo* ride over a winding all-weather coastal road, passing villages on stilts and night fishermen. Shared taxis cost Rp1200 pp (35 min.) for this run. From Donggala, small *kapal motor* embark N to Toli Toli, Rp12,500, 24 hours; S to Pare Pare (from where you can catch buses to Ujung Pandang, Rp12,500, 48 hours; W to E. Kalimantan (Samarinda, Balikpapan, or Tarakan). Ask at Donggala's *syahbandar's* office on the waterfront. It's also possible to board *kapal layar* for Sulawesi ports, or charter *prahu sunde* for inexpensive sightseeing, fishing, or crossing over to Pantaloan. Along the W coast, a road N leads to Sabang, 155 km. Gorontalo, N. Sulawesi, is 2 days by road, around Rp20,000 (meals included).

Vicinity Of Donggala
Climb **Bale Hill** for a good view of Donggala's harbor, full of sleek sailing vessels; there's a tiny village on top. For **Tanjung Karang Beach**, walk N 3 km (30 min.) along a rocky road. At the "Y" intersection, bear R and walk for 30 min. down to this long beach with beautiful white sand, waving *kelapa*, excellent snorkeling. There's a fishing village here, very relaxing. Take a *bemo* (Rp300) from Donggala and visit the villages of **Towaeli** and **Bonoge**.

NORTH SULAWESI

A beautiful land of vast coconut and clove planta-tions, active volcanos, lakes, hotsprings, ancient burial sites, picturesque villages, white-sand coral islands, and outstanding snorkeling and diving. Sula-wesi Utara, with an area of 27,515 sq km, lies on a nar-row peninsula over 772 km long by 103 km wide. To one side is the Maluku Sea with its gulfs of Tomini and Gorontalo. Along this peninsula are 6 extinct vol-canos, each towering 1,800-2,400 m. Two volcanos overlook Manado, but most of the time they're covered in clouds. Rich volcanic ash has blessed N. Sulawesi with extremely fertile land, and in the thinly populated narrow lowlands and valleys the area has been very successful agriculturally, producing rice, vanilla, nutmeg, corn, coconut palms, and cloves. Forest products include rattan, ebony, resins and gums. Valuable *cingke* (cloves — also known as "golden trees") are grown everywhere. Land not cultivated with this Christmas tree-like spice tree is planted with coconut palms for copra. This is the largest copra production area of Indonesia (18,000 tons exported per month). Everyone — including teachers, bankers and army colonels — tends his plot of coconut palms after hours.

The population of nearly 2.6 million is comprised of an ethnic mix of peoples from mainland SE Asia, In-donesia, the Philippines, and the colonial countries of Spain, Portugal, and the Netherlands. A heavily in-dustrialized province, Sulawesi Utara has a higher standard of living than most other regions of In-donesia. In fact, this very wealthy province even feels like a separate republic. And its geographic isolation from the rest of Indonesia, and its rebellious history, confirm this impression. The dry season is May to Oct., rainy season, Nov. to April. So near the equator is the Minahasan peninsula that telephone poles cast no shadows at noon.

History

Legends say that the original Minahasan tribe was divided by the god Muntu Untu at a huge boulder called Batu Pinabetengan (in the Tondano area). At Manado's intersections you'll notice numerous statues of ferocious, legendary warriors who once guarded the city. Portuguese traders were the first Westerners to arrive, as early as 1563. At Amurang are the remains of the fort the Portuguese built; they also used Manado Tua off the coast as a base. The Spaniards were next on the scene, converting the population to Catholicism and introducing horses. In

the mid-17th C., the Dutch were called by the Mina-hasans to help them expel the Spaniards. The Dutch proceeded to build a wooden fort in Manado in 1657, and the Spanish were driven out within 3 years. From 1679 until Indonesian independence 270 years later, the Sulawesi spice trade was monopolized by the Dutch. In the words of Alfred Russel Wallace, in the early part of the 19th C. this area was "a wilderness, the people naked savages, garnishing their rude houses with human heads." Then Dutch planters in the early 1800s started cultivating coffee here and the Minahasans began to make spectacular "progress" as agriculturalists. Because of the closeness of its religious, military, and economic ties with the colonial power, Minahasa soon became known as the "12th Province of Holland." The Minahasans even supplied mercenary troops for the colonial army, helping the Dutch quell indigenous anti-colonial revolts on other islands, earning the Minahasans the contempt of other Indonesians who called them *Anjing Belanda* ("Dutch Dogs").

During WW II, the Japanese occupied the region from Jan. 1942 to Aug. 1945, and Manado was heavi-ly damaged by Allied bombs in 1945. The Japanese left behind extensive cave systems (near Tondano, Kawangkoan, and Tomohon) where ammunition, medical supplies, food and weapons were stored. In the late 1950s, tensions between Jakarta and the Outer Islands increased in proportion to Sukarno's anti-parliamentarianism. Vice-President Hatta's resignation in December 1956 worsened the situa-tion. Finally, in early 1958, regionalist forces of N. Sulawesi seceded from the republic and established a government of their own. Finding common cause with the Revolutionary Government of the Republic of Indonesia (PRRI) established in West Sumatra, the so-called Permesta insurgents of N. Sulawesi de-manded greater regional autonomy and a more just distribution of national wealth. Sukarno charged that the rebels received American aid, which soured rela-tions with the U.S. and encouraged Sukarno to de-velop closer relations with China and the Soviet Union. By the end of July, however, the brief rebellion was crushed, except for guerilla activity in the moun-tains which lasted until mid-1961. The rebellion had several important consequences for North Sulawesi: Sukarno's hand was considerably strengthened, ushering in the era of Guided Democracy; officers from the armed forces were forced into retirement, making the officer corps more Javanese; Jakarta's central military authority was firmly established in the Outer Islands. The people here are still forced to grow food crops to supply Java.

The People

The Minahasans, the largest component of N. Sulawesi's population, are a polite and gracious people. They were appreciated by the Dutch for their administrative abilities, Protestant work ethic, soldiering, maritime skills, and as teachers. There is still a considerable Eurasian admixture in the population, and the Minahasan region is virtually 100% Christian. Strong historical and cultural ties to the Philippines are also evident, the area having been partly settled from the north, and the 2 Minahasan dialects are related to Filipino languages. This far northern peninsula, together with the Sangir-Talaud archipelagos, forms a natural bridge to the Philippines, which has provided for the movement of people and cultural traits back and forth.

Christian Minahasans are especially hospitable to Westerners. Their houses reflect European tastes with rose bushes out front, surrounded by spathodea trees in full bloom; hibiscus, bougainvillea, citrus and gardens bright with flowers. Window sills and porch railings are lined with potted plants; garden and yard vegetation is lavishly tended. Other distinct groups of Sulawesi include the Gorontalo of the Gorontalo plain between Bolaang Mongondow and Toli Toli, virtually all Muslim, and the peoples of the Sangihe and Talaud islands N of Minahasa.

Religion

In the 1820s, Dutch colonialism brought in its wake overbearing reformist Protestants who began missionary work. By 1860, nearly the entire population had been converted. By virtue of education in Christian and Dutch schools, established very early in comparison to the rest of Indonesia, the Minahasans and Manadenese were widely employed in the Dutch civil service and colonial army prior to independence in 1950. Today, N. Sulawesi Province is the most heavily Christianized province in Indonesia, that religion followed by 90-95% of the population, of which 15-20% are Catholic, the remainder Protestant. The excellent education system in place here can be attributed to the intense competition among the different church schools, plus a lot of church money. The Minahasans take Christianity just as seriously as the Makassarese and Bugis practice Islam in the south. Christmas is celebrated joyfully and with great pageantry in Manado and surrounding areas.

Waruga

Dating from the 10th C. (but mostly from the 17th C. and later), stone graves *(waruga)* were built to contain bodies in a sitting position; some may have contained a number of corpses. The Minahasans' pre-Christian belief was that the human baby is born in this sitting position in the mother's womb, and in this position he must pass on to eternity. Looking like miniature Chinese temples, the largest *waruga* are less than 3 m tall. Engravings on the headstones depict the cause of death, the deceased's hobby, character, and occupation. These include a woman giving birth, hunters, families, respected officials, children pulling a man's ears, and fighting cocks. Originally, each family had its own burial ground, but since 1817 the local government has ensured that all *waruga* are gathered in one communal burial ground. This was for reasons of health and also for protection against grave robbers. When a person died it was usual for him to take with him his earthly riches. See *waruga* at Airmadidi (19 km SE of Manado) and at Sawangan (6 km from Airmadidi).

Waruga, *Airmadidi.*
Waruga *were once common all over Minahasa but with the spread of Christianity, they were either destroyed or forgotten.*

Music, Dance And Crafts

The end of the harvest *(panen)* — from Oct.-May. — is the festive season when thanksgiving celebrations *(pengucapan)* are held all over Minahasa. There is pre-Christian dancing, conch-shell jug bands, as well as performances of the mesmerizing wooden xylophonic *kolintang* orchestra, as exciting a sound as the wildest Jamaican blue beat. In the villages, the music usually takes place on Sundays. The *Maengket* is a typical Minahasan cultural dance consisting of 3 styles: *Owey Kemberu,* performed during harvest time; the *Marambak* staged at the inauguration of a newly built house; and the *Lalayaan,* performed at a party when a man announces his fiance. Buy tapes of traditional music *(kolintang)* at **Toko Terang** on Jl. Pierre Tendean, Manado. Traditional dances can be chartered in Tara Tara, 40 km from Manado or 15 km from Tomohon (Rp400 by *oplet)* for around Rp50,000.

The Minahasans are not that adept at handicrafts. "Maybe because the Lord gave us cloves" is one explanation offered. Basketry is an active craft, and the Sangir Group is known for its woodcarving such as ebony galleons. From the Bolaang Mongondow district comes Karawang cross-stitch fabrics and garment. (The Guam flight has been discontinued) In Manado, you'll find antiques, clothes, kitchenware, woodcarvings, local coffee and vanilla, and even carved wooden beds ready to dismantle and ship back home.

Events

On 23 Sept., the anniversary (in 1964) of the official establishment of N. Sulawesi Province is celebrated throughout the province. In Manado, there are costume shows and cultural performances, as well as horse racing and bull racing. Don't miss the Chinese Taoist festival of *Tai Pei Kong* in Manado which is held 2 weeks after the lunar New Year. Although this celebration has been greatly reduced in size and splendor due to restrictions imposed by the local government, it remains the largest of its kind in SE Asia. The festival dates to a time more than 200 years ago when a small band of Chinese settlers, braving rough seas, arrived in Manado's harbor with their swords, daggers, and effigies.

Food

Minahasans enjoy their own rather spicy cuisine. Enormous goldfish *(ikan mas)* are served at special roadside restaurants built out over fishponds surrounded by lotus blossoms. A kitchen hand catches the live fish, which is then served spiced and glowing a rich golden-brown (eat *ikan mas* slowly as there are many sharp bones). Another delicacy of the region are papaya leaves; the fruit itself is fed to the pigs, but the leaves are served up as cooked greens. Other regional dishes include: *kawaok* (fried field rats), *rintek wuuk* (spiced dog), *kelalawar pangang* (bat stew), and

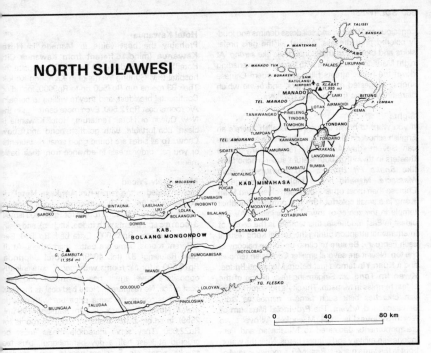

NORTH SULAWESI

tinoransak (a pork dish). Out in the small towns, restaurants specializing in Minahasan cooking are the best and cheapest places to sample these flavorful delicacies.

Getting There

Access from the Philippines is prohibited, and Garuda inexplicably cancelled their intriguing flight from Guam in early 1988. Coming up from the S, it's possible to travel by road now from Parigi, C. Sulawesi, onto the N. Sulawesi peninsula, then up to Manado via Gorontalo. However, this approach is still quite challenging. Easier is to fly from Palu to Gorontalo and

travel the remaining 520 km overland to Manado. Or fly from Gorontalo to Manado with Bouraq (Rp42,800), or fly directly from Palu to Manado (Bouraq, Rp93,000). Make Manado your base of operations. Yet another way is to cross Teluk Tomini via the Togian Is. by boat from Poso, Ampana, or other small towns along the western peninsula of C. Sulawesi to Gorontalo on the southern coast of N. Sulawesi. One can also take kapal motor or kapal layar from Palu's Wani or Pantaloan harbors to such northern peninsula ports as Toli Toli, Leol (a port near Toli Toli), Kwandang, and even as far as Manado. See appropriate sections for more detailed information.

MANADO

The capital of N. Sulawesi Province, this port city of 265,000 people is prosperous, progressive, and Protestant. Right away you'll notice the lack of sharp class distinctions—most everyone is middle class, and there's little evidence of extreme poverty here. This is modern, upwardly mobile Indonesia—one of the most Westernized cities in Indonesia—and it's pleasant to see after all the squalor of the major islands. Although the city is built on gentle hills sloping down to a beautiful bay, with high mountains and a volcano in the background, Manado holds little of

interest to the visitor; there are no historical sights, no cultural centers or museums of note, and no nightlife. But this might change. It was a big day for group tourism to Manado when Garuda flights from Guam were inaugurated in 1986; Guam travel agents even sold packages of 6 nights and 7 days for US$523. Why Garuda discontinued this service is one of the great mysteries of life. With the gross exception of the waterfront, the city is clean and tidy, and there is a reasonable selection of hotel accommodations and restaurants available. The shops are quite Western-conscious and trendy, and sell dress denims and loudly colored print dresses. Almost all the girls prefer skirts and blouses to traditional dress like *sarung*. At night Manado comes alive with throngs promenading down the hectic streets filled with modern Chinese shops, congested movie theaters, and *bemo* which blare tinny music from outside speakers.

Sights

If you want to brush up on your English, there's an English school on Jl. Walanda Maramis where American Seventh-day Adventists teach. Many movie theaters in town (Rp1000) feature super-macho films like *Snake Pit Horrors* and *Kommando Raid Massacre*. Manado has a higher percentage of Chinese than most other Indonesian cities. **Ban Hian Kong** is a small colorful 19th C. Confucian-Buddhist temple in the center of town (Jl. Panjaitan 7A). The oldest in East Indonesia, this temple is the center of international attention during the Tai Pei Kong festival each February. Be sure to climb up to the balcony at the top. Near it are several smaller Confucian temples and a **Kuan Yin** temple just before Megawati Bridge. **Kwan Im Tong**, Jl. Singamangaraja, is one of the oldest temples in Manado. The city's numerous Christian churches bear such familiar names as Zion, Bethesda, and Advent. The **Provincial Museum of North Sulawesi** is on Jl. Maengket. All over town are monuments dedicated to Minahasan and Pan-Indonesian military and cultural heros. Near the waterfront is the large market, **Pasar 45,** a motley sprawl of semi-permanent shops (also a *bemo* station). Visit **Jenki fish market** by the river.

ACCOMMODATIONS

Cheapest is **Peng. Keluarga**, Jl. Singkil by the bridge—Rp1500 s, Rp3500 d, with a balcony overlooking the busy street—a very central place popular with travelers but almost never empty. A little better, down a few doors, is **Losmen Kotamobagu** (Rp2500 s, Rp5000 d) but also usually full. Superior to either of these is the **Flamboyan** in between, over RM Flamboyan, which offers a quite adequate but basic row of rooms for Rp2500 s, Rp5000 d. Friendly people, good eats downstairs, and balcony over the rather noisy street. **Hotel Tenterum**, Jl. Sarapung 8 (tel. 3127) is a family-style hotel with lots of atmosphere near the center of town; Rp5000 s, Rp10,000 d. This is Manado's oldest existing hotel; it was founded in 1947 and before that was a Dutch hotel. Jeanne is a nice lady. No meals served, unless special ordered. Rooms in front are bigger but noisier. Lots of taxis and *oplet* in front, and the Garuda office is just up the street. At Jl. Yos. Sudarso 103 (tel. 3454) is the **Ahlan City Hotel;** 12 Economy Class rooms go for Rp8250 but outside *mandi;* rooms with *mandi*, Rp12,000-13,000. A well-run place, secure, clean sheets.

Hotel Kawanua

Probably the best value in Manado is **Hotel Kawanua** (mind, different from Kawanua City Hotel!), Jl. Yos. Sudarso 40 (tel. 3842), opposite the hospital (RM Gunung Wenang) in Kampung Kodok. Their 33 rooms run Rp7500 up to Rp9000, including Continental breakfast, and they're willing to bargain. A/c rooms cost Rp12,500. Even more central than the New Queen or Hotel Tenterum, Hotel Kawanua is clean, comfortable, with goldfish pond and Chow Chow. To all sides are found good small restaurants or you can order meals in advance from their basic menu.

Moderately Priced

Higher priced is the family-run **Angkasa Hotel**, Jl. Soegiono 2A (tel. 2039), with commodious standard rooms for Rp16,000, suite rooms for Rp25,000 (small 3-room a/c apartments with fridge, kitchen), and really big suite rooms, Rp35,000. Extra bed: Rp3500. See different rooms; some are better than others. At Jl. Sam Ratulangi 37 (tel. 4049) is **Hotel Jeprinda**, Rp16,500 s for a/c rooms with *mandi*, conveniently opposite a travel agent, near downtown and main post office. No restaurant. Not a bad deal as the New Queen has rooms for same price but with outside *mandi*. **Hotel Minahasa**, Jl. Sam Ratulangi 199 (tel. 2559), in an old Dutch mansion, rents a/c rooms for Rp22,000. They serve incredible meals (must be ordered at least half a day beforehand), plus tea snacks, *zirzak*, etc. Excellent people, good service. **Hotel Ricardo,** perched on a hill a short way from city center, is in the Rp20,000-45,000 range. If you have reservations, they provide free transport from the airport.

High Priced

Manado's number one and the city's only 3-star hotel is the **Kawanua City Hotel**, Jl. Sam Ratulangi 1 (tel. 52222), in the center of town near the business district. With central a/c, elevators, 2 restaurants, lounge, travel agent, shops, large swimming pool, American breakfasts, and sanitized toilet seats, they are trying very hard to be a Holiday Inn—and nearly succeeding. Patronized by Guamian, German, Japanese, and Singaporean tourists, they charge Rp44,530 s before discount. Read newspapers and relax in the a/c lobby. The pool is open 0600-1800. All credit cards accepted. The **New Queen Hotel** is a small "big" hotel, very service-oriented and efficient; Rp16,500 s, Rp23,100 for standard, all the way up to Rp39,600 d for superior, plus Rp49,500 d for superior, plus 21% service and government tax. Credit cards accepted. Good restaurant (but bad coffee), and they overcharge a bit for laundry. Garuda pilots and stewardesses stay here. From the roof there's a sweeping view over the whole neighborhood and the ocean. Also check out the **Garden Hotel**, Jl. Supratman 1 (tel. 51688/52688); US$15 s, US$18 d for stan-

1. Terminal Calaca
2. Warung Vendje
3. Pasar 45
4. Kawanua City Hotel
5. Gunung Wenang Hospital
6. Angkasa Hotel
7. Wisma Mustika
8. Ahlan City Hotel
9. Terminal Paal 2
10. Pelni office
11. Hotel Kawanua
13. Garuda office
14. post office
15. Bouraq office
16. telephone office
17. Hotel New Queen
18. Merpati office
19. Wisma Minahasa
20. tourist office
21. immigration office
22. terminal for buses to Gorontalo, Palu, Poso, etc.

MANADO

TELUK MANADO

NOT TO SCALE

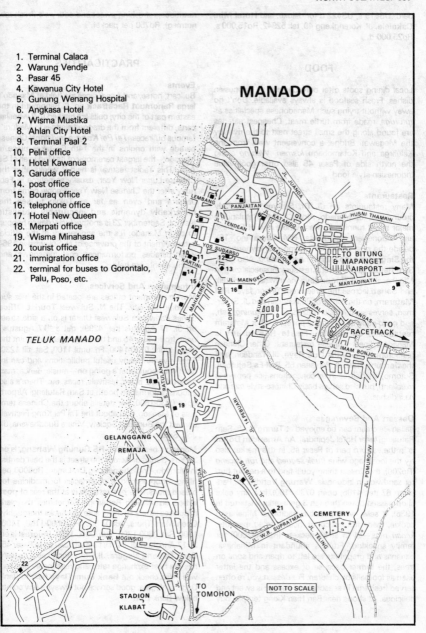

dard, US$19 s, US$22 d for deluxe; and **Hotel Mini Cakalele**, Jl. Korengkeng 40, tel. 52942; Rp15,000 s, Rp25,000 d.

FOOD

Local dining spots offer only Chinese or Indonesian dishes. Fresh seafood is always available. Don't go away without trying such Manadonese specialties as *tuturuga*, made from turtle meat. Cheapest eateries are found along the small street next to the river by the Megawati Bridge, a convenient walk from the Keluarga and Kotamobagu *losmen*. *Warung* along the north side of Pasar 45 also offer good-value Indonesian-style food.

Restaurants

Many restaurants on Jl. Dr. Sutomo, particularly around Bioskop Manado. Along Jl. Sam Ratulangi, a major street running S, are a whole row of Chinese and Indonesian restaurants: **RM Surya** (no. 16), beside the post office, for a filling *nasi campur;* and the **Singgalang** (no. 127) for *nasi padang.* Also on Jl. Sam Ratulangi are several restaurants specializing in Minahasan food: **Tinoor Jaya** (near Minahasa Hotel), and **Sehati** (across the street from Tinoor Jaya). **RM Mataram**, on the corner of Jl. Tendean and Jl. S. Parman, serves such Muslim dishes as *nasi kuning*, fish, and *gado-gado* at *very good* prices; 2 other Mataram restaurants are nearby. **Fiesta Restaurant** is Manado's finest Chinese restaurant. Other Chinese restaurants include the **Due Raya**, Jl. Tandean; and the **Jantung Hati**, Jl. Panjaitan 55. **RM Es Sejuk**, Jl. Sutomo, specializes in *es* concoctions (ice papaya is excellent), but also serves basis Chinese-style *mie* and *nasi* dishes.

Dessert And Beverages

Italian ice cream can be enjoyed at **Turing** on Jl. Sam Ratulangi (near Hotel Jepindra). An **American Donat** is in the eastern part of Pasar 45. In this market also try the local sago wine *(tuak saguer)* and *roti kacang* (Rp200), the closest thing you'll find to a peanut butter sandwich in Indonesia. **Warung Vendje**, Jl. Panjaitan 67 (tel. 4105, open 0730-2100), is a tiny cake shop passed down through 3 generations (started in 1936). It sells every possible traditional Minahasan cookie, made from coconut, rice, nutmeg, peanuts, *kenari* nuts—all in small packets (Rp400-2000) for family snacking. Fruit is abundant in Minahasa; bananas and grapefuits are left to ripen and spoil on trees, the former because of excess and the latter used as footballs by children. For dessert you're often served fresh fruit in season; local papaya is sweet and delicious. At shops near Ban Hian Kiong temple, buy nutritious, refreshing sweet and sour *pala* (fresh raw nutmeg), Rp750 per packet.

PRACTICALITIES

Events

Bullcart, horse, and *bendi* races are held at Manado's large **Ranomuut Racetrack** on Jl. Ranomuut in the eastern part of the city; bulls are hitched to 2-wheeled carts, different from the dragged sledges in Madura's famous bullraces. *Tai Pei Kong*, a traditional Chinese parade with origins in the 14th C., takes place in Manado—the largest ceremony of its kind in all of SE Asia. This Taoist festival is held 2 weeks after the Chinese Lunar New Year, usually sometime in February after the Chinese New Year. People come from Jakarta and even as far as Tokyo to see this remarkably dynamic and inscrutably ritualistic festival. September 23 is another lucky day to happen to be in Manado: it's the anniversary of the official establishment of the province of N. Sulawesi in 1964 when parades, performances, costume shows, and racing events are held.

Information And Services

Most government offices are located in the hills surrounding the city. The N. Sulawesi **Tourist Office** (Dinas Pariwisata Sulawesi Utara) is on a side street off Jl. 17 Agustus (tel. 4299); get a "17 Agustus" *oplet* from Pasar 45 and the passengers will point the way. Hours: 0700-1400, Fri. until 1100, Sat. till 1230. They give out many useful publications and can inform you about what's going on—music, dance, martial art shows, plays, festivals, races, etc. There's also a tourist information booth at Sam Ratulangi Airport, open 0830-1600. For details about the Chinese temples of Manado, and about the Tai Pei Kong Festival, contact the Buddhist Society, Vihara Buddhayana, Jl. Jos. Sudarso 8.

Manado's best hospital, **RS Gunung Wenang**, is on Jl. Yos. Sudarso. Across the street is the best dentist in Manado, English-speaking Dr. Limen; Rp6000 per filling. Shop around at pharmacies for medicine for prescriptions. The *pos restante* is at the rear of **post office** on Jl. Sam Ratulangi. Sometimes the clerk misplaces letters so make sure he checks thoroughly. Open Mon.-Thurs. 0800-1600, Fri. 0800-1100, 1400-1600, Sat. 0800-1300, Sun. 0800-1200. **Imigrasi** is on Jl. 17 Agustus (tel. 3491); take an *oplet* from Pasar 45. **Bank Dagang Negara**, Jl. Dotulolong Lasut, usually has the best exchange rates and reasonably fast service. Also check out **Bank Bumi Daya** next to Bank Dagang Negara; good service but always a few points below Bank BDI.

TRANSPORT

Getting There

Although the Trans-Sulawesi Highway has been "completed," it's difficult to connect by road to the far NE tip of this long, thin, rugged peninsula. By bus from Palu (W coast of C. Sulawesi), it's around Rp25,000 (2 days) to Manado; from Gorontalo, it's Rp8,500 (18 hours). If you approach by ship and dock at the large port of Bitung, 46 km E of Manado, get a *bis umum* to Manado, Rp800. For airfares to Manado, see "From Manado" below. Always check first with Bouraq, as they provide the widest range of cheap fares from Jakarta, Ternate, Kalimantan, Palu, and Ujung Pandang. Mandala has a cheap flight from Surabaya to Manado for only Rp167,000. Garuda's direct flight from Guam has been tragically put to death. In May 1987, flights were initiated from Darwin (Australia) to Kupang, Ujung Pandang, and Manado twice weekly. Arriving by air, Sam Ratulangi Airport is 15 km from Manado in Mapanget, Rp250 by *oplet* or Rp5000 fixed price by taxi (20 min.) to town. Taufik Moki, a very helpful man in charge of the airport tourist info office (open 0800-1630), gives out pamphlets and free color postcards.

Getting Around

No *becak* in Manado. What are called *"bemo"* in other places are called *"oplet"* here. Swarms of them (Rp150) run frequently to and from Pasar 45, Manado's main *oplet* station. Terminal Paal Dua, near the corner of Jl. Sudirman and Jl. Martadinata, is another busy station for *oplet;* this is the terminal for Bitung. *Bendi* are little horse-drawn carts that carry passengers and goods around town; you might think you're in New Orleans! Hire one for Rp150-200 for short rides within the city, Rp100-250 outside the city, or charter one for Rp3500-4000 per hour. If you're short on time (and long on *rupiah),* charter a taxi (minimum: 3 hours) for Rp3000 per hour (Rp3500-4000 with a/c) and hit all the nearby hotspots: Airmadidi, Bitung, Lake Tondano, Tomohon, Tinoor, and back to Manado, about 5-6 hours RT.

A private tour guide, F.F. Ticoalu (or just "Mr. Tico" for short) can be contacted through the tourist office, Kawanua City Hotel, or Pola Pelita Tours & Travel (Jl. Sam Ratulangi 113). Tico does private tours of Manado, charging from US$5 to US$12 per day, depending upon length and complexity. He'll show you letters from satisfied clients who vouch for his honesty and reliability. Sooner or later you'll run into the energetic and irrepressible Mr. Tico!

FROM MANADO

By Road

For destinations in Minahasa and northern Sulawesi, there are 3 bus stations in Manado, which are also collection points for minibuses and *oplet.* From the Terminal Calaca (N of Pasar 45) on Jl. Sisingamangaraja, board *oplet* for the airport (Rp250, 30 min.), and for Airmadidi (Rp350), or by bus to Bitung (Rp800). Terminal Paal-Paal is at the end of Jl. Martadinata, with buses to: Bitung (Rp800), Likupang (Rp800), Kemo (Rp550), and many other easterly destinations. From the Karombasan Terminal, board *oplet* to: Kotamobagu (Rp3500, 4 hours), Tondano (Rp600), Tomohon (Rp450), Kawangkoan (Rp700), Belang (Rp1400), Amurang (Rp1400), and Inobonto (Rp2500). For Gotontalo, take a Sario Bahu *oplet* from Pasar 45 to Terminal Gorontalo (near the sea) where you can catch a bus for Rp8500, 16-18 hours (3 river crossings).

By Ship

The city's harbor terminal and most of its shipping offices are N of Pasar 45 and the Calaca *oplet* station. The principal deep-water port for northern Sulawesi, however, is at Bitung on the eastern coast of the peninsula, 48 km from Manado. To sail anywhere outside of Sulawesi you often have to go to Ternate (N. Maluku) first. Pelni (tel. 2844), a 5-min. walk S of the Kawanua City Hotel on Jl. Sam Ratulangi, sells tickets for several of its ships calling at Bitung. For example, the KM *Kambuna* does the Medan-Padang-Jakarta-Surabaya-Ujung Pandang-Balikpapan-Pantoloan-Bitung-Medan loop. Another Pelni ship, the MV *Umsini,* does only Jakarta-Surabaya-Ujung Pandang-Bitung-Ternate-Ambon-Jayapura. Sample Pelni Economy Class fares from Bitung: Balikpapan, Rp32,400; Ujung Pandang, Rp36,100; Surabaya, Rp55,700; Jakarta (Tg. Priok), Rp66,600. Pelni has another office in Bitung on Jl. Jakarta, tel. 226.

By Boat

From Manado's harbor, *kapal motor* leave for such northern and central Sulawesi ports as Kwandang (Rp8000), Paleleh (Rp12,000), Leok (Rp15,000), Toli Toli (Rp20,000), and Pantoloan (Palu's harbor), Rp30,000. **PT Putra Utara** lines, Jl. Pelabuhan 111, tel. 52524 (near harbor entrance), has boats 3 times weekly for Kwandang. Also try **PT Tabera Raya,** Jl. Sisingamangaraja (near Pasar Jengki). About every 1½ weeks, there are boats from Manado Harbor (or Bitung) to Ternate for around Rp15,000, 36 hours. **to Sangir Islands:** PT Dau Marine, Jl. Toar (near Bank

Pembangunan Indonesia), has boats to Siau (Rp11,500) and Tahuna (Rp11,500) from Manado Harbor. Also try PT Putra Utara (tel. 52524), Jl. Pahlawan 111 (near harbor entrance).

Flights

Merpati's office is at Jl. Sam Ratulangi 138, tel. 4027; take a Sario- or Wanea-bound *bemo* from Pasar 45 down Jl. Sam Ratulangi. Open Mon.-Sat. 0800-1500, Sun. 0900-1200. **Garuda:** Jl. Diponegoro 1, tel. 4535; open Mon.-Sat. 0700-1600, Sun. 1000-1600. **Bouraq:** Jl. Sarapung 27, tel. 2757. Merpati has flights to Ambon, Rp118,000; Gorontalo, Rp42,800; Poso, Rp102,100; Palu, Rp93,500; and Ternate, Rp44,900. Garuda flies daily to: Ujung Pandang, Rp131,700; Surabaya, Rp196,500; Jakarta, Rp259,400; and Denpasar, 178,300. Bouraq (Jl. Sarapung 27B, tel. 2757/2675) flies to Gorontalo, daily at 0700, Rp42,800; Palu, daily at 0700, Rp93,000; Balikpapan, twice daily at 0700 and 0830, Rp132,400; Ternate, 4 times weekly at 1400, Rp 44,900; Surabaya daily at 0830, 167,000; Jakarta, daily at 0830, Rp220,500. **Mandala** (Jl. Sarapung 17, tel. 51743/51324/51824) has a flight to Surabaya for only Rp167,000. There have been no flights from Manado to Davao, Philippines, since 1978. Take a *bemo* 15 km to Manado's

Sam Ratulangi Airport from Stasiun Calaca; Rp250. Allow one hour to get to the terminal and then out to the airport. Or charter an *oplet* for Rp3000-4000, 20-30 minutes. Airport tax: Rp1800.

Tour Companies

Since rental cars, motorbikes, and tourist guides are still not generally available, most visitors use the services of a tour agent. Two good ones are **Pandu Express,** Jl. Sam Ratulangi (tel. 51188), and **Pola Pelita Express,** Jl. Sam Ratulangi 113 (tel. 52231). Both offer tours of Manado and the surrounding countryside where coconut plantations and spice-processing plants may be toured. Pola Pelita offers the 4-day "Manado Fantasi Tour" which takes in the Minahasa highlands; US$115-145 pp. The "Minahasan Highland Circle Tour" (4 days, 3 nights) visits the Pinabetengan stone, volcanic mountains, lakes, hot springs, *waruga,* and the Bunaken sea gardens. Even longer excursions can be arranged, such as their 7-day Mountain-Lake-Beach Tour for US$190-250 pp. For groups of 6 or more, a welcoming party at the airport, a cultural performance, and a dinner party are thrown in free. These tours are generally very good value.

VICINITY OF MANADO

An 18-hole golf course is at **Kayuwatu** (means "stone wood," in reference to the ancient Minahasans' first golf clubs!), 5 km from Manado, its well-tended fairways set amidst towering coconut palms. At **Lotak,** 7 km S of Manado (turn off at Pineleng), is the tomb of Imam Bonjol (b. 1791), one of Indonesia's most famous freedom fighters. In W. Sumatra, Imam Bonjol led the Padri War against Dutch tyranny. The Dutch captured and exiled him in 1841 to Lotok, where he died in 1864. The village of Pineleng is descended from Imam Bonjol's family. A Catholic seminary is in the middle of this village. Also visit copra plantations in this area; it seems *everyone* has their hand in the copra (and clove) business. Thick coconut plantations cover all the coastal areas, while cloves are grown in the highlands. For Lotak, get an *oplet* from Pasar 45 in the Pineleng direction. **Tasik Ria** is a well-known beach for sunbathing and canoeing, 25 km W of Manado; take an *oplet* from near Terminal Gorontalo, Rp500. Entrance: Rp200.

Airmadidi

The name means "hotsprings," even though there aren't any here. In this mountain village, 19 km SE of Manado, you see the best example of *waruga,* old pre-Christian tombs of the ancestral Minahasans. Hewn from single blocks of limestone, *waruga* are

shaped like small Chinese temples with enormous roof-shaped covers. Often lavishly decorated with intricate animal and anthropomorphic carvings, Portuguese gentlemen in 18th C. attire, or showing features of important Minahasans. Corpses were buried inside in a squatting position along with household articles, gold, and Asiatic porcelain dating back to the Ming Dynasty. Once common over a large area of Minahasa, as Christianity spread *waruga* were either forgotten or destroyed. Because they contained valuables, many have been plundered. Now they have been all collected and assembled in places like Airmadidi. Airmadidi is Rp350 by *oplet* from Manado's Terminal Calaca; you arrive at the Airmadidi *oplet* station from where it's just a 15-min. walk to the *waruga.* A small museum here is open 0800-1700.

Vicinity Of Airmadidi

The **PT United Coconut Tina Indonesia** is a few kilometers from Airmadidi in the vicinity of Sukur village, the source of most of Manado's fruit. This factory for processing dessicated coconut is worth a visit. At **Taman Waruga Sawangan,** 144 ancient *waruga* have been beautifully restored within the confines of a tranquil terraced garden. Take an *oplet* from Airmadidi to Sawangan (Rp100, 6 km). Other *waruga*

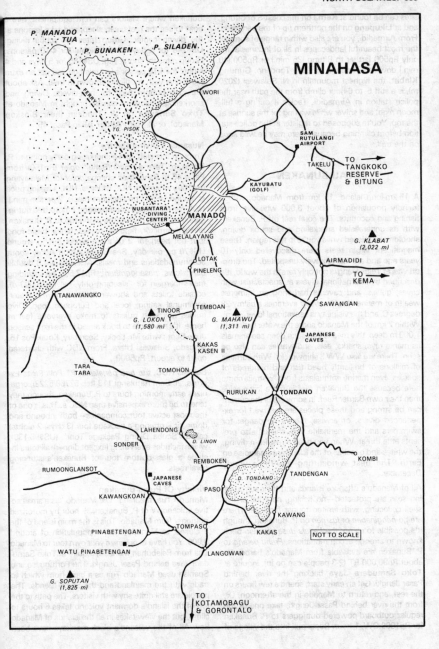

MINAHASA

P. MANADO TUA

P. BUNAKEN

P. SILADEN

FERRY

TG. PISOK

NUSANTARA DIVING CENTER

WORI

SAM RUTULANGI AIRPORT

KAYUBATU (GOLF)

TAKELU

TO TANGKOKO RESERVE & BITUNG

MANADO

MELALAYANG

G. KLABAT (2,022 m)

LOTAK

PINELENG

AIRMADIDI

TO KEMA

TANAWANGKO

TINOOR

TEMBOAN

SAWANGAN

G. LOKON (1,580 m)

G. MAHAWU (1,311 m)

KAKAS KASEN II

JAPANESE CAVES

TARA TARA

TOMOHON

RURUKAN

TONDANO

LAHENDONG

D. LINON

SONDER

REMBOKEN

KOMBI

RUMOONGLANSOT

JAPANESE CAVES

PASO

D. TONDANO

TANDENGAN

KAWANGKOAN

KAWANG

PINABETENGAN

TOMPASO

KAKAS

NOT TO SCALE

WATU PINABETENGAN

LANGOWAN

G. SOPUTAN (1,825 m)

TO KOTAMOBAGU & GORONTALO

sites can be found at **Kema** on the coast S of Bitung, and at **Likupang** on the northern tip of the peninsula. From Airmadidi, you are also within range of some of the most beautiful landscapes in all of Indonesia. It's only Rp500 farther to Bitung (35 min.) or Rp500 (40 min.) down to Tondano on Lake Tondano. **Gunung Klabat,** the highest mountain in N. Sulawesi (2020 m), is a stiff 5- to 6-hour climb from the path near the police station in Airmadidi. Tackle it during a full-moon night and shiver while waiting for the sunrise at the top. You're supposed to register at the police station before climbing because there may be wild *anoa* on the trail.

PULAU BUNAKEN

A 15-km-long island, 15 km from Manado, with a friendly population of about 3,000 who live from fishing and coconuts. The coral reef off P. Bunaken, with its unparalleled snorkeling and scuba diving, shouldn't be missed while you're in this region. These magnificent virgin reefs were discovered only 10 years ago and are still relatively unspoiled. The drop-off wall at Teluk Liang is not only rare in the world, it's described by international divers as spectacular with caves, gullies, and caverns harboring an immense wealth of marine life. The water averages a balmy 28 degrees C. and the visibility is sensational (over 30 m). Within 2 km of the Manado shore the water is already 1,000 m deep; this means that such deep-sea animals as manta rays, sharks, eels, and whales can also be seen. There are also WW II shipwrecks. With curtains of millions of brilliantly hued fish and hundreds of species, even marine enthusiasts from Australia come here because the Bunaken reef is more impressive than their own Barrier Reef. In some areas the current can be strong and these places are reserved for experienced divers; otherwise, there's no danger for swimmers and the marinelife (e.g. sharks) also presents little threat. When you need a rest from diving, the white-sand beaches of the island are a paradise on Earth. The best windsurfing month is windy December.

All of Manado's offshore islands and their surrounding seas are protected—no fishing, no coral or live shell collecting, with limited tourist facilities. There are no *penginapan* or *losmen* on P. Bunaken, though it's possible to camp; the *kepala desa* has also been known to arrange accommodations. *Prahu pelang* to P. Bunaken are available from Manado's harbor for about Rp90,000 RT (2-3 people can go in). Inquire at **Toko Samudera Jaya** backing the river behind Pasar Jengki. Get an early start, spend a few hours on the reef, and return to Manado in the afternoon. Or, from the river behind Pasar Jengki, take one of the regular outboard-powered outriggers to P. Bunaken for Rp1000 OW, 1 hour. Boats pull into the village of Bunaken where visitors can rent equipment, hire a boat to see the reefs, eat, sleep, and take lessons at the diving center. Group rates for scuba diving: US$245 for 5 days and 4 nights for 4-10 persons. Group rates for snorkeling: US$185 for 5 days and 4 nights for 4-10 persons (on this one you get an extra night dive with spotlights thrown in free). Ask about the glass-bottom boat for non-divers. Diving and snorkeling equipment can be bought in Manado at **Toko Senayan** on Jl. Tendean (near Bioskop Manado), or at **Toko Akbar Ali** in Pasar 45.

Nusantara Diving Centre

Through this club, join a snorkeling party going to P. Bunaken. Take a "Sario/Bahu" *oplet* (Rp150) from Pasar 45 to Bahu, then change *oplet* for Melalayang (Rp150), where the NDC office is. NDC's asking price is around US$50 pp (includes meals, 2-person min.). NDC has 60 tanks, 2 compressors, 7 motorized outriggers. For scuba diving, the *prahu* trip to P. Bunaken, diving instructor, flippers, masks, tanks, basic food (but not beer) for 2 or more works out to around US$70 pp per day. See Bapak Anton Adrey about accommodations and meals. Available are 8 double bungalows *(pasanggrahan);* Rp17,500 pp including meals (bargain for "sleeping only," at Rp15,000 d), outside toilets and shower facilities, no hot water, communal eating, local and European food. Dive guides mix with guests to make everyone feel at home. It's advisable to book ahead in the high season June-Sept.; write Mr. Locky, Secretary, Kotak Pos 15, Manado, Sulawesi Utara. From NDC with chartered *oplet* to airport, Rp5000.

Besides NDC, the *biro perjalanan* PT Pola Pelita Express, Jl. Sam Ratulangi 113 (tel. 52768/5223), organizes early-morning tours to P. Bunaken, though they tend to be more expensive than NDC's. This is one of the most active tour companies—both inbound and domestic—offering a package tour (3 days, 2 nights) called "Scuba Diving Package Tour" (US$95-130), which includes everything (except dinner); all tours include a glass-bottom tour of Bunaken's stunning coral reefs.

Vicinity Of Pulau Bunaken

Manado Tua, meaning "Old Manado," is a small active volcano W of P. Bunaken, ½ hour by motorized outrigger from Manado. This is the main island of the 3 closest to Manado, with a population of around 3,000. You have to organize your own tour to Manado Tua from Pelabuhan Manado; inquire at Toko Samudera Jaya behind Pasar Jengki. The Portuguese and Spanish used Manado Tua as a base from which to trade with the mainland and the Spice Islands. The people are still quite shy with visitors. The path to the top of the island's dormant volcano takes 6 hours to climb, but the view takes in all the islands of Manado Bay. All of the volcano's black monkeys have been hunted and killed. Today, its coral reefs are almost totally unspoiled, superb for snorkeling and skin diving. The volcano rests on a plateau, where the water is at most 3 m deep — ideal for coral and sponges. The bed is a mixture of white sand and coral formations; sponges grow as big as a meter in diameter. At the edge of the reef, the plateau drops off to a depth of 2,000 m — a whole new underwater world. Barracuda, tuna, *kakap,* and other enormous species (but few sharks) such as parrot fish can often be sighted. Take a picnic lunch. Two hours by motorized outrigger to the NE is **P. Mantehage,** also famous for its sea gardens. Another island, **P. Siladen,** is 1½ hours by boat from Manado, also has good diving and snorkeling and beautiful white-sand beaches with many shells.

BITUNG

A major port on the E coast, 1 hour (48 km) by regularly departing *oplet* (Rp800) from Manado's Terminal Paal-Paal. Bitung's harbor, from which timber, coffee, cloves, and copra are exported, is well protected by **P. Lembeh,** a large island just offshore. Within the harbor complex on Jl. Jakarta is the Pelni office (tel. 226/152). **Aertembuga,** a few km from Bitung, is the fishing center of N. Sulawesi. There's excellent skindiving and snorkeling from islands off Bitung. The traveler's favorite place to stay is **Yordan,** Jl. H.V. Worang Kadoodan (tel. 239), 5 rooms, fan; Rp7500-10,000 d. **Peng. Samudera Jaya,** Jl. Sam Ratulangi 2 (tel. 114), charges Rp8000 s or d, but not worth the extra money. A Pelni agent is right next door. Eat at **Hawaii** or **Virgo** (Jl. Yos. Sudarso Madidir Ure) restaurants. South of Bitung, on the southern side of the northern peninsula, is **Kema,** an important seaport in Portuguese times and the site of a Portuguese fort; take a *bemo* from Bitung (Rp200).

Gunung Dua Saudara National Park

This 3,000-ha nature reserve (also known as the Tangkoko-Batuangus Reserve), 30 km S of Bitung, was established around the peaks of **G. Dua Saudara** (1,351 m) and **G. Tangkoko** (1,109 m), and includes coastline and coral gardens offshore. A real cross-section of Sulawesi's endemic animal life lives here: tarsiers, crested macaques, monkeys, cuscus, *anoa, babirusa, maleo* (jungle fowl), hornbills, cockatoos, inhabiting a geologically fascinating area of hotsprings and volcanic craters. Bring your own food. First obtain a permit (Rp1000) and the latest info on visiting the reserve from the PPA office on Jl. W.R. Supratman, Rika Atal, Manado (near Hotel Garden). One way is to take a jeep from Manado (Rp75,000, 4-5 hours), walk 3 hours through the jungle, have lunch and return; inquire at Manado's Pola Pelita Express (Jl. Sam Ratulangi 113). Another option is to take a

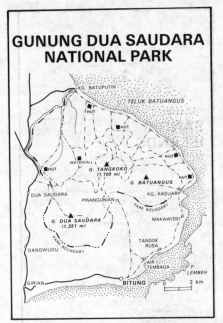

GUNUNG DUA SAUDARA NATIONAL PARK

minibus from Bitung up to Girian (Rp150), then an old Chevrolet taxi via Danowudu (where you get your permit stamped by the *camat)* and Dua Saudara village to Kampung Batuputih, 20 km, 1 hour, Rp1000 pp (or Rp1500 if you sit in front). Or in Bitung hire boats directly to Kampung Batuputih, 25 km. In Kampung Batuputih, on the reserve's NW border, stay in PPA's simple guest bungalows. Trails also lead into the reserve from Kampung Kasuari on the reserve's SE border, where guides can also be hired. Blinds have been set up so you can observe wildlife. From Kasuari, villagers will ferry you by *prahu* around a small cape to Teluk Batuangus. Gunung Tangkoko (1,109 m) can be climbed in about 3 hours.

SANGIR-TALAUD ISLANDS

An archipelago that stretches from the northern tip of N. Sulawesi nearly all the way to Mindanao, the large southern island of the Philippines. Not only physical features but also the languages spoken in Sangir-Talaud are closely related to those spoken in the Philippines. Before the arrival of the Portuguese, the Islamic sultanate of Ternate ruled over Sangir-Talaud. The Dutch occupied the islands in the late 17th C., eventually converting most of the population to Chris-

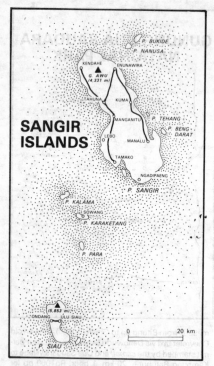

SANGIR ISLANDS

P. BUKIDE
P. NANUSA
KENDAHE
ENUNAWIRA
G. AWU (4,331 m)
TAHUNA
KUMA
MANGANITU
P. TEHANG
LEBO
MANALU
P. BENG-DARAT
TAMAKO
NGADIPAENG
P. SANGIR
P. KALAMA
SOWANG
P. KARAKETANG
P. PARA
(5,853 m)
ONDANG
ULU SIAU
P. SIAU
0   20 km

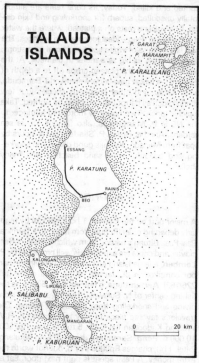

TALAUD ISLANDS

P. GARAT
P. MARAMPIT
P. KARALELANG
ESSANG
P. KARATUNG
RAINIS
BEO
KALONGAN
LIRUNG
P. SALIBABU
MANGARAN
P. KABURUAN
0   20 km

tianity. The principal industries today are copra (exporting around 30,000 tons a year) and clove production. The total population of the islands is around 300,000. The light-complexioned natives, famous for their delicate carving of black mahogany, are believed to have originated from somewhere in northern Polynesia. Though the northernmost islands of the Talaud group are only 120 km from Mindanao—the closest point to the Philippines in Indonesia—you can't get to the Philippines from here (except perhaps during Easter and Christmas).

These islands present a quietness and beauty of their own. There are sandy beaches, coral reefs, and small fishing *kampung* out of time. Like so many islands in the Moluccas, this is a highly volcanic chain with a number of both inactive and active volcanos. Gunung Awu (elev. 4,331 m) on P. Sangir (also called P. Sangihe) has a long record of explosions and loss of life and property dating back to 1711, with the most recent occurring in 1966. The ground on this island is very shaky. Gunung Ruang, G. Karanggetang, and G. Banua are also highly active. Many rare and distinctive palms, notably the *kavesu* and *sago barok*, grow in the region.

Tahuna

The capital of the Sangir-Talaud group is the town of Tahuna, situated on the main island of Sangir. Here is the best TV reception in N. Sulawesi where Filipino and even Malaysian stations can be picked up! Stay at **Tagaroa**, Jl. Malahasa 1, which has 7 rooms with private bath, running water and flush toilets; Rp17,500 s, Rp25,000 d, VIP room with a/c, Rp37,500 s, Rp56,500 d. Cheaper is **Wisma Anugah**, 200 m from downtown, about Rp10,000 pp; also serves meals. There are at least 7 restaurants, **Yenny, Al Fajar, Madorosa,** etc. There is no beach far enough away from a village where you won't be bothered by village children, and the whole coast is dotted with villages! For a beach holiday? Disappointing.

Pulau Siau

The largest of the southern islands in the Sangir group, P. Siau has historically fallen under the administrative control of the Manado district of N. Sulawesi. Its large, active volcano, G. Awu (5,853 m), has the same name as the mountain on P. Sangir. It erupted in 1974, forcing the evacuation of the island's entire population of 42,000 to Minahasa. For information on climbing G. Awu, inquire at the volcanologist office in Tahuna.

Getting There

Merpati flies directly from Manado to Naha Airport (21 km from Tahuna on P. Sangir) for Rp52,700. Or you can fly with with Merpati from Manado to Melanguane Airport on P. Karakelang (in the Talaud Group, NE of the Sangir Is.), twice weekly, Rp66,200. A cheaper way is to catch small cargo boats leaving Manado Harbor every other night. The *Agape* sails 3 times weekly; the faster, better, express *Pan Marine* sails 3 times weekly from Manado's harbor to the Sangir Is. for Rp21,000 RT 1st Class, Rp15,000 Economy; 2 days and 2 nights. Even in the 1st Class cabin, 17 people will be staring at you the whole time, so for more privacy you might want to pay Rp20,000 extra for the captain's cabin. Boats also depart from Bitung about 5 times weekly. Boats stop at different ports such as Beo and Lirung for 12-36 hours, depending upon how many supplies have to be loaded or unloaded. Inquire about latest prices and schedules at the shipping agency **PT Putra Utara**, Jl. Pelabuhan 111 (tel. 52524) near the gate to Manado's harbor terminal, or **PT Holpers**, also on Jl. Pelabuhan.

TOMOHON AND VICINITY

Tomohon (elev. 780 m) is a pretty, windy, sunny town with still-active G. Lokon (1,580 m) towering in the background, and the sea visible beyond. The smell of sulphur can be very strong. The town has a pleasantly cool climate, not unlike a European summer. Known as *Kota Kembang* ("Flower City"), every wooden house seems to be draped with orchid plants, while household gardens burst with enormous zinnias, dahlias, marigolds, and glorious perennial gladiolas. A center for Christian mission groups and the location of a Christian theology school (at nearby **Bukit Inspirasi**, "Hill of Inspiration"), Tomohon hosted the 9th grand assembly of the World Council of Protestant Churches in 1981, attracting 25,000 people.

Take the road by the Christian University leading up to Bukit Inspirasi, from where you can see the Lokon Volcano and Manado City; take the steps back down. A fine market (Tues., Thurs., and Sat.) features broasted dogs (their burnt carcasses, set in rigor mortis, are laid out on rough wooden tables), giant roasted rats, snakes, and bats. A mission *polyklinik* here charges only Rp300 per consultation. Tomohon is also known for its wheelwrights, who supply most of the wheels for the *bendi* (pony traps) of Manado; Tomohon's streets echo with the sound of horses' hooves. People are very friendly. From Tomohon, take an *oplet* to Tondano (Rp300, 30 min.), and Kawangkoan (Rp350, 45 min.).

From Manado's Terminal Karombasan, take a public bus or minibus direct to Tomohon (Rp450). Pass by wonderful views of the city and at night see strings of lights below. Honky-tonk beer joints and restaurants perch on the side of the road all the way up. Buy *durian, langsat*, mangos, and other monsoon fruits at Pineleng, a village just above Tomohon. The bus continues to climb up through the plantations between the volcanos of Lokon and Mahawu. At **Temboan Tinoor**, halfway up the mountain to Tomohon (16 km from Manado), experience real ethnic Minahasan cooking: mice, dog (very peppery hot), wild pig *(babi hutan)*, and a gin called *cap tikus*, Rp100, plus sago wines *(tuak saguer)* of varying potencies. The food is heavily spiced, and visitors who don't like hot food should ask for their food *tidak pedas*. Superb views of Manado and the bay. Approaching Tomohon, there are many fish ponds on the L where *ikan mas* (goldfish) are raised.

Vicinity Of Tomohon

This is a lovely area, comparable with the mountain towns of Java, with many places to visit. An oft-expressed greeting, when you meet people in upcountry Minahasa: *Pakatua'an Wo Pakalawiren!* ("Wishing you long life and health!"). Because of the rich *cingke* cash crops, the people in surrounding villages are comparatively well off. Virtually every house has flower pots, gardens, and flowering trees. This pine-forest region has one of the highest concentrations of hotsprings in Indonesia. Many horsecarts, so plenty of transportation (Rp100-250 per ride). Two km out of Tomohon on the road to Tara Tara are WW II Japanese ammunition caves. In **Kinilow**, 5 km before Tomohon, is a large modern swimming pool, Indraloka (Rp250 entrance), plus natural hotsprings and public baths with hostesses, rubdowns, and cottages for rent (Rp 18,000 a night). At **Kakaskasen I**, a few km beyond Tinoor and 3 km before Tomohon, dances are sometimes held on Sat. night (Rp250 admission) from 2000 to late. The boys dance with the boys during the disco numbers while the girls dance with the boys during the slow numbers! Girls here are vacuum packed until marriage!

Kakaskasen II is overshadowed by the 2 volcanos G. Lokon and G. Mahawu. Both have crater lakes of considerable beauty, duck-egg blue and smoking, within 1½ hours walk of this village. Lokon is usually considered to be the more beautiful of the 2 and the casual climb should be no problem for anyone in reasonable condition. Guides (for around Rp5000) may be found with the help of the *kepala desa*. The walk takes you through fields of corn and *enau* (palm oil trees). The final 30 min. follows the frozen lava flow which has formed a rock river holding freshwater rain pools for refreshment. The steaming crater lies 600 m below the peak of the mountain. The lake is about 60 m deep, crusted with yellow sulphur. It threatens to erupt every 10 years (last erupted in 1971). Start from Kakaskasen II no later than 0700, arriving at the Lokon crater while the morning is still cool and the sun has just filled the crater.

Sonder

This clove village, 20 km SE of Tomohon, consists of one main street with 3 churches (Minahasa, Seventh-day Adventist, Catholic). During the harvest (July-Oct.), one can hardly drive through the streets because of the *cingke* which people have put out to dry on mats (their yards are already overflowing!). Even stilted traditional-style homes built of wood sport color TV sets, kitchen gadgetry, and expensive furniture. With a per capita income of US$5500, this is one of the richest towns in Asia.

Rurukan

A colorful 900-m-high mountain village perched halfway between Tomohon and Tondano, 5 km up a twisting, rough mountain road. From the center of the village, take the road to Kumelebuag. Turn R after 400 m, follow a dirt path down for 100 m, then turn L and go straight along a jungle path to reach some fine hotsprings. Backtracking to the village, follow the main road down to Tondano, another 6 km; this is a beautiful walk with a panoramic view of Lake Tondano. After reaching the outskirts of Tondano, take a *bendi* (Rp250) or walk 2 km to the end of Tonsea Lama village. Descend from the road to the R to see the powerful 40-m-high waterfall. Then take a *bendi* (Rp200) to the *stasiun* and back to Tomohon (Rp300), or continue along to Manado from Tonsea Lama.

Tara Tara

30 km SW of Manado. In Tomohon, turn R at the ticket office and either walk 8 km or take an *oplet* (Rp300). A traditional windmill is located toward the end of the road to the right. Powered by a fast-running stream at the bottom of a small ravine, the immense water wheel drives an intricate maze of belts, pulleys, and wooden gears whose final achievement is the vertical operation of a group of heavy log pounders that pulverize the grain. It's possible to travel along this road to Tanawangko, then circle back to Manado. In Tara Tara, contact the *hukum tua* to charter extraordinary dances for around Rp50,000: *Maengket, Kebesaran* (War Dance), old Portuguese, harvest, and Christian dances. The headman just raises the microphone and dancers suddenly appear wearing macaque ape helmets! Music is provided by a group of 5 or 6 *kolintang* players, using homemade instruments made of bamboo and brass, very lively and characteristically Minahasan—more pleasing to the Western ear than most Asian tunes. You may have to send an *oplet* to pick up more dancers. Be sure to give a donation to the village. Stay at the Tamaska.

Lahendong

A few km S of Tomohon on the main road to Langowan, Rp200 by *oplet.* There's a hotsprings on the R before Lahendong village, but it's a real commercial operation. Better to get off just after the bridge on the edge of the village where there's a huge lava flow with small, bubbling, steaming craters, and a hot-springs along the side of the river which cuts through it. Interesting to walk around this area. In addition to the hotsprings, there's D. Linow, a small, highly sulphurous lake, which bubbles at the edges and has steam jets. The lake's colors change depending upon the light and viewing perspective: shades of light blue, green, turquoise, etc. Hundreds of large white birds and beautiful small songbirds are in residence—a fairy-tale environment! Sticks set up with strings in the water attract dragonflies, which the local youths capture at night, then fry and eat! Bathe in the hotsprings by the side of the lake near the power project. Take an *oplet* to Lahendong, get off at the KANTOR VULKANOLOG sign, and walk 700 m to the lake.

TONDANO AREA

Tondano is a large market town located in the middle of a fertile rice-growing plateau. Catch a minibus or *oplet* from Tomohon (Rp300), or from Manado's Terminal Karombasan (Rp600). Stay at the excellent, clean, and cool Asri; Rp15,000 per room includes breakfast, tea and coffee. (Also check out the Nusantara, in Tounkuramber.) Eat at the Pemandangan or Fireball restaurants on the main road, Jl. Raya Tomohon. From Tondano, continue on to other resort towns surrounding D. Tondano, a large, scenic lake, beautifully situated between paddyfields and the Lembean Mountains. This 50-sq-km lake, about 30 km SE of Manado, is 700 m above sea level and is the largest lake in the region. Its abundant fish provide a livelihood for the native population. The waterfall of Tondano was famous for its spectacular beauty. The tiny island in the middle is known as Likri. From Tondano village, Tomohon is Rp300, 30 min., by *oplet.*

Vicinity Of Tondano

From Tondano take the road to Airmadidi, which carves its way through thick plantations of endless coconut, following the Tondano River, with dramatic views of the Klabat volcano and evening mists filling the valley. See extensive Japanese-made caves about 1-hour's walk on this road. From Tondano, pay Rp500 to travel around the W or E side of the lake. Eastbound, stop in at Tandengan and Eris, both with nice views of the lake. Remboken, on the W side, has a better selection of pottery than Manado; also hotsprings at the Taman Wisata. At Paso, bathe in large steaming concrete tanks; ask for *air panas umum* (Rp500). Stay at Tempat Pemandian Florida,

Rp10,000. From Paso there are lovely views of Lake Tondano across steaming fields of hotsprings amongst the rice.

By taking either direction S from Tondano, you wind up in **Kakas** at the bottom of Lake Tondano. No *losmen* here, but contact the *kepala desa* who'll turn you on to some accommodation if you're willing to speak English. From Kakas take a small *prahu* across the lake to Kawang (Rp250), a regular ferry run for villagers who live in Kakas and own clove gardens and property in Kawang. Five km SW of Kakas is **Langowan**, a mountain village with hotsprings, *sawah*, and virgin forests.

Kawangkoan

Located between Langowan and Amurang, Kawangkoan is a crossroads village reached by *oplet* (Rp800) from Manado's Pasar Karombasan. Eat at **Restaurant Harmoni**. Local coffee and hot *biapong* (soft pastry cakes with a meat and vegetable filling) can be enjoyed at **RM Kopi Gembira**, a locally well-known coffee shop open from 0500 to 2100. This village is known for bullcart racing, celebrated *kolintang* performances, and underground Japanese fortress and storage caves (on the road to Kiawa, Rp200, 3 km, by *oplet* or Rp500 by *bendi* from Kawangkoan). Eat in the restaurant opposite the caves. The *Maengket* dance can be chartered in **Tompaso**. From Kawangkoan, return to Manado by *oplet* (Rp800) or continue on toward the western end of N. Sulawesi. The flaming red and yellow gladioli (*bunga mas*) of **Pinabetengan** village 5.5 km to the S are the most beautiful of all Minahasa's 1500 colorful villages. Minahasans claim gardening as their main leisure preoccupation.

Watu Pinabetengan

A megalithic stone of the ancestors near Kawangkoan, its surface covered in crude, mysterious line drawings and scripts which have never been deciphered. According to Minahasan history, this is the place where the ancestors first divided up the land between the people (*Watu Pinabetengan* means "the stone of discussion about the division"). This memorial boulder, 2 m high and 4 m long and shaped like the top part of a *waruga*, has served as a political gathering place for the Minahasan elders since time immemorial. There have been at least 6 major discussions at the stone: the first division of the tribes; a reconciliation of the differences between the tribes; a resolution in the 17th C. to drive out the Spanish; a defense meeting to defend Minahasa against attackers from Bolaang Mongondow in the S; a demand for Indonesian independence in 1939; and a blessing for the new Indonesian Republic in 1945. Though each of the 6 Minahasan tribes speaks its own dialect, they are today all united as one people (*Mina Esa* means "become one" or "united").

Watu Pinabetengan is located 40 km from Manado and 5 km from Kawangkoan. First take an *oplet* from Manado's Terminal Karombasan to Kawangkoan (Rp800, 2 hours). From Kawangkoan, take a *bendi* 3 km (Rp300, 30 min.) to Desa Pinabetengan. Then walk 2 km along an upgraded road to the site in a beautiful forest on the slopes of a mountain commanding a majestic view over Minahasa. Unfortunately, the government has buried the sacred stone in an ugly concrete crypt, like a white-tiled grave! It should've been situated on a lovely grass hillock for everyone to see and enjoy. To make it worse, the concrete roof makes it even darker, and birds who live under the roof shit on the revered object. A pity, as the site has the potential of an important tourist attraction. Don't visit it during the first part of the year: thousands of people converge on the memorial stone during the month of January. Bathe in the hot springs nearby.

BOLAANG MONGONDOW DISTRICT

KOTAMOBAGU

An attractive, clean Muslim town in the middle of the mountains, Rp4000, 4 hours, and 218 km by bus from Manado's Karombasam Bus Terminal. Friendly people. Kotamobagu is the cultural center and capital of the Bolaang Mongondow District, located in the upland plateaus between the Minahasa and Gorontalo districts. The Bolaang are a coastal people who merged with the inland and earlier settled Mongondow. Villages, formerly made up of longhouses, are strung out along roads. Village heads (*kepala desa*) here are called *Sangadi*. Primarily an agricultural region with rice, sago, maize, yams, and cassava grown, coconuts, coffee, and rice are the cash crops. Islam, which replaced the indigenous ancestor cult, dates from around 1830. Protestant missionaries have also made inroads.

Accommodations And Food

Losmen Lely is the cheapest at Rp5000; **Losmen Tenteram** and **Losmen Widuri** are Rp10,000-15,000. **Hotel Ramayana**, Rp5000-10,000, is a traditional homestay with bamboo buildings just down the road from Lely and Tenteram. **Wisma Kabela**, on Jl. Soetoyo, has a swimming pool and a nice garden out in back, but grotty rooms, hot and airless, with no view and the 40 geese have turned the place into an evil-smelling pond. Asking price for the new rooms is a ridiculous Rp15,000, old rooms Rp5000, but bargain. One of the most delightful hotels in all of Indonesia is the **Hotel New Plaza** on the L-hand side only a 5-min. walk farther up the road. Lovely situation overlooking mountains and *sawah*, beautiful swimming pool, excellent service. Bungalow rooms with fan (no need for a/c because nights are cool) and breakfast, coffee or tea on arrival and throughout the day cost Rp15,000, while a/c rooms go for Rp25,000 (only 4). Lots of market stalls for budget eating. **Nasional Restaurant** for Chinese-style food and drink. Also check out the **Sahabat Jujur**, Jl. A. Yani.

Vicinity Of Kotamobagu

From Kotamobagu, catch a local bus for Amurang, to connect with an excellent, wide, smooth Korean-built highway which now stretches between Amurang and Gorontalo. From Kotamobagu to Doloduo is Rp1000 (57 km). A nice day-trip is to picturesque **Bilalang** village, 3 km N of town, Rp300 by *oplet*. More enjoyable might be to take a *bendi* there for Rp600. Every Sun. a 1,000-m horserace (with betting on the side) takes place at Togop, 3 km N of Kotamobagu; free entry. Ten km NE of Kotamobagu (or 3 km from Tobonon) is Modayag, a cool, high goldmine village. Stay at the *pasanggrahan*.

Gunung Ambang National Park is only a 30-min. drive (27 km) from Kotamobagu. This reserve offers crater lakes, montane forests, sulphur fumaroles, and hot mudpools. The park, lying at an altitude of 1,100-1,800 m above sea level, is filled with *Pigafetta* palms, tree ferns, and flowering shrubs. There are good trails, which the locals use to hunt rats, bats, and snakes to spice up their diet. From Kotamobagu's bus terminal, take a bus to **Bong Kudai Baru**, a beautiful drive on a good road through coffee plantations. In Bong Kudai Baru, where the road bends sharply to the R to Modoinding, go straight on a cobblestone track. After about 100 m, there's a PPA hut on the R (children will show you the way). A permit obtained in Dumoga may be required, but the guardian is so slow-witted that one can probably enter without a *surat*. Take the narrow path immediately L after the PPA hut through vegetable fields until the wider track at R-angle. Turn R on this track and then L again, past bamboo clumps and 2 huts in the fields on L-hand side until the edge of forest. Steep climb up through the forest, just follow the path, then through the tunnel of 3-m-high *alang* grass to a cliff from where you can see and hear sulphur fumaroles. It's about a half-hour climb in all from the PPA hut to the fumaroles.

Imandi

Buses leave for Doloduo every morning before 0900; Rp600. The route passes through 50 km of splendid river and mountain country over a good, sealed road. Stop in at Imandi, a small quiet village, and an ideal place just to relax. Stay at **Peng. Ingat Budi**, Rp5000 per bed. **Peng. Sweetheart**, right in the village itself,

charges Rp5000, or Rp8000 full board; better food than at Ingat Budi. From Imandi, walk or take a *bendi* 7 km to **Desa Werdhi Agung** (pop. 600), a Balinese *transmigrasi* colony, where you'll find heart-shaped Balinese faces, one *pura* (temple), a *gamelan* orchestra, Balinese *bubur* rice cakes, and *Legong* dances on occasion of the big Balinese festival, *Galungan*. Crafts are also made here. Another smaller Balinese *kampung*, **Desa Merta**, is only 3 km from Imandi.

Doloduo

There are irrigation systems just like on Bali 7 km beyond Imandi in Doloduo. Stay at **Losmen Sabar Menanti** which also provides meals. From Doloduo to **Molibagu**, it's a 20-km walk over a small mountain range through a beautiful forest with lots of butterflies. Meet people walking in both directions. Plan on about 4 hours, and you can make the RT in one day. From Molibagu, boats embark for Gorontalo or Bitung at least 3 times weekly, but try to find out in Doloduo when the next boat is because there's no *losmen* in Molibagu (only an 8-room *pasanggrahan* where you could possibly stay). One of the local policemen usually puts Westerners up but his hospitality is embarrassing — 3 huge meals a day while his family watches. Best to arrive the day before the boat sails. Boats are either *prahu* with outboards and outriggers or big fat 15- to 20-m-long boats with large outriggers and diesel engines. To Gorontalo it's Rp5000-7000, 12 hours, an overnight trip (but might not be operating July-Sept. due to big seas and easterly winds).

Taman Nasional Dumoga Bone

From Kotamobagu, take a bus to Doloduo (Rp1000). Ask the driver to drop you off at the entrance to this remote and fascinating national park, 4 km beyond Doloduo. Walk to park office and ask permission to stay in the guesthouse, Rp1500 pp (no food provided). If your purpose is "rekreasi," NOT "scientific research," Mr. Palete will give permission. Take your own tea and coffee plus breakfast; eat in the *warung* by the dam for Rp1000. At present 2 Dutch ornithologists (Dr. Dekker and Dr. Vermeulen) are in residence in the guesthouse. They will show you the nesting site of the *maleo*, a bird the size of a large chicken which lays 250-gram eggs in hot volcanic soil some 20-40 cm below the surface. The young dig themselves out and if they survive ants, monitor lizards, and dogs, take themselves off into the forest without ever seeing their parents. You also have a good chance of seeing the famous Celebes Ape *(Macaque Nigra)*, which is not really an ape but a tailless monkey, feeding at the forest edge behind the guesthouse. The great hornbill, many species of kingfishers, and a number of other bird species endemic to Sulawesi are also denizens of the park, but you'll be lucky to see them.

Inobonto

A small Muslim port town along the Korean highway from Manado to Gorontalo. A pleasant place to hang out, quiet and relaxing. Like Mexico, sleepy and lazy. Only a dozen travelers a month come this way. **Hotel Kotabuan**, 500 m from the harbor, is the best place to stay. **Hotel Tepi Laut** ("Edge of the Sea") is so close to the harbor that you can hear the waves. **Losmen Haji Idrus** right around the corner is cheaper and has better food but the lighting leaves you a little in the dark. Eat local food at one of the eating places at **Air Anjing**, 12 km to the northeast. Boats out of Inobonto are becoming rarer since goods are now transported speedily along the new Trans-Sulawesi Highway, but it's still possible. Have tea with the harbormaster on his porch on the beach and find out what boats he is expecting. You might have to wait 3-4 days, but he'll send a boy to your *losmen* when a boat comes in. It won't leave for hours anyway. Boats W to Kwandang stop in small Muslim coastal towns like Bintauna, Baroko, Buko; pay no more than Rp5000-6000 through to Kwandang. If you speak Arabic along this western section of Bolaang Mongondow, you're in. Boats also carry copra between Inobonto and Bitung; ride along for around Rp7500.

Vicinity Of Inobonto

The tiny isolated village of **Labuhan Uki**, 40 km from Inobonto, has clear water and a white-sand beach. Go first SW to Lolak (stay in **Losmen Sederhana**), then walk 8 km along the beach or 9 km by road. There are no vehicles to Labuhan Uki. You can see the bare patches on the mountain slope across the bay where timber for boatbuilding has been cut down. Several families live on the white untouched beaches of **Pulau Molosing**, tending palm plantations. At **Bintauna**, 60 km W of Inobonto, are ruins of an old Portuguese fort. To experience Sulawesi scenery at its finest, take the Rp1500 bus trip from Inobonto on the Korean highway over the mountain NE to **Poigar** village. Visit Poigar's Minahasan village on the far bank of the river for fresh fish or spiced dog. Select your dog in a cage; the black ones supposedly are the tastiest.

GORONTALO

The 500,000 Gorontalese include the population of Gorontalo as well as those of the surrounding district of Gorontalo (between Toli Toli to the W and Bolaang Mongondow to the NE). Nearly all Gorontalese are Muslim. The women use colorful *sarong* as veils and shields from the sun and heat. The port of Gorontalo, on the S-central coast of the northern peninsula, is the main town of the Gorontalo District and the second largest town (pop. 85,000) in N. Sulawesi. It has only recently been connected to the rest of N. Sulawesi by road. The city has a rich local culture, history, and handicrafts. Dutch architecture is still in evidence, fine specimens being the **Saronde Hotel** and the **RS Umum** (public hospital). Although a spread-out town, all the important offices, hotels, and eateries are within a small central business district. It's an easy walk from downtown to the **Pasar Sentral** and the bus station in the northern part of this small city. *Oplet* run from the station across from Pasar Sentral all over town, Rp200 flat fee. There are also hundreds of *bendi* (Rp150-200). The harbor is in the eastern part of town, Rp300 by *oplet*.

Accommodations

Dutch-built **Peng. Teluk Kau**, Jl. Jen. Parman 42 (tel. 785); Rp4500 s, Rp8000 d, is roomy and a good deal for the price, with gigantic canopied double beds and high ceilings. Down the street at no. 461, and about the same price and standard, is **Peng. Shinta**, Jl. Jen. Parman 35 (tel. 461). A nicer place to stay is **Hotel Melati** on the road to the harbor about 400 m from the town area next to the Ideal Theater and across the road from the playing field. A beautiful big old colonial house, great veranda, large rooms with old paintings and artifacts, but in the Rp15,000 d range. Another Dutch-built villa, converted to a hotel, is **Hotel Saronde**, Jl. Walanda Maramis 17 (tel. 735); Rp7500 s up to Rp16,500 d with a/c and TV. The **Indah Ria**, Jl. A. Yani, is the city's top hotel, clean, and with the most privacy.

Food

The cheapest, best-value eating is in the *warung* in or near Pasar Sentral market: *nasi campur* or *nasi kuning* for as little as Rp500. Around the *bioskop* in Gorontalo's center is another collection of inexpensive *warung*. Across the street from the *bemo* station, 15 min. walk from Peng. Teluk Kau, is a good fruit and vegetable market. Meals at Teluk Kau's restaurant are a slight rip-off. The **RM Dirgahayu** and **RM Mana Lagi**, both on Jl. Pertiwi, specialize in tasty goat dishes like *sate*, curry, and soup. For Padang-style food, head for **RM Padang** on Jl. Sam Ratulangi.

Getting There

From Manado, take a minibus to Amurang (Rp1400) from where the N coast road leads via Lolak to Kwandang. From Kwandang, take a minibus (Rp1000) one hour S to Gorontalo (in the rainy season it's more difficult to reach). Or you can take a *kapal motor* from Manado's harbor down the N coast to Kwandang. Another possibility is to take a bus Manado-Inobonto-Kotamobagu, then a minibus farther to Dumoga, Imandi, and Molibagu on the coast from where it's Rp5000-7000 by motorized *prahu* to Gorontalo. Gorontalo can also be reached by bus from Palu, C. Sulawesi; Rp12,000, 36 hours.

FROM GORONTALO

By Bus
Bus offices and ticket agencies are at the bus station. Buses to Manado leave regularly (Rp8500), pulling into Terminal Gorontalo 12-14 hours later. Buses also travel the terrible road down to Palu, C. Sulawesi; Rp12,000, 24-36 hours.

By Boat
Take a horsecart (30 min., Rp400) or an *oplet* (15 min., Rp300) to the harbor. As you trundle by, shout *"Ke mana?"* down the long row of boats to find out where they're sailing. Ships heading for ports along the northern arm of Sulawesi embark from the port of Kwandang, 2 hours and Rp1000 by bus from Gorontalo. From Gorontalo's harbor, there are also many ships of all sizes to Bitung, Rp10,000-12,000, 20 hours; and sometimes ships to Kendari. Pelni (Jl. 23 January 31, tel. 20-419) has a fairly regular boat to Poso, Kendari, then Ujung Pandang. Another shipping line to check out is PT Gapsu on Jl. Mayor Dullah (tel. 198) in the harbor.

From Gorontalo's harbor, there are at least 2 small *kapal motor* weekly to the other (southern) side of Teluk Tomini. The easy way is to take a boat to Parigi, then travel by *oplet* or minibus to Palu or Donggala. You can fly out of Palu, or take a boat or ship from Donggala (C. Sulawesi) S to Pare Pare or Ujung Pandang. Alternatively, take a boat from Gorontalo's harbor, 2-3 days, to either Bunta, Pagimana, or Ampana on the S shore of Teluk Tomini. Ampana is perhaps your best bet as there's a *losmen* and a few places to eat. From Gorontalo, PT Lamala has boats departing to all these points and is the cheapest company. From any of these villages there are boats or minibuses departing for Poso on the southernmost shore of Tomini Bay but be prepared for a wait as departure times are irregular. Sometimes you can get a boat direct from Gorontalo to Poso for around Rp18,500 Deck Class, 48 hours, with stops in the Togian Is. en route.

By Air
Merpati (Jl. Jen. S. Parman 45, tel. 143) has service to: Manado, daily Rp37,200; Palu, Rp43,700; Poso, Rp57,800; Surabaya, Rp138,400; Toli Toli Rp50,400; Ujung Pandang, Rp97,600. Bouraq (Jl. A. Yani 34, tel. 70-870) has flights to: Balikpapan, daily at 0815, Rp93,000; Banjarmasin, daily at 0815, Rp138,100; Jakarta, daily at 0815, Rp218,300; Manado, 10 times weekly, Rp42,800; Palu, daily at 0815, Rp50,000; Tarakan, daily at 0815, Rp165,000; Ternate, 4 times weekly, Rp87,700; Ujung Pandang, daily, Rp106,600. The Bouraq people will come to your hotel pick you up. It costs Rp5000 and takes 45 min. by taxi out to Gorontalo's airport 32 km north.

GORONTALO DISTRICT

Most travelers who visit N. Sulawesi usually fly out without seeing Gorontalo, though this area is fascinating for its conservative and isolated Islamic culture. Lying between Bolaang Mongondow and the Toli Toli districts, the Gorontalo plain is made up of a number of different ethnic groups, the Buol, Limboto, Kwandang, Soewawa, Attingola, etc. The district is 95% Muslim. Four dialects are spoken here which in the W are closer to Torajan, while in the E are distinctly Filipino. Governed from the Ternate sultanate, a federation of all the different principalities was formed in 1673. The district came under Dutch control in the 1890s. Swidden rice, maize, and sago are the staples of the region, while on Lake Limboto nets, traps, and harpoons are used to catch fish.

Lake Limboto Area
Dahawalolo, 13 km from Gorontalo (Rp400 by *bemo),* has a hotsprings inside a concrete complex. Not too clean, not too hot (thermally), obnoxious kids, but best view of Lake Limboto. Lake Limboto (only 3 m deep!) is a fertile rice-growing area only 5 km NW of Gorontalo. Hire a *prahu* from boys to visit small lakeside fishing villages. Other places to see in this upland plain are: Utapato, a bathing place and view over the lake; Batudia, bathe in steaming water; Lombongo, another hot bathing spot, but in the jungle. Check out the travel agencies in Gorontalo to arrange budget travel to hotsprings around Kwandang, Limboto Lake, river travel along the north coast, pigeon-hunting, swimming, and jungle walks. Near the school in Dembe is a recently renovated Portuguese fortress called Benteng Otanaha. Three crumbling towers on a hill are all that remain, but a superb view of Lake Limboto. Take a *bendi* (Rp600) or an *oplet* (Rp200) from Gorontalo to the start of the path up the hill (see the sign).

Kwandang
A port since Portuguese times, Kwandang lies N of Gorontalo (Rp1200, 1 hour by bus). This small coastal town consists of a police station, school, Pelni office, one hotel, and several foodstalls. From Kwandang, take cattle and cargo boats to Taraken (E. Kalimantan), departing about once weekly; Rp7500 Also *kapal motor* W to Toli Toli or NE to Manado. From Kwandang to the harbor, it's Rp200 by *bemo.* Just before the beginning of town is an old Portuguese fortress, Benteng Ota Mas Udangan, with just a tower and wall segments remaining. This fort was once on the sea, which has now receded. Another Portuguese ruin, Benteng Oranje, is NE of town on the road to Manado; the path begins on the L just after the bridge.

MALUKU

Jan Pieterszoon Coen
(1587-1692)

*T*he first discovered and most famous of all Indonesian islands, today the Moluccas are the most undiscovered and least developed. These were the original "Spice Islands" of Dutch colonial history that spurred Columbus to cross the Atlantic and discover America. Fought over by Spanish, Portuguese, British, and Dutch merchant fleets for nutmeg and cloves to preserve meat, their fabulous wealth changed the world's balance of power. This 25th province of Indonesia stretches over an area 50% greater than Kalimantan, yet its thousand islands make up less than 4% of Indonesia's total land area. Only about 1.5 million people live here, many of them skilled agriculturalists and seafarers. Animists—Papuan, proto-Malayan, and Negrito—live in the interiors. The most visited islands are Ambon, Ternate, Tidore, and the Bandas, in that order. The only real urban center in the whole of Maluku is Ambon City (or Amboina) on P. Ambon. If you're into goodly portions of adventure, ethnology, and history, these scattered islands are for you.

INTRODUCTION

Maluku Province, with its provincial capital at Ambon, is divided into 3 administrative districts: North Moluccas (Maluku Utara, consisting of Ternate, Tidore, Halmahera, Morotai, Bacan, Sula, and Obi); Central Moluccas (Maluku Tengah: Ambon, Ceram, Buru, and the Bandas); and Southeast Moluccas (Maluku Tenggara, comprising Kai, Tanimbar, Aru, Babar, Wetar, Leti, Damar, etc.). Militarily, the Moluccas are of vital strategic importance, guarding the shortest sea and air lanes N from Australia to the Philippines and Japan. The Dutch navy had its second largest base in the Indies in Amboina harbor, which the Japanese neutralized very early in the war. Maluku is also a transition zone between Asian and Australian flora and fauna, as well as between the human cultures of Melanesia and SE Asia.

The Land

The total land area of these 1,000 or so islands is 87,100 sq km (about two-thirds the size of Java); its territorial waters comprise 294,946 sq km. To the E the Moluccas are bordered by Irian Jaya, to the S by Nusatenggara, to the W by Sulawesi and to the N by the Philippines. Surrounded by coral reefs, the 5,000-m-deep Moluccan Sea adds to their geographical remoteness. The islands vary in size from tiny uninhabited atolls, the tops of submerged volcanos, up to Halmahera, Buru, and Ceram, each over 4,000 sq km. The best known—Ternate, Tidore, Banda, and Ambon—range in size from 40 to 480 sq km. Most of the northern and central islands have dense tropical jungles, active volcanos, deserted beaches, spectacularly colorful coral gardens, wild, rugged mountainous interiors. Some island groups (the Arus, for example) have such a low elevation that they consist mainly of great stretches of mangrove swamps, tidal salt marshes, and vast areas of sea-grass. Other islands, particularly in N. Maluku, are volcanic in origin; mountains on Halmahera and Ceram reach heights of over 3,000 m. Lying right in the middle of the great chain of volcanos known as the "Ring of Fire," Maluku is a volatile territory, with 70 eruptions recorded in the last 400 years; earthquakes are not uncommon on Ternate, Ambon, and the Bandas.

Climate

Wet, humid, and tropical, though tempered by fresh sea breezes. Temperatures vary from 24-29 degrees C during the dry season (Sept.-March), 19-22 degrees C in the rainy season. The wet season everywhere else in Indonesia is Oct.-April, but in Maluku it's April to August. The sea is too rough during this time for small boats. Lying near the equator, monsoons blow over Maluku less regularly. Rainfall is heavy throughout the year, the volume dependent upon the height and orientation of the mountain chains. The best season for sea travel, known as *musim teduh*, is Sept.-March when the seas are calm and inter-island shipping is more frequent. This is also the fishing season, which means abundant seafood.

coconut-eating crab (Birgus latro): *This giant crab climbs up coconut palms at night and cuts off the nuts, which fall to the ground. The crab then descends, tears off the husks, breaks open the nuts, and eats the white meat.*

FAUNA AND FLORA

In spite of the unremitting pressures of the timber concessions and human settlements, the Moluccas still offer the naturalist a striking example of the luxuriance and beauty of tropical animal life. In the 19th C., Alfred R. Wallace developed his theory of evolution here, which later greatly influenced Darwin's work. A transition zone between the Asian and Australasian/Papuan plant and animal kingdoms, many unique species are found here. The Aru and Kai islands have marsupials, such as a dwarf species of tree kangaroo only 30 cm tall, and the tree-living cuscus (a small opposum-like animal). About 90 species of butterflies are found in the Moluccas, 25 of which are endemic, including gaily colored birdwing species as large as small birds. There's a rich variety of other rare insects, and an indigenous species of frilled lizards. Yet, in spite of the unbroken chain of islands which seems to link the Moluccas with the Asian continent, there is a conspicuous absence of land mammals. Wild deer, wild pigs, and the tiny shrew have reached certain parts of the Moluccas (these most likely were introduced by man). There are monkeys on P. Bacan, and the Sulawesi black baboon and *babirusa* have reached as far as the Sula Islands. Ornamental fish, shellfish, and other marine forms abound in extraordinary variety.

Before traveling extensively in the Moluccas, read A.R. Wallace's *The Malay Archipelago* (Graham Brash Pte. Ltd., Singapore), still the most complete book in English on the area's natural history. Also, in Karangpanjang, a suburb of Ambon, is a lush garden where you can find a great variety of Moluccan flora,

including endemic orchids, and the Siliwama Museum there has natural history exhibits showing Moluccan forms.

Birds

The region's profuse birdlife, particularly plumage birds, shows great affinity to New Guinea species. There are many kinds of honeyeaters, 22 species of parrots, the famous racket-tailed kingfisher, the giant red-crested Moluccan cockatoo, 4 species of nutmeg-eating pigeons, and even 2 species of bird of paradise (on Aru). The region is well known for its parakeets and other vividly colored birds such as black-capped, purple, and green lories. Ceram has dazzling white fruit pigeons, and on Morotai and Halmahera are a multitude of gay parrots. As Australia is proud of its black swans, the Moluccas are equally proud of their black cockatoos. Yet there's a widespread absence of such common Asian species as woodpeckers, thrushes, jays, tits, and pheasants. In all of these eastern islands, people keep lorikeets and king parrots as pets; you'll see them on front porches, in houses, *warung,* everywhere. The large, mound-building megapode bird lays its eggs in uniquely constructed mounds of rotting vegetation in which the heat generated eventually hatches the eggs. This curious bird, sometimes called the jungle fowl or *maleo,* is found on Ceram, Buru, and Haruku. On Ceram and the southern islands lives the huge, nearly wingless cassowary. The brown booby is also common in the Moluccas.

Flora

The vegetation of Maluku is extravagant, with many Australian forms intermingled with the predominating Asiatic. Cloves, used by Egyptians to embalm their dead over 2,000 years ago, is found all over C. Maluku, particularly on Ceram and the Liassers. Nutmeg is also cultivated throughout C. Maluku. Other products include copra, damar resin, and hardwood timber such as the red and white *meranti.* Kayuputih *(cajuput)* oil is derived from the region's eucalyptus trees, while the all-important sago tree provides the main staple in the Moluccan diet as well as bark to make walls for houses and leaves to make roof thatch. An indigenous orange prune-like fruit, the *gandria,* grows in Poka and Rumahtiga on Ambon. A curious species of banana, the red-brown *pisang tongka langit,* does not hang down but grows up. Wild forest orchids are found on the Tanimbars and Kais.

HISTORY

Early History

Nutmeg and cloves have brought trade to these islands since at least 300 B.C. They were known by

Chinese, Javanese, Gujerati Indians, and Arabs long before the Portuguese "discovered" the Moluccas in 1498. Chinese Tang literature of the 7th C. mentions *Mi Lu Ku*. In A.D. 846, Ibn Khordadhbih wrote about some "Spice Islands" 15 days' sailing off Java. The Moluccas were always treated as satellites by various Javanese kingdoms and port cities on the N. Java coast: the 13th C. Singosari Dynasty prospered hugely on the spice trade with the Moluccas. From the 14th C. the spice trade in the islands was dominated by powerful Muslim sultans on Ternate, Tidore, and Djailolo (Halmahera). When the Portuguese captured Melaka in the late 16th C., Maluku was known as *Jazirat-al-Muluk*, the "Land of Many Kings."

The Search

In 15th C. Europe, the preferred way to preserve and improve the flavor of meat was to use nutmeg and cloves. These spices also went into the making of incense, lotions, perfumes, and medications to relieve gout, colic, and rheumatism. Other spices were prized for their aphrodisiacal qualities. Aristocratic ladies wore nutmeg in gold and silver brocades around their necks and sweetened their breath with spices. Gentlemen added zest to their grogs and soups with grated nutmeg which they carried in small fancy cases equipped with tiny graters. At that time the Moluccas were the only place in the world where these precious aromatic spices were grown. For centuries, Europeans could obtain the spices only through Arab traders. European monarchs dreamed of controlling the source and thus capturing their untold wealth.

Starting in the second half of the 15th C., various European nations launched expeditions in search of these legendary islands, the "Indies." Christopher Columbus was searching for a shorter, westerly route to the Indies when he stumbled upon the Americas in 1492, calling the inhabitants "Indians." Spices were the main incentive behind Magellan's voyage of discovery; he too was looking for a shortcut to the Indies when he discovered the Straits of Magellan and finally crossed the Pacific to the Philippines. It is a testament to European greed and perseverance that ruins of 400-year-old European fortresses litter scores of Moluccan islands today.

The Portuguese Era

Portuguese rule (1512-1605) was cruel and brutal. The Portuguese navigator Albuquerque captured Goa (India) in 1510 and Melaka (Penisular Malaysia) in 1511. Soon after, he also captured an outstanding map of all the smaller islands N of Java, from which the Portuguese were able to trace the origin of nutmeg and mace to the Banda Islands, and cloves to Tidore, Ternate, Halmahera, Bacan, Makian, and Moti. By 1512 the Portuguese were in the C. Moluccas in force, busi-

ly converting the inhabitants to Catholicism. Magellan's crews arrived in Ternate mad with joy in 1521, after a journey of 27 months. Antonio Galvao established economic control over the Moluccas in 1529, monopolizing the spice trade in Ambon and the Bandas. By 1550 it was claimed that 9 missionaries had converted 20,000 souls on Halmahera and Ternate, and another 20,000 on Ambon. In 1570, when a nephew of Captain Sancho de Vasconcelos murdered Sultan Hairun, the people of Ternate attacked and routed the Portuguese. The Portuguese later returned to neighboring Tidore, but their fortunes had taken a bad turn. They were forced out of Hitu in 1601, and driven entirely out of Tidore and Ambon by 1605.

The Spanish Era

By virtue of Magellan's passage around Cape Horn, the Spanish laid claim to the Moluccas under the Treaty of Tordesilas. Early Spanish influence was eclipsed by the Portuguese but the Spanish and their Filipino lackeys sent expeditions from Manila and finally subdued Ternate in 1606 after a hard fight, also grabbing some islands off Tidore and parts of Halmahera. In 1616 another expedition was mounted to drive out the Dutch, but its commander died en route and it was called off. The Spanish finally evacuated the northern Moluccas in 1663.

The Dutch Era

The Dutch period lasted from around 1605 to 1942. Beginning in the 17th C., the Dutch tried to create a world monopoly of the valuable nutmeg, cinnamon, and clove trade in this region. In 1607 they gained power by signing a treaty with the sultans of Tidore and Ternate, stating that the price of cloves was to be fixed, that the Dutch would "defend" Ternate against the Spaniards, and that the sultan would pay the Dutch back for the cost of all battles fought on his behalf. At the time the Moluccans were generally grateful to the Dutch for driving out the Portuguese and Spanish, and for the fact that they offered such high prices for their spices. But the Dutch soon revealed their true motives, imposing a ruthless system of forced cultivation which remained in place for hundreds of years. Plantations were laid waste and production reduced to keep profits high. Anyone caught buying or selling even the smallest parcel of spices was executed. On the basis of the spice trade, the Netherlands East India Co. was established and prospered until rampant corruption and intense competition drove it into bankruptcy in 1799. The Dutch government took over its affairs at the beginning of the 19th century. During the 19th and 20th C. colonial wars, eastern Indonesia was a traditional supplier of military manpower on the side of the Dutch against popular ethnic uprisings in Java and Sumatra.

The Decline

At the end of the 18th C. the world demand for cloves and nutmeg fell drastically. Coffee, tea, and cacao were the big money crops and the value of spices gradually declined. At about the same time the British and French smuggled out seedlings and succeeded in planting clove and nutmeg trees in their colonies in India and Africa, breaking the back of the monopoly. The Moluccas soon became an economic backwater. Ambon, Ternate, and the Bandas were opened to foreign shipping in 1854, but it wasn't until 1863 when a liberal constitution was adopted in Holland that forced cultivation at last ceased and all monopolies were terminated.

Modern History

The Moluccas were taken by the Japanese in Jan.-Feb. 1942, and recaptured by the Allies in 1945. After Indonesia declared its independence in 1945, civilians and former military members (KNIL) of the Dutch colonial army created—with Dutch backing—the Republik Maluku Selatan in 1947 which broke off ties with Indonesia in 1949. When the Dutch refused to continue to back the new republic in 1950, the secessionist attempt was abandoned and some 40,000 sympathetic Moluccans were evacuated to the Netherlands. Today a sizable number of Moluccans make up the Indonesian population of Holland, many of whom have never seen their homeland. Those disappointed with life in Holland returned to Indonesia in the 1970s to face yet other problems of readjustment and cultural conflicts with the Ambonese who never left. Some Moluccans in Holland still harbor the futile dream of returning and liberating their country, a dream which exploded in violence in 1977 when a band of youthful Moluccan malcontents seized the Indonesian Consulate and hijacked a commuter train in Holland, killing one passenger and holding the rest hostage.

ECONOMY

In the golden days of the spice trade, the Moluccas were the richest commercial region in the Dutch East Indies. Today, foreign investors and the government joint ventures are extracting tin, asbestos, and important oil deposits. Timber is the big growth industry with mills on Buru, Ceram, Halmahera, Taliabu, and Mongole. Plywood, which is exported to Japan, Singapore, and Hong Kong, is processed at plants in Batu Gong near Passo on Ambon, and a larger one at Waisarisa on Ceram. Besides timber, agriculture, and fishing, the mainstays of the local economy are raising sheep and goats, and in Christian villages, pigs.

Agriculture

Copra, cacao, coffee, rice, sago, maize, sugarcane,

and fruit are important agricultural products. Copra is one of the chief money crops. Rice is grown on Ceram, eucalyptus oil is produced on P. Buru. Paradoxically, the islands' most important products are no longer exotic spices, though cloves, nutmeg, and resins are still cultivated on some islands. Cloves *(buah cengkeh)* are sun-dried buds of the clove tree. The trees require very little maintenance and each carries 30,000-50,000 buds which when dry yield 3 kg of cloves selling for around Rp8000-9000 per kg. The clove tree flowers 10 years after it is planted and keeps blossoming for another 75 years. The spicy smoke of Indonesian cigarettes *(kretek)*, wafting through the *kampung* or *pasar* and now popular around the world, are in part made from cloves. Cloves are also used in pharmaceuticals. Nutmeg *(pala)*, produced only in Ambon and the Banda Islands, comes from the inner seed of the nut from the nutmeg tree. The lacy scarlet flesh surrounding the shiny chestnut-colored seed is used in the making of mace. Nutmeg trees reach a height of 12-15 m. They begin to bear fruit after 5 years, attain full maturity after 20 years, and blossom for another 80 years.

Fishing

In Maluku are some of the richest fishing grounds in Indonesia, especially for shrimp, crab, *trepang* (sea cucumber), and tuna. The province's surrounding oceans are at present being criminally raped by the Japanese. The government has established a frozen fish packing plant in Galela (Halmahera), and near Kate Kate and Rumahtiga on Ambon are frozen shrimp processing plants, a joint Japanese/government venture. Fish mills have also opened up in the Arus in SE Maluku. Pearls (both half and round pearls) are cultivated in Kao Bay (Halmahera) and the Kai and Aru islands. If you get the chance, it's great fun to make the rounds at night on the mudflats with a Moluccan crabber. Carrying a torch, he plunges a cylinder of split bamboo over the scuttling *kepiting*, placing each in a sack slung around his shoulders.

Tourism

In Dutch times these islands were so remote they were called *Groote Oost* ("The Great East"), a term which applied to all the small archipelagos between Sulawesi and New Guinea. Because of lack of transportation, no one but a few Dutch officials ever visited the region. But now with Merpatis' expanded air network, coupled with the more liberal 60-day visa policy instituted in 1984, more travelers and tourists are turning up in Ambon and to even the more far-flung island groups—nearly 6,000 domestic and foreign tourists in 1985. Marine tourism holds almost unlimited promise: the skin diving in gin-clear waters from Ambon to Ternate is unbelievable (bring your own snorkel and fins), even less spoilt than Bunaken (N. Sulawesi) or Maumere (Flores). The local *adat* *(sasi)* protects Maluku's ecological resources. The province's sandy beaches are beautiful and often empty, and the maritime climate splendid. Although the people are friendly and helpful, working against tourist development is the lack of funds to develop tourism facilities.

THE PEOPLE

The Moluccas is a fascinating ethnographic, linguistic, and anthropological environment. With a total population of 1.5 million, the average population density of these many scattered islands is around 13 per sq km. The islands are inhabited by a number of distinct, relatively isolated ethnic groups: the Alfuros, dark-skinned frizzy-haired proto-Malays (or Australoids), the original inhabitants of the Moluccas; lighter-skinned straight-haired deutero-Malays (or Mongoloids) who arrived many centuries later; minority groups like Chinese, Arabs, Javanese, and Moluccans of European descent who trace their lineage from Spanish, Portuguese, and Dutch colonists. One of the major ethnic groups is the Ambonese, living along the coastal areas of the islands of Ambon, Saparua, Nusa Laut, and western Ceram. Roving colonies of "sea gypsies" (Orang Laut) follow a marine economy and moor their boats in the many ports of the archipelago.

The Alfuros

Alfuros is the collective name for all of the indigenous peoples living usually in the interior mountainous areas of Maluku. Foreign traders—whether European, Javanese, or Chinese—have always settled the coastal areas of Maluku, forcing inland the dark-complexioned aborigines of the islands, called by the Portuguese Alifuro, meaning "uncouth, savage, pagan." The Spanish were not able to subjugate them on the islands of Buru and Ceram, and even as late as 1890 they were still described as headhunting savages, dressed only in a cidako which covered the genitals. With government encouragement and support, many of these isolated inland tribes have been relocated to the coasts where they continue their more forest-oriented gathering of coconuts rather than taking up the Malay-style livelihood of fishing. The term Alfuro, still in use, has to this day an unfavorable stigma. The Alfuros do not inhabit Ambon, Haruku, Saparua, or Nusa Laut.

Religion

European Catholic and Protestant missionaries started proselytizing in this region over 100 years ago. In C. Maluku, Christians and Muslims are equally divided. Generally, Muslims outnumber Christians in N. Maluku, while Christians predominate in the south. But like so many of Indonesia's ethnic groups, the locals also govern themselves by local adat customary law. Many tribes, particularly in the SE

islands, also believe strongly in supernatural and ancestor spirits, both benevolent and malevolent. All over eastern Indonesia there is a widespread belief in witches (swangi).

ARTS AND CRAFTS

Music And Dance

Maluku has a rich traditional music; many popular Indonesian folk songs originated here, especially from Ambon. The special type of gamelan played here is called totabuang. Bamboo flutes are played unceasingly by schoolkids. There are a number of original dances, many containing elements imported from abroad: in the Bambu Gila Dance, bamboo poles about 2-2½ m long are placed crosswise and clicked rhythmically together. As the tempo gradually speeds up, dancers step between and around the poles without getting their feet caught. A dukun puts a spell on the bamboo and can order it to go anywhere he commands; 7 men are powerless to hold it back. The Badapus Dance is similar to the Balinese Kris Dance; men stab themselves with sharp weapons but their flesh isn't pierced. Even the spectators who take part cannot harm themselves. Also performed is the slow and hypnotic Handkerchief Dance.

Crafts

On Ambon and Ternate, model ships and houses are built completely out of cloves; clove artifacts have been tourist souvenirs at least since the 19th century. For handwoven fabrics, each Moluccan island has retained its own artistic styles, motifs, and dyeing methods. The tribes of Ceram make the finest woven crafts. On the Kai Islands, unique earthenware with arabesque and curlicue designs are produced. Freed from hard labor thanks to the widely available and easily harvested sago palm, Moluccans are excellent boatbuilders and seamen and have traditionally embarked on long trading expeditions. Notice the wide use of outrigger canoes which indicates that you are on the periphery of Melanesia.

GETTING THERE

Ambon (the provincial capital) is the gateway to Maluku from Java and Ujung Pandang, Ternate is the gateway to Maluku from Manado, N. Sulawesi. Garuda flies to Ambon from Jakarta for Rp222,900 and from Surabaya for Rp193,000. Merpati flies from Ujung Pandang to Ambon for Rp79,100 or from Manado daily to Ternate for only Rp39,000. Bouraq and Mandala airlines also have regular flights to Ambon from Ujung Pandang, and Bouraq has direct service 3 times weekly from Jakarta to Ternate (Rp258,700), stopping at Balikpapan (Kalimantan), Palu, Gorontalo, and Manado en route. One "Outer Island" loop is to fly from Surabaya to Ujung Pandang, then head overland up through Sulawesi (visiting Torajaland on the way) to Poso, take a boat across Teluk Poso to Gorontalo, travel overland to Manado, fly or take a boat to Ternate, then fly or take a boat to Ambon and back to Ujung Pandang or Java. Some travelers, on the Los Angeles to Jakarta flight, get off at Biak (Irian Jaya) and fly down to Ambon for Rp107,600 (1 hour, 3 flights weekly). Or, from the other direction, fly from Manado (N. Sulawesi) over to Ternate and work your way down through Maluku from there. For only Rp169,700 1st Class, Ambon is also accessible from Jakarta on Pelni's luxurious KM *Rinjani*, plying the route Tg. Priok-Surabaya-Ujung Pandang-Bau Bau-Ambon.

GETTING AROUND

By Road
Of only about 1,800 km of roads, less than 500 km are paved. The main road systems are on Ambon (150 km); Saparua; Kailolo (Haruku); Masohi/Amahai, Kairatu (Ceram); Namlea (Buru); Ternate; Soa Siu (Tidore); Tual (Kais); Tobelo, Galela, and Jailolo (Halmahera); Daruba (Morotai); Sanana (Sulas); Labuha (Bacan). Minibuses and *bemo* travel the main roads, with the main terminals usually in the center of town near the *pasar* or *stanplatz*. Roads are virtually nonexistent in the interiors of the Outer Islands, where you should expect to walk practically everywhere along coastal paths linking villages or on footpaths high into the mountains.

By Air
The most expedient but costliest way to see the Moluccas. In order to create a more equitable distribution throughout Indonesia, in 1980 Merpati pioneered flights to the smaller islands in the "Outer" Moluccas. Merpati has a very useful flight from Ternate to the small airstrips of Bacan and Halmahera; it also offers a service from Ambon to Ceram, Banda, and such main towns in SE Maluku as Saumlaki (Tanimbar) and Langgur (Kai). Using mostly Britten-Norman Islanders, Merpati now serves: Ternate, Galela (Halmahera), Labuha (Bacan), Ambon (Ambon), Nalea (Buru), Sanana and Amahai (Ceram), Bandaneira (Banda), Langgur (near Tual, Kais), Saumlaki (Tanimbars), and Mangole (Sula). Sample fares: Ambon to Langgur, Rp84,600 (stopping in Banda on the way); Ambon to Ternate, Rp63,600. Ambon has the only jet-length runway in the province.

By Sea
Between the main ports of call, the only regular sea links are provided by the government-run Pelni and Perintis ships which carry people and cargo from one island group to another at approximately 3-week in-

tervals. This means that you must either explore the island of your choice while the ship is in harbor, or disembark to await the next ship. The deep-water harbor of Ambon is Maluku's principal port. Pelni's KM *Baruna Bhakti* departs for Ternate and the northern Moluccan ports, returning to Ambon, every 3 weeks; the KM *Niaga X* does the 3-week southern loop (Banda, Tual, Saumlaki, etc.), and back to Ambon. Regular ships also connect Ternate to Bitung, the main port on Sulawesi's northern peninsula. Fares are cheap; for example, the 14-hour voyage from Banda to Ambon on the *Nusantara Daya* costs only Rp5000. It's possible to rent a space in a cramped crewmember's cabin with a small fan for Rp20,000-25,000 (a whole cabin goes for Rp60,000!).

It's fairly easy to hitch a ride on a local boat working up and down the coasts. Most native settlements are coastal and transport between them is traditionally by boat—from *kapal motor* right down to small dugouts with 15-hp motors! Regional craft are called *prahu, jungku, arombai,* or simply *bot.* Inter-island ferries are also widely available, especially during the dry season (Sept.-March). For example, a regular ferry leaves Langgur (Kai Kecil) to Elat (Kai Besar) in the morning and returns that same afternoon, costing only Rp1000. Local, inexpensive ferries connect Ambon to its neighboring islands of Saparua and Nusa Laut. And at least 4 vessels depart twice weekly from Ambon to coastal villages on Ceram (Rp7500-15,000) and to Buro (Rp8000-12,5000). Ideally, though, this is a region that should be explored in your own self-contained, seaworthy craft with plenty of time. Be prepared for adventure!

Accommodations
Ambon and Ternate offer a number of modern, comfortable hotels (Rp15,000-35,000) with a/c, plus *wisma,* (Rp10,000-20,000) and even *losmen* (Rp5000-8000). Prices often include 2 meals per day. Although prices tend to be at least twice those on Java and Bali, in Maluku you might be able to stay with a family for much less than in a hotel. This is a quality experience; ask at the tourist office which family in town offers guestrooms. In SE Moluccas (Tual and Dobo), it's possible to stay with missionaries and at priests' residences *(pastoran)* for as little as Rp2000 pp per day including meals. If they don't ask for any money, be sure to give a donation. Take along lots of cash in a moneybelt. Your VISA or MasterCard is absolutely useless in the Moluccas; they either ignore it, laugh, or just say "No." Travelers cheques can even be difficult to cash and they are of little use in places like Dobo in the Arus.

Food
Minang-style restaurants are found in Ambon, but otherwise the regional food is quite basic. Fish is the main source of protein; for seafood lovers, there's an

abundance of crab, shrimp, and tuna. In the villages, meat and fowl are generally eaten only at feasts or celebrations. One of the main sources of carbohydrates is a meal extracted from the heart of the sago palm, a tree which grows wild. The sago provides not only food, but its fronds are also used to thatch huts, while the leaf midrib is utilized to build walls and ceilings. Sago bread comes in the form of a

giant waffle. A unique dish of this region is *papeda*, prepared by pulverizing and straining the pulp from the trunk of a sago palm. This "flour" is then boiled to form a tasteless, jelly-like mass eaten hot or cold. *Papeda* has the consistency of, and even looks like, wallpaper paste. If you don't swallow it straightaway, you think you're drowning. Thankfully, *papeda* is often served with a flavorful fish curry soup which

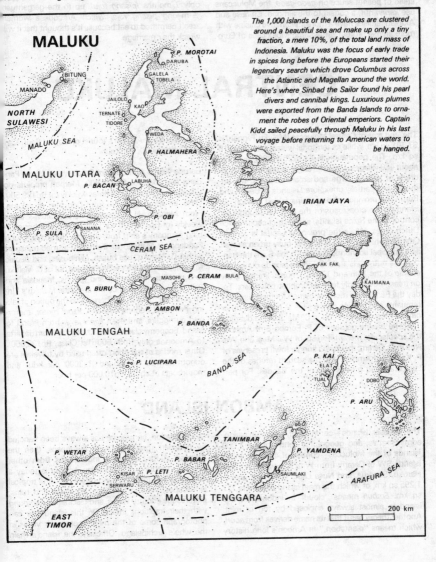

MALUKU

The 1,000 islands of the Moluccas are clustered around a beautiful sea and make up only a tiny fraction, a mere 10%, of the total land mass of Indonesia. Maluku was the focus of early trade in spices long before the Europeans started their legendary search which drove Columbus across the Atlantic and Magellan around the world. Here's where Sinbad the Sailor found his pearl divers and cannibal kings. Luxurious plumes were exported from the Banda Islands to ornament the robes of Oriental emperors. Captain Kidd sailed peacefully through Maluku in his last voyage before returning to American waters to be hanged.

makes it almost palatable. This sago diet is supplemented by cassava and sweet potatos. Other popular regional dishes include boiled sweet potatos, roast fish *(ikan bakar)* and sour sauce, all served of course with sago cakes.

In N. Maluku, a yellow saffron-flavored rice *(nasi kunyit)*, accompanying *sate* and curry, is delicious. Instead of peanut sauce on *gado-gado*, the Moluccans use *kanari* nut, a cousin to the almond. Chinese and Arabian families have a more imaginative cuisine with more animal protein served, and Moluccans of European descent follow European-style eating habits, serving such dishes as red-bean soup and pig's feet There's the full range of fruits found everywhere in Indonesia: *salak, papaya, durian, mangga, langsat, duku, jambu,* etc. One regional fruit is the *gandaria,* an orange-colored prune. Over 22 varieties of bananas grow throughout these islands, including one tiny species which grows to maturity in only 7 months *(pisang tuju)*, up to the gargantuan ½-m-long *pisang raja,* which Ambonese women aren't permitted to eat because it's thought that it will wreck their marriage.

CENTRAL MALUKU

The land area of Central Moluccas (Maluku Tengah) is 37,701 sq km, while its territorial waters total 265,316 sq km. The population is 443,225 (1986), living in about 480 villages. Maluku Tengah is made up of hundreds of islands, large and small, including the immense and partially unexplored islands of Ceram and Buru. The province also contains fabled Ambon, an island on the crossroads of the colonial struggle for control of the Spice Islands, and district capital since Dutch times. While the provincial capital is Ambon City, Masohi on Ceram is another busy urban as well as a principal economic center. To the S are the Bandas, the nutmeg islands. On these islands during the course of the 16th and 17th C., money literally grew on trees, though only for the European colonizers. Today the Bandas are more renowned for their historical remnants and pristine diving sites. A number of other natural reserves are found in C. Maluku: the dazzling 1,000-ha marine gardens of P. Pombo E of Ambon; the spectacular *meranti* forests of Wai Mual and Wai Nua in C. Ceram; the *maleo* (jungle fowl) preserves of P. Kasa N of Ambon; and the seabird refuges of the Lucipara-Penju groups SW of the Bandas. For permits, inquire at Ambon's tourist office, 1st floor, Kantor Gubernor, Jl. Pattimura.

Garuda flies to Ambon from Surabaya via Ujung Pandang each day for Rp222,900. Merpati propjets do this same flight at least 3 times weekly for Rp189,500. Other air approaches are from Denpasar or Jakarta. From Manado, N. Sulawesi, Merpati flies 3 times weekly for Rp118,000. Or take a Pelni or other shipping company's ship from Jakarta, Surabaya, Ujung Pandang, or Manado via Ternate. For road transport within C. Maluku, use buses, minibuses, and *becak.* Merpati provides inter-island service out of C. Maluku to a number of distant island groups; Mandala and Pelita airlines also service the area (see Maluku's "Intro" chapter for details). There's also the option of taking Pelni and Perintis coasters, *kapal motor,* motorized outriggers, and even *kapal layar* from island to island. Economy class on the KM *Rinjani* from Jakarta to Ambon is only Rp55,500 (1st Class, Rp135,800). Other modes of transport often used by travelers are dugout canoes for around Rp3000 per hour and motorboats at about Rp10,000 per hour.

AMBON ISLAND

The Uliasser Islands—commercial, communication, administrative, and geographic center of the 1,000 islands of the Moluccas—consist of 4 mountainous islands SW of Ceram: from W to E they are Ambon, Haruku, Saparua, and Nusa Laut. Their total area is 1,295 sq km, of which the main island Ambon is 777 sq km. *Embun* means "cloud" in Indonesian; this island is almost always enclosed by fog or mist. Another theory has it that its name derives from *apon,* which means "plantation." In Ambon's long history of exploitation, commerce has always been handled by outsiders, beginning with Europeans, then the Chinese, Arabs, and now Indonesians from other islands. Predominantly Christian Ambon is today a sort of "mini-Moluccas" and offers beautiful tropical landscapes, historic buildings, churches and ruins, picturesque country walks, and fascinating *kampung* with their traditions intact. On this island you can photograph some of the most spectacular vistas in the whole archipelago. Officially, the island's main

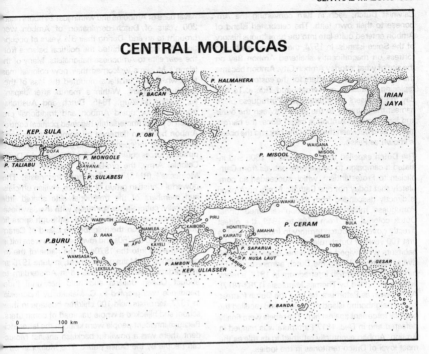

CENTRAL MOLUCCAS

P. HALMAHERA

P. BACAN

IRIAN JAYA

KEP. SULA

P. OBI

DOFA

P. MONGOLE

SANANA

P. TALIABU

P. SULABESI

WAIGANA

MISOOL

P. MISOOL

WAHAI

WAEPUTIH

PIRU

D. RANA

NAMLEA

KAIBOBO

HONITETU

AMAHAI

P. CERAM

BULA

P. BURU

W. APU

KAIRATU

HONESI

TOBO

KAYELI

P. SAPARUA

WAMSASA

TIFU

P. AMBON

NUSA LAUT

P. GESAR

LEKSULA

KEP. ULIASSER

MARUKU

0   100 km

P. BANDA

---

city is called Amboina, although nobody much uses the name anymore—both the island and city are called Ambon. There is tight control on visitors; on arrival you are signed in at the airport's *imigrasi* office and your hotel also has to register you with the police.

The Land

This horseshoe-shaped (48 km X 22 km) island is divided into **Hitu**, the northern peninsula, and **Leitimor**, the southern peninsula. It's believed that Ambon was once 2 separate islands; seabed movements and shifting sands connected them. Within the loops of land created by these peninsulas nature has created an excellent harbor which can accommodate large spice and copra ships. Ambon has 2 beautiful bays, **Teluk Ambon** and **Teluk Baguala**. The entire island is very mountainous; **G. Horiel** in Leitimor rises to nearly 580 m; the highest point, **G. Latua** is nearly 915 m. Both mountains are volcanic in origin, although activity ended long ago. The island, however, is still subject to earthquakes, and sulphur beds and hotsprings are common.

Ambon's rich soil gives rise to nutmeg, cloves, cinnamon, betelnut, and palm plantations; a variety of orchids grow wild on shrubs and trees. Although a profusion of tropical blossoms sprout outside of windows, plastic flowers are prized, found in every home, hotel lobby, and hotel room. The main staples are sago, tubers, vegetables, and cassava, which grows wild in swampy areas. Fish provides the main protein, though the Ambonese do not fish on a commercial scale. Cloves and nutmeg are still among the primary cash crops, though not nearly on the scale seen in the past. Swidden crops such as squash and other gourds, plus spinach, are also cultivated; the Ambonese preference for root crops betrays their Melanesian origins.

HISTORY

Early History

The ancestors of the present inhabitants of C. Moluccan villages migrated from W. Ceram or from Makian Island near Ternate no later than the 15th C.; this is evident in their *adat*. Divided into small kinship groups, the Ambonese were originally slash-and-burn cultivators. They were first dominated by the Islamic kingdom of Ternate to the N, which forcibly eradicated headhunting, propagated Islam, and introduced a political rather than a tribal form of social organization. Next came the Catholic Portuguese, then the

Calvinist Dutch, each in turn converting the Ambonese to their own faith. The celebrated island of Ambon entered quite late into the tumultuous history of the Spice Islands. In 1574, the Portuguese built a fortress on magnificently sheltered Ambon Bay on the site of what is today Ambon City. Ambon became the Portuguese headquarters for the eastern islands, replacing fortresses on Ternate and Tidore. To this day the Uliassers are littered with Portuguese place names: the entrance to the strait between the outer and inner bays of Ambon is called Boca, the narrow strip of land between the top of the bay and the ocean is known as Passo.

The Dutch expelled the Portuguese in 1605 and initiated a campaign to convert the natives from Catholicism to Protestantism, which succeeded so completely that today not one Catholic family on Ambon is directly descended from those first converted by Portuguese missionaries. Ambon remained under Dutch colonial rule from 1606 to 1949, the oldest directly governed Dutch territory in Indonesia. In the first 100 years of Dutch rule, one-third of Ambon's inhabitants were wiped out by either diseases or punitive expeditions. When the Dutch administration returned after the British interregnum in 1817, a rebellion broke out led by Thomas Matulesia (1783-1817). Also known as Pattimura, he took the Dutch fortress on the neighboring island of Saparua and repelled the colonial force sent against him. The rebels were finally defeated and in Dec. 1817 Pattimura was hanged in Ambon. Ambon eventually returned to its role as the most loyal of Dutch territories in the Indies.

Patasiwa And *Patalima*

These traditional Ambonese military defense organizations were famous for their raiding forays. The military tradition and love of martial spectacle attracted the Ambonese to the Royal Netherlands Army (KNIL), which endowed them with preferred status. For centuries the Dutch used Ambonese mercenaries to help them police the archipelago, according them better wages and privileges than other Indonesian soldiers received. Brave, strong, intelligent, obedient, the Dutch kept many thousands of these native sons combat-ready to suppress uprisings by other ethnic groups and troublesome sultans on Java and Sumatra. The Ambonese today are still fond of parades and marches, goose-stepping and arms swinging. Ambonese also served in the Netherlands Indies civil government as teachers, foremen of native workers, and as sailors crewing Dutch vessels. During the 1930s, the Dutch turned the island into the administrative seat and a major naval bastion for all the eastern islands. Ambon also became the center of educational and missionary activity for the region.

WW II And Independence

On 31 Jan. 1942, Japanese bombers attacked the naval base of Amboina and within just 24 hours nearly 300 years of Dutch domination of Ambon were brought to an end. During their 3½ years of occupation, the Japanese shifted the political balance from the *adat* elite to Ambonese nationalists. Many of the island's Muslims welcomed their new colonial masters, while the Christians mourned the loss of their Dutch supporters. Within a month after Japan' capitulation in Aug. 1945, Dutch and Australian troops had occupied Ambon and traditional pro-Dutch loyalists immediately regained political control. Ambon has been flattened by bombs 3 times since WW II. After independence and before Javanese republican forces could be sent out to replace the Dutch Colonial Army, the pro-Dutch "Republic of South Moluccas" (RMS) seceded from Indonesia. This powerful Christian group of soldiers, civilian officials and members of the traditional elite shared little ethnically, culturally, or spiritually with the Javanese. Resistance was crushed in 1950, although sporadic guerilla fighting on the neighboring island of Ceram continued into the '60s and reverberations were felt in Holland even into the 1970s. In the name of the Independence for Maluku Movement, in June 1975 an extraordinary plot was uncovered in Amsterdam to abduct Queen Juliana and hold her until independence was granted to C. Maluku by Indonesia. In 1977, terrorists held 100 children hostage in their school and hijacked a whole trainload of commuters. Because innocent people were killed in the latter incident, there was a powerful backlash against Moluccan people by the Dutch public. The Moluccan emigres in Holland have since quieted down but their dream lives on.

Aftermath

The violent suppression of the RMS in 1950 was probably the worst possible way for Ambon to become integrated into the Indonesian Republic and has made for a sharply polarized society with little regional autonomy. Leaving a legacy of divisiveness and mistrust, the Javanese have never really forgotten that this island once revolted against their centralist government and the Javanese now occupy Ambon, holding the whole island in a sort of house arrest. One predictable result has been the dramatic change in the fortunes of the island's Muslims, who are no longer dominated by Christians. Islamic schools and the Muslim religion have received much support and funding from Indonesia's Muslim majority which controls the national government. All top administrative positions, except for a cosmetic pro-Java governor, are Javanese-filled. While only 9 Dutch policemen maintained order here before the war, now it takes thousands of Javanese soldiers to control the island. Although you can discreetly talk to Ambonese about their feelings, the less you say about politics in public anywhere on Ambon, the better.

THE PEOPLE

A very striking people, the Ambonese have mixed racially with Portuguese, Alfuros, Malays, Javanese, and Dutch, creating a sort of creole Moluccan culture. This amalgam is most obvious in the lighter-skinned coastal villagers; interior peoples have darker complexions with more pronounced Melanesian features. A strong Melanesian element is also evident in the urban population as people from surrounding islands (from as far away as Buton) arrive in Ambon to seek work. (This also makes for a large group of hungry young men in Ambon City who always try to squeeze an extra Rp100-200 out of you.) The Ambonese tongue is classified as belonging to the Ambon-Timor group of Malayo-Polynesian languages. European languages have made a deep impression. For example, Portuguese lives on in Ambonese: *mui* from *muito* for "very much"; religious terms such as *perdeos, komunyan,* and *nyora* for "Mrs." In some families and among the elderly, Dutch is still spoken as a second language. More Ambonese (largely political refugees) live in Holland than on Ambon.

Village Organization

The majority of Ambonese live in villages lining the coasts of the island. Each Ambonese village is either *patasiwa* or *patalima,* "Nine Divisions" or "Five Divisions"—territorial quasi-political partrilineal federations *(uli)* which date from the 15th century. These federations protected the Ambonese against war and colonial repression. The Dutch later abolished the federations and made each village politically independent and governed by a ruling council. From this native elite a village headman (called by the pompous title of raja) is chosen or inherits the title. Other traditional officers who help govern the village are the head of the *soa* (administrative subdistrict), the Lord of the Land *(Tuan Tanah),* the *adat*-chief, the war leader *(kapitan,* now a purely ceremonial office), the chief of the forest police *(kepala kewang),* the village messenger *(marinyo),* and the village priest *(mauwang).* Each of the important lineages on the island has an honorific title, belongs to a sacred spring, and maintains its own cultivated plots *(dati).* Many villages also maintain an ancestral memorial stone in an "original settlement" *(negeri lama)* in the hills.

Adat

Although the villages on Ambon are either Christian or Muslim, they are all nearly identical in their social and cultural fabric. Scratch the skin of a Muslim or a Christian and you find *adat.* Socially approved *adat* behavior is equated with the will of the ancestors, and violation of *adat* could incur the wrath of ancestral spirits. Village councils enforce the *adat* and carry out temporal punishment of offenders, if necessary. One classic example of living *adat* is the *pela* system. This ritual, myth-form of truce between villages which were once at war dates back to the 15th and 16th centuries when Christianity and Islam were introduced into the Moluccas. Over 50 *pela* confederations were formed to avoid the harmful mistrust which could develop between villages adhering to different religions. When several or more villages have adopted a *pela* alliance, this common law is even stronger than blood relationships. To avoid conflict, the youngsters of *pela* villages are strictly forbidden to marry, a union which is looked upon as a form of incest. Sometimes Christians help their Muslim neighbors build a mosque and Muslims help their Christian neighbors build a church; *pela* villages also help each other plant and harvest crops, share the financial burden of funerals, weddings, and together celebrate national and religious holidays. Despite the experience of the rebellious RMS movement in the 1950s—in which Christian soldiers victimized Muslims, deeply dividing the two communities—the alliances are still strong. Even the sizable Moluccan exile communities living in the Netherlands practice *pela!*

Religion

Ambon's Christian community is a product of European contact, while the island's Islamic community came into being as a result of early trading with Ternate, Makassar, and Java. Saint Francis Xavier established a mission on Ambon as early as 1547; by the start of the 17th C. there were as many as 50,000 Catholics in C. Maluku. Today, Christianity and Islam are equally represented on Ambon to the extent that sometimes you see a mosque and a church in the same *kampung.* These modern religions have largely replaced the indigenous animism. But since Islam is the state religion of Indonesia, most public offices are held by Muslims. Identifying and allying themselves so strongly with the Dutch, the Christians for decades had a decided advantage in education, local government positions, etc. But after the RMS misadventure of the 1950s, the Muslims are now the favored majority, receiving direct financial support and perks from the government. This makes for less harmonious, albeit more equal, relations between the followers of both faiths. The many *haj* on the island sponsor constant loudspeaker calls to prayer, the refrains beginning to drown out the choruses of Christian singers. The church and mosque congregations exert a powerful social and moral force in village life.

SHOPPING

Although more expensive than Java or Bali, you can find about anything you might want if you are willing to wander around. Ambon City has hundreds of (mostly) Chinese-owned shops. The city market is fascinating, but the crowds are heavy. Black coral bracelets *(akar bahar)* or turtle shell bracelets (Rp1500), *gigi duyung* (seacow teeth), Rp5000 or more. Great Ming platters, Rp150,000-300,000; the Naulu people of Ceram have loads of 16th C. Ming cheaper, but you have to really hike for it. Stuffed sea turtles run Rp30,000-40,000. Big bottle of Johnny Walker, Rp12,000. Pulau Buru is the origin of *kayu-putih* oil, which is processed and sells quite cheaply on Ambon at Rp500 for a small bottle, Rp900 for a large bottle. *Runut* is the local name for the tissue which covers the young leaves of a coconut tree. In the past it was used as a sieve for sago washing, but its contemporary use is as a basic material for fans, bags, and wall decorations.

Moluccan clove ship

Clove Artifacts

Ambon's oldest craft, sold to Dutch tourists for generations. The first designs were of the *kora kora*, the Moluccan gondola, built entirely out of cloves. The art was invented by the Mustamu family of Mardika (Kota Ambon), the skill passed down from father to son. Nowadays, clove artifacts are also produced in Latuhalat but sometimes their stock is depleted because they sell mostly to retailers. Designs now include baskets, flowers, birds, cigarette and cigar boxes, and whole ships mounted in glass cases and built completely out of cloves with tiny seamen, oars, and lanterns on deck: Rp10,000-15,000 depending on size and workmanship involved. Also try the shops along Jl. A.Y. Patty.

Shops

Craft shops are along Jl. Mr. J. Latu Harhary and A.Y. Patty in Ambon City. In Rumahtiga village, visit Frans C. Tita's **Salawaku Art Shop**, a shell-crafts cottage industry. Board a ferry or outrigger from near Galala, NE of Ambon, to Rumahtiga across Ambon Bay, Rp150. **Batumerah** is a section of Ambon, and the center of production for attractive pearl- and tortoise-shell articles. Bracelets run Rp1500-2000, rings Rp500-1000, hair clasps about Rp3000 or more; also wall decorations.

Garments

Moluccan shirts and jackets are either painted or em-broidered with beautiful designs of traditional Moluc-can decorative patterns. Ambonese Christians have been known, since Dutch times, for their black clothing worn to church. Women wear a black jacket and shawl *(kain pikul)* and sometimes go barefoot (especially in the village); men wear a black coat with white shirt and shell buttons. Young women's festive dress comes in all shades of red, while older women wear more subdued blue and violet colors. These Moluccan-style garments are available at hotel gift shops such as **Hotel Wisata** and **Amboina Hotel**; also ask the tourist office which tailors in town pro-duce the traditional jackets and blouses.

EVENTS

Most of the Ambonese *adat* ceremonies have fizzled out, but a few are still practiced. For example, when a new *baileo* (communal meetinghouse) is constructed, there's a purification ceremony by village headmen and elders called *cuci baileo*. This cleansing festival is also carried out on old consecrated *baileo* such as the one in Soya, SE of Ambon City, on the second Fri. of December. Newly elected rajas have inauguration ceremonies. Try to get in on an infant baptism and a Christian confirmation ceremony, both of which re-tain a number of pre-Christian indigenous features. **Kunci Tahun Baru**, meaning "locking in the New Year," is celebrated by feasting on sago, sweet pota-tos, and wild game. Ambonese funerals are conduct-ed by the village priest or elder. At the gravesite ser-vice flutes are played and sometimes graveside vigils are held on the third and 40th days after interment.

At Ambonese weddings, spiritual, civil, and *adat* prac-tices come into full play. The marriage first is perform-ed before the village raja, at his home or office, then at the church, then the *adat* rituals are carried out. The groom's relatives carry the bride's dowry (textiles, brandy, Chinese porcelain, money, motorscooter) to the bride's family. Formerly, heads were offered up in payment for the bride. Sudden elopements and mock wife-stealings, to avoid paying the bride price, are fre-quent and encouraged by parents because of the costs saved from not having a wedding.

Sports

The famous Darwin-Ambon International Yacht Classic Race started in 1976 with only 6 yachts; in 1986 there were 26. Yachts from Australia, New Zealand, Germany, and the U.S. take part, and even Ambon's tourist office has its own yacht! It costs around A$4000 to equip a yacht for the race, plus A$300 for the entry fee. Local sailing competitions and *arumbai manggurebe* or gondola-rowing con-tests are also popular. *Pencak Silat* (martial arts) is also widely practiced. The N coast town of Mamala practices a sport called *sapulidi* (also called *baku*

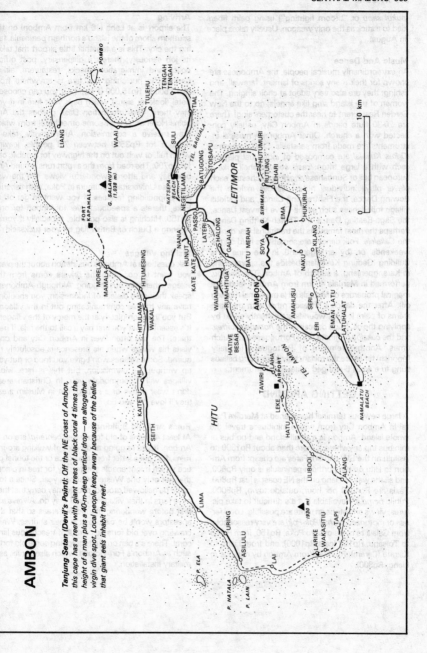

AMBON

Tanjung Setan (Devil's Point): Off the NE coast of Ambon, this cape has a reef with giant trees of black coral 4 times the height of a man plus a 40-m-deep vertical drop — an altogether virgin dive spot. Local people keep away because of the belief that giant eels inhabit the reef.

pukul sapu or "broom fighting") using palm fibers tied to a stick as the only weapon. Usually takes place in August.

Music And Dance

An extraordinarily musical people, the Ambonese are known for their many songs of lament, farewell, and fishing; they are also very adept at choir singing. The women of the island sing like angels; go to the New Garden Restaurant to hear the customers sing! There are 20-30 flute bands in Ambon City, usually connected with a church. Other Ambonese musical instruments are made from seashells. Shell orchestras (Orkes Kulibia) are composed of individual players, each with a large triton (casis cornita) shell. Like a European bell or Sundanese angklung orchestra, each player plays individual notes. Dances include the Rowing Dance, the Fishtrapping Dance, and various village folk dances such as the Clove Harvest Dance, the Sago-Beating Dance, the Thatch-Knitting Dance. Perhaps the most famous is the traditional war dance, the Cakalele. Folk dances are sometimes held on the weekends or (by arrangement) in the Fine Arts Building (Gedung Kesenian) beside the sports arena in Karangpanjang, a suburb of Ambon. The Sasapu, performed in Mamala 40 km from Ambon, lauds the magical properties of Mamala oil (a medicinal rubbing oil). After the dancers hit each other with the hard stems of palm leaves, wounds are instantly cured by applying the oil. Such dances as the horlapep, katreji, and the cakaiba originate from Portuguese and Dutch times. Another remnant of Portuguese (actually Moorish) times are the melancholy Keroncang ballads sung to a small 5-stringed guitar-like instrument.

GETTING AROUND

A large new bus terminal has opened at Mardika Pantai in Ambon City from where minibuses travel the whole island. Ambon is a small island and no bus or minibus trip anywhere is more than about Rp1300 (to Asilulu on the SW corner). Fares are cheap: from Ambon to Hitu on the northern peninsula is only Rp600, and all the way to Liang on the NE coast is just Rp800. Taxis are Rp4000 per hour; outside town, Rp5000. Public bemo are available but it's difficult to take pictures; views and stops en route are possible. Local ferries or motorized prahu (Pok-Pok) are very reasonable; from Galala to cross over to Poka, Rp150; from Passo to Toisapu, Rp150 (cars Rp1000), and from Liang to Kairatu (Ceram), Rp2500 (from Ambon by minibus to Liang, Rp800).

Arriving

The airport is at Laha (46 km from Ambon) on the southern shore of the island's northern peninsula, facing the city. This is a together little airport that takes its job seriously; there's a dispensary, post office, police and immigration checks, restaurant, airline desks. The punishing taxi fare is anywhere from Rp12,500 to Rp15,000 (1 hour). Or you can choose a hotel (look for signs) which pays your fare in if you stay there. The Information Desk pushes the Amboina Hotel on you, or some other hotel from which they receive a commission. Alternatively, take a minibus for Rp3500 between 7-8 people, leaving when full, or wait out on the highway for a public one for Rp700. The road from the airport runs around Ambon Bay and affords wonderful views. On the way you pass Universitas Pattimura in Poka, with fisheries and shipbuilding facilities. If you want to get off at Poka, there's a speedboat over to Ambon for only Rp150. Hitching is also possible, especially if you're wearing a Dutch or British flag on your rucksack!

Visiting Villages

Ask questions at Ambon's bus station about the place you want to go; often the drivers come from the village where the bus is going. Although Ambonese speak their own dialect of Indonesian, you shouldn't have any trouble communicating out in the villages. But you'll be completely at the mercy of the villagers. It's essential that you first pay a call to the raja, if he's there. The raja often lives in Ambon City and only visits his village when his presence is absolutely required. Some villages won't give you food or put you up without his permission, but this is rare. Most villages will accommodate you. In Christian areas don't wear a kain or a sarung, but in Muslim areas they'll love it if you do.

Ruins And Old Buildings

At least 40 ruins of old fortresses (benteng) are on P. Ambon. If you're going to do a lot of walking around ruins, first get a letter from the police or the tourist office which might enable you to stay for free in places that get only one Western visitor a year. Since a fort could be hallowed ground, people may deny that they have forts in their villages even if they do. Always ask first before wandering around out-areas so that the ancestors won't be disturbed in their shrines. While crawling over old forts be careful of treacherous land coral. There's a ban on photographing some old forts, such as Ambon's Fort Victoria, which also serves as a military installation.

AMBON CITY

The administrative capital of Maluku Tengah (pop. 207,702 in 1986), a disparate collection of government offices and closely knit *kampung*, this is the most important Indonesian city between Ujung Pandang and Jayapura. On a high, rocky coastline on Leitimor, the southern peninsula, the city is in a lovely setting divided by steep ravines. One long street has well-stocked shops and an impressive *stanplatz* used for both grazing cattle and soccer matches. Walk around town during siesta time in the afternoon when families relax on their front verandahs sipping tea. Join in a Christian service on Sun. in one of the town's numerous churches, a real window into Ambonese culture. The Islamic community lives in the SW of town around Mesjid Besar.

Food, accommodations, and transport in this fair-sized city are as expensive as Bandung, but the pace is slower. You see few foreigners here except missionaries and occasional Dutch, Australian, or New Zealand tourists. As a foreigner you'll be the object of constant attention, but there are enough friendly Ambonese around to make your stay worthwhile. Music is everywhere; all the latest Western tapes pulsate from shopfronts, transistors, and taxi buses, guitars are played on porches and street corners, and everyone owns and exchanges cassettes. Ambon is one of the few places in Indonesia where you see drunks on the street, especially on Sun. afternoons and in the evenings. The city has a tough new mayor now who's really into cleanliness and discipline. A pair of cops stand on nearly every street corner checking drivers' licenses and handing out tickets for jaywalking.

History

This city has had a hard history since the Portuguese first established a fort here 400 years ago, the start of Ambon's modern era. Because of the worldwide popularity of its spices, Ambon has been caught in the crossfire and destroyed many times. Before the arrival of Europeans, the land now occupied by town was called Honipopu, which consisted of 4 villages. Ambon was for centuries an important waystation for the spice traffic between Ternate and the Banda Islands. The great blind Dutch naturalist, Rumphius (1628-1702), was buried in the garden of his former home in Ambon but his grave has long since disappeared (a Catholic school and library are named after him). Rumphius worked for over 50 years in and around Ambon collecting hundreds of new tropical species. This extraordinary figure worked with such zeal that he became known as "the Blind Pliny of the Indies." Rumphius' uncanny illustrations of the region's biota still stand today as some of the finest

and most beautiful ever drawn. Known all over the Indies as "Beautiful Amboina," pre-war Ambon had spacious squares with tall trees, shady cobblestone streets, promenades and gardens, a charming tree-lined waterfront, with the white houses of the Dutch mingling with the natives' palm houses. The town was all but demolished by Allied bombs in 1945. In 1950, just 4 months after the formal transfer of sovereignty from Holland (Dec. 1949), there was a fierce counter-revolution by the Ambonese to break away from the authority of the new Indonesian government. Declaring its independence from the rest of Indonesia under the banner of Republik Maluku Selatan (RMS), the rebellion was bloodily crushed by Java-centralist troops by Sept. 1950. A new administrative center, with many government buildings and official residences, was built in the 1970s in the suburb of Karangpanjang—the "Brasilia" of Ambon.

SIGHTS

Historical

The statue with the upraised sword in the town park is of **Kapitan Pattimura** who fought against Dutch oppression. The statue is located on the spot where this guerilla leader was hanged by the Dutch. His last words to his captives were "Have a pleasant day." Pattimura's most famous action was leading an assault on Fort Duurstede on P. Saparua, E of Ambon, on 5 March 1817. The memorial to freedom-fighter **Martha Christina Tiahahu**, in the suburb of Karangpanjang, overlooks the whole of Ambon City and Ambon Bay (both day and twilight views are superb). Tiahahu and her father served in Pattimura's guerilla forces; she died on a ship to Java with other POWs. Near the statue is the Provincial House of Assembly where elected members meet periodically. Other colonial-era remnants, all on Jl. Pahlawan Revolusi, include: the mausoleum of **Sunan Pakubuwana VI** (a Solonese ruler who died here in exile in 1849); the former Dutch governor's mansion; and the former home of the Javanese **Prince Diponegoro** (exiled here for several years). See the huge mural in the church on Jl. A. Rhebok depicting the holy cross as a stairway to heaven.

Cemeteries

In the suburb of Tantui just E of Batumerah, about 2 km from downtown Ambon, an **Allied Forces Cemetery** was established to consecrate the British, Dutch, and Australian servicemen captured, tortured, and killed in Moluccas and Sulawesi during WW II. One of the best-maintained war cemeteries in Indonesia, ceremonies are held each year on 23 April to celebrate ANZAC Day, Australia's equivalent of America's Memorial Day. The official Australian entourage, accompanied by a warship, includes the Australian ambassador and a medical and technological team who lend islanders assistance for a week. The Indonesian **Heroes Cemetery** *(Makam Pahlawan)* is nearby. The authorities committed the deadly sin of destroying the town's old cemetery, informing the residents to come and get their family's tombstones. The **Christian Cemetery**, in Soya Kecil, should be seen for its inscriptions and oddly shaped tombstones.

Libraries

Next to the Chinese Cemetery in Benteng is a *perpustakaan* with open (Dutch and reference books) and closed (English and Indonesian) stacks. Open until 1330. Bishop Sol at the **Keuskupan**, the bishop's house on Jl. Raya Pattimura, also has an outstanding collection of antiquarian Dutch, English, and German books on the Moluccas, very possibly the largest and most complete in existence. One volume contains an account of a German scientist (Embrik Strand) who collected spiders on the Kai and Aru islands back in 1908! Bishop Sol, who runs the library, is extremely knowledgeable about Maluku and speaks quite good English.

Siwalima Museum

A regional museum in Batu Cipeo containing historic, craft, and ethnographic objects from all over the province, a suprisingly good collection with many fascinating exhibits: *ikat,* wonderful protective and ancestor statues, woodcarvings, boat models, ceramics, etc. Donation: Rp1000. Nus will show you around. Open 0800-1400; closed Mon. and Fridays. No cameras allowed, but pamphlets, postcards, and photos available. The museum's catalog (Rp3500) contains thorough descriptions of exhibits. Ask to visit the library on the second floor of the building next door. The museum, high on a hill overlooking the harbor, is a steep and pretty walk up from the road to Amahusu in the southern outskirts of Ambon. Board a minibus from the Terminal Mardika Pantai, get off at the turnoff, then walk 10 min. up to the museum; ask anyone for directions. Or take a taxi for Rp3000 each way.

Fort Victoria

On Jl. Selamat Riadi in the town center, across from the Pattimura statue, the original fortress was built by the Portuguese in 1575 and named Fort Kota Laka. The Dutch overran it in 1605, ending Portuguese control of the Spice Islands. To stamp out Portuguese prestige, the Dutch reduced the fort nearly to its foundations, renamed it Fort Victoria, then expanded and updated the complex over the next 350 years. You can still recognize the symbols of the various towns

and provinces of Holland on the different crests on the fort walls. The fort in the 17th C. was near the beach, and the town of Ambon grew up around it, steadily expanding inland. Now the military occupies the site and only the gate, a few old buildings, and the large bulwarks along the sea remain of the original fort. To enter, get permission from the fort commander. Don't take photographs without a permit or your film will be confiscated. Fort Hollandia, overgrown with grass, is next to Fort Victoria.

ACCOMMODATIONS

Since accommodation is expensive and the city's airport is 46 km from town, Ambon City is not the place for just an overnight stop. The few hotels are in high demand by a constant stream of incoming businessmen, government officials, and other travelers. Rates in most of the hotels in Ambon include meals. One nice touch are a number of family-run hotels in "somebody's home," where you mix right in with the family's life and are likely to learn much about the Ambonese customs. These accommodations, such as Hotel Eleonoor and Wisma Game, are excellent value. Sometimes a hotel will ask you to register with the police, but most of the time they will do it on your behalf. Watch the 10% tax which some hotels add onto you bill.

AMBON CITY

1. Hotel Cendrawasih
2. Hotel Josiba
3. Wisata Hotel
4. Lawamena Haulala (army base)
5. *bemo* Terminal Pelita
6. church
7. Gereja Maranatha (Protestant)
8. Governor's Office
9. Hotel Transit/Rezfany
10. Bank Expor-Impor Indonesia
11. Bank Indonesia
12. Bank Dagang Negara
13. Pondok Asri
14. Wisma Game
15. cinema
16. Amboina Hotel
17. Hotel Silalou
18. Hotel Sela
19. Hotel Eleonoor
20. Palopa
21. New Garden Restaurant

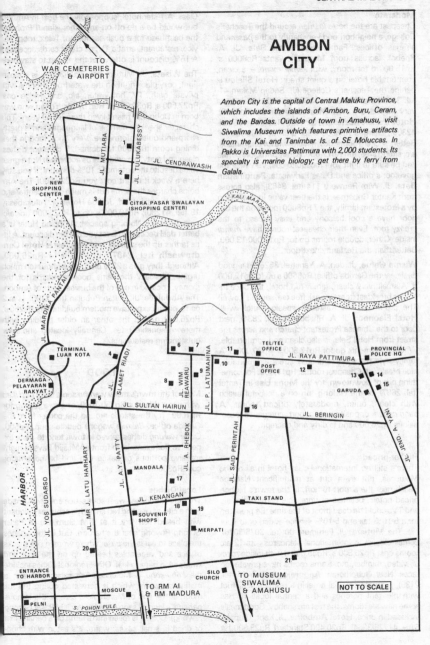

AMBON CITY

Ambon City is the capital of Central Maluku Province, which includes the islands of Ambon, Buru, Ceram, and the Bandas. Outside of town in Amahusu, visit Siwalima Museum which features primitive artifacts from the Kai and Tanimbar Is. of SE Moluccas. In Pakko is Universitas Pattimura with 2,000 students. Its specialty is marine biology; get there by ferry from Galala.

TO WAR CEMETERIES & AIRPORT

JL. MUTIARA

JL. TULUKABESSY

JL. CENDRAWASIH

KALI MARDIKA

NEW SHOPPING CENTER

CITRA PASAR SWALAYAN (SHOPPING CENTER)

JL. MARDIKA PANTAI

TERMINAL LUAR KOTA

DERMAGA PELAYARAN RAKYAT

JL. SLAMET RIADI

JL. WIM REAWARU

JL. P. LATUMAHINA

TELITEL OFFICE

JL. RAYA PATTIMURA

PROVINCIAL POLICE HQ

POST OFFICE

GARUDA

JL. JEND. A. YANI

JL. SULTAN HAIRUN

JL. BERINGIN

HARBOR

JL. A. RHEBOK

JL. SAID PERINTAH

MANDALA

JL. KENANGAN

TAXI STAND

JL. YOS SUDARSO

JL. MR J. LATU HARHARY

JL. A.Y. PATTY

SOUVENIR SHOPS

MERPATI

ENTRANCE TO HARBOR

SILO CHURCH

TO MUSEUM SIWALIMA & AMAHUSU

PELNI

MOSQUE

S. POHON PULE

TO RM AI & RM MADURA

NOT TO SCALE

Moderate

Cheapest are the basic *losmen* around the Teacher's College, a neighborhood very handy to the *pasar* and airlines offices: Family-style **Hotel Sela**, Jl. A. Rhebok (across from Merpati), wants Rp8000 s, Rp15,000 d for rooms with *kamar mandi*— a clean, comfortable hotel on a quiet street. **Hotel Silalou** is behind the Teacher's College (Jl. Sedap Malam 41, tel. 3197); Rp7000 s, Rp14,000-18,000 d. Run by a very helpful old man. Meals also served (Rp7000). **Hotel/Transit Rezfanny**, Jl. Wim Reawaru 115 (tel. 42300), charges Rp8000 s for drab upstairs rooms. Better, slicker rooms downstairs with *mandi* inside, a/c, sitting area, run Rp17,000. Barely drinkable coffee and be sure to light your mosquito coil. Very near the governor's office and Dinas Pariwisata. **Penginapan Beta**, Jl. Wim Reuwaru 114 (tel. 3463), also across from Kantor Gubernor, is the best value in town. Run by a Protestant family, the 7 Rp8000 rooms on the top floor have a cool balcony and easy access to the breezy roof. Even their cheapest rooms have *mandi* inside. Other, double rooms go for Rp12,000-13,000. Better than the Rezfanny next door.

Wisma Game, Jl. Jen. A. Yani (tel. 3525), is a good deal near the Garuda office; Rp6600 s up to Rp12,000 d. A small, very clean, family-run hotel, the price includes breakfast (toast, eggs), free tea, sandals, towel. The proprietor Mr. Kasturian speaks Dutch well. **Hotel Eleonoor**, Jl. A. Rhebok 30 (tel. 2834), next door to the Chinese Protestant church and across the street from Hotel Sela, is also clean and comfortable. Whole apartments go for Rp17,500 s, Rp30,000 d. A family-style place on semi-busy street, comfortable, nice breakfast. Cheapest rooms: Rp11,000. For something out of downtown, try the **Mona Lisa** in Tantui (tel. 2667), or the **Halong Inn** on a peaceful beach with clean, quiet, moderately priced rooms. A *penginapan* opposite the airport charges a scandalous Rp26,000 and is dirty and decrepit.

Higher-priced

There's still no international-class hotel in all of the Moluccas, not even out at magnificent Natsepa Beach near the airport turnoff. In the town's higher-priced hotels, because of unreliable current, the a/c and TVs could be dead most of the time. Be prepared for a 5-10% tax and 5-10% service added onto your bill. The **Mutiara**, Jl. Pattimura 90 (tel. 3075/3076), comes closest to international standards—its 12 a/c rooms cost Rp25,500 s, Rp35,000 d with inside *mandi*, video, minibar, etc. Some rooms have private terraces. Near Gubernoran. **Anggrek**, Jl. A. Yani (tel. 2139), is an old colonial hotel in a residential district with pleasant porches and a central location. Has some new a/c rooms, the rest are shabby. Good meals included in price. **Hotel Amboina**, Jl. Kapt. Ulupaha 5 (tel. 41725/3354); Rp20,400 Standard, Rp28,800 1st Class. A 1-star hotel, supposedly the best in Ambon but would be a rip-off on any other island! Probably the best base for a businessperson. Telex, room service, restaurant, erratic TV, all credit cards accepted. A 15% discount is offered at the airport to stay here.

The **Wisata**, Jl. Mutiara (tel. 3293/3567), is a close, tight, cozy place right on the waterfront. Rooms with private bath, TV, hot water, a/c, and fridge cost Rp27,500 s, Rp30,000 d. Run by Mr. Yunan who was born in Dobo, but hasn't lived there for 50 years. This character speaks a number of languages and is pretty sharp and quite informative. Very good food in their dining room (Rp6000 for dinner); 9 different dishes clean and tasty. No credit cards accepted. Not a great value despite the automatic 10% discount; if you stay here a week it might cost you Rp228,500! The Amboina charges the same but is much more central and close to the taxi stand. **Josiba Hotel**, Jl. Tulukabessy 19 (tel. 41280); Rp10,000 s up to Rp25,000 (for a/c) plus 20% tax. Nothing special; Amboina Hotel is a better deal because at least you get the discount. A little farther up the same side of the street is **Hotel Cendrawasih** (tel. 2487); Rp10,500 to Rp26,000. Although they give a 20% discount without too much urging, basically the same poor standards for the money. Located in one of the busiest parts of Ambon. The **Abdulalie**, Jl. Sultan Bubulah (tel. 2796), is in 2 parts, one an expensive modern building (Rp16,250 s, Rp26,500 d) and the other an older building with more reasonable rates. Centrally located and near outstanding restaurants.

FOOD

Most of the town's many *warung* serve tasty *nasi ikan* with vegetables for Rp750-1000, or a *mie goreng* for Rp1000. Try the stands around the corner from the Garuda office. *Bakmie* wagons peddle soup, Rp500. Other *warung* dishes served in town tend to more expensive; for example, in front of Mesjid Raya at night massive portions of baked fish and baked potatos cost Rp3000.

Local Dishes

Try the Ambonese sweet-sour sauce *colo-colo,* made with a citrus base and red chilis; it's especially piquant with baked fish (try it at **RM Sumatra** in Pasar Gotong Royong near the harbor). Out in the villages the place to eat is the *pasar* where women sell snacks of rice and vegetables heated up on the spot and wrapped in banana leaf. Other regional dishes include the *kohu-kohu,* a Moluccan fish salad; and *laor,* a marine seaworm which is harvested during the full moon at the end of March. Also sample the famous *papeda,* a kind of sago porridge (try it in Pasar Gotong Royong). Cold, it is rolled into a lump on a banana leaf or dried in small cakes; warm, it's eaten with chop-ticks *(gata-gata),* served with a fish sauce *(kuah ikan),* or cooked with *cili* (Spanish peppers) or shellfish.

Restaurants

Dining out is not a big tradition with the Ambonese, who prefer family-style homecooking, but because of the influx of immigrant workers a number of *warung* and restaurants have sprung up. Head for the *rumah makan* along Jl. A.Y. Patty and around the harbor, as well as several more on Jl. Said Perintah, and 3 good ones in a row on Jl. Sultan Hairun. One, **Halim Restaurant,** Jl. Sultan Hairun SK 3/37 (tel. 97126), beside Kantor Gubernor, has a full menu: crab soup, Rp3000; the best *mie goreng,* Rp2000; also known for its ice cream. Nice open-air sitting area. Also try the **Tip Top** next door. For Java-*asli* food such as *Ayam Goreng Kalasan,* Yogya-style, eat at **Restaurant Sakura** next to the Tip Top. Several good *nasi padang* restaurants, such as the **Minang Jaya** on Jl. Kemakmuran, are at the *stasiun bis.* The hotel restaurants serve simple but good food; don't expect gourmet dishes. Because of lack of pasture land, most meats have to be imported.

Several wonderful Madurese eateries **(RM Makan Ai** and **RM Madura)** face each other in the Muslim quarter on Jl. Sultan Babulah close to Hotel Abdulalie. As an Eagles tape plays in the background, feast on a full range of genuine Islamic-Indonesian dishes such as *gado gado* with super fresh vegies (Rp600), perfect *Soto Ay Madura* (Rp1000), plus a selection of ice juices. A lot of life too, as *sate* smoke wafts through a crowded, noisy room. Both are open 0700-0100. Nearby, the **Abdulalie Coffee Shop & Restaurant** has sirloin steak, spaghetti, all kinds of soup, and ice cream—a popular place with the city's affluent (buy *kayuputih* oil here). The **New Garden Restaurant** on Jl. Pahlawan Revolusi is the best Chinese restaurant in town—even on Mon. nights it's crowded! Classical Mandarin fare, with dishes in the Rp3000-5000 range, while an organ and vocalist perform for your dining pleasure—a fun place!

Fruits, Desserts, And Drinks

Pineapple (Rp1250, but much less in season in December) and *durian* (Rp1500, cheaper in May) are unbelievably expensive, so stick with the cheaper indigenous fruits like *pala gula,* sweet-and-sour raw nutmeg; Rp250 for a 1-ounce bag. Exquisite fruits such as *rambutan* and *mangosteen* are available in season. The island's bananas—all 22 varieties—are famous throughout the archipelago for their size and flavor. *Nasi goreng* here is made with plantains cut into very small cubes to resemble rice and prepared the same way as fried rice. Used for baby food, the largest grow 50-75 cm (20-30 inches) in length and grow upwards instead of down. *Gandaria,* 10 for Rp500, is a sweet orange plum found only on Ambon. *Ucapi* are yellow, peach-like fruits with translucent pulp—similar to *duku* in taste—10 for Rp250. *Tomi-*

tomi are small, sour cherries. *Kutu katak* are branches of bitter berries. This island's alcoholic *sopi* is a potent palm wine served in backroom places. The best is made in Latere. *Sopi rusa* has a 2-month-old deer fetus in the bottle; supposedly has curative and strengthening powers. It takes about 4 glasses, at Rp150 per glass, to get a good buzz going. A brandy and *avokat* cocktail is Rp200. Cold Bintang beer, Rp2000 per bottle.

OTHER PRACTICALITIES

Entertainment

A number of small movie houses are scattered around town; the one opposite the *stanplatz* has Sat. midnight showings. There are at least 4 nightclubs in and near town; the **Santa Bar & Restaurant** has a restaurant, cafeteria, live band, and hostesses. Music and other performances are occasionally held at the **Gedung Kesenian** beside the sports hall in Karangpanjang.

Events

Pattimura Anniversary is celebrated on 15 May each year: runners arrive from Saparua carrying lighted torches which are used to ignite a huge bonfire in front of the Pattimura Monument. Each Aug. the **Darwin-Ambon sailing race** finishes at Galala up the coast NE of Ambon City. Celebrations commemorating the founding of Ambon City (in 1575) take place each 17 Sept. at which time there is *arumbai mangurebe* (boat racing).

Shopping

Crafts and souvenirs are generally expensive. The only reasonable items are pretty tortoise-shell rings, fans, bracelets, and hair clasps. Ships and *prahu* are dominant themes: inside bottles, with sails made of shells, small ships made out of tortoise shell (Rp30,000), and boats made entirely of cloves—in all shapes and sizes, Rp8500-30,000. Flowers and baskets are also made of cloves. You also find bracelets, necklaces, pendants, wall hangings, flower arrangements, hairpins (Rp3500), etc. made from *kulit mutiara* (mother of pearl). For local crafts, it's better to locate the source and buy directly, though the island's craft villages are getting hip to the prices in the stores now. Compare before you buy. Go to **Rumahtiga** for shell and other indigenous crafts. Peddlers will come around the hotels selling pearls for Rp175,000 before bargaining; if they're harder than your teeth, they're real pearls.

The city has 12 souvenir shops. Up to 50% of the crafts come from Tanatoraja, Bali, or other islands, so ask before you buy. **Noorman Art Gallery,** Jl. Latu Harhary 88 (tel. 3163), specializes in shellwork, clove crafts, *sarung, kayuputih* and *lawang* oil. Visit the

Chinese antique shop **Toko Lima**, Jl. Mr. J. Latu Harhary A/III/5, for exquisite blue-and-white ceramics. Also check out the souvenir shops along Jl. Pattimura and Jl. A.Y. Patty; **Toko Sulawesi** on Jl. A.Y. Patty has a very complete selection of souvenirs. **Tempat Masyarakyat Maluku Tenggara** is a cottage industry inside Kampung Skip where Tanimbar-style weaving is produced; Rp40,000 (high) is the average price. **Kantor Perindustrian**, inside Wisma Ria, also sells crafts. Although neighboring P. Buru is the source for *kayuputih* oil, it's processed and bottled on Ambon. This oil is used as a surface balm for itching and may be swallowed for a stomach ache. It's most attractively packaged by **Abdulalia** on Jl. Sultan Abdulalie; Rp500 for a 25-cc bottle, larger bottles for Rp900. They also sell *Minyak Kulit Lawang,* which is twice as expensive; this is a hot oil for itching, rheumatism, and heals cuts quickly.

Services

The **tourist office**, Dinas Pariwisata Dati I Maluku, is on the ground floor of Kantor Gubernor on Jl. Pattimura. Open Mon. to Thurs. 0800-1400, Fri. until 1130, Sat. until 1300, closed Sundays. The officer for tourism *(Kepala Dinas),* Mr. Oratmangun, can answer your questions and make it easier for you to visit places that present bureaucratic difficulties. Get the booklet, *Guide to Maluku;* postcards (when available) can be bought at Rp175 apiece. Dinas Pariwisata also rents snorkeling equipment and masks: full tanks (Rp12,500 per day), fins, and masks (Rp2500). The best doctors work in **RS Umum** where there are specialists (one internist has been trained in Italy); also good doctors and service at **RS Tentara,** the military hospital. One-hour photo service for Kodak, Agfa, Fuji, etc., at **Union Color Photo Service,** Jl. A. Y. Patty 3 (tel. 3349/3569); Rp200 per print.

Change U.S., U.K., or Australian currency at **Bank Dagang Negara**, Jl. Antoni Rhebok. Compare their rates with those of **Bank Expor Impor Indonesia** just down from the post office, also on Jl. Raya Pattimura. You'll have trouble changing any other currency. Open Mon. to Fri. 0800-1300; Sat. 0800-1100. The **post office** is on Jl. Raya Pattimura; the Tel/Tel office is opposite. **Kantor Imigrasi** is on Jl. Dr. Kaijadu, a new building opposite a small church; get there by *bemo* from the *stanplatz,* Rp100. Another small immigration office at the airport stamps your passport upon arrival. Your hotel registers you with the police, instead of you having to do it (takes an hour!). Some travelers don't even bother registering and get clean away with it.

Getting There

The Pelni boat *Rinjani* sails about every 2 weeks from Jakarta via Surabaya, Ujung Pandang, Bau Bau, Ambon, Sorong. It arrives in Ambon every other Sun. at about 1100, leaves for Sorong at 1700 the same day,

returns to Ambon on Tues. at 1100, then sails again to Jakarta at 1700 the same day. To Ambon the economy fare is Rp169,000 from Jakarta, Rp264,300 from Belawan, Rp130,000 from Surabaya, Rp45,000 from Sorong, Rp81,900 from Ujung Pandang, and Rp59,800 from Bau Bau. In front of Terminal Lua Kota (or Terminal Mardika Pantai) on Jl. Mardika Pantai is the small boat harbor of Dermaga Palayaran Rakyat where small *kapal* from other Moluccar islands call.

Ambon is the gateway to the Moluccus. Garuda flies to Ambon from Surabaya via Ujung Pandang every day for around Rp193,000. Merpati propjets do this same flight 3 times weekly for Rp164,100. From Manado, N. Sulawesi, Merpati has flights 6 times a week, Rp118,000. The airport, at Laha, is 46 km from Ambon City. Take a minibus, *bemo* (Rp600), or taxi (Rp12,500, 1 hour) over the narrow road from the airport via Passo, or take the vehicle ferry from Rumahtiga over to Ambon City (Rp150). The Merpati bus might take you into the city office for free.

Local Transport

Made up of only a half dozen main streets, and stretching out along the waterfront for 3 km, you can easily walk to most places worth going to. The harbor is at northern end of Jl. Pahlawan Revolusi. Thousands of *becak* are color-coded red, yellow, and white and are only permitted to carry passengers on the days designated for each color (except Sundays). As the competition is ferocious, *becak* prices are the same as on Java (Rp300-400 for 1-2 km). *Bemo* go to the suburbs from the *stanplatz* on Jl. Raya Pattimura. Sample distances and fares: Air Salobar, 4 km, Rp100; Karangpanjang, 4½ km, Rp125; Ahuru, 6 km, Rp150; Batumerah, 2 km, Rp100; Tantui, 3½ km, Rp100; Dermaga (ferry to Rumahtiga), 4½ km, Rp125. The bus fare is Rp100 to anywhere in town—Lin I, Lin II, etc. Taxis are available at the taxi stand down from the Amboina Hotel (Rp3500-4000 per hour).

FROM AMBON

By Road

Bemo and buses leave often from the *stanplatz* at the end of Jl. A.Y. Patty on the corner of Jl. Sultan Hairum, called Terminal Bemo Pelita. For destinations outside the city minibuses depart from the new terminal at Mardika Pantai. This 48-X-22-km island has only around 200 km of asphalted roads. Sample fares **from Ambon N to:** Hila (Rp890, 45 km); Hitulama (Rp550, 30 km), Wakal (Rp600, 32 km), **to the NE to:** Waai (Rp550, 29 km), Liang (Rp750, 41 km), Tulehu (Rp450, 24 km); **to the SW to:** Latuhalat (Rp325, 17 km), Amahusu (Rp150, 8 km), Eri (diving) (Rp200, 10 km). To get to Soya, take a bus (Line I) from Terminal Pelita to Batumeja (Rp100), then take a minibus up to Soya (Rp150, 6 km).

By Air

Merpati, the most active carrier in the region, flies to: Ternate (N. Maluku), Rp73,100; Amahai (P. Ceram), Rp32,100; for Galela (P. Halmahera) you first have to fly to Ternate (Rp73,100), then fly from Ternate to Galala (Rp35,100); Bandaneira (Banda Is.), Rp48,100; Manado, Rp102,600, daily (20-min. fuel stop in Ternate); Tual (Kai Is.), Rp82,100; Saumlaki (Tanimbar Is.), Rp87,100. During the wet season (April-Aug.), many of the small unsurfaced landing strips on Maluku's outer islands are unfit for aircraft. Long-distance flights from Ambon: Jakarta, Rp161,100 (twice weekly); Surabaya, Rp139,500; Ujung Pandang, Rp82,000; Biak, Rp91,500. Garuda is the only airline that flies to Jayapura, Rp155,750; Biak, Rp85,250; Sorong, Rp59,750. Two Garuda flights per week head to Timika on the S coast of Irian Jaya, which continue to Jayapura. Mandala flies to Ujung Pandang (Rp90,800), Surabaya (Rp163,800), and Jakarta (Rp189,300); Merpati does these runs 4 times weekly for roughly the same prices.

If you miss your plane, there's a *penginapan* at the airport for Rp26,000 d, but it's shitty. Instead, camp on the pretty beach of Air Manis in Laha village, only 2 km from the airport. Airlines offices: Garuda, Jl. Jen. A. Yani (tel. 2481); Merpati, Jl. A. Rhebok (tel. 42480/3480); Mandala, Jl. A.Y. Patty SH 4/18 (tel. 2444). Get out to the airport at Laha (46 km from Ambon) by taking a bus (14-16 people) from Terminal Mardika Pantai; Rp700 (1 hour). Or hire a taxi for Rp8000-10,000 (some want Rp12,000-15,000) from the taxi stand off Jl. Said Perintah. Domestic airport tax is Rp1400.

Travel Agencies

Both of Ambon's 2 travel agencies do local and intra-island nature/cultural tours. For groups of 3 to 5, **Sumber Budi Tour & Travel**, Jl. Mardika 2/16 (tel.

3205), does a 3-day, 2-night sightseeing tour of Ambon City and nutmeg and clove plantations (US$194 pp); a 3-day, 2-night snorkeling, skin diving, and safari fishing tour (US$395 pp); a 6-day historical tour of the Banda Is. (US$510 pp). But their most creative tour is the all-day wild lobster-catching excursion off Saparua (US$525 pp); you get to eat your catch afterwards! See Mr. J.G.B. Nanlohy. **Natrabu Tour & Travel**, Jl. Rijali 53 (tel. 3537), offers such exotic group tours as: Babi Island Diving (US$537.50 pp); Amboina City Tour (US$21.50 pp for 2 person group); tours to Waai (US$29.50 pp) and Soya, Sirimau, Ema (US$62.50). Most prices include transfer service from airport, guide, a choice of accommodtions, breakfast and lunch, airfare from Ambon, and all transport costs. For ticketing, go to **PT Daya Patal**, Jl. Said Perintah SK. 11/27A, tel. 3529/41136, telex 73140 DPAB.

By Boat And Ship

Ambon is a center for inter-island sea transport on either small *kapal motor* or bigger ships to Central, North and SE Maluku. For the latest fares and ships, go down to the **Dermaga Pelayaran Rakyat** at the northern end of Jl. Sultan Hairun and ask the friendly harbormaster *(syahbandar)*. Also inquire at the Pelni office, Jl. Pelabuhan 1 (tel. 34). Timetables change constantly. During the monsoon season (May-July), sea travel is restricted in S. Moluccas, though the weather doesn't hinder the larger seagoing vessels. Larger boats have more reliable departures and more comfortable passages. For the smaller boats, March-April is the best time to travel around Banda, Kai, and the Tanimbars. Clove boats to E. Ceram and other central and northern Moluccan ports mostly travel during the clove season Sept. to Dec. when seas are calm. Listed below are all vessels departing from Dermaga Pelayaran Rakyat twice weekly:

VESSELS SAILING FROM AMBON

Vessel	DWT	Capacity	Route from Ambon	Fare
KM *Wahai Star*	150 (tons)	100 (people)	To Taniwel (Ceram)	Rp7,500
			To Wahai (Ceram)	Rp12,500
			To Bula (Ceram)	Rp15,000
KM *Suliati*	150	100	As Above	As Above
KM *Taman Pelita*	150	100	As Above	As Above
KM *Tiga Berlian II*	75	60	As Above	As Above
KM *Wahai Star*	150	100	To Namlea (Buru)	Rp8,000
			To Airbuaya (Buru)	Rp12,500
KM *Suliati*	150	100	As Above	As Above
KM *Tiga Berlian II*	75	60	As Above	As Above
KM *Dewi Jaya*	150	100	As Above	As Above
KM *Usaha Baru III*	60	60	To Leksula (Buru)	Rp7,500
KM *Siane III*	60	60	As Above	As Above

For Ceram

From Dermaga Pelayaran Rakyat, catch boats to **Taniwel** (Rp7,500, 8 hours) and other Ceramese ports. From Tulehu on Ambon's E coast, boats depart to many locations on Ceram. For example, board *spetbot* to **Kairatu** (Rp5000, 1½ hours), diesel-powered boats to **Amahai** (Rp5000, 3 hours). Boats from Tulehu to **Tehoru** leave irregularly except during clove season. Charging Rp10,000, the vessels sail right through the night (8 hours), an uncomfortable but exciting voyage. Between Tulehu and Waai there's now a new harbor called **Hurnala** for the big fast boats to Pararua and points on Ceram (Amahai, Tehoru). From Hitu, catch *prahu* and motorized *prahu* (more expensive) to **Waiputih, Whu, Waijase,** and **Piru.**

For Banda And Maluku Tenggara

The Kai, Tanimbar, and Banda islands can be reached by small boat from Ambon; allow at least 10 days RT. Perintis may have ships sailing from Ambon to Banda, Tual, Elat, Dobo, or Larat—depending on demand for cargo. Pelni has 2 ships running regularly. KM *Niaga XII* has the long route: Ambon-Banda-Tual-Elat-Dobo-Larat-Saumlaki-Tual-Banda-Ambon for Rp23,250 Deck Class RT. There are 3 other *Niagas*, some of which have the "shorter" route: Ambon-Banda-Tual-Elat-Dobo-Larat-Saumlaki-Tual-Banda-Ambon for Rp17,500 Deck Class. Be aware that on these boats people are packed like beetles under miserable hygienic conditions, though some relief can be had in crew cabin space rented out at steep prices.

Other Destinations

For **Namlea** on P. Buru, take *kapal motor* from Ambon's Dermaga Pelayaran Rakyat (Rp7500), leaving every night at 2000. Merpati also flies once weekly on Sun, Rp35,200, **to Ternate:** There are twice-monthly Perintis ships: *Baruna Bakti* and the smaller, longrouted *Pendulu*. Other rustbuckets (Rp15,000 to Ternate), such as the KM *Tolsuti,* are rare. **to Ujung Pandang and Surabaya:** Pelni's KM *Rinjani* runs twice a month between Ambon, Bau Bau (Kendari), Ujung Pandang, and Surabaya; Rp130,000 Economy Class to Surabaya. Takes 10 days, leaving Ambon at 1700 on Tues. for Bau Bau (Rp59,800); Ujung Pandang (Rp81,900); Surabaya (Rp130,000). The ship arrives at Tg. Priok (Jakarta—Rp169,700) on Sat. afternoon. **to Irian Jaya:** Pelni's KM *Rinjani* sails every other Sunday at 1700 from Ambon to Sorong for Rp45,000 Economy Class; Jayapura, Class III is about Rp15,000 more, Class IIB is Rp20,000 more, Class I is about twice as much.

AROUND AMBON ISLAND

Gunung Nona

Take a *bemo* to Benteng, then turn R and climb 2 hours up to the top of this small mountain for relie from the noise and heat of the city. Useful words yo might need on this climb: *pemancar televisi* (T tower), *kebon kasbi* (cassava patches), *kubura* (cemetery).

Air Salobar

A sometimes quiet beach, rocky shoreline, and fish ing village here. Close by, near the sea and 5 km from Ambon, is *Batu Capeo,* a gigantic hat-shaped cora rock along a small beach. Legend has it that a mai lost his top hat on the sea and it returned to land form ing this rock. Aloha Bar & Restaurant is just minute down the road. Chat with hostesses flown in from Surabaya. Saturday night tariff: Rp12,900.

Kusukusu

The largest cave on Ambon, well known and a fairl easy walk from the city; take a minibus out to the *rumah sakit* (hospital), then turn down Jl. Mangga Dua. It's an hour's walk from the hospital to the cave There are 11 or so bridges to cross before Kusukusu village. From the main entrance down into the cave is a steep descent, but once inside it's mostly level Some useful vocabulary: *gua* (cave), *tangga* (stairs) *jalan dalam gua* (passageway, entrance), *sente* (flashlight), *jembatan* (bridge), *kalong* or colloquia *burung* (bat). Yes, there's a few bats inside, but not menacing. Expect a muddy floor.

Batumerah

A suburb NE of Ambon City on the road to Passo, Rp150 by *bemo*. At a bend in the road a small house sells *minyak cengkeh*, bottles of powerful, burning-hot oil made from clove leaves. A small 10-cc bottle costs Rp650. Claimed to be the exclusive source for all of Maluku. Tortoise-shell and other crafts are made nearby. See the old mosque in this Muslim village.

Galala

Check out the scores of tuna boats moored at Galala, Rp250 (6 km) from Ambon by *bemo*. From Galala, take the relaxing Rp150 ferry ride across Ambon Bay to Rumahtiga, leaving when full. A car and passenger ferry also does the crossing from Galala to Pokka, the location of Pattimura University. A oceanographic research station was established here by the Russians and abandoned in the mid-1960s when communism gained such a bad name in Indonesia. Buildings and machinery now lie rotting and overgrown. Try the local specialty, smoked tuna, sold at *warung*. At Rumahtiga, drop in at Frans C. Tita's, Gang Sehati 7. Working alone, he produces shell crafts, including animals with shell feet and eyes (Rp600). A Chinese family also produces crafts here. **Waiame** is a white-sand, clear-water beach W of Rumahtiga. Nice view of the city, particularly at dusk. Accommodations available.

Halong

from Ambon Rp200 (7 km) by minibus. This village has an *Angkutan Laut,* the finishing point for the 6-day Darwin-Ambon sailing race held annually in August. A bar and restaurant are also here, plus 18 army-owned cottages for rent, called **Halong Inn**; Rp15,000 pp. The spit of land opposite Halong is called the Marthafons Cape where there are Pertamina cottages for rent, as well as other accommodations. At this point it's only 1½ km across the bay as the fish swim; it's over 30 km if you follow the shore road.

Passo And Baguala

Twin towns located on opposite sides of the narrow isthmus joining Ambon's 2 peninsulas, 12 km from Ambon City. **Natsepa Beach**, just E of Baguala and 14 km from Ambon (Rp500, 45 min. by minibus) is a large, beautiful, white-sand beach with a view over Leitimor. It seems that all of Ambon empties out to bathe and picnic here on Sundays. **Toisapu** is a more secluded beach on the opposite shore of Teluk Baguala, 18 km from Ambon; get there by *prahu* or motorboat from Passo.

Amahusu

In this village, 8 km SW of Ambon City, are radiant marine gardens only a short distance from the beach. Hire an outrigger. Good swimming too, and a panoramic view of Hitu Peninsula. Farther to the SE, 26 km from Ambon, is **Namalatu**, with clear, calm water surrounded by a white sandy beach and coral reefs. Good bathing and fishing. Coconut trees along the beach provide shade and refreshment. There's a motel here too.

Latuhalat

A Rp325, 45-min. (17 km) minibus or *bemo* ride from Ambon's Terminal Luar Kota along a bumpy, snake-like road. On the way between Amahusu and Eri, notice the numerous Japanese WW II pillboxes. Latuhalat, on the S coast of Leitimor Peninsula, features a beautiful secluded beach next to Batu Bicara, coral reefs, and good scuba diving and snorkeling (wear thongs because of razor-sharp coral). Best time to visit is Sept. to Dec. when the seas are calm. Ships made of cloves are made in at least 6 houses in this village. However, they'll want more for them than at the souvenir shops in town. Children could be pesky.

Eman Latu

Farther up the coast from Latuhalat, here you can see up to 15 m below water. Don't need a mask, only a snorkel. Or just stick your head under the water; it's like swimming inside an aquarium! Visit other villages such as **Naku, Ema,** and **Kilang** along the southern peninsula.

Rutung

On the S coast of Leitimor, this village is a 24-km walk from Ambon right across the center of the peninsula. Pass through avenues of eucalyptus trees, over rolling rhododendron-blanketed hills, dense forests with beautiful mauve orchids growing out of giant tree trunks, clear streams at the bottom of ravines. At last there's a chain of hills before the coast and an incredible panorama of the Banda Sea and long sweeping stretches of yellow beaches. Then descend down to the village. **Hutumuri**, a bit NE of Rutung, has a complete shell orchestra. Hire an outrigger, *kapal layar,* or motorboat (expensive) to take you from Rutung to Passo, passing limestone cliffs and caves, tiny bays, sea gardens of pink coral, amber seaweed, and multicolored tropical fish along the way.

HITU PENINSULA

Tulehu

By *bemo* Rp450 (24 km) from Ambon, Tulehu's small harbor is the departure point for *kapal motor* to Ceram (Amahai and Tehoru), and to Saparua and the Haruku Islands. Coming into town, the first structure you see is Tulehu's silver-domed mosque. From Tulehu you can see P. Haruku in the distance. Curative hotsprings are located along the beach just S of Tulehu. A hotel is nearby.

Waai

A friendly, well-off Christian village, Rp550 by minibus (31 km) from Ambon, where there's a sacred pool over a 60-m-high waterfall. Holy fish come from under the sea. A 10-year-old girl "calls" a giant eel by thumping on the water, then feeds it eggs. If the eel shows up, it means a bright future for all who see it.

Liang

This journey, Rp750 (41 km) by minibus from Ambon, takes you along the coast via Galala, Passo, Tulehu, and N where at low tide you can see rusting wrecks of ships transformed into sea gardens covered with grass, brilliantly colored flowers, and even trees. Liang is known for its friendly people, good beach, and swimming.

Hitulama And Vicinity

Thirty km N of Ambon, this is the oldest Islamic *kampung* on the island; some believe it was founded as early as the 11th C. by Arab or Javanese traders who had driven the native Alfuro tribespeople into the mountains. In the 16th C., Hitu is where the Portuguese landed; you can still see the ruins of their first trading post. The *kapal motor* for northern Ceram (Piru, etc.) leaves from Hitulama. The section of coastline to the E of Hitu to Liang is very rugged; a fairly good road leads E to **Mamala** where an unusual traditional event takes place each year at the end of *Ramadan*. Now a form of ritualized warfare, in *sapulidi* (broom-fighting), combatants whip each other with coconut-fiber brooms. A *dukun* treats the open wounds with Mamala oil which is said to have almost magical curative qualities. From Mamala, proceed NE to **Morela**. Though there doesn't even seem to be a trail along parts of this coast, persist. East of Morela is the old stone fortress of **Kapahala** which was captured by the Dutch in 1646; follow the track into a hilly area past weirdly shaped caves and bizarre rock formations, finally ascending stone stairs up to the fortress which is protected on 3 sides by a precipitous drop. Inside are graves of Kapahala's suicidal defenders.

Hila

A village of long traditions 12 km W of Hitulama on a bumpy road, or a Rp825 (45-km, 1½-hour) minibus ride from Ambon. The air is heavy with the scent of mace, nutmeg, and cloves, laid out on *tikar* in the streets to dry. The people of Hila venerate several Portuguese helmets, looking upon them as protective mascots and sources of strength. The entire village and its 300 screaming kids adopt you ("Misteer! Misteer!"). See Prasasti Mosque, built in 1414 on G. Wapaue. It was moved (the legend says "dragged") to Tehalla, 6 km away, before being moved to its present location in Hila in 1664. Visit it on Fri. afternoons or other worship times when old ladies, clad from head to foot in white gowns, congregate inside. Also a Christian church here, built in 1772, with Dutch-inscribed plaque.

Kaitetu

In neighboring Kaitetu, visit the blockhouse, **Nieuw Amsterdam,** which has an unfortunate location (next to a grade school) along the bay; schoolkids throng around you. It's not certain how much of this trading post was of Portuguese and how much of Dutch construction. A fantastically contorted banyan tree grips the insides of the structure and nothing is left but the walls. Several old cannon lie in the nearby school's garden. Near the blockhouse is the oldest church on Ambon, still in use, dating from 1780 with a Dutch-inscribed plaque. Kids will paddle you down the coast for more ruins. Or just start walking. From Kaitetu, walk along a dreamy pebble beach where the giant island of Ceram looms in the distance. Reach the clove plantations by climbing high up into the hills behind Hila. One km W of Kaitetu the road ends (it's being extended); follow the trail to a *kampung* through clove groves and (sometimes) along the beach. To prevent another devastating Hitu War in the 16th C., the Dutch built Fort Rotterdam in **Lima**, 16 km SW of Hila. It's presently in a dilapidated condition.

Alang

A Christian coastal village on the SW tip of the island,

reachable mornings by ferry from Ambon's Pasar Ikan pier (Rp1000). Only larger boats can do the passage during the "east season" (April-July) when high winds and waves make the sea hazardous. For over 400 years Alang has guarded the entrance to Ambon Bay. The village sits unsteadily on the rocky terraced slopes rising steeply from the bright green sea. Because of the lack of level space, its houses are built very close together on just a few streets. Nutmeg and cloves are the main crops; Alang is also known for its *kanari* nuts. People in this village love to sing, especially folk songs. Listen to the choirs and flute orchestras in the large well-maintained church with great rough-hewn beams.

SOYA

Soya has long traditions and an air of mysticism. It's said that the last 32 Portuguese families in the Moluccas were driven to this mountain village in the early 17th C.; they held onto their Catholic faith until finally they converted to Protestantism. The old church in Soya was built by the Portuguese in 1817. Nearby are huge boulders surrounding a square, once a *baileo* (meeting place). From the church, turn L and follow a small, twisting footpath, keeping to the R for 15 min. to the top of G. Serimau. If you find the right vantage point, the view from here takes in the long inlet that separates the 2 peninsulas. On G. Serimau, there's a foot-high sacred stone chair surrounded by a hedge, believed to be where the first raja sat. The trench surrounding the throne area was dug by the Dutch. A WW II concrete pillbox, overlooking Ambon Bay, stands 10 m away. In a slope in back of the throne is the *tampayang keramat*, a clay water urn which never goes dry (even in the dry season). It is visited by locals seeking good fortune, a cure for illness, or a perfect marriage partner. If a local plans to leave the area, he will take some water from the urn with him to give himself protection wherever he goes. The original urn was stolen in 1980, and replaced by the present one.

To get to Soya, take a *bemo* from Ambon's Terminal Luar Kota to Batumeja (Rp150), then continue to Kayuputih and Soya (Rp200). If you want to walk, a red clay path leads SE of Ambon up to this village (2 hours' walk) through a countryside full of steep-sided valleys, rainy hills covered in buffalo grass, jungle, palm groves, and higher up, Amboina conifers. Useful vocabulary: *gereja yang lama* (old church), *kursi batu* (stone chair), *tempayan* (urn), *pala* (nutmeg), *air terjun* (waterfall).

Vicinity Of Soya

Naku is a village with long Portuguese traditions about 15 min. farther along the path from Soya. Descendants of the Portuguese still live here. The name of the neighboring village, **Hatalai,** is very close

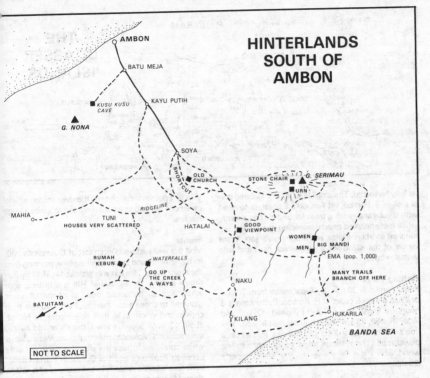

HINTERLANDS SOUTH OF AMBON

AMBON
BATU MEJA
KAYU PUTIH
KUSU KUSU CAVE
G. NONA
SOYA
SHORTCUT
OLD CHURCH
STONE CHAIR
G. SERIMAU
URN
RIDGELINE
MAHIA
TUNI HOUSES VERY SCATTERED
HATALAI
GOOD VIEWPOINT
WOMEN
MEN
BIG MANDI
EMA (pop. 1,000)
RUMAH KEBUN
WATERFALLS
GO UP THE CREEK A WAYS
NAKU
MANY TRAILS BRANCH OFF HERE
TO BATUITAM
KILANG
HUKARILA
BANDA SEA

NOT TO SCALE

in spelling to the town of Atalaia in Ribatejo, Portugal. The shirts the men wear are in the same style as those worn in Ribatejo, and the *kapitan* of Hatalai, Antonio Parera, will perform an old dance uncannily similar to the 17th C. *fandango* of the Ribatejo district. Another way to get to Hatalai is to take a *bemo* from Ambon to Kayuputih (Rp300), then walk up the hill. A fantastic waterfall is located along the path from Naku to **Batuitam.** Take the path to Batuitam, cross the river, and then the next river has the waterfall. You can also reach Batuitam from Kusukusu via Mahia, then return to the city via Hatalai. It's also possible to walk on a jungle path from Soya to Ema; on the way you pass a point on G. Serimau where you can see the whole S coast. **Ema** is a friendly village on top of the mountain. From Ema walk down to the coastal villages of **Hukurila** or **Lehari.**

AMBON'S OFFSHORE ISLANDS

Pulau Pombo And Pulau Kasa

Pombo and Kasa are 2 small unprotected island reserves near Ambon. Both have undeveloped, unprotected marine reserves as well as nesting sites for seabirds, megapodes, and an endemic species of lizard *(Hydrosaurus amboinensis)*. Pulau Kasa has the larger and better reefs (2,000 ha compared to Pombo's 1,000 ha), but both have suffered from fishing with explosives, said to have been learned from the Japanese during the war. Whatever you take onto the islands, please take it out again. Info and a visitor's pass should first be obtained from the Oceanographic Institute at Pattimura University in Pokka. A small rundown shelter exists on P. Pombo, but there's no fresh water on either island. Camping is easy and pleasant with no mosquitos. Maluku's eccentric (for Indonesia) rainy season (May-Oct.) applies here; rough seas are associated with this period along all coasts exposed to the SE trades.

Kasa (60 ha) is the larger of the 2 islands, still well forested despite continued disturbance by local fishermen and wood collectors. Found here are the megapode bird and numerous pigeons (from where P. Pombo gets its name, "Pigeon Island"). The megapode builds its mound of leaves and other bits of vegetation which, in the process of rotting, provide sufficient heat to incubate its eggs. In order to dig themselves out, the chicks hatch fully clawed, as well

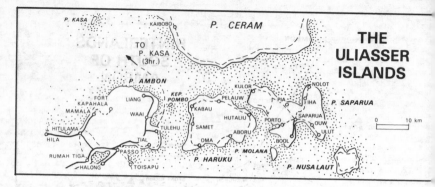

THE ULIASSER ISLANDS

as fully feathered. The small (4.6 ha), uninhabited coral atoll of P. Pombo, off Ambon's E coast, is covered with shrubs and nesting trees for birds; it has a sandy white reef-sheltered beach, sweeping panoramas, untouched snorkeling sites, and stunning sunsets. In the center of the island lies a pool which rises and falls with the tides.

Getting There

Pulau Pombo is 30 min. by *kapal motor* from Tulehu or Waai on the E coast of P. Ambon. Pulau Kasa is 3 hours by *kapal motor*. Tulehu (Rp450, 42 km) and Waai (Rp550, 29 km) are easily accessible from Ambon's Terminal Luar Kota (Jl. Mardika Pantai) on a paved road. The minibus takes you straight to the wharf where the ferry over to the island departs (20 min.).

SAPARUA

A small coral isle of 202 sq km, 74 km E of Ambon. Population in 1986 was 43,933 in 25 villages. There's a big clove plantation in the center and many other plantations dot the coast (clove season is Nov. and Dec.). Saparua is very hilly, rising steeply from the sea. The island's main city and capital, Saparua, has a big market Wed. and Saturdays. There are 2 ruins and an old church (at Ouw) on the island. A 15-min. *bemo* ride from the ferry landing is a nice hotel, in front of which swim tame herbivorous sea cows (dugongs).

History

As a center of nutmeg and clove cultivation, Saparua has a torrid history. Spice has been traded from coastal villages on this and adjacent islands for more than 500 years. Old Dutch fortifications litter the coasts, most obliterated. Saparua was the site of a revolt under the leadership of Thomas Matulessy (alias Kapitan Pattimura); the island still celebrates "Pattimura Day" in memory of this national hero. A flaming torch is carried by relay runners from each village it passes through until it arrives for the official ceremony in Ambon where it is used to ignite a huge bonfire.

Sights

Visit the well-restored Dutch fort of **Duurstede** with its battlements and cannon still in place, pointing over the rocky shore. This fort was attacked in 1817 by Pattimura and his forces. **Saniri Hill** is a historic spot where *kapitan* (warlords) from all of the Uliassers gathered to chose a commander. Pattimura was then chosen and sworn in as their new leader. At **Nolot**, about 13 from Saparua town, there's an old *baileo*, the traditional Moluccan meetinghouse. **Waisisilia**, a white coral beach, was the site of a decisive battle between Pattimura and the Dutch. In **Haria** village, Pattimura's battle dress is in the custody of a village elder, Manuhutu, and may be viewed upon request. **Ouw** is a big traditional pottery center which turns out most of the island's distinctive earthenware. This is not art pottery, but pots, water urns, and sago molds, etc. for everyday use.

Getting There And Around

Get ferries from Tulehu on P. Ambon (Rp1250), at least 2 boats per day but leaving usually only in the mornings (first at 0600, arriving at around 1200). This comfortable passage takes you past islands with Ceram in the background. The boat from Tulehu docks at Porto, from where you can get a *bemo* to Ouw to the other side of the island. From Saparua (the capital), the road is very bad, up and down hills. Boats to Saparua also leave from Waai, E coast of Ambon, but less often.

Lovely beaches and curative hotsprings are found on **Nusa Laut**, an island SE of Saparua and the most westerly of the Uliassers. The isle of **Haruku** (in 1986 pop. 23,467 in 12 villages) is 7 km E of Ambon, between Saparua and Ambon. Once an important clove-growing island, there are ruins of Portuguese fortifications as well as nice views and hot sulphur springs (at Oma) esteemed for curing skin diseases.

CERAM

This primitively beautiful island is 340 km from E to W, with an area of 17,354 sq km—about half the size of Holland. It's also the 2nd largest (after Halmahera) and one of the least known islands of the region. Ceram is very wooded, watered, and mountainous (but nonvolcanic). The island's mountains rise over 2,000 m; the highest peak in the center (G. Murkele Besar) is 3,027 m. Some of its central forests are impenetrable and have never been explored. Ceram's northern coasts are covered in long stretches of swamplands, while its southern coasts are steep and rocky. Luckily, Ceram's inaccessible and difficult terrain has prevented extensive exploitation of its land and timber resources. Its rivers are almost useless for navigation and there are few big towns and few natural harbors. A rough and wild place, Ceram was of little value to the Dutch colonists. The island's coasts were settled early by Malays; its indigenous population, the Alfuros, primitive and indomitable head-hunters, lived in the interior. The Dutch maintained 4 trading posts, and at Wahai were European coffee and cacao plantations. European fortresses are now all in ruins and smothered in vegetation. The most popular ruin to visit is 17th C. Fort Campelo, built by the Dutch on the western tip of the island (Little Ceram). The first man to go around the world was an Alfuro (native Ceramese) slave named Henry, a member of Magellan's crew whom Magellan had taken to Europe on his first voyage.

From a traveler's standpoint, there are 2 reasons to visit Ceram: its clean white beaches on the S coast, many reachable from Masohi; and the unforgettable walk through the center of the island from Hatumetan to Wahai. But you don't need to take the trans-Ceram trek to see native life; just get away from the coasts and you'll start to find the indigenous people. Be sure to ask permission before photographing women. Expensive hotels and a few less expensive *losmen* are found in Amahai and Masohi. Inland, places to stay are few and far between. You may stay with missionaries, and if you're in a real bind the police will always put you up or turn you on to a place. Out in the villages fruits, including pineapples and *durian*, are as cheap as you'll ever find in Indonesia. Rice cultivation, except by the *transmigrasi* settlers, is unknown. As rice is imported you'll generally find the village people eating *papeta* and other sago products, tapioca roots or potatos, and vegetables.

Climate

This island has different weather entirely from Ambon's; if it's clear on Ceram, it's probably rainy on Ambon. Most of Maluku has—for Indonesia—a unique rainy season (May-Oct., with the heaviest rain in July) but in the central part of Ceram rainfall is fairly even throughout the year, averaging 2,000 mm. The best season for visiting the inner valleys is June to Oct. though if traveling to Ceram by sea avoid the S coast during July and August. Also, the N coast is exposed to strong winds Jan.-March.

Flora And Fauna

Ceram's steep hills, sharp ridges, and deep river valleys have protected most of its endemic flora and fauna from excessive hunting, export, or loss of habitat. As in neighboring Irian Jaya, there are few native mammals—no monkeys, cats, or squirrels—and only several marsupial species (mainly cuscus and bandicoots). There are 13 species of fruit bats, 11 insectivorous bats, 3 phalangers, and 2 species of mongoose. Some mammals have been introduced by man; in E. Ceram wild pigs come down to the beach to hunt for crabs. Numerous deer roam the forests around Sawai (N. Ceram) where beaters and dogs force them to jump from granite cliffs into the sea where they are retrieved by other hunters in rowboats. The island's birdlife, however, probably the most colorful in all of the Moluccas, more than makes up for its lack of mammals: bright-colored lories, parrots, cockatoos, kingfishers, and pigeons as well as cassowaries, megapodes, hornbills, friar birds, honeyeaters, and white eyes. The pigeons here are particularly eye-catching, especially the golden Nicobar pigeon which lives deep in the forest; it has bright green feathers contrasting with a snow-white tail. Another remarkable species is the racket-tailed kingfisher whose head, nape, and shoulders are light blue, beak a brilliant coral, back and wings a rich purple, with 2 long tailfeathers fanning out like a spoon at the tip. There are also tree-climbing fish along Ceram's shores, rare purplish pythons in jungle shadows, crocodiles and lizards splashing in estuaries. Ceram is also famous for its bright butterflies; be on the lookout for the striking *Papilio ulysses* (the Blue Mountain butterfly), which ranges all the way from Ceram to the Solomon Islands.

Economy

Ceram's principal source of income are petroleum products. Before the oil slump of 1986, it was hoped that oil revenues would dramatically increase with the exploitation of additional oil deposits on the island's eastern coastal shelf. With its virgin forests and hundreds of kilometers of wilderness coasts, the island's biggest potential growth industry is tourism. But visitors are rare. Except for limited employment at the

Bula (pop. 5,421 in 1986) oil center on the NE coast, not many opportunities exist for earning a living. Its principal products are resin, coral, fish, rice, maize, sugarcane, spices, coconuts, and fruits. The native peoples of the interior still depend upon forest products such as roots and wild sago, cultivate coconuts, and sell copra and Agathis resin (damar), cockatoos and lories. Some natives earn a secondary cash income by the cultivation of spices and vegetables. The best information about the native economy is R. Ellen's book *Nuaulu Settlement and Ecology* (1978, The Hague, Martinus Nijhoff). Ellen has also published a number of essays on the topic, some of them listed in the bibliography of the book.

THE PEOPLE

An ethnologically rich island, Ceram's local name is *Nusa Ina* ("Mother Island"), possibly alluding to the fact that the founding aristocratic families of Ambon and other central Moluccan islands originated here. In the E live the tribal peoples; the W part of the island has more Malays. The bulk of the island's total population of 111,813 (1986) today live in the coastal areas; successive waves of alien ethnic groups pushed the original Ceramese inland, yet today a considerable admixture is evident among the coastal peoples. Among the most notorious headhunters in the old Dutch East Indies, the native Ceramese proved very difficult for the Dutch to govern. The reason why many indigenous groups live nowadays on the coast is that the Dutch administration wanted to control them and so resettled many villages from the inaccessible interior to the coast. The Dutch introduced this strategy in the course of the 19th C. and this is why only comparatively few people live in the interior.

The inland villagers, courteous and friendly to travelers, are completely different from coastal ones. Also the aborigines have a different physiognomy from the other native peoples of the archipelago. In the W and along the southern coasts live the largest concentration of these Deutero-Malay groups, and on the far W coasts there are even completely ethnic Javanese villages. At 90-140 people per sq km, Ceram's southern coast is one of the most densely populated areas of the Moluccas.

Tribal Peoples

The collective name for the native tribes in the interiors of all the larger Moluccan islands is Alfuros, from the Portuguese *alifuro,* meaning "uncouth, savage." When the Portuguese arrived in the region in the late 16th C., they found the natives living only in the mountain regions. Today, all interior tribes (such as the Borera and Nuaulu peoples) live in fairly permanent settlements and practice shifting cultivation which provides for more than half of their subsistence needs. These indigenous people have a tripartite

mode of production in which hunting and gathering still plays a surprisingly large role. Some of the best stick and staff fighters in Indonesia, the bow and arrow is still commonly used by the mountain people of western Ceram—a tall, excitable, dark-complexioned people of the Papuan and Melanesian physical type.

Until relatively recently, the taking of heads was apparently an essential part of the ceremonial life of some tribes. The number of heads determined a man's status in the community and was indicated by black rings on the belt of his *tjidako.* Heads were given in essence to the Lord of the Heavens, portrayed in the form of concentric circles symbolizing the sun. The Alfuro reputation for savagery persists, undeservedly, to this day. Every so often a rumor spreads that they're seeking a head to be used, for example, in a bridge-dedication ceremony. Resident Westerners will then post guards in their living rooms, and people stay in at night. Even on neighboring Ambon, the Ambonese are a bit concerned and will tell you that they all feel more secure when the rainy season cuts Ceram off from the mainland for several months. The central districts of Ceram are sparsely inhabited by mixed Alfuro tribes, with less warlike traditions. The marshes and hills of eastern Ceram shelter a Veddoid people, the Bonfia, who are shy, peaceful, and almost untouched by any cultural influence from the outside world.

Religion

In the past, the religion of most of the tribespeople was a form of animism, a belief that stones, trees, forests, and mountains are populated by spirits, often the souls of the dead *(nitu nitu).* Their religion was similar to the old religion of the Bataks of N. Sumatra. Ceram was famous for its village *kakihan* societies made up exclusively of adult males. These groups practiced periodic initiation of pubescent boys by means of ritually "devouring" the initiates by a crocodile figure, sacrificing pigs on stone altars, and issuing frightening noises from the spirit houses—strikingly similar to certain New Guinea rites. Later Islamicization, combined with the inexorable Indonesianization of the territory, has made deep inroads into these native religious systems. Though Ceram does retain its socio-religious institutions to a higher degree than anywhere else in C. Maluku, out of a total native population of around 60,000, today 16,000 are Islamic, 12,000 Christian. The remainder are animists.

SIGHTS OF CERAM

From Ambon's Dermaga Pelayaran Rakyat, catch a minibus to Tulehu (Rp550, 24 km) from where you catch a boat to Amahai (Rp5000, 3 hours). The *kampung* where the boat docks is **Soahuku,** and it costs Rp200 to get up to Masohi. The government head-

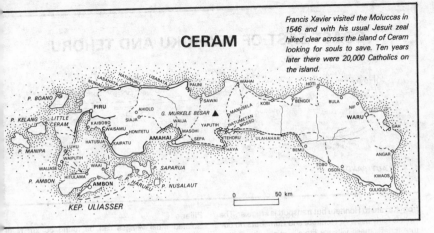

CERAM

Francis Xavier visited the Moluccas in 1546 and with his usual Jesuit zeal hiked clear across the island of Ceram looking for souls to save. Ten years later there were 20,000 Catholics on the island.

quarters for the *kabupaten* of Ceram is at Masohi which has 2 costly accommodations: **Mess Ole-Sio** (Jl. Salahutu) and **Losmen Maharani** (Jl. Kesturi). From Masohi, take minibuses to: Sehati, 4 km, Rp100; Makariki, 6 km, Rp125; Sion, 8 km, Rp150; Transad, 13 km, Rp250; Kantor Camat, 27 km, Rp500; Usliapan, 34 km, Rp625.

Between Soahuku and Masohi is Amahai, consisting of only a school, post office, a few houses, and a stretch of fields and woods. Stay in the town's *penginapan*. Amahai can be very bureaucratic; you might register at one police station, then a cop will come around and complain that you didn't register at his station too. People might even approach you on the street to ask to see your passport, pretending to be police. *Kantor pos* are found in Amahai and Masohi; do your posting at either of these because there are no more for a long way east.

MASOHI-AMAHAI AREA

NOT TO SCALE

From Amahai

Nice walks in this area: a short one out around **Tanjung Kwako** (wear shorts and thongs or you'll never get the vicious grass seeds out of your clothes), and a longer one up to **Lake Itu Allah** (not for the novice trailfinder). Here there's a sago swamp; the lake itself is at the end of a long, swampy meadow. **Kawa Pool** is located roughly between Amahai and Masohi, easily reached from either town. The pool, which runs down to the sea via a small stream, contains what are believed to be sacred fish and eels. You can also take a minibus from Amahai for Rp450 (24 km) to Sepa (or Rp550 from Soahuku) and beyond. On this road E you pass through the villages of **Rutah** and **Rohoa** where some Nuaulu tribesmen live, descendants of the aborigines. Sample minibuses fares from Amahai to: Rutah, 7 km, Rp150; Hatuheno, 15 km, Rp275; Januelo, 12 km, Rp225; Rohua, 29 km, Rp550; Tamilu, 36 km, Rp675.

With its thousand-kilometer coastline, many beaches are scenic and suitable for swimming and fishing. Among the more accessible are **Kwako Cape** (Tanjung Kwako), **Rutah, Uneputi, Piru, Elpaputih, Soleman**, etc., all in S. Ceram and reached by minibus from Amahai or Masohi. **Marsegu** is a coral atoll in the W part of the island, 60 km from Ambon, where 33 species of sea lilies are found, probably the largest variety of any habitat for this attractive aquatic family.

Kairatu

Population 31,284 in 1986. Take a coaster from either Amahai's dock or from Tulehu on Ambon. From Kairatu's port into town is Rp300 by minibus. There's a *pasanggrahan* here run by a woman whose children force open the louvres so they can peer in; it's next to a school full of rowdy and curious kids; Rp6000 pp with meals, Rp3000 without. A road has been built

COAST EAST OF SOAHUKU AND TEHORU

from Kairatu to Honitetu but transport is irregular. The walk is fairly easy. At Honitetu and Rumahtita no culture is left; these villages literally stink with Rp300 *durian* in season (Jan.-March); from here it's about a 2-day walk to aboriginal areas on a difficult up-and-down trail.

The Walk East

Popular also with travelers is the walk E along the fascinating coastal track from Sepa to Haya, Tehoru, Saunulu, Yaputih, and Hatumetan; allow at least one week. Faster is to take regular motorboats which do the run to Tehoru from Masohi. The road goes as far as Tamilu, 36 km and Rp675 by minibus from Soahuku. From Sepa you can walk along the beach, or sometimes on a parallel track through the coconut plantations all the way to Tehoru. From Sepa E to Rohoa is 5 km; Nuaulus live around **Rohoa. Tamilu,** a big *kampung* with many stores and nice peanut pancakes, is 8 km beyond Rohoa. **Empera** is 5 km farther; in Empera are the last stores until Haya, 40 km farther.

From Sepa all the way to Tehoru is 70 km. There's enough water (needs purifying, of course) and the rivers can be forded easily in the dry season. Camp or stay with the *bapak raja.* **Namasula** is a Muslim village where they ask Rp400 for a bunch of bananas (they don't know to cheat there well). **Salamaha** and **Misa** are 2 very friendly Christian towns where they might treat you to *kelapa muda* if you're thirsty. **Haya** is a big town with 9 Catholics, 67 Protestants, and 2,500 Muslims. Twelve km later, the trail ends at **Tehoru** (pop. 23,441 in 1986) which is the *camat's* headquarters but has no post office. Luxury items such as ice blocks or a box of matches are expensive (Rp400 each). From Tehoru, take a *prahu* across the bay (if you try to walk, you'll have to cross an estuary) to Mosso. For the interior, follow trail descriptions below.

Piliano

Isolated tribal villages can be found 30 km N of Yaputih but the trail leading from Yaputih is too difficult; take trails N either from Hatumetan or from Hatu. Piliano is a ½-day walk uphill from just W of Hatu. From Hatumetan, 2 trails lead to Piliano but to avoid a big ford walk W from Hatu and turn inland just before the first large stream after passing through a graveyard. Cross the river a bit beyond on a log. Farther along are 2 main forks—go right (the L heads for Yaputih). Take the best-used trail inland after this. Go down to the big river and cross a stick bridge *(titian),* then climb up through clove groves to Piliano.

TRAIL TO PILIANO

NOT TO SCALE

MANUSELA RESERVE

There are 2 approaches to this 100,000-ha forest reserve. From the S, first take a motorboat (departing 3 days a week) from Masohi to Tehoru (pop. 16,000), then another motorboat to Saunulu (10 km, 1 hour). Or walk from Masohi to Sepa, Haya, Tehoru, Saunulu, Hatumetan, etc. along a coastal track. Remember, no stores are found on this S coast in the central section until Haya (from Tamilu or Empera). From Hatumetan to Manusela about 3 days. **Wahai**, the main town on the N coast just outside the reserve, has no airstrip but 4 coasters from Ambon call twice weekly. The *Wahai Star* leaves Ambon for Wahai on Wed. at 1200 and returns to Ambon on Thurs. at 2400. The *Tiga Berlian* leaves Ambon on Sat. at 1200 and departs Wahai on Sun. at 2400. Both *kapal motor* charge Rp12,500 OW or Rp30,000 pp for berths and the passage takes 30 hours. Get a permit to the reserve at Air Besar, near Wahai. Walking from Wahai to Manusela village takes 5-8 days. The main tracks are shown on the accompanying maps. There are no facilities in the reserve park. Officials or villagers hire themselves out as guides for as little as Rp2000 per day.

The Land

The reserve consists of a section across the middle of Ceram. In the N, the reserve is intended to protect the headwaters of the Toluarang, Mual, and Isal rivers, all of which are to be dammed for the important Pasahari irrigation and *transmigrasi* scheme, as well as the Sariputih River farther east. This northern part is flat up to the foothills 50 km from the coast. The southern part is contrastingly very steep and mountainous, with high ridges isolating the inner valley. The small villages of this valley, of which Manusela is the largest, are accessible only by foot. Preserves have been set aside for the protection of the cassowary and other birds; also fine lowland and montane forests, especially between Kanikeh and Roho. **G. Murkele Besar** (3,027 m), on the reserve's eastern border, is Ceram's highest mountain.

Walk Across Central Ceram

The starting point for this trip is Tehoru, the seat of the *camat*. Pack food in or you might have to content yourself with eating biscuits for the 2-3 days it takes to reach Manusela. In Tehoru you must register (again) with the police; the chief might be summoned back from another village in order to register you. The chief might even arrange your passage (for free) on a boat across the bay to Mosso, or you can hire a *prahu* for around Rp10,000-15,000. There are 2 trails N, from Hatumetan or Wolu. The latter is very poor and seldom used. From Hatumetan, it's a 2-day walk to Manusela, with no habitation in between, over a

2,050-m-high pass. The trail is easy to follow once past the cultivated areas at the start, but it's pretty rough walking and there are few campsites. The first critical junction is where an indistinct track turns E through a small valley with huge taro plants. Further on, there are several campsites (no water nearby), then from a nice rock shelter the trail heads N crossing and recrossing the Wae Walala River 4 times in rapid succession (could be difficult after raining).

The entire trip N across the island via Manusela might take a week. After Manusela, you might need a guide for at least 1 day to take you through the Roho-Wasa section which is mostly flat and swampy (except for 2 mountains), plus another guide for a few hours through a maze of rivers W of Kanikeh. You'll probably meet very few people on the trail, and no stores. West of Roho is the *kampung* of **Huaulu** inhabited by some Nuaulu-type aborigines. Ask to stay with the *bapak raja*. On the way you might come across natives packing a *lopa-lopa*, a carrying case made from sago fronds, commonly used throughout the interior of Ceram. Parrots live around G. Pinang. The trail ends in Wahai (pop. 1,500), the first post office since Amahai. From Wahai, catch a boat to Ambon (Rp12,500, 30 hours).

Manusela

A Nuaulu village of several hundred souls with an active and friendly *bapak raja*. The church here was constructed of materials—tin roofing, aluminum drainpipes, eaves, windows, etc.—carted over the mountains. Rice will be scarce but the *bapak* might serve delightful heaps of boiled potatos and eggplant with deer jerky. From Manusela, there are 2 trails to the N coast. Take the one via Maraina to the west. Between Manusela and Kanikeh the journey is sometimes right up the rivers, sometimes on trails. Huaulu is another Nuaulu town W of Roho, on a side trail.

Wahai

About 1,500 people live here. There's a police station, a *kantor camat*, and a post office. In the same Chinese store that sells tickets to the boats, they sell *dendeng rusa* or fried deer meat for about R1500 per kg. No *losmen* in Wahai, but you can stay at Tan Tok Hong's house, Jl. Sinar Indok (Rp10,000 d, including meals). The KM *Wahai Star*, KM *Wuliati*, KM *Taman Pelita*, and KM *Tiga Berlian II* all do the Ambon-Taniwel-Wahai-Bula-Ambon loop twice weekly on different days. From Wahai, it costs Rp12,500 (or Rp30,000 for a cabin) to Ambon, stopping at innumerable places along the way. At Sawai there's a dock so you may go ashore and wander around town awhile before reboarding. The sea journey can take up to 2½ days because the captain might not want to sail around the W side of Ambon in the afternoon when the seas are very high.

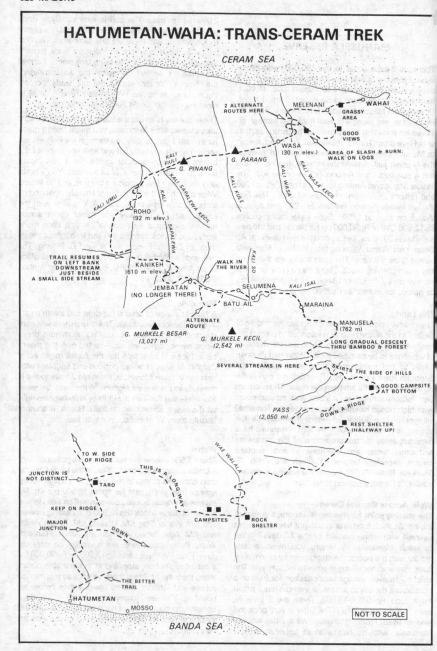

HATUMETAN-WAHA: TRANS-CERAM TREK

CERAM SEA

2 ALTERNATE ROUTES HERE

MELENANI

WAHAI

GRASSY AREA

GOOD VIEWS

WASA (30 m elev.)

AREA OF SLASH & BURN: WALK ON LOGS

KALI FIULI

G. PINANG

G. PARANG

KALI KULE

KALI WASA

KALI WASA KECIL

KALI UMU

KALI SAPALEWA KECIL

ROHO (92 m elev.)

KALI SAPALEWA

TRAIL RESUMES ON LEFT BANK DOWNSTREAM JUST BESIDE A SMALL SIDE STREAM

KANIKEH (610 m elev.)

WALK IN THE RIVER

KALI SO

SELUMENA

KALI ISAL

JEMBATAN (NO LONGER THERE)

BATU AIL

MARAINA

ALTERNATE ROUTE

MANUSELA (762 m)

G. MURKELE BESAR (3,027 m)

G. MURKELE KECIL (2,542 m)

LONG GRADUAL DESCENT THRU BAMBOO & FOREST

SEVERAL STREAMS IN HERE

SKIRTS THE SIDE OF HILLS

GOOD CAMPSITE AT BOTTOM

PASS (2,050 m)

DOWN A RIDGE

REST SHELTER (HALFWAY UP)

WAE WALALA

TO W. SIDE OF RIDGE

THIS IS A LONG WAY

JUNCTION IS NOT DISTINCT

TARO

KEEP ON RIDGE

MAJOR JUNCTION

DOWN

CAMPSITES

ROCK SHELTER

THE BETTER TRAIL

HATUMETAN

MOSSO

BANDA SEA

NOT TO SCALE

TRANSPORT

Getting There

Fly once weekly (Mon.) from Ambon to Amahai with Merpati for Rp14,000. Merpati also flies between Amahai and Langgur for Rp85,100. From Waai (P. Ambon), get boats to Kamal, Nurue, Waisamu, Hatusua, Karatu (on Ceram's W coast). From Tulehu on Ambon there are boats to Seruawan, Tihulale, Kairatu (Rp5000), Kamarian, Rumahkai, Latu (W. Ceram), Liang, Waraka, Makariki, Masohi (Soahuku Harbor, for Rp5000), Sepa, Rutah, Tamilu, and Tehoru (S coast of Ceram). Popular with travelers is to take the regular boat over from Tulehu on Ambon to Amahai on Ceram, then take a minibus and walk along Ceram's southern coast to Hatumetan where they hike 5 days up through the center of the island to Wahai from where they take another boat back to Ambon (Rp12,500, 2 days, at least 4 boats weekly).

Getting Around

Plan on walking; motorized transport is scarce. You need 3 months to really get into the island. Ceram's traditional culture is only found deep in the interior. Roads (only about 40 km) are restricted to the immediate area around the principal towns of Amahai, Masohi, and Wahai. Travel by truck from Wahai E to Kalisonta and W from Wahai to Rumah Sokat. A small road follows the S coast from Amahai to Tamilu. Few travelers make it over to the E which is quite remote and inaccessible. A trans-Ceram highway to the N coast is in the early stages of construction; it will greatly aid development of the N coast of the island. In other places, land travel in the interior is entirely over tracks. To get to nearby coastal villages from Amahai, you can also take *prahu*, though not all boats run daily. If you want to head for the eastern part of the island, allow 4-5 days. If there's no intra-island boat transport, return to Tulehu on P. Ambon, then depart again for another point on Ceram.

BURU

Buru is a large, magnificently wild island W of Ceram. One of Maluku's 3 largest islands, it has an area of 8,806 sq km (slightly larger than Bali). The island is surrounded by coral barriers, covered in impenetrable eucalyptus forests, elephant grass, and vine-shrouded nonvolcanic mountains. The soil is poor, with some savannahs. Coastal areas are flat and marshy, dotted with impoverished fishing villages. There are very few roads; only one river is navigable by small boats. In the western part of Buru is 670-m-high **Lake Wakolo**, with a 60-km circumference. In the NW corner is the **Kaku Palatmada** mountain range, with a volcanic peak rising over 2,100 m. Dense forests crowd right down to the sea.

Although the VOC built a fort on Buru as early as 1657, most of the island has only recently been explored. A third the size of Holland, Buru was ruled by a single Dutch Resident during the later colonial era. In 1861, the indefatigable A.R. Wallace spent May and June here wading barefoot through the island's muddy swamps where he "discovered" no less than 17 new species of birds. Since independence, the island's main claim to fame is as the penal colony for mostly Javanese prisoners suspected of involvement in the 1965 "communist" coup.

Buru produces timber, its principal industry, as well as *kayuputih* oil derived from a species of eucalyptus tree. This oil has been exported since Portuguese times. The main town is **Namlea**, a dusty village on the NE coast composed of Chinese shopkeepers, natives, Arabs, and Javanese. Some *transmigrasi* settlements have been established here, especially since the island's 13,000 political prisoners were sent home. Now that the prisoners are gone, no special military clearance is required to visit the island.

Buru's population (around 63,000) is divided between the animist and Proto-Malayan Gebmelia of the interior and mixed racial groups along the coasts known as Gebmasin, of both Christian and Muslim faiths. Until 1969 cannibalism was still practiced deep in the island's rugged interior. Isolated aboriginal tribes around the Lake Wakolo region—the Rana, Waeloa, Waetenum, and Waejapo—number about 3,000. These first-wave inhabitants hold on to their hunting and foraging culture but are dying out fast.

The Prisoners

From 1969 to 1979, Buru was the "rehabilitation center" for political detainees (called *tapol*) suspected of complicity in or sympathy with the nearly successful coup of 1965. During this period P. Buru was a forbidden island, sealed off from the rest of Indonesia and the world by the *Kopkamtib* (State Security Agency). The giant center, located inland from Namlea on the Wai Apu River, held as many as 13,000 prisoners (of Indonesia's 100,000 total) by the end of 1975. Prisoners attended compulsory indoctrination lectures, the aim being to replace communist ideology with the government *Panasila* philosophy. Detainees were forced to faithfully attend a mosque or church (hundreds of communist voices singing "Jesus is my Shepherd" resounded eerily through the Buru jungles!). The wet rice cultivation introduced by the government failed miserably. There were no newspapers, movies, radios, or TV. Prisoners lived under harsh conditions, were sometimes tortured, deprived of water, and fed salted food. The many

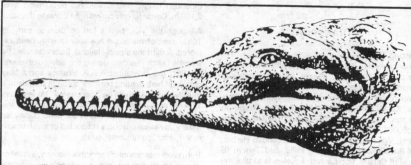

crocodiles: This giant reptile is distributed from the Asian mainland to northern Australia. Maximum length is 9 m. The crocodile of Irian Jaya is quite distinct. In Africa crocodiles lay their eggs in mud, usually in two layers with sand in between. The heat of the sun hatches the eggs. But since the rivers of New Guinea are often surrounded by dense forests right down to the water's edge, the sun's heat can't be used to incubate eggs. So New Guinea crocodiles drag leaves and plants together and lay their eggs in the center of a ½-meter-high heap. The heat of the mouldering vegetation hatches their eggs. The female usually lies on top or at the side to guard the eggs. These crocodiles, if not hunted with firearms, prey on man.

writers, artists, and other intellectuals confined to the camps as "prisoners of conscience" read like a cultural "Who's Who" of Indonesia: Subronto Admojo, one of the Indonesia's leading composer-conductors; Basuki Effendi, Indonesia's foremost film director (he was the camp violinist and instrument-maker); and probably Indonesia's greatest prose writer, Pramoedya Ananta Toer (who had spent 2 years in a prison fighting the Dutch), all imprisoned without a trial after the abortive coup. There were no watchtowers or barbed wire, and camp guards weren't armed. They didn't need to be. Buru was an ideal isle of exile, from which no prisoner ever escaped alive. Thirty-eight escaped the camp in 1974 only to perish of exposure in the jungles within days.

The Release

Finally, under pressure from foreign governments and such humanist organizations as Amnesty International, plans were made in 1975 to begin releasing the prisoners. With the collapse of the anti-communist regimes in S. Vietnam, Cambodia, and Laos, and the financial bankruptcy of its state oil company Pertamina, Indonesia felt more conciliatory toward its Japanese, American, and European allies. With the election of President Jimmy Carter and his human rights policies in 1976, conditions began to improve and the pace of the release process quickened. By 1979, all prisoners had gone home, replaced for the most part by *transmigrasi* settlers who are exploiting the millions of dollars the government spent on Buru and the work started by the *tapol,* who had hacked their settlement literally right out of the jungle.

Transport

The Pelni and Perintis ships, the KM *Bedalu* and the KM *Baruna Bakti,* stop at Buru in their passages to and from Ambon and Ternate. More regular are the ships KM *Wahai Star, Suliati, Tiga Berlian II, and Dewi Jaya,* which all sail from Ambon to Namlea (Rp8000) and Airbuaya (Rp12,500) twice weekly. The KM *Usaha Baru III* also sails from Ambon to Leksula on Buru for Rp7500. Merpati flies from Ambon to Namlea on Thurs. at 1310 for Rp30,600 (30 min.). The plane lands close to Namlea on a coral airstrip still pockmarked with bomb craters from the 1950 Indonesian attack on the forces of the Republic of S. Moluccus. There are a few roads around Namlea; but on the rest of the island are only muddy jungle tracks.

The "PKI resurgence:" During the latter half of 1988, there was an extraordinary increase of reports in Indonesia's news media of former PKI operatives having infiltrated the government, the armed forces, academia, and the state school system. Many felt that the real purpose behind these almost daily published reports about the communist menace was to ensure that the state security arm, Kopkamtib—which has since been dismantled—would continue to function. Others theorized that the reports were aimed at particular officials. The commie-baiting headlines also sold very well. Since March of 1988, the circulation of the daily newspaper *Jayakarta* soared to 80,000. In June 1988, all copies of Pramoedya Ananta Toer's new historical novel, *Rumah Kaca,* were seized. *Jayakarta* subsequently bragged that it had initiated the campaign to ban *Rumah Kaca.* The Attorney General's prohibition against communist literary works constitutes the government's first step in a "zero tolerance" policy against books which they feel smack of communism.

THE BANDA ISLANDS

Nine small volcanic islands 160 km SE of Ambon on the NE fringe of the Banda Sea, the Banda Group was world famous from the 17th-19th centuries as the original Spice Islands of the Dutch East Indies. These islands played a gigantic role in Indonesia's early history. To acquire control of the nutmeg trade, in 1619 the ruthless 31-year-old Dutch Governor-General Jan Pieterszoon Coen exterminated Banda's indigenous population—one of the blackest days in Dutch colonial history. Now comprising the southern-most islands of the Central Maluku District and governed from Ambon, the 2 main islands are close together and you can get around them easily by *prahu*. There is magnificent scenery, beautiful sandy beaches, puffing volcanos, easygoing accommodations, planters' ruined mansions with marble floors, crumbling Dutch forts, one of the finest harbors in the archipelago, and peerless coral gardens and reefs. The Bandas get a trickle of travelers and odd adventurers—the lone Australian or German, a pair of New Zealand women, or a few yachties. Wealthy senior tourists, retracing "the footsteps of Magellan," arrive on the luxury cruise ship *Lindblad Explorer*. As yet uncorrupted by tourism, there're only 2 trucks, 6 motorbikes, and 3 cars on the islands, one of which meets you at the airport. Theft is practically unknown. Electricity is very sporadic; the generator is turned on at 1800 or 2100 (you never know) and it's always turned off again by 0600!

The Land

The early romantic vision of the Bandas was a jewel-like cluster of forgotten tropical islands surrounded by crystal waters, brilliant coral reefs, hills lined with aromatic spice trees on which perched flocks of green and red parrots, all presided over by a still-active volcano which resembles Mt. Fuji in miniature. This vision is also the reality. The group consists of 4 main islands—Lontar (Banda Besar or "Great Banda"), Neira (on which sits the principal town, Bandaneira), Run, and Ai, in addition to 5 smaller islands, all volcanic in origin. (Since 1586, eruptions have been reported on an average of once every 21 years.) Covering a total of some 45.6 sq km, the largest of the Banda Group is the 32-sq-km P. Lontar. Considered the most beautiful cluster of islands in the Moluccas, the forests are remarkably green and surrounding waters so clear that coral and even minute objects can be seen to depths of up to 8 fathoms.

Fauna

Deer and pig have been introduced to the islands; also inhabiting them are big nutmeg pigeons, *Ducula concinna*, a species distinct to the Kai, Banda, and

Watabela islands. The Bandas are also fortunate to have their own 2,500-ha marine reserve based on the coral gardens in the lee side of P. Lontar. The actual reserve area no longer contains the best coral, but **P. Suanggi**, Bandas' farthest outlier, has the most extensive coral reefs, the finest sand beaches, and is a nesting site for boobies and other seabirds. In all, 167 fish species are found in these sheltered waters, including the magnificent flashlight fish *(Photoblepharon bandanensis)* and 24 species of butterfly fish. Watch out for lurking sharks. Tiny fluorescent algae also live in the waves of the sea, turning the water sparkling white. This "milk sea" is at its weakest in June and July, but is very pronounced in August. The **Penju Is.**, 200 km SW of the Bandas, are nesting grounds for giant sea turtles.

Flora

Banda is home of the best-known commercial species of nutmeg, *Myristica fragrans*. The tree, which can grow 8-12 m in height, is always in bloom. The fruit ripens year-round. When mature and yellow the 5-cm fruit splits open, revealing a dark red aril surrounding a crimson seed. The aril is carefully stripped off and dried, in which state it forms mace. The seed is a thin, hard shell around a wrinkled kernel. When dried, this kernel is the nutmeg. Plantations of these handsome trees still cover large areas of P. Lontar. Harvested twice each year, the islands remain the most important world producer of nutmeg, exporting about 500 tons per year. Ironically, while the rest of the world considers nutmeg a delicacy, the inhabitants of these islands reputedly have never used it as a condiment themselves.

HISTORY

To really appreciate Banda it helps to have a keenly developed sense of history. Before going, borrow a copy of Willard A. Hanna's *Indonesian Banda* (Institute for the Study of Human Issues) from a well-stocked Asian Studies library; copies are also available at Bandaneira's museum and Hotel Laguna. The only detailed study of the islands' culture and history over the past 400 years, this is an engrossing and provocative book of not only the colonial system in microcosm but also the whole evolution of modern Indonesia.

Spice

These islands derive their name from the Javanese word *Bandau*, meaning "United"; another interpretation traces the origin to *Nusa Banda*, "Islands of

Wealth." Spices are bound up inextricably in the history of these islands. For centuries the Bandanese had been selling their spices to such traditional regional trading partners as Bugis, Chinese, and Arabs in exchange for medicine, and ceramics, and *batik* and other textiles. Scholars believe that Hindu-Javanese merchants were the first to introduce nutmeg and mace in the international emporia, the commodities reaching Europe around A.D. 500. The demand for spices as preservatives accelerated in Europe to such an extent that by the 16th C. expeditions were dispatched in search of the source. The Portuguese captain Antonio d'Abreu discovered the Bandas in 1511, inaugurating a profitable Bandanese-Portuguese trade which lasted for nearly 100 years. Atypically, the Portuguese did not leave a trail of intrigue and exploitation in the Bandas as was the case in the other Moluccan clove islands of Ambon, Tidore, and Ternate, which they had annexed. The Portuguese kept a tenuous hold on the islands until the arrival of the Dutch in the early 17th century.

Early Dutch Expeditions

The Dutch first attempted to lure the Bandanese away from the politically and economically bankrupt Portuguese. In 1599 the Dutch Vice Admiral van Heemskerk arrived with 2 ships and 200 men to barter iron goods, heavy woolens and velvets, gunpowder, mirrors, and trinkets. For these inappropriate and unwanted goods, the Dutch demanded the island's entire crop of nutmeg and mace. The village elders signed a written treaty under pressure, not realizing that the Dutch considered the document to carry the full force of the law. After signing, the Bandanese ignored the treaty and went back to freely selling spices to their traditional buyers, which included the English on the island of Run. When the Dutch found out, they were outraged, threatened reprisals, and demanded even more stringent agreements. Finally, under the auspices of the Dutch East Indies Co., in 1609 Admiral Pieter Verhoeffe sailed a war fleet of 13 ships and a thousand men into Bandaneira's harbor to impose an airtight monopoly on all spices leaving the Bandas. After cursory negotiations, the admiral began constructing a massive fort upon the foundations of a former Portuguese fort—a premature and provocative act. Under pretense of further negotiations, the Bandanese lured the unarmed Dutch into an ambush in which the admiral and 45 of his entourage were killed. This escalated the pace of events, unleashing a catastrophe.

Dutch Conquest

After the ambush, the chiefs and much of the population deserted the spice gardens around the fort and fled into the hills. In retaliation, the Dutch survivors blockaded the islands, attempting to persecute and starve the Bandanese into submission. Punitive expeditions were launched against the islanders, but the stubborn Bandanese resisted, expelled the Dutch from the island of Ai, and continued to trade with the English. The Dutch were getting nowhere in this war of attrition, and at last decided to take more drastic measures. Their choice of a commander, the ruthless Jan Pieterszoon Coen, had witnessed the murder of Verhoeffe during the 1609 expedition. This man, of whom Dutch historians have said "his name reeks of blood," gave no quarter. Invading the Bandas from Batavia with a force of 2,000 men, Coen's mercenaries rampaged through the islands razing villages, burning boats, raping, and looting. Two-thirds of the population were wiped out, the remainder sold into slavery or driven into the hills to die of exposure. Only 1,000 Bandanese survived in the archipelago out of an original population of 15,000.

Monopoly

In Coen's attempt to impose a monopoly once and for all in the Bandas, British factories and forts first had to be destroyed, stocks of spices confiscated, and their merchants and seamen beaten and thrown into chains. Coen began setting up a closed horticultural preserve to control the growing and sale of spices. To keep the supply down and prices up, nutmeg groves on all but the 2 main islands were destroyed. Coen carved up the remaining gardens into 68 concessions, or *perken,* which were offered free to Dutch planters called *perkeniers*—mostly rogues and drifters. In order to work the nutmeg trees on these now unpopulated islands, each land grant was provided with 1,500 imported slaves from other islands—Timorese, Papuans, Javanese, Makassans, Siau Islanders, and Chinese. The Dutch East Indies Co. controlled demand and fixed prices, assuring a guaranteed income for the *perkeniers* and astronomical profits for the company.

English Fortunes Fall And Rise

Continued English interference in the region led to the "Amboina Massacre" in 1623 in which merchants and their Javanese guards were beheaded. This convinced the English of the futility of maintaining a presence in Maluku; finally, in the Treaty of Breda (1667) the English relinquished all claims to the Bandas in exchange for the small and insignificant Dutch island of Manhattan in the Americas. The British returned in 1795 and by a mere show of force took the islands to protect them from Napoleon, restoring them to Dutch rule in 1803. In 1811 during the Napoleonic Wars the English again seized the Bandas, returning them again in 1817.

Isles Of Obscurity

The monopoly system begun by the Dutch eventually declined as a result of widespread corruption. The *perkeniers* enriched themselves further by smuggling and selling subsidized supplies on the black market, eventually growing degenerate and lazy, detested by their slaves and Dutch officials alike. Many of these planters took slave girls as mistresses and wives, evidenced by the fascinating racial blends seen on the islands today. During the Napoleonic Wars the English, with great foresight, transplanted prime nutmeg seedlings in their colonies at Sumatra, Penang, Colombo, and Calcutta, which eventually broke the back of the Dutch monopoly. The price that nutmeg and mace could command on the world market was thus drastically reduced, and trade in these spices dwindled to a trickle. Production plunged from 2,000 tons to 300 tons a year, and the Bandas became an economic backwater. The rampant graft and larceny finally drove the Dutch East Indies Co. into bankruptcy in the 1790s with a staggering debt of 12 million guilders (equal to US$50 million in today's money).

The Colonial Era

When the new Dutch colonial administration took over the affairs of the shattered company in the early 1800s, it began to institute long overdue reforms. Slavery was abolished in 1862, the plantation workers replaced with imported convicts and gangs of Javanese coolies. The *perkeniers* gained title to their landholdings in the 1870s but managed their finances so poorly that their *perken* were bought up at rockbottom prices by Chinese and Arab competitors, and by an official government agency created for the purpose. The late 19th and early 20th centuries saw the Dutch colonialists sponsoring churches, schools, and public works. In contrast to its stormy beginnings, these tiny islands, under the paternalistic rule of the Dutch, returned to a state of relative peace and prosperity which lasted up to the mid-20th century. The tiny and once-famous Bandas became a remote and nearly forgotten outpost of the empire.

Isles Of Exile

With the nationalists' demand for self-determination gaining momentum through the 1920s and '30s, all was not as peaceful elsewhere in the archipelago. In the 1930s Banda was chosen as the isle of exile for several of Indonesia's most popular revolutionary leaders, Sutan Sjahrir and Mohammed Hatta (cofounder of the Indonesian republic). Transferred from the infamous Boven Digul detention camp in West New Guinea, these famous visitors arrived on 11 Feb. 1936. Their presence immediately made a subtle impact on the Bandanese, who felt they were once again put on the map. The fervent revolutionaries rented ex-colonialist quarters, mingled with and endeared themselves to the townsfolk, ordered books from Batavia and the Netherlands, and even started tutoring the local children—all under the watchful eye of the Dutch warden who occupied the jail next to their dwellings. The nationalists swam, fished, and hiked in what amounted to a delightful exile in an idyllic tropical setting, which was to end abruptly in 1942 with the Japanese invasion. Fearful lest they should fall into Japanese hands and be used for propaganda purposes, the Dutch flew Hatta and Sjahrir out of Bandaneira on 31 Jan. 1942 to Java, just before the Japanese attacked. When the Republic of Indonesia was proclaimed in 1945, Hatta became vice-president and Sjahrir later became prime minister.

The Japanese Occupation

During WW II, the Japanese military had little interest in developing spice commodities and thus nutmeg production virtually ceased. Forced to fend for themselves, the Bandanese reverted to a subsistence economy, planting cassava and sweet potatos and trading fish for sago from Ambon. Later the Japanese used Bandaneira as a rendezvous point for their warships when other ports in the Banda Sea were being strafed by Allied bombers. Just before the return of the Dutch in early 1945, American bombers flying out of New Guinea occasionally bombed and strafed Bandaneira. On one occasion, a stray bomb landed in the middle of a wedding party, killing 100 people and injuring hundreds more. The old pre-war Bandaneira pier, where stately KPM ships once tied up to unload cargo and passengers, is now a twisted mass of iron, a grotesque memorial to this tragedy. The doomed wedding procession is now buried under the floor of Bandaniera's church.

The Post-war Years

By the end of the Japanese occupation, the once beautiful and high-yield nutmeg estates had fallen into sad disrepair. The *perkenier* were demoralized, and no new planting had taken place for years. The increasing use of refrigeration to keep meat fresh further eroded clove and nutmeg markets. The Dutch at last gave up their Indonesian possessions in 1949 and the Banda Is. lost their importance in the international trade arena forever. During the Sukarno era, the Bandas were associated with the Central Moluccan rebellion instigated by the Ambonese, and the nutmeg gardens were nationalized. The whole spice enterprise, rife with corruption, fell into even further neglect. The industry has been only partially rehabilitated during the Suharto regime.

ECONOMY

Bandaneira has always been an entrepot for the Tanimbar and Aru islands as well as for the coastal towns of southern Irian Jaya. But this historical trade has always been small scale: its production of *trepang*, tortoise shell, and sharks' fins is modest, and what fruit and vegetables are grown can only supply the local market. Employment opportunities are dismal. As soon as the youth of Banda are able they migrate to Ambon. Finding jobs there almost as nonexistent as in Banda, they move on to Ujung Pandang, and inevitably, wind up in the streets of Jakarta, adding to the already swollen mass of that city's jobless. Seldom do they ever return.

Nutmeg and mace are both derived from the fruit of the dioecious nutmeg tree (Myristica fragrans). The fleshy, yellow-brown fruit, which resembles an apricot, is about 5 cm (2 inches) in diameter. As the nutmeg ripens the pulp breaks open to reveal the nut encircled by a network of crimson mace.

The Nutmeg Industry

Ever since VOC times, Banda has been run like one big nutmeg plantation, with little economic development in any other sector. On the decline for decades, the depression of the 1930s brought on even more deterioration in the nutmeg industry and WW II and the political and social turbulence of the '40s and '50s nearly killed it for good. But Bandanese spices, still considered peerless in quality, might yet stage a comeback. It is with this in mind that the government has begun to allocate redevelopment expenditures to revitalize the nutmeg industry. The principal trading partner for the spice is, ironically, Holland, where Dutchmen still like to sprinkle the spice over their vegetables. And all over the world, unadulterated prime nutmeg and mace are still considered essential in gourmet cooking. In Indonesia itself, Sulawesi and Java have outstripped Banda in production, while Grenada in the West Indies also is a major producer. Nutmeg brings in about US$2400 and mace about US$3000 per ton. One of the largest enterprises in the islands is the CHV, the walled-in headquarters for the

state-run nutmeg cooperative. Here the nutmeg is processed, then shipped (usually) to Ambon, from where it is exported to other domestic and international ports.

Fishing

Besides tourism, the only other sector of the island economy which shows any promise is fishing. These seas are a rich reservoir of high-quality swordfish, tuna, garupa, etc. Although Bandanese fishermen put out to sea in over 20 arumbai (traditional Bandanese fishing vessels), so far only the Japanese have exploited these waters to any commercial extent. Their wanton robbery of the waters of the Banda Sea, to absolutely no enrichment of the region's inhabitants, has raised vehement protests, but to little effect. Fishing remains a small, indigenous industry which barely supplies the local market: when there's a surplus it's dried, salted, and exported to Ambon. Plans by the government to modernize fishing fleets and canning facilities have never gotten off the ground. And the chance of this ever happening in such a provincial economic backwater is unlikely.

THE PEOPLE

The Banda Islands have lost their aboriginal population. Two-thirds of the original Bandanese people were wiped out by the Dutch in the 17th C., who then imported Makassarese convicts, Javanese coolies, and Papuan and Timorese slaves to work the nutmeg plantations. These were joined later by an influx of Europeans, Eurasians, Chinese, Buginese, Arab merchants, and other immigrants. The contract laborers in time earned their freedom, and many of the present-day inhabitants of the Bandas are descended from them. All these variegated races, languages, and religions eventually produced today's homogenous, highly distinct, and complex Bandanese people. In 1986, the total population was 12,635. In some of these islands an archaic dialect is spoken which is not used anywhere else in Indonesia. Although utterly devoid of any productive employment opportunities for the young, Banda does offer its inhabitants a good number of blessings, even dignity. Banda islanders do not share the grinding poverty of Java's urban poor, housing quality is above standard for Indonesia, and the people are able to feed themselves adequately with the help of government subsidies. The 7 schools of the group have an enrollment of over 1,000 students at the primary and secondary levels, though they are ludicrously underequipped and understaffed.

Events

Before the Dutch finally expelled the Portuguese from the Bandas, the latter had already been here for over 100 years; the local dances still show a distinctive Portuguese flavor. The Cakelele dance is put on whenever the *orang besar*, Des Alwi, asks for it. Des is the owner of the island's premier hotel. In this war dance, village men dance around a large bronze drum decorated with leaf offerings. In other Portuguese-derived dances, old costumes, blunderbusses, helmets, and shields are worn. Another dance one sometimes sees in Bandaneira resembles the Chinese dragon dance, in which children dress up in sackcloth costumes with papier-mache masks. Also, the *Mako-Mako* and *Maru-Maru* dances are still held on occasion in the Bandas.

BANDANEIRA

The principal town on P. Neira, Bandaneira is perched on the edge of a gigantic crater. This quiet, peaceful town, today just a few short streets filled with Mediterranean-style homes and shops, was once the Dutch administrative center for the whole region, famous all over the Dutch East Indies for its beauty. Bandaneira's dilapidated buildings, though reflecting the turbulent history they have seen, have a mysterious air of decay about them. The town has an old Dutch church (Jl. Gereja), ancient Fort Nassau (built in 1621), and along Jl. Pelabuhan are grand mansions of the *perkeniers*. Around town are other examples of gracious Dutch colonial architecture, most left to crumble into ruin. All the historical sites may be toured, and since there aren't many tourists you really get the A-treatment. Two resident cassowaries prance down the middle of the main street—no traffic, so why not? A few years ago Holland dug 35 wells; now the holes are all there, but only 5 pumps have survived. The show at Bandaneira's single cinema (Rp1000 admission) is the town's main event at night. On a plateau above Bandaneira, backed by a 240-m-high rock, is massive Fort Belgica, commenced in 1611, which has survived numerous earthquakes. Bandaneira's landlocked harbor, with no visible outlet, was one of the finest in the Indies. The wharf faces the narrow strait in the middle of which sits the imposing G. Api volcano. Between P. Neira and P. Lontar are sea gardens of colorful fish and every variety of coral.

Dutch Reform Church

Located in the center of town, this church (1852) overlooks the neglected park which surrounds Fort Nassau. The lovely church (150 member congregation) is a severe structure which replaced an earlier building destroyed by an earthquake. The church has a clock that doesn't work; apparently it clicked its last the very moment of the Japanese invasion 47 years ago. Near the church are a Christian and a Chinese cemetery with lichen-covered inscriptions; probably one of the most fascinating collections of old tombstones in all of Indonesia. The Dutch governor of Banda is buried here. The Bandaneira's old **Catholic** church (50-member congregation) has a clockface with only 8 numbers on it, and no hands—a haunting touch even for the Bandas. Services are held here only once a week, but the church is well cared for; see caretaker Julius who will show you around. Ask to see the church service, a whole set of 17th C. pewter that would probably fetch $100,000 at auction in London.

Kantor Bupati

The magnificent *bupati's* residence was once the Dutch *controlleur's* mansion, built in the 1820s with giant granite paving slabs, bright floor tiles, shiny marble, heavily carved beams, huge wooden doors, and shuttered windows. Although the building is still used as Banda's administrative headquarters, the top *kabupaten* administrator nowadays uses Ambon as his base. (Indonesian *pegawi* consider getting posted to Banda to be the bureaucratic equivalent of exile.) Behind the building in the garden is a statue of the Dutch King Willem III. Ask to see the inscription by a 19th C. French prisoner who scratched a lament on the wall. A stern, heavy, colonial air still pervades this building.

Middenstraat

This residential street that runs along the waterfront, adjacent to the *bupati's* residence, is now called Jl. Pelabuhan. On Middenstraat are the giant *perkeniers'* stone mansions, though the majority are in serious disrepair. These buildings are occupied now by the military or police. One of the grandest of these waterfront buildings is the former **Harmonie Club**, the center of Dutch social life where the *perkenier* set would socialize with their fat wives in the cool of the evening, smoking cigars, drinking Bols gin, and playing cards. There were often balls and banquets as well as musical or theatrical performances by traveling troupes. Today the Harmonie Club is in ruins. Another big Dutch villa is being converted into a bank.

Museums

The **Mohammed Hatta Museum** is in a building once occupied by the freedom-fighter Dr. Mohammed Hatta (1902-80) who, together with the nationalist Sutan Sjahrir (1909-66) was exiled to Banda during the 1930s. It contains exile memorablia, the desk and pens he used, etc. Hatta eventually became the first vice-president of the new Indonesian republic and Sjahrir went on to form the Partai Socialis Indonesia in 1945. The **Rumah Badya** museum, formerly a *perkenier* mansion converted into a mosque, is now the home of the Baadillah family, who claim descent from Arab sea captains. The head of the family, Des Alwi, runs 2 hotels in Bandaneira and also rents out snorkeling and diving equipment. This historical museum (which also rents rooms in the back) contains artifacts tracing the whole nutmeg culture, plus paintings, big ceramic vases, old coins, etc.

Forts

Fort Belgica is a pentagonal-shaped Dutch fort built in 1611 on the ruins of a 16th C. Portuguese fort, above Bandaneira about 500 m from the harbor. Although overgrown, the structure is still standing and in fairly good condition (but not for long if they don't do something). It was last restored in 1935! Cannons point out over Bandaneira's sleepy harbor. Climb up to one of the towers for a sweeping view over the town, volcano, and nutmeg groves. Remains of a moat are still visible. Also visit the overgrown, crumbling walls of **Fort Nassau**, below Fort Belgica near the church. Just a gateway, a rusting cannon, and 3 walls remain of this fort built in 1609 by the Dutch. In the repressive atmosphere of Banda's plantation system in the 17th and 18th C., the major reason for building these fortifications was to protect the white population against slave uprisings.

Skin Diving

Some dazzling coral gardens are found in the straits between P. Neira, G. Api, and P. Lontar, a body of water which constitutes a large, broken-up crater lake. The configuration of these 3 main islands has created one of the most beautiful natural harbors in Indonesia. The Banda Sea is very deep blue, and the colors of the sand, rocks, and sky vivid and bright, while objects at the bottom of the transparent sea are visible for many meters. You could find yourself swimming in the middle of a school of 100 dolphins frolicking in the water! Diving equipment can be hired from Des Alwi at Hotel Complex: snorkel, mask and fins, Rp2000 per day, tank for Rp12,000 per day. Motorboats, going for around Rp15,000 per hour, are preferable. Smaller canoes, although quite maneuverable and able to travel great distances, usually capsize when you attempt to climb back in. While snorkeling, be careful of stonefish and angelfish. The most beautiful coral reefs are found surrounding **P. Karaka** which lies off G. Api. The paddle canoe from Bandaneira's harbor costs Rp3000-4000 per hour to get out here (1 hour each way). There's only one, very friendly old man living on the island.

Volcanos

Meaning "Mountain of Fire," the main harbor of the Bandas is dominated by the **Gunung Api** volcano rising 676 m out of the sea. Though its main crater is thought to be extinct, it is constantly puffing away and has a treacherous history. On 2 April 1778, a violent eruption was accompanied by an earthquake, a hurricane, and a *tsunami*. Fires flared up all over P. Neira, destroying 500,000 nutmeg trees and nearly obliterating the town of Bandaneira. In 1820 another eruption occurred. Today the rim of the crater can be reached by first taking a motorboat (or canoe) from Neira's harbor, then climbing up a 500-m-long footpath (2 hours RT). From the top is a splendid view over the town and the whole Banda chain. Some outstanding snorkeling is found off G. Api in the shallow coral groves opposite **Taman Laut** on P. Neira, and on P. Karaka (also known as P. Sareer; see above).

Also climb P. Neira's 250-m-high mountain, **G. Papenberg**, on a poorly maintained trail, some sections of which have stone steps. The trail begins beyond town and anyone can show you the way. On the side of G. Papenberg are the ruined mansions and sheds of the rich Lans family, as well as the dilapidated estates of 2 other *perkenier* families. Ask the locals about the springs on G. Kele, known locally as **Airmata Cilubintang**.

PRACTICALITIES

Accommodations

The cheapest places to stay in Bandaneira, both run by friendly people, are **Peng. Delfika** in an old *perkenier* mansion, Rp15,000 s or d. Also check out **Peng. Selecta**, for the same price. More expensive is the **Hotel Laguna**, the principal tourist hotel (which everyone tries to steer you toward). Costing Rp35,000 s with bath/wc, or Rp60,000 pp d full board plus 10% tax, use the CB radio to talk to the Arab owner in Jakarta and try to get the price down to Rp25,000 d. They expect you to take all your meals there (fresh fish, tea, etc.); Rp10,000 for 3 meals per day (they also pack a lunch if you go out for the day). The Laguna rents out canoes, motorboats, snorkeling equipment, arranges tours and marine excursions.

Also try the pricey **Hotel Mulana** on the waterfront, **Hotel Complex** (rent diving gear here), the peaceful **Rumah Badya Hotel** (Rp10,000 pp, in back of the museum), and the **Naira Hotel** (Jl. Pantai), each about the same price as Hotel Laguna. But the best is to ask around and try to stay with a Bandanese family which will not only put you up but also act as guide and counselor. Inquire at the police station which family puts up travelers, and they will send out a courier; expect to give a donation of around Rp7500 per day (try Abdulrahman's). Elsewhere on the islands, stay with the *kepala kampung*.

Food And Services

Except at Hotel Laguna, there are no refrigerators in town so food can't keep. Bandaneira is chronically short on vegetables, eggs, and even rice is expensive here. At the *pasar*, near the CHV compound (government nutmeg cooperative), buy fruits, vegetables, and fish, but it's only open when a ship is in. Try such fruits as *zirzak*, *nangka*, citrus, and *taliu*, a cigar-shaped fruit having the taste of a *kanari*, in stalls selling fruits and fried fish snacks. The police come around the hotel restaurants to sponge free beer (which the hotel pays for). There's one *rumah makan*, **RM Nusantara**, with good *nasi campur* and *ikan bakar*. The price of fish depends upon how big the catch was. Dog is still eaten on Banda and even a skinny one fetches Rp10,000; the locals will tell you that for some illnesses, you have to have *sate anjing*.

There are no banks, fancy restaurants, or nightclubs on Banda. Avoid any dealings with the local *imigrasi* office; real sonsabitches, absolutely the worst in all of Indonesia, with nothing to do but hassle you. Banda-

neira's *rumah sakit umum*, with its Indonesian doctor, can handle minor ailments and injuries but for anything serious go to Ambon.

Getting There

Until the late 1970s, only 100- to 200-ton *kapal motor* or *kapal layar* connected the islands with the outside world (Ambon) by irregular schedules. Now a small

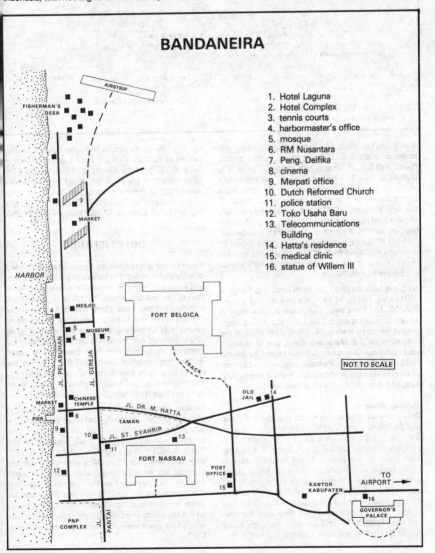

BANDANEIRA

1. Hotel Laguna
2. Hotel Complex
3. tennis courts
4. harbormaster's office
5. mosque
6. RM Nusantara
7. Peng. Deifika
8. cinema
9. Merpati office
10. Dutch Reformed Church
11. police station
12. Toko Usaha Baru
13. Telecommunications Building
14. Hatta's residence
15. medical clinic
16. statue of Willem III

NOT TO SCALE

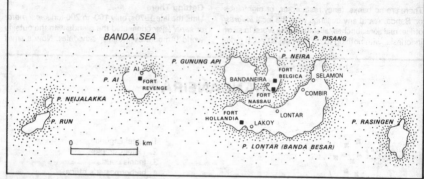

THE BANDA ISLANDS

BANDA SEA

P. PISANG

P. GUNUNG API

P. NEIRA

FORT BELGICA

BANDANEIRA

SELAMON

P. AI

Al

FORT REVENGE

COMBIR

FORT NASSAU

P. NEIJALAKKA

FORT HOLLANDIA

LONTAR

P. RUN

LAKOY

P. RASINGEN

0   5 km

P. LONTAR (BANDA BESAR)

airstrip has been built. The Merpati flight from Ambon to Banda costs Rp50,500, departing 2 times weekly (Wed. and Sat., if enough passengers). You're only allowed to take 10 kilos pp, but you can leave your stuff with your hotel proprietor in Ambon. This flight continues on to Tual and Langgur in the Kais (SE Maluku). Buy only a OW ticket as you might be able to get a boat back to Ambon. Buy return tickets at the Merpati agent's office on Jl. Pelabuhan, Bandaneira. Arriving in Banda, a car meets you at the airport to drive you into town for Rp2000. Or walk into town in about 20 min. if you take the shortcut which comes out beside Rumah Badya.

Frequent coasters also leave from Ambon to Banda, a 200-km trip taking 14-16 hours and costing around Rp5000. The Pelni ship, KM *Niaga X,* sails every 3 weeks for a swing around the entire Banda Sea, stopping at Banda on both ends. Some other ships of the line, such as the *Nusantara Daya,* are of dubious seaworthiness. Crews rent out their cabins for around Rp10,000. Also check Perintis Lines, which has vessels to Banda from Ambon about every 3 weeks. The best, of course, is to visit by private yacht.

Getting Around

Only a few vehicles are found on the island of Neira and the island's only road leads from town to the airport. Do like the natives: walk or ride bicycles. The principal roadway on the island is the one leading from town to the airport. Some very picturesque tracks lead from Bandaneira around the island. Boats are the way to see the other islands in the group. The seas are calm Sept.-Dec., although in March and April it's also possible (the rainy season is May-Oct.). The charter rate for motorboats (find them near the market) runs Rp30,000-75,000 per day; figure on about Rp150,000 to P. Ai and back. Cheaper is to hire or bor-

row from the locals canoes and other types of rowing vessels at Rp3000-4000 per hour (useful for getting out to G. Api from Bandaneira, a 10-min. paddle!). For other islands in the province, about every 3 weeks either Pelni or Perintis ships call at Bandaneira, providing transport to: Tual, Rp7000; Elat, Rp7500; Dobo, Rp12,250; Larat, Rp17,300; Saumlaki, Rp22,250.

OUTER ISLANDS

Pulau Lontar (also known as Banda Besar) is located directly S of P. Neira. The largest of the Banda Group, this long, thin island is covered in nutmeg orchards. During the days of forced cultivation it supported half a million nutmeg trees. Plantations still thrive under the shade of the island's remaining *kanari* trees, whose leafy umbrella spreads out at a height of 35 m, nearly blotting out the sun. Lontar is reachable by chartered motorboat from near Bandaneira's *pasar.* At first the boatmen want Rp15,000 RT, but the school boat goes over at around 0900 (Rp2000 pp) and returns at around noon, ample time for you to get up to see **Fort Hollandia,** the island's main attraction.

Located on the central spine of the island near the village of Lontar, a steep flight of steps leads up to the overgrown hilltop fortress. This once huge fort, devastated by an earthquake in 1743, was built by the Dutch in 1621 during a punitive visit by the redoubtable Jan Pieterszoon Coen. Nice view of the volcano from the top. Near Tanjung Burang is an underwater holy urn, **Tempayang Keramat,** said to be watched over by a white tortoise and holy fish. Reachable by canoe or motorboat from Bandaneira. **Laci** is a well on P. Lontar renowned for its purification ceremonies which take place every 13 years; the next will be in 1989.

To reach any of the outer islands of the Banda Group, a motorboat must be chartered from Bandaneira. **Pulau Ai** is a small island to the W of G. Api, 21 km from Bandaneira (2 hours by motorboat); its name means "water" in Bandanese. Pulau Ai was conquered by the Dutch in 1616; they built a fort and a blockhouse here called "Revenge." Made of coral-lime, the structure rises straight up from the sea. During the Napoleonic era, the island was occupied by the English who grew cloves here. To the SW, **P. Neijalakka** was also a British stronghold until the Ambon Massacre of 1623. **Pulau Suanggi,** a favorite habitat for seabirds 125 km NW of Bandaneira, has gorgeous natural panoramas and pristine white sandy beaches. **Pulau Manuk,** a volcanic island 80 km S of the Banda Group, is an untouched nesting ground for seabirds. Also has beautiful marine gardens for skin diving and snorkeling.

Lucipara-Penju Groups

Isolated, uninhabited groups of reefs, sandy beaches and coral cays 200-230 km SW of the Bandas, about a 14-hour sea voyage from Bandaneira. Nestling among the Lucipara Group, surrounded by a huge platform reef holding a veritable treasury of sealife, is P. Mai. Like famed Almeira in the Indian Ocean, this island is one of few on the planet in its primeval state. With the exception of a few coconut palms, P. Mai supports a natural flora undisturbed by man. Also inhabiting the island are a distinct species of mound-building megapodes, incubating their eggs in sand containing layers of decomposing vegetaton. Pulau Mai's reef edge is one of the most spectacular drop-offs anywhere, plunging to a depth of over 900 m. These islands are also breeding grounds for a huge colony of sea turtles.

NORTH MALUKU

The fabulous spice islands of Maluku Utara have been lauded in literature and fable from as early as 1667 when Ternate and Tidore were alluded to in Milton's *Paradise Lost.* The 353 islands of the district had a total population of 418,582 in 1986, with an average density of only 17 people per sq km. Its land area is 32,000 sq km, while its sea territory covers 207,381 sq km. Most of the islands are volcanic in origin, and immense areas of the district's larger islands—Halmahera, Morotai, Bacan, Obi, Sulabesi, Mongole, and Taliabu—are covered with dense rainforests. Commercial crops include cloves and nutmeg. Sago and a great variety of forest orchids grow all over the district.

The forests of Halmahera, Obi, Bacan, and Sula provide the best opportunities for wildlife observation. Birdlife, particularly on Halmahera, is profuse: the *anggang, kasumba, maleo,* parrot (Halmahera and Obi), giant crestless cuckatoo, orange-crested cockatoo, and gong bird (P. Obi). Wild animals include deer, cuscus, the Bacan monkey of P. Bacan, lizards on P. Obi and Halmahera, and a wide variety of butterflies all over N. Maluku. In its seas are ornamental fish, colorful corals, seashells, and the *kenari* crab. Maluku Utara has about the same rainy season as the rest of Indonesia. The administrative seat and capital of the *kabupaten* is Ternate.

History

Islam was brought to N. Maluku by Javanese traders probably during the 15th century. Before the coming of the Europeans in the early 16th C., the 2 rival kingdoms of Tidore and Ternate had long been engaged in almost continual war with each other over

control of the lucrative spice trade. Their domains once stretched as far as Cebu (Philippines), Flores, and Sulawesi. For hundreds of years these and other nearby sultanates traded with Chinese, Arabs, and Javanese merchants. The first factual account of the islands comes from the Portuguese Barbosa in a manuscript dated 1516. The adjacent islands became well known in Europe during the 16th and 17th C. as the sole supplier of cloves. In the hopes of wresting this monopoly away from the 4 sultanates of the region, the Portuguese established themselves on Ternate in 1521. However, eventual conflict with the sultans led to their expulsion from Ternate in 1574 and from Tidore in 1581.

The Dutch, arriving in N. Maluku at the start of the 17th C., were first welcomed by the sultan of Ternate who was anxious to keep the Spaniards and Portuguese in check. Granting the Dutch a spice monopoly, it was the sultan's intention to extend his power, with Dutch help, over not only the Moluccas but beyond to Makassar in southern Sulawesi. But the colonialists bolstered the power of the sultanates only as long as it suited their purposes. When the Dutch decided to confine clove cultivation to Ambon, under the merciless leadership of Arnold de Vlamingh they destroyed the clove gardens of the northern Moluccas and brought all illegal smuggling to a halt. Although these harsh measures caused widespread revolt throughout the islands of the region, the Dutch prevailed, shearing the sultan of all his power. Ruins of colonial forts—Portuguese, Spanish, English, and Dutch—can be found today on every major spice-producing island in the area.

Economy

The economy of N. Maluku centers on timber, fishing, copra, and spices. The islands of the Sula and Obi archipelagos are important timber-producing areas, while prime-quality cacao is produced on P. Bacan. Ternate, Tidore, Makian, and Moti are still major clove-producing islands which have enjoyed a resurgent prosperity due to the new-found popularity of clove cigarettes around the world. The district today has 465,000 *cengkeh* trees with nearly 3,000 ha under cultivation.

Transport

Ternate is the focus of air and sea transportation in the region. Merpati provides service from Ambon 11 times weekly (Rp63,600) and from Manado (N. Sulawesi) twice daily (Rp39,000). Bouraq flies from Balikpapan, Rp177,300; Tarakan, Rp249,300; Manado, Rp44,900; Jakarta, Rp258,700; Surabaya, Rp204,100. Within Maluku Utara, Merpati flies from Ternate to: Galela (Rp31,200) and Kao (Rp23,000) on neighboring Halmahera 3 times weekly, as well as to other out-of-the-way islands such as Mongole in Kep. Sula once weekly (Rp61,600), Morotai once weekly (Rp36,100), Sanana on P. Sulabesi twice weekly (Rp52,300). If traveling by road within N. Maluku, take *bendi* (Rp300-400 pp within Ternate), public *bemo* (Rp200 in urban areas), and island buses. Roads circle the islands of Ternate and Tidore, and there are small road systems around Jailolo and Galela on Halmahera, Sanana on P. Sulabesi, and Labuha on P. Bacan. Sea transport is well developed in the district. Public motorized *prahu* and motorboats travel between all the main administrative and market centers. Pelni and Perintis coasters connect the main ports of N. Maluku to N. Sulawesi as well as to Ambon and elsewhere in Maluku Province. For only around Rp10,000 pp, Pelni's KM *Baruna Bhak* does a loop every 3 weeks from Ambon to Ternate, stopping at many island ports during the 10-day passage.

TERNATE ISLAND

The northernmost of a series of 7 islands off the W. coast of Halmahera. Ternate's small area—only 65 sq km with a width of only 9.7 km—is all out of proportion to its tempestuous 500-year history. Scores of overgrown and ill-maintained Portuguese and Dutch fortifications litter the island, which is occupied almost entirely by the active volcanic cone of G. Gamalama (1,721 m). This lofty mountain is made up of 3 peaks (Madina, Arfat, and Kekan), a grotesque shape brought about by numerous deadly eruptions. Within the last 4 centuries there have been no less than 70, mostly affecting the northern half of the island. The worst took place in 1763, which devastated the prosperous seaport of Fort Takome on the NW coast and so obliterated one slope that it has since been known as Batu Angus (Burnt Corner). Another eruption in 1840 destroyed every house in Ternate City. The island is still very geophysically unstable, with frequent earth tremors. All this volcanic history assures that most of its towns are coastal, connected by a road around the island. The loop around the island costs only Rp500 and takes 2 hours.

History

At one time Ternate, Tidore, Moti, Mare, and Makian were the world's only suppliers of cloves. A traditional power center for all the northern Moluccas, the Portuguese entrenched themselves here in 1521 with the aim of turning Ternate into one of their chief spice-producing centers. In their attempts to monopolize the spice trade, they assassinated Sultan Hairden in 1570. The hatred generated by this murder led to their expulsion and eventually cost them the East Indies. The Spaniards, who founded Manila in 1570, moved S and captured the weakened Portuguese garrison in Ternate in 1574. Sir Francis Drake called at Ternate in 1579 and took on 5 tons of cloves. The English buccaneer was much impressed by the thriving port and the sultan's fabulous wealth. Although warmly received, Drake's visit was never followed up by future trade.

The island's history took a new turn in 1599 with the arrival of the opportunistic Dutch. Relying on Dutch assistance against the Portuguese and Spanish, and bent on expanding his control over adjacent islands, the sultan granted the newcomers a spice monopoly. For more than 80 years Ternate rose in power until the Dutch decided to confine clove production to Ambon, voiding all contracts with Ternate in 1683. In one stroke the Ternate sultanate lost control of many northern Moluccan islands, vast territories which henceforth were administered by the Dutch. The sultan and his descendants were thus reduced to titular rule, pensioned off by the Dutch. Before WW II, Ternate was a regular port of call for Dutch pocket steamers, a service entirely disrupted by the Japanese invasion of 1942.

Economy

Much of the island is still densely wooded, and the timber trade is an important source of revenue. The volcanic, fertile land produces sago, bananas, cassava—the staples—supplemented by a little rice, maize, vegetables, and sugarcane. Copra, cacao, and coffee are important cash crops. The scent of cloves and nutmeg can still be picked up in the air. Coral is found everywhere along the coast and there are some outstanding dive sites for pearls.

The People

The native population (70,000 in 1986) is of very mixed blood with the Malay physical type predominant. Because of the extensive trade contacts with Arab merchants and other Islamic groups, the population today is 90% Muslim. These northern islands have a very strong orthodox Islamic presence; groups of young schoolgirls in white veils and sky-blue blouses are frequently seen in Ternate's streets. There's a tiny Christian community, the *Orang Seracci*, descendants of natives converted in the 17th C. by the Portuguese. The bell in Ternate's only church is believed to have been presented by St. Francis Xavier himself. Witch-craft *(keswange)* is widespread; mediums are capable of communication with spirits called *manganitu* and may function as healers who perform many rituals in the life of an individual.

TERNATE CITY

This town, now the administrative center for N. Maluku, has clung to the side of a smoking volcano since the 1500s. Lying on a flat strip of land on the SE side of the island, Ternate is a picturesque seaport, the volcano rising majestically above the main street filled with *bemo* and *bendi*. Formerly the capital of the most powerful sultanate E of Ujung Pandang, Ternate today (pop. 45,672 in 1986) is the second largest town in eastern Indonesia (behind Ambon) and a major shipping center. Though Ambon is more cosmopolitan, Ternate is quieter and more relaxing (except for the earth tremors at night). Ternate's fervent Muslims are in general generous, warm, and friendly. You will also encounter less "Hello Misters!" here than in other places. Wander down to the harbor in the southern end of town from where you can easily make out the island of Halmahera. South of the harbor area is **Bastion**, where you catch boats over to the neighboring island of Tidore.

The Sultan's Palace

Located above the town on Jl. Babulluh past Benteng Oranye on the road to the airport. Also known as the *kedaton*, the palace has now been converted to a museum and is open to the public. The original structure dates from 1234. Designed by an English architect, the palace thus resembles a European country villa. Get a *bemo* from the Jl. Pahlawan Revolusi station (Rp100), then walk up the majestic flight of steps to the verandah. If the gate to the museum is locked, try to locate the curator (who doesn't ever seem to be there!). Among the royal regalia and heavy atmosphere of decay, you can still see by special request the extraordinary "jeweled" crown that Drake described in his 1579 visit, though all the priceless jewels and ornaments have been replaced by cheap glass stones.

Exhibits are scanty, just some Portuguese cannons, lamps, old books, Dutch swords and shields, some Chinese ceramics. The *pendopo* in the rear of the palace is now used as a *balai* for town meetings. A short bus ride out of Ternate via Laguna and up the mountain, **Foramadiaha** was the site of the Ternate sultan's original court. Today only remnants of the palace foundations and some sultans' tombs have survived. The last sultan (d. 1974) was an outrageous playboy called Butch who used to take Lindblad cruises and thrill all the old ladies onboard by playing 1930s Cole Porter songs on the ship's piano. Butch wore a magical ring set with a very large ruby, a description not dissimilar to Sir Francis Drake's account of the powerful and wealthy Ternate sultan of the 15th century.

Ruins

There are more forts per square meter in and around Ternate City than in any other locale of similar size in Indonesia. These crumbling, overgrown ruins once guarded the valuable clove plantations. In addition to the ruins below are the Spanish **Fort Santo Pedro**, 6 km from Ternate City, dating from 1522, and **Fort Gamalama**, 20 km from Ternate City, dating from the 14th century.

Benteng Oranye is a big fortified trading post right on the edge of town opposite the *bemo* station. Built by the Dutch architect Madeliede in 1606-07, it is now a military complex. The original garrison once stretched over a huge area with the town of Ternate growing up around it. The stately fort still has mounted cannon and its VOC seal intact. Informal tours are conducted by the soldiers.

From Benteng Oranye, it's a pleasant 2-km walk N of town, or a Rp300 *bemo* ride, to **Benteng Toloko** just past Desa Dufa Dufa on the right. This small, well-maintained Portuguese fort, erected on a hill by d'Albuquerque in 1512, is located on the road to the airport. Inside you'll get a sweeping panorama of Ternate City. The structure is in such splendid condition that the 16th C. official seal is still quite visible. The inscription and coat of arms at its entrance, however, are Dutch, placed there by one of the first Dutch governors of Ternate, Peter Boit, who in the inscription makes the false claim that he built the fort. Benteng Toloko is shaped so much like a male sexual organ that this must have been the architect's intention. The shape of Benteng Kayu Merah represents the complementary female sexual organ, but here the similarity is not as obvious.

It's Rp300 by *bemo* along the road in front of Peng. Yamin to serene, unfinished **Benteng Kayu Merah** in the S of town. Complete with a moat, the edge of the sea laps at the walls of the fort built in 1510. North of Kayu Merah is Pelabuhan Bastion where you catch *kapal motor* to Tidore. Another 2 km S of Kayu Merah, a heap of old stones is what's left of **Kota Janji**, a fortress where the Portuguese murdered Sultan Hairden in 1570.

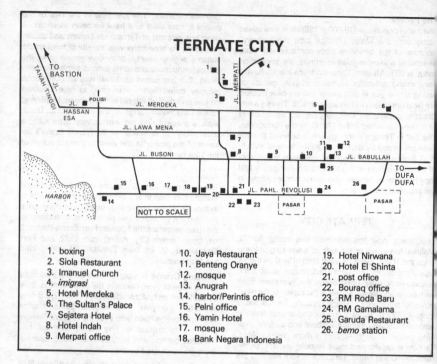

TERNATE CITY

TO BASTION

JL. TANAH TINGGI

JL. POLISI
JL. MERDEKA
HASSAN ESA

JL. LAWA MENA

JL. BUSONI

JL. MERPATI

JL. BABULLAH

JL. PAHL. REVOLUSI

HARBOR

NOT TO SCALE

TO DUFA DUFA

PASAR   PASAR

1. boxing
2. Siola Restaurant
3. Imanuel Church
4. *imigrasi*
5. Hotel Merdeka
6. The Sultan's Palace
7. Sejatera Hotel
8. Hotel Indah
9. Merpati office

10. Jaya Restaurant
11. Benteng Oranye
12. mosque
13. Anugrah
14. harbor/Perintis office
15. Pelni office
16. Yamin Hotel
17. mosque
18. Bank Negara Indonesia

19. Hotel Nirwana
20. Hotel El Shinta
21. post office
22. Bouraq office
23. RM Roda Baru
24. RM Gamalama
25. Garuda Restaurant
26. *bemo* station

A 15-min., 11-km *bemo* ride from town down a lovely road to Kastela (or Rp200 past Kota Janji) is **Benteng Kastela**, erected by the Portuguese captain Antonio de Brito in 1522. Named after the Portuguese castle nearby, this wrecked fortification's gateways still stand. More than just a fort, Kastela was the center of a town called Ave. The remains of the hospital can be seen in thick undergrowth and an old Portuguese well nearby is still used by the locals. The ramparts at the circumference of the town are also clearly visible. Fort Kastela, thought at the time to be impregnable, was abandoned only 50 years after it was built; it now protects a papaya patch and the main road around the island dissects it. From the shore of the village you can see P. Maitara between Ternate and Tidore.

PRACTICALITIES

Accommodations

At least 15 places to stay, mostly on the expensive side. Many hotels might be booked up, or might not accept foreigners. Usually there are separate rates for rooms with meals and rooms without; be sure to establish rates, and if there are any hidden taxes, in advance. A good deal is **Wisma Alhilal**, Jl. Monunutu

2/32 (tel. 21404), charging Rp7500 s, Rp15,000 d. This family, which serves outstanding meals, is used to travelers and is very helpful. Although family-style **Wisma Sejahtera**, Jl. Lawamena 21, has small rooms, it is quite comfortable and homey; Rp7500 s, Rp9500 with meals; Rp10,000 d, Rp17,500 with meals. **Penginapan Yamin,** just outside the harbor gates, is one of the cheapest at Rp6000 s, Rp8000 d. Other hotels to try are **Anda**, Jl. Ketilang 49; **Massa**, Jl. Busouri 27; **Merdeka**, Jl. Merdeka 19; **Thamrin**, Jl. Merdeka 28; and **Nusantara**, Jl. Lawamena 18A– all charging around Rp5000 s, Rp85-10,000 with meals.

In the higher-priced category, down near the harbor is **Hotel Nirwana**, Jl. Pahlawan Revolusi 58 (tel. 21787, see Mgr. Paulus Polar); Rp12,500-15,000 s with meals. The **El Shinta**, next to Hotel Nirwana, charges up to Rp40,000 d without attached bathrooms. **Hotel Merdeka**, Jl. Monunutu, charges Rp12,500 for big rooms including meals. Also check out also **Hotel Chrysan**, Jl. A. Yani (tel. 377/210); Rp12,000 s, Rp23,250 d; **Hotel Anda Baru**, Jl. Ketilang 49 (tel. 155); Rp10,000 s. **Hotel Indah**, Jl. Bosouri 3 (tel. 21334), in the middle of Ternate, has no private bathrooms but is quite good value at Rp16,500 full board. Their a/c rooms are almost twice the price. The **Angin Mamiri**, Jl.

Babullah 17 (tel. 21245), offers Rp7500 s and Rp15,000 d rooms (also higher-priced a/c rooms); meals cost extra, Rp4000 pp for lunch or dinner.

Food

Experience such traditional N. Moluccan dishes as *kenari* crab, *mamuya* (lobster eggs), yellow rice, *bagea*, *dabu-dabu*, and cassava cakes. Also try *ikan bakar* (roasted fish) with *coloh-coloh* sauce — a specialty here. Local food can be enjoyed in the town's *warung*. Several good *es jus* street stalls are along Jl. Pahlawan Revolusi. During Jan. and Feb. the streets and markets are literally flooded with *durian* at Rp1500-2000 apiece. There are many good places to eat: **RM Anugerah**, on Jl. Busouri across from the *bemo* station, has meals for Rp800-1000; **RM Gamalama**, Jl. Pahlawan Revolusi, offers inexpensive meals and specializes in *Coto Ternate*. For Padang-style food, go to the **Jaya**, Jl. Busouri, and the **Roda Baru**, Jl. Pah. Revolusi. For Chinese food, the **Garuda Restaurant** on Jl. Babullah opposite the *bioskop* is the place. The **Fujiama**, Jl. Pahlawan Revolusi (next to the post office), is the swankiest and priciest restaurant in town.

Crafts

During the golden age of the spice trade, Ternate's markets overflowed with fantastic merchandise. A few shops sell tortoise-shell bracelets, *kulit mutiara* (mother of pearl) articles, jewelry, and perhaps a lady might come up and try to sell you *batu bacan* and other semi-precious stones at inflated prices. In the markets green, red, or dazzling white *krakatua raja* (king parrot) and big blue pigeons are for sale. Beware of vendors of old coins as there's lots of fake casting going on. Test if it's silver by dropping it against concrete and listening to the ring. Douglas Capp, at Calvari Mission (Pentecostal) in Ternate City, is an avid shell collector.

Events

Sultan Nuku's birthday celebration each year consists of traditional ceremonies and a parade of the sultan's troops, attired in uniforms from the time of Napoleon. See the *Soya Soya* Dance if you hear of it, performed by 13 men. For information on where to see the esoteric Muslim rite of self-mortification with knives (called *Badubus*) as well as local magic acts such as the *Gambu Gila* contact friendly Haji Ulmar, a part-time tourist guide, at the mosque in Kampung Falajawa just before the harbor.

Services

Three banks on the main street change money but **Bank Dagang Negara** on Jl. Nukula does it with the least hassles. **Bank Negara Indonesia** and **Bank Expor Impor Indonesia** on Jl. Pah. Revolusi (adjacent to the harbor) also changes U.S. dollar TCs; open Mon.-Fri. 0800-1100, Sat. 0800-1000. The **post office** is on Jl. Pahlawan Revolusi next to the Fujiama Restaurant and near Bank Negara Indonesia. The tourist office, **Kantor Pariwisata**, on the main street has scant information! With luck you might get a map of the Moluccas. **Kantor Imigrasi** is on Jl. Merpati, a road up above the town. Here you must apply for a *surat jalan* in order to visit any of the out-islands of Maluku Utara.

TRANSPORT

Pelni's KM **Umsini** sails from Jakarta to Ternate for Rp68,000 Economy, Rp168,700 1st Class. Flying into Ternate is spectacular. From **Ba Ullah Airport** at Tarau, walk out to the main road and flag down a *bemo* into town, Rp300. Or take a taxi, Rp3000. No *becak* on Ternate, *bemo* cost Rp150 to anywhere in town. A ring road runs entirely around the island, passing through all the coastal villages; without stops the complete circuit can be accomplished in about 2 hours. Suggested itinerary for a round-the-island circuit: Dufa Dufa, for 16th C. Fort Toloko; "Burnt Corner" for the lava flow Batu Angus; Sulamandaha, a small village, the northernmost point on the island, with a black-sand beach opposite P. Hiri; the villages of Loto and Taduma; Kastela village, the site of another historical ruin; Akerica, a sacred spring; Aftador, the scene of a Japanese WW II atrocity; Kulumata, another ruined fortification; and Kayu Merah; yet another ruin; and finally to Bastion and back to Ternate City.

From Ternate By Air

Frequent *bemo* go back and forth to the airport in Tarau, 5 km from town, Rp300. You can also take a taxi (Rp3000), or charter a whole *bemo* for Rp2000-3000 out to the airport. From Ternate, Merpati flies to: Ambon, Rp63,600, daily; Galela (Halmahera), Rp31,200, 3 times weekly at 0700; Gebe, Rp48,100, Sat. at 0820; Kao (Halmahera), Rp23,000, Tues., Thurs. and Sat. at 0900; Labuha (P. Bacan), Rp29,900, Mon. and Wed. at 0700; Manado, Rp39,000, daily at 1610; Sanana, Rp52,300, Mon. and Wed. at 0700. Bouraq flies 3 times weekly to: Balikpapan, Rp177,300; Jakarta, Rp258,700; Manado, Rp44,900; Surabaya, Rp205,200; Ujung Pandang, Rp147,000. **airlines offices:** Merpati, Jl. Bousori (tel. 314); Bouraq, Jl. Pahlawan Revolusi 58 (tel. 21787).

From Ternate By Sea

P.T. Premut's ships *Semangap*, *Pulau Mas*, and *Gunung Mas* sail N to Doruba (Morotai), and Galela and Tobelo, on Halmahera, Rp8000. Futuru Jaya's ships *Morotai Star* and *Kasratu Indah* also do this trip for about the same price; other companies go as well. Pelni, whose office is just inside the harbor at Jl. A. Yani 1, offers irregular Economy Class service to Kendari, Rp22,275; Luwuk, Rp28,280; Poso, Rp25,870; Gorontalo, Rp22,330; Ujung Pandang, Rp31,730;

Surabaya, Rp55,240; Tanjung Priok, Rp68,000; Bitung, Rp5700. Perintis Lines sails to Bitung, Rp11,000; Jailolo, Rp4500; Tobelo, Rp7000; Sorong, Rp11,250; Sausapor, Rp8,905; Manokwari, Rp11,150; Biak, Rp12,700; Jayapura, Rp35,900; and other locations. Sri Wijaya (swing R just before the harbor gates and follow the road in the direction of Kastela) has ships to Ujung Pandang, Rp26,850; Surabaya, Rp53,850; and Jakarta (Tg. Priok), Rp59,850; departing for these destinations via Ujung Pandang once monthly.

From Ternate's harbor (or from the port of Bastion), *kapal motor* and motorized *prahu* leave regularly for ports on surrounding islands: Makian, Rp3500; Rum on Tidore, Rp1000; Labuha (Rp7500) and Gebe on P. Bacan; and Jailolo (Rp3500) and Patani on P. Halmahera, as well as other destinations such as P. Morotai N of Halmahera. The *syahbandar's* office, Jl. A. Yani 1 (tel. 21214/21206), down on the waterfront, will inform you of which boats go where on which market days. To charter a boat to see the volcano on P. Maitara it costs as much as Rp50,000; try to negotiate with a fisherman to take you for less.

Boats To Ambon

Other than Perintis, boats are rare. Perintis Maluku's *Baruna Bhakti* takes 10 days to Ambon (Rp8500) via Lubuha (P. Bacan)-Lawui-Falabisahaya-Dofa-Bobong and Sanana (P. Sulabesi). If you take this boat, you can count on wall-to-wall passengers, tropical songbirds, minimal sanitary facilities, but beautiful scenery. A test of endurance. Meals are sold on the boat for Rp750 each. It's possible to rent a space in a cramped cabin with a small fan for Rp18,000-25,000, while a whole cabin goes for Rp65,000. This boat also sails N to Doruba, Bere-Bere, Galela, and Tobelo before returning to Ternate and Ambon. Perintis' *Bendulu* also sails to Ambon but is smaller, has more stops, and takes longer; their office is opposite Pelni's in the harbor.

AROUND THE ISLAND

Dufa Dufa is a fishing village 3 km from town and the site of Fort Toloko erected in 1512 (see "Ruins" above). Nice white-sand beaches around this village. **Cengkeh Afu,** 4 km from town in Kampung Maliaro and 650 m above sea level, is the world's oldest clove tree (as of 1988, it was 375 years old). Over 36 m high, almost 2 m wide, and 4.26 m in diameter, 3 men can't join their arms around it. This tree yields up to 600 kg of cloves each year. It is from Cengkeh Afu that a seed was first smuggled to Mauritius by a Frenchman, breaking the Dutch clove monopoly in the 18th century. See others nearly as huge in the clove plantations nearby, and on the road between Ternate and Kayu Merah.

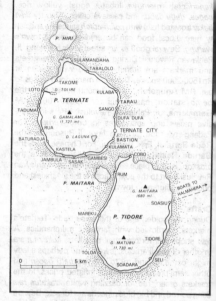

TERNATE AND TIDORE

Gunung Gamalama

An active volcano (1,721 m) with 3 craters on the island's northern side. The central crater has collapsed, forming a lake with vertical sides 80 m high. Gunung Gamalama, also known as Ternate Mountain, rises over the town of Ternate. Extremely unstable geophysically, an eruption occurred in Sept. 1980 when two-thirds of Ternate's inhabitants evacuated to neighboring Tidore. The last eruption was in 1983. The volcano can be climbed on foot from Ternate City, but before setting out consult with Udin at Hotel Sejahtera. First take a *bemo* or hike up a steep road 3 km to Desa Marikrubu. From there, it's another 3 km to the Cengkeh Afu tree. Take particular care crossing the bamboo bridge as one of the poles may be rotten. From the clove tree, it's 2-3 hours up to the top and back. It can be quite dangerous on the rim; there's a sheer drop into the cavernous crater. If you throw a rock into it, no sound. At the top you must walk on hot marble-sized stones, the residue of a 1737 eruption.

Batu Angus

"Burnt Corner." To the N between Tarau and Kulaba (catch a *bemo* from Tarau), this site is where a river of ava from G. Gamalama plowed its way down to the ea in the 18th century. A Japanese war memorial tands nearby. This ravaged N coast has always borne he brunt of Ternate's devastating volcanic activity, tanding out in contrast to the luxurious forests and egetation found in the eastern and southern coasts of he island.

akes, Beaches, Reefs

nland are 2 volcanic lakes, covered in lotus flowers. Beautiful, inviting, spring-fed **Lake Laguna** is 7 km S f Ternate City. Past Laguna, the road leads up the nountain to Foramadiaha (see "Ruins"). **Lake Tolire** s just a 10-min. walk off the main road, about 24 km

from Ternate City; catch a *bemo* to Takome, then walk. The locals are afraid to swim in this deep, green-shaded lake as they claim its waters are populated by crocodiles and demons.

Bastion Beach is 3 km from Ternate town. **Ngade** is a white-sand beach 7 km from town. **Sulamandaha Beach** is 16 km away; good swimming spot. The whole stretch of coast on the NE between Tabalolo and Dufa Dufa has white-sand beaches and splendid reefs; no sharks, but watch the very strong currents. Averaging only about 2 m deep, direct sunlight goes straight to the bottom where you see black lava piled upon black sand, with white coral on top of this.

TIDORE

With an area of about 78 sq km, slightly larger than its sister island, Tidore lies just 1.5 km southwest. Both slands are just volcanic cones emerging from the sea. The southern part of the P. Tidore is occupied almost entirely by an extinct volcanic peak, **G. Matabu** (1,730 m). The soaring peaks of Tidore and Ternate are only 2 of 10 conical volcanos which form a line off the W coast of Halmahera. Below the 300-m level coffee, fruit, and tobacco are cultivated in very fertile soil. The northern half of Tidore consists mostly of hills, with a few level strips along the coast.

With its relaxed people, many skilled smithies, and craftsmen, Tidore (pop. 33,717 in 1986) has a completely different feel to it than Ternate. The natives, originally of Alfuro stock, have intermixed considerably with outsiders. Even though Islam arrived relatively late (around A.D. 1430), the Tidorese are now Muslims all. The *tarian adat* is the *Sulit Sulit*. The only accommodation on the island is in the main town of Soasiu, but you could probably make arrangements to board in a private home. The best days to visit Tidore are the market days (Tues. and Sat.) when the island's towns are a spectacle of color, and transportation is plentiful.

History

Like Ternate, Tidore was the seat of an ancient and once-powerful sultanate which ruled over immense areas of eastern Indonesia as far as New Guinea. European contact began in the 16th century. After Magellan was killed in the Philippines, his crew reached Ternate in 1521. The Portuguese fought the sultans of both Tidore and Ternate, destroying the palaces and alienating the people. Later, the Spaniards took over the island and helped the Tidorese maintain their independence from the sultan of Ternate and the Dutch. In 1654, the Dutch finally conquered the island, but subsidized the sultan and allowed him to rule his subjects and retain his rank and title. During the period of Dutch rule in the 18th C., a young French adventurer

(Pierre Poivre—the "Viper") stole, from right under the noses of the Dutch, young clove tree seedlings which he successfully transplanted on the tiny French island of Mauritius in the Indian Ocean. The Japanese occupied Tidore in 1942.

Magellan's Voyage: The day after Magellan's death in April 1521, 27 men of the expedition were lured ashore and executed at Mactan in the southern Philippines of Cebu. Two ships then fled the scene, the *Trinidad* and the *Victoria*. Arriving at Tidore on 8 Nov. 1521, the crew, mad with joy, discharged all their artillery, giving thanks to God. They had searched for the fabulous Spice Islands for 27 months. After 6 weeks of trading for cloves they put off again, but the *Trinidad* sprung a leak, so the *Victoria* sailed on alone to Europe in the first circumnavigation of the globe.

Sights

Rum is the island's main port, where the boats arrive from Ternate. A short *prahu* ride from Rum is **P. Maitara** (pop. 500) and about a 25-min. walk from Rum's *pasar* are the ruins of a Portuguese fortress. Shop and eat in Rum's many bamboo market stalls; Sun. is market day when ships made out of cloves are sold. The S coast village of **Seli** consists of a row of houses made of bamboo and volcanic rock along the sea. From Seli, **P. Moti** (famed for its cloves) and **P. Mare** are visible. The road from Rum all the way to Seli is well maintained.

Soasiu, with G. Tidore serving as its backdrop, is the largest and most important town on Tidore. Soasiu was the Indonesian headquarters for the West New Guinea campaign during the Republic's clash with the Dutch over that territory in 1965. Nearby are 2 overgrown ruins of Spanish forts: one sits above the road high over the sea as you enter town. Children will lead you up a difficult trail to see a mountain fortress, a maze-like complex, its walls crumbled long ago. The old sultan's palace, also taken over by vegetation, sits above the town, and there's also a restored mosque. Stay in **Losmen Gebura**, Rp4500 s.

Getting There

No airstrip as yet — you must take one of the numerous motorboats from Bastion to Rum, Rp750. Crossing, on the L you can see Halmahera's huge shadowy form. This scenic trip takes only 30 min. and there are many boats, especially on Soasiu's market days of Tues. and Sat., when boats also arrive aplenty from Halmahera. From Rum, take a minibus 45 min. to Soasiu, Rp800. One can also occasionally take a motorboat from Ternate's harbor over to **Cobo** (Rp750, 30 min.) or Tidore's far northern tip. On the road from Rum to Soasiu near Soadara, see where the lava from G. Matubu slid over the road in a 1968 eruption, which killed 11 people. Since then, an entirely new town has been built on the ash and rubble of Soadara.

OUTER ISLANDS

THE SULA ISLANDS

An island group in the SW region of Maluku Utara, between P. Buru and Sulawesi. Combined, the 3 large islands and innumerable smaller ones have an area of nearly 13,000 sq km. For the most part, the Sulas are nonvolcanic with hilly interiors and low-lying swampy coasts. The population of 67,453 (1986) is mainly proto-Malay, with some primitive semi-nomadic groups still living along the coasts and animists inhabiting the interiors. Rice is grown on these islands, while the forests are worked by Japanese and Filipino timber companies. In the eastern part of P. Taliabu, in the interior NE of Bobong, live animist tribes. From Bobong it's about a day's walk to **G. Godo** where the Mangai and Sibojo people live. The villages of Kadai, Mange, and others have wonderful *adat* houses with *atap* roofs. The Mangai and Kadai people also live on P. Mongole. The least interesting of the group is **P. Sulabesi**. By Sanana's harbor is an old fort, dating from Portuguese times, ruined but in good condition with cannon lying in the entrance and a wildflower garden inside.

The Sulas are difficult to reach by sea, but Pelni's KM *Baruna Bhakti* stops in Sanana (P. Sulabesi) on its Ambon-Ternate voyage. Other ships often stop in Sanana to unload cargo. For P. Mongole: first get a ship from Ternate for Rp12,000 to Sanana, then take a small motorboat to Dofa for Rp3000. From Sanana to Bobong it's 1 day by *kapal motor* (Rp7500), departures daily. From Bobong on P. Taliabu, ships operate farther to Banggai, Kep. Banggai, then from Banggai catch a *kapal motor* on to Kendari or Luwuk, SE Sulawesi. Merpati flies from Sanana to: Ambon, twice weekly, Rp50,700; Labuha, Rp45,300; Morotai, Rp88,400; and Ternate, Rp52,300.

THE BACAN ISLANDS

The 80 Bacan Is., off the SW tip of Halmahera, have a combined area of 1,600 sq km, with a population in 1986 of 40,101. The islands are green, hilly, volcanic in origin, and covered in forests. The sultanate of Bacan was formerly powerful; he traveled in a gorgeous cabined barge with gilded roof, fluttering flags, and bravely clad rowers. Although the island contains gold, copper, and coal, its mineral wealth has never

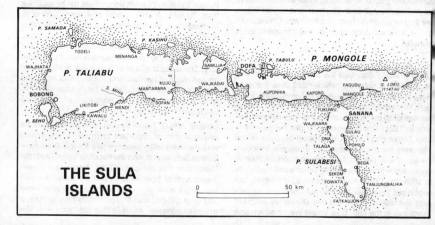

THE SULA ISLANDS

0   50 km

een exploited. On the main island cacao and copra re produced, plus there's a Japanese-run pearl farm. he Bacanese Malay natives are mostly Islamic with nly a few hundred Christians *(Orang Sirani)* on the slands, descendants of the Portuguese. In addition, here are small groups of people from Galela (Halmaera), as well as descendents of Tomore colonists, rought from Sulawesi at their own request to escape nter-tribal warfare. To get to Labuha, the main town, y with Merpati at 0700 on Mon. and Wed. for Rp29,900 from Ternate. Or take a daily *kapal motor* for p12,000 from Ternate Harbor. Two Pelni boats, coming and going on the Ternate-Ambon run, also stop ere for 2 hours.

Dutch **Fort Barnevald** (1615) is only a half-hour's walk from Labuha harbor. It is said that the fort is haunted by soldiers who were formerly stationed there; during the full moon you can hear cadence be-ing called and the shuffling footsteps of soldiers drilling. The sultan's palace, 30% of which is still intact, dates back to the 13th century. **Air Belanda,** a former bathing place of the Dutch, is 3 km from Labuha. Climb the main island's G. Sibela for a marvelous panorama over the surrounding islands.

In Labuha, stay at **Wisma Eka Endar**, Jl. Usman Sjah, which has 4 double rooms with private bathroom for Rp9500 full board (a very good price). Also check out **Wisma Harmonis**, rooms without bathrooms, Rp9000 pp. The *warung* near the pier is clean and friendly. A limited number of Bacan's famed *batu bacan* (semi-precious stones) can be purchased at un-marked **Toko Sibela** near Labuha's harbor. Or look for the stones in nearby *perusahaan* (workshops)—they come in translucent red and white, as well as other striking color combinations.

HALMAHERA

This grotesquely shaped island, largest and northern-most of the Moluccas, is about 322 km long with an area, including smaller satellite islands, of a staggering 16,835 sq km. In shape and geography just a smaller version of Sulawesi, the island's 4 tentacles are high, densely forested mountain chains which tumble to-gether into the center. These peninsulas enclose 3 great bays (Kao, Buli, and Weda), all of which open toward the east. The isthmus connecting the northern peninsula is only 8 km wide. The northern peninsula is volcanic with 3 active and 2 semiquiescent peaks; the other sections are nonvolcanic. Tidal waves caused by volcanic eruptions have wiped out whole coastal vil-lages as late as 1969.

So far from Jakarta, the island is a well-kept travelers' secret. It remains economically and agriculturally undeveloped. Mother of pearl and *trepang* are harvested from the sea. Many pearl divers live on Kao Bay, in particular in the Magaliho Is., reachable by motorboat from Tobelo. Rice is grown on the plain S of Galela. Sago is also an important subsistence crop. Cash crops include damar, copra, wild nutmeg, forest hardwoods. Halmahera's heavy tropical forests con-tain a great variety of trees including the ironwood *(Nania vera)*, as well as such botanical wonders as the trumpet-shaped, pure white, 7.5-cm-wide *fagraea* flower.

History

Settled first by Malayan sea gypsies *(Orang Laut)*. The Portuguese and Spanish were better acquainted with Halmahera (called "Moro" at the time) than with many other parts of the archipelago. In the Middle Ages, a native state evolved on the Bay of Jailolo. This sul-tanate prospered until it was supplanted by Ternate in 1380, but even these powerful ursurpers were able only to control the coastal regions of the island. The Dutch first secured a footing on Halmahera with the sultan of Ternate's aid, but since Halmahera grew only negligible quantities of lesser-grade spices and pos-sessed few other marketable commodities, it was ne-glected by the colonial administration. In WW II, the Japanese occupied Halmahera, using their big base on Kao Bay as their command headquarters for the whole SW Pacific. In Kao Bay (about an hour's walk from Dodinga or take the bus), you can still find many downed Japanese planes in the jungle and at the bot-tom of the sea, plus wrecked landing craft and am-phibious tanks rusting on the beach.

The People

The population of over 100,000 is made up of im-migrants and merchants from other islands, Malayan fishermen, and in the interior hybrid Melanesian (Alfuro) stock. The vast majority of Halmahera's in-habitants are Islamic, though missionary efforts in the N have converted as many as 10,000 to Christianity. The approximately 30 distinct tribes of inland Hal-mahera have remained untouched by the more sophis-ticated sultanate islands such as Ternate and Tidore, and unexploited by competing merchant fleets. Thus, much of their traditional culture remains intact. These mixed Papuan-Malay types, called *Orang Primitif* by other Halmaherans, have crisp, wavy hair, light skin, strong builds—a true forest people, some semi-nomadic. Several groups live in the Galela and Tobelo areas. These people have tall, muscular Polynesian physiques with oval faces, high open brows, aquiline noses, cinnamon skin, and thick beards. Formerly, this tribe hunted with barbed ironwood spears and bows and arrows, built and maintained temples *(sabuas)*, and believed in an afterlife. One theory has it that they

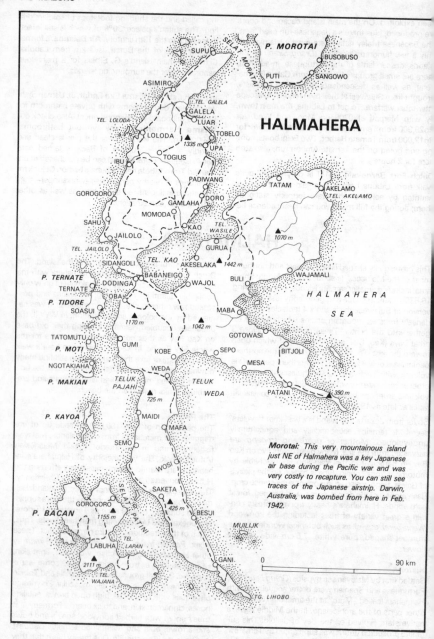

HALMAHERA

P. MOROTAI

Morotai: This very mountainous island just NE of Halmahera was a key Japanese air base during the Pacific war and was very costly to recapture. You can still see traces of the Japanese airstrip. Darwin, Australia, was bombed from here in Feb. 1942.

0   90 km

are remnants of Caucasian groups migrating across the Pacific in prehistoric times.

Ask one of these natives to make you a palm-leaf cup, a unique souvenir. The Tobelo, Galela, and Tabau tribes in the northern part of this island produce amazingly intricate plaited mats and decorated bark fabrics given as marriage gifts or used at mortuary festivities. Sleeping mats 2 m long are made of *pandanus* leaves. Some pieces take years to complete, especially the ornamental display mats.

SIGHTS

The following route takes you from Dodinga, where the *kapal motor* from Ternate pulls in, to the more accessible areas of the island. **Dodinga**, on the western side of the northern peninsula facing Ternate and Tidore, is reachable by boat (Rp3500) from Bastion, just a Rp100 *bemo* ride S of Ternate. From Dodinga buses leave for Babaneigo on Teluk Kao, Rp3500. From Babaneigo, take boats N to Tobelo. From Dodinga E to Buli on Teluk Buli, it's a 2-day walk. Northwest of Dodinga is **Sidangoli** with white sandy beaches, beautiful coral marine gardens, and breathless panoramas. **Maba**, S of Buli, is the heaviest black-magic area.

Jailolo

Boats from Ternate do the 2-hour trip to Jailolo (pop. 25,037 in 1986) at least once daily for Rp1000; buy your ticket on the boat at Bastion. Unusual regional *adat* houses in this town. Take a motorboat out to the 13th C. ruins of the sultan's palace. From Jailolo, it's Rp200 by *bemo* to Bubaniego. The aboriginal areas of the Tobelo and Ibu tribes are a 70-km walk inland.

Tobelo

In 1878, the Dutch launched a successful expedition against the pirates of Tobelo. In 1986 the population was 29,957. Stay in **Toko Megaria**, 3 double rooms with private baths (outside the bedroom), Rp12,500 pp including meals; upstairs rooms are cheaper. **Hotel Pantai Indah**, 7 rooms with bathrooms, charges Rp13,500 pp. **Wisma Sibua Lamo**, 5 rooms with bathrooms, charges Rp12,500 pp with meals. A large hospital here run by a church group *(Gereja Masehi Injili Halmahera)* also operates a coconut plantation on the side. The New Tribes Mission is also based here.

About once a week ships travel from Ternate's Pelabuhan Bastion to Tobelo, Rp6000. From Tobelo, take a bus to Galela, Rp1500; Upa, Rp200. It's about a 30-km 1-day, 1-night walk to the villages of **Desa Pickwang** and **Kusuri** where aborigines live. Or take a minibus, Rp1000 to Kusuri.

Galela

This town (pop. 17,392 in 1986) is famous for the 5 lakes in its vicinity. **Lake Duma**, with its lovely surroundings, is especially worth visiting. Climb 930-m **G. Mamuja**, an active volcano that emits rivers of lava. Travel 16 km from town by road and then hike 3 km to the top. There's a hotspring at **Kalimede**, out of Galela. Fly from Galela with Merpati to Ternate, Tues., Thurs., and Sat. at 0800; Rp31,200. From the airport into town is Rp400 by *bemo*. Or you can take a coaster to Ternate for around Rp6000.

Loloda

Pop. 17,745 in 1986. A magnesium mine here is run by a joint local government/Japanese venture. One of Halmahera's longest and most interesting rivers is the **Loloda**, coming down the mountains and emptying into the Bay of Loloda. Hire a motorized *prahu* to the 3 islands in the southern part of Loloda Bay. These amazing islands rise straight up from narrow beaches, forming pinnacles of rock up to 90 m high clothed with dense vegetation clear to their tops. Caves and tunnels dug out by the waves, and the exposed rocks of the cliffs themselves, sculptured by tropical rains, combine to create some of the strangest scenery on the island.

Transport

The easiest is to board a *kapal motor* at Bastion's harbor, S of Ternate City, to Dodinga on P. Halmahera (Rp1000, 45 min.). From Dodinga, get a minibus for Babaneigo on Teluk Kao (Rp2000), then a coaster N to the town of Kao (Rp4000); stay at the only *losmen* in town, Rp5000 pp. From Kao, there's a daily motorboat to Tobelo. From Tobelo buses leave for Galela, Rp3500. Pelni's vessels stop at Jailolo, Galela, Tobelo, and Wada, together with Doruba on P. Morotai. Merpati flies from Ternate to Galela for Rp31,200.

There were once more bureaucratic hassles and formalities on P. Halmahera than on most other islands of Maluku Utara, requiring that you report to the police, then *imigrasi*, filling out forms in triplicate and projecting your itinerary. But lately, it has been easing up. Still, take along extra passport photos. With no good navigable rivers, and roads only around the principal towns, travel in the rugged interior is arduous. It is fairly easy to travel from Dodinga up to Galela; anywhere else you have to walk or take boats along the coasts. The missionaries, mostly based on the northern peninsula, are a valuable source of info.

Pulau Morotai

To the NE of the northern peninsula of Halmahera lies this 1,600-sq-km island, more than 80 km long and from 20-42 km wide. Some mountains, such as the

Sabotai Range, reach 1,130 m high. The strait separating Morotai from Halmahera is only 16 km or so wide; Wallace concluded that they must have been connected in some remote epoch. Pulau Morotai today is a big copper-producing island with tens of thousands of coconut palms waving in the wind. Other main crops include chocolate, damar gum, and rattan. The island is populated (34,850 in 1986) by a mixture of races, with Papuans predominating (Moro-

tai is only about 320 km W of Irian Jaya). Morotai was a big Japanese airbase during WW II. It was from here that Japanese bombers raided Darwin, northern Australia. During the Pacific campaign, **Doruba** served as a temporary headquarters for MacArthur. The island experienced heavy fighting during the war; Doruba's harbor is full of old wrecks. Doruba boasts a good market. A Pelni ship also stops here, Rp12,500 from Ternate.

SOUTHEAST MALUKU

This remote district extends from Wetar, off the eastern tip of Timor, to the Aru Group, only 240 km from the underbelly of Irian Jaya. The territorial waters of the region are immense, totaling 320,470 sq km, while its land area is only 28,000 sq km. In all there are 287 islands and islets, 199 inhabited, stretching in a long chain on the edge of the Arafura Sea between Australia and Irian Jaya. Most of the islands are hilly to mountainous, some are volcanic in origin, and others (such as the Arus) have extensive marshlands and lowland swamps. The economy of the region centers on fishing, logging (kayu besi), forest products (rattan), and pearls. Isolated from the main currents of Indonesian culture and economy, Maluku Tenggara is a forgotten place: difficult to get to and travel around in. Tourism is nil. Accommodations, food, and transport are expensive or difficult to come by. However, travel here is rewarding because, as a direct result of their inaccessibility, native customs, crafts, dress, and traditions are still very much alive.

Fauna And Flora
The fauna and flora of the region show marked affinity to species found in Australia and New Guinea, including a profuse variety of butterflies; marsupials such as cuscus and miniature kangaroos on Aru and Kai; wild buffalos on the islands of Yamdena, Moa, and Luang; wild goats on Wetar; several species of cockatoo, green parrots (in the Dobo area), and several species of the bird of paradise (P. Baun). Marinelife includes sea turtles which nest on the island of Enu, a dazzling array of ornamental fish off the islands of Luang and Sermata, shrimps W of Yamdena, pearls in the Arus, sea cucumbers around the islands of Selaru, Seira, Toyando, and the Arus, octopus in all the seas, and a huge variety of shellfish. The sea is also home to akar bahar (black coral), sea kasuari, agar agar, seaweeds, etc. Wild orchids (lelemuku) bloom on Tanimbar at least 4 months of the year; other varieties of orchids such as macan tutul, and macan kumbang are found on Kai and in the far southern islands. Exotic woods like

meranti and salamoni (black ironwood) grow in scattered locations. Ordinary ironwood is found on the Kais, a few sago forests on Aru and Tanimbar.

Ecological Devastation
Far from natural paradises as they were in the good old days, wild animal life in Maluku Tenggara, on both land and sea, is in danger of extinction. This region is no different from any other area of Indonesia being raped — it just started a bit later than most in the process. Officially, a number of nature reserves have been established on the Tanimbars, Arus, and other islands, but these are a joke. Just like everywhere else in Indonesia, the Arus and the other islands are rapidly being stripped of fish, shrimp, turtles, sharks, trees, birds, etc. On Kai Kecil there are almost 30 villages whose populace is chopping down trees as fast as they can, planting whatever they think will grow, killing whatever they can eat, and just generally raising hell with the environment. It is almost impossible to get away from coconut palms, tapioca, bananas, and sago fields. People in Ambon are willing to pay Rp100,000 for a white cockatoo (the ones with the yellow crest) so there are any number of people eager to supply the market (even if their share of the loot is only Rp2000!). The Japanese and Taiwanese have their typical fishing factories on the scene, so in Dobo it is nearly impossible to find fresh shrimp or any variety of the many fish that supposedly are plentiful everywhere in Aru waters. Since shark fins are worth as much as Rp50,000 per kilo (sales mostly to Hong Kong and Japan), everything that floats is out reaping the harvest with nets extending as much as one kilometer from the fishing boats. How long it will continue nobody knows for sure.

History
Southeast Maluku has been little influenced by the outside world. Even Portuguese and Dutch colonial-

sts saw little economic significance in this remote group and paid it scant attention. Still, there are ruined Dutch forts in the Tanimbars and the Arus. Late in the 19th C. missionaries began proselytizing with great success in the region, and today the majority of SE Maluku's inhabitants are at least nominally Protestant or Catholic. Christianity has made the deepest inroads on Leti, Kisar, and Tanimbar (Kisar-Babar are Protestant, Tanimbar and Kai mainly Roman Catholic), though animism still pervades the lives of the people, particularly the interior tribes. In coastal areas, Islamic communities predominate.

The People

Southeast Maluku has a population of around 250,000 (1986), living in 523 villages. Of mixed proto-Malayan and Papuan races, Melanesian features become more noticeable in the eastern islands (Aru and Tanimbar), and are less pronounced in the W (Kisar and Wetar). The region has long been known for the ferocity and hostility of its tribes, with accounts of headhunting and even cannibalism reported. Even up until the early 1960s, most communities in the islands between Alor and Kai were divided into 3 fixed hereditary castes— nobility, commoners, and slaves. The nobility were often of mixed Malay-indigenous origin, the commoners of indigenous races, while the slaves were curly-haired natives imported or indentured from New Guinea. A hereditary land-owning class still holds much power while dark-skinned Papuan types are found lower on the social ladder. Life is centered on the sea, and some villages are even laid out in the form of a boat as seen from above. No systematic ethnographic study has ever been made of the cultures of this isolated region, and anthropological literature is scarce.

The main diet on the islands of Kisar-Babar is maize; on the volcanic islands of Damar, Teun, Nila, and Serua, it's *pisang* (bananas); on Tanimbar the root products *ubi* and cassava are the staples; on the Kais cassava, and in Aru sago. On Tanimbar and Babar you find some dry-rice cultivation. Cassava is becoming introduced more and more over the whole area.

Arts And Crafts

Although the SW and SE Moluccan islands are racially and culturally mixed, their arts are rather homogeneous. A good many of their traditions—woodcarving, weaving, and pearl-diving—are largely intact. Primitive woodcarving is a living art, especially in the Tanimbars, and is seen in statuary, on doorposts, and on prows of local *prahu*. The art of the peoples of Alor-Kai (but *not* the Aru Is.) can be traced back as far as the ornamental Dongson-style of Annam. This style incorporates numerous Oriental motifs, as seen in their small carved wooden ancestor statues. At present nearly all the old ancestor statues, sculptures, carvings, and figurines have either been burned by fervid

Ambonese *pendeta* (ministers) or sold to foreign "collectors." You'll find a great number of beautiful specimens in the Siwalima Museum in Batu Cipco, P. Ambon, a visit to which is an excellent introduction to the art of the area. New figurines, resembling the old sculptures, are made by a few Tanimbarese and Babarese living in Ambon. The best islands for traditional architecture, in homes and public meeting halls, are Tanimbar, Babar, Kisar, and Serwaru. Antiques found in the region are chinaware, swords, shields, and ancestral carvings.

spirit-totem

Except for the Kais, *ikat* backstrap handloom weaving is done on every island. The motifs and colors have much in common with those used on Sawu, but are quite different from those produced on Sumba and Timor. Factory-made cotton and artificial dyes are gaining more and more currency. Prices vary from Rp25,000 up to Rp75,000, depending on size, age, and patterns.

Local musical instruments include shell-horns, *totobuang* (of Hindu-Javanese origin), *tifa*, gongs, bamboo flutes, and violin (of Portuguese origin). See many work dances (weaving and fishermen's dances), social dances (the *Sul Sawat* from the Kais, the *Angkosi* and *Badendang* from the Tanimbars), war dances (the *Tnabar Ilaa*, the *Cakalele*, etc.), and traditional dances (the *Rubai Dab* and the *Tiwa Nam*).

TRANSPORT

Getting There

If you don't have the time to journey by sea, fly Merpati from Ambon to Saumlaki, twice weekly (Rp75,700) or to Langgur, once daily (Rp84,600), both

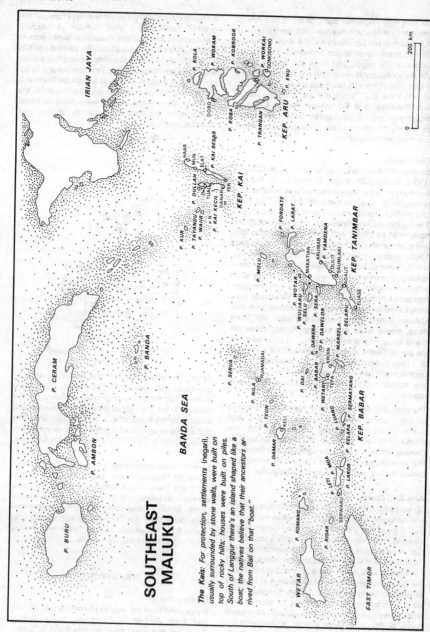

SOUTHEAST MALUKU

The Kais: For protection, settlements (negari), usually surrounded by stone walls, were built on top of rocky hills; houses were built on piles. South of Langgur there's an island shaped like a boat; the natives believe that their ancestors arrived from Bali on that "boat."

BANDA SEA

IRIAN JAYA

P. CERAM

P. BURU

P. AMBON

P. BANDA

P. SERUA

P. NILA — RUAMADAI

P. TEUN — GELI

P. DAMAR

P. DAI

P. BABAR

P. WETANG

P. MARSELA

P. DAWERA

P. DAWELOR

P. SERMATANG

KEP. BABAR

P. ROMANG

P. WETAR

P. KISAR

P. LETI

P. MOA

P. LAKOR

P. KELAPA

SERWARU

EAST TIMOR

P. WULIARU

P. SELU

P. SERA

P. MOLU

P. YAMDENA

ARUBAB

MAKATIAN

OLILIT

SAUMLAKI

ADAUT

SELARU

ELIASE

KEP. TANIMBAR

P. FORDATE

P. LARAT

P. KOBROOR

P. KOBA

P. KOLA

P. WOKAM

P. ENU

GOMOSOMO

WORKAI

P. TRANGAN

KEP. ARU

DOBO

P. KUR

P. KAI KECIL

P. KAI BESAR

KEP. KAI

HAAR

YUN

ELAT

DANAR

FER

P. DULLAH

P. TAYANDU

WAIIR

0 200 km

in the Tanimbars. Then from Saumlaki or Langgur, take a Pelni ship or some other boat to outlying islands. The mission boats went bankrupt in 1980; the remaining regular approaches to Maluku Tenggara are by plane to the Tanimbars and Kais or by overcrowded, filthy but cheap Pelni-Perintis ships from Ambon or Kupang, sailing about once every 3 weeks. They pile 250-300 passengers on regularly, and the ships are a disaster area 95% of the time. The sanitary conditions are disgusting, people sit and lie everywhere, they cook, care for their pets and kids as best they can, and patiently endure the whole thing as there is no other way to travel.

The KM *Dukuh* does the short route from Ambon (Ambon-Banda-Tual-Dobo-Saumlaki-Tual-Banda-Ambon) twice monthly, while the KM *Niaga XIV* does the extended one (Ambon-Banda-Tual-Kroin-Tepa-Sermatang-Lakor-Moa-Leti-Kisar-Wetar-Romang-Damar-Tepa-Saumlaki-Tual-Banda-Ambon) a month. The short route is called *route Tenggara dekat*, the long route *route Tenggara jauh* (which takes 15 days to reach the terminus at P. Wetar). Sample ticket prices: Ambon-Tual, Rp16,000; Ambon-Tepa, Rp25,500. Cabins (one or 2 beds) are Rp25,000 per day; single beds (lower deck), Rp12,000 per day; meals Rp600 per day, *nasi ikan* only. You can hire a crew member's bunk for Rp20,000-30,000 (4 bunks to a room).

Getting Around

Since few minibuses or buses exist, most of the villagers cover the distances between villages on foot; hire rowing, sailing, or motorized vessels along the coasts, or take one of the local ferries. For example, the local boat from Langgur to Elat is only Rp1000, going over in the mornings and coming back the same afternoon. You can get a ship to almost anyplace in SE Maluku if you hang around long enough — which might mean a week or so! Boats are more frequent to Ambon and Banda than they are to Babar, Kisar, and Wetar, and some outliers can only be reached by chartered boat. The mission ships have been sold, so at present missionaries use small motorized *prahu*. In the wet season (May-Aug.), there are very few boats. At other times of the year, nobody ever seems to postpone or cancel a sea voyage because of weather.

Accommodation is limited, and proper hotels are only found in the administrative/commercial centers such as Tual, Saumlaki, and Dobo. Everywhere else, ask the missionaries or police to put you up for suitable remuneration, or stay on the boat you arrived on.

THE KAI ISLANDS

Two fairly large and many tiny islands covering a total area of about 900 sq km. Not known until 1886, the islands once had 18 rajas. With heavy forests and rugged mountains, these nonvolcanic islands are singularly picturesque. Their coasts rise hundreds of meters above the sea, forming an arc of uplifted coral reefs along with the Watubelas to the N, the Arus to the E, and Timor, Sawu, and Sumba to the south. With bays of dazzling white sand, magnificent butterflies and beetles, many species of pigeon and exotic other birds, the Kais used to be a real discovery for the naturalist and for the traveler with the time and money to get there. Today, the islands are on the brink of an ecological doomsday. **Tual**, on P. Dullah, is the principal town and administrative center of SE Maluku. **Elat** on Kai Besar is the capital of the Kai Is., seat of the Dutch *controlleur* during colonial times.

The Kai islanders cultivate taro, yams, maize, rice. Sago is collected from the swamps. Regional dishes include *embal* or cassava cakes. Mango stones (seeds) are soaked in brine for 3-7 days to soften and pickle them, then they are boiled or made into cakes to supplement the diet during the dry season. Much of the Kais' cash income is derived from timbering, boat-building, producing copra, and collecting *trepang*. All but 2 villages are coastal.

The People

The inhabitants of the Kais are Papuan in origin. Although the original population has become more mixed with later immigrant groups, the Melanesian strain that A.R. Wallace observed in the 19th C. is still very much in evidence. "The loud, rapid, eager tones, the incessant motion, the intense vital activity manifested in speech and action are the very antipodes of the quiet, unimpulsive, unanimated Malay," he wrote in his journal in 1860.

Three classes or status-groups of people make up this society: the aristocrats or ruling lineage *(mel mel)*, the common people *(ven ven)*, and the ex-slaves *(hiri hiri)* who still live with the stigma of slavery. The most important kin group is the *fam* or patrilinear clan which lives in a few closely packed villages. The village head is called the *rat*. Other village functionaries are the *kapitan* (war chief) and the *marinjo* (village crier). Descent is patrilineal. Bride prices are often paid, though the groom has the option of substituting bride price service *(nafdu)*. The bride price could be reciprocated by a gift from the girl's parents.

Religion

About one-third are animist. There are deities of the sun *(duan lerwuan)*, moon *(duan luteh)*, sea *(Hejan*

Suwat), agriculture (Lir Majoran), as well as spirits of the dead (nitu). The remainder of the population is equally divided between Islam and Christianity. To counter the spread of Islam introduced by Buginese missionaries, the Dutch brought in Protestant and Catholic missionaries and by the turn of the century large numbers were being converted. Some state their religion is Agama Hindu; on Kai Besar a few villages are said to be Hindu. Today the Kais' population of around 90,000 (1986) is actually declining because of the very high incidence of malaria and cholera, which kill hundreds each year.

Kai Islands pottery

Arts And Crafts

Besides Ambon, Kep. Kai is the most musical of the Moluccas. These islanders also turn out wooden bowls, statues, and pottery. On **P. Tayandu**, a small island W of Kai Kecil, pottery made from local clay is a thriving cottage industry. Pieces are sold for a song to passing boats. The Kai islanders were once noted boatbuilders, but since the islands' forests have been so plundered the art is declining. Wallace observed magnificent long canoes, with the bow and stern rising up in a peak several meters high, decorated with shells and waving plumes or cassowary hair. These prahu, made without a nail or piece of iron, could hold 60 men and 20-30 tons of cargo, able to sail on any sea to Singapore. To this day the islands' harbors are always full of prahu weighing 5-200 tons, and islanders still fish at night from elaborate and skillfully built dugout canoes and plank outriggers.

Getting There

Merpati Twin Otters fly daily from Ambon to Langgur in the Kais for Rp84,600. Excess baggage is expensive, so travel light! You'll land at Banda on the way to Langgur; landings are pretty rough! Flights also depart from Saumlaki (Tanimbar) to Langgur on Tues. and Fri. at 1220 for Rp44,900. You'll land at Dumaatuban Airport just outside of Langgur on and you must cross a bridge to reach Tual, 5 km away on P. Dullah.

Another approach is by sea; first fly to Kaimana on the southern coast of Irian Jaya from Nabire (Rp41,300),

then take a kapal motor or sailing prahu to Tual, Rp12,500 or thereabouts. A brisk trade goes on between Kaimana and the Kais so boats are frequent. On the way they sometimes stop in the Mengawitu Islands. These small boats seldom venture out over open seas during the rainy season (April-Aug.), though this doesn't stop the Pelni and Perintis ships, the KM Dukuh and the KM Niaga XIV, which stop in Tual, Kai Kecil, about once every 3 weeks year-round (Rp16,500). Be prepared for the ship being up to 1 week late. See "Getting There" in the Introduction for intineraries.

Getting Around

Transport on Kai Kecil (P. Dullah and P. Nuhuroa) is surprisingly developed with beautiful new minibuses arriving from the willing Japanese makers. The roads may not be perfectly smooth, but they're definitely passable at all times and traffic is steady in all directions. Fares are cheap; from Langgur to Tual (5 km) is Rp100 and if you want to go to the southern villages (such as Danar), it's only Rp500. Road systems are less developed on Kai Besar where to the more distant villages you must walk on trails. You need to have at least a rudimentary knowledge of Indonesian. Don't drink the water. If you don't take anti-malaria pills, you'll probably catch malaria though the hospital in Langgur will treat you. Motorized prahu are of course available for charter at expensive prices. You can get a ship to almost any place in SE Moluccas if you hang around long enough. In the dry season there are kapal motor to Kaimana, Irian Jaya.

KAI KECIL

Pulau Dullah and Kai Kecil are 2 islands W of Kai Besar. Generally flat, they consist mostly of swampland and coconut palm groves, with some ironwood forests. **Tual**, on P. Dullah, is the main town and chief population in 1986 was 52,249. About a dozen Dutch missionaries and teachers live here. There's a good road system on both islands with minibuses heading everywhere, or you could also possibly borrow a bicycle from the mission. Villages consist of big houses containing several nuclear families. In some villages, large squatting wooden statues representing hero ancestors are found; others have thick defensive stone walls. Along sea cliffs are inscribed paintings of natives and their prahu; nothing is known of these paintings except that they are very old.

Sights

Just outside of Tual is an open-air museum of belang (prahu) right on the shore. **Pasir Panjang Beach** is 3 km long with deep blue water and nice coral. **Ohdideer**, 12 km from Tual, is a white sandy beach ideal for swimming and rowing, also nice diving in marine gardens. Pulau Dullah also has superb marine gardens. At he far end of Ohdideer Beach is sacred **Luat Cave** which contains strange, undeciphered inscriptions. **Difur**, about 13 km N of Tual, is a center for traditional pearl cultivation. **Wearblel Lake** is a 3-sq-km lake with a depth of 21 m; good fishing. At **Danau**, a pond surrounded by grass meadows and *cemara* trees, watch wild animals come down to drink. Clear, blue **Mas II** reservoir provides drinking water for the town of Tual. The traditional-minded people from the island of **Ur**, W of P. Kai Kecil, are quite different from other Kai people. They keep themselves isolated, though they have a kind of marriage-exchange system with the nearby island of Kai-Tanimbar.

KAI BESAR

Known as "Great Kai," this is the largest island in the Kais, about 80 km long and very narrow. Total population in 1986 was 37,080. Part of the spectacular limestone arc system of eastern Indonesia, scenic Kai Besar's topography is quite mountainous; the highest peak is G. Dab (688 m). Very few roads on Kai Besar so you have to walk. **Elat**, on P. Kai Besar, is the capital of the subdistrict. In Banda-Elat and Eli on Kai Besar live the (Muslim) descendants of the survivors of the Dutch genocide on the Banda Islands in the 17th century. They produce fine boats, woodcarvings, silver- and goldwork.

Most villages on the E coast are animistic. **Onoilim** is on a small hill, a primitive *kampung gunung* which shows signs of influence from the Aru Islands. **Ohewait**, also on the E coast, is a sacred village; a

footpath connects it with the W coast. **Haar** is a tiny village on the NE tip which is divided into 3 *kampung*: you've got your Catholic church, your Protestant church, and your Islamic mosque, with only about 6 meters separating each community which have little to do with each other.

Accommodations And Food

Best place to stay is the Catholic Mission (Pastoran Katolik), 200 m from the airport; Rp2000 with meals for a nice room with access to the priestly sanitary arrangements. The food is quite acceptable and you'll eat with the father and brothers while listening to highly amusing accounts of the day's religious events. The **Linda Mas** in Tual, 5 km down the road, costs Rp18,000 per night including meals. The rooms are small, the beds impossible (unless you find a layer of packed felt irresistible), and the typical Indonesian *mandi* has a weird stool-type toilet. There's also a *pasanggrahan* for government officials which you may stay in if there's a vacancy.

Transport

Tual is the center of trade and shipping for Kep. Kai. From Ambon to Tual (landing at Langgur) fly Merpati daily for Rp71,400. Minibuses travel often (Rp100, 5 km) between Langgur and Tual. From Tual there's a daily boat to Elat on W coast of P. Kai Besar; Rp1000 (3 hours). About once every 3 weeks there's a Pelni ship to Dobo in the Arus; Rp3500 for Deck Class (but you can rent a crew member's cabin for around Rp20,000). Buy tickets at the Pelni office at the docks or on the boat itself.

Glory of the Seas (Conus gloriamaris): *One of the world's rarest shells is found in Indonesia, this cone by the name of Glory of the Seas. Usually selling for US$1000-2000, depending on the size and how fine the specimen is. For over 200 years this shell was the costliest and most coveted in the world. Its long spire and finely reticulated color pattern made it so lovely and elegant that just to see one was a privilege, to hold one was an honor. The earliest record of the species was found in the collection of a Dutchman in 1757. The Hoehler specimen, found in the Solomon Islands, was bought for US$2000 in 1963. The theft of a Glory of the Seas was the central theme in a novel written by Miss Fanny Steele, and numerous papers have been written on it. There are only about 50 specimens known to exist. They have been stolen, crushed to pieces by jealous owners, lost. See one in the British Museum or in the Academy of Natural Sciences, Philadelphia. Nowadays, certain shells of the mollusc family are considered rarer.*

THE TANIMBARS

The Tanimbar Islands, with a total land area of 5,568 sq km, are made up of about 66 nonvolcanic islands, though only 7 are inhabited. Total population in 1986 was 64,494. Located 675 km SE of Ambon, this isolated group is the southernmost of the Moluccas, accessible by air and sea. The Tanimbars offer numerous empty beaches, pristine coral reefs and sealife, a strong traditional culture, unique flora, and superb scenery. The islands are world famous among botanists for the *Larat* orchids which grow only here, and in fact another name for the Tanimbars is *Lelemuku*, the local word for "orchid." Saumlaki is the largest town, located on the southern coast of **P. Yamdena**, the largest island of the group.

History

The Buginese and Makassarese were trading rice, iron, copper coins, ivory, and guns for slaves, sago, and textiles in the Tanimbars as early as the 16th century. The Dutch established a fortified factory here in 1645. They abandoned it within several years, returned in the late 19th C. to settle the islands, but were given a hostile reception. Wearing magnificent battle costumes and headdresses, native Tanimbarese have had a long history of savage internecine warfare, headhunting, and cannibalism. The Dutch were not able to pacify the islands until they sent in an expedition in 1907, building a garrison and bolstering their police force.

The People

The Tanimbars are composed of a mix of peoples: Irianese, Negritos, Melanesians, *Orang Maluku*. Papuan physical features (frizzy hair and dark skin) predominate. A number of subgroups are scattered throughout the islands, each speaking its own mutually unintelligible dialect. Slaves once existed but they could marry into a higher class and gain their freedom. The Alfuro aborigines have for the most part retained their traditional culture and animist religion; on some islands shark cults are still practiced. It's an ancient custom for village elders to occupy ancestral stone seats, like the boat-shaped one at **Aruibab** (E coast of P. Yamdena) to indicate their origins and reinforce their right to rule. The Alfuro are some of the best spearmen in Indonesia, who still use blowpipes but only as a hunting weapon with hunting dogs. Maize is the staple dish, supplemented by cassava, yams, and taro baked in a Polynesian-style pit oven. Fowl and pig are eaten on special occasions. *Tuak* is very popular; along with tobacco and betelnut it's an important component of rituals.

Crafts

In the Saumlaki (P. Yamdena) and Larat (P. Larat) areas you can find high-quality plaiting and *ikat* weaving decorated with symbolic traditional patterns. *Tikar* weaving, shell jewelry, coil pottery, and metallurgy (copper coins worked into ornaments) are also widespread and well-developed crafts. Wood- and some stonecarvings are also exported. Carvings can also be seen on *adat* houses as well as on the bows of the large *belang*, a gondola-like vessel used by the local rajas. Tanimbarese are skilled boatbuilders, fashioning their own plank boats and dugout canoes with outriggers, which you see drawn up on the beach in Yamdena coastal villages. Traditional dwellings *(das* on Yamdena) have steep, thatched gable roofs with buffalo horn decorations placed at the ridge poles. Inside are small compartments in which an extended family of up to 20 people sleep. Sometimes there is a separate men's and boys' building *(lingat)* where headhunting raids were once prepared but which now serves as an eating and gathering place.

Economy

Except for several timber companies, a subsistence economy exists on these islands. The soil is worked by the slash-and-burn method and food staples are typically Melanesian: maize, yams, taro, cassava, with some rice also cultivated under the supervision of an *adat* foreman. During droughts or food shortages, the islanders hunt and collect sago. In the dry season one dish is particularly popular; it is made from mango pits which are soaked in saltwater for days, then boiled and eaten. Fish supplements the diet; the Tanimbarese practice torchlight fishing using harpoons and lines.

Transport

Perintis has a ship out of Ambon for the SE Moluccas about once every 3 weeks: to Larat, Rp14,500; Saumlaki, Rp18,600. Merpati flies from Ambon on Tues. and Fri. at 0800 to Saumlaki; Rp75,700. There are also flights from Saumlaki to the Kais for Rp44,900. In the islands themselves, there are few vehicles, so count on walking. Rowing canoes, outriggers, and *kapal motor* are available between the islands of the group. If you don't know the magic, be aware of sharks in these waters.

YAMDENA ISLAND

The largest island of the Tanimbars. The language *(Yamden)* spoken along the E coast is related to Tetum in the Timor Archipelago. *Fordat,* spoken on the islands W and N of Yamdena, is more closely affiliated with the other Moluccan languages. From Saumlaki, walk through the villages up the E coast. But take care; herds of wild bulls kill about 15 people per year on this island. **Lakateri Beach** has white sand and coral gardens. The **Bangruti, Bangdas,** and **Weritubun** caves have stalactites and stalagmites. Natural salt mines are found between the villages of **Otimmer/Selwasa** and **Wowonda,** in the center of P. Yamdena, where salt lies 30 cm thick on the ground and covers an area of 4 hectares.

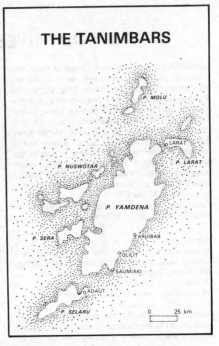

THE TANIMBARS

P. MOLU

LARAT

P. NUSWOTAR

P. LARAT

P. YAMDENA

P. SERA

ARUIBAB

OLILIT

SAUMLAKI

ADAUT

P. SELARU

0   25 km

Saumlaki

The largest town in the Tanimbars. There's a nice mission where you can always get a bed or take a bath; Rp4000 full board. Also one good small hotel, the **Ratulel,** run by kind people; Rp15,000 pp with food. Visit the delightful harbormaster, chief of police, and Odilon, the amicable Chinese merchant. He'll tell you how simple the people are, yet so happy. The *ikat* weaving center is in **Olilit,** N of Saumlaki.

Transport

About every 3-4 weeks a Pelni ship — the only dependable intra-island transport — stops at Saumlaki and then departs for Babar, Sermatang, Kisar, etc. to the southwest. Pelni's KM *Dukuh* does the "short route" from Ambon, stopping at Banda, Tual, Dobo, Saumlaki, then back to Tual, Banda, and Ambon (Rp3500 from Dobo to Saumlaki). Sometimes *kapal motor* also sail for Aru and Kai. From Saumlaki you can also catch *prahu* to the southern end of Selaru and its main town of Adaut for 2 packs of good tobacco or Rp4000. Pulau Selaru is a poor island, low and bushy. There's not a lot of food; meals of only dried fish cost Rp400-600. Trade a bottle of beer for a black coral bracelet *(akhar bahar).* The surrounding islands are known for their pearl-diving (both white and black pearls) and gorgeous coral reefs.

THE SOUTHWESTERN ISLANDS

Located SW of Banda off the NE coast of Timor, this group can be divided into 2 main archipelagos: the northern arc of islands (Serua, Nila, Teun, Damar, and Romang), mostly volcanic and wooded; and the southern arc (Weter, Kisar, Leti, Moa, Lakor, Luang-Sermatang, and Babar), generally less fertile with savannah-like landscapes. All these islands share cultural and historical similarities emanating from a common cultural capital, **P. Luang**, in roughly the geographic center of the region. The Dutch established themselves in these SW islands in the 17th C.; since the 1800s the islands have been administered from Ambon. All the SW islands are noted for their plaiting and weaving; the Babar, Leti, and Damar groups are the haunt of anthropologists.

The People

Natives were notorious for their savagery and head-hunting; today the inhabitants are a mixture of Papuan, Malay, Negrito, and Arab peoples. Most are Christian, although features of the old paganism are still in practice: the veneration of a male sun god and female earth goddess, and the belief in fictive hero ancestors and spirits of maize, rice, bees, and stones. Ancestor spirits are depicted in wood and bone, and religious chiefs perform a renewal festival *(Porka)*

every 7 years; at one time *Porka* rites involved public orgies and taking heads. Originally, a rigid caste system was in force; the Dutch, however, instituted administration by local rajas who ruled with the help of appointed headmen and hereditary *adat* chiefs.

Adat villages today often contain a communal council house in front of which stands a wooden ancestor statue of the village founder. Single nuclear family dwellings are now replacing the large raised extended family dwellings everywhere. As is typical of elsewhere in Maluku Tenggara, the people have a heavy starch diet of maize, rice, sweet potatos, cassava, and millet. Inhabitants of some islands such as Kisar, Babar, Romang, and Damar subsist on sago. In the Romang-Damar group, breadfruit, bananas, and coconut are the rule, and on Wetar wild honey is an important commodity of exchange.

THE BABAR ISLANDS

An isolated group of 6 economically unimportant islands, with a combined area of about 650 sq km, named after the largest central island of Babar (570 sq km). The islands of the group are nonvolcanic, high, and rugged. The natives are an amalgam of Papuan

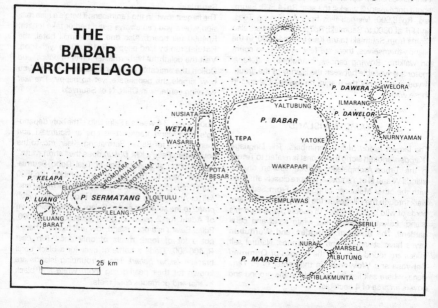

THE BABAR ARCHIPELAGO

Native girls of SW Moluccas onboard an explorer's ship early this century. South Moluccan islanders are of mixed proto-Malay and Papuan stock with Papuan features more noticeable in the E near New Guinea (Tanimbar and Aru) and becoming less evident farther W (Kisar and Leti).

and proto-Malayan races. About one third of the group's population (approx. 17,578 in 1986) lives in Tual, Ambon, Dobo, and Ceram, looking for jobs, education, medical help. Although Christianized, these nearly inaccessible islands still maintain a phallic-animist religious structure (as do the Leti Is. and Wetar to the west). Be sure to see Babar's unique *bero;* islanders sail as far as Tanimbar in these canoes with one outrigger. During festivities, the traditional circle dance *seka* is performed; accompanied by the *tifa* drums, these dances last all night.

Arriving in Tepa (P. Babar), the administrative center, you must report to the *camat,* police, and military office. In every village you may stay in the *kepala desa's* house; give him Rp1500-2000 per day for food, and bring some cigarettes. A footpath around Babar connects all the villages, which takes 3-4 days to complete. Be careful: if you're on your own, an innocent chat with an unmarried girl will make the Babarese *toli belik* ("beat a tin drum") which may mean that you're obliged to marry her!

Sights

Near **Tepa** at Watrorona is a 150-m-high stone staircase at the base of a steep mountain; climb up to the top for the view. A natural geyser which shoots water high into the air at high tide is 10 km from Tepa. Near the villages of **Yatoke** and **Wakpapapi** (P. Babar) are guarded sacred caves containing skulls and other artifacts of the ancestors. The islands of **Dawelor** and **Dawera** have similar sacred caves. The sandy beaches on **P. Sermatang** (Mahaleta, Romdara, Rot-

nama, Elo, and Gerwaly), W of P. Babar, are covered with rust iron and green-black colors.

Pulau Wetan, a few km W of P. Babar, has sacred caves near the villages of **Lektupang** and **Nusiata** which are ancestral burial places. The "skull cave" near **Pota Besar** is an old defensive stronghold, fenced in by human skulls. **Pulau Marsela,** SE of P. Babar, is the weaving and plaiting center of the group. *Seka* dances in traditional costumes are performed in the villages of **Ilbutung** and **Marsela**. This island is well known for its mildly alcoholic *sopi* distilled from the juice of the *lontar* (here called the *koli)* tree.

Pulau Luang

The Luang Is. (Luang, Sermatang, and Kelapa) have a combined area of 389 sq km. Luang was once the cultural heart of the Leti and Babar islands. The languages of Leti and W. Babar are similar, more or less dialects of Luangese. Half the proto-Malayan Luangese profess Christianity, the other half Islam, while animism is the strongest among the Sermatangs. Luang's goldsmiths once traveled all over the region to make gold earrings which are still used in the bride price. Today Luang is well known for its marine products *(hasil laut),* its ideal fishing grounds, and *ikat* weaving for which they charge Rp40,000 (and up) per piece. The island is overgrown with olive trees, and some areas are inhabited by wild buffalos. Its marine gardens extend way out to sea; at ebbtide you're able to walk from P. Luang to the uninhabited island of P. Kelapa.

THE OUTER ISLANDS

The Leti Group
East of Kisar and Timor, the Letis have an area of around 900 sq km and a population of about 30,000. They are nonvolcanic and comparatively infertile. The proto-Malay natives are half Christian, half Muslim. *Porka* festivals are held every few years with phallic rites (also on Moa and Lakor islands). The famous Leti sculptures are all gone. **Tutukei** village, the pottery, basketry, and weaving center, is the only link to Leti's past; it's on a hilltop near Serwaru (the administrative center). From Serwaru it's not that difficult to find a

fishing boat over to East Timor. Since that portion of Timor is now closed to tourists, you'll need a *surat jalan* before they'll take you across the Wetar Strait.

Pulau Kisar
East of P. Wetar, this 250-sq-km island supports a population of around 9,000. The landscape is hilly, almost denuded of trees, and the soil infertile. Ninety percent of the Kisarese are Islamic, the remainder Christian. Proto-Malays live here except for one district inhabited by descendants of Dutch soldiers and Kisarese women—over 100 years ago the Dutch maintained a garrison on the island. Although they still have Dutch names and do not mix with the island's aborigines, they no longer speak Dutch.

THE ARU ISLANDS

The unusual Aru Islands, in the middle of the Banda Sea, consist of several large islands surrounded by many small close-packed ones. Formed by low-lying limestone formations, the islands share a similar topography to the Kais. Most of group's 21 islands are flat and swampy, their extensive marshes broken by low hills. Lying about 640 km SE of Ambon and only 240 km from the coast of West New Guinea, the Arus probably once formed part of that giant island-continent. Between these islands are deep, narrow channels known locally as *tanah besar* or "big land," while the numerous islands and islets on the Great Aru Bank to the E are called *belakang tanah* or "beyond the land." These saltwater straits give rise to numerous and beautiful waterfalls. Essentially an unknown region, monsoonal forests cover the interiors, for the most part growing directly out of limestone rock with very little in the way of topsoil, and there are endless white-sand beaches. The main town and principal trading and shipping center for the district is Dobo, on the small island of Wamar off the W coast.

Fauna
The Arus are an overlapping distribution area where the fauna of Asia and Australasia meet. There is small game, deer, cuscus, wallabies, kangaroos, crocodiles, monitor lizards, an amazing variety of insects, and wonderful birdlife: lories, rainbow lorikeets, parakeets, cassowaries, and the great black palm and yellow-crested cockatoos which live on the *kanari* nuts other birds are unable to crack. Two species of bird of paradise reach full plumage in the courting season (May-Sept.). At least on Wamar, all species are today in great danger of extinction. One day when I was out walking not too far from Dobo, I met a man bringing home a pheasant-type bird which he had downed with a bow and arrow, and which would grace his table that evening. Under unremitting pressure from human set-

tlement, birds (of any kind) are scarce on Wamar. Wildlife on the *belakang tanah* islands to the E is said to be the least disturbed.

In the 1850s, Wallace was forced to recuperate here from inflamed insect bites and write down for the first time all his thoughts on the faunal differences which he had observed during 7 years of travel. He and Darwin jointly announced to the world their Theory of Evolution in London in 1858, but because Darwin had emphasized man's evolution more he received the lion's share of the fame. Once a paradise for the naturalist, Wallace went ecstatic in the Arus, filling many rhapsodic pages describing Aru's flora and fauna. Except for its general geographic location, Dobo bears no resemblance to Wallace's trading village. Both Wallace and Strand were able to start collecting all manner of fascinating and unusual things just on the walk from Dobo to Wangil on P. Wamar; now you are never out of the sight or sound of village life.

History
Dobo has been for centuries a famous native trading station in which every house was full of outside commodities traded for marine products and exquisite bird of paradise skins. Chinese traders would come from as far away as Goram and Makassar, and pirate Malay *prahu* from the Sulas or elsewhere would occasionally attack and burn villages. To guard their spice monopoly in the southern Moluccas, the Dutch finally built a fortress on P. Wokam in 1659. Dutch trade declined in the second half of the 18th C., and the Makassarese and Buginese quickly filled the vacuum. In 1882, the Dutch reopened trade with the establishment of an administrative settlement in Dobo. By 1904 they had gained control over the islands, though the Dutch commissioner would visit only at long intervals to hear complaints and adjust matters. (Today the trade is mainly back in the hands of the Makassarese and

Buginese.) Dobo was one of the few places in the Indies where Japanese were numerous before 1941 — engaged primarily in pearl production. In the 1960s the Arus played a strategic role in the war of liberation in Irian Jaya. In Dobo you can see the commemorative column where Yos Sudarso, who perished in the battle of Trikora while the Indonesians were attempting to wrench Irian Jaya away from the Dutch.

Economy
Vast quantities of marine wealth come from these isolated waters: *agar-agar*, turtle shell, *trepang*, and edible birds' nests. Although illegal, collection of bird of paradise skins is still active. The *trepang* which used to lie so thickly on the banks have now become hard to find, and shark fishing with imported nets has greatly increased the catches of dugong, one of the rarest of sea mammals. Dugongs are chiefly valued for their ivory teeth, especially those of the female. Made into cigarette holders, they are an important status symbol in Indonesia. These islands were once famous for their pearls, of great purity and high value, but today the pearl and mother of pearl "industries" are languishing, to say the least.

The People
The ethnic groups of the Arus resemble those of the Kais and the Tanimbars; pure Papuan Alfuro communities now live only in the interior of P. Wokam — primitive, nomadic bands that seldom come in contact with outsiders. Inhabitants of the western coasts have mixed more with Malayan immigrants, are lighter skinned, and tend to look down upon the E coasters. But unlike the neighboring Tanimbarese, the peaceful Arus rarely warred among themselves. Because of their changeable terrain, these flat islands are among the most sparsely inhabited regions of Indonesia. At high tide many areas are under water even though the land, being so densely forested by mangroves, appears to be *terra firma*. Since clearings for cultivation are often washed out, the scattered native Alfuros are often on the move. In the southern islands they gather sago and paddy melons, harvest wild mangosteens and honey, practice some slash-and-burn agriculture, and in times of food shortages hunt pig, deer, cassowary, and tree kangaroo. Although today the islanders are a mix of Christian and Muslims, animism persists.

Crafts
The Arus share many historical and cultural affinities with New Guinea; their plastic arts reflect this association. In the Arus the finest mother of pearl in the world is found. The islands are a production center for shell artifacts, tortoise shell, *akar bahar*, dugong- and crocodile-teeth pipes, cassowary eggshell crafts. The Catholics are trying to revive the making of native pottery, striking painted and engraved clay dishes and

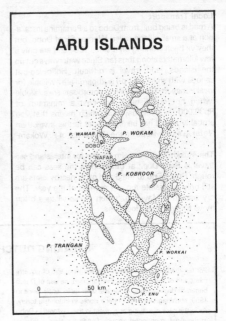

pots. Large squatting ancestor statues are set up in centers or at entrances to villages and on mountaintops.

Getting There
There's only one airstrip on the Arus, in a small village S of Dobo called Bendjina, where a navy patrol plane (looking for fishing poachers) drops in whenever it feels like it. One could conceivably hitch a ride on that plane (either direction from Ambon), but don't bank on it. They are supposedly working on some kind of regular air service to Dobo, but for the moment the nearest civilian airport is at Langgur (5 km from Tual) on Kai Kecil. For the traveler without the time for a lengthy sea voyage, the Langgur airstrip is a real boon because it at least gets you within striking distance of the Arus.

The only reliable way to reach the Arus is by Pelni ship about once every 3 weeks on the "long route" out of Ambon, which stops in the Kais en route. The regular port of call for ships in the Arus is Dobo on P. Wamar. From Tual (Kai Kecil) to Dobo takes about 24 hours by Pelni boat, usually leaving in the afternoon and arriving at Dobo early the next morning. The ship has a canteen on it so you can buy sandwiches, candy, drinks, etc., but carry boiled water, hard candies, salted peanuts, or whatever else for snacks. The basic fare is Rp3500; buy your ticket either on the boat or at the Pelni office on the dock in Tual. Coasting vessels also call at Dobo from Kaimana (Irian Jaya).

Local Transport

A road is being built from Dobo to a Pertamina installation at a small village called **Wamar** SE of Dobo, but they've been working on it since 1984 and are only a few kilometers along thus far. Since waterways cut up the islands, land travel is difficult. Hollowed-out canoes with small (15 hp!) outboards are available for local transport. Occasionally, motorboats are available (when not out fishing) but cost a minimum of Rp30,000 for a half-day trip, which means that you probably would not be able to get farther away than **Nafar**, a small village on the SW corner of P. Wokam.

The *Musim Teduh* or calm season for inter-island sea travel is Sept.-Dec.; at other times the seas can be rough. **Pulau Enu** to the S and other nearby islets are still only accessible those 4 months of the year. The dry season is May-Aug., when whole villages often move to streamside locations.

Accommodations And Food

For accommodations and guides, avail yourself of the *camat*, village head, traditional lineage heads, or *orang kaya*. There's no hotel in Dobo, so most travelers stay at the **Pastoran**; Rp2000 per day including meals. A woman comes in during the day to wash up, do the laundry and housekeeping, but only cooks rice. The food comes from a local restaurant and consists of several dishes of fish, vegetables, occasional meat (almost always venison), and soup. For the evening and morning meals you eat warmed-up leftovers. A young Indonesian seminarian, Fr. Segers, is an all-around assistant to the priest, a kind, 71-year-old Hollander who has responsibility for about 20 village churches scattered all over the Arus. Sometimes he makes 7-8 day trips to visit several of these churches, even as far as to P. Workai (Baimoen village), and you could possibly hitch a ride with him. This would probably be your only opportunity to see the real Aru jungle.

SPEAKING DUTCH IN INDONESIA

For hundreds of years Dutch was the language of government and of the ruling elite. Even though the use of Dutch began to decline when Indonesia won its independence in 1950, speaking Dutch still opens doors in Indonesia today. As in the case of staying as a guest in the *pastoran* in Dobo in the Arus (mentioned above), Dutch travelers will have ample opportunity to speak their mother tongue in Indonesia. It's a wonderful experience for Dutch visitors to meet Dutch-speaking Indonesians, particularly those who lived in Indonesia during the 1920s and 1930s. Speaking Dutch, you can actually have a conversation of real depth and substance, not just your usual bus station banter and small talk which is often the case when you can't speak Indonesian well.

You could meet anyone anywhere in Indonesia who is still able to speak Dutch — zoo curators, Papuan seminary students, Eurasian shopkeepers on Lombok, Chinese in Ujung Pandang — you never know. Indonesians who speak fluent Dutch are a storehouse of information, local lore, and historical information. The owners of Wisma Esther and Wisma Delima in Jakarta are only several examples of numerous hotel proprietors across Indonesia who can speak Dutch. And many older Indonesians will tell you very readily and proudly which high school in Holland they attended and who their teachers were. You sometimes even meet Indonesians in their twenties who can speak Dutch fluently, the language having been spoken traditionally in their homes.

Ambonese families, for example, often speak Dutch among themselves.

Travelers from other countries will also learn that Hollanders make invaluable traveling companions. They can translate for you what is vividly told them by older folk; they can read plaques, old books and inscriptions, and tell you stories of their relatives' experiences in the old Netherlands East Indies in the *tempo doeloe*, literally the "time before" or loosely translated as "the good old days."

Some Dutch expressions sound a bit funny to native Dutch ears. Indonesians speak an archaic, almost biblical form of Dutch, using old terms and expressions which have long been outdated in Holland itself. "Indonesian- Dutch" is more polite and formal than streamlined, modern Dutch. There are, in fact, fewer differences between Dutch and Indonesian-Dutch than between the Dutch spoken in the N of Holland aand that spoken in the S of Holland. Though Indonesians tend to overpronounce the Dutch "r," it's still pure unaccented Dutch. Like the voice of the *dalang* in *wayang kulit*, the island flavor comes through in their intonation. As Indonesians sing a little in their own regional languages, so do they in Dutch also. In another 10-15 years there will be very few fluent Dutch speakers as the old people are dying off and all the young people now want only to learn English.

IRIAN JAYA

*P*olitically a part of Indonesia since 1969, Irian Jaya is Indonesia's most spectacular region for tourism. It's the biggest and most intact natural history museum in existence—all 260,000 sq km of it (the same size as Spain or California!). This province comprises roughly the western half of the island of New Guinea, the second largest island in the world after Greenland (785,000 sq km). Papua New Guinea (PNG), the eastern ½ of the island (pop. 3 million), became independent from Australia in 1975. Irian's provincial capital, Jayapura, is 3,520 km from Jakarta. Although the province makes up 22% of Indonesia's total land surface, only 1% of the nation's people live here; it's the least visited, least populated, most remote Indonesian province. Decades behind Java, it's also the country's least economically developed territory. With the exception of large coastal cities like Sorong, Manokwari, Jayapura, and Merauke, the vast land mass of Irian Jaya is punctuated by just a dozen or so frontier towns connected only by air or sea. Between these posts stretch thousands of kilometers of mountains and jungle, most of it isolated and primitive.

INTRODUCTION

There is no land entry into Irian Jaya. A route popular with travelers is to depart from Cairns (Australia) for Port Moresby (PNG) where they apply for a tourist visa for Indonesia. From Port Moresby, they fly or make their way overland to Vanimo (northern PNG), then hop over to Jayapura. See "Paperwork" below for more information. Jayapura is expensive to reach (Rp260,000 from Jakarta with Merpati); if flying from the states, get off at Biak and fly to Jayapura from there (Rp45,600). Ujung Pandang is a favorite jumping-off point for Biak, Jayapura, and other destinations in eastern Indonesia. The best months to travel in Irian Jaya are June and July not only because of the drier weather, but because students are on holidays and themselves traveling around, making it easier to find guides among them.

THE LAND

Irian Jaya has wilder landscapes and more impenetrable, treacherous jungle than any other tropical region, including the Amazon Valley, and central white-sand beaches lined with coconut palms, wild forest streams plunging down rock faces, snowfields, jewel-like turquoise and green lakes strewn with glacial debris, heaths and yellow marshes with head-high grass, stands of pine trees, wild sugarcane meadows, casuarina groves, and moss-carpeted forests with bright flowers growing riotously. There are

silences you will remember. The greater part of its land mass is mountainous with a high central backbone extending for 650 km, dividing Irian Jaya into the S and north. Some mountains are so high that planes must fly between them to avoid turbulence; the highest, Puncak Jaya, is 5,039 m. Although situated just 4 degrees below the equator, some mountain tops are permanently covered in snow and ice. This system of central ranges compares in structure and relief to the Swiss Alps, but communication problems in this undeveloped territory are immense. High mountain regions are broken up by coarse grassy valleys and rainforests. Soil is generally poor in the S, but rich in the north. The most untouched part of Irian Jaya is between Wamena and the border of PNG—just you, them, and the jungle.

Climate

It's hot and humid on the coastal fringes, however mountain areas above 1,800 m are warm in the daytime but cold during the night, sometimes with frosts. The climate varies through the highlands; one valley might experience a dry season, an adjacent one a rainy season, while yet a third nearby valley may have rainfall evenly distributed throughout the year! The Baliem Valley and others to the N are broad and receive more sunshine than the steep, narrow valleys to the south. There are no well-defined seasons, but Dec. and Jan. are generally warmer, while Aug. and Sept. are more misty and cold. The southern low-

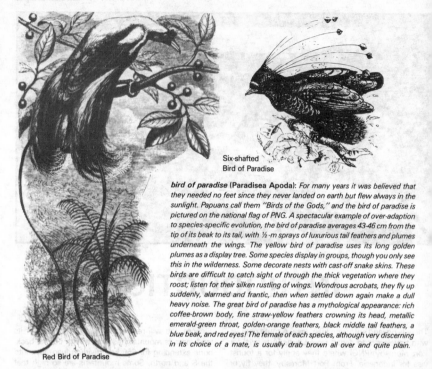

Six-shafted
Bird of Paradise

bird of paradise (**Paradisea Apoda**): *For many years it was believed that they needed no feet since they never landed on earth but flew always in the sunlight. Papuans call them "Birds of the Gods," and the bird of paradise is pictured on the national flag of PNG. A spectacular example of over-adaption to species-specific evolution, the bird of paradise averages 43-46 cm from the tip of its beak to its tail, with ½ -m sprays of luxurious tail feathers and plumes underneath the wings. The yellow bird of paradise uses its long golden plumes as a display tree. Some species display in groups, though you only see this in the wilderness. Some decorate nests with cast-off snake skins. These birds are difficult to catch sight of through the thick vegetation where they roost; listen for their silken rustling of wings. Wondrous acrobats, they fly up suddenly, alarmed and frantic, then when settled down again make a dull heavy noise. The great bird of paradise has a mythological appearance: rich coffee-brown body, fine straw-yellow feathers crowning its head, metallic emerald-green throat, golden-orange feathers, black middle tail feathers, a blue beak, and red eyes! The female of each species, although very discerning in its choice of a mate, is usually drab brown all over and quite plain.*

Red Bird of Paradise

lands, however, have a very distinct dry season; in Merauke sometimes it doesn't rain for 5 months straight.

Because of its phenomenal rainfall (as great as 550 cm per annum), Irian Jaya possesses some of Indonesia's largest rivers. Originating in the mountains, these mighty watercourses flow like undulating snakes through evergreen forests down to the lowlands. In the S and SW, they have created mosaic river systems snaking through one million sq km of mangrove swamps, casuarina groves, and tidal forests. The great Baliem, Memberamo, Tariku, Taritatu and Digul rivers have many rapids and waterfalls in the gorges and long valleys through which they pass.

Fauna
The whole territory holds immense fascination for the naturalist. Freshwater and terrestrial vertebrates are nearly all of the Australian type (particularly from NE Australia). Many species may occur in one locale of Irian Jaya but not in another, possibly due to the varying amounts of rainfall between the lowlands and the highlands. Except for freshwater eels, fishing is restricted to the coastal regions. Recently, small fishponds have been introduced in the villages. Some

highland tribes have never seen a fish, only eels, freshwater crayfish, and tadpoles with flattened heads attached to rocks of fast-flowing streams. The province is also host to fabulously colored butterflies, some exceedingly rare. The coral islands E of the Bird's Head Peninsula in Cendrawasih Bay are famous as feeding grounds for sea turtles and dugongs, and serve also as important nesting sites for seabirds.

On land there are cuscus, bandicoots, bats, rats, mice, snakes, tortoises, crocodiles, frilled lizards, and giant monitor lizards. Irian Jaya has the world's largest tree-climbing water rat. The spiny anteater is a nocturnal marsupial with a long beak-like snout, small black eyes, a powerful set of claws, no tail or teeth, but a very long thin tongue with which it catches ants, termites, and other insects. It has one exit for both solid and liquid excreta; the only other animal like it is the platypus, which is absent from New Guinea. Tree kangaroos with gray-brown coats live in the higher regions. The phalanger has fox-like ears and a long bushy tail. The marsupial cat, presumably, chases marsupial mice. Other marsupials include possum which vary in size from the mouse-like flying possum to the furry cuscus, the largest of the possum family.

Birds

This island is renowned for its exquisite, colorful, and still-plentiful birds which number more than 650 species. Having developed in isolation, species here are unique and spectacular. These include at least 80 protected species of the exotic bird of paradise. The males have a brilliantly colored, luxuriant spray of tail feathers. Sometimes you'll see a flash of color as they dart by deep in the forest. Other birds include parrots, lovely green pigeons, honeyeaters, plumed herons, and other lowland birds. The blue-gray *mambruk* (crown pigeon), named for its crown of tufted down, inhabits the coastal marshes, as does the multihued kingfisher. The male bowerbird dances and parades before females on a display ground made of a layer of moss surrounded by a one-m-high wall made of moss and brightly decorated with flower petals, leaves, fruit, and berries. Japen Island in northern Cendrawasih Province is the source for most bird skins and exotic live specimens.

HISTORY

Negritos settled New Guinea beginning perhaps 30,000 years ago. Some believe that the original mountain Papuans came from the great plains to the S or even from as far as Australia; their features and languages are similar to those of Australian aboriginals. During Neolithic times the Melanesians arrived from the east, bringing with them the bow and arrow, the ax blade, pottery, crop plants, the calendar, cowrie shells for money, tattooing, betel-chewing, decorative woodcarving, outrigger canoes and seagoing vessels, the dog and the pig, men's and women's clubhouses, ritualized cannibalism, and warfare.

The subsequent discovery and coastal exploration of western New Guinea came about because of the Moluccan spice trade. Arab, Chinese, and Malay traders were the island's first explorers. The Portuguese arrived in 1512, the Spanish in 1526, and in 1605 the first Dutch ship, captained by William Janz, reached the mainland where 9 of his crew were eaten by tribesmen while fetching water. When early 17th C. European navigators saw snowcapped peaks from their ships, they thought they were clouds. In 1623, the Dutch captain Jan Carstensz first glimpsed the glacier that was later to be given his name: Carstensz Toppen.

The Spanish, British, and Germans all tried to establish colonies in the territory, but most ended in disaster. Western New Guinea was officially annexed by the Dutch in 1848; they built their first capital at Manokwari in 1898, then garrisoned men at Fak Fak on the W coast and at Merauke on the SW coast in 1902. The present Jayapura was founded in 1910, a political move: the town was located 22 km from the

New Guinea border, laying real claim to this half of the island and keeping it from the Germans, who at the time controlled land to the E of the border. The highlands of western New Guinea were not penetrated until 1933 when Roman Catholics, Lutherans, and Seventh-day Adventists went in, and well into this century maps of Netherlands New Guinea still had great blank patches in the center where no white man had ever penetrated. By 1938 Hollandia (as Jayapura was then called), had a population of only 800 Indonesians, 400 Dutchmen, and the natives.

World War II

The war swirled furiously around this island. By spring of 1944, General Douglas MacArthur's forces had captured most of the Bismark Archipelago and the Admiralty Islands and neutralized the advance Japanese base at Rabaul, successively penetrating Japan's rear barrier zone of defense in the SW Pacific. MacArthur then moved westward on the island of New Guinea to prepare for his next step: the Philippines. American forces stormed the beach near Jayapura one April morning in 1944 and met only token resistance. Over the coming months, Hollandia became a gigantic staging area. Since MacArthur had obliterated most of the coastal towns during the war to uproot the Japanese, as a war reparation gesture he built a new town on this N coast in 1944. In MacArthur's airy hilltop residence, which overlooked the whole magnificent harbor, he planned the liberation of the Philippines. By Oct., a huge armada of over 500 ships rendezvoused in Hollandia's harbor. Eyewitnesses reported that the fleet, interconnected by catwalks with thousands of glowing lamps, looked like a great city floating on the water. U.S. Army camps which once bivouacked whole divisions now lie smothered in jungle, and a few rusting landing barges on the beach at Hamadi are the only remnants of the war. Most of the hulks were long ago turned into spatulas and eggbeaters by Hong Kong merchants.

The Dutch Colony

After the surrender of Japan in 1945, West New Guinea was handed over by the Allies to the Dutch again. While the rest of the archipelago was lost to them piece by piece, the Dutch eventually grew to look upon West New Guinea as the one last pearl in their former island empire. The Dutch openly encouraged Papuan nationalism and sought to prepare the territory for self-government by training the Irianese in the necessary administrative and technical skills. The chances of the colony ever supporting itself were poor; Holland's purpose in continuing to hold on to the territory was more a matter of emotion and prestige. Holland believed that its settlements in New Guinea would prove politically invaluble if the Indonesian Republic started breaking up.

Ironically, the Dutch refusal to pull out brought the young Indonesian nation together even more. All

the Dutch in Indonesia: By governing through local leaders, a tiny mercantile seafaring nation on the other side of the world in cold northern Europe came to dominate a sprawling archipelago in the tropical East Indies for over 350 years. The Dutch established the first estate crops and thus the first economic wealth of Indonesia. They used the considerable wealth generated from the Indonesian land and raw materials to increase agricultural export and trade, and to support manufacturing development in Holland. They upset the eco-logical balance by introducing new health schemes so Indonesians lived longer; population growth in Indonesia for 100 years after 1830 was stupendous (growing to 60 million). But by bringing to bear their organizational skills, by importing technology, European education, egalitarian ideas and ideologies, the Dutch eventually made themselves superfluous and brought about their own extinction in the area. Their last pearl in this necklace of islands—West New Guinea—they gave up in 1969.

through the 1950s and early 1960s as the Indonesian Republic seemed to be tottering, its economy in shambles, with regional rebellions flaring up on Sumatra, Sulawesi, and Maluku, the specter of the Dutch bogeyman was held up to the Indonesian masses. Sukarno appeared to hold the whole wobbly state together by vehemently accusing the Dutch of plotting to reconquer Indonesia from their base in West New Guinea. Dutch imperialism was godsent, probably the most powerful cohesive force in welding the new republic together. And when the "Irian Question" was settled and the territory finally handed over by the Dutch, it put Indonesia on the road to political chaos.

"Self-determination"

The Indonesian Republic's claim to the territory was based on the historic half-truth that West New Guinea once was under the suzerainty of the sultan of Tidore in Maluku to the west. The Indonesians also argued that *all* of the former Netherlands East Indies had been promised to the republic by truce agreements. After years of futile haggling, in the early 1960s Sukarno at last launched his *konfrontasi* campaign to oust the Dutch. With the mission of leading Irianese villagers in rebellion and sabotage against the Dutch, more than 2,000 Indonesian soldiers parachuted into wild jungle or put ashore in various parts of the Dutch-held territory. Sukarno boasted that the Irianese kept Indonesian flags hidden in their homes, ready to be raised once the war of liberation for the territory began. Actually, few educated Irianese wished to become part of Indonesia—or the Netherlands, for that matter. The majority wanted total independence

from both. Most of Indonesia's military forays into the area ended in catastrophe and hundreds of Indonesian troops were captured and killed (you can see some of their graves in Abepura, near Jayapura). World opinion, power politics, and a fateful meeting between Bobby Kennedy and Sukarno—not military ferocity or prowess—did more to force the Dutch out.

The so-called New York Agreement between Holland and Indonesia in 1962 called for the Irianese to be given an opportunity to vote so that their joining the Indonesian Republic be an "Act of Free Choice." But in the year this vote was to be held (1969), Jakarta waived the referendum and selected only 1,025 delegates to do the voting. These government-appointed representatives, plied with favors and promises, voted to join Indonesia without a single dissenting vote. The Indonesians failed to consult the remaining 800,000 or so people in the interior, partly because of the very real communication difficulties. In Aug. 1969, Dutch West New Guinea became a part of Indonesia. The Indonesians renamed the territory *Irian Jaya*, meaning "Victorious Irian."

POLITICS

The OPM

With the formal approval of the United Nations, the changeover from Dutch colony to Indonesian colony took place during a period of severe repression under Indonesian military occupation. Believing that the Irianese are Melanesian and not Asian, Papuans have never had any feelings of strong cultural or historic affinity with Indonesia. These feelings of opposition have been compounded by the way Papuans have been treated at the hands of the Indonesians. Since the 1960s, West Papuans have suffered numerous violations of their rights: racial discrimination, arrest and detention, torture, disappearances, and extra-judicial killings. As a result, a liberation movement called the *Operasi Papua Merdeka* (Free Papua Movement) has taken root. Since 1969, the year the Indonesian Republic failed to make good on its promise of self-determination, small ragtag forces of guerillas have based themselves in dense jungle lowlands near the northernmost joint boundary with Papua New Guinea. Although ambushes of Indonesian army patrols occur and Indonesian civil servants are now and then assassinated, most incidents are successfully hushed up. Many thousands have been killed as a result of the military operations to suppress this movement. Political troubles brought on by the elections in May 1977 led to uprisings in the central highlands in which Danis attacked police posts with spears and pounded stakes into airfields to prevent reinforcements from landing. Fighting flared up again in the Wissel Lakes region in 1981, and border skirmishes were reported as recently as 1984, with thousands of refugees pouring into PNG border areas. The OPM today is essentially contained and doesn't constitute a real threat to the present Indonesian administration. Indonesians have used a combination of military repression, tight political control, economic development, co-opting Irianese radicals, as well as stepping up their nationalistic education policy, all aimed at instilling in the Irianese a sense of belonging to the Indonesian nation. Obliteration has become the fate of an entire people: cultural obliteration as well as the obliteration of their cause through neglect by the world community. Because the dominant minority is not white, it is an issue which has hardly ever been raised in the UN.

Indonesian Occupation

The government claims to be spending more money per capita (about US$50 in 1984-85) in Irian Jaya than in even the Java provinces. But bear in mind that Irian Jaya's average population is only 6 people per sq km and most of the money goes to improve transportation and communication links to solidify the political infrastructure and to make it easier for the military to control the territory. Much emphasis is put on education/indoctrination, taking a full one-third of the province's development budget since the early 1980s. About one-third of the civil service is employed by the Education Department. Cendrawasih University in Jayapura was one of the first projects the Indonesians completed, and about 1,500 bachelor of arts and 200 master of arts students had graduated from there by 1984. Vocational schools for high school-age students are being built or expanded, and a trickle of Irianese are sent to Java for technical training. Indonesians generally have a paternalistic attitude towards

the Irianese, whom they seem to regard as inferior, and they tend to enforce change too quickly. But harsh early "civilizing" policies, such as attempts to get the Irianese of the hinterlands to wear clothes instead of their traditional penis gourds, have been replaced by a more realistic, humane approach which utilizes education and wage labor as the means to instill a more "Indonesian" lifestyle in the natives.

Transmigrasi

A great source of friction between Melanesians and Indonesians is the government's transmigration scheme. Papuans are little amused by the argument that their sacrifice will alleviate population pressure on overcrowded Java. At present, Asian-Indonesians occupy for the most part coastal settlements and the main urban centers. But the government's ultimate aim seems to be to have Asian-Indonesians outnumber the whole Papuan populace by the close of the century. Using tactics ranging from outright cash payments through legal hocus-pocus to strongarm eviction, the government is working hard to set up the unassimilated isolated tribesmen of the interior in housing estates where it can keep a better eye on them. Unfortunately for Indonesians, the OPM finds this *transmigrasi* policy its most effective recruiter. Officials have stated that the Irianese have no right to lay claim to land that is not being "used." They obviously do not consider the collecting of wild food and the hunting of game as valid and productive uses of the land.

THE ECONOMY

Crucial to an understanding of Indonesia's determination to hold on to and develop Irian Jaya is the fact that it contains the world's richest copper deposit, some of Indonesia's largest oilfields, as well as important gold, uranium, and timber resources. Standard Oil Company was already drilling for oil in West New Guinea as early as the 1930s. Since 1969, when the territory passed into the hands of Indonesia's central government, the Javanese have laid big plans for Irian's inland and offshore wealth. The Japanese are robbing its deep seas to the N by paying off influential politicians. Although its soil is generally poor, this province produces rattan, copra, and the finest and widest variety of timber in Indonesia, including tough, weather- and borer-resistant ironwood *(kayu besi)*. Luckily, marketing and logistical problems continue to keep Irian's timber industry in its infant stages. All these mineral, petroleum, ocean, and forest resources are being exploited with little benefit to the Irianese, providing employment for only about 10,000 people—an infinitesimal fraction of the total workforce. The Papuan population, as a rule, get very little spin-off from foreign investments: not only political positions but most economic enterprises are filled by outsiders. Except as laborers, native sons aren't employed by these companies, and the higher-echelon company personnel are also drawn from outside.

No fabulous gold strike happened here as it did in PNG, but copper deposits discovered in 1936 at Tembagapura in the Ertsberg Mountains in the S-central region are reported to be among the largest in the world. Starting with nothing, and in the middle of a Stone Age culture, Freeport Minerals Co. in the '70s put in tramways to transport ore to the mill and a slurry pipeline—the longest on earth—to carry the concentrate through the mountains down to the sea. A huge processing mill, a modern loading port, and a 112-km road from the coast up to the mountains were also built. With the severe drop recently of the world copper price, had all the basic infrastructure not already been in place the project would now be operating at a loss. Since the early 1970s, the enclave and export nature of the Freeport venture has brought few local economic rewards.

THE PEOPLE

Irian Jaya's native Papuans are divided into the Negroids of the high valleys and plateaus whose skins are brown and black, and the coastal and foothills Papuans, a blending of the Melanesian and Negroid races. Papuans have little ethnic, linguistic, historic, or spiritual relationship with other Indonesians. There's a giddy variety of tribes and over 700 distinct languages spoken, with no one language intelligible to more than 150,000 people. Some languages are spoken by as few as 2,000. Since the 1950s, children all over Irian Jaya have been taught the national language, *Bahasa Indonesia*. While Irian Jaya's mountain people cultivate gardens, its coastal peoples are basically hunters and gatherers whose staple diet is sago, either formed into large balls and roasted, made into porridge, or mixed with coconut milk and flattened into pancakes. Coastal dwellers, like the Asmat, traditionally paddle their canoes in the standing position and are masterful woodcarvers. Headhunting and cannibalism were once rife but now have been all but stamped out by the efforts of the Indonesian government and the missionaries.

Some tribes continue to resist any contact with the outside world. Negritos of the purest blood, and a few little-known, extremely isolated pygmy tribes, still live in the rough Sudirman Range, raising crops and pigs on land as high as 3,000 m. The majority of the Papuans in the central mountain regions live in small clans kept isolated by terrain, dialect, and customs. These upland Irianese generally possess more complex social, spiritual, and family structures than the coastal peoples. Indonesians from Sulawesi, Java, Maluku, and many other islands live in trading and

fishing communities and in oil and timber centers along the coasts, rivermouths, and on the satellite islands off western New Guinea. These immigrants have mixed with coastal natives and since annexation in 1969 have established thriving local businesses.

Highland Tribes

Central highlanders still largely live a Stone Age existence. In high, fertile valleys such as the Baliem, the native Dani have for centuries constructed arduous irrigation systems. Fields are generally cleared by men, though planting and harvesting are done by women. Each wife has her own garden plot. In the higher regions, tribesmen slash and burn forests to grow vegetables. They terrace and cultivate mountain slopes that lie at as much as 50-degree angles, far above the frost line as high as 2,800 m. Dani women wear a traditional grass skirt with a net-bag over the head and back, while the men wear penis sheaths *(koteka)* made from dried gourds. The illiteracy rate among the Dani is low, but in areas outside of the central Baliem Valley literacy is nonexistent. The Grand Valley of the Baliem is one of the longest settled of the interior upland areas and the Dani over the years have become highly skilled at playing rival missionaries and the civil authorities against each other.

Highland Irianese don't look upon you as superior to them; they accept you as you are and have no eye avoidance. Known for their wide grins, they let out little yelps of delight, walk with you through the valley, take you back to their villages, and may play a bamboo jew's harp for your entertainment. In really remote interior areas, blond hair fills the natives with amazement. They'll stroke a Caucasian's hair because it's so soft and smooth, wanting to keep locks of it for decoration. They might lift up your trouser leg to make sure you're white and hairy underneath. When you shave or brush your teeth Irianese might run away, thinking that you've gone mad with foam coming from your mouth!

The staple diet of the highlands is sweet potatoes, roasted or steamed. The pig is all-important in the highlanders' ceremonial and economic life, a crucial part of their social organization, and a major source of protein. Parts of the pig are used in ornamentation and for making tools. Pork is essential for feasts, as payment of personal debts, and tribal reparations are also made with pigs. A man's main interests are pigs and women—new wives are purchased with *rupiah* and fat pigs—and his social status is determined by how many of each he owns.

Population

With a population of about 800,000 in the interior, 70,000 on the coasts, and around 200,000 in the Jayapura urban area, Irian Jaya is Indonesia's most sparsely populated province. Only the areas around Manokwari on the E coast of the Vogelkop (the

by angry natives. Despite the deaths, the missionaries persisted. Fearless missionaries were the first outsiders to enter the interior and attempt settlement in the 1950s. Today, 25 different Christian denominations have established themselves in Irian Jaya. The majority of missionaries are sensitive, intelligent and dedicated. They have built over 4,000 schools, 130 hospitals, 240 first-aid posts, and their private air services are the most extensive on the island. There are important Protestant and Catholic agricultural projects at Mulia, Angguruk, Soba, and Ninia, as well as an agricultural program at the Bible and Vocational Institute at Sentani. Due to their efforts and those of the Indonesian government, schools all over the central highlands now teach *Bahasa Indonesia*.

Success in conversion has varied from tribe to tribe. In some cases, Christian doctrines were force-fed to Papuans who already practiced their own integrated and proud spiritual beliefs. Sometimes spectacular shifts to Christianity occurred; other times the missionaries were pretty much ignored. The greatest successes were achieved in establishing peace and putting an end to cannibalism. Only after an area was rendered "safe" by the missionaries would government officials and soldiers arrive. On the deficit side, to the lament of historians and anthropologists, there have been instances where priceless works of art, fetishes, and handicrafts have been destroyed. The missionaries also brought with them diseases. A large portion of the money flowing into Irian Jaya from followers overseas goes to aggrandizing the missionaries' comfortable way of life and not to the direct administration of welfare for the Irianese. But the missionaries remain extremely important change agents between the Irianese and the Indonesian authorities. The missionaries have been training natives gradually to take over mission work as Westerners phase out. For background reading on mission work and thinking, read some "missionary classics" from the "Booklist."

"Bird's Head" in Dutch), the Schouten Is. in Geelvink Bay, the N coast near Jayapura, and several fertile highland valleys (Paniai Lakes and the Baliem Valley), have relatively high population densities. A few inland valleys have 10-15 people per sq km, though most regions fewer than 6 people per sq km, or are totally uninhabited.

Of the total population today, 79% are Irian-born. The rest are immigrants, mostly ethnic Javanese, plus Bugis, Butonese, and Makassarese from Sulawesi. Immigrants have made important contributions to the growth of the local economy since 1969, establishing construction industries, cheap minibus transport in all the major towns, thriving market gardens, and makeshift consumer markets such as Pasar Ampera in Jayapura. To some extent the Irianese have copied the trading practices as well as farming, fishing, and other skills of the immigrants, but the latter have severely limited the level of Irianese employment. The civil service sector remains the major source of income for urban Irianese. Most key government officials are still recruited from outside the province.

The Missionaries

In the early days European, Australian, and American missionaries made tremendous sacrifices to bring a message that is still barely comprehensible to the Irianese. Since 1855 when the Dutch opened up the first mission station at Manokwari, 168 missionaries (mostly Indonesian) and 68 converts have been killed

CRAFTS AND SHOPPING

Irianese crafts are less affected by commercialism than in PNG. The Asmat of the Casuarina Coast in the S carve striking wooden shields, ancestoral and serpent totem poles, dugout canoes, prows and paddles, masks, soul ships, ironwood shields and spears, sago pounders, and grub trays. Colors used originally were red, black, and white only. Formerly they carved using only animal teeth and shells, and stone axes obtained through trade with the mountain people, but since the war metal tools have been used. The Asmat also work with bone to a lesser degree. An UN-financed handicraft project promotes and protects Asmat art; visit their outlet at Agats. Mailing crafts back surface post from Jayapura is too much of a bureaucratic hassle, so wait until Ujung Pandang or Denpasar.

In the highlands, any of the following implements may be offered for sale by natives from the moment you step off the plane in Wamena. The women's bark-string bag *(noken)* is made from rolled bark fibers, often dyed in red and purple stripes. The *noken* hangs down the back, supported by a strap around the forehead. In it, women carry heavy loads of sweet potatoes, babies, piglets, and tools — sometimes all at once! When empty, it's worn over the shoulders and down the back to keep a woman warm in the cold mornings and evenings. The yellow penis gourd, *koteka* or *peka* pipe, is common all the way from Telefomin on the Sepik River in PNG to Teluk Bintuni S of the Bird's Head. Measuring 7½ cm up to ½ m long, the *koteka* is made from the outer rinds of an elongated pumpkin-like gourd. Men wear no clothing except for this penis sheath, which seems to accentuate their nakedness all the more. Each man has a wardrobe of several sizes and shapes, according to what he feels like wearing that day. A very short *koteka* is used when a man goes boar-hunting; an elongated one serves for festive occasions. It may be decorated on top with a tassel of fur, strips of colorful fabric, or a spiky cocoon. In some mountain tribes the penis sheath is also used as a betelnut container or a place to keep money. Uplanders also make stone axes by cracking a cliff-face with fire high on a scaffold or by hammering on cold rock: methods at least 30,000 years old, but now dying out.

PAPERWORK

Visas

Because Jayapura, the provincial capital of Irian Jaya, is not counted among the official tourist gateways into Indonesia, a special internal visa is required to visit the territory if you're flying into Jayapura from another country. However, foreign tourists may enter the territory via Biak, an island off the NW coast, and receive the usual 60-day tourist pass. From Biak fly with Merpati to Jayapura for Rp45,600. Ever since the start of the US$1000 Los Angeles-Jakarta flight via Biak in 1986, Indonesian authorities have loosened up on issuing tourist passes and travel permits to and within Irian Jaya. It costs US$800 Los Angeles to Biak, the easternmost gateway to Indonesia.

If you intend to enter Jayapura from Papua New Guinea, a 60-day Indonesian visa is usually easy to obtain from the Indonesian consulate in Port Moresby (PNG). But relations between Indonesia and PNG are up and down; you never know what the consulate's latest policy is until you actually arrive in Indonesia. Don't believe what any consulate abroad says. Sometimes the Indonesian consulate in Port Moresby will not issue a visa, or you may be restricted in the number of days you can stay in Jayapura. By the same token, if you are on a 60-day tourist pass, you

cannot officially leave Jayapura for Wewak (PNG) even though there are flights there. However, you can leave the country from Biak because it's an international gateway.

Surat Jalan

When in Irian Jaya itself, you need a *surat jalan* from the police in Biak or Jayapura to visit such places as the Baliem Valley, Agats, Nabire, Oksibil, Merauke, and anywhere near the border with PNG. Without proper documentation, travelers are put right back on the plane. The *surat jalan* can be obtained simply, quickly, and cheaply in Jayapura from the police station on Jl. Jen. A. Yani or in Biak at the main police station on Jl. Selat Makassar. You'll need 4 extra passport photos and Rp1000; takes 30 minutes. Another option is to get your *surat jalan* for Irian Jaya's interior in Jakarta (Direktorat Pengamanan Politik, Departemen Dalam Negeri, Jl. Merdeka Utara 7). Travel agents (Tunas and Pacto) in Jakarta can also get the permit for you in 2-4 days, but will charge you plenty for it. All areas you might visit should be written on the *surat jalan;* the police in Jayapura can give you information on which areas are off limits to travelers. The length of validity of the *surat jalan* should not exceed the expiry date of your tourist pass. With your *surat jalan* check in immediately with the police upon arrival in each town or village. The police in Wamena (Baliem Valley) are said to be more lenient about allowing visits to more remote central highland areas, so wait until you get there for your *surat jalan* to such places as Ninia and Soba. However, you can't get permits in Wamena for Illaga, Enarotali, and Oksibil; these must be acquired in Jayapura.

GETTING THERE

By Air

If flying from PNG into Irian Jaya, stock up on about US$20 in Indonesian *rupiah* at the Wespac Bank in Wewak, then change the rest of your money at Sentani Airport or in Jayapura banks, which offer better rates. Garuda has flights from: Jakarta, Rp352,800; Manado, Rp194,100; Surabaya, Rp347,500. Garuda also flies to Biak from Jakarta, then take another flight to Jayapura for Rp61,800. Biak is also accessible with Garuda from Ujung Pandang (Rp193,200) and Denpasar (Rp249,900). Merpati flies to Jayapura from: Ambon, Rp120,700; Biak, Rp45,600; Jakarta, Rp260,800; Surabaya, Rp256,800; Ujung Pandang, Rp198,300. Once in Jayapura, you can reach just about any other worthwhile destination in Irian Jaya via Merpati or missionary aircraft.

From foreign countries, Air Niugini flies from Honolulu to Port Moresby each Sun. evening at 1830

US$709 OW with 30 days advance purchase requirement. Another Garuda flight from Honolulu to Bali passes through Biak (9 hours from Honolulu); Biak is only 3½ hours from Bali. Qantas flies from Cairns (Australia) to Port Moresby for A$191 OW Economy; Air Niugini flies from Brisbane (A$320 OW) and Sydney for (A$392 OW). It's quite possible to crew on a yacht out of North Queensland to Port Moresby. Once in Port Moresby, travel up through PNG, then take the weekly Air Niugini hop from Vanimo to Jayapura (US$150), the plane returning to Vanimo the same day. One can also fly direct to Jayapura from Port Moresby (US$275) or Wewak (US$142) in PNG. Using this "back door" approach into Indonesia, it's possible to hop down to Bali via Ujung Pandang (although Darwin-Kupang-Mataram-Denpasar is cheaper).

Arriving

From Sentani Airport to Jayapura (45 km) is Rp1000 by minibus (one changeover), leaving from about ½ km down the road in front of the airport, or take a taxi into town for Rp10,000 (not the Rp15,000 they first ask!). Instead of spending the night in noisy and unglamorous Jayapura, you might as well just stay in more agreeable Sentani village, particularly if you're flying on to Wamena. You do have to go into Jayapura to get your *surat jalan*, but this you can do in one morning by minibus (Rp1000 OW). On the way back, hit the museum and the Batik Irian Center in Abepura, then fly out of Sentani for Wamena the next morning at 0700. Returning from Wamena, you'll be flying out of Sentani anyway. You can even get the *pas foto* required for your *surat jalan* in Sentani in the photo shop next to RM Virgo. Or, even better, get your *surat jalan* in Biak and save yourself from going into Jayapura at all.

By Sea

Irian Jaya's smaller coastal towns lack regular shipping services, but Pelni's new liner services to such major towns as Biak, Sorong, and Jayapura provide a reliable and cheap way to cover great distances. Departing the main ports of Java, Pelni calls at points in Irian Jaya about every 2 weeks. From Tg. Priok (Jakarta), the KM *Umsini* charges Rp93,900 Economy, Rp226,500 1st Class to Jayapura; Rp72,600 Economy, Rp173,200 1st Class to Sorong. On the way to Jayapura or Sorong, Pelni stops at such principal ports as Bitung (N. Sulawesi), Tarakan (E. Kalimantan), Ambon (C. Maluku), and Ternate (N. Maluku). Don't count on Pelni schedules or itineraries to be exact. Other shipping lines also have vessels embarking for Moluccan and Irianese ports from Java. The harbormasters' offices in Tg. Perak (Surabaya) and Tg. Priok (Jakarta) are the best places to inquire. It's also possible to take a ship from the Kai Is. (SE Maluku) to Kaimana on Irian Jaya's S coast, but once you arrive in Kaimana the authorities won't let you take a missionary aircraft or walk up into the mountains without a *surat jalan*, which you must fly to Biak or Jayapura to obtain!

GETTING AROUND

Road networks only exist around urban centers such as Biak, Jayapura, and Merauke. None of the province's district capitals are linked by road, nor are the highlands connected by road to the coast. The government is building a road from Wamena to the N coast to be finished in 5-10 years so better get to the Baliem quick if you want to see it unspoiled. Because road construction is so staggeringly expensive, planes are about the only means of travel in the interior. Garuda offers flights from Jayapura to Biak (Rp61,800), Sorong (Rp132,100), and Timika (Rp111,100). But the cheapest and widest selection of flights within the province is offered by Merpati with daily flights (incl. tax) from Jayapura to: Wamena, Rp37,400; Kaimana, Rp122,000; Nabire, Rp75,000; Manokwari, Rp97,200; Serui, Rp75,500; Merauke, Rp92,000; Fak Fak, Rp168,000; Batom, Rp28,500. You could fly in a 20-year-old Viscount or a Dakota (spare parts to which are still being manufactured by specialist firms in the USA), but most likely you'll fly in a small fixed-wing aircraft in which you sit like paratroopers on canvas chairs.

Missionary Aircraft

Using light fixed-wing aircraft and helicopters, missionary organizations fly to tiny, remote missionary stations, but are costlier. One of the largest organizations is Missionary Aviation Fellowship (MAF) which serves the Protestant missions and uses 185 airstrips all over Irian Jaya. Associated Missions Aviation (AMA) is smaller and serves the Roman Catholic missions. Both carry passengers, cargo, and accept charter business, and most all missionary groups have offices at Jayapura's Sentani Airport. Be sure to arrange for your *surat jalan* to destinations *prior* to flying into the interior or you'll be returned to Jayapura at your own expense. It's also wise to reserve flights in advance. Other missionary groups operating in Irian Jaya:

ABMS—Australian Baptist Missionary Society;
APCM—Asian Pacific Christian Mission;
CAMA—Christian Missionary Alliance;
RBMU—Regions Beyond Missionary Alliance;
SIL—Summer Institute of Linguistics;
TEAM—Evangelical Alliance Mission;
UFM—Unevangelized Fields Mission;
UNCEN—Cendrawasih University;
ZGK—Netherlands Reformed Church.

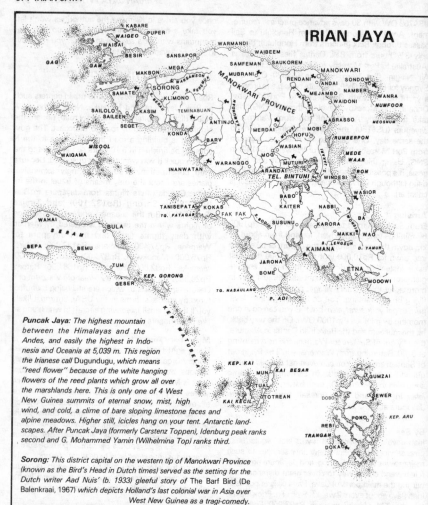

IRIAN JAYA

Puncak Jaya: The highest mountain between the Himalayas and the Andes, and easily the highest in Indonesia and Oceania at 5,039 m. This region the Irianese call Dugundugu, which means "reed flower" because of the white hanging flowers of the reed plants which grow all over the marshlands here. This is only one of 4 West New Guinea summits of eternal snow, mist, high wind, and cold, a clime of bare sloping limestone faces and alpine meadows. Higher still, icicles hang on your tent. Antarctic landscapes. After Puncak Jaya (formerly Carstensz Toppen), Idenburg peak ranks second and G. Mohammed Yamin (Wilhelmina Top) ranks third.

Sorong: This district capital on the western tip of Manokwari Province (known as the Bird's Head in Dutch times) served as the setting for the Dutch writer Aad Nuis' (b. 1933) gleeful story of The Barf Bird (De Balenkraai, 1967) which depicts Holland's last colonial war in Asia over West New Guinea as a tragi-comedy.

history of Irian Jaya: Third Century Bronze Age objects from Indochina have been found as far E as Lake Sentani on the northern coast of West New Guinea, but the civilization responsible has long since vanished. This island was first discovered by Portuguese navigators in the 16th C. and named Papua which is early Malay for "black, fuzzy hair." Jan Carstenz sailed along the S coast of Irian Jaya in 1623, writing in his ship's log abouth very high mountains which appeared covered in snow (this was Puncak Jaya). When he returned to Europe, he was laughed at. The whole of the interior was terra incognito until the 1930s when a Dutch expedition first penetrated and reported finding a chain of "ice mountains." They named the highest peak after Carstenz, who had first seen them.

flora of Irian Jaya: Many species of liana, beech trees, tree ferns, tree orchids, and the so-called "ant-house plants," which are potato-shaped and honeycombed with tunnels inhabited by biting ants, tree frogs and lizards. From the lagenaria come gourds used by the Irianese as bottles, dippers, and other containers. Libodedrus is an incense tree found at high elevations. At night the mold of the rainforest floor glows and flickers in the dusk from the decomposing bacteria it contains.

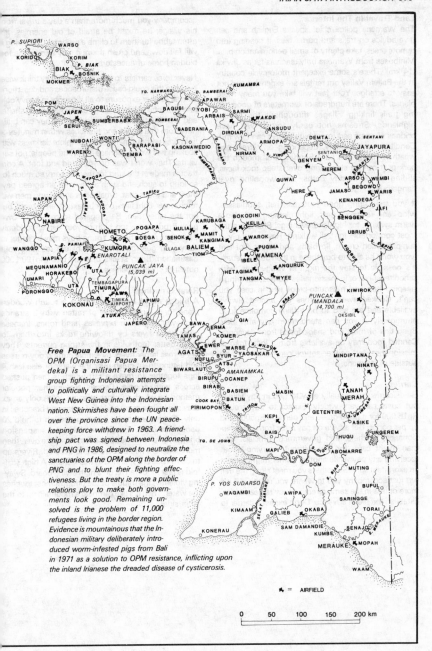

Free Papua Movement: *The OPM (Organisasi Papua Merdeka) is a militant resistance group fighting Indonesian attempts to politically and culturally integrate West New Guinea into the Indonesian nation. Skirmishes have been fought all over the province since the UN peacekeeping force withdrew in 1963. A friendship pact was signed between Indonesia and PNG in 1986, designed to neutralize the sanctuaries of the OPM along the border of PNG and to blunt their fighting effectiveness. But the treaty is more a public relations ploy to make both governments look good. Remaining unsolved is the problem of 11,000 refugees living in the border region. Evidence is mountainous that the Indonesian military deliberately introduced worm-infested pigs from Bali in 1971 as a solution to OPM resistance, inflicting upon the inland Irianese the dreaded disease of cysticerosis.*

$\star$ = AIRFIELD

0   50   100   150   200 km

Land Travel In The Interior

The Wamena police chief speaks English and can give advice on trails and porter fees. If heading into remote areas, take plenty of small denomination bills. Minibuses from Wamena only reach as far as Jiwika (14 km). There's some excellent motorcycle country in the Baliem Valley but rentals are expensive and not easy to arrange. Your feet will take you many more places. There are hundreds of kilometers of good hiking trails linking villages throughout the central highlands. Streams not easily forded will have bridges of some sort (most highlanders can't swim!). Conditions vary widely, depending on terrain and weather. Hiking can be a Sunday stroll though the park or it can be clambering over steep rock faces, sliding down muddy paths, and wobbling over dangerous bridges.

If you trek, bring good footwear, hat, sunglasses, wind- and rainproof gear, light clothing and also a warm sweater for highland evenings. Shorts are the most comfortable for trail walking. Have a supply of sun-protection cream, lip balm, and insect repellent (you won't be able to buy these in Irian Jaya). Usually it's possible to stay the night in village huts, with schoolteachers, or in missionaries' homes, but bring a sleeping bag and mosquito-proof tent in case you can't. Cooked sweet potatoes are almost always available and are said to be a fairly complete food nutritionally, if you can stand them day after day. Bring tins of meat and snack foods from Jayapura. Canned food may be available from a local *toko* or missionaries, but neither source can be counted on outside of Wamena.

Carriers

Guide/carriers are usually easy to find in any village but costs can vary widely. Expect to pay around Rp15,000 for a good guide and perhaps Rp5000 and up per porter. Get advice on pay rates from local missionaries, teachers, and government officials. One man might carry for you without worrying about receiving any pay while another carrier might expect an exorbitant sum. Still others you meet along the trail will just accompany you to where you're going if it's more or less in the same direction they're headed for. Establish the fee in advance. Don't expect a carrier to accompany you much more than a day's travel from his village; he might be afraid of old enemies. It's often taboo for them to climb a mountain, believing it will fall down and crush them; it may also be the forbidden home of ancestors.

Never force carriers to walk later than they think wise because this could cause disturbances and desertion as well as over-exposure to all if caught in heavy cold rain. Mountain Irianese know best where good shelter and plentiful firewood can be found. They can build huts from tree trunks and branches within minutes or light fires without matches in complete darkness with soaking wet wood. Irianese are proud people, not servants. They won't wait on you hand and foot. A contract is made at the start for them to carry so much for so long to such and such a place for an agreed payment and that's that. Small boys and young men will fetch water, light fires, cook breakfast, erect tents, but not the older men. Be prepared to carry your own pack if prices are too high or your carrier suddenly decides to return home. Young boys may be eager to carry your gear but often tire before reaching your destination. Bring stacks of small bills (Rp100-1000 notes) to cover expenses.

River Crossings

A bridge might be a slippery log, a rough wooden plank, or a single strand of rattan with 2 strands somewhat higher to serve as hand ropes. Irianese cross small rivers by throwing rocks into them to make better footholds in the strong currents. They get across larger rivers by simply cutting down trees and letting them crash over the water or else lash 4 logs together to make a raft which is then pushed across with a pole. Canoes are another popular method by which to cross streams. With only an ax they can build a crazy bridge of rattan and branches in only 30 min. and make it strong enough to hold 20 people at once. For more elaborate suspension bridges, an arrow shoots the first *liana* vine over, then more lines are hauled across and secured. Rivers up to 60 m wide are spanned in this fashion. A high scaffold is first mounted as on a high diving board. Swaying violently, the middle of the bridge almost touches the water. Then it's like climbing a mountain up to the other side!

THE NORTHERN DISTRICTS

JAYAPURA

Known as Hollandia during Dutch times, this city was the capital of the Netherlands New Guinea—at that time a small, attractive town in an amphitheater-like setting with red-tiled roofs, inhabited by 8,000 Dutch civil servants. The Dutch were here to stay: they put in permanent hardtop roads, expensive dock facilities, and sturdy public buildings. The town has changed its name many times. When Irian Jaya fell into the hands of the Indonesian Republic it became Sukarnopurna, then Kota Baru, and when the territory was finally "liberated" in the 1960s, it was renamed Jayapura, (means "City of Victory"). Located on the NE coast of Irian Jaya, this provincial capital has a brilliant blue picture-postcard harbor surrounded by perpetually green hills. Access roads to the city are hewn from steep rock walls and lights of ships shine up from the harbor at night. Most houses are built on the slopes, while the administrative portion lies in a flat area between them. This portion has all the worst features of a modern Indonesian city—noisy, dirty streets, too much traffic at night, garish blaring tape cassette shops.

Inhabited by gentle Melanesians, immigrant laborers from other islands, and Indonesian bureaucrats (mostly Javanese), here is where SE Asia and the Pacific meet. On Jayapura's streets you'll see tribesmen, vendors with Javanese-style *pikulan*, Minang merchants, expatriate oil men, Bugis fishermen, sailors from Makassar, and a trickle of travelers. The town is dead from 1200-1600 when most shops and offices close. In the evenings there are about 4 main streets pulsating with life. Prices for food, accommodations, and transport are relatively high and it's difficult to bargain.

Accommodations

All the following rates are quoted without tax, which may add 10-20%. The price of the room may include meals so try to bargain a room rate without meals and eat in the *pasar*. Cheap hotels (Wisma Asia and Losmen Hamadi) are also found in Hamadi just over the hill (see Hamadi section below), or at Sentani 32 km inland. In Jayapura, **Losmen Jayapura**, Jl. Olah Raga 4 (tel. 21216), asks Rp7000 for upstairs rooms (no fan) or downstairs rooms for Rp8000 (wall fan). All right for one night (quieter than Losmen Irian Indah). **Losmen Irian Indah**, Jl. A. Yani (upstairs over some shops), wants at first Rp10,000 s or d for front rooms (with one continuous balcony) but can sometimes be talked into Rp8000. If you don't mind noise, this hotel is ideal for crashing for one night because it's right up from the police headquarters where you get your obligatory *surat jalan* for Wamena. **Losmen Sederhana**, Jl. Halmahera 2 (tel. 21291/22157), Rp11,000 s or for a/c rooms upstairs Rp13,000 s, is located in a lively area opposite the night market, yet quiet at night.

A small, cheap, clean, friendly hotel on the main road just down the street from the big new Bank Indonesia is **Mess GKI**. Jl. Sam Ratulangi (tel. 503); Rp12,000 without meals, Rp16,200 with meals (good food). Although they have no cheaper rooms, the garden environment, ping pong table, and central location recommend it. The supposedly top-drawer downtown Hotels Triton and **Dafonsoro** (Jl. Percetakan, tel. 21870/22285) are in the Rp20,000-Rp35,000 range and real holes for the amount you're asked to pay for their mediocre rooms. **Hotel Triton**, Jl. Jen. A. Yani 52 (P.O. Box 33, tel. 21218/21171), offers free pick-up and drop-off at the airport. Spare and smelly economy rooms go for Rp17,500 plus 20% tax, which includes breakfast (egg, bread, coffee).

Food

Basic Indonesian dishes are available, though they're expensive because most foodstuffs are imported from Java and Sulawesi. Stick to the street *warung*, which don't charge that much (Rp1500 and up). In front of the Pelni office, around the *mesjid*, and next to the *kantor pos* are all congregation points for *warung*: soups run Rp400; *lontong* (spring rolls with beansprout filling), Rp100; *sate*; small prawn tortillas, Rp100; tasty *gado-gado*, Rp600. Several excellent *mie goreng* (Rp1500) tents are on Jl. Percetakan. The **Pasar Malam** (open 1700-2300), 2 blocks behind the Ekspor-Impor Bank and near the *bemo* terminal, has many eating tents with delicious charcoal-grilled fish *(ikan bakar)* and vegetables for Rp2500—about the best deal in town (6 stalls in front of **Losmen Sederhana**). There are also half a dozen restaurants serving European, Indonesian, and Chinese food. Recommended are the **Cahaya**, Jl. A. Yani, and the restaurants along Jl. Percetakan such as the **Sayang** and the **Flamboyan**, where full meals run Rp4000-5000.

Shopping

There are 3 markets in Jayapura, a main market in Hamadi, and another in Abepura where you can buy anything from a motorbike to tailored trousers. Called

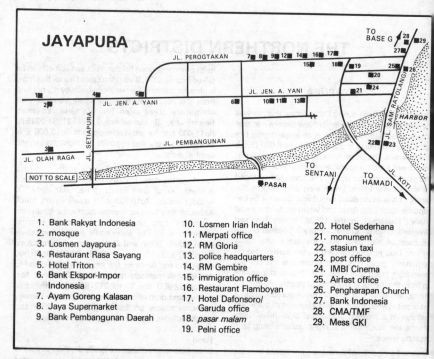

JAYAPURA

1. Bank Rakyat Indonesia
2. mosque
3. Losmen Jayapura
4. Restaurant Rasa Sayang
5. Hotel Triton
6. Bank Ekspor-Impor Indonesia
7. Ayam Goreng Kalasan
8. Jaya Supermarket
9. Bank Pembangunan Daerah
10. Losmen Irian Indah
11. Merpati office
12. RM Gloria
13. police headquarters
14. RM Gembire
15. immigration office
16. Restaurant Flamboyan
17. Hotel Dafonsoro/ Garuda office
18. *pasar malam*
19. Pelni office
20. Hotel Sederhana
21. monument
22. stasiun taxi
23. post office
24. IMBI Cinema
25. Airfast office
26. Pengharapan Church
27. Bank Indonesia
28. CMA/TMF
29. Mess GKI

here supermarkets, Jayapura's department stores—Yohan, Maju Makmur, Bintang Mas, Jayapura, etc.—are crammed with consumer goods and shoppers. Jalan Jen. A. Yani, the city's main shopping street, brings out thousands of people at night. At the airport, crafts and souvenirs are sold at the CAMA shop and at the *kantin*. **Lake Sentani** natives carve intricate panels with raised surfaces painted black and white. **Teluk Yos Sudarso** is well known for its bark paintings of fish and monitor lizards, and woodcarving in the round showing kneeling and standing figures.

Services

The **tourist office** (Dinas Pariwisata) is in the Kantor Gubernor on Jl. Soasiu, Dok II Bawa. Change money at the **Ekspor-Impor Bank**, Jl. Jen. A. Yani. Hotel Dafonsoro on Jl. Percetakan might also change US and Australian travelers cheques but at a bad rate. Get *lots* of small bills if heading into the interior. You can also change *kina* to *rupiah* at MAF just outside the airport at Sentani; you'll see their offices on the left. Departure tax from PNG is 10 *kina*. **Imigrasi** is centrally located on Jl. Percetakan; open Mon.-Thurs. 0730-1430; Fri. 0730-1100; Sat. 0730-1300. Close to the Merpati office on Jl. A. Yani is the main **police station**, where you get your permit to visit points in the interior such as Illaga, Oksibil, Enarotali, and Wamena in the Baliem Valley. (Take note that permits to the first 3 places are not issued at Wamena.) See T. Prayitno in Room 30 (open at 0800), who might ask you a number of irrelevant questions like what is your religion. You'll need to fill out a number of forms, hand over 4 passport photos and Rp1000. In the photo shops in town have your 5 *kilat* ("lightning") passport photos made for Rp6000.

Getting There

Even though there are flights between PNG and Jayapura, you can only officially enter Irian Jaya from PNG if you have a 60-day tourist pass, obtainable in Port Moresby. Check with the Indonesian Embassy in Port Moresby for the latest regulations as they seem to change all the time. The latest is that upon arrival at Sentani (Irian Jaya), you're issued a 45-day "transit pass" which they claim is extendable anywhere but actually is not. You can also change money at the Westpac Bank in Wewak, although Jayapura banks give better rates.

Garuda flies to Jayapura from: Biak, Rp61,800; Jakarta, Rp352,800; Manado, Rp194,100; Merauke,

Rp91,500; Sorong, Rp132,100; Surabaya, Rp347,500; Timika, Rp111,100. **Merpati** flies to Jayapura from: Jakarta, Rp260,800, once weekly; Biak, Rp45,600, 10 times weekly; Ambon, Rp120,700, 3 times weekly; Sorong, Rp114,900, once weekly; Ujung Pandang Rp198,300, 3 times weekly. Or take the Pelni ship KM *Umsini* from Tg. Priok to Jayapura every 7 days, stopping at ports in Sulawesi and Maluku along the way, from Rp39,900 Economy up to Rp226,500 1st Class.

No Customs check when coming into the airport at Sentani, from where it's a 32-km (one-hour) drive along the western shore of Lake Sentani to Jayapura. Taxis want Rp10,000 into town, but just walk ½ km from the terminal to the main road where you can catch a minibus for around Rp1000. The MAF office is in the hangar near the airport terminal; open all week 0530-1200 and 1400-1600. They can change small amounts of *kina* if you're arriving from PNG. You must go into Jayapura for airline offices, a *surat jalan*, *imigrasi*, and cheaper store food.

Getting Around

Jayapura's central business district is small enough to walk anywhere. Take minibuses or *bemo* around town and beyond (Rp200-750) from the terminal near the Ekspor-Impor Bank on Jl. Jen. A. Yani; minibuses also run up and down Jl. Jen. A. Yani looking for fares. Sample fares from Jayapura: Hamadi, Rp250; Abepura, Rp400; up to the N end of town (Dok IX and Base G), Rp500; Sentani Airport, Rp1000 (or Rp10,000, one hour, by taxi). Taxi fares around town average Rp1000, but expect to be ripped off from time to time.

FROM JAYAPURA

By Ship

Pelni and other lines sail to Ujung Pandang, Jakarta (Rp93,900 Economy), or Surabaya (Rp89,500 Economy) every 7-10 days. By ship is a relaxed way to experience Outer Island Indonesia. It takes a slow-moving 4-5 days to Ujung Pandang and another 1-2 days to Surabaya. There are calls en route at Sorong, Ternate, and Bitung. You usually spend 1-2 days at sea, then have 1-2 days to walk around port or go swimming. But you have to hang out near the ship as departure times are often changed. Inquire at the Pelni office on the waterfront in downtown Jayapura (Jl. Halmahera 1, tel. 21270), or at the *syahbandar's* office (tel. 21923) on Jl. Koti.

By Air

Garuda flies from Jayapura to: Biak, Rp61,800; Sorong, Rp132,100; Ambon, Rp163,300; Ujung Pandang, Rp255,000; Jakarta, Rp352,800; Denpasar, Rp311,700; Merauke, Rp91,500; Manado, Rp194,100. Be sure to book in advance at the Garuda office and be

at the airport 1 ½ hours before flight time as flights are heavily booked and lines are long. Merpati flies to: Wamena, Rp31,300, 10 times weekly; Biak, Rp45,600, 10 times weekly; Manokwari, Rp83,800, 5 times weekly; Sorong, Rp97,700, on Fri.; Merauke, Rp79,600, on Mon.; Serui, Rp78,800, 3 times weekly; Nabire, Rp64,300, on Mon. and Wed.; Oksibil, Rp49,300, on Wed.; Karubaga, Rp51,100, on Sat.; Tanah Merah, Rp30,000, on Mon.; Timika, Rp82,100, on Thursdays. Air Niugini (PNG's national carrier) has flights every Wed. to Vanimo and on to Wewak and Port Moresby. There are reports of getting a 10% discount if you go out to Sentani Airport and wait for the Jayapura-Vanimo (PNG) flight on a standby basis (also inquire about student discounts).

Airline Offices

Merpati, Jl. Jen. A. Yani 15 (tel.21327/21810/21913/21111); open Mon.-Thurs. 0700-1400, Fri. 0700-1100, Sat. 0700-1400, Sun. and holidays 1000-1200. Garuda's office is in Hotel Dafonsoro, Jl. Percetakan 20 (tel. 21220); open Mon.-Fri. 0800-1230 and 1330-1600, Sat. 0800-1300, Sun. closed.

Heading For PNG

If you're on a 60-day Indonesian tourist pass and traveling to PNG, you cannot officially leave Irian Jaya through Jayapura even though there are flights to PNG. However, you can from Biak. Sometimes this regulation is very tight, sometimes loose. In addition, no one tells you before check-in that you have to have a valid cholera vaccination—not older than 6 months, not younger than one week—before flying to PNG. Get the shots (2 within 8 days) in Jayapura at *immunasi* next to the police station. If you show up at the airport without an International Health Certificate, they'll give you a note to take to *imigrasi* stating that you could not board the plane. *Imigrasi* will give you a one-week extension (Rp5000 stamp fee).

VICINITY OF JAYAPURA

Go to the end of the bus line to **Ankasa** (Rp300) and get off and walk around; good views of the city. Buses leave every hour until noon, then no buses until 1600. Also visit the *transmigrasi* settlement, **Genyem**, at Nimboran S of the city. Share the charter of a minibus up to **Pemancar Stasiun TVRI**, a steep 2-km climb from the highway to the top of a mountain between Jayapura and Hamadi. This TV relay station affords magnificent views over Jayapura and its harbor.

Bestiji (Base G)

From the terminal at the harbor end of Jl. Percetakan, take a minibus (Rp300) to Bestiji, an Indonesianization of the name of the wartime American military "Base

G." After a successful amphibious assault in April 1944, General Douglas MacArthur established his Pacific HQ here on a hill overlooking the beautiful harbor. You can still see his old command post. The huts are now used for a fish farming enterprise. The site can be visited with permission from the military. From Bestiji, walk 10 min. to a poor, partially deserted beach.

Hamadi

A satellite town over the hills about 5 km to the E of Jayapura; catch a minibus (Rp300, 15 min.) near Jayapura's Ekspor-Impor Bank. A war memorial in Hamadi marks the spot where Allied forces landed on 22 April 1944. See rusting wartime amphibious landing craft and a Sherman tank down a nearby beach. Visit the fish market. Hire a hollowed-out tree trunk *prahu* with an outboard motor from Hamadi's market over to the beach at Holteken, then follow the marshy path which leads up the hill behind the houses built for the New Zealand logging firm. In Hamadi, stay at **Losmen Hamadi Jaya**, the cheapest at Rp6500 s, Rp8000 d; breakfast and free tea is included in the price but it could be noisy. Right next door is a studio where you can have 5 photos made for your *surat jalan* (Rp1500, takes one day). Close to Pasar Sentral is **Wisma Asia**, Jl. Perikanan 18 (tel. 22277); Rp8500 s, Rp13,000 d. Adequately clean, quiet, fan, towel, sitting area, reasonably priced (although you can now find rooms in Jayapura even cheaper).

Cendrawasih University

Some of the most accomplished pieces of recent Irianese art can be seen at the anthropological museum on the university grounds. It's in Abepura on the way into the city from Sentani Airport, or from Jayapura take a minibus 6 km to Abepura, Rp500. The museum, called **Gedung Pengabidian**, also exhibits artifacts like a fantastic alligator skin drum from Fak Fak, Lake Sentani sculpture and pottery, plus garments, spears, masks, baskets, boats, etc. from other Irianese tribes. John D. Rockefeller donated a large part of the exhibit. Captions and the museum's catalog are all in Indonesian. Open 0800-1200 every day except Sun., it's right next to the administration building. At the university is also a 45,000-volume library (Perpustakaan Wilayah), 3 km toward Jayapura from the museum. Also in Abepura is the **cemetery of national heroes** where Indonesian casualties of the militarily disastrous (but politically successful) Irian campaign of the early '60s are buried. South of Abepura is **Proyek Batik Khas Irian Jaya**, 2 km off the main highway, where Irianese-style *batik* is produced.

Sentani

A small town lying on a plain W of Jayapura. From Jayapura, you have to change minibuses 2 or even 3 times and spend a total of Rp1500 and 1½ hours (45

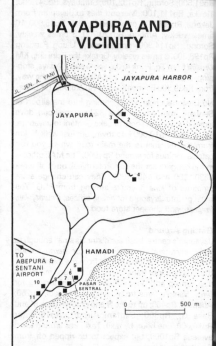

JAYAPURA AND VICINITY

1. Stasiun Taxi (minibus terminal)
2. harbor entrance
3. *Warung*/Restaurant & Garuda Agent
4. *pemancar stasiun TURI*
5. Wisma Asia
6. mosque
7. monument to Allied landing
8. landing vehicles
9. church
10. *pasphoto* (*surat jalan* photos)
11. Losmen Hamadi Jaya

km) out to this town. Having the feel of a small village, Sentani is a more agreeable place to spend the night than Jayapura, and many travelers stay here their first night in Irian Jaya, then take a minibus into Jayapura the next morning to get their *surat jalan* for the interior. Taxis run from 0500-2200 (Rp1200); take a taxi to Abepura (Rp600, to see the museum and the *batik* factory), then another taxi into Jayapura's Stasiun Taxi (Rp600). Return to Sentani that evening with your *surat jalan* and fly out to Wamena the following

...ay. You can even get your *pas photo* done in Sen-
ani, next to RM Virgo.

Pleasant **Losmen Mensapur Rani**, Jl. Yabaso Sen-
ani (200 m from the airport), charges Rp7000 per
night. The police paperwork at this *losmen* is massive
(3 forms), taking 10 min. to fill out. Cool water to drink
all the time. See the lazy street life go by outside. Mr.
Bernard, the owner, is a real character. Mediocre
breakfast costs Rp1000. **Losmen Minang Jaya**, 500
m from the airport, is not worth the Rp10,000 they
charge. Eat at **RM Virgo**, right on the Sentani-
Jayapura highway after the bridge on the left. Full
menu with ice juices; average meal is Rp2000. Even
the Catholic missionaries eat here. Across the street
are 2 Javanese restaurants, **Lili** and **Sari**, serving *nasi
gudeg* and *gado-gado* (Rp700).

Lake Sentani

Located on the other side of the airstrip, the water's
edge only 1½ km from Losmen Mensapur Rani. The
shores of this lake—the home of around 15,000
shoredwellers—are very picturesque, especially from
the air. The lake sprawls in all directions, with sleepy
rows of stilted houses lining the bottom of the hills
where they meet the water. See fishtraps set below
the water for seawater fish which enter the lake. It is
the women's job to retrieve the catches. Lake Sentani
is also known for its pottery, a craft not found in abundance in Irian Jaya. To tour the lake, see Mr. Bernard
of Losmen Mensapur Rani. Motorized *prahu* rent for
Rp20,000-25,000 per hour; unmotorized canoes for
only Rp5000 per hour. The nearest picturesque village is **Netar**, just 2½ km from the airstrip. Visit the
strange group of stones at **Doyo**; U.S. soldiers van-
dalized this site during WW II. The largest stone is
only ½ m high, but check out the engravings on nearby boulders—figures with jutting chins and small
noses. At **Abar** village see craftsmen who carve tree
bark and make clay pottery. Tribal chiefs' houses
have human, crocodile, fish, bird, and snake carvings
on them.

BIAK

Hot and bright, like glittering sequins, another name
for Biak (pop. 80,000) is *Kota Karang* (Town of Coral).
Just one degree S of the equator on an island of the
same name 200 km from Irian Jaya's N coast, Biak is a
travelers' way station and the easternmost international gateway to Indonesia. On the Garuda flight
from Los Angeles to Jakarta (US$1000), some trav-
elers get off at Biak (US$800) in order to start their
tour of Indonesia, working their way W through Maluku and Sulawesi to the Greater Sundas. The city also
serves as a big Indonesian naval base, a supply center
for offshore oil rigs in the Sorenarwa Straits and Irian
Bay, and it's also a major port for Irian Jaya's tuna in-

dustry. One of the stepping stones from then-Dutch
New Guinea to the Philippines, Biak played an important role in General MacArthur's island-hopping campaign through the southwest Pacific area.

Biak today is a typical middle-sized Outer Island town
with cinemas, restaurants, and Chinese supermarkets. The post office you pass on the road (Jl. M.
Yamin) in from the airport. The police station, where
you get a *surat jalan*, is on Jl. Selat Makassar. On the
corner of Jl. Iman Bonjol and Jl. A. Yani is the new
Bank Ekspor-Impor (open Mon.-Fri. 0800-1400, Sat.
0800-100, Sun. closed) which cashes travelers
cheques. Biak is a bird-smuggling center and you can
see all manner of exotic birds at Pasar Panir, including
"protected" bird of paradise skins from Serui on the
island of Japen; also for sale are live lorikeets and
ravens from other New Guinea islands. Biak woodcarvings are sold at the airport terminal shop and at
workshops that have sprung up in the village of
Swapodibo.

War Relics

Exploiting the successes of the Hollandia campaign,
on 27 May 1944 the Hurricane Task Force of the U.S.
Sixth Army landed at Bosnik on Biak Island. The
Japanese defense was based on the brilliant use of
the unfriendly terrain. Facing little initial opposition,
the Japanese purposely withheld their main forces
until U.S. troops had advanced to the rugged limestone hills beyond the beaches. Then, from the cliffs
and caves overlooking the advancing Allied columns,
the Japanese launched a savage counterattack and,
aided by 5-ton tanks, succeeded in driving a block
between the beachhead and the invading force. After
a week of bitter, heavy fighting, the Japanese
retreated to a network of enormous interlocking
caves known in American military annals as The
Sump. During the night the Japanese left their cave
positions to make harassing attacks while by day mortars fired on the newly captured airdromes. The
Americans finally poured aviation gas and TNT down
the long tunnel, incinerating thousands of Japanese
soldiers alive. The cave system is now a tourist attraction, with a long flight of steps leading down into it.
Once a year, Japanese come to pay homage at the
cave entrance to the 6,000 who died. To see both
Bosnik and The Sump, charter a taxi at the airport for
Rp5000 per hour (for 2 hours). Or you can reach the
caves by walking up a path from the far side of the airport. More war relics still lie all over the beaches and
highlands of Biak. Rusted hulls of trucks, jeeps, tanks,
and planes remain where they were abandoned, covered now by flowering creepers. A line of tanks,
covered with shells and coral, has been pressed into
service as a pier. Bunkers on cliffs face the beaches of
the Mokmer Airdrome, and a nearby Quonset hut
houses a large family.

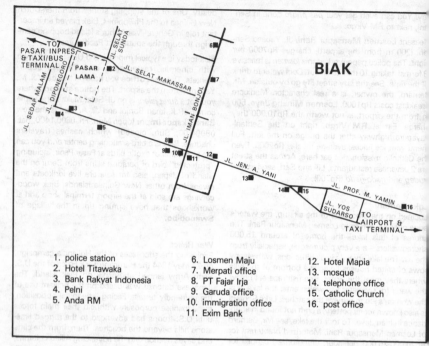

BIAK

TO PASAR INPRES & TAXI/BUS TERMINAL

TO AIRPORT & TAXI TERMINAL →

1. police station
2. Hotel Titawaka
3. Bank Rakyat Indonesia
4. Pelni
5. Anda RM
6. Losmen Maju
7. Merpati office
8. PT Fajar Irja
9. Garuda office
10. immigration office
11. Exim Bank
12. Hotel Mapia
13. mosque
14. telephone office
15. Catholic Church
16. post office

Accommodations And Food

The cheapest is **Losmen Maju**, Jl. Iman Bonjol (tel. 21218), at Rp6000 s, Rp12,000 d (no meals) with *kipas angin* and attached *mandi*. Laid-back **Hotel Mapia**, Jl. Jen. A. Yani (tel. 21383/23961), charges Rp14,500 for rooms with meals; economy rooms are Rp8500 with meals. One of Indonesia's handsomest hotels and a great set for a B-grade American movie is **Hotel Irian** (tel. 21839/21139), just opposite the airport and only a 20-min. walk into town. Built of solid teakwood by KLM in 1952, this single-story hotel has a 30-x-20-m dining room, all original fittings and furnishings, a seaside garden, and 80 rooms (most with verandas), all within earshot of the thundering surf. Rooms with fan and *mandi* cost Rp18,000 d without food and Rp25,000 with, a/c rooms are Rp30,000 with food. With few guests and marginal service, its purpose seems to be to supply passing Merpati planes with food. Other higher-priced accommodations include the **Titawaka**, Jl. Wolter Monginsidi (tel. 21885/21835); Rp27,000 s, Rp32,000 d with a/c and all meals. On a small hill facing the sea, their buses will pick you up and drop you off at the airport.

Visit the covered market where you can buy dozens of varieties of fruit (watermelon, taro, durian) as well as *gado-gado*. Eat in the *warung* which open up at night in front of Hotel Mapia. Catering to the town's mixed population, a number of restaurants (**Megaria, Anda,** etc.) serve plentiful seafood and succulent prawns. **Restaurant Kleopatra** on Jl. A. Yani has all the standard Indonesian dishes like *nasi campur* and *gado-gado*.

Getting There

Garuda has one flight daily (at 0500) from Jakarta via Ujung Pandang to Biak's Frans Kaisiepo Airport for Rp318,100. Other Garuda fares to Biak from: Denpasar, Rp249,900; Manado, Rp165,900; Sorong, Rp73,300; Surabaya, Rp285,800; Ujung Pandang, Rp193,200. Merpati also flies from Jakarta direct to Biak via Surabaya and Ujung Pandang for around Rp257,400. Arriving, walk easily from the airport down Jl. Prof. M. Yamin into town or hitch or take a minibus (Rp400) on the public road right outside the airport. Or from the airport 5 km to town by taxi is Rp5500. Biak town is small enough that you can walk anywhere within 5-10 minutes. Catch minibuses from Jl. M. Yamin or from Jl. A. Yani out to the airport.

From Biak

Garuda flies to: Timika, Rp61,800; Ambon, Rp107,600 (one hour, an easy way to get to Maluku) and Manado, p165,900. Consider using Biak as your base rather ¬an Jayapura because Biak is an important air hub for ¬ian Jaya. Merpati Twin Otters fly to and from: ¬orong, Rp62,300; Manokwari, Rp43,900; Serui, ¬p22,200; and Nabire, on the N coast, Rp45,900; Fak ¬ak, Rp137,300; Kaimana, 79,400; and Merauke, on ¬he S coast, Rp144,000. The daily flight to Jayapura, ¬p45,600, is dramatic, with the jungle coming right ¬own to the sea on the R and the endless Micronesian ¬cean to the left. **airline offices:** Garuda: Jl. Jen. A. ¬ani (tel. 21331/21457); open 0700-1200 and 1300-¬600. Merpati: Jl. Iman Bonjol (tel. 21386/21336).

¬iak is an oil base and there is heavy sea traffic to and ¬rom the island. Take note that monsoons begin in ¬ug. and last for 1 ½ -2 months; there are more ships ¬hen the seas are not so rough (Nov.-July). The Pelni ¬ffice is near the harbor entrance on Jl. A. Yani, op-¬osite the bus and taxi terminal. All sea journeys ¬eading W travel via Maluku. Inquire at P.T. Fajar Irja ¬opposite Merpati office) and at the *syahbandar's* at ¬the harbor about crowded coasters to Serui, Manok-¬wari (via P. Numfoor), Fak Fak, Sorong (Rp7500), etc. *Prahu* with outboard motors are also available to such ¬traditional islands as P. Japen to the S of Biak.

Vicinity Of Biak

Rent taxis in town for Rp4000 per hour, outside town Rp5000 for per hour. The upper third of this 72-x-32-km island is mountainous while the remaining third is essentially flat. Biak's economy is mainly based on agriculture, which has helped preserve the virgin beaches and unpolluted waters of the district. From Biak town, take a minibus 26 km to Bosnik (Rp600) on the E coast, the first Dutch capital of Biak. Beautiful beach here, from where you can see the islands of the Owi Group to the southeast. **Korim Beach** is on the N coast, 40 km by taxi from town. Ride on a well-paved road through tropical land-scapes of Melanesian hill villages, tunnels of butter-flies, and tall dead trees with orchids perched on top. Sleep in the house on the beach, or ask the *kepala kampung* for a bed. Also on the N coast, accessible by dirt track, is the **Biak Nature Reserve,** which pro-tects species of cockatoos and parrots. On **P. Sipiori,** 2 hours away by boat, is another sizeable nature reserve. Together with the big islands of Supiori and Numfoor, 43 islands make up Cendrawasih (meaning "bird of paradise") District for which Biak is the capital.

CENDRAWASIH DISTRICT

The NE peninsula of West New Guinea was known as *Vogelkop* ("Bird's Head") in Dutch times. The in-habitants of this coastal district are a striking mixture of Irianese, Buginese, Filipino, and Chinese. There has also been much contact with the people of Maluku, the native languages here have a connection with those of N. and S. Halmahera. Along Cendrawasih's coasts are many picturesque small towns with fishing and sawmill operations. Though remote from main sea lanes, this region has many natural harbors. His-torically, the wiry little mountain men of the Arfak Mountains—the Moiray, Hattam, and Meach clans—were the most notorious headhunters of western New Guinea. Ancestors' skulls were often worn as charms or kept in an honored part of the house. Dur-ing WW II, these tribes fought the Japanese (and ate them) with rifles dropped from Allied planes. Some tribes living deep in the interior still shun all contact with outsiders, refusing to move down to the War-mare settlement.

Manokwari

At Dore, near present-day Manokwari, the English built a fort in 1790, but so many died of beriberi and starvation that they pulled out by 1795. Caves (actual-ly just passages) excavated by the Japanese during WW II are all over town. Though only covering a small area, the land in this district is very rich and supports a population of around 85,000. Mountains come right

down to the sea. The taxi from the airport is Rp3000. Stay at the **PKN,** Rp30,000 pp. **Hotel Arfak,** Jl. Brawijaya, is Rp20,000 pp. **Universitas Cendrawa-sih,** specializing in agriculture and forestry, is at **Am-ban,** 3 km S of Manokwari's harbor. Lovely beaches **(Pasir Putih)** are found on the N side of the Manokwari Peninsula. On the hill (G. Ajamberi) be-tween the beaches and town is a beautiful forest reserve where there are still hornbills and other rare birds. Remains of the area's first mission (1855) is found on **P. Manisam,** about 150 m offshore. Take a 2-day hike up into the **Arfak Mountains** from Maripi, S of Manokwari. From Manokwari there are ferries twice a week to Ransiki (Rp5000) and weekly to Wasior (Rp7000); they leave from the wharf near the market and minibus terminal. From the large cacao plantation at Ransiki you can hike up to the **Anggi Lakes** in 3 days. Missionaries work among the natives of this area.

Sorong

A big Pertamina oil and timber base with a population of around 45,000. This high-priced capital of Sorong District lies at the very western tip of the Bird's Head. The oilfield at Sorong was first drilled in 1932. There's a beautiful seaside in front of Sorong, but not much else to see or do except drink Johnny Walker and bed down with Manado hostesses from the several night-clubs around Hotel Cendrawasih. Stay at **Batanta,** Jl.

Barito 1 (tel. 21569); Cendrawasih, Jl. Sam Ratulangi 28 (tel. 21966); or at the Mamberamo, Jl. Sam Ratulangi (tel. 21564)—all in the Rp14,000-21,000 range. For alternate accommodations, contact Daniel Loupatty in Kampung Baru (tel. 140). Head over to Doom Island (Rp300 from dock), a nice place to visit for a few hours. There's a trail around it, an hour's walk through villages and a graveyard, with lots of children for company.

About once every 2 weeks Pelni's KM Umsini stops at Sorong on its way from Java to Jayapura; Rp72,600 Economy, Rp173,200 1st Class from Tg. Priok. From Sorong, rent dugouts for Rp5000 per hour for island-exploring. Pulau Salawati, one of the closest, is the home of the 12-wired bird of paradise, an endemic myra, orange lori, and white-crowned koel. A long-boat without floats (2 engines) can be chartered for Salawati, but for islands farther out, larger motorized craft are recommended, especially during the rough seas of the NW monsoons (Nov.-March). On this coast outboard motors are given as part of the dowry, so if you want to start a family bring a Johnson or an Evinrude.

Sorong's Jefman Airport is on a small island 20 km offshore; the regular daily airport ferry is a real rip-off (Rp5000 OW), but there's no other way to get into town. From Sorong there are regular connections to

Biak (on Sun., Rp54,100) and Jayapura (on Fri. Rp97,700). Other Merpati fares, with flights leaving 3 times weekly: Fak Fak, Rp47,700; Teminabuan Rp15,500; Manokwari, Rp62,600. Garuda fares: Denpasar, Rp205,300; Jakarta, Rp255,800; Manado, Rp119,100; Surabaya, Rp241,000; Ujung Pandang, Rp159,300. Merpati/Garuda office: Jl. Jen. A. Yani 81 (tel. 21344).

Kaimana

A small, expensive town on the underside of the Bird's Head Peninsula, capital of the Fak Fak District. In 1828, the Dutch built a fort on Triton Bay (where Utarom Airstrip, near Kaimana, is today) but nearly the whole contingent died of malaria, starvation, beri beri, and native attacks. Stay at the pasanggrahan or in the mission station (Rp3000 per day with food). The mission has maps to point the way for some good walks in the surrounding jungle, though there are few native villages left. Walk all the way to Teluk Bintuni in about 1 week. In the dry season there's a small boat to Kokonau on the S coast, where there's a mission station; from Kokonau get a plane farther to Timika (Rp21,400, on Thurs.). Merpati has flights from Kaimana to: Biak, Rp69,000, on Wed.; Enarotali, Rp56,300, on Mon.; Fak Fak, Rp38,200, 5 days weekly; Nabire, Rp41,300, Mon. and Fri.; and Timika, Rp56,500, on Fridays.

CENTRAL HIGHLANDS

Puncak Jaya

Irian Jaya's highest peak (5,039 m) is also known as Carstensz Toppen, named after the Dutch sea captain who first gazed upon its snowcapped peak in the 17th century. Several neighboring peaks are also over 4,000 m; the best known of these are Carstensz Timor (4,880 m) and Naga Pulu (4,862 m). Rumor has it that 4 climbers reported killed climbing Puncak Jaya in 1987 were actually abducted and executed by the OPM. This explains why it's now almost impossible to obtain permission to climb the peak. Even when climbers arrive from Nabire with a surat jalan, the local police turn them back at Illaga because they don't want to be responsible for them. Then they go up to Jayapura and waste a week trying to get permission there.

If your group does manage to get permission to climb Puncak Jaya, prepare for an expedition in which all your supplies must be brought with you. The usual starting point is Illaga. Merpati flies to the strip at Illaga from Nabire each Wed. at 0755 for Rp23,00; small missionary aircrafts sometimes fly from Jayapura, Wamena, and possibly other towns as well. Carriers can be hired in Illaga for the 4- to 5-day hike to the mountain base camp. Routes to the summit vary

greatly in difficulty. In general the easiest routes are up the southern faces. Expeditions must obtain permission to use Timika Airport near Kokonau, as well as the road up to Tembagapura which belongs to the huge Freeport Mineral Co. copper mine there. The northern face of Puncak Jaya is the most challenging of all the peaks. Climbers need winter gear to protect against sub-freezing temperatures and possible high winds. No technical hardware is needed on the easier routes. May to Nov. is the best (driest) season.

Freeport Copper Mine

The town of Tembagapura is the supply base for the Freeport Copper Mine, 10 km from the mine site (elev. 3,658 m) and mill at G. Bijh (means "Mineral Mountain"). Discovered in 1936 by Dutchman Jean Jacques Dozy, this is one of the world's largest outcrops of base metal, literally a whole mountain of solid copper lying SW of Puncak Jaya in the Paniai Lakes District. In the early 1970s, with the Suharto regime actively wooing foreign investment after the tumultuous Sukarno years, an agreement was reached with Freeport Copper Co. to develop the gigantic project. The mining town of Tembagapura is nicely laid out with modern homes for the expats and

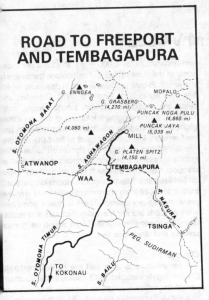

ROAD TO FREEPORT AND TEMBAGAPURA

start of the longest slurry pipeline on earth, as well as the world's longest (762 m) aerial tramway over one of the most inaccessible terrains this side of Antarctica. Tramway cars carrying the rich ore pass through clouds and over ghostly 500-m-high waterfalls, dumping their loads at the mill to return up to the mine in never-ending procession. At the mill the ore is crushed to a fine powder to prepare it for the flotation process which separates the valuable minerals to produce the concentrate to flow in the slurry pipeline. This pipeline runs for 120 km to the port of Amamapare on the Arafura Sea on the S coast of Irian Jaya, where it's dehydrated for the monthly 20,000-ton shipment to Japan.

Paniai Lakes

Glorious scenery. Discovered by a Dutch flier, Wissel, in 1936 while making an aerial survey for an oil company. These enchanted lakes are entirely surrounded by blue mountains. The most spectacular, **Lake Paniai**, is 24 km long by 18 km wide with sloping hills rising from it. There are 2 smaller, olive-green lakes. None contain fish, only freshwater shrimp. No mosquitos here. Women seine at night from log boats, building fires in them to keep warm. A heavy mist comes in low over Paniai's waters in the early morning and from 0900 clouds start to obscure the mountain walls around the lake. The surface is calm until 1100 when a strong wind sweeps across it and breakers crash against the shore. This area is the home of the Moni and the Ekagi tribes. The **Ekagi** (or Kapaukus) are a healthy, muscular, black-skinned pygmy people less than 1½ m tall. One of the first Europeans who visited Paniai described them as "childlike, carefree, undependable, selfish, deceitful, transparent, credulous, superstitious, fairly industrious, timid, but not without racial pride." **Enarotali**, on a high plateau near the lakes, is accessible by air from: Biak, Rp54,900, each Fri.; Manokwari, Rp94,100, each Fri.; and Nabire, Rp18,900, on Mon., Wed., Fri. and Sundays. AMA also operates flights connecting Enarotali with Nabire, Illaga, Kokonau, Timika (near Kokonau), and Agats.

dormitories for the 2,000-plus mineworkers from Biak, Java, the Philippines, Sulawesi, and Irian Jaya. The town sits on a mountainous slope under the vertical face of Mt. Zaagham; after a hard rain, at least 50 waterfalls sprout out of the tropical vegetation and bare rocks of its uppermost slopes. Facilities include schools, tennis courts, clubs, indoor sports complex, football field, latest video movies, commissaries, and bars. Towering over everything is glacier-packed Puncak Jaya, the highest peak between the Himalayas and the Andes.

The all-weather road from Tembagapura is only 10 km long, but you climb 1,066 m in elevation, passing through a 900-m-long tunnel up to the mine site. At the processing mill see the highest refinery and the

THE BALIEM VALLEY

The valley was discovered by a wealthy American explorer during his botanical and zoological expeditions in 1938, who first reported that this 1,600-m-high valley appeared to be inhabited by a lost civilization. When the clouds cleared, the expedition members beheld a vast, beautifully tended garden of checkerboard squares with neat stone fences, clean-cut networks of canals, and meticulously terraced mountain slopes. (Read of this discovery in the March 1941 issue of *National Geographic*.) The Grand Valley of the Baliem received worldwide publicity in 1945 when a sightseeing plane out of wartime Hollandia crashed and its survivors had to be rescued in a daring glider operation. An American nurse in this group called the valley a Shangri-La. The first outsiders to settle here were missionaries landing by float plane on the Baliem River in 1954. The Dutch established a settlement at Wamena in 1956, bringing in schoolteachers, new breeds of livestock, modern clothing, and metal tools. Wamena continued under their control until Indonesia wrested West New Guinea from Holland in 1962.

Although Indonesians took over the valley in 1969, their "Indonesianization" campaign is not yet total. Even in the main town of Wamena about 20% of the men and 33% of the women still wear traditional dress. The villages and gardening systems are still much as they were, although steel tools have replaced the polished wood, stone, bone, or sharpened bamboo implements of only 10 years ago. Children are not, however, taught about their own history, culture, and environment, but are indoctrinated with the pan-Indonesian national mentality. The valley has magnificent scenery and unlimited tourist potential. However, the increasing number of military personnel is putting a strain on the surviving forests on the valley sides (particularly around Wamena), which are being cut down for timber. Environmental problems are already looming.

The Land

The Grand Valley is 72 km long by 16-32 km wide. It is inhabited by tribes of Neolithic ex-warrior farmers, the Baliem Dani, who number over 100,000. The Baliem River, which has its source in the G. Trikora mountains, runs like a snake through a valley of stony riverbeds, jungled ravines, *kampung* of round houses, plots of green cultivated fields, and stone walls. This river and its tributaries provide water for the Danis' elaborate chessboard-patterned drainage and irrigation systems, which remind one more of New England farmlands than the home of Stone Age man for perhaps 25,000 years. Practicing pig-raising

and horticulture for 5,000 years, the Dani are today some of the most skilled and meticulous gardeners in the world. Excess produce is sold in Jayapura, which has little agricultural land around it. Droughts and pests are uncommon. Sweet potato *(erom)*, cultivated only with digging sticks and grown on raised plots, is their staple crop. Bushes are planted to prevent erosion, leaf mulch is used to heat the soil, and casuarina trees are planted to siphon off some of the loam's excessive moisture. Ditches are also used as compost heaps, so that each new crop can take root on fertilized soil. Steep mountain slopes are terraced, mud is scooped from channels to build more planting areas, forests are cleared. There is now a good network of roads around the valley, but cars and motorbikes are expensive to hire. There are no dangerous animals and disease is rare.

Climate

The temperature is mild and the rainfall moderate (though highly variable). If it's raining in the southern part of the valley, it might be sunny in the north—or vice versa. September through Oct. is the season of high winds, usually rising in the afternoon. It's frequently cloudy except in the early morning when all the surrounding mountains are in clear view.

WAMENA

This settlement, like Katmandu, is surrounded by cloud-wreathed mountain peaks. The plane fare from Jayapura is about Rp37,400 (45 min.) and is money well spent. Wamena is a small town with row upon row of mission offices, schools, and what seems like hundreds of government offices, all sprawling across the flat Baliem Valley floor. Wamena gets about 1,000 tourists per year. As everything—gas, foodstuffs, goats and cows, trucks, building materials, steel girders for bridges, and anything else manufactured—is flown in, prices are some of the highest in Indonesia. You can cut down on your costs if you eat in the market and stay in the nearby villages. The market, bustling with farmers selling their sweet potatoes, bananas, carrots, and other produce, is the town's premier tourist attraction. This is also the place to view Wamena's extraordinary mixture of cultures and customs—craggy Dani tribesmen, tall stately Minangs, Western-attired Javanese, curly-haired Ambonese. For additional entertainment, the military shows movies every night (Rp2000) and you can even bring your own portable TV; there are regular broadcasts!

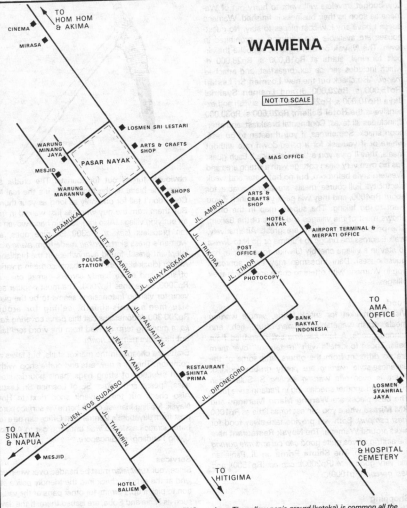

WAMENA

NOT TO SCALE

TO HOM HOM & AKIMA

CINEMA

MIRASA

LOSMEN SRI LESTARI

WARUNG MINANG JAYA

ARTS & CRAFTS SHOP

PASAR NAYAK

MESJID

MAS OFFICE

WARUNG MARANNU

SHOPS

ARTS & CRAFTS SHOP

JL. AMBON

HOTEL NAYAK

JL. PRAMUKA

JL. LET S. DARWIS

JL. TRIKORA

AIRPORT TERMINAL & MERPATI OFFICE

POLICE STATION

JL. BHAYANGKARA

POST OFFICE

JL. TIMOR

PHOTOCOPY

JL. PANJAITAN

BANK RAKYAT INDONESIA

TO AMA OFFICE

JL. JEN. A. YANI

RESTAURANT SHINTA PRIMA

JL. JEN YOS SUDARSO

JL. DIPONEGORO

LOSMEN SYAHRIAL JAYA

JL. THAMRIN

TO SINATMA & NAPUA

MESJID

TO & HOSPITAL CEMETERY

HOTEL BALIEM

TO HITIGIMA

Crafts are less affected by commercialism than in the PNG half of the island. The moment you step off the plane in Wamena, implements will be offered for sale by natives. The string bag (noken) is made from rolled bark fibers, often dyed in red and purple stripes. It is supported by a strap around the forehead. In it, women carry sweet potatos, babies, piglets, and tools—sometimes all at once! When empty, it's worn over the shoulders and down the back to keep the woman warm in the cold even-

ings. The yellow penis ground (koteka) is common all the way from the Sepik River in PNG to Teluk Bintuni S of Manokwari Province. Measuring from 7½ cm up to ½-m-long, it's made from the outer rinds of an elongated pumpkin-like fruit. Men wear no clothing except for their penis sheath, which accentuates their nakedness all the more. Each man has a wardrobe of several shapes and sizes: a very short koteka is used when he goes boar hunting, an elongated one serves for festive times, etc.

Accommodations

Low-budget travelers will want to hurry out of Wamena as soon as their business is finished. Wamena doesn't have any low-cost places to stay. No guesthouses are available and camping is prohibited in town. The **Nayak** on Jl. Angkasa, opposite the airport terminal, starts at Rp18,000 s, Rp28,000 d, which includes service tax, breakfast, and attached *mandi.* Also check out the new **Losmen Sri Lestari** (Rp15,000 s, Rp20,000 d) and **Losmen Syahrial Jaya** (Rp10,000 s, Rp20,000 d). More stylish and expensive is the **Hotel Baliem;** Rp20,500 s, Rp30,000 d, includes all taxes, Continental breakfast, and afternoon snack. Sometimes, if you threaten to go elsewhere or if you ask for a pared-down rate without meals, they'll give you a "special price." Each guest has his own very clean cottage with a sitting area and Western-style bathroom, but no hot water and weak electricity. Full-course meals are also available for about Rp4000, and they will pack you a lunch if you want to go hiking. The superb map in the office shows most of the villages and rivers of the Baliem. The people working there are great. Alternatively, walk E across the bridge to Pugima or go N to Jiwika to stay in a village cheaply (Jiwika, for example, has guesthouses). Dani tribesmen may even approach you in Wamena with offers to come and stay in their villages.

Food

Visit the market for snack foods, simple *warung* meals, fresh vegetables, *durian,* fruit, fish, and canned goods. A few *kakilima* sell deep-fried flour balls. Those foodstalls with "restaurant" over them are no different than the others, and some of the Javanese-style *warung* are pretty grubby looking. There is even one *warung* serving S. Sulawesian cuisine and another specializing in Padang-style food. The best places are **Warung Mario Marannu** and **RM Mirasa** where you can eat for as little as Rp1000 *(nasi campur).* Both will provide take-away food for hikes around Wamena. The **Nayak Restaurant** near the airstrip serves quite good *cap cai* and *mie goreng* but not cheap. The **Shinta Prima** on Jl. Panjaitan has very good *sate* (Rp2000), *cap cai* (Rp1500), and *nasi goreng* (Rp1000).

Shopping

The local market, Pasar Nayak, is an unbelievable hodgepodge of foreign and domestic goods. Stone axes *(kapak)* sell from Rp5000-10,000, the cost depending upon the type of stone used, the size, and the labor involved. The cheaper variety is sold in the market stalls. Ax blades sold now are mostly the common black variety but green stone is the hardest and considered the finest. The Dani have become aware that a lot of money can be had for such things and some specimens look filed or lathed on machines and

Dani kapak

obviously turned out for tourists. The cruder and larger the blade is, the more likely it's the real Mc-Coy—don't fall for one only as long as your thumb! Buy them from the guy who has just walked in from an outlying village. Also look for thin hand-woven rattan bracelets *(sekan),* Rp300 for nice ones, and women's grass skirts *(yokal)* made from *alang-alang* (elephant grass), found everywhere in the highlands. *Noken* (cloak-like bark-string bags) come in a variety of sizes and make handy carriers—small ones are Rp3000, large ones Rp7000. The most popular souvenir for visiting Indonesians seems to be the giant-size men's penis-sheath, selling for around Rp200-300. Indonesians call this penis covering *koteka,* a mocking term derived from the word for "tail," but its native name is *holim.*

Crafts are cheaper in the market stalls, but fakes are common. There's a new arts and crafts shop, with a good selection of string bags, penis gourds, stone axes, spears, and *sekan,* SE of Losmen Sri Lestari. Also check out the souvenir shop next to Hotel Nayak. Mailing Irianese crafts home via surface parcel post from Jayapura's Central Post Office can be a real bureaucratic hassle, so wait until you get to Ambon, Ujung Pandang, or Singapore.

Services

Since your *surat jalan* must be handed over when you land at the airport, check into the friendly police station to pick it up. Permits for other parts of the valley, such as Ninia and Soba, are issued there. If the Jayapura police gave you the Baliem Valley but not more remote central highland areas, apply for those here as the Wamena police are said to be more lenient. The cops frequently ask to hold your passport while you're hiking about. The post office (Jl. Timor) is open Mon.-Thurs. 0800-1200, Fri. 0800-1000, Sat. 0800-1100. Change money at **Bank Rakyat Indonesia** close to the airstrip (open Mon.-Fri. 0800-1300, Sat. 0800-1100). The rate is lower than normal: Rp1555 = US$1 as opposed to Rp1635 = US$1.

n Wamena, you can use Rp5000 and Rp10,000 bills, but when you get just a couple of hours' walk away, they want just the red ones (Rp100). People expect Rp100 per photo so you'll need lots.

Getting There
Obtain your *surat jalan* at Jayapura's police station, then take the Merpati F-27 flight (Rp37,400, 45 min.) out of Jayapura's Sentani Airport, leaving with passengers once daily on a rather flexible schedule. Or fly with Airfast or some other charter group which charges a little more. Mission aircraft are more expensive still but may be your only choice if flying to Wamena from an out-of-the-way place. Because the clouds and mists come over in the afternoon both at take-off and at landing, the morning flight could be crowded. There are 2 other flights to Wamena from Sentani, but they only take cargo. Sometimes the only 2 passes into the Baliem accessible to non-pressurized aircraft are closed. Be prepared: this is a fantastic flight. A siren chases all people and animals off Wamena's runway when a plane is about to land! The only transport from the airport to town is your feet. No problem because one hotel is quite near the airstrip, while the other is only a 20-min. walk. Strapping Dani boys will stride off to your hotel with your luggage, with you trotting behind trying to keep up!

From Wamena
The Merpati flight to Jayapura (Rp37,400) leaves at 0830 and arrives in time to connect with onward flights to Ujung Pandang and Surabaya. Buy tickets 2 hours before departure at their office (open Mon.-Fri. 0530-1700, closed Sat. and Sun.) adjacent to the airport terminal. Other sample fares from Wamena: Bokondini, Rp18,500; Ewer, Rp21,500; Merauke, Rp60,500. Also inquire at the MAF and AMA air service offices at the airport for flights out. Using only small Cessnas, these missionary airlines usually offer only air service within the highlands. A week's notice is preferred so that you can be worked into their schedule, otherwise there could be a long wait (pilots are always in short supply). MAF even has a helicopter for really remote places.

The first roads of the Baliem were put in to provide not only lanes of transport but also to serve as neutral territory between warring tribes. By using just the roads, sticking to the exact center, the tribesmen could then walk safely to and from Wamena. Now the government intends to build a road from the Baliem all the way N to Jayapura on the coast. The first leg has already reached slightly beyond Jiwika, but given the high mountain ranges that block the way, it will probably take 20 years to complete. It took the survey party almost a month to complete the journey on foot! Now minibuses run between Wamena and Jiwika.

Hiking From Wamena
Walking on the numerous and generally well-maintained dirt footpaths and hard-gravel roads of this valley is an invigorating and unforgettable experience, and almost the only way to go. It is difficult to find vehicles or even motorbikes to charter, and if you do the cost is just too high. But many people in Wamena do have motorbikes and you may be able to come to some agreement; numerous tracks such as from Wamena to Hom Hom and to Musatfak can easily be handled by a motorcycle. The climate is ideal for walking, though rains can turn the trails slippery. The people are friendly and welcoming everywhere, approaching you on the paths and offering a handshake. Women are generally too weighed down under loads of sweet potatoes, piglets, or babies and tend to walk past you with averted eyes. Greet men with *"Narak!"* followed by a handshake; to women, shout *"La'uk!."*

In most villages you could stay the night in simple huts, or perhaps with the village teacher or pastor (expect to donate about Rp3000 per night). In the bigger villages, it is possible to sleep on the floor of the schoolhouse or church, or sometimes with missionaries. When staying in village huts, determine first if there's a charge. You could be presented in the morning with an itemized bill for Rp5000, just for a few potatoes and sleeping in a *honnay*. The Danis may be naked but they are not stupid. Most of the missionaries of the Baliem are happy to help travelers, including offering accommodations and meals either free or at low cost. However, some travelers have marred the reception for those who follow by taking help for granted, disregarding private property, and helping themselves to missionaries' supplies. Don't blow it for the rest of us.

Indonesian is now widely known and many younger Danis can read and write. Bring good footwear, hat, sunglasses, mosquito repellent, lip balm, wind and rain gear, and light clothing but also a warm sweater for highland evenings. If camping, bring a sleeping bag and mosquito-proof tent in this high, cleared, rainy, and heavily irrigated valley. Unfortunately, there are no places to hire camping gear in Wamena, so you have to stick close to civilization for accommodations. For info on serious hiking, see "Getting Around" in the introduction to Irian Jaya.

Guides And Porters
The Baliem Hotel can help with charters, guides, and porters for the longer walks. A good man to speak to about hiking in the area is Justinius Daby, a security officer who will probably meet you at the airport. Justinius asks Rp25,000 per day; a porter costs another Rp5000 per day. He speaks pretty good English, knows the area well, and can arrange trips to anywhere. Specializing in the Baliem and the Asmat

area, he has relatives on the S coast and takes small groups to Asmat villages once a year. If he's already booked, he can direct you to another English- or Indonesian-speaking guide at probably less (Rp5000 per day for two?). Having someone along to translate between Indonesian and the local language makes for a far more rewarding trip.

THE BALIEM DANI

Like *Dayak* of Kalimantan, *Dani* is a generic term applied to all of the tribes of the Baliem Valley, deep in the highlands of western New Guinea. The exact origin of the tribes is not known. All have Negroid features and dark brown skin, but each tribe's language, customs, and even physical appearance can be quite distinct. The Dani peoples practice a high degree of social organization and an extraordinarily sophisticated form of agriculture, and an advanced engineering skill in constructing rattan bridges and dwellings. They have a complicated system of trading and bartering, importing bird of paradise feathers, *scere*-bird plumes, cowrie shells, and the finest spearwood from distant villages. The Danis spend most of their lives working their fields—cleaning, draining, pruning vines, weeding beds, and scooping up the rich, dark soil to enrich their gardens—so their strength is phenomenal. Watch one run through the forest barefoot or walk 20 km with a man on his shoulders. Seven Javanese can't hold a Dani down on the ground. Yet the Danis have the gentlest handshake you'll ever experience, and appear fearless—their most striking characteristic.

Clothing, Body Ornament
The loincloths of other tribes and clothing of white men are repugnant and rude to the rural Dani. Except for the rolled grass or reed skirts for the women and tube-like yellow gourds over the genitals of the men, no clothing is worn. Apart from the ringbeards and beehive-hairdos, Dani men find hair on the rest of the body repulsive and untidy, so they diligently remove it from the arms, legs, chest, back, and all other parts of the body with tweezers made of twigs of the araucaria. Body decorations worn every day are hairnets, cowrie shell necklaces, and armbands of pigs' scrotums which they believe ward off ghosts. Dani men also put ballpoint pens, drinking straws, boar tusks, or pieces of tin cans through their noses, and insert anything from cigarettes to diaper pins into their pierced earlobes. Danis don't believe in washing but smear their bodies with a soot and earth mixture, a thick layer of rancid pig fat, or red or white clay to keep themselves warm in the often cold climate. In the chilly mornings, Dani men stand with their arms wrapped around their necks to keep themselves warm. For festive occasions (and formerly during bat-

tles), men are elaborately adorned—headdresses of cassowary whisks, white egret feathers, anklets of parrot feathers; all make them appear ready to take flight! Penis sheaths *(holim)* are made from gourds of various sizes cultivated for that purpose. Some villagers in the N of the valley wear brightly colored bands of cloth on their penis gourd; these men have much thicker gourds, the size of a piece of large bamboo. Money is carried in the gourd when they come to market.

Crafts
Tourism preserves and develops Dani crafts and also serves to introduce a cash economy to the people. Dani are enthusiastic craftsmen, designers of tools and dwellings; they also use shells, feathers, and other organic articles for self-adornment and for sale. Men in this society are the creators, women are the producers. Powerful warriors who hunt wild boar with spears can sit for hours making delicate skirts or orchid-fiber necklaces for their wives. Men make arrows, spears, axes, shields, paddles, canoes, and use bone awls and needles for weaving. Spider webs are harvested in the forest and hung around the throat in unique, woven patterns. Men also produce the ancestor sculptures, musical instruments, and sacred ritual objects of veneration which are kept in the men's ceremonial house, often referred to as the center of the cosmos.

Economy
Traditionally, most of the fieldwork was done by the women, leaving the men free to guard them and go on periodic raiding parties. But since these have been prohibited by the government, the men now work the fields. A Dani man's status is reckoned by how many pigs and wives he owns. Pigs and shells are still media of exchange and circulate freely at weddings, funerals, and feasts; salt and pigs are still traded for the forest products of other tribes. Magnificent gardeners, plots are skillfully irrigated and drained by an intricate network of ditches. With their fertile and self-sufficient gardens and herds of fat pigs, the Dani are potentially a prosperous people. Only sugar and bananas are native to the region; all other produce—taro, sago, cabbage, sweet potatoes, coconuts, and yams—were brought in by Papuans relatively recently (5,000 years ago). Since 1954, the missionaries and both the Dutch and Indonesian governments have introduced a variety of vegetables into the fertile valley. Although the Dani grow these vegetables, they rarely eat them themselves but rather sell them to the transmigration populace in the daily Wamena market or export them by air to Jayapura. This is the only way they are able to raise the cash to buy the influx of electronic, plastic, and metal goods. Rambutans, apples, mangos, mangosteens, and *durian* were introduced from E. Java in the early 1970s.

Village Life

Designed originally as mini-fortresses, the Danis live in villages with U-shaped courtyards (not unlike African *kraal*), guarded by a swing door which can be easily defended. A typical settlement is also surrounded by a sturdy fence which keeps the *kampung's* pigs in and the neighbors' pigs out. Straw-thatched, dome-roofed, windowless roundhouses, plus a long-house for the women, are grouped around the open space. Nearby are taro, tobacco, and banana gardens. Gourd vines grow under the roof eaves. Dani buildings are held together with only rattan vines or elephant grass *(logob)*. Roofs may be made of juniper tree bark or pandanus leaves which are interlocked into each other like roof tiles, making the structures water- and windproof. Long tunnel-like passages sometimes connect the structures to avoid moving outdoors on cold nights.

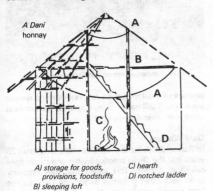

A Dani honnay

A) storage for goods, provisions, foodstuffs
B) sleeping loft
C) hearth
D) notched ladder

A village contains a ritual men's house *(iwool)* which only initiated males may enter. The round grass men's house *(honnay)* is used by all males over age 8 for sleeping naked at night. Divided into a lower level with a firepit and an upstairs sleeping section, the upper story is like a cozy hayloft; coals from the first floor fireplace give even heat throughout the whole structure. What smoke doesn't escape through the bamboo slats keeps down the mosquitos, which are horrendous. A small door, giving the only light, is barred at night with heavy wooden planks. Women, children, and pigs live in the long women's houses *(wew umah)*. Inside, heated rocks are placed around to sit on and the sweet, acrid smell of ashes permeates the air.

Family Life

Men and women lead altogether separate lives and the major divisions of labor follow the lines of age and sex. Men cut wood, construct buildings and fences, shape tools, and clear land for cultivation. Women have a definite market value; previously they were purchased with pigs and cowrie shells, today with pigs and *rupiah*. After the day's work, the men gather to chat, joke, and work in the communal *honnay*, while the women cultivate sweet potato gardens, tend children, or cook in the women's smaller round hut *(ebeai)*. Dani babies aren't weaned until 4-5 years old and during all that time on the breast a man may not sleep with his wife. When asked why this is necessary, the Danis reply that the ghosts demand it. Polygamy, practiced only by those who are well off such as chiefs, witch doctors, or teachers, is thought to have evolved as a result of this custom. Where there are many wives, their sequence dictates their dominance. The first wife is the highest ranking and can demand help from the others. Although the different wives utilize a common kitchen, each woman has her own hearth, and prepares food for herself and her children. The women alternate feeding the husband. Until they marry, Dani girls wear grass skirts as are found on other Pacific islands. When a man buys a wife, the bridegroom's village drapes her with a married woman's skirt made of seeds strung together and worn just below the abdomen. Though her breasts are exposed, her buttocks are always scrupulously covered. She also wears a long warmth-giving knotted net bag around her head and down her back. Babies, piglets, belongings, and food are all carried together in it, and it also protects the women's backs from ghosts.

Diet And Feasts

Although women cook the daily meals, the men take over at festivals, including the serving of the meal. There are no regular eating times; the Danis eat when they're hungry. Sweet potatoes, of which there are 70 different varieties, compose 85-95% of their diet. Eaten skin and all, along with the protein-rich leaves, at least twice a day, sweet potatoes are usually roasted directly on the embers of the fire, but are steamed at festivals. The Danis don't store or plant seeds but plant instead vegetative parts such as sprouts, tubers, rootstocks, and slips. Ginger, yams, cucumbers, spinach, beans, bananas, and tobacco are also grown. The Danis eat almost anything else they can lay their hands on: roots, dragonfly larvae, mice, raw tadpoles, frogs, caterpillars, spiny anteater and other marsupial entrails. No knives or forks or cooking vessels are used, just round water gourds.

The Pig

Pigs, one of the few indigenous mammals of New Guinea, are the most highly valued animals. Pigs were formerly used as a means of "living currency" and are still used today as part of the bride's price. The Dani believe that pigs possess a soul similar to that of man. Pigs are raised as members of the family. They are called by ancestors' names, fed in the kitchen, take their rightful place around the hearth, and are stroked and fondled by their masters. Piglets share the same string net as babies, are carried about together by the women, and human babies must sometimes compete with hungry orphaned piglets for mother's milk. Tamed pigs walk alongside the Danis without a leash or are leashed by a rope tied to their hind legs. Adult pigs consume daily the same quantity of sweet potatoes as a man does, so they provide the women with an equal amount of work. Although raised by the women, pigs are owned by the men. Each family cuts holes or notches on their pigs' ears so they are immediately recognized. The word for pig fat may not be pronounced in the presence of women; using it is a man's prerogative.

Pig flesh is eaten only on festive occasions such as mass marriages or funerals. Whereas in former days a man reached the status of "Big Man" by his brave deeds as a warrior or hunter, today he acquires that prestigious title as a successful wild boar hunter and by the number of large pig feasts he has sponsored during this lifetime. Try to get in on one of these big pig feasts, which usually coincide with the ripening of taro roots served with the steamed pork. Pigs are slaughtered by tying them to a stake and shooting them with arrows. Their flesh is eaten with vegetables cooked in big pits covered by layers of hot stones and steaming grass. Bamboo knives are used to cut up the meat. The Danis smash bones with rocks to get at the marrow, suck flesh from the jaws, nibble at vertebrae, gnaw at the kidneys — the whole pig vanishes. On the spiritual level, consuming their endeared pets symbolizes the incorporation of the pigs' spirit into the spirit of the human host. Spoons are later made from pig pelvic bones.

Death

Cremation is the customary method of disposing of a corpse. If the stature of the deceased warrants it, his body is sometimes dried and displayed; see mummified remains in Akima and one hanging on a building at Blai on the Kemabu River to the W of the Grand Valley. After a death, the whole village mourns and wails. Sometimes women try to throw themselves on the funeral pyre, and women commonly smear their upper bodies and faces with yellow clay to show their grief. Once the mud dries, it turns the skin a bluish-white, which gives a mourning woman a ghostly pallor. In former times, female relatives of the dead, starting at about 12 years old, had their fingers amputated up to the second joint. The wound was dressed in banana leaves and husks, then bound with a mixture of clay and ashes. It was then proudly displayed around the village. Now prohibited, this

fingerless women outside honnay

practice of ritual mutilation continues only in remote areas. You'll still notice many fingerless women (and some men) over 40 years old.

Dani Warfare

Broken up into a number of fierce clans, until about 25 years ago the Danis practiced what anthropologists call ritual warfare. This meant that they regularly faced each other in formal battle. The Dani did not fight a war *(weem)* for an ideology, or in order to annex land or to dominate people, but only to avenge ghosts of dead warriors. Battles were called out in the mornings, one alliance in the valley against another. If the battle was not cancelled because of rain, about 200 men would enjoy the fight. If a Dani did not want to participate, he was not called a coward or made to suffer. Sallies were highly ritualistic, not intended to wreak carnage. Frontline fighting seldom lasted for more than 10-15 minutes. The main force relaxed on a hill nearby, watching, smoking, gossiping, and meeting friends participating from other areas. When darkness came and the battle was almost over, warriors on both sides would hurl abuse and taunts at each other, causing much laughter. Rarely did a man die unless he was clumsy or stupid. If a death did occur, the rectum and ventral base of the dead man's penis were plugged with grass to prevent bad magic from entering. When a Dani clan learned later that an enemy had died of wounds, they would congregate on hilltops to sing pitched, victorious choruses and yodels, sounding somewhat like cheers from a football stadium.

The Indonesian government and the missionaries have now eliminated all warfare between tribes. Consequently, the chiefs now have less and less of a basis for their authority—they became chiefs partly because they were fearsome and skilled warriors. Before they were torn down by the Indonesian authorities, watchtowers once stood along the perimeters of cultivated areas so the no-man's-land beyond could be watched and enemy raids seen before they happened. Each tower was the responsibility of those men who had gardens in the immediate vicinity. While women worked in the gardens during the day, men took turns as sentries in the towers. Messages and challenges were yodelled from one tower to the other.

Memories are long. Recently when the men of Jiwika wanted to open up new gardens it was necessary for them to fetch some tools from Wamena. No porters could be obtained for the trek because the tribesmen feared for their lives. Twenty-five years ago the tribe around Wamena was their enemy! As long as 5-8 years after a group of tribes had been defeated they might recover, rally, and secretly plan revenge. When the time came these usually peaceful men became bestial, attacking villages at night, burning down huts, raping women, and killing as many men and boys as they could find. Famine, starvation, and sickness followed.

One of the last skirmishes to take place in the valley was in 1971 when the American anthropologist Wyn Sargent married Chief Obahorok in order to observe at very close quarters the tribal habits of the Dani. The story goes that Obahorok, egged on by Sargent, staged a tribal war for his bride's benefit. When the Indonesians learned of the marriage, they expelled the American and Obahorok become the object of worldwide curiosity. It is because of this incident, and pressure from the OPM, that the police and military in the Baliem are still extremely wary of journalists. It is still a good idea not to say you're a writer when filling out forms or answering questions.

SHORT WALKS FROM WAMENA

Sinatma

A Protestant mission one hour's walk W of Wamena. Near Sinatma, 2 suspension bridges, made of vines and rough wood, cross over a tributary of the Wamena River.

Pugima

An easy walk from Wamena E across the Baliem River on a 2-strand rope hangbridge which sways as you cross. Walk S on the road beside the airport for about ¾ of the runway length, then turn L on a path over rocks polished by bare feet, cross the runway (being alert for planes and the warning siren). Jog L, then continue E on the trail to the river. The rickety 30-m-long bridge is about ½ km downstream to the right. River waters here are deep and calm enough for swimming. The woods across the river can be used for camping. Follow the trail a short distance longer to the village, where the chief sells ornately carved arrows at about the same prices they sell for in Wamena.

Woruba

A nice 3-hour walk to the E of Wamena via Pugima. This is a pretty walk because you go over a rope bridge, then along the river, then up over hills to a point where you can look out over the valley. Not a flat walk like many in the valley, the scenery really changes along the way.

Akima

At the end of a 2-hour walk N from Wamena is the infamous smoked mummy of Akima. Walk NW on the compacted gravel road from Wamena, turning L at the intersection, past the jail to **Hom Hom**. Turn down to the river and cross the bridge. Continue on the dirt road to Akima. A tourist sight, it costs Rp10,000 per group to view the decorated mummy, so if you want to see it take others along with you. The mummy is not for sale, not even an arm; it's the chief's grandfather. These are the Soka people, so don't call them Dani. Akima is also accessible by minibus from Wamena—the models were specially chosen to fit over the tiny, swinging 1½-m-wide hangbridge between Wamena and Akima!

Jiwika

Pronounced "yi-WEE-ka." An easy 5-hour (15-km) walk N from Wamena. **Baliem Huts Yiwika** (Rp5000 s, Rp10,000 d) is run by the local schoolteacher and his wife; meals are an extra Rp5000. Another *losmen* costs Rp10,000 s, Rp20,000. An alternative is the traditional Dani village huts (without the pigs); see Tinus Daby at the airport. The price is reasonable: Rp3000 s, Rp5000 d, including light breakfast. For other meals you have to pay extra. Meet Kurulu Mabel, chief of the Jiwika confederation of villages and paramount chief of the NE side of the Baliem River. He has 65 wives. His first wife and 2 sons were killed in a field by a raiding party, so he started a war, captured the murderers, and ate them. If you ask how they tasted, he'll smile.

Consider using Jiwika as a base or rest stop from which to see the NE end of the valley. It's an agreeable place to recover from the aches and pains received from sleeping in village *honnay* and trekking waist-deep in mud! From this village of modern-style houses walk to nearby *kampung* to see dome-shaped *honnay;* in several nearby villages you can also see some smoke-cured ancestors. Steep paths lead into the hills to the villages of **Wosi** (2½ hours from Jiwika or 8 hours and 30 km from Wamena), **Bugi**

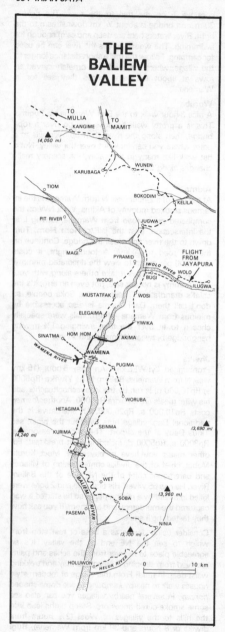

THE BALIEM VALLEY

TO MULIA

TO MAMIT

KANGIME

(4,050 m)

WUNEN

KARUBAGA

TIOM

BOKODINI

KELILA

PIT RIVER

JUGWA

MAGI

PYRAMID

FLIGHT FROM JAYAPURA

IWOLO RIVER

WOLO

WOOGI

BUGI

ILUGWA

MUSTATFAK

WOSI

ELEGAIMA

YIWIKA

SINATMA

HOM HOM

AKIMA

WAMENA RIVER

WAMENA

PUGIMA

WORUBA

HETAGIMA

SEINMA

(3,690 m)

(4,240 m)

KURIMA

BALIEM RIVER

WET

(3,960 m)

SOBA

PASEMA

NINIA

(3,700 m)

HOLUWON

HELUK RIVER

0   10 km

(5-6 hours from Jiwika or 12 hours and 40 km from Wamena), and **Wolo** (1½ hours beyond Bugi). At **Woogi**, 6-7 hours' walk N of Wamena or one hour W of Wosi, see splendid dances, such as the wedding ceremony dance. To photograph a funeral or dancing it's best manners to pay Rp3000-5000.

The Salt Pools

One hour's walk up a steep hillside path in a valley behind Jiwika you can see a centuries-old process of collecting salt. Banana leaves are first pounded to a pulp and then carried up the hill on shoulder poles. Next, the banana leaves are dipped into a pool of natural saline water from a spring and squeezed and prodded until saturated. Then the pulp is spread on rocks to dry some before being folded up and carried back down the path. Women carry up to 70-kg stem sections back to be further dried and then burned. The ashes are collected and used as salt.

Bat Caves

Another walk, 2½-3 hours N of Jiwika, takes you to a whole series of magnificent bat caves known simply as **Goa**. Little kids will light torches and take you down into them to see stalactites and stalagmites. Climb out through the back of the cave for some really impressive views of the valley.

Pyramid

About a 7- to 9-hour walk N on a vehicular road which leads all the way from Sinatma via Elegaima to this mission station and airstrip. With its beautiful panorama, this site is named after a mountain here shaped like a pyramid. If walking, take the track leading from Wamena to Hom Hom, Musatfak, Woogi, and Pyramid.

Hetagima

From Wamena, head S down Jl. A. Yani, cross the bridge, and Hetagima is an easy 3- or 4-hour walk (15 km). After 2 hours of walking, a track turns off toward the village which you can see in the distance. Ask directions along the way. Stay as a guest in one of the beehive huts of the village. Saltwells are a little beyond the village.

Kurima

Beyond Hetagima and near the entrance to the Baliem Gorge is Kurima, a 6- to 7-hour walk S from Wamena (25 km). This track, through cultivated flatlands, has lost some of its charm to visitors now that it's accessible by motorbike. Stay with the Catholic nuns at Kurima. The Baliem Valley abruptly ends here and a narrow canyon of soaring rock walls begins.

Southern Baliem Valley Loop

A 2- to 3-day walk which loops through Pugima, Seinma, Kurima, and Hetagima. Wamena to Pugima is an easy 2-hour walk on a good trail. Pugima to Seinma takes 6-7 hours, wandering through limestone country of sinkholes and small rounded hills. Trail and terrain are confusing here. Either have a guide, a compass, or get lost. The Baliem River is not fordable at this point so continue downstream from Seinma 1½ hours to a suspension bridge. Cross the bridge and turn R for the 7-hour walk back to Wamena via the Kurima and Hetagima turnoffs. A worthwhile side trip from Kurima would be to walk an hour or so downstream after crossing the suspension bridge to see the canyon and raging river.

LONGER WALKS FROM WAMENA

Wolo Valley

A scenic side valley of the Baliem with friendly people (everyone wants to shake your hand!) and a good trail. From Wamena head N following the main trail through Jiwika and Wosi and on to the Wolo River. Don't cross but follow this small river about 2 km upstream to Bugi, a 12-hour (or an easy 2-day) walk from Wamena. Bugi would be just a few hours from Pyramid if there were a way across the Baliem River. Hiking upstream along the Wolo River you pass impressive high cliffs, many gardens, several caves, and superb panoramas. The flight from Jayapura to Wamena often enters the Baliem by this side valley. About 3 hours beyond Bugi is Wolo village's school and airstrip. Another mission station, Ilugwa, is higher still and 3 more hours' walk.

Karubaga

This 4- to 6-day hike actually leaves the Baliem Valley and crosses over a spectacular divide to the N side of the range running across New Guinea. Due to the 1977 rebellion here the government still maintains a large presence. You'll likely need a *surat jalan* from Wamena. Always check in at police stations to lessen the chance of suspicion. Most of the travel is through the land of the western Dani people, who tend to be exceptionally friendly and open to visitors. Mission work has been unusually successful here and now the western Dani themselves are carrying "The Word" throughout West Irian. Trails are generally excellent, wide, and well-graded despite the mountainous terrain. No signs or maps for hiking; a guide (Rp15,000 a day) is a wise investment.

From Bugi (see previous hike) rejoin the track along the Baliem River and follow it north. When the river turns W continue straight and begin the long climb to the pass. From the top descend steeply to **Kelila**, a mission station with an airstrip. It's a long 8- to 9-hour walk here from Bugi. **Bokodini** is 3- to 4-hours' easy walk W of Kelila. An MAF pilot, airstrip, and a school for Western missionary children are based here. Karubaga is 12 hours and a lot of ups and downs farther west. A good place to stop midway is **Wunen**, a village with an airstrip and a large new school. Karubaga has a mission hospital, airstrip, hydro station, and several missionary families. From Karubaga possibilities include: (1) flying back to Wamena with MAF; (2) walking over rough trails S to **Tiom** in the upper Baliem Valley; (3) continuing W to Mulia, Illaga, Enarotali, etc.; (4) making a side trip N to **Mamit**, a one-day hike.

Soba, Ninia, And Holuwon

This 5-day OW hike SE of Wamena enters a whole new world. Gone are the sunny open valleys of the Baliem and western Dani regions. Now cold gray mists swirl among the mountain peaks and raging streams roar at the bottom of steep-walled valleys. Trails tend to be narrow, winding, and a bit muddy. Life is harder here; potatoes grow slowly in the meager soil and insufficient sunshine. But the sun does break through to reveal enchanted moss forests, gardens, villages, towering green-clad mountains, and countless waterfalls. Near Holuwon you can sight down the Baliem River to the flat, humid lowlands stretching below to the horizon. In 1968 Australian Stan Dale and American missionary Phil Masters were killed by angry cannibals in the Seng Valley E of Ninia, but for fear of the consequences of eating white men's flesh, the bodies were cremated and not devoured. Read of their misadventure in *Lords of the Earth* by Don Richardson, exciting, "must" reading for any visitor to the area!

Enter the Baliem River Gorge at the S end of the Baliem Valley near Kurima. A suspension bridge spans the river at the gorge entrance. Walk down along the W side of the river, cross a second suspension bridge, then follow the meandering trail S as it climbs high above the Baliem River. Ask where the trail to Soba branches off, or better yet, hire a guide. Soba is a 2-day walk from the entrance of the gorge. Ninia is a full day's walk E of Soba over a high pass. Holuwon is a long 9 hours SW of Ninia. MAF flies to all 3 missions from Wamena. Holuwon seems to receive the most flights. It is easiest to have a carrier (Rp5000-6000 per day) but you can find your way without one—just expect to get lost occasionally. MAF will take you to Ninia or Holuwon for Rp30,000 OW from Wamena if there's room. Sometimes MAF will make room by delaying their own cargo, if you are willing to pay a higher fare.

THE SOUTH COAST

Merauke And Vicinity

A forlorn place on the SE coast, Merauke is the most easterly major town in Indonesia. With its dry spells, the climate here is different from that of other parts of Irian Jaya. Stay in the reasonably priced government *pasanggrahan* on Jl. Biak, in **Hotel Asmat**, or in **Hotel Gedung Putih**. Eat at **RM Bahagia** near the Gedung Bina Ria (movie theater). *Warung* are also set up near the Kores police station. Merauke is accessible from Jakarta by Pelni ship for Rp73,300 Economy, or fly Merpati from Jayapura for Rp92,000 or from Biak (on Fri.) for Rp125,200.

Inland there are sago palm swamps and white-barked eucalyptus trees. Landscapes are very similar to Australia, with giant antheaps 4-5 m high, kangaroos thumping through the shrub, wild pigs and deer (venison dishes are common). During the dry season, drive through large savannahs with 1- to 2-m-high elephant grass, kingfishers, flocks of wild cranes, storks, wild horses, unclaimed cattle, and in the shrub forests cassowaries. Up the Maro River to the village of **Erambo** see herons, sandpipers, wimbrels, parrots, and crowned pigeons as large as geese flying overhead. Red eyes of crocodiles shine in flashlight rays at night (for eating, boil the hind legs and tail; tastes like fishy chicken). **Pulau Yos Sudarso**, just off the coast, can be reached by small boat from Mapi and Merauke. There's a government station in Kimaam on the Selat Mariane Strait. Most villages are inaccessible during the dry season (June-Oct.). The island is very flat and swampy so the natives live on artificial islands where they grow yams and other root crops.

Tanah Merah

Means "Red Clay." Take a riverboat from the mouth of the Digul River (near Mapi) 3 days to this jungle outpost over 300 km upriver. Or fly with Merpati from Merauke on Mon. at 1125 for Rp25,000; from Jayapura on Fri. at 0805 for Rp30,000; or from Biak on Fri. at 0805 for Rp75,600. Called Boven Digul in Dutch times, this was originally a large internment camp built on a malarial swamp. During revolutionary times (1926-48), notable Indonesian political personalities were exiled here—Hatta, Bondan, Sukarno—and numerous others. In 1926, many of the Communist leaders of the Madiun Rebellion were sent here by the Dutch. There were never any successful escapees; all were invariably eaten by cannibals and died before they reached the coast. During the post-independence era, it was a nationalist status symbol to have been interned in this notorious penal settlement. The present Indonesian government imprisons most opponents of its regime on Nusakambangan off Cilicap, C. Java.

THE CASUARINA COAST

A swampy stretch of coast in SE Irian Jaya between the Barai and Trikom rivers, so named because of its huge casuarina trees, an Australasian species with jointed leafless branches. At dusk the sky fills with thousands of flying foxes which swarm down to feed on the trees' ripe fruit. Here lives the largest of the New Guinea parrots, the *kakatua raja*, or king parrot.

Once known for their cannibalism, some of the most untouched tribes of New Guinea live here. Human meat was prepared like pig meat: the body was cut up into pieces by women and roasted over a fire. In fact, humans were called "long pigs," though human flesh is juicier. Before heading for this coast, read *Where The Spirits Dwell: An Odyssey in the New Guinea Jungle* by Tobias Schneebaum (Grove, 1988) which gives a vivid picture of Asmat tribal life.

River travel can be very hazardous because unbelievably strong river currents cut away at the ground, ripping out trees and chunks of earth. Riverbanks are choked with bush, trees, ferns, gnarled roots, and flowers. Going upriver you spot freshwater turtles, crocodiles, white herons, Indian sea eagles, kingfishers, parrots, and slow-flapping hornbills. At night trees are brilliantly lit by fireflies. Pass by red flowering trees hidden in the jungle and little villages hugging the banks, their houses usually on stilts. When inhabitants are unhappy in a location they pack up the whole town and move elsewhere, so never expect a village you've heard about to still be there.

The Asmat

A tribespeople who live along the Casuarina Coast, untouched by civilization until recent times. Barely 2 generations removed from headhunting, Dutch outposts, missionary settlements, and foreign expeditions finally made inroads on this isolated culture during the '50s and '60s. Vast mangrove, sago, and bamboo forests crowd their swampland environment, home for approximately 70,000 Asmat scattered in some 100 villages. Formerly, the families of the entire tribe resided together in houses up to 28 m long called *yeus*. Today, in such coastal villages of **Basiem** and **Agats**, families occupy separate dwellings built on pilings. Catwalks or log paths are necessary to cope with the spongy terrain and an estimated 5,100 mm of rainfall per year. *Yeus* are still used, but now only by men as clubhouses where only the bachelors sleep. Upriver Asmat still live in longhouses, and some even build houses in treetops. The Indonesian government encourages nomadic Asmat to settle in permanent villages and has built schools and clinics to attract them downriver.

The Asmat stand up to paddle long narrow canoes with 3-m-long paddles. Fish and shrimp are caught in large hoop nets. They live on sago (their staple diet), mussels, snails, and collect fat insect larvae from decaying stumps of sago palms to be eaten to the accompaniment of throbbing drums and ritual dances. These larval feasts might last for 2 weeks. Dead ancestors' spirits are invited to attend festivities, but only for a night, after which they are driven away. Almost every household article is given the name of a dead person. Implements of war were traditionally also named after dead relatives to remind the owner of his obligation to take revenge. In the upper river reaches, tribes wrap their dead in bark and lay them out on scaffolding only a few meters away from the house. The bodies are left there to rot until only the skeleton is left. Then the bones are brought into the house. A man might wear the skull of his mother around his neck in order that she give him protection in death as she did in life. Wife swapping (Papisj) system) is practiced by some tribes as a ritual to increase bonds between men in times of stress, and some men have an "exchange friend" (lover) in addition to his wife.

This whole estuary region is famous for its carvers. Much of the Asmats' highly original art is symbolic of warfare, headhunting, and warrior-ancestor veneration. In the 1950s when tribal warfare was outlawed and the warrior's way of life started to disappear, it threatened to curtail the artistic production of the people. For example, their huge bisj (phallic ancestor poles) were carved solely to commemorate forebears mighty in battle. Fortunately, in 1969 under a project financed by the UN to revive local handicrafts, old master carvers were located in each major village and encouraged to train promising young carvers. A purchasing depot was set up at Agats where good-quality carvings brought in from outlying villages were sorted, selected for display, and purchased from the carvers for cash or barter goods. See some spectacular pieces of Asmat art in the Museum of Primitive Art in New York City.

Agats

The starting point for visiting Asmat villages in the area, Agats gets about 10 groups each year from Holland and Germany. The missionaries started a timber mill here and raised wooden walkways all over town which have now fallen into disrepair—quite dangerous in places. Not very good warung, just shops with seats outside. Agats' main attraction is its unique museum of primitive woodcarvings, weaponry, etc. run by the Catholics. Carvings made from ironwood (kayu besi) produced around this coastal village

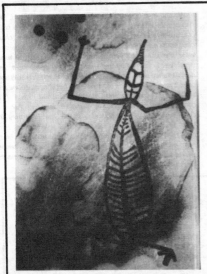

Cape Abba: On the S shore of Teluk Bintuni (S of the Bird's Head). There are many caves and galleries in this area with rock wall drawings executed by prehistoric artists 400-1,000 years ago in high coastal cliffs accessible only by sea. The Abba cave has one whole wall covered in silhouettes of hands with red ochre spat around them. A wild chaotic, multicolored collection of stenciled footprints, figures of men and sea animals, lizard gods, fish, turtles, birds, boats, crescent moons, solar eclipses, and setting suns. See a hornbill with its ribs x-rayed! Some are hauntingly drawn, others just scribbled. In these marvelous paintings artists show their very close relationship with the sea and the cosmos. Other cave paintings are found near Kokas (NW of Fak Fak) and Kaimana.

include hafts for stone axes, 1- to-2-m-tall ceremonial shields, sago bowls, copulation figurines, solid wood human heads, arabesque panels, çanoe paddles. Knives and necklaces are made from thigh bones and vertebrae of the giant cassowary bird. *Prahu* are painted in bright colors and ornamented with superb carvings.

The Ewer Airstrip near Agats on the Per River can take only small Islanders or Cessnas. For inland trips, go with the missionaries who operate motorized *prahu*

which travel upriver. A Pelni ship makes the 2-week Merauke-Sorong run once a month. It stops at really out-of-the-way places like Agats, Pirimopon, Mimika, Kaimana, Fak Fak, and Teluk Bintuni. Calls are also made at Tual in the Kai Is.; Tual-Kaimana is an 18-hour trip. The ship tends to be overcrowded on the run to Sorong, carrying people looking for work. Conditions can be pretty filthy; you'll be hard-pressed to find a place to sleep, while the food and toilets come in the usual Pelni fashion.

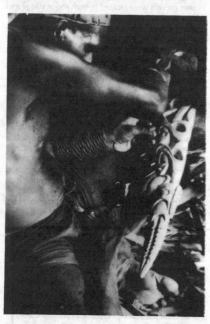

Asmat woodcarving: The Asmat live on an enormous plain between the sea and Irian Jaya's central mountain range, a vast expanse of muddy lowlands intersected by a network of rivers and covered in tropical rainforests. For centuries the Asmat were preoccupied with the necessity of appeasing ancestor spirits, producing a wealth of superbly designed shields, canoes, sculptural figures, and drums used in their

rituals and in everyday life. Carving in freshly cut wood, the Asmat paint them with only 3 colors (red, white and a little black) derived from mixing crushed shells, lime, earth, charcoal, and water. Until the end of WW II, the only tools utilized were shells, animal teeth, tusks, and precious stone axes which were obtained by trade with the mountain people. Today, flattened nails set into wooden handles and iron axes and chisels have replaced the old-style tools but shell and bone are still used for scraping and smoothing finished pieces. The general design is first traced by a single incised line, then the detail is carved out in deep relief. Visit the Small Industries Artifact Shop in Agats where hundreds of small figures and bowls are churned out for sale. For authentic ancestor poles, paint-mixing vessels, grub-trays, soul-ships, paddles, canoe prows, shields, spears, masks, drums, and personal ornaments you must travel inland or down the coast.

Looming ecological disaster: Unconscionable timber concessionaires have caused serious damage to the forests and environment of the Asmat people. The 70,000 Asmat have a territory of 27,000 sq km; an area a little larger than the Netherlands. Asmatters are very dependent on the approx. 20,000 sq km of forests which surround them, using the land as a hunting ground which provides a livelihood for families. The Asmat also gather forest products such as rattan. Their whole area has now been alloted to concessionaires who employ the Asmat to do the felling and stripping of trees, sliding them into the rivers and floating them in a raft for the concessionaires to collect. No reforestation is taking place. The types of saleable hardwood tropical trees are decreasing and the overlogging is taking place farther and farther away from the rivers. Even more serious is the process of land erosion which the uncontrolled felling has caused. The sloping territory of the Asmat was formed from mud sediments over millenia. The brackish swampland has no stones whatsoever. This means that several large rivers from the Jayawijaya Range such as the Frinskap, Berasa, and Tor will completely submerge the region, turning it into sea again within 10 years. Something must be done quickly to stop this ecological and social devastation!

BAHASA INDONESIA

Any seasoned traveler will tell you that the ability to speak the language of the country you're visiting has a huge effect on the quality of your experience while there. You don't have to commit to memory hundreds of complicated sentences. A basic grasp of such simple, everyday phrases as "Good morning," "Thank you," and variations of the theme "I want to eat/sleep" will help you tremendously to explain what you want, make friends, find your way, learn correct prices, and generally make your stay more enjoyable. You'll be amazed at how much you can say with only a 500-word vocabulary, so don't worry so much about grammar and sentence construction at first. Just concentrate on memorizing the most important commonly used words and phrases in this appendix, all of which have been selected for their value to travelers. Your emphasis should be on effective, speedy communication for use in your daily activities. The most important phrase in this section is *Saya belum lancar di Bahasa Indonesia.* ("I'm not yet fluent in Indonesian.") After saying this, you can then ask your question. If you don't first get the idea across that you are a non-speaker of the language, your inquiry is likely to produce an outpouring of verbiage impossible for you to comprehend.

At first, Indonesian might appear extremely simple. It's a non-tonal language with no tense suffixes or prefixes, no case genders or definite articles, no declensions, no conjugations, not even a verb "to be!" In actuality, however, the very lack of obvious rules makes it difficult to speak the language correctly or to express yourself in a natural way. To speak enough Indonesian to get by is easy—easier than English. But to speak Indonesian well is another matter; it is as difficult and sophisticated as any of the world's great languages. But the surprised expressions and smiles of those you address will be your just reward! *Selamat belajar!*

SPELLING

Bahasa Indonesia is written in Latin script and has 21 letters. Spelling is strictly phonetic and small children after only 2-3 years at school can read adult literature aloud to their grandparents. In 1972 Indonesia simplified its spelling *(ejaan yang disempurnakan)*, making revisions in the language to conform to Malay, though the pronunciation remains the same. Sometimes the old spelling is still used on road signs, maps,

in publications, and in dictionaries. In the "new" spelling, every "j" becomes "y" (as in "yarn"), every "dj" changes to "j" (as in "jam"), every "tj" to "c" (as in "chair"), "ch" to "kh," "nj" to "ny," and "sj" to "sy." To make matters even more confusing, there are spelling variations everywhere you go, depending upon the island or even upon the *district* of the island. Words from other major languages of Indonesia have influenced the Indonesian language. Many Javanese words change "o" for "a" when translated into Indonesian; Diponegoro becomes Dipanegara and Solo becomes Sala. Some Indonesians spell *tolong* (please) as *tulang*, and so forth. Up to about 1947, Indonesian words on signs, maps, and other materials were transcribed using Dutch sounds—e.g., BANDOENG (Bandung) and BOEKOE (buku), and you'll still come across these archaic spellings. But people's names—being sacred—never change.

ACCOMMODATIONS

Where's a hotel? Where's a losmen?
   Dimana ada hotel? Dimana ada losmen?
Which is the best hotel/*losmen*?
   Hotel/losmen mana yang terbaik?
Recommend me a good first-class hotel.
   Tunjukkan hotel kelas satu yang baik.
I want a quiet, small hotel.
   Saya ingin hotel yang tenang dan kecil.
That hotel is near the town square, far from the airport.
   Hotel itu terletak dekat lapangan, jauh dari pelabuhan udara.
Please take me to Wisma Borobudur.
   Tolong antar saya ke Wisma Borobudur.
Do you have a room available? Sorry, there aren't any rooms .
   Ada kamar kosong? Ma'af, tidak ada.
Can I have a room for one night?
   Bisakah saya dapat kamar untuk semalam?
We have a reservation. We want to reserve a room.
   Kami telah memesan kamar. Saya ingin memesan kamar.
How long are you staying?
   Berapa lama anda akan tinggal disini?
I will stay two days. On Tuesday I travel to Malang.
   Saya akan tinggal dua hari. Hari Selasa saya terus ke Malang.

One or two persons, sir? I'm alone.
Untuk satu atau dua orang tuan? Saya sendiri.
Single, please. Two (three) of us, one room.
Untuk satu orang. Dua (tiga) orang, satu kamar.
One room, two beds. Clean and tidy.
Kamar dengan dua tempat tidur. Bersih dan rapih.
Have you a room with a private bath?
Apa ada kamar yang pakai kamar mandi tersendiri?
hot and cold water
air panas dan dingin
How much for one night? One person?
Berapa harga satu malam? Satu orang?
What is the rate per day? Week? Month?
Berapa taripnya se hari? Minggu? Bulan?
Does the price include breakfast? It includes three daily meals.
Apakah sewanya termasuk sarapan pagi? Termasuk tiga kali makan.
What time do I have to check out?
Jam berapa saya harus keluar?
May I see the room first? What's my room number?
Bolehkah saya melihat kamarnya dulu? Nomor berapa kamar saya?

I'm leaving tomorrow midday.
Saya berangkat besok siang.
Here is the key to your room. The door's open.
Ini kunci kamar Tuan. Tidak dikunci.
Is it safe here? First floor. Second floor.
Amankah disini? Lantai pertama. Lantai kedua.
Is there a bathroom on this floor? Where's the toilet?
Apa ada kamar mandi di lantai (tingkat) ini? Mana WCnya?
Please spray my room. It has mosquitos.
Tolong semprot kamar saya. Ada nyamuk didalam.
The mattress is too hard. I want to change rooms.
Kasurnya terlalu keras. Saya mau ganti kamar.
I want a better room/cheaper room.
Saya minta kamar yang lebih baik/kamar yang lebih murah.
larger room/smaller room/quiet room
kamar yang lebih besar/kamar yang lebih kecil/kamar yang tenang
Have you anything cheaper? Have you anything better?
Adakah yang lebih murah? Adakah yang lebih baik?
I'll take this one. It'll do.
Saya ambil yang ini. Boleh juga.
Please put out the light (oil lamp), I want to sleep.
Tolong padamkan lampunya, saya mau tidur.
Please turn down the radio, it's loud.
Pelankan radio itu, suaranya terlalu keras.

HOTEL SERVICES

Just ring for service. May I have...?
Telpon saja untuk pelayanan. Bolehkah saya minta...?
I want another pillow. Another blanket.
Saya ingin bantal lagi. Satu selimut lagi.
Dutch wife/hot water/ice/ice water
bantal guling/air panas/es/es batu
Please clean my room. To make a bed
Tolong bersihkan kamar saya. Membereskan tempat tidur
soap/toilet paper/towel
sabun/kertas toilet/handuk
I want to speak to the manager.
Saya mau bicara dengan pengurus.
May I deposit my passport with you?
Boleh saya titip paspor saya dengan Saudara?
May I use your telephone?
Bolehkah saya meminjam telpon?
Is there a message for me? I'm sorry, you were out.
Ada pesan untuk saya? Maaf, anda sedang tidak ada disini.
I need a porter. Will you please fetch my suitcases.
Saya memerlukan seorang portir. Tolong ambil kopor-kopor saya.
Please call a taxi.
Tolong panggilkan taxi.
Can I have breakfast in my room?
Bisakah saya makan pagi di kamar?
Please send my breakfast up.
Tolong kirimkan sarapan saya keatas.
Is there someone who washes clothes? Please wash these clothes.
Ada orang yang mencuci pakaian? Tolong cucikan pakaian ini.
Can I have them back tomorrow? Yes, all these are mine.
Apakah bisa selesai besok? Ya, ini semua punya saya.
Please wake me up at 0600. Before sunrise. Very early.
Harap bangunkan saya pukul enam pagi. Subuh. Pagi-pagi.
Don't wake me up.
Jangan bangunkan saya.
I want to check out now. Give me my bill, please.
Saya mau keluar sekarang. Saya minta rekening saya.
I will return next week.
Saya akan kembali minggu yang akan datang.
Can you store my things for five days?
Bisakah anda menyimpan barang-barang saya untuk lima hari?

CONVERSATION, SMALL TALK

Where are you from? I'm from the U.S.A.
> *Anda berasal dari negara mana? Saya berasal dari U.S.A*

My nationality is Australian/American/Dutch.
> *Saya berkebangsaan Australi/orang Amerika/orang Belanda.*

How old are you? I'm twenty years old.
> *Umur berapa Tuan? Saya berumur duapuluh tahun.*

Are you a tourist? What's your address?
> *Adakah Tuan seorang wisatawan? Dimana alamat anda?*

When did you arrive here? How long have you been here?
> *Kapan Tuan tiba disini? Sudah berapa lama anda disini?*

I've just arrived in Indonesia.
> *Saya baru datang di Indonesia.*

Have you ever been here before? Where are you going?
> *Apakah Tuan sudah pernah kemari sebelum ini? Mau kemana?*

Will you stay long in Indonesia? No, just a couple of months.
> *Tuan akan tinggal lama di Indonesia? Tidak, hanya beberapa bulan.*

Have you already been to Bali? Yes, already.
> *Sudah pernah ke Bali? Ya, sudah.*

No, I've never been to Torajaland.
> *Belum, saya belum pernah ke Tanatoraja.*

How do you like the climate of Indonesia? The climate is wonderful!
> *Bagaimana tentang iklim Indonesia? Iklimnya baik sekali!*

Do you smoke? May I have a light (for a cigarette)?
> *Anda suka merokok? Boleh saya minta korek api?*

What's your ocupation?
> *Apakah pekerjaan anda?*

I'm a businessperson. I'm a student.
> *Saya adalah seorang pengusaha. Saya seorang pelajar.*

My occupation is artist/sailor/teacher/writer.
> *Pekerjaan saya seniman/pelaut/guru/penulis.*

What's your religion? I'm a Christian/Jew/Muslim.
> *Agama apa anda? Saya orang Kristen/orang Jahudi/orang Islam.*

Are you married? Yes, I am. Not yet. Do you have children?
> *Apa anda sudah kawin? Ya, sudah. Belum. Sudah punya anak?*

Do you like Indonesian cooking?
> *Apakah Tuan suka makanan Indonesia.*

Yes, but some dishes are too hot for me.
> *Ya, tetapi sebagian masakan pedas bagi saya.*

Will you be free this evening?
> *Anda tidak akan sibuk malam nanti?*

Would you like to come to my house?
> *Maukah Anda datang ke rumah saya?*

Where shall we meet? Let's meet in front of...
> *Dimana kita akan jumpa? Kita jumpa saja di depan...*

Okay, no problem. I'm sorry, I can't.
> *Baiklah, tidak ada persoalan. Ma'af, saya tak dapat.*

AT THE RESTAURANT, AT THE MARKET

I'm hungry. I'm going to go to a downtown restaurant.
> *Saya lapar. Saya akan pergi ke restoran di pusat kota.*

Where's a good restaurant?
> *Restoran mana yang baik?*

Can we stop for lunch/dinner?
> *Dapatkah kita berhenti untuk makan siang/makan malam.*

Let's have lunch. Who'll join me?
> *Mari kita makan siang. Siapa ikut saya?*

This is the best foodstall here.
> *Ini warung yang terbaik disini.*

I'm a vegetarian, I don't eat any meat. Vegetables only.
> *Saya seorang vegetaris, saya tidak makan daging-dagingan. Sayur saja.*

I want Indonesian food.
> *Saya mau makanan Indonesia.*

What time is breakfast? It's served at seven o'clock.
> *Jam berapa waktu makan pagi? Makan pagi dihidangkan pada pukul tujuh.*

Waiter! I want a table for five persons.
> *Pelayan! Saya ingin meja untuk lima orang.*

I'm sorry this table is reserved.
> *Ma'af, meja ini sudah dipesan.*

Give me tea instead of coffee.
> *Berilah saya teh untuk gantinya kopi.*

Do you take sugar and milk?
> *Tuan pakai gula dan susu?*

Is this water drinkable? No, it's not drinkable.
> *Apa air ini bisa diminum? Tidak, itu tak bisa diminum.*

I'm thirsty. Please get me a glass of ice water.
> *Saya haus. Tolong ambil segelas air es.*

Please give me some hot water. I want boiled water (for drinking).
> *Tolong beri saya air panas. Saya minta air matang (untuk minum).*

May I see the menu? What's the specialty in this restaurant?
> *Boleh saya lihat daftar makanan? Apa keistimewaan rumah makan ini?*

We're in a hurry, please bring our orders quickly.
Kami terburu-buru, tolong cepatkan pesanan kami.

When will it be ready? What's the price?
Kapan siapnya? Berapa harganya?

That's too expensive. Have you got Indonesian dishes?
Itu terlalu mahal. Apakah anda menyajikan makanan Indonesia?

Let's have some satay. Don't make it too spicy!
Mari kita makan sate. Jangan terlalu pedas!

What is that/this? I'd like another helping. Is there more?
Apa itu/ini? Saya mau tambah lagi? Ada lagi?

Please bring us some hot chili sauce. Bring me coffee.
Bawakan kami sambal. Bawakan untuk saya kopi.

Bring me another glass. What do you have for dessert?
Ambilkan untuk saya gelas yang lain. Apa yang anda punyai untuk makanan pencuci mulut.

I have had enough. I want a banana.
Saya sudah kenyang. Saya ingin pisang.

I want to wash my hands. Where's the toilet?
Saya mau cuci tangan. Dimana kamar kecil?

Good. Waiter, please bring me the bill.
Bagus. Bung, saya minta bonnya.

Can you change a 10,000-rupiah bill?
Bisakah anda menukar sepuluh ribu rupiah uang kertas?

at the same time/each person/if there is any/finished
pada waktu yang sama/setiap orang/kalau ada/habis

to like very much/really delicious/enjoy your meal!
suka sekali/enak sekali/selamat makan!

a little/too little/a little more
sedikit/terlalu sedikit/sedikit lagi

fresh/clean/dirty/to taste
segar/bersih/kotor/mencicipi, merasa, mencoba

lukewarm/hot/underdone/well done
hangat/panas/mentah/matang

cold/hot (temperature)/hot (spicy)
dingin/panas/pedas

to cook/one serving/forbidden (for Muslims)
memasak/satu porsi/haram

to boil/to fry/to slice/to squeeze (fruit)
merebus/menggoreng/mengiris/memeras

salty/sour/vinegar/sweet/honey/bitter (or plain)
asin/asam/cuka/manis/madu/pahit

plastic bag/bottled drinking water
kantong plastik/botol air minum

fork/spoon/knife/glass/plate/bowl/cup
garpu/sendok/pisau/gelas/piring/mangkok/cangkir

rice (after cooking)/rice noodles/sticky white rice
nasi/bakmi/ketan

beans/fermented white soybeans/soybean curd/shrimp paste
buncis/tempe/tahu/terasi

soup/noodle soup/curried chicken/fried rice/fried noodles
sup/mie kuah/ayam kari/nasi goreng/mie goreng

fish/prawns/squid/crab/carp/lobster/eel
ikan/udang/cumi/kepiting/ikan mas/udang karang/belut

meat/liver/heart/beefsteak/water buffalo/frog legs
daging/hati/jantung/bistik/daging kerbau/kaki kodok

beef/chicken/lamb/mutton/pork
daging sapi/daging ayam/daging domba/daging kambing/daging babi

vegetables/tomato/onion/cabbage/corn/potatos/sweet potato/carrots/avocado
sayur/tomat/bawang/kol/jagung/kentang/ubi/wortel/apokat

salt/ginger/chili/cinnamon/pepper/cloves/garlic/lemon
garam/jahe/cabe/kayu manis/merica/cengkeh/bawang putih/jeruk

beer/rice wine/water/cordial/ice/orange juice/soda water
bir/tuak/air/strop/es/air jeruk/air soda

bread/toast/cake/cracker/spring rolls
roti/roti bakar/kue/biskuit/lumpia

butter/cheese/cream/milk/ice cream
mentega/keju/kepala susu/susu/es krim

egg/fried egg/omelet/boiled egg/soft-boiled egg
telur/telur mata sapi/telur dadar/telur rebus/telur setengah matang

snacks/peanuts/candy/shrimp chips
makanan kecil/kacang tanah/gula-gula/krupuk udang

Where can I buy fruit? Where's the market?
Dimana saya bisa beli buah-buahan? Pasar dimana?

apple/coconut/citrus fruit/papaya/pineapple/fried banana fritters
apel/kelapa/jeruk/pepaya/nanas/pisang goreng

to pick out good ones/ripe/remove the skin
pilih yang baik/matang/kupas

How does one eat this? Peel it and then you can eat it as is.
Bagaimana cara makannya? Dikupas, lalu bisa dimakan begitu saja.

HEALTH: DRUGSTORES, HOSPITALS, CLINICS

Where is the nearest drugstore? Hospital?
Dimanakah apotik (toko obat) yang terdekat? Rumah sakit?

What's your ailment? I need medicine for diarrhea.
Sakit apa? Saya perlu obat untuk berak-berak.

Do you have something for an upset stomach?
Insect bites?

Apakah ada obat untuk gangguan perut?
Gigitan serangga?

My throat is very sore. Can you make up this prescription?

Tenggorokan saya sakit sekali. Tolong buatkan resep ini?

"enter wind" (to catch a cold or flu)/dry cough/ itching

masuk angin/batuk kering/gatal

I have a splitting headache/stomachache/sore eye/disease

Saya pusing sekali/sakit perut/sakit mata/penyakit

earache/toothache/backache/stomach cramp

sakit telinga/sakit gigi/sakit punggung/kejang perut mules

infection/malaria/cough (n.)/cough (v.)

infeksi/malaria/batuk-batuk/batuk

healthy/seriously sick

sehat/sakit keras

broken arm/leg

lengan patah/kaki patah

I don't sleep well. I have a cough/fever.

Tidur saya tidak nyenyak. Saya batuk/demam.

take medicine/take a pill

minum obat/minum pil

How many pills shall I take a day? Three times daily.

Berapa tablet harus saya makan sehari? Tiga kali sehari.

Take three teaspoonfuls before/after meals.

Minumlah tiga sendok teh sebelum/sesudah makan.

on getting up/on going to bed/sleepy

waktu bangun tidur/jika mau tidur/ngantuk

I'm sick. I want to see a doctor.

Saya sakit. Saya mau pergi ke dokter.

Where is there a doctor who speaks English?

Dimana ada dokter yang bisa berbicara Bahasa Inggeris?

doctor's consulting hours/patient

jam bicara/pasien

Please call a doctor. That wound/cut needs dressing.

Tolong panggilkan dokter. Luka itu perlu dibalut.

How long have you had this cold? About a week.

Sudah berapa lama anda menderita masuk angin? Kurang lebih satu minggu.

You're very pale. Is your temperature still high?

Anda pucat. Apakah suhu badan anda masih tinggi?

Where's the pain? How's your appetite?

Dibagian mana yang anda rasakan sakit?
Bagaimana nafsu makan anda?

I'll write you a prescription.

Saya akan menuliskan resep untuk anda.

Wash the cut in boiled water.

Basuh luka itu dengan air panas.

medicine/alcohol/antiseptic cream/aspirin

obat/alkohol/krem antiseptik/aspirin

bandage/plasters/cotton/injection

perban/plester/kapas/suntikan

cough medcine/laxative/ointment/powder

obat batuk/obat peluntur/salep/bedak

sedative/sleeping pill/talcum powder/tranquilizer

obat untuk meredakan sakit/obat tidur/bedak talek/obat penenang

stool specimen/to rub (with salve)

contoh buang air/menggosok

NUMBERS

0	*nol*
1	*satu*
2	*dua*
3	*tiga*
4	*empat*
5	*lima*
6	*enam*
7	*tujuh*
8	*delapan*
9	*sembilan*
10	*sepuluh*
11	*sebelas*
12	*duabelas*
15	*limabelas*
20	*duapuluh*
30	*tigapuluh*
40	*empatpuluh*
100	*seratus*
200	*duaratus*
500	*limaratus*
1,000	*seribu*
3,000	*tigaribu*
10,000	*sepuluh ribu*
100,000	*seratus ribu*
268	*duaratus enampuluh delapan*
150	*seratus limapuluh*
307	*tigaratus tujuh*
537	*limaratus tigapuluh tujuh*
11,347	*sebelas ribu tiga ratus empatpuluh tujuh*
first	*pertama, kesatu*
second	*kedua*
third	*ketiga*
fourth	*keempat*
fifth	*kelima*
sixth	*keenam*
seventh	*ketujuh*
eighth	*kedelapan*

ninth	kesembilan
tenth	kesepuluh
eleventh	kesebelas
twelfth	keduabelas
½	setengah
¼	seperempat
¾	tigaperempat
1 ½	satu setengah
2½ %	dua setengah persen
⅓	sepertiga
⅔	dua pertiga
a fifth	seperlima
a tenth	sepersepuluh
divide	bagi
multiply	kali
to slice	iris, potong
one slice	satu iris, satu potong
a dozen	duabelas/satu lusin
to cut	potong
number	nomor
total/quantity	jumlah
plus/add (v.)	tambah
minus/subtract	kurang
more (quantity)	lagi
approximately	kira-kira
how many/much	berapa
many/much	banyak
too	terlalu
too many	terlalu banyak
few	sedikit
enough	cukup
if you can flip it:	helai
if you can count it:	biji or buah
Exceptions are animals	ekor
and units or items like a bag	satu (se)kantong
a handful:	segenggam
a spoonful:	satu sendok penuh

fix two slices (pieces) of meat
   bikin dua iris (potong) daging
buy four fish
   beli empat ekor ikan
I need five eggs. I need five shirts.
   Saya perlu lima biji telur. Saya perlu lima helai baju.
sheets of (paper, cloth)
   helai (kertas, kain)
three sheets of paper
   tiga lembar kertas

PHOTOGRAPHY

May I take photographs here?
   Bolehkah saya mengambil foto disini?

I have a camera. Cameras prohibited.
   Saya punya tustel (fototustel). Dilarang memotret.
Where is the nearest photo studio?
   Dimanakah foto studio yang terdekat?
Where can I get photographic materials?
   Dimana saya bisa memperoleh bahan-bahan fotografi?
Can I buy a film? Please develop this film.
   Dapatkah saya membeli satu rol film? Tolonglah cuci film ini.
I want to have my photo taken.
   Saya ingin difoto.
I want to have this film developed and printed.
   Saya mau mencuci dan mencetak film ini.
Can you enlarge this photo? I want this size.
   Dapatkah anda memperbesar foto ini? Saya mau ukuran ini.
Let me have a proof, please.
   Coba lihat contohnya.
When will it be ready? Can you make it earlier?
   Kapan selesainya? Bisa lebih cepat?
What type of paper do you use (to print a film)?
   Kertas produksi apa yang anda pakai (untuk mencetak film)?

GREETINGS, POLITE EXPRESSIONS

Selamat may be used in conjunction with almost any action word. Together they form a phrase which translates as "may your (action) be prosperous, blessed!" Thus, *Selamat tinggal* means literally "May your remaining be prosperous." *Selamat tidur* means "Sleep well"; *Selamat bekerja* means "Enjoy your work." By itself, *Selamat* means "Congratulations" or "Good luck" (lit. "Health").
Good morning/Good afternoon/Good night
   Selamat pagi/Selamat siang/Selamat malam
Where are you going? (a common greeting)
   Mau kemana? or Pergi ke mana?
I'm taking a walk. (a common answer)
   Jalan-jalan.
please/go right ahead
   silahkan
Come in please. Please sit down.
   Silahkan masuk. Silahkan duduk.
Hot today, isn't it? It will rain soon.
   Panas sekali, ya? Sebentar lagi (hari) mau hujan.
It's a beautiful day, isn't it? Nice day, isn't it?
   Harinya indah, ya? Harinya enak, ya?
Nice view, isn't it?
   Pemandangannya indah sekali, ya?
pleased/be happy
   senang
Thank you/Excuse me (Pardon me)
   terima kasih/Ma'af
Good appetite! Bon apetit! This food is delicious.
   Selamat makan! Makanan ini nikmat sekali.

Happy Hari Raya! Merry Christmas! Happy New Year!
Selamat Hari Raya! Selamat Hari Natal! Selamat Tahun Baru!

Thanks for the invitation.
Terima kasih atas undangan saudara.

Have a good trip.
Selamat berjalan.

Welcome (lit.: "Good fortune on arrival").
Selamat datang.

very interesting/very beautiful (of buildings, monuments)
sangat menarik/bagus sekali

INTRODUCTIONS

How are you?/What's new?
Apa kabar?

Fine, thanks, and you?
Kabar baik, terima kasih, dan Tuan?

Don't be shy.
Jangan malu-malu.

Do you know Mr. Ali?
Apakah saudara kenal Tuan Ali?

I'm glad to meet you. (lit. "Good fortune on meeting.")
Saya senang bertemu denganmu.

I want you to meet my father/mother.
Saya perkenalkan anda dengan ayah/ibu saya.

This is Mrs. Ahmad.
Ini Nyonya Ahmad.

Hello, what's your name? My name is Mohammad.
Halo, siapa namamu? Nama saya Mohammad.

Do you know Mr. Panggabean? I know him well.
Saudara kenal Tuan Panggabean? Saya kenal baik dia.

Are you Mr. Jones? Where are you from?
Apa saudara bernama Jones? Dari mana asal saudara?

I'm from New York. Here is my card.
Saya berasal dari New York. Ini kartu saya.

May I offer you something to drink or eat?
Anda ingin minuman atau makanan?

Perhaps no. Are you sure?
Mungkin tidak. Apakah anda pasti?

You are very hospitable. It's very kind of you.
Anda sangat ramah tamah. Anda baik sekali.

Excuse me. Come again.
Permisi (asking for permission to leave).
Silahkan datang lagi.

TELEPHONE

May I use the telephone?
Bolehkah meminjan telpon Anda?

I want to make a long-distance call.
Saya ingin menelpon untuk interlokal.

How much is a long-distance call to...?
Berapa ongkos interlokal ke...?

Can I dial direct?
Dapatkah saya menelpon langsung?

What number are you calling?
Saudara minta nomor berapa?

the line is busy/out of order
telponnya sedang bicara/tilpon ini rusak

hold the line/there's no answer
tunggu sebentar/tidak ada jawaban

He's not in. Who's speaking?
Ia tak ada di tempat. Siapakah ini?

Is this telephone directory still new?
Buku telpon ini masih baru?

wrong number/the line was interrupted
salah sambung/hubungan telpon terganggu

May I speak with...?/Wait a minute.
Boleh saya bicara dengan...?/Tunggu sebentar.

I want to speak to Mr. Sujono.
Saya mau bicara dengan Tuan Sujono.

AT THE BANK

Where's a bank? Where's the nearest bank?
Dimana bank? Dimanakah bank yang terdekat?

What time does the bank open?
Jam berapa bank buka?

Where can I cash travelers cheques.
Dimana boleh saya menguangkan cek perjalanan turis?

Is there a wire transfer for me?
Ada kiriman uang untuk saya?

I'm sorry, it hasn't arrived yet.
Ma'af, belum datang.

Please contact the Jakarta branch for me.
Tolong hubungi cabang Jakarta untuk saya.

I want to change some American dollars.
Saya mau menukar dolar Amerika.

What's the exchange rate for the dollar?
Berapa kurs uang dolar?

One thousand six hundred and thirty-five rupiahs for one dollar.
Seribu enamratus tigapuluh lima rupiah untuk satu dollar.

Give me five thousand-rupiah notes.
Beri saya uang lima ribuan.

I want to change this into small money.
Saya ingin tukar ini uang kecil.

AT THE POST OFFICE

I'm looking for the post office.
Saya sedang mencari kantor pos.

Where can I mail this? Do not fold!
Dimana saya dapat mengirimkan ini? Jangan dilipat!

Please post this letter/parcel for me.
Tolong poskan surat/bungkusan ini untuk saya.

I want to send this letter via regular mail/airmail.
Saya mau mengirim surat ini biasa/pos udara.
I want to register this letter.
Saya mau surat ini surat tercatat.
This is a special-delivery letter.
Ini adalah surat kilat.
Airmail to New York is Rp800.
Pos udara untuk New York Rp800.
Please weigh this letter/packet.
Tolong timbang surat/paket ini.
Please give me postage stamps/aerograms/postcards.
Saya mau beli perangko/warkatpos udara/kartu pos.
This package is overweight.
Paket ini terlalu berat.
Do you want a return receipt?
Tuan ingin surat tanda terima?
to tie with nylon string/to wrap with paper/tape
mengikat dengan tali/bungkus dengan kertas/isolatip

RECREATION AND SIGHTSEEING

Where's the theater/moviehouse/music hall?
Dimana gedung sandiwara/gedung bioskop/gedung musik?
What kind of play (movie) would you like to see?
Sandiwara (film) apa yang anda suka?
What's on at the Jakarta Theatre tonight? What's showing?
Film apa di Jakarta Theatre malam ini? Film apa yang diputar?
Is there a matinee today? What's the admission?
Adakah matinee hari ini? Berapa harga karcisnya?
Please reserve two tickets for Friday.
Saya mau pesan dua karcis untuk hari Jum'at.
What time does it start? It will start at 1800.
Jam berapa mulainya? Mulainya jam 6 sore.
Let's sit in the first row. This is a good seat.
Mari kita duduk dibaris depan. Disini baik juga.
Sorry, all tickets have been sold out. Sorry, the house is full.
Ma'af, karcis sudah habis terjual. Ma'af, kami sudah penuh.
Where can we go to dance? Is there a discotheque in this hotel?
Dimana kita bisa berdansa? Ada diskotik di hotel ini?
I'd like to dance to live music. Is there a nightclub here?
Saya suka berdansa dengen diiringi band. Ada kelab-malam disini?
Would you like to dance?
Maukah anda berdansa?

Is there a lot to interest tourists around here?
Apakah disini banyak pemandangan yang menarik untuk turis?
Can you give me advice on what to see around here?
Pemandangan apa yang bisa dilihat di daerah ini?
Is there a tourist office near here?
Apakah ada kantor pariwisata di sekitar ini?
What's the fare for a roundtrip to the Loksado area?
Berapa ongkos pulang-pergi ke daerah Loksado?
What will we see on that trip?
Apa saja yang akan dilihat di perjalanan itu?
What shall we bring on the trip?
Apa saja yang harus kita bawa?
How much do you charge per hour? What's included in the price?
Berapa taripnya sejam? Termasuk apa saja itu?
What time does the bus leave? What time do we get back?
Jam berapa bisnya berangkat? Jam berapa kita kembali?
I want a guide who speaks English.
Saya ingin seorang petunjuk-jalan yang bisa bicara bahasa Inggeris.
Is it all right to take photographs?
Bolehkah memotret?
What's that building? Where can I see good paintings?
Gedung apa itu? Dimanakah saya bisa melihat lukisan-lukisan yang baik?
Is there a cave near here? Where's the waterfall?
Ada gua dekat sini? Dimana air terjun?
I want to climb to the peak of that volcano.
Saya mau naik kepuncak gunung itu.
From where can one start the climb? From a village to the north.
Dari mana bisa berangkat? Dari desa ke utara.
How long (time) to the top?
Berapa lama keatas?

Is it safe to swim here? Yes, it's shallow here.
Aman berenang disini? Ya, disini dangkal.
Don't swim too far. It's very calm/rough/deep/dangerous.
Jangan berenang terlalu jauh. Tenang sekali/berombak/dalam/bahaya.
There's a bathing spot on the river.
Di sungai itu ada tempat pemandian.
I only want to sunbathe. Is there a quieter beach?
Saya hanya mau berjemur. Ada pantai yang lebih sepi?
I'm a good swimmer. I like big waves and white sand.
Saya perenang yang baik. Saya suka ombak besar dan pasir putih.
I want to hire a mat/sailboat/tent.
Saya mau menyewa tikar/perahu layar/tenda.

May I go fishing? What time is high/low tide?
    Bolehkah saya memancing? Jam berapa air pasang/surut?

Note: Banners on buildings, stretched out over streets, and hanging from fences and walls announce current and upcoming events, performances, dramas, movies. Keeping an eye on banners is one of the best and quickest ways to keep abreast of the cultural goings-on in a town or city.

concert/solo concert/recital
    konser/konser tunggal/pertunjukan

theater/play/movie/art exhibition
    teater/sandiwara, drama/bioskop/pameran kesenian

SHOPPING

I want to buy... Where can I buy...?
    Saya mau beli... Dimana saya bisa beli...?

Where's the shopping center in this town? How do I get there?
    Dimanakah pusat pertokoan di kota ini? Naik apa saya pergi kesana?

Do you sell arts and crafts here? May I see some batik?
    Tuan ada menjual barang kesenian dan kerajinan tangan di sini? Boleh saya lihat batik?

I'd like to buy silver crafts.
    Saya mau membeli barang-barang kerajinan perak.

I'm just looking around.
    Saya hanya melihat-lihat.

I'd like to look at blouses. Which one (do you) want?
    Saya ingin melihat-lihat blus. Mau yang mana?

Do you have many kinds? I only want this one.
    Punya banyak macam? Saya hanya mau yang ini.

Do you have it in other colors?
    Apakah ini ada warna yang lain?

I prefer something of better quality. These are better.
    Saya lebih suka kwalitas yang lebih baik. Ini lebih baik.

I want one which is new. Can you show me something else?
    Saya mau yang baru. Tolong tunjukkan yang lainnya?

May I try on this dress? Where is the fitting room?
    Boleh saya mencoba baju? Dimana kamar pasnya?

Will it fade/shrink? Where are these goods made?
    Ini bisa luntur/menyusut? Barang-barang ini dibuat dimana?

Those are bad. Same or different? Is there enough?
    Itu Jelek. Sama atau lain? Apakah cukup

What is the price of this? May I bargain?
    Ini berapa harganya? Boleh ditawar?

That's too expensive. Do you have a cheaper one?
    Itu terlalu mahal. Ada yang lebih murah?

Can you come down in price? No, the price is fixed.
    Bisa saudara kurangkan harganya? Tidak, ini harga pasti.

I'll just buy them another time.
    Saya beli lain kali saja.

When will it be ready? Can you deliver it to my hotel?
    Kapan selesainya? Bisa anda antarkan kehotel saya?

I'll take it with me.
    Saya akan membawanya sendiri.

How much is it altogether? May I have a receipt, please?
    Berapa jumlah semuanya? Boleh saya minta tanda terimanya?

Please wrap this with thick paper.
    Tolong bungkuskan dengan kertas yang agak tebal.

Let's go to the market.
    Mari, kita pergi ke pasar.

What is this? What are you making?
    Apakah ini? Sedang bikin apa disini?

Do you sell mosquito nets? Yes (there is), sir.
    Jual kelambu? Ada, Tuan.

How much is this mosquito net?
    Berapa harga kelambu ini?

Twenty-five hundred *rupiah*, Sir.
    Duaribu limaratus rupiah, Tuan.

Don't give me a crazy price! I've seen some that are cheaper.
    Jangan beri harga gila! Saya pernah lihat ada yang lebih murah.

I'll come back later.
    Saya akan kembali lagi.

I can only pay one and a half thousand.
    Saya hanya bisa bayar seribu limaratus rupiah.

If you want it for eighteen hundred *rupiah*, just take it.
    Kalau Tuan mau seribu delapan ratus rupiah, ambil saja.

Last price. It's up to you.
    Harga akhir. Terserah Tuan.

Here is one and a half thousand rupiahs. Is it enough?
    Ini seribu limaratus rupiah. Cukup?

Please wrap it up for me. Please make a very strong package.
    Tolong bungkuskan. Tolong bungkuskan yang kuat sekali.

for sale/to pick out/to point out
    untuk dijual/memilih/menunjukkan

cheap/expensive/to make a profit
    murah/mahal/membuat untung

to pay/to pay cash
    membayer/membayar kontan

there is/there is not/as much again
ada/tidak ada/sekali lagi
big and little/little (not much)/same
besar dan kecil/sedikit/sama
on top of/in front of
diatas/dimuka, didepan
maker or doer/merchant or shopkeeper/antique dealer
tukang/pedagang, penjual/pedagang antik

DO YOU SPEAK INDONESIAN?

Can you speak Indonesian?
Dapatkah anda berbahasa Indonesia?
I don't speak Indonesian.
Saya tidak bicara Bahasa Indonesia.
Please speak slowly.
Tolong bicara pelan-pelan.
Yes, a little. Just enough to make myself understood.
Ya, sedikit. Hanya cukup untuk dimengerti.
Where did you learn it? I learned it by myself.
Tuan belajarnya dimana? Saya belajar sendiri.
Your Indonesian is fluent. Your pronunciation is good.
Bahasa Indonesia anda lancar. Ucapan kata-kata anda baik.
How long have you been studying Indonesian?
Sudah berapa lama anda belajar Bahasa Indonesia?
Do you speak English? May I practice my English with you?
Apa saudara dapat bicara Bahasa Inggeris?
Boleh saya praktek Bahasa Inggeris pada kamu?
I'm very sorry. Perhaps another time.
Ma'af sekali. Mungkin lain waktu.
What is the name for this? What does this word mean?
Apa namanya ini? Apa arti kata ini?
What do you call this? What is this (that) called in Indonesian?
Ini namanya apa? Apa namanya ini (itu) dalam Bahasa Indonesia?
How do you spell it? How do you pronounce it?
Bagaimana mengejanya? Bagaimana mengucapkannya?
What did he (she) say? Please repeat. Say it again.
Apa katanya? Coba ulangi lagi. Sekali lagi.
I understand. I don't understand.
Saya mengerti. Saya kurang mengerti.
What is *"pembangunan"* in English?
Apakah arti "pembangunan" dalam Bahasa Inggrisnya?
How do you translate *"jam karet"* into English?
Bagaimana terjemahan "jam karet" dalam Bahasa Inggris?

TIME, SEASONS, MEASUREMENTS, COLORS

What time is it?
Jam berapa?
I was ten minutes late.
Saya terlambat sepuluh menit.
How long? It takes only ten minutes.
Berapa lama? Itu hanya sepuluh menit.
When? What time does it start?
Kapan? Jam berapa mulai?
earlier/already/ago/recently
tadi/sudah/yang lalu/baru-baru ini
now/once again/just now
sekarang/sekali lagi/baru saja
immediately/quick
segera/cepat
later/afterwards
nanti/kemudian or *sesudah*
to be late/already late (in the day)
terlambat/hari sudah siang
not yet/nearly finished
belum/hampir habis or *hampir selesai*
a few hours/minutes ago
beberapa jam/menit yang lalu
just a moment longer
sebentar lagi, segera
it's not going to happen/it won't come about
tidak jadi/tidak akan terjadi
very flexible schedule; "rubber time"
jam karet
When did you leave Sydney?
Kapan anda meninggalkan Sydney?
I arrived here only yesterday.
Saya sampai disini kemarin.
many times/just this once
seringkali/baru sekali ini
for the first time
untuk pertama kali
I saw him a week ago.
Saya ketemu dia seminggu yang lalu.
I left San Francisco two months ago.
Saya pergi dari San Francisco dua bulan yang lalu.

0500-0700 (5-7 a.m.)
pagi pagi
0700-1200 (7-12 a.m.)
pagi
1200-1500 (12-3 p.m.)
siang
1500-1900 (3-7 p.m.)
sore

today/yesterday/the day before yesterday/the day after tomorrow
hari ini/kemarin/kemarin dulu/lusa

tomorrow/the day after tomorrow/tomorrow morning
besok/lusa/besok pagi

two more days/in the daytime
dua hari lagi/di siang hari

next month
bulan yang akan datang or *bulan depan*

day off/every day/nowadays
hari libur/tiap hari/sekarang ini, saat ini

midday/later in the afternoon
tengah hari/nanti sore

last night/tonight/the whole night/midnight
tadi malam/malam ini/semalam suntuk/tengah malam

thirty minutes
tigapuluh menit

second
detik

hour/o'clock
jam/pukul

past/after
lewat

quarter past five
jam lima lewat seperempat

six-thirty
setengah tujuh

Just seven o'clock
Tepat pukul tujuh

It's seven ten.
Sekarang pukul tujuh lewat sepuluh menit.

quarter to eight
jam delapan kurang seperempat

twenty to nine
jam sembilan kurang duapuluh menit

It's eleven thirty.
Jam setengah duabelas.

week/last week/next week
minggu/minggu yang lalu/minggu depan

once a week/in a week
seminggu sekali/seminggu lagi

Monday/Tuesday/Wednesday
Hari Senin/Hari Selasa/Hari Rabu

Thursday/Friday/Saturday/Sunday
Hari Kamis/Hari Jum'at/Hari Sabtu/Hari Minggu

What day is today? Monday morning.
Hari apa ini? Senin pagi.

Tomorrow is Tuesday.
Besok hari Selasa.

It's Friday, the twenty-second.
Ini hari Jum'at, tanggal duapuluh dua.

Yesterday was Sunday.
Kemarin hari Minggu.

January/February/March/April
Januari/Februari/Maret/April

May/June/July/August
Mei/Juni/Juli/Agustus

September/October/November/December
September/Oktober/Nopember/Desember

What date is today?
Tanggal berapa hari ini? or *Tanggal berapa sekarang?*

It's the sixteenth of July.
Hari ini tanggal enambelas Juli.

What date was it yesterday?
Kemarin tanggal berapa?

Do you have a calendar?
Apa saudara punya tanggalan?

May 17, 1941.
Tujuhbelas Mei, sembilanbelas empatpuluh satu.

this year/for years and years
tahun ini/bertahun-tahun

season/dry season/hot season/rainy season
musim/musim kemarau/musim panas/musim hujan

wind/humid/nice day/beautiful weather
angin/lembab/hari bagus/cuaca bagus

clear/cloudy/cool/hot/foggy
terang/mendung/sejuk/panas/berkabut

measurement/distance
ukuran/jarak

to weigh/width/length
timbang/lebarnya/panjangnya

to measure (for size)/to measure (for volume)
mengukur/menakar

depth/height/bigger than that
dalam or *kedalaman/tinggi* or *ketinggian/lebih besar dari itu*

black/white/yellow/red/blue/green/brown/orange
hitam/putih/kuning/merah/biru/hijau/coklat/oranye

TRANSPORTATION

What are the tourist places I should visit?
Apa nama tempat pariwisata yang harus saya kunjungi?

There are two caves near the hotsprings.
Ada dua gua dekat sumber air panas.

Is it safe to swim here?
Aman berenang disini?

Where do you want to go?
Anda mau pergi ke mana?

I want to go to Yogya.
Saya mau pergi ke Yogya.

When are you leaving?
Kapan anda berangkat?

I depart tommorrow/today.
Saya berangkat besok/hari ini.

not sure/not certain
belum tentu/belum pasti

I'm worn out.
Saya agat capek.

How far is it from here? Is it near?
Berapa jauh dari sini. Dekat?
Far from here. This way/that way. Which way?
Jauh dari sini. Kesini/kesana. Kemana?
Turn left at the corner.
Belok ke kiri di prapatan.
Go straight ahead and turn to the left/right.
Jalan terus dan kemudian belok kekiri/kekanan.
Go back to the intersection, then follow the sign.
Kembali kepersimpangan jalan, lalu ikuti tanda arah.
My address is.../I live on Melati Street.
Alamat saya.../Saya tinggal de Jalan Melati.
Straight ahead. On the right. On the left.
Terus. Disebelah kanan. Disebelah kiri.
Cross here. Wait here. Stop here.
Di sini menyeberang. Tunggulah disini. Berhenti disini.
to back up, go backwards/to go forward, advance
mundur/maju
To search for. Where can I find a post office?
Mencari. Kantor pos dimana?
Please show me the way to the highway.
Tolong tunjukkan ke jalan raya.
I want to find this address. I am lost.
Saya mau mendapat alamat ini. Saya tersesat.
Please show me on this map.
Tolong tunjukkan dipeta ini.
What is the name of this street?
Apa nama jalan ini?
What town does this road lead to?
Jalan ini menuju kekota apa?
Where can I catch a... ? Where can I rent a...?
Dimana saya akan naik...? Dimana bisa menyewa...?

How many kilometers is it to Rantepao?
Berapa kilometer ke Rantepao?
What's the best route to follow?
Jalan mana yang terbaik?
This road is under repair.
Jalan ini sedang diperbaiki.
This road is very slippery. Look out.
Jalan ini sangat licin. Hati-hati.
My car has broken down. Where can I find a mechanic?
Mobil saya mogok. Dimana saya bisa dapat seorang montir?
I have a flat tire. Will you please repair the tire?
Ban saya kempis. Tolong pompakan bannya?
What's wrong with the engine? Switch off the engine.
Apa yang rusak pada mesin ini? Matikan mesin-nya.
The engine won't start. Is there enough gasoline?
Mesin ini mogok. Apakah bensinnyacukup?
Fill it up please. Check the oil.
Tolong diisi penuh. Periksa olinya.

at the bus/train station
di stasiun bis/stasiun kereta api
Where is the ticket window?
Dimana ada loket?
How long does it take from here to Bogor?
Berapa lama perjalanan dari sini ke Bogor?
Where's the airport?
Dimana lapangan terbang?
How much does a taxi to the airport cost?
Berapa tarip taxi kepelabuhan udara?
Please help me with my luggage.
Bung, tolong bawakan barang-barang saya.
There are three pieces.
Semuanya ada tiga barang.
Where is the passport and customs checkpoint?
Dimana tempat pemeriksaan paspor dan barang?
Which gate do I go to for the plane for Singapore?
Saya harus pergi kepintu mana untuk naik pesawat ke Singapura?
When is the next flight?
Jam berapa ada penerbangan berikutnya?
When is the next flight to Jambi?
Kapan ada penerbangan lagi ke Jambi?
At what time does the plane for Ambon leave?
Jam berapa pesawat terbang ke Ambon berangkat?
Is there a nonstop flight between Jakarta and Samarinda?
Apakah ada pesawat langsung antara Jakarta dan Samarinda?
What's the fare to Solo?
Berapa ongkosnya ke Solo?
I want a single/return ticket.
Saya mau beli karcis sejalan/pulang pergi.
Stewardness, are we near Kupang?
Pramugari, apakah kita sudah dekat dengan Kupang?

Where is the railway station?
Dimana stasiun kereta api?
Where is the railway information desk?
Dimana tempat bertanya?
Where is the baggage room?
Dimana kamar bagasi?
I want a ticket to Bandung. What's the fare?
Saya mau beli karcis ke Bandung. Berapa ongkosnya?
Which class do you want? First Class or Second Class?
Kelas berapa yang Tuan mau? Kelas satu atau kelas dua?
How much is a First Class roundtrip ticket to Bogor?
Berapa harga karcis kelas satu pulang-pergi ke Bogor?
Is it half price for a child?
Apakah anak-anak setengah harga?

I want to reserve two seats to Bandung on Monday.

>	*Saya mau pesan dua kursi untuk ke Bandung pada hari senin.*

What time is the first train for Banyuwangi?

>	*Jam berapa kereta-api pertama menuju Banyuwangi?*

is this seat taken? Sorry, already full.

>	*Apakah kursi ini kosong? Ma'af, sudah ada orang.*

There's room for one more. Take a seat, please.

>	*Ada tempat untuk satu orang lagi. Silahkan duduk.*

How long does the train stop here?

>	*Berapa lama kereta-api berhenti disini?*

What time does the train arrive?

>	*Jam berapa kereta api datang?*

Does this train go to...?

>	*Apakah kereta api ini ke...?*

We will arrive in Cilacap at around noon.

>	*Kita akan sampai di Cilacap kira-kira tengah hari.*

time of arrival

>	*waktu kedatangan/jam datang*

What time will the ship be sailing?

>	*Jam berapa kapal ini akan berangkat?*

Where do I get the boat to Balikpapan?

>	*Darimanakah dapat saya naik kapal ke Balikpapan?*

Perhaps on Monday.

>	*Barangkali hari Senin.*

Which class are you traveling?

>	*Perjalanan Tuan di kelas berapa?*

First Class (or cabin)/Economy Class

>	*Kelas Satu/Kelas Ekonomi*

It's time to go onboard.

>	*Sekarang ini waktu untuk naik ke kapal.*

to take a *becak*/call a *becak*

>	*naik becak, berbecak/panggil becak*

Turn to the right/left.

>	*Belok ke kanan/kiri.*

What is the *becak* fare there?

>	*Berapa ongkok becak ke sana?*

Don't pay more than Rp400 *rupiah.*

>	*Jangan bayar lebih dari empatratus rupiah.*

Driver, take me to Losmen Matahari.

>	*Bung, bawa saya ke Losmen Matahari.*

Two thousand! How is it possible nowadays, sir!

>	*Duaribu! Mana bisa sekarang ini, pak!*

Better just call another *becak.*

>	*Lebih baik, panggil saja becak lain.*

All right, make it one thousand.

>	*Ayo, seribu!*

What time will the bus leave? Let's get on the bus.

>	*Jam berapa bis ini akan berangkat? Mari kita naik bis.*

Are there buses that go there? How long from here to there?

>	*Apa ada bis yang ke sana? Berapa lama dari sini kesana?*

Which bus will take us downtown?

>	*Bis yang mana yang akan ke kota?*

Does this bus go directly to Bukittinggi?

>	*Apakah bis ini pergi langsung ke Bukittinggi?*

Are there any empty seats? No standing room!

>	*Ada tempat duduk yang kosong? Tak ada tempat untuk berdiri!*

Where shall we get off? Let's get off the bus here!

>	*Dimana kita akan turun? Kita turun disini!*

At the next stop, please let me off.

>	*Saya akan berhenti dipemberhentian berikutnya.*

Shall we take a taxi? We have to take a taxi.

>	*Perlu kita naik taksi? Kita harus naik taksi.*

call a taxi/please get me a taxi

>	*panggil taksi/tolong panggilkan saya taksi*

Where is the taxi stand? Is this taxi taken?

>	*Dimana tempat taksi? Apakah taksi ini ada yang pakai?*

How much is this taxi per hour? The taxi has a meter.

>	*Berapa sewa taksi ini per jam? Taksi itu pakai meter.*

Taxi! To the airport!/Drive me to...

>	*Taksi! Ke lapangan terbang!/Antar saya ke...*

Take me to a cheap/expensive hotel.

>	*Antarkan saya kehotel yang lebih murah/mahal.*

I want to see the city. Please drive me around for sightseeing.

>	*Saya ingin melihat kota. Tolong antar saya berkeliling lihat-lihat kota.*

Drive a bit faster. I'm in a hurry.

>	*Cepat sedikit. Saya buru-buru.*

Please slow down. Please drive more slowly.

>	*Kurangi kecepatan. Jalan pelan-pelan saja.*

Stop here. What's the fare, driver?

>	*Berhenti disini. Berapa ongkosnya, Bung?*

STREET SIGNS

Parking	*Parkir*
No parking	*Dilarang parkir*
Cross here	*Menyeberang di sini*
Women/Men	*Wanita/Laki-laki*
Keep Out	*Dilarang Masuk*
Entrance	*Pintu Masuk*
Exit	*Pintu Keluar*
Caution	*Awas/Hati-hati*
Open/Closed	*Buka/Tutup*
Danger	*Bahaya*
Waiting Room	*Ruang Tunggu*
Information	*Penerangan*

Up/Down	*Naik/Turun*
Push/Pull	*Dorong/Tarik*
Police	*Polisi*
Police Station	*Kantor Polisi*
Headquarters	*Kantor Pusat*
Branch	*Cabang*

USEFUL PHRASES

yes
> *ya* (Dutch spelling and pronunciation)

no
> *tidak* (with an adjective or verb) or *bukan* (with a noun)

this, that
> *ini, itu* (after the noun)

I do not have...
> *Saya tidak punya...*

There is... There is not...
> *Ada... Tidak ada...*

Yes, you're right.
> *Ya, Tuan benar.*

It seems wrong. It's not necessary.
> *Rupanya salah. Ini tidak penting.*

In my opinion. That's right.
> *Saya rasa, saya kira, menurut saya. Itu betul* or *Itu benar.*

As much as possible
> *Sebanyak mungkin*

I'm tired/hungry/thirsty
> *Saya lelah/lapar/haus*

I want... Do you want...? I'm looking for...
> *Say mau... Anda mau...? Saya mencari...*

I'm interested (in)... to like...
> *Saya tertarik... suka...*

I need... I like... I hope so.
> *Saya perlu... Saya suka... Saya harap begitu.*

I want to borrow... Do you have...?
> *Saya mau pinjam... Anda punya...?*

Don't... I don't like it that... I don't want.
> *Jangan... Saya tidak suka itu... Saya tidak mau.*

I like Indonesia. Fine, okay.
> *Saya suka Indonesia. Baik.*

I know. I don't know.
> *Saya tahu. Saya tidak tahu.*

I think so. I don't think so.
> *Saya kira begitu. Saya kira tidak begitu.*

I have... Of course.
> *Saya punya... Tentu saja.*

an expression of surprise/pain
> *Wah!/Aduh!*

in the future... in this manner... in that manner
> *pada masa yang akan datang... begitu... begini...*

Yes, you're right. You're wrong.
> *Ya, anda benar. Anda salah.*

It's possible. It's not possible. To be able.
> *Mungkin. Tidak mungkin. Bisa, dapat (may), boleh*

I'm glad to hear it.
> *Saya senang mendengarnya.*

Thanks for the gift. It's very kind of you.
> *Terima kasih atas hadiah anda. Anda baik hati sekali.*

Excuse me for being late. Excuse me for interrupting.
> *Maafkan, saya terlambat. Maafkan, saya mengganggu.*

Excuse me for a moment. May I be excused?
> *Maafkan saya sebentar. Bolehkah saya tidak ikutserta?*

I beg your pardon.
> *Saya mohon maaf.* or *Maafkan saya.*

Excuse me, what did you say?
> *Ma'af, apa yang anda katakan?*

I'm sorry, I can't help you.
> *Ma'af, saya tidak dapat menolong anda.*

TROUBLES, DIFFICULTIES, HASSELS

Indonesia is not a violent environment and you very seldom hear of muggings, rapes, fights. But by virtue of its huge population base, there is an element of the population who are illbred and rude (*kasar*, in Indonesian). If anyone is ever bothering you or touching you indecently, it's usually enough to say *Jangan begitu, itu tidak biak.* ("Don't act like that, it's not nice.") This is sufficiently firm, yet polite, and will cover most unpleasant situations.

Please help me for a moment. I've missed the train.
> *Tolonglah saya sebentar. Saya ketinggalan kereta api*

I've been robbed. I've been held up. What a pity!
> *Saya baru dirampok. Saya baru di todong. Kasihan!*

My money has been stolen. Our bags are missing.
> *Uang saya dicuri orang. Barang-barang kami halang*

I've lost my passport. All my IDs are gone.
> *Paspor saya hilang. Semma surat-surat pengenalan saya hilang.*

Where's the police station? Please call the police.
> *Dimana kantor polisi? Tolong panggilkan polisi.*

Can I speak with the manager? I am angry.
> *Bisakah saya bicara dengan pengurus? Saya marah.*

Let's talk the problem over with....
> *Marilah, kita bicarakan persoalan ini dengan...*

Is there anybody here who speaks English?
> *Ada yang bisa berbahasa inggeris disini*

Can I have a translator, please?
Ada penterjemah disini?
Where's the information desk? Where's the moneychanger?
Dimana "information desk?" Dimana tempat menukar uang?
Don't be angry with me. Don't be ill mannered.
Janganlah marah kepada saya. Jangan kurang ajar.
Don't do that. Absolutely not!
Jangan bikin itu. Sama sekali tidak!
Don't talk nonsense. Don't bother me.
Jangan omong kosong. Jangan ganggu saya.
Excuse me, I must be going now.
Maaf, saya harus pergi sekarang.
I am angry. I want to go away from here.
Saya marah. Saya ingin pergi dari sini.

Will you please leave me alone? Please go away. Go away!
Sudikah anda membiarkan saya sendiri? Pergilah! Pergi!
Be patient, please! Don't disturb me. Leave her alone.
Sabarlah sebentar. Jangan mengganggu saya! Jangan ganggu dia.
What's the matter? Be careful of him.
Ada apa? Hati hati sama dia.
His manners are very vulgar. He's ill-mannered (impolite/rude).
Dia tidak sopan. Dia kurang ajar.
Never mind. That's all right. Forget it!
Tidak apa-apa. Itu tak mengapa. Lupakan saja

GLOSSARY

acar—cucumber pickle salad

adat—traditional law or custom; unwritten rules of behavior covering such matters as inheritance rights; land ownership; cooking and eating; ceremonies of birth, marriage, and death; times and methods of sowing rice; building houses; praying for rain; courtship; activities a menstruating woman may participate in, etc. *Adat* is the real law of the land, the oldest and most respected.

Airlangga—an E. Javanese hermit-king who ruled from A.D. 1019-1049, during the Golden Age of Indonesia. His reign saw the flowering of intense literary and artistic activity and marked the beginning of a distinct E. Javanese style of art and architecture. During his rule, Airlangga achieved the unification of nearly all of Java.

air panas—literally means "hotsprings," but could also be a medicinal springs or health spa

alun-alun—the main town square, playing field, and/or town park where public meetings, festivals, and sports events take place. The park-like expanse of lawn is often dotted with grazing goats. Facing the *alun-alun* are the public buildings: mosque, church, local government offices, post office, banks, schools.

alus—a term used to describe the most refined cultural traits in real life, as well as in characters in the *wayang* theater forms. All gestures, judgments, behavior, or temperaments which are smooth, gracious, pure, polite, noble, subtle, civilized, sophisticated, exquisite.

Amir Hamzah—the prophet Mohammed's uncle. During the rise of Islam on Java in the 15th C., the Amir Hamzah tales—derived from 7th C. Persian history—became Indonesianized. They tell of battles, wars and love affairs of the warrior-missionaries *(wali)* of Java. Stories from this play make up some of the most popular *wayang golek* episodes of C. and W. Java.

angklung—a rattle instrument, dating from Neolithic times, used in W. Java by the Sundanese to accompany folk dances. Hollow bamboo tubes cut to graduated lengths are suspended in a wooden frame. When the frame is shaken these tubes hit each other, producing a strange xylophonic sound.

anoa—a timid animal that resembles a miniature buffalo, its horns sloping straight back from its head. Indigenous only to the high mountain forests of Sulawesi, there are 2 species: the lowland *(Buba-*

lus depressicornis) and the highland *(Bubalus depressicornis quarlesi)*.

apem—a thick doughy pancake spread with sugar and crushed nuts or coconut, then folded over

arak—distilled rice brandy; about Rp1200 a bottle in the markets

Arjuna Wiwaha—a play composed by Mpu Kanwa in A.D. 1035. One of its more famous scenes describes the hero Arjuna meditating in the Himalayas to gain strength. To test his will, Shiva sends heavenly nymphs to dance near him, but his concentration holds. This play, inspired by the Hindu *Mahabharata,* was first translated into Old Javanese during the reign of King Airlangga.

ASEAN—Association of South East Asian Nations (Singapore, Thailand, Malaysia, Indonesia, Philippines), a political/economic/military organization founded in 1968 to check the perceived tide of communism in SE Asia.

ASKI—Akademi Seni Kerawitan. Dance academies found in all the major ethnic cultural centers of Indonesia

asli—native, original, authentic; also could mean high-born or noble

asram—a student dormitory or student flats. Only in its broadest sense does it mean "retreat" or "school" in Indonesian.

ASTI—Akademi Seni Tari Indonesia. Government-sponsored undergraduate-level performing arts schools

atap—palm thatch

Atoni—the native people of Indonesian Timor, living mainly in the inland mountain areas

babirusa—an Indonesian mammal, the "hog deer" *(Babirousa babirussa)* indigenous only to Sulawesi

badak—Javan or Sumatran rhinoceros

bahasa—language, dialect

Bahasa Indonesia—the national language of Indonesia

bajai—a motorized, 3-wheeled *becak* used in Jakarta; Rp1000-1500 is the average fare

bajigur—a delicious drink made of coconut milk, thickened with rice and sweetened condensed milk

bale—platform; also written *balai*

Bali Aga—the aboriginal pre-Hindu inhabitants of Bali

banci—female impersonators or transsexuals, found particularly in Jakarta, but also in such diverse places as Ujung Pandang and Tanatoraja. Also called "sister boys." The polite word is *waria,* a combination of *wanita* (female) and *pria* (male).

bandrek—a Sundanese drink made from ginger milk, coconut, and brown sugar

banteng—the wild cattle *(Bos javanicus)* of Indonesia; looks like a cow but has longer legs. In both sexes the rump is white, darkening to tawny-red in the cows and calves, deep black in the older bulls. *Banteng* graze on cooler well-drained foothills and grasslands and usually travel in herds of 1-2 bulls with several cows and their young. Lone bulls rejected by the herd can be dangerous, so stay clear. The *banteng* symbolizes freedom and nationalism for the masses.

banyan—a fig or *waringan* tree with writhing arteries which spread out 10-15 m. Buddha's Bo Tree, under which he received enlightenment, was a *banyan.* Found on Indonesia's coat of arms, its sturdy trunk, umbrella-shaped crown, and cool shade symbolize physical protection and divine blessing. The banyan is believed to never die, replenishing itself from seedlings which drop from its branches. It may never be cut down for powerful spirits may dwell in it.

bapak—father, headman, leader, male teacher, department head, boss

Bapparda—Badan Perkembangan Pariwisata Daerah or Local Tourist Development Board.

Barong Dance—the most violent and dramatic of Balinese dances; used often as an exorcism. Two demonic characters, Rangda and Barong, feature in this mythological story. Also called the *"Kris Dance."*

Batak—a proto-Malayan people of N. Sumatra, one of the Ancient Peoples of Indonesia

batik—a traditional way of decorating cloth by the wax-resist or "negative" painting method

becak—Indonesia's bicycle trishaw. Carries 2 or more, plus goods. Rarely used for distances longer than 2-4 km; average fare is Rp500-1000.

Bedaya Dance—a sedate court dance of the C. Javanese *kraton;* also seen in the palaces of a few river kingdoms of E. Kalimantan. This dance dates back to the ancient Majapahit and Sriwijaya empires and is traditionally performed by 9 women costumed as brides. Related to the sultan, the dancers are part of the sacred regalia of the court. The *Bedaya* was inspired by a 17th C. love affair between a sultan and the South Sea Goddess, Nyai Loro Kidul. Attended by invitation only.

bemo—a small, 3- or 4-wheeled covered vehicle. The driver sits in front with 1 or 2 passengers and there are seats in back for 6-8 more passengers and their wares. Costs Rp200-400 for a 2- to 5-km ride. Often much cheaper to charter than taxis.

bendi (or "dog carts")—a versatile horse-drawn 2-wheeled cart. They're not fast or comfortable, but they're cheap (Rp500/km or less). A *bendi* offers the best visibility for sightseeing and has a canopy to ward off the sun or rain. Used extensively in rural Java and W. Sumatra.

benhur—a pony cart used for local transportation on Sumbawa

benteng—an old fortress, either Portuguese, Dutch, Indonesian, or English. Today *benteng* are frequently occupied by the Indonesian army.

Bersih Desa—an annual village cleansing festival which takes place after the harvest to rid a town of evil

Bharta-yuddha—a lyrical masterpiece begun by the court poet Mpu Sedah in A.D. 1157. The poem describes a tremendous 18-day epic battle in Indian mythology between 2 family groups, the 5 Pandava brothers (the 5 Senses of Man) pitted against their hundreds of evil cousins, the Korawas. The most popular stories and figures in today's *wayang* plays are based directly on this involved Javanized story.

bhikku (female: *bhikksuni*)—the *Pali* form for "religious hermit." On Java it means "Hindu or Buddhist teacher."

Bhinneka Tunggal Ika—a Sanskrit term attributed to a 13th C. poet and now Indonesia's official motto. It means "We are many, but we are one," or, more commonly, "Unity in diversity." The 14th C. Majapahit prime minister, Gajah Mada, was the first to use this Indonesian phrase.

Bima—a warrior-lover of the Hindu *Ramayana* epic poem. One of the 5 Pandava brothers, the biggest and the baddest, the black-headed giant hero. Also the name of a fast a/c train that runs between Surabaya and Jakarta.

bioskop—movie theater, cinema

bis air—a river ferry used in Kalimantan and Sumatra

bis kota—city bus

bis malam—special, fast, more expensive buses which travel long distances at night on Java, Bali, S. Sulawesi and Sumatra

blimbing ("star fruit")—a crispy, watery, thirst-quenching sour fruit which looks like a starfish. Usually yellow, but there are white and green varieties too. Wedged pieces smoothed over with salt is one favorite way to eat *blimbing.*

bonze—a Buddhist monk

Bouraq—an Indonesian airline which flies to many remote places on Sulawesi, Kalimantan, Nusa-tenggara, and Maluku

Brahma—the 4-headed Hindu God of Creation who gave birth to the Hindu castes; the head of the Hindu Trinity. Brahma appears in white robes and rides a goose. Once thought to be the greatest and most revered of all the Hindu gods because he set the universe in motion, he faded in importance with the rise of Shiva and Vishnu. Brahma was seldom worshipped in Indonesia.

Brahman—on Bali, a member of the highest Hindu caste

breadfruit—related to figs, the breadfruit *(artocarpus)* grows all over Indonesia and Polynesia. The massive, globose fruit (weighing up to 20 kg) must be cooked before eating. Breadfruit wood is easily worked and its inner bark was once used to make *tapa* cloth.

brem—fiery Balinese wine made from fermented black rice; tastes a bit like sweet sherry and should be served cold

bubur—Indonesian porridge, a soft semi-liquid food made from rice, coconut, or beans. Served usually in a glass with ice or sometimes steaming hot in a bowl. Comes in all shapes: snake-like curls, balls, pellets, or a pulpy mash. Colors range from bright green to chartreuse. Quite cheap, it's a common *kampung* dessert. The Chinese add chicken, pork, and pork rinds.

bupati—a local native chief or government district officer appointed by the minister of internal affairs. The Dutch called them "regents" and governed through them. The *bupati* is the embodiment of traditional elite culture and the focus for rural popular politicals. In large towns his function can be compared to the position of mayor.

camat—civilian assistant head of a district, second in command after the *bupati*

candi—a Hindu or Buddhist tomb-temple. The term is commonly applied to all ancient monuments and ruins on Java and Sumatra, irrespective of their particular purpose or religious orientation.

canting—an implement used for drawing (waxing) *batik* designs. The *canting* has a short bamboo handle and a tiny kettle on one end with a spout at the bottom where the wax comes out.

cap—a tin or copper stamp, the size of a small book, used in the hand-stamped *batik* process. *Cap*-printed *batik* is less time-consuming (and much less expensive) than hand-drawn *batik*.

cap cai—Indonesian vegetable and/or meat chop suey

casuarina—a tough, fire-resistant tree prevalent in the drier eastern islands of Indonesia. Sometimes called the "Australian pine," it has dense, needle-like branches that serve as leaves. In Indonesian, it's called *cemara*.

cecak—small household lizards, formidable killers of mosquitos

cella—a niche in an ancient stone temple in which a divinity, or his or her symbol, a reincarnated king, or a nobleman or noblewoman, is placed

cemara—see casuarina

ciku—a sweet, soft, egg-shaped fruit, brown outside and in. To eat it, the skin must be sliced off. Its smooth flesh almost melts in your mouth, but be careful of the smooth doe-eyed stones inside.

colt—Pronounced "coal," this is a Mitsubishi van or minibus. Used all over Indonesia to transport passengers quickly from town to town. About one-third more expensive than buses but faster, the closest thing to an "express" service you can find.

copra—coconut meat dried in the sun until it looks like soles of shoes, curled by the heat and tinged with mold. Oil extracted from it is used in cooking oil, beauty lotion, soap, nitroglycerin.

cuscus—a nocturnal marsupial with soft fur, sharp claws and teeth, living a solitary existence except during the mating season. The female is frequently solid gray-brown while males are spotted. The *cuscus* keeps to the trees where it lives on leaves and fruits. Found in Irian Jaya, its satellite islands, and Maluku.

dagob—the highest pinnacle of a *stupa*

dalang—the *wayang* puppeteer who either manipulates the puppets and speaks the words, or narrates a plot for live actors. He is the playwright, producer, director, singer, and poet who jokes, cues the *gamelan*, philosophizes, impersonates. In essence, he is the star of the show.

Damar Wulan—a Majapahit hero found in E. Javanese theater forms

Darul Islam—a murderous rebellion which took place around Bandung from 1948 to 1962. Its goal was to set up an Islamic state.

datu—a Batak medicine man, priest, prophet, or physician

debus (or *dabus*)—an awl-like dagger with which participants in mystical ceremonies, after reaching a state of trance, inflict wounds upon themselves

delman—a large, horse-drawn wagon carrying up to 6 people

dermaga—pier, loading-stage, quay-wall

desa—a small agrarian village. On Java, a *desa* consists of farmhouses, barns, community meeting places, ricefields, fishponds, forests, houses. On Bali, a *desa* may also have a central square, temples, market, *waringan* tree, and an alarm-drum tower.

Dewi Sri—the Rice Goddess. From the time of rice-planting to harvesting, ceremonies are held all over Java and Bali in her honor.

dokar—a light, 2-wheeled horse carriage, usually with 2 seats for 4-6 passengers. Corruption of the English "dog cart."

duku—ping-pong ball-sized fruits, sweet with a sour tinge. Each wedge of the translucent white flesh is enclosed in a light-brown shell containing a hard, greenish center which might taste bitter if you take too deep a bite. To open, just squeeze.

dukun—could be a folk doctor, witch doctor, black magic advocate, herbalist, druggist, village healer (using incantations), ritual specialist (employing simple prayers or amulets), chronicler, bard, diviner, or a conjuror and spiritual leader of great prestige

durian—the outside of this odorous fruit is spiked like the ball of a mace. The inside consists of 3 or 4 compartments where the cream-colored fruit surrounds large pods. Suck the mushy custard-like pulp from the pods. Tastes like vanilla ice cream with onions, Camembert cheese and nectarines, brandied eggnog with radishes, and other such wild combinations.

empu—the *kris*-maker

erong—graves hung from high cliffs in Torajaland, S. Sulawesi

es—ice. Could also mean sweet, frozen fruit-flavored water on a stick, Rp100-200.

es buah—a mixture of fruit with shaved ice and sweetened condensed milk, coconut, *bubur*, and chocolate syrup on top

es jus—a combination of fruit, crushed ice, and sweet syrup mixed in a blender

fahombe—a stone-jumping sport of the Nias Islanders. Once used to train warriors for battle and to prove a young man's fitness to take a wife, now it's a tourist spectacle which you must pay to see.

gado-gado—a national dish of steamed green beans, soy beans, potatoes, cabbage, or bean sprouts and covered in a rich, tangy peanut sauce. The best is found in Jakarta.

Galungan—a Balinese festival during which the gods come down to visit the island for a week. Celebrated also by Balinese communities all over Indonesia.

gamelan—a Javanese or Balinese percussion-type orchestra. Made up of bronze and wooden xylophones shaped like discs, cylinders, keys, or bulbous hollow bowls and beaten with hammers.

Ganesha—in Hindu mythology, the fat-bellied elephant-headed son of Shiva and Parvati; the God of Household, Learning, and Prosperity. Beloved Ganesha is worshipped before every undertaking to assure success.

gang—alleyway, small lane, path, or street

ganja—marijuana

garuda—a legendary bird, like a combination eagle and supernatural roc. Garuda, the mount of Vishnu, tried to rescue Sita midflight during her abduction by the devil-king Rawana, but died in the attempt. The *garuda* is a common motif in Indonesian art, the official emblem of the Republic, as well as the name of the government-run international airline.

genggong—a Balinese jew's harp

gotong royong—village socialism. A traditional village practice of mutual cooperation in planting, irrigation, and harvesting. This is the actual means by which a new school gets built, a local industry started, an irrigation canal dug—not by a masterplan from Jakarta. It's encouraged by the government because it makes its job easier and helps fight inflation.

gringsing—in E. Bali, the *ikat* "flaming cloth" weaving design

gudeg—a Yogyanese culinary specialty combining rice with boiled young jackfruit, chicken, egg, and a spicy coconut cream sauce. Sometimes served with boiled buffalo hide.

gunung—mountain. Gunung Merapi means "Mount Merapi."

guru—in the Indonesian sense, anyone who teaches

haj—the pilgrimage made by Muslims to Mecca, which some 40,000 Indonesians undertake each year. A *haji* is a man who has made the pilgrimage; he wears the white skullcap called a *peci*. *Hajah* is the feminine form. The honorific title *Haji* or *Hajah* may precede a person's name.

Hari Raya (or *Idul Fitri*)—the Islamic New Year, with several days of festivities ending the month-long Muslim fast, *Ramadan*. Celebrated by Muslims all over Indonesia with ear-splitting firecrackers, mass prayers in mosques and public places, followed by visits among relatives and friends when new clothes are worn and gifts exchanged.

helicak—a small, motorized 3-wheeled vehicle which carries 5-8 passengers. Average fare, Rp200-600.

hukum tua—in Minahasa, N. Sulawesi, the head of a village

huta—a Toba-Batak settlement, a small group of houses standing like an island in the midst of a ricefield. A great number of Toba-Batak family names have *huta* as a prefix: *Hutagalung, Hutabarat*, etc.

ibu—mother. Also a deferential or affectionate title used when addressing any older woman such as a landlady, washerwoman, cook or *warung* proprietor.

Idul Fitri—*Leberan* day, the feast at the end of the fasting month

ikan bakar—baked fish

ikat—a tie-dye technique. Thin coconut fibers are wound tightly around cotton thread to prevent the bound parts from absorbing color when they're dipped into a dye bath. By changing the wrappings after dyeing, various colors and patterns can be applied to the unwoven threads. *Ikat* can be applied to the warp, the weft, or (rarely) to both.

imigrasi—Kantor Imigrasi is the immigration department or office where foreigners must go to renew visas or work or residence permits.

istana—a palace or castle; usually precedes a proper name, i.e., "Istana Bogor"

jambu-air—the rose apple *(Syzygium jambos)*. A juicy, pink, light-green, or white bell-shaped fruit about the size of a large strawberry. A popular way of eating *jambu-air* is to first break it by squeezing it between the palms of the hands and then dip the pieces into a mixture of black soy sauce, sugar, and sliced chilies. The whole fruit is edible.

jambu-batu—a guava *(Psidium guajava)*, a pear-shaped, smooth, very seedy fruit. Eat the green outer layer, the pulp, or the whole thing.

jamu—herbal medicines made from a mixture of roots, barks, and grasses, usually steeped in hot water and drunk; other *jamu* are eaten or applied to the skin

jeruk—citrus fruits. In some parts of Indonesia it means orange or mandarin, in other parts, a grapefruit or lemon.

jimmy—a small, powerful, energy-efficient Suzuki vehicle which rents on Bali for about Rp30,000 per day. Also spelled *jimny*.

joget (or *joged*)—social, not religious, dancing. On Bali this dance form is a licensed, socially sanctioned flirtation dance in which a young dancer entices boys from the audience to dance with her.

juru kunci—caretaker or "Keeper of the Shrine." You must go to this man to be let into a temple, museum, historical or tourist site. He frequently produces a guestbook to sign and asks for a small donation.

kabupaten—a regency of a province. Kantor Kabupaten is the office or residence of the head of the regency.

kain—a length of material (2.75 m X 1.2 m) worn by both men and women, fastened at the waist by a sash. A *kain* is what the Western-dressed civil servant changes into when he or she gets home from work. *Kain kebaya* is the national dress of Indonesian women.

kakawin—a classical poetry style of ancient Javanese courts

kala—literally "badness" or "evil," but in the figurative sense it is the demon himself who invisibly causes evil. A symbol of coarseness and malice, he haunts desolate places like seashores, deep forests, cemeteries, or crossroads. *Kala* can go into people's bodies and make them idiotic or insane. A *kala*-head is the carved stone head of a monster over temple gates and recesses to magically ward off demonic forces; looks like a stylized lion's or dragon's head.

kamar mandi—bathroom, washroom

kampung—a village, neighborhood, homestead, family, or migrant living compound in the country or city. In the city, *kampung* are really villages transplanted into the metropolis, each one reflecting the ethnic background and origins of its inhabitants. This poor man's sector is made up of hundreds of shanties separated by narrow lanes or footpaths, very crowded and often without paved roads or electricity. Sometimes up to 3,000 people are jammed together in a single housing unit with just palm matting walls separating households.

kanari—a nut similar to an almond

kancil—also called the "mouse-deer." The *kancil* is not a true deer and has no antlers. Smallest of all hoofed, cud-chewing mammals, it stands no more than ½ m at the shoulders, with a soft brown coat and undersides. In folk tales, it is represented as a shy, seemingly helpless creature who uses cunning and its razor sharp teeth to outwit stronger enemies.

kantor—office

Kantor Camat—office of the *camat* (district head)

Kantor Kabupaten—*bupati's* (regent's or mayor's) residence or office

Kantor Pariwisata—tourist office

kapal laut—a seagoing ship

kapal motor—a small motorized vessel capable of traveling along coasts, up rivers, and across channels or straits

kapok—a silky, waxy fiber taken from the pods of the *kapok* tree which grows on higher slopes. *Kapok* resists vermin and moisture and is as good as cork as a filler for life preservers. Oil from its seeds is used in munitions, food, soap.

kasar—a term used to describe rough, uncivilized, ungracious, impolite, coarse, blunt traits or attributes in objects, people, or skills. Also could mean in poor taste, inappropriate. Includes things like poorly played music, stupid jokes, cheap pieces of cloth, blotchy paintings.

kauman—the orthodox Islamic quarter of a city, known for its strict adherence to Islamic customs and traditions, where visitors are expected to be on their very best behavior

Kawi—Old Javanese, the classical literary language of early Javanese and Balinese poetry (*kawi* means "poet"). Nine out of 10 words in it are Sanskrit. Very rich, flowery, and archaic, well suited for singing and chanting and musical meter. *Kawi* is now kept more alive on Bali than on Java.

kayu besi—ironwood *(Metrosideros petiolata Kds)*

kayuputih oil—a panacea derived from the *kayuputih* tree *(Eucalyptus alba)*. Drink diluted or rub on full strength for stomachaches, headcolds, rashes, etc.

kebaya—a Chinese long-sleeved blouse with shaped bodice worn by Indonesian women. Most commonly made of cotton (the wealthy sometimes use silk, velvet, or brocade), it has a swooping decolletage and finely embroidered edges.

Kecak—a seated choral dance-drama performed by Balinese men. Also called the "Monkey Dance" because of its characteristic staccato chorus ("chaka, chaka, chaka") with the dancers' arms shooting up and bodies contorting as in a hypnotic voodoo rite.

kecamatan—subdistrict, the administrative unit that comes under the *kabupaten*

kecap—ketchup

kecapi—a plucked stringed musical instrument used in the Buginese and Makassarese areas of S. Sulawesi; similar instruments are found in the Batak and Gayo areas of northern Sumatra

kedai kopi—coffee shop, a local gathering place for men. In the cities, they could serve meals, in the villages just biscuits and *pisang goreng*.

Kediri—an E. Javanese dynasty (A.D. 1049-1222) known mainly for its poetry. Though few of its permanent monuments remain, such a large number of literary works were produced that this period is known as Indonesia's Golden Age of Literature.

keelong—a raised fishing platform used by fishermen all over the archipelago

kelapa—both the coconut tree or its fruit. The coconut has a wide variety of uses: food, drink, oil, wine, leaves for thatching, fiber for matting, its shells for water vessels and dippers, etc.

Ken Arok—a historical 13th C. Javanese king about whom a classic of *Kawi* literature was written: the story of "The Magic Kris." This rapist-bandit-charmer-parvenu became ruler by murdering the king, then marrying his beautiful wife. It's a story of intrigue, assassinations, curses, and black magic—a high drama of medieval Java.

kepala desa—village leader or headman. Other names are *lurah, kepala kampung, kepala negeri,* and *penghulu kampung.* See also *lurah.*

Keroncang—see *kroncong*

ketingting—a small canoe with a swivel-mounted motor designed for shallow river travel in Kalimantan's interior

Ketoprak—a Javanese folk play. Though this village entertainment has less polished dancing, it's now so popular that it rivals *wayang orang* in costuming, staging, and music. Its stories are based on Javanese history and ballads.

klotok—a specialized, canopied river craft of Kalimantan. Has an outboard motor and sounds like a chorus of bullfrogs ("klotok, klotok, klotok").

kolintang—a wooden xylophonic orchestra used in the Minahasa area of N. Sulawesi. Sounds somewhat like *gamelan*.

Konfrontasi—the period (1962-65) when Sukarno's regime threatened Malaysia with military intervention because of Malaysia's alleged neo-colonialist policies. Indonesian raiders were put ashore on the Malaysian peninsula and attacks were launched from Kalimantan into British-administered northern Borneo. *Konfrontasi* ended abruptly with Sukarno's overthrow in 1965.

korupsi—corruption, graft

kraton—a walled and fortified palace city. Derived in part from India, *kraton* were the supreme centers of religious worship and culture in the Hindu-Javanese system of rule. The *kraton,* and not the villages, became the bearers of Hinduism and Islam in Indonesia. They are now more or less museums. The highest ranking are located in the heart of Java in the sultanate cities of Yogya and Solo.

kretek—sweet, clove-flavored cigarettes, named after the crackling sound they make when smoked

kris—a Javanese or Balinese double-edged dagger. Designed for thrusting, its blade twists and winds like a snake. Simultaneously a weapon, an ornament, a cultic object (said to have magic powers), and the finest example of Indonesian metallurgy.

Krishna—the dark-skinned Hindu god of human form, the eighth incarnation of the god Vishnu, but worshipped by the masses in his own right. Krishna is a popular hero in the *Bhagavad Gita* who could lift elephants at 4 years of age; he later became a magnificent warrior and a great lover.

kroncong—gentle melancholy music played in Nusatenggara and in Jakarta. Derived from the popular lute music of 16th C. Portugal.

krupuk—fried prawn or fish crisps; Indonesian bread. Looks like a giant misshapen cracker.

Kuda Kepang—a flat hobby horse made of painted bamboo *(kuda* means horse; *kepang* is plaited bamboo) used in a trance-dance of the same name. Performed by men simulating the actions and antics of horses.

kulkul—a drum tower found in Javanese and Balinese villages, from which an alarm is sounded or people are called to meetings

ladang—slash-and-burn shifting cultivation. Using simple tools such as digging sticks and axes, plots are first cleared by burning, then crops (most often upland rice, sweet potato, or corn) are cultivated on the ashes for several years. The farmer then moves and clears a new plot, leaving the old one fallow for 2-20 years. Vegetation meanwhile restores and regenerates the earth, when he or his descendants return to begin the cycle again. Prevalent in the Outer Islands.

lahar—lava or mud emitted from active volcanoes. *Berlahar* means to erupt.

lakon—the content or plot of a *wayang* play. It's like the first draft of a scenario—very standardized.

The *lakon* includes an organized list of scenes, where the action is going to occur, names of the leading characters, what they talk about and why. Seldom is there any written dialog. There are 4 main groups of scripts: early history, the *Arjuna,* the *Ramayana,* and the *Pandava* cycles.

lapangan—field, square, park, shopping plaza

Leberan—see *Hari Raya*

Legong—a classical Balinese dance performed by 2 young girls. Training begins at 4-5 years old; they retire at around 13 or once they begin menstruation. Considered by many the most beautiful and graceful of the Balinese dance ballets.

leyak—on Bali, an evil spirit that haunts dark, lonely places. *Leyak* can assume any shape, devours the entrails of babies and corpses, casts spells, and drinks blood from the necks of sleeping people.

liana—a species of palm tree whose fibers are used in binding. It grows virtually everywhere, though it's hard to keep as an indoor plant. Quite expensive, about Rp10,000 for one band.

liang—gravesites hewn out of cliffs by the Torajans of S. Sulawesi

lingga—a Hindu religious symbol in the form of an upright, phallus-shaped stone column. A *lingga* is a symbol of male virility and manliness, the phallic emblem of Shiva. *Yoni* is the female counterpart, a vagina-shaped symbol of fertility.

loket—train or bus ticket window or office

longbot—a long, thin, motorized river craft capable of high speeds; sometimes propelled by as many as 3 outboard motors. Used in Kalimantan.

longsat—a small round fruit with a yellowish-white skin and sweet white meat

lontar—a species of palm tree *(Corypha gebanga).* Life-giving, especially in the eastern part of the archipelago, providing food, shelter, utensils, and ornaments. Its fan-like leaves are used to plait sacks, as fishing nets, food covers, baskets. Much Indonesian literature and history have been inscribed over the years on 3.5-X-30-cm strips of this palm. "Volumes" are made by threading them together with a string, like venetian blinds. Texts and pictures are engraved with an iron stylus and filled in with a mixture of soot and oil.

lontong—glutinous rice wrapped in *pandanus* leaves

Loro Ratu Kidul—the South Sea Goddess, called also Nyai Loro Kidul. Said to be the legendary wife of a 16th C. Mataram ruler, she is still venerated along the S coast of Java.

losmen—rooms to let, found in even the smallest towns. Cheaper than hotels but quite adequate. On Bali and Lombok, *losmen* are usually native-style houses, a family-run inn.

Ludruk—a theater form, created in this century, popular in the big cities of Indonesia, especially in E. Java. Comparable to musical comedy or burlesque shows in the West.

lurah—a village head on Java, elected formerly by secret ballot. First among equals, the *lurah* must mediate at meetings to see that everyone comes to some agreement. Once these local leaders were the only officials to be elected by the people, but now they are appointed and salaried by the government. See also *kepala desa.*

lurik—a locally made finely woven striped textile of Yogya and Solo, C. Java; often used as cheaper *batik* material.

MAF—Missionary Aviation Fellowship, a missionary airline serving the interior of Irian Jaya, Maluku, and Nusatenggara

Mahabharata—a Hindu epic containing 100,000 couplets—the longest epic poem in the world. It recounts a tremendous 18-day battle between 2 family groups in the legendary state of Bharat during the Vedic Age in India (1500-500 B.C.). Translated into the high language of *Kawi* in the Middle Ages, this Indian masterpiece plays a gigantic part in Indonesian literature, art, and theater.

Majapahit—an ancient E. Javanese empire which held power over much of what is now Indonesia from A.D. 1292 to 1398. Majapahit, the mightiest indigenous kingdom in Indonesia's history, was finally dissolved by Islamic princes around A.D. 1520.

makara—a mythical aquatic animal in old Javanese sculpture, combining the features of a dolphin with those of a crocodile. The *makara* has a trunk, large teeth, feet, and a tail that often transforms itself into a foliated scroll. Corresponds to the zodiacal sign of Cancer.

maleo—the junglefowl *(Megapodiidae).* The ground-dwelling *maleo* lays its eggs in large mounds of vegetation, to be hatched by the heat of the fermentation. Other species lay their eggs in black volcanic sand to be hatched by the heat of the sun.

mambruk—the crown pigeon, found only in Maluku and Irian Jaya. A large bluish-gray bird with a purplish-brown breast, wings marked by 2 bars, and a tuft of finely ramified feathers on its head. Poor fliers, they live and forage mostly on the forest floor or feed in coastal marshes, flying up to low trees only to roost or when disturbed. Papuans eat the *mambruk,* and its crest feathers are very much in demand, so this bird is now protected.

mandala—an ancient magic circle or shrine, symbolic of the universe, designed for meditation. Its historical source is India. Also the name of an army-owned and -run airline operating on Java, Sumatra, and Sulawesi.

mandau—the traditional sword of the Dayak of Kalimantan

mandi—a cement, palm, or bamboo bathroom containing a large cement tub from which you throw water over yourself with a dipper, elephant-fashion. The tub is not meant to be climbed into and its water is not for drinking.

mangosteen—a round purple-black fruit with a whorl of green sepals on the top. Inside, white, sweet-sour juicy segments huddle into a ball. Comes into season Jan. to March.

martabak—a thin, fried Arabian pancake stuffed with meat, egg, and/or vegetables. Sold over the counter at foodstands for around Rp1000. Best eaten with green chilies *(lombok)*, slices of cucumber, and a cold Bintang Beer.

MAS—Malaysian Airline System

Mataram—a Hindu empire which reached its apogee in the 16th and 17th centuries, represented today in the sultanates of Yogya and Solo. Though it professed Islam, Mataram retained a Hindu-Buddhist state structure. Some of Mataram's kings are buried in highly venerated royal tombs at Imogiri and Kota Gede near Yogya.

Menak Jonggo—a deadly enemy of the Majapahit hero Damar Wulan; a very evil literary character used as a central theme in *wayang golek.*

menhir—a prehistoric monument consisting of one large upright stone

merdeka—freedom

Merpati—a government-run airlines which operates mainly domestic flights. Merpati offers the most extensive network of any of the domestic airlines.

meru—a Javanese (and Buddhist) mountain-of-heaven. The legend of this sacred mountain originates in India. *Meru* is also a pagoda-like thatch roof found on Bali.

mesin becak—a motorized *becak* with a side car

mesjid—mosque

mie—noodles

mie goreng—fried noodles with meat and/or vegetables; for Rp300 extra it's topped with a fried, boiled, or scrambled egg.

muezzin—in the Islamic world, these men call the faithful to prayer from high towers on the mosques. In many places they have been replaced by loudspeakers which reach farther than the human voice, startling you awake at 0500 or earlier.

muncak—a small graceful variety of deer *(Muntiacus muntijak)* found on Timor and Java. Also known as the "barking deer."

muara—mouth of a river; estuary

naga—a Hindu mythological serpent charged with magic powers. Most snake symbols, encountered frequently in SE Asia, are derived from this legendary creature.

nangka—jackfruit. A sweet, refreshing, fibrous, segmented fruit weighing up to 20 kilos. On the tree it hangs like a heavy green water bag. Under the thick, tough outer layer, the golden pulpy fruit is both juicy and chewy. A cousin of the *nangka* is the smaller and creamier *cempedak.*

nasi—rice

nasi campur—eggs, vegetables, meat, or fish and sauce on a heap of steamed rice. At Rp800-1500, it's a good bargain meal all over Indonesia.

nasi liwet—a Solonese (C. Java) specialty of rice cooked in *santen* with garnishes

nasi padang—rice with many side dishes, usually spicy hot *(pedas)*. This style of cooking originated in W. Sumatra but is now found everywhere in Indonesia.

nasi pecal—a breakfast dish similar to *gado-gado* with boiled vegies such as papaya leaves, tapioca, bean sprouts, string beans, and fried *tahu* (soybean cake) and *tempe,* plus fresh cucumbers, soybeans, coconut shavings, peanuts. Peanut sauce could be added on top.

negeri—district

Negritos—the first known human inhabitants of Indonesia, entering the archipelago about 30,000 years ago. A pygmy people similar to African Negroids in facial features but with thick wooly hair, rounder heads, and smaller statures. Genetic traces of this stock are still detectable in the interiors of large islands, particularly in eastern Indonesia.

oplet—a small, covered pickup truck with side benches in back, used to cheaply transport passengers in cities and between nearby villages and towns. In Sumatra, it could be a small bus seating 25 or more people. *Oplet* is derived from the Dutch for "to flag down."

Orang Laut—aboriginal nomadic sea gypsies or fishermen

owa—This monkey is easily recognized by the hood of fine tufted white hair ringing its face. The tailless *owa* are fantastic tree climbers with long spider-like arms, and have a shrill, piercing call. Gray, yellowish, brown, and black varieties are found in Sumatra; in Kalimantan and W. Java the gray *owa* is more common.

Padri War—a violent Muslim reform movement in the Minangkabau region of W. Sumatra (1821-38)

pala—sweet-sour fruit of the nutmeg tree of Maluku and N. Sulawesi

pamong—in Solo, a "guide" for spiritual development. Could also mean caretaker, supporter, mentor, educator, teacher.

panakawan—grotesque figures found in *wayang* performances to give comic relief. Semar and his sons Petruk, Gareng, Bagong, and Nala, are equivalent to the medieval court jesters, the scholar-disciples of the heros. With their paunches, short legs, flat noses, and flabby breasts, they are a distinctive Javanese addition to the Hindu epics.

Panca Sila—a Sanskrit phrase meaning "The Five Principles." This political philosophy was put forth in 1945 by Sukarno to provide a constitutional basis for the Republic. They are: belief in one of the 4 universal religions; nationalism; Indonesian-style "guided" democracy; humanitarianism; and a just and prosperous society. These principles are meant to be a point of social and political reference, a touchstone for the state. National education is aimed at producing citizens morally responsible to the principles. Surmounted by a proud eagle, the *Panca Sila* plaque can be seen over the entrance archways of even the smallest villages throughout Indonesia.

pandanus—fibrous leaves of a tree native to Indonesia. Used in building, making utensils, wrapping, or for clothing. *Pandan* in Indonesian.

pangeran—literally prince, lord; an honorific term for a saint, royal personage, or nobleman

pangolin—anteater *(Manis javanica); trenggiling* in Indonesian

***Panji* Cycle**—an extensive cycle of Javanese stories, with many different written and oral versions. Originating in the 15th C., the stories focus on Panji's reunion with his elusive bride. The vowel rhymes are based on the Indonesian language and are more in tune with the native ear than the courtly *kakawin* poetry. Staged often at wedding parties, this cycle provides themes for mask and puppet plays.

parang—chopping knife, machete, cleaver

pasanggrahan—government lodge, resthouse, or forestry hut which might accept travelers for a modest price or for free if there's a vacancy. Sometimes it is a commercial venture, a hotel.

pasar—market. For much of rural Indonesia it's the whole focus and center of a village.

pas jalan—see *surat jalan*

patong—carved posts, statues, or totems; also *patung*

peci (or *kopiah*)—an Indonesian felt or velvet cap, usually black; an Islamic religious symbol of tradition and power. Resembling the old overseas cap or the service cap in the U.S. military, the *peci* could also be worn by non-Muslims since it's also the national headwear of Indonesia and of the Malaysian culture.

pedanda—a high priest of the Bali-Hindu religion

pegawai—a white-collar worker, functionary, staff, or employee, most often a civil servant or a government official

Pelni—Pelayaran Nasional Indonesia, the reasonably priced state shipping line of Indonesia with an extensive inter-island network

pemangku—curators of the village temple; temple priests

pemuda—young man; youth. During the 1945-50 independence struggle, groups of *pemuda* were synonymous with "revolutionary bands."

pencak silat—the Indonesian national self-defense art, a sort of stylized combat. It's both a lethal fighting skill and a graceful artform designed for both empty-handed combat and for the use of weapons. Though indigenous to Indonesia, it's a synthesis of many fighting arts with origins mainly in China. When practiced with percusssion accompaniment it looks like dance, and in fact many dances have borrowed movements from it and vice versa.

pendopo—a traditional, ornate, open-air pillared pavilion with a low pyramidal overhanging roof, found usually in a *kraton* or in front of a Javanese nobleman's house. Serves for audiences, receptions, rituals, and celebrations accompanied by entertainments. Nowadays, many productions of amateur dance associations are performed on *pendopo*.

penghulu—a headman in a Batak village of N. Sumatra. This term is also used in Sumbawan villages.

penginapan—a cheap hotel with plain facilities, abbreviated "Peng."

penjaga—guard or watchman at a temple site, building, bank, residence, hotel

perkutut—turtledove; a Javanese singing bird with a pale blue head and rosy breast. Outside houses on Java there's often an 8-m-high pole on top of which is a *perkutut* in a cage, trilling blithely. The bird is hoisted by pulley to the top of the pole at dawn, then hauled down again at dusk.

Pertamina—Indonesia's mammoth state-owned and -run oil company

pesarian—a school of Islamic studies

pikulan—a pole which looks like an archer's bow that rests on the shoulders of a laborer or a peddler on the move. Up to 25 kg of bricks, water, and other burdens can be suspended from each end.

pisang—banana

PKI—Partai Komunis Indonesia. The Communist Party of Indonesia (founded by a Dutchman in 1914) exercised considerable social and political power in Indonesia during the later years of the Sukarno regime (1960-65). Dissolved on 12 March 1966 by order of President Suharto.

plangi—a tie-dye technique practiced in Lombok, Palembang (S. Sumatra), and in the eastern districts of Java and Bali. Motifs are first drawn or stamped on the fabric, then the figures are sketched in outline with a tacking thread. When the threads are pulled tight small loops come up. When the fabric is dipped into the dye vat, the areas that were covered with the string don't absorb the dye, forming a design according to the pattern stitched. A broad range of shades can be applied to one fabric. This technique probably reached Indonesia by way of India.

polisi—police

pondok—a cottage, hut, cabin, hotel, or a Muslim boarding school

PPA—Perlindungan dan Pengawetan Alam, the Indonesian Forestry Service

prahu—a swift, strong, wooden sailing vessel or outrigger of Malay origin. Often built entirely without metal or nails, a *prahu* shows a very high level of traditional technology. Some weigh as much as 250 tons.

priyayi—the established aristocratic administrative class of Java. This upper middle class is roughly the successor of the old Hindu *Satriya* caste and today they are generally the intelligentsia and the new business group: senior officials, military officers, corporate presidents, university professors, doctors, lawyers, engineers, architects, politicians, writers. The term is also used to describe a cultured person or cultured behavior.

puak—tribe, ethnic group, or clan

puputan—Balinese ritual suicide

pura—a Balinese terraced temple consisting of 3 tiers enclosed by walls. A gateway, often lavishly sculpted and decorated, leads to the terraces. The third terrace is usully the most sacred, where you find recesses for offerings, shrines, and *meru*-roofed structures.

puri—on Bali, a prince's palace

pusaka—sacred heirlooms passed down from dynasty to dynasty or from generation to generation in families

rafflesia—a giant flower of Sumatra; named after the English governor-general of Indonesia, Sir Stamford Raffles (1781-1826) who first recorded it.

raja—a prince, lord, or king. On Bali it may still be used to refer to male Hindu royalty. In C. Maluku, a raja is the aristocratic head of a village or district. In W. Timor, a raja is the head of one of the 10 traditional Atoni princedoms.

raksasa—a mythical giant from Hindu mythology. Sculptures and reliefs of *raksasa* figures often guard entrances to temples. Fierce, moustached, with long canine teeth sticking out through his cheeks like a boar's tusks, and armed with a large club, he wards off evil forces.

Ramadan (or *Puasa*)—the Muslim month of fasting which takes place on the ninth month of the Javanese-Muslim calendar. From dawn to dusk, devout Muslims abstain from drinking, smoking, eating, sex, and other earthly pleasures. They rise at 0300 or 0400 and eat a meal which must last them through all the daylight hours. The fast is broken each sunset with a whistle, a siren, the firing of a cannon, or the beating of the mosque drum. The intensity and spiritual tension builds up as the month progresses. At the appearance of the new moon *Ramadan* is over and a week-long celebration *(Hari Raya)* begins.

Ramayana—an Indian poem composed of 18 books and 24,000 verses divided into 500 songs, all about an Aryan king of the Indian Vedic Age. The hero Rama (Vishnu reincarnated) defeats the wicked King Rawana of Ceylon who has stolen his consort and who is generally troubling the world. This story is known throughout SE Asia and all over Indonesia wherever Hindu culture penetrated. The *Ramayana* provides the story line for almost all Indonesian theater as well as inspiring much of its art: fabric design, painting, sculpture, etc. Shops, companies, trains, and even toothbrushes are named after its characters and you can see reliefs depicting this story on ancient temples throughout Java and Bali. Written over 2,000 years ago, the *Ramayana* epic is as old as Homer's *Iliad* and also incorporates the same legend: the abduction of a great beauty followed by a terrible war to rescue her.

rambutan—a hairy, red-skinned fruit with sweet white juicy meat; tastes like a very sweet grape

rante—a ceremonial field for funeral ceremonies in Torajaland, S. Sulawesi

rawon—rice with spiced sauce. Some versions are a spicy-hot beef or buffalo meat soup with fried onions sprinkled on top and served with *lontong.*

rebab—a one-stringed violin of Arab-Persian origin

rempeyek—round peanut crisps fried in spiced batter

rendang—spicy-hot beef in a thick rich sauce made from a Minangkabau recipe of W. Sumatra. Traveling food, it can last without refrigeration for as long as a month.

Reyog—a form of *wayang topeng,* a masked dance with a small number of performers, including a ferocious tiger with a peacock standing on top of it, a red warrior figure, and a giant. Often big, heavy, decorated headpieces are worn. This involved, 4-hour trance-dance is not commonly seen, but is very popular. Ponorogo, C. Java, is one of the centers.

ristaffel—means literally "rice table" in Dutch. A tropical smorgasbord, a banquet specialty. Though the food is Indonesian, the way of presenting it is Dutch. Plan to overeat. Boiled rice is the base with 20-40 individual spicy side dishes: meat, fish, eggs, and vegetables in various curries and sauces, dried, pickled, and fresh fruit, coconuts and nuts, and on and on.

romusha—slave laborers used by the Japanese during WW II

ronde—a warm Javanese drink sold in *warung* and by street vendors, made from ginger syrup, peanuts, fruit slices *(kolang kaling)*, one ladle of hot water, and yellow balls of glutinous rice at the bottom of the bowl or glass. Many variations on the theme. Costs Rp400-600, with egg Rp800.

rotan—rattan, a tough pliable vine from which handicrafts and furniture are made. Can grow up to 100 m in length.

rumah adat—a traditional native-style house, usually old

rumah makan—eating place, restaurant, cafe

rumah sakit—hospital or clinic

rupiah—the Indonesian monetary unit; US$1 = Rp1635

rusa—deer (Cervus timorensis)

sago—a starchy, low-protein food extracted from the sago palm, the staple food of many of the rural populations of the eastern islands. Sago is relatively tasteless, but plentiful and indestructable. Stems are cut off the palm and then slivers beaten with water into pulp. When washed, the fibers float away and a flour remains. A single sago palm trunk will yield hundreds of kilos of sago in return for a day's work. The pith resists mold and can be kept up to 12 months.

salak—a pear-shaped, plum-sized sour fruit with a brown snake-like skin; comes from a palm tree. To avoid tartness, peel the inner membrane before eating.

sambal—a spicy-hot chili sauce whose basic ingredients are fresh chilies, garlic, sugar, salt, vinegar, and onions

sambar—a deer (Cervus unicolor) with a set of 3-pointed antlers. Related to the European red deer and the American elk. Used synonymously with rusa.

sampan—a small sailboat used over short distances in western Indonesia

Sangyang Dedari—Balinese trance-dance performed by 2 untrained young girls who dance in unison on top of men's shoulders

santri—a Muslim who embraces the ethics and values of orthodox Islam. Historically, these devout Muslims have been merchants and traders. In many Javanese towns, santri live in their own neighborhoods called Kaum.

sarung—a kain with both ends sewn together, used by men, women, and children. Worn with a tight sheath-like effect, the slack of this long skirt is folded and tucked in. A sarung is ultra-chic when worn by a Javanese priyayi woman, ultra-useful when worn by workers of the land. It is well suited for carrying, sheltering, and binding. Indonesian men's sarung often have simple designs, mostly combinations of stripes and checks, while Indonesian women generally prefer more floral, intricate, and colorful designs.

sasando—plucked bamboo tube zither of Roti, Timor, and surrounding islands

sate—a national dish much like the Arabic kebab. Chicken, beef, pork, mutton, seafood, or entrails are threaded on thin bamboo skewers and grilled over a charcoal fire. After roasting, sate is frequently served with a sharp peanut sauce, a small plate of raw onions, and chilies. Sate sellers carry their kitchen on their shoulders, balanced on a pikulan. For you he sets his kitchen down, fans the charcoal embers, prepares sate to taste, then jogs off looking for more customers.

sawah—flooded fields of rich, deep mud, artificially constructed (often terraced) and continuously cultivated with a specialized crop, usually rice

sawo—the sapodilla plum, a fruit shaped like a potato but with the texture and flavor of sweet bread

Seketan—Mohammed's birthday. Celebrated with special week-long ceremonies and festivals in Yogya and Solo. There are big fairs, continuous prayer, processions carrying beehive-shaped "mountains of rice," and a parade of royal guards and palace officials.

sekotang—a spicy-hot herb-flavored tea

selimut raja—the finest of the handmade ikat burial blankets woven on the island of Sumba

Serimpi—any of the dances of the C. Javanese palace courts characterized by fluttering scarves and straight-backed dancers. Dating from Hindu times, Serimpi is performed by groups of even-numbered dancers and lasts for about 45 minutes.

serow—the goat antelope (Capricornis sumatraensis) of Sumatra. Adapted to life in high grassy mountain areas, this member of the ibex family is short horned and long legged with pointed hoofs.

Shiva—in the Hindu galaxy of gods Shiva is one of the mightiest, the Destroyer of the World. Shiva is still the most venerated of the gods of India. His emblem is the phallus (lingga).

siamang—a black monkey (Hylobates syndactylus) found on Sumatra and in W. Malaysia. It's difficult to tell the siamang from the owa, but the siamang's throat puffs up when it cries out.

Simalungun—one of the 5 Batak clans of eastern N. Sumatra

Singosari—an ancient, ruthless E. Javanese dynasty whose official faith was a Buddhist-Shivaite syncretism. Though it ruled for only 71 years (A.D. 1222-93), Singosari initiated a new sculptural technique in its temple reliefs, the so-called wayang kulit style.

sirih—betelnut, in use in Indonesia for over 2,500 years. Considered the equivalent of European snuff, these scarlet seeds are chewed mostly by older people all over Indonesia, their teeth becoming rust-colored after years of chewing. Betelnut contains a natural alkaloid, similar to psylocybin, which causes a mildly euphoric stimulation. Betelnut serves important ritual functions in restoring harmony and peace between individuals or within a community.

slendang—a long narrow shawl or shoulder cloth, also worn around the breast. The *slendang,* worn folded or wound, does not require any tailoring or fasteners. It could be used as a sling for carrying babies and burdens on the back, or as a cushion for a heavy basket on the head, but is generally thrown over one shoulder or wrapped around the head for warmth or fashion.

SMAC—Sabang Merauke Air Charter, a small airline servicing Jambi, Aceh, and other remote areas of Sumatra

songket—a gold-threaded fabric woven by the floating-weft technique. *Sarung songket* is the traditional *sarung* for Indonesian bridegrooms.

sopi—an alcoholic drink, Indonesian gin. *Sopi manis* is liqueur.

soto—a spicy soup found all over Indonesia. Served with rice or *lontong,* soybean sprouts, chicken, mutton, or beef, and garnished with fried or green onions.

soto ayam—Javanese chicken broth

soto madura—a rich, coconut milk soup full of noodles, bean sprouts and other vegetables, plus chicken

spetbot—a long motorboat with an outboard motor used in western Indonesia

Sriwijaya—an empire which may have flourished in southern Sumatra near present-day Palembang during the 12th century. Some scholars theorize that Sriwijaya's power centered on mainland SE Asia (Thailand and Indochina).

stanplatz—a bus, *oplet, bemo,* minibus or taxi station; an assembly point for all of these conveyances. Taken from the Dutch, the word is still widely used on Java.

stasiun kereta api—railroad station

stempel—a long narrow river craft of Kalimantan which travels at high speeds and rides so close to the water that you often get wet

stupa—a bell-shaped burial place for the remains or relics of Buddha, one of his disciples, or of Buddhists.

subak—the village water board in southern Balinese villages which controls the flow of water, irrigation, canal building, drainage, and maintenance

Subud—a religious, commercial, non-denominational (but embraces Islamic philosophy) association on Java. *Subud* has centers all over the world. Its leader, called simply *Pak* ("Father"), died in 1987.

suling—flute

Sunan—the titular and spiritual head of Solo's Kraton Hadiningrat. Also the title of a *wali* and the name of his burial place.

Sundanese—the main ethnic group of W. Java. Fifteen percent of all Indonesians, the Sundanese are the next largest single group of Indonesians after the Javanese. They generally practice a more orthodox form of Islam than the C. and E. Javanese.

surat ijin—see *surat jalan*

surat jalan—a letter or travel permit that you may be required to present to army, police, forestry, immigration, or customs officials obtained from a PPA office, the local police station, or *camat's* office. Also called *surat ijin.*

surau—a Minangkabau (W. Sumatra) meeting house for men and boys where they study cooking and the Koran; the village male "clubhouse"

syahbandar—the harbormaster. The word dates from the 14th C. Hindu Majapahit kingdom when it employed Muslims as *syahbandar,* or chiefs, of some of their ports. *Syahbandar* are found in every port in Indonesia where there are ships, from Wangi Wangi to Telukdalam. See him about ship and boat schedules and fares.

tanuk—tapir, a prehistoric pig-like mammal that still exists in the forests of Sumatra and Kalimantan. Predominantly black with white hindquarters, it reaches a length of nearly 2½ m and can weigh up to 450 kg. The tapir's nose and lips are longer than a pig's and movable, resembling a short trunk, thus it's sometimes called *babi gajah,* or the elephant-pig.

tau-tau—lifesize statues representing the dead placed on balconies outside cliffside graves in Torajaland, S. Sulawesi

tegalan—a permanent, unirrigated garden or field

tempe—a tasty, protein-rich cake made from fermented soybeans

Tempo Doeloe—roughly translates as "the Old Days"; refers to the time of the colonial Netherlands East Indies

THR—Taman Hiburan Rakyat ("People's Parks"), entertainment complexes found in towns and cities all over Indonesia

toko mas—gold shop

tongkonan—a special ceremonial house used for religious activities, burials, marriages, and for sleeping; built by upper-class Torajas of S. Sulawesi

transmigrasi—a government resettlement program aimed at relieving the population pressure on Java and Bali by relocating individuals or communities to the Outer Islands to set up farming colonies under government sponsorship and supervision

trapel cek—travelers cheques

trepang—smoked and dried sea cucumber which the Chinese use in making soups

tritik—a process in which designs are stitched on a fabric, then the thread is pulled tightly so that only the exposed areas are dyed, leaving the areas underneath the threads and tucks colorless until restitched in a different pattern or re-dyed. While the *ikat* technique is applied to the thread before weaving, the *tritik* method is used for dyeing finished fabric. The finest *tritik* is produced in Solo.

tuak—rice, palm *(arin)*, or *sago* beer. *Tuak* is most often made from glutinous rice. The grain is first cooked, cooled, mixed with a number of powdered roots and yeasts, and then put into a large earthenware jar to brew. Before the brew is served water and sugar are added to dilute the mash.

tugbot—a long, slow, flat-bottomed, motorized river craft with a shelter used in Kalimantan

tukang—artisan, workman, skilled laborer; one who does something, i.e., *tukang portret* (photographer), *tukang listerik* (electrician)

ulos—an oblong fabric made by the *ikat* process, worn in the Bataklands of N. Sumatra by both men and women. Dull deep colors are characteristic.

Vishnu—in the Hindu pantheon of gods, Vishnu functions as the Guardian of the World. On Java, kings and other historical personages such as Sukarno were frequently regarded as incarnations of Vishnu. This Hindu god was personified symbolically in many creatures such as fish, tortoises, and in the Hindu epics as Krishna and Rama.

VOC—Vereenigde Oost-Indische Compagine. A unique Dutch institution established in 1602 by the merger of a number of Dutch trading concerns with the aim of establishing a ruthless monopoly of the spice trade.

wadian—female shaman of the Dayak regions of Kalimantan

wakil—a government agent, representative, deputy; the civilian counterpart of a military commander

wali—one of the 9 legendary holy men who introduced Islam to Java. Worshipped as saints, their graves (indicated by the title *Sunan*) are looked upon as sacred places and are usually located on mountaintops.

waringan—*see* banyan

waruga—pre-Christian Minahasan (N. Sulawesi) burial sacrophagi shaped like prisms

warung—a poor man's restaurant; a foodstall or portable kitchen. Many also sell coffee, soft drinks, cigarettes, canned foods, *sirih*, etc.

wayang—a dramatic puppet theater. In the strict sense it means flat, carved-leather rod puppets of the shadow play, but in its broad sense it could mean any dramatic performance.

YHA—Youth Hostel Association. In Indonesia youth hostels are usually more expensive than cheap hotels or *losmen*.

yoni—a stylized vagina usually carved out of stone, the Hindu symbol of female life-giving force

zirzak—custard apple. Derived from the Dutch word meaning "sour bag." Though it tastes heavenly, don't overeat this rich, sweet-sour fruit with a creamy texture—too many will give you a bellyache.

BOOKLIST

ANTHROPOLOGY

Coppel, Charles A. *Indonesian Chinese in Crisis.* Singapore: Oxford University Press, 1983. An examination of the historical background to Indonesia's "Chinese problem," and the various attempts of the Chinese community to accommodate itself to the ebb and flow of national politics. The best study on this subject so far.

Denslow, Julie Sloan, and Christine Padoch, eds. *People of the Tropical Rainforest.* University of California Press and Smithsonian Institution, 1988. Contributors explore diverse ways in which people use rainforest land around the world. Discussed are the transmigrants of Indonesia and the Bugis migration to Kalimantan forests.

Dumarcay, Jacques. *The House in South-East Asia.* Singapore: Oxford University Press, 1987. Covers domestic architectural forms from the earliest reconstructions of the Dongson culture through the different regional variants of the archipelago. Lavishly illustrated with color plates and line drawings by the author, a noted French architect.

Koentjaraningrat, ed. *Villages in Indonesia.* Ithaca, New York: Cornell University Press, 1967. A collection of comprehensive surveys of 13 villages all over Indonesia derived from firsthand experiences of Indonesian, Dutch, and American anthropologists. Although oftentimes dry reading, this book goes part of the way in presenting the giddy ethnic diversity found throughout Indonesia.

Lebar, Frank M., ed. *Ethnic Groups of Insular Southeast Asia.* New Haven: Human Relations Area Files Press, 1972. One of the very few systematic surveys of the people and cultures of insular SE Asia. Most of these very descriptive ethnographic summaries are accompanied by bibliographies and ethnolinguistic maps.

Wertheim, W.F., ed. *The Indonesian Town: Studies in Urban Sociology.* Amsterdam: The Royal Tropical Institute, 1958. A study by Dutch scholars of pre-war urban communities, dated but interesting.

Wallace, Alfred Russel. *The Malay Archipelago.* Singapore: Graham Brash Pte Ltd., 1983. A reprint of the 1869 classic. Represents 7 years of research by this great British naturalist on the flora, fauna, and ethnology of numerous Outer Islands of Indonesia. Still a brilliant, exhaustive, and valid study of natural phenomena as well as an exciting travelogue.

ARTS AND CRAFTS

Barbier, Jean Paul. *Indonesie et Melanesie.* Geneva: Collection Barbier-Muller, 1977. Excellent b/w photos of Batak, Dayak, eastern island, and other tribal artifacts. French text.

Bodrogi, Tibor. *Art of Indonesia.* London: Academy Editions, 1973. A detailed geographical, chronological description; Bodrogi even finds a cultural pattern in this incredible jumble of cultures and islands called "Indonesia."

Brackman, Agnes de Keijzer. *Cook Indonesian.* Singapore: Times Books International, 1984. Quick and easy-to-follow cooking methods from a long-time Indonesia resident.

Coomaraswamy, Ananda K. *History of Indian and Indonesian Art.* New York: Dover Publications, 1985. Most of this study deals with Indian art, but Indonesia and the peripheries of SE Asia are covered where they reflect Indian influences. The major focus is on architecture and sculpture.

Draeger, Donn. *Weapons and Fighting Arts of the Indonesian Archipelago.* Rutland, Vermont: Charles E. Tuttle, 1972. If martial arts is your interest, this book is not only well-researched and written, but it's the only one on the subject. Also incorporates entertaining travel anecdotes.

Elliott, Inger McCabe. *Batik: Fabled Cloth of Java.* New York: Clarkson N. Potter, 1984. A sumptuous, unique book of color photos of 120 extraordinary *batik* pieces as well as extensive b/w photos and text covering the history, motifs, and methods of production of *batik* in Yogya, Cirebon, Pekalongan, Lasem, and other towns along Java's N coast.

Feldman, Jerome. *The Eloquent Dead.* Los Angeles: UCLA Museum of Cultural History, 1985. Contains 270 b/w photos, 23 color plates, and essays on the ancestral art of the Nias, Batak, Dayak, Torajan, Lesser Sundas, Moluccas, and Biak areas of Indonesia as well as other linguistically related areas of SE Asia.

Fraser-Lu, Sylvia. *Indonesian Batik: Processes, Patterns and Places.* Oxford: Oxford University Press, 1986. Describes the traditional *batik* of C. Java as well as those of the N coast. Thirty color plates, 10 b/w photos, and 100 line drawings cover the processes, designs, and regional differences.

Frey, Edward. *The Kris: Mystic Weapon of the Malay World.* Oxford: Oxford University Press, 1986. The various aspects of this mysterious weapon are examined by a leading expert in Malay weaponry. Its possible origins, salient features, and craftsmanship are all interestingly handled.

Hering, B. *Candi and Pura: A Pictorial History.* Australia: Centre for Southeast Asian Studies, James Cooke University, 1985. A unique collection of photos which vividly depict the most striking examples of early medieval Indonesian monumental art, accompanied by plate descriptions and introductory chapters on history and religion.

Hitchcock, Michael *Indonesian Textile Techniques.* Aylesbury, UK: Shire Publications, 1985. A short but concise volume on the complex and fascinating textile traditions of Indonesia. Covers everything from the harvesting and spinning of cotton to the versatility of looms.

Holt, Claire. *Art in Indonesia: Continuities and Change.* Ithaca, New York: Cornell University Press, 1967. The best on this very broad subject. A modern classic written more for the student of art than for the academic. Covers her researches and personal observations while exploring Java and Bali's ancient ruins, as well as the performing and plastic arts.

Horridge, Adrian. *The Prahu: Traditional Sailing Boat of Indonesia.* Oxford: Oxford University Press, 1985. The most complete study of the indigenous vessels of Indonesia yet published. This expanded second edition features 41 color photos and 70 line drawings.

Horridge, Adrian. *Sailing Craft of Indonesia.* Oxford: Oxford University Press, 1986. A 92-page introduction to the various types of sailing craft used in Indonesia; includes 34 color photos and 25 line drawings.

Kartomi, Margaret J. *Musical Instruments of Indonesia.* Melbourne: Indonesian Arts Society, 1985. An excellent illustrated survey of the full range of musical instruments used in the many island regions of Indonesia, from xylophones and gongs to bowed strings and jew's harps. Alphabetical format.

Kempers, Bernet. *Ancient Indonesian Art.* Amsterdam: D.P.J. van der Peet, 1959. The be-all, end-all book for this subject; over 350 pages. Very scholarly, accurate information. Know your Hindu mythology before starting.

Krannich, Ronald L. and Caryl Rae, and Jo Reimer Jo. *Shopping in Exotic Places.* Manassas, Virginia: Impact Publications, 1987. The newest and most comprehensive shopping guide to Asia. The authors offer sound, detailed advice on practicalities of travel in Asia, how to locate quality shops, select alternative products, bargain for the best prices, avoid scams and rip-offs, and shipping your purchases home.

Marks, Copeland and Mintari Soeharjo. *The Indonesian Kitchen.* New York: Atheneum, 1981. With its well chosen and clearly written recipes, this is one of the best books on Indonesian cooking. Includes explanatory, cultural, and historical headnotes. Good value.

Mitchell, Kenneth. *A Taste of Indonesia.* Hong Kong: Oracle Book Distributors, 1982. A modest selection of popular Indonesian recipes illustrated with full-color photos. Nice souvenir.

Paintings and Statues from the Collection of Dr. Sukarno, President of the Republic of Indonesia. Peking: People's Fine Arts Publishing House, The People's Republic of China, 1956. A record of President Sukarno's collection of paintings in the Istana Bogor, W. Java. Most of the paintings are the works of Indonesian artists after independence. Quite evident is the preoccupation Sukarno had with Asian women.

Rawson, Philip. *The Art of Southeast Asia.* New York: Frederick A. Praeger, 1967. A comprehensive, authoritative account of SE Asian art in every category from tiny bronzes to large architectural complexes, including essential background information on the history, traditions, social organization, and religious beliefs. Seventy-five pages out of 278 are devoted to Indonesia.

Spee, Miep. *Traditional and Modern Batik.* Kenthurst, Australia: Kangaroo Press, 1982. Covers all aspects of *batik* from its ancient origins to modern forms. Includes background information on *batik* culture, recipes for dyeing, detailed instructions on most *batik* processes. A useful handbook for beginners with many b/w and color photos.

Stohr, W. *Art des Indonesiens Archaiques.* Geneva: Musee Rath Geneve, 1981. Outstanding b/w photos of the artifacts, sculpture and statuary of the Niaser, Batak, Torajan, Dayak, Nusatenggaran, and Moluccan peoples. French text.

Volkman, Toby Alice. *Film on Indonesia.* New Haven: Yale University Southeast Asia Studies, 1985. The most comprehensive annotated catalog available of films on Indonesia. Unfortunately, the catalog is already out of date and an updated version is not even in the planning stages.

Wagner, Frits A. *Indonesia: The Art of an Island Group.* New York: Greystone Press, 1967. Useful general account covering art, literature, dance, and drama from prehistoric times to independence. Flowery, art auction-style writing, but some broad-view insights lucidly written.

Willetts, William. *Ceramic Art of S.E. Asia.* Singapore: S.E. Asia Ceramics Society, 1971. Though difficult to find, this book is one of the best on the subject, with ample color illustrations, what and what not to look for.

BALI

Bali. Singapore: Times Editions, 1986. Vivid full-color photos depict every facet of Balinese daily life and culture; would make a neat souvenir.

Bali. Singapore: APA Productions Ltd., 1986. One of the "Insight Guides" series, this fascinating photographic overview of Bali has been a classic from the day it left the presses in 1970. Designed by Hans Hoefer, text by Star Black and Willard A. Hanna, updated by Made Wijaya.

Baum, Vicki. *A Tale From Bali.* Singapore: Oxford University Press, 1984. First published in 1937, this historical novel portrays the events leading up to and surrounding the famous *Puputan* death charge of Balinese royalty in 1906. Also a remarkable study of Balinese character, customs, and way of life.

Coast, John. *Dancers of Bali.* New York: G.P. Putnam's Sons, 1953. After joining with the Indonesian nationalists to help expel the Dutch, Coast immersed himself in the study of Balinese music and dance. He was the first dance impresario to organize a tour of Balinese dancers and musicians to Europe and America.

Covarrubias, Miguel. *Island of Bali.* Oxford University Press, 1972. Written by a Mexican painter who lived and worked in Belahluan, Bali, for 2 years in the 1930s collecting material for this artistic classic of traditional Balinese culture, the scope of which makes fascinating reading. Covarrubias was one of the first to call what the Balinese were living and creating "art." He rendered the drawings, his wife shot the photographs.

Covernton, Mary. *Bali & Lombok—A Travel Survival Kit.* Victoria, Australia: Lonely Planet Publications, 1986. A popular travel guide to Bali and the neighboring island of Lombok.

Daniel, Ana. *Bali: Behind the Mask.* New York: Alfred A. Knopf, Inc., 1981. During several extended stays in Bali, the author/photographer documented her experiences studying dance under one of Bali's last great classical dancers, I Nyoman Kakul.

Djelantik, A.A.M. *Balinese Paintings.* Singapore: Oxford University Press, 1986. A concise survey of Balinese painting styles. Each volume of OUP's excellent "Images of Asia Series" is written by an authority of the subject for the non-specialist reader. Extensively illustrated.

Eiseman, Fred B., Jr. *Bali.* Scottsdale, Arizona: Fred B. Eisman, Jr., 1986. Volumes 1 and 2, with a third volume due out in 1988. A collection of fascinating magazine articles and essays grouped together in different volumes, each written in different lengths, styles, and degrees of scholarship. With more than 25 years spent on the island, Eiseman writes with uncommon perspicacity on such topics as Balinese witchcraft and magic, cricket fighting, seaweed farming, and the spices of Bali.

Gorer, Geoffrey. *Bali and Angkor.* Singapore: Oxford University Press, 1986. A 1930s pleasure trip to Sumatra, Java, Bali, Thailand and Cambodia. An observant travel writer analyses the role art and religion play in the life of the Balinese. Gorer's writing has great style.

Kempers, A.J. Bernet. *Monumental Bali.* Netherlands: Van Goor Zonen Den Haag, 1977. A good introduction and guide to Balinese archaeology, concentrating on the mysterious early period of the island's history but with many connections to later Balinese culture.

Kertonegoro, Madi. *The Spirit Journey to Bali Aga, Tenganan Pegringsingan.* Bali: Harkat Fondation, 1986. An unusual book which collects the traditions,

ceremonies and lost legends of Tenganan village, E. Bali, the home of the "original" Balinese.

Koke, Louise G. *Our Hotel in Bali.* New Zealand: January Books, 1987. How 2 young Americans made a dream come true by opening one of the first Balinese-style tourist hotels on Kuta Beach, in the 1930s. The architectural style they pioneered flourishes today as does the surfing they introduced to Bali. Their adventure lasted until the Japanese invasion in 1942.

Lueras, Leonard and Ian R. Lloyd *Bali: The Ultimate Island.* New York: St. Martin's Press, 1987. A spectacular picture essay of Bali with old historical b/w photos, everyday portraits, and coverage of contemporary arts and crafts, everyday ceremonies, workers of the land, and commerce. A good buy at US$35.

Mabbett, Hugh. *In Praise of Kuta.* New Zealand: January Books, 1987. From slave port to fishing village, Kuta Beach today is one of the most popular tourist resorts in the world. More than 50 exuberant full-color photos.

———. *The Balinese.* New Zealand, January Books, 1985. An excellent introduction to all elements of Balinese life with chapters on everything from family and village life to cremations and religion, from music and dancing to wildlife and the effects of tourism.

McPhee, Colin. *A House in Bali.* Singapore: Oxford University Press, 1985. This account of a young American composer's stay in Bali prior to WW II is an amusing and sympathetic look at Balinese society and a rare look at the importance of music in Balinese life.

Neka Museum: Guide to the Painting Collection. Ubud Bali: The Neka Museum, 1986. An illustrated history of Balinese painting by Neka, a respected painter and gallery owner in Campuan, Bali. Full-color photos, b/w sketches, and biographies of both Balinese and foreign painters.

Powell, Hickman. *The Last Paradise.* Singapore: Oxford University Press, 1986. Another American's "discovery" of Bali in the 1920's. A description of Bali's inhabitants, customs and beliefs before the advent of modern tourism.

Pucci, Idanna. *The Epic of Life.* New York, Alfred Van der Marck Editions, New York, 1985. The extraordinary paintings in this large format art book grace the ceiling of the Palace of Justice, Gerta Gosa, in Bali's former royal capital of Klungkung. Opposite each full-color reproduction is a vivid recounting of the section in the Hindu epic, the *Mahabharata,* which corresponds to the scene.

Ramseyer, Urs. *The Art and Culture of Bali.* Singapore: Oxford University Press, Singapore, 1986. This large-format book explains the social, religious, and philosophic concepts that rule the lives of the Balinese and find their expression in their paintings, temples, folk art, ritual offerings, music, dance, and dramatic arts. Magnificently illustrated.

de Zoete, Beryl and Walter Spies. *Dance and Drama in Bali.* New York: Harper and Brothers Publishers, 1939. Best introduction to the traditional dances and dance dramas of Bali. Out of print.

GENERAL

Indonesia: A Country Study. United States Government, 1983. One of a continuing series of books written by the Foreign Area Studies, The American University, under the government's Area Handbook Program. Five authors describe and analyze the historical setting, the society and its environment, the economy, the government and politics, and the national security of Indonesia. A good broad introduction with useful maps.

Indonesia From The Air. Jakarta and Singapore: PT Humpuss and Times Editions, 1985. A spectacular record of a team of photographers who traveled from Sumatra to Irian Jaya taking photos of Indonesia from helicopters and fixed-wing aircraft, from the edges of volcanos and from the tops of cliffs. One of the few books to capture the breathtaking patterns and rhythms of the entire Indonesian archipelago.

Introducing Indonesia. Jakarta: American Women's Association, 1975. Aimed at the expat community, this guide to Jakarta covers such topics as deciding what to take, shipping pets, learnign the dos and don'ts, choosing a house, assembling household staff, arranging utility service, leaving Indonesia, etc. The shopping section, "The Jakarta Directory," is outstanding; the travel chapters on the rest of Indonesia are superficial.

Blair, Lawrence. *Ring of Fire: Exploring the last Remote Places of the World.* New York: Bantam Books, 1988. The story of 2 brothers who, for a period of 12 years starting in 1973, penetrated and filmed some of the most remote regions of Indonesia. The film became a 4-part cycle which opened PBS television's *Adventure* series in May of 1988.

Dekker, N.A. Douwes. *Tanah Air Kita.* The Hague: W. Van Hoeve Ltd. (no year given). A wonderful pictorial mosaic of 350 b/w and 16 color photos taken in the 1950s. Although many of the photos appear staged, this large-format book is a valuable record of postwar Indonesia.

Draine, Cathie, and Barbara Hall. *Culture Shock! Indonesia.* Singapore: Times Books International, 1986. An excellent guide to interacting with Indonesians at all social and business levels. Includes sections on the character of the people, their social etiquette, customs, world view, and expectations.

Fischer, Louis. *The Story of Indonesia.* New York: Harper and Row, 1959. A definitive work which blends history and personal journalism to give an overall picture of Indonesia in the 1950s. Fisher's portraits of the leading political and military leaders of the day are compelling, and his scholarship is honest and meticulous.

Huen, Kurt G. *Indonesia: Hildebrand's Travel Guide.* Frankfurt: K & G, Karto-Grafik Verlag MBH, 1985. A small guidebook to Indonesia with scores of maps, 40 b/w and color illustrations, and a fold-out map. Awkward translation.

Jones, Howard Palfrey. *Indonesia: The Possible Dream.* New York: Harcourt Brace Jovanovich, Inc., 1971. A study-and-memoir to Indonesia by a former U.S. ambassador to Indonesia. His 8-year relationships with the dynamic Sukarno and other political and military leaders, as well his account of the explosive aftermath of the 1965 coup, make for the best reading.

Kayam, Umar. *The Soul of Indonesia: A Cultural Journey.* Baton Rouge: Louisiana State University Press, 1985. A 3-month journey across Indonesia to record selected traditional arts—how they prosper, adapt, or struggle—of Aceh, Nias, W. Sumatra, Java, S. Sulawesi, E. Kalimantan, Bali, and Irian Jaya.

Kipp, Rita Smith and Susan Rodgers. *Indonesian Religions in Transition.* Tucson: The University of Arizona Press, 1987. Original essays which examine such subjects as mantric Islam among the Javanese, Sufism among the Highland Gayo, new syncretisms formed from *adat,* and the transformation of "primitive" religious rituals by the expanding tourist industry. Erudite and fascinating.

Neill, Wilfred T. *Twentieth-Century Indonesia.* New York: Columbia University Press, 1973. A very thorough survey of Indonesia's physical environment, history, and culture. The flora, fauna, and sealife chapters are particularly well-written.

Oey, Eric. *Indonesia.* Singapore: APA Productions, 1986. With 250 color photos and 10 color maps, this artistic and thorough guide presents the Indonesian archipelago in all its compelling beauty and diversity. Makes you want to go.

Owen, Norman G. *Death and Disease in Southeast Asia: Explorations in Social, Medical and Demographic History.* Singapore: Oxford University Press, 1987. Shows how the study of death and disease can enhance our understanding of the SE Asian past.

Palmier, Leslie. *Understanding Indonesia.* Hampshire, England: Gower Publishing Co., 1985. Revised versions of a lecture series given at Oxford in 1983. Chapters include Introduction, Industrial Development and Trade, National Integration, Drama and Society, Attitudes to the World.

Southall, Ivan. *Indonesia Face to Face.* Singapore: Malaya Publishing House. The experiences of Australian and New Zealand technical aid volunteers in the 1960s. The volunteers spent 2 years in various parts of Indonesia, living in Indonesian homes and hostels and receiving Indonesian rates of pay.

Steinberg, David, ed. *In Search of Southeast Asia.* New York: Praeger Publishers, 1971. Written by 6 leading SE Asian scholars in the U.S., this is one of the best introductory social histories of SE Asia yet published. Deals with the period from 1800 to publication.

Stewart, Ian Charles. *Indonesians: Portraits from an Archipelago.* Singapore: Concept Media Pte Ltd., 1983. A spellbinding photographic essay consisting of 280 full-color photos of the most ethnically diverse people in the world. Covers all the main geographic and culture regions of Indonesia.

Wilhelm, Donald. *Emerging Indonesia*. London: Quiller Press, Ltd. 1985. Indonesia's dynamic pace of development examined against the critical political events of the past 40 years. Individual chapters cover topics such as national ideology, culture, foreign investment, industrial/agricultural development, transmigration, and the problems of youth and human rights. Supplemented by photographs.

HISTORY

Adams, Cindy. *Sukarno: An Autobiography as Told by Cindy Adams*. New York Bobbs-Merrill Company, Inc., 1965. Shows conditions in Indonesia during Dutch rule. Makes you feel Sukarno's charisma; his demogogic energy jumps from every page.

Benda, Harry J. *The Crescent and the Rising Sun: Indonesian Islam Under the Japanese Occupation 1942-1945*. The Hague: W. van Hoeve, 1958. An excellent treatise on Islam in Indonesia, studied from its first appearance in the islands. The war years are given the most detailed treatment.

da Franca, A. Pinto. *Portuguese Influence in Indonesia*. Jakarta: Gunung Agung, 1970. The author has traveled from Sumatra to Timor to research his unique perspective on Indonesian history.

Day, Clive. *The Dutch in Java*. New York: Oxford University Press, 1966. Though some of the material is historically inaccurate, this history makes you really interested in the period.

Frederick, William H. and John H. McGlynn. *Reflections on Rebellion*. Athens, Ohio: Ohio University Center for International Studies, 1983. True stories from the Indonesia political upheavals of 1948 (the Madiun Affair) and 1965 (the alleged communist coup).

Hall, D.G.E. *A History of South-East Asia*. New York: St. Martin's Press, Inc., 1981. This work is especially valuable for visualizing Indonesia in its larger setting. The chapters and references on Indonesia are comprehensive and reliable.

Hanifah, Abu. *Tales of a Revolution*. Australia: Angus and Robertson Pty Ltd., 1972. A record of an Indonesian's personal experiences during the struggle for independence against the Dutch.

Hughes, John. *Indonesian Upheaval*. New York: David McKay Company, Inc., 1967. Describes the circumstances surrounding the alleged communist coup of 1 Oct. 1965 and the ensuing events that reached final resolution in March 1967 when Sukarno finally transferred political authority to General Suharto. Written by the first American newspaper correspondent to arrive in Jakarta after the coup, this is one of the journalistic accounts, but essentially an unfair interpretation. Hughes was a communist-hater and his book typifies a mid-fifties preoccupation with the red bogeyman. But the material, despite its bias, is valuable and written in a suspenseful, tight style.

Kahin, Audrey. *Regional Dynamics of the Indonesian Revolution*. Honolulu: University of Hawaii Press, 1985. Essays on the Indonesian social revolution in 8 diverse areas of Indonesia which pitted Indonesians against Indonesians in the scramble for power during the postwar years.

Lovestrand, Harold. *Hostage in Djakarta* Chicago: Moody Press, 1967. A missionarys' experience of imprisonment and trial in Indonesia during the political turmoil in the 1960s.

Mack, Vice Adm. William P. and William P. Mack Jr. *South to Java*. Baltimore, Maryland: The Nautical & Aviation Publishing Company of America, Inc. 1987. Gut-wrenching naval combat fiction set in WW II during the deadly Battle of the Java Sea.

Masselman, George. *The Cradle of Colonialism*. New Haven: Yale University Press, 1963. The author puts a new perspective on the early history of the Netherlands East Indies by utilizing long-neglected Dutch archives.

McCoy, Alfred. *Southeast Asia Under Japanese Occupation* New Haven: Yale University Southeast Asia Studies, 1985. Nine essays which reassess the thesis of the late Harry Benda that the "Japanese interregnum" formed a distinct and decisive epoch in SE Asian history.

Mossman, James. *Rebels in Paradise*. London: Jonathon Cape, 1961. A journalist's view of Indonesia's Civil War (1958) in which N. Sulawesi and W. Sumatra declared themselves separate states. War, Indonesian-style. A clear, expertly written window onto Indonesian character.

Raffles, Thomas S. *The History of Java*. Vols. I and II. London: Black, Parbury, and Allen. A monumental work written in the early 19th C. between the Napoleonic Wars by the English governor-general. Includes a description of Raffles' times in Indonesia.

Reid, Anothony. *The Indonesian National Revolution*. Hawthorn, Victoria: Longman, 1974. A concise account of the Indonesian revolution and the formation of the Indonesian state.

Ricklefs, M.C. *A History of Modern Indonesia*. Bloomington: Indiana University Press, 1981. Indonesia's troubled history, from the coming of Islam ca. 1300 to the present day, is described in this comprehensive work.

Shimer, Barbara Gifford, and Guy Hobbs. *The Kenpeitai in Java and Sumatra*. New York Cornell Modern Indonesia Project, 1986. Authentic memoirs of the Japanese military police during their WW II occupation of Indonesia. Highlights cases where individuals among them understood native norms and brightened the lives of oppressed Indonesians.

Simatupang, T. *Report from Banaran: Experiences During the People's War*. New York: Cornell University Southeast Asia Program, 1972. Deals with the period from the beginning of the Dutch police action on 19 Dec. 1948 to the return of General Sudirman to Yogyakarta on 10 July 1949. The first full-length book in any language devoted to the oddly-neglected climax of the revolution.

Steinberg, David Joel. *In Search of Southeast Asia: A Modern History.* Honolulu: University of Hawaii Press, 1986. Six leading historians study SE Asian history, politics, and society since the 18th century.

Tantri, K'tut. *Revolt in Paradise.* London: Heinemann, 1960. A passionate book by a young British-born American woman who went to Bali in the 1930s, was adopted by a Balinese *raja*, thrown in prison and tortured by the Japanese, and fought with Indonesian guerillas for independence against the Dutch after WW II.

Toussaint, Auguste. *History of the Indian Ocean.* Chicago: University of Chicago Press, 1966. The history of the emergence of Asian and European contact in the Indian Ocean.

Van Heekeren, H.R. *The Stone Age of Indonesia.* Amsterdam: M. Nijhoff, 1958. One of the best studies of Indonesia's prehistory. See also the companion volume, *The Bronze Age of Indonesia* by Van Heekeren.

Wilson, Greta O. *Regents, Reformers, and Revolutionaries.* Honolulu: Asian Studies of Hawaii no. 21, University Press of Hawaii, 1978. An anthology of selections by prominent Indonesian spokesmen illustrating diverse aspects of early 20th C. Indonesian social change.

IRIAN JAYA

Harrar, Heinrich. *I Come From the Stone Age.* London: R. Hart-Davis, 1964. A famous explorer's account of his mountain-climbing expedition to West New Guinea. Maps and color illustrations.

Hayward, Douglas. *The Dani of Irian Jaya Before and After Conversion.* Sentani Press, 1981. A missionary book on the western Dani. Very readable anthropology.

Hitt, Russell T. *Cannibal Valley.* New York: Harper and Row, 1962. Experiences of missionaries in the Baliem, Enarotali, and Ilaga regions of West New Guinea from 1954 to the late 1950s.

Merrifield, Gregerson, and Ajamiseba. *Gods, Heroes, Kinsmen.* Dallas: International Museum of Cultures, 1983. Ethnographic studies of the spirits and belief systems of 7 different tribes of Irian Jaya.

Mitton, Robert. *The Lost world of Irian Jaya.* Melbourne: Oxford University Press, 1985. A pictorial study by an Australian geographer and anthropologist. From 1971 until his death in 1977, Mitton took notes and hundreds of color photographs of the cultures and environments of 5 distinct groups living along the Baliem River.

Pospisil, Leopold. *The Kapauku Papuans of West New Guinea.* New York: Holt, Rinehart and Winston, 1963. A case study of a complex Papuan society in its pristine aboriginal state.

Schneebaum, Tobias. *Where the Spirits Dwell.* New York: Grove Press, 1988. The story of Schneebaum's adventures with the Asmat tribe of SW Irian Jaya in which he entered into a sexual relationship with an "exchange friend" or male lover. Humane, loving, precise in detail.

Temple, Philip. *Nawok.* London: J.M. Dent, 1962. A New Zealand expedition (1961) into Irian Jaya's highest mountain ranges.

White, Osmar. *Parliament of a Thousand Tribes: A Study of New Guinea.* Indianapolis: The Bobbs-Merrill Co., Inc., 1965. A study of race relationships in West New Guinea by an Australian newspaper reporter with 30 years experience in the southwest Pacific. Eight pages of photos and a fold-out map.

JAVA

Abeyasekere, Susan. *Jakarta: A History.* Oxford: Oxford University Press, 1987. A rich, pioneering document, the first general history of Jakarta, with maps and photos excellently presented. In spite of its charitable treatment of the new regime, this book is banned in Indonesia.

Banner, Hubert S. *Romantic Java* Philadelphia: J.B. Lippincott, 1927. An early 20th C. description of Java's peoples, customs, arts, and natural beauty. Sample chapters include: Superstitions about Animals, Native Servants and Their Ways, Sidelights on Commercial Life, etc. Photos and line drawings throughout.

Bennett, Richard, and Sheila Bennet. *Bandung and Beyond.* Bandung: Aneka Karya, 1980. A detailed guide to the hills, volcanos, rivers and springs, forests and lakes, ruins and curiosities in the environs of Bandung with ideas for longer trips in W. Java.

Carpenter, Frank G. *Java and the East Indies.* New York: Doubleday, Page and Company, 1923. One of the "Carptenter's World Travels Series," this travelogue covers Java (mostly), Sumatra, Sulawesi, the Moluccas, Borneo, and West New Guinea. Includes 125 original photos and 2 color maps.

De Wit, Augusta. *Java: Facts and Fancies.* Oxford: Oxford University Press, 1987. Travels in Java at the outset of the new Dutch "Ethical Policy" during the first decade of this century. An important social document and a good read. Includes 160 b/w photos.

Dumarcay, Jacques. *Borobudur.* Oxford: Oxford University Press, 1985. A complete examination of one of the largest religious monuments in the world, incorporating the most recent research and summarizing the different theories held by scholars.

– – –. *The Temples of Java.* Oxford: Oxford University Press, 1986. A study by a noted architectural scholar of all the main Hindu and Buddhist monuments of C. and E. Java constructed between the 7th and 15 centuries by a noted architectural scholar.

Fowler, George A., Jr., Cale, Roggie and Joe C. Bartlett. *Java: A Garden Continuum.* Hong Kong: Amerasian Ltd., 1974. The authors trace the development of Javanese civilization from its earliest beginnings through the rise of Hinduized empires, the Islamization of Java, the advent of Dutch rule, and the role of Java in present-day Indonesia.

Geertz, Clifford. *The Religion of Java.* Chicago: University of Chicago Press, 1976. A reprint of a 1961 classic. Still a goldmine of highly readable details of Javanese religion, customs, and values. Pare, E. Java ("Mojokuto"), was Geertz's working model.

Hatley, Ron J. Schiller, A. Lucas, B. Martin-Schiller. *Other Javas Away From The Kraton.* Australia: Monash University, 1984. Four papers which examine Java's relative place in Austronesia, the status of *priyayi* on Java's N coast, 3 revolutionary biographies, and the facets of life in a central Javanese mountain village.

Heuken, Adolf. *Historical Sites of Jakarta.* Jakarta: Cipta Loka Caraka, 1982. This book guides the reader into Jakarta's past, to Old Batavia — its ancient mansions, churches, mosques, temples, palaces. It gives not just descriptions of the buildings but detailed historical background as well.

Hoadley, M.C., and M.B. Hooker. *An Introduction to Javanese Law.* Tucson: University of Arizona Press, 1981. An introduction to the oldest Javanese law text, Javanese legal thought and history.

Hutton, Peter. *Insight Guides: Java.* Hong Kong: APA Productions, 1984. One of APA's trilogy of guides to Indonesia. Contains hundreds of color and historical photos, dozens of maps and charts, and a section of travel information.

Lindsay, Jennifer. *Javanese Gamelan: Traditional Orchestra of Indonesia.* Oxford: Oxford University Press, 1986. An introduction for the layman which provides a listening framework so that the exotic sounds of the *gamelan* can be given musical and cultural sense. Includes explanations of the instruments and the form of the music, plus a list of places to go to hear *gamelan.*

Scidmore, E.R. *Java: The Garden of the East.* Oxford: Oxford University Press, 1986. A late 19th C. travel book written by an American visitor offering unique glimpses of various aspects of Javanese and Dutch-Javanese life in the heyday of colonial rule.

Smithies, Michael. *Yogyakarta: Cultural Heart of Indonesia.* Oxford: University Press, 1986. An erudite yet practical guide to the history of Yogya, the monuments and sights in and around it, its people and the arts and crafts practiced there.

Taylor, Jean Gelman. *The Social World of Batavia.* Madison: University of Wisconsin Press, 1983. A comprehensive analysis of Old Batavia's extraordinary social world, with an emphasis on the Dutch-Eurasian ruling elite. Illustrations, photos, maps, and genealogical charts.

Van Ness, Edward C., and Shita Prawirohardjo. *Javanese Wayang Kulit.* Oxford: Oxford University Press, 1985. Written for the general reader, the authors give a lively account of *wayang kulit*'s traditions, characters, plots, and the medium's importance in the everyday life of the Javanese. An excellent primer.

KALIMANTAN

Ave, Jan B., and Victor T.King. *Borneo: The People of the Weeping Forest.* Leiden, Netherlands: National Museum of Ethnology, 1986. The best introductory book on the island. Outstanding treatment of the land and people, Dayak tribal life, and the deep ecological and social changes on the island of Borneo. Color and b/w photos throughout.

Barclay, James. *A Stroll Through Borneo.* London: Hodder and Stoughton, 1980. A 5-month trek across Borneo starting in Sarawak and crossing the border into Indonesian Kalimantan. A sympathetic picture of such tribes as the Penans, Ibans, and Kayans.

Beeckman, Captain Daniel. *Voyage to Borneo.* New York Harper and Row 1973. A reprint of a travelogue first published in 1718 which records the 1713 voyage of the *Eagle Galley* to Banjarmasin in SE Borneo. Beeckman's detailed eye-witness acounts of the Banjarese and Dayaks of the time continue to fascinate present-day anthropologists.

Hansen, Eric. *Stranger in the Forest: On Foot Across Borneo.* Boston: Houghton Mifflin Company, 1988. In 1982, Eric Hansen hiked for 7 months through the Kalimantan jungle. He lived and hunted with the Punan, one of the last surviving rainforest dwellers in the world.

MacKinnon, John, et.al.*Borneo* Amsterdam: Time-Life International B.V., 1975. A magnificent book which explains with ample text and intriguing photos the plants, lifeforms, geology, and history of this jungle island. More than just a beautiful coffee table book.

Miller, Charles C. *Black Borneo.* New York: Modern Age Books, 1942. Heart-thumping adventures from the "come back alive" school of explorer. Miller, born on Java, made many trips to Borneo in the company of his father, a captain in the Dutch East Indies Army. The story climaxes in the Apo Kayan region of E. Kalimantan.

O'Hanlon, Redmond. *Into the Heart of Borneo.* New York: Random House, 1984. An exuberant, hilarious narrative of a hazardous 1983 journey on foot and by boat into the center of Borneo.

Vredenbregt, Jacob. *Hampatong: The Material Culture of the Dayak of Kalimantan.* Jakarta: PT Gramedia, 1981. A pictorial, annotated survey of Dayak statues carved from wood or bone.

LANGUAGE

Almatsier, A.M. *How to Master Bahasa Indonesia.* Jakarta: Penerbit Djambatan, 1974. A short-term course for English-speaking foreigners. Sold all over Indonesia (Rp4000-5000).

Dardjowidjojo, Soenjono. *Sentence Patterns of Indonesian.* Honolulu: University of Hawaii Press, 1978. A comprehensive presentation of the linguistic system of Indonesian, with particular emphasis on the language's complex system of affixes. Each chapter also includes sections on pronunciation and useful notes on behavior.

Echols, John and H. Shadily. *An Indonesian-English Dictionary.* Ithaca: Cornell University Press, 1975. First published in 1961 and extensively revised and enlarged in 1963. A well-balanced register of the Indonesian vocabulary with the main derivations and clear, accurate definitions. Where necessary, definitions are accompanied by sample sentences that illustrate usage. None better for the serious English-speaking student.

— — —. *An English-Indonesian Dictionary.* Ithaca: Cornell University Press, 1975. With 25,000 head-words, the only truly comprehensive modern English-Indonesian dictionary. Includes modern idioms and slang, many abbreviations, technical terms, cross references, especially to irregular verb forms and noun plurals. Complements the authors' previous work (above). This is the Big Artillery, the best available.

Kramer, A.L.N. *Van Goor's Indonesian Dictionary.* Rutland, Vermont: Charles E. Tuttle Co., 1986 (17th printing). This easy-to-use bilingual dictionary features colloquial usages, clear, easy-to-read type, multiple definitions, pronunciation aids. Sturdily clothbound for heavy travel, it's one of the best compact dictionaries available.

Kwee, John B. *Teach Yourself Indonesian.* Kent, England: Hodder and Stoughton, 1984. Carefully graded lessons take the student through pronunciation and word order, parts of speech and grammar, to the point where he or she will be able to take part in everyday conversation and read simple texts. Distributed in the U.S.A. by David McKay Co., 2 Park Ave., New York, NY 10016.

Sarumpaet, J.P. *Modern Usage in Bahasa Indonesia.* Carlton, Australia: Pitman Publishing Pty. Ltd., 1980. Whereas bilingual dictionaries offer a confusing variety of translations, this book is a guide to correct spelling, nuances of meaning, situations in which a word might be taboo, and whether the word is a regional variety.

Wolff, John U. *Say it in Indonesian.* New York: Dover Publications, Inc., 1983. No other phrasebook contains these features: 2,100 up-to-date practical entries, easy pronunciation transcription, every entry numbered and indexed, quick word substitution for every need, handy bilingual glossary.

LITERATURE

Alberts, A. *The Islands.* Amherst:The University of Massachusetts Press, 1983. Library of the Indies Series. An original collection of stories by an outstanding Dutch writer on Indonesia.

Aman, Dra. S.D.B. *Folk Tales From Indonesia.* Djambatan, Indonesia, 1982. Popular myths and legends from all over Indonesia.

Aveling, Harry. *Contemporary Indonesian Poetry.* Australia:University of Queensland Press, 1975. Poems in Indonesian and English by such modern poets as Rendra, Rosidi, Heraty, Sastrowardjo, Ismai.

Beekman, E.M. *The Poison Tree.* Amherst:The University of Massachusetts Press, 1981. Selected witings of the renowned Dutch naturalist Rumphius (1628-1702) on the tropical flora, shellfish, minerals, and precious stones of the Dutch East Indies. Also an intriguing and erudite sourcebook on the native use of plants, native customs, lore, religion, and historical information of the period.

Couperus, Louis. *The Hidden Force.* Amherst: University of Massachusetts Press, 1985. A masterpiece of psychological fiction by one of Holland's greatest novelists. Although written 45 years before Indonesian independence, it reveals many of the reasons why the Dutch colonial empire was destined to fail.

Dekker, Douwes. *Max Havelaar.* Amherst: University of Massachusetts Press, 1982. Library of the Indies Series. First published in 1860. The "Uncle Tom's Cabin" of the Dutch colonial period and one of the greatest works of Dutch literature. Describes the exploitation of the Javanese peasant under the control of the rapacious Dutch colonial policy and the greedy Javanese regents in the time of the infamous *Cultuur Stelsel* period. This book did more to bring this period to an end than any other efforts. Takes place in Lobok District, W. Java.

Dermout, Maria. *The Ten Thousand Things.* Amherst: University of Massachusetts Press, 1983. Set in the Moluccas, this haunting, offbeat novel draws on the author's rich memories and knowledge of Indonesian customs and folklore while an ominous current of violence pervades the whole story.

Forbes, Anna. *Unbeaten Tracks in Islands of the Far East.* Oxford:Oxford University Press, 1987. The experiences of 'an unassuming, resourceful Victorian woman who traveled from Batavia to Sulawesi, Moluccas and Timor in the late 19th C. Anna was the wife of the distinguished naturalist Henry O. Forbes, who wrote *A Naturalist's Wanderings in the Eastern Archipelago* (1887).

Hendon, Rufus S. *Six Indonesian Short Stories.* New Haven: Yale University Southeast Asia Studies, 1968. Samples of work produced by Indonesian short-story writers in the 1940s and early 1950s, a high point in the development of Indonesian fiction and the refinement of the Indonesian language as a literary vehicle.

Kartini, Raden Adjeng. *Letters of A Javanese Princess.* Lanham, Maryland: University Press of America, 1985. One of the earliest modern Indonesian literary masterpieces, written (in Dutch) by the daughter of the regent of Rembang. The first Indonesian nationalist, Kartini argued that all Indonesian women have a right to be educated, but not to the exclusion of their domestic duties. Vivid atmosphere of Javanese court life at the turn of the century.

Koch, C.J. *The Year of Living Dangerously.* New York: Penguin Books, 1978. A complex drama of loyalty and betrayal played out in the eye of the political storm of 1965.

Lubis, Mochtar. *Twilight in Djakarta.* Oxford: Oxford University Press, 1986. Basically about political corruption in post-independence (1950s) Indonesia. One of the best documents of daily life in the capital, especially its underbelly: the *becak* drivers, the derelicts, the prostitutes. Finished in 1957, a year after he was jailed by Sukarno. This book goes on and off the banned books list.

———. *The Indonesian Dilemma.* Singapore: Graham Brash Pte.Ltd., 1983. A distillation of an electrifying 3-hour critique Lubis delivered on 6 April 1977 at the TIM in Jakarta in which the author focuses on what he feels are weak character traits of the Javanese people.

———. *A Road With No End.* Singapore: Graham Brash Pte.Ltd., 1982. A story set between the time of the re-occupation of Indonesia by the Dutch in 1946 and the First Police Action of 1947.

———. *The Outlaw and Other Stories.* Singapore: Oxford University Press, 1987. Spanning the 30 years between the 1950s and the 1970s, this selection of tragic stories is representative of Lubis at the peak of his literary career.

Moore, Cornelia Niekus. *Insulinde: Selected Translations from Dutch Writers of Three Centuries on the Indonesian Archipelago.* Honolulu: University Press of Hawaii, 1978. Mainly autobiographical short stories centering on the Dutch experience in Indonesia during their colonization.

Nieuwenhuys, Rob. *Mirror of the Indies: A History of Dutch Colonial Literature.* Amherst: University of Massachusetts Press, 1982. The definitive literary history of the colonial Dutch East Indies, this study covers works on natural history to religious sermons to pamphlets and the accounts of travelers from the 17th to the 20th centuries.

de Nijs, E. Briton. *Faded Portraits.* Amherst: University of Massachusetts Press, 1982. A fictionalized memoir of family life in the colonial Dutch East Indies. Reminiscent of the literature of the American South, this book wistfully records an era that was passing.

du Perron, E. *Country of Origin.* Amherst: University of Massachusetts Press, 1984. Second only to *Max Havelaar* as an important Dutch work on Indonesia, this novel teems with the atmosphere of the tropics and evokes the colonial scene in great detail.

Savage, Victor R. *Western Impressions of Nature and Landscape in SE Asia.* Singapore: Singapore University Press, 1984. Popular non-fictional literature by Western sojourners and travelers who have written of their experiences in Indonesia over the centuries. Savage asserts that romantic perceptions of SE Asia were a major factor influencing the spread of colonialism in the region.

Toer, Pramoedya Ananta. *The Fugitive.* Hong Kong: Heinemann Educational Books (Asia) Ltd., 1975. Set in Aug. 1945, immediately after the declaration of independence from the Dutch. Pramoedya himself was captured and tortured by the Dutch and *The Fugitive* was smuggled out of prison by sympathetic Dutch intellectuals.

Van Schendel, Arthur. *John Company.* Amherst: University of Massachusetts Press, 1983. A vivid, panoramic sea journey during the early years of the Dutch East Indies company.

Vuyk, Beb, and H.J.Friedericy. *Two Tales of the East Indies.* Amherst: The University of Massachusetts Press, 1983. An autobiographical novel set on the island of Buru in the Moluccas, and the story of the relationship between a young Dutch government official and an older and wiser administrator in southern Sulawesi in the 1920s.

Ward, Philip. *Indonesian Traditional Poetry.* New York: Oleander Press, 1975. An annotated anthology of Indonesia's folk chants and ritual songs in English and the regional languages.

Watson, Lyall. *Gifts of Unknown Things.* London: Hodder and Stoughton, 1983. A fascinating book which records the mystical happenings on a small volcanic island, somewhere in Indonesia.

MALUKU

Deane, Shirley. *Ambon: Island of Spices.* London: John Murray, A description of *adat* customs in Ambonese society through the author's own experience living on Ambon in the early 1970s.

Hanna, Willard A. *Indonesian Banda: Colonialism and its Aftermath in the Nutmeg Islands.* Philadelphia: Institute for the Study of Human Issues, 1978. Hanna deftly demonstrates how the Dutch became their own worst enemies, creating a monopoly system in the Bandas that eventually declined into economic chaos. Full of interesting detail. Explodes many Maugham-created fantasies.

NATURAL PHENOMENA

Beekman, E.M. *The Poison Tree.* Amherst: The University of Massachusetts Press, 1981. Selected writings of the renowned Dutch naturalist Rumphius (1628-1702) on the tropical flora, shellfish, minerals, and precious stones of the Dutch East Indies. Also an intriguing and erudite sourcebook on the native use of plants, native customs, lore, religion, and historical information of the period.

Donner, Wolf. *Land Use and Environment in Indonesia.* Honolulu: University of Hawaii Press, 1987. Presents a thorough survey of scientific research, of experience gained through fieldwork, and of political strategies that deal with Indonesia's natural environment in connection with land use.

Elisofon, Eliot. *Java Diary.* Toronto: Macmillan Company, Toronto, Canada, 1969. An adventure-packed diary of the author's experiences in the Ujung Kulon Nature Reserve of W. Java, recording in 130 b/w and 17 color photos the fauna typical of the Greater Sunda Islands.

Farrelly, David. *The Book of Bamboo.* San Francisco: Sierra Club Books,1984. A complete and inspiring sourcebook of the bamboo culture, including illustrated descriptions of its hundreds of uses, plus how to cultivate, maintain, and harvest this astonishing plant.

Kavanagh, Michael. *A Complete Guide to Monkeys, Apes and Other Primates.* New York: The Viking Press, 1983. Written by an expert primatologist, this is a complete, up-to-date, fully illustrated guide to all the world's living primates. Understandable and fascinating for the general reader, yet authoritative and detailed enough for the specialist. Includes distribution maps and full-color photos illustrating every genus.

Kusumadinata, K., ed. *Data Dasar Gunungapi Indonesia.* Bandung: Republic of Indonesia, 1979. The most comprehensive volcanological survey of Indonesia yet published. Included are historical notes on eruptions and climbs by explorers and geologists. Written in Indonesian.

Maple, Terry L. *Orang-utan Behavior.* New York: Van Nostrand Reinhold Co., 1980. A discussion of the natural history, broad behavioral patterns, expression and emotion, sexuality, birth, development, parental bahavior, captive habitat management, and conservation of the orangutan.

McNeely, Jeffrey A., and Paul Spencer Wachtel. *Soul of the Tiger: Searching for Nature's Answers in Exotic Southeast Asia.* New York: Doubleday, 1988. Two American conservationists and adventurers, with over 20 year's experience in the area, give fascinating, bizarre, and humorous accounts of the vital connections between Southeast Asians and their animals.

Merrill, E. *Plant Life of the Pacific World.* Rutland, Vermont: Charles E. Tuttle Co., Rutland, Vermont, 1981. A well-organized overview of the plantlife of the whole Pacific region, a distillation of Dr. Merril's 42 years of botanical research in the area. First published in 1945.

Planet Earth: Volcano. Alexandria, Virginia: Time-Life Books, 1982. A thorough discussion of how volcanos are formed, histories of famous Indonesian eruptions like Tambora on Sumbawa and Toba on Sumatra, and the rise of modern volcanology, etc. Full-color photos, b/w photos, maps.

Veevers-Carter, W. *Nature Conservation in Indonesia.* Jakarta: PT Intermasa, 1978. Sponsored by the Indonesian Wildlife Fund. An island-by-island guide to the nature reserves of Indonesia.

— — —. *Land Mammals of Indonesia.* Jakarta: PT Intermasa, 1979. Contains drawings, field notes, distribution, and zoological data for all Indonesian mammals. Written by an American anthropologist.

NUSATENGGARA

Attenborough, D. *Zoo Quest For A Dragon.* Oxford: Oxford University Press, 1986. A vivid and entertaining account of travel to Bali, Java, the interior of Borneo, and Komodo (to acquire a Komodo dragon for the London Zoo).

Auffenberg, W. *The Behavioral Ecology of the Komodo Monitor.* Gainesville, Florida: University Presses of Florida, 1981. Reporting the findings of the author's 13-month field study of the ecology and behavior of the spectacular Komodo dragon. A pioneer book in predation studies.

Budiardjo, Carmel, and Liem Soei Liong. *The War Against East Timor.* Zed Books Ltd., London, 1984. Analyses Indonesia's military and political strategy to subjugate and integrate East Timor since Suharto's invasion of this former Portuguese colony in 1975.

Fox, J. *The Flow of Life.* Cambridge: Harvard University Press, 1980. Erudite essays by international scholars on the social anthropology of eastern Indonesia.

Kessler, C. *Lombok—Just Beyond Bali.* Jakarta: PT Indira, 1984. A picture essay on Lombok with short sections on historical background, the people, and the land. One of very few books in print on Lombok and for sale only on the island and in Jakarta.

Traube, E. *Cosmology and Social Life.* Chicago: University of Chicago Press, 1986. An ethnographic study of ritual life in an eastern Indonesian society, that of the Mambai of East Timor.

Wheeler, Tony. *Bali and Lombok.* Melbourne, Australia: Lonely Planet, 1986. A popular travel guide to Bali and its neighboring island. Eight pages of color photos.

POLITICS AND ECONOMY

Cho Oon, Khong. *The Politics of Oil in Indonesia.* England: Cambridge University Press, 1986. A book-length discussion of the Indonesian petroleum industry: the impact of foreign investment, the form and content of agreements, provisions for national control, problems of negotiation.

Cho, Suharto, McNicoll, and Mamas. *Population Growth of Indonesia.* Honolulu: University Press of Hawaii, 1980. An analysis of fertility and mortality based on the 1971 census.

Geertz, C. *Agriculture Involution: The Processes of Ecological Change in Indonesia.* Los Angeles: University of California Press, 1963. An incisive account of Indonesian agricultural history, primarily covering the period of Dutch control from 1619 to 1942.

Hamish, McDonald. *Suharto's Indonesia.* Australia: Fontana Books, 1981. The author first explains the dynamics of the Javanese culture and against this background describes the rise of Suharto, the nature of his powerbase, his restructuring of the Indonesian economy, the rise and fall of Pertamina, the takeover of E. Timor, and the fate of Indonesia's political prisoners. The best introduction to Indonesian politics of the 1970s.

Jenkins, David. *Suharto and His Generals: Indonesian Military Politics.* Ithaca, New York: Cornell Modern Indonesia Project, 1984. An exhaustive examination of the army's involvement in Indonesian political life. Included are interviews with former and current military leaders.

Legge, J.D. *Sukarno: A Political Biography.* Allen and Unwin Ltd., London, 1972. A standard biography and one of the best introductions to Sukarno yet published. Also gives some flashes into a wide spectrum of Javanese life, while suggesting that Sukarno incorporated archetypical Javanese character traits.

Lubis, Mochtar. *The Indonesian Dilemma.* Singapore: Graham Brash Pte Ltd., 1983. A revised version of a famous 3-hour lecture which sparked reactions all over Indonesia, Lubis defines the Indonesian character and encourages Indonesians to reassert their ethical values to achieve national security.

MacAndrews, Colin. *Central Government and Local Development in Indonesia.* Singapore: Oxford University Press, 1986. Written by specialists in their fields, these essays focus on how government works in Indonesia and how development policies are implemented at both the central and local levels. Also provides an up-to-date analysis of such important policy areas as transmigration, agriculture, rural industrialization, and transportation.

May, Brian. *The Indonesian Tragedy.* Singapore: Graham Brash Pte Ltd., 1984. May concludes that the major impediment to progress in Indonesia is cultural. He asserts that the country's main "tragedy" is the ruling junta's blind attempt to force a Western economic model on a backward and superstitious people.

Penders, C.L.M., and Ulf Sundhaussen. *Abdul Haris Nasution: A Political Biography.* Australia: University of Queensland Press, 1985. One of the architects of the guerilla war against the Dutch and later an outspoken critic against the New Order, this book contains material on Nasution's early life, his experiences during the Japanese occupation, his views on military strategy, his experiences as a civilian politician, and his basic political and moral values.

Pye, Lucian W. *Asian Power and Politics: The Cultural Dimensions of Authority.* Cambridge, Massachusetts: The Belknap Press of Harvard University, 1985. A broadly gauged analysis of contemporary Asian politics. Pye shows how Asian societies, confronted with the task of setting up modern nation-states, respond by fashioning paternalistic forms of power that satisfy their deep psychological craving for security.

Roeder, O.G. *The Smiling General: President Soeharto of Indonesia.* Djakarta: Gunung Agung Ltd., 1969. A biography of Suharto by a former correspondent for German and Swiss newspapers. Follows the rise of an unknown officer from obscurity to the position of acting president in less than 2 years. Some useful information.

SUMATRA

Errington, Frederick. *Manners and Meaning in West Sumatra.* New Haven: Yale University Press, 1984. An engrossing analysis of how the Minangkabau conduct and interpret their lives and an exploration of the contrasts between Minang consciousness and Western. A beautifully written and richly illustrated book.

Freidus, Alberta. *Sumatran Contributions to the Development of Indonesian Literature, 1920-1942.* Honolulu: University Press of Hawaii, 1977. A tribute to the genius of Minang poets and writers in the development of a modern Indonesian literature.

Frey, Katherine. *Journey to the Land of the Earth Goddess.* Jakarta: Gramedia Publishing Division, 1986. A panoramic view, in color photos and text, of the Minangkabau culture of W. Sumatra: their myths, customs, practice and worship of Islam, archaeology, contemporay life, rituals and ceremonies.

Graves, Elizabeth. *The Minangkabau Response to Dutch Colonial Rule.* Ithaca, New York: Cornell University Southeast Asia Program, 1981.

A study of 19th C. Minangkabau society and its interaction with Dutch political and economic power, particularly within the context of the Padri Movement (1784-1830).

Marsden, William. *The History of Sumatra.* Oxford: Oxford University Press, 1986. A reprint of the esteemed 1811 edition, this "history" includes authenticated facts in the fields of geography, linguistics, botany, and zoology.

Salim, Leon. *Prisoners at Kota Cane.* Ithaca: Cornell Modern Indonesia Project, 1986. A memoir, from the Indonesian perspective, of the final days of Dutch colonial rule on Sumatra in 1942.

Stoler, Ann *Capitalism and Confrontation in Sumatra's Plantation Belt.* New Haven: Yale University Press, 1985. This fascinating ethnographic history analyzes how popular resistance actively molded both the form of colonial expansion and the social, economic, and political experience of the Javanese laboring communities on Sumatra's 19th C. plantations.

Szekely, Ladislao. *Tropic Fever.* Oxford: Oxford University Press, 1979. A remarkable semi-autobiographical account of a planter's life in Sumatra during the first 2 decades of this century. First published in 1937.

Whitten, A., D. Sengli, A. Jazanul, and H. Nazaruddin. *The Ecology of Sumatra.* Yogyakarta: Gadjah Mada University Press, 1984. A comprehensive overview of the impact of a wide range of agricultural, social, and industrial developments on the man-made and natural ecosystems of Sumatra and its surrounding islands.

Whitten, Tony. *The Gibbons of Siberut.* London: J.M. Dent and Sons Ltd., 1982. The first full-length, popular account of gibbon life as well as a study of Siberut Island's botany, wildlife, and people.

TRAVELOGUE

Clifton, V. *Islands of Queen Wilhelmina.* London: Constable & Company Ltd., 1927. A Victorian lady's adventures in the Outer Islands in the early 20th century. Beautifully written.

Clune, Frank. *Isles of Spice.* New York: E.P. Dutton and Co., Inc., 1942. An extensive pre-WW II journey through the Dutch East Indies, Indochina, and North Australia.

Dixon, Gale. *Indonesian Ports: An Atlas-Gazetteer.* Committee of Southeast Asian Studies Monograph series. Australia: James Cook University of North Queensland, 1985. Covers a larger number of Indonesian ports than has previously been available from a single source. Gives name, latitude, longitude, pilot reference, maximum draft in harbor, minimum depth alongside, total length of wharfage, port services, etc. Invaluable reference for the mariner.

Fairchild, D. *Garden Islands of The Great East.* New York: Charles Scribner's Sons, 1943. A botanist's hunt in a Chinese junk for exotic plants in the far-flung isles of the East Indies in the 1930s. Fairchild introduced into the United States 200,000 named species and varieties of plants from all over the world.

Gibson, A. *The Malay Peninsula and Archipelago.* London: J.M. Dent and Sons Ltd., 1928. About one-third of this travelogue is devoted to "Insulinde," or the Dutch East Indies.

Greenfield, Darby. *Indonesia: A Traveler's Guide.* Vol. I, *Java and Sumatra.* Vol. II, *Bali and the East.* New York: The Oleander Press, 1976. The author traveled over 200,000 km by air, sea, river, jeep, car, and on foot in every one of Indonesia's provinces (except Timor Timor) to collect material for these travel guides.

Hanbury-Tenison, R. *A Pattern of Peoples.* New York: Charles Scribner's Sons, 1975. The author spent 3 months traveling through the Outer Islands reaching a wide cross section of peoples from the highly cultured Torajans of Sulawesi to the Stone-Age Dani of the Baliem Valley in New Guinea. Color photos.

Hilton, J. *The Story of Dr. Wassell.* Boston: Little, Brown and Company, 1943. A true story of an American Navy doctor who got his wounded men out of Java through the turmoil of the Japanese invasion in WW II.

de Leeuw, Hendrik. *Crossroads of the Java Sea.* New York: Garden City Publishing Co., 1931. A travel narrative by a Dutch-American describing the strange customs and other interesting data he came across on Java, Sumatra, Borneo, Sulawesi, and Bali.

Mackellar, C.D. *Scented Isles and Coral Gardens.* London: John Murray, 1912. A collection of letters written in the 1890s which describe at firsthand the author's travels in the Indies. The extensive b/w photos are unique.

McDougall, W. *Six Bells Off Java.* New York: Charles Scribner's Sons, 1948. The fast-moving story of the author's wartime escape from Shanghai to Palembang and ultimate capture and imprisonment by the Japanese.

Pelzer, D. *Trek Across Indonesia.* Singapore: Graham Brash Pte Ltd., 1982. Pelzer, with an architect's degree from MIT, traveled to remote and primitive villages all over Indonesia to gather a photographic record of traditional house forms.

Schreider, H. and J. *The Drums Of Tonkin.* New York: Coward-McCann, Inc., 1963. An account of a young couple's 13-month journey across the Indonesian archipelago in a seagoing jeep. A first-rate tale of adventure.

Stevenson, W. *Birds' Nest in Their Beards.* Boston: Houghton Mifflin Company, 1963. A journalist's coverage of the turbulent period beginning with the first Afro-Asian conference held in Bandung in 1955 and ending 8 years later at the Moshi conference in Africa.

Southall, I. *Indonesian Journey.* Melbourne: Lansdowne Press, 1965. A book for young readers of the author's travel experiences.

INDEX

Learning to use the index well has a very practical application. Looking up a city, town, or region in the index is the fastest way to find a place to sleep that night, learn what arts and crafts are available in a given area, what museums, sights, and cultural performances are to be seen, what transportation to take when first arriving, and the easiest way to get farther down the road.

Page numbers in **boldface** indicate the primary reference to a given entry. Page numbers in *italics* followed by **c**, **i** or **m** indicate information in a caption, illustration, or map. An italicized **c** could also refer to lists, tables, charts, legends; **i** also refers to photographs. A **p** following a page number means that references are found here and there.

Please see abbreviations' key on page 1058

ABBREVIATIONS

MEASUREMENTS

All prices in this book are in Indonesian currency, the *rupiah,* unless otherwise stated. All hotel and restaurant prices are pp (per person), per day, or per meal. To avoid confusion, all clock times appear according to the 24-hour airline timetable system, i.e., 0100 is 1:00 AM, 1300 is 1:00 PM, 2330 is 11:30 PM. From noon to midnight, merely add 12 onto regular time to obtain airline time. Indonesians operate on *jam karet* ("rubber time"). Since this book is used by people from all around the world, the metric system is employed throughout. Here are the equivalents:

1 inch	=	2.54 centimeters
1 foot	=	.3048 meters (m)
1 mile	=	1.6093 kilometers (km)
1 km	=	.6214 miles
1 nautical mile	=	1.852 km
1 fathom	=	1.8288 m
1 chain	=	20.1168 m
1 furlong	=	201.168 m
1 acre	=	.4047 hectares (ha)
1 sq km	=	100 ha
1 sq mile	=	2.59 sq km
1 ounce	=	28.35 grams
1 pound	=	.4536 kilograms (kg)
1 short ton	=	.90718 metric ton
1 short ton	=	2000 pounds
1 long ton	=	1.016 metric tons
1 long ton	=	2240 pounds
1 metric ton	=	1000 kg
1 quart	=	.94635 liters
1 U.S. gallon	=	3.7854 liters
1 Imperial gallon	=	4.5459 liters

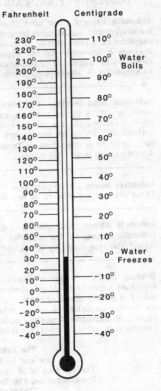

Unless otherwise indicated, north is at the top of all maps. When using official topographic maps you can determine the scale by taking the Representative Fraction (RF) and dividng by 100. This will give the number of meters represented by one centimeter. For example, a map with an RF of 1:10,000 would represent 100 m for every cm on the map.

To compute Centigrade temperatures, subtract 32 from Fahrenheit and divide by 1.8. To go the other way, multiply Centigrade by 1.8 and add 32.

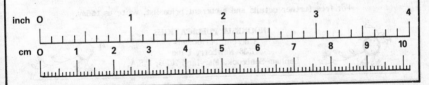

INDONESIA PUBLICATIONS

INDEPENDENT PERIODICALS ON CONTEMPORARY INDONESIA IN ENGLISH

Indonesia Reports. Our most cited periodical. Features a daily log of news stories translated and summarized from the Indonesian-language press. Plus five article supplements titled Politics, Human Rights, Culture & Society, Books & Biblio, and Business & Economy. All five supplements appear in every issue. Each issue carries 70-80 solid pages of information, about equally divided between the log and supplements. A subscription covers 12 monthly issues.

Indonesia News Service. Our best-seller. It's like a news wire. Published twice a week, it gets a lot of news—almost twice as much as appears in **Indonesia Reports** log—to readers shortly after events occur in Indonesia. **INS** concentrates on key articles in such major newspapers as **Kompas, Suara Pembaruan,** and **Jawa Pos** and such major news magazines as **Tempo, Editor,** and **Panji Masyarakat.** Plus a lot more. A subscription covers 104 issues.

Indonesia Issues. A 12-page newsletter. Each copy probes a single topic in depth. These articles are written by non-Indonesian authors. A subscription covers 12 issues.

Indonesia Mirror. Our other 12-page newsletter. Using the same article format as **Indonesia Issues,** all the material is instead written by Indonesians and selected to reflect the true diversity of opinion within Indonesia. A subscription covers 12 issues.

Briefing Books. Looseleaf compilations of analytic and documentary materials on important topics from all our various periodicals. The **Briefing Books** are particularly useful in quickly becoming current on a subject area and in providing helpful readings for courses on Indonesia. Each **Briefing Book** is regularly updated as relevant items appear in **Indonesia Reports** supplements, **Issues,** and **Mirror.** Compilations do not overlap each other in content. **Briefing Books** available include these titles:

The Indonesian Military Elite
Law and Political Liberty in Indonesia
The Petition of 50 Group and the Tanjung Priok Incident
Transmigration, the Environment, and Indigenous Peoples
Political Islam in Indonesia
Irian Jaya
East Timor
Indonesia's Economy
Recent Dissertations on Indonesia

For free further details and a current price list, write us today.

INDONESIA PUBLICATIONS
Current Periodicals
7538 Newberry Lane
Lanham-Seabrook, Maryland 20706, U.S.A.

Did You Enjoy This Book?
Then you may want to order other
MOON PUBLICATIONS titles.

Like the guide you're holding in your hands, you'll find the same high standard of quality in all of our other titles, with informative introductions, up-to-date travel information, clear and concise maps, beautiful illustrations, a comprehensive subject/place-name index, and many other useful features. All Moon Publications' guides come in this compact, portable size, with a tough Smyth-sewn binding that'll hold up through years of hard traveling.

INDONESIA HANDBOOK by Bill Dalton. The most comprehensive and contemporary guide to Indonesia, covering island by island the cheapest places to eat and sleep, ancient ruins and historical sites, wildlife and nature reserves, spiritual centers, arts and crafts, folk theater, and dance venues. Color and b/w photos, illus., maps, charts, booklist, vocabulary, index. 1100 pages. **$17.95**

SOUTH KOREA HANDBOOK by Robert Nilsen. A land of haunting beauty, rich culture, and economic promise, South Korea neatly weaves the warp and woof of tradition and modernity. This definitive travel guide to the once-hidden "Hermit Kingdom" leads you into the heart and soul of the country. Color and b/w photos, illus., maps, charts, place names translated into Korean characters, Korean glossary with useful notes on speaking and reading the language, booklist, index. 600 pages. **$14.95**

JAPAN HANDBOOK by J.D. Bisignani. Packed with money-saving tips on travel, food, and accommodation, this comprehensive guide dispels the myth that Japan is too expensive for the budget-minded traveler. A useful encyclopedia on every facet of Japanese life. 8 color pages, 200 b/w photos, 92 illus., 29 charts, 112 maps and town plans, appendix on the Japanese language, booklist, glossary, index. 504 pages. **$12.95**

SOUTH PACIFIC HANDBOOK by David Stanley. Here is paradise explored, photographed, and mapped — the original comprehensive guide to the history, geography, climate, cultures, and customs of the 19 territories in the South Pacific. No other traveler knows the South Pacific like David Stanley. 12 color pages, 195 b/w photos, 121 illus., 35 charts, 138 maps, booklist, glossary, index. 588 pages. **$13.95**

MICRONESIA HANDBOOK by David Stanley. Midway, Wake, Saipan, Tinian, Guam — household words for Americans during WW II, yet the seven North Pacific territories between Hawaii and the Philippines have received little attention since. Enjoy the world's finest scuba diving in Belau, or get lost on the far-flung atolls of the Gilberts. *Micronesia Handbook* cuts across the plastic path of packaged tourism and guides you on a real Pacific adventure. 8 color pages, 77 b/w photos, 68 illus., 58 maps, 12 charts, booklist, glossary, index. 238 pages. **$8.95**

FINDING FIJI **by David Stanley.** Fiji, everyone's favorite South Pacific country, is now easily accessible either as a stopover or as a whole Pacific experience in itself. This guide covers it all—the amazing variety of land and seascapes, customs and climates, sightseeing attractions, hikes, and beaches, even how to board a copra boat to the outer islands. Packed with practical tips, everything you need to know in one portable volume. 4 color pages, 35 b/w photos, 78 illus., 26 maps, 3 charts, Fijian glossary, index. 127 pages.   **$6.95**

BLUEPRINT FOR PARADISE: How to Live on a Tropic Island **by Ross Norgrove.** Ever dreamed of living on a tropic island? *Blueprint For Paradise* explains how to make that dream a reality. Derived from personal experiences, Norgrove describes: choosing an island, designing a house for tropical living, transportation, installing electricity and water systems, adapting to the island lifestyle, successfully facing the elements, and much more. As entertaining as it is practical. 8 color pages, 40 b/w photos, 3 maps, 14 charts, appendices, index. 202 pages.   **$14.95**

NEW ZEALAND HANDBOOK **by Jane King.** New Zealand is nature's improbable masterpiece, a world of beauty and wonder jammed into three unforgettable islands. Explore whitewater rapids and silent fjords, ski the slopes of a smoldering volcano, fly fish for monstrous trout in an icy stream—only in New Zealand. 8 color pages, 99 b/w photos, 146 illus., 82 maps, booklist, index,512 pages.   **$13.95**

HAWAII HANDBOOK **by J.D. Bisignani.** This definitive guide takes you beyond the glitz and leads you to a genuine Hawaiian experience. With a comprehensive introduction to Hawaii's geography, history, arts, and events, plus the best sights, lodging and food, entertainment, and recreation. 12 color pages, 318 b/w photos, 132 illus., 74 maps, 43 graphs and charts, appendix, booklist, Hawaiian and Pidgin glossaries, index. 788 pages.   **$15.95**

MAUI HANDBOOK: Including Molakai and Lanai **by J.D. Bisignani.** Here is "no fool-'round" advice and budget-shaving tips on Maui's full range of accommodations, eateries, rental cars, shopping, tours, and transport, plus a comprehensive introduction to island ways, geography, and history. 6 color pages, 50 b/w photos, 62 illus., 27 maps, 13 charts, booklist, glossary, index. 300 pages.   **$10.95**

GUIDE TO THE YUCATAN PENINSULA: Including Belize **by Chicki Mallan.** Explore the mysterious ruins of the Maya, plunge into the color and bustle of the village market place, relax on unspoiled beaches, or jostle with the jet set in modern Cancun. Here is all the information you need to explore every corner of this exotic land. 4 color pages, 154 b/w photos, 55 illus., 53 maps, 68 charts, appendix, booklist, glossary, index. 400 pages.   **$11.95**

GUIDE TO JAMAICA: Including Haiti **by Harry S. Pariser.** Colorful Jamaica is one of the most beautiful islands in the Caribbean, and arguably the world. No other guide treats the island and its people with more depth and cultural sensitivity. 4 color pages, 51 b/w photos, 39 illus., 18 maps, 10 charts, booklist, glossary, index. 174 pages.   **$7.95**

GUIDE TO PUERTO RICO AND THE VIRGIN ISLANDS: Including the Dominican Republic by Harry S. Pariser. *Terra incognita* to most of us—now discover these beautiful islands for yourself. Pariser turns up good-value accommodations, dining, entertainment, and many travel bargains. This guide is proof that "budget" travel means getting more for your money—not less. 4 color pages, 55 b/w photos, 53 illus., 35 maps, 29 charts, booklist, glossary, index. 225 pages. **$8.95**

ARIZONA TRAVELER'S HANDBOOK by Bill Weir. This comprehensive guide contains the facts and background to make Arizona accessible and enjoyable. It's all here—the state's history and natural features, places to go, directions, hours, phone numbers, as well as motel, restaurant, and campground listings. 8 color pages, 250 b/w photos, 81 illus., 53 maps, 4 charts, booklist, index. 448 pages. **$11.95**

UTAH HANDBOOK by Bill Weir. Three states rolled into one, Utah has the pristine alpine country of the Rockies, the awesome canyons of the Colorado Plateau, and the remote mountains of the Great Basin. Take in cosmopolitan Salt Lake City, ski Utah's "greatest snow on earth," and explore the spectacular rock formations of Utah's many national parks. Weir gives you all the carefully researched facts and background to make your visit a success. Color and b/w photos, illus., maps, charts, booklist, index. 460 pages. **$11.95**

ALASKA-YUKON HANDBOOK: Including the Canadian Rockies by David Stanley and Deke Castleman. *Alaska-Yukon Handbook* gets you to and around the 49th state and western Canada by car, bus, thumb, ferry, cruise ship, and plane. It guides you to North America's tallest mountains, wildest rivers, greatest glaciers, largest wilderness parks, and most abundant wildlife. The *inside* story, with plenty of well-seasoned advice to help you cover more miles on less money. 8 color pages, 26 b/w photos, 91 illus., 94 maps, booklist, glossary, index. 398 pages. **$10.95**

GUIDE TO CATALINA and California's Channel Islands by Chicki Mallan. A complete guide to these remarkable islands, from the windy solitude of the Channel Islands National Marine Sanctuary to bustling Avalon—a world of vacation opportunities right in Southern California's back yard. Recreation, entertainment, and travel info, plus a comprehensive listing of marinas and boating facilities. 8 color pages, 105 b/w photos, 65 illus., 39 maps, 32 charts, booklist, index. 275 pages. **$8.95**

CALIFORNIA DOWNHILL by Stephen Metzger. Gives complete, detailed listings of all of California's 39 downhill ski areas, from the bunny slopes of Big Bear to the near-vertical faces of Squaw Valley. Includes resort hours, rates, facilities, and how to get there; deals and discounts; lodging and dining close to the slopes; day-care and baby-sitting services; and facilities for cross-country and disabled skiers. 4 color pages, 37 b/w photos, 21 illus., 30 maps, 41 charts, index. 144 pages. **$7.95**

BACKPACKING: A Hedonist's Guide by Rick Greenspan and Hal Kahn. This humorous, handsomely illustrated how-to guide will convince even the most confirmed naturophobe that it's safe, easy, and enjoyable to leave the smoggy security of city life behind—and "rough it" in style. 90 illus., annotated booklist, index. 199 pages. **$7.95**

IMPORTANT ORDERING INFORMATION

1. **Prices:** All prices are subject to change. We always ship the most current edition. We will let you know if there is a price increase on the book you ordered.

2. **Domestic orders:** We ship UPS or US Postal Service 1st class. Send $3.00 for first item and $.50 for each additional item. Please specify street or P.O. Box address, and shipping method. Please include a daytime phone number. We will inform you of any delay in shipping your order.

3. **Foreign orders:** All orders which originate outside the U.S.A. **must** be paid for with either an International Money Order or a check in U.S. currency drawn on a major U.S. bank based in the U.S.A. For International Surface Bookrate (8-12 weeks delivery), send U.S. $3.00 for the first book and U.S. $1.00 for each additional book.

4. **Telephone orders:** We accept Visa or Mastercharge payments. **MINIMUM ORDER U.S. $15.00.** Call in your order: (916) 345-5473. 11:00 a.m. – 5:00 p.m. Pacific Standard Time.

A new concept in moneybelts. Made of heavy-duty, water-resistant Cordura nylon, the *Moonbelt* offers maximum protection for your money and important papers. This pouch, designed for all-weather comfort, slips under your shirt or waistband, rendering it virtually undetectable and inaccessible to pickpockets. Many thoughtful features: 1-inch-wide nylon webbing, heavy-duty zipper, and a 1-inch high-test quick-release buckle. No more fumbling around for the strap or repeated adjustments, this handy plastic buckle opens and closes with a touch, but won't come undone until you want it to. Accommodates travelers cheques, passport, cash, photos. Size: 5 x 9 inches. Available in black only.   **$8.95**

ORDER FORM
(See important ordering information on opposite page)

Name: _____ Date: _____

Street: _____

City: _____

State or Country: _____ Zip Code: _____

Daytime Phone: _____

Quantity	Full Book Title	Price

Taxable Total	
Sales Tax (6%) for California Residents	
Shipping and Handling Costs	
TOTAL	

SHIP TO: ☐ address above   ☐ other _____

_____

_____

Make checks payable to:

_____

MOON PUBLICATIONS 722 Wall St. Chico CA 95928 USA tel. (916) 345-5473

WE ACCEPT VISA AND MASTERCHARGE!
To order: CALL IN YOUR VISA OR MASTERCHARGE NUMBER, or send written order
with your Visa or Mastercharge number and expiry date clearly written.

CARD NO.   ☐ VISA ☐ MASTERCHARGE

☐☐☐☐☐☐☐☐☐☐☐☐☐☐☐☐☐☐☐☐

SIGNATURE_____ EXPIRATION DATE_____

MINIMUM CREDIT CARD ORDER: US$15